PHAIDON ENCYCLOPEDIA OF ART AND ARTISTS

PHAIDON ENCYCLOPEDIA OF ART AND ARTISTS

PHAIDON

Phaidon Press Limited
Littlegate House, St Ebbe's Street, Oxford

Published in the United States of America by E. P. Dutton, New York

This edition first published 1978

Adapted from the *Pall Mall Encyclopedia of Art*, 1971
Original French edition, *Dictionnaire Universel de l'art et des artistes*

ISBN 0 7148 1513 6
Library of Congress Catalog Card Number: 77-89312

Printed in Great Britain by BAS Printers Limited, Over Wallop, Hampshire

Picture origination and colour printing by De Lange/Van Leer NV, Deventer, Netherlands

PREFACE

The purpose of this book is to provide, within reasonable limitations of space, a comprehensive and authoritative reference guide for both student and general reader, as well as a lively appreciation of the history of world art.

In 1971 the five-volume *Pall Mall Encyclopedia of Art* was published jointly in the U.K. by the Pall Mall Press, an imprint later absorbed into the Phaidon Press, and in the U.S. by Praeger Publishers Inc. The five-volume work was, in its turn, based on the *Dictionnaire Universel de l'art et des artistes*, published in three volumes in 1967 by Fernand Hazan, Paris, and edited by the distinguished French art historian and critic Robert Maillard. When the English-language version was undertaken the contents of the French edition were fully revised and updated, and many new articles were added, chiefly in the areas of American and British art. This encyclopedia is based on the contributions originally written for the much larger work, abridged, brought up to date and adapted to suit the format of a single volume.

The encyclopedia is composed of three categories of articles. There are biographies documenting the work of painters, sculptors, graphic artists and architects active in the West from medieval times to the present. These are complemented by articles on periods, styles, schools and movements, and by surveys of the art of civilizations whose individual artists are mainly unknown, at least in the West. Such surveys are broken down whenever possible, so that there are items on peoples of the Far East, Middle East, and pre-Columbian America who have been revealed to have a distinct culture and art-forms of their own. Longer articles are divided into sections covering the various aspects of the particular subject. Appropriate cross-references ensure that all material relating to any single subject is easily accessible.

A considerable debt of gratitude is owed to Robert Maillard and the team who compiled the French edition; to Fernand Hazan; and to David Bell, the editor of the 1971 English-language edition, and an editorial team on both sides of the Atlantic. Dr Lucia Wildt, Dr I. Grafe and Mrs Rosemary Blott undertook the updating and adaptation for the present volume.

The publishers also wish to thank the museums, libraries, galleries, public and private foundations, and collectors who have kindly consented to the reproduction of works of art in their possession and acknowledge the copyrights held by S.P.A.D.E.M. and A.D.A.G.P., Paris.

A

AACHEN, Hans von (1552, Cologne—1615, Prague), one of the principal German Mannerist painters. He made the journey to Italy in 1574 and remained for a time in Venice, where he enthusiastically viewed the work of Tintoretto and Correggio. After a long stay in Rome he returned to Germany, where we find him in 1588 at Cologne, then at Munich and Augsburg. In 1592 he was called to Prague and appointed Painter to the Bedchamber of Emperor Rudolf II. On the death of Rudolf the artist was confirmed in his office by Emperor Mathias. He painted mythological scenes, but had several portraits to his credit also. His *Bathsheba Bathing* (Vienna, Kunsthistorisches Museum) is considered his masterpiece.

AALTO, Alvar (b. 1898, Kuortane, Finland—d. 1976), Finnish architect. Although his first important works were built between 1927 and 1933, they are more reminiscent of Frank Lloyd Wright than of the protagonists of European functionalism. The range of his work is one of the widest of 20th-century architects: industrial architecture (Toppila, 1930–31; Sunila, 1936–39); hospital (Paimio, 1929–31); cultural and civic (Viipuri library, 1931–35; Senior Dormitory, Massachusetts Institute of Technology, 1947–48; Town Hall, Säynätsalo, 1950–52; Cultural Center, Helsinki, 1955–58); domestic (Villa Mairea, 1938–39; his own house on the island of Muuratsalo, 1952); administrative buildings (Rautatalo office, Helsinki, 1953–55; National Pensions Institute, Helsinki, 1952–56); religious buildings (churches at Vuoksenniska, 1957–59, and Seinäjoki, 1958–60); town planning (Sunila, 1936–39 and 1951–54; Kauttua, 1938–40; regional plan, Imatra, 1947–53); design of mass-produced furnishings: chairs (from 1927), vases, and lighting accessories.

The outstanding characteristics of style common to these projects is freedom of ground plan and volume design. Neither a geometric nor any other kind of preconception hampered Aalto; apart from his artistic instinct, he was guided entirely by the nature of the site and the function of the interior. His work is distinguished by an intense feeling for materials and a treatment of them that is sensual; some of his favorite materials were brick, which he used with remarkable surface effects, and various kinds of woods, to which modern chemistry has given a new life. Copper (for covering), slate, and marble are also found in his work.

Aalto worked in the United States, where he concentrated on university building; in Iraq, where he designed the museum and post office at Baghdad; and in Europe. The great French art collector and picture dealer Louis Carré asked him to design his country house (Bazoches-sur-Guyonne, 1956–59), and several German municipalities, reacting against the impersonality of the International Style that spread over Germany following World War II, invited him to build civic and cultural centers (Cultural Center at Wolfsburg, 1959–62; Essen Opera House, 1965; municipal blocks of flats in Berlin and Bremen).

ABBASID ART. *See* **ISLAMIC ART.**

ABBATE, Niccolò dell' (*c.* 1509/12, Modena—1571, Fontainebleau), Italian painter and decorator. We know very little about his work in Italy. In 1546 he painted frescoes for the Palazzo Comunale at Modena, now in the Palazzo dei Musei, Modena; and in 1547 he did others at the Palazzo Poggi and at the university, both in Bologna. The most important part of his career was spent decorating the château of Fontainebleau, as Primaticcio's assistant, from 1552 until his death, but his landscape painting is more easily distinguished and appreciated (*Landscape with Figures*, Rome, Galleria Borghese; *Landscape with Orpheus and Eurydice*, 1557 (?), London, National Gallery; *Rape of Persephone*, 1557 (?), Paris, Louvre). The *Chastity of Scipio* (after 1552; Louvre) shows Niccolò handling a type of figure painting quite different from the Fontainebleau decoration; it is characteristic of northern Italian Mannerism, with soft modeling that derived from Correggio.

ABBEY, Edwin Austin (1852, Philadelphia—1911, London), American etcher and painter. His work was published in *Harper's Weekly* as early as 1870, and an association with this magazine lasted throughout his life. He was influenced by the English artists (Frederick Leighton, George Frederic Watts, Sir John Everett Millais, John Brett) who participated in the Centennial Exhibition, Philadelphia, and made his first trip to England in 1878. By the early 1880s Abbey was well entrenched in British art circles; he became friendly with Sir Laurence Alma-Tadema and J. A. M. Whistler, and began exhibiting at the Royal Academy in London. By 1889 he concentrated more on oil painting. His decorations for the Boston Public Library (*Quest of the Holy Grail*, 1902) are typical of his painting style, as are other large commissions, such as those for the Pennsylvania State Capitol (1902–11) and the *Coronation of Edward VII* (1902–4; London, Buckingham Palace). The enthusiastic reception of the library murals influenced a change in some of his late graphic works, which often become laden with a pomp and theatricality related to the style of the Pre-Raphaelites.

ABILDGAARD, Nicolai Abraham (1743, Copenhagen—1809, near Fredericksdal), Danish painter who played a considerable part in the Neoclassical movement at the end of the 18th century. He worked in Rome from 1772 to

Alvar Aalto. Carré house, Bazoches-sur-Guyonne. 1956–59.

Abstract Art. Constantin Brancusi. *Prodigal Son. c.* 1914. Louise and Walter Arensberg Coll., Philadelphia Museum of Art.

1777, making studies from the antique and from Raphael, Michelangelo, and Titian. His first work on a Classical theme was the *Philoctetes* (1775; Copenhagen, Statens Museum for Kunst). In 1778 he was appointed to the teaching staff of the Copenhagen Academy and, between 1780 and 1791, he carried out a vast decorative scheme at Christiansborg Palace. This was considered his masterpiece, but the paintings were destroyed when the palace was burned down in 1794. Abildgaard occasionally did architectural and decorative work, as well as sculpture in metal, and he exercised considerable influence at the Copenhagen Academy, where he was director from 1789 to 1791 and again from 1801 until his death.

ABSTRACT ART. After half a century of existence—and of vicissitude and controversy—abstract art, despite its now universal presence, still raises historical and aesthetic problems that no account, however brief and objective, can dismiss. Architecture and music are accepted, of course, as abstract arts, whereas poetry, painting, and sculpture are regarded as representational arts. Should this traditional distinction be retained, or can all the arts make claim to the same internal autonomy as music and architecture?

PAINTING

Abstract painting seems to have been engendered by just such a desire to compete on its own ground with the suggestive power of music, as Wassily Kandinsky did, or with the formal ideal of architecture, as was Piet Mondrian's aim. The term "abstract" is itself equivocal and open to discussion. "I call abstract art," said Michel Seuphor, one of the leading interpreters of the movement, "any art that contains no reference to, no evocation of reality, whether or not this reality was the artist's point of departure." This subsidiary distinction corresponds to two historically discrete periods of abstract art: an initial period (1910–16), in which abstraction represented the culmination of an antinaturalistic process, and a second period, which began in 1917 with the De Stijl movement and is still continuing, in which abstraction *per se* is presented at the outset as an absolute principle. It would perhaps be desirable to refer to art of the first kind as "abstract" and to use the term "nonfigurative" for the second.

Kandinsky's first consciously abstract watercolor was painted in 1910; in the same year he wrote his basic theoretical work, *On the Spiritual in Art*, an aesthetic defense of his new orientation and one of the key writings in the history of abstract art. Kandinsky received his impetus from visual experiences; but it was in music that he discovered the principle of his aesthetic. It is significant that he called his sketches *Improvisations* and his completed works *Compositions*. In 1912 the Czech Frank Kupka also exhibited abstract paintings directly inspired by music: *Fugue in Red and Blue, Hot Chromatics*, etc. He was the precursor of the Musicalists, who formed a group with Charles Blanc-Gatti and Henri Valensi (1883–1960) around 1920. Another pioneer was Francis Picabia, whose *Rubber* of 1909 was already non-figurative, while Robert Delaunay, the founder of Orphism, also raised the lyrical potentialities of pure color to the point of abstraction. Color, he said, is both "form and subject." Inspired by his example, the American painters Morgan Russell and Stanton Macdonald-Wright founded the Synchromist movement in Paris and Munich in 1913. But it was in Russia, from about 1913, that the limits of abstract art were systematically explored, in the Rayonism of Mikhail Larionov and Natalia Goncharova, the Nonobjectivism of Alexander Rodchenko, and the Suprematism of Kasimir Malevich. Indeed most of the pioneers of abstract art were of Russian origin, including the Lithuanian composer Mikolojus Ciurlionis (1875–1911), who began painting abstract compositions that were the attempted equivalents of music as early as 1905–6.

The other field of expansion of abstract art was Holland, where, in 1917, in opposition to the organic, lyrical tendency that had entered the art of Kandinsky from Fauvism and Expressionism, Mondrian and the De Stijl movement (Theo van Doesburg, Bart van der Leck), gave shape to the intellectual and geometrical tendency derived from Cubism, thus effecting a shift from "abstraction" to "nonconfiguration." Mondrian's new direction, Neoplasticism, signaled his abandonment of abstraction, with its absolute plastic relationships, and a movement toward the purity and universality of mathematics. At about the same time a number of artists in Zurich, including Jean Arp and Sophie Taeuber-Arp, began to explore the possibilities of free, irrational forms, through which Dada was to make its essential contribution to abstract art. In Florence, *c.* 1915, Alberto Magnelli produced a series of rigorously abstract pictures with strong, flat colors.

A backward glance at the situation of painting as a whole at the end of World War I will show abstract art in a position to become the dominant mode. But the movement lost some of its momentum; and, with its rejection by the great Cubists, it became obvious that its time had not yet come. The emergence of Surrealism in 1924 made the existence of abstract art especially precarious, and the period between the wars was one of alternate eclipse and resurgence for abstraction. While Picabia and Delaunay returned to figuration, new abstractionists emerged, beginning in 1920, including the Germans Otto Freundlich and Friedrich Vordemberge-Gildewart; the Hungarian László Moholy-Nagy, who taught at the Bauhaus; the Dutch painter César Domela (b. 1900), who joined the De Stijl group; the Belgians Victor Servranckx and Jozef Peeters; Kurt Schwitters and Willi Baumeister after 1923; the painter-typographer Hendrick Werkman (1882–1945) in 1926; former Cubists such as Sergei Charchoune (active 1912), Alfred Reth, and Auguste Herbin in 1930; and, from 1933, Magnelli in a geometric style and Hans Hartung in a lyrical mode. In April 1930 the first international exhibition of abstract art was organized in Paris by Michel Seuphor and Joachim Torrès-Garcia under the auspices of the revue *Cercle et Carré*, which had been founded in the same year. In 1932 the Abstraction-Création group was formed to continue the work of *Cercle et Carré* and, like its predecessor, published an annual album (until 1936) and organized regular exhibitions. The year 1937 was an important one for art in the United States: it saw the first exhibition of the American Abstract Artists Foundation and the

Abstract Art. Julio Gonzalez. *Standing Figure.* 1931. *Photo Galerie de France, Paris.*

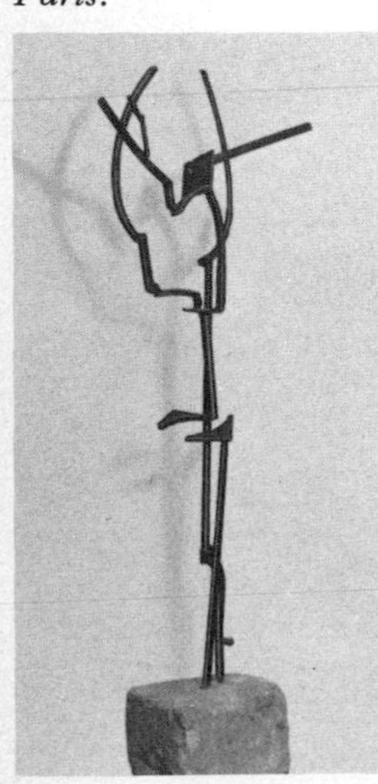

creation of the Museum of Non-objective Painting, the latter directed by Hilla Rebay. Nevertheless, abstract art seemed to have lost its initial impetus. With the outbreak of the Spanish Civil War, followed by World War II, Expressionism revived and became the dominant movement in art. Obviously the war made a break, in art as in everything else, and when it was over a very new situation existed. Paul Klee had died in 1940, Delaunay in 1941, Freundlich in 1943, Kandinsky and Mondrian in 1944. New, hitherto unknown names made their appearance; and from 1945, in every country, abstract art spread rapidly. This explains the importance of the Salon des Réalités Nouvelles, which opened in Paris in 1946 and, containing more than 1,000 contributions, represented the first official international exhibition of nonfigurative art. Finally, the publication in April 1949 of Michel Seuphor's *L'Art abstrait, ses origines, ses premiers maîtres* confirmed the historical importance of the movement and its creators.

It would be impossible to provide a complete survey of recent developments in abstract art. In France, one might mention such different and incompatible names as Hartung and Roger Bissière, Jean Fautrier and Jean Bazaine, Alfred Manessier and André Lanskoy, Nicolas de Staël and Maria Elena Vieira da Silva, Maurice Estève, and Wols (Wolfgang Schulze), Serge Poliakoff and Pierre Soulages, Jean Atlan (1913–60), and Bram van Velde (b. 1895). In Belgium, Louis van Lint, Anne Bonnet (1908–60), Gaston Bertrand (b. 1910), and Jo Delahaut (b. 1911) have met with success. Pierre Alechinsky (b. 1927), a Belgian, settled in Paris after founding the Cobra movement with the Dane Asger Jorn and the Dutchman Karel Appel. Germany has seen the growth of a school of abstract art led by such artists as Ernst Wilhelm Nay, Theodor Werner (1886–1969), Fritz Winter (b. 1905), Julius Bissier, and K. R. H. Sonderborg (b. 1923). In Britain, despite the pioneering work of Ben Nicholson and Paule Vezelay before World War II, the artistic climate was hostile to abstraction, and it was not until after the war that it slowly took root. Victor Pasmore was the first painter of any distinction to turn abstract in the postwar period—sculptors adopted the new style more readily—and after 1950 he was followed by a number of others, Brian Wynter (1915–1975), Roger Hilton (1911–1975), and Ivon Hitchens among them. There was little nonfigurative art in Italy between the early experiments of Giacomo Balla and Magnelli around 1915 and the emergence of Atanasio Soldati (1896–1953) and, around 1931–34, of Enrico Prampolini and Mauro Reggiani (b. 1897). Not until the end of World War II did a coherent movement begin to emerge, with Afro Basaldella (b. 1912), Emilio Vedova, Antonio Corpora (b. 1909), Giuseppe Capogrossi, Alberto Burri, and Giuseppe Santomaso. The abstract movement reached Spain, Scandinavia, Yugoslavia, Poland, Brazil, and Japan. But the greatest revelation was undoubtedly the American school, which created an entirely original style in the work of such representative but varied artists as Mark Tobey, Hans Hofmann, Arshile Gorky, Jackson Pollock, Willem de Kooning, Bradley Walker Tomlin, Franz Kline, Robert Motherwell, and Mark Rothko.

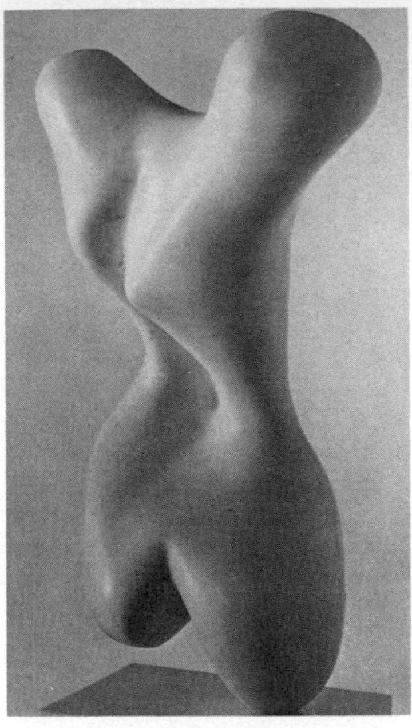

Abstract Art. Jean Arp. *Torso.* 1931. Coll. Müller-Widmann, Basel.

SCULPTURE

In degree of abstraction, sculpture is now fully on a par with painting but, in the early stages of its development toward abstraction, it owed much to the attempts of painters to free themselves from the rules of imitation and from traditional concepts of form. In this respect the influence of Cubism and Futurism was decisive, enabling sculptors like Henri Laurens, Alexander Archipenko, Jacques Lipchitz, Ossip Zadkine, Umberto Boccioni, and, in a more direct way, Raymond Duchamp-Villon, Constantin Brancusi, and Julio González to set modern sculpture on its irresistible course toward freedom from the object. These pioneering efforts were seconded by incursions into sculpture on the part of the painters themselves; the contributions of Picasso, Matisse, Georges Braque, Léger, and Max Ernst were often bold and vitalizing. But it is in relief, often polychrome, that the last links with naturalism were broken. It appears to have been a Russian, Vladimir Tatlin, who first took this decisive step: as early as 1913 he was making purely geometrical compositions of various materials that he suspended at the intersection of two walls. In 1915 another Russian, Jean Pougny (1894–1956), who was also a painter, adopted similar methods in his compositions of colored cardboard. These were the beginnings of the movement that was later to be given the name of Constructivism, a first cousin of Malevich's Suprematism. Artists who joined it later were Schwitters, Moholy-Nagy, the Rumanian Marcel Janko, and Arp.

Constructivism found its leading exponents and theorists in Naum Gabo and his brother Antoine Pevsner, who later took part in the activities of the Abstraction-Création group in Paris. Artists who could also be described as "Constructivists" (in the wider meaning of the term) are the Belgian Georges Vantongerloo; the Frenchman Jean Gorin (b. 1889); the Swiss Max Bill; the American Alexander Calder; his compatriots Harold Cousins (b. 1916) and Richard Lippold; the British sculptor Kenneth Martin; the Italian Berto Lardera; the Argentinian Francesco Marino di Teana (b. 1920); the German Norbert Kricke (b. 1922); the Hungarian Nicolas Schöffer, who, in Paris, invented "spatiodynamism," an animated synthesis of sculpture, painting, and cinema; and the Swiss Jean Tinguely, with his kinetic constructions.

Sculptors of an Expressionistic tendency include the Italians Umberto Mastroianni, Roberto

Abstract Art. Antoine Pevsner. *Developable Column. Photo Masclet, Paris.*

Crippa (b. 1920), and Francesco Somaini (b. 1926); the Argentinians Pablo Manès (b. 1891) and Alicia Penalba; the American Seymour Lipton; and the Swiss Robert Müller. A kind of exasperated Baroque would seem to characterize the work of the Dutchman Willem Couzijn (b. 1912) and the Americans Theodore Roszak, Louise Nevelson, and, in a younger generation, Shinkichi Tajiri (b. 1923), John Chamberlain, and Richard Stankiewicz. Chamberlain and Stankiewicz use scrap metal, like the Frenchman César (César Baldoccini), the Belgian Roël d'Haese (b. 1921), and many others who seem to be obsessed by destruction, either natural or deliberate.

What was most lacking in nonfigurative sculpture was monumental power. The architectural revolution that took place after World War II created a spirit of emulation among sculptors and architects. The buildings designed by Oscar Niemeyer for Brasilia and Le Corbusier's chapel at Ronchamp in France are really sculptures on an architectural scale. Inversely, Henri-Georges Adam's *Signal* in front of the museum at Le Havre; Étienne-Martin's *Demeures* ("Dwellings"); Jacques Zwobada's mausoleum at the Mentana Cemetery near Rome; the sculpture-habitations of André Bloc (1896–1966), Gérard Manoni (b. 1928), or Constantino Nivola; the works of the Japanese-American Isamu Noguchi intended for gardens—all show clear signs of a movement toward a synthesis of the arts that may be regarded as one of the most striking phenomena of 20th-century sculpture.

ACADEMICISM, according to Louis Hautecoeur, is "a form of pharisaism: a respect for the letter while sinning against the spirit." Critics usually apply the word "academicism" to the phenomenon of sclerosis, which attacks artistic movements that become too dependent on stereotyped formulas or on a blind obedience to rules. Certain historians would like to confine this term to a definite historical reality, that is, to the numerous academies that were founded in Europe from the 16th century. The earliest academies, such as the Accademia di S Luca at Rome; the Guild of St. Luke at Antwerp; and the Maîtrise des peintres et sculpteurs de la Ville et de la banlieue de Paris, which was founded in 1260 and which in 1649 became the Académie de St-Luc, presided over by Simon Vouet, were really outgrowths of the medieval guilds. On the other hand, the drawing up of a body of doctrine and its subsequent teaching were the aims pursued by the Accademia degli Incamminati, set up by the Carracci in Bologna about 1585–86 to revive the conscientious study of the nude and develop the intelligent imitation of masterpieces.

Some would apply the term academicism to the powerful and unified style created in France by the Académie Royale de Peinture et de Sculpture, founded in 1648 through the initiative of the chancellor Séguier and the painter Charles Le Brun. From 1671 the Académie was enlivened by the "Quarrel of Color Versus Drawing" between the *poussinistes* (followers of Poussin) and the *rubénistes* (followers of Rubens). The period that followed the supremacy of Le Brun was certainly not one of academicism. Although the aesthetic norms remained the same, although many painters remained faithful to the rationalist spirit of the 17th century, a healthy breeze of innovation continued to blow through the Académie. A number of provincial academies were established on the model of the Paris academy, and other European capitals followed its example also: the Antwerp Academy, established in 1663 by Philip IV and David Teniers the Younger; the Berlin Academy, founded in 1697; the Academia de San Fernando in Madrid, which was planned by Velázquez and founded in 1752 by Philip V and the sculptor Giovanni (or Juan Domenico) Olivieri (1708–62); the Royal Academy in London, founded by George III in 1768, with Sir Joshua Reynolds as its first president. All these institutions organized their exhibitions and instruction along similar lines, but none of them deserved the charge of academicism leveled at them by Louis David as a term of abuse when, in 1793, he demanded that the Convention abolish the Académie Royale.

At the beginning of the 19th century, when public taste favored Neoclassicism, the Académie was reluctant to accept Romanticism and Realism. Yet a painter like Eugène Delacroix, who was shunned for years by his colleagues, was elected, seven years before his death, to the chair that had been occupied by Hippolyte Delaroche for 24 years. On the other hand, in the second half of the 19th century, the members of the Institut appointed the holders of the chairs at the École des Beaux-Arts, controlled the distribution of the Prix de Rome, and selected the exhibitors in the annual Salon. They instituted a decadent regime based on restrictive teaching and outdated traditions. All independent activity was severely condemned; painters such as Monet and Cézanne were systematically rejected and the *peintres maudits* ("pariah painters") were born. For quite some time the *pompiers* ("stuffed shirts," conventionalists) continued to win honors and fortune in the face of the Salon des Refusés. They trained attentive disciples to imitate them, and the walls of the Salon des Artistes Français were covered with replicas of William Bouguereau and Léon Bonnat. The École des Beaux-Arts at that time really was a prize example of historic academicism, but this period in the history of art is no longer of sufficient interest to merit the exclusive use of the term academicism.

Academicism. Annibale Carracci. *Astronomer*. Cabinet des Dessins, Louvre, Paris. *Photo Josse-Lalance, Paris.*

Achaemenian Art. Ruins of the palace of Darius I, Persepolis. 6th–5th century B.C. *Photo Roger-Viollet, Paris.*

ACHAEMENIAN ART. The capture of Nineveh (612 B.C.) by the combined efforts of the Neo-Babylonians (Nabopolassar) and the Medes (Cyaxares) was followed by a division of western Asia between the two conquerors: a Median Empire from Anatolia in the west to the borders of Iran in the east; and a Neo-Babylonian Empire from the Persian Gulf to the Mediterranean. In the midst of the Median lands was a small kingdom whose ambitious ruler, Cambyses, of the tribe of Parsua, claimed descent from Achaemenes. To strengthen his authority, he married the daughter of his suzerain, Astyages. The offspring of this marriage was Cyrus. He overthrew his grandfather (553 B.C.) and established the Perso-Achaemenid dynasty, which, with its 11 sovereigns, subdued Babylon and held sway over an immense territory, stretching from the Indus to Upper Egypt. Had the Achaemenids contented themselves with Asia and Egypt, they would no doubt have reigned a long time. Their mistake was to cross the Hellespont and provoke the Greeks. The reaction of the latter took a century to come, but when it did, it was decisive: Alexander the Great conquered Persia by a series of victories in pitched battle, pursuing its last sovereign, Darius III Codomannus, as far as Bactria, where he was assassinated (330 B.C.).

This rapid historical survey enables us to better understand the sources of Achaemenian art: it was influenced at various stages by Ashur—a vanished city that still lived in its monuments—Babylon, Thebes, and even Athens. Thus it is composite in character, but by no means is it completely unoriginal.

Persian monumental art has survived in the ruins of palaces built in the royal cities: Pasargadae (Cyrus the Great), Persepolis (Darius I, Xerxes I, Artaxerxes I), and Susa (Darius I, Xerxes I, Artaxerxes II Mnemon). Pasargadae already exemplifies the typical arrangement of a series of independent buildings, isolated from each other but grouped within the same precinct. The arrangement was repeated on a gigantic scale at Persepolis, with a massive use of columns, an obvious borrowing from Egyptian hypostyle halls. On the other hand, the idea of porticoes must have come from the Greeks. Susa is different; nearer to Mesopotamia, it adhered to the more Oriental conception of a court with halls and apartments around it.

Ornament was an integral part of Achaemenian architecture, and it is here that foreign influences are most clearly in evidence. The gatehouses at Pasargadae and Persepolis were guarded by enormous stone bulls, winged and human-headed, in imitation of those at Sargon's palace in Khorsabad. Carvings similar to the Assyrian war reliefs are to be seen at Persepolis, with the important difference, however, that actual warfare does not appear. Only the results are shown: the arrival of the vanquished with tribute, or the various peoples of the empire supporting the royal throne with their outstretched arms. The army is not absent, but it is shown in its ceremonial function and in static formations, like the soldiers along the stair ramps at Persepolis, or the archers, "Immortals" of the royal guard, at the palace of Susa. In contrast to Pasargadae and Persepolis, the decoration at Susa shows animal friezes not to be seen elsewhere: lions, winged griffins, horned lions, and winged lions with human heads. There is no doubt that the antecedents here are Babylonian (Processional Way, Gate of Ishtar, palace; *see* BABYLONIAN ART).

The capitals crowning the slender columns of Achaemenian buildings were an original creation. They consisted of two animal protomas back to back: bulls, sometimes with human heads, or griffins. This original feature was combined with borrowed elements: the Aegean fluting of the columns and the Egyptian entablature, particularly the cavetto characteristics of the Nile Valley.

The Achaemenids seem to have done very little sculpture in the round, apart from the animal protomas for capitals. Their greatest artistic achievement was their metalwork. At the royal table, the plate was worthy of the master of the world: sumptuous rhytons, dishes, and cups in gold and silver. The winged ibexes of nielloed gold and silver, originally jar handles (Paris, Louvre; Berlin, Staatliche Museen), the gold dagger from Ecbatana (New York, Metropolitan Museum), jewelry, torques, bracelets, earrings—all these prove the technical virtuosity and the taste of the artists who made them.

ACTION PAINTING. This term, generally attributed to the American art critic Harold Rosenberg, is used to denote the form of Abstract Expressionism practiced since World War II by the New York School. Painters such as Jackson Pollock, Willem de Kooning, Franz Kline, Clyfford Still, Adolph Gottlieb, and Mark Rothko felt the need for a closer link between the man and his work and tried to express the pressure of their impulses, the violence of their feelings, and, at a higher level, the dynamism of life in the raw. They sometimes abandoned the easel and even the usual tools of their art for new techniques such as "dripping," in which paint was dropped onto a flat canvas from perforated cans. Others, such as Kline and Rothko, developed a more ordered, more premeditated form of Expressionism.

ADAM, family of French sculptors from Lorraine, whose most notable members were the three sons of Jacob-Sigisbert Adam (1670–1747), sculptor to Leopold I, Duc de Lorraine.

LAMBERT-SIGISBERT, *called* ADAM THE ELDER (1700, Nancy—1759, Paris), was trained by his father in Nancy, and in Paris by François Dumont (1687–1726). He was awarded the Prix de Rome in 1723, and spent 10 years in Italy. He played a major role in the Rococo decoration of Hôtel Soubise, Paris, but his most important work, in which he was helped by his brother Nicolas-Sébastien, was the *Triumph of Neptune and Amphitrite* for the Neptune Fountain, Versailles (1735–40).

NICOLAS-SÉBASTIEN, *called* ADAM THE YOUNGER (1705, Nancy—1778, Paris), trained in Paris and worked briefly in Montpellier before joining his eldest brother in Rome. Returning to France in 1734, he assisted Lambert-Sigisbert on several works. Later, on his own, he sculptured the tomb of Queen Catherine Opalinska of Poland in the Chapelle de Bon-Secours, Nancy (1747–49). His commissions included many sculptural groups and the decorative programs for a number of palaces and town houses. His *Prometheus Bound* (1762) is in the Louvre, Paris.

FRANÇOIS-GASPARD (1710, Nancy—1761, Paris), third son of Jacob-Sigisbert, also received the Prix de Rome. In his early years he worked with his brothers, and he later made a career for himself at the court of Frederick II of Prussia. He spent 13 years (1747–60) decorating the gardens of Sanssouci with all the mythological figures of Olympus.

Robert Adam. Portico, Osterley Park, Middlesex. Remodeled 1761–80. *Photo Country Life, London.*

ADAM, family of architects of Scottish origin. The Adam brothers were architects by profession at the time of the English Renaissance, but as outstanding decorators they gave their name to a decorative style that drew on Classical art and the Roman Renaissance. Their father, William Adam (1689–1748), was the most popular architect of Edinburgh in the first half of the century. After settling in London, the brothers were patronized and admired by the aristocracy—among their clients were George III and Queen Charlotte—and from 1759 to 1775 they were often called upon to embellish the ancestral homes of dukes, earls, and gentlemen. In addition to their structural remodeling, which featured rooms of different sizes, heights, and shapes, domed ceilings, and expansive interior vistas, the Adams believed in a whole integrated decorative scheme, and to this end they designed furniture, carpets, tapestry and embroidery, upholstery, mirrors, silver plates, door furniture, and fire-grates to complement their wall and ceiling stuccowork. They also designed new buildings.

ROBERT (1728, Kirkcaldy, Scotland—1792, London), the most gifted of the family, received preliminary training from his father and set off on the Grand Tour in 1754. During this period French and English architects were making a close study of Classical ruins and evolving their own Neoclassical styles from them. Robert Adam, in his turn, wanted to make a reputation for himself in the same way, and he found a subject in the antiquities of Dalmatia. Adam left Italy (Venice) on July 11, 1757, with the French architect Clérisseau and two Italian designers and headed for Spalato (now Split, Yugoslavia), the Illyrian capital of Diocletian, where the group remained for five weeks sketching ruins. In 1764 Adam's luxurious *Ruins of the Palace of the Emperor Diocletian at Spalato in Dalmatia* was published in London, and was so well received that a second edition appeared in 1778.

On his return to England, he found that his reputation had preceded him. He settled there in 1759 with his brothers, and the team was an immediate success. Robert was the creative member of the group.

JAMES (1730, Kirkcaldy—1794, London), a skillful draftsman who had introduced the Palladian spirit of the Earl of Burlington and William Kent into his father's firm, interpreted Robert's ideas. William, the youngest brother, looked after financial matters, while John, the eldest, administered the family property, in addition to his independent architectural work in Scotland.

Syon House, Isleworth (1762–69), the seat of the dukes of Northumberland in Middlesex, provides a striking illustration of the Adams' concept of total interior design, applied to their remodeling of an ancient building. Similar refined decoration can also be seen in the reception rooms at Shardeloes (1759–61), the library at Kenwood, Hampstead (1767–68), and the music room at Harewood House, Yorkshire (1759–71). At Osterley Park, Middlesex (1761–80), which was remodeled by Robert, a double row of unfluted Ionic columns forms the entrance to the inner court; the arabesques in the Etruscan Room are less reminiscent of Renaissance decorations by the Zuccari and Polidoro da Caravaggio (seen, for example, in the Kenwood library ceiling) than of the tomb sculpture along the Appian Way. At Bowood (1761–64), the seat of the Earl of Shelburne in Wiltshire, Robert Adam's archaeological passion inspired the Diocletian Wing, which bears a certain resemblance to the crypto-porticus at Spalato. The interior decorating scheme and the design of the monumental southern façade of Kedleston Hall, Derbyshire (*c.* 1765–67); Mersham-le-Hatch, Kent

(1762–72); Newby Hall, Yorkshire (*c.* 1767–85), and its museum of antiquities; and Compton Verney, Warwickshire (*c.* 1761–65), are some of the Adams' many masterpieces. The brothers are credited with some 100 works altogether. A large collection of their drawings is preserved at Sir John Soane's Museum, London.

In London, where they built the screen wall to the Admiralty (1760) early in their career, the Adams bought a large group of fashionable houses on the left bank of the Thames, which they called the Adelphi (1768–72), after their fraternity ("adelphi" comes from the Greek for "brother"). These buildings, the most notable—and famous—examples of the Adam style in London, were demolished in 1936, except for No. 7 John Adam Street. In addition, they were responsible for the south and east sides of Fitzroy Square (*c.* 1790–1800) and Portland Place (1776–*c.* 1780), London, which Nash later incorporated into his town-planning project stretching from Regent's Park to St. James's Park.

Around 1777, the Adams undertook large public works like the church at Mistley, Essex (1776), Edinburgh University (begun 1789–91; completed 1815–34, to modified designs), and Charlotte Square, Edinburgh (designed 1791; executed with modifications 1792–1807), the largest architectural project by the Adams that has survived.

The brothers' influence was enormous. The publications of their own designs, *Works in Architecture of Robert and James Adam* (1773–79; 3rd volume, 1822), and collections of engraved designs by the English decorators Mathias Lock (active mid-18th century), Mathias Darly (1754–78), Thomas Chippendale the Younger (*c.* 1750–1822/23), and George Richardson (1736?–1817?) popularized their style all over England and the continent.

Dankmar Adler and Louis H. Sullivan. Auditorium Building, Chicago. 1886–89. *Chicago Architectural Photo Co.*

ADAM, Henri-Georges (1904, Paris—1967, Perros-Guirec, Brittany), French sculptor. After studying at the École des Beaux-Arts, he began a career that encompassed sculpture, engraving, and tapestry. He became known to the public in 1943, when he designed the décor and costumes for *Les Mouches*, Jean-Paul Sartre's first play, and he attracted the attention of Picasso with the famous *Gisant*, which he exhibited at the Salon de la Libération. Picasso encouraged Adam and lent him his Paris studio and his house at Boisgeloup, where in 1949 Adam executed the *Grand Nu*, later acquired by the Musée National d'Art Moderne, Paris. The *Monument to a Political Prisoner* (1952) showed Adam moving toward a synthesis of sculpture and architecture that found remarkable expression with *Signal* (1960), in the square of the new museum at Le Havre, and especially with the *Swan* (1964), at the Porte de Vincennes, Paris.

ADLER, Dankmar (1844, Weimar—1900, Chicago), German-born architect of the Chicago School. His name is associated with that of Louis Sullivan, and it is as difficult to think of one without the other as it is to state the exact contribution of each to their collective work. On the technological plane, Adler was not responsible for any innovation in construction comparable, for example, to those of William Le Baron Jenney: he revealed a personality complementary to the more capricious and artistic one of Sullivan. After joining Adler in 1879 as office manager, Sullivan became his partner in 1881. The first important work of the partnership was the Auditorium Building, Chicago (1886–89). It was especially remarkable for the spatial and acoustical qualities of its theater (capacity 4,237), with a curved floor and parabolic ceiling attributable to Adler. With the exception of the Gage Building (Chicago, 1898–99) and the Schlesinger and Mayer (now Carson Pirie Scott) Department Store (Chicago, 1899–1904), Sullivan's best works, notably the Guaranty (now Prudential) Building (Buffalo, 1894–95), with its famous pile supports, were built during his partnership with Adler, which ended in 1895.

AEGEAN ART. To avoid duplicating material in the separate entries on Cretan and Mycenaean art, we shall limit our discussion here to those cultural phenomena of the 3rd millennium B.C. in continental Greece (Thessaly), the islands, and north-west Asia Minor, to which the emergent Cretan and Mycenaean cultures of the beginning of the 2nd millennium trace their origin.

With the Neolithic period came the first rudimentary (but technically assured) examples of that glazed pottery that was to have such a magnificent development in succeeding centuries. From the beginning hand-shaped vessels were thin-walled and well fired. Often polychrome, they presented varied, subtly toned colors, enhanced by brilliant glazes. The only sculptures dating from this period were female effigies in terra cotta or stone, for religious use, evoking the mysteries of fecundity by their simplified contours.

This primitive civilization received the first waves of Indo-European migrations, and with the invaders came new forms made possible by metalworking techniques. This transformation was centered in northwest Asia Minor and spread to the neighboring islands. It is conjured up by a single name: Troy. In Troy I and II, the deepest levels at this site, may be found the most evocative remains of the period beginning *c.* 2600 B.C. and extending through the debacle late in the 3rd millennium B.C. A violent destruction is revealed by a thick layer of ashes and debris, and not until Troy VI and its Mycenaean constructions and furnishings do we find a new period of prosperity, corresponding to the descriptions of the *Iliad.*

The architecture of Troy I and II was imposing. The citadel was surrounded by a wall approximately $16\frac{1}{2}$ to $19\frac{1}{2}$ feet wide at its base and standing to a height of about $27\frac{1}{2}$ feet, constructed of rough but solid stone and flanked by bastions and towers. Several carefully guarded gates gave access to the palace, the plan of which, the megaron, was to recur in the famous palaces of Mycenae and

Aegean Art. Cycladic idol. Naxos, 2500–2000 B.C. Ashmolean Museum, Oxford.

African Art. Ibo bronze stand or altarpiece. Nigeria.

African Art. Baule loom heddle pulley. Detail. Ivory Coast.

African Art. Bakuba wooden goblet. Congo.

Tiryns and, much later in its noteworthy career, to serve as the basis of the Classical Greek temple.

The prosperity of this civilization may be seen even more readily in its rich gold and silver work. In a hiding place in the wall, the German archaeologist Heinrich Schliemann found a treasure of gold and silver cups, golden ornaments, silver bars, and bronze weapons that had been secreted at some critical moment in the siege. The workmanship was meticulous and incorporated the Mesopotamian process of granulation. The ornaments were made of plaquettes and small chains, decorated with spirals, volutes, and a variety of geometric designs.

Whereas everyday pottery was still coarse and hand-molded, the wheel was used for sacred vessels, which were transformed into human effigies by the addition of separately modeled pieces, a novelty for the time.

After a gap of time the civilization called Helladic made its appearance on the Greek mainland. The question of whether the stimulus for this culture came from Troy II or new migrations is still unresolved, but it is possible to trace its development through archaeologically determined periods up to the fall of Mycenae at the close of the Late Helladic era. At first architectural forms were extremely varied, with circular and apsidal shapes alongside the megaron. No measurable progress was made in architectural techniques until the Mycenaean period. Pottery showed great richness of form and decoration. Play of geometric lines and contrast of color provided the décor, which was sometimes in light on dark and sometimes in darker colors on the natural clay.

In the Cyclades cultural evolution was not a mere adjunct to Trojan or Helladic development, despite demonstrable contacts among these regions. Cycladic art had many parallels with Helladic, but it was more hermetic and more enduring. An important original contribution was made to the history of plastic art by the Cyclades, in the form of marble vases and idols. The vases were often left unadorned, their quality depending on beauty of material. In form they resembled terra-cotta vessels, but the latter had a quite different decorative program in which sea and shore were evoked by volutes, spirals, and undulating lines.

The milky, sometimes translucent, marble idols of the Cyclades are even more famous, for they are flattened and vigorously stylized in a way that appeals to modern taste. The idols accompanied ritual and funerary offerings and represented the great goddess, protector of life, but the symbols of fertility are only indicated by a few incised features and protuberances that are hardly noticeable.

AERTSEN, Pieter (1508, Amsterdam—1575, Amsterdam), Dutch painter. Nicknamed "Lange Pier," he became a Master at Antwerp in 1535 and a burgher in 1542. His activity in the city was primarily on behalf of churches and the merchant Rauwaerts, and his nephew Joachim Beuckelaer was his pupil there. From 1557 until his death he lived in Amsterdam. He signed his works with his initials and a trident, symbol of his father's clothworker's card. Three of his sons, Pieter Pietersz (*c.* 1543–1603), Aert Pietersz (*c.* 1550–1612), and Dirck Pietersz (*c.* 1558–1602), were also painters. Between 1543 and 1552 Aertsen painted altarpieces in the spirit of Jan Gossaert (*Crucifixion*; Antwerp, Musée des Beaux-Arts); popular scenes of contemporary mores suggestive of Van Hemessen but not satiric (*Farm Woman*, 1543; Lille, Museum); and still lifes (*Butcher's Stall*, 1551; Uppsala University). He next turned to compositions with many small figures, influenced by Jan van Amstel and in their turn influencing Bruegel (*Fair*, 1550, Vienna, Kunsthistorisches Museum; *Christ Carrying the Cross*, 1552, Berlin; *Statue of Nebuchadnezzar*, Rotterdam, Museum Boymans-van Beuningen). Between 1554 and 1562 he moved toward a grander style and learned to assimilate Italian formulas while keeping his Northern vigor. From this period date his large altarpieces, which were nearly all destroyed in the iconoclastic upheaval of 1566. His masterpieces are the two pictures of a *Cook* at Brussels (1559 and 1561) and the *Egg Dance* (1557; Rijksmuseum)—admirably painted genre scenes, perceived with deep yet discreet lyricism. Aertsen influenced the Flemish painters of the 17th century, the Italian Bartolomeo Passarotti, and the Spaniards Juan del Castillo and Velázquez in their *bodegónes*, or kitchen scenes. At the close of his career he yielded to extravagance. A market scene or a man peeling vegetables became pretexts for painting fruit, vegetables, food of all kinds heaped to overflowing (*Cooks*, 1569, Stockholm, Coll. Count Hallwyl; *Vegetable Seller*, Museum Boymans-van Beuningen). In such works he shows himself to be one of the great virtuosos of still-life painting.

AFRICAN ART. Because of the diversity of their techniques, their styles, their uses, and the ways in which they have entered African history, the arts of Africa are not easy to classify. The expression "primitive art" is no definition of an art characterized by a long evolution, technical refinements, and expression of traditional values. And if we restrict ourselves to a single type of creation, wood sculpture, we at once appreciate the difficulty when we need to identify and characterize the different "schools." Rather than preserve superficial, if convenient, analogies, it is preferable to indicate the regional groupings among which the great sculptural arts are found. The Sudan is the home of the stylistic austerity of the Bambara, the symbolic vitality of the Dogon, and the creative exuberance of the Senufo. The region of Guinea, that is, the coast of the Gulf of Guinea, is the meeting place of a glorious past, exemplified by Ife and Benin, and a present rich in works of art and still preserving elements of excellence, of which the Yoruba, Ashanti, Baule, and Agni peoples are the exponents. But the most marked diversity is found in the Congo and the surrounding territory, which embraces the monumental art of the Bamileke, the magically potent sculpture of the Fang, the aristocratic works of the Bakuba, and the classical ones of the Baluba.

The exercise of political power, expressed by ceremonial and ritual, is in most cases an incentive to vigorous artistic creativity. Effigies, chairs and thrones, royal drums, and decorated cloths reserved for the aristocracy all combine to emphasize the mythical bases of authority and to sanctify it. The sphere of religion is, more than any other, the sphere of art. The images of ancestors and the masks worn by members of the initiation societies bear witness to this.

The African arts make use of all available materials and all modes of expression within the reach of the artist's technical capability. Grasses and other vegetable matter are utilized with a more or less marked aesthetic intention in the velours and basketwork of the Bakuba of the Congo and the cotton materials decorated with mythical themes by the Senufo of the Ivory Coast. Wood—sculpted, polished, colored, overlaid with precious metals—remains the most important material; it can be directly carved and is preferred by Africans above all other materials. This does not mean that it is used exclusively. In various places in western Africa and in the Congolese basin, soft stone is sculpted. Ivory is everywhere in demand; its polish and patina have an immediate aesthetic appeal and its commercial value makes it precious. Terra cotta is widely found, but pottery statues seem to be somewhat rare, although sometimes, as in the examples found at Ife, they reach the level of masterpieces. Brass, bronze, and copper have enabled Africans to show their talents as casters and provided the civilizations of Benin with the means of showing their greatness, just as gold afforded to those of the Gold Coast the opportunity of demonstrating their excellence.

European study of the arts of Africa received an impetus in 1871, when Dr. Scheinfurt chanced to find in central Africa some sculpted statuettes whose beauty stirred him. Thereafter he made it his mission to collect, study, and publicize the work of the craftsmen and artists of Africa; in 1875 he issued his *Artes Africanae*. Later, Leo Frobenius, working to an exacting system, carried the search further. But the African "curiosities" first became impressed upon the mind of a wider public through the influence of the Fauvist and Cubist painters and a few writers, such as Guillaume Apollinaire and Blaise Cendrars.

It was after 1918 that enthusiasm for African sculpture became inflammatory in Europe. In 1919 the Devambez Gallery organized the first exhibition of African and Oceanic works. In April 1920, the journal *Action* published a number of comments on Negro art. The movement was launched. It had its undiscriminating propagandists, such as the critic and dealer Paul Guillaume, and its detractors, such as Jean Cocteau.

The researches of the ethnographers led to a second discovery in the sphere of African arts: the revelation of the diversity of styles. Studies focused attention on the environments from which the works derive their full significance and brought into being the view of African art as a language, conveying meanings to a special degree in the absence of writing, and as a means of pleasure as much as an instrument of ritual.

However recently appreciated, and however perishable the works may be, the arts of Africa are ancient. Rock paintings and engravings are found not only in the Sahara region but also in east Africa, where they are of indifferent quality, and in South Africa, where they have probably been made from the late Palaeolithic era until the present day, and where the art of animal painting has been brought to perfection. Archaeologists in Africa are beginning to uncover the products of the great lost civilizations, such as that of Nok (2nd half of the 1st millennium B.C.) in Nigeria and that of Sao (10th–16th century) in the Chad district. They enrich the panorama of the past, which is dominated by the enigmatic, massive ruins of the Zimbabwe in southern Rhodesia. But the most inspiring discoveries are still those of the terra cottas and bronzes of Ife (before the 1st decades of the 13th century) and the bronzes and ivories of Benin (12th–17th centuries). They prove the existence in early times of great civilizations on the shores of the Gulf of Guinea and are evidence of an art of high sophistication that belongs to the common treasury of mankind.

AGOSTINO DI DUCCIO (1413, Florence—1481, Perugia), Italian sculptor whose calligraphic low reliefs display singular lyricism and delicacy. His first certain works, four reliefs (signed and dated 1442), made for an altar and now mounted on the outside of Modena Cathedral, suggest a North Italian—possibly Paduan—background. He next appears at Rimini in 1449, working with Matteo de' Pasti on the interior decoration of the Tempio Malatestiano (then being rebuilt by Leon Battista Alberti), for which he executed a large number of reliefs and made the tomb of Sigismondo Malatesta's ancestors and that of Isotta degli Atti. In 1457 Agostino moved to Perugia, where he executed most of the sculpture—mainly in low relief—on the façade of the Oratory of S. Bernardino. After visiting Bologna in 1462, he returned to Florence, where he entered the guild and worked for the cathedral. In 1470 Agostino went back to Perugia; little of importance survives from his last years. Some *Madonna and Child* panels carry on the low-relief style of his Rimini work, achieving great delicacy and charm in a decorative and linear style.

Agostino di Duccio. *Musician Angels.* 1458–59. Oratory of S. Bernardino, Perugia. *Photo Boudot-Lamotte, Paris.*

AKKADIAN ART (*c.* 2340–2180 B.C.). Akkad, or Agade, was a city in central Mesopotamia, south of Baghdad, perhaps on the site of Deir, where the Euphrates and the Tigris flow closest to one another. It was the capital of the kingdom founded in the 24th century B.C. by Sargon, an officer of obscure descent. His dynasty had 11 kings who reigned, according to scholars, for a total of either 181 or 197 years. The dynasty collapsed in the 22nd century B.C. under attacks of the Guti, nomad invaders who arrived from the northeast and rapidly overran Mesopotamia.

Numerous Akkadian monuments show the Sumerian artistic heritage. In their victory steles the

Akkadian Art. Head of King Sargon (?). Nineveh, *c.* 2300–2200 B.C. Baghdad, Iraq Museum. *Photo Schneider-Lengyel, "Univers des formes," Gallimard, Paris.*

Akkadians at first continued the Sumerian principle of division into horizontal registers to facilitate reading of the narrative. The influence of the Sumerian helmet of Meskalamdug (Baghdad Museum) is seen in the extraordinary royal head in bronze found at Nineveh (*c.* 2300–2200 B.C.; Baghdad, Iraq Museum), which a number of archaeologists think may represent Sargon himself. At Mari, on the middle Euphrates, and in the Diyala region, modern excavation has uncovered Akkadian statuary, amulets, beads, and script samples identical with those of the (Sumerian) Early Dynastic period.

Akkadian originality and boldness are given free expression in the *Victory Stele of Naram-Sin* (2nd half of 3rd millennium B.C.; Paris, Louvre), which commemorates the victory of Sargon's grandson over the Luluhi. Sumerian division into registers is no longer retained. The king, wearing the horned crown of gods, is supersized and stands isolated above his men to denote his sovereignty. Striding on the conquered, he marches at the head of his troops up wooded, mountainous ground toward the summit and the sky. Victors and defeated number no more than 15 figures altogether, yet the repetition of their stance gives the effect of mass advance by a whole army. In contrast to the strict arrangement of the earlier Sumerian *Stele of the Vultures* (Louvre), with its ordered chronological narrative contained by rigid ground lines, the *Victory Stele of Naram-Sin* is a flamboyant carving of mobile figures in active poses. It is the earliest known monument glorifying a conqueror in action, and no other surviving piece embodies the originality of Akkadian art to the same degree.

Akkadian Art. Victory stele of Naram-Sin. Susa, second half of the 3rd millennium B.C. Louvre, Paris. *Photo Giraudon, Paris.*

There is the same vitality in the glyptics, where, as in earlier art, we see the multifarious activity of a pantheon that, despite the change in names, is based on the Sumerian pantheon. The compositions remain realistic and hieratic—the cylinder-seal of Sharkalisharri (son of Naram-Sin) shows a highly controlled organization—but there is a non-Sumerian animation in the mythological scenes, which, without texts, we can understand only superficially, and in the epic encounters with wild beasts, lions, and buffalo by the legendary hero Gilgamesh. It is here that Akkadian art shows its most characteristic feature: dynamism.

No important Akkadian architecture remains, and sculpture in the round survives only in badly mutilated statues. Manishtusu's robe and Naram-Sin's feet (both in the Louvre) are mere fragments, but the few heads that have come down to us are a credit to the mastery of artists who reached beyond schematized formulas to living portraiture.

ALBERS, Josef (1888, Bottrop, Germany—1976, New Haven, Connecticut), American painter and designer. His first lithographs and woodcuts (1916–19) were done in Essen, Germany, in the Expressionist tradition. While at the Munich Art Academy during the following years, he studied with Franz Stuck. At the age of thirty-two Albers entered the Bauhaus school in Weimar, first as a student and later as a teacher. There, during the early 1920s, he was occupied by the creation of stained-glass windows, and also began a series of glass paintings that gave the first evidence of his use of the square as a distinct form. He also designed furniture, using the principles of smooth surface, uniform texture, and hard, durable substances, creating the first bent laminated chair intended for mass production.

In 1933, upon the closing of the Bauhaus, Albers was one of the first of its teachers to emigrate to the United States, where he became one of the most influential propagators of Bauhaus ideas on design reform and methods. At Black Mountain College in North Carolina, where he taught from 1933 to 1949, he opened a textile class; from 1938 to 1948 he worked on masonite, evolving geometric forms, with the square finally emerging as his dominant theme. Moving on to Yale University in 1950, where he became chairman of the department of architecture and design, he began his renowned series of paintings and lithographs, which have been given the generic title *Homage to the Square*. His exploitation of the fact that chromatically proximate colors can produce the illusion of a third color also made him a precursor of the Op artists, who experiment with visual perception.

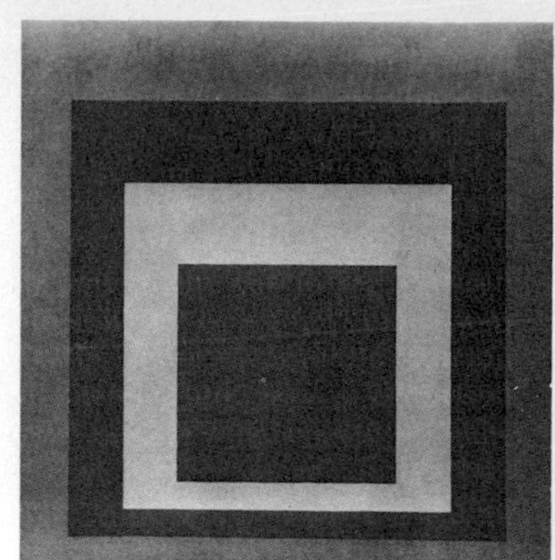

Josef Albers. *Homage to the Square: "Ascending."* 1953. Whitney Museum of American Art, New York. *Photo Geoffrey Clements.*

ALBERT, Calvin (b. 1918, Grand Rapids, Michigan), American sculptor. Albert studied art in Grand Rapids; at the Art Institute of Chicago; and, from 1937 to 1940, with Alexander Archipenko, Lázló Moholy-Nagy, and Gyorgy Kepes (b. 1906) at the Chicago Institute of Design, where he later also taught. In 1947 he settled in New York, where he taught at the Pratt Institute. In 1953 he was a winner in the competition on the theme of the Unknown Political Prisoner, sponsored by the London Institute of Contemporary Art, and in 1960 he had a major retrospective at the Jewish Museum in New York.

Albert emerged as an important American sculptor in the early 1950s, with his work in open-form, direct-metal sculpture. He developed and patented a durable, lightweight, and highly flexible lead alloy that he called Modalloy. The artist can mold this material directly with his hands and an applied-heat modeling tool; the finished sculpture can be treated with a variety of patinas. Albert's sculpture retains the fluid effect of molten metal, often drawn out into spiky, surrealistic extensions or fragile, weblike threads. The result is an Abstract Expressionist style, with a perfect fusion of the imagery, derived from still-recognizable organic forms, and the direct handling, which allows for a rough, unfinished-looking surface (*Seated Chair*, 1956).

ALBERTI, Leon Battista (1404, Genoa—1472, Rome), Italian architect, writer, and scholar. The son of an ancient family that had been banished from Florence, he studied the liberal arts at Padua, probably at the school of the humanist Gasparino Barzizza, and law at Bologna. When the decree of banishment was revoked, the young man was able to visit Florence with the suite of Pope Eugenius IV in 1434; there he discovered the first masterpieces of the artistic revival.

Yet Alberti did not remain in his city, because he had obtained (1432) the office of abbreviator in the Papal Chancery at Rome, for which he was qualified by his Bologna doctorate. He was personally attached to the popes, from Eugenius IV to Pius II, and for 30 years he divided his time between the duties of his office, artistic activity, largely in the field of architecture, and his work as a writer and humanist. His *Della pittura* was written in 1435. Its plan and rhetoric were influenced by Cicero, but its ideas were based on the practice of Brunelleschi, Donatello, and Masaccio, and on Alberti's admiration for modern Florentine art and architecture. The author explains the principles of linear perspective, just discovered by Brunelleschi, and his definition, "the painted surface is a cross section of the visual pyramid," dominated the development of the theory of perspective down to the middle of the 16th century. In 1450 he wrote his great aesthetic and technical treatise, *De re aedificatoria*, which was circulated in 1452, printed in 1485, and translated from Latin into French by Jean Martin and published by Kerver in 1553. It is divided into 10 books, on the model of Vitruvius' *De architectura*, and discusses the problems of the resistance of materials, the effect of climate, the flow of water, the organization of work on sites, the design of the architectural orders, and the various types of buildings, their decoration and their situation in the town. Steeped in the philosophy of Pythagoras, he attached supreme importance to numbers, and subordinated the building's design to three kinds of relations, or means: arithmetic, geometric, and musical. Besides the quantitative values (*numeri*), the qualitative value of certain pre-eminent forms (*figurae*), like the right angle, the circle, and the hexagon, had to be recognized in the architect's projects. Finally, Alberti turned his attention to the distribution of these figures over the interior of the building and its emplacement on the site (*collocatio*).

While he was working out his ideal, the princes Lionello d'Este, Sigismondo Malatesta and Luigi Gonzaga, and a Florentine merchant, Giovanni Rucellai, gave Alberti the opportunity to realize it in actual buildings. The Arco del Cavallo (partly destroyed) and the cathedral campanile (*c.* 1443) at Ferrara seem to have been Alberti's first attempts, and they anticipate one of his masterpieces, the Tempio Malatestiano at Rimini (1446–55). He enclosed the old church of S. Francesco in a marble shell, giving its exterior the appearance of a Classical temple. Inside, he retained the arrangement of the chapels, which the sculptors Agostino di Duccio (1418–98) and Bernardo Ciuffagni (1381–1457) decorated with graceful ornamentation. The upper part of the temple was not completed, but a medal by the architect Matteo de' Pasti (1446–67) gives an idea of the project (1450).

Alberti probably had the assistance of Bernardo Rossellino in erecting several buildings in his native Florence. The palace built (1446–1551) for Giovanni di Paolo Rucellai follows the requirements prescribed by Alberti in his treatise: "The nobleman's house should be finely decorated and look attractive rather than proud."

Giovanni Rucellai's generosity enabled Alberti to finish a work that had been begun in the previous century, the façade of S. Maria Novella in Florence (*c.* 1456–70). Here, as in the little Rucellai Chapel in S. Pancrazio, the effect of materials in contrasting colors shows a successful continuation of a Tuscan tradition.

Again in Florence, Alberti, acting less as architect than as general adviser, helped with the work on the Annunziata, where the octagonal choir and cupola were begun by Michelozzo under the patronage of Cosimo de' Medici and finished by Antonio Manetti (1423–97) at the expense of Luigi Gonzaga. But at Mantua, the seat of the Gonzaga, Alberti designed two churches. S. Sebastiano, built on the Greek-cross plan, has an imposing interior. Unfortunately, the modifications of his executants, the disappearance of the dome, and finally the absurd restoration of 1925 have all combined to change the nature of his designs. His plans for S. Andrea at Mantua were accepted in preference to those of Manetti, who was Brunelleschi's favorite pupil, but the church was not begun until the year of Alberti's death. In spite of its decoration at a later period, the interior, with its spacious and harmonious proportions, is irresistibly attractive. The layout

Leon Battista Alberti. *Self-Portrait.* Cabinet des Médailles, Louvre, Paris. *Photo Jean Roubier, Paris.*

Leon Battista Alberti. Church of S. Francesco (Tempio Malatestiano), Rimini. Executed by Matteo de' Pasti after Alberti's designs. 1446–55. *Photo Brogi-Giraudon.*

shows such profound judgment that 100 years later Giacomo da Vignola could still draw inspiration from it for his celebrated plan for Il Gesù in Rome. From 1470 to 1710 the architects Luca Fancelli, who was Alberti's pupil, Anton-Maria Viani (1636–1700), who partially executed S. Andrea at Mantua, and the Bolognese architect Giuseppe Torri (1655–1713) continued to give material form to the last ideas of one of the pioneers of modern architecture.

ALBERTINELLI, Mariotti (1474, Florence—1515, Florence), Italian painter, He was taught by Cosimo Rosselli at the same time as Fra Bartolomeo. Together the two pupils painted several pictures signed with a cross between two rings, including the *Annunciation* of 1497 in the cathedral at Volterra. Their collaboration ended in 1500, when Bartolomeo became a Dominican. Albertinelli's manner reveals a general contemporary Florentine interest in atmospheric effects and airy composition, stimulated by the work of Leonardo and Perugino. The Uffizi *Visitation* of 1503 and the *Crucifixion* fresco in the Certosa of Val d'Ema offer rhythmically satisfying unities.

ALBRIGHT, Ivan Le Lorraine (b. 1897, North Harvey, Illinois), American painter. Before World War I he studied architecture at Northwestern University and at the University of Illinois; during the war he was attached to a medical unit and made surgical drawings whose clinical precision was echoed in his later paintings. Afterward he enrolled at the École des Beaux-Arts in Nantes, and from 1919 to 1923 studied at the Art Institute of Chicago. In the early 1920s Albright began to achieve notoriety for his morbidly meticulous renderings of reality. His painting *That Which I Should Have Done I Did Not Do* (1931–41; Chicago, Art Institute) won a medal as the best entry in the 1942 Artists for Victory Exhibition held at the Metropolitan Museum in New York. In it one sees a gnarled door, a funeral wreath, and a sepulchral hand enshrouded in an aura of decay and horror.

Like his contemporary Hyman Bloom or the group of painters known as the Magic Realists, Albright was interested in revealing that each particle of life—even if depicted as withering flesh—is shimmeringly alive. For the most part, however, the viewing public was repulsed by his preoccupation with putrescent themes, while still impressed by the artist's technical abilities in recording them. Major restrospectives of Albright's works were held at the Art Institute of Chicago in 1964 and at New York's Whitney Museum of American Art in 1965.

ALDEGREVER, Heinrich (1502, Paderborn—1560, Soest), German engraver and painter whose real name was Trippenmeker. He left no less than 290 copperplate engravings and finds a natural place alongside those successors of Albrecht Dürer usually classified as the "little masters": the brothers Barthel and Hans-Sebald Beham and Georg Pencz. In his engravings of ornament intended mainly for the goldsmith's use—he was himself a goldsmith—Aldegrever draws heavily upon these artists for inspiration. His best period seems to have been the decade 1530–40, his most justly celebrated prints being those of the *Marriage Dancers* (1538), almost Baroque in their monumental exuberance.

ALEIJADHINO, António Francisco Lisboa, *called* (b. 1738, Ouro Preto, Minas Gerais—d. 1841), the greatest architect and sculptor of 18th-century Brazil, nicknamed *Aleijadhino* ("little cripple") because of a disfiguring disease, perhaps leprosy, that he contracted in middle age. He was a mulatto, the illegitimate son of Francisco Lisboa and a Negro slave girl. Aleijadhino was trained by his father and worked in the rich mining state of Minas Gerais, where he created a unique Rococo style of architecture, called Aleijadhino, a combination of elaborate embellishment applied to restrained and simple designs. In 1763 he finished the plans for the remodeling of the parish church of Morro Grande; in 1766 he designed the chapel of the Third Order of São Francisco at Ouro Preto; and in 1772, also at Ouro Preto, he was responsible for the sanctuary of the Brotherhood of São José. In 1810 he designed the frontispiece of the church of Tiradentes. His most famous work is at Congonhas do Campo, where the sanctuary of the Bom Jesus de Matazinhos was built in imitation of the one in Braga. He probably designed the terraces (1780), and he carved the epic group of the *Prophets* (soapstone) that decorates them (1800–5). He or his workshop carved the *pasos* (wooden processional figures in scenes from the Passion) for the six chapels on the Via Sacra of this sanctuary. In later years Aleijadhino's hands became so crippled that he had to have tools strapped to his arms. Nevertheless, his sculpture is distinguished by its technical proficiency, as well as its powerful strength and directness, and, when warranted by the subject, by great decorative skill.

Aleijadhino. *The Prophet Isaiah.* Church of Bom Jesus de Matazinhos, Congonhas do Campo. *Photo Marcel Gautherot, Rio.*

ALESSI, Galeazzo (*c.* 1512, Perugia—1572, Perugia), Italian architect. It is not known who gave Alessi his architectural training, but he evidently studied the work of Michelangelo. He succeeded the architect Giuliano da Sangallo at the Rocca Paolina (destroyed 19th century) in Perugia, then spent several years in Rome, and finally settled at Genoa, where from 1548 he worked almost without a break in the service of the great Sauli family. He built the church of S. Maria in Carignano in the form of a Greek cross. It was begun in 1552 and was not finished until 1603. At the same time, Alessi was building the Villa Cambiaso (begun 1548) and the so-called Villa delle Peschiere (1560–72), which has two rows of pilasters surmounted by a balustrade. He first built the Palazzo Sauli

(1555–56; very little now remains), then the Palazzo Cambiaso (*c.* 1565) and the Palazzo Lercari (begun 1567) in the Strada Nuova, now Via Garibaldi. He founded a lasting tradition in Genoa: among the splendid mansions attributed to him, some are by his pupils and were built after 1600. He also worked at Milan, where he was consulted by the Opera del Duomo and provided plans and drawings for the Certosa di Pavia. The Palazzo Marino, Milan (1558–60), with its façade comprising three orders, is a fine example of Alessi's architecture and of the lavish Mannerist decoration that was a feature of his style.

ALGARDI, Alessandro (1595/98, Bologna—1654, Rome), after Bernini, the most important Italian sculptor of the 17th century. Algardi's art is closely linked to the Classical tendencies that flourished in Rome at the same time as the High Baroque style and that were illustrated in painting by Poussin, Andrea Sacchi, and Domenichino.

The date of Algardi's birth has been much disputed. Certainly he went to Rome as a young man and was there by about 1625, but before this date he had studied under the aged painter Lodovico Carracci and had imbibed the principles of the Bolognese Academy. In Rome he became a friend of the Bolognese painter Domenichino, and also secured the patronage of another Bolognese, Cardinal Ludovisi. Domenichino was responsible for getting him the commission to make two statues in stucco, a *St. Mary Magdalene* and a *St. John*, for the church of S. Silvestro al Quirinale. They were executed around 1628 and they show that, at this early stage of his style, Algardi had come under the influence of Bernini, whose *S. Bibiana* dates from 1624–26. But the influence of antique art also is notable in his portraits of this period, for example the *Cardinal Mellini* (*c.* 1629; Rome, S. Maria del Popolo). His portrait of *St. Philip Neri* (1640; Rome, S. Maria in Vallicella) is an imaginative recreation of the founder of the Institute of the Oratory, who had died in 1595, but the characterization in such works as the *Cardinal Zacchia* (1626; Berlin) and the *Bracciolini* (London, Victoria and Albert Museum) shows that he was capable of scrupulous realism when he had the sitter before his eyes. Algardi's monument to Leo XI in St. Peter's, finished in the late 1640s, is a simpler and chastened version of Bernini's tomb of Urban VIII. The Algardi tomb is entirely in white marble, unlike the mixture of white and colored marble, bronze, and gilding used by Bernini. Algardi became head of the Academy of St. Luke in 1640; in effect, this amounted to a recognition of his leadership of the Classical school. In 1644 he directed the construction of the Villa Doria-Pamphili, on the Janiculum. Under the pontificate of Innocent X (1644–55), Bernini was out of favor and Algardi received a number of important commissions, including his only large relief, the *Attila* (1645/46–53) in St. Peter's. Late in life Algardi retired to Bologna, where there are works by him.

Alessandro Algardi. *Beheading of St. Paul.* 1641–47. Church of S. Paolo, Bologna. *Photo Alinari-Giraudon.*

ALLAN, David (1744, Alloa, Scotland—1796, Edinburgh), Scottish painter of portraits, conversation pieces, and genre scenes. In 1764 he went to Italy, where he stayed for 13 years, painting portraits, of which the most charming is that of *Sir William Hamilton and His First Wife* (1770; London, Coll. Earl Cathcart; other versions extant), and engraving scenes of the Roman carnival. He is said to have painted a number of history pieces, but nearly all have disappeared. One that survives is the *Origin of Painting* (1773; Edinburgh, National Gallery of Scotland), which won the gold medal of the Academy of St. Luke in 1773.

After a brief spell in London (1777–79), Allan returned to Scotland and worked for several years as an itinerant painter in the houses of the nobility. For his patrons, he painted large group portraits in the style of Johann Zoffany and Arthur Devis: the *Atholl Family Group* (1780; Blair Atholl, Coll. Duke of Atholl); the *Halkett Family Group* (1784; Edinburgh, Pitfirrane House); the *Hunter Blair Family* (1785; Blairquhan, Maybole, Coll. Sir James Hunter Blair).

In 1786 Allan succeeded Alexander Runciman (1736–85) as director of the Trustees Academy of Art in Edinburgh, where he lived until his death 10 years later. His last years were occupied with works for publishers: he illustrated Allan Ramsay's *Gentle Shepherd* in 1787 and a selection of Robert Burns's lyrics in the early 1790s. Also in these years, he produced his most successful paintings: *The Connoisseurs* (Uckfield, Sussex, Coll. Mr. and The Hon. Mrs. Basil Ionides) and the *Penny Wedding* (1795; New Brunswick, Beaverbrook Art Gallery), which has the distinction of having inspired Sir David Wilkie to paint his famous picture of the same title.

ALLEGRI, Antonio. *See* **CORREGGIO.**

ALLORI, Alessandro (1535, Florence—1607, Florence), Italian Mannerist painter. Orphaned at the age of five, he grew up in the house of his uncle Agnolo Allori, better known as Bronzino, who gave him his earliest training in painting. Later Allori became a pupil of Giorgio Vasari; then, in Rome (1554–56), of Michelangelo, who had a strong influence on his treatment of form and movement. He returned to Florence, where he won the esteem and patronage of the Medici. He painted portraits (*Bianca Cappello*, Florence, Uffizi); some famous religious pictures (*Sacrifice of Isaac*, Uffizi; the *Woman Taken in Adultery*, 1577, Florence, S. Spirito); and in 1598 decorated the cloister of S. Maria Novella and some of the chapels of the Annunziata. In 1580 he decorated the Palazzo Cepperello, Florence (now the seat of the Banca Toscana) with scenes taken from Homer's *Odyssey*. In 1590 he published his *Dialogo sopra l'arte del disegnare le figure*

("Treatise on the Art of Drawing Figures").

CRISTOFANO (1577, Florence—1621, Florence), son and pupil of Alessandro. He painted religious pictures and very competent portraits. His most famous work is *Judith and Her Servant Girl* (Florence, Palazzo Pitti), Mannerist in style and skillfully colored. The model for this picture was his very beautiful mistress, whom he also represented in a passionate and sensual *Penitent Magdalen in the Desert* (Uffizi).

ALLSTON, Washington (1779, Georgetown, South Carolina—1843, Cambridge, Massachusetts), American Romantic painter. In 1796 he entered Harvard University, from which he later graduated as poet of his class. His interests then turned toward painting, and by 1800 he had decided to sail for England. In London he studied at the Royal Academy with his compatriot Benjamin West, and was fascinated by the wild visions of the Swiss-born Romantic painter, Henry Fuseli. In Paris by 1804, Allston absorbed the art in Napoleon's newly formed Louvre collections; for the next four years he lived in Rome, where he met the English Romantic poets Samuel Coleridge and William Wordsworth. In 1808 Allston returned to the United States, but he went to England again three years later. While in England, he enjoyed a successful professional and social career, painting eclectic Biblical and allegorical works. Upon his return to America in 1818, he was elected to the American Academy of Fine Arts in New York.

Allston's first paintings show that a major influence was Nicolas Poussin. His later paintings, such as *Moonlit Landscape* (1819; Boston, Museum of Fine Arts), foretell Albert Pinkham Ryder's similar nightmarish forebodings, and are often considered as having inaugurated the American school of Romantic landscape. As early as 1806 Allston gave American art its first coloristic style, breaking with the Neoclassical academic tradition being practiced then on the Continent. His landscapes emphasized amorphous shapes rather than an objective comprehension and rendition of realistic forms. His most famous, although perhaps least inspired, work is *Belshazzar's Feast* (painted over a long period: 1817–43).

ALMA-TADEMA, Sir Laurence *or* Laurens (1836, Dronrijp, Friesland—1912, Wiesbaden), Dutch-born painter of the English School. Alma-Tadema was trained in Antwerp, where—after a period at the Academy—he worked as an assistant to Baron Hendrik Leys (1815–69), a history painter whose meticulous style he imitated. By 1870, the year he settled in England (he became a naturalized British subject in 1873), Alma-Tadema had achieved a considerable reputation with his many history paintings on ancient Egyptian, Greek, and Roman life, of which a typical example is the *Pyrrhic Dance* (exhibited at the Royal Academy in 1869; now in the Guildhall Art Gallery, London). The huge success that Alma-Tadema enjoyed in his own lifetime (he became a Royal Academician in 1879 and was knighted in 1899) seems hard to understand today, but the very qualities in his work that appear so damning now—the cold and meticulous finish, the lifeless accuracy of the settings, and the partiality for coy anecdote (as in *A Hearty Welcome*, 1878; Coll. Sir Henry Thompson)—appealed to the Victorians' passion for facts and to their deeply engrained sentimentality.

Sir Laurence Alma-Tadema. *The Visit.* 1868. Victoria and Albert Museum, London.

ALMOHAD ART. *See* **ISLAMIC ART.**

ALMORAVID ART. *See* **ISLAMIC ART.**

ALSLOOT, Denis van (1570, Brussels—1628, Brussels), Flemish painter of landscapes and genre scenes, court painter to Archduke Albert and Archduchess Isabella. He was long known only by the remaining pictures in a series of scenes from the *Ommeganck Procession of 1615 to Notre-Dame-du-Sablon* (London, Victoria and Albert Museum; Madrid, Prado), painted for Isabella in 1616 and hung at Tervueren in 1619. Since 1948, a number of works painted between 1608 and 1620 have been grouped with his *Abbaye de la Cambre* (1609; Nantes, Museum) and show Alsloot, as a pupil of Gillis van Coninxloo, to have been the first landscapist of the forest of Soignes in the 17th century and the founder of the Brussels school of landscape. His medium-sized panels, in delicate shades of brown, pink, or green, always show the same charm, at once mysterious and familiar, and a personal, unspoiled feeling for the natural scenery of Brabant.

Denis van Alsloot. *Winter Landscape.* Louvre, Paris. *Archives photographiques, Paris.*

ALTDORFER, Albrecht (*c.* 1480, Regensburg, Bavaria—1538, Regensburg), German painter and engraver. In addition to holding the appointment of city architect,

Albrecht Altdorfer. *Battle of Arbela.* Detail. 1529. Alte Pinakothek, Munich.

he is known to have purchased houses in 1513 and 1532; to have been elected to a seat on the Councils of Regensburg in both 1519 and 1526; and further, to have refused a nomination as burgomaster of the town. A will, made in 1538, also attests to an enviable degree of affluence; his estate included many works of art.

His dated works begin about the year 1506—paintings, wood-engravings and drawings—the last by no means the least, for he was a keen and accomplished draftsman. His curious painting, the *Family of Satyrs* (Berlin, Staatliche Museen), dates from 1507. The subject itself is not unusual; families of satyrs or savages were ever popular with German painters. What is new, and peculiar to Altdorfer, is the very minor importance given to the figures in comparison to the landscape setting; here the clumps of trees are the real subject. He was to carry this even further in the very small *St. George in the Forest* of 1510, painted on parchment (Munich, Alte Pinakothek), in which the knight, slaying a rather tame dragon with exemplary tranquillity, is literally overwhelmed by the forest; a forest more idyllic than mysterious, moreover, where every leaf is detailed with the precision of a miniaturist.

Also dating from 1510 is one of the most universally admired of Altdorfer's paintings, the *Rest on the Flight into Egypt* (Berlin, Staatliche Museen). The Holy Family has stopped by an elaborate fountain of Italianate design, and around the fluted stone basin little winged putti, so beloved of Altdorfer, are at play.

In 1511 he journeyed through the Tyrol and doubtless into Austria, marking the route of his travels with drawings of the Danubian scene; drawings that, even more substantially than the forest in the *St. George* painting, constitute a major foundation of landscape art. On this journey, too, he was probably influenced by the work of Michael Pacher.

It must have been shortly after his return home that Altdorfer entered the service of the Emperor Maximilian I. Around 1515 he decorated parts of the emperor's *Prayer Book*. Pages with his border drawings in colored inks, showing a delightful variety of knights, satyrs, barnyard animals, rustic folk, and fantastical scenes, randomly mixed with angels and religious subjects, are preserved in the Bibliothèque Municipale, Besançon.

In the *Holy Family* (1515; Vienna, Kunsthistorisches Museum) there are signs of a new preoccupation with amplitude and monumentality. Preferable, and probably of about the same date, is the charming nocturnal scene of the *Nativity* (*c.* 1512; Berlin, Staatliche Museen). Even more enchanting is the *Birth of the Virgin* (Munich, Alte Pinakothek), probably a little later in date.

In scale and in scope Altdorfer's major works are undoubtedly the two series of paintings dealing with the life of St. Florian. One of these, of 1518, is preserved in the monastery of that name, near Linz, and undoubtedly formed part of an altarpiece. It is executed with the minute precision and the rather limp correctness we have come to expect of Altdorfer's human figures, and there is more than a suspicion of coldness in the total effect. The second series consists of six panels, now distributed between the museums of Florence (Uffizi) and Nuremberg (Germanisches Museum), and a private collection in Augsburg.

After this Altdorfer seems to have done fewer paintings. *Susanna at the Bath* (1526; Munich, Alte Pinakothek) presents a fantasia of Renaissance architectural elements framing a swarm of activity. His two greatest paintings were done at the end of his life. In 1528 Duke Wilhelm IV of Bavaria commissioned from a number of painters a series of "histories," both Classical and Christian, for the decoration of his country retreat. Altdorfer's contribution, which far outshines the others, was his *Battle of Arbela*, also known as *Alexander's Victory* or the *Battle of Issus* (1529; Munich, Alte Pinakothek). Here the artist's visionary faculty unites the many disparate elements, and the minutiae, which so often mar his work, serve him well.

This visionary faculty, which, even with Altdorfer, is only occasionally apparent, seems to have exerted very little influence on German art. However, his miniaturist style on the one hand, and his concept of landscape—so fresh, so direct, and so thoroughly localized—on the other, attracted many artists, particularly the engravers and the draftsmen, rather than the painters, of the

Albrecht Altdorfer. *Men of the Forest.* 1510. Albertina, Vienna. *Photo Walter Dräyer, Zurich.*

Danube School, of which Wolf Huber is the principal exponent.

AMMANNATI, Bartolommeo (1511, Settignano, near Florence—1592, Florence), Italian architect and sculptor. He served his apprenticeship in these disciplines in the workshop of Baccio Bandinelli in Florence; but he soon left this artist to continue his training with Jacopo Sansovino in Venice. His first works were executed at Padua for the jurist Benavides, whose tomb he erected at the Church of the Eremitani. Later he worked in Pisa, Urbino, and Naples. In Rome he collaborated with Giorgio Vasari and Giacomo da Vignolo at the Villa Giulia, for Pope Julius III. Summoned back to Florence by Cosimo I, future Grand Duke of Tuscany, Ammannati was engaged from 1558 to 1570 on the enlargement of the Palazzo Pitti. Also in Florence he built his masterpiece, the Ponte S. Trinita on the Arno (1567–69, perhaps after a plan by Michelangelo; destroyed 1944, rebuilt 1957). In the same city he constructed, in collaboration with Giorgio Vasari, the magnificent staircase (completed in 1559) of the Laurentian Library, after Michelangelo's designs. In the Piazza della Signoria he built the Fountain of Neptune (1576), dominated by a rigid statue of Neptune surrounded by charming figures in bronze, not all of which are by Ammannati's hand. At Lucca he undertook the construction of the Palazzo della Signoria, which was not completed until the 18th century. In Rome he built the Negretti and Ruspoli palaces (*c.* 1580) and designed the austere College of the Jesuits (Collegio Romano, 1583–85).

AMORITE ART. *See* **BABYLONIAN ART.**

AMSTEL, Jan van (1500, Amsterdam—*c.* 1542, Antwerp), Dutch-born painter who worked in the Flemish style. He was admitted a Master at Antwerp in 1528 and made a burgher of the same city in 1536 under the name of Jan van Amstel Aertssonne. Van Amstel's signature has been identified as that of the Brunswick Monogrammist, an artist active in the second quarter of the 16th century, who painted the *Feeding of the Five Thousand* (Brunswick, Braunschweigisches Landesmuseum) and several small paintings, either Biblical subjects, or brothel scenes hitherto wrongly attributed to Jan Sanders van Hemessen. Attempts to attribute some of these works to Marie Bessemers (also known as Mayken Verhulst, *c.* 1520–*c.* 1600), a miniaturist, the wife of Pieter Coecke and mother-in-law of Pieter Bruegel the Elder, met with serious objections. As a precursor of Bruegel, Van Amstel shows a poetic sensibility in his handling of landscape and in his treatment of light. His influence appears to have been wide: in perspective and piling up of landscape masses, Pieter Bruegel's famous *Calvary* (Vienna, Kunsthistorisches Museum) owes much to Van Amstel's Louvre representation of the subject. Pieter Aertsen and Gillis Mostaert (1534–98) were others whose art derived something from Van Amstel's work.

ANDHRA PERIOD. *See* **INDIAN ART.**

ANDREA DEL CASTAGNO, Andrea di Bartolo di Bargilla, *called* (*c.* 1421/23, Castagno, near Florence—1457, Florence), Italian painter. He probably worked with Fra Filippo Lippi and had the opportunity of studying Masaccio before executing, at the Palazzo del Podestà in Florence, a *damnatio* of Cosimo de' Medici's adversaries hanged by their heels (1440). In 1442 he was in Venice, where—together with a certain Francesco Faenza—he decorated the apse of the old church of S. Zaccaria with energetic frescoes representing God the Father, the four Evangelists, St. Zacharias, and St. John the Baptist. Castagno then returned to Tuscany (probably in 1443) and, in the chapel of the Castello del Trebbio in the Val delle Sieci, painted a fresco of the *Madonna and Child* (Florence, Coll. Contini Bonacossi), who are shown with St. John the Baptist, St. Jerome, and the children of the donor against an extraordinary background of brocade. Between 1445 and 1450 he decorated the monastery of S. Apollonia, Florence, with the *Last Supper* and three scenes from the Passion—monumental frescoes that created a sensation. He also painted portraits—the *Portrait of a Man* (Washington, D.C., National Gallery) is no doubt by him—and gave a new impulse to secular painting. In a loggia of the Villa Carducci Pandolfini at Legnaia he depicted, under a painted frame, a series of over life-size *Famous Men and Women* (they have since been removed to the refectory of S. Apollonia). From 1451 Andrea continued the frescoes at S. Egidio abandoned five years earlier by Domenico Veneziano. But it was at the Annunziata in 1454–55 that he gave evidence of the full measure of his artistic force, with a *St. Julian* that recalls somewhat the light tones of Veneziano; a *Trinity*, represented in an extraordinary foreshortening; and, in the chapel of Ottaviano de' Medici, a fresco of *Lazarus, Martha, and the Magdalen* (lost). In 1456 he executed for S. Maria del Fiore (Florence Cathedral) an equestrian portrait of Niccolò da Tolentino as a pendant, on the same wall, to Paolo Uccello's equestrian portrait of *Sir John Hawkwood* painted 20 years earlier. The portrait marks the apogee of his style, a late stage of which is exemplified in the tense and moving *Crucifixion* of the Convento degli Angeli (now in the Cenacolo di S. Apollonia, Florence). Andrea died in mid-career, struck down by the plague in 1457.

Andrea developed with greater consistency than Uccello, though not without certain limitations, the plastic principles of the new style. The energy and the relief of the recently restored frescoes in Venice derive clearly from Masaccio and Donatello. He gave careful emphasis to the movement of bodies and to facial expression: the tension in his scenes is always as dramatic as that of his faces. The *Famous Men and Women* provide a good example of the resulting force and solidity: his *Dante* and *Pippo Spano* are not easily forgotten. Their type derives as much from the pictorial tradition as from statuary.

ANDREA DEL SARTO, Andrea d'Angiolo, *called* (1486, Florence—1531, Florence), Italian painter who, with Raphael and Leonardo da Vinci, was one of the most significant representatives of Florentine Classicism. Son of Angiolo di Francesco, a tailor, whence the name Sarto, Andrea began as a goldsmith's apprentice and was then taught for several years by Piero di Cosimo. Like all Florentines, he studied the cartoons of Leonardo and Michelangelo and learned a great deal from the soft and veiled transitions practiced by the former. Andrea's earliest work is the grave and sustained *Noli me tangere* (*c.* 1510) at the Uffizi, Florence. In 1510 he decorated the walls of the entrance to the Annunziata with the *Miracles of S. Filippo Benizzi*. But his first major commission was to decorate in *terra verde* the little Chiostro dello Scalzo, Florence. He began in 1511 with the *Baptism of Christ* and finished in 1526 with the *Birth of St. John the Baptist*. In 1517 he painted for the nuns of the convent of S. Francesco the *Madonna of the Harpies* (1517; Uffizi). Invited to the French court by François I in 1518, Andrea did a portrait of the dauphin and painted the Louvre *Charity*, which reflects again the same slightly melancholy ease. In 1521 he attempted the grand manner by painting a historical fresco, *Caesar Receiving Tribute*, for Poggio a Caiano, followed in 1524 by the *Deposition* (Florence, Palazzo Pitti), and in 1525 by the *Madonna del Sacco* (Florence, Chiostro dei Morti), an exceptionally skillful composition. In the Pitti *Assumption of the Virgin* (1530) Andrea begins to exaggerate the effects of drapery and reflected light. Finally, mention should be made of his penetrating portraits (*Self-Portrait*, 1486; Palazzo Pitti), which reveal, in all their modesty and earnestness, the personality of the artist as much as that of his sitters.

ANDREA DI BARTOLO. *See* **BARTOLO DI FREDI.**

ANDREA DI CIONE. *See* **ORCAGNA.**

ANDREA PISANO, Andrea da Pontedera, *called* (*c.* 1290, Pontedera, near Pisa—1348, Orvieto), Italian sculptor, architect, and goldsmith, son of a lawyer, Ugolino Nini. We know nothing of his activities before 1330, when he was invited to Florence to cast the south bronze door of the Baptistery (1330–36), but he was probably trained at Pisa as a sculptor and goldsmith. In 1340 he was put in charge of work at the duomo in Florence, and in 1347 he was given the same appointment at Orvieto Cathedral. The last document in which he appears is dated 1348; in it his functions are devolved on his son Nino.

Andrea's reputation rests on the famous bronze door of the Baptistery and the bas-reliefs that decorate the base of the Campanile (the construction of which he supervised from 1337 to 1343) of Florence Cathedral. The Baptistery door comprises 28 panels, 14 on each leaf. The 20 upper panels illustrate scenes from the life of St. John the Baptist, a subject taken directly from the mosaics of the Baptistery itself, while the eight lower panels represent the Cardinal and Theological Virtues. Andrea's art, with its grace and charm, has the refinement of a goldsmith's work. At the Campanile, where he deservedly succeeded Giotto as *capomaestro* (master of the works), Andrea respected the general design of the old master, who had planned an encyclopedic ensemble in the French manner, grouping together 54 scenes from Genesis, allegories of the Sciences, Arts, and Crafts on the lower register, and of the Planets, Virtues, Liberal Arts, and Sacraments on the upper register. It is generally agreed that Andrea did not put his hand to the reliefs of the upper register, even those executed during his supervision as architect. On the other hand, there are grounds for attributing to him the 21 reliefs of the lower register; of these, Agriculture, Sculpture, and the Art of Weaving are among the most celebrated and satisfying achievements of Florentine sculpture. Influenced by the precious style of French 14th-century ivories, Andrea Pisano succeeded in bringing an incomparable technical perfection to the service of plastic beauty.

Andrea Pisano. *Art of Weaving.* 1337–43. Campanile of Florence Cathedral. *Photo Alinari-Giraudon.*

ANDROUET DU CERCEAU, family of French architects of the 16th–18th centuries, whose principal members were:

JACQUES THE ELDER (*c.* 1510, Paris?—*c.* 1585, Geneva or Annecy?). None of his known works has survived. He was primarily an engraver and draftsman who did numerous drawings based on the ancient buildings that he had studied enthusiastically during a stay in Italy from 1530 to 1534. One of his best-known publications is *Les plus excellents bâtiments de France* (1576 and 1579), which contains views of the principal châteaux of the time. There is good reason to suppose that Jacques was able to realize some of his projects. An example is the château of Verneuil-sur-Oise (1565–75) for Count Philippe of Boulainvilliers, which anticipated the great architectural complexes of the 17th century. The château at Charleval is another, begun for Charles IX in 1571 but left unfinished. His work represents an aspect of French Mannerism characterized by an excessive use of ornamentation, as can be seen in his engravings for Verneuil and Charleval.

BAPTISTE (1544/47–1590), eldest son of Jacques, worked with his father on the château at Charleval in 1575. He drew up the plans for the Pont-Neuf, Paris, which was not completed until after his death. He was appointed chief superintendant of buildings for Henri III at the death of Jean Bullant, and in 1578 he succeeded Pierre Lescot as superintendant of the Louvre buildings. Baptiste worked at the château of Verneuil and has often been credited with the construction in 1578 of the Hôtel d'Angoulême (now the Hôtel Lamoignon), Paris.

JACQUES THE YOUNGER (*c.* 1550–1614), second son of Jacques. In 1594 he was appointed

Jean Androuet du Cerceau. Horseshoe staircase at the château of Fontainebleau. 1632–34. *Photo Jean Roubier, Paris.*

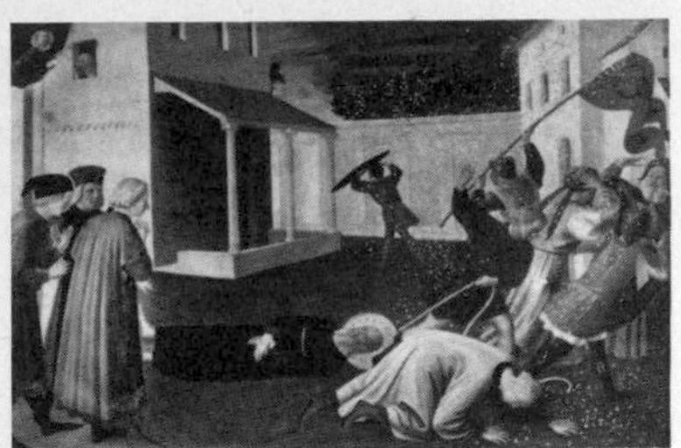

Fra Angelico. *Martyrdom of St. Mark*. Predella, Linaiuoli Altarpiece. Detail. 1433. Museo di S. Marco, Florence. *Photo Anderson-Giraudon.*

Fra Angelico (and pupils). *The Meal of S. Domenico Served by Angels*. Predella, altarpiece on the Coronation of the Virgin. *c.* 1430–40. Louvre, Paris.

Fra Angelico. *Birth and Calling of St. Nicholas of Bari*. Predella, Perugia Altarpiece. Detail. 1437. Vatican Museum. *Photo Anderson-Giraudon.*

Fra Angelico. *Lamentation of Christ*. 1440–45. Museo di S. Marco, Florence. *Photo Giraudon, Paris.*

architect of the Louvre and, in fulfillment of his functions, seems to have been put in charge of building the western part of the Grande Galerie from the Pavillon de Flore to the present Pavillon de Lesdiguières (1594–1607; Louis Métezeau is probably responsible for the eastern part). Jacques shared his father's work at Charleval and Verneuil.

JEAN (*c.* 1590–*c.* 1650), son of Baptiste. In 1617 he was appointed architect to the king. He worked on the walls of Paris and was put in charge of building the Pont-au-Change (1639). He constructed some of the finest mansions of Paris at the beginning of the 17th century, notably the Hôtel de Bretonvilliers in the Île St-Louis (1637–43; destroyed), the Hôtel de Mayenne (*c.* 1613), and the Hôtel Sully (1624–29). He also built the splendid horseshoe staircase at the château of Fontainebleau (1632–34). In the tradition of his family, his work gives great prominence to decorative elements.

ANGELICO, Guido di Pietro, *called* Fra Giovanni da Fiesole *or* Fra (*c.* 1400, Vicchio, Tuscany—1455, Rome), Italian painter. Guido di Pietro was born in the valley of the Mugello in Tuscany. In 1407 he and his brother Benedetto entered the Dominican convent in Fiesole. After a year's novitiate Guido took the vows under the name of Fra Giovanni da Fiesole.

In 1449 he became prior of his convent with the full assent of Cosimo de'Medici; he held this office for three years.

The earliest record of Fra Giovanni as a painter dates only from 1432, when he painted an *Annunciation* for the Servi in Brescia (lost), and the circumstances of his training remain obscure. The following year the sculptor Lorenzo Ghiberti was engaged in designing the marble frame for the altarpiece commissioned from Fra Giovanni by the Arte dei Linaiuoli, or Linen Guild (*Linaiuoli Madonna*; Florence, Museo di S. Marco). This imposing work shows to what extent Fra Angelico was receptive to new ideas in Florence: the majestic and firm silhouettes of the two St. Johns are no less revealing in this respect than the clear spatial articulation of the scenes in the predella. The same applies to the series of altarpieces he painted between 1435 and 1440, with their now traditional arrangement of the Virgin flanked by saints—as, for example, the altarpiece for S. Domenico in Cortona, very similar to the Linaiuoli one, or that for S. Domenico in Perugia (1437; Perugia, Galleria Nazionale dell'Umbria). Three works, now in the Museo di S. Marco, datable to the years after the return of Cosimo de' Medici and illustrating the theme of the *sacra conversazione*, show an even more solid organization of space: the one intended for the convent of S. Vincenzo d'Annalena (Museo di S. Marco), where it was not installed until 1453; that for the high altar of S. Marco, with the Virgin flanked by eight angels and eight saints; and that for a Franciscan church at Bosco ai Frati (before 1445). The *Coronation of the Virgin* in the Louvre, Paris (*c.* 1430–40), and the *Annunciation* at Cortona (Museo del Gesù), with its magnificent rhythm, are thought to be from the same period. The large *Deposition*, painted around 1440 for S. Trinita (Museo di S. Marco), with its landscape, its figures, and its architectural décor, shows the artist at his most ambitious.

When the convent of S. Marco was restored, it fell to Fra Angelico to supervise its decoration, cell by cell; he is likely to have employed several assistants. Summoned to Rome in 1447, probably by Eugenius IV, to paint a chapel in the Vatican, Fra Angelico took with him several assistants, among whom was Benozzo Gozzoli. He also agreed to spend his summers in Orvieto to paint a *Last Judgment* in the chapel of S. Brizio. But he went only once, and then returned to Florence to minister to the needs of his convent. He died in 1455 in Rome, where he was buried in the Dominican church of S. Maria sopra Minerva. The humanist Lorenzo Valla wrote the epitaph: "For some works I shall survive on earth and for others in heaven."

Fra Angelico's earliest training was probably as a miniaturist and illuminator. He seems close to Lorenzo Monaco in the delicacy of his colors and a candor that does not exclude preciousness. There is even a "Gothic" aspect in works such as the reliquary from S. Maria Novella (mentioned by Vasari), with its background of gold guilloche and its elongated figures, or the Vatican *Madonna*. He delighted in arabesques and delicate

Fra Angelico. *Annunciation. c.* 1440–47. Convent of S. Marco, Florence. *Photo Bulloz, Paris.*

contours but was no less alive to volume and amplitude. In the *Coronation of the Virgin*, for instance, the figures are not arranged vertically but in depth, along a sharp curve; the elongated silhouettes and the stylized drapery seem to take on a new value. The same applies to the *Virgin Enthroned with Eight Angels and Eight Saints* (S. Marco), in which the throne of the Virgin stands against a spacious background of greenery in the Garden of Paradise.

Though his training gave him a greater affinity with Masolino, after 1430 Fra Angelico was influenced by Masaccio's frescoes in the Brancacci Chapel and retained something of Masaccio's gravity. In the Linaiuoli Altarpiece, with its Virgin who is both sculptural and pretty, he is close to the style of Ghiberti. Architectural features contribute to the firm composition of the Cortona *Annunciation*. The picture shows a loggia whose thin columns recall Michelozzo, Cosimo de' Medici's architect. The perspective of the portico reveals a regular succession of intervals that frame the figures and expand the space around them. The effect created by the even diffusion of light justifies a comparison with Domenico Veneziano, who was working at S. Egidio about 1440 and whose *Madonna di S. Lucia* probably dates from 1445.

In the 15th century it is almost a rule for the panels of the predella to show a more spontaneous manner, sometimes even a popular note. The greater freedom of the artist here encouraged invention and Fra Angelico, like any good Tuscan storyteller, often made delightful improvisations.

The S. Marco cycle is enough to remind us how wrong it would be to interpret Fra Angelico's art outside its Dominican context. Here he was not speaking to the world at large but to those withdrawn from it. The themes treated in the cycle, which is largely the work of studio hands, are deliberately reduced and neutralized. In S. Marco, Fra Angelico is still obviously attached, in spite of the setting, to Trecento narrative; the contrast between the externally "modern" forms and the emotional tenderness of the figures emphasizes his isolation and his originality.

ANTOINE, Jacques-Denis (1733, Paris—1801, Paris), French architect, from a family of Parisian artisans. The circumstances of his apprenticeship are not known. In competition with other architects he was chosen to construct the Hôtel des Monnaies (the Mint) in Paris, defeating his brilliant colleagues François Dominique Barreau de Chefdeville (b. 1725) and Étienne-Louis Boullée. The building was erected between 1768 and 1774.

The success of this building brought Antoine many commissions in France and abroad. From 1782 he assisted Pierre Desmaisons (1724–1800) in the reconstruction of the Palais de Justice, Paris, which had been destroyed by fire four years earlier. He remodeled the Salle des Pas Perdus (waiting hall), and built the grand staircase and the archives depository. Still extant in Paris are his Hôtel de Narbonne (*c.* 1785), as well as a long row of buildings unified by a common order in Rue St-Honoré. He also built the beautiful Château de Herces, near Houdan (1772); the Château de Buisson d'Osmoy, Eure (1781); the Mint in Bern (1790–92); and parts of the Duke of Berwick's palace in Madrid.

ANTONELLO DA MESSINA (*c.* 1430, Messina, Sicily—1479, Messina), Italian painter of the Early Renaissance, unique in his stylistic fusion of Flemish feeling for detail with Italian amplification of form. Trained in Naples and thus exposed to a variety of artistic influences, Antonello early traveled to Milan, where he remained until about 1456, and where he perhaps came into contact with Petrus Christus, heir to the traditions of the Van Eycks. The *Crucifixion* now at Sibiù, Rumania, dates from this time. Between 1465, when he executed the *Salvator Mundi* (London, National Gallery), and 1473, the date of the *Polyptych of S. Gregorio* (Messina, Museo Nazionale), the only securely dated work is the *Ecce Homo* of 1470 (New York, Metropolitan Museum). It is the first of a series of pictures on this theme; another is in Vienna (1474; Priv. Coll.). Concurrently, Antonello painted a remarkable set of male portraits, including those in Cefalù, Pavia (Museo Malaspina), and New York (Metropolitan Museum, Altman Coll.). The *Portrait of a Condottiere* at the Louvre is signed and dated 1475, the *Portrait of a Man* in Turin (Coll. Trivulzio), 1476. In both, the manly face, painted with great authority, acquires strength by its contrast with the dark background. During the period 1465–73, he probably visited Rome, where he may have come in contact with the work of Piero della Francesca. In 1474 he was commissioned to paint an *Annunciation* (now at Syracuse, Museo di Palazzo Bellomo) for the church of S. Maria dell'Annunziata in the Palazzo Acreide. The following year he was in Venice, where in 1475–76 he executed a large altarpiece for the church of S. Cassiano, today known only from fragments and copies in Vienna (Kunsthistorisches Museum). He is documented as spending his final years in Messina.

Antonello trained in Naples with Colantonio (active 1440–70), whose work shows Flemish, Provençal, Spanish, and French influences. In particular, the pupil acquired a grounding in the Flemish style, which included a thorough knowledge of the art of Van Eyck. Northern influence is clearly discernible in the robust naturalism, articulation of space, and figures of the Sibiù *Crucifixion*. Perhaps the most important technique Antonello learned from his Northern masters was painting in oil, which he probably introduced to Italy. His mastery of the new medium is responsible for the exquisite finish of his pictures.

The Flemish elements become less pronounced during the period of Antonello's greatest activity, when he was attempting to give his compositions a more Italianate monumentality and to simplify his forms, probably under the influence of Piero della Francesca. In the *Salvator Mundi* he broke with the Flemish tradition. His changes in composition led to a new harmony, which found magnificent expression in the *Madonna and Child* (London, National Gallery). The well-known Palermo *Virgin of the Annunciation* (Galleria Nazionale) is stylistically close to the *Salvator*, especially in the perspective rendering of the hands; this suggests that they were painted about the same time. The intense light and the violent relief of the forms almost anticipate Caravaggio.

The force of Expressionist inspiration in Antonello can be seen in his treatment of the theme of the *Ecce Homo*. He made it the image of suffering by stamping it with the unchanging, universal features of human distress, to the smallest detail. The series of male portraits offers a parallel illustration of Antonello's increasingly reductive style and the growing skill of his psychological analysis. In the *Polyptych of S. Gregorio*, perspective is used to organize the composition. The three main figures appear in a unified space. The Syracuse *Annunciation* appears to have been inspired by Van Eyck. Antonello's interest in Flemish motifs has returned and can also be observed in the pictures painted after his arrival in Venice in the spring of 1475: the *Crucifixion* (Antwerp, Musée Royal des Beaux-Arts) and the powerful *Pietà* (Venice, Museo Correr). In the famous *St. Sebastian* (Dresden, Gemäldegalerie), the monumentality of the saint's figure is emphasized by its central position and the reductive modeling, which recall the techniques of Piero and Giovanni Bellini, both of whom were influenced by Antonello and who, in turn, left their mark on his later work. In the London *Crucifixion* the placement of architectural forms in the landscape background is handled with particular smoothness. Antonello's remarkable feeling for synthesis appears in a less purely intellectual manner than Piero's. This lesson was not lost in Venice, where it was adopted and perpetuated into the mainstream of European painting by the Bellini and their followers.

ANTONIO VENEZIANO, Antonio Francesco da Venezia, *called* (before 1340, Venice—after 1387, Florence?), Italian painter. He came to Florence in his youth, after receiving some training in his native town, and was the pupil of Taddeo Gaddi. In 1370 he was paid for some paintings in Siena Cathedral. Antonio went to Pisa in 1384 to work on the decoration of the Camposanto (south wing) and, from 1384 to 1386, completed a cycle on the *Legend of St. Raynerius*, begun by Andrea da Firenze and interrupted since 1377. The three scenes painted by Antonio are in the lower register; they were already damaged and altered by repainting before World War II, and suffered from the incendiary raid in 1943. Without rejecting the Giottesque tradition, Antonio gave it a more popular and naturalistic direction.

ANUSKIEWICZ, Richard (b. 1930, Erie, Pennsylvania), American painter. He received his degrees and his training in art at the Cleveland Institute of Art and at Yale University in New Haven, Connecticut, where his studies with Josef Albers were instrumental in defining the direction he was to take as a painter. Anuskiewicz painted precise geometric abstractions in which the chromatic combinations often derive their bewildering retinal effects from the artist's own preoccupation with and exploration of scientific optics. This style has been called Op art because its flat colors and geometric patterns are employed in ways that deliberately activate and confuse the visual response.

Anuskiewicz tended to favor either unmodulated black-and-white patterns, or the dynamic properties of contrasting and juxtaposed reds, turquoise, and chartreuse. *Convexity II* (1966; New York, Sidney Janis Gallery) is typical of his painting of graphlike striations in red, blue, and green. In this work, he causes a rhomboid placed within a square to appear to project out beyond the plane surface by the particular deployment of the lines, and by the degree of brilliance of the colors. In 1967 Anuskiewicz augmented his paintings on canvas and board with a series of three-dimensional painted cubes set on mirror bases. In these new works, he extended the buckling and warping effects of the surface patterns into both actual and illusory space.

APPEL, Karel (b. 1921, Amsterdam), Dutch painter. After studying for three years at the Royal Academy in Amsterdam (1940–43), Appel sought to develop an impulsive formal language based directly on life, in reaction against the geometric academicism inherited from the De Stijl movement. In 1948, with Guillaume Corneille (Cornelis van Beverloo) and Constant (Constant Nieuwenhuys, b. 1920), he founded the "experimental group" and the revue *Reflex*, which were soon to be absorbed into the Cobra movement. It was in Paris—where he exhibited for the first time in 1949 and settled the following year—that Appel mastered his creative power. In his work, gesture is never gratuitous or uncertain, but has its basis in a natural violence that may be seen in its most naked form in a group of figures dating from 1961, hewn with a hatchet from twisted chunks of olivewood and smeared with paint. This aggressive polychromy is not confined to sculpture, but is used just as brutally in Appel's canvases: red or blue nudes, tragic figures abandoned to the fury of color, or a flaming landscape eviscerated by the sun, exposing the moving, sensual matter of which it is composed. An action painter, Appel gives full rein to his violent Expressionism in numerous mural compositions and also in stained-glass windows.

APPIANI, Andrea (1754, Milan—1817, Milan), Italian Neoclassical painter. His frescoes, commissioned by the Archduke Ferdinand for his villa at Monza in 1789, and his colossal figures in the dome of S. Maria presso S. Celso in Milan (1792–98) brought him fame. As painter to Napoleon I (in his capacity as king of Italy), Appiani made a number of effigies of the emperor and a series of frescoes at the Palazzo Reale in Milan (1808), depicting four Virtues—*Fortitude, Justice, Wisdom,* and *Temperance*. His portraits and his history paintings of scenes from antiquity place him at the head of the Italian Neoclassical school.

ARABIAN PRE-ISLAMIC ART. In contrast with the desert country of central Arabia, southern Arabia (now consisting of Yemen, the Aden Protectorate, Hadhramaut, and Oman) is an ancient center of civilization. It was at the end of the 19th century that archaeologists began to discover the monumental ruins and the lapidary inscriptions that revealed the importance of the ancient kingdoms of Saba, Ma'in, Qataban, and Hadhramaut, which once flourished there. The buildings we know to have existed were at first dated too early and are now

Arabian Pre-Islamic Art. Alabaster statuette of Ammiram. Abyad Kar, 1st century B.C. University Museum, Philadelphia.

Arabian Pre-Islamic Art. Stele depicting a funerary banquet scene. 2nd or 3rd century A.D. Louvre, Paris. *Photo André Vigneau-Éditions Tel, Paris.*

regarded as evidence of a civilization that existed from the 5th century B.C. They represent a high point of prosperity derived from the development of trading by caravan and the production of aromatics for a world that now stretched from one end of the Mediterranean to the other. Internecine wars between Jewish sympathizers and Christians led to the intervention of the Ethiopians, then of the Persians, between the 5th and 6th centuries A.D. As a result there was a decline in the prosperity of this civilization, which was systematically annihilated with the arrival of Islam in the 7th century A.D.

In northwest Arabia, on the caravan route that linked the southern Arabian towns (and, through them, India and east Africa) to the Mediterranean via Petra and the port of Gaza, the kingdoms of Dedan and Lihyan developed at an undetermined time between the 6th century B.C. and the beginning of the Christian era. At Dedan, now the oasis of el-Ula, was found a large statue of a king, in an Egyptian-influenced style; and the rupestrian tombs of Khereybe, its necropolis, differ specifically from the Nabataean rupestrian tombs (*see* HELLENISTIC ART; ROMAN ART), which were common even in this region, particularly at Hejra, Madyan, and Quaraiya.

South Arabian art is infinitely richer. During the 10 centuries covered by our documents, we see peripheral influences having a profound effect on the indigenous art, which included altars for incense or libations; funerary steles, or the mask and carved head that were placed in a niche hollowed out of a high stele; votive objects (effigies of bulls, camels, or horses; statues of sitting or standing figures); inscribed plaques offered to the gods, decorated with carved friezes representing the symbolic animals of divinities (ibex, bucrane).

In the ancient period, a Greek-influenced style appeared in the execution of monumental inscriptions and in the Athenian type of coinage; but architecture, like sculpture, was mainly influenced by Persian Achaemenid models (*see* ACHAEMENIAN ART). This became increasingly apparent when the American excavations of 1952 at Marib, the capital of Saba, discovered the portico of the great oval temple and its propylaea. The Persian decoration with blind windows found there includes elements that were to be widely exploited in all southern Arabian art, becoming gradually more complicated, and that are very characteristic: a group of receding panels with transverse bands composed of a number of horizontal grooves, bordered with a line of denticles at the bottom.

The Hellenistic influence appeared in the 1st century A.D. in statuary and architectural decoration, but in a style borrowed at second hand from Syria and the Parthian regions. The Hellenistic flowering of the 2nd century A.D., with its tall bronze statues and vine-leaf decoration (sometimes even cupids and bacchic animals), was followed in the 4th century A.D. by a new style that derived from the eastern taste for decorative effect. The champlevé technique, with deep shadows hollowed out between motifs left flat and then line-drawn, developed into a precursor of the Byzantine style. The bas-relief with figures was introduced in the Hellenistic period; but from the 3rd century A.D., the modeling and drawing became rather barbaric; the decoration of the votive or funerary steles was now descriptive and depicted figures in the midst of their everyday activities: children, caravan drivers, camel riders, warriors.

The minor arts, which have been insufficiently studied, are represented by alabaster utensils, gold jewelry, seals of different Mesopotamian styles, and, most remarkable of all, the small bronze oil lamps with their leaping ibexes.

ARABO-MUSSULMAN ART. *See* **ISLAMIC ART.**

ARAMAEAN ART. The Aramaeans, first mentioned in tablets from Mari (18th century B.C.), were of Semitic stock, originally nomads in the Syro-Arabian desert; gradually they settled into several distinct groups. One of these occupied the area in Lower Mesopotamia that was later to be Chaldaea; another annexed a region known as Bit-Adini on the middle Euphrates in Aram-Naharaim. Under Ben-Hadad (9th century B.C.), Damascus became the seat of a powerful dynasty, as did Hamath on the Orontes. Finally, after the fall of the New Hittite Empire, there appeared the kingdom of Samal with Zincirli as its center (8th century B.C.). This fragmentation proved disastrous and, in the 8th century B.C., all the territories under Aramaean control fell to the Assyrians, then passed successively to the Neo-Babylonians, the Achaemenids, and finally the Seleucids.

An opinion of what is properly Aramaean art can be formed only after the rejection of all monuments obviously marked by foreign influences—such as a number of reliefs from Bit-Adini. It is between Aleppo and Damascus, in the heart of Aram, that one can expect to find indisputably Aramaean work.

Genuine examples include a stone head from Qatna (near Homs); a headless torso from Sfira (near Aleppo); and particularly the head of a god from Djabbul (near Aleppo), a high-ranking divinity with tense features, thin lips, and lined cheeks (2nd half of the 2nd millennium B.C.; Paris, Louvre). Sheikh Saad, a small village south of Damascus, is the provenance of a lion (early 1st millennium B.C.) of rare authority and power, so skillfully has the sculptor rendered the slow, irresistible advance of the animal on its prey (Damascus,

Aramaean Art. Hazael, king of Damascus. Found at Hadatu. 9th century B.C. Louvre, Paris. *Photo Josse-Lalance.*

Aramaean Art. Head of a divinity. 2nd half of the 2nd millennium B.C., Djabbul, near Aleppo. Louvre, Paris.

Alexander Archipenko. *Carrousel Pierrot.* 1913. Solomon R. Guggenheim Museum, New York.

Museum). The same compact force characterizes the bulls from Hadatu (8th century B.C.), much more convincing in this respect than the lions from that site. Rougher in treatment are the statue of King Idrimi from Alalakh (London, British Museum), probably Aramaean in spite of its cuneiform inscription, and the stele of Melkart discovered near Aleppo.

Also Aramaean are the stele from the kingdom of Samal (8th century B.C.), with King Barrekub represented in the Assyrian manner (Berlin, Vorderasiatisches Museum), and two steles from Neirab (near Aleppo), with the figures of Sinzirban and Agbar, priests of the moon god (7th–6th century B.C.; both Louvre).

Skillful as stonecutters, the Aramaeans were also excellent sculptors in bronze, producing statuettes of gods in large numbers. One of the best of these, found at Qatna, portrays a high-ranking divinity sitting in a long bordered dress (Louvre).

The Aramaeans also displayed great talent in ivory work. In 1928 the ruins of the palace at Hadatu yielded a remarkable set of ivory decorations for furniture, many of which are now in the Louvre. Their provenance is established by an Aramaic inscription on one of the panels, which mentions the name of Hazael, king of Damascus. If Damascus is the place of manufacture, the artistic derivation is composite, with many foreign themes—Egyptian (sphinxes, two divinities protecting the Horus child with their wings, two winged gods binding a sheaf of papyrus); Aegean (the "woman at the window," a cow licking its young); and Anatolian (lion heads). On the other hand, a long-haired, bearded personage with hands clasped, shown in a full-faced view (Louvre), can only be an Aramaean and might well be King Hazael himself. Thus with its reliefs, its bronzes, and its ivories, ancient Syria, the Aram of history, finds itself amply documented.

ARCHIPENKO, Alexander (1887, Kiev—1964, New York), Russian-born American sculptor noted as creator of "sculpto-painting" and other new techniques. After studying at the Kiev Art School, he went to Paris in 1908. He opened new paths in sculpture by piercing the mass so that space could penetrate it (*Walking Woman*). The influence of Cubism was translated into geometric, often triangular forms that were linked by harmonious curves; a typically elegant example is the *Gondolier* of 1914. With his *Medrano* constructions, Archipenko began to use a variety of materials (wood, glass, metal) and to paint the base and forms in brilliant colors.

In 1914 Archipenko began to develop his "sculpto-painting," in which some parts are in relief, others painted. In his pure sculpture, however, his constant preoccupation remained the contrast between convex and concave forms, volume and hollow.

Archipenko spent the years 1921–23 in Berlin, then went to the United States, where he became a citizen in 1928. He invented mobile works called "Archipentura" in 1924: canvases divided horizontally into narrow slats set in motion by hidden motors. He taught at the University of Washington in 1935–36 and later at the New Bauhaus in Chicago. In 1939 he settled in New York, where he operated a highly regarded school of sculpture.

ARCIMBOLDO *or* **ARCIMBOLDI,** Giuseppe (1527/30, Milan—1593, Milan), Italian painter. In the early part of his career (1549–58), he is recorded as having worked on Milan Cathedral, where he was engaged on such tasks as the repainting of the façade (1557). From 1562 he was employed, in succession, by the Hapsburg emperors Ferdinand I, Maximilian II, and Rudolf II, working in Vienna and Prague until 1587, when he returned to Milan. Arcimboldo is best known for his fantastically composed heads, in which the shape of the face is suggested by the skillful combination of fruits, vegetables, fishes, and shells, as well as all sorts of everyday objects. The earliest signed and dated examples are the allegories of *Summer* and *Winter* (both 1563; both Vienna, Kunsthistorisches Museum). The same museum possesses allegories of *Fire* and *Water*, both dating from 1566. He also designed costumes for various types of court pageants and festivities. The Gabinetto dei Disegni e Stampe in Florence's Uffizi has about 150 of his lightly colored ink drawings, done in 1585 for a winter tournament and dedicated to Rudolf II. Several of Arcimboldo's most interesting works were portraits of members of the imperial court and their servants; these include *The Librarian* and *The Gardener*, or the *Portrait of Rudolf II in the Guise of Vertumnus* (both Skokloster, Sweden, Coll. Baron Von Essen).

Giuseppe Arcimboldo. *The Librarian.* Coll. Baron Von Essen, Skokloster, Sweden.

ARDEMÁNS, Teodoro (1664, Madrid—1726, Madrid), Spanish architect and painter. Since he had an aptitude for the sciences, he studied mathematics, but he also learned painting under Antonio de Pereda and Claudio Coello and studied architecture. Although he was appointed painter to the king in 1704, he did not produce much in this capacity; the *Battle of Lepanto* (1721; Madrid, Bishop's Palace) and *St. Barbara* (1723; Madrid, Museo Lázaro Galdiano) have been identified as his. He was essentially an architect, and in that capacity an important official of the court and city of Madrid. This explains how he came to write two works that do him great credit: *Declaración y extensión sobre las ordenanzas de Madrid, que escribió Juan de Torija, y de las que se practicaban en Toledo y Sevilla* ("Statement and Discourse on the Laws of Madrid, written by Juan de Torija, and On Those Practiced in Toledo and Seville"), 1719, and *Fluencias de la tierra y curso subterráneo de las aguas* ("River Sources of the Earth and the Subterranean Flow of Waters"), 1724. He was the architect for the cathedrals of Toledo and Granada (1689–91), and for the Town Hall (1700) and Alcázar in Madrid

(1702). About 1690 he reconstructed the doorways and towers of the Ayuntamiento of Madrid. In 1722 he submitted his designs for the church of S. Millán. He was also commissioned to supervise Pedro de Ribera's construction of the Toledo Bridge across the Manzanares, to the west of the capital (1719). Ardemáns built the original palace at la Granja (1721–23), which has survived through all the later reconstructions. To the west, facing Segovia, he set an important chapel, inspired by the Alpajés Church at Aranjuez. (The present façade is not his; it was erected by an Italian, Andrea Procaccini [1671–1734] between 1729 and 1734.)

ARMENIAN ART. The monuments of pagan Armenia have almost entirely disappeared; the only important remains are the ruins of the Ionic peripteral temple at Garni and the foundations of a palace, also at Garni, where a pavement mosaic representing water divinities and bearing Greek inscriptions was recently uncovered. With the establishment of Christianity in the beginning of the 4th century A.D., religious architecture made rapid strides. The oldest extant buildings (5th and 6th centuries A.D.) are vaulted basilicas in the Syrian style, with one or three aisles. The excavations under the cathedral of Echmiadzin have revealed, however, that the earlier church, erected in the 5th century A.D., was already in the form of a cross inscribed in a square, with projecting axial niches. From the end of the 6th century A.D. the centralized domed church, with a conical roof over the dome, was the normal type.

The plans and elevations offer numerous variations. The simplest form is that of the square with a dome on squinches over the central part abutted by four vaulted niches, as at Agrak, near Tekor. By an increase in the number of niches, this quatrefoil became an almost circular polygonal building (Zoravar church near Eghvard). Elsewhere, subsidiary niches on the diagonal axes increased the number of supports of the dome, while small rooms at the four corners of the church stressed the rectangular plan (Echmiadzin, St. Hrip'simé). When the dome rested on free-standing supports, it was abutted by barrel vaults, rather narrow at Bagaran, but wider in churches with a cross inscribed in a rectangle (Cathedral of Mren) or in a trefoil (churches at T'alin).

New modes of construction appeared at the end of the 10th century. At the cathedral of Ani, built by the architect Trdat, who was invited to Constantinople to restore the fallen dome of Hagia Sophia, the pillars that support the dome on pendentives have clusters of engaged columns; and the vaults as well as the arches are pointed. The Shepherd's Chapel at Ani is one of the earliest examples of an ogival structure. In succeeding centuries, powerful intersecting arches supported the stone ceiling in the vast porches of the churches or the refectories of the monasteries.

The severe aspect of the façades is alleviated by the carved decoration, and the important place assigned to monumental sculpture constitutes one of the essential points of difference between Armenian and Byzantine churches. Floral and zoomorphic motifs and geometric ornament surround the doors, windows, and blind arcades of the façades, becoming extremely complex in the 10th century. Figural representations appeared at the same time: busts of saints in medallions; images of Christ and of the Virgin; portraits of the founders of the churches, and at Zvart'nots, even those of the architect and the masons holding their tools. This sculpture reached its highest point in the 10th century at the church of the island of Aght'amar in Lake Van, a unique example in the art of this period—East or West—of a church entirely covered with low relief. In the course of the following centuries, figural representations appeared inside the churches, usually in the form of carved slabs; occasionally figures in high relief stand against the columns. The decoration included also a number of carved steles, the oldest of which date from the 5th and 6th centuries A.D.

There remain but few examples of monumental painting, so the evolution of Armenian painting must be studied in the illuminated manuscripts. The only extant illuminations from the early period are the 6th-century A.D. leaves to be found at the end of the *Gospel of Echmiadzin* of A.D. 989 (Erivan, Armenian S.S.R., Matanderan Government Archives, No. 229); but there is an almost uninterrupted series of works, dated and often signed, from the 10th to the end of the 17th century. In Armenia proper the best examples date from the 10th and 11th centuries. A strong Byzantine influence may be seen in richly decorated 11th-century Gospels produced after the annexation of large sections of the Armenian territory by the Byzantine Empire. In the following centuries the foremost centers were in the new kingdom established in Cilicia, and the art of miniature painting reached its apogee there in the 13th century. In the same period, this activity, interrupted by the Seljuk conquest, revived in Armenia proper, and new schools were established in the mother country as well as in the Armenian settlements abroad. Each school had its own personality, and some produced work of considerable merit, in particular those of the provinces of Siunik' in the 14th century and those of Khizan, south of Lake Van, in the 15th century.

Armenian Art. *Christ.* Relief on west façade, church of Aght'amar. 915–21. *Photo Josephine Powell, Rome.*

Armenian Art. Cathedral of Ani, Turkey. 989–1001. Built by the architect Trdat.

ARMITAGE, Kenneth (b. 1916, Leeds), English sculptor. He studied at the Slade School, London (1937–39), and later was head of the Bath Academy of Art (1946–56). Bronze is Armitage's chosen medium. For him the human figure engaged in unheroic everyday activities remained the proper study of sculpture. He regarded humanity with affection, bringing to it an observation that is detached, compassionate, and at times whimsical and playful. He made his subject the group, shown as a single flattened slab, sometimes resembling a folding screen, each panel of which represents one individual. From this screen emerge impersonalized, knoblike heads, as well as breasts and attenuated limbs (*Seated Group Listening to Music*, 1952). In his later sculpture, Armitage worked increasingly in the round.

ARMORY SHOW. Properly called the International Exhibition of Modern Art, the show was held at the 69th Regiment Armory in New York from February 17 to March 15, 1913. The idea for this now famous exhibition originated with the 1910 Independents Show in New York, which was an unjuried exhibition of American painting that attempted to provide a showcase for native artists who were being neglected by an art market still limited to the Old Masters and to certain established American and foreign painters. In 1911 the artists Walt Kuhn, Jerome Myers, and Elmer Livingstone MacRae (1875–1955) began discussing the possibility of a large invitational exhibition with their dealer, the landscape painter Henry Fitch Taylor (1853–1925). Later that year the idea was realized with the formation of the Association of American Painters and Sculptors, an organization whose original members included both conservative academicians and realists as well as radically oriented artists. As its president, the society chose Arthur B. Davies, who was familiar with both European and American modernist tendencies. Walt Kuhn became the group's publicist, and thus the association had two leaders committed to a program that would guarantee an exhibition with an international scope and liberal leanings.

The Armory Show was actually two exhibitions in one. The American section included works by the organizers of the show, as well as paintings by some of the more conservative native painters. John Sloan's *Sunday, Women Drying Their Hair* (1912; Andover, Mass., Addison Gallery of American Art, Phillips Academy), William Glackens' *Family Group* (1911; Washington, D. C., Coll. Mr. and Mrs. Ira Glackens), and Alfred Maurer's *Autumn* (before 1913; Coll. Mr. and Mrs. Ira Glackens) were among some of the more notable of the American entries. The European section was meant to demonstrate that the 19th-century French tradition of J. A. D. Ingres, Pierre Puvis de Chavannes, Eugène Delacroix, and Jean-Baptiste Camille Corot was the evolutionary foundation for contemporary modernist developments, and the works exhibited clearly indicated that the Europeans were far more advanced than their American colleagues. Works by Henri Matisse, Odilon Redon, Paul Cézanne, Georges Braque, Pablo Picasso, Wassily Kandinsky, and Marcel Duchamp were major attractions. The European section was predominantly French; German Expressionism was almost completely neglected, other omissions being Italian Futurism and Orphic Cubism. Sculpture was also poorly chosen, although pieces by Auguste Rodin, Aristide Maillol, Constantin Brancusi, and Wilhelm Lehmbruck were included. Thus the show provided a somewhat incomplete panorama of modernist developments.

Critical and public response to the Armory Show was inflammatory and outrageous. The ultimate effect of the exhibition was to force American artists to come to terms with a living tradition and to discard academicism in favor of a new and independent formal order; contemporary art could no longer be neglected and ridiculed in America. Although the museums still largely ignored modernism and the colleges and art schools did not update their curricula, the Armory Show did educate the public and helped to stimulate and expand the art market. In the year immediately following, new galleries opened in rapid succession and American collecting expanded. Before the mid-20th century most of these collections were institutionalized or opened for viewing, making available a permanent showcase for modernism to a once outraged public.

ARNOLFO DI CAMBIO (*c.* 1245, Colle di Val d'Elsa, near Siena—1301/2, Florence), Florentine architect and sculptor, *capomaestro* of Florence Cathedral (S. Maria del Fiore). He is first mentioned in 1265 as assisting Nicola Pisano on the famous pulpit of Siena Cathedral. He seems to have left Nicola's workshop about 1269, and in 1277 he is documented in Rome in the service of Charles d'Anjou. Before that date he had completed the monument of Cardinal Annibaldi (1276; Rome, S. Giovanni in Laterano), and the tomb of Pope Adrian V (d. 1276) in S. Francesco, Viterbo. In 1281 Arnolfo was in Perugia working on a fountain near the Fontana Maggiore of Nicola Pisano (fragments in Perugia, Galleria Nazionale dell'Umbria). The monument of Cardinal de Braye (d. 1282) in S. Domenico, Orvieto, dates from the following year. Arnolfo also worked on the ciboria of the high altars of S. Paolo fuori le Mura (1285) and S. Cecilia in Trastevere (1293), Rome.

After beginning the monument of Boniface VIII (Grotte Vaticane; now dismembered) in 1296, he returned to Florence and started the Palazzo Vecchio, while supervising the early work on the Duomo. The sculptures he executed for the façade are now dispersed: *Dormition of the Virgin* (Berlin), *Birth of the Virgin* (Florence, Uffizi), and *Virgin and Child* (Florence, Opera del Duomo). Two Florentine churches—S. Croce and the Badia—are attributed to Arnolfo.

ARP, Jean *or* Hans (1887, Strasbourg—1966, Locarno), Franco-Swiss poet, painter, and sculptor. Arp published his first

Arnolfo di Cambio. Tomb of Pope Boniface VIII. 1296. Grotte Vaticane. *Photo Leonard von Matt, Buochs.*

Jean Arp. *"Moustache des Machines."* 1965. *Photo E. Bertrand Weill, Paris.*

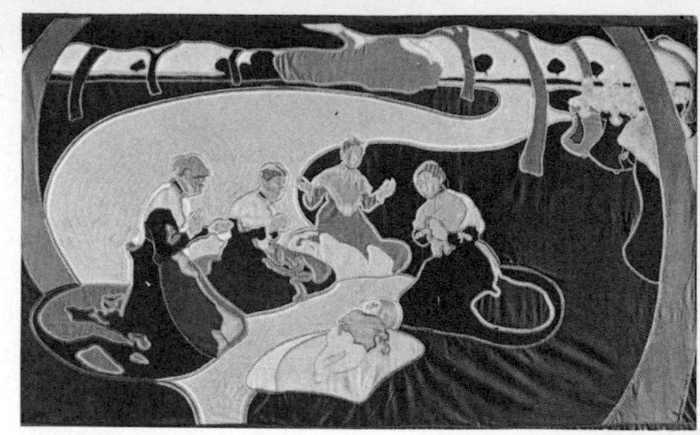

Art Nouveau. Henry van de Velde. *Vigil of the Angels.* 1893. *Photo Kunstgewerbemuseum, Zurich.*

volume of poetry, which strongly shows the influence of German romanticism, in 1904, the year he became a student at the School of Decorative Arts, Strasbourg. After further training in Weimar, he traveled to Paris in 1908 to enroll in the Académie Julian. Within a year he was producing paintings that were almost completely abstract in design. In 1912 he visited Kandinsky in Munich and briefly joined the Blaue Reiter. The following year his abstract work was shown at the first Autumn Exhibition organized by Herwarth Walden, founder of the progressive and influential review *Der Sturm.* Returning to Paris in 1914, he became friendly with Max Jacob, Picasso, Modigliani, and Robert Delaunay. He went to Switzerland at the outbreak of World War I, and there founded the Dada movement with a number of refugee artists and writers among whom were Tristan Tzara, Richard Hulsenbeck, Marcel Janco, Emmy Hennings, and Sophie Taeuber. During this time Arp was producing his first painted wood reliefs, which, with their bold, clean shapes emphasizing line and contour, were highly significant for the future of sculpture. He also executed collages.

After the war Arp brought Dadaist ideas to Cologne. In 1921 he married Sophie Taeuber, and four years later he settled permanently in Meudon, outside Paris, where he took part in the activities of the Surrealist circle for a short period. In 1930 he joined the Cercle et Carré and a year later, the Abstraction-Création group. The beginning of World War II found the artist in Grasse. He again took refuge in Zurich, where, in 1943, Sophie Taeuber died. At the end of the war, he returned to his studio at Meudon.

Arp's few paintings all date from before 1914. In his Dada and Surrealist periods, he concentrated on collages, ink drawings, and reliefs in painted or perforated wood or designed with wool. In 1930 he made his first *papiers déchirés* ("torn papers"), followed some 12 years later by the *papiers froissés* ("crumpled papers"). Arp became irresistibly drawn to sculpture in his mature years, and it was with sculpture that he made his most important artistic contribution. During the 1930s he evolved a series of works of remarkable purity and concentration from very simple motifs—a torso, a bud, a column. To these solid forms, with their undulating contours and dense volumes, he added, after 1959, the hollowed bronzes cut from smooth, flat slabs of metal. He also continued to produce *papiers déchirés, papiers froissés,* and painted reliefs, sometimes substituting duraluminum for wood. His untiring activity extended to engraving, tapestry, and poetry.

ARPINO, Giuseppe Cesari, *called* Cavaliere d' (1568, Arpino, Frosinone prov.—1640, Rome), Italian Mannerist painter. His rise to fame was rapid. From 1588 to 1591 he was in Naples, where he decorated the cupola of the sacristy in the Certosa di S. Martino. In 1596 the Roman Senate commissioned him to decorate the great hall in the Palazzo dei Conservatori; this he did not finish. Among his other Roman works the best known are the painting of *Christ with St. John the Evangelist* in S. Giovanni in Laterano (between 1597 and 1601) and the rather undynamic fresco cycle in the Paolina Chapel of S. Maria Maggiore. The Cavaliere's style is not the product of a deliberate and successful eclecticism, but derives from the decorative Mannerism of the Zuccari, Scipio Pulzone (before 1550–98) and others.

ART NOUVEAU. This term was originally taken from the name of a gallery opened in Paris in December 1895 by Siegfried (known as Samuel) Bing. In the German-speaking countries, the same movement came to be known as the *Jugendstil*, from the name of the Munich review *Jugend* ("Youth"; founded January 1896).

Art Nouveau is a resurgence of an essentially decorative, Romantic, Baroque style that aims at exploiting the ornamental value of the curved line, whether its origin is predominantly floral (Belgium, France, Spain) or geometrical (England, Scotland, Germany). Although it appeared primarily as an architectural and decorative style, its influence on painting and the graphic arts has been far greater than formerly admitted. The sinuous line, used either expressively or decoratively, is found throughout Toulouse-Lautrec's work, and had a decisive influence on the early work of Edvard Munch, Ferdinand Hodler, and Oskar Kokoschka.

The origins of the movement go back in part to the English writer John Ruskin, whose ideas were modernist as well as inspired by nature. These ideas first influenced the applied arts: William Morris' textiles and wallpapers (1880), the wood engraving by the young architect and decorator Arthur H. Mackmurdo (1851–1942) for the frontispiece of his *Wren's City Churches* (1883), Émile Gallé's decorative glass (1884), and the furniture designed in 1891 by Gustave Serrurier-Bovy (1858–1910). *La Plante et ses applications ornementales* ("The Decorative Applications of Plant Forms"), published in 1896 by Eugène Grasset (1845–1917), provided influential stylized floral designs. The movement had also spread to architecture. The first building worthy of mention in this

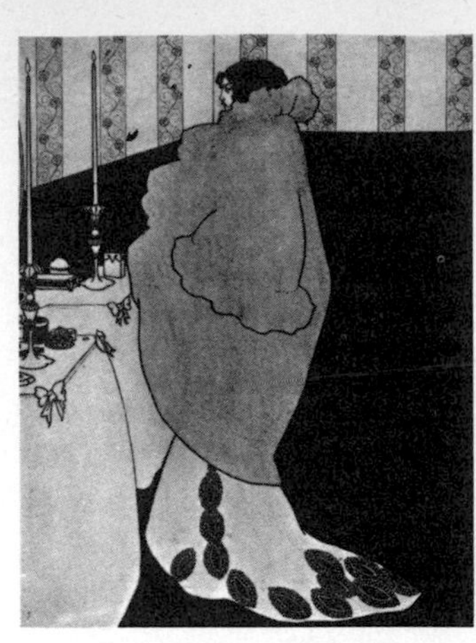

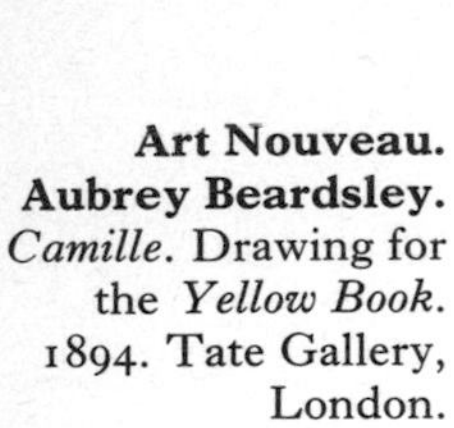

Art Nouveau. Aubrey Beardsley. *Camille.* Drawing for the *Yellow Book.* 1894. Tate Gallery, London.

respect was the house designed by Victor Horta for the engineer Dr. Van Tassel in Brussels (1892–93). Representative examples of the new style include the houses built by Paul Hankar (1859–1901) in Brussels between 1893 and 1900; Hector Guimard's Castel Béranger (1898), métro stations (*c.* 1900), and his auditorium for the Humbert de Romans building (1902; destroyed), all in Paris; Horta's Maison du Peuple (1896–99) and the old Hôtel Solvay (1895–1900), both in Brussels; August Endell's Elvira photographic studio in Munich (1896–98; destroyed); and the Folkwang Museum at Hagen, redesigned by Henry van de Velde (1900–1902).

The situation in the plastic arts was quite different, and it is extremely difficult to distinguish the specifically Art Nouveau style from a number of Expressionist and Symbolist tendencies. Symbol, decoration, expression: these were the fashionable key words of the day. The most striking fact was perhaps the revival of drawing and engraving in all its forms and a new interest in mural composition and in the new techniques of illustration. The hero of the new style in England was the Mannerist prodigy Aubrey Beardsley, the illustrator of works by Oscar Wilde and of the *Yellow Book* (April 1894), whose art, through Whistler and Japanese prints, was related to the work of William Morris and Walter Crane. In France, Art Nouveau was a particularly important element in the revival of the minor arts, largely through the school at Nancy founded by Émile Gallé (1846–1904), whose glassware was inspired in shape and decoration by organic forms and Japanese prints. Guimard's decoration of the Paris métro station entrances may have been the most typical example of the 1900 style, but it was in the poster, one of the most dynamic creations of the period, that it attained its highest and most significant expression, especially in the work of Henri de Toulouse-Lautrec and his rivals Théophile-Alexandre Steinlen (1859–1923), Jules Chéret, and Leonetto Cappiello (1875–1942).

In Belgium, the most influential and most interesting figure was Henry van de Velde, a Post-impressionist painter who, about 1890, left the easel in order to devote himself exclusively to the decorative crafts (decoration, wallpapers, bookbinding, furniture, textiles) and to architecture. Around him there gathered an Art Nouveau group more socially conscious than elsewhere, which included the architects Paul Hankar and Victor Horta as well as the painters Adolphe Crespin, Henri Evenepoel, Théo van Rysselberghe, and Alfred William Finch (1854–1930).

In Spain it was at Barcelona, the center of the Spanish cultural revival, amid Antoni Gaudí's fantastic architecture with its exclusively vegetal decoration, that Art Nouveau flourished remarkably. A whole group of artists became disciples of the new forms, including Santiago Rusiñol (1861–1931), Ramón Casas Carbó (1866–1932), and Isidro Nonell y Monturiol (1873–1911).

But the most active centers of Art Nouveau were undoubtedly Munich and Vienna. In 1892 the Secession of Munich was formed by Franz von Stuck (1863–1928), Wilhelm Trübner (1851–1919), and Fritz von Uhde (1848–1911), who still remained heavily influenced by Arnold Böcklin. In 1897 Max Klinger became its president. In January 1896 the review *Jugend* was published by Georg Hirth; it included contributions by the best German painters and draftsmen. In 1899 Fritz Erler (1868–1940), Angelo Jank (1868–1940), and Leo Putz (1869–1940) formed the group called *Die Scholle* ("The Soil"). Wassily Kandinsky, who had been in Munich since 1896, was greatly attracted to this group before he opened his own school of art. In 1899 the Berlin Secession, whose president was Max Liebermann, was formed. From 1895 to 1900 the review *Pan*, edited by the art critics Otto Julius Bierbaum and Julius Meier-Graefe, published drawings by Beardsley, wood engravings by Félix Vallotton, etchings by Munch, and lithographs by Toulouse-Lautrec.

It was in the cosmopolitan and refined Vienna of the turn of the century that the *Jugendstil* came to its full flowering. The undisputed leader of the movement was Gustav Klimt, who designed the famous decoration of the University (1900–03), which is inlaid on the wall like mosaic. He remained president of the Secession until 1905. In January 1898 the review *Ver Sacrum* appeared. Its exhibitions (notably that of Hodler in 1904) enjoyed great success, and on November 12, 1898, the review's own building, designed in the new style by Josef Maria Olbrich, was opened. Poets and musicians, including Hugo von Hofmannsthal, Peter Altenberg, and Gustav Mahler, also contributed to the group's atmosphere of refined culture and precious aestheticism. The same spirit informs the group's furniture, jewelry, and *objets d'art*, produced in the Wiener Werkstätten ("Viennese studios"), which were founded in 1903 and saw some of the earliest work of the young Kokoschka, who had been a fellow student of Egon Schiele at the School of Decorative Arts and a friend and protégé of the famous architect Adolf Loos. In 1908 Kokoschka exhibited the illustrations to his book *Die träumenden Knaben* ("The Dreaming Boys"), which reveal the dual influence of Klimt, to whom the book is dedicated, and of Hodler. It is perhaps the masterpiece of the *Jugendstil*, with its delicate drawing and decorative use of color.

ARTS AND CRAFTS MOVEMENT. A movement initially launched with the founding and first show in London of the Arts and Crafts Exhibition Society in 1888, brought about largely through the efforts of C. R. Ashbee (1863–1942), an architect and designer, and Walter Crane (1845–1915), the first president. Exhibitors included William de Morgan, potter; W. A. S. Benson, metal designer; and Ashbee himself. Between 1861 and 1888, a number of associations had grown up with the same aims as those of the designer William Morris, who had attacked industrial production for introducing into daily life nothing but ugliness and artificiality, where beauty and truth should reign. In practical terms, however, the cost of labor immediately priced the articles produced by hand beyond the means of the very people whose lives Morris had intended to enrich.

Like Morris, Crane and Ashbee promoted the revival of artistic craftsmanship and loudly opposed machine production. At a time when mechanization was already well advanced, however, their aims could not hope to succeed. Nevertheless, the Arts and Crafts ideals of individual design, fitness for use, and attention to the nature of materials and of fabrication in producing objects for everyday use link the movement with industrial design and 20th-century architecture, making it inseparable from the birth of modern design.

ASAM, Cosmas Damian (1686, Benediktbeuern, Bavaria—1739, Weltenburg, Bavaria) *and* Egid Quirin (1692, Tegernsee, Bavaria—1750, Mannheim), German architects and decorators. It is convenient to consider the Asam brothers as a unit, since the two worked in close collaboration, carrying out typically Baroque decorative schemes. Cosmas Damian Asam was certainly one of the greatest decorative and illusionist German Baroque painters in fresco, while Egid Quirin concentrated on sculptural stuccowork.

We find both brothers in Italy from 1712 to 1714, where Cosmas Damian studied under the caricaturist Pierleone Ghezzi (1674–1755). Working with his brother, who executed the stucco sculpture, he demonstrated his mastery of illusionist techniques and the delicacy of his palette in a series of decorated ceilings. The principal examples of Cosmas Damian's decorative work are at Weingarten (1717 and the years following), Freising (*Madonna and Child,* 1720), Einsiedeln in Switzerland (*Birth of Christ,* 1724–26), Breunau, near Prague (*Banquet of St. Günther,* 1727–28), Ettlingen (*Legend of St. John Nepomuk,* 1732), Osterhofen (*Legend of St. Norbert,* 1733), Weltenburg (1733 and the years following), and Ingolstadt (1736). In addition to these religious works, he did ceiling paintings of secular subjects in the castles and palaces of Mannheim, Altegloffsheim and Bruchsal.

Asam Brothers. Church of St. John Nepomuk, Munich. 1733–46. *Photo Franz Stoedtner.*

As for architecture, it is usual to attribute the monastic church of Rohr (1717–25) to Egid Quirin. In the chancel is a sculptured *Assumption of the Virgin* in which life-sized figures of the apostles are thrown into wildly gesticulating wonder at the spectacle of the Virgin being carried heavenward by angels. The Benedictine abbey of Weltenburg (begun 1718), is probably by Cosmas Damian, and here again in the chancel is a stunning vision: a silver stucco St. George with a sword of flame lunging toward the spectator from a dazzling radiance of light provided by hidden windows (after 1718). The dragon and the princess are silhouetted in the foreground in gold. The Asams' use of concealed lighting and their approach to church design and decoration are directly inspired by the work of Gian Lorenzo Bernini. The two brothers worked together to create the tiny but magical church of St. John Nepomuk in Munich (1733–46), which represents the full flowering of their remarkable talents.

ASPLUND, Erik Gunnar (1885, Stockholm—1940, Stockholm), foremost Swedish architect of the first half of the 20th century. He made a historic transition from a Neoclassical to a modern conception of architecture by fully exploiting the possibilities of glass and steel in the construction of the pavilions of the Stockholm Exhibition in 1930. In the years preceding this important event, his outstanding works were the Skandia Cinema (1922–23) and the Stockholm City Library (1924–27), two buildings that were typical of the tendencies of the period, the first because of the equilibrium and regularity of its lines, the second because of its austere symmetry.

The pavilions of the Stockholm Exhibition inaugurated a better understanding of the problems of his time, evident, for instance, in his Bredenberg store (1933–35) and State Bacteriological Laboratory (1933–37) in Stockholm, and in the Göteborg Law Courts extension (1934–37). The crematorium, surrounded by woodland, in Stockholm's south cemetery (1935–40), which is generally regarded as his masterpiece, is an even better illustration of the modern principle behind his work.

ASSEMBLAGE. An extension of the Cubist collage, assemblages are composed of patently non-art natural or manufactured items as well. "Assemblage" has been used to designate a wide range of productions, from Marcel Duchamp's non-creations—the "assisted" (i.e., joined together by the artist) and "unassisted" ready-mades (such as his 1914 *Bottlerack* [Paris, Coll. Man Ray], simply removed from its familiar context and declared a work of art by the artist)—to combinations of "found objects," such as the American sculptress Louise Nevelson's wall-sized boxes filled with broken furniture parts, wooden gears, and bar bells (*Nightscape,* 1959; Zurich, Gimpel and Hanover Galerie), or the American painter Robert Rauschenberg's "combine paintings," which include his *Satellite* (1955; Chicago, Coll. Mrs. Claire Zeisler), with its stuffed rooster attached to the top of an expressionistic collage.

In 1912 Picasso's *Still Life with Chair Caning,* which was the first Cubist collage, initiated tendencies that would lead to assemblage. Later both Georges Braque and Juan Gris, fellow Cubist painters, joined Picasso in his experiments by affixing labels, cards, mirrors, and other objects to their picture surfaces.

The print-collages of the Futurists in the 1910s, the works of the Dadaists, which focused on negative values, and the Surrealists'

Egid Quirin Asam. *Assumption of the Virgin.* 1718–22. Monastic church, Rohr. *Hirmer Fotoarchiv, Munich.*

Assyrian Art. *Assurnasirpal hunting a lion.* Kalakh (Nimrud), 9th century B.C. British Museum, London.

combinations of unrelated entities in incongruous situations, arbitrarily composed, were all absorbed by assemblagists. The American sculptor Joseph Cornell's glass-covered compartmented boxes were begun in the 1930s. By the late 1940s and early 1950s some of New York's Abstract Expressionist painters, including Willem de Kooning and Jackson Pollock, were incorporating torn newspapers, glass, keys, cigarette butts, and other foreign matter into their compositions, although these materials were nearly buried under the artists' lavish application of pigment. A resurgence of assemblage followed Rauschenberg's combine paintings and Jasper Johns's painted targets of the 1950s. Several sculptors, such as the Americans John Chamberlain and Richard Stankiewicz and the French Jean Tinguely, with his machine spoofs, combined welding techniques with the assembling of found objects. Nevelson's elegant and often monumental monochrome agglomerations of wooden or plastic components and Edward Kienholz's (b. 1927) gruesomely ironic tableaux mark both the formal and conceptual limits to which assemblage was pushed in the 1960s.

ASSYRIAN ART. Assyria lies in Upper Mesopotamia, on either side of the Tigris. As early as the 3rd millennium B.C. the region was culturally under Sumerian influence. However, Assyria as a distinct political entity dates from a later period, beginning in the 13th century B.C. and ending in 612 B.C. These two dates mark off the hegemony of a race that achieved universal dominion by force of arms.

The kings ordered the mass production of narrative reliefs in alabaster and gypsum that illustrated the outstanding events of their reigns on hundreds of yards (if not miles, as at Khorsabad) of the façades of their residences. It was an official art, with its repetitive scenes conforming to prescribed patterns. A greater thematic originality was shown in the relief of *Sennacherib at the Siege of Lachish* (690 B.C.; London, British Museum); the *Feast in a Garden*, showing Assurbanipal resting under a vine, telling his queen of his victories over the Elamites (7th century B.C.; British Museum); or the relief showing the meeting between Shalmaneser and Mardukzakir-shumi. There are also differences in scale: gigantic dimensions under Sargon II, more human ones under Sennacherib, and a further reduction under Assurbanipal, with emphasis on detail. Assurbanipal left an extraordinary epic in stone, a series of hunting scenes (7th century B.C.; British Museum) in which Assyrian art transcends its limitations to reach an unprecedented peak of achievement.

Beside this profusion of low relief, it is surprising that there is so little sculpture in the round, hardly 20 pieces. The list is soon exhausted: Assurnasirpal frozen in a hieratic stance (9th century B.C.; British Museum); two seated and two standing effigies of Shalmaneser; two statues of the god Nabu; six divinities carrying boxes; six others holding a flowing vase, from Khorsabad; and a headless woman from Nineveh (11th century B.C.; British Museum).

Great and prolific sculptors, the Assyrians also numbered many painters. Unfortunately, the products of this art were given little attention in the early excavations and have been only infrequently recorded; moreover, they are poorly preserved. We do know, however, that the royal palaces were copiously ornamented with murals. Sargon's residence at Khorsabad and even the provincial residence at Tell Ahmar (Til Barsip) each had several halls decorated with painting. The subjects were similar to those of the stone reliefs—warfare, tribute, and hunting.

The Assyrians also carved in ivory (the finds at Nimrud have been a revelation in this respect) and showed skill as metalworkers in bronze figurines and especially in decorative bronze revetments for doors, notably those from Balawat (9th century B.C.; British Museum). The inspiration here is entirely military, an account of Shalmaneser's campaigns, detailed and consequential enough to gladden a historian's heart. Assyrian art did not live long enough to decay. It was cut off in its "classical" phase when, in 612 B.C., the political power whose capital was then Nineveh collapsed before the coalition of the Medes and the Babylonians.

The models for Assyrian religious building were the temples and ziggurats of the Babylonians. Evidence of a more original secular architecture is found in excavations of the palace of Sargon II at Dur Sharrukin (dedicated 706 B.C.). The palace reflects the majesty of the king in its myriad apartments, courts, and temples but above all in the stone reliefs that relate his exploits.

AUBERJONOIS, René (1872, Montagny-sur-Yverdon, Vaud—1957, Lausanne), Swiss painter. His father was Swiss and his mother French. After Classical studies in Switzerland and Germany, he went to England, studying at the Royal College of Art, London. In 1897 he went to Paris, where he worked in the Luc-Olivier Merson studio. At the outbreak of war in 1914, he settled in Lausanne. He joined the Cahiers Vaudois group, and in 1918 designed the sets and costumes for *L'Histoire du Soldat* with music by Igor Stravinsky and text by Charles Ferdinand Ramuz. For some years Auberjonois, a violent opponent of naturalism, practiced a kind of broad divisionism. His strict, stark composition sometimes reflects the geometric bias of Cubism. Auberjonois was a first-rate draftsman, and his use of line reflects an acute sensitivity as well as poetic gifts that may be

Assyrian Art. The god Nabu. 9th–8th century B.C. British Museum, London.

appreciated in striking transmutations. Auberjonois executed two mural compositions: one (1936) for the abbey at Dézaley in the Lavaux district, Vaud; the other (1934) for the Musée Géologique Cantonal in the Palais de Rumine, Lausanne. A fine collection of his works can be seen at the Basel Kunstmuseum.

AUDUBON, John James (1785, Les Cayes, Haiti– 1851, New York), American artist and naturalist. Brought up as a wealthy bourgeois in France during the revolutionary years, Audubon went to the United States on business in 1803 and three years later made it his home. It was only after his frontier store in Kentucky failed that he turned to portrait painting. His overriding passion, however, was ornithology. Today his name is associated primarily with the major published result of his observations, *Birds in America* (1827–38). This work appeared in four volumes, illustrated with 435 engravings of Audubon's most famous studies and accompanied by a text in five octavo volumes, *Ornithological Biography* (1831–39). His studies of birds posed dramatically on branches or among plants seem very tightly and dryly rendered, although the silhouetting of angular and characteristic animal and plant forms against the unarticulated white of the paper is appealing for the freshness of the design. While Audubon's talent is often judged by the engravings that illustrate his books, in his original studies (432 of which are in the collection of the New-York Historical Society), closely examined and sensitively suggested details appear to be the result of a devoted approach to his work and subject matter rather than of objective duplication. Audubon combined media; he often drew textures, such as feathers and details of markings, with pencil and pastel lines over large areas of watercolor. His duality of vision—large, emphatic shapes on one hand, and an almost decorative elaboration of minuscule details on the other—lends a distinctive personal quality to his art.

AUSTRALIAN ABORIGINAL ART. All the Australian aborigines depended entirely on hunting and collecting for their subsistence, and this generally necessitated a wandering life without permanent settlement to take advantage of local abundances, with the result that their material culture is very simple. The inspiration of practically all their art is religious. Each small social group believes itself to be mystically associated with an animal or plant species known as the "totem." Women and boys are excluded from totemic ceremonies and must never see the ceremonial objects; however, most of the bark paintings, some rock paintings and carvings and, of course, the decoration applied to weapons and implements, such as wooden bowls and baskets, may be seen by anyone.

The weapons of the aborigine include clubs, boomerangs, spears, and spear throwers, all of which are decorated. Their surfaces often show parallel flutings, an effect seen also on other kinds of wood objects. Sometimes they are colored all over with red ocher; sometimes, especially in the north, they have in addition bands of white and yellow. Spear throwers and boomerangs, having relatively flat surfaces, lend themselves to more elaborate incised ornament; this is found especially in southern Queensland and southeast Australia, and sometimes shows European influence in its subject matter and style. Shields, which are even more elaborately decorated, have highly stylized patterns representing the totem or some object associated with it. The shields of northwest Australia have distinctive, carved zigzags colored red and white.

Many tribes of central, western, and northern Australia make sacred objects of two distinct but similar kinds: churingas (*tjuringas*) and bull-roarers. Churingas are flat, oval, elongated, or occasionally circular slabs of wood, or, in the central districts, of stone, incised on one or both sides with conventional patterns that refer to the myths and the totem animals. They are usually red-ochered. In the deserts of western Australia, where they are of wood, the churingas have angular patterns of incised lines with a similar significance, and they may exceed 9 or 10 feet in length. To the north they are often painted only and are decorated for ceremonies with feathers made to adhere with human blood. Bull-roarers are similar in appearance; they are made of wood and are generally not more than about 12 inches long. At one end a hole is pierced to take a cord by which the bull-roarer is whirled around, making a moaning noise that the women and uninitiated boys believe to be the voice of a spirit.

The bark paintings of the north and northwest are among the most impressive products of aboriginal art. They are usually made on the bark sheets that form the covering of the crude shelters, and are therefore visible to all. The subjects and styles vary considerably in a relatively small area. Western Arnhem Land is the home of the "X-ray" style, in which both the external appearance and the internal organs of animals are portrayed. In the east of Arnhem Land the subjects are often mythical beings and the tales associated with them, and spaces are filled in with close crosshatching in several colors.

The Kimberley district of north-west Australia produces two distinctive types of decorated objects. Pearl-shell phallocrypts, used as men's initiation ornaments, are incised with meanders formed of parallel lines and also, largely due to European influence, with naturalistic animals, human beings, and foliage. They are traded far afield. Baobab nuts are decorated by scraping the surface to form naturalistic figures of animals and plants or geometric patterns.

Much of the finest Australian art is found among the paintings or engravings on rock surfaces. It would be misleading to call this "cave art," for much of it is in rock-shelter sites where the overhang protects it from the weather;

Australian Art. Stone churinga. British Museum, London. *Photo Fine Art Engravers, London.*

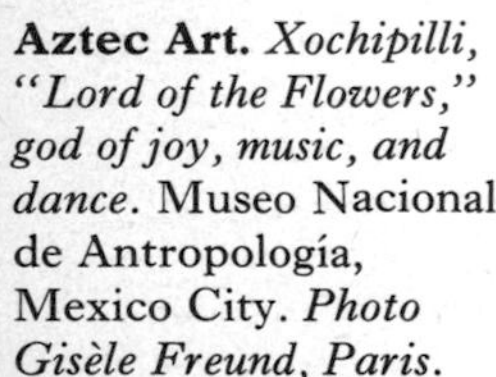

Aztec Art. *Xochipilli, "Lord of the Flowers," god of joy, music, and dance.* Museo Nacional de Antropología, Mexico City. *Photo Gisèle Freund, Paris.*

unlike European Palaeolithic art, it is never found in the depths of caves away from daylight.

The engravings have been made by several techniques. In some cases the subject is shown in simple outline. Huge figures of human beings and animals in this style are numerous in the soft sandstone of the Sydney district and at Port Hedland in northwestern Australia. Sometimes the whole figure is pounded, so that its rough pitted surface contrasts with the smooth rock face; in central Australia the rock has a brown patina against which the pounded area shows white. The styles range from apparent abstraction to relative naturalism. Geometric elements—circles, concentric circles, straight or meandering lines used singly or in groups—occur very widely and are the only form found in Tasmania. Certain styles and techniques have a wide distribution; these include monochrome outlines and silhouettes, geometric motifs, and stencils. The stencils, most commonly of hands, but also of arms, feet, weapons, and tools, may have been made simply for amusement, but they sometimes had religious significance as marking the physical presence of the maker in a sacred place and thereby bringing him into communion with it. In eastern Australia, from north Queensland to central Victoria, paintings are relatively uncommon; they generally represent stylized human beings, weapons, or animals. A style that shows human beings with thin bodies (the "stick figures") in vigorous and graceful activity, hunting, fighting, dancing, is found in south and central Australia. In central Australia geometric motifs resemble those carved on the churingas and have similar significance; but there are also large paintings representing mythical creatures (snakes, etc.), which are very sacred. They are repainted by initiated men, a ritual believed to bring about the increase of the totem species.

The finest and most complex rock painting is found in the north and northwest, from eastern Arnhem Land to the Kimberley district. Some of the X-ray figures are almost 10 feet long and are made up of thousands of lines in several colors. In Arnhem Land the subjects include human and mythical figures, animals, fishing and hunting scenes, weapons, and geometric and unidentifiable elements. Many caves are not sacred and the paintings may be seen by any aborigine. Knowledge of the Wondjina paintings of the Kimberleys and of similar paintings of the Lightning Brothers farther east in the Northern territory, on the other hand, is strictly limited to initiated men. The Wondjinas are portrayed as large static anthropomorphic figures; their heads are surrounded by red, halolike zones and they always lack mouths. They are creator heroes, each regarded as the ancestor of the local clan, yet in a sense all aspects of one being. They are repainted each year, in order to bring the monsoon rains and general fertility.

AVERCAMP, Hendrick (1585, Amsterdam—1634, Kampen), Dutch painter. A pupil of Pieter Isaacsz (1569–1625), he was a distant follower of Gillis van Coninxloo and of Pieter Bruegel. Avercamp evokes the vast silent horizons of the Dutch plain and the canals locked in winter snow and ice. His drawings (Windsor, Royal Library; Hamburg, Kunsthalle) and his small paintings, horizontal in format, are uniform but spirited representations of Dutch outdoor scenes (*Winter Scene on a Canal*; Toledo, Museum of Art), illustrating the simpler popular entertainments. He exploited a fashion but remained a prodigious colorist whose vermilions ring out among a web of indeterminate grays and golden or pinkish whites (*Winter Landscape*, 1608; Bergen, Museum). Avercamp's subtle lighting reproduces the Dutch atmosphere, and his figures maintain a touching reserve and solitude in the midst of their common pleasures.

AVERY, Milton (1893, Altmar, New York—1965, New York), American painter. Starting in 1930, Avery demonstrated a marked Fauvist influence in his work (*Mother and Child*, 1944; New York, Grace Borgenicht Gallery), although he always retained a personal style that was seemingly naive and childlike in its outlook. It is partly through Avery that American painters assimilated Henri Matisse's teachings concerning space and flat patterns of decorative equal-valued colors. Cubism did not play an important part in Avery's development, unlike many other American artists of his generation.

Avery contributed to the progress of 20th-century American painting, his works heralding the radical streamlining of form that was employed in the 1950s by New York's Abstract Expressionist painters. Many of his paintings are bold, stark seascapes reminiscent of those of Albert Pinkham Ryder and John Marin. In *Green Sea* (1954; New York, Metropolitan Museum), Avery used remarkably simple geometric forms that foreshadow the hard-edge style in abstract painting of the late 1960s. His earlier *Evening at Home* (1940; New York, Coll. Curt Valentin), like most of his paintings, is a small canvas that becomes curiously monumental, with its bizarre, hulking shapes suggesting an enormity of space beyond their own scale.

AYYUBID ART. *See* **ISLAMIC ART.**

AZTEC ART. After the fall of Tula in A.D. 1168, the high plateaus of central Mexico were invaded by several tribes who had come from the northwest in search of agricultural land. Known to the ancient inhabitants of the territory as Chichimeca, or barbarians, these tribes soon adopted the culture of the Toltec peoples they had conquered. The Aztecs, who arrived last, in less than 200 years (1324–1521) succeeded in dominating Mexico from the Atlantic to the Pacific and as far south as Guatemala. At first, they entrenched themselves on a boggy island by the shores of Lake Texcoco where, in about 1324, they founded their capital, Tenochtitlán, on the site of present-day Mexico City. To ensure the independence of their city, the Aztecs negotiated an alliance with Netzahualcóyotl, the statesman, legislator, and prince of the city of Texcoco, on the eastern shore of the lake. Subsequently, they became masters of the entire valley and created a civilization that was as brilliant as it was terrible. From 1440 to 1525 seven sovereigns—absolute monarchs—ruled, the most notable being Montezuma I, Tizoc, Montezuma II, and Cuauhtémoc, the last of the line, who was executed by Cortés and the conquering Spaniards.

Aztec society was a military theocracy, dominated by religion, with common ownership of land and no hereditary classes. It is certain that in their struggles against the other peoples, the Aztecs drew their strength not only from their skill and discipline in combat, but from the fact that for them war was a religion, in the true sense of the term. They believed that the continuing life of the sun, earth, moon, and gods depended on a perpetual offering of human hearts, and war became the principal means of obtaining victims for the sacrifice. (Death by sacrifice was an expected end for the Aztecs themselves, also.) The example provided by the gods could hardly fail to strengthen the belief that death was not an end to be feared but an honor to be sought after.

The Spaniards described their amazement when for the first time they entered Tenochtitlán, a vast town stretching for nearly two miles and covering an area of about 2,471 acres. Since the city had grown up from a small island, it rested on earth-platforms, and the buildings were separated by a whole network of canals, as in Venice. Three raised roads had been built over the lake, and an aqueduct, which was the work of Montezuma I, brought drinking water from the springs of Chapultepec. The main building materials were volcanic stone or bloodstone, unbaked clay, wood, and mortar. According to the chronicler Bernardino de Sahagún, the center of Tenochtitlán, where religious ceremonies took place, consisted of an imposing group of 25 temples, altars, houses for the priests and chiefs, baths, arsenals, ball courts, and a great many other buildings of lesser importance.

Also in the center stood the Great Pyramid, and it was on this site that the Spanish, after razing the whole area to the ground, built a cathedral. The pyramid was scaled by three flights of stairs of 120 steps each, and was crowned at its summit by twin temples, one painted blue and white and dedicated to Tlaloc, the rain god, the other decorated with skulls painted in white on a red background, dedicated to Huitzilopochtli ("Hummingbird-on-the-Left"), god of the sun and war. The pyramid at Tenayuca (*c.* 1200–*c.* 1507), also spared, is a superstructure of five massive stories, with a platform at the summit for twin temples. These are reached by double staircases about 90 feet high. Typical of the severe art of the Aztecs, the pyramid was not embellished with sculpture. The only decoration is a frieze of serpents at the base.

Like the architecture, the sculpture was massive and powerful. In the bas-reliefs or freestanding sculpture, what is immediately striking is the accumulation of elements and meanings, each work containing a multitude of symbols in one compact and perfectly unified whole. Moreover, some of the sculpture is covered with iconographical details whose purpose is to explain the sculpture itself. It is difficult to define a single Aztec style; as so often happens with conquerors, they adopted the ideas and made use of the techniques of the people they dominated. Thus a great many statues follow Toltec or Mixtec models and certain motifs, such as snakes and eagles engraved or carved on tools and weapons, appear to have originated on the shores of the Gulf of Mexico. A giant statue of Coatlicue, goddess of the earth, which decorated the great temple of Tenochtitlán, was discovered in 1790 near the city site (now in Mexico City, Museo Nacional de Antropología): nearly 9 feet high, she has a face formed by two snake heads facing one another, while her skirt is made of a mass of entwined reptiles; around her neck she wears a chain of hearts and severed hands. Equally disturbing are the effigies of Xipe Totec ("Our Lord the Flayed One"), god of the spring and of harvests but also of sacrifice and purification. He is generally represented as an officiating priest, dressed for the occasion in the skins flayed from the victims offered in sacrifice. However, the Aztec pantheon included less fierce figures and in addition to Quetzalcoatl, the Plumed Serpent, symbol of the union of the heavens and the earth, divine protector of the arts and sciences, there were the seated figures of Xochipilli ("Lord of the Flowers"), the god of joy, music, and dance, who is conceived as a serene, much more naturalistic figure, and whose image reveals a kindlier side to Aztec art.

The enormous carved monoliths were another characteristic product of the Aztecs. The Stone of Tizoc, the Teocalli of Sacred War (the commemorative stone of the temple dedicated to the Sun in 1507), and especially the Great Calendar—a block of porphyry $11\frac{1}{2}$ feet in diameter—are examples of these monoliths. The Great Calendar is really a finely engraved zodiac, with the image of the sun in the center, surrounded by the four ages of the world and the divisions of the year—a summation of Aztec cosmogonic concepts.

Animals are a common subject in Aztec art (coiled snakes, monkeys, rabbits, and grasshoppers), and they provide a very rich range of expression, from a strictly naturalistic art to the creation of fantastic, supernatural beings such as Xiuhcoatl, the Fire Serpent (London, British Museum), which is supposed to represent thunder. Basalt is one of the commonest materials used, but a great many statuettes, masks, and ornaments are carved in semiprecious stones such as jadeite, obsidian, opal, cornelian, and onyx—even rock crystal. Some of the more exceptional pieces include the "regalia" in turquoise mosaic, the pectoral ornaments, and other ceremonial objects (some of them made of feathers) that were given to Cortés and sent to Emperor Charles V.

Aztec pottery was not particularly original and did little more than continue the techniques and styles of other peoples, particularly the Mixtecs. Dishes, urns, conical goblets for drinking pulque (an alcoholic beverage), generally decorated with realistic motifs, either animals or flowers, have been unearthed; the design is usually black or white on an orange-yellow background.

Quite a considerable number of Aztec manuscripts have survived. Like those of the Maya, they are formed of long strips of paper made from vegetable fibres and coated with white. The Aztecs had no written language; since they used a system of pictographic signs, paintings and drawings had to be comprehensible in themselves and all aesthetic considerations were subordinate to clarity. We can learn something of the nature and rules of this art from manuscripts such as the Mendoza Codex, which was compiled at the beginning of the colonial period. The approach is more conceptual than impressionistic. Objects are represented frontally or in profile. Sacred objects are shown in outline, so that their nature can be recognized at once. There is a total absence of perspective, paint is used without shading, and the brightness of the colors is heightened by the black outlines around each form.

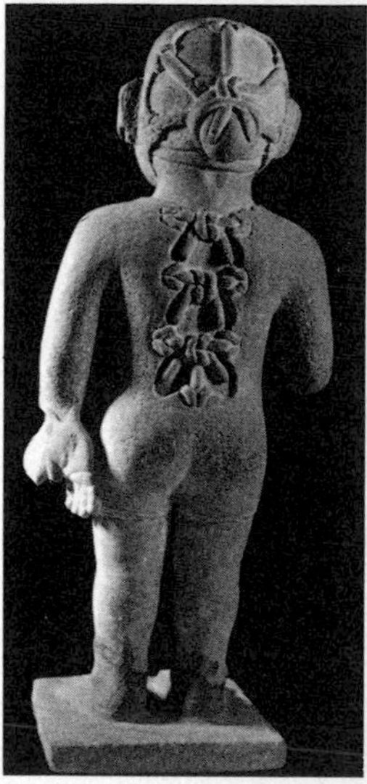

Aztec Art. *Xipe Totec, "Our Lord the Flayed One."* Coll. Salomon Hale, Mexico City. *Photos Gisèle Freund, Paris.*

B

BABYLONIAN ART. Babylon lies on the banks of the Euphrates, in the middle of the palm grove, some 50 miles south of Baghdad, the present capital of Iraq. The city had two periods of greatness, from the 19th to the 16th century B.C., and from 625 to 539 B.C.

First under Akkadian, then under Sumerian hegemony, Babylon emerged as a power in its own right under Sumu-abum (reigned 1894–1881 B.C.), but the most celebrated sovereign of the dynasty, called Amorite or Babylonian, was Hammurabi (reigned 1792–1750 B.C.). Warrior and statesman, he is known above all as a legislator through his code, the 282 laws of which are engraved in cuneiform on the two faces of an irregular stele of black basalt found at Susa and now in the Louvre, Paris. At the top is a relief in which the sovereign is represented standing in front of the throne of Shamash, the god of justice.

Babylonian Art. *Code of Hammurabi*. Detail. 18th century B.C. Louvre, Paris. *Photo André Vigneau, Paris.*

Babylonian art is to be found in the ruins of Mari, the capital of the Middle Euphrates, which enjoyed a 30-year period of prosperity under the Amorite king Zimrilin before its capture by Hammurabi. The royal palace has yielded statues of Ishtup-ilum, the governor of Mari, of the goddess with a flowing vase, of Tura-Dagan-Puzaur-Ishtar, and of Iduilum; as well as wall paintings, especially the "Investiture" cycle. In Mari, perhaps better than anywhere else, one can observe the transformation of Neo-Sumerian art in a specifically Semitic milieu. The Sumerian hardness has been radically softened—Ishtup-ilum alone preserves it—and the static Sumerian world is sometimes uplifted by Semitic dynamism. This is the impression given by the bronze statuette of a man kneeling, dedicated to the god Amurru for the life of Hammurabi, found at Larsa.

The second and last great period of Babylon is called Neo-Babylonian or Chaldaean. After the Kassites and the Assyrians, independence was regained under Nabopolassar, who founded a dynasty of which Nebuchadnezzar II (reigned 604–562 B.C.) was the most distinguished representative. Babylon was again the proud capital of a kingdom, bent on recovering the splendors of its Sumerian past. Building on an unprecedented scale was undertaken throughout Mesopotamia, with Babylon itself well in the lead: fortifications, palaces, sanctuaries, spacious thoroughfares, the famous hanging gardens, and, towering above all, the seven-story ziggurat of Etemenanki ("house of the foundation of heaven and earth"), which was probably the Tower of Babel mentioned in the book of Genesis. Contrary to expectations, the ruins of the royal city have yielded no great art treasures. Destruction by war and pillage no doubt account for this. All that has survived is the glazed brick decoration of the Ishtar Gate, the processional way, and one hall in the royal palace. This decoration comprises symbolic animals (bulls, dragons, and lions), rosettes, and palmettes, in yellow, rose, and white on a blue ground. The lack of stone explains the absence of anything similar to Assyrian reliefs. The material was baked, molded, and glazed brick, and the Babylonian architects and artists put it to a variety of uses with consummate skill. All this came to an end when, in 539 B.C., Cyrus entered Babylon (*see* ACHAEMENIAN ART), while its last sovereign, Nabonidus, having turned the throne over to his son Belsharusar (Balthasar), took refuge in Teima, in the heart of Arabia, and became a hermit.

Neo-Babylonian Art. Processional way to Babylon. 7th–6th century B.C. *Photo Goldner, Paris.*

BACHIACCA, Francesco Ubertini Verdi, *called* (1494, Florence—1557, Florence), Italian painter. Bachiacca was trained at a time when Florentine painting was turning to the pursuit of the singular and the rare; this is reflected in his strange pair of panel paintings, *Benjamin Brought Before Joseph* and *Joseph Receiving His Brothers* (both 1515–20; both London, National Gallery), commissioned by Pier Francesco Borgherini for a room that Andrea del Sarto, Francesco Granacci (1469–1543), and Jacopo Pontormo also helped to decorate. About 1525 Bachiacca was in Rome with Giulio Romano and Benvenuto Cellini. Later he entered the service of Cosimo de' Medici and produced brilliant cartoons for tapestries—the *Months* (1552–53) and *Grotesques* (1549), both in the Uffizi, Florence. Part painter, part artisan, Bachiacca was one of those artists who carried the Florentine naturalist tradition into Mannerism.

BACICCIA *or* **BACICCIO,** Giovanni Battista Gaulli, *called* (1639, Genoa—1709, Rome), Italian Baroque painter. He received his complex early training in Genoa, where he studied the work of Pierino del Vaga (1501–47), Frederico Barocci, and Rubens; this was followed after 1657 by a study of the great Roman masters (Raphael and, above all, Pietro da Cortona). Baciccia's style is superficial, but his portraits are perceptive and sincere (*Pope Clement IX*, *c.* 1667; Rome, Galleria Nazionale), and his religious compositions have a fine moving spirit (*St. John the Baptist Preaching*; Dijon, Musée des Beaux-Arts). Above all, in his great decorative works we find some of the best expressions of Baroque illusionism (*Christian Virtues*, church of S. Agnese in Piazza Navona, 1668–71; and the ceiling in the church of Il Gesù, 1672–83/85, with its dazzling fresco on the *Triumph of the Name of Jesus* in the nave; both in Rome).

BACKOFFEN, Hans (*c.* 1470, Sulzbach, near Saarbrücken—1519, Mainz), German sculptor. He worked primarily in stone, which he handled with great virtuosity. He is responsible for some of the archbishops' tombs in Mainz Cathedral, including those of Berchtold von Henneberg (1504) and Ulrich von Gemmingen, who is shown kneeling between his patron saints, St. Martin and St. Boniface, beneath a Crucifixion. The folds of the draperies are animated, the faces long and scowling, and the fingers knotty—evidence that the art of Backoffen remained completely untouched by the Italian Renaissance. Also typical of his style are the Crucifixion groups in the churchyard of St. Peter's, Frankfurt (1508), and in the parish church of Wimpfen am Berg (*c.* 1511). The influence of Backoffen extended throughout the entire Rhineland.

BAÇO, Jaime, *called* Jacomart (*c.* 1410, Valencia—1461, Valencia), Spanish painter. He worked mainly in Valencia, where he had an important workshop, and was painter to the court of Alfonso V and Juan II of Aragon. In 1440 he was summoned by Alfonso to Naples, where he spent several years, returning there in 1446. Living at a time when Spanish painters were learning to use oils and beginning to be influenced by the Quattrocento, Baço successfully combined a Flemish technique with elements from the Italian Renaissance. He painted a triptych showing Sts. Anne, Augustine, and Ildefonso with Cardinal Borgia, the future Pope Calixtus III (1444–55; collegiate church of Játiva); a *St. Martin* altarpiece (1447 or 1457; episcopal palace of Segorbe); and a *Last Supper* altarpiece, now in the Diocesan Museum in Segorbe.

BACON, Francis (b. 1909, Dublin), self-taught English painter who began by designing interior decorations. Incongruous, half-realized images suggestive of undefinable horror (*The Magdalen*, 1945–46; Batley, Bagshaw Art Gallery) in his early work were soon replaced by a single head or figure, almost invariably inspired by photographs, press cuttings, or reproductions of paintings. Certain subjects recur: the business executive, popes (*Study after Velázquez's Portrait of Pope Innocent X*, 1953; New York, Coll. Mr. and Mrs. A. M. Burden), the Crucifixion. The isolation and terror of the human condition was his continuing theme; the hotel bedroom, curtained space, or focusing lines that appear to form a glass cage emphasize the void surrounding the single figure. In the 1960s Bacon's settings became simplified and the horror was concentrated in distortions of features and the nude body (*Lying Figure with Hypodermic Syringe*, 1963; London, Priv. Coll.).

BAIZERMAN, Saul (1889, Vitebsk, Russia—1957, New York), American sculptor. In Russia, Baizerman briefly attended the Imperial Art School in Odessa. In 1910 he emigrated to New York and studied for a year at the National Academy of Design and, until 1920, at the Beaux-Arts Institute of Design, under the sponsorship of the architect Lloyd Eliot Warren (1868–1922).

Until the mid-1920s, Baizerman worked primarily with small sculptures, based on the observation of ordinary people, as in the series *The City and the People* (1920–25). This series initiated Baizerman's work in hammered metal, which became the distinctive mark of his style and resulted in his major oeuvre of hammered copper reliefs. His primary subject became the nude human figure on a heroic scale, ranging from single images to group motifs recalling Classical friezes, which he called "sculptural symphonies" (*March of the Innocents*, 1931–39; *Exuberance*, 1940–49). The musical titles he often chose indicate the lyrical, subtle, and harmonious quality of his work, which attains a universality through frequent references to Classical motifs and through the anonymity of the figures, rarely particularized with faces or detailed limbs.

BAKST, Lev Samuilovich Rosenberg, *called* Léon Nicolaevich (1866, St. Petersburg—1924, Paris), Russian painter, a militant pioneer of modern art in his native country and an early and prominent member of the *Mir Iskusstva* ("World of Art") group. Bakst went to Paris in 1893, studying under the Finnish master Albert Edelfelt (1854–1905). However, it is as a designer of sets and costumes for Sergei Diaghilev's celebrated Ballets Russes that he became famous in the years prior to World War I. His art was based on an elegant and refined eclecticism, inspired as much by Aubrey Beardsley as by Greek vase painters or Persian miniaturists, and was infused with his Oriental heritage of vivid color and exoticism. Bakst is best remembered for his sets and costumes for the ballets *Cléopâtre* (1909), *Schéhérazade* (1910), *Le Spectre de la Rose* (1911), *L'Après-midi d'un Faune* (1912), *Daphnis and Chloë* (1912), *Le Martyre de St. Sébastien* (1911), and *Les Femmes de bonne humeur* (1917).

BALDOVINETTI, Alesso (1425, Florence—1499, Florence), Italian painter. Baldovinetti was a pupil of Domenico Veneziano; from 1450 he was occupied as a decorator and mosiacist at the baptistery in Florence. In 1453 he was commissioned to decorate with mosaic the soffits over the north door, and in 1455 those over the Doors of Paradise. Another interesting mosaic is that with St. John the Baptist on the tympanum over the south door of the duomo in Pisa (1467). In 1454 Baldovinetti was working in Florence with Andrea del Castagno at the Ospedale di S. Maria, where he painted an *Inferno*. The spacious *Nativity* for the cloister of the Annunziata (1460–62) and the *Annunciation* for S. Miniato (1466), where he also decorated the Chapel of the Cardinal of Portugal with large and luminous figures of Prophets, Evangelists, and Doctors of the Church, are perhaps his best works. The panel with Sts. John the Baptist, Catherine, Lawrence, and Ambrose, for the church of S. Ambrogio, and the *Trinity with St. Benedict and St. Giovanni Gualberto* (Florence, Accademia) date from about 1470. The frescoes for the choir chapel in S. Trinita (1471–97), covered up in 1760, have been partly retrieved.

Baldovinetti became one of the leading mosaicists in Florence at a time when the city had replaced Venice as the leading center of that art. The favor mosaic came to enjoy was such that Lorenzo de' Medici could think it was suitable for decorating the entire cupola of S. Maria del Fiore, the cathedral of Florence. The large scale of Baldovinetti's compositions was well adapted to this medium. Finally, there is a great simplicity in his Madonnas and a remarkable sensitivity in his calm and luminous landscapes. The Louvre *Virgin and Child* and the *Nativity* at the Annunziata are perhaps the two best examples.

BALDUNG GRIEN, Hans Baldung, *called* Hans (*c.* 1484, Gmünd, Swabia?—1545, Strasbourg), German painter and engraver. After serving his time as a journeyman, he went to Nuremberg, hoping to study with Dürer, whose pupil he became about the year 1503. The master's influence is felt much more in the drawings and engravings than in the paintings; from the beginning Baldung shows himself more of a colorist than his teacher, as one may see in the small painting in the Louvre, Paris—*Knight, Death, and the Maiden*, believed to have been executed between 1503 and 1505. In 1507 for the choir of Halle Cathedral he painted two altarpieces: the *St. Sebastian* (Nuremberg, Germanisches National-

Hans Backoffen. *St. Benedict.* Liebieghaus (Städtische Skulpturensammlung), Frankfurt. *Foto Marburg.*

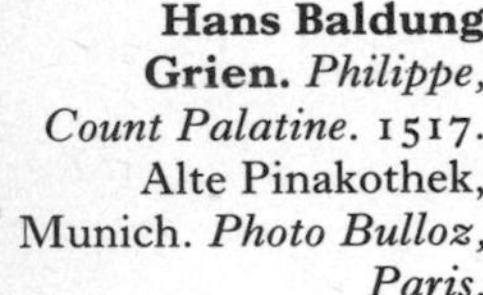

Hans Baldung Grien. *Philippe, Count Palatine.* 1517. Alte Pinakothek, Munich. *Photo Bulloz, Paris.*

museum) and the *Adoration of the Magi* (Berlin, Staatliche Museen). At this time Baldung also made a great many drawings to illustrate books coming off the presses of Ulrich Pinder, in addition to his numerous designs for stained glass. In 1509 he was granted citizenship in Strasbourg, and from this period comes a *Crucifixion* (Staatliche Museen), painted in 1512, probably on the eve of his departure for Freiburg im Breisgau, where he remained for about five years.

During his stay in Freiburg, Baldung was occupied mainly with two altarpieces for the cathedral, which can still be seen in their original positions. The Schnewlin Altarpiece, probably started by Baldung and finished by another hand, contains one fragment of outstanding quality: *St. John the Evangelist on Patmos* (*c.* 1514), with its luminous central figure in a landscape reminiscent of Grünewald. More important, however, is the painting that adorns the high altar, finished in 1516. Open, it presents a *Coronation of the Virgin* in the center and the *Twelve Apostles* on the wings; closed, the *Annunciation*, the *Visitation*, the *Nativity*, and the *Flight into Egypt*. Finally, on the reverse, we have the *Crucifixion, St. Jerome and St. John the Baptist*, and *St. Lawrence and St. George*. The color throughout is refined to a degree never attained by Dürer; Baldung's use of whites was particularly skillful.

Several of the painter's finest portraits also date from this time: *Count Ludwig zu Löwenstein* (1515; Berlin, Staatliche Museen), *Margrave Christoph von Baden* (1515; Munich, Alte Pinakothek), and *Philipp, Count Palatine* (1517; Alte Pinakothek). Baldung's approach to portraiture was intensely personal and entirely that of a painter: he never lost sight of his total concept while occupied with the individual features of the sitter. Some of his most dramatic woodcuts are probably also from this period, such as the *Lamentation of Christ* (1515), or, more particularly, the strange *Body of Christ Borne by Angels* (1515–17).

Again in Strasbourg, where he remained for the rest of his life, Baldung painted the *Altarpiece of St. John* for the Dominican church of Frankfurt (1519; Frankfurt, Städelsches Kunstinstitut) and a *Stoning of St. Stephen* for Archbishop Albrecht von Brandenburg (1522; Strasbourg). These are the last two altarpieces painted by Baldung; after this his religious compositions are comparatively rare and of modest dimensions, such as the *Nativity* of 1520 (Munich, Alte Pinakothek), notable for its light effects. The artist turned to the production of more and more nudes and mythological subjects. At times, as in the paintings of *Two Witches* (1523; Städelsches Kunstinstitut) and *Judith* (1525; Nuremberg, Germanisches Nationalmuseum), he aimed at a solidity of form approaching that of sculpture in the round. But it is in the allegorical paintings *Truth* and *Music* (1529) that Baldung's female nudes are most seductive (both Munich, Alte Pinakothek). In *c.* 1530 he produced a number of paintings illustrating Classical myths, with the figures in contemporary dress. His colorism in the *Pyramus and Thisbe* (*c.* 1530; Berlin, Staatliche Museen) is outstanding. This painting is perhaps Baldung's only unqualified masterpiece.

In a few of the late wood engravings the hidden springs of Baldung's enigmatic personality are most fully expressed: there is a series of three prints dated 1534, depicting wild horses kicking, biting each other, and even relieving themselves. In one of these the artist has included himself as a spectator, half hidden by a tree. No less unusual is the print called the *Bewitched Stableboy* (*c.* 1544), in which the boy is drawn in audacious foreshortening.

Baldung's style shows the influence of many masters, yet is peculiarly his own. His was one of the most original minds in German Renaissance art.

BALLA, Giacomo (1871, Turin—1958, Rome), Italian painter. Balla is Futurism's most astonishing manifestation. During a brief stay in Paris he discovered Impressionism and Divisionism and developed a passion for problems of light and color. On his return to Rome he made the acquaintance of Gino Severini and Umberto Boccioni, and imparted the new creed to them. In 1909 he was converted to Futurism by the art critic Filippo Tommaso Marinetti. Three years later his picture *Dog on a Leash*, now in the Museum of Modern Art, New York, was received with derision by a public still hostile to avant-garde tendencies.

From 1913 to 1916 he painted an entire series of paintings, among them *Mercury Passing Before the Sun* (1914; Milan, Priv. Coll.), that contains some of the most abstract works that Futurism has given us. Balla succeeded in giving an original and finished plastic form to the sensations, the movement, and the "states of soul" that Futurism, at first analytical, afterward sought to synthesize in a single and unique expression, taking its example from Cubism. If we consider not the intention but the results, it must be recognized that Balla, unwittingly perhaps, went beyond the limits of Futurism to take his place alongside the leading masters of abstract art. Unfortunately, this period of authentic invention, which found no response in a world entirely preoccupied with war, was of brief duration. His pioneering work remained almost unknown until mid-century.

BALTHUS, Balthasar Klossowsky, *called* (b. 1908, Paris), French painter of Polish origin. Born into a family of artists, he was still a child when the German poet Rainer Maria Rilke encouraged him to become a painter. He had no master in any

Balthus. *Patience.* 1943. Pierre Matisse Gallery, New York.

real sense of the term, and although influenced by the work of his contemporaries, he avoided membership in any group or school. His canvases are marked by a strict economy in the use of deliberately muted color and an innate feeling for composition, whether of isolated figures or of groups conceived on a vast scale, as in *The Mountain* (1937; New York, Coll. Mr. and Mrs. Pierre Matisse) or *Le Passage du Commerce Saint-André* (1952–54; Meudon, France, Coll. Claude Hersent). The sometimes strange and even morbid atmosphere of his subjects conceals an art that, in fact, aims at providing a perfectly objective and impersonal vision of reality. Balthus has also designed sets for the theater: Albert Camus' *L'État de siège* (1948) and Ugo Betti's *L'Île des chèvres* (1953).

BANDINELLI, Bartolomeo, *called* Baccio (1493, Florence—1560, Florence), Italian sculptor, son of a goldsmith in the service of the Medici, and himself a protégé of that illustrious family. He first learned his father's profession, then trained as a sculptor with Giovanni Francesco Rustici (1474–1554). His career began in 1515, upon the return of the Medici to Florence, with a commission for a statue of St. Peter for the duomo. In 1531 Alessandro Medici entrusted him with the block of marble that Michelangelo was to have used for a companion group to his *David*. Bandinelli carved from it a *Hercules and Cacus* (1534; Florence, Piazza della Signoria). Cosimo I commissioned from Baccio a monument for his father, Giovanni delle Bande Nere (1540; now in Florence, Piazza S. Lorenzo). Bandinelli's most colossal work is the choir screen for the duomo in Florence (1540–60), which comprised 80 statues. Artistically a failure, it was removed in 1842 (now in the Museo dell'Opera del Duomo). His most successful work is probably *Nicodemus Supporting the Dead Christ*, begun shortly before his death with his son's assistance. Toward the end of his life he was patronized by Eleanor of Toledo, who commissioned two statues for the Grotta del Buontalenti in the Boboli Gardens, Florence.

BARBARELLI, Giorgio. *See* **GIORGIONE.**

BARBARI, Jacopo de', *also called* Jacob Walch (*c.* 1440, Venice—*c.* 1516, Brussels?), Italian painter. He probably met Albrecht Dürer in Venice in 1494 or 1495 before he produced the admirable view of Venice (1500), which is still one of the masterpieces of the art of wood engraving. A short time later he was in the service of Emperor Maximilian. Then, between 1503 and 1505, he worked for the elector of Saxony; in 1505 he moved to Weimar, and finally to the court of Archduchess Margaret, regent of the Netherlands.

The Berlin *Virgin and Child with Saints*, one of Jacopo's earliest paintings, shows the influence of Alvise Vivarini. In the Dresden *Galatea* (Gemäldegalerie) and the Weimar *Christ* (Staatliche Kunstsammlungen Weimar) he moves away from the sustained style established by Antonello da Messina. The *Still Life with a Gauntlet* (1504; Munich, Alte Pinakothek), perhaps an emblematic picture, is rendered with a masterly assurance and has a precise realism unique for its time. Finally, Jacopo can be credited with genre scenes in a Northern manner, and with elaborate allegories (*Naked Couple* on the back of the *Portrait of a Man*, Berlin), from which engravings were also made.

BARBARIAN ART. The arts and crafts of the time of the Great Migrations in Europe (*c.* A.D. 360–*c.* 560) through the 8th or 9th century A.D. were the product of a revolution, one of the most far-reaching of the many revolutions that have shaken the Western world throughout the ages.

In the West, about A.D. 400, the Roman Empire was a huge body sapped of vitality. Meanwhile, a large part of the Asiatic world, the steppes region, was still profoundly disturbed by violent attacks, movements of entire peoples, who, setting out from the Far East, spread across Asia to the plains of southern Russia and Hungary: the Turco-Mongol world—the race of the Huns—was advancing on the Iranian world of the Sarmatians (Alans, Jazygen, Roxolani tribes), who in turn were being driven westward.

This Asiatic migrant world came into conflict with the Germanic world, which itself was in the throes of movement and transformation. In the 3rd century A.D. the Goths settled in southern Russia and joined forces with the Alans; in the 4th century A.D. it was the Franks, the Suevians, the Alamanni, and the Saxons who threatened the western frontiers of the Empire. All were irresistibly attracted by the wealth of the Empire; on December 31, A.D. 406, the Suevians, Alans, and Vandals, who were being attacked from behind by the Huns, crossed the frozen Rhine: the Great Migrations had begun.

Barbarian Art. Tombstone of Niederdollendorf. Rhineland-Westphalia. Frankish, 7th–8th century. Rheinisches Landesmuseum, Bonn.

As a result of a massacre (A.D. 408) of the dependants of barbarian troops serving in the Roman army, Alaric's Visigoths invaded Italy and in 410 sacked Rome. They later crossed into Spain, which was lost to the Empire in A.D. 447. Meanwhile, the Salian Franks moved down toward Cambrai (A.D. 430–40) and the Ripuarian Franks crossed the Rhine. Rome was thus assailed on all sides, when, in A.D. 451, Attila and his Huns surged toward Gaul. The latter were defeated, but they had broken through the last defenses, and their onrush gave the final blow to the Empire.

Britain, deprived of troops since the revolt of the usurper Constantine III (A.D. 407), had become the prey of Picts and especially Saxons. Under Clovis and his sons, the Franks seized the whole of Gaul. Italy was in the hands of the Ostrogoths. After the short-lived "reconquest" by Justinian (A.D. 533–55), it was seized by the Lombards, who also made incursions into Gaul across the Alps between A.D. 569 and 575. Further to the north, the Alamans were

Barbarian Art.
Gilded silver fibula from Gummersmark, Denmark.
Scandinavian, *c.* 500.
National Museum, Copenhagen.

defeated by Clovis, but they infiltrated into Lorraine during the 6th and 7th centuries A.D. and into the Franche-Comté through Porrentruy in the 7th.

The Germanic world, composed of various peoples, settled down over the ruins of Rome. But its victory was to be no more than a temporary one, for the barbarian gradually came to worship the civilization he had ravaged.

The art that emerged from a revolution of such scope was singularly complex. The contributions of the populations occupying territory at the time of the Great Migrations is particularly evident in Gaul, where the ancient Celtic influence reappeared, as it also did in Ireland, and in Central Europe, where the ironsmiths of Celtic origin taught the secrets of their craft to the invaders. The Germans were a poor and relatively uncultured people at the beginning of their migrations and were not in themselves very creative, but they excelled at adapting to their own purposes the decorative styles and techniques that they encountered. The contribution of the steppe peoples is fairly complex. The Huns, and later the Avars, brought with them traditions not only from the Far East but also from Siberia; the Sarmatians, who were in contact with India, developed a taste for cloisonné in gold and silver, which they prized highly for personal adornment. They were also in contact with the outposts of the Greek world around the Black Sea, with the goldsmiths of Olbia and Panticapaeum, who taught them remarkably subtle techniques. These techniques were transmitted by them to the Goths, then to the other Barbarians. The cultures of the eastern Mediterranean were diffused westward through colonies of peoples from the Near East; Byzantium (which was itself more than half orientalized) exercised a constant influence, especially on the ruling classes. The legacy of Rome became increasingly apparent as time went on, and eventually its influence became dominant in most phases of life, except the military.

Based on an extremely clever juxtaposition of metals of different hues (iron and various grades of steel), the metallurgy of the time of the Great Migrations revived and improved techniques of protohistoric times. It was probably the ironsmiths of Noricum who first succeeded in making the swords with pattern-welded blades, with carbonized edges that were case-hardened and tempered, the fanciscs, or throwing axes, with most of the head of ordinary iron and the cutting edge formed of a curved strip of tempered steel, soldered by an inner groove onto the head; and also the scramasax (straight sabres), with backs that were sometimes laminated, which had carbonized edges that were often extremely hard.

It was above all in the working of metal that craftsmen, who were both artists and technicians, expressed themselves. Architecture and sculpture were in decline, with the possible exception of decorative wood carving. Artistic activity was centered on the minor arts, particularly jewelry, and, apart from certain variations, the same fashions spread through Western Europe.

Jewelry involved gold- and silver-work, damascening, and bronzework. The work in precious metals is notable for its brilliant use of color: the white of base silver, the black of niello, the polychromy of garnets, chrysoprases, glass beads, and glass paste, and, of course, the glow of gold itself. It included a great variety of fibulas, either cloisonné or set with filigree and stones mounted in paste, or, less often, embossed. The large pins, rings, and belt buckles were decorated in the same way; the rings often bore monograms and were used as signet rings. From the end of the 5th century A.D. and especially in the 7th, several very fine belt bosses appear, which are similarly decorated. Gold and silver were used in clothes and hangings, embroidered with gold thread and made "entirely of silk," according to Gregory of Tours. Their decoration is Byzantine; the silk itself came from China by the "silk route," and later, after the 6th century A.D., it was transported from Byzantium; it was usually decorated in the weaving with Sassanid designs.

Inherited from the Syrian barbarians who worked in Gaul, damascening—the art of plating or encrusting a metal with a small quantity of another metal, either a more precious or a more common one—became extraordinarily popular, particularly in the 7th century A.D. Innumerable iron belt bosses damascened with silver or brass have been found in the graves of this period.

The decorated bronzework consists of belt bosses, often plated, and also of fibulas, ornamented discs for adornment, rings, belt buckles, pins, and a number of receptacles, some from Coptic Egypt, decorated with embossed patterns. Brass, equal in quality to the finest of our own time, was used to imitate gold, particularly in the embossing of remarkable round brooches.

The art of glasswork was practiced with extraordinary mastery in the 4th century A.D., notably by the Syrian glassworkers of the Cologne school, and the glassworks of the Rhineland and Moselle continued in the 6th and 7th centuries A.D. to produce muslin glass (which contains only small amounts of basic oxides), made according to the Syro-Egyptian technique.

The decoration of jewelry had a religious or magical purpose. Many of the patterns are geometrical, but most of them share a common characteristic, at least at the beginning: the use of motifs derived from solar symbols, among which the most common are the wheel—later the S-shaped sign—the swastika, and the quadrilobate. Representations of animals are common and allude to myths and beliefs. In addition to the deer, which has been honored by a number of very different civilizations, there was the horse, which was adopted as a totem by the nomads; the bull, symbol of strength and fecundity; the boar, which was sacred to the Germanic peoples; the fish, emblem of water; the cicada, a symbol of immor-

Barbarian Art.
Head of an Ostrogothic king.
6th century.
Formerly Peirce Coll. *Photo Giraudon, Paris.*

tality; the eagle, either double- or single-headed, the image of the supreme deity, which is linked with the myth of the tree of the world and may have been borrowed from Siberian tribes; and, finally, the mythical monsters: griffons looking behind them, imbricated monsters, chthonian-type entwined dragons—an inheritance of beliefs drawn from the Middle East that was almost as old as the world.

The human figure is found less often. In the form of the human mask, it was originally pagan and represented the supreme deity. But in the 7th century A.D., it became the Holy Face anointed by chrism or accompanied by the *Immanuel* inscription. In the same period, the man praying between two confronting animals became Daniel or St. Menas, who prefigure Christ, or occasionally Christ himself. Coptic Egypt, Syria, and the Middle East were frequently the sources of these figures that decorate belt bosses; the bosses, often transformed into reliquaries, had protective qualities that were regarded as essential by men who lived dangerously. Italy and southern Gaul also produced a few sculptures on stone or stucco (altar fronts and particularly sarcophagi), with subjects of Christian and late Roman inspiration. Similarly, Christian iconography was used to illustrate the manuscripts executed by monks throughout Western Europe.

In fact, it was the monk in the spiritual sphere, and the craftsman devoted to his art in the temporal, who prevented society from becoming completely barbaric; they prepared the way for the time of the great cathedrals.

BARBIERI, Giovanni Francesco. *See* **GUERCINO.**

BARBIZON SCHOOL. The name derives from the village of Barbizon, about 30 miles southeast of Paris, the meeting place for a group of independent French landscape painters of the second half of the 19th century, who were united by a common desire to paint "on location" undisturbed, and by their passion for the Forest of Fontainebleau as a subject. Several of these painters only occasionally came to Barbizon, to meet Rousseau. The Barbizon "School" thus refers not to a school of art but rather to the more

Barbizon School. Jean-Baptiste Camille Corot. *Environs of Barbizon. Photo Bibliothèque Nationale, Paris.*

or less random gathering of all those painters—adhering to no common set of artistic theories—who even for a short time stayed in the village.

Théodore Rousseau left Paris in 1848 to retire into solitude. Combining English Romanticism with Dutch realism and a mystical feeling for nature, he painted majestic foliage and open skies (*Forest Clearing at Fontainebleau*, 1848–50; Paris, Louvre). Charles Jacque (1813–94), an animal painter and amateur farmer, soon joined him: his works were poetic scenes of herds of sheep or cattle grazing in the undergrowth (*The Old Forest*, c. 1850–60; New York, Brooklyn Museum). Jean-François Millet turned his back on rocks and trees to look out into the plain, at the steeple of the church of Chailly, at the fields and the orchards (*Spring*; Louvre). In his best paintings he depicted the daily toil of peasants, which had previously been unacceptable as a subject (*The Gleaners*, 1857, and *The Angelus*, 1859, Louvre; *Woodcutters*, London, Victoria and Albert Museum). Diaz de la Peña, whom the journalist Jules Claretie called "the Correggio of Barbizon," evoked the green moss of rocks, the autumnal red woods, and the glittering reflections of ponds with a virtuoso's brush that gave phosphorescent tints to his canvases (*Heights of Jean-de-Paris*, 1867; Louvre). Many artists came to Barbizon to share in the arguments between painters and to try to glean some advice from the pioneers there; such writers as Henri Murger and the Goncourt brothers were also among the visitors. Jean-Baptiste Camille Corot, who often lived in the neighborhood, sought the different values of tones and bathed his trees in a silver mist (*Forest of Fontainebleau*, 1846; Boston, Museum of Fine Arts). Jules Dupré (1811–89), a sensitive observer of storm and wind effects, sometimes let his style be inspired by Rousseau's, although he preferred to work at Compiègne (*Sunset after the Storm*, 1851; Louvre). Charles-François Daubigny gave proof of a peaceful talent; his work is notable also for his early use of Impressionist effects. Jacques Raymond Brascassat (1804–67) and Constant Troyon (1810–65) painted oxen standing on the edge of woods, while Antoine Barye painted solemn imaginary beasts of the jungle lying among the rocks. Honoré Daumier, an occasional visitor, as was Jean-Baptiste Carpeaux, shared Millet's gift for rendering striking poses and a sense of volume. Barbizon also attracted Gustave Courbet and such foreigners as the Rumanians Ion Andreesco (1850–82) and Nicolae Grigoresco, the Belgians Camille van Camp (1834–91) and Victor de Papelen (1810–81), the Swiss Karl Bodmer (1809–93), and the American William Morris Hunt. All left under the influence of Rousseau and Millet. It is only in this sense that we may speak of a school, for Rousseau refused to define how his conception of painting differed from that of official art as praised by the juries.

BARLACH, Ernst (1870, Wedel, near Hamburg—1938, Rostock, Mecklenburg), German sculptor, graphic artist, and dramatist. The son of a country doctor, Barlach studied at the Hamburg School of Arts and Crafts (1888–91), went on to the Dresden Academy (1891–95), and then spent a year in Paris at the Académie Julian. A visit to Russia in 1906 had a

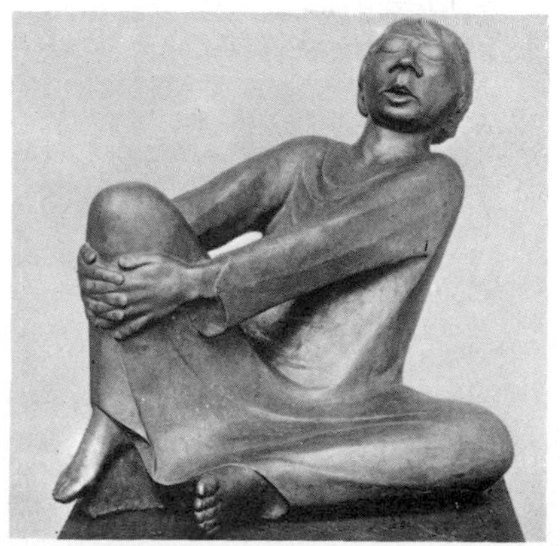

Ernst Barlach. *Man Singing.* 1928–30. Kunsthalle, Hamburg.

decisive influence on his artistic development. From 1907 to 1908 he worked in Munich as an illustrator for the satiric journal *Simplizissimus*, and in 1910 he settled at Güstrow, Mecklenburg. In the army from 1915 to 1916, he became a member of the Berlin Academy of Fine Arts four years after his discharge. The Viennese Secession made him an honorary member in 1936. During the period of the Nazis' power, when great numbers of art works were branded "degenerate," a total of 341 works by Barlach was withdrawn from public collections and confiscated. Imprisoned in Güstrow in 1938, he died in the same year, perhaps from starvation. After World War II his work returned to favor and was exhibited in Germany and abroad.

Barlach should be regarded as an Expressionist. He wanted to combine Cubist structure with a highly dramatic expression, rooted in Gothic-style design and composition. His style is characterized by cubic form, swept through and vitalized by a single motion, as, for example, in *Avenger* (1914; Hamburg, Priv. Coll.) and *Fugitive* (1920; Hamburg, Priv. Coll.), whose weighty mass seems to be raised by some superhuman force. Another characteristic of his art is his frequent use of several figures merged together in the expression of a single emotion (*Women Singing*, 1911; *Panic*, 1912; *Abandoned*, 1913; *Death*, 1925). For the Güstrow memorial (*Hovering Angel*, 1927; Güstrow Cathedral), he conceived a daring composition with a recumbent figure, which, like some spirit of the dead, is suspended from the ceiling over the graves. In 1934 the collector Herman Fuerchtegott Reemtsma encouraged the artist to complete the *Listeners' Frieze*, a semicircle of nine figures carved from oak, originally intended for a commemorative monument to Beethoven. Barlach's popularity rests mainly on his sculptural and, to a lesser extent, his graphic work, although he made an important contribution to the theater as a writer of Expressionist drama.

BARNARD, George Grey (1863, Bellefonte, Pennsylvania—1938, New York), American sculptor. While still in his teens, he went to Chicago to study at the Art Institute, and in 1883 left for Paris, where he remained for 12 years. After his return to the United States in 1896, Barnard gave an exhibition in New York, and in 1913 he was represented by five sculptures in the Armory Show.

Barnard worked primarily in marble and did most of his marble-cutting himself. As a student he had been strongly influenced by Michelangelo, and some of his earlier work, such as the *Struggle of Two Natures in Man* (1894) or the *Hewer* (1902), shows a Michelangelesque sense of physical vitality, as well as careful modeling, contrasted to a rough-hewn background; his late work took on a softer quality. Most of his sculpture consists of ideal figures, often conceived as group sculptures.

Barnard's collection of medieval art, housed in the former Cloisters in New York's Washington Heights and opened to the public by the sculptor in 1914, forms the nucleus of the present Cloisters, a division of the Metropolitan Museum in Fort Tryon Park. A memorial collection of his work is at Swarthmore, Penn.

BAROCCI *or* BAROCCIO, Frederico (*c.* 1535, Urbino—1612, Urbino), Italian Mannerist painter. One of the great personalities of the latter half of the 16th century in Italy, Barocci is today one of the least known. He served an apprenticeship in Rome, which he completed after returning to Urbino by a careful study of Correggio, from whom he took his shadowy contours and the delicately mannered grace of his figures. His intimate compositions, however, have a slightly affected charm (*Rest on the Flight into Egypt*, 1573; Vatican Museum); of higher quality are the great religious works, which are enlivened by an amazing manipulation of space (*Martyrdom of St. Vitalis*, 1580–83; Milan, Brera) and inventive, delicately fashioned accessories (*Circumcision*, 1590; Paris, Louvre). Barocci was considered by the German scholar Hermann Voss (*Die Malerei der Spätrenaissance in Rom und Florenz*, 1920) as an important forerunner of the Baroque in his spatial dynamism, with figures linked in chains of diagonal countermovement, and in his shimmering, iridescent colorism.

BAROQUE ART. The word "baroque," of uncertain origin, was first used as an adjective meaning bizarre or irregular. As a noun it seems to have gained currency toward the end of the 18th century through such writers as Francesco Milizia: "Baroque," he wrote, "is the ultimate in the bizarre, the ridiculous carried to extremes." But in the writings of German historians the term gradually lost its pejorative connotation. From about 1887 or 1888, the term can be said to have been in common use in Germany as a designation for the period following the Renaissance.

The word has in fact two distinct meanings. One is aesthetic: Baroque is defined in relation to Classicism, as a reaction against it. Movement was its distinctive characteristic in opposition to stability. A separation of the arts was alien to the spirit of Baroque; theater and festivals were the preferred means of expression because they united them. Baroque art was analogous to rhetoric; unreal, it sought illusion in *trompe-l'oeil*. Classicism and Baroque, especially the latter, never exist in a pure state: every style has in it a Classical and a Baroque element. In different periods of art history one or the other is preponderant: the Pergamum Altar is Baroque in relation to the Parthenon, German sculpture of the 15th century is Baroque in relation to that of the Renaissance. In a narrower sense, Baroque is a chronological rather than an aesthetic term. It designated a particular age covering roughly the whole of the 17th century and the 18th up to about 1750, when a Neoclassical reaction arose in Rome.

Baroque Art. Gian Lorenzo Bernini. Baldacchino in St. Peter's, Rome. 1624–33. *Photo Boudot-Lamotte.*

The Baroque age was born in Rome toward the end of the 16th century in reaction to the post-Renaissance stylistic development called Mannerism (*q.v.*). It has been represented by certain scholars as the style of the Counter Reformation. According to this theory, the chief propagator of the new style was the Society of Jesus, the newly founded (1540) order of the Jesuits. Perhaps by chance the Baroque spirit coincided with intense architectural activity on the part of the papacy in Rome—the erection of numerous churches and Carlo Maderno's addition of the nave and façade to St. Peter's (1612). However, recent research has shown that the influence of the clergy, including the Jesuits, on the style of their churches was far from decisive. The term Baroque has also been given a sociological interpretation. According to some scholars, it is related to a monarchical form of society, while others see it as an expression of a feudal, peasant culture, and the reaction to it as that of a bourgeois structure.

Mannerism lasted until about 1590–1600; it is a style so essentially different that it cannot properly be considered as a kind of proto-Baroque, as it has been by some critics. Scholars have emphasized its metaphorical character, the predominance of certain forms—especially those of a flowing, supple, feminine order—its artifice, and its frequent eroticism. Finally, it should also be noted that Mannerism tended to be of provincial origin.

The initial impetus of Baroque, on the other hand, came from Rome, where a new type of church, with single nave, side chapels, domed transept, and pedimented façade, had developed toward the end of the 16th century, when Giacomo da Vignola and Giacomo della Porta built the church of Il Gesù. Roman Baroque is represented principally by three men: a sculptor, Gian Lorenzo Bernini; an architect, Francesco Borromini; and a painter, Pietro da Cortona. The style found its supreme expression in Bernini's groups of figures (*Rape of Proserpina*, 1621–22; *Apollo and Daphne*, 1622–25; *David*, 1623–24; all in Rome, Galleria Borghese), followed by his Baldacchino in St. Peter's (1624–33) and, above all, by the Cathedra Petri in the same basilica (1656–66). Bernini's exterior architecture, which always drew its inspiration from antiquity, is less typically Baroque. But the work of Borromini, who was exclusively an architect, represents a complete break with that of his predecessors; he showed great inventiveness in his decoration, created forms of amazing boldness, and rejected the rather timid tendencies of Carlo Maderno, whose façades for the churches of S. Susanna and St. Peter were nevertheless important.

In painting, the problem is more complex; there were at least three different currents (Realism, Classicism, Baroque), which may be exemplified by three major works in Rome: Caravaggio's paintings in S. Luigi dei Francesi (*Calling of St. Matthew* and *Martyrdom of St. Matthew*, both *c.* 1600), with their startling contrasts of light and shade, represent the realistic current; Annibale Carracci's ceiling decorations for the Galleria in the Palazzo Farnese (1597–1604), frescoes that were later described as Classical, but that in fact differ considerably less from the work of Caravaggio than has been said; and Pietro da Cortona's later ceiling of the Gran Salone in the Palazzo Barberini, which was not completed until 1639, and whose continuous expanse of painting had a decisive influence on all 17th-century decoration. In other Italian centers, Baroque sometimes assumed such a different character that there almost seem to be several Baroque styles rather than one. In Naples, Jusepe de Ribera dominated painting with his Caravaggesque followers; in southern Italy (especially in Lecce) and in Sicily, a Spanish influence can be detected in the architecture. In the north, Venice was rather in a class of its own with Baldassare Longhena, who built S. Maria della Salute (begun 1631), while the special glory of Genoa was its magnificent palaces, which won the admiration of Rubens. Turin possessed in Guarino Guarini one of the most original architects of the whole Baroque movement. Guarini was succeeded by Filippo Juvarra, whose theatrical designs, along with those of the Bibiena, are the quintessence of Italian Baroque; Juvarra, however, showed in the Superga (1717–31), a mountain sanctuary near Turin, that he was also capable of using Classical restraint.

Baroque Art. Étienne Martellange. Church of St-Paul–St-Louis, Paris. 1627–41. *Archives photographiques.*

In its partial conquest of Spain, the Baroque was preceded by the Plateresque style, an art with a profusion of minute detail. The Baroque was to be found not so much in architectural exteriors, nor in the great painting of Spain's golden age, in which Velázquez and Zurbarán showed little enthusiasm for the more excessive tendencies of the Baroque; it was found rather in the huge retables with their superabundant and apparently unordered decoration: Narciso Tomé's Transparente in Toledo Cathedral, with light flowing over the streaming gold, is perhaps the supreme expression of this type of work. The Baroque is also found in polychrome sculpture: Pedro Berruguete, a direct pupil of Michelangelo, gave his work a particularly Spanish imprint. All this culminated in the art of the *pasos*, those excessively and almost unbearably realistic statues that were drawn on rolling platforms in Holy Week processions and were sometimes dressed in real clothes, the *imagines de vestir*. In Portugal, decorative proliferation was not, as in Spain, carried to the point where it interfered with the architectural form, but was confined mainly to gilded wood carvings inside the churches, the finest examples of which are found in a number of churches in Oporto (São Bento, São Francisco). The tendency toward ornamentation reached its culmination in Brazil, particularly at Salvador and Ouro Prêto, where at the end of the 18th century Aleijadhino (Francisco Lisbôa) produced his exceptionally fine work—perhaps the most typical of colonial Baroque, which was even more vehement than that of the metropolis. The transplantation of the

Churrigueresque style to New Spain gave it a special flavor of its own. Among the more typical examples of this new incarnation of the Baroque are the Sagrario Metropolitano (1749) and cathedral of Mexico City (begun 1653), the unparalleled splendor of the façade of Zacetecas Cathedral (dedicated 1752), and the nave of S. Domingo at Oaxaca (1657).

In northern Europe, Rubens and his school, led by Jacob Jordaens, were the only serious rivals of the Italians. Rubens gave the Baroque one of its most lasting forms of expression. In architecture, the spread of new forms met with no resistance, but in fact it remained fairly superficial, since architects were content merely to apply Baroque decoration to Gothic structures (the Grand' Place in Brussels, Rubens' house in Antwerp). This was not the case in sculpture, where Rubens had a strong influence on such sculptors as Luc Faydherbe (1617–97). The style hardly penetrated into Holland. Although unquestionably Baroque traits appear in Rembrandt, his work contains personal features of so distinctive a character that the Baroque is scarcely recognizable. In Britain it had a cool reception also; Inigo Jones and his followers had made Andrea Palladio the predominant influence there, and Palladio could not be called Baroque on any count. The scholarly Sir Christopher Wren, connoisseur of French architecture, never demonstrated more than a slight attraction for the Baroque. With the Adam brothers, Britain was one of the first countries in Europe to rediscover the significance of Classical antiquity.

Baroque Art. Johann Balthasar Neumann. Staircase of the Residenz, Würzburg. 1719–44. *Photo Erich Müller, Kassel.*

In France, well known as the home of Classicism, matters were less simple than is usually thought. There existed a sort of French proto-Baroque art known as the Louis XIII style, which in the field of decoration was a kind of amplification of the art of Fontainebleau; but it did not in fact spread very far. Around the middle of the 17th century, an architect of genius, François Mansart, tried to found a peculiarly French Classicism by using the antique orders with the French-style high roof. It is a curious fact that Mansart, who is not known to have gone to Italy, should have built in Paris the church of the Val-de-Grâce (begun 1645), which is certainly, together with Étienne Martellange's St-Paul—St-Louis (begun 1627), the closest to Roman Baroque.

In French painting the situation was hardly less ambiguous. Nicolas Poussin became the paragon of Classicism, but the artist who brought the Classical tendency of the Carracci to its final development was Charles Le Brun, the apostle of Poussinism. Pietro da Cortona was Le Brun's inspiration for the decoration of the Galerie d'Apollon in the Louvre (1663) and the state apartments at Versailles (1671–81).

The Baroque style spread at a rather late date into Germany, but it found there a particularly fertile terrain. Like France, Germany had had a proto-Baroque period, with an even wilder ornamental style, paralleled by great heaviness in its architecture. Protestant Prussia possessed at a very early date a great Baroque sculptor and architect, Andreas Schlüter, who appears to have been a direct follower of Bernini. In the Catholic areas of south Germany there were a great many centers, the most important undoubtedly being Austria, which boasted some notable architects at that time. Vienna was amply adorned with palaces designed by Johann Bernhard Fischer von Erlach and Johann Lukas von Hildebrandt, while Jakob Prandtauer, a self-taught architect of genius, built abbeys, and Balthasar Permoser carved an *Apotheosis of Prince Eugene of Savoy* (1718–21; Vienna, Österreichisches Barockmuseum) that is the very essence of Baroque. In Bavaria, where the Jesuits erected (1580–97) their first church (Michaelskirche, Munich), the Italianate Asam brothers created a Berninesque theatrical art in which light was an important element. Pilgrimage churches, such as Dominikus Zimmermann's Die Wies (1745–54), were built at this time. Bavaria also produced the Dientzenhofer family, who took the Baroque into Bohemia. In Saxony Matthäus Pöppelmann produced the Zwinger (begun 1709), a series of seven pavilions in Dresden, an architectural ensemble of a fantastic kind, which was paralleled in sculpture in the work of Permoser. The same period saw the Frauenkirche (1725–43) of George Bähr (1666–1738), with its seven rows of interior galleries surmounted by a high stone dome, and Johann Balthasar Neumann's episcopal Residenz at Würzburg (begun 1719), the most sumptuous of the princely palaces. The whole of south Germany was soon given over to the Baroque, but it produced what were perhaps its greatest masterpieces when its stuccoworkers, whose virtuosity was incomparable, renewed their zest with the adoption of French Rococo ornamentation (*see* ROCOCO).

BARRA *or* **BARRAT,** Didier. *See* **MONSU DESIDERIO.**

BARRY, Sir Charles (1795, London—1860, London), British architect, one of the most eminent representatives of the official (revivalist) style during the first half of the 19th century and designer of the Houses of Parliament, Westminster, London. After a three-year architectural tour of Greece, Italy, Egypt, and Palestine, Barry settled in London in 1820. His work was extremely eclectic: he adopted an Italianate manner for three of his London buildings—the Travellers' Club, Pall Mall (1829–31), the Reform Club (1837–41), and Bridgewater House (1847–49), a magnificent private residence. His King Edward VI's School in Birmingham (1833–37) is a Gothic Revival structure. He also provided the plans for Manchester's Royal Institute of Fine Arts, a Greek Revival work (1824–35); the Athaeneum, Manchester (1837–39); the Halifax Town Hall (1859–62); and Covent Garden Opera House in London (1857), which had been destroyed by fire. Barry's fame rests mainly on his plans for the Houses of Parliament (constructed 1840–c. 1860), which he was commissioned to execute after winning a competition in 1836. He devoted the rest of his life almost entirely to this work, for which he made some 8,000 drawings, assisted by Augustus W. Pugin, one of the leaders of the Gothic Revival in Great Britain. At his death the buildings were not finished, and it was his son, Edward Middleton Barry (1830–80), also an architect, who supervised the completion of the work.

BARRY, James (1741, Cork—1806, London), Irish history painter. He arrived in Dublin in 1763 bearing a group of historical compositions that impressed Edmund Burke, who summoned him to London the following year. Burke also financed a journey to Italy, where Barry stayed from 1766 to 1771, studying antique marbles, Michelangelo, and Titian. He was made a member of the Royal Academy in 1773, although he did not exhibit there after 1776. Barry was appointed professor of painting at the Royal Academy in 1783 but was dismissed from that institution in 1799 for abusing his colleagues in his lectures. He died in poverty.

Barry's finest achievement was his decoration (1777–83) of the Great Room of the Royal Society for the Encouragement of Arts in London with six allegorical canvases. A kind of exalted romantic Neoclassicism is apparent in the first three paintings of the series: *Orpheus Reclaiming Mankind from Its Savage State; A Harvest Home or Thanksgiving to Ceres and Bacchus*; and the *Victors of Olympia*. This spirit declines in *Navigation, or the Triumph of the Thames* and the *Distribution of Premiums in the Society of Arts*, and becomes an unresolved Shakespearean mixture in *Elysium, or the State of Final Retribution*.

The "Shakespearean" element in Barry is expressed not only in scenes on Shakespearean subjects, such as the *Death of Cordelia* (London, Tate Gallery), but also in such portraits as *Hugh, First Duke of Northumberland, in Garter Robes* (c. 1784; Isleworth, Syon House), with its dramatic lighting and pose.

BARTHOLDI, Frédéric Auguste (1834, Colmar, Haut Rhin—1904, Paris), French sculptor, whose academic style and taste for the grandiose brought him many official commissions during his career. He is remembered primarily for two works. In 1880, after five years' work, he completed the *Lion of Belfort*, a gigantic sculpture of red sandstone, 72 feet long and 36 feet high, poised on the high expanse of rock on which the ancient town of Belfort was founded, guarding the fortress of the castle. Bartholdi's second famous work is the *Statue of Liberty*, a gift from France to America, which stands at the entrance to New York harbor. Bartholdi began work on a model of the *Liberty* in 1876. The first stone for the pedestal was set in New York eight years later, and in 1886 the statue was cast in copper. The dedication ceremony took place the same year, with the artist personally supervising the proceedings.

BARTHOLOMÉ, Albert (1848, Thiverval, Seine-et-Oise—1928, Paris), French sculptor, one of the most famous in Paris at the end of the 19th century and a figure of national esteem following receipt of the grand prize for sculpture at the Centennial Exposition of 1900. He had been a painter until 1886, when, following the death of his wife, he turned definitively to sculpture on the advice of the painter Edgar Degas, his lifelong friend. Each year at the Salon he exhibited separate parts of a great funerary composition, the entire maquette of which was to meet with great success in 1894. The city of Paris and the French government jointly commissioned Bartholomé to erect his imposing and poignant *Monument to the Dead* in the cemetery of Père-Lachaise (completed in 1899). He also sculpted the female figures on the *Monument to Jean-Jacques Rousseau* (1912) in the Panthéon, Paris, and a number of war memorials.

BARTNING, Otto (1883, Karlsruhe—1959, Darmstadt), German architect. Bartning studied at the Technical School of Art, first in Charlottenburg, then in Karlsruhe, and subsequently at Berlin University. From 1928 to 1930 he was director of the State College of Architecture, Fine Arts, and Crafts in Weimar, after which he settled in Berlin. In 1951 he was made president of the Association of German Architects. Among his most revolutionary works were the steel church in Cologne (1928), his circular Church of the Resurrection in Essen (1930), and the temporary church buildings constructed from prefabricated wooden sections that he designed for use by evangelical relief teams (design 1946). Important secular buildings include the Wylerberg House, near Cleve (1924), administrative offices for the Red Cross in Berlin (1925), exhibition buildings for the German government in Milan (1926), and the Rittberg Children's Hospital in Berlin-Lichterfelde (1928).

BARTOLO DI FREDI (c. 1330, Siena—1410, Siena), Italian painter. In 1353 Bartolo di Fredi Battilori opened a *bottega* (at the same time a shop and a workshop) in partnership with Andrea Vanni (c. 1332–1413). Later Luca di Tommè (c. 1330–89) and Bartolo's son Andrea also worked there. At San Gimignano he first worked at the Collegiata (Old Testament scenes, 1356–67) and later (1390) at the church of S. Agostino, which he decorated with a *Life of the Virgin* (only the *Birth of the Virgin* and the *Dormition* survive). Other important works are the Montecalcino *Descent from the Cross* (1382), a polyptych of 1388 (partly in Montecalcino, partly in Siena, Pinacoteca), and a *Madonna* (Florence, Uffizi). In his old age he became sensitive to the influence of French or Franco-Flemish miniatures and joined the mainstream of European Gothic. The principal works of his last period are the *Adoration of the Magi* (1930s; Siena, Pinacoteca), the *Presentation in the Temple* (Paris, Louvre), and the triptych in the Perugia Museum. His manner is characterized by a somewhat rough realism and vivid, varied colors with sharp contrasts. ANDREA DI BARTOLO (c. 1360,

Sir Charles Barry, assisted by **Augustus W. Pugin.** Houses of Parliament, Westminster, London. 1840–c. 1860. *Photo Martin Hürlimann, Zurich.*

Frédéric Auguste Bartholdi. *Statue of Liberty.* 1886. Entrance to New York harbor. *Photo Refot-Rapho.*

Antoine Barye. *Lion Crushing a Serpent.* 1833. Louvre, Paris. *Archives photographiques, Paris.*

Siena—1428, Siena), Bartolo's son, produced less important work, little of which has survived. We know that he painted altarpieces for several chapels in Siena Cathedral, but they have been lost. Extant works are an *Annunciation* in the church of SS. Pietro e Paolo in Buonconvento and a signed *Assumption* painted for Pienza Cathedral (New York, Metropolitan Museum).

BARTOLOMEO, Baccio della Porta, *called* Fra (1472/75, Florence—1517, Florence), Italian painter. After an apprenticeship in the workshop of Cosimo Rosselli, Bartolomeo became a Dominican in 1500, under the impact of Savonarola's preaching. From his very earliest works, the *Annunciation* (1497) in the duomo at Volterra, painted jointly with Mariotto Albertinelli, and the portrait of *Savonarola* (1514–17; Florence, Museo di S. Marco), his style was restrained and severe. In 1504 he was commissioned to paint the *Vision of St. Bernard* (Florence, Accademia), full of subtle effects and exquisite harmonies. A short stay in Venice gave him a certain taste for color (the *Eternal Father with Mary Magdalene and St. Catherine of Siena*, 1509; Lucca, Pinacoteca). Back in Florence, he resumed his association with Albertinelli. He then painted large compositions of mystical dialogues in a calm and simple, rather gray manner, such as the *Marriage of St. Catherine* (Paris, Louvre, and Florence, Uffizi). Bartolomeo's last works are marred by grandiloquence—witness the *Madonna della Misericordia* (1515; Lucca, Pinacoteca)—or by an obvious imitation of Raphael filtered through the veiled shadows of Andrea del Sarto—the *Salvator Mundi* (1516; Florence, Palazzo Pitti). The intervention of an assistant, Giuliano Bugiardini, becomes noticeable in these pieces, especially the Pitti *Pietà* (*c.* 1516–17). The fresco *Noli me tangere* is in a class apart; it lacks assurance but the conception is noble. Bartolomeo painted it in 1517 for the chapel of the convent of S. Maria Maddalena near Le Caldine, where he retired shortly before his death.

BARYE, Antoine (1796, Paris—1875, Paris), the greatest animal sculptor of the French School. His early training as apprentice to his father, a goldsmith, was to prove useful throughout his career: in fact, he tooled the casts that he produced by the cire-perdue method.

Barye's *Tiger Devouring a Gavial* (Paris, Louvre), exhibited in the Salon of 1831, aroused amazement and admiration but also adverse criticism that doubled on the exhibition of his *Lion Crushing a Serpent* (1833; Louvre). However, the Duc d'Orléans commissioned a table centerpiece composed of hunting groups; but the jury of the 1837 Salon rejected the first groups of the centerpiece, and the death of the Duc d'Orleans prevented completion of the project. He executed the symbol of victory for Louis-Philippe's July Monarchy, a *Striding Lion* for the Bastille Column (1840). The Republic of 1848 rewarded him feebly with appointments as head of the casting workshop of the Louvre, as drawing teacher at the Muséum National d'Histoire Naturelle (1854), and as a member of the jury of the Exposition Internationale (1855), which saw the triumph of his masterpiece, the *Jaguar Devouring a Hare* (bronze; Louvre) executed five years earlier. Although his favorite models were wild animals, he composed (1854–60) four superb groups for façades of the Denon and Richelieu pavilions of the new Louvre (*Peace, War, Force,* and *Order*), that are unsurpassed by any figures in the Classical tradition. When he was seventy-two, he was given the supreme official honor of a seat in the Institut.

Barye's knowledge of animals and his enthusiasm for Classical myths enabled him, quite as much as his desire to enter the Institut, to compose two beautiful groups—the *Centaur and Lapith* (also called *Theseus and the Centaur Bianor*, 1846–48; New York, Metropolitan Museum and Puy, Musée Crozatier) and *Theseus Fighting the Minotaur* (1846–48; Musée Crozatier)—that revive the disturbing power of ancient legend. Finally, Barye's paintings and watercolors, executed in the forest of Fontainebleau, further enhance the artist's reputation. There are three almost complete collections of Barye's work in the United States: at the Walters Art Gallery, Baltimore; the Maryland Institute of Art, Baltimore; and at the Corcoran Gallery of Art, Washington, D.C.

BASCHENIS, Evaristo (1617, Bergamo—1677, Bergamo), Italian painter. There is an unbroken record of the Baschenis family from 1400. Evaristo was its most illustrious member, a man of genius. He worked at first with his father, and seems to have been well acquainted with Cremonese art. About 1647 he entered the clergy. He left a battle scene in the style of Jacques Courtois (1621–76), and a few religious subjects, but his fame rests on his still lifes, especially those with musical instruments (*Still Life*, after 1650; Brussels, Musées Royaux des Beaux-Arts). He also painted kitchen scenes and excelled in rendering gleaming silk ribbons. The scholar Charles Sterling believes that Baschenis' style—restrained, carefully outlined, and characterized by beautiful, well-rounded, and simple volumes—was influenced by Caravaggio. The best collection of Baschenis' works is in the Accademia Carrara in Bergamo.

BASKIN, Leonard (b. 1922, New Brunswick, New Jersey), American sculptor and printmaker. Baskin's art education began with the Rumanian-born sculptor Maurice Glickman (b. 1906), from 1937 to 1939, and continued at Yale University in New Haven, Connecticut, the New School for Social Research in New York (B. A., 1949), the Académie de la Grande Chaumière in Paris, and the Academy of Fine Arts in Florence. Thereafter he became a teacher of printmaking at the School of the Worcester Art Museum, Worcester, Massachusetts, and a professor at Smith College, Northampton, Massachusetts.

Baskin was preoccupied in his art with both physical death and spiritual decay. He took up the theme of mortality in 1950, after seeing the sculptured tombs of the past in Europe. Working in stone, wood, or bronze, he created a series of massive, ponderous human figures that are either physically or spiritually dead. His effigies of the dead, such as *Dead Poet*, a portrayal of John Donne in a winding sheet (1955; Newton Centre, Mass., Coll. Mr. and Mrs. Arthur Vershbow), or *The Great Dead Man* (limestone, 1956), suggest death as the natural state of man. Other images, however, including *Poet Laureate* (bronze, 1956) and *The Guardian* (limestone, 1956), show a decadent smugness through suggestive physical characteristics: small, pig-like eyes and an obese awkward nude body. Baskin frequently also used symbolic animal images, particularly birds, either in combination with the men, or in direct fusion with their bodies (*Birdman*, 1961; New York, Grace Borgenicht Gallery).

BASSANO, family of Italian painters, known as Bassano from the name of the village near Venice where they were born.

JACOPO *or* GIACOMO (1510, Bassano—1592, Bassano) was the son of a village artist, Francesco Bassano the Elder (1470/75—*c.* 1541), from whom he received his training. Jacopo arrived in Venice around 1534 and there established contact with Lorenzo Lotto, Palma Vecchio, and Titian. The study of Parmigianino's etchings was then the fashion of the day and Mannerism in vogue; Jacopo reflects this trend in his *Madonna Between St. James and St. John the Baptist* (Munich, Alte Pinakothek). In the *Deposition* for the church of S. Luca in Crosara, he imitated Pordenone. *Samson* (*c.* 1538; Dresden, Gemäldegalerie) is perhaps his most representative work of this period. The results of his study of Parmigianino, Titian, and German engravers between 1540 and 1550 can be fully appreciated in the *Adoration of the Shepherds* (*c.* 1550; Hampton Court, Royal Collection) and in the *Beheading of the Baptist* (*c.* 1550; Copenhagen, Nationalmuseet). About 1560 Jacopo adopted a new manner, tensely emotional and with a dark tonality and various contrivances: the *Crucifixion* for S. Teonisto in Treviso (1562; now in the Museo Civico there). When El Greco reached Venice, Bassano was inventing a nocturnal world, scintillating, rich, and confused. The example of Tintoretto, from 1572 onward, contributed further to this development. Works such as *Susanna* (Nîmes, Musée des Beaux-Arts) or *St. Jerome* (Venice, Accademia) preserve some solidity of form under the effect of light, but the rural strain asserts itself and converts every picture into a deeply felt pastoral. Tintoretto's oblique perspective appears everywhere: the *Martyrdom of St. Lawrence* (1571; Belluno, Duomo) or *St. Paul Preaching* (1574; Marostica, church of S. Antonio). His last works, in which he was helped by his sons, Francesco the Younger and Leandro (1557–1622), are typical products of the family atelier. Their success is another indication of how much the Bassano did to popularize luminism in painting.

FRANCESCO THE YOUNGER (1549, Bassano—1592, Venice), Jacopo's eldest son, trained with his father, in whose workshop he remained for most of his career. Between 1570 and 1580 Francesco turned to Biblical and pastoral subjects with a more narrative character. In 1579 he devoted himself to historical painting. His success, at first throughout Italy, then throughout Europe, was probably due to pictures of small format, such as the series of *Seasons* in which he gave a paler version of the pastoral manner learned in the family workshop. He took part in the decoration of the Sala del Maggior Consiglio and the Sala dello Scrutinio in the Palazzo Ducale after the fire of 1577. The large canvases (1583–87) with scenes from Venetian history (*Pope Alexander III Presenting the Blessed Sword to Doge Ziani*) lack originality and distinction. While Francesco specialized in crowded compositions and used his father's chiaroscuro, Leandro and the other brothers specialized in the genre scenes of crafts and seasons, beloved of northern taste.

Jacopo Bassano. *Penelope.* Museum, Rennes. *Photo Giraudon, Paris.*

BAUCHANT, André (1873, Châteaurenault, Indre-et-Loire—1958, Montoire-sur-le-Loir, Loir-et-Cher), French painter. It was not until the age of forty-six that this horticulturist from Touraine turned to painting in celebration of the trees, flowers, fruit, and birds of his birthplace. In 1921 he sent nine paintings to the Salon d'Automne. They were noticed by artists and intellectuals; by the Russian impresario Sergei Diaghilev, who commissioned him to do sets for Stravinsky's *Apollon Musagète*; and by the dealer Jeanne Bucher, who organized his first one-man show in 1927 and championed his work for some 15 years. Bauchant's bouquets of flowers, scenes of work in the fields, his *Ganymede* (1924; Paris, Coll. Jeanne Bucher), *Battle in the Forest of Châteaurenault* (1930; New York, Coll. Catesby Jones), and his *Fifth Day of Creation* (1942; Paris, Coll. Maximilien Gauthier), all retain the bucolic tone and sense of poetic realism that endow even his heroic or epic subjects with a gentle, almost angelic purity. Bauchant was actually a rather awkward draftsman, but he instinctively knew how to compose forms in a monumental space. His style was that of the fresco, with stately arrangements, light colors, and absence of shadows. He had a very original way of interpreting grass, leaves, and trees; rock formations or mountains attained a fantasy and grandeur that constitute the finest aspect of his work.

BAUDRY, Paul (1828, La Roche-sur-Yon, Vendée—1886, Paris), French painter, one of the most famous representatives of official painting at the end of the 19th century. He suppressed the original elements in his art to conform to the academic style necessary for an official career, and he had a great fashionable success with his opalescent nudes (*Toilette of Venus*, 1859; Bordeaux, Musée des Beaux-Arts; *Abduction of Psyche*, 1884, Chantilly, Musée Condé). In 1864, after decorating the Hôtel Fould (1854) and the Hôtel Galliera (1863), both in Paris, he was commissioned by Charles Garnier to decorate the foyer of the Paris Opéra. He went to Italy to study Michelangelo and Raphael, then worked 10 years on this project, which was too vast and exhausted

Baugin. *Dessert with Wafers.* Louvre, Paris. *Photo Giraudon, Paris.*

him physically but earned him membership of the Institut in 1870. At the time of his death in 1886, Baudry was doing preparatory work for a *Life of Joan of Arc* commissioned for the Panthéon in Paris. He was a prolific portraitist throughout his career.

BAUGIN (documented *c.* 1630, Paris), French painter. He was, with Jacques Linard, Louise Moillon, and Bizet, one of the most engaging still-life artists in France at the beginning of the 17th century. Only three signed works by Baugin are known: the *Five Senses*, also called *Still Life with Chessboard* (before 1630; Paris, Louvre), an assemblage of objects of symbolic meaning, rich in painterly qualities despite its Cartesian rigor; a *Still Life with a Candle* (1630; Rome, Galleria Spada); and above all the *Dessert with Wafers* (Louvre), which shows that he knew how to subordinate beauty of texture to elegant simplicity and a sense of economy. These three still ifes, signed merely "Baugin," are credited by some scholars to Lubin Baugin, a painter of religious themes in the Mannerist style; it is by no means certain, however, that Lubin Baugin is the author of these still lifes or that he is even the same artist as the painter who signed his canvases "Baugin."

BAUGIN, Lubin (*c.* 1610/12, Pithiviers, Loiret—1663, Paris), French painter of whom only about 20 works have survived. He achieved renown in Paris during the regency of Anne of Austria. Baugin's *Holy Families* and his more ambitious compositions, now dispersed, for chapels in Notre-Dame Cathedral in Paris show his reputation to have been deserved. In his work one finds discreet references to earlier masters (Correggio, Raphael, Leonardo), the Fontainebleau Mannerists, and contemporary Italian painters (Baugin was nicknamed the "Little Guido," after Guido Reni).

According to some art historians, Lubin Baugin should be credited with the three famous *Still Lifes* (two in the Louvre, Paris; a third in Rome, Galleria Spada) that are simply signed "Baugin" and that are among the most subtle masterpieces in this genre and period.

BAUHAUS. In 1915 Walter Gropius was invited by the Grand Duke of Saxe-Weimar to take over the direction of the Art Academy and the Polytechnical School at Weimar, in the latter case as successor to Henry van de Velde. One of the first steps taken by the young architect on assuming his post in 1919 was to combine the two schools into one under the name Das Staatliche Bauhaus—the German word *Bau* meaning "construction." The Bauhaus, bound to the historical and social conditions of defeated Germany, reflected a desire for positive and rational reorganization, in reaction against Expressionist individualism. Its conscious ambition was to re-establish the lost unity of all the arts under the primacy of a modern architecture that would meet the concrete needs of industrial civilization. Gropius favored teamwork, not only in architecture but also in the production of furniture, ceramics, and all the arts that could be integrated into building: "The final although distant goal of the Bauhaus is the unified work of art—the Great Construction—in which there is no distinction between monumental and decorative art."

With this end in view, the program of the school consisted of two parallel courses: one devoted to the knowledge of materials and the different artistic techniques (*Werklehre*), the other to design and the theory of form (*Formlehre*). A course in architecture, culminating in a diploma, completed this training. As long as the Bauhaus remained in Weimar, the courses continued on two planes simultaneously, and each student had two teachers—an artist and a master craftsman. The Bauhaus was an incomparable center of artistic training and culture; for, apart from Gropius himself, the principal teachers were first rank painters: Lyonel Feininger (1919–33), Paul Klee (1920–30), Oskar Schlemmer (1921–29), Wassily Kandinsky (1922–32), and Laszló Moholy-Nagy (1923–28), all of whom gave their major attention to the Bauhaus during their years of activity there. Klee taught theory, then tapestry and painting on glass, which suited his style. He summed up his method in his *Pädagogisches Skizzenbuch* (*Pedagogical Sketchbook*), which appeared in 1925. Kandinsky also gave lessons in general theory, as well as specializing in abstract composition and mural painting. Schlemmer and Moholy-Nagy were responsible for reviving, in the spirit of the Bauhaus, metalworking and other plastic crafts and the arts of the theater and of ballet, photography, typography, advertising, etc. But it was undoubtedly Feininger, faithful to the Bauhaus throughout its existence, who best represented the Constructivist aesthetic tendency, in all its purity and flexibility.

In 1923 the Bauhaus organized an exhibition of the work of its first four years: the feature of the exhibit was a model house, the Am

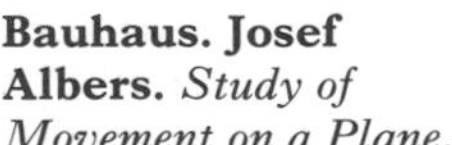

Bauhaus. Josef Albers. *Study of Movement on a Plane.*

Bauhaus. Walter Gropius. Bauhaus at Dessau. 1926. *Bildarchiv Foto Marburg.*

Horn, built and furnished entirely by the school's workshops. Despite the success of the exhibition, the Bauhaus was forced to close its doors on April 1, 1925, under pressure from the more conservative elements in the city, allied with the provincial government of Thuringia. The Bauhaus was invited by the city of Dessau to make its home there in premises that the mayor asked Gropius himself to design. Work began in the autumn of 1925 and was completed in December 1926. The complex of buildings is particularly remarkable for the use it made of reinforced concrete and glass, and is one of the major European works of architecture of the 1920s. The programs were reorganized, and the method of instruction with two teachers was abandoned. The theoretical and practical courses could now be entrusted to a single teacher, since a number of former pupils had joined the staff: Josef Albers, Herbert Bayer, Marcel Breuer, Hinnerk Scheper, and Joost Schmidt. The basic principles were reaffirmed; but more attention was paid to experimental work and the development of prototypes for industrial production, leading to the design of many accessories of daily living still in use today.

In 1928 Gropius resigned as director in order to devote himself more freely to his own work, and he was succeeded by the Swiss architect Hannes Meyer. In June 1930, following a disagreement with the municipal authorities, Meyer too resigned. He was succeeded by Mies van der Rohe, but only for a short time: in April 1932, the Nazis came to power in the government of Saxe-Anhalt, and the Bauhaus was forced to move, this time to Berlin. There, too, it had to shut down, in 1933.

In 1937 Gropius and Feininger went as refugees to the United States, where they both had distinguished careers, Gropius as head of the department of architecture at Harvard, and Feininger as a painter. They were joined shortly thereafter by Moholy-Nagy, who tried to revive the tradition of the movement by founding the New Bauhaus in Chicago in 1937, which he directed until his death in 1946. The movement was the subject of two important retrospective exhibitions, the first in New York in 1938, the second in Munich in 1950.

BAUMEISTER, Willi (1889, Stuttgart—1955, Stuttgart), German painter. His personal style began to appear in 1919 in mural compositions with planimetric forms, in which he used a mixture of plaster and sand. Fixed into the walls without frames, they suggest space in the same way as the work of the Cubists, which Baumeister discovered during his first visit to Paris in 1914. An article about him appeared in 1922 in the periodical *L'Esprit Nouveau*, which attracted the attention of Le Corbusier, Ozenfant, and Léger. His Constructivism disappears in the works painted after 1930 on grounds of sand, in which the figures are contracted into calligraphic diagrams. From this point, signs dominate his painting, assuming their most enigmatic forms in the *Ideograms* (1937).

In Paris, he contributed to the Cercle et Carré exhibition (1930) and to the shows of the Abstraction-Création group. He illustrated the Sumerian epic of *Gilgamesh* (1942–53; 150 versions, including drawings, lithographs, and silkscreen prints) and the Biblical stories of *Saul* and *Esther* (both 1944), using mythical figures among the hieroglyphs and fragments of architecture. In other series, the *African Pictures* (1942–55; over 60 versions) and the *Metaphysical Landscapes* (1946–54; 73 versions), he varied the means of expression from calligraphic relief, molded or inscribed in sand, to signs covered by transparent layers, from cuneiform characters to simple patches and bands of color. In *c.* 1948 his earthy, somber tones lightened, and his forms became more restrained and more geometric. Beginning in 1953 Baumeister produced his most important works, two series called *Montaru* (1953–55; 53 versions) or *Monturi* (1953–54; 16 versions) according to whether the heavy central masses, rising like submerged continents, were black or white. During the same period he executed his more somber *Safer* series. The significance of Baumeister's title for this group is unknown.

When he returned to Stuttgart after the war, he was appointed to teach at the Academy of Fine Arts. In 1954 a huge retrospective exhibition of his work was held in the town, where he died the following year. He was one of the few painters who remained in Germany under the Nazi regime to have a profound influence on the artists of the post-war generation.

BAZAINE, Jean (b. 1904, Paris), French painter. He studied sculpture at the École des Beaux-Arts in Paris but was increasingly attracted to painting, and in 1932 had his first private showing. Ten years later Bazaine's style had crystallized; at this time his method consisted of stripping objects of their ordinary appearances, fragmenting them, and enabling them to break open, to escape from their isolation and blend more fully with their surroundings. By about 1947 the objects were no longer identifiable. Although his painting was now nonfigurative, nature was still his point of departure, and he interpreted the reality that impressed him (*Sea Wind*, 1949, Paris, Priv. Coll.; *Child and Night*, 1949, Paris, Priv. Coll.; *Clearing*, 1951) with vivid or delicate colors and a network of boldly drawn and strongly rhythmic lines. In the mid-1950s draftsmanship became less important in his pictures and he turned increasingly to expression in terms of juxtaposed or blended patches of color. Bazaine also worked in stained glass (baptistery windows of the church at Audincourt) and mosaic (church at Audincourt, 1951; UNESCO headquarters, Paris, begun 1958). His works are among the most interesting contributions of modern art to these media.

BAZHENOV, Vassili Ivanovich (1737, Dolskoy—1799, St. Petersburg), Russian architect. After studying at the St. Petersburg Academy, he was sent to Paris, where he completed his studies (1760–62) under the direction of Charles de Wailly. He visited Rome, returning to Russia in 1765. Then, at the request of Empress Catherine II, he drew up plans for rebuilding the Kremlin in Moscow in a classical style. His original drawings, which are preserved in the Bibliothèque de l'Arsenal in Paris, and especially the wooden model, which is still in Moscow, enable us to imagine what this new Kremlin would have looked like. In Moscow Bazhenov built the Pashkov Palace (1784–86), now the Rumyantsev Museum. The plans of St. Michael's Castle, where Czar Paul I was assassinated, are also attributed to him. The actual construction was completed by Vincenzo Brenna (1745–1820).

BAZILLE, Frédéric (1841, Montpellier—1870, Beaune-la-Rolande, Loiret), French painter. Shortly after his arrival in Paris in 1862, Bazille, who came of an old Protestant family from Languedoc, became friendly with Monet, Renoir, and Sisley. Although quite a talented artist himself, he played an important role in the birth of the Impressionist movement mainly because of his friendships with his fellow painters and the financial aid he gave them. Killed in action at Beaune-la-Rolande in the Franco-Prussian War at the age of twenty-nine, he left a body of work characterized chiefly by its variety, bright color, and limpid atmosphere, but somewhat lacking in firmness and authority. It is difficult to say whether Bazille died before reaching maturity as a painter or whether he had already attained his full powers. His major work, the *Family Reunion* (1867; Paris, Louvre), seems to lack personality when compared to the great canvases of Renoir and Monet.

BAZIOTES, William (1912, Pittsburgh—1963, New York), American painter. He came to New York in 1933, and studied at the National Academy of Design with Leon Kroll (1884–1974). During the next several years (1936–41) he worked for the WPA Federal Art Project, both as a teacher and painter. In 1948, along with Robert Motherwell, Barnett Newman (d. 1970), and Mark Rothko, he co-founded a school called "The Subject of the Artist." Out of this grew "The Club," which held weekly meetings and discussions among New York's avant-garde artists. Baziotes worked in relative obscurity until 1944, when his work was shown at Peggy Guggenheim's important gallery, Art of This Century.

Baziotes' art was linked to an interest current among several New York artists at the time, namely the universal basis of primitive forms and mythological themes as a valid content for their works. Despite a high degree of abstraction in his later work, he remained deeply involved with subject matter, although content was not always explicit or obvious, even when recognizable forms emerged. He favored amoebalike biomorphic shapes, which traced back to the creations of Arp, Miró, and the psychic automatism of the Surrealists. Baziotes never developed the bravado Expressionism or painterly style of his contemporaries, and throughout the development of his mature style, he flattened forms into decorative patterns, floating them in a misty atmosphere (*Red Landscape*, 1957; Minneapolis, Institute of Arts). *Primeval Landscape* (1953; Philadelphia, Museum of Art) and *Pompeii* (1956; New York, Museum of Modern Art) are characteristic of his exceptional gifts as a subtle colorist, and indicate his method of conjuring up amorphous configurations.

BEARDSLEY, Aubrey Vincent (1872, Brighton—1898, Menton), English illustrator who epitomized to a greater degree than any other English artist of his time the *fin de siècle* spirit embodied in the Art Nouveau style. Three phases have been detected in Beardsley's work. In the first, the influence of the Pre-Raphaelites, Sir Edward Burne-Jones, and Puvis de Chavannes was predominant. The second, extremely decorative, phase—in which he demonstrated a superb command of compositional mass and scale—was influenced by Japanese prints. Beardsley's final phase owed much to the art of 18th-century France, and showed signs of a return to greater naturalism.

A precocious and talented child, Beardsley was already gaining recognition for his drawings at the age of eighteen, and in 1891—on the advice of Burne-Jones and Puvis de Chavannes—abandoned his job in a London architect's office to attend the Westminster School of Art. His first important commission came from the Dent publishing firm, for which Beardsley produced more than 500 drawings for a two-volume edition of Sir Thomas Malory's *La Morte d'Arthur* (1893–94). In 1894 he became art editor of the *Yellow Book*, a short-lived periodical devoted to the arts; subsequently he joined the staff of the *Savoy*, a magazine to which he contributed several poems as well as many drawings. Chief among the works Beardsley illustrated were Oscar Wilde's *Salomé* (1894), Alexander Pope's *The Rape of the Lock* (1896), and, shortly before his death, Ben Jonson's *Volpone* (1898). His output between 1892 and 1898 was prodigious.

BEAUDIN, André (b. 1895, Mennecy, Seine-et-Oise), French painter. He trained at the École des Arts Décoratifs in Paris and in 1921 met Juan Gris, who was to have a profound influence on him. Beaudin remained faithful to the spirit of Cubism throughout his career. Distortions in perspective, effervescent lines, and formal tensions were already apparent in his *Four Elements* (1924; Priv. Coll.) and the *Sleepers* series of 1925; in the fluid figures and still lifes of 1927–32; in the dancing shapes that followed; then, from 1937, in the series of Equidae and Bovidae, birds, open windows, Seine bridges, galloping horses, village houses, trees, and aquatic plants. Whatever his subject, Beaudin decomposes and recomposes it to suit himself, stripping the world of its external characteristics, its inertia and weight, and replacing them with a subtle, coherent ensemble of line and color.

In 1961 Beaudin decorated the ceiling of the church of St-Jean-Marie-Vianney at Rueil. His work also includes tapestries, etchings, lithographs, sculptures, and illustrations for the works of a number of poets. Although his career developed in an unobtrusive way, his reputation steadily grew. In 1962 he was awarded the Grand Prix National des Arts.

BEAUNEVEU, André (*c.* 1335, Valenciennes—1403/13, Bourges), the most famous French painter and sculptor of his day. In 1360 he worked for Yolande de Bar in Flanders, and the following year for the city of Valenciennes. In 1364 he went to Paris, where Charles V appointed him his personal stone carver and commissioned him to design the tombs of his grandfather Philippe VI and his father Jean le Bon, as well as his own mausoleum. All were erected in the basilica of St-Denis, where they may still be seen today. At the same time, Beauneveu had another statue of Philippe VI executed in his studio for Philippe's tomb in the Church of the Jacobins in Paris (1365; Paris, Louvre). He then worked on several tombs for Louis de Mâle, Count of Flanders, in the collegiate church of Courtrai (1374–77). He probably worked on the "Beau Pilier" of the chapel of St. John the Baptist in the northwest corner of the cathedral of Amiens; then, having entered the service of Jean, Duke of Berry (1386), he supervised work on the duke's favorite residence, the sumptuous castle of Mehun-sur-Yèvre.

Beauneveu executed illuminations for the library of the duke. In his Psalter of Jean de Berry (before 1402; Paris, Bibliothèque Nationale), sculpturally conceived figures of apostles and prophets are represented in grisaille against brightly colored backgrounds. Although the equal of his contemporary Claus Sluter, he is less highly regarded today. His talent outweighs his reputation, however; he was the last of the great itinerant artists in the medieval tradition.

BECCAFUMI, Domenico di Pace, *called* Domenico (*c.* 1486, Arbia, near Siena—*c.* 1551, Siena), Italian painter. A peasant's son who tended his father's sheep as a child, he was adopted and educated by his father's employer, Lorenzo Beccafumi. Vasari thought highly of his painting but, during the following centuries, Beccafumi gradually fell into worse and worse disfavor. Later and less prejudiced critics realized that his Mannerism and his unusual light effects heralded the greatest achievements of the next century. Beccafumi is no longer part of the Sienese School in that he discarded its dying traditions and benefited instead from the teachings and discoveries of Michelangelo, Raphael, Fra Bartolomeo, and even Sodoma. On the other hand, his use of bright, vivid colors belongs to the best Sienese tradition. Moreover, he always remained faithful to his native town; he opened a workshop there and returned after his visits to Florence, Rome, Pisa, and Genoa. His main works are: *St. Catherine Receiving the Stigmata* (1513; Siena, Pinacoteca), the *Worship of the Golden Calf* (1538–39; Pisa Cathedral), the *Trinity* (1513) and the *Mystic Marriage of St. Catherine* (1528), both in the Siena Pinacoteca, where we also find the two masterpieces of his mature period, the *Christ in Limbo* and the *Birth of the Virgin* (1544).

BECKMANN, Max (1884, Leipzig—1950, New York), German painter and graphic artist. Although of the generation of Ernst Ludwig Kirchner and Franz Marc, Beckmann remained outside both the Brücke and the Blaue Reiter groups; at a time when Expressionism was asserting itself, he was working in an Impressionistic manner, under the influence of Lovis Corinth. A transformation came as a result of World War I. Shaken by events and anxious to express his disquiet, his pessimism, and his protest, he adopted a style at once drier and more incisive. In order to emphasize that his figures were embodiments of feelings and of mental attitudes rather than individuals in their own right, he gave them a somewhat doll-like appearance. Further, he constructed for them an exiguous space in which they appear cramped and ill at ease.

In 1923 Beckmann began a series of portraits, spanning more than a decade, that show he was by then able to look on humanity with a less horrified and more conciliatory eye. But when the Nazis came to power in Germany and when, in 1937, he emigrated and settled first in Holland (1938–47), then in the United States, he reverted to his pessimistic trend of thought. This is apparent above all in the series of great triptychs that he began to paint in 1932, which embody ideas, symbols, and "literature" rather than painterly values. Although the form is fuller than in work of the years 1920–22, the color, which aims at richness, often is merely crude and strident. Outstanding among the triptychs is the enigmatic *Departure* (1932–35; New York, Museum of Modern Art).

Max Beckmann. *Self-Portrait.* 1944. Bayerische Staatsgemäldesammlungen, Munich.

BEECHEY, Sir William (1753, Burford, Oxfordshire—1839, London), British portraitist. In 1772 he entered the Royal Academy Schools, where he may have studied with Johann Zoffany. He first sent a picture to the Royal Academy in 1776, exhibiting regularly from that date.

Beechey spent the years 1782–87 in Norwich, then returned to London and rapidly devised a portrait formula that would be pleasing to London taste. His portraits of the *Children of the Duke of Buccleugh* (1789; Bowhill, Coll. Duke of Buccleugh) have a simple, wind-blown charm that hardened into a fairly elaborate prettiness in the *Dashwood Children* (1790; Toledo, Museum of Art). Some of his best effects, such as the silhouetting of a single figure against a low horizon or a dramatic sky, were taken from Sir Thomas Lawrence (*Master James Hatch*, 1796; San Francisco, California Palace of the Legion of Honor). Beechey became an Associate of the Royal Academy in 1793 and in the same year painted a full-length portrait of Queen Charlotte, who appointed him her official portrait painter.

By the mid-1790s Beechey, John Hoppner, and Lawrence monopolized fashionable portraiture. A mild dash of Romanticism in Beechey's temperament enabled him to paint such picturesque works as *King George III Reviewing the Tenth Dragoons* (1794–98; Royal Collection), and the portrait of the *Prince of Wales* (1798; Royal Collection) silhouetted against a lowering sky. He was made a Royal Academician in 1798 and was knighted in the same year.

BEGAS, Karl (1794, Heinsberg, near Aix-la-Chapelle—1854, Berlin), German painter of historical subjects and portraits. After a youth spent in Cologne and Bonn, he entered the studio of Gros in Paris in 1813. From 1822 to 1824 he was in Italy, where he fell under the spell of the Nazarenes and associated himself with the Neoclassical sculptor Bertel Thorvaldsen. In 1824 he settled in Berlin, where he was appointed professor in 1826. His later paintings of Romantic subjects (*Lorelei*, 1835; Hannover, Provincial Museum) enjoyed great popular success, but he was at his best in his portraits, two notable examples of which are a self-portrait painted while he was still in Gros's studio and the double portrait of his parents (1826) in the Wallraf-Richartz-Museum, Cologne.

REINHOLD (1831, Berlin—1911, Berlin), the best-known son of

Karl. A sculpture student of Christian Daniel Rauch (1777–1857) at the Berlin Academy, he went to Rome in 1856. From his return to Berlin in 1858 until his death, he was constantly occupied with official commissions, including those for the pediment to the Berlin Stock Exchange (1859), the statue of Schiller (1864–71), the fountain of Neptune at the Royal Palace of Berlin (1891), the monument to Emperor Wilhelm I (1892–97), the monument to Bismarck, which stood in front of the Reichstag (1901), and a number of statues in the Siegesallee (Avenue of Victory)—all in Berlin. In terms of artistic accomplishment, certain of his portrait busts, notably that of the painter Adolf von Menzel, are superior to his monuments. His brothers, Oskar (1828–83) and Karl (1845–1916), were respectively a painter and a sculptor of some distinction.

BEHRENS, Peter (1868, Hamburg—1940, Berlin), one of the leaders of the architectural revolution in Germany. He had a very real influence on the younger generation because one of his goals was to cooperate with industry and no longer to separate the professions of architecture and engineering. He applied these principles to far more than architecture; in 1898 he was one of the first artists to design models of bottles for mass production, and this was the start of a specialized activity that has come to be known as industrial design. In 1907 his inventive ability led to an invitation from the Allgemeine Elektricitäts-Gesellschaft (AEG) to direct not only the artistic side of the company's entire manufacturing output, but also the advertising, packaging exhibitions, and the design of warehouses, workshops, and offices of the organization.

Until about 1898, Behrens was merely a mediocre painter interested in the graphic arts: his early wood engravings, his bookbindings, and title-page designs reflected the decorative Jugendstil, the name given the Art Nouveau movement in Germany. But in 1899 he took part in the Die Sieben ("the seven") group, which had been organized by the Grand Duke Ernst Ludwig at Darmstadt, with the aim of fostering active cooperation among all branches of the plastic arts. It was there, in 1901, as part of a large group exhibition organized on the Mathildenhöhe, that Behrens made his debut as an architect by building his own house, entirely equipped by himself, in the artists' community that was founded on this occasion. He was then invited to become director of the Düsseldorf School of Arts and Crafts (1903–7). Gradually he rationalized and laid the basic principles of a style that he had derived from Henri van de Velde and Charles Rennie Mackintosh by adhering more closely to a functionalist approach. His strict methods achieved an impressive monumentality in the construction of the AEG gas-turbine plant, Berlin (1908–9), in which the glass walls of the main hall are enclosed in a steel framework. As chief architect of the AEG industrial group, following the same principles, he went on to build a high-tension factory (1910), a plant for small electric motors (1910–11), and a group of buildings for the accommodation of workers at Hennigsdorf, near Berlin (1911). Subsequently Behrens' architecture became more monumental, as seen, for instance, in his German Embassy in St. Petersburg (1911–12), and to a greater degree in the administrative buildings of the Mannesmann Corporation in Düsseldorf (1911–12), or of the Farbwerke (dye plant) at Höchst, near Frankfurt (1920–25), one of his most important constructions in the period following World War I. Some of the greatest architects of our time—Walter Gropius, Le Corbusier, and Mies van der Rohe—studied at his studio in Berlin.

Peter Behrens. Entrance hall of the administrative buildings. Farbwerke Höchst, near Frankfurt. 1920–25.

BELL, Vanessa (1879, London—1961, Sussex), English painter of landscapes, portraits, and still lifes. The elder sister of novelist Virginia Woolf, she studied painting, first under Sir Arthur Cope (*c.* 1899–1900), then at the Royal Academy Schools (1901–4). Her early work (*Iceland Poppies*, 1909; Coll. Duncan Grant) was in the discreet tradition of the New English Art Club, where she exhibited. After the revelation of the two Postimpressionist exhibitions organized by Roger Fry in London in 1910–11 and 1912, she came under the influence of the Fauves and—to a lesser extent—of Toulouse-Lautrec and Van Gogh. The coloring in her work became brighter and the design more abstract (*Portrait of Iris Tree*, 1915; Coll. Richard E. Morphet, England). After World War I, however, she reverted to the rather conventional form of Impressionism that she continued to favor until her death. Her participation in a heroic phase in the history of English art and letters and her association with the Bloomsbury Group at least provided her with some fascinating sitters: among others, she painted portraits of the writers Virginia Woolf, E. M. Forster, Lytton Strachey, Roger Fry, and Aldous Huxley.

BELLEGAMBE, Jean (*c.* 1470, Douai—1535, Douai), Netherlandish painter. The first documentary evidence of his presence in Douai dates from 1504; by that time he was married, and was a burgher and a Master. Jean Bellegambe worked for the town and its chief citizens, for the churches and, in particular, for the Benedictine and Cistercian abbeys of the district: Anchin, Flines, Marchiennes, and St-Amand.

A contemporary of Jan Massys, Bellegambe limited his activity to altarpieces; his was a Walloon art based on a strange mixture of conservatism and iconographic daring. Of his early works only a *Lamentation* (Warsaw) and a *Virgin with a Donor* (Angers, Museum) are known. His full development may be seen in the fine triptych painted in 1509 for Jeanne de Boubais, abbess of Flines, the *Retable of Le Cellier* (New York, Metropolitan Museum). In this work Bellegambe first used a formula that was later to vary only in the degree of subtlety or grandiloquence with which it was applied. The best examples are the polyptych of the *Trinity* (Douai, Museum), painted about 1509–14 for the abbot of Anchin; the *Virgin and Female Saints* (*c.* 1515; parts in Brussels, Musées Royaux des Beaux-Arts, and Baltimore, Walters Art Gallery); the *Annunciation* (*c.* 1518; Leningrad, Hermitage), painted for the abbot of St-Amand; the *Immaculate Conception* (1526; Douai, Museum); the *Mystical Bath of Souls* (*c.* 1505–10: Lille, Palais des Beaux-Arts); the *Last Judgment* (Berlin); the *Adoration of the Christ Child* (1529; Arras Cathedral); and *Christ with the Executioners* (Arras Cathedral).

These altarpieces, executed in a beautiful, light color scale of which the keynote is a delicate violet gray, are the work of an artist of great talent, a bold yet sensitive painter of the landscape around Douai, a skilled portraitist, a virtuoso in the rendering of texture, a man amused by childish games.

BELLINI, famous family of Italian Renaissance painters, whose important members were Jacopo and his two sons, Gentile and Giovanni. To a large extent the Bellini determined the course of Venetian painting in the 15th and 16th centuries.

JACOPO (*c.* 1400, Venice—1470/71, Venice) is mentioned for the first time in 1424. He trained with the Late Gothic International Style artist Gentile da Fabriano, in whose honor he christened his eldest son. In 1436 he was invited to Verona by Bishop Guido Memmo, where he painted a *Crucifixion* (1436) for the chapel of St. Nicholas in the duomo. In 1441 he was in Ferrara at the court of Este, where, according to the sonnet by Ulisse Alioti, he competed with Pisanello for the best portrait of the young Lionello d'Este. Also in 1441, he painted a *Virgin and Child* (Paris, Louvre), with a small donor figure of Lionello d'Este. By the middle of the century, Jacopo was a painter in vogue. Gentile and Giovanni were soon helping him in his workshop, and the paintings of the 1460s were frequently joint productions.

Many of his works have disappeared, and thus it is difficult to trace the development of his art. What paintings survive show him to have been strongly influenced by Fabriano's decorative International Style, although Jacopo's rather weighty figures look forward to the Early Renaissance. The signed *Christ on the Cross* (Verona, Museo Civico) is dry and hard in draftsmanship, but it has a remarkable luminosity. The same applies to the Verona *St. Jerome* and the *Annunciation* of S. Alessandro, Brescia (which was attributed for a long time to Fra Angelico). Jacopo painted many Madonnas, including the signed *Virgin and Child* at the Accademia in Venice; the beautiful signed Madonna in Lovere (near Brescia); and a small Madonna found in a church near Imola, and now at the Brera, Milan, dated 1448.

Jacopo's originality and greatest artistry appear in the two volumes of drawings (both undated; the earlier in London, British Museum; the later [between 1440 and 1450?] in Paris, Louvre), which he perhaps compiled for his sons. They contain an extraordinary assortment of documents, including copies after the antique and, in the Paris notebook, advanced studies in spatial composition, possibly influenced by Leon Battista Alberti. Jacopo was fascinated by perspective and experimented with it in unusual ways, with results that are often similar to stage design. These notebooks are his major artistic legacy.

GENTILE (1429, Venice—1507, Venice), probably the elder of the two sons, trained as an apprentice with his father. The earliest work bearing his signature, dated 1465, is the large tempera at the Accademia, Venice, portraying the first patriarch of the city, Lorenzo Giustiniani. In 1466, Gentile was working with his father, Francesco Squarcione, and Bartolomeo Vivarini on a series of paintings for the Scuola di S. Marco. Soon afterwards he attained a position as official portraitist, painting Emperor Frederick III during the latter's visit to Venice in 1469, and a portrait of Cardinal Bessarion (1472; now lost) for the Scuola della Carità. From September 1479 to November 1480 he stayed in an official capacity at the court of Constantinople, where he was exposed to Eastern currents that significantly affected his art. The celebrated *Portrait of Mohammed II* (*c.* 1480; London, National Gallery), painted during his stay, is a remarkable historical document and, with *Lorenzo Giustiniani*, shows Gentile at his height as a portraitist.

Apart from portraiture, Gentile specialized in gold-filled panoramic scenes of Venetian activities, particularly parades and ceremonies. In 1474 he began a cycle of history paintings in the Sala del Maggior Consiglio in the Doges' Palace. The work was taken over by Giovanni when Gentile went to Constantinople in 1479, but fire destroyed these sumptuous evocations of Venetian feasts (*Reception of Alexander III*) and dramatic scenes (*Sea Battle of Salvore*) in 1577. For the Scuola di S. Giovanni, Gentile did three works in a cycle relating the Miracle of the True Cross—the

Giovanni Bellini. *Orpheus.* Widener Coll., National Gallery of Art, Washington, D.C.

celebrated *Procession of the Reliquary of the Cross in the Piazza S. Marco* (1496), the *Miracle of the True Cross at the Ponte S. Lorenzo* (1500), and the *Miraculous Healing of Pietro de' Ludovici* (1501; all now Accademia). In 1492 Gentile agreed to replace the large works by his father and brother in the Scuola di S. Marco that had been destroyed in the fire of 1485. He began the first of these, *St. Mark Preaching in Alexandria* (Milan, Brera), in 1505, but the work was interrupted by illness and finished by Giovanni.

GIOVANNI (*c.* 1430, Venice—1516, Venice), *also called* Giambellino, has always been considered the younger son, although his exact birth date is not known. His name appears next to Gentile's after their father's on the altarpiece the three did for the basilica of S. Antonio in Padua. Giovanni generally followed the techniques learned in his father's workshop for some time. Beginning in the 1460s a personal style gradually emerges in his Madonnas; the early ones, the *Correr Madonna*, the *Davis Madonna*, and the *Crespi Madonna*, with their elongated hands, recall Byzantine icons. Mantegna's influence does not appear until quite late, about 1465–70, in the *Madonna* (Berlin, Staatliche Museen) and in the *Transfiguration* (Museo Correr), with its energetically chiseled landscape. The panels devoted to the theme of the Passion are no less vigorous: the *Blood of the Redeemer* (1464; London, National Gallery), the *Pietà degli Avogadori* (Doges' Palace), the *Crucifixion* (Museo Correr), the *Dead Christ* (1464; Milan, Museo Poldi-Pezzoli), and *Christ Blessing* (1464; Louvre). Giovanni's work is rich with suggestions of new and deeper insights into these themes. His *Agony in the Garden* (1464; London, National Gallery), for instance, is similar to Mantegna's, but filled with a new kind of spirituality. This gift for expression achieves yet greater results in the *Pietà* at the Brera.

By the mid-1460s Giovanni had his own workshop, and his artistic development thereafter can be traced in his series of commissioned altarpieces. Those for the Carità (1460–64; now Accademia), for SS. Giovanni e Paolo (*St. Vincent Ferier*, 1464), and finally, for S. Francesco at Pesaro show all that he learned from Antonello da Messina. In the altarpiece for S. Giobbe (1487?; now Accademia), the perspective creates a two-way movement of light that is reflected by the gold mosaic of the apse. In the *Transfiguration* (*c.* 1480; Naples, Museo di Capodimonte), the light is concentrated in Christ's white robe. In 1488, he signed two works: the triptych for S. Maria dei Frari, one of his finest pieces, and the *Madonna with the Doge Agostino Barbarigo* for the convent of S. Maria degli Angeli, Murano.

The extraordinary vitality of the aging painter can be seen from his reaction to the work of his pupils Giorgione and Titian; his portrait of *Doge Loredano* (1488; London, National Gallery) shows his receptivity to the fresh spirit and colorism of the two artists, both of whom were more than 40 years younger than their master. His light is even richer and his accents sharper in the *Baptism of Christ* (1502; Vicenza, S. Corona) and two late versions of the *Madonna* (Rome, Galleria Borghese, and Venice, Accademia). In his late work, the altarpiece with three saints in S. Giovanni Crisostomo, Bellini again displays the special feeling of intimate magnificence that he had developed in his works of the 1470s.

The Bellinis were particularly alive to the problems of the day. Jacopo knew that the traditional formulas were no longer valid and that reform would have to be radical. Giovanni faithfully reproduced the atmosphere of the Byzantine churches of the Lagoon. His long career made him the dominant figure in the second half of the century.

BELLOTTO, Bernardo, *also called* Canaletto the Younger (1720, Venice—1789, Warsaw), Italian painter, nephew and pupil of Antonio Canaletto, to whom some of his paintings have been mistakenly attributed. Shortly after leaving Canaletto's studio, he went to Rome and painted the *View of the Tiber with Castel Sant' Angelo* (*c.* 1740; New York, Metropolitan Museum). Bellotto was the great traveler among the Venetian *vedutisti*, or view painters. His peregrinations began in 1745, at first in Italy (*Turin from the Gardens of the Palazzo Reale*; Turin, Galleria Sabauda); then, summoned by August III, king of Poland and elector of Saxony, he went to Dresden, where he was court painter (1747–59) and where he returned after a few years in Vienna and Munich (*Vienna from the Belvedere*, 1759–60; Vienna, Kunsthistorisches Museum). Finally he settled in Poland, at the court of Stanislas II Poniatowski.

BELLOWS, George Wesley (1882, Columbus, Ohio—1925, New York), American painter, a descendant of early settlers in America. In 1909, after studying art in New York for several years, he took a studio across the street from the athletic club that staged the prize fights he loved to paint. He spent most of his short life in New York, combing its parks and byways for material for his work. Ordinary people in everyday situations interested him, and he treated them sometimes humorously, sometimes satirically. After 1916 some of his most effective efforts were lithographs. A group of hallucinatory, morbid images in this medium, his despairing reaction to World War I, recall Goya. Bellows' best-known paintings were inspired by the ringside. A fine example is *Stag at Sharkey's* (1909; Cleveland, Museum of Art). More numerous than the athletic pictures are Bellows' portraits. While he sacrificed the personal identities of the boxers in emphasizing their expressive motions, the individual, often introspective personalities of Bellows' portrait subjects dominate these canvases. The group portrait of the artist's family, *Emma and her Children* (1923; Boston, Museum of Fine Arts), for instance, is a particularly touching, melancholy image.

BELLUSCHI, Pietro (b. 1899, Ancona, Italy), Italian-born American architect and educator, Dean of the School of Architecture and Planning at the Massachusetts Institute of Technology from 1951 to 1965. Belluschi was educated in Rome and went to the United States in 1923. Two years later he settled in Portland, Oregon, where he joined the firm of A. E. Doyle, becoming its chief designer in 1927. His earliest works were primarily houses, executed in the native woods (fir and hemlock) of the Pacific Northwest. His celebrated sleek glass slab for the Equitable Savings and Loan Association building in Portland (1946–48) is consonant with his commercial style.

Belluschi was particularly concerned with the iconography of architecture, having developed for each functional type the particular form and structure that would suit its purpose most logically and beautifully. He is best known for his religious buildings, in which there is a typically straightforward use of traditional materials—wood, stone, and brick.

BENEDETTO DA MAIANO (1442, Florence—1497, Florence), Italian architect and sculptor. His earliest works were carved altars, often in chapels built by his brother, the architect Giuliano da Maiano, such as the altar of S. Fina (1475) in the cathedral at S. Gimignano, or the S. Savino tomb (1476) in Faenza Cathedral. His masterpiece in sculpture is the superbly decorated pulpit in S. Croce, Florence (probably 1472–75), which is entered by a flight of stairs that pierces the pier supporting the pulpit. After 1481, without leaving Florence, he completed the tomb of Mary of Aragon, begun by Antonio Rossellino, for S. Anna dei Lombardi in Naples; for the same church he also

Benedetto da Maiano. *Bust of Pietro Mellini*. Museo del Bargello, Florence. *Photo Alinari, Florence.*

executed the splendid Mastrogiudice altar (finished by 1489), on a design similar to the nearby one by Rossellino. Finally, he executed the tomb of Filippo Strozzi in S. Maria Novella (1491), as well as a portrait bust of Strozzi (Paris, Louvre). Though his work does not have Donatello's emotional force or the lyricism of Desiderio da Settignano, Benedetto was an artist of high order.

Benedetto's major work of architecture was the Palazzo Strozzi in Florence. He belonged to the generation influenced, to some extent, by Giuliano da Sangallo, to whom the Strozzi Palace has also been ascribed. Begun in 1489, it is one of the grandest of all Florentine palaces; it was completed by Cronaca by the addition of the magnificent cornice. Benedetto also designed the elegant portico outside S. Maria delle Grazie at Arezzo, as well as executing decorative work in the Palazzo Vecchio, Florence, and at the Santuario at Loreto.

BENJAMIN, Asher (1773, probably Greenfield, Massachusetts—1845, Boston), American architect and writer. During his youth in the Connecticut Valley he was trained as a carpenter, and soon became a successful builder working on many projects in the region, including Charles Bulfinch's Connecticut State House (1792). In 1797 he published *The Country Builder's Assistant*, the first builder's handbook written in America and designed specifically for American needs, reinterpreting, in carpenter's terms, the work of such English writers as Batty Langley (1696–1751) and William Halfpenny (d. 1755). In 1803 Benjamin moved to Boston and soon came completely under the influence of Bulfinch. His second book, *The American Builder's Companion* (1806) proclaimed a "New System of Architecture."

Benjamin's personality is less vivid in his architecture than in his writings. In Boston he built the West Church (1806) and the Charles Street Church (1807). He designed the Rhode Island Union Bank Building in Newport (1817) and made the design for Center Church in New Haven, Connecticut (built 1813–15 by his student, Ithiel Town), and for the First Church in Northampton, Massachusetts (somewhat altered and built 1810–12 by Isaac Damon, who was probably also his student).

BENOIS, Alexander Nikolaevich (1870, St. Petersburg—1960, Paris), Russian painter, set designer, and art critic of French descent. He was one of the founders, with Sergei Diaghilev, of the *Mir Iskusstva* ("World of Art") group and although Diaghilev was the principal organizer of the movement, Benois was its guide and spokesman.

Benois, with Léon Bakst, was the artist with the greatest influence on the creation of Diaghilev's Ballets Russes and on the artistic style it adopted. He, more than any other, was responsible for the importance of painting in the productions of the Ballets Russes. His sets for *Le Pavillon d'Armide* (1909), *Giselle* (1910), and *Petrushka* (1911) contributed a great deal to the dazzling effects that the Ballets Russes had, first on Parisian audiences, then on the whole of Europe, at the beginning of the 20th century—an effect in which fantasy and reality, poetic inspiration and popular tradition appeared side by side in a theatrical and artistically coherent display.

BENTON, Thomas Hart (1889, Neosho, Missouri—1975, Kansas City), American painter. Born into a politically prominent family, Benton first saw formal art in Washington, D.C., where his father was a member of Congress. He spent three years (1908–11) in Paris, at that time the center of controversial developments in modern art. The lasting impression of this experience, however, was not so much an understanding of modern French painting—Benton's later art emphatically rejects modernist tendencies—as an appreciation of Spanish art, particularly the work of El Greco. After World War I Benton traveled throughout the United States, sketching the subjects that were to stimulate much of his artistic production, subjects drawn from the American scene, especially the rural people and their occupations. During the 1930s he became famous for his semi-historical murals (1933, University of Indiana, Bloomington; 1936, State Capitol, Jefferson, Mo.), which were controversial for their mid-western "regionalist" subjects and popular native imagery. During World War II he temporarily abandoned this aspect of his art to concentrate on the *Perils of War* (Columbia, Missouri Historical Society), a series of paintings intended to "help awaken the people to the dangers of the moment." Social comment gradually disappeared from Benton's work in the 1940s and 1950s, when his art also evolved stylistically.

BÉRARD, Christian (1902, Paris—1949, Paris), French painter and designer of stage sets. In 1920 he joined the Académie Ranson, where he studied mainly under Édouard Vuillard. His painting, informed by a deep feeling for modernity and for the inner life of the individual, is limited almost exclusively to human scenes: the uneasy poetry of sleeping or pensive faces and of towns and beaches whose backgrounds dissolve in a mist of washtints or thin oil color; the fleeting poetry of the worlds of fashion and the stage. It was in the ephemeral world of the theater that Bérard's art found its finest expression: he produced the décors for Jean Cocteau's *La Voix humaine*, 1930, and *La Machine infernale*, 1934; Molière's *L'École des femmes*, 1936, and *Don Juan*, 1947; and for Giraudoux's *La Folle de Chaillot*, 1945. He also designed sets for ballets (*La Symphonie fantastique*, 1936; *Les Forains*, 1945) and films (Cocteau's *La Belle et la Bête*, 1945).

BERCHEM, Nicolaes *or* Claes Pietersz. (1620, Haarlem—1685, Amsterdam), Dutch painter, son of the still-life painter Pieter Claesz. A pupil of Jan van Goyen and a Master in 1642, Berchem was in Rome from 1642 until 1645. He painted some large canvases (*Education of Bacchus*, 1648; The Hague, Mauritshuis), but he preferred a small scale on wood or canvas. Berchem's pastorals—*The Ford* (Paris, Louvre), *Flocks* (1656; Amsterdam, Rijksmuseum), *Ford in Italy* (1661; The Hague, Mauritshuis)—had a great success in France during the 18th century and were an inspiration to both François Boucher and Jean-Baptiste Oudry. The realistic animals and myths, as well as the work, play, and loves of the shepherds living in an idyllic Arcady, are portrayed in landscapes in which conventional formulas are combined with freshly observed details from nature. A highly prolific, successful, and hard-working artist, he was responsible for some 800 paintings, 500 drawings, and over 50 etchings; he also added figures to the canvases of other artists.

BERCKHEYDE, Dutch painters, brothers, both of whom specialized in urban landscapes.

JOB (1630, Haarlem—1693, Haarlem), the elder brother, entered the painters' guild in 1654. He was at first less highly esteemed than his younger brother, but he is now considered the more accomplished artist. From his slender output (*Old Exchange at Amsterdam*, 1669, Rotterdam, Museum Boymans-van Beuningen; *Interior of the Church of St. Bavo at Haarlem*, 1688, Haarlem, Frans Halsmuseum), the most striking evidence of his great gifts is the *Oude Gracht at Haarlem* (1666; The Hague, Mauritshuis), a view of the quays and canal with a bridge in summer.

GERRIT (1638, Haarlem—1698, Haarlem), the younger brother, entered the guild in 1660 and is the better known. He painted numerous views of Haarlem, of The Hague, and of Amsterdam (*The Spaarne*, 1661, Douai, Museum; *The Great Market*, 1671, Haarlem, Frans Halsmuseum; *The Dam*, 1672, Amsterdam, Rijksmuseum; *The Fishmarket*, 1692, Frans Halsmuseum), sometimes with a sharpness akin to Pieter Saenredam, sometimes with a more supple freshness.

BERLAGE, Hendrik Petrus (1856, Amsterdam—1934, The Hague), Dutch architect. His best-known work is the Stock Exchange, Amsterdam (1897–1903), which is regarded as the starting point of modern architecture in Holland.

Berlage's activity extended well beyond architecture and town planning: in particular, he designed furniture and wallpaper, showed great interest in handicrafts, and published a number of writings. Moreover, he was one of the first European architects to adopt the new American building methods, which he studied on a visit to the United States in 1911.

Job Berckheyde. *Interior of the Church of St. Bavo at Haarlem*. Detail. 1688. Frans Halsmuseum, Haarlem.

BERNARD, Émile (1868, Lille—1941, Paris), French painter, poet, and art critic. When he was sixteen he went to the École des Beaux-Arts in Paris, in the studio of Fernand Cormon (1845–1924), where Toulouse-Lautrec was his fellow student. At eighteen, he had already made friends with Van Gogh and Gauguin, and was a trusted friend, too, of Cézanne and Odilon Redon. The correspondence he carried on with all these leading painters has been invaluable to historians of modern art. Two years after the suicide of Van Gogh, he organized an exhibition in Paris of 16 of his paintings, which helped to establish Van Gogh's reputation. Gauguin's debt to him was even greater, for it was Bernard who converted Gauguin to cloisonnism, although Gauguin has been claimed as its originator. Gauguin painted his *Yellow Christ* (1889) three years after the *Yellow Christ* of Émile Bernard, who also painted the Synthetist *Pouldu Landscape* in 1886, before his first meeting with Gauguin. Bernard left Paris in 1894 and went to live in Egypt; he did not return to France until ten years later. During his long stay away, he fell under the spell of Venetian art—to a degree that diluted his own forceful style—and became increasingly absorbed in writing, which occupied more and more of his time. Thus the painting of his later years, which did not live up to the promise of his early work, has been forgotten.

BERNINI, Gian Lorenzo *or* Giovanni Lorenzo (1598, Naples—1680, Rome), Italian Baroque painter, sculptor, decorator, and architect, whose name epitomizes the artistic activity of the papacy in the 17th century, one of the most prosperous periods in the church's history. Bernini's precocious genius made its first appearance in sculpture. The success of such works as the *Goat Amalthea with the Infant Jupiter and a Faun* (1615; Rome, Galleria Borghese) and the *Martyrdom of St. Lawrence* (*c.* 1616–17; Florence, Coll. Contini-Bonacossi) gained for the young Gian Lorenzo the favor of Cardinal Scipio Borghese. One of the most original characteristics of the artist is apparent in several works executed for the cardinal: his ability to capture in stone the moment of highest drama, such as David's gesture as he loads his sling against Goliath (1623–24; Galleria Borghese), Proserpina's doomed struggle to escape from her captor Pluto (1621–22; Galleria Borghese), or the incipient metamorphosis in one of his earliest masterpieces, the *Apollo and Daphne* (1622–25; Galleria Borghese). At this early period, Bernini had already begun a portrait series: the most majestic of these are *Pope Urban VIII* (*c.* 1640–42; Spoleto Cathedral) and *Francesco I d'Este, Duke of Modena* (1650–51; Modena, Galleria Estense). In his bust of *Costanza Buonarelli* (*c.* 1635; Florence, Bargello), his sole informal portrait, Bernini portrayed the features of his Roman mistress. Also unique of its type is the bust of *Antonio Negrita* (Rome, S. Maria Maggiore), the Negro ambassador from the Congo, carved in black marble with incrustations in the eyes. Bernini's secular commissions were followed by ecclesiastical ones spanning many years, during which one can recognize the spiritual evolution of the artist. His range covered every nuance of religious emotion: the ardor and confidence of prayer in the *St. Jerome* holding the crucifix to himself (*c.* 1661–63; Siena Cathedral), the tender beatitude of *St. Bibiana* with the martyr's palm (1624–26; Rome, S. Bibiana), the dying rapture of the *Blessed Ludovica Albertoni* (1674; Rome, Altieri Chapel, S. Francesco a Ripa). In the *Ecstasy of St. Teresa* (1645–52; Rome, Cornaro Chapel, S. Maria della Vittoria), the masterpiece he executed while temporarily out of favor with Pope Innocent X, Bernini attempted the difficult subject of spiritual ecstasy.

At a time when scenic illusion was supremely important, a decorator as brilliant as Bernini rose effortlessly to the position of architect, and, from his early thirties on, he was entrusted with the planning of buildings. For

Gian Lorenzo Bernini. *Ecstasy of St. Teresa.* 1645–52. Cornaro Chapel, S. Maria della Vittoria, Rome. *Photo Alinari, Florence.*

Gian Lorenzo Bernini. Colonnade of St. Peter's, Rome. 1656–67. *Photo Ministero della Difesa Aeronautica, Rome.*

Rome's Palazzo Barberini, where he succeeded Carlo Maderno and collaborated for a time with Francesco Borromini, his great rival in architecture, Bernini designed the façade (1628–33), in which three stories of arcades and loggias are superimposed upon each other. The Palazzo di Montecitorio (designed 1650) and the Palazzo Chigi-Odescalchi, both also in Rome, are his greatest secular buildings, but Bernini devoted more of his time to churches. He treated the central plans of S. Tomaso di Villanova at Castelgandolfo (1660) and S. Maria dell'Assunzione at Ariccia with great simplicity. S. Maria is severely classical, with an interior—as Bernini explained during his stay in France—that had at first seemed rather cramped but appeared wider by a third when the dome was completed. Bernini used a similar device in S. Andrea al Quirinale, Rome (1658–78): the two rounded arms project forward in a kind of welcoming gesture and focus attention on the subtle façade. The interior oval space is articulated by a running entablature, supported by composite pilasters, and ringed by nine chapels. On the shortest axis, directly opposite the entrance and thus the spectator's first and most immediate view, is the high altar; here the entablature carries a broken pediment that encloses a statue of St. Andrew ascending from the earthly church body toward the heavenly dome. By combining the literal with the symbolic, Bernini created a complete religious experience. Despite its small size, he considered this church his most accomplished work. The delicate polychromy, the ribs and caissons of the vaults, and the flights of the cherubs reveal Borromini's influence.

When he succeeded Maderno, Carlo Fontana, and the great masters of the 16th century at St. Peter's, most of the construction had been completed. Bernini's major task was to harmonize the various parts, designed over several generations; his arrangements, both inside and outside the church, express the spirit of a single period and the unity of a single inspiration. Bernini swung the two arms of the elliptical colonnade around the piazza to compensate for the overemphatic effect of the horizontals by leading the eye to the central part of the building.

For the transept of the basilica Urban VIII commissioned the Baldacchino (1624–33), which was to replace the temporary scaffolding of wooden beams and canvas that had previously sheltered the Blessed Sacrament (the alleged remains of St. Peter's grave) with a structure of marble and bronze as high as Palazzo Farnese. Behind the Baldacchino, Bernini erected another splendid composition—a fusion of architecture, sculpture, and stained glass—the Cathedra Petri, or chair of St. Peter, the visible symbol of Peter's role as Christ's vicar and as the first pope (1657–66).

Like the Baldacchino, which was copied throughout the Catholic world, the two papal tombs in St. Peter's also became prototypes of a new Christian representation of death. These works are inspired by an over-all dramatic concept complementing their function as funerary monuments. The tomb of Urban VIII (finished in 1647) is the earlier of the two; the pope sits at the summit, wearing his triple tiara and giving his blessing to the world. At his feet the winged skeleton of Death, having emerged from a black marble sarcophagus, writes on a tablet the name of the man who can no longer elude his call. In the second monument, carved 25 years later (1671–75), when Bernini was in his seventies, Alexander VII is shown kneeling bareheaded, and a wraithlike Death emerges with an hour-glass, ready to carry off the person of the pontiff wrapped in his jasper drapery.

Bernini spent almost his entire career in Rome, with one notable exception: Cavalier Bernini was invited—or rather summoned—to Paris by Louis XIV in 1665. The inadequacy of the French plans for the completion of the Louvre and the desire to execute a power play at the expense of Alexander VII caused Louis XIV and his finance minister Colbert to take this step. A medal struck in 1665, engravings, and drawings preserved in Paris and Stockholm help us to reconstruct Bernini's plans for the Louvre. Altogether, Bernini devised four projects for it, none of which was carried out.

While in France the sculptor carved a bust of Louis XIV from life (1665; Versailles, Museum). But his coolness toward French building style and French painting annoyed his hosts, and it was this opposition, in addition to financial considerations, that led Louis XIV to abandon Bernini's plans when the great artist returned to Italy. On taking his leave (1665), the master offered the king his portrait bust and received 10,000 golden crowns as recompense.

Bernini spent his final 15 years in Rome. His later works, beginning perhaps with *Truth Revealed by Time* (1646–52; Rome, Galleria Borghese), display a highly personal style, more spiritual and meditative than before. Among the finest of these are the two statues he designed for the Chigi Chapel in S. Maria del Popolo: *Daniel in the Lion's Den* (1655–57) and *Habakkuk and the Angel* (1655–71). Others, of increasing emotional intensity toward the end, are the famous angels on the Ponte S. Angelo (1667–69) and the *Blessed Ludovica Albertoni*. These final offerings reveal a high sense of the dramatic and a deep religious faith—qualities that, to a greater or lesser degree, are central to Bernini's entire oeuvre.

BERRUGUETE, Pedro de (b. Paredes de Nava?—d. before 1504), the first great Spanish Renaissance painter. He was exposed early to the Hispano-Flemish atmosphere in Castille, the Palencia region, Burgos, and Valladolid, where the tradition set by Jan van Eyck's followers prevailed. This background was not at variance with his experience in Italy, which he visited about 1447, since he spent some time at Urbino, where Flemish painting was appreciated. While in this town he took part in the decoration that Federigo da Montefeltro had commissioned for his palace: many of the portraits painted for the duke's study (some now in the Louvre, Paris) are attributed to him, and he is credited, too, with the group portrait of *Federigo da Montefeltro and His Court* (Windsor Castle). He definitely acquired his own particular feeling for light during his trip to Italy, since he enriched his Hispano-Flemish training by studying the works of Piero della Francesca and the Venetian School; he also brought back to Spain a knowledge of Quattrocento architecture and decoration, particularly as they were practiced at Urbino. At Paredes de Nava he painted the *Evangelists* and the Retable of the Holy Cross (church of S. Juan) and the *Life of the Virgin* (main altarpiece in the church of S. Eulalia). At S. María del Campo he depicted the *Beheading of St. John the Baptist* in a Renaissance setting, and he devoted the great altarpiece of the church of S. Tomás, Ávila, to the life of that saint; the arms of the *crucero* (transept) show episodes from the life of St. Dominic and St. Peter Martyr (mostly in Madrid, Prado). The altarpiece in the choir of the cathedral at Ávila (1499–1506) might have been his masterpiece, but he completed only two parts: *Christ in the Garden of Olives*, together with the intensely pathetic *Flagellation*, at the top on the left; and the paintings of the predella, showing the *Evangelists and Church Fathers* surrounding the presence of Christ in the Eucharist in the center. Apart from these large groups, the *Annunciation* in the Carthusian monastery at Miraflores displays a brilliant use of light. Berruguete not only combined the Hispano-Flemish tradition with what he had learned in Italy, but he tempered the realism of the period with an aristocratic elegance, an inner serenity, and a restrained tone. These various qualities appear in the artist's *Self-Portrait*, which gives a sympathetic picture of the man and suggests his genuine talent (Madrid, Museo Lazaro Galdiano).

ALONSO DE (*c.* 1488, Paredes de Nava, near Valladolid—1561, Toledo), his son, was a sculptor, painter, and architect. He received his early training from Pedro and at first wanted to follow in his footsteps as a court painter. However, he studied in Italy, notably in Florence and Rome, from about 1508, and was clearly very much influenced by the years he spent in that country, where he admired the *Laocoön* in the Vatican collections and came under Michelangelo's influence. Alonso's temperament seemed to harmonize instinctively with the Florentine Renaissance style of the sculptors Ghiberti and Donatello. Although he undoubtedly did a number of paintings in Italy, the only one known with certainty is the *Coronation of the Virgin* (Paris, Louvre). After his return to Spain he was appointed painter to King Charles I around 1518. While at Saragossa (1517–18), he worked on the tomb of Juan Selvagio in the church of S. Engracia (fragments in Saragossa, Palacio de Museos). The relief of the *Resurrection* dates from the same period (Valencia Cathedral). Although nominally court painter, he received very little royal support, and so he set up as a sculptor in Valladolid. The altarpiece for the monastery of La Mejorada, Olmedo (1525; Valladolid, Museo Nacional de Escultura), on the theme of the Passion, is already typical of his style, with its disregard for "correctness," its agonized poses, and the importance placed on the inner life. The following are thought to have been executed at the same time: the *Ecce Homo* in the church of S. Juan, Olmedo; *Christ at the Pillar*, in the church of Guaza (province of Palencia); and the *Virgin and Child*, in the church of S. Eulalia, Paredes de Nava. The S. Benito altarpiece (1526–32) constitutes the crowning achievement of Berruguete's work at Valladolid. The quality of the scenes in relief (*Mass of St. Gregory*, the *Virgin Giving the Chasuble to S. Ildefonso*, the *Life of Christ*, and *S. Benito*) is generally inferior to that of the statues or groups in the round—the *St. Sebastian* or the *Sacrifice of Isaac*, for instance—which show an extraordinarily powerful expressivity. The great altarpiece in the Colegio de los Irlandeses, Salamanca (1529), has been reconstructed, but magnificent sections of it are still preserved: the *Calvary*, the *Virgin of Pity, St. Bartholomew, St. Andrew*, and *St. Peter*. The *Adoration of the Magi* in the church of Santiago, Valladolid (1537), follows the pattern of the altarpiece in the Capilla del Condestable of Burgos Cathedral, in which scenes from the lives of Christ and the Virgin are arranged around the central subject.

In Toledo Cathedral, to which he had been summoned by Cardinal Tavera, Berruguete carved figures from the Old and New Testaments above the choir stalls. He was responsible for the *Transfiguration* in alabaster, which dominates the throne, and for the three reliefs in painted wood, which decorate it—the *Crossing of the Red Sea*, the *Brazen Serpent*, and the *Last Judgment*. It is likely that he

Alonso de Berruguete. *Messenger sent by King Totila to S. Benito.* Detail from the S. Benito altarpiece. 1526–32. Museo Nacional de Escultura, Valladolid. *Photo Martin Hürlimann, Zurich.*

Albert Besnard. Ceiling of the Théâtre-Français, Paris. Detail. 1910–13. *Archives photographiques, Paris.*

executed the altarpiece of St. Ursula, also at Toledo. The *Transfiguration* in the cathedral inspired him to another similar piece of work in painted wood in the church of El Salvador, Upeda, which was unfortunately badly damaged in 1936. Death overtook the artist while he was working on his patron's tomb at Toledo (Hospice of S. Juan de Bautista).

BERTHOLLE, Jean (1909, Dijon—1970, Dijon), French painter. After studying at the École des Beaux-Arts in Lyons and Paris, he set out to develop a personal idiom, passing from a sensual Impressionism influenced by Renoir to a tormented Expressionism reminiscent of Soutine. Later, Bertholle abandoned realism for an allusive style (1948), then for nonfigurative painting (*Composition*, 1955; Paris, Musée National d'Art Moderne), with clearly defined forms, carefully articulated composition, and sober, somewhat solemn color. Some works in this mode express religious feelings (*Magnificat*, 1958), while others are inspired by the external world (*Venise* and *La Ville*, both 1957).

BERTOIA, Harry (b. 1915, San Lorenzo, Italy), American sculptor. He came to the United States in 1930, and studied art at the Detroit Society of Arts and Crafts and at the Cranbrook Academy of Art in Bloomfield Hills, Michigan, where he also taught (1937–41). Bertoia established a reputation not only as a sculptor, but also as an interior designer, furniture designer, and graphic artist, for he considered all these disciplines to be related. While working as a sculptor-designer for Knoll Associates in New York City during the early 1950s Bertoia designed a wire chair; due to his particular interest in the integration of sculpture and architecture, he created much architectural sculpture for public buildings, of which one of the most successful examples is the 70-foot metal screen commissioned by Skidmore, Owings & Merrill for the Fifth Avenue Branch of the Manufacturers Trust Company, New York (1954).

BESNARD, Albert (1849, Paris—1934, Paris), French painter. In 1866 he entered the École des Beaux-Arts, where he studied under Alexandre Cabanel. He showed little enthusiasm for the academic training there but came into his own in 1874 as the recipient of the Prix de Rome and exhibitor of a highly successful female portrait in the Salon. Besnard spent the years 1879–81 in London, where he painted several portraits of British aristocrats. In Paris his decorations for the École de Pharmacie (*Convalescence*, 1883; *Gathering Medicinal Herbs*, 1884) express the poetic grandeur of science. One may question the quality of his *Evening of Life* (1887; Paris, Mairie of the 1st arrondissement) and *Life Reborn from Death* (Paris, Sorbonne), but not the originality of the bold lighting and play of reflections in decorations for the dome of the Petit Palais and for the ceilings of the Hôtel de Ville and Théâtre-Français, all in Paris. The same experiments appear in his portraits (*Madame Roger Jourdain*, 1886; Paris, Louvre) and in his easel compositions (*The Happy Isle*, 1900; Paris, Musée des Arts Décoratifs), together with an obtrusive overlay of Art Nouveau. Besnard was director of the École Français in Rome (1914), then of the École Nationale des Beaux-Arts (1922), and a member of the Institut de France. In 1924 he was elected to the Académie Française.

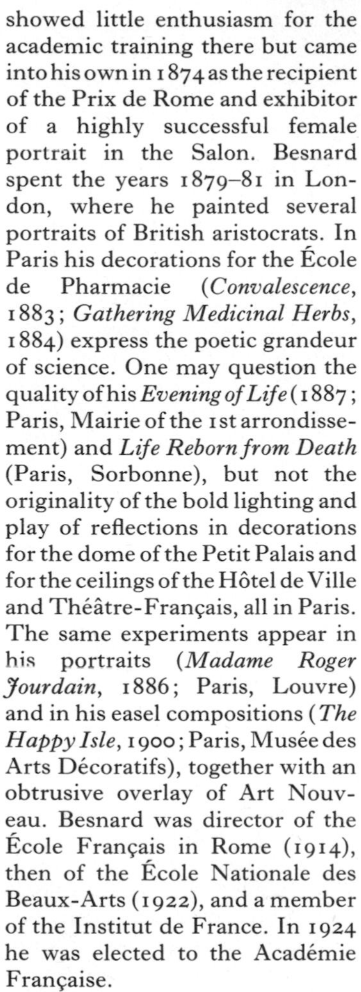

BEUCKELAER *or* **BUECKELAER,** Joachim (*c.* 1530, Antwerp—*c.* 1573, Antwerp), Flemish painter of still lifes, often with New Testament scenes introduced into the background. He became a pupil of his uncle Pieter Aertsen in 1542, and a Master in 1560. His numerous works, which appeared in nearly all Flemish collections of the 17th century, are dated from 1561 to 1571. He was a follower of Aertsen, from whom he took such subjects as the *Kermesse* (1563; Leningrad, Hermitage), various market scenes (*Peasants with Poultry, Butter, and Eggs*, 1567; Vienna, Kunsthistorisches Museum), and culinary scenes (*Kitchen Scene with Christ in the House of Mary and Martha*, 1567; Stockholm, Nationalmuseum). A master of still life, he showed an extreme virtuosity as a painter of fruit (*Market Woman*; Antwerp, Musée Royal des Beaux-Arts), game, and fish (*Fish Market with Ecce Homo*, 1570; Stockholm, Nationalmuseum).

BEWICK, Thomas (1753, Cherryburn, near Newcastle—1828, Cherryburn), English wood engraver. In 1767 he was apprenticed to Ralph Beilby (1744–1817), a Newcastle copperplate engraver, and he worked with his master on the illustrations to an edition of Gay's *Fables*. He settled in London shortly after his apprenticeship expired in 1774, but in 1777 returned to Newcastle, where he entered into partnership with Beilby. Bewick's own *General History of Quadrupeds* was published in 1790 and immediately established his fame as a wood engraver of the first rank. A second edition appeared in 1791, and an eighth in 1824. In conjunction with his brother John, Bewick supplied woodcuts for William Bulmer's editions of *Poems by Goldsmith and Parnell* (1795) and Somerville's *Chase* (1796).

Bewick's crowning achievement was his *British Birds*. The first volume, with written descriptions by Beilby, appeared in 1797; the second volume, *British Water Birds*, published in 1804, was the work of Bewick alone. The exquisite drawings, the best of which are in the Hancock Museum and the public library in Newcastle, were done from life; details of feathers and plumage in the British Museum, London, attest Bewick's supreme delicacy and naturalism. A prolific worker, Bewick also supplied numerous illustrations for current publications, such as *The Sportsman's Friend* of 1801. In 1818 his last important illustrated work, *Fables of Aesop and Others*, appeared; here the cuts are in oval frames and have a more condensed look. In 1822 Bewick began to write a *Memoir* for his daughter, which contains a lively account of his youth and his religious and political opinions. The work was finished a week before his death in 1828.

BIBIENA, Galli da, a family of Italian architects, stage designers, inventors, and decorators descended from Giovanni Maria Galli, who became known as Bibiena from the name of the village near Florence where he was born in 1625. He was a painter, and after training under Francesco Albani, he worked mainly in Bologna, where he died in 1665. The most famous members of the family were:

FERDINANDO (1657, Bologna—1743, Bologna), son of Giovanni Maria Galli, and the most prolific of the Bibiena. He studied both painting and architecture and worked first as an architect in the service of the Farnese family in Parma. In 1708 he was invited to Barcelona to create decorations for the marriage of the future Emperor Charles VI. Ferdinando then went to Vienna, where he designed settings for court festivities and opera productions.

FRANCESCO (1659, Bologna—1739, Bologna), brother of Ferdinando. He specialized in the design of theater buildings, many of which are no longer standing. He worked at Piacenza, Parma, Rome, and then in Mantua as architect to the Gonzaga family. After staying for some time in Genoa and in Naples, he was called to Vienna to build an opera house. Sometime between 1712 and 1720 he also designed the Teatro Filarmonico in Verona.

ALESSANDRO (1687, Parma—1769, Mannheim), eldest son of Ferdinando. In 1719 he was in the service of the Elector Palatine Karl Philipp, who appointed him superintendent of his buildings and ennobled him in 1740. He is best known for the north wing of the palace and the Opera in Mannheim (1737; destroyed by fire in 1795) and for the Jesuit church there.

GIUSEPPE (1696, Parma—1756, Berlin), second son of Ferdinando. The most accomplished artist of the family, he was famed for his opera sets. While still very young, he accompanied his father to Barcelona and then to Vienna, where he settled and organized the most splendid entertainments for the Hapsburgs. In 1747 and 1750 he worked on the new Dresden Opera House (destroyed by fire in 1849) and in 1748 on the lavish Italian Baroque interior decoration of the theatre in Bayreuth.

ANTONIO (1700, Parma—1774, Milan), third son of Ferdinando. A theatre architect, he worked in Siena, Florence, and Bologna, where he built the municipal theater (1756–63), one of the finest Baroque theaters in Italy. He decorated many churches and was employed by the court in Vienna.

CARLO (1728, Vienna—1787, Florence), son of Giuseppe. He worked throughout Europe, being the last of the Bibiena to devote himself to the theater.

BIEDERMEIER, a literary and, particularly, artistic style of late bourgeois classicism that existed in Germany, Austria, and Scandinavia between 1814 and 1848. The term is derived from the name of a comic character created by the 19th-century German poet Ludwig Eichrodt, and was at first used wholly pejoratively. The subjects of Biedermeier painting are drawn from the more pleasant everyday incidents of bourgeois life; the technique is realistic and precise but generally pedestrian. The chief representatives of this style were Georg Friedrich Kersting (1785–1847), Ludwig Richter (1803–84), Moritz von Schwind (1804–71), who employed a half-sentimental, half-fantastic treatment; Josef Danhauser (1805–45), a more dramatic artist; Carl Spitzweg (1808–85) and Theodor Hosemann (1807–75), with their rather stiff sense of humor; and Ferdinand Georg Waldmüller (1793–1865), one of the most lyrical of the Beidermeier landscape painters. In literature, Beidermeier writers cultivated a bourgeois coziness, a taste for the trivial and sentimental, and very conservative and moralistic notions. In the decorative arts the term is applied particularly to interior decoration: Beidermeier furniture is comfortable, graceful, and gay.

BIERSTADT, Albert (1830, Solingen, North Rhine-Westphalia—1902, New York), German-born American landscape painter. He came to the United States as a child, and grew up in New Bedford, Massachusetts. In 1853 he went to study at the Düsseldorf Academy. He continued his training in Rome, and in 1857 returned to America, settling in New York in 1861. Some time later he moved his studio to Irvington on the Hudson, but later lived again in New York.

Although Bierstadt's Düsseldorf training had not prepared him to paint the American landscape, the scale and inspiration of the great West enabled him to transcend these former limitations. In his *Merced River, Yosemite Valley* (1866; New York, Metropolitan Museum), one sees his broad handling of these vast and grandiose spaces—the almost Alpine mountain ranges, exaggeratedly tall, sweep down majestically to the small and intimate figures in the encampment. Bierstadt's small field sketches are more admired today than some of his paintings, for they show an inspired and spontaneous—yet artful—approach, the difference between creative artist and mere craftsman.

BILL, Max (b. 1908, Winterthur), Swiss architect, painter, sculptor, and writer. He studied at the School of Arts and Crafts in Zurich, then from 1927 to 1929 at the Dessau Bauhaus, where the teaching profoundly influenced his artistic development. There he absorbed a thorough knowledge of different materials and their functions, as well as the conception of a synthesis of the arts centered in architecture. He settled in Zurich as an architect in 1930, and he also extended his activities to sculpture, painting, and the applied arts.

Like Georges Vantongerloo, Bill often based his painting on straight lines and geometric patterns, designed with a rhythmic order that varied according to the theme. The same order appears in his sculptures composed of multiple elements, such as the *Construction with Thirty Identical Elements* (1938–39). With the *Unending Band* (1935) he tackled the problem of continuous movement in sculpture. The same theme reappears in *Infinite Surface in the Form of a Column* (1953), a

Max Bill. *Construction.* 1958–59. Théâtre du Parc, Grenchen, Switzerland.

slender blade of brass that rises like an arrow in rotation. In his paintings after 1950 Bill tried, according to mathematical formulas, to give visual form to notions of the indefinite and immeasurable. He gave up restrictive lines and surfaces for color zones transformed through luminous tones into fields of energy, acting one against the other. He was cofounder of the Hochschule für Gestaltung at Ulm, which he directed from 1951 to 1957, and designed its architectural layout to harmonize with the undulating ground.

BINGHAM, George Caleb (1811, Augusta County, Virginia—1879, Kansas City, Missouri), American painter. His artistic talents were revealed when he tried sign painting, and he soon turned to portraiture. After studying art for a few months in Philadelphia, he realized that Easterners were fascinated by life in what was then the West. His lighthearted genre paintings of life on the Missouri River were widely acclaimed. The most lyrical version of his river subjects, *Fur Traders Descending the Missouri* (1845; New York, Metropolitan Museum), captures an eternal moment in which the mirror-like surface of the water doubles the silhouette of figures and objects in a boat and extends to the edges of the canvas the golden glow of hazy sunlight. Serenity also characterizes Bingham's landscapes, unpeopled except for placid cows. More activity and noise enter his political subjects (*Stump Speaking*, 1854; St. Louis, Boatman's National Bank). In the most successful of these, Bingham was able to unite large crowds by using carefully controlled patterns of light and dark. In quest of further refinement for his art, Bingham went to Düsseldorf, Germany, during the 1850s, and his once spontaneous and occasionally poetic imagery never recuperated from the infusion of studied artificiality and garish color.

BIROLLI, Renato (1906, Verona—1959, Milan), Italian painter. After studying at the Accademia Cignaroli in Verona, he went to Milan in 1928. In 1938 he helped to found the Corrente Group, and both in his work and writing he put up a vigorous resistance to the academic and official art of the Novecento. He was then persecuted by the regime and twice imprisoned. In 1947 he was one of the organizers of the Fronte Nuovo delle Arti, which grouped together the postwar Italian avant-garde; five years later he took part in the group called the Eight Italian Painters. Influenced initially by Van Gogh, Birolli came for a time under the influence of Picasso (*Girl with Bread*, 1948; Brescia, Coll. Achille Cavellini); then, in 1952, his art culminated in a highly colored and completely nonfigurative expressionism (*Fire*, 1956, Rome, Coll. Campilli. *In Search*, 1956, Rome, Coll. De Luca).

BISSEN, Herman Wilhelm (1798, Schleswig—1868, Copenhagen), Danish sculptor. He first studied painting, then joined the Copenhagen Academy of Fine Arts (1816–23) to study sculpture. He worked in the Roman studio of the Neoclassical sculptor Bertel Thorvaldsen from 1824 to 1834, and was appointed professor of sculpture at the Academy of Fine Arts in Copenhagen in 1840. His masterpiece is probably the Soldier's Monument (1850) in the cemetery at Fredericia, Jutland, which clearly shows the break with Thorvaldsen, who never abandoned the canons of Classical beauty. Among Bissen's other works, mention should be made of the portrait bust of *King Frederik VI* (1856), the *Anger of Achilles* (1861), and the huge frieze—144 feet in length—in the castle at Christiansborg, representing the *Triumph of Bacchus and Ceres* (1835–41). He was given a great many commissions, notably for the magnificent portrait of *Bishop J. P. Meyer* (1835–36) and for the statues of Apollo and Athena that decorate the entrance hall of the University of Copenhagen.

BISSIER, Julius (1893, Freiburg-im-Breisgau, Germany—1965, Ascona, Switzerland), German painter. Although he attended courses at the Academy of Fine Arts in Karlsruhe (1913–14), he was essentially self-taught. In 1919 Bissier met the Sinologist Ernst Grosse, who introduced him to the art and civilizations of the Far East. He abandoned figurative painting after 1930 to begin the quest for a few signs, as concentrated and stark as possible, to serve as the basis for "psychograms," or calligraphic equivalents for particular feelings. He confined himself exclusively to black and white until 1947, when he began to use color for his monotypes. In 1956 Bissier began a series of miniatures, painted in an oil-and-egg tempera that not only gave his style greater breadth, but also marked a return to visual appearances reduced to simple transparencies.

BISSIÈRE, Roger (1886, Garonne—1964, Boissiérettes, Lot), French painter. He studied at the École des Beaux-Arts in Bordeaux, then went to Paris in 1910. He exhibited for the first time at the Salon d'Automne of 1919; became the friend of André Lhote and Georges Braque; contributed to *L'Esprit Nouveau*, a review founded by Amédée Ozenfant and Le Corbusier; and taught at the Académie Ranson from 1925 to 1938. In 1939 he retired to his ancestral home in Boissiérettes (Lot). Blinded by glaucoma, he nevertheless executed, with the aid of his wife, tapestries consisting of bits of fabric sewn together. In 1948 he underwent an operation and regained his sight. From that date his exhibitions became more frequent. In 1952 he was awarded the Grand Prix des Arts; in 1959 the Musée National d'Art Moderne in Paris organized a retrospective of his works.

BLAKE, William (1757, London—1827, London), English poet, mystic, engraver, and painter. In 1767 Blake entered the drawing school of Henry Pars (1742–82), and in 1772 began a seven-year apprenticeship to the engraver James Basire (1730–1802) in Lincoln's Inn Fields; part of this time was spent in drawing busts, tombs, and monuments in Westminster Abbey and other London churches. After his apprenticeship expired, Blake continued his studies at the Royal Academy Schools, where his friends included James Barry, Henry Fuseli, John Hamilton Mortimer (*c.* 1741–79), John Flaxman, and Thomas Stothard (1755–1834). The influences of the latter three are discernible in one of Blake's earliest works, the *Penance of Jane Shore*, in pen and watercolor (1778–80; London, Tate Gallery).

In 1782 Blake married, and two years later he set up a print shop in Broad Street with James Parker (1750–1805), a fellow student at Basire's. For three years Blake engraved his own designs and those of others. This continuity was broken in 1787, when his brother Robert died, and a new mysticism, together with a sense of being "directed," entered Blake's life. He became associated with the Swedenborgians, whose first chapel was opened in London in 1788; he was highly excited by the fall of the Bastille and was friendly with the radical republicans Price, Thomas Paine, and Mary Wollstonecraft, and with the anarchist William Godwin. About 1794 when the radical London Corresponding Society was put down, he turned his attention from political agitation to "spiritual strife." Blake was enormously active both as a poet and engraver. An early book of *Poetical Sketches* had been printed in 1783, but a prospectus of 1793 lists *Songs of Innocence; Songs of Experience; America, a Prophecy; Vision of the Daughters of Albion; The Book of Thel;* and *The Marriage of Heaven and Hell*. These books were printed in an entirely original manner. Each page was engraved like a picture on a copper plate, but Blake wrote the words and drew the image in a liquid impervious to acid, then applied acid to eat away the rest of the plate, leaving the words and pictures in relief. Ink or color wash was then applied, the pictorial part being then finished off by hand with watercolor. This combination of poetry and painting, the one inseparable from the other, is at its most attractive when the text is short, as, for example, in the title page of *The Book of Thel* or the page entitled *The Lamb* from *Songs of Innocence* (both 1789; London, British Museum). Blake's illuminated painting culminated in a series of large color plates of 1795, of which the *Newton* and the *Nebuchadnezzar* (both Tate Gallery) are the most important.

To the years 1794–99, when Blake was living in Lambeth, belong *Europe, a Prophecy*, which has as its frontispiece *The Ancient of Days* (British Museum), *Urizen, Ahania, Los*, and *The Song of Los*. The theme of all these books is the struggle between reason and imagination.

In 1800 Blake moved to Felpham in Sussex on the invitation of the poet William Hayley, who asked him to engrave illustrations for his *Life of Cowper*. In Felpham the *Four Zoas* were written, largely to be converted into *Milton* and *Jerusalem*. On his return to London in 1803, Blake entered upon a period of apparent failure. In 1808 his illustrations to Blair's *Grave* were attacked as "libidinous." An exhibition that he held in 1809 attracted only one notice, and that was hostile; and in 1815 he was reduced to engraving vases and tureens for Josiah Wedgwood the Younger's private catalogue. His main, indeed only, patron at this time was Thomas Butts, for whom he painted his first temperas as well as more than 100 watercolors on subjects from Milton and the Bible. *Jerusalem* (1804–*c.* 1818) and *The Book of Job* (*c.* 1818–20) were composed at this time. The last three years of Blake's life were occupied with the illustrations to *Dante* and were comforted by the admiration of a number of younger painters such as John Varley (1778–1842), John Linnell (1792–1882), and Edward Calvert.

Blaue Reiter. August Macke. *At the Zoo*. 1912.

BLAKELOCK, Ralph Albert (1847, New York—1919, New York), American painter. Although he was largely self-trained as an artist, the influence of the French Barbizon School painters Théodore Rousseau and Jean-Baptiste Camille Corot are discernible in his landscapes, which are also related to those of the Hudson River School of American landscapists.

Blakelock's early paintings were small, frequently repetitive landscapes; he then turned to American Indian themes after taking a trip to the West in 1869–72. He is best known for his moonlit landscapes, in which the sky is partially covered by delicately silhouetted branches and trees, painted in mottled darks against the richly glowing light of the dusk or the full moon (*Brook by Moonlight*, *c.* 1885; Toledo, Museum of Art). Blakelock often relied on musical improvisation to infuse his paintings with the mysterious or pastoral mood he wished to evoke, and he reputedly sometimes alternated between playing the piano and painting in order to achieve the kind of rhythmical visual nuances he desired (*Pipe Dance*; New York, Metropolitan Museum).

In 1899, following a nervous breakdown, Blakelock was committed to an asylum and his work was largely forgotten; but in 1916 his paintings were rediscovered and he was released, only to gain a measure of fame and success when it was already too late for him to benefit from it.

BLAUE REITER, one of the most fertile artistic movements of Germany prior to 1914. It was long believed that its name was derived from a small painting by Wassily Kandinsky, dated 1909 and actually entitled *Der blaue Reiter* ("the blue rider") or *Improvisation No. 3* (Munich, Coll. Strangl). But in 1930 Kandinsky himself explained how the name came to be adopted: "Franz Marc and I chose this name as we were having coffee on the shady terrace of Sindelsdorf. Both of us liked blue, Marc for horses, I for riders. So the name came by itself." At the beginning of the 20th century Munich was one of the main centers of German artistic activity. In January 1909 Adolf Erbslöh (1881–1947), Alexej von Jawlensky, Kandinsky, Alexander Kanoldt, Alfred Kubin, Gabriele Münter (1887–1962), Marianna von Werefkin (1860–1938), Heinrich Schnabel, and Oskar Wittenstein formed the New Artists' Federation of Munich, holding their first exhibition at the Tannhäuser Gallery from December 1909 to January 1910. Other artists joined the movement and Picasso, Derain, Rouault, Vlaminck, Braque and Van Dongen were invited to take part in the exhibitions.

This vast group with no definite program had no aim other than to unite all the young artistic forces. To show its importance and its variety, Marc and Kandinsky took it upon themselves, in July 1911, to prepare a collective volume of aesthetic studies and numerous illustrations under the title of *Der blaue Reiter*. But even before it appeared, Kandinsky, Kubin, Marc, and Münter left the association. On December 18, the first exhibition of the new Blaue Reiter group was held, showing 43 pictures by Henri Rousseau, Delaunay, Elizabeth Epstein, Eugen

1.

2.

3.

1. **Andrea del Castagno.** *David. c.* 1450–57. Widener Coll., National Gallery of Art, Washington, D.C.
2. **Andrea del Sarto.** *Portrait of Lucretia, wife of the painter.* Prado, Madrid.
3. **Albrecht Altdorfer.** *Susanna at the Bath.* Detail. 1526. Alte Pinakothek, Munich. Photo Kempter, Munich.
4. **Fra Angelico.** *Deposition. c.* 1440. Museo di S. Marco, Florence.
5. **Andrea Pisano.** *Baptism of Christ.* Baptistery door, Florence. 1330–36.
6. **Mariotto Albertinelli.** *Adoration of the Infant Jesus.* Detail, predella of the Visitation. 1503. Uffizi, Florence.

4.

5.

6.

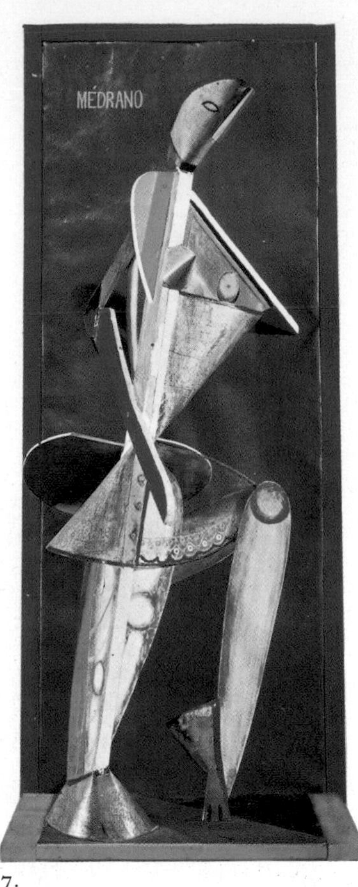

7.

8.

9.

10.

11.

7. **Alexander Archipenko.** *Medrano II*. 1914. Solomon R. Guggenheim Museum, New York.
8. **Giuseppe Arcimboldo.** *Summer*. 1563. Kunsthistorisches Museum, Vienna.
9. **Jean Arp.** *Painted wood*. 1917. Coll. artist.
10. **Andrea Appiani.** *Parnassus*. 1810. Villa Reale, Monza.
11. **Hendrick Avercamp.** *Winter Landscape*. Detail. Rijksmuseum, Amsterdam. Photo Eds. Tisné, Paris.
12. **Karel Appel.** Sketch for cover of review *Du*. Zurich. 1963.
13. Opposite: **Antonello da Messina.** *Portrait of a Man*. Detail. *c*. 1475. National Gallery, London.

12.

14.

15.

16.

17.

14. **Frédéric Bazille.** *Family Reunion.* 1867. Louvre, Paris.
15. **André Bauchant.** *Father Truffaut.* 1925. Private Coll., Paris.
16. **Hans Baldung Grien.** *Three Graces. c.* 1540. Prado, Madrid.
17. **Jacopo Bassano.** *Crucifixion.* 1562. Museo Civico, Treviso.
18. **William Blake.** *Dante and Virgil at the Entrance to Hell,* from the "Divine Comedy." 1824–27. Tate Gallery, London.
19. **Giovanni Bellini.** *Madonna of the Trees.* 1487. Accademia, Venice.
20. **Giacomo Balla.** *Mercury Passing Before the Sun.* 1914. Private Coll., Milan.

18.

19.

20.

21.

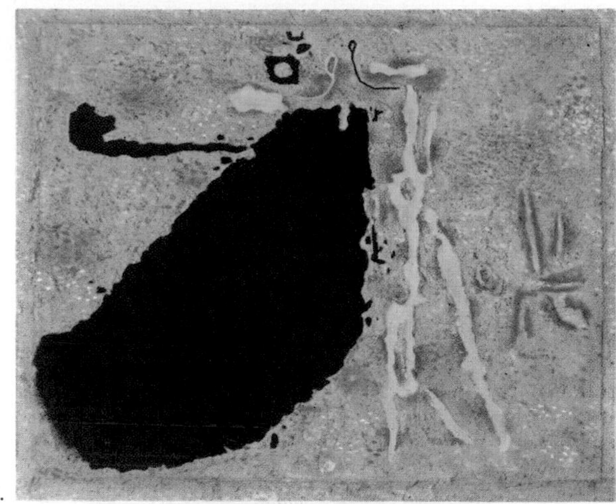

22.

21. **Francis Bacon.** *Man and Child.* 1963. Marlborough Fine Art Ltd., London.
22. **Willi Baumeister.** *Safer with Pipe.* 1953. Galerie Bucher, Paris.
23. **Jean Bazaine.** *Noon, Trees, and Rocks.* 1952. Private Coll., Zurich.
24. **Aubrey Beardsley.** *Isolde. c.* 1890. Fogg Art Museum, Harvard University, Cambridge, Mass.
25. **Arnold Böcklin.** *Isle of the Dead* (first version). 1880. Gottfried Keller Coll., Kunstmuseum, Basel. Photo Walter Dräyer, Zurich.
26. **Umberto Boccioni.** *Elasticity.* 1912. Private Coll., Milan.

23.

24.

25.

26.

27.

28.

29.

27. **Camille Bombois.** *Girls Bathing*. Private Coll.
28. **Hieronymus Bosch.** *The Garden of Delights*. Detail from central panel of triptych. Between 1485 and 1505. Prado, Madrid.
29. **Pierre Bonnard.** *La Toilette*. *c.* 1922. Musée National d'Art Moderne, Paris.
30. **Sandro Botticelli.** *Pietà*. Early 1490s. Alte Pinakothek, Munich.
31. **Richard Parkes Bonington.** *View of the Parterre d'Eau at Versailles*. 1825. Louvre, Paris.
32. **François Boucher.** *Young Girl Resting (Louise Murphy)*. 1752. Alte Pinakothek, Munich.
33. Opposite: **Pieter Bruegel the Elder.** *Wedding Banquet*. Detail. *c.* 1566. Kunsthistorisches Museum, Vienna.

30.

31.

32.

34.

35.

36.

37.

38.

34. **Eugène Boudin.** *Beach at Trouville.* 1863. Private Coll., Paris.

35. **Georges Braque.** *Musical Forms.* 1913. Louise and Walter Arensberg Coll., Philadelphia Museum of Art.

36. **Dirk Bouts.** *Justice of Otto: Ordeal by Fire. c.* 1473. Musées Royaux des Beaux-Arts, Brussels.

37. **Bernard Buffet.** *Canal St-Martin.* 1956. Private Coll., Paris.

38. **Sir Edward Burne-Jones.** *Love Song.* Metropolitan Museum of Art, New York

Kahler (1882–1911), August Macke, Albert Bloch (b. 1882), composer Arnold Schönberg, David Burliuk (b. 1882), Jean Bloé Niestlé (1884–1942), Münter, Kandinsky, Marc, and Heinrich Campendonk (1889–1957). A second exhibition, confined to drawings and engravings (in black and white), and comprising 315 items altogether, took place at the Goltz Gallery three months later, in February 1912. The circle was enlarged by the inclusion of the Brücke group of Dresden, the New Secession of Berlin, the French artists Braque, Derain, Picasso, La Fresnaye, Vlaminck, Robert Lotiron (1886–1966), and Paul Véra (1882–1958), and the Russians Natalia Goncharova, Mikhail Larionov, and Kasimir Malevich. Paul Klee, moved by the works of Marc, Delaunay, and Kandinsky, joined the group and exhibited his poetic watercolors.

The Blaue Reiter yearbook gives a fairly good picture of the scope of this movement, which embraced all the arts and its revolutionary enthusiasm. "Traditions," said Franz Marc, "are a fine thing, but what is really fine is to *create* a tradition, and not just live off one." Kandinsky, prime mover and fighting theoretician, contributed an article on the problem of form, a sequel and conclusion to his basic work, *Vom Geistigen in der Kunst* (1912), which had appeared shortly before (English translation by Michael Sadleir, *The Art of Spiritual Harmony*, 1914). Marc wrote a study of the different tendencies in modern art in Germany, Burliuk of tendencies in Russia. The French critic Roger Allard introduced Cubism; the German critic Erwin von Busse wrote about Delaunay. The composers Theodor van Hartmann and Schönberg dealt with modern music. In the writings of these men, there was no formulation of any aesthetic rule. There can be found, however, a consistent aversion to academic formulas, and a faith in what Kandinsky called the "inner necessity." This was the simple declaration that appeared on the title-page of the inaugural catalogue: "We do not seek to propagate any precise or particular form: our aim is to show, through the variety of forms represented, how the inner desire of the artist expresses itself in different ways." Expressionism, Cubism, Orphism, and abstract tendencies were there in a generous fraternity of romantic inspiration.

The war dispersed the efforts and energy of the Blaue Reiter. Macke was killed in 1914, Marc in 1916. Klee and Kandinsky went to the Bauhaus at Weimar and later at Dessau. A retrospective exhibition of the movement was arranged in Munich in 1949.

BLECHEN, Karl (1798, Cottbus, Brandenburg—1840, Berlin), one of the principal painters of the German Romantic School. He became friendly with the landscapist Caspar David Friedrich, and attracted the attention of the architect Karl Friedrich Schinkel, who commissioned him to paint stage designs. The landscapes he brought back with him from an Italian journey (1828–29) and those painted after his return to Berlin, where he taught at the Academy, are remarkable for their luminosity, vivacity of color, and the atmospheric lightness of their skies (*Gulf of Spezia, c.* 1829–30; Berlin, Verwaltung der Schlösser und Garten). Other works include the dramatic *Mountain Gorge in Winter* (1825; formerly Berlin, Nationalgalerie) and *Cave on the Gulf of Naples* (1829; Cologne, Wallraf-Richartz-Museum). An untimely death prevented Blechen from showing the full measure of his gifts.

BLOEMAERT, Abraham (1564, Gorinchem, Holland—1651, Utrecht), Dutch painter. He was probably a pupil of Gerrit Splinter (active 1569–86) and Joos de Beer (died before 1595). His art combines the Mannerism of Frans Floris and Jacopo Bassano with Caravaggist influences and an academicism inspired by Guido Reni.

BLONDEL, François (1618, Ribemont, Aisne—1686, Paris), French architect, military engineer, mathematician, and diplomat, the all-powerful theorist of French Classicism. When Colbert founded the Académie Royale d'Architecture in 1671, he naturally chose Blondel as director.

The Porte St-Denis in Paris (1671) remains Blondel's most important work. It is a triumphal arch freely adapted from the antique, intended to glorify the king's victories in allegorical terms. He also built the Porte St-Bernard (1670; demolished 1787), and doubtless inspired Pierre Bullet, designer of the Porte St-Martin. In the eyes of posterity, Blondel the theorist is more important than Blondel the builder, and it is as such that he remains one of the great names of the *Grand Siècle*.

BLONDEL, Jacques-François (1705, Rouen—1774, Paris), French architect, nephew of Jean-François Blondel (1683–1756), who had built a number of private homes in Geneva and country houses on the banks of Lake Leman (Lake Geneva). Jacques-François Blondel was doctrinaire, like Louis XIV's illustrious architect, François Blondel, to whom he was not related. He admired the "ancients" but had even greater praise for the "moderns," and was also an enthusiast of Gothic. He achieved eminence in his time by opening a private school of architecture, authorized by the Académie d'Architecture, then all-powerful and very jealous of its privileges, and by publishing the theoretical and practical lectures he gave there from 1742. The four volumes of his *Architecture française* (1752–56) constitute an enlightened defense of academicism, a critique of Rococo decoration, and an appeal in favor of a return to "the good taste of the last century" along with respect for the rules.

At a mature age Blondel found the opportunity to put his views fully into practice, in the Hôtel de Ville at Metz. Begun in 1764 and completed a year after the architect's death, this superb building has a discipline and severity worthy of the *Grand Siècle.*

BLOOM, Hyman (b. 1913, Latvia), American painter. He emigrated to the United States in 1920 and settled in Boston. A visit to the Museum of Modern Art in New York gave Bloom the opportunity of discovering the Expressionist paintings of Georges Rouault and Chaim Soutine. After working for the WPA Federal Art Project during the Depression, Bloom had his first major show at the Museum of Modern Art's "Americans 1942" exhibition. His preoccupation with his Jewish origins was revealed in *Synagogue* (1940; New York, Museum of Modern Art) and in later series of paintings on Jewish themes.

In 1945 Bloom began his so-called *Corpse* series, strongly influenced by Soutine's violently distorted representations of slaughtered oxen. *Female Corpse, Back View* (1947; New York, Durlacher Brothers) created a controversy when it was exhibited at the Virginia Museum Biennial of American Painting, due to its bold display of a visceral, morbid subject. Bloom's works from the 1950s onward continued to dwell on the theme of decay and mortality (*Autopsy*, 1953; and the *Anatomist*, 1953; both New York, Whitney Museum). In later scenes of dissection this sense of horror is still largely present. Bloom's subsequent style evokes Rembrandt and the Baroque masters he had examined as a student, as well as the sweeping brushstrokes and brilliantly impasted coloration of Théodore Géricault.

BLUEMNER, Oscar (1867, Hanover, Germany—1938, South Braintree, Massachusetts), American painter. He was trained as an architect and portrait painter in Germany, and after emigrating to America in 1892 maintained an architectural office in New York. Bluemner exhibited in the 1913 Armory Show, was a member of Alfred Stieglitz' influential 291 Gallery, and actively participated in the Forum Exhibition of 1916.

Bluemner is known particularly for his expressionistic and irrational use of color. Although influenced by the Cubists, he worked in an independent vein, and unlike them was concerned with a simplification of reality rather than a complex dissection and rearrangement of forms. As a color theorist, he derived his concepts as much from Byzantine mosaics, medieval stained glass and illuminations, or Oriental painting, as from the ideas of Robert Delaunay and the American Synchromists. However, Bluemner differed from these colorists in that he chose to reject pure abstraction. Inner emotion and a mystical romanticism motivated his art, and his working aim was to find some symbolic-realistic form for his daring use of color. This he sought in a geometricized version of landscape, in which sharp contrasts of light and shade define his characteristically cubic forms (*Old Canal Port*, 1914; New York, Whitney Museum). Bluemner's almost exclusive concentration on the landscape genre tended to limit his repertory of forms; but this often allowed for a bold intensification of color moods and surprising configurations within a dense and compact visual fabric.

When he verged on abstraction—as in the visionary watercolor *Moonrise* (1928) or the strident 1929 oil painting *Red Glare* (also called *An American Night*), both of which are in the Graham Gallery in New York—Bluemner endowed color with some of its most original and luminous effects.

BLUME, Peter (b. 1906, Russia), American painter. He was brought to America when he was five, and received his early training in New York at the Art Students League and the Beaux-Arts Institute of Design. Blume's first major works were based on the lessons of Cubism, but in the early 1930s he turned toward Surrealism, achieving widespread recognition when his painting *South of Scranton* (1931; New York, Metropolitan Museum) won first prize at the Carnegie International Competition of 1934. Here one sees for the first time the artist's use of floating, mystical figures frozen in motion against skies painted like theatrical backdrops.

In 1932 and 1936 Blume was in Italy on Guggenheim Fellowships. It was during this period that he began his most famous work, the *Eternal City* (1934–37; New York, Museum of Modern Art). In this canvas Blume undertook a social statement against Fascism, using complex symbolism, satire, and a highly polished technique aimed at capturing the smallest details. Satire is seen too in *Light of the World* (1932; New York, Whitney Museum), in which the artist comments on the awe-struck neighbors who stand in the back yards of a typical rural town, compulsively viewing some miraculous modern contraption. His later works are a faithfully detailed transcription of reality.

BLUMENTHAL, Hermann (1905, Essen—1942, Russia), German sculptor. After serving an apprenticeship as a stonemason in Essen from 1920 to 1924, Blumenthal worked for a year in that city as an ornamental mason and began to study sculpture. He then moved to Berlin, where he continued his studies at the Vereinigte Staatsschulen für freie und angewandte Kunst, working under Wilhelm Gerstel (1879–1963) and Edwin Scharff (1887–1955). A prize from the Prussian Academy of Art enabled him to spend a year in the Villa Massimo in Rome (1931–32), followed by visits to Nowawes and Essen before returning to Berlin, where he joined the studio community on the Klosterstrasse (1934). In 1936 Blumenthal revisited Italy on a traveling scholarship, and worked both in Florence (Villa Romana) and Rome (Villa Massimo). He returned to Berlin and was awarded Düsseldorf's Cornelius Prize the following year. In 1940, however, his work was brought to a sudden end when he was conscripted for military service.

Blumenthal's artistic roots lay in the German Neoclassical sculptural tradition but, like Gerhard Marcks (b. 1889) and Ludwig

Oscar Bluemner. *Old Canal Port*. 1914. Whitney Museum of American Art, New York.

Kaspar (1893–1945), he sought new forms of expression. The emotional restraint, strictly controlled gestures, and static organization of Blumenthal's work are the result of a rigorous, archaic structure. Typical of his work, usually under life size, are his *Adam* (1931–32), *Thinker* (1929–30), and *Kneeling Figure* (1929–30). All of them have their origins in the working-class milieu from which Blumenthal himself had emerged.

BLYTHE, David Gilmore (1815, near East Liverpool, Pennsylvania—1865, Pittsburgh), American painter and engraver. Little is known of the early influences on his art, and it is assumed that he had little or no formal artistic training. From 1832 to 1835 he was apprenticed as a wood carver. Two years later the young artisan enlisted in the United States Navy, traveling from Boston to the West Indies. After naval duty Blythe returned to Pennsylvania in 1841, working as an itinerant portrait painter for several years. In Uniontown, where he settled from 1846 to 1851, he carved a statue of General Lafayette for the county courthouse.

Blythe set about recording the Pittsburgh of his period, in a style not unlike that of William Hogarth in England. Although he painted portraits and landscapes, Blythe remains best known for his satirical treatment of commonplace scenes and occurrences. His humor and unusual handling of distortion are clearly seen in his portrait of *Lincoln Writing the Emancipation Proclamation* (New York, Harry S. Newmann Gallery).

BOCCIONI, Umberto (1882, Reggio Calabria—1916, Sorte, near Verona), Italian painter and sculptor. One of the signatories (with Giacomo Balla, Gino Severini, Luigi Russolo, and Carlo Carrà) of the "Manifesto of Futurist Painters" in February 1910, Boccioni was the real theoretician of the group. His primary concern as painter and sculptor was the expression of movement. In his various manifestoes, including *Futurist Painting and Sculpture* (1914), he declared that it was necessary to universalize the "Impressionist moment." By this he meant that, while the Impressionists painted the object at a particular moment, the Futurists meant to "synthesize all moments of time, place, form and color" and to express them in a single painting or sculpture. The Futurists also reacted against the objectivity of Cubism, believing that a picture should express feelings and moods; it is true that a painting like Boccioni's *Elasticity* (1912; Milan, Priv. Coll.), a synthesis of a horse's movements in a race, expresses a dimension that a Cubist picture of the time does not. Banishing horizontals and verticals, Boccioni invented the "line of force," that is, a representation of the energy with which every object reacts to light and shade and that is itself a generator of forms and color-forces. These new relations between matter and space perhaps found their finest expression in his sculpture, particularly in his famous *polimaterici* (sculptures composed of different materials: iron, wood, glass, etc.), which he exhibited in 1913. At the outbreak of World War I, Boccioni was mobilized; he died at the age of thirty-four of injuries sustained in a fall from his horse.

Umberto Boccioni. *Development of a Bottle in Space.* Kunsthaus, Zurich.

BÖCKLIN, Arnold (1827, Basel—1901, San Domenico, near Fiesole), Swiss painter. Intending to become a landscape painter, he frequented the studio of Johan Wilhelm Schirmer in Düsseldorf between 1845 and 1847. Böcklin's paintings of this period are somewhat reminiscent of Caspar David Friedrich. The next years were *Wanderjahre*, during which the artist visited Brussels, Antwerp, Zurich, Geneva and Paris. Then he went back to his native Basel until 1850, when he left for Rome, which was to be his center of activity until 1857. There he painted low-keyed views of the Roman Campagna, adorned with mythological scenes. He returned briefly to Basel, then went to Germany. To earn a living, Böcklin found it necessary to practice portraiture, a genre in which he produced some of his best work. With *Pan Among the Rushes* (Munich, Neue Pinakothek), exhibited in Munich in 1859, he first became known to the public; this work also attracted the attention of several collectors, in particular the wealthy patron Graf von Schack. In 1860 Böcklin was appointed to a teaching post at the Weimar art school; his financial situation now secure, he returned to Rome, visited Naples and Pompeii, and acquired a passing interest in the technique of encaustic painting. In 1864 and 1865 he painted his first truly popular works, two brightly colored *Villas by the Seashore* (both Munich, Schackgalerie). When he returned to Switzerland (1866), he carried out mural paintings in the Basel Kunstmuseum and also carved—for he practiced all the arts—a number of grotesque masks for the Kunsthalle of the same city. In Munich he painted a large number of mythological scenes, such as the *Battle of the Centaurs* and the *Marine Idyll* (*c.* 1871–74; Schackgalerie), in which he intensified an already discordant colorism.

Italy again attracted Böcklin; and, except for a brief sojourn in Zurich, he lived continuously in Florence from 1874, surrounded by a circle of admirers, among whom were the critic Hugo von Tschudi and the sculptor Adolf von Hildebrand. Some of his best-known paintings date from this period: the *Elysian Fields* (1878; Berlin, Nationalgalerie) and five versions of the *Isle of the Dead* (first version 1880; Basel, Kunstmuseum). Böcklin's seventieth birthday was made the occasion for great celebrations in Germany, Switzerland, and Italy. His last years were darkened by an ill-health that was reflected in his work. A well-known example is *The Plague*, rather cold in color, begun in the spring of 1898 and left unfinished (Basel, Kunstmuseum).

BOFFRAND, Germain (1667, Nantes—1754, Paris), French Rococo architect and decorator. His artistic style was formed by Jules Hardouin-Mansart. A prolific architect of princely residences and aristocratic houses, he showed restraint in the design of his buildings but decorated his rooms with a graceful and expansive elegance, making great use of

Germain Boffrand. Elevation of the Foundling Hospital, Paris. Detail. *Photo Josse-Lalance, Paris.*

rocaille ornament (curved decorative forms originally based on shell motifs). Boffrand began his career in Paris, where he constructed a series of residences that includes the imaginative Hôtel Amelot de Gourney (1695), with its unusual courtyard entry. For the De Rohan family, he enlarged and decorated the Hôtel Soubise (1734–40), which today houses the Archives Nationales. Perhaps his most important work in Paris was the Foundling Hospital (later demolished), notable for the great dimensions of its façades and for its chapel, painted by the decorators Paolo Antonio Brunetti (d. 1783) and Charles Natoire (1700–77). On becoming first architect to the Duc de Lorraine in 1708, Boffrand rebuilt the Château de Lunéville, near Nancy, in partial imitation of Versailles, and in the countryside of Lorraine (near Laval), on medieval foundations, he built the Château de Crâon, one of his major works.

BOGARDUS, James (1800, Catskill, New York—1874, New York City), American architect, inventor, manufacturer of machinery, and publisher of the pamphlet *Cast Iron Buildings: Their Construction and Advantages* (1858), in which he describes himself as "Architect in Iron." His five-story front for the John Milhau Apothecary (1848) was New York City's first cast-iron façade. His own factory, also in downtown New York, designed in 1848 and erected the following year, was a full-scale, three-dimensional advertisement for the material: it apparently had interior structural members of iron as well as an iron and glass envelope.

Bogardus produced an extremely inventive project for the New York World's Fair, 1853, consisting of a circular hall surrounding a 300-foot tower, the hall to be roofed by sheets of iron suspended between its iron outer walls and those of the tower.

BOILLY, Louis Léopold (1761, La Bassée, Nord—1845, Paris), French genre painter, the best reporter of everyday life from the reign of Louis XVI to that of Louis-Philippe. Son of a sculptor and painter, Arnold Boilly (active 1764–79), he tired of the building trades and went from Douai to Arras, then to Paris, painting portraits for a living, catering to the current taste for gallant images and other frivolities. He did portraits of *Lafayette* on his return from America (1788) and of his fellow townsman *Robespierre* wearing a dress coat, chamois vest, and nankeen knee breeches (1789; Lille, Palais des Beaux-Arts). He flattered the Revolutionaries by taking as models *Lucile Desmoulins* (Paris, Musée Carnavalet) and *Madame Danton*, and struck a licentious note for the curious sightseers at the Young Painters' Salon (1791) with the *Venal Love* and *Precocious Pleasures*, bringing him a denunciation for indecency. But he regained favor with a *Triumph of Marat*, painted in a few days (*c.* 1794; Lille). The Directory brought Boilly freedom in an easygoing society. For 40 years he was to record the most varied scenes of Parisian life: *Arrival of the Stagecoach* (1803; Paris, Louvre); the *Galleries of the Tribunate* (Salon of 1804), where agitators mingled with demimondaines; *Isabey's Studio* (1798; Paris, Louvre); *Houdon's Studio* (1804; Paris, Musée des Arts Décoratifs), which shows the sculptor modeling his bust of the mathematician Gaspard Monge; and the *Departure of the Conscripts* (1808; Musée Carnavalet).

BOL, Hans (1534, Mechlin—1593, Amsterdam), Flemish landscape artist, miniaturist, engraver, and decorator. After studies in his native town, Bol went to Heidelberg, where he worked for the elector for two years (1550–52). He then returned to Mechlin, where he was made Master in 1560. After several relocations he finally settled in Amsterdam, where he became a citizen in 1591. Although there are very few extant oils, several important works by Bol have survived. The Musées Royaux des Beaux-Arts in Brussels possess his only signed work, a *Panoramic View of Antwerp* (1572). A fine illuminated manuscript, the Duke of Brabant's Book of Hours (1582), is in the Bibliothèque Nationale, Paris. Bol also executed designs for a series of prints called *Venationis, Piscationis, et Avcupii tipi* ("Illustrations of Hunting, Fishing, and Fowling"), the first edition of which was published in 1582. He is also supposed to have executed tapestry cartoons.

BOLDINI, Giovanni (1842, Ferrara—1931, Paris), Italian painter. Boldini began painting in his father's studio, and later went to Rome and then to Florence, where he studied at the Academy of Fine Arts. While in Florence, where the discussions of the Macchiaioli group in the Caffè Michelangelo were at their height, Boldini early rejected official teaching. In 1867 he went to Paris, where he was deeply impressed by the work of Manet, but he expended his virtuosity on fashionable portraits and brilliant interpretations of Parisian scenes and townscapes. In 1869 Boldini arrived in London and became the favorite portraitist of the aristocracy: he portrayed such well-known persons as Whistler (New York, Brooklyn Museum), the Duchess of Marlborough, and Princess von Hohenlohe. But it was in Paris, where he returned in 1872, that most of his best painting was done (particularly the portraits of *Count Robert de Montesquiou*, 1897, Paris, Musée National d'Art Moderne; and of the dancer *Cléo de Mérode*, 1901; New York, Coll. Daniel Wildenstein). He was renowned as a colorist and technician, but his increasingly refined manner did not always avoid affectation and facility.

BOLOGNA, Giovanni, *also called* **GIAMBOLOGNA** (1529, Douai—1608, Florence), Italian Mannerist sculptor and architect known in France as Jean Boulogne or Jean Bologne. He was trained at Mons in the atelier of Jacques du Broeucq (1505–84), then went to study in Italy and was in Rome for two years, where he was influenced by Michelangelo. He intended to go back to Flanders, but on his return journey he stopped at Florence (*c.* 1556) and remained there for the rest of his career. Giambologna first made his mark in the competition for the Fountain of Neptune (1560), although his model was rejected as too costly in favor of Bartolomeo Ammannati's. Little is known about his earlier works. His first major achievement was the Fountain of Neptune in Bologna, commissioned by Pope Pius IV (1563–67). At the same time he did a number of statuettes of *Mercury* for various patrons. The climax of the series was the statue of the god sent in 1565 to Emperor Maximilian II of Germany and, in 1580, the "flying" or *Medici Mercury* (Florence, Bargello), celebrated for the elegance of its aerial movement. His simultaneous preoccupation with movement and expression is evident in *Florence Triumphant over Pisa* (gesso model, 1565, Florence, Accademia; marble, 1570, Bargello) and *Samson Slaying a Philistine*, commissioned by Francesco de'Medici (1565–68; London, Victoria and Albert Museum). For the Piazzale dell' Isolotto, in the Boboli Gardens, Florence, he carved the Fountain of Oceanus (1567–76). The *Apollo* in Francesco de' Medici's *studiolo* at the Palazzo Vecchio, Florence, also dates from this period. Akin to this figure in their refined voluptuousness are the *Venus* at the Villa della Petraia, near Florence (1567?), and the more restrained *Grotticella Venus* in the Boboli (1570).

Giambologna's first important religious work was the marble Altar of Liberty in Lucca Cathedral, with its unusual, very Apollonian Christ (1577–79), followed by bronze reliefs for the Grimaldi Chapel in Genoa (1579–85; now at Genoa University) and the Salviati Chapel at S. Marco, Florence (1579–89). Giovanni's constant striving for the harmonious group caught in an aerial equilibrium culminated in what is his most celebrated sculpture, the *Rape of the Sabines* (1579–83; Florence, Loggia dei Lanzi), a complex three-figure work carved from a single block of marble. His desire for sculpture in a natural setting of greenery and water led to the colossal *Apennine* (*c.* 1580), a piece of Humanist fancy, in the park of the Villa Demidoff at Pratolino. Toward the end of the century he executed the group of *Hercules and the Centaur* (1594–99; Loggia dei Lanzi) and the equestrian statue of Cosimo I (1581–95; Florence, Piazza della Signoria), which earned the artist further commissions for similar monuments: equestrian statues of Ferdinando I de' Medici (1601–8; Florence, Piazza SS. Annunziata), Henri IV, ordered by Marie de Médicis for the Pont-Neuf in Paris (begun 1604; fragments in Paris, Louvre), and Philip III of Spain (begun 1606). Finally, mention may be made of the very ornate decoration of his own sepulchral chapel at the Annunziata (1594–99). Giambologna is the only 16th-century sculptor whose original working models have survived (study for the *Rape of the Sabines*; Victoria and Albert Museum).

BOLTRAFFIO, Giovanni Antonio (1467, Milan—1516, Milan), Italian painter. Boltraffio was trained in the Bergognone tradition and was influenced by Vincenzo Foppa and Bernardo Zenale (1436–1526). He was soon attracted by Leonardo and became one of his most devoted disciples. When Leonardo had to leave Milan, he put Boltraffio in charge of his workshop. In 1515, in the church of S. Onofrio in Rome, Boltraffio painted frescoes in which the Leonardesque elements are more in evidence than the Lombard tradition. He is best known for his excellent portraits, such as the *Portrait of the Poet Girolamo Casio* (before 1500; Milan, Brera) and the *Portrait of a Youth* (1505–10; Philadelphia, Johnson Collection). The *Two Kneeling Worshipers* (1516; Brera) is in fact the lower part of a large altarpiece, possibly the *Casio Family Virgin* (Paris, Louvre), commissioned in 1500 for a Bolognese church, in which we see Girolamo Casio and his father being presented to the Virgin by their patron saints. Notable also are the *Madonna and Child* (Milan, Museo Poldi-Pezzoli) and the *Narcissus* (Florence, Uffizi). Boltraffio, with his elegant, aristocratic style, is among the finest Lombard painters of the Renaissance.

BOMBOIS, Camille (1883, Venarey-les-Laumes, Côte-d'Or—1970, Paris), French painter. The son of a mariner, he had very little schooling. At sixteen he began to draw, recording with naïve honesty the varied episodes of his life as a wrestling champion, circus boxer, roadmender, and, in Paris, a ditchdigger. For seven years he worked evenings in a printing works, in order to paint during the day. In 1922, despairing of ever being able to show his paintings in public, Bombois decided to exhibit them in the street. They were noticed by a few collectors, a dealer, and by the German critic Wilhelm Uhde, who had discovered and patronized other naïve painters. Success was not very long in coming, and Bombois settled in a small house in the Paris suburbs. His main subjects were derived from personal experience: athletes at fairs, circus dancers and horseback riders, buxom farmers' wives, canals reflecting trees, villages, hills, landscapes, and still lifes. Bombois employed a color that is sober, limpid, and delicate, and also demonstrates an acute sense of spatial depth. When he took special pains with his work, he verged on academicism, but when painting those people and things he loved, Bombois often attained an exquisite naturalness.

BONANNO OF PISA (active 1174–86), Italian sculptor, bronze founder, and architect. He was responsible for the decoration (1180) of the main door of the cathedral at Pisa, but the panels were destroyed by fire in 1595. There has survived, however, his door for the S. Ranieri Portal (opening into the south transept, 1180), with 24 compartments in which are represented the principal scenes from the life of Christ. He also executed the folding door of Monreale Cathedral in Sicily (1186).

BONDOL, Jean de, *called* Hennequin *or* Jean de Bruges (b. Bruges), Flemish painter, active in Paris between 1368 and 1381, according to archival evidence, and probably for an even longer period. His miniatures for a *Bible Historiale* dedicated to Charles V (The Hague, Rijksmuseum Meermanno-Westreenianum) prove that from 1371, the date of the manuscript, he had a perfect knowledge of the Parisian manner of Jean Pucelle. In this *Bible* and in other illuminated manuscripts from his workshop, he renewed the tradition of Pucelle by infusing it with a new heightened feeling for

Giovanni Bologna. *Venus.* 1567? Villa della Petraia, near Florence. *Photo Alinari-Giraudon.*

the tactile quality of forms and a more exact definition of space.

Jean de Bondol dominated Parisian painting in the time of Charles V, whose official painter he became, and was associated with the execution of the largest cycle of mural decorations that survive from the period, the famous set of *Apocalypse* tapestries in the Château d'Angers. The breadth and variety of the program (the work originally comprised some 90 scenes, of which over 70 have been preserved), the elegance and poetic power of each segment, and the harmony of the ensemble make the *Apocalypse* one of the great works of the Gothic period.

BONINGTON, Richard Parkes (1802, Arnold, near Nottingham—1828, London), English painter of landscape and genre subjects. He spent the greater part of his short working life in France and was perhaps as influential as John Constable in introducing the English landscape formula into French Romantic painting. He moved with his family to Calais in *c.* 1817 and began his career by sketching in the streets of that city then studied for a few months with Louis Francia (1772–1839). Bonington later moved to Paris, armed with a letter of introduction to Delacroix, whom he met in the Louvre. He studied at the École des Beaux-Arts and, about 1820, entered the studio of Baron Gros, who expressed great admiration for his watercolors.

In 1822 Bonington had a great success in the Salon with views of Lillebonne and Le Havre, which he had toured in the preceding year. In 1823 he went on a second tour of northern France (including French Flanders) that inspired the two fine paintings of the *Market Tower at Bergues* (1822; London, Wallace Collection) and the *Abbey of St. Bertin, Saint-Omer* (1823; Nottingham, City Art Gallery). In 1824 he provided lithographs for the Normandy volume of Baron Taylor's *Voyages Pittoresques dans l'ancienne France*, and in the same year he exhibited in the famous Salon that contained Constable's *Hay Wain* and Delacroix' *Massacre at Chios*. In 1825 Bonington went to England, where he worked with Delacroix, who was also on a visit; he was deeply impressed by Turner, whose influence was decisive on his last landscapes, as was that of Rubens on his late costume pieces. A second journey to England, in 1827, brought him into contact with Sir Thomas Lawrence, with whom he shows marked similarities of handling. But undoubtedly the most important journey of his last years was undertaken with Baron Rivet at the beginning of 1826, when he made a tour of Italy, where his painting acquired a new brilliance on exposure to the views and sunlight of Venice. His career was brought to an abrupt end when he died of consumption in 1828.

Richard Parkes Bonington. *Self-Portrait with Easel. Photo Giraudon, Paris.*

Owing to his close connection with Delacroix, Bonington is often considered an Anglo-French or even a French artist. Certainly he had a great influence on later French painters, notably Corot. But Bonington was a fundamentally English painter, whose landscape style was clearly in the line of development from Girtin to Turner. He was also a fundamentally English Romantic, with a taste for muted medievalism and careful Gothic detail: his *Interior of Senlis Cathedral* (1822; Coll. Mr. P. M. Turner) was one of the earliest Gothic interiors of the Romantic movement. His mature manner may be said to date from this picture, and his later journeys in northern France and Flanders only strengthened this placid, poetic, topographical approach (the *Institut, Paris, from the Quais*, 1827; London, British Museum). Only after his visit to England in 1827 is the broader manner of Turner adopted, for example in the *English Landscape with a Timber Wagon* (1828; Wallace Collection), and it is true that the pictures painted in Venice have greater brightness of color and more emotional freedom.

BONNARD, Pierre (1867, Fontenay-aux-Roses, Seine—1947, Le Cannet, Alpes-Maritimes), French painter. He entered the École des Beaux-Arts in 1888. The following year he succeeded in selling a poster design, *France-Champagne*, for 100 francs and, encouraged by this, he decided to become a painter. He gave up his legal post and immediately joined the Nabis, a group influenced by the ideas of Paul Gauguin and Paul Sérusier. He exhibited with them at the Salon des Indépendents and contributed rather unenthusiastically to the Symbolist periodical *La Revue Blanche*. Turning his back on the Symbolist theories of Sérusier and Denis and soon free of the decorative Synthetism taught by Gauguin, Bonnard became fascinated by Japanese prints. Following Japanese style, he avoided modeling, used flat tones, and composed with juxtaposed planes (*Terrasse Family, c.* 1893, Priv. Coll.; *The Parade*, 1890, Switzerland, Priv. Coll.) From 1893 to 1895 he executed many lithographs, and drawings in charcoal, pencil, and pen, and worked on the décors and costumes for the Théâtre de l'Oeuvre. In 1896 his first one-man show took place at the Durand-Ruel Gallery, Paris. In 1898 he illustrated his first book, *Marie*, a novel by Peter Nansen, and the Parisian art critic Ambroise Vollard then asked him to illustrate Paul Verlaine's *Parallèlement* (1900). About 1898 he gave up the use of flat areas of color and sought to situate the object in space as affected by light. He neglected neither draftsmanship nor composition, which he handled more audaciously than Degas or Toulouse-Lautrec. For example, in a painting of Madame Bonnard, the artist shows his wife leaning over an oval table whose shape emphasizes the rigid rectangular frame; elsewhere, the vertical lines of a door shear the sinuous arabesques of a naked woman in motion (*Nude Leaving Bath*, 1910; Mexico City, Priv. Coll.); or a boldly lifted horizon and distant features of a Provençal landscape fall onto the foreground in a cascade of blues, greens, yellows and purples.

At this point, Bonnard was so obsessed by color that he gave up his graphic art for some years. After providing illustrations for *Daphnis et Chloë* (1902) and Jules

Renard's *Histoires Naturelles* (1904), he ceased working for writers until 1920, when he turned to engraving and lithography to illustrate André Gide's *La Prométhée mal enchaîné* (1920), Octave Mirbeau's *Dingo* (1924), and Vollard's *Sainte Monique* (1930). In 1911 he sent three decorative panels, commissioned by the Russian collector Morosov, to the Salon d'Automne.

After the war, Bonnard painted the *Abduction of Europa* (1919; Toledo, Ohio, Museum of Art), *Luncheon* (1927; New York, Museum of Modern Art), and *Low Tide* (*c.* 1922), *La Toilette* (*c.* 1922), and *View over Le Cannet* (1924), the last three in the Musée National d'Art Moderne, Paris. In 1925 he bought a villa at Le Cannet (near Cannes), where he often stayed and, as a result, his color became heightened and increasingly incandescent. In his still lifes, landscapes, seascapes, nudes, and interiors, the tones reached an incredible degree of intensity, but an intensity always veiled with a gentle tenderness.

In 1942, with the death of Madame Bonnard, who had been his only model, the artist refused to leave his retreat at Le Cannet. His art blossomed forth with magnificent works. He took such liberties with reality in his *Circus Horse* (1946; Fontainebleau, Coll. Charles Terrasse) and *Ox* that the advanced wing of contemporary art referred to them to justify some of its experiments. Finally, just as Monet had offered the best of his genius in his *Water Lilies*, so during the months before his death Bonnard was able to sum up the ideal of his entire life in a work embellished with all the dreams of his youth. In his series of large *Mimosas* Bonnard penetrated to the essence of painting. Through progressive abstraction these became a flowing of melted gold, a sumptuous drapery fringing the upper part of the painting, a fanfare of yellows, praising the song of an existence.

BONNAT, Léon (1833, Bayonne—1922, Monchy-St-Éloi, Oise), one of the most famous French painters of the Third Republic. Enormously successful at the Salon, he was lavishly rewarded by the state and was made a member of the Institut in 1881. At Madrid, where his father was a bookseller, he attended the studio of the painter Frederico Madrazo (1815–94). The city of Bayonne later sent him to Paris to study with Léon Cogniet (1794–1880). He abandoned his Spanish-inspired religious painting to devote himself to official portraiture (*Victor Hugo*, 1879; *Cardinal Lavigerie*, 1888, Paris, formerly Musée du Luxembourg; *Thiers* and *Loubet*, Musée Bonnat). He was a skillful draftsman but strove for photographic representation and persisted in painting purplish-blue skin against bituminous backgrounds. The *Martyrdom of St. Denis* (1885; Paris, Panthéon) has a sadness that, while solemn, is hardly religious. In his lifetime Bonnat was immensely fashionable. Today he is generally scorned: his influence on Toulouse-Lautrec, Dufy, and Othon Friesz, as well as the beauty of some of his female portraits (*Madame Pasca*, 1874, Paris, Louvre; *Madame Erhler*, 1880, Paris, Petit Palais) have been too often forgotten.

BONTECOU, Lee (b. 1931, Providence, Rhode Island), American sculptor. She studied with William Zorach and John Hovannes (1900–73) at the Art Students League in New York from 1952 to 1955, then worked in Rome from 1957 to 1958 on a Fulbright Fellowship, and, in 1959, received an L. C. Tiffany Grant. Bontecou's early sculpture, of the mid-1950s, included birds, animals, and human figures in terra cotta and metal; the human images in particular were formed by slightly separated, armorlike plates revealing dark cavities beneath. These sculptures were the forerunners of Bontecou's canvas constructions, characterized by faceted planes punctured by large dark orifices, which she began making in 1959. Most of these constructions are wall reliefs—although some are freestanding—and constitute some of the earliest and most successful examples in American art of the shaped canvas. Grayish, generally monochromatic tarpaulin, cut into abstract and irregular geometric shapes, is fastened onto the frame with wires that protrude as sharp dangerous barbs. These geometric planes converge toward one or more black, gaping holes that are sometimes equipped with jagged, tooth-like elements or with bars, creating a surrealistic contrast to the otherwise rather severely formal conception.

Lee Bontecou. *Untitled*. 1961. Museum of Modern Art, New York. *Photo Eric Pollitzer, New York.*

BORDUAS, Paul-Émile (1905, St-Hilaire, Quebec—1960, Paris), Canadian painter. He began his career around 1920 by assisting the painter Ozias Leduc (1864–1955) in the mural decoration of churches. After studying at the École des Beaux-Arts in Montreal, Borduas began teaching art in the Montreal schools in 1927. He went to Paris in 1928 and studied briefly with Maurice Denis. On his return in 1930 he opened a studio for mural decoration in Montreal. By 1937 Borduas was teaching at the École du Meuble in Montreal. He exhibited his first abstract and Surrealist paintings in 1942, and, in 1944–45, he gathered about him a group of artists who became known as Les Automatistes. In 1948 they published an anarchistic manifesto, *Refus global* ("Total Refusal"), which resulted in Borduas' dismissal from his teaching post. A difficult period ensued, and the artist moved first to New York (1953), where he met Franz Kline and other Abstract Expressionists, and two years later to Paris. With Alfred Pellan he was founder of the Montreal School of the 1940s and 1950s.

BORÈS, Francisco (b. 1898, Madrid), Spanish painter. From 1922 Borès took part in the avant-garde activities of the Ultraist Group, and in 1925 his work was exhibited for the first time, in the Exposicíon de Artistas Ibericos at Madrid. In the same year he settled in Paris. At first Borès was an admirer of Juan

Francesco Borromini. Façade of S. Carlo alle Quattro Fontane (S. Carlino), Rome. Detail. 1667. *Foto Marburg.*

Gris, but before long he broke with the geometric discipline of the Cubists. His experiments then led to the selection, for each of his pictures, of a single background color that created the atmosphere of the work and on which a whole repertoire of familiar objects, such as fruit, functioning as symbols, usually allusive, were sketched or inscribed in the manner of a filigree. This manner culminated in vast compositions in which references to the real world merged imperceptibly with imaginative details. Later, by purifying his color, Borès was able to take a nude, a simple still life, or a single figure as his point of departure and create a perfectly homogeneous world of poetic feelings in which, under a uniform lighting, each form creates its own space.

BORGLUM, Gutzon (1867, Bear Lake, Idaho—1941, Chicago), American sculptor. His early art education was in California, mostly in lithography, fresco painting, and oil painting. In the early 1890s, he studied in France, exhibited both paintings and sculpture at the Paris Salon, and formed a friendship with Auguste Rodin. He also spent an important year in Spain; and, after a period in California from 1893 to 1896, he left for England, where his art was especially well received.

During the late 1890s, Borglum turned increasingly to sculpture and, after his return to the United States in 1902, he concentrated on sculpture almost exclusively. His more successful work includes a colossal bronze sculpture of Lincoln seated on a park bench (Newark, New Jersey, courthouse); an over life-size head of Lincoln (Washington, D.C., the Capitol); and the bronze *Mares of Diomedes*, one of the earliest sculptures by an American artist purchased by the Metropolitan Museum in New York. Borglum is probably even more famous for his two most ambitious monuments: the unfinished memorial to the Confederate Army carved on the side of Stone Mountain in Georgia; and the four Presidential heads (Washington, Jefferson, Theodore Roosevelt, and Lincoln) on Mount Rushmore in the Black Hills of South Dakota.

BOROVIKOVSKI, Vladimir Lukich (1757, Mirgorod—1825, St. Petersburg), Russian painter of Ukrainian origin, the fashionable portraitist of women during the reign of Czar Alexander I. In 1788 he settled in St. Petersburg, where his art developed under the influence of three foreign artists who visited Russia: Madame Vigée-Lebrun; Giovanni Battista Lampi the Elder (1751–1830), who was his teacher; and the Swede Alexander Roslin (1718–93), who had visited Russia from 1775 to 1777. He even came to know Catherine the Great in 1787 and left an informal portrait (1795; Moscow, Tretyakov Gallery) of the old empress, wearing a quilted satin wrap and strolling with her favorite greyhound in the park at Tsarskoe Selo. But Borovikovski really belongs to the reign of Alexander I. There is already a touch of sentimental Romanticism in his portraits of women, such as that of *Madame Marie Ivanovna Lopouchine* (1798; Tretyakov Gallery), their languorous grace recalling Prud'hon and the masters of the English School, whose works he may have known from engravings.

BORROMINI, Francesco Castelli, *called* Francesco (1599, Bissone, near Lugano—1667, Rome), the most original architect of the High Baroque in Rome. After humble beginnings as a stonecutter and ornamentalist, first in Milan, then in Rome (after 1621) under the supervision of Carlo Maderno, his Lombard compatriot and foster brother, Borromini collaborated briefly with Bernini on the Palazzo Barberini (until 1633), where the parts that each designed may still be compared. This was the start of a long rivalry between the two men to secure papal favor.

Borromini's independent building activity took place entirely in Rome. The first work for which he was completely responsible was S. Carlo alle Quattro Fontane (S. Carlino), a tiny church and cloister in which he immediately demonstrated his technical mastery; 30 years later his career ended with the completion of its façade and that of the neighboring convent. The Oratory (1637–40) and Library (1642–43) of S. Filippo Neri, adjoining S. Maria in Vallicella, anticipate his masterpiece, the church of S. Ivo della Sapienza (1642–50). Based on the highly unusual star hexagon plan, this work is extremely original throughout, particularly in its spiral dome, which was perhaps inspired by a Babylonian ziggurat. Contemporary with some work on the Spada, Pamphili (Piazza Navona), and Carpegno palaces are the interior decoration of S. Giovanni in Laterano (1647–49) and the design for S. Maria dei Sette Dolori, built for the Augustines at the foot of the Janiculum (begun 1650s; façade unfinished at Borromini's death). In a brief moment of official favor at the end of the pontificate of Innocent X, he designed the façade for Carlo and Girolamo Rainaldi's partially completed S. Agnese in Agone in Piazza Navona (1653–61). Borromini then devoted himself to his last great palace, the Collegio di Propaganda Fide (1662–66), the external decoration for the cupola of S. Andrea della Fratte, the design for its bell tower at the corner of Via Due Macelli and Via Capo le Case, and finally the S. Carlino façade (1664–67). In the summer of 1667 he fell ill; in a fit of delirium he stabbed himself with his sword, dying the next day, after repenting his action. At his request, he was buried beside Maderno in S. Giovanni dei Fiorentini, Rome.

In addition to the high originality of his over-all conceptions, Borromini's inventive solutions to problems of structural and decorative detail are in great part

Francesco Borromini. Courtyard and church of S. Ivo della Sapienza, Rome. 1642–50. *Photo Leonard von Matt, Buochs.*

responsible for the individuality of his buildings. At an early age he was thoroughly trained in stonemasonry, and with this solid grounding he multiplied cantilevers and overhangs in the S. Andrea della Fratte bell tower to give an impression of lightness as well as elegance. The technical master who seemed in this way able to defy gravity never overlooked any means of creating optical illusions or awakening the idea of the miraculous, as he skillfully contrived the "accelerated" perspective in the Palazzo Spada gallery (1634–36) and the indirect daylight in the side chapel of S. Agnese. Nor did the creator of the delightful rotunda in S. Giovanni in Oleo (1658) neglect refinements—he had an abundance of exquisite decorative details, including quantities of cherubim and seraphim, who fill the S. Ivo cupola with their fluttering wings, support the architraves in the aisles of the Lateran, and fold their wings in a mischievous "on guard" position in the S. Andrea della Fratte bell tower—apparitions full of joy in Borromini's monuments of a highly wrought, arbitrary, and precious art.

BOSCH VAN AKEN, Hieronymus (*c.* 1450, 's Hertogenbosch, Brabant—1516, 's Hertogenbosch), highly original Flemish painter of the late Middle Ages. Seven references in archives and seven signed works (which include the significant *Temptation of St. Anthony*) are the only certain elements known of this extraordinary artist who lived at 's Hertogenbosch (Bois-le-Duc) at the end of the 15th century and who signed himself "Jheronimus Bosch." He was the son, grandson, and nephew of painters, a friend of the architect Alaert du Hameel, who engraved his works, and he was married to a rich patrician, Aleid van der Meervenne; he was also a member of the jury of the Confrérie of Notre-Dame, which gave theatrical performances. Bosch undertook decorative works and altarpieces and made designs for stained glass. Celebrated in his own lifetime, he was referred to as *insignis pictor* ("distinguished painter") at his death in 1516. Later, highly favored by Philip II of Spain, his work stimulated such a craze for fantastic *diableries* at the end of the 16th century that it has required a great deal of labor to distinguish his 40 probable paintings from numerous imitations.

Works attributed to his youthful period (*c.* 1480), and already conceived in a monumental style, are the *Seven Deadly Sins* (Madrid, Prado) and the *Conjurer* (St-Germain-en-Laye, Museum), this last an image of the credulity that leads to heresy. The following probably belong to the period 1485–1505: *Ship of Fools* (Paris, Louvre); *St. John on Patmos* (Berlin, Staatliche Museen); and the great triptychs, the *Hay Wagon* (Prado), the *Garden of Delights* (Prado), and the *Temptation of St. Anthony* (Lisbon, Museu Nacional de Arte Antiga). The more restrained works date after 1505: the *Epiphany* (Prado); two versions of the *Crowning with Thorns* (London, National Gallery; Prado), which have a harsher tone, reflected particularly in the faces; and the *Prodigal Son* (Rotterdam, Museum Boymans-van Beuningen), in which the figure of a beggar, dispassionately conceived, attains the grandeur and pathos of a new humanism.

Bosch's enormous individuality derives from his unusual powers of invention and his unique vision of the world. His compositions are disconcerting, anarchic, alive and teeming. In carefully chosen subjects his fantasy is developed in a multitude of strange forms—monstrosities—composed of dislocated elements of real beings. By referring only indirectly to the world of man and everyday objects, he opens up a world of fantasy, made more graphic and chilling by his allusions to the real. For his nightmare beings or dream creatures are always associated with undistorted forms of fruit, birds, and young women. Bosch also makes use of symbols from astrology, sorcery, and alchemy, probably inspired, at least in part, by the traditions of illumination and choir-stall sculpture. Each detail takes on a symbolic significance within the whole, which is itself some kind of allegory. The unique assembly of forms, with their perplexing interpretations, always clearly expresses the same central idea, the illustration of the Christian life under its two guises: the guilt of sin, the forgetfulness of the message of Christ, and too great an attachment to earthly pleasures, or Vanity, on the one hand; the divine Truth taught by the Savior of the world, the force of Faith against Evil, and the virtues of asceticism on the other. But since Bosch lived in the troubled period at the end of the Middle Ages, and since he considered himself a militant artist, the play of fancy and mystical ardor are almost always exceeded in his work by the anguish he induces by the predominance of images of hell. The *Temptation of St. Anthony*, a vision of repulsive nightmares endured in desperation, and the *Garden of Delights*, a beautiful but disquieting image of avidly culled desires, of sensual pleasures and dreams, are two poles of his fantasy; for him the gratification of obscenity, lust, and heresy are all aspects of the same obsession that afflicts the pleasure-hungry world. For all this, his world is full of beauty.

Hieronymus Bosch. *The Errant Fool.* Detail. Exterior of Hay Wagon triptych. *c.* 1505. Prado, Madrid.

BOSSCHAERT THE ELDER, Ambrosius (*c.* 1573, Antwerp—1621, The Hague), Netherlandish still-life painter known to have worked in Antwerp, Middelburg, Utrecht and Breda. He was one of the first artists to paint flower and fruit arrangements in the descriptive style adopted at the beginning of the 17th century by Osias Beert (*c.* 1570–1624) and Clara Peeters (*c.* 1594–after 1657) (*Flowers in a Faïence Vase*, 1619; Amsterdam, Rijksmuseum; *Glass*

Hieronymus Bosch. *Paradise,* from the Garden of Delights triptych. Between 1485 and 1505. Prado, Madrid. *Photo Giraudon, Paris.*

of Flowers in a Niche, 1618; Copenhagen, Statens Museum for Kunst). With the same precision, clarity, and virtuosity, Ambrosius also painted some very fine still lifes of fruit (*Dish of Fruit with a Siegburger Jug*, before 1615; Paris, Priv. Coll.). Like Jan ("Velvet") Bruegel, he was in the habit of placing a butterfly or a cyclamen flower near the edge of his paintings. He had a fine sense of texture, volume, and of pure, luminous color. Ambrosius had three sons, AMBROSIUS THE YOUNGER (1609–45), JOHANNES (1610/11–after 1626), and ABRAHAM (1613–after 1643), all of whom were also flower and fruit painters. Ambrosius is the most famous, his paintings being more varied than those of his brothers (*Flowers in a Glass Beaker*, 1634; England, South Walsham Hall, Coll. Hon. Henry Rogers Broughton).

BOSSE, Abraham (1602, Tours—1676, Paris), French engraver and draftsman. His views on perspective, which he was the first to teach, ultimately brought about expulsion both from his seat in the Academy and his teaching post (1661).

Bosse came to Paris at the age of twenty-six; there he worked for a fellow Calvinist, a print dealer whose shop he eventually bought. At this time he was also in contact with the engraver Jacques Callot, whose techniques he adopted. These included the combining of etching and engraving in a single work and the use of a harder varnish, which allowed even, dependable biting. Bosse produced more than 1,500 plates, mostly after his own drawings. He depicted every aspect of the French social system under Louis XIV with the cold objectivity of a moralist. Such works as the *Palace Shopping Gallery* (1637–38), the *Theater of the Hôtel de Bourgogne* (1634), the *Infirmary of the Hôpital de la Charité* (1641), the *City Wedding* (1633; 6 plates), the *Burial*, the *Bloodletting*, the *Schoolmaster* (1635?), and the *Cries of Paris* give us a detailed picture of the French capital under Richelieu, drawn with uncompromising honesty and exactitude.

BOTH, Andries (*c.* 1608, Utrecht—1641, Venice), Dutch painter and engraver, son of Dirk Both (d. 1664), a painter on glass, and pupil of Abraham Bloemaert. He painted scenes of popular genre in the style of Adriaen Brouwer (*Cardplayers*; Amsterdam, Rijksmuseum). JAN (*c.* 1618, Utrecht—1652, Utrecht), brother of Andries, was also a pupil of Bloemaert. He visited Italy and came under the influence of Claude Lorrain. In 1640 he returned to Utrecht, where he became famous as a landscape painter and contributed to the development of Karel Dujardin and Michael Sweerts. He initiated a taste for the pastoral and a style of idyllic and ornamental landscape that soon became highly fashionable. Jan was particularly fond of sunny landscapes. His sensitivity and charm are apparent in a number of landscapes with muleteers, and in a *View on the Tiber, near the Ripa Grande, Rome* (London, National Gallery); a *Picturesque Site in Italy* (Rijksmuseum); and the *Sunken Road* (Paris, Louvre). An interest in classical composition may be seen in his *Landscape with the Judgment of Paris* (London, National Gallery), in which the figures are by Cornelis van Poelenburgh.

BOTTICELLI, Alessandro di Mariano Filipepi, *called* Sandro (1444/45, Florence—1510, Florence), one of the greatest Italian Renaissance painters, who created a wholly personal and independent style that was both linear and volumetric. Sandro was the son of a tanner from Borgo Ognissanti. His rise seems to have begun in a goldsmith's workshop in Florence. He probably received his training in painting from Fra Filippo Lippi, which might explain his fondness for portraying the Madonna. By 1470 Sandro already had his own workshop, and in 1472 Lippi's son, Filippino Lippi, was working as his assistant. The influence of Andrea del Verrocchio and, later, of Antonio Pollaiuolo, is also apparent in the works of Botticelli's youthful period. By the mid-1470s, however, his style was becoming increasingly personal, and in his late works the iconography, to a large extent, was personal as well.

One of Botticelli's earliest paintings is the allegorical representation of *Fortitude* (1470; Florence, Uffizi), for the hall of the Arte di Mercanzia, Florence, which displays the linear vigor of Pollaiuolo, with whose workshop Botticelli was briefly associated. Soon afterward he came under the patronage of the Medici and in 1476–77 Cosimo de' Medici and his family appeared as the magi in the *Adoration of the Magi* (Uffizi), which he executed for the S. Maria Novella, Florence. In July 1478 Botticelli received a commission that was openly political: to paint the *damnatio* ("condemnation") of the Pazzi and their accomplices (conspirators against the Medici); in a fresco (1478; destroyed 1494) over the Porta della Dogana, he showed the traitors hanged. During the same period he produced several portraits that are outstanding for the precision and strength of their drawing and that show Botticelli's deepening awareness of the sitter's personality. The posthumous effigy of Giuliano is one of these (*c.* 1475–76; Washington, D.C., National Gallery).

A more revealing indication of Botticelli's unique position in the Florentine milieu, specifically his contact with the Medici and their circle, are the important allegorical tableaux he was commissioned to paint for the Medici villas: the *Primavera* (Uffizi), generally dated *c.* 1478, and the *Birth of Venus* (Uffizi), of the early 1480s, which is perhaps Botticelli's most widely known work. The panel of *Mars and Venus* (early 1480s; London, National Gallery), probably executed to commemorate a marriage, is stylistically related to these.

In 1480 Botticelli proved his mastery of fresco techniques in the superb *St. Augustine* (Florence, Ognissanti), an example of the strength and masculinity of a style more often praised for its delicate linear qualities. In 1481 he had the honor of being invited, with a group of Tuscan and Umbrian artists, to decorate the walls of the Sistine Chapel at the Vatican. Botticelli's important contri-

Sandro Botticelli. *Judith with the Head of Holophernes.* 1470s. Uffizi, Florence.

Sandro Botticelli. *La Derelitta.* Between 1490 and 1497. Galleria Pallavicini, Rome. *Photo Anderson-Giraudon.*

butions were scenes from the lives of Christ and Moses, including two brilliantly handled compositions showing Jethro's daughters, and the tragic punishment of Korah, Dathan, and Abiram for their rebellion against Moses and Aaron (1481–82).

Again in Tuscany, Botticelli participated in the decoration of Lorenzo's Villa dello Spedaletto, near Volterra (*c.* 1483; frescoes now ruined). There are also the two celebrated marriage allegories (early 1480s; Paris, Louvre), perhaps honoring the wedding of Giovanna degli Albizzi and Lorenzo Tornabuoni, from the Villa in Chiasso Marcerelli (later Villa Lemmi), near Florence. The allegorical *Calumny of Apelles* (*c.* 1494; Uffizi), based on Lucian's description, is another testimony to the scholarly leanings of Botticelli and his patrons.

The artist was also in demand for religious works. He painted the *St. Barnabas* altarpiece (mid-1480s?; Uffizi), and the *Coronation of the Virgin* (1488–90; Uffizi) for a chapel in S. Marco. Here the frenzied angels perhaps indicate the beginning of the religious crisis that was to upset Botticelli's life and profoundly influence his art. His workshop specialized in paintings of the Madonna and Child: *Madonna of the Magnificat* (*c.* 1485; Uffizi); *Madonna of the Pomegranate* (1487; Uffizi); *Madonna with Angels* (1490s; Milan, Ambrosiana).

In the 1480s and 1490s, entombments and scenes of martyrdom are numerous: two *Pietàs* (both early 1490s; Milan, Museo Poldi-Pezzoli, and Munich, Alte Pinakothek), both of which show the effects of Botticelli's reaction to Savonarola; episodes from the life of St. Zenobius (Dresden, London, New York), etc. It is, no doubt, the religious crisis of his last years that explains the deep change in his art after 1498 and that inspired the paintings charged with allusions to contemporary afflictions, such as the *Mystic Nativity* (between 1490 and 1497; London, National Gallery) and the *Mystic Crucifixion* (*c.* 1496; Cambridge, Mass., Fogg Art Museum). Another highly personal undertaking, and Botticelli's supreme achievement as a draftsman, is the series of illustrations on parchment for Dante's *Divine Comedy* (between 1490 and 1497; now divided between the Staatsbibliothek, Berlin, and the Vatican Library). The project was financed by Lorenzo di Pierfrancesco, a cousin of Lorenzo the Magnificent, who seems to have supported Sandro in this period.

BOTTICINI, Francesco di Giovanni (1446, Florence—1497, Florence), Italian painter. In 1459 he became a pupil of Cosimo Rosselli and Verrocchio; he was also influenced by Botticelli. Most of Francesco's works have now been recognized through the judicious attributions of Bernard Berenson (*Madonna and Child in Glory*, Paris, Louvre; *Coronation of the Virgin*, Turin, Museo Civico), although Berenson may have been too generous in his list of attributions.

Francesco's style derives its rather dry craftsmanship from Neri di Bicci, its technique from Cosimo Rosselli, certain of its powerful silhouettes from Andrea del Castagno, and the delicacy of its Madonnas from Fra Filippo Lippi. Finally, his angels combine the influence of Botticelli's faces with the precious attitudes and brilliant colors of Verrocchio (*Madonna with Angels*; Florence, Palazzo Pitti).

BOUCHARDON, Edmé (1698, Chaumont, Haute Marne—1762, Paris), French sculptor who broke with the Rococo style of his contemporaries and restored classical art to favor. Son of the sculptor Jean-Baptiste Bouchardon (1667–1742) and pupil of Guillaume I Coustou, he won the Prix de Rome in 1722 and remained in Rome for 10 years. His reputation there was so high that he was given commissions for busts of Pope Clement XII, the Duc de Polignac, and the Duchess of Buckingham. He was particularly praised for an admirably executed copy of the *Barberini Faun* (1726–30; Paris, Louvre).

On his return to Paris, Bouchardon obtained three successive official commissions. The first, for the *Fountain of the Seasons* in Rue de Grenelle (1739–45), came from the city of Paris. He designed both the sculpture and the general plan. He had a defender in the Comte de Caylus—traveler, lover of antiquity, son of the Marquise de Caylus, the famous writer of memoirs. The Comte de Caylus extolled Bouchardon's talent against the defenders of the Rococo style and obtained for his protégé a commission for a statue of *Cupid Carving his Bow from the Club of Hercules.* The artist spent more than 10 years on this work (1739–50). Exhibited in the Salon d'Hercule at Versailles, it obtained a mild critical success. The singularity of the model's pose, borrowed from a Mannerist painting by Parmigianino (*Amor, c.* 1532–33; Vienna, Kunsthistorisches Museum), worked to its disadvantage.

The third project, still more grandiose, occupied him for 14 years (1748–62): an equestrian statue of Louis XV that stood in the Place de la Concorde, Paris, until its destruction at the time of the French Revolution. The artist made a thorough study of the horse, and 300 of his preparatory drawings still exist. He was unable to complete this work, having exhausted himself in its execution; and he died before its installation. He failed to finish the allegorical

Edmé Bouchardon. *The Marne River.* Louvre, Paris. *Photo Boitier-Connaissance des Arts, Paris.*

figures of the Virtues designed to stand at the four corners of the pedestal: they were executed by Jean-Baptiste Pigalle.

JACQUES PHILIPPE (1711, Chaumont—1753, Stockholm), the brother of Edmé, was sculptor to the Swedish court in Stockholm. He worked for the chapel of the Royal Palace in Stockholm and executed many busts, including one of Charles XII.

BOUCHER, François (1703, Paris—1770, Paris), the most representative French painter of 18th-century *art galant*. His career was long and happy. Although he won a Prix de Rome at the age of twenty, Boucher was unable to go to Italy until 1727. While there, he was influenced only by Tiepolo, and borrowed only mythological subjects from the Italians. Back in France, he devoted himself to Venus, whose historiographer he became. His first painting of the goddess, *Venus Asking Vulcan for Arms for Aeneas* (1732; Paris, Louvre), shows him already master of a facile talent.

A tireless worker who never stopped painting until his death, Boucher led a life that combined labor and pleasure. In 1733 he married a delightful Parisian who was to play an important role in her husband's art by becoming his model, as the Murphy sisters were to do later on. His wife is seen in *Rinaldo and Armida* (1734; Louvre), which he painted for his reception into the Academy, and reigns in the famous *Triumph of Venus* (1740; Stockholm, Nationalmuseum). Boucher earned money for his family by designing and engraving the plates for the *Cries of Paris*, a collection showing the picturesque street sellers of the time, and by illustrating some of the most beautiful books of the century, such as the 1734 edition of Molière's plays. He became the most fashionable painter in France, adapting his "pastorals" to all decorative schemes, setting a style that the 18th century was to reproduce to the point of abuse. His shepherds in knee breeches and pumps charmed his aristocratic clientele, and his "pastorals" and "hunts" were also the subjects of tapestries for the Beauvais factory, of which he was director: *Venetian Fetes* (1736), *Story of Psyche* (1739), *Chinese Fetes* (1743), *Loves of the Gods* (1744), *Noble Pastoral* (1755).

François Boucher. *Rustic Luncheon.* Detail. *Photo Boudot-Lamotte, Paris.*

After the death of Jean-Baptiste Oudry, Boucher went to the Gobelins factory, where he had the *Metamorphoses* and the *Amynthus* woven for the château of Belleville, residence of Madame de Pompadour, whose protégé he became. The favorite painter of the marquise, her artistic adviser and even her drawing teacher, he painted several full-length portraits of her—at her harpsichord, in her park, on a sofa (1758; Vienna, Kunsthistorisches Museum), or even at her dressing table. In 1754 he received commissions for two more paintings for Belleville, a *Sunrise* and *Sunset* now in the Wallace Collection, London. Painter to the king in 1765 and director of the Academy, he could have left a less conventional image of his time, as is proven by *La Marchande de Modes* (1746; Stockholm, Nationalmuseum) or the *Luncheon* (1739; Louvre). But to these one may prefer the most beautiful of nudes, the adorable *Young Girl Resting* (*Louise Murphy*, 1752; Munich, Alte Pinakothek), which scandalized the prudish Diderot, or the *Bath of Diana* (1742; Louvre). A universal artist of prodigious fecundity, Boucher made the mistake of reflecting too perfectly the taste of his time. His vogue scarcely survived him, and Davidian Neoclassicism rejected his delicate art, which did not regain favor until the middle of the 19th century.

BOUDIN, Eugène (1824, Honfleur, Calvados—1898, Deauville), French painter. Boudin's father had a bookshop in Le Havre and exhibited his son's paintings in the window. They were discovered by Millet, who encouraged him to devote himself completely to painting. In Le Havre he made the acquaintance of Baudelaire, Courbet, Monet, and Jongkind, who had a decisive influence on his work. Boudin is the painter of the sea and sky over the English Channel, of aerial transparency, of the delicate, shifting light that quivers over the water and gives a sparkle to the hoop-skirted women grouped along the iridescent, wave-lined beaches. His rapidly executed sketches are, however, even finer than his carefully done canvases; in these, he rendered with admirable freedom and spontaneity the shifting and receding forms intervening between the horizon and the painter's eye. A charming example is *Beach Scene* (1865; St. Louis, City Art Museum). Boudin's paintings are well represented in the collections of the Musée de l'Impressionnisme, Paris, and the Musée Eugène Boudin, Honfleur; the artist willed over 6,000 sketches, pastels, and watercolors to the Cabinet des Dessins (Paris, Louvre).

BOUGUEREAU, Adolphe William (1825, La Rochelle—1905, La Rochelle), French painter. Judging from the extraordinary success of his works and the influence of his teachings, Bouguereau should be regarded as one of the masters of academic painting, which dominated French artistic life at the end of the 19th century. He entered the École des Beaux-Arts in Paris in 1846 and in 1850 was awarded the Prix de Rome. He attracted a wide public with his allegories and mythological compositions (*Youth and Love*, 1877; Paris, Louvre). The line is firmly drawn, but the modeling is wooden, and the paint so smooth and glossy that Degas and his friends damned any canvas that was overpolished as being *bouguereauté* ("bouguerated"). After decorating (1869) the ceiling of the Grand Théâtre in Bordeaux, the artist decorated the chapels of several Paris churches: that of St-Louis at Ste-Clotilde (1859), those of St-Pierre—St-Paul and St-Jean Baptiste at St-Augustin (1866), and that of the Virgin at St-Vincent-de-Paul (1888). He also painted religious compositions in a superior Pre-Raphaelite style (*Virgin of Consolation*, 1877;

Louvre). Bouguereau was showered with honors and in 1876 was elected to the Institut. With Alexandre Cabanel, he reigned over the annual Salon, keeping it within the bounds of official academicism and systematically rejecting the experimental painting of Manet and the Impressionists.

BOULANGER, Louis (1806, Vercelli, Piedmont—1867, Dijon), French Romantic painter. The protective but soon overwhelming friendship of the poet and novelist Victor Hugo led Boulanger, himself a poet, to produce work that was highly literary. Boulanger's technical mastery in handling Romantic themes is evident in his lithographic illustrations (*Phantoms*, 1829), as well as in paintings inspired by the writings of Hugo (*Scene of an Orgy*, 1866; Dijon, Musée des Beaux-Arts). The imaginative freedom of his best works—exemplified by a painting called *Mazeppa* (1827; Rouen, Musée des Beaux-Arts)—and a sensitivity to atmospheric effects recalls the landscapes of Paul Huet and even anticipates the strivings of Eugène Boudin.

BOULENGER, Hippolyte (1837, Tournai, Hainaut—1874, Brussels), Belgian painter of French extraction. In 1863, he discovered the beauty of the forest of Soignes and founded the realist School of Tervueren, the Belgian equivalent of the French Barbizon School. The group made its mark at the 1866 Salon in Brussels, creating a scandal with its crude colors. Its triumph came in 1872, when the gold medal of the Salon was awarded to Boulenger's *Avenue of Elm Trees* (1871; Brussels, Musée d'Art Moderne). Boulenger dominated the group by the lyrical sensitivity of his work, which can be seen in *Spring at Boitsfort* (1873; Tournai, Musée des Beaux-Arts). His *Study of Clouds* (1869; Brussels, Musée des Beaux-Arts d'Ixelles) anticipates the freedom and coloring of the Impressionists.

BOULLÉE, Étienne-Louis (1728, Paris—1799, Paris), French architect. He was a pupil of Jean Laurent Le Geay (active 1732–86) and one of the supporters of the return to Classicism in the middle of the 18th century. Most of his numerous constructions have disappeared, with the exception of the Hôtel Alexandre, later the Hôtel Suchet, Paris, in which he used Ionic columns to support an upper story on the courtyard side, while pilasters of the same order adorn two stories overlooking the garden. Although Boullée was a skilled and prolific architect, for him the conception of a work was a nobler act than the actual building. As a theoretician, he expected the most beautiful geometrical forms from nature to inspire lofty sentiments, for, 100 years before the Symbolists, he believed that form and feeling were united by a mysterious bond. He thus resolved the artistic conflict of his day between ideal beauty, which inspired the Neoclassical style, and expressive power, shown by the pre-Romantics.

BOURDELLE, Antoine (1861, Montauban, Ille-et-Vilaine—1929, Le Vésinet, Seine-et-Oise), French sculptor, painter, and designer. After studying with Alexandre Falguière (1831–1900) and Jules Dalou in Paris, Bourdelle entered the studio of Rodin, whose influence on his artistic output was lifelong. Bourdelle became Rodin's assistant in 1890. His earliest works express the Romantic strain that never left him. His first successes—an early *Beethoven* with wind-swept hair (1893; he executed some 21 likenesses of Beethoven during his career), and *Hercules Drawing His Bow* (1909)—are popular in their appeal, and their "message" is more striking than their sculptural value. The *Memorial to the Dead* at Montauban (1902) is marred by similar excesses. Bourdelle's too-faithful memory sometimes led him to produce works with archaic overtones, such as the *Dying Centaur* (1914) or *Penelope* (1912). His *Virgin of Alsace*, which stands at the summit of the Vosges, is reminiscent of Romanesque art, while *Mickiewicz Walking* (1928) is clearly Romantic in inspiration. The Mannerist elongation of his *France Greeting America* (1926) appears to derive from Jean Goujon. The bas-reliefs that decorate the Théâtre des Champs-Élysées, Paris (1912), and that complement its architectural style are somewhat less flamboyant. One of his most successful works is the *Monument to General Alvear* (1914–19; Buenos Aires), an equestrian statue of the liberator of Argentina, surrounded by the four giant symbolic figures of Liberty, Strength, Victory, and Eloquence. Bourdelle's prolific output also includes busts (Anatole France, James Frazer [1919], Auguste Perret, and Charles-Louis Philippe), as well as drawings, illustrations, paintings, and ceramics. His works can be seen at the Musée Bourdelle in Paris, formerly his studio.

Antoine Bourdelle. *Sappho.* 1887. Musée Bourdelle, Paris. *Photo Bulloz.*

BOURGEOIS, Louise (b. 1911, Paris), American sculptress. Her education included studies in Paris at the Sorbonne, the École du Louvre, the Académie des Beaux-Arts, and a number of private studios, including that of the painter Fernand Léger; in New York City, where she moved in 1938, she studied at the Art Students League. She taught at the Louvre and the Académie de la Grande Chaumière in Paris and at Brooklyn College in New York. She emerged as an important modernist sculptress in the early 1950s with her wood constructions, usually uniformly painted in either black or white. Around 1949, she experimented with images that represented tall

Louise Bourgeois. *One and Others.* 1955. Whitney Museum of American Art, New York.

and thin, abstract, anonymous personages, related to the sculpture of David Smith and Isamu Noguchi, and meant to be grouped around the viewer; works from this period include *The Blind Leading the Blind* (painted wood, 1949). A few years later Bourgeois organized her forms into compositions suggesting landscape or architecture, as in *Garden at Night* (painted wood, 1953). In the 1960s, she turned away from constructions to modeling forms in plaster, intended for casting in metal.

BOUTS, Dirk (*c.* 1415, Haarlem—1475, Louvain), Flemish painter. Following Robert Campin, Jan van Eyck, and Rogier van der Weyden, Bouts gave a Gothic interpretation of the divine, man, and nature. Resident in Louvain in 1448, he there married Catherine van der Bruggen; his two painter sons, Dirk the Younger (*c.* 1448–91) and Aelbrecht (*c.* 1460–1549), imitated his style. The possibility that he was a pupil of Van der Weyden in Brussels has been conjectured from the works attributed to his youth (*Virgin*, Madrid, Prado; *Descent from the Cross*, Granada Cathedral, Capilla Real, and Paris, Louvre; *Entombment*, London, National Gallery). Bouts may have gone to Haarlem between 1448 and 1457. When he reappeared at Louvain, in 1457, it was as a Master, a burgher, and an educated man who conversed with theologians. From that time, documents and texts relative to his commissions show an uninterrupted activity at Louvain until his death in 1475.

Bouts can be appreciated in the following authentic works: the *Martyrdom of Erasmus* (Louvain, St-Pierre); the *Last Supper* (1467, St-Pierre), which is his masterpiece; the wings of the *Last Judgment*, painted in 1470 (*Paradise*, Lille, Palais des Beaux-Arts; *Hell*, Louvre); and the *Ordeal by Fire* (Brussels, Musées Royaux des Beaux-Arts), a panel painted about 1473 on the theme of the *Justice of Otto*. To these may be added the *Martyrdom of St. Hippolytus* (Bruges, St-Sauveur) and a *Portrait of a Man* (1462; London, National Gallery). Less secure are the *Virgin of Sorrows* (Louvre), the *Christ as Savior* (Rotterdam, Museum Boymans-van Beuningen), and the admirable *Adoration of the Magi* (Munich, Alte Pinakothek), called the "Pearl of Brabant" and wrongly attributed to Bouts' son Dirk, a triptych that aroused great enthusiasm among the Romantics, who admired the sunset (*St. Christopher* wing), the poetic landscape (*St. John* wing), and the presence of a kingfisher and of a stream among the flowers. These pictures show the artist's impressive skill.

The art of Dirk Bouts is one of gravity, reserve, and an apparent coldness. A disquieting painter, he created his own aesthetic of silence and immobility. He controlled his effects by precise calculation but was all the more moving for his avoidance of obvious pathos. There is a total integration of the divine into the human and real, explaining the attraction felt by Bouts for beautiful objects, as in the Louvain *Last Supper*. The still life motifs of this work are a prelude to the genre paintings of the following century; but in Bouts they form only a complementary part of pictures in which objectivity conceals a discreet tenderness, a quivering force, and a deep religious feeling.

BOYLE, Richard, Earl of Burlington (1694, London—1753, London), English architect—important not so much for his work as a designer and innovator as for the far-reaching influence he had on the rise and spread of Palladianism in England. He already took a passionate interest in architecture when he set off on the Grand Tour to Italy (1714–15), and on his return he employed Colin Campbell to redesign Burlington House, London (begun *c.* 1717), on the model of Palladio's Palazzo Porto-Colleoni at Vicenza. His patronage of Campbell, and more important, his lifelong friendship with William Kent, whom he took on his second visit to Italy (1719) to study architecture, did much to popularize Palladianism. Burlington himself designed about a dozen buildings, nearly all houses for his friends or public buildings under his patronage. Except for the functional block of the dormitory of Westminster School (1722–30), he adhered strictly to the principles and practice of the two paragons of the Palladian movement, Palladio himself and Inigo Jones. His two most important works are his own villa at Chiswick (*c.* 1725), which bears a certain resemblance to Palladio's Villa Rotonda, with features borrowed from Inigo Jones, and the Assembly Rooms at York (1730), an exact model of Palladio's Egyptian Hall.

BRAMANTE, Donato di Pascuccio di Angelo, *called* (1444, Monte Asdrualdo—1514, Rome), leading Italian architect of the High Renaissance, active particularly in Rome, who numbered Raphael among his pupils. Born in the region of The Marches, Bramante received his early education in the brilliant city of Urbino. By 1482 he was in Milan, where he stayed for almost 20 years, frequently in the service of the Sforzas, and it was in Milanese territory that he increased his knowledge of building before settling in Rome (1499) to serve the extravagant ambitions of Pope Julius II.

In the cultivated environment of Urbino, where Leon Battista Alberti had met Piero della Francesca, at the time when Luciano Laurana and Francesco di Giorgio Martini were building the Palazzo Ducale for the Montefeltro family, Bramante, in the course of a double apprenticeship as painter and architect, absorbed the pure and logically ordered style of these inspired geometers. His earliest documented works are some frescoes in Bergamo, painted in 1477. In Milan, his great fresco figures on the walls of the Palazzo Panigarola (now in the Brera) remain the most important evidence of a talent that could have put him on a level with the great Lombard painters, had not his activities as an architect soon taken precedence over his work as a decorator. Also in Milan, the apse of S. Maria delle Grazie and the sacristy of S. Satiro are the buildings in which the architect Bramante first showed himself responsive to the Lombard environment. In the Milanese church of S. Maria presso S. Satiro he used false perspective in the painted apse to provide the feeling

Bramante. Cloister, S. Maria della Pace, Rome. 1504. *Photo Anderson-Giraudon.*

of illusory depth—the first such use of this device in architecture. More significant among his works in Lombardy is the great arch of the façade of the cathedral of Abbiategrasso (1497), conceived as a high niche in two stories framed by twin columns, in which reminiscences of St. Mark's in Venice and of Alberti's S. Andrea in Mantua are combined, heralding the complex works at the Vatican.

With the fall of Ludovico il Moro in 1499, which ended the most brilliant period of the Renaissance in the duchy of Milan, Bramante traveled to Rome, where the two splendid pontificates of Julius II (1503–13) and Leo X (1513–21) were to follow. In the city which at that time was experiencing the fever of archaeological discoveries, Bramante quickly freed himself from Lombard affectations; the sight of Roman monuments increased in him the feeling for vast perspectives and space composition that he had absorbed from his masters at Urbino. One of the first signs of this is the Tempietto of S. Pietro in Montorio—a small, domed rotunda surrounded by Doric columns, which he built on the Janiculum, in the cloister of the Franciscans (1502), on the spot where St. Peter was believed to have been crucified. Elegantly simple in its proportions and making extensive use of antique sources, it is one of the constructions that define the style we call High Renaissance.

With Cardinal della Rovere's elevation to the papacy as Julius II, Bramante was given a commission that allowed him greater scope than ever before. On the slope of the Vatican Hill, on a site 300 yards long, he was to plan a monumental ensemble that would join the Belvedere of Pope Innocent II (a small summer house) with the medieval Vatican Palace. Following the example of the Roman temple of Fortune at Praeneste (Palestrina), Bramante exploited all the opportunities offered by the sloping ground. On one of the long sides he screened the old buildings with three tiers of arcades and joined together three successive courts with magnificent tiered landings. The huge exedra of the Belvedere crowned the vista with tremendous spaciousness.

A more grandiose idea was under way at the Vatican—the rebuilding of Constantine's basilica of St. Peter. Bramante's plan, famous although frequently a subject of controversy after his time, envisioned a building in the shape of a Greek cross surmounted by a cupola over the crossing. It was to be flanked in the angles of the cross by four subsidiary chapels, buttressed by campaniles, and also cross-shaped. On the outside the building would show a similarity of appearance from all sides, symbolic of Catholic universality. Bramante died without being able to push the execution of his plan far enough to force his successors to carry it out. But it seems likely that Raphael, in designing the architectural background for the *School of Athens* fresco (Vatican), used an interior view of the projected basilica.

Bramante developed the theme of the centrally planned building on a more modest scale in the churches of SS. Celso e Giuliano and S. Biagio della Pagnotta, Rome. His influence, if not his own participation, is apparent in S. Maria della Consolazione, built on a splendid site beneath the walls of the Umbrian city of Todi. Although completed at the beginning of the 17th century, it is nevertheless considered the religious building that most perfectly exemplifies the Renaissance style.

BRAMANTINO, Bartolomeo Suardi, *called* (*c.* 1465, Milan—*c.* 1530, Milan), Italian architect and painter. Apart from a short stay in Rome (1508), where, according to Vasari, he met Perugino, Pinturicchio, and Sansovino and worked in the Vatican Stanze, Bramantino lived and worked in Milan. He was both painter and architect for the Trivulzio family, for whom he drew up the plans of the Gian Giacomo Trivulzio chapel in the church of S. Nazaro Maggiore and designed a series of tapestries mentioned in the account book of Magno Trivulzio. In Milan Bramantino painted a *Deposition* (1513) for the Carthusian monks of Chiaravalle and worked for the duomo (1519). In 1530 he was appointed by Francesco II Sforza as architect and painter to the court.

Trained by Bernardino Jacopi Butinone (before 1436—after 1507), Bramantino was influenced by Vincenzo Foppa in his use of color, and more decisively by Bramante, who gave his style its grandeur. The works painted by Bramantino between 1485 and 1505 show the evolution of his style toward final artistic freedom: for instance, the Boston *Madonna* (Museum of Fine Arts), the Sansepolcro *Nativity* and *Pietà* (Milan, Biblioteca Ambrosiana), and the *Adoration of the Magi* (London, National Gallery), in which there are distant reminiscences of Leonardo da Vinci.

Bramante. *Christ at the Pillar*. Brera, Milan.

BRANCUSI, Constantin (1876, Pestisani, Rumania—1957, Paris), Rumanian sculptor whose entire career was spent in Paris. He received a scholarship to the School of Fine Arts in Bucharest in 1898. In 1903 he began wandering through Europe, but after a year he decided to settle permanently in Paris. Although he studied at the École des Beaux-Arts, Brancusi was also exposed to the influence of Rodin, who was then at the height of his career. In 1906 he exhibited for the first time at the Société Nationale des Beaux-Arts.

Brancusi then went his own way, making his own discoveries, rejecting both classical naturalism and the impressionist fragmentation of Rodin, both the sensualism of Maillol and the intellectualism of the Cubists. No one eliminated superfluous details more severely than he. Through a series of reductions, he attained primordial form, the essential form, or better still, the embryo, the nucleus, the original ovum, the oval that is both concrete and abstract. This development can be seen in the many versions of his *Sleeping Muse*, the *Prometheus* (1911), the *Newborn* (1915), the *Beginning of the World* (1924), the *White Negress* (1924), and the many variations of the bust of *Mademoiselle Pogany*, sculptured between 1913 and 1933. In his desire for great simplification and starkness of form, he polished and repolished his marbles and bronzes, lovingly and endlessly smoothing the contours and surfaces until solid metal and stone became a translucent medium for the idea enclosed within. Whether in the curve or the straight line, in the gracefully elongated oval or the square geometricity of the block, there is always the same concision, the same starkness of form, and the same intensity of feeling, interiorized in the material, the grain of the marble, the molecule of metal.

In 1907 Brancusi moved to 54 Rue de Montparnasse. He became friendly with a number of artists in the district, notably Amedeo Modigliani and Henri Rousseau, for whose tomb he was to carve a cippus and to engrave in the stone Guillaume Apollinaire's famous poem. His reputation grew, and he received commissions from abroad. In 1913 he sent five works to the Armory Show in New York and three more to the Allied Artists Exhibition in London. Then in New York, in 1914, his first one-man exhibition took place, at Alfred Stieglitz's Gallery 291.

Between 1914 and 1918 Brancusi made a series of wood carvings, the *Prodigal Son*, the *Witch, Caryatid*, and *Chimera*, which he carved in oak with a hatchet. After the war, his wood carvings became more abstract, as demonstrated by *Adam and Eve* (1921; New York, Solomon R. Guggenheim Museum), *Socrates* (1923), *The Leader* (1925), and the *Endless Column*, whose final proportions were the product of an exhaustive study. This work is nearly 100 feet high and is composed of uniform elements symmetrically repeated to a virtual infinity. It was executed in gilt steel and erected in 1937 at Targu-Jiu, in the artist's native region, at the foot of the Carpathians.

Constantin Brancusi.
Cock. 1941. Musée National d'Art Moderne, Paris.

A close affinity united the sculptor with the hidden forces of nature and he instinctively found, among the profuse vocabulary of its forms, the one that summarized them all. An illustration of this abstraction can be appreciated in *Girl's Torso* (1922), *Leda* (1924), *Cock* (1941), *Flying Tortoise* (1943), *Seal* (1943), and *Bird in Space*, which he repeated between 1924 and 1949 in a series of variations that were increasingly simplified, dense, and reductive. Brancusi rediscovered the themes and forms that have haunted man for thousands of years, the eternal archetypes that constitute the indissoluble depository of the ages and have never ceased to inspire great sculpture. His *Golden Bird* can be related to ancient Egypt, *Mademoiselle Pogany* to some Cycladic idol, his *Sophisticated Girl* to the Venus of Lespugue, or one might see in his *Gate of the Kiss* a transposition of the Gate of the Sun at Tiahuanaco.

In 1925 the artist moved to 11 Impasse Ronsin, where he worked until his death in proud and disdainful solitude, indifferent to honors and rewards and refusing to take part in the Venice and São Paulo biennales. He stopped sending anything to the various Paris salons. He agreed to exhibit his works only in the United States (at the Brummer Gallery in New York in 1926 and 1933; at the Guggenheim Museum in 1955), where his earliest buyers lived, and he made several visits to America himself, in 1926, 1928, and 1939. In 1937 he went to India to direct the building of the *Temple of Deliverance*, which had been commissioned from him by the Maharajah of Indore, but the prince fell seriously ill and the plans were not carried out. The model is still in existence, however (1933; Paris, Musée National d'Art Moderne). This design, the *Caryatid*, the *Gate of the Kiss*, the *Endless Column*, and the *Spirit of the Buddha* (1937; Guggenheim Museum) are Brancusi's most successful experiments in architectural sculpture.

BRAQUE, Georges (1882, Argenteuil—1963, Paris), outstanding 20th-century French painter. He was eight years old when his father, a house painter, settled in Le Havre. In 1900 he went to Paris and entered first the École Nationale des Beaux-Arts and then the Académie Humbert. After a summer at Honfleur (1904), he became attracted to Fauvism, which had found an enthusiastic practitioner in Othon Friesz, Braque's friend from Le Havre. In 1906 the two young artists went to Antwerp, and the following summer to La Ciotat. Braque returned to Paris with some distinctly Fauvist canvases. However, Cézanne's influence was evident in an equilibrium and a conciseness that heralded a new artistic course. With Picasso, Braque was evolving the fundamentals of what was to be known as Cubism, a pictorial language the necessity of which was simultaneously felt by both artists, although neither had conceived or practiced it previously. Braque is thus the only master to have experienced and illustrated the two most important aesthetic adventures of the early 20th century.

His *Large Nude* of 1907 (Paris, Coll. Mme. Marie Cuttoli) is a clear step in his passage from Fauvism to Cubism; and a more energetic awareness of form is emphasized in *Houses at l'Estaque* (1908; Bern, Marguerite and Hermann Rupf Foundation), *Still Life with Musical Instruments* (1908; formerly coll. artist), and *Le Château de La Roche-Guyon* (1909; Stockholm, Coll. Rolf de Maré).

At the end of 1909, Braque was separating the volumes into geometrical elements. In close collaboration with Picasso, he immediately began applying his experiments to the human figure and to still life. He experimented with combinations of angles and lines, overlapping planes, and the simultaneous projection of various disconnected parts of the object on the picture surface. This mode of working could not but lead to abstraction, and around 1911 Braque's art seemed destined to break all links with the real. The process did not go further, however, for of all the Cubists, Braque was the first to react against the austerity and hermeticism of the Cubist works, beginning with his own. Indeed, it was during 1911 that he first introduced in one of his canvases (*The Portuguese*; Paris, Priv. Coll.) a reference to the world of appearances—an inscription in printed letters; he also began to apply fragments of various materials—paper, bits of wood or cloth, sand—to the canvas. Thus he developed the so-called *papier collé : Still Life with Playing Card, Bottle, Newspaper, and Tobacco Packet : "Le Courrier"* (1913; Philadelphia, Museum of Art); *Aria de Bach* (1914; Paris, Coll. Mme. Marie Cuttoli).

Until 1914 Braque and Picasso were inseparable. When war was declared Braque was sent to the front. Seriously wounded in 1915, he had to be trepanned. After long months of convalescing, he began to paint again in 1917, without Picasso. Light, which had not previously been his concern, began to occupy Braque increasingly. He became more respectful of the object than formerly and strove to cast his inspirations in more stable, durable form.

Beginning in 1925, the less angular, more colorful, and less conceptual Cubism of *Café-Bar* (1919; Basel, Kunstmuseum) and *Mantelpieces* (1922–23) gave way to the neo-realism of the *Canéphorae* ("basket holders," partially draped female nudes, often with fruit baskets; 1923–26), the

Georges Braque. *Cabins.* 1930. Private Coll. *Photo Galerie Maeght, Paris.*

first plaster reliefs, the etchings for Hesiod's *Theogony*, the *Guéridon* ("table") series (1926–30), the small seascape series, and the still lifes made of objects divided lengthwise into light and dark sections.

The next five years were among the most fertile of his career, although not copious in output. It was the period during which he brought together in an assured equilibrium a distillation of all the resources of his genius and the results of his experimentation. From this time date his most sumptuous still lifes (*Red Tablecloth*, 1933, Paris, Coll. Aimé Maeght; *Yellow Tablecloth*, 1935, St. Louis, Coll. Mr. and Mrs. Richard K. Weil). He also applied his system of contrasting planes to the human figure, notably in *Woman with a Mandolin* (1937; New York, Museum of Modern Art), the *Duo* (1937; Paris, Musée National d'Art Moderne), and *Painter and Model* (1939; New York, Coll. Walter P. Chrysler, Jr.). During World War II his painting became richer and acquired a spiritual quality, its objects arranged in a more open and less involved space, freed of the backgrounds charged with ornamental motifs: *Black Fish* (1942; Musée National d'Art Moderne), *Red Table* (1942; U.S.A., Priv. Coll.), and the *Salon* (1944; Musée National d'Art Moderne). Increasingly economical in his means, Braque gave his style a more and more monumental grandeur. The *Billiard Table* series, begun in 1944, led to the *Studio* series (1949–56), and finally to the *Birds* series (1955–63), in which he found the greatest harmony between inspiration and technique.

Braque also left an important body of sculpture (animals, birds, and fish in bronze and in lead; human profiles; engraved and colored plaster reliefs) and lithography. He designed décor for the theater (*Les Fâcheux*, 1924; *Zephyre et Flore*, 1925, for the Ballets Russes) and tapestry cartoons, and executed three decorations on a grand scale, one for the ceiling of the Henri II gallery in the Louvre (1952)—great black birds encircled with white against a blue background—and the other two for the Fondation Maeght at St-Paul de Vence (1954). In 1953–55 he executed some stained-glass windows for the small church of Varengeville, a village in Normandy where he had spent every summer, beginning in 1930. In 1962 he made jewelry designs.

BRAUN, Matthias Bernhard Braun von (1684, Ötz, Austria—1738, Prague), Czech sculptor. Braun was born in the Tyrol but spent most of his working life in Bohemia, particularly in Prague, where he was made a freeman of the city in 1710. He was one of the most influential figures of Czech Baroque sculpture.

We know very little of Braun's life as a young man; he probably studied in Italy and saw the sculptures of Bernini, whose influence on his work appears to have been profound. In 1704, at Bolzano (Bozen), he met Count Franz von Sporck, a rich patron of the arts, who wanted to build a spa at Kuks. For this estate Von Sporck commissioned Braun to execute a large-scale sculptural group based on Cesare Ripa's *Iconology*; the most successful pieces were the series of *Virtues* and *Vices* (*c.* 1719). In Prague Braun carved two works for the Charles Bridge, the *Vision of St. Luitgard* (1710), a sculptural group, and the statue of *St. Ivo* (1711). He was then commissioned to decorate the Clam-Gallas Palace, built 1713–19 by Johann Bernhard Fischer von Erlach. He later sculptured a group without precedent in the "New Forest" of Betlam, on Von Sporck's estates near Kuks—statues (originally painted), many of colossal size and carved out of the living rock, that rise out of the ground in the middle of the forest. Each has a symbolic meaning, part of a program that had been worked out in detail by Von Sporck.

BRAUNER, Victor (1903, Piatra-Neamt, Rumania—1966, Paris), Rumanian painter whose career was spent in Paris. He first visited the French capital in 1925, and when he returned to settle there five years later, he had already participated in the avant-garde movements in his own country. He was soon on close terms with his compatriot Constantin Brancusi and later became friendly with Alberto Giacometti and Yves Tanguy, who introduced him to André Breton. It was Breton who patronized his first Paris exhibition in 1934. Brauner became deeply involved in the Surrealist movement; his art took on a visionary quality and became a medium for the exploration of the secret world of dreams. This is the period (*c.* 1938–40) of his chimeras—diaphanous creatures with the head of a woman, huge staring eyes, and a body that ends in bird claws or the paw of some wild animal. After the war Brauner continued to develop his symbolic language, adapting it to the creation of a fabulous world of fresh, vivid color, alive with animals and plants, unknown gods and strange characters, such as *Strigoï the Sleepwalker* (1946), the *Metal Charmer* (1947), or the *Knight of the Bond* (1949). His art mingles nonsense with tenderness, anxiety and lucidity with irony, and is remarkable for its originality and independent development.

BREGNO, Andrea (1421, Osteno, near Como—1506, Rome), Lombard sculptor and architect. His style—rather cold, but of Classical elegance—is seen to advantage in his sumptuous tomb designs, which were inspired by triumphal porticoes. There are several examples of these in Rome, including the monument of Cardinal Labretto (d. 1465; S. Maria in Aracoeli), the relief from the tomb of Cardinal Nicholas of Cusa (d. 1464; S. Pietro in Vincoli), and the tomb of Cardinal Coca (d. 1477; S. Maria sopra Minerva). The church of SS. Apostoli, also in Rome, contains Bregno's monuments of Cardinal Pietro Riario (1475–77) and the tomb of Raffaello della Rovere (d. 1477). Particularly notable are his Borgia altar (1473) and the monument of Cristoforo della Rovere (d. 1479), both in S. Maria del Popolo, Rome. As an architect, he is credited with the Palazzo Riario, later called the Cancelleria, in Rome, erected by Giovanni della Rovere, nephew of the pope, who had been named prefect of the city. This building is outstanding for its clarity of design and its grandeur.

Georges Braque. *Yellow Bouquet.* 1952. *Photo Galerie Maeght, Paris.*

Georges Braque. *Profile.* 1939–40. *Photo Walter Dräyer, Zurich.*

Rodolphe Bresdin. *Bather and Death. Archives photographiques, Paris.*

BRESDIN, Rodolphe (1822, Ingrande, Maine-et-Loire—1885, Sèvres, Seine-et-Oise), French engraver. His oeuvre consists exclusively of drawings, etchings, and lithographs, with the exception of one small painting. His first etchings and lithographs, which were often tiny but very meticulously executed, immediately revealed his taste for the fantastic and strange, which he maintained and cultivated throughout his career, and which he displayed equally in landscapes and Biblical scenes (the *Good Samaritan*, 1861; lithograph). The artist, whose imaginative powers are abundantly evident in his work, apparently dreamed of the simple, happy life evoked by the scene he described in versions of the *Flight into Egypt*, and left Paris on several occasions for Tulle, Toulouse, and Bordeaux. Around 1871 he won a trip to America as a prize for his design of an American banknote, and from there he went to Canada, returning penniless to France in 1876. The quintessential Bohemian artist while he lived, Bresdin died in poverty in a garret.

Bresdin's vision was dominated by nature, primeval in force. On one of his visits to Toulouse, he created the *Holy Family Beside a Rushing Stream* (1853?; lithograph), a variation on his *Flight into Egypt* theme. In another vein, the *Forest of Fontainebleau* (etching) is a particularly beautiful and fresh evocation of nature, largely because it lacks his usual macabre undertones.

Bresdin's incredibly delicate and detailed lithographs were probably copied from preliminary etchings, since his fine craggy lines are characteristic of the etcher's needle and not of the lithographer's crayon. As such, they are virtuoso pieces, and good impressions are rare.

BRETT, John (1830, Bletchingley, East Surrey—1902, Putney, London), English landscape painter. He entered the Royal Academy Schools in 1854, and soon came under the influence of the Pre-Raphaelites, exhibiting with them in 1857. The painting that earned him fame was the *Stonebreaker* (1857–58; Liverpool, Walker Art Gallery), in which the figure is almost incidental to the brilliant and meticulous rendering of scenery at Box Hill in Surrey; its realistic style had by then been made both fashionable and popular by William Holman-Hunt and Sir John Everett Millais. The painting was shown in 1858 at London's Royal Academy, where it attracted the attention of the critic John Ruskin, who set great store by photographic realism. The admiration and support of the leading critic of the day proved, however, to be a mixed blessing: after the Royal Academy exhibit in 1859 of the *Val d'Aosta* (Coll. Sir William Cooper), Brett produced little work of quality, his style becoming dry and mechanical. There is evidence to suggest that Ruskin was partially and indirectly responsible, his repeated exhortations breaking the painter's nerve.

BREUER, Marcel (b. 1902, Pécs, Hungary), American architect, one of the masters of contemporary domestic architecture. At the age of eighteen he enrolled at the Academy of Fine Arts in Vienna but was disappointed by the teaching there; at the end of 1920 he moved to the Bauhaus in Weimar as one of its youngest pupils. He soon joined the teaching staff; in 1924, when still only twenty-two, he was chosen by Walter Gropius to direct the furniture department. In 1925 he created the first metal tubular chair adapted to mass production; over the next three years, using the same principle, he designed a whole range of simple but boldly conceived furniture, used first in the homes of the teachers at the second Bauhaus at Dessau and reproduced 20 years later for the UNESCO building in Paris. Meanwhile his interest in architecture grew; when he left the Bauhaus in 1928, he settled in Berlin as an architect and decorator. During the next eight years, he designed several bold and practical dwellings in which he showed himself to be a fervent adherent of the functional principles of the new architecture (Harnischmacher House, Wiesbaden, 1932; Dolderthal apartments, Zurich, 1934). At the same time, he pursued theoretical studies in town planning and completed a wide range of projects for factories, theaters, and hospitals.

When the Nazis came to power, Breuer emigrated first to Britain, then to the United States in 1937, in response to Gropius' invitation to teach at Harvard. He worked with Gropius (1938–41) on a number of projects, including the Defense Housing Project for aluminum workers at New Kensington, Pennsylvania (1941). He became a naturalized American citizen in 1944. In 1946 he settled in New York, where he opened his own office and designed suburban residences of distinction, adapted to the requirements of American living and ranking, with the works of Frank Lloyd Wright and Richard Neutra, among the most original achievements of modern architecture. His reputation spread when he was commissioned, with the Italian Pier Luigi Nervi and the Frenchman Bernard Zehrfuss, to design the UNESCO building in Paris (1953–58). Many other commissions followed, often for buildings on a monumental scale: the church of St. John's Abbey for a Benedictine monastery at Collegeville, Minnesota (1953–61); a lecture hall for New York University, University Heights (1956–61); the De Bijenkorf Department Store, Rotterdam (1953–57); the IBM Research Center at La Gaude, near Nice (1960–62), a huge building on pilotis in the form of opposed "Y"s; and the new Whitney Museum of American Art, New York (1964–66).

Marcel Breuer. Lecture hall, University Heights Campus, New York University. 1956–61. *Photo Ben Schnall.*

Marcel Breuer is one of the last representatives of functionalism, a doctrine calling, in his opinion, for the expression in form and materials, of the function that each part of a building is to occupy within the whole.

BREUGHEL. *See* **BRUEGEL** *or* **BREUGHEL.**

BRIANCHON, Maurice (b. 1899, Fresnay-sur-Sarthe), French painter. From 1920 he exhibited in the Salon d'Automne. His first pictures—interior scenes, nudes, and landscapes—show the influence of Bonnard and Manet. Apart from his canvases, his extremely varied work includes mural decorations (Palais de Chaillot, 1936; Conservatoire National de Musique, with his wife Marguerite Louppe, 1942), tapestry cartoons, and theatrical and ballet designs, including *Grisélidis* (1922) and three ballets of the Paris Opera: *Valses nobles et sentimentales* (1938), *Sylvia* (1941), and *Les Animaux modèles* (1942). Brianchon's art has great unity; it is based on a mat technique that strives neither for textured effects nor the delights of spontaneous brushwork, and rejects anything savoring of affectation. Yet texture and brushstroke are indeed elements in his painting; no surface is completely flat and inert, no color is polished. Everything in the picture vibrates with subtle, delicately composed harmonies.

BRILL, Paul (1554, Antwerp—1626, Rome), Flemish painter and engraver. Although he spent most of his life in Rome, where he came under strong Italian influences, his northern temperament always prevailed in his works. He was one of the finest landscapists of his time, and after abandoning his youthful Mannerist approach to nature produced some of the earliest landscapes to anticipate the Classical vein of Baroque landscape painting (*Rocky Landscape*, 1602; Glasgow, Art Museum). Brill first worked as a decorator of clavichords at Antwerp and in 1580 joined his brother Mathys in Rome to paint frescoes. He decorated several great houses there, including the Palazzo Rospigliosi, and worked in the Vatican for Pope Sixtus V, painting views of the Roman Campagna. He also painted on panel and canvas, and later on copper; these late works are numerous and were sold for high prices. At first Brill remained faithful to the style of Gillis van Coninxloo (*Wooded Landscape*, 1591, Florence, Uffizi; *Deer Hunt*, Paris, Louvre). Between 1600 and 1610 he began to infuse a Virgilian sentiment into his Italianate landscapes (*Flock of Goats*; Louvre). Attracted by the luminous effects of Adam Elsheimer and also by the lyricism of the Venetians, he turned toward a more sensitive interpretation of landscape (*Landscape with Goatherds*, between 1615 and 1625; Indianapolis, Herron Museum of Art).

BRIULLOV, Karl Pavlovich. *See* **BRÜLLOV** *or* **BRIULLOV,** Karl Pavlovich.

BRONZE AND IRON AGES. *See* **PREHISTORIC ART.**

BRONZINO, Agnolo Torri, *also called* Angiolo (1503, Florence—1572, Florence), Italian Mannerist painter. The official portraitist to the Florentine ducal court belongs to the second generation of Tuscan Mannerism—cold, refined, impeccably cultured, with an extraordinarily high level of technical proficiency. Bronzino learned the controlled Tuscan technique of drawing as an apprentice to Raffaellino del Garbo (*c.* 1470–1524), but he owes his most influential training to Jacopo da Pontormo, whom he assisted in the Certosa di Val d'Ema at Galluzzo (1522–25) and whose clear colors and supple forms left their mark in the two tondi of the *Evangelists* in the Capponi Chapel at S. Felicita, Florence, which are attributed to Bronzino. The artist was expelled from Florence in 1530 by the bishop and entered the service of Guidobaldo II, duke of Urbino. During his sojourn away from home, he painted a portrait of the duke (1530–32; Florence, Palazzo Pitti) and decorated the Villa Imperiale at Pesaro. He was able to return to Florence in 1532 and again helped Pontormo, who was then working at Poggio a Caiano. In 1539 he was commissioned to decorate the chapel of Eleonora of Toledo, the duke's wife, at the Palazzo Vecchio in Florence, and thereafter he rose rapidly to the position of court painter. He painted a large number of portraits that captured the reserved and formal court atmosphere and gave him an immense reputation: *Cosimo I de' Medici in Armor* (1545); *Eleonora of Toledo and Her Son Giovanni* (*c.* 1545); and *Bartolomeo and Lucrezia Panciatichi* (*c.* 1540)—all in the Uffizi, Florence. In 1546–47 he was invited to Rome and painted several eminent persons there, including *Giannettino Doria* (1546–47; Rome, Palazzo Doria).

For Eleonora's chapel, which was not completed until 1564, Bronzino executed a very affected *Pietà* (1545; Besançon, Musée des Beaux-Arts) and rather confused scenes from the *Life of Moses* (after 1548; Florence, Palazzo Vecchio). Compositional sophistication is similarly exaggerated in the allegory of *Venus, Cupid, Folly, and Time* (*c.* 1542–45; London, National Gallery). Bronzino also took over the fresco work of Pontormo (who died in 1558) at S. Lorenzo in Florence, and completed Pontormo's *Martyrdom of S. Lorenzo* in 1569. His last piece, the *Trinity* for the Cappella dei Pittori at the SS. Annunziata in Florence, dates from 1571.

Of greatest interest in Bronzino's work is the over-all conception and brilliant brushwork of the portraits. Their firmness comes from a balanced construction in which direct light has a precise value and a specific role. In the portrait of *Guidobaldo* the form is admirably compact. *Ugolino Martelli* (*c.* 1537–38; Berlin, Staatliche Museen) has a concentration that is reminiscent of Pontormo. The play of cold tones, greens, and violets is as calculated as in Lorenzo Lotto, but here it is combined with a vigorous contour. In the portrait of *Eleonora of Toledo and Her Son Giovanni* the brocades and silks dominate the composition and govern the pose: the personage becomes a splendid mannequin, an unforgettable costume. The same is true of *Lodovico Capponi* (1550–55; New York, Frick Collection), although the subject was only a youthful page at the Medici court.

BROOKS, James (b. 1906, St. Louis, Missouri), American Abstract Expressionist painter. In 1926 he came to New York, where he studied at the Art Students League (1927–30). During the early 1930s he began to paint in the genre of Social Realism and from 1936 to 1942 executed murals for the WPA Federal Art Project. Brooks's style falls into two phases: naturalism prior to 1945 and a lyrical kind of abstraction after that time. In 1946, while working under the influence of Synthetic Cubism, he became aware of the drastic spatial and pictorial deviations from this mode that were occurring in the abstract paintings of Bradley Walker Tomlin and Jackson Pollock. Thereafter, he changed his own style to one based increasingly on a swift, "automatic" notation. From 1952 he composed large-scale works in alternating color systems, either merging closely keyed half tones or emphasizing a major chromatic scale of pure spectrum color in flat, discrete shapes (*Ainlee*, 1957, New York, Metropolitan Museum; *Rasalus*, 1959, New York, Whitney Museum). Important to the evolution of his style was the method of attaching painted swatches of paper to the canvas surface. Brooks's concern, like that of many of his colleagues in the New York School, was with a chain of spontaneous formal reactions between the artist and his painting, ultimately resulting in the picture's independent existence from its creator.

BROUWER *or* **BRAUWER,** Adriaen (1605, Oudenaarde—1638, Antwerp), Flemish painter. He was a cultivated artist, influenced by Pieter Bruegel and Frans Hals (but outside the circle of influence of Rubens). At Antwerp his pupil was Joos van Craesbeeck (*c.* 1605–*c.* 1665), a baker.

A painter of works of small dimensions, Brouwer limited himself to a few subjects: *Smokers* (*c.* 1626; Paris, Louvre; Budapest, Museum of Fine Arts); *Drinkers* (Louvre; Nantes, Musée Municipal; Rennes, Museum); *Peasant Interiors* (Rotterdam, Museum Boymans-van Beuningen); and *Tavern Brawls* (Munich, Bayerische Staatsgemäldesammlungen). He painted these truculent heroes in the spirit of Bruegel, more attentive to bodies, masses, movement, and atmosphere than to faces, but concerned with satire and morality. Brouwer's brilliance came from Hals. He had an exquisite sense of light and, using a rich but light impasto, achieved moving contrasts between saturated, earthy local colors and more delicate shades of gray. In landscapes that are now greatly prized (*Twilight*, Louvre; *Dune Landscape*, painted toward the end of his life, Vienna, Akademie der Bildenden Künste), his miserable, downtrodden creatures are painted in country settings by twilight or moonlight, lost in an inimical nature whose tragic atmosphere Brouwer rendered by a palette limited to brown, ocher, yellow, or black, lightened by white.

Libéral Bruant. Hôtel des

BROWN, Ford Madox (1821, Calais—1893, London), English painter of religious, literary, and genre pictures. He may be safely considered the father of the Pre-Raphaelite movement, although he was never officially a member of the Brotherhood. As a youth, he lived and studied art in Belgium, until, in 1840, he moved to Paris. His earliest important work, the *Execution of Mary Queen of Scots* (1842; Coll. Henry Boddington), is close to that of Hippolyte Delaroche.

In 1844 Brown settled in England; the following year he undertook a journey to Italy that was to be of crucial importance to him. He became acquainted with, and undoubtedly influenced by, the German Nazarene painters Peter Cornelius and Friedrich Overbeck, in Rome; he reached the Eternal City via Basel, where he greatly admired the paintings of Holbein, and henceforth decided that he would be "the Holbein of the 19th century." A picture painted on his return to England, *Chaucer at the Court of Edward III* (1845–51; Sydney, Australia, National Gallery), is extremely German in feeling and contains all that love of literary detail and brightly colored folklore that was to pass through William Holman Hunt and Sir John Everett Millais to William Morris and Sir Edward Burne-Jones. Another specifically Pre-Raphaelite picture, *Wickliffe Reading His Translation of the Bible to John of Gaunt* (1847; Bradford, City Art Gallery and Museum), with its overt piety and Orcagnesque grouping, owes an obvious debt to the Nazarenes.

In 1848 Brown met Dante Gabriel Rossetti, who insisted that he be taken as a pupil. Brown communicated the ideas of the Nazarenes to him, and they thus became Pre-Raphaelite currency. Brown's two most important pictures are *Work* (1852–63; Manchester, City Art Gallery) and *The Last of England* (1852–55; Birmingham, Art Gallery). *Work* purports to illustrate laborers digging up part of Heath Street, Hampstead, watched by passers-by and spectators who include Thomas Carlyle and the theologian Frederick Denison Maurice. *The Last of England*, a much more successful work, shows the sculptor Thomas Woolner, a member of the Pre-Raphaelites, and his wife emigrating to Australia to join the gold rush.

This virile mood passed and was replaced by the influences of Burne-Jones and William Morris. In 1865 Brown became associated with the latter's firm, Morris, Marshall, Falkner, and Co. The most important undertaking of his later years was the decoration of the Manchester Town Hall with twelve huge frescoes illustrating the history of that city (1878–93). He attained some distinction as a landscape painter, notably in the *Pretty Baa-Lambs* (1851; Birmingham, Art Gallery), which was painted in the open air, a practice which Brown pioneered, and the nostalgic *English Autumn Afternoon* (1852–54; Birmingham, Art Gallery).

BRUANT, Libéral (*c.* 1635, Paris—1697, Paris), French architect. He belonged to a prolific family of architects: his father, Sébastien (d. 1670), was master architect and carpenter to the king; his brother Jacques (d. 1664) is known chiefly as the architect of the entrance pavilion of the drapers' hall in Paris (now in one of the courtyards of the Musée Carnavalet); his two sons, Libéral-Michel (1663–1725) and François (1679–1732), also followed the family profession under Louis XV.

Two buildings of the first order are the work of Libéral Bruant: the church of the Hospice de la

Salpêtrière (*c.* 1670) and the Hôtel des Invalides (1670–77), with its so-called Soldiers' Church, onto which Jules Hardouin-Mansart grafted the church of the Dôme. Earlier, Bruant had built Richmond Castle (1662) for the Duke of York (the future James II), and collaborated in the building of Notre-Dame-des-Victoires, then the church of the monastery of the Petits-Pères (1671–79). In 1683 he built his own house, still standing in the Marais district of Paris.

BRUCE, Patrick Henry (1880, Virginia—1937, New York), American painter. In 1907 he settled in Paris, where he worked in Matisse's studio. He was later associated with Robert Delaunay's Orphist movement. Bruce was very concerned with structural solidity, and painted assemblages of colored and contrasting planes with a palette knife. Despite the attention paid him by the poet and critic Guillaume Apollinaire, he met with as little success in France as in the United States, and from 1920 painted in almost complete isolation. It was during this later period that he did his most original works: still lifes, in which geometrical planes intermingle in vivid colors, flat tints, and volumes. The luminous atmosphere and the severity of the forms give these works an austere spirituality. In 1933 Bruce destroyed all his canvases, except for 15 that he left to his friend Henri-Pierre Roché, of which six paintings from his Orphic period are today in the Société Anonyme collection of modern paintings at the Yale University Art Gallery in New Haven, Connecticut. Also remaining are a number of works from his early Impressionist period.

BRÜCKE, Die ("the bridge"), federation of German Expressionist artists founded in 1905 by Fritz Bleyl (b. 1881) and a group of pupils of the Dresden Technical School—Ernst Ludwig Kirchner, Erich Heckel and Karl Schmidt-Rottluff. One of the aims of the Brücke was to attract to itself all the revolutionary elements of the period. Thus, in 1906, Emil Nolde and the Swiss Cuno Amiet (1868–1961) who was an old friend of Gauguin at Pont-Aven, and who exhibited at the Arnold Gallery in Dresden, were invited to join the movement. Max Pechstein and the Finn Axel Gallen-Kallela (1865–1931) joined the same year. From 1905, regular exhibitions were held and meetings took place in Kirchner's studio, a converted shop in the Berliner-strasse that he had adorned with frescoes, wood sculptures, and furniture made out of packing cases, and where members worked together from the same models. The last painter to join was Otto Müller (1874–1930), who was admitted in 1910, a few months before the group moved to Berlin. But rifts had already begun to appear. Nolde left in 1907, Bleyl in 1909; Pechstein was expelled in 1912. The Brücke was officially dissolved in 1913. This movement, which marks the beginning of modern art in Germany, represented, for that country, the more or less contemporary equivalent of French Fauvism, from which it drew its main inspiration (Van Dongen was the significant link), but with an Expressionist and social emphasis strengthened by the example of Edvard Munch and expressive Nordic anguish. The first style of the Brücke group is characterized by a strong similarity of technique, made even stronger by their working together, that runs through all the different media: painting, sculpture, wood engraving, posters, and fabric printing. Dramatic landscapes and nudes, mystical and visionary compositions, scenes of the countryside, the streets, the circus, the cafés-dansants, and the demi-monde were their principal themes. After the transfer to Berlin of the already divided group, individual styles became more pronounced. In the nervous atmosphere of the big city, Heckel and Kirchner began to evolve in the direction of an Expressionism intensified by sharp, broken forms and dissonant and darkened colors. On the eve of World War I the group dispersed, each one setting out on his own artistic way.

BRUEGEL *or* **BREUGHEL,** a family of Flemish painters of whom Pieter Bruegel the Elder was the first in time and remained the first from every point of view. No less than 12 painters bore this name; the last were recorded in Italy, in the 18th century, as flower painters.

PIETER I, *called* THE ELDER (*c.* 1525, Brögel—1569, Brussels), Flemish painter. In 1551 he became a Master at Antwerp, where his family may have resided before settling in the village of Brögel, in Belgian Limburg. He brought back remarkable drawings of the Alps from a journey to Italy in 1552. He first worked in Antwerp in the engraving workshop of Hieronymus Cock. In 1563 he married Maria Coecke van Aelst and settled in Brussels. Bruegel was painting in the troubled period of the "century of Beggars" (rebels, mainly Protestant, against Spanish dominion); though probably not a member of a heretical sect, he was deeply affected by the national calamities. Despite his training by two artists sympathetic to Italy, Pieter Coecke van Aelst and Hieronymus Cock, he rejected the fashions of the day, the nude, and great historical subjects with Roman architectural settings. He used the lessons of the great primitives, of the German engravers, of Bosch, of the Benings; but his art was above all a continuation of the somewhat Italianate experiments of such masters of genre as Lucas van Leyden, Jan Sanders van Hemessen, and Pieter Aertsen and such painters of spirited landscapes as Cornelis Massys, Henryck met de Bles (*c.* 1500–*c.* 1554 or *c.* 1584?), and Jan van Amstel. All the themes chosen by Bruegel the Elder had already been used by other painters with happy results; stylistically and iconographically formularized, they were nevertheless transformed and exalted by the power of Bruegel's genius. Bruegel's first works were landscape drawings from nature and satirical drawings in the manner of Bosch (*Cardinal Sins, Virtues*). He came to painting late, though a *Christ Appearing to the Apostles* (Priv. Coll.), dated 1553, has recently been attributed to him.

Pieter Bruegel the Elder. *Self-Portrait.* *c.* 1565. Albertina, Vienna. *Photo Walter Dräyer, Zurich.*

Pieter Bruegel the Elder. *Fall of Icarus.* Between 1562 and 1565. Musées Royaux des Beaux-Arts, Brussels. *Photo A.C.L., Brussels.*

His earliest certain works, in 1559 and 1560, were folklore subjects that gaily mock human folly (*Netherlandish Proverbs* or the *Blue Cloak*, Berlin; the *Battle Between Carnival and Lent*, 1559, and *Children's Games*, 1560; both Vienna, Kunsthistorisches Museum). The swarming of the motley crowd is a vivid expression of Erasmian satire.

After 1562, Bruegel's landscapes become wider; in his panoramic compositions, crowds move in circular rhythms around a fixed point; the color scheme achieves greater unity by the repetition of a vivid dominant tone in splashes on gray. This is the period of the *Fall of Icarus* (between 1562–65; Brussels, Musées Royaux des Beaux-Arts, and New York, Coll. D. M. Van Buuren); of the *Tower of Babel* (1563) and the *Procession to Calvary* (1564; both Kunsthistorisches Museum); of the *Triumph of Death* (Madrid, Prado); of the *Dulle Griet* (Antwerp, Musée Mayer van den Bergh), visions of hell in the manner of Bosch. In Brussels in 1565, in his tranquil home in a less turbulent town, Bruegel became calmer, meditating like a Renaissance poet on the relation of man to nature, and achieving a classical grandeur in his paintings of the *Months* for the financier Niclaes Jonghelinck. This series, an epic of rural life and the fate of man linked to the rhythm of the seasons, is a powerful representation of a nature observed in its changing aspects but recomposed in a heroic mode. The horizon is lowered, and wide spaces bring a sense of air into the picture. A few figures remain in the foreground, symbols of a task or of a spiritual state. But the painter of the *Hunters in the Snow* (1565), of the *Dark Day* (1565), of the *Return of the Herd* (1565; all Kunsthistorisches Museum), of *Haymaking* (Prague, National Gallery), and of the *Harvest* (Metropolitan Museum), also entrances by his use of color, by symphonies of brown, white, and golden yellow that evoke the atmosphere of the season. Between 1565 and 1567, Bruegel also painted forest scenes (*St. John the Baptist Preaching*; Budapest, Museum of Fine Arts); the sea (*Storm at Sea*; Kunsthistorisches Museum); and effects of snow and ice under a leaden sky (*Skaters*, Brussels, Coll. F. Delporte; *Adoration of the Magi*, Winterthur, Coll. Oskar Reinhart; *Numbering at Bethlehem*, Brussels, Musées Royaux des Beaux-Arts; *Massacre of the Innocents*, Kunsthistorisches Museum). These works date from the period of the iconoclastic crisis and Spanish repression, whose impact on Bruegel may be seen in references to clandestine sermons, wartime taxes, and the exactions of soldiers. On looking, however, at his *Wedding Banquet* or *Peasant Dance* (both Kunsthistorisches Museum)—those realistic but burlesque interpretations, in a palette of red and gold, of motifs from Dürer and Tintoretto, preludes to Jordaens—one might think that he was seeking escape; but the wild faces animated with greedy gaiety are not images of peace. A disenchanted bitterness appears in 1567 in the *Land of Cockaigne* (Munich, Alte Pinakothek), which is a return to the indirect expression of the *Proverbs*. This outlook brought him to the hallucinatory expressionism of the works of 1568, monumental despite their small size: the *Bird Nester* (Kunsthistorisches Museum); the *Magpie on the Gallows* (Darmstadt, Landesmuseum); and the *Beggars* (Paris, Louvre), which are almost impressionistic in touch, painted in vivid tones replete with minute accents, and with exquisitely delicate landscape backgrounds. The bitterness becomes most marked in two works in distemper on canvas, the *Misanthrope* and the *Parable of the Blind* (both 1568; Naples, Museo di Capodimonte). The subject is taken from a Flemish proverb and from an example by Bosch; but, in Bruegel, horror has become the overwhelming symbol of the human condition, and the composition has the grandeur of a Sophoclean drama. As a young painter, Bruegel was amused by human stupidity; in his late works he is rent by the irremediable blindness of humanity, sunk in misery and poverty. Indifferent to ideal beauty, preferring to paint the common people, he defines the totality of a form by its mass and its dynamism, but primarily by its color, which for him creates the form. His imagination, seeking universal significance, is wedded to a Flemish taste for exact detail, yet observation and sensibility are always subordinated in his work to the power of thought.

PIETER II, *called* HELL BRUEGEL (*c.* 1564, Brussels—1638, Antwerp), eldest son of Pieter Bruegel the Elder, was a pupil of Gillis van Coninxloo, and a Master at Antwerp in 1585. His work is still little known, and it is difficult to distinguish the numerous free copies that he made of his father's work from works by his son Pieter III (b. 1589) and from copies by other hands of the work of Bruegel the Elder. He collaborated with

Pieter Bruegel the Elder. *Tower of Babel.* Detail. 1563. Kunsthistorisches Museum, Vienna.

Josse de Momper. The *Abduction of Proserpina* (Madrid, Prado); a *Census at Bethlehem* (1610; Brussels); the *Inn at St-Michel* (Cachan); *Attack on a Snow-Covered Village* (Douai, Museum); and a *Crucifixion* (Paris, St-Nicolas-du-Chardonnet) have been attributed to him. He earned his nickname from his predilection for painting fires and visions of hell, as in his *Burning of Troy* (Besançon, Musée des Beaux-Arts) and *Aeneas in the Underworld* (Bordeaux, Priv. Coll.).

JAN, called VELVET BRUEGEL (1568, Brussels—1625, Antwerp), Flemish painter. The second son of Pieter Bruegel the Elder, born some months before the death of his father, he was brought up by his grandmother, Marie Bessemers, widow of the miniaturist Pieter Coecke. She probably taught him to paint, and he may have learned from her the subtle coloring and delicate touch that earned him his nickname. Jan traveled in Italy, where Cardinal Federigo Borromeo became his patron, and he was appointed court painter to the archdukes of Austria in 1610. He was a friend and assistant to Rubens, who became the guardian of his son Jan and his daughter Anne, the future wife of David Teniers. The activities of his numerous descendants, who were minor painters in Flanders and Italy, are known down to the 18th century. Some of the work of Velvet Bruegel was done in collaboration with Rubens (*Virgin with a Garland*, Madrid, Prado; Brussels, Musées Royaux des Beaux-Arts; Paris, Louvre) and with Hendrick van Balen (1575–1632), Frans Francken II, and Josse de Momper. He was an excellent flower painter (*Large Bouquet*, The Hague, Coll. Turkow; *Garland and Vases with Flowers*, Oxford, Ashmolean Museum) and of still lifes (*Bowl with Jewels*, 1618; Brussels, Musées Royaux des Beaux-Arts). His reputation rests above all on the fertile imagination shown by his charming paintings of idyllic landscapes. The world in its smallest details filled him with wonderment and a sense of its abundance: animals, birds, shells, flowers, fruit, and jewels appear in profusion in his fine landscapes. Among his best works are the *Battle of Arbela* (1610; Paris, Louvre), *Paradise* (The Hague, Mauritshuis), the *Garden of Eden* (Windsor Castle and Mauritshuis), the *Elements* (Louvre), and the *Embarkation* (Nantes). The Prado possesses 50 of his paintings, including the marvelous series of the *Five Senses*, painted 1617–18. With charming originality and imagination, a scantily clad goddess appears in each of the paintings, surrounded by little cupids and the worldly goods she cherishes. Ingenuity, a profusion of motifs arranged in studied disorder, coloring of the greatest subtlety, a palette in which the cerulean blue possesses exquisite nuances, and the touch of an illuminator—all these impart the most subtle, imaginative values to Velvet Bruegel's creations, at the dawn of the great century of Flemish painting.

ABRAHAM (1631, Antwerp—1690, Naples), Flemish painter, the grandson of Jan (Velvet) Bruegel. He pursued his career in Italy under the patronage of Prince Antonio Ruffo di Messina. He seems to have gone to Italy at an early date; his paintings were already in the prince's collection by 1649. In any case, he worked in Rome between 1660 and 1671, then settled in Naples, where he founded a school of painting.

BRUGES, Hennequin *or* Jean de. *See* **BONDOL,** Jean de.

BRÜLLOV *or* **BRIULLOV,** Karl Pavlovich, *also known as* Charles Bruleau (1799, St. Petersburg—1852, Marciano, near Rome), Russian Romantic painter. In 1833 he had an enormous success with a large melodramatic picture, the *Last Day of Pompeii* (Leningrad, State Russian Museum), which he painted in Rome. When the Scottish novelist Sir Walter Scott, then an old man, was staying in Rome, he wrote to Brüllov that his picture was "an epic," and Edward Bulwer-Lytton took up the theme in his famous historical novel, *The Last Days of Pompeii*. Today, this pseudo-historical reconstruction has been supplanted in favor by Brüllov's less pretentious subjects: charming portraits of Countess Samoilov in riding habit or wearing a ball gown; the *Boat Trip*, showing the painter with his two daughters; or a *Self-Portrait* (1848; Moscow, Tretyakov Gallery).

BRUNELLESCHI, Filippo (1377, Florence—1446, Florence), Italian Renaissance architect and sculptor. Although it would seem from the years of his birth and death that Filippo di Ser Brunellesco belonged to the Middle Ages, he was in fact the earliest modern architect and one of the initiators of the Renaissance, on an equal footing with his fellow citizens Donatello and Masaccio.

Filippo Brunelleschi. Dome of the cathedral of S. Maria del Fiore, Florence. 1420–36. *Photo Alinari-Giraudon.*

He first expressed himself successfully in sculpture, and probably visited Rome with Donatello. In 1401 he took part in the now-celebrated competition for the decoration of the north bronze door of the Florentine Baptistery. The bronze entered by Lorenzo Ghiberti received the most votes, due to its elegant composition and polished execution. In a later rivalry, Donatello himself pronounced the superiority of Brunelleschi's wooden Crucifix for the Gondi Chapel (S. Maria Novella) over his own at S. Croce. His greatest success, however, came from his architectural efforts. His churches and porticoes in Florence were the first in more than a thousand years to be inspired structurally by the Classical art of Rome; to equip himself technically, he made a careful study of Roman building methods and materials. In 1418 he was awarded the commission to construct the dome of S. Maria del Fiore, the cathedral of Florence, and his fame as an architect rests primarily on his bold realization of this dome, a feat previously believed incapable of execution.

The construction of the dome, begun in 1420, was finished in 1436, except for the lantern, which his successors completed after his death following his model. Above the octagonal crossing built by the architects of the 14th century, Brunelleschi placed a drum with large circular windows on each of its eight sides, which lightened its weight without reducing its strength. On this support two stone shells, closely tied together by cross ribs, form the dome, which, on account of its pointed shape, could be mistaken for a survival from the Middle Ages. The shape was determined, of course, by the parts of the building already completed; the Classical-minded Brunelleschi would no doubt have preferred a circular drum. The same type of structure had been successful in pre-Renaissance baptisteries at Cremona and Pisa, but on a much smaller scale. The huge size of Brunelleschi's dome displayed a technical mastery and daring unrivaled by his contemporaries.

Work on the dome was contemporary with Brunelleschi's outdoor loggia for the Spedale degli Innocenti, the first foundling hospital in the world, where, perhaps for the first time, Roman Classical columns were harmoniously united with round arches. He chose the *bambini*, medallions of foundlings by Andrea della Robbia, to decorate the spandrels. In his mature works, Brunelleschi frequently and liberally used the medallion, sometimes to exploit the decorative talents of Donatello, sometimes to challenge his own ingenuity (the decoration of the Pazzi Chapel is thought to be his).

The old Sacristy of S. Lorenzo (1420–28) and the Pazzi Chapel at S. Croce (after 1430) are significant for the parallelisms in their structures and for their internal organization. Both are examples of a centralized scheme, based on the cube. Pilasters, stylobates, and entablatures frame and divide the wall surface, and are resolved in the upper part by the curves of arcades, medallions, pendentives, and ribbed shell domes. Plane and solid geometry were equally a part of Brunelleschi's equipment, and he "discovered" the rational principles of linear perspective, by which, applying mathematical ratios, he reduced the manipulation of space in architecture to a system of rules. He used with great skill the colored materials traditional in Tuscany, and the contrast of the dark *pietra serena*, which was used to articulate the structural members on the rough plaster of the walls, combined with the effects of light and shade to animate his creations.

A similar inspiration is seen in the churches of S. Lorenzo (1424–46) and S. Spirito (begun 1436), which are basilical Latin crosses in form, with a nave and two aisles covered by a coffered roof. The plan of S. Spirito, in particular, demonstrates the Pythagorian discipline that the aging architect, ever more exacting, imposed upon himself. But the timidity of his successors prevented the completion of the plan as Brunelleschi had envisioned it.

The palace of the Guelph party (begun in 1419; partly restored after damage during World War II) and the Palazzo Pazzi are among Brunelleschi's other works. His religious buildings include the cloister of S. Maria Novella and the Barbadori Chapel at S. Felicità (begun 1418). Although he completed only its foundations, the church of S. Maria degli Angeli, which he designed in 1434, is historically significant, for it represents one of the first modern expressions of the central plan. Work on the church lasted only a short time, however, and it is known only from Giuliano da Sangallo's drawings.

Filippo Brunelleschi. Pazzi Chapel, S. Croce, Florence. After 1430. *Foto Marburg.*

BRUSSELMANS, Jean (1884, Brussels—1953, Dilbeck), Belgian painter. After studying at the Brussels Academy, he was drawn toward Fauvism and Impressionism until, at the beginning of the twenties, he adopted the kind of constructivist Expressionism that enabled him to evolve the essentials of his mature work. While the visible world was always his starting point, painting was for him above all an organization of forms, of which the regularity and austerity belong more to geometry than to the world of objects (*Marine Dorée*, 1939; Brussels, Col. Gustave van Geluwe). Each being, each thing—the reaper as well as the sheaf of corn, the tree in blossom, the jug, or the lamp—is subordinated to the tyrannical demands of his formal design (*La Moison*, 1934; Liège, Musée des Beaux-Arts).

BRUYN, Willem de (baptized 1649–d. 1719, Brussels), Flemish architect trained in Italy. He was appointed architect to the city of Brussels in 1685 and supervised the reconstruction of the Grand-Place there. (The guild houses had to be rebuilt after the bombardment of Maréchal de Villeroy in 1695.) De Bruyn allowed Jan Cosyn and Cornelis van Nerven (active 1696–1717) to rebuild the houses on the north side as they pleased, in a joyfully imaginative vein. He himself designed Maison des Brasseurs and the huge Maison des Ducs de Brabant (1698), in which Doric and Corinthian pilasters are superposed on the façade, ornamented with a convex pediment in the Italian manner.

BRYGGMAN, Erik (1891, Turku—1955, Turku), Finnish architect, graduate of the Helsinki Polytechnic School. One of the leaders of Scandinavian functional architecture, he was responsible, with Alvar Aalto, for the exhibition organized to celebrate the 700th anniversary of the city of Turku (1929). His masterpiece is the chapel of the cemetery (1938–41), outstanding for the magical lightness of its interior space and combining a strictly functional approach with a touch of romanticism.

BUCHSER, Frank (1828, Feldbrunn, near Soleure—1890, Feldbrunn), Swiss painter. While he was still very young, he made his way to Rome, where his brother was working, but poverty forced him to enlist in the Swiss Papal Guard. In 1849 he became a follower of Garibaldi, then went to Paris. The rest of Buchser's life was spent in ceaseless foreign travel, interspersed with visits to his own country, where in 1864 he founded the Society of Swiss Painters. He visited Spain, England, Holland, Morocco, and Dalmatia. From 1864 to 1871 he traveled in America, where he painted some of his finest portraits. Buchser has been compared with Gustave

Courbet in his taste for realism, which sometimes tended toward the anecdotal (*Negro Hut in Charlottesville, c.* 1870; Basel, Kunstmuseum); in the close attention he pays to light effects, he might occasionally be mistaken for a pupil of Édouard Manet.

BUFFET, Bernard (b. 1928, Paris), French painter. Buffet won the attention of both critics and public at an unusually early age. His first one-man show took place in 1947, and in the following year he was awarded the Prix de la Critique (Critics' Prize). His work at this time was frankly realistic; motifs included interior scenes and still lifes, morbid and despairing in mood, painted in an elegantly rhythmic style with simplified, bold drawing and a use of muddy grays or faded whites (color appeared some time later). Buffet subsequently applied this style to the most varied subjects, thereby attracting, despite the boldness with which he treated certain themes, a good deal of adverse criticism: scenes from the *Crucifixion* (1951; Coll. Maurice Garnier), the *Horrors of War* (1954; Coll. Pierre Bergé), the *Circus* (1955), *Paris Townscapes* (1956–57), the *Life of Joan of Arc* (1957–58), *Birds* (1959). He also worked as an illustrator, notably for Jean Cocteau's *La Voix humaine* (1957), and produced a fine series of dry points on the theme of the *Passion* (1954).

BUGIARDINI, Giuliano di Piero di Simone (1475, Florence—1554, Florence), Italian Cinquecento painter. He received his formal training in Domenico Ghirlandaio's workshop. He then became assistant to Mariotto Albertinelli, whose type of Madonna he copied in his *Virgin with Sts. Magdalen and Bernardino* (1503; Florence, Museo di San Marco dell'Angelico). In 1508 Bugiardini was called by Michelangelo to Rome, where his figures became fuller and where a greater coloristic contrast entered his art (*Holy Family with St. John*; Leningrad, Hermitage). In Bologna (1527–30) his art reached its zenith with such works as the *Madonna with Sts. Anthony and Catherine* (Bologna, Pinacoteca). Bugiardini eventually returned to Florence, where he adopted the soft contours of Andrea del Sarto and, with Michelangelo's help, solved compositional problems on—and finally completed—his most ambitious work, begun 12 years before, the *Martyrdom of St. Catherine* (Florence, S. Maria Novella).

BULFINCH, Charles (1763, Boston—1844, Boston), American architect. He was a major figure in New England during the important transitional phase known as the Federal period. Bulfinch created a notable series of public buildings in Boston in the last years of the 18th century: the Hollis Street Church (1788), the Boston Theater (1793; rebuilt 1798), the Massachusetts State House (1787–1800), and the Franklin Crescent (1793). He was one of the few major architects of his time who was not European-born and trained, his only contact with the architectural models of Europe having been a trip (1785–87) through England, France, and Italy, made after his graduation from Harvard. Memories of buildings by the Adam brothers, William Chambers, James Wyatt, and Sir Christopher Wren influenced his work, supplemented by later contacts with New York architects and with Benjamin Latrobe's circle in Philadelphia. His enormous oeuvre included the Leverett Street Almshouse (1799–1801), the United States Bank (1798), Holy Cross Roman Catholic Church (1803), the rebuilding of Faneuil Hall (1805), the New North Church (1804), the Federal Street Church (1809; an early essay at Gothic), Boylston Hall (1810), India Wharf (*c.* 1806), the New South Church (1814), Massachusetts General Hospital (1816–18), and a host of private houses, all in Boston.

In 1817 Bulfinch was appointed architect to the Capitol in Washington, D.C., replacing Latrobe. Here his job was mainly to complete work begun by others, and only the details of the west front show his personal stamp. While in Washington, he built the Unitarian Church (1822) and designed the Maine State House at Augusta (1829–31). In 1829, the Capitol finished, he returned to Boston to find his own style abandoned for the Greek Revival. He spent his last 15 years in retirement.

BULLANT, Jean (*c.* 1510/15, Amiens?—1578, Écouen), French architect, probably the son of Jean I Bullant, master mason at

Bernard Buffet. *Interior.* 1950. Musée National d'Art Moderne, Paris. *Photo Giraudon, Paris.*

Amiens. When his apprenticeship was completed, he set out for Italy, where he remained until about 1537. On his return to France, the high constable of Montmorency asked him to draw up plans for his château at Écouen. Bullant is known to have directed the work there in 1542; construction was not completed until 1552. He remained the architect at Écouen for the rest of his life, residing there as well. In collaboration with Jean Goujon, who did the sculpture, he built the chapel and the porticoes that decorate the north and south wings of the castle. In 1557, on the recommendation of the Montmorency family, he was appointed Henri II's superintendent of buildings and was responsible for the extensions to the château at Chenonceaux, for which he was complimented by Catherine de' Medici in 1560. In 1570 the Queen Mother asked him to take over the construction of the château at St-Maur and to add two pavilions to the existing buildings of the Tuileries. He also appears to have worked at the châteaux at Fontainebleau and Chambord (1571–74) and on the chapel at Vincennes (1574–78).

BULLET, Pierre (1639, Paris—1716, Paris), French architect and town planner of the reign of Louis XIV. Bullet's major work in town planning was his rebuilding of the Quay Pelletier in Paris, which, with the renovation of the entire surrounding district, occupied him for two years, beginning in 1673. In 1674 he assisted his master, Nicolas-François Blondel, in building the Porte St-Denis in Paris, and in the same year, following his own plans, he undertook the Porte St-Martin. Bullet rebuilt several town houses in Paris, generally along Classical lines; the Hôtel de Vouvray, the Hôtel Le Pelletier de St-Fargeau (1687; now the Bibliothèque Historique de la Ville de Paris), and the Hôtel de Crozat (completed 1702) are still standing. Some time after

Above left: **Jean-Baptiste Bullet de Chamblain.** Château de Champs-en-Brie. *Photo Boudot-Lamotte, Paris.*
Above right: **Bartolommeo Buon.** Ca' d'Oro, Venice. 1422–34. *Photo Martin Hürlimann, Zurich.*

1675 he designed two chapels for the Parisian church of St-Germain-des-Prés, and in 1682, began the choir and nave of the church of St. Thomas Aquinas, also in Paris (the work was not completed until 1760).

BULLET DE CHAMBLAIN, Jean-Baptiste (1667, Paris—1737, Paris), his son, was an architect and decorator, an exponent of the Regency style. Around 1727 he undertook the construction of the Hôtel Dodun, Paris, following the designs of his father, and in the same period planned and built the beautiful Château de Champs-en-Brie (Seine-et-Marne), a residence of Madame de Pompadour.

BUNSHAFT, Gordon (b. 1909, Buffalo, New York), American architect who participated in some of the most important projects of the firm of Skidmore, Owings & Merrill, of which he became a partner in 1946. His strong personality can be felt in his project for Lever House, New York (1952), the first of the curtain-walled skyscrapers rising on a low podium, which subsequently enjoyed international popularity. This approach to the building, as an elegant glass box unrevealing of its contents, is more directly derived from the late work of Mies van der Rohe. It was carried even further in the Pepsi-Cola Building (New York, 1958–59), a small, beautifully proportioned structure carried on *pilotis*, in which even the contrast between base and tower has been eliminated. The simple perfection of this style was, in a sense, a dead end, and with his design for the Rare Book Library at Yale University, New Haven, Conn. (1962–64), Bunshaft abandoned the purism of the fifties. A certain mannerism was introduced into the external structural elements, the cubic form of the building resting on a huge Vierendeel truss supported by four concrete *pilotis* at the corners.

BUON *or* **BON,** Bartolommeo (*c.* 1374, Venice—1464/67, Venice), Italian sculptor. He was the son of the sculptor Giovanni Buon (*c.* 1355–*c.* 1443), and between them they ran the largest and most important Venetian sculpture workshop of the first half of the 15th century. He worked extensively at the Ca' d'Oro, the masterpiece of Venetian Gothic architecture, between 1422 and 1434; there he executed, among other things, the large wellhead, in collaboration with the sculptor Rosso, who may have been the Florentine Nanni di Bartolo. Buon also worked on the Porta della Carta (between the Doges' Palace and St. Mark's) from 1438 to 1442, and did the tympanum for the Scuola di S. Marco in 1437; he succeeded his father in 1443 as head of the workshop, which was active until his own death.

BUONTALENTI, Bernardo (1536, Florence—1608, Florence), Italian architect, painter, and decorator. Ultimately his style derived from Michelangelo, but it was more placid, less dynamic than that of his great predecessor. He did not indulge in the decorative extravagances of his Mannerist contemporaries; the ornamental sculpture on his buildings lacks the dramatic chiaroscuro of theirs. His first important commission was the villa of the Grand Duke Francesco de' Medici at Pratolino, near Florence (demolished 1800). Duke Francesco's town house, the Casino di S. Marco, begun in 1574, is remarkable for the Mannerist decoration around the doors and windows, contrasting with the plain façade. In 1575 he began to remodel the Villa della Petraia, near Florence. The façade of S. Trinita (1593) is his most interesting design; its two orders, clearly divided, show a stirring of Baroque in an otherwise traditional Florentine design. Fort Belvedere (1590–95), on a steep hill overlooking Florence, marks Buontalenti as the first of a distinguished line of Italian military engineers who built fortifications in Italy, Germany, and Hungary. His work as a painter and miniaturist is negligible.

BURCHFIELD, Charles (1893, Ashtabula Harbor, Ohio—1967, New York), American painter. As early as 1917, in a series of watercolors that he called conventions for abstract thought,'' Burchfield had worked out a set of archetypal pictographs for basic states of mind (fascination with evil, dangerous brooding, fear, etc.), which he was to use extensively in his later, more truly representational paintings.

Burchfield's style from 1920 to 1940 tended to be rather conservative, although the emotional emphasis was still on the sinister, as he recorded the gloomy and oppressive mood of small Ohio towns (*Six O'Clock*, 1936; Syracuse, Museum of Fine Arts). In this period his work relates to that of Edward Hopper, who was similarly concerned with the barren loneliness in America's cities and rural towns. Their interest in the American scene was to develop later into the Regionalist movement of the early 1930s and the Social Realism of the 1940s.

After 1940 Burchfield turned increasingly toward nature in order to reveal its mysterious, basic forms. *An April Mood* (1955; New York, Whitney Museum) is typical of this late landscape style.

BURCKHARDT, Carl (1878, Lindau, near Zurich—1923, Lignoretto, Ticino), Swiss sculptor. It was in Munich, where he lived from 1897 to 1904, that his career began. Between 1900 and 1904 he visited Italy several times, and his subsequent paintings show the influence of Hans von Marées and a distinct leaning toward the monumental. At this time he began to produce sculpture. It was not until 1910, however, after a stay in Rome, that he opted definitely for this new means of expression.

His work is characterized by a preference for simple forms; for sober, solid constructions, and compact masses. His sculptures show traces of Archaic Greek influence—Burckhardt's initial inspiration—which he adapted to the demands of his time. One of the most important of his finished works is the group of figures he executed for the fountains of the Baden Station (Gare Badoise), Basel (1914–21), but his best works are perhaps the *St. George* (1923) and the *Amazon* (1923), his last sculpture, which guards one of the bridges over the Rhine.

BURGHAUSEN, Hans von (*c.* 1360, Burghausen, Upper Bavaria—1432, Landshut, near Munich), German mason and architect. The seven churches that he is known to have built exhibit extraordinary variety within the framework of a Late Gothic style. The earliest was the Carmelite church at Straubing (begun 1378), a hall church with an aisleless choir. Hans tended to favor churches of this general type throughout his career. The church of St. Martin at Landshut, his most important, was constructed of brick; the choir was built first (1392—1407), and was followed by the nave (from 1407). A net vault, similar to that at Prague Cathedral, is carried on extremely slender piers, while the two side aisles have plain star vaults. The façade is quite flat, but the exterior is distinguished by a very tall tower that was not completed until the early 16th century. Hans produced a smaller version of St. Martin's in his church at Neuöthing. The church was begun in 1410, but the nave was only constructed between 1484 and 1510, although the original plan seems to have been retained. The Spitalkirche in Landshut (completed 1497) is again a hall church, this time with a hall choir. Here he used the motif of a central pier in the apse that, in a somewhat different form, was also to appear in the choir of the Franciscan church at Salzburg (begun 1408).

BURGKMAIR THE ELDER, Hans (1473, Augsburg—1531, Augsburg), German painter and engraver. He probably received his early training from his father, who had an engraver's workshop. Very little is known of his output until 1501. He may have worked on illustrations for the books issued by the printing shop of Erhart Ratdolt, who was a very active publisher in Augsburg at the time.

In 1501 Burgkmair received his first important commission. The convent of St. Catherine in Augsburg had been granted by Rome the privilege of the same indulgences earned by pilgrims to the seven basilicas. The nuns commissioned paintings representing each of these basilicas. Burgkmair executed three of them, all now in the Gemäldegalerie at Augsburg: *St. Peter's* (1501), *St. John Lateran* (1502), and the *Holy Cross of Jerusalem* (1504). One can follow the artist's progress in these paintings as his facility increases, particularly in the direction of anecdotal composition. With the completion of these works, Burgkmair's reputation was assured, and the Elector Frederick the Wise commissioned a triptych from him for the Schlosskirche of Wittenberg (1505; Nuremberg, Germanisches Nationalmuseum). The artist took another decisive step forward with two versions of the *Madonna and Child*, dated 1509 and 1510 (both Germanisches Nationalmuseum); the earlier, of a fully Italianate monumentality, is particularly important, for here Burgkmair shows himself completely freed from the flat angularity of the primitives.

He retained his traditional style, however, in the numerous sketches for illustrations he supplied to the printing shops of Augsburg, notably those for the works of the preacher Johannes Gailer von Kaiserberg (whose portrait he had painted in 1490; Augsburg, Gemäldegalerie). The portraits of *Hans Schellenberger* and his wife *Barbara* (both 1505; Cologne, Wallraf-Richartz-Museum) are also in the Northern manner. In 1505 he began to associate with the Humanists of Emperor Maximilian's court, and in 1508 a superb woodcut appeared (executed from Burgkmair's design by Jost von Negker, *c.* 1485–1544) representing the mounted emperor in armor, matched by an equally resplendent *St. George* in the same year. From this time on, Burgkmair's activities were almost entirely devoted to Maximilian's projects until the emperor's death in 1519. Between 1509 and 1512, he provided the 92 woodcuts for the genealogy of Maximilian and illustrated the historico-allegorical romances of the emperor. In 1515, Burgkmair collaborated in the decoration of 12 pages for the emperor's prayer book (Besançon, Bibliothèque Municipale), and the following year he made a substantial contribution of 61 woodcuts to Maximilian's *Triumphal Procession* (which appeared in 1526).

Toward the end of his service for the emperor, Burgkmair again turned his attention to painting large altarpieces, producing two triptychs in rapid succession, both of which are today preserved in the Alte Pinakothek, Munich: *St. John the Evangelist* (1517) and, more importantly, a *Crucifixion* (1518), in which Burgkmair used brilliant colors and a style strongly reminiscent of the Venetians.

During the remaining 12 years of his life, Burgkmair was less productive. The altarpiece of the *Rosary*, somewhat overly detailed and fragmented in composition, was painted in 1512 for the chapel of St. Roche in Nuremberg, and reveals a certain lassitude. Later he received two commissions from Elector Wilhelm IV of Bavaria: *Esther Before Ahasuerus* (1528; Munich, Alte Pinakothek), dry and encumbered with Oriental motifs, and a historical painting, the *Battle of Cannae* (1529; Schleissheim, Staatsgalerie).

The development of Burgkmair's graphic works approximately parallels that of his painting. He produced several series around 1519–20: the Christian, Jewish, and pagan *Heroes*; the *Heroines*; and the *Follies of Love*, including Samson, David, Solomon, and Aristotle. He did a group of illustrations for Martin Luther's translation of the *Old Testament* in 1523.

BURLINGTON, Richard Boyle, Earl of. *See* **BOYLE,** Richard, Earl of Burlington.

Burmese Art. Above left: Ananda, principal Buddhist temple at Pagan. Late 11th century. Above right: detail of terra-cotta panel illustrating the life of the Buddha. Mingalazedi temple, Pagan. *Photos Louis Frédéric, Paris.*

BURMESE ART. Burma was for a long time divided between the Pyus, a people from central Asia who had settled in the north of the country, and the Mons, who lived in the south; it was not unified until the 8th century A.D. In an attempt to guarantee the unity of the new kingdom, a capital was founded in A.D. 847 at Pagan, on the left bank of the Irrawaddy, about 88 miles from present-day Mandalay. Buddhism was introduced by Indian colonists, who had been settling on the Burmese coast from the 1st century, and gradually became the dominant religion. Pagan was sacked in 1287 during the terrible invasions of Kublai Khan and never rose again from its ruins. During its 400 years of existence the city had covered itself with an incredible number of temples, pagodas, and monasteries. Even today there are some 500 of these buildings, though their state of preservation varies considerably.

The oldest sanctuaries date from the 10th century A.D. The Nathlaungkyaung temple, one of the few surviving Hindu buildings (the other temples were Buddhist), can be dated from A.D. 931. It was not until the reign of Anawratā (1040–77), however, that the great artistic flowering began. There were two main categories of buildings: the stupa, which contained relics, and the temples, which were consecrated to the Buddha. Notable among the temples are the Tilominlo (1218), a two-storied structure decorated with sandstone; the Mahābodhi temple, which was consecrated in 1215 and is a copy of the sanctuary of Bodhgaya in India; lastly, the most famous of all, the Ananda, founded by Buddhist monks and consecrated in the 11th century by King Kyanzittha (1084–1112). Its ground plan is in the shape of a Greek cross, the arms formed by huge porticoes rising against the four sides of the central structure, an imposing square mass that supports several terraces rising in graded tiers, the last of which serves as a base for the main tower, or sikhara, which has a slightly convex roof. Burma, in fact, was the only country in southeast Asia to adopt this exclusively Hindu type of roof. Two concentric corridors at the level of the terraces enable the worshiper to walk around the inside of the building and to meditate before the 30-foot statues of the Buddha in the four chapels situated on the axes of the porticoes.

Another important building in Pagan is the Mingalazedi (1274), a huge stupa whose circular, multistoried base rests on a wide, square platform itself built of three terraces. With its arrangement of receding terraces and the circular shape of its upper stories, this sanctuary bears a closer affinity to Javanese building and may be compared with the gigantic stupa of Borobudur (*see* JAVANESE ART).

The Pagan buildings are made almost entirely of brick and mortar—stone was used very sparingly—and all are covered with stucco work that, over doors and windows, takes the form of very delicately chiseled arcades whose general design is flamelike—hence the florid, precious quality so typical of Burmese art. The interior walls were covered either with paintings or with terra-cotta panels, usually varnished, illustrating in naive style the main events of the Buddha's life. The sculptors, breaking with the traditional principle of continuous narration, chose to treat each episode in a single panel. A certain schematization may have resulted, but the narration as a whole gained in clarity, vitality, and grace. For the simplicity of their style, these works must be numbered among the best examples of classical Burmese sculpture. Unfortunately, this brief flowering was followed by a rapid decline; and immediately after the invasions of the 13th century there appeared images of the Buddha, carved in marble, that are travesties of the classical model.

BURNE-JONES, Sir Edward Coley (1833, Birmingham—1898, London), English Pre-Raphaelite painter. While a student at Exeter College, Oxford, he formed a close friendship with William Morris and saw the work of Dante Gabriel Rossetti, John Everett Millais, and William Holman Hunt in the collection of Thomas Combe, the director of the Clarendon Press. He especially admired Rossetti, whom he met in London in 1855 and on whose advice he left the university. In 1856, Burne-Jones's artistic career began. He was almost entirely self-taught, although he had a few lessons and constant advice from Rossetti. In 1858 he returned to Oxford to collaborate with Rossetti and others on a scheme of decoration for the reading room of the Union.

In 1859 Burne-Jones went to Italy and seems to have studied the second great influence on his work, Botticelli. He paid a second visit in 1862, this time to Milan and to Venice with Ruskin, for whom he copied Tintorettos. He became an Associate of the Royal Society of Painters in Water Colour in 1863 and exhibited with them until 1870. The opening of the Grosvenor Gallery in 1877 was marked by an important representation of his works, which established him in the public eye. The following year he submitted works to the Paris Exhibition, with great success; and in 1882 he and Lord Leighton were the only two British artists invited by the French government to represent their country at the International Exhibition of Contemporary Art. His fame was consecrated in 1890 when Agnew's exhibited a series of paintings, known as the *Briar Rose*, based on the story of Sleeping Beauty and now in the drawing room at Buscot Park, Gloucestershire. He was made a baronet in 1894 and died in London in 1898.

The sources of Burne-Jones's paintings and watercolors are medieval ballads, classical myths, Morris' *Earthly Paradise*, the poems of Chaucer and Spenser, and, intermittently, the Bible. Technically labored and intensely literary, his work shows great continuity of style. The influence of Rossetti is very clear in early works, such as the *Merciful Knight* (1863; Worcester, Trustees of Sir John Middlemore), and that of Morris, less consistent, in the decorative and stylized *Sidonia von Bork* of 1860 (Witley, Coll. W. Graham Robertson). The full force of the Italian experience comes through in works such as the *Golden Staircase* (1876–80; London, Tate Gallery); and *King Cophetua and the Beggar Maid* (1884; Tate Gallery), in which the female type is lifted straight from Botticelli's *Primavera*.

BURNHAM, Daniel Hudson (1846, Henderson, New York—1912, Heidelberg, Germany), American architect, one of the leading members of the Chicago School. He collaborated with John Wellborn Root, whose partner he became in 1873, in designing Chicago's Monadnock Building (1889–91), a 16-story skyscraper—the last to be built in masonry—and Reliance Building (1890–94), the prototype of American steel-framework construction, anticipating the most daring achievements of the mid-20th century in its almost exclusive use of glass and metal. Burnham was commissioned to organize the World's Columbian Exposition in Chicago (1893) and later turned to a kind of academic eclecticism.

BURRI, Alberto (b. 1915, Città di Castello, near Arezzo), Italian painter. Until 1940 he practiced as a doctor and painted in his spare time, carrying out color experiments that were similar to those being made by Scipione and Mario Mafai (1902–65). After the war he gave up medicine to devote himself to painting. His early experiments with abstraction in 1949 led to two series of pictures, *Mildew* and *Blacks* (*c.* 1949–50), both of which received considerable critical acclaim when they were exhibited in 1952. Two later series were *Irons* (1959) and *Plastics* (1961–62). His art is characterized by the grouping or collage of raw materials carefully chosen from scrap heaps (planks of wood, rags, torn canvases, iron plates), sometimes enlivened by a thick application of black or red paint.

BUSCH, Wilhelm (1832, Wiedensahl—1908, Mechtshausen), German draftsman, caricaturist, and painter, trained at the academies of Düsseldorf, Antwerp, and Munich. Beginning in 1858, his drawings appeared in *Die Fliegende Blätter*, a humorous journal to which he continued to contribute until 1871. In 1865, the publication of *Max and Moritz*—a series of drawings relating to the escapades of two scamps—brought him overwhelming success. *Max and Moritz*, which was translated into countless languages, including Japanese, was followed by other stories of the same variety, among them *Die fromme Helene (Pious Helen)* and *Pater Filucius* (both 1872). Busch's art here foreshadows the animated cartoon and he displays quite a mordant wit—rather anti-clerical, and very much centered around the "little man." His drawing is elliptical, full of rounded forms, and very assured. Sceptical and pessimistic, Busch early withdrew from artistic circles and ceased to produce anything. His painting, which became known only after his death, proved to be of unusual interest. It derives from the Dutch and particularly from Adriaen Brouwer, whose influence is also noticeable in his drawings. The jocular *Celebrating the Harvest* is an example.

BUSCHETO (d. *c.* 1080, Pisa), Italian architect. A funerary inscription on the façade of Pisa Cathedral designates Buscheto as its master architect; this building, following the victory of the Ghibelline city over the Saracens, inaugurated the Pisan school of Romanesque architecture. The cathedral was begun in 1063 and consecrated in 1118, but it was not completed until the end of the 12th century, when a certain Rainaldo extended the nave and designed the façade, thereby altering considerably the earlier conception of the structure. Nevertheless, the originality of the cruciform plan adopted by Buscheto remains evident, and the style of the cathedral was imitated not only in other buildings at Pisa, but also at Pistoia and Lucca.

BUTLER, Reg (b. 1913, Buntingford, Hertfordshire), English sculptor. An architect by training and practice, he began sculpting in earnest in 1944, having learned how to work iron as a blacksmith during World War II. His open, wrought-iron sculpture, first made in 1948, was in the tradition of Julio Gonzalez (*Woman*, 1949; London, Tate Gallery), and for some years he was among the most original sculptors of his generation in England. In 1953 Butler won first prize in the international competition for a monument to the *Unknown Political Prisoner* (1951–52; Berkhamsted, Hertfordshire, Collection artist). He abandoned wrought-iron the following year, when his first sculptures in shell bronze appeared: taut human figures in movement. The tension in these figures gradually slackened during the following years into a flaccid academicism, but a series of small bronzes (1963) and towers (*Tower*, 1962), showed a complete renewal through primitive and African art.

BYZANTINE ART. The most salient feature of Byzantine art is its close connection with the historic circumstances of its birth, and with the nature and structure of the state that brought it to maturity. Both the unity and the originality of this art is due to its being the art of the Byzantine Empire.

The prejudice that has for too long attributed to Byzantine art the characteristic of hieratic immobility must be dropped: it was in fact complex, varied, and changing. However, throughout its millennial development Byzantine art retained certain permanent features; they shall be distinguished here.

Religious Art

Above all, Byzantine art was a Christian art and existed to serve the Church. Illustrations to sacred texts were simply another way of revealing the truths contained in the accompanying text. The mosaics and frescoes that covered the churches were not placed there to delight the eye, they were the

Edward Burne-Jones. *The Golden Staircase*. 1876–80. Tate Gallery, London.

Reg Butler. *Head of Ara*. 1960–62.

expression of faith or dogma, a commentary on the words pronounced from the ambo (a raised pulpit from which the Epistle and Gospel were read) or on the liturgy performed around the altar. The Byzantine artist made use of an almost uniform type, without personal interpretation. While the Western artist appealed to the heart, the emotions, the Byzantine addressed the mind, intending a commentary. The former remained on the level of humanity, whereas the latter strove toward abstraction of the divine, and toward what may perhaps be called pure religion.

This had various consequences. The first was that Byzantine works of art were anonymous, for the artist made no claim to be shaping a personal work. Another consequence was that the choice and arrangement of subjects, and even the composition of each scene, were not left to the artist's discretion. Gradually a scheme was worked out for the painted decoration of a church, establishing which scenes and figures had to take what place in the various parts of the building, according to the symbolic meaning of each part.

Such dependency on, and submission to, the Church was hardly favorable to progress, and in fact the very idea of progress was foreign to that theocratic and conservative art. The result was a certain impression of monotony, increased by the Byzantine artists' habit of copying models due to a conviction that the first images of the participants in the story of Christ's Passion were actual portraits that dated miraculously from the time those personages were alive. Moreover, it was believed that the efficacy of the image, its power to grant or to protect, was linked with its fidelity to the primitive type.

Byzantine art also had another characteristic: it was an imperial art. The reason for this resides in the very nature of the Byzantine monarchy; the emperor was an Eastern sovereign, an incarnation of the Divinity, and His representative on earth. Scenes in which an emperor is shown crowned by Christ, or in which he is presiding over a council, are religious scenes. Imperial portraits, of which the best known are those in the basilica of S. Vitale in Ravenna, are sacred figures.

Art of the East

Insofar as it was both religious and imperial, Byzantine art might be characterized as Oriental. Further Oriental features are found in its techniques and forms.

The first of these features entailed the substitution of color for relief. Sculpture in the round, which had provided Classical art with its most perfect means of expression, disappeared in the Byzantine era. Under Oriental influence, flat, colored patterns were substituted for forms modeled in space. Even architectural structures were conceived as carefully balanced masses of materials that were tractable but far from noble and to which was added, both inside and out, a brilliantly colored mantle.

Another Eastern characteristic of Byzantine art had to do with the passion for ornament, which took the place of a pursuit of form. Compare the wonderful forms the Greek potter was able to give vases, often covered with nothing but plain black slip, with heavy Byzantine pottery, so clumsy in form, but covered with brilliant glaze. Byzantine artists tended everywhere to see plain surfaces as ready to receive some luxurious decoration, in which complicated ornament played a more important part than any of the figures represented.

It is not surprising that as it lost its sense of plasticity and form, Byzantine art also lost its sense of the human body. The human figure was no longer represented for its own sake, but as the dwelling place of a thought or a faith. It was essentially a spiritual art, preoccupied with the divine and eternal, not with the earthly and transitory, with the universal rather than the particular.

THE FORMATION AND EVOLUTION OF BYZANTINE ART

Christian art of the first three centuries, known chiefly through the pictures in the catacombs, was a symbolic art. Forced concealment had necessitated the expression of Christian subjects only through images borrowed from secular art: the fish, the dove, the garden of flowers, and the Good Shepherd with his flock. It was, moreover, a charming form of art, full of the freshness of youth and able to revive and invest with new meaning the pictorial compositions of the Greek East and Alexandria.

The triumph of the Church in the 4th century A.D. changed that situation entirely. The appearance of art was altered: it was now triumphant and sumptuous. Churches of grandiose proportions arose throughout the Empire. Their interior walls were covered with rich mosaic decoration that for some time preserved the pastoral motifs, plants, animals, garlands, and rinceaux that had been adopted in the art of the catacombs. But by the end of the 4th century A.D. the spirit of this decoration was changing. There arose an idea that art could be given a higher aim, that of instructing and edifying the faithful. Subjects were sought in the sacred texts, and gradually there was formed that body of historic and monumental decoration with which Byzantine art really began.

Effacement of Rome and Predominance of the East

Because the Empire from Constantine to Justinian was still the Roman Empire, for a long time its art was regarded as a continuation of that of Rome. But what Rome was thought to have bequeathed to Byzantium was really what Rome itself had borrowed from the East.

In the 4th and 5th centuries A.D., the East was distinguished by two regions: the first comprised Greece itself and the coastland of the eastern Mediterranean, where there developed a sort of common language, striking in its uniformity; the second region included the continental parts of the Balkan peninsula and Asia Minor, as well as Egypt, Mesopotamia, Armenia, and Persia. Unlike the coastal districts, these countries had no unity; in fact, the differences between them were profound. But most shared one

Byzantine Art. *Christ symbolized by O*

common feature—that they resisted the penetration of Greek thought and art, and were deeply affected by Iranian and Semitic influences. Of course, between the two regions there was a natural crossing and mixing of the Greek and Eastern influences. In the formative period of Byzantine art (the time between Constantine and Justinian) all those diverse elements played their part.

Role of Constantinople

It was at Constantinople that these elements fused and Byzantine art came to maturity. Residence of the emperor and the court, and the seat of government, Constantinople was an extremely busy commercial center, and so attracted a wealthy and cosmopolitan society, patrons of the arts and of luxury industries. As a university city, it soon came to be regarded as the intellectual capital of Byzantium, and later as the religious capital also. Its past, geography, and even the language of its inhabitants made it a Greek city, and to it the art of the Christian East was soon to owe all that it still retained of Hellenism, as well as a certain spirit of moderation that tempered the excesses of both provincial and Oriental art.

The Great Ages of Byzantine Art

It was under Justinian in the 6th century that Byzantine art attained its first classic age. Its most striking characteristic lay in the fact that it was an imperial art: influenced by the sovereign's strong will, it spread through every province, expressing the ideas of authority and unity that were the guiding principles of Justinian's policy.

Within the Empire, the 7th century A.D. brought a swift decline in culture and the arts. But beyond its frontiers, the prestige of the previous century's art still exerted its influence: this was true in Armenia, in the Arab-conquered provinces of Palestine and Syria, and in Rome—where there were many colonies of Eastern monks, and where, in the 7th century A.D. and the first half of the 8th, there were as many as 13 popes of Greek and Syrian origin.

Iconoclasm's first effect was to destroy many monuments of the first golden age. It put in their place purely decorative ornament, plant and animal motifs, or pictures of secular or historic subjects. Most of its monuments were subsequently destroyed as sacrilegious after the triumph of the iconodules. But an art emerged with new characteristics after that troubled period. A theological doctrine concerning images inculcated reverence for the model, the prototype, which might be sought in the old illuminated Gospels that had escaped destruction by the iconoclasts. From then on, Byzantine art was theological and Eastern, for it was in the East—in Syria—that many of the manuscripts copied had been illuminated; and even after the Arab conquest, monks in Byzantium remained in close contact with monasteries in Syria and Palestine.

Byzantine Art enjoyed a second golden age during the reigns of the Macedonian emperors and the Comnenes. There were, as previously mentioned, two distinct tendencies: one was the aristocratic, official art, showing a keen taste for Greek antiquity, and gladly accepting those secular subjects that had been favored by the iconoclasts; there was also the art of the Church, monastic in spirit and Eastern in inspiration, with an inclination to make of religious art something fixed forever and subservient to dogma. From the time of the Comnenes, the Church prevailed. In the 12th century, the diffusion of the influence of Byzantium was widespread—to Venice, southern Italy, and Norman Sicily, and also to those parts of Russia ruled by the princes of Kiev, to Bulgaria, and to Serbia.

Venetian trade expansion, the Crusades, the conquest of Constantinople, and the establishment there of a Latin Empire for half a century—all these factors sapped the strength of Byzantium beyond recall. Nevertheless, a real artistic renaissance took place in the 14th century, making that the last great age of Byzantine art. Especially in the paintings and illuminated manuscripts, this century left us many interesting works in a new, freer, and more natural style, more open to sentiment and even to pathos. Its most beautiful works are not sumptuous showpieces in precious materials but the wall paintings on Mount Athos and at Mistra.

ARCHITECTURE

Although perhaps until the middle of the 3rd century A.D., Christians were content to celebrate their worship in subterranean galleries or in a room in some friendly house, they did not wait until the Church's triumph before erecting special buildings. In the long period between the persecution of Decius (A.D. 250) and Diocletian (A.D. 303), there was certainly an elaboration of the edifice intended for Christian worship, and by Constantine's reign that structure's essential features were fixed.

The Hellenistic Basilica

A splendid flowering of grandiose buildings marked the triumph of Christianity. Constantine himself contributed to these edifices, with St. John Lateran, St. Peter's, and S. Paolo fuori le Mura, all in Rome; the first churches of Hagia Sophia, of St. Eirene, and of the Holy Apostles, in Constantinople; and many buildings in Palestine, of which the most famous was the church of the Holy Sepulcher. These monuments may be divided

Byzantine Art. Exterior view of Hagia Sophia, Istanbul (formerly Constantinople). Between 532 and 537. The minarets date from 1453, during the Turkish period. *Photo G. E. Kidder-Smith, New York.*

Byzantine Art. Church of St. Theodore (Brontocheion), Mistra. Late 13th century. *Photo Marburg.*

into two main categories: buildings with central or radial plan, and those with basilican plan. The former tend especially to be martyria, or baptisteries. A martyrium was a place intended for commemorative worship, and was built either at the tomb of some famous martyr whose relics it contained, or at some other place with particularly moving associations for a Christian. These early Christian monuments with central plan include the octagonal church at Antioch, the church on the Mount of Olives in Palestine, the round church of the Holy Sepulcher, and the round church of S. Constanza in Rome.

The basilican plan was preferred for the ordinary meeting place of the faithful and the celebration of daily worship. A basilica was a complex building: its essential parts included first the atrium, generally provided with a fountain, or phiale, for ritual ablutions. From the east side of the atrium several doors opened into the narthex, a long gallery separating the atrium from the basilica proper, where the catechumens and the penitents were allowed to remain during the services. The basilica proper opened off the east side of the narthex; it was an oblong hall divided by rows of columns into a nave and two side aisles, and terminated at the east end by a semicircular apse. The altar, with a stone canopy, or ciborium, above it, was separated from the congregation by the barrier that shut off the sanctuary. In the nave in front of the sanctuary there was an ambo, a stone platform approached by one or two steps, for the use of readers and preachers. The basic plan might be complicated by the addition of a transept. The whole was covered by a wooden roof with a double slope, except for the apse, which had a vault.

Byzantine Building Methods

Byzantine architecture was brick architecture, with vaults and domes built of this material. Brick architecture spread from the East to Byzantium; and it was also from the East, where wood was rare, that Byzantium learned to build vaults without centering. Finally, it was in the East, notably in those Sassanian palaces of Firuzabad (A.D. 450) and Sarvistan (A.D. 350), that the Byzantines found brick domes built over a square plan.

Such were the methods that permitted Byzantine architects to build great structures in which the thrusts of domes and vaults were skillfully balanced. There was variation in the plans. Some buildings, such as S. Vitale in Ravenna (A.D. 526–47) and Sts. Sergius and Bacchus (6th century A.D.) at Constantinople, had circular plans, while others had the cruciform plan previously used in the mausoleum of Galla Placidia in Ravenna (mid-5th century A.D.), a plan also used for the Church of the Apostles in Constantinople, rebuilt by Justinian (destroyed in the 15th century). But the most common plan, elaborated in the 5th century A.D. and characteristic of the age of Justinian, was the domed basilica, which can be divided into two types.

In the first type, the basilica properly so called remained. But a dome supported on massive pillars was placed between the end of the nave and the apse. That, for instance, is the plan found in a large 6th-century A.D. basilica that has been excavated at Philippi, in Macedonia.

In the second type the union between basilica and dome is achieved in the vertical plane, the dome being superimposed on the basilica without interrupting it. That type is found nearly fully developed in a very beautiful monument in Isauria, Hodja Kalesi (probably 6th century A.D.), and in a monument at Meriamlik (late 5th century A.D.). It is also found in Hagia Sophia in Constantinople, Kasr-ibn-Wardan in northern Syria (6th century A.D.), S. Sophia in Salonika (iconoclastic period?), and the Church of the Dormition in Nicaea.

Hagia Sophia in Constantinople (A.D. 532–27) is not the clearest example of the domed basilica: that vast building used novel solutions to many problems. But it is the masterpiece of Justinian's architecture, and indeed of all Byzantine architecture, and is the monument in which the spirit of that architecture can be recognized most clearly. Justinian entrusted the work to two Greek architects from Asia Minor, Anthemius of Tralles and Isidorus of Miletus, and he put immense resources at their disposal.

Some basilicas of the Paleo-Christian type were still being built in the 6th century. For instance, in Ravenna there was S. Apollinare Nuovo, founded under Theodoric but completed under Justinian, as well as S. Apollinare in Classe. Also, domed basilicas were still being built long after the 6th century, and among that type were some churches in Constantinople later turned into mosques. But this type, however interesting, was only a stage in the evolution of Byzantine architecture. The combination of basilica and dome was in a sense an impure form: the basilican plan is by definition opposed to the central plan. The dome, which exerts the same thrust at every point on its circumference, calls for a central plan to absorb that thrust evenly.

Byzantine architects found the solution to that problem when they developed the Greek-cross plan that was to remain typical of Byzantine architecture for many centuries. In that scheme the dome is buttressed by four barrel vaults at right angles to each other. The exterior walls of the four barrel vaults (of approximately equal length), together with the dome over their point of intersection, form a cross with equal arms, from which the name of the plan derives. As the plan developed, the dome was placed on an increasingly high polygonal drum. Often a small dome was placed on each of the four arms of the cross. There was usually a narthex, but no atrium. This type appeared in complete, although still clumsy, form in the 9th century A.D., in the well-preserved church of Skripou in Boeotia. It finally reached perfection in the 10th century A.D., in a number of churches in Constantinople (later the mosques of Budrum, Kilisse, Zeirek, and Fetiye) and in Salonika (Theotokos, St. Pantelemon, St. Catherine, and the Holy Apostles). In spite of provincial variations and the survival of earlier types, it can be said that the Greek-cross church prevailed from the time of the Macedonian dynasty until the fall of Constantinople.

Secular Architecture

While there are many Byzantine ecclesiastical monuments, only a very imperfect idea can be had of the secular architecture. Almost all secular buildings have vanished. Only literary allusions and, very rarely, illustrations in illuminated manuscripts afford any idea of Byzantine houses. So too, one must read the accounts of writers, travelers, and pilgrims for a picture of Constantinople over the centuries, with its rich merchants' quarters, splendid aristocratic districts, imperial palaces, Senate, hippodrome, and theater; its great streets, porticoes, squares, and forums; the acropolis, the capitol, and the golden mile; the baths of Zeuxippos and Arcadius; the innumerable convents, with their outbuildings, guest quarters, and hospitals; the specialized markets; the Tower of the Winds, the lighthouses, arsenals and ports.

SCULPTURE

In Byzantine art—sensitive to color and indifferent to plastic values—sculpture in the round lost importance and very soon disappeared. It was essentially reduced to the role of a decorative technique at the service of architecture.

Relief

Relief, which is simply ornament applied to a flat surface, survived better than sculpture in the round. Historical relief was an Eastern art form adopted by Rome to glorify the concept of empire. The reliefs on Trajan's Column in Rome are the best-known examples. Both Theodosius and Arcadius erected columns around which a spiral frieze carved in stone recounted their exploits. These works have perished, but some reliefs that have survived show how this art had degenerated.

Relief carving found its last home inside the churches. There it ornamented the columns of the ciborium, the lintel over the entrance door, the ambo, and the parapets closing intercolumniations. Sarcophagi may be added to these, since the types of ornament are analogous.

The only important group of sarcophagi that has survived is at Ravenna: dating from the 5th and 6th centuries A.D., they show obvious Eastern influences and have nothing in common with Roman funerary art.

In every Byzantine church there were a great number of marble panels that were used as parapets for the galleries, as dividers between nave and aisles, or—most frequently—between church and sanctuary. Usually only one face was carved, the one visible from the nave. But these panels can hardly be called reliefs, for soon every trace of modelling disappeared and the enamelist's champlevé technique took over. In that process shallow carving, following a pattern sketched on the stone, produced hollows that were filled with dark mastic, contrasting with the light areas of the raised marble surface.

Architectural Ornament

The evolution of architectural ornament is best understood by studying the capitals. The first type of capital in use in Byzantine art was the Corinthian, in both simple and composite forms. From the 5th century A.D. on, a new technique modified its appearance profoundly. The thornless acanthus was replaced by a jagged, thorny one, and this was only roughly sketched with the chisel, leaving the drill to finish the work: this is called the Theodosian capital. Then the Classical architrave or lintel course was replaced by the arch, and the carrying surface of the capital had to be made much bigger. That was sometimes done by inserting an impost block between the capital and the springing of the arch, but the scheme generally preferred was to give the capital a heavier, massive almost cubic appearance (basket capital). The ornament around that powerful mass lost all modeling and became more like a piece of stone lacework applied to the body of the capital; it was carved in the Oriental *à jour* technique in which the background of the design was pierced through, allowing passage of light between the solid motifs. The champlevé technique, noted in connection with reliefs, was also used for capitals and cornices. This technique was used in the great 11th-century churches—Hosios Lukas and Daphni—and later in many churches in Athos and Mistra. In St. Mark's in Venice, some heavy capitals whose form roughly resembles the Ionic impost are decorated with rinceaux that stand out against a background of dark mastic; their surface however is perfectly flat.

IVORIES

There are a great many Byzantine ivory carvings, and they form a natural transition between sculpture and painting: their technique is that of sculpture, but their iconography that of painting. Owing to the many problems still without final solution, any division into schools would appear premature. It is enough to distinguish two basic periods: the 4th to 6th centuries A.D., and the 10th to 12th centuries A.D.

In the first period, the workshops of Constantinople produced a group of ivories (mostly of secular subjects) including consular diptychs. It was the custom for the consuls, on the day they entered into office, to send to their friends, to the leaders in the capital, and to the emperor diptychs made of two leaves of ivory that were decorated more or less elaborately in accordance with the recipient's rank. Great numbers of them have been found, and they form a well-dated series from the beginning of the 5th century A.D. until the consulate was abolished in the middle of the 6th.

The use of diptychs extended to personages other than consuls, and to occasions other than entry into office, such as appointment to any high post or a family ceremony. No doubt the famous Barberini ivory in the Louvre belongs to the series of works made in Constantinople.

On the other hand, ivories with religious subjects were made in Alexandria, Antioch, and in workshops in the area of the great Palestinian sanctuaries. This group, called Syro-Egyptian, was very important for the origins of Christian art; it includes two masterpieces, the Trivulzio plaque and Maximian's chair in Ravenna (Archiepiscopal Museum). The plaque in the Trivulzio Collection

Byzantine Art. Proto-Byzantine colossal bronze statue of a Christian emperor. Barletta, Italy. *Photo Boudot-Lamotte.*

Byzantine Art. Capital. S. Vitale Ravenna. 6th century. *Pl Anderso*

Byzantine Art.
Ariadne. 6th century. Musée de Cluny, Paris. *Photo Giraudon, Paris.*

is one of a group with scenes of the Passion, and it is tempting to connect them with the great places of pilgrimage in Palestine. There is no doubt that the magnificent ivory episcopal chair in Ravenna dates from the time of Justinian (mid-6th century A.D.). It is the best illustration of the complex influences that helped to form Christian art, and it shows how a still living Hellenic tradition was being gradually replaced by Eastern contributions.

MOSAICS AND FRESCOES

It must be remembered that the great monuments of secular architecture have vanished, along with their mosaics and frescoes. It is therefore only in churches that original works exist that give an impression of Byzantine painting. Byzantine artists paid little heed to the decoration of the exterior; but showed real creative power when it came to decorating the churches' interior walls. For a long time it was the rule to decorate the lower part of the walls with panels of colored marble in varied designs. Mosaics, when there were any, were on the upper parts by the windows, where they received good light, or on the curved surfaces of domes, apses, and vaults, where it would have been hard to affix marble slabs. That type of ornament was extremely costly, and increasing poverty during the later centuries of the Empire explains why painting, which had always been used in less important buildings, came to take the place first of mosaics on the upper parts of the churches, and then of the marble revetments on the lower parts.

Symbolic Decoration

The first churches were decorated, as the catacombs had been before, with motifs borrowed from the pagan repertoire but endowed by the imagination with a symbolic meaning. A striking example of such types of decoration, at once picturesque and symbolic, lies in the mosaics of the building in Rome incorrectly called the mausoleum of S. Costanza (A.D. 330).

Principles of Historical Decoration

A change took place in Christian art during the 4th century A.D. as an explicitly religious iconography was formed. A letter written at the end of the 4th century A.D. by St. Nil to the exarch Olympiodoros suggests that the sign of the cross should be painted in the sanctuary, and that on the walls there should be scenes from the Old and New Testaments, "so that for the illiterate, unable to read the Holy Scriptures, the paintings may serve as a reminder of the actions of the faithful servants of God and spur the public to imitate them." That provided both an aim for religious art—the edification of the faithful—and a program, the illustration of the Old and New Testament narratives.

Clearly, painting could not fulfill the role of creating a historical style and still be content with the symbols that had been held sufficient until then. Here is the very clear decision of one of the councils: "In some holy pictures the Precursor is represented pointing to a lamb . . . the symbol of Christ our God . . . we ordain that in holy pictures, in place of the accustomed lamb painters represent the Lamb who took upon Himself the sins of the world, Christ our God, in His human form." That interesting passage clearly marks the transition from symbol to the real image; it explains the evolution of Christian art that began in the 4th century A.D. and that reached its consummation when artists dared to handle the Crucifixion in fullest detail.

The First Monuments

It is in Syria and Palestine that it appears one should look for the real origin of Christian iconography. In the land where the events took place, on the walls of the great sanctuaries built to commemorate them, artists developed their illustrations of the Gospel story. If they had not been destroyed, such scenes would be seen to form the prototypes of those great themes to be repeated an infinite number of times on the walls of Byzantine churches. But in Palestine, Syria, and Mesopotamia, Oriental influences predominated, and it was certainly from that milieu that the illustrations of the Gospel story of Christ's life were derived. The type of Christ was also Syrian—older, bearded, of dusky complexion, and with hair straight and centrally parted, taking the place of the young, unbearded Christ with long, curly hair.

The Great Ensembles of the 5th and 6th centuries A.D.

Although we are badly informed about those countries where Christian art was a really creative force, more is known about some of the great cities where the new style was elaborated and, so to speak, consecrated.

Constantinople is in truth disappointing. The mosaics in Hagia Sophia, at last freed from Turkish whitewash, were drastically altered over the centuries. But we are more fortunate when it comes to Thessalonica, where the round church of St. George has preserved the striking 5th-century mosaics in its dome.

However, it is in Ravenna that are found the masterpieces among Byzantine mosaics of that period: in the mausoleum of Galla Placidia and the Baptistery of the Orthodox, both dating from the 5th century A.D.; in S. Apollinare Nuovo, whose decoration extended in time from Theodoric to Justinian; and in S. Vitale, which was purely Justinian.

The Transitional Period

Very few works of art remain from the 7th century A.D., a critical period in Byzantine history. However, in the West—safe from the hands of the iconoclasts—some works did survive: in Ravenna, where some of the mosaics of S. Apollinare in Classe were clearly inspired by S. Apollinare Nuovo and S. Vitale; and especially in Rome, where there are many works, Byzantine in style and technique, dating from the 6th to the 9th centuries A.D. These include mosaics in the apse of S. Agnese fuori le Mura (7th century A.D.), the chapel of St. Venantius in the Lateran (mid-7th century A.D.), and the oratory in St. Peter's, built in A.D. 705 by Pope John VII, a Greek, in honor of the Virgin; frescoes in S. Maria Antiqua, at the foot of the Palatine hill, which spanned the 7th to 10th centuries A.D., and from the 9th century A.D., the lovely mosaics in the chapel of S. Zeno in the church of St. Praxed.

Meanwhile, in the East, religious painting did not vanish, but was transformed. Control fell into the hands of the monks—the bitter, and finally victorious, enemies of the iconoclasts. It is illuminated manuscripts that provide the most information about this iconodulic art; as for important mosaics, there is only that in the apse of S. Sophia at Salonika, which is thought to date from the end of the 8th century A.D. The earliest of the frescoes in the rock churches of Cappadocia also date from the iconoclastic period. These are coarse works, but they provide much information about popular monastic art, which, it is interesting to note, embraced everything most opposed to the great Byzantine tradition. There are, for example, many episodes derived from the Apocryphal Gospels; in some scenes the characterization is realistic and highly dramatic; worship of the Virgin and saints plays a considerable part; inverse perspective is used, so that figures behind are larger than those in the foreground.

The New Iconography

It would be a great mistake to suppose that iconoclasm was fatal to artistic creation. On the contrary, that period was one of intense and fruitful activity, and it has been fairly said that the second golden age owed its essential attributes to iconoclasm.

Naturally, secular art gained by the new imperial favor. But religious art, defending itself against attacks and criticism, was driven to justify itself by a formulation of doctrine concerning images that was to become the accepted aesthetic doctrine of Byzantium.

The Cappadocian frescoes have already been mentioned; most of them—and there are hundreds—date from the 10th and 11th centuries A.D. These works, although clumsy and unattractive, have the merit of giving us some idea, distorted certainly but still recognizable, of the great painting that flourished in Byzantium. The same can be said of the frescoes in the chapels and caves of southern Italy, which was in truth a province of Byzantine art. Arab conquest and iconoclast persecution had led many Greek monks to settle there, and the 9th-century A.D. Byzantine conquest made it Magna Graecia again for several centuries.

Much is known about the mosaics of the 11th century from a number of scattered works, and especially from the great ensembles in the churches of Hosios Lukas and Daphni on the Greek mainland, the monastery of Nea Moni on the island of Chios, and S. Sophia in Kiev. In Italy, the very extensive mosaics of St. Mark's in Venice and those in the cathedral of nearby Torcello were created over many centuries. In Sicily, the monuments of Palermo, Monreale, and Cefalù are as valuable for the 12th century as those of Ravenna are for the 6th.

For the 11th century, we will confine our attention to Daphni. The church has a Greek-cross plan with a dome resting on squinches. Mosaics cover the dome and squinches, the four arms of the cross, the chapels of the prothesis and diaconicon flanking the sanctuary, and the narthex. The quality of the mosaics, the judiciousness and elegance of the compositions, make them the undoubted masterpieces of the second golden age, and one of the few monuments of Byzantine art whose beauty really touches the modern viewer.

At Torcello, the Last Judgment is a very fresh and original composition. At St. Mark's, only a part of the vast tapestry of mosaic covering the walls was executed in the late 11th century and by Byzantine artists: the Christ, Ascension, and Pentecost in the three domes, and the cycles of the great feasts, the miracles of Christ, and the life of St. Mark on the walls. Another group of mosaics dates from the 13th century and was in part the work of local craftsmen trained by the Byzantines; in particular, there is the great Genesis cycle in the narthex, which derived its inspiration from originals of the 6th century. The mosaics in the baptistery are of the 14th century.

The Norman kings of Sicily were great builders, and they followed Byzantine fashions in the decoration of their buildings. The finest ensembles of 12th-century Byzantine mosaics are those in the churches of Sicily. The earliest is in the apse of Cefalù Cathedral, founded by Roger II. The church in Palermo called the Martorana, which was founded by the admiral George of Antioch, is completely Byzantine both in plan and in decorative scheme. In Palermo the Capella Palatina, built by Roger II in 1132 as the chapel of the royal palace, is covered with extremely rich and complex ornament. The mosaics in the dome, apse, and sanctuary are still Byzantine; but in those of the nave and aisles a different style, Latin inscriptions, and figures of saints of the Latin Church make it seem likely that they are the work of Italian pupils. The cathedral of Monreale, founded by William II and decorated toward the end of the 12th century, is covered with mosaics measuring no less than 64,560 square feet.

The Renaissance under the Palaeologi

After the disasters of the Crusades and sack by the Latins, it looked as though Byzantium would be unable to form a new school of art. However, the time of the Palaeologi did see a true renaissance in painting in Constantinople itself, in mainland Greece (especially in Mistra), in Macedonia, and on Mount Athos, and its influence extended into Russia, Bulgaria, Rumania, and especially Serbia.

There was a change in the technique of painted ornament. Fresco tended to take the place of mosaic, no doubt partly for reasons of economy, but perhaps also because that technique allowed more suppleness of drawing and variety of color, better corresponding to the spirit of the new age. And, frescoes being painted quickly and at little cost, it now became possible for the first time to extend the decorated area to cover the walls of the church completely. Compositions became both more numerous and more complex: pictures were invented to illustrate even prayers, psalms, and hymns.

Under constant menace at Constantinople, Byzantine Hellenism found its last refuge in Mistra, which enjoyed a period of brilliance under the Palaeologi. The frescoes painted over a span of 150 years in the churches there are the finest examples of the painting of that age. The most outstanding churches are the Metropolitan (early 14th century), the Peribleptos (late 14th century), and the Pantanassa (early 15th century). The earliest frescoes in the Metropolitan belong to the Macedonian school. But the rest must be the work of the same school of artists as made the mosaics in the Kahrie Djami, for the fantastic and elaborate architectural backgrounds, crowded figures, freedom of movement,

Byzantine Art. *John the Bapt*
11th–early
century.
St. Ca
Sin
P

concern to render living reality, and tender or dramatic pathos in such scenes as the Last Judgment are the same in the frescoes as in the mosaics. The frescoes in the Metropolitan are usually regarded as the first masterpiece of the Cretan school; it is known that the best artist working in that style was Theophanes the Cretan, who lived in the 16th century.

At roughly the same time the Macedonian school of painting, which owed less to Byzantium and more to the East, flourished in Greek Macedonia, Serbia, and also in the Russian city of Novgorod. In that school, the subjects were placed into one continuous frieze instead of being divided into separate pictures. This method was used in many of the churches on Mount Athos, at least until the 16th century; for it was in about the middle of that century that the famous Panselinos of Thessalonica painted the frescoes of the Protaton of Karyes. In the end the Cretan school supplanted the Macedonian school in Serbia and Russia from the 15th century, and on Mount Athos in the 16th.

MINIATURES

European libraries and Eastern monasteries contain thousands of manuscripts with miniatures on a gold background or simple colored vignettes. For some periods, from which hardly any frescoes or mosaics survive, there are extant at least some illuminated manuscripts. There are also miniatures, inspired by now vanished works, which reflect the originals. Moreover, because they attracted less attention than large-scale works, miniatures escaped certain strict forms of control. And being easy to reproduce and carry about, they spread throughout the Empire those iconographic themes that they either originated or copied.

The Earliest Manuscripts

The art of illustrating manuscripts, both in the earlier form of the papyrus roll (rotolus) and in the later parchment book (codex), is known to have been well advanced always in Egypt. In illustrating innumerable manuscripts of Homer and Virgil, the artists of Alexandria created a complete secular iconography, which was known and copied throughout the ancient world. There is in the Vatican Library a roll (some 33 feet long) with a continuous frieze illustrating the exploits of Joshua, and therefore known as the *Joshua Roll* (Ms. gr. 431). That manuscript may not be earlier than the 7th century A.D., but it is a copy of an original that may have dated from the 5th and was certainly completely Alexandrian. It would seem that frequently scenes were cut out from the long frieze of a roll in order to provide illustrations for a codex. An example of such an occurrence may lie in the *Vienna Genesis* (Vienna, Nationalbibliothek), a fragmentary but very beautiful manuscript written in letters of silver and gold on a background of purple parchment. In this 5th-century A.D. manuscript, scenes from the Old Testament are illustrated in a Hellenistic and completely pagan decorative idiom. The *Christian Geography of Cosmas Indicopleustes* (Ms. gr. 699, Vatican Library) is another famous manuscript. Its author was a 6th-century A.D. Alexandrian, and the various manuscripts that survive of his work are copies of the 6th-century A.D. edition. One finds in them a curious mixture of secular and Christian subjects.

The practice of illustrating the Gospels arose later, and from the beginning there were two schools: that of Alexandria, which remained faithful to the taste for the picturesque and to the elegant nobility of Hellenistic art; and that of Antioch, which was more Eastern, more realistic, and also nearer to what we have called the historical and monumental style. None of the ancient Alexandrian manuscripts survive, and only evidence of a later date can prove the existence and character of that school. More information is available about the beginnings of the Syrian school. The famous Syriac *Rabula Gospel* (Florence, Biblioteca Laurenziana), illustrated by the monk Rabula in A.D. 586, is as remarkable for its decidedly Eastern taste for ornament as it is for the historical character of the Gospel scenes, the monumental style of the great compositions, and the attempt to base the figures on observation of real people (it contains the earliest "portraits" of the Evangelists). Even more famous is the *Rossano Codex* (Rossano Cathedral, Italy), written in silver letters on a purple ground and dating from the end of the 6th century A.D.

Miniatures of the Iconoclast Period

Illustrated manuscripts of the iconoclast period make up to some extent for the absence of the great monuments that were destroyed. A distinction must be made between two types of manuscript: those that counted as official art and obeyed the interdictions against images; and those coming from monastery workshops, which reacted against official policy by multiplying the number of religious images and indulged, too, in satirical pictures aimed against the iconoclasts.

There are a fairly large number of secular manuscripts in the first class. It is interesting to point out how a 9th-century A.D. manuscript of *St. Gregory Nazianzen* (Milan, Biblioteca Ambrosiana) retained only a few of the religious scenes, but added a number of secular subjects and also mythological and allegorical ones. It is also very significant that one finds a manuscript such as the 9th-century A.D. Gospel, *Parisinus 63*, which has nothing but purely linear ornament; in it the Eastern influence—

one of the principal characteristics of iconoclast art—is quite marked.

Meanwhile the monasteries used miniatures as a means to assert their feelings. To them is due the most original invention of Byzantine miniaturists: the psalter with marginal illustrations, of which a manuscript formerly in the Chludov Collection (called the *Chludov Psalter*) is a typical example. It contains no large compositions but a great number of vignettes in the margins, distinguished by their lively drawing and sober colors. Of greatest interest are those in which the iconoclasts are depicted crucifying Christ, destroying or whitewashing images, and holding councils.

Miniatures at the Time of the Macedonians and the Comnenes

The age of the Macedonian emperors and the Comnenes was the great age of Byzantine miniatures. Spurred by their recent victory, the monasteries were busy centers for manuscript production.

The monastic psalter with marginal illustrations continued in fashion: there is a good 11th-century psalter from the Studion workshop (Add. Ms. 19352, British Museum), and the *Barberini Psalter* in the Vatican Library is a fine 12th-century example. But there is also a group of "aristocratic psalters"—luxuriously decorated works containing a few very fine miniatures filling whole pages. The earliest and finest example, executed for an emperor in the 10th century in Constantinople, is now in the Bibliothèque Nationale, Paris (Ms. gr. 139). It contains 14 large miniatures with subjects taken from the sacred text.

Miniatures under the Palaeologi

For this period there is no great manuscript to compare with those of the preceding age. There are, however, a good number of manuscripts, including secular ones reflecting the form of humanism that was in fashion at that time. But taken as a whole, the miniatures of the age of the Palaeologi attest to a period of decadence.

TEXTILES

Figured textiles were an important branch of Byzantine art. Rich fabrics with complicated designs and startling colors gave full scope to the virtuosity of Constantinople's craftsmen, skilled in every luxury technique. In the churches, embroidered materials were used for the priests' vestments and the appurtenances of the Liturgy, as well as for the curtains of the ciborium, and hangings between columns and in doorways. In private houses they were used for every domestic requirement—to complete the furnishings and, extensively, for clothing. Famed throughout the medieval world and easy to transport, these sumptuous fabrics greatly helped in the diffusion of Byzantine art. There are still many of them in Western church treasuries, where they were brought by pilgrims and crusaders, or sent as gifts by emperors; on account of their beauty, they have often been chosen to cover relics. There are fine examples in the Sancta Sanctorum in the Lateran, and in Sens Cathedral in France.

GOLD AND ENAMEL

No account of Byzantine art would be complete without some mention of goldsmith's work and enamel, which enjoyed great favor as luxury crafts. An early example is the strange collection of little flasks (ampullae) preserved in the treasury of Monza Cathedral. The scenes in repoussé with which they are decorated have a special interest, as they are thought to derive their inspiration from the decoration of the great churches in the Holy Places.

The silver objects, and no doubt the gold jewels too, found at Kyrenia on Cyprus, also came from Syrian workshops: the most notable among these is a series of plates in repoussé (6th century A.D. ?) with scenes from the story of David. Another object from Syria is the great repoussé silver paten (inlaid with gold) found at Riha, near Antioch. It is in a different style, less free and almost monumental; on it is one of the earliest examples of the beautiful scene known as the Communion of the Apostles. Many silver vases and other objects, dispersed in various museums, certainly come from the same Syrian workshops as the vase from Emesa (Homs) in the Louvre. Finally, mention must be made of the silver chalice found at Antioch and now in the Kouchakji Collection in New York: it probably dates from the 4th or 5th century A.D., and is another brilliant example of the virtuosity of the Syrian school of silversmiths.

Scattered literary references do not do much to make up for the shortage of original works. Chroniclers have described the richness of Justinian's throne and the dinner service that he had made out of the Vandals' gold. But there is greater interest in the description of the altar of Hagia Sophia, for which Justinian had assembled every sort of precious material, "melting those that could be liquefied and joining them to those that were solid." That quotation has been interpreted as a reference to enamel technique, and perhaps to champlevé enamel. Constantinople learned from the East very early the technique of cloisonné enamel. If a cloisonné enamel cross in the Lateran is correctly dated in the 6th century A.D., it must be the earliest Byzantine object in that technique that has been preserved.

It is only from literature that anything is known of Theophilos' marvelous goldwork in the imperial palace: a golden plane tree spread its branches over the throne, and on them perched golden birds that moved and sang as ambassadors entered; golden lions and griffins guarded the throne and stood up wagging their tails or roaring. We know from Constantine Porphyrogenitus and from the accounts of ambassadors

Byzantine Art. Quadriga. 6th or 7th century. Silk textile. Musée de Cluny, Paris. *Photo Giraudon, Paris.*

Byzantine Art. Silver chalice from Antioch. 4th or 5th century. Coll. Kouchakji, New York. *Photo Giraudon.*

Byzantine Art. Weight representing an empress. Benaki Museum, Athens. *Photo Hassia, Paris.*

that the luxury of the palace under the Macedonian emperors was prodigious. Some objects are still preserved in Eastern monasteries, while large numbers were brought by crusaders to the West; they include reliquaries, little boxes, covers of Gospels, crosses, frames of icons, enameled plaques, and chalices. The treasury of St. Mark's in Venice is particularly rich in such things, of which the most famous is the unique *pala d'oro*. It is a plaque measuring some 10 feet by 6½ feet and composed entirely of enamels set in gold and silver, studded with precious stones. It was commissioned in Constantinople in the 10th century by a doge, but it was refashioned in the 12th century, and then after 1204 it was enriched with the great enamel plaques plundered from the convent of the Pantocrator in Constantinople; it was restored again in the 14th century.

It is no surprise to find that, in this field more than in any other, the age of the Palaeologi was a time of decadence. Hardly anything deserves mention except a few church ornaments, preserved mostly in the monasteries on Mount Athos, to which the emperors presented them.

THE DIFFUSION OF BYZANTINE ART

In the previous discussions, Byzantine art was classified as the art of those lands subject to the authority of the Byzantine Empire. But that has left out two aspects of Byzantine art: in the first place, there was the spread of Byzantine art to countries linked to Constantinople by some political, economic, or religious tie before the fall of the city in 1453; then there was its prolongation after 1453 as the form of art appropriate to Orthodoxy.

The second category may easily be ignored here. "Byzantine" art, from the moment it lost the support of that Empire with which it was so intimately linked, became limited to a monotonous repetition of ancient themes. Nevertheless, its radiation during the continuance of the Empire, in domains beyond its rule, is a more rewarding subject of study.

The effect was quite different in the East from the West. In this context, one must exclude from the West some parts of Italy, like Ravenna, that came nearer to being actual provinces of Byzantine art than centers of radiated influence. It is more surprising to find Rome strongly under the influence at the time when the crises of the 7th and 8th centuries A.D., the Arab conquests, and the iconoclast dispute might have been expected to weaken Byzantium's influence. But it was just at that time that basilicas with galleries were built in Rome (S. Agnese fuori le Mura, for example) and that one found there "Byzantine" mosaics such as those in the chapels of St. Venantius in the Lateran, of John VII in St. Peter's, and in St. Praxed's and the oratory of S. Zeno. It is known that Venice and Torcello were centers of Byzantine art, and that artists summoned from Constantinople worked there. This tendency reached its height under the Norman kings of Sicily, who ruled lands that had long been Greek and whose history was intimately linked with that of Byzantium. Like the monuments of Ravenna, those in Monreale, Palermo, and Cefalù took their style of decoration and sometimes also their methods of construction from Byzantine models.

Because the Slav lands became Orthodox, they were inevitably stamped with the artistic heritage of Byzantium. The beginning of the story is well known: in A.D. 863 two Greek brothers from Salonika, Cyril and Methodius, translated the holy books into the Slavic language, inventing for this purpose the Glagolithic alphabet, and thereby supplied the Slavic world with both alphabet and literary language; they also permanently won it over to orthodoxy. Two subsequent events are of particular importance: in A.D. 864 the Bulgarian Czar Boris, and then in A.D. 989 Vladimir, Grand Prince of Kiev, were converted to Orthodoxy and had all their people baptized. After Bulgaria and Russia, Serbia and then the principalities of Moldavia and Walachia entered the religious sphere of Byzantium.

In Bulgaria, the influence of Byzantine art was apparent from the 10th century on. It was important in the 12th century, the date of the paintings of Batchkovo; in the 13th, with those at Bojana; and in the 14th, when those at Zemen and Tirnovo were painted. In Russia, the presence of Greek artists was continually mentioned by the chroniclers of each age, but their influence was particularly strong beginning in the 11th and 12th centuries; in Kiev, the paintings in S. Sophia are the outstanding example, and the Greek Theophanes is known to have lived in Moscow, too, where he was collaborator with, if not the master of, Andrei Rublev, the most famous Russian painter at the beginning of the 15th century. In Serbia, it has been possible to identify several schools in which there was a combination of borrowings from Dalmatia in the West, from Greece, from Byzantium, and from the East. But the Greco-Byzantine influence continually increased, especially in Serbian Macedonia, becoming predominant at the end of the 13th and first half of the 14th centuries, in the reigns of Milutin and Dushan. At Gratchanitsa, Greek inscriptions appear in the paintings; the same is true at Nagoritchino, where the signature of the painter Eutychios is found with the date 1317. In 1349 one finds another Greek signature at Lesnovo, and one can follow the Byzantine influence in the monastery of Marko, in the many churches around lakes Prespa and Ochrida, and on Mount Athos, where Chilandari and other churches were rebuilt, repaired, or decorated by Serbian czars. Finally, those principalities beyond Bulgaria and Serbia in what was later to be Rumania came, rather tardily perhaps, under Byzantine influence. This was particularly marked in Walachia, where both the cruciform plan and the incrustation of Byzantine churches appeared. For the 14th century, a good example is the church of St. Nicholas of Curtea at Ardjech: most of its inscriptions are Greek, and the paintings, in spite of some traces of Italian influence (arriving through Serbia), are of Byzantine inspiration.

To conclude, Byzantine art does not seem to have radiated as strong an influence as one might have expected from its long prestige, its uncontested superiority during so many centuries, and its powerful originality. In the West if one excludes the Byzantine provinces in Italy, such influence was both ephemeral and superficial. That this influence was permanent and deep in the Slavic lands was due in part to the fact that the czar corresponded to some extent to the basileus (a ruler of the Eastern Roman Empire), and that Orthodoxy was the accepted religion.

CABANEL, Alexandre (1823, Montpellier—1889, Paris), one of the most fashionable French painters in the Paris of the late 19th century. In 1845 he was awarded the Prix de Rome and was elected to the Institut in 1863; together with William Bouguereau, he organized the annual Salon, thus assuring the survival of conventional academicism. Cabanel's allegories of the *Months* for the Hôtel de Ville in Paris (1853; destroyed 1871) were followed by the *Five Senses* (1858) and the *Hours* (1864) for the Hôtel Pereire and the *Death of St. Louis* for the Panthéon (1878), both also in Paris. These decorations, though skillfully composed, are somewhat banal in conception; the drawing is weak and the color lacking in harmony. Cabanel shows more power in his portraits (*Alfred Bruyas*, 1846, and *Self-Portrait*, 1852; both Montpellier, Musée Fabre); and there is a certain grace in the equivocal nudity and languid poses of his female figures (*Birth of Venus*, 1863; Paris, Louvre).

CADMUS, Paul (b. 1904, New York), American painter. Cadmus took an interest in art while still a youth, since his father was a commercial lithographer and water-colorist and his mother an illustrator. He studied at the National Academy of Design and then at the Art Students League, both in New York. Between 1934 and 1937 he executed murals for the WPA Federal Art Project and for the U.S. Treasury Department.

Cadmus developed a delicately detailed style, but his graphic portrayals of sex or horror often shocked. Because he combined a perverse vision of everyday life—as in *Fantasia on a theme by Dr. S.* (1946; New York, Whitney Museum)—with a precise technical manner, Cadmus was characterized as one of the Magic Realists, a group that included such painters as Ivan Albright and Peter Blume.

CAFFIERI, Jean-Jacques (1725, Paris—1792, Paris), French sculptor, descendant of a family of sculptors of Neapolitan origin. A recipient of the Prix de Rome in 1748 and an Academician in 1759, he exhibited in the Paris Salons from 1757 to 1789. Taught by his father Jacques (1678–1755) and by Jean-Baptiste Lemoyne, Caffieri acquired an interest in the rendering of the human face and specialized in portrait busts done from life or from his collection of portraits, engravings, and casts of illustrious figures. His portraits of Pierre Corneille (1777) and the dramatist Jean Rotrou (1783) are in the foyer of the Comédie-Française or Théâtre Français in Paris. His finest portraits, however, were those done from the model, for Caffieri had an incomparable gift for animating the expression of a human face. Unforgettable are the dry coldness and affected smile of his *Rameau* (1761; destroyed in a fire at the former Opéra, Paris; plaster copy in Bibliothèque Ste-Geneviève); the Burgundian face and twinkling eyes of *Piron* (1762; Dijon, Museum); and above all his masterpiece, the gay and kindly countenance of the astronomer *Canon Pingré*, lively in spite of his age, his eyes sunken in folds of flesh and sparkling with malice (1789; Paris, Louvre).

CAILLEBOTTE, Gustave (1848, Paris—1894, Gennevilliers, Seine), French painter, best known as one of the principal patrons of the Impressionists. From 1876 to 1882 he took part in five of the exhibitions of the Impressionist group. His portraits (*Henri Cordier*, 1883; Paris, Louvre) and landscapes may have been influenced by Degas, but his views of Paris (*Snowy Rooftops*, 1878; Louvre) and realistic scenes of working-class life (*Workmen Planing a Floor*, 1875; Louvre) are highly personal in expression. In his will Caillebotte left his collection, comprising no less than 65 Impressionist works, to the State, which, however, rejected it. After three years of negotiations and a campaign in the press, 38 of the pictures were accepted. It was not until 1928 that these works—including Renoir's *Swing* and *Moulin de la Galette*, and Pissarro's *Red Roofs*—finally entered the Louvre.

CALDECOTT, Randolph (1846, Chester, England—1886, St. Augustine, Florida), English graphic artist and illustrator. He settled in London in 1872 and, although he was active as a painter and sculptor, his real métier was illustration. He made his debut in *Punch* in June 1872, and was soon busy working for such popular journals as *London Society*, the *Graphic, Pictorial World*, and the *American Daily Graphic*. In 1878 he began to provide the colored illustrations for children's books on which much of his fame rests: *The House That Jack Built*, *John Gilpin* (both 1878); *Babes in the Wood* (1879); *The Great Panjandrum* (1885); and so on. In these illustrations he exploited his two great assets—a vein of sentimental charm, partially reminiscent of Thomas Stothard's (1755–1834) work, and a keen eye for humorous and lively incident.

CALDER, Alexander (b. 1898, Philadelphia—d. 1976), American sculptor. Having trained and begun to practice as an engineer, Calder went to evening classes in 1922 in New York to learn drawing, then studied painting at the Art Students League. He went to Paris in 1926, where he made a small circus composed of acrobats, clowns, and tiny dancers of wood and metal revolving on a ring, then went on to create his first wire sculptures in the same style. These small figures and comic animals were among the ingenious mobile toys that Calder exhibited in 1927 at the Salon des Humoristes. The following year he held his first one-man exhibition in New York. On his return to Paris in November 1928, he began to make zoomorphic figures in wood and then portraits out of wire. In 1931, after joining the Abstraction-Création group, Calder exhibited his first abstract sculptures as well as assembled forms set in motion by a motor. A short time afterward, however, he removed all mechanical sources of energy and created works that were only set in motion by currents of air, which Jean Arp termed "mobiles."

Jean-Jacques Caffieri. *Canon Pingré*. 1789. Louvre, Paris. *Photo Giraudon, Paris.*

Above left: **Alexander Calder.** *Red Construction.* 1945. *Photo Galerie Carré, Paris.* Above right: **Jacques Callot.** Detail from *Siege of the Île de Ré.* 1630. *Photo Bulloz, Paris.*

In 1933 Calder set up his studio on a farm in Roxbury, Connecticut. Notable among the works produced from this time are the famous *Mercury Fountain* for the Spanish Pavilion at the Exposition Internationale, Paris (1937), book illustrations (*Fables* of La Fontaine, 1946), and stage sets. When he returned to Paris after World War II, he was commissioned (1951) by the Théâtre National Populaire to design the décor for Henri Pichette's play *Nucléa*; UNESCO commissioned the monumental mobile that was placed on the grounds of its headquarters at Place Fontenoy, Paris, in 1958.

Calder's mobiles, which at our approach stir gently and glide, rise, fall, and turn at varying speeds and in different directions, define by their movements alone an intangible contour and create an endless variety of rhythms. Other qualities are revealed in the "stabiles," which, because they are immobile, must communicate through line, structure, mass, and proportion. Those that Calder constructed between 1937 and 1947 seemed rudimentary combinations of sheet-metal plates that had been previously cut out. The stabiles exhibited in 1959 at the Galerie Maeght, Paris, were quite different in character. He had never before produced forms of this size, weight and breadth.

CALLOT, Jacques (1592, Nancy—1635, Nancy), one of the most celebrated French engravers of his time, whose influence on the history of engraving was immense. He learned the technique of engraving from Philippe Thomassin (1561/62—*c.* 1649), a well-known craftsman, and signed his first work in 1611. Called to Tuscany, which was ruled at the time by a Lorraine-born duchess, he perfected his technique and experimented with applying to the copper plate the hard glaze used by lute makers in place of the traditional soft engraver's glaze. This allowed repeated and dependable bitings and enabled Callot to combine engraving with the delicate effects of etching. He became a virtuoso technician.

He then produced his *Caprices* (1617), a series of 50 small plates depicting beggars, bandits, gentle folk, duelists, *commedia dell'arte* figures, and even horses and cityscapes, all captured with great spirit. While on holiday south of Florence, he created the celebrated *Fair of Impruneta* (1620), a composition remarkable for the handling of a multitude of figures enacting an endless variety of scenes.

After the death of Cosimo II de' Medici, Callot, in considerable prosperity, returned to Nancy. He held no official post at this time, and used the sketches made during his travels for the series of 25 *Beggars* (1622)—engravings of vagabonds, thieves, beggars, hunchbacks, and tramps, depicted with a cutting realism, yet with a fantasy that delighted the Romantics. This group was followed by 12 portraits collectively entitled the *Nobility of Lorraine* (1623). Called to the court of the Infanta Isabel of Flanders in 1625, he was present at the siege of Breda and began a six-part drawing of the battle, which was printed on the famous presses of the firm of Christophe Plantin (1628). This was the most dramatic of the three sieges he depicted. His others, the sieges of the *Île de Ré* (1630) and of *La Rochelle* (after 1631), commissioned by the French court, were not published during his lifetime, as the queen mother, who had been his patron, fell from favor. While passing through Paris he made views of the *Louvre* and the *Pont-Neuf* (both 1629), and acquainted the French graphic artists with his use of the hard glaze. The subsequent invasion of his native Lorraine by the troops of Louis XIII inspired the vengeful pages of his *Troubles of War* (1633) and powerful and moving *Tortures* (1634). His last great work was the *Temptation of St. Anthony* (1634).

CALS, Adolphe-Felix (1810, Paris—1880, Honfleur), French painter. He trained first as an engraver and then went on to study painting at the École des Beaux-Arts, Paris. His training was therefore both that of a craftsman and an academic painter. Cals favored the theme of peasant life, which he handled in a spirit reminiscent of Millet (*Woman and Child in an Orchard*, 1875; Paris, Musée de l'Impressionnisme). At the same time his sense of atmosphere; his leaning toward a subjective art; his friendship with the Dutch painter Johan Barthold Jongkind; and, from 1873, when he settled at Honfleur (*Sunset at Honfleur*, 1873, and *Lunch at Honfleur*, 1875; both Musée de l'Impressionnisme), his relations with the painters of the Ferme St-Siméon, a small fishing inn near Honfleur where Boudin used to stay—all these factors make Cals as much a precursor of Impressionism as Daubigny.

CALVERT, Edward (1799, Appledore, Devon—1883, London), English landscape painter. As a young man he lived in Plymouth; in 1824, following his marriage, he moved to London, where he first exhibited at the Royal Academy in 1825. During the years from 1827 to 1831 he came into contact with William Blake and his circle, especially Samuel Palmer, who became a close friend. He produced very little and destroyed many of his works, apparently finding it difficult to reconcile his mystical tendencies with the aesthetic aspects of painting. His landscapes, in the tradition of Giorgione and Claude Lorrain, have an almost Symbolist appearance (*Olympus*, Manchester, Whitworth Art Gallery; *Amphion with the Flocks of His Brother Zethus*, London, British Museum). After a visit to Greece in 1844, Calvert painted one of his few highly finished oils, a *Classical Landscape* (Oxford, Ashmolean Museum). More vivid and personal are his engravings on wood and copper, of which the finest is perhaps *The Bride* (1828; British Museum).

CAMBIASO, Luca (1527, Moneglia, near Genoa—1585, Madrid), Italian painter. At the age of fifteen Luca helped his father to paint the *Roman Stories* in the Palazzo Saluzzo, Genoa. Two years later, with Lazzaro Calvi (1502–1607), he decorated the Palazzo Doria (now Spinola) in Genoa. In February 1547, with his father and Francesco Brea (active 1530s–1540s), Luca worked on the Taggia *Resurrection* and on the frescoes of S. Maria del Canneto. His close friendship with the architect Galeazzo Alessi probably dates from that period; they worked together at S. Matteo in Genoa, then in the Lercari Chapel of Genoa Cathedral (1567). A journey to Emilia around 1560 accounts for the influence of Correggio and Parmigianino apparent in many of his works. In 1562 Luca painted the figures of *St. Benedict, St. John the Baptist*, and *St. Luke* in the church of S. Caterina; in 1580, *St. Augustine Surrounded by Saints* at S. Bartolomeo di Vallecalda. In 1583 he left Italy with Lazzaro Tavarone (1556–1641), who had been called to Spain by Philip II to decorate the vault of the sacristy in the Escorial. He remained at the Spanish court until his death.

Luca Cambiaso. Drawing after studio mannequins. Gabinetto dei Disegni e Stampe, Uffizi, Florence.

CAMDEN TOWN GROUP, English school of painting largely inspired by Walter Sickert and by the part of London he most admired. It was founded in 1911, after the Postimpressionist exhibition held in London in the winter of 1910–11. Its aims were based on those of the New English Art Club of 1886, namely an attempt to import the more enlightened French vision into English art. The principal members, after Sickert, were Lucien Pissarro (1863–1944), Charles Ginner (1878–1952), Harold Gilman, and Spencer Gore, all of whom did in fact create a form of Postimpressionism in England.

CAMPAÑA, Pieter de Kempeneer, *called* Pedro de (1503, Brussels—1580, Brussels), Flemish-born Mannerist painter, active in Spain. A member of the Kempeneer family, whose name he bore at first, he is documented in Bologna in 1529, at work on a triumphal arch for the visit of Emperor Charles V. He is said to have accompanied Cardinal Grimani to Venice, and there is evidence that he saw Raphael's Vatican frescoes in Rome, but as early as 1537 he went to Andalusia to work at Seville Cathedral. (Seville, a leading artistic center, maintained close contact with Spanish Flanders.) He settled there and became famous under the name of Pedro de Campaña.

His art combines Flemish realism of detail with Mannerist figural elongation and dramatic spatial effects. Pedro painted two versions of the *Descent from the Cross*, now in the museum at Montpellier (*c.* 1540) and in Seville Cathedral (1547). The altarpiece of the *Purification* (1555; Seville, Cathedral) and the altarpieces in S. Ana of Triana, Seville (1557; with the collaboration of native artists)—showing scenes of the Virgin, St. Joachim, and St. Anne—and Cordova Cathedral (1556), with scenes from the life of Christ, are also by his hand. In 1563 Pedro de Campaña went back to the country of his birth and spent the end of his life making tapestry cartoons for Brussels factories.

Jacob van Campen. The Huis ten Bosch, The Hague. 1647. *Photo Dutch Tourist Office.*

CAMPBELL, Colen *or* Colin (b. Scotland—d. 1729, London), Scottish architect. Nothing is known of Campbell's early life. In 1718 he was appointed Chief Clerk of the King's Works and Deputy Surveyor, and in 1725 he described himself as architect to the Prince of Wales. The three volumes of his *Vitruvius Britannicus* were published successively in 1715, 1717, and 1725; they consisted of engravings of English country houses in the classical style, including some of his own. The book had a great influence, giving impetus to Palladianism, which was a twofold revival of Palladio, the 16th-century Italian architect, and his English admirer, Inigo Jones; an early convert was the Earl of Burlington. Only one of Campbell's three most influential buildings was strictly modeled after Palladio: Mereworth Castle, Kent (*c.* 1722–25), a close imitation of Palladio's Villa Rotonda, near Vicenza; in fact, Mereworth's tall dome is based on the master's original design, which was flattened by the builders. The other two—Wanstead House, Essex (1715–22; demolished 1822), and Houghton Hall, Norfolk (built for Sir Robert Peel, 1721–30; towers and other modifications added by James Gibbs)—were the prototypes of the English country house for a century to come. Campbell remodeled Burlington House, Piccadilly (*c.* 1717–19), for the earl, basing its design on Palladio's Palazzo Porto-Colleoni at Vicenza, but borrowing the details from Inigo Jones.

CAMPEN, Jacob van (1595, Haarlem—1657, Randebroek, Amersfoort), Dutch architect who gave decisive form to Dutch Classicism. After Hendrick de Keyser and before Philips Vingboons (1614–78) and Adriaen Dortsman (d. 1682), Van Campen built a number of the middle-class stone houses along the canals of Amsterdam. In 1647 he supervised the decoration of the Oranjezaal, the main hall of the Huis ten Bosch ("House in the Woods") at The Hague, which had been commissioned by Amalia von Solms, the widow of the Prince of Orange. In 1633 he designed the Mauritshuis, also at The Hague (built by Pieter Post), one of the first examples in the Netherlands of a palace in the Classical style. From 1648 to 1665 the grandiose Town Hall (now the Royal Palace) at Amsterdam was built according to his plans and partly under his supervision.

CAMPENDONK, Heinrich (1889, Krefeld—1957, Amsterdam), German painter. Campendonk accepted an invitation from Franz Marc to join him at Sindelsdorf in Upper Bavaria, and later that year (1911) exhibited with the Blaue Reiter in Munich. From 1914 to 1916 he served with the German forces, then settled in Seeshaupt on the Starnbergersee, where he produced woodcuts and *verres églomisées*, the latter influenced by Bavarian folk art. In 1920 Campendonk visited Italy, discovering Giotto and Fra Angelico. In 1923 he joined the staff of the Industrial School of Art in Essen, then in 1925 transferred to the Düsseldorf Academy where he taught painting. Following his dismissal by the Nazis in 1933 as a "degenerate artist," Campendonk moved to Belgium, and subsequently to Holland, where he taught at the Rijksakademie in Amsterdam from 1935 until shortly before his death. In 1937 at the International Exhibition in Paris he was awarded a Grand Prix for his stained-glass windows. Campendonk's style was formed during the period of his association with the Blaue Reiter. Franz Marc and Marc Chagall exerted the strongest influence on his romantic and dreamlike early paintings, which revealed a decorative tendency (*Cowshed*, 1920; New York, Priv. Coll.). His later pictures are more abstract, two-dimensional, and dispassionate. A large part of his output consisted of stained-glass windows, watercolors, and woodcuts.

CAMPIGLI, Massimo (1895, Florence—1971, St. Tropez), Italian painter. Campigli began to paint in Paris, working according to the plastic laws set out in Amédée Ozenfant and Le Corbusier's review, *L'Esprit Nouveau.* "In the manner of a bee," wrote the critic Jean Paulhan, "Campigli begins by enclosing his characters in their cells." Painting on canvas as though on a wall, he created work that is, in certain respects, reminiscent of Etruscan and Roman painting. His women, shaped like amphoras, with slender waists and arms that stand out from their sides like the handles of a vase, have a grace at once ancient and novel. At a time when the painters of his generation were constantly in search of rejuvenating innovations, Campigli remained faithful to himself and to the poetic, painted world of his dreams.

CAMPIN, Robert, *also called* Master of Flémalle (*c.* 1378, Valenciennes—1444, Tournai), Flemish painter. He settled in Tournai, where he became a Master in 1406 and a burgher in 1410. As a painter he achieved considerable importance, the extent of which has been realized only recently. There is now no doubt concerning his identity as the so-called Master of Flémalle, one of the truly revolutionary artists of the Flemish School. "Master of Flémalle" is an inaccurate name designating the painter of four panels in the Städelsches Kunstinstitut, Frankfurt, who was thought to have been from an abbey at Flémalle-lez-Liège, which in fact never existed. He is also known as the Master of the Mérode Altarpiece after a triptych now in the Cloisters, New York, which was long in the possession of the princes of Mérode. Campin's identification with this painter has been the subject of one of the greatest of art historical arguments. At the end of the 19th century, the Mérode triptych and other panels were attributed in turn to a number of minor masters, including Jacques Daret (*c.* 1404–*c.* 1470). In 1909 they were attributed to Campin, and by 1928 a passionate argument had developed, but the more objective historians were inclined to support the Campin attribution, since the works in question were spread over two decades and clearly demonstrated a most original personality. The works are hypothetically dated as follows: between 1420 and 1430, the *Marriage of the Virgin*, with *St. James the Greater* and *St. Claire* in grisaille on the reverse (Madrid, Prado), the *Nativity* (Dijon, Museum), the Mérode *Annunciation* (The Cloisters), a *Madonna* (Leningrad, Hermitage); between 1430 and 1435, the *Virgin in Glory with Saints* (Aix-en-Provence, Musée Granet), the *Trinity*, two panels representing a *Madonna* and *St. Veronica*, and a *Crucified Thief* (all Städelsches Kunstinstitut), and *Portrait of a Man* and *Portrait of a Woman* (both London, National Gallery); between 1435 and 1440, a *Crucifixion* (Berlin), and *St. Barbara, St. John the Baptist, and a Donor* (Prado).

Campin may be considered one of the early innovators of the Flemish School. He was responsible for its transition from the Gothic International Style to a poetic representation of actual life and of objects. Using a more opaque paint than Van Eyck and painting in a less inspired, more archaic and more incisive style, Campin saw the terrestrial world as an image of the heavenly world and expressed its poetry through symbols borrowed partly from mystical literature and through a narrative sweetness that has something of the quality of a fable. The Dijon *Nativity*, which is still characterized by refined elegance and a relative indifference to perspective, presents a landscape that is certainly symbolic but nonetheless closely observed and lively, rural, and rich in picturesque detail. In the Mérode *Annunciation*, set in a bourgeois home, a charming and realistic narrative form is ennobled by a sacred subject. In others of his works (*Virgin and Child Before a Fire Screen*, London, National Gallery; *Madonna*, Städelsches Kunstinstitut), Campin emulates the sculptors of Tournai and expresses himself in plastic values as yet unknown in Northern painting. He is a painter capable of expressing the greatest pathos and also a remarkable portraitist: *Portrait of a Woman* (London, National Gallery) is painted in carefully defined volumes against a flat background; and its subject—fresh, wholesome, and clear-eyed—has a soul.

CAMPOLI, Cosmo Pietro (b. 1922, South Bend, Indiana), American sculptor. Campoli studied at the Art Institute of Chicago, receiving the diploma in sculpture in 1950. For the next two years he

Robert Campin. *St. Veronica*. Between 1430 and 1435. Städelsches Kunstinstitut, Frankfurt. *Photo Busch-Hauck.*

worked in Europe, and in 1954 he received first prize in the Sixteen Chicago Sculptors show. From 1953 he taught in Chicago at the Institute of Design of the Illinois Institute of Technology and at the Contemporary Art Workshop, which he founded in 1950.

Campoli's purpose in his sculpture is to express the universal and archetypal aspects of humanity; from around 1949 on, he concentrated on motifs of birth, death, nourishment, and the mother-child relationship, both in human and animal figures. His imagery most often expresses terror or pain, as in *Jonah and the Whale* (lead, 1953), in which the moment of entrapment and death is shown rather than rebirth. Campoli's forms are solid, closed, and enveloping, and like his symbolism, they express a cyclical perpetuity; a particularly successful example of the fusion of image and form is *Mother and Child* (plaster, 1949), in which the seated mother is identified with the chair and is thus a symbol of the lap or womb.

CANALETTO, Antonio Canale, *called* (1697, Venice—1768, Venice), Italian painter. Canaletto's father was a theatrical designer and he began by working with him. In 1719 Antonio was in Rome and it was there, it seems, that he rapidly acquired the special skill that was to make him celebrated as a painter of *vedute*, or city views. Specialization in this genre was a remunerative pursuit in the 18th century, when travelers were numerous in Italy and expected to take back with them souvenirs of the places they had visited on the Grand Tour. By 1720 Antonio was a member of the painters' guild in Venice; he found effective patrons and protectors, especially among the large colony of Englishmen staying in the city. Owen McSwiney, impresario and agent for collecting works of art, recommended him to the Duke of Richmond, and from 1736 he was assiduously patronized by Joseph Smith, English consul in Venice, a keen admirer and collector of Canaletto's works. Smith was probably responsible for the painter's three visits to England (1746–50; 1751–53; 1754–55). In 1763 he became president of the Venetian Academy.

Canaletto's *vedute* are precise without ever being dry; they show an exceptional sense of harmony, which nothing is allowed to impair. The Venetian skies are generally depicted as cloudy, sometimes almost leaden. Architecture is always scrupulously rendered, almost as if with a ruler. For the first rapid outline of his compositions, the artist often used a *camera obscura*, noted the colors to be used on the leaves of his sketchbooks, and indicated lighting by broadly treated hatchings. More than 140 of these drawings, and over 50 paintings were collected by Smith, and later acquired for the English Royal Collection. The tiny figures that appear in these *vedute* are drawn with great vivacity.

CANDELA, Felix (b. 1910, Madrid), Spanish-born Mexican architect known for his concrete shell structures. Candela fought on the Republican side during the Spanish Civil War and emigrated to Mexico in 1939. He had trained as an architect at the Escuela Superior de Arquitectura, Madrid, and toward the end of his training period had watched the construction of one of Eduardo Torroja's buildings, incorporating the use of shell concrete. Upon obtaining Mexican nationality, he at first worked in another architect's office, then set up an independent practice with his brother Antonio. His first important shell structure was the Cosmic Rays Pavilion at Ciudad Universitaria in Mexico City (1951), which is covered with a hyperbolic paraboloid that measures no more than $6\frac{1}{4}$ inches at its thickest point. He was also asked to produce a traditional design for the church of the Virgen Milagrosa (Miraculous Virgin) in Mexico City, erected 1954–55.

Candela created more strictly contemporary shapes in the double curved vault (a shell made from the intersection of two paraboloids) over the main hall of the Bolsa de Valores (Stock Exchange), Mexico City (1955), the Chapel of Nuestra Sẽnora de la Soledad, Coyoacan (1955); the huge concrete umbrellas of the Great Southwest Corporation's industrial community (1958) between Dallas and Fort Worth, Texas; and the Manatiales Restaurant, Xochimilco (1957–58), where the traditional elements of roof and walls are abolished in a single eight-petaled concrete membrane, undulating up and down from the ground like some exotic flower, which Candela himself considered his most significant structure.

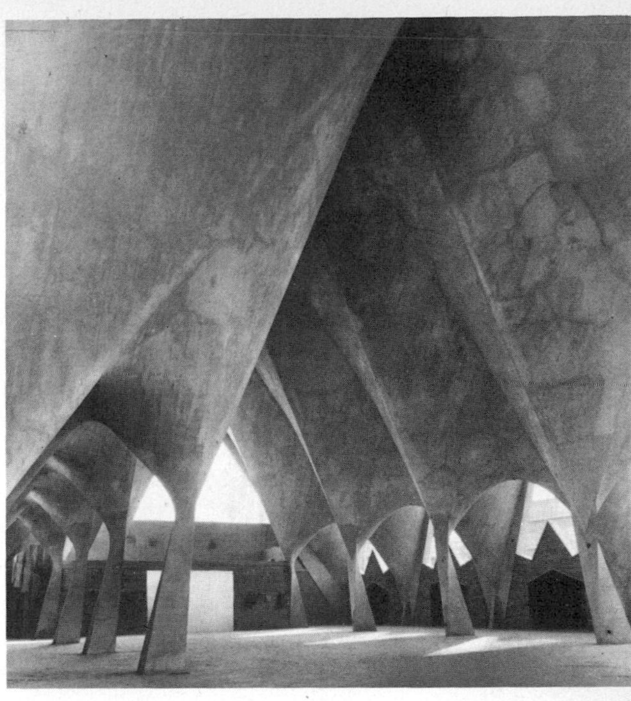

Felix Candela. Church of the Virgen Milagrosa, Mexico City. 1954–55.

CANDILIS, Georges (b. 1913, Baku, U.S.S.R.), French architect. After studying at the National Technical University of Athens, he worked with Le Corbusier (1945–51) and was strongly influenced by him. He designed a number of buildings in Morocco and Algeria, where he devoted himself to the special problems of Moslem living conditions. He then supervised the new housing development (1956–59) at Bagnols-sur-Cèze, a suburb of Nîmes, one of the outstanding French postwar architectural complexes, and worked on the construction of a pilot district in a town of 100,000 inhabitants at Toulouse-le-Mirail. Mention should also be made of the La Tour-l'Évêque complex at Nîmes (1961) and his development, in cooperation with Jean Balladur (b. 1924), of the Languedoc-Roussillon littoral. His various works have been executed in collaboration with his associates Paul Dony, Alexis Josic (b. 1921), and Shadrach Woods (b. 1923).

CANO, Alonso (1601, Granada—1667, Granada), Andalusian painter, sculptor, and architect. Cano was first trained in the workshop of his father, Miguel, a *maestro ensamblador* ("master joiner") who settled in Seville in 1615. In that town the young man studied under the sculptor Juan Martínez Montañes; from 1616 to 1621, he was a pupil of the painter Francisco Pacheco, as was Diego Velázquez. He settled in Madrid in 1638, but was imprisoned as a murder suspect in 1644. After his release he fled to Valencia, where he hid in the Carthusian monastery of Portacoeli for 18 months. In 1652 he was appointed *racionero de musica* at Granada Cathedral, but was expelled in 1656. Four years later he made his peace with the chapter and became *maestro mayor* ("chief master") of the cathedral in 1667.

As an architect, in 1667 he submitted a design for the façade of Granada Cathedral. It was not carried out until after the death of its creator, and in the 18th century carved scenes above the doors and statues on the cornice were added to Cano's original design.

In sculpture Cano was the foremost representative of the classical Spanish Baroque—classical in his choice of non-flamboyant subject matter and in his avoidance of overdramatic or realistic effects, but Baroque in his mode of expression; his characters are animated by an inward fire reminiscent of El Greco. Among many other sculptured works, Cano executed the large altarpiece in S. María, Lebrija (1629–31), of which the carved *Madonna* is particularly outstanding, the statues of Franciscan saints (with the help of Pedro de Mena) and the head of *St. John of God* in the Granada Museo Provincial de Bellas Artes; and, in the cathedral of the city, the *Immaculate Conception* (1655), a child *St. John the Baptist*, and the three busts of *St. Paul*, *Adam*, and *Eve*. (The last two works were completed after the artist's death.)

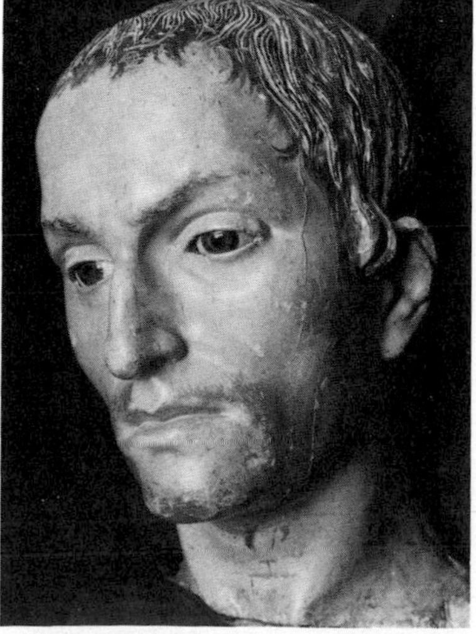

Alonso Cano. *St. John of God.* Museo Provincial de Bellas Artes, Granada. *Photo Mas, Barcelona.*

Cano's paintings are numerous. The *St. Agnes* in the Dresden Gemäldegalerie dates from his training period in Seville and shows traces of Zurbarán; *Descent into Limbo* is another relatively early work (1637–40; Los Angeles, County Museum). His later paintings are looser and lighter and foreshadow some of Velázquez's atmospheric effects. In Madrid, among many other works, he painted *St. Isidore's Miracle of the Well* (1645–46) and *St. John on Patmos* (both Prado). Later, settling in Granada, he executed the seven *Mysteries of the Virgin* for Granada Cathedral (1652–54), and after 1660, the *Virgin of the Rosary* (Malaga, Cathedral) and the *Immaculate Conception* (1663; Granada, Cathedral). He also produced a great number of drawings.

CANOVA, Antonio (1757, Possagno, near Treviso—1822, Venice), Italian sculptor, one of the leading exponents of the Neoclassical style. He moved to Venice as a boy and received his early training there in the years around 1770. His early works show more of the spirit of French 18th-century portraiture than of the antique, and his first statue of a specifically Neoclassical subject was the *Icarus* of 1779 (Venice, Museo Correr), but even in this the treatment of the heads is naturalistic. Toward the end of 1779 Canova went to Rome; in 1780 he went south to Naples and Pompeii, and this revelation of classical antiquity seems to have determined his future career. From 1781 he lived in Rome, where in 1782 he received his first major commission, the monument to Pope Clement XIV in the church of SS. Apostoli.

In 1787, Canova was commissioned to do *Genius of Death*, to be placed next to the sarcophagus of Clement XIII in St. Peter's, completed in 1792. During this period he also made his famous *Cupid and Psyche*, the marble of which is now in the Louvre, Paris. The element of sentimental eroticism is characteristic of late 18th-century Neoclassicism and prefigures French Romantic painting of the 1830s. The French invasion of Italy caused him to go to Vienna, where he received a commission for a large monument; but in 1799 he returned to Rome, where he was made a member of the Academy of St. Luke (1800). In 1802 he was invited to Paris by Napoleon, of whom he made a plaster bust. In 1806, he was commissioned to make an equestrian statue of Napoleon for Naples. But the most remarkable of his portraits of the emperor are the two colossal standing figures that represent him as a Roman hero holding an orb in his right hand and with an imperial toga over his arm but otherwise entirely nude. This extraordinary representation was repeated; the bronze version of 1811 stands in the courtyard of the Brera, Milan, while that in marble, captured by the Duke of Wellington probably in 1815, stands in the Wellington Museum in London.

Antonio Canova. *Pauline Bonaparte as Venus.* 1808. Galleria Borghese, Rome. *Photo Alinari-Giraudon.*

Another similar transformation was effected in *Pauline Bonaparte Borghese as Venus* (1808; Rome, Galleria Borghese), which transfigures a portrait statue with clearly recognizable features into an antique Venus of a Roman rather than Greek type. In 1816, during his visit to London, Canova was able to study the sculptures from the Parthenon acquired by Lord Elgin and *Theseus and the Centaur* (1805–19; Vienna, Kunsthistorisches Museum) may possibly reflect their influence. In 1819 Canova received a commission from the British government to erect the huge memorial in St. Peter's, Rome, in memory of the exiled Stuarts—the last of the Stuarts, Henry Cardinal of York, having died in 1807. In 1819 he also began the construction of the temple in his own honor in his native village of Possagno, which still has the largest collection of sketches and plasters of his works.

CANTERBURY, family of eminent English masons of the 13th and 14th centuries, who were the first to develop the ogee arch and diaper patterns based on it. They were also the originators of the "London" type of canopied tomb, which appears to be inspired by goldsmiths' work and in its turn exerted a wide influence both in England and abroad.

MICHAEL OF CANTERBURY (active 1275–1317) was almost certainly responsible for the tomb of Edmund Crouchback, Earl of Lancaster, in Westminster Abbey (1295–1300). Michael is regarded as progenitor of both the Flamboyant and Perpendicular styles. He was working at Canterbury from about 1275, but he was also engaged on the Prior's House at St. Mary-le-Bow in Cheapside, London, between 1275 and 1280. He settled in London about 1291. He was master of the works at St. Stephen's Chapel in the palace of Westminster, from 1292; but only the crypt chapel, dedicated to Our Lady, would have been started at that time. Other works attributed to Michael are the Cheapside Eleanor Cross (1291–94) and the tombs of Archbishop Peckham (d. 1292) and Bishop William of Louth (d. 1298). The attribution of the tomb of Aveline of Lancaster (d. 1276), wife of Edmund Crouchback, to Michael seems doubtful; but the Church of St. Etheldreda in Ely Place, London, is in his style.

WALTER OF CANTERBURY (active 1319–27) succeeded Michael as master of the works at St. Stephen's Chapel, but only after an interval of several years (1320). By 1323, if not before, Walter had become master of the king's works. In this capacity he rebuilt part of the outer wall of the Tower of London between 1324 and 1325. He probably furnished plans for the tomb of Aymer de Valence (d. 1323), which is similar to work in St. Stephen's crypt. He may be the Walter whose death is recorded in 1330.

THOMAS OF CANTERBURY (active 1324–36) is first heard of as a mason working under Walter in St. Stephen's crypt and in the passage leading to the Painted Chamber (1324). In 1326 he was engaged in rebuilding the chapel of the London Guildhall. There is a record of his "first coming to Westminster" in May 1331, which refers to his starting work on the upper chapel at St. Stephen. His work represents a final florescence of the Decorated Style. Thomas introduced reversed cusps and initiated a new type of tracery known as "Kentish," which was a development of the Curvilinear phase and a step in the direction of Perpendicular. Closely related to the style of St. Stephen's Chapel are the tomb of John of Eltham (d. 1334) at Westminster, the stone screen surrounding the tomb of Archbishop Meopham (1333) at Canterbury, and the great window in St. Anselm's Chapel, Canterbury (1336).

CAPOGROSSI, Giuseppe (b. 1900, Rome), Italian painter. After living in Paris from 1927 to 1932, he returned to Rome and founded the Gruppo Romano with the painters Corrado Cagli (b. 1910) and Emanuele Cavalli (b. 1904). Then, after World War II, he founded the Origine group, of which he remained a member until 1951. From a strictly figurative style of art that included landscapes, still lifes, and groups of dancers, he passed almost without transition to complete abstraction (1949–50). From that time, all Capogrossi's work was dominated by a single theme; adopting a motif having the form of a claw or trident, he constructed, in one painting after another, the most varied compositions, first in black and white, then in color. The danger of constantly using one limited form is repetitiveness and Capogrossi did not always avoid this. Nevertheless, the rhythmic pattern covering the surface of his canvases creates, in his best work, a tension that has deeper appeal than simple decoration (*Composition*, 1953; Rome, Coll. Argan).

CAPPELLE, Jan van de (*c.* 1624, Amsterdam—1679, Amsterdam), Dutch painter and collector. His inherited wealth enabled him to build one of the largest collections of paintings of the 17th century, which included marines by Simon de Vlieger (*c.* 1600–53), Jan Porcelis (*c.* 1585–1632), and Jan van Goyen, and portraits by Frans Hals and Rembrandt. Van de Cappelle was himself a notable marine artist of estuaries (*River Scene with a Dutch Yacht Firing a Salute*, *c.* 1665; London, National Gallery), ports, and ships anchored off shore; the waters are invariably painted in a calm mood. Early morning and evening were the artist's favorite times; clouds, the translucent reflections of sails, and hulls in the water (*State Barge Saluted by the Home Fleet*, 1650; Amsterdam, Rijksmuseum), and the subtle lavender and golden tones of sunsets were as important an element in his paintings as the great sailing ships themselves.

CARAVAGGIO, Michelangelo Merisi *or* Amerighi, *called* (1573, Caravaggio, Lombardy—1610, Port'Ercole, Tuscany), Italian painter who introduced a new conception of light and a realistic iconography to the art of Italy.

Caravaggio's first major commission (*c.* 1597), which brought him immediate fame, was for the Contarelli Chapel in the Roman church of S. Luigi dei Francesi; he shared it with the Mannerist painter Giuseppe Cesari, known as the Cavaliere d'Arpino. The first painting done by Caravaggio for the series, *St. Matthew and the Angel* (formerly in Berlin, now destroyed), caused a scandal and was rejected. The artist replaced it with another version and proceeded to paint the *Calling of St. Matthew* and the *Martyrdom of St. Matthew*.

Earlier than this spectacular exploit, or contemporary with it, are the fat and fleshy *Bacchus* at the Uffizi, Florence, the one at the Galleria Borghese, Rome, and the *Medusa*, also at the Uffizi. The *Rest on the Flight into Egypt* and the *Repentant Magdalen* (both Rome, Galleria Doria Pamphili), the *Fortuneteller* (Paris, Louvre), and the *Amor Victorious* in Berlin (Staatliche Museen), reveal an artist who, if not complaisant, was at least at peace with himself, hardly the man to cause a revolution in painting. The revolution occurred suddenly with Caravaggio's works for S. Luigi dei Francesi. Their success among artistic circles was complete; the public was partly won over, partly scandalized. The reasons for this can be summed up in two words:

Caravaggio. *Calling of St. Matthew. c.* 1598. Contarelli Chapel, S. Luigi dei Francesi, Rome. *Photo Alinari-Giraudon.*

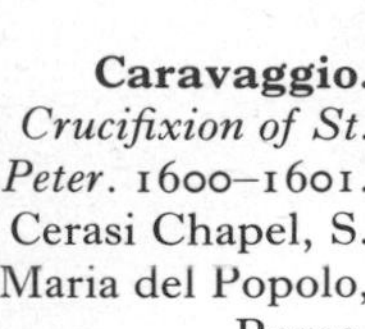

Caravaggio. *Crucifixion of St. Peter*. 1600–1601. Cerasi Chapel, S. Maria del Popolo, Rome.

light and realism. Almost black, opaque shadows are contrasted without transition with equally stark artificial lighting. There is no modulation in outline or detail. The light is not natural and seems to anticipate modern electrical projectors. The background is almost always black, which gives the forms a strikingly plastic effect. Caravaggio reduces his compositions to the barest essentials, with neither landscape nor ornament to distract one's attention. As for realism, Caravaggio made a point of introducing common, even coarse people into his religious scenes. At least three of his works were refused by the ecclesiastical authorities who had commissioned them: the *St. Matthew and the Angel* for the Contarelli altar, showing the saint with his legs crossed and the dirty sole of his left foot turned outward in the foreground; the *Conversion of St. Paul* (1600–1601; Rome, S. Maria del Popolo); and the *Death of the Virgin* (*c.* 1605–7; Paris, Louvre). There is not only realism here but bravado as well. The principal figures in the *Martyrdom of St. Matthew* are the fierce-looking naked executioner and the fleeing child with its mouth open in a shrill cry, two unforgettable types that recur in a whole series of pictures by Baroque artists, particularly in scenes of martyrdom, for which the Contarelli paintings served as a model. Close in date (1600–1601) and manner to the Contarelli works are the vast canvases in the Cerasi Chapel at S. Maria del Popolo, Rome: the *Crucifixion of St. Peter* and the *Conversion of St. Paul*.

Caravaggio's life was no less shocking than his art. From 1600 to 1607 he engaged the constant attention of the police and the law courts for his brawls, sword fights, ill-treatment of prostitutes, outrageous behavior toward some of his fellow painters, and suspect friendships with others. All this ended with Caravaggio's murder of a man in 1606.

During all these tumultuous episodes he went on painting without interruption; paradoxically, the pictures dating from these years are among the most peaceful of his whole career. In 1604 he completed for the Chiesa Nuova in Rome (S. Maria in Vallicella) the most moving of his religious paintings, the *Deposition of Christ*, now in the Vatican Museum: taut, compact, inscribed in a triangle, without a trace of the former bravado. Conceived in the same spirit are the two roughly contemporary Virgins: the *Madonna di Loreto* (Rome, Sant'Agostino) and the *Virgin and Child with St. Anne* (Rome, Galleria Borghese). In the latter, also called the *Madonna dei Palafrenieri*, the Child, one of the most delightful nudes of Caravaggio, places his foot on his mother's to help her crush the serpent.

Probably also from this period is the *David* holding the severed head of Goliath (Galleria Borghese). It is thought, with some reason, to be a self-portrait. Another work that can be assigned to the Roman years is the *Death of the Virgin*, one of Caravaggio's most remarkable paintings, notable for its effects of color, with the cinnabar red of the Virgin's dress harmonizing with the rusty hue of garb of the crying woman. At Naples, where Caravaggio had fled in 1607, he painted the *Flagellation*, now in S. Domenico Maggiore, Naples, and the *Seven Works of Mercy* (Naples, Monte della Misericordia), in which the light from a torch creates deep contrasts. But he did not stay in Naples for long. Soon we find him in Malta, where on July 14, 1608, he received from the Grand Master, Alof de Wignacourt, the Cross of the Knight of Grace. Caravaggio's celebrated portrait of Wignacourt, now in the Louvre, is a consummate study of the reflection of light on armor, with a livid, helmeted page wearing a coat with a red facing. The masterpiece of the artist's Maltese period is his *Beheading of St. John the Baptist* (1608), in the cathedral at Valetta.

At the end of 1608, Caravaggio was in Syracuse, Sicily, where he painted the *Burial of St. Lucy*, now in ruinous condition, for the church of S. Lucia. He went on to Messina, where the Museo Nazionale has an *Adoration of the Shepherds* and a *Raising of Lazarus*, large pictures with stronger contrasts, it seems, than the *Burial of St. Lucy*; but they have suffered a great deal from early restorations. Caravaggio's last canvas is another *Adoration*, executed in Palermo for the Oratorio di S. Lorenzo, and also sadly damaged.

CARLES, Arthur Beecher (1882, Philadelphia—1952, Chestnut Hill, Philadelphia), American painter. Carles studied at the Pennsylvania Academy of the Fine Arts in Philadelphia intermittently between 1901 and 1907. During his travels to Europe in 1905 and 1907, he became acquainted with several of the important young painters in Paris—Matisse, Picasso, Robert Delaunay, Hans Hofmann, and the American John Marin. Several years later, Carles exhibited his own works at Alfred Stieglitz' Photo-Secession Gallery, and also in the 1913 Armory Show in New York. During the 1920s and 1930s, he evolved a decorative yet representational style that became increasingly abstract, providing an alternative to Cubism, but still within a modernist context. Throughout his development, Carles made very personal use of chromatic relationships, based on an appreciation of the plastic potentialities of color; in certain of his works the picture surface and its images contain literally hundreds of hues. One of his earliest works, *L'Église* (*c.* 1910; New York, Metropolitan Museum), reveals a clear Fauvist influence in its organization of clearly delineated areas of saturated color. Between 1937 and 1941, when he finally stopped painting, Carles created works, often on mural scale, whose spontaneously brushed surfaces and violent rhythms anticipate the Abstract Expressionism of American painting in the 1950s.

CARLEVARIS, Luca Antonio (1663, Udine—1729, Venice), Italian painter. Orphaned at the age of six, Carlevaris was brought to Venice in 1679, where he resided until his death. The Zenobio family of Venice became his generous patrons, and in recognition the artist signed his work "Luca da Ca' Zenobio." Abbé Moschini's statement that Carlevaris visited Rome as a young man and made several sketches of its buildings and ruins is probably true; some of these ruins are recognizable in his *capricci* of harbors, landscapes, and shipyards. But Carlevaris was above all the painter of Venetian views, called *vedute*. His compositions for two of the subjects that provided themes for this popular genre—the splendid civic welcome given by the Venetian republic to a foreign dignitary (*Earl of Manchester's Embassy*, 1707, Birmingham, City Art Gallery; *Count Colloredo Visiting Venice as Imperial Ambassador*, 1727, Dresden, Gëmaldegalerie) and the regatta on the Grand Canal—became the model for later *vedutisti*.

CAROLINGIAN ART. *See* **ROMANESQUE ART.**

CAROLUS-DURAN, Charles Durand, *called* (1837, Lille—1917, Paris), French painter of the late 19th century who enjoyed enormous success as a portraitist of the Parisian aristocracy and rich bourgeoisie. After studying in Lille, he went to Paris in 1853 and frequented the Académie Suisse. In the early 1860s he went to Italy, and, later in the decade, to Spain, where he was profoundly impressed by the works of Velázquez. He had a brilliant career, rewarded by international commissions, Salon medals, and considerable official recognition. In 1905 he was elected to the Institut and later became director of the Académie de France, with headquarters at the Villa Medici in Rome. In addition to mediocre decorations (*Glory of Marie de Médicis*, 1878; ceiling in the Louvre, Paris) and banal, Spanish-inspired compositions (the *Assassination Victim*, 1866; Lille, Palais des Beaux-Arts), he produced sensitive and well-composed portraits (*Madame Feydeau*, 1869, Lille, Musée Palais des Beaux-Arts; *Lady with a Glove*, 1869, Louvre, a portrait of his wife).

CARON, Antoine (*c.* 1527, Beauvais—1599, Paris), French painter. Personal attendant to Catherine de Médicis, an erudite artist, and a fervid member of the Catholic League, he began his career at Fontainebleau under Primaticcio, from whom he derived the Mannerism of his style. He executed a series of drawings on the *Story of Artemis*, commissioned by the apothecary Nicolas Houel; these were later reproduced in tapestry (Paris, Mobilier National; 28 pieces). Caron painted subjects such as the *Triumph of Summer* (*c.* 1569; New York, Wildenstein & Co.), the *Triumph of Winter* (*c.* 1569; Paris, Coll. Jean Ehrmann), and the *Tournament of the Elephant* (*c.* 1590; Paris, Priv. Coll.). The figures in these works, and those that followed, were comments on contemporary events and reflect the taste for allegory of Jean Antoine de Baïf's academy of poetry and music, to which Caron probably belonged. His two versions of the *Massacre of the Triumvirs* (1562, Dijon, Museum; 1566, Paris, Louvre) were commentaries on the struggles of the Catholic triumvirate formed by the Guise family, and they foreshadow the massacre of St. Bartholomew's Day in 1572. The *Martyrdom of Sir Thomas More* (*c.* 1591; Blois, Museum) was conceived in a similar spirit. The *Astrologers Watching an Eclipse* (*c.* 1575; London, Coll. A. F. Blunt) recalls the eclipse of 1574 that coincided with the death of Charles IX. *Augustus and the Tiburtine Sibyl* (*c.* 1580; Louvre) employs a scene from Virgil to prophesy the ultimate triumph of the true faith. *Abraham Invested by Melchisedec* (*c.* 1598; Paris, Priv. Coll.), celebrates Pope Clement VII's absolution of Henri IV following the French king's abjuration of Protestantism.

CAROTO, Giovanni Francesco (*c.* 1480, Verona—*c.* 1555, Verona), Italian painter, the leading artist of his time at Verona. Caroto was very susceptible to a variety of influences and successively followed a number of models: Andrea Mantegna, whose pupil he was; Liberale da Verona (*c.* 1445–*c.* 1529); the Lombard artists (he worked for a long time in Lombardy); and finally Correggio. These tendencies, more or less assimilated with the Veronese coloristic tradition, resulted in a skillful but sometimes affected eclecticism. Caroto often revealed these qualities in his landscape paintings, such as those in S. Maria in Organo. There are a great many of his works at Verona, in the museum and in churches (*Madonna in Glory with Saints*, 1528; S. Fermo Maggiore). His brother Giovanni (*c.* 1488–*c.* 1566), a subtle and individual colorist, was active in Verona throughout his career, and is believed to have been Veronese's first master.

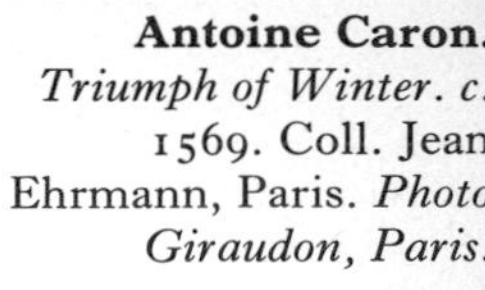

Antoine Caron. *Triumph of Winter. c.* 1569. Coll. Jean Ehrmann, Paris. *Photo Giraudon, Paris.*

CARPACCIO, Vittore (1450–55, Venice—1525–26, Venice), Italian painter whose contribution as painter-chronicler of Venice is outstanding. As a young man, he may have traveled to Dalmatia and the Near East. Thereafter it is easy to follow his career, because of his fondness for painting dated *cartellini* ("little cards") on his canvases. One of these appears in the *Arrival of St. Ursula in Cologne* (1490)—his earliest dated work and the first of a large series of paintings for the Scuola di S. Orsola, Venice, completed in 1498 (all now in Venice, Accademia). Commissions subsequently were regular: from 1502 to 1508 he executed a series of panels illustrating the *Lives of Sts. George, Jerome, and Tryphonius* for the Scuola di S. Giorgio degli Schiavoni; a cycle for the Scuola degli Albanesi (now dispersed in Milan, Venice, and Bergamo); large compositions such as *Pope Alexander III at St. Mark's* and the *Meeting between the Pope and the Doge in Ancona* for the Doges' Palace in 1507 (all destroyed in the fire of 1577); the St. Thomas altarpiece for S. Pietro in Murano (1507; now in Stuttgart, Staatsgalerie); the *Presentation in the Temple*, very Belliniesque in its apse setting (1510; Accademia); and in 1514 the *S. Vitale on Horseback*, the great altarpiece for S. Vitale, which is still in the church. His allegory of

Vittore Carpaccio. *Legend of St. Ursula: Dream of St. Ursula.* Accademia, Venice.

Vittore Carpaccio. *Two Courtesans. c.* 1510. Museo Correr, Venice.

the *Meditation on the Passion of Christ* (*c.* 1485; New York, Metropolitan Museum) and the *Preparations for the Entombment of Christ* (*c.* 1505; Berlin, Staatliche Museen) are considered quite early paintings, as indicated above, although neither is dated.

Carpaccio's stylistic outlook varied little throughout his career. In Venice, for the Scuola di S. Stefano, he painted the life of the saint (1510–20; pictures now dispersed in Berlin, Milan, Stuttgart, and Paris); *St. Roch and Donor* (1514; Bergamo, Galleria dell'Accademia Carrara), part of a polyptych for the church of S. Fosca, Venice; the *Martyrdom of the Ten Thousand* (1515; Accademia; much restored), originally in the church of S. Antonio di Castello, Venice (destroyed 1807). He also did work for provincial centers: the *Madonna Enthroned with Saints and Angels* for S. Francesco in Pirano (1518), a *St. Paul* for S. Domenico in Chioggia (1520), and, one of his last recorded works, organ shutters for the Cathedral at Capodistria. A document dated June 26, 1526, refers to Carpaccio as dead.

His early style was without any doubt influenced by Gentile Bellini, the ancestor of the *vedutisti* (painters of scenic local views). Carpaccio contributed something unique—Northern tapestry ensembles are perhaps a parallel—with his cycles for the Venetian *scuole* (confraternities or beneficent societies). The subject of the earliest of these cycles, the *Legend of St. Ursula* (1490 98) was popular both in northern and southern Europe. Carpaccio adheres closely to the text of the *Golden Legend* by Jacobus de Voragine.

Carpaccio was also interested in portraiture. Several contemporary faces appear in the procession of the *Martyrdom of the Ten Thousand* and in the groups of the *Betrothed Greeted by the Pope in Rome* (between 1492 and 1494). The same interest is observable in the panel known as the *Two Courtesans* (*c.* 1510; Museo Correr).

The sense of tonal color and of color harmonies that unifies the composition was clearly a lesson learned from Antonello da Messina and Giovanni Bellini. These influences are obvious in pictures with such traditional themes as the *Blood of the Redeemer* (1496; Udine, Museo Civico), the *Meditation on the Passion of Christ* and the *Sacra Conversazione* (*c.* 1500; Caen, Musée des Beaux-Arts).

The cycle in the Scuola di S. Giorgio degli Schiavoni consists of nine canvases illustrating the lives of the Dalmatian patron saints George, Tryphonius, and Jerome. Here too the story is taken from the *Golden Legend*, with, again, close attention to accurate and realistic detail: the celebrated scene known until recently as *St. Jerome in His Study*—the subject is in fact St. Augustine receiving the vision of St. Jerome, and the work is now called the *Vision of St. Augustine* (*c.* 1502)—is strikingly original in its precision and in the entirely Flemish intimacy of its Humanist interior.

CARPEAUX, Jean-Baptiste (1827, Valenciennes, Nord—1875, Courbevoie, Seine), French sculptor. In Paris he studied first with François Rude, then with François-Joseph Duret (1804–65), acquiring an excellent technique. In 1854 he was awarded the Prix de Rome and left for Italy. He was immediately enchanted by the Sistine Chapel of Michelangelo, whom he described as "thundering with character." The first piece he submitted to the Academy, *La Palombella* (1856; Paris, Musée du Petit-Palais), portrayed a delightful Trasteverine. Next came his *Little Fisherman with a Seashell* (1858; Paris, Louvre), inspired by Rude's *Fisherman* but endowed with a more nervous grace. His third was *Ugolino and His Children* (1860; Louvre), inspired by a passage in Dante's *Inferno*. It astonished the art lovers of Rome but in Paris it was very coldly received. Fortunately, the press gave it wide publicity, and Princess Mathilda, a cousin of Napoleon III, took Carpeaux under her wing. Hector Lefuel (1810–81), the architect in charge of work on the Louvre, commissioned him to do the central group on the new Pavillon de Flore.

Carpeaux's project (*Triumph of Flora,* 1863–66) involved him in distressing squabbles with Lefuel, for Carpeaux's spirited relief disturbed the harmony of the façades. Nevertheless, the work was generally admired for its power—"More alive than life itself," said the writer Théophile Gautier.

Next came two major works, the first being the statues of the *Four Parts of the World* for the fountain of the Observatoire (1867–72), on which four allegorical nymphs are grouped about the celestial sphere. Carpeaux's group symbolizing the *Dance*, on the façade of the Paris Opéra (1869; original in the Louvre), is his masterpiece.

CARR, Emily (1871, Victoria, British Columbia—1945, Victoria), Canadian painter. She studied first at the San Francisco School of Art (1889–*c.* 1895), then at the Westminster School of Art in London (*c.* 1899–1904), returning to Canada occasionally to teach painting and to paint the Indian villages of the British Columbia coast. During the years 1910–11 she was in Europe, studying at the Académie Colarossi in Paris, sketching in Brittany, and traveling in Sweden. After her return to Victoria, Carr held her first exhibition and began to paint in a

Jean-Baptiste Carpeaux. *Portrait of Charles Garnier.* Louvre, Paris.

Fauvist style. She experienced difficult times, and to support herself she made carpets and pottery with Indian designs. Encouraged by Mark Tobey and Lawren Harris (1885–1970), she began her most characteristic work in the late 1920s (*Blunden Harbor*, 1929; Ottawa, National Gallery of Canada). In the 1930s and 1940s, she evolved her style into a personal and powerful expression of nature, using spiraling forms and intense colors (*Rushing Sea of Undergrowth*, 1936; Vancouver, Art Gallery). Emily Carr wrote a number of autobiographical books, including *Growing Pains* (1946).

CARRÀ, Carlo (1881, Quargnento, Piedmont—1966, Milan), Italian Futurist painter. He borrowed from Cubism its structure and limited palette, and tried, at the same time, to insert into its austere construction the movements of crowds so dear to Futurist dynamism. When, in 1916, he made the acquaintance of Giorgio de Chirico, the originator of Pittura Metafisica, Carrà believed he had at last found his true vocation, to rediscover the magic of painting by means of the representation of the simplest objects. This magic was one of the effects of perspective and of the relationship between full and empty spaces in the composition of a picture. It was therefore through perspective that De Chirico and Carrà wanted to renew the miracle of the Renaissance artists. Carrà's paintings of this period, less known outside Italy than De Chirico's, are often more elaborate than those of his friend, to whom he obviously owes his first ideas. Notable among his paintings are the *Metaphysical Muse* and the *Enchanted Room* (both 1917; both Milan, Coll. Emilio Jesi). Carrà rejected everything that De Chirico borrowed from the French and the Germans, and took his inspiration from Giotto, though not without a certain heaviness.

CARRACCI, a famous family of Italian painters from Bologna who were active during the second half of the 16th century. Its leading members were:

LODOVICO (1555, Bologna—1619, Bologna), first cousin of the more noted Annibale Carracci and five years his senior. He grew to maturity in the late Mannerist atmosphere then prevailing in Bologna. At first, perhaps, he tended to play the part of the leader in the joint undertakings of the family, such as the frescoes in the Palazzo Fava (1584) and the foundation of the Accademia degli Incamminati (1585–86), both in Bologna, with which the Carracci imposed a new taste in that city for classically inspired painting. But his *Conversion of St. Paul* (1587–89; Bologna, Pinacoteca), with its dramatic violence and its investigation of the problems of light, his *Virgin Enthroned with Saints* (1588; Bologna, Pinacoteca), which recalls both Tintoretto and Veronese, and his *Preaching of St. John the Baptist* (1592; Bologna, Pinacoteca), rich in color contrasts, all show a definite leaning toward the brilliant palette and animated composition of the Venetian painters.

AGOSTINO (1557, Bologna—1602, Parma), cousin of Lodovico and elder brother of Annibale. It was Agostino who provided, with his *Communion of St. Jerome* (early 1590s; Bologna, Pinacoteca), the most complete and the most generally admired illustration of the classicistic ideals of the Accademia degli Incamminati. He was summoned to Rome when Annibale undertook the decoration of the Galleria in the Palazzo Farnese, but was unable to get along with his brother. The Farnese family attracted him to Parma, where he began a career that was prematurely interrupted by his death. Agostino's work is somewhat overshadowed by that of his brother Annibale and his cousin Lodovico, but his reputation, so long upheld by a large collection of prints, has benefited by the reappraisal of the Carracci family by art historians of the mid-20th century.

ANNIBALE (1560, Bologna—1609, Rome), by far the most important painter in the family, served his apprenticeship in Bologna together with his cousin Lodovico and his brother Agostino. The prevalence there of Late Mannerism explains Annibale's ready acceptance of the work of Correggio when he visited Parma (*c.* 1585), and of Venetian colorism and lighting effects, during a stay in Venice (1585–86). The *Charity of St. Roch* (1595; Dresden, Gemäldegalerie), with its vigorous structure and narrative eloquence, proves fully the mastery already attained by Annibale at the time of his arrival in Rome (1595). Cardinal Odoardo Farnese commissioned him to paint the so-called Camerino (*Story of Hercules and Ulysses*, 1595–97) in his palace there and then entrusted him with the decoration of the famous gallery. Annibale's decorative work in the Palazzo Farnese was of supreme importance in the history of European painting. His last works, *Vénus aux Amours* (Chantilly, Musée Condé) and the grandiose *Pietà with St. Mary Magdalene and St. Francis* (Paris, Louvre), emphasize the urge toward monumental power that informed all his work without, however, excluding the frankest of realism (the *Bean-Eater*; Rome, Galleria Colonna), nor the subtle analysis of landscape (*Sacrifice of Isaac*, Louvre; *Rest on the Flight into Egypt*, Princeton, N.J., Princeton University Museum). He invigorated Mannerist theories by a firm and robust Classicism during the same years that Caravaggio was turning toward a realistic appraisal of nature in order to reject Mannerism and create a fresh idiom.

Annibale Carracci. *Polyphemus and Acis.* 1595–97. Palazzo Farnese, Rome. *Photo Anderson-Giraudon.*

CARREÑO DE MIRANDA, Juan (1614, Avilés—1685, Madrid), Spanish painter. In 1623 he arrived in Madrid, where he studied drawing under Pedro de las Cuevas (1568–1635) and painting under Bartolomé Román (1596–1659). On showing exceptional talent, he was soon given important commissions in Madrid for the now-destroyed cloister of the Colegio de Doña María de Aragon, where he depicted the *Life of St. Augustine,* and for the Convento del Rosario. In 1646 he signed a *St. Anthony Preaching to the Fishes* for the nuns of the Caballero de Gracia (Barcelona province, Balaguer de Villanueva y Geltrú Museum); and in 1656 he

Benvenuto Cellini. *Danaë with Young Perseus*. Detail from Perseus with the Head of Medusa. 1545–54. Loggia dei Lanzi, Florence. *Photo Jeiter, Hadamar*.

painted another *St. Anthony* (Madrid, Coll. Joaquin Paya). Patronized by Velázquez, Carreño became painter to the king in 1669 and, two years later, Pintor de Cámara to Charles II. In 1674 he was entrusted by Queen Mariana with the arrangement of the paintings in the royal apartments of the Escorial. He showed great skill in fresco work, particularly on three occasions when he collaborated with Francisco Rizi (1608–85): at Madrid in the Alcázar's hall of mirrors under Velázquez' guidance (1659) and on the vault of S. Antonio de los Portugueses, and at Toledo Cathedral in the chapel of the Sagrario (1665–70; restored in 1788 by Mariano Salvador Maella, 1739–1819).

Carreño's art is clearly influenced by Velázquez. He chose models similar to those used by Velázquez when he painted the fool *Francisco Bazán* and the hideous dwarf *Eugenia Martínez Vallejo* (Madrid, Prado). He was Velázquez' very worthy successor in the portraits of *Doña Inés de Zuñiga, Countess of Monterrey* (1665?; Madrid, Museo Lázaro Galdiano); *Queen Mariana* (Prado; Madrid, Academia de San Fernando); and *Charles II* (*c.* 1673, San Francisco, Legion of Honor; other versions in Prado; Toledo, Casa del Greco; New York, Hispanic Society).

CARRIERA, Rosalba (1675, Venice—1757, Venice), Italian painter. She was introduced to miniature painting by Jean Stève (active later 17th century), a Frenchman who painted snuffboxes, and her earliest known portrait is a pastel of an unknown woman, which dates from 1700. In 1705 she was already a member of the Accademia di S. Luca in Rome. From 1708 she devoted herself entirely to the medium of pastel. All the members of fashionable society passed through her Venetian studio; Elector Augustus of Saxony was a keen admirer of her portraits, as a result of which many of her works are now in Dresden.

CARSTENS, Asmus Jakob (1754, St. Jürgen, Schleswig—1798, Rome), Danish Romantic-Classical painter. After a childhood and youth clouded by poverty, Carstens studied briefly in Copenhagen before visiting Berlin. In 1792 he went to Mantua and then to Rome, where he remained for the rest of his life. In 1795 Carstens exhibited his pictures at the Studio Buttoni in that city, and received favorable reviews from the critic Karl Ludwig Fernow, who later became his biographer. After Carstens' death, in 1798, Goethe bought part of his estate for the Weimar Collection.

Carstens took the subject matter of his paintings from Greek legends, the Greek pantheon, especially Hesiod's *Theogony*. He invariably set the action of his pictures against a bleak background, and his characters have relatively undifferentiated physiognomies. The body contours are extremely smooth, and no attempt has been made to introduce tonal values, the colors being purely local and arranged in a precise pattern with the object of producing strong contrasts. *The Heroes in Achilles' Tent* (1794; Weimar, Schlossmuseum) is a good example of this technique. The spirituality of Carstens' work, which is particularly evident in his *Night with its Children, Sleep and Death* (1795; Weimar, Schlossmuseum), sometimes enables us to forget his definition of art as the "portrayal of ideas."

CARUS, Karl Gustav (1789, Leipzig—1869, Dresden), German painter and theoretician. He was a highly gifted physician, who, after graduating in 1811 and accepting a post as university lecturer, was invited to join the staff of the Dresden Academy of Surgery as a gynecologist. Shortly afterward, in 1818, Carus published his *Manual of Zootomy*. He was a friend of Johann Wolfgang von Goethe, becoming one of his early biographers (*Goethe*, 1843). But Carus was also one of the leading art theorists of Romanticism, and his aesthetic writings (*Letters on Landscape Painting*, 1831) exerted a powerful and fruitful influence on contemporary painters, especially Caspar David Friedrich. He himself attended classes at the Leipzig Academy in his student days; he also took lessons with Friedrich August Tischbein (1750–1812) and taught himself to paint in oils. Examples of Carus's work include an *Alpine Landscape* (1822; Düsseldorf, Kunstmuseum); *Mountain Landscape* (Essen, Museum Folkwang); and the *Temple of Juno of Agrigentum* (Dortmund, Museum für Kunst und Kulturgeschichte).

CASORATI, Felice (1886, Novara, Piedmont—1963, Turin), Italian painter. He was originally a student of music and law at Padua. From 1907, the date of his first exhibition (at the Venice Biennale), until the 1920s, he participated in the activities of the Italian avant-garde. With Carlo Carrà, Romolo Romani (1884–1916), Luigi Russolo, and especially Alberto Martini (b. 1876), he was in the vanguard of the Symbolist movement in Italy. This movement, less literary than its French counterpart, was inspired both by the Viennese Secession and by the work of English engravers of Aubrey Beardsley's generation and was to pave the way for Futurism and Metaphysical Painting. In this connection, Casorati's paintings and engravings of the first two decades of the 20th century have a real historical interest.

CASSATT, Mary (1845, Pittsburgh, Pennsylvania—1926, Mesnil-Beaufresne, Oise), American painter, printmaker, and pastelist. Descended from a French family that had emigrated to America in the 17th century, and raised in an atmosphere of veneration for French cultural and artistic tradition, she lived in Europe from 1866, studying in the great museums of the Continent, and settled in Paris in 1872. That same year, she first exhibited in the Paris Salon, where her work attracted the attention of Degas, who introduced her to the Impressionists, with whom she exhibited several times, beginning in 1879 (the *Cup of Tea*, 1879; New York, Metropolitan Museum). Her portraits of mothers with children have delicacy and distinction and are done with remarkable technical skill, but they are also rather precious, and the repetition of subject is tiresome. Her best work was perhaps done after the great exhibition of Japanese prints held in Paris in 1890: the color print series of 1891, and paintings such as *Young Women Picking Fruit* (1891; Pittsburgh, Carnegie Institute), in which she emphasized line and pattern to great effect.

CASTAGNO, Andrea del. *See* **ANDREA DEL CASTAGNO.**

CASTIGLIONE, Giovanni Benedetto, *called* Il Grechetto (*c.* 1610, Genoa—1665, Mantua), Italian painter. According to one of his biographers, he was deeply influenced by Van Dyck, but it is obvious that the work of Bernardo Strozzi (1581–1644) also made an impact on him. From 1639 to 1661 he was in the service of Charles II of Nevers, duke of Mantua. The chronology of his works cannot be based on known dates and has to be worked out from a stylistic study, though his masterpiece, the *Crib* in the Church of S. Luca in Genoa, bears the date 1645. It is a typically Baroque composition, in which still life elements are less important than in his other works, where they are usually treated with more emphasis than the subject itself, as for instance in *Christ Driving the Moneylenders from the Temple* (Paris, Louvre), one of his best pictures. Castiglione presented all his subjects in the same way, whether they were religious, like *Abraham's Journey* (Genoa, Palazzo Rosso); mythological, like the *Faun* (Rome, Galleria Nazionale d'Arte Antica); or pastoral.

CATLIN, George (1796, Wilkes-Barre, Pennsylvania—1872, Jersey City), American painter who has left an invaluable record of America's Indians as they appeared in the early frontier days. He began as a portrait painter, but in 1822—stimulated by Charles Wilson Peale's portraits of Indians, and the experience of seeing an actual delegation of prairie chiefs returning to Philadelphia from Washington, D.C.—he became determined to record these people before their heritage disappeared. Catlin traveled West both as an explorer and a painter, and went along on the expedition of General William Clark, who negotiated treaties with the Indians. By 1837 the diligent painter had amassed enough work (45 tribes were depicted in all, in a meticulously realistic yet highly romanticized style) to hold an extremely popular exhibition of his Indian subjects in New York's Clinton Hall. Subsequent to this success, he hired exhibition halls in Philadelphia, Baltimore, and Washington, D.C. In 1839 Catlin left for England, to tour the Continent with his "Gallery of Indians." In time, however, he encountered failures and even had trouble selling the collection. It was offered to the Smithsonian Institution in 1846, but was not accepted until 1879 (it is now housed in the Smithsonian's United States National Museum).

CAVALLINI, Pietro (13th–14th century), Italian painter. Giorgio Vasari calls him "a Roman painter," but we have no proof that he was born in Rome. The dates of his birth and death are also uncertain. We only know that he died very old, about the middle of the 14th century. His first documented work,a mosaic (*Life of the Virgin*) in Rome's S. Maria in Trastevere, dated 1291, shows the masterful touch of a mature artist.

Around 1293 Cavallini decorated the church of S. Cecilia in Trastevere with frescoes of which only a fragment of the *Last Judgment* is extant. These paintings, without backgrounds but with large, empty surfaces that convey a sense of space, have, like the mosaics of S. Maria in Trastevere, a classical majesty. Equally remarkable are the brightness of the colors, the wide range of tones, and the use of shading, which gives modeling to the faces. In 1308 Charles of Anjou called Cavallini to Naples. Back in Rome, he worked at S. Paolo fuori le Mura (*c.* 1315), where he made the mosaics on the façade (now replaced). A year later, Cavallini returned to Naples. Works attributed to him or to his school—for he had many pupils—are the fresco on the tomb of Cardinal Matteo d'Acquasparta (d. 1302) in S. Maria in Aracoeli, Rome, and the frescoes in S. Maria Donnaregina, Naples (1316–20).

CELLINI, Benvenuto (1500, Florence—1571, Florence), celebrated Italian goldsmith, sculptor, and writer. To escape the consequences of a brawl, Cellini fled to Rome, where he worked until Charles V sacked the city in 1527. During this terrible episode he took part in the defense of Rome, and claimed to have fired the shot that killed one of the leaders of the imperial forces, the constable of Bourbon. After the Sack he worked in Mantua and Florence, from where he fled during the siege of 1529 to return to Rome and the patronage of Pope Clement VII, for whom he made a great morse (now lost) for the papal cope and dies for a new coinage, which established his reputation. In 1537 he went to France to work for Francis I; disappointed in the patronage he received, he returned to Rome, only to be imprisoned on an accusation of stealing papal jewels during the Sack. Eventually he was released through the intervention of the French ambassador, and he returned to France. The great work of this period (1540–45) was the famous gold saltcellar, finished in 1543 (Vienna, Kunsthistorisches Museum); among other works, now mostly lost, he also made the bronze model for the bas-relief of the *Nymph of Fontainebleau* (1545; Paris, Louvre).

His first works in free-standing sculpture were busts, such as *Cosimo I de' Medici* (1546–47; Florence, Bargello). In 1545 he began the *Perseus with the Head of Medusa*, unveiled in Florence's Loggia dei Lanzi (where it still is) in 1554. His last 20 years are a record of bitter quarrels with the sculptor Bartolomeo Bandinelli, and the writing of treatises on goldsmithing and sculpture and of his great *Autobiography*.

Benvenuto Cellini. *Ganymede*. Museo del Bargello, Florence. *Photo Boudot-Lamotte, Paris.*

CELTIC ART. In the strictest sense of the term, Celtic art has no restrictive geographical boundaries, since the Celts never formed a unified, politically organized nation. They were a barbaric people sharing a common language, economy, as well as a material and social culture. Their civilization originated in the first centuries of the last millennium B.C. in west-central Europe, and it eventually stretched from Ireland

Celtic Art. Ritual chariot. 1st century B.C. Musée des Antiquités Nationales, St-Germain-en-Laye.

Celtic Art. Figure of a god, from Bouray. 3rd–1st century B.C. Musée des Antiquités Nationales, St-Germain-en-Laye. *Photo Belzeaux-Zodiaque.*

and western Spain to Anatolia, and from northern Germany to central Italy. During the second Iron Age, in the 5th century B.C., there was a vast reorganization of wealth and power among the Continental Celts, and this gave rise to new artistic achievements. The new trends are classified as the La Tène art style, or the La Tène culture (lasting until the 1st century B.C.), after the site in Switzerland where many objects have been found.

Celtic art inherited from the preceding Hallstatt period (*c.* 700–500 B.C.) the accomplished metalwork techniques of engraving, openwork, and *repoussé*, and also a range of abstract geometric and rectilinear motifs. But more important than this inheritance was the transformation it underwent in the art of the La Tène Celts. Although the Hallstatt peoples had contacts with Greek and Italian works, it was not until the Celtic La Tène art that these works became a potent source of artistic inspiration. The earliest such wave of foreign influence dates back to the mid-6th century B.C. and was brought with the wine trade from the peoples of the Greek colony of Massilia (Marseilles) and the Etruscans to the Celts of Burgundy, the Middle Rhine, and the Upper Danube, the area that first produced the fine La Tène art. Evidence for this exchange has been discovered in the Rhodian bronze wine jugs found in graves at Kappel-am-Rhein, Baden; Greek black-figured drinking cups from Heuneberg, Camp de Château in the Jura, and Mont Lassois in Côte-d'Or; and the remains of brick fortifications excavated at Heuneberg, showing clearly Mediterranean construction methods. The second wave of influence was stylistically more important. About 500 B.C. the Scythians invaded central Europe from central Asia and, although they were soon driven back beyond the Dnieper, their decorative styles remained in the art of the Celts. They were skilled metalworkers, and the spiraling, interwoven, curving, and countercurving linear patterns generally considered characteristically Celtic, as well as stylized animal motifs, can be traced to central Asiatic art: the pair of confronted bulls' heads terminating the magnificent torque, or neck ornament found at Trichtingen (Stuttgart, Landesmuseum) is an Achaemenid motif.

The essential qualities of Celtic art are unmistakable. The spiral, curve, and countercurve were dominant motifs. Designs were sometimes in relief, otherwise incised deeply or lightly engraved. Human, animal, and plant forms were absorbed into two-dimensional abstract patterns, and their elements—the parts of an animal's body or the features of the human face—treated in purely graphic terms, and the whole was transformed into an elaborate arrangement of flowing curves and geometric pattern. The Greek palmette and other Classical motifs were used, but changed to conform with Celtic design. The carved stone pillar from Pfalzfeld (Bonn, Rheinisches Landesmuseum), and the jewelry from the graves of the Marne and those at Reinheim in the Saarland, offer excellent examples of the style.

CERANO, Giovan Battista Crespi, *called* (*c.* 1575/76, Cerano—1632, Milan), Italian painter of the Lombard School. He was an architect, sculptor, and engraver, as well as one of the leading Milanese painters of his time. Cerano went to Rome (1585–95), where he studied the works of Federico Barocci, Gaudenzio Ferrari, and the Tuscan Mannerists, and then settled in Milan, which was at that time the center of artistic currents from Venice, and open to the influence of Florentine, Emilian, and northern Mannerism. In 1621 Cerano was appointed director of the art academy established by Cardinal Federico Borromeo, who had a deep interest in the artistic life of Milan. In 1629 he was put in charge of the statuary of Milan Cathedral, and his *modelli* (Milan, Museo del Duomo di Milano) for the sculptures over the façade doors show a skillful management of confined space. Cerano executed a number of commissions for churches in the region: four large pictures illustrating the life of S. Carlo Borromeo for the duomo, Milan (1602), the *Baptism of St. Augustine* for S. Marco, Milan (1618), and the *Mass of St. Gregory* for S. Vittore, Varese (1615–17), one of his most significant works and one that, in its audacious composition, is reminiscent of some of Tintoretto's paintings.

CERUTI, Giacomo (active 1724–38), Italian painter. He was probably born at the end of the 17th century, perhaps in Brescia, where he seems to have spent most of his life. Besides the portraits (*Portrait of a Man*; Milan, Brera) and genre scenes, in which he was at his best, Ceruti painted mediocre religious compositions. His nickname, "Il Pitocchetto," probably refers to his practice of painting scenes of low life, only one of which is dated: *The Beggar* (1724; Bergamo, Coll. Bassi-Rattgeb). In 1728 he painted 15 symbolic portraits for the Broletto (the town hall of Brescia), commissioned by the podestà and vice-captain of that town. Ceruti painted the usual subjects of genre painting as well as beggars, artisans, and representations of the worst physical deformities in portrayals of low life that seem strangely modern by their restrained and straightforward treatment. His rustic subjects, which look like a new version of some of Caravaggio's themes, and revive the great European current of realism in art, have rightly been rescued from oblivion by modern art critics who consider them his most original works.

CESAR, César Baldaccini, *called* (b. 1921, Marseilles), French sculptor. He studied at the École des Beaux-Arts in Marseilles and then in Paris, where he learned modeling, wood carving, and stone carving. In 1952, however, he found in metal and scrap metal a means of creating an image of present-day alienations and of expressing more fully the tragic force of life in our age. The use of detritus in sculpture has become commonplace; the emotional effect of such a work depends largely on the extent to which the found objects retain their identity. They remain intact in the assemblages of Richard Stankiewicz, in which each found object communicates its separate associations to the work as a whole. Other sculptors, such as Louise Nevelson and Robert Muller, integrate the objects into the whole, almost obliterating their identity in the process of welding them together. César belongs to this second group. His integration of familiar scrap-iron objects into an unfamiliar form has a surrealistic effect, either sinister—a nightmare creation of the machine age (*Grand Duchess*, 1955)—or dignified and almost noble (*Man of St. Denis*; London, Tate Gallery).

CESARI, Giuseppe. *See* **ARPINO,** Giuseppe Cesari.

CEYLON, ART OF. *See* **SINGHALESE ART.**

CÉZANNE, Paul (1839, Aix-en-Provence—1906, Aix-en-Provence), French painter, the most outstanding innovator of the 19th century. Cézanne—who came from a middle-class banking family—enrolled at the law faculty in Aix-en-Provence in 1859. However, he soon showed far more interest in drawing than in his law studies and simultaneously began to take courses at the School of Design in Aix. Then, with the support of his mother and one of his sisters, he managed to overcome his father's objections to an artistic career, and went to Paris in 1861. There he studied at the Académie Suisse and frequented the Louvre, paying particular attention to Caravaggio and Velázquez. He ran into Émile Zola, and made the acquaintance of Armand Guillaumin, who introduced him to Camille Pissarro. The hubbub of the big city did not suit Cézanne, however, and he returned to Aix, discouraged to the point of accepting a job in his father's bank. He concurrently painted a number of portraits and decorated the walls of the Jas de Bouffan, an estate his parents had bought in 1859.

Cézanne returned to Paris in November 1862 and began to frequent the Impressionists. Nevertheless, he much preferred the work of Courbet and Delacroix, as he felt himself to be a strongly sensual romantic; he advocated painting, as he said, "with guts." In the evenings, he would be seen at the Café Guerbois in Paris, which served as a meeting place for Zola, the novelist Léon Cladel, the critic Louis Edmond Duranty, Renoir, Manet, and Sisley, and would then disappear for days and weeks at a time. In 1869 he met Marie-Hortense Fiquet, a young model, who followed him to L'Estaque in 1870, when he fled to evade the mobilization order.

When the Franco-Prussian war was over, less than a year later, Cézanne returned once more to Paris. He was thirty-two years old, and had not yet produced anything of particular interest, although his work clearly demonstrated a revolt against academic strictures; he had not begun to lay the groundwork for the revolutionary experiments of his maturity. The early *Temptation of St. Anthony* (1867–69; St-Germain-en-Laye, Coll. Alphonse Kahn), *Nègre Scipion* (1866–68; São Paulo, Museu de Arte Moderna), and *A Modern Olympia* (1870; Paris, Louvre) contributed little to his future development. In 1872 Marie-Hortense Fiquet gave birth to a son, who was named after his father, Cézanne now settled for two years in Auvers-sur-Oise, where he worked with Guillaumin and Pissarro, and began to change his art. However, *House of the Hanged Man* (1873; Paris, Musée de l'Impressionnisme), *Dr. Gachet's House* (1873; Basel, Kunstmuseum), and *Landscape in Auvers*, which he exhibited in 1874 in the first Impressionist Salon, received their share of gibes and sarcasm. Cézanne painted a few more Impressionist canvases and then, in 1876, his true personality began to emerge. The light brushstrokes, division of tones, and experiments with effects of light disappeared, and he began to accentuate volume, to compose through manipulation of mass, and to perfect the unity of his compositions. In 1877 he took part in the third Impressionist exhibition, but with no more success than in 1874. He then abandoned the idea of the group show and spent the remainder of his life in solitude. He retired to Aix and remained in Provence, leaving only on a few indispensable trips to Paris, or to visit Renoir at La Roche-Guyon in 1883, or Victor Chocquet, an admirer, at Hattenville in 1886.

Cézanne married Marie-Hortense Fiquet in 1886, and two years later his father died, leaving him a handsome heritage. He had quarreled with Zola, Monet, and a number of other artists and, although he maintained contact with Émile Bernard, Gauguin, and Van Gogh, their relationships were neither cordial nor trusting. The first attacks of diabetes, which followed upon a series of public failures, accentuated his hypochondria. In 1894 the government rejected the Caillebotte estate, which included a number of Cézanne's paintings, because it contained so many Impressionist and Postimpressionist works. A year later the Parisian art dealer Ambroise Vollard organized Cézanne's first one-man show. Although these events served to enhance Cézanne's reputation among younger artists, they revived the academicians' hostility toward him.

No period of his work, however, proved more fruitful and assured than the decade 1885–95. These were the years in which he produced the series of portraits of Madame Cézanne, the *Blue Vase* (1883–87; Louvre), *Boy in the Red Waistcoat* (1890–95; one version in Merion, Pa., Barnes Foundation), *Mardi Gras* (1888; Moscow, State Museum of Modern Western Art), the *Card Players* (1890–92; versions in Louvre; Courtauld Institute, London; Barnes Foundation), and the many *Baigneurs* and *Baigneuses*, which he treated as geometrical problems. L'Estaque, the Jas de Bouffan, Gardanne, and the Montagne Ste-Victoire, near Aix, served as inspiration for many landscapes.

As the years passed Cézanne's lyricism intensified. In his paint-

Paul Cézanne. *House of the Hanged Man.* 1873. Musée de l'Impressionnisme, Paris. *Photo Giraudon, Paris.*

Paul Cézanne. *Card Players. c.* 1890–92. Coll. Pellerin, Paris. *Photo Bulloz.*

ings and admirable watercolors of Château-Noir and the Montagne Ste-Victoire, particularly the works done after 1900, he expressed himself wholly through the deployment of planes and colors. In 1905, after seven years of work on it, he completed the *Grandes Baigneuses* (Philadelphia, Museum of Art) in the studio he had built on the Chemin des Lauves in Aix.

He attempted to build a world of a permanence and universality that would be ensured by form, color, and structure—"to make Impressionism into something solid and durable, like the art in the museums." From this art of the museums, which he so venerated, he nevertheless unhesitatingly eliminated chiaroscuro, modeling, transitional color values, and traditional perspective. He treated his figures like still lifes, and structured the sky, sea, earth, and vegetation of his landscapes as firmly as rocks and houses. In order to suggest depth on the flat, two-dimensional canvas surface, Cézanne shifted the angles of vision, raised the horizon line when necessary, and cut horizontals with verticals and oblique lines. Once the feeling of space had been thus obtained, the problem became one of rendering objects in the light that colored them, with all its atmospheric modifications. Rejecting the conventions then prevalent, Cézanne made a discovery that was to have incalculable consequences. For natural light, with its variations traditionally rendered through degrees of light and shade, he substituted an invented light expressed through the use of pure color. Shadow was eliminated and modeling was replaced by the juxtaposition of color tones; values were rendered through chromatic relationships. This conception led Cézanne to a completely new interpretation of form and line, for, as he himself said, "When color is at its richest, form attains its plenitude." The object is then defined by an autonomous ensemble of lines and colors, articulated planes and harmonies, contrasts of warm and cool tones, and volumes whose density stimulates the sense of touch.

Cézanne thereby made of the painting an autonomous object, a complete and coherent world, a specifically plastic creation that owed nothing to literature, anecdote, psychology, or symbol. Consequently, he is at the source of almost every innovating movement of the 20th century. He prepared the way for the Fauves and was the first of the Cubists; his late work influenced nonfigurative painting. Every modern artist is indebted to him, and if painters today seem to run with such speed, it was Cézanne who taught them to walk.

CHABAUD, Auguste Élisée (1882, Nîmes—1955, Graveson, Bouches-du-Rhône), French artist, one of the best representatives of modern Provençal painting. In his early period (1902–12) he followed in the wake of the painters of the post-Impressionists by his choice of themes (the circus, *café-concert*, dancing, night life); but stylistically he adhered to Fauvism, both in its early stages and in the later flowering of the movement. Indeed Chabaud must be recognized as one of the initiators of Fauvism. For several years he divided his time between Paris and Graveson, his family home, where he took up permanent residence in 1912, there renewing the fine Provençal tradition of such painters of light as Paul Guigou in vigorous landscapes still richly Fauvist in their vehemence but distinguished by a genuinely classical note. His remarkable *Moulin de la Galette* (1905) is in the Musée National d'Art Moderne, Paris.

CHADWICK, Lynn (b. 1914, London), English sculptor. He trained as an architect. After World War II he specialized in designing, and his first sculptures were mobiles, originating as decorations for display stands. *Idiomorphic Beast* (1953) was his first solid sculpture and one of the most powerful and original works by the postwar generation of artists in England. His technique of welding an armature of straight rods into tetrahedral cages and filling them with a compound of gypsum and iron filings determined the faceted, geometric character of all his series: the evocative *Seasons* (1955; London, Arts Council of Great Britain) and *Moon of Habana* (1957; Paris, Galerie Cordier); the disquieting *Maquette for Two Winged Figures* (1956); and the more contemplative *Pyramids* (1962; Coll. artist) and *Inner Eye* (1962; New York, Museum of Modern Art). In 1956 Chadwick was awarded the International Sculpture Prize at the Venice Biennale.

CHAGALL, Marc (b. 1887, Vitebsk, Russia), French painter of Russian Jewish origin. After an apprenticeship with the painter Pen, an honest portraitist of the notables of the town, Chagall went to St. Petersburg in 1907, where he was admitted to the Imperial School of Fine Arts. But the teaching there was poor, and the atmosphere depressing and dreary when compared with the school newly founded by Léon Bakst, the theatrical designer. Chagall, admitted to this studio, found the teaching there a revelation. When he returned to Vitebsk, he had already developed a style of his own—still somber and heavy, but with flashes of light. He used it in scenes that are beyond the realm of direct observation and that represent the beginnings of an effort toward synthesis. Chagall returned to St. Petersburg and gained the patronage and friendship of a deputy of the duma, who offered him a small grant enabling him to go to Paris.

Upon his arrival in Paris in 1910, Chagall became an intimate of the poets Blaise Cendrars, Max Jacob, and Guillaume Apollinaire, and of the painters Roger de La Fresnaye, Robert Delaunay, and Amedeo Modigliani. This was a highly productive period for the artist; it was in Paris—to use his own expression—that he washed his eyes. His ideas and his instinct for geometrical composition were confirmed by the experiments he saw going on all about him. But whereas the Cubists sought to interpret everyday objects, such as

Marc Chagall. *Portrait of Bella in Green.* 1934–35. Stedelijk Museum, Amsterdam.

Marc Chagall. *Blue Violinist.* 1947. Coll. Reverend and Mrs. James McLane, Los Angeles.

a pipe or a guitar, in their very essence, Chagall applied this methodical organization to a description of the elements of reality as seen through his imagination or his memory. Since, for him, reality always contained projections into the past and the future, his work unfolds on several spatial planes, and the laws of gravity do not apply to his people and objects. Each detail is fully autonomous and contains within itself every potential for beauty and grace. Chagall's great canvases of this period—*I and the Village* (1911; New York, Museum of Modern Art), *To Russia, Donkeys, and Others* (1911; Paris, Musée National d'Art Moderne), *Self-Portrait with Seven Fingers* (1911; Amsterdam, Stedelijk Museum), *Drinking Soldier* (1912; New York, Solomon R. Guggenheim Museum), and *Pregnant Woman* (1912–13; Stedelijk Museum)—all reveal a pure vision of a unique inner world, which the artist succeeds in transmitting without distortion or weakening, giving it an external existence, beyond the realm of time.

Chagall had just returned to Russia when World War I broke out. Drafted into a camouflage unit, he remained in St. Petersburg, and in 1915 married Bella Rosenfeld. During this period he acquired a heightened awareness of the tragic reality of his inner world. Hitherto, he had expressed its sadness, its horror, and its poetry with vehemence, by means of intense lines and colors. Now he perceived it differently, painting it in delicate pinks, acid greens, and transparent blues.

When the Russian Revolution came, Chagall was appointed commissar for the fine arts in the district of Vitebsk by Lunacharsky, whom he had known when the latter was an exile in Paris in 1912. The new regime encouraged the most advanced forms of modern art. Chagall founded an academy, in which he welcomed the participation of all art movements. He invited Casimir Malevich to teach there, but after a disagreement with Malevich, who was not so liberal, Chagall resigned. In Moscow he joined Alexis Granowsky, director of the Yiddish Theater, who commissioned him to paint murals for the auditorium and foyer of the theater. When he was asked also to design the scenery and costumes (notably for Sholem Aleichem's *Agents* and Nikolai Gogol's *The Marriage*), he helped with the production and gave the characters themselves a new dimension, transforming them into a gallery of representative types.

In 1922 Chagall decided to return to France. It was then that the French art dealer Ambroise Vollard, having noticed one of his paintings, suggested that he do some illustrating. Selecting Gogol's novel *Dead Souls*, Chagall made 96 etchings (not published until 1949). In 1926 he illustrated the *Fables* of La Fontaine with 100 etchings (published in 1952).

In 1941 Chagall decided to go to the United States, at the invitation of the Museum of Modern Art in New York. Tragically alert to all that was happening in Europe, he found powerful and renewed inspiration in the misfortunes of his race and the threats to human liberty. In 1944 the artist's wife Bella died, and moving evocations of the past and future began to appear in his work. He completed the great composition entitled *Around Her* (Paris, Musée National d'Art Moderne), which he had begun in 1937, and which became a synthesis of all his favorite themes, grouped around the evocation of Bella.

Chagall returned to France permanently in 1947 and settled in Vence in 1949. Late in his career, as his importance grew, Chagall concentrated on large-scale projects involving architectural decoration. These included his designs for the monumental group of twelve stained-glass windows (symbolizing the twelve tribes of Israel) for the synagogue of the new Hadassah Medical Center in Jerusalem, which were put into position in 1962; the new ceiling of the Paris Opera (unveiled 1964); and murals for the façade of the new Metropolitan Opera at Lincoln Center in New York (1966).

CHAMBERLAIN, John (b. 1927, Rochester, Indiana), American sculptor. Chamberlain was trained in Chicago. His early sculpture, influenced by David Smith, was linear and open, constructed largely from iron pipes; later, developing the possibilities of twisted metal sheets, he emerged as an important sculptor in the late 1950s and early 1960s with assemblages made from the discarded metal of wrecked automobiles (*Johnnybird*, 1959). Since they revive the concept of colored sculpture, his assemblages are related to the action painting of Willem de Kooning in their bold and slashing color, which in Chamberlain's case is inherent in the material but intensified by a coating of lacquer. The grand scale and the suggestions of violence and energy in his work also could be compared with action painting, but Chamberlain's approach differs in its dependence for materials on the environment, specifically the environment of the discarded and the damaged.

CHAMBERS, Sir William (1723, Gothenburg, Sweden—1796, London), English architect. Long years of study and extensive travel prepared William Chambers for the position of official architect to the English court, which he occupied toward the end of the 18th century. In Paris, about 1750, he probably made the acquaintance of Jacques-Germain Soufflot, and became the friend of the architects Joseph Peyre and Richard Mique (1728–94), who worked with him under Jacques-François Blondel. After spending five years in Italy, Chambers returned to England, where his reputation was established by his book *Designs of Chinese Buildings* (1757) and his important *Treatise on Civil Architecture* (1759). From 1760 to 1773 he built private houses such as Duntish Court, Dorset (after 1760), Charlemont House, Dublin (1763), and in London, Albany House, Piccadilly (1771–73), and Carrington House, Whitehall (1765; demolished 1886), the last with a staircase in imitation of Genoese examples by Bartolomeo

Sir William Chambers. Pagoda in Kew Gardens, Surrey. 1761. *Photo Kersting, London.*

Bianco (before 1590–1657), and Gregorio Petondi. But the most curious of Chambers' constructions at this period of his career were those he built for the Dowager Princess of Wales in Kew Gardens: the Roman arch, the pagoda, and various temples and pavilions, which, in engravings (published 1763), had an influence on French art. After the death of the Palladian architect Henry Flitcroft (1697–1769), Chambers became Comptroller of His Majesty's Works and was entrusted with the construction of Somerset House, one of the largest buildings in England. This great structure is less remarkable for its general composition than for the quality of its decoration, which was the expression of wide learning and a cultivated eclecticism.

Promoted in 1782 to Surveyor-General (a ministerial appointment that no architect had occupied since the time of Sir Christopher Wren), invested with the Swedish Order of the Polar Star, and knighted by George III, Chambers used his favorable social position to promote the founding of the Royal Academy of Arts.

Martin Chambiges (?). Tower of St-Jacques, belfry of the church (destroyed) of St-Jacques-de-la-Boucherie, Paris. *Photo Jean Roubier, Paris.*

CHAMBIGES, family of French architects and master masons active throughout the 16th century. Its leading members were:

MARTIN (late 15th century, Paris—1532, Beauvais), master builder of the city of Paris. In 1489 he provided plans for the transept of Sens Cathedral, on which he began work in 1490. He is also thought to have begun the cathedral's north porch. He designed the façade of Troyes Cathedral, on which he worked until 1516, when he left the construction in the charge of his son-in-law, Jean de Soissons (d. 1531), who officially succeeded him in 1518. He also provided plans for the transept of Beauvais Cathedral, which were executed by Jean Wast (d. 1524). Lastly, he was present in Senlis in 1504 and 1515, and furnished plans for the façade of the cathedral transept, carried out by his son Pierre. Martin is also credited with the tower of St-Jacques-de-la-Boucherie in Paris, the façade of St. Pierre at Senlis (1515), and the porches of the churches at Marissel and Rumilly-les-Vaudes.

PIERRE I (d. 1544, Paris), son of Martin. After assisting his father at Troyes and Beauvais (1511–18), he worked independently at Chantilly (1527) for Anne de Montmorency; at Fontainebleau under Gilles Le Breton (d. 1552); and in 1539–42 at the château and hunting lodge (La Muette) at St-Germain-en-Laye. He was a master builder of the city of Paris and from 1534 to 1544 took part in the building of the Hôtel de Ville under the direction of Domenico Boccador. He also worked as master builder to the king at the bailliage of Senlis, where he completed the work begun by his father. He is credited with the château of Challuau, near Moret, which François I had built for the duchess of Étampes.

PIERRE II (*c.* 1545–1616), son of Pierre I. He took part in the preparatory work on the Pont-Neuf, Paris. He was also connected with the Louvre, where his role seems to have been merely that of a contractor. He was a sworn expert to the king and was frequently consulted on projects.

CHAMPAIGNE, Philippe de (1602, Brussels—1674, Paris), painter of Flemish origin who became a naturalized Frenchman. A pupil of Jacques Foucquières (1580/90–1659), he was brought to Paris by his master, who was working at the Luxembourg Palace. Champaigne, in collaboration with the young Nicolas Poussin, did some painting there himself, under the direction of Nicolas Duchesne, whose position as painter to the Queen Mother Marie de Médicis he acquired in 1628, when he married Duchesne's daughter.

Champaigne became the favorite painter of Cardinal Richelieu, who valued his piety as much as his talent, and he painted canvases for the gallery in the Palais Royal, as well as a series of portraits of great men. The most famous of these, *Gaston de Foix* (1635; Versailles, Museum), is based on the design by Giorgione. He came to enjoy the confidence of Louis XIII, who commissioned several historical pieces, including the *Reception of the Duc de Longueville into the Order of the St-Esprit* (1634; Toulouse) and the *Vow of Louis XIII* (1638; Caen, Museum), in which the king is seen dedicating his kingdom to the virgin. Portraiture was his favorite genre, in which his honesty, psychological insight, and Flemish palette were seen to full advantage. His most famous achievement is his full-

Philippe de Champaigne. *Omer Talon.* Detail. 1649. Samuel H. Kress Coll. National Gallery of Art, Washington, D.C.

length portrait of *Cardinal Richelieu* (1635; Paris, Louvre), which reveals the influence of Rubens and Van Dyck.

Champaigne was appointed official court portraitist, and all the celebrities of the day—Mazarin, Turenne, Mansart, Perrault—posed for him; the women who wished to be flattered on canvas stayed away. Soon after his wife's death, he became involved with the Jansenists at Port Royal (1643); this experience profoundly influenced his art. He became the community's regular painter, reaching the summit of his art in portraits of the Jansenists. A great personal blessing prompted him to paint a masterpiece: his daughter, who had been paralyzed since 1660, was healed miraculously on the day of Epiphany, 1662, after a novena begun the preceding Christmas; Champaigne then painted his famous ex-voto, *Mère Agnès and Sœur Catherine de Ste-Suzanne Praying* (1662; Louvre).

JEAN-BAPTISTE (1631, Brussels—1681, Paris), nephew of Philippe, was also Flemish born. History painter and portraitist, he worked in a vein similar to that of his uncle, whose Jansenist beliefs he shared. He was naturalized as a French citizen in 1655, and was received into the Academy in 1663. As a decorator, he probably worked in the apartments at Versailles, notably in the Salon de Mercure.

CHANDLER, Winthrop (1747, Woodstock, Connecticut—1790, Woodstock), American painter. Chandler, who spent his entire life in rural northeastern Connecticut, except for a brief stay in neighboring Worcester, Massachusetts, painted some of the earliest (1769) examples of still life done in America before the Revolution. His earliest landscapes were used as interior decoration—many were set into mantelpieces—and thus emphasize his grounding in the crafts rather than the fine arts. After 1775 he referred to himself as a limner, in this way marking himself as a humble though specialized Colonial artist. (He actually made his living as a housepainter.)

Chandler's portraits, his most important work, are vigorously designed, although they are as obviously patterned as the decorative arts from which his technical training was derived. He broaches on an understanding of three dimensions only in his most ambitious paintings. One of these, *Mrs. Ebenezer Devotion* (1770; Brookline, Mass., Historical Society), an incisive character study, falls short of achieving an effectively pictorial sense of atmosphere or the placement of forms in natural space, but its compositional elements—curtains and clothing—are pleasingly articulated and colored. At the same time these individual details are subordinate to Chandler's strong sense of over-all design.

CHANTREY, Sir Francis Legatt (1781, Norton, Derby—1841, London), English sculptor. The son of a carpenter, Chantrey studied carving in Sheffield, although his small local reputation was made as a portrait painter. After moving to London, where he began studying at the Royal Academy in 1802, he continued for a while as a portrait painter, but from 1807 devoted nearly all his time to sculpture, and in particular to the portrait busts with which he made both fame and fortune. He became a Royal Academician in 1818, and was knighted by William IV in 1835. His style was based on Neo-classical principles but was always more circumstantial in detail, and in his finest busts—such as that of Sir Walter Scott at Abbotsford, Scotland—he combined an acute observation of flesh and clothing with a strong sense of dignity and decorum.

Jean-Baptiste Chardin. *Still Life with Turkey Hen.* Museum of Fine Arts, Budapest.

CHARDIN, Jean-Baptiste Siméon (1699, Paris—1779, Paris), French master of the art of still-life painting. He began working in his father's carpenter workshop but was rescued by Noël-Nicolas Coypel, who, following the practice of using assistants to paint accessories in portraits, asked Chardin to paint a gun as realistically as possible. His employer was so satisfied that he recommended him to Jean-Baptiste Van Loo, who needed collaborators for the restoration of the Grande Galerie at Fontainebleau. A surgeon who was a friend of his father asked him to paint a sign for his shop. Instead of painting a shaving dish and lancets, the traditional emblems of the profession, it occurred to Chardin to execute a street scene showing the surgeon caring for a wounded duelist lying on his doorstep. The painting attracted the attention of crowds and established the artist's reputation.

Chardin exhibited for the first time in 1728, at the Exposition de la Jeunesse, held in the Place Dauphine for just one morning each year, on Corpus Christi Day. His entries were the *Rayfish* and *Buffet* (both Paris, Louvre), which were so successful that he was admitted to the Académie Royale two months later. In 1731 Chardin married. He submitted 16 paintings to the Exposition of 1734; since he worked slowly and with difficulty, we may assume that these had been painted over a long period of time. Now a past master of still life, he wanted to try his hand at another genre and turned to subjects "in the taste of Teniers," as the *Mercure de France* put it. The results included his *Lady Sealing a Letter* (1733; Berlin, Staatliche Museen), *Washerwoman* (*c.* 1733; Stockholm, Nationalmuseum), and *House of Cards* (1734–35; Louvre), all scenes of middle-class mores. His entries in the Salon of 1737 were greeted with surprise and admiration and were so successful that Chardin temporarily limited his production to domestic scenes. He sent nine paintings to the Salon of 1738, including the *Scullery Maid* (formerly Coll. Baron H. de Rothschild, Paris; destroyed in England, 1940), *Young Draftsman* (Berlin, Staatliche Museen), and *Boy with a Top* (Louvre), a portrait of the younger son of the jeweler Godefroy. Aristocratic art lovers plagued him with commissions that he was unable to satisfy; his Salon entries were all sold in advance, and he was even forced to paint several replicas of each. At the Salon of 1739 he showed *Back from Market* (Staatliche Museen), at that of 1740 he exhibited *Saying Grace* and the *Industrious Mother* (both Louvre), intimate scenes whose delicate good nature pleased philistines and connoisseurs alike.

Jean-Baptiste Chardin. *Saying Grace.* Museum Boymans-van Beuningen, Rotterdam. *Photo Giraudon, Paris.*

Chardin's wife died in 1735; nine years later he married a neighbor, Marguerite Pouget, a wealthy bourgeoise of whom he left many portraits. With the exception of the *Lady with a Bird Organ* (exhibited 1751; New York, Frick Collection) and the *Blind Man of the Quinze-Vingts* (exhibited 1753; formerly Paris, Rothschild Collection), he quickly returned to the still lifes of his early years: game, fruit, luncheons, and instruments of all kinds, the most successful of which are the *Attributes of the Arts* and *Attributes of Music*, painted for the château of Choisy (1765; Louvre). In the last years of his life, weakened by illness, he worked exclusively in pastel, a more rapid medium in which he produced three masterpieces: *Self-Portrait with Spectacles* (1771), *Self-Portrait with Eyeshade* (1775), and *Madame Chardin* (1775), all in the Louvre.

CHASE, William Merritt (1849, Williamsburg, now Nineveh, Indiana—1916, New York City), American painter. Chase first studied in Indianapolis and then at the National Academy of Design in New York (1869). After a short time there, he left for Munich in 1872 to paint at the Royal Academy, where he met Frank Duveneck, who was to popularize the bravura manner of the Munich School in America at the end of the 19th century. Chase also spent time in Venice, and by the time he returned to New York in 1878 to teach at the Art Students League, he had already gained recognition. He was subsequently elected president of the newly founded Society of American Artists (1879) and later made a National Academician (1890).

Chase always remained a realist, hardly altering his style throughout his career. After his arrival in New York, he passed through a brief Impressionist-influenced phase, but he never progressed far from the style of his early works, which were done in the dark tonalities characteristic of the Munich School. However, contacts with the paintings of Frans Hals and Velázquez did prompt Chase to adopt a more highlighted, almost Whistlerian manner (*Alice in the Mirror*; Southampton, N.Y., Parrish Art Museum). He made the acquaintance of James McNeill Whistler in London, 1885, when he painted a *Portrait of Whistler* (1885; New York, Metropolitan Museum). Chase was renowned for his figure studies, completed in three hours and executed entirely while standing before an assembled student body. He is perhaps best known for his small still lifes of fish (*Still Life with Fish*; Metropolitan Museum, and *English Cod*, 1904; Washington, D.C., Corcoran Gallery).

Jules Chéret. Poster for the Palais de Glace in the Champs-Élysées. 1894. Bibliothèque des Arts Décoratifs, Paris. *Photo Giraudon.*

CHASSÉRIAU, Théodore (1819, Samaná, Santo Domingo—1856, Paris), French painter. His father, a native of La Rochelle, was consul in Puerto Rico, and his mother was a Creole; the family settled in Paris in 1822. He was very precocious, and when only eleven became a cherished pupil of Ingres. At the end of 1834, when he was fifteen, his master went to Rome, and Chassériau prepared his first Salon entry by himself (1836). At the age of nineteen he submitted his *Susanna at Her Bath* to the Salon of 1839; it now hangs in the Louvre, Paris. The smaller *Marine Venus* (1838; Louvre), similar in conception, was a nonchalantly graceful companion piece at the Salon. At the end of 1840, Chassériau joined Ingres in Rome, only to realize that he no longer saw eye to eye with his master and that, though still Ingres' disciple as a draftsman, he had become a Romantic in his use of color. This attractive combination is evident in his *Andromeda* (1840; Paris, Coll. A. Chassériau). While in Rome, he painted the portrait of *R. P. Lacordaire*, represented in the cloister of S. Sabina, and dressed in the homespun robes of the Dominican Order (1840; Louvre). In 1842 Chassériau's *Esther Adorning Herself to Be Presented to Ahasuerus* (Louvre) caught the attention of the writer Théophile Gautier, who noted "her hieratic beauty and the nostalgic languor in a smile like that of a barbarian captive." At the Salon of 1843 he showed the portrait of his *Two Sisters*, Aline and Adèle (Louvre). Degas considered this double portrait to be the best of the 19th century. An artist who conceived painting in such plastic terms was destined to decorate large surfaces: in 1841 Chassériau was asked to decorate the chapel of Ste-Marie l'Égyptienne in the church of St-Merri, Paris, and in 1844 to execute a decorative ensemble for the *Cour des Comptes* (destroyed by fire in 1871). In 1854 he executed a mural ensemble for a chapel at St-Roch and the hemicycle of St-Philippe-du-Roule, both in Paris.

At the invitation of his model, the caliph of Constantine, the painter went to Algeria in 1846. He was fascinated by the country and brought back many sketches and notes that he utilized in later works: *Moorish Woman* (1850); *Arab Horseman* (1850; Louvre); *Jews of Constantinople* (1851; Nice, Coll. Rex Ingram); and *Harem Interior*, which is unfinished (1856; Louvre). He exhibited eight paintings at the Salon of 1850, including the *Sleeping Bather* (Avignon, Musée Calvet), which was unanimously admired by the critics and showed its painter to have been the Titian of the Romantic period in his cult of the beautiful nude. Chassériau died at thirty-seven, exhausted by work and pleasure, after finishing his large *Tepidarium* (1853; Louvre).

CHÉRET, Jules (1836, Paris—1932, Nice), French poster designer and decorative painter. When he gained recognition in 1858 with a three-color poster for Offenbach's *Orphée aux Enfers* (*Orpheus in the Underworld*), Chéret had already produced a large number of lithographic vignettes for plays produced for special occasions and for book jackets. He lived in London from 1859 to 1866, illustrating books for the publisher Cramer and designing posters. On his return, he opened a printing establishment that produced many famous posters now avidly sought by collectors. His dancing figures, painted with airy lightness, often in acid pastel tones, enlivened the gray walls of Paris with their iridescence (*Le Bal du Moulin Rouge*, 1889; *Loïe Fuller aux Folies-Bergère*, 1893; *L'Eldorado*, 1894). After using broad areas of flat tints under the influence of Toulouse-Lautrec, Chéret returned to a kind of Impressionism after 1900. The Musée Chéret in Nice possesses a large collection of his posters and a number of his pastels and paintings.

CHILLIDA, Eduardo (b. 1924, San Sebastian), Spanish sculptor. After three years in Paris (1948–51), he took up metalwork, in the age-old tradition of northern Spain. In the 1950s he bent the metal into rigid ribbons, jagged strips, spikes, and twists (*Borderline Uproar* series, 1956–59), into sharp ridges and blades or the short, trenchant outlines of *Dream Anvils* (1960). In the 1960s these dynamic, slim shapes were succeeded by masses articulated by asymmetrical or balanced blocks. The powerful frames of narrowly convergent and imbricated volumes in *Abesti Gogora* (1962–64) capture and seal the interior space, which is treated as a positive volume, in an austere, bare hermeticism.

CHINESE ART. In the vast land of China the earliest surviving works of art date back more than 3,000 years. Down the centuries, sculpture, architecture, and painting came into being, flourished, and then atrophied. Foreign influences were often felt, but Chinese civilization was able to absorb everything brought in from outside, and itself exerted a powerful influence on neighboring lands. Of course, some links are lacking in so long a story, but archaeological discoveries and the labors of art historians have provided a better understanding of the main developments in China's art.

The Chinese built for the span of only one lifetime; and, except in later centuries, the emperors did not preserve the palaces of their predecessors. Wood was universally used as the building material, but before the 9th century A.D. there is no ancient wooden building preserved, nor is there even a faithful reconstruction of one, unless an exception is made for 6th-century A.D. Japanese buildings that were constructed after Chinese models and have been faithfully restored down the centuries. Ch'in Shih-huang-ti's 266 palaces and those of the Han, T'ang, and Sung emperors, celebrated by the poets, are no more than memories. Only tombs, pagodas, ramparts, and bridges were built to last. The earliest surviving pagodas in brick hardly date back beyond the 6th century.

At An-yang, the old Shang capital, the remains of solid walls with watch-towers have been found, as well as the site of the platforms on which the principal building was erected, with stone bases for wooden pillars. For the Chou period, we must rely on literary sources to provide an idea of the splendid palaces, shrines, and houses.

The short-lived Ch'in Dynasty, which unified China, is famed for the palaces built by its founder, Ch'in Shih-huang-ti, of which we can read astonished descriptions, and for the Great Wall that follows the crest of hills for nearly 2,000 miles. In some regions this great fortification is no more than a high bank and ditch; but in others the walls are built of blocks of stone and are as much as 29 feet thick, with bastions 13 feet higher than the ramparts. However, the wall in its present form is probably not more than 500 or 600 years old.

The first Han emperor built his new capital at Ch'ang-an in Shensi with walls, palaces, and immense audience chambers entirely of wood. Paintings and carvings in tombs and small pottery models give us an idea of Han constructions with low over-hanging roofs, the prototypes of classical architecture in wood; of the future pagoda there existed only the central mast and a tier of canopies under a single roof. Though the principle of vaulting was known, it was not used except for temples.

With the spread of Buddhism in the period of the Six Dynasties, the construction of sacred buildings assumed great importance. The temples were built in the Chinese fashion, with halls, galleries, and surrounding walls. The pagoda, a new form, appeared with three stories in the 4th century A.D., rising to five or more in the 6th.

There were great advances in Buddhist architecture under the Sui and the T'ang until the proscription of A.D. 845, when many sacred buildings were destroyed. The pagodas became more completely Chinese: generally a pair of pagodas was built, the Chinese principle of symmetry being more important than the original conception of a reliquary; but, at the end of this period, single pagodas became once again the norm. All the surviving T'ang pagodas are of brick; whether of brick or wood, they were square in shape. The Ta-yen Pagoda (also known as the Great Pagoda of the Wild Geese) at Hsi-an in Shensi (A.D. 652), with its imitation beams and seven stories, and also the neighboring Little Pagoda of the Wild Geese, with its fifteen stories indicated by brick projections, are the last survivors of a brilliant period. The only wood building that survives is a 9th-century A.D. hall, that of Fo-kuang-ssu on Mount Wu-t'ai Shan in Shansi, a great edifice with many columns, open on the outside, like many buildings in Japan, in particular those of Tōshōdaiji monastery at Nara and Daigoji near Kyoto.

After the time of troubles of the Five Dynasties, the Sung rebuilt K'ai-fêng on a strict plan, made it their capital, and built palaces there. A great architect from Hang-chou, Yü Hao, was put in charge of this work, and he produced a classic of wooden construction. A state architect, Li Chiai, wrote a treatise, the *Ying-tsao Fa Shih* (published 1103), which has been preserved and includes discussions of geometry, carpentry, and work in stone and terra cotta. Sixty hexagonal or octagonal pagodas still exist, their keynote being simplicity. The finest examples are at K'ai-fêng: the slender Iron Pagoda with 13 stories, its height being 184 feet and its width only 31 feet; and the square Magnificent Pagoda, of which only three stories, with their beautiful external decoration, survive. The Northern Pagoda at Suchou is exceptional in terminating in a cupola. As for wooden architecture, there are great ensembles at Chêng-ting in Hopei, with pavilions more elaborately carved than those of T'ang times and with higher and more regular intersections. In the Southern Sung period, we find that the great Taoist temple, the Yüan-miao-kuan at Soochow in Kiangsu, is already simpler.

The northern barbarian empires were interested in imitating the ways of the defeated Chinese emperors. But the Liao type of octagonal brick pagoda is an innovation: its base is divided into carved registers, the body of the structure is decorated with Buddhist groups, and there are 13 superimposed roofs.

The Yüan, the Mongol invaders who conquered China, brought no considerable modifications to architecture. Apparently it was in their time that the Tibetan bottle-shaped stupa, the *chorten*, was introduced into China; this was the type used much later, in 1652, by Emperor Shun-chih (1644–61) when he built the White Pagoda at Peking.

The Chinese emperors of the Ming Dynasty were anxious to revive ancient traditions. They tried to restore the Southern Sung style, but architectural decadence clearly set in. Emperor Yung-lo (1403–24) moved the capital to Peking and within the town he began to build the Imperial City; inside that in turn was the Forbidden City, with its succession of terraces, palaces, parks, lakes, and porticoes. South of the town he built the Temple of Heaven (1420) and the Temple of Agriculture (1422). Chia-ching (1522–66) built the Temples of the Earth and the Moon and, in the Tibetan style, the Temple of the Lamas.

Under the Ch'ing, the only original constructions were the Lamaist temples and imperial palaces at Peking. The Forbidden City had been burned when the Ming fell. K'ang-hsi (1662–1722) started to rebuild it, and Yung-cheng (1722–35) carried on the work, which was finished by Ch'ien-lung (1736–96), who rebuilt the Temple of Heaven. The ensemble still stands today, converging on the throne room, the T'ai-ho-tien, which was the center of the ceremonial life of the empire. But the Ch'ing emperors not only restored Ming work: with the assistance of the Jesuit priests Castiglione and Attir, they also

Chinese Art. Ta-yen Pagoda (Great Pagoda of the Wild Geese), Tz'u-en Monastery, Hsi-an, Shensi. *c.* A.D. 652–704.

Chinese Art. Shang bronze. Vessel of the *yu* type, in form of owl. 12th–11th century B.C. Cleveland Museum of Art.

Left: **Chinese Art.** Chou bronze. Ritual vessel of the *hu* type. 8th–6th century B.C. Musée Guimet, Paris.

Above: **Chinese Art.** Chariot model. Late 6th or 7th century A.D. William Rockhill Nelson Gallery of Art, Kansas City.

built the Summer Palace in imitation of Versailles (destroyed in 1860 at Lord Elgin's orders).

SCULPTURE

If we are to understand the main lines of the evolution of sculpture over more than 3,000 years, we must include in that category everything made of stone, wood, bronze, or pottery. Excavations at An-yang, the Shang capital in Honan, have added much to our knowledge of the Shang Dynasty. Some of the objects found date back as far as 1300 B.C. The most remarkable finds are the bronzes, which show extraordinary technical mastery. Such achievements clearly presuppose centuries of striving, but we can as yet only guess at what went before. The forms of the vessels had already been established. There were also zoomorphic vases in the shape of elephants or owls, teeming with decorative motifs and, despite their stylization, organic in form.

Under the Han, large-scale statuary, carved bas-reliefs and steles, and pottery figurines flourished. The tomb of General Ho Ch'ü-ping in Shensi, dating from 117 B.C., contains the oldest known large-scale Chinese sculpture, which consists of a horse trampling a fallen soldier under foot, a buffalo, and a tiger. A new taste for naturalism is characteristic of the age. The bas-reliefs in the tomb chambers of Shantung and Honan are in some cases incised; in others the stone is cut away, so that the figures stand out in relief. The most impressive feature of Han art is the sudden flowering of pottery tomb figures. Besides models of houses and farms, there are pottery figures of all manner of human types: dancers, acrobats, and female figures whose forms, decorated with a few incised lines, achieve an exquisitely majestic presence. Even more lively perhaps are the figurines of familiar animals, whether depicted in a gay and friendly spirit, as with the pigs, ducks, owls, and dogs, or with nobility, as with the horse.

The anarchy that followed the downfall of the Han did not prevent a varied development of sculptural forms in the time of the Six Dynasties. Funeral steles were erected in the neighborhood of the towns; the tombs of emperors and high officials, particularly those in the vicinity of Nanking, were guarded by huge stylized animals, winged lions, and massive chimeras.

Meanwhile Buddhist sculpture made its appearance in China, as Buddhist iconography traveled along the silk road through Kashgar, Tur-fan, Kucha, and Khotan to Tun-huang. Niche-like caves of varying size were hollowed out of mountain flanks. Yün-kang (A.D. 460–536) in Shansi, Lung-mên (A.D. 494–759) in Honan, and T'ien-lung Shan (A.D. 684–755), also in Shansi, to mention only the main sites, are like splendid cathedrals that bear witness to the faith of generation after generation of anonymous sculptors.

From the beginning of the 4th century A.D., traces of Hellenistic, Gandharan, Indian, Persian, and central Asian influence may be seen in small gilt bronzes; at the beginning of the following century, these influences recur in colossal statues of Buddha at Yün-kang. But contact with China transformed Buddhism: at Buddha's side stand the bodhisattvas Maitreya, Amitabha, and especially Avalokiteshvara the Compassionate, who by a strange avatar becomes the goddess Kuan-yin.

The emperors of the Wei Dynasty were fervent Buddhists, and under their rule, after the lively art of the caves of Yün-kang, a more purified style prevailed at Lung-mên; the forms were slender and elongated, and an inner smile appeared on the faces. The same calm serenity is found not only in cave statues, but also in small gilt bronzes and stone steles.

Baroque tendencies became more marked under the Northern Ch'i (A.D. 550–77), and the influence of Indian Gupta art stimulated a fresh humanism. Under the Sui, who restored the unity of the empire, a hieratic element reappeared in sculpture; but there was a human sweetness in the features, as we see in the statues at T'o Shan and Yü-Han Shan in Shantung, as well as a grave humanity in the smiling head and the body revealed by the drapery.

This tendency is carried further under the T'ang in the last great age of Chinese Buddhist sculpture; at Lung-mên and T'ien-lung Shan there is not a trace of frontality in the supple figures. Large-scale secular sculpture reemerged in the powerful horses

Chinese Art. *Bodhisattva.* Wei Dynasty, early 6th century A.D. Metropolitan Museum of Art, New York.

carved in bas-relief on the tomb of Emperor T'ai-tsung (A.D. 637) in Shensi, which recall the painting of the time and may have been based on drawings by Yen Li-pên.

Under the Sung, sculpture fell into a decline. There was still a demand from the faithful for cult statues carved in wood or modeled in pottery, and artists sought to give feminine beauty to Kuan-yin, the goddess of mercy, and an appropriately ascetic look to those saintly Buddhist devotees, the lohans; but their expressive power had faded.

PAINTING

The origin of fresco painting is attributed to the mythical Yellow Emperor in 2700 B.C. The earliest surviving picture, *Noble Lady with a Phoenix and a Dragon* (Peking, Historical Museum), is on silk and dates from the 3rd century B.C. Paper was invented in A.D. 105. Down the centuries the walls of palaces and sanctuaries were decorated with frescoes—those of the Han period illustrate the life of men, great battles, and mythological scenes with precision and grace. But it was Chinese painting on paper and silk—an art very close to calligraphy—that developed a technique and a style of representation markedly different from those of the West.

The first painter of whom we have, if not an original work, at least a very old copy, is the 4th-century A.D. artist Ku K'ai-chih (A.D. 345?–406?), a realistic and candid painter. Hsieh Ho (late 5th century), none of whose works has been preserved, was the great theorist of the following century: his *Six Principles* for assessing the merits of paintings have been interpreted down the centuries to suit the taste of each successive age.

Yen Li-pên (d. A.D. 673), at the beginning of the T'ang Dynasty, continued to follow the tradition of studied realism. The reign of Emperor Ming Huang witnessed a great flowering of Chinese painting, with grandiose beginnings in the art of the landscapist Li Ssu-hsün (A.D. 651–716), whose work was carried on by his son, Li Chao-tao (active *c.* A.D. 670–730), the leading exponent of the Northern School of landscape painting. For Wang Wei (A.D. 699–759), recognized as the great master of the Southern School, reality was best suggested by blurred, monochromatic shapes in which the black ink achieved its maximum effect. The technical skill of Wu Tao-tzu (*c.* A.D. 699–759), the "prince of painters," became legendary, but no work of his survives. Han Kan (A.D. 720–80?) was the great painter of horses. The court painters Chang Hsüan (active *c.* A.D. 713–42) and Chou Fang (active A.D. 780–810) painted the life of the palace ladies in a most charming fashion.

During the troubled time of the Five Dynasties after the collapse of the T'ang, landscape became transformed, partly because so many artists had taken refuge in the countryside and partly through the influence of Taoist and Buddhist ideas. Kuan T'ung (early 10th century A.D.) and Tung Yüan (A.D. 907–60) gave a more powerful expression to natural forms; Li Ch'êng (active *c.* A.D. 960–90), the "master of distant, horizontal planes," favored monochrome in his deliberately composed and very individualized works.

Under the Northern Sung Dynasty, landscape was intellectualized, and Kuo Hsi, in his *Advice on Landscape Painting*, created a system and forms to which later centuries were continually to have recourse. Li Lung-mien (1040–1106) was a high official who painted mythological scenes and animals in a precise style. Huang Ch'üan is famous for his enchanting animals, while Shih K'o painted scenes of Ch'an Buddhist inspiration in the *i-p'in*, or "untrammeled" style. Emperor Hui-tsung (1101–25) gave encouragement to artists and was himself a skilled painter of birds and flowers.

After the loss of north China the Southern Sung empire established its capital at Hang-chou. The Academy was re-established, with Li T'ang (*c.* 1049–1130) and his follower Li Ti (*c.* 1100–92) to assure continuity. The two masters of the age were the academicians Ma Yüan (active *c.* 1190–1230) and Hsia Kuei (active 1180–1230), who together give their names to the Ma-Hsia school and practiced the kind of asymmetrical composition known as "all-in-one-corner," in which the main theme is compressed and empty space achieves a remarkable importance. Their monochromatic landscapes were intended to suggest rather than to represent.

Parallel to official painting, the incorrectly styled Ch'an School developed. Its practitioners were monks of the Buddhist Ch'an sect, but it was not specifically religious. The monks rejected the old rules and worked freely. The greatest of them, Mu-ch'i (1220?–80?), had a lightning brushstroke and an astonishing economy of means. Liang K'ai (1140?–1210?), an academician who abandoned official life to live in a monastery, first excelled in the Ma-Hsia style and then went on to "untrammeled" painting, capturing a violent scene or the character of an individual with a few strokes of his brush. Also working with a few sure lines, Yin-t'o-lo could convey the essence of a vivid scene, and Ying Yü-chien could conjure up an impressionistic landscape from mist by a few well placed blots. Ch'ên Jung (active 1235–60) was the great painter of dragons, a subject of religious as well as cultural significance.

A reaction set in when the Mongol Yüan Dynasty came to power. Some artists, among them Chao Mêng-fu (1254–1322) and Kao K'o-kung (1248–1310), rallied to the invaders. Others retreated into the country and resumed a direct contact with nature, but each in his own way looked back beyond the painters of the Southern Sung School to the masters of the Five Dynasties and of T'ang times. Each of the "four great Yüan masters" has his own personality: Huang Kung-wang (1296–1354) painted the familiar countryside; Wu Chên (1280–1354) practiced a careful realism; Wang Mêng (1309–85) painted imaginary, tragic landscapes; but the most original of all was Ni Tsan (1301–74), who, by means of pale tones and a few spare lines, constructed a frozen world with no place for man. Other masters were Kung K'ai (active *c.* 1260–80), with his exquisite

Chinese Art. Tz'u-Chou stoneware vase. Sung Dynasty (A.D. 960–1279). Metropolitan Museum of Art, New York.

Chinese Art. Kuo Hsi. *Early Spring in the Mountains.* 1072. National Palace Museum, Formosa.

brushwork; Ch'ien Hsüan (*c.* 1235–90/1301), with his attractive flowers and insects; and Jên Jên-fa (1st half of the 14th century), who compares favorably with Chao Mêng-fu as a painter of horses.

The Ming was a Chinese dynasty, and painters set about documenting the great masters of the past. Encyclopedias were composed; rules were established; a pictorial language was elaborated; and academicism held the field. Emperor Hsüan-tê (1426–35) was himself a painter of distinction. Two schools emerged: that of Chê, founded by Tai Chin (active 1st half of 15th century), who, with his disciple Wu Wei (1459–1508), adhered to reality, which he interpreted with a baroque charm; and that of Shên Chou (1427–1509), the founder of the Wu School, who sought inspiration from the Southern Sung and Yüan masters. The most distinguished scholar-painter was Tung Ch'i-ch'ang (1555–1636), whose erudition and technique were faultless, but who also lacked feeling; he was the great theorist of his age.

The Manchu rulers of the Ch'ing Dynasty were determined to adopt Chinese cultural patterns, and indeed to become Chinese. The emperors Shun-chih (1644–61), a painter himself, K'ang-hsi (1662–1722), and Ch'ien-lung (1736–95) patronized painters, formed collections, and had encyclopedias compiled. Painting remained academic, however, and the rules of the *Painting Manual of the Mustard Seed Garden* (1679) became obligatory. Six painters are traditionally recognized as great: the four Wangs (Wang Shih-min [1592–1680], Wang Chien [1598–1677], Wang Hui [1632–1717], Wang Yüan-ch'i [1642–1715]), Wu Li (1632–1718), and Yün Shou-p'ing. Yet for all their talent, they could not save Chinese painting from academic decadence.

The great painters of the age were the individualists in revolt against official art and sometimes against the government itself. The first, Hung-jên (1603–63), led an austere existence pursuing the ideal of pure painting. Pa-ta Shan-jên (1626–*c.* 1705) was an eccentric who gave monochrome painting a new power in the flowers and animals he sketched with a few brushstrokes on the white page. Shih-t'ao (1630–1717), a man of learning and a poet, rejected all the old techniques and created a new, living, uniquely powerful style of landscape painting. Shih-ch'i (*c.* 1610/25–*c.* 1693/1700), with his mysterious landscapes, seems the most religious; Kung Hsien (1660–1700), a hermit, brought a new breath of tragedy into painting.

CHIRICO, Giorgio de (b. 1888, Volo, Thessaly), Greek-born Italian artist who developed the Metaphysical school of painting. In Paris, where he settled in 1911, de Chirico soon won admirers among avant-garde poets and writers. Guillaume Apollinaire, of whom he painted a famous portrait in 1914 (Paris, Coll. Madame Guillaume Apollinaire), was to be his most ardent champion. The Surrealists found in de Chirico a painter who shared their preoccupation with mystery, the unknown, the unconscious, and the dream. A troubling atmosphere pervades his canvases, which are filled with strange, rigid architectural forms as well as impersonal objects. Then, from 1915, appeared mannequins and caryatid statues with ovoid heads, marked by the mathematical sign of infinity. This was also the period of one of de Chirico's most famous paintings, the *Disquieting Muses* (1916–17; Milan, Coll. Gianni Mattioli), whose enigmatic silhouettes stand against the crenelated towers of the Castello Estense in Ferrara.

Giorgio de Chirico. *Melancholy.* 1912. Private Coll., London.

At the same time the artist began his series of *Metaphysical Interiors*, hermetic rooms littered with the fetishes of civilization. On his return to Paris from Italy in 1924, de Chirico immediately joined the Surrealist group, participating in their first exhibition in 1925 and exerting a deep and continuing influence on them. He undertook new themes (horses, gladiators); wrote *Hebdomeros* (1929), a dreamlike novel with Promethean pretensions; and, at the same time, designed sets and costumes for the Swedish Ballet, Diaghilev's Ballets Russes de Monte-Carlo, and the Kroll-Oper of Berlin. In 1933 he painted a series of *Bathers* (Rome, Priv. Coll.), by which time he had already returned to a sterile academicism.

CHRISTUS, Petrus (b. Baerle, near Ghent—d. *c.* 1473, Bruges), Flemish painter. Master at Bruges in 1444, mentioned as working at Cambrai in 1454 and at Bruges in 1463, Petrus Christus left some 20 works, of which eight are signed and five dated. An eclectic artist, he was successively influenced by Jan van Eyck, as seen in his *St. Jerome* (1442; Detroit, Institute of Arts) and his *Crucifixion* (Dessau, Staatliches Museum), Rogier van der Weyden (*Deposition*; New York, Metropolitan Museum), and, finally, by Dirk Bouts. He had a fine technique and brought to his work highly personal inflexions. These are perhaps due to a stay in Italy, or to a temperament open to the secrets of men and to the mystery of the spirit, whose solitude he felt

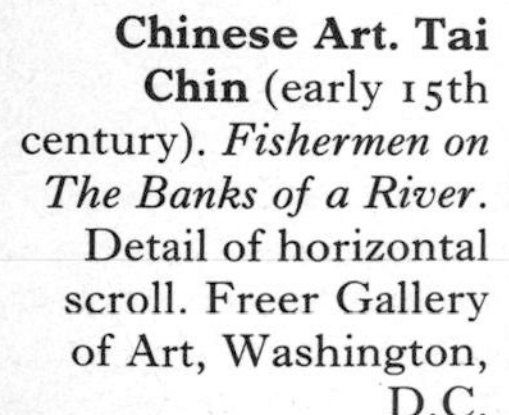

Chinese Art. Tai Chin (early 15th century). *Fishermen on The Banks of a River.* Detail of horizontal scroll. Freer Gallery of Art, Washington, D.C.

and expressed. This sensitivity characterizes his best works. In the *Deposition* (Brussels, Musées Royaux des Beaux-Arts) the figures are dispersed in a lyrical landscape. The *St. Eligius as a Goldsmith Presenting a Ring to an Engaged Couple* (1449; New York, Coll. Robert Lehmann) may depict an episode from the legend of St. Godeberta or merely the visit of an engaged couple to a jeweler, but it is rendered as a picturesque genre scene, dry in drawing but with a beautiful and rich coloring that brings green, carmine, vermilion, and gold brocade into a harmonious arrangement. Each figure appears self-absorbed. Petrus' best-known work is the highly original and exquisitely finished *Portrait of a Young Woman* (*c.* 1446; Berlin, Staatliche Museen). The youthful, secretive figure has a most refined elegance. The black velvet, the deep blue of the dress, and the delicate porcelain tones of the face, on which the shadows are faintly blue, stand out strongly against a finely modulated gray background.

CHURCH, Frederick Edwin (1826, Hartford, Connecticut—1900, New York), American painter of the Hudson River School. From 1844 to 1846 he studied with the Romantic landscapist Thomas Cole in the Catskills and the Berkshire mountains. From 1855 until 1875 the gifted artist was the leading member of the Hudson River School. In the early 1850s he traveled in Maine, along the Mississippi River, and to Niagara Falls and South America, gathering impressions for his dramatized view paintings. From 1867 to 1869 Church traveled throughout Europe and the Middle East, and upon his return to the United States, as the mood of the country changed, he turned away from grandiose landscapes to the painting of Old World reveries based on these later travels. The *Heart of the Andes* (1859; New York, Metropolitan Muscum) and *Niagara Falls from the American Side* (1856–57; Washington, D.C., Corcoran Gallery) gained wide fame both in America and in Europe, and were the first paintings to truly embody the cosmic enthusiasms of their era. Their broad visual scope was balanced by the lushness and multiplicity of careful detail. The essence of Church's art was its theatricality, and its purpose was to excite wonder. His chief heroic themes—such as Niagara Falls, the wilderness, and the Arctic—were epic representations of the New World's classic image.

CIMABUE, Cenni di Pepi, *called* (1240/50, Florence—1302?, Pisa), Italian painter. The only certain documented work by Cimabue is the mosaic in the apse of Pisa Cathedral, particularly the figure of St. John, for which there are documents of 1301 and 1302.

Practically every deduction made about Cimabue is based on the attribution to him of the very large *Maestà* originally from the church of S. Trinita in Florence and now in the Uffizi. This painting shows that he derived elements of his style from earlier Florentine painters such as Coppo di Marcovaldo (*c.* 1225–after 1274), from whose work (*Madonna del Bordoye*, 1261; Siena, S. Maria dei Servi) he borrowed the use of a network of gold lines to provide highlights and a decorative linear rhythm. It is usually thought that the *Maestà* dates from about 1285, as it is held to be contemporary with the *Rucellai Madonna* (Paris, Louvre) of that year. Some of the mosaics in the baptistery at Florence are also attributed to him, but thc only other works generally accepted as his are two large crucifixes and a number of frescoes, now almost entirely ruined, in the Upper and Lower Churches at Assisi. In the Upper Church there are numerous frescoes in the transept and choir, including two *Crucifixions* and a series of scenes from the *Life of the Virgin*. The vault of the Upper Church also contains a number of frescoes attributed to Cimabue.

The two large crucifixes are the one in S. Domenico, Arezzo, and that formerly in the church of S. Croce, Florence. The Arezzo crucifix is probably an early work (perhaps *c.* 1260/65), since it relates to similar works by Coppo di Marcovaldo. The S. Croce crucifix (Florence, Museo dell'Opera di S. Croce; gravely damaged by floodwaters in 1966) is far more advanced, both in the modeling of the body and in the rendering of a pathetic effect through the somewhat exaggerated curve given to the body of Christ. Cimabue's passionate intensity of feeling, expressed by means of outline and facial expression, determined one of the leading characteristics of Florentine art and must be seen as an indispensable preliminary stage in the dramatic and realistic art of Giotto.

Petrus Christus. *Deposition.* Detail of landscape. Musées Royaux des Beaux-Arts, Brussels. *Photo A.C.L., Brussels.*

CIMA DA CONEGLIANO, Giovanni Battista Cima, *called* (*c.* 1459, Conegliano, Veneto—1517/18, Conegliano), Italian painter, active in Venice. A conservative artist, he resisted the excitement of Giorgionesque romanticism, but was touched by the muted colorism and monumental vision of Giovanni Bellini. This is already apparent in the calm rhythm and simple articulation of his *Madonna of the Pergola*, painted in 1489 for S. Bartolomeo in Vicenza (now Museo Civico).

Frederick Edwin Church. *Heart of the Andes.* 1859. Metropolitan Museum of Art, New York.

Cima da Conegliano. *Madonna of the Orange.* Accademia, Venice. *Photo Brogi.*

In 1493 he painted the great altar panel for the duomo in Conegliano, for which he also executed a *Sacra Conversazione* (1493). In the same year he moved to Venice and began to supply Venetian churches with signed and frequently dated altar-pieces: the *Baptism of Christ* for S. Giovanni in Bragora (1494), the *Annunciation* for the Zeno Chapel in S. Maria de' Crocicchieri (Leningrad, Hermitage), the large altar-piece for the Carità (1496–99; Venice, Accademia), and the *St. Peter Martyr*, with its architectural setting opening out into landscape in the background, painted for the church of Corpus Domini (1509; Milan, Brera). The *Incredulity of Thomas* (London, National Gallery) was executed in 1502 for the duomo of Portogruaro, and the *St. Catherine* for S. Rocco in Mestre (London, Wallace Collection).

Cima's manner changed little. He retained throughout an astonishing calm with interesting undertones of rusticity and a certain tendency to be solemn. In his little anecdotic scenes Cima combined exotic color with Carpacciesque costumes. He is at his best in clear and gentle landscapes with distant views suffused by a calm light: the *Madonna of the Orange* (Venice, Accademia), where the forms are smoothly finished, the tones saturated, and the space ample, and the *Madonna with St. John the Baptist and St. Mary Magdalene* (Paris, Louvre).

Matteo Civitali. *St. Sebastian.* National Gallery of Art, Washington, D.C.

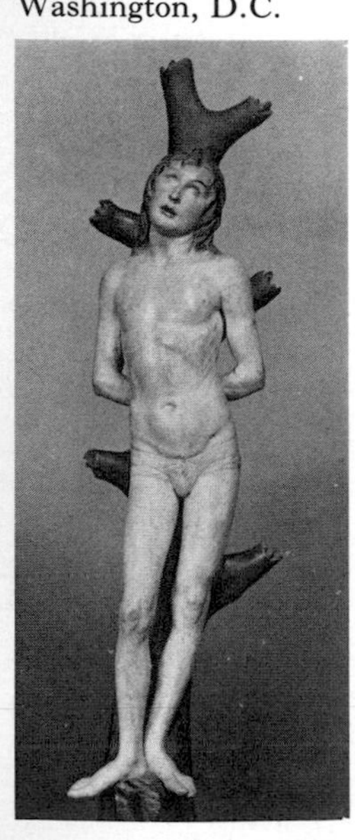

CIVITALI, Matteo di Giovanni (1436, Lucca—1501, Lucca), Italian sculptor, medalist, and architect, an associate of Antonio Rossellino, at whose studio in Florence he was trained. He also introduced printing in Lucca. His earliest known works are effigies of Humanists—the marble medallion of Pietro d'Avenza (d. 1475) and the tomb of Pietro da Noceto (1467–72), both in Lucca Cathedral. His chief patron was Domenico Bertini, who commissioned a *Virgin and Child* with the Bertini blazon (1479; Lucca, S. Michele) and, in the same year, a funeral monument for himself and his wife, which Civitali decorated with an exquisite bust of Donna Bertini. Bertini also commissioned the high altar (1473–after 1476), the choir screen (1478), and the celebrated chapel of Volto Santo (1481–84) in Lucca Cathedral, and it is for the same patron that Civitali executed his most popular work, the rustic *Madonna della Tosse*, or *Madonna of the Cough*, unusual for its air of bourgeois intimacy (1480; Lucca, S. Trinita). Next commissioned by Niccolò da Noceto, he designed (1484–85) and carved the altar of S. Regolo for Lucca Cathedral. In 1498 Civitali went to Genoa, where he carved statues of Adam and Eve, Elizabeth and Zacharias, and Isaiah and Habakkuk for the chapel of St. John the Baptist in the duomo.

CLAESZ., Pieter (*c.* 1597, Burgsteinfurt, Westphalia—1661, Haarlem), Dutch still-life painter, a pupil of Floris Van Dyck (1575–1651) and father of the landscape painter Nicolaes Berchem. His most characteristic subjects were tables laid for a meal or containing remnants of a meal. At first Claesz. followed the dry still-life style of Floris van Schooten (active 1605–55), in which objects and earthy or metal colors were juxtaposed in disorder (*Still Life with Glass of Beer*, 1627, Switzerland, Priv. Coll.; *Musical Instruments*, Paris, Louvre). After 1630, perhaps under the influence of William Claesz. Heda, he began to integrate his forms more closely, to seek a unity of impression, and to construct geometric schemes based on the Golden Section. From 1640, the tones became warmer, the paint lighter, the tonality more transparent, and the arrangement of curving and straight lines more subtle (*Luncheon with Pewter Jug*, 1643, Brussels, Musées Royaux des Beaux-Arts; *Still Life with Pitcher*, 1644, The Hague, Mauritshuis; *Still Life with a Pâté*, 1647, Budapest, Museum of Fine Arts; *Still Life*, 1643, Minneapolis, Institute of Arts; *Large Glass*, 1649, Amsterdam, Coll. Dr. H. A. Wetzlar). The most beautiful effects are undoubtedly seen in the *Still Life with Drinking Vessels* (1649; London, National Gallery), in which the browns and ochers are enlivened by pure whites and restrained reds. Such works show Claesz. to be a painter who exhibits, by the sobriety and intimacy of his forms, color, and light, a poetic sense that unites delicacy of feeling with rigorous discipline of thought and probity of sensation.

CLASSICISM. This term, used to designate both an artistic tradition and an aesthetic attitude, is one of the most confusing concepts in art history. The tradition to which it refers was born in Greece and Rome and continued in subsequent periods when antique works were used as prototypes. This is the "Classical" tradition, and in this sense Classicism is a constant feature in the art of almost all post-Classical periods. The more restricted aesthetic use of the term applies only occasionally within this long tradition, referring to styles, or phases of a style, marked by such qualities as clarity, order, and balance. In this sense Classicism is a feature of one period of ancient art, that of Greece in the 5th century B.C., as well as of Italy in the High Renaissance, and of France both in the 17th and late 18th centuries A.D.

In discussions of art from the Renaissance onwards, the concept is often used in a comparative sense to signify those works that, within the context of a given style, most exhibit the aesthetic qualities associated with Classicism. During the Renaissance, artists desired to improve their social position and to liberate themselves from the old, repressive craft guilds. To support their claim, they had to give art rational justification, which was achieved by referring to such ancient authorities as Aristotle and Horace. It remained for the 17th century to formulate a coherent artistic doctrine that used the categories of literary Classicism as yardsticks of artistic excellence. With reference to the art of the 16th century, this theory condemned Venetian, Flemish and Dutch painting for its "naturalism" and lack of clarity. The most exemplary works were held to be those produced in Rome in the first decades of the 16th century, especially by Raphael and his followers. For the 17th century, the works of Nicolas Poussin were considered to be among the finest examples of Classicism. Modern art historians, using their own aesthetic criteria, also consider Raphael and Poussin the most Classical artists in later Western art. In this case modern aesthetic standards coincide with classic intellectual criteria, but aesthetics and theory do not always reach the same conclusions.

MEDIEVAL CLASSICISM

During the reign of Emperor Charlemagne there was a deliberate attempt to restore the Classical past. This period, extending from A.D. 771 to 877, is known as the Carolingian revival. Architecture provides a revealing example of Carolingian Classicism. The three-arched gateway (*c.* 800) to the monastery at Lorsch, Germany, in its elements (columns, pilasters, capitals) and in its over-all form (deriving ultimately from a Roman triumphal arch), uses the Classical "language" of architecture.

During the Romanesque period (1050–1200), Classical details abound in architecture, and the Roman technique of vaulting large, longitudinal units reappeared. Around 1150 the Romanesque style began to yield to the Gothic, which was the most important and widespread of medieval artistic developments.

Classicism. Donatello. Equestrian statue of Gattamelata, Padua. *c.* 1445–50. *Photo Alinari—Art Reference Bureau.*

Gothic architecture makes use of many of the same Classical details found in Carolingian and Romanesque buildings. In the sense of the term, however, referring to that point in the development of a style at which its aesthetic potential is most fully realized, certain Gothic buildings have been called Classical, such as the nave of Amiens Cathedral (completed 1236). Gothic sculpture and painting, on the other hand, are directly related to Classicism, through the use of ancient models. Classicism is also seen in Gothic art in the grace and Classical equipoise of many figures, as in the *Visitation* portal (*c.* 1230), at Rheims Cathedral.

RENAISSANCE CLASSICISM

A determined effort on the part of artists to revive the antique was made in Italy in the early 15th century. As we have seen, Classical antiquity did not have to be discovered; but it was only in the Early Renaissance—from about 1400 to 1475—that artists attempted to revive Classical antiquity by studying the principles of its art. For instance, Donatello's equestrian monument of *Gattamelata* in the Piazza del Santo, Padua (*c.* 1445–50), was inspired by Roman examples, which had also led to the creation of equestrian figures in Carolingian and Gothic times. There is an ancient setting, with a huge triumphal arch, in Andrea Mantegna's fresco of *St. James Led to Martyrdom* in the Church of the Eremitani, Padua (*c.* 1455; since destroyed), and the figures wear Roman costumes. In Renaissance architecture it was no longer simply a question of using the Classical orders and other details, but of discovering or reformulating the principles used by ancient builders. Such was the achievement of Leon Battista Alberti in the façade of S. Andrea at Mantua (*c.* 1470). He used Classical systems—a triumphal arch and a temple front—but interpreted and adapted them to the form of a Christian church.

In general it may be said that in the Early Renaissance a knowledge of Classical subjects and competence in their production had been achieved. During the High Renaissance (*c.* 1475–1520) an aesthetic program was incorporated into the antique style of the Early Renaissance. Two of the finest examples of High Renaissance Classicism are Leonardo's *Last Supper* (*c.*1495–98; Milan, S. Maria delle Grazie) and Raphael's *School of Athens* (*c.* 1510–11; Rome, Vatican). Discrete figures and groups compose a whole that, in the German critic Heinrich Wölfflin's terms, achieves a carefully balanced "unity in multiplicity." These are the normative qualities of Classicism from the High Renaissance on. In the period known as Mannerism, art has been characterized as anti-Classical when it deliberately flouts the Classical principles with which these artists were thoroughly familiar.

Classicism. Andrea Mantegna. *St. James Led to Martyrdom. c.* 1455. Formerly church of the Eremitani, Padua (destroyed). *Photo Alinari—Art Reference Bureau.*

BAROQUE CLASSICISM

In the 17th century an intellectual and aesthetic program associated with Classicism was formulated by the Italian connoisseurs Giovanni Battista Agucchi and Giovanni Pietro Bellori and accepted by artists and critics in the French Royal Academy of Painting and Sculpture. Directed against the fantasy of Mannerist artists, the naturalism of Caravaggio, and the "realism" of Northern artists, it

Classicism. Leon Battista Alberti. Basilica of S. Andrea, Mantua. *c.* 1470. *Photo Alinari—Art Reference Bureau.*

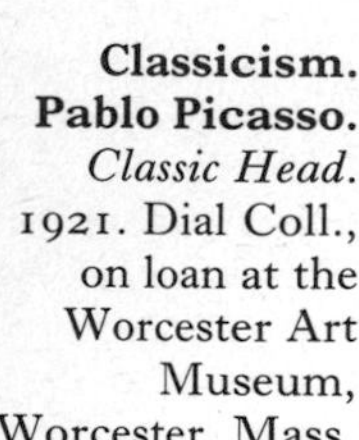

Classicism. Pablo Picasso. *Classic Head.* 1921. Dial Coll., on loan at the Worcester Art Museum, Worcester, Mass.

aimed to restore High Renaissance ideals and emphasized the achievement of Raphael. In Italy Annibale Carracci was seen as heir to Raphael, while the French Academy considered Nicolas Poussin to be his modern counterpart. Francesco Duquesnoy's *St. Andrew* (1629–40; Rome, St. Peter's) has been called Classical, although its emotional intensity is clearly a Baroque quality. Compared with the works of the great Baroque sculptor Gian Lorenzo Bernini, however, it is seen to have a Classical restraint. Poussin was influenced by works of Baroque Classicism, such as those of Annibale Carracci and his successor, Domenichino (1581–1641), but he was inspired principally by the works of Raphael.

NEOCLASSICISM AND MODERN CLASSICISM

By the mid-18th century there was a reaction against Rococo frivolity and sensuality and a renewed admiration for the antique. The resulting style, known as Neoclassicism, was anticipated in the writings on "Greek" art by the German critic Johann Joachim Winckelmann, who described the newly discovered Herculaneum. Winckelmann used Greek literature as his model to define the essential qualities of Greek Classicism: the simplicity and grandeur of the art of the 5th century B.C. He considered Raphael and Poussin to be the greatest of the moderns, since they based their styles on the best antique models. The *Oath of the Horatii* (1784; Paris, Louvre) by Louis David was considered the fulfillment of these ideals when it was unveiled in 1785. After David, Classicism became infused with Romanticism; the Classical ideals of harmony and perfection had to coexist with, or were completely replaced by, new ideals of the exotic and expressive.

A striking, and in many ways characteristic, example of modern Classicism is a "Classic" *Head of a Woman* by Pablo Picasso (1921; Worcester, Mass., Art Museum). In some sense an antique prototype was used, but here is an honest attempt to recapture the heroic qualities of ancient art that, in its distortion, reverses all the eternal values of Classicism. The Classical tradition may have lived on in the 20th century, but the aesthetic ideals of Classicism are dead.

CLAVÉ, Antoni (b. 1913, Barcelona), Spanish painter and theatrical designer who settled in Paris in 1939. With his settings for Garcia Lorca's play, *House of Bernarda Alba* (1951), an operatic production of the *Marriage of Figaro* (1952), and, in particular, for the Ballets de Roland Petit—*Carmen* (1949), *Revanche* (1951), and *Deuil en 24 heures* (1953)—he emerged as one of the freshest minds designing for the contemporary stage. Clavé's paintings of figures, which are both realistic and hieratic, and his still lifes are less well known. His draftsmanship is bold, and he overlays thick applications of rich, deep color with bright blues and reds (*Black Warrior*, 1958; Coll. artist). The same controlled exuberance is seen in his lithographs for editions of Prosper Mérimée's *Carmen* (1946) and Rabelais' *Gargantua* (1955). Clavé also worked in sculpture and designed the sets for the film *Hans Christian Andersen* (1952).

CLOISONNISM, a style of painting invented by Émile Bernard and Paul Gauguin, characterized by sinuous, strongly marked arabesques surrounding large areas of pure color, which are juxtaposed without tonal transitions. The term derives from the similarity of the final effect to cloisonné enamel, in which the sections of colored enamel are separated by thin metal partitions (*see* PONT-AVEN).

CLOUET, Jean, *also called* Janet (1486, Flanders—*c.* 1540, Paris), French painter of Flemish origin, a specialist in royal portraits. He moved to Paris no later than 1529 and devoted himself to his acutely individual, intimately constructed court portraits. Two entire aspects of his work (religious paintings and tapestry cartoons), mentioned in documents, have been lost. As for his portraits in oil, there are few that can be attributed to him with certainty; among these are the recently found *Guillaume Budé* (*c.* 1535; New York, Metropolitan Museum), *François II as Dauphin* (Antwerp, Musée des Beaux-Arts), and unquestionably the great state portrait of *François I* (*c.* 1520–25; Paris, Louvre). However, some 125 portrait drawings, executed in black and red chalk with colored highlights, constitute a regular portrait gallery of the first Valois court. These drawings were intended merely as preliminary sketches for paintings completed in Clouet's studio. Nevertheless, they are actually direct, eyewitness observations drawn from life, and are highly expressive.

FRANÇOIS (*c.*1522, Tours—1572, Paris), painter, and son of Jean, was also called Janet by his contemporaries. Trained in his father's studio, he took charge of it in 1542 and achieved even greater fame. François was painter to four kings, François I, Henri II, François II, and Charles IX. His earliest known portrait is that of the *Duchesse de Bouillon* (1550), a pencil sketch of which is in the collection of the Musée Condé. Like his father, François was a prolific painter of royal portraits; his large, full-length portrait of *Henri II* (1559; Paris, Louvre) is painted in the ceremonial style that was just making its appearance in France. Clouet, however, preferred half-length portraits; we have 54 of his pencil drawings and 13 paintings, two of which are

François Clouet. *Lady in her Bath (Diane de Poitiers?). c.* 1550. Samuel H. Kress Coll., National Gallery of Art, Washington, D.C.

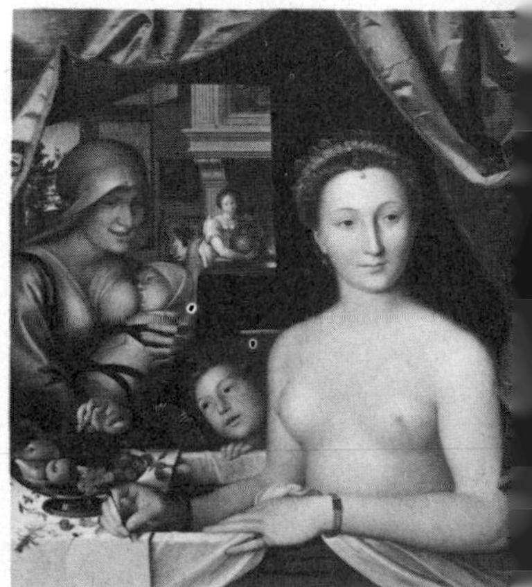

signed and dated. These two, both half-lengths, are the portraits of *Pierre Quthe* (1562; Paris, Louvre), and the lovely, bare-breasted *Lady in her Bath* (*c.* 1550; Washington, D.C., National Gallery). According to tradition, she is Diane de Poitiers, although it is possible she represents Marie Touchet, mistress of Charles IX. Clouet's loveliest portraits are those of *Charles IX as a Child* (1561; Vienna, Kunsthistorisches Museum), the *Duchesse de Roannais* (1563; Louvre), *Jeanne d'Albret* (1570; Musée Condé) and *Elisabeth of Austria*, the wife of Charles IX (1571; Louvre). His most striking pencil drawing is of Henri IV's future wife, *Queen Marguerite as a Child* (*c.* 1560; Musée Condé). His drawings became increasingly popular and Queen Catherine de Médicis collected them until her death. At her death she owned 200; the collection is now divided between the British Museum, London, and the Musée Condé.

COBRA, a 20th-century international painting movement whose name was formed from the initial letters of the names of the three capitals (copenhagen, BRussels, Amsterdam) that were the homes of its members. Cobra is now regarded as one of the most important artistic groups to emerge after World War II. Its foundation was the climax of a long development and its influence is still felt. Under the direction of Asger Jorn, the Danish abstract surrealist group, reacting against the academicism produced by Cubism and Neoplasticism, developed a kind of Baroque style in which reminiscences of Art Nouveau were mingled with popular Viking motifs. In 1948 its members noticed that there were similar ideas behind the Dutch Experimentele Groep and its review *Reflex*, published by Corneille (Cornelis van Beverloo), Karel Appel, and Constant (b. 1920). About the same time, in Brussels, the poet and critic Christian Dotremont, assisted by Pierre Alechinsky (b. 1927), united these groups in a magazine (called *Cobra*) and in an "International of Experimental Art," which opened the way for group showings.

There were two large exhibitions of Cobra: the first in the Stedelijk Museum in Amsterdam in 1949, the second in the Palais des Beaux-Arts at Liège in 1951. Cobra acted as a crucible in which the most expressionistic art of our time was developed: the visionary, lyrical imagery of Corneille (*Dreams*, 1949); the impulsive, visceral calligraphy of Alechinsky; the chromatic, sensual violence of Appel; and the romantically unrestrained gestures of Jorn.

COCK, family of painters from Antwerp that included Jan Wellens (before 1490–*c.* 1527), a follower of Bosch, Master at Antwerp in 1503, and his sons, Matthys Wellens (*c.* 1509–1548) and Hieronymus. As painters and engravers, known for their very fine drawings, the members of the Cock family hold an intermediary position in landscape art between Joachim Patinir (*c.* 1480–1524) and Henryck met de Bles (*c.* 1500–*c.* 1554).

HIERONYMUS (JEROON) WELLENS DE (1507, Antwerp—1570, Antwerp) entered the guild in 1545 and is celebrated as a publisher of engravings and as a picture dealer. After his return from Rome he propagated a taste for the antique: he employed the Italian engraver Giorgio Ghisi (1520–82), published engravings after Raphael, Michelangelo, Titian, and Parmigianino, and took Lambert Lombard and Frans Floris as collaborators. Hieronymus also disseminated engravings of the work of Bosch, encouraged genre painters of earthy subjects, and published German engravings; Bruegel the Elder worked for him for a considerable time both before and after his own Italian journey.

COECKE VAN AELST, Pieter (1502, Aelst—1550, Brussels), Flemish painter, sculptor, and designer of tapestry and stained glass, a pupil of Bernaert van Orley and a Master at Antwerp in 1527. Coecke was a well-known figure in Brussels, particularly as a theorist and as the head of a large workshop. In 1533 he went to Constantinople on behalf of a tapestry manufacturer, and from this journey he brought back drawings and a book, *Manners and Customs of the Turks*. In 1539 he translated Serlio's *Tutte l'Opere d'Architettura e Prospettiva* (*Complete Works on Architecture and Perspective*; first English edition 1611) into Flemish. Coecke organized the decoration of Antwerp for the entry of Emperor Charles V in 1549, became court painter, and helped disseminate the style of Raphael. In 1544 he married Maeyken Verhulst; their daughter married Pieter Bruegel the Elder in 1563. Coecke has been identified as the Master of the Last Supper, whose works are dated between 1527 and 1550 (*Last Supper*, Liège, Museum, and Brussels, Musées Royaux des Beaux-Arts; the *Woman Taken in Adultery*, Ghent, Museum voor Schone Kunsten). His influence was considerable.

Cobra. Pierre Alechinsky. *Badigeon.* 1950. Private Coll.

COELLO, Claudio (1642, Madrid—1693, Madrid), Spanish painter. He worked first with his father and later in Francisco Rizi or Ricci's (1608–85) studio. The painting of *Christ's Entry into Jerusalem* (Valladolid, Coll. Doña Rosa del Valle) can probably be traced back to his formative period. His work also reveals a profound knowledge of Italian art, which left its mark on one of his earliest paintings, the *Child Jesus at the Temple Gate* (1660; Madrid, Prado). Coello completed the *Triumph of St. Augustine* for the convent of the Agustinos Recoletos at Alcalá de Henares in 1664 (Prado). Two years later he painted the altarpiece for the church of S. Cruz at Madrid, the central panel of which represented the *Discovery of the Cross*; and in 1668, for the S. Plácido Benedictine monastery in the same city, he painted the side altarpieces (*St. Gertrude* and *Sts. Benedict and Scholastica*) and also the main altarpiece (an *Annunciation*). The three altarpieces are still in position. The *Virgin and Child Between the Theological Virtues and Saints* (Madrid, Prado) and the *Virgin and Child Worshiped by St. Louis, King of France* (Prado) date from 1669. Other notable works include the *Virgin of Succor* (1681; Santiago de Compostela, S. Martín Pinario sac-

Sir William Coldstream. *Bolton.* 1938. National Gallery of Canada, Ottawa.

risty); *St. Catherine* (1683; London, Apsley House); *S. Rosa de Lima* and *S. Domingo de Guzmán* (both Prado); the *Virgin Appearing to S. Domingo* and the *Franciscan Jubilee* (Madrid, Academia de San Fernando); the *Miracle of St. Peter of Alcantará* (Munich, Alte Pinakothek); the *Communion of St. Teresa* (Madrid, Museo Lázaro Galdiano); and two paintings representing the *Immaculate Conception* (Madrid, church of S. Jerónimo and Museo Lázaro Galdiano).

From 1685 to 1690 Coello worked on his masterpiece, the *Sagrada Forma* (1690; Escorial), which represents the adoration of the miraculous Host of Gorkum in the presence of Charles II and his court. He not only grouped the composition admirably, but gathered together an amazing portrait gallery. In 1691–2 he painted *St. John of Sahagún* and *St. Thomas of Villanueva* for the convent of the Carmelitas de Abajo at Salamanca; in 1693, the *Martyrdom of St. Stephen* for the Dominican monastery of S. Esteban, also in Salamanca.

Coello was Pintor del Rey, later Pintor de Cámara (1685). He painted portraits of *Don Juan de Alarcón* (Bilbao, Coll. Valdés); *Padre Cabanillas* and *Queen Mariana of Austria* (both Prado); the queen's minister, *Valenzuela* (Madrid, Coll. Don Luís Levison); *Charles II* (Frankfurt, Städelsches Kunstinstitut); and *Doña Nicolasa Manrique* (Madrid, Instituto Valencia de Don Juan).

COENE, Jacques. *See* **MASTER OF THE BOUCICAUT HOURS.**

COLDSTREAM, Sir William (b. 1908, Belford, Northumberland), English painter of portraits and landscapes, and from 1949 director of the Slade School of Fine Art in London. Coldstream exhibited with the New English Art Club and the London Group between 1929 and 1934; in 1934 he abandoned painting for three years to be an assistant in a documentary film unit. In 1938 he opened a School of Drawing and Painting with Claude Rogers (b. 1907) and Victor Pasmore in London, and in 1949 was appointed Slade Professor at University College, London.

Coldstream's subtle and distinguished style, in which Classical and realist elements are mingled, runs counter to all contemporary trends and has inspired comparisons with David, Cézanne, and Seurat. Only the last comparison is apt, for there is indeed an abstract quality even about Coldstream's most traditional official portraits (*Miss Helen Darbishire*, 1938, Oxford, Somerville College; *Sir Ifor Evans*, 1959, London, University College). His landscapes are more straightforward: pictures such as *Bolton* (1938; Ottawa, National Gallery of Canada) are among the most remarkable British achievements in this field in this century.

COLE, Thomas (1801, Bolton-le-Moors, Lancashire—1848, Catskill, New York), American painter. When he was seventeen years old Cole persuaded his bankrupt father to take his family to the United States. In his new homeland he worked for two years as a journeyman woodblock engraver. Then, fascinated by the productions of an itinerant portrait limner, he set out on foot to make his fortune painting "likenesses." When this venture failed he turned to landscape painting. Cole was torn between the need to base his art upon the scrutiny of nature and a desire to elevate such naturalism with "imagination." In his real views, of which the *Oxbow*, or the *Connecticut River near Northampton* (1836; New York, Metropolitan Museum) is probably the greatest, such heightening is achieved through dramatic effects of lighting and swirling vapours. But Cole preferred to paint imagined, often Italianate scenes, peopled with tiny figures and conveying a moral idea (the *Course of Empire* of 1835–36, a series of five paintings in the New-York Historical Society).

COLIN *or* **COLYNS,** Alexander, *called* Colin of Mechlin *or* Colin de Malines (1526, Mechlin—1612, Innsbruck), Flemish architect and sculptor of the Brabantine school, who specialized in woodcarving. He was invited to Innsbruck in 1561 by the painter Florian Abel (d. *c.* 1565) to carry out, in marble, Abel's designs for the tomb of Holy Roman Emperor Maximilian I in the Franciscan church (Hofkirche). For the tomb of Maximilian, which was also decorated with colossal bronze statues by Peter Vischer, Colin executed (before 1566) 20 marble reliefs illustrating events in the emperor's life, the most famous of which is the *Submission of the Duke of Guelders*. He also sculptured the statue of Maximilian and four Cardinal Virtues. In the Silver Chapel of the Hofkirche he decorated the tomb of Archduke Ferdinand II with four battle scenes carved in black and white marble. Colin's masterpiece, also in the Silver Chapel, is the tomb of Philippine Welser, wife of the archduke (1581).

COLLINS, Charles Allston (1828, Hampstead, North London—1873, London), English painter and author. Brother of the novelist Wilkie Collins, he studied at the Royal Academy Schools, and showed his first painting at the Academy in 1847. In the late 1840s he became involved in the Pre-Raphaelite movement, adopting several of its tenets, such as strong, clear colors, meticulous observation, and an attempt to create a rarefied, pseudomedieval mood. These traits appear in both the *Pedlar* (1850; Manchester, City Art Gallery) and *Convent Thoughts* (1851; Oxford, Ashmolean Museum).

COLLINSON, James (1825, Mansfield, Nottinghamshire—d. 1881), English genre and history painter. The son of a bookseller, he entered the Royal Academy Schools, where he became friendly with his fellow students, Holman Hunt and Dante Gabriel Rossetti. Rossetti was impressed by the detailed and highly finished style of the *Charity Boy's Debut* (1847; present whereabouts unknown), and it was partly on the strength of this that he invited Collinson to become one of the seven founding members of the Pre-Raphaelite Brotherhood. He maintained the meticulous finish that was one of the chief tenets of Pre-Raphaelite aesthetics in such works as *Answering the Emigrant's Letter*, exhibited at the Royal Academy in 1850 (Manchester,

City Art Gallery) or the *Renunciation of Queen Elizabeth of Hungary*, shown at the National Exhibition in 1851 (Johannesburg, Art Gallery).

COLOMBE, Jean (d. 1529, Bourges), French miniaturist, brother of the sculptor Michel Colombe. Working in the style of Jean Fouquet, Jean was largely responsible for the revival of the Bourges workshops in the second half of the 15th century. Between 1485 and 1489 he was commissioned by Blanche de Montferrat, the wife of Charles I of Savoy, to complete the manuscript of the *Très Riches Heures du Duc de Berry* (Chantilly, Musée Condé), which had been begun by the Limbourg brothers. Colombe executed the illuminations of the second half: his darker colors, thick-set figures, and generally heavier style impart a rustic flavor to his painting. Colombe's art, which falls between Gothic and Renaissance styles, finds perhaps its best expression in his *Histoire de la Guerre de Troie* (*c.* 1490–1500), now in the Bibliothèque Nationale, Paris.

COLOMBE, Michel (*c.* 1430, Bourges—*c.* 1512, Tours), French sculptor, brother of the miniaturist Jean Colombe. He settled in Touraine in 1490 and became official sculptor to Anne de Bretagne in 1501; he designed and executed the tomb of her parents, Duke François II and Marguerite de Foix, in the church of the Carmelites in Nantes (1502–7; now in Nantes Cathedral). The recumbent figures are still essentially Gothic, while the decoration is Italian; the great innovation of the tomb are four life-size statues of Virtues, standing at the corners of the monument and detached from it; they were posed for by charming young girls of Touraine. In 1509, when Colombe was nearing eighty, he completed the marble high relief of *St. George* (Paris, Louvre), commissioned by Cardinal d'Amboise for the chapel in his Château de Gaillon. This work, completed by Colombe in his workshop in Tours, shows the undiminished suppleness of his technique.

COLVIN, Marta (b. 1917, Chillán, Chile), Chilean sculptress. After studying sculpture at the School of Fine Arts in Santiago, she went to France in 1948 and later visited Britain, her European masters being Ossip Zadkine, Henry Moore, and Henri Laurens. On her return to Chile Colvin was appointed to a teaching post at the Santiago School of Fine Arts. However, it was in France, where she later settled, that she produced the works that are most deeply influenced by the spirit of South America, whose rock formations and ancient myths she translated into plastic terms. In her earlier works Marta Colvin was inspired by processes of organic growth, the form emerging as if by a kind of germination (*Humus*, 1954; *Manutara*, 1957; *Southern Star*, 1960). Gradually, her form rose up and became the image of the Andes in aerial structures and in ascending spatial frameworks (*Towers of Silence*, 1960). Finally, Marta Colvin constructed, out of an enclosure of pillars without walls, of shafts as hieratic as caryatids, the figure of an empty space, haunted by an abstract presence. Rooted as it is in an elemental world to which it owes its basic themes, the art of Marta Colvin reconciles within itself the monumental severity of primitive works and the most polished lyricism.

CONDER, Charles (1868, London—1909, Virginia Water, Surrey), late 19th-century English painter. At the age of fifteen Conder went to Australia, where he was employed as a draftsman for the *Illustrated Sydney News*. He was converted to a mild form of Impressionism by the painter Tom Roberts and exhibited a number of "impressions" in Melbourne in 1889. Conder's style, however, did not really crystallize until his visit to Paris in 1890. There he attended the Académie Julian and the Atelier Cormon and was influenced by Toulouse-Lautrec and the Nabis (*Moulin-Rouge*, Manchester). He also had a nostalgia for Antoine Watteau and Gabriel de Saint-Aubin, and his paintings on silk, which he began to produce in the mid-1890s, hark back in spirit to the 18th century. A draftsman in the tradition of Honoré Daumier, Conder produced illustrations for many contemporary magazines, including *The Savoy, The Studio*, and *The Yellow Book*. The art dealer Samuel Bing also commissioned him to decorate a room in his Maison de l'Art Nouveau in Paris.

CONINXLOO, family of Belgian painters active in the 15th, 16th and 17th centuries.

CORNELIS VAN (d. *c.* 1560), surnamed Scernir or Schernier, was active in Brussels, where he decorated the collegiate church of Ste-Gudule. He painted a number of Madonnas in the Italian manner, including the *Genealogy of the Virgin* (1526; Brussels, Musées Royaux des Beaux-Arts).

GILLIS VAN (1544, Antwerp—1607, Amsterdam) was by far the most distinguished artist of the family. Belgian born, Coninxloo fled his native land in 1585 to escape religious persecution and lived for a short time near Frankfurt. In 1595 he settled in Amsterdam. Considered an outstanding landscapist by his contemporaries, including Karel van Mander (1548–1611), Coninxloo was a lyrical interpreter of wild life and a sensitive specialist in forest hunting scenes. The true subject of his works is nature: human figures and human activities are almost lost in the deep space of his paintings and are dwarfed by his overpowering trees, with their sinewy, aggressive roots and blanket of foliage that almost obliterates the sky. Little natural light penetrates his private forests. His woodland views (*Wooded Landscape with Huntsman Crossing Bridge*, 1598, Vienna, Liechtenstein Palace; *Landscape with Judgment of Midas*, 1588, Dresden, Gemäldegalerie) combine fine effects of lighting with traditional coloring and precisely detailed treatment of foliage. His influence was widely felt in Flanders and is particularly evident in the work of Hercules Seghers, who studied with Coninxloo, and Jan Bruegel.

Michel Colombe. Figure of Prudence from the tomb of François II and Marguerite de Foix. 1502–7. Nantes Cathedral.

Marta Colvin. *Solar Sign.* 1962. *Photo Bertrand Weill, Paris.*

John Constable.
Wivenhoe Park, Essex. 1816. Widener Coll., National Gallery of Art, Washington, D.C.

CONSTABLE, John (1776, East Bergholt, Suffolk—1837, London), with J. M. W. Turner, one of the two great English landscape painters of the 19th century. His father was a miller, and the genesis of his growth as an artist may be traced quite simply to environment and example: in the first place, Constable was deeply attached to the spectacle of the English countryside, and in the second, his mother arranged an early introduction to Sir George Beaumont (1753–1827), a connoisseur, amateur painter, and a great admirer of Claude Lorrain, whose *Hagar and the Angel* he carried around with him. Sir George recognized Constable's raw talent, but urged much-needed lessons in technique; Constable enrolled at the Royal Academy Schools in 1799. He studied the works of other painters, notably Jacob van Ruisdael, Claude Lorrain, Richard Wilson, Annibale Carracci, and Rubens. The absolute simplicity of his vision was in total contrast to the febrile pre-Romantic tastes of his times.

Constable's life was singularly uneventful. For a brief period he consented to follow his father's profession, but a visit to London in 1795 put him in contact with the etcher John Thomas Smith (1752–1812), who sent him a correspondence course of subjects and models to copy. On a second visit in 1799, a letter of introduction to Joseph Farington (1747–1821), a pupil of Richard Wilson, was instrumental in getting him into the Royal Academy Schools. In 1802 he showed a landscape at the Royal Academy summer exhibition. In 1804 he was back in Suffolk, copying or painting portraits for local patrons. Two years later he made a tour of the "sublime" Lake District countryside (*Borrowdale* series of watercolors, 1806; London, Victoria and Albert Museum) but, characteristically, he preferred flat river valleys to the drama of the mountains, which he found "depressing." Suffolk, together with Salisbury, which he first visited in 1811, Hampstead, and Brighton, where he lived after his marriage, remained his favorite subjects. In 1816 he married Maria Bicknell after a long courtship; his extremely happy life with her coincided with his greatest period as a painter and her death in 1828 was followed by fits of depression and an increasing somberness and expressionism in his work. He was elected an Associate of the Royal Academy in 1819 and a full member in 1829. In his later years he lectured on landscape painting at Hampstead and at the Royal Institution, London.

Constable aligned himself with the Northern naturalists (Ruisdael, Meindert Hobbema) rather than the classicizing idealists such as Wilson. He did, however, broaden his range considerably; for example, *Malvern Hall, Warwickshire* (1808; London, National Gallery) has the tranquility of the finest paintings by Thomas Girtin, while the *Flatford Mill* (1817; Tate Gallery) attempts the all-embracing exhilaration of Rubens, nine of whose landscapes were exhibited at the British Institution in 1815. His oil sketches, which were done in the open air, have abounding freshness and excitement, seen for instance in *Brighton Beach* (1824) and his numerous studies of clouds (all in London, Victoria and Albert Museum).

Constable tried to exhibit a large picture every two years at the Royal Academy. He cautiously allowed one of these, the *Hay Wain* (1821; London, National Gallery), to be sent to the Paris Salon of 1824, together with two other landscapes. The originality of the picture, which had already been noted by the French writer Charles Nodier in his *Promenade de Dieppe aux Montagnes d'Écosse,* had a historic effect on Delacroix. Its dense vitality was acknowledged by most French critics, who nevertheless criticized the coarseness of the execution. This technical weakness became pronounced in Constable's later works: his unhappiness after his wife's death was expressed in greater violence of pigment, more strokes with the palette knife and occasionally, as in *Hadleigh Castle* (1829; London, Tate Gallery), a palpable expressionism that was to be emulated by Théodore Rousseau and Narcisso Diaz de la Peña.

John Constable.
Salisbury Cathedral. *c.* 1827. National Gallery, London.

CONSTRUCTIVISM, sculptural and architectural program that was formulated by the sculptor brothers Naum Gabo and Antoine Pevsner and published in Moscow in 1920 as the *Realist Manifesto.* The term "Constructivism" derives from the authors' desire to "construct" in art. The principles of their manifesto are as follows: since space and time are the essential factors of life, art must be created in their image. It follows therefore that volume, in so far as it is incapable of conveying the depth and transparency of space, should be abandoned, as well as static rhythms, which are incapable of expressing real time.

Gabo first applied his theories in "kinetic sculptures," as well as in transparent plastic reliefs with merging lines and planes. Later he worked in curved structures composed of tubes or superimposed transparent wires, followed by compositions in which crystal, alabaster, and various metals were combined in "astonishing marriages of curved and angular forms". Antoine Pevsner, like his brother, strove to capture the indefinite expansion of space and time in works composed of strips of metal merging in an eddying *perpetuum mobile.*

In architecture in the strict sense of the word, the Constructivists operated within the framework of a functional aesthetic, using geometrical forms stripped of all ornamentation, and based solely on the relations of plane and mass, space and volume. The Constructivists also recommended the use of the most modern materials—steel, glass, and plastics. In 1922, in Berlin, a Constructivist International was founded by El Lissitzky and Theo van Doesburg. The manifesto, produced for the occasion and published in *De Stijl*, expounded a philosophy that was closer to formal abstraction than to

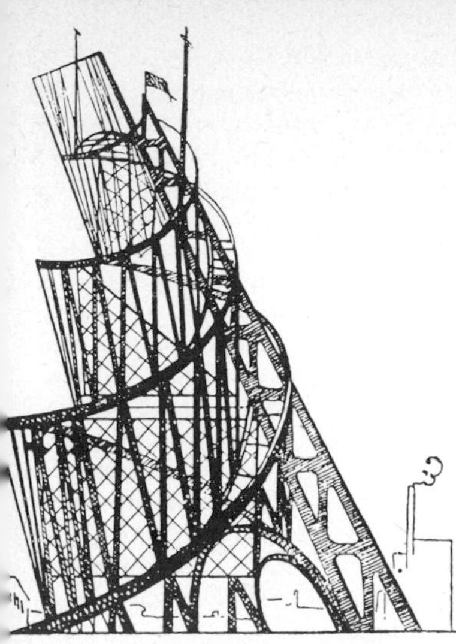

Constructivism. Vladimir Tatlin. Project for the Monument for the Third International, Moscow. 1920.

Cubism. Besides Van Doesburg, several other members of the Dutch De Stijl group of artists and architects were associated with the movement, including Piet Mondrian, Mart Stam (b. 1899), and Georges Vantongerloo. There was an element of fantasy in Constructivist architecture; it is unfortunate, but hardly surprising, that many of its designs remained as projects: office blocks hoisted onto colossal piers across a city street, known as "Cloud Props," by Lissitzky and Stam (1924); project for a theater at Kharkov, by Marcel Breuer (1930); and a book of futuristic designs for imaginary buildings, *Architectural Fantasies* (1933), published in Leningrad by Iakov Chernikov (1887–1951). Architecture and sculpture were often combined, as in Tatlin's great steel spiral (the unrealized project for the *Monument for the Third International*, 1920) or in Gabo's enormous construction for the Bijenkorf Department Store in Rotterdam (1952).

COOPER, Samuel (1609, London—1672, London), English miniaturist, known to his contemporaries as "the Apelles of England" or "the Van Dyke of miniature painting." He was trained by his guardian and uncle, John Hoskins, and spent the years 1636–42 on the Continent, probably in France and Holland. His earliest documented miniature dates from 1642, though a certain number of works precede this. Cooper's reputation abroad was more illustrious than that of any other British painter of his time and after his restoration Charles II lost little time in seeking out Cooper and sitting for him. From 1660 until his death Cooper was called upon to provide portraits of leading members of the Court and of men and women prominent in other spheres of society. Of supreme competence, he was able to match his style to the uncompromising seriousness of *Oliver Cromwell* (*c.* 1657; Coll. Duke of Buccleuch), or to the uneasy swagger of *Charles II* (1665; Sussex, Coll. Trustees of Goodwood House), and he imparted considerable depth to his portrait of *Barbara Villiers, Duchess of Cleveland* (Northamptonshire, Althorp, Coll. Lord Spencer). Less well known are his exquisite drawings, which bear comparison with those of Isaac Oliver; an outstanding example is *Thomas Alcock* (*c.* 1655; Oxford, Ashmolean Museum).

COPLEY, John Singleton (1738, Boston—1815, London), American painter. Shortly after 1750, he established himself in Boston as a painter and engraver, and with considerable rapidity evolved a highly personal portrait style suited to the temper of his New England patrons. In such portraits as those of *Mrs. Nathaniel Appleton* (1763; Cambridge, Fogg Art Museum, Harvard University) and *Governor and Mrs. Thomas Mifflin* (1773; Philadelphia, Historical Society of Pennsylvania), Copley displays his debt to the fashionable elegance of European Rococo portraiture.

In 1766 Copley sent to London a portrait of his half-brother for exhibition at the Society of Artists. This work, the *Boy with a Squirrel* (Priv. Coll.), impressed Sir Joshua Reynolds and Benjamin West to such an extent that West wrote to Copley advising him to come to Europe. This he finally did in 1775, making a tour of Italy, Austria, Germany, Holland, Belgium, and France. In Italy he preferred to imitate Raphael and the Carracci, and produced an *Ascension* (1775; Boston, Museum of Fine Arts), which was closely modeled on Anton Raphael Mengs. A portrait of *Mr. and Mrs. Ralph Izard*, also painted in Italy (1775; Boston, Museum of Fine Arts), shows Copley's rather touching eagerness to adopt European Neoclassicism: the subjects, with unadorned American faces, sit at a heavily carved table and share the stage with a Greek vase, a statue of Orestes and Electra, and a view of the Colosseum.

The year 1775 marks a natural break in Copley's style. He was to oppose tradition when commissioned by Brook Watson, a merchant who had had his leg bitten off by a shark in Havana Harbor, to commemorate this occurrence. The result, *Brook Watson and the Shark* (1778; versions in Boston, Museum of Fine Arts, and London, Christ's Hospital), is said to have violated the accepted rules of history painting even more than West's *Death of Wolfe*. In 1779–80 Copley commemorated the *Death of the Earl of Chatham* in the House of Lords (London, Tate Gallery), in which the massed scarlet robes and the more skillful compositional climax inaugurate a type of modern history painting that is the forerunner of Louis David's *Tennis Court Oath*. This was followed in 1783 by his masterpiece, the *Death of Major Pearson* (London, National Gallery), a much more weighty combination of Romantic color and Neoclassical gesture, and in 1791 with the *Repulse of the Floating Batteries at Gibraltar* (Tate Gallery), a rather less successful venture along the same lines.

COPTIC ART. Copt, deriving from an Arabic corruption of the Greek Aigyptios, is the name given to Egyptian Christians. The most illustrious are Anthony, Paul (the first Christian hermit), Macarius, and Pachomius, who among them created Christian monasticism. Christianity spread rapidly in Egyptian territory during the 1st, 2nd, and 3rd centuries A.D. However, in A.D. 451 the Copts broke away from the Western Church, rejecting the doctrines of the Council of Chalcedon and accept-

Samuel Cooper. *Thomas Alcock. c.* 1655. Ashmolean Museum, Oxford.

ing Monophysite teaching. This independence, and the gradual assertion of Egyptian nationalism, strengthened the movement and led to the individuality and maturity of Coptic art by the 6th century A.D., chiefly in the monastic communities.

Endowed with an undeniable feeling for ornament, the Copts extracted a certain picturesqueness from Egyptian motifs, as in the decoration of the great monasteries of Bawit, of Sohag (White Monastery and Red Monastery, both *c.* A.D. 430), Memphis, and in the pilgrimage town of St. Menas near Lake Mareotis. Columns with basket capitals, round arches, niches with triangular pediments, all in white limestone, form admirably pure outlines. Festoons, meanders and scrolls carved in stone stand out starkly against backgrounds heightened by dark colours. Christ, his saints, and the first heroes of monasticism, motionless and frontal, are grouped in frescoes painted with thick strokes of yellow ocher and red against bright backgrounds.

Few cultures have left such a rich legacy of craftwork. The Copts were bookbinders (they are credited with the invention of modern binding in the 4th century A.D.), joiners, bronzesmiths, glassmakers skilled in the chemistry of colors, ivory carvers and, above all, extremely skillful dyers and weavers with a mastery of both figure composition in large-scale tapestries (either monochrome or woven with multicolored threads) as well as of the meticulous geometrical ornamentation in the decorative bands (*clavi*) and panels sewn onto tunics. Textiles were perhaps the finest product of Coptic art. Crude Hellenistic figures in cloths woven by the peasants were still produced as late as the 5th century A.D., but the highly organized textile guilds had begun to design Biblical and Christian subjects by the end of the 4th. In the mid-5th century A.D. oriental styles and sometimes compositions (hunting scenes) appeared. Coptic textiles were exported in large quantities, and masterpieces of Egyptian craft are to be found in cathedral treasuries throughout western Europe.

After the Persian invasion at the beginning of the 7th century A.D. (which caused greater damage and destruction than the Arab conquest of A.D. 640), the Christian monasteries were fortified with outer walls and provided with a central dungeon. White limestone was replaced by unburned brick; the art of sculpture was lost. Painting changed from the old linear designs with white backgrounds to mystical portrayals seen darkly through a sea of blue, purple, and black. One of the finest examples of this style (which adopted Coptic subject matter, although its practitioners were often Syrian, Armenian, and even Ethiopian) decorates the old church of St. Anthony in the Red Sea Desert. Cavalcades of military saints transfixing demons with their lances appear beside rows of bearded hermits, while at the east end Christ enthroned is surrounded by the 20 elders and the 4 beasts of the Apocalypse. One is reminded of medieval Catalan painting.

Coptic Art. *Horus stabbing a crocodile.* 5th–6th century A.D. Louvre, Paris. *Photo Walter Dräyer, Zurich.*

CORINTH, Lovis (1858, Tapiau, East Prussia—1925, Zandvoort, Holland), German painter and graphic artist, a leading member of the *Sezession* group. His studies took him to Königsberg, Munich, Antwerp, Amsterdam, and Paris, where he worked mainly under William Bouguereau. Later, when he settled in Berlin (from 1900), he was described as a "German Impressionist". In his highly subjective portraits, his nudes, and his historical or mythological subjects, Corinth seized upon reality with a rather heavy hand and with sensual impetuosity.

In 1911 an apoplectic stroke gravely impaired his health and brought about, if not a radical reorientation of his art, at least a more deeply felt creative effort. A note of torment appeared along with a breathless and agitated animation, which dematerialized objects and scattered them over the canvas. This visionary Impressionism is apparent in the portraits as well as the still lifes, the flower pieces (*Red Roses*, 1925; New York, Coll. K. Gutman-Rosin), and the religious subjects (*Ecce Homo*, 1925; Basel, Offentlich Kunstsammlung), but is displayed with the maximum freedom in the huge landscapes that Corinth painted after 1918 on the banks of Walchensee Lake in Bavaria, using predominantly cold colors. He also executed a number of graphic works, primarily etchings and lithographs, which are among his most Expressionistic productions (*Self-Portrait*; 1924, etching).

CORNEILLE, Cornelis van Beverloo, *called* (b. 1922, Liège), Dutch painter. In 1948, at the age of twenty-six, with Karel Appel and Constant Nieuwenhuys (called Constant, b. 1920), he founded the avant-garde 'Experimental Group," an anti-academic association that favored spontaneity and free expression, and the revue *Reflex*, both of which were preludes to the Cobra movement, founded later that year in Paris. Corneille exhibited for the first time in 1949 in Paris, where he settled the following year, and where he began to develop a more personal style. Through his own work, and his influence within the Cobra movement, Corneille made significant contributions to the development of modern painting and graphic techniques. He traveled a great deal—notably in Africa and America—and his colors and texture are imbued with his impressions of those continents, conveyed not as transpositions of specific sites but as poetic bird's-eye views of geological landscapes whose light reveals internal structure and sudden florescences (*Sun Rising Above Rocks*, 1957; Paris, Coll. Sauvage). Corneille's work is closely linked to popular feeling, and is based on a whole system of signs (birds, clouds, sun, trees, stones) whose logical sequence creates a new language.

CORNEILLE DE LYON (*c.* 1510, The Hague—*c.* 1575, Lyons), painter of Dutch origin who became a naturalized Frenchman in 1547. Following his arrival in Paris, he managed to accompany the French court when it moved to Lyons, where he is first documented in 1540. By 1544 he belonged to the suite of the Dauphin, the future

Henri II. When Henri ascended the throne, Corneille became his official painter and personal valet (1551) and he retained the title of king's painter under Charles IX. In 1564, when Catherine de Médicis was passing through Lyons, she visited his studio She admired the series of little portraits of the entire court painted 20 years earlier, including one of herself and another of her daughters, and she was amused by the out-of-date clothing. Most of these portraits were engraved in medallions in a book called *Promptuarium Iconum* ("Collection of Portraits"), published in Lyons in 1553. The series of small portraits generally ascribed to him are painted on wood, with each face set against a flat background of blue or green. Their charm lies in an exquisite sense of color and a dexterity with the brush that improved steadily through countless repetitions of the same theme. Among the many portraits ascribed to him, some of the most noteworthy are those of the *Dauphin François* (Chantilly, Musée Condé), *Clément Marot* (Paris, Louvre), *Madame de Pompadour des Cars* (Versailles, Museum), *Gabrielle de Rochechouart* (*c.* 1547; Chantilly), *Monsieur de Randan* (Versailles), and *Madeleine de France* (Blois).

CORNELIUS, Peter (1783, Düsseldorf—1867, Rome), German painter. After studying at the Düsseldorf Academy, he went to Rome (1811), where he joined the Nazarene painters. When, in 1816, Bartholdy, the Prussian consul general, entrusted the Nazarenes with the decoration in fresco of one of the state rooms in the Palazzo Zuccaro, Cornelius carried out the best compositions of the ensemble: the *Interpretation of Pharaoh's Dreams* and the *Recognition of Joseph by His Brothers* (now in Berlin, Staatliche Museen). In 1819 Cornelius was called to Munich by the heir to the throne of Bavaria, the future King Ludwig I, to decorate the Glyptothek. This project, completed in 1830, was to bring the artist great personal success. In 1821 he assumed direction of the Düsseldorf Academy; then, in 1824, of the Munich Academy. He came into conflict with the architect Leo von Klenze over the decoration of the Alte Pinakothek in Munich and, in compensation, was entrusted with that of Friedrich von Gärtner's (1792–1847) Ludwigskirche in Munich, but the work did not meet with great public approval. In 1841 King Friedrich-Wilhelm of Prussia called Cornelius to Berlin, where the painter's efforts were engaged mainly in preparatory work for a vast cycle of frescoes, never realized, to decorate a Berlin cemetery on the model of the Camposanto in Pisa.

CORNELL, Joseph (b. 1903, Nyack, N.Y.—d. 1973), American sculptor. Cornell began painting, without any formal training, during the Depression and had his first exhibition in New York in 1932; he continued to have one-man shows in the United States, including a major retrospective in 1967 at the Guggenheim Museum, New York.

Cornell is best known for his enclosed constructions assembled of various objects and clippings within picture-frame boxes; the unexpected juxtapositions of the materials seem surrealistic, yet the constructions are controlled by a remarkable precision, order, and a sense of stillness. There is a remote and nostalgic quality about Cornell's boxes, with their allusions to both geographical and temporal distances, achieved by historical references (*Medici Slot Machine*, 1942; *Taglioni's Jewel Casket*, 1940) or through cosmological elements, as in the *Sun Box* and *Eclipse Series* of the early 1960s. In a number of ways Cornell utilized theater and film conventions, with which he was familiar through his own experiments in film-making. His work marks a stage in the development of collage and assemblage in the 20th century between Dadaism and later large-scale assemblages, such as Robert Rauschenberg's combines.

COROT, Jean-Baptiste Camille (1796, Paris—1875, Paris), French landscape painter. In 1822 he entered the studio of the academic artist Jean-Victor Bertin (1775–1842) at the École des Beaux-Arts, Paris. His father agreed to subsidize a trip to Italy on the condition that he paint a self-portrait before leaving; *Corot at His Easel* (1825; Paris, Louvre) shows a tall, strapping fellow, calm and vigorous, but with anxious eyes and necktie askew.

In March of 1826, while in Rome, he painted the *Colosseum* (1826; Paris, Louvre) in 30 sittings in the Farnese Gardens. To the Salon of 1827 Corot sent the *Bridge of Narni* (Ottawa, National Gallery of Canada), a landscape following academic canons. Returning to Paris in 1828, he painted carefully prepared portraits of his relatives and friends, for he did not wish "to leave indecision in any object."

Jean-Baptiste Camille Corot. *Cathedral of Chartres*. 1830. Louvre, Paris. *Photo Giraudon, Paris.*

Fleeing his native city in 1830, Corot painted the *Cathedral of Chartres* (1830; Louvre) in an unexpectedly rustic setting, bathed in the golden atmosphere of the surrounding plain of the Beauce. In 1834 he returned to Italy, adding each day to the number of sketches from which he was later to draw the elements of the "souvenirs" he would send to successive Salons. He then resumed his wanderings through France. He felt obliged to continue to send to the Salons dancers, shepherds, fauns, and monks, but he placed them in country scenes taken from his sketchbooks. If Corot became an innovator, it was instinctively and without intending to do so. However, he left at least one masterpiece in the classical style, *La Toilette* (1859; New York, Coll. Wildenstein), evocative of both Virgil and Giorgione. The press began to praise him during the Salon of 1840, to which he sent a *Little Shepherd* (Metz, Museum), purchased by the state, and a *Flight into Egypt*. Finally in 1846, in recognition of his *View of the Forest of Fontainebleau* (exhibited 1831; Washington, D.C., National Gallery) he was awarded the Legion d'Honneur. In 1848 he was made a member of the Salon jury; thereafter he was represented each year by a view of Ville d'Avray accompanied by souvenirs of his travels.

Correggio. *Leda and the Swan. c.* 1530. Staatliche Museen, Berlin-Dahlem. *Photo Walter Steinkopf, Berlin.*

Corot worked up to the very end of his life, and his last pictures are among the most beautiful: *Souvenir of Mortefontaine* (1864), the *Church of Marissel* (1867), and above all the *Belfry of Douai* (1871), the *Road of Sin-le-Noble* (1873), and the *Cathedral of Sens* (1874), all in the Louvre.

CORPORA, Antonio (b. 1909, Tunis), Italian painter. After studying at the Tunis Academy, he went to Florence to study the masters in the Uffizi, and then settled in Milan, where he came into contact with artists of the abstract avant-garde. Between the wars he often visited Paris, where he was noticed by the art dealer Leopold Zborowski, a friend of Amedeo Modigliani. In 1945 he settled in Rome; there—with the painters Renato Guttuso and Giulio Turcato (b. 1912), and the sculptor Pericle Fazzini—he founded the Neo-cubist group. In 1947, with Renato Birolli, Emilio Vedova, and Giuseppe Santomaso, he took part in the Fronte Nuovo delle Arti group. He was one of the eight Italian painters who exhibited at the Venice Biennale in 1952. Corpora resisted abstraction for some time and his development from figurative painting occurred over an extended period. Taking the principles of Cubism as a point of departure, he chose a form of abstraction that rejected both geometricism and Tachism. Austere, somber, and reserved, his works are remarkable for the solidity and richness of their paint, which appears to have been applied in depth to produce an effect that is alternately opaque and iridescent (*Mediterranean Scene*, 1953; Brescia, Coll. Achille Cavellini).

Correggio. "*Madonna della Scodella.*" *c.* 1530. Pinacoteca, Parma. *Photo Alinari-Giraudon.*

CORREGGIO, Antonio Allegri, *called* (between 1489 and 1494, Correggio, Reggio Emilia—1534, Correggio), Italian painter. A group of works, attributed to Correggio's early years, including a fresco of the *Deposition* at S. Andrea, Mantua, appears to suggest a thorough artistic education at Mantua itself, in a milieu permeated by examples of Mantegna's art. But the vehemence and harshly chiseled volumes of Mantegna's work are already softened by a delicate sfumato betraying the influence of painters such as Lorenzo Costa, and no doubt an echo of the experiments of Leonardo. Correggio's first authenticated altarpiece, the *Madonna with St. Francis* (1514–15; Dresden, Gemäldegalerie), embodies a series of traditional motifs that possess a facility of composition due perhaps to the influence of Raphael's *Sistine Madonna* (hung in Piacenza *c.* 1513; now in Dresden, Gemäldegalerie). A series of half-length figures of the Virgin (Hampton Court; Milan, Castello Sforzesco) attributed to the years 1514–17 show the same care in imparting movement to broad and softly modeled forms.

At the convent of S. Paolo in Rome the *camera*, or chamber, of the abbess (*c.* 1519), with its umbellated vault and its delicate trellis of leaves and fruit, assuredly betrays the influence of Mantegna, but the grisailles of the lunettes (*Adonis*, the *Three Graces, Juno Chastized*) already contain those beautiful nudes with rather shortened proportions whose wholly sensual seductive appeal is inevitably to suffuse even his ecclesiastical paintings. Begun in 1520, the cupola of S. Giovanni Evangelista, Parma, creates a stable and luminous composition in which the religious theme appears to yield to an impassioned hymn in praise of the human body, which draws inspiration from Michelangelo. The cupola of the cathedral, dedicated to a representation of the *Assumption of the Virgin* (1524–30), adopts and amplifies the same theme.

Correggio's compositions show a predilection for sweeping diagonals (the *Madonna della Scodella*, *c.* 1530; Parma, Pinacoteca) or for floating rhythms (the *Deposition*, *c.* 1522; Parma, Pinacoteca), accentuating the insubstantial draperies and unstable poses. The artist experimented with spatial compositions of ever increasing complexity and subtlety (allegories of *Vice* and *Virtue*, *c.* 1532–33; Paris, Louvre). At times, grace of expression verges on worldly suavity (the *Madonna with St. Jerome*, known as *Day*, *c.* 1525, Parma, Pinacoteca; the *Mystic Marriage of St. Catherine*, *c.* 1525, Louvre) and even an affected rhetoric (the famous *Madonna with St. George*, *c.* 1531; Gemäldegalerie). In the series of mythological canvases done in the early 1530s this is redeemed by an avowed sensuality ranging from the false innocence of adolescence (*Leda and the Swan*, *c.* 1530; Berlin, Staatliche Museen) to languid voluptuousness. The great masterpieces—the *Danaë* of 1530–32 in the Galleria Borghese in Rome, and *Jupiter and Antiope* in the Louvre—represent the cry of desire itself. Correggio's art seems to renounce the experiences of the great Renaissance geniuses, reflecting instead each seductive nuance of feeling from coquetry to voluptuousness. This very renunciation entailed the discovery of a new world and a new language, the repercussions of which were immense: in the work of Parmigianino, Baroccio, or Lodovico Carracci its influence was direct; at the beginning of the 19th century it was pushed to the point of plagiarism by Pierre-Paul Prud'hon; and its spirit permeated all of Baroque art of the 17th and 18th centuries.

COSSA, Francesco del (*c.* 1435, Ferrara—*c.* 1478, Bologna), Italian painter. Formed in the same artistic milieu as Cosimo Tura, who was slightly older, Cossa benefited from the latter's experience and the example of Borso d'Este's miniaturists. However, his style is completely original in the major works of his Ferrarese period—the frescoes painted for Borso d'Este in the Hall of the Months in the Palazzo Schifanoia, Ferrara (1470). Cossa was largely responsible for three of the twelve frescoes in this cycle. What remains of the others was the work of Ercole de'Roberti and less important artists, including Baldassarre Estense (before 1441–1504). Cossa represented *March, April,* and *May* in three superimposed registers with scenes glorifying Duke Borso; several signs of the Zodiac (*Aries, Taurus, Gemini*); and the triumphs of *Minerva, Venus*, and *Apollo*. These important works comprise one of the most successful of all the secular decorative cycles of the period. Cossa here shows himself the equal of Tura in his plastic force, the implacable energy of the figures and contours, and the enamel-like brilliance of his colors; but there is a certain courtly good humor and a more relaxed prosaic note. He went shortly afterward to Bologna, where he found new clients. There he made stained-glass windows (one is today in the Musée Jacquemart-André, Paris), frescoes that have since disappeared, and altarpieces, of which three survive: the *Annunciation* (Dresden, Gemäldegalerie); a *Madonna with St. Petronius and St. John* (1474; Bologna, Palazzo Comunale); and a huge polyptych, now dispersed, painted for the Griffoni Chapel in S. Petronio (1473). Before dismemberment, there was, at the center, in front of imaginary, brightly lit landscapes, a *St. Vincent Ferrer* (London, National Gallery), flanked by *St. Peter and St. John the Baptist* (Milan, Brera); on an upper level a harsh and terrible *Calvary* was flanked by *St. Florian* and *St. Lucy* (Washington, D.C., National Gallery). The predella and pilasters were the work of Ercole de' Roberti, who at this time was collaborating with Cossa. With the Roverella polyptych, painted by Tura at the same period, the Griffoni polyptych constitutes one of the summits of the poetic and plastic genius of Ferrara.

COSTA, Lorenzo (1460, Ferrara—1535, Mantua), Italian painter. Costa worked in Bologna from 1483 to 1506; then, until his death, at the court of Mantua, where he succeeded Andrea Mantegna. Although receptive to Venetian influences, he was primarily a follower of the great Ferrarese style, particularly that of Ercole de' Roberti, and he produced a modified version of it during his most original period, which extends from about 1485 to the closing years of the 15th century. The mural paintings in the Bentivoglio Chapel of S. Giacomo Maggiore (1488–90) and the large altarpieces in S. Petronio (1492) and S. Giovanni in Monte (1497), all in Bologna, reveal a stately classicism that is delicate yet substantial, and show too his remarkable qualities as a portraitist and landscape artist. He did not always avoid a certain lifelessness, but he is often redeemed by a real narrative gracefulness, as in the *Allegories* for the *studiolo* of Isabella d'Este (Paris, Louvre), by a tender melancholy in facial expressions, and by an occasional elegance of line, which anticipate the refinements of Mannerism.

COSTA, Lúcio (b. 1902, Toulon, Var), French-born Brazilian architect; and one of the leading figures in modern Brazilian architecture. In 1924 he received his diploma from the National School of Fine Arts in Rio de Janeiro, and he then entered into partnership with Gregori Warchavchik (b. 1896), one of the pioneers of modern building methods in Brazil. In 1931, a year after the Vargas revolution, Costa was appointed director of the School of Fine Arts, which included the School of Architecture. He also worked for the National Historical and Artistic Patrimony Department from its foundation in 1937, producing a number of studies and supervising the restoration of monuments. When Costa was commissioned to design the Ministry of Education and Health in Rio (1937–43), he at once formed a group of young assistant architects and invited Le Corbusier to act as consultant. Having introduced modern ideas into the architecture of his country, Costa was made responsible for the Brazilian Pavilion at the New York World's Fair (1939). He is most famous for his town planning of the new city of Brasília (1956), which provided a starkly modern and appropriate setting for the public buildings designed by Niemeyer and placed Brazil in the forefront of modern architecture.

COSWAY, Richard (1742, near Bampton, Devon—1821, London), English miniaturist. He was sent to London before he was twelve years old and studied under Thomas Hudson (1701–79) and at William Shipley's (1714–1803) drawing school. In 1769 he was accepted as a pupil at the Royal Academy Schools; he was made an Associate in 1770 and a full member in 1771. In 1781 he married Maria Hadfield (1759–1838), a miniature painter trained in Italy. Cosway seems to have participated to the full in the social life of his time and was an intimate friend of the Prince of Wales. He is best known as a miniaturist, a field in which he was extremely competent, achieving a fresh naturalism that has a bloom of high fashion (the *Prince Regent*, Coll. Countess of Portarlington). He also painted a number of portraits in oils that show greater seriousness, as, for example, his *Self-Portrait in Van Dyck Costume* (Coll. Lord Berwick). Certain of Cosway's drawings, such as that of *Henry, 7th Duke of Beaufort* (Coll. Duke of Beaufort), are supreme expressions of the panache of the Prince Regent's circle.

COTES, Francis (1726, London—1770, London), fashionable 18th-century English portraitist. He was a pupil of George Knapton (1698–1778), and may have completed his studies abroad. There is a striking dependence on Rosalba Carriera in Cotes' *Princess Caroline Matilda* of 1766 (Brunswick); on the other hand, he could have seen many examples of Rosalba's work in England, notably at Horace Walpole's estate Strawberry Hill (Twickenham, Middlesex). The main influence on his mature style, that of Jean Étienne Liotard, can be explained by Liotard's extremely successful visit to England in 1753–55.

From the 1750s Cotes was in competition with Sir Joshua Reynolds and Allan Ramsay, and this three-sided rivalry ended only with the death of Cotes in 1770. He worked mainly in pastels until about 1763 and in oils thereafter. He was named one of the 24 directors of the Society of Artists when it was incorporated by Royal Charter in 1765, and in 1768 was a foundation member of the Royal Academy.

Cotes' extremely attractive style is at its best in works in which he is free of the desire to emulate Reynolds. His portraits of *Francis Burdett* (1764; Hull, Ferens Art Gallery), *Mrs. Samuel Allpress* (1769, Coll. Marquess of Crewe), and *John Adam* (Blairadam, Coll. Capt. C. K. Adams) are fresh, intimate, lively, brightly colored, and free of the more obvious hallmarks of "fashion."

Francesco del Cossa. *Month of March*. Detail: *Tree Pruning*. 1470. Palazzo Schifanoia, Ferrara.

Robert de Cotte. Palace of Cardinal de Rohan-Soubise, bishop of Strasbourg. Façade on the Ill River. 1731. *Photo E. Glasser—Service du Tourisme, Strasbourg.*

COTMAN, John Sell (1782, Norwich—1842, London), English watercolorist. He went to London about 1798 and, the following year, became associated with Dr. Thomas Monro. Cotman's closest and most influential contact was Thomas Girtin, whose artistic heir he became—at least to some extent—after the latter's death in 1802.

In 1806 Cotman returned to Norwich. To the Norwich Society's exhibition of 1807 he sent 20 works; to that of the following year, 67. From 1810 to 1822, he was active primarily as an etcher of architectural antiquities. This activity was financed by Dawson Turner, a banker and amateur antiquarian, who became Cotman's close friend on Cotman's removal to Yarmouth in 1812. The most important series of etchings were: *Etchings of All Ornamental Antiquities in Norfolk*, 1812–19; *Sepulchral Brasses of Norfolk and Suffolk*, 1814–19; *Norman and Gothic Architecture in the County of Norfolk*, 1816–18; and *Architectural Antiquities of Normandy*, 1822, for which J. M. W. Turner wrote the text.

In 1834 Cotman was appointed drawing master to King's College, London, where his pupils included Dante Gabriel Rossetti. This period saw a sudden burst of Romanticism in Cotman's art. *The Gateway of the Abbey of Aumale, Normandy* (1832; Norwich, Castle Museum) has a brilliance of color and an intense interest in the medieval picturesque that bear witness to the example of Richard Bonington.

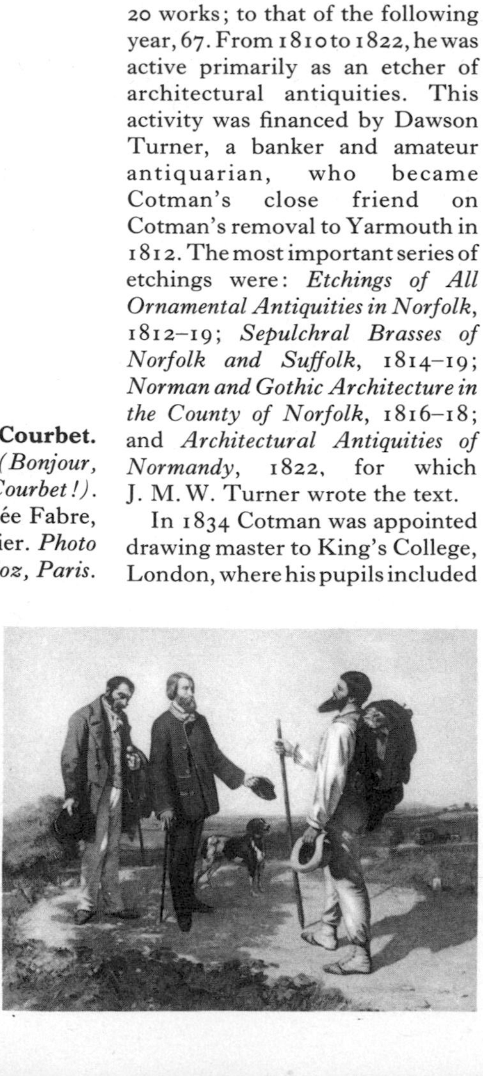

In 1841 Cotman paid a final visit to Norwich. The drawing entitled the *Wold Afloat* (London, British Museum) and the unfinished painting *From My Father's House at Thorpe* (Castle Museum) reveal the artist's intense and almost naturalistic pantheism, which he had previously held in check by his rigorous sense of form.

Cotman's preoccupation with flat color wash and geometric form gave his work an abstract intellectual quality that was entirely ahead of its time. This quality, unique in British art, can best be appreciated in works such as *Greta Bridge, Yorkshire* (1810; Castle Museum), with its characteristic washes of blue and yellow. The *Window Between St. Andrew's Hall and the Dutch Church, Norwich* (1807; Melbourne, National Gallery of Victoria), exquisite in its finesse, combines the delicate tracery of the Gothic window with a feeling for the broadness and solidity of the wall. It is this ability to combine the general and the particular, together with a matchless understanding of the relationship of architecture to landscape, that makes Cotman an artist in the highest category.

COTTE, Robert de (1656, Paris—1735, Paris), French architect. His career began under the reign of Louis XIV with a period of brilliant activity while he was working with his brother-in-law, Jules Hardouin-Mansart, who, when dying, charged him with completing his work.

De Cotte's designs (1699–1710) for Versailles (the vestibule of the chapel, the Salon d'Hercule, and the Grand Trianon) and his decoration for the chancel of Notre-Dame de Paris (1708–14) were still animated by the spirit of Hardouin-Mansart. The example set by the master was also the basis for many of De Cotte's designs for private dwellings in Paris. Many of these houses were unfortunately destroyed, but the Hôtel d'Estrées on Rue de Grenelle (1713; now the embassy of the U.S.S.R.), and the Hôtel de Bouvallais (*c.* 1717) still give an idea of their scope.

From 1708, in the immediate vicinity of the capital, De Cotte undertook the reconstruction of the Abbaye de St-Denis, which was completed after his death. His fame reached Flanders, the Rhineland, Alsace, Piedmont, and Spain. For Elector Joseph Clemens of Bavaria, he continued work on the Castle of Bonn (1715). He succeeded Enrico Zuccali as architect for Max Emmanuel's castle of Schleissheim, near Munich (1719); he was also the architect of the Thurn und Taxis Palace in Frankfurt (1732–41), and around 1734 he drew up plans for the Cabinet of the Furies at the royal palace in Madrid.

Two of De Cotte's finest surviving works are the bishop's palaces at Verdun (1724) and Strasbourg (1731). The horseshoe courtyard at Verdun is reminiscent of the royal stables at Versailles, while the palace at Strasbourg, built for the Cardinal de Rohan, is an imposing quadrilateral whose more ample façade, crowned by a squared dome in the tradition of Jacques Lemercier and Louis Le Vau, is reflected in the waters of the Ill River.

COURBET, Gustave (1819, Ornans, Doubs—1877, La Tour-de-Peilz, near Vevey, Switzerland), French painter, and exponent of realism. At the age of twenty, Courbet went to Paris, supposedly to study law; but he turned instead to painting, which he pursued in the Louvre, copying two supreme models, Giorgione and Velázquez. He worked relentlessly, and submitted a recollection of the hunt to his first Salon (*Courbet with a Black Dog*, 1842; Paris, Petit Palais). The Salon of 1846 accepted only one of his eight entries, but in Courbet's opinion this Salon marked the beginnings of his style, termed realist by the painter and his friends. After the Revolution of 1848, the Salon was open to all contributors. He showed six of his paintings in 1848, and the critics began to take notice of his singular talent. His entry for the Salon of 1849, the *Man with a Leather Belt* (Paris, Louvre), was another self-portrait, but "in the Venetian manner." The government bought Courbet's *After Dinner at Ornans* (Lille, Palais des Beaux-Arts), which depicts his family gathered around the still-laden

Gustave Courbet. *The Meeting (Bonjour, Monsieur Courbet!).* 1854. Musée Fabre, Montpellier. *Photo Bulloz, Paris.*

Gustave Courbet. *The Atelier.* 1854–55. Detail. Louvre, Paris. *Photo Giraudon, Paris.*

table. Returning to Ornans in October, 1849, he painted the *Stone Breakers* (destroyed; formerly Dresden, Gemäldegalerie), whom he had met on the road.

In December 1848 Courbet began the painting that was to confirm him in his role of leader of a school and make him famous at the age of thirty, *Burial at Ornans* (Louvre); in it he portrayed the people of his village gathered in the cemetery—50 life-size figures standing against a distant background of bluffs. The picture seemed shocking and blasphemous to the horrified bourgeoisie, who accused him of painting in an ugly and subversive manner. To disconcert his judges, Courbet submitted a work of incomparable freshness and harmony to the Salon of 1852, the *Demoiselles du Village* (New York, Metropolitan Museum), who were none other than his three sisters in summer dress, in the most verdant of valleys. Rewarded by sarcasm, he retaliated by undertaking the subject sacred to academicism, the nude, for the following Salon (the provocative *Bathers*, Musée Fabre). It was to this canvas that he owed his closest friendship, that of a Montpellier collector named Alfred Bruyas, who commissioned a portrait of himself and asked Courbet to paint their meeting on the road to Montpellier, where the painter had gone at his invitation. The result was the famous *Meeting*; also known as *Bonjour, Monsieur Courbet!* (1854; Musée Fabre), lampooned by the poet Théodore de Banville in humorous verse.

During his frequent visits to the south of France, Courbet lightened his palette. This became apparent when he returned to Ornans and painted the *Winnowers* (1854; Nantes, Musée des Beaux-Arts), in which his sister Zoé, in a red dress, is seen sifting grain. He returned to Paris and began his *Atelier* (Louvre), a "real allegory," the most important manifesto of realist art, which he exhibited in 1855, together with 40 earlier canvases, in a temporary building that he had constructed on Avenue Montaigne, following the rejection of the *Atelier* by the jury of the Exposition Internationale.

In his *Demoiselles des Bords de la Seine* (1856; Petit Palais), Courbet poked fun at admirers of boudoir scenes. The years that followed were filled with trips to Belgium, Germany, and the south of France, in the enjoyment of a reputation that had spread throughout Europe. In the five years preceding the fall of the Second Empire in 1870, he alternated winter landscapes and marines (he had been taken to Honfleur and Trouville by Eugène Boudin and there discovered the sea) with portraits and nudes, more sumptuous than ever (*Woman with a Parrot*, 1866, Metropolitan Museum; *Sleepers* or *Slumber*, 1866, Petit Palais). At the Salon of 1866, he had an unqualified success with the *Deer Cover* (Louvre). Following the *Kill* (Besançon, Musée des Beaux-Arts) in 1867, he prepared a second one-man show at the Rond-Point de l'Alma. In 1869 he made another trip to Munich, where he had his last great success and dazzled his German colleagues by the virtuosity of his portrait of the painter Wilhelm von Kaulbach's maid, the marvelous *Woman of Munich*, worthy of Velázquez.

COUSTOU, family of French sculptors from Lyons, descended from François Coustou (documented 1657–90), a wood carver who married the sister of Antoine Coysevox, a sculptor in the service of royalty. The principal members of the family were:

NICOLAS (1658, Lyons—1733, Paris), son of François. He won the Prix de Rome in 1682. On his return to France he worked constantly in the royal workshops at the châteaux of Trianon, Versailles (*France*, Chambre du Roi, 1701; J-B. Colbert, 1716), and above all Marly. The *Nymph with a Quiver of Arrows* and *Venus with a Dove*, saved from the wreckage of Marly, are now in the Tuileries, Paris, while *Meleager Killing a Boar* (1706) is at Versailles, and *Adonis Resting from the Hunt* (1710), the most successful, is in the Louvre, Paris. Nicolas executed a figure of *Louis XV as Jupiter* (Louvre) for the château of Petit-Bourg and began the sepulchral figure of *Cardinal de Farbin-Janson* in Beauvais Cathedral (completed by Guillaume).

GUILLAUME (1677, Lyons—1746, Paris), brother of Nicolas, a pupil of Coysevox. He worked in Rome with Pierre II Legros (1616–1719) and later collaborated in all of his brother's works. He was sole author, however, of a statue of *Louis XIII Kneeling*, found opposite the *Louis XIV* by Coysevox in Notre-Dame, Paris. Guillaume's portrait sculpture includes the funerary statue of *Cardinal Dubois* in the church of St-Roch, Paris; a terra-cotta bust of his brother *Nicolas* (Louvre); and a statue of *Maria Leszczynska as Juno* (1731; Louvre), a masterpiece of Rococo freedom and vivacity. His final work, two sculptural groups known as the *Horses of Marly* (1742–45), is his crowning achievement; originally carved for Marly, the statues were transferred to the entrance to the Champs-Élysées at the Place de la Concorde in Paris, becoming pendants to Coysevox's earlier *Horses of Marly* (completed 1702).

COUTURE, Thomas (1815, Senlis—1879, Villiers-le-Bel, Seine-et-Oise), best known of the mid-19th century French academic painters. He studied painting first in the Paris studios of Baron Antoine-Jean Gros and Hippolyte Delaroche, and then in Rome (1837). He met with some success in the Salon (the *Lust for Gold*, 1844; Toulouse, Musée des Beaux-Arts), and in 1847 his *Decadent Romans* (Paris, Louvre) brought him fame. He showed greater pictorial sense in his *Promises* (preparatory study in Minneapolis, Walker Art Institute), a study for a huge canvas on *Volunteers Enrolling*, which he never completed. One of Manet's teachers, he published his theories in *Entretiens d'atelier* ("Studio Topics").

Guillaume Coustou. *Bust of Nicolas Coustou.* Louvre, Paris. *Photo Jean Roubier, Paris.*

COX, David (1783, Deritend, near Birmingham—1859, Harborne), English watercolor painter. From

1804 to 1813 he made his home in London; in 1805 he paid his first visit to northern Wales, with which his name is so closely associated.

The chronicle of Cox's life consists mainly of a series of sketching trips throughout England, with visits to Belgium and Holland in 1826 and to France in 1829 and 1832. His journeys to Wales were resumed in 1842; thereafter he paid an annual visit to Bettws-y-Coed. Many of his finest works are associated with Welsh sites and scenery.

Works such as the *Hereford* (Birmingham, City Art Gallery) and the *Ghent* (Manchester, Whitworth Art Gallery) follow the pattern made popular by Samuel Prout (1783–1852). But Cox has traits that rescue him from anonymity. An early oil of *All Saints Church, Hastings* (1812; Birmingham, City Art Gallery) has a kind of ardent freshness and sparkling quality that is peculiarly his own. The rain-washed *View in Paris* (London, Tate Gallery) is free of any literary or historical associations and for this very reason is more modern than similar subjects by Richard Parkes Bonington, whose indirect influence may be read into the watercolors inspired by Cox's visits to France (*Calais Harbor*; London, British Museum). In 1836 Cox discovered a rough Scottish wrapping paper that exactly suited his technique; his later works have a corresponding vitality far removed in feeling from the well-bred daintiness of his early watercolors. An excellent example is the *Sun, Wind, and Rain* of 1845 (Birmingham, City Art Gallery).

COYSEVOX, Antoine (1640, Lyons—1720, Paris), French sculptor. Son of a wood carver, he arrived in Paris at the age of seventeen. There, through the offices of André Le Nôtre, he became the apprentice of Louis Lerambert (1620–70), a sculptor who worked at Versailles and was highly regarded at court. In 1676 he went to Paris to accept membership in the Académie Royale and was induced to stay by promises of advancement extended by Charles Le Brun. At Versailles, the Cour de Marbre, Grande Galerie, and Salon de la Guerre (with the *Glory of Louis XIV*, 1683–85), and, above all, the Escalier des Ambassadeurs, destroyed during the reign of Louis XV, owed their best decorative elements to Coysevox, notably the bust of Louis XIV in Roman attire (1678–80), which survived the destruction of the ensemble. It was in the gardens, however, that his influence was particularly apparent: in the *Chariot of Triumphant France* (1683), the *Vase of War* (1684), the bronze *Garonne* and *Dordogne* on the Parterre d'Eau (1685), and in the copies of antique sculpture: the *Nymph with a Shell* (1683; Paris, Louvre), *Kneeling Venus* (1686; Louvre) and *Castor and Pollux* (1702; Versailles).

Antoine Coysevox. Tomb of Cardinal Mazarin. Detail. 1689–93. Marble. Institut de France, Paris. *Foto Marburg.*

Le Brun's death (1690) brought a liberation from a somewhat constraining supervision and enabled Coysevox to display his fullest powers at the Château de Marly. The *Horses of the Watering Trough* (1701–2; now at the entrance of the Jardin des Tuileries); the groups for the artificial river at Marly, notably the *Seine* (1706; Louvre) and the *Flora* (Tuileries), were inspired by eclogues and pastoral poetry. The masterpiece of this mythological idyll is the statue of *Marie-Adélaïde de Savoie as Diana* (1710; Louvre); it was the first of those "mythological portraits" that were to enjoy an ever increasing popularity.

Coysevox' true genius, however, is to be seen in a dazzling series of portrait busts that created the image of an age. First and foremost are the portraits of Louis XIV, some 10 in number, showing his transition from royal youth to moribund old age. The most impressive is the statue of the king kneeling in the choir of Notre-Dame, Paris (1715). The busts of the *Great Condé* (1686; Louvre); the courtly *Cardinal Melchior de Polignac* (1718; Paris, Coll. Mme. de Polignac); and those of the artists *Le Brun* (1679; Louvre), *Le Nôtre* (*c.* 1701; Paris, Église St-Roch), and *Mansart* are all masterpieces.

There remain the funeral monuments, in which Coysevox excelled. He executed the mausoleums of the Marquis de Vaubrun (1680; Château de Serrant), Colbert (1685–1712, Paris, St-Eustache), Mazarin (1689–93; Paris, Institut de France), and Le Brun (Paris, St-Nicolas-du-Chardonnet). In his late sculpture, Coysevox anticipated the 18th century, whose sculptors were all trained either by himself, his nephews—the Coustou family—or by their pupils.

COZENS, Alexander (1717, St. Petersburg, Russia—1786, London), one of the most original of the 18th-century English watercolor painters, the son of a shipbuilder in the service of Czar Peter the Great.

Cozens' "systems" were the main source of his fame among his contemporaries. The earliest was a book of 32 different species of tree, semi-diagrammatic in treatment, published in 1771. In 1772 Cozens conceived a system entitled *Morality*, to consist of illustrations of human virtues and vices treated in a fairly epic manner. Other systems considered types of facial beauty and varieties of sky. But undoubtedly his most famous system was his *New Method of Assisting the Invention in Drawing Original Compositions of Landscape*, published in 1785. Here he developed an idea popularized by Leonardo da Vinci. In order to fix the attention on a general outline of composition rather than a mere assemblage of details, the artist should stain or blot a piece of paper with a large brush and convert this into a landscape. Figures and animals could then be added in pencil and finally a system of lighting superimposed. The process relies a great deal on an acute visual memory, such as Cozens himself possessed, and many of his blots in the British Museum, London are very near in appearance to Chinese painting, in which the same technique is used for different reasons. The insistence on bold brushwork rather than a detailed pencil is undoubtedly an innovation in the history of English watercolor. The lonely grandeur of his landscape sketches, evident in *Rocky Island* (Manchester, Whitworth Art Gallery) and *Sun Breaking*

Through Clouds (British Museum), also gives his work a Rousseau-esque quality.

JOHN ROBERT (1752, London—1797, London), son of Alexander, was also a watercolorist. In 1773 he etched and signed eight *Views of Bath*, and in 1776 he exhibited at the Royal Academy a picture of *Hannibal Crossing the Alps* (now lost). In the same year Cozens traveled through Switzerland to Italy, possibly as draftsman to the collector Richard Payne Knight, and remained in Italy until 1779. A second and more elaborate journey to Italy, via Cologne, Augsburg, and the Tyrol, was made in 1782 in the company of William Beckford.

John Robert Cozens' watercolors may be related almost without exception to his two journeys to the Alps and Italy. The earlier watercolors are delicate, simple, and impersonal, with a complete absence of visual "effects." The drawings and watercolors of the second Italian journey are richer in color, and here indeed it is possible to see an adumbration of Turner. There is also a greater emotional content, conveyed in broad bands of light and shade, that might tentatively be described as proto-Romantic (*View from Mirabella*; London, Victoria and Albert Museum).

CRAM, Ralph Adams (1863, Hampton, New Hampshire—1942, Boston), American architect. Cram worked in Boston, studied in Europe, then returned to Boston in 1889. He formed a partnership with Charles Wentworth (1861–97) that was joined in 1891 by Bertram Goodhue, and on the death of Wentworth by Frank Ferguson (1861–1926). After Goodhue's departure in 1914, the firm continued as Cram and Ferguson. Cram's work (largely institutional architecture) included buildings for the U.S. Military Academy (West Point, N.Y., 1908); Rice Institute (Houston, Tex., 1913); Wheaton College (Norton, Mass., 1918); Sweetbriar College (Lynchburg, Va., 1930s); Rollins College (Winterhaven, Fla., 1931); and Princeton University (Princeton, N.J., 1913). Cram also achieved great success in church design, particularly when, in 1911, he was appointed to continue the Cathedral of St. John the Divine in New York. He published more than 20 books, including *Church Building* (1901), *The Gothic Quest* (1907), *The Substance of Gothic* (1917), *The Catholic Church and Art* (1929), and *The End of Democracy* (1937).

CRANACH THE ELDER, Lucas (1472, Kronach, Franconia—1553, Weimar), German Renaissance painter and engraver. In 1503 he is documented in Vienna, where he painted portraits of two Humanists, *Doctor Reuss* (Nuremberg, Germanisches Museum) and *Doctor Cuspinian* (Winterthur, Coll. Oskar Reinhart), with their wives. His *Crucifixion,* destined for the Scottish Monastery of Vienna (now in the Kunsthistorisches Museum), with its three ferocious horsemen, was probably painted *c.* 1500. Another *Crucifixion* (Munich, Alte Pinakothek), dated 1503, makes use of less markedly criminal types and produces a highly dramatic effect, with the Christ at the extreme right of the composition looming against a stormy sky. From 1504 comes the charming idyll of the *Flight into Egypt* (formerly Berlin).

In the same year the Elector Frederick the Wise called Cranach to Wittenberg, where he was to serve, with exemplary fidelity, three successive electors: Frederick the Wise, who died in 1525; John the Constant, until 1532; and finally John Frederick the Magnificent, whom he followed into captivity in Augsburg (1550) after the disastrous battle of Mühlberg. He made a journey to the Low Countries in 1508, and in the same year he was granted the armorial crest of a winged dragon, which became the signature for the output of his very fashionable workshop, carried on even after his death by his son.

In 1506 Cranach made a woodcut, *Venus and Cupid*, and in 1509 he painted the *Venus* now in the Hermitage, Leningrad, both of which display a feeling for ample form. These two Venuses inaugurate a series of female nudes—including several versions each of *Nymph at the Spring* (1518, Leipzig, Museum der Bildenden Künste; 1534, Liverpool, Royal Institution), *Venus* (1530, Braunschweig, Herzog-Anton-Ulrich-Museum; 1532, Rome, Galleria Borghese; 1532, Frankfurt, Städelsches Kunstinstitut), and *Lucretia* (*c.* 1530, Munich, Alte Pinakothek; 1532, Vienna, Akademie der Bildenden Künste)—in which the somewhat equivocal type favored by Cranach emerges even more clearly. The draftsmanship, despite its audacious distortion, is wonderfully fluent. Cranach turns his back, more and more decidedly, on realism in all its aspects. These mannered nudes are at the same time sensual and, when he brings them together in a mythological scene, such as the *Judgment of Paris* (1529; New York, Metropolitan Museum), he finds means of further accentuating this characteristic by adorning one of the goddesses with an immense hat, while by contrast, the armor in which Paris is encased gives him the appearance of a large, articulated scarab. In the princely *Hunts*, a series of anecdotal works, the artist's eccentricity can be appreciated even more clearly. The earliest (1529), and probably one of the best, is that of *Frederick the Wise and Maximilian* (Vienna, Kunsthistorisches Museum). Other *Hunts* include those in Moritzburg, near Dresden (1540; Barockmuseum Schloss Moritzburg), Vienna (1544; Kunsthistorisches Museum) and two in Madrid (1544 and 1545; Prado).

Throughout his career Cranach was a great portraitist: the demands of his sitters and the visual support of a model restrained him from his free flights into fields of curious experiment with their sometimes disappointing results. On the other hand, two painted *Portraits of a Young girl* (*c.* 1508, Zurich, Kunsthaus; *c.* 1529, Paris, Louvre) show him in command of a touching simplicity. Elsewhere, notably in his full-length portraits, he used the alternating stripes of color produced by the slashed costumes to give the painting the flat appearance of a playing card. Examples of this are found in the companion portraits of *Henry the Pious of Saxony* and his wife, *Catherine of Mecklenberg* (both 1514; Dresden, Gemäldegalerie), in which the yellows dominate, contrasting with the reds and blues.

The great number of his paintings is matched by an extremely large body of engraved work, consisting in great part of woodcuts from his own drawings, in which he frequently shows himself the equal of Dürer. Some engravings, notably those reproducing the features of the great reformers, have a more popular flavor.

LUCAS, *called* THE YOUNGER (1515, Wittenberg—1586, Weimar), his

Lucas Cranach the Elder. *Venus and Amor*. Detail. 1531. Musées Royaux des Beaux-Arts, Brussels. *Photo A.C.L., Brussels.*

Cretan Art. Throne room of the palace at Cnossos. Late Minoan. *Photo Loirat-Rapho, Paris.*

son, was also a painter and directed the workshop after his father's death. The output declined somewhat in quality, but there are still great beauties to be found, for instance, in the high altar of the church at Weimar, in which Lucas the Elder can have had no great hand, although the work, at least in part, is dated 1552, a year before his death.

The attribution of paintings from the Cranachs' workshop is still difficult, and various pictures once assigned to the father are now believed to be the son's, among them *Fountain of Youth* (1546, Berlin) and the *Nymph at the Spring* (*c.* 1537; Kassel, Museum).

CRESPI, Giovan Battista. *See* **CERANO,** Giovan Battista Crespi.

CRESPI, Giuseppe Maria, *called* Lo Spagnuolo (1665, Bologna—1747, Bologna), Italian painter. An apprenticeship begun very early in the Bolognese workshops and continued in Venice, Modena, Parma, and Urbino encouraged Crespi to cultivate a chiaroscuro technique in which a few splashes of saturated color enliven dark and tawny shadows. During his long and laborious career at Bologna he was engaged on large-scale decorative works (the *Gods and the Seasons*, 1691; Bologna, Palazzo Pepoli) and altarpieces (*Communion of St. Stanislaus*; Ferrara, Chiesa del Gesù), but a large proportion of his time was devoted to genre scenes (*Flea Catcher*; Florence, Uffizi). His style shows an attempt to abandon Guercino's type of lyricism for an almost photographic reality. Crespi's realism is blended with effects of strong light and shade that often invest a common subject with faintly morbid mysteriousness (*Portrait of Fulvio Grati*; Bologna, Priv. Coll.).

CRETAN ART. The originality of Cretan culture is outstanding among the pre-Hellenic societies. Not until the remarkable findings of 20th-century archaeologists was the existence of this civilization known. Perhaps the most spectacular single discovery was the excavation of the enormous palace at Cnossos, initiated by Sir Arthur Evans in 1899, the first clue to the Minoan heritage to be uncovered. Subsequently the remains of similar structures were brought to light at Phaestus and Mallia.

The Cretan palace, which in idea and form was borrowed from the Orient during the middle Minoan period, translated into a complex structure the flexible and creative spirit of Minoan society. The island thalassocracy had little need for defense other than its fleet, so the palaces of Phaestus and Mallia are without ramparts and there are no more than vestigial traces of fortifications at Cnossos. The Minoan palace has an essentially non-centralized plan; it is a collection of elements of independent origin, which came to be grouped around a rectangular central court. Its large size is perhaps explained by the absence of temples, suggesting that the palace served a religious as well as administrative function.

Minoan is a sinuous and adaptable form of architecture, linear rather than massive, and more concerned with the amenities of life indoors than with over-all design. Large square blocks of stone are not much used except for thresholds and doorjambs, as corner-stones, and in the construction of pilasters. The walls were built of rough blocks of stone, held by cob mortar and clamped together with a framework of wood, which, of course, disappeared in the fires that apparently destroyed each of the palaces in turn (*c.* 1400 B.C.). Thus, the outer casing of the walls was of great importance. Additionally, they gave opportunities for decorating.

Fresco painting provided a wide and valued field for the diverse talents of Cretan artists and it is there that the apparently contradictory elements that constituted their originality stand out most clearly: delight in colors, combined with a sure understanding of their relationships; an exuberant fantasy that does not exclude a careful observation of detail; an appreciation of movement that renders precise poses in the most stylized forms, explicit action captured in purely decorative line. The technique of true fresco—that is to say, painting on the damp plaster—was well adapted to so spontaneous an art. It was probably at the beginning of the 2nd millennium B.C. that representations of living things were introduced into the large panels of color that had at first been the only decoration of the walls. The artists' immediate mastery of color and draftsmanship is remarkable. The famous *Saffron Gatherer* from Cnossos (*c.* 1500 B.C.; now Heraklion, Archaeological Museum) is blue, the color complementary to the traditional background red; and the blue monkey and a blue bird with outstretched wings, in a dream landscape, illustrate the same color harmonies. Although the colors are fantastical, the gestures and movements are realistic, the poses momentary, like the cat behind a bush, ready to spring at a bird that is just about to fly away (*c.* 1500 B.C., Hagia Triada; now Heraklion).

As social life developed, and with it a taste for festivals and religious ceremonies attended by a large audience, the crowd scene, treated in the manner of a miniaturist, became an additional subject. Cretan games are recorded in a more linear graphic style, of which perhaps the best example is the astonishing scene of an acrobat leaping over the horns of a charging bull and landing between two women.

Pottery offered boundless possibilities for color and pattern, but Minoan potters never adapted the fresco painters' human figures to their purposes. The charm of the first style, known as Kamares (Early and Middle Minoan), lies in the simple interplay of supple sinuous lines and in the glisten of the brown, red, buff, and black glazes. The patterns vary from a simple spiral twirl to the suggestion of the calyx or corolla of a flower. There is great variety and audacity in the work of these potters; the shapes of cups, goblets, mugs, ewers, and jars, of thin and exquisite pottery, are in

Cretan Art. Terracotta vase with polychrome decoration. Kamares style. First palace at Phaestus, Middle Minoan. Archaeological Museum, Heraklion.

harmony with their linear ornament. At the beginning of the Late Minoan period the introduction of patterns based on the fauna and flora leads to greater naturalism, although the feeling for decorative stylization remains.

The aesthetic genius of the Cretans was less suited to sculpture than to painting; but the painted and especially the molded reliefs on pottery and metalwork and the carved reliefs on stone vases deserve their high reputation. Two of the stone rhytons, the *Harvester Vase*, recording a boisterous rustic procession, and the *Wrestler Vase*, decorated with several scenes from the public games arranged in bands (both at Heraklion, Archaeological Museum) represent some of the finest art of the Minoan civilization. Realistic gestures and a feeling for vivid detail and for essential and vital movement have given us masterpieces like the Vaphio cups (*c.* 1500 B.C., Vaphio, Laconia; now Athens, National Museum). There are also small figures of priestesses, dancing girls, and acrobats, executed in materials that, like these subjects, are decorative in themselves.

As one would expect, this taste for linear composition stimulated the art of gem carving. Minoan gems are not only a delightful series of tiny masterpieces, but also provide much valuable evidence concerning the religious ceremonies of the Minoans and many aspects of their public life.

CRIVELLI, Carlo (b. 1430/35, Venice—d. 1493 or 1495), Italian painter. Crivelli's career can only be understood in terms of a distinctive artistic culture that developed in the townships of The Marches. Expelled from Venice after an elopement in 1457, he took refuge in Dalmatia (he was still at Zara in 1465), then returned to Italy. In 1468, at Massa Fermana, he completed a polyptych, the *Madonna Between Four Saints* (S. Silvestro); then, in Ascoli Piceno, a vast ensemble with two tiers and a predella for the duomo (1473), and two others for S. Domenico, the 13 parts of which have been reassembled under the name of the Demidoff Altarpiece (1476; London, National Gallery). The *Annunciation* with St. Emidius and the Angel, also in the National Gallery, showing the saint holding a model of Ascoli, is dated 1486. The admirable *Coronation of the Virgin* for S. Francesco di Fabriano (1493; Milan, Brera) marks the conclusion of a career punctuated by a series of great *montages* of panels fashionable in Italy at the time. Crivelli also painted small devotional panels for private chapels, such as the curious *Madonna with the Instruments of the Passion* (*c.* 1460?; Verona, Museo di Castelvecchio), or the exquisite *Madonna and Child* (1480?; Ancona, Museum).

Crivelli's work is a wonderful illustration of the strong decorative and plastic tendencies of the last third of the 15th century. His originality lay in associating the rich gofferings and exquisite jewelry with the delicate expression of emotions, which can be studied in his figures of young female saints (*Mary Magdalene*; Amsterdam, Rijksmuseum) and in the small panels. But his style had no future: with the contemporary Pietro Alemanno and Vittore Crivelli (d. 1501/2), Carlo's brother, his manner sank to the level of a provincial convention.

CROME, John, *called* Old Crome (1768, Norwich—1821, Norwich), English landscape painter. He is known to have copied pictures by Richard Wilson (the early *Temple of Venus at Baiae*; Norwich, Castle Museum) and possibly Gainsborough's *Cottage Door,* then in the collection of Thomas Harvey of Norwich, who also possessed Dutch and Flemish paintings, including landscapes by Meindert Hobbema. Wilson, Gainsborough, and Hobbema were the main influences on Crome's mature style.

The *Norwich Directory* of 1801 makes mention of "John Crome, Drawing Master," and it was in this capacity that he earned his living until his death. In 1803 Crome founded the Norwich Society. The group met once a fortnight for the study of prints and drawings, and from 1805 to about 1825 an annual exhibition was held. Crome's contribution to the Society's exhibition of 1806 included "a sketch in Gainsborough's manner," but there is little overt Gainsborough influence in Crome's work of this time, which is very Dutch in character and contains echoes not only of Hobbema but also of Aert van der Neer (1603–77; *Moonrise on the Marshes of the Yare,* 1808–10; London, National Gallery) and Jan van der Heyden (1637–1712; *New Mills, Norwich, c.* 1810–11; Castle Museum).

In 1814 Crome went to Paris; a letter to his wife mentioned an impending visit to the Neoclassicist David. The Castle Museum contains two animated and atypical pictures inspired by the French visit: *Boulevard des Italiens* and *Fishmarket at Boulogne* (both 1820). Crome continued his uneventful life in Norwich, contributing intermittently to the exhibitions of the Royal Academy until 1818. His finest works were done in his later years, notably the *View on Mousehold Heath* (*c.* 1815; London, Victoria and Albert Museum), which triumphantly vindicates his admiration for Gainsborough, and the magnificent *Poringland Oak* (1817–21; London, National Gallery), which is a quiet refinement on the naturalism of Constable. He had also tried his hand, not too successfully, at etching: the 31 plates of *Norfolk Picturesque Scenery* were published in 1834.

CROPSEY, Jasper Francis (1823, Rossville, Staten Island—1900, Hastings-on-Hudson, New York), American painter. He began studying architecture while very young, and was apprenticed to the office of the architect Joseph Trench for five years. Ill-health forced him to stop working and, in 1841, during a period of recuperation in the country, he began to paint the surrounding landscape. Because architectural commissions were scarce, Cropsey turned more and more to his painting, depicting the Catskills, the Hudson River, the White Mountains, and the area around New York City with a skill marked by vigorous drawing, the evocation of vivid local colors, and an eye for careful detailing as well as for the panoramic view. After his marriage in 1847 he went to Europe for three years, touring the Continent and working in Rome in the former studio of Thomas Cole. On his return to America in 1849, Cropsey was elected to the National Academy of Design. He lived in England from 1856 to 1863, during which time he gained a considerable reputation, his paintings being favorably compared to those of Turner and Constable.

Cropsey devoted himself mainly to painting autumnal scenes

Carlo Crivelli. *Annunciation.* Detail: *St. Emidius and the Angel.* 1486. National Gallery, London.

(*Autumn on the Hudson River*, 1860; Washington, D.C., National Gallery). His aim was to capture the typically American scene, but his style shows that he learned certain conceptual mannerisms from Dutch Baroque landscapists such as Jacob van Ruisdael or from the Neapolitan Baroque painter Salvator Rosa, who was popular in America during the 19th century. *Washington Headquarters on the Hudson* (1857?; Washington, D.C., Corcoran Gallery) is characteristic of Cropsey's work in general.

CROSS, Henri-Edmond (1856, Douai—1910, St-Clair, Provence), French painter. Cross went to Paris from Lille where, for two years, he had attended the École des Beaux-Arts. His painting, influenced by that of his teacher, François Bonvin, was at the time somber, bleak, and somewhat vulgar in its realism. By the time he exhibited with Seurat and Signac at the first Salon des Indépendants (1884), he had already adopted divisionism, whose faithful practitioner he remained, and had also greatly lightened his palette. A man of intuition rather than of reason, basically a colorist rather than a painter of light, he anticipated some of the Fauves' innovations. His flexible line, supple arabesques, and even his palette were carefully observed by Matisse, who worked near Cross's studio in the Midi in 1904. On the whole, however, divisionism was constraining rather than stimulating to Cross, and this undoubtedly explains his inability to carry through his experiment with the discipline it required. His watercolors were executed with greater freedom than his oils and communicate the warmth of his personality. Thanks to them, Cross's reputation has survived, and in the mid-20th century his work enjoyed a revival of interest.

Cubism. Pablo Picasso. *Girl with a Mandolin.* 1910. Roland Penrose Coll., London.

CRUIKSHANK, family of English graphic artists.

ISAAC (*c.* 1756, Leith, Scotland—*c.* 1811, London) was the son of a Lowland Scot. He went to London in the late 1790s, and became a book illustrator, watercolorist, and a political caricaturist in the tradition of James Gillray and Thomas Rowlandson. His political prints, such as the *Watchman of the State* (1797), enjoyed considerable popularity.

GEORGE (1792, London—1878, London), Isaac's younger son, was the most distinguished artist of the family. Beginning as an illustrator of children's books and song sheets, he turned to political satire in 1811 with his drawings for the periodical *The Scourge, a Monthly Expositor of Imposture and Folly* (1811–16). In the period 1811–15 his political caricatures seriously rivaled those of Gillray. But it was in the field of book illustration (primarily etchings or wood engravings) that he made his name. Cruikshank's mature style, with its strong elements of the grotesque, the dramatic, and the humorous, made him in some ways the ideal illustrator for the writings of Charles Dickens (*Sketches by Boz*, 1836–37; *Oliver Twist*, 1838) and Harrison Ainsworth (*Jack Sheppard*, 1839; *The Tower of London*, 1840). Many of his illustrations appeared in books and periodicals that Cruikshank published himself, as *George Cruikshank's Comic Almanack* (1835–54). He became an eager propagandist for temperance reform during the 1840s, as may be seen in two series of etchings—the *Bottle* (1847) and the *Drunkard's Children* (1848)—and in a large canvas, the *Worship of Bacchus, or the Drinking Customs of Society* (1862; London, Tate Gallery).

ISAAC ROBERT (1789, London—1856, London), George's elder brother, was trained by their father. After a short period as a sailor, he became a successful painter of miniatures. Impressed, however, by the success of his brother's prints, he turned to etching satirical and humorous subjects, stressing the foibles and scandals of contemporary society in particular. He collaborated with his brother on several series of etchings.

CUBISM, stylistic name given to the aesthetic and technical revolution in art brought about by Pablo Picasso, Georges Braque, Juan Gris and Fernand Léger between 1907 and 1914. Henri Matisse and André Derain also contributed to the formation of this movement, which influenced the majority of avant-garde artists during the years that preceded World War I.

The history of the development of Cubism falls into three phases: a Cézanne phase (1907–9), an analytical phase (1910–12), and a synthetic phase (1913–14). A favorable climate for its growth had been prepared in Paris by the vogue of Negro sculpture and primitive art, the Seurat retrospective exhibition in the Salon des Indépendants of 1905 and, particularly, the Cézanne retrospective in the Salon d'Automne of 1907. In the spring of 1907 Picasso completed *Les Demoiselles d'Avignon* (New York, Museum of Modern Art); the right-hand section, violently simplified and merely sketched in without the use of chiaroscuro, marks the beginning of Cubism. He met Braque, whose natural evolution he accelerated. That autumn, Kahnweiler opened, in Rue Vignon, Paris, the gallery that was to become the home of Cubism. In 1908 the famous Bateau-Lavoir ("boat washhouse") group—which took its name from the Montmartre tenement where its members, including Picasso, the writer and painter Max Jacob (1876–1944), and Juan Gris went to live—was formed. It also included the poet Guillaume Apollinaire, the critics André Salmon and Maurice Raynal, Gertrude and Leo Stein, and others. Braque, fresh from his experiments with Impressionism and Fauvism, began to control his color by an austere sense of form; Picasso, the instinctive draftsman, also tried to introduce color into his work. They made a study of the fundamental problem of painting: the representation of colored three-dimensional volumes on a flat two-dimensional surface. The history of Cubism is that of the successive solutions discovered to resolve this difficulty.

In 1910 Braque gave up landscapes for figures and still lifes, moving on, in his own words, from visual space to tactile and manual space. Picasso left the Bateau-Lavoir group for the Boulevard de Clichy, also in Montmartre, where he painted a series of heads and portraits. The second phase of Cubism, described as analytical by Juan Gris because of the increasing breakdown of form, is characterized by the use of simultaneity. Several views of the same object are put together on a single canvas. Thus, the object appears fragmented, displayed from all angles, and opened from the inside. The problem of simultaneity has always preoccupied artists who, in the imitative and visual phase of painting, from Van Eyck to Manet, have been unable to find any better means of representing multiple views than by reflections in a mirror. This period of extreme analysis and systematic experimentation within the Cubist movement was not without a certain danger of "hermetism," which Braque and Picasso proposed to remedy by the use of sized paper and real materials (such as sand, glass, newspaper, and cloth) inserted in the canvas to stimulate perception. This combination is known as collage. During this period Cubism was widely publicized, thanks to the publication of the doctrinal book by Albert Gleizes and Jean Metzinger, *Du Cubisme* ("On Cubism"), in 1912. The movement also became divided into many tendencies, of which the principal two were Orphism and the Section d'Or, the precursors of abstraction and Purism.

In the following year, 1913, Apollinaire published *Les Peintres Cubistes* ("The Cubist Painters"), in which he spoke already of conceptual painting. In 1911 Juan Gris had begun to break down the object methodically in his paintings, but he reversed the procedure in the summer of 1913, during his decisive stay at Céret with Braque and Picasso. The multiple representation of the same object on a canvas had made that object difficult to understand and distorted its rhythm, even though it remained representational. In the synthetic phase of Cubism the break with traditional naturalist representation practiced since the Renaissance is complete. The new method discarded completely all imitative processes, and used freely invented plastic "signs" comparable to the metaphors of poets. Cubism ceased to be a point of view, an empirical technique, and became a conceptual aesthetic philosophy, an objective ordering of the world represented in its essence rather than in its appearance. In line with the evolution of science and contemporary thought, a new plastic language had been created, whose rigor fostered individual impulses without restrictions of any kind. The collective exaltation of the years from 1907 to 1914 was shattered by the advent of World War I, which caused the creators of Cubism to disperse, each following his own artistic destiny.

CURRIER, Nathaniel (1813, Roxbury, Massachusetts—1888, New York), *and* **IVES,** James Merritt (1824, New York—1895, Rye, New York), American lithographers and partners in the printing firm of Currier & Ives. Currier was apprenticed to the Boston lithographers William S. and John B. Pendleton. He then worked with M. E. D. Brown (active 1832–96) in Philadelphia until he transferred to New York City, where he formed a partnership with the lithographer Adam Stodart. When Currier and Stodart dissolved their firm in 1835, Currier established his own printing house. In 1837 he joined with James M. Ives to form the famous firm of Currier & Ives, which prospered until 1907. Currier retired in 1880 and Ives a few years later, but the business was carried on by their sons. Ives worked as a lithographer in New York City before 1852, and Currier originally hired him as a lithographer. Five years later he attained the status of partner and for almost 40 years he served as the firm's business manager. From 1857 to 1907 Currier & Ives published 7,000 prints, including cartoons; reproductions of oil paintings; scenes depicting disasters and shipwrecks, land and naval battles, clipper ships and whalers, sporting and hunting events, railroads, fires and portraits of presidents.

CURRY, John Steuart (1897, Dunavent, Kansas—1946, Madison, Wisconsin), American painter and muralist. After five years as an illustrator, he went to work in Paris for a year. His realistic study of an American subject, *Baptism in Kansas* (1928, New York, Whitney Museum), focused national attention on him. The painting depicts a radiant moment as Plains people perform their simple religious rites. This was followed by other popular scenes of Midwestern farm life, including *Hogs Killing a Rattlesnake* (1930; Chicago, Art Institute). By the 1930s Curry had become the leading figure among the American regionalist painters, who also included Thomas Hart Benton and Grant Wood. From 1936 until his death, he was professor of art at the University of Wisconsin. His most powerful achievements are the murals he painted (1938–40) for the state capitol in Topeka, Kansas. One depicts the lonely expanse of Kansas prairie lands. Another is dominated by the turbulent figure of the abolitionist John Brown, flanked by Union and Confederate soldiers; on the outer edges dynamic pillars formed by a tornado and a buffalo hunter surround the frenzied scene.

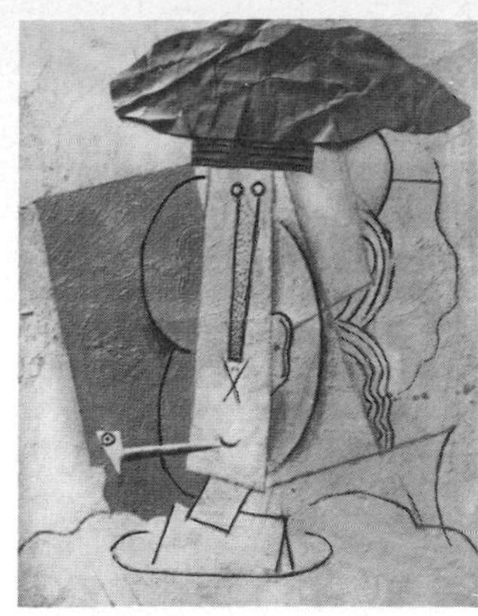

Cubism. Pablo Picasso. *Student with a Pipe.* 1913–14. Private Coll., Paris.

CUYP, family of Dutch painters that included JACOB GERRITSZ. (*c.* 1594, Dordrecht—1652, Dordrecht), best known as a portraitist, and AELBERT (1620, Dordrecht—1691, Dordrecht), his son, a noted painter of animals, particularly cows. Although trained by Jan van Goyen in the tradition of peaceful bourgeois interiors, landscapes, and marines, and imitative of Van Goyen's monochromatic manner in his early work, Aelbert Cuyp proved to be more strongly influenced by the Italianized taste of the Utrecht School, and after about 1648 his canvases are drenched in an Italianate golden sun. He painted idyllic encounters of shepherds, cowherds, and graceful milkmaids, set in fine landscapes of meadows and riversides, which included placid animals and which were often bathed in the warm light of a setting sun. *Young Horseman Riding Out* (Paris, Louvre) combines the vivid colors of the costume with enchanting vistas suffused in a dreamlike atmosphere of light.

D

DADA, a movement that flourished from 1915 to 1922—that is, between the splintering of Cubism and the appearance of Surrealism—forming the negative, preparatory stage for the second movement, and appearing almost simultaneously in Zurich, New York, and Paris. Switzerland's neutrality during World War I had turned it into a refuge for political exiles. Among them were the Rumanian poet Tristan Tzara, the Alsatian sculptor Jean Arp, and the German writers Hugo Ball and Richard Hulsenbeck. The Dada movement was formed in February 1916, when these four artists founded the Cabaret Voltaire in Zurich. This was a club for artists, equipped with a stage and an exhibition hall, and was the scene of a whole series of lectures and activities. Tzara is reputed to have named the movement by sticking a pin into the word "dada" (the French equivalent of "hobbyhorse") on a page of a Larousse dictionary he had opened at random.

As early as 1915, in New York, Marcel Duchamp had given a foretaste of the principles of Dada by exhibiting the most ordinary and most preposterous objects, the so-called ready-mades, as works of art. In the same year, with Man Ray, the critic Marius de Zayas, and the art patron Walter Arensberg, he founded the review *291*, the organ of the so-called anti-painting movement, published by Alfred Stieglitz. At this point Picabia arrived in New York and became a close friend of Duchamp. In January 1917, after his return to Barcelona, Picabia founded the review *391*. A year later he was in Switzerland, where he met with the Dada movement and contributed to the review *Dada*, which Tzara had begun to edit in 1917.

In 1919 Tzara went to Paris, accompanied by Picabia, and was enthusiastically welcomed by the group centered in the magazine *Littérature* (so named by antiphrasis), which included the writers André Breton, Louis Aragon, Philippe Soupault, Paul Éluard, Georges Ribemont-Dessaignes, Benjamin Péret, and Arthur Cravan. In 1921, however, Picabia broke away from the group and was soon followed by Breton. Dada and the newborn Surrealism, which had been united in the beginning, separated, and the Dada movement disintegrated because of quarrels.

In Germany, with its climate of defeat and social crisis, Dada found a fertile field for its activities. The German branch of the movement had three main centers: Berlin, where the group included George Grosz and had been led since 1917 by Hülsenbeck; Hanover, under Kurt Schwitters; and Cologne, where Max Ernst, now joined by Arp, was making his collages. The Cologne group came to an end in 1922 with the departure of Max Ernst for Paris.

Basically the absurd humor of Duchamp and Picabia and the violence of the whole movement expressed a desire for purity that demanded the destruction of the ethical and aesthetic foundations of a society in the throes of change. They also, however, opened art to the cult of the irrational, which took the place of the old logical values. By remaining faithful to its principles and refusing to be absorbed by a new school, Dada perished from its own negation. But its negation was fruitful, since it led directly to Surrealism.

Dada. Francis Picabia. *Portrait of the Poet Tristan Tzara.* 1920.

DALI, Salvador (b. 1904, Figueras, Catalonia), Spanish painter. His father was a native of the village of Cadaquès, whose scenery was to remain Dali's true spiritual home. Through art reviews he became keenly interested in Cubism, Futurism, and Metaphysical painting. Nevertheless, in his respect for an exact realism, Dali resorted to *trompe l'oeil* and photography, the extraordinary possibilities of which he was to emphasize much later in such films as *Le Chien Andalou* (1929) and *L'Age d'Or* (1931), produced with Luis Buñuel. The paintings that he showed in Barcelona in 1925, and in Madrid in 1926, were already based on strangeness and contrast. He made contact with Surrealism and in 1929 he organized a triumphant exhibition at the Galerie Goemans in Paris. The same year he married Gala, the former wife of the poet Paul Eluard. A newcomer to the Surrealist group, Dali was one of its most flamboyant and convinced members. Using a rich philosophical terminology, he elaborated a new method of creation, which he defined as "paranoiac-critical activity." He knew very well how to use visionary experiences, interpretations of memory, and all the mental distortions that he came across in his systematic, conscious study of psychological derangement and pathological accidents.

Salvador Dali. *Mae West.* 1936. Art institute, Chicago.

In his Surrealist work, however, Dali remained faithful to his initial mythology, pushing to the extreme only the pathological and morbid distortions to which he subjected his materials. In 1937–38, when he began to take his inspiration from Italian Renaissance art, and to prepare for the return to Classicism that marked his later work, he was on much less sure ground. He was disowned by his friends, and the Surrealist leader, the poet André Breton, denounced his technique as ultrareactionary and academic. Nevertheless, he had considerable success in the United States, where he went to live in 1940. He now gave his models a so-called "atomic" interpretation, and undertook religious themes. When he returned to Spain after the war, at Cadaquès he found nourishment for his basic pictorial realism, and also the elements of a Baroque tradition that seemed better suited to his temperament than the austerity of a classicism derived from Raphael. Some of his best known and most frequently reproduced works are the *Crucifixion* (1951; Glasgow Art Gallery), in which the figure hangs over the world, and the *Last Supper* (1955; Washington, D.C., National Gallery). Salvador Dali the man is even more of an enigma than Dali the painter. Although he was very lavish with his secrets in his writings (*The Secret Life of Salvador Dali*, 1942; *Fifty Secrets of the Art of Magic*, 1948), Dali assumed so many masks and poses that his true personality remains obscure. One can, nevertheless, discern elements of authenticity and continuity in his temperament. This applies particularly to the physical presence of the landscapes of his childhood; the hills of Ampurdan, stretches of sand, and the shores of Cadaquès, bleached white by the sun.

DALLE MASEGNE, Jacobello *and* Pier Paolo (active 14th century, Venice), Italian sculptors and architects whose activity is documented between 1383 and 1409. Nothing is known of them before they appeared in Emilia, where they designed the tomb of Giovanni da Legnano (1383; Bologna, Museo Civico). In Venice they came under the influence of Nino Pisano, which is particularly apparent in their complex and detailed high altar for the church of S. Francesco, Bologna, built in 1388–92. In 1394 they sculptured their most important work, the iconostasis (choir screen) in St. Mark's, Venice, which includes marble statues of the Virgin and the 12 apostles in a new simple and unrefined style. In 1399 they went to Milan to work on the new cathedral. Jacobello was then commissioned by Gian Galeazzo Visconti to work on the Castello Visconteo at Pavia, and the two separated. In 1400 Pier Paolo returned to Venice, where he carved a *Virgin and Child* for the funerary monument of the Doge Antonio Venier (SS. Giovanni e Paolo). He then designed and began to execute the large windows of the balcony of the south façade of the Doges' Palace in 1402, but he died the following year, before completing the work. Jacobello remained in Milan, where he survived his brother by six years. He belonged to a consultative commission concerned with the building of the cathedral, but his name disappears in 1409. The brothers' most important contribution was their introduction of northern Gothic naturalism into the traditional idealism of Italian sculpture.

DALOU, Jules (1838, Paris—1902, Paris), one of the greatest French naturalistic sculptors of the late 19th century. During the Commune he joined the Fédération des Artistes, headed by Courbet, and was appointed a curator at the Louvre. With the fall of the Commune he fled to London, unimpeded by the government of Adolphe Thiers; in 1874 he was condemned *in absentia* to hard labor. Dalou gained great recognition in London, where he was appointed to a teaching post at the Royal College of Art. His very naturalistic statues of women were deservedly admired (*Woman Taking Off Her Stockings*, *c.* 1870–80, London, Tate Gallery; bust of *Céline Chaumont*, 1879, Paris, Petit Palais). Dalou took advantage of the amnesty of 1879 to enter a grandiose sketch in a competition organized by the city of Paris for a *Triumph of the Republic*. His entry was unsuccessful but was later accepted by the municipal council for the Place de la Nation. The monument was finally unveiled 20 years later, in 1899. In the same period Dalou completed his *Mirabeau Replying to Dreux-Brézé* (1883; Paris, Palais Bourbon); his *Monument to Delacroix* (1890; Paris, Luxembourg Gardens); and the tombs of Louis Auguste Blanqui (1885; Paris, Père-Lachaise cemetery) and of Victor Hugo (1886; Paris, Panthéon). Maquettes of workers and peasants, modeled from life (Petit Palais), were studies for the *Monument to the Workers* that Dalou had only just begun at the time of his death. Only one sturdy life-size figure of a peasant, in the spirit of Millet, had been finished and could be cast in bronze (1902; Paris, Louvre).

DANTI, Vincenzo (1530, Perugia—1576, Perugia), Italian goldsmith and sculptor, the eldest son of the goldsmith Giulio Danti (1500–75); both his brothers, Girolamo (*c.* 1547–80) and Ignazio (1536–86), were painters. Vincenzo, however, was the most famous member of the family. In 1556 he finished the casting of a seated statue of Pope Julius III, which was placed outside Perugia Cathedral. In 1557 he left Perugia, and settled in Florence, where he worked at the court of Cosimo I de' Medici. In 1567 Danti published his *Primo libro del trattato delle perfette proporzioni* ("First Volume of the Treatise on Perfect Proportions"). From 1561 he followed the dictates of fashion and devoted himself entirely to statuary. He executed the very Michelangelesque group of *Truth Triumphant over Falsehood* (*c.* 1561; Florence, Bargello) and his masterpiece, the *Beheading of St. John the Baptist* (1569–71; over the south door of the Florentine Baptistery), in a theatrical yet balanced Mannerism that anticipates the Baroque. He returned to casting with his bas-relief of *Moses and the Brazen Serpent* (Bargello), and the bronze of *Venus Anadyomene* (after 1570) in the *studiolo* of the Palazzo Vecchio, Florence. And he returned to marble with his *Venus* (Florence, Palazzo Pitti) and *Leda and the Swan* (London, Victoria and Albert Museum), both executed in the same period as the *Venus Anadyomene*. One of his best-known and later works is his statue of Duke Cosimo I (after 1568; Bargello).

DANUBE SCHOOL, name given to a group of painters, graphic artists, sculptors, and architects, who, from 1500 onward, were active in the Austro-Bavarian territories flanking the Danube, the Salzach, and the Inn rivers. The school's style was derived from the new sense of form evolved by certain Late Gothic artists, especially Lucas Cranach the Elder during his sojourn in Vienna. It reached its peak in the second and third decades of the 16th century, when it penetrated into Bohemia and Hungary in the northeast, and the territories of the Upper Rhine and Switzerland in the southwest. Its foremost representatives in painting and the graphic arts were Albrecht Altdorfer of Regensburg and Wolf Huber of Passau (after 1480–1553), while the sculptor Hans Leinberger of Landshut (active early 16th cen-

Jules Dalou. *Candor.* *c.* 1875. Petit Palais, Paris. *Photo Giraudon, Paris.*

Vincenzo Danti. *Venus Anadyomene.* After 1570. Palazzo Vecchio, Florence.

tury) and the architect Benedikt Ried of Prague led the movement in their respective fields. The members of the Danube School were intimately involved with nature and portrayed the native landscape with a curious mixture of topographical fidelity and poetic license. It was the painters of the Danube School who first raised the genre of landscape to the status of an independent art (Altdorfer, *Danube Landscape*, *c.* 1522; Munich, Alte Pinakothek). The human figure, although of secondary importance in their landscapes, was also characterized by movement and transformation in the work of the Danube painters; in this respect they were directly opposed to Albrecht Dürer, the champion of classical form in figure composition, from whose rich store of motifs they frequently borrowed. Their graphic view of art was also shared by the sculptors and architects of the Danube School.

DASBURG, Andrew Michael (b. 1887, Paris), American painter. He first studied at the Art Students League in New York with Kenyon Cox (1856–1919) and Frank Vincent DuMond (1865–1951), and took some additional night classes under Robert Henri, who greatly stimulated the young painter. In Paris in 1909, Dasburg was impressed by showings of the work of Cézanne, Matisse, Derain, Braque, and Picasso. In 1913 he exhibited three paintings and a sculpture in the Armory Show in New York. In 1914 he went again to Paris and London, and three years later made his first visit to Taos, New Mexico, where he settled permanently.

After some efforts directed by Synchromist color principles around 1916 or 1917, Dasburg returned to a more realistic style—a simplified treatment of nature (*Chantet Lane*, 1926; Denver, Art Museum) and, less frequently, of the human figure. By 1930 he had adopted a Cézanne-like handling of form, using subjects principally as agents through which he projected his own reactions to shape and color (*Autumn Fruit*, 1934; Albuquerque, University of New Mexico Art Museum). At this time he began to live in Taos, but was unable to paint from the mid-1930s until 1946 because of a crippling illness. He returned to his art after 1946 and his new body of work found its inspiration in the New Mexico landscape (*Autumn Desert*, 1952; Los Angeles, Coll. Mrs. Amalio M. de Schulthess).

Honoré Daumier. *Rue Transnonain, 14 April, 1834.* 1834.

DAUBIGNY, Charles-François (1817, Paris—1878, Paris), French landscapist of the Barbizon School. In 1835, having received a small scholarship, Daubigny went to Italy, where he spent an unproductive year. In 1840 he entered the competition for the Prix de Rome for landscape painting as a pupil of Paul Delaroche; but, after submitting a sketch that was ranked third, he was disqualified for failing to appear at the meeting at which the definitive subject was to be announced. He earned his living by doing engravings for books and regularly sent to the Salon landscapes of peaceful rivers with misty horizons or ponds with wading ducks. At first he painted in a highly detailed style, with a great respect for nature.

As a successor to Jean-Baptiste Camille Corot, Jules Dupré (1811–89), and Théodore Rousseau, Daubigny attracted the attention of the critics at the Salon of 1848 with five landscapes of the Morvan, in which he paid special attention to effects of light (*Valley of the Cousin*, 1847; Paris, Louvre). In 1853 his *Harvest* (1851; Louvre) was bought by the government. Gradually he began to sacrifice detail, painting with broad strokes and covering large areas at a time. After a meeting with Corot in 1852, he began to envelop the carefully constructed outlines of his trees with atmosphere. In 1857 his success became established with his *Spring* and *Great Valley of Optevoz*, a site in the Dauphiné (both Louvre). But the place he loved best was the village of Auvers-sur-Oise, to which he returned every year. Aboard his barge, the "Bottin," a floating studio that Manet imitated a few years later at Argenteuil, he sometimes went down the Oise and the Seine as far as Pont-de-l'Arche. In 1865 he spent the summer with Courbet, Monet, and Boudin at Trouville. As time went on, Daubigny's manner became lighter and freer, with hatched backgrounds; his last canvases reflect the spirit of the Impressionists if not their technique, especially the *Mills of Dordrecht* (1872; Detroit, Institute of Arts) and *House of Mother Bazot* at Valmondois (1874; Hague, Mesdag Museum), the home of his childhood nurse, whom he often visited. A fine work of his classic period is the *Garden of the Prince Imperial* (1860; Paris, Ministère des Finances).

DAUCHER, Hans (1486, Ulm?—1538, Stuttgart), German sculptor and medallist. In 1500 his uncle, the sculptor Gregor Erhart (late 15th–early 16th century), took him on as an apprentice in his Augsburg workshop. It seems probable that he then lived with his father, the sculptor Adolf Daucher (1460/65–1523/24)—who had him registered as a master craftsman in Augsburg in 1514—until 1522, during which time they may have shared the same workshop. In 1528 Daucher visited Vienna, after which nothing is known of his activities until 1536, when he was listed as a member of Duke Ulrich of Württemberg's household. Daucher's earliest known work, which is both dated and signed, is a relief of the *Virgin* (1518; now in Vienna, Schatzkammer). At about the same time (*c.* 1517–18) he completed the altarpiece for the Fugger Chapel in the church of St. Anna in Augsburg, which is one of the major works of German sculpture from the period in which Albrecht Dürer's style predominated. In it the suffering Christ is depicted in the round as a standing figure supported by Mary, Joseph, and an angel. There are three reliefs on the socle: *Christ Carrying the Cross, Descent from the Cross*, and *Descent into Hell*.

DAUMIER, Honoré (1808, Marseilles—1879, Valmondois), French painter, lithographer, and caricaturist. His signature first appears in 1830, beneath a drawing in *La Silhouette*, a satiric weekly. In the same year he was hired by Charles Philipon, founder of *La Caricature*, a newspaper of the liberal opposition. Daumier served a six-month prison sentence (August 1832–February 1833) for a caricature of Emperor Louis-Philippe as Gargantua published in that paper. But this misadventure did not discourage the cartoonist, who painted watercolors while in prison. After his release, Daumier began his series of "masks" and "portraits". He attended sittings of parliament, and on his return home modeled clay busts that served as a basis for his drawings—for he never worked from nature, but from memory. In 1834 Daumier published four lithographs of unequaled violence and satiric force: the *Legislative Belly, Freedom of the Press, La Fayette's Funeral*, and the outstanding *Rue Transnonain, 14 April, 1834,* which shows an episode of contemporary history in all its terrible and trivial reality. In 1835 *La Caricature* was suppressed, putting an end to the first phase of Daumier's career, the phase linked with current politics. He turned then to social satire in *Le Charivari*, founded in 1832 by Philipon, to which he contributed for 40 years. All the living monstrosities, the shameful secrets, the evil or farcical characters to be found in a great city were grist for his mill, but his preferred model and the one he treated most pitilessly was the kind of banal and ridiculous bourgeois portrayed in the comedies of the contemporary dramatist Eugène Labiche. He stigmatized lawyers and, in the famous *Robert Macaire* lithograph of 1836 (a fictitious rogue who was the hero of a popular play), lambasted the legal profession. In 1848 Daumier turned his talents once more to the defense of liberty, now threatened by Bonapartist agents. These he personified in the immortal *Ratapoil* (1850; Paris, Louvre), a sculpture depicting one of the starveling remnants of Napoleon's army. Tiring of journalistic work, he was dismissed from *Le Charivari* and from 1860 to 1863 devoted himself exclusively to painting, dealing with popular themes devoid of all satiric intent. In 1875 Daumier, ill and nearly blind, retired to Valmondois and was saved from misery by Jean-Baptiste Camille Corot, who so admired him that he bought and presented to him the house where Daumier was to spend his last days.

In 1878 an exhibition at the Durand-Ruel gallery brought together the best of Daumier's oeuvre: 200 drawings selected from among the 4,000 lithographs he had done, and 100 paintings. Slender as it is, his production in this second field impresses us with its exceptional intensity and sense of modernity. Yet nothing illustrates better his prodigious powers of synthesis and evocation than the various versions, done late in his career, of *Don Quixote* and *Sancho Panza*. These veritable symbols of the universal human condition unite the grotesque with the sublime and reveal the variety of Daumier's talents. Another aspect of his art is that even the smallest of his works amaze the viewer by their monumentality of composition. His coloring, always muted, is less important than the eloquence of gesture, as revealed in the *Print Collector* examining a rare find (1869; Paris, Petit Palais); the *Lawyers* exchanging hypocritical greetings after the court session (Lyons, Museum); and the *Washer-woman* hoisting a heavy load of wet clothes onto her back (*c.* 1861; Louvre).

DAVID, Gerard (*c.* 1460, Oudewater—1523, Bruges), Flemish painter, the last great artist of the 15th century in Bruges. Trained at Haarlem, perhaps with or under Geertgen tot Sint Jans, and a member of the Bruges guild in 1484, David was at first an eclectic who borrowed motifs from Jan van Eyck and Rogier van der Weyden, and, to a lesser extent, Dirk Bouts, and Hans Memlinc. After the latter's death, he became the official painter of Bruges, where he died; he perhaps journeyed to Genoa in 1511 and definitely made a trip to Antwerp in 1515. Although he is credited with a number of canvases on stylistic grounds, only three of his paintings are documented. Two of these—companion panels representing the *Judgment of Cambyses* (Bruges, Musée Communal)—are also dated: 1498. The new spirit of the Renaissance is reflected in the Italianate decorative details, in the figures reminiscent of Pinturicchio or Leonardo, and in the taste for intimate genre shown in the well-known *Virgin with the Milk Bowl* (Brussels, Musées Royaux des Beaux-Arts).

In the altarpiece of Jean des Trompes at Bruges (*c.* 1502–8; Musée Communal), in the *Virgin with the Milk Bowl*, and in the *Landscape* at Amsterdam (Rijksmuseum), very modern effects of light can be seen on a river, in undergrowth, and in clearings in a wood. Reserve and sobriety (*Marriage at Cana*, after 1503, Paris, Louvre; *Marriage of St. Catherine*, between 1501 and 1511, London, National Gallery) are, however, still the dominant characteristics of an artist who achieves monumentality in his masterpiece and third documented work, the *Virgo Inter Virgines* (1509; Rouen, Museum).

Gerard David. Right wing of the altarpiece of Jean des Trompes: the donors. *c.* 1502–8. Musée Communal, Bruges. *Photo A.C.L., Brussels.*

DAVID, Jacques-Louis, *called* Louis (1748, Paris—1825, Brussels), French painter. He received a humanistic education, but his taste for drawing determined his career. On the advice of François Boucher he entered the studio of the latter's pupil Joseph-Marie Vien (1716–1809), initiator of the taste for Pompeian decor. In 1774 David won the Prix de Rome after three successive failures; in 1775 he left for Rome with Vien, who had just been appointed director of the Académie de France there. In the course of several months, David accumulated volumes of drawings after monuments and statues. Returning to France in 1780, he exhibited at the Salon of 1781 a large preparatory drawing (1778; Paris, Louvre) for a canvas he never actually painted, the *Funeral of Patroclus*. In 1784 he was made a member of the Académie Royale de Peinture et de Sculpture and began work on the *Oath of the Horatii* (Louvre), considered from the very beginning to be the profession of faith of the new school. He went to Rome to complete the picture, accompanied by six of his pupils. The painting had a sensational success in Rome, followed by a triumph two months later in the Salon of 1785 in Paris. On commission, he then executed the *Death of Socrates* (New York, Metropolitan Museum), which had as tumultuous a success at the Salon of 1787. In the Salon of 1789 David's painting of the *Lictors Bringing Brutus the Bodies of His Sons* (Louvre) so alarmed the royal authorities because of its revolutionary theme, that they tried in vain to prevent its exhibition.

Louis David. *Oath of the Horatii.* 1784. Louvre, Paris. *Photo Giraudon, Paris.*

Louis David. *Empress Josephine.* Detail from the *Coronation of Josephine.* 1805–7. Louvre, Paris. *Photo Boudot-Lamotte.*

David was then forty years old and renowned, consorting with such illustrious figures as the statesman Charles Maurice Talleyrand. During the first four Revolutionary years he was the artistic director of the new regime, for he believed in Robespierre as he did in Plutarch. As deputy and twice president of the Convention and a member of the Committee of Public Safety, David was at the peak of his political commitment. The Jacobins asked David to paint the *Tennis Court Oath* (1791–92; Versailles, Museum): the canvas was never carried beyond a sketch, but the preparatory drawing (Versailles; another study in Cambridge, Mass., Fogg Art Museum) was exhibited in the Salon of 1791, where it was received with great enthusiasm. On presentation of a report that he inspired, the Académie Royale was abolished in 1793; David then received full powers to organize artistic instruction and institutions on a more liberal basis. Having voted for the death of the king, he glorified the martyrs of the Revolution in three paintings: *Michel Le Peletier de Saint-Fargeau* (1793; destroyed); the *Death of Marat* (1793; Brussels, Musées Royaux des Beaux-Arts), a masterpiece, "one of the greatest curiosities of modern art," in the words of Baudelaire; and *Joseph Bara* (1794; Avignon, Musée Calvet), a brave little hussar who was shot at Cholet, and whom legend changed into a drummer. Thus it was hardly surprising that, when Robespierre fell, David's enemies were relentless in their accusations. He was arrested and imprisoned in the Luxembourg Palace; from his cell he painted a delightful view of the Luxembourg Gardens (1794; Louvre). David was liberated in December 1794, imprisoned again in May 1795, and finally amnestied in October of the same year.

In 1795 David was free, rich and at the head of a celebrated studio. He finished what he considered his masterpiece, the *Sabine Women* (1799; Louvre), whose theme, the reconciliation of enemy brothers, had occurred to him during his imprisonment. This extraordinary composition caused a sensation, with its nude warriors and horses without bits or bridles. David attached such importance to the *Sabines* that he kept it on exhibition for four years. Napoleon himself went to see the picture and criticized various aspects of it, particularly the immobility of the figures; but on his return from Egypt, the First Consul paid a brief visit to David, posing for a striking portrait (1797–98; Louvre) on which David based a romantic equestrian version showing *Bonaparte Crossing the Alps* (1801; Versailles, Museum). As the Revolution had done, the Empire roused David from his classical dreams. Napoleon ordered four huge pictures, of which only two were painted: the *Coronation of Josephine*, also known as *Le Sacre* (1805–7; Louvre), and the *Distribution of the Eagles* (1810; Versailles). Repeatedly interrupted by official commissions, it took him four years (1810–14) to complete his new "Greek painting," *Leonidas at Thermopylae* (Louvre), in which the erudite coldness of the *Sabines* was even more in evidence. His glory was then without equal; his pupils had included J. A. D. Ingres, Antoine-Jean Gros, Jean-Baptiste Isabey, François Granet (1775–1849); François Gérard, and Girodet-Trioson. But, with the return of the Bourbons, he had to go into exile as a regicide. He settled in Belgium, where his art suffered a sharp decline.

His greatest works are his groups of portraits. His manner of painting, which progressed from broad flat surfaces to the wonderful modulations of the portrait of *Madame Récamier* (1800; Louvre), lent exceptional grandeur to simple human effigies. His technical mastery was unparalleled; he was just as successful in painting a simple *Maraîchère* (*Market Gardener*; Lyons, Museum) or a member of the Convention (*Édouard Jean-Baptiste Milhaud*, 1793; Louvre), as in painting the *Marquise d'Orvilliers* (1790), *Madame de Verninac* (1799), or *Pope Pius VII* (1805; all three in the Louvre). David's greatest achievements are perhaps his portraits of subjects he knew well, the Pécouls (1783; Louvre) or the Sériziats.

DAVID D'ANGERS, Pierre-Jean David, *called* (1788, Angers—1856, Paris), French sculptor. In 1808 he went to Paris, where he studied with the painter Louis David and the sculptor Philippe Laurent Roland (1746–1816). He won the Grand Prix de Rome in 1811 and spent five years in Italy, where he met Antonio Canova. On his return to France (1816) he completed the model for a monument to *Le Grand Condé*, the brilliant 17th-century militarist, which Roland had left unfinished at his death (since 1827 in the Cour d'Honneur at Versailles). To his contemporaries, David d'Angers seemed the Romantic sculptor par excellence. He was commissioned to decorate the pediment of the Paris Panthéon, on which he represented the *Nation Distributing Crowns to Genius* (1837), a bas-relief in a strict classical style. Among his most successful works were his portrait busts, including the diabolical *Paganini* (1830), the Olympian *Goethe* (1831), and the somber *Lamennais* (1838). His approximately 500 medallions (most in the Louvre, Paris), which constitute a portrait gallery of his era for which he traveled throughout Europe to gain material, have also stood the test of time. David d'Angers' masterpiece is perhaps the *Child with Grapes* (1845; Louvre), for which his four-year-old son served as model. The Musée des Beaux-Arts at Angers houses the greater part of his production.

David d'Angers. *General Bonaparte.* 1838. *Photo Jean Roubier, Paris.*

DAVIES, Arthur Bowen (1862, Utica, New York—1928, Florence, Italy), American painter. In

1880 Davies went to Mexico as an engineering draftsman. Upon his return to the United States, he studied at the Art Institute of Chicago, but by 1886 he had shifted his attention to New York, where he enrolled at the Gotham School and the Art Students League. Davies then settled in Congers, New York, painting and doing magazine illustrations to earn a living. In 1893 the art dealer William Macbeth persuaded the philanthropist Benjamin Altman to finance a European trip for the young Davies; as a consequence, he came under the influence of the Venetian painters, the German Romantics, the English Pre-Raphaelites, J. A. M. Whistler, and Puvis de Chavannes.

The early works of Davies are pastoral scenes, using rich color and heavy impasto, but by 1903 he had formulated a more characteristic style, as seen in the *Unicorns* (1906; New York, Metropolitan Museum) and *Crescendo* (1910; New York, Whitney Museum). In these idyllic paintings the landscapes project an almost mystical calm, which is also reflected in the artist's favorite figures of enigmatic and ethereal female nudes. His mysterious *Dream* (*c.* 1908; Metropolitan Museum) is akin to the elusive mythological and visionary subjects of Odilon Redon.

In 1913 Davies was elected president of the Association of American Painters and Sculptors, and was also chosen to play a major role in the organizing of the Armory Show, along with the painter Walt Kuhn. The works he helped to assemble for this exhibition prompted Davies to try several modernist-formalist experiments of his own (*Intermezzo*, *c.* 1913; New York, Graham Gallery), but it is primarily for his earlier romantic reveries that he is remembered.

DAVIS, Alexander Jackson (1803, New York—1892, West Orange, New Jersey), American architect. Davis began his career as an artist in New York in the 1820s but soon turned to architectural drawing. He worked as a draftsman for Josiah Brady (*c.* 1760–*c.* 1832), and also designed for builders on a freelance basis. Davis was well-known as a renderer, and his presentation drawings and views of buildings were engraved and published: they are a valuable source of information today about the architecture of the time. He soon became a member of the advanced circle that centered around the architectural firm of Martin E. Thompson (1789–1877) and Ithiel Town. Davis joined the firm, and when Thompson eventually left, he and Town formed a partnership. Among the works generally associated with Davis' name are the New York Custom House (Town, Davis, and others, begun 1833); the North Carolina Capitol (Town, Davis, and David Paton, begun 1833); the Illinois State Capitol (Town and Davis, 1837); Colonnade Row, New York (Davis, 1831); "Sachem's Wood," New Haven, Connecticut (Davis, 1828); and "Glen Ellen," Towson, Maryland (Davis, 1832).

Town retired in 1835, collaborating only occasionally thereafter, and Davis' work from this time on became more varied. His output was large and versatile, including academic buildings (Davidson College in North Carolina, 1850–52); palatial private houses (Stevens House, New York, 1845); country houses of classical serenity (remodeling of "Montgomery Place," Barrytown-on-Hudson, 1843); Italian villas (E. C. Litchfield House, Brooklyn, 1853); Gothic cottages (Drake Villa, Hartford, Connecticut, 1845); and castles (Harral House, Bridgeport, 1846).

DAVIS, Stuart (1894, Philadelphia—1964, New York), American painter. In 1909, after a year of high school, he abandoned his studies to attend Robert Henri's art classes in New York. In 1910 he exhibited in the Independents' show that included The Eight and other artists rejected by the National Academy and did satirical illustrations and covers for the leftist review *The Masses*. But the Armory Show (1913) opened his eyes to broader horizons, and after World War I he adopted a concise, epigrammatic style strongly influenced by Fernand Léger.

His reflections on modernism culminated in the famous *Eggbeater* series of abstractions of 1927–28, during which time he retreated to his studio and nailed an eggbeater, an electric fan, and a rubber glove to a table; they remained his exclusive subject for a year.

In 1928 Davis traveled to Paris, where he remained for two years. There he painted views of the city that contain recognizable forms removed from context—kiosks, café tables, Paris façades with their lettered signs—as elements in otherwise abstract compositions. These visible "signposts" remained in his artistic vocabulary after his return to America, but after a time they began to break up into fragments, organized in monumental compositions of increasing complexity, such as *Hot Still-Scape for Six Colors* (1940; New York, Coll. Mrs. Edith Gregor Halpert), whose innumerable brilliantly colored scraps allude to landscape and urban forms without suggesting them explicitly.

DE CHIRICO, Giorgio. *See* **CHIRICO,** Giorgio de.

DE CREEFT, José (b. 1884, Guadalajara, Spain), American sculptor. De Creeft's experience with sculpture began at a very young age; at twelve he worked as an apprentice in a bronze foundry; at sixteen he became an apprentice in Madrid to Don Agustín Querol (1863–1909), the official government sculptor; and at twenty-one he was in Paris, studying at the Académie Julian. The academic approach to sculpture dissatisfied him, however, especially the customary practice of having the sculpture carved by professional stonecutters. In 1911 he went to work as a craftsman in a stonecutters' workshop in order to learn carving himself. This training enabled him to copy his own plaster casts in stone, but in 1915 he abandoned this process and began direct carving. His contribution to American sculpture, after his arrival in the United States in 1929, was his strong position in the renewal of direct carving, which became prominent in America in the 1920s and 1930s.

When De Creeft began direct carving, he made an intense study of Oriental philosophy and sculpture as general models for his own work; his female heads and figures, which constitute his most typical subject matter, have the strong, rounded, and sensuous forms of Eastern, and sometimes pre-Columbian, sculpture. De Creeft's work tends toward the monolithic and the monumental, and usually shows an interest in texture. Polished and rough surfaces are frequently juxtaposed so that the smooth forms often appear to be enveloped by or emerging from a

Edgar Degas. *Fourteen-Year-Old Dancer. c.* 1880. *Photo Leonard von Matt, Buochs.*

rough background. Characteristic examples of his stylistically rather uniform oeuvre are *Maya* (black Belgian granite, 1935) and *Emerveillement* (serpentine, 1941); less typical but sometimes more remarkable are his experiments with hammered lead, such as the portrait head of *Sergei Rachmaninoff* (1943).

DEGAS, Hilaire Germain Edgar de Gas, *called* (1834, Paris—1917, Paris), French painter. Degas entered the École des Beaux-Arts in 1855; in 1856–57 he made a study of Quattrocento painting while in Rome, Naples, and Florence. His early work comprised history paintings (*Semiramis Building Babylon,* 1861; Paris, Musée de l'Impressionnisme) and primarily portraits, influenced by the linear style of J. A. D. Ingres, which were exhibited at the Salon. In 1864 he executed several portraits of his friend Manet; in 1865 he painted the *Lady with Chrysanthemums* (New York, Metropolitan Museum), in which for the first time he employed the asymmetrical compositional style he had learned from the Japanese masters. Degas soon lost interest in historical subjects, and his avid curiosity swiftly led him to explore the world of theater and the dance. These, together with scenes of the racecourse, were to become his favorite subjects.

Degas accompanied his brother to the United States in 1872 and returned to France the following year with a canvas representing the *Cotton Exchange in New Orleans* (1873; Pau, Musée des Beaux-Arts). The artist suddenly acquired an intense feeling for the modern, a taste for unconventional composition, and for themes, forms, and rhythms taken from everyday life. He began to explore the possibilities of color, his intellectual and aesthetic interests bringing him now into contact with the writers and painters who gathered at the Parisian Café Guerbois in the company of Manet, Monet, and Renoir.

Edgar Degas. *At the Races—Before the Stands.* 1869–72. Musée de l'Impressionnisme, Paris. *Photo Laniepce, Paris.*

Degas took an active part in the first Impressionist show of 1874, and exhibited 10 canvases, including the *Dancing Class* and the *Ballet Rehearsal* (both in Paris, Musée de l'Impressionnisme). He contributed other paintings of dancers and horse races to the next two exhibitions, as well as a few naturalistic scenes, among them *At the Seaside* (1877; London, National Gallery) and *Women Seated at a Café Terrace* (1877; Musée de l'Impressionnisme). The series of *Dancers on Stage* and the portrait of *Duranty* (1879; Glasgow, Art Gallery) belong to this period, at which time Degas was also trying his hand at engraving, as were Mary Cassatt and Pissarro. At the sixth exhibition of the Indépendants (the name by which the Impressionists were known after 1879), he showed his first sculpture, a small wax figure of a dancer (1881), for he was now beginning to compensate for his weakening sight by his sense of touch.

Other themes made their appearance in Degas' pictorial work: in *Women Ironing*, the *Milliners* (1882–83), and *Women at their Toilette* (1885–98), silhouettes are sketched from life and arrested in fleeting attitudes. His studies of the human body, generally seen from the rear, served as pretexts for a skillful exploration of plastic forms, linear arrangements, and light (the *Tub*, 1886, and *After the Bath*, 1898, both in Paris, Musée de l'Impressionnisme; the *Bath, c.* 1890, Chicago, Art Institute). As his sight dimmed, Degas was obliged to give up oil painting and consequently executed fewer subjects requiring naturalistic details, using instead pastel, pencil, gouache, and distemper.

After numerous travels throughout France between 1889 and 1892, Degas returned with impressions he transcribed into 40 superb little landscapes, consisting of tinted monotypes, pastels, and charcoal sketches touched up with gouache—all recording with gusto the dreams that passed before his weakened eyes. These endearing scenes were assembled for exhibition in Degas' first and last one-man show, which was held at Durand-Ruel in Paris (October 1892).

Although recognized as the leader of the Impressionists, Degas rejected their aesthetic, just as he rejected academic convention. He worked only in the studio, from imagination or memory, and scorned the idea of painting in the open air or after sketches, as practiced by Monet and his friends. "Drawing," he said, "is not what one sees, but what one must make others see." His landscapes are precise, subtle, and superbly colored, and suffused with an incomparable poetic quality. Whereas the Impressionists dissolved forms in light, Degas accentuated them, using—and sometimes misusing—artificial illumination, such as the footlights and spotlights of the theater. Degas strove, finally, to reconcile the fluidity of Impressionism with the precision of classicism, and compositional logic with improvisational spontaneity.

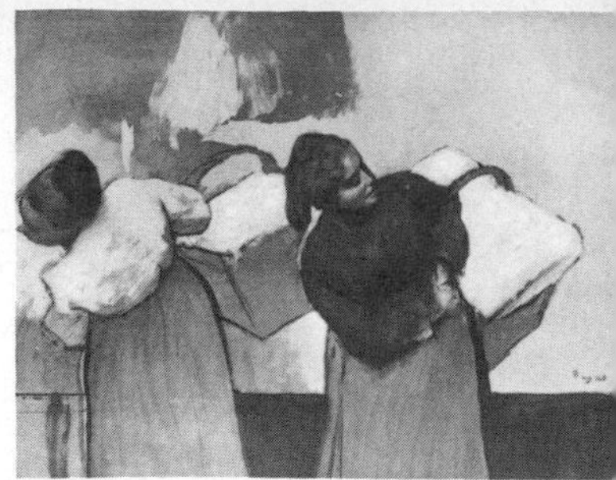

Edgar Degas. *The Laundresses.* 1876–78. Coll. Mr. and Mrs. Howard J. Sachs, Stamford, Conn.

DELACROIX, Eugène (1798, Charenton-St-Maurice—1863, Paris), French painter, leader of the Romantic school. On the advice of his uncle, Henri-François Riesener (1767–1828), himself a painter, Delacroix entered the studio of Pierre-Narcisse Guérin in 1815, although he would have preferred to study with Antoine-Jean Gros. There he met Théodore Géricault, whose elegance and genius he admired. Delacroix's first entry in the Salon was the *Bark of Dante* (1822; Paris, Louvre), inspired by the Italian poet's *Divine Comedy* (*Inferno*, Canton VIII); it shows the influence of Géricault's subdued palette, and also reveals a powerful plastic imagination. The painting drew a laudatory article in the journal *Le Constitutionnel*, signed by Louis Adolphe Thiers, who was later minister and president but was then unknown and approaching politics by way of journalism. There is reason to believe that

Delacroix was actually the son of Talleyrand. Among the many factors pointing to a relationship between the prince and the painter, the most revealing was their startling physical resemblance, which it is said shocked Delacroix when he first saw a miniature of Talleyrand on his mother's desk.

His success in 1822 having brought him fame, Delacroix for a time led a busy social life. He was a friend of Richard Parkes Bonington, who frequented the studio of Gros, and he became acquainted with Thales Fielding (1793–1837). At this time Delacroix work feverishly on the masterpiece of his early years, the *Massacre at Chios* (1824; Louvre). Tradition has it that after seeing one of Constable's landscapes at a Parisian art dealer's, in the four days remaining before the opening of the Salon Delacroix repainted entirely the background landscape of his picture, introducing half tones, broken color, and glazes, which give his canvas its incomparable brilliance.

The *Death of Sardanapalus* (1827; Louvre), a poetic dream of voluptuousness and death, provoked a scandal; however, this did not prevent Charles X from commissioning Delacroix to paint a *Battle of Nancy* (1831; Nancy, Museum) or the Duchesse de Berry from ordering a *Battle of Poitiers* (1830; Louvre); these works foreshadowed Delacroix's masterpieces in the genre of battle painting—the *Battle of Taillebourg* (1837; Louvre) and the *Taking of Constantinople by the Crusaders* (1840; Louvre), the latter a painting "of essentially Shakespearean beauty," according to the poet Charles Baudelaire.

The Revolution of 1830 brought into power Delacroix's protectors—the Duc d'Orléans as king, Thiers as minister, Talleyrand as ambassador—and inaugurated his most brilliant period. It is not without reason that in his *Liberty Leading the People* (1830; Louvre), shown in the Salon of 1831, the artist depicted himself as a student brandishing a gun on a barricade: he too was sure of his powers and was the great victor in that Salon. The State bought the canvas for 3,000 francs. Subsequently, the French government decided to negotiate a treaty of friendship with the sultan of Morocco and entrusted the mission to the Comte de Mornay who took Delacroix along as attaché. He brought back seven albums of watercolors and sketches, from which he was to draw the subject matter for more than 100 canvases. These are probably among his most original works, and include the *Women of Algiers* (1834; Louvre), the *Moroccan Kaid* (1837; Nantes, Musée des Beaux-Arts), the *Jewish Wedding in Morocco* (*c.* 1839; Louvre), and the *Sultan of Morocco and His Entourage* (1845; Toulouse, Musée des Augustins).

After 1833 Delacroix yielded entirely to his imagination, refusing to use a model and plunging further and further into his dream. He alternated a series of decorative projects with a return to certain themes that were dear to him, themes taken from Byron, such as the *Combat of the Giaour and the Pasha* (1827; Chicago, Art Institute), the *Shipwreck of Don Juan* (1840; Louvre), and the *Fiancée of Abydos* (1849; Lyons, Musée des Beaux-Arts); or such Dantesque themes as the *Justice of Trajan* (1840; Rouen, Musée des Beaux-Arts) and the *Two Foscari* (1855; Chantilly, Musée Condé); or subjects taken from Shakespeare, for example *Hamlet and Horatio in the Graveyard* (1839 and 1859; both Louvre) and *Othello and Desdemona* (1847–49; New York, Coll. E. V. Thaw). He treated his great official decorations in Paris as an heir of Titian and Rubens: the Salon du Roi and library of the Chamber of Deputies in the Palais Bourbon (1833–47), the library of the Luxembourg Palace (1840–47), and the ceilings of both the Gallery of Apollo at the Louvre (1850–51) and the Salon de la Paix at the Hôtel de Ville (1852–54; destroyed 1871). He made numerous sketches and preparatory studies for the famous series of *Lion Hunts*, of which the finest examples are in Bordeaux (1855; Musée des Beaux-Arts), Boston (1858; Museum of Fine Arts), and Chicago (1861; Art Institute). In these canvases the influence of Rubens a result of several trips to Belgium—joins with memories of Delacroix's Moroccan journey.

Eugène Delacroix. *Combat of the Giaour and the Pasha.* 1827. Art Institute of Chicago.

DELAROCHE, Hippolyte, *called* Paul (1797, Paris—1856, Paris), one of many French academic painters in the early 19th century who based their careers on the public taste for historical scenes. He was a pupil of Antoine-Jean Gros and received the friendly encouragement of Théodore Géricault. Delaroche began painting scenes of contemporary events (*Storming of the Trocadero*, 1827; Versailles, Museum), but very soon "he won fame with a flair for choosing moving, pathetic subjects": *Lady Jane Grey Executed at the Tower of London* (1834), the *Little Princes in the Tower* (1831; Paris, Louvre). From 1832 Delaroche occupied the place in the Institut that Delacroix received after his death. By treating the Romantic themes dear to Delacroix in an academic, bourgeois spirit, Delaroche made large-scale historical composition respectable (*Assassination of the Duc de Guise*, 1835; Chantilly, Musée Condé) and paved the way for Thomas Couture and Jean-Paul Laurens (1838–1921). But his very real talent for dramatic effects does not redeem his works, which are arid in execution, of stiff draftsmanship and dull color.

DELAUNAY, Robert (1885, Paris—1941, Montpellier), French painter. In 1904 Delaunay executed paintings in the style of Gauguin, and was subsequently attracted by Neoimpressionism, his admiration for Seurat leading him to Eugène Chevreul's studies on simultaneous contrasts in colors. From 1908, after showing an interest in the work of Cézanne, he was influenced by Cubism, most conspicuously in three series of paintings, *St-Séverin* (1909); the *Tours de Laon* (1910–12); and the

Eugène Delacroix. *Sleeping Odalisque, or Woman with a Parrot.* 1827. Musée des Beaux-Arts, Lyons. *Photo Giraudon, Paris.*

Villes, notably the huge composition of the *Ville de Paris* (1910–12; Paris, Musée National d'Art Moderne). But his lyricism was too vital, his passion for color too sensual to bow to the intellectual discipline of a Georges Braque or a Juan Gris. This is already apparent in the three large paintings of the *Tour Eiffel* dating from 1910 (Basel, Kunstmuseum; New York, Guggenheim Museum; Germany, Priv. Coll.), in which the picture space is increased tenfold by mere play of colors and their contrasts. Delaunay's first purely abstract paintings were executed in 1912; yielding to his violent need for expression, he produced his admirable series of *Windows*, in which he offered a dynamic perception of the world of light, radically at variance with any realistic vision of nature.

As early as 1911, then, Robert Delaunay had worked out a precise conception of nonrepresentation in the visual arts. At the same time as Kandinsky, Mondrian, and Malevich, and perhaps even earlier, he was a pioneer in nonfigurative painting. Naturally enough, Kandinsky invited him to participate in the first Blaue Reiter exhibition held in Munich in 1911; and the following year Paul Klee, August Macke, and Franz Marc visited him in Paris. Delaunay was in fact the initiator of an entirely new art, to which Guillaume Apollinaire gave the name of Orphism. Delaunay's lyricism now attained an extraordinary intensity, not only in the harmonic organization of color, but also in the abstract juxtapositions of flashing, whirling circles or disks. His intense love of rhythm stimulated an interest in sporting events: the *Cardiff Team* (1912–13; Eindhoven, Stedelijk van Abbe-Museum); *Homage to Blériot* (1914; Grenoble, Museum); and the dazzling series of the *Sprinters* (1924–26). Ultimately it led him to pure rhythm or total abstraction, to which he devoted himself with fervor from 1930, reviving the kinetic motif of *Homage to Blériot* in plays of multicolored disks and giving monumental breadth to his nonobjective compositions (the series of *Rhythms* and *Eternal Rhythms*). He also produced polychrome reliefs of casein paint, cork, cement, plaster, and sand, with which he would have liked to cover the walls of drab habitations and cities. He did in fact have the satisfaction of executing several major decorative projects for exposition pavilions, including colored bas-reliefs for the Pavillon des Chemins de Fer at the Exposition Internationale of 1937 (*Air, Iron, and Water*, now in Grenoble, Musée de Peinture et de Sculpture).

DELAUNAY, Sonia Terk (b. 1885, Ukraine), French painter of Russian origin. After a childhood spent in St. Petersburg, she went to study in Germany (Karlsruhe), then to Paris, where she studied at the Académie de la Palette. She was influenced at first by Gauguin and Van Gogh and experimented in the intensification of color (the *Dressmaker Philomena*). She exhibited in the art dealer Wilhelm Uhde's gallery and met Robert Delaunay, whom she married in 1910. At this stage she developed a mode of expression that combined the experiments of Cubism and those of Orphism (*Le Bal Bullier*, 1913; Paris, Musée National d'Art Moderne). In 1913, at the Berlin Herbstsalon, she exhibited about 20 objects (bookbindings, fabrics) and pictures, including the first "simultaneous book," Blaise Cendrars's *La Prose du Transsibérien*, with illustrations whose structure and emotive power have their source in the juxtapositions, or "simultaneous contrasts," of prismatic colors. A stay in Spain and Portugal (1915–20) inspired large, brilliant compositions (*Market at Minho*, 1915; Paris, Musée National d'Art Moderne) and a series of abstract watercolors based on local folk dances. On her return to France, Sonia Delaunay applied her painting experiments to fashion design: her work revolutionized textiles and also exercised a great influence on decoration everywhere, especially in the theater and films. Her originality and architectonic power were brilliantly displayed in huge compositions for the Pavillon de l'Air and Pavillon des Chemins de Fer at the Exposition Internationale of 1937 (in collaboration with her husband). After the death of Robert Delaunay in 1941, Sonia Delaunay entered a new phase in her artistic development. While living at Grasse she painted a series of gouaches showing great refinement in their color relations; her work also acquired an even greater economy, but never at the expense of richness or originality.

DELL'ABBATE, Niccolò. *See* **ABBATE,** Niccolò dell'.

DELLA PORTA, Giacomo (*c.* 1540, Rome—1602, Rome), Italian architect. His prolific career was spent entirely in Rome except for the period 1565–70, when he lived in Genoa. He dominated the Roman architectural scene during the last quarter of the century, which saw intense activity in building because Pope Sixtus V was replanning the layout of the city. Della Porta was Giacomo da Vignola's pupil, and he took over a number of unfinished projects after his master's death (1573). One of the first was the design of the dome and façade (*c.* 1575–84) of Il Gesù in Rome. Two other Della Porta façades, both familiar to tourists in Rome, are those for Trinità dei Monti (1579) and S. Luigi dei Francesi (1589). When he succeeded Vignola as architect of St. Peter's he modified Michelangelo's design for the dome and replaced it with a more steeply rising form, constructed (1585–90) with the help of Domenico Fontana, the other leading Roman architect of the day. Della Porta's secular works in Rome include the Piazza del Campidoglio (1578) and the Palazzo del Senatore (1573–98), both modifications of Michelangelo's designs,

Robert and Sonia Delaunay. Bas-relief. Entrance hall, Pavillon des Chemins de Fer, Exposition Internationale, Paris. 1937. Musée de Peinture et de Sculpture, Grenoble.

and the Palazzi Chigi and Aldobrandini. He also designed the Villa Aldobrandini at Frascati, famous for its splendidly planned gardens and fountains (1598–1603).

DELLA QUERCIA, Jacopo. *See* **JACOPO DELLA QUERCIA.**

DELL'ARCA, Niccolò. *See* **NICCOLÒ DELL'ARCA.**

DELLA ROBBIA, Luca. *See* **ROBBIA,** Luca Della.

DELORME, Philibert. *See* **L'ORME,** Philibert de.

DELVAUX, Paul (b. 1897, Antheit, near Huy), Belgian painter. He was nearly forty when de Chirico and Magritte guided him toward Surrealism, the style to which he owes his fame. Like de Chirico he loved deep perspective, and like Magritte he practiced a meticulous realism in the painting of objects. Nevertheless, Delvaux asserted his own personality both in his choice of subject and in his style. He is the painter of impossible encounters. The girls who people his canvases with their pale nudity and wasted grace have the faces of sleepwalkers, despite their wide-eyed gaze: submerged in their solitude, they pass without seeing each other (*Hands*, 1941; Choisel, Coll. Claude Spaak). They walk, stand, or recline in front of Greek temples, Italian palaces, well-kept gardens, luxurious interiors, or melancholy waiting rooms. Sometimes they brush past sad-looking bureaucrats who ignore them; and they always seem to be waiting rather anxiously for the event that will awaken and deliver them (*Phases of the Moon*, 1939; New York, Museum of Modern Art).

Delvaux's images are less aggressive than those of Magritte: they have more atmosphere and "logic," and disturb without jarring. His concept of form is in the realistic tradition, but his use of color is more modern. His pictorial gifts may be appreciated in watercolor landscapes, in which he is not only more relaxed than in his ambitious Surrealist compositions, but also more subtle and vibrant.

DEMUTH, Charles (1883, Lancaster, Pennsylvania—1935, Lancaster), American painter. After studies at the Pennsylvania Academy of the Fine Arts, he visited Europe in 1907 and again in 1912, when he remained for two years. Demuth's early work was influenced by the Fauves, especially Matisse, as well as by Cézanne and John Marin. In his watercolor landscapes of 1912–17 (*Trees and Barns, Bermuda*, 1917; Williamstown, Mass., Williams College Museum of Art) Demuth combined Cubistic analysis with the free brushwork and the space-defining color of the Expressionists. He began working in several styles, each associated with a different kind of subject matter. His fruit and flower studies, for instance, were done in watercolor, his preferred medium (*August Lilies*, 1921; New York, Whitney Museum). In these works mild influences of Cézanne and perhaps of Odilon Redon are transformed into something quite personal: delicate, oblique, sophisticated, with a hint of mystery also. These qualities are predominant in Demuth's illustrations as well, and in his studies of circus and cabaret performers—his most important works, despite their seemingly fragile and ephemeral character. Chief among his illustrations are those for Émile Zola's *Nana* (1915–16) and *L'Assommoir*, Frank Wedekind's *Die Erdgeist*, and Henry James' *The Turn of the Screw* and *The Beast in the Jungle*. Finally, Demuth's curious studies of modern factories (*Machinery*, 1920; New York, Metropolitan Museum) are close in their prismatic technique to the urban landscapes of Lyonel Feininger and Charles Sheeler.

DENIS, Maurice (1870, Granville, Manche—1943, Paris), French painter, decorator, and engraver. After brilliant secondary studies, he entered the Académie Julian in Paris in 1888. Through Paul Sérusier, he was soon introduced to Gauguin's Symbolist-Synthetist art, as shown by the *Muses* (1893; Paris, Musée National d'Art Moderne). Intelligent, cultivated, and an excellent writer, Denis became the theorist and an exponent of a group of painters who called themselves Nabis (after the Hebrew word for prophet). Their work is characterized by simplified drawing without modeling, which emphasizes the two-dimensionality of the canvas, and by accent on line and arabesque, stressing pattern, which gives their paintings a highly decorative quality. Maurice Denis is also credited with having explained and justified the great works of the 19th century. His own painting, however, did not match the intellectual audacity of his theories.

Maurice Denis. *Hommage à Cézanne.* 1900. Musée National d'Art Moderne, Paris. *Archives photographiques.*

After two visits to Italy, in 1895 and 1897, Denis abandoned Symbolism for the style of the Sienese and Florentine Quattrocento. His figures, posed in volumetric space, took on weight and amplitude (decorations—including easel paintings, murals, and stained-glass windows—for the church of Vésinet, 1895–1903). He continued to produce paintings and huge murals, notably for the Théâtre des Champs-Elysées (begun 1912) and the Petit Palais (1924–25), both in Paris. Denis had been attracted by Christian themes from his youth, and in 1919, with the painter Georges Desvallières (1861–1950), he founded the studio-school called the Ateliers d'Art Sacré in Paris, which trained pupils as collaborators on religious commissions.

Denis' most famous painting is probably *Hommage à Cézanne* (1900; Paris, Musée National d'Art Moderne). His writings on art include *Théories: Du Symbolisme et de Gauguin vers un nouvel ordre classique*, 1912; and *Nouvelles Théories sur l'art moderne et l'art sacré*, 1922.

DE PREDIS, Giovanni Ambrogio (*c.* 1455, Milan—1517, Milan), Italian painter. In 1483 he and his brother, Evangelista, began work with Leonardo da Vinci for the Confraternity of the Immaculate Conception in Milan, on an altarpiece that included the *Virgin of the Rocks* (London, National Gallery), which is his most famous work in collaboration with the master. The project was not completed until 1508, and Ambrogio ultimately became Leonardo's most faithful follower and achieved great success as a portrait painter. Some of his works are so like Leonardo's that a few of his portraits have been attributed to his master, including the *Gentleman* (Milan; Brera) and *Girl with Cherries* (New York, Metropolitan Museum). On the other hand, he sometimes returned to the old Lombard tradition of profile portraits, as in the portrait of *Francesco Brivio* (Milan, Museo Poldi-Pezzoli). His position as court painter to the Sforza family, which he attained in 1482, provided him with famous sitters: he painted the portraits of *Ludovico*, the *Duchessa Caterina*, several versions of *Bianca Maria Sforza* (1493, Washington, National Gallery; Paris, Louvre), and her husband *Holy Roman Emperor Maximilian I* (1502; Vienna, Kunsthistorisches Museum).

DERAIN, André (1880, Chatou, Seine-et-Oise—1954, Garches, Seine-et-Oise), French painter. At the age of eighteen he entered the Académie Carrière, where he met Matisse. He struck up a friendship with Maurice de Vlaminck, who also lived in Chatou. They exhibited with Matisse, Rouault, and Henri-Charles Manguin at the 1905 Salon d'Automne, which introduced Fauvist painting to the Parisian public. Derain was a Fauve through and through, bringing to the movement not only his youthful impetuosity, but also a lucidity stemming from a keen intellect and a broad culture. He was particularly receptive to the new dogma of "form through color," which he illustrated in the 1905 series of landscapes of Collioure and the London scenes of 1906 (*A Corner of Hyde Park*, Troyes, Pierre Lévy Collection; *Westminster Bridge*, Paris, Priv. Coll.; *London Bridge*, New York, Museum of Modern Art). But, although he shared the Fauves' passion for color, Derain felt a need to organize the turmoil of his sensations and curb a freedom that had become self-intoxicated. His ambitions were boundless; in particular, his *Bathers* of 1908 (present location unknown) represents an attempt to combine the discoveries of his predecessors, from Manet to Cézanne, and to reconcile them with his own requirements.

Derain broke with Fauvism in 1908, when he came under the influence of Cézanne. There followed a period of Cubist stylization, especially in such paintings as the *Old Bridge at Cagnes* (Washington, D.C., National Gallery), the powerful *Still Life with Pitcher* (Paris, Priv. Coll.), and the *Black Castle*. These three works, dating from 1910, are remarkable for their inflexible lines, sober coloring, and construction through superimposed planes. Then, as though frightened by his own daring, as though already disillusioned, Derain sought security in the examples provided by museums and art books. He was attracted successively by Nicolas Poussin (the *Salt Flats of Martigues*, 1912–13; Bern, Priv. Coll.), by the Italian primitives (the *Billiard Table*, 1913), and by African masks and the Fayum portraits (the *Two Sisters*, 1914; Copenhagen, Statens Museum for Kunst). After 1920 he was influenced by the Quattrocento painters and the decorations of Pompeii.

Derain painted works of undeniable quality: *Harlequin and Pierrot* and the *Kitchen Table* (both 1924, present location unknown); the *Still Life: Dead Game* (Pittsburgh, Carnegie Institute), which was awarded the Carnegie Prize in 1928; several landscapes of Gravelines and St-Maximin (*Vue de St-Maximin*, 1930; Paris, Musée National d'Art Moderne). He worked in other media besides painting, often with great success. His woodcuts for Guillaume Apollinaire's *Enchanteur Pourrissant* (1909), Ovid's *Les Héroïdes* (1938), and Rabelais' *Pantagruel* (1943) will never be forgotten, and his sculptures in stone and bronze have a delightfully archaic flavor. He also designed sets and costumes, e.g. for the Ballets Russes (*La Boutique Fantasque*, 1919).

André Derain. *Female head.* 1939–53.

DESIDERIO DA SETTIGNANO (1430, Settignano—1464, Florence), one of the major Florentine sculptors of the mid-15th century, born of a family of stonemasons. Only two of his works—both in Florence—can be dated with any certainty: the Marsuppini tomb in S. Croce, begun after 1453, and the altar of the Sacrament in S. Lorenzo, finished in 1461. The Marsuppini tomb follows the form established by Bernardo Rossellino in the Bruni tomb (*c.* 1444/47) on the opposite side of the nave, but it is rather more decorative in detail and diffuse in its elements. The execution is softer and more delicate, achieving in the *putti* supporting shields that flank the sarcophagus an extraordinary transparency and tenderness of handling. Several portrait busts have been attributed to Desiderio, only one of which seems, on stylistic grounds, to be connected with him: the marble bust of a young woman in the Bargello, Florence. Its sensitiveness and refinement link it with the ethereal candle-bearing angels flanking the tabernacle of the S. Lorenzo altar. Despite his short career, Desiderio is important in that he reaffirms, in the face of the harsh and strongly dramatic emotion and forceful realism of Donatello's late works, the parallel Florentine current of grace, a tender conception of beauty, and a rather mannered elegance inherited from Ghiberti.

Desiderio da Settignano (attributed). Bust presumably of Marietta Strozzi. Staatliche Museen, Berlin-Dahlem.

DESJARDINS, Martin van den Bogaert, *called* Martin (1640, Breda, Netherlands—1694, Paris), Dutch sculptor who worked mainly in Paris. After studying in Antwerp he settled in Paris, where he was first appointed a teacher (1675), then rector (1686) at the Académie Royale de Peinture et de Sculpture. He worked on a number of buildings in Paris (Collège des Quatre-Nations; Porte St-Martin, 1673) and took an active part in the decoration of the park at Versailles (*Thetis*, 1670; *Diana*, 1680). Marshal de La Feuillade commissioned a statue of Louis XIV (1686), to be erected in the Place des Victoires, Paris. The statue (now in the Orangerie, Versailles) pleased the king so much that the marshal gave it to him and ordered another from Desjardins. The second version, much more elaborate, was erected in 1686 and destroyed during the Revolution; but some fragments have survived: bas-reliefs in the Louvre, Paris and corner statues (*The Conquered Nations*) in the Parc de Sceaux. In 1691 Desjardins set up an equestrian statue of the Roi Soleil in the Place Bellecour, Lyons; a presumed maquette for this work is in the Musée des Arts Décoratifs, Lyons. He also executed tombs and some very fine busts (*Édouard Colbert*, 1693; Louvre).

DESNOYER, François (1894, Montauban, Tarn-et-Garonne—1972, Séte), French painter and sculptor. He is referred to as a Cubo-Fauvist, a description that places him aptly enough between the contradictory movements that he seems to reconcile in his art, in which the lyricism of pure color does not preclude a Cézanne-like concern for the discipline of form. Desnoyer's sense of form derives primarily from the same sensual imagination that makes him an excellent sculptor; his ability to organize simple, vigorous compositions may be credited to a sound knowledge acquired by copying works of Bruegel, El Greco, Goya, Delacroix, and Courbet. His art, which is balanced and straightforward but also emotional, warm, and filled with *joie de vivre,* protests against the impositions of the intellect. During the course of his career Desnoyer adopted a lighter manner, particularly in his watercolors. He never, however, lost a monumentality that can be appreciated in his mural paintings in the ballroom of the town hall at Cachan, near Paris, as well as in his light-filled landscapes (*Transporter Bridge at Marseilles*, 1940; *Pleasures of the Beach*, 1949; both Paris, Musée National d'Art Moderne); his penetrating portraits; and his great luxuriant nudes, whose forms have the undulating contours of Baroque architecture.

DESPIAU, Charles (1874, Mont-de-Marsan, Landes—1946, Paris), French sculptor. Although he professed great admiration for Auguste Rodin and assisted him in 1907, Despiau differed greatly from the creator of the *Burghers of Calais*. His art is characterized by its reserve, its calm, and its rejection of dramatic gesture. His male nudes are closer to those of Classical Greece than to those of Rodin. The female nudes are even fuller in form, with smooth surfaces and undulating contours (*Eve*, 1925; Paris, Musée National d'Art Moderne).

If most of Despiau's portraits are of young women, it is not because he sought prettiness for its own sake, but because he preferred to present faces whose full freshness had been only lightly marked by life. All his figures look contemplative. His busts of *Line Aman-Jean* (1925), *Mademoiselle Bianchini* (1929), the *Princesse Murat* (1934), or *Maria Lani* (1929)—which is the richest in inner life—portray women who seem self-absorbed, as if listening to the beating of their hearts and trying to capture their most imperceptible feelings. He gives no hint of the storms that might trouble the calm eyes of his figures, purse their lips, or disturb the serene purity of their brows. They are always endowed with a grave and dignified air, and with much charm.

DESPORTES, François (1661, Champigneulle, Haute-Marne—1743, Paris), French painter who specialized in still life and animal painting. In 1695 he was called to Warsaw by King Sobieski, to whom he became court portraitist. He returned to France the following year and in 1699 entered the Académie as an animal painter, although his reception piece was his *Self-Portrait as a Hunter* (1699; Paris, Louvre). Louis XIV named him painter to the royal hunt, and in this capacity he decorated a number of the king's residences (the Ménagerie of Versailles, Marly, La Muette) as well as those of courtiers. Desportes' hunting pictures are now scattered in various museums: the *Fox Hunt* (Angers, Museum); the *Wolf Hunt* (Rennes, Museum); the *Boar Hunt* (Lyons, Museum); the *Deer Hunt* (Grenoble, Museum, and Rouen, Museum). He depicted the animals in precise landscapes; for, like Corot and Sisley, Desportes went out into the countryside to paint, using a cane with a steel tip and frame as support for his portfolio. His landscapes, now to be found at Compiègne, were unique in the 17th century. In 1735 Desportes received an important commission from the Gobelins factory, on which he was engaged from 1737 to 1741: the design for the splendid tapestry of the *New Indies* (Rome, Palazzo Quirinale), a work of exotic richness.

Charles Despiau. *Greek Woman*. 1944. Private Coll. *Photo Giraudon, Paris.*

DEUTSCH, Niklaus Manuel. *See* **MANUEL DEUTSCH,** Niklaus.

DEUTSCHER WERKBUND, German association of designers, manufacturers, and businessmen, founded October 6, 1907, through the efforts of the German architect Hermann Muthesius (1861–1927), who was then superintendent of the Prussian Board of Trade for Schools of Arts and Crafts. Its aims were to encourage the highest standards in materials and craftsmanship in the applied arts, particularly manufactured goods, and to establish a center for all who sympathized with these objectives. The inspiration for the Deutscher Werkbund came from William Morris' Arts and Crafts Movement: Muthesius had studied the designs of Morris and his followers during a six-year stay in England, and through his writings he had already done more than anyone else to make the work of the British group known in Germany. The impact of Muthesius' ideas and their forceful propagation can be appreciated from the fact that just after the Werkbund's foundation, several industrialists began to hire architects and graphic designers as consultants.

Apart from Muthesius, the most representative members of the association were architects like Theodor Fischer (1862–1938), Richard Riemerschmid (1868–1957), Hans Poelzig, Josef Hoffmann, and Henry van de Velde. From the beginning, the philosophy of the organization diverged fundamentally from William Morris' position. Morris remained hostile to the machine to the end of his life; Muthesius never shared this attitude, and the Werkbund, soon after its founding, not only accepted the machine as an inevitable fact, but welcomed it as a means of producing quality goods on a large scale. The exhibition organized by the Deutscher Werkbund in Cologne in 1914 enjoyed an unprecedented success. From the architectural point of view the most remarkable work was the model factory designed by Walter Gropius and Adolf Meyer. Other architects, such as Van de Velde, Behrens, Josef Hoffmann, and Bruno Taut (1880–1938) contributed designs that became landmarks of modern architecture because of their use of steel, concrete, and glass. To judge merely from the associations that took the Werkbund as a model (Austrian Werkbund, 1910; Swiss Werkbund, 1913; the Design and Industries Association in Britain, 1915), the movement had a considerable influence abroad.

The great postwar event in the history of the Werkbund was the exhibition of Domestic Design held in the Weissenhof quarter of Stuttgart (1927), which was organized by the association's vice-president, Mies van der Rohe. Those taking part included Behrens, Gropius, Hans Scharoun, Ludwig Hilberseimer (1885–1967), Max Taut (1884–1938), Jacobus Oud, and Le Corbusier. All the possibilities of the new architecture were demonstrated. The Werkbund was so successful that it represented Germany at the 1930 Exposition Universelle in Paris, and only the rise of Nazism interrupted its activities.

DE VRIENDT, Cornelis *and* Frans. *See* **FLORIS.**

DEWING, Thomas Wilmer (1851, Boston—1938, New York), American painter. In 1895, with John Twachtman, J. Alden Weir, Childe Hassam, and others, he formed The Ten, a group whose members were American painters opposed to academic tradition and in favor of individual artistic experimentation.

Dewing applied his lyrical and poetic Impressionism to elegant genre scenes of fashionable ladies in drawing rooms and gardens. His unique qualities as a painter take the form of extraordinary spatial arrangements and atmospheric contexts. In the *Recitation* (1891; Detroit, Institute of Arts) he suspends figures and chairs in seemingly unreal bands of space. The dreamlike figure in *Young Women with Violoncello* (*c.* 1905; Chicago, Art Institute) could as easily exist outdoors as in an interior. Dewing's treatment of space is thus curiously unlocalized and is one of the most distinctive features of his work.

DE WINT, Peter (1784, Stone, Staffordshire—1849, London), English watercolor painter. In 1802 he went to London and was apprenticed to the mezzotinter John Raphael Smith (1752–1812), with whom he remained for four years; then, with his fellow apprentice William Hilton (1786–1839), he took rooms in the painter John Varley's house in Broad Street. Varley introduced him to the painter Dr. Thomas Monro (1759–1833), and he attended several of Monro's famous evening classes in Adelphi Terrace. The main influence on De Wint's work at this time was that of Thomas Girtin, who is the inspiration behind several broad, calm, architectural watercolors (*High Bridge, Lincoln*; London, Victoria and Albert Museum).

De Wint earned his living mainly as a teacher, but from very early in his career he found an easy sale for his watercolors. As a sideline and a source of additional income he prepared travelers' sketches for engraving: Major Light's *Sicilian Scenery* appeared in 1823, and John Hughes' *Views in the South of France* in 1825.

Watercolors such as *Gledstone Hall, Yorkshire* (Bedford, Cecil Higgins Art Gallery) or *Gloucester* (1840; Lincoln, Usher Art Gallery) show his style at its most literal and serene. Slightly more interesting are those long, low, horizontal harvest scenes (*Canterbury*; Coll. Lord Ashton of Hyde), in which he almost consciously underlines his Dutch ancestry by following the compositional plan of Philips Koninck (1619–88). De Wint was also an effective painter in oils and in this medium occasionally achieved a depth that suggests the influence of Turner (*Chelsea Old Bridge*; Leeds, City Art Gallery).

DIAZ DE LA PEÑA, Virgilio Narcisso (1808, Bordeaux—1876, Menton, Alpes-Maritimes), French painter. The son of a Spanish refugee, and an orphan early in life, Diaz was apprenticed to a printer and then to a potter, but on making the acquaintance of Jules Dupré (1811–89) and Auguste Raffet (1804–60), he decided to take up painting. The decisive event of his career, however, was his meeting Théodore Rousseau, the founder of the Barbizon School. Diaz realized that Rousseau's paintings of the forest of Fontainebleau had brought a fresh impetus into art, drawn from John Constable and the 17th-century Dutch school. Eventually he joined Rousseau and his friends and became one of the leading Barbizon artists, exhibiting for the first time at the Salon of 1831, the same year as Dupré. Settled in Barbizon, he turned to pure landscape, concentrating on effects of light and shade and exercising a baroque taste for dramatic contrasts of natural phenomena as seen in *Approaching Storm* (1871; Moscow, Pushkin Museum) and *Landscape* (Cambridge, Fitzwilliam Museum).

DICKINSON, Preston (1891, New York—1930, Spain), American painter. He is noted mainly as a pioneer of Cubism in America. Influenced by the 1913 Armory Show in New York, Dickinson also relied on Japanese prints and later on Cézanne for his pictorial inspiration. His personal translation of Cézanne's methods, in which he used the discordance of Fauvist color to enliven his compositions, was Expressionistic rather than structural. Practicing a Cubist-Realist simplification of form (called Precisionism in America), he produced a number of lively, though fragile pictures of industrial and urban sites (*Industry*, before 1924; New York,

39.

40.

41.

42.

43.

39. **Vittore Carpaccio.** *Legend of St. Ursula: Reception of the English Ambassadors.* Detail. *c.* 1496–98. Accademia, Venice.

40. **Annibale Carracci.** *Bean-Eater.* Galleria Colonna, Rome.

41. **Caravaggio.** *Lute Player. c.* 1595. The Hermitage, Leningrad.

42. **Carlo Carrà.** *Metaphysical Muse.* 1917. Coll. Emilio Jesi, Milan.

43. **Canaletto.** *The Bucintoro Returning to the Molo on Ascension Day. c.* 1730. Crespi Coll., Milan.

44.

45.

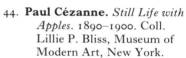

46.

47.

44. **Paul Cézanne.** *Still Life with Apples.* 1890–1900. Coll. Lillie P. Bliss, Museum of Modern Art, New York.
45. **Mary Cassatt.** *The Toilet.* 1891.
46. **Felice Casorati.** *Still Life.* Private Coll.
47. **Jean-Baptiste Chardin.** *The Cellar Boy.* 1738. Hunterian Museum, University of Glasgow.
48. **Marc Chagall.** *Purim.* 1917. Coll. Louis E. Stern, New York.
49. **Philippe de Champaigne.** *Cardinal Richelieu.* 1635. Louvre, Paris.
50. Opposite: **John Constable.** *View of Dedham (Stour Valley and Dedham Village).* Detail. *c.* 1815? Wm. W. Warren Fund, Museum of Fine Arts, Boston.

48.

49.

70.

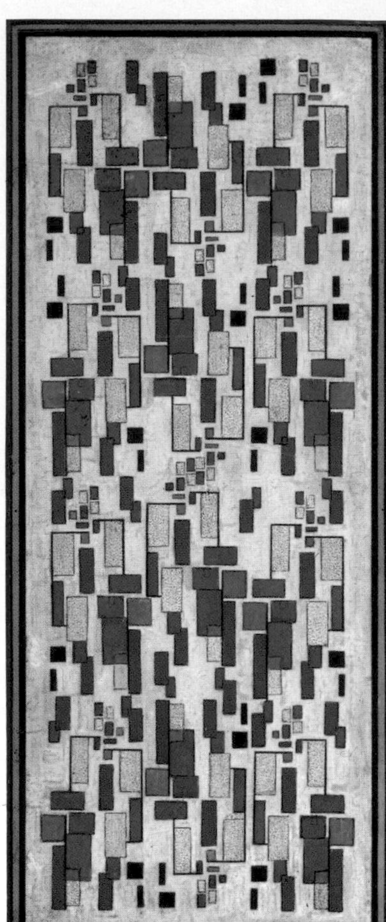

71.

72.

73.

74.

75.

70. **François Desportes.** *Landscape.* Musée National du Palais de Compiègne, Oise.
71. **Theo van Doesburg.** *Composition VI.* 1917. Private Coll., Meudon.
72. **Charles Demuth.** *Acrobats.* 1919. Museum of Modern Art, New York.
73. **André Derain.** *The Dancer.* 1906. Statens Museum for Kunst, Copenhagen.
74. **Arthur G. Dove.** *Anonymous.* 1942. Metropolitan Museum of Art, New York.
75. **Jean Dubuffet.** *Extremus Amibolis.* 1956.

Whitney Museum), still, however, relying on oriental design.

In his *Still Life with Yellow-Green Chair* (1928; Columbus, Ohio, Gallery of Fine Arts), Dickinson is perhaps at his most original. Although the arrangement of objects recalls the work of the Spanish painter Joan Miró, he created a colossal, ponderous space, coupled with an unusual disposition of ordinary objects

DIEBENKORN, Richard (b. 1922, Portland, Oregon), American painter. In 1946 he enrolled in the California School of Fine Arts in San Francisco, where he taught from 1947 to 1950, along with Clyfford Still, Mark Rothko, and others who offered him encouragement. Diebenkorn's earliest work consisted of still lifes, interiors, and figurative paintings; but, after some contact with American painting of the mid-to-late 1940s in New York, he began to work in a nonobjective, action-charged style. Diebenkorn made a rapid transition from geometric abstraction to a freer, expressionistic style, looking to Willem de Kooning for a use of vigorous, calligraphic line (*Albuquerque*, 1951; Albuquerque, N.M., University of New Mexico Art Gallery).

Until 1955, Diebenkorn's work remained abstract; then, encouraged by his friend, the painter David Park (b. 1911), he began to experiment with representational painting again, distrusting the hyperemotionalism of his previous canvases. He turned slowly to figures, landscapes, and still lifes, attempting to organize Abstract Expressionist brushwork into the recognizable forms of representational art (*Man and Woman in Room*, 1957; New York, Coll. Joseph H. Hirshhorn). He showed particular interest in asymmetrical compositions (*Corner of Studio—Sink*, 1963, New York, Poindexter Gallery; and *Girl Smoking*, 1963, San Francisco, Coll. Mr. & Mrs. Peter A. Selz), and in an organization of pictorial space into negative, open areas, balanced by a positive concentration of incidents in smaller sections of the canvas.

DILLER, Burgoyne (1906, New York—1965, New York), American painter and sculptor. In the late 1930s, Diller belonged to the American Abstract Artists group, which included Fritz Glarner, Ilya Bolotowsky (b. 1907), Lee Krasner (b. 1911), Willem de Kooning, Josef Albers, David Smith, and other artists who generally worked within the conventions of Neo-plasticism or based their style on that of Picasso's studio interiors of the late 1920s. From 1935 to 1940, Diller was head of the mural division of the New York Federal Art Project, a position that made it possible for him to help many young painters—such as Jackson Pollock, Adolph Gottlieb, Mark Rothko, and Ad Reinhardt—to continue painting during the Depression years.

In the late 1940s, Diller began to activate his canvas with complex, ladderlike configurations consisting of narrow, intersecting horizontal and vertical bars. The influence of Mondrian's New York paintings (1944) can be seen in these syncopated compositions. In his later works, Diller turned to simpler arrangements, in which a few rectangles are suspended freely on the colored grounds that characterized an earlier manner. Also dating from this later period is a series of blocky formica structures, such as the lustrous black *Project for Granite, No. 6* (New York, Coll. Noah Goldowsky and Richard Bellamy).

DINE, James, *called* Jim (b. 1935, Cincinnati, Ohio), American painter, considered by some critics a Pop artist. He began painting in the 1950s and first exhibited in New York in 1960, at which time he had also been involved for some years in the phenomena known as Environments and Happenings. He produced four of these during 1959–60: *Smiling Workman, Jim Dine's Vaudeville, Car Crash*, and the *Shining Bed*. After 1960 he returned to painting.

Dine owed a great deal to the climate created by Robert Rauschenberg and Jasper Johns, who raised the problem of combining objects and painting into a single entity. New York Dada, particularly the work of Marcel Duchamp, is also considered an important influence in his development. He was concerned with what is permissible aesthetically in a work of art, and he consistently included real objects in his paintings, displaced and dissociated from their everyday context, in a theatrical manner that is sophisticated in its frivolity (*Two Palettes in Black with Stovepipe*, 1963, New York, Sidney Janis Gallery; *Shoes Walking on My Brain*, 1960, New York, Coll. Dr. A. Solomon). In the mid-1960s Dine enclosed objects, such as garments, within glass boxes, cast lifesize feet, boots, and hands (*Double Right-Handed Doorway*, 1965; Sidney Janis Gallery), made plywood hearts, and executed collages.

DI SUVERO, Mark (b. 1933, Shang-hai, China), American sculptor. In 1941 Di Suvero's family emigrated to California, where he later studied at San Francisco City College and the University of California at Berkeley, majoring in philosophy. He moved to New York City in 1957, and three years later had his first one-man show there.

Di Suvero's early sculpture showed a violent expressionism, but in the early 1960s he began making small constructions that developed into his major, giant compositions of old wooden beams and planks, tires, chains, and other scrap materials from junkyards and demolished buildings (*Hank Champion*, 1960; New York, Coll. Mr. and Mrs. Robert C. Scull). Thus, like John Chamberlain and Richard Stankiewicz, Di Suvero drew upon the environment for his materials, and was interested in the formal possibilities of his assemblages. His work is on a colossal scale, and in the long, energetic strokes that the beams of his constructions cut through space, it resembles the Abstract Expressionist paintings of Franz Kline. His constructions are generally characterized by oblique, centrifugal lines of force and by a tension that holds the various suspended elements in a seemingly precarious balance. In some of Di Suvero's works there are mobile seats—usually old rubber tires— in which the viewer is invited to sit and thereby become directly involved in the space of the construction by moving around and through it.

DIVISIONISM. *See* **NEO-IMPRESSIONISM.**

DIX, Otto (1891, Untermhausen, near Gera, Thuringia—1969, Singen, Baden-Württemberg), German painter. In 1927 Dix was appointed to a teaching post at the Dresden Academy, but was dismissed by the Nazis in 1933. He lived at Hemmenhofen on Lake Constance from 1935, except for a period in 1945–46 when he was a

Theo van Doesburg. *Counter-Composition.* 1924. Stedelijk Museum, Amsterdam.

prisoner-of-war in France. Immediately after his demobilization, he turned to Dadaism, revolting against traditional art and the morality of a society that had caused the holocaust of war and its aftermath. His Dadaism took the form of montages with beads, colored paper, and cutouts from poetry albums; but he was soon swept into the German Neue Sachlichkeit ("new objectivity"). The branch to which Dix belonged was the social Verism of George Grosz, which depicted surface reality with meticulous clarity but so distorted form and perspective that the final result was grotesque. This was a powerful technique in which Dix executed violent paintings of protest against the horror of war, the cripples, whores, and tycoons, all of which were also the subject of Grosz's bitter drawings. His book of engravings, *War* (1944), is equally forceful. In the 1950s Dix abandoned Verism for a broader, Expressionistic style.

DOBSON, William (1610/11, London—1646, London), the most distinguished native-born English portraitist of his age. The main influences on his style were the Venetian paintings he was able to study in Charles I's collection. A brief interest in the school of Utrecht inspired the curious *Executioner with the Baptist's Head* (Liverpool, Walker Art Gallery), a canvas with which, according to tradition, Dobson refused to part. His name is inextricably associated with the establishment of the Royalist court at Oxford. Most of his portraits were painted during this period (1642–46) and are brilliant reflections of the worldly but overcast temper of the Royalist generals (*John, 1st Lord Byron, c.* 1644; Coll. J. Leicester-Warren).

Dobson's richest and most splendid portraits include the *Charles II as Prince of Wales* (Edinburgh, Scottish National Portrait Gallery) and the *Endymion Porter* (London, Tate Gallery), with their warm, brilliant coloring and full complement of draperies, columns, thunderclouds, marble busts, dogs, and attendants. Less impressive but infinitely more subtle is the melancholy oval of *Prince Rupert* (Coll. Earl of Dartmouth), while the full-length portrait of *James Compton, 3rd Earl of Northampton* (Coll. Marquess of Northampton) has an integrity that raises it far above the general level of 17th-century English portraiture. It is probably accurate to regard this picture as the finest native English portrait before Hogarth set a new standard with his *Captain Coram* (1740).

Domenico Veneziano. *St. John the Baptist in the Wilderness. c.* 1445. Predella, altarpiece of S. Lucia de' Magnoli. Samuel H. Kress Coll., National Gallery of Art, Washington, D.C.

DOESBURG, Christian Emil Marie Küpper, *called* Theo van (1883, Utrecht—1931, Davos, Switzerland), Dutch painter, decorator, and art critic. A writer of fables, plays, and articles, he originally planned a career in the theater. In 1913 he began his investigation into the unification of painting and architecture and in 1915 published an article in praise of Mondrian, whom he later met. From this time, his own painting tended to abstraction. In 1917, with Mondrian, Vilmos Huszar (1905–60), Bart van der Leck, Georges Vantongerloo, and several Dutch avant-garde architects, Van Doesburg founded the review *De Stijl,* which had considerable influence on the development of the arts, particularly in Germany. After an exhibition of the De Stijl group in Paris in 1923 (Galerie de l'Effort Moderne), Van Doesburg abandoned the strict principles formulated by Mondrian and embarked on a new direction that he was later (1926) to call Elementarism, which sought greater dynamism by the use of inclined planes (*Color Sketch,* 1924–25; Paris, Coll. François Arp). In 1927 he decorated a number of rooms in the Aubette dance hall at Strasbourg, where Arp and Sophie Taeuber were also working. This, his main work, has unfortunately been destroyed.

Of Doesburg's many writings, the most important are his *Classique, Baroque, Moderne* (Paris, 1921) and *Grundbegriffe der neuen gestaltenden Kunst* ("Basic Principles of the New Plastic Art"), published by the Bauhaus in 1924.

DOMENICO VENEZIANO (*c.* 1400, Venice—1461, Florence), Italian painter. Domenico's career is illuminated by two important documents: the much quoted letter to Piero di Cosimo de' Medici, dated April 1, 1438, from Perugia, in which the artist asks to be recommended to Piero's father and compares himself to Fra Angelico and Fra Filippo Lippi; and a record of payment, dated September 7, 1439, for fees owing from the Ospedale di S. Maria Novella for frescoes painted in the choir of S. Egidio by Domenico and his assistants (Piero della Francesca is mentioned among them). The *Madonna* from the altarpiece of S. Lucia de' Magnoli, a signed work now at the Uffizi, Florence, is generally thought to be later (*c.* 1445); the predellas are dispersed in various museums (Cambridge, Fitzwilliam Museum; Berlin, Staatliche Museum; Washington, D.C., National Gallery). About 1460 Domenico painted scenes from the lives of St. Francis and St. John the Baptist at S. Croce; one fresco survives, with superbly expressive figures of the two saints. We do not know whether Domenico came to Florence before 1439 or whether his influence had already made itself felt there; for his light, clear color was a contribution to Florentine painting that modified the style of painters who had been influenced by Masaccio's monumentality. The altarpiece of S. Lucia reveals the strong personality of the artist in his mature period. Here, we can see at once, is the starting point of Piero della Francesca. The *Carnesecchi Tabernacle*, a fresco painted about 1440 on a street tabernacle in the Via de' Cerretani in Florence and transferred to canvas in 1851 (now in London, National Gallery), shows other qualities and other influences. The standing *putto* recalls Gentile da Fabriano. The

Donatello. *Miracle of the Mule.* 1445–48. High altar of St. Anthony, Padua. *Photo Alinari-Giraudon.*

massive, rigidly perfect treatment of the Madonna and the plunging view of God the Father suggest interests and preoccupations that would not have been foreign to Paolo Uccello. It is also usual to attribute to Domenico the superb tondo with the *Adoration of the Magi* (Berlin, Staatliche Museen).

On the basis of the altarpiece of S. Lucia, scholars have attributed to Domenico the portraits of *Matteo Olivieri* (Washington, D.C., National Gallery) and *Michele Olivieri* (New York, Priv. Coll.), the elegant and clear *Profile of a Noblewoman* (Boston, Isabella Stewart Gardner Museum), and a number of decorative panels.

DONATELLO, Donato di Betto Bardi, *called* (1386, Florence—1466, Florence), the most important Italian sculptor of the 15th century in Florence. He exerted a decisive influence on most of the sculptors of his own generation, and on the course of painting, both in Florence and, through Andrea Mantegna, in northern Italy as well. He was also one of the main sources of inspiration for Michelangelo, who was taught by Donatello's pupil Bertoldo (*c.* 1420–91). The earliest record of Donatello shows that he was working for his compatriot Lorenzo Ghiberti on the first set of Baptistery doors in 1403; by 1406 he had left Ghiberti's shop and was employed on the decoration of Florence Cathedral. His connection with the cathedral lasted many years and one of their commissions first made his name: this was the seated figure of *St. John the Evangelist,* which was carved between 1413 and 1415. But before the *St. John,* Donatello had already made two important marble statues. The earlier of these, and the earliest work of his that can be discussed with certainty, is the marble *David* now in the Bargello, Florence, which was carved for the cathedral about 1408: it has a grace of line that is clearly in the tradition of the International Gothic style and of Ghiberti in particular. The decisive departure from this rather elegant style to the more heroic conception typical of Donatello can be seen taking place in the *St. John the Evangelist*, already mentioned, and in the figure of *St. Mark*, carved in 1411–12 for one of the niches on the façade of the church of Or San Michele, Florence. This more Classical, and more valid, conception of the human figure becomes the dominant characteristic of his style and can perhaps best be seen in the series of *Prophets* (1427–36), carved over a long period for the campanile of Florence Cathedral. The most famous of these is the one known as *Zuccone* ("Baldhead," 1435–36).

One of his most important innovations, the statue of *St. George* (1415–16), was carved for one of the niches of Or San Michele and is now in the Bargello. In order to better integrate the statue with the building, Donatello carved on the base a very low relief of *St. George and the Dragon*, which exhibits strict obedience to the newly rediscovered science of perspective. His bas-relief marks an important stage in Renaissance art, the pictorial possibilities of the medium having been brought to such a point as to summarize the later development of painting. Donatello was to develop the pictorial possibilities of very low relief in a number of works executed mostly in the mid-1420s and again toward the end of his life. About 1425 he went into partnership with the architect and sculptor Michelozzo; in 1427 they were engaged on a number of important works, including the tombs of the antipope John XXIII (Florence, Baptistry) and Cardinal Brancacci (Naples, S. Angelo a Nilo). Later they also made the outdoor pulpit of the cathedral at Prato. The Brancacci monument—with its low relief of the *Assumption*—illustrates particularly well the pictorial and dramatic possibilities of shallow relief. Perhaps the most important of the low-relief designs in which the dramatic possibilities of perspective are fully explored is the *Feast of Herod,* completed for the baptismal font of Siena Cathedral in 1427.

The next major event in Donatello's career was his journey to Rome, where he spent some 18 months between 1431 and 1433, very probably in the company of the architect Brunelleschi, the two thus renewing their acquaintance with Classical Roman art. There can be no doubt that as a result Donatello's subsequent style became even more influenced by late antique and early Christian work. This is confirmed by the famous reliefs of the *Dancing Children* on the Cantoria (Singing Gallery) in Florence Cathedral, commissioned on his return in 1433 and completed in 1439. It is probable also that the bronze *David* (now in the Bargello) dates from some time after his return from Rome. The idea of such a statue and the Christian interpretation of the form indicate the period 1433–43, that is, between Donatello's stay in Rome and his departure for Padua. The

Donatello. *Judith and Holofernes.* Detail. 1457–60. Piazza della Signoria, Florence. *Photo Alinari-Giraudon.*

elaborate perspective of his stucco bas-reliefs in Brunelleschi's Old Sacristy at S. Lorenzo, Florence, as well as the dramatic realism of the figures on his bronze doors there, also indicate a date in the years immediately before his departure for Padua.

Donatello went to Padua in 1443, stayed there 10 years and executed two major works: the bronze equestrian statue of the condottiere *Gattamelata* (1447–53) in the Piazza del Santo and the high altar of the basilica of S. Antonio, which seems to have been begun in 1444 with a commission for a crucifix. The high altar has been rebuilt and its original form is still a matter of considerable controversy; but the individual statues, and above all the reliefs, exerted a decisive influence on all Paduan and Venetian painters of the next half century. The large reliefs of the *Miracles of St. Anthony* (1445–48) exploited his earlier discoveries in perspective and combined them with a forceful and almost melodramatic figure style. This style was continued in his last Florentine works, most particularly in the bronze reliefs on the two pulpits in S. Lorenzo, Florence; the bronze relief of the *Lamentation of Christ* (London, Victoria and Albert Museum); *Judith and Holofernes* (1457–60); and the carved wooden statue of *St Mary Magdalene* (*c.* 1456) in the Baptistery, Florence. In its exploration of the possibilities of extreme ugliness it exercised a profound influence on all later Florentine art, in particular that of Andrea del Castagno.

DONGEN, Cornelis T. M., *called* Kees van (1877, Delfshaven, near Rotterdam—1968, Monte Carlo, Monaco), French painter of Dutch origin. He was enrolled by his father in a school of decorative art in Rotterdam and at the age of twenty went to Paris, where he worked as a market porter, house painter, and itinerant sketcher in the sidewalk cafés. The life of Montmartre, the quarter in which he lived, so fascinated him that all trace of his Dutch background disappeared from his paintings. In 1906 he became an ardent Fauve; he was the most faithful and perhaps the most gifted of the group. The paintings of the next six or seven years were dominated by the recurring image of a woman with immense eyes and flaming hair, her flesh streaked with vibrant yellows, greens, blues, and vermilions (*Woman with Jewels*, 1905, Switzerland, Priv. Coll.; *Woman with a Black Hat, c.* 1908, Leningrad, Hermitage).

After World War I, Van Dongen was sought after by aristocratic society, not because his portraits were flattering, but because his sarcastic images made no attempt to disguise moral and physical defects. He created a feminine type that was half drawing-room prostitute, half sidewalk princess; her murky eyes, livid face with blood-red mouth, spindly arms, and exaggeratedly thin body adorned with sparkling jewels and veiled in silk or tulle, or cynically stripped nude, brought the painter a certain notoriety. Van Dongen also produced portraits in a less provocative, less taut style that were touching in their simplicity (*Gilbert Pétridès*, 1951; Paris, Coll. P. Pétridès). The paintings inspired by his trip to North Africa (*Fellahs*, *c.* 1912; Paris, Musée National d'Art Moderne); his scenes of Paris (*Lake of the Bois de Boulogne*, *c.* 1912; Musée National d'Art Moderne; *Pont Alexandre III*, Amsterdam, Priv. Coll.) or Versailles; and his Deauville seascapes attain an almost miraculous technical richness in their extreme concision. With two colors and a single arabesque, he could obtain striking effects that efface the memory of the superficiality, softness, and preciosity of the paintings commissioned by his cosmopolitan clientele. His improvisatory verve and his insolent dash will long be remembered. His portraits of *Dr. Rapport* (1913; Rotterdam, Museum Boymans-van Beuningen), *Anatole France* (1917; Paris, Coll. Dr. Roudinesco), and *Boni de Castellane* (1927; Monaco, Priv. Coll.) will outlast his too ingratiating portraits of society women, dethroned kings, and maharajahs.

DORÉ, Gustave (1832, Strasbourg—1883, Paris), French painter, draftsman, and lithographer. He produced his first lithograph at the age of thirteen. Two years later he accompanied his parents to Paris, where he showed his drawings to Charles Philipon, who was beginning to publish his *Journal pour rire*. Doré loved music, the theater, the circus, and the legends of Alsace and the Black Forest, subjects that lent a dreamy power to the illustrations and lithographs that made him famous. In 1853 he illustrated an edition of Rabelais with drawings of grandiose verve, followed two years later by illustrations for Balzac's *Contes drolatiques* (*Droll Stories*), his masterpiece. With the illustrations to the *Wandering Jew* (1856) of Eugène Sue, the first phase of Doré's career came to a close.

His next projects were illustrations for Dante's *Inferno*, published at his own expense (1861), Perrault's *Contes* (1862), and Cervantes' *Don Quixote* (1863), books that provided particularly suitable material for an artist who excelled at giving form to chimeras and dreams. He was fascinated by the

Gustave Doré. Illustration for Balzac's *Contes drolatiques.* 1855. Bibliothèque Nationale, Paris. *Photo Giraudon, Paris.*

stories of the Queen of Sheba, Balthasar's Feast, and the Tower of Babel, which he interpreted in his illustrations for the Bible in 1866; next came the *Fables* of La Fontaine in 1867. His powerful imagination made him a master of the grandiose exaggeration of satire and mystery.

DOSSO DOSSI, Giovanni di Lutero, *called* (*c.* 1490, Ferrara—1542, Ferrara), Italian painter. Dosso spent the major part of his fertile career in Ferrara, but his visits to Rome (where he probably met Raphael) and especially to Venice were very important for his art. In his early days in Ferrara he was influenced by Venetian painting, and above all by Giorgione and Titian. The latter, moreover, worked in Ferrara, where Dosso must have seen his paintings. Dosso introduced Giorgionesque romanticism to the school of Ferrara, but augmented it with a pictorial freedom and energy learned from Titian. He was an excellent colorist and bathed his representations of the *Madonna and Saints* (Modena Cathedral; Rome, Galleria Nazionale) in a bright atmosphere, rich in warm contrasts and shimmering effects. The imaginary or familiar landscapes are largely responsible for the charm of the allegorical and mythological scenes that the artist made his specialty. The *Witches* (Rome, Galleria Borghese; Washington, D.C., National Gallery), the *Rustic Idylls* (New York, Metropolitan Museum), the *Argonauts* (National Gallery), the *Apollos with Musical Instruments* (Galleria Borghese), and the symbolic but passionate nudes bring to life again in some way the unexpected fantasy and magic of the great Ferrarese painters of the 15th century. Like them, Dosso also left portraits of vital intensity.

DOUGHTY, Thomas (1793, Philadelphia—1856, New York), American painter of the Hudson River School. He worked in his native city as a leather currier until 1820, at which time he embarked upon a career in painting. Among the earliest of American artists to specialize in the landscape genre, Doughty soon won recognition for his serene views of the Pennsylvania and New York countryside (*On the Hudson*, 1821; New York, Metropolitan Museum). In 1824 he was elected a member of the Pennsylvania Academy, and also exhibited a number of paintings illustrating James Fenimore Cooper's novel *The Pioneers*, published the previous year. Two years later he had his first major exhibition at the National Academy of Design in New York, and between 1837 and 1846 made several trips to Europe.

Doughty was a popular and financially successful artist in his day, although at present his paintings seem almost primitive in their charming simplicity. Nevertheless, in such landscapes as *In Nature's Wonderland* (1835; Detroit, Institute of Arts), he managed to record a tender and fleeting moment in the scenic history of America, when its countryside was still largely pure and untamed.

DOVE, Arthur G. (1880, Canandaigua, New York—1946, Centerport, New York), American painter. After studying at Hobart College and Cornell University, Dove began working as an illustrator for such magazines as *Scribner's* and the *Saturday Evening Post*. In 1907 he went to France, where he spent 18 months. During a stay in Cagnes he produced landscapes and still lifes influenced by Cézanne.

Dove's true personality did not emerge until he returned to New York, where, in 1910, he painted six nonfigurative canvases that marked his shift to abstraction. The following year he continued this trend with a series of abstract pastels (*Sails*, 1911; New York, Coll. Philip L. Goodwin). His abstraction is the result of a methodical process of elimination and selection—far removed from Kandinsky's romanticism—that consists in discovering the exact color and shape of each object, in order to determine the relationship of objects and thus the form and nature of painting itself.

Once Dove had developed his own style, it changed little, although the paintings of his last years, during which he was ill and beset by financial worries, are often somber and peopled by tense, hieratic shapes: *Long Island* (1940), *Parabola* (1943) and *That Red One* (1944; all New York, Downtown Gallery).

DUBREUIL, Toussaint (*c.* 1561, Paris—1602, Paris), French painter. We know from documents that Dubreuil, first painter to Henri IV, provided the designs for the pictorial decoration of a number of large-scale projects: the Petite Galerie in the Louvre, the Galerie des Cerfs and the Galerie des Chevreuils at Fontainebleau, and the royal apartments at St-Germain-en-Laye. Nothing remains of the Louvre and Fontainebleau projects, and only a few fragments of the St-Germain cycle survive (*Sacrifice*, Paris, Louvre; others at Fontainebleau); added to a fine collection of drawings (most of them in the Louvre) and a number of tapestries woven from his cartoons, however, they enable us to form a judgment of his work. Dubreuil emerges as the most personal artist of the Second School of Fontainebleau. He was strongly influenced by the masters of the first school: he acquired their elegant Mannerism, a certain feeling for romance and fantasy, and a firm grasp of large-scale composition. But Dubreuil's concern for clarity and naturalness, his attention to everyday details, and the harmony he establishes between landscape and figures reveal a new taste that was to become one of the sources of 17th-century French Classicism.

Dosso Dossi. *Diana and the Nymph Callisto.* Detail. Soon after 1538. Galleria Borghese, Rome. *Photo Anderson-Giraudon.*

DUBUFFET, Jean (b. 1901, Le Havre), French painter. It was only in 1942 that Dubuffet decided to devote himself to painting. His first paintings were violently colored views of Paris and of its Métro. They were followed in 1946 by his *Mirobolus, Macadam & Cie., Hautes Pâtes* ("thick impastos"), with graffiti-like figures incised in a monochromatic, muddy paste mixed with sand, gravel, or tar. In 1947, after a visit to the Sahara, Dubuffet gave an exhibition of wildly imaginative portraits of his friends, including Henri Michaux, Antonin Artaud, and Paulhan (*Maast with Long Hair—Portrait of Jean Paulhan*, 1946; Chicago, Coll. Mr. & Mrs. Arnold H. Maremont). In 1949, at

Duccio di Buoninsegna. *The Maestà.* 1308–11. Museo dell'Opera del Duomo, Siena.

the Galerie René Drouin, he held the first exhibition of *Art Brut*, a now well-known label explained by the essay he wrote for the catalogue: *L'art brut préféré aux arts culturels* ("Crude art in preference to the cultural arts"). The exhibition featured the work of amateur artists and mental patients, in whose art Dubuffet found a heightened and unspoiled creativity.

After two further visits to the Sahara came the *Paysages grotesques* of 1949 and the *Corps de dames* of 1950, whose violent Expressionism emerges from textures that are not only mineral but also human and vegetal. The wide, opaque reliefs *Sols et Terrains* (1951–52), were followed by *Terres Radieuses*, a collection of ink drawings whose proliferating lines foreshadow the continuous homogeneous space of the *Assemblages d'empreintes* (*Imprint Assemblages*—cutouts decorated with India ink) and *Impressions lithographiques*. The same spirit animates the sculptures composed from 1954, which consist of fragments of plaster, sponge, papier mâché, silver paper, and other materials. But Dubuffet's lyricism reached its highest expression in the period marked by his *Topographies* and *Texturologies* (both 1957–59). Subsequently, in *Beard of Uncertain Returns* (1959; New York, Museum of Modern Art), the distinctive face of man reappeared, misty like a landscape, blue like a pebble polished by the tide. With the *Matériologies* series (begun 1959), the painter extended his expressive range still further by using crumpled and painted silver paper, vinyl plastics, or polyester resins.

DUCCIO DI BUONINSEGNA (*c.* 1255, Siena—*c.* 1318, Siena), Italian painter. His name appears in records for the first time in 1278, at which time he was decorating manuscript binding. In 1285, in Florence, he was given his first important commission. His works can be divided into three main periods: 1278–90, 1290–1308, and after 1308.

On April 15, 1285, the Florentine Brotherhood of the Virgin Mary, the Compagnia dei Laudesi, commissioned from Duccio a large altarpiece for the Rucellai chapel in the Florentine church of S. Maria Novella; the altarpiece, usually called the *Rucellai Madonna*, is now in the Uffizi, Florence. The attribution of this work raises a problem. If, as Giorgio Vasari claims, it is by Cimabue, we must suppose that the painting commissioned from Duccio has been lost. Father Vincenzo Fineschi was the first, in his *Memorie Istoriche* of 1790, to disagree with Vasari and recognize Duccio's hand in the *Rucellai Madonna*. This attribution seems likely and is widely accepted today. But one observes that, in this youthful work, Duccio is still very near Cimabue. On the other hand, the Sienese painter shows a more sensitive approach, particularly noticeable in the more supple movements of the figures, the elegant folds in the materials, and the bright ornaments and subtle color effects.

During the second period (1290–1308), Duccio's artistic personality developed and his fame spread. Several polyptychs are by his own hand, among them the *Virgin Surrounded by St. Peter, St. Paul, St. Augustine, and St. Dominic* (Siena, Pinacoteca).

Several outstanding pictures painted either by Duccio himself or under his supervision belong to his last period: the so-called London triptych (London, Royal Collection) with the *Crucifixion* at the center, the *Annunciation* and the *Virgin Enthroned* on the left, and the *Coronation of the Virgin* and *St. Francis Receiving the Stigmata* on the right. But none of these works equals the large Siena *Maestà*, which is not only the painter's masterpiece but one of the masterpieces of 14th-century Italian art. Commissioned in 1308 for the cathedral, it was completed in 1311. A large wooden panel, painted on both sides, each with a predella, it showed on the side facing the congregation the *Madonna Surrounded by Saints*, and on the other side a number of individual scenes from the *Life of Christ*. The panel was later sawn through and its two sides are now juxtaposed, in the Opera del Duomo, Siena. It has been preserved almost intact: only a few fragments from the predella are missing or scattered through various collections in Europe and America (*Annunciation, Christ Healing the Blind*, and *Transformation,* London, National Gallery; *Nativity*, Berlin; *Temptation of Christ*, New York, Frick Collection; *Nativity*, and the *Calling of St. Peter and St. Andrew*, Washington, D.C., National Gallery). In the general organization of the panel and in the use of gold for the background, something of the Byzantine manner remains, but the flatness is replaced by receding planes and depth is suggested by chiaroscuro. The forms are more supple, the sinuous outlines more elegant.

DU CERCEAU. *See* **ANDROUET DU CERCEAU.**

DUCHAMP, Marcel (1887, Blainville, Seine-Inférieure—1968, Neuilly-sur-Seine), French painter and sculptor, the brother of Jacques Villon and Raymond Duchamp-Villon. After a number of Fauvist pictures (1908–10), he turned to experimental work in which he revealed his own highly original talent. His *Nude Descending a Staircase, No. 2*, painted in 1912 and exhibited in 1913 at the Armory Show in New York, caused a scandal. This work is related to Futurism in its attempt to represent movement, incorporating as it does five silhouettes, almost superimposed upon one another, descending a spiral staircase in such a way that five successive movements are represented in a single image, as in a photographic film. Duchamp anticipated Dadaism with his "ready-mades" and with the publication of *291*, an "anti-painting" magazine, on which he worked with Man Ray, the critic Marius de Zayas, and the art patron Walter Arensberg. Between 1915 and 1923 he worked intermittently on *The Bride Stripped Bare by Her Bachelors, Even*, a "mystico-mechanical epic of human desire" in two parts, the Bride's Domain in the upper section, the Bachelor Apparatus in the lower (oil and lead wire on glass). This work, enthusiastically acclaimed by the Surrealists, was Duchamp's masterpiece, never followed by a work of comparable impact. He remained closely associated with the Surrealists, creating the coalsack ceiling for the 1938 International Surrealist Exhibition in Paris, and also the so-called Rain Room for the Surrealist Exhibition in 1947 at the Galerie Maeght, Paris.

DUCHAMP-VILLON, Raymond (1876, Damville, Eure—1918, Cannes), French sculptor, brother of Jacques Villon and Marcel Duchamp. After studying medicine, he turned to sculpture around 1900. He was self-taught, using Rodin's work as his model. About 1910 he discarded all influences and chose to work in geometricized volumes that he strove to make increasingly synthetic. His head of *Baudelaire* (1911; Paris, Musée National d'Art Moderne) is circumscribed in an oval; although the hollows of the eyes, the projection of the nose, and the modeling of the cheeks and mouth are clearly delineated, the purity of the line remains unspoiled. For all its starkness, the work is a living portrait that conveys the particular character of the poet's face and the complexity of his mind. Shortly afterward, Duchamp-Villon modeled a bust, *Maggy* (1912; Musée National d'Art Moderne), in which the form acquired even greater autonomy. It is less the head of a woman than an idol, one of the first idols of modern art. When he created his work, Duchamp-Villon was counted among the followers of Cubism; from 1911, he had been a member of the Puteaux group, which included, as well as his two brothers, Roger de La Fresnaye, Fernand Léger, Albert Gleizes, and Jean Metzinger.

Raymond Duchamp-Villon. *Baudelaire*. 1911. Musée National d'Art Moderne, Paris. *Photo Galerie Louis Carré.*

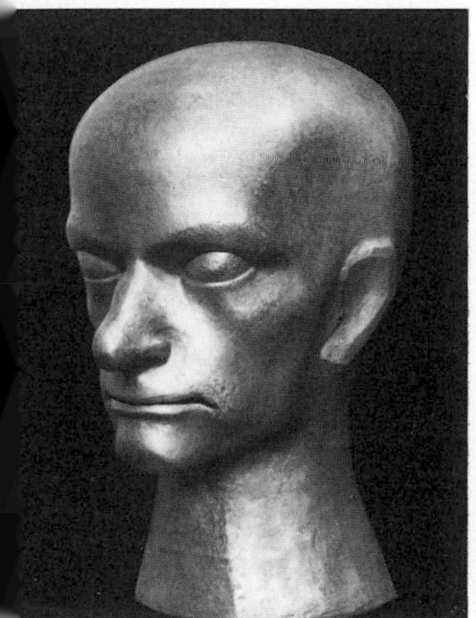

Duchamp-Villon's most daring and original sculpture was the famous *Horse* of 1914 (Musée National d'Art Moderne), half animal and half machine. Some parts, rigid and mechanical, seem to have come from a locomotive; others, curved, flexible, but taut, suggest the spring of a leaping horse. The work is thoroughly abstract, a completely autonomous organism quivering with a powerful dynamism. World War I unfortunately interrupted this brilliant career: Duchamp-Villon was mobilized and in 1916 caught an infectious disease from which he died two years later.

DUECENTO. The Byzantine influence felt in Italy from the early Middle Ages was particularly strong during the 13th century. The history of Italian painting during the Duecento might be considered as both the history of the domination of Byzantine art and the liberation achieved by Giotto at the beginning of the 14th century. The first tentative steps in the direction of a return to antiquity were made by the sculptor Nicola Pisano. In Rome and Latium, where vestiges of the Classical tradition always remained, this new pre-Renaissance style was given special impetus.

Roman paintings of the 13th century stem from the cycles of S. Clemente (Rome) and Castel Sant'Elia, near Nepi. The frescoes of Anagni Cathedral, probably painted between 1231 and 1255, are the most important examples of Roman painting of the time. They constitute a narrative cycle stretching from the Old Testament to more recent hagiography. Toward the end of the century a few major artists, whose works stand out because of their use of bright colors, benefited from the experience of both Roman painting and the Byzantine style. These artists included Pietro Cavallini (mosaics of S. Maria in Trastevere, 1291, and frescoes at S. Cecilia, 1293), Jacopo Torriti (Assisi, 1280, and S. Maria Maggiore, Rome, 1295), and Filippo Rusuti (S. Maria Maggiore, façade mosaic, 1308).

Duecento. Cimabue. *Crucifix. c.* 1285–88. S. Croce, Florence. *Photo Alinari-Giraudon.*

In Tuscany a similar evolution took place, but it is more difficult to follow than in Latium because there were so many artistic centers. In Florence various tendencies were either combined or in conflict. The mosaic in the choir of the baptistery of S. Giovanni shows Venetian influence. The Florentine painted crosses of the second half of the century (Florence, Accademia; San Gimignano, Museum) do not differ from those painted in Pisa or Lucca. Lastly, Coppo di Marcovaldo, a Florentine who settled in Siena, is one of the precursors of Cimabue. The first Sienese master of the century was Guido da Siena; the last, Duccio, held a place similar to that of Cimabue in Florence or Cavallini in Rome.

Judging from the number of works that have survived, Pisa and Lucca were the most active 13th-century artistic centers not only in Tuscany but in all Italy. Painting on wood is characteristic of these schools and there are three favorite themes: the Virgin enthroned, otherwise known as the *Maestà*; the painted Crucifix on a rectangular or cross shaped panel, both decorated with compartmentally arranged narrative scenes; and the *paliotto*, or altar frontal, dedicated to one saint, whose full length portrait occupies the central panel, with scenes from his life or legend told on the side panels and predella: The third theme is characteristic of Italian art of the Duecento: the central character varies from one *paliotto*

Duecento. Above left: Façade of S. Lorenzo Cathedral, Genoa. Late 13th century.
Above right: S. Maria Novella, Florence: nave, 1278. *Photos Alinari-Giraudon.*

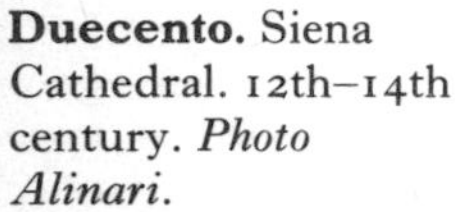

Duecento. Siena Cathedral. 12th–14th century. *Photo Alinari.*

to the next; St. Francis (pala in S. Francesco, Pescia, by Bonaventura Belinghieri) is depicted most frequently, but we also find representations of St. Mary Magdalene and St. Michael.

The situation was slightly different in northern Italy. Venice, which remained in the 13th century the largest market for Byzantine art, was also a living center where new works were created. The decoration of the basilica of St. Mark's was continued, especially in the atrium, with the *Creation* mosaics, whose iconography is entirely Byzantine. From Venice, Byzantine art spread to all of northern Italy.

In southern Italy, from the 11th century, a so-called Benedictine art developed. Most of the paintings from that time have been destroyed, but there remain the large frescoes of S. Angelo in Formis, near Capua (11th–12th centuries), and the *Last Judgment* frescoes (*c.* 1340) in S. Maria del Casale, near Brindisi, painted by Rinaldo da Taranto (active 14th century).

Although the Duecento was not one of the greatest centuries of Italian painting, it was a decisive turning point in its history. This is evident to an even greater extent, in architecture and sculpture. In architecture, the Romanesque tradition had supplanted Byzantine influence everywhere except in Venice. The Romanesque tradition was widespread even when, at the end of the century, the Cistercian monks introduced the Gothic style. The abbey of Fossanova, near Rome, consecrated by Pope Innocent III in 1208, was the first Cistercian church in Italy. A few years later, in 1217, Pope Honorius III consecrated the abbey of Casamari, east of Rome. This abbey served as the model for the architects of S. Galgano (*c.* 1224–88; now in ruins), not far from Siena. From its starting point in Latium, Gothic had finally reached Tuscany. However, it was not until Giovanni Pisano, architect and sculptor, began working on Siena Cathedral that Gothic found a genuinely Italian expression. It is important to remember that this new style did not continue without resistance, evidenced by the reappearance of the pediment in façades (S. Andrea, Vercelli, 1219–27; S. Antonio, Padua, 1232–1307), or the use of marble facing in bands of alternate colors in the Pisan manner (cathedral of S. Lorenzo, Genoa, late 13th century). All the charm of S. Francesco in Bologna (1236–63) lies in the subtle compromise established between the Romanesque and Gothic styles. S. Francesco at Assisi, founded by Gregory IX in 1228, does not avoid these contradictions either. Similarly, this surrender to the canons of the new order reappears in S. Maria Novella in Florence. In Rome, the church of S. Maria sopra Minerva (1280) stands as a unique example of the Gothic style.

The situation at the cathedral of Siena (begun 1249) was quite different. At first the Sienese were content to follow plans that had been tried out at S. Galgano under the direction of Giovanni Pisano, who had been entrusted with designing the façade in 1284. This inflection of the Gothic style toward a typically Italian mode of expression was parallcled at the same time in Florence by the work on the cathedral of S. Maria del Fiore, begun in 1296 under the supervision of Arnolfo di Cambio, who worked there until his death in 1302. Though certain aspects of Gothic architecture were accepted, the proportions were fashioned in another spirit. A new equilibrium was established between vertical ascension and spreading horizontal lines, and was emphasized by the bareness of the walls and the restrained decoration. This spatial expansion was even more evident at S. Croce in Florence (1294), a work that tradition has long attributed to Arnolfo di Cambio. In this structure, the Gothic vault, the major element of the style, was abandoned in preference to a ceiling with an open timber roof.

The solutions to architectural problems were no less original in secular building. In the second half of the century Emperor Frederick II of Hohenstaufen, king of Naples and Sicily, was responsible for the Castello Maniace at Syracuse (*c.* 1240), and especially for the Castel del Monte (1240–46) in Apulia. The second half of the century witnessed the erection of an impressive series of public buildings and princely residences throughout the country. In 1225 construction was begun in Florence on the Palazzo del Podestà (or Palazzo del Bargello), and in 1298 on the Palazzo della Signoria (probably under the direction of Arnolfo di Cambio). The Palazzo Pubblico in Siena was erected between 1289 and 1309. Perugia, Viterbo, Piacenza (Palazzo Comunale begun in 1281), and Orvieto—the latter with its superb Palazzo del Popolo—vied with each other in their bold inventiveness.

The development of sculpture during the Duecento was even more momentous for the future. From the beginning of the century the transition could be observed from the sturdy Romanesque forms and the style of Benedetto

Antelami to the quivering precision of the Gothic in the series of the Months in Ferrara Cathedral. Out of these complex and contradictory currents grew the art of Nicola Pisano (*q.v.*), whose powerful personality encouraged the transition toward fresh forms. Nicola's workshop was the training ground of the two great masters who dominated the century, his son Giovanni Pisano and Arnolfo di Cambio, both already mentioned as architects.

DUFRESNE, Charles (1876, Millemont, Seine-et-Oise—1938, La Seyne, Var), French painter. He exhibited at the Société Nationale des Artistes Français and at the Salon des Indépendants from 1905; his first important works, dating from 1908, followed an extended visit to Italy. In the course of two years spent in Algiers (1910–12), Dufresne found purity of form and violence of color in the Mediterranean light. Later, in a studio filled with strange objects brought back from his travels, he reconstructed a fabulous world, exotic and intensely alive. He also painted religious scenes that earned him the admiration of younger painters such as Francis Gruber. In addition, he executed theatrical designs (settings for *Antar*, a ballet with music by Rimsky-Korsakoff, at the Paris Opéra, 1921); designs for tapestries; and mural decorations (*Le Théâtre de Molière* for the Palais de Chaillot, Paris, 1937).

DUFY, Raoul (1877, Le Havre—1953, Forcalquier, Basses-Alpes), French painter. In 1900, when he had completed his military service, a municipal scholarship enabled him to go to Paris. He entered Léon Bonnat's studio at the École des Beaux-Arts, and found the stimulation he needed in galleries, viewing Cézanne at Ambroise Vollard's, and Monet and Pissarro at Durand-Ruel's. Although Dufy's first paintings were frankly inspired by the Impressionists, he quickly became attracted to the works of Matisse. Without the least transition, he then adopted the Fauvist style, and—together with Albert Marquet and Friesz—began painting a brilliant series of Normandy ports and flag-decked streets (*Beach at Ste-Adresse*, 1906, Paris, Coll. Fize; *Old Houses at Honfleur*, 1906, Paris, Coll. Roudinesco). He was next attracted to Cubism, under the combined influence of Cézanne and Braque, whom he followed to L'Estaque. Forsaken by the collectors who had taken an early interest in him, the young artist began making woodcuts, and in 1911 illustrated the first edition of Guillaume Apollinaire's *Bestiary*. This edition has become one of the most sought-after of rare books. Paul Poiret, the famous dress designer, admired Dufy's woodcuts so much that he offered him a credit of 2,500 francs a month to enable the artist to set up a textile design studio on Avenue de Clichy, Paris. Dufy also designed textiles for the Lyons silk firm of Bianchini-Férier.

After World War I, he courageously took up painting again, having, however, already abandoned the Cubist style, which was so unsuited to his impulsive character. His experience in designing textiles, and later ceramics and tapestries, helped him to find a personal mode of expression between 1922 and 1925. This consisted of a quick, airy, and allusive draftsmanship, composed of nothing but commas, curlicues, zigzags, and other little strokes; light, clear, and sparkling colors; and a pert and free composition.

Though Dufy may have made an occasional concession to the superficial and facile side of his extraordinary talents and to the taste of his patrons, he redeemed himself immediately with a number of highly accomplished works: the *Nice Casino* (1927; Geneva, Coll. Georges Moos); the *Bay of Angels at Nice* (1927; Brussels, Coll. Dotremont); *Deauville Harbor* (1935; Geneva, Priv. Coll.); *Atelier with Grapes* (1942; Paris, Priv. Coll.); *Glorious Sunday* (1943; Paris, Louis Carré Gallery); the *Yellow Console* (1947; Paris, Louis Carré Gallery); and the *Black Freighter* (1952; Paris, Priv. Coll.) are all paintings with admirable formal qualities and great brio. Dufy seemed to have set himself the most difficult problems merely for the sake of solving them and communicating to others the pleasures he derived from this game. Witness the swarming composition of the *Cowes Regatta* (1934; Paris Louis Carré Gallery) or the *Races* (1935; Coll. Prince Aly Khan).

Dufy's production also included watercolors; book illustrations (Mallarmé's *Madrigals*, 1920; Apollinaire's *Assassinated Poet*, 1926; Montfort's *Beautiful Child*, 1930); and stage sets for plays (Salacrou's *Fiancés of Le Havre*, 1944) and ballets (De Beaumont's *Palm Beach*, 1933). In 1929 he was commissioned by the Beauvais tapestry mills to design coverings for a set of drawing-room furniture. He also painted one of the largest murals ever executed (nearly 6,400 square ft.), an object of astonishment for visitors to the Palace of Electricity at the 1937 International Exposition in Paris.

Raoul Dufy. *Artist and His Model in the Studio at Le Havre.* 1929. Dauberville-Bernheim Jeune Coll., Paris. *Photo Giraudon, Paris.*

DUNOYER DE SEGONZAC, André (1884, Boussy-St-Antoine, Seine-et-Oise—1974, Paris), French painter, engraver, and illustrator. In 1908 he first exhibited at the Salon d'Automne, where two years later he attracted great notice with his painting of the *Drinkers* (formerly Paris, Coll. Paul Poiret). He exhibited at the Salon des Indépendants for the first time in 1909. In 1933 he was awarded the Carnegie Prize; the following year, the Grand Prize of the Venice Biennale.

Although a friend of Apollinaire, Max Jacob, Signac, Dufy, and Vlaminck, Dunoyer de Segonzac never joined any of the great aesthetic movements of the early 20th century. He was sufficiently sure of himself and of the direction he had taken to remain faithful to realism, although he was never enslaved by it. He used a limited range of earthy colors and showed a marked preference for massive forms and thick, compact paint (*Landscape at St-Tropez*, 1927; *Still Life with Bread and Wine*, c. 1936; both Paris, Musée National d'Art Moderne). His excellence as a draftsman is particularly apparent in his pen drawings, engravings, and watercolors, which are sharper, more graceful, and more vital than his paintings of still lifes, nudes, and landscapes, in which he succeeded neither in discarding tradition nor in discovering its secrets. A catalogue of his prints would comprise some 2,000 items, including such series as *Paysages du Morin* (1923), *Plages* (1935), and *De Joinville à Bougival* (1936). His work as an illustrator includes some of the finest books of modern bibliophilism: *Les Croix de bois* (1921) by Roland Dorgelès, *Tableau de la Boxe* (1922) by Tristan Bernard, Virgil's *Georgics* (1947), and *Quelques Sonnets de Ronsard* (1956).

DUQUESNOY, Francesco *or* François, *called* Il Fiammingo (1594, Brussels—1643, Leghorn), Belgian-born Baroque sculptor, active in Italy, the son and pupil of Jérôme Duquesnoy (before 1570–1641). He lived in Rome from 1618 until just before his death, when he agreed to return to France to work for the crown; he died en route. In 1627–28 Duquesnoy worked for Bernini on the baldacchino in St. Peter's, where his much admired contributions led to the commission for the huge *St. Andrew* (1628–40) in one of the niches under the dome. In 1629 he began his masterpiece, the *St. Susanna* for the choir of S. Maria di Loreto in Rome, which occupied him until 1633. His tombs for Adrien Vryburch (1629) and Ferdinand van den Eynde (1633–40) in S. Maria dell'Anima are small-sized marbles, and contain his favorite and recurrent motif of the *putto*. With these figures of small children, derived at first from Titian and later strongly influenced by Rubens, Duquesnoy achieved great celebrity. Perhaps his most famous interpretation in this genre is the relief of music-making *putti* on an altar by Francesco Borromini in the Cappella Filomarina in SS. Apostoli, Naples (1642).

Francesco Duquesnoy. *St. Andrew.* 1628–40. St. Peter's, Rome. *Photo Anderson-Giraudon.*

Duquesnoy's style is characterized by an expression of sweet devotion and repose, of dignity and reticence, constituting the antithesis of Bernini's Baroque ecstasy and movement, jagged silhouettes, and intense chiaroscuro. Duquesnoy's work exhibits the powerful influence of the antique (the Classical *Urania* inspired his *St. Susanna*) and of the Bolognese Classicist Domenichino.

JÉRÔME (1602, Brussels—1654, Ghent), Francesco's brother, was trained, like him, in their father's studio. After a long stay in Spain in the service of Philip IV, he traveled to Florence in 1640 and a year later settled in Rome with his brother. On Francesco's death he returned to Brussels, where he carved several statues of the apostles for the cathedral of St-Michel, notably a *St Thomas*, and where he also executed a *St. Ursula* for the Église de la Chapelle. Among his best works are the group of *St. Anne with the Virgin,* and particularly the funerary monument of Bishop Triest (completed 1654) in the cathedral of St-Bavon, Ghent, a powerful and pensive conception.

DURAND, Asher Brown (1796, Jefferson Village, now Maplewood, New Jersey—1886, Jefferson Village), American painter. Having studied engraving for five years (1812–17), Durand pursued this career until 1835. Although he established a reputation as a master engraver, his interest in painting soon lured him away from his early profession. First he turned to portraiture, then to landscape painting, becoming a leading figure in the so-called Hudson River School. His landscapes may be divided into two general categories: intimately detailed, objective, and painterly studies of trees and rocks; and exhibition pieces, more tightly painted and elevated in sentiment and mood. One may sense near-mystical overtones in the glowing light (suggestive of Claude Lorrain) that emanates from the core of many of Durand's paintings (*Old Oak*, 1844; New York, Historical Society).

Albrecht Dürer. *Self-Portrait at the Age of Thirteen.* 1484. Albertina, Vienna.

DÜRER, Albrecht (1471, Nuremberg—1528, Nuremberg), German painter and engraver, generally recognized as the greatest German artist and an equal of the masters of the Italian Renaissance. His father was a Hungarian goldsmith who settled in Nuremberg. Dürer was apprenticed at the age of fifteen to Michael Wolgemut, the most highly respected painter-engraver in town. Having, like most of the artists of his time, a lively sense of his own importance, the young artist carefully preserved a silverpoint drawing of himself (1484; Vienna, Albertina) made two years before entering on his apprenticeship, which shows his extreme precocity as a draftsman. While still in his master's studio, in 1490, he painted a portrait of his father (Florence, Uffizi).

In 1490 Dürer set off to work his time as a journeyman. Not surprisingly, his steps turned in the direction of Colmar, the birthplace of Martin Schongauer, for whom he left on record his unwavering admiration, an admiration apparent in his own engravings. When he reached Colmar in 1491, Dürer found that Schongauer had just died, but three of his brothers were keeping the studio going. We find Dürer next at Basel, where a fourth brother of Schongauer lived, and with him Dürer appears to have collaborated on illustrations for certain of the city's book publishers. On his return to Nuremberg, Dürer married: the Louvre possesses a *Self-Portrait* painted in tempera on parchment at the time of his engagement in 1493. Immediately after his marriage, Dürer made the first of his journeys to Italy (1494–95), which is illustrated by several admirable landscapes in watercolor executed on the way.

After his return, his activity redoubled. The year 1498 saw the appearance of the *Apocalypse*, a collection of woodcuts, and of the first great copperplate engravings, in which the nudes are a credit to his technical ability, his knowledge of the female form, and his familiarity with Italian art. Also in 1498, he painted a *Self-Portrait* (Madrid, Prado), in which he is again dressed with the elegance of a dandy. Several supremely vigorous portraits followed, including that of *Oswolt Krel* (1499; Alte Pinakothek), and the *Young Man Wearing a Cap* (1500; Alte Pinakothek), who, according to tradition, was the painter's brother Hans. Meanwhile Dürer was also painting religious subjects. The Paumgärtner altarpiece (*c.* 1503; Alte Pinakothek) consists of a central panel containing a *Nativity*, and wings containing representations of *St. George* and *St. Eustace*, who are actually portrait figures of Lucas and Stephen Paumgärtner. Another distinguished religious painting is the pristine *Adoration of the Magi* (Uffizi), dated 1504. In these early years of the 16th century, Dürer already enjoyed a great reputation. The most popular, though not the best, of the self-portraits (Alte Pinakothek), in which Dürer appears to see himself as a Christ figure, bears the date 1500, but this is recognized to be false, and dates of 1504 and 1505 have been suggested.

In 1506 Dürer went again to Italy. In Venice he received a commission from the Fondaco dei Tedeschi to paint the *Feast of the Rose Garlands* (1506; Prague, National Gallery), now unfortunately in a very ruinous state. The first effect of this journey was a renewal of the Italian influence, which is evident in the two panels of *Adam* and *Eve*, painted in 1507 (Prado). In the *Adoration of the Holy Trinity* (1511; Vienna, Kunsthistorisches Museum), Dürer surpassed himself in brilliance and clarity, though at the cost of some harshness in the color harmony. After this there is an interlude in the succession of paintings, the years 1510 to 1516 being devoted almost entirely to engraving. In 1511 Dürer completed and published several series of wood engravings begun much earlier: the *Great Passion*, the *Little Passion*, and the *Life of the Virgin*; he also engraved the large copperplates, so famous as to have become almost legendary, of *St Jerome in His Study* (1514), *Knight, Death, and the Devil* (1513), and *Melancholia* (1514).

From 1515 to 1520 he was heavily engaged in the great undertakings of Emperor Maximilian, decorating several pages of his prayer book with spontaneous and entertaining drawings and providing designs for woodcuts for the *Triumphal Arch* and the *Triumphal Procession*. From 1519, however, comes a painting, now in the Metropolitan Museum, New York, the subject of which is familiar in German art: *the Virgin and Child with St. Anne*. The drawing is strong and the masses powerful, but the color lacks warmth.

In 1520–21 Dürer made a triumphal journey through the Low Countries: all the painters went to see him and pay homage to his genius. On the way, he produced a great many drawings and also kept a diary, a priceless record, which he illustrated in silverpoint. On his return he appears to have been largely preoccupied with religious speculation—like his friend Pirkheimer, he had become an ardent follower of the Protestant reformer Martin Luther—and with the writing of theoretical treatises (*On the Mensuration of Lines and of Whole Bodies*, 1525; *On the Fortification of Cities, Castles and Small Towns*, 1527; and *Four Books on the Proportions of the Human Body*, 1528). In 1526, however, a renewed activity resulted in the production of several of his best portraits, and above all of the solemn, monumental *Four Apostles* (Alte Pinakothek), which is a masterpiece in its handling of drapery, its profundity, and its simplicity combined with grandeur, and which may also stand as his testament of faith.

DUVENECK, Frank (1848, Covington, Kentucky—1919, Cincinnati, Ohio), American painter. His formal studies began in 1870 at the Munich Academy, under Wilhelm von Diez (1839–1907); there he met and befriended his American compatriot, William Merritt Chase. It was in Munich also that he painted his *Portrait of an Old Woman* (1871; New York, Metropolitan Museum). In 1873 Duveneck was forced to return to America due to a cholera plague, and two years later became an instant success when several of his canvases were shown at the Boston Art Club. Soon after he was back in Munich for several more years of study. Following a trip to Italy with Chase in 1878, he opened schools of his own in Munich and Venice, which were quite successful.

Albrecht Dürer. *St. Jerome in His Study.* 1514. Galleria Corsini, Rome. *Photo Anderson-Giraudon.*

In 1888 Duveneck returned to the United States, settling in Cincinnati, where he became an influential teacher at its art academy. Both as a teacher and as a painter he was an exponent of the loose painterly style of the Munich School, which stressed a dark palette and a brilliant and spontaneous display of brushstrokes. Duveneck was also drawn to the Spanish 17th-century painters, as may be seen in his *Turkish Page* (1876; Philadelphia, Pennsylvania Academy of the Fine Arts), which recalls the realistic images of low life by Jusepe de Ribera and Bartolomé Esteban Murillo.

DYCE, William (1806, Aberdeen, Scotland—1864, Streatham, Surrey), English religious and historical painter who anticipated the principles of the Pre-Raphaelites in many important ways. He visited Rome in 1825 and in 1827–29, studying fresco painting, which he later sought to revive in England. He also came into close contact with the German Nazarene painters Peter Cornelius and

Johann Overbeck and copied their style faithfully in works such as *Joaz Shooting the Arrow* (1844; Hamburg, Kunsthalle) and especially the Raphaelesque *Madonna and Child* of 1845 (England, Royal Coll.). Dyce must thus be considered a legitimate forerunner of Ford Madox Brown and William Holman Hunt. He received several government and church commissions, including the decoration of the House of Lords (*Baptism of King Ethelbert*, 1845–47) and the Queen's Robing Room (*Vision of Sir Galahad and His Company*, 1848), both in the Houses of Parliament, London.

Dyce's best work was done under the influence of the Pre-Raphaelites, and in this vein he produced some of the most charming pictures of the entire movement: the minutely detailed *Pegwell Bay* (1859–60; London, National Gallery) and the ravishing *Titian's First Essay in Color* (1860; Aberdeen, Art Gallery). He became head of the Government Schools of Design, and in 1844 Associate of the Royal Academy, then a full member in 1848. Resident in Edinburgh in the 1830s, Dyce became an Associate of the Royal Scottish Academy in 1835.

DYCK, Sir Anthony van (1599, Antwerp—1641, London), Flemish painter. No portrait tells more about this artist than *Van Dyck with a Sunflower* (London, Coll. Duke of Westminster), in which Van Dyck—with a finger twisted in his golden neckchain, and pointing to the large flower—turns his proud glance toward the spectator.

The son of a rich Antwerp merchant, he was apprenticed in 1609 to Hendrik van Balen the Elder (1575–1632), becoming a Master in 1618. As may be seen in the admirable *St. Martin* for the Saventhem Pfarrkjrche (*c.* 1621), he understood and profited by the lessons of Rubens, with whom he worked around 1619 and whose verve and capacity for the Grand Manner he assimilated. From this period date such mythological and Biblical pictures as the *Drunken Silenus* (Brussels, Musées Royaux des Beaux-Arts); and *Samson and Delilah* (Vienna, Kunsthistorisches Museum). Since 1955 several paintings formerly attributed to Rubens have been ascribed to him: art historians have seen Van Dyck's style in the double portrait of *Jean Charles de Cordes and His wife Jacqueline de Castres* (1617–19; Brussels, Musées Royaux des Beaux-Arts). At the age of twenty-one, he accepted the invitation of the Count of Arundel to work for the court of England. He arrived in London at the end of 1620, but left for Italy a few months later. There he was reunited with his patroness, the Countess of Arundel, with whom he visited Mantua, Turin, Milan, and Genoa in 1622–23. During his stay in Italy, which ended in 1627, he was successively the guest of Cardinal Bentivoglio in Rome and of the great Genoese families of Spinola, Brignole Sale, and Durazzo. The portraits of *Paolina Adorno*, the *Marchesa Brignole Sale with Her Son*, and the *Marchesa Elena Grimaldi Cattaneo* (all *c.* 1625; Washington, D.C., National Gallery) are monumental in composition and sober and delicate in color, with a faithful rendering of facial expressions. With Van Dyck's return to Antwerp, there began a period of intense activity (1627–32). Accepting numerous commissions for churches at Antwerp (*Ecstasy of St. Augustine*, 1628; Augustijnenkerk), Courtrai (*Raising of the Cross*, 1631; church of Notre-Dame), Ghent (*Crucifixion, c.* 1630; church of St. Michael), Mechlin, and Dendermonde, he emerged as a painter with a shimmering, gentle Baroque style. In the same period he adopted the Flemish formula of half-length portraits and painted spirited likenesses of *Count Hendrik van den Bergh* (*c.* 1630; Madrid, Prado), *Anna Wake* (1628; The Hague, Mauritshuis), and *Adriaen Stevens and His Wife* (1629; Leningrad, Hermitage).

Van Dyck settled in England in 1632 as chief painter to Charles I, who was extremely kind to him. During the next seven years, he painted all the members of the court, over whom the shadow of a tragic destiny already hovered. At the end of his stay, Van Dyck married (1639) Mary Ruthven and in 1640, immediately after the death of Rubens, returned to Antwerp, where on October 18 the guild of artists received him with ceremony. In January 1641 he was in Paris, where he hoped to receive a commission from the court. He became ill and quickly returned to England, where he witnessed the birth of a daughter on December 1; eight days later he died. Van Dyck's last period (after 1632) was of uneven quality. Nevertheless, he sometimes achieved incomparable feats of insight and distinction. His palette became lighter and more refined, his paint thinner, and his silver and golden lights emerged from warmer shadows. He was a virtuoso in the rendering of the white of a satin, the blue of a silk, or the crimson of a velvet. Impressive indeed are the portraits of *Charles I in Three Positions* (*c.* 1637; Windsor Castle, Royal Collection), *Philip, Lord Wharton* (1632; Washington, D.C., National Gallery), *Thomas Killigrew and Thomas Carew* (1638; Windsor Castle, Royal Collection), the *Three Sons of Charles II of England* (Galleria Sabauda), *Prince William II of Orange and His Young Wife, Princess Mary Stuart* (1641; Amsterdam, Rijksmuseum), and *James Stuart, Duke of Lennox and Richmond* (after 1632; London, Kenwood, Iveagh Bequest). His masterpiece is the portrait of *Charles I* (1635; Louvre), which emphasizes the proud and elegant grace of the extravagant king.

Sir Anthony van Dyck. *William II of Nassau and Orange. c.* 1640. Mellon Coll., National Gallery of Art, Washington, D.C.

Sir Anthony van Dyck. *Portrait of James Stuart, Duke of Lennox and Richmond.* After 1632. Iveagh Bequest, Kenwood, London.

EAKINS, Thomas (1844, Philadelphia—1916, Philadelphia), American painter. His art education reflected his strong scientific inclination: not only did he attend drawing classes at the Pennsylvania Academy of the Fine Arts (1861–66), but he concurrently pursued anatomical studies at a medical college. The results of these studies included a scientific paper on muscles and some of the finest figurative American paintings. His painting the *Gross Clinic* (1875; Philadelphia, Jefferson Medical College) combines a startling objective realism—in the detailed depiction of an operation in progress—with a psychologically penetrating realism—in the portrait of the surgeon. His interest in science extended beyond anatomy to the construction of space and volumes, and he often combined theoretical perspective with observations of both constructed models and real objects. A painting such as *Max Schmitt in a Single Scull* (1871; New York, Metropolitan Museum) is the result of a combination of such methods, with its sunlit landscape, studio-lit figure, and carefully constructed space. In his later portraits, however, Eakins' scientific interests were overshadowed by his penetrating psychological insights. Observations of light on textures and forms in space are gradually subordinated and finally disappear as the artist focuses on just a head and, by implication, a state of mind. These late portraits (*Mrs. Edith Mahon*, 1904; Northampton, Mass., Smith College Museum of Art) are Eakins' most intense and haunting images.

EARL, Ralph (1751, Worcester County, Massachusetts—1801, Bolton, Connecticut), American painter. A portraitist in New Haven, Earl's loyalist sympathies obliged him to flee to England (1778), where he probably studied with Benjamin West. Back in America in 1785, he continued to paint in his earlier, somewhat severe and archaic style, now only slightly softened and chromatically enlivened. Indeed, one of his most commanding portraits (*Roger Sherman, c.* 1775–77; New Haven, Yale University Art Gallery), predates his European experience. Earl was one of the first American artists to paint the scenery of his native land. In some of his portraits, such as *Mrs. William Mosely and Her Son Charles* (1791; Yale University Art Gallery), somewhat schematized but convincing sunlit views of the Connecticut countryside are almost more interesting than their reserved and stolid inhabitants.

EARLY CHRISTIAN ART. The term Early Christian does not refer to a style, but rather to the art produced by Christians during roughly the first five centuries A.D. In particular, this includes the clandestine 2nd- and 3rd-century A.D. catacomb art, and the art that developed openly after A.D. 313—when the Edict of Milan recognized Christianity—up to the Carolingian period in the West and to the reign of Justinian in the East (*see* BYZANTINE ART).

There are few extant remains of the Christian art of the first two centuries, at least few such traces as might differentiate it from contemporary pagan art. Certain catacomb frescoes and a large number of objects from Roman and Coptic Egypt are not definitively identifiable as Christian. Christian art of the East in the 3rd century is documented by a single site, the city of Dura-Europos on the Euphrates, which was destroyed by the Persians in A.D. 256. The buildings of the town included a house used for Christian worship, which was decorated with mural paintings depicting such scenes as Adam and Eve, the Good Shepherd, and the Women at the Sepulcher. In the West, apart from terra-cotta lamps, which are especially frequent in Roman Africa, and liturgical accessories in bronze, numerous underground remains have been found in Rome of houses in which the Eucharist was celebrated. However, the most important documents of Early Christian art are Italian and Provençal sarcophagi, and paintings in catacombs.

These suburban underground cemeteries are important for the themes used in their decoration—symbolical themes designed to convey indirectly the mysteries of the new faith: the anchor with a dolphin entwined stands for the cross, the fish for Christ, the dove for the soul, and the peacock for the immortality of the soul; loaves of bread, vine twigs, and flasks of wine allude to the Eucharist, which is also signified by banquet scenes (catacomb of Priscilla, Rome).

At roughly the same time typological scenes appear, primarily based on the parallelisms between the Old Testament and the New. Except for some of the miracles, scenes from the life of Christ are less frequent and occur later: the Passion is avoided, particularly the Crucifixion itself, which was still a common form of execution for slaves.

The catacombs were used as cemeteries after the Edict of Milan established toleration of Christianity throughout the empire. Their decoration became richer and more independent of Greco-Roman art.

Sculpture was confined to sarcophagi, of which the earliest, found in Provence, seems to date from the end of the 2nd century A.D. The main sculpture workshops in the 4th and 5th centuries A.D. were in Rome, Arles, and along the coast of Catalonia (Tarragona, Tarrasa, Barcelona) in Spain. In the sarcophagi reliefs Christian elements mingle with pagan, and figure decoration is seen side by side with arabesques (Good Shepherd sarcophagus, 2nd half of the 4th century A.D.; Vatican, Museum). Greek influence is evident in the frequent scenes from nature. In the representation of Christ, both in sculpture and in painting, the young beardless type is based on Greek models. A bearded Christ, of Syrian derivation, appears on a sarcophagus from Arles. For some time the two representations of Christ continued side by side—they both appear in the brilliant mosaics in S. Vitale, Ravenna (A.D. 526–47)—until finally the second became dominant and established a tradition.

Christian architecture did not come into its own until after the Edict of Galerius (A.D. 311). It flourished under Constantine: the secular basilica (a rectangular hall often divided into three or five aisles by rows of columns) became

Early Christian Art. *The Good Shepherd.* 3rd century. Catacomb of the Giordani, Rome. *Photo Leonard von Matt, Buochs.*

the model for the great edifices raised by the emperor, his mother, and other members of the imperial family. Churches sprang up all over the empire: in Italy, at Ostia, Capua, and Naples; in the East, at Tyre, Antioch, Bethlehem, Jerusalem, and Constantinople. A basilica was raised on the Vatican hill, on the site of St. Peter's tomb (A.D. 324–344; destroyed 15th century) and another on the site of St. Paul's tomb, in Via Ostiense (S. Paolo fuori le Mura, rebuilt at the end of the 4th century A.D.); the Lateran Basilica, dedicated originally to the Savior and, after the 10th century restoration, to St. John, was radically altered by Francesco Borromini (1646–49). S. Maria Maggiore, built after Constantine's death, and S. Sabina, both in Rome, have survived as the best examples of basilical architecture, the beauty of which resides in the harmonious proportions. They still retain mosaics on the walls, especially the apsidal walls, where they offer visions of Paradise.

The basilical plan was not the only pagan structural form taken up by Christian architects in the 4th century A.D. There was also the centralized plan, which derived from both the circular *martyrium* and the Roman mausoleum. The most interesting examples—all of which are in Rome—are the mausoleum of S. Helena, and that of Constantina (today called S. Costanza), decorated with mosaics of Hellenistic inspiration; also the baptistery at S. Giovanni in Laterano (4th and 5th centuries A.D.), and S. Stefano Rotondo (5th century A.D.). S. Lorenzo in Milan (4th century A.D.) has a circular plan organized around a central square.

Early Christian Art. *Christ as Teacher*. A.D. 350–60. Museo Nazionale Romano, Rome. *Photo Leonard von Matt, Buochs.*

EECKHOUT, Gerbrandt van den (1621, Amsterdam—1674, Amsterdam), Dutch painter, draftsman, and engraver. His father, a goldsmith, was rich enough to pay the very high fees necessary for him to study (1635–40) under Rembrandt, in whose circle he remained until the master's death in 1669. Eeckhout's early works, primarily Biblical scenes and portraits, reveal the profound influence of his famous teacher, particularly the *Woman Taken in Adultery* (Amsterdam, Rijksmuseum), the *Expulsion of Hagar* (1666; Raleigh, North Carolina Museum of Art), and *Isaac Blessing Jacob* (1642; New York, Metropolitan Museum). Indeed, many of his pictures were for a long time attributed to Rembrandt: one of these was the *Raising of the Daughter of Jairus* (Berlin). Eeckhout's range of subjects was wide, and his work shows the influence of such artists as Pieter de Hooch and Gerard Terborch, in addition to that of Rembrandt. There are also some remarkable pieces of goldsmith's work signed with his name (in its French form: G. du Chesne).

EGG, Augustus Leopold (1816, London—1863, Algiers), English painter of genre and history subjects. After studying at Sass's Art School (1834), Egg entered the Royal Academy Schools, and made his official exhibition debut at the Academy in 1838. In the previous year he had joined the "Clique," a group of painters united in their hostility toward the Royal Academy's organization and artistic policy; though it was an important prototype for the Pre-Raphaelite Brotherhood, the group came to nothing, its members being far too independent in their purely aesthetic aims. Egg's early works were, for the most part, illustrations of popular poets (*Launce's Substitute for Proteus's Dog*, inspired by Shakespeare, and shown at the Royal Academy in 1849; now Leicester Art Gallery) and novelists such as Sir Walter Scott. But after the pre-Raphaelites had become established, Egg adopted their interest in realistic subjects, and also began to produce scenes from modern life. The most famous of these is *Past and Present* (shown at the Royal Academy in 1858; now London, Tate Gallery), which is actually a trio of paintings in serial form, showing the decline and fall of a faithless wife.

EGYPTIAN ART. Dynastic Egypt—beginning with the 1st Dynasty around 3000 B.C. and ending with the 30th in 330 B.C.—was an immensely prolific workshop in which all, or nearly all, of the objects produced bore a distinctive hallmark. Before about the year 3000 B.C., art in the prehistoric Nile Valley could only be described as a variant of the type of work common in primitive societies. After the 5th century A.D. a complete break with idolatrous traditions appears in the arts wherever Nilotic Christianity expresses itself in a wholly Egyptian idiom. The Pharaonic style was a reflection of a corporate body in which the king was the supreme mouthpiece and the scribes were the backbone. It originated at the same time as hieroglyphic script, that is, toward the period when the legendary Menes is thought to have founded the 1st Dynasty, and it reached its first peak in the Pyramid Age (the period of the 4th Dynasty), when the bureaucratic patterns of the state were definitively established. The style became moribund when Hellenic influences began to permeate the Egyptian upper classes during the Ptolemaic Period, and the triumph of Christianity was its deathblow.

There can be no argument that in dynastic Egypt, more than at any other period or in any other country, the fine arts (architecture, sculpture, painting) and the applied arts (from goldsmiths' work to weaving) form an integrated whole, finding their fullest expression in the temples and tombs. But in this context Egyptian art is functional, concrete, concerned with everyday matters, materialistic—in other words, human and earthbound. The art of the Pharaohs is intuitive rather than intellectual: it "identifies itself with the cosmos," but only in accordance with beliefs that the Egyptians held about the world in which they had to live. They felt

Egyptian Art. Façade of the small temple at Abu Simbel. 19th Dynasty. *Photo UNESCO-Laurenza.*

that the building of temples would lend substance to the insubstantial universe around them. Architecture would reproduce in simplified form the structure of the universe, from the lowest level of the foundations (which, according to Egyptian myths of the creation, represented the primordial ocean) to the starry ceilings supported by columns in the shape of plants. Scenes of the eternal rites protected, sustained, and extolled in artistic terms the gods on whom everything depended. Portraits of the Pharaoh were repeated there with monotonous regularity, in the same way that his statues were copied again and again on façades and in courtyards: thus art was able to assure the gods of the Pharaoh's constant attendance upon them. No one could fill the Pharaoh's place as a sorcerer, for he was held to be the equal of the gods and, as such, was depicted on the same scale. Likenesses of private persons were also made for the temples: statues were carved showing the subject at prayer, so that the devout might "dwell in the house of God for ever." The same applied to the tombs. Statues of the deceased were placed in the chapel to receive offerings, while those in the burial vault preserved the youth, beauty, and incorruptibility of his body. Colored reliefs or mural paintings describing the labors of field and workshop, with the owner's servants on parade and his family gathered around him, would carry the cheerful atmosphere of a manorial estate into the deceased's mortuary chapel; in the burial chamber itself, impressive pictures and inscriptions would raise him to the rank of a blessed spirit endowed with supernatural powers.

A visitor with little time to spare often brings away from some great museum an impression that Egyptian art marked time, as it were, for more than 3,000 years—that is to say, for a period at least as long as that which elapsed between the Geometric style of post-Mycenaean Greece and the abstract art of our own day. The most convincing appreciation of Egyptian art can hardly be based upon praise for its variety, for in the fashion of most Oriental and primitive communities, Egypt cared little for abrupt changes, in her visual arts as well as in many other aspects of life. Her great artists, far from asserting themselves blatantly, preferred to express their imagination, creative instincts, and personal talent by more subtle means. Character and gesture, people and objects, animals and plants could be captured in form and color, in an effort to perpetuate life. With this end in view, artistic effort proceeded on lines that, by general consent, had been proven by experience. The Egyptians were satisfied with their rules in the same way that they were content to fashion their statues of stone in a cubic and monolithic form, and in the same way that they believed their gods to be immortal and monarchy to be part of the natural law.

A passive allegiance to certain hallowed principles ought not, on the other hand, to be held directly responsible for the traditionally hieratic quality of Egyptian art. The Pharaonic liking for order expressed itself theoretically through the ideal of calm repose, and in practice by a contempt for uncontrolled movement. The identification of sacred order with serenity and of infernal disorder with unrest goes far to explain why Egyptian hunters, oarsmen, and warriors, painted in all the heat of their exertions, suggest energy but not motion. Symbols of order are given prominence by being arranged in a geometric setting of frames and friezes, and of lines or columns of hieroglyphs that serve as captions for the scenes. On the other hand, symbols of disorder are frequently sprawled in a riotous tangle across vast confused spaces: battlefields covered with contorted bodies, green thickets where waterfowl exchange shrill cries, hilly hunting grounds where hound and quarry are at each other's throats. A paradox in the art of ancient Egypt is, if one may so express it, that the dead are dynamic while the living remain static. In stone, wood, gold, or bronze, the sculptor rigidly invested his gods, kings, and nobles with the calm courtesy that was his guiding principle. The character of the person commemorated in the statue was certainly made known—inscriptions were in fact carved to perpetuate it—but it might be eclipsed by the personality of the king (whom his subjects resembled) or by the attributes inherent in the sitter's function. From the Old Kingdom onward, it was customary to be represented with "fair round belly"—a sign of affluence; and from the time of the Middle Kingdom with the severe lined features of an old man—the sign of experience. A high proportion of the portraits that have come down to us are thus not truly

Egyptian Art. Ushabti of Tut-ankh-amon found in his tomb in the Valley of the Kings. Egyptian Museum, Cairo. *Photo Hassia, Paris.*

realistic, but the products of a convention. The sculptor remains aloof, accepting the national conformity, but one feels in an indefinable way that he has disclosed some revealing feature of his model in the carved face, perhaps a sulky mouth or an expression in the eyes.

The serene consistency of the Pharaonic mood embraces a chronological sequence of styles. It is not simply a matter of the orders of sacred architecture, the repertoire of subjects treated, or such details as fashions in clothing, but also of the changes in taste that are revealed with the passing of time. Let us consider, for example, the case of the funerary statuettes called ushabtiu, or "answers." These little figures in the form of mummies clutching agricultural implements to their bodies used to be placed in burial chambers. Originally the magic text that one often sees inscribed on the figurines was supposed to be "recited before an effigy made from wood of the tamarind or jujube tree in the likeness of the owner as he was on earth." Sheer instruments of magic, hidden away in the vaults, they were certainly not showpieces. Nevertheless, no material, no workmanship, no ornament was too elegant for those ushabtiu commissioned by persons of high rank: hard dark stone in the Middle Kingdom; polished wood in the Tuthmoside period; bright blue or delicate violet-patterned beige glazed porcelain under the Ramessides; stiff bronzes from the Tanite tombs; the renowned faïences from Deir el Bahari; serpentine in the time of the Ethiopian kings; or the variegated greens of innumerable faïences of the Late Period. Yet in hard times men of substance (and the poorer classes in periods of prosperity) contented themselves with having for "answerers" rudely carved stumps or ill-defined shapes modeled in clay. The power of the word alone was thus sufficient to carry out, in place of the deceased, the forced labors that the kingdom of the dead prescribed for its subjects.

Pharaonic art was almost a nationalized industry in the service of an idealized monarchy credited with divine powers, and as such its fortunes fluctuated with those of the state. Thus the history of Egyptian art unfolded according to the same chronology as the economic, social, and political history of the country. After the Prehistoric Period, when it was still unformed, and the Thinite period, when it began to take permanent shape, it was to achieve great heights under the three kingdoms, while faltering during the three Intermediate Periods. There ensued a final renaissance, ending ultimately in an enfeebled version of the national style that managed to survive under the colonial regime of Greco-Roman times. Within each golden age a considerable number of well-defined styles evolved that were attributable to such influences as the ruling Pharaoh's personality, prevailing religious beliefs and practices, fashions in dress, and the current climate of public feeling.

PREHISTORIC PERIOD (before 4000 B.C.)

As already noted, this era yields only primitive works, but it enables us to witness the origins of many technical processes destined to be used with undiminished success in the time of the Pharaohs. From the 4th millennium and throughout the Tasian (still Neolithic), Badarian, and Nagadian (Copper Age) periods, the population of Upper Egypt increased its output and improved its skill in all the arts. Huts of wood, reed, and mud were erected for divinities. Flint tools were used to fashion bone, ivory, and horn into combs, pins, statuettes, and amulets decorated with outlines of animals or human figures reduced to their barest essentials. Glazed soapstone beads from this prehistoric period give a hint of the future achievements of Egyptian faïence-makers. The craft of the coppersmith, imported from Asia, made it possible to manufacture delicate ornaments and fine utensils. The modeling and firing of clay had long been making good progress: innumerable vases of various shapes are found in the oval pits where the dead were laid, and along with them mysterious female figures with arms uplifted in a motionless dance, casting a spell to ensure success for hunters and prosperity for husbandmen. Among the more luxurious vessels is the polished red earthenware with whitish patterns that is typical of the Amratian subdivision of the Nagadian period; the later Gerzean culture is characterized by purplish decorations on mushroom-colored pottery. These surfaces

Egyptian Art. Stele of the Serpent King. Abydos, 1st Dynasty. Louvre, Paris.

present a miniature painted world, sometimes abstract in design (spirals and waves) and sometimes figurative (boats, dancers of both sexes, and birds). There are even complete scenes, such as a hunting party setting out (shown on the bottom of a bowl), a hippopotamus hunt, a sailing event, and a troupe of dancers. The latter scene, painted on a linen shroud, is the oldest "canvas" in the history of the world.

It is not in the field of ceramics but in the making of beads, carving of palettes, and especially in the shaping of vases that one sees a promise of the Egyptian sculptors' future mastery over the hardest rocks. The time had almost come when the Predynastic Age would produce craftsmen who were to hammer out of marble, diorite, and breccia a plentiful supply of thin-walled, capacious vessels of simple and dignified form. These were polished with abrasives and their interiors hollowed out by a drill.

Shortly before the beginning of the 3rd millennium B.C., the Age of Copper suddenly became the Predynastic Period (*c.* 4000–*c.* 3000 B.C.). Burial pits were lined with

Egyptian Art. Votive palette of King Narmer, sovereign of Upper Egypt. 1st Dynasty. Egyptian Museum, Cairo. *Hirmer Fotoarchiv, Munich.*

bricks, and then paved and covered with planks of wood. Fortresses and palaces were surrounded by high ramparts with redans. Ivories were decorated with grand processions of animals or other lively subjects. Large palettes of schist were covered with delicate and skillfully composed reliefs, sometimes accompanied by a commentary in hieroglyphs. On monuments of the Scorpion King (one of the last predynastic rulers) and Narmer (the first king of the 1st Dynasty) the true characteristics of the Pharaonic style can be detected under appearances that are still somewhat crude. Unfortunately, it is impossible to be explicit about the conditions that prompted this almost miraculous step forward. Contributory factors no doubt included the arrival of artistic prototypes and craftsmen from Mesopotamia, a combination of circumstances favoring civilized pursuits, and the sudden awakening of a national consciousness in the Egyptians.

THINITE PERIOD
(1st and 2nd Dynasties,
*c.*3000–2800 B.C.)

The term for this era originates from the unidentified town of Thinis, near Abydos. The funerary monuments of Abydos, the splendid tombs of Saqqara, and the more modest graves of Helwan allow us to follow the various developments of Thinite architecture. Bricks were used more extensively and with improved effect in the building of the large oblong superstructures called mastabas, which covered the graves of the more privileged classes. The fittings became increasingly elaborate, and included stairways and vaulted ceilings. The shafts for the actual graves were sunk progressively deeper, and from the original vast vault there was a growing trend toward the endless subterranean galleries of the 2nd Dynasty. Blocks and slabs of stone acted as facings for certain walls and floors.

In sculpture, statues of King Khasekhem provide evidence of the progress made in the best workshops during the first two dynasties. The effigy of the carpenter Bezmes (London, British Museum), on the other hand, indicates that workshops patronized by private citizens were still in the apprenticeship stage. But in both cases one can see the traditional iconography taking shape. Similar inconsistencies are met with in the art of relief: beautiful royal stelae such as that of the Serpent King, mediocre ones of eminent citizens at Saqqara and Helwan, and deplorable ones of servants at Abydos, all testify in their own way to the emergence of attitudes, customs, and graphic conventions.

To compensate for a decline in the art of pottery, the manufacturers of hard-stone vases carried their art to its highest peak by their manual dexterity, the impressive abundance of their output, and a taste that verges on virtuosity and tends, in fact, to be overrefined. Actually it is the applied arts—ornaments of gold or faïence, caskets, spoons, chess pieces, bed legs, and other objects of ivory—that best recall the discreet luxury and elegance of the Thinites and that compensate for the scarcity of treasures in the fine arts. This period represents the vigorous adolescence of Egypt, during which national prototypes were being invented, improved, disciplined, and permanently established. While this vigorous style was pursuing its leisurely course toward perfection, the invention of an architecture built entirely of stone inaugurated a new era.

OLD KINGDOM
(3rd–6th Dynasties,
c. 2800–2300 B.C.)

In a sense, the period of King Zoser, which witnessed the magnificent climax of Thinite development, possesses a style of its own, although simultaneously representing the beginning of Memphite supremacy. In piling several mastabas on top of each other for the royal tomb, Imhotep—high priest of Heliopolis and perhaps "carpenter, sculptor, maker of stone vases"—erected the oldest of the pyramids at Saqqara. He used small stones that could be handled like bricks to build this so-called step pyramid, as well as the vast bastioned wall that surrounded it and the complex of temples grouped inside this enclosure. Imhotep's rivals were able to deduce the techniques of a sound and feasible architectural system from his pioneering efforts.

The typical art style and renewed vigor of the Memphite state becomes evident in the reign of Sneferu (4th Dynasty), under whose good-humored but powerful rule arts and crafts were given a new impetus. He is memorable for having launched expeditions to the turquoise mines and for opening up alabaster quarries at Hat-nub. His name seems to be attached to no less than three pyramids: the South or Bent Pyramid at Dahshur, a rhomboidal monument with its gradient at two different angles; the North Pyramid at Dahshur, which is the first true pyramid in the geometrical sense of the word; and the temple at Medum, a structure originally terraced but later cased in to give it the classic pyramidal form.

Almost nothing remains of the great city temples that must have been built in the same style during the Old Kingdom, but a spectacular display of all the arts of the period is preserved for us in the burial grounds of Medum, Dahshur, Saqqara, Giza, and Abu Roash. The Memphite plain is the heart of Egypt, and it was in these so-called pyramid towns dotted along its whole length that the style we call Memphite originated. The most skilled masons and artisans created the Memphite style for the kings and courtiers of three dynasties. The rise to paramount importance of the Sun God and the growing popularity of the Osiris cult played their part in the modification of ritual concepts and practices, which in turn influenced artistic inspiration and conditions of patronage.

Even when the resources of the monarchy diminished, even when an element of whimsy began to prettify the reliefs of everyday life,

Egyptian Art. *Hippopotamus.* Thinite period. Ny Carlsberg Glyptotek, Copenhagen.

Egyptian Art. Step pyramid of King Zoser at Saqqara. 3rd Dynasty. *Photo Audrain-Samivel.*

Egyptian Art. *Birdcatcher.* Mastaba of Nefer-her-n-ptah, Saqqara. End of 5th–early 6th Dynasty. *Photo Hassia ("Chefs-d'oeuvre de la peinture égyptienne," Hachette).*

even when sculptors lowered their standards to suit middle-class tastes and purses, even in its early rough-hewn and provincial manifestations, the Memphite style established in its purest form the ideal vision of Egypt: a robust nobility that seems for a brief time under the rule of Cheops and Chephren to tend toward architectural megalomania; a calm assurance that is not without a certain good humor; a harmony of straight lines and broad symmetrical masses, which somehow does not conflict with a marked relish for bright colors and elegant decoration; and, underlying everything else, a desire that the earthly life be carried forward into eternity, happily preserved from change and decay—all these factors cause Memphite art to waver between geometry and naturalism.

The entire royal quarter in the Memphite necropolis sums up at a glance the structure of society and the history of architecture. The most advantageous site is occupied by the king's pyramid, colossal up to the time of Chephren, and noticeably smaller afterward. With its back against this mound is an upper temple faced with fine blocks of stone; a long causeway joins it to a lower temple that is level with the area outside the necropolis. A sober liturgy in stone, the pyramid contains little besides corridors and a vault. The royal temples, increasingly complex in plan, represent a more versatile form of art, especially during the 5th Dynasty, which was responsible for the most beautiful examples of columns, based on papyrus and palm motifs. The nobles are buried around the pyramid in mastabas above a vertical shaft leading to a vault. Occupying the core of the mastaba is a mortuary chapel that in the 5th and 6th Dynasties develops into an apartment containing several rooms. In the cliffs of Middle Egypt the most impressive hypogea were constructed. The hypogeum consisted of a corridor and a chapel from which a shaft led to a vault. By their dimensions and the magnificence of their decorations, those of the princes at Meir, Deir el Gebrawi, and Aswan (dating from the 6th Dynasty) illustrate the development of a major provincial school.

It seems that painting was relatively little practiced in its own right between the time of Sneferu (the *Geese of Medum* in the Egyptian Museum, Cairo is the classic example of painting in this period) and the end of the Old Kingdom, whereas the custom of employing painted relief in the royal tombs and more elaborate mastabas became quite widespread. From the time of Zoser until the beginning of the 6th Dynasty, the wealth and variety of illustrations increase in proportion with the verbosity of decorative inscriptions, ritual texts, and hieroglyphic captions. Solemn encounters between king and gods, ritual offerings, stereotyped evocations of triumphs over the barbarians—all these themes provide scope for grandiose treatment. While such subjects belong almost exclusively to the domain of temple art, picturesque representations of an eternal life similar to life on earth are the usual themes in Memphite mastabas and provincial hypogea as well as in the royal temples. The subject matter is extended in the 5th Dynasty to include a brilliant assemblage of people, domestic and wild animals, furniture, tools, and other objects such as are found in the so-called Chamber of the Seasons in the Sun Temple of King Ne-user-ra at Abu Gurob, and in the tombs of Ti, Ptah-hotep, Mera, Kagemni, Idut, and Mahu at Saqqara. Draftsmen sometimes introduced new themes or hitherto unrecorded historical incidents, which were then repeated from monument to monument.

Always in matters of style, and sometimes in the choice of themes, the royal monuments set the standard. The style of the best relief sculptors developed almost imperceptibly with each successive reign. Until the beginning of the 5th Dynasty some elements survived of those broadly treated and boldly projecting reliefs that were contemporary with the great pyramids, but the treatment of surface detail gradually became more refined in relief art from this time onward. For a fleeting period the art of relief culminated in a delicacy of handling, a subtle gradation in the levels of projection, and a high degree of finish. However, a tendency toward hasty workmanship becomes evident in backgrounds that are left uneven around the figures (which themselves have grown less smooth in texture) and in coarsened details.

As the Old Kingdom period advances, an evolution comparable with that of the reliefs can be

Egyptian Art. *King Chephren* (detail). Giza, 4th Dynasty. Egyptian Museum, Cairo. *Hirmer Fotoarchiv, Munich.*

Egyptian Art. Right and far right: *Nofret and her husband, General Rahotep.* From his mastaba at Medum. Early 4th Dynasty. Egyptian Museum, Cairo. *Photos Hassia, Paris.*

observed in sculpture, demonstrating a noble classicism that is succeeded later by a degree of vulgarization. The seated figures of the couple Rahotep and Nofret from the chapel at Medum (now Egyptian Museum, Cairo), the statue of Chephren with a falcon (Egyptian Museum), the busts of Prince Ankh-haf (Boston, Museum of Fine Arts) and the powerful vizier Hemiunu (Hildesheim, Pelizaeus Museum), the so-called reserve heads (which probably were placed in the burial chamber as a more permanent substitute for the head of the mummy should it suffer damage), and the statues of Mycerinus flanked by two goddesses attest to the glory of the 4th Dynasty, which represents Egyptian sculpture at its zenith. The diversity of style exhibited by its portraiture in the round is remarkable, and its restraint, while ceasing to be archaic, has not yet become academic. A similar treatment, broad in handling, continues to be characteristic of all the colossal statuary of this period, which develops along lines parallel to that of architecture in the grand manner. The sphinx at Giza (built *c.* 2500 B.C. and said to represent Chephren) is an early masterpiece of this type. It does not suffer in the least by comparison with the colossus of Userkaf and Sphinx A 23 in the Louvre, which must surely be ascribed to the Old Kingdom, and which have a massiveness that is architectural rather than sculptural.

By the time of the 6th Dynasty, sculpture was no longer what it had been. Here and there in the tombs, smaller painted limestone statues are not lacking in craftsmanship. Taken separately, these scribes clad in their brief loincloths, these citizens in their clinging robes, these appealing little groups provide a fairly accurate impression of what the average Egyptian was like. Wood sculpture of this period is less rigid and more sensitive.

During the Pyramid Age the applied arts followed Thinite precedents in matters of decoration; by this time techniques had been almost perfected. In the furnishings belonging to Queen Hetep-heres, mother of Cheops, the skilled joinery of the chairs, the exquisite delicacy of the canopy, the precision of the inlaid hieroglyphs and encrusted emblems are quite unlike the powerful stone structures with their unbending severity. Even so, the essential characteristics of the Memphite style—stark integrity, austerity in ornament—are still present in the hard-stone vases and in several sturdy alabasters. However, the art of carving stone vases declined and finally lost its greatness with the end of the Old Kingdom.

FIRST INTERMEDIATE PERIOD
(7th–early 11th Dynasties,
c. 2300–2050 B.C.)

By observing the breakdown of old customs and practices and the emergence of new ones, the historian can follow the progressive weakening of the Memphite regime and the rise of the feudal system. In reliefs of the time of Pepy II, one detects beneath the careful academic finish a certain decadence of style and regrets the way in which sculpture pandered to middle-class demands. Yet good traditions and a high degree of competence still survived in the capital and managed to flourish in the provinces. It is possible that the kings of the 9th and 10th Dynasties preserved some elements of Memphite classicism in their capital of Heracleopolis—the small private stelae of their officials at Saqqara do in fact prolong the forms and types of the 6th Dynasty—but the rising provincial schools in Upper and Middle Egypt did little to keep the old traditions alive.

As far as we know, there was no further construction of royal architecture on the grand scale; instead the period is represented by the comparatively simple hypogea of Assiut, the barbaric hypostyle hall at Mialla (near Luxor), and later the tiny chapels, crowned with miniature pyramids, of the first Theban rulers. The harshly colored, crudely modeled reliefs on the stelae at Naga ed Der or at Gebelein, striking though they sometimes are, represent only a feeble attempt to repeat the style of earlier periods.

There was no more great sculpture, unless one counts some of the wooden effigies of nobles from Middle Egypt, such as that of Nakht in the Louvre. However, the first stages in the development of a pleasant minor genre did arise: it consisted of small models made from neatly fitted miniature planks and scraps of wood, all carved with a light touch and painted in lively colors to represent a funerary boat, the occupant's household retinue, the work of the farm, various trades, and forms of entertainment. The warriors from the tomb of Mesehty and, dating from the end of the period, the collection of models from the tomb of the chancellor Meketra, ought to figure at the head of any anthology that might be compiled of the history of dolls' houses and wooden soldiers.

MIDDLE KINGDOM
(11th–13th Dynasties,
c. 2050–1780 B.C.)

Due to his military strength, the Theban ruler Mentuhotep I assured the triumph of the Theban 11th Dynasty over the Heracleopolitan 10th Dynasty, thus extending his authority as far as the Libyan and Arabian extremities of the delta. In art as well as in all other aspects of life, the Middle Kingdom inaugurated by Mentuhotep reached its apogee under the Amenemhats and the Sesostris of the 12th Dynasty, then declined in the course of the 13th Dynasty. As soon as the unity of the kingdom was restored, a rapid and intentional return to the noble examples of the Old Kingdom ensued, and techniques were perfected anew. A relative uniformity of style was set by the best workshops attached to the court, but this did not prevent the occurrence of a duality in the art of the two capitals (with a school of Lisht in the north and a school of Thebes in the south) or the exercise of a certain independence by artists in the provinces. The precedents for several iconographic themes and for various types of objects characteristic of this era can be found in the First Intermediate Period. On the other hand, the upward mobility of the lower strata of officials, employees, and tenants must have been attributable to some factor connected with the collapse of the Old Kingdom; in all the provinces this upgrading of the

Egyptian Art. *The beer brewer.* End of 4th Dynasty. Egyptian Museum, Cairo. *Photo André Vigneau-Éditions Tel, Paris.*

Egyptian Art. *Head of Sesostris III in his old age.* 12th Dynasty. Egyptian Museum, Cairo. *Photo André Vigneau-Éditions Tel, Paris.*

ordinary citizen was maintained in varying degrees, reaching its climax toward the end of the 12th Dynasty and during the 13th Dynasty. This popularization of the arts is at the same time closely associated with a new spirit in the liturgy of the dead. The popular acclaim of Osiris, patron of the mummified and reanimated dead, and of his sacred city of Abydos, together with the adoption of a new eschatology (based on an afterlife in the underworld instead of in the sky), had consecrated or initiated new traditions in ritual art during the First Intermediate Period. These included the custom of placing statuettes of the dead in the actual vault (not only, as hitherto, in the chapel), and the use of anthropoid coffins in which the properties of statue and mummy were combined, and the employment of ushabtiu.

Because it is the sum of several heritages, the style peculiar to the Middle Kingdom is among the most difficult to define. It displays heterogeneous tendencies in degrees varying with the different artistic disciplines: the naturalism of the tomb paintings may be contrasted with the formalism of votive statuary; the forceful muscularity of royal colossi with the broad masses of Osiride images; and the formalized and abstract modeling of attenuated bronzes with the lifelike immediacy of animal statuettes made by artists specializing in this genre. Similarly although Sesostris III is portrayed with inhuman stiffness in his official statues, he is revealed in other portraits as having a careworn countenance pitiable in its human frailty.

Under Mentuhotep I there was a sudden renaissance of sacred architecture in the grand manner. In its size and magnificence, the mausoleum of Mentuhotep himself revives the stately splendors of the Old Kingdom, but it is in the nature of an original creation and not merely a pastiche. Mortuary chapels for the rulers who preceded Mentuhotep had been built into the hillside at Dra abu'l Nega; they were partly cut out of the rock, and partly built in the open air, faced with porticoes and surmounted by a modest pyramid. For the glory of the king who had united Upper and Lower Egypt, a new site was chosen: the foot of a tall line of cliffs that hemmed in the long valley of Deir el Bahari. The idea of using a mortuary temple (for the reception of the body) with an excessively long approach was borrowed from the tombs of Memphite kings, while the concept of a monument topped by a pyramid and embedded in the rock was derived from the Intefs, Mentuhotep's immediate predecessors. This tomb was imitated much later in the temple of Queen Hatshepsut, built in the 18th Dynasty in the same valley. After Amenemhat I founded a new place of residence near Lisht, in the southern part of the Memphite plain, the kings of the 12th Dynasty were buried in that city and later in the vicinity of Dahshur. In a comparatively economical manner the original style of Memphite sepulchral monuments was revived. Thus the tomb of Amenemhat III at Dahshur consists of an upper temple, a ramp, and a lower temple. But the masterpiece of his reign, according to Greek and Roman writers, was a second mausoleum, with numerous galleries and courtyards, which he had built in the province of the Fayum and which attained fame under the name of the Labyrinth.

By the beginning of the 12th Dynasty, the restoration of a single centralized monarchy had brought back the custom of grouping mastabas of officials around the royal pyramid. These mastabas were kept to a fairly simple pattern. The survival of manorial estates in the provinces ensured the continued and extended construction of fine porticoes and handsome pillared halls, chiefly in Middle Egypt. Eventually the prosperity of minor officials and the spread of the Osiris cult caused the proliferation around the town of Abydos of humble brick mastabas sometimes topped with a miniature pyramid—an obvious sign that at least one of Pharaoh's former sepulchral prerogatives had become democratized.

It is only from the Middle Kingdom onward that secular architecture makes its appearance in Egyptian history manifested in the so-called soul houses (small-scale models in wood and pottery found in the tombs) and especially in the city of Sesostris II at Lahun and the fortresses of Sesostris III in the Sudan. It is an architecture already sophisticated, extremely well-planned, and effective.

The renaissance in religious, royal, and funerary architecture brought with it a complementary renewal in the art of mural decoration. The production of low relief had been mediocre during the First Intermediate Period—except perhaps in the area of Heracleopolis, where it preserved (at Assiut) something of the adroitness that characterized the 6th Dynasty. At Thebes, under the three kings called Intef, there was an attempt at careful workmanship and orderly composition. A royal school of competent craftsmen favoring ample forms developed far from Memphite sources. After the reunion of the Two Lands (Upper and Lower Egypt) contact was resumed with what remained of the ancient capital city of Memphis. From the time of Mentuhotep, and more particularly under Sesostris I, ancient themes were mingled with those that had originated during the Intermediate Period. The modeling of reliefs and treatment of details became more precise, more delicate. Under Mentuhotep II (at Tod, Erment, and Elephantine), Sesostris I (in his jubilee shrine at Karnak), and Sesostris III (at Medamud), the bold relief is of excellent quality; it becomes colder and more conventional in those rare royal monuments of the 13th Dynasty that are presently known to us. A comparable stylistic evolution is visible in the private stelae, whose quality varies in accordance with the importance of the site and the rank of the subject. During the 12th and 13th Dynasties the workshops of Abydos produced prodigious numbers of stelae for those people who wished to leave a record of their names near the shrine of Osiris although they could not actually be buried there. This output, amounting almost to an industry, is wearying in its mediocrity, but one cannot omit a reference to it because these stones—arched at the top and depicting whole families of little people sitting, standing, praying, or participating in their ritual meal—are found in nearly all museums and collections.

During the 13th Dynasty the great hypogea of the governors of Upper and Middle Egypt were richly decorated with scenes comparable in subject matter with those of Memphite mastabas, but more varied and executed in colored low reliefs or flat painting. Examples may be seen at Beni Hasan, Deir el Bersheh, Meir, Assiut, Qaw el Kebir, Thebes and Aswan.

The revived royal patronage of reliefs, the desire to restore discipline in all things, and at times a direct return to the best Memphite precedents led to more care in workmanship, more organization of composition, and greater skill in coloring. On the walls of the earliest chapels at Meir, where scenes and details were copied from tomb to tomb, some fine reliefs (and others of poorer quality), carved with only a slight projection, renew the tradition of the mastabas; but they incorporate vagaries in draftsmanship and in the proportions of the human figure, traits which reveal the legacy of the Intermediate Period. At Beni Hasan, paintings of uneven quality provide not only a chronicle of the Hare nome but also a comprehensive collection of scenes from everyday life. In an almost cinematic manner, painting gradually becomes emancipated from the art of relief. Some coffins of prominent citizens at Bersheh, in full polychrome, provide splendid evidence of this trend toward the end of the 12th Dynasty, as may be seen in the famous group of the daughters of the nomarch Djehuty-hotep III (Egyptian Museum). The chapel of Ukh-hotep III, the last great overlord of Meir, must have seemed an enchanted palace when his presumptuously regal portraits were still intact and its gay paintings had not yet suffered the ravages of time.

There is a remarkable contrast between the heavy gloom of royal statues in the reign of Sesostris III and the graceful style of painting dating from the same period. The development of sculpture is nevertheless parallel with that of the graphic arts: it springs in an already vigorous form from the First Intermediate Period, achieves a severity worthy of the ancient dynasties, and develops its own complex mode of expression. Some statues of kings and nobles, beginning with the celebrated figure of Mentuhotep I with his skin painted black and his garments white (Egyptian Museum), are typical products of early Theban sculpture, simple, massive, rude, and archaic in appearance. Later, at Lisht, the white limestone statues of Sesostris I represent the first results of an attempt to recapture the spirit of the Old Kingdom. The realistic Theban school of sculpture expresses itself with full force only during the reign of Sesostris III. As in the north, the formula for royal images exalts the sovereign's divine power according to a canon less rigid than that of the Old Kingdom. Nevertheless, the chief renown of the masterpieces at Medamud, Deir el Bahari, and Karnak lies in the taut, uneasy manner in which the highly individualized face of Sesostris is carved out of the dark stone.

The more idealized style of Lisht reappears in the Fayum under Amenemhat III, the successor of Sesostris III. It is evident in the figure of Amenemhat at Hawara and in numerous other statues that exhibit every shade of variation from a rather characterless form to the life-like features of the extraordinary human-faced lions at Tanis. One glance is enough to show that archaeologists who try to assign a date to them are faced with a considerable problem: framed as they are in their manes, the faces seem so alien that at first they appear to be portraits of a foreigner, one of the Hyksos kings. The massive lines of these creatures enthroned on lofty foundations, as well as the stranded locks of hair in their luxuriant manes, are not devoid of certain archaic characteristics, a fact that has prompted one pioneering thesis to attribute these so-called Hyksos monuments to the 3rd Dynasty. If their archaism can be considered genuine, it would seem that the prototype of the human-faced lion (hitherto datable to the 6th Dynasty by virtue of one minute figurine) ought to be regarded as of even earlier origin. In fact, support for such a theory can be found in the reappearance of this type in the reigns of Hatshepsut and the Kushite Taharqa, two reigns during which artists consciously adopted an archaistic style. However, if we overlook the leonine elements in the heads of the Tanis lions, we shall recognize in them robust variations of the features of Amenemhat III, three of which show a man still young while the other three represent the same subject at a more advanced age. Given our present state of knowledge, we can only guess that the sculptors of the 12th Dynasty revived an ancient model of a sphinx whose style appealed to the taste for the monolithic that marked their private statuary.

The functions of private statuary, especially in the first part of the 12th Dynasty, were still dictated by precedents of the First Intermediate Period. For example, statues in mortuary chapels showed the dead seated in glory and clad in the royal loincloth; but the fine wooden statuettes in the vaults were succeeded by bronze figurines attenuated and formalized beyond all naturalistic bounds, or by ushabtiu in the form of mummies. In fact, sculpture

Egyptian Art. *Sesostris III at the jubilee festival (Sed festival).* Medamud, 12th Dynasty. Egyptian Museum, Cairo. *Hirmer Fotoarchiv, Munich.*

began to veer toward an abstract formalism. The prevailing fashions in clothes—long loincloths and enveloping cloaks—lent themselves to these effects of unencumbered mass. Instead of limestone painted in naturalistic colors, highly polished hard stones became the vogue. The static impression created by the style of the Middle Kingdom corresponds admirably with the ancient Egyptians' desire to be eternally "close to the god" or "in the city of the dead." The ushabtiu in the vaults and the statuettes and family groups in the temples were designed to fulfill these aims. The nature of the stone, its high degree of polish, the unbending stiffness of the poses, and the prescribed gravity of the facial expressions cause several statues of dignitaries in the 12th and 13th Dynasties to be ranked among the finest masterpieces of conceptual sculpture.

With few exceptions, the applied arts of the Middle Kingdom were related to painting: the same charm emanates from the jewelry of princesses found at Lisht, Illahun, and Dahshur as from the ladies in the paintings from Bersheh and Meir. While sculpture grew more circumscribed than ever in its official or ritual preoccupations, the decorative arts were becoming more precious and frivolous than in Memphite times. Under the Sesostris family, the Egyptian Empire extended beyond the third cataract of the Nile, and exerted its influence as far as northern Syria—a factor that caused a lively exchange of products and techniques. The kings of Byblos (a port in Syria) took to their graves the gifts of Pharaoh and weapons of Egyptian pattern made in their own workshops. An Egypto-Sudanese art was evolved in the trading post of Kerma in Dongola province. Aegean motifs such as spirals and volutes were introduced into the decoration of mats and pottery. In addition to these, at the very moment when the style of ritual statuary tended toward an abstract formalism, there appeared a genre of sculpture on a smaller scale—terra cottas, ivories, and especially faïences—that was in an entirely different vein. After the discoveries at Lisht and Heliopolis, a cache of faïences found at Byblos illustrates almost single-handedly all the liberties and fantasies that the makers of statuettes allowed themselves toward the end of the 13th Dynasty. Statuettes of docile sheep, cats crouched ready to spring, mongrels on the alert or relaxing, comic baboons, grotesque dwarfs, and even an unfortunate cook sprawled beside his fire fanning the embers—all recall that a lighthearted naturalism and outbursts of earthy humor always flourished in Egyptian art beneath a surface of hieratic formalism.

SECOND INTERMEDIATE PERIOD
(13th–17th Dynasties,
c. 1780–1570 B.C.)

This period is the despair of the historian. Several unfinished pyramids south of Memphis, a multitude of royal names known to us by means of a few stones and by a host of small objects, even a whole treasure-trove of private stelae fail to explain how the institutions of the Middle Kingdom fell into decline, or how the invading Hyksos from Asia imposed their dominion as far as Middle Egypt. During the 13th Dynasty and even the 14th Dynasty, royal statues (whose formulas underwent a startling change), the rare temple reliefs, the stelae, and the private statues of Abydos at times retain the characteristics of an efficiently geared industry; but the royal works become vitiated as the period advances and the votive stelae of Edfu and Hierakonpolis grow progressively worse. The archaeologist must content himself with analyzing on innumerable scarabs the changing phase of a decorative art that was often haphazard in execution. According to documentation—if not in actual fact—Egyptian art does not really flourish again until the 17th Dynasty, when the kings of Thebes succeeded in breaking the power of the Hyksos, and by which time the New Kingdom had virtually begun.

NEW KINGDOM
(18th–20th Dynasties,
c. 1570–1085 B.C.)

Once the Hyksos were expelled, Egypt again became a major power; during almost the whole of the New Kingdom it was to be a leading figure. This brilliant period is the one from which the greatest number of works has come down to us. Its political history is sufficiently well known to allow us to distinguish three periods that can serve as a rough framework for the art historian. The 18th Dynasty, during which the Tuthmosids and Amenhoteps reigned, saw the Egyptian Empire reach its most extensive limits, ranging from the northern part of the Sudan to the north of Syria. The Amarna Period, that strange interlude of Akhenaten's heresy, marks the end of the 18th Dynasty. In the Ramesside Period, which corresponds with the 19th and 20th Dynasties, Egypt began by maintaining her political ascendancy: Sety I, Ramesses II, and

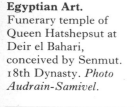

Egyptian Art. Funerary temple of Queen Hatshepsut at Deir el Bahari, conceived by Senmut. 18th Dynasty. *Photo Audrain-Samivel.*

Ramesses III, although unable to salvage Northern Syria, at least retained their hold on Palestine and repelled the invasions that menaced the Nile Valley. Under the last of the Ramessides, however, Egypt slowly foundered.

18th Dynasty
(*c.* 1570–1370 B.C.)

To a great extent, information concerning the monuments surviving from the first kings of this dynasty (such as that of Amenhotep I at Karnak) is still unpublished; and since the evidence they provide is so scanty, one must be resigned to an imperfect knowledge of how the restored Egyptian state re-created the patrician workshops and how the way was prepared for its third classic period, which probably sprang from the tradition of the 12th Dynasty preserved or rediscovered at Thebes, and that of the Old Kingdom unearthed at Memphis. This dual source is, as it were, transfigured by the appearance of a new sensibility, for it is no longer a spirit of vigor that animates the major works, but rather one of elegance—an elegance somewhat cold at first but becoming more graceful and culminating in ostentation. The monuments of the reign of Hatshepsut furnish an illustration both of the double return to earlier sources and of the new sensibility. The first example is the temple of the god Amon, that was built at Karnak (on the right bank of the Nile in the Theban region) to honor both the dynastic divinity and Queen Hatshepsut, who set herself up as Pharaoh. This temple is the best preserved and most renowned example of Tuthmosid architecture. On the river's left bank stands the temple of Hatshepsut on the site of Deir el Bahari. The achievement of a single reign, the Deir el Bahari complex is magnificent in its setting and is a work unique in its general conception, if not in the detail of its fittings.

After Hatshepsut's reign (as well as before it) the Pharaohs had a temple erected at the foot of the Theban necropolis, dedicated simultaneously to the god Amon and to their own cult. The mother house of the cult of Amon, it was embellished by each king of the 18th Dynasty. They refurbished and extended the original monument, erecting pair after pair of impressive obelisks. They inserted doorways and chapels, and added buildings around the outskirts, along with new courtyards and pylons. If Deir el Bahari reveals what Egyptian genius could create out of virgin soil, then Karnak—in spite of the ruin of its older parts—represents an even more unusual facet of the Pharaonic spirit. The temple was in a perpetual state of construction: it was partly demolished and repaired by underpinning, its extent was modified, old blocks of stone were used again, and it was rededicated.

Sculpture and painting also demonstrate how another style came to be substituted for the comely graces of the time of Hatshepsut and Tuthmosis III. A more showy kind of elegance triumphed under Amenhotep III. His overseers designed immense concentrations of buildings such as the temple of Soleb in the Sudan (now sadly ruined) and the funerary temple of Kom el Heitan. The latter surpassed in dimensions all the royal temples of Thebes, though scarcely any of it remains standing now except the twin Colossi of Memnon. This pair of Nubian sandstone giants was dug out of the quarries in the Aswan mountains north of Cairo and transported upstream against the current under the direction of a favorite minister of Amenhotep III. This eminent man, the son of Hapu, was also called Amenhotep; during his own lifetime he was awarded the privilege of a funerary temple, and was worshipped later as a god. The taste for colossal effigies, so well suited to the function of proclaiming before the people the superhuman glory of kings, became particularly developed in the time of Amenhotep III (and that of Ramesses III at a later date). The elegance of the Tuthmosid era persisted, however, and may be seen in the temple of Amon at Luxor, which is the work of the brothers Suti and Hor.

In the New Kingdom era, the custom of erecting vast funerary temples as tombs for the Pharaohs was replaced by burial in sloping underground tunnels in the Valley of the Kings. The graves of Theban nobles were simple chapels hollowed out of the hillside and surmounted by a small pointed pyramid. In itself, therefore, the funerary architecture of the New Kingdom has little to claim our admiration. If experts and amateurs alike make their way to Qurneh, Dra abu'l Nega, Guret, Murai, and Deir el Medina, it is to look at the paintings and reliefs that enliven the chapels and vaults. The 18th Dynasty witnessed a marvelous florescence in the two techniques used in mural decoration—relief and painting—with magnificent scenes in the temples and intimate scenes in the tombs telling anew the story of daily life in Egypt. In the temples, one finds not only the eternal ritual pictures of oblations, but also spectacular scenes of annual ceremonies and certain national festivals. In private tombs, a larger part is played by specifically religious themes than was customary in earlier times, and paintings begin to appear showing the owners of the tombs praying before the gods. By contrast, certain sacred acts such as the traditional offering to the dead, the communal meal that reunites the family at the time of the "great feast of the valley," and the funeral ceremonies themselves are treated with an easy familiarity that mitigates the severity of the ritual.

For recording all these subjects, low relief was used regularly in the

Egyptian Art. Second court of the temple at Luxor, lined with a double row of papyriform columns. Reign of Amenophis III. *Photo Gaddis, Luxor.*

great temples. It was also widely employed in the hypogea of Thebes whenever the quality of the rock was suitable, as well as at Memphis, where the walls of richly endowed chapels were faced with limestone. At the beginning of the 18th Dynasty, the reliefs of some tombs—with their clean lines and air of understatement—often recall the best works of the Middle Kingdom; but in the temples, artists began to suggest tactile values by the use of modeling. At the time Deir el Bahari was being decorated, a new style appeared; expressive but never overemphatic, and full of restrained vitality, it was a result of artists having derived their patterns from certain great ritual scenes in the repertoire of the Old Kingdom temples. Later the trend toward fantasy that is indicated in painting also affects relief, and expresses itself in that medium in a more graceful and sensuous treatment, together with a virtuosity that enables craftsmen to render all the pretty fripperies of fashionable costume (as in the tomb of Ramose).

However, at all those levels of the Theban hillsides where the rock threatened to crumble at the touch of a chisel and where it had to be faced with roughcast, painting on a flat surface pursued its own course of glory. After the reign of Hatshepsut, the forms became lighter and more flexible, and the groups more varied and animated (notably in the tomb of Rekhmira); the chromatic range is wider than in the past, a greater freedom of handling asserts itself, an unstudied grace transfigures the traditional dignity, and the colors—set against a beige background—become less sharply defined. This style is at its most charming in the tombs of Nakht, Menna, and other contemporaries of Tuthmosis IV, in which humorous touches steal into the settings. The freedom of this Theban school of painting was not of long duration.

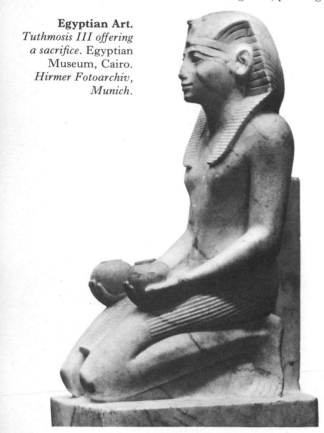

Egyptian Art. *Tuthmosis III offering a sacrifice.* Egyptian Museum, Cairo. *Hirmer Fotoarchiv, Munich.*

In royal statuary, one can observe from the beginning of the 18th Dynasty (in the naive statue of Queen Teti-sheri in the British Museum, for example) that refinement of features and forms marking the Tuthmosid period. It is hardly surprising that the feminine reign of Queen Hatshepsut should, by a subtle adaptation of Middle Kingdom prototypes, have retained and developed this graceful tendency; but it is a curious fact that the statues of Tuthmosis III and Amenhotep II should continue to present these hardy athletes and redoubtable warriors in a bland and youthful guise. The types of royal statues also seem to multiply progressively. Statuettes of precious woods and metals were included in the furnishings of temples and were carried in processions as symbols of the Pharaoh's participation in the sacred rites. In keeping with the increasing complexity of theology and ritual, the royal poses, headdresses, and emblems were all varied. Soon the first figures of this type in limestone, sandstone, granite and wood began to appear in life-size scale and even larger. At least as early as the 18th Dynasty the small cult objects used in the solemn consecration of the olibanum (an aromatic resin employed as incense) were often in the form of a king prostrate on his knees and pushing in front of him the vase containing the precious substance. Just as often the king assumes the aspect of an anthropocephalic lion holding the container between his paws, which are occasionally replaced by human arms. This type of object needed only to be transposed into stone for the type

Egyptian Art. *Offering of the royal family to Aton.* Amarna, Atonist period. Egyptian Museum, Cairo.

of the so-called offering sphinx to be created. There we have a revealing instance (and by no means an isolated one) of the way in which Egyptian religion engendered new art forms and posed new problems for artists.

Under Amenhotep III, the peak of the Tuthmosid period was marked by a superabundant, varied output and new tendencies in royal sculpture as well as in other branches of the arts. The enormous productivity of the period included numerous royal colossi, a series of deities in blue granite that were carved on the occasion of royal jubilees, and hundreds of seated or standing lion-headed goddesses. A fresh spirit began to animate some of the master sculptors, who were developing new methods: the creation of several gigantic faces hewn out of quartzite allowed them to push to its limits the art of colossal portraiture by a skillful juggling of the planes of the face rather than by simply enlarging a portrait of natural dimensions. In quite another direction, certain small figures—such as the Amenhotep now in the Brooklyn Museum—show all the physical imperfections of the subject, and yet the gentle melancholy of the expression tempers the harshness of the realism. One finds this contemplative expression in an even purer form in several private statues of the reign of Amenhotep III (such as that of Amenhotep, son of Hapu), where it replaces the rather insipid smile of earlier works. Private statuary in the earlier years of the dynasty began by reviving the restrained style of the Middle Kingdom, but not without transforming it in two radically opposed ways: either by an increased plasticity or by an even sterner use of monolithic effects. The increased number of religious concepts gave rise to new types of effigies, such as men holding before them an idol of their chosen divinity (called naophori) or the dead kneeling to salute the rising sun (called stelephori and orants).

The pleasing style associated with the Tuthmosids and Amenhoteps is naturally at its best in the decoration of secular architecture and in the ornamentation of *objets de luxe*. The residence of Amenhotep III in Thebes yields attractive mural paintings with amusing demons guarding the harems, elegant volutes, clouds, and white pigeons. Scenes of the marshes, the countryside, and other naturalistic settings that were later to brighten the walls of numerous palaces in Amarna with unprecedented dash and imagination also provided the favorite subject matter for ornamenting faïences, paterae (flat dishes used for pouring libations), and such toilet accessories as unguent spoons. Depictions of lotus and papyrus forms, swimmers, huntresses, frail rowboats, lively animals, musicians, and petite foreign servant girls, all convey an impression of freshness, youth, and luxury.

Amarna Period

(*c.* 1370–1350 B.C.)

This is unquestionably the only episode of folly in the whole course of Egyptian history. It is also the most emotionally engaging, for which reason its historical interpretation is more disputed than that of any other period. Amenhotep IV, the son and successor of Amenhotep III, repudiated the pantheon of his ancestors and acknowledged as his only god the visible disk of the sun, called the *aten* in Egyptian. He began by constructing a vast temple for this new cult at Karnak, near the temple of Amon (who was renounced and anathematized). Soon Amenhotep IV abandoned his own name and became known as Akhenaten. He installed himself and his court at a new city that he called Akhetaten ("the horizon of the aten"), now Tel el Amarna. His reign was destined to end in obscurity, with his son-in-law Tutankhaten returning to Thebes to reign under the name of Tut-ankh-amon.

This shattering interlude was a heresy in art as well as in religion. Breaking with accepted tradition, a Pharaoh and his whole entourage seized upon certain concepts, isolating and exalting them to excess. Temples became a vast series of open spaces and enclosed courtyards linked by means of doorways with broken lintels; these areas were the setting for serried ranks of altars. The hollow reliefs preserved the best elements of Theban inventiveness. Vivid anarchy of composition, a lively taste for movement—which is similarly unleashed in the paintings from the palaces of Amarna—and sometimes carelessness in execution gave to the designs of this period a special verve that accentuates still more the peculiar anatomy of the figures. The exclusive exaltation of the king's personal religion had the effect of generalizing the royal pattern to excess. Everyone—from Queen Nofretete and the young princesses and courtiers to the humblest subjects—presents a protruding jaw, epicene breasts, a slack stomach, sloping shoulders, and rather emaciated limbs.

The Amarna sculptors who carved the colossi of Karnak with such broad handling launched out into a determined ultrarealism that must have seemed exaggerated even to the heretics themselves. But this style gave way eventually to a more moderate so-called Amarna style. Even if it remained abnormal, the appearance of the body became merely unusual instead of monstrous, and the modeling of the face tended toward a spiritualization of expression.

Ramesside Period

(*c.* 1350–1085 B.C.)

During the period of the Amarna heresy, Egyptian pre-eminence in the Near East, already tottering at the end of the reign of Amenhotep III, crashed in ruins. The old order was firmly re-established by general Horemheb, followed by his colleague and companion in arms, Ramesses, who founded a new dynasty. Of the earlier Ramessides, Sety I and Ramesses II (19th Dynasty) were warlike kings and lavish builders; Ramesses III (beginning of the 20th Dynasty) was cast in the same mould. Under them Egypt remained a power to be reckoned with, her workshops prospering and an appreciable standard of craftsmanship being maintained. In the reign of Sety I artists seem to have picked up the threads left loose at the end of Amenhotep III's reign, and thus recreated a style that was elegant in spite of its academic tendencies. Under Ramesses II and again under Ramesses III there was a vast output of works, some of which are outstanding, and all bearing witness to the current taste for size and weight. In architecture, the megalomaniacal trend of the Ramessides began to manifest itself as early as the reign of Sety I, who played an important part in the erection of the hypostyle hall at Karnak, with its solid monostyle columns ranged on both sides of lofty axial bays. As for the contemporaneous temples of Qurneh and Abydos, a certain restraint is preserved: the plan is spacious and the decoration in good taste. A number of temples in the style characteristic of the period of Ramesses II have survived in a fairly good state of repair. They are of cumbersome proportions, stupendous dimensions, have ponderous square pillars supporting clumsy heavy-footed colossi, thick monostyle columns, towering pylons, long walls decorated with battle scenes on a gigantic scale, friezes, and bands of huge hieroglyphs. These features are best seen in the Theban funerary temple known as Ramesseum; the rock-hewn temple (or speos) at Abu

Egyptian Art. *Colossus of Akhenaten*. Detail from the temple of Aton at Karnak. Atonist period. Egyptian Museum, Cairo. *Photo Hassia, Paris.*

Egyptian Art. *Ramesses II*. Museo Egizio, Turin.

Simbel; and the earlier buildings at Luxor. Ramesses III had built an even more grandiose version of the Ramesseum at Medinet Habu, and at Karnak laid the foundations of the small temple of the god Khons.

In the temples (such as those at Abydos) and the tombs (such as that of Pasar) the art of relief achieved a wonderful subtlety of touch between the time of the restoration of orthodoxy and the accession of Ramesses II. In the reign of Ramesses II, who abandoned raised relief in favor of hollow relief for mural decorations, and under his successors relief sculpture gained in vigor what it lost in elegance. It is not altogether surprising that this period of kings whose origin was military should have left us the most extensive and the most evocative scenes of war. The external walls of Karnak and Medinet Habu show a genuine mastery of composition in their panoramic scenes of the triumphs of Pharaoh, who in all his mettlesome might crushes underfoot the picturesque heaps of defeated barbarians. In private tombs, the Theban school of painting has left us a dull repertoire of commonplace religious imagery during the period of Ramesside decadence. Earlier, however, a sort of cheerful vulgarity continued to lend interest to scenes of daily life (in the tomb of Ipy, for example), and although these progressively gave way to an occult funereal iconography the painters had a brilliant flair for enlivening their figures of divinities and deceased persons with rich clothing and jewels.

Egyptian Art. Interior court and colonnade of the temple of Ramesses II, Luxor. 19th Dynasty. *Photo Audrain-Samivel ("Trésor de l'Égypte," Éditions Arthaud).*

Power and wealth, the two dominant traits in Ramesside architecture, are just as much in evidence in royal sculpture. Ramesses II commissioned a prodigious number of colossi bearing his own traits, statues on a heroic scale, and standard-bearers wearing loincloths and burdensome crowns. The "pillar stelae" of the eastern delta, the engaged statue grouped against a background (which are more in the technique of high relief than of sculpture), and the statues of private individuals in the form of stone slabs, all testify that the style of Ramesses II should not be condemned, as it often is, as a complete collapse of taste. It did produce a certain concept of beauty that renders it an interesting phase of Egyptian art. Under the 20th Dynasty a reaction can be detected, marked by a return to the more supple modeling that was the glory of the 18th Dynasty.

THIRD INTERMEDIATE PERIOD
(21st–24th Dynasties,
c. 1085–715 B.C.)

The two influences that contributed to the downfall of the New Kingdom were the military leaders turned priests of Amon and the Libyan warriors. Kings of Tanis and the so-called priest-kings of Thebes reigned during the 21st Dynasty, and Libyan rulers during the 22nd and 23rd Dynasties. A divided Egypt was no longer a great power and, just as in the two previous Intermediate Periods, artistic production was on the whole scanty and mediocre. Nevertheless, studies so far attempted on the rare works of those ill-fated centuries show unmistakably that all these works are not to be despised by any means, and that they may even enable us to conjecture how the styles and methods of the Late Period were dimly foreshadowed. The small cache of ushabitiu found at Deir el Bahari has long been famous for its high quality, and the gold masks, silver coffins, jewels, and utensils used in royal and aristocratic Tanite burials prove that applied arts maintained this quality.

Sculpture did not die out altogether. Original pieces that can be attributed with certainty to the 21st and 22nd Dynasties are of the utmost rarity, but in at least one of them—the kneeling *Osorkon*—one can detect a worthy attempt on the part of the Tanite workshops to recover the splendors of bygone days. The rather taut grace of the face and the supple articulation of the body correspond exactly to the message contained in the inscription on the stele the king pushes in front of him: "Osorkon appeals to his god." Toward the end of the 9th century B.C., while two royal houses were disputing over their rights to rule the country, the Theban aristocrats once more set up their own effigies at Karnak. The type and even the treatment of these private statues are, as a rule, copies from the Middle Kingdom or the beginning of the 18th Dynasty, and indicate the first step toward a renaissance. On the other hand, a peculiarity of the Libyan period that certainly deserves comment is the sudden appearance of notable bronze statuettes, sometimes richly adorned with chiseled and inlaid emblems, such as those of Queen Karomama in the Louvre and the Lady Takushit in the National Archaeological Museum, Athens. The formula is often new, but sometimes, as in the Louvre's Mosu, archaizing tendencies are evident—the technique, however, is faultless. The increasing importance of bronze heralds the Late Period, during which time bronze statuettes of the gods enjoyed a considerable vogue.

Egyptian Art. Remains of the first columned hall of the Ramesseum, Thebes. *Photo Henri Stierlin, Geneva.*

FROM THE KUSHITE AND SAITE
REVIVAL TO THE ROMAN PERIOD
(715 B.C.–A.D. 392)

There were two mainsprings in the renaissance of Egyptian art that became evident, if not fully established, by the time the kings of Napata founded the 25th Dynasty (known as Kushite or Ethiopian; 715–664 B.C.). The legacy of the Ramessides and antiquarian researches instigated by Theban sculptors and certain draftsmen of Lower Egypt during the 8th century B.C. combined to provide the necessary impetus. Artists continued to draw inspiration from early Theban sculpture, but there was also a tendency to go back even farther to Old Kingdom sources: reliefs on ancient Memphite temples were traced off in almost servile copies. Simplicity of form and rejection of nonessentials again became the rule and remained so throughout the Saite period (26th Dynasty, 664–525 B.C.), which witnessed the reestablishment of Egypt's unity, independence, and colonial expansion. One might say of this Egyptian renaissance that its output is characterized by the great reverence with which it regarded the distant past, but a reverence that was not based exclusively on antiquity. This applies to the Kushite period, when certain new types of monuments and a kind of realism hitherto unseen made their appearance, but it is even more true of the Saite period. Particularly where sculpture was concerned, new modes of feeling and expression soon came to light. Under the first Persian domination (27th Dynasty, 525–401 B.C.), all traces of antique prototypes seem to have been thoroughly watered down. During the last indigenous dynasties (28th–30th, 401–330 B.C.), Egypt was endowed with a renewed form of art prefiguring that of Greco-Roman times. In fact, under the Ptolemies (330–30 B.C.), who were Hellenistic in manners and culture but recognized by the Egyptian priesthood as authentic Pharaohs, and later under the Romans (30 B.C.–A.D. 392), Egypt was to preserve not only her religious beliefs but the traditions of her art. It is true that some aspects of the latter soon disappeared (such as the great funerary architecture), and that others lingered on precariously (such as low relief) or forfeited their national character (such as jewelry and other industrial arts with a cosmopolitan appeal). But in the construction of temples and in sculpture, then at the height of its prestige among the major arts, Egyptian inspiration and skill were not exhausted for a considerable period of time.

The colonnade of the Kushite king Taharqua at Karnak, the naos (or sanctuary) of the Saite king Amasis at Mendes, and the descriptions of certain monuments as seen by Herodotus seem to indicate that the 25th and 26th Dynasties had not entirely renounced the idea of sacred architecture on a vast scale. Of the major temples relating to the Saites in the Delta, little remains except scattered blocks from which it is impossible to reconstruct the stages of evolution culminating in a monument such as the temple of Darius, which owes its survival to its isolated position in the heart of the Khargeh oasis. Under foreign influence, great restoration schemes that had been initiated during the 30th Dynasty were carried through to a successful conclusion in several towns of Upper Egypt (Edfu, Dendera, and Philae, as well as Kalalsheh and Dakka in Nubia) where, by chance, some important buildings have been preserved almost intact. The structure of Ptolemaic temples recalls Theban counterparts but certain new elements should be noted: façades with saddleback copings, adjoining *mammisis* (annexes built onto the great sanctuaries in the Late Period for the annual ritual of the birth of the child-god), kiosks, and an enclosing outer wall, which transforms every major temple into a great stone box.

The progress of funerary architecture in Lower Egypt was also brilliant, but did not last as long as sacred architecture. It suffices to compare the charming chapels of the divine consorts of Amon at Medinet Habu with the colossal palaces of Mentuemhat and Petamenopet in the flat country of the Asasif to realize that a pleasing manner and an arrogant manner coexisted in Kushite Thebes.

At Hermopolis in Upper Egypt, one last funerary monument, whose general appearance is that of a chapel for divine worship, was built for the sage Petosiris at the beginning of the Hellenistic period. Between the 26th and 30th Dynasties, immense burial pits were dug at Memphis and were cleverly planned to outwit marauders.

Official low reliefs, which had consistently adhered to ancient standards both for hollow and raised carving, underwent remarkable changes. In the proportions and spacing of its figures, in its restrained detail and carefully chiseled inscriptions, the Kushite revival had re-created a style that was austere and stripped of nonessentials. The Saite Renaissance, while preferring more elongated outlines and more angular hieroglyphics, continued along the same lines, but toward the end of the 6th century B.C. an unexpected reversal took place. Subtle planes and discreet suggestion were replaced by an overstated plasticity in the modeling. This sensual style is far from being displeasing, for it survived on the liveliness of its inspiration, the novelty of its subject matter, and the virtuosity of its sculptors. These conditions ceased to be fulfilled under Greek domination when, confined to the mechanical repetition of ritual scenes, the beauty of Egyptian relief ended in corruption.

Hundreds of Saite bronzes and faïences of good quality testify to the survival of the old traditions in

Egyptian Art. Bas-relief showing the distribution of golden collars to the seamstresses of a weaving studio. 26th Dynasty. Egyptian Museum, Cairo. *Photo Hassia, Paris.*

Egyptian Art. *Statuette of a cat.* Saite period. Louvre, Paris. *Photo André Vigneau-Éditions Tel, Paris.*

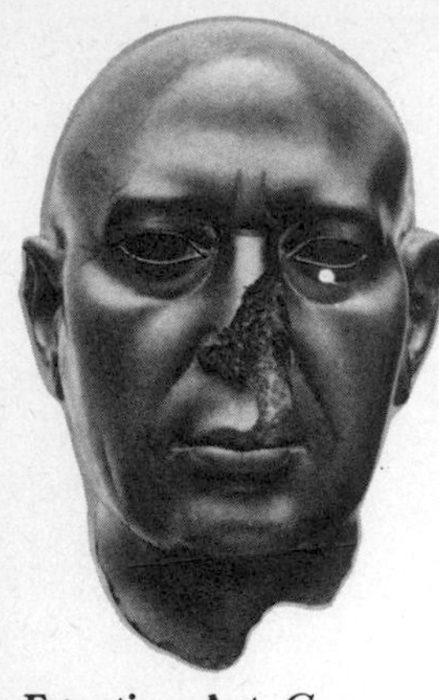

Egyptian Art. *Green head.* Mid-4th century B.C. Staatliche Museen, Berlin-Dahlem. *Photo Walter Dräyer, Zurich.*

the applied arts, but the most astonishing revelation of the vitality of latter-day dynastic Egypt is found in the various phases undergone by large-scale sculpture. In this field an interplay of converging and diverging currents and of innovations and archaisms is revealed. The treatment of royal sculpture no longer has the variety of New Kingdom examples: as in Old Kingdom sculpture, the king wears little but a loincloth and a headdress. On the contrary, the private statues—which are exclusively sepulchral effigies—may be cubiform or naophorous as in the New Kingdom, but the repertoire of attitudes and raiment is severely simplified under the Saites and later becomes impoverished, in spite of the appearance (at the end of the 6th century B.C.) of statues showing Egyptian dignitaries in Persian costume. The modeling and finish of the figures is enhanced by the quality of the materials then popular—the hardest and darkest stones that could be found in the Egyptian deserts. In the conception of the faces, Saite sculptors exhibited a surprising variety, practicing simultaneously an attractive idealization of the features, a conventional attribution of the marks of age, and sometimes a more or less relentless realism. In the time of the Persian dominations there also appeared the true portrait, observing not only the spirit but also the individual particularities of the model. The Psamtik-sa-neith from Cairo (4th century B.C.), the Pikhaas from Tanis (1st century B.C.), and, among other so-called green heads, that in Boston's Museum of Fine Arts—all are splendid bust portraits revealing the vigor and creative power of sculptors who kept Pharaonic art alive in the centuries when Egypt had become nothing but a colony to be exploited by alien dynasties.

Gustave Eiffel. Garabit Viaduct over the Truyère River, Cantal. 1880–84. *Photo Jean Roubier, Paris.*

EIDLITZ, Leopold (1823, Prague, Czechoslovakia—1908, New York), American architect. He emigrated in 1843 to the United States, where he entered the office of Richard Upjohn in New York. After leaving Upjohn, Eidlitz was largely responsible for the completion of St. George's Episcopal Church, New York (1848). He designed St. Peter's, Westchester (1851); the Broadway Tabernacle (1859; demolished), and the Emanuel Synagogue (1868; demolished), in New York; as well as Christ Church, St. Louis (1867), one of his best-known works. His secular architecture included the City Hall, Springfield, Massachusetts (1855; demolished); the American Exchange Bank (1857), the old Produce Exchange (1860), and the Dry Dock Savings Bank (1875), all in New York; and many other buildings in and near that city. His major commission was the redesigning and completion, in cooperation with Henry Hobson Richardson and Frederick Law Olmsted, Jr., of the State Capitol at Albany, begun in 1875. Eidlitz was the author of numerous magazine articles and a book, *The Nature and Function of Art* (1881).

EIFFEL, Gustave (1832, Dijon—1923, Paris), French engineer and builder. Eiffel realized the potentialities of rolled iron and steel and understood the necessity of rethinking traditional forms and construction methods in terms of the new materials. When, in 1867, he set himself up as a consultant engineer, he already had a wealth of practical experience behind him, and the commissions soon flowed into his workshops from all over the world. Time and again he proved the flexibility of the building methods he had developed, the most characteristic of which is the lattice beam. His enormous output was crowned with his three masterpieces: the Maria Pia Bridge over the Douro, near Porto, Portugal (1877–78; span 530 ft., height 200 ft.); the Garabit Viaduct over the Truyère River, Cantal (1880–84; arch span 550 ft., height 408 ft., total length 1,667 ft.); and the 1,000-foot tower in the Champ-de-Mars, Paris, known as the Eiffel Tower (1887–89). These three giants are all based on the same principle, which Eiffel had discovered in his use of the lattice beam: all the bearing elements are formed of three-dimensional structures consisting of arrangements of small, standard angle-irons or flat irons.

The architectural significance of the Eiffel Tower is that it established the potential dynamism of an engineering-based architecture. It also showed that entirely new forms could be conceived in harmony with mathematical requirements. But it was 20 years before artists (the painter Robert Delaunay and the sculptor Antoine Pevsner), and still longer before architects, realized the implications of Eiffel's work: that space could be treated in a purely dynamic manner, conceived as a complex and unstable network of nuclei and fields of force. The action of the wind was a significant problem for the stability of his structures, and from 1900 Eiffel devoted himself increasingly to aerodynamics research, publishing his results in *Air Resistance and Aviation* (1913 and 1914).

EILSHEMIUS, Louis Michel (1864, Newark, New Jersey—1941, New York), American painter. His early work is Impressionistic in its focus, but later a more personalized inspiration takes over. In 1908 Eilshemius met Albert Pinkham Ryder, whose visionary paintings became the prime influence on his own often naive-looking art.

Although a prolific painter, Eilshemius received little recognition until he was acclaimed by Marcel Duchamp and other American artists at the Independents show of 1917; this was followed by his first one-man show in 1920 at the newly formed gallery of the Société Anonyme. In *Jealousy* (1915; formerly New York, Curt Valentin Gallery) one sees the artist's tortured forms at their most typical: ghostly shapes of women sprawl threateningly in a room whose mood is filled with evil portents. The round painted corners of the canvas, which Eilshemius frequently used to create an illusionistic frame around his pictures, give this work a strikingly theatrical effect. In *Afternoon Wind* (1899; New York, Museum of Modern Art) female nudes float dreamily through a silvery landscape, joined together in erotic, hybrid shapes.

ELAMITE ART. Elam was a region to the east and northeast of Babylonia, stretching from Hamadan to the Persian Gulf, roughly corresponding to the modern Iranian province of Khuzistan. It was the seat of several powerful dynasties, and what might justly be called an Elamite culture existed from the 3rd millennium B.C.; its most brilliant center was at Susa (modern Shush). The excavation of this city did not yield an architecture corresponding to this period, although objects dating from it were found. One must be wary of regarding as Elamite those monuments that are in fact Mesopotamian or that are war trophies brought back to Susa by sovereigns of the 13th and 12th centuries B.C.

After a proto-Elamite civilization (the ceramics of Susa I and II), a specifically Elamite phase can be distinguished beginning at the time of the fall of Ur (*c.* 2015 B.C.). Excavations carried out at Choga Zambil revealed a magnificent five-story ziggurat and palaces (13th century B.C.), built by Untash-Huban, king of Susa. Also from this period are the famous statue of Napir-Asu, wife of Untash-Huban, cast in bronze and finished with the chisel, and the great stone stele depicting the king, the queen, and genii holding streams of flowing water to their breasts. The Mesopotamian influence is apparent in the mural decoration of fired bricks in the sanctuary of Shushinak at Susa. The bull-god protecting the date palm is recognizable, although rather clumsily stylized, and the goddess Ninhursaga, elbows flexed and hands supporting her chin, is also recognizable. This decoration, which dates from the 12th century B.C., bears a strong resemblance to that of the temple built at Uruk by the Kassite king Karaindash. Indeed, the two arts—Kassite and Elamite—are closely related (*see* KASSITE ART).

Objects that are specifically Elamite include the gold and silver statuettes of offering bearers, the bronze tablet of *Sit Shamshi*, a maquette of a sacred place, and several terracotta heads of bearded men (all discovered at Susa; some now in the Louvre, Paris). But perhaps the most remarkable of these objects is a bronze head (New York, Metropolitan Museum) said to be from the Lake Urmia region. The features are marked by a serene and meditative gravity; the hair is flattened beneath a turban tied tightly over the forehead and the curly beard encroaches well over the cheekbones; the thin, tight lips express a reserve that must also have been shown in the eyes, which were originally inlaid but are now empty.

With the neo-Elamite periods (9th–8th century B.C.) there was a great increase in the production of glazed pottery: receptacles, pyxides ornamented with figures (sphinxes, griffins) or geometrical motifs (rosettes or checkered patterns), and tiles used for mural decoration. There were also various objects in bronze, in particular situlae with *repoussé* decoration.

Elamite Art. Head of dignitary. Said to be from the Lake Urmia region, Iran. Late 2nd millennium B.C. Metropolitan Museum of Art, New York.

ELEMENTARISM, movement in 20th-century Dutch art founded by Theo van Doesburg, an offshoot of Mondrian's Neoplasticism. In an article-manifesto published in 1926 in the Dutch review *De Stijl*, Van Doesburg, who in 1916 had been Mondrian's first follower, defined Elementarism as partly a reaction against an overly dogmatic application of Neoplasticism and partly a consequence of Neoplastic ideas themselves. It retained the right angle, which was the exclusive form of Neoplasticism, but rejected its obligatory horizontal-vertical position in favor of inclined planes that would produce dynamic instability. Van Doesburg was followed by Cesar Domela (b. 1900) and Friedrich Vordemberge-Gildewart, who had also been followers of Mondrian.

ELLIOTT, Charles Loring (1812, Scipio, New York—1868, Albany), American portrait painter. From 1830 to 1840 Elliott worked in many parts of central New York State and, after 1840, he settled in New York, where he was a leading portraitist. In the 1850s, during the most successful period in his career, he was the local artist of William Street, and dashed off portraits of the cotton merchants who did their bargaining there. Like many painters of the time, Elliott felt that he had to compete with photography, and he copied many of his later paintings from photographs, a common practice of the day.

Although Elliott's portraits are often uninspired, they do possess a certain penetrating realism. The few full-length portraits that he painted are inferior to his smaller works. A typical, but noteworthy, example of his depersonalized handling of portraiture is his *Matthew Brady* (1857; New York, Metropolitan Museum).

ELSHEIMER, Adam (1578, Frankfurt am Main—1610, Rome), German painter and engraver. A pupil of Philipp Uffenbach (1566–1636) in Frankfurt, he was also exposed to the art of pure landscape painting through contacts with the Frankenthal artists, settlers from the Low Countries. He later traveled to Munich, and then to Venice, where he studied with Hans Rottenhammer (1564–1625) and became acquainted with the work of Tintoretto, particularly his experiments with light effects. Elsheimer's early work shows the effects of his varied training (*St. John the Baptist Preaching*; Munich, Alte Pinakothek). In 1600 he went to Rome, where he remained for the rest of his life, and where he belonged to the intimate circle of Rubens and Paul Brill. His figures took on a new amplitude, and he began to concentrate on

Elamite Art. Ziggurat of Choga Zambil, near Susa. Mid-13th century B.C. *Photo Roger-Viollet, Paris.*

Reginald Ely. Chapel of King's College, Cambridge. 1446–1515. *Photo Kersting, London.*

Italian Classical subjects. He also did some landscapes in which the figures are dwarfed by magnificent foliage (*View of Tivoli with the Temple of the Sibyl*; Prague, National Gallery). He studied closely the lighting in the works of Caravaggio, executing many studies of night effects (*Flight into Egypt*, 1609; Alte Pinakothek) and experimenting particularly with lighting from a single local source (a candle, a lamp, fire, etc.) that gave off a glow in the darkness. The effect is especially striking in his etchings and dry-points, which anticipate the richness, mystery, and breadth of those of Rembrandt. Elsheimer's experiments played an important role—far greater than his apparent achievement—in the development of chiaroscuro. His influence on Claude Lorrain and on a certain number of Italian painters is beyond question and, without a doubt, it also extended to Rembrandt and, in the 19th century, to the German Romantics.

ELY, Reginald (active from 1438—d. 1471), English master mason, one of the leading figures in 15th-century English architecture. Most of his working life, for which there is documentary evidence spanning a third of a century, was spent in Cambridge; but one may infer from bequests in his will that he was a native of Norfolk. His use of curvilinear tracery (which survived late in that county) supports this theory.

The first mention of Ely at Cambridge is in 1438–39, when he was building a staircase at Peterhouse. In 1443 he is recorded as working at King's College; he may well have been there since the first foundation in 1441. He was the first of the four masons responsible for King's College Chapel (1446–1515), one of the major monuments of the Perpendicular style. In a patent of 1444 he was commissioned as "chief mason of our royal college of the blessed Mary and St. Nicholas of Cambridge." He retained this title until 1461, when the work, initiated by Henry VI, came to a standstill following Edward IV's seizure of the throne.

In 1449 Ely was employed at King's Hall, Cambridge, a college that later became part of Trinity College. On stylistic grounds, there is strong evidence for associating him with a number of other buildings. These include the churches of St. Edward (enlarged 1446) and St. John the Baptist (rebuilt *c.* 1453), both in Cambridge; the kitchen buildings at Peterhouse (1449–50); the library at Pembroke College, Cambridge (1452; destroyed 1875); the north porch of Thaxted Church, Essex (*c.* 1445), to which he made a bequest in his will; and the church at Burwell, north of Cambridge (*c.* 1464), which is attributed by village tradition to "the architect of King's College Chapel."

EMPIRE STYLE. The artistic life of France under the Empire can no more be separated from that of the Revolution than can the Empire itself from the revolutionary situation that it stabilized. The art of the Empire period was dominated by two exceptional individuals, the Neoclassical painter Louis David and Napoleon I. From 1789 to 1814, David exercised complete control over the development of French painting, while Napoleon, by virtue of his extraordinary power over people, annexed the arts in their entirety to his own greater glory. On the eve of the French Revolution, the students at the Académie de France in Rome (both painters and architects) eagerly adopted ideas on ideal beauty derived from the aesthetic theories of the archaeologists Antoine Quatremère de Quincy and Johann Joachim Winckelmann. This dogmatic conception of painting emerged victorious from revolutionary upheavals: it was defended by David up to the time of the Convention, when—having been elected a deputy for Paris—he succeeded in getting the Académie Royale de Peinture et de Sculpture (which opposed the new doctrine) dissolved. Freed at last from all constraint, David gathered his disciples in his studio—Eustache Langlois (1777–1837), Georges Rouget (1784–1869), François-Xavier Fabre (1766–1837), Anne-Louis Girodet-Trioson, and, above all, Baron Antoine-Jean Gros and Baron François Gérard—and henceforth directed the development of French art toward an ideal beauty, sought assiduously through the imitation of Greek art. Almost at once, however, David found that he had to sacrifice this search in favor of the obligatory visual commemoration of the great events of the French Revolution. The inspiration for such themes constituted an attempt to rival the stoicism and generosity of spirit of the ancients. In opposition to the dominance of David was the studio of his great rival, Jean-Baptiste Regnault (1754–1829). But most of Regnault's pupils—and especially the most famous of them, Pierre-Narcisse Guérin—were also strongly influenced by the example of David's school.

The confirmed Neoclassicists suggested contemporary events by choosing parallel events from Roman history. Thus, in 1799 Guérin painted the *Return of Marcus Sextus* (Paris, Louvre), which alluded to the return of the French *émigrés* and which pleased the public because of its political overtones. Similarly, David's *Sabine Women* (1799; Louvre) expressed the general desire for

Empire Style. Louis David. *Napoleon Crossing the Alps.* 1801. Versailles Museum.

national reconciliation. Gros alone, who had met Bonaparte in Milan and joined his entourage, recognized as early as 1796 that the young general's bold victories in the Italian campaign offered a new and epic subject matter, such as he portrayed in *Napoleon on the Bridge at Arcola* (1796; Louvre). From the beginning of Bonaparte's Consulate, French painters acknowledged their new leader, and celebrated him either in heroic portraits, or in scenes depicting dramatic military episodes.

As First Consul, Napoleon set about institutionalizing artistic matters. He reaffirmed the changes brought about by David under the Convention, and fixed, for more than a century, the organization of the Institut des Beaux-Arts. After 1804 Napoleon subsidized painters, decorated them, and occasionally even ennobled them. He commissioned David to paint the *Coronation of Josephine* (1805–7; Louvre) and the *Distribution of the Eagles* (1810; Versailles), both huge pictures that occupied the artist for several years. Girodet similarly glorified the emperor with *Napoleon Receiving the Keys of the City of Vienna* (Versailles), Gérard with the *Signing of the Concordat*, and Gros with *Napoleon at the Battle of Eylau* (1808; Louvre). Painters were also the regular iconographers of the new court. Besides portraits of the emperor (by David and Girodet), of the empresses Joséphine (Prud'hon) and Marie-Louise (Gérard), of the king of Rome (Jean-Baptiste Isabey), and of Laetitia Bonaparte (Gérard), there exists an almost complete record of the important persons of the time, from marshals to courtesans.

The Revolution was a fallow season for French architecture, since most available money was spent on an endless succession of foreign wars. It was not until the Empire period that more ample funds provided the means for new architectural projects. These mainly took the form of urban improvements in Paris (the Pont d'Iéna, the metal footbridge of the Pont des Arts, the Cour du Carrousel, and the Rue de Rivoli), aqueducts and fountains, and a number of utilitarian buildings (the Bourse, the Halle au Blé). When the renovation of Malmaison was completed, Napoleon undertook the systematic restoration of the main royal residences (Louvre, Tuileries, Fontainebleau, Compiègne, St-Cloud). In Paris he built the Arc de Triomphe du Carrousel (1806–8) and the Colonne Vendôme (1810), began the Arc de Triomphe de l'Étoile, and had plans drawn up for the future Palais du Roi de Rome, which was to occupy the hill of Chaillot. Most of these buildings were entrusted to the same pair of architects, Charles Percier and Pierre François Fontaine, but Napoleon also supported the talents of Alexandre Théodore Brongniart (the Bourse, begun 1808), Pierre-Alexandre Vignon, 1763–1828 (the Madeleine, begun 1806, which was conceived as a Temple of Glory), and Jean-François Chalgrin (Arc de Triomphe de l'Étoile, 1806), because of their Classical ideas inspired by Greco-Roman art. This did not, however, prevent him from giving his support to François Bélanger (1744–1818), who had new ideas on iron structures (Halle au Blé, 1807).

Between 1789 and 1802 sculpture vegetated undisturbed. Jean-Antoine Houdon, before taking Napoleon as his sitter, sculpted busts of Charles Dumouriez, the great revolutionary general, and Antoine Barnave, who prevented the royal family's escape at Varennes. Under the Consulate and the Empire, however, sculpture became very important, discovering a new ferment in the extraordinary creative power of ancient statuary and of its brilliant Venetian imitator, Antonio Canova. French sculptors such as Joseph Chinard (1756–1813), Denis Antoine Chaudet (1763–1810), and Pierre Cartellier (1757–1831) created their own school, in which dignity and craftsmanship were the essential qualities. Some sculptors executed maquettes of bronzes for interiors or unglazed Sèvres porcelain, and worked with cabinetmakers to produce a severe but sumptuous style of furniture, which reflected the imperial desire for a court atmosphere of stiff solemnity. The emperor himself encouraged and supervised the factories producing fabrics and tapestries, and, above all, the Sèvres porcelain factory (directed by Brongniart and Percier), which was included in the Civil List as early as 1804. The ten years of this imperial reign, which proved so important for the organization of the country, also saw the richest art collection of Europe housed in the Louvre, under the direction of Vivant-Dominique Denon (1747–1825). It included works preserved from royal and aristocratic French collections, as well as ancient sculptures and paintings by the great masters which had been brought back from Italy or Spain as tribute, or had been forcibly donated—through vari-

Empire Style. Far left: **Jean-Baptiste Regnault.** *The Three Graces.* 1799. Louvre, Paris. Left: **Baron Antoine-Jean Gros.** *Napoleon on the Bridge at Arcola.* 1796. Louvre, Paris. *Photo Giraudon, Paris.*

Empire Style. Above: **Joseph Chinard.** *Bust of a Young Man. c.* 1802. Musée Municipal d'Art et d'Industrie, St-Étienne. *Photo Giraudon, Paris.* Below: **Charles Percier and Pierre Fontaine.** *Arc de Triomphe du Carrousel*, Paris. 1806–8. *Photo Chevojon, Paris.*

James Ensor. *Ray.* 1892. Musée Royal des Beaux-Arts, Brussels. *Photo A.C.L., Brussels.*

ous treaties—by the states that passed under Napoleon's rule.

ENDELL, August (1871, Berlin—1925, Breslau), German architect. While in Munich, he was closely associated with two of the leading designers of Art Nouveau, Hermann Obrist (1863–1927) and Richard Reimerschmid (1868–1957). His most celebrated work was the Elvira Photographic Studio in Munich (1897–98; destroyed by Hitler's orders as an example of "decadent" art), which was remarkable not only for the Rococo decorations within and the extraordinary dragonlike shape splayed over the façade, but also for its asymmetrical door and window openings. In the Elvira Studio Endell was experimenting with his original theories on the emotional effect of certain architectural proportions, discussed in his essay, *Formenschönheit und dekorative Kunst* ("Beauty of Form and Decorative Art"), published in the periodical *Dekorative Kunst* (1898). He remodeled the Buntes Theater, Berlin (1901), an old dance hall, with a curving proscenium arch and Art Nouveau decoration at its most fantastic. The department stores and other buildings he subsequently built in Breslau and Berlin were more subdued. Endell also designed jewelry, furniture, and textiles. In 1918 he was appointed director of the Breslau Academy of Fine and Applied Arts.

ENSOR, James (1860, Ostend—1949, Ostend), Belgian painter and engraver. At the age of nineteen and while still a student at the Brussels Academy, Ensor was already producing paintings that inaugurated the style of his first maturity. His subjects at this time included portraits, middle-class interiors, and some landscapes and still lifes. He was more concerned with light than with objects and faces, creating a light that enriched the work of this period with delicate and exquisite nuances (*Afternoon at Ostend*, 1881; Antwerp, Musée Royal des Beaux-Arts).

Toward 1884 Ensor had adopted the palette of the French Impressionists, to whom he was also linked by his deep veneration of light. Nevertheless, the freedom with which he interpreted the color of objects in order to enhance their quality, or to render them more uncommon, ties him less to the Impressionists than to Bonnard, particularly the post-1910 Bonnard. Understandably, he allowed himself the fullest freedom when painting the sea or the sky of Ostend, or in such scenes as *Carnival on the Beach* (Quarengnon, Coll. Madame Van Weyenbergh).

But Ensor was not solely a poet of light. Although increasingly estranged from reality, he remained interested in people, even if he no longer treated them with the respect shown earlier; nevertheless, he saw in man above all a grotesque creature that excited his irony and his satiric sense. Time and again Ensor stages a show of clown faces or of skeletons draped in absurd, tawdry, and multicolored rags (*Skeletons Warming Themselves at a Stove*, 1889; Dallas, Coll. Windfhor). There is one that stands out above the others, at least by its dimensions (*c.* 9 ft. × 12 ft.) and its spectacular character: the *Entry of Christ into Brussels* (1888; Knokke-Zoute, Belgium, Casino Communal). Under a broad red banner bearing the inscription "Vive la Sociale" ("long live the Social State"), a motley crowd of tatterdemalions with jeering clownish faces jostle and push in the uproar of a fairground, forming an escort to Christ mounted on an ass. The color is pure, impassioned, truculent, strident, and dissonant as a blare of trumpets. The touch is broad, the drawing summary and a little coarse.

To grasp the full significance of this painting, one must remember that Ensor painted it in 1888, which is to say that his vision at that time was as "advanced" as Van Gogh's and more forward-looking than Gauguin's. He was unquestionably one of the initiators of the non-representational painting that ultimately dominated the 20th century, as well as being one of the precursors of Expressionism.

EPSTEIN, Sir Jacob (1880, New York—1959, London), English sculptor, born of Russo-Polish parents. In 1907 he carved 18 statues for the British Medical Association Building, London, and the acute controversy these aroused, on grounds of indecency, was a foretaste of the abuse and sensationalism that Epstein was to attract throughout his life. In 1911 he was commissioned to execute the tomb of Oscar Wilde in the Père-Lachaise cemetery, Paris. For some time he was attracted to Vorticism (an offshoot of Futurism) and later he became one of the founding members of the London Group (*c.* 1914). From that time on, however, Epstein followed his own inclinations, remaining outside the great contemporary movements. Indifferent to technical innovation, he continued to work concurrently in two styles, carving directly in stone on a colossal scale, and, in his more intimate works, modeling in bronze with great freedom of touch. His large-scale sculptures—*Rima* (1925), *Genesis* (1931), *Ecce Homo* (1935), *Adam* (1939), *Lazarus* (1949), and *Monument to the Dead of the Working Class* (1959)—often offended the general public for what appears to be their deliberate brutality.

Epstein's portraits, on the other hand, always found favor with the public. They are brilliantly executed, with great flair and an almost painterly concern for light, shade, and texture. He was the major portraitist of the great men of the 20th century: among those who sat for him were *Einstein, Shaw, Conrad, Somerset Maugham, Nehru,* and *Paul Robeson.*

Epstein also produced bronzes of a monumental nature, for example, the *Visitation* (1926), *Lucifer* (1945); *Christ in Majesty* (1957), for the cathedral of Llandaff, near Cardiff, Wales; and *St. Michael* (1962), for the new cathedral at Coventry. His *Madonna and Child* (1950–52), for the Convent of the Holy Child Jesus in Cavendish Square, London, is considered by many to be the finest work of public sculpture to have appeared in London in the 20th century.

ERICHSEN, Thorvald (1868, Trondheim—1939, Oslo), Norwegian painter. He was deeply affected by Impressionism and for some time, like Monet, painted series of pictures of the same subject under varying atmospheric conditions. His color lacks Monet's brilliance and his objects are less immaterialized, for he uses light to model them, as a realist painter would, rather than to dissolve them. His art, which later showed Bonnard's influence (*Interior*, 1930; Coll. J. Sejorsted Bødtker), is rich and varied. Erichsen was a highly sensitive but impressionable painter who remained an isolated figure throughout his life.

ERNI, Hans (b. 1909, Lucerne), Swiss painter. Although he was trained as an architect and worked as a commercial artist, he went on to a career as a painter. In 1928–29 he visited Paris for the first time, attending classes at the Académie Julian and visiting the Louvre assiduously. He then discovered contemporary painting and joined the Abstraction-Création group. Erni's enormous output includes work in practically every field of painting, and in a number of styles, including a rather hard-edged dry manner, often in tempera, and a looser pen-and-ink technique. He did several important murals (*Three Graces of Lucerne*, 1935, Lucerne, Railroad Station; *Creative Energy*, 1946, London, Royal Institute of British Architects; *Conquests of Man*, 1954, Neuchâtel, Musée d'Ethnographie), posters, book illustrations, and lithographs. His art lacks neither technique nor compositional sense, but rather the energy necessary to fulfill his high ambitions.

ERNST, Max (1891, Brühl, near Cologne—1976, Paris), naturalized French painter of German origin, one of the leading Surrealist artists. After completing studies in philosophy at the University of Bonn (1911), he decided to devote himself to painting. In 1914 he met Jean Arp at the Werkbund exhibition in Cologne. After World War I, he founded the Dada group of Cologne with Johannes Theodor Baargeld (d. 1927); together with Arp and Baargeld he published the single issue of the review *Die Schammade* (1920). This was also the period of his first collages, so different from those of the Cubists, particularly the famous *Fatagaga* series, begun with Jean Arp.

In 1922 Ernst settled in Paris, collaborated on the review *Littérature*, and became friendly with the poets André Breton, Paul Éluard, Louis Aragon, Philippe Soupault, Robert Desnos, René Crevel, Benjamin Péret, and other members of the future Surrealist group, all of whom figured, together with Raphael and Dostoevski, in a painting of 1922, *Au Rendez-vous des Amis* (Hamburg, Coll. Dr. L. Bau). He also participated in the first exhibition of the Surrealist group at the Galerie Pierre, Paris, in 1925 and soon perfected the technique of *frottage*: by placing pieces of paper haphazardly on flooring and then rubbing them over with a pencil, Ernst produced imprints that became mysterious works peopled by strange animals and disturbing landscapes (published in a portfolio, *Histoire Naturelle*, 1926). Soon the artist extended this rubbing technique to a variety of materials. Thus were born the artist's astonishing "Surrealist reveries," of which the *Vision Inspired by the Nocturnal Aspect of Porte St-Denis* (1927; Brussels, Coll. Mabille) remains one of the most striking.

Ernst's activities increased. He collaborated on the sets for *Roméo et Juliette* for the Ballets Russes (1926) and *Ubu enchaîné* for the Comédie des Champs-Elysées (1937); published the collage-novels *La Femme 100 Têtes* (1929) and *Une Semaine de Bonté* (1934); and executed strange lunar sculptures. In 1936 his style of painting underwent a transformation with the themes of the *Nymph Echo* (1936; New York, Museum of Modern Art) and *Ville entière* (1936; Carcassonne, Coll. James Du Cellier), showing tangled, stifling forests of uncontainable growth. With World War II Ernst was forced to take refuge in the United States, where he edited (1942–44) the review *V V V* with Breton and Marcel Duchamp and worked on Hans Richter's film, *Dreams That Money Can Buy* (1945).

In 1953 he returned to Paris with Dorothea Tanning, whom he had married in 1946; he was by then a famous artist. The Venice Biennale awarded him its Grand Prize in 1954, and he was a jury member of the Prix de Rome in 1961. In his later years Max Ernst became a truly excellent painter. When he sought to communicate his obsessions, he was convincing despite an expression that was more literary than plastic. Such works as *Un peu de Calme* (1939), *Europe After the Rain* (1940–42; Hartford, Wadsworth Athenaeum), and *La Nuit rhénane* (1944; Priv. Coll.) wove their spell, taking us back to prehistoric times of fossils, river deposits, decaying flora, and monsters.

ESKIMO ART. It is generally thought that, like the other "aboriginal" inhabitants of America, the Eskimos came from Asia across the Bering Strait. Their livelihood depends mainly on fishing and hunting the great sea mammals, although the hunting of various land animals, particularly caribou, is also highly developed. Their art is limited by their way of life to the decoration of clothing, which is made of different-colored strips of fur; the engraving of tools, most of which are made of ivory from the tusks of walruses or from antler tines or bones; and small sculptures carved from the same materials and also stone. Many of their utilitarian objects, such as toggle pins and arrow straighteners, are shaped like animals of the region. The earliest known traces of Eskimo activity are mainly stone implements dating from about 2000 B.C. (the Denbigh Culture). Much later, around the beginning of our era, three main cultural streams made their appearance, two in the western region and a third covering the whole of the eastern region. The western traditions are unquestionably the more interesting. The decoration of tools originally consisted of incised parallel lines (the Kachemak Culture, 500–1000 A.D.), and sculpture was limited to small, roughly carved human figures; but Eskimo art suddenly advanced greatly, with an extensive production of

Jacob Epstein. *Madonna and Child.* 1950–52. Convent of the Holy Child Jesus, Cavendish Square, London.

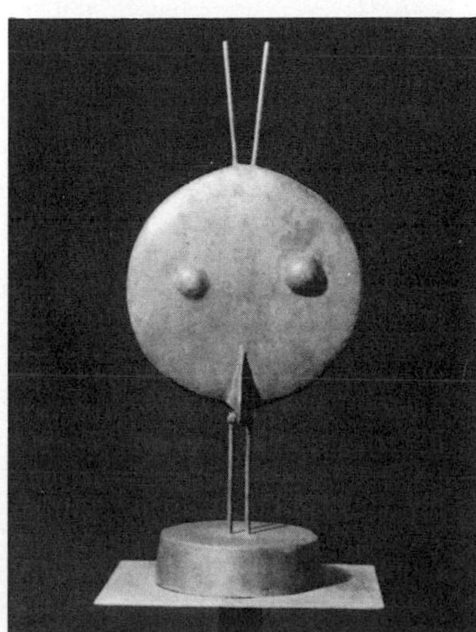

Max Ernst. *La Belle Allemande.* 1934. *Photo Walter Dräyer, Zurich.*

Eskimo Art. Salmon inua. Southwest Alaska. Coll. André Breton, Paris. *Photo Jean Lavaud, Paris.*

naturalistic representations of animals in ivory and of masks carved from wood or bone. The special quality of these masks is their intimate mixture of the realistic, imaginative, and supernatural elements characteristic of Eskimo art in general. The most striking of the many types in use are the *inua*: used in religious ceremonies as a means of communicating with the supernatural world, they are relics of a time when man and animals had not yet become entirely separate concepts. At the same time, the art of incising and engraving was enriched by a new kind of decoration, that of circles traced with a primitive compass, permitting new motifs: concentric circles, a point and circle.

The other branch of western Eskimo art was indigenous to northern Alaska. The main cultures were the Okvik, centered in the island of St. Lawrence, south of the Bering Strait, and the Old Bering Sea Culture (early 1st millennium A.D.). Here too the technique of engraving was widespread: everyday objects such as harpoons, axes, and the needle-boxes were decorated in a curvilinear style, with clusters of parallel lines, circles, and ellipses drawn freehand. One of the distinctive features of the ancient culture of the Bering Sea is its numerous spiral motifs. Without precedent in Eskimo art, they recall the Scytho-Siberian decorative style. Besides decorative work, these cultures produced some remarkable stylized human figures, notable examples of which are the so-called Okvik Madonna (College, Alaska, University of Alaska Museum) and Okvik Venus (Washington, National Museum). Near Point Hope traces have been found of a culture known as the Ipiutak (*c.* 2nd–7th century), closely related to the Old Bering Sea Culture but richer in invention and materials. Pieces of iron of probable Asiatic origin have been found, as well as bones arranged in rings, which are almost certainly a replica in organic matter of an original metal model. Sculpture in the strict sense of the word includes not only masks but also zoomorphic statuettes. With the Punuk period (*c.* 600–13th century and later), there was a noticeable stiffening, particularly in the engraving, which became more schematic; but it was accompanied by pictographic decoration representing hunting scenes, in which the modeling of the animal forms seems close in inspiration to the Paleolithic art of Europe. Painted scenes were rare, however; among the most curious are those used to decorate the drums of medicine men.

The eastern branch of Arctic art is undoubtedly less interesting. The Dorset Culture (2nd century A.D. to close of the 1st millennium) was centered in Hudson Bay, though traces of it have been found as far north as Baffin Island and as far south as Newfoundland. Its peoples do not appear to have been influenced by the ideas that reached the Eskimos of Alaska from Siberia. For their miniature sculpture they used wood or bone, sometimes ivory, modeling coarse effigies with broad faces and thickset figures. The Thule Culture (*c.* 900–1800) in Canada and the Inugsuk (*c.* 1400) in Greenland are the immediate sources of modern Eskimo civilization. Surviving evidence of these cultures consists mainly of simply formed everyday objects, but animal and human figures were also produced. The Angmassalik region in east Greenland produced a more distinctive art, however, comprising realistic wooden masks that were often exaggerated to the point of caricature.

In our own time, both in the east and the west, the Eskimos have continued to make statuettes of men and animals; particularly successful are representations of birds used as dice in a game of chance. Under the influence of missionaries and traders, the Eskimos turned to sculpture in steatite. Animated by the elemental qualities that dominate the lives of the Eskimos, these sculptures, though hybrid, retain an impression of mass and vigor.

ESTÈVE, Maurice (b. 1904, Culan, Cher), French painter. Although he attended the free studios of Montparnasse, his real artistic training took place in the solitude that was to be his preferred milieu for creation. In 1923 Estève visited Spain, where he directed the design studio of a weaving mill in Barcelona.

From 1924 to 1929, Estève showed an interest in the innovations of Van Gogh, Cézanne, and the Surrealists; later he was attracted by the work of Fernand Léger. But from 1935 his vision became more subjective, more detached from naturalistic formulas; by 1938 he had built up a highly personal repertoire of forms and colors in which the human figure was linked to everyday objects within a firmly constructed composition (the *Interiors* of 1942). Then, around 1944, the structure of his paintings became more flexible, without losing any of its firmness. From 1947 his forms, though cohesive and linked by strong, fluid articulations, lost their dependence on the world of appearances to become subject to the logic of purely formal considerations (the *Lithographer*, 1950; Paris, Coll. Mr. and Mrs. Jean Fossez). From a vision and technique in a perpetual state of renewal, he produced a body of work that reconciled opulence and sensual beauty with economy and an almost unparalleled intellectual discipline.

ETHIOPIAN ART. The oldest surviving buildings date from 500 B.C., and belong to an Ethiopian civilization related to the Sabaean culture of southwest Arabia. A

Eskimo Art. Shaman mask (?). Alaska. Coll. Georges Duthuit, Paris. *Photo Jean Lavaud, Paris.*

succession of towns and temples stretched across the high plateaus from the port of Adulis to the capital, Aksum. Inside the ruins of temples, statues have been found that show impassive, seated figures draped in togas. Also discovered were votive thrones decorated with bas-reliefs, incense altars, and inscriptions in Sabaean letters that are as pure as those of Greek epigraphy. The prosperity of Aksum is indicated by the remaining foundations of its great palaces, and especially by the funerary steles, monoliths of hard gray stone that once lined the white limestone terraces. Only one remains standing today: known as the great stele of Aksum, it is about 70 feet high, and dates from the 5th century B.C. The occasional bronze figurines and pieces of decorated pottery that have been uncovered make clear how regrettable it is that so much should have been lost of a past that owed nothing to Pharaonic Egypt, and that marked a radically new and original departure from its south Arabian parent culture.

From the 3rd to the 9th century A.D., the emperors of Aksum, whose powers extended as far as Arabia, struck coins that bore their forceful images. In the 4th century A.D., one of these rulers, Ezana, was converted to Christianity. Ethiopia has always remained faithful to that conversion, and has dedicated its art to the expression of this religion. The oldest churches, with façades combining timberwork and stone, resemble the pagan temples that preceded them. The two churches near Aksum, built on the site of the tombs of Emperor Caleb (514–42) and his son and successor, Gabra Maskal, as well as the venerable monasteries of Debra Damo and Abba Mata, both at Ham (the latter, unfortunately, destroyed in 1961), are further examples of this type of construction.

Ethiopian ecclesiastical art reached its peak in the 12th century, under the short-lived Zagwe dynasty. During this period, King Lalibela (1182–1220) had built nearly a dozen monolithic churches in the city that today perpetuates his name. Carved out of solid rock, they display an extraordinary variety of design.

After 1270 (the year in which the Solomenid emperors returned to the throne), a large number of convents and monasteries were built. The most magnificent of these churches were destroyed in the Moslem invasion of 1530–31. All that survived were manuscripts, whose iconography conforms to Syrian or Armenian models; their linear stylization is admirable, and their warm colors recall the effects achieved in stained glass or tapestries.

Ethiopia was devastated by the Moslems, but rose again. In 1541 a Portuguese force disembarked in Ethiopia and contracted an alliance with the Ethiopians to drive out the Moslems. The Portuguese built a number of churches, and brought with them a new architectural style as well as Syrian and Indian craftsmen. From 1632, the new capital of Gondar boasted castles whose towers, crenellated walls, and balconies are very similar to Renaissance architecture of the West. Gondar's numerous churches had interiors adorned with hundreds of scenes from Biblical and Christian history. This period saw the building of the first of those circular churches that even today are one of the main attractions of the Ethiopian landscape; many abbeys also sprang up on the islands of Lake Tana. Manuscript illustrations of the time show a marked interest in groups of figures, in movement, and in the picturesque details of stories and costumes. After being abandoned for a century, Gondar was laid waste in 1888 by the dervishes from Sudan. Everywhere else in Ethiopia, artists continued to paint the interior walls of churches, supplementing Old and New Testament subjects with scenes from Ethiopian history.

The tradition of religious pomp lives on today in Ethiopia, and may be seen even in its folk art, which is rich in pious images. The variety of present-day Christian jewelry is also extraordinary, epitomizing every style that has existed in Ethiopia over the last several thousand years.

ÉTIENNE-MARTIN, Martin Étienne, *called* (b. 1913, Loriol, Drôme), French sculptor. He went to Paris in 1933 and worked at the Académie Ranson under the influential direction of Charles Malfray (1887–1940). Called up in 1939, Étienne-Martin was taken prisoner in 1940 and released in 1942; he settled at Dieulefit in the Drôme, then, in 1944, at Mortagne in the Orne with the painter Alfred Manessier. A great admirer of the Baroque and of the Surrealists, Étienne-Martin revealed this in his art by a tendency toward convulsive and ecstatic creations. Wood, in the form of large blocks of knotty roots, remained one of his favorite materials (*Great Dragon*, 1945; *Of Them*, 1956). But in 1948 he began a series of sculptures in fabric similar to those of nomads' tents. From 1950 he devoted most of his time to the series of *Dwellings*, huge labyrinthine constructions that seem to abolish all distinction between notions of void and volume.

ETRUSCAN ART. If one is to believe Herodotus (5th century B.C.), the Etruscans came by sea from Lydia; other hypotheses repeat the assertion of Dionysius of Halicarnassus (1st century B.C.) that they were an autochthonous people, and the question of their origin remains unresolved. In the realm of art, the Etruscans developed an original culture profoundly reflective of their religious beliefs. In the 7th century B.C., the Etruscan civilization succeeded the so-called Villanovan culture, and experienced its greatest expansion in the 6th and 5th centuries B.C., disintegrating only with its gradual incorporation into the Roman sphere (beginning with the town of Veii in 396 B.C.), a process that was accompanied by considerable Etruscan influence on Rome.

From their first appearance, Etruscan art and artifacts betray their Oriental origin by a taste for precious materials such as gold, silver, ivory, and bronze; by the use of such meticulous techniques as filigree and granulation, no

Ethiopian Art. Great stele. Aksum. 5th century B.C. *Photo Toni Schneiders, Lindau.*

Etruscan Art. Cinerary urn. Sarteano, late 7th century B.C. Museo Archeologico, Florence. *Photo Walter Dräyer, Zurich.*

Etruscan Art. Head of a warrior. Orvieto, 530–20 B.C. Museo Archeologico, Florence. *Photo Walter Dräyer, Zurich.*

doubt borrowed from Syria, Mesopotamia, and Asia Minor, where they were practiced; and especially by a choice of motifs in which decorative values are predominant. The Etruscans' lively imagination led them to multiply lines and scrolls, to juxtapose volutes and spirals, and to stretch out linear patterns. They clearly enjoyed producing regular rows of lions, sphinxes, and birds, which we find even on their jewelry: most notable are the charming rows of birds, ducks in particular, on Etruscan pins and brooches. A taste for linear decoration led the Etruscans to adopt the technique of incision, which produced pieces of great beauty when used on objects of bronze. These include mirrors with scenes from mythology and from domestic life, and cists, of which those made at Praeneste are best known. One masterpiece in this genre of illustration portrays the legend of the Argonauts in great detail and with a fine sense of design, composition, and attitude.

Monsters, fantastic animals, and all the equivocal creatures that an unbridled imagination could invent, figure in Etruscan painting and sculpture. The bronze chimera from Arezzo (5th century B.C.), now in the Museo Archeologico, Florence, has a lion's body with a tail turning into a snake, which snaps at the horns of a goat springing out of the lion's back. This triumphant delight in the irrational is a common theme both on vases and in tomb paintings.

On the other hand their sense of realism and observation of living models make their representations of animals the most accurate of ancient times. They observed birds and fishes, delineating them in a wide variety of poses that revealed impressive powers of observation. The famous Roman wolf of bronze, whose full udders are well displayed by the cunning placement of the hind legs and whose flanks are expertly modeled under the taut skin, is a masterpiece of 5th-century B.C. Etruscan art.

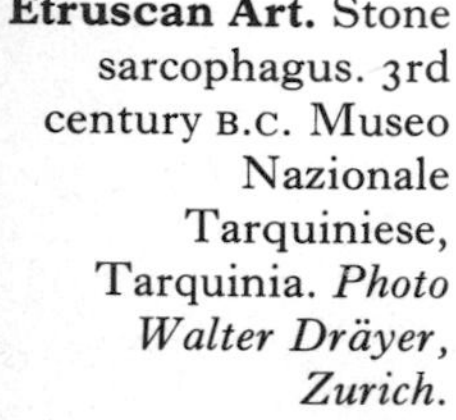

Etruscan Art. Stone sarcophagus. 3rd century B.C. Museo Nazionale Tarquiniese, Tarquinia. *Photo Walter Dräyer, Zurich.*

There is the same marked contrast, not to say contradiction, in other fields of Etruscan art. Architecture, as far as one can judge, seems to have been governed by concerns of a practical order. The town walls of the 4th century B.C., solidly built of large quadrangular blocks set in a regular pattern, follow the natural undulations of the ground. The same practical considerations are evident in the temples, whose squat proportions are accentuated by the length of the façade, which had to allow room for the three cellae obligatory in the Etruscan tradition. As the Etruscans very often built in wood and brick, no fine buildings have been preserved, and we have to fall back on adaptations in the famous tombs of Tarquinia, Cerveteri, and Chiusi. These tombs, carved out of soft rock in the region stretching from the Arno to the Tiber, preserve the layout and the elements (pillars, capitals, friezes) of Etruscan religious and domestic architecture. But the creative imagination of the Etruscans can be seen again in their temples, which were decorated with figures in relief or in the round and heightened by color.

Plaques were decorated with friezes of animals, intended as a protection against evil and derived from Oriental sources. In southern Etruria, files of marching warriors or galloping horsemen were more usual: a frieze of this sort, found on the Esquiline in Rome, represents gods and heroes mounting chariots drawn by winged steeds. The beam-ends of temple corners were reserved for Gorgonic heads, except where—as at Veii and Capua—graceful figures of divinities sprang from a spreading palmette. There are some famous works among the groups and free-standing figures from pediments or roof tops. For example, the two winged horses found shortly before 1939 at Tarquinia were sculptured in relief on a plaque that filled a pediment space. Their style resembles Greek art of the 4th century B.C., and they give a very lively impression of horses pawing the ground ready to start. From a different period comes the famous terra-cotta Apollo from the great temple at Veii, which is influenced by mid-6th century B.C. Ionian sculpture. It came from a group representing Apollo and Heracles in the presence of Hermes, quarreling over a slaughtered deer.

Their natural taste and their religious preoccupations made Etruscan artists turn away from idealization of human features. The Etruscans believed that when the dead man was represented on his tomb, his individual features should be recognizable, so that the deity could identify him. This is the reason for the great number of funeral masks and statues found in tombs.

The magnificent frescoes from the tombs of Tarquinia and Cerveteri also reveal a spirit that is both free and profoundly conservative. They are richly colored, with varied shades of green, blue, light yellow, and ocher added to the fundamental red, black, and white. The subjects are taken from mythology or from domestic life. Nothing could be more evocative of subtlety, creative vigor, and a sense of life and movement than the banqueting scenes and groups of musicians and dancers that were intended to bring delight into the monotonous days of the occupants of the so-called Tomb of the Leopards at Tarquinia.

ETTY, William (1787, York—1849, York), English painter of mythological nudes. In 1807 he became a student at the Royal Academy Schools and a pupil of Sir Thomas Lawrence, whose brilliant, warm technique he faithfully copied. In 1815 Etty went to France, and in the following year to Italy. Returning via Paris, he entered the studios of Jean-Baptiste Regnault (1754–1829), but stayed only about a week. Regnault's influence is apparent in the picture with which Etty gained recognition, *Cleopatra's Arrival in Cilicia* (1821; Port Sunlight, Lady Lever Art Gallery). Further visits to France and Italy in 1821–23 gave him an opportunity to study painters whom he was temperamentally inclined to follow: Pierre-Narcisse Guérin, Rubens, Titian, Van Dyck, and Giulio Romano. Meanwhile, he continued to attend the life class and to exhibit highly finished mythological scenes at the Royal Academy (*Youth on the Prow and Pleasure at the Helm,* 1832; London, Tate Gallery).

Etty's pictures seem to present a contradiction in terms: extreme physical sensuality combined with complete emotional vapidity. On the rare occasions when he succeeds in his compositional schemes, the result has a warmth and weight unusual in British art (*Hero's Farewell to Leander*, 1827, Tate Gallery; *Britomart Redeems Fair Amoret*, 1833, Lady Lever Gallery). He presents superficial resemblances to Delacroix, notably in the strength of his color and the occasional liquid brilliance of his handling; but his painting of *Venus and Her Satellites* (1835; London, Coll. A. Devas), with its superb torsos and simpering attitudes, stamps him irrevocably as a follower of Guérin and Pierre-Paul Prud'hon.

EUSTON ROAD SCHOOL, association of teachers and pupils founded in London in 1937 as a painting school by Sir William Coldstream, Victor Pasmore, and Claude Rogers (b. 1907). The group, which ceased to be an educational establishment in 1939, also included Lawrence Gowing (b. 1918) and Graham Bell (1907–43). Although their aims were never very clearly formulated, the members were united in their opposition to the extreme tendencies of modern art and in their attempt to restore the validity of representational painting and the commonplace subject. The use of muted colors and a consciously unobtrusive technique are characteristic of the Euston Road School.

EVENEPOEL, Henri (1872, Nice—1899, Paris), French painter of Belgian origin. He spent his youth in Brussels, then settled in Paris in 1892 to continue his artistic studies. He entered the studio of Gustave Moreau in the École des Beaux-Arts, where he became friendly with Rouault, Matisse, and Albert Marquet. He paid close attention to the work of Toulouse-Lautrec and Jean-Louis Forain (1852–1931), whose influence may be seen in his paintings of the Parisian scene. Evenepoel soon became enthusiastic about the art of Manet, whose example he followed in his portraits, the genre in which he produced his most remarkable work.

In 1897 Evenepoel spent several months in Algeria, where his palette became a little brighter and warmer but hardly brilliant. His tender melancholy found expression in discreet and rare harmonies like those of the Nabis, with whom he also shared an interest in the sights of the streets and parks of Paris.

EVERGOOD, Philip (b. 1901, New York—d. 1973), American painter. Educated in England at Eton and Cambridge at the insistence of his parents, Evergood was later drawn to painting. He painted for a short while at the Académie Julian in Paris, but he was disappointed with the teaching methods there, and began a long period of self-training. He returned to America in 1926, yet remained there only three years before traveling to Europe again. He went back to the United States in 1931 during the depths of the Depression, which had much to do with the turn his painting would take shortly after. In 1933 he enrolled in the Federal Public Works of Art Project, and in the next few years he produced his most militant social protest paintings. These works also relate him to the social realist trend that was characteristic of American painting during the 1930s (*New Lazarus*, 1927–54; New York, Whitney Museum).

Evergood's propagandistic style was tempered in time, and he eventually returned to his earlier themes of bizarre fantasy. Yet even in a gay and seemingly innocent work such as *Lily and the Sparrows* (1939; New York, Whitney Museum), his preoccupation with the sordid conditions of life remains evident.

EWORTH *or* **EWOUTSZ,** Hans (b. Antwerp; active 1545/49–1575, England), Flemish artist who worked in England, mainly as a portrait painter. Although many of his works are extant, little is known of his life beyond the fact that he enjoyed the patronage of the English court from around 1554. At its best, his style is firmly rooted in the tradition of Holbein, with vigorous references to Jan van Scorel and Quinten Massys, as in his portrait of *Lady Dacre* (*c.* 1555; Ottawa, National Gallery of Canada), inset with a portrait of the sitter's husband in the style of Holbein. What enlivens Eworth's style is a taste for Mannerist allegory that must stem from a purely Flemish source. One of his earliest dated portraits, that of *Sir John Luttrell* (1550; Somerset, Dunster Castle, Coll. G. F. Luttrell), shows the subject naked to the waist, plunging through a stormy sea with a broken ship in the background; he raises a clenched fist that is embraced by a pseudo-classical figure of peace with her attendants. Less spectacular but more ambitious is the portrait of *Queen Elizabeth Confounding Juno, Minerva, and Venus* (1569; Middlesex, Hampton Court Palace), an unexpected version of the Judgment of Paris. His more straightforward portraits, notably the several versions of *Mary Tudor* (one in Windsor, Royal Collection), are considerably less cluttered in their settings and are probably conscious emulations of the work of the queen's favorite painter, Antonio Moro.

EXPRESSIONISM, term denoting both a style in art and a 20th-century art movement in northern Europe. Whereas the terms Impressionism, Fauvism, Cubism, Futurism, and Surrealism apply to clearly defined contemporary groups or movements, Expressionism refers as well to a permanent tendency in art that is characteristic of the Nordic countries in times of social stress or spiritual disturbance. Considered

Philip Evergood. *The New Lazarus.* 1927–54. Whitney Museum of American Art, New York. *Photo Oliver Baker Associates, Inc., New York.*

Expressionism. David Alfaro Siqueiros. *Peasant Mother.* 1929. National Museum of Fine Arts, Mexico City. *Photo Giraudon, Paris.*

in its strictest terms, Expressionism constitutes the present tragic phase of Romanticism, bound to the anguish of our times and to the resurgence of the Slavic and Nordic spirits. Unlike the painters of the School of Paris, who wanted to create an international language, Expressionist artists favored individual and ethnic distinctions.

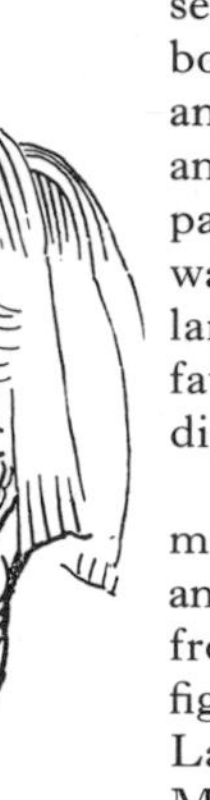

Expressionism. Oskar Kokoschka. *Portrait of Herwarth Walden.*

The first Expressionist movement, incorporating Symbolist and Art Nouveau influences, lasted from 1885 to 1900. Its leading figures were Van Gogh, Toulouse-Lautrec, James Ensor, Edvard Munch, and Ferdinand Hodler. Their subjectivism expressed itself in obsessional and dramatic themes, and through intensity of color, monumentality of forms, and the violence and sharpness of their drawing.

Hodler, Munch, and Ensor figured in the second wave of Expressionism, which arose around 1905 in Germany with the creation of the group called the Brücke, and in France with the decisive contributions of Rouault, Picasso (blue and Negro periods), Matisse, and the Fauves. Munch, a Norwegian, was the central figure of Nordic Expressionism, and left his mark both in Germany and Scandinavia, where his influence is comparable with that of Cézanne in France. The Secession movement, which included numerous Expressionist artists who rejected participation in exhibitions sponsored by the academies, soon spread to Munich, Vienna, and Berlin.

Expressionism took firm root in the Brücke group, nurtured by Munch, Van Gogh, and Negro sculpture; in a general way it permeated the various currents in Germany up to the formation of the Blaue Reiter group in Munich on the eve of World War II. Emil Nolde and Ernst Ludwig Kirchner, specifically Germanic temperaments, rebelled against the art of Paris. In Vienna, at the very moment when Freud, in the same city, was developing psychoanalysis, Egon Schiele and Oscar Kokoschka executed striking series of portraits resembling flights into the subconscious. A new ferment was brought into art through the nostalgia, anguish, and tenderness of such exiled artists as Chaim Soutine, Jules Pascin, and Marc Chagall, who settled in Paris before 1914. Expressionism reached the United States in about 1908 through Max Weber.

The interim period between the two wars stabilized itself into a kind of Neoclassicism, interrupted by only one revolutionary art movement, Surrealism. But the great masters of Expressionism—Munch, Ensor, Rouault, Nolde, Soutine, Kokoschka, and Weber—continued on their own, each perfecting his own work, while national forms of Expressionism developed in other countries, notably in Belgium, with the school of Laethem-St-Martin (Constant Permeke, Gustave de Smet, Fritz van den Berghe—1883–1939); in Brazil (Lasar Segall, Candido Portinari), and particularly in Mexico (Diego Rivera, José Clemente Orozco, David Alfaro Siqueiros, Rufino Tamayo) in the monumental and popular form of the fresco. Defeated Germany tried desperately to react against its instinctive Romanticism, but the so-called New Objectivism group (*Die Neue Sachlichkeit*), graced with the presence of artists such as Otto Dix, George Grosz, and Max Beckmann, dominated the last phase of Expressionism, endowing it with such trenchant realism and social violence that it was condemned by the Nazis. Beckmann took refuge in Holland, where Expressionism evolved in a parallel manner (Jan Sluyters, Jan Toorop). After the 1929 crisis, Expressionism gained many recruits in the United States, notably Ben Shahn, Ivan Albright, Abraham Rattner (b. 1895), and Karl Knaths. The Civil War in Spain and World War II caused Picasso to adopt a new Expressionist style of hitherto unheard of violence, of which the masterpiece is *Guernica* (1937; New York, Museum of Modern Art). This brought in its wake a general revival of Expressionism—in Europe (1935–50), in Latin America, and especially in the United States, as a result of the direct influence of Beckmann and the various Germanic tendencies.

At the end of World War II, the idea of Expressionism, which had until then been reserved exclusively for figurative art, found itself associated with purely abstract experiments pursued by a whole segment of the painting world, particularly the members of the American movement known as Abstract Expressionism. The term was sufficiently flexible to embrace painters as different as Hans Hartung or Wols (Wolfgang Schulze) in France, Emilio Vedova in Italy, and Jackson Pollock in the United States. However, so broad an interpretation admits as Expressionist everything that is not pure geometric abstraction, as derived from Mondrian or the Constructivists.

The very exaggeration of such a definition, the breadth and variety of the styles it encompasses, is enough to render it useless. Thus it would seem preferable to limit this already ambiguous term to the generation of American painters who, encouraged by the experiments of the Surrealists, began to turn to the exploration of the subconscious and the expression of the irrational. This generation, grouped around Jackson Pollock (the creator of action painting), included among its most influential members Willem de

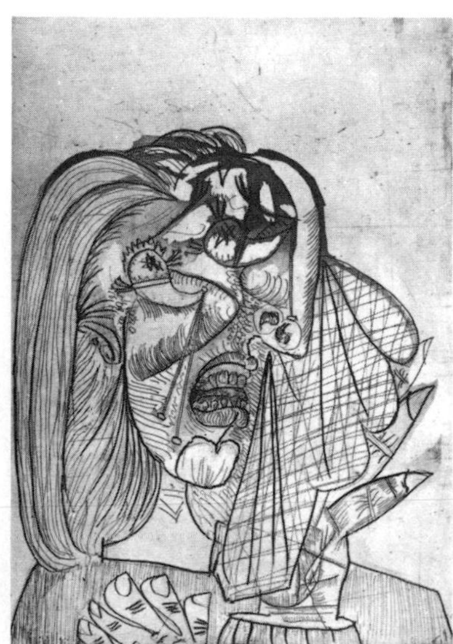

Expressionism. Pablo Picasso. *Weeping Woman.* 1937. Penrose Coll., London.

Kooning, Mark Rothko, Franz Kline, Clyfford Still, and Robert Motherwell.

EYCK, Jan (*c.* 1390, probably Maaseik, Limburg—1441, Bruges) *and* Hubert (?) van, Flemish painters. There is some doubt that Hubert, the elder brother, ever existed. We know that Jan had a brother, not a painter, whose name was Lambert. The tradition that arose after 1565 concerning Hubert's existence is a confused one. A partly indecipherable quatrain on the frame of the altarpiece of the *Mystic Lamb*, designating Hubert as painter of the polyptych, actually postdates the execution of the work, if one is to believe the microchemical examination. As for the slab in the lapidary museum at Ghent, supposedly from Hubert's grave, its inscription, dated 1426, was appended in the 16th century. However, Hubert has eminent partisans among art historians, and the grand debate, begun in 1930, is so little resolved that a recent author claimed to see portraits of the brothers in the figures of the two burghers, one with his back turned, who gaze at the landscape in the *Virgin of Autun*, more popularly known as the *Madonna of Chancellor Rolin* (*c.* 1433–34; Paris, Louvre).

The *Virgin of Autun* offers problems of documentation. It was known to have been painted by Jan about 1430–35 for the Chancellor Rolin; in 1956, however, a reputable critic put forward a theory that the landscape is a very exact view of Liège at a certain moment of history, and dated the work at around 1410–20. At the same time he rejected the traditional identification of Chancellor Rolin. The eminent art historian Erwin Panofsky nevertheless accepts the traditional identification, and dates the work *c.* 1433–34.

Few of the Van Eycks' works are signed and still fewer well documented; but the biographical facts concerning Jan are more certain. He was in the service of John of Bavaria, count of Holland, at The Hague (1422–24). He was perhaps trained at Liège; the background in his early *Virgin in the Church* (Berlin, Staatliche Museen) contains a view of the interior of the old cathedral of Liège. At the death of the count Jan entered the service of Philip the Good, duke of Burgundy (1425), and settled in Lille. He was sent on diplomatic missions to Spain (August 1426) and Portugal (October 1428), settled definitively in Bruges in 1430, married there in 1434, and died on July 9, 1441. For modern viewers Jan is regarded above all as the painter of the great polyptych in the cathedral of St Bavon in Ghent, called the altarpiece of the *Mystic Lamb* (1426–32). Even more than Jan's early works, the polyptych makes a decisive break with the prevalent International Gothic style by its large size (over 9 by 15 feet), by the new artistic ambitions it reveals, and by its masterly handling. The Christian dogma it illustrates extends over the 12 panels of the open altarpiece. In the center of the upper register is the Triumphant Christ with divine attributes, surrounded by the Virgin and St. John the Baptist, on either side of whom are groups of angelic musicians, and, in the panels on the extreme left and right, Adam and Eve, the first couple, whose transgression was redeemed by the suffering of Christ. The lower register portrays the concrete reality of earthly life. In the center the radiant Lamb, its blood flowing into a chalice, stands on an altar in the axis of the figure of Christ, related to the upper register by the Dove of the Holy Ghost. The Christian martyrs advance from the back of the central panel; in the left foreground, the prophets and patriarchs of the Old Testament are gathered, with the confessors and apostles, followed by the popes, bishops and the faithful, on the right. The defenders of the faith—the soldiers and just judges—ride forward in the 2 lower panels of the left wing, while the pilgrims and hermits advance on foot in the right. The images of the closed altarpiece, painted for the most part in grisaille or in *trompe-l'oeil*, complete this vast evocation of redemption by relating pagan premonitions (those of the Erythraean and Cumaean sibyls) and Biblical prophecies (Zachariah and Micah) to New Testament events and personages (the Annunciation, St. John the Baptist, St. John the Evangelist). In the outermost panels of the lower register, the donors, Josse Vijdt and his wife, are shown in attitudes of prayer.

Hubert (?) and Jan van Eyck. *Polyptych of the Mystic Lamb* (closed). 1426–32. St-Bavon Cathedral, Ghent. *Photo A.C.L., Brussels.*

Apart from the technical qualities, of which the sources still remain obscure, it is van Eyck's acceptance of life, his total humanism, that constitutes the "Eyckian miracle." It is felt in the portraits of the donors, in the costume and features of the sacred figures, in the angel who plays the organ, and in the figures of Adam and Eve, which are the earliest nudes in Northern painting. Van Eyck's originality consists in expressing the poetry of the world by style and fantasy combined with illusionism, in avoiding preciosity while retaining the qualities of an illuminator. These characteristics and the beauty of the colors, whether soft or enameled, translucent or opaque, are found in a number of paintings created after 1430, both portraits and religious works, which have been authenticated by a date or a signature. These are the *Portrait of a Young Man* (also called *Timotheus*, 1432; London, National Gallery); the so-called *Ince Hall Madonna* (1433; Melbourne, National Gallery of Victoria); the portrait of a *Man in a Turban* (1433; London, National Gallery); and the *Madonna with Canon van der Paele* (1436; Bruges, Groeningemuseum). In 1437 Van Eyck painted *St. Barbara*, a brush drawing on chalk background (Antwerp, Musée Royal des Beaux-Arts) and in 1439 the excellent portrait of his wife, *Margaret van Eyck* (Groeningemuseum). His finest works, apart from the *Mystic Lamb*, are the *Arnolfini Wedding Portrait* (1434; London, National Gallery) and the *Virgin of Autun*. The subject of the first picture is still uncertain, and some critics believe it to be a portrait of Van Eyck and his wife.

F

FABRITIUS, Carel (*c.* 1620, Midden-Beemster, near Amsterdam—1654, Delft), Dutch painter. He was the most gifted pupil of Rembrandt, and began working at Delft in 1647. Although at first he imitated his master in the large *Raising of Lazarus* (*c.* 1643; Warsaw, National Museum), he had sufficient talent to free himself from his influence and to express his own thoughtful and vigorous vision. From the few works that have survived, it is clear that Fabritius' interests lay in the intellectual aspects of painting, in the study of perspective in limpid light, in careful composition, and in managing his naturally thick and heavy handling of paint with the greatest firmness (the *Soldier*, 1654; Schwerin, Staatliches Museum). His best work, the *Goldfinch* (1654; The Hague, Mauritshuis), has an immediate appeal because of its illusionistic effects.

BARENT (1624–1673), Carel's brother, was also a painter, and is best known for his Biblical scenes, many of which are in the Rijksmuseum, Amsterdam.

FALCONET, Étienne-Maurice (1716, Paris—1791, Paris), French sculptor. Son of a journeyman joiner, he studied with Jean-Baptiste Lemoyne, from whom he learned how to achieve the spark of life that animated his works. Falconet admired Pierre Puget and declared himself a partisan of sculpture that was "living, animated, passionate." He had known Madame de Pompadour when she was still only Madame d'Étioles, and for her château at Bellevue he carved in marble an allegorical figure of *Music* (1751; Paris, Louvre), representing the beautiful royal favorite in the title role of the opera *Eglé*, which she had interpreted for the king. In 1754 he presented his *Milo of Crotona* (Louvre) as a reception piece at the Académie Royale de Peinture et de Sculpture. His reputation was assured by the two marble figures he sent to the Salon of 1757, *Love Threatening to Strike*, commissioned by Madame de Pompadour, and his famous *Bather* (both Louvre), a subject to which he often returned. Madame de Pompadour then asked Falconet to direct the sculpture studio in the Sèvres porcelain factory and, until 1767, he furnished about 100 models, copied from François Boucher or created by himself—children, mythological nudes, dancers, or amatory groups inspired by the *Contes* of La Fontaine. His *Pygmalion and Galatea* (1763) was a triumph acclaimed by Denis Diderot, who considered it a supreme masterpiece. The artist's renown reached Russia, and Catherine II asked him to execute a monument to Peter the Great in St. Petersburg. Falconet spent 12 years (1766–78) on this enormous task: his equestrian statue of the czar is one of the most important works of the 18th century.

Étienne-Maurice Falconet. Equestrian statue of Peter the Great, Leningrad. 1766–78. *Photo Martin Hürlimann.*

FANTIN-LATOUR, Ignace Henri Joseph Théodore, *called* Henri (1836, Grenoble—1904, Buré, Orne), French painter. Although he was on friendly terms with the Impressionists, Fantin-Latour remained apart from them in his work; he was more at ease in the warmth of his studio than in the open air. Trained first by his father, Théodore (1805–72), a pastel painter, and later at the drawing schools of Lecoq de Boisbaudran in Paris, Fantin-Latour exhibited in the Salon of 1861, although in 1863—with Manet and Whistler—he was relegated to the Salon des Refusés. Working in the tradition of intimate realism, he produced group portraits such as *Homage to Delacroix*, 1864; *A Studio in the Batignolles Quarter*, 1870; *Table Corner*, 1872; and the *Dubourg Family*, 1878 (all in Paris, Musée de l'Impressionnisme), in which he pictured his friends Whistler, Baudelaire, Zola, Manet, Monet, Renoir, Verlaine, and Rimbaud, among many others. Fantin-Latour is probably best known for his bouquets of flowers, done to suit the taste of the middle-class collector and displaying his sensitive handling of color harmonies. In his lesser known compositions inspired by the program music of Schumann and Berlioz, and particularly by Wagnerian mythological cycles, as well as in some of his many lithographs, Fantin-Latour's imaginative treatment and filmy, muted style approach the Symbolist world of Gustave Moreau and Odilon Redon.

FATTORI, Giovanni (1825, Leghorn—1908, Florence), leading Italian painter of the 19th century. He trained at the Academy of Fine Arts in Florence (1846–48), and in 1855, turning to a fresh and increasingly free expression, he became the leading spirit of the Macchiaioli, a group of Italian Impressionists. Instead of large paintings of battle scenes he soon preferred scenes of military life, which he executed with a power and a lack of polish unprecedented at the time (*Patrol*, *c.* 1885; Rome, Coll. Marzotto), and landscapes of the Maremma in which he spaced with discernment his light cavalry, bulls, and keepers. Fattori also painted some portraits, but broad, sweeping landscapes and intimate corners of the countryside remained his most congenial subjects (*La Rotonda di Palmieri*, 1866; Florence, Galleria d'Arte Moderna). In 1875 he went to Paris, where he greatly admired the Impressionists without, however, changing his own style. Far from being a formula, the patch (*macchia*) technique appealed to Fattori's temperament: it enabled him to give drama and vitality to large spaces and to reconcile the need for pictorial structure with the desire to express the quivering fugacity of emotion.

FAUTRIER, Jean (1898, Paris—1964, Châtenay-Malabry), French painter. Fautrier spent his childhood in London, where he joined the Royal Academy Schools at the age of fourteen. After his return to Paris he painted the *Sunday Walk* (1921), which, with its ambiguous naiveté, was perhaps a criticism of both society and painting. Around 1923 he met the art dealer Jeanne Castel, who organized an exhibition for him, and by 1926 dealers were fighting for his work. Fautrier's painting tended to be allusively representational and fluid (*Flowers*, *c.* 1927; New York,

Museum of Modern Art). In 1928, at the request of André Malraux and the publisher Gallimard, he executed a series of lithographs illustrating Dante's *Inferno*, which were never actually published, but which were exhibited in 1939. Around 1928 he gave up oil painting and tried to find, first with pastel and then with tempera, a more impulsive way of expressing reality. He returned to oils just before World War II. He used paper instead of canvas, and created on it a rough, uneven surface to which inks and powdered colors were applied, producing the effect of extraordinary vitality (*Bare Breasts*, 1945; Paris, Coll. André Malraux). This ceaseless concern for technical perfection could be appreciated at two exhibitions at the Galerie René Drouin, Paris: one in 1943, organized by the art critic Jean Paulhan; the other in 1945, in which André Malraux prefaced the catalogue for the famous series of *Hostages*, inspired by the victims of Nazi brutality. The painter's powers and his self-imposed limitations appeared here clearly. In 1960 Fautrier won the first prize for painting at the Venice Biennale.

FAUVISM. The first artistic revolution of the 20th century, Fauvism was based on the glorification of pure color and did not constitute a school with a particular system and theory. At the Salon d'Automne of 1905, in Paris, a dozen painters influenced by Henri Matisse exhibited together publicly. They showed together again at the Salon des Indépendants of 1906, and in both cases public reaction was virulent.

The movement crystallized around the dominant personality of Matisse, whose ideas were adopted during the pioneering years by three main groups from different areas: the group from Gustave Moreau's studio and the Académie Carrière, Paris (Albert Marquet, Henri Manguin, Charles Camoin—1879–1965—and Jean Puy); the painters from Chatou, a Paris suburb (André Derain, Maurice de Vlaminck); and the last to join, the group from Le Havre (Othon Friesz, Raoul Dufy, Georges Braque). These three groups were joined by an independent, Kees van Dongen.

First Georges Rouault, then Matisse, Marquet, Manguin, and Camoin were students at the École des Beaux-Arts, Paris, in the studio of Gustave Moreau. When he died (1898), his students scattered. In 1899 Matisse returned to Paris from visits to Corsica and Toulouse with a collection of small landscapes vigorously sketched with pure tones in a pointillist technique. In the same audacious style as his landscapes, he painted figures in pure blue and brilliant scarlet and orange still lifes. He was closely followed in these experiments by Marquet. In 1899, at the Académie Carrière, he met Puy, Pierre Laprade (1875–1932), Auguste Chabaud, and, of greater import, Derain, who, with the self-taught Vlaminck, was making parallel experiments in a more summary and even more intense style. Thus, the first wave of Fauvism (1899–1901) was led on one side by Matisse and Marquet, under the influence of Cézanne's structural composition, and on the other by Derain and Vlaminck, under the impact of Van Gogh's Expressionism.

In 1902–3 Matisse and Marquet painted interiors and views of Paris, stressed the graphic element in painting, and returned to the somber color range of the early Manet. Vlaminck indulged his passion for the use of brilliant colors, a trend he later claimed to have initiated. The group united again in the Salon des Indépendants of 1903 (Matisse, Marquet, Puy, Manguin, Camoin, Friesz, and Dufy), but it did not attract the public's attention. Matisse had a strong influence over Friesz, and when he exhibited *Luxe, Calme, et Volupté* at the Salon des Indépendants of 1905 his effect on Dufy was equally decisive. Both gave up Impressionism and adopted Matisse's "pictorial mechanism." Derain joined Matisse at Collioure, and from their stimulating contact the first true Fauve paintings were executed. These created a sensation at the 1905 Salon d'Automne, which included works by Marquet, Manguin, Puy, Louis Valtat (1869–1952), Vlaminck, Friesz, and Rouault.

The Salon des Indépendants of 1906, which showed works of Braque—the last of the painters from Le Havre to be converted to Fauvism—and the Salon d'Automne of the same year, which was dominated by Gauguin's decorative style, and to which Van Dongen contributed,

Fauvism. Henri Matisse. *Pink Onions*. 1906. Statens Museum for Kunst, Copenhagen.

marked the zenith of Fauvism, the essential principles of which can be summed up as follows: color constructs space and is the equivalent of light; the whole plane surface should flame with color without any modeling or illusionist chiaroscuro; purity and simplification of means; an absolute correspondence between expression (emotive suggestion) and decoration (the formal order of the picture) through composition. By the end of 1907, the collective paroxysm of Fauvism collapsed in the face of the rise of Cubism, which, moreover, Matisse and Derain, as well as Braque helped to form. Each of the Fauves went his different way: Matisse alone, and perhaps Dufy in another mode, preserved to the end the eternal youth of Fauvism.

FAYUM PORTRAITS, funerary portraits discovered in the Egyptian tombs at the oasis of Fayum, executed by Greek and Roman artists from the 1st to the 4th century A.D. Showing head and bust, they were painted on small wooden tablets or on linen with either distemper or encaustic, or a combination of the two techniques; they were placed on the sarcophagus at the height of the dead person's face, so that his features would be perpetuated in the life beyond. The union of hieratic and realistic styles apparent in earlier Egyptian art (especially of the 18th Dynasty) appears once again in these portraits, but with a greater concern for

Fauvism. Raoul Dufy. *Bay of Angels at Nice*. 1927. Dotremont Coll., Brussels. *Photo Giraudon, Paris.*

Fayum Portraits. *Funerary portrait of a young girl.* 2nd century A.D. Louvre, Paris.

expression of character. The faces are mature, untouched by the ravages of age, with the large eyes set in a fixed stare of great intensity, conveying a certain inquietude of inner life. The portraits offer evidence of a spirit that later welcomed Christian mysticism with such fervor. Studies have shown, moreover, that these portraits, with their immense, obsessive eyes, were the prototypes of the first Byzantine icons of the 5th century A.D.

FEININGER, Lyonel (1871, New York—1956, New York), American painter. The son of a violinist of German origin, Feininger studied the violin himself, leaving the United States at the age of sixteen to further his studies in Germany. But drawing attracted him even more than music, and he entered the School of Decorative Arts in Hamburg while awaiting a place in the Berlin Academy. In Berlin, he worked as an illustrator and cartoonist for newspapers and satirical reviews. In 1907, during a stay in Paris, he turned to painting. In 1911, once again in Paris, he made the acquaintance of Robert Delaunay and discovered in Cubism the first inkling of the style he was to make his own. A year later, in Berlin, he produced the first of the Constructivist compositions in which his originality clearly asserts itself.

What distinguishes Feininger is the sharpness and strict control of his draftsmanship: whether he was painting architectural subjects, boats, or clouds, he defined each object with the rigor of geometry. His work is partitioned off and subdivided, even to the light spreading across the sky, which is so directed as to impart a crystalline quality to the world of appearances (*Church of the Minorites*, 1926; Minneapolis, Walker Art Center).

In 1919 Feininger became a teacher at the Bauhaus in Weimar. He followed the school when, in 1926, it moved to Dessau, where it was later closed by the Nazis (1932). Five years later, the hostility that the Hitler regime showed toward modern art drove him to return to the United States. Impressed by the skyscrapers of Manhattan, he began in 1940 to produce a series of paintings dominated by vertiginous verticals, in which the lines are no more than a slender bone structure, and in which the color is even more transparent and more immaterial than before. He also painted, often in watercolor, landscapes and seascapes (*Blue Boat*, 1944; Boston, Museum of Fine Arts) in which swift, fine lines are combined with delicate tints.

Lyonel Feininger. *Gelmeroda.* 1923.

FELIXMÜLLER, Conrad (b. 1897, Dresden), German painter and graphic artist. He began to study painting at Dresden in 1912, then came into contact with Ludwig Meidner and Raoul Hausmann (1886–1971). In 1919 he became a founding member of the Dresden Secession, and also joined the Novembergruppe. After 1934 Felixmüller lived in Berlin, until he was invited to teach painting and drawing at the University of Halle/Saale (1949). In 1961 he again took up permanent residence in Berlin. Felixmüller achieved rapid success, but his reputation was shortlived, for he soon opted for a thoroughly traditional form of realism. Nevertheless, as far as his early period is concerned, he may be regarded as one of the successors to Die Brücke. The pictures of people going about their daily tasks, as well as those of circus life, portraits (*Georg Kind*, 1915; and *Raoul Hausmann*, 1920, both Altenburg-Poschwitz, Städtisches Gablentz-Museum) and self-portraits from those early years were all painted in the style of Die Brücke with just a hint of the techniques developed by the Blaue Reiter group and of the Expressionism of Emil Nolde. A typical work from this, his most creative period, is the picture of the *Father and His Sons* (1919; Stuttgart, Neue Staatsgalerie). In the 1920s Felixmüller moved toward the expressive realism of Otto Dix and George Grosz but did not join the New Objectivity group (*Lovers in the Spring Woods*, 1926; Städtisches Gablentz-Museum). His realism then strayed on to naturalistic paths. Felixmüller also produced a large body of graphic work.

FERBER, Herbert (b. 1906, New York), American sculptor. While studying dentistry at Columbia University, New York (D.D.S., 1930), Ferber studied sculpture at night at the Beaux-Arts Institute of Design (1927–30), and subsequently maintained both careers.

Ferber's sculpture shows a long line of development from closed to open form—from sculpture as object to sculpture as environment. His early work, from the 1930s, is generally massive, and carved in wood or stone. In 1940 he made his first open wood sculpture, and through the 1940s worked for greater openness, partly influenced by Henry Moore. At the same time, Ferber's sculpture became strongly vertical, often resting on a single point (*Flame*, lead and brass rods, 1949). His subject matter became increasingly abstract, moving from the human figure, through abstracted organic forms, to the abstract "roofed sculptures" and "cages" after 1954. These were paralleled in full scale by the room commissioned in 1961 by the Whitney Museum of American Art, New York, called *Sculpture as Environment, Interior,* consisting of a room-size construction through which the spectator could move, thus participating in the spaces of the sculpture. In the 1960s his work became increasingly simplified and formal, best seen in the series of *Calligraphs*.

Ferber also showed notable originality in technique. Around 1945 he began soldering repousséd sheets of lead together at their edges to create hollow forms, and later used also copper and brass, which required a natural change to welding in 1950. In addition to using these techniques for constructing his sculpture, Ferber also used them to texture the surfaces with molten metal, another important innovation in contemporary sculpture, which he shared with such sculptors as Ibram Lassaw, Seymour Lipton, and Theodore Roszak.

FERNÁNDEZ *or* **HERNÁNDEZ,** Gregorio (1576, Sarria?, Galicia—1635, Valladolid), Spanish Baroque sculptor. Fernández is first documented as a student in Valladolid, where he spent his entire career. It was in this town that he made a reputation as the most distinguished representative of the Castilian school of polychrome sculpture in the early decades of the 17th century. As artistic heir to Alonso Berruguete and Juan de Juni, Fernández was obliged to look for originality in new directions—in Baroque realism. His sculpture—many-paneled altarpieces, single statues, and *pasos* for Holy Week processions—expresses contemporary Spanish piety.

The *pasos* were dramatic portrayals of various episodes of Christ's Passion, which were carried in procession on floats during Holy Week. The Museo Provincial de Bellas Artes, Valladolid, preserves the *St. Veronica* and *Simon of Cyrene* from the *paso* that Fernández devoted to the *Ascent to Calvary*, executed in 1614 for the church of La Pasión in the town. Of those commissioned for the church of Vera Cruz, also in Valladolid, the *Descent from the Cross* remains intact, but only *Christ at the Column* has survived from the *Flagellation* (1623).

Possibly the best known of the artist's altarpieces are those in the Colegiata de S. Pedro, Lerma (1615), in the Convento de las Huelgas, Valladolid (1616), and in S. Miguel, Vitoria (1624–34); perhaps his greatest is the high altar of Plasencia Cathedral (1624–34). Fragments of several others are in the Museo de Escultura Religiosa at Valladolid. The devotional preferences of his contemporaries are shown also in the individual statues Fernández carved: the *Immaculate Conceptions* in the Vera Cruz, Salamanca (1620), and in the convent of the Encarnación, Madrid, which also possesses a *Christ at the Column* and a *Dead Christ*. These themes were treated repeatedly by the artist, often with only the slightest variations.

Gregorio Fernández. *St. Veronica*. 1614. Museo Provincial de Bellas Artes, Valladolid. *Photo Mas, Barcelona.*

FERRARI, Gaudenzio (*c.* 1475, Valduggia, Piedmont—1546, Milan), Italian painter whose art owes much to the great Lombard tradition of Bergognone (*c.* 1455–1523/35), Vincenzo Foppa, Andrea Solario, and Giovanni Boltraffio. His first important work was in the church of S. Maria delle Grazie in Varallo. There, during the first years of the 16th century, he painted scenes from the *Life of Christ* in a style imbued with characteristics of the Quattrocento and reminiscences of Perugino. At the Sacro Monte in Varallo, he painted a large cycle of pictures and sculptures treated with a remarkable verve and freedom. Particularly in the large *Crucifixion* fresco (1520–23), he displayed his ability to combine imaginative decorative elements with lively anecdotal material.

He contributed to the paintings in the church of the Assumption and S. Lorenzo at Morbegno in the Valtellina between 1520 and 1526; his style here is so personal that it has encouraged art historians to attribute similar works to Ferrari, such as the S. Abbondio altarpiece in Como Cathedral. The artist evidently was influenced by Dürer's engravings, particularly those of the *Little Passion*. Ferrari settled in Milan in 1439 and painted the frescoes of the S. Corona Chapel in S. Maria delle Grazie, in which the forms and attitudes appear exaggerated. However, the late frescoes of S. Maria della Pace in Milan display the beauty and freedom of handling of his mature works, whose rich manner anticipated the Baroque in their drama and movement.

FETTI *or* **FETI,** Domenico (*c.* 1589, Rome—1624, Venice), Italian painter. A pupil of Lodovico Cigoli (1559–1613), he was exposed to a variety of influences. Contact with Orazio Borgianni (d. 1616) drew him toward the milieu of Caravaggio, and the work of Adam Elsheimer led him to paint Biblical subjects in the guise of small-scale genre scenes, such as the *Lost Piece of Silver* (Florence, Palazzo Pitti), which is also a study of single-source lighting. Other works inspired by Biblical subjects include *Multiplication of the Loaves*, a fresco cycle (Mantua, Museo Civico), and the *Lost Sheep* (Dresden, Gemäldegalerie). Fetti became a court painter in Mantua in 1613 and executed a number of frescoes for the cathedral there. In 1621 he moved to Venice, where he remained until his death. The full-fleshed and lavishly appointed *Melancholia* (Paris, Louvre) shows to what extent he continued the Venetian tradition, while the small *Good Samaritan* (*c.* 1622; New York, Metropolitan Museum), with its loose, paint-laden brushwork, is equally characteristic of another side of his artistic personality, which also derived from the Venetian manner.

FEUERBACH, Anselm (1829, Speyer—1880, Venice), German painter. He studied first in Düsseldorf, then in Munich and Antwerp, but mainly in Paris, where he spent three years in Thomas Couture's studio. He went to Italy in 1855 and, on the advice of Couture, to Venice; from 1873 to 1876 he taught at the Vienna Academy; then, after brief stays in

Heidelberg and Nuremberg, he returned to Venice, where he died.

Feuerbach's work may be divided into three groups: large paintings with numerous figures, strongly influenced by Couture; paintings of characters from classical mythology, which were greatly admired in Germany; and portraits. His paintings of *Iphigenia* gazing out over the sea (1871; Stuttgart, Staatsgalerie) or of *Medea* (1870; Mannheim, Kunsthalle) have a certain nobility and grandeur but also a coldness and a photographic quality. His model for the *Iphigenia* series was a lovely Italian from Trastevere, Nanna Risi, who worked for him for part of his career. The various unidealized portraits of this very beautiful model—such as the one in Stuttgart (1861)—probably represent the height of Feuerbach's achievement.

FIELD, Erastus Salisbury (1805, Leverett, Massachusetts—1900, Leverett), American painter, active largely in western Massachusetts. In his early work Field combined the traditions of sign painting and studio art in his use of simplified forms defined by hard edges and bright local colors. He lived in Massachusetts and Hartford, Connecticut, from 1832 to 1842, and during this time recorded the region's prim country inhabitants. His portrait of *Miss Margaret Gilmore* (Boston, Museum of Fine Arts) exhibits all the characteristic elements of his style: the stiff, mannered pose; flatly stenciled floor patterns; a rich sense of color. Except for faces, in which he captured much of the New England personality, Field's portraits were executed according to a standard formula, with furniture, bodies, and poses frequently interchangeable.

Later, forced by the popularity of the daguerreotype to give up painting likenesses from nature, Field did portraits from photographs. During and after the Civil War he attempted more ambitious, imaginative paintings, such as his grandiose architectural fantasy, the *Historical Monument of the American Republic* (*c.* 1876, Priv. Coll.; engraving by E. Bierstadt in Springfield, Mass., Museum of Fine Arts), filled with elaborate towers and other details derived from architect's manuals. In his later years he favored Biblical and mythological subjects, such as *He Turned their Waters into Blood* (*c.* 1845; Washington, D.C., National Gallery), in which doll-like figures stand in awe beneath Egyptian pillars as the blood-red Nile churns past them.

FIELDING, Copley (1787, East Sowerby, Yorkshire—1855, Worthing, West Sussex), British watercolor painter. He was taught by his father, the portraitist Theodore Fielding (active 1775–1818), but it was as a landscape painter that he made his name. In Paris, where he exhibited at the 1824 Salon, he won a gold medal. He excelled especially in sky studies and seascapes: the latter, in particular, seem to have had an influence on the French Romantics of the school of 1830 (Delacroix, Géricault) similar to that of Richard Parkes Bonington. The Victoria and Albert Museum, London, owns many of his works.

FILARETE, Antonio di Pietro Averlino, *called* (*c.* 1400, Florence—*c.* 1469, Milan), Italian architect and sculptor, among those Florentines most deeply imbued with Quattrocento humanism. He began by assisting in the workshop of Lorenzo Ghiberti on the famous bronze doors of the baptistery of Florence, which led directly to his being chosen by Pope Eugene IV to make the great bronze doors for St. Peter's, Rome. These, begun in 1439, were installed in 1445. Francesco Sforza in Milan employed him to build the Castello Sforzesco (1451–54) on the site of the Visconti stronghold. This work was extensively remodeled in later years. Filarete was responsible for the plans of the vast Ospedale Maggiore in Milan, founded by Francesco Sforza, although he built only the right wing (1457–65). The building was not completed until the 18th century (after his designs). He also provided the plans for Bergamo Cathedral. His most important contribution, however, is his 25-volume *Treatise on Architecture*, which he dedicated to Piero de' Medici (*c.* 1464). It contains an extraordinary mixture of architectural fantasies and imaginative monuments, overburdened with turrets and pediments, for a model city—La Sforzinda—furnished by his vast erudition with elements borrowed from the pagan (Plato's *Republic*) and Christian worlds.

Filarete. Detail of the façade of the Ospedale Maggiore, Milan. 1457–65. *Photo Alinari-Giraudon.*

FINI, Leonor (b. 1908, Buenos Aires), painter and theater designer of Italian origin. An artist with an unusual personality, sensitive to the gracefulness of life but also capable of producing the most bizarre creations (*Shepherdess of the Sphinx*, 1941; Venice, Coll. Peggy Guggenheim) and painting with the most exquisite nuances (*Silence Enveloped*, 1955; New York, Coll. Alexandre Iolas), she designed several settings and costumes for the Paris theater: *Le Rêve de Leonor* (Ballets des Champs-Élysées, 1945); *Le Palais de Cristal* (Opéra, 1947); *Les Demoiselles de la Nuit* (Ballets de Paris, 1948); *Bérénice*, for Jean-Louis Barrault (1955); and Jean Genet's *Les Bonnes*. She also worked for the cinema (*Romeo and Juliet*, 1953). Her imaginative portraits of famous personalities (*Jean Genet*, 1949, Turin, Coll. Cavalli, and *Anna Magnani*, 1949, Rome, Coll. Anna Magnani) are outstanding. The subtle quality of her art appears equally well in drawing, sometimes heightened by washes or watercolor, and in richly colored, smooth-textured oil painting (the *Secret Festival*, 1965).

FISCHER, Johann Michael (1691, Burglengenfeld, Upper Palatinate—1766, Munich), German architect. His epitaph in the Frauenkirche in Munich honors Fischer as builder of "32 churches, 23 monasteries, and many palaces." Although it is impossible to verify the accuracy of these figures, Fischer was certainly prolific and, like Dominikus Zimmermann, was one of the greatest ecclesiastical architects of Bavaria during the Baroque period.

From the choir of the monastery of Niederalteich (1724–26) to the parish church of Altomünster

(1763–66), a dozen or more churches show him to have remained faithful to a few structural types, which he carried to perfection in their various applications. He built some churches with a long nave, especially when the foundations of an earlier building made this a necessity, but his own preference seems to have been for a centralized ground plan. At times he united the two alternatives by inserting a vast rotunda at the crossing of the nave and choir. An extremely successful example of churches with naves is his masterpiece at Ottobeuren (1737–66), where the abbey's cupolas rest on pendentives covering the bays. The church of St. Michael in the Munich suburb of Berg-am-Leim (1727–37), on which Fischer seems to have collaborated with Jean François de Cuvilliés, and the churches at Aufhausen (1736–51) and Rott-am-Inn (1759–63) show the centralized arrangement. Each has a cupola, accompanied by four auxiliary chapels delimiting the diagonal axes, inscribed within either a rectangular or octagonal space.

FISCHER, Theodor (1862, Schweinfurt—1938, Munich), German architect. After studying at the Munich Polytechnic Institute, Fischer set up as an independent architect in Dresden in 1889, remaining there for the next three years. He then worked with Paul Wallot (1841–1912) on the Reichstag Building in Berlin, and also collaborated with Gabriel von Seidl (1848–1913) in Munich. In 1901 he was appointed professor at the Technical College in Munich, but transferred to the Technical College in Stuttgart within the year, where he held the chair until he returned to Munich in 1908. Together with his compatriot Peter Behrens, Fischer was one of the foremost architects of the first decade of the 20th century. His buildings were designed primarily in terms of functional requirements. Appearance was not an overriding consideration, although a certain air of monumentality is in fact a characteristic feature of his work. Public, residential, and ecclesiastical structures formed the greater part of his output. In 1908 he completed the University of Jena, and between 1908 and 1911 built the garrison church in Ulm, which was to make a crucial contribution to the development of modern church architecture. In these first two decades of the 20th century, which was such a fertile period for him, Fischer also designed public buildings (Police Station, Munich, 1911–14), theaters (Stadt-theater, Heilbronn, 1912), and museums (Landesmuseum, Kassel, 1909–12; and Landesmuseum, Wiesbaden, 1912–15), as well as residential buildings.

FISCHER VON ERLACH, Johann Bernhard (1656, Graz—1723, Vienna), Austrian sculptor and architect who worked to create a national art free from the influence of the Italian masters who had dominated Austrian art until that time. At Salzburg, the city that had harbored Italians for so long, Gasparo Zuccalli (1667?–1717) was forced to give up his post of court architect to the young Austrian, and later Fischer's plans for the Karlskirche in Vienna were chosen by the emperor in preference to those of Ferdinando Galli da Bibiena. It was the knowledge Fischer had acquired during a 14-year stay in Italy (1670–84), as much as his double status as sculptor and architect, that gained for him the patronage of the house of Hapsburg.

Fischer's earliest training was in sculpture. That he was at first receptive to the influence of Borromini may be seen in such sculptural and decorative works as the triumphal arches honoring Emperor Joseph I in Vienna (1690) and the mausoleum of Ferdinand II at Graz (1687), and still more obviously in his work for church authorities in Salzburg between 1694 and 1707. The earliest of his religious commissions in Salzburg is the Dreifaltigkeitskirche (Holy Trinity), 1694–1702, modeled after Borromini's S. Agnese in Piazza Navona, Rome (1653–57). Next came the Kollegiankirche (collegiate church) of the Benedictine University (1696–1707). The church of the Hospital of St. John (commissioned 1695), the church of the Ursulines (commissioned 1699), and the high altars of the churches in Mariazell (1693) and Stassengel also number among the architect's most interesting achievements in his first period. Fischer then undertook several secular projects, including a palace for Count Michael II Althan at

Johann Michael Fischer. Abbey church at Ottobeuren. 1737–66. *Photo Schmidt-Glassner, Stuttgart.*

Frain (Vranov nad Dyji) in Moravia (1690–94). Here, as in his Schloss Althan at Rossau, near Vienna (designed *c.* 1690), Fischer was already using schemes that he later developed both in royal country homes near Vienna and in palaces in the capital. In the first category belong the Villa Strattman (later Bartoli, then Schwarzenburg, 1691–93) in Neuwaldegg, the Belvedere of the Villa Liechtenstein, in Rossau, and the first Schönbrunn of Joseph II (1700), completed later by Antonio de Pacassi. Of the impressive group of Vienna town palaces built during the second stage of Fischer's career, Batthyány Palace, completed about 1700 (later Schönborn), the Dietrichstein-Lobkowitz Palace (begun 1710), and the important palace for Prince Eugene (1695–98; enlarged by Johann Lucas von Hildebrandt in 1708) should be mentioned.

About 1715 Borromini's influence and a predilection for exuberant decorative sculpture gave way in Fischer's work to a sort

Johann Bernhard Fischer von Erlach. Church of the Holy Trinity, Salzburg. 1694–1702. *Bildarchiv Nationalbibliothek, Vienna.*

of eclecticism based on borrowings from Roman antiquity and French Classical architecture. With the help of the learned scholar Karl Gustave Heraeus, he wrote a book particularly notable for its illustrations of the architecture of many different countries, *Entwurf einer historischen Architektur in Abbildung unterschiedener berühmter Gebäude des Altertums und fremder Völker*, presented to Emperor Charles VI in 1712 and published in enlarged form in 1720 (English edition, *A Plan of Civil and Historical Architecture, in the Representation of the Most Noted Buildings of Foreign Nations, Both Ancient and Modern*, published 1730). The Karlskirche (church of St. Charles Borromeus, 1716–32) in Vienna marks a vital point in the development of Fischer's new style, and was undoubtedly influenced by his research in the field of archaeology.

Shortly before his death Fischer undertook the building of the Imperial Library at Vienna (1722), a work that is considered by some scholars as the culminating achievement of Austrian Baroque. The Library, together with the Spanish Riding School and the Imperial Chancery, was part of an immense scheme to enlarge the imperial complex of the Hofburg, the most ancient parts of which had been scheduled for demolition. It was left to his son JOSEF EMMANUEL FISCHER VON ERLACH (1693, Vienna—1742, Vienna), whom he brought up to work on a grand scale, to give this series of royal buildings the appearance by which it is known today. Throughout his life Josef Emmanuel carried on his father's tradition and completed the buildings he had left unfinished, not without making occasional modifications. Among his independent works are Schloss Austerlitz (remodeled 1731–32) and Schloss Neuwartenburg (1730–32), the Military Pensioners' Hospitals in Prague-Karolinenthal (designed before 1730) and Budapest, and several parts of the beautiful abbey of Klosterneuburg (designs, 1730).

Frans Floris. *Feast of the Gods.* Detail. 1550. Musée Royal des Beaux-Arts, Antwerp. *Photo A.C.L., Brussels.*

FLANNAGAN, John Bernard (1895, Fargo, North Dakota—1942, New York), American sculptor. Flannagan's artistic development began with painting: from 1914 to 1917 he studied painting at the Minnesota Institute of Arts, and in the early 1920s painted in a wax technique he learned from Arthur B. Davies. During these years he also began to carve, at first in wood, but then, after 1928, only in field stone. To Flannagan the material and the sculpture were of the highest importance, with the artist functioning mainly as a means to an end. At the same time, Flannagan's carve-direct sculpture, with no intermediary process between the artist's touch and the final result, remains personal and intimate, especially considering its small scale: he always shunned the monumental. The recurrent motif in his work is birth or development, as in *Triumph of the Egg* (granite, 1937), *Jonah and the Whale: Rebirth Motif* (bronze, 1937), and a number of mother and child images. Yet, his solid forms turn in on themselves in a circular, self-contained manner, as if toward death or in eternal flux.

Flannagan's first one-man show in New York was in 1927, and this was followed by others on a regular basis. In the early 1930s he spent two years in Ireland, the second time on a Guggenheim Fellowship. After 1939, when he suffered a near-fatal accident, he had to give up the strenuous work of carving, and thus turned to cast sculpture, drawings, and watercolors.

FLAXMAN, John (1755, York—1826, London), English sculptor, son of a maker of plaster casts who also worked for the potter Josiah Wedgwood (1730–95). He first exhibited in 1767; in 1770 he entered the Royal Academy Schools, where he met William Blake, who introduced him to Gothic art. About 1771 he also met George Romney, who had just returned from Italy, and the two men influenced him profoundly in the direction of Neoclassic theory. From 1775 Flaxman produced many quasi-antique reliefs for Wedgwood ware (the *Dancing Hours*), as well as portrait medallions. His Neoclassic tendencies were confirmed during his seven years in Rome (1787–94). While still in Rome he received important commissions for monuments, notably that to Lord Chief Justice Mansfield (1795; London, Westminster Abbey). After his return to London in 1794 he made over 170 monuments in some 30 years. His great European reputation—perhaps greater than that of any other British artist—was founded on the pure outline drawings engraved as illustrations to the *Iliad* and *Odyssey* (Rome, 1793). They were followed by *Aeschylus* (1795) and *Dante* (1802). The austere linearism of these drawings appealed greatly to the taste of his contemporaries: Ingres and the Nazarenes were influenced by him and Goethe praised him.

FLINCK, Govert (1615, Cleves, Germany—1660, Amsterdam), Dutch history and portrait painter. He was Rembrandt's pupil for a year, painted his portrait at the age of thirty-three (1639; London, National Gallery), and imitated his master's style so closely that he is said to have sold some of his paintings as Rembrandt's. In the early 1640s he changed to a lighter manner, modeled after Bartholomeus van der Helst (1613–70), with the result that he became the favorite painter of Amsterdam's notables. Flinck painted three large group portraits of militia: the *Amsterdam Musketeers* (1642), the *Company of Captain Albert Bas* (1645), and the *Banquet of the Civic Guards*, to celebrate the Peace of Münster (1648), all of which are today in the Rijksmuseum, Amsterdam. Two months before his death, the municipality gave him the largest commission ever offered to a Dutch artist: 12 paintings for the Town Hall, illustrating the struggle between the Batavians and Romans. The commission was divided among a number of artists after Flinck's death.

FLORIS *or* **FLORIS DE VRIENDT,** Cornelis (1514, Antwerp—1575, Antwerp), Flemish architect, sculptor, and engraver of "grotesque" decorations, an exponent of the Flemish taste for Italianate art. The Town Hall in Antwerp, which he designed (1561–65), is conceived as a Roman palace. Among his sculptures are the tomb of Jean de Mérode at Geel and the monumental tabernacle of St. Léonard at Léau (1552), which rises in a spire 40 feet high, with 10 stories bearing statues and reliefs that are partly Gothic, partly Renaissance in style. He also built the tabernacle at Suerbempde, near Diest, and the jube of the cathedral at Tournai (1573).

FRANS (1516, Antwerp—1570, Antwerp), brother of Cornelis, was a Mannerist painter. He was a pupil of Lambert Lombard at Liège and became Master at Antwerp in 1540. On an extended visit to Italy (1541–47) he made red chalk drawings from Classical art and from Michelangelo's *Last Judgment*; returning to Antwerp, he opened a celebrated studio through which passed Marten de Vos (1532–1603), Lucas de Heere (1534–78), and Frans Pourbus the Elder (1545–81), and which disseminated the Mannerist style in Flanders for 20 years. Floris received numerous commissions, including the decoration for the house of the financier Nikolaus Jonghelinck in 1554 (scenes from the *Labors of Hercules* and allegories of the *Liberal Arts*), and he executed many religious paintings (*Fall of the Rebel Angels*, 1554, Antwerp, Musée Royal des Beaux-Arts; *Adoration of the Magi*, 1571, Brussels, Musées Royaux des Beaux-Arts, and Dresden, Gemäldegalerie; *Last Judgment*, 1566, Brussels, Musées Royaux des Beaux-Arts) and Ovidian mythological scenes (*Feast of the Gods*, 1550, Antwerp, Musée Royal des Beaux-Arts; *Venus Mourning the Dead Adonis*, *c.* 1550, The Hague, Mauritshuis).

Frans Floris may be considered the Primaticcio of Flemish painting, nearer to that painter and to Parmigianino and Vasari than to Michelangelo. Although very much in tune with the taste of the times, he was an artist of greater depth than his Mannerist compositions alone suggest. His portraits show considerable talent: they include a *Falconer* (1558; Brunswick, Herzog Anton-Ulrich-Museum) and a *Portrait of an Old Lady* (1558; Caen, Musée des Beaux-Arts).

FONTAINEBLEAU, School of. In 1526 François I decided to remodel the château of Fontainebleau in the Italian style. He attracted some well-known Italian Mannerist artists—Rosso Fiorentino (in 1530), Francesco Primaticcio, and Niccolò dell'Abbate—to the new center of operations, and when he put these three painters in charge of his teams of decorators, François I founded the first School of Fontainebleau. An original style grew up under the Italians' guidance that was admittedly a branch of international Mannerism, but also a blend of the artists' Italianate style, their French surroundings, and the Northern influences they were absorbing. Most of the important works of this first school are lost: only drawings, copies, a handful of identifiable paintings, and a few, often damaged frescoes (presently being restored), were preserved.

Rosso Fiorentino directed the Fontainebleau workshops for 10 years. He decorated the Galerie François I (1533–40) with frescoes and highly ornamental stucco-work.

Primaticcio practiced an engaging Mannerism, influenced by Michelangelo's *forma serpentinata* and the studied elegance of Pontormo and Parmigianino. After Rosso's sudden death in 1540, Primaticcio succeeded him as director of works at Fontainebleau and decorated the Chambre du Roi (1533–35), the Galerie d'Ulysse (1541–70)—both of which have unfortunately been destroyed—and the Salle de Bal (1551–56, much restored). His frescoes were often enhanced by stucco frameworks of garlands and graceful, finely drawn feminine nudes (bedroom of the Duchesse d'Étampes).

Primaticcio was the artistic dictator at Fontainebleau for 30 years and imposed his style on a whole generation of painters and craftsmen who helped to embellish the château in the middle of the 16th century. In 1552 he called in the assistance of Niccolò dell'Abbate, who was obsessed with problems of color and landscape, and exercised a considerable influence over the School of Fontainebleau by introducing a strain of theatricality and fantasy. Primaticcio employed a number of Italians who are still little known, including Antonio Fantuzzi (*c.* 1508–after 1550), Luca Penni (1500–56), Rugiero de Rugieri (d. 1596), and perhaps the Master of Flora, who did several amusingly sensual works (*Birth of Love*, *c.* 1560; New York, Metropolitan

School of Fontainebleau. Francesco Primaticcio. Stucco decoration in the bedroom of the Duchesse d'Étampes, Fontainebleau. *c.* 1541–45. *Photo Jean Roubier, Paris.*

Museum). Better known are those French artists who worked in the style of the school, such as Jean Cousin the Elder (*c.* 1490–*c.* 1561) and his son Jean Cousin the Younger (*c.* 1525–*c.* 1594), François Clouet, and Antoine Caron, the protégé of Catherine de Médicis. Several anonymous paintings also belong to this period: these are presently considered to be the work of French painters, but one day they may be attributed to Flemish artists. It would be a mistake, in fact, to consider the art of the first School of Fontainebleau as a graft of Italian influence onto French stock, and to reject the Northern contributions because so little is known about them.

On the other hand, it would be just as misleading to define the Second School of Fontainebleau (late 16th–early 17th century) as the supremacy of Flemish painters over the royal enterprises. After Henri IV of France renounced his Protestant faith and was crowned king in 1589, peace was re-established and the work of decoration could be resumed. Whether the directing artists were French (Toussaint Dubreuil and Martin Fréminet—1567 1619) or Flemish (Ambroise Bosschaert, known as Dubois—*c.* 1543–1614), Italian influence remained dominant, because the artists of Fontainebleau had studied the work of such painters as the Zuccaro brothers and Bartholomaeus Spranger at Rome and as a result were stylistically a part of the last stages of international Mannerism. When Dubreuil died in

Carlo Fontana. Façade of S. Marcello al Corso, Rome. 1682–83. *Photo Alinari-Giraudon.*

1602, Dubois, who already had a reputation in France, became director of the Fontainebleau projects. He decorated the Chambre de la Reine and, more important, the Galerie de Diane (destroyed). Although adhering to the main outlines of the previous program, he painted scenes from chivalrous romances instead of nudes. His art, less mannered than that of his predecessors, was characterized by such effects as fluttering draperies, hard light, and rather mawkish sentiment. Martin Fréminet succeeded him in 1614. He had been trained in Italy, was summoned back to Paris in 1603, and later was put in charge of decorating the chapel of the Trinité at Fontainebleau (1608–19). His strained Mannerism, with its exaggerated foreshortenings and strident colors, belonged to an outworn style. When he died in 1619, the decoration of Fontainebleau was abandoned, but its influence on the following centuries was conspicuous.

Domenico Fontana. Façade of the Palazzo Reale, Naples. 1600–32. *Photo Alinari-Giraudon.*

FONTANA, Carlo (1638, Rancate, Como—1714, Rome), leading Baroque architect of the Roman School. He arrived in the Eternal City around 1650, where he studied under the guidance of Pietro da Cortona and Carlo Rainaldi and for 10 years was Bernini's faithful assistant. Fontana worked for the Chigi family on the Palazzo Odescalchi in Rome (1664) and on the Villa di Cetinale, which they were building near Siena. He also designed a series of chapels and churches in Rome, which earned him the honor of election as Principe of the Accademia di S. Luca in 1686 and again in 1691–1700: the Ginetti Chapel in S. Andrea della Valle (1671), the magnificent incurving façade of S. Marcello al Corso (1682–83), and the Cibo Chapel in S. Maria del Popolo, with its painted decorations (1683–87). After Bernini's death, he supervised the work on the Baptismal Chapel in St. Peter's (1692–98), which he decorated with sculptures, and also executed the rather severe portico of S. Maria in Trastevere, Rome (1702). Fontana was not only a great architect: the prolific schemes of his versatile mind filled 28 volumes, now in the Royal Library at Windsor. His functions as an engineer included the supervision of Rome's waterways and pipelines; he also designed the gardens in the Quattro Fontane district and studied various projects for town planning and acoustics.

FONTANA, Domenico (1543, Melide, Switzerland—1607, Naples), Italian architect. As soon as he arrived in Rome (1563), he won the protection of Cardinal Montalto, the future Sixtus V, who, on becoming pope in 1585, planned to modernize Rome and turn it into a fitting capital of Christendom. Fontana became one of the leading architects for the various papal projects; his work exemplifies the last phase of an uninspired and academic Mannerism. It includes the Vatican Library (1587–90), the Sistine Chapel in S. Maria Maggiore (1586), and the Lateran Palace (1587), his most important undertaking in Rome. In his capacity as town planner of the Eternal City, Fontana plotted the lines of six large thoroughfares radiating in a star from S. Maria Maggiore; had the Obelisk of Caligula erected in St. Peter's Square (1586); and supervised the transportation of the colossal statues of the Dioscuri, discovered in the Baths of Constantine, to the Piazza del Quirinale. Forced into exile by intrigues against him after the death of his patron Sixtus, Fontana went to Naples in 1592 and was appointed royal engineer to the Spanish Viceroy. In his new post, he built the Palazzo Caraffa della Spina (1598) and the majestic Palazzo Reale (1600–32), as well as several other buildings in Naples.

FONTANA, Lucio (1899, Santa Fé, Argentina—1968, Varese, Italy), South American-born sculptor and painter, taken by his parents to Italy at the age of six. Rejecting his academic training at Milan's Brera Academy, he maintained an uncompromising demand for artistic freedom, and in 1934 joined the French Abstraction-Création movement without, however, subscribing to its dogmas of "geometricism." From 1939 to 1946 Fontana lived in Argentina, where in 1946 he published his *Manifesto Blanco* ("White Manifesto"), in which he outlined the new aesthetic that he defined in his *Manifesto tecnico di spazialismo* ("Technical Manifesto on Spatialism"), the following year. This manifesto explained the ideas of the Spazialismo movement, which Fontana founded in 1947 in Milan; it combines the ideas of formal art with the uninhibited experiments of Dadaism. He was advocating a synthesis that would abolish the demarcation, not only between painting and sculpture, but also between nature and art (*Spatial Concepts*, 1957; bronze). Fontana further developed his "concept of space" in a series of paintings, often monochrome, with surfaces enlivened by perforations—a scattering of holes or slashes like gaping wounds.

FOPPA, Vincenzo (*c.* 1427, Brescia—1515, Brescia), Italian painter. He is generally considered to be the founder of the Milanese school of painting and, according to Vasari, was trained in Padua. It is now thought that the more precise influences on his work were Stefano da Verona (1374–after 1438) and Jacopo Bellini. His activity was centered in Genoa, Pavia, Milan, and Brescia. In 1468 he went to Milan and painted the frescoes in the Portinari Chapel of

S. Eustorgio, dedicated to St. Peter Martyr. After about 1470 Foppa's visits to Genoa became frequent, allowing him to have numerous contacts with Flemish and Provençal art. After 1480 his style matured and became receptive to Renaissance art under the influence of Leonardo and particularly Bramante. In 1488 he painted an altarpiece for the Cappella Fornari in S. Maria di Loreto, Savona, and the large polyptych commissioned by Cardinal Giuliano della Rovere, later finished by Ludovico Brea (*c.* 1450–1522/3), for Savona Cathedral (1490). After his final return to Brescia, Foppa seems to have been attracted by the new stylistic discoveries of the Renaissance, which he combined with his own deeply felt seriousness, as for instance in the *Epiphany* (London, National Gallery) and the *Annunciation* (Milan, Coll. Borromeo). His last dated work is the *Orzinuovi Standard* (1514; Orzinuovi, Chiesa dei Morti).

FOSTER, Myles Birket (1825, North Shields, Northumberland—1899, Weybridge, Surrey), English landscape painter and book illustrator. From 1841 to 1846 he worked for the engraver Ebenezer Landells (1808–60), a one-time pupil of Thomas Bewick, and contributed to such magazines as *Punch* and *The Illustrated London News*. In 1846 Foster went to work for Henry Vizetelly (1820–94) as an illustrator, and during the 1850s the landscapes, vignettes, and genre scenes that he provided for a large number of books (Longfellow's *Evangeline*, 1850, and *Hyperion*, 1853; Goldsmith's *The Traveller*, 1856; and *The Poetical Works of Edgar Allan Poe*, 1858) brought him a considerable reputation with the public.

Landscape remained Foster's first love, however, and during the 1860s he virtually gave up black-and-white illustration. His landscapes, which are for the most part in watercolor—although from 1869 to 1877 he preferred working in oils—are highly finished in technique and rather sentimental in character, as in the *Milkmaid* (1860; London, Victoria and Albert Museum). Foster first exhibited at the Royal Academy in 1859; he was made an associate in 1860 and, later (1862), a full member of the Old Water-Colour Society. In 1876 he was elected a member of the Royal Academy in Berlin.

FOUQUET, Jean (*c.* 1425, Tours—1477/81, Tours), the most famous French painter of the 15th century. Fouquet spent some time in Italy, where he is recorded in 1447. He made friends with the architect and Humanist Filarete, with whom he was able to examine some of the works in which the new principles had been applied. The monuments Fouquet saw in Rome are recognizable in his later miniatures.

By 1448 Fouquet was married and living in Tours. From Italy he brought back the rigorous theories of perspective that were still unknown to the French, a new conception of space, and a feeling for monumental, weighty figures that permitted him to achieve a new interpretation of everyday life. For all these reasons it is barely probable that the portrait of *Charles VII* (Paris, Louvre) dates from this time, despite the inscription on the frame referring to "the most victorious king of France." The scholar and critic Charles Sterling has rightly pointed out that this could easily refer to the Truce of Arras (1444) rather than the victorious end of the Hundred Years' War at Formigny in 1450. The work would then precede the trip to Italy, and this would explain its archaic touches. The miniatures of the Hours of Étienne Chevalier probably date from the 1450s. Forty-seven of the presumed original sixty sheets have been found, the majority preserved in the Musée Condé, Chantilly. These are full views of Paris, which give a fascinating documentary picture of the city in the time of Charles VII, with the cathedral of Notre-Dame, the Louvre, Ste-Chapelle, the Temple, the Bastille, and even the gallows of Montfaucon.

On the death of the king's mistress Agnès Sorel (1450), Étienne Chevalier, king's treasurer and executor of her estate, commissioned from Fouquet the famous Melun Diptych: it shows St. Stephen presenting the treasurer to the Virgin, whose features appear to be those of Agnès. This work counts among the most beautiful creations of the 15th century. The portrait of *Guillaume Juvénal des Ursins* (Louvre), executed somewhat later, around 1455, must have been part of a similar diptych: here the figure praying before the Virgin is represented against a rich background, taken directly from the decorative repertory of the Italian Renaissance. At the same time, Fouquet was illuminating manuscripts, notably a *Decameron* (Munich, Bayerische Staatsbibliothek) and the *Great Chronicles of France* (Paris, Bibliothèque Nationale). With the death of Charles VII (1461), he began to play a more important official role. He became director of court ceremonies, celebrations, entertainments, and mystery plays, as well as a sculptor of tombs and designer of stained-glass windows. Louis XI took up residence in Tours and Fouquet did a portrait of the king, of which only a bad copy remains (New York, Brooklyn Museum). Fouquet's masterpiece and the most certain of his works dates from the period 1470–76: the *Judaic Antiquities*, painted for Jacques d'Armagnac, Duc de Nemours, which shows a consummate mastery in the handling of parades and crowd effects. Fouquet shows wide landscapes bathed in a peaceful light, real architecture, and living scenes. This breadth of vision has led art historians to attribute to him the *Descent from the Cross* (*c.* 1470–80) in the parish church of Nouans, Indre-et-Loire.

In its long development, Fouquet's work embraces the transformation of French art over 50 decisive years. Born a miniaturist, he attained grandeur.

Below left: **Jean Fouquet.** *St. John on Patmos*. Miniature from the Hours of Étienne Chevalier. *c.* 1450. Musée Condé, Chantilly. *Photo Giraudon, Paris.*

Below right: **Jean Fouquet.** *Descent from the Cross. c.* 1470–80. Parish church, Nouans.

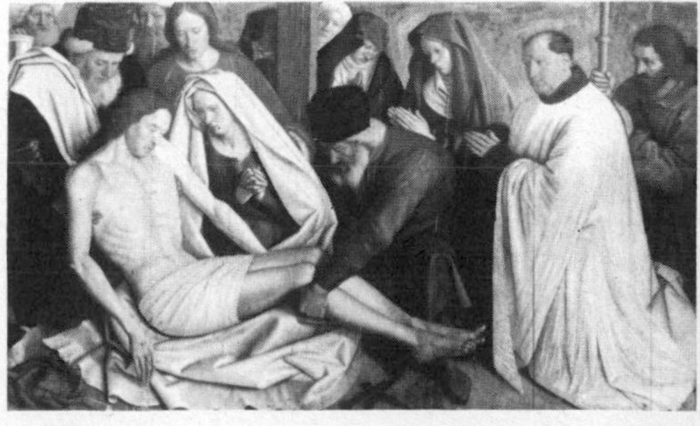

Jean-Honoré Fragonard. *The Toy Sellers*. Detail from the Fête at St-Cloud. 1775. Banque de France, Paris. *Photo Giraudon, Paris.*

FRA ANGELICO. *See* **ANGELICO,** Guido di Pietro.

FRAGONARD, Jean-Honoré (1732, Grasse, Alpes-Maritimes—1806, Paris), French painter, draftsman, and etcher. In 1747 he studied with Jean-Baptiste Chardin, to whom he had been referred by François Boucher. The following year Boucher accepted him as a pupil; later he studied with Carle van Loo. In 1752, at the age of twenty, he won the Prix de Rome. In 1756 he went to Italy where he reserved his admiration for Francesco Solimena and Giambattista Tiepolo. Very sociable, he became friendly with Jean-Baptiste Greuze, Hubert Robert, and with the charming Abbé Richard de Saint-Non. With the Abbé, Fragonard returned to France via Bologna and Venice in 1761. For his reception piece at the Académie Royale de Peinture et de Sculpture he chose an antique subject, *Coresus Sacrificing Himself to Save Callirhoe* (1765; Paris, Louvre), a stunning canvas that was received enthusiastically and was purchased by the Marquis de Marigny for the Gobelins Factory. Boucher introduced him to collectors, notably the financier Bergeret, who was to become his Maecenas. Fragonard's reputation as a painter was made by a picture commissioned by the Marquis de Saint-Julien, the *Swing* (1766; London, Wallace Collection).

Jean-Honoré Fragonard. *Boy as Pierrot*. 1789–91. Wallace Coll., London.

Tax collectors, lords, and actresses deluged Fragonard with commissions, which he carried out rapidly in the intervals between social engagements. Paintings that can be assigned to this period (1765–72) include the *Stolen Shift*, or *Cupid Undressing a Girl Lying on a Bed* (Louvre), the *Girl Making Her Dog Dance on Her Bed* (Priv. Coll.), and the *Longed-For Moment* (Priv. Coll.), works that would be considered risqué were they not redeemed by the artist's lightness of touch and innocent grace. Painting more and more hurriedly as time went on, he produced mere studies, but studies that are more alive than finished pictures (*Women Bathing*, 1775, and *Sleeping Bacchante*, 1765–72; both Louvre). On June 17, 1769, he married Anne-Marie Gérard, the seventeen-year-old daughter of a perfume distiller of Grasse. She bore him a daughter, Rosalie, and a son, Évariste (1780–1850), who became a painter. Fragonard's oeuvre was henceforth to be enriched by such simple, moving themes as his family, his house, and his garden. Madame du Barry asked him to paint four panels on the theme of "the progress of love in a young girl's heart." He painted four marvels: the *Pursuit*, the *Meeting, Love Letters*, the *Lover Crowned* (all 1771–72; all New York, Frick Collection); not broad enough for Louis XV, they were replaced by the labored vulgarity of Joseph-Marie Vien (1716–1809). Meanwhile Fragonard's protector Bergeret, who had talked for 20 years of going to Italy, decided to make the trip and took along Fragonard and his wife (1773). The travelers went through Florence, Naples, and Venice and returned via Vienna, Prague, Dresden, and Frankfurt, arriving in Paris at the end of 1774. In 1775 Fragonard was commissioned by the Duc de Penthièvre to furnish a decorative painting for his residence in Paris, the Hôtel de Toulouse; the result was a masterpiece, the *Fête at St-Cloud* (Paris, Banque de France), the most dazzling evocation of nature he ever committed to canvas. It was his last landscape: henceforth he painted only portraits or genre figures of women, girls, and children, or allegorical and sentimental scenes. Fragonard glorified family life in a series of intimate scenes, including the *Visit to the Foster Mother* (1777–79; Washington, D.C., National Gallery); the adorable *Boy as Pierrot* (1789–91; London, Wallace Collection); and *Child With a Curio* (1780–88; Portland, Oregon, Art Museum), whose subject is presumed to be the young Évariste. He even emerged as a forerunner of Romanticism in the unexpected chiaroscuro of various paintings of literary inspiration (the *Fountain of Love*, c. 1790, Wallace Collection; *Votive Offering to Love*, 1780–88, Orléans, Museum). But he had already lost his clientele; and, with the Revolution, he was ruined. He retired temporarily to Grasse, then returned to Paris in 1791. Meanwhile his son Évariste had become a pupil of Louis David. Through David's influence, Fragonard was made president of the Conservatoire du Museum des Arts in 1796 (he had been a member since its foundation in 1794). In 1794 he stopped painting; in 1805 he was expelled from the Louvre along with the other artists who lodged there, and the following year he died, forgotten.

FRANCESCA, Piero della. *See* **PIERO DELLA FRANCESCA.**

FRANCESCO DI GIORGIO MARTINI (1439, Siena—1502, Siena), Italian architect, engineer, painter, and sculptor. He won greatest renown as an architect, although only one major building of his construction is documented—the church of the Madonna del Calcinaio, near Cortona, commissioned in 1484. His position as a major architect of the Renaissance, therefore, rests on two debated attributions, the designs of the Palazzo Ducale at Urbino and of the neighboring church of S. Bernardino.

It is certain that Francesco di Giorgio was invited to Urbino in 1477 by Federigo da Montefeltro, but Giorgio Vasari is mistaken in awarding him the honor of building the Palazzo Ducale singlehandedly. Luciano Laurana had almost finished it when he left Urbino in 1472. Francesco planned a hanging or terraced garden, and began building a new courtyard; his style is also thought to be recognizable in the upper part of the two towers. There are grounds for believing that Francesco, in fulfillment of one of Duke Federigo's last wishes (he died in 1482), built the church of S. Bernardino. He supervised the building of the Palazzo Ducale at Gubbio, begun in 1470 on Laurana's designs, and the Palazzo della Signoria at Iesi (1486–98; greatly altered since). At Siena an old tradition credits him with the church of S. Maria della Nevi (1471). Some critics have connected him with the Palazzo della Cancelleria in Rome (begun 1485), which is traditionally attributed to Bramante although it was largely finished before Bramante arrived in the city. Francesco di Giorgio was also a military engineer and in this capacity worked on the walls of Lucca and, in The Marches, built fortresses at Sassocorvaro, Mondavio, Cagli, S. Leo, and Iesi. He was in Urbino when Signorelli invited him to build the Madonna del Calcinaio at the foot of the town. This little church, one of the most perfect of the Quattrocento, in the form of a Latin cross, is crowned at its transept by an octagonal cupola, erected at the beginning of the 16th century by an architect who obviously respected the master's intentions.

As a painter of altarpieces, Francesco revealed himself a true pupil of Vecchietta in the *Annunciation* and the *Coronation of the Virgin* (1472; both Siena, Pinacoteca). But after he had met Signorelli and perhaps admired the works of Botticelli, Francesco painted a *Nativity* (*c.* 1490; Siena, S. Domenico), an exquisite work that harmonizes the spirits of Siena and Florence and shows the painter's interests as an archaeologist and architect.

The two candle-bearing angels (1497) in Siena Cathedral are among Francesco's best-authenticated sculptures. Here the linear refinement of the Sienese School is blended with overtones from Donatello, whose *rilievo schiacciato* ("very low relief") Francesco had imitated in his *Descent from the Cross* (*c.* 1474; Venice, S. Maria del Carmine). In the architectural background of the *Flagellation* relief (Perugia, Galleria Nazionale), Francesco found solutions derived from Donatello bronzes for his problems of perspective.

Francesco's speculative reconstructions of ancient buildings (MS. 148, Turin, Biblioteca Reale), his sheets of sketches (Florence, Biblioteca Nazionale), his book of travel notes (Florence, Uffizi), and his *Trattato di architettura civile e militare* (*c.* 1482) throw light on the intentions behind his buildings and reveal some of his main preoccupations.

FRANCIABIGIO, Francesco di Cristofano Bigi, *called* (*c.* 1482, Florence—1525, Florence), Italian painter, a pupil of Mariotto Albertinelli and Piero di Cosimo. Early in his career his work reveals an assimilation of the misty, dissolving contours and compositional style of Leonardo da Vinci. He shared the fresco work in the cloister of SS. Annunziata, Florence, with Andrea del Sarto, where he was responsible for the *Marriage of the Virgin* (1513). Also in Florence, he painted the *Last Supper* in the Chiostro dello Scalzo, again associated with Del Sarto, with whom he also worked on the vast and grandiose decorative scheme for the *salone* at the Medici villa at Poggio a Caiano, near Florence. Franciabigio's contribution was a *Triumph of Cicero*, in which his talent appears rather strained. Franciabigio was evidently dominated by two masters of grace and subtle expression: *Triumph of Hercules* and *Job* (both Florence, Uffizi) reveal Leonardo's continuing influence; the essence of the *Young Man* (Paris, Louvre) and the *Holy Family* (between 1510 and 1520; Vienna, Kunsthistorisches Museum) can be traced to Raphael. The chief merits of Franciabigio's not very considerable output are the grace of his figures, the freshness in his color, and his airy landscapes.

FRANCIS, Sam (b. 1923, San Mateo, California), American painter. During the late 1940s he studied under Clyfford Still in San Francisco, painting his first abstract compositions in 1947. For several years he lived in Paris, where he first gained a considerable reputation, and then began to divide his time between Switzerland and the United States. Unlike most of his contemporaries, he was more influenced by the free, open style of Jackson Pollock than by the relatively dense, worked canvases of Willem de Kooning. The technique of dripping, flicking, and splattering the paint onto the canvas stamps his compositions with a paradoxically controlled abandon that is a part of his dynamic and meditative nature (*Summer No. II*, 1957; New York, Martha Jackson Gallery). As background for his brilliant splotches of color, Francis leaves large areas of the canvas bare, which gives his work a light and airy openness (*Blue on a Point*, 1958; Rye, N.Y., Coll. Mrs. Harry Doniger). The vibrating delicacy of his painting action has something in common with Mark Tobey.

Francesco di Giorgio Martini. *St. Jerome in the Desert.* National Gallery of Art, Washington, D.C.

FRANKENTHALER, Helen (b. 1928, New York City), American painter. She studied art with the Mexican painter Rufino Tamayo and, after considerable Cubist training and exercise with Paul Feeley (b. 1913) at Bennington College, was led to her own style of Abstract Expressionism through the work of Arshile Gorky and early paintings of Kandinsky. In 1950 Frankenthaler worked with Hans Hofmann. She saw Jackson Pollock's work in 1951, at which point she was also looking at Willem de Kooning's paintings. She soon began to recognize more possibilities for herself in Pollock's vocabulary than in the De Kooning-Gorky idiom. She responded particularly to a certain surreal element in Pollock—the understated image that was present beneath his webs of interlaced line. Frankenthaler was also interested in Matisse and, especially, in Miró, in whom she discovered the same associative qualities that attracted her to Pollock's paintings. In 1958 she married the Abstract Expressionist painter Robert Motherwell.

The initial step in a painting by Helen Frankenthaler is the exploration of various color and shape combinations, although these may change midway through the work. Her lyrical and sensitive approach to color allowed a unique interpretation of Pollock's methods. In 1952 she painted *Mountains and*

Freake Limner. *Mrs. Elizabeth Freake and Baby Mary.* 1674 (?). Worcester Art Museum, Worcester, Mass.

Sea (Coll. artist; on loan to the Metropolitan Museum), whose fragile blues and pinks defined a new approach to the staining of unsized, unprimed canvas with thin liquid pigment. In 1953 this painting attracted the attention of the painters Morris Louis and Kenneth Noland, who were soon converted to Frankenthaler's working methods, which they saw as a means to achieve a maximum opticality in their own work. Frankenthaler subsequently used stronger, although no less original, coloration, in more solid-looking shapes than her earlier diaphanous trails and pools.

FRAZEE, John (1790, Rahway, New Jersey—1852, Crompton, Rhode Island), American sculptor. Frazee's experience in sculpture began with stonecutting; in 1814 he established a shop with a partner in New Brunswick, New Jersey, and in 1818 opened another shop in New York City, where he specialized in mantelpieces and tombstones. Around 1825 Frazee began carving portrait busts: his first, of the lawyer John Wells, was probably also the first marble bust made in America and no doubt the first done by a native artist. In 1831 he carved a bust of Chief Justice John Jay for the United States Congress, and around 1834 he made a series of portrait busts for the Boston Athenaeum, which included those of Daniel Webster, John Marshall, and Judge Joseph Story. In addition, Frazee left an interesting plaster model for a self-portrait (1829). The first successful exponent of a tradition of marble sculpture in America, Frazee looked to Classical models for his style, and he was a forerunner of the later 19th-century Neoclassical school in America.

FREAKE LIMNER (active 2nd half of 17th century, New England), American artist identified only by his two paintings of the Freake family of colonial New England, *John Freake* and *Mrs Freake and Baby Mary* (both dating from 1674; both Worcester, Mass., Art Museum). This is the earliest known group of New England paintings, of which the masterpiece is *Mrs. Freake and Baby Mary*. Although lacking a successful rendering of weight and depth, the painting is animated by the purposeful patterning of colors and textural contrasts. The rigidly placed puppetlike figures are as flat as pressed flowers, and thus relate to the last vestiges of medieval art, more alive in the English motherland than on the Continent. The composition, with its sharply edged areas of local color, also recalls inherited conventions in the very widely practiced trade of sign painting. In this work, as in three portraits of the Gibbs children (all 1670; *Henry Gibbs* and *Margaret Gibbs* in Charleston, W. Va., Coll. Mrs. David M. Giltinan), which are also attributed to the Freake Limner, effects of light are largely ignored. Instead, particularly in the young *Margaret Gibbs*, we see an inward rather than an outward source of radiance. Margaret's hair, her arms, her silver necklace and bows are all depicted with an awkward flatness. But despite the artist's inability to render either three-dimensional forms or naturalistic space, technical weaknesses are more than offset by the painting's remarkable decorative design.

FRENCH, Daniel Chester (1850, Exeter, New Hampshire—1931, Stockbridge, Massachusetts), American sculptor. His first commission was the *Minute Man* at Concord, Massachusetts (bronze, 1875). His large oeuvre, mainly in bronze or marble, includes numerous portrait busts and statues of prominent Americans, both historical and contemporary—Washington (1900), Lincoln (1912), Ralph Waldo Emerson (1879; 1914), General Lewis Cass (1886), and others. French also received many commissions for ideal figures for public buildings, such as the *Four Continents* (1907) at the United States Customhouse in New York City and the *Alma Mater* (1903) at Columbia University in New York City. In 1893, for the Chicago World's Fair, he made a colossal 65-foot gilded female allegorical figure called *The Republic*, as well as four group sculptures symbolizing American life, in collaboration with Edward Clark Potter (1857–1923). His most famous and imposing work is the seated marble figure of Abraham Lincoln inside the Lincoln Memorial in Washington, D.C., completed in the year 1922.

FREUNDLICH, Otto (1878, Stolp, Pomerania—1943, Lublin-Maidanek, Poland), German painter and sculptor. It was only at the age of twenty-seven, during a stay in Florence, that he decided to devote himself entirely to art. Briefly tempted by the ornamental graces of Art Nouveau, he began to practice a more constructive art in 1908, in experimental canvases composed of broad areas of pure color, intense to the point of lyricism but clearly organized and separated. In 1909 Freundlich settled in Paris, where he had a studio in the Bateau-Lavoir quarter of Montmartre. He began his first sculpture while continuing to practice painting. In 1914 he returned to Germany, where he remained for the next 10 years. From this period date his first works in stained glass and his first

Otto Freundlich. *Mountain-Sculpture.* 1934. *Photo Giraudon, Paris.*

Caspar David Friedrich. *Wreck of the "Hoffnung."* 1821. Kunsthalle, Hamburg.

mosaics, as well as experimental work in new materials; his first uncompromisingly non-figurative paintings were executed in 1919. In 1924 Freundlich returned to Paris, where he exhibited successively at the Salon des Indépendants and the Salon des Surindépendants and joined the Cercle et Carré group. The Nazis destroyed much of his work after featuring his sculpture, *The New Man*, on the cover of the catalogue of their exhibition of so-called degenerate art.

Freundlich's highly original work avoids geometrical coldness by the density of its light, the radiating power of its color, and its sustained lyricism. His rigorously abstract pictures are first seen as broad areas of bright color, then gradually decompose in subtle gradations by means of an arrangement of rectangles of unequal surface and value. But it was perhaps in such sculptures as the *Mountain-Sculpture* of 1934, which he dreamed of reproducing on a gigantic scale, that Freundlich's constructive discipline found its fullest expression.

FRIEDRICH, Caspar David (1774, Greifswald, Mecklenburg—1840, Dresden), German painter, one of the most typical exponents of German Romantic landscape. Although he attended the Copenhagen Academy in 1794, he was mainly self-taught. In Dresden, where he arrived in 1798, he moved in the Romantic circle that revolved around the writers Johann Ludwig Tieck and Novalis, and in 1801 he made the acquaintance of Philipp Otto Runge. Friedrich had a predilection for the island of Rügen and for the vast, melancholy landscape of Pomerania, where he had spent his childhood. One often finds in his paintings the motif of the ruined monastery of Eldena, on the edge of the Greifswald. His first characteristic composition is the *Cross on the Mountain* (1807; Dresden, Gemäldegalerie), a lonely landscape under a beautiful evening sky. Other typical subjects were cemeteries in the snow, a man and a woman gazing at the moon, and a seashore at dusk. All his scenes are forcefully "re-created" by his precise technique (*Wreck of the "Hoffnung,"* 1821; Hamburg, Kunsthalle). His paintings have the polished brilliance of a mirror.

It seems that in his own time Friedrich did not achieve the reputation he deserved and it was not until 20th-century Germany discovered its own image in his paintings that he came into his own. His spontaneous watercolors and sky studies would seem to have been unjustly neglected.

FRIES, Hans (*c.* 1460, Fribourg—*c.* 1518, Bern), Swiss painter. In 1488 Fries became a member of the Corporation du Ciel, the Basel painters' guild. He then reappears in Fribourg, where he held the office of town painter and for several years was a member of the Great Council. In 1517 he moved to Bern. Six panels from the *Life of the Virgin* (1512) in the Basel Kunstmuseum, as well as two additional panels from the same series (Nuremberg, Germanisches Nationalmuseum) constitute his most important work in terms of size. Also in the Germanisches Nationalmuseum are two fragments (1514) that originally belonged to a triptych from the commandery of St. John in Fribourg. Fries' earlier paintings—such as a *Martyrdom of St. Barbara* and a *St. Christopher* (1503; both Fribourg, Musée d'Art et d'Histoire) and two panels from an *Apocalypse* (Zurich, Kunsthaus)—seem, however, to show greater originality. Over the years the artist's color, which had been harmonious, grew vulgar. Nevertheless, Fries holds an eminent place in the history of Swiss painting.

FRIESZ, Othon (1879, Le Havre—1949, Paris), French painter. Like Raoul Dufy, Friesz was born in Le Havre, and he studied under Dufy's teachers, Charles Lhuillier (1824–98) at the local art school, and Léon Bonnat at the École des Beaux-Arts in Paris. Also like Dufy, Friesz joined the Fauves, was influenced by Cézanne, and flirted with Cubism. From 1905 to 1907, in La Ciotat, Falaise (with Dufy), and Antwerp (with Georges Braque), Friesz painted canvases in which color took the place of line and form. This color was not so violent or heavy in contrasts as that of his fellow Fauves, and his line was not as elegant as that of Dufy or Matisse, but heavier and more exuberant. By 1908 he had left the Fauves. Cézanne's work attracted him for a time, until he drifted toward a Baroque style after a trip to Portugal in 1911. Friesz, who painted the admirable *Portrait of Fernand Fleuret* (1907; Paris, Musée National d'Art Moderne) and displayed such lyric strength in the *Portrait of Madame Friesz* (1923; Musée National d'Art Moderne), then began to develop in a completely unforeseen fashion. He limited his palette to ochers, earth colors, and whites, and an almost animal sensuality, a bent for eloquence, paradoxically linked to a marked preoccupation with composition, gave his still lifes and landscapes the somewhat ambiguous aspect of "ordered chaos."

FRITH, William Powell (1819, Aldfield, near Ripon, Yorkshire—1909, London), English painter of literary, historical, and contemporary genre subjects. After a period at Henry Sass's Academy in London, he studied at the Royal Academy Schools, and made his debut at the Royal Academy in 1840 with a scene from Shakespeare's *Twelfth Night*. In

William Powell Frith. *Derby Day*. 1856–58. Detail. Tate Gallery, London.

the 1840s there was a great vogue for elaborately reconstructed scenes from popular history and literature, and Frith followed the taste of the day with considerable success (scene from Molière's *Le Bourgeois Gentilhomme*, shown at the Royal Academy in 1846; reduced replica in London, Victoria and Albert Museum). He had no sympathy for the "revolutionary" Pre-Raphaelites (or, later, for the Impressionists), but it was probably the Pre-Raphaelites' widely publicized attention to minute detail and interest in modern subject matter that encouraged Frith to embark on the panoramic scenes from contemporary life by which he is now best known (*Ramsgate Sands*, shown at the Royal Academy in 1854, Royal Collection; *Derby Day*, shown in 1858, London, Tate Gallery; and the *Railway Station*, 1862, Coll. Royal Holloway College, Egham, Surrey). They achieved enormous popularity through the medium of engraving. An associate of the Royal Academy in 1845, Frith was made a full Academician in 1853, when he was chosen to fill the vacancy left by Turner's death.

FROMENTIN, Eugène (1820, La Rochelle—1876, La Rochelle), French painter, novelist, and art critic. The son of a doctor, he devoted himself to painting at an early age and was the pupil of Charles Rémond (1795–1875), and then of Louis Cabat (1812–93). The works of Delacroix and of the orientalist Prosper Marilhat (1811–47) inspired him to make a brief trip to Algeria in 1846 and a longer one in 1848. In 1847 he exhibited the pictures he had brought back from his first trip; in 1852 he embarked on a third journey and stayed for two years, going as far as Laghouat. He brought back not only a large number of drawings, but also two books that are masterpieces of descriptive writing: *Un Été au Sahara* ("A Summer in the Sahara"), 1857, and *Une Année dans le Sahel* ("A Year in the Sahel"), 1858. In his painting he chiefly treated aristocratic hunting themes, as in his *Falcon Hunts* (1863; Paris, Louvre) and *Gazelle Hunts* (Nantes, Musée des Beaux-Arts). Fromentin had greater gifts as a writer than as a painter, and the views he expressed in his *Maîtres d'autrefois*, 1876 (*Old Masters of Belgium and Holland*, 1882) reveal a penetrating and cultivated mind.

FROST, Arthur Burdett, Jr. (1887, Philadelphia—1917, New York?), American painter. Contacts with the American Synchromist painters (Stanton Macdonald-Wright, Patrick Henry Bruce, Morgan Russell) in Europe, and with other modern French painters, turned Frost away from his early academic training. Frost studied first at the Pennsylvania Academy of the Fine Arts in Philadelphia and in 1905 attended William Merritt Chase's school in New York. Robert Henri was also an important influence at this time. The following year he worked at the Académie Julian in Paris. Acquaintance with Bruce gained Frost an introduction to the circle of avant-garde artists who frequented the Paris home of Gertrude and Leo Stein. Through them he was made aware of Impressionism and of the newest trends in European painting. His earliest works from this period (1907) suggest the influence of Pierre Auguste Renoir. Bruce also introduced Frost to Henri Matisse, whose teachings brought the art of the Neoimpressionist Paul Signac and of Paul Cézanne to the young artist's attention. The principles of simultaneous color contrasts and harmonies found in Michel Eugène Chevreul's writings and in Ogden Rood's *Modern Chromatics* (1879) preoccupied Frost, although he also learned more intuitive approaches to optical color mixture from Matisse and from the Orphic Cubism of Robert Delaunay and his followers. *Harlequin* (1912; Priv. Coll.) displays Frost's exploration of these coloristic effects while remaining within a semifigurative style.

In 1914 Frost returned to New York, where he worked actively to bring recognition to Bruce and Delaunay. Although this mission proved unsuccessful, Frost was finally given a showing himself in New York at the Montrose Gallery in 1917 (*Colored Forms*, 1917; present location unknown).

FULLER, George (1822, Deerfield, Massachusetts—1884, Brookline, Massachusetts), American painter. In 1838 he completed his scanty education and turned to landscape and portrait painting. Two years later Fuller went to Albany, and in 1842 he went to Boston, where he lived for six years. In 1847 he traveled to New York to study at the National Academy, to which he was elected a member a decade later. In 1860, after spending three years in the South working on studies of Negro life, Fuller visited Europe for a few months. While there, he became friendly with the English Pre-Raphaelite painters Dante Gabriel Rossetti and William Holman Hunt, and was greatly influenced by their work. At his father's death, Fuller was forced to become a farmer in order to support his two brothers; for 15 years he struggled at this occupation, until a crop failure made him sell some of his paintings.

An exhibition that followed this period included work Fuller had done while isolated on his New England farm, and was quite successful, so that he was able to devote himself to painting once again. From then until his death, he painted some of his finest works and exhibited frequently at the National Academy. In *Girl with Turkeys* (1884; Worcester, Mass., Art Museum), one observes Fuller's debt to the French painter Jean-François Millet, but the figure of the girl and the lively flock of turkeys are treated flatly, revealing an early tendency for abstract design in 19th-century American painting.

FULLER, Richard Buckminster (b. 1895, Milton, Massachusetts), American builder noted for his large-scale geodesic structures. As early as 1927, he developed his own version of Le Corbusier's "machine for living," the Dymaxion House (dynamism plus maximum efficiency); unlike European avant-garde architecture, such as Le Corbusier's Villa Savoye (1929), this building had no aesthetic pretensions whatsoever and was basically an arrangement of technical equipment and living space. Some years later, around 1932–35, Fuller produced a motorized version of his project with his three-wheeled Dymaxion Auto. He then began to study structures and became famous with his geodesic domes—polyhedric frameworks of steel ribs covered with standardized elements, tetrahedric or octahedric in form, made of metal, plastic, or even cardboard. Fuller's most typical works include the Ford Rotunda (1953), a geodesic aluminum dome on the circular build-

Richard Buckminster Fuller. Auditorium, Honolulu. 1956. *Photo American Cultural Center.*

ing of the Ford Motor Company at Dearborn, Michigan; the Union Tank Car Company dome (1958) at Baton Rouge, Louisiana, with a diameter of 384 feet, and the United States dome at Expo '67 (1967, Montreal). These domes are space-frame structures of a continuous tension-compression type, in which each member functions in both capacities. Fuller has also experimented with tensegrity (a contraction of Tensional Integrity) structures, a system differentiating tension from compression elements that was discovered by the sculptor Kenneth Snelson (b. 1927), a former pupil (examples shown in 1960 at the Museum of Modern Art, New York).

FURNESS, Frank (1839, Philadelphia—1912, Philadelphia), American architect. After a period as a draftsman in the architectural office of Richard M. Hunt in New York, Furness returned to his native Philadelphia, and in 1867 commenced joint practice with John Fraser (1838–98) and George Watson Hewitt (1842–1916). From 1869 to 1877 the partnership was continued as Furness and Hewitt; the major buildings of those years were the Pennsylvania Academy of the Fine Arts (1872–76) and the Guaranteed Safe Deposit and Trust Company (1875), both in Philadelphia. After Hewitt left the firm in 1877, Furness took another partner, Allen Evans (1849–1925), with whom he continued to practice until his retirement. Among the structures of this later period—all in Philadelphia—were the Livingston House (1881); the Penn National Bank (1882); the National Bank of the Republic (1884); the library on the campus of the University of Pennsylvania (1888); and the Broad Street Station (1892–94; demolished 1953).

Furness combined structural rationalism with vigorous detailing and cyclopean massing to produce buildings whose forcefulness merits comparison with that of his contemporary, H. H. Richardson, although Furness' influence was neither so wide nor so lasting.

FUSELI, Henry, *born* Johann Heinrich Füssli (1741, Zurich—1825, Putney Hill, London), Swiss painter, who spent most of his career in England and adopted the Anglicized form of his name after 1764. Raised in an intellectual atmosphere, he received instruction from his father, Johann Caspar Füssli (1706–82), a painter and art critic. He studied theology and aesthetics, and in 1764 translated into English Johann Joachim Winckelmann's *Gedanken über die Nachahmung der griechischen Kunst* ("Reflections on the Imitation of Greek Art"). A sojourn in Italy from 1768 to 1778, and particularly his stay in Rome, where he drew from the antique and made copies after Michelangelo, laid the ground-work for his career as a painter. On returning to England, he threw himself into both literary and artistic work. On the advice of Sir Joshua Reynolds, he began to devote himself solely to painting. His canvases, which brought him considerable recognition, were grandiloquent and rather artificial (*The Nightmare*, 1781; Zurich, Kunsthaus); nevertheless, he was an important positive influence in the incipient Romantic movement, both for his choice of literary subject matter and his highly individual treatment of the scenes, rich with Gothic fantasy. At the same time, his observance of the traditional rules of formal composition and the heroic scale of his canvases link him closely with late 18th-century Neoclassicism. Around 1780 he produced a curious series of fashion plates with a distinctly erotic flavor, in which women of Michelangelesque proportions are shown in various stages of dress and undress. At about the same time he made the acquaintance of William Blake, upon whom he had a marked influence. In the course of his successful career, Fuseli was elected a Royal Academician and appointed to an Academy professorship.

FUTURISM, a movement that appeared in 1909 as a reaction on the part of a number of Italian poets and artists against a static art that in their view was unsuited to represent the modern world and express its dynamic and transient poetry. Its strength lay in its cult of energy, which was seen as a property not only of objective phenomena, but also of mental states. According to the Futurist aesthetic, it was not enough merely to represent in a single space, *simultaneously*, the successive movements of a woman walking in the street accompanied by a dog on a leash (Giacomo Balla, *Dog on a Leash*, 1912; New York, Museum of Modern Art); it was also necessary for the artist to express the feeling, memories, and associations of ideas with which, for him, the subject was enveloped. For the Futurists, then, space is no longer optical and purely plastic, but is extended by an intuitive depth that Umberto Boccioni called a fourth dimension.

This program was opposed, in spirit and form, to Cubism and Fauvism, both of which were quite alien to the Futurists' will to power. But this did not mean that the Futurist painters advocated a complete break with earlier styles and techniques: Gino Severini, for example, adapted Seurat's use of

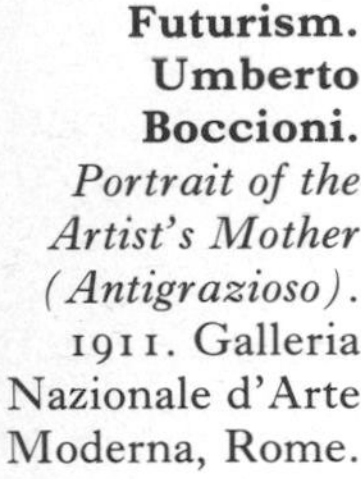

Futurism. Umberto Boccioni. *Portrait of the Artist's Mother (Antigrazioso).* 1911. Galleria Nazionale d'Arte Moderna, Rome.

pure color to Futurist purposes, Carlo Carrà used the gray tonalities of the Cubists, and Boccioni was influenced by Picasso's "realism."

The movement, originally concerned only with poetry (Marinetti's *Manifesto of Futurist Poetry*, 1909), soon spread to painting. In Milan, at the beginning of 1910, Carrà, Boccioni, and Luigi Russolo worked out a program of action with Marinetti, the result of which was the *Manifesto of Futurist Painting*. It was followed in April by a *Technical Manifesto of Futurist Painting*, then, in February 1912, by an exhibition at the Galerie Bernheim-Jeune in Paris, the introduction to which was also something of a manifesto. From 1908 to 1916, the rallying point and the "voice" of the movement was *La Voce*, a periodical published in Florence. Ardengo Soffici, who joined the movement in 1913, and the writer and critic Giovanni Papini founded the review *Lacerba* in the same year. The movement was joined by a great many artists, including Mario Sironi, Ottone Rosai and Enrico Prampolini. The death, in 1916, of Umberto Boccioni, the real mind behind the group, and the enormous increase in membership, hastened the disintegration of the movement, which became more and more politically oriented.

Futurism had also reached sculpture (Boccioni's *Technical Manifesto of Futurist Sculpture*, 1912). Boccioni's own works are among the best produced by the movement. Futurism eventually invaded the theater, music (Russolo's concerts on the "rumorharmonium," an instrument of his own invention), and, much later, architecture. The most important representatives in this field were Mario Chiattone (1891–1932), and Antonio Sant' Elia (1888–1916), a bold, impassioned theoretician. Their Città Nuova ("city of the future") exhibition at Milan in 1914 broke the bounds of architectural academicism (skyscrapers with external elevators, traffic at different levels, etc.). Sant 'Elia wrote a preface to the catalogue, in which he forcefully defended the new approach to architecture and town planning. Fourteen years passed before the question of Futurist architecture was raised again. In 1928, under Mussolini's patronage, the only exhibition claiming adherence to the movement (Prima Mostra di Architettura Futurista) was opened; it included architectural, decorative, and advertising projects. The 1932 Mostra della Rivoluzione Fascista (Exhibition of the Fascist Revolution) marked not the apotheosis, but the total regression of an aesthetic that was Futuristic in name only.

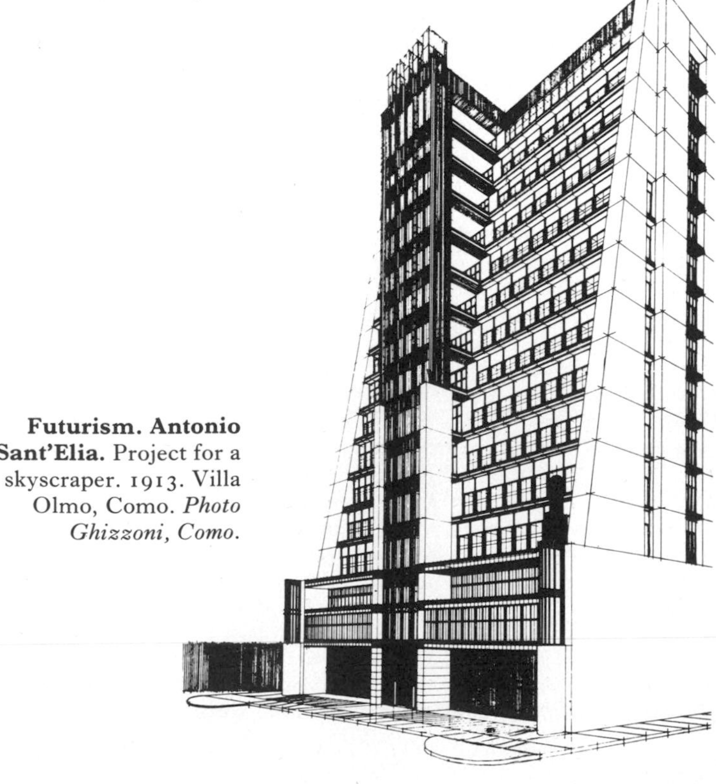

Futurism. Antonio Sant'Elia. Project for a skyscraper. 1913. Villa Olmo, Como. *Photo Ghizzoni, Como.*

FYT, Jan (1611, Antwerp—1661, Antwerp), Flemish painter, preeminent among the Baroque still-life specialists of Flanders. A pupil of Frans Snyders in 1621, a Master in 1629, he traveled for 10 years in France, Italy, and Holland before settling in Antwerp in 1643. His works are dated between 1638 and 1661. He painted flowers, hunting scenes (Brussels, Musées Royaux des Beaux-Arts; Madrid, Prado), groups of birds, fruit, and particularly dead game (1651; Stockholm, Nationalmuseum). Fyt modified Baroque animation into something more sober and introverted and sought to render plasticity rather than decorative effects. He preferred to construct his pictures using a square canvas divided according to the golden section, arranged his objects in depth, and distributed his masses in luminous planes, stressing volume and modifying local color. He constantly varies the tones of the local color and skillfully conveys the suppleness of fur and feathers at the moment when life has just been extinguished. In *Still Life with Mushrooms* (Musées Royaux des Beaux-Arts), gray greens and vivid yellows stand out from a warm harmony of browns. In *Dog and Game* (Paris, Louvre) a lilac red and fine grays are enveloped in a golden light. The *Dead Peacock* (Rotterdam Museum Boymans-van Beuningen) is a masterpiece of color composition, light, and handling the royal-blue plumage splashed with warm brown, violet, green and gold has a sumptuous splendor.

G

GABO, Naum (1890, Briansk—1977), Russian sculptor. His real name was Pevsner, but he soon changed it to Gabo to avoid being confused with his brother Antoine. His studies in mathematics and physics in Munich and his several trips to Italy and Paris (1912–14) brought him into contact with various avant-garde movements. World War I broke out while he was in Stockholm, where, in 1915, he began his first sculptures—heads and busts—constructed in the Cubist manner, with bent surfaces that cut sharp lines into space. Using sheets of metal, wood, cardboard, and celluloid, he sought to express the contemporary spirit in substances other than academic stone and bronze. Gabo brought some of his constructions to Russia when he returned in 1917; he joined the group of Kasimir Malevich, Tatlin, and Alexander Rodchenko in Moscow. In 1920 he issued the famous *Realist Manifesto*, which was also signed by his brother, and in which he stated his position in the controversy between the partisans of a free and independent art and those who demanded that art be applied to utilitarian aims. In 1920, Gabo executed his first "kinetic sculpture," a simple blade of steel 30 inches high that, when set in motion by an electric motor, multiplied its volume in space (*Kinetic Model*; U.S.A., Coll. artist). Moving elements were found again in the glass and bronze *Monument for the Institute of Physics and Mathematics* (1925; never executed).

Naum Gabo. *Female Head.* 1916. Museum of Modern Art, New York.

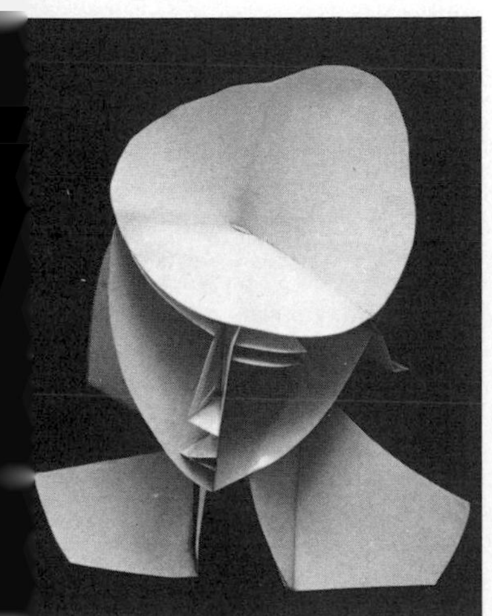

In 1922 Gabo left Russia for Berlin, where he spent 10 years with El Lissitzky and Laszlo Moholy-Nagy, contributing to the spread of Constructivist ideas. After making drawings and models of *Towers*, he produced an astonishing *Column* (1923; New York, Museum of Modern Art), which is a purely geometrical construction of glass, metal, and plastic. In 1927 Gabo and Pevsner designed the sets and costumes of *La Chatte* for Diaghilev's Ballets Russes, and in 1932 the artist settled in Paris, where he took part in the activities of the Abstraction-Création group. Three years later he went to England, where he undertook a series of constructions in which angular designs were replaced by curved, modeled surfaces of unbroken, continuous rhythm.

Later Gabo created extraordinary combinations of curved and angular forms, in which such materials as aluminum, bronze, steel, and gold wire were used together. He went so far as to use color—brick red, for example—in contradiction to one of the principles stated in his *Manifesto*, requiring the artist to adhere to the specific tones and substances of the materials used. In 1946 Gabo settled in the United States, where he began executing monumental constructions in light-weight materials. In 1952, for the Esso Building in Rockefeller Center, New York, he designed a monument of plastic and iron wire—a luminous column enclosed by curves—that would rise in a diamond shape over 15 feet high (never executed). The same spirit is seen in the huge monument he built for the Bijenkorf Department Store in Rotterdam (1957) in the form of a tree with splayed branches, enclosed protectively in a light steel framework.

GABRIEL, family of French architects active in the 17th and 18th centuries, the best-known members of which are:

JACQUES IV (after 1636, St-Paterne, near Tours—1686, Paris). He built the château in the Parisian suburb of Choisy for the Grande Mademoiselle (Louise de Montpensier).

JACQUES V (1667, Paris—1742, Fontainebleau), sometimes known as Gabriel Père, was the son of Jacques IV. He was related through marriage to the architects Jules Hardouin-Mansart and Robert de Cotte, succeeding the latter as first architect to Louis XV in 1735. He often entrusted the decoration of his buildings to the Rococo sculptors Jacques Verberckt and Michiel van Voort (1704–77). The Hôtel Biron (1728–30) in Paris was built with the assistance of Jean Aubert; now the Musée Rodin, it owes a good deal of its charm to two oval salons that project on either side of the garden façade.

After the fire of 1720 that caused great destruction in Rennes, Gabriel and the engineer Robelin were commissioned to replan and rebuild that city. The plan of the Hôtel de Ville, or Town Hall (1726–44) is original: a hemicycle, dominated by a clock tower at its center, curves inward between a block, occupied on the left by the Hôtel de Ville proper and on the right by the Présidial. At the center is a niche formerly containing a full-length statue of Louis XV (it was destroyed during the French Revolution). Gabriel was more traditional in his designs for the Place Royale in Bordeaux (1731–55), in which the Hôtel des Fermes, or Customs House (1735–38) and the Bourse, or Stock Exchange (begun 1741) form a semi-octagon opening onto the Garonne estuary. Gabriel Père also designed the Episcopal Palace at Blois, the staircase leading to the Salle des États in the Palais des États at Dijon; and the plans for La Rochelle Cathedral, which was not completed until 1862.

JACQUES-ANGE (1698, Paris—1782, Paris), the son of Jacques V, succeeded his father as first architect to the king (1742) and as director of the Académie d'Architecture (1742). He erected some of the most important buildings in 18th-century France, and the Classical discipline of the Louis XIV style survives more strongly in his work than in that of any other architect of the period.

Like most of the architectural plans intended to glorify the French monarch, the Place Louis XV (now the Place de la Concorde) was originally proposed by the city authorities, but a vast piece of land outside the walls was offered to the city of Paris by Louis XV, an act that enabled Gabriel to be called in. At this time the taste for natural beauty was growing, and Gabriel was careful not to allow his buildings to obscure the view of the

Seine. He designed an octagonal esplanade surrounded by a moat, bordered with balustrades, and divided by low buildings alongside the river. After some hesitation, it was decided to build two palaces, separated by a new street whose axis (later extended by the Pont Louis XVI) would intersect the axis of the Champs-Élysées and the Tuileries Gardens, which had been laid out in the 17th century by André Le Nôtre. Gabriel's plans included the two palaces; the buildings in Rue Royale facing the church of the Madeleine, which was then under construction; and the Hôtels de la Reynière and de la Vrillière, flanking the palaces and the entrance to the two adjacent streets.

The building of the École Militaire, intended for the training of officers, was just as complex. Gabriel's first plans were rejected as being too expensive, but in 1753 a new plan was drawn up for an imposing structure, near the Champ-de-Mars, to consist of five pavilions linked by low buildings. This project was considerably reduced when the expulsion of the Jesuits left room for another military school in the former Collège de la Flèche.

Apart from these two great buildings in Paris, Gabriel worked for 40 years on a number of royal residences, which he either built or redesigned. At Fontainebleau he rebuilt the Galerie d'Ulysse (1737), the Pavillon des Poêles, and decorated the state and private apartments of the royal family. At Versailles, Gabriel decorated the apartment of the dauphin, the private apartments of the queen and of Madame du Barry, as well as the boudoir of Madame Victoire and the king's library. But his most important work at Versailles was the building of the Opera house, a 15-year project. Returning to some of Mansart's ideas about "good design," Gabriel wanted to rebuild the palace at Versailles so that its center would be surmounted by a dome. His plans were begun, and the result was the Pavillon Gabriel, to which a pendant was added later by Napoleon.

For the château at Compiègne, Gabriel triumphed over a double difficulty: the different ground levels created by the presence of the old rampart between the courtyard and the gardens, and the acute angle formed by the main façades, which he disguised on the inside by a clever piece of planning. At Choisy only his two pavilions and the small château remain. But we still possess his Ermitage at Fontainebleau (1749), the Pavillon Français in the Trianon gardens, the Pavillons de la Muette and du Butard and, of course, the Petit Trianon at Versailles (1762–68). The latter is undoubtedly the most accomplished example of his work.

Jacques-Ange Gabriel. Petit Trianon, Versailles. 1762–68. Courtyard façade. *Photo Jean Roubier, Paris.*

GADDI, Taddeo (d. 1366, Florence), Italian painter. Taddeo owed much of his training to Giotto, who, according to Vasari, had held him at his baptism, and under whom, according to Cenino Cennini, Gaddi worked for 24 years. His first dated work is a triptych of 1334, showing the *Madonna and Child with Saints* (Berlin, Staatliche Museen); but in 1332 he had already started working on the frescoes of the Baroncelli Chapel in S. Croce, Florence, which he finished in 1338. Taddeo, although more concerned with picturesque and narrative details, was nonetheless the most faithful follower of Giotto and the best representative of a tradition of narrative painting that lasted until the end of the 14th century. His experiments with light in the Baroncelli Chapel are striking (*Annunciation to the Shepherds*). After completing the S. Croce frescoes, Taddeo worked at S. Miniato al Monte, then in Pisa (church of S. Francesco, 1341–42). Later he painted an altarpiece for the church of S. Giovanni Fuorcivitas, Pistoia (1353), and a *Madonna*, signed and dated 1355 (Florence, Uffizi).

AGNOLO DI TADDEO (late 1340s, Florence—1396, Florence), the son and pupil of Taddeo, was first mentioned in 1369, among the painters working at the Vatican for Pope Urban V. In 1380 he decorated the Loggia de' Lanzi in Florence (the frescoes are lost); then, between 1380 and 1390, the choir of S. Croce (*Legend of the True Cross*); and finally, the Cappella della Cintola in Prato Cathedral, 1394–96. Agnolo was trained in the Giotto tradition and continued painting in the narrative manner of the Florentine Trecento, but is nearer to Simone Martini than to Giotto.

GAINSBOROUGH, Thomas (1727, Sudbury, Suffolk—1788, London), English landscapist and portraitist, the most poetic illustrator of the English personality since Sir Anthony van Dyck. Gainsborough began his career as a landscape painter in his native Suffolk, under the influence of such Dutch landscapists as Jan Wynants (1625–84) and Jacob van Ruysdael.

The young man arrived in London about 1740 and there became an assistant to the French-born engraver Hubert François Gravelot (1699–1773). He also worked with the painter Francis Hayman (1708–76) on the decorations for London's Vauxhall Gardens, and thus became indirectly acquainted with the Rococo pastoral style. At the same time he was employed by art dealers to copy and restore paintings by the Dutch little masters. The dichotomy between these two styles was resolved by the format Gainsborough adopted for his early portraits: *Mr. and Mrs. Robert Andrews* (*c.* 1748; London, National Gallery) shows simple, unpretentious little figures faintly reminiscent of Watteau, but they occupy considerably less of the pictorial space than the broad cornfield that surrounds them. Gainsborough was, in fact, more advanced in landscape than in portraiture, as may be seen in his *Charterhouse* (1748; London, Foundling Hospital Offices).

In 1748 Gainsborough returned to his native Sudbury; in 1750 he moved to Ipswich, and in 1759 settled in Bath. There is no doubt that from this time he set out to earn his living as a portraitist, although his early exercises in this field are a little timorous. In 1759, he renewed his acquaintance with the works of Van Dyck, the portraitist who was to be the major influence on his mature style, and whose pictures he had seen at Wilton. Gainsborough's greatest portraits show gentlemen relaxing in landscape settings (*Mr William Poyntz*, 1762; Althorp, Coll. Earl Spencer) and ladies musing in glades or forests, their miens often ennobled by poignant light effects, great facial beauty, and imperceptible adaptations of Van Dyckian costumes. Van Dyck is the only master Gainsborough ever acknowledged, yet the latter's handling—lighter and sketchier than that of the Flemish master—gives his work a more wistful, less pretentious appeal. The climax of Van Dyck's influence came, not unexpectedly, after Gainsborough moved permanently to London in 1774, and may be seen at its most brilliant in the portraits of *Lady Margaret Fordyce* (*c.* 1776; Dalmeny, Coll. Earl of Rosebery) or the *Honourable Mrs. Graham* (1775; Edinburgh, National Gallery of Scotland).

By 1780 he had gained the patronage of the royal family, who preferred his style to that of Reynolds: his portraits of King George III and Queen Charlotte (now at Windsor Castle) were exhibited at the Royal Academy in 1781. Gainsborough's sitters, whatever they may have looked like in real life, are transmuted on the canvas into ethereal creatures of exquisite sensibility. After a dispute with the Royal Academy in 1784, Gainsborough exhibited his works only in his studio. His portraits became more glamorous, more poignant, more theatrical in presentation (*Mrs. John Douglas*, 1784; Waddesdon, Buckinghamshire, Waddesdon Manor), and more purely imaginative. These very late works hark back to that idyllic world celebrated in such landscapes as the *Harvest Wagon* (1771; Birmingham, Barber Institute of Fine Arts).

In the 1780s Gainsborough began to paint in another genre, that of the "fancy picture." These, of which the best known is the *Country Girl with Dog and Pitcher* (1785; Russborough, Coll. Sir Alfred Beit), rely heavily on the wistful charm of Murillo's late style, with perhaps an overtone of Jean-Baptiste Greuze, yet the landscapes are darker, more sublime in character, and remind us that the Romantic era of the Picturesque is at hand.

GARGALLO, Pablo (1881, Maella, Aragon—1934, Reus, near Tarragona), Spanish sculptor. In 1911, during his second stay in Paris, Gargallo, overwhelmed by Picasso's Cubist paintings, began to turn toward modern art. The change was obviously made with certain reservations; throughout his career, Gargallo's clay, stone, and marble sculptures demonstrated his unmistakable allegiance to the realist tradition. His creations in iron, lead, or copper, however, were conceived in a more daring vein. The first works carried out in these materials are masks (from 1911). Later he tackled more complex problems, forging *Christ on the Cross* (1923), *Dancer* (1924), *Harlequin with Flute* (1932), and *Prophet* (1933). Although his conceptions remained basically naturalistic, he often replaced convex volumes with hollows, flat surfaces, or voids circumscribed by lines.

GARNIER, Charles (1825, Paris—1898, Paris), French architect. The son of a Parisian blacksmith turned coachmaker, Garnier studied at the École des Beaux-Arts, Paris, and won the Grand Prix de Rome at the age of twenty-three. He returned to Paris after five years spent traveling in Italy, Greece, and the Near East. This long absence abroad left the future creator of the Paris Opéra with the memory of an opulent, sensual, and joyful world.

In 1861 Garnier won a competition arranged by Napoleon III for the building of a great opera house in Paris. All his other buildings are overshadowed by this colossal undertaking, which was imitated throughout the world and may well be regarded as the masterpiece of 19th-century architecture. Work began in 1862, but the building was not completed until 1875. Garnier was genuinely Baroque in temperament and gave full rein to an imagination and a love of splendor that suited the imperial regime perfectly; but he never allowed the decoration to obscure the logical conception that such a building required. The decoration is brilliant and exuberant in its use of polychromatic materials and in the abundance of the statuary, both outside the building and in the entrance hall, the staircase, the bar, and the auditorium itself. But the arrangement of the various elements in this huge theater remains completely rational. The balance of the side façades, whose sturdy masses form a harmonious frame for the main façade and its splendid loggia, and the proportions of the broad dome, dominated by the flattened gable of the stage end, reveal the architect's mastery and invention quite as much as his system of contrasting elements. His Baroque effects find their culmination in the staircase, Garnier's finest achievement.

An analysis of Charles Garnier's other buildings—the Casino at Monte Carlo, the Observatory of Mont Gros at Nice, the Cercle de la Librairie and the Théâtre Marigny, both in Paris—show that he remained faithful to his own principles. He could also be severe when necessary, notably in his own villa at Bordighera, near San Remo, and in the few public buildings he designed on the Italian Riviera.

Thomas Gainsborough. *Mary and Margaret, the Artist's Daughters. c.* 1758. Victoria and Albert Museum, London.

Charles Garnier. Opéra, Paris. 1862–75. Grand staircase. *Foto Marburg.*

Antonio Gaudí. Church of the Sagrada Familia, Barcelona. 1884–1926. Nativity façade with towers. *Photo Mas, Barcelona.*

GARNIER, Tony (1869, Lyons—1948, La Bédoule), French architect. Garnier's career began dramatically with his project for a Cité Industrielle (1901–4), which he designed in the Classical shade of the Villa Medici, during his stay there as a winner of the Prix de Rome (1899). Not only did Tony Garnier formulate in this early work some of the principles that have subsequently determined the course of modern town planning, but he also included in it a remarkable number of concrete proposals for the solution of specific problems in modern urban development that he was later able to use in the great achievements of his maturity. Most of these belong to the vast program of redevelopment begun by the city of Lyons well before 1914. They include the La Mouche slaughterhouse (1909–13); the Olympic Stadium (1913–16), a masterpiece of reinforced concrete built to seat 20,000 spectators; the Grange-Blanche Hospital (1915–30); and the États-Unis district (1928–35). The Town Hall of Boulogne-Billancourt (1931–34), which he designed with Edouard-Bernard Debat-Ponsan (1847–1913), was a prototype for numerous later administrative buildings, derived from the Cité Industrielle project.

The underlying idea of this project was quite revolutionary. His conception was of an urban organism (with neither military barracks nor churches) capable of fulfilling all the needs of modern industrial man. With exceptional originality, he proposed to construct all the buildings of reinforced concrete, a material that until then had been used only in a few industrial buildings. At the same time he conceived a number of forms that exploited this material to the full, forms that have become basic to 20th-century architecture: a continuous line of window, glass walls, stilts, roof terraces, and cantilevers. Equally original were the arrangement of the buildings and the articulation of the different sectors of the town: residential districts without enclosed courtyards, but with uninterrupted stretches of greenery and traffic-free pedestrian precincts, houses with inner courtyards, one-story schools spreading freely in open space, hospitals planned in separate blocks, enormous playing fields, and even a civic center, which was a new idea at the time.

GATCH, Lee (1902, Baltimore, Maryland—1968, Trenton, New Jersey), American painter. Gatch first studied art with Leon Kroll (1884–1974) and John Sloan at the Maryland Institute of Fine Arts in Baltimore (1920–24). He continued his training in France (1924–25) at the American School in Fontainebleau and at the Académie Moderne, Paris, where his teacher was the Cubist painter André Lhote. During his stay in France, Gatch came to know and admire the Nabis painters who later influenced his own style.

Gatch's paintings are abstractions from nature that reveal his strong interest in formal relationships, texture, and symbolism. His early works in the 1920s were oriented toward Cubism, reflecting his training in Paris. In the 1930s and 1940s he developed a more personal style, employing the figure in abstract compositions and experimenting with paintings based on variations of a single color (*Pleasure Garden*, 1945; New York, Coll. Mr. and Mrs. Lionel Bauman). Gatch's compositional devices often included sweeping circular shapes and large rectangular elements placed diagonally within the picture frame, especially as his designs increased in simplicity and freedom (*Night Gothic*, 1957; Boston, Museum of Fine Arts). The surface texture, however, increased in richness, and in contrasts between thin, translucent passages and thick, mat areas of paint. The use of symbols, often with religious connotations, is also prevalent in Gatch's later work (*The Lamb*, 1954; New York, Coll. Joseph H. Hirschhorn).

GAUDÍ, Antonio Gaudí y Cornet, *called* Antonio (1852, Reus, Tarragona—1926, Barcelona), Spanish (Catalan) architect. Gaudí is undoubtedly one of the major figures in the architectural interpretation of Art Nouveau, although this is only one aspect of his work. He was a fervent admirer of the Gothic genius, particularly for its flamboyance and overstatement. Nevertheless, he was a modernist of a very daring sort: elements in his works could almost be mistaken for creations of the 1950s.

He received training at an architecture school in Barcelona, and was apparently a nonconformist even at a young age. His earliest independent work was the Casa Vicens, Barcelona (1878–80), a large villa in which Gaudí already allowed his fantasy free play, decorating the exterior with polychrome tiles. In 1884 he was put in charge of the work on the enormous neo-Gothic Church of the Sagrada Familia in Barcelona, which occupied him for the next 40 years. At his death, in addition to the crypt (which was not his design) and the outer walls of the chevet, only one transept façade (the so-called Nativity façade) with four spires had been completed. The most original work on the church belongs to Gaudí's mature style, from the late 1890s on. The structure—in both conception and detail—defies methodical description. It is indeed architecture treated as sculpture, as can be seen in the four towers of the façade and, above all, in the three porches that seem to derive, as if through a distorted mirror, from those of Rheims. These porches contain an entire complex world of animals and plants in a kind of Baroque delirium. Lastly, the pediments, carved of stone, are covered with an imitation of snow from which emerge sculptures representing events from the life of Christ.

Toward the end of the 19th century, Gaudí came under the patronage of Eusebio Güell y Bacigalupi, a Catalan industrialist. The Parque Güell (1900–14), a landscaped park with playgrounds, promenades, and some small buildings (now the Municipal Park of Barcelona), appears still more arbitrary in design than the Sagrada Familia, and no less astonishing. His major secular works, the Casa Batlló, which he remodeled (1905–7), and the Casa Milá, his original design (1905–10)—both apartment buildings in Barcelona—are further proof of his extraordinary creative genius. In the Casa Milá, particularly, he carried his originality to its utmost limits; there are no straight lines at all. In both buildings, interior and exterior, he used highly plastic, curvilinear walls, which appear to undulate like waves, giving the effect of motion throughout.

GAUGUIN, Paul (1848, Paris—1903, Atuana, Dominica, Marquesas Islands), French painter. Gauguin was the son of a Republican journalist, Clovis Gauguin, and of Aline Chazal, the daughter of Flora Tristan, a militant Saint-Simonian and an eccentric woman of letters. At the age of seventeen Gauguin joined the navy, and he visited Rio de Janeiro and Bahia, Brazil, as well as Scandinavia. On the death of his mother in 1871, he joined a stockbroker's firm in Paris, where he met Émile Schuffenecker, who introduced him to painting. In 1873 he married Mette Sophie Gad, a young Danish woman of bourgeois background; they were to have five children. Gauguin then began to frequent artistic circles and became a close friend of Camille Pissarro. He took part in the Impressionist exhibitions of 1880, 1881, and 1882, then suddenly announced to his wife that he was leaving the Stock Exchange. She became very worried about the future, and decided to take the children and live with her parents in Copenhagen. Gauguin went with them, but he soon felt himself an intruder in his wife's family. In 1885 he returned to Paris with his son Clovis. He put Clovis in a boarding-school and in June 1886 set off for Brittany, where he spent the summer at Pont-Aven. In 1887, with Charles Laval, he set sail for Martinique; but they soon fell ill and had to return to France. In 1888 Gauguin again visited Pont-Aven, where Émile Bernard, whom he had met two years earlier, was living. This meeting proved decisive. Gauguin broke with the Impressionists, whose realistic fallacy he condemned, and formulated a new approach to painting. He called for a return to simplified, solid, well-defined forms, lighting without shadows, and flat colors. An example of the new style is the painting *Vision after the Sermon*, or *Jacob Wrestling with the Angel* (1888; Edinburgh, National Gallery of Scotland). Gauguin summed up these principles in one word, Synthetism. As a system, it was very close to the Japanese aesthetic, which he discovered through Van Gogh during the two months he spent with his friend at Arles (Nov.–Dec. 1888). During this stay he also produced a number of paintings, including *Les Alyscamps* (Paris, Musée de l'Impressionnisme) and the famous portrait of *Van Gogh Painting Sunflowers* (Laren, Coll. V. W. Van Gogh, on loan to the Stedelijk Museum in Amsterdam). In 1889 he exhibited a number of paintings which made a strong impression on young artists. Thus when in April 1889 he returned to Pont-Aven, a dozen of them accompanied Gauguin and their group became known as the school of Pont-Aven. But Gauguin settled in an inn at Le Pouldu, another village in Brittany; he was followed by his most faithful companions, Charles Filiger, Armand Seguin (1869–1903), Isaac Meyer de Haan (1852–95), Henry Moret, Maxime Maufra, and Paul Sérusier.

It was there, among the Breton calvaries, that Paul Gauguin became fully convinced of the aesthetic of Synthetism and its vision of the world, which was inspired by Japanese prints, medieval stained glass, folk imagery, and primitive sculpture. See, for example, his *Yellow Christ* (1889; Buffalo, Albright-Knox Art Gallery), and his *Portrait of a Woman with a Cézanne Still Life* (1890; Chicago, Art Institute). It was not by chance, therefore, that on his return to Paris in December 1890, Gauguin joined the Symbolist writers who met at the Café Voltaire. But literary circles and their endless talk, together with financial difficulties, exasperated him and he set off on April 4, 1891 for Tahiti. He went to live among the natives at Mataiéa, and it was there that he painted some of his finest pictures: *Two Women on the Beach* (1891; Paris, Musée de l'Impressionnisme), *Vahine no te Tiare*, or *Woman with a Gardenia* (1891; Copenhagen, Ny Carlsberg Glyptotek), *Reverie*, or *Woman in a Red Dress* (1891; Kansas City, Mo., Nelson Gallery of Art), *Tahitian Women on the Beach* (1892; New York, Coll. Robert Lehman), *Nafea Faa Ipoipo*, or *When Are You Getting Married?* (1892; Basel, Kunstmuseum), *Manao Tupapau*, or *The Spirit of the Dead is Watching* (1892; New York, Coll. A. Conger Goodyear). Penniless and exhausted by worry and overwork, Gauguin returned to France in April 1893.

His uncle had died, leaving him about 10,000 francs, with which he organized riotous parties, presided over by Annah, "La Javanaise," whom he painted in an unforgettable portrait. Degas arranged an exhibition of Gauguin's Tahitian works at the Galerie Durand-Ruel (Nov. 1893). Financially, this exhibition was a catastrophe, but it aroused the enthusiastic admi-

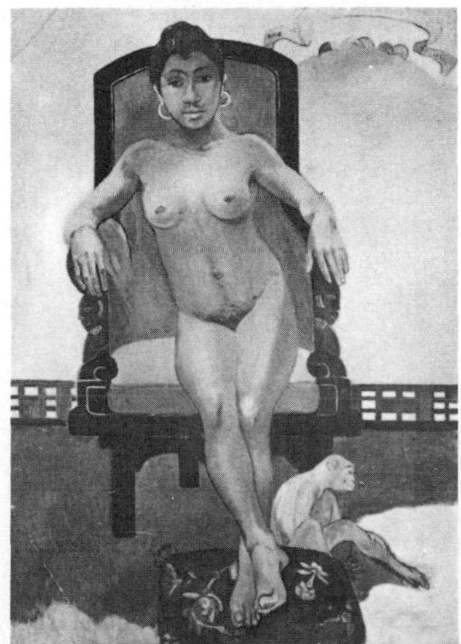

Paul Gauguin. *Annah the Javanese.* 1893. Private Coll., Winterthur, Delaware.

Paul Gauguin. *Where Do We Come From? What Are We? Where Are We Going?* 1897. Museum of Fine Arts, Boston.

ration of Pierre Bonnard, Édouard Vuillard, and Maurice Denis. A series of misfortunes made Gauguin decide to return to the South Sea islands. A sale at the Hôtel Drouot proved disastrous. Nevertheless, he embarked for Tahiti and arrived there in July 1895.

He soon settled in the north of the island, in a hut, where he worked heroically. His health began to fail and in 1897 he had to enter a hospital. But he continued to paint and produced some of his finest masterpieces: *Nevermore* (1897; London, Courtauld Institute Galleries), *Tahitian Women with Mango Blossoms* (1899; New York, Metropolitan Museum), and, above all, the great work, *Where Do We Come From? What Are We? Where Are We Going?* (1897; Boston, Museum of Fine Arts). His manuscript, *Noa-Noa*, appeared in the *Revue Blanche* (beginning Oct. 15, 1897). Revolted by the attitude of the whites toward the natives, he published satirical papers that aroused the hostility of the local authorities. In August 1901, he settled at Fatu-Iwa, on Dominica, one of the Marquesas Islands, in a rustic dwelling that he called the "Maison de Jouir" ("House of Pleasure"). It was there that he painted *And the Gold of their Bodies* (1901; Paris, Musée de l'Impressionnisme), *Tales of the Savages* (1902; Essen, Folkwang Museum), and *Riders on the Beach* (1902; two versions: Essen, Folkwang Museum; New York, Coll. Stavros Niarchos).

By returning to the vital sources of inspiration and language, Gauguin attained through the immobility of his figures, the gravity of their attitudes, the systematic use of arabesque and flat areas of color, the solemn grandeur of ancient and primitive art. He brought fresh life to the art of painting: the Nabis, particularly Bonnard, Vuillard, and Félix Vallotton, felt his influence, and the Fauves were his direct descendants.

GAUL, August (1869, Gross-Anheim, near Hanau—1921, Berlin), German sculptor. Gaul attended the Academy of Drawing in Hanau, then the Industrial School of Art and the Academy of Fine Arts in Berlin. From 1893 to 1897 he was the assistant of Reinhold Begas (1831–1911), the Neo-Baroque sculptor. While in Italy (1897–98), Gaul joined Adolf von Hildebrand's circle and became acquainted with the new ideas being put forward by Hans von Marées, which called for simplicity, unity, and universality in sculptural design. Upon returning to Germany he settled in Berlin, where his bronze *Lioness* brought him acclaim at the Secession exhibition in 1899. A later bronze *Lion*, done in 1906, is equally monumental (Hamburg, Kunsthalle). Gaul was one of the best German animal sculptors in the early 20th century. In his sculptures, he sought to establish a pure form of classical simplicity that was devoid of sentimentality, a quality that appears also in his pencil studies (*Tigers*, 1890).

GAULLI, Giovanni Battista. *See* **BACICCIA.**

GEERTGEN TOT SINT JANS (b. *c.* 1465, Leiden—d. *c.* 1495), Netherlandish painter. Very little of his life is known: Karel van Mander (1548–1611) states that he died at the age of twenty-eight. He was a pupil of Albert van Ouwater, a master of some renown, in Haarlem, and his work anticipates that of Jan Joest van Calcar (1455/60–1519), Quinten Massys, Bosch, and Lucas van Leyden. Geertgen spent most of his short life as a lay brother in the monastery of St. John, Haarlem. In two surviving panels from a large triptych of the *Crucifixion* (*Burning of the Bones of St. John* and *Pietà*; *c.* 1484, Vienna, Kunsthistorisches Museum), and in a *Man of Sorrows* covered with blood (Utrecht, Aartsbisschoppelijks Museum), he reveals Expressionist tendencies. His *Adoration of the Magi* (Amsterdam, Rijksmuseum) already has something of the troubled mysteriousness of Bosch; the *Madonna* (Berlin) shows the influence of wood carving. His tiny *Nativity* (London, National Gallery) is a beautiful nocturnal scene, a study of the effects of artificial light. The *Virgin in Glory* (Rotterdam, Museum Boymans-van Beuningen) is an instance of his use of delicate color and sensitive tonal values. *St. John in the Wilderness* (Berlin, Staatliche Museen) is seen in a tender dawn light that reveals the fresh and flowery landscape in which the saint meditates. The greens and blues of this landscape are subtly linked with the saint's brown robe by the blue cloak in which he is enveloped. In all of Geertgen's work, the landscape is a positive compositional element, far from simple background. Curiosity about man and the world, originality of expression combined with a kind of realism, a lively compositional sense, brilliant coloring, and a scientific treatment of light characterize other works attributed to him, which include the *Holy Kinship of the Virgin*, *Martyrdom of St. Lucy*, *Tree of Jesse* (all Rijksmuseum), and *Life of Christ* (Brussels, Musées Royaux des Beaux-Arts).

GEISER, Karl (1898, Bern—1957, Zurich), Swiss sculptor. A self-taught sculptor, Geiser lived briefly in Berlin before settling in Zurich in 1922. He began his career with a series of heads and figures of boys, and he was a talented and conscientious craftsman: it took him 10 years

Gentile de Fabriano. *Miracle of St. Nicholas.* 1425. Samuel H. Kress Coll., National Gallery of Art, Washington, D.C.

Artemisia Gentileschi. *Judith and the Servant*. Palazzo Pitti, Florence. *Photo Anderson-Giraudon.*

(1926–36) to execute two monumental groups for the Gymnasium in Bern. The cold austerity characteristic of Geiser's earlier work was replaced by a new warmth and vitality in his numerous figures of women (executed from 1943 to his death), in which the heavy, full forms are reminiscent of the works of Aristide Maillol. At his death, a *David* (begun 1944) for the town of Solothurn, near Basel, and a *Monument to the Glory of Labor* (begun 1952) remained unfinished.

GELLÉE, Claude. *See* **LORRAIN,** Claude.

GENTILE DA FABRIANO, Gentile di Niccolò di Giovanni di Massio, *called* (*c.* 1370, Fabriano, The Marches—1427, Rome), Italian painter, trained in the local tradition of his birthplace. In 1408 he was recorded in Venice, where, the following year, he painted frescoes (destroyed) for the Palazzo Ducale. He was in Florence from 1422 to 1425, then in Siena, and arrived in Rome in 1427 to decorate S. Giovanni in Laterano (frescoes, destroyed in the 17th century). He was one of the rare artists before Piero della Francesca to have synthesized the art of the main centers of culture in Italy. In Venice Gentile influenced Jacopo Bellini, Jacobello del Fiore (1394–1439), and Michele Giambono (active 1420–62), each of whom must have developed a different aspect of the master's art: the agility of his line, his elegance, the sumptuousness of his flutings and arabesques. The few portraits known to be from his hand are masterly. Gentile was thus one of the leading painters of the International Gothic style in the early 15th century, introducing, even into large pictures, a courtly refinement and an exquisite romantic atmosphere, together with "naturalistic" inventions. The most characteristic example of Gentile's winning manner is the altarpiece of the *Adoration of the Magi* (1423, Florence, Uffizi; predella in Paris, Louvre), painted for the S. Trinita in Florence. With its aristocratic silhouettes, gold and silver highlights, elaborate detail, magic pageantry, and fine indifference to realism, it represents the summit of an art that had already been transcended by Masaccio.

GENTILESCHI, Orazio Lomi, *called* Orazio (*c.* 1565, Pisa—1639, London), Italian painter. By the time he reached Rome in 1585, he had been trained by his brother, Aurelio Lomi (1556–1622), in the tradition of such Mannerist painters as Agnolo Bronzino and Jacopo Pontormo. He was one of the first to understand the importance of Caravaggio, whom, however, he interpreted with a great deal of freedom. Gentileschi was in Genoa from 1621 to 1623, then in France. From 1626 he lived in England as court painter.

The chronology of Gentileschi's work is uncertain. *David and Goliath* (Dublin, National Gallery) and *St. Cecilia and the Angel* (Rome, Galleria Corsini), still predominantly Caravaggist, are tentatively dated about 1610. In 1623 he painted the *Annunciation* (Turin, Galleria Sabauda), a replica of the one executed for S. Siro, Genoa. The *Lute Player* (Vaduz, Liechtenstein Collection) and the *Rest on the Flight into Egypt* (known in two highly similar versions, at the Louvre, Paris, and in the Kunsthistorisches Museum, Vienna, with a third at the Birmingham City Art Gallery) seem datable to about 1626.

ARTEMISIA (1597, Rome—after 1651, Naples), daughter of Orazio, pupil of her father and of Agostino Tassi (1565–1644). One of her earliest works, *Susanna and the Elders* at the castle of Pommersfelden, bears the date 1610 (unless it should be read 1619); but her artistic personality is indistinguishable at this stage from Orazio's. Artemisia left Rome with her father in 1621 and settled in Florence, where she painted a *Judith and Holophernes* (Florence, Uffizi). Also dating from the Tuscan period are paintings of *Judith and the Servant* in the Palazzo Pitti, Florence, and the Museo di Capodimonte, Naples, the latter revealing an interest in the night effects of the Tenebrist painters. After visits to Rome and Naples, Artemisia joined her father in London (1638/39), where she outshone Orazio. In 1640 she returned to Naples and seems to have been influential among the Caravaggists. She was awarded a commission, highly coveted by Neapolitan painters, for three paintings for the choir of Pozzuoli Cathedral.

GÉRARD, Baron François (1770, Rome—1837, Paris), French painter. He was a pupil of the Neoclassical master Louis David, who helped him to obtain a commission to illustrate editions of the works of Virgil and Racine. At the Salon of 1795, Gérard exhibited a picture painted in the sentimental taste of the time, *Belisarius Bearing a Child Stung by a Snake*. Despite its success, the work found no other buyer than Jean-Baptiste Isabey, who bought it to encourage the painter. In recognition of this, Gérard painted a magnificent portrait of Isabey and his daughter descending the staircase of the Louvre with their dog (1795; Paris, Louvre). Disappointed by the criticism aroused by the mythological painting he entered at the Salon of 1798 (*Psyche Receiving the First Kiss from Cupid*; Louvre), Gérard decided to devote himself to portraiture. A skillful diplomat and a perfect courtier, he succeeded in winning the approval of Napoleon, who commissioned him to paint all the official portraits of the Bonaparte family, of court

Baron François Gérard. *Madame Récamier*. 1802. Musée Carnavalet, Paris. *Photo Giraudon, Paris.*

Théodore Géricault. *Light Cavalry Officer Charging*. 1812. Louvre, Paris. *Photo Giraudon, Paris.*

dignitaries, and foreign princes. He was particularly gifted in female portraiture, and in 1802 painted a fine study of Madame Récamier (Paris, Musée Carnavalet). After Napoleon's downfall, Gérard's friend, the statesman Talleyrand, presented him to Louis XVIII, whose official painter he became. His subsequent portraits included those of Czar Alexander I, the king of Prussia, the duke of Wellington, Charles X, and Louis-Philippe. In 1819 Louis XVIII awarded Gérard the title of baron.

GÉRICAULT, Théodore (1791, Rouen—1824, Paris), French painter, draftsman, and lithographer. From his youth he showed a taste for drawing and for horses. He left the lycée in 1808 for Carle Vernet's studio, where he met an elegant, witty, and worldly group gathered around the master, himself an eccentric dandy. Two years later Géricault left to study in Guérin's studio, where a more reasonable atmosphere prevailed. At the 1812 Salon he exhibited a *Light Cavalry Officer Charging* (Paris, Louvre), which was placed opposite Gros's *Murat*. At the next Salon (1814), however, his *Wounded Cuirassier* (Louvre) was unfavorably received. With the return of the Bourbons, he impulsively enlisted in the king's musketeers at Versailles, and in March 1815 accompanied Louis XVIII on his flight to Ghent. Géricault left for Italy in September 1816: he visited Florence and Rome, admired the Sistine Chapel and the work of Caravaggio, and brought back a picture, the *Race of the Riderless Horses* (1817; Louvre). He painted his grooms in Classical nudity and gave his horses a grandeur and rhythm recalling Greek bas-reliefs. Géricault returned to Paris in the fall of 1817 and lived in a house his father owned on the heights of Montmartre, next to Horace Vernet's studio. The wreck of the frigate "Medusa" off the coast of Senegal, which caused a political scandal, led him to paint an enormous Michelangelesque canvas—the *Raft of the Medusa* (1818–19; Louvre)—that was a naturalistic and journalistic document of a current event in French history. At the Salon of 1819, Géricault's *Medusa*, which the catalogue prudently listed as a *Shipwreck Scene*, was noticed only because of its political significance. This uniquely powerful painting combined a pyramidal Classical composition with bold, vehement Baroque chiaroscuro. From this period may also date his friendship with Dr. Georget, who later commissioned an extraordinary series of portraits of insane patients at the Salpêtrière (1822–23; Ghent, Musée des Beaux-Arts; Lyons, Museum).

In 1820 Géricault, discouraged and exhausted, went to England, where an impresario named Bullock agreed to sponsor a traveling exhibition of the *Medusa*; Géricault's share of the proceeds financed a two-year stay in London, where he executed several series of lithographs and painted the *Epsom Derby* (1821; Louvre). Shortly after returning to France (1822), he fell from a horse, suffering a spinal injury that was to prove fatal.

GHIBERTI, Lorenzo (1378, Florence—1455, Florence), Florentine sculptor whose fame rests on the two great bronze doors of the Baptistery in Florence. Active as a sculptor, goldsmith, writer, and architect, he was one of the most notable figures of the Early Renaissance. Toward the end of his life Ghiberti wrote his *Commentaries*, the second of which contains his autobiography, the earliest by an artist to come down to us, and the principal source of knowledge concerning the Trecento. The autobiography naturally contains details concerning Ghiberti's works, so that there are almost no problems connected with the attribution of his major undertakings. Ghiberti left Florence as a young man, in 1400, only to be summoned back to the city to take part in a competition held in 1401 to decide the awarding of the commission for a second pair of bronze doors for the Baptistery (the first doors had been installed by Andrea Pisano in 1336). Seven sculptors took part in the competition, the subject being the sacrifice of Isaac. Two of the competition reliefs are extant, those of Filippo Brunelleschi and Ghiberti (both in the Museo del Bargello, Florence). Ghiberti won the competition and began work in 1403. His doors, which were closely modeled on the Pisano doors, have 28 scenes from the New Testament, and were completed in 1424. In 1425 Ghiberti was commissioned to make another pair of doors and to decorate them with reliefs of scenes from the Old Testament. These were completed in 1452 and are very different from the earlier scenes. There are only 10 reliefs, treated in an entirely new and different style. The stylistic changes between the two sets of doors reflect the traditional Trecento Gothic style on the one hand and the new humanistic art of the Renaissance on the other. Not only does the second pair of doors make extensive use of pictorial means and of the newly discovered laws of perspective; Ghiberti also employs high relief, medium re-

Below left: **Lorenzo Ghiberti.** *The Annunciation*. Panel from north portal of Baptistery, Florence. 1403–24. *Photo Jean Roubier, Paris.*

Below right: **Lorenzo Ghiberti.** *The Story of Abraham*. Panel from Doors of Paradise. 1425–52. Baptistery, Florence. *Photo Alinari.*

76.

77.

78.

79.

76. **Albrecht Dürer.** *Hare.* 1502. Albertina, Vienna.
77. **Duccio di Buoninsegna.** *Adoration of the Magi.* Panel, Maestà altarpiece. 1308–11. Museo dell'Opera del Duomo, Siena.
78. **Marcel Duchamp.** *Nude Descending a Staircase, No. 2.* 1912. Louise and Walter Arensberg Coll., Philadelphia Museum of Art.
79. **Raoul Dufy.** *The Regatta.* 1938. Stedelijk Museum, Amsterdam.
80. **André Dunoyer de Segonzac.** *The Rowers.* 1914. Private Coll., Paris.

80.

81.

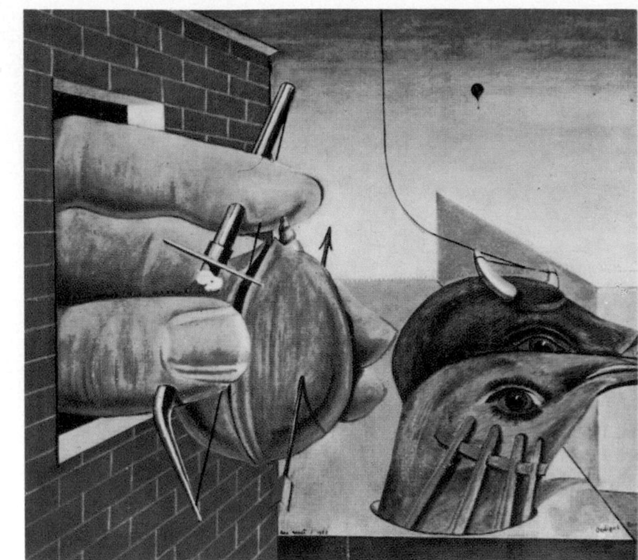

82.

84.

83.

85.

86.

87.

88.

89.

90.

91.

92.

81. **Sir Anthony van Dyck.** *Portrait of Charles I, King of England.* 1635. Louvre, Paris.
82. **Max Ernst.** *Oedipus Rex.* 1921. Coll. Hersaint, Paris.
83. **James Ensor.** *Ostend Rooftops.* 1898. Coll. P. Pechère-Wauters, Brussels.
84. **Henri Evenepoel.** *The Spaniard in Paris.* 1899. Museum voor Schone Kunsten, Ghent.
85. **Jan van Eyck.** *Arnolfini Wedding Portrait.* 1434. National Gallery, London.
86. **Jean Fautrier.** *Anything Else But Love.* 1960. Coll. artist.
87. **Carel Fabritius.** *Goldfinch.* 1645. Mauritshuis, The Hague.
88. **Henri Fantin-Latour.** *Engagement Still Life* (so called). 1869. Musée de Peinture et de Sculpture, Grenoble.
89. **Leonor Fini.** *The Secret Festival.* 1965. Photo Galerie Iolas, Paris.
90. **Domenico Fetti.** *The Lost Piece of Silver.* Palazzo Pitti, Florence.
91. **Lyonel Feininger.** *Schooner in the Baltic.* 1924. Coll. Richard Doetsch-Benziger, Basel.
92. **Vincenzo Foppa.** *Madonna of the Book.* Castello Sforzesco, Milan.

93.

94.

95.

96.

97.

98.

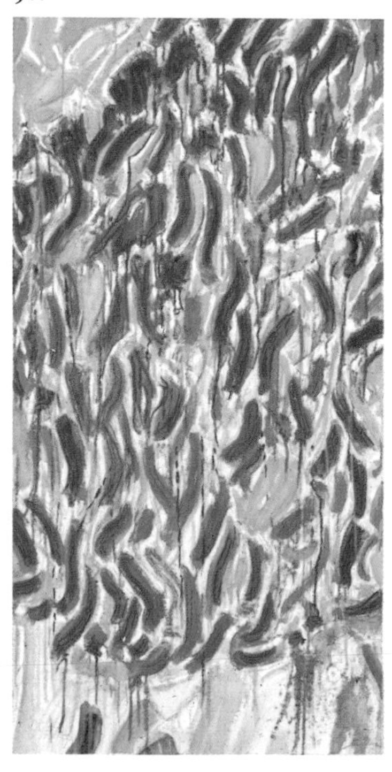

93. **Jean Fouquet.** *The Announcement of Saul's Death to David.* From the "Judaic Antiquities." *c.* 1470–76. Bibliothèque Nationale, Paris.
94. **Henry Fuseli.** *Succubus.* 1810. Kunsthaus, Zurich.
95. **Caspar David Friedrich.** *Morning Light.* 1808. Folkwang Museum, Essen.
96. **Othon Friesz.** *Portrait of Fernand Fleuret.* 1907. Musée National d'Art Moderne, Paris.
97. **Otto Freundlich.** *Composition.* 1930. Private Coll., Paris.
98. **Sam Francis.** *Red and Yellow.* 1955. Private Coll.
99. Opposite: **Jean Honoré Fragonard.** *The Swing.* Detail. 1768. Wallace Coll., London.

lief, and low relief in creating the illusion that some figures are nearer the spectator than others. The doors, whose beauty caused Michelangelo to praise them as the "Doors of Paradise," were heavily gilded to create a still richer pictorial effect.

The abruptness of the change between the two sets of doors can be explained in terms of the evolution of Ghiberti's style in the intervening years, and above all, in response to the influence of Donatello and Classical sculpture. His statue of St. John the Baptist (1414; Florence, Or San Michele) is still an entirely Gothic work; the St. Matthew (1419–22; Or San Michele) is much more Classical; and the reliefs (1417–25) for the baptismal font of Siena Cathedral show a pictorial handling similar to that of the second pair of doors and obviously derived from Donatello.

GHIRLANDAIO, Domenico di Tommaso Bigordi, *called* (1449, Florence—1494, Florence), Italian painter. His two younger brothers, Benedetto (1458–97) and Davide (1452–1525), also distinguished themselves, in painting and mosaic respectively. The three set up a *bottega* (workshop) that became very active under the patronage of a restricted middle-class clientele. Its output was considerable, and there is hardly a church in Florence without a Ghirlandaio altarpiece. After the decoration of the chapel of S. Fina in the Collegiata at San Gimignano (1475) came a series of commissions for the cathedrals of Pisa and Lucca, and for the Ognissanti in Florence. Domenico's *St. Jerome* (1480) in the latter church is a somewhat feeble partner to Botticelli's brilliant *St. Augustine*, but his fresco of the *Last Supper* (1480) in the refectory is a success. In 1481–82, Domenico belonged to the team of painters commissioned to decorate the Vatican's Sistine Chapel. He contributed the *Resurrection* (lost) and *Christ Calling St. Peter and St. Andrew*. Back in Florence, he worked on the decoration of the Sala dei Gigli in the Palazzo Vecchio. Francesco Sassetti engaged Domenico to paint frescoes on the *Life of St. Francis* and an altarpiece with the *Adoration of the Shepherds* (1485) for the family chapel in S. Trinita, while Giovanni Tornabuoni commissioned the artist to decorate the choir of S. Maria Novella with frescoes (1486–90) on the *Life of the Virgin* and the *Life of St. John the Baptist*. The output of the Ghirlandaio *bottega* was uneven. The tondo of the *Adoration of the Magi* (1487; Florence, Uffizi) is successful, as is the restrained and likeable *Visitation of* 1491 (Paris, Louvre); but the 1488 version of the *Adoration of the Magi* for the Ospedale degli Innocenti in Florence betrays the hands of assistants. The well-defined gifts of Domenico are clearly present in the portrait of *Giovanna Tornabuoni* (Lugano, Coll. Thyssen) and in the *Old Man and His Grandson* (Louvre). The Ghirlandaio workshop produced the *Annunciation* mosaic over the Porta della Mandorla of Florence Cathedral (1490), and several mosaic panels by Davide are still extant, including a *Madonna Enthroned with Angels* (Paris, Musée de Cluny).

Domenico was obviously aware of Flemish art: the extreme realism of the *Old Man and His Grandson* and the minute detail of the *St. Jerome* at the Ognissanti are, in fact, Northern in spirit. The *St. Francis* cycle at S. Trinita and that of *St. John the Baptist* at S. Maria Novella offered exceptional opportunities for anecdote, which Domenico exploited with great success by placing contemporary personages, undisguised, in the midst of sacred happenings.

Domenico Ghirlandaio. *Old Man and His Grandson.* Louvre, Paris.

GIACOMETTI, Alberto (1901, Stampa, Grisons, Switzerland—1966, Chur, Grisons), Swiss sculptor, son of the painter Giovanni Giacometti. He modeled his first bust at the age of thirteen. In 1919 he entered the School of Arts and Crafts in Geneva, then spent a year in Italy, where he was able to study the masterpieces of previous centuries. In 1922 Giacometti settled in Paris, where three years of study with the sculptor Antoine Bourdelle convinced him that one could never capture "the whole of a figure" by following the model too closely. He began to create imaginary, symbolic sculptures, elementary in form, out of roughly modeled, incised blocks (the *Couple* and *Spoon Woman*, both 1926). About 1930 he joined the Surrealist movement, whose influence is evident in such works as the *Suspended Ball* (1930–31) and the *Palace at 4 A.M.* (1932–33): open cages with strange objects enclosed by a void.

From 1935 to 1945, he experienced one of the most critical and anguished periods in his career. His long, laborious experimentation led him to model statuettes that became ever smaller, until they reached matchbox size, as in a bust of his brother Diego, a work to which he returned repeatedly. Later the figures became tall and slender, their fragile bodies anchored solidly to enormous feet. Giacometti added and removed plaster until the volume was transformed into a cracked mass and the surface became a kind of rough bark. The transitory aspect of his work was heightened by movement, as in *Falling Man* (1950–51) or *Walking Man* (1960). Concurrent with his single figures, he began to model groups, establishing the proper relations between the figures by variations in distance and proportion. As if to justify their scale, he would sometimes place a head beside them (the *Forest*, 1950) or surround them with a network of twigs to delimit their universe (the *Cage*, 1950–51). During the last years of his life he returned time and again to the faces of Diego and his wife Annette, the models through whom he expressed all the pain and experience of his art.

GIACOMETTI, Augusto (1877, Stampa, Grisons—1947, Zurich), Swiss painter. A member of the avant-garde at the beginning of the 20th century, he studied at the School of Decorative Arts in Zurich and is best known for his large-scale decorative work. He experimented with color values, publishing a book on the subject, *Die Farbe und ich* (1933); in the early 1900s he did a series of pastel compositions on the theme of the square, some of which are reminiscent of Giacomo Balla's early Futuristic work. Giacometti is

Alberto Giacometti. *Large Head of Diego.* 1954. *Photo Rapho–Ernst Scheidegger, Zurich.*

regarded as a precursor of Tachism: he often applied color in thick strokes on a smooth background, left partially bare to introduce an effect of lightness (*Climbing Piz Duan*, 1912; Zurich, Kunsthaus). In addition to mosaics (Zurich University) and stained glass (churches of Chur, Davos, Stampa), Giacometti executed large-scale decorations that are remarkable for their expressive power, compositional control, and mastery of bold colors (New Stock Exchange and entrance hall of the Town Hall, Zurich).

GIACOMETTI, Giovanni (1868, Stampa, Grisons—1933, Glion-sur-Montreux, Vaud), Swiss painter. He was one of the great champions of Impressionist painting in Switzerland, and a close friend of the Italian genre painter Giovanni Segantini from 1894 until Segantini's death in 1899. After studying at the School of Fine Arts in Munich, Giacometti spent three years in Paris, where he was awarded a silver medal at the Exposition Universelle of 1900. He took part in several exhibitions in Munich (1896–1910), Rome (1911 and 1925), Paris (1925), and Venice (1926). Showing a strong preference for luminous colors, Giacometti drew on the themes provided by his native region and produced a powerful, original body of work with affinities to both Impressionism and Expressionism (the *Lamp*, 1912; Zurich, Kunsthaus).

GIAMBOLOGNA. *See* **BOLOGNA,** Giovanni.

GIBBONS, Grinling (1648, Rotterdam—1721, London), the most famous English sculptor of the 17th century. He was born in Holland of English parents and worked entirely in England. His figure sculpture, which gradually changed from a moderate Baroque to a determined and stiff Classicism, is rarely of high quality. The figures in his relief carvings tend to be jerky, and there is little narrative interest. Gibbons' real importance is as a decorative wood carver of fruit and flowers. Important sources of his style are the carvings of the Fleming Artus Quellin and the works of still-life painters of his day; his baskets of flowers in Petworth House, Sussex, seem to come directly from the flower painter Jean-Baptiste Monnoyer. At Windsor, under the influence of the painter Antonio Verrio (*c.* 1639–1707) and the architect Hugh May (1622–84), who were restoring the apartments, Gibbons' wood carvings became freer and more extravagant, setting the pattern for the English Baroque interior.

GIBBS, James (1682, Footdeesmire, near Aberdeen—1754, London), Scottish architect. A pupil of Carlo Fontana during a stay in Rome in the early part of the century, Gibbs occupies a singular position in the development of English architecture during the first half of the 18th century. His two masterpieces, St. Martin-in-the-Fields, London (1721–26), and the Radcliffe Library at Oxford (1739–49), show that his style was equally dissociated from the archaeological intentions of Nicholas Hawksmoor, the dramatic effects of Sir John Vanbrugh, and the Palladian academicism of Colen Campbell. The influence of Sir Christopher Wren, however, is apparent in the interior of St. Martin's. But while Wren treated the towers of his City churches as adjuncts, Gibbs made the St. Martin's spire emerge through the roof behind a Corinthian peristyle, an integral part of the main building. The circular plan, which Gibbs had unsuccessfully proposed in a preliminary project for this church, was adopted in his Radcliffe Library. The very personal church of St. Mary-le-Strand in London (1714–17), the Senate House (1722–30) and Fellows' Building (1724) at King's College in Cambridge, the cathedral of Derby (1725), and the private residences of Sudbrook Lodge in Petersham (*c.* 1718) and Ditchley in Oxfordshire (1720–22) are among the most remarkable of Gibbs' works, which, although generally regarded as conservative, were highly influential and inspired numerous imitations. His elaborately illustrated *Book of Architecture* (London, 1728) was widely used in America and in the British colonies until the end of the 18th century.

GIBSON, Charles Dana (1867, Roxbury, Massachusetts—1944, New York), American illustrator and painter. He received his basic art education at the Art Students League in New York, and furthered his studies in Paris (1888) at the Académie Julian. When he returned to America, Gibson did illustrations for such magazines as *Scribner's, The Century*, and the various Harper publications. Toward the turn of the century an interest in social commentary and New York society resulted in a large production of works lampooning American mores, wealth, and social practices. His wife, Irene Langhorne Gibson, often served as his model for the now-famous "Gibson Girl." Among the fruits of these social observations were his illustrations for such publications as *The Education of Mr. Pipp* (1899) and *The Weaker Sex* (1903). After mastering pen and ink, Gibson revisited Europe to study painting. He returned home to head the government's Pictorial Publicity Division during World War I, and in 1920 became editor of *Life Magazine*.

GIBSON, John (1790, Conway, Wales—1866, Rome), English sculptor, one of the leading exponents of Victorian Neoclassicism. A portrait bust by Gibson was accepted for the Royal Academy exhibition in 1816, and in the following year he was finally able to realize his ambition to go to Rome, where he lived for the remainder of his life. He was only persuaded to return to London in 1844 and 1850

James Gibbs. Senate House. 1722–30. King's College, Cambridge. *Photo Kersting, London.*

John Gibson. *The Wounded Warrior*. The Royal Academy of Arts, London. *Photo C. Cooper & Sons Ltd., London.*

in connection with royal commissions.

In Rome Gibson came into contact with the two masters of Neoclassical sculpture—Antonio Canova, with whom he studied briefly, and Bertel Thorvaldsen, who gave him advice and instruction. Neoclassicism, with its restraint and emphasis on refinement of detail and purity of finish, became the decisive influence on his life's work. Gibson's success in his own day was considerable: his clients included the English royal family, the emperor of Russia, the king of Bavaria, and members of the English aristocracy.

In one important respect, Gibson departed from the strictest Neoclassical principles: beginning in the late 1830s, he frequently added color to his sculptures. Although he invoked the Greeks as the source of this innovation, his work was received with mixed feelings. Nevertheless, the famous *Tinted Venus* (*c.* 1850; Coll. P. J. Dearden) created a sensation when it was exhibited in London in 1862.

GIFFORD, Sanford Robinson (1823, Greenfield, New York—1880, New York), American painter. The main influences on his artistic development were Thomas Cole's dramatic landscapes, which often portrayed the grandeur of his own familiar surroundings. In the 1850s Gifford traveled and studied in Europe and also visited Greece and Egypt. He later visited the Far West, like his Hudson River School colleagues Frederick Church and Albert Bierstadt, but was more interested in capturing certain effects in nature—particularly light and atmosphere—than he was in painting spectacular, romantic, or exotic landscapes celebrating the myth of the American continent.

To achieve the effect of an atmospheric veil in paintings such as *Mountain Landscape* (1860; Albany, Coll. Fillin), Gifford applied thick coats of varnish to the surface of the canvas. It is interesting that although the French Impressionists were working with similar means at the same time as Gifford, the latter, who did not work directly from nature as they did, was not influenced by their work. Instead, Gifford executed his paintings from small drawings (done on the spot) that aimed not so much to imitate nature, but to describe its effects in terms of color and light.

GILBERT, Sir Alfred (1854, London—1934, London), English sculptor. He studied in London and Paris, and from 1878 to 1884 worked in Rome. He exhibited at the Royal Academy from 1882, was made an Associate in 1887, and a full Academician in 1892 (he resigned in 1909 but was re-elected in 1932). The seated bronze statue of Queen Victoria at Winchester (1887) was Gilbert's first important commission. Thereafter he produced memorial statues and portrait busts, as well as ornamental work, which was often in the sinuous Art Nouveau style. His best-known work, begun soon after 1887 and unveiled in 1893, is the Shaftesbury Memorial Fountain in Piccadilly Circus, London, known popularly as the Eros fountain because it is surmounted by a statue of the god of love.

GILBERT, Cass (1858, Zanesville, Ohio—1934, Brockenhurst, England), American architect who specialized in monumental public buildings. He studied at the Massachusetts Institute of Technology and in 1880 made the requisite architectural tour of Italy, France, and England. Upon his return that same year he joined the firm of McKim, Mead & White, but left in 1882 to form a partnership in St. Paul, Minnesota with James Knox Taylor, which lasted 10 years. In 1896 Gilbert won the competition for the Minnesota State Capitol, St. Paul (completed 1903). This started him in a career of governmental commissions that included city halls and courthouses, the New York Customs House (1899–1907), the Treasury Annex in Washington, D.C. (1918–19), the West Virginia State Capitol (1924–31), and the U.S. Supreme Court building, Washington, D.C., begun in 1933 and completed by his son in 1935. His heavy, richly ornamented earlier works suggest Roman Baroque architecture; the later buildings derive from the styles of 18th-century Europe.

Despite the predominance in Gilbert's work of a Classically oriented eclecticism, his most renowned and impressive building is the Woolworth Tower, New York (1911–13), which initiated the vogue for Gothic skyscrapers. It astonished contemporaries not only by its height of 792 feet, but also by its magnificent expression of that height.

GILIOLI, Émile (b. 1911, Paris), French sculptor. After a childhood spent in Italy, he went to the School of Decorative Arts in Nice (1928) and then, in 1931, to the École des Beaux-Arts in Paris, where he studied under Jean Boucher (1870–1939). Influenced by Constantin Brancusi, Henri Laurens, and Raymond Duchamp-Villon, Gilioli soon discovered Cubist sculpture. In 1940 he settled in Grenoble. Although he rapidly developed an abstract style, he continued to learn from Egyptian, Greek, and Roman sculpture. He used un-

Émile Gilioli. *Captive Bird*. 1958. Galerie Carré, Paris.

usually colored precious materials, such as gilt bronze, Carrara marble, onyx, and agate to create elementary and harmonious volumes with highly polished surfaces, enlivened by the play of light resulting from subtle asymmetries and sudden breaks (*Caterpillar*, 1957, Paris, Coll. Louis Carré; *Captive Bird*, 1958, Paris, Galerie Louis Carré). Gilioli's later sculptures are remarkable for a meditative quality, an austere grace not found in his earlier works, and a tendency toward monumentality (*Beggar Woman*, 1962). These characteristics were already apparent in his *Voreppe Memorial* (1946), his *Monument to the Deportees of Grenoble* (1950), and his *Recumbent Statue* at Vassieux in the Vercors.

GILL, Irving John (1870, Syracuse, New York—1936, Carlsbad, California), American architect. He first worked as a draftsman (1890–92) for Dankmar Adler and Louis Sullivan in Chicago. In 1893 Gill left the Midwest and established his own practice in San Diego, California. His early work included eclectic half-timbered houses in Coronado, California, as well as Shingle Style resort homes on the East Coast. From 1908 to 1916 Gill advocated a new architecture of "bare honesty" and "chaste simplicity." In his California buildings for Bishop's School at La Jolla (1909–16), and in the Ellen Scripps House (1916; now the La Jolla Art Center), he employed the clean cubic masses and the sheer unornamented wall planes that characterized his mature period.

Gill also endeavored to simplify interior design and construction methods. He experimented with concrete two-by-fours, developed a fire-retarding solid lath and plaster wall, and refined a tilt slab fabrication system, first used extensively in the Women's Clubs of La Jolla in 1913. A Christian Science church in Coronado, and a combined city hall, fire and police station in Oceanside were his only major commissions after 1916.

GILLES, Werner (1894, Reydt, Rhineland—1961, Essen), German painter. In 1914, shortly after enrolling at the Academy of Art in Kassel, Gilles was called into the army. After the war he returned to the Academy, but soon transferred to the Bauhaus in Weimar, where he studied under Lyonel Feininger from 1919 to 1921. Gilles then spent a year in Italy, and upon his return to Weimar joined Oskar Schlemmer's class. After receiving the Palazzo Massimo award, Gilles went to live in Rome (1931). From then until 1941 he spent the major part of his time in Italy, finally returning to Germany, where in 1944 he was conscripted into the army. Settling in Munich for two years in 1949, Gilles thereafter divided his time between that city and Sant' Angelo, Ischia. Along with Werner Heldt and Eduard Bargheer (b. 1901), he belonged to the circle of Ischia painters.

Gilles was a poetic visionary, and his dreamlike, mythical scenes with their legendary figures of shepherds, fishermen, angels, and deities—inspired by Greek mythology, the Bible, and the poetry of Hölderlin, Rimbaud, and Rilke—were symbolic, abstract compositions characterized by bright colors and a light touch. Best known of his works are the two cycles on the *Legend of Orpheus*, including *Song of Orpheus* (1947; Hamburg, Kunsthalle), executed in 1947 and 1949. Other paintings by Gilles include *Stormy Night* (1948; Berlin, Coll. Markus Kruss) and *Landscape* (1947; Hanover, Coll. Sprengel), which was dedicated to Hölderlin.

GILLOT, Claude (1673, Langres, near Dijon—1722, Paris), French painter and decorator. Gillot painted scenes of everyday life that combine the frolicsome art of the Dutch little masters with the more sober genre tradition of the French Le Nain brothers. More original are those paintings that derive their subject matter and cast of characters from the pantomimes and marionette shows of the Italian *commedia dell'arte*, such as the *Two Coaches* (Paris, Louvre) and the *Tomb of Maître André* (*c.* 1707; Louvre). Gillot was also one of the most admired decorators of his generation, designing illustrative vignettes for the *Fables* of Antoine Houdar de La Motte (1719), tapestry cartoons, and costumes for the opera. Today his chief importance rests on the fact that he was the teacher of Watteau, who worked in his studio from 1703 to about 1708, and who drew inspiration for his *fêtes galantes* from the theatrical themes of Gillot.

GILLRAY, James (1756, Chelsea, London—1815, London), English political and social satirist. He was apprenticed as an adolescent to a publisher of bank notes and maps, Harry Ashby (1744–1818); but his profession did not please Gillray, who joined a group of strolling players. By 1775, when his first caricatures were published, he had returned to London. Thereafter, until 1807, when his health gave way, he produced a series of prints in both color and black and white, often elaborate in style, satirizing all aspects of contemporary life, particularly in England and France. A "caterpillar on the green leaf of reputation," he was merciless in his exposure of political ineptitude and social foibles. *Dido in Despair* (1901), with its pointed references, by close analogy, to Lady Hamilton's adulterous affair with Lord Nelson, is typical. Gillray's last years were clouded by mental illness and, from 1811 until his death, he produced no work at all. His caricatures represent a spirited continuation of the Hogarthian tradition.

James Gillray. *Dido in Despair*. 1801. British Museum, London.

GILMAN, Harold (1876, Rode, Somerset—1919, London), English portrait and genre painter. In 1896 he became a pupil at the Hastings Art School, and from 1897 to 1901 studied at the Slade School in London under Frederick Brown, Philip Wilson Steer, and Henry Tonks (1862–1936). In 1904 he went to Spain, which provided him with the most important influence on his early works, namely that of Velázquez. In London he came into the circle of the English Impressionist painters Walter Sickert and Charles Ginner (1878–1952), who introduced Gilman to the French Postimpressionist theories of Gauguin, Cézanne, and Van Gogh. The second Postimpressionist exhibition in London, organized by the critic Roger Fry and held from November 1910 to January 1911, as well as a subsequent visit to Paris, completed Gilman's artistic education. The result was a resolutely English form of Postimpressionism relying heavily on Van Gogh (the *Canal Bridge*, 1912; London, Tate Gallery) and Ker-Xavier Roussel (1867–1944). A change in Gilman's style occurred around 1910: his later works are flat and brilliantly colored in the Postimpressionist manner. His masterpiece in this later style is generally acknowledged to be the portrait of *Mrs. Mounter* (1917; Liverpool, Walker Art Gallery). Even more French in character are his heavily pointillist drawings. Gilman helped to found the Camden Town Group in 1911, and was the first president of the London Group in 1913.

GILPIN, Sawrey (1733, Carlisle, Cumberland—1807, London), English animal painter. The son of an amateur artist, he went to London (1749), where he was apprenticed to Samuel Scott (*c.* 1702–72). Gilpin specialized in painting horses (*Horses Frightened in a Thunderstorm,* 1798; London, Royal Academy), which he would often endow with quasi-human emotions. He collaborated with other artists, on occasion providing the figures and horses in the landscapes of George Barrett (1728–84), and of William Marlow (another of Scott's pupils), as in their joint work, shown at the Society of Artists in 1771, depicting the *Duke of Cumberland Visiting His Stud at Windsor* (now in the Royal Collection). From 1786 Gilpin exhibited at the Royal Academy, of which he became an Associate in 1795 and a full Academician in 1797.

GIMMI, Wilhelm (1886, Zurich—1965, Chexbres, Switzerland), Swiss painter. He was much admired by the painters of the School of Paris between 1910 and 1940, and was one of the most important figures in 20th-century Swiss art. He studied at the Académie Julian in Paris, but he learned at least as much from Masaccio's frescoes in Florence and those of Piero della Francesca in Arezzo; but the decisive influence on his work was Cézanne. In 1919 his first entry in the Salon d'Automne attracted a great deal of attention. Gimmi's sound, firmly structured work combines vigor of composition with subtle coloristic harmonies, particularly remarkable in his landscapes of the Île St-Louis and the Île de la Cité (*Pont Marie*, 1927; Paris, Musée de l'Impressionnisme) and in his scenes of cafés and of the foyer at the Opéra. While in Paris Gimmi also painted several portraits of the Irish novelist James Joyce, for whom he professed great admiration. The second phase of his career unfolded in Switzerland. He painted several mural decorations for official buildings in Zurich and was awarded the city's Grand Prix for painting in 1962.

GIMOND, Marcel-Antoine (1894, Tournon, Ardèche—1961, Nogent-sur-Marne), French sculptor. Gimond studied first at the School of Fine Arts in Lyons and then successively with Aristide Maillol and Jean Renoir. He went to Paris in 1920, and in 1924 was awarded the Prix Blumenthal. He gave up monumental sculpture, such as the *Girl Standing* (1934; Paris, Musée National d'Art Moderne), and devoted himself to the more intimate, more subtle form of the portrait. His many busts are modeled with force and clarity, but are sometimes lacking in vitality (*Gabriel Fauré*, 1931, Tournon, Museum; *Frédéric Joliot-Curie*, 1960, St-Denis, Museum). Gimond's figures of women and girls are more sensitive in execution (*Madame Vincent Auriol*, 1956; Musée d'Art Moderne de la Ville de Paris). He succeeded in conveying gravity and tenderness through the rather severe medium of portrait sculpture. Maillol discovered "a feeling of grace" in these placid dreamy faces (for example, *Mademoiselle Ferrandier*, 1938; Tournon, Museum).

Marcel-Antoine Gimond. *Bust of a Woman. Photo Marc Vaux, Paris.*

GIORDANO, Luca (1632, Naples—1705, Naples), Italian Baroque painter. He was called *Luca fa presto* ("Luca the Speedy") as much in admiration as in contempt: according to contemporary estimates, his oil paintings totaled 5,000. Giordano is thought to have studied with Jusepe de Ribera in Naples, but the influences he underwent were so complex and his visual memory so retentive that it is difficult to distinguish the strands in his artistic make-up. When he was barely thirteen, he left his native city for Rome, where after having executed many copies and perhaps even forgeries, he was engaged (about 1650) as assistant by Pietro da Cortona, who initiated him into the grand style of decoration. Back in Naples, Giordano was immediately given important commissions, both for easel paintings and frescoes. In 1665 Giordano became Master in the painters' guild. About 1677 he was at the monastery of Monte Cassino, decorating a vault that is now destroyed. His presence in Venice is confirmed by his paintings in the church of S. Maria della Salute. Cosimo III de' Medici summoned

Luca Giordano. *Feast of Herod.* Museo di Capodimonte, Naples.

him to Florence, where, between 1684 and 1686, he painted the vast ceiling in the gallery of the Palazzo Medici-Riccardi (*Apotheosis of the Medici*). Then, at the invitation of King Charles II of Spain, Giordano went to Madrid, arriving in 1692 to execute gigantic paintings in the Buen Retiro palace; later he worked in the monastery of S. Lorenzo at the Escorial, and in the sacristy of Toledo Cathedral. The Prado in Madrid possesses approximately 50 of his works. The accession of Philip V brought him back to Naples (1702), where he reached the height of his fame with the *Story of Judith*, painted on the ceiling of the Certosa di S. Martino (1704).

GIORGIONE, Giorgio Barbarelli, *called* (1477/78, Castelfranco Veneto, Treviso—1510, Venice), Italian painter. Factual knowledge about Giorgione's career is scant and uncertain, the catalogue of his works incomplete and conjectural. The first reliable document, dated 1508, records a disagreement concerning the fee for his fresco cycle (since ruined) on the façade of the Fondaco dei Tedeschi, Venice. In 1510 Isabella d'Este inquired about a "nocturne" left behind by the painter, recently deceased: this is our evidence for the date of Giorgione's death. But the most important information was supplied by the art lover and collector Marcantonio Michiel, who 15 years later, toured the collections of Venice and Padua, and counted 13 pictures by "Giorgio del Castelfranco." Vasari, in the second edition of his *Lives* (1568), described the rapid development of Giorgione: a period of solitary training, followed by an apprenticeship with Giovanni Bellini, then the discovery of Leonardo.

Giorgione. *Adoration of the Shepherds.* Samuel H. Kress Coll., National Gallery of Art, Washington, D.C.

The catalogue of Giorgione's works includes only about 20 items. First are the *Trial of Moses* and a work of less certain attribution, the *Judgment of Solomon* (both Florence, Uffizi). The *Adoration of the Shepherds*, sometimes called the *Allendale Nativity* (Washington, National Gallery), a cardinal work, is difficult to date. Another group comprises the *Boy with a Flute* (Hampton Court Palace); the *Boy with an Arrow* (Vienna, Kunsthistorisches Museum); the Benson *Holy Family* (Washington, National Gallery), and the *Adoration of the Magi* (London, National Gallery), the last finished, no doubt, by another hand. From about 1500 dates the Leningrad *Judith* (Hermitage), transferred from wood to canvas in 1838 and attributed until the end of the last century to Raphael. An altarpiece of 1504, the *Madonna with Sts. Francis and Liberale*, in the duomo of Castelfranco Veneto, concludes the early phase of Giorgione's development. To the following years are assigned the *Laura* (dated 1506; Kunsthistorisches Museum); the *Portrait of a Man* (San Diego, Fine Arts Gallery); the *Tempest* (Venice, Accademia); the *Three Philosophers* (Kunsthistorisches Museum); the *Madonna Reading* (Oxford, Ashmolean Museum); the *Portrait of a Man* in a violet tunic, standing before a parapet inscribed with the initials "VV" (Berlin, Staatliche Museen); the *Sleeping Venus* (Dresden, Gemäldegalerie); and the *Concert Champêtre* (Paris, Louvre). The frescoes on the façade of the Fondaco Dei Tedeschi, Venice (1508)—known through engravings made by Antonio Maria Zanetti the Younger in 1760–71—mark, it seems, the beginning of a new, more monumental phase. To the two final years of Giorgione's life are assigned the *Self-Portrait* (Brunswick, Herzog Anton Ulrich-Museum), a fragment of a larger picture known through an engraving of 1650 by Wenzel Hollar; the *Two Singers* (Rome, Galleria Borghese); the *Portrait of an Old Woman* holding a streamer inscribed "Col tempo" (Venice, Accademia); and *Jesus and the Thieves* (Venice, Scuola di S. Rocco).

Some art historians, such as Roberto Longhi, have discerned an Emilian influence in Giorgione's early works. Their sweetness and formal equilibrium derive, it would seem, from central Italy. The landscape is more sensitive and more supple than the figures, until a softening of contours and a refinement of values create an effortless fusion of figure and landscape, which becomes pure vibration. This new development reveals the influence of Bellini, to whose style Giorgione brought new concentration, and possibly also that of Leonardo. In the Castelfranco altarpiece, the vibrancy of the atmosphere, which suggests third dimension without perspective devices, is a transposition of Leonardo's *sfumato* into a peculiarly Venetian luminosity of color. This strange vision was paralleled by an important new technique. According to a tradition recorded by Vasari, Giorgione used color directly, without any preparatory drawing. His palette included dark reds, golden yellows, browns, and above all, dazzling whites like vibrations of light, conveying the quality of a surface of water, of a piece of cloth, or of crystal. His audacity pointed the way for the entire Venetian School.

Giorgione. *Concert Champêtre.* Louvre, Paris. *Photo Giraudon.*

Giorgione's vision can be both realistic to the point of verism, as in the *Two Singers* or the *Portrait of an Old Woman* (which recalls Northern masters), and dreamlike. The two tendencies coincide in the *Concert Champêtre*, in which every element sustains a melancholy reverie: the close relations between the female nudes and nature; the harmonious continuity between the curve of a hip and the slope of a hill; the music, twilight, and the pastoral setting. It was probably Giorgione who invented and fused the two great themes of modern painting, the female nude and landscape.

The artist's early death, combined with the habit prevalent in

Renaissance workshops of completing work left unfinished, has made the problem of attributions virtually insoluble in many instances. There is no doubt that Sebastiano del Piombo, Titian, and Palma Vecchio, mentioned by the early chroniclers, set their hands to Giorgione's last canvases.

GIOTTO, Giotto di Bondone, called (1266/67 or 1276/77, Colle di Vespignano—1337, Florence), Italian fresco painter, renowned as the founder of modern painting. Traditionally, Giotto is said to have been a pupil of Cimabue, and it is likely that he was also much influenced by Cavallini and perhaps even more by the sculptor Nicola Pisano and his son Giovanni. In the art of Giotto, for the first time, human beings become the sole vehicle for the expression of deep emotions that are Christian in content. The Fall of Man and the Redemption are seen as dramatic human events. Giotto's monumental figures are set in a background that adds the force of naturalism to the Christian message they express.

Until the 19th century it was universally believed that Giotto was responsible for the great narrative series of 28 large frescoes on the *Life of St. Francis* in the vast basilica of S. Francesco at Assisi, where the saint is buried. Several modern art historians maintain that this cycle is not by Giotto, but by some unknown artist. Their view is based on the alleged impossibility of reconciling the style of the St. Francis scenes with the fresco cycle, certainly by Giotto, in the Arena Chapel at Padua.

The Scrovegni Chapel in the church of S. Maria Annunziata dell'Arena was consecrated on March 25, 1305. The frescoes were probably begun soon after, and were certainly finished by about 1309–10. The entire west wall is occupied by a huge *Last Judgment*, including a portrait of the donor accompanied by angels and holding a model of the church. The rest of the nave (but not the choir) is covered with four tiers of frescoes. The top tier contains scenes from the lives of St. Joachim and St. Anna. The Incarnation is symbolized on the chancel arch by the *Annunciation* and the next two tiers are taken up with scenes from the Life and Passion of Christ. The main cycle ends with the *Pentecost*, and the fourth and lowest tier is devoted to allegorical figures of the Virtues and Vices in grisaille.

Apart from the Assisi frescoes, there are several other works that can be attributed to Giotto and that may be dated prior to the Arena Chapel cycle or even before 1300. It is likely that Giotto studied in Rome, where he is known to have worked for Cardinal Stefaneschi as well as in Old St. Peter's, but there are only three Roman works that may be attributed to him. The first, and by far the most important, is the huge mosaic of the so-called Ship of the Church (*La Navicella*). This, though certainly Giotto's own work, was almost entirely remade in the 17th century. However, two fragments seem to show the original style. A fresco fragment of *Boniface VIII Proclaiming the Jubilee* in S. Giovanni in Laterano in Rome has been attributed to Giotto; recent cleaning shows that it has affinities with the Assisi frescoes. The third and most problematical work is the polyptych in the Vatican Museum, the *Stefaneschi Altarpiece*, taken from Old St. Peter's. At least three other works are signed: the altarpieces in the Louvre, Paris, in Bologna, and in S. Croce at Florence; but they too are much inferior to the Paduan frescoes. On the other hand, the *Ognissanti Madonna* (Florence, Uffizi) is neither signed nor well documented, yet it is universally accepted as an autograph work. The *Dormition of the Virgin* (Berlin, Staatliche Museen) has also been held, on stylistic grounds alone, to be by Giotto.

Two other controversial works must be mentioned, the *Crucifix* in S. Maria Novella and the *Madonna* in S. Giorgio alla Costa, both in Florence. The former is perhaps the finest of all these attributed works.

Giotto's later style is generally agreed to be found in two sets of frescoes in S. Croce, the main Franciscan church in Florence, where he is thought to have decorated four chapels. The Bardi Chapel contains a series of scenes from the life of St. Francis; the Peruzzi Chapel contains scenes from the lives of St. John the Baptist and St. John the Evangelist. Both cycles may be expected to shed new light on Giotto's style in the near future. No dates can be assigned to these works with any confidence. Giotto was in Naples in the early 1330s. In 1334 he was made overseer of the cathedral works in Florence (on account of his fame as a painter and not because he was an architect) and began to build the Campanile, which was altered after his death.

Giotto. *Meeting of Joachim and Anna at the Golden Gate.* 1305–6. Scrovegni Chapel, S. Maria Annunziata dell'Arena, Padua. *Photo Anderson-Giraudon.*

GIOVANNI DA MILANO (active 1346–69), Italian painter. Originally from Como, he was trained in Lombardy, probably by Stefano and Giusto de' Menabuoi, who taught him the principles of Giotto's art. He settled in Florence in 1350, becoming a citizen in 1366. He had achieved prominence by 1365, when he was awarded a commission from the *capitani* ("overseers") of Or San Michele for frescoes in the Rinuccini Chapel in S. Croce, representing the lives of the Virgin and of Mary Magdalene. Other notable works by Giovanni da Milano include a *Pietà* (Florence, Accademia) and the polyptych from the church of the Ognissanti (Florence, Uffizi). His lyricism and sensitivity anticipate the Sienese painter Sassetta, with whom he has been confused, and other Tuscan masters of the International Gothic style. The beauty of his color, his poetry—at once intimate and inspired—and the vigorously rhythmic space of

Giotto. *Death of St. Francis. c.* 1318. Bardi Chapel, S. Croce, Florence.

Giovanni di Paolo. *Adoration of the Magi.* Mellon Coll., National Gallery of Art, Washington, D.C.

his compositions, in which Lombard influences are combined with Sienese charm, make Giovanni da Milano the greatest of 14th-century Lombard painters.

GIOVANNI DA UDINE, Giovanni di Francesco Ricamador, *called* (1487, Udine—1564, Rome), Italian painter. He was captivated by the gracious and appealing style of Raphael and became his regular assistant. Giovanni's great opportunity came in the Vatican Logge where, under Raphael, he was allowed to develop his *grotteschi* (1517–19). Here he created a bizarre and fantastic world of great ornamental force by covering his stucco surfaces with a mass of motifs in relief derived from the Domus Aurea, or Golden House, of Nero in Rome. The ornament became fashionable, and Giovanni was given commissions at the Villa Madama (1520) and the (Villa) Farnesina in Rome, and at the Palazzo Vecchio in Florence. He carried the formulas of Raphael's workshops to the palaces of Udine, Venice (Palazzo Grimani), and, with the painter Pierino del Vago (1501–47), of Genoa.

Giovanni Pisano. *Massacre of the Innocents.* Pulpit in Pisa Cathedral. 1302–10. *Photo Alinari-Giraudon.*

GIOVANNI DI PAOLO (*c.* 1400, Siena—*c.* 1482, Siena), Italian painter. He never left his birthplace, where his name is mentioned for the first time in 1423. The influences during his formative years were those of the Sienese painters Paolo di Giovanni Fei (1372–1410), Taddeo di Bartolo (*c.* 1362–1422), and Sassetta, and also Gentile da Fabriano; but, in the course of his long life, his artistic personality became increasingly individualized. For a long time he was regarded as an inferior painter, but he is now considered one of the great Sienese masters of the 15th century. The critic Bernard Berenson called Giovanni di Paolo the "El Greco of the Quattrocento". His nervous draftsmanship, violent colors, and vigorous and poetic interpretation of reality have caused the terms Expressionism and Surrealism to be used in connection with his art; his paintings are in fact imbued with a dreamlike atmosphere. Giovanni di Paolo's principal works are a *Madonna and Child with Angels* (1426; Castelnuovo Berardenga, Propositura); a polyptych of the *Madonna and Child with Saints* (1445; Florence, Uffizi); a *Presentation of Christ in the Temple* (1447–49; Siena, Pinacoteca); the extraordinary *Miracle of St. Nicholas of Tolentino* (small panel from a predella, *c.* 1455; Philadelphia, Museum of Art); the *Last Judgment, Heaven, and Hell* (*c.* 1460–65; Siena, Pinacoteca); and *Six Scenes from the Life of St. John the Baptist* (Chicago, Art Institute).

GIOVANNI PISANO (b. *c.* 1245/50, Pisa—d. after 1314), Italian sculptor and architect, son and pupil of Nicola Pisano. He began his career by working with his father on the pulpit of Siena Cathedral (1265–68), and also completed the fountain known as the Fontana Maggiore at Perugia (1278), begun by Nicola. Later he carved the busts and statues on the coping of the Pisa Baptistery. The pieces that have survived (Pisa, Opera del Duomo) show a surprising energy and exuberance, marking a decisive break with the serenity of antique sculpture. From 1284 he worked on the duomo of Siena, where he was *capomaestro* ("master of the works") from 1287 to 1296; in addition to his functions as architect, he also carved a number of tall figures along the west façade and extending around the north and south sides.

Giovanni was the only Italian architect capable of treating a façade as an organic, planned whole like those of the French cathedrals. In 1301 he completed the hexagonal pulpit in the church of S. Andrea at Pistoia, begun in 1297; the statues and bas-reliefs reflect the passion and love of movement in his art. His chief work at this time was the pulpit for Pisa Cathedral (1302–10), in which one of the figures at the feet of St. John is believed to be a self-portrait. This circular structure, as complicated as a reliquary and Baroque in its exuberance, is particularly famous for its balustrade, decorated with nine reliefs whose subjects—the *Massacre of the Innocents*, the *Passion*, the *Last Judgment*—gave Giovanni the opportunity to crowd excited, angry mobs within the narrow framework, their faces distorted by passion or violence. His last work, which dates from 1313, is the monument of Margaret of Luxembourg in the church of S. Francesco di Castelletto at Genoa (dismembered; some fragments are in Genoa's Palazzo Bianco).

In the course of his career, Giovanni Pisano carved a number of free-standing statues of the Virgin and Child in the French manner. Notable examples are to be found above the entrance to the Pisa Baptistery (*c.* 1295); in the Scrovegni Chapel, Madonna dell'Arena, Padua (*c.* 1305); and in the Cappella della Cintola in Prato Cathedral (*c.* 1312). Giovanni Pisano was the most powerful creator of forms in his time: with astonishing skill he succeeded in harmonizing the demands of the Late Gothic style with the forms of antique statuary.

GIRARDON, François (1628, Troyes—1715, Paris), the French sculptor most representative of the art of Versailles. Son of a master founder, he attracted the attention of Chancellor Séguier, who sent him to Rome at his own expense. On his return in 1652, Girardon worked for the royal residences under Charles Le Brun's direction and generally contented himself with carrying out the projects conceived by Le Brun. His first important work for Versailles was the group of *Apollo Served by the Nymphs* (1666–75)—on which he collaborated with Thomas Regnaudin—for the grotto of Thetis, placed in the Bains d'Apollon by Hubert Robert in the 18th century. Next he carved the *Bath of the Nymphs* (bas-relief, 1675) in the Allée de l'Eau, a masterpiece of delicacy reminiscent of Domenichino's painting of the *Hunt of Diana*, and represented *Winter* (1686), for the Northern Parterre, as a noble, hooded beggar. His last work for Versailles, the *Rape of Persephone* (1694–99) in the grove of the Colonnade, was inspired by Giovanni Bologna's *Rape of the Sabines* in Florence. In addition to his statuary for Versailles, Girardon carved a number of creditable busts, including those of *Lamoignan* (1673; Versailles, Museum); *Boileau* (Paris, Louvre); *Mignard* (Paris, church of St-Roch); and *Arnauld* (Paris, Bibliothèque Ste-Geneviève). His bronze equestrian statue of *Louis XIV* (1683–99), which stood on the Place Vendôme, Paris, was destroyed during the French Revolution; a model is preserved in the Louvre. Lastly, Girardon was the author of a number of tombs, the most imposing being that of Cardinal Richelieu in the church of the Sorbonne (1675–94).

François Girardon. *Bath of the Nymphs* (left half). 1675. Park of Versailles. *Photo Roger-Viollet, Paris.*

GIRODET-TRIOSON, Anne-Louis Girodet de Roucy, *called* (1767, Montargis, Loiret—1824, Paris), French painter. He entered Louis David's studio in 1785, and soon became the master's favorite pupil. He won the Prix de Rome in 1789, and spent five years in Italy. In 1793 Girodet sent to the Salon a surprising *Sleep of Endymion* (Paris, Louvre). Back in Paris, he painted a number of portraits and had a *succès de scandale* at the Salon of 1799 with a painting of a well-known beauty, the actress Mademoiselle Lange, as *Danaë* (Leipzig, Museum der Bildenden Künste) receiving a shower of copper coins instead of gold. In 1801 the architect Pierre François Fontaine (1762–1853) asked Girodet to execute a decoration for the Château of Malmaison on a theme from Ossian, whose poetry (actually the work of the Scottish poet James Macpherson) Bonaparte greatly admired. He painted the *Shades of French Heroes Received by Ossian in the Paradise of Odin* (sketch in Louvre). In 1808 Girodet turned to the writings of Chateaubriand for his inspiration and painted the *Entombment of Atala* (Louvre). He drew his inspiration increasingly from literature, illustrating editions of Virgil, Anacreon, Racine, and even Bernardin de Saint-Pierre's *Paul et Virginie*. His two incursions into the field of contemporary history painting, *Napoleon Receiving the Keys of the City of Vienna* (1808; Versailles, Museum) and *Revolt at Cairo* (1810; Versailles), have only documentary interest.

GIRTIN, Thomas (1775, London—1802, London), English watercolor painter. He was a pupil of the draftsman and topographer Edward Dayes (1763–1804) from 1789 to about 1791 or 1792, and was employed by him to apply watercolor wash to engravings. His further education took place at the academy of Dr. Thomas Monroe (1759–1833) in the company of Girtin's friend and contemporary, J. M. W. Turner. Here the main influence was that of the watercolorist John Robert Cozens, whom both young artists copied.

From 1792 to 1793 Girtin provided watercolors for engravings appearing in the antiquarian James Moore's book, *Monastic Remains and Ancient Castles in England and Wales*. By 1799 he was sufficiently important to become the leader of a group known as the Brothers, or Girtin's Sketching Club (the group was revived in 1802 as the Drawing Society, under the leadership of John Sell Cotman). Girtin paid his only visit to the Continent in 1801, when he went to Paris and painted 20 watercolor views of the city for a volume of engravings (published posthumously by his brother in 1803).

Girtin's achievement in the medium of watercolor is out of all proportion to the short span of his working life. Few drawings are known before 1792. Some, such as *Lichfield Cathedral* (London, Coll. Thomas Girtin), exhibited at the Royal Academy in 1795, although showing great competence, present no radical departure from the stock 18th-century topographical formula. A watercolor of the same year, *Lincoln Cathedral* (London, Coll. Thomas Girtin), shows the topographical element to be in abeyance and a more picturesque approach gaining ground. The *Village of Jedburgh* (*c.* 1800; Armidale, New South Wales, Coll. Dangar) shows a complete dissolution of the 18th-century topographical vision into something more complex, more modern, more infinitely personal. The astonishing *White House at Chelsea* (1800; London, Tate Gallery) vindicates Turner's generous tribute, "If Tom Girtin had lived, I should have starved." The Paris scenes (*Rue St-Denis*, 1801–2; Norwich, Coll. Sir Edmund Bacon), as impersonal and objective as the early cathedral views, have that cast of maturity and modernity that prefigures the watercolors of Richard Parkes Bonington.

GISCHIA, Léon (b. 1903, Dax, Landes), French painter and decorator. Gischia studied in Paris under Othon Friesz, but in 1927, after a crisis of conscience, he suddenly stopped painting. It was not until 1936, when he was stimulated by meeting Fernand Léger and André Beaudin, that he began to paint once more. He exhibited for the first time in 1938 at the Galerie Jeanne Bucher, Paris. In 1941 he took part in the exhibition "Jeunes peintres de tradition française," which was a landmark in the revival of revolutionary painting in France. With the end of World War II, he began to work for the Théâtre National Populaire in Paris, and provided some of their finest theatrical settings, notably for T. S. Eliot's *Murder in the Cathedral*, George Büchner's *Death of Danton* (1948), Corneille's *Le Cid* (1949), Heinrich von Kleist's *The Prince of Hamburg* (1951), Alfred de Musset's *Lorenzaccio* (1952), and

Victor Hugo's *Ruy Blas* (1954). Of an intransigent turn of mind, Gischia was suspicious of emotion and spontaneity; his work is lyrical but controlled, and far removed from any trace of rhetoric.

GIULIO ROMANO, Giulio Pippi, *called* (1492 or 1499, Rome—1546, Mantua), Italian Mannerist painter, architect and decorator. As Raphael's favorite pupil, he was given the task from 1515–16 of executing some of the master's cartoons for the Vatican Stanze (in particular those in the Sala dell'Incendio) and was in charge of the group of artists engaged on the decoration of the Logge. Raphael also employed him at the Villa Farnesina in Rome, where Giulio painted six of the groups in the spandrels surrounding the main fresco in the Loggia di Psiche (1518–19). He even had a hand in certain of the master's paintings, such as the *Holy Family of Francis I* (1518; Paris, Louvre). After Raphael's death, Giulio was made responsible for completing the Sala di Costantino in the Stanze. But it was in Mantua, the capital of the Gonzaga princes, that he spent the greater part of his short career. It was Giulio Romano who gave Mantua its street plan, its cathedral, and the general layout preserved to this day.

The artist's masterpiece is the Palazzo del Tè, a summer pleasure house built for Duke Federigo Gonzaga II on the outskirts of the city. Its architecture marks an important stage in the spread of Roman Classicism, while its decoration reflects the restless Mannerist spirit of the generation of artists that emerged in Italy after Raphael's death. The palace was built between 1525 and 1535.

Two great decorative cycles stretch through the apartments of the Palazzo del Tè, consisting of frescoes, oil paintings, and stucco friezes. To the northeast, a suite of rooms is decorated with amorous subjects. This is repeated around the hall, in which Giulio Romano illustrated the story of Psyche with 22 scenes (1527–31) chosen from *The Golden Ass* by Apuleius. In the southeast apartment, a second symbolic group illustrates the military virtues and the imperial idea: a tribute to Charles V, who twice visited the palace and conferred the title of duke on Federigo. The most spectacular room in this part of the building is the one that is painted from floor to ceiling with frescoes representing the *Fall of the Giants* (1532–34).

After Federigo Gonzaga appointed Giulio Romano inspector of water works and buildings in Mantua, the artist supervised the construction of the porticoes of the city's *Pescheria* ("fish market"); the transformation of the abbey church of S. Benedetto Po; the Palazzo Colloredo; and other patrician residences in that city, including the artist's own house (1544). Working in the Palazzo Ducale from 1538–1539, he decorated the Appartamento di Troia, the bridal suite of the duke's wife Margherita Paleologa (destroyed in 1899), and perhaps the Cortile delle Cavallerizze. After the death of Giulio Romano, Giovanni Battista Bertani (1516–76) made use of his plans for Mantua Cathedral; Bertani respected the basilical arrangement of the naves, but the choir and portal, built in 1755, depart from Giulio's original conception.

Giulio Romano was a prolific artist. Other aspects of his varied genius are to be found in his altarpieces (the *Stoning of St. Stephen*, 1523; Genoa, S. Stefano); in his frescoes in the Villa Madama in Rome (1520–21); and his cartoons, scattered throughout England, for the *Fructus Belli* series of tapestries. The architects Sebastiano Serlio and Andrea Palladio borrowed a number of motifs from him and, in his design of the Palazzo dei Banchi in Bologna, Vignola successfully imitated the arcades, rustication, and coping of Giulio's Palazzo del Tè. Francesco Primaticcio, who had worked with Giulio Romano on the Palazzo del Tè, was to propagate his master's decorative Mannerist style at Fontainebleau in the 1530s.

GLACKENS, William (1870, Philadelphia—1938, New York), American painter. In 1891 Glackens met Robert Henri, who persuaded him to take up painting and who remained a major influence in his career. At this time he was illustrating for the Philadelphia *Press*, together with George Luks, John Sloan, and Everett Shinn. In 1895 Glackens worked in Paris, where he showed at the Salon. In the years following his return he continued to work as an illustrator for the New York *Herald* and New York *World* newspapers, as well as for *McClure's Magazine*, where his work drew critical acclaim for its freshness and immediacy. By 1900 all of his Philadelphia friends had gathered in New York, where, eight years later, they organized an exhibition at the Macbeth Gallery, calling themselves The Eight. This show grew out of their failure, in spite of Robert Henri's position as judge, to gain admission to the National Academy.

Glackens' range of subject matter included portraits, still life, and scenes of middle-class life—boating, bathing, park- and cityscapes. Even in his portraits, however, he usually took a disinterested point of view, preferring the typical rather than the individual qualities of his sitters. In *Chez Mouquin* (1905; Chicago, Art Institute)—the title referring to a

Giulio Romano. Palazzo del Tè, Mantua (courtyard façade). 1525–35. *Gabinetto Fotografico Nazionale, Rome.*

restaurant where The Eight frequently met—Glackens paid homage both to Édouard Manet's *Bar at the Folies-Bergère* (1881–82; London, Courtauld Institute), and to Renoir, whose manner especially influenced his later works.

GLARNER, Fritz (b. 1899, Zurich—d. 1972), American painter of Swiss origin. He spent his youth in France and in Italy, where he studied painting in Naples, Rome, and Milan. In 1922–23 Glarner settled in Paris. His earliest pictures were naturalistic in conception but, by a slow, disciplined process, he transcended this style. He began his abstract works around 1930, and in 1933 joined the Abstraction-Création movement. In 1936 he settled in New York. He became a close friend of Piet Mondrian, who emigrated to the United States in 1941, and was with the Dutch painter during his last moments. Glarner was deeply influenced by the method and spirit of Mondrian's Neoplasticism but remained true to his own personality. Features of his art, which he called "relational painting," were the introduction of obliques into the strict arrangement of the orthogonal system (*Relational Painting*, 1947–48; New York, Museum of Modern Art); a fondness for the circular format, reminiscent of the tondo of the Italian Renaissance; and the use of a wide variety of grays.

GLEIZES, Albert (1881, Paris—1953, Avignon), French painter and theorist. Though influenced at first by Impressionism, he soon became aware of its limitations, and in 1907 took up Cubism. In 1911 he exhibited in the now-famous Salle des Cubistes in the Salon des Indépendants, and also at the Salon d'Automne, where his *Portrait of Jacques Nayral* (1911; La Flêche, France, Coll. Commandant Georges Houot) achieved a somewhat notorious success. He took an active part in the meetings of the Section d'Or, held in Jacques Villon's studio at Puteaux. Whether or not we accept his claim to be the founder of Cubism, Gleizes was undeniably the movement's theorist. In 1912 the publication of his treatise *Du Cubisme* gave him a reputation beyond the borders of France. Drafted in 1914, he was soon demobilized and went to the United States in 1917. He returned to Europe two years later, a convert to religion and concerned, as ever, with technical problems. In 1923 he formulated the results of his experiments and his meditations in *La Peinture et ses lois*. Gleizes published several pamphlets and books, including *La Forme et l'histoire* (1932), in which he preached the "return to Christian man"; in his paintings he tried to express the symbolic rhythms of the art of the Middle Ages.

The work of his early years remained his most successful: *Football Players* (1912–13; New York, Priv. Coll.), *Lorraine Pitcher (La Cruche Lorraine*; Kitchawan, N.Y., Coll. Herbert M. Rothschild), and *Brooklyn Bridge* (1915; New York, Solomon R. Guggenheim Museum).

GOES, Hugo van der (*c.* 1440, Ghent—1482, Rouge-Cloître, near Brussels), Flemish painter. He was a Master at Ghent in 1467, and dean of the guild in 1474. In 1475 he entered the monastery of Rouge-Cloître, where Holy Roman Emperor Maximilian I honored him with a visit. After his return from a visit to Cologne in 1481, he became mad but continued to paint until his death. An exceptional painter who preferred the example of Jan van Eyck to that of Rogier van der Weyden—though the latter was more fashionable at the time—Van der Goes displays a strong feeling for the monumental and theatrical in his art. His work, which is still inadequately studied, is well illustrated by the tumultuous *Adoration of the Magi* (*c.* 1478; Berlin, Staatliche Museen); the *Death of the Virgin* (Bruges, Musée Communal), a work predominantly in cold blue tones; and the Portinari Altarpiece, the central panel of which represents an *Adoration of the Shepherds*. Some 18 feet long, this triptych was painted around 1476 for Tommaso Portinari, the Medici agent in Bruges, and given by him to the church of S. Maria Nuova in Florence (it is today in the Uffizi, Florence). The work shows a boldness in its iconography, and a color scheme based on strong tones of vermilion, ultramarine, and green. The still life of irises, lilies, and columbines in the foreground, as well as the three rough shepherds demonstrate his realism and precision of draftsmanship.

Hugo van der Goes. *Portinari Altarpiece*. Left wing: *St. Anthony and St. Thomas with Tommaso Portinari and his Two Sons.* Right wing: *St. Margaret and St. Mary Magdalene with Maria Portinari and her Daughter.* *c.* 1476. Uffizi, Florence.

GOGH, Vincent van (1853, Groot-Zundert, Holland—1890, Auvers-sur-Oise, France), Dutch painter. One of his uncles was an art dealer, who in 1869 got the boy a job with the Goupil Gallery in The Hague. Later Vincent went to work for the gallery's London branch, and then, in 1875, for their main branch in Paris, but he was soon fired. By 1877 he was working as a clerk in a bookstore in the Dutch town of Dordrecht. Increasingly subject to crises of mysticism, Van Gogh went to Amsterdam to prepare for the entrance examination to the theological seminary there. After his first failure, he went to Brussels to attend a Protestant school. In November 1878, he arranged to be sent as a missionary to the Borinage region of Belgium, intending to bring its miners back to Christ, but his overzealous behaviour earned him the distrust of the miners and the enmity of the clergy. In July 1879, Van Gogh was dismissed.

In 1880 Vincent began drawing figures of miners after works by François Millet. In October he moved to Brussels, where his brother Theo, who was now working for Goupil in Paris, sent him enough money to pay for a few lessons in anatomy and perspective. From April to December he stayed in Etten, where his parents and sister were then living. His conflicts with his father were aggravated by his love for his cousin Kee. She rejected him heartlessly, and Vincent went to The Hague to work under the supervision of his painter-cousin, Anton Mauve. This chosen path, however, held many more misfortunes in store. He quarreled with his father, who disapproved of his artistic intentions; he broke with Mauve; wandered along the coast, making drawings and paintings of seascapes and fishermen; and went to the moors of Drenthe, where he drew his inspiration from thatched cottages, hamlets, and the peasant folk. When his money ran out, Vincent sought refuge in the parsonage at Nuenen, where his father had just been appointed. He spent two years there, displaying a passion for his work that amazed those around him. A brief romance with a neighbor and the sudden death of his father in no way diminished the impetus of his work. Soon he tackled oil painting with the same furious passion. The *Potato Eaters* (1885; Laren, Coll. V. W. van Gogh) dates from this active period.

Vincent van Gogh. *Cornfield.* June 1888. J. W. Böhler Coll., Lucerne.

Van Gogh spent the winter of 1885 in Antwerp, attracted by the harbor and the wharfs, impressed by the grandiose paintings of Rubens, fascinated by the Japanese prints he discovered in a local shop. A new world of light and balance suddenly opened up before him. He produced a few more canvases in the dark, sad style of Nuenen, such as *Daughter of the People* (1885) and the *Shoes with Laces* (1886), both in the V. W. van Gogh Collection in Laren. In February 1886, Vincent left for Paris, where he was welcomed by his brother Theo.

Vincent immediately enrolled in the studio of Fernand Cormon (1845–1924), and there struck up a friendship with Toulouse-Lautrec. Outside the school, Van Gogh experienced a great revelation when he viewed the works of the Impressionists. Using a brighter palette and broken brushstrokes, he painted views of Montmartre and the suburbs, a few still lifes, portraits, and self-portraits above all. Obsessed with Japanese prints, he copied three of them. When winter set in, his creative fever subsided, and, acting on the advice of Toulouse-Lautrec, he departed for the warmth and sunlight of Arles on February 20, 1888.

Everything about Provence entranced Van Gogh: from that moment on, he abandoned Nordic realism and Parisian Impressionism. His hand had never been so sure as now, when all at once he turned from his preoccupation with light to that of color. Suddenly, Vincent's canvases sparkled with vermilion, emerald green, Prussian blue, and yellow—that sacred yellow emblematic of the sun. Over a period of 15 months (February 1888 to May 1889), displaying a haste as feverish as it was deft, Van Gogh painted some 200 canvases, including *Orchard in Blossom*, the *Drawbridge at Arles*, a *View of Arles with Irises*, the *Plain of La Crau, Boats on the Beach, Sunflowers* (all in the V. W. van Gogh Collection, Laren), and the *Café at Evening* (Otterlo, Kröller-Müller Museum). Landscape followed upon landscape and one portrait succeeded another: the *Postman Roulin* (Boston, Museum of Fine Arts), *Lieutenant Milliet* (Kröller-Müller Museum), *Madame Ginoux*, also called *L'Arlésienne* (New York, Metropolitan Museum), *Armand Roulin* (Essen, Folkwang Museum), and portraits of Vincent himself. Everything that Vincent produced in Arles attests to his aspiration for order, health, and serenity—the very things that life denied him at a time when he was achieving them in his art.

Vincent van Gogh. *Self-Portrait with a Severed Ear.* 1889. Leigh B. Block Coll., Chicago.

Hardships and excesses, together with the arrival of Paul Gauguin in 1888 and the ensuing conflicts between the two artists, finally brought about the dramatic events of December 23: Van Gogh tried to strike Gauguin, and then cut off his own ear. Gauguin fled, Vincent was taken to the Arles hospital. Released two weeks later, he painted the two famous versions of his *Self-Portrait with a Severed Ear* (London, Courtauld Institute; Chicago, Coll. Leigh B. Block), the portrait of *Doctor Rey* (Moscow, Pushkin Museum), and the *Old Willow Trees* (London, Coll. Alex Reid and Lefevre)—all at the beginning of 1889. He began to suffer from hallucinations. When the attacks grew more frequent, he was again interned in the Arles hospital and then, at his own request, in the asylum at Saint Rémy. Between attacks, Van Gogh worked: from that awful period date the *Field of Irises* (New York, Coll. Charles S. Payson), *Yellow Cornstalks with Cypress Trees* (London, Courtauld Institute), *Starry Night* (New York, Museum of Modern Art), *Vincent's Room* (Laren, Coll. V. W. van Gogh), and the *Hospital Park* (Essen, Folkwang Museum)— altogether some 150 paintings in which the wavy lines, disjointed forms, and whirling arabesques are the signs of an exalted imagination, not to say a characteristic pathological delirium.

In May 1890 Vincent placed himself under the care of Doctor Paul-Ferdinand Gachet in Auvers-sur-Oise. At this time he painted the doctor's portrait (Paris, Louvre) and that of his landlady, *Mademoiselle Ravoux* (U.S.A., Priv. Coll.), as well as the *Church at Auvers* (Louvre), the *Town Hall on Bastille Day* (Chicago, Coll. Leigh B. Block), and the *Cornfield with Crows* (Laren, Coll. V. W. van Gogh). On July 27, 1890, Van Gogh shot himself in the chest with a pistol. On the 29th, he died with Theo by his bedside. Six months later his brother followed him to the grave, after going insane himself.

GÓMEZ DE MORA, Juan (1586, Madrid—1648?, Madrid), Spanish Baroque architect. He was the nephew and pupil of Francisco de Mora (*c.* 1546–1610) and, in 1611, was appointed master of the works at the Alcázar and at the Pardo in Madrid. At the convent of the Encarnación in Madrid (1611–16), he combined reminiscences of Mora's S. José in Avila with those of Bernini's S. Bibiana in Rome. In 1617 he designed the Clerecía, the large Jesuit seminary in Salamanca; but, owing to alterations made by succeeding architects, we can best see his hand in the plan and the interior of the church. The Plaza Mayor in Madrid, which he built between 1617 and 1619, was also altered later. The cloister of Zamora Cathedral, which he had designed, was finished in 1621. Between 1619 and 1627, Gómez de Mora transformed the Alcázar in Madrid, building a majestic façade on the south side. In his later works, particularly the façade of the church of the Jesuits at Alcalá de Henares (1602–25), his style became more complicated. In Madrid, he built the Quinta de la Zarzuela (1634–37) and the Palacio del Ayuntamiento, or Town Hall (from 1640; much altered by Teodoro Ardemáns).

GONCHAROVA, Natalia (1881, Ladyzhino, Russia—1962, Paris), Russian painter. After studying in Moscow, she visited several European countries. On her return to Russia, she contributed actively to the artistic revival. In 1908, in the first "Golden Fleece" exhibition in Moscow, she exhibited a number of well-constructed paintings in which the stylization of the forms reflected a sort of Cubism. About 1911, Mikhail Larionov, her lifelong companion whom, however, she married only at the end of her life, invented Rayonism; Goncharova fully developed his ideas. This movement advocated a poetic expression of nature in which not the objects themselves, but their relations to each other formed the important element. Such pictures as *Electric Lamps* (*c.* 1912) and, more particularly, *Cats* (*c.* 1911; New York, Guggenheim Museum) were among the first nonfigurative paintings.

The Russian impresario Sergei Diaghilev commissioned her to design the settings and costumes for the ballet *Le Coq d'Or*, which was produced at the Paris Opéra in 1914. That same year Goncharova settled in Paris with Larionov. Apollinaire wrote the preface for the exhibition she held, also in 1914, at the Galerie Paul Guillaume. The Cubist method, along with reminiscences of Russian icons and Iberian art, inspired the series of *Spanish Women* and *Women Carrying Oranges* (1915–25). She continued to work for Diaghilev's Ballets Russes, and her settings for Igor Stravinsky's *Les Noces* (1923) were universally admired.

GONTARD, Karl Philipp Christian (1731, Mannheim—1791, Breslau), German architect. He was appointed director of public works at the court of Bayreuth in 1749. In the following year Gontard was sent by the margrave to complete his training in Paris, where he was introduced to neoclassicism by Jacques-François Blondel. In 1752 he returned to Bayreuth and in 1756 was made captain of engineering. His private buildings in Bayreuth include the Reitzenstein, Spindler, and Athenaris palaces, as well as his own residence. Gontard entered Frederick the Great's service in 1764. He designed several important installations in Potsdam, including the impressive building for the "Communs" with its link colonnade (1765–69); the Guardhouse; the Antique Temple, Temple of Friendship, and Chinese Dragon House in the park (all between 1765 and 1777); the Salt Store (1770); as well as the Noack House (1770) and Military Orphanage (1771–77) in the city. In 1779 Gontard was sent to Berlin, where he designed the twin churches on the Gendarmenmarkt in 1780, and the Oranienburg Gate in 1786. When he succeeded to the throne, Frederick William II retained Gontard's services, and in 1787 commissioned him to build the Marble Palace in Potsdam. One of his last works was the conversion of the king's chambers in the Berlin Castle.

GONZÁLEZ, Julio (1876, Barcelona—1942, Arcueil, near Paris), Spanish sculptor. At Barcelona, in the workshop where his grandfather and then his father had exercised their trade of goldsmithery, he learned the techniques of metalworking. He also studied drawing and painting at the Barcelona School of Fine Arts. In 1900 the González family settled in Paris. There González exhibited with his brother Jean, also a painter, at the Salon des Indépendants and the Salon d'Automne. Jean died in 1908. In his grief, Julio lost all interest in his work for several months. When he emerged from this dark period, he gave up painting and began to sculpt, using the techniques he had learned in his youth. His first works were masks in hammered metal. In 1927 he produced his first works in wrought iron, a series of

Juan Gómez de Mora. Plaza Mayor, Madrid. Built 1617–19. *Photo Mas, Barcelona.*

Julio González. *Montserrat.* 1936–37. Stedelijk Museum, Amsterdam.

Cutout Masks and *Still Lifes*. He had shaken off the influence of Cubism, perceptible in his bronzes, and, using the process of oxyacetylene welding, which he had learned while employed at the Renault factory in 1917, he produced the greater part of his oeuvre in a few years.

González discovered, through his skill in forging, riveting, welding, and hammering metal, the plastic qualities of iron; and he restored distinction and purpose to this material, hitherto used for minor or industrial work. Through a phenomenon familiar in the world of art, his choice of a material that had hitherto been despised led to the development of a suitable technique, which in its turn gave rise to an appropriate style. That is why, although González was misunderstood in his day, his importance as an innovator is now unquestioned. Sometimes he created forms that were immediately intelligible, like his *Masks* (1927), *Don Quixote* (1929), *Montserrat* (1936–37) — that monumental masterpiece acquired by the Stedelijk Museum of Amsterdam—sometimes shapes that were boldly transposed, like the *Kiss* (1930), *Maternity* (1933), *Woman with a Mirror* (1936), and the series of *Cactus-Men* (1939–40). During the winter of 1941, González began a huge plaster figure, but only finished the head. This was *Montserrat II*, inspired by the horrors of war.

GOODHUE, Bertram Grosvenor (1869, Pomfret, Connecticut—1924, New York City), American architect and decorative designer. He had no academic training but at fifteen began his apprenticeship in the office of James Renwick in New York. In 1891 he moved to Boston to work for Ralph Adams Cram, and later became his partner in the firm of Cram, Goodhue & Ferguson. Cram was an important influence at the beginning of Goodhue's career, supplying the theory and impetus for a Neo-Gothic ecclesiastical style that Goodhue interpreted superbly in such churches as St. Thomas (1906) and the Chapel of the Intercession (1912), both in New York City. The firm's buildings at the U.S. Military Academy, West Point (1903–8), with their fortress-like walls and reticent trim, set the standard for 20th-century collegiate Gothic.

As he became increasingly independent of Cram, Goodhue began to turn away from the Gothic, seeking new inspiration in Spanish colonial architecture, which he had studied and written about. As advisory and consulting architect, he chose that ornate Baroque style for the 1915 Panama California Exposition at San Diego, and designed the permanent structures there—the Fine Arts Building and the California State Building—to reflect the Spanish-Mexican heritage of California.

Beginning in 1920 Goodhue tried to break away from historical precedent to create a modern idiom that could be integrated with decorative work by contemporary sculptors and painters. In that year he won the competition for the Nebraska State Capitol at Lincoln (completed posthumously in 1929), with a design that featured a tower rising from the center of a three-story base of offices. In his entry in the competition for a new Chicago Tribune Building (1922; rejected) and his Los Angeles Public Library (completed 1925), Goodhue went even further in stripping all ornament from the body of the building, concentrating it as a climactic feature at the top.

GORDIN, Sidney (b. 1918, Chelyabinsk, Siberia), Russian-born American sculptor. Gordin began his artistic career as a painter, but in the late 1940s turned to sculpture. His earliest sculpture consists of open-form, precise, rectilinear metal constructions (*No. 8*, 1952; brazed silver, polished brass, San Francisco, Dilexi Gallery). In slightly later work, he shifted his emphasis to the possibilities of metal rods in twisted and curved configurations that suggest freer, more organic forms, such as trees (*6-24-58*, 1958; welded steel, Dilexi Gallery). From this point on, Gordin's art reflects an increasing interest in two-dimensional forms and frontality, first in small-scale constructions of painted flattened and hammered metal, and after 1965, in wall-mounted wood reliefs with compositions of projecting curvilinear shapes (*5-65*, 1965; wood and acrylic, Dilexi Gallery). The reliefs are often painted white, with some of the forms accented in color.

GORE, Spencer Frederick (1878, Epsom, Surrey—1914, Richmond, Surrey), English painter. He studied at London's Slade School from 1896 to 1899. In 1904 Gore visited Dieppe and met the English painter Walter Sickert, under whose guidance he discovered the world of the French Impressionists. The influence of Sickert remained evident in his works (*Nude Woman on a Bed*, 1910; Bristol, City Art Gallery) until about 1910, when it was replaced by a somewhat muted imitation of Gauguin and Van Gogh, whose paintings Gore had seen in London's first Postimpressionist exhibition in 1910. A form of subdued Intimism followed, as seen in such works as the *Gas Cooker* (1913; London, Tate Gallery) and *North London Girl* (1911; Tate Gallery). Gore also produced a number of suburban landscapes derived from those of Camille Pissarro. In 1911 he became the first president of the Camden Town Group, an organization of British painters dedicated to French Postimpressionist principles.

GORKY, Vosdanig Adoian, *called* Arshile (1904, Hayotz Dzore, Turkish Armenia—1948, Sherman, Connecticut), American painter. Gorky played an important historical role in the birth of the New York School of Abstract Expressionism. It is in fact owing to his receptiveness that American painters of Jackson Pollock's generation were indirectly subjected to a series of European influences: not only Cézanne, Picasso, and Miró, but also Kandinsky, whose colors and rhythms Gorky sometimes borrowed, and Matisse, whose freedom he emulated.

Gorky lived in the mountain forests of his native country until 1914, then emigrated to Russia, where, from 1916 to 1918, he studied at the Polytechnic Institute of Tiflis. In 1920 he went to the United States. From 1925 to 1931, he studied and taught at the Grand Central School of Art in New York. Like most American artists of his generation, he worked for the WPA Federal Art Project during the Depression (1936–38), and he reached artistic maturity in this period.

When he painted *The Artist and His Mother* (1926; New York, Whitney Museum), Gorky was still influenced by Picasso's pre-Cubist period. He then went through a Cubist phase himself, followed by the influence of

Kandinsky's first abstract paintings. In the development of his own style, his meeting in 1939 with the Surrealists (particularly with Roberto Matta) was decisive. His point of departure was always the observation of nature, but the process of abstraction and dislocation led him paradoxically to the creation of a subjective and symbolical world. He constructed his paintings by the interpretation of lines and forms and by color, which was always keyed to the dominant tone of the background, on which a few brilliant splashes acted like a source of light. The bright colors used about 1944, when *The Liver is the Cock's Comb* (Buffalo, Albright-Knox Art Gallery), was painted, were muted in the series of masterpieces produced in 1947–48, just before Gorky's suicide: *Agony* (1947; New York, Museum of Modern Art); *The Betrothal II* (1947; Whitney Museum).

GOSSAERT *or* **GOSSART,** Jan, *also called* Mabuse (*c.* 1478, Maubeuge, Hainault—*c.* 1536, Antwerp), Flemish Mannerist painter. After a journey to Italy (1508–10) that took him to Florence, Rome, and Venice, Gossaert became a keen student of Classical antiquity and introduced the pagan spirit of Italian art into 16th-century Flemish painting, becoming one of the leading Antwerp Mannerists. His paintings, drawings, and tapestry cartoons were frequently based on erotic mythological themes (*Neptune and Amphitrite*, 1516, Berlin, Staatliche Museen; *Danaë*, 1527, Munich, Alte Pinakothek). In compositions having elaborate architectural settings (the *Malvagna Triptych*, after 1510; Palermo, Galleria Nazionale della Sicilia) or in his numerous variations on the theme of *Adam and Eve* (versions in Berlin's Charlottenburg Palace and England's Hampton Court Palace), Gossaert makes every form a pretext for exhibiting his virtuoso knowledge of the new sciences of anatomy, perspective, and the interaction of moving bodies in space. He concentrates on firm modeling and an exaggerated delineation of muscles in the manner of Michelangelo, combining memories of the art of Dürer and the Italians with the native Flemish qualities of brilliant technique, dense coloring, and lively sensuality.

GOTHIC ART. The term Gothic was first used during the Renaissance, by Italian painters and writers such as Raphael and Giorgio Vasari, to refer to the art that flourished throughout Christian Europe for more than three centuries, from about 1150 until 1500. They used it in a derogatory way because the only standards of beauty they could imagine were those of Classical art. The climate of opinion they established prevailed to such an extent that throughout the 17th and 18th centuries minds that were considered enlightened had nothing but scorn for that art. The enthusiasm of the Romantic movement was needed to revive Gothic art.

In the style that followed the Romanesque period, architecture occupied a predominant place. Gothic architecture was essentially French for it developed in the Île-de-France and was represented there by a proliferation of monuments as early as the 12th century. When the style spread to other countries, from the 13th century, it was varied in certain respects but its basic character remained the same.

The trend of Gothic architecture was away from Romanesque heaviness and sobriety and toward lightness, grace, and even fragility. In sculpture and painting realism was sought: figures were given expressive faces and lifelike poses. In the minor arts perhaps more than in any other sphere, the fastidious tastes for luxury and refinement are reflected.

ARCHITECTURE

The essential character of Gothic architecture lies in the manner of its construction. Vaults do not rest on thick walls, as in previous styles, but are supported on piers. This new system of building was made possible by the use of the ribbed vault. This developed out of the groin vault, which had been employed in Romanesque times. It was produced by the addition of two diagonal ribs, probably for reinforcement, formed from two arches that make up a framework within the vault by springing diagonally from one transverse arch to another and intersecting at the crown. These supporting ribs, or ogives, carry the weight of the vault, relieve part of the pressure on the crown where a counteraction of forces occurs, and distribute the thrust to the four corners and so on to the piers. Further, diagonal ribs divide the vault into four compartments or separate cells that can be of light construction. At a later date the formeret or wall rib began to be used also. This lateral rib engaged in the thickness of the wall partially relieves the wall of the weight of the vault by supporting the cells at the side. It also completes the framework of the bay, making each bay an independent unit.

The first true ribbed vaults that can be securely dated are those in the cathedrals of Durham (choir aisles, *c.* 1093–96) and Winchester (transept aisles, immediately after 1107), the abbey church of Notre-Dame at Jumiège (chapter house, 1101–9), Évreux Cathedral (1119), and the abbey church at Lessay (ribbed vault, *c.* 1100). The ribbed vault seems to have been used first in Anglo-Norman architecture, where many other early (but undated) ribs are found.

The sexpartite vault originated in Normandy, in the abbeys of St-Étienne and Ste-Trinité at Caen, both of whose naves were vaulted about 1110–20. This type of vault was divided into six cells by a supplementary rib parallel to the transverse arches. The four strong corner piers carried nearly all the weight of the vault.

The first ribbed vaults had semicircular transverse and supporting arches, but the arches of the nave were often wider and therefore higher than those of the aisles. The thrust of these umbrella-shaped vaults was absorbed by the transverse arches and lateral walls, and therefore the walls would have had to be very thick, as in Romanesque churches. But instead the pointed arch was employed: it could be made as steeply pointed as was necessary to equal the height of the diagonal

Jan Gossaert. *Jean Carondelet.* 1517. Louvre, Paris. *Photo Giraudon, Paris.*

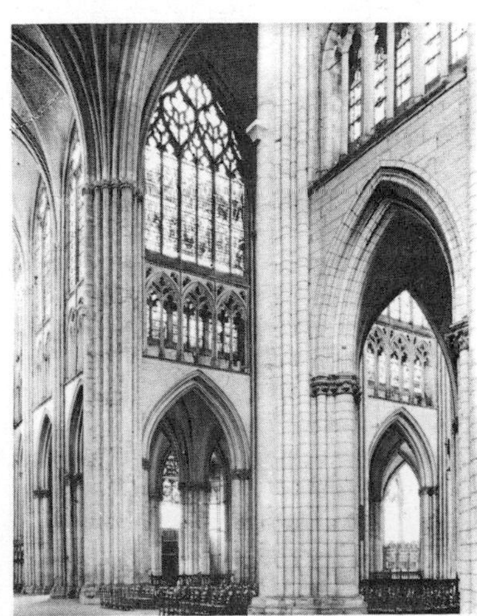

Gothic Art. South transept, Troyes Cathedral. 1206–40. *Photo Jean Roubier, Paris.*

Gothic Art. Double nave divided by columns, Church of the Jacobins, Toulouse. 1230–92. *Photo Yan, Toulouse.*

ribs. The weight of the vault was thereby distributed among the transverse, diagonal, and wall ribs, and this made it possible to diminish the thickness of the walls and to make large openings in them. The pointed arch was not imposed all at once on Gothic art: the semicircular arch was still used for apertures, and only toward the mid-12th century was it replaced by the pointed arch in windows, triforia, and portals.

The supports of the Gothic ribbed vault scarcely differed from those of the Romanesque vault. In the 11th century, the round pier was still used but in a more slender form. An alternating rhythm of massive and slender piers corresponded with the structure of the sexpartite vault, for transverse arches were carried on the massive piers while the slender piers supported supplementary ribs. Compound piers, used more and more frequently, were of colonnettes corresponding to the ribs or even the tracery of the vault. In the 15th century, the piers often lacked capitals. Buildings with several aisles of unequal height required a means of buttressing the nave, since piers are only capable of supporting a vertical thrust. This function was fulfilled by the flying buttress, a quadrant arch detached from the rest of the structure, which leans against the exterior wall of the nave, spans the side aisles, and transmits the nave's thrust to an external buttress pier. But even the simplest form of flying buttress was not yet in use with the first ribbed vaults. The earliest means of support for the nave was a series of buttressing walls constructed above the transverse arches of the aisles. These walls were liable to crush the transverse arches of the aisles. In an attempt to make them lighter, they were pierced with quadrant-shaped openings on the part nearest the nave. It was by enlarging these openings that the flying buttress was eventually developed. The first place in which it was fully exposed to view was along the nave of Notre-Dame Cathedral in Paris (the nave was begun in 1180).

The Gothic style evolved slowly over a long period. Its phases overlap, but for purposes of study, it is possible to distinguish a transitional period, up to about 1140; an Early Gothic style, about 1140–94; a High or Rayonnant Gothic style (the period of the great French cathedrals), about 1194–1280; and a Late or Flamboyant Gothic period, about 1280–1500.

Religious Architecture in France

Transitional and Early Periods. During the 12th century, ribbed vaults and other elements of Gothic construction began to appear in Romanesque buildings with thick walls, narrow windows, wide transverse arches, and Romanesque decorative elements. The east end of the Romanesque abbey church at Morienval was given a ribbed vault in 1125, and St-Étienne at Beauvais also combined Romanesque and Gothic elements. The west porch of St-Pierre at Moissac has the first vault built entirely on pointed arches, although the ribs have no supporting function. Impetus was given to the new architectural movement with the building of Sens Cathedral and the abbey church of St-Denis, both of which were begun about the same time (*c.* 1140 and *c.* 1135, respectively). St-Denis, built under Abbot Suger (*c.* 1081–1151), is considered the first Early Gothic building. Norman influence can be detected in the façade and the diagonal ribs have triple moldings; but in each of the radiating chapels a fifth rib extends from the keystone of the vault to a console between the two windows. Sens Cathedral constitutes another important stage in the development of the Gothic style. Still Romanesque in many details, it nonetheless shows a unified conception in certain sections that may well be called Gothic.

North of the Loire river, one after another of the great 12th-century cathedrals began to be built. Noyon (1145) had a nave with alternating massive and slender piers and (before the fire of 1293) a sexpartite vault. The transept had rounded ends—a Romanesque echo found also in the cathedrals at Tournai and Soissons. On an eminence commanding the town of Laon is the cathedral of Notre-Dame (begun *c.* 1160), with a four-story nave under a sexpartite vault carried on piers of equal strength.

In 1163 Pope Alexander III and Bishop Maurice de Sully laid the foundation stone of the cathedral of Notre-Dame in Paris; the vaults of the chevet were completed in 1177 and the choir was consecrated in 1182. It was still archaic in feeling, with thick walls, and its small windows and double aisles made it dark. The façade (begun 1200) unites grace and power in the harmony of its symmetrical apertures and of its two galleries. The great flying buttresses, with their exceptional span nearly 50 feet in radius, endow the apse exterior with a remarkable beauty.

Bourges Cathedral was begun under Guillaume, bishop of Bourges from 1200 to 1209. It comprises five aisles and a double ambulatory, and has no transept interrupting the longitudinal axis. Five portals correspond to the nave and four aisles, which are of unequal height, the outermost being lowest (*c.* 30 ft.) and the nave the highest (*c.* 121 ft.). The vaults are sexpartite, but their weight is distributed equally among the piers.

High or Rayonnant Gothic. In the 13th century the Île-de-France—vital center of Gothic art—produced four cathedrals that embody the French High Gothic style: Chartres, Amiens, Rheims,

Gothic Art. Arcaded flying buttresses, apse exterior. Chartres Cathedral. 1200–60. *Photo Josef Jeiter, Hadamar.*

Gothic Art. Vaults of the ambulatory, Bourges Cathedral. 1209–60. *Photo Jacques Boulas, Orléans.*

and Beauvais. The new style was adapted to very diverse plans, but certain general tendencies asserted themselves. The walls are pierced more and more, and the rose window became very common. The choir became unusually large, as at Chartres; the radiating chapels were placed close together, and the central one was often made deeper than the others. From the mid-13th century, the choir was frequently separated from the nave by a rood screen (most screens were destroyed in the 18th century). The height of the vaults continued to increase. Sexpartite vaulting was gradually abandoned in the Île-de-France, Picardy, and Normandy in favor of the ribbed vault on an oblong plan in which each bay of the nave corresponds with one bay of the side aisles.

Several types of arches were used: the three-centered, the equilateral pointed, the lancet, and the cusped arch. Round piers and clusters of small columns were replaced more and more by cruciform piers that derived their form from four colonnettes attached to the shaft at right angles. Galleries were formerly found either alone, or surmounted by a triforium, but in this period they were omitted to allow for longer clerestory windows and higher aisles. The triforium was soon united with the high clerestory windows by a common system of colonnettes; at the same time, the triforium was opened to the exterior. The separate, narrow, lancet windows of the preceding period were at first grouped together under large arches and divided by sections of wall called *trumeaux* (for example, at Soissons Cathedral). In the 13th century the group became less solid in appearance: the *trumeau* was reduced to a mullion, and the tympanum of the arch was perforated with circles (called plate tracery) and curvilinear and multifoil tracery. Round windows known as roses appeared in façades and transepts.

The High Gothic style is said to have been born at Chartres. The cathedral had been ravaged by a fire in 1194 that spared nothing but the beautiful sculptured west portal executed not long before (*c.* 1145–70) and the south tower built in the mid-12th century. The new church was erected over an 11th-century crypt and consecrated in 1260. It had a three-story elevation of ground arcades, triforium, and clerestory, and was covered by a quadripartite ribbed vault. Radiating chapels open off the double ambulatory. The nave is very wide, short, and high, and there are only two side aisles. The Romanesque west façade admits light through a rose window and is flanked by two towers surmounted by spires.

The cathedral of Notre-Dame at Rheims was also rebuilt after a fire (1210), and the old cathedral at Amiens was destroyed by fire in 1218. In 1220 Bishop Evrard de Fouilloy laid the foundation stone of the new building. With its west front partly completed, the cathedral was opened for worship in 1236. The nave of Notre-Dame at Amiens, the largest French cathedral, has been regarded as the purest work of classic Gothic architecture. Elements of the façade are borrowed from the cathedrals of Laon and Paris.

Many excellent artists of the Middle Ages are anonymous. But documents relating to some of them have survived. William of Sens (d. 1180), creator of Canterbury Cathedral, is known to have worked on the last stages of Sens. Jean d'Orbais and Jean le Loup built the choir and transept of Rheims Cathedral (1211–13), while Bernard de Soissons and Robert de Coucy (d. 1311) were responsible for the nave (1255–1311). Pierre de Montreuil (1200–66) rebuilt the nave of St-Denis in Paris after 1231; no doubt

Gothic Art. West façade with Royal Portal, Chartres Cathedral. *c.* 1134–1216. *Photo Josef Jeiter, Hadamar.*

the open triforium there was also his creation, and he designed the rose windows for the transepts; he is also credited with the Ste-Chapelle in Paris (*c.* 1245–48). Jean de Chelles (d. 1258) lengthened the transept of Notre-Dame, Paris, illuminated by two rose windows over 40 feet in diameter. The architects of Amiens were, successively, Robert de Luzarches, Thomas de Cormont, and the latter's son Renaud. Strasbourg Cathedral was built by Erwin von Steinbach (d. 1318), Clermont-Ferrand Cathedral by Jean des Champs, and St-Nicaise at Rheims by Hugues Libergier (d. 1263). Eudes de Montreuil (d.

Gothic Art. West façade, Amiens Cathedral. 1220–36. *Photo Jean Roubier, Paris.*

Gothic Art. East end and south porch with Flamboyant style canopy, Ste-Cécile Cathedral, Albi. *Photo Yan, Toulouse.*

1289) was active during the reign of Louis IX (St. Louis).

Flamboyant or Late Gothic. The last phase of Gothic architecture was not marked by a structural change but by the use of decorative features. To the piers were attached a multitude of colonnettes that were continuations of all the elements of the ribbing. Capitals were no longer used and the colonnettes thus soared up into the ribs in one unbroken line. But before long the colonnettes merged with the pier itself, which resumed the cylindrical shape that had been current in the 12th century. The most characteristic arch was the ogee, formed by two curves and two reverse curves united at the top.

In the 15th century, important porches were built in front of church entrances, at the side of the church, or even jutting out in front like a gigantic baldachin. It was also the period for fine façades, ornamented and carved almost to excess. Towers became more massive, and spires were transformed into stone lacework.

French Gothic Schools. In every French province, monuments were built under the influence of the style that had originated in the Île-de-France. But each region adapted it to its own individual character and to the requirements of its own culture and resources.

The school of the Île-de-France, which had produced so many masterpieces from St-Denis to the Ste-Chapelle, continued to be active in the 15th century. The school of Champagne scarcely differed from that of the Île-de-France. It retained the sexpartite vault and the gallery at clerestory level for a longer period. At times it dispensed with the ambulatory. The Burgundian school was dominant in eastern France, extending as far as western Switzerland. Burgundian Gothic was slow to evolve from the very austere Romanesque style of Cistercian architecture. The Cistercians, however, adopted the ribbed vault very early, and were instrumental in the diffusion of Gothic art. Burgundian architects used sexpartite vaults in the naves of churches and groined vaults in the side aisles. On the exterior, lantern towers and semicircular portals remained in favor for a long time. Among the monuments of the Burgundian school are the cathedrals of Nevers, Dijon and Auxerre, Geneva and Lausanne.

The Norman school engaged in reciprocal architectural exchanges with the Île-de-France, to which it gave the ribbed vault. Before the end of the 13th century, Norman Gothic developed its own features: a choir surrounded by an ambulatory with radiating chapels; a large chapel on the axis of the nave, dedicated to the Virgin; an elevation of two or three stories; a wall passage at the sill level of the windows; lancet arches; and a lantern tower at the crossing of the transept. English influence is seen in the presence of a large arched window piercing the façade in place of a rose, and in portals flanked by columns. Notable examples are two churches in Rouen (St-Ouen and St-Maclou), the choir of Mont-St-Michel, and the spire of Notre-Dame church at Caudebec-en-Caux. The school of Anjou prevailed in western France and extended its influence to Portugal and Scandinavia. Architects of Anjou combined the dome and the ribbed vault in a system of deeply concave, or domical, vaults. In Anjou, the aisleless church became popular.

The school of the south does not include all Gothic buildings in that area, but those within a certain style that is easily identified. They are usually brick with tiled roofs, and have a nave with no side aisles. They have ribbed vaults resting on interior buttresses that form partitions between the side chapels; the nave is almost as wide as it is high. An imposing example is the cathedral of Ste-Cécile at Albi (begun 1282), a fortresslike church crowned with a belfry that resembles a keep. The nave is almost 98 feet in width and in height. Southern France also produced another type of church, with two equal aisles divided by tall columns. A fine example is the Jacobin church at Toulouse, where the ribs of the vault fan out from the supports like the branches of a palm tree.

Religious Architecture Outside France

The new architecture that was created and perfected by France in the 13th century spread throughout the Christian West, the Near East, and even the colonial empires founded by Spain and Portugal in the 15th and 16th centuries. Most countries eventually created their own Gothic styles out of the French and other forms that they assimilated.

England. The ribbed vault was known in England at a very early date. Anglo-Norman master masons applied it to Romanesque buildings: Durham Cathedral was given ribbed vaults between 1093 and 1133, while in France work was only beginning on the construction of the abbey church of St-Denis. English Gothic architecture thus appears to have developed ahead of the Continental schools and independent of them. Cistercian influence was less marked in England than elsewhere. It

Gothic Art. Triforium of Angel Choir. 1256–1320. Lincoln Cathedral. *Photo Kersting, London*

Gothic Art. Nave, St. George's Chapel. Windsor Castle. *Photo Kersting, London.*

appears chiefly in the use of the square east end in churches and in certain aspects of their plans. Some English churches are related to those in France. When William of Sens rebuilt the choir of Canterbury Cathedral (begun 1175), he modeled it on the choir of the cathedral at Sens. The chevet of Lincoln Cathedral was reconstructed (1192–1200) by a French architect; and Westminster Abbey, London (begun 1245), was built on a French plan even though in an English style.

In the early 13th century, England developed its own brand of Gothic, which evolved through three stages: Early English (*c.* 1200–1300), Decorated (*c.* 1300–75), and Perpendicular (*c.* 1375–1500). Early English is characterized by ribbed vaults with very pointed arches, elaborate moldings, a flat chevet pierced by a large window or by a series of lancets, a double transept, and a west façade pierced by a window. The interior has a three-story elevation. On the exterior, a lantern tower covers the crossing of the transept, and there are towers on the west front (as in the cathedrals of Lincoln and Salisbury, and York Minster). A rapid evolution of forms led to the development of the Decorated style. In the vaults, the liernes and tiercerons that had appeared at Lincoln Cathedral in 1233 were multiplied and the system of ribbing became more and more complex, as in York Minster, Exeter Cathedral, and the choir of Gloucester Cathedral. Window tracery was marked by curves and reverse curves, anticipating the Flamboyant style that later spread through France (15th century). A further change resulted in the most typical form of English Gothic, which was called the Perpendicular style. Characteristic of this style are flattened stone vaults supported by ribs that fan out (as in the cloister at Gloucester Cathedral), and a more ornate treatment of the timbered roof already in use in the Decorated period. The windows, on the other hand, became more austere: they were divided by long vertical mullions set very close together and interesecting with horizontal mullions. It was this quality in the window tracery that gave the style its name. The principal monuments include the chapels of the oldest colleges at Oxford and Cambridge (for example, King's College Chapel, Cambridge), Norwich Cathedral, Henry VII's chapel at Westminster Abbey, and St. George's Chapel at Windsor Castle. This style of Gothic was peculiar to England and had no influence elsewhere.

The Low Countries. The Low Countries were open to French influence from the beginning of the Gothic period. In Belgium, Soissons Cathedral served as the model for reconstructing the choir of Tournai Cathedral (1242–55), as well as for the cathedral at Ghent and for Notre-Dame at Bruges. In Holland, Soissons was also copied at Utrecht Cathedral. St-Martin at Ypres, whose nave and aisles date from 1254, was the first purely Gothic Belgian church. The choir of St-Gudule in Brussels (1225–51) was influenced by the cathedrals of Laon and Cambrai. The Cistercians, followed by the Benedictines, built in the styles of Burgundy and the northern French provinces, but their abbeys are in ruins. From the Flamboyant period until the 16th century, Gothic churches proliferated; they were in a heavier style than was customary in France. Examples include Notre Dame du Sablon in Brussels, St-Jacques and Notre-Dame in Antwerp, and the abbey church of St-Jacques at Liège (1513–38).

Germany. German Gothic art drew all its inspiration from France, but Germany was rather late in adopting the new style (*c.* 1250–1550). At the beginning of the 12th century, buildings otherwise entirely Romanesque replaced their old roofing with ribbed vaults. The Cistercians brought Burgundian influence; even when their churches retained the Romanesque plan, they were covered with ribbed vaults. Later, German builders imitated the great French cathedrals: Bamberg Cathedral, while preserving its Carolingian plan with two apses, was inspired by the façade of Laon Cathedral; the same is true of Naumburg Cathedral. Magdeburg Cathedral was inspired by the cathedrals of both Laon and Noyon. The church of St. Elizabeth at Marburg (begun 1235) has a nave and side aisles of equal height, recalling the churches of Poitou. It combines the style of Soissons Cathedral—in its choir with neither ambulatory nor chapels, but with two stories of windows—with a transept ending in two apses that is reminiscent of the round transept arms of Noyon Cathedral. The type of building that places nave and aisles under one roof and dispenses with flying buttresses was very popular in Germany; it is known as the hall church (Hallenkirche) and was particularly prevalent throughout Westphalia and in the Baltic regions. Cologne Cathedral was begun in the mid-13th century (1248); it was continued in the 14th but remained incomplete and was finished only in the 19th. Strasbourg was built on the plans of Erwin von Steinbach; it was begun in 1277 and continued by his sons and other masters; the north tower dates from the 15th century. The brick monuments of northern Germany have a character all their own, with very high windows and numerous bell turrets; the cathed-

Gothic Art. East end, Church of St. Elizabeth, Marburg. 1235–83. *Foto Marburg.*

rals of Lübeck and Danzig are examples.

Italy. Although the ribbed vault was used in the churches of Lombardy—even at S. Ambrogio in Milan—as early as the 11th century, Gothic architecture was not brought to Italy until the 13th century, when it was introduced by the Cistercians. Its first essays there were scarcely more than a form of Romanesque covered with the ribbed vaults: examples are the abbeys of Fossanova (1187–1208), Casamari (1203–17), and S. Galgano. Few examples are found in central and southern Italy: in Rome there is only the Dominican church of S. Maria sopra Minerva; in Naples, French architects worked on S. Domenico Maggiore (begun in 1239), and this church still retains its nave, single aisles, and pointed arches.

In Tuscany is the Dominican church of S. Maria Novella, Florence (1278–1360), with ribbed vaults, a flat chevet in the Cistercian manner, and a nave and two side aisles with a reduced number of piers. This church marks the birth of Florentine Gothic, which is characterized by the pursuit of interior space and marked horizontality: here the width and height of the building are equal. The Franciscan church of S. Croce, also in Florence (begun in 1252), has a Cistercian-style east end, but any vertical effect is cut short by the timber roof. The cathedral of Orvieto, with a nave and two side aisles, is covered with ribbed vaults in the chevet and transept; its façade, the work of Lorenzo Maitani (*c.* 1275–1330), Andrea Pisano, and Andrea Orcagna, features the French arrangement of three portals; however, the masonry in alternate bands of black and white, which is also found at Siena and Genoa cathedrals, removes any resemblance to French cathedrals. In the majority of Italian churches, the façade is not an integral part of the main building, which is usually enclosed by a plain wall at the west front; the façades, differing in period and style, are superimposed on the wall and are generally much larger. Siena Cathedral is one of the most complex examples: the only Gothic parts are the restorations carried out under the direction of the Cistercian monks of S. Galgano, the façade by Giovanni Pisano, and the baptistery.

In Umbria, a church dedicated to St. Francis was begun at Assisi in 1228. The upper church of S. Francesco consists of a simple rib-vaulted nave of four bays. The church of S. Chiara (1257), also in Assisi, has flying buttresses and a rose window. The cathedral of Perugia (*c.* 1230), with a nave and two side aisles of equal height, has affinities with churches in southern France. In Bologna, the church of S. Francesco (begun 1236) is close to the French Gothic style. S. Petronio was built during the Flamboyant period (begun 1390) and is an imposing Gothic church with a nave and two side aisles, and side chapels set in the buttresses. At the same time in Milan, work began on the enormous marble cathedral, supervised in the early stages by French and German master masons, and later by the Milanese themselves.

Spain and Portugal. Gothic architecture, widely disseminated in Spain, was introduced by the Cistercians in the first half of the 12th century and established successively in Catalonia, Castile, and Navarre. The first Cistercian foundation, the monastery of Moreruela, goes back to 1130; the church (1170–90) had side aisles and an ambulatory covered with ribbed vaults. Many of their monasteries had churches whose naves were covered with ribbed vaults. The church at Santas Creus (*c.* 1174–1225) is typically Cistercian in plan, being massive and crenellated like a fortress; it is illuminated by an immense pointed window in the façade, and a lantern tower rises at the crossing of the transept. Cistercian influence is seen in the cathedral of Tarragona (begun 1174), with a rib-vaulted interior and ogival portal, and a cloister that is almost a replica of the one at Fontfroid. Of similar influence are the cathedrals of Lérida (1203–78) and Valencia (founded 1262), which are little more than Romanesque churches with ribbed vaults.

Burgos Cathedral (*c.* 1221–60), built on a cruciform plan, has a nave and two side aisles and a chevet with nine radiating chapels. The very tall lantern tower over the *crucero* (crossing of the transept) was not built until the 16th century. The two towers of the façade are given extra height by spires that also date from the 16th century. Toledo Cathedral, begun sometime before 1224, is one of the most spacious Gothic churches. It has two aisles on either side of the nave, an ambulatory from which

Gothic Art. León Cathedral. 1255–1303. *Photo Boudot-Lamotte, Paris.*

Gothic Art.
Below left: **Giovanni Pisano.** Façade, Siena Cathedral. Begun 1284. *Photo Anderson, Rome.*
Below right: Interior of upper church. Church of S. Francesco, Assisi. 1228–39; revaulted 1253. *Photo Alinari-Giraudon.*

originally radiated 15 chapels, and a triforium opening onto the transept. León Cathedral (1255–1303) has a purity and elegance reminiscent of Rheims and Amiens cathedrals. In Navarre, Pamplona Cathedral is outstanding for its beautiful cloister (1317); the cathedral of Tudela is in the transitional style (begun 12th century). In Catalonia, the cathedral of Barcelona (1298–1450) has an apse with 11 radiating chapels. The nave appears to be the same height as the two side aisles, although it is not. It is a good example of Catalan Gothic, which tends to minimize the division between nave and side aisles by reducing the number of supports. At Gerona Cathedral, the feeling for space led to the construction of an aisleless nave (1416) covered by a vault with a span of over 75 feet and without intermediate supports. At Seville Cathedral, in Andalusia, the Flamboyant style appears in the vaulting at the crossing of the transept.

In Portugal, Gothic buildings worthy of note include the monastery of Alcobaça (1158–1220), whose church has ribbed vaulting over the nave; the cloisters of the cathedrals of Oporto and Lisbon; and the church of Batalha (begun 1387), a great ensemble of Gothic architecture combining the styles of English Perpendicular, French Flamboyant, and various other elements, pointing up the fact that there was no true Portuguese Gothic style by that time.

Northern and Central Europe. The influence of Gothic architecture extended north as far as Scandinavia. In Sweden, French influence was strong at first (cathedral of Uppsala, begun in 1287 by a French architect), and then a more German Gothic prevailed. The cathedral of Trondheim in Norway (mostly 13th century) shows English influence, while in Denmark the cathedral of Roskilde (begun mid-12th century) is stylistically related to French cathedrals. The churches of Cracow, in Poland, developed a local type of Gothic with a preponderant use of brick and a profusion of bell towers. Bohemia was directly dependent on French art; Charles IV sent for Mathias of Arras (d. 1352) to build the cathedral of St. Vitus in Prague, which follows the plan of Narbonne Cathedral. Very few monuments remain intact in the former kingdom of Hungary, although the Benedictines and Cistercians built abbeys there that reproduced French types sometimes mingled with German elements. It is known that Villard de Honnecourt was summoned to Transylvania.

The Aegean and the Near East. The Romanesque style persisted in the kingdom of Jerusalem, and therefore few Gothic works were built. In the kingdom of Cyprus, the Gothic style is seen in S. Sophia at Nicosia, in the remains of the cathedral of Famagusta, and in those of the abbey of Lapäis. Rhodes also has many Gothic monuments.

Civil and Military Architecture

Military and civil structures were almost inseparable in the 12th and 13th centuries, and emerged as distinct types only slowly in the course of the 14th century. Nor was religious architecture independent of them, since monasteries had to include living quarters, and many fortified churches were built; castles also had chapels.

France. In the 13th century, before they became luxurious residences, castles were still strongholds. Richard Coeur de Lion built the Château-Gaillard at Les Andelys, in Normandy, and King Philip Augustus constructed or reconstructed Gisors, Falaise, Verneuil, and other castles on the western borders of his domain. Soon the castle was organized to serve as a dwelling. In the Château-Gaillard (begun in 1196), the outer wall of the keep had served as a support for buildings leaning against it. In the 13th century, castles without keeps began to appear (such as Boulogne). In the 14th, stone walls were built with machicolations (stone corbels alternating with openings through which missiles could be dropped on attackers), and these were often crowned with crenellated parapets in the 15th century. But the development of artillery in the course of the following century made defense from a height impossible and even dangerous; the walls were therefore made lower as well as thicker to increase their resistance to fire—over 72 feet thick in the castle of Salses, in Roussillon. Gothic residences, part fortress and part palace, emphasized either one of these aspects. All the monuments have disappeared, except for the château of Vincennes: begun by St. Louis and fortified and transformed by Charles V (1336–73), it had a rectangular keep with round corner towers, and two rectangular enclosures flanked by towers and lookout posts; a reliquary chapel was added later.

The French popes marked their stay in their native land with the construction of the castle of Villandraut (Gironde), a magnificent example of military architecture built by Clement V (Bertrand de Got) in 1306–7; and the Palace of the Popes at Avignon, one of the most extensive feudal castles. The old part of that palace was built under Benedict XII (the Cistercian Jacques Fournier) in 1334–42. The new section of the palace, built under Clement VI in 1342–52, extends south and east of the earlier part, around the Grande Cour.

The royal princes were also great builders. Under Jean de Berry were constructed the fortresses of Usson and Nonette in Auvergne; the beautiful palace at Mehun-sur-Yèvre (1367–90) by Guy de Dammartin (d. 1398), known only from a miniature in the *Très Riches Heures du Duc de Berry* (begun *c.*

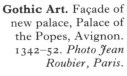

Gothic Art. Façade of new palace, Palace of the Popes, Avignon. 1342–52. *Photo Jean Roubier, Paris.*

Gothic Art. Limbourg Brothers. *Les Très Riches Heures du Duc de Berry : Château of Mehun-sur-Yèvre. c.* 1416. Musée Condé, Chantilly. *Photo Giraudon, Paris.*

Gothic Art. Façade, Town Hall, Bruges. Begun 1377. *Foto Marburg.*

1416; Chantilly, Musée Condé); and a number of other vanished castles. Louis d'Orléans built Pierrefonds, restored by Viollet-le-Duc, as well as La Ferté-Milon (1392–1407), left unfinished.

The 13th century marked a change in the art of urban fortification. The best example is the citadel of Carcassonne. Its Gallo-Roman fortifications and Visigothic towers made it the chosen strong point of the French kings for keeping turbulent Languedoc in submission. St. Louis surrounded the town with an exterior wall provided with towers. His son, Philip III, finished the work and constructed the Porte Narbonnaise, reinforced by the Tour du Trésau, and opposite, on the bank of the Aude, he erected the square Tour de l'Évêque. Another fortified town was Aigues-Mortes. It was the port from which St. Louis left for the Crusades; its ramparts, finished by Philip the Fair, surround a quadrilateral dominated by a tower to the southwest.

Aigues-Mortes and Carcassonne were among many new towns that were built in the south and south-west of France from the 11th to the 14th century. Founded by both French and English kings, by lords, bishops, and monasteries, they were most often built in the face of an enemy. Among them were French and English *bastides* in Aquitaine; the royal town of Villeneuve-lès-Avignon; and many a "Villefranche" and "Villeneuve," as well as names famous for other reasons—Granada, Pamplona, and Fleurance (Gers).

Few private houses of the 13th and 14th centuries remain in France. In northern France they were constructed of wood, in the Île-de-France and Burgundy they were of stone, and in the south brick was used. A charming survival from this period is the town of Cordes (Tarn), which has been called the "Dame de Pierre". More urban architecture has survived from the Late Gothic period. At Bourges is the beautiful house of Jacques Coeur (1443–51); in Paris is the Hôtel de Cluny, built in a restrained style for Jacques d'Amboise, abbot of Cluny, with a chapel known for its beautiful lierne vaulting, and the Hôtel de Sens, rebuilt by Archbishop Tristan de Salazar.

Few examples of town halls have survived from before the 16th century. The town hall at La Réole dates from the late 12th century, but the finest are found in the northern provinces, at Douai (1463), St-Quentin, Compiègne, Arras (1463–94), and Noyon (1485–1523). In the central and southern areas are the former Hôtel de Ville at Bourges, the old town hall of Toulouse (14th-16th century), the one at Libourne and, in the east, that of Colmar. Although it was built in the 16th century, the Palais de Justice at Rouen is among the finest examples of Flamboyant Gothic.

Flanders. Flemish civil architecture showed more originality than the religious monuments, and in the Gothic period fine structures were built that were a source of civic pride. The first town halls go back to the 13th century (for example, the one at Alost); that of Bruges, begun in 1377, is illuminated by high windows and has the silhouette of a church nave. The most beautiful is that of Brussels (1402–55), which incorporates a belfry surmounted by an elegant openwork spire. The town halls of Ghent (1527–80), Oudenaarde (1515–30), and Courtrai are among the most outstanding. In Holland, those worthy of mention include Middelburg, with the most northerly Flamboyant town hall (16th century), and the smaller building at Kampen.

Italy. Italy, like Flanders, attached considerable importance to its municipal buildings. The city of Florence erected the Palazzo del Podestà, also known as the Bargello (1254–1346), with its severe tower and beautiful courtyard and staircase; and the square, massive Palazzo Vecchio (1298–1314). The building is crowned by a crenellated sentry parade from which a tower rises more than 300 feet. The tower (Torre del Mangia) at the side of the Palazzo Pubblico in Siena reaches a height of nearly 335 feet above a building less lofty but more extensive than its Florentine counterpart; it is the highest tower in Italy. Piacenza has preserved a Lombard Gothic Palazzo Pubblico of the 13th century (1281); Perugia has the Palazzo dei Priori (13th–14th century); and in Bologna is the Palazzo del Podestà of the 12th century, rebuilt in the 15th.

Venice gave its Gothic buildings an accent of lighthearted elegance. The waterfront façade of the Doges' Palace was constructed in the second half of the 14th century. Along the Grand Canal, among marble palaces of many styles are several Gothic ones: the Ca' d'Oro (begun 1421), the Palazzo Pisani, and the Ca' Foscari (both 15th century).

In Naples, the imposing mass of the Castello Nuovo, or Maschio Angioino (1279–83), commands the port; constructed for Charles I of Anjou by Pierre de Chaulnes, it was altered in the 15th century for Alfonso V of Aragon. Further south, in Apulia, is the castle of Trani, built about 1249 for Frederick II by Philippe Chinard and remodeled in the 15th and 16th centuries. The same architect built the mountain stronghold of Castel del Monte for Emperor Frederick II in about 1240. On an octagonal plan with corner towers, the

Gothic Art. Façade facing the sea, Doges' Palace, Venice. Second half of 14th century. *Foto Marburg.*

building is a combination of Gothic and Romanesque.

Spain. Spain gave a very personal note to its civil architecture. The *lonja*, or exchange, offers one example. That of Palma in Majorca, called the Lonja del Mar (1426–50), has a fine vaulted hall divided into three aisles and supported by spiral piers; on the exterior, the corners are marked by graceful colonnettes. This building inspired the Lonja de la Seda, built in Valencia at the end of the 15th century. In Barcelona, the earliest buildings line the streets of the *barrio gótico*, or Gothic quarter; next oldest are the surviving parts of the old town hall (Ayuntamiento) of the 14th century, particularly one of its interior courts, as well as the two adjoining palaces of the Deputación and of the Audiencia, with the patio of the orange trees. In Majorca, near Palma, is the castle of Bellver, built by royalty in the 14th century and enclosing a beautiful circular court surrounded by a gallery with two stories of arcading. At Valencia is the 15th-century palace of the Generalife and, of greater interest, the Puerta de Serranos (1349), a gateway flanked by two polygonal towers that is a good example of 14th-century military architecture.

Germany. Notable among German civic structures are the buildings that house the exchanges, as well as the Hanseatic towns. Also worthy of mention are the town halls of Munster, Cologne, and Brunswick (begun 1302).

Bohemia. In Bohemia, mention must be made of the castle of Charles IV (mid-14th century) and the tower of the Charles IV Bridge, both in Prague, as well as the castle of Carlstein, built about 1348 by Mathias of Arras (d. 1352).

Levant. Military architecture of the Levant is known to have been the source of Gothic castles in the West; to this day, the original state of numerous ruined or vanished castles is hinted at by the imposing remains of the Château de Saône and the Krak des Chevaliers.

SCULPTURE

Sculpture in France

Transitional Period. A period of transition from Romanesque to Gothic in about the second half of the 12th century was characterized by perfection of workmanship, a restrained mode of expression, and direct observation of nature. Simpler capitals were freely ornamented with naturalistic renderings of ivy, acanthus, and artichoke foliage.

Gothic sculpture was essentially monumental and formed an integral part of the architecture: portals especially were designed as settings for it. The earliest statues, attached to the columns and following their rigid and attenuated lines, were like caryatids; the garments appeared to be molded on their simplified forms and were fluted with parallel or concentric folds. Abbot Suger was responsible for the first achievement in the new style, the abbey church of St-Denis, near Paris, which formed the prototype of all Gothic portals.

From St-Denis evolved the Royal Portal of Chartres Cathedral (*c.* 1145–55). Constructed by the artists of St-Denis for the narthex of the original Romanesque cathedral, the portal follows the same plan in a more developed form. It was the first masterpiece of Gothic sculpture, even though certain Romanesque elements are still visible; its entirely new grace is striking. Each of the three portals has its own tympanum. The jambs are adorned with 24 statues attached to columns, representing figures from the Old Testament.

The Royal Portal set the pattern for numerous other portals, which borrowed from it all or part of their tympanum sculpture and statuary. Among this group are the south portal of Le Mans Cathedral (*c.* 1158), with its tympanum of Christ in Majesty and its jamb figures; the west portal of Angers Cathedral (*c.* 1160); the Portail Ste-Anne of Notre-Dame Cathedral in Paris (after 1163), with its Virgin in Majesty; and the south portal of Bourges Cathedral (*c.* 1170?). About 1185, a new theme appeared on the lintel of the west portal at the cathedral of Senlis: the Death and Assumption of the Virgin. It was depicted in two successive scenes, and the second was full of lively movement, grace, and charm. Senlis served as a model for the portals of the cathedrals of Mantes (*c.* 1190); Laon, with its Coronation of the Virgin on the tympanum (early 13th century); Chartres (the central doorway of the north portal, *c.* 1195–1200); and Lausanne (where examples of large statues are found).

The Thirteenth Century. In the 13th century Gothic sculpture attained Classical perfection. It was modeled after nature, but forms were ennobled and idealized. Ornaments consisted of familiar plants. The Old Testament would be studied first, with its great personages and events pointing to the Coming of Christ. And then scenes from the New Testament would depict the Nativity of Christ and the sad but consoling account of the Passion. Included would be representations of Good and Evil, in the form of a Triumph of the Virtues. The Last Judgment figured on the tympanums of many churches, and the lives of the saints were depicted as a form of encouragement. Profane history—not without points of contact with sacred history—was also included in this didactic scheme, as were the Signs of the Zodiac, the Seasons, and the Labors of the Months, along with personifications of the seven Liberal Arts and Philosophy.

Everywhere capitals assumed the form of widemouthed baskets decked out with curled leaves and buds. Gables, pinnacles, and spires were crowned with finials, and most of the statues were sheltered under canopies rather like sentry boxes fortified with crenelations and turrets. At this time statues lost their stiffness and acquired a beauty comparable to that of Greek sculpture. They were given lifelike proportions and natural poses and gestures. Faces became more expressive, and

Gothic Art. *Queen of Sheba between David and Solomon.* Jamb figures of the Royal Portal, Chartres Cathedral. *c.* 1145–55. *Photo Jean Roubier, Paris.*

Gothic Art. *Resurrection of the Dead*. Detail from the Last Judgment, Rheims Cathedral. *Photo Jean Feuillie, Paris.*

Gothic Art. *Virgin.* Trumeau, north portal, Notre-Dame Cathedral, Paris. *c.* 1250. *Photo Alinari.*

figures more lifelike: at Chartres, as early as about 1230, the statues of St. Theodore and St. Gregory embody perfectly the types of knight and doctor of the Church.

The Last Judgment was given its definitive form in the central doorway of the south portal of Chartres Cathedral (1205–15). Statues of the Apostles line the doorjambs. This type of portal appears also at Notre-Dame in Paris, in the central doorway of the west front (*c.* 1220). At Amiens, in the central portal of the west façade (*c.* 1225–36), the arrangement is more complex. On the *trumeau* is the figure of Christ known as the Beau Dieu, the most famous statue in Amiens. At Rheims, the tympanum of the Last Judgment appears on the left portal of the north transept, as an initial plan for the west front (*c.* 1220) was superseded by another project in which the tympanums would be replaced by stained glass.

The cult of the Virgin, which was very widespread during the 13th century, is magnificently illustrated in the sculpture of Gothic churches. The portal of the Virgin appears not only in churches dedicated to her (Notre-Dame), as at Laon, Senlis, Paris, Amiens, and Rheims, but also in those erected in honor of a saint—St-Etienne at Bourges, Sens, and Meaux, and St-Jean at Lyons. Various reliefs represent the Death of the Virgin, others feature the Burial of the Virgin, still others show the Assumption of the Virgin. Portals with the Coronation of the Virgin combine with the actual crowning the scenes of death, burial, and resurrection.

Many portals were erected in honor of saints, especially the patron saints of the diocese. At Sens Cathedral, the left portal of the west front is dedicated to St. John the Baptist, and the central doorway to St. Stephen. The south façade of Chartres contains the Porte des Martyrs, with scenes of the martyrdom of St. Stephen, and the Porte des Confesseurs, with scenes from the lives of Sts. Martin and Nicholas. Notre-Dame in Paris has the Porte St-Étienne, on the south façade. An interesting feature is the occasional combination of the three themes in a single façade.

The Fourteenth Century. At the end of the 13th century, sculpture was freed from the monumental order: decoration became less a part of the structure, and the sculptor less submissive to the architect. Ornament assumed restless forms; portals were decorated to excess, gables were built increasingly higher, and tympanums were often replaced by windows; façade statues were made smaller and were set in niches under canopies. Small reliefs covered the lower part of the doorjambs. At the Portail de la Calende (south front) in the cathedral of Rouen, they represent the lives of various Saints, while on the Portail-aux-Libraires (the north portal of the same cathedral), these quatrefoils are interspersed with scenes from Genesis (the Labors of Adam). At Auxerre Cathedral numerous small scenes, full of vitality, combine Scriptural themes with symbolic representations drawn from pagan antiquity (for example, Heracles or Eros). Related to these reliefs are the small, separate scenes on the north wall of the choir of Notre-Dame in Paris: they must have been executed between 1310 and 1320. The scenes on the Portail St-Étienne on the south transept of the same cathedral are said to record incidents from student life: they are in a style inspired by antique art.

A new genre of sculpture appeared in screens enclosing choirs. One of the most beautiful is that of Notre-Dame in Paris, which is close in style to the art of the 13th century. The work was begun by Jean Ravy about 1318 or 1320, who worked until 1344 or 1346; in 1351 it was finished by Jean le Boutellier (d. 1370). The two sides were joined at the front by a rood screen, the work of Pierre de Chelles in 1300–18: it features scenes of the Passion and the Resurrection.

Refinement in sculpture was sometimes carried to a degree that approached Mannerism; pleasant expressions, elegant poses, and complicated draperies swelling at the hip were much in favor. Besides the tendency toward refinement, another contrary current existed: the realism that appeared in the figures of Apostles at the Ste-Chapelle and in the St. Joseph at Rheims became accentuated about 1340 in the extraordinary statues of Apostles from the chapel of Rieux (now in Toulouse, Musée des Augustins), as well as in funerary monuments. The first portrait carried out in this way in France was the statue on the tomb of Philip the Bold (*c.* 1300). In the abbey of St-Denis there is a similar series of effigies on the tombs of Bertrand du Guesclin, Marie de Bourbon, Philip VI, and John the Good. André Beauneveu (active 1360–1403) was responsible for a number of these effigies. Statues of Charles V and his wife, Jeanne de Bourbon, were made about 1375 for the portal of the chapel of the Hôpital des Quinze-Vingts (now in the Louvre). The sculpture of

Gothic Art. *Scene of student life.* Detail from the Portail St-Étienne, Notre-Dame Cathedral, Paris. *Archives photographiques, Paris.*

Claus Sluter, with its heavily dramatic form of realism, grew out of a similar trend.

The Fifteenth Century. This century was dominated by a dramatic art that was best represented during the first 50 years by its Holy Sepulchres and Virgins of Compassion, or *Pietàs*. In funerary sculpture, realism was pushed to its limits, as in the figure known as the monument of Cardinal Lagrange (Avignon, Musée Calvet), a decrepit and decayed body. In the second half of the century, artists also worked in a more serene style, producing Virgins smiling tenderly upon the Child at play, such as the charming Virgin of Marthuret at Riom, and the Virgin from Écouen (now in London, Victoria and Albert Museum).

Sculpture outside France

Spain. The sculpture of the Portico de la Gloria at Santiago de Compostela represents an inspired interpretation of French sources. The portal of the Sarmental at Burgos, a masterpiece of its kind, contains echoes of Notre-Dame in Paris and Amiens Cathedral; but its Christ in Majesty is of quite a different character. In the north portal and entrance to the cloister, the influence of Rheims can be felt. The cathedral of León presents a magnificent ensemble of sculpture that is French in style but with an exuberance that is entirely Spanish.

In Navarre, the cloister of Pamplona was decorated by French sculptors; the tomb of Charles the Noble is a Burgundian work. In the provinces of Aragon are the carved portals of Tarragona and of Palma in Majorca, the door of the Apostles in the cathedral of Valencia, and some notable funerary monuments including those of King Pedro III (d. 1285) and his son Jaime II (d. 1327), and of Lope Fernández de Luna, archbishop of Saragossa.

Italy. Italy was further removed from French influence, and its sculptors tended to seek their models in antiquity; examples of Italian Gothic sculpture are a Last Judgment at Ferrara Cathedral; a Deposition at Lucca Cathedral (*c.* 1250); a Resurrection of the Dead at Orvieto Cathedral (*c.* 1350), with similarities to the one at Bourges; and the Arts and Labors of Man on the campanile in Florence. But here one is already at the dawn of the Renaissance (*see also* DUECENTO; TRECENTO).

Gothic Art. West façade, Wells Cathedral. 1230–55. *Photo British Tourist Office.*

England. English sculptors borrowed little from the great French ensembles. Their façades were arranged differently: they were adorned with statues placed under arcading in superimposed registers, and the geometric tendency was in accord with that of the mullions in the great windows. This is the arrangement prevailing in the cathedrals of Lichfield, Salisbury (very much restored), Exeter, and Wells (first half of the 13th century).

Sepulchral monuments are numerous and well preserved: the deceased is often represented in a lively attitude, far removed from the repose of French effigies. These tombs were supplied with weeping figures well before their appearance in Burgundy.

Germany. In Saxony, Thuringia, Franconia, and on either side of the Upper Rhine, in regions where stone was available, Germany borrowed widely from French sculpture. Proof is found at Strasbourg, where the tympanum of the Death of the Virgin and the statues of the Church and the Synagogue on the south portal (*c.* 1230) were obviously influenced by the style of Rheims. The west front, decorated at a later date, has drawn inspiration from French models for its arrangements and its iconography. Strasbourg was the source of the Last Judgment at Freiburg im Breisgau and on the portals of Magdeburg Cathedral. The earlier "Golden Portal" at Freiburg (1235) combines the iconography of the Virgin with that of the Last Judgment.

The two most famous ensembles are those of Bamberg and Naumburg. The sculpture at Bamberg reflects that of Rheims, but its hard and heavy qualities make it essentially Germanic. Especially famous is the Visitation group, which derives from the classical workshop at Rheims. The originality of Naumburg is seen in the 12 statues of founders placed in pairs around the periphery of the cathedral choir: in many ways—their secular character, their profoundly individual and realistic aspect, and their garments falling in heavy folds—they herald the art of Albrecht Dürer.

STAINED GLASS

Stained glass was to Gothic art what mural painting was to Romanesque: it continued on the church interior the teaching dispensed outside by the sculpture of the portals. The use of stained glass for windows goes back to the very early Christian basilicas; its existence was recorded by the Church Fathers in the 4th and 5th centuries, but there seems to be no surviving stained glass dating with certainty from before the late 10th century. In the Romanesque period windows were generally small and it was unusual for them to be fitted with stained glass. With the coming of Gothic building techniques, there ceased to be any obstacle to enlarging the window openings. Thus the art of stained glass was deployed over increasingly vast spaces.

The technique of stained glass began with the manufacture of the glass itself, out of a paste made

Gothic Art. Great rose window. North transept, Notre-Dame Cathedral, Paris. *c.* 1257. *Photo Jean Roubier, Paris.*

from silica and potassium, following the formula set down by the monk Theophilus (pseudonym of Roger of Helmershausen) in his *Treatise of Divers Arts*, about 1120. The glass was colored in bulk by fusion with a medium of metallic oxides. Uncolored glass was greenish white; if the smelting process was prolonged, the glass took on a warmer tone.

The window having been designed, it was divided into sections separated by a lead armature. A red-hot iron was used to cut the glass to the required shapes, in accord with a pattern. Then it was painted. The Gothic glass-painter followed the form and the graphic style of the Romanesque painters: he added in grisaille the features of the face, drapery folds, and shadows, in broad, free strokes, using a brown paste of ground glass and an oxide of iron or copper. When this was dry, he accented the highlights and adjusted the modeling by removing or adding pigment. Then the whole pane of glass was fired again so that the paint fused with the glass surface. The pieces were finally set in place and grooved lead strips fitted around them and soldered at the joints on both sides.

Gothic Art. *Nativity*. Detail from the Childhood of Christ. Late 12th century. Chartres Cathedral. *Archives photographiques, Paris.*

Among the oldest extant groups is that of the abbey of St-Denis, contemporary with the dedication of the choir (1144). The ensemble was almost entirely destroyed at the time of the French Revolution, but the remaining fragments were remounted in a modern framework. The iconography, of major interest, is symbolic and concerned with the interpretation of Biblical types. There is no doubt that the workshop of St-Denis was also responsible for the stained glass of the façade at Chartres. Completed in 1170, it consists of three large windows in which the sky-blue background is enlivened with red, yellow, orange, and white arranged in perfect harmony. The scenes are enclosed in medallions with wide borders of foliage and strapwork.

In the cathedral of Le Mans are four panels of an Ascension, purely Romanesque in style and very close in feeling to contemporary wall paintings; they can be placed between 1134 and 1158. Three windows in the cathedral at Angers (*c.* 1160–70) are in the tradition of St-Denis and Chartres. Romanesque art still dominated in the late 12th-century great window in the chevet of the cathedral at Poitiers. In limpid blues and gleaming reds it depicts a Crucifixion surmounted by an Ascension.

In the first half of the 13th century, stained glass seems to have been dominated by the great ensemble of Chartres, of which a considerable part of the original glass has survived, even though not fully intact. The ensemble is remarkable in its conception and in the clarity with which its meaning is conveyed in an unencumbered composition: it is the most beautiful work of its kind bequeathed by the Middle Ages.

The second most important ensemble of stained glass is that at Bourges Cathedral, although it is less beautiful than that at Chartres. Two workshops can be distinguished in this group—one in which red glass, bright tones, and a vigorous design predominate (windows of the Passion and the Apocalypse), and another in which the workmanship is more delicate and the style more developed (windows of the Old and the New Covenant, and of the Last Judgment). The works of these two ateliers are interspersed, giving coherence to the ensemble. In the cathedral of Sens, three windows belong to the first quarter of the 13th century and were connected with the school of Chartres and Bourges. Few of the original elements remain in the west rose window of Notre-Dame in Paris (*c.* 1220). This work is very close in style to that of Chartres, but there is no way of knowing which influenced the other.

The style of Chartres spread to countries outside France, notably England, where it appears in Trinity Chapel at Canterbury Cathedral (*c.* 1225), in Lincoln Cathedral, and in work produced by the ateliers responsible for York Minster and the cathedrals of Salisbury and Peterborough. In Germany, there are examples of the style at Cologne, Marburg, and Regensburg.

A new phase in the history of stained glass began in the middle of the 13th century. It seems to have been initiated by the Paris workshops that produced the stained glass in the principal chapel of the Ste-Chapelle and the rose windows of Notre-Dame, and before that the ensemble in St-Germain-des-Prés (dispersed in the 19th century). The Ste-Chapelle is made up of 15 stained-glass windows separated by slender colonnettes, and a rose on the west front representing the Apocalypse (altered in the 15th century). These windows comprise no less than 1,134 scenes. The little figures are drawn with a firm outline, and their forms are elegant and supple. Their simplicity and the few accessories that accompany them contribute to the clarity of this illustrated Bible.

Among the great cathedrals, Beauvais has preserved almost none of its 13th-century glass, while Amiens has only fragments, apart from the window of Bishop Bernard d'Abbeville (1269). Rheims has lost its magnificent stained glass that dated from the 13th and early 14th centuries. Despite a skillful restoration by Jacques Simon, the original effect is lost. Only part of the glass in the choir has survived and, in the nave, only 8 of the 20 figures of kings of France, placed above images of the bishops who consecrated them.

The art of stained glass was never cultivated in Italy to the extent that it was in France, but one must not overlook the great ensemble at Assisi, made between 1240 and 1250 after cartoons by Cimabue and Pietro Cavallini. In Spain, French influence is evident in the medallions of the cathedral windows at León.

During the 13th century, windows had become larger; they comprised several lancets divided by mullions, the panes of glass being set directly into a lead armature. In the 14th century, a number of changes were made: the lancets were made taller and narrower, and the armature was therefore replaced by simple transverse bars of iron. The height of the lancets required that the figures represented on them be elongated; but that was not sufficient to fill the space, so the figures were raised on pedestals and surmounted by high canopies. The glass painters painted the architectural details in grisaille and sometimes added a new color, a yellow produced by applying silver salts and then firing the glass (*jaune d'argent*). This technique became very popular in the 14th and 15th centuries for the treatment of hair, haloes, drapery folds, and other details in which pale shades were desired. A reaction against this tendency set in about the middle of the 15th century, and warm colors returned to favor.

The stylistic development of stained glass paralleled that of painting. Studied elegance was the rule: the refined draftsmanship and charming figures prettily disposed reflected a form of Mannerism, while foregrounds and backgrounds were naturalistic.

The stained glass produced in Germanic countries during the 14th century was characterized by beautiful colors and a variety of attitudes in its figures. Interesting ensembles include those at Königsfelder (in Switzerland), Altenberg, Regensburg, Prague, Augsburg, Cologne and Ulm. In England, the 14th century was a great period. For a long time, panes of glass had been imported from France, and relations thus established were maintained with Normandy and with Rhenish workshops. In the 14th century, English craftsmen produced a quantity of glass cut regularly into small panels containing one figure each. This was the plan adopted at Merton College, Oxford, and in Exeter Cathedral at the beginning of the century. *Jaune d'argent* came into use in 1330 at Wells Cathedral and appeared next in the cathedral at Gloucester against colored backgrounds. The glass at New College, Oxford, and at Winchester Cathedral, made in the last decades of the 14th century, belongs to the Perpendicular style, the most beautiful expression of which was the great window in the choir of York Minster (1405). There is little Italian stained glass worthy of mention besides some panels in Bologna (S. Petronio), in Florence (Or San Michele, S. Croce, S. Maria Novella), and in Venice (SS. Giovanni e Paolo).

France had some prolific regional schools in the 15th century. That of Bourges produced the pale-colored windows of the Ste-Chapelle of the dukes of Berry, consecrated in 1405; the glass in the chapel of Jacques Coeur (1448–50); and several examples in other chapels. The ateliers of Normandy continued the series begun at Rouen, Évreux, Le Mans, and extended their influence as far as the cathedral of Quimper, in Brittany. The work of Parisian glass painters is especially well represented by the clerestory windows in St-Séverin (*c.* 1475).

Of work produced by the ateliers of Dijon, very few pieces remain. Lorraine and Alsace were under German influence. The cathedral of Metz has some panels with large figures dating from the late 15th century. Strasbourg (a center as important as Cologne), Sélestat, and Saverne, all in France, mark stages in the activity of Pierre d'Andlau, who also worked in Germany at Ulm, Augsburg, Nuremberg, and Munich, and as far as Innsbruck in Austria. The works of this master offer some of the finest interpretations of the realism of the Flemish school and of contemporary German painters and engravers.

PAINTING

The passage from Romanesque to Gothic was much more abrupt in painting than in architecture and sculpture: it seems to have taken place with no period of transition. In a comparison of Gothic painting with Romanesque, the most striking feature is the abandonment of that antique majesty and simplicity that prevailed until the 12th century. Compositions became richer and more complicated: they lost their former monumentality. Figures were no longer treated in a uniform manner: they were gradually given distinguishing features, and faces began to reflect personality. Reality was given greater attention in depicting plants, trees, and flowers, and their species became recognizable. A profusion of accessories, anecdotes, and minor incidents surrounded the central episode. Perhaps the most important change was the introduction of the third dimension into the picture. Thus, in the *Maestà* (1308–11) of Duccio, whose general order still recalls what the Renaissance called the "Greek style" (meaning Byzantine), one can already distinguish graduated planes of recession and some modeling of chiaroscuro.

The advent of Gothic was also marked by an important change in subject matter. Gothic painters concentrated on the Life of Christ, notably episodes of the Passion treated with a realism that becomes more marked as the 15th century approached. The most mournful scenes became as frequent as they were rare in earlier centuries. In the same spirit, the *Danse Macabre* and Triumph of Death proliferated toward the end of the Middle Ages.

The renewal and development of the cult of the Virgin was expressed in a growing number of representations. More than half of all Sienese paintings were Madonnas. Even more noticeable,

Gothic Art. *Tree of Jesse*. Detail. 1522–24. Beauvais Cathedral. *Photo Jean Feuillie, Paris.*

Gothic Art. *Gouvernement des Princes : medieval street.* 15th century. Bibliothèque de l'Arsenal, Paris.

perhaps, is the way episodes in the life of Mary were treated, and the place granted her above all other beings. In pictures of the Annunciation, for example, the angel Gabriel was shown kneeling before her—an attitude that was never depicted in the Romanesque period.

Gothic painting raised complex historical problems. The chronology of the style varied from one country to another, and even from province to province, in accordance with the early appearance or late survival of Gothic forms. Its golden ages did not coincide. In France, the 13th century was a great period for miniatures; a whole repertory of new forms developed, including architectural backgrounds inspired by contemporary buildings. In the 15th century, Paris and Dijon became important artistic centers. In Italy, the Sienese painters were at their height in the first half of the 14th century, but they sustained a vigorous tradition of Gothic painting well into the 16th century. Avignon, influenced by both Italy and northern France, was the center of an artistic florescence toward the mid-14th century. The altarpiece of the *Mystic Lamb* in Ghent (1432) by Hubert and Jan van Eyck marked the beginning of a golden age in Flemish painting that continued until the first years of the 16th century in the work of Hieronymus Bosch.

Certain features were common to all painting of this period, notably an attention to minute details and a refined sense of decoration, which reveals itself as much in the architectural backgrounds as in the delightful settings of trees and flowers. In so far as all painters stressed these general characteristics, they are said to belong to an International Gothic style, as opposed to national schools. In Italy, a purely Italian form of Gothic was created by such masters as Giotto, Duccio, Pietro and Ambrogio Lorenzetti, and Simone Martini, while Antonio Pisanello and Gentile da Fabriano were interpreters of International Gothic.

ILLUMINATED MANUSCRIPTS

The political and cultural ties that existed between France and England after the Norman Conquest in 1066 were paralleled in art. Throughout this period there existed an Anglo-French school of manuscript painting that still influenced the scriptoria of Burgundian abbeys in the 12th century. In France, under St. Louis, a new style was born that had its main center in Paris (until the end of the 15th century). Manuscripts were no longer produced solely in monastic scriptoria, but were made also in lay guilds that began to flourish in the mid-13th century.

One of the earliest examples of works produced at the time of St. Louis is the *Psalter of Blanche of Castile* (*c.* 1230; Paris, Bibliothèque de l'Arsenal, Fr. 1186), in which the influence of stained glass is seen in the inclusion of the miniatures in medallions, although the style is that of the English illumination. The *Psalter of St. Louis* (*c.* 1256; Paris, Bibliothèque Nationale, Lat. 10525) is evidence of the prevailing taste for architectural and floral decoration that began to invade the margins. Another noteworthy group is that of the illustrated moralized Bibles, in which a reduced text is accompanied by overflowing imagery. The *Moralized Bible* in the Bibliothèque Nationale (Lat. 11560) presents on each page a detailed illustration of the text set out in eight medallions in two columns; it was illuminated for St. Louis in Paris between 1230 and 1250.

In the 14th century, the miniature assumed its definitive form and artistic autonomy. Master Honoré and Jean Pucelle headed flourishing ateliers. The latter workshop, which produced Pucelle's *Belleville Breviary* in 1343 (Paris, Bibliothèque Nationale, Lat. 10484), introduced symmetrically patterned backgrounds that became the rule in Charles V's reign. In the *Grandes Chroniques de France* (before 1380; Bibliothèque Nationale, Fr. 2813), the numerous scenes stand out against extremely varied checkered backgrounds. The oldest known versions of the *Grandes Chroniques* (Paris, Bibliothèque Ste-Geneviève, 782) was created a century earlier; in 1274 it was presented to Philip the Bold by the monk Primat, author of the *Chroniques*. This manuscript, from which Charles V's copy was transcribed, was similarly decorated with paintings.

The illuminators from the 15th century on can generally be identified by name and style. André Beauneveu, Jacquemart de Hesdin, and the Limbourg brothers worked for the Duc de Berry; Simon Marmion, Jean Le Tavernier, and Philippe de Mazerolles for the duke of Burgundy; Jean Fouquet, Jean Bourdichon, and Jean Colombe, who contributed to the *Heures de Laval*, brought fame to the school of Touraine. Certain very great miniaturists remain unidentified, including the creator of the *Grandes Heures de Rohan* (1425; Bibliothèque Nationale, Lat. 920), which contains a series of remarkable full-page paintings.

In England, 13th-century abbeys produced works that are difficult to distinguish from those of northern French monasteries. For example, the *Psalter of Queen Ingeborg* (*c.* 1210; Chantilly, Musée Condé), with its fine backgrounds of burnished gold, seems from its calendar to be the work of a Parisian illuminator, while from the style of its miniatures, it would appear to be a work of the English school. The famous *Queen Mary's Psalter* (London, British Museum, Royal Ms. 2 B. VII), so named because it was presented to Mary Tudor in 1553, was made in the first half of the 14th century for some member of royalty, perhaps Edward II. It is one of the masterpieces of English painting; its miniatures are framed in architecture on a gold background, and it also includes decorated initials, pen drawings grouped in pairs on each page, and a profusion of tinted drawings in the lower margins.

Germany's production of Gothic illuminated manuscripts was not outstanding. The best example is the *Manuscript of Manesse*, illustrating the lyric ballads and poems of the minnesingers: it is of documentary interest for the history of armor and costume.

As in other types of painting, the art of illumination in Italy broke away slowly from Byzantine and Romano-Byzantine forms. The *Epistolary* attributed to the miniaturist and calligrapher Giovanni Gaibano, executed in 1259 and preserved in the Capitular Library at Padua, is a noteworthy example of an art harking back to Byzantium. Only at the very end of the 13th century and the beginning of the 14th did the first interpretations of International Gothic appear, in Lombardy and Emilia: these were the miniatures by Neri da Rimini in the *Antiphonary* of 1314 (Bologna, Museum). From the same period is the *Pantheon of Godfrey of Viterbo* (a 12th-century chronicler), with decoration by Milanese artists (Paris, Bibliothèque Nationale). At the end of the century (*c.* 1385), the *Book of Hours of Gian Galeazzo Visconti* was made, probably by the workshop of Giovannino de' Grassi (d. 1398). Its somewhat heavy floral ornament in the margins, characteristic of Italian manuscripts, contrasts with the delicate colors in the central picture, as is seen in the beautiful decorated initial of the Magnificat.

WALL PAINTING

Gothic wall painting was relegated to the lower walls of churches, the walls separating chapels, castles where bare walls were no longer in favor, and Romanesque churches where artists continued not only to paint plain walls, but also to repaint areas previously decorated with frescoes that appeared outmoded. Enough remains of these works to give an idea of the development of Gothic wall painting and its reflection of the general features of Gothic art. In it is seen the typical abandonment of the Byzantine linear tradition, of Romanesque pictography, and of classic moderation in the interpretation of subjects, and the adoption in their place of increasingly sensitive modeling and a more realistic and anecdotal interpretation of iconographic themes. Gothic wall painting was strongly influenced by stained glass.

A new iconography appeared in the 13th century, at the same time as the new style. Among the new subjects in wall painting was the Coronation of the Virgin, inspired by the sculpture on the portals. The finest example seems to be that in the old church at Vernais (Cher), of the late 13th century. This was one of the first churches to offer another new theme, the Choir of Angels: below the Coronation, six angels play stringed instruments. At the end of the 14th century, the dome of the former chapel of the château at La Clayette (Saône-et-Loire) was painted with angels with outstretched wings, playing various musical instruments in a circle around the image of Christ.

The 15th century ushered in a new theme, the *Danse Macabre*: it was characteristic of Western art at the end of the Middle Ages, and was a product of the same mood as the Triumphs of Death and the Meetings of Three Dead Men and Three Living. The earliest *Danse Macabre* represented in France was that in the Cemetery of the Innocents in Paris, executed in 1424, but no longer extant. The best known is that of the abbey church of La Chaise-Dieu (*c.* 1460–70; Haute-Loire).

The evolution of manuscript and wall painting in the direction of the easel picture is illustrated by the decoration of the chapel in the Château de Dissay (Vienne), built by Pierre d'Amboise, bishop of Poitiers. The paintings were executed about 1493; those of the upper register are well preserved and comprise five pictures, four of which are borrowed from the Old Testament scenes. The fifth scene, which depicts the Fountain of Life, forms the center of the decoration.

Court painting was important during the Gothic period. At the château of Pernes-les-Fontaines (Vaucluse), the Tour Ferrande was decorated a little after 1266. But the first great decorative paintings of secular subjects were those at Avignon. The hunting scenes of the Chambre du Cerf in the Palace of the Popes (painted 1343–44) have a strong resemblance to tapestry in their backgrounds of greenery. Formerly considered the work of French artists, these famous paintings are now attributed to Matteo di Giovanetto da Viterbo (active 1343–66), who was summoned there by Clement VI. The same artist must have worked also in the chapel of St. Martial (1345) and in the audience chamber (1353), which were also in the palace, as well as in the chapel of the charterhouse at Villeneuve-lès-Avignon (decorated between 1354 and 1362).

PANEL PAINTING

Panel painting occupied an important place in the Gothic period; it was not unknown to Romanesque painters, but it was seldom practiced. Only in the 13th century did altarpieces begin to be produced in quantity. This was the case everywhere in the West, especially in Italy, where a host of known artists were at work. Outside of Italy, several important works were produced. The altarpiece on the *Life of the Virgin* (Paris, Musée de Cluny), painted about 1350, contains the checkered backgrounds characteristic of miniature painting at that period. Other noteworthy examples include four panels representing scenes of the Passion on gold backgrounds (Besançon, Museum), and the reredos from the church of Heiligenkreuz (Vienna, Kunsthistorisches Museum). The genre of the altar picture—reredos and frontal—flourished particularly in Catalonia (for instance, the *retablo* of the Mangraña at Perpignan) and throughout northern Spain.

From the 14th century, the Spanish *retablo* sometimes assumed gigantic proportions, and was to a certain extent a continuation of wall decoration; its disposition was monumental. The reredos representing the Pentecost in Manresa Cathedral, executed in 1394 by Pedro Serra, comprises no less than 58 panels giving the

Gothic Art. *Danse Macabre. c.* 1460–70. La Chaise-Dieu, Haute-Loire. *Photo Jean Feuillie, Paris.*

Gothic Art. *Scene by a pond.* Chambre du Cerf, Palace of the Popes, Avignon. 1343–44.

beholder a complete course in theology. The altarpiece was to Spanish art what the fresco was to Italy and stained glass was to France.

TAPESTRY

Tapestries were known in the earliest civilizations, and enjoyed a sort of "golden age" in the West during the 14th and 15th centuries. They were employed as wall coverings to lessen the cold and damp in private dwellings, and they were also hung in churches, where their office was not only protective and decorative but also devotional.

Workshops were set up in Paris about 1300. In the course of the century, they progressed from the reproduction of geometric designs and armorial bearings to that of animals, then to naturalistic scenes in which secular subjects were shown beside religious themes. During the reign of Charles V, there was a considerable vogue for tapestry, thanks to the patronage of the king and his brothers and the talent of Nicolas Bataille (active 1363–1400), the weaver responsible for the oldest extant French tapestry, the justly famed ensemble of the *Apocalypse* at Angers (Musée des Tapisseries). This hanging was ordered from him by Louis I, duke of Anjou, and carried out between 1375 and 1381, following patterns supplied by Hennequin de Bruges (Jean de Bondol; active 1368–81).

Among other productions of Nicolas Bataille or his workshop, the only ones that compare with this masterpiece are the *Presentation in the Temple* in the Musée Royal de L'Armée et d'Histoire Militaire in the Palais du Cinquantenaire in Brussels, and the sequence of the *Nine Heroes* in the Cloisters of the Metropolitan Museum, New York.

The workshops of Arras were perhaps as old as those of Paris, but while the latter almost disappeared under the English occupation after 1420, the former continued to enjoy great prosperity until the mid-15th century. The weavers of Tournai, who produced, among other works, some beautiful *verdures* (backgrounds of trees and flowers), suffered a decline after 1500. The Franco-Flemish regions knew many other workshops, the most celebrated being that of Brussels, which developed especially in the 16th century.

GOTTLIEB, Adolph (1903, New York—1973, New York), American painter. Gottlieb received his initial training in 1920 at the Art Students League, New York, under John Sloan and Robert Henri. Later he traveled through Europe, and then returned to New York. By 1930 his first exhibition of Expressionistic figures and landscapes had been held at the Dudensing Gallery in New York, and in 1935 he again traveled to Europe. Gottlieb was one of the founding members of the "Ten," a group that also included Lee Gatch, Mark Rothko, and Ilya Bolowtowsky (b. 1907). In 1936 Gottlieb worked as an easel painter for the WPA Federal Art Project, painting in a representational style influenced by Milton Avery's soft coloristic manner. His early style, whether manifested in still lifes, figure paintings, sea- or landscapes, contained Surrealistic overtones derived from Salvador Dali.

In 1941 Gottlieb's mature style began to evolve with a feeling of rebellion against American provincial realism and European geometric abstraction. Along with other Abstract Expressionists—Mark Rothko, Jackson Pollock, Clyfford Still, Theodoros Stamos—Gottlieb came into contact with the European expatriate Surrealists in New York during World War II. Freudian psychology and a long-standing association with primitive and Indian art of the Northwest Coast also helped form the basis for his series of *Pictographs*, sustained from 1941 until 1951. Gottlieb did not intend to illustrate such themes, however, and for him the pictographic process was one of free association. The more overt allusions to Freudian psychology (masks, blind eyes, fragmented faces) were later transformed into abstracted signs and themes in which the grid still functioned as a working skeleton (*Romanesque Façade*, 1949; Urbana, Ill., University of Illinois, Krannert Art Museum). The years 1951 to 1956 marked a departure into the *Imaginary Landscape* series, whose obvious horizontal divisions between a "sky" zone punctuated with frozen suns or astral forms, and a loosely brushed "ground" area were later eliminated and dissolved in the fluid fields of the *Burst* series, which was begun in 1957.

Jean Goujon. *Caryatids.* 1550–51. Musicians' Gallery, Louvre, Paris. *Photo Ionesco-Réalités, Paris.*

GOUJON, Jean (*c.* 1510, Normandy—1564/68, Bologna), major French Renaissance sculptor. He is first known to have worked in 1540 on columns of the organ loft in the church of St-Maclou, Rouen. Somewhat later he arrived in Paris and worked on the rood screen for the church of St-Germain-l'Auxerrois (1544–45): two bas-reliefs from this rood screen, the *Entombment* and the *Four Evangelists*, are now in the Louvre, Paris. About this time Goujon began working with Pierre Lescot, with whom he collaborated fruitfully for the rest of his career. His definitive style was already set; formal problems were to be his primary concern. Goujon's engravings for the first French translation of Vitruvius, by Jean Martin (1547), led Martin to cite him as a true scholarly authority along with the Italians Leon Battista Alberti and Sebastiano Serlio. He was named sculptor to the king in 1547 and, under Lescot's direction, decorated the Hôtel de Ligneris in Paris (now the Musée Carnavalet), where the visitor may admire his allegorical statue of *Summer*.

The famous *Nymphs* of the Fountain of the Innocents in Paris, renowned for the undulating grace of their bodies and the fluidity of their draperies, were commissioned by Lescot (1549). They are surrounded by bas-reliefs of se divinities at play—the same figure overused by the school of Raphael, but lightened and more finely modeled by Goujon. In 1549 Goujon began the long undertaking at the Louvre that he was not to interrupt until he fled Paris after the massacre of his fellow-Protestants at Vassy (1562). He decorated Lescot's beautiful façade in the Louvre's Cour Carrée with allegories of *History* and *Victory, War* and *Peace, Glory* and *Renown*. The undulant bodies, veiled by tunics, show Goujon's decorative talents and Classical leanings to great advantage. He further developed these tendencies in his *Caryatids* (1550–51) of the Musicians' Gallery (Louvre), which were to recapture in a Mannerist rhythm the sovereign grace of the statues of young girls at the Erechtheum in Athens.

GOYA Y LUCIENTES, Francisco José de (1746, Fuendetodos, near Saragossa—1828, Bordeaux), Spanish painter and graphic artist. He studied in Saragossa at the Escuela Pía of Padre Joaquín, and also worked in the studio of the painter José Luzán (1710–85). Goya undertook a journey to Italy in 1770–71, possibly staying in Naples. In 1771 he received second prize from the Parma Academy for his entry in a painting competition. In Parma Goya studied Correggio's paintings and frescoes in the cupolas of the city's churches. On his return to Spain in 1771, Goya went to Saragossa, in Aragon, and painted the *Gloria* in the small chancel of the cathedral (1772) and a series of frescoes in the Carthusian monastery of Aula Dei, near Saragossa (1771–72).

Francisco Goya. *Lovely Advice.* Etching from *Los Caprichos.* 1793–98.

Upon settling in Madrid in 1773, Goya married Josefa Bayeu, whose brother, the painter Francisco Bayeu (1734–95), introduced him to the Neoclassical painter Anton Rafael Mengs and other painters at the Spanish court. Between 1776 and 1791 Goya prepared 43 cartoons for tapestries to be woven at the royal factory of Santa Bárbara and destined for the apartments of the Pardo and Escorial palaces. Notable among these cartoons, which display a lively anecdotal sense, are: the *Picnic* (1776), the *Parasol* (1778), the *Crockery Seller* (1779), the *Injured Mason* (1786), and *Blind Man's Buff* (1788)—all of which are in the Prado, Madrid.

In 1780 he became painter to King Charles III, and a rather uninspired *Crucifixion* (Prado) won his admission to the Academy in that year. In 1785 he was appointed assistant director of the tapestry factory of Santa Bárbara, and in 1789 painter to the royal chamber. Goya's religious commissions became numerous: he worked for the Basilica of Nuestra Señora del Pilar in Saragossa (the *Queen of Martyrs*, 1780); for the church of San Francisco el Grande in Madrid (*St. Bernardino Preaching Before the King of Aragon,* 1784); for the cathedral of Valencia (*St. Francis Borgia*, 1788–89); and for the convent of Santa Aña at Valladolid (*Death of St. Joseph,* 1787). He became an admirable portrait painter who soon developed an original style of his own, marked by a stark simplicity of representation, a subtly varied richness of tone, and an acute analysis of character. Goya's interpretation of the *Family of the Infante Don Luis* (1783; Florence, Priv. Coll.) is imbued with a tender humanity; his *Charles III* dressed as a huntsman (1786; Prado) is inspired by the royal portraits of Velázquez.

In 1792 Goya fell gravely ill at Cadiz, and thereafter was afflicted with almost total deafness. In 1793, immediately after his illness, Goya painted 11 cabinet pictures for the Academy of San Fernando in Madrid. These pictures differ from Goya's preceding works in their altered tone, suddenly imbued with a tragic intensity; the artist's palette is also new, with gray tones against which clear colors shine like flames, and his brushstroke has become swift and nervous. *Los Caprichos* ("The Caprices"), a series of etchings executed between 1793 and 1798, are intellectually inspired by the philosophical spirit of the time.

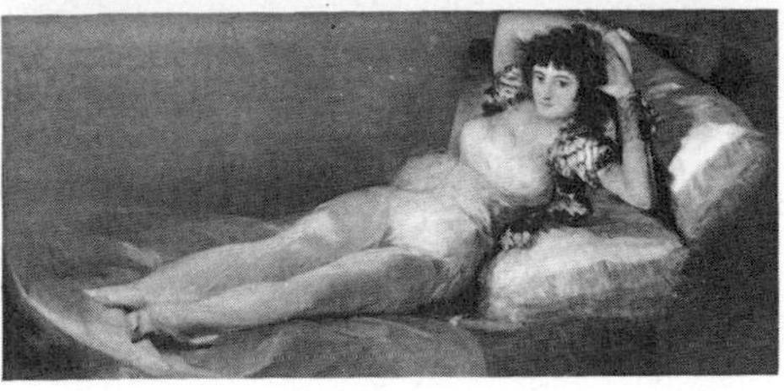

Francisco Goya. *The Naked* and *Clothed Majas. c.* 1804. Prado, Madrid.

In 1795 Goya was appointed director of painting at the Academy of San Fernando, and in 1799 first painter to the royal chamber. In this latter capacity, he was called upon (1798–1801) to execute various commissions for the court. He painted individual portraits of *Charles IV* and *Maria Luisa on Horseback* (both 1799; both in the Prado), as well as the *Condesa de Chinchón,* an exquisite and melancholy figure (1800; Madrid, Coll. Duchess of Sueca). In the group portrait of the *Family of Charles IV* (1800; Prado), the influence of Velázquez is reduced to the presence of the portrait painter himself, seen in the upper left corner of the picture.

Aside from his royal portraits, Goya produced a number of other outstanding portraits during this period: *Doña Tadea Arias de Enríquez* (1793–94, Prado); *Francisco Bayeu* (1975, Prado); the *Condesa of Fernán-Núñez* (1803; Madrid, Coll. Duchess of Fernán-Núñez); the actor *Isidro Maiquez* (1807, Prado); and *Doña Isabel Cobos de Porcel* (1806; London, National Gallery). The *Duchess of Alba* was painted in a black costume (1797; New York, Hispanic Society of America) and in red and white (1795; Madrid, Coll. Duke of Alba). It is, however, a mistake to connect the duchess with the *Naked Maja* or the *Clothed Maja* (both *c.* 1804; both in the Prado) as has been frequently attempted.

In 1808 there began a train of political events that had a profound effect on Goya's life and work. Charles IV was obliged to abdicate in favor of his son, Ferdinand VII. Napoleon I, however, was determined to impose as sovereign of Spain his own brother, Joseph Bonaparte. On May 2, 1808, the people of Madrid rose against the Napoleonic forces. The insurrection was put down the next day by French troops who executed the Spanish patriots they had taken prisoner; this violent scene was commemorated by Goya in the *Shooting of May 3, 1808* (1814, Prado). The subsequent reign of Ferdinand VII—who was restored to the throne in 1814—was marked by a pitiless and despotic repression of liberals and French partisans. As a protest against all war, Goya produced *Los Desastres de la Guerra* ("The Disasters of War"), a series of etchings (1810–14) abounding in horrible details. In a similar vein are his engravings of *La Tauromaquia* ("Bull-fighting"), 1815–16, and *Los Proverbios*—also known as *Los Disparates*, or "The Follies"—of *c.* 1813–18. The numerous frescoes that Goya painted in his house, the Quinta del Sordo ("deaf man's house"), including the famous *Saturn Devouring His Children* (after 1818; transferred to the Prado), reveal a nightmarish world.

In 1824, fearing the effects of the absolutist reaction, Goya obtained permission to go to France, and after a short stay in Paris settled in Bordeaux. He revisited Spain in 1826, but spent his last years in Bordeaux, where he painted the famous *Milkmaid of Bordeaux* (1828; Prado). The astonishing body of work Goya left at his death illustrates all the stages in the evolution of modern painting, from the elegant, worldly Rococo style of the 18th century to 19th-century romanticism and Impressionism.

Benozzo Gozzoli. *Lorenzo de' Medici.* Detail from the Procession of the Magi. 1459. Palazzo Medici-Riccardi, Florence. *Photo Anderson-Giraudon.*

GOYEN, Jan van (1596, Leiden—1656, The Hague), Dutch landscape painter. He traveled widely in Europe before settling in The Hague in 1631. Van Goyen's best landscapes, whether on panel or canvas, are datable after 1640. His work shows a transition from a placid vision to a romantic feeling for nature, from a varied color range to a monochromatic palette, from restrained effects of light to a bold chiaroscuro. Sometimes a ray of golden light pierces his silvery grays and light ochers and is surrounded by brown and green shadows; at other times the effect is centered in half tones in an ensemble of bister, sepia, and muted green. But these experiments, as varied as the times of day and the motives that inspired them, are simply the means by which Van Goyen expressed the unique atmosphere of the sites and skies of his native land. He needed only a small range of subjects: a *River Scene* (1636; Cambridge, Mass., on loan at Fogg Art Museum); *Two Oak Trees* with their twisted branches (1641; Amsterdam, Rijksmuseum); or a townscape, most often *Dordrecht* (1633; The Hague, Mauritshuis).

GOZZOLI, Benozzo di Lese, *called* Benozzo (1420, Florence—1497, Pistoia), Italian painter. He began as a goldsmith's apprentice, then worked with Lorenzo Ghiberti on the baptistery doors in Florence. Later he assisted Fra Angelico, whom he followed to Rome and Orvieto. He spent some time in central Italy, where he painted a cycle of frescoes for the Franciscans at the church of S. Fortunato in Montefalco, and another for the nuns of S. Rosa in Viterbo (lost). His reputation as a decorator was sufficiently established by 1459 for the Medici to engage him to paint the chapel in their new palace in Florence, the Palazzo Medici-Riccardi; this continuous frieze of wall frescoes was Gozzoli's most spirited and imaginative work. He was less original in altarpieces such as the *Virgin and Child Enthroned Among Angels and Saints* (1461; London, National Gallery), painted for the Compagnia di S. Marco in Florence. In San Gimignano he decorated the church of S. Agostino (1463–65) and the Palazzo del Popolo. From there Gozzoli went to Pisa, where he covered an entire wall of the Camposanto with Old Testament subjects and remained for 17 years.

Gozzoli's art is that of the storyteller, graceful and witty rather than stylistically inventive. In the Medici Chapel, the *Procession of the Magi*, making its way through a dreamlike Tuscany, is composed, in accordance with tradition, of people of all ages, in festive headgear and exotic clothes.

GRANT, Duncan James Corrowr (b. 1885, Rothiemurchus, Inverness-shire, Scotland), English painter, decorator, and designer of textiles, pottery, and theater décor. Grant studied under Jacques-Émile Blanche (1861–1942) in Paris (1906), and at the Slade School in London. A cousin of the writer Lytton Strachey, he soon became a member of the Bloomsbury group, which included Roger Fry, Clive and Vanessa Bell, and Virginia Woolf. From 1913 to 1919, he worked with Fry at the Omega Workshops. He was influenced by those works of the Fauves and of Cézanne that were included in Fry's London Postimpressionist exhibitions of 1910–11 and 1912. The Tate Gallery in London has a representative series of his paintings. His early portraits, among the most interesting of all his works, include *J. M. Keynes* (1908; Cambridge, King's College), *Virginia Woolf* (1911; England, Coll. Mrs. David Garnett), and *Lytton Strachey* (1913; England, Coll. Mrs. Bagenall).

GRANT, Sir Francis (1803, Edinburgh—1878, Melton Mowbray, Leicester), Scottish portrait painter. After making his debut at the Royal Academy in 1834, he achieved a considerable reputation with his hunting scenes. His success was based on a fluent, straightforward style without affectations. In the 1840s Grant became the most fashionable British portrait painter of the day, patronized by the royal family and the aristocracy. An Associate of the Royal Academy in 1842 and a full Academician in 1851, he was made its president in 1866, succeeding Sir Charles Eastlake. *Sir Walter Scott with Two Staghounds* (1831; Edinburgh, Scottish National Portrait Gallery), the equestrian portraits of Queen Victoria and Prince Albert (1846; Horsham, Christ's Hospital School) and the portrait of Lord Macaulay

(1854; London, National Portrait Gallery) are characteristic of Grant's style.

GRAVES, Morris (b. 1910, Fox Valley, Oregon), American painter. He first gained recognition when he was awarded a prize from the Seattle Art Museum in 1933; this was followed by a one-man show there three years later. Like many other American artists, Graves was supported during the Depression by the WPA Federal Art Project.

Oriental art and the manner in which the West Coast painter Mark Tobey used it influenced Graves early in his career, as did his interest in Zen Buddhist and Vedanta (Indian) philosophy. Around 1937 he gave up the use of oil to work with tempera, wax, ink, and gouache on thin papers, employing methods and techniques that were related to Japanese and Chinese scrollwork. In 1942 he received critical acclaim for some of his first works in this manner with a show at the Museum of Modern Art, New York. The images of blind birds, pine trees, and waves bounded by lines of white tracery are common in Graves's paintings. The *Little Known Bird of the Inner Eye* (1941; New York, Museum of Modern Art) evokes his mystical attitude toward nature, and while it does not imitate Oriental art per se, the delicacy of its colors and definition reveals his interest in the East.

GRECO, Domenikos Theotokopoulos, *called* El (1541, Candia, Crete—1614, Toledo), Spanish Mannerist painter. Born on the island of Crete, El Greco went to Italy around 1560, at first staying in and around Venice and frequenting the circle of Titian, Tintoretto, and Jacopo Bassano. In 1570 he was in Rome. It is not known whether El Greco collaborated in the works of Titian's old age, or whether he returned to Venice after leaving Rome in 1572. It seems logical, however, to suppose that the influence of Titian, and later that of Michelangelo, must gradually have supplanted the Byzantine influence evident in El Greco's earliest works. These include the *Modena Polyptych* (*c.* 1568–69; Modena, Galleria Estense); *Christ Healing the Blind Man* (*c.* 1570; Dresden, Gemäldegalerie); *Christ Expelling the Merchants from the Temple* (*c.* 1575; Minneapolis, Institute of Arts); and the portraits of *Giulio Clovio* (*c.* 1570; Museo di Capodimonte) and *Vincentio Anastagi* (1576; New York, Frick Collection).

During the years 1576–77 El Greco was in Madrid and Toledo. The year 1577 brought El Greco two important commissions in Toledo: the altarpiece for the church of S. Domingo el Antiguo, and the *Espolio* (*Disrobing of Christ*) for the sacristy of Toledo Cathedral. Of the S. Domingo ensemble, the central panel with the *Assumption of the Virgin* is now in the Chicago Art Institute; the *Holy Trinity* from the upper portion is in the Prado, Madrid, as is a flanking panel representing *St. Benedict*. Still in their original setting in the church are the *Holy Face, St. John the Baptist, St. John the Evangelist*, and the side panels of the *Adoration of the Shepherds, St. Jerome*, and the *Resurrection*.

More precious to El Greco than these commissions in Toledo was the coveted patronage of King Philip II. In 1580 he painted for the king the *Adoration of the Name of Jesus* (known popularly as the *Dream of Philip II*) and the *Martyrdom of St. Maurice* (both in the Escorial). The last-named picture displeased the king, and was not placed in the chapel for which it had been commissioned.

Having failed to satisfy Philip II, El Greco was obliged to restrict his ambitions to Toledo, which at that time still enjoyed capital importance in the economic, social, and intellectual life of Spain. Here El Greco won a great reputation, being treated with much esteem until his death. His own artistic predilections adapted themselves readily to certain forms of Spanish art, such as altarpieces containing numerous sculptured figures and paintings; figures of saints, presented singly or in pairs; and series of images of the apostles, called *apostolados*. His saints and martyrs, often disproportionately elongated, but always majestic and hieratic, conform to a static rhythm that recalls that of Byzantine mosaics.

The chronology of the great commissions entrusted to the artist near the end of his life is known to us. In 1586 he painted for the church of S. Tomé in Toledo the *Burial of the Count of Orgaz*: the altarpiece is still in its original setting. Tradition has it that the count had been honored at his death with miraculous obsequies, St. Stephen and St. Augustine having descended from Heaven to bury him with their own hands. The scene depicting this miracle occupies the lower part of the painting, while the upper part shows the soul of the dead count being received into Heaven. Of the three altarpieces painted by El Greco for the chapel of S. José in Toledo (1597–99), the principal one—showing *St. Joseph Leading the Child Jesus* and the *Coronation of the Virgin*—remains intact; the panels of the side altarpieces (the *Virgin with St. Agnes and St. Thecla* and *St. Martin and the Beggar*) are now preserved in the National Gallery, Washington, D.C. After 1603 El Greco suffered poverty and was obliged to accept commissions that were frequently beyond his strength. To the year 1603 are assigned the altarpiece for the College of S. Bernardino at Toledo and the important paintings for the church of the Merced in Illescas: the *Nativity, Annunciation, Coronation of the Virgin*, and *Apparition of the Virgin to S. Ildefonso*. The tendency toward pathetic contemplation that is so evident in the great commissioned pictures mentioned above is found also in the *Vision of the Apocalypse* (*c.* 1610; Zumaya, Zuloaga Museum), and above all in the numerous paintings of *St. Francis of Assisi*, one of El Greco's favorite

Morris Graves. *Little Known Bird of the Inner Eye*. 1941. Museum of Modern Art, New York.

El Greco. *Christ Expelling the Merchants from the Temple*. National Gallery, London.

El Greco. *Portrait of Cardinal Niño de Guevara.* *c.* 1598–1600. Metropolitan Museum of Art, New York.

subjects (versions in Madrid, Lille, and elsewhere).

El Greco's portraits owe their rare power of suggestion to the absorbed expressions of the models and their somber dress. Great spiritual intensity is seen in the portrait of *Cardinal Niño de Guevara* (*c.* 1598–1600; New York, Metropolitan Museum), an extraordinary composition that may have influenced Velázquez when he painted the portrait of Pope Innocent X. El Greco endowed Toledo with a burning soul akin to his own in his only landscape, the *View of Toledo* (1608; Metropolitan Museum).

GRECO-ROMAN ART IN THE MIDDLE EAST. The Hellenistic period in the Middle East began immediately following the death of Alexander the Great in 323 B.C. The terminal date adopted here is the year 64 B.C., which marked the arrival of the Romans in the Middle East and the establishment of the Roman province of Syria. In its cultural development, the East had suffered from internal struggles and rivalries between Lagides and Seleucids. The Romans brought to the Middle East their own national virtues of order, regularity, and clarity, thus creating a milieu favorable to artistic activity. Under their protection, art flourished in the great Eastern capitals and produced a number of spectacular achievements. The Romans themselves had to defend these monuments against the Parthians (between 93 B.C. and 226 A.D.) and against the Sassanids, but eventually they fell into the hands of the Arabs (638 A.D.).

It is extremely difficult to date with any degree of certainty a piece of sculpture, produced on Phoenician territory between the 4th and 1st centuries B.C., that has no inscription on it. However, it is in the latter half of the 4th century B.C. that scholars usually place the extraordinary series of sarcophagi in Parian marble that was discovered in 1887 in the necropolis at Sidon. These Hellenistic works have been given various arbitrary names, such as the Alexander Sarcophagus, the Weeping Women Sarcophagus, the Satrap Sarcophagus, and the Lycian Sarcophagus. It might be possible to date the Satrap and the Lycian sarcophagi as works of the 5th or even 6th century B.C., whereas the Alexander and Weeping Women sarcophagi seem to belong to the 4th century B.C.

But it was in Greco-Roman art that the East was most productive. On the hill of Nimrud-Dagh, in Commagene (the ancient Syrian region between the Taurus mountains and the Euphrates) one can still see the huge statues erected near the tomb of Antiochus I (69–34 B.C.). Baalbek, built against the snow-capped hills of present-day Lebanon, was justly famous for its temples. The city's origin and early history were Semitic. It was raised to the status of a colony during the reign of Augustus, and it was probably at this time that work began on the restoration of the temple of Hadad (the god of fertility and the elements), which later was known as the Great Temple. It was not until the reigns of the emperors Antoninus the Pious (A.D. 138–161), Septimius Severus (A.D. 193–211), and Caracalla (A.D. 211–217) that the colossal extensions to the temple of Hadad began. On the acropolis, two sanctuaries stood side by side: the Great Temple was rededicated to the Heliopolitan triad (Jupiter, Venus, and Mercury); the second was probably dedicated to the Semitic goddess Atargatis.

Halfway between Damascus and the Euphrates, in the middle of the Syrian desert, was Palmyra. This caravan town, known in the Bible as Tamar or Tadmor, was also Semitic in origin and had been forced from the 1st century A.D. to accept Roman control. After becoming a "free city" and later a Roman colony, Palmyra won its independence in the 3rd century A.D. under the Odeinat family. Until she was defeated by Emperor Aurelian, Palmyra's Queen Zenobia had provided the city with an unprecedented degree of prosperity. With its temples (those of Bel and Baal-shamin were the most celebrated), its broad streets flanked by colonnaded porticoes, its theater, and its agora, Palmyra was once a symbol of wealth. Hundreds, perhaps thousands, of busts of its citizens and their wives were carved. Many of them are faithful portraits that have preserved for us the features of Palmyra's inhabitants in a style strongly influenced by the unidealized realism of Roman portraiture.

Leaving Palmyra, and going due east as far as the Euphrates, the traveler arrived at Dura-Europus. This city was entirely Hellenistic in foundation, since it was built by the Macedonians under Seleucus Nicator (312–280 B.C.). Dura was a Greek city, planned on a square grid, but it was the meeting point of several civilizations and therefore of several schools of art. The influences came from both the West (Greeks, Romans, Palmy-

Greco-Roman Art. Below left: Alexander Sarcophagus. 4th century B.C. Archaeological Museums, Istanbul. Below right: Ruins of a Corinthian colonnade, Palmyra. *c.* A.D. 200. *Photo George Rodger-Magnum.*

Greco-Roman Art. El-Dair ("the temple"), Petra. 1st century A.D. *Photo George Holton, New York.*

renians) and the East (Parthenians and Sassanians). Dura was the center of a remarkable syncretism in both art and religion—to such a point, indeed, that painters in turn decorated the temple of the Palmyrenian gods with a fresco on the *Sacrifice of Conon* (1st century A.D.; today in Damascus, National Museum); a synagogue with frescoes from almost the entire Old Testament (245 A.D., Damascus); a Christian chapel; and a mithraeum (a sanctuary dedicated to Mithra). The same situation existed in the sculpture. For example, a charming and delicate masterpiece, such as the *Aphrodite with a Tortoise* (Paris, Louvre), which is imbued with Hellenic grace, existed side by side with a *Zeus-Kyrios*, a *Hadad*, and an *Atargatis*, showing Semitic gods in Roman dress.

The city of Petra was almost as impressive as Palmyra as a center of artistic activity. It was a base for merchants and caravans, and stood between the Dead Sea and the Gulf of Aqaba, surrounded by a magnificent array of red rocks. The Edomite city of Sela, which was also a trading base, had existed since the 6th century B.C. A Nabataean dynasty won its independence at the end of the 2nd century B.C., that is, in the middle of the Hellenistic period. One of the sovereigns, Aretes the Philhellene (87–62 B.C.), gave Petra the scale and magnificence of a capital. The temples, palaces, baths, nymphaea, and theater (mid-2nd century A.D.) at Petra were built in his reign and that of his successor, but many of them have almost completely disappeared. In 106 A.D. Emperor Trajan incorporated Petra into the Roman province of Arabia. Although no longer independent, the city continued to be prosperous, as can be seen from the increasingly magnificent tombs covering the cliffs of Petra, with their façades decorated by columns, pediments, and statues. Their style may be a decadent one, as seen in the decorative complexities of El-Khazna or El-Dair (1st-century A.D. funerary temples carved out of the rock), but it emphasizes the boldness of their architects and the virtuosity of their craftsmen. Thus Petra, along with Baalbek and Palmyra, remains one of the most astonishing achievements of Greco-Roman art in the Middle East.

GREEK ART. Any attempted short definition of the role of Greek art in the history of plastic forms is bound to have as its basis the concept of man himself: Greek plastic art was first of all the study and expression of man, and so everything needed to be on a human scale. By "man" was meant the Platonic idea of man, of which individuals are incomplete incarnations, but less so if they are part of a social group or political community. From its very beginnings the evolution of Greek plastic art must be seen within this frame of reference. Amid all variations of time and place this underlying humanity and the basic human proportions of Greek works of art form a fundamental element of unity throughout the history of Classical art. The artist's function was to bypass individual characteristics and to find a form appropriate to the expression of an idealized and abstract humanity.

ORIGINS OF PLASTIC ART

No doubt it was the Greek feeling for form that led the potters of the 10th century B.C. gradually to modify the inherited Mycenaean shapes. Originally, however, the ornament was purely linear and geometric, without reference to the actual world of animals and vegetation. Curving, sinuous lines at first, then straight lines and broken ones, triangles, checkerboards, chevrons, and finally meander patterns, Greek crosses, and swastikas formed the whole repertoire of the earliest phase of Greek pottery, which is the first basic revelation of the Hellenic spirit. The shapes, clay, and decoration of the pottery from Athens were the best, but the same purely abstract ornament was found on the islands, on Crete, on the Ionian coast, and even in Anatolia.

It was in Athens at the turn of the 9th century B.C. that the human silhouette first broke into this cold world of geometric patterns. To be sure, this silhouette was very stylized: the head was merely a circle balanced on a line that linked it to an inverted triangle representing the torso; a bulge indicated the buttocks, while the limbs were spindles bent at acute angles. Such a silhouette easily fitted into one of the traditional zones of the geometric ornament, usually on the belly of the vase. The vase's function determined the choice of theme. To begin with, only funeral scenes were depicted. The black silhouettes stood out against the beige or reddish ground of the vase; not a single extra line or incision was used to add the smallest detail to face or figure, and no suggestion of a third dimension enlivened it.

Greek Art. Attic amphora. 8th century B.C. National Museum, Athens. *Hirmer Fotoarchiv, Munich.*

Greek Art. Cycladic pitcher. Aegina, 1st half of 7th century B.C. British Museum, London.

But the break with the pure geometric scheme had been made, and nothing would be able to halt that revolution, with its profound consequences. The fundamental Greek attachment to man and life led to a swift evolution of themes and subjects: in the course of the 8th century B.C. the concept of decoration was transformed. Lively scenes were painted on vases other than amphoras and funeral urns; craters and hydrias for domestic use came to be decorated with scenes of the wanderings of Ulysses or the battles before Troy; animals, particularly man's faithful companions the horse and dog, appeared first; later, toward the beginning of the 7th century B.C., with the advent of the so-called Orientalizing style, the decorative repertoire was enriched by exotic sphinxes, lions, and every sort of deer. It was about that time, before the middle of the 8th century B.C., that the first pottery and bronze figures appeared in Greek art.

It was again at the shrines—at Olympia, Delphi, and Sparta—that, after a break of several centuries, so-called Geometric figures began to reappear; they were offerings that were either images of the worshiper himself (a warrior or athlete) or models of rams, bulls, horses, or other victims that the faithful could not always afford to sacrifice. They show the same spirit of simplification and abstraction as do the figures painted on the pots. They are of very small dimensions, flat, with angular contours and no volume, with simplified heads and linear limbs, leaving no place for realistic qualities or a taste for exact detail.

Greek Art. Archaic torso. Megara Hyblaea, Sicily. 1st half of 6th century B.C. Museo Archeologico Nazionale, Siracusa. *Photo Leonard von Matt, Buochs.*

Greek Art. Temple of Hera I, called the Basilica, Paestum. Doric. *c.* 530 B.C. *Photo Henri Stierlin, Geneva.*

ARCHAIC PERIOD

In about the middle of the 7th century B.C. a new age in the history of plastic form began, for then life-size sculpture made its appearance and architectural forms came to flower. At the same time the old unity of the Geometric world was breaking up under new historic, economic, and social pressures. It was an age of intense activity and astonishingly vigorous creative drive in both the newly settled and the older parts of the Greek world.

Various factors were responsible for that flowering of the Hellenic creative genius. First there was the great movement of expansion, following social and economic difficulties, when Greek colonies were planted in central and southern Italy, in Sicily, along the west coasts of the Mediterranean, in Africa, and in southern Russia. Busy trade between one Greek city and another, and also between Greeks and neighboring civilizations, led not only to the exchange of objects, but also to travels by artists, who saw and appreciated new forms of expression.

Meanwhile, the new cities were growing rich, and were eager to build bigger and better structures than the old metropolises; they also felt themselves in competition with the native cultures with which they came in contact. All of this favored artists, enabling them to rely on increased material and technical resources; consequently, important projects, buildings of vast dimensions, and other undertakings to match the available resources began to attract the creative imaginations of various types of artists.

The evolution of ideas and religious beliefs in these new historic circumstances led to the birth and rapid growth of temple architecture and cult or votive sculpture.

If one is to believe Classical literary sources, the first cult statues, the xoana, were made of wood in a rudimentary style. The figure, hardly distinct from the primitive pillar, remained with its body sheathed, only the schematic features of head and face being carved. The first temples were of modest size and various shapes. Archaeological remains and some pottery models from Argos, Perakhora, and Samos allow us to form some idea of the shape of those temples, which were often simple rectangular chapels with the roof supported by a row of internal columns; there might be an apse at one end and a small projecting roof might form a porch on the façade. In the end the scheme inherited from the Mycenaean palace—the megaron—prevailed, with its rectangular plan, entrance on one of the shorter sides, and porch with portico. It was around that core that architects elaborated the definitive shape of the Greek temple, but there were important regional variations.

Between the mid-7th century B.C. and the last quarter of the 6th, two main tendencies came to be differentiated as the Ionic and Doric spirits; they were not rigid categories, being without question two aspects of a single aesthetic conception, but the two types stood out with some distinctness in the plastic arts. The difference was more one of temperament and of an aesthetic world view than any distinction of race, of techniques employed, or of geographical distribution. For artists with a Doric turn of mind, a sense of mass, a taste for balanced force, athletic qualities, and a respect for geometry counted most, while the Ionians were more appreciative of grace, of slight and slender proportions, and they did not hesitate to sacrifice the spirit of geometry to decorative values.

Ionia and the Islands

Ionia here means more than the central part of the coast of Asia Minor: it includes the large islands of Samos, Lesbos, Chios, and part of the Cyclades. It was the area in which the Greek world came in touch with the civilizations of the East, and therefore where foreign influences left the deepest mark. All the fauna of the East—bulls, lions, and every sort of deer—file proudly across the vases of Rhodes and frolic on the 7th-century B.C. pots from Paros and Naxos.

Sculpture developed more freely, coming under somewhat different Eastern influences on the coast and in the islands. The 7th-century B.C. ivory offerings to Artemis at Ephesus have the rather soft shapes and heavy blurred features of Oriental types; and though they are more slender, the figures carved on the lowest drums of the columns of the Artemision are of the same sort.

However, the contemporary sculptors of Samos and Chios had transformed the Eastern heritage, refining shapes and enlivening features; all the island vivacity comes out in the gaiety of the expressions and the skillful arrangement of the drapery. The masterpiece of Ionian sculpture of this time comes from Samos: it is the Hera dedicated by Cheramyes (Paris, Louvre). The Archaic sheath has become a finely pleated dress, which is also a well-conceived column leading up to, supporting, and contrasting with the harmonious shape of the bust; the decorative value of the drapery has been used to bring out the plastic value of the body. There are *korai* at Delos, caryatids from the treasuries at Delphi, and scenes on the frieze of the Treasury of the Siphnians there that well illustrate the full charm of Ionic sculpture.

It was in architecture that the Ionians were able to give free reign to both their imagination in decoration and to that taste for the grand and monumental that their power enabled them to indulge. In this case, too, they sought models abroad. Tradition says that the Samian architects Rhoikos and Theodoros traveled to Egypt and returned to Greece with the knowledge of how to use colonnades, divide space with successive groups of interconnected columns, and make columns soar upward by the use of slender flutes with a luxuriant molding below or even, as at Ephesus, with elaborately carved figures, and the entire column blossoming out at the top into the supple volutes of the capitals. The splendor of these imposing buildings was increased by the richness of the material used—a white or bluish marble.

The Peloponnesus

Geometric order prevailed here, as did the simplicity, not to say severity, of the Doric style, even though Lacedemonian austerity had been very appreciably modified down to the mid-6th century B.C. by the summoning of Ionian artists (such as Bathycles of Magnesia). It was in the northeast—at Argos, Corinth, and Sicyon—that a powerful school of sculpture developed. The well-known figures of *Cleobis* and *Biton* (Delphi, Archaeological Museum), attributed to Polymedes, are representative of Argive work, geometric in design, in very clear contrast to the graphic and linear tendencies of Ionian art. A statue from Tenea and many bronze figurines provide an insight into the sculpture of 6th-century B.C. Corinth. The athletic type represented is lithe and spare, having shed the excessive weight of the solid Argive works. There is a more robust and dynamic sense of movement, in spite of a certain roughness and schematic dryness such as one notes in the frieze of the Sicyonian Treasury at Delphi. Crossing lines and volumes emphasize the geometry of these carvings, but the works also give an impression of contained strength and of irresistible movement.

The same tendencies were at work in architecture, but the invention of painted pottery revetments, traditionally associated with Corinth, introduced a brighter element. We know the outline of the columns of the Temple of Apollo, which dominated the ancient town at Corinth; a patina has formed over the tufa from which they were carved, and their solid, squat forms are planted on a substructure integrated with the rock.

Athens

At no great distance from these Peloponnesian centers Athenian artists were forging the means of expression for a very different world—a world in which Dorian severity gave way to the carefree and exuberant gaiety of the Ionians, and in which balance and discipline were natural and unconstrained. During the 6th century B.C. the creative power of the Athenians was at work in every field of plastic art.

The potters invented new shapes and improved old ones, making more slender amphoras and hydrias and deeper cups; lekythoi were made for the first time. Ornament, with new motifs introduced from the East, was brought under control and organized to suit the vase's shape and the surface to be decorated; at the same time technique was transformed by using contrasting black and red, a combination of colors made possible by the nature of Attic clay.

Sculptors were busy both with freestanding figures and with carving on buildings. The quality and originality of Archaic sculpture in Athens are known from the *korai* excavated from the debris used to level part of the Acropolis after the Persian invasion, and from *kouroi* found much later in Attica. While the types of both *kouros* and *kore* clearly were introduced from Ionia, there were great differences in conception and treatment: the handling was pre-

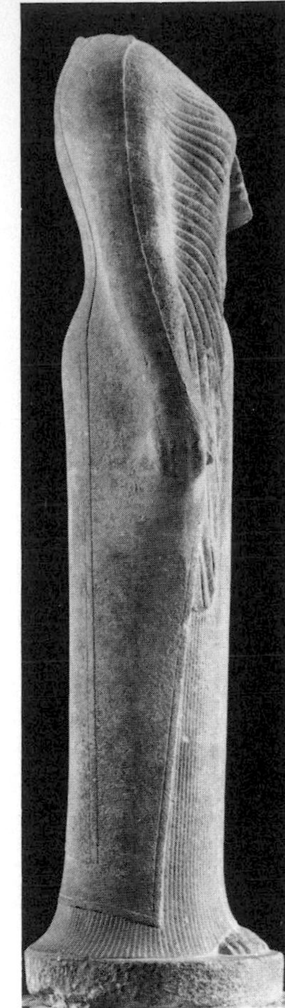

Greek Art. *Hera of Samos. c.* 550 B.C. Louvre, Paris. *Photo André Vigneau-Éditions Tel.*

Greek Art. *Aphrodite, Artemis, and Apollo.* Fragment of the east frieze from the Treasury of the Siphnians, Delphi. *c.* 550–525 B.C. Delphi, Museum. *Hirmer Fotoarchiv, Munich.*

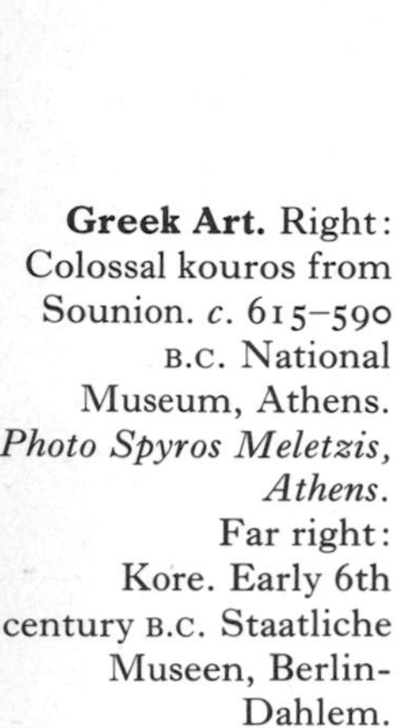

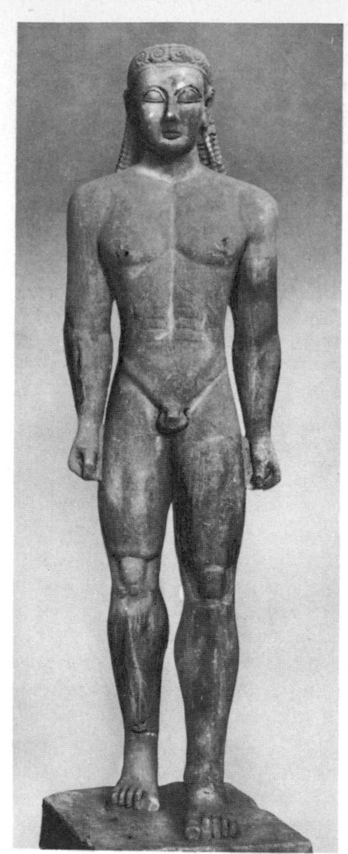

Greek Art. Right: Colossal kouros from Sounion. *c.* 615–590 B.C. National Museum, Athens. *Photo Spyros Meletzis, Athens.* Far right: Kore. Early 6th century B.C. Staatliche Museen, Berlin-Dahlem.

cise and accurate with no exaggerated muscles or superfluous flourishes; the tendency was toward generalization and the expression of a type rather than an individual.

It would seem that one difficult problem of architectural sculpture was first faced in Athens, namely carving to fit the triangular pediment of a temple façade. The megaron plan for a temple involved a roof sloping down left and right from the center, so that on the façade one straight and two oblique lines left a narrow space to be filled: from the beginning of the 6th century B.C. sculptors began to fill it with freestanding or semi-attached figures. They chose subjects from legends of heroes in combat with animals or monsters, the elongated human bodies conveniently filling the corners of the pediment. Thus in the Acropolis Museum are found fragments of tufa pediments taking their names from the Olive Tree, Hydra, and Triton—all naively shaped, but already strongly drawn and brought vividly to life by the use of bright reds and blues, for no strict ideas about realism hampered Attic sculptors from choosing the gayest and most decorative colors.

There is no trace of grandiose architectural conceptions in the buildings on the Acropolis; it was not until the age of Peisistratos in the second half of the century that any important building activity occurred in Athens. But even then there was nothing original: the vast dimensions of Peisistratos' Olympieion were influenced by Ionian buildings; when he added an external colonnade to the Temple of Athena on the Acropolis, he was only following the example of western Greek architects at the beginning of the century, who had enlarged old temples at Thermos and Syracuse with such peristyle colonnades.

Western Provinces

The western Greek cities first showed a distinct aesthetic personality in their architecture. For the vigor of those colonies planted along the trade routes of the West is apparent both in their architectural designs and in the carved or colored ornament of their buildings.

The builders of the first temples in Elis, Acarnania, and on Corfu derived both technique and decorative themes from Corinth; the pottery revetments on wooden or soft stone buildings at Calydon, the painted metopes at Thermos, and the sculptures at Corfu were the products of a still primitive art, but they were vigorous and energetic, with a taste for themes of battle and strife. The Dorian inspiration of Sicilian artists is even clearer, and in architecture the Doric order prevails. The oldest of the temples is that of Apollo at Syracuse, which was given its massive, squat stone colonnade supporting a thick and heavy entablature in the first years of the 6th century B.C.; the subsequent series of temples at Selinous, Syracuse, and Agrigentum continues in the same tradition. It is the number of such buildings, rather than any increase in size, that bears witness to the prosperity of those cities. In the second half of the century, Ionian influences began to infiltrate the Doric tradition of central and southern Italy. At Locri an exclusively Ionic temple was begun, but elsewhere the attempt was to soften Doric ruggedness by the introduction of Ionic themes. In temples at Silaris and Paestum there are interesting efforts to introduce Ionic elements at every level, but especially in the entablature.

The sculpture we know best from this time is architectural in origin—the metopes from Selinous and those from the sanctuary of Silaris, now on view in the Paestum Museum. Both the somewhat geometrical compositions from Selinous and the less austere figures at Paestum have in common an instinct for movement, *mise en scène,* and the theatrical presentation of people and themes, which is thoroughly in character with the dominant Greek interest in the theater.

CLASSICAL PERIOD

After the close of the Archaic period, that is to say from the last quarter of the 6th century B.C. and down to the time of the Persian Wars, there was a lull in the intense

Greek Art. Berlin Painter. Athenian crater: *Ganymede.* *c.* 480–470 B.C. Louvre, Paris. *Hirmer Fotoarchiv, Munich.*

activity of creative exploration, while discipline was imposed. Some centers of production fell into the background or disappeared; after 470 B.C. nothing new came from the cities of Sicily; Ionia and the islands were slow to recover from the devastation by Persian armies followed by the rough hegemony of Athens, and it was not until the 4th century B.C. that they again stamped Greek art with their original contribution. Only the workshops of Athens and the Peloponnesus, with their very different characteristics, had the creative force to maintain the lead in the Hellenic world. A period of unity succeeded one of dispersion.

Painters, sculptors, and architects sought to profit from every intellectual, moral, and spiritual endowment of mankind to build a bridge to lead man back to his divine origin. Just such a great and noble encounter is recorded in the frieze of the Panathenaia that Phidias' (*c.* 500–430 B.C.) sculptors carved around the cella of the Parthenon: the Athenian people, duly assembled, visit Olympus to be received by the serene assembly of the gods.

Artists were glad to show off their knowledge of the human body and their technical accomplishment. The metopes of the Treasury of the Athenians at Delphi are a good example of that interest in anatomy; in particular, the figure of Heracles struggling to bring down the hind is a remarkably intelligent study of the body in movement, a direct representation of muscles in action. Simplification set in and the sculptures of the Temple of Aphaia at Aegina (Munich, Glyptothek) might almost be described as dry. In both pediments the scenes are presumably from the Trojan War, with Athena as the dominating figure.

The Temple of Zeus at Olympia has suffered much from the ravages of time and the poor quality of the porous limestone, originally concealed by stucco that is made to appear like marble. We know from Pausanias that Libon of Elis was the architect, but its fame now rests chiefly on its sculptured decoration. The plan was on the most traditional Doric pattern, with a cella surrounded by a peristyle of six columns in front and thirteen on the sides: columns, capitals, and moldings all have supple, full, and vigorous outlines. Moreover, the poverty of the local stone used for walls and columns was compensated by the splendor of the marble which was used not only for the sculptured decoration, but also for gutters and tiles. Within, the natural contrast of black stone in the center surrounded by white marble made a worthy setting for the astounding statue in gold and ivory on its pedestal of dark stone.

But it is the splendor of the sculpture that first strikes us. The pediment figures carved in the round comfortably fill their triangles. On the eastern façade, the central figure of Zeus presides over the triumph of the young couple Pelops and Hippodamia over her parents, Oinomaos and Sterope. The river gods Alpheus and Cladeos in the angles indicate the scene's location. There is a majestic dignity in all the figures, whether nude or draped, which most happily combines a sense for sculptural mass and composition with architectural balance. The composition of the western pedi-

Greek Art. Temple of Concord, Agrigentum. Doric. *c.* 450–440 B.C. *Photo Henri Stierlin, Geneva.*

Greek Art. *Pallas Athena.* West pediment of the Temple of Aphaia, Aegina. *c.* 410 B.C. Glyptothek, Munich. *Photo Leonard von Matt, Buochs.*

Greek Art. *Procession of the Panathenaia.* Fragment of the east frieze of the Parthenon, Athens. *c.* 442–438 B.C. Louvre, Paris. *Photo André Vigneau-Éditions Tel, Paris.*

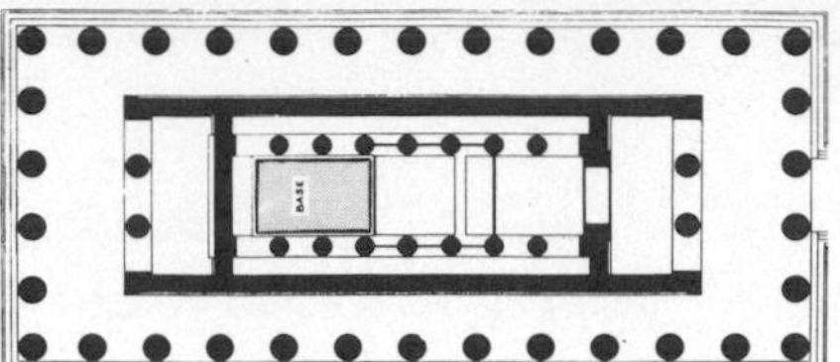

Greek Art. Temple of Zeus, Olympia. Plan. *c.* 470–460 B.C.

ment may be less original, for its subject—the battle of Centaurs and Lapiths—was a familiar theme in vase painting, but as sculpture it is assured and masterly.

The metopes in groups of six at each end of the Doric cella illustrated the Twelve Labors of Heracles, and the carving is as masterly as that of the anonymous sculptor of the pediments. Thus, both for its architecture and for its sculpture, the Temple of Zeus at Olympia marks one of the highest points in Greek art.

This vein of feeling was further explored by Phidias with finer subtlety, more complex symbolism, and an even greater power of idealization: it is to this tradition that the sculptures embellishing the Parthenon belong. The majesty and power of the Phidian creation gave expression in terms of harmonious, assured, and serene sculpture to the spirit of an age and to some of the profoundest intuitions of the Athenian soul at a moment when technical mastery and control of material, whether marble or bronze, was complete. But that should not allow us to forget the continuation of a pre-Classical way of seeing the world by Myron (active 1st half of 5th century B.C.), Polycleitus (*c.* 480/75–420 B.C.) and others. The desire to study man and man's body in every mood and activity was pursued in neighboring workshops that were even rivals of those of Phidias. Myron's way of seeing was never forgotten, and its influence was very soon manifest once more at the beginning of the 4th century B.C.: witness the marked feeling for movement in free space that we find in the funeral monuments of this time, a concern that was to be taken up again and carried further in Hellenistic sculpture.

HELLENISTIC REVIVAL

In the art and architecture of the 4th century B.C. and later there developed the most fundamental element in Greek art, an element that lay dormant for a time: the conquest of space and the play of shapes therein, by which means space was both defined and limited. Once again political evolution played a useful part: Hellenic civilization had spread beyond its traditional bounds, and the Classical unity had been broken up by contact with the arts, conceptions, feelings, and religious beliefs of the Orient. As in the 6th century B.C., one is again aware of the aesthetic individuality of different lands, centers, and schools. Athens maintained her primacy in intellectual life, but in the plastic arts the most significant activity was elsewhere, and new centers in the Peloponnesus, Pergamum, Rhodes, and Alexandria attracted artists increasingly. Moreover, the patronage of individuals began to play a more active part: Hellenistic princes and kings had workshops that were exclusively their own, and artists of all sorts would travel great distances to enter their service and to paint, carve, and build monuments commissioned to enhance their glory. Mausolus and his family in Caria, the Attalids at Pergamum, and the Ptolemies at Alexandria simultaneously or successively attracted the finest artists of their day to the aesthetic centers they created. That tendency was already beginning in the third quarter of the 4th century B.C., and it continued down to the end of Hellenistic times.

Architectural forms became more slender and elegant, but there was no break with Classical norms. In the Argolid and at Alexandria, some effort was made to bring ornament into greater prominence, thus leading to the triumph of the Corinthian order. But the really significant innovation in Hellenistic architecture was the creation of ensembles,

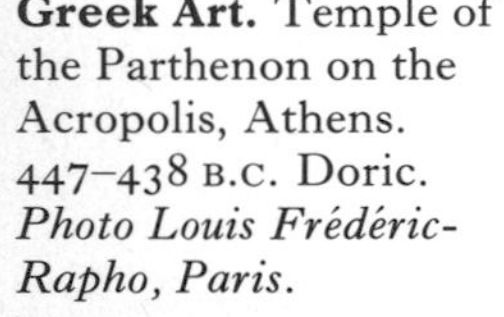

Greek Art. Temple of the Parthenon on the Acropolis, Athens. 447–438 B.C. Doric. *Photo Louis Frédéric-Rapho, Paris.*

Greek Art. Myron. *Discobolus. c.* 460–450 B.C. Roman replica. Museo Nazionale Romano, Rome.

of which the buildings on the Acropolis gave a first taste, with architectural masses disposed and organized within space that has itself been defined, limited, and brought under control. The triumph of this new spirit was embodied in the mid-4th century B.C. by the Mausoleum at Halicarnassus, and then by the great buildings at Pergamum and the Asklepieion at Cos. Unquestionably, the acropolis at Pergamum is the masterpiece of Hellenistic architecture: each succeeding terrace, from the agora up to the arsenals and palaces at the top, has been treated individually, with its own function and character, yet all are interlocked and articulated in a fan around the theater, and the plan of the theater itself has been given stability by a portico some 722 feet long and several stories high, with powerful vertical buttresses built on the lower slopes of the hill to sustain them. It is astonishing how traditional the orders remained: Doric or Ionic porticoes or colonnades were always the basic element forming the backdrop against which the main buildings, the temples in particular, stood out. Consequently, there evolved an architectural type for a sanctuary, of which the third terrace of the Asklepieion at Cos and the Temple of Zeus at Priene are the most typical examples: the temple is integrated with its surrounding porticoes, and only the façade stands out in front of the colonnade, which forms the background of the composition and which is no longer independent.

Greek Art. *Youth.* Detail of bronze statue found in the sea near Antikythera. *c.* 350–330 B.C. National Museum, Athens. *Photo Spyros Meletzis, Athens.*

One psychological element played an essential part in the evolution of art at that time. Political instability and the weakening of the city-state, which had always provided the normal framework of social life, combined with wars and expanding commercial traffic to produce a liberating influence on individuals. Inevitably the restlessness of the time found expression in sculpture, which grew increasingly preoccupied with the state of the individual soul and with the feelings of isolated human beings. From the 4th century B.C. on, portraits became the most important part of the sculptors' output: orators, philosophers, writers, princes, and kings came to be studied for interest in their individual characters. The great 4th-century B.C. masters—Scopas, Praxiteles, and Lysippus—all felt the profound restlessness of the age, although they had uniquely different ways of expressing it.

Art assumed a more important place within the house: there was greater living space inside a Hellenistic house, comfortably encircling its mosaic-ornamented peristyle court; sculptors and painters were invited to decorate apartments. Indeed, this practice must have been widespread to account for the large quantities of bronze, marble, and terra-cotta statuettes that have been found. No account of Greek sculpture would be complete without mentioning the terra-cotta workshops, especially those of Myrrhina in Asia Minor and Tanagra in Boeotia. Of course the technique was not new. Large works such as the Zeus and Ganymede recently discovered at Olympia prove the skill and artistry of 6th-century B.C. craftsmen. In Hellenistic times a completely new genre developed, having as its keynote a taste for the picturesque, the intimate details of life, and feminine charm. Archaic Boeotian terra cottas had provided realistic studies of the coarse Theban peasantry and laborers; but the Tanagra figurines are all grace and charm, and are concerned with the facile elegance of a luxurious life. In passing from the 5th century B.C. to Hellenistic times, Greek sculpture became more homely and individual: in effect it left the lofty Olympian heights of the pediment of the Parthenon and descended into the earthly realm of the ordinary citizen's home. Perhaps it lost its majesty thereby, but not its vitality, and in harmony with its deepest natural instincts it became more intimately human.

Greek Art. Tanagra figurine: *Woman Walking.* Late 4th–early 3rd century B.C. Louvre, Paris. *Photo Éditions Tel.*

GREENE, Charles Sumner (1868, Cincinnati, Ohio—1957, Carmel, California) *and* Henry Mather (1870, Cincinnati, Ohio—1954, Altadena, California), American architects. Both brothers attended the Beaux-Arts-influenced architecture school at the Massachusetts Institute of Technology (1888–92), worked briefly in Boston after graduation, and in 1894 established a partnership in Pasadena, California.

Influenced by Japanese construction, they emphasized the structural skeleton of their architecture by articulating each rafter, beam, and post. Joints were painstakingly notched, pegged, or strapped with metal bands and wedges. Timber ends and edges were rounded or smoothly carved. Natural or stained California redwood was used for the framing and the shingle siding. Redwood was often set against local cobblestone or clinker-brick masonry for contrast.

The Greenes broke from the Romantic movement to develop a new residential form, the California bungalow. The informal and spacious plans of the Arturo Bandini house in Pasadena (1903) and the C. W. Hollister house in Hollywood (1905) sought greater communication between indoors and out.

GREENOUGH, Horatio (1805, Boston—1852, Somerville, Massachusetts), American sculptor. Greenough belonged to the first generation of 19th-century American Neoclassical sculptors, and was the first of many Americans to study and work in Italy, where he went in 1824. His work includes many marble portrait busts, a few reliefs, small single- or group-figure sculptures, and large public commissions. Greenough's major commission was the colossal statue of *George Washington* (1832–41) in marble, ordered for the U.S. Capitol and now in the Smithsonian Institution, Washington, D.C. Another important commission was the design for the *Bunker Hill Monument* (1877; Boston). His smaller pieces are less pretentious than his large work, and may be considered more attractive (*Forest Children*, 1835–37; marble, Boston, Massachusetts Historical Society).

Jean-Baptiste Greuze. *Village Bride*. 1761. Louvre, Paris. *Photo Giraudon, Paris.*

GREUZE, Jean-Baptiste (1725, Tournus, Saône-et-Loire—1805, Paris), French painter. Greuze gained recognition by combining two types of painting much in favor at the time, namely the intimate genre style of Jean-Baptiste Chardin and the erotic gallantries of François Boucher. His first contribution to the Salon (in 1755), a *Grandfather Reading the Bible to His Family* (Leningrad, Hermitage), was immediately popular, and won the approval of the Academy, to which he was admitted in 1769. Thereafter he sent painting after painting to the annual Salons with the same success: the *Village Bride* (1761; Paris, Louvre), the *Father's Curse* (*c.* 1765; Louvre), the *Son Punished* (1781; Louvre), and the *Paralytic Tended by His Children* (1763; Hermitage). The moralizing tone of these pictures is precisely the aspect of Greuze's art that alienates modern viewers, for despite their beauty of detail, the paintings lack truthfulness: his poor were painted for the rich, his coy village brides for great lords, his seductive ingénues for roués. When he abandoned his moralistic and literary pretensions he was a capable painter, as in certain fine portraits, such as *Étienne Jeaurat* (1769; Louvre).

GRIEN, Hans Baldung. *See* **BALDUNG GRIEN,** Hans.

GRIGORESCO, Nicolas (1838, Piatra—1907, Campina), Rumanian painter. He was apprenticed at the age of ten to an icon painter. He executed mural paintings for the churches of Zamfira (1856) and Agapia (1858–61). In 1861 he went to Paris, where he worked briefly in the studio of Sébastien Melchior Cornu (1804–70), but he soon settled outside the city, in Barbizon from 1862 to 1867 and then for two years in Marlotte. He then returned to Rumania, took part in its war of independence (1877–78), and painted a number of battle scenes. In 1880 he went back to France and exhibited in Paris at the Galerie Martinet in 1886, just prior to returning home. He opposed academicism with his open-air painting, which is Impressionist in manner and possesses great spontaneity and vivacity of execution. His subjects are usually of Rumanian peasant life: picturesque villages, dusty old country roads, and the characteristic beauty of his native countryside (*Among the Trees; Little Shepherd; Sleeping Calf*; all Bucharest, Museum Simu).

GRIPPE, Peter (b. 1912, Buffalo, New York), American sculptor. Grippe studied art at the Albright Art School and the Art Institute, both in Buffalo. He received numerous awards for his work, which is represented in New York at the Museum of Modern Art, the Metropolitan Museum, and the Whitney Museum (*Three Furies, II*, 1955–56; bronze), as well as in the Philadelphia Museum and many other public and private collections.

Grippe's stylistic development is rooted in the series of terra-cotta *Cities* that he began in 1939. In these he fused the images of the figures and the buildings to express movement and to show man's relationship to his environment. During the early 1940s this series changed direction, as Grippe reduced the detail, separated the figures from their background, and aimed at transparent, open sculpture. Named "Space Figures" by the artist, these sculptures, together with Ibram Lassaw's constructions, formed the first American examples of cagelike sculpture. Seeking a clearer articulation of space, Grippe began to explore the lost-wax process of bronze casting, a technique he perfected until his intricately interwoven forms could be cast in one piece. Major new influences on his work resulted from a rereading of the classics around 1952 and a visit to Europe in 1953, when he was particularly impressed by Romanesque sculpture, Gothic cathedrals, and Auguste Rodin's *Gates of Hell*. A new series of *Cities* begun at this time expressed a greater violence than before (*Three Figures, II*, 1955–56; Whitney Museum), and in the late 1950s a series of *Mephistopheles* was suggested by Goethe's *Faust* (*Mephistopheles, 2*, 1958; New York, Nordness Gallery).

GRIS, José Victoriano Gonzalès, *called* Juan (1887, Madrid—1927, Boulogne-sur-Seine, near Paris), Spanish painter. He was a highly gifted draftsman and soon began to contribute to illustrated news-

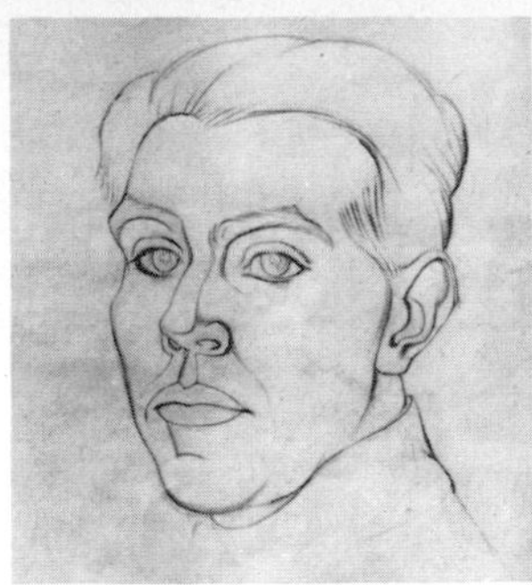

Juan Gris. *Self-Portrait.* 1920. *Photo Galerie Louise Leiris, Paris.*

papers, while trying his hand at painting. In 1906 Gris left for Paris. Attracted by the nascent glory of Picasso, he settled near his compatriot in the Bateau-Lavoir where he remained for 15 years. In order to earn a living he did drawings for the satirical press. In 1912 Gris exhibited in the Section d'Or and at the Salon des Indépendants and joined the Cubists, although he found their technique excessively analytical. Like Braque and Picasso, Gris rejected the ambiguity of values, chiaroscuro, and the complicated overlapping of planes (*Lampe à pétrole, c.* 1912; Otterlo, Rijksmuseum Kröller-Müller). Sometimes, to achieve a decorative effect, he added sand and ash to his palette; but rhythm and, above all, composition were the dominant preoccupations of this inflexibly rigorous sensibility.

The still lifes painted before 1915 were somewhat mannered in their stylization, but soon they were distinguished by a sober, assured technique and a balanced distribution of line and color (*The Violin*, 1916; Basel, Kunstmuseum). Gris began to use a process that had been invented by Braque, that of simulation of wood or marble, assimilating such fragments of reality into the canvas. He composed collage paintings with *papier collé* (*Breakfast*, 1914; New York, Museum of Modern Art), which Braque and Picasso used primarily in their drawings. Ever more demanding, he began to dream of a calm, rational, static art. However noble his aspirations, his work lost in strength and liveliness—the Harlequins, Pierrots, portraits, and still lifes painted after 1919 lack emotional warmth. Although undermined by ill-health in the last four years of his life, he accepted several commissions from the Russian impresario Sergei Diaghilev, notably one for the sets and costumes of the ballet *Les Tentations de la Bergère* (1924). Juan Gris' intransigent handling of the flat composition and colored surfaces, his simplified expression of the many-sidedness of the object, and his almost scientific skill in expressing his intellectual schema in a persuasive formal language endowed the Cubist revolution with Classical virtues.

GROMAIRE, Marcel (1892, Noyelles-sur-Sambre, Nord—1971, Paris), French painter and decorator. Even in his earliest works he was in full possession of his basic style and subject matter. Instead of developing these later, he merely simplified them and emphasized their dramatic force. The severe outlines of his drawing inscribe the forms within their basic masses. Gromaire's color is somber, powerful, and wonderfully mellow; it is always limited in range, even when, as in stained glass, it is enlivened by broad strokes of red, blue, ocher, and pale yellow. His feeling for synthesis and his great craftsmanship made Gromaire one of the great decorators of his time, particularly in tapestry. By exploiting the natural potentialities of that medium, he succeeded in creating monumental works with the most economic means, namely a narrow color range and a stylization of form (*Woodcutters of Mormal*, 1941; Paris, Musée National d'Art Moderne).

As he moved further away from the particular (*Fairground Lottery*, 1923; Musée National d'Art Moderne), Gromaire emerged above all as a creator of myths. His half-fairy-like, half-terrifying views of New York (*View of New York Looking Out to Sea*, 1950; Paris, Coll. Louis Carré) became magnified into quintessential representations of the city. Gromaire produced a considerable body of engraved work in addition to his paintings and tapestries.

Marcel Gromaire. *View of New York Looking Out to Sea.* 1950. Coll. Louis Carré, Paris.

GROPIUS, Walter (1883, Berlin—1969, Boston), German architect, undoubtedly one of the leading architects of the 20th century. He studied in Munich (1903–5) and then in Berlin until 1907, when he joined the office of Peter Behrens. In 1910 Gropius set up his own practice as an industrial designer and architect. His first important project was for the Fagus factory, which he built (1911) in collaboration with Adolf Meyer (1881–1929) at Alfeld an der Leine, Lower Saxony, and which is remarkable for its extensive use of glass and steel. Similarly radical methods were used in the Model Factory and Administrative Office Building that Gropius designed, also with Meyer, for the famous Deutsche Werkbund Exhibition at Cologne in 1914.

Walter Gropius and Adolf Meyer. The Fagus factory, Alfeld an der Leine. 1911.

Antoine-Jean Gros. *Napoleon Visiting the Plague-Stricken at Jaffa.* Detail. 1804. Louvre, Paris. *Photo Giraudon, Paris.*

World War I interrupted Gropius' work. As early as 1915 he had been appointed by the Grand Duke of Saxe-Weimar to succeed the Belgian architect Henry van de Velde as director of both the Grossherzogliche-Sächsische Kunstgewerbeschule and the Grossherzogliche-Sächsische Hochschule für Bildende Kunst at Weimar, but he did not take up his post until 1919. He merged the two institutions into a completely new establishment that he called the Bauhaus (House of Building), whose deep and lasting effect is universally acknowledged. Gropius was director of the school for eight years before resigning to devote himself exclusively to his own work. Of his many projects dating from this period, the Bauhaus building itself at Dessau (1925–26) is one of the most important. Mention should also be made of his designs for the Municipal Theater at Iena (1923), in collaboration with Meyer, and of the revolutionary project for a "Total Theater" (designed in collaboration with the Berlin producer Erwin Piscator) which could be transformed according to the requirements of each play. The model was exhibited at the 1930 Exposition Universelle in Paris, but the theater was never built.

Gropius wanted to be not only an architect and industrial designer, but also a sociologist. Toward the end of his term as director of the Bauhaus he worked on plans to improve living conditions in populous urban centers. His ideas were partially realized by the Dammerstock housing project near Karlsruhe (1927–28), and, above all, in the Siemensstadt estate near Berlin (1928), of which Gropius was chief architect.

With the rise to power of the Nazis in 1933 the situation became extremely difficult for avant-garde architects: in 1934 Gropius left Germany and settled in London, where he formed a partnership with Edwin Maxwell Fry (b. 1899), a distinguished British architect of the younger generation. Together they designed the laboratories of London Film Production at Denham (1936) and the Impington Village College near Cambridge (1936).

At the beginning of 1937, Gropius went to the United States, where he had been offered the Chair of Architecture at Harvard University. Soon afterward he formed a partnership (dissolved in 1941) with the Hungarian-born architect Marcel Breuer, who had studied and taught at the Bauhaus. They designed a number of private homes, as well as a working-class housing development at New Kensington, near Pittsburgh (1941). Thereafter Gropius resumed the experiments he had begun in 1932 on the construction of houses from prefabricated units, and with Konrad Wachsmann (b. 1901) perfected a type of house that was erected all over California.

Gropius was always an enthusiastic advocate of group work and in 1945 founded the T.A.C. (The Architects' Collaborative) with a number of young American architects. The work of this firm included the Junior High School in Attleboro, Massachusetts (1948); the Harvard University Graduate Center in Cambridge, Massachusetts (1949–50); the McCormick Office Building in Chicago (1935); a block of flats for the Berlin Hansa Quarter (built for the Interbau Exhibition of 1957); the U.S. Embassy in Athens (1957–61), and the new commercial and administrative center at Back Bay, Boston (1953).

The work of Gropius, unrivaled in imaginative power and scope, has had a world-wide influence. Throughout his long career he invariably produced solutions of startling brilliance and simplicity. But however important his work as an architect was, his influence as a theoretician and teacher was perhaps even greater.

GROPPER, William (b. 1897, New York), American painter. His career began in 1919 with political cartoons for the Sunday section of the *New York Tribune*. He was particularly active as a cartoonist in the 1920s, contributing to such American newspapers and magazines as *The Dial, The Quill, Pearson's Magazine, Broom, New York World, Morning Freiheit*, and the *New York Post*. By the late 1920s Gropper had established himself as a well-known illustrator and cartoonist, and a book of his cartoons was published (1930) by the A.C.A. (American Contemporary Art) Gallery, New York. The drawings he made on a visit to Russia in 1927 were also published in 1930.

In addition to graphics, Gropper did serious easel and mural paintings. He began to paint around 1921, but his first exhibition was not held until 1936 at the A.C.A. Gallery, New York. The themes of his paintings reflected interests similar to those evident in his journalistic art; with his attitude of social concern and support of liberal causes, his most frequent subjects were politics, war, peasant life, American folklore, and Jewish village life (*The Senate*, 1935, New York, Museum of Modern Art; *Farm Hand, c.* 1942, Minneapolis, Walker Art Center). During the 1930s Gropper was active in mural painting; his commissions included murals for the Detroit, Michigan, Post Office (1939), and the New Interior Building, Washington, D.C. (1938).

GROS, Baron Antoine-Jean (1771, Paris—1835, Meudon, near Paris), French history painter. At the age of fourteen he became a pupil of the great Neoclassical painter Louis David, who helped him to obtain a passport for Italy (1793). He visited Florence, Genoa, and then Milan, where he was introduced to Josephine Bonaparte, who in turn presented the artist to her husband. Napoleon agreed to pose for Gros after his victorious Italian campaign, and the result was *Bonaparte on the Bridge at Arcole* (1796; preparatory sketch in Paris, Louvre, painting in Versailles, Museum). Gros traveled throughout Italy, following Napoleon's army, all the while studying Rubens, whose sensuous Baroque influence soon began to counterbalance the Davidian Neoclassicism Gros had previously adopted.

On his return to France, he sent his somewhat Romantic *Bonaparte* to the 1801 Salon. To celebrate General Andoche Junot's victory in Nazareth, Bonaparte organized a competition for the best painting of the battle. Gros won the competition, but his picture never got beyond the preparatory stage (1801; Nantes, Museum). Bonaparte asked the artist to paint a picture of his visit to the sick soldiers in Jaffa. The resulting *Napoleon Visiting the Plague-Stricken at Jaffa* (1804; Paris, Louvre) was a triumph for Gros, who continued thereafter in the same vein of epic realism. In 1808 he produced another masterpiece, *Napoleon on the Battlefield at Eylau* (Paris, Louvre). This picture marked the climax of his career, and led to his being decorated at the Salon by the Emperor himself.

The fall of Napoleon, the death of Josephine, and David's exile were hard blows to the artist, and his inspiration began to weaken. Retaining his admiration for David, Gros nevertheless was torn between opposing Romantic and Neoclassical loyalties. Uncertain of his true course, he returned to the Davidian subjects of Greek tragedy. Fortunately, two official paintings—*Louis XVIII Leaving the Tuileries* (1817; Versailles, Museum) and the *Duchesse d'Angoulême Embarking at Pauillac* (1819; Bordeaux, Museum)—allowed him to return to contemporary subjects. On the death of David, he felt morally obliged to perpetuate the now-outdated principles of his master. But his pupils were deserting him for J. A. D. Ingres, and after the Revolution of 1830 he became the chief target in the aesthetic disputes of the avant-garde. He was too weak to resist the hostility of his colleagues and the desertion of the younger generation of artists. On the morning of July 26, his drowned body was found in the Seine at Bas-Meudon.

GROSS, Chaim (b. 1904, Kolomea, Austria), Austrian-born American sculptor. Gross's art education began in Budapest and Vienna after World War I; in 1921 he went to New York, where he studied first at the Educational Alliance Art School, then with Elie Nadelman at the Beaux-Arts Institute of Design (1922–26), and in 1927 with Robert Laurent at the Art Students League. He gave his first one-man exhibition in New York in 1932.

Gross's major and almost sole subject was the human figure in action or play, most often used in rhythmical, vertically balanced compositions of circus performers or of a mother playing with her children (*Handlebar Riders*, 1935, lignum vitae, New York, Museum of Modern Art; *Family of Three*, 1948, Mexican tulipwood, New York, Coll. Joseph H. Hirshhorn). Gross was primarily concerned with form rather than subject and, because of his preference for direct carving and his respect for the inherent qualities of his medium—primarily wood—the forms of his figures are dictated by the cylindrical shape of the block. In 1958, however, Gross also began to model in clay for casting in bronze, a method that allowed for more open and angular forms and rougher surfaces than in his carved wood sculpture.

GROSZ, George (1893, Berlin—1959, Berlin), German-born painter, draftsman, and lithographer who became a naturalized American citizen in 1938. He began to paint as early as 1911, but his drawings constitute his major oeuvre. Haunted by the condition of society around him, this incisive draftsman and savage satirist first depicted the evil, absurd face of war; then, after 1918, the buffoonery of the postwar years (*Trio*, 1919; pen and ink, from *Ecce Homo*). In 1918 Grosz was a member of the Dada group of Berlin, which had a radical political orientation; then, in 1925, he turned toward the realism of the Neue Sachlichkeit. In 1932 he was invited to teach at the Art Students League in New York, where he remained as professor until his return to Germany in 1959, shortly before his death. In America, a romantic and idyllic note appeared in his painting (*Approaching Storm*, 1940; New York, Whitney Museum); but his satire was still alive. He first directed it against the materialism of the middle classes; then, after World War II, on a broader basis, in nightmare visions like the fantastic series of *The Stickmen* (1947–48), emaciated, insect-like symbols of nihilism.

GROUP OF SEVEN, circle of 20th-century Canadian painters who instituted the first important national movement in Canadian painting. The leaders, both of whom were in Toronto by 1913, were the English-born J. E. H. MacDonald (1873–1932), a graphic designer in the Art Nouveau tradition who had turned to landscape painting (*Spring Breezes, High Park*, 1912; Ottawa, National Gallery of Canada), and Tom Thomson (1877–1917). In 1910 Lawren Harris (1885–1970) was painting the shabbier streets of Toronto in what was called a "socialistic" style. Arthur Lismer (1885–1969) and Frederick Varley (1881–1969), who had emigrated from their native Sheffield in 1912, joined the ranks of the commercial artists who by now also included Franklin Carmichael (1890–1945) and Frank H. Johnston (1888–1949). The group was complete when Alexander Young Jackson (1882–1974) arrived in 1913.

George Grosz. *Couple.* 1930. Tate Gallery, London.

The group became acquainted with the North Country of Ontario while on sketching trips to Georgian Bay and Algonquin Park in 1912–13. In Algonquin Park in 1914, Jackson and Thomson arrived at a new method of painting the wild forested country by using bold colors and emphatic flat designs. Examples of this style are Jackson's *Red Maple* (1914; National Gallery of Canada) and Thomson's *Pointers* (1916–17; Toronto, Hart House, University of Toronto). World War I scattered the group, and Thomson was drowned in Algonquin Park in 1917. The survivors reassembled in Toronto in 1919, and in 1920 held their first joint exhibition, calling themselves for the first time the Group of Seven. For these early group shows they painted large exhibition pieces in which they employed the common motif of a tree set against sky and water, as in Varley's *Georgian Bay* (1920), Lismer's *September Gale* (1921), and Harris' *Lake Superior* (1924)—all in the National Gallery

Francis Gruber. *Homage to Jacques Callot*. 1942. Coll. Jacques Bazaine, Paris.

of Canada. MacDonald, Harris, Jackson, and Lismer extended their field of work very widely throughout Canada during the 1920s and 1930s; Varley eventually turned to figure painting (*Vera*, 1930; National Gallery of Canada); Johnston dropped out of the Group in 1922, and MacDonald died in 1932. Three new members joined: Alfred Joseph Casson of Toronto (1898–1976) in 1926, Edwin Holgate of Montreal (b. 1892) in 1931, and L.L. (Lionel Lemoine) FitzGerald of Winnipeg (1890–1956) in 1932, thus widening the Group's representation geographically, and increasing their number to eight. In 1933 the Group of Seven changed its name to the Canadian Group of Painters.

GRUBER, Francis (1912, Nancy—1948, Paris), French painter. He benefited from the advice of Roger Bissière and Georges Braque, who lived in studios near him in Paris, and in 1928 he entered the Académie Scandinave, where he became the favorite pupil of Othon Friesz and Charles Dufresne. His success at the Salon d'Automne and the Salon des Tuileries exhibitions was such that at the age of eighteen he was already one of the most well-known characters in the artists' quarter, Montparnasse. He was a devoted worker, meticulous in technique, and he was also a remarkable draftsman. He conceived his painting on a large scale; every one of his works, from the vast mural composition he executed for the Lycée Lakanal (*Homage to Le Nôtre*, 1936) to the smallest of his still lifes, is resolutely monumental in conception. Although he gradually withdrew from all groups and all Salons, he worked unremittingly, painting large figures, portraits, and still lifes with birds or impaled lizards. He also painted a tragic *Homage to Jacques Callot* (1942; Paris, Coll. Jacques Bazaine), in which he expressed all the distress of a world reduced by war to the state of a cadaver. His last paintings are nudes with angular silhouettes, imprisoned within an enclosed, suffocating world that is rigorously simplified to red hangings, stark walls, and the gray floor of the studio; or large canvases inspired by the movement of trees, with young, slim bodies in imaginary forests that resemble pure and uncluttered architectural forms.

Matthias Grünewald. *Meeting of St. Erasmus and St. Maurice*. Detail. *c.* 1524. Alte Pinakothek, Munich.

GRUNEWALD, Isaac (1889, Stockholm—1946, Oslo), Swedish painter. He began to study painting in Stockholm in 1905, the year of his first exhibition. The following year he went to Paris, where he entered the Académie Matisse. From 1921 to 1931 he lived almost entirely in France, where he had several exhibitions. Grunewald's greatest influences were Edvard Munch, Paul Cézanne, and Henri Matisse. His use of earthy colors and the construction of volumes by means of subtle geometrical indications give his later paintings (*Snöljus*, 1939; Stockholm, Nationalmuseum) and his mural compositions (in Stockholm's Town Hall and Nationalmuseum) a sustained monumental breadth and an intensity of spiritual feeling. Grunewald painted many portraits (*Jules Pascin*, 1921, Göteborg, Konstmuseat; *Mrs. Ellen Hoppe*, 1930, Stockholm, Nationalmuseum) and self-portraits, as well as still lifes, flowers, and landscapes; he also designed the sets and costumes for several theatrical productions and did graphic and ceramic work.

GRÜNEWALD, Matthias (*c.* 1460 or 1475–80, Würzburg?—1528, Halle, Saxony), German painter. The artist for so long known to us under this name is in fact—on the authority of his first biographer, Joachim von Sandrart (1606–88)—recorded in documents as Mathis Nithart, or Mathis Gothardt Neithardt, though it would seem that he adopted the latter form rather late in his career. The artist's early life is veiled in obscurity and presents many problems to the biographer. Some authorities place his birth date at about 1460, making him Dürer's senior by 10 years; others favor a later date, between 1475 and 1480. The later dating, however, would make it impossible to identify him with a certain Master Mathis of Aschaffenburg, whose name appears in documents of this town from around 1480. On the other hand, if one places his birth at about 1460, the problem arises of finding works to furnish the years of activity preceding the altarpiece in the Lindenhardt church—which is dated 1503 and quite convincingly attributed to Grünewald. Once Grünewald settled in Seligenstadt, on the Main river, where his name appears in the rate books from 1501 to 1525, his career can be followed with greater accuracy. In 1509 he became court painter to the Elector of Mainz, Archbishop Ulrich von Gemmingen, who employed him on the reconstruction of his palace in Aschaffenburg. On the death of Ulrich in 1514, he passed into the service of the Elector Albrecht von Brandenburg. But Grünewald, who was in difficulties—probably of a religious nature, despite the great tolerance of Albrecht—fled to Frankfurt and, in 1527, to Halle, where he died.

Grünewald's connection with Dürer is an interesting one: the two artists actually met in 1520 at Aachen for the emperor's coronation, at which time Dürer gave Grünewald some of his engravings. Grünewald's work suggests some familiarity with that of Dürer, but his own temperament drew him in the opposite direction from those ideals of classic equilibrium which the Nuremberg master pursued. Although Grünewald seems to have been quite familiar with the work of certain Italian artists, displaying an assured grasp of the scientific proportions of the human figure and of its foreshortening in perspective, he remained profoundly Gothic in feeling, totally immune to the example of Classical antiquity and an ardent romantic all his life.

Grünewald's masterpiece is the Isenheim Altarpiece (Colmar, Unterlinden Museum), on which he was engaged from about 1512 to about 1515. It stood in the church of the Order of St. Anthony at Isenheim until 1794, when it was removed to Colmar. The principal part of this complex ensemble consists of the wooden figures of St. Anthony enthroned, flanked by St. Augustine and St. Jerome, which were carved by the Strasbourg sculptor Nicholas of Haguenau, who completed the work about 1505. The rest of the altarpiece consists of two fixed wings and four movable ones, which were commissioned from Grünewald by the abbot of Isenheim, Guido Guersi. During Lent, the wings were to be closed, showing an implacably realistic *Crucifixion*. Two fixed wings show, on the left, St. Anthony Abbot, and, on the right, St. Sebastian. When the outer movable wings were opened for Easter, Christmas, and other triumphal feasts, the scenes—from left to right—would reveal the *Annunciation, Concert of Angels, Nativity*, and *Resurrection*. When open on the feast of St. Anthony, patron saint of the convent, the central compartment of the inner movable wings shows Nicholas' carved figures. Grünewald's painted wings present, left, *St. Anthony and St. Paul in the Desert*; right, the *Temptation of St. Anthony*.

The sublimity of the Isenheim Altarpiece, which is created largely by the intensity of expression and handling of light, was never surpassed, or even equalled, by Grünewald. His other crucifixions, of which the most important is in the Karlsruhe Kunsthalle (*c.* 1525), are weaker versions of the Isenheim example, again showing the body of the Savior scarified and pierced by thorns.

Grünewald's charming *Virgin of Stuppach* (1519; Stuppach, Pfarrkirche), with its exquisite still life, and the delightful narrative panel representing the *Miracle of the Snow* (1517–19; Freiburg-im-Breisgau, Augustinermuseum) were brief lyric interludes in his otherwise lifetime tendency toward a searing Expressionism. The only other painting that reveals a different spirit from that of the Isenheim panels is the *Meeting of St. Erasmus and St. Maurice* (*c.* 1524; Munich, Alte Pinakothek).

GUARDI, Francesco (1712, Venice—1793, Venice) *and* Giannantonio (1699, Vienna—1760, Venice), Italian painters. The Guardi are a good example of a *bottega* (half studio, half shop) in the Venetian tradition. The family came from the Trentino; Domenico, the father (1678–1716), was the founder of the painting workshop. The elder son, Giannantonio, probably trained his brother Francesco, the *vedutista* (painter of views); and the two worked together until Giannantonio's death in 1760.

The two artists seem to have worked jointly on a series of eight paintings illustrating Tasso's *Gerusalemme Liberata* and on paintings decorating the organ parapet of the church of Angelo Raffaele, Venice, which illustrate, through a luminous haze, the *Story of Tobias* (after 1753). The *Ridotto* (*Gaming Room*) and the *Parlatorio delle monache* (*Visitors' Room of the Nuns*; both Venice, Ca' Rezzonico) are more commonly attributed to Francesco. They were probably painted around 1745–50. After this Francesco seems to have devoted himself primarily to the painting of *vedute* (*The Piazzetta*, Venice, Ca' d'Oro), but fell far short of the success of Canaletto. A true Impressionist, Francesco differed profoundly from his senior and rival. His lines, instead of being dry and, in buildings, as straight as though traced with a ruler, seem to vibrate in a diffuse atmosphere. He planted his figures with a verve that is quite foreign to Canaletto. One simple stroke, unerringly placed, sufficed to indicate a silhouette or a movement. Francesco's sepia wash drawings render the shimmering atmosphere of the city with an incredible lightness, and they show an extraordinary feeling for groups. Four paintings belonging to the Gulbenkian Foundation, Lisbon, are among his masterpieces: *View from Mira over the Brenta Canal*, 1760; *Festival on the Piazza S. Marco*, *c.* 1770; *Regattas on the Grand Canal*, *c.* 1770; and *S. Pietro di Castello*, 1770–75.

Francesco Guardi. *Strollers at Venice.* Drawing.

GUARINI, Guarino (1624, Modena—1683, Milan), the most important Baroque architect of northern Italy before Filippo Juvara. In 1639 Guarini entered the Theatine Order of Modena, and first took up the study of building construction in collaboration with a fellow priest, Bernardo Castagnini. He had already become Superior of his monastery in Modena when various difficulties with the court there obliged him to leave that city; he spent the 10 following years teaching and designing buildings in Parma, Guastalla, Messina, Paris, Munich, and perhaps Lisbon also. Some time after 1666, he settled in Turin, where he built several of his finest works for Duke Carlo Emanuele II. Appointed Superior of the Theatine monastery in Turin in 1679, he was

Guarino Guarini. Palazzo Carignano, Turin. Begun 1679/80. *Photo Alinari-Giraudon.*

Guercino. *Venus and Adonis.* Musée des Beaux-Arts, Bayonne. *Photo Musées Nationaux.*

recalled to Modena in 1683, but died before returning there.

A considerable body of the architect's work, both religious and secular, survives in Turin. The Theatine church of S. Lorenzo (1668–87) has a square plan circumscribing an octagon whose sides curve inward toward the center. Across the dome stretch eight elliptical ribs, which intersect to form a web that is silhouetted against the bright lantern crowning the dome. An equally original conception is displayed in the chapel of the SS. Sindone, or the Holy Shroud (1667–90), at the east end of the cathedral of S. Giovanni in Turin.

In addition to these two buildings and the Torinese church of Sant'Andrea (1679–1705), Guarini undertook several secular projects in Turin. The most splendid of these is the Palazzo Carignano (begun 1679/80), built for Prince Philibert of Savoy. This masterpiece shares with the Jesuit Collegio Nobile (1678; the present-day Academy of Sciences) and the Palazzo Provana di Collegno (built posthumously, in 1698, after his designs)—both in Turin—a place among Guarini's best works, in which his use of brick and stucco often results in a rough and unfinished appearance that yet has tremendous power.

Guarini's book, *L'architettura civile* (published posthumously in 1737 by the Piedmontese architect Bernardo Vittone), includes some geometric experiments and also provides some information about numerous architectural projects of his that have disappeared or that were never completed. One of these was the church of Ste-Anne-la-Royale in Paris, offered to the Theatine Order by Cardinal Mazarin, whose death in 1661 caused an interruption in its construction; it was resumed on a more modest scale in the 18th century by the architects Liéven and Pierre Desmaisons (1724–1800). The church was destroyed in 1822, but one of its chapels remains.

GUERCINO, Giovanni Francesco Barbieri, *called* Il (1591, Cento, near Bologna—1666, Bologna), Italian painter of the High Baroque. He was a pupil of Lodovico Carracci, from whom he learned a skill with lighting effects that was made surer by a visit to Venice (1618); to this he added a robust naturalism that was the typically Bolognese counterpart to Caravaggio's realism. Arriving in Rome in 1621, Guercino established his reputation with a series of huge works, including the *Aurora* fresco (1621; Rome, Casino of the Villa Ludovisi) and the *Burial of St. Petronilla* (1621; Rome, Palazzo dei Conservatori, Pinacoteca Capitolina). Little by little, however, the powerful drama of his compositions gave way under the influence of Guido Reni and the Classicist circles in Rome to a calmer style, in which his forms achieved more stability, and even a certain gracefulness. This refined style is most noticeable in the painter's later decades, when he returned to set up his workshop at Bologna (1642). Throughout Guercino's work, however, we find an almost romantic inspiration that fires not only his grandiose decorations but also the most unpromising religious subjects with imagination. Stirring episodes from the Bible (*Christ at the Column*, 1657, Rome, Palazzo Chigi) and pagan scenes (*Death of Dido, c.* 1630; Rome, Galleria Spada) were similarly treated in a dramatic manner.

GUÉRIN, Baron Pierre-Narcisse (1774, Paris—1833, Rome), French painter. He was a pupil of the Neoclassical painter Jean-Baptiste Regnault. Political events prevented him from competing for the Prix de Rome before 1796, and from going to Italy after he had won the prize the following year. Nevertheless, he began to produce paintings inspired by Greco-Roman themes: the *Return of Marcus Sextus* (1799; Paris, Louvre), depicting a fictitious episode in Roman history, was interpreted as an allusion to the return of the *émigrés* who had left France during the Revolution, and at once made Guérin famous. He was presented to Napoleon, who decorated him. All his subsequent work was in the same vein as this first success, based on ancient history and interpreted according to the Neoclassical aesthetic of Louis David (*Aeneas Recounting to Dido the Misfortunes of the City of Troy*, 1813; Louvre). Guérin was the most gifted of David's followers. His intelligence made him a teacher who respected the natural qualities of his pupils, among whom were the great Romantic painters Théodore Géricault and Eugène Delacroix.

GUILLAUMIN, Armand (1841, Paris—1927, Paris), French painter. Guillaumin was an important member of the Impressionist School. His circle included Claude Monet, Camille Pissarro, Paul Cézanne, and Paul Signac, whom he did much to help. Most of Guillaumin's landscapes are imbued with a truly joyful lyricism, and his artistic vision is particularly direct and objective. His work has a technical authority, and a certain vigor in the brushstrokes, which in his later style comes near to that of the Fauves. In 1863 he exhibited at the Salon des Refusés, and in 1874 he participated in the first Impressionist exhibition at the studio of the photographer Nadar. Thereafter he took part in all the group's exhibitions, except those of 1876 and 1879. During these years he often stayed in Auvers-sur-Oise as the guest of Dr. Paul Gachet, the patron of many Impressionists. In 1887, however, he discovered a more favorable region for his work at Crozant, in the Creuse. At this time Guillaumin also became friendly with Vincent van Gogh. From 1892 he traveled widely in France, and in 1904 he spent two months in Holland. Whether he took his subjects from the various places he visited in his travels (*Sunset at Ivry*, 1873, and *View of Agay*, 1895; both in Paris, Musée de l'Impressionnisme), or from the numerous quarters of Paris (*Quai de Bercy*, 1881; Geneva, Oscar Ghez Modern Art Foundation), Guillaumin was one of the greatest landscape painters of his time.

GUIMARD, Hector (1867, Lyons—1942, New York), French architect and decorator. He was the most important architect of the Art Nouveau movement in France. One of his principal preoccupations was to escape the dangers of excessive rationalism, which he regarded as inseparable from industrial civilization. He adopted a combination of the latest building techniques and the naturalistic decoration already advocated by Viollet-le-Duc, John Ruskin, and Sir Edward Burne-Jones, and he rejected the old ornamental paraphernalia derived from Classicism. Disliking pastiche, Guimard exploited and handled with great mastery the peculiarly Baroque play of curve and counter-curve in his limitless variations on floral and vegetal motifs. His apartment building, Castel Béranger (built 1894–98), in Paris, is one of the finest examples of the Art Nouveau style and of his own powers of invention, particularly the highly decorative ironwork gates. A similar love of decoration characterized his famous Métro station entrances in Paris (*c.* 1900), with their cast-iron risers and railings, sometimes surmounted by glass awnings, in which he combined glass with cast iron, wood, and ceramic. Among Guimard's other works, the Humbert de Romans concert hall (1902), with its metal framework, and the reinforced concrete synagogue (1913), both in Paris, are notable.

GUSTON, Philip (b. 1913, Montreal, Canada), American painter. He grew up in Los Angeles, where in 1930 he began his studies at the Otis Art Institute. He worked as a muralist for the WPA Federal Art Project in New York from 1936 to 1940. Guston achieved his initial success as a figurative painter, and his first one-man show took place in 1944 at the Midtown Gallery, New York. He taught in many universities and art schools, such as Pratt Institute and Yale University, and traveled in Spain, France, and Italy. He received the Prix de Rome in 1948 and a Guggenheim Fellowship in 1968.

Guston eliminated representative or figurative references from his work around 1947–50 and began to paint abstractly. His own version of Abstract Expressionism, often termed Abstract Impressionism, fluctuated between a characteristically sensuous, lyrical, and subtly tinted manner and a more sober, discordant, less elegant style. In a typical painting from the mid-1950s, such as *Altar* (1953; New York, Coll. Morton Feldman), with its small, hatched brushstrokes of pale peach on a white ground, one observes the artist's more lyrical bent. After 1954 color became rawer and more expressionistic, with paint applied in bold and forceful strokes. This increasing density is also indicative of Guston's study of Andrea Mantegna and Piero della Francesca while in Italy (1960).

GUTTUSO, Renato (b. 1912, Palermo), Italian painter. In 1931 he went to the Italian mainland to study painting. He began his career in Naples and Milan as a painter of nudes and landscapes. In 1935 he settled in Rome and, inspired by Courbet and Van Gogh, turned his attention to more dramatic subjects: *Execution in the Countryside* (1938), a homage to the Spanish poet Federico García Lorca; the *Flight from Etna* (1938; Rome, Galleria Nazionale d'Arte Moderna). His *Crucifixion* (1940–41) was highly controversial: it depicted a naked woman at the foot of the Cross and a multicolored town in the background, and was obviously intended to arouse powerful emotion. In 1947 Guttuso helped to form the Fronte Nuovo delle Arti, which proclaimed the need to link art with a cultural and social revolution. When this group split, Guttuso became the leader of its figurative faction and one of the founders of Italian Socialist Realism. He communicated human and social truths in such huge canvases as the *Occupation of Uncultivated Land in Sicily* (1949–50; Berlin, Deutsche Akademie der Künste) and *Battle at the Ponte Ammiraglio* (1951–52), with its breath of popular epic.

GUY, Francis (1760, Lorton, England—1820, Brooklyn), American painter. Guy was a silk-dyer and calendar-maker in London before he came to America in 1795. Unsuccessful at these occupations in Philadelphia and New York, he went to Baltimore three years later and there began to paint landscapes. He painted nature as a domesticated setting for human and animal existence; his work often represented peaceful scenes of villages, the ordered arrangement of buildings, and cultivated fields with figures engaged in various activities. Guy painted some English landscapes from sketches made while still in England. His most notable extant pictures belong to a series of snow scenes painted between 1817 and 1820, which depict small towns with snowy roofs, smoking chimneys, and streets gaily filled with animals, children, and men and women going about their daily business (*Winter Scene in Brooklyn, c.* 1817; New York, Brooklyn Museum). The detail in many of these works, despite Guy's crude manner, is so accurate that numerous figures may actually be identified as the historical inhabitants of Brooklyn, where the scenes were located.

Hector Guimard. Métro station entrance, Paris. *c.* 1900. *Photo René-Jacques, Paris.*

Renato Guttuso. *Studio interior.* 1960. Coll. Mrs. Augusta McRoberts, England.

H

HADZI, Dimitri (b. 1921, New York), American sculptor. In 1950–51 he studied as a Fulbright Fellow at the Athens Polytechneion and at the Museo Artistico Industriale in Rome, where he eventually settled permanently. Hadzi received several major prizes and important commissions, including one for Philharmonic Hall, Lincoln Center for the Performing Arts, New York. His first one-man exhibition was held at the Galleria Schneider, Rome, in 1958, and was followed by others there and in New York, Munich, Düsseldorf, and the Massachusetts Institute of Technology in Cambridge (retrospective, 1963); in 1956 and 1958 his sculpture was included in the Venice Biennale.

Hadzi's imagery is generally derived from Classical motifs, battles, and armor. His earliest sculptures are fairly literal allusions to mythological figures, but after 1958 his work became more abstract in a series based on shields and helmets (*Elmo-M.I.T.*, 1963; bronze, Cambridge, Massachusetts Institute of Technology). Although he also carved, Hadzi worked primarily in bronze, making his models in specially prepared wax.

HAGUE, Raoul (b. 1905, Constantinople, Turkey), American sculptor. Hague arrived in the United States in 1921 and studied at Iowa State College (1921), at the Chicago Art Institute (1922–25), and at the Beaux-Arts Institute of Design in New York (1925–27). He began direct stone carving in the early 1930s and exhibited this early work in a group exhibition at the Museum of Modern Art (1932) and at the New York World's Fair (1939). By around 1947, however, his interest had shifted to wood, which had become his most satisfying medium: his first one-man show of carved wood sculpture in New York was held in 1962. Hague's mature style is characterized by massive and monolithic asymmetric forms that tend to be abstract; the natural character of the grain and the surface of the wood remain evident and essentially unaltered in the sculpture (*Angel Millbrook Walnut*, 1964; New York, Egan Gallery).

Hague School. Johan Barthold Jongkind. *Sunset, Port of Antwerp.* 1868.

HAGUE SCHOOL, Dutch school of painting of the late 19th century. The leader of the school was Jacob Maris (1837–99), around whom were grouped the painters Bernardus Blommers (1845–1914), Johannes Bosboom (1817–91), Paul Gabriel (1828–1903), Jozef Israëls (1824–1911), Johan Barthold Jongkind, Willem (1844–1910) and Matthijs (1839–1917) Maris, Anton Mauve, Hendrik Willem Mesdag (1831–1915), Willem Roelofs (1822–97), and Jan Hendrik Weissenbruch (1824–1903). The Hague School is well represented in the "Realist" rooms of the Rijksmuseum in Amsterdam and the Rijksmuseum H. W. Mesdag at The Hague, which was established in 1903 around the collection of Mesdag and his wife. The Hague School was the center in Northern Europe of a Realist art inspired by the French painters Camille Corot, Charles-François Daubigny, and Gustave Courbet; and its artists developed a half objective, half lyrical style of landscape and animal painting. They were sensitive to the poetry of humble life, and the best of them, like Weissenbruch and Jongkind, brought a fresh, poetic interpretation of light to Dutch painting. The school contributed to the formation of George Hendrik Breitner (1857–1923), the painter of Amsterdam, and Vincent van Gogh, whose *Potato Eaters* was based on a painting by Israëls.

HAHN, Hermann (1868, Kloster-Veilsdorf, Germany—1942, Pullach), German sculptor. After training at the Munich Academy, he traveled and studied extensively in Holland, Belgium, France, England, and Greece, then settled for a long period in Italy. The great influence on him was the art of Adolf von Hildebrand. When he returned to Munich, Hahn continued the tradition of Hildebrand's Classicism and, in his turn, had a considerable influence on the young generation of German sculptors, many of whom trained in his studio. Among the monuments he created was one to the composer Franz Liszt, in Weimar, and another to the poet Johann Wolfgang von Goethe (1914), in Chicago. He also left a number of fine portrait busts, including one of the art historian Heinrich Wölfflin (Munich, Bayerische Staatsgemäldesammlungen).

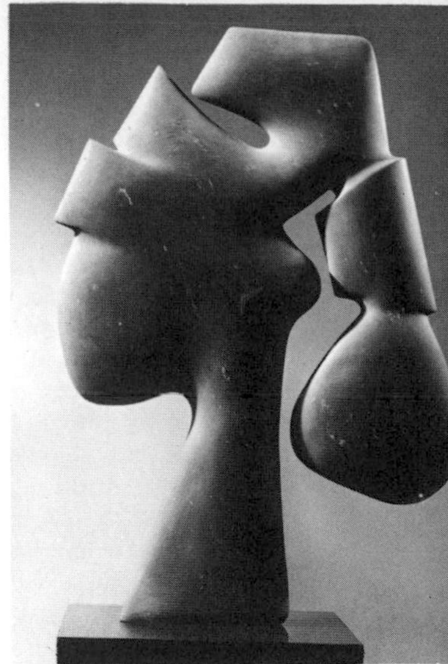

Étienne Hajdu. *Head.* 1966. Galerie Knoedler, Paris.

HAJDU, Étienne (b. 1907, Turda, Rumania), French sculptor. The son of Hungarians living in Rumania, he went to Paris in 1927 and for three years attended the studios of the sculptors Antoine Bourdelle and Paul Niclausse. In 1930 he became a naturalized French citizen. Around 1934 he began to work in an abstract idiom, but he was later attracted to Expressionism; his first exhibition (at the Galerie Jeanne Bucher, Paris, in 1939) revealed both tendencies. Demobilized in 1940, Hajdu spent the years of the Occupation working as a marble mason in a factory in the Pyrenees; this experience in stone carving is apparent in his precise studies of insects (*Cricket*, 1942; *Stag-Beetle*, 1942–43). On his return to Paris, he began to work on huge aluminum or beaten copper bas-reliefs (*Machine Rhythm*, 1948; *Homage to Béla Bartók*, 1949). His art attained its fullest expression from 1951, when he settled at Bagneux in a house that he had built himself. Hajdu's art alternates between two kinds of creation: first, the bas-reliefs, with their orchestrations of convex and concave elements across a continuous background. Secondly, he created two-dimensional figures, delicately notched and usually in marble.

HALS, Frans (1580, Antwerp or Mechlin—1666, Haarlem), Flemish-born portrait painter of the Dutch school. In 1600 he became the pupil of Karel van Mander (1548–1611) in Haarlem, where he later entered the Guild of St. Luke (1610). He remained in Haarlem for the rest of his life, except for a brief visit to Amsterdam in 1633. His output consisted primarily of portraits, and even his genre scenes may be considered portraits in so far as they show a trait or temperament more than a study of manners. Hals excels in the rendering of a smile, a hearty laugh, or a sly grimace: the masterpieces in this vein are the *Gypsy Girl*, also called *La Bohémienne* (*c.* 1628; Paris, Louvre) and *Malle Babbe* (*c.* 1630–33; Berlin, Staatliche Museen). This joviality even enlivens portraits of Dutch burghers, such as those of *Stephanus Geraerdts* (*c.* 1650–52; Antwerp, Musée Royal des Beaux-Arts) and *Isabella Coymans* (*c.* 1650–52; Paris, Coll. Edmond de Rothschild). A scrupulous truthfulness is combined with liveliness in the full-length standing portrait of *Willem van Heythuyzen* (*c.* 1625; Vaduz, Liechtenstein Collection).

The finest works by Hals are a series of eight group portraits (spanning the years from 1616 to 1666) preserved today in the Frans Halsmuseum in Haarlem. These pictures presented the painter with certain problems. He had to place each sitter in a suitable position, while striving at the same time for a coherent and lively grouping with a community of feeling. But in these commemorative groups, which are almost a form of history painting, a degree of nobility and magnificence was also necessary. Hals achieved this with perfect ease, effortlessly creating a sense of harmony between figures, costumes, materials, and accessories. In this respect, the *Banquet of the Officers of the Company of St. Hadrian* (*c.* 1627; Haarlem, Frans Halsmuseum) is a masterpiece of truth and gaiety, a riot of glittering color in full light, and a balanced composition despite what appears to be the most lively disorder. The height of this dazzling art of group portraiture is reached in the painter's last two works: the *Governors* and the *Women Governors* of the Haarlem almshouses for the aged (both *c.* 1664; both Frans Halsmuseum). Here, in a new and deliberate sobriety of effect is to be found another kind of genius altogether, for this time the soul, and not merely the temperament, has been painted.

Frans Hals. *Malle Babbe.* *c.* 1630–33. Staatliche Museen, Berlin. *Photo Walter Steinkopf, Berlin.*

HAMILTON, Gavin (1723, Lanarkshire, Scotland—1798, Rome), Scottish history painter and antiquarian. Although most of Hamilton's paintings are lost and are now known only through engravings, it seems incontestable that he was the most important British painter in the Neoclassical style, indeed one of the most important painters of the entire movement.

In 1742 Hamilton went to Rome, where he studied with the history painter Agostino Masucci (*c.* 1691–1758). In 1752 or 1753, he visited England, where he worked as a portrait painter for about two years. In 1754 he returned to Rome and became a dealer in old master paintings and Classical sculpture. At this time he frequented the Neoclassical circle of Anton Raphael Mengs and the German art scholar Johann Joachim Winckelmann, and in the 1760s painted a series of illustrations for Homer's *Iliad*, which he sent for exhibition to the Royal Academy and to the Society of Artists in London, and which were widely circulated through engravings by Domenico Cunego (1726–1803). Little is known of his later life.

The importance of Hamilton's contribution to European painting hinges on the fact that he was the first artist of any nationality to subordinate his subject matter to the stringent Classical ideal that was later codified by the critic Winckelmann in his *Geschichte der Kunst des Altertums*, 1764 ("History of the Art of Antiquity"). Credit for pioneering Neoclassicism in painting has been equally divided between Joseph-Marie Vien (1716–1809) and Mengs, but a portrait by Hamilton, *William Hamilton of Bangor* (before 1754; Scotland, National Portrait Gallery), antedates both Mengs's paintings at the Villa Albani in Rome and Vien's Grecianizing works submitted to the Paris Salons of 1761 and 1763. Hamilton's series of Homeric subjects are austere but crowded compositions depending directly on Poussin, and occasionally on Charles Le Brun. These works anticipate the Neoclassical compositions of Louis David, and were emulated with surprising fidelity by the aged Vien in 1783–85.

Hamilton is also important as an antiquarian who undertook numerous excavations.

Frans Hals. *Portrait of a Couple.* 1622. Rijksmuseum, Amsterdam.

HAPPENING, a participational art form initiated in America (and practiced as well in Japan and Europe), consisting of a synthesis of environmental situations, composed and unplanned theater events, the visual arts, and extra-artistic materials. Its origins are multiple, although its development as a viable form of "total theater" dates from the period around 1957–59 in New York. At that time a number of painters and artists affiliated with the Reuben Gallery were experimenting with perishable urban subject matter (termed "gutter art" by some) and were concerned with extending the

Happening. Kurt Schwitters. *"Schnurchel en largeur."* 1923. Coll. Hannah Höch, Berlin.

Jules Hardouin-Mansart. Place Vendôme, Paris. Begun 1699; construction completed 1720.

possibilities for the performance and exhibition of new art forms. Happenings actually grew out of painting, and might be seen historically as the theatrical counterpart of the kinesthetic "action" notions inherent in Abstract Expressionist painting. The painters Allan Kaprow, Claes Oldenburg, Jim Dine, Red Grooms, Robert Whitman, and Al Hansen all helped originate the earliest Happenings—the name of which derives from Kaprow's "18 Happenings in 6 Parts," performed at the Reuben Gallery in October 1959. Assemblage, collage junk-sculpture, and such combine-constructions as Robert Rauschenberg's early work or even Kurt Schwitters' Merz theater serve as sources for the Happenings as well. Everyday items and surroundings are united in a large-scale time-space continuum that aims to eliminate the customary barriers that exist between audience and performer in traditional theater. The composer John Cage (who had been one of Kaprow's teachers) was a crusader for chance methods of arrangement and composition, and also contributed to the theoretical and practical background of these first Happenings.

HARDING, Chester (1792, Conway, New Hampshire—1866, Boston), American painter. He began his artistic career while in Pittsburgh (1817), where he worked as a painter of signs and houses. Like many other early American artists, Harding learned the rudiments of portraiture from an itinerant limner. He traveled through Cincinnati, St. Louis, and Kentucky, gaining considerable recognition with his paintings, despite their crude execution. In 1826 he settled in Boston, where his popularity brought him more work than he could handle. He painted many portraits of contemporary political celebrities of the period, such as *Daniel Webster* (several versions, including one exhibited 1831; Boston, Athenaeum), *Henry Clay* (several, including one *c.* 1820; Amherst, Mass., Amherst College), *General William Tecumseh Sherman* (*c.* 1866; New York, Union League Club), and *Stephen van Rensselaer* (1835–39; New York, Metropolitan Museum). *John Randolph of Roanoke* (1829; Washington, D.C., Corcoran Gallery) displays the painter's characteristic concentration on the head and face, a trait due to his lack of training in the complexities of human anatomy.

HARDOUIN-MANSART, Jules (1646, Paris—1708, Marly-le-Roi, near Paris), French architect. Son of a painter and descendant of the sculptor Germain Pilon, Jules Hardouin was much more the pupil of Libéral Bruant than of his uncle François Mansart, who did not esteem him. He was twenty at the death of his uncle, whose name he added to his own in 1668. Having achieved success in the rebuilding of the small Château du Val, near St-Germain, Hardouin-Mansart replaced Antoine Lepautre in the rebuilding of the Château de Clagny. He had already replaced Bruant as architect of the Invalides, and Daniel Gittard at Chantilly, when, in 1676, he obtained the office of first architect, which had been vacant for six years after the death of Louis Le Vau.

Even his critics admitted that Hardouin-Mansart had a good eye, was quick in making decisions, and had "lofty conceptions." Moreover, the very name of Mansart seemed to be the guarantee of a French tradition as opposed to the Italian influence that was apparent earlier in the work of Le Vau and on the wane since the rejection of Bernini's plans for the Louvre, Paris (1665). This Gallic spirit in architecture was manifested after the Treaty of Nijmegen (1678–79) by the creation of a "French Order," incorporating designs such as the cock and the sun in the capitals of columns; the introduction of French marbles, and the manufacture of French mirrors according to secret formulas stolen from the works at Murano.

This was the framework for the creation of the Galerie des Glaces, or Hall of Mirrors at Versailles (1678–84), its construction necessitating an alteration of the façade on the park side, which was carried out in a spirit of simplification and repose. When an extension toward the park was considered, Mansart's suggestion of two long wings to the north and south of the central unit (1678–89) was adopted in preference to a plan for a second "envelope" put forward by Le Vau. Between 1680 and 1686, Mansart built the Salon de la Guerre, the Salon de la Paix, and the Queen's Staircase; completed the wings of the forecourt; and constructed the Grand Commun (Hôpital Larey), the large and small stables, the Orangery, and the Hundred Steps. In the park he built the colonnade and the groves of the Dômes and of Fame, and replaced the ornamental flower bed that Le Nôtre had planned with a lake.

At about the same time he produced plan after plan for French towns and the residences of princes and courtiers. Among these were the châteaux of Dampierre, Choisy, Navarre, Boufflers, Villette, and Haras du Pin; the girls' school of St-Cyr, near Versailles (1686; military academy from 1808); the bridge at Moulins; and the new façade of the palace and the Place des États at Dijon. In Paris he built the Place des Victoires (1685) and one of his greatest masterpieces, the Place des Conquêtes (1699–1720; now Place Vendôme).

In religious architecture the following churches and chapels reveal in the variety of their designs and construction Mansart's versatility and imagination: the Chapelle de la Communion at St-Séverin; the churches at Chantilly and Marly; Notre-Dame at Versailles; and the Vaubrun Chapel at Serrant, rhythmically articulated by a funeral arangement of black marble pilasters. In the chapel of Versailles (1698–1710), Mansart adopted a plan on two levels: the lower part for the court, the upper galleries giving access to the royal apartments. The Invalides (1679–1706) offers one of the most perfect examples of the central plan.

Two palaces crowned Mansart's grandiose achievement. The ensemble at Marly, no longer standing, included 12 pavilions representing the signs of the zodiac, arranged as a cortège to the royal château and surrounded by terraces, waterfalls, and lakes arranged in tiers—a marvel created by

Mansart during Le Nôtre's long stay in Rome. The other palace, which has been preserved, is the Grand Trianon or Trianon de Marbre, which replaced D'Orbay's Trianon de Porcelaine at Versailles. Its pink marble peristyle was the fruit of a collaboration between Mansart and Robert de Cotte, one of the master's most brilliant assistants in the latter part of his career.

JACQUES, *called* HARDOUIN-MANSART DE SAGONNE (1703 or 1709, Paris—1776, Paris), architect, grandson of Jules Hardouin-Mansart. He designed the cathedral of St-Louis at Versailles (1743–54), whose façade, with its two orders, its triangular pediment, and its twin towers with bell turrets, is an accomplished example of the Louis XV style.

HARE, David (b. 1917, New York), American sculptor. Hare spent most of his early life in the Southwest. With no formal training in art, he first worked in color photography, publishing a portfolio of color photographs on the American Indian for the American Museum of Natural History (1940), and exhibiting his work in New York (1940–41). From 1942 to 1944 he was editor of the Surrealist magazine *VVV*. Hare's interest shifted seriously to sculpture around 1943, and he began exhibiting in New York soon after.

Although Hare worked in other media, he is known primarily for his sculptures in welded metal. As his style emerged in the 1940s, it was marked by an emphasis on line and open form, as well as Surrealist qualities in treatment and subject matter. Hare's sculptures often juxtapose prominent structural rods with smaller, weblike or spiky forms. He used figurative elements in such pieces as *The Eaters* (1952; New York, Kootz Gallery); *Juggler* (1950–51; steel, New York, Whitney Museum); and *Man Running* (1954; welded steel and bronze, New York, Museum of Modern Art). In the 1950s motifs of natural and celestial phenomena were also explored: *Sunrise* (1955; steel, bronze, and alabaster, Buffalo, Albright-Knox Gallery), and *Sunset I* (1953; stone and painted wire, New York, Museum of Modern Art).

David Hare. *Sunrise.* *c.* 1954–55. Albright-Knox Art Gallery, Buffalo.

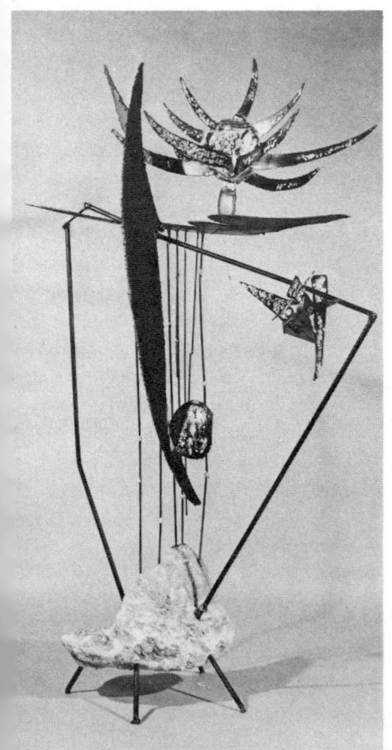

HARNETT, William Michael (1848, Clonakilty, Cork—1892, New York), Irish-born American still-life painter. He was brought to the United States in infancy. He learned the engraver's trade and became a skilled silverware decorator. He did not try oil painting until 1874, and gave up engraving to become a still-life painter the following year. Harnett entranced the public, including the purchasers of art, by the realism of his images. Viewers were at once surprised and delighted to find that the violin they tried to lift from the wall, or the burned matches they tried to pull off the table edge, were only paint. Harnett was most concerned about the selection of objects, preferring them old and mellowed. He is almost unequaled in the ability to differentiate textures, being especially adept at suggesting the thin, crinkly quality of paper. Harnett's most famous work, *After the Hunt* (1885; San Francisco, California Palace of the Legion of Honor)—painted during a stay in Europe (1880–86) and exhibited at the Salon of 1885 in Paris—shares with his best paintings a masterfully controlled abstract composition; remarkable verisimilitude of textures; and the device most conducive to the *trompe-l'oeil* effect, namely a minutely described background wall, close to and parallel with the picture surface, in front of which the apparently three-dimensional objects seem to penetrate the real space of the spectator.

William Michael Harnett. *After the Hunt.* 1885. California Palace of the Legion of Honor, San Francisco.

HARRIS, Harwell Hamilton (b. 1903, Redlands, California), American architect and educator. He taught at many American colleges, including the University of Texas, North Carolina State College, the University of Southern California, Columbia University, and Yale University. Harris worked under Richard Neutra from 1929 to 1932. One year later he established his own practice in Los Angeles. Harris' architecture was largely residential (the Dallas Unitarian Church, 1964, is an exception). His early houses (1934–40), for example, the Marion Clark House in Carmel, California (1938), were small and low-cost. Plans were compact, but rooms were spacious and arranged for relaxed living. Large areas of glass, usually sliding panels or swinging doors, permitted easy access to outdoor terraces and balconies. His houses after 1940 were larger and more sprawling. Several, such as the dramatic Weston Havens House (1941) overlooking the San Francisco Bay area from Berkeley, were set on steep hillside sites with sweeping views.

HARRISON, Peter (1716, York, England—1775, New Haven, Connecticut), often called "America's first professional architect," although, in fact, he practiced without remuneration. He first arrived in the American colonies in 1739. On a trip back to England in 1747–48 Harrison became acquainted at first hand with the recent Palladian movement, which had transformed

Hans Hartung. *Engraving*. 1953.

18th-century English architecture, and also acquired at that time a magnificent library of architecture books, including folios of designs by Palladio, Inigo Jones, James Gibbs, and William Kent, which provided the basis for many of his own buildings.

His earliest executed work was the Redwood Library in Newport, Rhode Island (1748–50; existing in altered form today), which was the first building in America to reflect contemporary Old World taste. His other Newport buildings are the Brick Market (1761–72), which was based on Inigo Jones's Somerset House, and the Touro Synagogue (1759–63).

In Massachusetts Harrison designed King's Chapel, Boston (1749), and Christ Church, Cambridge (1759–61). The former was in use by 1758 but its Ionic portico was not added until 1787 (after Harrison's drawings), and it never received the steeple and spire he planned for it. Unfortunately, Harrison's avowed royalist sympathies led to the burning of his architectural drawings and library by irate patriots shortly after his death, and the buildings cited above are the only documented records of his talent, although other work in the colonies has been attributed to him.

Childe Hassam. *Washington Arch in Spring*. 1890. Phillips Coll., Washington, D.C.

HARRISON, Wallace Kirkman (b. 1895, Worcester, Massachusetts), American architect. After training at the École des Beaux-Arts in Paris and the American Academy in Rome, he began his career as a draftsman with McKim, Mead & White (1923–25). His own firm was one of three organizations participating in the construction of Rockefeller Center in New York (1931–47). His partner on the project was Jacques André Fouilhoux (1880–1945). With the Alcoa Building (1952) in Pittsburgh, he proved his mastery of the steel-and-glass architecture of the International Style; but he replaced glass by an even more precious material: the façade consists of panels of pressed aluminum, each the height of one story. The Corning Glass Building in New York (1959), a perfectly finished industrial product consisting of 28 stories of colored glass, is in the tradition of Gordon Bunshaft's Lever House (1952), New York, for Skidmore, Owings & Merrill, and may be considered a culmination of this style. Finally, Harrison was co-ordinator of the Lincoln Center complex in New York, where he built the new Metropolitan Opera (1960–66) with an interior reminiscent of a traditional European opera house.

HARTLEY, Marsden (1877, Lewiston, Maine—1943, Ellsworth, Maine), American painter. In 1909, at Alfred Stieglitz's 291 Gallery, Hartley had his first show, consisting of so-called black landscapes. In 1912 Stieglitz and the painter Arthur B. Davies helped to send him to Europe. In Paris Hartley met Gertrude Stein and admired the work of the Cubists, but he soon moved on to Munich, where the Expressionist paintings of Franz Marc and Wassily Kandinsky were destined to have a much greater effect on his work. In 1914 he embarked on a series of abstractions (*Portrait of a German Officer*, 1914; New York, Metropolitan Museum) that owed little to Parisian influences. Teeming with boldly outlined forms, violent in color, aggressively painted, they created a strong impression when they were exhibited in Berlin. Hartley remained in Berlin and Dresden during the first years of World War I. Shortly after his return to America, he began to evolve a figurative style of his own, borrowing a tendency toward abstraction and an idiomatic treatment of volumes from the Cubists and strong emotive colors from the Expressionists in order to paint simplified interpretations of the violent scenery of New Mexico or the New England coast (*Granite by the Sea*, 1937; New York, Whitney Museum).

HARTUNG, Hans (b. 1904, Leipzig), French painter of German origin, one of the leading representatives of abstract art. He began to paint at an early age, and these youthful attempts, produced under the influence of the Expressionists Emil Nolde and Oskar Kokoschka, already anticipate his first nonfigurative ink or chalk drawings and watercolors of the years 1921–22. From 1924 to 1928 Hartung studied art history and philosophy; anxious to acquire a deeper technical knowledge of painting, he also attended classes at the academies of Leipzig and Dresden. He then traveled in Italy, Holland, Belgium, and above all France, where he haunted the museums and painted several copies of the old masters. In 1935 he fled from the Nazi regime in Germany and settled in Paris. It was during the years immediately preceding World War II that his first important abstract paintings appeared. Hartung developed his own linear style, in which a scratched line, a bold brushstroke, or an inkstain was superimposed on a background of colored planes.

At the outbreak of World War II he joined the French Foreign Legion, and after demobilization made his way through Spain to North Africa, where he joined the Legion again in 1943. Seriously wounded on the Alsace Front, Hartung had one of his legs amputated, but he took up painting once more after his return to Paris. His artistic development then followed an unbroken, logical course. Gradually, his work grew calmer, the elements were loosened, and the surface became dominated by a dark play of lines. Gathered in sheaves, these lines pursue an ordered movement or are spread out in space like stalks shaken by the wind (*T. 1957–8*, 1957; Paris, Galerie de France), with different degrees of black standing out against the luminous background through transparent layers of paint. The refinements of his late technique give his drawings the appearance of delicate engravings. Hartung—who in 1960 was awarded the Grand Prix for painting at the Venice Biennale—had a decisive influence on painters of the younger generation, particularly in France and Germany.

HASSAM, Frederick Childe, *known as* Childe (1859, Dorchester, Massachusetts—1935, East Hampton, New York), American painter and illustrator. Hassam declined a college education in favor of studying art. In 1883 he went to Europe, where he stayed only a few months and attempted no formal schooling. He returned to Boston, where he studied art seriously for three years and worked with a wood engraver as an illustrator. In 1886 he made a second trip abroad to obtain further training.

In 1890 Hassam began to work in a more obviously Impressionistic style. He approached Impressionism in the pointillistic technique of Claude Monet—a technique he perfected by 1891. He came closer to Monet's style than any of the other Americans working in this mode; he painted directly from nature, taking delight in the common scenes of New York City (*Washington Arch in Spring*, 1890; Washington, D.C., Phillips Collection) and the surrounding Connecticut countryside. The particular quality of sunlight in Hassam's work developed out of Monet's art and also from his admiration for Jean-François Millet, Jean-Baptiste Camille Corot, and J. A. M. Whistler. In a *Landscape* (1903; Albany, New York, Coll. Fillin) the high-keyed palette of pure emerald greens, blues, gold, and amber reds is typical of Hassam's work.

In 1898, along with Weir, Hassam founded the Ten American Painters, a group that was the closest approach in America to a formal organization of Impressionists. Hassam remained an essentially 19th-century painter and his death marked the end of Impressionist painting in America.

HAVILAND, John (1792, Somerset, England—1852, Philadelphia), British-born architect of the American Federal and Greek revival periods. In London, as the apprentice of James Elmes (1782–1862), he absorbed the prevailing Regency style, and received a thorough technical training. After two years in the Imperial Corps of Engineers in St. Petersburg, he went to Philadelphia (1816), where he opened a school of architecture with Hugh Bridport (1794–1837). Two years later he published the first American book of the Greek Revival, *The Builder's Assistant*, with superb engravings by Bridport. Although it gave the orders correctly, its designs were not literal copies of Greek models. Haviland's work was always inventive, a free mixture of a very personal form of Greek detail and Regency planning.

His best-known buildings, mostly in Philadelphia, include: the First Presbyterian Church (1820), St. Andrew's Episcopal Church (1822; now St. George's Greek Orthodox Church), the Deaf and Dumb Asylum (1824), the Walnut Street Theater (1828), the Arcade and the Franklin Institute (both 1826), the Blight House (1828), and Colonnade Row (1830). Perhaps most famous was his Gothic Revival design for the Eastern State Penitentiary in Philadelphia (1821–29).

HAWKSMOOR, Nicholas (1661, Ragnall?, Nottinghamshire—1736, London), English architect. Hawksmoor worked with Wren in London when he built the Royal Hospital, Chelsea (1682–90), Kensington Palace (1691–1715), and Greenwich Hospital (1696–1729). He also designed Sir John Moore's Writing School at Christ's Hospital under Wren's direction (1692–93). His activities with Vanbrugh (after 1690) did not prevent Hawksmoor from undertaking independent work that included six London churches, the country house of Easton Neston, Northamptonshire (completed 1702), and university buildings. He was appointed Surveyor under the Act for Building Fifty New Churches (1711), and the six he built in London constitute the greater part of his independent work. Like Wren, Hawksmoor abhorred the long Gothic nave, and his plans always begin with the concept of a square within a square. The distortions forced upon this elegant system by nonformal requirements illustrate the Classic-Gothic conflict in Hawksmoor's work. At St. Anne's, Limehouse (1714–24), and St. George-in-the-East (1715–23), Hawksmoor used Wren's four-column plan to articulate the center, although the main spaces were of equal height. But at St. Mary Woolnoth (1716–27) and St. George's, Bloomsbury, the central square is higher than the outer one so that the nave is lit from high clerestories. His façades often use gigantesque proportions, and the peculiar complexities and contradictions of adjacent surfaces (as at Christchurch, Spitalfields, 1823–29) mark him as one of the most "Mannerist" of the English Baroque architects. Hawksmoor's Gothic designs for All Souls College, Oxford (1715–40), were preferred to the Italianate plans put forth six years previously by William Talman (1650–1720). In contrast, at Queen's College, Oxford (1709–38), he adopted the plan of a French *hôtel* for the south courtyard. His Classicism is evident in the somber mausoleum of the Carlisle family (1729–36) in the grounds of Castle Howard, Yorkshire. It is a circular building with a double range of blind arcades, surrounded by a high crown of Doric columns. Although his independent output is small, and his individual contribution to collective work difficult to isolate, Hawksmoor emerges as perhaps the most talented English architect of the period.

Nicholas Hawksmoor. Mausoleum of the Carlisle family in the grounds of Castle Howard, Yorkshire. 1729–36. *Photo Kersting, London.*

Henri Hayden. *Portrait of Moïse Kisling.* 1914. Oscar Ghez Modern Art Foundation, Geneva.

HAYDEN, Henri (1883, Warsaw—1970, Paris), French painter of Polish origin. In 1907 he went to Paris, intending to stay for a year, but he remained in France for the rest of his life. In 1909 Hayden began to paint at Le Pouldu and Pont-Aven in Brittany. In 1911 he came under the influence of Cézanne (*Pianist*, 1911), then turned increasingly toward Cubism, eventually gaining the friendship of the sculptor Jacques Lipchitz and the painters Juan Gris, Picasso, and Gino Severini. His Cubist period (*Three Musicians*, 1920, Paris, Musée National d'Art Moderne; *Woman at a Pedestal Table*, 1920) came to an end in 1922. Working in the south of France, in Brittany, and in the Lot, he returned to a more direct perception of nature. About 1949, Hayden found a new creative *élan*. While remaining faithful to reality, he used the lessons of the Cubists to achieve a synthetic transposition of nature. He revealed a highly personal vision, a remarkable knowledge of plastic translation, and a style of increasing purity and confidence (*Beige Still Life with Sauceboat*, 1959, Paris, Coll. Suillerot; *Plage de Dielette at Cherbourg*, 1962).

Stanley William Hayter. *Horse.* 1931. Rosenwald Coll., National Gallery of Art, Washington, D.C.

HAYTER, Stanley William (b. 1901, London), British engraver and painter. Hayter trained as a research chemist and worked for the Anglo-Iranian Oil Company in Persia (1922–25), painting the countryside in his spare time. In 1926, following a successful exhibition of his work organized by this company, he went to Paris to train as a painter. Hayter soon began to specialize in engraving, a medium to which he had been introduced by Jacques Villon. In 1927 he founded Atelier 17, where he pursued his graphic research. He was a member of the Surrealist group from 1934 to 1940. In May 1940, Hayter transferred his studio to New York, where Marc Chagall and Jacques Lipchitz studied and worked with him, as they had done previously in Paris. He returned to France in 1950.

Having abandoned figuration early in his career, Hayter developed an impulsive, sharp, labyrinthine line in his engraving; in his etching technique, the use of materials sensitive to acid implied a conscious exploitation of the accidental. The development of Hayter's engraving was paralleled by his painting, particularly in his use of violent colors that sweep through space as if expressing its latent forces.

HEADE, Martin Johnson (1819, Lumberville, Pennsylvania—1904, St. Augustine, Florida), American painter. Heade traveled widely in Europe, especially in Italy, during his early twenties, returning to the United States in 1839. He spent time in various parts of the country, including Philadelphia, St. Louis, Chicago, Rhode Island, and Maine, first painting portraits, then turning to landscapes. Along with Fitz Hugh Lane, Heade is one of the forgotten mid-19th-century American landscapists whose style differed from the freer, more theatrical manner of the Hudson River School. His subtle, precise technique and extreme realism offered an alternative view of the American countryside.

Head experimented briefly with Impressionism, but his great powers of observation and poetic imagination ultimately led him in another direction. Both his many studies of orchids and hummingbirds (*Hummingbird and Passionflowers*; New York, Metropolitan Museum) and his landscapes reveal a special sensitivity to the qualities of American light; every nuance of mist, sunshine, or storm was rendered in a meticulous and polished realistic style. The luminism that is characteristic of his work was to influence such painters as Winslow Homer and Eastman Johnson. *Approaching Storm; Beach Near Newport* (Boston, Museum of Fine Arts) is perhaps more romantic in feeling than his other paintings, but like *Spring Shower, Connecticut Valley* (1868; Museum of Fine Arts), the beautiful rhythms of light that bathe the scene imbue the work with an appealing formal harmony.

HECKEL, Erich (b. 1883, Döbeln, Saxony—d. 1970), German painter. Heckel was, with Ernst Ludwig Kirchner and Karl Schmidt-Rottluff, one of the founders of the Brücke group of Expressionists who gathered in Dresden in 1905. Like them, he was influenced by Van Gogh and Edvard Munch and, about 1907, began using bright colors and a violent style. Heckel specialized in landscapes and nudes tinged by a certain melancholy. In 1910 his line began to be less rapid and more angular, while his color darkened. This tendency was accentuated in 1911 when, like Kirchner, he went to live in Berlin. There he painted grave, anxious, sometimes anguished figures that seem to belong to the world of Dostoevski (*Two Sisters*, 1911; Priv. Coll.). Heckel's meeting in 1912 with Lyonel Feininger, Franz Marc, and August Macke led him to a greater concern with form and light. After World War I, he moved toward a calmer style. Nevertheless, his most engaging works are his engravings and the paintings of his Expressionist period.

HEDA, Willem Claesz. (*c.* 1593, Haarlem—*c.* 1680, Haarlem), Dutch still-life painter. After painting a few portraits and religious works, he began to specialize in still-life painting; in fact, his earliest dated work is a

Vanitas (1621; The Hague, Museum Bredius). Together with Pieter Claesz., he was the great painter of laden tables or the remains of a meal. His works are to be found in nearly all the museums of Europe. Heda occasionally painted rare materials and aristocratic, sumptuous compositions like those of Willem Kalf (1619–93) of Amsterdam (*Still Life*, 1648, Leningrad, Hermitage; *Still Life with Ham*, 1656, Budapest, Museum of Fine Arts), but he preferred the table settings of bourgeois homes. The *Still Life with Tobacco* (1637; Dordrecht, Coll. Rédelé) skillfully combines the grays and greens of a shadowed zone, in which a pewter pitcher stands, with the beige-gray of the luminous area, where a white pipe stands out brilliantly. But Heda is rightly celebrated as a painter of "monochrome" still lifes that owe their effect to refinement of values, half tones, and transparent glazes on a single color. For the *Dessert* (1637; Paris, Louvre), he used a delicate scale and ashy and silver grays; for the *Still Life with Wine, Tobacco, and Watch* (1637, Dordrecht, Coll. Rédelé), subtle effects of gold on gold.

HEEMSKERCK, Marten van (1498, Heemskerck, near Haarlem—1574, Haarlem), Dutch Mannerist painter. Heemskerck was deeply impressed during his stay in Italy (1532–36) by the muscular nudes of Michelangelo and by the ruins of antiquity, of which he made many drawings in his so-called Roman Sketchbook (now in Berlin's Kupferstichkabinett). He also admired the works of the Mannerist painters Jacopo Pontormo and Francesco Parmigianino, and upon his return to Haarlem in 1537, became one of the leading Northern practitioners of Italianate Mannerism. Such mythological compositions as the *Venus and Cupid* (1545; Goteborg, Konstmuseum) and the *Erythraean Sibyl* (1564; Amsterdam, Rijksmuseum) show evidence of his humanistic learning and of his ability to render the female nude with fashionable grace. Heemskerck's religious paintings—among them *Aaron and Moses with the Brazen Serpent* (1551; Haarlem, Frans Halsmuseum) and the huge triptych of the *Passion* (1540; Sweden, Linkoping Cathedral)—combine Mannerist refinement with Michelangelesque power. His crowded compositions, with their elegantly elongated figures and brilliant colors, at times seem devoid of true emotion. Yet, like so many Northern artists, Heemskerck was a sober and precise portraitist, capable of restrained color harmonies and able to convey the spirit of his sitters within their natural setting. Thus the pendant portraits of *Pieter Bicker* counting his money and of his wife *Anna Codde* at her spinning wheel (both 1529; both Rijksmuseum) prove that Heemskerck was able to preserve the Dutch sense of realism despite his admiration for the Italianate style.

HEILIGER, Bernhard (b. 1915, Stettin), German sculptor. He trained at the Stettin School of Arts and Crafts, then at the Berlin Academy. Heiliger first attracted the attention of the public in the mid-1940s and in 1950 was awarded the Fine Arts Prize of the City of Berlin. His work combines natural, organic forms with poses derived from Classical statuary (*Seraph I*, 1950; bronze). His sculptures drew further and further away from human prototypes, acquiring characteristics of both animal and plant forms (*Vegetative Figure*, 1955); but through all their metamorphoses, they retained a vertical movement suggesting growth. This dynamism was coupled with a concern for equilibrium, notably in the *Two Figures* (1954; asbestos cement) in Darmstadt and the *Ferryman* (1956; bronze) on a bridge over the Neckar River near Esslingen. Heiliger was also an excellent portrait sculptor (the actor *O. E. Hasse*, 1959; cement).

HELD, Al (b. 1928, New York), American painter. After serving in the Navy (1945–47), he returned to New York to study at the Art Students League, where he produced figurative paintings with a political-social slant. In 1950 he worked at the Académie de la Grande Chaumière in Paris under Ossip Zadkine. Before he arrived in Europe Held had seen the mural-size "drip" paintings of Jackson Pollock, and while in Paris he attempted to reconcile his own approach with the influences of Pollock and Piet Mondrian. Upon his return to America in 1952, he became involved in the Abstract Expressionist style then current. In 1956 he helped found the Brata Gallery on Tenth Street, New York, where a number of second-generation Abstract Expressionist painters held exhibitions.

Willem Claesz. Heda. *Dessert.* 1637. Louvre, Paris. *Photo Giraudon, Paris.*

In about 1959 Held found that he had to make his paintings more sharply structured and less ambiguous. He continued to paint with a thick impasto, and began to evolve a series of oversized alphabet-letter paintings, using acrylic paint. His concern with the scale and emphatic presence of his forms became increasingly apparent. Although he did not use modeling and had a preference for strong flat colors, many of the paintings seem to possess volumetric density. In *Dowager Empress* (1965; New York, Whitney Museum), for example, a bulging red circle that overlaps an inscribed black rectangle seems to burst the confines of the already large-scale canvas. Later in the decade Held continued to explore the aggressive, expansive feeling of his gigantic letter series (1963–65).

HELDT, Werner (1904, Berlin—1954, Sant' Angelo, Ischia), German painter. In 1940 Heldt joined the German armed forces and was taken prisoner. Upon his release in 1946, he settled in West Berlin, but spent the winter months on the island of Ischia, where he joined the group of artists that included Werner Gilles and Eduard Bargheer (b. 1901).

Heldt was the painter of Berlin and its streets. During his early period, he used deep-toned colors and usually portrayed the streets at night with gas lights, coaches, and members of the working class standing outside taverns. Later, when he came under the influence of Italian Metaphysical painting and the New Objectivity, his streets became unreal, even dreamlike, more sparsely populated, and dramatized by a deep perspective treatment. After 1930, however, and due to Maurice Utrillo's influence, Heldt began to

Jean Hélion.
Grande Journalerie.
1950.

employ a less somber palette. During the Third Reich, his output was restricted almost entirely to drawings. Then in 1946 he began the long series of street scenes on which his reputation today chiefly rests.

HÉLION, Jean (b. 1904, Couterne, Orne), French painter. In 1929, after exhibiting his first nonfigurative paintings, he helped to found the nonobjective Art Concert group, whose theorist was Theo van Doesburg; then, from 1932 to 1934, he shared the activities of the Abstraction-Création group. Before World War II, he was one of the masters of abstract art, which was for him the "idiom of clarity" and the means of constructing an ideal world. Hélion lived in the United States for four years, then returned to France at the beginning of World War II. When he was a prisoner of war in Germany (1940–42), the forms of the real world forced themselves into his consciousness, so that, after he had succeeded in escaping and reaching the United States at the end of 1942, he abandoned pure abstraction, introduced figurative elements into his constructions, and gradually became a painter of everyday life. Form was schematized, and his hieratic figures were placed in severe settings in which public benches, newspapers, and umbrellas were endowed with an enigmatic, almost mythological presence (*Man with a Newspaper*, 1943). In 1946 Hélion returned to Paris, where he painted a series of Everyday Allegories and eliminated all vestiges of abstraction.

Robert Henri.
Dutch Girl in White. 1907.
Metropolitan Museum of Art, New York
(Arthur H. Hearn Fund, 1950).

HELLADIC ART. *See* **AEGEAN ART.**

HELLENISTIC ART. *See* **GRECO-ROMAN ART IN THE MIDDLE EAST; GREEK ART.**

HEMESSEN, Jan Sanders, *called* Jan Sanders van (1500, Hemessen, near Antwerp—1565, Haarlem), Flemish painter. In Antwerp, a city always receptive to new artistic ideas, Van Hemessen attempted, with the help of Italianate formulas, to gear the native Flemish feeling for life and the Erasmian humanism first expressed by Quinten Massys toward the grand manner of painting. His pictures of daily life, tavern scenes, and satires on lust or greed (*Prodigal Son*, 1536; Brussels, Musées Royaux des Beaux-Arts) are well known. In these semi-caustic, semi-jovial genre scenes, a tendency toward Mannerism is already apparent, along with echoes of Leonardo da Vinci and Agnolo Bronzino, and a taste for contrapposto poses and facial expressions that go beyond mere amused observation. Between 1540 and 1550 his works displayed extremes of Expressionist emotion (*Mocking of Christ*, Linz; *St. Jerome*, Prague, National Gallery) or calm grandeur with harmonious and luminous color (*Madonna and Child*, 1544; Stockholm). His later paintings tended toward an almost frenzied violence, and to grandiose compositions in which the earlier half-figures gave way to full-length forms—all knit together, nevertheless, by a unity of color and movement. Thus, such late works as *Tobias Healing His Father* (1555; Paris, Louvre) and the *Expulsion of the Merchants from the Temple* (1556; Nancy, Museum) herald the Baroque style by their coarseness, their use of chiaroscuro, and, above all, by their excessive animation.

HENNEQUIN DE BRUGES. *See* **BONDOL,** Jean de.

HENRI, Robert (1865, Cincinnati—1929, New York), American painter. He is notable less for his own art than for his spirit as a teacher and crusader against academic conservatism, in favor of a new democratic humanism in both art and life. Henri himself received a traditional training in art at the Pennsylvania Academy of the Fine Arts in Philadelphia, as well as the Académie Julian and the École des Beaux-Arts in Paris. In 1891 he settled in Philadelphia, where he became acquainted with the newspaper illustrators Glackens, Shinn, Luks, and Sloan, introducing them to the works of such European masters as Manet, Goya, Hals, and Velázquez. When he returned from a trip to Europe in 1901, Henri began teaching at the Chase School in New York, where he was joined by his four Philadelphia friends. But Henri soon became disenchanted with the stuffy attitudes encouraged by the Academy in the art schools and started his own school, where Edward Hopper, Rockwell Kent, Morgan Russell, Bellows, Kuniyoshi, and Stuart Davis studied. Although his own work did not fulfill the radical implications of his principles, his teaching inspired independence and aesthetic progress, opening new and formerly unacceptable areas of life as subjects for art. In 1908, after being rejected by the Academy, Henri and his friends staged the now-famous independent exhibition of The Eight at the Macbeth Gallery in New York. In 1910 he also helped organize the first Independents Show; although it was an unjuried forum with no prizes, it gave young Americans a chance to show their work.

Henri's earliest paintings were sober scenes of Paris and New York. His travels in Europe influenced him to paint portraits in a style emulating the rapid and brilliant brushwork of Manet, Hals, and Velázquez (*Laughing Child*, 1907; Whitney Museum). With sharp observation, but rather facile surface effects, Henri painted Irish peasants, society ladies, young girls, and Spanish dancers (*Dancer with Castanets*, 1904; New York, Coll. artist's estate).

HENRI IV STYLE. Henri III (1551–89; reigned from 1574) did no more than continue the work already begun by François I and Henri II at the Louvre Palace, Paris, and at Fontainebleau. The queen mother, Catherine de Médicis, continued with building the palace of the Tuileries, which she had approved in 1564. Philibert de l'Orme, with Pierre Lescot the major architect of 16th-century France, had drawn up plans for the building and designed the external decoration, which he derived from Italian Mannerism. The death of the kingdom's leading architects (De l'Orme in 1570, Lescot and Jean Bullant in 1578) put a stop for a time to work on the Petite Galerie of the Louvre and on the Tuileries.

Similarly, at Fontainebleau, the death of the painters Primaticcio (1570), Niccolò dell'Abbate (1571), and François Clouet (1572) robbed the first School of Fontainebleau of its leaders. Portraiture and portrait-drawings continued to be highly favored in Paris, where François Bunel and François Quesnel rivaled the famous brothers Étienne (*c.* 1520–1603) and Pierre (*c.* 1524–1600) Dumonstier in both fields.

After the assassination of Henri III by Jacques Clément (1589), the new king of France had to face war and internal dissension, pacify rivals, and re-establish peace before he could concentrate on the reconstruction of the nation. Henri IV of Navarre (1553–1610) was perhaps a less serious art-lover than the Valois, but he realized his need for a prestige policy of urban redevelopment and for the glory of completing the decorative splendor of Fontainebleau. He was wise enough to leave the execution of this policy to his ministers: Maximilien de Béthune, Duc de Sully, and the economist Barthélemy de Laffemas. Henri's marriage to Marie de Médicis resulted in increased royal patronage of the arts. After his assassination in 1610, Marie, as regent for the young Louis XIII until 1615, continued the program begun by her husband with the completion of work at Fontainebleau and the building of the Luxembourg Palace (designed by Salomon de Brosse, 1615).

Henri IV was above all a builder. Between 1599 and 1616 the Pont-Neuf was completed, probably after designs by Androuet Du Cerceau, Des Illes, and Guillaume Marchand (*c.* 1531–1605); Henri III had laid the foundation stone on May 31, 1578. Next Henri IV wanted to create a residential square and accordingly built the Place Royale (1605–12; today Place des Vosges). He probably adopted the plans of Claude de Chastillon (1547–1616) for the general arrangement and used Louis Métezeau's designs for the façades. The Place Dauphine, at the end of the Île de la Cité, was planned in 1606 according to a similar idea based on the symmetry of forms. These squares were soon imitated in the provinces (Place Ducale, Charlesville, by Clément Métezeau for Charles de Gonzague, 1608) and the construction methods were adopted for certain royal châteaux (Château-Neuf, St-Germain-en-Laye, by De l'Orme, *c.* 1557) and princely houses (château at Rosny-sur-Seine, for the Duc de Sully, 1595–1610). For the Cour des Offices (Stable Court) at Fontainebleau, probably built by Rémy Collin (active 1601–31) and completed in 1609, which was the principal addition to the château under Henri IV, the decorative surface pattern of the Place des Vosges houses was reversed, with brick moldings set off by white façades.

When Marie de Médicis decided to build the Luxembourg, she commissioned the design from Salomon de Brosse (*c.* 1565–1626), whose work was important to the development of 17th-century French Classicism. He imitated the rusticated garden façade of the Palazzo Pitti and toned down the Mannerist tendencies, so that his architecture looks forward to the style of Louis XIII.

Henri IV's desire to embellish his new buildings had a revitalizing effect on French painting: he not only patronized native artists, but also attracted Flemish painters to France. These had visited Italy and studied in Rome, and onto a grounding in Italian Mannerism they grafted northern European elements, producing what might be called an international Mannerism. Its major manifestation in France was the Second School of Fontainebleau, which included a number of painters, working under the direction first of Toussaint Dubreuil (until 1602), then of Ambroise Bosschaert (called Dubois) and Martin Fréminet (1567–1619). Almost all that survives of their work at Fontainebleau, unfortunately, are decorations in the Roman style by Dubois, based on the romance by Heliodorus (Cabinet de Théagène et Chariclée, *c.* 1608; today Salon Louis XIII) and episodes from Tasso's *Jerusalem Delivered*, also by Dubois (Cabinet de Clorinde).

Henri IV Style. Place des Vosges, Paris. 1605–12.

Paris was gradually laying the foundations for its future as an artistic capital. Thriving studios were set up by such painters as Ferdinand Elle (*c.* 1580–1637) and Georges Lallemant (d. *c.* 1635). Thomas de Leu (active in Paris 1576–1614), engraver to Henri IV, executed bold but rather stiff portraits; Quentin Varin painted pictures for Parisian churches; and the Flemish Frans Pourbus the Younger (1569–1622), who settled in the capital from 1609 to 1622, painted official portraits as well as beautifully simple, restrained religious pictures. Of the many other foreigners who visited France at this time, the most famous was Rubens, active in Paris, who painted for the queen the extraordinary cycle of the *Life of Marie de Médicis* for the Galerie de la Reine in the Palais du Luxembourg (1622–25; now in the Louvre).

In Nancy, from 1600 to 1617, Jacques Bellange developed a fantastic and highly personal Mannerist art, particularly in his etchings, and he also executed

Henri IV Style. Frans Pourbus the Younger. *Portrait of Henri IV.* 1606. Musée Condé, Chantilly. *Photo Giraudon, Paris.*

Barbara Hepworth. *Forms with Right Angles and a Circle.* 1963. Coll. artist. *Photo British Council.*

some official commissions. Jean Chalette (1581–1645) was active in Toulouse, painting portraits of local officials. This was also the period of the early works of the Lorrainese artists Jacques Callot and Claude Deruet (1588–1660), who were to become widely known during the reign of Louis XIII.

In sculpture the scene was lackluster. Roman and Tuscan influence remained dominant. Certain artists continued to work in the style of Primaticcio, but others adopted a more sturdy realism in their court sculpture to glorify the monarch. Examples include the full-length statues of the king, one in the Louvre by Barthélemy Tremblay (1568–1629), and another, dated 1608, by Nicolas Cordier (1567–1612); the equestrian bas-relief by Mathieu Jacquet (called Grenoble, active from 1590; d. before 1610) for the Belle Cheminée at Fontainebleau (1599; now in Louvre); and the famous equestrian statue of Henri IV, commissioned by Marie de Médicis in 1604/5 and finally erected in 1614 on the Pont-Neuf. The horseman, which has disappeared, was cast by Giovanni Bologna and Pietro Tacca, and the four slaves in chains (Louvre), which surrounded the corners of the pedestal, by Pierre de Francheville (1548/53–1615).

Henri IV's importance in promoting and defending the French luxury industries should not be overlooked. In 1608 he housed Girard Laurent and Maurice Dubout (active in Paris 1584–1636) in the Grande Galerie of the Louvre, and guaranteed a market for their work by the edicts of 1599 and 1601 concerning the importation of tapestries *à bocages* (designs of natural and stylized foliage with animals). In 1607 he also encouraged two Flemish artists, François de la Planche (or van den Planken; d. 1627) and Marc de Comans (d. 1643), to settle in the Gobelins district of Paris by giving them patent letters on condition that they operate 80 tapestry frames. Similarly, Henri IV helped in the setting up of the Italian faïence factory at Nevers by the privilege he granted in 1603 to the ceramists Augustin (d. 1612), Baptiste (d. before 1618), and Dominique (active 1578–1638) Conrade, whose works include the decoration of the Château de Gloriette.

HEPWORTH, Barbara (1903, Wakefield, Yorkshire—1975, St. Ives, Cornwall), English sculptress and draftswoman. She studied at the Leeds School of Art (1920) and at the Royal College of Art in London (1921–24). She then won a scholarship that allowed her to spend nearly three years in Italy. Hepworth received numerous commissions, including one for the two large sculptures (*Turning Forms,* 1950, Hertfordshire, County Council; *Contrapuntal Forms,* 1950, Essex, Harlow New Town) for the Festival of Britain (1951), as well as *Vertical Forms* (1951) for the Technical College in Hatfield, Hertfordshire, and *Meridian* (1959) for State House, London. In 1953 she won a second prize in the International Sculpture Competition held at the Tate Gallery, London, for her version of the monument to the *Unknown Political Prisoner.* Examples of her work are included in the collections of the Tate Gallery (*Forms in Echelon,* 1938), the Museum of Modern Art in New York, and the Kröller-Müller Museum in Otterlo, Holland, as well as in many other public collections throughout the world.

It is easy to draw comparisons between the work of Barbara Hepworth and that of Henry Moore. Until the mid-1930s, and at various times afterward, their artistic evolutions progressed in parallel directions. Both Hepworth and Moore tended to open up their sculptural masses by piercing them and hollowing them out. Hepworth's idiom, however, is colder and more enigmatic than Moore's; her sculptures are static rather than dynamic. The sculptor Constantin Brancusi and the painters Piet Mondrian and Jean Arp exerted decisive influences on her work as did, to a lesser degree, Walter Gropius, Naum Gabo, and Laszlo Moholy-Nagy when they were in England before World War II. Most of Hepworth's work was nonfigurative and, after 1934, references to humanity, at least in her sculpture, were rare.

In 1939 she settled permanently in St. Ives, Cornwall, where she lived and worked. The Cornish landscape released fresh impulses in her art and, between 1943 and 1947, she produced some of her most lyrical works.

After around 1947 a renewed interest in the human figure led her to create a series of representational drawings of surgeons and doctors working in operating theaters. Human allusions also crept back intermittently into her sculptures, which often, however, revealed an unresolved dichotomy. In 1951 she produced some small-scale groups of monolithic figures that create an equally uncomfortable impression of being neither human beings nor dolmens. She then returned once more, and with great success, to non-figurative sculptures of a less compact nature, often on a considerable scale.

HERBIN, Auguste (1882, Quiévy, Nord—1960, Paris), French painter. Herbin occupies an unusual position in relation to the artistic ideologies of the 20th century: he always remained on the fringe without actually committing himself to any one of them. In Cubism, for instance, he found a means of ordering his intense and unruly color in large still lifes and very firmly structured landscapes. He pursued a slow process of purifying his forms which, in 1917, led him to abstract compositions. These works, together with the parallel experiments of Juan Gris, are probably Cubism's most interesting attempt to formulate a new art, based on geometry and

Auguste Herbin. *Domestic scene.* 1909. Oscar Ghez Modern Art Foundation, Geneva.

divorced from the figural fragmentation of Picasso and Braque. In 1931, with Georges Vantongerloo, he founded the Abstraction-Création group, an organization of artists that included followers of Surrealism, Constructivism, Kandinsky's Abstract Expressionism, and the De Stijl principles of elemental forms. His color became pure energy, with a tension, contrast, and harmony that produced strictly calculated variations. The forms were taken from plane geometry—circles, various triangles, squares, rectangles, or rhombuses—to which color added dynamism and planar interaction (*Spring*, 1955; Paris, Galerie Denise René). Herbin was able to create an idiom of the greatest precision, the laws of which he formulated in a theoretical work, *L'Art non-figuratif non-objectif* ("Nonfigurative, Non-objective Art"), published in Paris, 1949.

HERLAND, Hugh (active 1360–1405), the greatest of English carpenters. His father William (active 1347–75) became King's Chief Carpenter in 1354, and the two Herlands are considered to have been the creators of the type of canopied choir stall seen at Lincoln (*c.* 1370) and Chester (*c.* 1390) cathedrals. Hugh first appears in the records in 1360; but he must already have been in the royal service for some years, for in 1366 he was granted a life pension for his "long service." He succeeded his father in 1375, and in 1378 was appointed carpenter and controller at Rochester Castle until 1386–87. The tester over the tomb of Edward III in Westminster Abbey (one of the masterpieces of Gothic woodwork) must date from about this time. Other works in his style are the tester over the tomb of Philippa of Hainault (date unknown) and the roof of the Abbot's Hall at Westminster (*c.* 1375). In 1379 Herland was appointed one of the King's Master Carpenters, and was in charge of work at Leeds Castle in Kent. In 1383 he resigned from this office because he was "verging on old age"; but he worked for William of Wykeham in Hampshire from 1387 onward.

He designed the timberwork of New College, Oxford (founded by Wykeham in 1380), and was undoubtedly also the author of the timber vault of Winchester College Chapel, which still survives. His greatest opportunity came when Richard II decided to rebuild Westminster Hall and appointed Herland carpenter and controller. The roof that he designed is the first hammer-beam construction to which we can ascribe a definite date. A landmark in the history of art, it is the finest work of its kind and has the largest span of all medieval roofs. Herland was probably engaged on this work from about 1393 until after 1400.

HERRERA, Juan Bautista de (1530, Mobellán, Santander—1597, Madrid), Spanish Renaissance architect. In 1558 he joined the court of Philip II in Madrid, and in 1563 began to assist the official court architect, Juan Bautista de Toledo, with the construction of the Escorial on the outskirts of Madrid. After Toledo's death in 1567, Herrera was put in charge of that vast project. His major contributions were the main façade of the monastery—taller than Toledo had planned, and with emphasis on the central part—and the adjoining church, which is reminiscent of St. Peter's in Rome. Apart from his work on the Escorial, Herrera provided the designs for the alteration of the royal palace at Aranjuez (*c.* 1564); for the south façade of the Alcázar at Toledo, constructed by Jerónimo Gili (active 1567–79) and Diego de Alcántara, in 1571–85; and for the Lonja, or Exchange, at Seville, built by Juan Bautista de Minjares (1583–93). Around 1589 he also conceived a grand plan for Valladolid Cathedral: the project was never completed, however, and Herrera's plans were virtually ignored by successive architects.

HERTERVIG, Lars (1830, Tysvaer, near Stavanger—1902, Stavanger), Norwegian painter. After studying at Stavanger and Oslo, he went to Düsseldorf in 1852, there becoming a pupil of the Norwegian painter Hans Fredrik Gude (1825–1903). Hertervig occupies a unique position in Norwegian art, his pictures standing midway between reality and dream. They are directly inspired by natural phenomena; but they go beyond these into an unreal, visionary world, made up of an accumulation of strange and disturbing details, always severely contained within a firm composition. In particular, his art shows a definite predilection for the juxtaposition of horizontals and verticals; his color is always rich and subtle. Hertervig's work was completely unknown during his lifetime, but is now regarded as one of the peaks of Norwegian painting. He is represented in the Nasjonalgalleriet, Oslo, by a number of works, including *Lake in the Forest* (1865) and two *Self-Portraits*.

HESSELIUS, Gustavus (1682, Falun, Sweden—1755, Philadelphia), Swedish-born American painter. After leaving his native Sweden—where he had received some artistic training—he went to America via London in 1712, and was one of the first artists in the colonies to paint professionally and to be awarded a commission to decorate a building. His work may be divided into three main categories: religious themes, Classical mythology, and portraiture. In 1721 he was commissioned to paint an altarpiece of the *Last Supper* (1721–22; now Fredericksburg, Va., Coll. Mrs. Rose Henderson), which, in addition to being the first commission of any public distinction done in America, was also one of the first compositions executed during the colonial period to contain more than one figure. Hesselius is noted above all for his portraits of Indians commissioned by John Penn (*Chief Lapowinska*, 1735; Philadelphia, Historical Society of Pennsylvania Museum). In 1734 the artist went to Philadelphia, where he painted the woodwork in Independence Hall and became a good friend of Benjamin Franklin. In 1746 he built the first pipe organ in America for a Moravian congregation in Bethlehem, Pennsylvania, thus establishing himself as a pioneer in instrument making as well as in painting. Other paintings with mythological themes, such as *Pluto and Persephone* (also called *Bacchus and Ariadne*; *c.* 1742, Detroit, Institute of Arts) and *Bacchanalian Revel* (*c.* 1742; Philadelphia, Pennsylvania Academy of the Fine Arts), reveal that he was influenced by engravings of works by Paolo Veronese and Nicolas Poussin.

JOHN (1728, Maryland—1778, Annapolis), Gustavus' son, was also a portraitist. Although John was a more prolific portrait painter than his father, he was not quite as accurate as the latter in respect to detail. Whereas Gustavus possessed a modest skill in modeling

Adolf von Hildebrand. Hubertus Fountain, Munich. *Photo Bruckmann, Munich.*

by soft chiaroscuro contrasts, John was awkward and uneasy dealing with volumetric representation; nor was he as adept as his father in the art of making faces come alive. His portrait of *Richard Sprigge* (*c.* 1761; Winston-Salem, N.C., Museum of Early Southern Decorative Arts) reveals a much cruder touch in the rendering of costume details and a less tutored eye for capturing the sitter's personality. The painting *Charles Calvert and a Colored Slave* (1761; Baltimore, Museum of Art) is, however, a charming example of his work at its best.

HICKS, Edward (1780, Attleborough, now Langhorne, Pennsylvania—1849, Newtown, Pennsylvania), American painter. Most of the pictures painted by this most famous 19th-century American "primitive" artist were of the same pacifist-Biblical subject, the *Peaceable Kingdom*, of which Hicks painted about 100 very similar versions: examples may be found in the New York State Historical Society, the Brooklyn Museum in New York City, and in many other public and private collections in the United States. In the *Peaceable Kingdom*, wild animals are shown living peacefully with tame ones and with children: lions, tigers, wolves, and leopards stare out at the observer with frighteningly transfixed gazes that seem to hint at their former savage existence. Hicks remained a primitive in his flattened, stylized shapes, decoratively combined, which he intensified and personalized with glowing, jewel-like colors and a seemingly infinite precision of drawing and modeling.

HILDEBRAND, Adolf von (1847, Marburg—1921, Munich), German sculptor. In Munich, he studied under Kaspar von Zumbusch (1830–1915), whom in 1867 he accompanied to Rome, where he became friendly with the art historian Konrad Fiedler, later his patron, and the painter Hans von Marées. From the beginning of his career as a sculptor, he produced work that was remarkable for its maturity, and for the clarity and balance of its forms. In 1872 he returned to Italy and stayed for two and a half years. During that time he assisted Hans von Marées with frescoes for the Stazione Zoologica in Naples. On his return to Germany he settled in Munich, where he designed the Wittelsbach Fountain (1891–94) and built himself a house (1897). From that time he lived alternately in Munich and Florence. He was a sculptor more of single statues, conceived over a long period, than of ambitious monuments. However, the equestrian statues of the prince regent Luitpold in Munich (1903–13), and especially of Bismarck in Bremen (1907–10), are skillfully constructed. His busts and plaques are particularly fine. A reflective artist, Hildebrand developed his theories in *Problem der Form in der bildenden Kunst*, 1893 ("The Problem of Form in Plastic Art"), which played an important role in the reaction of German sculptors against naturalism, and he had a considerable influence on aestheticians such as Heinrich Wölfflin and Josef Strzygowski.

HILDEBRANDT, Johann Lucas von (1668, Genoa—1745, Vienna), one of the greatest exponents of Baroque architecture in Austria. He grew up in Italy, where he was a pupil of the architect Carlo Fontana and also received early training in engineering and town planning. Hildebrandt began his career as an engineer in the imperial army and served in Italy under Prince Eugene of Savoy. According to Hildebrandt himself, he took up architecture as early as 1692. He settled in Vienna, where he became Imperial Councilor in 1698 and *Hofbaumeister* ("court architect") in 1700. One of his first works was the House of the Singing Bird, built at Breslau in 1705. The following year, on the Laudongasse, just outside Vienna, he began work on a summer palace (1706–17) for Friedrich Carl von Schönborn, one of the Schönborn family of prelates and princes who remained his powerful protectors throughout his life. Hildebrandt also built a country palace at Göllersdorf (1710–17) for them, and was one of the architects summoned by Elector Lothar Franz von Schönborn to build Schloss Pommersfelden, to which he contributed the staircase (1711–18). About the same time, he built a residence in Vienna for Count W. P. Daun, now called the Daun-Kinsky Palace (1713–16).

The Belvedere, built in 1714–24 for Prince Eugene in Vienna, is remarkable for its general plan of two palaces that face each other and

Johann Lucas von Hildebrandt. Upper Belvedere, Vienna. 1721–24. *Photo Bundesdenkmalamt, Vienna.*

for the arrangement of the terraced gardens linking them on the side of a hill. The Lower Belvedere was the first to be completed (1714–16); it comprised a ground floor with strongly accentuated horizontals, broken only by a single projecting bay with an additional story. A more dramatic silhouette is that of the Upper Belvedere (1721–24), a series of pavilions of unequal height and width, linked together by the entablature of the graceful piano nobile (second floor) that runs uninterrupted around the whole building.

Hildebrandt could be magnificently extroverted, as in the funerary chapel of the Schönborns at Schloss Göllersdorf; he could also be more subdued, as in the Priesterseminarkirche ("seminary church") at Linz (1717–25). Following an introduction by Friedrich Carl von Schönborn, the Imperial Vice-Chancellor, to Abbot Gottfried Bessel, Hildebrandt undertook the reconstruction of one of the largest abbeys in Austria, Göttweig Abbey, which had been almost completely demolished by fire. The rebuilding was begun in 1719 on a site overlooking the Danube valley. Though the work remained unfinished, the magnificence of its conception is undeniable.

The qualities of the Belvedere reappeared, after 1720, in other princely residences: Schloss Bruck on the Leitha, the Harrach Palace in Vienna (in front of which there is a concave arrangement of railings and gate that is reminiscent of Schloss Göllersdorf and of the gardens of the Belvedere), and above all, at Schloss Mirabell in Salzburg. In Mirabell, as in the grand staircase at Göttweig Abbey and in a number of Hildebrandt's other decorative designs, there is an almost Mozartian grace and lightness, and an elegance that is perhaps unique in the splendid wealth of Baroque architecture in central Europe. Hildebrandt's career ended with two huge projects. The first of these was the rebuilding of the Hofburg, Vienna, according to plans that were altered shortly afterward by the Fischer von Erlachs, father and son. The second was the rebuilding of the Würzburg Residenz, where—while the powerful Friedrich Carl von Schönborn was alive—the influence of Hildebrandt prevailed over that of his partner, Balthasar Neumann. In this building the art of the two masters may be compared: Neumann Classical and restrained, Hildebrandt elegant and richly ornate.

HILLIARD, Nicholas (1547, Exeter—1619, London), English miniaturist who was the greatest native-born painter of the Elizabethan age. He was the son of an Exeter goldsmith, and was himself apprenticed to a jeweler and goldsmith. In 1570 he was recorded in the Goldsmiths' Company, and at an unknown date was appointed limner and goldsmith to Queen Elizabeth I. An undated but obviously early portrait (Welbeck Abbey, Coll. Duke of Portland) shows the queen in a frontal position, wearing a great deal of meticulously painted jewelry. In 1584 he designed the second Great Seal for the queen. On his accession to the throne in 1603, King James I confirmed Elizabeth's patronage of Hilliard, subsequently granting the artist a 12-year monopoly on court portraiture (1617). Hilliard was the author of *The Arte of Limning*, a treatise in which he states that he based his art on that of Holbein.

Hilliard was at all times a straightforward portraitist, and within these limits remained attached to his earliest training as a goldsmith. His mature style is already visible in the *Portrait of a Man of Twenty-Four* (1572; London, Victoria and Albert Museum). His later *Self-Portrait* (1577; Victoria and Albert Museum), however, indicates that his style gradually became looser, nervous, and even more brilliant. Hilliard's most poetic portraits are of men, such as the elegant and love-sick *Young Man Leaning Against a Rose Tree* (*c.* 1588; Victoria and Albert Museum); the full-length Renaissance portrait of *George Clifford, 3rd Earl of Cumberland* (*c.* 1590; Greenwich, National Maritime Museum); or the *Unknown Man Against a Background of Flames* (Victoria and Albert Museum). His best Jacobean works are generally tighter and drier in handling, as in the miniature of *Queen Elizabeth of Bohemia* (Knowsley Hall, Coll. Earl of Derby).

HIQUILY, Philippe (b. 1925, Paris), French sculptor. After studying (1947–51) in the studio of the sculptors Marcel-Antoine Gimond and Alfred Janniot at the École des Beaux-Arts in Paris, Hiquily abandoned figurative Classicism and began to work in soldered metal. He created a world that was both threadlike and substantial, in which he pushed to its utmost limits the possibilities of a strange, yet delicate and comical Mannerism, strongly impregnated with eroticism. Hiquily's semi-human, semi-animal forms are the result of his style of organic exaggeration that contrasts with his preference for elongated and elliptical shapes (*Venus of Shanghai*, 1964; *Stripteaser*, 1958, New York, Guggenheim Museum).

Nicholas Hilliard. *Unknown Man Against a Background of Flames.* Victoria and Albert Museum, London.

HIRSHFIELD, Morris (1872, Poland—1946, New York), American painter. As a child he sculpted and painted a large ornamental stand showing two lions holding between them the Ten Commandments for the cantor's prayer box in his village synagogue. He went to New York at the age of eighteen and worked in the garment district, eventually founding a highly successful women's slipper factory, which he called the "E. Z. Walk Company." Illness forced him to give up work for an extended period, during which his business went so badly that he was obliged to retire. Only then, in the mid-1930s, did he return to painting. Hirshfield's hallucinatory and naive canvases were discovered in 1939 by the American art dealer Sidney Janis, who included his works in the exhibition of "Contemporary Unknown American Painters" held in the same year at the Museum of Modern Art, New York.

Hirshfield's figures are rigid and hieratic and have a dreamlike

Hittite Art. Zoomorphic vase. 15th century B.C. Archaeological Museum, Ankara.

intensity. He painted his first work, *Beach Girl* (1937), over an old canvas, using a face from the original painting for his figure, who stands in a naively abstracted landscape of sea, sand, and sky. Other remarkable paintings by him include *Angora Cat* (1937), *Lion* (1939; New York, Coll. Sidney Janis), *Nude at the Window* (1941), *Tiger* (1940), and *Girl in a Mirror* (1940; both New York, Museum of Modern Art).

HITCHENS, Ivon (b. 1893, London), English landscapist. He studied in London at the St. John's Wood School of Art and at the Royal Academy Schools, and was a member of the London Group and of the short-lived Seven and Five Society (founded 1919). In 1925 Hitchens had his first one-man show in London, and thereafter exhibited regularly in that city. He was also represented in major exhibitions in Paris and Venice. His style is characterized by a typically English compromise between a pastoral naturalism and abstraction, and temperamentally he was related to William Blake's follower, Edward Calvert. The main influences on his work, however, were the paintings Henri Matisse produced during the 1920s. Although Hitchens had a narrow technical range, he exploited his popular and well-proven idiom of a personal and contemplative lyricism. There have been several retrospective exhibitions of his paintings, including one in the British Pavilion at the 1956 Venice Biennale.

Hittite Art. *King Tudhalia IV protected by the god Sarrumma.* Yazilikaya, near Bogazkoy. 13th century B.C. *Photo Yan, Toulouse.*

HITTITE ART. The Hittites were a people of Indo-Germanic origin who settled in Anatolia at the beginning of the 2nd millennium B.C. They found there a civilization that was already highly developed, as we know from the discoveries made in 1935 in the royal tombs of Aläjä Hüyük (2300–2100 B.C.), 56 miles from Khattusas (now Bogazkoy, Turkey). This is confirmed by the bronze or silver statuettes found at Horoztepe, the stone idols of Kültepe, and the much older earthen statuettes of Hacilar, which are the earliest representations of the mother-goddess. To these could be added the mural paintings discovered at Catal Hüyük, which date from prehistoric times. The civilization, and therefore the art, of the Hittites was the result of a fusion of two elements: what might be termed a *Hatti* basis and a *Hittite*, or Indo-Germanic, contribution. In addition, there were external influences, Mesopotamian and Egyptian in particular.

Hittite art is divided chronologically into the same divisions as its history: the Ancient Empire (1800–1450 B.C.), the New Empire (1450–1200 B.C.), and the Neo-Hittite period (12th–8th centuries B.C.). It is a curious fact that, apart from ceramics, we possess very few objects that date with any certainty from the Ancient Empire. A small bronze statuette found at Khattusas, representing a seated, bearded god, and a few lead idols (single divinities, or ones shown in couples or trios) are practically the sole surviving iconographical evidence from the Ancient Empire period.

The New Empire, on the other hand, is abundantly represented, mainly in its capital, Khattusas, with its impressive fortress, its city walls, and its two monumental gates. At Aläjä Hüyük, the city walls were also pierced by a gate that was guarded by two magnificent sphinxes, while inside the city there were a great many reliefs showing processions of worshipers or warriors, as well as scenes of libation, worshiping, hunting, and frolicking deer. But even this work is excelled by the sculpture at Yazilikaya, an open-air sanctuary not far from Khattusas, where more than 80 figures are carved out of the cliff. A double procession of male and female deities are seen moving toward each other. Mention might also be made of the rupestrian sculptures of Sirkeli, of Karabel, of Fasillar, and of Sipylos, where the fertility-goddess rises to a height of 20 feet.

Such monumentality provides a striking contrast with work in glyptics, which reveals an incomparable delicacy of carving, as in the Tyszkiewicz cylinders at Aydin; the Louvre cylinder referred to as AO, 20138, which is no more than 1¾ inches high; and the seals of Bogazkoy or of Aläjä Hüyük. The same technical perfection is also found in ceramics, where the more luxurious utensils are extraordinarily elegant.

Around 1200 B.C., Anatolia, like the whole of western Asia, was submerged beneath the attacks of the "Sea Peoples" and the empire of the Hattusils, Mursils, Tudhalias, and Suppiluliummas was swept away. However, the Hittite civilization was to survive for some time in the small states that reappeared on the periphery—at Malatya, Maras, Carchemish, Senjirli, Sakce Gözü—and also in cities whose political pretensions were either less ambitious, as in the case of Kara Tepe, or non-existent, as in Taïnat. A revival took place in these centers, and the Neo-Hittite period (12th–8th centuries B.C.) was to continue until the Assyrians had completed their conquest.

The artistic production of these new centers is considerable. The finest example of Neo-Hittite architecture is Samal (Senjirli), at the foot of the Amanus. The city was strictly circular in shape and surrounded by a double wall. It was dominated at its center by a citadel or acropolis, in which were concentrated the temples and palaces. The buildings were of unbaked brick on stone foundations: the bottom of the façades was set off with carved stones known as orthostates (war scenes, banquets, soldiers, deities); the bases of the columns consisted of two sphinxes or two lions side by side, with a cushion on their back to support the shaft. The same ornamentation was found at Mal

118.

119.

120.

118. **Antoine-Jean Gros.** *Napoleon on the Battlefield at Eylau.* Detail. 1808. Louvre, Paris.

119. **Benozzo Gozzoli.** *Dance of Salome.* 1461–62. Samuel H. Kress Coll., National Gallery of Art, Washington, D.C.

120. **El Greco.** *View of Toledo.* 1608. Metropolitan Museum of Art, New York.

121. **Juan Gris.** *Breakfast.* 1914. Museum of Modern Art, New York.

122. **Matthias Grünewald.** *Crucifixion.* From the Isenheim Altarpiece. *c.* 1512–15. Unterlinden Museum, Colmar.

121.

122.

123.

124.

125.

126.

127.

123. **Armand Guillaumin.** *Melting Snow in the Valley of the Creuse.* 1898. Oscar Ghez Modern Art Foundation, Geneva.

124. **Francesco Guardi.** *Feast of the Ascension in St. Mark's Square, Venice. c.* 1770. Gulbenkian Foundation, Lisbon.

125. **Frans Hals.** *Banquet of the Officers of the Company of St. George. c.* 1627. Frans Halsmuseum, Haarlem.

126. **Hans Hartung.** *Watercolor.* 1922. Private Coll.

127. **Meindert Hobbema.** *The Avenue, Middelharnis.* 1689. National Gallery, London.

atya, where incidents in stag or lion hunting were represented, as well as ritual scenes. At Carchemish there are also more complex compositions, such as the one commemorating the presentation by King Arara of the princely heir Kamana in the presence of the entire royal family—the queen and eight children, the youngest of whom is being held in its mother's arms. From Maras have come several steles, one of which is secular in inspiration, depicting a man holding scales and a woman holding on her knee a child whose left hand is gripping a rope tied to the feet of a falcon. Lastly, one must mention the guardian lions with their gaping, grimacing jaws, placed at the gates of Sakce Gözü and Taïnat; they are perhaps the finest of their kind. Although less fully represented, freestanding sculpture is also of great quality: the divine statue at Carchemish, whose base is composed of two lions linked by a genie having the head of a bird of prey; the armed god at Samal; and the colossal statue of a king at Malatya.

In the field of rupestrian reliefs, mention should be made of the sculpture of Ivriz (17 feet high), in which King Warpalawa advances toward the god of vegetation, who is holding thorns in one hand and heavy bunches of grapes in the other (8th century B.C.). Also dating from the 8th century B.C. are the monuments of Kara Tepe, on the foothills of the Taurus mountains in southern Turkey, which were discovered in 1947–49.

There is no doubt that Hittite art spread beyond the frontiers of the state, but in so doing it came into conflict with Aramaean power, and therefore with its art. This artistic confrontation is apparent at Aleppo, Alalakh, and Til Barsip (modern Tell Ahmar). From the latter site comes the stele of the storm-god Teshub (Paris, Louvre), a work of the early first millennium B.C.

Hittite Art. *Hunting scene.* Malatya, 9th century B.C. Archaeological Museum, Ankara. *Photo Walter Dräyer, Zurich.*

HOBBEMA, Meindert (1638, Amsterdam—1709, Amsterdam), Dutch painter. With Jacob van Ruisdael, his teacher and later his rival, Hobbema is the most celebrated Dutch 17th-century painter of landscapes. Of his life we know only that he signed his first picture at the age of twenty; married a serving maid in 1668 and had three children; and, after 1669, held the position of municipal inspector of weights and measures. Hobbema's numerous works, well represented in European public collections, depict scenes in the eastern Gelderland. His masterpiece, *The Avenue, Middelharnis* (1689; London, National Gallery), painted in beautiful tones of brown, gray, red ocher, and muted blue, is a characteristically Dutch invitation to escapism. But Hobbema was more often a painter of friendly landscapes and limited horizons, with a thatched cottage, a red roof, or a mill as welcoming shelters. He particularly liked rivers in wooded country and was the painter of watermills. With incisive draftsmanship he analyzed forms and noted the details of foliage. A lover of picturesque effects, he placed the foreground in shadow, used clumps of oak trees as a screen, girded groves and cottages with semicircular paths, and projected his lighting on a mill, a pond, or the bend of a stream in the center of the composition. His special qualities—which may be appreciated in the *Sunny Landscape* (Rotterdam, Museum Boymans-van Beuningen); the *Ruins of Brederode Castle* (1671; London, National Gallery); and especially in the *Watermill* (Paris, Louvre)—are a sure technique, more secure than that of Ruisdael; clarity of form; agreeable color; subtle lighting; and the charm of transparent or gently clouded skies.

HODLER, Ferdinand (1853, Gürzelen, Bern—1918, Geneva), Swiss painter. Hodler was one of the most important figures in modern Swiss painting. At seventeen, he left the Bernese Oberland for Geneva, where he lived in great poverty, trying to earn a little money by painting portraits, scenic views, and butchers' shop signs. But before long he met his benefactor, Barthélemy Menn (1815–93), who was a friend of Corot, an admirer of Ingres, and a teacher at the Geneva School of Fine Arts. He gave Hodler methodical instruction in painting, and taught him the rules governing the application of geometry to art. These principles had a profound effect on his work, which was based on clarity of proportions, parallelism, symmetry, and rhythm.

His first works were inspired by Corot, but he soon freed himself from this influence. Hodler was of a mystical turn of mind, obsessed with his search for the ideal. This tendency found expression in a series of monumental mural compositions in a Symbolist manner: the famous trilogy *Weary of Life, Disappointed Souls*, and *Eurythmy* (1891–95; Bern, Kunstmuseum); the *Retreat from Melegnano* (1896–1900; Zurich, Landesmuseum); *Day* (1900; Bern, Kunstmuseum); *William Tell*, the *Emotions*, and others. He also painted a series of very moving portraits and a great many landscapes of the Bernese Oberland and the Geneva region that possess great beauty, strength, and grandeur. This aspect of his work has perhaps suffered an unmerited neglect at the hands of critics, some of whom would like to include his Symbolist compositions under a German Expressionist label, while others see in them a more Latin spirit. In fact, Hodler's work is clearly dominated by "Latin clarity," and he is closer to the poetic approach of Puvis de Chavannes than to Germanic mythology and symbolism. Lastly, one should insist on Hodler's gifts as a draftsman, which link him to his great compatriots Urs Graf (*c.*

Ferdinand Hodler. *Day.* 1900. Kunstmuseum, Bern.

1485–1527/8) and Niklaus Manuel Deutsch.

HOFER, Karl (1878, Karlsruhe—1955, Berlin), German painter. During a prolonged stay in Rome (1903–8) he discovered the work of Hans von Marées, and was strongly influenced by its Classical idealism. The second lasting influence on his art was Cézanne, which began with his stay in Paris (1908–13). In 1913 Hofer settled in Berlin, where he achieved considerable success; in 1928 a large exhibition marked his fiftieth birthday. At the end of World War II he was appointed director of the Hochschule für Bildende Künste in Berlin. Hofer's painting is Expressionist in style, but it is more restrained and poetic than that of the Brücke painters: see, for example, his *Black Rooms* (first version 1928; second version 1943). His figures appear lost in the world of people and things, and express a strong feeling of isolation and pessimism. Hofer wrote several theoretical works, including *Wege der Kunst* ("The Ways of Art") in 1947 and an autobiography in 1952, *Aus Leben und Kunst* ("Life and Art").

HOFFMANN, Josef (1870, Pirnitz, Moravia—1956, Vienna), Austrian architect. Hoffmann was a pupil and follower of Otto Wagner, and in 1897 was one of the founding members of the Vienna Secession, a group of artists who continued the Art Nouveau style in Austria. In 1899 he began to teach at the Kunstgewerbeschule, and in 1903, with Koloman Moser (1868–1918), he founded the Wiener Werkstätte, a group of workshops devoted to the development of crafts that acquired an international reputation. Hoffmann's style was established in 1901 with his design for four villas on the Hohe Warte, with their cubic volumes and their contrast of black and white, and, in 1902, with his design for a hall in the Secession palace to provide a setting for Max Klinger's Beethoven monument. The convalescent home at Purkersdorf, outside Vienna (1903), a rational and sober building 20 years ahead of its time, firmly established his reputation as an architect. Hoffmann then designed a house in Brussels for the financier Adolphe Stoclet. The Stoclet House (1905–11) was his masterpiece: with its copper roof, its marble walls with ridges cased in chased bronze, and its silver interior decoration, it anticipated the advent of the International Style. After World War I he was principally occupied with the problem of inexpensive housing; in Vienna, where he was chief architect, he designed a series of working-class houses (1924–25).

HOFMANN, Hans (1880, Weissenburg, Bavaria—1966, New York), American painter. He received most of his training in Paris (1904–14), where he visited the studios of the Fauvist painters and was a close friend of Robert Delaunay. In 1915 he opened an art school in Munich. When he emigrated to the United States in 1932, he founded another school (1933–58). His influence on the younger generation, particularly on Clyfford Still and Jackson Pollock, was considerable; he also played an important part in the birth of Abstract Expressionism in New York. For Hofmann, a picture was a dynamic organism of colored planes whose secret life was based entirely on a complex of attractions and repulsions. He was a skillful exponent of gestural painting, but he placed no less importance on color, which he manipulated with inimitable boldness and vigor (*The Gate*, 1959; New York, Guggenheim Museum). The importance of his painting gained recognition (Venice Biennale, 1960) only after a long eclipse by his work as a teacher.

HOGARTH, William (1697, London—1764, London), English painter and engraver. Hogarth's position in English art is unique: he broke the domination of English taste by Continental painters. He began as an apprentice to Ellis Gamble (active 1712–18), an engraver of arms on silver plate. In 1720 he started his own engraving business. He is known to have enrolled as a student at the academy of John Vanderbank (1689–1727) in St. Martin's Lane, and later to have had private tutoring at Thornhill's house in Covent Garden. In 1729 he married Thornhill's daughter Jane, and the task of winning round his father-in-law, who disapproved of the match, may have determined him to succeed in the sphere of painting. His first efforts in this medium were portraits and conversation pieces which he endowed with tremendous animation (the *Wedding of Stephen Beckingham and Mary Cox*, 1729; New York, Metropolitan Museum). Orders poured in, a reconciliation with his father-in-law was effected, followed by a commission to paint the royal family in 1730 or 1731. Nevertheless, although a successful portraitist, Hogarth turned to moral subjects, and emphasized that in pictures of this sort he intended to proceed as a dramatist: certainly his sharp characterization and his ability to control narrative show an innate sense of theatricality. So great is the fame of Hogarth's "morality plays" that it is perhaps surprising to realize that he painted no more than three series of this type: the *Harlot's Progress*, engraved in 1732, of which the original paintings disappeared in a fire at Fonthill in 1755; the *Rake's Progress*, 1733, comprising eight paintings now in the Soane Museum, London; and the six scenes of *Marriage à la Mode* (1742–46) today in London's National Gallery.

William Hogarth. *Calais Gate.* 1748. Tate Gallery, London.

In 1734 Thornhill died and Hogarth inherited his academy, which he turned into one of the most important English art schools prior to the founding of the Royal Academy in 1768. In 1735 he decorated the staircase of St. Bartholomew's Hospital, London, with two huge religious compositions in the Classical European tradition. They failed to bring the artist commissions for history paintings, and in his disappointment Hogarth returned to portraiture, which he gradually freed from the stiffness of Sir Godfrey Kneller's tradition. Undoubtedly his finest portrait is that of his friend *Captain Thomas Coram* (1740; London, Foundling Hospital), in which Hogarth achieves a rare combination of European dignity and English directness.

In 1748 Hogarth paid a visit to France but was turned back at Calais, where he was seen sketching the fortifications and was thought to be a spy. He commemorated this event by painting *Calais Gate* (1748; London, Tate Gallery), in which the wicked, starving look of the French is compared unfavorably with the jovial rotundity of the English.

In 1749 Hogarth acquired a villa at Chiswick and retired there to work on his book of theory, *The Analysis of Beauty*. Published in 1753, it consisted of a long argument on the arbitrary premise that the essence of beauty lay in the serpentine line. Ironically enough, the book was well received on the Continent but made little impression in England. Yet his fame remained constant, and his originality was quickly recognized in France. In England he was eclipsed by the more spectacular success of Sir Joshua Reynolds; only historians were to understand how Hogarth, by ridiculing contemporary connoisseurship and the cult of the old masters, had purified English taste.

HOLABIRD, William (1854, Amenia Union, New York—1923, Evanston, Illinois) *and* **ROCHE,** Martin (1855, Cleveland, Ohio—1927, Chicago, Illinois), American architects. Holabird, after two years at West Point (1873–75), moved to Chicago, where he joined the engineer William Le Baron Jenney in 1875. Roche, with only a public school education, had entered Jenney's office in 1872. After a brief partnership (1881–83) with Ossian C. Simonds (1855–1931), a landscape gardener, the two architects formed the firm of Holabird and Roche.

The 13-story Tacoma Building (1888–89) by Holabird and Roche contained all the structural metals then in use—cast iron (columns), wrought iron (girders), and Bessemer steel (beams). It was the first building to utilize rapid and efficient rivet construction. The projecting bay window, used again in the Monadnock Building addition (1893), allowed more light and air to penetrate interior office space, but its bulging shape still obscured the simple box skeleton behind it. Under the influence of Sullivan, whose refined façade appeared side by side with two of their own buildings in the Gage group (1898–99), Holabird and Roche designed thinner, flatter, more expressive structures after 1900, especially in the Republic Building (1905–9) and the Brooks Building (1909–10).

After Holabird died, his son John Augur (1886–1945) maintained the office until Roche's death, when a new partnership was formed with John Wellborn Root, Jr. (1887–1963).

Hans Holbein the Elder. *Crossbowman.* Detail from the St. Sebastian altarpiece. 1516. Alte Pinakothek, Munich.

HOLBEIN THE ELDER, Hans (between 1460 and 1470, Augsburg—1524, Isenheim), German painter. Were it not for his illustrious son, Holbein the Elder would occupy a more honorable and less privileged place in German painting. Like Hans Burgkmair, whose senior he was and with whom he had much in common, Holbein executed competent but somewhat uninspired altarpieces that show his deep knowledge of Flemish painting. About 1500 or 1501, he painted, with the help of assistants, an altarpiece on the Passion of Christ (Frankfurt, Städelsches Kunstinstitut, and other collections) for the Dominicans of Frankfurt. In 1502, together with Burgkmair, he was among a number of artists commissioned by the nuns of the convent of St. Catherine to paint a group of pictures featuring the seven Roman basilicas. Holbein's contribution, representing St. Paul's Outside the Walls (*c.* 1504; Munich, Bayerische Staatsgemäldesammlungen), shows great ease of manner, while the altarpiece for the Dominicans seems rather violent and harsh. The panels for the Kaisheim altarpiece, depicting scenes from the life of Christ and the Virgin (1502; Munich, Alte Pinakothek), seem to have been painted after another visit to the Netherlands. In his last period, Holbein made considerable use of Italian decorative motifs. A number of these motifs are found in the Augsburg altarpiece of St. Sebastian (1516; Alte Pinakothek), particularly in the framing of the splendid figures of St. Elizabeth and St. Barbara on the wings. He used the same motifs again in the *Fountain of Life* (1519; Lisbon, Museu Nacional).

Hans Holbein the Younger. *Portrait of the Artist's Wife and Two Elder Children.* 1528/29. Kunstmuseum, Basel.

Holbein left a few portraits and a large number of silverpoint drawings. One of these (1511; Berlin, Kupferstichkabinett) represents his two sons, Ambrosius and Hans. Ambrosius (1494–*c.* 1519) was a member of the Basel painters' guild in 1518. His works are difficult to distinguish from those of his father and brother. However, two of his portraits of children (Basel, Kunstmuseum) are worthy of mention.

HOLBEIN THE YOUNGER, Hans (1497, Augsburg—1543, London), German painter. His beginnings are rather obscure. From 1515 he was in Basel, where his success seems to have been very rapid. A minor work, a schoolmaster's signboard in the Basel Kunstmuseum, dates from 1516; but a more important work of this period was a commission from the humanist Oswald Myconius to sketch illustrations (1515–16) for a copy of Erasmus' *In Praise of Folly*. In this way Holbein came into contact with the printer Johannes Froben, who overwhelmed him with commissions for frontispieces and illustrations for his books. In 1516

Holbein also painted the double portraits of the banker and burgomaster *Jakob Meyer* and his wife *Dorothea Kannengiesser* (Kunstmuseum). In 1517 he was in Lucerne, where he decorated the façade of the Hertenstein house (fragment of the fresco in the Lucerne Museum). In 1519 he joined the Basel painters' guild, probably in succession to Ambrosius, of whom all subsequent trace has been lost; and in 1520 he became a burgher through his marriage to the widow of the tanner Ulrich Schmidt. Holbein certainly did not lack commissions. The delightful, aristocratic portrait of *Bonifacius Amerbach* (1519; Kunstmuseum) is another distinguished work of this period. Through Jakob Meyer, he was commissioned to decorate the council chamber in the Basel Town Hall (1521–30; 11 fragments preserved in the Kunstmuseum).

The year 1523 was notable for Holbein's creation of the two profile portraits of *Erasmus*, one in the Kunstmuseum and the other in the Louvre, Paris. From this period also date religious paintings that admittedly contribute little to Holbein's reputation. Among these are the Oberried Altarpiece (*c.* 1520; inner sides of shutters in the university chapel of the cathedral at Freiburg im Breisgau) and the *Passion of Christ*, painted on four panels, possibly the fragments of an altarpiece (*c.* 1520; Kunstmuseum). In 1526 Holbein painted a portrait inscribed "Lais Corinthiaca" (Kunstmuseum), a picture of a courtesan counting her gold: the sitter is actually Magdalena Offenburg. Her outstretched hand is a copy of Christ's left hand in Leonardo da Vinci's *Last Supper*. It is a luminous painting, more colorful than his later manner. About the same time, Holbein painted another portrait of Magdalena, as Venus with Cupid at her side (Kunstmuseum). As a contrast to these portraits of a lady of doubtful morals, he painted the so-called *Darmstadt Madonna* (1528–30; Darmstadt, Grand-Ducal Castle), which depicts the Basel burgomaster Jakob Meyer and his family kneeling at the foot of the Virgin and Child. By the simplicity of the poses and its rich color, it is perhaps the finest work of Holbein's first period.

Holbein must have realized how precarious his own position might be in the midst of the religious controversies of the day. He asked Erasmus to recommend him to Sir Thomas More, Lord Chancellor to the king of England. It seems that Holbein was well received in the circle of Erasmus' friends, Archbishop Warham and Bishop John Fisher. Unfortunately, only the original sketch (Kunstmuseum) and various oil copies have survived of the admirable group of Thomas More and his family, begun in 1527. Holbein's draftsmanship gained in breadth in the portraits of *Sir Henry Guildford* (1527; Windsor Castle, Royal Collection) and the astronomer *Nicolas Kratzer* (1528; Louvre). Nevertheless, this first stay in England was not a long one; in 1528 he returned to Basel, and it was there that he painted a grave, admirable portrait of his family (1528/29; Kunstmuseum).

The situation at Basel was far from improved: the destruction of images by the Reformers was becoming more widespread than ever. Holbein set off once more, and, after a brief stay in Antwerp, arrived in London in 1532. Success did not come at once, for his former protectors were either disgraced or in prison. But he found generous patrons among the German merchants of the London Steelyard (the wool staple and the Hanseatic League). Apart from their own portraits, they commissioned two large compositions for their banqueting hall. Court patronage soon followed. Holbein then produced one of his most famous works, the *Ambassadors*, the double portrait of the French envoys Jean de Dinteville and Georges de Selve (1533; London, National Gallery), a superb display of the painter's craft in which the two men stand out against a subdued green background. There followed a number of portraits of Henry VIII, with the face of a suspicious sensualist, dressed in sumptuous brocade garments; one of the best versions is that in the Galleria Nazionale in Rome. Holbein became the king's favorite painter and was commissioned to paint the portraits of three of his wives, Jane Seymour, Anne of Cleves, and Catherine Howard. His portraits of courtiers can only be described as perfect. The subject is rendered with such intensity, with such control over detail, that the presence of the person himself could hardly be more striking (*Robert Cheseman of Dormanswell*, 1533; The Hague, Mauritshuis).

HOLLAND, Henry (1745, London—1806, London), English architect. His father was a builder who founded a prosperous construction firm in Fulham and also did a certain amount of designing. Henry, his eldest son, gained his architectural experience by working in the family business, carrying out the designs of such architects as Robert Adam and Lancelot ("Capability") Brown (1715–83), and later designing alterations and additions of his own. In 1771 he became Brown's assistant, and in 1773 married his elder daughter. Holland's first considerable undertaking was the layout of Hans Town, Chelsea, on 89 acres that he leased from Lord Cadogan in 1771. The few remaining houses are of the simple two- and three-story design, typical of much contemporary town building. Holland's Neoclassicism is distinguished by its refinement and the influence of contemporary French architecture, which was favored by members of the Whig circles, his chief patrons. His first important commission for them, Brooks's Club, London (1776–78), in a restrained Palladian style, led to his employment by the Prince of Wales for the rebuilding of Carlton House, London (1783–85; demolished in 1827–28). Holland tempered the grandeur of current styles with a more intimate strain of his own: he broke up the imposing length of the libraries in his major reconstructions at Althorp (1787–89) and Woburn Abbey, Woburn, Bedfordshire (1787–88), with rows of columns; and in the charming *chinoiserie* of the Woburn dairy he showed how successful he could be in small-scale work. The elegant French decoration in his country mansions and in the design of Drury Lane Theatre, London (1791–94), is characteristic of his work.

HÖLZEL, Adolf (1853, Olomouc, Czechoslovakia—1934, Stuttgart), German painter. Hölzel's historical importance depends not only on his work, but also on his theoretical writings and his teaching (his students included Oskar Schlemmer and Willi Baumeister). Between 1888 and 1906 he was the most outstanding artist of the Dachau group and directed the school of painting in Dachau. Hölzel was especially interested in color harmonies. With the other painters of the Dachau group, he abstracted flat, ornamental designs from the moorlands and, as early as 1906, he was experimenting with forming these into a self-contained picture. His writings were as influential as his teaching in propagating his ideas on color. The first article, published in 1904 for the review *Die Kunst für Alle* ("Art for All"), was entitled "Means of Artistic Expression and Their Relations with Nature and the Work of Art." In 1906 Hölzel succeeded Leopold Graf Kalckreuth as professor at the Stuttgart Academy. His main works are the stained-glass windows of the Stuttgart Town Hall and the Bahlsen factory in Hanover.

HOMER, Winslow (1836, Boston, Massachusetts—1901, Prouts Neck, Maine), American naturalist painter, lithographer, engraver, and watercolorist. From 1857 to 1875 he did illustrations for the periodicals *Ballou's Pictorial* and *Harper's Weekly*. In 1862 *Harper's* assigned him to cover the Civil War, and his first important oil painting, *Prisoners from the Front* (1866; New York, Metropolitan Museum), dates from this time. He visited France in 1866 and in 1867, and it was during his second stay there that he began to paint scenes of country life and to do portraits of country children, which became his favorite theme after he returned to the United States; his *Long Branch, New Jersey* (1869; Boston, Museum of Fine Arts) is a characteristic early work depicting rural life in America. In the 1880s, Homer's style changed: he began to do large-scale works, and turned to dramatic scenes of the sea, which he treated heroically and which he painted with great power (*Eight Bells*, 1886; Andover, Mass., Phillips Academy, Addison Art Gallery of American Art). In 1881 and 1882 he lived in England, at Tynemouth, Northumberland, on the North Sea, where he did drawings and watercolors upon which he later based many etchings and oils of rescues at sea. In 1883 he settled permanently in Prouts Neck, on the Maine coast, and produced a series of paintings of fishermen on the Grand Banks, off Newfoundland. The following year, in Nassau, he began doing watercolors of the West Indies (*Rum Cay*, 1898–99; Worcester, Mass., Art Museum). Thereafter he traveled and painted in the Adirondacks, Maine, Canada, and, almost every winter after 1898, in the West Indies or Florida. During this second phase of his artistic activity, he transformed man's struggle against the forces of nature into a pure symbol of natural violence (*Coast in Winter*, 1892, Worcester Art Museum; *Gulf Stream*, 1899, New York, Metropolitan Museum).

HONTHORST, Gerrit *or* Gerard van (1590, Utrecht—1656, Utrecht), Dutch painter and engraver. A pupil of Abraham Bloemaert, he became a follower of Caravaggio while in Rome (1619–21), where he specialized in nocturnal scenes and candlelight effects, thus earning the Italian nickname of Gherardo delle Notti. His *Adoration of the Shepherds* (1621; Florence, Uffizi) shows the Caravaggesque style—combined, however, with the native Dutch influence of Geertgen tot Sint Jans. After returning to Utrecht and becoming a Master in 1622, Honthorst began to use lighter colors and, not without echoes of Jan van Hemessen, to make a name for himself by painting variations on the themes of concerts, taverns, gypsies, and other everyday genre scenes with half-length figures (the *Merry Violinist*, 1623, Amsterdam, Rijksmuseum; the *Concert*, *c.* 1619–21, Rome, Borghese Gallery; the *Dentist*, 1622, Paris, Louvre).

Honthorst was also court painter at The Hague between 1637 and 1652. He produced paintings for the palace at Rijswick and some 15 extremely detailed portraits of the princes of Orange. That of *Prince Frederick Henry and Amalia von Solins* (*c.* 1648; The Hague, Mauritshuis) is a large double state portrait, with the prince in armor, wearing a blue sash, and the princess in a lace-trimmed black dress standing before red draperies with a view of a besieged town in the background. The portrait of their children, *William III and Mary of Nassau* (*c.* 1648; The Hague), has the freshness of a rustic scene.

Gerrit van Honthorst. *A Concert. c.* 1619–21. Borghese Gallery, Rome. *Photo Anderson-Giraudon.*

HOOCH, Pieter de (1629, Rotterdam—1683, Amsterdam), Dutch painter. A pupil of Claes Pietersz. Berchem, he worked at Delft, Leiden, and The Hague before finally settling in Amsterdam. Prior to the vast enthusiasm engendered for Vermeer by 20th-century art critics, De Hooch was considered the finest of the Dutch genre painters. He attached greater importance to interiors, to anecdotal themes, and to the linking of figures with their surroundings than did Vermeer, although both artists created the same atmosphere of bourgeois orderliness, cleanliness, silence, and calm. His palette, warmer than that of Vermeer, brilliantly interpreted the falling of sunlight on the warm, yellow, rough cast of walls or on the intense red of rooftops and brick floors. His least attractive works, painted after 1665—when he began attempting to rival Vermeer—depict fashionable gatherings and conversation groups set in wealthy interiors. De Hooch's best period (1656–65) is represented by a series of Dutch interiors (*Card Players*, 1658; London, Buckingham Palace) and courtyards (*Courtyard of a House*, 1658; London, National Gallery). His pictures are usually organized around a door that opens to reveal another room, which opens onto yet another, or onto a courtyard, gardens, or a passage seen vertically on the canvas and carrying the eye through to another house altogether.

HOOD, Raymond Mathewson (1881, Pawtucket, Rhode Island—1934, Stamford, Connecticut), American architect. Hood worked for the firm of Cram, Goodhue, and Ferguson in Boston before setting up his own practice in New York, which he maintained until 1927. He already had the American Radiator Building, a New York skyscraper (finished 1924), to his credit, when he made a name for himself by winning first prize in a competition organized by the Chicago Tribune for new offices. His Neo-Gothic Chicago Tribune Building (1923–25) was created at a time when Chicago, the fief of the

Edward Hopper. *Sunday at dawn.* 1930. Whitney Museum, New York.

Functionalist school, was developing a taste for pastiches of old styles, and it won high praise. In 1929 Hood drew up proposals for a series of bridges into Manhattan lined with blocklike apartment houses, although he still appeared as an ardent Neo-Gothicist in his Masonic Temple and Scottish Rite Cathedral, Scranton, Pennsylvania, of the same year. In the works immediately following, however—the Beaux-Arts Apartments (1930), the News Building (1930), and particularly the well-known McGraw-Hill Building (1930–31; with J. André Fouilhoux, 1879–1945), all in New York—he showed himself already in complete control of a cleaner-lined, more severe approach.

HOPPER, Edward (1882, Nyack, New York—1967, New York), American painter. In New York, where he lived for most of his life, he was a student (1900–5) of the painter Robert Henri, leader of The Eight group of urban realists. The lonely mood of the city became one of Hopper's favorite themes, as in *Early Sunday Morning* (1930; New York, Whitney Museum) and *Approaching a City* (1946; Washington, D.C., Phillips Gallery). His canvases often depict one or more nearly deserted buildings whose geometric character is emphasized by means of a harshly revealing light. Everyday scenes, radically simplified and devoid of nonessentials, thus become almost unearthly or surreal in aspect. Although Hopper's stress on solidly composed forms has sometimes been thought to ally him with the exponents of abstraction, his fundamental realism and interest in emotionally charged lighting effects relate him more closely to the 19th-century American landscape tradition.

Victor Horta. Hôtel Solvay, Brussels. 1895–1900. *Photo P. d'Otreppe, Brussels.*

HORTA, Victor (1861, Ghent—1947, Brussels), Belgian architect. He was one of the leading founders of Art Nouveau, and his work foreshadowed the development of modern architecture. His original decorative style started a craze that swept Europe. His development falls into two distinct periods. The first began with his Hôtel Tossel (1893) in Brussels, in which his principles are clearly apparent: modification of the traditional ground plan; replacement of the corridor flanked by uniform rows of rooms by an octagonal hall leading into rooms at various levels; the use of exposed iron as a structural material; and the primacy of the curved line. This flying "whiplash line" was used lavishly and with great originality by Horta in his ornamentation, which was inspired by vegetal motifs. However, it concealed nothing of the basic structure: on the contrary, overlaid with these sinuous curves, the bulbs of a chandelier, the hinges of a door, or the metal framework of a winter garden were incorporated into the total decorative effect. Horta's "whiplash style" reached its height in the Hôtel Solvay (1895–1900) in Brussels, for which he designed the furniture, the lighting, and the carpets with as much care as he gave to the proportions of the building as a whole. His ornamental lyricism became more restrained in the important Maison du Peuple (1896–99) and the Innovation store (1901), both in Brussels. His second period was marked by a far less flamboyant style, in which he used curves primarily structurally, subdued his ornamentation, and completely abandoned exposed iron. After Horta's visit to the United States (1916–19) and his appointment as director of the Brussels Académie des Beaux-Arts (1927–31), he undertook a reform of the teaching of architecture. But in the works of his maturity—the Palais des Beaux-Arts (designed 1914; built 1922–28), and the Gare Centrale (1938–45), both in Brussels—he remained faithful to the spirit of craftsmanship in building techniques advocated by Art Nouveau.

HOUDON, Jean-Antoine (1741, Versailles—1828, Paris), the most famous French sculptor of the 18th century. He began to carve at the age of nine, and in 1758 became a pupil of René-Michel Slodtz (1705–64). He won the Prix de Rome in 1761, and subsequently spent four of the most fecund years of his career in Italy (1764–68). There he studied anatomy as well as antique art, showing great enthusiasm for the discoveries at Portici and for the masterpieces of the Renaissance. He incorporated his morphological studies in his famous *Écorché* ("anatomical model"), 1767, originally a study for a statue of St. John the Baptist. This work brought immediate fame to its youthful author. While in Rome, he also showed his talent in a *St. Bruno* (1767) for the church of S. Maria degli Angeli, which was admired by Pope Clement XIV.

In 1773 Houdon was called to work for the duke of Saxe-Gotha, undoubtedly on the recommendation of Diderot, of whom he had exhibited a bust at the 1771 Salon (Paris, Louvre) and through whose influence he later received commissions from Catherine the Great. For the duke's gardens at Gotha, he carved his famous marble *Diana* (1780), a theme he had already handled in bronze in 1776 (Tours, Museum). For the residence of M. de Saint-Waast, he executed *Winter* (1783) and *Summer* (1785), an exquisite pair of figures now in the Musée Fabre, Montpellier.

According to Houdon, a sculptor's first duty was to preserve the truth of forms; in fact, he sometimes made moldings. Among the finest of his busts are those of the *Marquis de Méjanes* (Aix-en-Provence, Bibliothèque) and *Mirabeau* (1791; Louvre). Houdon's subtlety is most apparent in his female busts, notably those of the *Comtesse de Sabran* (1785; Berlin) and *Sophie Arnould*

Jean-Antoine Houdon. *Voltaire with Antique Drapery*. 1781. Comédie-Française, Paris. *Photo René-Jacques, Paris.*

as Iphigenia (1775). Also outstanding are his busts of intellectuals and artists, especially those of *Voltaire* (1778) and *Jean-Jacques Rousseau* (1779). His bust of Rousseau has the piercing little eyes of a hallucinated man: Houdon reconstituted the face from a death mask. As for Voltaire, the philosopher posed for the sculptor in Paris on the very eve of his death. Thus Houdon was able to give animation to the famous seated statue at the Comédie-Française (1781), which shows the sarcastic old man leaning forward to make one last quip. On the recommendation of his friend Benjamin Franklin, of whom he made a bust (1779; Louvre), Houdon was commissioned by the state of Virginia to execute a statue of *George Washington* in 1785.

HOWE, George (1886, Worcester, Massachusetts—1955, Philadelphia), American architect and educator. Howe was associated with various partners during his career: with Walter Mellor (1880–1940) and Arthur I. Meigs (1882–1956) from 1916 to 1928; with William Lescaze from 1929 to 1934; in 1935 with Norman Bel Geddes (1898–1958); with Louis I. Kahn from 1941 to 1942; then with Kahn and Oskar Stonorov (1905–1970) from 1942 to 1943; and with Robert M. Brown (b. 1908) from 1946 to 1955. During World War II Howe served as supervising architect for the Public Building Administration (1942–45). He later became chairman of the architecture department at Yale University (1950–54).

The light wooden frame and the concrete cantilevered construction of Fortune Rock, the Clare F. Thomas house (1939; near Somesville, Maine) marked a definite departure from Howe's heavy masonry residences with Mellor and Meigs, such as his own home, High Hollow (1914; Chestnut Hill, Pennsylvania). The multistoried Philadelphia Saving Fund Society Building (1930–32) stands as a synthesis of Lescaze's International Style formalism and Howe's Beaux-Arts rationalism.

Other notable works by Howe included Square Shadows, a cubistic residence for William S. Wasserman in Whitemarsh, Pennsylvania (1930); war housing with Kahn and Stonorov at Carver Court (1944; near Coatesville, Pennsylvania); the WCAU Radio and Television Station in Philadelphia (1952); and the Philadelphia Evening Bulletin Publishing Plant (1955), both with Brown.

HUASTEC ART. The Huastecs lived in the great coastal plain of the Gulf of Mexico, on a territory approximately covering the present-day Mexican states of Tamaulipas, San Luis Potosí (the eastern part), and Veracruz. They do not appear to have been much affected by the material and cultural developments that had taken place in the high Mexican plateau, and therefore almost every aspect of their civilization possesses archaic characteristics. From an ethnic and linguistic point of view, the Huastecs belong to the Maya family, from whom they had probably separated around 1000 B.C. Thereafter they evolved independently and preserved their own character, up to the arrival of the Spaniards in 1521.

The architecture of the Huastecs is related to the building of the pre-Classical age, as demonstrated by the pyramids of Tantoc in San Luis Potosí, which are even taller than those of the Toltecs at Teotihuacán, in central Mexico. One special characteristic is that the infrastructures of the Huastec temples and the bases of their altars follow a circular or even a "D" shape, which would relate them to the Aztec cult of Quetzalcoatl as the Wind God.

Huastec Art. *Old Man Carrying a Child.* Musée de l'Homme, Paris. *Photo Sougez, Paris.*

A common kind of Huastec sculpture was the stone stele, on which mythological scenes were inscribed in bas-relief in a restrained style (*Stele of Xolotl*, 11th–13th century A.D.; Mexico City, Museo Nacional de Antropología). The Huastecs' freestanding statues are two-dimensional, the volumes only slightly formed. The statues found at Pánuco in central Mexico are examples of this kind of work. But the greatest piece of Huastec art is perhaps the stone statue found at Tamuín in northern Mexico, representing a standing youth bearing a child on his back (after A.D. 1000; Mexico City, Museo Nacional de Antropología). This is an image of Quetzalcoatl as the Evening Star, with his son, the Setting Sun.

Frescoes have also been discovered at Tamuín that represent a whole series of deities wearing elaborate plumed costumes, al-

Huastec Art. *Stele of Xolotl.* 11th–13th century. Museo Nacional de Antropología, Mexico City.

Arthur Hughes. *April Love.* Tate Gallery, London.

though the figures are placed so close to each other that it is difficult to distinguish individual costumes. The general effect is of a rigid mosaic.

Ceramics underwent a constant, though irregular, development, from the three-footed goblets and bowls of the pre-Classical period to the later pieces, decorated with incised plant designs or geometric motifs. The post-Classical vases are distinguished by their elaborate baroque forms and their bold black decorations on a white ground.

HUDSON RIVER SCHOOL, group of mid-19th century American landscape painters, whose principal members were Asher B. Durand, Worthington Whittredge, John F. Kensett, Sanford Gifford, Thomas Doughty, and John W. Casilear (1811–93). They had an almost pantheistic love of nature, and their work consisted of representations of the Catskill Mountains of New York, the White Mountains of New Hampshire, as well as scenes of the Hudson River region. Following the lead of Thomas Cole, perhaps the first great American landscape painter, but working in a less Romantic and literary style, the Hudson River artists depicted in a highly realistic and at times even intimate manner the American wilderness, encouraged in their work by the current vogue for landscape paintings as parlor decorations. The second generation of the Hudson River School—including Albert Bierstadt, who painted panoramic and too often bombastic views of the American West, Frederick Church, who found his picturesque sites in Latin America and the Near East as well as in the Hudson River Valley, and Thomas Moran—contained some of the most impressive landscape painters of the entire group.

HUGHES, Arthur (1830, London—1915, Kew Green), English painter and book illustrator. His first exhibited painting, *Musidora* (shown at the Royal Academy in 1849; now Birmingham, City Art Gallery), was a traditional academic work. In 1850, however, Hughes read *The Germ*, the short-lived journal of Pre-Raphaelite art; he was converted to the new movement, and adopted the clear, bright colors and careful attention to detail that the Pre-Raphaelites advocated. To these he contributed his own delicate, yet intense, poetry. His best paintings are confined usually to one or two figures in a woodland or garden setting (*April Love*, 1856, London, Tate Gallery; the *Long Engagement*, 1853–59, Birmingham, City Art Gallery). Although never officially recognized in the 19th century as a major painter, Hughes at his best was the equal of the Pre-Raphaelites. Nevertheless, he had, by the late 1850s, withdrawn from the artistic life of London, and his powers declined in the 1860s. In his work as a book illustrator, however, Hughes was able to sustain his imaginative force rather longer, as evidenced by the set of drawings he made for Christina Rossetti's book of children's poems, *Sing Song* (1872).

HUGO, Victor (1802, Besançon, Doubs—1885, Paris), French poet and novelist, also a painter and draftsman. Hugo developed a personal style in the course of his first journeys (1839, 1840) through the Rhineland. The sketches he brought back from these trips revealed an architectural vision that at first conformed to the tenets of Romanticism (medieval ruins of small towns and moonlight). Soon, however, his vivid imagination transformed this early vision into a powerful and personal artistic conception. Some of his compositions are slightly overworked (*Burg with the Cross*, 1850; Paris, Musée Victor-Hugo), and his freer work, such as *Landscape with Three Trees* (1850; Musée Victor-Hugo), is often more appealing to modern tastes. Among Hugo's most successful works are his elaborate seascapes of the Channel Islands, Jersey and Guernsey; the travel sketches he executed "on the spot"; his post-exile landscapes, which reveal a perfect technical mastery and indicate that he was more concerned with the evocation of atmosphere than with the creation of gloomy effects; his series of caricatures for an album called *Théâtre de la Gaieté* (*c.* 1869); and a series of drawings called the *Witch's Trial* (*c.* 1874). Hugo also designed furniture to suit his own taste, and sometimes even built it with his own hands out of parts of older pieces. His experiments in interior decorating included various types of wall decorations, such as tiles, that he

Victor Hugo. *Castle on the Rhine.* Musée Victor-Hugo, Paris. *Photo Roger-Viollet, Paris.*

made and painted himself. He produced many sculptures that were praised by the French writers Théophile Gautier and Charles Baudelaire and that were sometimes, although not always justifiably, claimed by the Surrealists. He also designed the sets for several theatrical productions, and frequently produced illustrations for his own writings.

HUNDERTWASSER, Fritz Stowasser, *called* Fritz (b. 1928, Vienna), Austrian painter. Despite a brief period at the Vienna Academy of Fine Arts, Hundertwasser may be regarded as self-taught. The boldness and freshness of his color and the almost obsessional repetition of certain checkerboard and spiral forms make him a kind of "naive abstract" painter. But he also shows an awareness of the work of Egon Schiele and, more particularly, Gustav Klimt—the Viennese masters of the Jugendstil. After journeys to Italy and Morocco, Hundertwasser settled in Paris, where he developed his theory of "transautomatism," by which is meant a mode of creation that, through the different levels of the unconscious, succeeds in expressing, in continuous succession, images that are entirely freed from appearances. He began with totemic figures tinged with a certain humor, then went on to produce a series of cellular structures, followed by a circular configuration that soon became very characteristic of his manner.

HUNT, Richard Morris (1827, Brattleboro, Vermont—1895, Newport, Rhode Island), American architect. After early education in the United States, Hunt accompanied his family to Paris in 1843. In 1844 he spent a brief period in the atelier of the architect Samuel Darier (1808–84) in Geneva, then in 1845 entered Hector-Martin Lefuel's studio in Paris, and in 1846 was admitted to the École des Beaux-Arts. In 1855 Hunt returned to the United States and began work on drawings for the Capitol building, Washington, D.C., under Thomas Ustick Walter. But by 1857 he had moved to New York, where in 1858 he opened an atelier of his own and established a permanent practice. Among his major works were the Stuyvesant Apartments (1869), the Tribune Building (1873), the Tenth Street Studio (1856), and the main entrance section of the Metropolitan Museum (built 1900–1902), all in New York; the National Observatory in Washington, D.C.; the Fogg Museum at Harvard University, Cambridge, Massachusetts; the Divinity School at Yale University, New Haven, Connecticut; and the Theological Seminary and Memorial Chapel at Princeton University, New Jersey. Hunt also designed numerous houses, including the Marshall Field house (1879) and the Borden house (1884), both in Chicago; the Vanderbilt house (1880) and the Astor house (1893) in New York; as well as a great country house in the Italian manner for Cornelius Vanderbilt ("The Breakers"; 1892–95) at Newport, Rhode Island, and another for George W. Vanderbilt ("Biltmore"; 1890) at Asheville, North Carolina.

HUNT, William Holman (1827, London—1910, London), English painter of religious and literary subjects, and member of the Pre-Raphaelite Brotherhood. In 1843 he began to attend lectures at the Royal Academy Schools, where he met Sir John Everett Millais, who became a close friend, and who joined Hunt and Dante Gabriel Rossetti in 1848 in founding the Pre-Raphaelite Brotherhood. Hunt's laborious, highly linear, and minutely detailed style, combined with his unswerving moral aim, made him the key figure in the movement. Although the Brotherhood was extinct by 1852, Hunt continued to paint Pre-Raphaelite pictures for the rest of his life.

In 1849 he went to France and Belgium, where he discovered a natural affinity with the work of the Flemish primitives, whose methods he emulated in *Two Gentlemen of Verona* (1851; Birmingham, City Museum and Art Gallery). In 1854 and again in 1892 Hunt visited Egypt and Palestine, where he painted his two great religious works: the *Finding of Christ in the Temple* (1854; Birmingham, City Museum and Art Gallery) and the *Scapegoat* (1854; Port Sunlight, Cheshire, Lady Lever Art Gallery). The latter is—along with the *Light of the World* (1854; Oxford, Keble College)—the most famous of Hunt's religious paintings, all of which are characterized by an infinitely detailed symbolism.

William Morris Hunt. *The Bathers*. 1877. Worcester Art Museum, Worcester, Massachusetts.

HUNT, William Morris (1824, Brattleboro, Vermont—1879, Isle of Shoals, Scotland), American painter. At first Hunt intended to be a sculptor and worked with Henry Kirke Brown (1814–86) in Rome. He then entered the Düsseldorf Academy, where he studied painting briefly before returning to Paris. In France he painted under Thomas Couture for five years (1847–52), during which period he was also influenced by the Barbizon School and became a close friend and disciple of Jean-François Millet.

Hunt returned to America in 1855, and in 1862 settled in Boston, where he established himself as a teacher of the newest Parisian method of painting. His teaching and his position as a patron of the arts had great importance for such painters as John La Farge and Childe Hassam. The *Bathers* (1877; Worcester, Mass., Museum of Art), in which a nude male figure balances on his fellow bather's shoulders like a pillar of light amid the dark shady recesses of a pool, reflects the coloristic softening and tonal moderation of Hunt's Düsseldorf training, tempered by Millet, while it also demonstrates his interest in capturing the effect of a suspended moment. An undated (probably late) painting, *American Falls* (Washington, D.C., Corcoran Gallery), is almost Impressionistic in its handling of a rapidly brushed, roughly impasted surface of pastel hues penetrated by a luminous rainbow arc.

HURRITE ART. The Hurrites appeared in the middle of the 3rd millennium B.C. and occupied a region between the Upper Tigris and the Upper Euphrates, between the Hittite territories and Assyria. They were non-Semitic in race and Asian in language, and they founded a state—the kingdom of Mitanni—whose history is extremely difficult to reconstruct. The Mitannians exploited the rivalries between the great powers and at first became the allies of the Pharaohs against the Hittites. They continued to play the role of arbiters until they were wedged in by the Hittites and the Assyrians, and were condemned to disappearance as an influential political faction (14th century B.C.).

One of the oldest and most beautiful pieces of Hurrite art is a small bronze lion (late 3rd millennium B.C.; Paris, Louvre), holding in its front paws a bronze plaque placed on a white limestone tablet. An inscription on the tablet bears the name of Tisari, king of Urkish. This votive piece is both graceful and realistic, but most other works are less well preserved and more naive in inspiration. There is, for example, the terracotta support found at Tell Chuera: the decoration, which is on three levels, depicts (somewhat confusedly) lion-headed eagles, with outspread wings and surrounded by rosettes; various four-legged animals; and a "master of the animals."

Hurrite Art. *Lion with foundation tablet.* End of 3rd millennium. Louvre, Paris. *Archives photographiques, Paris.*

Hurrite Art. *Goddess with long braids.* Tell Halaf. Early 1st millennium B.C. Destroyed in 1943. Cast in the Museum, Aleppo.

From the evidence of the monuments at Tell Halaf (which are neither Hittite nor Aramaean) we assume that the influence of Hurrite art lasted for a long time. One of these buildings (*c.* 11th century B.C.)—which was the work of King Kapara—contained an extremely strange collection of sculptural figures, their divine faces reflecting a world of terror and mystery. But the finest piece of all is the large female statue found walled up in a mass of unbaked brick masonry: a fascinating and provocative deity whose face, with its frozen smile, is flanked by two long braids that hang down to her breasts (beginning of the 1st millennium B.C.; cast in Aleppo, Museum). Naturally, its style is very close to that of certain ivories discovered at Nimrud (early 1st millennium B.C.), but which were certainly not executed in the Assyrian capital. The theory that these ivories were of Hurrite origin, or at least a product of Hurrite tradition, is well worth consideration. Similarly, Hurrite deities have been found carved in the rocks of Yasilikaya, in Hittite territory.

HUYS, Pieter (1520, Antwerp—1584, Antwerp), Flemish painter and engraver. Brother of the engraver Frans Huys (1522–62) and son of a landscapist, Huys became a Master at Antwerp in 1545. He began as an engraver of Bosch's work while in the studio of Hieronymus Cock. Later he worked for the printer and publisher Christophe Plantin in Antwerp, engraving the plates for the *Royal Bible* of 1566. He lived at Tournai after 1581. Huys—a witty and anecdotal minor master—expresses the diverse curiosities of an age when Boschian fantasy, satire, and Italianate decoration were in fashion. His paintings are still confused with those of Jan Mandijn (1502–60) or Jan Sanders van Hemessen. The only authenticated paintings bearing his signature are the *Battle of Angels and Demons and Torments of Hell* (1570; Madrid, Prado), and two versions of the *Temptation of St. Anthony* (1547, Paris, Louvre; and 1577, Antwerp, Museum Mayer van den Bergh).

HUYSMANS, family of Flemish painters of the 17th and 18th centuries.

JACOB (1663, Antwerp—1696, London) was an able portraitist at the court of King Charles II in England, where he settled shortly after 1660, and where he became known as Jacob Houseman. Among his portraits is one of *Izaak Walton* (1691; London, National Portrait Gallery).

JAN BAPTIST (1654, Antwerp—1716, Antwerp) worked primarily in Mechlin as a landscapist (*Ruins of a Corinthian Temple*, 1695, Munich, Alte Pinakothek; *Landscape with Cattle and Two Herdsmen*, 1697, Brussels, Musées Royaux des Beaux-Arts).

CORNELIS (1643, Antwerp—1727, Mechlin), the brother of Jan Baptist, specialized in Italianate landscapes of Brabant and the forest of Soignes (*Washerwomen and Cows at a Watering Place*, Nantes, Museum; *Edge of the Forest*, Paris, Louvre). The best-known member of the Huysmans family, he borrowed motifs from the landscapes of Jacques d'Arthois (1613–88) and Titian, giving them a romantic touch. His paintings are well composed, with masses illumined against hazy blue distances, precise details, and tiny animated figures.

HYRE, Laurent de la. *See* **LA HYRE,** Laurent de.

I

IBBETSON, Julius Caesar (1759, Farnley Moor, Leeds—1817, Masham, Yorkshire), English painter, primarily of landscapes. In the late 1770s, Ibbetson fled to London, where he earned a precarious living by making copies and forgeries of 17th-century Dutch landscapes and of works by Thomas Gainsborough and Richard Wilson. His own style was influenced by what he was called upon to copy (*Landscape with a Disabled Soldier*, 1784; England, Priv. Coll.), but this in no way inhibited his progress. Having made his debut at the Royal Academy in 1785, he was appointed (in 1787) official draftsman to the first British Mission to the Imperial Court of Pekin.

Back from the Far East he worked in Liverpool, Scotland, and in the Lake District of northwest England. In 1805 he settled at Masham in Yorkshire. Although his subject matter was sometimes Romantic (*Phaeton in a Storm*, 1798; Leeds, City Art Gallery), Ibbetson's style retained its 18th-century character. His small, full-length portraits in a rustic setting evoke the style of the young Gainsborough. Apart from conventional oil paintings, he also produced book illustrations (for the 4th edition of *Modern Times, or the Adventures of Gabriel Outcast*, 1789, written anonymously) and even interior decoration (for the Music Room at Kenwood House, Hampstead, *c.* 1795–96).

IMPRESSIONISM, artistic movement that flourished in France from the 1860s through the 1880s. From April 15 to May 15, 1874, a group of young independent painters—including Paul Cézanne, Edgar Degas, Armand Guillaumin, Claude Monet, Berthe Morisot, Camille Pissarro, Pierre Auguste Renoir, and Alfred Sisley—constituted themselves the "Société Anonyme" and exhibited outside the official Parisian Salon in the studio of the photographer Nadar on the Boulevard des Capucines, Paris. The exhibition caused an uproar, and the journalist Louis Leroy, writing in the April 25th issue of the satirical magazine *Le Charivari*, jeeringly called the exhibitors "impressionists," after a canvas by Monet called *Impression—Sunrise* (1872; Paris, Musée Marmottan). This name, which was accepted by the painters themselves, soon became popular and was universally adopted.

The Impressionist painters were all born between 1830 and 1841. These young innovators, who came from different environments, met in Paris around 1860. They soon left the confines of their respective Parisian art schools for the nearby forests of Fontainebleau. From there they went to the Seine estuary and the Channel beaches, where the light-filled atmosphere and water-saturated air inspired Monet to evolve a style of painting that became more and more fluid, ethereal, and highly colored. Pissarro and Sisley remained close to Jean-Baptiste Corot's style. Cézanne and Degas had no part in this pre-Impressionist phase. Manet, because of the modernity of his subject matter and his *succès de scandale* in 1863 at the Salon des Refusés, became the standard-bearer of the young school that met at the Café Guerbois in Paris. In 1869 Monet and Renoir painted together at Bougival, a small village on the Seine. Each did several versions of the picturesque wharf of the Grenouillère. In their endeavor to convey the dynamism and joy of this spectacle, which constantly stimulated them, they spontaneously discovered what ultimately became the technical principles of Impressionism: the division of tone and the use of shimmering spots of color. Although the Impressionists' style had not yet attained unity—it did not become a truly conscious one until 1873—the freshness of these first Impressionist canvases was never surpassed.

The Franco-Prussian War of 1870 dispersed the Impressionist group just when their artistic experiments were taking shape. Manet, Renoir, Degas, and Bazille (who was killed in battle) were called up and went to war; Monet, Pissarro, and Sisley took refuge in London, where Charles-François Daubigny introduced them to Paul Durand-Ruel, the art dealer who was to become their chief defender. Their discovery of J. M. W. Turner and John Constable hastened their technical evolution. In 1872 Monet at Argenteuil (near Paris) and Pissarro at Pontoise (Seine-et-Oise) began painting the new type of open-air landscapes. Monet worked on a grandiose, universal scale and his paintings, which were dominated by the spell of water and by the phantasms of light, attracted Renoir, Sisley, and Manet; Pissarro's work, which was bucolic and earthy, placed greater stress on structural values and influenced Cézanne and Guillaumin. With the conversion of Manet, Cézanne, and, to a limited extent, Degas to light-colored painting in 1873, the Impressionist style spread and became more generally understood. The painters of the group now systematically lightened their palettes and actually used colors to create shadows. The Impressionists made light the dominant principle of their art: they exalted it and made it vibrate, simultaneously abandoning contour, modeling, chiaroscuro, and overprecise detailing. The overall composition retained the vigor of a sketch and created an incomplete, schematic impression that shocked their contemporaries. In 1874,

Julius Caesar Ibbetson. *A Phaeton in a Storm.* 1798. City Art Gallery, Leeds.

Impressionism. Edgar Degas. *Cotton Exchange in New Orleans.* 1873. Musée des Beaux-Arts, Pau. *Photo Giraudon, Paris.*

Impressionism. Paul Cézanne. *"Le Nègre Scipion."* 1866–68. Museu de Arte Moderna, São Paulo. *Photo Giraudon, Paris.*

Impressionism. Pierre Auguste Renoir. *Portrait of Paul Durand-Ruel.* 1910. Private Coll.

with the exception of Manet, who remained faithful to the official Salon, the whole group faced the public under a barrage of insults and taunts. Seven joint Impressionist exhibitions followed, at intervals, until 1886. On the occasion of the third group exhibition (1877), at Renoir's suggestion, the critic Georges Rivière published a small periodical called *The Impressionist*, in which he commented intelligently and warmly on his friends' artistic efforts, emphasizing their conquest of pictorial autonomy. In 1878 the writer and art critic Théodore Duret published *Les Peintres Impressionnistes* ("Manet and the French Impressionists," 1912); this work, together with the writer Louis Duranty's *La Nouvelle Peinture* ("The New Painting," 1876), was the first study of the movement as a whole. The defection of Monet, Renoir, and Sisley in 1880, at the time of the group's fifth exhibition, revealed a profound crisis, both personal and aesthetic. After a heroic decade, precisely when Impressionism was about to win recognition for itself it ceased to exist as a spontaneous ideal. Each of the original Impressionist painters reached artistic maturity and went his own way; each, however, remained faithful to the common beliefs that had drawn them together in the first place: the principles of truth to nature and freedom of technique.

At the time of Manet's death in 1883, a new generation of artists (Georges Seurat, Vincent van Gogh, Paul Gauguin, Henri de Toulouse-Lautrec) had matured. These new painters were influenced by Impressionism but reacted against it; their appearance coincided with the complete break-up of the initial group. By the mid-1880s, geographical dispersion was accompanied by a divergence in their aesthetic principles. Renoir and Cézanne, carried along by their genius, fulfilled themselves without faltering, in a continuous upward surge. Monet, Sisley, and Pissarro, however, the three landscapists most closely linked to Impressionism, experienced many vicissitudes and produced uneasy and uneven work, sometimes merely decorative. After 1895 Pissarro regained an astonishing creative vigor, and his last masterpieces, characterized by their cosmic spirit, vibrating light, and their communication of a direct emotional response to nature, were—like those of Monet, Renoir, and Cézanne—in the widest sense derived from Impressionism.

The Impressionist painter depended on his intuition alone and could only rely on his sincerity. Each of his paintings was an act of creation that was not the result of technical mastery and, as such, each canvas was a new beginning, a reinvention of painting. From the perspective of the mid-20th century, the Impressionist experiment appeared to have fitted naturally into the pictorial tradition that developed from the Renaissance and to have pursued with increasing faithfulness the optical expression of reality. Under the dominant influence of Gustave Courbet, Impressionism developed in a more or less realistic tradition and was intensified to the point where it was overthrown only to be replaced by the departure from reality characteristic of modern painting.

INCA ART. The Incas are the best known of all the ancient peoples who inhabited Peru. Like the Aztecs of Mexico, they were comparatively late arrivals: no traces of their culture predate 1200 A.D. By the time of the Spanish Conquest (1532), however, they had subdued the peoples of Peru, Bolivia, and the equatorial regions, and extended their dominions as far as the deserts of Chile. The Incas had no system of writing, so some of their history is known to us through the tales and traditions recounted by the Inca *harawek*, or official narrators, and transcribed by Spanish chroniclers. The first eight kings of Inca tradition were at least partly legendary, particularly Manco Capac, founder of the dynasty (around 1200 A.D.), who was a kind of demigod, and was transformed into a statue at the end of his life. Their career of conquest began under their ninth ruler, Pachacuti Inca Yupanqui (reigned 1438–71), when they overran the state of Tiahuanaco in 1445, and continued under Pachacuti's son, Tupac Inca Yupanqui (reigned 1471–93). They extended their sway with amazing rapidity, but in 1532 they were themselves overcome by the Spaniards, and their last monarch, Atahualpa, was put to death by Pizarro.

The Inca empire was a strange mixture of theocracy and primitive communism, producing the most powerful class of civil servants and government officials that the New World had ever known. The pyramid of society was headed by the emperor—or Inca—himself, who was regarded as a descendant of the sun and as a most sacred personage. His senior officials and army officers were drawn exclusively from the ranks of the Inca race, and the lesser posts were allocated on an ever-widening basis. Land and most agricultural produce was the property of the state, which was responsible for sharing it among the people; one part went to the ruler and his family, another to the nobles and priests, and the last to the workers. As each citizen was obliged to do a certain amount of work for the state, in lieu of tax, important public works were undertaken throughout the country. In this way, a network of excellent roads was built, with a postal system maintained by relays of runners. Perhaps the most astonishing aspect of this civilization was that such a strict control of the population and its activities could be maintained without a written language. The sole method of calculating and keeping records was by using knotted strings or *quipu*, which were deposited in a central archive at Cuzco.

Inca civilization was a stone and bronze one, and maize was its staple crop. Houses were conglomerate structures rather like modern single-story barracks, with one room to a family. The Incas were among the greatest architects of pre-Columbian America: the aqueducts, canals for irrigation, suspension bridges, enormous terraces for cultivation, fortresses, and palaces are the work of remarkably well-trained and organized technicians.

There were several building styles, characterized by the use of stones of different sizes. These included the cyclopean stone blocks, each weighing several tons, used in the walls of fortresses and cities, as well as for temples and palaces (the fortress at Sacsahuamán with its system of concentric walls is one of the most imposing ruins of Cuzco); small polygonal blocks, often irregular in shape, which were combined with larger blocks the size of paving stones, all so carefully hewn and placed together—without mortar—that, five centuries later, the thinnest knife blade cannot be inserted between them; and lastly, the large rectangular blocks with convex outer surfaces, like cushions, that can also be seen at Cuzco. The architectural layout of this capital city was unique, as it was the Inca practice to erect a new palace for each successive ruler. The cities of the high plateaus, such as Machu Picchu, 50 miles north of Cuzco, perched like eagles' nests on the mountaintops, are more remarkable for their romantic location than for architectural worth. By contrast, the layout of the lowland city of Ollantaytambo, in the Urubamba River valley, is obviously the result of a rigid and symmetrical advance design that called for a central plaza surrounded by rectilinear streets. Although Inca buildings harmonize perfectly with the landscape, the architecture is severely utilitarian. There seems to have been almost no sculptural ornamentation, and the walls were decorated mainly with tapestries.

There was very little statuary in the accepted sense of the term, although there are remains showing relief decoration on utensils and tiny stone offertory vessels in the shape of llamas. It is easy enough to account for this lack from the writings left to us by the Conquistadores, who remarked on the profusion of gold leaf, beaten or engraved with ritual figures and scenes that covered the walls of important rooms. The Spaniards also reported the existence of gardens filled with gold and silver models of trees, plants, and birds. Unfortunately, most of the marvelous gold and silver wares were melted down into ingots to fill the Spanish kings' treasure chests. All that now remains of this former splendor are a few vases, some precious ornaments, and small models of men and llamas found in tombs.

As in other Peruvian civilizations, the essence of Inca art is found in its ceramics and textiles. There were five standard forms for vases and vessels, of which the most typical was an "aryballoid" shape, with a conical base and slender neck. Pots were made in several sizes and seem to have been used for a variety of purposes. Among other wares, dishes with birds' heads, cups, and goblets are particularly noteworthy. Decoration was confined to a few simple geometrical themes (crosses, lozenges, angular scrolls) combined with stylized fern patterns, pleasant enough but limited and lacking in vitality.

Inca Art. Silver figurine. Peru. Musée de l'Homme, Paris. *Photo Sougez, Paris.*

INDIAN ART. More than that of any other region of Asia, the art of India has from its beginnings been dedicated to religious ends. Throughout millennia, Indian artists were anonymous craftsmen

Inca Art. Ruins of the city-fortress of Machu Picchu, Peru. *Photo Serraillier-Rapho, Paris.*

Indian Art (Indus Civilization). Limestone head. Mohenjo-Daro, late 3rd–early 2nd millennium B.C. Central Asian Antiquities Museum, New Delhi. *Photo Louis Frédéric-Rapho, Paris.*

serving the faiths of Hinduism, Buddhism, and Jainism. Their procedure in architecture, painting, and sculpture was always traditional; following fixed laws of craftsmanship, they created objects for worship and for the revelation of the unseen supernatural world. The goal of the plastic arts was neither realism nor physical beauty: it was the abstract perfection of the form, with its bland, masklike face and smooth, tubular limbs, that was calculated to inspire devotion.

Elements of natural scenery, when they do appear in painting or sculpture, are usually simply backdrops for the activity of the human or divine figures. Animals receive a more sympathetic treatment, however. Since early times, they had been thought of as embodiments of natural forces; some had even come to symbolize the four cardinal directions. Their associations with the earlier lives of the Buddha, who considered them, as sentient beings, worthy of his compassion, led to a far more naturalistic depiction. But, as in all Asian art, the artists were more concerned with life and movement than with a faithful description of a particular specimen.

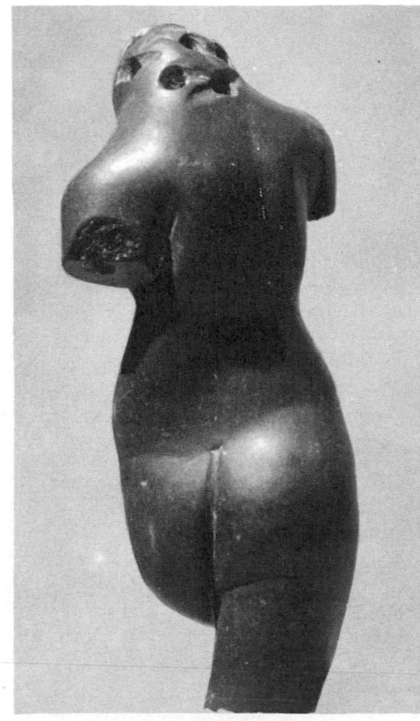

Indian Art (Indus Civilization). *Dancing god of Harappa.* 2400–2000 B.C. National Museum of India, New Delhi. *Photo Larkin Bros. Ltd., London.*

Buddhism produced an art that was often descriptive, sometimes even realistic, but always serene, as if detached from the passions of the world. With the triumph of Hinduism after the Gupta Period, a new vigor and dynamism appeared, and the iconography was modified. Hindu art affirmed the cosmic grandeur of the deity; colossal scale and epic compositions full of dramatic action were outstanding characteristics. After the "medieval" period, this dynamism spread to popular iconography, which ultimately took on a romantic, even sentimental coloring, with its attachment to the cult of Krishna and his loves.

Indian art has always been concerned with the absolute, and striven to suggest another world beyond that of forms. Certain symbolical devices of Indian art, such as the multiplicity of heads and arms in representations of divinities, must be accepted as parts of a sacred visual language of didactic intent.

INDUS VALLEY PERIOD
(*c.* 2500 B.C.–*c.* 1500 B.C.)

From approximately the middle of the third millennium B.C. until at least 1500 B.C., western India was the site of a great prehistoric civilization known as the Harappa Culture or the Indus Valley Period. The centers of this civilization extended from the mouth of the Indus northward to the Punjab. The principal cities were Mohenjo-Daro, about 250 miles from the mouth of the Indus, and Harappa on the banks of the Ravi.

Architecture

The great urban centers of this period were probably only extensions of the small village cultures of Baluchistan that existed contemporaneously with Mohenjo-Daro and Harappa, and survived their fall. Both cities were built on many levels, probably as a result of periodic destructions by floods. At each site, an acropolis or citadel contained the temples and public buildings; below these artificial

Indian Art. Steatite seal: rhinoceros. Mohenjo-Daro, 3rd millennium B.C. National Museum of India, New Delhi. *Photo Walter Dräyer, Zurich.*

mounds, the city proper was laid out in a plan of broad intersecting avenues dividing the quarters into regular blocks. Kiln-fired bricks of uniform size were employed in all of the Indus cities. The houses, sometimes of two or more stories, were invariably built around a central courtyard. Since the windows of the houses opened onto these courts, the street façades presented a monotonous expanse of blank walls. Little architectural decoration was employed. The principal architectural monument at Mohenjo-Daro was a great public bath, suggesting the tanks of modern Hindu temples, and, like them, undoubtedly used for ritual ablutions. A vast granary was the most impressive public building at Harappa. Perhaps the most advanced feature of the public architecture of the Indus cities was the elaborate system of drains and sewers, more efficient than any such municipal sanitary arrangement before the Romans.

Sculpture

Excavations carried out at the Indus cities have revealed a handful of statuettes and a great number of intaglio seals or talismans, but no evidence of monumental sculpture. A few limestone heads found at Mohenjo-Daro might seem to reflect the hieratic canons of Mesopotamia; but a more interesting group of figurines from Mohenjo-Daro and Harappa anticipates the canons of Indian art of the historical periods. One such work, a fragmentary dancing figure from Harappa (New Delhi, National Museum of India), is of extraordinary interest from the aesthetic and iconographical point of view. The statuette originally had three heads, and was apparently ithyphallic. The torso is twisted in a violent *contrapposto*, and one leg is raised as though in the performance of a dance. Carved between 2400 and 2000 B.C., this figure foreshadows the dynamic conception of the Dancing Siva of later Hindu art.

The carvers of the Indus civilization were masters of conceptual naturalism in their portrayal of animals. Their extraordinary skill may be studied in the representation of such beasts as the elephant, the rhinoceros, and the urus ox on the steatite seals that were the special emblems of the merchants of Mohenjo-Daro and Harappa.

MAURYA DYNASTY
(322 B.C.–185 B.C.)

The art of the millennium after the collapse of the Indus civilization around 1500 B.C. has been totally lost, owing to the use of perishable materials, but in terms of religious and historical development, the Maurya Period is of great interest. Its literary monuments include the *Vedas*, the hymns of the Aryan conquerors, and the great Hindu philosophic texts, the *Brahmanas* and the *Upanishads*. The 6th century B.C. witnessed the appearance of the historical Buddha and his foundation of one of the great Oriental religious systems. Jainism also came into being in this century. An event of great importance for later Indian history was the invasion of Alexander the Great in the late 4th century B.C. His establishment of Greek satrapies in Iran and Bactria in northern Afghanistan introduced Hellenistic culture to the Eastern world.

Not long after Alexander's withdrawal, the powerful Maurya Dynasty came into power in India under Chandragupta (322? B.C.–298 B.C.), who forced Alexander's successors to withdraw beyond the Hindu Kush Mountains, and ruled an India united from the Kabul River almost to the southern tip of the peninsula. Maurya art, like the political and social structure of the Maurya Empire, was closely related to that of India's western neighbors, Iran and the Hellenistic empires of the Near East. The greatest Maurya emperor was Asoka (reigned 272–232 B.C.).

Sculpture

A considerable number of surviving monuments testify to Asoka's support of Buddhism. Asoka is remembered, too, for his edicts enjoining the people to follow the Buddhist doctrine. Sometimes these proclamations were engraved on the face of cliffs, but more often on towering stone pillars erected at sites connected with the Buddha's earthly mission. One of these columns or lats stood in the Deer Park at Sarnath, where Sakyamuni had first expounded his doctrine of the Eightfold Path to salvation. The principal remnant, a finely carved sandstone capital (Sarnath Museum), shows official Maurya art to have been a combination of foreign forms and Indian iconography. Four animals are represented on the plinth of the capital—the lion, bull, elephant, and horse—alternating with four rayed discs. Above are four lions back to back; they once supported an enormous wheel as an emblem of the Buddha's law or dharma.

Indian Art (Maurya Period). Lion capital from the Pillar of Asoka. Deer Park at Sarnath, mid-3rd century B.C. Sarnath Museum. *Photo Louis Frédéric-Rapho, Paris.*

An indigenous popular taste rather than the official imperial style is seen in a group of colossal statues of yakshas, male nature spirits of wealth and fecundity, found at Patna and elsewhere. These over life-size images were invariably carved of the same sandstone used for the Asokan capitals, but their stylistic character is completely Indian. A typical example in the Indian Museum at Calcutta presents a gigantic form dressed in the Indian skirt or dhoti, with serpentine bracelets on his powerful arms.

Architecture

The architecture typical of the Maurya Period marked the resumption of a tradition of monumental building in permanent materials. Important architectural remains from the 4th to the 2nd century B.C. have been found at Patna. There are obvious borrowings from Achaemenid Iran, in the plan and elevation of this imperial site, where refugee craftsmen may have worked. The complex was surrounded by a towered wall with gateways, constructed of massive teak logs encasing a packed core of earth. One palace structure of great interest, apparently an audience hall, was highly similar in plan to the apadanas of Darius and Xerxes at Persepolis, with row upon row of columns supporting a flat roof.

The Buddhist emperor Asoka is credited with the foundation of innumerable stupas, but none has come down to us in its original state. His dedications also include a number of rock-cut cells for the use of hermits of the heretical ajivika sect in the Barabar Hills of Bengal. One of these, the Lomas Rishi cave, has a carved façade unmistakably based on freestanding models. This monument presents striking correspondences with wooden architecture: the tympanum is divided into two blind courses, one decorated with reliefs, the other with a carved trellis reproducing the wooden latticework of freestanding structures; in the interior, the beams and rafters of a wooden framework are suggested by stone projections from the vaults. This miniature example of carved architecture is a significant anticipation of the Buddhist sanctuaries of the Early Classic Period.

EARLY CLASSIC PERIOD:
ŚUNGA (185 B.C.–72 B.C.) AND
EARLY ANDHRA (*c.* 32 B.C.–*c.* A.D. 50)
DYNASTIES

With the collapse of the Maurya Empire in the early part of the 2nd century B.C., India was once more divided into a number of separate kingdoms, all of which promoted a basically Indian art. This division lasted until the advent of the Guptas in the 4th century A.D. The Śungas ruled the Ganges Valley and parts of central and western

Indian Art (Maurya Period). Large figure of yakshi. Patna, *c.* 200 B.C. Indian Museum, Calcutta.

India. Somewhat later, the house of the Andhras founded an empire extending across the waist of India from Bombay to Madras. Buddhism remained the dominant religion.

Architecture

The principal architectural remains from the Śunga and Andhra periods are the relic mounds or stupas and the cave temples or chaityas. The stupa was the most original creation of Buddhist architecture. Its usual form, perhaps based on earlier royal burial mounds, was that of a hemispherical tumulus set on one or more circular or square basement stories. Typical are the reliquaries of solid masonry from Sanchi in Bhopal State, dating from the 2nd century B.C. to the 1st century A.D. The largest of these, usually called the Great Stupa, was begun by Emperor Asoka and enlarged in the 2nd and 1st centuries B.C.

The stupa had a cosmological symbolism: the base represented the earth; and the hemispheric dome, the vault of the sky. The mast stood for the invisible axis of the world, the central pivot around which the cosmic universe was organized; the umbrellas were symbols of the various heavens and of the divinities governing the firmament. The Buddha, present in his earthly relics, thus appeared as the Master of the world. At Sanchi the sculptural decoration is concentrated on the uprights and crossbars of the portals. The relief carvings represent episodes from the career of the Buddha and from his earlier incarnations.

Rock Sanctuaries. The most spectacular examples of architecture of the Early Classic Period are the rockcut chaitya halls of western India. These cave temples exist in considerable numbers in the flanks of cliffs of the Western Ghats to the north and south of Bombay—at Bhaja, Karli, Nasik, and Kanheri (near Borivli). A few of the earlier sanctuaries at the famous site of Ajanta in the Deccan belong to this early type of architecture as well. The chaityas are, of course, not structural architecture but imitations of freestanding buildings, carved into the rocky core of lonely hillsides. As may be seen in certain unfinished cave temples at Ajanta, the grottoes were hollowed out by tunneling into the rock at the top of the façade, gradually removing material to shape the vault of the roof, and then working downward and leaving as freestanding masses of stone the columns and other accessories of the interior. A typical early example of the chaitya hall is the cave at Bhaja, which may be dated in the early 2nd century B.C. Its façade is an enlargement of a type already seen in the Lomas Rishi cave.

The largest and most impressive of all the grotto temples is the chaitya at Karli, not far from Bhaja. Construction may have begun as early as 80 B.C., the date of an inscription at the site; but the monument was not dedicated until about A.D. 120, and is therefore the latest in the series. The entrance was originally adorned with a pair of carved pillars repeating the form of the Maurya columns at Sarnath (one column remains in place). A perforated stone screen, cut from the living rock, gives entrance to a narthex. The rear wall of this vestibule is carved with reliefs dating from the Kushan and Gupta periods.

Indian Art (Śunga Dynasty). *Jataka of the Deer*. Medallion from the balustrade, stupa at Bharhut. Early 1st century B.C. Indian Museum, Calcutta. *Photo Louis Frédéric-Rapho, Paris.*

The interior of the Karli chaitya is of great magnificence. The plan presents the usual tripartite division into nave and side aisles. The pillars are far more complicated than the shafts at Bhaja: each column rests on a lota or water jar, and the shaft is fluted into 16 facets. Above is a campaniform capital topped by an inverted stepped pyramid supporting groups of riders on elephants and horses. These figural groups, carved in high relief along the nave, suggest a triforium frieze. Attached to the stone vault are wooden ribs simulating the construction of the temple's freestanding prototypes in perishable materials. The massive stupa in the apse is ornamented with a wooden umbrella surviving from the time of dedication; the columns in the ambulatory behind this object of devotion are of the same simple octagonal type as the earlier columns at Bhaja.

Sculpture

The earliest known surviving example of Indian architectural sculpture is the carving of the railing of the stupa of Bharhut (near Satna), where one of the gateways has also been reconstructed. The carving may be

Indian Art (Śunga Dynasty). Great Stupa at Sanchi. 2nd century B.C.
Right: north gateway, or toran (1st century B.C.). *Photo Louis Frédéric-Rapho, Paris.*

dated to the Śunga Period (late 2nd and early 1st century B.C.). The ornamentation consists mainly of images of devatas (godlings) and yakshas, medallions with Buddhist legends, portrait busts of donors, and floral motifs. The archaic quality of the work is particularly apparent in the linear drapery, whose seams and borders recall the kore of the Acropolis in Athens.

The most striking figures of Early Classic sculpture are the yakshis or tree goddesses that were placed in the angles between the uprights and crossbars of each of the gates at Sanchi. A wonderful example is a yakshi from Sanchi (Boston, Museum of Fine Arts), originally shown suspended from the branches of a flowering mango tree.

The relief sculpture of the gateways of the Great Stupa at Sanchi displays many of the stylistic traits that will mark Indian carving for the next millennium. Contrasting with the archaic formalism of the Bharhut panels, the densely crowded scenes from the *Jatakas* (stories of previous incarnations of the Buddha) at Sanchi are cut in such depth that the forms in the foreground appear to swim against a dark well of shadow. The figures have a sensuous litheness and a swelling fullness that repeat, on a smaller scale, the canon of the famous yakshi at this site. All the participants, whether animal or human, are filled with a pulsating vitality.

Indian Art (Śunga Dynasty). Torso of yakshi. Sanchi, 1st century B.C. Museum of Fine Arts, Boston.

KUSHAN PERIOD:

GANDHARA ART (*c.* A.D. 50–500)

In the middle years of the 1st century A.D., the territories today included in modern Afghanistan and northwest Pakistan were conquered by an Indo-Scythian horde, the Kushans, whose distant homeland had been in Kansu in northwest China. The Kushans established their rule as far east as the Bengal Valley and westward into Sind. Their principal dynasty endured until the disastrous invasion by the Sassanian king of Iran, Shapur II, in A.D. 241. During the period of their greatest power in the first centuries of our era, the Kushans were in close diplomatic and commercial contact with the Roman Empire, accounting for the extraordinary Classical character of their art, called Gandhara from the ancient name of the heart of their empire. Under the rule of the Kushans, Buddhism enjoyed a period of great prosperity, especially under Emperor Kanishka.

The reign of Kanishka, which probably began in the late 1st or early 2nd century A.D., was the great period of Gandhara art, witnessing the first representations of the Buddha in human form and the development of a standard iconography for the illustration of the Master's life.

Sculpture

The first generations of artists who came to serve the Kushan monarchy were in all likelihood itinerant craftsmen from the Roman provinces of Egypt and the Near East. It was inevitable that these sculptors, when called upon to represent Sakyamuni, should fall back on the forms and techniques of their homelands. The earliest images of the Buddha are scarcely Indian at all: the head, crowned by a mass of wavy ringlets, is borrowed from a prototype such as the Greco-Roman Apollo; the voluminous robe is an adaptation of the Classical himation or the toga as we know it in effigies of Greek philosophers and Roman emperors. Such figures are really to be judged as provincial Roman works, and the inappropriateness of this completely humanistic type for the spiritual and metaphysical ideal of the Buddha is at once apparent. Many of the Gandhara

Indian Art (Gandhara School). Head of Buddha. 2nd–3rd century. Central Museum, Lahore. *Photo Walter Dräyer, Zurich.*

Buddhas have something of the hard schematic character of sculpture in Near Eastern centers that, like Parthia and Palmyra, had undergone Roman influence.

In the reliefs decorating the monasteries and stupas of Gandhara, the sculptors clearly reflect the deeply cut, pictorial style of imperial Rome. Following the Roman mode of heroic narrative, each event in the Buddha story was represented in a separate panel, in contrast to the earlier Oriental method of continuous narration, whereby several episodes from a story were combined in the same frame.

Both slate carving and stucco decoration were practiced at Gandhara. Stucco, probably introduced from Parthia or Alexandria, was employed as early as the 1st century A.D., and continued in use at least until the 5th century A.D., long after stone sculpture had been abandoned in the region. Stucco sculpture included heads of figures fashioned in local clay. Although based on late Roman models, the best of these, especially those from Hadda and the Peshawar region, achieve a combination of realism and spiritual pathos that is evocative of the Gothic sculpture of Rheims and Amiens.

Architecture

The architecture of Gandhara reveals the same combination of Indian and Greco-Roman forms characteristic of the sculpture of the region. The earliest monuments date from the period of Parthian domination in the 2nd and 1st centuries B.C., notably the temple at Jandial within the complex of the ancient city of

Taxila. This building originally had a pronaos with Ionic columns, and its plan resembles that of a peripteral temple. The columns of the porch were constructed of drums in Greek fashion, and the Ionic capitals recall provincial versions of this Greek order, in the temple of Apollo at Didyma.

Adjoining the Jandial temple is the city of Sirkap, dating from the period of Indo-Greek and Parthian occupation. It is believed to have been destroyed by the Kushans about A.D. 65. The foundation plans of its public buildings show a mixture of Indian and Western types.

The architecture of the Kushan Period in Gandhara is exclusively Buddhist and may be studied in innumerable monastic establishments and stupas. The arrangement of the Buddhist monasteries or viharas follows a more or less standardized plan, with a number of contiguous courts, some girdled by niches for the objects of worship, others surrounded by small cells for the habitation of the monks. A number of small dedicatory stupas were generally crowded in the center of the court of the images.

The masonry of the earliest structures in Gandhara, from the Greco-Parthian period to the 1st century A.D., was a rubble conglomerate faced with stucco. In the 1st century A.D., the walls were built of small boulders, with stone chips filling the interstices. This diaper-patterned masonry was replaced in the 2nd century A.D. by a type utilizing larger stones; and finally, in the 3rd century A.D., horizontal courses of cut stone alternated with layers of rubble ("semi-ashlar" masonry).

Indian Art (Gandhara School). Small stupa, Swat Valley. Indian Museum, Calcutta. *Photo Louis Frédéric-Rapho, Paris.*

Before the devastating invasion of the Huns in the 5th century A.D. and the later onslaughts of Mohammedan conquerors, the stupas of Gandhara must have been among the most impressive in all India. Unfortunately, little survives of the splendors described by Chinese pilgrims from the 5th to 7th century A.D. Many of these relic mounds, such as the Teppe-i-Rustam at Balkh and the Dharmarājīka Stupa at Taxila, were of colossal dimensions. The most famous of all was the great tower of Shāh-jī-kī-Dherī at Peshawar, erected by King Kanishka. The monuments of Gandhara were tall, with an emphasis on the crowning mast of umbrellas. The most striking feature of the Gandhara stupas was their decoration: a massive layer of sculptured stucco covered the base, the drum, and presumably the superstructure as well. The ornament consisted of a succession of niches filled with images, like the blind arcade of an Early Christian sarcophagus. Frequently, the base as well as the successive stories of the monument were supported by atlantes or couchant lions and elephants. The Gandhara stupa is a combination of the indigenous tumulus and a decoration that unites Roman and Indian elements. Only the Baroque richness of its decor is completely Indian.

KUSHAN PERIOD: KUSHAN ART AT MATHURA (c. A.D. 50–320)

While the foreign school of Gandhara flourished in the northern territories of the Kushans, the ancient Indian schools were perpetuated in the southern capital at Mathura, the modern Muttra, near Agra.

Sculpture

At the time when the first Indo-Roman images of Buddha were being carved at Gandhara, native Indian craftsmen at Mathura produced icons of the Buddha in a purely Indian style. Typical is a statue found at Sarnath, dedicated by a Friar Bala (Sarnath Museum). Like all Mathura sculpture, it was made of reddish sandstone and originally polychromed and gilded. In contrast to the cold, ideal model of the Gandhara School, this Mathura image has a typically Indian fullness and warmth, and shows a respect for canons of proportion going back to the Indus Valley Period.

Indian Art (Kushan Period). Mahābodhi Temple at Buddh Gaya. Probably founded 2nd century A.D., with many subsequent restorations. *Photo Martin Hürlimann, Zurich.*

At Mathura the ancient Oriental cult of kingship was followed to the extent of dedicating a special sanctuary to the effigies of sovereigns. Among the portraits discovered in the ruins of this building was one of the famous king and Buddhist patron Kanishka (Mathura, Archaeological Museum). The very idea of representing secular personages is un-Indian; we may suppose that the custom was borrowed by the Kushans from Rome and Parthia. The rigidly frontal character of the Kanishka image and its essentially linear rather than plastic character are distinctly reminiscent of the Parthian portraits of nobility found at Hatra (now Al Hadhr), Iraq.

Architecture

Unhappily, so thorough was the devastation by later invaders, and so disastrous the continued use of ancient sites as stone quarries, that no single architectural monument has survived intact from the Kushan Period at Mathura.

A sanctuary generally associated with the Kushan Period, at least in its primitive form, is the famous Mahābodhi Temple at Buddh Gaya. As early as the time of Asoka, a hypaethral shrine had been built around the Bodhi Tree, under which the Buddha had received enlightenment. Probably as early as the 2nd century A.D., this primitive dedication was replaced by a vast covered structure. A terra-cotta plaque discovered at Kumrahar, datable to the 2nd century A.D., presents a view of this building, whose rectangular podium supports a tower in the form of a truncated pyramid, itself surmounted by a spire. The exterior faces of the tower are decorated with niches, presumably for the reception of images. The monument underwent a number of restorations, one as early as the 11th century A.D. by the Burmese, and another even more complete renovation, again by the Buddhists of Burma, in the last decades of the 19th century. The statuary found *in situ* is all of the Pāla-Sena Period (A.D. 730–1197), as is, in all likelihood, the final exterior decoration. The tower is now topped by a massive lotiform member (amalaka), itself surmounted by a tapered spire. The building, with its converging lines, gives an impression of soaring grandeur enhanced by the angle towers (of uncertain date) that repeat the shape of the main tower in smaller scale.

LATER ANDHRA DYNASTY (*c.* A.D. 150–320)

The civilization of the Andhras, which was established as early as the 2nd century B.C. in the Kistna River region to the north of Madras, reached its period of greatest power and prosperity in the early centuries of our era. It came to an end with the rise of the Gupta Dynasty about A.D. 320. Buddhism was the dominant religion and the dedications to the faith made Amaravati one of the wonders of the Buddhist world.

Architecture

The most important monument at Amaravati was an immense stupa originally covered with a rich revetment of carved limestone slabs. The stupa itself, surrounded by a massive railed enclosure, was an enlarged version of the type already seen at Sanchi. Presumably, the portions of the dome that were not ornamented with marble carving were embellished with richly colored and gilded stucco. A number of slabs from the site are still extant, including representations of the monument in the days of its glory.

Sculpture

Although the eastern territories of the Andhras have been found to yield sculpture in the archaic style of Sanchi, the decorations of the Amaravati stupa belong to the period of final florescence, from the 2nd to the 4th centuries A.D. The beautiful and intricate style of Amaravati sculpture may be appreciated in the slab of the *Buddha's Triumph Over the Elephant Nālāgiri*. The story is related in a number of episodes following the convention of continuous narration, but the individual figures and groups are filled with a new dynamic movement. Their pliant elegance anticipates the final realization of the Indian ideal in the Gupta Period.

Indian Art (Later Andhra Period). *Buddha's Triumph over the Elephant Nālāgiri*. Medallion from the balustrade, Great Stupa at Amaravati. 2nd century. Government Museum, Madras. *Photo Goloubev-Musée Guimet, Paris.*

GUPTA DYNASTY (A.D. 320–600)

The Gupta Dynasty's foundation in A.D. 320 saw India united as she had not been since the days of the Mauryas. This period, sometimes referred to as the golden age of Indian culture, saw an unparalleled florescence in all the arts: painting, sculpture, architecture, literature, music, and the dance. The art of the Gupta Period provided models for all of Buddhist Asia. The prevalent form of Buddhism was Mahayana, or the Great Vehicle, a theistic enlargement of the early faith, in which the Buddha was regarded as an immortal divine personage, assisted by a host of bodhisattvas or archangels who ministered to the sufferings of humanity.

Sculpture

A truly magnificent example of Gupta sculpture is a relief from the ruins of Sarnath, representing the Buddha's first preaching in the Deer Park (Sarnath Museum). The Buddha is seated, his legs folded beneath him in the posture of yoga meditation; his hands form the Dharmacakra Mudra, the gesture signifying the Turning of the Wheel of the Law. Below, on the plinth, are two deer kneeling to the right and left of the symbolic wheel, and, with them, the Buddha's earliest disciples. A magnificently carved halo ornamented with foliate designs is placed behind the Buddha's head.

This statue marks a complete return to Indian ideals: only the anthropomorphic conception is dependent on the Roman school of Gandhara. The image has a crystalline perfection of form, due largely to the suppression of anything resembling naturalistic muscular structure; it seems completely self-contained and static, a suitable embodiment of the serenity and inner spiritual power of the Buddha.

Architecture

The Gupta Period, without doubt the age of the ultimate achievement of an Indian aesthetic, reveals the same development of canonical types in architecture as in sculpture and painting. The Indian temple assumes the form that, with few modifications, it will maintain for all later periods of religious building. Typical is the very simple Temple 17 at Sanchi,

Indian Art (Gupta Period). *Buddha: his first sermon in the Deer Park*. Sarnath, 4th or 5th century. Sarnath Museum. *Photo Louis Frédéric-Rapho, Paris.*

Indian Art (Gupta Period). *Faces of women.* Mural painting from Vihara ("monastery") no. I, Ajanta Caves. Mid-6th century. *Photo Musée Guimet, Paris.*

consisting of a closed block-like cella or *garbha griha* intended to house a cult or image, preceded by a pillared portico or *maṇḍapa.* The temple achieves an almost classic refinement through the essential closed shapes of its walls and the austere relieving decoration. Another site famous in the annals of Indian building is Aihole in Mysore, where a number of Gupta shrines still stand. All follow the plan of the temple at Sanchi, but have a distinctive conical spire or sikhara above the holy of holies and a number of vestibules between the porch and the entrance to the cella. The distinctive feature of the *maṇḍapas* is the roof, built in a succession of shallow stepped terraces and crowned by an amalaka finial at the summit. Although the *maṇḍapas* of temples in Orissa are generally enclosed, in other parts of India, as at Osia, near Jodhpur, these porches take the form of open colonnades. The essential features of the Orissan temples may be found in the famous shrine at Konarak, while the towered sanctuaries of Khajuraho typify the architectural style of central India.

Painting

Included among the masterpieces of Indian painting are the mural decorations of the Buddhist cave temples at Ajanta in the Deccan. The earliest of these wall paintings, which at one time completely covered the interior surfaces of the grottoes, date from the 1st century A.D.; the latest is from the 7th century A.D. Although the late wall paintings were executed after this part of India came under the rule of the Chalukya Dynasty (A.D. 550–642), their style is a perpetuation of Gupta ideals.

The technique of Indian wall painting is quite different from the European mode of fresco. In murals like those at Ajanta, the rock wall was covered with a thick layer of earth mixed with a binding medium like chopped straw or animal hair, then smoothed to receive a thin slip of white clay or gypsum that, once dry, provided the ground for the actual drawing and painting. On completion of the decoration, a burnishing process was employed to provide a final, even luster.

A great monument of Gupta painting is the representation in Cave I of Avalokiteshvara, the Compassionate Lord and chief of the bodhisattvas. In this painting, the Bodhisattva manifests himself in human form to a group of ecstatic worshipers. The figure of this divine being is a painted counterpart to Gupta sculptural ideals. As in the art of the Early Classic Period, the body is bent on its axis in a violent *contrapposto.* This pose, so vibrantly elastic, and the flower-like gestures of the hands, are derived from the vocabulary of the Indian dance.

A fixed convention of Indian wall painting, the establishment of the principal figure as a dominant axis around which the secondary elements are deployed, may be observed in this painting of Avalokiteshvara. There is no uniform suggestion of space; indeed, behind the central figure is a flat area filled with heraldic floral forms, so unreal and abstract that they heighten a supernatural aura.

The flat ceilings of assembly halls and viharas (monasteries) such as Cave I at Ajanta were originally painted with a rich, textile-like network of panels with mythological subjects, themselves framed by panels with simpler motifs (floral and vegetal forms, real and imaginary beasts). These decorations show great inventiveness, a sense of vitality and pliant growth, and reveal a rococo lightness and movement in pure design that are unmatched in Asiatic art.

Indian Art (Pallava Dynasty). Detail from the *Descent of the Ganges,* Mahabalipuram. 7th century A.D. *Photo Louis Frédéric-Rapho, Paris.*

PERIOD OF THE HINDU DYNASTIES (7th–16th centuries A.D.)

When the Gupta empire came to an end in the 7th century A.D., India was once more divided into a number of separate kingdoms, which, under various local dynasties, endured until the Mogul conquest. This age is sometimes referred to as the Medieval Period, but the designation of Period of the Hindu Dynasties is more descriptive of political and artistic conditions. As its name implies, the period saw the reestablishment of Hinduism as the dominant Indian religion; and Buddhism, originally a heretical Hindu sect, was gradually absorbed and eventually entirely replaced by the Brahmanic faith.

Sculpture

The last chapter in the history of Buddhist art in India can be dated from the dynasty of the Pālas (A.D. 730–1197), who were the successors of the Gupta emperors in the Bengal Valley. The Buddhism of this period is known as Tantrism, an esoteric cult similar to Hinduism. The great center of the Buddhist learning was Nalanda University at Baragaon. Its countless monasteries and stupas represent a development of earlier plans, and the elaborate stucco decoration is a dry perpetuation of the Gupta style. Great quantities of votive sculptures were carved at Nalanda University and elsewhere from a local stone varying from bluish gray to a basalt-like black. Even at their best, these icons are no more than mechanical repetitions of Gupta canons. A few surviving fragments of Pāla manuscripts reveal essentially the same characteristics, and may be regarded as the antecedents of the religious painting of Tibet and Nepal.

One of the great periods in the history of Indian art was during the reign of the Pallava Dynasty (*c.* A.D. 600–900) in eastern India. The Pallavas were the successors of the Andhras in the region around the modern city of Madras; and their art, dedicated entirely to Hinduism, was in some respects a dynamic outgrowth of the sophisticated style of Amaravati. A magnificent memorial to the craftsmen of this period is the group of monuments at Mahabalipuram, where a number of freestanding temples or raths were carved in an enormous outcropping of granulitic rock. It was from seven small shrines, visible far out to sea, that the site was named Seven Pagodas by seamen in the East India trade. The 7th-century A.D. complex includes a stone carving covering the entire surface of a giant boulder on the beach, representing the Descent of the Ganges. The style is markedly different in the celestial and terrestrial zones. The figures of the devas flying through the air have the most elegant, attenuated proportions, with long tubular limbs that seem only a step removed from the canon of Later Andhra art. The animals in the lower zone—the herd of elephants, lions, and deer—are carved with a telling naturalism that concerns itself with only the essentials of structure and movement, avoiding textural distractions. Unlike earlier reliefs of the Andhra and Gupta periods, the carving is unconfined by a frame, but flows in baroque fashion over the entire surface of the gigantic stone. One is struck not only by the titanic scale of this work—the elephants are life-size—but the feeling of expansive volumes and surging dynamic movement that informs the whole composition.

The magnificent style of Mahabalipuram was transferred to western India and the Deccan by the Chalukya Dynasty, which was overthrown by the Rāshṭrakūṭas in A.D. 750. The great temple of Siva (the Kailāsanāth Temple) at Ellora, hewn from the living rock, was a Rāshṭrakūṭa dedication. The continuing impact of the Mahabalipuram style may be noted in a Kailāsanāth relief devoted to the legend of Siva, presenting an episode from the *Ramayana*.

What is regarded as the final triumph of the Dravidian stone carvers is the decoration of the famous Rāshṭrakūṭa Temple at Elephanta, a charming island in Bombay Harbor. The interior of this rock-cut shrine contains a gallery of enormous reliefs illustrating episodes from the legend of Siva. In the very center of the sanctuary rises a colossal three-headed divinity, identifiable as Siva in the center, in his benign aspect of Mahadeva; at the left, the mask of Siva the Destroyer, with a skull in his crown; and, at the right, Umā, the feminine complement of Siva.

Bronze Sculpture. While stone carving underwent an unparalleled development through its close connection with architecture, bronze sculpture found a favorable ground for development in south India, and especially in the Deccan, in the 9th century A.D. All the gods of the Brahmanic pantheon were cast in bronze; but the most spectacular, and also the most famous, figures were those of Naṭarāja, that is, Siva as the God of the Dance. Siva is shown whirling in the eternal dance; his hands display various attributes of his divine power; his body is covered with the tiger skin and cobra, trophies of his victory over the fanatical rishis; and in his matted hair is the figure of the goddess Ganga, a symbol of the sacred river he bestowed on man. Although there are hundreds of representations of Naṭarāja from the 10th to the 19th century A.D., no two are exactly alike.

Erotic Sculpture. A special chapter in the plastic history of the Period of the Hindu Dynasties must be reserved for the erotic sculpture that has brought renown to sanctuaries in Orissa (Konarak) and central India (Khajuraho). At Konarak, the Sūrya Deul or Temple of the Sun has a continuous frieze of mithunas (couples either in normal embrace or performing various sexual perversions) decorating the porch of the shrine; similar motifs in great abundance adorn the temples at Khajuraho. To explain the inclusion of these erotic couples, it has been suggested that their sexual activities at Konarak symbolize the fructifying power of the sun or, as seems more plausible, that their presence there and at Khajuraho was dictated by Magian sects within Hinduism that advocated the performance of all manner of sexual acts as a means of achieving moksha (reintegration with the Absolute, the Divine). The figures, particularly at Khajuraho, are carved with an almost Mannerist elegance. At Konarak as at Khajuraho, the bands of lovers form a marvelously rich pattern of moving light and shade, covering the fabric of the shrine like a deep vegetal growth.

Architecture

Rock Sanctuaries. The tradition of rock-cut sanctuaries attained new and spectacular heights in the Period of the Hindu Dynasties. It is at Ellora, with its shrines to various religions of India (Buddhism, Hinduism, Jainism) that late developments of this architecture can best be appreciated. The most justly famed structure is the Kailāsanāth Temple, a dedication of Krishna I (A.D. 757–83) of the Rāshṭrakūṭa Dynasty. This enormous shrine was conceived as an architectural representation of Mount Kailas, the fabled seat of Siva in the Himalayas and the goal of countless thousands of pilgrims. Carved from a single quarry of rock were the sanctuary proper, standing more than 90 feet high; a subsidiary temple; a massive entrance porch; and an ensemble of galleries and grottoes around a court dominated by two life-sized carvings of elephants. The main temple has a cruciform plan, with three porches or *maṇḍapas*, and the fourth arm occupied by the holy of holies. Above this cella rises a stepped pyramid or *prāsāda* terminating in a bulbous dome or

Indian Art (Chola Dynasty). *Siva Naṭarāja*, or *Siva Dancing*. Early 12th century. Museum Rietberg, Zurich.

Indian Art (Chandella Dynasty). Group of erotic sculptures, or mithunas, Khajuraho. 11th century. *Photo Louis Frédéric-Rapho, Paris.*

Indian Art (Orissan style). Sanctuaries at Bhubaneswar. In the center: Lingarāj Temple. 11th century.

stupika, which is repeated in smaller scale at various levels of the elevation.

The famous cave temple on the island of Elephanta, also dedicated to Siva, may be dated in the 8th or 9th century A.D. Its form is that of a pillared hall, with six rows of columns "supporting" the flat roof of the cave. The arrangement of this sanctuary follows the plans of earlier Gupta shrines.

Freestanding Architecture. Between the 5th and 9th centuries wood was gradually replaced by brick or trimmed stone, durable materials that permitted considerable development in freestanding construction. The use of horizontally corbeled courses produced, according to the material used, two main types of roof: the stone pyramid, with steeply diminishing stages, or brick curvilinear roofs. Both modes presuppose the use of a square plan. The field of architecture in the Period of the Hindu Dynasties, roughly from the 7th to the 16th century, is so vast that its development can only be indicated by representative types widely separated in time and space.

An accomplished example of curvilinear roofing of a square-plan building is the Liṇgarāj Temple at Bhubaneswar in Orissa. Building at this pilgrimage site began in the 8th century A.D. and continued until the 11th. The Liṇgarāj, which dates from the 11th century A.D., may serve to illustrate this entire group. The most striking feature of the elevation is the conical beehive tower or sikhara that rises more than 120 feet behind a series of porches. The plan is simply an enlargement of that of the Gupta temple, with the *garbha griha* (cella) covered by a spire and the porch or *maṇḍapa* continued by a series of identical vestibules. The rib-like members that encase the tower curve inward to unite in the amalaka, a conventionalized lotus form like a cogwheel in shape, resting on the building like the lid of a jar. Above it is a bottle-shaped finial or *kalasa* surmounted by Siva's trident.

Belonging to this renaissance of Orissan architecture is the famous Sūrya Deul or Temple of the Sun at Konarak. Only the porch decorated with a frieze of erotic reliefs and the stump of the sikhara survive. Related to this style of building are the shrines of Khajuraho in Bundelkhand. Elements that were separate at Bhubaneswar, such as the porch, are integrated into the building's mass.

The sanctuaries built in western India, in Kathiawar and Gujarat, the holy land of the Jains, have been compared with the temples of Khajuraho, to which they are related in structure. The most famous examples, the Dilwara Shrine and Tejpal Temple, are in Abu. They were built from the 10th century A.D. in white marble and are unequaled for the richness of their decoration, which is spread over the walls and ceilings like a vast stone lacework.

Architecture in southern India reached a climax under the Chola Dynasty (*c.* A.D. 907–1053), notably during the reign of Rajaraja the Great (A.D. 985–1014). The principal monument to this sovereign is the Rājrājeśvara Temple dedicated to Siva at Tanjore about A.D. 1000. The shrine is dominated by a towered pyramid, rising 190 feet above a two-storied cella. This spire is really an enlargement of the old sikhara form, divided into 13 stories. It is crowned by a domical finial, really an immense *stupika*, topped by a single stone weighing 80 tons. Many details, such as the volute cornices, are survivals from the Pallava style. The decoration of the basement, with figures set in deep niches, recalls the temples of Mahabalipuram. The lowest zone of the podium is decorated with an inscription chronicling the victories of the royal donor. The plan of this sanctuary, consisting of the *garbha griha* under the spire, preceded by a pillared porch, is only an extension of the simplest form of Indian shrine.

The last phase of Dravidian architecture may be illustrated by the Great Temple at Madura, a dedication of the Nayak Dynasty in the 17th century. The temple is a true city, its precinct enormously expanded in conformity with the demands of an enlarged Hindu ritual. An enclosing wall with gateways surrounds an immense court for the accommodation of worshipers and religious processions. The entire complex is dominated by gigantic portal towers (gopuras), concave in profile and crowned by hull-shaped roofs. They are covered from top to bottom with a host of stuccoed images of Hindu divinities. The central shrine is approached through a maze of covered courts and porticoes, an effect not unlike the approach to the inner shrine of an Egyptian temple. The one architectural novelty that appears in these late south Indian temples is a tank or basin for ritual ablution, surrounded by a colonnaded cloister.

MOSLEM INDIA

From the 8th century A.D. onward, the Moslems had begun to exercise pressure on India, gradually encroaching on territory in the north. A new era began with the proclamation in 1206 of the constitution of the Sultanate of Delhi, which incorporated the whole northern half of the country. A hundred years later, even the Deccan passed into Moslem rule. From that time, India was covered

Indian Art (Moslem Period). The Qutb Minar (minaret), Delhi. Begun early 13th century. *Photo Louis Frédéric-Rapho, Paris.*

with mosques and minarets, mausoleums, palaces, and fortresses that followed the canons of Islamic art more closely than Indian. This official art gave India an architecture of rare elegance, beginning with the Quwwat-Islam, the first mosque to be built on Indian soil (early 13th century), and the Qutb Minar at Delhi, a minaret that stood nearly 250 feet high as a proud symbol of the victory of Islam. Other notable structures included the tomb of Ghiyas-ud-din Tughlak at Delhi, built in 1325 of red sandstone and white marble, with skillfully inclined walls surmounted by a simple dome, and, also at Delhi, the beautiful tomb of Isa Khan, an octagonal building surrounded by an arcaded gallery and crowned by a principal dome with bell turrets. This first Moslem empire was vast and loosely organized, and it soon broke up into independent kingdoms that coexisted with the Hindu states. As a result, regional Indo-Islamic styles were born. The most important buildings of these sultanates are to be found in Ahmadabad in Gujarat (the Sidi Sayyid Mosque) and, above all, in Bijapur. The masterpiece of Bijapur is the tomb (Gol Gumbaz) of Mohammed Adil Shah (1660), a perfect 200-foot cube surmounted by an enormous dome 143 feet in diameter. But this building already shows the influence of the Mogul style.

Indian Art (Mogul Period). Tomb of Humayun, Delhi. 1566. *Photo Louis Frédéric-Rapho, Paris.*

THE MOGUL PERIOD (1526–1707) It was not until the 16th century, under Baber (1526–30), the founder of the Mogul dynasty, and his son Humayun (1530–56), that the Moslem empire regained its unity and splendor. The tomb of Humayun, which was erected in 1566 by his widow, marks the radical beginning of a new style. It represents, in fact, the introduction of Persian architectural forms into India. But it was only with Emperor Akbar (1556–1605), the grandson of Baber, that Mogul art really began.

Architecture

Many of the Mogul buildings show the disinterested efforts of Akbar to create a universal religion based on Buddhism and Zoroastrianism as well as Islam. His chief enterprise was the foundation of a new capital, Fatehpur Sikri, a strange city of red sandstone, built between 1569 and 1583 and abandoned at the beginning of the 17th century because of its climatic unwholesomeness and lack of water. The plan of the city itself, and even that of its Great Mosque, were based on Hindu geomantic practice and recall the earliest town plans of the Aryan period.

Nowhere are the mind and taste of Emperor Akbar revealed more completely than in his hall of private audience, the Diwan-i-Khas. The principal architectural and iconographic feature of this building is a lotiform pillar that rose at the center to support the emperor's peacock throne. From the capital radiated four railed balconies. Akbar sat in the center, with his ministers at the four corners, as a re-enactment of the ancient Indian concept of the Lord of the Four Directions.

One of the most impressive memorials at Fatehpur Sikri is the monumental portal of the quadrangle of the Great Mosque. Although Persian in its general form, this gateway is already peculiarly Mogul in its beautiful combination of red sandstone and white marble inlay, a form of decoration developed by Akbar's architects.

A notable monument from the reign of Jahangir (1605–27), Akbar's son, is the mausoleum of Itmad-ud-Daulah, the monarch's father-in-law. The gleaming white marble structure, incrusted with precious stones, is enhanced by a formal setting of lawns and cypresses. The mausoleum is a central-plan building with octagonal towers at the corners and a low pavilion above the roof.

The high point of Mogul architecture was reached in the reign of Akbar's grandson, Shah Jahan, in the Taj Mahal, erected at Agra as a tomb for his favorite wife, Mumtaz Mahall. Its principal designer was a Turk named Ustad Isa. The records of its construction reveal that the artisans employed at the site included architects, inlayers, metalworkers, and mosaicists from Multan in the south

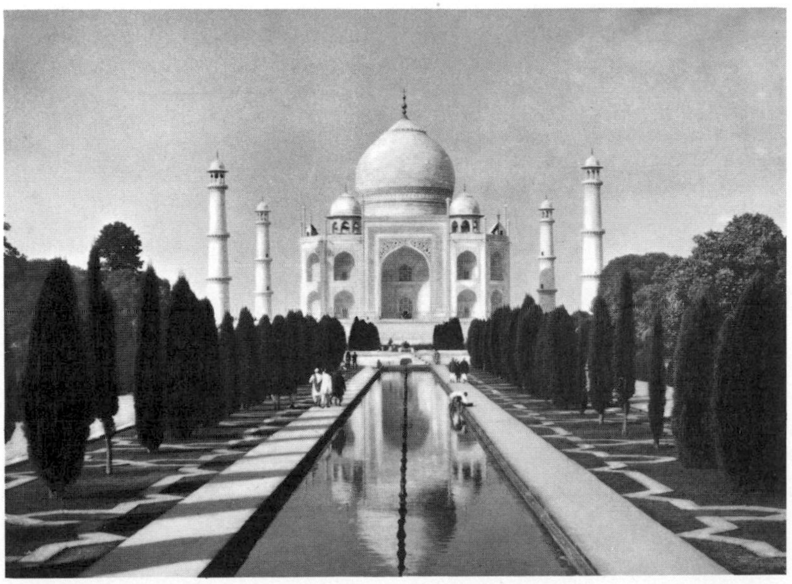

Indian Art (Mogul Period). Taj Mahal, Agra. 1632–47. *Photo Martin Hürlimann, Zurich.*

Punjab to Samarkand in Central Asia; but the vast majority were Hindu craftsmen like those who had labored on the projects of Akbar. We have here a final, harmonious blending of Persian and Hindu forms. The great welcoming arch of the main portal, with niches on either side to emphasize the scale, is a variation of the *iwan* of Iranian mosques; but the pearl-like central dome and its constellation of four smaller cupolas echo the five domes of the Hindu temple. The combination of arches and domes is not an original creation of Shah Jahan's architects, but a wonderfully harmonious reworking of the elevation of the tomb of Emperor Humayun (1566).

Painting

The Mogul School. Emperor Akbar wished to found a school of miniature painting, and decided to employ both Persian artists and painters of Indian origin. Mogul painting was an official, and therefore primarily secular, art. The artists' task was to record important events in the life of the court—scenes of the palace, the hunt, or battle—and to glorify the personalities of their patrons in splendid portraits. The result was an original art that soon lost its dependence on Iranian models. The paintings were usually a collective enterprise: one artist drew the main outlines, while others added the background and the color. The borders and inscriptions were the work of specialists in decoration and calligraphy.

The climax of Mogul painting, as in architecture, came in the reigns of Jahangir and Shah Jahan, when, through the influence of European paintings and engravings introduced by the Jesuits, Mogul court painting achieved a successful synthesis of Western realism and the traditional forms of Indian and Persian art. Portraiture had a particular appeal to Mogul artists and their patrons. A remarkable example of this art is the portrait of *Shah Jahan* (1631; London, Victoria and Albert Museum) by the famous court artist Bichitr.

One of the most remarkable examples of realistic painting under the Moguls is the *Dying Opium Addict* (1618; Oxford, Bodleian Library), whose painter seems to have caught the precise appearance of approaching death. The victim seems completely unconscious, cut off from everything except his own approaching end in the quiet room. The harsh realism of the figure is set off not only by the colossal pillows that support him, but also by the simplicity of the wall and its balancing pictures.

One of the most esteemed artists in the studio of Jahangir was Mansur, who painted the many exotic species of fauna that filled the gardens of the sovereign. As we can see in his magnificent representation of a *Turkey* (1610; Victoria and Albert), he was more than a realist; like Audubon, he was able to impart a universal character to his subjects.

OTHER INDIAN PAINTING

Few Indian paintings have survived from the 6th to the 14th century. Fragments of a distorted, nervous style of figure painting, dating from the 8th century, appear on the porch ceiling of the Kailāsanāth Temple at Ellora. These paintings are a linear, mannered version of the classic mode of Ajanta and are the stylistic ancestors of the illuminations of Jain scripture (the *Kalpa Sutras*) in western India in later centuries. The Jain miniatures are invariably planned as flat designs and executed in a limited range of bold primary colors. The style of these naive miniatures, executed mostly in Gujarat, exercised a profound influence on the beginnings of the great Rajput School of painting.

The term Rajput painting is used to denote the court art of the Hindu states that maintained a precarious sovereignty in the centuries after the Mohammedan destruction of the great Hindu empires. There were as many schools of Rajput painting as there were principalities; but the principal centers were in western India, the Deccan, and the Himalayan states to the north of the Punjab. The principal subjects of the Rajput painters were portraiture; the chivalric prowess of princes; and, above all, the new popularized cults of Hinduism, which, fostered by the rise of a vernacular literature, presented a simple religion to the common man, with an emphasis on the personalities of Radha and Krishna. Some Rajput painters undoubtedly learned their craft in the service of the Mogul court, with its strong traditions of Persian and Western painting. Other styles developed out of the Jain manner of miniature painting, which flourished in Gujarat in the 13th and 14th centuries. A page that illustrates the transition from the style of Gujarat to that of the Rajasthani School (the Rajput school of the plains, established in Rajputana) is a painting of a lady worshiping a phallic emblem of Siva, executed in Mandu about 1550 (Victoria and Albert).

The last and most exquisite flowering of Rajput painting was the Kangra School. Subjects ranged from everyday village life to religious themes, with a corresponding stylistic diversity. Some works are painted in bright, harsh colors, while others reveal subtle harmonies. The masterpieces of Kangra painting combine, in a particularly lyrical style, the meticulous observation of the Mogul School and the idealized sensuality of Ajanta. The great period of Kangra painting came during the reign of Sansar Chand (1775–1832), a ruler devoted to the arts and to the cult of Krishna as a symbol of romantic love. A beautiful page from this period is *Radha and Krishna in the Grove* (*c.* 1785; Victoria and Albert), which seems to echo the forms of the lovers.

A single painting from Tehri-Garhwal will illustrate the local school of this remote hill state in the late 18th century. The *Lady Caught in a Storm* (*c.* 1780; London, British Museum) presents the usual theme of passionate desire. In this picture, the fragile figure of a girl hastens through the jungle night as lightning blazes in the sky and cobras slither on the ground. The drawing and color are a mannered version of the Kangra style. Every shape looms as a palpable sensuous emblem; the serpents echo the curves of the maiden's figure and accelerate her movement, just as the ribbon of lightning provides a celestial orchestration to her flight. The attenuation of the girl's body is a convention of the Kangra and Garhwal schools, as are the classic profile and the large eye that seems to swim with love.

Although schools of painting survived in Kangra and other Himalayan centers until the present century, their history in the period of Sikh and British dominion was one of slow decline into a dry and lifeless echo of the great masters of the latter part of the 18th century.

INDIANS OF NORTH AMERICA, Art of the. Since aboriginal American art developed in almost complete isolation and remained cut off from the cultures of the Old World, the question of how such vast territories came to be populated has aroused a great deal of speculation. Recent discoveries have led to the conclusion that the first settlements took place some 15,000 years ago and that the settlers came mainly from northern Asia by way of the Aleutian Islands or across the Bering Straits. Apart from such ethnic infiltrations by this route, the New World developed free of all foreign influences until its discovery by Christopher Columbus. For several centuries the whole continent was peopled almost entirely by tribes of bison hunters, who were of necessity nomadic and who left few traces of their existence and no art. The cultural level of these peoples was rudimentary, and remained that way in several regions until the arrival of the white man. As it has so far proved impossible to give precise dates to prehistoric objects found in North America, any attempt at chronology must depend largely on conjecture; no firm dates can be given for any period before the 10th century A.D.

The immense area of North America may be divided into six artistic regions:

Arctic. Homeland of the Eskimos, this region ranged from Alaska to Greenland. As they also live in Siberia, the Eskimos are the only people belonging simultaneously to both the Old and the New Worlds. Also noteworthy is the fact that they have never tried to make contact with the Indian tribes. Their art has remained faithful to traditions going back thousands of years (*see* ESKIMO ART).

Southwest. Extending from the north of Mexico to the southern foothills of the Rocky Mountains, this was the territory of the Pueblo Indians. They appeared about A.D. 700, succeeding the Basket Makers, and rapidly developed a prosperous society that was distinguished by its large communal settlements (*see* PUEBLO ART).

Eastern Plains. This term is generally said to include the whole area between the Mississippi and the Atlantic, from the Great Lakes to the Gulf of Mexico. The geographical variety of the region gave rise to many different cultures. Despite this, permanent village settlements were established throughout the entire region, clustered around great mounds that were used either for burial or as bases for temples; thus the generic term Mound Builders serves to designate all these cultures (*see* MOUND BUILDERS, Art of the).

Northeast and Great Lakes. Little archaeological information is available for this area; most of the objects that have been found date from the 18th century and after. One of the most important tribes was the Iroquois. They were expert wood carvers, and most of their domestic utensils were decorated in order to have prestige value. The most interesting sculptures they produced were wooden masks, which were usually painted and adorned with horsehair. Several types of mask can be distinguished: one type is fabricated from corn husks and belongs to the Society of Husk Faces; the best-known are those of the brotherhoods of medicine men known as the False Face Societies. Far more common than their sculpture was embroidery with porcupine quills, an art in which the Iroquois showed consummate skill. Another material frequently used was moose hair, which they colored in the same way as porcupine quills, with vegetable dyes, before mounting them on deerskins. Still another form of decoration used on clothing was shell beads, for which they later substituted glass beads obtained from trade with European settlers. The use of moose hair in embroidery and of dyed porcupine quills also prevailed among Indians of the Great Lakes area. In addition these tribes practiced the unique art of plaiting with basswood and reeds, generally in making carrying bags. With French influence in the area, the designs of these bags later came to be influenced by 17th-century French tapestries.

Great Plains. This area, situated between the Mississippi and the Rocky Mountains and stretching from the Gulf of Mexico far into Canada, is the one that produced the stereotyped image of the Redskin. The Plains region was unsuited to primitive agricultural methods and became a favorite hunting ground for bison, especially after the Spaniards introduced the horse into America. Their continual movement from place to place discouraged serious pottery making, basketwork, or weaving, and even their work in wood and stone was mostly limited to the indispensable manufacture of bows and arrows. The only real opportunity for stone carving was in the creation of pipe bowls, of which many fine examples exist. The various tribes of the Plains, such as the Blackfoot, the Dakota, and the Sioux were unrivaled at the dressing of skins. Apart from tepees, they were used for clothing, footwear, shields, and a whole range of equipment from pouches and vessels to boxes and even

Indians of North America (Mound Builders). The Wilmington Tablet. From Adena, Ohio. 500–900. Ohio Historical Society, Columbus.

Indians of North America (Nootka). *The Thunderbird settling on an orc; a wolf and thunder snake.* From the Northwest Coast. *c.* 1850. American Museum of Natural History, New York.

Indians of North America (Haida). *The Bear Mother suckling her child.* From Queen Charlotte Islands. 1884. Smithsonian Institution, Washington, D.C.

coffers. The skins were painted directly or else embroidered with porcupine quills and, later, glass beads. All the handiwork produced by the women of the tribes, such as the decoration of belts with wampum or the making of ornaments and domestic utensils, shows a strong tendency toward geometric, abstract patterns. On the other hand, the men painted the skins used for tepees, shields, and robes for the chiefs; hunting and war scenes were common, as well as religious pictures, and often these drawings had a propitiatory purpose, having been designed to assure the protection of the owner.

Northwest Coast. The inhabitants of this region were fishermen whose livelihood was assured by the abundant supply of such fish as salmon and halibut. Vast tracts of pine and cedar forests gave them the timber necessary to build houses and fishing boats. The land provided abundant game as well as food plants. This prosperity and the leisure gained from their easily won food supply allowed the Indians to engage in a very special and rather fierce kind of competition for social prestige, called the potlatch ceremony. If on an important occasion (a dedication or celebration of the winter dances, for example) the chief of a clan decided to give a feast, he was obliged to invite his rival and to press all his worldly goods upon him as a gift. The rival, at the risk of being discredited, then had to repay the compliment by giving a feast in his turn and giving back more than he had received. Under these conditions, it is easy to understand the importance attached to works of art, and their abundance, richness, and splendor—features that were an important part of the exchange ritual. The custom of the potlatch was largely responsible for some of the finest sculpture in American Indian art, especially masks and totem poles, which were unrivaled for their expressive power.

The masks are of fantastic design and are among the most intricate in existence, for they often represent several different personages or several aspects of the same divinity. Some of the most striking were movable, consisting of several hinged sections that could be manipulated to give an element of dramatic surprise to ritual ceremonies. Thus while a mask when closed might represent the head of the mythical crow, with its four hinged flaps opened it would reveal a previously concealed human face. All were painted bright colors, adorned with cloth, leather, or fur, and incrusted with mother-of-pearl or sometimes animal teeth. The totem poles, carved out of cedar trunks, were generally decorated with well-known myths along with the family history symbolized by its crest—a superposition of fantastic totem animals. It is known that each tribe, or clan, venerated a particular totemic animal. The poles were set up as burial, memorial, or commemorative objects.

Frequent commercial exchanges between the tribes led to a mixing of motifs and techniques, and it is now extremely difficult to make clear distinctions between styles. Kwakiutl art is among the most impressive. It is distinguished by an unusually vivid imagination, and the liveliness of the figure carving is only equaled by the boldness of the painting, whose main colors were red, green, blue, and white. Haida art appears to be the work of more assured craftsmen, with a noteworthy sense of detail and form. They seem to have been less concerned with immediate effect than were the Kwakiutl artists, but their work appears more sensitive; one of the finest examples of Haida carving is the famous "Bear Mother" statuette from the Queen Charlotte Islands (1884; Washington, D.C., Smithsonian Institution). A third important group is the Tlingit tribe. They excelled in all techniques and proved themselves very accomplished artists. Their art manages to be expressive without being violent and shows a rare understanding of design and composition.

Apart from the masks and totem poles, these tribes produced an immense variety of objects, mostly in wood but sometimes in walrus ivory or animal horns; stone was rarely used. A number of iron and copper objects have been found, such as masks and daggers. The northwest coast tribes were the first Indians to work these metals. Mention should also be made of the astonishing coverings woven by the Chilkat women out of goat hair and cedar bark fibers. The predominant colors were black, white, gray-blue, and yellow, and the patterns were mostly based on animal forms. These works perhaps more than any others reveal the primitive artist's gift for abstracting his subject and representing appearance as well as its profound reality.

INDIANS OF SOUTH AMERICA, Art of the. The enormous continent of South America is divided physiographically into four parts: the great mountain chain of the Andes; a narrow coastal strip between the mountains and the Pacific Ocean; the tropical rain forest area, drained by the Orinoco and Amazon rivers; and the grassy plains of the pampas in the extreme south of the continent. Only the first two of these areas appear to have provided the proper conditions for the birth and development of genuine civilizations.

The rain forest area was, and still is, populated largely by primitive

Indians of North America (Chilkat). Man's shirt, from Cape Prince of Wales, Alaska. 1890–1900. Museum of the American Indian, New York.

Indians of South America (Diaguite). Funerary urn. Musée de l'Homme, Paris. *Photo Sougez, Paris.*

tribes who live precariously by hunting, fishing, and at times by rudimentary agriculture. Living as they do along the banks of rivers, they are compelled to lead a seminomadic existence that is hardly suited to the development of art. Their dwellings are open-sided huts with thatched roofs, and their furniture usually consists of hammocks and stools carved out of a single block of wood, and figurines modeled in clay. Most of the Amazon basin tribes show genuine inventiveness in the way they use such fragile materials as feathers, which were mounted on sticks and used either as head-dresses, ceremonial robes, necklaces, or ear ornaments. Apart from these strictly artisan industries, however, traces of a rather higher (though still primitive) culture may be found on the island of Marajo, on the lower Amazon, and in the immediate neighborhood. These remains consist of large artificial mounds containing elaborate funerary urns of red clay, ornamented with intricate combinations of narrow and wide incised lines and stylized animal figures (usually amphibians). These urns are like the pottery both of the Jivaro Indians of the Ecuador highlands and the West Indies. This civilization may well represent settlers from outside the area who, once they moved into this difficult environment, succumbed to nature for lack of technical knowledge, as the Vikings did in Greenland.

The pampas in the south were the home of nomadic hunters subsisting on game pursued with that peculiar South American weapon, the bola. Here, too, conditions were not conducive to the development of a superior art. It was only in the Andes and in the adjacent strip of sandy plain along the Pacific coast that any high culture evolved (*see* INCA ART).

In the north, however, in Colombia and Ecuador, less advanced tribal cultures existed that nevertheless did reach a fairly high degree of proficiency in the arts. Indeed, it was from this area that the legend of El Dorado, the Golden Man, arose. The origin of this legend lay in the religious rites of the Chibcha tribe, in the course of which its ruler coated himself with gold dust before bathing in front of his assembled people in the sacred Lake Guatavita. This custom did not fail to attract the cupidity of the Spanish conquerors, who plundered an enormous amount of treasures. Most of these are today in Bogotá's unique Museo del Oro, devoted exclusively to ancient goldsmith's work. Among the more curious objects are the nose ornaments (*narigueras*), which range from a simple ring to crescent-shaped strips of metal that were sometimes as long as 8 inches and completely concealed the lower part of the face. Notable, too, are the innumerable jewels, ceremonial ornaments, and ritual objects shaped like shells, snakes, crocodiles, or birds; their exact purpose remains a mystery.

Pottery is equally abundant and sufficiently differentiated from one area to the next to make the task of locating it a fairly easy one. Thus the Quimbaya made considerable use of "negative" painting, in which the motifs stand out in light color against a dark ground. The Quimbaya also practiced the rather rare technique of champlevé enamel, engraving the piece after firing it. Their huge anthropomorphic vases, like those of the Chibcha, have extremely stylized facial features in which the mouth and eyes are reduced to thin horizontal slits. Lastly, the Mosquitos produced large oval funerary urns, their lids bearing the figure of a naked man or woman, seated with the hands placed on the knees. In the region of San Agustín, near the sources of the Rio Magdalena, the remains of a megalithic civilization have been discovered. These consist of dolmen-shaped temples carved out of the rock or cliff faces, or in the rock-beds of torrents. In addition, some 300 stone statues have been found, whose style ranges from the realistic (warriors and animals) to the symbolic (half-human, half-feline deities). Not far from this area, at Tierradentro, underground rooms have been discovered perched atop high hills.

This brief sketch of the Andine tribes would not be complete without mention of the various populations living in the cordilleras of Chile and the Argentine, beyond the southern boundaries of the Inca empire. They consisted of two main groups: the Atacamenos, or inhabitants of the Atacama desert, and the Diaguite of the northwest Argentine. The principal remains of their civilization are wooden objects, such as syringes and trays for snuff, and copper pectoral plaques ornamented with reliefs of human figures and animals. Their pottery hardly differs from the usual forms, but it includes a particularly large number of funerary urns for children (who seem to have occupied a special place among the Diaguite), with boldly stylized decorations that combine the disjointed features of the human face with geometric motifs.

Indians of South America (Chibcha). Terra-cotta anthropomorphic vessel. Colombia. Museo Nacional de Antropología, Bogotá.

INGRES, Jean-Auguste-Dominique (1780, Montauban, Tarn-et-Garonne—1867, Paris), French Neoclassical painter. In 1791 his father sent him to the academy of Toulouse, where he studied painting and music, and in 1797 he went to Paris to train under Louis David. In 1801 Ingres won the Prix de Rome with his *Envoys from Agamemnon* (Paris, École des Beaux-Arts); but the condition of the state finances did not allow him to depart for Rome until 1806. Meanwhile, he remained in Paris and painted a number of portraits, including that of *Bonaparte as First Consul* (1804; Liège, Museum), which, with the portraits (1805; Paris, Louvre) of *Philibert Rivière, Madame Rivière*, and especially that of *Mademoiselle Rivière*, revealed an extraordinary ability to convey the individual quality of a face. Nevertheless, the five pictures that Ingres exhibited at the Salon of 1806—the three portraits of the Rivière family; *Napoleon I on the Imperial Throne* (1806; Paris, Musée de l'Armée); and *Self-Portrait at the Age of Twenty-*

Indians of South America (San Agustín culture). Warrior mounted by a demon. National Park, San Agustín, Colombia. *Photo Musée de l'Homme, Paris.*

Four (1804; Chantilly, Musée Condé)—were strongly criticized.

Ingres remained at the Villa Medici in Rome from 1806 to 1810, and corrected the teaching he had been given by a study of the Italian primitives and particularly of Raphael, for whom he always had a special devotion. After a portrait of *Madame Devauçay* (1807; Musée Condé) and another of the painter *François Marius Granet* (1807; Aix-en-Provence, Musée Granet), he started work on the paintings he intended to send to the Académie des Beaux-Arts in Paris, *Oedipus and the Sphinx* and the *Bather of Valpinçon* (both 1808; Louvre). Once again he was badly received by the critics, who complained of his energetic modeling and his rejection of conventional beauty. For his last submission to the Académie, wishing to surpass himself, he painted *Jupiter and Thetis* (1811; Musée Granet), which contrasts the languorous grace of the Nereid with the Olympian majesty of the god. This time the Académie des Beaux-Arts commented that he "used his talent only to debase himself." The year 1814 saw three important works, the *Great Odalisque* (Louvre); the portrait of the *Vicomtesse Madame de Senonnes* (Nantes, Museum); and the first version of the *Sistine Chapel* (Washington, D.C., National Gallery). The failure at the Salon of 1819 of his *Roger Freeing Angelica* (Louvre) did nothing to reconcile him with France; and, in 1820, he settled in Florence, at the home of his friend the sculptor Lorenzo Bartolini (1777–1850). It was there that he received the commission for the *Vow of Louis XIII* (Montauban, Cathedral), a painting heavily indebted to Raphael's *Sistine Madonna*. When it was finished, in 1824, he decided to go to Paris himself to present it and to leave Paris at once if it was not a success.

Jean-Auguste-Dominique Ingres. *Portrait of Monsieur Bertin.* 1832. Louvre, Paris.

In fact, it was a triumph; the public believed that Ingres had rediscovered the touch of the Renaissance masters. He was made a member of the Académie des Beaux-Arts in 1825, and opened a studio in Rue Visconti. His prestige was considerably enhanced by his *Apotheosis of Homer* (1827), which he painted for the ninth room of the Charles X Museum in the Louvre. He then began work on his *Martyrdom of St. Symphorian* (1834) for Autun Cathedral. In this extremely powerful work, he finally rejected David's influence and, as a result, was unanimously attacked by the Classicists. Ingres, despotic by nature and subject to fits of anger, applied for the post of director of the French Academy in Rome, which he secured.

From 1835 to 1841, he lived at the Villa Medici. Apart from his teaching and administrative functions, he worked on the *Odalisque with Slave* (1839; Cambridge, Mass., Fogg Art Museum); the *Virgin with the Host* (1841; Moscow, Pushkin Museum); and, above all, *Antiochus and Stratonice* (1840; Musée Condé). This picture, commissioned by the Duc d'Orléans, was exhibited at the Palais-Royal in Paris and attracted a crowd of enthusiastic admirers.

On his return to Paris, Ingres received reparation for past criticism. King Louis-Philippe invited him to Versailles and Neuilly. The Duc de Luynes commissioned him to decorate one of the galleries in the Château de Dampierre. Ingres took up residence there in 1843 and began work on the allegory of the *Golden Age*; but he was disappointed by the duke's attitude and in 1847 abandoned the project. He completed a number of portraits that he had abandoned years before, such as that of *Madame Moitessier*, of which he made two versions (1851, Washington, D.C., National Gallery; 1856, London, National Gallery). He was constantly solicited to paint portraits, whose psychological penetration was achieved only through unremitting labor. His innumerable sketches for the portrait of *Monsieur Bertin* (1832; Louvre), the founder of the *Journal des Débats*, are proof of his thoroughness.

Ingres produced some of his freshest work in his old age, particularly his nudes. In the limpid innocence of the *Source* (1856; Louvre), he revived a theme that he had explored earlier in his *Venus Anadyomene* (1848; Musée Condé), that of youthful womanhood. At the age of seventy-nine, he completed the *Turkish Bath* (Louvre); he returned to this picture in 1863, inscribing it in a circle instead of a square. His last pencil drawing, done shortly before his death, was a tracing of *Christ at the Tomb* by Giotto.

Jean-Auguste-Dominique Ingres. *The Turkish Bath.* 1859–63. Louvre, Paris. *Photo Giraudon, Paris.*

INNESS, George (1825, near Newburgh, New York—1894, Bridge of Allan, Scotland), American painter. In 1841 he was apprenticed to the Sherman & Smith firm of map engravers in New York, and in 1844 he studied in the Brooklyn studio of the French-born painter Régis François Gignoux (1816–82). Inness then took advantage of a patron's offer, and in 1847 went to Europe to study the paintings of the old masters. In 1850 he traveled to Paris, where he came in contact with the Barbizon painters Jean-Baptiste Camille Corot and Jean-François Millet. He made another trip to Europe in 1854, and when he returned to America he lived in several New England cities. From 1870 to 1874 he lived in Italy and France, and upon his return home finally settled in Montclair, New Jersey. In 1894, to recuperate from an illness, he made a final trip to the Continent, and died in Scotland.

Inness was a contemporary of the generation of Hudson River School painters. To a certain extent he inherited the tradition of moralistic or epic naturalism established by painters such as Thomas Cole, Asher B. Durand,

and Frederick Church, but Inness' pictorial aims were much more modest: rather than making accurate or instructive records of the countryside, he painted what he called "civilized landscapes." He rejected spectacle and moral edification for a more intimate view of landscape based on the desire to give visual form to a mood and to create a subtle communication with the spectator through nuances of light and tone.

The meadows and mossy glens in his pictures convey the sense of a broad, serene, and yet intimate vision of nature. In *Peace and Plenty* (1865; New York, Metropolitan Museum) one observes Inness' relation to the Hudson River painters in terms of a pictorial and conceptual heritage. Later in his career Inness moved away from the more literal transcriptions of his early years; his paintings of the 1880s and 1890s reveal his growing preoccupation with evocative formal generalities and monochromatic tonal moods. The misty softness and blurred focus of both light and detail in a work such as *Sunset in the Woods* (1891; Washington, D.C., Corcoran Gallery) are typical of this last period.

INTERNATIONAL STYLE. This name, which has now become a generally accepted architectural term, was first used by the scholar Henry-Russell Hitchcock and the architect Philip Johnson in their book *The International Style: Architecture Since 1922*, published in 1932. In the absence of anything more appropriate, it is used to designate the new style of architecture that appeared in Europe during the years 1920 to 1930, and gradually came to be accepted through the work of a small group of creative minds who have since become the leading architects of the 20th century. Hitchcock and Johnson went on to distinguish three main characteristics of the style: architecture was now conceived in terms of volume rather than mass; axial symmetry was replaced by the key concept of distributing the architectonic elements logically; and all arbitrary decoration was eliminated. The term "International Style" should be limited to the period immediately after World War I, when architects realized that their work could lean neither on historical traditions nor on national characteristics, but had to reflect the universal needs of men and the potentialities of the new materials.

The movement sprang up simultaneously in various parts of Europe. In Austria it took the form of an abrupt rejection of ornament and a new emphasis on structure, both of which are noticeable in the last works of Otto Wagner, those of Josef Hoffmann, and in the houses of Adolf Loos (Steiner House in Vienna, 1910). In Germany it was born with Peter Behrens' factories, paradigms of functional elegance for the following generation. Walter Gropius became a master of the International Style with his buildings for the Dessau Bauhaus (1925–26) and for residential estates such as Dammerstock-Karlsruhe (1927–28). Mies van der Rohe contributed to the International Style with his projects of 1921 to 1925, including two skyscrapers with glass façades for Berlin, an office block with a ribbon window design, the German pavilion for the International Exhibition at Barcelona (1929), and especially the Tugendhat House at Brno, Czechoslovakia (1930). In Holland, Theo van Doesburg invented "antiarchitecture," and the "viaduct city" (1922–23), in which he advocated the logical distribution of volumes. Gerrit Rietveld, beginning with the shop he designed for a jeweler in the Kalverstraet in Amsterdam (1921), and J. J. P. Oud with his housing scheme for workers at the Hook of Holland (1924–27) followed similar aims. Although the precursor of the International Style in France was Auguste Perret, and other examples can be found in the work of Robert Mallet-Stevens and André Lurçat, the decisive stimulus was provided by Le Corbusier. The project for the Maison Citrohan (1920–22), the Villa Stein at Garches (1927), and the Villa Savoye at Poissy (1929) are notable examples of his fertile ideas. A reaction to the International Style began to develop around 1930 in those countries where it had begun, but by this time it had already started to spread to neighboring lands: to Italy with Giuseppe Terragni (1904–42); to Finland with Alvar Aalto; to Denmark with Arne Jacobsen; and to the United States with Eero Saarinen, whose General Motors Technical Center at Warren, Michigan (1950–55), was built according to Miesian principles and was perhaps their final embodiment.

International Style. Ludwig Mies van der Rohe. Residential block, Weissenhof housing estate, Stuttgart. 1927.

IPOUSTÉGUY, Jean-Robert (b. 1920, Dun-sur-Meuse), French sculptor. Ipoustéguy first established a reputation as a painter, and as such worked on the decoration of the church at Montrouge (1947–48). Then, from 1949, he devoted himself exclusively to sculpture. He met the sculptor Henri-Georges Adam, who encouraged and, like Picasso and Constantin Brancusi, influenced him. For almost 10 years, his work was abstract in tendency (*The Rose*, 1956); but he later returned to a representational idiom in which the human figure became increasingly important, as in *David* (1959) or *Man* (1963), with its outstretched arms, whose presence seems to be multiplied by the repetition of the left leg, seized in two different stages of the act of walking. Ipoustéguy often used cement as an experimental medium, but preferred plaster, finding in this material a greater potential for precision and rigor.

IRANIAN ART. From its origins to the battle of Nehavend (A.D. 642), which saw the defeat of the Sassanids at the hands of the Arabs and the establishment of a Moslem culture, Iran amassed an artistic heritage covering some 7,000 years. Iran had long been represented mainly by Susa, that is, by the Mesopotamian borderland, but important finds in the northern regions, in the area around the Caspian Sea and, above all, in Azerbaijan, near the Lake of Urmia, indicate flourishing—and artistic—civilizations.

Although the earliest works of art—female and animal figurines that date from about 6000 B.C.—have been found in Kurdistan, at Tepe Sarab, a greater number of very early ruins have been found at Tepe Sialk, near Kashan, about

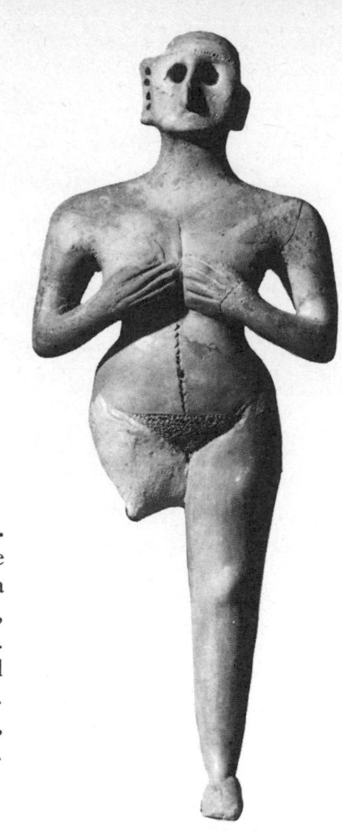

Iranian Art. Neolithic. Figurine of goddess in terra cotta. Turang Tepe, mid-3rd millennium. Archaeological Museum, Teheran. *Photo Walter Dräyer, Zurich.*

150 miles south of Teheran. The site yields evidence of decorated pottery from Neolithic times. About the middle of the 4th millennium B.C., Susa, Sialk, Giyan, Damghan, and Tell Bakun appear as centers of civilization. A very fine example of work from Susa, capital of the Elamite kingdom, is a tall goblet of terra cotta (mid-4th millennium B.C.; Louvre) with ornamentation that combines naturalism (galloping salukis) and various degrees of stylization (a graceful, long-necked ibex). The Iranian art of this period was not confined to painted pottery; glyptic art was also highly developed (first seals, then cylinders); common scenes are of hunting, agriculture, and war, treated in a rich, concentrated style.

Western Iran was to lose its independence when Sumer passed under the domination of the Akkadians (24th century B.C.). Certain cylinders of the latter half of the 3rd millennium B.C. are stylistically interchangeable with Mesopotamian cylinders. Similarly, there is no doubt that the rock relief of Sar-i Pul, in which King Anubanini is shown triumphing over the Lullubi tribe, was inspired by the victory stele of King Naram-Sin (*see* AKKADIAN ART).

The Elamite raids of the 12th century B.C. brought back to Susa a mass of trophies, including the stele of Naram-Sin, the Code of Hammurabi, and a number of Kassite *kudurrus* (boundary stones used to mark off property). But the Elamite kings could also boast of specifically Iranian achievements: in architecture, the ziggurat of Dur-Untashi (modern Choga Zambil), founded by Untash-Huban in the 13th century B.C. (destroyed by Assyrians, *c.* 640 B.C.); in metalwork, innumerable masterpieces such as the statue of Napirasu, wife of Untash-Huban (13th century B.C.; Paris, Louvre); the extraordinary head of an official now in the Metropolitan Museum, New York; and the two bearers of offerings in gold, silver, and electrum found at Susa.

But Iran was to reveal many more artistic riches, first in Luristan, then in the northwest region. It was there, in the late 1920s, that clandestine excavations uncovered thousands of bronzes of great variety. There were weapons (axes and daggers), bits and harnesses, pins with large round heads, idols, ensigns, and jewelry. Only two properly conducted excavations have taken place: one in 1937 at Surkh Dum and one in 1963 by a Danish expedition. Neither of these solved the mystery that surrounds these objects, nor threw any more light on the problem of their date, which would appear to be between the 15th and 8th century B.C. (*see* LURISTAN BRONZES).

Another equally mysterious discovery, and one of tremendous historical and artistic importance, is that of the so-called Ziwiye treasure (7th century B.C.), found in 1947 in Saqqiz, on the border between Azerbaijan and Kurdistan. This is a bronze urn containing a mass of particularly valuable objects in gold, silver, and ivory, including pectorals, bracelets, torques, and necklaces. Stylistically, the pieces are varied; sometimes there is a clear Assyrian influence, at others the work seems closer to that of the art of the steppes (Cimmerian or Scythian), with its vigorous portraits of animals, full of exuberant movement.

Iranian Art. Figure of the god Sraosha (?). Luristan, 8th century B.C. Coll. Foroughi, Teheran. *Photo Walter Dräyer, Zurich.*

Although the stylistic disparity in the Ziwiye treasure probably reflects an unstable political situation, the rich materials confirm that prosperity must have reigned in northern Iran at the beginning of the 1st millennium B.C. The additional discovery of a magnificent 10th-century B.C. bowl with lion heads in the round and a dagger, both in gold (Teheran, Archaeological Museum), at Kalardasht in Gilan, near the Caspian Sea, indicates that the prosperity was fairly widespread. In 1958 John Dyson, excavating at Hasanlu, south of the Lake of Urmia, discovered a golden bowl decorated with strange scenes that were difficult to interpret (Teheran, Archaeological Museum). To a perhaps less mysterious, but infinitely more elegant art belongs a goblet now in the Louvre, decorated with a two-headed winged monster, holding two gazelles in his paws, which have

Iranian Art. Brown terra-cotta rhyton in form of stag. Amlash, 9th–8th century B.C. Coll. Foroughi, Teheran.

human hands; this motif is repeated three times. The Hasanlu bowl and the Louvre goblet probably date from the 12th or 11th century B.C.

In the early 1960s the Western antiquities market was supplied with large shipments of new objects, which reputedly came from the region of Amlash, southwest of the Caspian Sea, not far from Kalardasht. They included animals in fine red pottery, particularly humped bulls, with the hump strongly emphasized, bronzes, and very fine pieces of goldsmith's work. In 1961 an official excavation, led by Dr. E. O. Negahban of the Teheran Archaeological Museum, at a site called Marlik (Gilan), also in the Amlash region, uncovered a necropolis, probably a royal one, in which were found some very fine pieces of goldsmith's work, and also a great many humped bulls, which confirmed the authenticity of those already found in the clandestine excavations. Marlik also yielded male and female figurines of a curious style, with heads surmounted by a cylindrical hairstyle, eyes formed by two concentric circles, no mouths, and curved hips.

The discoveries in the Gilan and Azerbaijan provinces, although incompletely understood, are important not only for their artistic value, but because they provide evidence that helps to determine the origins of what was later to become Median art, the direct forerunner of Achaemenian art. With the reappearance of the treasures of northern Iran, particularly those of Azerbaijan, the splendors of the Achaemenid, Parthian, and Sassanian civilizations that followed seem less inexplicable (*see* ACHAEMENIAN ART; PARTHIAN ART; SASSANIAN ART).

ISABEY, Jean-Baptiste (1767, Nancy—1855, Paris), French painter, the most brilliant miniaturist of his time. He first showed in the Salon of 1793 and continued to take part in official exhibitions until 1841. Isabey's finest miniatures date from the Directory (1795–99). An early friend of the revolutionaries, he later became the official painter and draftsman to the government of Napoleon. In this capacity he documented Napoleon's activities, and he was also in charge of the official entertainment at the Tuileries, St-Cloud, and Malmaison. In addition, he designed the court uniforms and coats of arms for the new nobility. Isabey was so politically adaptable that he was successively painter to Louis XVIII, Charles X, Louis-Philippe, and Napoleon III. In 1814 Talleyrand took him as official painter to the Congress of Vienna, whose participants, along with several ruling heads, he painted in a series of individual miniatures (some portraits of royalty in Morgan Library, New York). About 40 of his miniatures are owned by the Wallace Collection, London, including four portraits of Napoleon and likenesses of Wellington, Jérôme Bonaparte, king of Westphalia, and Louis XVIII. Isabey was the last French miniaturist of consequence before this medium was eclipsed by photography.

EUGÈNE (1804, Paris—1886, Lagny, Seine-et-Marne), his son, a genre painter and lithographer, was a charming minor master of the Romantic period. Inheritor of his father's diplomacy in court circles, he was named draftsman for the expedition to Algiers (1830). The watercolor landscapes, and particularly the marines that he executed toward the end of his career, anticipate Impressionism (*Low Tide*; Paris, Louvre).

ISLAMIC ART. Through 13 centuries of history, the Islamic countries—which, at the height of Islam's power, included Egypt, India, Spain, and parts of North Africa, as well as the Middle East—saw the growth of a number of clearly diversified artistic schools. Nevertheless, an Islamic art exists as an entity, easily definable as the art of one civilization. This civilization first appeared in the heart of Arabia, shortly before A.D. 622, when Mohammed began to preach a new religion. It soon spread over an immense area, which was organized at first in the form of a huge conquering empire, but which later broke up with the rise of regional centers and with successive internal changes of a political nature. Throughout the Islamic world there subsisted a common faith and religious practice that linked and vitalized modes of life and thought.

Among the cohesive forces in the Islamic empire, the most important was the constant presence of a type of personal, autocratic government, which favoured the development of a sumptuous and opulent art. It is this art that can be found throughout the Islamic world, even though it derived its vitality from the activities of a local bourgeoisie of merchants and craftsmen, who were bound by local ties and who were directly influenced by the customs and traditions of their different regions. Another unifying factor in Islamic art is the rigidity, flavored with legalism, that has always characterized religious doctrine in Islamic countries. This rigidity has contributed to the formation of Islamic architecture and craft-

Islamic Art (Abbasid period). Mosque of Ibn Tulun, Cairo. 876–79. *Photo Henri Stierlin, Geneva.*

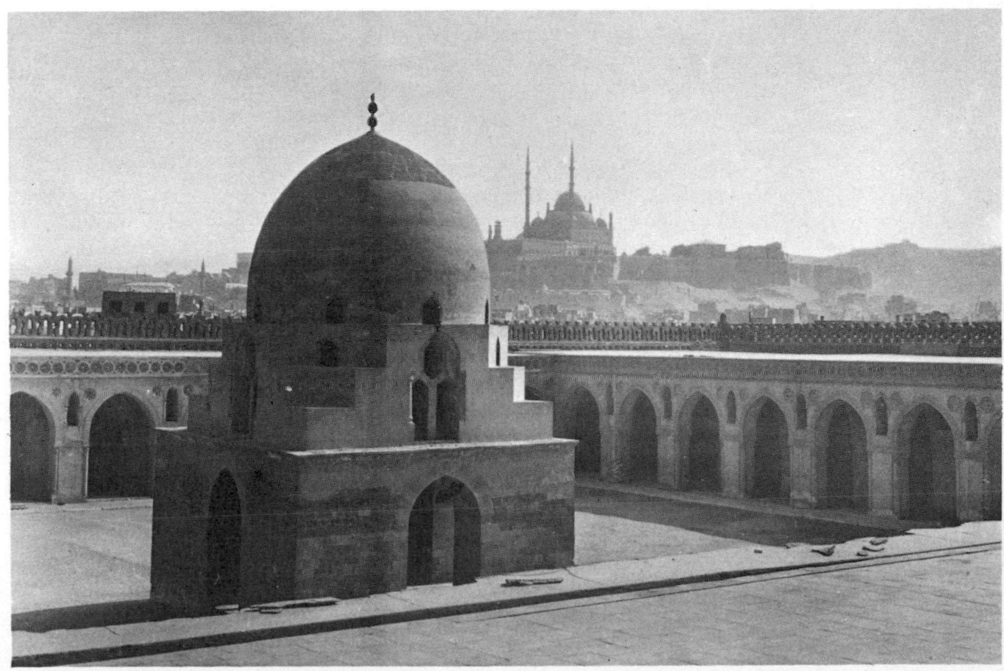

work, ranging from the mosque to the town house, and including the decorative variations of stylized plant arabesque and strictly geometrical strapwork.

In view of this strict control, it is easy to understand why there were considerable limits to the individuality of the various adaptations that characterized Islamic art. Such adaptations were integrated into it with a degree of ease that depended on the region or period; for instance, in the course of a power struggle between rival Moslem princes of differing backgrounds, the elements from previous artistic heritages often merged with the tendencies introduced by new ethnic groups.

These adaptations explain the rich variety of the Islamic artistic heritage. They also explain the succession of styles that correspond to the various local revivals brought about by spatial and temporal fragmentation. But a deeper unity prevails over the complexity of this chronological and geographical compartmentation.

PRINCIPAL CHRONOLOGICAL STAGES

First of all, we must emphasize the fundamental importance of the two caliphal dynasties, the Umayyads and the Abbasids, that reigned successively over the Near East in the golden age of Islam (from the 7th to the 13th centuries A.D.). The first of these had its capital in the ancient Syrian city of Damascus (conquered by the Arabs in A.D. 635); the second had for its capital the city of Baghdad, which was created by the Abbasids on a new site in A.D. 762, and was to become an important urban and commercial center of almost legendary splendor.

The Umayyads, who were Syrians by adoption, reigned in Damascus for nearly a hundred years (A.D. 660–750). They encouraged the first stirrings of Islamic civilization at the very moment when it was becoming conscious of itself; that is, after the extraordinary military expansion of the preceding years and after profound changes had taken place in the organization of the Moslem state. It was not surprising that Umayyad rulers of the extensive Arab empire should produce a culture that was markedly more self-assured and in some ways more original than the cultures of which it was composed.

Later, and in a similar way, the Abbasids, who held the caliphate from A.D. 750 to the capture of Baghdad by the Mongols in 1258, were at first the respected rulers of an empire that was almost as imposing as that of the Umayyads. During the Abbasid caliphate, the art of Baghdad and of Samarra (another of the caliphs' Mesopotamian residences) dominated artistic activity in the most distant provinces, while labor and raw materials flowed into Iraq to supply the caliphs' workshops and to satisfy a population avid for luxury articles. This period also saw the establishment of the decorative, and even structural, idiom to which Moslem artists and craftsmen in every part of the Islamic world have remained faithful, even to the present.

But the centrifugal forces that had always operated within such a far-flung empire soon brought about the breakup of the empire into a number of small principalities in both east and west. The earliest of these was the Umayyad emirate of Andalusia, which was founded at Cordova in A.D. 756 by a survivor—Abd al-Rahman—of the massacre of the Umayyad caliph and his family in Damascus at Abbasid hands. This was shortly before the foundation in North Africa of the independent kingdoms of the Rustamids (A.D. 761–907), the Idrisids (A.D. 788–828), and the Aghlabids (A.D. 800–909). The last-named dynasty, which ruled over the province of Ifrikiya, a territory that was roughly equivalent to present-day Tunisia, was responsible for buildings that are still considered among the most representative of Abbasid architecture. Similarly, there appeared in Egypt the state of the Tulunids (A.D. 879–905), whose founder, the Turkish officer Ahmed ibn Tulun, gave his name to one of the finest mosques at Cairo. The Ikhshids (A.D. 935–69) then followed, while in Syria the Hamdanids (A.D. 926–1016) encouraged a new artistic center that grew up around Aleppo. In Iran the emergence of the kingdoms of the Tahirids (A.D. 820–73) and Safawids (A.D. 873–902) was followed by the more important and lasting rule of the Samanids (A.D. 902–99). This period also saw the establishment of the Turkish state of the Ghaznawids (A.D. 977/78–1186), which at the height of its power produced a rich, eclectic architecture that can still be seen in the buildings of the ruined sites of Bust and Ghazni (both in Afghanistan). At the same time the Buwayhids (A.D. 945–1055) established their power in Baghdad itself and encouraged the rise of an original style that was particularly successful in its application to the minor arts.

The 10th century A.D., then, saw a powerful resurgence of local rule that finally destroyed the old unity. Iran and Iraq were now in the hands of Turkish or Persian dynasties whose power was universally acknowledged. At the same time, Moslem Spain was also becoming increasingly isolationist, and its autonomy was formally established when the great ruler Abd al-Rahman III (A.D. 912–61) took the title of caliph. More important still, another power that was to prove extremely aggressive, that of the Fatimids (A.D. 910–1171), had appeared in Africa in 894. Their descendants reigned in Tunisia as caliphs until their conquest of Egypt (A.D. 973), where they founded their new capital, Cairo. In the course of their rule, the Fatimids extended their influence as far as Syria, although they lost control of the Maghreb territories, where their former governors had become independent rulers of small Berber kingdoms. These included the Zirids (A.D. 973–1167) of Kairouan and the Hammadids (A.D. 1015–1152) of Kal'a, in the heart of the Hodna Mountains.

During the first half of the 11th century A.D., the empires of the Almoravids (A.D. 1053–1147) and the Almohads (A.D. 1162–1269) extended their power on both sides of the Straits of Gibraltar.

The appearance of the Seljuk empire (*c.* A.D. 1040/55) marked the beginning of a profound transformation of Moslem society in the east, which for centuries afterward was dominated by the non-Arab dynasties. Later, in various regions of the Islamic world, states were established as important as that of the Seljuk Turks in Anatolia (in the 12th century A.D.), or those of Zankids and Ayyubids in Syria and Egypt. The main preoccupation of all these states was the struggle against the Franks, who had been ruling the Holy Land since the capture of Jerusalem during the First Crusade in A.D. 1099. Despite

128.

129.

130.

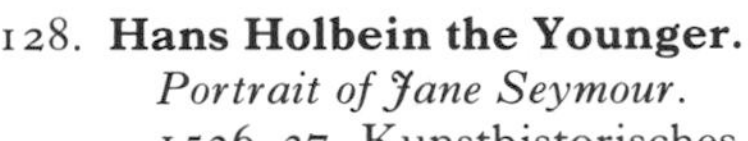

128. **Hans Holbein the Younger.** *Portrait of Jane Seymour.* 1536–37. Kunsthistorisches Museum, Vienna.

129. **Winslow Homer.** *In the Bermudas.* 1899. Metropolitan Museum of Art, New York.

130. **Karl Hofer.** *Nude with Basket of Fruit.* 1928. Wallraf-Richartz-Museum, Cologne.

131. **Edward Hopper.** *Nighthawks.* 1941–42. Art Institute of Chicago.

131.

132.

132. **William Hogarth.** *The Shrimp Girl.* *c.* 1760. National Gallery, London.

133. **Fritz Hundertwasser.** *Memory of a Painting that was the Memory of a Period that was the Memory of Something Personal.* 1960. Coll. Poppe, Hamburg.

133.

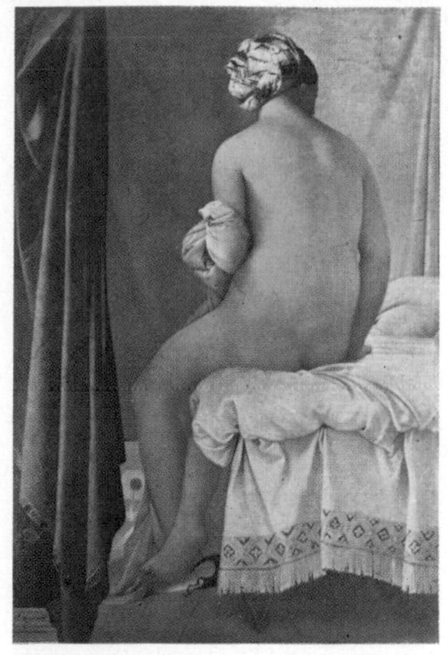

134.

135.

136.

137.

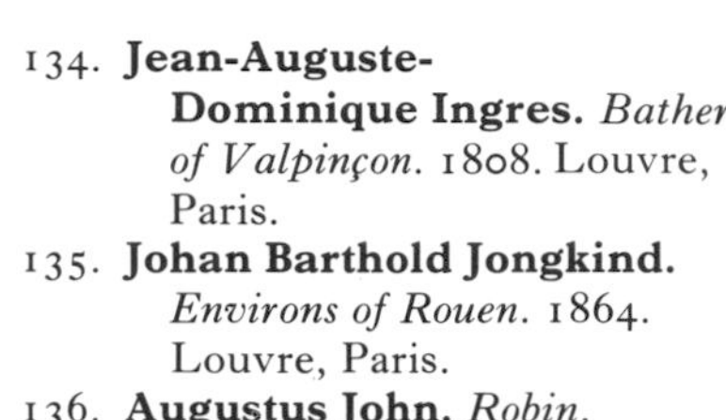

134. **Jean-Auguste-Dominique Ingres.** *Bather of Valpinçon.* 1808. Louvre, Paris.

135. **Johan Barthold Jongkind.** *Environs of Rouen.* 1864. Louvre, Paris.

136. **Augustus John.** *Robin.* *c.* 1909. Tate Gallery, London.

137. **Alexej von Jawlensky.** *The Peonies.* 1909. Städtisches Museum, Wuppertal.

138. **Jacob Jordaens.** *Allegory of Fertility.* *c.* 1625. Musées Royaux des Beaux-Arts, Brussels.

139. **Asger Jorn.** *The Sun Wearies Me.* 1961. Galerie Rive Gauche, Paris.

138.

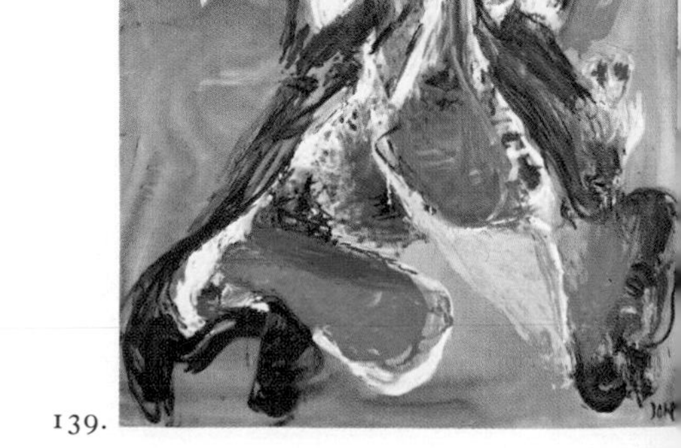

139.

the changing fortunes of war, the Zankids, during the reign of their pious sovereign Nur al-Din (A.D. 1146–73), and the Ayyubids under their no less famous Saladin (A.D. 1169–93), founder of the dynasty and chivalrous rival of Richard Coeur-de-Lion in the battles of the Third Crusade, were probably at the height of their power. At the same time there grew up, in the Iranian provinces bordering India and Turkestan, the powerful but ephemeral empires of the Ghurids (A.D. 1100–1215) of Afghanistan and of the Khwarizm-Shahs (A.D. 1077–1231), which were swept away by the Mongol hordes under Genghis Khan. The creation of cultural centers in the Iranian provinces shows admirably how methods of construction and decorative styles spread over an enormous area during this period and brought fresh life to the art of the whole Islamic world.

The Almoravid and Almohad empires did not undergo such a profound revolution, but nonetheless they too had a lasting effect on the westernmost regions. The main characteristics of Hispano-Moresque art, which developed under their rule, were perpetuated in the small states that emerged from the dismemberment of their empires: the Nasrids (1238–1492) of Granada, who still enjoy a romantic celebrity from the ruins of their palace, the Alhambra (largely built 1238–1358; extensive later rebuilding and restoring); and in North Africa, the Hafsids (1229–1574) of Tunis, the Abd al-Wadids (1236–1550) of Tlemcen, and the Marinids (1196–1428) of Fez, as well as the later Moroccan dynasties of the Sa'dis (1548–1654) and the Alawids (from 1665), under whom artistic motifs that had been used for centuries finally lost all vitality.

In the eastern part of the Islamic world, however, spectacular changes had taken place, the most important of which was caused by the 13th-century Mongol invasion. The only successful opposition to the Mongol advance was made by the new state established by the Mamluks in Cairo on the ruins of the Ayyubid kingdom. But on the other side of a frontier that more or less corresponded to that of present-day Iraq was the huge Asiatic empire built by Genghis Khan, which stretched from the Caucasus to China. This empire was divided into four independent states, one of which, that of the Ilkhanids of Iran (1254–1385), evolved along an undeviating line, altered neither by the later fragmentation of the country, nor by its reunification under the new conquest of Timur or Tamerlane (1370–1405). This new unity was again destroyed from within, and the last of the Timurids was left with greatly reduced possessions. This situation lasted until the rise, in the early 16th century, of the three last great Moslem empires—the Safawid, the Mogul, and the Ottoman.

The Safawids in Persia (1501–1736) represented a genuinely national state that derived its strength from ancient indigenous traditions and that prepared the way for the modern Iranian revival. Meanwhile, further east in India, the power of the great Moguls, established in 1526, had increased. Finally, in the regions closer to the ancient centers of Moslem civilization, the state that had been established with such difficulty by the Ottomans within the anarchy of post-Seljuk Anatolia had continued to develop since the 14th century. Not only had the capture of Constantinople in 1453 strengthened the Ottomans' position as champions of the Moslem faith against Christendom, but the formerly Byzantine city of Istanbul became the seat of government of an enormous empire, which extended its power over Syria, Egypt, Iraq, and Arabia, as well as over the Balkans and the distant regions of Tunisia and Algeria. This expansion was accompanied by a brilliant flowering of Turkish and Moslem civilization in which Islamic art found one of its most typically national expressions.

The historical development of the Islamic world is paralleled by the development of Islamic art, which is often categorized by such ethnic terms as Arabic, Persian, Indo-Persian, and Hispano-Moresque. These terms, which at different times have overlapped, nonetheless have the advantage of expressing the heterogeneity of the traditions that emerged from the Islamic melting pot.

Arabic or Arabo-Moslem Art
The first of these terms must certainly be used with care. It would be incorrect to speak of an indigenous artistic development in the Arabia of the Hedjaz, either before or after the coming of Islam. Arabia produced no luxury object or architecture worthy of attention either during Mohammed's lifetime or during the reign of his four direct successors. On the other hand, some of the products of the Umayyad period (which followed the reigns of Mohammed's successors) may be confused with those produced in the Byzantine or Sassanian periods.

The relatively cautious use of the term Arabo-Moslem, if not of Arabic, may be justified as a means of suggesting the circumstances in which the oldest Moslem culture developed in a Semitic and Hellenized Near East that became Arabized with remarkable rapidity. The empires of the Umayyad caliphs and Abbasids were therefore essentially Arabic, profoundly affected by an Arabo-Moslem mentality based both on the text of the Koran and on an even more ancient national pride, which encouraged the development of an essentially Arabic literature and made Arabic the obligatory language, not only for administrative purposes, but also for all learning.

The art that developed could not fail to be impregnated by Arabism as well. This is admirably illustrated by the importance given in the decoration of buildings and all kinds of objects to motifs based on the regular, embellished forms of the archaic Arabic characters. In the same vein, one can relate certain types of abstract ornamentation, which made their appearance in the Umayyad period, to the spirit that animated some kinds of Arabic poetry and prose of the golden age.

Such statements, however, should be made with the greatest care, bearing in mind the part other

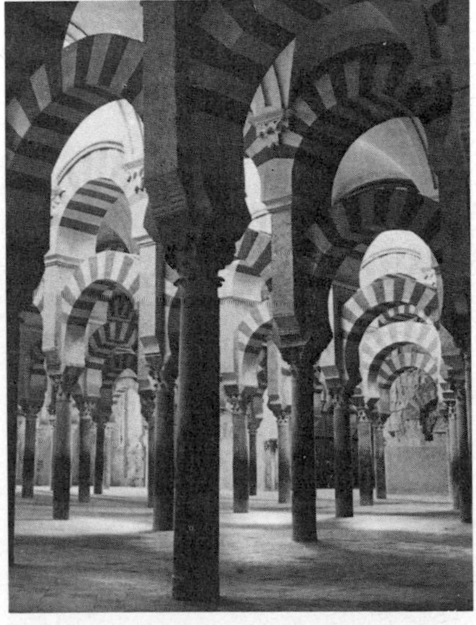

Islamic Art (Umayyad period). Interior of Great Mosque, Cordova. Late 8th–10th century. *Photo Roger-Viollet, Paris.*

ethnic temperaments played in these artistic and literary developments. Above all, conclusions valid only for the Arabo-Moslem world of the first centuries should not be extended unduly to later periods. The use of the term Arabic to describe a work of art becomes even more problematic after the initial period of Arab conquest, a period in which, as we have seen, the term was already ambiguous. Furthermore, the maintenance of Arabic as the principal language in certain regions, while it was replaced in others by national languages such as Persian and Turkish, in no way implies that the art of these Arab-speaking regions preserved the specifically Arabic characteristics to any greater degree. Islamic art was constantly being revitalized by the most varied kinds of influences, and did not, like literature, make any attempt to remain faithful to an Arabic tradition.

Persian Art

On the other hand, the term Persian art is associated in the European mind with luxury and elegance. The Safawid period produced the marvelous pottery and goldsmith's work, the miniatures, and above all, the brocades and carpets that soon were featured in the collections of European kings and princes and that often constitute a large part of the Oriental collection in museums. It would be tempting to conclude that, beginning in the early 16th century, at the time of the Safawid dynasty's struggle to unify their territories under the Shi'i faith and to establish the powerful state that reached its height under the great Shah Abbas I (1571–1629), a distinctive and original Persian style had developed. But such a conclusion would not be accurate. From the time of its conquest by Arab invaders in the 7th century A.D., Iran had formed an essential part of the Umayyad and Abbasid empires. Its material and cultural contributions to their organization were of primary importance.

In fact, at a very early date, as early as the Umayyad period, Iranian characteristics had appeared in Islamic art. For example, all the iconographical themes exalting the person of the caliph, the motifs of fantastic flora and fauna that decorate the walls of buildings, building methods, and the secret processes used in the making of precious objects had already originated in eastern Mesopotamia and were crystalized under the patronage of the Sassanian rulers—each called a "king of kings." (The Sassanian dynasty ruled in Persia from A.D. 226 to 641.)

Yet despite such an all-prevailing Persian influence, it would be difficult to find among the earliest Moslem productions any works that were specifically Persian, because the art of Iran was at this time so completely assimilated by that of the Arab empire, and because the artists and craftsmen were more concerned with emphasizing their Moslem character than their membership in any particular ethnic group or geographical area.

It was not until the 10th century A.D., when the collapse of Abbasid power facilitated the growth of small, semi-independent Iranian states, that a specifically Persian tradition emerged. This renaissance, which was genuinely Iranian in character, gained new strength when the Seljuk Turks invaded and dominated Persia in the 11th century A.D. They made Persia the center of a new expansionist empire, with Isfahan as the favored residence of the Grand Sultan Malik-shah (ruled A.D. 1073–92), and their architectural tastes and patronage exercised a lasting influence on all their possessions in the Near East. The so-called Seljuk art that developed not only reflected the profound cultural changes brought about by the accession to power of the Turkish sovereigns but it also showed how dominant were the ancient Persian traditions in the art of Islamized Iran. Its buildings of fired brick, in which the decoration served to emphasize the structural value of the volumes, and its simple bronze objects, in which the modeling supported the rhythm of the arabesques, represented within Islam a vital Iranian national art no less worthy of the name than that of the Safawid period, but one that has received less than its due because of the fortuitous destruction of much of its work.

Islamic Art (Seljuk period). Bronze perfume brazier. Iran, 12th century. Coll. E. Rabenou, New York. *Photo Walter Dräyer, Zurich.*

The elegant art of the Ilkhanid (1254–1385) and Timurid (*c.* 1370–*c.* 1490) periods should also be regarded as an original Persian manifestation. The art of these two dynasties was affected first by the upheavals in Iran caused by the disasters of the Mongol invasions, then by the break that occurred in the 13th century between the Arab countries (spared by the hordes of Genghis Khan) and the Persian territory, which was annexed to the central Asian world and thereby exposed to eastern influences, notably from China.

Indo-Persian Art

Yet another example of the fertility of invention that has characterized the art of Iran throughout its history is Indo-Persian art, an offshoot that derived from Iranian traditions and transposed them with an unparalleled sense of grandeur, while adhering with scrupulous fidelity to the basic teachings of Islamic doctrine. It was, in fact, the product of a bold symbiosis, effects of which can be observed from the early 11th century, when the Ghaznawid conquerors had more or less completely Islamized northern

Islamic Art (Safawid period). Rinceaux decoration on glazed faïence. 1617. Masjid-i-Shaykh Lutf Allah, Isfahan.

India. Its most impressive achievements belong to the 16th and 17th centuries, when the Mogul dynasty was represented by such illustrious names as Akbar, the philosopher-emperor, or Shah Jahan, his grandson, who built the Taj Mahal at Agra (1632–47).

Hispano-Moresque Art

In its broadest extension, Hispano-Moresque denotes the art of the Iberian peninsula and the Maghreb throughout their history or, in a narrower sense, this art from the 12th century, when the contribution of Moors proper brought a marked change in its development. Of these two uses the second is the more accurate. But it must not be forgotten that the most obvious characteristics of the ancient Berber empires of the Almoravids and the Almohads had always belonged to these regions, which tended to self-sufficiency and fierce local patriotism. Indeed, it was too great a fidelity to this earlier heritage, remolded without any radical change under the expansion of the Almoravid and Almohad dynasties, that led to the sterility of art in later periods and its incapacity to produce anything but endlessly repeated copies to satisfy the demands of the small local dynasties. The same impoverished style has persisted without interruption to the 20th century.

Turkish Art

Contemporary with the decline of Hispano-Moresque was the artistic revival taking place in the Moslem Near East. The various manifestations of this revival are often grouped together under the term Turkish art, and while such a term fails to take account of the actual complexity of the phenomena involved, it serves to link these to the rise of Turkey, a fact that was to have profound consequences for the later development of the Islamic world.

The art of the Ottoman Empire developed from the art of the Seljuks of Rum in the 12th and 13th centuries, which was related to the contemporary arts of the Zankids and Ayyubids in the Syro-Egyptian countries. Ottoman Turkish art was a remarkable flowering of splendidly conceived and skillfully executed works, which fulfilled in a formerly Byzantine setting the needs of a new expression of the Moslem genius, at once European and Asiatic, and which preserved in fact a number of specifically Turkish characteristics. This is apparent in its sense of balance in the decoration and in its exceptional capacity for organizing large architectural complexes for practical purposes.

ARCHITECTURE

If we now return to Islamic art as such—that is, to permanent tendencies that always survived local variations—one of the first points to note is that this art was, in all times and places, an art of building. However, the Moslem builders often used materials that were not very durable and they were unable to expend on their buildings the necessary care and technique, which explains why so many famous buildings have disappeared, why others look mediocre at the present day, and why, until very recently, this aspect of Islamic art was largely ignored in the West.

The building of huge places of worship, which at first were places of assembly, continued throughout the Islamic world to be the principal preoccupation of its rulers. Similarly, the construction of new palaces for kings and princes, often on the site of a new capital, always accompanied the progress of a victorious dynasty. Thus the taste for these monumental creations influenced an art of building whose ruined examples—frequently reduced to mere archaeological remains—are often our only evidence of its flowering.

Naturally, the stylistic tendencies shared by Moslem architects, from India to the most westerly part of Africa, did not prevent them from using different construction methods according to the natural resources and the local customs. The movements of skilled workers and the spread of characteristic practices from one Islamic empire to another led to the simultaneous use of these various methods and to a heterogeneity of form and structure with a corresponding heterogeneity in the methods of decoration.

However, the principal Islamic buildings retained a number of unchanging characteristics throughout their history, from the splendid creations of caliphs or noblemen to the more modest buildings of the traditional Moslem city, which soon became stereotyped. To the first category belongs the huge *jami* (great mosque), an edifice that was both communal and royal in character. It formed the central element in each city and included the princely residences and sometimes, too, the mausoleums. To the second group belong the small madrasahs, innumerable private houses, with their low apartments arranged around an inner courtyard or garden, and public structures such as the *sabil* or fountain, *hammam* or steam baths, the *maristan* or hospital, a covered market known as a *suk* or *bazaar*, and the caravanserai (guest house), known as a *khan*.

Religious Architecture

The religious architecture perhaps expresses more clearly than any other the peculiar character of the environment in which it was conceived. As we have seen, it covers a whole range of building from the urban great mosque, built by a caliph or governor, to the humble *masjid* (from which our own word mosque derives).

Great Mosques. Among the many mosques built throughout the Islamic world the great mosques, or "mosques for the Friday address," are the most magnificent and the most revealing. These structures still retain much of their original nobility and charm, and furnish us a means of following the successive stages of a continuously evolving art.

The structural and stylistic developments in famous *jami* built between the 7th and 9th centuries A.D. at Damascus, Jerusalem, Fostat, Kairouan, and Cordova illustrate the rather disordered growth of an architectural style that originated in the Umayyad empire and reached full maturity under the Abbasids. The Great Mosque at Damascus, or Mosque

Islamic Art (Ottoman period). Architect: Sinan. Domes of Shahzade Mosque, Istanbul. 1543–48. *Photo Martin Hürlimann, Zurich.*

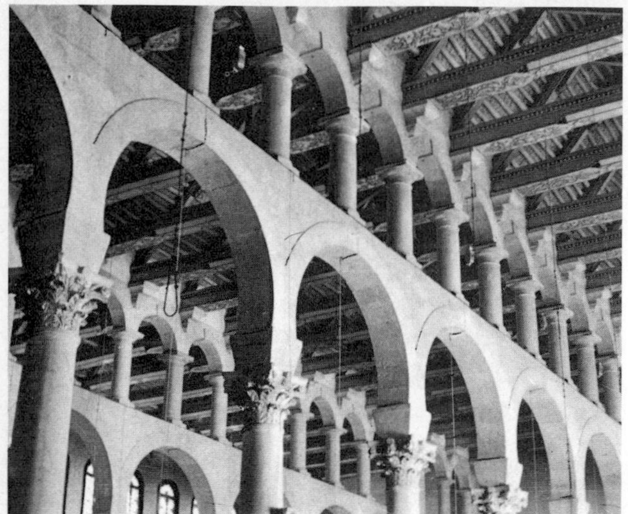

Islamic Art (Umayyad period). Great Mosque of Damascus. 705. *Photo Enrico Mariani, Como.*

Islamic Art (Aghlabid period). Great Mosque at Kairouan, Tunisia. 836–63. *Photo André Martin, Paris.*

Islamic Art (Safawid period). Masjid-i-Jami (Great Mosque), Isfahan. 1088. *Photo Georges Bourdelon, Paris.*

of the Umayyads, was built by the Caliph al-Walid in A.D. 705 and still retains its plan and parts of its original construction. Admirable mosaic panels, in which the complex influences of Roman, Greek, and Byzantine traditions can be detected, still stand out from the gilt walls of the portico, whose perfectly harmonious proportions have often been praised.

Despite successive restorations and extensions carried out between A.D. 833 or 848 and 987/88, the Great Mosque at Cordova (A.D. 784/85–786/87) is no less perfectly balanced in its lines. What first strikes the visitor to this mosque is its forest of columns; there are 1,200 of them supporting a double range of arches, one on top of the other. Its immense height, and its 11 aisles and doubled arches have been explained as the effect of regional influences that have already been absorbed into Visigothic art.

With its solidity and strength, the Great Mosque of Kairouan, Tunisia, built between A.D. 836–63 by the Aghlabid masters of eastern Berbery, is reminiscent of the later masterpieces of European Romanesque architecture. Nor could one remain unmoved by the silent purity that still invests the mosque built at Cairo in A.D. 876/77–79 by Ahmad ibn Tulun for the princely district of al-Katai, which he had founded.

Although these buildings were constructed by varied methods, all were an interpretation of the same, pre-established architectural scheme, which was imposed on the builders of the first monumental mosques. They were obliged, in fact, to combine the idea of the modest shelter at Medina, where the first believers met in the courtyard of the Prophet's house, with a splendor and monumentality that would compare favorably with the places of worship in pre-Islamic times, and provide suitably imposing structures for political meetings, state occasions, and the weekly rite of solemn prayer. Similarly, the decorators remained faithful to the requirements of this program when in their carved bas-reliefs, stucco facings, and colored designs they used geometrical and floral motifs drawn from different sources, or when they executed the first examples of what was to become typically Islamic strapwork and arabesque.

The great mosques of later periods also offer a number of extremely revealing architectural plans. These include the Seljuk mosques of the 11th and 12th centuries, built on or near the Iranian plateau, which combined with the earlier schemes such regional peculiarities as the *iwan* (large hall, barrel-vaulted and enclosed on three sides), the pavilion with a dome resting on four pillars, and the central, cruciform plan of a courtyard surrounded by four *iwans*. These are the first examples of the mosque-madrasah and mosque with central pavilion, which were extensively used in the building of the Mongols and Timurids and, shortly afterward, in the brilliant architecture of Safawid Persia and Mogul India. From the 14th century onward, a faint memory of these forms can be seen in the more traditional types of the Mamluk mosques of Egypt. Equally original innovations are to be found in the revolutionary designs of the great Ottoman architects, who after the conquest of Constantinople in 1453 set out to fill the Turkish city of Istanbul with magnificent sanctuaries.

A few examples are sufficient to illustrate these tendencies. The splendid Masjid-i-Jami at Isfahan reveals 20 different structures, dating from the 11th to the 18th century; nevertheless, it is largely a Seljuk building, constructed between 1072 (the court, *iwans*, and sanctuary) and 1088 (the north dome, called the Gunbad-i-Kharka). It can be compared to another in the same architectural tradition, an enormous Mongol construction at Tabriz, the citadel of Ali Shah (also known as the Mosque of Arg) built 1312–22. The great mosque of Shahjahanabad at Delhi (17th century), whose huge esplanade is dominated at its western end by five festooned arches and the three onion domes of its sanctuary, forms an arresting contrast with the tall structures of the mosques of Istanbul, such as the Sulaimaniye, the masterpiece of the architect Sinan. Built in 1550–56 for Sulaiman the Great, it still impresses the visitor with its huge central dome and the luminosity of its interior space. Notable also is the skillful arrangement and picturesque appearance of the contemporary Persian and Turkestan mosques, such as the Masjid-i-Shah (Royal Mosque, 1612–38) built by the Safawid Shah Abbas at Isfahan on the south side of the Maidan-i-Shah (Royal Square), which rise on all sides of their central courtyards in glittering rectangular panels of faïence, deeply indented by the arches of their *iwans*. In the West, there are the very different mosques of Egypt and North Africa. These are less ambitious in scope, although the Ayyubids and Mamluks, on the one hand, and the Almoravids and Almohads, on the other, had been great constructors of religious buildings. Despite a growing taste for the Baroque and excessive decoration, archaic traditions still remain in them. In all these buildings the central element is the huge meeting hall, which sometimes—though rarely—became an area open to the sky. A number of subsidiary elements became permanent and easily recognizable features because they were required by the form of worship.

One of these elements was the *mihrab*, an empty niche set in the middle of the *kibla*, or back wall in the prayer hall, which appeared in the early 7th century. Originally, it commemorated the prince or imam (priest), or represented the place where Mohammed led the believers in prayer. It became a focal point of the mosque and it gradually grew larger, becoming distinguished by a particularly rich ornamentation that sometimes contrasted sharply with the simplicity of the surrounding wall.

Another element is the minaret, or call tower, from which the muezzin announced the hour of prayer. Quadrangular towers for this purpose were first built during the Umayyad period and were probably an imitation of the bell towers of Syrian churches or the Pharos lighthouse at Alexandria. The minarets were the first examples of structures that early became indispensable to a sanctuary of any importance, though they later took the most varied forms. The same word describes both the archaic types of cubic minaret preserved in the Maghreb or in Andalusia—the tower of the Giralda at Seville (1184–96) or the Hassan Tower at Rabat, for example—and the cylindrical constructions of the Khurasian minarets or their later post-Seljuk Oriental developments. These later buildings range from the huge, delicately de-

Islamic Art (Safawid period). Masjid-i-Shah (Royal Mosque), Isfahan. 1612–38. One of the four *iwans*. *Photo Lénars-Altas.*

Islamic Art (Ghurid period). Minaret at Jam, Afghanistan. 1194. *Photo Délégation Archéologique Française en Afghanistan—Marc Le Berre.*

Islamic Art (Almohad period). Giralda Tower, Seville. 1184–96. Belfry built 1568. *Photo Martin Hürlimann, Zurich.*

Islamic Art (Mogul period). Pearl Mosque, Agra Fort. 1650. *Photo Martin Hürlimann, Zurich.*

corated tower built in 1194 on the Ghurid site of Jam in Afghanistan to the pairs of cylindrical shafts with brick foundations that flank the Safawid *iwans*, the Ottoman minarets already mentioned, or the Baroque superpositions of stories with different sections that were built for the last foundations of the Mamluks in Egypt or Syria.

Another subsidiary element is the *midaa*, the annex preceding the prayer hall, which was used for lesser ablutions and thus always contained a fountain. The *midaa* was generally built as a porticoed courtyard next to the large covered hall.

Certain types of mosque furniture, too, were regularly used, causing minor modifications to the architecture. The most typical is the *minbar*, a kind of throne that had been used by Mohammed. Its use as a simple pulpit gradually made it an indispensable feature of a mosque. It was a raised, often transportable seat, found in every prayer hall, to the right of the *mihrab*, and was accessible by a short, straight flight of steps. The *maksura* was a special place formerly reserved for the sovereign, sometimes surrounded by simple wooden railings, but sometimes very elaborate. During the Abbasid period, for example, it led to the sumptuous decoration of the whole length of the *kibla* wall. Again, during the Seljuk period, the *maksura*, in the form of a lavish domed pavilion, was built in front of the *mihrab*.

Islamic Art (Ottoman period). Hospital of Bayazid II, Edirne. *Photo Eduard Widmer, Zurich.*

The Masjid, Madrasah, and Theological School. The *masjid* was a small oratory in which daily prayers were said and sermons heard, but which was unsuited to the address and official prayer on Friday. It had always been the custom to have *masjids* inside palaces or in any other private building intended in some way or other to mark the owner's devotion to Islam. There were many examples of this in earlier times, and some remarkable specimens from the 11th century. The most outstanding *masjids*, however, are probably those of the Mogul period; the small Moti *masjids* (Pearl Mosques) built inside the forts of Agra and Delhi are masterpieces.

The oratories came to be associated with religious building of all kinds, from the madrasah to the tomb of a saint or the sanctuary marking a pilgrimage site of obscure origin. The madrasah was a state institution, founded during the dominion of the Great Seljuks for training officials and for the study of every aspect of the law in a properly orthodox fashion. The students were fed and lodged on the premises; each school consisted of a number of cells: *iwans* in which the lessons were given, an oratory, which was either distinct from or was simply one of the *iwans*, a courtyard, and various outbuildings. One characteristic of the madrasah's architecture survived for a long time, especially in the East: the arrangement of the *iwans* around a central courtyard in a cross plan. The Zankid and Ayyubid schools that sprang up in Damascus and Aleppo during the 12th and 13th centuries followed this plan, and the tradition continued to flourish in Cairo, notably in the admirable Mamluk madrasah built in 1356–62.

The various types of madrasah, developed in other provinces, departed from this plan only very gradually. The original plan is still the basis of 13th-century Seljuk buildings in Anatolia, where the central courtyard is often replaced by a domed hall. There were local variations of numerous Marinid madrasahs in Fez. Generally speaking, the madrasah, like the great mosque, illustrates the conservatism that characterizes the architectural history of every important type of Islamic building.

The characteristics that appeared so clearly in the development of the madrasah appear again in that of the *Dar al-Hadith*, a school devoted to teaching sacred traditions; in the simple Koranic school or *kuttab*; and in the hospital known as the *maristan* in some regions, which consists of rooms for the patients and domed halls or *iwans* in which consultations were given; these characteristics are also seen in the monastery, with its cells arranged around a courtyard and its prayer hall. The latter type of buildings first appeared in the early years of Islam, when they were used as military monasteries, or *ribats*, and were occupied by warriors who had dedicated themselves to fight in the Holy War. From the 12th century, however, these buildings were again used as monasteries for mystics or Sufis (known in the East as *khanakah* or *tekie* and in the West as *sawiya*). The Ottoman Empire of the 16th and 17th centuries produced what were probably the finest examples, such as the hospital of Bayazid II at Adrianople (now Edirne) or the multiple buildings of the university surrounding the Istanbul mosques of Fatih and Sulaiman.

The mausoleums attached to imposing buildings were not always objects of pilgrimage. Some belonged instead to the tradition of the princely tomb—*turbe* or *kubba*—which first appeared in Iran in the 10th century and included such buildings as the domed tomb of Ismail Samani at Bukhara and the impressive Gumbat-i-Qabus, the tomb tower of Qabus ibn Washmgir (1006–7) in Gurgan, near the Caspian Sea. The Seljuk, Mongol, and later mausoleums show that they continued to enjoy considerable favor in Iran. The best-known examples of these are the mausoleum of the Seljuk Sindjar (d. 1157) in Merv, that of the Ilkhanid Uldjaitu Khudabanda (d. 1316) in Sultaniya, and the Gur-i Mir at Samarkand, whose brilliant outline marks the site of the tomb of the famous Timur, or Tamerlane.

Other Islamic sovereigns who sponsored the building of pious institutions for the community also became fond of funerary architecture, which helped to encourage not only the types of architectural complexes already mentioned, but also the proliferation of tomb-towers that were direct imitations of Iranian models. These were scattered throughout Anatolia after the Turkish conquest; but the best example of this type of building is the Green Turbe (after 1421) at Bursa, Turkey. Comparable to this structure are the 17th-century masterpieces built in India by the Great Moguls, of which the Taj Mahal at Agra is the supreme example, although the majestic tomb of Humayun (ruled 1508–56) at Delhi is also impressive.

The Kaba. Of this type of sanctuary, there are only two extant examples that possess any architectural interest, for the thousands of small *kabas* dotted over the landscape of the Moslem countries today are virtually valueless from an artistic point of view. These buildings, known in the East as *walis* and in the West as *kubbas* (sometimes wrongly called "marabouts"), reflect the growth of popular religious feeling toward sacred remains. The first and earliest of these buildings, the Kaba of Mecca, is not strictly speaking a building at all. Underneath the *kiswa* (a black brocaded cloth or "Holy Carpet") is a simple windowless rectangular building, 40 feet long, 35 feet wide, and 50 feet high, that encloses the Black Stone, a pre-Islam Arab treasure. Before becoming the most sacred of all Moslem sanctuaries, it was the center for local religious activities, and was organized in the manner of the ancient sacred enclosures of the northern Arabs.

The Dome of the Rock. This second surviving sanctuary is, by contrast, a complex and sophisticated building. It was erected by the Umayyad Caliph Abd el-Malik around 691 on the rock that lies in the center of the Temple area of Jerusalem, which is known as the Haram as-Sharif. The rock was sanctified by traditions connected with Biblical incidents and with episodes in the life of the Prophet. The Dome of the Rock (a translation of the Arabic term *kubbat as-Sakhra*, which should replace the incorrect name of Mosque of Omar), is built on a plan that is a later development of the circular plans adopted in Byzantine churches. The Dome's solid octagonal base encloses two octagonals within, formed by columns, above the innermost of which rises the dome. Some of the mosaics are close imitations of Byzantine work; others derive from Sassanian prototypes. The mosaics with the sumptuous bronze or copper facings on the tie beams and the building's marble columns made it a splendid rival to the Christian rotunda of the Anastasis (Jerusalem).

Secular Architecture

Side by side with these various buildings there existed the nonreligious architecture, the most important of which was the courtly construction. The Moslem conquerors, intent on equaling the successes of the older masters, produced works of high quality in this field.

Palaces and Princely Residences. Among the remains of the royal residences of the great Umayyad and Abbasid dynasties—whose members actively encouraged the arts—is a series of the first royal or aristocratic residences of the Syro-Palestinian steppe. Such residential complexes were built behind the defensive walls that were divided by semi-circular towers, and were arranged in a regular manner around a central, porticoed courtyard. The apartments followed a uniform plan: four small rooms enclosing a larger one, reception rooms that are sometimes very spacious, and baths that continued the tradition of Roman and Greek thermae. An over-all ornamentation, with extremely varied motifs, covers the parts of the building intended for the use of the prince; it also emphasizes the importance of the monumental entrance, which articulates the central axis of the complex. The delicate stone tracery decorating the façade and the cool paintings that cover the walls of the bath of the palace at Qusayr Amra (724–43) provided impressive evidence of the luxuriousness of this type of dwelling when they were discovered at the end of the 19th century.

These buildings were incorrectly called "desert castles" when first discovered in the midst of what was by that time little more than a desert. In fact, they were luxurious mansions, well fortified, and surrounded by irrigated gardens, that had been built in a lavish style by the early Umayyad caliphs as hunting lodges. Although they could not yet be classed as "royal towns," they do show the architectural beginnings of the type of palace that the Abbasid builders later developed with such splendor. They also reveal the degree to which, even at the beginning of Islam, the ceremonial of official audiences and the rigidity of their minutely prescribed etiquette had already developed in the princely residences as well as in the mosques.

This knowledge helps us to understand the various combinations and sizes of basilical halls and rooms surmounted by magnificent domes. The most typical example is at Mshatta, and belongs to a tradition that dates back to Greco-Iranian aulic art, which also inspired the development of the plan of the great mosque.

The Abbasid golden age saw the construction of magnificent residences with numerous courtyards, dwellings, and state rooms and bearing celebrated names that evoked the splendors of paradise or the brilliance of famous constellations. Specifically Eastern structural elements, such as the *iwan* preceding a domed hall, similar to those in the ancient Sassanian palaces, were used to satisfy the demands of ceremonies that were more than ever imperial

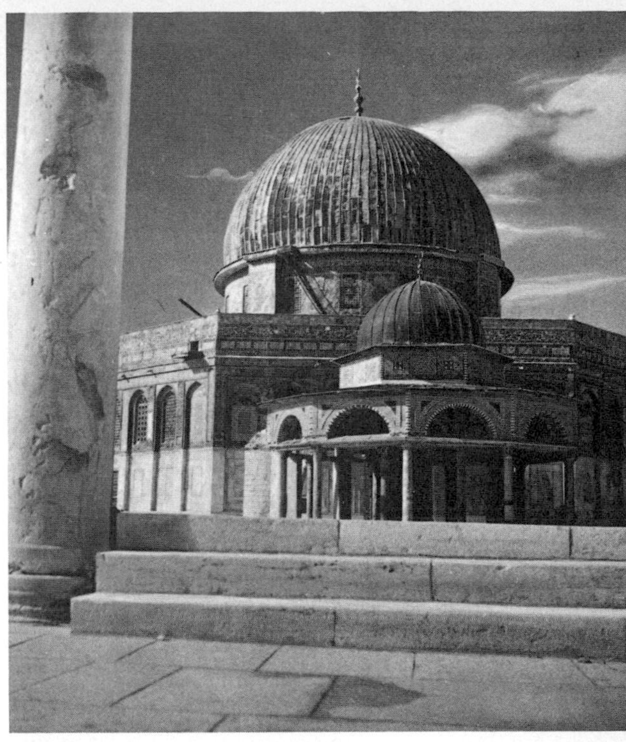

Islamic Art (Umayyad period). Dome of the Rock, Jerusalem. *c.* 691. *Photo Roger-Viollet, Paris.*

in scope. At the same time ever larger extensions were added—parks planted with trees and adorned with pools where private festivities were celebrated, esplanades where troops paraded for military reviews, and hippodromes in which the finest horsemen trained for polo.

However, neither this increase in the building area, nor the proliferation of outbuildings to house the servants and mercenaries (the courtiers had their own palaces in the neighborhood) altered the principle of rigid symmetry that had been established in earlier, more modest buildings. The strict axial arrangement of the Jausak al-Khagani (*c.* A.D. 836) is still apparent; its triple *iwan*, which dominates the Tigris from its high terrace, is preceded by a succession of ruins stretching for almost three-quarters of a mile. The layout of Samarra's Balkuwara Palace (*c.* A.D. 850) around a cruciform median hall is a further example of this simple type of planning. The same principle dominated contemporary town planning, which took the prince's throne as the central pivot, not only of the various parts of the palace, but also of the residential quarters occupied by the functionaries. The whole complex was confined within the fortified walls that protected the caliph and his court from the outside world. Such, for example, was the plan of the famous Round City, built within a circular wall by al-Mansur, one of the earliest Abbasid caliphs, in A.D. 762 when he founded his capital on the deserted site of Baghdad. Unfortunately, the Baghdad of al-Mansur has survived only in the descriptions of contemporary chroniclers, on which the rather uncertain reconstructions of modern historians and archaeologists have been based. Even the astonishing remains of Samarra and, related to them, a little further north, another of the caliph's temporary capitals, Raqqa on the Euphrates, whose 23 miles of ruins are scattered along the Tigris, have provided no more than fragmentary information. In the West, the same fate was shared by the Aghlabid palaces at Kairouan, erected beside huge artificial lakes, which today are all that remains of them, and by the Tahirid palaces at Merv in Transoxiana, which were also inhabited before long by independent princes after being occupied by the Abbasid caliph al-Mamun and his court.

The 10th century, at which time separate Moslem states, each with its own capital, began to establish themselves, produced not only the now completely vanished splendors of the Fatimid residences of Tunisia and Cairo, but also a number of princely citadels that have been partially preserved. Among these are the castles of Lashkari Bazaar in what is now southern Afghanistan, which survived the destruction of the Ghaznawid dynasty and whose imposing outlines still rise on the abandoned banks of the Hilmand River. Other reflections of past splendors are the remains recently excavated in Algeria on the site of the Kala, once the capital of the Hammadid empire, and above all those in Andalusia, where archaeologists discovered the ruins of Madinat al-Zahra (978–79), a royal residence built at the gates of Cordova by Abd al-Rahman III, the greatest of the Umayyad caliphs of Spain. In Sicily there was another group of palaces, which, although of a rather later date, belong to the same architectural tradition. Although they were considerably diminished by the almost total destruction of the Castello della Favara and the Cassaro at Palermo, the remains of the badly preserved reception halls in the Cuba Pavilion (1180) and the Zisa Palace (1154–60; both Palermo) reveal a fully developed architectural style.

But these are still incomplete remains; much more recent works—Hispano-Moresque palaces, of which the Alhambra of Granada is undoubtedly the finest example; Safawid Persian palaces; Ottoman seraglios; and Mogul residences in India—have fortunately been preserved and still retain much of their mural decoration and their appointments. The famous Nasrid patios of the Alhambra, enclosed with delicate arcades like the Court of the Lions, or filled by a mirror of water like the Court of the Myrtles, as well as the halls decorated with stucco panels and stalactite vaults and columns that catch the light, and the massive towers of the ramparts, open to the horizon with their twin bays—all show the almost excessive delicacy of the surroundings in which the last dynasty of Moslem Spain expired shortly before the reconquest of Granada in 1492.

The high-columned loggias and the faïence decoration of the palaces of Ali Qapu, built at Isfahan at the beginning of the 17th century by the great Shah Abbas I, give us some idea of the splendor of the courts of the Safawid princes. The superb collections of manuscripts and works of art in the Topkapu Sarai palace reflect over 400 years of successive contributions to a complex and exceptionally rich architecture.

The most magnificent examples of Moslem palace architecture are perhaps the "red forts" (built of sandstone) of the Mogul sultans at Delhi, Agra, and Lahore. The Diwan-i-Am (Hall of Public Audience) at Delhi is distinguished by the majestic alignment of the red sandstone arcades, and the Diwan-

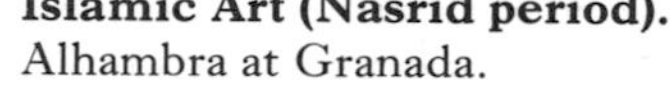

Islamic Art (Nasrid period). Alhambra at Granada. 1238–1358. Left: Court of the Lions. Below: Hall of Judgment. *Photos Anderson-Giraudon* and *Martin Hürlimann, Zurich.*

i-Khas (Hall of Private Audience) in the admirable residence built in 1638 by Shah Jahan, also at Delhi, is notable for the white marble ornamentation inlaid with colored stone. An emperor of the same dynasty, the great Akbar, who lived there from 1570 to 1585, built the most complete extant example of the Islamic royal city, Fatehpur Sikri, near Agra. Its various palaces, mosques, and bazaars, which quite clearly bear Indian stylistic influences, are now deserted but still perfectly preserved behind the city's outer walls, with their monumental porch that welcomes the visitor from the height of an equally monumental staircase.

Islamic Art (Ottoman period). Cinil Kiosk, Topkapu Sarai, Istanbul. Built 1472 by Mehemmed II. *Photo Martin Hürlimann, Zurich.*

These Mogul buildings are partly a reflection of a somewhat idealized image of the Abbasid palaces on which they were modeled, but they also indicate the gradual transformation of this palace architecture. The part of the palace intended for solemn receptions was situated opposite the monumental entrance leading up to it. Similarly, the four courtyards that can still be seen inside the seraglio at Istanbul were placed in such a way as to compartmentalize formally, in a specific order that had been established for a long time, first the outbuildings, then the apartments where public ceremonies took place, then those reserved for envoys of some importance, and finally the buildings occupied by the various caliphs who lived in the palace. This is seen in the Baghdad Kiosk (17th century) and that of Sofa (18th century).

The immutability of these elements, required by the type of government maintained for centuries in all the Moslem territories, accentuates all the more clearly the changes that had gradually affected princely life in these same regions. An increasing love of elegance and affectation gradually penetrated all classes of society and was strong enough to transform earlier attributes. This development of taste and sensibility was largely responsible for the appearance of kiosks, or pavilions, whose design was a combination of the *iwan* and the veranda, and which offered the greatest possible enjoyment of the gardens surrounding them.

Although large, unenclosed, vaulted halls had long been in use, new possibilities presented themselves when it was decided to arrange such *iwans* behind a deep columned loggia, or around a domed hall, and to isolate these edifices simply by adding sloping roofs on slender supports, which further emphasized the impression of lightness. The whole building could either be arranged in a strictly rational way, as in the Cinil Kiosk, Topkapu Sarai, Istanbul, finished by Mehemmed II the Conqueror in 1472, or it could be conceived with an attractive touch of fantasy, like the famous Safawid pavilion of the Chihil Sutun or Pavilion of the Forty Columns (*c.* 1598; restored 17th century) at Isfahan.

Citadels, Precincts, and City Walls. This softening of palace architecture was not the only change to be brought about in this field of Islamic architecture. The sovereign who gave audiences and diverted himself within his private domain could not do without the protection of a strong outer wall. Even in the periods of great imperial unity the palace retained some of the characteristics of a military camp; in more troubled times impressive fortresses were built, particularly in Egypt and Syria during the wars of the Crusades. Citadels of this kind, of which the finest examples, both militarily and aesthetically, are those of Damascus, Cairo, and, above all, Aleppo, are undoubtedly among the masterpieces of Moslem art. They show what a degree of perfection and effectiveness the builders of military constructions had reached. They also show that this science of fortification possessed—at its height in the 13th century—an exceptional nobility and grandeur conferred by its colossal proportions and excellent building materials.

City walls, both newly constructed and restored, have the same defensive and aesthetic attributes as these citadels. Their former grandeur can still be appreciated in the monumental gates that are often all that remain of the medieval Islamic cities. Thus the severe fortified gates of Cairo, built in the 11th century and known today as Bab al-Nasr, Bab al-Futuh, and Bab Zuwaila, symbolize the power of the city that the Fatimid caliphs chose as their capital after their victorious entry into Egypt (A.D. 969), and whose fame survived the dynasty itself. Similar surviving monuments are the carved stone gates that create the effect of many triumphal arches in the cobwork ramparts of Moroccan cities such as Rabat (Bab al-Ruwah) or Marrakesh (late 12th century). These gates express the sober magnificence of the Almohad sovereigns and their concern with spreading their decorative style through the territories, generally in buildings that were both aesthetic and utilitarian.

Town Planning. Apart from their defences, early Islamic cities had few public buildings, except for the "communal house" (the earliest mosques). It was only in the Safawid period, with the remarkable efforts—in the first years of the 17th century—of Shah Abbas I to make Isfahan a capital worthy of his authoritarian power, that any real attempt at town planning was made. First, a magnificent arterial road was constructed, the Chahar Bagh or Avenue of the Four Gardens. This broad avenue stretches for over two miles and is lined with rows of plane trees,

Islamic Art (Abbasid period). Plate in glazed faïence. Nishapur (?), 10th century.

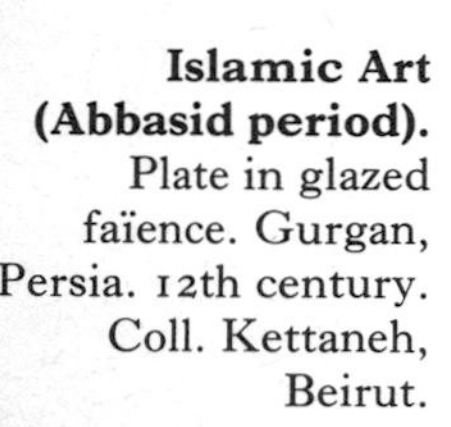

Islamic Art (Abbasid period). Plate in glazed faïence. Gurgan, Persia. 12th century. Coll. Kettaneh, Beirut.

Islamic Art (Seljuk period). Plate from Rayy, Persia. 12th century. Staatliche Museen, Berlin.

Islamic Art (Ottoman period). Turkish clock. Topkapu Sarai Museum, Istanbul. *Photo Yan, Toulouse.*

kiosks, and pools of running water. At the heart of the city the famous Maidan-i-Shah (Royal Square) was laid out. Around its long rectangle were rows of shops placed behind a series of arcades, and in the middle of each side were more imposing elements—the entrances of the palace of Ali Qapu, the Masjid-i-Shah, the Mosque of Sarutagi, and the Qaysariya, or imperial bazaar.

Previously, the sovereigns had not concerned themselves with the area outside the confines of the "royal city," which in spite of its often extraordinary size, was nothing more than their own private residence; the real city—the center of artisan and commercial activity—expanded in an extremely disordered fashion. Indeed, all urban development in Islamic countries was conducted with the utmost freedom, and the contrast between the poor quality of private buildings, which remained undecorated, and the lavish religious buildings standing beside them is quite striking. The ancient Hellenistic cities little by little lost the regularity of their original layout, and the antique buildings became less and less classical in appearance as a result of extensive reconstruction and alteration. Examples of this abound in the ancient cities, such as Aleppo or Damascus.

The Moslems' hydraulic works, however, indicate their profound interest in problems of urban water supply and land irrigation. Their hydraulic installations show the ingenuity displayed in this sphere by the Moslem master masons, who often scientifically improved upon the techniques inherited from previous civilizations.

Suks, Baths, Khans, and Bazaars. The absence of civic activity in cities that never possessed any municipal organization did not prevent them from erecting certain buildings that were indispensable to the economic and social life of their inhabitants. Public and private *hammams* (fountains), which were works of art as well as necessities, were a common feature. Covered markets, warehouses, and hostelries for tradesmen and merchants were among the most important civic buildings. None of these constructions, however, were remarkable examples of Islamic architecture. It was not until the Ottoman period that we find really large urban *khans*, connected with equally imposing country caravanserais that were placed at intervals along the principal trading routes, with baths, public fountains, and huge markets, all of which were remarkable for the logical clarity of their plans and the high quality of their materials and decoration.

Some examples of earlier constructions have survived. Among these are the *suks*, or markets, planned as commercial streets, bordered with identical small shops covered by barrel vaults; remains of these from the 12th and 13th centuries are still standing at Aleppo, Fez, and Tunis. There are also the public baths built at this period in the Syro-Egyptian cities, next to the madrasahs and hospitals with which they shared certain features of construction and decoration. Finally, there are the caravanserais: some of these follow the usual Iranian model, with a central courtyard and four *iwans*, which had been current in that country since the Seljuk period, as, for example, the ruins of Rabat-i-Sharaf in Khurasan, still recognizable beneath the refinements of the Safawid architecture. Others belong to the simpler type, in which galleries and cells were arranged inside a regular quadrilateral around a central courtyard.

But these works can in no way compare with the designs of the Ottoman architects in Turkey, who—with their attention to sound construction and logical planning—achieved within a utilitarian design monumental civic compositions comparable with those of their most majestic mosques and seraglios. An example is the astonishing great Bazaar of Istanbul, parts of which date back to Mehemmed II and Sulaiman I the Great, that is, to the 15th and 16th centuries. Its plan as a kind of merchant city with innumerable alleys becomes clear when one distinguishes two main divisions: first, the enclosed halls covered with small cupolas, surrounded by shops and selling only precious stuffs and jewelry, like a later version of the *qaysariyas* of the first centuries; secondly, covered markets called *arastas*, whose lengthwise arrangement is exactly like that of the *suks* that earlier had existed throughout the Moslem world.

Similarly, it is the soundness of the initial conception, combined with skillful execution in fine stone, that makes the innumerable examples of Ottoman *khans* so exceptional. The lodgings were comfortable and the shops were arranged in two stories around a central courtyard, sometimes covered by a system of cupolas on pendentives. Likewise, public baths reached a high degree of development at this time in the interior plan and the exterior balance of the buildings, as, for example, in the very original Haseki Hurem Hamani of Istanbul (1556), with its two exactly symmetrical parts. Finally, the public fountains, originally simple decorative arches against a wall, became in the 18th century real kiosks of imposing dimensions, which were soon modeled and curved with refined elegance.

Ottoman houses, however, crammed together in narrow, winding streets that often finished as dead ends, possessed in their picturesque confusion all the defects that for centuries had been those of the typical Moslem house. The purpose of the house was to safeguard the privacy of home life, and, as a result, its exterior aspect was little more than an anonymous wall and sometimes even a blind façade, which did nothing to improve the architectural appearance of the city. In the Ottoman period lighter materials, particularly wood, were introduced, and the low structures with peristyles of the traditional Mediterranean house were being replaced by the overhanging stories of the Turkish house, which originated in Istanbul and was imitated throughout the empire, as far away as North Africa. This development made domestic buildings still more fragile, even the large houses of the rich citizens.

DECORATION, FURNITURE, AND ORNAMENTATION

There is frequently little distinction made between the decoration of a building of huge dimensions and a small-scale object; the decorative motifs, for example, on a huge wall panel and on the lid of a box or the belly of a ewer can derive from the same source. This explains the development of a unique aesthetic that to some extent underplayed variety in structural form to emphasize a spiritual unity, manifested in the common ornamental repertoire that was used, irrespective of place or period, by craftsmen practicing the most diverse techniques.

The remarkable household objects have long been admired for their sumptuous combinations of line and color, for the rhythmic flow of their designs, and for the subtle harmonies drawn from the juxtaposition of flat tones or by the play of light and shade on low relief. The iridescence of the metallic gold luster pieces produced in the Abbasid period with a technique that once brought fame to the potters of Baghdad, Fatimid Egypt, and Iran survived for centuries, glittering in the ceramic tiles of Rayy and Kashan after the Mogul conquest and in the dishes of Málaga and Valencia in Mudejar Spain. On some ancient specimens the decoration is painted in black beneath a turquoise glaze, or in deep purple against a creamy white background. Other examples have designs incised from enamels in all shades of brown, yellow, and green. These productions were followed by the refined techniques of the Seljuk *minai* or polychrome pieces, and finally by Ottoman work in which strong colors, dominated according to the series by tomato red or manganese violet and a fine range of blues, contrast with plain light grounds. At the same time, the motifs became more varied and differed according to period and region; sometimes they had the crude vigor of an often abstract stylization, sometimes a delicate outline that emphasized the elegance of the subjects, in other cases a linear vitality that made many of the scenes depicted look like small genre paintings, or a charming attention to naturalism, as in Ottoman ceramics.

Enough survives of Islamic textiles to indicate how splendid they once were. Outstanding are the linen and silk, embroidered with now-faded colors, that were produced in the Abbasid period. Later, in the Safawid and Ottoman periods, the commercialized production of brocades with more graceful but still endlessly repeated subjects became one of the main industries of Iran and Turkey. The softness and skillful blending of their colors are excelled only by the knotted carpets. The art of carpet making did not reach its peak until the 15th century, but carpets then became the indispensable luxury of every well-to-do home.

Works carved in wood, stone, rock, crystal, and ivory, or cast in bronze and copper before being

Islamic Art (Mamluk period). Mosque lamp. 14th century. Staatliche Museen, Berlin.

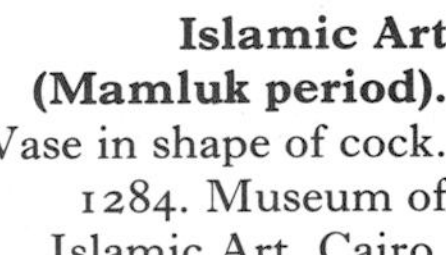

Islamic Art (Mamluk period). Vase in shape of cock. 1284. Museum of Islamic Art, Cairo.

Islamic Art. *Lion.* Bronze fountain (?). 11th-12th century. Staatliche Museen, Berlin. *Photo Walter Dräyer, Zurich.*

Islamic Art (Mongol period). Faïence tile. Iran, 13th–14th century. Art Museum, Seattle.

Islamic Art (Mongol period). *Deer.* Persian miniature from a treatise on natural history. 13th century.

chiseled and, from the 12th century, sometimes inlaid with gold or silver, are among the most meticulous achievements of artists living in Moslem territory. Surfaces were often divided into compartments with bands, medallions, and more complicated strapwork, which on woodwork was made up of little panels arranged in attractive geometric patterns.

The same motifs were repeated in illuminated book decoration, which, with calligraphy and the other applied arts in the Islamic world, began to flourish during the same period. The delicacy, richness, and variety of the calligraphy, the often extremely beautiful bindings, and the excellent miniatures made these books among the most remarkable productions of their kind. Our knowledge of the miniatures is still imperfect, but the reputation of Persian art in the West is very largely based on its miniature painting.

Decorative Motifs

This proliferating decoration of every kind of object, which developed with the emergence of the plastic and artisan arts in the Moslem Middle Ages, was of a single type—the same used for the walls of buildings. It had two fundamental characteristics: an avoidance of empty space and an abstraction that was usually linear.

The foreign origins of motifs, borrowed as early as the Umayyad period from Byzantine and Sassanian art, had little significance. The essential character of Moslem decoration was hardly modified by the frequent addition of new elements, from the sinuous volumes introduced during the Abbasid period under the influence of the art of the steppes to the peony flowers and Chinese clouds that were widespread in the Mongol period. The first palm leaves, derived from the acanthus leaf and Classical pampres, and the earliest interpretations of the trees of life, taken from Oriental art, were absorbed into a decorative idiom that also contained more realistic flora, enlivened on occasion by a direct imitation of nature.

Similarly, the arabesque passed in succeeding periods from vigorous and composite patterns in the mosaics and stuccoes of the Umayyad period to the freedom seen in Persian carpets or in Ottoman faïence, with its decoration of tulips and carnations. There is, for example, the continuity of soft, abstract curves drawn on the plasters of Samarra by a combination of incision and low relief, and the sober fullness of the 12th-century plant forms, which reached their maturity in the Ghurid and Ayyubid East and the Almoravid and Almohad West. Yet the arabesque retained its essential rhythm, which determined the development of Islamic floral decoration, and reappeared in the arrangements of polygons, which—beginning in the 11th century—provided the basic pattern for most of the ornamental compositions. When the motif was fully developed, the simple schemes based on squares, hexagons, or octagons were replaced by stars having an increasing number of points, and having lines that always possessed an inner dynamic movement radiating from each partial center and leading the beholder's eye beyond the limited fragment it embraces at one glance. The same movement dominated the pattern of the bands that divided the various decorated sections on both artifacts and buildings. There are also 13th- and 14th-century bowls and ewers in which animals, human figures, floral motifs, and calligraphic inscriptions are integrated into the geometric organization of the whole object.

Examples of this can be seen in the lively compositions with animals and human figures that were carved on ivory and bronze objects, such as the caskets of Umayyad Spain or the various metal utensils made in post-Seljuk Iran and the Near East. Then there are the scenes painted on Egyptian dishes of the Fatimid period, or, from an earlier time, the frescoes of the Umayyad castles of Syria or the Abbasid palaces of Samarra, in which the scenes anticipate many later masterpieces of the so-called Arab and Persian miniatures.

The similarity of the bands of epigraphic decoration to the arabesques and geometric strapwork that entwined with them or served as their background has sometimes been exaggerated. They still conformed to the linear spirit that had already produced Arabic writing, which was the only graphic element in the art of the Islamic countries until modern times.

This writing did not acquire an identity separate from the scripts out of which it was derived until its characters were linked to each other systematically on a regular base line. The continuity of the inscribed line became increasingly emphatic. Beginning in the 10th century, the same process can be observed in Kufic (an early Arabic alphabet) writing on archaic lapidary inscriptions, where it is decorated with flowers and entwined stems without ever losing its angular character; or again in

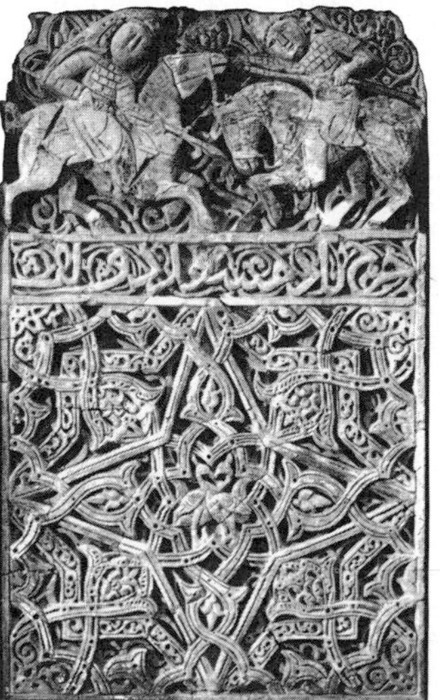

Islamic Art (Seljuk period). Stucco panel. Rayy. 13th century. Art Museum, Seattle.

Islamic Art (Ottoman period). Mosque lamp on a decorative relief. 1357. Museum of Islamic Art, Cairo.

the decorative transformations of the cursive writing familiar to the copyists, which later, in the 12th century, was used on buildings. It is perhaps in the unique and strange success of anthropomorphic writing—for example, in the inscriptions of a number of 13th-century Iranian bronze objects, in which the gestures of the small figures, arranged in the most varied attitudes, form a succession of legible words—that we can best feel this dynamism, linking and animating human shapes that would at first seem quite unsuited to representing letters, but which are at the same time completely dehumanized.

The regularity of this rhythm and the uniformity of the style it produced are the predictable result of decoration based on an extremely limited idiom, but one that was applied ubiquitously, from mosques to domestic utensils. Its aesthetic effect depends entirely on the play of lines and colors over a surface. This explains the connection between the stylized decoration, and the aniconism (opposition to the use of images) inherent in the art of Islam.

Islamic art is the perfect expression of the antihumanist outlook that always characterized the Islamic civilization. This supreme detachment from man as an object of study and contemplation was responsible for the absence of a whole category of works, both literary and plastic, that is abundantly represented in other civilizations.

PAINTING

Although it has often been remarked that the Moslem religion hampered the development of painting in the Islamic world, especially of figurative subjects, this certainly is not the case. The Koran and the oldest traditions of Islam formulated no precise doctrine regarding images. Over the centuries, however, several factors led the Moslem legists to formulate an iconoclastic theory of images. This interdict was accepted, in principle, by all of the sects and factions of Islam, but there always remained an intellectual minority who challenged it and who limited, rather than prohibited, the activity of the figure painter. The representation of God was formally forbidden, and it was only in history books (such as the *Universal History* by Rashid al-Din) or tales (such as a *Varqeh and Gulshah* of the 13th century) that a few images of Mohammed and other personages belonging to the sacred history of Islam appeared. The only notable exceptions to this ruling are the Turkish and Persian manuscripts of the *Miraj-nama*, which describe the mystical Ascension of the Prophet.

There is no doubt either that the extraordinary development of calligraphy and manuscript illumination and even the large frescoes and ceramic compositions that decorate the mosques of Iran and Turkey often owe their effects, whether austere or flamboyantly rich, to the inspiration of the Moslem faith. It is nonetheless true that Islamic painting was generally secular, especially princely, in character. The princes of the great Moslem dynasties were the patrons of artists. Although popular painting may have existed in the Islamic world before the 19th century, we know nothing about it. Another general characteristic of Islamic painting was its literary character. Mural paintings, of which there were many, have not survived except for a few rare examples; illustrated manuscripts form the bulk of extant Islamic painting; in fact, it seems that the most celebrated artists devoted themselves to these.

The documents of Islamic painting can be divided into five principal groups: the first centuries of Islam, that is from the 7th to the 12th; the Arab school; the Persian school; the Turkish school; and the Mogul school.

First Centuries

Our knowledge of Moslem painting during the first six centuries of Islam is so fragmentary that it is difficult to trace its history. During the Umayyad period the palaces of the princes were partly decorated with mural paintings, of which only a few fragments remain. Those at Khirbat al-Mafjar are hard to interpret, but at Qusayr Amrah Alois Musil, a Czech priest, was still able to have most of the scenes copied at the end of the 19th century. They include scenes of princely life, images symbolizing power, erotic figures of women, purely decorative designs, and a remarkable scientific representation of celestial space. The stylistic origins of the paintings at Qusayr Amrah are varied: Persian and even Hindu elements, and especially late Classical art, appear. The same applies to the two

Islamic Art (Buwayid period). Ring of ibexes. Persia, 998. Art Museum, Cleveland.

frescoes discovered on the floor of the palace at Qasr al-Hayr in Syria (*c.* 728). One of these, probably a copy of a mosaic, depicts Gaea, goddess of the Earth, and is Romano-Byzantine in manner; the other, which is more Oriental in feeling, shows musicians and a hunter of Sassanian type. The Umayyad mosaics in the Dome of the Rock at Jerusalem, the Great Mosque of Damascus, and the floors of the Palestinian palaces Khirbat al-Mafjar (724–43; near Jericho) and Khirbat al-Minyah are among the finest that survive from the first centuries of Islam. The sources of their style and motifs are almost exclusively Mediterranean. In short, Umayyad painting is remarkable not so much for its originality as for the variety of its origins, for its rich, sometimes excessive decoration, and for an iconography that was calculated to add luster to a young, conquering dynasty.

So few examples have been preserved from the centuries following that it is difficult to piece together their history. At Samarra excavations have brought to light several 9th-century frescoes, executed in a flat linear style that seems to indicate Persian or even central Asian origins. They contain purely decorative motifs and scenes from the princely life.

Outside Abbasid Iraq, there appear to have been two principal centers of painting. The first, in Egypt, was probably active from the 10th century. Our knowledge of it is limited to references in texts, a few fragments of mural paintings, and a large number of illustrations on papyrus and paper. The subjects can rarely be identified with certainty, and the quality of most of the surviving examples is mediocre. An exception is the ceiling of the Capella

Islamic Art (Abbasid period). Miniature from a *Materia Medica* by Dioscorides. Baghdad, 1222. Louvre, Paris.

Palatina at Palermo, painted for a Norman prince in 1154. The old themes of royal life reappear here once more, as well as narrative illustrations, landscapes, and a whole decorative bestiary. Their style derives from Egypt and Iraq, and they are the best known examples of Fatimid painting.

A second center of painting existed in Iran, and was particularly active from the 10th century. Fragments of frescoes have been discovered at Nishapur and Lashkari Bazaar. Too few examples are preserved to enable us to define precisely the style of these paintings, but it seems that the linear tendencies of Iranian art were maintained. These are found in one of the rare illustrated manuscripts of the period, an astronomical treatise, dated 1008 and preserved in the Bodleian Library, Oxford.

The Arab School

The end of the 12th and the first half of the 13th century were the great periods of Arab painting. A series of phenomena, which have yet to be studied, created a surge of painting linked to a clearly identifiable milieu, both social (the wealthy middle class and the aristocrats) and geographical (the great cities of the Fertile Crescent). It was primarily an art of the miniature; the illustrated books were scientific treatises or tales. Some of the most remarkable examples of illustrated books produced during this first period of Arab painting are the following: the *Kalila and Dimna* (Paris, Bibliothèque Nationale); the *De Materia Medica* (1229; Istanbul, Topkapu Sarai Library); the Pseudo-Galen of the Bibliothèque Nationale, Paris, dated 1199; a dispersed *Dioscorides*, dated 1224; the *Maqâmât* by Al-Harîrî, in the Bibliothèque Nationale (the famous manuscript known as the Harîrî Schefer, dated 1237 and painted by Al-Wasiti); and the *Maqâmât* in the Oriental Institute, Leningrad. These manuscripts show, in varying degrees, the influence of disparate origins, particularly Byzantine. The manuscripts are especially interesting for the amazing realism in the scenes of everyday life.

The second half of the 13th century did not produce works of comparable quality, but under the Mamluks of Egypt, in the 14th century, there is again a group of Maqâmât manuscripts, the best example of which is in Vienna's Nationalbibliothek, and is dated 1334. Although they are less inventive than the works of the preceding century, these miniatures have a high quality of execution. Toward the end of the 14th century, Arab painting produced only a popular style of mediocre quality.

The Persian School

Like the Arab school, the development of Persian painting can also be followed from the 12th century. The Rayy and Kashan ceramics show that a whole iconographic idiom and range of styles existed before the appearance of illuminated manuscripts. Texts also refer to numerous examples of mural painting, but the Persian school is primarily known for the illustration of books. With the first examples, such as the *Varka and Gulshah* (Istanbul, Topkapu Sarai Library) of the 13th century, there appears a keen sense of decorative effects, especially in the transformation of the backgrounds into tapestries of color.

The establishment of Mongol rule at Tabriz and the conversion of the Mongol princes to Islam mark the real beginnings of the great period of Persian painting. There came together, in one place and at a single moment, the techniques of Chinese painting, a considerable influx of persons and ideas from the West, and a great literary and spiritual rejuvenation in Iran. The painting of the first half of the 14th century reflects these events. A series of illustrations of the *Shah-nama* allows us to codify the major iconographic themes of Persian legend, while the famous manuscripts of the *Universal History* by Rashid al-Din show the Persian artists' assimilation of styles and techniques from many parts of the world, particularly China. The interaction of this new wealth of forms and styles with an interest in the Iranian legends explains the masterpiece of the period, the so-called Demotte manuscript of the *Shah-nama*, whose 55 miniatures can be dated around 1330. In it we find represented in a single work a keen sense of drama that sometimes achieves real feeling and considerable psychological subtlety, with an astonishing variety of compositions and a stylistic versatility that make this manuscript unique in Iranian art.

The end of the 14th century and the first half of the 15th saw the development of Classical Persian painting, perhaps under the influence of painters such as Abd al-Hayy who were trained in the earlier style. Under the Timurids there developed a more lyrical art, in which poetic or even mystical subjects replaced the epic and created a new style. The British Museum manuscript of Khwaju Kirmani's *Divan*, painted by Junayd in 1396, and especially the manuscripts commissioned by Baysunghur Mirza in the beginning of the 15th century, invented or refined a new Iranian landscape characterized by high horizons, gold and blue backgrounds, and small figures set in a world of natural forms eternally in flower.

The second half of the 15th century is dominated by what is generally described as the Bihzadian revolution, after a Persian painter, Kamal al-Din Bihzad, who enjoyed great renown in his lifetime, but about whom we know little. The *Bustan*, in the Egyptian National Library at Cairo and the *Khamsa* (1494) in the British Museum, illuminated manuscripts to which Bihzad contributed the miniatures, indicate that this revolution consisted primarily of

Islamic Art (Timurid period). *Warrior Seated beside a Flowering Shrub*. 15th century. Museum of Fine Arts, Boston.

the rediscovery of human detail and the greater complexity in composition.

With Bihzad opens the most brilliant and richest period of Persian painting. A *Zafar-nama* in the Imperial Library, Teheran, Nizami miniatures in the British Museum, and a large *Shah-nama* in a private collection in New York represent the high points of Persian painting. Great painters such as Mīr Musavvir, Muhammadi (active *c.* 1580), Mir Ali al-Harawi, and many others lend a personal touch to many of these miniatures, although they worked within the general conventions of the period.

At the end of the 16th century and in the 17th century a new development took place in Persian painting. Aqa Riza and Riza Abbasi, among others, created the art of the court portrait and often gave it a touch of social satire that toward the middle of the century led to several examples of realistic cruelty. The succeeding centuries produced few masterpieces, although the great mural painting of the Kajar dynasty (18th century) displays a certain primitive charm.

The Turkish School

Turkish painting is still relatively unknown. Before the establishment of the Ottoman Empire, it is often difficult to determine exactly what is precisely Turkish in paintings that are generally described as Iranian. Nevertheless, a series of drawings at Istanbul, the so-called "Album of the Conqueror" (15th century; Istanbul, Topkapu Library), by Ahmed Musa and Mehmet Siyah Kalem is quite unlike the Persian work in style. These drawings consist of scenes of nomadic encampments in which the people, animals, and landscape are treated in a particularly vivid, virile, and realistic manner. In the 16th, 17th, and 18th centuries, there was also a court style that depicted the outstanding feats of the sultans. Many of these paintings are in a traditional Iranizing style, but always with greater realism of detail than in Persian painting. The masterpiece of this descriptive genre is a *Sur-nama* (1720–22) painted by Levni, which illustrates the festivities in Istanbul on the occasion of the circumcision of Ahmed III's sons.

The Mogul School

From the point of view of Islamic painting, the most important of the numerous schools in Moslem India flourished under the great Mogul emperors. They imported painters from Iran, in whose manuscripts and portraits Persian subjects and styles were gradually transformed by the traditions of Indian painting and later by certain Western conventions. The major difference between Persian and Mogul art lies in the use of color. The pure tones of Persian painting, applied without shading, became infinitely varied and graduated in Mogul work, which gradually took on a convincing illusion of space and atmosphere (*see* INDIAN ART).

ISRAELITE ART. It is customary to apply the terms Hebrew, Israelite, and Jewish to three successive historical periods: the first covers the period from the arrival of Abraham in the land of Canaan to the settlement of Jacob and his children in Egypt; the second, from the Exodus (*c.* 1200 B.C.) to the taking of Jerusalem (6th century B.C.); and the third, from the return from captivity (6th century B.C.) to the final destruction of Jerusalem, with the second revolt under Bar Kokhba (A.D. 132).

Nothing is known of the Hebrew art of the patriarchal period. For this entire age, during which the Israelites led a nomadic life, only the art of the original Canaanite inhabitants is known in any way.

The Israelite period encompasses the time of Moses (late 13th–early 12th century B.C.), the Judges (*c.* 1250–1050 B.C.), and the Kings, through the various historical vicissitudes—the united monarchy from Saul (who became king *c.* 1025 B.C.) to Solomon (reigned *c.* 973–933 B.C.), the schism—with Israel going to Samaria, and Judah to Jerusalem—the fall of Samaria (under the attacks of the Assyrian king Sargon II, in 721 B.C.), and the fall of Jerusalem (under the prolonged attacks of the Babylonian king Nebuchadnezzar, in 586 B.C.). It is well known that, from the beginning, any artistic expression was seriously limited by the prohibition in the Ten Commandments. But the words have been interpreted as prohibitions against the making of images for the purpose of worship; even the most pious sovereigns took certain liberties with this prohibition. The Ark of the Covenant in Jerusalem, within the

Israelite Art. *Cherub.* Ivory plaque from the palace of Achab, Samaria. 8th century B.C. Palestine Archaeological Museum, Jerusalem.

Temple of Solomon itself, was placed under the protection of two gilded cherubim (I *Kings* 6:23–28). Moreover, the bronze bases of the same sanctuary were decorated with lions, oxen, and cherubim (I *Kings* 7:29), while the precious woods with which the rooms of the Temple were paneled were also ornamented with cherubim, together with palms and garlands of flowers (I *Kings* 6:29). After the schism, the first king of Israel, Jeroboam (reigned *c.* 933–912 B.C.), installed two golden calves in the temples at Dan and Bethel (I *Kings* 12:28–29). When Solomon decided to build the Temple, about 959 B.C., he called in foreign craftsmen whose work naturally reflected the methods and styles of their own countries. The tripartite plan of the sanctuary (porch, main hall, and Holy of Holies) probably reproduced Canaanite prototypes. The decoration may well have originated in Phoenicia, whose art is known to have been strongly influenced by that of Egypt.

The same might be said of the ivories found at Samaria, capital of the kingdom of Israel, which decorated the wall paneling and furniture of leading citizens (*Amos* 6:4). The luxury and power of the state were reflected in the palace architecture. The Temple of Solomon (170 × 100 ft.) was an example of extraordinary wealth placed at the disposal of skilled craftsmen. The same was true of the official civil buildings of Jerusalem, of which nothing remains but a list (I *Kings* 7:2–12), and of the architectural achievements of Ahab, king of Israel (reigned *c.* 875–850 B.C.), which included the stables of Megiddo and the walls of Samaria—the finest piece of masonry excavated in Palestine. In the minor arts,

Israelite Art. Seal of "Shema servant of Jeroboam." *c.* 775 B.C. Department of Antiquities, Ministry of Education and Culture, Israel.

equally, a great many outstanding works were produced: among the surviving seals is that of Shema, the servant of Jeroboam II, with its roaring lion (c. 775 B.C.).

Just as Samaria had fallen to the Assyrians, Jerusalem fell to the Neo-Babylonians in 586 B.C. The city was completely pillaged. The two 30-foot high bronze columns—Yakin and Bo'az—that flanked the portal of the Temple (I *Kings* 7:21) were broken, as were the supports of the famous bronze water container.

The period of Jewish art began with the edict of Cyrus in 538 B.C., which brought the Babylonian Captivity to an end, and continued throughout the Achaemenid, Seleucid, and Roman periods up to the destruction of Jerusalem in A.D. 132. In the field of religious architecture, it is again the Temple that stands out as the most noteworthy example. The sanctuary that was destroyed in 586 B.C. was not rebuilt until 520 B.C., when Joshua and Zorobabel ordered work to begin (*Ezra* 6: 6–15). For the first time there appeared a seven-branched candelabrum, which replaced the ten-branched one of Solomon's time.

It was not until the reign of Herod the Great, who was made king by the Romans in 37 B.C., that the Temple regained its former splendor. Work was begun about 20 B.C., but was still unfinished by the time of Christ (*John* 2: 20). The building was one of the wonders of Jerusalem: it was still tripartite in plan, and was of white stone ornamented with gold plating, the roof dotted with gold needles. Herod also ordered his architects to modernize Samaria, renamed Sebaste; to honor the Ramet el-Khalil, the site of Abraham's encampment, by erecting a modern wall; and, above all, to erect over the cave of Macpela, which contained the Graves of the Patriarchs, at Hebron, a building worthy of their memory.

Israelite Art. *Spoils from the Temple in Jerusalem: Golden Candelabra.* Relief on the Arch of Titus, Rome. A.D. 70.

The funerary architecture that preceded and followed the time of Christ is also well documented at Jerusalem, with the tombs of the Valley of the Kidron; these show a definite imitation of Phoenician buildings, especially those at Amrit. The Tombs of the Kings and the tomb of Herod's family are good examples of tombs hollowed out of rock. The apocryphally named Tombs of the Judges (or Sanhedrin) and Retreat of the Apostles are decorated with naturalistic motifs (garlands, rosettes, finials, and bunches of grapes), which are also found in great profusion among acanthus leaves on ossuaries. The decoration of these ossuaries was based on that of the sarcophagi, which were also of stone.

Further evidence of Jewish architecture has come to light through the Israeli excavations on the site of Masada, the center of Jewish resistance from A.D. 66 to 73, situated in desert country on the western shore of the Dead Sea. Herod had a palace built there, with mosaics and paintings that created the illusion of marble; but this residence was even more a fortress, with an arsenal, stores, and cisterns of huge capacity.

Herod the Great was also responsible for the foundation of Caesarea Maritima on the Phoenician site known as Strato's Tower. Excavations have revealed monuments of the Roman period; a theater and an acephalous statue of Artemis of Ephesus. As at Samaria, Jewish art was completely impregnated with the Greco-Roman civilization. Apart from sections of the substructure, which includes the still visible Wailing Wall, nothing remains of the Temple of Jerusalem, not "one stone upon another" (*Mark* 13: 1–2). Of the seven-branched candelabrum and the sacred trumpets, all that remains is a representation on the triumphal Arch of Titus in Rome (A.D. 70). This is probably the most spectacular example of Jewish ritual art (*see* JEWISH ART).

Israelite Art. The tomb of Zechariah. 1st century A.D. Valley of the Kidron, Jerusalem. *Photo Goldner, Paris.*

ITTEN, Johannes (1888, Süderen-Linden, Thun—1967, Zurich), Swiss painter. Through his work and his teaching, Itten was one of the pioneers of 20th-century art. From 1913 to 1914 he studied under Adolf Hölzel at the Stuttgart Academy and was considerably influenced by his theories of color harmony. Successively, from 1916, he directed an art school in Vienna, taught under Walter Gropius at the Weimar Bauhaus (1919–23), established a weaving studio in Switzerland, and directed the Krefeld School of Textile Art. Finally, from 1938 to 1953, he took over the direction of the Zurich School and Museum of Applied Art. Itten formulated his ideas in several published works, notably in *Kunst der Farbe*, 1961 (*Art of Color*, 1961) and *Mein Vorkurs am Bauhaus*, 1963 (*Design and Form*, 1964). His earliest abstract compositions made original use of Cubist ideas (*Meeting*, 1916; Zurich, Kunsthaus). Subsequently a horizontal-vertical checkerwork characterized his search for expression through color, for a concrete painting that is both rational and sensual (*Horizontal-Vertical*, 1916; *Modulation Orange-Green-Blue*, 1964).

J

JACOBSEN, Arne (b. 1902, Copenhagen), major Danish architect of the 20th century. His first important work was the Bellavista Housing Estate (1933) at Klampenborg, near Copenhagen, where the terraced arrangement of each unit gave the individual apartments a view over the sea. Jacobsen avoids all extraneous effects and is concerned only with the impression of the architectural mass; for a long time his work was influenced by Le Corbusier. However, the group of individual yellow-brick houses he built between 1950 and 1955 at Søholm shows a diversity in handling these masses. The Jesperson Building (1955) in Copenhagen, like the Rødovre Town Hall (1954–56), owes its purity of line to a subtle use of the so-called curtain wall—lightweight walls of transparent surface, freed from the function of support by modern materials and building methods. In Copenhagen's first skyscraper, the SAS Building (1959), Jacobsen used a reinforced concrete mass as a podium or substructure to a steel and curtain wall structure. In addition to his architectural activity, Jacobsen designed the interior decoration of the SAS Building; his many industrial designs, for furniture, cutlery, and textiles, for example, brought him international recognition.

JACOBSEN, Robert (b. 1912, Copenhagen), Danish sculptor. Jacobsen's earliest works were in wood, and their hieratic Expressionism has much in common with images of primitive magic, with which his sensibility had deep affinities. In his iron figures called *Dolls* (1949–56) and *Cosmonauts* (1962) he created a humorous parody of these early images. In 1941 he joined the Surrealist-influenced Danish group, Host. The sculptural problem of space was, however, already his major preoccupation, and it reappeared in all his later works. He settled in Paris in 1947, and began to use iron as the medium for his spatial structures, finding it suitable for the severe requirements of his design as well as the fantasy of his inspiration. He achieved subtle effects of opposing rhythms in his reliefs, and finally created geometric treelike forms projecting into space (*Message to Space*, 1962). In Jacobsen's late works the iron is oxydized, corroded, twisted, and knotted into extremely varied shapes (*Spatial Graphism*, 1962). In his reliefs of *Cosmonauts*, he even introduced painted surfaces, whose dark or bright tones bring out the conflicts and dissonances of the forms.

JACOMART. *See* **BACO,** Jaime.

JACOPO DELLA QUERCIA (1374/75, Siena—1438, Bologna), Italian Renaissance sculptor. He first appears among the contestants in the famous competition held in Florence in 1401 for the execution of the reliefs on the Baptistery Doors. His entry has not survived, and his first certain work is the tomb of Ilaria del Carretto in the cathedral of S. Martino, Lucca (*c.* 1406). It has been asserted by some scholars that Della Quercia was aware of Northern Gothic sculpture, in particular the works of the Burgundian Claus Sluter, and certain aspects of his Fonte Gaia reliefs, for instance, support this. Jacopo's other early works were a *Madonna and Child* (1406; Ferrara, Museo dell'Opera), and his first work in Siena itself, the Fonte Gaia (portions of which are now in Siena's Palazzo Pubblico). The latter, a fountain, was commissioned in 1409, but not executed until 1414–19.

The tombs and altar Jacopo provided for the Trenta Chapel in the church of S. Frediano, Lucca, were begun after 1416 and finished in 1422. The sculptured retable is notable in that its figures are not freestanding, as they appear to be, but are in high relief, while the predella panels (carved in low relief) exhibit the typical Gothic attitude toward pictorial space. The figures themselves show a new sense of unity and a grave simplicity in the features, which remind one irresistibly of works by the young Michelangelo.

From 1417 to 1431 Jacopo worked on the font in the baptistery of S. Giovanni, Siena, for which he carved one of the gilt-bronze reliefs—*Zaccharias in the Temple* (1427–30)—after the completion of Donatello's panel of the *Feast of Herod* (1423–27), which greatly influenced Della Quercia by its realistic interpretation of pictorial space. Later, Jacopo was commissioned to complete the marble upper part of the font, for which he carved the small *Prophets* in niches, as well as the crowning figure of *St. John the Baptist*. Jacopo's final important work, which occupied him for the rest of his life, was the decoration of the door of S. Petronio in Bologna, executed from 1425 onward, although he also undertook various other works in the same years. Today the S. Petronio door consists of a tympanum containing a freestanding *Madonna and Child*, flanked by statues of *St. Petronius* and *St. Ambrose* (the latter by another hand); around the door are 15 Old Testament narratives in low relief, all that was executed of a more ambitious project. These reliefs are extremely striking. In the iconography and in the bulky rhythmic forms of the draperies, they look back to Northern Gothic art; in their use of anatomy, of a rational scale between figures in the same composition, and in their masterly handling of very low relief, they reflect the most recent experiments of Lorenzo Ghiberti and Donatello; and finally, in their grandeur, directness, lack of intrusive decorative detail, and single-minded concentration on the meaning of each episode, they anticipate Michelangelo.

JANCO, Marcel (b. 1895, Bucharest), Rumanian painter. In 1915 he went to Zurich to study architecture at the Kunstgewerbeschule. There he met Jean Arp and a compatriot, the poet Tristan Tzara, and took part in the meetings of the famous Cabaret Voltaire, where Dadaism was born. From that time Janco moved toward an art that eschewed all figuration, and he sought to establish relations between abstraction and architectonic elements in his reliefs and paintings. His paintings on sacking (*Sun, Bright Garden*,

Jacopo della Quercia. *Creation of Adam.* Central portal of S. Petronio, Bologna. 1425–38. *Photo Anderson-Giraudon.*

1918; Priv. Coll.), his polychrome plaster reliefs, and later his oils and collages use rough, worn materials arranged in layers. In 1918, with Arp, Augusto Giacometti, and others, he helped found the Radical Artists group in Zurich, which published a review of the same name. A visit to Paris (1921) helped him to see in what ways his art differed from the Dadaists and future Surrealists. In 1922 Janco returned to Rumania, where he founded the review *Contimporanul*, whose varied activities continued until 1940. In 1942 he arrived in Tel Aviv as a Jewish war refugee. During the 1940s he largely abandoned his earlier abstract tendencies and the fresh-toned figurative art he had developed in the 1920s and 1930s, replacing them with Expressionist visions of the subject matter around him (*Arab Café, Yellow*, 1947; Los Angeles, Coll. Kline). During the 1950s and 1960s he returned to abstraction, this time in a more serene and lyrical vein. As opposed to his work of the 1920s, his late abstractions were based on natural forms (*Flight 607*, 1957).

Japanese Art (Yayoi period). *Haniwa warrior*. 5th century A.D. National Museum, Tokyo.

JAPANESE ART. The history of Japan reveals to a unique degree the ability of a highly gifted people to assimilate cultural patterns, religious beliefs, and technology from foreign sources, and to adapt them successfully to their own needs, thereby producing a remarkable fusion of native and foreign elements that is truly Japanese in every respect.

The origins of the Japanese people cannot be accurately or fully defined; we are fairly certain, however, that the Japanese archipelago was inhabited as far back as the Upper Paleolithic period. The evidence of several structural similarities between the huts on the Siberian coast and those of the first inhabitants of the archipelago suggests that these early settlers came from northern Asia. This archaic period is divided into two main phases: the first, the so-called Jōmon period, is characterized by a pottery style that was already well developed when it first appeared in Japan and that dates from at least the 6th century B.C.; the second, which began around the 3rd century B.C. with the appearance of Yayoi pottery, probably developed on the island of Kyushu, whence it gained ground rapidly in the rest of the archipelago. The use of bronze and iron spread at the same time. The origin of the Japanese people goes back in fact to these periods, which saw successive invasions of the islands from the coasts of northern and southeastern Asia.

HISTORICAL DEVELOPMENT

Prehistory

A characteristic feature of the Iron Age, from about the 1st or 2nd century A.D., were large families formed on a patriarchal pattern—a phenomenon that soon led to the development of rival clans. The most powerful of these were possibly the men of Yamato—considered ancestors of the present day Japanese—who organized themselves into a veritable state in the region of what is today Nara. A number of terra-cotta figurines called *haniwa* date from this period. These figures were funerary in nature, and were placed in rows around the great tombs.

The outstanding features of the period that extends from the 4th to the 6th century A.D. are due to the preponderant influence of the Yamato clan and to the quarrels of its rulers with the kingdoms of Korea. By the end of the 5th century A.D., Koreans and Chinese were settling on the Japanese archipelago, bringing with them the new techniques of weaving, metal casting, silkworm breeding, and calligraphy. During the period from the mid-6th to the mid-7th century A.D., known as the Asuka period, the introduction of Buddhism took place, an event of far-reaching consequences in the development of Japanese culture. At first the new faith met with some resistance, but with the regency of Prince Shōtoku Taishi in A.D. 593, Buddhism became established as the state religion. Great monasteries were built as centers of learning and community life.

Nara Period (A.D. 645–784)

In A.D. 645 a major reform in the government, called the *Taika* ("great reform"), brought about the introduction of certain political innovations modeled after the Chinese system of government. As a result of foreign influences, Japanese civilization made rapid progress: legal codes were promulgated, and education and literacy were spread by Buddhist monks. A substantial body of literature, although written in Chinese, gave the Japanese a national consciousness. Painting, sculpture, and architecture were given every encouragement, while the arts of weaving, silk making, lacquerwork, and metalwork also developed. This relatively short period is of paramount importance in the history of Japan, because it saw foreign techniques and styles used as a basis for the elaboration of forms peculiar to the national genius of the Japanese people, and for the formation of a spirit whose traces can still be found today—a spirit the Japanese call *Yamato* ("Japanese").

Japanese Art (Heian period). Five-storied pagoda at Daigoji, Kyoto. A.D. 951. *Photo Enrico Mariani, Como.*

Heian Period (A.D. 784–1185)

This began with a move of capital from Nara to Nagaoka, and then in A.D. 794 to Heian Kyo (modern Kyoto), where a new capital was patterned after the plan of the Chinese city of Ch'ang-an. Since the country had now been pacified and organized, with a ruler (Emperor Kammu, A.D. 781–806) who possessed unquestioned power, a golden age came into existence in Japan. Numerous new temples and monasteries were founded. Painting and sculpture enjoyed an exceptional flowering because of patronage from the court and from chiefs of such great families as the Fijiwara. The provincial governments, however, were vitiated by corruption early in this period. The clan leaders fought each other, and one of them, Minamoto Yoritomo, established a military government, or *bakufu*, at Kamakura. This was the beginning of the shogunate, which remained the instrument of government in Japan until 1868.

Kamakura Period (1185–1392)

While Yoritomo instituted a military dictatorship throughout the country, new Buddhist sects that were Japanese in conception arose, and the Zen sect was introduced from China; austere in spirit, these sects preached stringent military virtues. The popular tongue supplanted Chinese as the literary language, and epic narratives replaced folk tales. Art also experienced the effects of this change: architectural forms were simplified; sculpture became realistic again; warlike scenes predominated in painting; and the decorative arts enjoyed a fresh impetus. Every samurai had to cultivate moral and physical qualities that conformed to a strict moral code. These qualities were tested in 1274 and again in 1281, when the Mongols tried to invade Japan and were finally repulsed. The *bakufu* was unable to pay its troops, however, and Emperor Godaigo seized his opportunity to overthrow the military regime. This brought about a short-lived restoration of imperial rule (1334–35). Soon another civil war brought the warriors back into power under the leadership of Ashikaga Takauji, who established a new government at Kyoto, appointing a second emperor after Godaigo's flight from the capital. Finally, in 1392, the two governments were reunited in Kyoto, but the power remained in the hands of the shogunate.

Muromachi Period (1392–1573)

Far from practicing the austerity of the Kamakura shoguns, those of Kyoto began to indulge in the luxurious life of the capital, and gradually real power passed to the provincial chiefs, who soon waged bloody struggles for supremacy. A long series of civil wars followed, beginning in 1467. The arts nevertheless continued to develop in spite of the disorders, particularly at Kyoto. The arts of the tea ceremony and flower arranging were codified; the decorative arts, lacquerwork, embroidery, and inlaid metalwork reached a high level of refinement; and the search for perfection in these endeavors, encouraged by the spirit of Zen, continued unabated.

Momoyama Period (1573–1615)

The next period, beginning with Oda Nobunaga's accession to power, did not bring any fundamental change in the arts, but the relative peace allowed them to develop more freely. This precarious equilibrium, however, was threatened by Oda Nobunaga's suicide in 1582. One of his generals, Toyotomi Hideyoshi, succeeded him and continued his peaceful policy. The arrival of European traders and missionaries introduced the use of firearms, which modified methods of fighting and enabled the government to further enforce its authority.

Civil and military architecture was radically modified during this time. The interiors of houses began to be arranged on simple plans in which the proportions of component parts were of primary importance. A taste for works of art spread, and there was introduced into domestic architecture the use of the *toko-no-ma*, an alcove in which a painting or flowers were displayed.

Edo Period (1615–1868)

This stage began when Ieyasu Tokugawa seized power and the capital was changed once again, this time to Edo, present-day Tokyo. Japan was ruled as a feudal state by a shogun and its isolation became reinforced. In 1543, however, the Portuguese had persuaded the Japanese government to open the ports of Nagasaki and Hirado to Western trade. Japanese ships traveled to China, the countries of southeast Asia, and even to New Spain (Mexico) on trading expeditions, but foreigners were still forbidden to enter Japan and Christianity was regarded with suspicion if not open hostility. In spite of this, the natural curiosity of the Japanese people finally caused them to accept a number of European techniques, while Japanese art, under the influence of the Chinese Ming style, entered its Baroque phase. Painting became somewhat democratic, and this period saw the beginning of the popular genre of *ukiyo-e*, or colored prints, which enjoyed an immense vogue. Along with this technical expansion and with the introduction of new styles, there were several attempts to return to traditional forms and patterns of life, especially as the nationalistic Japanese grew more exasperated at the reiterated demands of Europeans to open their ports to trade. At last in 1854 the first treaty of friendship was signed by the shogun with the United States, then with Great Britain, Russia, and Holland. In 1868 Emperor Meiji mounted the throne with full powers of government in his hands.

Modern Period

Two wars, one with China in 1895, the second with Russia in 1904–5, ending in victory for Japan, helped to raise the country to the rank of a great power. Art was also affected, but it was not long before it assimilated Western ideas and transformed them to suit Japanese taste, while continuing to develop the traditions of the Edo period. After the beginning of the Tasho era in 1912 and Japan's involvement in two world wars, there followed a period of intensive industrialization. A cultural exchange with the West took place that coincided with the internationalization of art in general.

One of the essential factors for an understanding of Japanese art is the close correspondence that has always existed throughout Japanese history between political and artistic periods. To the Western mind the Japanese spirit is the quintessence of refinement in its cultivation of the ephemeral: the planning of a tea ceremony, the essence of which is gesture; the arrangement of a bouquet of flowers, whose formal interrelationships are as subtle as they are evanescent; the calligraphy of a poem, describing an instant or a state of mind on paper so fragile that a breath of air can carry it away. Yet the Japanese spirit is a rigid spirit as well, as is evident in the conceptions governing its own life and death, and in its infinite patience in the search for perfection.

ARCHITECTURE

The principal characteristic of Japanese architecture before the modern period was its frequent use of wood. Excavations have revealed wooden Neolithic huts of the pit-house type, structures that were half sunk into the earth and then covered with a saddle roof resting directly on the ground. These primitive buildings already show the primary importance of the components of roofs in Japanese architecture. In Japan, as in China, the roof is first raised on pillars, which mark the habitable space and which are placed on the ground without foundations. Between these pillars, partitions of wood or paper are stretched, supporting nothing and acting more as screens than as elements of building construction. The numerous *haniwa* terra-cotta models of dwellings that have survived from the archaic period have enabled us

Japanese Art. Great Torii of the Shinto sanctuary of Itsukushima, Miyajima. *Photo Sakamoto, Tokyo.*

to reconstruct the various types of roofing common during the 5th century A.D., some of which are the direct antecedents of buildings in the primitive Shinto style. At this period, the spaces between the pillars may have been filled with low mud walls or bamboo hurdles coated with lacquer or clay. Decorations on mirror backs and bronze bells prove that, alongside these houses, there existed pile dwellings similar to those still found in southeast Asia. Other archaic houses illustrated by *haniwa* models are shown built in terraces, but with each wing having individual roofs—a type of layout common in all periods.

The styles of Japanese architecture cannot be categorized in quite the same way as European styles; indeed, only two major orders can be distinguished: the Shinto and the Buddhist, each of them comprising not only a variety of styles or fashions, but also different systems of construction. A study of these factors requires a dual approach: either a consideration of types of construction (pagodas, prayer halls, outbuildings) or an examination of the elements of construction (the form and number of the roofs, forms of porches, and the decoration). The Japanese architect experimented freely and increasingly with a certain number of elements. This explains the apparent unity that makes it impossible to recognize a particular period or style except through an investigation of the constituent parts of each building.

Shinto Order

All buildings belonging to the Shinto religion, made of wood, possessed a plan that was generally quite simple, consisting of a single room (sometimes divided by a movable partition) surrounded by a balustraded gallery. The most characteristic types are to be found at the shrines at Ise and Izumo. These monuments have massive corner pillars supporting the roof beams without the intermediary cushion of capitals; a raised floor surrounded by a gallery; and a thatched saddle roof whose gables are decorated with scissor-shaped finials called *chigi*. A crest of rounded billets (*katsuogi*) lies crosswise on the ridge beam and presumably had a function at one time, but is now purely decorative. The Shinto temples are generally situated within a triangular space enclosed by four successive hedges. The *torii* (ceremonial gateways) stand before the actual entrances to the temples, which are simple porches. There are six main types of Shinto temples—one or more examples of each type still exist—all of which date from the Nara and Heian periods. After these, Shinto architecture gradually adopted many of the features of Buddhist architecture.

Japanese Art (Nara period). Yakushiji pagoda, near Nara. 710. *Photo Shosuke Takemura.*

Asuka and Nara Periods

The Buddhist monks from Korea brought with them a style and method of building adapted to the requirements of the new religion. The console constructed on the simple capital of a column was copied from the Chinese, but was transformed by Japanese architects to support the enormous weight of the new roofs. The building of the numerous monasteries began in the reign of Empress Suikō (A.D. 593–628). The oldest wooden structures in the world, the Hōryūji monastery complex near Nara, date from this period. These monasteries were generally built on a square plan surrounded by a double enclosure. Inside this precinct were two pagodas containing the relics, the principal hall housing the Buddha's image, the lecture hall (*kōdō*), and two small buildings, one used as a library, the other as a bell tower. The structures themselves were entirely of wood, built with pillars containing a slight convexity in the middle, which supported roofs of varying complexity. The roofs were typically Chinese, with upcurved forms and tile rather than thatch covering. Sometimes a sanctuary was enlarged by adding a covered gallery (called a *mokoshi*) with widely projecting eaves supported by pillars. The Yakushiji pagoda near Nara has one of the most striking examples of *mokoshi*. The only

Japanese Art (Nara period). Yumedono, or Hall of Dreams, of the Hōryūji Temple, Nara. 8th century. *Photo Sakamoto, Tokyo.*

surviving buildings of the period are the pagodas at Yakushiji and Hōryūji (the latter in Nara), the *kondō* (prayer hall) and *yumedono* of the Hōryūji, the pagoda of the Hokiji, some parts of the Shitenōji temple near Osaka, and the *kondō* of the Tōshōdaiji at Nara.

Heian Period

The introduction of new Buddhist sects and the establishment of their monasteries led to a modification in the layout of religious buildings. The arrangement of the buildings in the mountain monasteries followed more or less the natural formation of the ground and the enclosures were abandoned altogether. The monasteries on more level land remained faithful to the traditional plans but the enclosures were gradually replaced by passageways that connected the different buildings to one another. The pagoda alone remained isolated. There were hardly any changes in construction methods. Like the Japanese system of government borrowed from China, the symmetrical plan of the audience courts of the imperial palace complex or Chōdōin at Kyoto also stemmed from Chinese sources. One of the most important buildings of the entire complex, the Hall of State in the Chōdōin, was quite large and imposing, resting upon a series of red pillars rising from a stone platform. Leading to this monumental structure is a series of courts, surrounded by corridors as in the Buddhist monastery complexes, and with isolated buildings arranged symmetrically on either side of a central axis. To the south-east of the Chōdōin was the imperial residence of Kōkyō, composed of a group of buildings decidedly asymmetrical in plan. Just beyond the entrance to the Kōkyō was the only court of any size, to the south of which was located the large audience hall, called the Shishinden, which can be seen today in a 19th-century reconstruction at Kyoto. Like the Hall of State, this structure rises upon a series of pillars creating a veranda leading to the throne chamber itself. Behind the Shishinden were two somewhat smaller halls of the same length. To the west of these buildings was the actual residence, and to the east an alternate residence and other buildings having specific purposes, such as the preserving of the sacred imperial mirror, etc.

Japanese Art (Heian period). Hōōdō, or Phoenix Hall, of the Byōdōin Temple, Uji, near Kyoto. 1052–53. *Photo Enrico Mariani, Como.*

The houses were wooden; those of the nobility were raised slightly above the ground upon low piles, while humbler buildings were built over cavities. Continental techniques began at this time to influence Shinto temples, which were embellished with corridors. Good examples of this development can be seen in the Sumiyoshi Jinsha just outside Osaka, and in the Kasunga Jinsha at Nara. The pagoda of Daigoji at Kyoto and the Phoenix Hall, or Hōōdō, at Uji are remarkable survivals of this golden age.

Kamakura Period

During this period, the new *tenjikuyō* method of construction was imported from China, its special feature being the use of bracketing, which consisted of pieces of wood inserted one above the other, rising in tiers from the bodies of the main pillars to the roof. The reconstruction of the gigantic hall and south gateway of the Todaiji temple at Nara is the most typical example of this kind of tiered console. It should be remembered that after this time the *tenjikuyō* system was seldom used alone but rather in combination with the Sino-Japanese style that was already traditional and with the *karayō* system, which was the third method of construction imported from China by the Zen monks during this period, and the most commonly used in the Zen monasteries. The relic hall of the Engakuji monastery at Kamakura, built about 1282, and the Kaisandō, a memorial chapel at Eihōji, built in 1352, are classic models of this elaborate yet rather austere style.

Muromachi Period

The final syncretism of Shinto and Buddhist architecture was realized in this period. Pavilions adorned with gilding were set in the midst of splendid gardens (such as the Kinkakuji, the golden pavilion at Kyoto, 1397), and in their design there was an attempt to harmonize traditional ideas with the new developments. The walls were ornamented with multilobated windows; roofs became more and more curved, and seemed lighter.

Momoyama Period

Oda Nobunaga's example in building the first fortified castle in 1576 at Azuchi was immediately followed by several other clan chiefs, notably Toyotomi Hideyoshi, who built the castles at Osaka (1583) and Fushimi (1594). Other castles built during this period include those at Matsumoto (1594) and Himeji (1608), the

Japanese Art (Kamakura period). Shariden, or Engakuji relic hall, Kamakura. *c.* 1282. *Photo Sakamoto, Tokyo.*

Japanese Art (Muromachi period). Kinkakuji, or Golden Pavilion, Kyoto. 1397. *Photo Louis Frédéric, Paris.*

latter castle being today the best-preserved. Between the massive keep and the imposing walls surrounded by broad moats, there were luxurious pavilions and gardens. This was a new style called *shoin-zukuri*, imitated from the Buddhist temples but built for pleasure and comfort, and containing a great profusion of ornamentation. Private urban dwellings were constructed in long rows along the streets in the cities. These buildings were thatched and built of wood with only two or three bays on the façade. An elegant simplicity spread everywhere, becoming the hallmark of the period.

Edo Period

Temple architecture underwent a slight change around the year 1600. While each unit of the monastery complex formerly had its individual roof, architects began to group the various rooms under a single roof, abandoning the exterior passageways. The roofs became increasingly elaborate—as at the Hachiman temple in the monastery of Saidaiji at Nara and in the Kitano shrine at Kyoto (1607)—and the most visible parts of the building were adorned with sculpture, decorative panels, and were painted in bright colors, as was the fine memorial chapel at Eihoji. Decoration, directly inspired by Chinese motifs of the Ming Dynasty, became quite luxurious or even excessively ornamented, as in the gateway to Tokugawa Teyasu's mausoleum at Nikko. In the towns, the houses began to be built of plaster and covered with tiles because of the frequent fires, while the concentration of population and consequent lack of space forced architects to design buildings of several stories.

Japanese Art (Momoyama period). Matsumoto Castle. 1594. *Photo Sakamoto, Tokyo.*

Modern Period

Since the restoration of Emperor Meiji in 1868, Western influence has weighed heavily on Japanese architecture, except in the case of religious buildings, which have remained traditional. Blocks of flats and business establishments were built in imitation of European styles, or else incorporated elements of European styles in traditional Japanese forms. Because concrete is more resistant than either wood or plaster, it has been used extensively since the disastrous earthquake of 1923, which destroyed half of Tokyo. In recent years a number of Japanese architects, such as Hideo Kosaka (b. 1912), Kenzo Tange (b. 1913), and Kunio Mayekawa (b. 1905), have begun to develop a modern style that makes excellent use of materials developed by the latest technological advances, seen in Tange's Sogetsu Hall (1960) and Mayekawa's Harumi Flats (1957), both in Tokyo.

PAINTING

While the European artists have employed fresco and oil predominantly as the media of their paintings, the Japanese have for the most part limited themselves to watercolor and gouache. Japanese pictorial technique was, at least in the beginning, essentially Chinese. India ink or wash color was applied on paper or silk with the same kind of brush that was used for calligraphy. Originally, the artist was limited by the nature of his format—either the panel or the scroll. The latter eventually became the most commonly used, in the form of the *kakemono* or vertical scroll and the *makimono* or horizontal scroll, held in the hand and read from right to left. Early Japanese painting was exclusively religious (specifically Buddhist) in inspiration. Only gradually were certain subjects treated for their own sake rather than for their religious significance. This change is noticeable in the Heian period, with the development of a mature secular art and its division into the traditional subjects: the portrait, landscape, flowers and birds, narrative, and genre painting. Beyond their similarity in subject matter and materials, the major distinction between Japanese and Chinese painting was in their approach: while the Chinese artist was realistic, the Japanese artist idealized and gave free reign to his natural and often lyrical imagination. This explains why there soon appeared a specifically Japanese style, the *yamato-e*, in which outward appearance is reduced to its essential elements and is treated in a way that can be described as romantic.

Asuka and Nara Periods

The introduction of Buddhism into Japan during the second half of the 6th century A.D. brought with it a flood of immigrants, particularly artists who specialized in Buddhist themes. The only work of any importance dating from the Asuka period is the *Tamamushi Zushi*, the Beetle-wing shrine, kept in the monastery of Hōryūji. It is a model palace standing on a high base whose panels are decorated with various sacred scenes and figures, including some from the *Jataka* stories (stories of self-sacrificing Bodhisattvas), painted in red, yellow, and green on a black background. The paintings lack perspective and correct proportion, and several successive scenes are illustrated on the same panel, a characteristic of the later *yamato-e* style. In the 8th century A.D. Buddhism became the official religion and the art that served it experienced a golden age, coinciding with the transfer of the government to Nara in A.D. 710. At the time that the capital was being moved, the walls of the *kondō* (Golden Hall) of the Hōryūji monastery were decorated with a large group of paintings that unfortunately were almost completely destroyed by fire in 1949. These paintings consisted of 12 panels depicting the Buddha and various Bodhisattvas. Another famous work of this period, the *Portrait of Prince Shotoku* (Tokyo, Imperial Household Collection), resembles in style the portraits from Turfan, Sinkiang. The *Edakumi-ryō*, or Painters' Bureau, was established in 728 in Nara, its function being to decorate temples and to produce sacred images. Its workshop employed about 60 artists, each of whom was a specialist in executing backgrounds, in outlining, in applying color, and so on. Some of its notable productions were illustrations of the sutras, such as the *Causes and Effects*, dealing with the life of Buddha. Among the works of art surviving from this period, the treasures of the Shōsōin, a storehouse in Nara, are of considerable interest. The most famous of the paintings preserved there include the portrait of a *Woman Under a Tree* and the *Bodhisattva Banner*, a pen-and-ink drawing of a Bodhisattva on a cloud. The works from the Shōsōin reveal a new tendency in Japanese art; the figures are no longer seen frontally but instead are drawn in the three-quarter position, and the use of shading creates the illusion of relief.

Heian Period

The seat of government was transferred to Kyoto in an attempt to escape the growing domination of the Buddhist priesthood, and Buddhism itself underwent certain changes under the stimulus of the Tendai and Shingon sects. The adherents of these sects preferred painted figures to sculptured images, and a great number of paintings have survived from this period. Two subjects are outstanding: the mandala, a complex and schematized diagram of Buddhist deities, and pictures of the Guardians of the Faith, such as the *Red Fudo* of Myōōin on Mount Koya, with its fierce three-quarter view. Buddhist iconography of the period also included portraits of priests and monks, such as the *Monk Jiondaishi* (11th century; Nara, Yakushiji monastery), and innumerable pictures of the Amida Buddha, whose cult spread at the end of the Heian period. Then, *c.* A.D. 1000, the *yamato-e*, or painting in the Japanese manner, apeared as a recognizable style, stressing depictions of landscapes, towns, seasonal activities, and scenes from Japanese tales. Indeed, the *yamato-e* was the first deliberately secular art. The most famous work of this kind is the *Genji Monogatari* ("Tale of Genji") by Lady Murasaki, a narrative concerning the members of the Heian court. The most original feature of these scroll paintings is the unusual treatment of perspective: all the scenes are viewed from above, with the roofs of the buildings eliminated in order to enable the observer to look within. Although the coloration is brilliant, the general impression left by the *Genji Monogatari* is one of calm and serenity. The scrolls of *Animal Caricatures* (late 11th century; Kyoto, Kozanji Temple) ascribed to the priest Tōba Sōjō possess liveliness and humor in their satirical treatment of human foibles and deeds, and constitute another distinct type of scroll painting of the late Heian period.

Kamakura Period

While Kamakura art remained faithful to the styles of the preceding period, it revealed a marked tendency toward realism and dramatic—even violent—action, particularly in religious paintings, in which scenes of hell are represented in an imaginative manner.

The same realism is noticeable in portraiture, in which the painter was expected to produce a likeness. The portrait of *Minamoto no Yoritomo* (Takao, Jingoji Temple) by Fujiwara no Takanobu (1142–1205), for example, is a vivid character study. Another equally expressive portrait is of the monk *Myōe-shōnin* by Enichi bō Jōnin (early 13th century; Kyoto, Kozanji Temple), which represents the holy man sitting in a forest in an attitude of profound meditation. The Emaki (a horizontally opened hand scroll) of *Thirty-Six Immortal Poets* (three fragments are in Washington, D.C., Freer Gallery), a collection of poems accompanied by the portraits of the poets, was painted by Fujiwara no Nobuzane (*c.* 1177–1265), the son of Takanobu.

Notable among the religious works of the time is the *Life of Ippen*, illustrated by Eni (1299; Kyoto, Kankikoji Temple). The military tales are among the finest of the secular works. Some of the best-known examples are the scrolls of the *Heiji Monogatari* ("Tales of the Heiji Insurrection"), such as the *Attack on the Sanjo Palace* (Boston, Museum of Fine Arts), dealing with the Heiji civil war of 1159. These scenes, with their drama and violent movement, belong to a type of painting that is typically and traditionally Japanese.

Muromachi Period

Under the influence of the newly introduced Zen Buddhist cult, the traditional Buddhist iconography was neglected in favor of subjects that were considered more congenial to contemplation: barren landscapes and colorless, extremely austere portraits of Zen priests. Consequently, there spread through the 14th century a style of wash drawing called *suiboku*, executed with india ink alone. The leading practitioners of the *suiboku* technique were Mokuan, a Japanese painter who had settled in China, and the monk Kaō. They were succeeded by such artists as Bompō (1344–1420) and Chō Densu, whose work anticipated the great painters of the 15th century—Shūbun, Nōami (1397–1471), his son Geiami (1431–85), and Geiami's son Soami (*c.* 1472–1525). None of these, however, could rival Sesshū (1420–1506), the first Japanese artist to achieve complete mastery of the *suiboku* style. The modeling of his brushstrokes and the quality of his tones produced some of the most striking examples of the wash technique; his landscape entitled *Haboku Sansui* (1495; Tokyo, National Museum) is considered one of his finest works. Sesshū's most important followers were Bunsei, Sesson (*c.* 1504–89), and Jasoku. Kanō Masanobu created a style that combined the atmosphere and technique of the *yamato-e* with the expressive character of the Chinese *suiboku*. The compositions of landscapes and flowers on screens, panels, and scrolls were quite vigorous and were often colored, resulting in a style that was perpetuated by the Kanō school well into the 18th century. The authentic *yamato-e* style, however, continued to develop alongside that of the Kanō school, and Tosa Mitsunobu (1435–1525) of the Imperial Academy gave it a new vitality with his precise line and fresh color. This return to tradition, which was continued by his successors, who formed the Tosa school, survived until modern times.

Momoyama Period

During a period whose outstanding feature was the construction of fortified castles, artists began to employ an exuberant style featuring the lavish use of gold and brilliant colors. The great master of this exciting and splendid style was Kanō Eitoku (1543–90), the grandson of Kanō Motonobu (1476–1559), whom the shogun Nobunaga commissioned to de-

Japanese Art. Detail from the *Emaki of the Animals*. Late 12th century.

corate the seven stories of his castle at Azuchi, near Kyoto. It seems that at that time the Kanō school practically monopolized the decoration of castles and possibly of monasteries as well. The Tosa school remained completely overshadowed until Nonomura Sōtatsu (d. 1643) re-established its popularity at the beginning of the 17th century. The outstanding feature of Sōtatsu's work was his use of the *tarashikomi* technique, which consisted of applying the pigment on a surface that had been previously covered with paint and was still damp.

Edo Period

During this long period of stability and prosperity, the middle class shared with the nobility the latter's once exclusive privileges as patrons and arbiters of art. The nobles favored only the traditional schools of Kanō and Tosa, which were dedicated to the imitation of ancient models, while humbler people encouraged the appearance of several new types of art that had a common concern for the human personality. Kanō Tanyū (1602–74), Eitoku's grandson, was so successful that his own brothers' descendants were elevated to the status of official painters, mainly on his merit alone. Their work for the great feudal lords as well as for the government spread the Kanō style throughout Japan. During this time, the painters of the Tosa tradition were for the most part mediocre, but Tosa Mitsuoki (1617–91), the grandson of Mitsuyoshi (1539–1613), raised the prestige of the school to a slight degree. Classical subjects and style, however, found a brilliant exponent in Ogata Kōrin (1659–1716). Kōrin excelled as a painter of landscapes, flowers, and animals, treating these in a bold decorative style in which line was less important than color, as is clearly evident in one of his masterpieces, *Irises* (Tokyo, Nezu Art Museum). A realistic tendency is specially marked among the painters of the Shijō-Maruyama, founded by Maruyama Ōkyo (1733–95), who had studied Western perspective and understood how to render even the most fleeting phenomena (*Pine Tree in the Snow*, 1765; Tokyo, National Museum). In contrast are the lavish and somewhat stylized screen paintings by such artists as Kanō Sanraku (1559–1635) (*Plum Tree and Pheasant*, *c.* 1631–35; Myōshinji, Tenkyuin Temple), and Ogata Kōrin the painter, whose spectacular and surprisingly abstract *White and Red Plum Trees* (Shizuoka-ken, Atami Museum) may have exerted an influence on Western artists during the early 20th century.

The fondness of the cultivated classes for Chinese painting led to the importation of paintings of the Ming and Ch'ing dynasties, and of a number of illustrated books. It was at Nagasaki, where this fashion was most prevalent, that there arose the *nanga*, or Southern style of painting, also known as *bunjinga* ("art of literary men"). Two of the masters were Yosa no Buson (1716–83) and Ikeno Taiga (1723–76). There were a number of other talented painters in the school, each of whom had his own personal style: Gyokuran, Tanomura Chikuden (1777–1835), and the eclectic Tani Bunchō.

With the rise of the lower classes, genre painting became increasingly important. It began in the Momoyama period with large scenes painted on screens for the houses of the wealthy, and it ended during the Edo period with the proliferation of those small vertical scrolls that could be found even in the humblest dwellings. The scenes were all taken from the everyday life of the people and were treated in a more subjective manner than before. At Edo, the style was called *ukiyo-e* ("painting of the ephemeral world"). The first painter to put down his brush in favor of the engraver's burin was Hishikawa Moronobu (*c.* 1618/25–94), whose chosen subjects were especially appealing: scenes from the Kabuki theater and portraits of women and actors. Countless artists followed his example, among them Kiyonobu (1664–1729), his son Kiyomasu II (active 1690–*c.* 1720), Kiyomitsu, Okumura Masanobu (1686–1764), and Ishikawa Toyonobu (1711–85). Suzuki Harunobu's (1725–70) prints were, however, a landmark in the development of Japanese graphic art. Until then, only the outline had been printed and the artist had been required to brush in the color afterward. Harunobu invented the process of polychrome printing, which could reproduce up to 10 colors, including half tones. The art of portraiture was represented by Torii Kiyonaga (1752–1815), Saitō Sharaku (active 1794–95), and especially Kitagawa Utamaro (1753–1806), the great painter of women, whose psychological penetration of the feminine soul can be seen in such works as *Melancholy Love* (Tokyo, Coll. Shibui Kiyoshi). The landscape genre had been rather neglected until Katsushika Hokusai (1760–1849) raised it to the level of portraiture with his famous panoramas, such as the *Thirty-Six Views of Mount Fujiyama* (*c.* 1825–31). His success encouraged many artists to follow his example, among whom were Utagawa Kuniyoshi (1767–1861) and Andō Hiroshige (1797–1858—*Miidera Temple*; Boston, Museum of Fine Arts).

The present age has witnessed Japan's entry into the main currents of international life, and painting, like other art forms, has felt the influence of Western art in a dramatic way. From the beginning of the 20th century, countless movements have sprung up that are stamped to a greater or lesser degree with that influence, among them the Sōzō Bijutsu ("Creative Art") movement of the 1930s. Since the end of World War II, Western abstractionist tendencies have won a number of adherents, such as Kumi Sugäi (b. 1919), without in any way submerging past traditions.

SCULPTURE

Japanese sculpture, with very rare exceptions, was carved, assembled, or modeled into shape, rather than being really "sculptured" in the Western sense. Wood was most commonly used. Except for early works that were carved from the solid blocks, wooden sculpture was assembled from separate pieces and was often hollow. Bronze was widely used at all periods. Bone

Japanese Art (Jōmon period). Terra-cotta idol. 1st millennium B.C. National Museum, Tokyo. *Photo Sakamoto, Tokyo.*

ivory, hard stones such as agate, and some fine-grained woods were used for small works. The history of sculpture more or less follows the development of the other arts, and can be studied according to the same periods.

Origins and Pre-Buddhist Period

Jōmon pottery, the earliest form of Japanese pottery known to us, included human figurines in terra cotta, whose stylized forms have recently become a source of inspiration for modern Japanese art. About the 3rd century A.D. during the so-called Age of the Great Tombs, countless clay cylinders (*haniwa*) were placed in rows around the royal tombs. The *haniwa* could be sunk into the soil and were very often decorated with or modeled in the form of human figures (women, warriors, children), animals, houses, boats, and various other objects. Somewhat idealized and abstract, these *haniwa* figures mark the emergence of an authentically Japanese art.

Asuka Period

The introduction of Buddhism in the 6th century A.D. brought with it the beginning of religious statuary produced by Korean artists. One of the first Japanese sculptors was Kurat-sukuribe-no-Tasuna. He carved a large 15-foot statue of the Buddha that has unfortunately disappeared. A famous work by Tori Busshi, the son of Tasuna, is the beautiful bronze Shaka Triad (A.D. 623; Hōryūji Temple, Nara), whose style is very similar to that of the sculpture in the Chinese grottoes at Lungmên. Most of the works of this period were made of gilded bronze or painted camphor wood. They were frontal statues possessing a strict symmetrical arrangement; their proportions were excessively elongated, their eyes wide open and mouths gently smiling; surrounding their heads were huge haloes shaped like inverted pipal leaves.

Nara Period

The beginning of this period saw the increasing importation and imitation of new models (Chinese art of the T'ang dynasty; Mathura and Gupta art from India). Treatment of the human anatomy became more realistic; the figures were fuller, but the strict frontality and symmetry persisted. Two works illustrate perfectly the tendencies of this transitional period: the bronze Shō Kwannon in the Tōindō Hall of the Yakushiji pagoda at Nara, and the remarkable bronze head of Buddha, the Yakushi Nyorai, at the Kōfukuji Temple, also at Nara. An original, independent style also developed, which was profoundly idealistic, in spite of the decidedly turbulent character of some of its sculpture. As bronze was now reserved for large statues, cheaper materials were usual for lesser works, notably clay and dry lacquer, which was either built over a solid core of wood or around a hollow armature. Secular subjects, particularly portraits, took full advantage of these new techniques, which show as well a deliberate attempt to liberate Japanese sculpture from continental models.

Heian Period

It was not until the Heian period and the establishment of the esoteric Buddhist sects, the Shingon and Tendai, that Japanese sculpture acquired a certain amount of independence. Clay and lacquer techniques were replaced by wood carving. The style tended to become increasingly unrealistic, and in its massive form began to assume an overwhelming impression of power; the austere, impersonal faces became more abstract, as in the figure of *Ichiji Kinrin* (Hiraizumi, Chūsonji Temple). Several styles existed at the same time; these are evident in the imitations of T'ang sculptures in sandalwood, in the continuation of the Nara style, and in the rise of Shinto sculpture, with its realistic tendencies.

It was only under the Fujiwara rule in the last part of the Heian period that Chinese influences were completely absorbed into the Japanese culture. Sculpture then reached its maturity, a maturity that is seen in its correct proportions, harmonious forms, beauty of ornament, delicacy of expression, and sense of measure. The most famous sculptors were Kōshō, his son Jōchō (d. 1057—*Amida Nyorai*, 1053; Uji, Phoenix Hall), and their descendants, who formed family workshops. Jōchō gave quintessential expression to the Fujiwara style, endowing his figures with a massive body, a dignified attitude, and a more comely face than found in earlier styles. Sculpture gained in subtlety and delicacy, but otherwise was characterized by a rigidity and repetition of traditional forms in the works by Jōchō's followers. Only portraiture was able to preserve a certain degree of originality and nobility, as in the painted wood statue of *Prince Taishi Shōtoku* by Enkai (1069; Nara, Edono Hall, Hōryūji Temple).

Kamakura Period

Both the warlike character of this period and the influence of Chinese sculpture of the Sung Dynasty encouraged the realistic strain in Japanese sculpture that had been growing stronger since the Nara period. Facial expressions were humanized until they became exceedingly lifelike, with the eyes formed by a piece of crystal or glass. Besides traditional schools,

Japanese Art (Asuka period). Shaka Triad by Tori Busshi. A.D. 623. Hōryūji Temple, Nara. *Photo Sakamoto, Tokyo.*

Japanese Art (Heian period). *Kichijōten, goddess of happiness.* Jōruriji Temple, Kyoto. *(From "Sept siècles de sculpture japonaise," by Hachette.)*

Japanese Art (Kamakura period). *The patriarch Mujaku* by Unkei. Early 13th century. Hokuendō Hall, Kōfukuji Temple, Nara. *(From "Sept siècles de sculpture japonaise," by Hachette.)*

a new school began with Unkei and his two sons, Kōben and Tankei (1173–1256). These artists created a remarkable body of work that included the colossal statues of the *Niō* (1204), found alongside the south gate of the Tōdaiji Temple, the *Mujaku* statue (1208; Nara, Hokuendō Hall, Kōfukuji Temple), and the *Yuima* and *Kongōrikishi* by Jōkei, also at Kōfukuji. The portraits were especially notable for the vitality and conviction of their expressions and for the realism of their poses. Masks of the Nō theater began to appear at this time, inaugurating a style of their own, while the Gigaku and Bugaku masks followed the stylistic tendencies of the period.

After the Kamakura period, sculpture experienced a sharp decline when it lost its religious function; painting superseded sculpture almost completely. Therefore nothing original was produced, and sculptors turned to gardening, landscaping, painting, and calligraphy. During the modern period, little has been done to reverse this situation, and the contemporary Japanese school of sculpture is unable to rival its Western counterparts, nor can its work be compared with the creations of the past.

JAVANESE ART. Although there is evidence of Indian settlements in Java as early as the 4th century A.D., no remains of any actual monuments before the 8th century A.D. survive. The earliest buildings still standing are the eight Hindu temples on the Dieng plateau, which date from the early 8th century A.D.; a typical structure is Candi ("temple") Bhīma. With its rather square cella, preceded by an almost separate shallow porch, or *mandapa*, it essentially repeats the form of the Indian temples of the Pallava and Chalukya periods. Above the sanctuary rises a sikhara tower, with the stones, recessed in a step pattern, divided by conventionalized lotus quoins, as in many Orissan shrines (*see* INDIAN ART). The specifically Javanese elements of the building are its location on a raised base, its construction without mortar, and its solid plastic appearance, strongly articulated and sober in line. Other temples, such as Candi Pawon, near Borobudur, are decorated with floral motifs and carvings of real and mythical animals. The dominant feature of Javanese art is the balance maintained between the various architectural elements, and the restrained decoration, which never obscures the lines of the initial structure.

The greatest period of art in Java occurred in the 8th and 9th centuries A.D., when Indonesia was ruled by the Śailendra dynasty. Mahāyāna Buddhism was introduced at the same time, displacing Hinduism as the state religion. Buddhist temples were built throughout Java, the greatest of which is the stupa, or relic mound, of Borobudur, probably built between 800 and 850 by Śailendra. This monument is a giant realization of the *mandala*, or diagram of the cosmic system, which was a common source of inspiration in the art of Southeast Asia. The pyramidal base represents the "world mountain" Meru, which is encased within the hemispherical dome of the stupa, or sky. On entering, the worshiper was able to perform the rite of circumambulation on the consecutive levels of the building, and while ascending to follow in the reliefs of the galleries the journey of Bodhisattva toward nirvana. Numerous images of Buddhas of the Four Directions occupy deep, cavelike niches on the sides of the lower four galleries, while the fifth gallery and the circular terraces are devoted to the cosmic Buddha Vairocana. Proceeding upward, the worshiper at last emerges into the three upper platforms, with 72 reticulated bell-shaped stupas sheltering Buddha Vairocana, or Buddha of the Zenith, while at the very center, a single supreme Buddha, totally hidden, is believed to have been enclosed by a stupa of solid stone.

Placed side by side, the succession of carved reliefs, containing 2,000 scenes, would stretch for almost four miles. The reliefs on the lower levels, devoted to Jātaka stories and scenes from the life of Buddha, are carved with a naive naturalism appropriate to these folk tales. The decorations above, dealing with the careers of the great Bodhisattvas in the Mahāyāna pantheon, are more abstract; some are almost diagrammatic. There is a similar gentleness in the many statues of Dhyāni Buddha that adorn the monument (there are 504 altogether). They have the Indian abstract crystalline representation of form, and were undoubtedly carved according to the same canons of proportion that governed religious art throughout the entire Indian world.

About the middle of the 10th century A.D. the center of power

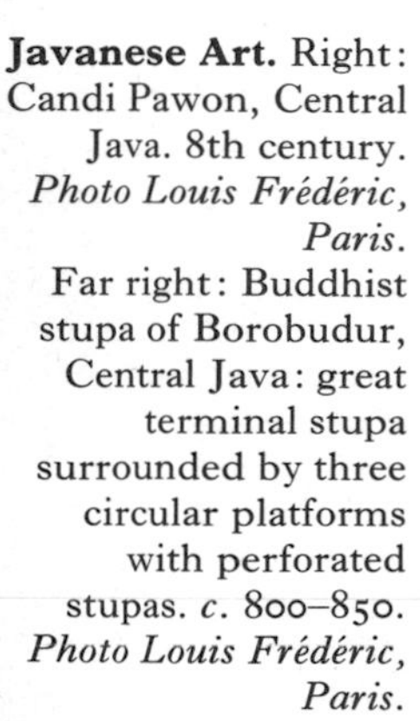

Javanese Art. Right: Candi Pawon, Central Java. 8th century. *Photo Louis Frédéric, Paris.* Far right: Buddhist stupa of Borobudur, Central Java: great terminal stupa surrounded by three circular platforms with perforated stupas. *c.* 800–850. *Photo Louis Frédéric, Paris.*

seems to have shifted from Borobudur to Prambanan, while Hinduism began to revive at the expense of Buddhism. Lara Jongrang, near Prambanan, is the site of a remarkable group of Hindu buildings, consisting of three large temples within a square outer wall; the most important of the three, the center one, is dedicated to Śiva (A.D. 860–915), the other two to Brahma and Vishnu. Opposite them are three subsidiary temples dedicated to the sacred animals that serve as steeds to the gods in Hindu mythology. The façades of the main building are decorated with very fine bas-reliefs of a rather precious, aristocratic grace.

A long period of political instability elapsed before the new artistic rebirth took place in the 13th and 14th centuries, centered around a new capital, Majapahit, in eastern Java. A typical example of the new art is the temple at Panataran (completed *c.* 1370). The square plan of the older temples is retained, but the proportions of the building are taller and thinner, and the pyramidal superstructure terminates in a cube that has not been seen before. It is the sculptural decoration, however, that has most changed, with the indigenous elements becoming more marked. The lintels are carved with gigantic monster masks, and the reliefs reveal a flat, patternized style in which the attenuated and wiry figures suggest the puppets of the Javanese shadow play.

Javanese Art. *Episode in a sacred dance.* Borobudur stupa, Central Java. *Photo Louis Frédéric, Paris.*

JAWLENSKY, Alexej von (1864, Kuslovo, Russia—1941, Wiesbaden), Russian painter. In 1896 he went to Munich, where he continued the studies that he had begun in 1889 at the St. Petersburg Academy. He saw works by Van Gogh and Cézanne, visited Ferdinand Hodler, and in 1905 met Matisse; these were all to be formative influences. Between 1905 and 1913, Jawlensky's painting was clearly related to that of the Fauves. Whether he painted landscapes, still lifes, or figures, he displayed his bright colors in simplified forms that were often circumscribed by a blue line.

In 1913 the influence of Cubism led Jawlensky to mute his palette and emphasize the geometrical aspects of his form. First he painted a series of variations on a landscape, in which he sought to achieve a balance of the colored masses. Then, from 1918, he executed the first of a series of faces based on a most elementary scheme: two horizontals or two curves for eyes, a vertical for the nose, a horizontal sometimes combined with an arc for the mouth, and an oval for the chin. This schematization became still more rigorous after 1921, when Jawlensky settled in Wiesbaden. He continued to repeat these faces with only slight variations for some years. Color alone differentiated the paintings, determining their significance and justifying their very varied titles: *Homer, Frost, Arabian Legend, Moonlight*, etc.

About 1934 his style became broader, more summary, his line more emphatic and less geometrical. But the faces that he executed were more directly expressive than earlier ones, though further removed from ordinary appearances. He called them *Meditations* and, in fact, their effect is to induce meditation.

JEAN DE BONDOL *or* **JEAN DE BRUGES.** *See* **BONDOL,** Jean de.

JEAN DE BOURGOGNE. *See* **BORGOÑA,** Juan de.

JEANNERET, Charles-Édouard. *See* **LE CORBUSIER.**

JEFFERSON, Thomas (1743, Shadwell, Virginia—1826, Monticello, Virginia), American legislator (prime author of the Declaration of Independence, July 1776), statesman (third President of the United States, 1801–9), and Neoclassical architect. Having acquired a taste for the architecture of Classical antiquity during a stay in Paris and a number of journeys to Provence between 1784 and 1789, Jefferson encouraged the development of a new official art in America that conformed to his ideal. The Maison Carrée, a 1st-century B.C. Greco-Roman temple at Nîmes, inspired his plans for the Capitol (1785–96) at Richmond, Virginia. The house he designed and had built for his retirement at Monticello (1770–84; 1796–1806) reflects his knowledge of the style of the 16th-century Italian architect Andrea Palladio. Jefferson also provided the plans for the campus of the University of Virginia at Charlottesville (1817–26), the Rotunda (1822–26) of which is reminiscent of the Pantheon in Rome. His Palladian-inspired plans for the White House in Washington, the new Federal capital, were somewhat modified by those of the Irish-born architect James Hoban (*c.* 1762–1831).

JENKINS, Paul (b. 1923, Kansas City, Missouri), American painter. Between 1948 and 1951 he worked at the Art Students League in New York under Morris Kantor (b. 1896) and Yasuo Kuniyoshi. Although Jenkins went to Paris in 1953 to live and work, he continued to maintain residence in New York, where his first one-man show was held in 1956 at the Martha Jackson Gallery.

From 1953 Jenkins painted with a liquid medium in order to obtain an effect of color in motion. In 1956 he returned to New York, where he first saw paintings by Helen Frankenthaler, Morris Louis, and Kenneth Noland, who had been working with poured, stained, and spilled paint on unprimed canvas. Three years later a voyage to Spain, during which he worked in watercolor, led Jenkins to a further involvement with transparent, flowing color. Avoiding the mark of the hand or brush, Jenkins worked by pouring paint from corner to corner, often pulling the canvas back on itself to create broadly flaring or tapering channels. Pictures such as *Phenomena Nearing Isthmus* (1962–63; Los Angeles, Coll. C. Martin) or *Phenomena Red Wing* (1962; New York, Coll. David Kluger), with its rich purple, pure red, and brilliant yellow forming a winglike configuration, often evoke—without describing—shapes or processes in the midst of flux and growth.

JENNEY, William Le Baron (1832, Fairhaven, Massachusetts—1907, Los Angeles), American architectural engineer. In 1868 Jenney settled in Chicago, where he built the first office building to have a steel frame. This was the Home Insurance Building (1883–85; now demolished), which was one of the prototypes of the 20th-century commercial style and prepared the way for the famous Chicago School of architecture. Jenney's other principal buildings in Chicago (designed in collaboration with his partner, William B. Mundie, 1893–1939) were the first Leiter Building (1879) and the second Leiter Building (1889–90), in which the façades are merely lightweight screens supported by the metal framework of the building.

JESPERS, Oscar (1887, Antwerp—1970, Brussels), Belgian sculptor. From 1927, he taught at the Graduate School of Architecture and Decorative Arts in Brussels. In his early work, he was influenced by Cubism; and his art continued to show a taste for geometric and simplified forms, even when, after World War I, he became a member of the Sélection group and briefly followed an Expressionist course. His economy of means and innate sense of monumentality may be appreciated in a number of large-scale works directly linked to architecture: the high relief in polychrome wood (1935) in the Gare Centrale in Brussels; the copper bas-relief for the Belgian Pavilion at the Exposition Internationale in Paris in 1937; and two large stone reliefs at the Postal Check Building in Brussels. Jespers' work is sober, even ponderous; but a group of sculptures dating from about 1937, inspired by the female figure, is outstanding for its balance and elegance.

Oscar Jespers. *The Prisoner*. Musées Royaux des Beaux-Arts, Brussels. *Photo A.C.L.*

JEWISH ART. It was long believed that the development of the visual arts among the Jews in antiquity was rendered impossible by their strict interpretation and enforcement of the prohibition of images in the ten Commandments and elsewhere in the Pentateuch (*Exodus* 20:4; *Deuteronomy* 4:10–18). Archaeological discoveries have made it apparent, however, that this was an ideal prescribed by certain teachers but not consistently observed in practice. It is now certain that even in antiquity, art had its place in Jewish life, even among Orthodox Jews. The most notable discovery was at Dura-Europos on the Euphrates, where in 1932–35 the ruins of a synagogue rebuilt in A.D. 245–246 were found in a remarkable state of preservation. The walls, some standing to full height, were covered with frescoes depicting scenes from the Bible, executed without restraint, in accordance with the usual Hellenistic technique used in this area. Traces of earlier frescoes appeared underneath these, and there is evidence that they were based on still earlier prototypes. The relationship between this Jewish Biblical art of the first centuries and primitive Christian art, which was similarly dependent largely on the Old Testament, is still being eagerly discussed. It is probable that similar decorations appeared in Palestinian synagogues at this period; but the only substantial remains found is the mosaic floor of Beth Alpha Synagogue dating from the early 6th century A.D. In a rather conventional manner it depicts the signs of the zodiac, the chariot of the sun with its driver, and the seasons personified by women. In contrast, the Biblical scene of the Sacrifice of Isaac contains surprisingly free representations of the human form.

The reliefs found in the catacombs of Beth Shearim near Haifa suggest that sculpture in the round was not wholly barred. There is every reason to believe

Jewish Art. So-called *Bezalel Haggadah*. Rhenish. Early 14th century. Bezalel National Art Museum, Jerusalem. *Photo Hillel Burger.*

that art for secular purposes had still fewer inhibitions than the art of the synagogue. The Jewish catacombs also give ample evidence of the existence of a Jewish pictorial and even sculptural art that can no longer be dismissed as outside of Orthodoxy.

Subsequently, however, Jewish art seems to have suffered an eclipse, which was due in part to the influences of the iconoclastic movement in the Byzantine Empire, and in part to the rise of Islam. Hebrew manuscripts that appeared in the Moslem world and the contiguous areas bore only elaborate decorations, with no representations of the human or animal form. Moreover the decorative elements tended to be separate from the actual Bible text, being concentrated in the preliminary pages and sometimes also in the supplementary ones. The tradition of Jewish pictorial art re-emerged in the Franco-German areas. The first evidence of this rebirth is a group of fine illuminated manuscripts of the 13th century; these, however, were obviously part of a firmly established tradition that reached back to a much earlier period. In some instances the artists responsible for this work are known to have been Jews, and their names are recorded. This seems to have been the case normally, although it is known that Hebrew manuscripts were occasionally illuminated by Christian artists.

Jewish Art. Stone sarcophagus. 2nd–4th century. From catacomb 20, necropolis of Beth Shearim, Israel. Department of Archaeology, Hebrew University, Jerusalem.

Of all illuminated Hebrew manuscripts of the Middle Ages, the best known are those containing the ritual for the domestic service on Passover Eve, the Haggadahs. These thin volumes were not taken into the synagogue, and so invited greater embellishment than usual, appealing especially to the women and children. Of the German Haggadahs, the most splendid is the Darmstadt Haggadah, executed in West Germany about 1430. The Spanish Haggadahs followed a different tradition, at least until the 14th or early 15th century: their text was left plain, while a series of illuminations depicting the story of the Exodus and the events leading up to it occupied the preliminary pages. The most famous is the Sarajevo Haggadah, probably a Catalan production of the mid-14th century. Other types of manuscripts that were illuminated were Bibles (generally sparsely), prayer books, and religious law books such as the Code of Maimonides. After the invention of printing, the tradition of the illuminated Haggadah was perpetuated in some memorable editions with lavish woodcut illustrations, such as the Haggadahs of Prague (1527) and Mantua (1560 and 1568), and with copperplate engravings, the first of which was that of Amsterdam (1695). Books of fables were also illustrated, in the style of folk art; among the most interesting is the *Meshal ha-Kadmoni* or "Ancient Parable," of Isaac ibn Sahula. Some of the engraved borders of early Hebrew printed books of the 15th century are of exceptional beauty, and in certain cases are known to have been the work of Jewish artists.

Illustrated Haggadahs continued to be produced throughout the 17th and 18th centuries. But the principal creations of that time were the illuminated Scrolls of Esther (extant only from the late 16th century, though they may have existed earlier), and the Marriage Contracts, some of which were quite beautiful, especially those produced in Italy. During this period there was a flourishing production of the elaborate brocades that hung before the Ark in the synagogue, the silver appurtenances that surmounted the Scrolls of the Torah read in the service, the silver and spice boxes used in the domestic ritual on the Sabbath, and the additional accessories used together with the Haggadah at the Seder service on Passover Eve, such as the majolica platters produced by a succession of Jewish manufacturers in and around Ancona, Italy in the 17th and 18th centuries. Plates were also produced in silver and pewter, appropriately decorated or engraved.

The names are known of a few Jewish craftsmen of the early 16th century, such as the engraver and medalist Moses da Castellazzo (d. 1527) and Salomone da Sesto, a metalworker famous for his swords and scabbards; both men worked for the dukes of Ferrara (among others). It was only in the late 17th and early 18th centuries that Jewish artists in the modern sense began to emerge, treating general subjects for a wide public. They were introduced to painting through two channels—as a development of metal engraving and gem cutting, which were common Jewish occupations; and as a secularization and broadening of their work in manuscript illumination. In the mid-19th century, a few Jewish painters of some merit began to distinguish themselves—Philipp Veit (1793–1877) and Eduard Bendemann (1811–80) in Germany, and Solomon Hart (1806–81) and the erratic Pre-Raphaelite Simeon Solomon (1834–1905) in England. As the century advanced, the number of Jewish artists increased, including men of first importance such as the Impressionist masters Camille Pissarro and Max Liebermann, and their great contemporary, Jozef Israëls (1824–1911), in Holland. Italy produced the highly renowned Amedeo Modigliani. In the 20th century, a sudden reawakening of genius occurred; leaving the Eastern European ghettos, numerous Jewish artists arrived in Paris, drawn by its flourishing artistic life. Marc Chagall, Moise Kisling, Chaim Soutine, Mané-Katz, and Jules Pascin were among them, and they were to play a prominent role in the development of the School of Paris. Elsewhere, too, Jews numbered among the foremost modern painters—Josef Herman (b. 1911) in England, Lasar Segall in Brazil, and Abraham Walkowitz, Ben Shahn, and Max Weber in the United States. Jews turned seriously to sculpture somewhat more tardily, but Mark Antokolski (1842–1902) was once a famous name in Russia, Chana Orloff was one of the outstanding women practitioners of the craft, and Sir Jacob Epstein was among the most gifted sculptors England ever knew. Nor should one omit the names of Jo Davidson (1883–1952), Arnold Zadikow (1884–1943), Jacques Lipchitz, Elie Nadelmann, Henryk (Enrico) Glicenstein (1870–1942), and Ossip Zadkine.

The revival of Jewish life in the State of Israel was accompanied by a significant surge in the activity of artists in all media, most of them born and trained abroad. Among the most significant may be mentioned Reuben Rubin (b. 1893), Mordecai Ardon (b. 1896), Nahum Gutman (b. 1898), Marcel Janc (b. 1895), and Moshe Castel (b. 1909). But there are as yet only faint signs that a characteristic school of Israeli art is emerging.

JOHN, Augustus Edwin (1878, Tenby, Wales—1961, Fordingbridge, Hampshire), British painter. From 1894 to 1898 he studied at London's Slade School, where he revealed his precocious gifts as a draftsman. In 1899 John visited Paris and was impressed by the paintings of Puvis de Chavannes in the Louvre; his *Lyric Fantasy* of 1911 (Coll. Hugo Pitman) reveals the extent of this influence. From 1901 to 1902 he worked as an art teacher in Liverpool, and in 1903 joined the New English Art Club. He became a Royal Academician in 1928. John's many compositions on

Jewish Art. Engraved silver case for the *Scroll of Esther*. *c.* 1700. Jewish Museum, London. *Photo Warburg Institute.*

Jasper Johns. *Green Target.* 1955. Museum of Modern Art, New York.

gypsy themes, done in an overly loose technique, are far inferior to his brilliant portraits. The obviously bravura qualities of *Madame Suggia* (1923; London, Tate Gallery) owe a great deal to the portrait style of John Singer Sargent, whose manner John continues in a certain sense. But more intimate likenesses, such as those of *Daphne* (1937; Great Bedwin, Coll. Lady Mary Campbell) and *Dylan Thomas* (*c.* 1938; Cardiff, National Museum of Wales), have an intensely modern and entirely personal verve.

GWENDOLEN MARY (1876, Haverfordwest, Wales—1939, Dieppe), his sister, studied at the Slade School in London from 1895 to 1898 and later in Whistler's studio in Paris, where she made her permanent home from about 1902. In 1906 she met the French sculptor Auguste Rodin, to whom she became deeply attached; other influential friends included Rodin's secretary, Rainer Maria Rilke, and the Catholic philosopher Jacques Maritain. In 1913 Miss John became a Catholic, and spent the last 25 years of her life in the Parisian suburb of Meudon, near a Dominican convent. Her finest portraits (*Self-Portrait, c.* 1900; London, Tate Gallery) have a spareness of technique and a directness of feeling far removed from the more feminine characteristics noticeable in the works of, for example, Mary Cassatt.

JOHNS, Jasper (b. 1930, Allendale, South Carolina), American painter. He studied at the University of South Carolina and came to New York to paint in 1952. The year 1955 marks the beginning of his mature work, a radical departure from the Abstract Expressionist painting then current. Johns began painting flags, targets, numbers, and alphabets—an iconography of predetermined common imagery treated in such a way that familiar meanings and specific identities were confused by such devices as painterly facture, neutralization of color, and violation of flatness. In works such as *Three Flags* (1958; Madison, Conn., Coll. Mr. and Mrs. Burton Tremaine) or *Target with Four Faces* (1955; New York, Museum of Modern Art) the flatness and focus of the image is equivocated by apparent spatial levels within the painting, or by the addition of three-dimensional compartments containing plaster casts of facial fragments. Gradually (1956–62) he shifted from the earlier emblematic images and subaesthetic common objects to more expressionistically painted works, but he was still concerned with this notion of ambiguity. Maps, words, and the act of painting itself became the subjects for his new pictures. In 1961 Johns began to attach real objects to the surface of his canvases, seeking an expanded vocabulary as he juxtaposed unexpected found materials, studio debris, or collaged fragments against painted fields. *False Start* (1959; New York, Coll. Mr. and Mrs. Robert C. Scull), one of his major works, is a web of visual (and even literary) puns and contradictions: stenciled labels are painted with the names of colors they are not, while bursts of bright red, blue, orange, or yellow are falsely identified by the names of the hues printed over them. Space is neither three-dimensional nor flat and the structuring is neither loose nor tight. In many lithographs and drawings Johns has explored the collage and imprint methods suggested in such a painting.

Like his theoretical forebear, Marcel Duchamp, Johns disassociates his art from artistic personality and self-expression, asking vital questions about the nature of seeing and conceiving.

JOHNSON, Eastman (1824, Lovell, Maine—1906, New York), American painter. In 1849 Johnson went to Europe to study at the Düsseldorf Academy. His work in Germany grounded him in the techniques of realistic rendition and gave him a taste for sentimental genre subjects. Between 1851 and 1855, while in The Hague, he made copies of the paintings of Rembrandt and other Dutch and Flemish painters. The following year he worked in Paris in Thomas Couture's atelier, where he was taught the tasteful arrangement of figures and a respect for literary content. Upon his return to the United States in 1855 he settled in Nantucket, Massachusetts, which became the scene of many of the genre paintings of his most active period (1870s and 1880s). After the 1880s Johnson turned chiefly to more lucrative portrait commissions.

Between 1859 and 1879 he painted primarily realistic narrative scenes and illustrations of traditional American subjects, such as *Corn Husking at Nantucket* (1860; Syracuse, New York, Museum of Fine Arts) or *In the Fields* (1870s; Detroit, Institute of Arts), as well as portraits of important historical figures and wealthy patrons. One of the distinguishing features of his work as a whole is his ability to describe and characterize his rustic or domestic subjects without oversentimentalizing or caricaturing them. Johnson's portraits, such as the *Funding Bill* (1881; New York, Metropolitan Museum) also possess a tempered dignity.

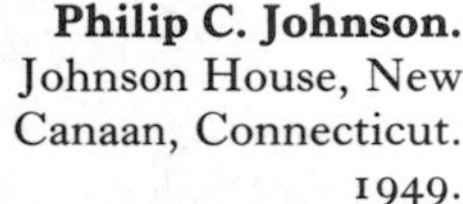

Philip C. Johnson. Johnson House, New Canaan, Connecticut. 1949.

JOHNSON, Philip Cortelyou (b. 1906, Cleveland, Ohio), American architect. An ardent propagandist and theorist of modern architecture, he first became widely known as the director (1930–36) of the Department of Architecture of the Museum of Modern Art in New York City. In 1932 he established a reputation as an art historian with a book written in collaboration with Henry-Russell Hitchcock, *The International Style:* its title became the standard designation for the architectural revolution that followed World War I. Although he studied with Marcel Breuer at Harvard University, his real master was Mies van der Rohe, on whom he wrote a brilliant monograph (1947). His first work was his own house at New Canaan, Connecticut (1949), which consists of a single undivided space, 56 feet by 32 feet, inscribed in a parallelepiped, with glass roof and walls and steel girders. Johnson's many subsequent experiments were variations on the same model (Rockfeller Guest House, New York City, 1950; the Wiley House, 1953, and the Boissonas House, 1956, both at New Canaan). But before long, he was drawn irresistibly to what he called "a greater creative freedom." The Temple Kneses Tifereth Israel (1955) at Port Chester, New York; the church (1960) at New Harmony, Indiana; the Sheldon Memorial Art Gallery (1962) for the University of Nebraska at Lincoln; the New York State Theater (1962–64) at Lincoln Center, New York City; and the Kline Science Tower (1964–67) at Yale University in New Haven, Connecticut—all illustrate, in the eclecticism of their forms, often inspired by the 17th and 18th centuries, the architect's new approach.

ONES, Inigo (1577, London—652, London), English architect nd scenographer. He replaced the Tudor style with an architecture ased on the Italian High Reaissance and Mannerist styles, of hich he was among the first of his ompatriots to have a direct and horough knowledge. He was the arliest English architect to achieve international stature.

In 1603, he appeared as a painter the service of the Earl of utland, whom he accompanied n his diplomatic mission to enmark. He had already visited Italy, where he had studied drawing and stage design, and he was an accomplished draftsman in the Italian manner. His culture and his courtesy won him the protection of Thomas Howard, Earl of Arundel, and of the Duke of Lennox and Prince Henry, heir presumptive to the throne. Ben Jonson's friendship and the court taste for theatrical spectacles gave Jones an opportunity to display his talent for production and the design of settings and costumes. His sketches for *Oberon* (1608), with their hunting attributes and grotesque elements, are still close to the Tudor style.

Through the medium of stage design, Jones was led on to architecture. In 1613, he paid a second visit to Italy, accompanying the Earl of Arundel, a trip that had a decisive effect on the development of his career and on the later development of English architecture. Throughout the journey he made sketches in his notebooks and annotated a copy of Palladio, now in the library of Worcester College, Oxford, with his own critical reflections. He visited Venice, Vicenza, Bologna, Florence, Siena and finally, in the winter of 1613–14, Rome. He completed the trip with second visits to Venice and Vicenza to study Palladio's own works further. In 1615 he was appointed Surveyor of the King's Works, the highest architectural post in England.

In the exercise of his official duties, which lasted from 1615 to the outbreak of the Civil War in 1642, Jones's architectural designs reflected his Italian experience. His most important commissions were the Queen's House, Greenwich (1616–18) and the Banqueting House in Whitehall, London (1619–22). The latter contains a large hall that is surrounded by an order of pilasters surmounted by a balcony, beneath a ceiling decorated with Rubens' painting of an apotheosis of James I, which he executed in 1635. The style of the façade reflects a critical interpretation of Palladio in which the models of the master appear transformed and stripped of their Mannerist characteristics.

In 1617 contemporaries were struck by the residence that the queen, Anne of Denmark, wife of James I, had commissioned to be built at Greenwich. The house consists of two rectangular main buildings linked by a bridge that crosses over a road. On the first story, overlooking the park, a loggia appears behind an Ionic colonnade flanked by two full wings. In another work designed for the queen—the chapel of St. James's Palace (1623; today Marlborough House Chapel)—the interpretation of Palladio already anticipates in its economy Claude-Nicolas Ledoux's Barrières in Paris.

From the chapel of Somerset House, built for Henrietta Maria of France, wife of Charles I (1630–35; much damaged by Parliamentarians), to the colossal Corinthian portico of St. Paul's Cathedral (begun 1630s; destroyed by fire 1666); and from the Prince's Lodging at Newmarket (begun 1619; later demolished) to the piazza at Covent Garden, bordered with arcades (designed by Jones, *c.* 1630; executed by Isaac de Caus, 1631; damaged by fire 1795, and rebuilt with alterations), Jones continued to produce works in which elements not

Inigo Jones. Queen's House, Greenwich (Now National Maritime Museum). 1616–35. *Photo Crown Copyright, London.*

Inigo Jones. Banqueting House, Whitehall, London. 1619–22. *Photo Kersting, London.*

Jacob Jordaens. *The Four Evangelists. c.* 1617–18. Louvre, Paris. *Photo Giraudon.*

only of Palladio, but of Giacomoda Vignola and Sebastiano Serlio were combined with Elizabethan traditions. During the Civil War the architect left London, and followed Charles I in his battles against the Roundheads. He reappeared under Cromwell, assisting the Earl of Pembroke in the rebuilding of Wilton House, Wiltshire (1647–52).

JONGKIND, Johan Barthold (1819, Lattrop, Holland—1891, Grenoble), Dutch painter. He was discovered by the genre painter Eugène Isabey, who helped him financially, took him to Paris in 1846, and introduced him to the landscape of the Channel coastline. From his travels in Normandy he brought back canvases, watercolors, and drawings in which he had captured—long before Monet and his friends—the play of light over water, sky, branches, and leaves. His spontaneity and technical skill might have aroused the envy of the Dutch 17th-century landscapists Jacob van Ruisdael and Jan van Goyen, his acknowledged masters.

Jongkind exhibited in the Salon des Refusés in Paris (1863), and achieved success in the years between 1865 and 1870, when he made several trips to his native Holland and to Brussels, Chartres, and Nantes. As a painter of atmosphere and of a changing, shifting nature, Jongkind stands as a precursor of Impressionism. He also produced rather prosaic canvases for a middle-class clientele, but his watercolors have great naturalness and originality (*Sunset on the Meuse, c.* 1866; Paris, Coll. G. Signac).

Jacob Jordaens. *The Painter's Family.* 1622–23. Prado, Madrid. *Photo Anderson-Giraudon.*

JORDAENS, Jacob (1593, Antwerp—1678, Antwerp), one of the great Flemish painters of the Baroque. Son of a cloth merchant, Jordaens was apprenticed in 1607 to a teacher of Rubens, Adam van Noort (1562–1641). Through van Noort, whose daughter he married, he became acquainted with the works of Jan Sanders van Hemessen and Pieter Aertsen. Between 1635 and 1655 he designed a series of cartoons, depicting proverbs and the stories of Ulysses, Alexander, and Charlemagne. His best work in tapestry design is the *Great Horses* (Vienna, Kunsthistorisches Museum, Waffensammlung). Jordaens placed his decorative talent at the service of the Church in such paintings as the *Four Evangelists* (*c.* 1617–18; Paris, Louvre); the *Martyrdom of St. Apollonia* (1628; Antwerp, St-Augustin); and the *Triumph of the Holy Eucharist* (Dublin, National Gallery of Ireland). He was also in the service of foreign courts, painting ceilings and walls for the queen of England and the king of Sweden. His masterpiece in this genre is the *Triumph of Frederik Hendrik* (1651–52), an immense composition entirely covering the walls of the Orange Room in the Huis ten Bosch ("House in the Woods"), a royal country house near The Hague. In this work the Baroque is given free reign in grandiose allegories filled with figures in tumultuous movement, the whole intensified by exuberant light and color.

The artist's early works (the *Painter's Family*, 1622–23; Madrid, Prado) are serious in tone and carefully finished. At first he used plebeian motifs sparingly, somewhat in the manner of Caravaggio (*St. Peter and the Tribute Money*, Copenhagen, Nationalmuseet; *Offering to Ceres*, Prado). His studies of facial expression probably derive from Hemessen; of his several *Heads of Apostles* (*c.* 1610), the most striking, executed with remarkably free brushwork, is at Douai (Museum) and shows some affinity with the contemporary work of Van Dyck. Beginning to concentrate on the more convivial pleasures, Jordaens did numerous variations on three subjects between 1620 and 1645: the *Satyr and Peasant*, based on one of Aesop's fables; the *Family Concert*, a domestic scene based on a local proverb; and the *King Drinks*, a scene from a folk tale and an evocation of Epiphany ceremonies. These works display Jordaens' increasing use of exuberant forms in a wide variety of poses, compositions crowded with figures and objects imbued with sensual vitality, and strong contrasts of light and color. He glorified the gods of plenty in his paintings of the Dionysiac myths (*Education of Jupiter*, Kassel, Staatliche Kunstsammlung, and Paris, Louvre; *Offering to Ceres*, Madrid, Prado; the *Triumph of Bacchus*, Kassel), and found a favorite theme in the *Allegory of Fertility* (*c.* 1617, Munich, Bayerische Staatsgemäldesammlungen; *c.* 1625, Brussels, Musées Royaux; Ghent, Museum voor Schone Kunsten; London, Wallace Coll.; *c.* 1645, Copenhagen, Nationalmuseet; *c.* 1650, Dresden, Gemäldegalerie). The version in Brussels is the finest, showing Jordaens' fine hand with color—vivid blues, brilliant reds and clear green blended with warm browns and pale golds. The very numerous fine works hold their own in originality and technical mastery with those of Van Dyck and Rubens, and are a proof of the astonishing variety and high level of Flemish painting in the 17th century.

JORN, Asger (b. 1914, Vejrun—d 1973), Danish painter. Jorn ap peared as the dominant personalit in the European Abstract Ex pressionist movement that came t be known under the name of Cobr (1948–51). Before that, durin World War II, he had played leading part in the Danish Abstrac Surrealist group, together wit Ejler Bille (b. 1910) and Egi Jacobsen (b. 1910). In 1955 Jor settled in Paris, and founded i turn the Movement for an Imag inist Bauhaus and the Ir ternational Situationist Move ment, both of which were directe mainly against Functionalism an Neo-Plasticism. Following th Jorn exploited the violent Ex pressionism that had been constant in his work, as was apparent in 1959 and again in 1962 when he exhibited paintings in a traditional style overlaid with animated signs of a strange mythology under the significant titles of "Défigurations" and "Nouvelles Défigurations" (*Les Enfants, c.* 1962; Paris, Galerie Rive Gauche). In the passion of his attack and by means of raw color (*In the Beatings of Swans' Wings*, 1963; Munich, Galerie Van den Loo), he expresses the violence of the mid-20th century and formulates solutions that have an immediate impact on the spectator and arouse in him a commitment similar to that of the artist.

JOURDAIN, Frantz (1847, Antwerp—1935, Paris), French architect of Belgian origin. From 1880 to 1910, Jourdain participated fervently in the modern movement in art and architecture. He also organized exhibitions, and in 1903 was one of the founders of the Salon d'Automne, where, two years later, the Fauves would hold their first exhibition. With the Samaritaine department store (1905), in Paris, he provided such a brilliant interpretation of the fundamental concepts of Art Nouveau architecture that for a time the "style Samar" was as highly regarded as Hector Guimard's "style Métro." The same provocative boldness is to be found in Jourdain's interiors, exhibition pavilions, and stage designs, but he never won the audience that his ingenious Samaritaine building deserved.

FRANCIS (1876, Paris—1958, Paris), his son, was a painter, decorator, and writer. At seventeen he entered Eugène Carrière's studio, and exhibited his first canvases at the Salon des Indépendants in 1897. In 1900 he decorated the Théâtre de la Loïe Fuller, Paris, for which he was awarded a gold medal. After several private exhibitions, he gave up painting in 1911 to devote himself to decorative art, in which he became a leader in the reaction against Art Nouveau. In 1912 he founded the Ateliers Modernes, which soon became a full-scale factory producing wallpaper, carpets, ceramics, and furniture of his own design. He designed the stage of the Théâtre du Vieux Colombier, Paris, for Jacques Copeau; a smoking car for the Paris-Orléans railway; and the director's office at the Collège de France, Paris. Problems of lighting, prefabrication, and living in a limited space preoccupied him until 1939, when he gave up decoration.

JOUVENET, Jean (1644, Rouen—1717, Paris), French religious painter. By 1661 he was in Paris, where he soon attracted attention and was engaged by Charles Le Brun as a collaborator at the Château de Versailles. He was accepted in the Academy (1675), where he filled a number of posts including that of rector (1707). Jouvenet's highly successful career established him, after the death of Pierre Mignard I (1695), as the most prominent master of the French School. His numerous commissions included the ceiling of the Parlement, Rennes (1694); four giant canvases for the church of St-Martin-des-Champs, Paris; and the figures of the 12 apostles for the dome of the Invalides, Paris. Jouvenet was a painter of great Baroque flair, gifted with a very personal sense of observation, whose work during the reign of Louis XIV foreshadowed the style of the Regency. The Louvre has 10 of his paintings, including the well-known *Descent from the Cross* (1697), which shows the strong influence of Rubens and the Carracci. Jouvenet's last work, the *Magnificat* (1716), which for two centuries hung behind the high altar of Notre-Dame Cathedral, Paris (today in one of the chapels), is considered one of the key paintings of French Baroque art.

JUGENDSTIL. It is by this name, derived from the review *Jugend* (Youth), founded in Munich in 1896, that the movement called Art Nouveau in Britain, France, and the United States, is known in the German-speaking countries (*see* ART NOUVEAU).

JUNI, Juan de (*c.* 1507, Joigny, Yonne?—1577, Valladolid), French-born sculptor active in Spain. Juni, who became one of the most distinguished Spanish polychrome sculptors, received his preliminary training in France. He reached León about 1533, and thereafter his presence has been traced in Medina de Ríoseco, Toro, Zamora, and Salamanca. He settled in Valladolid in 1541.

Juni's works are mainly but not exclusively marked by the emotional expression of religious sentiment. However, his turbulent temperament was modified by the influence of Renaissance Classicism. He drew on many sources, the work of Claus Sluter in Burgundy, for instance, as well as the northern Italian sculpture of Guido Mazzoni, and particularly the art of Jacopo della Quercia. There is, too, an obvious kinship between his work and that of Matthias Grünewald.

Juan de Juni. *Joseph of Arimathea.* Detail from the Entombment. 1541–44. Museo Nacional de Escultura, Valladolid.

At León, where he first worked, he helped to carve the stalls in the monastery of S. Marcos in the style of the High Renaissance (1536), and there are several of his works in the museum that now occupies the monastery. A remarkable polychrome Christ remains from his work for the choir screen of León Cathedral. For the church of S. Francisco, Medina de Ríoseco, he modeled the terra-cotta groups placed on either side of the high altar, the *Martyrdom of St. Stephen*, and a *Penitent St. Jerome* (both 1538). About 1540 he sculptured the tomb of the archdeacon Gutierre de Castro and a *Descent from the Cross* for the old cathedral in Salamanca. Later, in Valladolid, he made a magnificent seven-figure *Entombment* for the chapel of Fray Antonio de Guevara in the monastery of S. Francisco (1541–44); the statues are now in the city museum with a highly realistic and moving reliquary bust of *St. Anne* that dates from the same period.

Juni was commissioned to do a number of important altarpieces, notably a group for the high altar of the church of S. María la Antigua, Valladolid, which includes a statue of the Virgin radiating an intensely spiritual gentleness, a quality rare in his works (1545–62; now in Valladolid Cathedral). A *Purísima* from the monastery of Veruela, Saragossa, and the group of the *Virgin and Child with St. John* (so-called Virgen de las candelas) at S. Marina, León, were also done at this time, along with one of the sculptor's most Baroque but perhaps least profound works, *St. John the Baptist* (commissioned 1551; Valladolid, Museo Nacional de Escultura). In 1557 he produced one of his major efforts, the altarpiece dedicated to the Virgin in the chapel of the Benavente at S. María, Medina de Ríoseco. Among his last works at Valladolid are the *Christ* in the monastery of St. Catherine (before 1572), the altarpiece of St. Francis of Assisi in the monastery of S. Isabella, and the *St. Anthony of Padua* (Museo Nacional de Escultura).

Filippo Juvarra. Façade of the villa at Stupinigi, near Turin. 1729–35. *Photo Alinari-Giraudon.*

JUVARRA *or* **JUVARA,** Filippo (1678, Messina—1736, Madrid), one of the great Italian architects at the close of the Baroque era. He began as an engraver and theatrical designer and soon came to Rome, where he shone at the papal court. He applied himself to the Late Baroque, Renaissance, and Classical repertory. The designs he submitted on his admission to the Accademia di S. Luca and those prepared for an architectural competition sponsored by Pope Clement XI contain many of the ideas that Juvarra was later to expand for his large-scale works in Piedmont. He returned to Sicily in time to win the favor of King Vittorio Amedeo II, who was visiting his new realm after the Treaties of 1713.

Rejoining Vittorio soon afterward in Turin, with the title of First Architect to the King, Juvarra began to enjoy an international reputation. For his first work in Turin, the façade of S. Cristina (1715–28), he adopted the design of the portal of S. Marcello in Rome, built by Fontana. His own inventive and decorative skill was soon to emerge in numerous undertakings: in the interior refacing of the Trinità; in altars and chapels designed for S. Stefano, Corpus Domini, La Consolata, La Visitazione, S. Teresa, and the hospital of S. Giovanni, all in Turin; in the portal and vestibule for the Carthusian monastery of Collegno; and in other altars for Vercelli, Oropa, Bergamo, Lucca, and Chambéry.

Filippo Juvarra. Aerial view of the basilica at Superga, near Turin. 1717–31. *Photo Italian Embassy.*

The subdued Rococo style Juvarra preferred for secular decoration is illustrated by two elegant staircases in Turin: the Scala dei Forbici at the Royal Palace (1720), whose several flights are carried on flying stringers; and the more imposing flights that ascend parallel with the main façade of the Palazzo Madama (1718–21). The building of this façade coincided with a visit by Juvarra to France, and there are subtle echoes of the Classicism of Versailles in its basement and in the rhythm of its arched bays.

Two major works stand out among the architect's many achievements: a church attached to a royal monastery, and a palatial hunting lodge. The basilica and monastery of Superga (1717–31) are situated on the peak of a hill 5 miles from Turin. The domed central-plan church is flanked by two campanili; behind it lie the monastery buildings. The church is circular externally, but the nave is octagonal, opening into the second smaller octagon of the sanctuary. There is very little Baroque turbulence in Superga, which seems to herald the return of Classical traditions into Italian architecture. Juvarra was to use the central plan again for the seminary and church of S. Croce (begun 1718). The Carmine (1732–36) is the sole example in Juvarra's work of a long nave with side chapels over which are tall niches and a balcony that holds the elaborate plan together.

Together with Superga, the hunting villa at Stupinigi, near Turin (1729–35), is Juvarra's most original creation. A half-moon piazza leads into a vast octagonal courtyard surrounded by low buildings, behind which rises the main structure, composed of four wings grouped in a St. Andrew's cross (cross-shaped like the letter X) around a large oval hall. Overhanging the great central hall, with its fresco decoration by Domenico (d. before 1771) and Giuseppe (d. 1761) Valeriani, are small rooms jutting out to form balconies interconnected by passages behind the walls.

Juvarra's prestige, increased again in Turin by the palaces he built for Birago di Borgaro, Martini di Cigala, Guarene and Richa di Covasolo, was such that he was summoned to Madrid to rebuild the Royal Palace (designs submitted, 1735; construction, 1738–64). He died there in 1736, leaving his pupils, including Benedetto Alfieri and Giovanni Batista Sacchetti (d. 1764), to continue his work in Spain and Piedmont.

K

KAHN, Albert (1869, Rhaunen, Rhineland-Palatinate—1942, Detroit), German-born architect and engineer. He applied industrial methods of standardization and team design to insure rapid and economic construction. The output of his Detroit-based firm was prodigious: in 1937, for example, it was responsible for 19 per cent of all industrial building in the U.S. During his lifetime Kahn was the architect for more than 1,000 buildings for the Ford Motor Company and 127 for General Motors. In 1928 the Soviet government commissioned his firm to design factories in connection with the Five Year Plan, and 521 were completed under his direction.

Kahn's family emigrated to the U.S. in 1880 and settled in Detroit. Some 15 years later he organized his own firm, which included his brothers Julius, Louis, and Moritz as associates. His first major commission, in 1903, was a factory for Henry B. Joy's infant Packard Motor Car Company. Two years later, in his tenth plant for Packard, also in Detroit, he used reinforced concrete for the frame. His encounter with Henry Ford proved prophetic, for he gave architectural expression to Ford's dynamic vision of assembly-line production. Kahn's straightforward acceptance of the functional and constructional demands of industry and his refusal to make his utilitarian buildings fashionably picturesque or "aesthetic" made him a forerunner of the Neue Sachlichkeit movement in Europe. While his work also included hospitals, offices, schools, and military installations, it was in the area of factory design that he made his greatest impact. Shortly before his death Kahn completed a number of colossal war plants, among them the giant Ford bomber plant at Willow Run, near Ypsilanti, Michigan.

KAHN, Louis Isadore (b. 1901, Saare, Estonia), American architect. During a stay in Europe in 1928–29, he visited Rome, San Gimignano, Siena, Athens, Carcassonne, and Albi, sketching and taking notes on the great works of the past. This training explains his taste for clean lines and Classical order.

Beginning in 1941 he worked in Philadelphia in partnership with George Howe; the following year Oskar Stonorov (1905–70) joined them. Kahn's originality did not fully emerge until his middle years, first with the Yale University Art Gallery at New Haven, Connecticut (1952–54), then with the Trenton, New Jersey, Bath House (1956). In 1955 he was appointed Professor of Architecture at the University of Pennsylvania, and his influence began to grow. His first masterpiece was the Alfred Newton Richards Medical Research Building of the University of Pennsylvania, Philadelphia (1958–60). This building, whose powerful volumes are slightly reminiscent of the towers of San Gimignano, provides a new image of modern architecture, linked both to the industrial age and to the splendors of the past. All Kahn's later projects, which include the new town-planning project for Philadelphia (1953–62), the Salk Institute of Biological Research (1959) in La Jolla, California, and the United States Consulate at Luanda (1962), are imbued with the spirit that has brought Kahn the reputation of being "a classic of the avant-garde." In 1962 Pakistan commissioned him to produce an over-all plan for an entirely new city, Dacca, the future capital of East Pakistan (construction begun 1963).

KANDINSKY, Wassily (1866, Moscow—1944, Neuilly-sur-Seine, near Paris), Russian-born painter, a naturalized French citizen, and one of the founders of abstract art. In 1886 he went to the University of Moscow, where he studied law and political economy. It was not until 1895, when he visited an exhibition of the French Impressionists in Moscow, that a painting by Claude Monet showed him his true vocation. The following year he gave up his legal career and went to Munich to devote himself entirely to painting. After traveling in Holland, Tunisia, and Italy, he settled for a year (beginning in June 1906) at Sèvres, near Paris. In 1909, after returning to Munich, he helped to found, together with Alexej von Jawlensky and Alfred Kubin, the Neue Künstlervereinigung. From his meeting with Franz Marc in 1911 the Blaue Reiter movement was born; the two exhibitions of this Expressionist group proved to be the major events in the development of modern German painting. With the outbreak of World War I, Kandinsky was forced to return to Russia, where in 1921 he founded the Academy of Artistic Sciences. At the end of that year he left Soviet Russia and settled in Germany, first at Weimar, then at Dessau, becoming one of the principal teachers at the Bauhaus from 1922 to 1933. When the Bauhaus was closed by the Nazis in the latter year, Kandinsky took refuge in Paris, where he lived until his death.

Up to the age of forty-three he painted narrative pictures of no great originality; it was only in 1909 that he began to depart from nature. Then followed his series of "Improvisations" and "Compositions," which were alternately figurative and non-figurative, the latter possessing an astonishing vivacity of invention. In fact, it was in 1910, with an entirely abstract watercolor, that Kandinsky emerged as an initiator of nonrealistic art. In that year he also wrote *Über das Geistige in der Kunst* (*Concerning the Spiritual in Art*, 1947), a prophetic treatise on the artist's inner life. The naturalistic elements soon disappeared from Kandinsky's work, replaced by furious lines and vehement colors clashing freely in a passionate, romantic disorder. Abandoning himself to lyricism, he then produced some of the most masterly and original compositions in the history of abstract art.

World War I coincided with a break in the development of Kandinsky's art, and the painter of *Black Arc* (1912; Paris, Musée National d'Art Moderne) and the great *Fugue* (1914; New York, Guggenheim Museum) accepted the discipline of the objective, rational, and severe style that became the symbol of the Bauhaus. The romantic superabundance of

Louis Khan. Alfred Newton Richards Medical Research Building, University of Pennsylvania, Philadelphia. 1958–60. *Photo Lawrence S. Williams.*

Wassily Kandinsky. *Freshness.* 1941. Galerie Maeght, Paris.

his previous style was replaced by a colder, more thoughtful, more calculated conception that produced geometric forms and architectural structures in which it is tempting to see a certain homage to the Constructivism of Kandinsky's rival, the Dutch painter Piet Mondrian. Kandinsky now set about translating his mental schemes into combinations of lines, angles, squares, and circles, and flat applications of color, but with an alacrity and animation of rhythm that are absent from the austere works of Mondrian. The Bauhaus period also accentuated Kandinsky's didactic tendencies: in his essay *Punkt und Linie zu Fläche* ("Point and Line in Relation to Surface"), published in 1926, it is as a theoretician that he lays down limitations to creative freedom.

Side by side with his paintings, Kandinsky also produced woodcuts and drawings, designed the settings and costumes for Mussorgsky's *Pictures at an Exhibition* for the Friedrich Theater at Dessau (1928), and executed the frescoes for a music room at the International Exhibition of Architecture in Berlin (1931). In December 1933 he took up permanent residence at Neuilly-sur-Seine, a suburb of Paris. His style underwent yet another change: his forms abandoned their geometric aspect, became suddenly more concentrated, and evolved again into indecipherable hieroglyphs and ornamental motifs. What was communicated, however, was the presence of a spiritual world with infinite reverberations, as in *Composition X* (1939) and *Tempered Élan* (1944)—both in the collection of Nina Kandinsky.

Kandinsky was one of the first painters to realize more completely than others that the naturalistic traditions in art were exhausted. He bore witness to the artist's right to express the imaginings of his inner world, and in so doing, created an art as far removed from the pure abstraction of Mondrian as was the poetic magic of Paul Klee or the bitter sensuality of Robert Delaunay. Because it is simultaneously that of a precursor, an inventor, and a master, Kandinsky's work is of such richness that its effect on the development of art cannot yet be calculated.

KANE, John (1860, West Calder, Scotland—1934, Pittsburgh), American Primitive painter. When he was nineteen he emigrated to Pittsburgh, where he became a house painter and carpenter, and took up picture painting as a hobby. In his scenes of the Pittsburgh townscape, Kane transforms the dreary industrial city into a gay metropolis by means of the naive perspectives and decorative patterns of the Primitive style (*Panther Hollow*, 1930–31; New York, Whitney Museum). His *Self-Portrait* (1929; New York, Museum of Modern Art) is probably his best-known painting: its hypnotically staring eyes, frontal pose, tautly restrained energy, and symmetrical composition suggest a kind of modern icon.

KANOLDT, Alexander (1881, Karlsruhe—1939, Berlin), German painter. From 1901 to 1911 he was a member of the New Artists' Association in Munich, and from 1913 to 1920 of the Munich Secession. After the war he met George Schrimpf (1898–1938) and Carlo Mense (1889–1965), developing the ideas advanced by the New Objectivity (*Neue Sachlichkeit*, first used in 1923 by G. F. Hartlaub to designate the new realism developed in reaction to Expressionism). Kanoldt began to teach at the Breslau Academy in 1925 and at the Berlin Academy in 1932, where he was one of the leading representatives of the New Objectivity. After experimenting with Cubism, his natural inclination for Classical art brought him into contact with the works of André Derain and Carlo Carrà, and with the ideas of the *Valori Plastici*, an Italian movement that emphasized a heightened realism with Classical overtones. He evolved a hard, plastic style of realistic representation, so evident in his *Still Life* (1925; Mannheim Kunsthalle), but he seldom achieved the poetic quality that characterized the work of the Italians.

KAPROW, Allan (b. 1927, Atlantic City, New Jersey), American painter, assemblagist, creator of Happenings, and theorist. Within a brief and intense early career, Kaprow progressed from an interest in Abstract Expressionism and many-leveled paintings incorporating collage to assemblage. He then moved away from the single art object or picture frame to environments and Happenings. Kaprow developed an "action-collage" technique in which he employed such materials as straw, wadded newspaper, twine, and flashing lights. He became a crusader for artist-spectator involvement over an extended field of operation. While he still made assemblages and painted such constructions as *Grandma's Boy* (1956; Pasadena, Calif., Museum), between 1956 and 1958 Kaprow was studying musical composition with the avant-garde composer John Cage. In 1957–58 he began to create environmental works that demanded audience participation (an idea stemming from Cage's experiments), and this integration of space, materials, time, and people eventually led to the more experimental pieces. The first such work was called "18 Happenings in 6 Parts"—presented in October 1959 at the Reuben Gallery on Fourth Avenue in New York. It is from this performance that the now-famous term "Happening" is derived (*see* HAPPENING).

After 1960 he devoted himself to publicizing, creating, and establishing the Happening as a viable form of art in America. His concern, like that of such early Pop artists as Robert Rauschenberg, Robert Whitman, Claes Oldenburg, and Red Grooms, with whom he originated this all-encompassing form of environmental theater, has been to break down the traditional distinctions between life and the categories of art. Many of the Happenings have been performed in such untraditional settings as lofts, stores, gymnasiums, and parking lots. *Yard* (1961), for example, consisted of a backyard full of rubber auto tires heaped randomly for viewers to climb in and around.

KASSITE ART. The Kassites, who are believed to have originated in the Zagros mountains of Iran, invaded Babylonia in the 2nd millennium B.C., probably in the 18th century B.C., and after initial setbacks, established rulership as the second Babylonian dynasty. The royal list "A" shows that Kassite kings occupied the throne over a period of 576 years. Their victory ended a dynasty that had been remarkable for its prosperous civilization and that had produced an art of exceptional quality, but although the break was a brutal one, it did not result in regression. The Kassite capital of Dur-Kurigalzu (modern Aqar Quf, northwest of Baghdad), with its temples, palaces, and the ziggurat temple complex is witness to the new rulers' achievements. In architecture, Kassite art is best known for the frieze of bricks molded in relief found at Erech (formerly Warka) in the temple of King Karaindash (15th century B.C.), and decorated with alternating gods and goddesses holding curved vases. In sculpture, the best known examples of Kassite art are the *kudurrus*, or boulders of hard stone, on which titles to property were engraved. On these stones representation of the gods in human form was rare: they were more frequently depicted with symbols. One of the most famous *kudurrus* is that of Melishipak II (12th century), decorated with five bands of pictures. Not all of its forms have been deciphered, but they include the celestial bodies—the crescent (Sin), the star (Ishtar), and solar disc (Shamash)—and the higher deities—Anu, Ninmakh,

Kassite Art. *Kudurru* of Melishipak II, showing gods and goddesses. Susa, 12th century B.C. Louvre, Paris. *Photo Éditions Tel, Paris.*

and Ea. Other figures are believed to represent lesser divinities, Ninhursag, Nergal, Zababa, Ninurta, Marduk, Nabu, and Gula, and, further down, Adad, Nusku, Ningirsu; in the lower part of the monument are Ishara and Ningizzida, presumably gods of the underworld. The engravers used both vegetal and animal motifs and often gave an important role to inscription. There is no doubt that the Elamites (*q.v.*), successors to the Kassites in the 12th century B.C., were inspired by their art. An exciting discovery occurred in 1964 at Thebes, the capital of Boeotia, with the unearthing of a collection of 36 cylinder-seals in lapis lazuli and agate, of Kassite period and origin, and, thanks to the inscriptions, securely datable to the 14th century B.C. One of them bears the name of Kidin-Marduk, an officer of Burnaburiash II of Babylon (1367–1346 B.C.). *See* IRANIAN ART.

KAUFFMANN, Angelica (1741, Chur, Switzerland—1807, Rome), Swiss painter of portraits, mythologies, and allegories, frequently identified with the English School. At the age of twelve she went to Como to paint a portrait of that city's bishop, and in 1757 assisted her father with the decorations for the parish church at Schwarzenburg, Switzerland. In 1762 Angelica was in Florence, and in 1763 in Rome, where she painted a portrait of the German archaeologist Johann Joachim Winckelmann (1764; Zurich, Kunsthaus). After a visit to Naples, she was in Venice in 1765, where she met Lady Wentworth, the wife of the British ambassador, whom she accompanied to London the following year. In London Angelica had not only a tremendous personal success, but also became a foundation member of the Royal Academy in 1768, and exhibited in every Academy show from 1769 to 1782. Her marriage, in 1781, to the Italian decorative painter Antonio Zucchi (1726–95) brought her into the circle of the architect and decorator Robert Adam. There is no doubt that she assisted Zucchi in much of his decorative work, although her share in the decoration of numerous houses in London is difficult to estimate. In 1781 the couple left for Italy, where they spent the remainder of their lives. Around 1786 she began to frequent the Goethe circle in Rome, where for a time she adopted the German poet's passion for the new Neoclassical style.

Angelica's popularity as a painter is not difficult to understand. Her easy, natural gifts and competent early instruction were combined in facile, graceful mythologies that required no intellectual effort on the part of the spectator (*Bacchus and Ariadne*, 1764; London, Messrs. J. Leger and Son). The complete consistency of her style can be judged from the *Cupid's Wound* (1793; Shrewsbury, Attingham, National Trust), which varies only slightly from the much earlier picture. Her manner is essentially feminine, and, with the exception of the Winckelmann portrait, she is at her best with female sitters whom she portrays in a style that anticipates the portraits of Madame Vigée-Lebrun (*Grace Burdett, Wife of the First Earl of Farnham*, 1771–72; Coll. Lord Farnham). Historically, Angelica is interesting for having painted a Romantic Ossianic subject as early as 1773 (*Trenmore and Imbaca*, shown at the Royal Academy in 1773; Coll. Earl of Home).

KELDERMANS, a family of Brabantine architects and sculptors, originally called Van Mansdale, who came from Mechlin (Malines). They introduced the Gothic style into Belgium and erected some of the country's finest buildings from the 14th to the 16th centuries.

JAN I (*c.* 1345–1425), the founder of the family, is recorded as working on the corbel sculptures for the house of the deputy mayor at Mechlin (1377–85), and some years later he executed the tomb of François van Haelen for the cathedral of St-Rombaut in Brussels (destroyed 1810).

JAN II (*c.* 1375–1445), his son, supervised work on the collegiate church of St-Gommaire in Lierre for 20 years (1424–45), during the construction of the transept, and also worked on the church of St-Pierre in Louvain from about 1397 until his death. He was also active in Mechlin, Brussels, and Hanswijck.

ANDRIES (*c.* 1400–81 ?), son of Jan II. In 1454 he became director of the work on the church tower at Zierikzee (today in Holland) and was probably responsible for its many Gothic features. Later in his career he was made master of works to the court.

ANTHONIS (*c.* 1440–1512), his son, completed the work begun by Andries at Zierikzee. In Flamboyant Gothic style he built the façade of the Town Hall at Middelburg (1514–18), which he decorated with colossal statues of the counts of Holland and mounted with a bell tower.

ROMBOUT (*c.* 1460–1531), son of Anthonis, worked in partnership with Dominicus de Waghemakere (1460–1542), who was himself the descendant of a family of architects. Notable among their works, which continued Flamboyant Gothic into the next century, were the Palais de Justice in Mechlin, begun in 1507 and completed by Guyot de Beauregard, the Ghent Town Hall (1516–38), the Maison du Roi on the Grand-Place in Brussels, and designs for the church of St. Paulus (1530–71) and the new Bourse, both at Antwerp (completed 1531). Rombout's finest achievement was the church of Ste-Catherine at Hoogstraten (1526–46), built from his plans at the request of the Comte de Lalaing, the favorite of Charles V.

KELLY, Ellsworth (b. 1923, Newburgh, New York), American painter. In the late 1940s Kelly made low-relief wood constructions laced with string, based on actual representational forms abstracted into formal relationships. These indicated familiarity with both Jean Arp's reliefs and the Surrealistic-biomorphic shapes developed by Joan Miró. Matisse's late *papiers collés* (cutouts) also helped form Kelly's hard-edge abstract manner. Kelly continued to draw his forms from nature, although their origins were finally obscured in unified and brilliant colored surfaces (*Blue on White*, 1961; Racine, Wis., Coll. Johnson).

When he encountered problems with figure-ground interaction in some of his bright two-dimensional images, he resolved them through a highly original form of curved planar sculpture. This brilliantly colored sculpture developed both from a sculptural screen commission for the Philadelphia Transportation Building (1956) and from his own monochrome paintings composed of joined sections (1966–67). The sculptures often seem more two- than three-dimensional (reminiscent of Alexander Calder's painted metal stabiles), since they usually consist of only two thin bent or flapped aluminum planes (*Pony*, 1969; New York, Janis Gallery).

Kelly later moved beyond these problematic figure-ground relationships in a series of separate but joined panel paintings shaped to suggest volumetric structures seen in perspective.

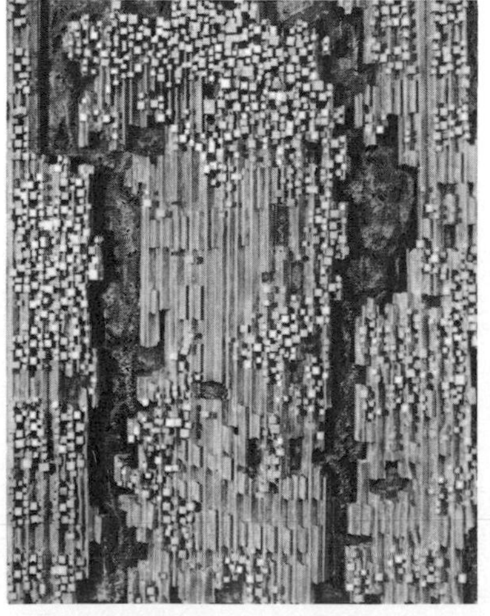

Zoltan Kemeny. *Elements in Freedom.* 1968. Kunsthaus Zurich. *Photo Walter Dräyer, Zurich.*

KEMENY, Zoltan (1907, Banica, Transylvania—1965, Zurich), Swiss sculptor of Hungarian origin. In 1927 he enrolled in the School of Fine Arts in Budapest. Between 1930 and 1940, he worked in Paris as an industrial designer; then, in 1942, he settled in Zurich, where he worked as a fashion illustrator. At the same time, he began to create sculptures of scrap metal and collages of rags and sand. Gradually, he restricted his production to copper or iron reliefs, sometimes formed into arrangements of rivets, letters, or numbers. Although these reliefs are fundamentally plastic, Kemeny himself regarded them as paintings. Each work was based on a type element from which, either by simple repetition or by variations of size and color, Kemeny drew hallucinating and always original effects. In 1963, for the foyer of the municipal theater at Frankfurt, he designed a huge suspended decoration, about 387 feet long, 33 feet high, and 40 feet wide, consisting entirely of a repetition of one of these type components. In 1964, at the Venice Biennale, Kemeny was awarded the Grand Prize for Sculpture for his powerful, restless, highly articulated work.

KEMPENEER, Pieter de. *See* **CAMPAÑA,** Pedro de.

KENSETT, John Frederick (1816/18, Cheshire, Connecticut—1872, New York), American painter. In 1840, he went to Europe, where he remained until 1847. He spent two years in England studying British painting and working on landscapes of the countryside. He also traveled in France, Italy, and Germany. In 1848, the year after he returned to America, Kensett opened a studio in New York City. In 1849 he was elected to the National Academy of Design.

Kensett took his subject matter from areas such as the Adirondacks, the Berkshires, the Catskills, and the Rocky Mountains. Although some of his paintings are done with precise realism, Kensett's pictures presage the same type of poetic interpretations of light and air as were later to be seen in the work of George Inness and William Morris Hunt. He worked from sketches rather than directly from nature, and consequently his paintings often have a more polished look than those of artists who worked outdoors. The *Mountain Stream* (1856; Albany, Institute of History and Art) displays his interest in dense tree growths on rocky ledges dripping with lichen, and is rendered with a literalness reminiscent of 17th-century Dutch landscapes. Kensett's canvases are rich in their treatment of surface and color. His skill in capturing the fresh and vibrant quality of nature earned him the reputation of being one of the foremost American landscape painters of the mid-19th century.

KENT, Adaline (1900, Kentfield, California—1957, Marin County, California), American sculptress. She worked and traveled in Europe, Yucatan, and Mexico until 1930, when she married the sculptor and painter Robert Boardman Howard (b. 1896) and established a studio in San Francisco. Kent had one-man shows in San Francisco, New York, and Paris; in 1939 she was commissioned to do a colossal statue, *Musician*, which represented Polynesia at the San Francisco World's Fair, and in 1956 she was included in the São Paulo Bienal.

Kent's sculpture is characterized by abstracted biomorphic imagery that simultaneously makes subtle references to human and geological forms, such as bones, shells, and rocks (*Finder*, 1953; magnesite, Toronto, Coll. Mr. and Mrs. Walter Landor). Her most common materials were terra cotta and hydrocal, which she sometimes painted with bold, colorful stripe patterns (*Universal Compass*, 1946; hydrocal), thus making a first step toward later American polychrome sculpture.

KENT, Rockwell (b. 1882, Tarrytown Heights, New York—d. 1971), American painter and illustrator. His artistic training came under the aegis of William Merritt Chase, Abbott Thayer, and—most significantly—Robert Henri. Kent and Henri organized an independent show to run concurrently with the more traditional exhibition held at the National Academy in the spring of 1910. His style at this time reveals an innate love of nature and an interest in light and shadow over broad planes (*Toilers of the Sea*, 1907; New Britain, Conn., Art Museum of the New Britain Institute). These works are close to the conceptions of Winslow Homer, although handled more freely and with a more loaded brush. Kent's early works are mainly landscapes and marine paintings. His admiration for William Blake is revealed in some of his later paintings (*North Wind*, 1919; Washington, D.C., Phillips Gallery), and especially in his book illustrations. Unlike Blake, however, are his emphatic contrasts of strong darks and lights and his solid geometricizing forms—two key features of his paintings after about 1920 (*Wake Up, America!*, c. 1942; Au Sable Forks, N.Y., Coll. artist). Among the published records of his life, work, travels, and philosophy are *Wilderness: A Journal of Quiet Adventure in Alaska* (1920), *Rockwellkentiana* (1933), *This is my Own* (1940), *It's Me, O Lord* (1955), and *Of Men and Mountains* (1959).

KENT, William (*c.* 1686, Bridlington, Yorkshire—1748, London), British architect, one of the leading exponents of Palladianism in England. In 1709 he went to Rome, where he studied painting for 10 years. Toward the end of this period he was persuaded to take up architecture by Lord Burlington, himself an architect. In 1719, Kent returned to London with Burlington, who remained his friend and patron for life. The two men collaborated on the plans for Holkham Hall, Norfolk (execution begun 1734 by Matthew Brettingham, 1699–1769). In addition to the main body of the building, there are four subsidiary wings housing the guest rooms, the chapel, the library, and the kitchens. The Treasury (1734), 17 Arlington Street (1741), and 44 Berkeley Square (1742–44), all in London, are notable mainly for their interior decoration. In 1732 and again in 1735–39 Kent submitted two sets of designs for new Houses of Parliament that strongly show the influence of Burlington (neither was executed). His last building, the Horse Guards, London (1751–58), was built after his death by John Vardy (d. 1765). In addition to his work as an architect, Kent was also a talented landscape gardener. His gardens at Carlton House, Chiswick, Stowe, and Rousham set the model for the promenade "à l'anglaise" that became fashionable throughout Europe at the end of the 18th century.

William Kent and Lord Burlington. Holkham Hall, Norfolk. Begun 1734 by Matthew Brettingham. *Photo Kersting, London.*

KERSTING, Georg Friedrich (1785, Güstrow—1847, Meissen), German painter. In 1808 he settled in Dresden, where he became acquainted with Luise Seidler (1786–1866) and Caspar David Friedrich. Kersting accompanied the latter on a walking tour across the Riesengebirge (1810), and painted his portrait in 1812 (*Caspar David Friedrich in His Studio*; Berlin, Nationalgalerie). He taught drawing in Warsaw in 1816, then two years later he settled permanently in Meissen, where he was the head of the painting division of the Meissen porcelain factory.

In his allegorical, religious, and historical paintings—especially the later ones—Kersting conformed to the dictates of the popular Düsseldorf school. But his real strength lay in small-scale paintings of interiors, which have something of the quality of portraits. His quiet, brightly lit rooms contain just a few elegant pieces of furniture and sensitive figures engrossed in simple tasks (*Man at a Secretary*, 1811; Weimar, Schlossmuseum). Kersting differs from the Romantics in his appreciation of the poetic qualities of ordinary objects and activities, of interest not for their symbolic (eternal) value but for their intrinsic (immediate) effect. His style developed from the geometrical compositions and transparent, tonal values of Danish Neoclassicism. In his early deep interiors, he used a soft, extremely delicate technique, with colors of greenish-brown running into gray. Later he adopted the Nazarene technique of painting large areas in cool, smooth colors, and also reduced the pictorial space by depicting sections of rooms instead of full interiors.

KEYSER, Hendrik de (1565, Utrecht—1621, Utrecht), Dutch architect and sculptor. He designed a number of churches in Amsterdam in the severest Protestant style. The Zuiderkerk or South Church (1603–11) is the simplest; the Westerkerk (built from his plans, 1620–38) is derived from the basilican plan and is dominated by a tower 278 feet high; and the domed Noorderkerk (1620) has a central plan radiating from the pulpit. Keyser built a number of houses, similar in design, that transformed the face of the city and still line the canals today. He also executed the tomb of William the Silent (1614–21) in the choir of the Nieuwe Kerk at Delft. This very fine monument was inspired by Primaticcio's tomb of Henri II in the basilica of St-Denis, near Paris, but is complicated by Baroque elements.

THOMAS (1596/97, Amsterdam—1667, Amsterdam), Hendrik's second son, was one of the most admired portraitists of the 17th

Khmer Art. Statue of queen as a goddess. Sambor style. 7th century. Musée Guimet, Paris. *Photo Leonard von Matt, Buochs.*

century. The art of Thomas, a fine painter who combined characteristics of Frans Hals and Rembrandt, is notable for its elegance of composition and sense of space, the quality of saturated tones dominated by luminous blacks, and subtlety and lightness of touch. Among Thomas de Keyser's paintings are the *Anatomy Lesson of Dr. Sebastian Egbertsz.* (1619; Amsterdam, Rijksmuseum); the *Companies of Harquebusiers* (Rijksmuseum); and portraits of *Constantijn Huygens and His Clerk* (1627; London, National Gallery), a *Dutch Family* (1640; Cologne, Wallraf-Richartz-Museum), and a *Seated Lady* (1626; New York, Coll. Hartog), which is a distinguished ceremonial portrait, monumental, poetic, and full of life.

KHMER ART. The Khmers, the direct ancestors of the present-day Cambodians, founded one of the most brilliant civilizations of South-east Asia. It developed toward the end of the 6th century A.D. and lasted roughly 700 years, in the region that is now Vietnam, Cambodia, and southern Thailand. From the 1st to the 7th century A.D., the period called pre-Khmer or Indo-Khmer, and earlier, these territories were inhabited by peoples of Sino-Tibetan origin who enjoyed very close relations with India and China. During this time Indian colonists brought Brahmanic civilization, with its different religions—Buddhism, Sivism, and Vishnuism—into the area. Since at first wood was the principal material used for both sculpture and architecture, almost no remains from the first 400 years survive.

Khmer Art. Temple-mountain of Bāksei Chamkrong, Angkor. 947. *Photo Louis Frédéric, Paris.*

SAMBOR STYLE

The art of the period (of which we have examples primarily from the 5th, 6th, and 7th centuries A.D.), with its strongly Indian foundation, is designated by the term "Sambor style," after the great architectural complex at Sambor (then Isanapura), a city founded by Isanavarman I (A.D. 616–627?) in Lower Cambodia. Architecture of this earliest period is a combination of forms and decoration of indigenous origin and elements imported from India. The sanctuaries are in the form of square towers, each with an entrance structure and a cella containing a cult image. Like the Indian *prāsāda*, these *prāsāt*, or conical towers, rise in gradually diminishing stories. The principal ornament consists of stone lintels, heavily decorated in wood-carving techniques, and low relief carvings in the panels framed by the pilasters of the ground story.

The sculpture of the pre-Khmer period, both Hindu and Buddhist, reveals an even closer indebtedness to Indian prototypes of the Gupta period. The finest examples may be dated approximately in the 6th or 7th century A.D. The Buddha statues are Cambodian variants of the Sarnath style, displaying the sheath-like garments and the plastic simplicity of the Indian masterpieces of the 4th and 5th centuries A.D. One of the great masterpieces of the pre-Khmer style is a statue of Harihara from Sambor (Phnom Penh, Cambodia, Musée National Vithei Ang Eng). In these early statues the precisely engraved definition of details of textural patterns and drapery serves to enrich the austerity of the form.

CLASSICAL PERIOD

(early phase, A.D. 800–1000; late phase, A.D. 1000–*c.* 1450)

In so far as we know from Chinese documents, after a century of strife and disorder (A.D. 700–800), the empire was pacified and unified by Jayavarman II (A.D. 802–50), a Javanese prince who laid the foundations of Khmer power. He was the first of a line of royal builders. With the appearance of new types of architecture and ornamentation at this time, the Classical period of Cambodian art may be said to begin. Jayavarman established the cult of Devarāja, or god-king, the ruler of the world. In order to emphasize the assimilation of the king to the god, this cult was practiced in a temple-mountain, which came to be the center of the kingdom. The temple thus became the temporal equivalent of the cosmos. These concepts implied two things: on the one hand, the need to build this temple on a mountain; or, in the absence of a mountain, to erect an artificial mound; hence the pyramids composed of superposed terraces, at the summit of which the cella was placed. The earliest surviving temple-mountain is the Bākong, built in A.D. 881 by Indravarman when he was resident at Roluos. The simplest and most eloquent example is the Bāksei Chamkrong (Angkor), dating from A.D. 947, in which a single tower of the Sambor type is placed at the summit of a five-storied pyramid, with flights of steps on all four sides. Another, already more complex example is the Phnom Bakheng (late 9th–early 10th century), a central temple of the first capital at Angkor. A natural hill was transformed into a huge pyramid of five levels, with five separated sandstone towers on the highest terrace and smaller replicas of these spires located on the lower levels. One can follow the development of the temple in the shrines that were built in the eastern zone of Angkor by successive kings: first Prē Rup in A.D. 961, and above all Takéo (early 10th century A.D.), which, with its five stories, its gallery surrounding the second story, and its eight towers at the top, directly anticipates Angkor Wāt.

Angkor Wāt

This monument is the most famous of all, and deservedly so. The huge structure, really a small city in itself, was the creation of Sūryavarman II (1112–52), who is identified here with Vishnu. Angkor Wāt was not only a temple dedicated to Devarāja; it was also the mausoleum of its founder. The building has a rectangular plan, surrounded by a moat nearly $2\frac{1}{2}$ miles in circumference and preceded by a continuous wall, pierced with gates. Its main entrance is approached by a causeway with balustrades in the form of giant serpents or Nagas that rear their gigantic hoods at the beginning of this boulevard. The cruciform portico or narthex leads the visitor into a gallery more than half a mile in circumference, decorated with tapestry-like reliefs from the legends of Vishnu and the realm of Yama, Lord of Death. Passing from the main portico through a square enclosing four small courts, the visitor emerges on the second level of the temple, which is a rectangular courtyard enclosed by colonnades and with towers at the four corners. The innermost shrine of the sanctuary rises from the center of this enclosure. It is a mountainous pyramid with stairways on all four sides, rising at a precipitous level to the highest platform, where a central spire is flanked by lesser towers at the angles of the arcaded cruciform plan. The individual towers at Angkor Wāt have a bombshell or pine-cone silhouette almost without precedent in earlier structures, and the auxiliary towers echo the shape of the central spire in smaller scale, enhancing the feeling of its magnitude. The effect of scale is further increased by a clever use of proportion.

The grandiose scale and the clarity of arrangement of Angkor Wāt are further enhanced by the great beauty of the sculptural decoration. Among the most beautiful carvings are the groups of celestial nymphs or *apsaras* (wives of the heavenly musicians). The most famous reliefs at Angkor cover the entire lower circumference of the building—a vast tapestry or scroll-painting in stone, executed in very shallow planes and with a strongly pictorial character that suggests derivation from wall-paintings.

The Bayon

Angkor enjoyed a final period of prosperity under Jayavarman VII (reigned 1181–*c.* 1218). He was a devout Buddhist and encouraged the spread of Mahāyāna Buddhism; the Hindu divinities were replaced by representations of the Buddha and of Lokeśvara. The king built a new capital, Angkor Thom, which he enclosed with a stone rampart that measured almost two miles on each side. The principal sanctuary of Angkor Thom was the Bayon, erected in its final form by Jayavarman VII during the late 12th and early 13th centuries. The central part of the sanctuary has the pyramidal elevation of many earlier structures. In this building, architectural symbolism played a more important role than ever and was charged with new significance. Similarly, each of the various chapels around the principal temple represents a province of the empire, and each is surmounted by a tower bearing four mammoth faces, representing the Bodhisattva Lokeśvara, "Lord of the World," in the guise of the king. But although the Bayon is still a temple-mountain in conception, it no longer possesses the strict layout and clarity of Angkor Wāt.

Khmer Art. Aerial view of the temple, Angkor Wāt. First half of 12th century. *Photo Claude Guioneaud, Biarritz.*

Sculpture

Sculpture attained a distinctly Khmer style somewhat earlier than architecture, namely in the late 8th and early 9th centuries A.D. During that period, it took on a new vitality; the silhouettes became more supple and the garments more natural. This harmony soon gave place to a more robust, but also a heavier style, and at the beginning of the 10th century A.D. the faces became harder and heavily incised by the horizontal line of the eyebrows and the strict frame of the various coiffures (tiara or cylindrical chignon); the garments became simple and austere to the point of being rigid and schematized. The result was a hard, impassive, distant art. At Angkor Wāt (first half of the 12th century), apart from the friezes of the *apsaras* already mentioned, the heads have a rather blocklike character, austere in a somewhat conventional way. The trend toward generalization and formalized hardness in the sculpture of Angkor Wāt culminated in the style of the Bayon (13th century). But although the sculpture of this period is marked by a masklike rigidity of expression, one is made more aware of the enigmatic, dreamy quality. The last era of Khmer civilization was one of titanic architectural programs that not only imposed mechanical mass production, but also completely exhausted the resources and strength of the realm. The end of this magnificent civilization came in the 15th century with the fall of Angkor to the Siamese, a disaster that brought about the complete disappearance of Khmer culture as such.

KIESLER, Frederick (1896, Vienna—1965, New York), Austrian-born American sculptor and architect. In 1923 he worked with Adolf Loos on the first city reconstruction projects in Vienna; in the same year he created the first architectural model for his "Endless House." After his emigration to the United States in 1926, he designed Peggy Guggenheim's Art of This Century Gallery in New York (opened 1942); directed the installations for the International Surrealism Exposition at the Galerie Maeght, Paris (1947); and designed the Festival Theater at Ellenville, New York (1955), and the World House Galleries, New York (1957). In Berlin Kiesler created extremely modern theater sets for Karel Capek's *R.U.R.* (1923) and Eugene O'Neill's *The Emperor Jones* (1923), both of which utilized motion pictures as backdrops and moved continuously in co-

Ernst Ludwig Kirchner. *The Amselfluh.* 1923. Kunstmuseum, Basel.

ordination with the play and the lighting. In the United States he was director of scenic design at the Juilliard School of Music, New York (1933–37), and designed sets for Juilliard productions and for the Metropolitan Opera, New York.

Around 1923 Kiesler became associated with the Dutch De Stijl group, and in the late 1930s and 1940s with the Surrealists. One of his main concerns was the expression of space and infinity, both in relation to natural and man-made forms. The first important example of this tendency was the architectural model for the "Endless House" (1923), which was originally intended for a "Space Theater," but was later gradually modified into a more sculptural form and was exhibited by the Museum of Modern Art, New York, in 1960. Kiesler's preoccupation with space and endlessness is also reflected in his sculpture, which is generally based on motifs from nature and the cosmos, such as the environmental *Galaxy* (*c.* 1950; wood) and *Marriage of Heaven and Earth* (1961–64; bronze), both in the Martha Jackson Gallery in New York. The latter work was part of a landscape series of 1961–64. Kiesler's art is strongly environmental and is, moreover, a fusion of different media—sculpture, painting, architecture, and theater. It is also a highly romantic art, resulting from his theories about the importance of time and space, as well as from his concept of creativity as a spontaneous, searching, and instinctive process.

Paul Klee. *Animals in the Full Moon.* 1927. Coll. F. C. Schang, New York.

KIRCHNER, Ernst Ludwig (1880, Aschaffenburg, Lower Franconia—1938, Frauenkirche, near Davos, Switzerland), German painter. When, in 1905, with Erich Heckel, Karl Schmidt-Rottluff, and Fritz Bleyl (b. 1881), Kirchner founded the famous Brücke group at Dresden, he was, like his friends, a student of architecture, and had done very little painting. But, like them, he was convinced that art was in need of renewal, and turned for inspiration to late medieval German woodcuts, Japanese prints, African and Oceanic sculpture, and the works of Edvard Munch, Van Gogh, and the Post-Impressionists. In his canvases of 1906, he applied pure, bright color with small brushstrokes. A year later, his color had not only increased in brilliance, but it was applied over large areas and enclosed with a bold line. His forms were elemental and powerful. The result was an Expressionistic art with a violent attack that revealed anxiety and revolt (*Self-Portrait with Model*, 1907; Hamburg, Kunsthalle).

In 1911 Kirchner settled in Berlin, and his painting underwent a profound transformation. The color became less strident, and the design firmer and more integrated (*Nude with Hat*, 1911; Cologne, Wallraf-Richartz-Museum). The impulsive artist was readily inspired by scenes on the streets of Berlin. He effectively projected the nervous animation, affected elegance, mannered gestures, and the artificiality in the lives of city inhabitants in *Five Women in the Street* (1913; Wallraf-Richartz-Museum).

In 1917 he left for Switzerland, where he took as subjects the mountains and the peasants and shepherds who lived on them (*Moonlit Winter Night*, 1918; Detroit, Institute of Arts). Although in these works he appears to have reached a profound understanding of nature, particularly in the paintings of 1921–25, he was unable to achieve the authority of his Berlin period. In 1938 he committed suicide, depressed over recurrent symptoms of illness and in despair over the situation in Germany. His work includes a number of remarkable engravings (usually woodcuts; *Peasants' Meal*, 1919) and some sculpture, in which he admitted to a debt to African art, in addition to a large body of painting.

KISLING, Moïse (1891, Cracow—1953, Sanary-sur-Mer, Var), French painter of Polish origin. He was introduced to modern French painting by Józef Pankiewicz (1866–1940), his teacher at the Cracow School of Fine Arts, who advised him to go to Paris in 1910. After World War I, which he spent as a volunteer in the French forces, he became a prominent figure in Montparnasse and one of the leading artists of the School of Paris, along with his friends Amedeo Modigliani, Chaim Soutine, Jules Pascin, and Marc Chagall. Kisling lived for a time at Céret, near Perpignan, at the same time as Picasso, Juan Gris, the poet Max Jacob, and the Spanish sculptor Manolo (1872–1945). Kisling's early style was strongly influenced by Cézanne, but his work later became increasingly fluid and vivid in color. Apart from his admirable nudes, he painted very moving portraits of children (*Small Boy in Striped Sweater*, 1937; Geneva, Oscar Ghez Modern Art Foundation), followed later by portraits of a number of figures from the world of the arts and letters. It is in his portraits of women, with their large, deep eyes, their supple necks, and their dazzling complexions, that Kisling expressed himself most completely.

KLEE, Paul (1879, Münchenbuchsee, near Bern—1940, Muralto, near Locarno), German painter. In 1898 he went to Munich, where he attended a private art school before entering the Academy. In 1902 he returned to Bern, and a year later produced his first engravings, which are also the first works in which his personality is clearly apparent.

In 1906 Klee returned to Munich, where he saw works by the Impressionists, Van Gogh, and Cézanne. In 1911 he met the Expressionists August Macke, Wassily Kandinsky, and Franz Marc, and the following year joined them in the third exhibition of the Blaue Reiter group. Also in 1912, he went to Paris, where he met Robert Delaunay and translated an essay on light by Delaunay for the Berlin review *Der Sturm*. In his own work, Klee progressed slowly and somewhat cautiously. In fact, it was not until he visited Tunisia in 1914 that he became convinced that he was "possessed by color" and that he was a painter.

Klee proved this to himself above all in his watercolors. Indeed, for a long time watercolor was more important in his work than oil painting. In those watercolors painted in Tunisia, the artist had not yet eliminated perspective space completely, but he was already tending to reduce everything to the flat surface of the paper. The colors are distributed in more or less rectangular compartments, which are juxtaposed and built up in a thoughtful but not too rigorous manner (*Motif of Hammamet*, 1914; Basel, Coll. Doetsch-Benziger). In the works that followed, Klee's vision became even more poetic, and the order of the external world was subjected completely to that of the picture. Yet however autonomous his work may be, and however great the element of imagination and fantasy, he never ceased to observe nature and to proclaim that it was indispensable to do so.

Toward the end of 1920, Klee became a teacher at the Weimar Bauhaus and then, until 1931, at the second Bauhaus in Dessau. His teaching was based on his own systematic study of the specific qualities of line, value, and color, for he believed that the painter should employ the utmost intelligence in the use of his means. However, the fact that Klee always favored a return to elementary principles did not mean that his own work lacked complexity and subtlety. On the contrary, few artists have produced a more refined, rich, and varied art than his.

In certain works, Klee expresses his vision primarily through line, which may be either thick or thin, slow or quick, nonchalant or decisive; it may either curve in upon itself, distend, meander, undulate, or stiffen and break. In other works, color may dominate—usually a delicate color that whispers rather than shouts, but one that may also be pure, bold, and sustained. Yet however varied Klee's works may be, there is nothing disparate about them, for they all bear the same unmistakable stamp of genius.

Paul Klee. *Family Outing*. 1930. Paul-Klee-Stiftung, Bern. *Photo Walter Dräyer, Zurich.*

This dedicated, unceasing speculation about artistic means does not prevent Klee's work from appearing delightfully naive, nor does it detract from its evocative power. And although the painter left the creative initiative entirely to his means, and advanced with no clear idea of where he was going, he could ultimately give his works such titles as the *Twittering Machine* (1922; New York, Museum of Modern Art), *Landscape with Yellow Birds* (1923; Basel, Coll. Doetsch-Benziger), *Woman's Mask* (1933; New York, Coll. F. C. Schang), *Flowering* (1934; Zurich, Private Coll.), *Flowering Harbor* (1938; Basel, Kunstmuseum), and *Drunkenness* (1939; Bern, Coll. Hans Meyer).

In 1928–29 Klee visited Egypt, which left as deep an impression on him as Tunisia, but he reacted to it in quite a different way. He was now closer to the underlying reality, both historical and contemporary, of the landscape before him, and he communicated his feelings and ideas in a more abstract way.

In 1931 he left the Bauhaus to take up a teaching post at the Düsseldorf Academy, remaining there for only two years. At the end of 1933 he was dismissed by the Nazis and returned to Bern, where he remained until the end of his life. During the 1930s his paintings became larger, his color brighter, his forms fuller, and his line thicker (*In Suspense*, 1930, Bern, Paul-Klee-Stiftung; *Two Fruits Forming a Landscape*, Bern, Coll. Félix Klee). In 1935 he began to suffer from scleroderma; treatment was unsuccessful, but nonetheless he produced a number of important and original works, including a magnificent series of pastels executed in 1937. The colors are applied to surfaces whose boundaries are sometimes emphasized by a thick line, and acquire sonorities that are either bright or muted, but always rich (*Struggle Harmonized*; Bern, Paul-Klee-Stiftung).

Klee's last paintings and drawings are increasingly elliptical in style. Although some of them seem to betray a certain tiredness, or even disquiet, the pain and nearness of death are not expressed in any obvious or dramatic way, since allusion and symbolism were always more important than direct expression for Klee.

KLEIN, Yves (1928, Nice—1962, Paris), French painter. He had a marked influence on his own generation, as much the result of his tempestuous life as of his theoretical writings and paintings. From 1946, his pictures were monochromatic, completely covered by an application of pure color. About 1957, blue came to replace all other colors. In 1957–59, he decorated the opera house in Gelsenkirchen, Germany, with blue monochrome panels and wall reliefs of natural sponge stratified with polyester. He then produced his *Anthropometries* (1958–60), imprints on paper of nude models coated with blue

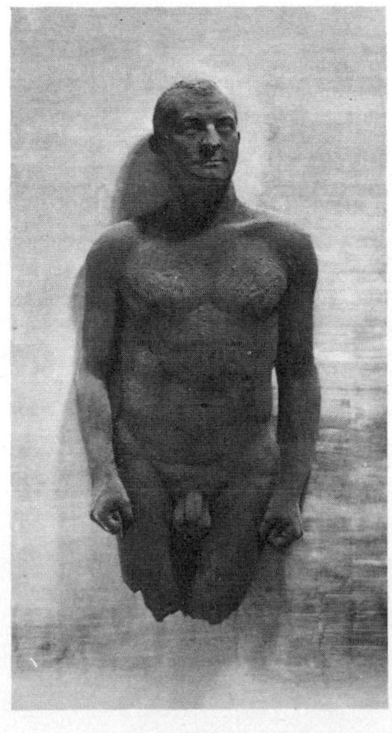

Yves Klein. *Portrait Relief of Arman.* 1962. *Photo Galerie Iolas, Paris.*

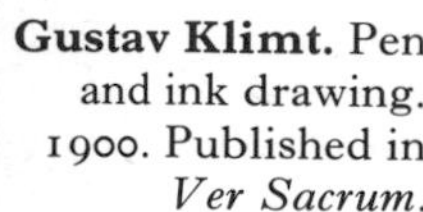

Gustav Klimt. Pen and ink drawing. 1900. Published in *Ver Sacrum.*

paint: "live brushes" operated by remote control. These were followed by the *Cosmogonies* (1960), a group of paintings executed with the help of natural elements, such as rain and wind; the *Planetary Reliefs*; and, from 1962, moldings taken from living models, of which only the *Portrait Relief of Arman* (blue on a gold ground) was completed. A year earlier, by directing incandescent gas jets onto asbestos boards, he had created his *Fire Paintings*. These experiments, for all their deliberate mystification, were the result of a logical process involving both intuition and premeditation. Their value lies not so much in the solution they offered as in the questions they raise. In 1962 Klein died of a heart attack at the age of thirty-four.

KLERK, Michael de (1884, Amsterdam—1923, Amsterdam), Dutch architect. He was the undisputed leader of a group of architects known as the Amsterdam School, who claimed to have no other aim than the expression of individual fantasy and a search for the picturesque at any price. After working as a draftsman in the firm of Eduard Cuijpers (1859–1927) and a period of study in Scandinavia, he returned to Amsterdam and designed the Hille Building (1911), marking the beginning of the Amsterdam School. Then he carried out Hendrik Berlage's plan for the residential district of Amsterdam-Zuid. In his Amsterdam apartment blocks—the Eigen Haard (1921) and the Dageraad (1920–22)—De Klerk revealed a kind of "dynamic" Expressionism, in which his love of innovation was reconciled with the traditional Dutch character.

KLIMT, Gustav (1862, Vienna—1918, Vienna), Austrian painter and decorator. In 1883 he and his brother Ernst opened an independent studio specializing in the execution of mural paintings (which they provided for theaters in Karlsbad and Vienna). In 1897 Gustav became one of the founding members of the Viennese Secession; he was its president until 1903 and contributed regularly to the movement's review, *Ver Sacrum*. Klimt's ornamental, linear technique is typical of the Jugendstil (the name by which the Art Nouveau style was known in Austria). His style is best exemplified by his series of portraits of fashionable Viennese matrons (*Madame Fritsa Riedler*, 1906; Vienna, Österreichische Galerie). The decorative panels he provided in 1902 for the exhibition of Max Klinger's statue of *Beethoven* (1886–1902; Leipzig, Museum der Bildenden Künste) at the Secession building in Vienna had a considerable influence. On the other hand, his monumental paintings of *Philosophy, Medicine*, and *Jurisprudence* for the ceiling of the Vienna University auditorium (1900–3; destroyed in 1945) were violently criticized by the public and administration alike. It was perhaps this failure that led Klimt to redirect his activity. He began a number of works for the Wiener Werkstätte, which had been founded by Josef Hoffmann in 1903. These included the ceramic decorations (*c.* 1909) in the dining room of Hoffmann's Stoclet House in Brussels.

KLINE, Franz (1910, Wilkes Barre, Pennsylvania—1962, New York), American painter. After studying at Boston University (1931–35) and at Heatherley's Art School in London (1937–38), Kline settled in New York in 1938. He was completely unknown until 1945, and earned his living by selling comic drawings and decorating bars. From about 1945 to 1950 Kline attempted to perceive reality in a fundamentally straightforward manner, as can be seen in the portrait of the Russian dancer Nijinsky in the role of Petrouchka (1948; New York, Coll. Mr. and Mrs. David Orr). In 1948, however, he produced a series of urban landscapes in which a more abstract vision is apparent. As with his friends Jackson Pollock and Willem de Kooning, this change led Kline to work only on a very large scale. His earlier forms collided and merged in his mature abstract style, leaving only signs, which appeared all the more dominant in that black was used to the exclusion of all other colors (*White Forms*, 1955; New York, Coll. Philip Johnson). Having arrived at a point of extreme tension between the black mass and the whiteness torn through it, Kline returned to color around 1957 (*Black, White, Gray*, 1959; New York, Metropolitan Museum), but in so doing, he did not abandon either the fury or the overwhelming lyrical power of his earlier compositions.

KLINGER, Max (1857, Leipzig—1920, Grossjena, near Naumburg), German painter, engraver, and sculptor. He espoused a total art that attracted the support of a small number of devotees, but left collectors indifferent. In 1893 he settled in Leipzig, where he remained except for a few lengthy visits abroad. Klinger left his most ambitious work, a statue in polychrome marble of a Jupiter-like *Beethoven* (1886–1902), to the Leipzig Museum der Bildenden Künste. This work, like his huge painting of *Christ on Olympus* (1897; Vienna), is a testimony to the artist's noble intentions, but it also reveals the inadequacy of his means. As an engraver, however, Klinger was not without merit (*Disgrace*, 1887). His technique in this medium was extremely subtle, and his teaching was praised by such men as Kandinsky.

KNATHS, Karl (b. 1891, Eau Claire, Wisconsin—d. 1971), American painter. Knaths was initially drawn to the work of the Impressionists, but soon felt that their coloristic exaggerations were overly sensual and superficial. Even after the impact of the 1913 Armory Show (which traveled to Chicago), in which Matisse's and Cézanne's paintings appeared,

Franz Kline. *High Street.* 1950.

Knaths still preferred a certain subdued and remote quality in the works of artists such as Millet, or in some rural scenes by Van Gogh. Knaths' version of abstraction always remained aloof from direct association with particular movements and schools. Abstract design and the poetic and spiritual possibilities of the simplest restructuring of nature were his primary concerns, and he tried to combine a deeply felt mystical attitude with an economical, though inventive, visual imagery. In 1919 Knaths settled in Provincetown, Cape Cod, often painting the seascapes around him (*Maritime*, 1931; Washington, D.C., Phillips Collection) in fresh, pure colors. His art clearly reveals an awareness of Cubism, especially of the work of Georges Braque and of the American abstractionists with whom he exhibited in the 1930s, yet it retains a particularly serene sensitivity to materials and subject matter throughout its range of forms and design.

KNELLER, Sir Godfrey (1646, Lübeck, Germany—1723, London), German-born portraitist of the English School. He attended Leiden University, and then went to Amsterdam. He went to Italy around 1672 and in 1675 he was in London, where a letter of introduction to Jonathan Banks led to commissions to paint portraits of the Banks family and their friend *James Vernon* (1677; London, National Portrait Gallery). The *Duke of Monmouth*, a brilliant full-length portrait of about 1677 (Sussex, Coll. Duke of Richmond and Gordon), gained Kneller an introduction to the king and caused his rise in popularity.

A group of highly successful and versatile portraits of 1685, including *Philip, Earl of Leicester* (Kent, Coll. Lord de l'Isle and Dudley) and a *Self-Portrait* (London, National Portrait Gallery), has an ease and an individuality of feeling that was soon to be lost. Later successful works are the 42 bust-length likenesses of members of the Kitcat Club painted between 1703 and 1713. In these works Kneller dispenses with studio props and achieves a new directness, as in the portrait of *Jacob Tonson* (1717; London, National Portrait Gallery), which shows a naturalization of the portrait formula leading directly to Hogarth. In 1688 he became one of the official painters to the English court, and continued to direct a vast studio until his death. Kneller's importance is historical rather than aesthetic, forming a prelude to the painting of Jonathan Richardson and Hogarth.

KNOBELSDORFF, Georg Wenzeslaus von (1699, Kuckädel, Poland—1753, Berlin), Prussian Baroque architect. For 20 years the baron of Knobelsdorff was associated with the major architectural enterprises of Frederick the Great. He trained in painting at the Prussian school of the Frenchman Antoine Pesne before becoming an architect. He must have shown himself capable of brilliant architectural conceptions, but his works were more often reconstructions than new creations, and many of them were disfigured or destroyed.

The summer residence of Sanssouci in Potsdam (1745–47) was the most elegant building of Frederick's reign. The name of Knobelsdorff is frequently mentioned in connection with this Prussian Trianon, but he was not its principal architect. The lavish one-story palace, crowned with a cupola, was actually built by Johann Boumann (1706–76) according to a design sketched by the king. Knobelsdorff was responsible for the fine semicircular Corinthian colonnade that encloses the courtyard. While at work on Sanssouci, Knobelsdorff and Frederick had their most serious quarrel, which resulted in the architect's permanent withdrawal from court circles.

In rebuilding the Potsdam Town Hall (1744–51), he provided columns and paired pilasters for the long façades, which were streaked with red, and later on with green, under the blue and gold roofs. In Berlin Knobelsdorff built the new wings for the palaces of Charlottenburg (1740–46) and, for the Queen Mother, of Monbijou (completed between 1740 and 1742); he also enlarged the castle of Rheinsberg (from 1737), which had been damaged by fire. The Berlin Opera House (façade 1741–43), the only work of which the sketched plans survive, shows the architecture adhering to the principles of Neoclassicism—the only time he did so—and attests his admiration for Palladio. This theater was to have been joined to the Royal Palace and the Academy of Science and Letters in a monumental ensemble, the Forum Fridericianum. However, the square was completed later with the erection of Prince Henry's Palace (now the University) and the Library, the work of Georg Christian Unger (1743–*c.* 1808) and the younger Boumann, Georg Friedrich (b. 1737).

After his accession in 1740 Frederick II continued to be guided by his own youthful taste; thus Knobelsdorff still displayed the graces of the Rococo in the Hall of Mirrors in the Charlottenburg, the Music Room and Hall of Bronzes in the Potsdam Town Hall, and the Flower Room and Library in Sanssouci. The vestibule and Oval Room of the latter palace are more Classical in style, which suggests that they were not decorated by Knobelsdorff.

Georg Wenzeslaus von Knobelsdorff. Colonnade, Sanssouci, Potsdam. 1745–47. *Foto Marburg.*

KOBELL, Ferdinand (1740, Mannheim—1799, Munich), German painter and etcher. In 1762 Kobell was encouraged by Elector Karl Theodor to join the Mannheim Drawing Academy, where he studied under Pieter Anton von Verschaffelt (1710–93). In 1764 he became a scene painter at the Court Opera House, and then went to Paris in 1768. Upon his return to Mannheim in 1771, Kobell was appointed court landscape artist. He was subsequently obliged to leave the city in order to escape French persecution, and settled in Munich in 1793. He was later appointed director of the Mannheim Collection in Munich (1798), which had been evacuated to that city. Kobell evolved a completely personal approach to nature and so became one of the pioneers of German Realism. In fact, he anticipated the 19th-century landscape in the splendid *Waterfall* (1779; Karlsruhe, Staatliche Kunsthalle), and in the views of Aschaffenburg and its environs, including the *Valley toward Goldbach in Unterfranken* (Munich, Neue Pinakothek), which he painted for Elector Erthal of Mainz in 1786.

KØBKE, Christen (1810, Copenhagen—1848, Copenhagen), Danish painter. In 1839–40 he traveled in Italy and Germany, and in 1845 painted the frescoes in the Thorvaldsens Muscum in Copenhagen. Købke was probably the most gifted of the Danish Romantics: his exquisite sense of color and the delicacy of his brushstrokes—sensitive to the slightest details—are apparent in his luminous, precisely rendered landscapes (*Castle of Frederiksborg*, 1835, Copenhagen, Hirschsprungske Samling; *Lakeside near Dosseringen*, 1838, Copenhagen, Statens Museum for Kunst), in his portraits, and in his sun-drenched church interiors with their simple, solemn charm. His healthy and forthright compositions reveal an almost pantheistic attitude toward nature, which was the prime source of his artistic inspiration. Købke's *Portrait of Frederick Hansen Sødring* (1832; Hirschsprungske Samling), a landscape painter (1809–62) and friend of the artist, is regarded as one of the masterpieces of Danish painting.

KOHN, Gabriel (1910, Philadelphia, Pennsylvania—1975, Los Angeles), American sculptor. After studying in New York at Cooper Union and the Beaux Arts Institute (1929–34), Kohn worked as a studio assistant to Herman MacNeil (1866–1947) and other sculptors, and from 1934 to 1942 as a sculptor and as a designer for the theater and films. In 1946–47 he studied with Ossip Zadkine in Paris and until the late 1950s worked primarily in France and Italy. In 1961 he moved to California, where he established a studio and taught in La Jolla and San Francisco.

Kohn's mature style emerged in the early 1950s, when he began to explore carved, and later, constructed wood sculpture. He was much concerned with the relationships between architecture and sculpture and in fact conceived of his work as architecture-sculpture. Kohn's forms are juxtaposed and balanced in oblique, projecting arrangements, with the weight distributed at unexpected points; the nature of the material and the process of construction remain visible in the laminations, the dowels, and the naturally finished, unstained, and unpainted surfaces (*Long Beach Contract, No. 1*, 1965; laminated redwood, Long Beach, California State College).

KOKOSCHKA, Oskar (b. 1886, Pochlarn, Lower Austria), Austrian Expressionist painter. From 1905 to 1909 he studied at the Vienna Kunstgewerbeschule and worked for the Wiener Werkstätte, which in 1908 published his illustrated poem *Die träumenden Knaben* ("Children Dreaming"). In 1910 he went to Berlin, where he also became a close friend of Herwarth Walden, editor of the Berlin review *Der Sturm*. In 1908 Kokoschka began a series of highly personal portraits that in themselves would have assured him a unique place among contemporary artists (*Marquis de Montesquiou*, 1909–10, Stockholm, Nationalmuseum; *Ernst Blass*, 1925, Bremen, Kunsthalle). Indeed, the interest he showed in the portrait was a sufficiently distinguishing feature of his art, for very few modern painters have shown any desire to render the particularities of a face. He displays their anxieties, complexes, and momentary impulses, revealing the fever that gnaws them from within and the decrepitude that threatens them. He pays almost as much attention to their hands as to their faces, and presents them in the most expressive positions (*Herwarth Walden*, 1910; Minneapolis, Coll. Samuel H. Maslon).

In Kokoschka's earliest works, color is less important than line, which is thin, tortuous, and incisive and the major vehicle of expression. About 1912, color increases in importance, and the brush is used for drawing as well as for applying the colors, which are now thicker and more sustained (the *Tempest*, 1914; Basel, Kunstmuseum). But the anguish and torment of the earlier works did not disappear. On the contrary, after Kokoschka was wounded in World War I, they increased in intensity.

In 1919 he took up a teaching post at the Dresden Academy, where he remained until 1924. During this period, he executed some of his most attractive landscapes. He left Dresden in order to spend the next 10 years traveling, not only in Europe, but in North Africa and the Near East. In the various places he stayed, Kokoschka painted huge, highly animated, panoramic landscapes—especially town views—having a portrait-like subtlety and precision (*Amsterdam*, 1925, Mannheim, Stadtische Kunsthalle; *Jerusalem*, 1929–30, Detroit, Institute of Arts). While continuing to express his own sensitive and highly charged inner temperament, Kokoschka showed a greater awareness of the light and atmosphere of the external world.

In 1934 the political situation in Austria and Germany forced the artist to move to Prague. Four years later he sought refuge in London, where he lived until 1953. He then settled at Villeneuve in Switzerland. His work became increasingly reminiscent of the Baroque decorative painters of Austria (*Thermopylae Triptych*, 1954; Hamburg, Hochschulbehörde). Although it is still possible to sense behind his late paintings the presence of an artist passionately preoccupied with the fate of man in the modern world, the poignant intensity of the earlier works is absent. It is these early works that place Kokoschka among the most important and most moving Expressionist painters of modern times.

KOLLWITZ, Käthe (1867, Königsberg, East Prussia—1945, Moritzburg, near Dresden), German graphic artist and sculptress. After studying painting and drawing in Berlin (1885–86) and Munich (1888–89), she settled in Berlin. She first gained recognition with two cycles of etchings, the *Weavers' Uprising* (1894–98) and the *Peasants' War* (1902–8), in which the influences of Edvard Munch, Honoré Daumier, and Vincent van Gogh are apparent. From 1914 to 1932 Kollwitz worked on a war memorial, which was also a tomb for her son Peter, who was killed in 1914. The result was her *Monument to the Dead* (1932), a simple grouping of two mourning parents, who are modern versions of medieval weepers. Reproduced in granite, these two effigies were finally erected in the cemetery of Eessen, near Dixmude, Belgium. A similar spirit animates her famous bronze statue *Pyramid of Mothers* (1937), which is a protest against all war. Her last sculpture, a *Pietà*, and a panel in high relief entitled *Lament*

Käthe Kollwitz. *The Father*. Figure from the Monument to the Dead. 1932. Eessen Cemetery, Belgium.

(both 1938) testify to her painful and moving resignation in the face of rising violence. Her major activity was graphic work, and the compassion and humanity that are the essence of all her art found their most moving expression in her drawings and lithographs. None is more touching than the last series of eight lithographs, *Death* (1934–36), in which the universal theme is all the more poignant for its fusion with the personal.

KOONING, Willem de (b. 1904, Rotterdam), Dutch-born painter, one of the leaders of the abstract art movement in the United States. In 1920 he discovered modern art, notably the geometric and non-representational work of the Dutch De Stijl group. A year in Belgium (1924) brought him into contact with Flemish Expressionism, which had a considerable influence on him for a time. In 1926 De Kooning went to the United States, where he settled permanently. His painting took on a symbolic, often surrealistic dimension, which became even more marked after his decisive meeting with the Russian-born abstractionist Arshile Gorky in 1928. This development was accompanied by a simplification of the artist's forms, which began to acquire a new weightlessness. Although he returned to a markedly figurative style in 1938, he continued at the same time to pursue a non-figurative development. Yet De Kooning, far from abolishing all relation to the real world in his canvases, grew preoccupied with the human figure. This concern became an exclusive one after 1945, and led him to capture appearances more directly (*Queen of Hearts*, 1943–46; New York, Coll. Joseph Hirschhorn). From these confrontations with nature there emerged a whole series of female figures (late 1940s to mid-1950s) whose derisory, monstrous forms, brutally stated in raw color, are the most tragic expression of an art carried to its extreme point of incandescence (*Woman I*, 1950–52; New York, Museum of Modern Art). From 1955 his paintings abandoned their anthropomorphic forms, and became a battlefield between the intrinsic dynamism of his material and color and the violence of his own handling of these elements (*Door to the River*, 1960; New York, Whitney Museum).

KOREAN ART. Located between the two great civilizations of China and Japan, Korea was the site of a genuine and remarkable flourishing of the arts. The influence of Chinese art on Korean painting, sculpture, and architecture was nevertheless decisive; many Korean artists went to China seeking inspiration. Other contacts resulted from the Chinese invasions of Korean territory, and the Chinese colony (founded 108 B.C.) during the Han Dynasty. Contacts with Japan were also numerous, culminating in the disastrous Japanese invasion of 1592–97.

Those examples of Korean art to survive the invasions of Chinese, Mongol, and Japanese armies, local wars, and the Korean War (1950–53) are nevertheless sufficient to establish the existence of a specifically Korean art, recognizable not simply because it developed within a limited geographic area, but because it possesses certain marked characteristics.

ARCHITECTURE

Chinese influence in architecture was predominant. An important building material was wood, used according to Chinese principles of construction. Because of the cold climate, the space between columns was filled with lime-covered fiber or wood, with brick or with stone. Pagodas, temples, fortifications, and castles were built of granite, but wars and time have left few ancient buildings standing.

The earliest era of Korean history is the Nan-shan period, about which little is known. The first Korean state, founded in 190 B.C., is known as Chosan, and had as its capital the city of Pyongyang. Culturally, this state represented a mixture of Chinese and northern Asian elements. The Chinese destroyed Chosan in 108 B.C., and founded a large colony divided into four provinces, the strongest and longest-lived of which was Lolang (destroyed A.D. 313).

At the time of the Three Kingdoms period (1st century B.C.–A.D. 668), which consisted of Koguryo in northern Korea, Paekche in the southwest, and Silla in the southeast, Buddhist influence led to the construction of pagodas, of which only the simple and elegant stone pagoda of Puyo, the former capital of Paekche, has survived. The magnificent tombs at T'ung-kou, capital of Koguryo, at Pyongyang, and at Uhyonni give some idea of the architecture of this time, with their mock beams and pillars. During the Great Silla Dynasty (A.D. 668–918), which began with the unification of Korea under the kingdom of Silla, architecture imitated T'ang models. At the temple of Bulkuksa (or Pulguksa), the stone structures, such as the classically constructed four-storied Sokka or Sākyamuni pagoda, and the granite Tabo or Prabhutaratna pagoda, provide authentic and valuable evidence for the Great Silla style and method of architecture, as do also the granite earth-covered caves of Sukkuam. During the Koryo Dynasty (A.D. 918–1392), the barbarian kingdoms of Liang and Yin in North China exerted their influence in competition with that of the Sung Dynasty. The vitality of Korean architecture at this time is evident in the temples at Pusoksa near Kyongju, and at Sudoksa near Yezan, where the earliest (11th century) Korean wooden building is preserved, as well as in the many-storied pagodas. Under the Yi Dynasty (1392–1910), there occurred the decline of Buddhism and the adoption of Confucianist methods and ideals, resulting in an extremely conservative, Chinese-oriented civilization. Decoration became the main concern of artists, and architectural forms were distorted, as can be seen in an extreme example, the Kyungbok Palace in Seoul (rebuilt 1867). The temples, pagodas, and palaces of this period reveal an architecture that, for all its interest and occasional beauty, was merely a learned imitation of past styles.

SCULPTURE

The development of Korean sculpture began with the arrival of Buddhism during the period of the Three Kingdoms (A.D. 372 in Koguryo, 384 in Paekche, and 528 in Silla).

The influence of the Chinese Northern Wei Dynasty was dominant in the bronze work, while the stone sculpture possessed a somewhat rough native strength. In the Koguryo kingdom, the sculpture is more massive than that at Paekche, where an austere style of sculpture developed. The *Kudara Kannon* (6th–7th century A.D.; Nara, Hōryūji Monastery), a wooden Bodhisattva from Paekche, is representative of the sculptural style that developed in that kingdom. But it is in the Silla kingdom in the 6th century A.D. that a new and typically Korean type made its appearance, with figures of Maitreya, the Buddha of the Future, in gilt bronze, head bent forward, with slender arms and a graceful body. The great *Maitreya* (beginning of the 7th century A.D.; Seoul, Duksoo Palace Museum of Fine Arts) has an evocative power and a beauty all of its own.

Korean Art. *Maitreya*. Three Kingdoms period (Silla), early 7th century A.D. Duksoo Palace Museum of Fine Arts, Seoul. *Photo Cernuschi Museum, Paris.*

During the Great Silla Dynasty, forms became more robust under T'ang influence. The only exception to this development is found in the caves of Sukkulam, near Kyongju. Here the sculptured figures are not cut out of the rock as bas-reliefs, but are carved separately from stone; they consist of Buddhas, naturalistic figures of the disciples, and figures of warriors guarding the entrance. Secular subjects at this time include guardian figures of animals at tombs.

Decadence set in during the Koryo Dynasty, despite the extraordinary development of Buddhism; spirituality, however, was replaced by an emphasis on naturalism. The Confucian emperors of the Yi Dynasty destroyed Buddhist works, and brought about the final eclipse of an art that was already in decline.

PAINTING

The earliest known Korean paintings date from the 5th century A.D., within the period of the Three Kingdoms. There is no doubt about the Chinese influence on the artists who painted the walls of the ancient tombs near T'ung-kou, Pyongyang, and elsewhere.

The first group of tombs near T'ung-kou on the Yalu river is decorated with representations of daily life, including hunting and banquet scenes, all painted in stylized and somewhat solemn silhouettes. These murals date from the 5th or early 6th century A.D. A second group of paintings, found near Pyongyang, marks an advance over that of T'ung-kou, and is of exceptional aesthetic quality. Deserving particular mention are depictions of a green dragon, a white tiger, and a black tortoise, encircled by a snake and a red bird (late 6th century A.D.). Paintings of the same type have been found in the kingdoms of Silla and Paekche, but they are inferior in quality to the work from Koguryo.

From the Great Silla Dynasty, we have a record of a Bureau of Arts, and the names of famous artists. The Koryo Dynasty, however, is the golden age of Korean painting—a period when the rulers encouraged the arts and assembled large collections. An Academy of

Korean Art. Chong Son. *Diamond Mountains*. 1734. Scroll. Museum für Kunsthandwerk, Frankfurt am Main. *Photo Cernuschi Museum, Paris.*

Art was created, but only a few Buddhist pictures from the end of this period have come down to us. These are elegant works, containing naturalistic elements.

Many works have been preserved from the Yi Dynasty, however. These paintings can be divided into two categories: those by the professional painters belonging to the Bureau of Arts, and those by scholar-painters who followed the example of the Chinese literati painters, and used their brushes for self-expression. By the former group we have many portraits of important figures, painted with incomparable finesse and realism (*Portrait of a Religious Figure*, 14th century; London, British Museum). In the 18th century there were artists determined to paint in what they called a "Korean" manner. These artists include Shin Yun-bok (1758–1820?) and Kim Hong-do (b. 1760), who painted the Korean landscape along with a number of humorous genre scenes. This Korean spirit is especially evident in the works of the animal painters, including Yi Am (b. 1499; *Dog with Puppies*, Seoul, National Museum of Korea), Cho Sok (b. 1595; *Bird on a Tree*, Seoul, Duksoo Palace Museum of Fine Arts), and Pyon Sang-Byok (beginning of the 18th century; *Cats and Swallows*, Duksoo Palace Museum of Fine Arts).

The earliest artists strove to imitate the Southern Sung masters of China, and painted scenes that, in spite of their admitted excellence, nevertheless lacked originality. Korean artists found more opportunity for self-expression when they began to imitate the Ming painters. Kim Duk-sin (1754–1822) and Sin Yun-bok, followers of the Wu school in China, painted lively rural scenes. But Chong Son (1676–1759), who energetically continued the experiments of the Wu school, was probably the greatest of all Korean masters. His *Diamond Mountains* (1734; Museum für Kunsthandwerk), which represents "twelve thousand slashed and rugged mountain peaks," is a close-knit and powerful composition, unique in Far Eastern art. His contemporary was Sim Sa-jong (1707–70), an eclectic painter, who executed *Landscape in Rain* (Museum für Kunsthandwerk) and *River by Night* (Seoul, National Museum of Korea), both scenes bathed in mist. Attributed to him is a vertical scroll of a *Tiger* (National Museum of Korea), a powerful and Classical representation of constrained fury.

During the 19th century Korean painting lost much of its strength and originality, a decline that continued unabated in the 20th century, as a result of Japanese annexation (1910–45) and the division of the country that followed World War II. Traditional techniques and themes, however, remained in use along with more international, Western-inspired methods of painting. Kam Zinchoon (b. 1928) is one of the traditionalists, whose vertical scroll of a *Bird on a Branch* (Oxford, Ashmolean Museum) is painted in a free, expressive manner that reveals the influence of the Chinese master Chu T'a (1626–1705).

Korean Art. Attributed to **Sim Sa-jong.** *Tiger*. Mid-18th century. Vertical scroll. National Museum of Korea, Seoul.

CERAMICS

The earthenware pottery of the Three Kingdoms period was somewhat crude in technique and form, and was often decorated with simple incised patterns. The Great Silla Dynasty witnessed no real change in the pottery, as can be seen in a stoneware funerary urn (8th–9th century A.D.; Washington, D.C., Freer Gallery) that is decorated with a similar, somewhat primitive incised design. It was during the Koryo Dynasty, however, that Korean ceramic ware reached a level equal to that achieved by the Chinese. Celadon ware, at first influenced by the Chinese Sung ware, became essentially Korean in form and design. While a celadon cup (11th–12th century) at the Freer Gallery retains a certain Chinese appearance in its decoration, two celadon wine vessels (11th–12th century; Duksoo Palace Museum of Fine Arts) reveal distinctively Korean forms in their elongated, tapered bodies and in their decorations. In the 12th century Korean potters introduced a method of decoration that made use of different colored clays resulting in black-and-white patterns, as seen in a water bowl decorated with peony designs at the Duksoo Palace Museum of Fine Arts. Yi ware consists of pale blue or green ware, called *pun ch'ong*; a somewhat rough but well-made celadon ware; a blue-and-white ware inspired by Ming pottery, though somewhat heavier than the Chinese prototypes and characterized by an extremely simple and sparse decoration; and, finally, in the 18th century, a ware whose technical inferiority to earlier work, according to the art historian Peter Swann, "is compensated for by vigorous designs on energetic shapes."

Korean Art. Funerary urn. Great Silla Dynasty, 8th–9th century A.D. Freer Gallery of Art, Washington, D.C.

KOWARSKI, Felicjan Szczesny (1890–1948), Polish painter. From 1923 he taught at the Cracow Academy, and from 1929 at the Warsaw Academy. Kowarski's work, which won him a great many disciples, is characterized by a tragic Romanticism, expressed in a strict Classical style of restrained monumentality. This is true whether his theme is the pathetic isolation of contemporary man, as in his gloomy landscapes peopled with sad-looking figures; the martyrdom of the Jewish people, as in his series of paintings produced under the Nazi occupation; or whether he is striving to express his social and political ideas, as in his large group portraits. Apart from his paintings, Kowarski left a number of sculptures and lithographs. Representative examples of his work include the painting *Electra* (1947; Warsaw, National Museum) and the bronze bust of *Marat* (1944; Warsaw, Coll. J. Kowarska).

KRAFT *or* **KRAFFT,** Adam (*c.* 1460, Nuremberg—*c.* 1509, Schwabach, near Nuremberg), German sculptor. Kraft was not influenced by the Italian style, but remained completely faithful to the Gothic spirit of the Middle Ages. His first sculptures, a series of reliefs (1490–92), appear to have been commissioned by Sebald Schreyer and Mathias Landauer for the exterior of the choir in the church of St. Sebald at Nuremberg. A contract signed in 1493 with the Nuremberg patrician Hans Imhof the Elder entrusted Kraft with the construction of a tabernacle to be placed near the high altar of the church of St. Lorenz in Nuremberg. Completed in 1496, it is slender and pointed, and rises 60 feet to the spring of the vaults. It includes some bas-reliefs that are rather badly set off by the complicated play of curves, and the

Adam Kraft. *Self-Portrait.* Detail from the tabernacle in the church of St. Lorenz, Nuremberg. 1493–96. *Photo Schmidt-Glassner, Stuttgart.*

whole structure is barely supported by two crouching figures, one of which probably represents Kraft himself.

The artist's works—the Pergenstörffer memorial (1498–99) and the Rebeck memorial (1500), both in Nuremberg's Frauenkirche—show a greater plastic sense. The second of these works depicts a large, well-balanced *Coronation of the Virgin*, with the figure of the Madonna placed between God the Father and Christ. The Rebeck memorial demonstrates how natural a sculptor Kraft could be when he was not trying to imitate painting.

Kraft's most important work—seven wayside reliefs in sandstone on the theme of the Passion, along the road from the city of Nuremberg to the outlying St. John's Cemetery—has suffered a good deal of damage. However, a substantial part of the reliefs have been rescued and are today in the Germanisches Nationalmuseum, Nuremberg. The group was executed near the end of the sculptor's life, showing that Kraft's late style underwent a marked simplification and purification.

KRALJEVIĆ, Miroslav (1885, Gospic, West Croatia—1913, Zagreb), Croatian painter. Along with the painters Josip Račić (1885–1908) and Vladimir Becić (1886–1954), he was one of the pioneers of modern Croatian painting. After studying under Baron Hugo von Habermann (1849–1929) at the Munich Academy, Kraljević lived for a time in Paris, where he was influenced by Édouard Manet. Although profoundly affected by Impressionism, he never completely adopted its color theory. In temperament and taste, Kraljević was closer to Gustave Courbet or Manet, whose use of somber colors highlighted with lighter tones particularly appealed to him. This is apparent in his two best paintings, *Self-Portrait with Pipe* and *Self-Portrait with Dog*, which are accomplished examples of his exceptional talent.

KROHG, Christian (1852, Aker, near Oslo—1925, Oslo), Norwegian painter. He was the leading representative of the naturalistic tendency that triumphed over Romanticism in Norway during the late 19th century. His art was vigorous, straightforward, and uncompromisingly realistic. Krohg took his subjects from the most ordinary, and sometimes the most somber and tragic, aspects of everyday life (*Mother and Child*, 1883; *Jossa*, 1886; both Oslo, Nasjonalgalleriet). The vividness of the paint and the vigor of the brushwork succeed in imbuing even the most banal subject with a subtle but powerful undercurrent of poetic feeling.

PER LASSEN (b. 1889, Asgardstrand, near Oslo), son of Christian, was also a painter. He studied in Paris, first at the Académie Colarossi, then in Henri Matisse's studio. In 1933 he left France and settled permanently in Norway, where he held a leading position in contemporary painting and taught at the Oslo School of Fine Arts. In his epic frescoes, he deals with the simple themes of daily life in town and country (murals in Oslo City Hall, completed 1949), or with the exaggerated rhythms of a mechanized world, peopled with robots and ravaged by violence and war (frescoes in Oslo Library, 1939). Whether he confines himself to a familiar detail of everyday life, or creates a composition of truly visionary power, he always expresses himself in formal constructions whose firmness and rather unexpected rigor are derived from Cubism.

KRSTIĆ, Djordje (1851, Stara Kanjiza, North Serbia—1907, Belgrade), Serbian painter. He studied at the Munich Academy in the 1870s, at which time the realism advocated by Gustave Courbet was becoming popular in Germany. Krstić's style is characterized by the use of warm, deep tones, somber colors, and chiaroscuro. He became the leader of the Serbian Realist school, and painted portraits (the *Anatomist*; Belgrade, National Museum), landscapes, and historical subjects (the *Fall of Stalac*, 1900; Belgrade, National Museum). At the turn of the century, Krstić's color became brighter and Impressionistic touches appeared in many works, including his landscape, *Topcider Wood*. For this reason his mature landscapes had a considerable influence on the younger generation of Serbian artists.

KUBIN, Alfred (1877, Litomerice, Czechoslovakia—1959, Zwickledt, Austria), Austrian draftsman and painter. After studying photography, he arrived in Munich in 1898 and entered the Academy, where he discovered the graphic work of Goya, Aubrey Beardsley, and Max Klinger, whose influence dominated his early style. In 1902 he exhibited at the Cassirer Gallery in Berlin. He then began to travel, and in Paris met Odilon Redon, for whose work he felt great sympathy. In 1906 he finally settled in the castle of Zwickledt, in Upper Austria. Although he was in close touch with the painters of the Blaue Reiter, his preoccupations were quite different. His art continued to explore a world of fantasy, and in this he remained isolated from his time. He illustrated the works of a number of Romantic writers, including Edgar Allan Poe, Fedor Dostoevski (*The Double*, 1913),

Per Lassen Krohg. *Kiki of Montparnasse.* 1928. Nasjonalgalleriet, Oslo.

Oscar Wilde, August Strindberg, and Barbey d'Aurevilly (*The Diabolists*, 1921). Kubin was a visionary draftsman, "haunted by the angel of the bizarre," and even published a fantastic novel, *Die andere Seite* ("The Other Side"), in 1909.

KUHN, Walt (1880, New York—1949, New York), American painter. Kuhn studied art in Paris and Munich, then traveled through Holland, Spain, Germany, and Italy, experimenting with the media and the many styles with which he came into contact. He was one of the few American realists able to absorb and adapt the new modernistic modes of painting that were introduced to America at the New York Armory Show of 1913. In 1912 he had helped organize the Association of American Painters and Sculptors, a group that formulated plans for the Armory exhibition. Along with his friend Arthur B. Davies, who was president of the Association, Kuhn was sent to Europe to collect avant-garde paintings. The works of the Fauvists Henri Matisse and André Derain, of Pablo Picasso, Paul Gauguin, and others had a decisive influence on the stylistic aspects of the painting he did upon his return. *Lavender Plumes* (1938; New York, Kennedy Galleries) is characteristic of the half-length, stoic frontal portraits of circus figures in makeup and garish costumes that he produced throughout his artistic career. From Matisse he borrowed the boldly distorted forms and the bright, almost gaudy colors, while the influences of Derain and Picasso are evident in the circus performers he loved to portray (*Blue Clown*, 1931; New York, Whitney Museum). In the 1920s Kuhn painted single figures on neutral backgrounds, deliberately limiting his focus to the starkly expressive human representation; during the 1930s he widened his repertoire to include flower studies, landscapes, and still lifes. Kuhn's friendship with Jules Pascin during the 1940s had strong effects on the graphic work he produced at that time.

KUNIYOSHI, Yasuo (1893, Okayama, Japan—1953, New York), Japanese-born American painter. He went to Seattle in 1906, began his art studies in Los Angeles, and continued them in 1916 at the Art Students League in New York. Kuniyoshi's early paintings of the 1920s often combined landscapes, figures (particularly children), and flowers in dreamlike compositions (*Child*, 1923; and *Landscape*, 1924; both New York, Whitney Museum). Ink drawings of the 1920s and 1930s showed more freely associated combinations, often related, however distantly, to Oriental aesthetic concepts (*Damp Place*, 1923; Whitney Museum). While in Europe in 1925 and 1928 Kuniyoshi was greatly impressed by the works of Chaim Soutine, Maurice Utrillo, Pablo Picasso and especially Jules Pascin, whose style had particular bearing on his later work. Like Pascin, Kuniyoshi concentrated on women and still lifes during the 1930s; *I'm Tired* (1938; Whitney Museum) shows a pensive female, recalling Picasso's Blue Period figures as well as Pascin's special regard for women's moods. Surrealism also seems to have influenced his production at this time, and sexual connotations prevailed in the paintings of the 1940s (*Upside Down Table and Mask*, 1940; New York, Museum of Modern Art). After 1948 the pictures of ruin and lonely desperation done during World War II in muted gray and earth tones (*Desert Woman*, 1943; Whitney Museum) were replaced by frescolike gayer scenes of carnivals and costumes, brighter in color and often more ironic than any of his earlier work (*Juggler*, 1952; Whitney Museum).

KUPKA, Frank *or* František (1871, Opocno, Bohemia—1957, near Paris), Czech painter, one of the originators of abstract art. In 1895 he went to Paris, where he lived for the rest of his life. In 1906 he was admitted to the Salon d'Automne; he adopted a highly developed technique to project the visions of his imagination and produced canvases that went much further than superficial appearances. The *Grand Nu*, or *Large Nude* (U.S.A., Priv. Coll.), exhibited in the Salon d'Automne of 1911, marked a decisive stage in his development. This painting was the bridge between a rationalized Fauvism and a Cubism that was on the verge of a new preoccupation with color. It was a rather hybrid composition, however, with elements drawn from different sources, and immediately thereafter Kupka changed his style. In 1911–12 he painted his first entirely abstract works—*Amorpha, Fugue in Two Colors* (Prague, National Gallery), which consisted of colored concentric rhythms on a white background; *Amorpha, Hot Chromatism* (U.S.A., Priv. Coll.); and *Amorpha* (Paris; Musée National d'Art Moderne). These paintings were exhibited at the Salon d'Automne in 1914 and were his initial abstract impulses; he went on to paint superimposed colored masses and chromatic blocks, piled one on top of the other or emerging from one another (*Vertical Planes*, 1913; Prague, National Gallery), and sometimes consisting of single lines like graphic motifs.

Frank Kupka. *Decision.* 1921.

At the outbreak of World War I, Kupka volunteered for the French army. In 1924 he exhibited his series of *Diagrams* and *Circling Arabesques* at the Galerie La Boétie in Paris, but the artistic trends of the times had changed direction and Kupka, a pioneer of nonobjective art, found himself practically neglected. He continued working with an uncompromising spirit until, influenced by Piet Mondrian, his art attained a purity and equilibrium suggestive of a philosophical architecture (*Three Blues, Three Reds*, 1930; *Connections*, 1934). In 1936 he regrouped his works into five broad categories—*Cycles, Verticals, Verticals and Diagonals, Triangles,* and *Diagonals*—for a large retrospective exhibition held at the Musée de l'Impressionnisme in Paris. In 1946 a retrospective of his works was organized at the S.V.U. Mánes Gallery in Prague, and the Czech government bought about 50 of his paintings to form a Kupka Museum. In 1958 retrospectives of Kupka's works were held at the Musée National d'Art Moderne in Paris and at the Museum of Modern Art in New York.

L

LABROUSTE, Henri (1801, Paris—1875, Fontainebleau), French architect. He won the Prix de Rome in 1824, and spent the next six years in Italy. On his return to Paris in 1830, he opened a studio in which he was to train a number of architects, including Anatole de Baudot (1834–1915).

His most famous work, the Bibliothèque Ste-Geneviève in Paris, built between 1843 and 1850, is a manifesto of his radical ideas. Its structure is entirely of iron, and its double nave is divided by a row of tall, slender cast-iron columns that support wrought-iron semicircular arches. The façade of the Bibliothèque Ste-Geneviève, decorated on its first story with garlands reminiscent of the festoons of the neighboring Panthéon, and pierced on its second story by broad bays, reveals a striking decorative sobriety.

Under Napoleon III, Labrouste was commissioned to rebuild the Bibliothèque Nationale; between 1862 and 1868, he built the nine metal cupolas that roof its large Salle des Imprimés (reading room). They are decorated with enameled faïence, and, as at Ste-Geneviève, are supported by strikingly slender cast-iron columns. Although the façades that Labrouste erected in Rue de Richelieu represent a movement toward the widespread eclecticism of the latter half of the 19th century, the Bibliothèque Nationale may be counted among the earliest masterpieces of modern architecture.

Henri Labrouste. Main reading room of the Bibliothèque Nationale, Paris. 1862–68.

LACHAISE, Gaston (1882, Paris—1935, New York), American sculptor. Lachaise was born in Paris, the son of a cabinetmaker. He studied at the École Bernard-Palissy and at the École des Beaux-Arts, where he was a fellow pupil of Charles Despiau. He then decided to emigrate to the United States, and, in 1906, settled in Boston, where he perfected his technique in the studio of a sculptor of commemorative monuments, Henry Hudson Kitson (1865–1947). In 1912 he moved to New York, where he began his heroic *Standing Woman* (bronze), which he did not complete until 1927; a later version (1932) is in the Museum of Modern Art, New York.

Gaston Lachaise. *Portrait of John Marin.* 1928. *Photo American Cultural Center.*

Lachaise is best known for his female nudes, but he also carved highly skillful animals, dolphins and peacocks. He executed a number of busts, including those of the painter John Marin (1928; Museum of Modern Art) and the poet E. E. Cummings (1924); bas-reliefs for the American Telephone and Telegraph Building (1921) in New York; and reliefs for the RCA Building at Rockefeller Center, New York. Lachaise was a meticulous craftsman and worked directly in stone. When he used bronze (his most successful medium), he polished it to an unnatural brightness. In his lifetime, Lachaise occupied a preeminent position among American sculptors; he is now regarded as a sensitive and powerful innovator, whose work was sometimes flawed by repetition and grandiloquence.

LAERMANS, Baron Eugeen (1864, Brussels—1940, Brussels), Belgian painter. He studied under the painter Jean Portaels and introduced the excitement of Expressionistic painting to the traditional, realistic art of Belgium. He frequently painted leave-takings, returns, wanderings, processions of workers on strike, emigrants, and stubborn peasants. He produced brutal forms by using earthy tones saturated and heightened with ultramarine, emerald, and dead white, and by creating strong lighting contrasts. The *Evening of the Strike* (1894; Brussels, Musée d'Art Moderne), *Emigrants* (1896; Antwerp, Musée Royal des Beaux-Arts), *Returning from the Fields* (1903; Brussels, Musée des Beaux-Arts d'Ixelles), and the *Intruders* (1903; Liège, Musée des Beaux-Arts) are extremely moving images of the human condition. More striking still is the *Dead Man* (1904; Brussels, Musée d'Art Moderne) that creates a weird impression with the powerful rhythm of the mournful group straggling along the bare wall by a canal. Toward the end of his career, Laermans' painting became less intense (*Bowls Players*; 1924, Brussels, Musée d'Art Moderne), but the plebeian inspiration and stylization remained unchanged.

LAETHEM-SAINT-MARTIN, School of. This school derives its name from a small village situated a few miles from Ghent, where the painter Valerius de Saedeleer settled at the end of the 19th century. In addition to its founder, the school comprised Gustave van de Woestijne, Albert Servaes (1883–1966), and the sculptor Georges Minne. In Laethem-Saint-Martin they found Albyn van den Abeele (1835–1918), who had begun, at the age of forty, to paint modest but penetrating works inspired by the life and landscape of the region.

This first colony of artists was succeeded, about 1910, by another, which included the painters Gustave and Léon (1881–1967) de Smet, Albert Saverys (1886–1964), Frits van den Berghe (1883–1939), Piet Lippens (b. 1890), Edgar Gevaert (b. 1891), Hubert Malfait (b. 1898), and, above all, Constant Permeke. The group reacted against both academic canons and the lack of vigor of latter-day Impressionism and Symbolism. Their desire to embrace concrete reality led them to restore to man a privileged position at the center of a soundly constructed world of harsh, powerful tonalities. Their robustness and dynamism enabled them to avoid the pathological aspects so often associated with Expressionism, and to achieve a humanity of vision worthy of the best Flemish traditions.

LA FARGE, John (1835, New York—1910, Providence, Rhode Island), American sculptor and muralist. In 1856 he went to Europe, visiting Paris and London, where he was influenced by the Pre-Raphaelites and William Morris' Arts and Crafts movement. Upon his return to America, he met William Morris Hunt, with whom he studied in Rhode Island and who encouraged him to begin painting professionally, impressing upon him the English notions of aesthetic reform and a revival of medieval crafts. He had studied the techniques of stained-glass designing in Europe and later devoted many years to it. In 1876 he was commissioned to execute the first large-scale American fresco project, the mural decorations for Trinity Church, Boston; his solution is decidedly Byzantine in feeling. Ten years later he collaborated with the sculptor Augustus Saint-Gaudens in designing the *King Sepulchral Monument* in Newport, Rhode Island. He then traveled to Japan and Samoa, where the lush scenery inspired him to execute many watercolor sketches. His most ambitious mural is the *Ascension of Our Lord* (1887; New York, Church of the Ascension), which blends well with the somber interior of the Greenwich Village church.

LA FOSSE, Charles de (1636, Paris—1716, Paris), French painter, son of a Parisian goldsmith. In 1658 he left for Italy, spending two years in Rome and three in Venice. After he returned to Paris, he earned, as a former pupil of Le Brun, a commission to paint the frescoes of the dome of the Church of the Assumption (1676). In 1673 he was received into the Académie de Peinture et de Sculpture, and in 1699 he became its director. He spent two years in London decorating Lord Montague's palace; his painted ceilings there (*Birth of Minerva, Fall of Phaëthon*) earned him the admiration of William III. Although originally commissioned to paint all the frescoes in the church of the Invalides, Paris, La Fosse executed only the cupola of the dome (*St. Louis Placing His Crown and Sword in Christ's Hands,* 1705) and the four pendentives of the *Evangelists,* which form a decorative whole of remarkable vigor and freshness of color. La Fosse proved the full scope of his powers in the monumental compositions he executed at Versailles (*Sacrifice of Iphigenia* in the Salon de Diane; *Sunrise* in the Salon d'Apollon), although it is perhaps in his smaller works, such as the *Finding of Moses* (1675–80; Paris, Louvre) and the *Triumph of Bacchus*, that his qualities as a painter are most apparent.

LA FRESNAYE, Roger de (1885, Le Mans, Sarthe—1925, Grasse, Alpes-Maritimes), French painter, illustrator, and sculptor. In 1908 he joined the Académie Ranson, studying under Paul Sérusier and Maurice Denis. His discovery of Paul Cézanne's art helped him find his personal idiom, which is characterized by a profound concern for forms, their geometric structure, and proper distribution over the compositional surface. Successful examples of paintings in this vein are the landscapes of 1911 painted at La Ferté-sous-Jouarre and Meulan (*Landscape*, 1911; Paris, Musée National d'Art Moderne), the *Man Drinking and Singing* (1910; Paris, Coll. Galeries Kleinmann et Cie), the *Cuirassier* (1912; Paris, Musée National d'Art Moderne), and *Jeanne d'Arc* (1912; Paris, Priv. Coll.). These inclinations prompted La Fresnaye to explore Cubism. After 1912 he exhibited with the Cubists at the Salon d'Automne, the Salon des Indépendants, and the Section d'Or, and sought in Cubism not so much an analytical representation of the object as a synthesis of line, color, and space. The achievement of this synthesis is evident in such works as the *Seated Man* (1914; Paris, Musée National d'Art Moderne), the *Conquest of the Air* (1913; New York, Museum of Modern Art), *Married Life* (1913; Minneapolis, Institute of Arts), and some excellent still lifes.

During the last years of his life his artistic activity was confined mainly to gouache, watercolor, and drawing. Except for two works, the *Portrait of Guynemer* (1921–23; Paris, Musée National d'Art Moderne) and *Landscape at Hauteville* (France, Priv. Coll.), the rare oils betray a return to naturalism or realistic traditionalism. On the other hand, his drawings resemble those of J. A. D. Ingres because of their purity and proud distinction. He produced some sculptures (*Eve*, 1910; Paris, Musée National d'Art Moderne) and illustrated such works as André Gide's *Paludes* (1921), Rimbaud's *Illuminations* (1949), and Paul Claudel's *Tête d'Or* (1950).

LA GUÊPIERE, Pierre-Louis-Philippe de (b. 1715–d. 1773, Paris), French architect. A pupil of Jacques-François Blondel, he worked almost exclusively in Germany, where he was one of the leading exponents of the French style in the 18th century. In 1752 he was appointed architect to Karl Eugen, Duke of Württemberg, at Stuttgart, where from 1754 to 1756 he completed the New Castle, begun by Leopoldo Retti. For Karl Eugen, he also decorated the apartments of the Castle at Ludwigsburg and carried out his two principal works, the château of Monrepos (1760–65), near the park of Ludwigsburg Castle, and the château of La Solitude (1763–67), near Stuttgart. These two buildings represent the transition from the Rococo to the Louis XVI style. Apart from his own buildings, La Guêpière had a considerable influence on the German architects of his time through two important publications: *Recueil de différents projets d'architecture*, 1752 ("Collection of Various Architectural Projects"), and *Recueil d'esquisses d'architecture*, 1760 ("Collection of Architectural Sketches").

LAGUERRE, Louis (1663, Versailles—1721, London), French-born painter of decorative schemes, historical subjects, and portraits. He studied for a short time with Charles Le Brun, and then in 1683 or 1684 went to England, where he worked for Antonio Verrio at Christ's Hospital in Horsham, Sussex, and at Chatsworth, Derbyshire. As an independent master, Laguerre executed commissions at Burghley House, Stamford, Devonshire House and Marlborough House (both in London), and at Blenheim Palace, Woodstock, where he decorated the salon (*c.* 1713), which is widely regarded as his masterpiece. With Verrio, Laguerre was the leading exponent of the elaborate decorative style, involving the painting of walls and ceilings—often illusionistically—which had been popular on the Continent for many years. Laguerre's training under Louis XIV's chief artist, Le Brun, gave him a particular insight into the problems involved in work of this kind. His portrait of *William, First*

Laurent de La Hyre. *Death of the Children of Bethel.* 1653. Musée Municipal, Arras.

Earl of Cadogan, is in the National Portrait Gallery in London.

LA HYRE, Laurent de (1606, Paris—1656, Paris), French painter. In 1635 and 1637 La Hyre was honored by the annual commission for a painting to be dedicated in the month of May in Notre-Dame de Paris; and, in the same period, he executed paintings for Cardinal Richelieu. In 1648 he was one of 12 founding members of the Académie Royale de Peinture et de Sculpture. His earliest extant works belong to the Baroque stream of painting, but reveal a discreet elegance and realism that gradually prevailed over rhetorical effect. His art, developing toward a tempered Atticism in which clarity and equilibrium were the dominant elements, paved the way for the Classical current that dominated Parisian painting during Anne of Austria's regency. Nevertheless, in his allegories of the liberal arts (*Allegory of Music*, 1648; New York, Metropolitan Museum), and in many details of his most Classical paintings, La Hyre offered a sincere description of simple reality. He was a highly gifted landscapist, sensitive to the most unspoiled aspects of nature; he set his religious and Classical scenes in the valleys and woods around Paris (*Landscape with a Flute Player*, 1647, Montpellier, Musée Fabre; *Laban Looking for His Idols*, 1647, Paris, Louvre).

Sir Edwin Henry Landseer. *The Old Shepherd's Chief Mourner*. 1837. Victoria and Albert Museum, London.

LAM, Wifredo (b. 1902, Sagua la Grande, Cuba), Cuban painter. Lam's father was Chinese and his mother Afro-Cuban, but his art is quintessentially Cuban. From 1938 to 1941 he lived in Paris, where he joined the Surrealist movement. In 1941 he returned to Havana, and the following year took part in the exhibition "First Papers of Surrealism" in New York. But Europe and Paris continued to attract him, and it was there that he finally settled. In Lam's paintings—*The Jungle*, a gouache (1943; New York, Museum of Modern Art); *The Shadow* (1952); or the *Tropic of Capricorn* (1961)—a tropical demonology combines the hieraticism of fetishes with a knife-edged luxuriance. Lam's world is a jungle inhabited by triangular creatures, bristling with spikes, adorned with manes, and armed with beaks, horns, and tusks.

LANDSEER, Sir Edwin Henry (1802, London—1873, London), English painter of animal subjects. Exceptionally precocious, Landseer was already exhibiting drawings of animals at the Royal Academy at the age of thirteen. In 1824 he visited Scotland with Charles Robert Leslie (1794–1859), and the fauna and wild terrain of that region were to become the main inspiration of his art. Landseer's early works (*Hunting of Chevy Chase*, exhibited R.A. 1826; now Birmingham, City Art Gallery) were solidly painted in a style influenced by Rubens and Frans Snyders. In 1831 he was made a member of the Royal Academy. In 1839 he painted his first portrait of *Queen Victoria* (Windsor, Royal Collection), who admired his work to such an extent that the royal family became both friends and patrons; he was knighted in 1850. Landseer's enormous popularity in the 19th century lay in his capacity to be extremely accurate in detail, and either sentimental or romantic in his approach to his subject matter. Pictures such as the *Old Shepherd's Chief Mourner* (1837; London, Victoria and Albert Museum) exploited the same vein of pathos as did Charles Dickens with the death of Little Nell. The humorous animal subjects, in which dogs and cats are given human attributes as in *Dignity and Impudence* (1857; London, Tate Gallery), deftly combined animal sentiment with a Punch-like vein of humor. Landseer declined the presidency of the Royal Academy in 1865. In 1867 the four lions that he modeled for the base of Nelson's Column in Trafalgar Square, London, were unveiled.

LANE, Fitz Hugh (1804, Gloucester, Massachusetts—1861, Gloucester), American painter and lithographer. Lane worked for various lithographic firms in Gloucester and eventually attracted the attention of the lithographer William S. Pendleton (1795–1879) of Boston, who invited him to become his apprentice. Lane worked in this capacity from 1832 until 1837, then did lithographic work for the Boston publishers Keith and Moore, and from 1845 to 1847 had his own lithographic firm. He returned to Gloucester in 1849.

Lane earned his living by making lithographs of scenes of Gloucester, one of the oldest American fishing ports, and selling them by subscription to the townspeople; these lithographs are of high quality and constitute part of Lane's finest achievement. His paintings, likewise, are mainly of harbor and marine scenes (*New York Harbor*, 1850, Boston, Museum of Fine Arts; *Off Mount Desert Island*, 1856, New York, Brooklyn Museum). They can be characterized during his best period, the 1850s, by a very precise visual description of the scene, a balanced composition, and luminous, carefully controlled effects of light and space. His later paintings, however (*Brace's Rock, Eastern Point, Gloucester*, 1863; Boston, Museum of Fine Arts), tend to have more dramatic and extravagant qualities, such as artificially balanced compositions and unsubtle use of color.

LANFRANCO, Giovanni, *also called* Giovanni di Stefano (1582, Parma—1647, Rome), Italian High Baroque painter. He was a disciple of the Carracci, and went to Rome in 1602 to work under the direction of Annibale Carracci on the decoration of the Palazzo Farnese. After Annibale's death, he went to Parma and Piacenza, absorbing the influence of Antonio Correggio. In 1612 Lanfranco returned to Rome, where he obtained the patronage of Pope Paul V, and where he produced arresting frescoes in the Palazzo Mattei (1615); the *Gods of Olympus*

(1624–25) in the Villa Borghese; and the *Virgin in Glory* (1625–27) in the dome of S. Andrea della Valle. For 13 years, beginning in 1633, Lanfranco lived in Naples. There he became a friend of the Spanish-born Jusepe de Ribera, and painted several large frescoes, including the *Dome of Paradise* (1641–43) in the S. Gennaro Chapel of Naples Cathedral. In 1646 he returned to Rome, where he painted a fresco of *St. Charles Borromeo in Glory* in the apse of S. Carlo ai Catinari. His skillful perspectives and bold foreshortenings (inspired by Correggio) make him one of the greatest Baroque decorators. Lanfranco was also an accomplished easel painter, as witnessed by his *Ecstasy of St. Margaret of Cortona* (*c.* 1620; Florence, Palazzo Pitti).

LANSKOY, André (b. 1902, Moscow—d. 1976), French painter of Russian origin. In 1921 he went to Paris, where he joined the Académie de la Grande Chaumière. Lanskoy soon became an enthusiastic admirer of Vincent van Gogh and Henri Matisse and met Chaim Soutine, whose influence can be detected in the portraits and still lifes he painted at the time. In 1924 the art critic Wilhelm Uhde introduced Lanskoy to the Galerie Bing in Paris, which organized his first one-man show the following year. Lanskoy conceived his painting in terms of a dominant color to which all the other elements of the picture were subordinated. After 1930, in fact, his artistic activity was a ceaseless endeavor to free color and to use it as his exclusive means of expression. It was not until 1941–43, however, that he succeeded in disengaging himself from all figurative structure. He laid on his color in generous amounts, and crushed it around a guiding line with an ascending movement that made it blaze into a rhythm. In this way, he subjected everything to the exultation of a particular tone. He used this technique in *Mourning Fiancée* (1953; Paris, Coll. Louis Carré) to communicate a sumptuous triumph of black.

LAPICQUE, Charles (b. 1898, Theizé, Rhône), French painter. From 1909 to 1917 he studied drawing at free schools and art academies in Paris and, in 1919, entered the École Centrale in Paris, where he received a scientific training, and where he later taught engineering. He took the opportunity, while he was an assistant (1931–43) in the Science Faculty at the Sorbonne, to do research in the field of color perception and, in 1938, he prepared his doctoral thesis on the *Optic of the Eye and the Vision of Contours*. After 1920, while pursuing his career as a scientist, he was also painting.

Paradoxically, the extremely learned Lapicque was an undogmatic painter who was readily drawn toward fantasy. After a Cubist phase (*Homage to Palestrina*, 1925; Paris, Coll. Galerie Jeanne Bucher) and a later Abstract period that he shared with his younger contemporaries such as Jean Bazaine and Maurice Estève, Lapicque returned, uncompromisingly, to figurative painting. This stylistic change was as surprising as everything else about him. His subjects included seascapes and regattas (1946; 1951–52), horseracing (1949–51), warriors (1950), mythological and heraldic figures (1953), Baroque Venice (1954–56), Classical and Christian Rome (1957–60), Chinese tigers (1960–61), and eternal Greece (1964).

LARDERA, Berto (b. 1911, La Spezia), French sculptor of Italian origin. Shortly before World War II, he took up sculpture following university studies; he worked in Florence until 1947, when he settled in Paris. From 1942, when he abandoned the representation of the human figure—the *Monument to the Partisans* [killed at Pian d'Albero], erected in Florence in 1945, is an exception—Lardera devoted himself to the arrangement of metal and space. Thus, in two-dimensional works in beaten copper or aluminum, first effigy-like, later (1944–48) consisting of geometric shapes joined by metal rods, he tried to free himself from blind mass. In 1948, when he returned to the third dimension, it was with the sole aim of dematerializing volume, piercing it, and opening it to the environment, with which it became integrated. From 1951, his *Dramatic Occasions, Heroic Rhythms, Cathedrals of Pain, Antique Goddesses, Miracles*, and *Dawns* affirmed their irreducible oppositions in dynamic structures in which iron and copper were cut with a blowpipe and soldered together, sometimes with bronze, in a three-dimensional calligraphy.

André Lanskoy. *Workshop for Musical Instruments.* 1961. Coll. Michel Couturier, Paris.

LARGILLIÈRE, Nicolas de (1656, Paris—1746, Paris), French painter. He spent his youth in Antwerp and was received as a Master of the Antwerp guild of painters in 1672; he then went to London (1674) to work in the studio of the portraitist Sir Peter Lely. The persecution of Catholics in England caused Largillière to return to Paris in 1682. On the advice of Adam van der Meulen (1632–90), the painter was introduced to Charles Le Brun, who aided him in establishing a successful career. When Largillière was elected to the Académie Royale de Peinture et de Sculpture in 1682, he repaid his debt by painting a magnificent portrait of Le Brun (1686; Paris, Louvre) as his reception piece.

Largillière's Flemish training taught him the secret of warm colors, lively flesh tints, and how to paint transparency and reflections. He painted group portraits in the Flemish manner and five huge compositions for the city magistrates of Paris, all of which have disappeared except one, an *Ex-Voto to St. Genevieve* (1696; Paris, St-Étienne-du-Mont). Largillière also painted some very fine still lifes, which show a masterly rendering of the texture of materials. His chief claim to fame, however, is as a portraitist. Among his finest works are the group portrait of the painter and his family (Louvre), *Louis XIV and the Royal Family* (1708; London, Wallace Collection), and his masterpiece, *La Belle Strasbourgeoise*

Berto Lardera. *Antique Goddess IV.* 1959. Städtische Kunsthalle, Mannheim.

(1703; Strasbourg, Musée des Beaux-Arts).

LARIONOV, Mikhail (1881, Tiraspol, Moldavian S.S.R.—1964, Fontenay-aux-Roses, near Paris), French painter of Russian origin. He painted at first with an Impressionist technique; then, in 1909, he exhibited at the Society of Free Aesthetics a painting influenced by Cubism, the *Glass* (New York, Guggenheim Museum), which represented one of the earliest experiments in non-figurative painting. In 1910 he showed his *Boulevard* at the Kraft Studio in Moscow, and mentioned, for the first time, his theories of Rayonism. He explained his ideas in a manifesto written in 1912 but not published in Moscow until a year later, when Rayonism had already passed its peak. Rayonism's brief career was limited to the work of Larionov and Goncharova, but it was one of the earliest examples of non-figurative art.

After contributing to the first Berlin Herbstsalon (1913), Larionov settled in Paris in 1914, and exhibited with Goncharova at the Galerie Paul Guillaume as soon as he arrived. The following year he accompanied the ballet producer Sergei Diaghilev to Italy and virtually abandoned painting to work with the Ballets Russes. He not only designed a number of successful sets—*Soleil de nuit* (1915), *Contes russes* (1917), *Chout* (1921), and *Renard* (1922)—but also provided choreography.

LASSAW, Ibram (b. 1913, Alexandria, Egypt), American sculptor born of Russian parents. Lassaw, who arrived in the United States in 1921, studied sculpture from the age of thirteen, principally at the Clay Club (1928–32) and at the Beaux Arts Institute of Design (1930–31) in New York. Beginning in 1933, he devoted himself exclusively to spatial abstraction. His sculptures, often polychromatic from 1937 (*Sing Baby Sing*, 1937), reveal a dual inspiration, oscillating between Surrealism and a more controlled rectilinear geometry. Around 1950, Lassaw achieved a synthesis of his experimental work of the past 20 years. His sculptures lead the spectator through a network of virtual planes, concretized by a continuous, curved, and soldered wire adorned with nodules of bronze and applications of acid-treated metals, minerals, or stones (*Procession*, 1956; New York, Whitney Museum). After 1953, he created several important architectural decorations, in particular the *Pillar of Fire* for Temple Beth El at Springfield, Massachusetts.

LA TOUR, Georges de (1593, Vic-sur-Seille, Alsace-Lorraine—1652, Lunéville, near Nancy), French painter. La Tour was the son of a baker at Vic. Almost nothing is known of his training, though he may have attended the studio of Claude Dogoz, the town's leading painter. In 1617 or 1618 he married Diane Le Nerf, the daughter of the silversmith to the duke of Lorraine. In 1620 the artist settled at Lunéville, where he took an apprentice and became the town's only "master painter."

In 1631 Lunéville was ravaged by the plague; the town then became the center of resistance to the French troops invading Lorraine. In 1633 Louis XIII took Nancy, and, while residing in that city, he was given one of La Tour's paintings of *St. Sebastian* (the saint invoked in cases of the plague), which he greatly admired. In 1638 Lunéville was set on fire and sacked. La Tour was as much affected as anyone else by this disaster, and in 1640 retired to Nancy, perhaps even to Paris. In 1642 he returned home, with the title "painter in ordinary to the king." At this time, Lorraine was being governed by the Duc de la Ferté, who wanted the town of Lunéville to give him some of La Tour's pictures. The artist took advantage of the situation by asking higher and higher prices, which had to be paid for by his fellow citizens by means of a special levy.

The chronology of La Tour's works is too imprecise to enable us to trace his stylistic development. A *Mocking of Christ* (Dordogne, Chancellery) is attributed to his earliest years as a painter, between 1620 and 1625. *The Magdalen at the Mirror* (Paris, Priv. Coll.) belongs to the period around 1628, while the later *Penitent Magdalen* (*c.* 1635–40; Paris, Louvre) shows his rigor of construction at its finest. The *Ecstasy of St. Francis* (Le Mans, Musée de Tessé) is remarkable for its rather theatrical contrast between the monk in prayer and the ecstatic saint. La Tour had a particular predilection for the theme of the Nativity, of which he made a gentle, rather melancholy version in the *Nativity* (*c.* 1650; Rennes, Musée des Beaux-Arts), and a more subtle, complex one in the *Adoration of the Shepherds* (Louvre). His *St. Sebastian Mourned by St. Irene* (*c.* 1650; Berlin, Staatliche Museen), is the most obviously Caravaggist of all his paintings. Among the works of his maturity, his genius is at its height in *Job Upbraided by His Wife* (Épinal, Museum), and in *Jesus and St. Joseph in the Workshop* (*c.* 1645; Louvre), which possesses an almost supernatural quality.

Many of La Tour's "daylight paintings" are religious in subject, as in the *Penitent St. Jerome* (*c.* 1620–25; Stockholm, Nationalmuseum). But there are others with secular subjects, such as the *Fortuneteller* (New York, Metropolitan Museum), *Hurdy-Gurdy Player* (Nantes, Musée des Beaux-Arts), which lay bare the logic of

Georges de La Tour. *Ecstasy of St. Francis.* Musée de Tessé, Le Mans. *Photo Giraudon, Paris.*

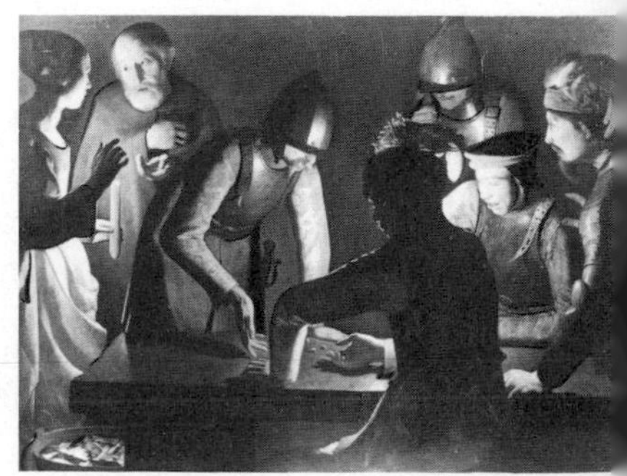

Georges de La Tour. *Denial of St. Peter.* 1650. Musée des Beaux-Arts, Nantes. *Photo Giraudon, Paris.*

his composition and technique. To the end of his career belongs the powerful *Denial of St. Peter* (Nantes, Musée des Beaux-Arts), which the artist himself dated 1650 (the only dated canvas by La Tour that survives) and which is one of the pictures painted for the Duc de la Ferté.

La Tour was not the first artist to paint night scenes—indeed, he learned much from such Caravaggisti as Carlo Saraceni (*c.* 1579–1620), and above all Gerard van Honthorst—but he is unique in the effects he obtained. His precise, uncluttered realism avoids all overemphasis; his skillful play with light and lengthened shadows becomes an expression of the inner life.

LA TOUR, Maurice Quentin de (1704, St-Quentin—1788, St-Quentin), one of the most distinguished of the French pastelists. The popularity of the pastels by the Venetian Rosalba Carriera probably encouraged him to adopt this medium, and success came quickly: in 1736, his reputation was great enough for Voltaire to commission a portrait. In 1737 he was elected to the Académie and exhibited two portraits at the Salon, the pretty *Madame Boucher* and a *Self-Portrait*, also called *L'Auteur qui rit* (Geneva, Musée d'Art et d'Histoire). The striking likenesses La Tour captured, and the strength of his drawing in an art that had previously been reserved for women, attracted a large circle of eminent patrons that included *Louis XV* (1748; Paris, Louvre), *Rousseau* (1753), the actress *Mademoiselle Favart* and the dancer *Mademoiselle Camargo* (portraits all in St-Quentin, Museum). However, his most successful portraits were those of his intimate associates, *Abbé Leblanc* (1747), *Abbé Huber* (1742), and the beautiful singer *Mademoiselle Fel* (1757), the artist's mistress (all in St-Quentin). Wishing to prove that pastel could rival oil painting, he sent his famous *Portrait of President de Rieux* (Geneva, Coll. Baron Édouard de Rothschild) to the 1741 Salon, and he produced a similar piece of technical bravura in 1755 with the full-length portrait of *Madame de Pompadour* (Paris, Louvre), shown seated at a table with sheets of music in her hand.

LATROBE, Benjamin (1764, Fulneck, Yorkshire—1820, New Orleans), English-born architect who worked exclusively in the United States. In 1796, after the death of his first wife, he left London for the United States. There he began his career by building the Bank of Pennsylvania (1798) in Philadelphia. This structure was universally acclaimed; with its Ionic order and its porticoes, it showed a unique application of the forms of Greek Classicism to modern architectural problems. For another important work, Baltimore Cathedral (1806–18), Latrobe submitted two designs, one Gothic and one Neoclassical; the second plan was accepted. Latrobe was an excellent engineer and an expert in the field of acoustics. From 1803 he played a leading part in the design of the Capitol in Washington, D.C. When this building was burned down in 1814, he supervised its rebuilding and himself designed the Senate chamber, the rotunda linking the two wings, as well as a part of the plan that was modified later by Charles Bulfinch, who in 1818 replaced Latrobe as supervisor of the Capitol's restoration.

LAURANA, Francesco (*c.* 1430, Vrana, near Zara, Dalmatia—*c.* 1502, Avignon), Italian sculptor, architect, and medalist of Dalmatian origin (born a Venetian citizen). For several years, beginning in 1453 or 1455, he directed work on the sculptures of the triumphal arch in the Castel Nuovo, Naples, some of which he also designed. Between 1461 and 1466 Laurana was in Provence at the court of King René of Anjou, where he introduced the style of the Italian Early Renaissance. Laurana was in Sicily from 1467 to 1471 or 1472 and there may have sculptured various reliefs and statues for the Mastrantonio Chapel in the church of S. Francesco d'Assisi at Palermo (1468–69), followed by a *Virgin* (1469) for the Palermo Cathedral, and the so-called *Madonna of the Snow* for the Church of the Crocifisso at Noso (1471). Other works that are generally attributed to him during his second sojourn in Naples (1472–75) are the beautifully simple and serene busts of *Beatrice of Aragon* (New York, Coll. Rockefeller) and *Battista Sforza* (1474; Florence, Bargello). The bust of *Isabella of Aragon* (Vienna, Kunsthistorisches Museum) was probably done during his third visit there, *c.* 1487. He spent his last years mostly in France, where he built the chapel of St-Lazare (1477–81) for the old cathedral of the Major in Marseilles.

Francesco Laurana. *Isabella of Aragon. c.* 1487. Kunsthistorisches Museum, Vienna.

LAURANA, Luciano (*c.* 1420, Zadar, Dalmatia—1479, Pesaro), Italian architect. His masterpiece was at Urbino, where Duke Federigo da Montefeltro had made his capital a great center of art and humanism. The ducal palace of Montefeltro was a medieval building that Laurana was asked to transform; thus it presents the combined characteristics of a country villa and a fortress. Two ancient towers frame three stories of loggias that look out over a hilly landscape of austere beauty. The inner courtyard, one of the most elegant of the Quattrocento, is surrounded by an arcaded portico supported by composite columns, while Corinthian pilasters adorn the first floor; inscriptions in Latin fill the friezes of both entablatures. The distribution of the unusually large apartments lent itself admirably to the sumptuous style of the ducal receptions. The death of Duchess Battista Sforza in 1472 interrupted the work of building, which was later continued by Francesco di Giorgio Martini. In the last years of his life, Laurana transformed the fortress of Pesaro.

LAURENS, Henri (1885, Paris—1954, Paris), French sculptor, illustrator, and graphic artist.

In 1911 he began his lifelong friendship with Georges Braque. Cubism was the major topic of the day and all the great creative artists felt its attraction. Laurens fell under its spell and, besides *papiers collés* (collages), made constructions of wood and colored metal, as well as some polychrome reliefs that were among the best of their kind (*Woman with a Mantilla*, 1918; *Man with a Clarinet*, 1919).

Meanwhile, he also became friendly with Picasso, who presented him soon afterward to the art dealer Léonce Rosenberg, who bought some sculptures from him in 1916 and who supported him until 1921, when the dealer Daniel-Henry Kahnweiler became his agent. Laurens drew, illustrated books with engravings, designed the décor for Darius Milhaud's *Le Train Bleu* (1924), performed by Diaghilev's Ballets Russes, carved a porch and fountain for the home of Monsieur Jacques Doucet (1923–25), and made a column and fireplace for the villa of the Vicomte de Noailles at Hyères. His geometric period ended in 1927, after which he began using curved lines, massive volumes, and voluptuously full forms. He did a series of *Reclining Women* (1928), followed by the series of *Ondines* (1932–33) and the wonderful *Mermaids* (1937). In 1937 he also created the *Great Amphion* (Paris, Musée National d'Art Moderne) and four high-relief panels: the first two, *Sea* and *Earth*, were done in sandstone for the Sèvres Pavilion at the 1937 Exposition Internationale in Paris; the second two, *Life* and *Death*, were done in plaster for the Palais de la Découverte, Paris.

After 1938 Laurens showed a strong lyrical quality in his works, and a closer union with the eternal laws and rhythms of life. In *Musician* (1938), *Flora* (1939), *Crouching Figure* (1941), and *Sleeping Woman* (1943), Laurens used only curves and rounded shapes and aimed at an expansion of his forms without, however, losing anything in concentration, massiveness or density.

Henri Laurens. *Mermaid.* 1945. Musée National d'Art Moderne, Paris.

With *Farewell* (1942), *Morning* (1944), *Large Mermaid* (1945), *Bather* (1947), *Deep Night* (1951), *Woman with a Bunch of Grapes* (1952), and a larger version of *Amphion* (1952), commissioned by the University City of Caracas, Laurens returned to graceful lines and a free composition, the same virile style and strength as his earlier sculptures; at the same time, however, they are marked by a calm, a restraint, and a controlled audacity and distinction. In 1953 he won the Grand Prize at the São Paulo Bienal. He illustrated several books, including *Les Pélicans* (1921), a play by Raymond Radiguet; *La Dernière Nuit* ("The Last Night," 1942), by Paul Éluard; and *Three Tales* (1953) by William Saroyan.

LAURENT, Robert (b. 1890, Concarneau, Finistère—d. 1970), French-born American sculptor. Laurent arrived in the United States in 1902 after spending his formative years studying and living in France and Italy. From the 1920s to 1960 Laurent taught successively at the Art Students League, New York; the Corcoran School of Art, Washington, D.C.; Vassar College, Poughkeepsie, New York; Goucher College, Baltimore, Maryland; and Indiana University.

Laurent was fundamentally a carve-direct sculptor with a strong regard for the nature of his materials—primarily alabaster, stone, and wood (which he exhibited as early as 1915, when it was considered a relatively unusual medium). His most frequent subject was the female figure (*Kneeling Figure*, 1935; bronze, New York, Whitney Museum), which was sometimes incorporated within a mother-child motif. Laurent also created numerous portrait heads (*Mimi*, 1928; bronze, Cape Neddick, Maine, Coll. Mrs. Robert Laurent) and received a number of public commissions (for the New York World's Fair, 1939; Fairmount Park, Philadelphia; and Indiana University).

LAWRENCE, Jacob (b. 1917, Atlantic City, New Jersey), American Negro painter. In 1930 Lawrence and his mother moved to the Harlem section of New York. There, he attended the Utopia Children's House after school. From 1932 to 1939 he often worked with the Negro painter Charles Alston (b. 1907). Painting under the auspices of the WPA in 1939, Lawrence gained from this experience a good deal of his artistic education, and at the same time became especially interested in Negro history.

In 1948 Lawrence illustrated the book *One Way Ticket* by the Negro poet Langston Hughes, an unusual commission for him since he was primarily a narrative painter rather than an illustrator. He executed several series of paintings, such as the immigration scenes of 1940–41, numbering about 40 works (*They Were Very Poor*; New York, Museum of Modern Art), the Harlem series of 1943, and the John Brown series of 1946 (*His Venture Failing Him, He Accepted Poverty*; Detroit, Institute of Arts).

LAWRENCE, Sir Thomas (1769, Bristol—1830, London), English portrait painter. In 1779, when his family moved to Oxford, he was already drawing portraits for money. In 1782 the family moved to Bath, and by 1786 or 1787 Lawrence had established himself in London. In 1789 he painted his first full-length portrait, *Lady Cremorne* (Cerne Abbas, Coll. Windham), a brilliantly sophisticated picture in the Reynolds idiom. On the strength of this work he was recommended to Queen Charlotte, whose portrait he painted in 1790 (it is today in Windsor Castle) and exhibited at the Royal Academy the same year, along with a portrait of *Miss Eliza Farren* (New York, Metropolitan Museum). This work earned him a compliment from Reynolds, whom he succeeded as Painter in Ordinary to the king in 1792. He became a Royal Academician at the age of twenty-five, in 1794, by which time he was established as the most fashionable portrait painter in London.

The early brilliance of the portrait of Miss Farren was maintained by a series of full-length portraits painted throughout the 1790s in which one becomes aware that an altogether more modern concept of the formal portrait has been grafted onto the Reynolds formula. A certain theatricality of presentation, as in the portrait of *Lord Granville Leveson-Gower* (1795–98; Coll. Earl Granville), reminds us that we are on the eve of the Romantic period. By 1806, however, he had consolidated and deepened his talent, as can be seen

Sir Thomas Lawrence. *Julius Angerstein and His Wife*. 1792. Louvre, Paris. *Photo Giraudon, Paris.*

from any of the male portraits of these years. Calmer, quieter, more solidly built half-length figures replace the glamorous full-length females of the earlier period. An opportunity to develop further in this vein came in 1815 when Lawrence, newly knighted, was commissioned to go to Vienna to paint a series of portraits of the heads of states that had been involved in the Napoleonic wars (the so-called Waterloo portraits, now in the Waterloo Chamber at Windsor Castle). This plan was frustrated by the Hundred Days, and Lawrence paid a brief visit to France (his first) to see the Louvre. In 1818, however, he set off for Vienna and then went to Rome, where he painted the portraits of Pope Pius VII and Cardinal Consalvi (both 1819; both Windsor Castle). He returned to England in March 1820, and succeeded Benjamin West as president of the Royal Academy. He paid a further visit to France in 1825 to paint portraits of Charles X and the Dauphin (both 1825; both Windsor Castle).

Lawrence was fundamentally an 18th-century artist who adapted and improved upon the formulas perfected by Reynolds. He was also sufficiently of the 18th century to base his portraits on Classical attitudes (*Elizabeth, Lady Conyngham, as Diana the Huntress*, 1802; Trustees of the Londesborough Estates). Yet Lawrence introduced significant modifications into the portrait tradition: his device of lowering the horizon so that his models are starkly silhouetted against a great vista of sky is undoubtedly more immediately effective than the naturalistic scale of portraits by Reynolds and Gainsborough.

LAWSON, Ernest (1873, San Francisco, California—1939, Miami Beach, Florida), American Impressionist painter. He went to New York in 1890 and became one of the members of The Eight, a group of realist painters that included Robert Henri, William Glackens, George Luks, and John Sloan, with whom he exhibited at the Macbeth Gallery in 1908. In 1913 he exhibited works in the controversial Armory Show.

Lawson confined himself almost exclusively to portraying urban realistic scenes of Manhattan. Although an exponent of the Impressionist style, he sought to preserve a greater degree of naturalism by imparting to his forms a fundamentally solid and stable outline. He did not, like the other members of The Eight, create figure paintings but rather specialized in landscapes of a serene nature. These include several paintings in the Whitney Museum of American Art in New York (*Winter on the River*, 1907; *Fishermen*, 1911; *High Bridge*, 1934) and in the Metropolitan Museum of Art, also in New York (*Winter*, 1914). Other works by Lawson are in the Barnes Foundation in Philadelphia, the Brooklyn Museum in New York, and the Art Institute of Chicago.

LE BRUN, Charles (1619, Paris—1690, Paris), French painter. He studied first under François Perrier, but was then placed in Simon Vouet's studio. At the age of nineteen, having composed a drawing glorifying Louis XIII, Le Brun was appointed painter to the king. In October 1642 the chancellor Séguier sent him to Rome in the company of Nicolas Poussin, with a pension and a recommendation to the Pope. Le Brun remained there for three years, studying the works of antiquity and benefiting from the advice of Poussin. At the time of his return to Paris, there was talk of founding a royal academy of painting and sculpture to assist artists in freeing themselves from the restrictions of the old apprenticeship system. Le Brun immediately supported the plan, becoming one of the 12 founding members of the illustrious institution, known as the Académie Royale de Peinture et de Sculpture. His reputation was growing rapidly, and soon the president of the Académie, Lambert de Thorigny, commissioned him to decorate the gallery of his town house (*c.* 1650). Le Brun's ceiling frescoes depicting scenes from the legend of Hercules received unanimous praise. In 1654 the artist was commissioned to paint six pictures for the seminary of St-Sulpice in Paris. He did not complete this series, for soon the finance minister Nicolas Fouquet made him his painter and *ordonnateur des fêtes* ("master of the revels") at Vaux. Le Brun settled at Vaux in 1658, where he decorated eight rooms in the château, supervised the design of the sculptures and ornaments, and organized the lavish theatrical shows staged there.

In 1662 Le Brun was raised to the peerage by Louis XIV. His title of first painter to the king was confirmed in 1664, and shortly afterward he was made royal equerry and curator-general of drawings and paintings to the king. In the meantime, he had also been appointed director of the Gobelins tapestry factory (1663). Painters, sculptors, goldsmiths, cabinetmakers, smelters, and weavers now worked directly under his supervision. At the Gobelins factory a team of painters and craftsmen carried out his designs for tapestries illustrating such series as the *Elements*, the *Seasons*, the *Battles of Alexander*, and the *History of Louis XIV*. His most famous decorative projects were those for the palace of the Louvre, where he decorated the Galerie d'Apollon (1661); and for the Château at Versailles, where he commanded a battalion of artists to construct the Staircase of the Ambassadors (1674–78; destroyed), and from 1678 to 1686 the Galerie des Glaces (Hall of Mirrors), the Salon de la

Charles Le Brun. *Hunt of Meleager and Atalanta*. 1658. Louvre, Paris. *Photo Giraudon, Paris.*

Le Corbusier. Villa Savoye, Poissy. 1929–31. *Photo Lucien Hervé, Paris.*

Guerre, and the Salon de la Paix. At the same time, Le Brun was able to devote his attention to the painting of such huge canvases as *Alexander the Great Entering Babylon* (1660–68; Louvre), part of one of the greatest epic series in French painting; and the *Pietà* (1642–46; Louvre).

After the death of Louis' finance minister Jean Baptiste Colbert (1683), Le Brun began to decline in status and power, and the rumor was spread that he was no longer capable of painting a picture himself. In response to these attacks, he executed the *Elevation of the Cross* (1685; Louvre) in a scant three months. When this work pleased the king, the painter repeated his exploit with *Moses Defending the Daughters of Jethro* (1686) and *Moses Marrying Sephora* (1687)—both now in the Galleria Estense in Modena. Le Brun then partially withdrew from public affairs, and near the end of his life worked on a series of paintings on the life of Christ, of which the last canvas to be completed, an *Adoration of the Shepherds* (1689; Paris, Louvre), is convincingly sincere in feeling. In 1689 he published a widely read treatise on the expression of the emotions: *La Méthode pour apprendre à dessiner les passions* ("The Method of Learning to Draw the Passions").

LECK, Bart van der (1876, Utrecht—1958, Blaricum, North Holland), Dutch painter. He first painted in a realistic style and, about 1908, began to model himself on Van Gogh. In 1910, however, his own personality began to emerge and his painting evolved toward representations in single-colored planes against a white background. His street scenes showed an emphasis on geometrical configuration rather than picturesque qualities (*Market*, 1913; *Work in the Docks*, 1916, Otterlo, Rijksmuseum Kröller-Müller). In 1917 Van der Leck joined the De Stijl group. His abstract period was rigorous, but it was graced by an immaterial elegance (*Composition*, 1918–20; Amsterdam, Stedelijk Museum). He moved away from Neoplasticism and returned to a finely balanced compromise between the figurative and the abstract. He became increasingly preoccupied with mural decoration (house at Hilversum, Netherlands, 1934), made pottery, and designed tapestries. At the end of his career, he made spectacular experiments with color in interior architecture (buildings of the Aeronautical School at Eelde, Netherlands, 1956–58).

LE CORBUSIER, Charles-Édouard Jeanneret, *called* (1887, La Chaux-de-Fonds, Switzerland—1965, Roquebrune, Alpes-Maritimes), French architect and city planner of Swiss origin. He met, in succession, almost all the architects who had anything to teach him: in 1907, in Vienna, Josef Hoffmann; in 1908, in Lyons, Tony Garnier; in 1908–9 he worked in Auguste Perret's studio in Paris and then, in 1910, in Peter Behrens' office in Berlin. During 1911–12 he was able to familiarize himself with the activities of the Deutscher Werkbund at Hellerau. His confrontation with Cubism finally came after he settled in Paris in 1917.

In Paris, Le Corbusier took up painting, which he never abandoned, and, with the painter Amédée Ozenfant, founded Purism, a post-Cubistic art movement. In 1918 they published a manifesto (*After Cubism*), which led Le Corbusier to define the basic requirements of style in a series of articles (*Rappels à Messieurs les Architectes*, "Warnings to Architects," 1920). In 1923 these articles, which had appeared in *L'Esprit Nouveau*, a magazine he had founded with Ozenfant in 1920, were published together as *Vers une architecture nouvelle* ("Toward a New Architecture," 1927). This book was followed in 1926 by *L'Art décoratif d'aujourd'hui* ("The Decorative Arts Today") and *Urbanisme* ("Town Planning"). During this period Le Corbusier produced a series of models and projects, as well as a number of revolutionary buildings: Maison Ozenfant, Paris, 1922; houses for Raoul La Roche and Albert Jeanneret in the Auteuil section of Paris, 1923; Housing Estate at Pessac, near Bordeaux, 1925; Villa Stein at Garches, near Paris, 1927; two houses in the experimental estate of Weissenhof in Stuttgart, 1927; and Villa Savoye at Poissy, near Paris, 1929–31. These studies, early constructions, and theoretical writings represent a coherent approach to architecture that might be summarized as follows:

1. All reminiscence of the stylistic forms of the past is eliminated. Volumes are reduced to the simplest geometrical shapes through the use of new structural elements such as the *pilotis* (columns of reinforced concrete),

Le Corbusier. Chapel of Notre-Dame-du-Haut, Ronchamp. 1950–55. *Photo Windstosser, Stuttgart.*

continuous metal-framed windows, glass walls, and roof terraces.

2. Le Corbusier's consciously provocative designs reflect the radical transformation of the home into a "machine for living in." The available living space is redistributed according to a new grouping of domestic functions and requirements. After 1922 the project for Immeubles-Villas (apartment blocks) offered a solution by which the regenerated living unit could be integrated into the collective housing system.

3. These Immeubles-Villas are only one of the many ways by which the archaic structure of a city could be adapted to the needs of modern life. With a plan for A Contemporary City of Three Million Inhabitants (1922), Le Corbusier dealt with the problem of the multipurpose metropolis, whose various functions were separated and grouped. He laid particular stress on the need for a three-dimensional approach to town planning.

The economic crisis of the 1930s drastically reduced the number of commissions Le Corbusier received, and, until the outbreak of World War II, he was forced to devote himself almost exclusively to research in town planning. During the same period he played a leading role in the work of CIAM (International Congress of Modern Architecture); in particular, he was largely responsible for the formulation and content of the Athens Charter (1943). Finally, in 1945, in his book *Les Trois établissements humains* ("The Three Human Establishments"), he provided a summary of his views concerning the ways in which man can dominate the ground.

Le Corbusier's projects for large public buildings, many of which were never realized, also date from the 1930s. The only projects actually built were the Centrosoyus, the central office of the cooperatives of the USSR in Moscow (1929–33); the Salvation Army Hostel in Paris (1929–33), since disfigured; the Swiss House at the Cité Universitaire, outside Paris (1930–32); and the Ministry of National Education and Public Health in Rio de Janeiro, built in collaboration with Oscar Niemeyer, Lúcio Costa, and other Brazilian architects (1936–45). His development toward greater plastic emphasis became increasingly apparent, especially after the war, in the Unités d'Habitation (large-scale housing blocks) at Marseilles (1947–52); Nantes-Rezé, Loire-Inférieure (1952–57); Berlin (1956–57); and Briey-en-Forêt, Meurthe-et-Moselle (1957–60). The application of the Modulor—a system of proportions developed by Le Corbusier from 1942 to 1948—gives these huge buildings a sense of lightness.

The other great works of the 1950s are as original as the Unités and, like them, are conceived so as to discourage imitators. The Capitol (1950–56) at Chandigarh, India, developed the theme of the community center with a lyricism and a breadth suitable to the situation and the role of the new capital of the Punjab.

The play of lines and curves on which the chapel of Notre-Dame-du-Haut at Ronchamp, Haute-Saône (1950–55), is constructed came as something of a surprise. Its curvilinear form, however, was the result of the complete rethinking of the building in terms of its function, and also in relation to the strict demands of what Le Corbusier called the "acoustics of the landscape." The architectural situations that Le Corbusier himself called the "phenomena of inexpressible space," have always abounded in his work; they give a unique nobility to the secular buildings of his last years: the Jaoul Houses in the Parisian suburb of Neuilly (1954–56); the Millowners' Association Building (1954) and the Museum of Knowledge (1956), both in Ahmadabad, North Bombay; the National Museum of Western Art in Tokyo (1957); the Brazilian House at the Cité Universitaire, Paris (1957–59), built in association with Costa; the Carpenter Center for the Visual Arts at Harvard University, Cambridge, Massachusetts (1961–64); the Youth and Art Center at Firminy, Loire (1956–65); projects for the church at Firminy; the Palais des Congrès in Strasbourg, Bas-Rhin; and the hospital in Venice (1964–65).

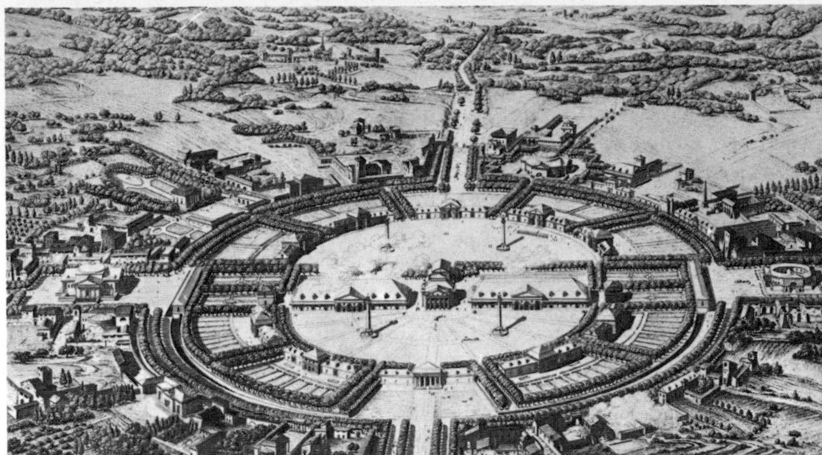

Claude-Nicolas Ledoux. Rock-salt mines and town of Chaux. Second plan. Bibliothèque Nationale, Paris.

LEDOUX, Claude-Nicolas (1736, Dormans, Marne—1806, Paris), French architect. A forerunner of our age in his social ideas as in his aesthetic, Ledoux was in his own time a famous architect with many clients; but his work has almost entirely vanished. After a short stay in the workshop of an engraver, he studied successively in the studio of Jacques-François Blondel and that of Louis François Trouard (1729–97), who obtained for him his first commissions (1757–64). In the first part of his career, from 1762 to 1774, Ledoux devoted himself primarily to private commissions. He constructed one of his rare surviving Parisian buildings, the Hôtel d'Hallwyl, in 1766; and for Madame du Barry he built a country pavilion on the enchanting site of Louveciennes and, at Versailles, monumental stables (1771–72). Numerous pavilions and town houses followed. All these residences have vanished; but we retain the grandiose Château de Bénouville, which he built in the countryside near Caen for the Marquis de Livry.

In 1774 he defended, in the presence of Louis XV, the plans of a whole town that he was planning to build around a rock-salt mine at Arc-et-Senans in Franche-Comté. The design was arranged in concentric ellipses; and, even though Ledoux was only able to carry out half the central ellipse, that achievement in itself remains impressive. In 1785, Ledoux had the idea of housing tollhouse administrative offices in some 60 monumental pavilions. These buildings, as expensive as they were unpopular, had nearly all been built when Ledoux's inevitable dismissal occurred. Meanwhile the architect had been able to express new ideas in the theater at Besançon, where for the first time the public in the pit had seats. The French Revolution soon interrupted the flow of this activity and Ledoux, imprisoned by mistake, devoted his period of captivity to the composition of a book of great artistic and social significance, which he published in 1804: *L'Architecture considérée sous le rapport de l'Art, des Moeurs et de la Législation*. After he was set free in Thermidor, Ledoux produced no more buildings. He died in 1806.

LEECH, John (1817, London—1864, London), English caricaturist. A child prodigy—like his great friend, Sir John Everett Millais—Leech was producing spirited sketches at the age of six. He was at Charterhouse School with the novelist William Makepeace Thackeray, whose aptitude for satirizing the foibles of the day he was to share—although, before he took up art, he studied medicine at St. Bartholomew's Hospital, London.

In the mid-19th century, the chief openings for a humorous graphic artist were in the fields of magazine and book illustration. In the 1840s, we find Leech contributing etchings to *Bentley's Miscellany* (from 1840) and the *Shilling Magazine* (1845), and providing illustrations for Dickens' *A Christmas Carol* (1844) and Gilbert Abbott Beckett's *Comic History of England* (1847–48) and *Comic History of Rome* (1852). A keen sportsman, Leech was the ideal illustrator for Robert Smith Surtees' successful *Handley Cross* novels, which appeared in the 1850s.

Leech was equally active as a wood engraver, and he became a regular contributor to the newly created *Punch* and *Illustrated London News*, which aimed to entertain and instruct an essentially middle-class readership. With a style that was gentler and less exaggerated than that of the great Regency satirist James Gillray, Leech hit precisely the right note: John Ruskin praised his caricatures as the "kindest and subtlest analysis of its [society's] foibles" that had yet appeared.

LEGA, Silvestro (1826, Modigliana Romagna—1895, Florence), Italian painter of the Macchiaioli group. He studied painting in Florence, where he came into contact with the Purist school of Luigi Mussini (1813–88), who advocated a return to the Italian masters of the Trecento and Quattrocento. The charming genre paintings of Lega's early manner, such as the *Pergola* (1868; Milan, Brera) or the *Visit* (1868; Rome, Galleria Nazionale d'Arte Moderna), betray an academicism of which he was to free himself later, especially when he retired to Pergentina, on the outskirts of Florence. It was there that Lega, together with Giuseppe Abbati (1836–67), Raffaello Sernesi (1838–66), Telemaco Signorini, and Odoardo Borrani (1834–1905), founded the so-called school of Pergentina, whose aim was to bring greater poetry and flexibility to the Impressionist doctrines of the Macchiaioli.

LÉGER, Fernand (1881, Argentan, Normandy—1955, Gif-sur-Yvette, near Paris), French painter. In 1903 he entered the École des Beaux-Arts, where he studied for a short time; in 1908 he moved into a studio in La Ruche. He became friendly with the Cubist writers Guillaume Apollinaire, Max Jacob, and Blaise Cendrars, and with the painters Albert Gleizes, Robert Delaunay, Henri Rousseau, Pablo Picasso, and Georges Braque. In the 1911 Salon des Indépendants, he exhibited *Nudes in the Forest* (1909–10; Otterlo, Rijksmuseum Kröller-Müller). Léger's *Wedding* (1911; Paris, Musée National d'Art Moderne) and *Woman in Blue* (1912; Basel, Kunstmuseum) marked a complete break with the past; with their tough, vigorous draftsmanship and the sharp contrasts of their rhythms and forms, they predicted the future direction of his art. Although Léger shared the Cubists' battle against traditional painting he felt much happier in the meetings of the Section d'Or group, whose members were more concerned than the Cubists with movement and color. In 1913 he began the abstract series of *Contrasts of Forms*, whose geometric patterns, logically and dynamically interlocked, immediately designated him as a bold innovator (*Contrasts of Forms*, 1913; Paris, Musée National d'Art Moderne).

Léger was mobilized in 1914, gassed at Verdun, and discharged in 1916. His experience of the harsh realities of mechanized warfare brought fresh life to his art. His idiom never varied from the *Town* (1919; Philadelphia, Museum of Art) to the *Mechanic* (1920; Paris, Galerie Louis Carré), or from *Disks* (1918; Paris, Musée des Beaux-Arts de la Ville de Paris) to the *Grand Déjeuner* (1921; New York, Museum of Modern Art). In all these paintings he created the same world of cogs, cranks, tubes, and robots, in movement or at rest. Soon, however, he began to paint still lifes again, and produced some uncompromisingly abstract murals (1924–26) in which he tried to suggest space by the interplay of colors alone. These interests were not new to Léger, who had already anticipated them in the settings and costumes he had designed for the Swedish Ballet (*Skating Rink*, 1921; *La Création du Monde*, 1922), in an abstract film (*Ballet Mécanique*, 1924), and in his mural decoration for the architect Le Corbusier's Esprit Nouveau pavilion at the 1925 Exposition des Arts Décoratifs. He solved the problems of reconciling plastic demands with the resources of color and of obtaining a synthesis of stability and movement in the same painting, by giving objects new functions and values (*Still Life with a Pipe*, 1928, and *Gioconda with Keys*, 1930; both Biot, Musée Fernand Léger). This contrast in motifs inevitably led Léger to create other contrasts in forms, rhythms, and colors, with the result that he always conceived a work in relation to a wall, whether it was a vast decorative scheme such as the *Transport of Forces* (1937) for the Palais de la Découverte in Paris, an easel painting such as the *Bather* (1931; Paris

Below left: **Fernand Léger.** *The Mechanic*. 1920. Galerie Louis Carré, Paris.

Below right: **Fernand Léger.** *Gioconda with Keys*. 1930. Musée Fernand Léger, Biot.

Coll. Louis Carré), or the monumental *Composition with Two Parrots* (1935; Paris, Musée National d'Art Moderne).

In 1940, when the approaching German forces scattered most Parisians, Léger temporarily settled in Marseilles. The sight of dockers swimming in the port inspired his series of *Divers* in 1941–46 (*Divers on Yellow Background*, 1941; Chicago, Art Institute). He escaped to the United States in November 1940; there, he painted his "figures in space" and also began to dissociate color from outline, a technique that he used for the rest of his life. When he returned to France in 1945 he brought with him a superb group of paintings that had been inspired by the industrial landscape of America; in Paris, he enlarged this collection by doing works in the same style (*Romantic Landscape*, 1946, Paris, Galerie Louis Carré; *Farewell New York*, 1946, Paris, Musée National d'Art Moderne). From this time, Léger's creativity seemed limitless and his artistic drive more powerful than ever before. In 1948–49 he completed his final version (*Leisure*, 1944–49; Paris, Musée National d'Art Moderne) of the series of *Cyclists* that he had begun in the United States in 1940. He then painted a series of *Builders* (*Constructors*, 1950; Musée Fernand Léger) and, in 1952–54, a series of *Country Outings*. In 1954 he also finished *Great Parade* (New York, Guggenheim Museum). During the same period, he designed sets for the theater (*Bolivar*, 1949; Paris, Opéra) and the ballet; stained glass for the church of Sacré-Coeur at Audincourt, Doubs (1951), for a church in Courfaivre, Switzerland (1954), and for the University of Caracas in Venezuela (1954); mosaics for the façade of the church of Notre-Dame-de-Toute-Grâce at Assy, Haute-Savoie (1949), and for the war memorial at Bastogne, in the Luxembourg province of Belgium (1950); a huge mural decoration for the auditorium of the United Nations General Assembly, New York (1952); and projects for decorative murals for the auditorium of the São Paulo opera house and a hospital in St-Lô, Manche (1954–56). At the same time, he also worked on tapestry cartoons, illustrations of the *Circus* (1949), and polychrome sculptures in ceramic (1950–55).

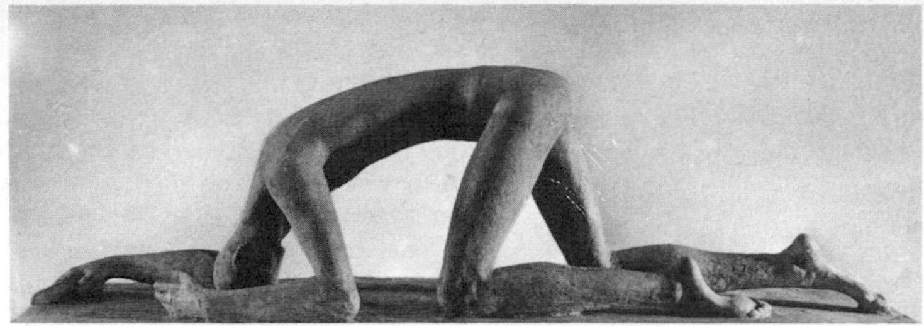

Wilhelm Lehmbruck. *Beaten Man.* 1915–16. *Photo Will Moegel, Stuttgart.*

LEGROS, Alphonse (1837, Dijon—1911, Watford, near London), French-born painter who became a British citizen. Legros was one of the most authentic of the French realist painters who followed Gustave Courbet. He entered the Dijon Academy of Fine Arts and then went on to study in Lyons and later in Paris. There, after a period in Armand Cambon's (1819–55) studio, where he met Henri Fantin-Latour, Whistler, Jules Dalou, and Rodin, he entered the "Petite École." Legros exhibited in the Salon of 1857 with his fine *Portrait of My Father* (Tours, Museum). In 1861 he painted his famous *Votive Offering* (Dijon, Musée des Beaux-Arts), and, in 1863, took part in the Salon des Refusés. His work was much appreciated by the most influential art critics, Champfleury and Baudelaire, but, impatient to sell, Legros went to London in 1860 at Whistler's invitation, and in 1863 settled there. He became a friend of the Pre-Raphaelites, married an Englishwoman, exhibited at the Royal Academy, and enjoyed success and official appointments. Legros was also an important engraver: he produced in all some 600 graphic works of exceptional quality, in which the influence of Rembrandt is apparent.

LEHMBRUCK, Wilhelm (1881, Meiderich, near Duisburg, West Germany—1919, Berlin-Friedenau), German sculptor. After studying at Düsseldorf (School of Decorative Arts, 1895–99; Academy of Fine Arts, 1901–7) and experimenting in the styles of Constantin Meunier and Auguste Rodin, he settled in Paris in 1910. He met Henri Matisse and Constantin Brancusi, and became a friend of Alexander Archipenko. A year later, Lehmbruck executed his first truly original sculpture, a *Kneeling Woman* (1911; New York, Museum of Modern Art). In this work he elongated the body, which seems not so much that of a real person as a symbol, the materialization of an idea, the incarnation of sensitivity, purity of heart, and devoted humility. In the male nudes of the next few years, he elongated the limbs still further, but even when they become thin, they retain their internal structure and vitality. Moreover, while a meditative gravity seems to envelop Lehmbruck's women, his men seem overcome by melancholy and tragically unfit for life. *Young Man Seated* (1918) is hardly less moving in his heavy solitude than the *Beaten Man* (1915–16) in his abandonment to pain. Even the *Young Man Standing* (1913; New York, Museum of Modern Art) is a prey to lassitude and doubt: the face conveys unmistakable anxiety and torment. The same is true even of the portraits, which usually present wounded or extremely vulnerable beings.

LEIBL, Wilhelm (1844, Cologne—1900, Würzburg), German painter. Leibl trained with Karl Theodor von Piloty at the Munich Academy and had already attained maturity as an artist when Gustave Courbet's visit to Munich in 1869 and his own stay of a year in Paris opened his eyes to new currents. Although particularly receptive to Naturalism, and also to Impressionism, he never lost his reverence for the old masters, whose technical excellence he made a part of his own art; in this respect his work recalls Vermeer. Although limited conceptually by his quest for realistic renderings, which took the form of exacting attention to detail, his technical command allowed him simultaneously to carry out controlled experiments with a number of styles and effects. He was master both of closed and of open, or painterly, form, and he was able to bring out either the linear understructure or the more sensuous aspect—the paint surface—of a work. He also experimented with effects of light and shade; some of his paintings are entirely structured by highlight and shadow (*Painter Sattler with a Hound*, 1870; Munich, Bayerische Staatsgemäldesammlungen).

LEIGHTON, Baron Frederick (1830, Scarborough, Yorkshire—1896, London), English painter. His artistic training was both comprehensive and thorough: he studied in Rome, Dresden, Berlin, Frankfurt, Brussels, and Paris.

His first great success in England was the painting of *Cimabue's Madonna Carried in Procession Through the Streets of Florence*, which was exhibited at the Royal Academy in 1855 and bought by Queen Victoria. Leighton was on friendly terms with the Pre-Raphaelites, but although he shared their interest in early Italian art, he never emulated their use of minute detail, always preferring broad effects. His paintings—with their often mythological subject matter, monumental compositions of a type recalling Raphael's Stanze, and the figures clad in Classical drapery (the *Captive Andromache*, shown at the Royal Academy in 1888, now in the Manchester City Art Gallery; the *Return of Proserpina*, shown there in 1891, now in the Leeds Art Gallery) are among the last examples of the grand traditional manner in European art.

The most satisfying of his works are those that reveal his very considerable powers as a designer and draftsman without unleashing the full force of his antiseptic imagination. *Flaming June* (shown at the Royal Academy in 1895, and now in Puerto Rico, Museo de Arte de Ponce), for example, depicts a single figure, with the pictorial interest lying in the rich color and in the careful interplay of limbs and drapery.

LELY, Sir Peter (1618, Soest, Westphalia—1680, London), English portrait painter of Dutch descent. Born Pieter van der Faes (Lely was a surname adopted by his father), he trained in Haarlem with the painter Pieter de Grebber (*c.* 1600–after 1692). The exact date of Lely's arrival in England is not recorded, but it was probably 1642 or 1643, shortly after Van Dyck's death. Van Dyck is certainly the influence behind Lely's first documented portrait, *Charles I and the Duke of York*, painted in 1647 for the Duke of Northumberland (Brentford, Middlesex, Syon House, Coll. Duke of Northumberland). Of the same date is the portrait of the *Children of Charles I* (Sussex, Petworth House). Its combination of coarseness of expression with depth of color was maintained by Lely in all his mature works. His technical progress can be judged by the portrait of the *Capel Sisters* (*c.* 1653; New York, Metropolitan Museum), or the even more brilliant undated portrait of *Abraham Cowley* (London, Dulwich College Picture Gallery), whose air of appealing languor is characteristic of Lely's portraiture.

The climax of Lely's career was reached in 1666, when he painted portraits for the Duke of York of those English admirals who had defeated the Dutch fleet in 1665. This series, known as the "Greenwich Flagmen" (Greenwich, National Maritime Museum), shows Lely at his best. At the same time he executed his most voluptuous and splendid female portraits, *Lady Byron* and the *Comtesse de Grammont* (both 1666; both Hampton Court, Royal Collection). These were to evolve in the late 1660s into the "Windsor Beauties," a series of portraits of the royal maids of honor commissioned by the Duchess of York (now in the Royal Collection at Hampton Court).

With the vast number of commissions and copies that came to him with his official appointment as court painter to Charles II in 1661, Lely demonstrated a steadily declining style. Nevertheless, his real gift to English painting was a new sensuousness of color and finish, and the introduction of a modified Baroque style on which Sir Joshua Reynolds was later to build his own portrait style.

LEMERCIER, Jacques (*c.* 1585, Pontoise, Seine-et-Oise—1654, Paris), French architect. He was the predecessor of Louis Le Vau as first architect to the king, and one of the founders of French Classicism under Louis XIII. His name and his work are associated with those of Cardinal Richelieu, for whom he built the Palais-Cardinal in Paris (begun 1633; now known as the Palais-Royal) and designed the small town of Richelieu (Indre-et-Loire), begun in 1631 beside the huge château that Richelieu envisaged as an eternal monument to his glory. The château has since disappeared, and the palace in Paris was almost completely rebuilt at the end of the 18th century. But the church of the Sorbonne (1635–42), another of Richelieu's foundations, remains one of the most expressive of Lemercier's creations.

At the Palais du Louvre, where Lemercier was commissioned to quadruple the original proportions of the Cour Carrée, he remained faithful to the style of Pierre Lescot's wing. In 1624 the first stone of the Pavillon de l'Horloge was laid; the ornamental richness of its upper stories was to influence successive architects of the Tuileries in Paris (under Louis XIV) and of the Louvre itself (under Napoleon III). Lemercier also built the wing to the north of the Pavillon de l'Horloge.

LE MOAL, Jean (b. 1909, Authon-du-Perche, Eure-et-Loir), French painter. After studying at the École des Beaux-Arts in Lyons, he went to Paris. There he worked first at the École des Arts Décoratifs, then at the Académie Ranson, where he met Roger Bissière in 1934. Between 1943 and the early 1950s he painted landscapes, interiors, and still lifes that showed the influence of both Fauvism and Cubism. In these works the structure is clearly defined, the light devoid of violence, and the color usually subdued (*Invitation au voyage*, 1945). From this point onward, he was almost exclusively inspired by landscapes: the harshness of Ardèche, a rocky coast, a flower-covered moor, and, most often, the sea and the clouds. He neglected the material details of reality in order to concentrate on the effects of light and color and, at the same time, he reduced the importance of line to such an extent that his paintings became vibrant juxtapositions of colored brushstrokes. As he developed he enlarged these splotches of color, distributed them with a greater sense of freedom, composed them according to broader rhythms, and made their tonalities more varied and sonorous (*Flora*, 1958–59).

LEMOINE, LEMOYNE, *or* **LE MOYNE,** François (1688, Paris—1737, Paris), French painter. The most highly regarded artist of the Regency period, he won the Grand Prix of the Académie Royale in 1711. He was received into the Académie in 1718, then in 172 went to Italy, where he was impressed by the boldness and

140.

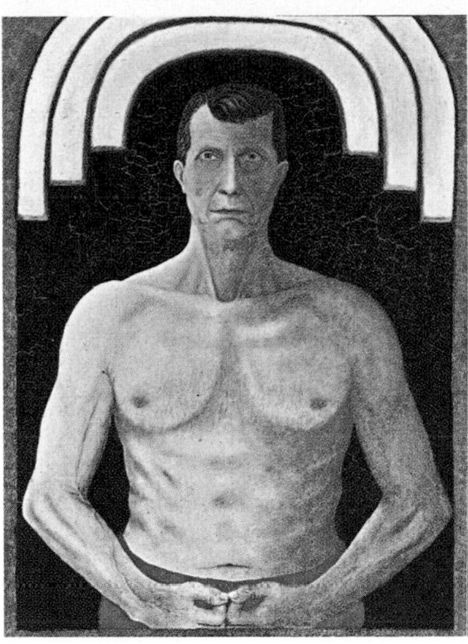

141.

142.

143.

144.

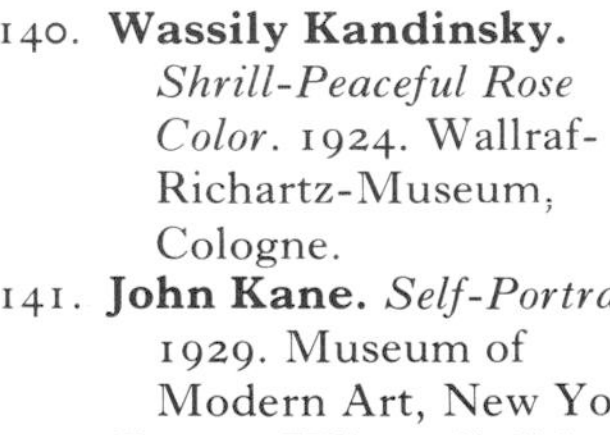

140. **Wassily Kandinsky.** *Shrill-Peaceful Rose Color.* 1924. Wallraf-Richartz-Museum, Cologne.
141. **John Kane.** *Self-Portrait.* 1929. Museum of Modern Art, New York.
142. **Gustav Klimt.** *Judith with the Head of Holophernes.* 1901. Österreichische Galerie, Vienna.
143. **Franz Kline.** *Green Vertical.* 1958. Sidney Janis Gallery, New York.
144. **Ernst Ludwig Kirchner.** *Young Girl on a Blue Sofa.* 1907–8. Minneapolis Institute of Arts.
145. **Oskar Kokoschka.** *Portrait of Herwarth Walden.* 1910. Coll. Samuel H. Maslon, Minneapolis.
146. **Paul Klee.** *Death and Fire.* 1940. Paul-Klee-Stiftung, Bern.

145.

146.

147.

148.

149.

150.

147. **Willem de Kooning.** *Merritt Parkway*. 1959. Sidney Janis Gallery, New York.

148. **Frank Kupka.** *L'Acier boit*. 1927–30. Private Coll.

149. **Roger de La Fresnaye.** *Conquest of the Air*. 1913. Museum of Modern Art, New York.

150. **Sir Peter Lely.** *Two Ladies of the Lake Family*. *c.* 1660. Tate Gallery, London.

151. **Antoine Le Nain.** *Three Young Musicians*. Los Angeles County Museum of Art.

152. **Maurice Quentin de La Tour.** *Portrait of Madame de Pompadour*. 1755. Louvre, Paris.

151.

152.

153.

154.

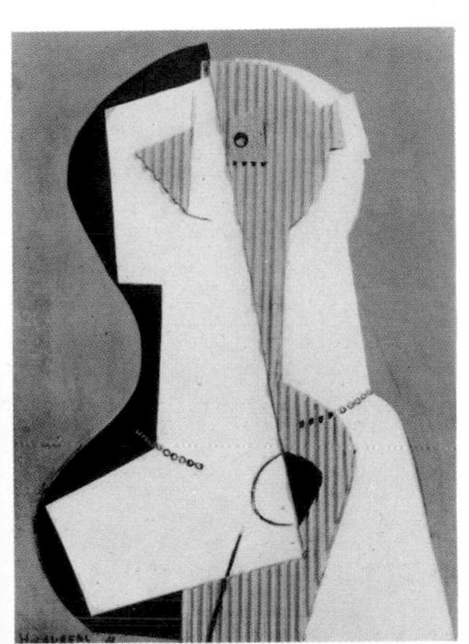

155.

156.

157.

153. **Charles Lapicque.** *Ulysses and Nausicaa.* 1964. Private Coll., Paris.

154. **Georges de La Tour.** *Nativity.* Rennes Museum.

155. **Henri Laurens.** *Woman with a Necklace.* 1918. Private Coll., Paris.

156. **Fernand Léger.** *Two Women with Flowers.* 1954. Tate Gallery, London.

157. **Charles Le Brun.** *Adoration of the Shepherds.* 1689. Louvre, Paris.

158.

159.

160.

161.

162.

163.

158. **Pol, Jehanequin, and Herman de Limbourg.** *The month of August, with the Château d'Étampes.* From the Très Riches Heures du Duc de Berry. 1415–16. Musée Condé, Chantilly.

159. **Filippino Lippi.** *Portrait of a Young Man.* National Gallery of Art, Washington, D.C.

160. **Jean-Étienne Liotard.** *Cup of Chocolate.* Gemäldegalerie, Dresden.

161. **Fra Filippo Lippi.** *Bartolini Tondo: Madonna and Child with Scenes from the Life of the Virgin.* 1452. Palazzo Pitti, Florence.

162. **André Lhote.** *Rugby.* 1917. Musée National d'Art Moderne, Paris.

163. **Pietro Longhi.** *Duck Hunting.* Galleria Querini-Stampalia. Venice.

164. Opposite: **Leonardo da Vinci.** *Portrait of a Lady with an Ermine.* Detail. 1483–4. National Museum, Cracow.

BELE FERONIERE

165.

166.

167.

168.

169.

170.

171.

172.

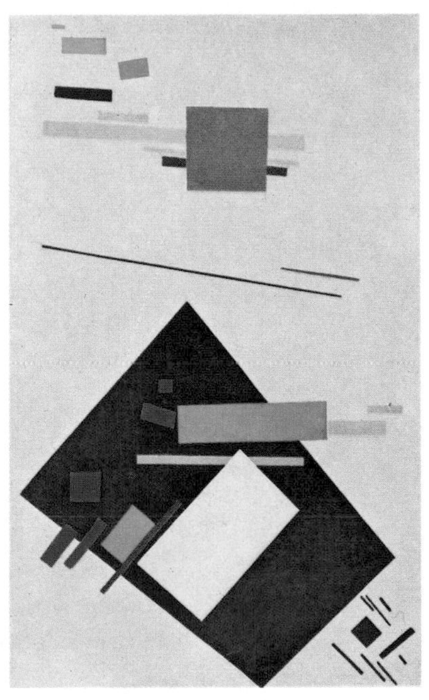

173.

174.

165. **Claude Lorrain.** *Landscape with Hagar and the Angel.* 1668. National Gallery, London.
166. **Lorenzo Lotto.** *St. Jerome in the Wilderness.* 1506. Louvre, Paris.
167. **Ambrogio Lorenzetti.** *Work in the Fields.* Detail from Good Government. *c.* 1338–40. Palazzo Pubblico, Siena.
168. **August Macke.** *Sunny Path.* 1913. Private Coll.
169. **Franz Marc.** *Blue Horse.* 1911. Coll. Bernhard Köhler, Berlin.
170. **Édouard Manet.** *Le Déjeuner sur l'Herbe.* 1863. Musée de l'Impressionnisme, Paris.
171. **Stanton Macdonald-Wright.** *Synchromy.* 1914. Private Coll., USA.
172. **René Magritte.** *Rough Crossing.* 1926. Coll. G. L. Niels, Belgium.
173. **Kasimir Malevich.** *Suprematist Composition.* 1915. Private Coll.
174. **Andrea Mantegna.** *Crucifixion.* Panel, S. Zeno altarpiece. 1456–59. Louvre, Paris.
175. **John Marin.** *Singer Building.* 1921. Philadelphia Museum of Art.

175.

176.

177.

178.

179.

180.

176. **Master of the Magdalen.** *St. Mary Magdalene.* Panel. *c.* 1250. Accademia, Florence.
177. **André Masson.** *Nude.* 1924–25. Coll. Peggy Guggenheim, Venice.
178. **Albert Marquet.** *Sergeant of the Colonial Army.* 1907. Coll. Robert Lehmann, New York.
179. **Master of the Life of Mary.** *Annunciation. c.* 1470. Alte Pinakothek, Munich.
180. **Quinten Massys.** *The Banker and His Wife.* 1514. Louvre, Paris.
181. **Masaccio.** *St. Peter Giving Alms.* Brancacci Chapel, S. Maria del Carmine, Florence.
182. **Master of Moulins.** *Madonna and Child Surrounded by Angels. c.* 1498/99. Panel of triptych. Moulins Cathedral.
183. **Simone Martini.** *The Blessed Agostino Novello Rescuing a Child Bitten by a Wolf.* Panel from altarpiece. *c.* 1333–36. Church of S. Agostino, Siena.

181.

182.

183.

grandeur of the decorative art of Pietro da Cortona, Veronese, and Parmigianino. When he returned to Paris, Lemoine painted the dome of the chapel of the Virgin in St-Sulpice (*Assumption of the Virgin*, 1731–32; sketch in Paris, Louvre) and the ceiling in the Salon d'Hercule at Versailles (*Apotheosis of Hercules*, 1733–36), which was not done in fresco, but on primed canvases, with a more precise treatment of details than is possible in mural painting. When shown to the public, it was universally acclaimed, and Lemoine was appointed first painter to the king (1736).

LEMOYNE, family of French sculptors of the 17th and 18th century.

JEAN-LOUIS (1665, Paris—1755, Paris), who was a pupil of Antoine Coysevox, was made an Academician in 1703 upon presentation of his bust of *Hardouin-Mansart* (Paris, Louvre). His fame as a portraitist was, however, soon eclipsed by that of his son.

JEAN-BAPTISTE (1704, Paris—1778, Paris) was a student of his father and of Robert Le Lorrain. He won the Prix de Rome in 1725 and entered the Academy in 1738. The official sculptor to Louis XV—of whom he left various portrait busts wherein one may trace the effects of age upon the monarch—Lemoyne had the most thriving studio of his day. Among his portrait busts of men one may cite those of the naturalist and physician *Réaumur* (1751; Louvre), the painter *Noël-Nicolas Coypel*, and above all the admirable *Montesquieu* (1760; Bordeaux), the finest image of that magistrate-philosopher. In his portraits of women, Lemoyne inaugurated the difficult genre of the flattering likeness, first with the busts of the *Comtesse de Brionne* (1763; Stockholm) and the beautiful *Hélène d'Egmont* (1767; Stockholm), who were favorites of King Gustave III of Sweden, and later with busts of the actresses *Mademoiselle Clairon as Melpomene* and *Mademoiselle Dangeville as Thalia* (both in Paris, Comédie-Française).

LE NAIN, family of French 17th-century painters consisting of three brothers—Antoine, Louis, and Mathieu. They formed a close partnership, and because they wished to conceal the part each played in the works produced in their studio, they signed them with their surname only. The brothers were all born in Laon, where their father was the collector of salt taxes. They were brought up among farmers, and the scenes of their childhood provided them with rustic subjects, which they handled with great authority. The brothers eventually went to live in Paris, where in 1629 Antoine was received as master painter at St-Germain-des-Prés, but they returned often to Laon. Their pictures are usually rather badly composed, but their realism gives them a compensating charm. Their figures may sometimes seem rather arbitrarily arranged, but all have admirably expressive faces. Their work was highly appreciated in their time, and in 1648 they were made members of the Académie Royale de Peinture et de Sculpture as "painters of *bambochades* (scenes of low life)."

ANTOINE (1588, Laon—1648, Paris), the eldest of the three, excelled above all as a miniaturist, his style being close to that of the Flemish minor masters. He executed miniatures on wood or copper, such as *Family Reunion* (1642; Paris, Louvre), *Children's Dance* (1643; Paris, Priv. Coll.), and *Portraits in an Interior* (1647; Louvre). In his *Saying Grace* (Paris, Priv. Coll.), one of the children taking part in the prayer is trying to suppress a laugh; such natural touches, naively expressed, are typical of Antoine. His hand is discernible in the *Studio* (*c.* 1630; London, Priv. Coll.), which probably represents the three brothers at home.

LOUIS (1593, Laon—1648, Paris) has always been regarded as the best painter of the three, his art having great seriousness and breadth. He was not afraid to work on large surfaces, and, unlike Antoine, preferred delicate nuances of grays and browns to brilliant colors. Louis liked to place man among nature, in open-air landscapes. Thus in the *Cart*, or the *Return from the Harvest* (1641; Louvre), he projects the light of a fine day onto a corner of a farm and produces an atmosphere imbued with bucolic poetry. Louis also painted rather serious interiors, such as the *Peasants at Supper* (c. 1645–48; Louvre), in which the figures in their worn clothes begin their frugal meal with due calm and dignity. Louis' *Saying Grace* (London, National Gallery) is much more serious than that of Antoine, and seems to confirm the theory that he began his career painting pictures for churches. His *Forge* (Louvre), depicting a family of craftsmen around the anvil, has been particularly highly praised.

Jean-Baptiste Lemoyne. *Bust of Crébillon.* Musée des Beaux-Arts, Algiers. *Photo Giraudon, Paris.*

MATHIEU (1607, Laon—1677, Paris) was influenced by Antoine, using what he learned very skillfully. His miniature on copper, the *Little Card Players* (Louvre) reveals a knowledge of chiaroscuro that Antoine did not possess. Mathieu was above all a portraitist; he was highly regarded at the French court, and in 1662 was made a knight of the Order of St. Michael. His verve, objectivity, and skill in composition are best seen in the *Guard* (1643; Paris, Priv. Coll.) and the *Backgammon Players* (Louvre), in which he shows himself to have been an attentive observer of his time.

LENBACH, Franz von (1836, Schrobenhausen, Upper Bavaria—1904, Munich), German painter. He was self-taught until about 1857, then trained in the Munich studio of the history painter Karl Theodor von Piloty (1826–86). In 1858–59 Lenbach was in Rome, where he became one of the German "Romanists." Shortly thereafter he painted his famous *Shepherd Boy* (1860; Munich, Schackgalerie). The artist returned to Munich in 1868, and spent the rest of his life in that

Louis Le Nain. *Peasants at Supper. c.* 1645–48. Louvre, Paris. *Photo Giraudon, Paris.*

André Le Nôtre. Gardens of the château at Versailles. 1661–68. *Photo Bulloz, Paris.*

city. In 1878 he was introduced to Prince Otto von Bismarck, whose favorite portraitist he became, painting no less than 80 portraits of the Prussian statesman. He also painted a number of court portraits (*Prince Ludwig of Bavaria and His Family*, 1882; Munich, Städtische Galerie im Lenbachhaus). In all, Lenbach produced around 4,000 paintings, but his speed hardly compensated for his lack of psychological penetration.

LE NÔTRE *or* **LE NOSTRE,** André (1613, Paris—1700, Paris), French landscape architect. His father was first gardener to the king at the Tuileries. In 1637 Le Nôtre succeeded to his father's position, and in 1656 he was appointed controller general of the royal building projects. The gardens of the château at Vaux-le-Vicomte, near Melun (*c.* 1655–1661), were his first masterpiece. They served as a model for his later plan for the park at Versailles (1661–68), and introduced the formal geometry of the so-called French, or Classical, garden. From then on, Le Nôtre's name was linked with some of the most important royal gardens—Meudon, Marly, St-Germain-en-Laye, Fontainebleau, St-Cloud, Chantilly, Sceaux—and with numerous private residences for the nobility, such as the château at Guermantes and the Château de Montjeu, near Autun.

A Le Nôtre garden is a vast theater in which the fountains, along with the geometrically disciplined rare flowers, parterres, bowers, and trimmed trees, all play a part in the well-regulated whole. Le Nôtre, employing the laws of optics as defined by Descartes, presents a new and intellectually rigorous concept of the art of landscape gardening, applying to it the scientific laws of perspective and of the refraction of light.

LEONARDO DA VINCI (1452, Vinci, near Florence—1519, Le Clos-Lucé, near Amboise), Italian painter. Heir to all the ideals of the Quattrocento, Leonardo also marked the beginning of the High Renaissance. He was admitted to Verrocchio's studio about 1469, where he was trained in all the various techniques and, according to tradition, distinguished himself by painting the left angel in the *Baptism of Christ* (*c.* 1475; Florence, Uffizi) and a small *Annunciation* (begun *c.* 1475; Paris, Louvre). From 1478 on, he began to receive important official commissions, such as the *Adoration of the Magi* (1481; Uffizi) for the monks of S. Donato a Scopeto, near Florence, which he left unfinished. This early period includes the *St. Jerome* in the Vatican and the portrait of *Ginevra de' Benci* (1474?; Washington, D.C., National Gallery). In about 1482 he left for Milan, offering his services to Ludovico il Moro.

On April 25, 1483, the Confraternity of the Immaculate Conception commissioned a painting for the church of S. Francesco, the *Virgin of the Rocks* (Louvre). In 1506 this painting was copied (London, National Gallery), and two panels with angels were added by a pupil, Ambrogio de Predis. The *Lady with an Ermine* (1483–4; Cracow, National Museum), and the unfinished *Portrait of a Musician* (*c.* 1485; Milan, Ambrosiana) date from that period. At this time Leonardo was concerned with problems of architecture: he took part in the discussions of the Milan Cathedral spire (1487) and later of the cathedral at Pavia. He was engaged on the famous fresco of the *Last Supper* for the refectory of S. Maria delle Grazie, Milan, from 1495 to 1497. From 1490 on, he started to develop his *Treatise on Painting* and his theoretical studies.

In February 1500, Leonardo was in Mantua at the court of Isabella d'Este, and in April he was in Venice, planning the defense against the Turks. On April 24, he arrived in Florence, where he stayed until 1506. In October 1503, he received the commission for the *Battle of Anghiari*, a fresco, intended to decorate the Palazzo Vecchio in Florence. (Drawings in the Royal Library, Windsor, and elsewhere, as well as drawn and engraved copies, including one by Rubens, are all that remain of the project.) It was during the same year that Leonardo must have started the *Mona Lisa*, or *La Gioconda* (Louvre), which was finished in 1507 and which he took to France. The *Madonna and Child with St. Anne* cartoon (London, National Gallery) may belong to about the same period.

In 1506 Leonardo responded to Charles d'Amboise's offer and returned to Milan, where he undertook a new sculptural project in the monument to Trivulzio, a condottiere under Louis XII of France. In 1512, however, when the French were driven out, Leonardo entered the service of Giuliano de' Medici, whom he followed to Rome. Giuliano died in 1515, and Leonardo decided to accept the invitation of the new French king, Francis I. He left for Amboise, where he settled in 1517. As engineer to the king, he drew up plans for the castle of Romorantin and organized several court masques. He died at Le Clos-Lucé on May 2, 1519.

We can understand Leonardo only by starting with Verrocchio, for it was under his influence that Leonardo began to develop his encyclopedic investigations. As painter and sculptor, he owed his

Leonardo da Vinci. *Mona Lisa.* 1503–7. Louvre, Paris.

Leonardo da Vinci. Study for *Leda and the Swan. c.* 1506. Royal Library, Windsor.

gentle technique and finish to the studio of this master.

In the *Virgin of the Rocks*, the traditional subject of the Madonna is given a personal interpretation; the meeting of the two children anticipates a theme taken up later in the *Madonna and Child with St. Anne* (London, National Gallery). Here Leonardo also developed the *sfumato* technique, which merged contour and volume in a new, more suggestive realism in which his newly discovered means of expression had full play.

Leonardo gave fresh life to perhaps the two most attractive aspects of painting: portraiture and landscape. He brought fundamental change to the conception of portraiture, especially of women, and at the same time showed his taste for the bizarre in his "caricatures," or studies of physiognomy. There are very few portraits in profile, but many full-face portraits exist: *Ginevra de' Benci*; the *Lady with an Ermine*; and the *Belle Ferronnière* (*c.* 1485–88; Louvre), whose attribution to Leonardo is sometimes disputed.

Leonardo arrived at some extraordinary results through meditating on landscape and its problems. His first landscape, dated 1473, was a drawing, a view of the Val d'Arno (Uffizi). In order to integrate the landscape with the picture successfully, he approached the problem through the details of foliage, plants, and pebbles; but he also approached it in a panoramic way, sometimes by a shadowy vault with glimpses of the far distance, as in the *Virgin of the Rocks*, and sometimes just with broad expanses of distance, as in the *Madonna and Child with St. Anne* and the *Mona Lisa*. Leonardo's pictorial output is accompanied by a quantity of notes and discussions of problems that indicate a mind open to every conceivable curiosity. There is nearly always a rare and strange slant to the artistic discoveries, a curiosity especially connected with the phenomenon of life accepted in its totality; there is a fascination for inextricably interlaced shapes, which ended after 1500 in numerous unfinished works, when the rough sketch became for Leonardo more important than the finished painting.

Immediately after his Florentine period, Leonardo's influence showed itself at work in Lorenzo di Credi and Piero di Cosimo. After his Milanese period, the growing part played by assistants makes attribution difficult. Giovanni Boltraffio, for example, stayed with the master all through the Milanese period; Ambrogio de Predis, Marco d'Oggiono, Bernardino Luini, and Andrea Salai remained in his orbit. Cesare da Sesto has to his credit the copies he made of the vanished *Leda*. Without Leonardo's precision, Raphael, Fra Bartolomeo, and Andrea del Sarto would not have achieved their noble, gentle, and disciplined art.

LE PAUTRE, family of French architects, decorators, and sculptors.

JEAN (1618, Paris—1682, Paris), engraver, devoted all his energies to the publication of collections of engravings in which his inexhaustible imagination was demonstrated in more than 2,000 architectural and decorative designs. Among these were: *Suite de lambris à l'italienne* (paneling), *Suite de vases à la moderne* (vases), and *Suite de clôtures de chapelle* (chapel screens). One might say that Jean Le Pautre, along with Charles Le Brun, actually created the Louis XIV style, since his works were so influential, not only in France, but also throughout Europe, where his collections were copied.

ANTOINE (1621, Paris—1691, Paris), architect and decorator, brother of Jean. One of his first works was the monastery of Port-Royal in Paris, built around 1646. Later, Madame de Beauvais commissioned him to build a town house in Paris, Antoine's best-known work. The Hôtel de Beauvais (1652–55) still exists and is admired for its ingenious use of an irregular and small site.

Antoine decorated the Hôtel de Guémenée (today the Maison Victor Hugo), and built the Château de Vaudreuil (1657) on an island in the Eure. He received the title of Controller of Building Works from the Duc d'Orléans who commissioned him to carry out important alterations at the Château de St-Cloud (1660).

PIERRE (1660, Paris—1744, Paris), sculptor, son of Jean. He was one of the most brilliant collaborators of Jules Hardouin-Mansart, who obtained for him a position as draftsman and engraver in the royal building works. Pierre studied in Rome, and is best known for his mythological groups.

LESCAZE, William (1896, Geneva—1969, New York), naturalized American architect. He was a pupil of Karl Moser (1860–1936), a Swiss architect, and gained a reputation in Europe before emigrating to the United States around 1930. The Savings Fund Society building in Philadelphia (1932), on which he collaborated with George Howe, marks the beginning of the revival of American architecture after the Depression. Its asymmetrical plan and spare façade, in which the architects exploited the structural materials rather than relying on ornamentation, mark the building as the first in America to display features of the European International Style. Lescaze was to retain his interest in refined surfaces, as can be seen in his CBS building in Hollywood, California

Jean Le Pautre. Study for a cartouche. Bibliothèque Nationale, Paris.

Eustache Le Sueur. *The Muses Clio, Euterpe, and Thalia. c.* 1647–49. Louvre, Paris. *Photo Giraudon, Paris.*

(1937–38). This was one of several radio and communications centers he built, which include the CBS studio in Chicago and Station WLW in Cincinnati, Ohio (1944).

LESCOT, Pierre (*c.* 1510, Paris—1578, Paris), French architect. Only one of his buildings is known, the Louvre of Henri II, which suffices to establish Lescot as a precursor of the French Classical style. Between 1541 and 1544, he erected the altar screen of St-Germain-l'Auxerrois, of which only some sculptures, from the hand of Jean Goujon, have survived. The collaboration of these two artists was to continue in the Louvre. François I commissioned Lescot to build "in his castle of the Louvre a large dwelling where at present is the great hall." François I died the the next year, but his successor Henri II confirmed Lescot in his functions.

The work at the Louvre, begun in 1546, occupied Lescot until 1556. The ground floor originally was to comprise two halls separated by a central staircase; but in 1549 Henri II asked Lescot to alter his plan. A larger apartment, the Hall of the Caryatids, replaced these rooms. The staircase was moved to the north of the building. This arrangement determined the style of the façade on the Cour Carrée. The façade presents two superimposed orders surmounted by an attic. Three projecting pavilions, with their columns framing niches, emphasize the rhythmic alternation of arcades and pilasters on the ground floor.

LESLIE, Charles Robert (1794, London—1859, London), English genre and history painter. He spent his childhood in Philadelphia and went to England in 1811. Two years later, Leslie began to study at the Royal Academy Schools, and for the next four years he concentrated on history paintings and portraits. After 1817, however, he turned to what was to prove a very popular type of genre painting, anecdotal and humorous in character, and usually inspired by episodes from the works of standard authors: *Sancho Panza in the Apartments of the Duchess* (1824; Sussex, Petworth House), from Cervantes, and *Le Malade Imaginaire* (1843; London, Victoria and Albert Museum), from Molière, are typical. Less typical, but more interesting, is the tiny *Scene in the Artist's Garden* (1840; Victoria and Albert Museum). Although successful and popular in his own day, he would probably be forgotten altogether had he not written one brilliant and important book, the *Memoirs of Constable* (1845), which contains a wealth of information on the great painter.

LE SUEUR, Eustache (1616, Paris—1655, Paris), French painter. At about the age of fifteen, he was admitted into Simon Vouet's studio. In 1648 he was one of the founding members of the Académie Royale de Peinture et de Sculpture.

In Le Sueur's earliest works, the style of Vouet is clearly discernible. But he freed himself from this influence by the time he executed his most famous works, the 22 paintings on the *Life of St. Bruno* (1645–48; Paris, Louvre) for the charterhouse of Paris. At about the same time, Le Sueur was commissioned to decorate the Hôtel Lambert in Paris: he painted seven pictures (now in the Louvre) for the Cabinet de l'Amour (*c.* 1646–47) and five for the Cabinet des Muses (*c.* 1647–49).

Le Sueur excelled in interpreting the more serene and private aspects of religious devotion, for which he came to be known as the "French Raphael." Of Le Sueur's abundant output for the churches of Paris and the monasteries of the provinces, particular mention should be made of his *St. Paul at Ephesus* (1649; Louvre) and the *Presentation in the Temple* (1652; Marseilles).

In 1654 he began a series of four pictures for the abbey of Marmoutiers, including the *Apparition of the Virgin to St. Martin* and the *Mass of St. Martin* (both Louvre). One of his last paintings, for the Parisian church of St-Gervais, represents *St. Gervais and St. Protais Refusing to Sacrifice* (Louvre), and reveals Le Sueur's exceptional mastery in historical composition.

LEU THE ELDER, Hans. *See* **MASTER OF THE CARNATION.**

LE VAU, Louis (1612, Paris—1670, Paris), French architect. Le Vau built many private houses, which helped prepare the way for the expansion of artistic work during the despotic rule of Louis XIV. The Hôtel Lambert, completed in 1644, is the most famous of these buildings, together with the Hôtel de Lauzun, built by Le Vau in 1656 for the arms supplier Gruyn des Bordes.

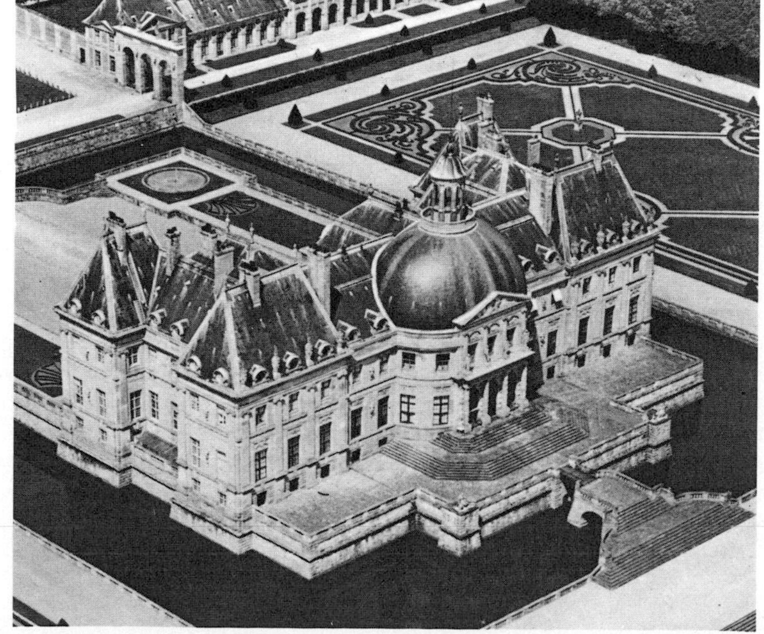

Louis Le Vau. Château de Vaux-le-Vicomte. 1657–61. *Aéro-Photo, Paris.*

The Hôtels Hesselin, Bautru, and d'Aumont, possibly the Château de Wideville, certainly those of Conflans, Dangu, and Le Raincy, and the central pavilion of Meudon were other important works that foreshadowed one of the masterpieces of this period: the Château de Vaux-le-Vicomte. Summoned by the luxury-loving Fouquet, Le Vau in 1656 undertook the construction of this residence that is known to have aroused the envy of Louis XIV. Surrounded by a moat, the château forms a rectangle with pavilions at each of its four corners. Its breadth is occupied by two rows of apartments, a novel arrangement for that time. Near the entrance are grouped the bedrooms, the study, and the baths. Overlooking the park, the reception rooms frame the large central hall. This oval salon, with its rounded end projecting in the middle of the façade, occupies the full height of two stories and the dome that crowns it dominates the whole building. Inside, under the cornice that extends around the springing of the dome, are carved eagles, lions, a crocodile, and a rhinoceros, as well as emblems of hunting, fishing, commerce, time, and love. This decoration is attributed to Nicolas Legendre (1619–71) and François Girardon. From 1648 on, an unobtrusive but very talented collaborator worked with Le Vau, François d'Orbay, whose hand must be recognized in a structure contemporary with Vaux, but of a very different character: Mazarin's new Château de Vincennes (1654–60). Colbert, the executor of Mazarin's will, chose Le Vau to build the Collège des Quatre Nations, a posthumous foundation set up by the cardinal, now the Institut de France.

The great royal building projects absorbed all of Le Vau's energy after 1655. For the Louvre he constructed the Rotonde and the Gallery of Apollo, the Courtyard of the Sphinx, and the north and south wings of the Cour Carrée. He constructed the façade facing the Seine, in front of which d'Orbay was to erect another. At Versailles, Le Vau built the wings of the forecourt, the first Orangerie (1661), and the Grotto of Thetys (destroyed in 1684). He lengthened the palace wall in the direction of the park and built new corner pavilions. Then in 1668 came the final transformation called the "enveloping" plan. On the park side, the new buildings projected beyond the corner pavilions and enclosed two lateral courtyards. Jules Hardouin-Mansart slightly readjusted Le Vau's design and extended it with the long wings to the north and south. Le Vau's plan of a second "envelope" was put into the hands of the builders shortly before his death; d'Orbay and André Le Nôtre, it is believed, intervened in time to prevent what already appeared to be a mistake. Nevertheless, Le Vau had done enough to appear to posterity as, to quote Voltaire, "one of the greatest architects of France."

LEVINE, Jack (b. 1915, Boston), American painter. Dr. Denman Ross of Harvard University acquainted the precocious Levine with the study of art history and with the paintings in local museums. Influences at first came from such artists as Degas, Daumier, and Rembrandt, while work subsidized by the WPA Federal Art Project in 1935 encouraged Levine's moralistic orientation. He was consistently concerned with the dehumanization and corruption in modern life, and such paintings as *The Trial* (1953–54; Chicago, Art Institute) and the *Gangster Funeral* (1952–53; New York, Whitney Museum) reflect this concern.

Levine's first one-man show was in 1939, and in 1955 a retrospective was held at the Whitney Museum in New York. His work is included in such major collections as the Museum of Modern Art in New York (*The Passing Scene*, 1941), the Metropolitan Museum (*Medicine Show*, 1955–56), and the Phillips Gallery in Washington, D.C. (*Under the El*, 1952).

LEVITAN, Isaak Ilich (1861, Kybartai, Lithuania—1900, Moscow), greatest Russian landscape painter of the 19th century. In 1889 he went to Paris for the International Exhibition and was exposed to the work of the French landscapists Camille Corot, the Barbizon masters, and the Impressionists. But although he assimilated their techniques, his interpretation of the Russian landscape remained a highly personal one. With penetrating emotion, he succeeded above all in rendering its more deserted, melancholy aspects, which accorded well with his elegiac temperament.

Louis Le Vau and Jules Hardouin-Mansart. Château de Versailles. 1668–90.

A favorite subject was large stretches of water, the flowing water of great rivers, and the stagnant water of ponds (*Neglected Pond*, 1887; Leningrad, State Russian Museum). Levitan preferred the soft twilight to the bright noon sun and the melancholy of autumn to the joy of spring (*Suburb, Golden Autumn*, 1889; State Russian Museum).

LEVY, Rudolf (1875, Stettin, now Szczecin, Poland—1944/45, Dachau or Auschwitz), German painter. After receiving an arts and crafts training in Berlin and Karlsruhe, he went to Munich to study painting. In 1903 he went to Paris where, together with Hans Purrmann and Oskar Moll (1875–1947), he helped form the nucleus of the Café du Dôme group. Through Purrmann, Levy met Henri Matisse, and from 1907 worked for many years in the latter's studio. However, he lived alternately in Berlin and Paris from 1931 until 1933, when he emigrated from Germany, eventually settling in Italy (1937). In 1943, however, he was seized by the Gestapo in Rome and deported to a concentration camp in Germany.

Levy was a member of the so-called German Matisse school led by Purrmann, and in his artistic development progressed from a Cézannesque treatment of form to a Matisse-like emphasis on color and pattern. In his best work Levy reveals a dense and rich organization of color and form, combined with a spontaneity and brilliance that make him one of the most exciting, though relatively little known, followers of Matisse. An example of his work is a *Still Life with Notes* (1942).

LEWIS, John Frederick (1805, London—1876, Walton-on-Thames, Surrey), English painter. He began by painting animal subjects, which he exhibited in the 1820s at London's Royal Academy

Wyndham Lewis. *Composition.* 1913. Tate Gallery, London.

and at the British Institution. A visit to Spain (1832–34), however, helped to transform his art; after this journey, he produced a large number of church interiors, street scenes, and bullfights, often in watercolor, in a style notable for brilliant color and minute attention to detail.

From 1842 to 1850, Lewis settled in the Middle East, living in Cairo. In 1850 he sent the *Harem* (London, Victoria and Albert Museum) to London for exhibition at the Old Water-Colour Society. Its exotic Oriental theme caused a sensation. The following year, Lewis returned to England and to success: in 1856 he was made president of the Water-Colour Society, and in 1865 he became a Royal Academician. He continued to paint Middle Eastern subject matter (*Door of a Café in Cairo*, 1865; London, Royal Academy), which he treated in an entirely straightforward manner that helps to explain his popularity.

LEWIS, Percy Wyndham, *called* Wyndham (1882, Nova Scotia—1957, London), English painter, novelist, and art critic. Lewis grew up in England, and after studying (1898–1901) at the Slade School of Art in London, he traveled widely in Europe, returning to London in 1910 to throw himself into the polemical battle for modern art. With a circle of friends that included the poet Ezra Pound, the philosopher T. E. Hulme, the writer Richard Aldington, and the sculptors Sir Jacob Epstein and Henri Gaudier-Brzeska, he formed a group that was to be associated with Vorticism, a movement founded by Lewis in 1914. Vorticism, derived in part from Cubism and in part from Futurism, was a dynamic and aggressive weapon, as explosive as the title of its periodical, *Blast: Review of the Great English Vortex.* Its aim was to thrust Britain into the Continental European avant-garde.

World War I failed to inhibit Lewis' activities. In 1914–15 he completed *Tarr*, his first major novel; published a folio of 20 drawings on the theme of the problems of modern life, entitled *Timon of Athens*; and did his first portrait of Ezra Pound (now lost; a 1938 version is in the Tate Gallery, London). In 1914 the first Vorticist exhibition was held at the Doré Gallery in London and the second issue of *Blast* appeared. In the 1920s Lewis produced many incisive, marvelously constructed pencil portraits that reveal his powers of visual analysis at their most lucid. In 1924 he published a magazine called *The Tyro*; it was followed in 1927 by his book *Time and Western Man*, and in 1930 by his best-known book, *The Apes of God.*

Lewis was a born painter, and the dominant characteristic of his art is an innate sense of construction. After 1914 his work was rarely entirely abstract. Often, Lewis' paintings seem to be pre-eminently geometric or rhythmic speculations; in addition to their sculptural qualities, they invariably have a totemic character that transforms them into magical objects with souls and lives of their own. *Sunset Atlas* (1934), on the other hand, with its Cubistic structure and fluid atmosphere, sums up rather well the characteristics of the Vorticist Movement. The Tate Gallery in London contains several works that are representative of his art: the *Surrender of Barcelona* (1936); *Red Scene* (1933), a composition painted in somber, flat tones in a masterly geometric construction; and his *Portrait of Edith Sitwell* (1923–35), with a vertical, metallic, and powerful aspect. His *T. S. Eliot* (1938; Durban, South Africa, Museum and Art Gallery) shares these characteristics.

André Lhote. *Reclining Woman. Photo Marc Vaux, Paris.*

LEYDEN, Lucas van. *See* **LUCAS (HUGENSZ.) VAN LEYDEN.**

LHOTE, André (1885, Bordeaux—1962, Paris), French painter. It was through reading Eugène Delacroix's *Journal* and Baudelaire's *Curiosités esthétiques* that he came to painting. In 1908 he left Bordeaux and went to live in Paris. At that time he seemed an adherent of Fauvism (*Women Around a Table*, 1910), but his devotion to Cézanne and his intellectual vigor turned him toward Cubism. His love for analysis and construction is already apparent in the *Widow* (1910) and more evident still in *Port of Call* (1912; Paris, Petit Palais). Pictures such as *Rugby* (1917; Paris, Musée National d'Art Moderne) exemplify Lhote's method: geometric transcription of figures or objects, clear articulation of the planes by means of contour or color, subtly hierarchized composition, calligraphic intelligibility. He applied the same method to his large-scale decorations for the Pavillon du Gaz at the Exposition Internationale of 1937 in Paris and for the Bordeaux Faculté de Médecine in 1955.

André Lhote taught a whole generation of painters in his school in Rue d'Odessa in Paris. He held the post of art critic of the *Nouvelle Revue Française* for a number of years and was the author of several highly esteemed works, the *Traité du paysage*, 1939 (*Treatise on Landscape Painting*, 1950) and the *Traité de la figure*, 1950 (*Theory of Figure Painting*, 1954), which have become classics.

LICHTENSTEIN, Roy (b. 1923, New York), American painter and sculptor. He worked in a non-figurative Abstract Expressionist mode before 1957; then he began to use loosely handled cartoon images from bubble-gum wrappers, also reinterpreting paintings of the old West by Frederick Remington and others. Conscious of the Happenings initiated in the early 1960s by Claes Oldenburg, Jim Dine, and his Rutgers colleague Allan Kaprow, Lichtenstein shared their concern with making art from the materials and products of the industrial environment. He was particularly interested in the lack of sensitivity in mass-produced, often perishable images and merchandizing art, which prompted him to mimic such aspects of the public landscape in his own work. Comic strip characters are extracted from their narrative context, blown up in size and reproduced with the same typographic screen techniques (Ben Day dots) with which they were printed, thus becoming an emblematic parody of the original (*Good Morning, Darling,* 1964; New York, Leo Castelli Gallery).

In his reproductions of corny popular romance characters, travel poster vulgarizations of Classical ruins (*Temple of Apollo*, 1964; Pasadena, Calif., Coll. Mr. and Mrs. Robert A. Rowan), comic book war heroes, advertising fragments (*Girl with Ball*, 1961; New York, Coll. Philip Johnson), or stylized landscapes, Lichtenstein contrasts what is already a travesty of emotion, scene, or object with his unemotionally banal rendition. He also uses the discredited styles and mannerisms of earlier periods, such as his paintings and sculptures (1967–68) based on the once popular 1930s "modern," a corrupt and ornamental version of Cubism. *Modern Painting With Yellow Interweave* (1968; Leo Castelli Gallery), and the curved brass or chrome, tinted glass, and marble slabs of his elegant sculptures evoke the taste and style of that period.

LIEBERMANN, Max (1847, Berlin—1935, Berlin), German painter and graphic artist, the major exponent of German Impressionism. After training in Berlin and Weimar, he moved to Munich and in 1884 to Berlin, where he lived for the rest of his life.

Groups of men and women at work were the principal subjects of his large compositions. *Women Plucking Geese* (1872; Berlin), his first important painting, which was dependent on the style of Jozef Israëls (1824–1911), created an uproar. After his first trip to Holland, he began to see figures and objects through a moist atmosphere suffused with light, influenced by the vision of Frans Hals, whom Liebermann studied and copied.

It was not until 1890 that he discovered Manet. His palette then became brighter, and there was more light and movement in his painting; landscapes and scenes in the street and on the beach gained a new unity of tone and color (*Polo Players*, 1902; Hamburg, Kunsthalle). A few years later, the influence of Degas appeared in more dynamic and nervous drawing and greater originality in the poses of the figures. Liebermann's style changed little during the last 30 years of his life, in which he concentrated on portraits (*Minister Luther*; Essen, Folkwang Museum), self-portraits (*Self-Portrait*, 1909; Hamburg, Kunsthalle), and views of his garden at Wannsee.

LIMBOURG, Pol, Jehanequin, *and* Herman de (b. late 14th century—d. *c.* 1416), Flemish miniaturists. The exact dates of their birth are still not known, but it has been established that they were the sons of a sculptor from Nijmegen, Arnold van Limburg. On the death of their father in 1399, Jehanequin and Herman, the two youngest, were apprenticed to a Parisian goldsmith. Around 1402 Pol and Jehanequin were working at Dijon, where they were attached to the Burgundian court, in the service first of Philip the Bold, then of John the Fearless. In 1410 the three brothers were first mentioned as being at the court of the Duc de Berry, where they succeeded the miniaturist Jacquemart de Hesdin (*c.* 1350–1410).

Only two works, authenticated by documents, can be attributed to the Limbourg brothers with certainty: the *Belles Heures*, also known as the *Heures d'Ailly* (between 1403 and 1413; New York, Cloisters), and above all the *Très Riches Heures du Duc de Berry* (1415–16; Chantilly, Musée Condé), undisputably their masterpiece. The execution of the *Très Riches Heures* was interrupted by the deaths of the duke and of the Limbourg brothers, and the work was only completed in 1485–89 by Jean Colombe of Bourges. Unprecedented powers of observation; taste for accurate, everyday detail; and a feeling for the narrative scene make the *Très Riches Heures* one of the finest expressions of the art of the miniature. Particularly admirable are the landscape backgrounds, in which many of the buildings of the period are rendered in minute detail.

Pol, Jehanequin, and Herman de Limbourg. *The Louvre under Charles V*. Miniature from *Les Très Riches Heures du Duc de Berry*. 1415–16. Musée Condé, Chantilly. *Photo Giraudon, Paris.*

LINARD, Jacques (*c.* 1600–1645), French painter. He was one of the most important of the masters of French still-life painting in the 17th century. From 1627, he was in Paris, working in the Île de la Cité, and later in the quarter of St-Nicolas-des-Champs. About 20 of his still lifes, signed and dated from 1627 to 1644, have survived. They usually depict dishes of fruit (*Plums and Pears on a Pewter Dish*, 1629; Athens, National Picture Gallery) or baskets of flowers, with arrangements of primroses, tulips, and anemones (*Basket of Flowers*; Paris, Louvre). Linard also executed several pictures whose highly concentrated organization reveals an ambition to raise the still life to a symbolic level (*Five Senses with a Landscape*, 1638; Strasbourg, Museum). His sober execution and his use of subtly harmonized colors against a dark background distinguish him clearly from the more flamboyant Flemish still-life painters.

LINNQVIST, Hilding (b. 1891, Stockholm), Swedish painter. His earliest influences were Edvard Munch and Ernst Josephson, but he owed his own concrete lyricism to the Swedish peasant primitives of the 18th and 19th centuries. From the *Square at Chinon* (1921–22) to his later mural paintings, it is this lyricism that gives his complex, large-scale works their unity. A plastic action—with episodes juxtaposed and articulated on the bold perspectives of a vast panorama of forms, figures, rhythms, and colors—unfolds around a balancing central theme in an enchanted world of Mediterranean light. Apart from sets for Richard Strauss's opera *Ariadne auf Naxos* (1944) and Mozart's *Magic Flute* (1956), Linnqvist's work consists mainly of monumental de-

Jacques Linard. *Basket of Flowers.* Louvre, Paris. *Archives photographiques, Paris.*

corations (*Life at the Riverside*, 1951, for the electricity works at Hjälta; the *Legend of Sweden*, 1952–53, a fresco for the entrance hall of the Solliden restaurant at Skansen) and a number of mosaics and tapestries (*Disa's Dream*, Aubusson tapestry, 1958–59).

LINT, Louis van (b. 1909, Brussels), Belgian painter. In 1939, with Anne Bonnet (1908–1960) and Gaston Bertrand (b. 1910), he was onc of the founders of "La Route libre," a figurative group that sought to reveal psychological truth through expressive deformations. His interiors, with their subtle coloristic contrasts and balanced composition, alternated with more imaginative, more caustic paintings. In 1949, with a series of paintings suggesting scaffolding, Van Lint moved toward abstraction: the arrangement of ropes and planks was reduced to a play of verticals and horizontals. After a somewhat frenetic period, he returned to nature, specializing in "abstract landscape" (*Forest Fire*, 1958; *Cumulus*, 1959).

LIOTARD, Jean-Étienne (1702, Geneva—1789, Geneva), Swiss painter and draftsman. Following an apprenticeship in Geneva, Jean-Étienne spent three years in Paris working under the miniaturist Jean-Baptiste Massé (1687–1767). In 1736 he began traveling, first to Rome, then to Naples and the Greek islands, and finally to Constantinople, where he lived for five years, painting several portraits of Turks and members of the English colony there. In Vienna, where he arrived in 1743, he won the favor of the public, and in Paris, where in 1748 he was welcomed as the "Turkish painter," his popularity was even greater. Living in London from 1753 to 1756, Liotard specialized in portraits of society women. He finally settled in Geneva in 1757. His *Tronchin Family* and *Madame Epinay* (both 1758; both Geneva, Musée d'Art et d'Histoire) are among the finest portraits of the period. He worked primarily in pastel, which he used with exceptional boldness and energy, avoiding *sfumato* effects. In addition to a few still lifes, Liotard painted elegant and refined genre scenes, including the well-known *Cup of Chocolate* (Dresden, Gemäldegalerie).

Jacques Lipchitz. *Prometheus Strangling the Vulture*. II. 1944–53. Philadelphia Museum of Art.

LIPCHITZ, Jacques (1891, Lithuania—1973, Capri), French sculptor of Polish-Jewish origin. He studied engineering in a state high school in Vilna, Lithuania (1906–9), and in 1909 decided to go to France. When he arrived in Paris he attended the classes of the sculptor Jean Antoine Injalbert (1845–1933) at the École des Beaux-Arts. He also attended the Académie Julian, the Académie Colarossi (where he studied drawing), and the municipal college on the Boulevard Montparnasse. In 1913 he produced sculptures that were influenced by Cubism. This influence, however, involved merely a simplification of planes and volumes and the reduction of real shapes to geometric constructions. Soon Lipchitz' search for a new idiom became his way of thinking about and creating form. Even when he portrayed human figures, he created a stiff, austere sculpture from which he eliminated every unnecessary detail (*Head*, 1915–16).

Around 1925 he began to look for a lighter sculptural form and, instead of being concerned with volume, he was preoccupied with the arabesque; he produced a series of *Transparent Sculptures* (begun 1925) that were small bronze figures in which the contours and their superpositions were the most important parts. Between 1930 and 1935, at the peak of his artistic development, he began to reintroduce emotional values into his sculptures. In such works as the *Return of the Prodigal Son* (1931; Coll. artist), the *Couple* (1928–29; Otterlo, Rijksmuseum Kröller-Müller), and the *Song of the Vowels* (1931–32; Zurich, Kunsthaus), form was not only the solution of a sculptural problem, but also the expression of an emotion.

Lipchitz gradually softened the rigidity of his contours. *Prometheus Strangling the Vulture*, which he did for the entrance to the Palace of Discovery and Inventions at the 1937 Exposition Internationale in Paris, was one of the first versions of a new theme that he continued to develop until 1943–44, when he used this subject for the façade of the Ministry of National Health and Education in Rio de Janeiro.

After 1941 Lipchitz lived in the United States. He modeled small-scale clay sculptures that were the embodiment of his genius for metamorphizing objects: these were either light sculptures, projected into space with points, ribbons, and shrublike shapes (*Blossoming*, 1942, New York, Museum of Modern Art; *Spring*, 1943, Cleveland, Museum of Art); or compact masses, rising out of a procreating world (*Prometheus Strangling the Vulture, II*, 1944–53, Philadelphia, Museum of Art). The *Notre Dame de Liesse* (1946–48) for the baptismal font of the church of Notre-Dame-de-Toute-Grâce at Assy in Haute-Savoie, for example, belongs to this group of sculptures.

LIPPI, Filippino (*c.* 1457, Prato—1504, Florence), Italian painter. He was the son of Fra Filippo Lippi and Lucrezia Buti. His father trained him, and then, as early as 1472, he was in Botticelli's workshop. In 1483 Filippino was commissioned to do two *Annunciation* tondi for the Palazzo Comunale in San Gimignano, and in the same year Lorenzo de' Medici invited him to decorate the Villa Spedaletto, near Volterra, in collaboration with his friends Botticelli, Ghirlandaio, and Perugino. About 10 years later, he decorated another Medici villa, the one at Poggio a Caiano (unfinished *Laocoön* fresco). He was not considered unworthy of completing the frescoes in the Brancacci Chapel in S. Maria del Carmine in Florence (1483–84); next to Masaccio's frescoes, he painted scenes representing St. Peter and St. Paul. About 1480–81 or a few years later, he painted for Piero del Pugliese's chapel in the monastery of the Campora, Florence, the *Vision of St. Bernard*

(Florence, church of the Badia), a powerful and sensitive masterpiece.

In 1487 Filippo Strozzi made a contract with Filippino to decorate the family chapel in S. Maria Novella. The work (the *Story of St. Philip and St. John*) was completed only in 1502, for Filippo Strozzi the Younger: it is the most important decorative scheme painted in Filippino's late style. In 1488 he had been called to Rome, where he decorated the Caraffa Chapel in S. Maria sopra Minerva with Dominican allegories, including the *Triumph of St. Thomas Aquinas*. He was then enjoying considerable popularity, and was asked to replace the *Adoration of the Magi* commissioned from Leonardo da Vinci in 1481 by the monks of S. Donato a Scopeto, and left unfinished. Filippino delivered the picture in 1496 (Florence, Uffizi). Filippino was more and more attracted by the picturesque: weapons, costumes, and archaeological settings copied out of his notebooks. In the Strozzi Chapel, the same characteristics appear in the *Meeting of Joachim and Anna* (Copenhagen, Statens Museum for Kunst), signed and dated 1497; in the *Marriage of St. Catherine* (1501) for the church of S. Domenico in Bologna; and in the large *St. Sebastian* for the church of S. Teodoro in Genoa (1503; Genoa, Palazzo Bianco).

LIPPI, Fra Filippo (*c.* 1406, Florence—1469, Spoleto), Italian painter. Fra Filippo joined the Carmelites in Florence at the age of eight, took orders in 1421, and was first recorded as a painter in 1431; thus he knew the work of both Masolino and Masaccio. In 1434 he was in Padua, where he painted the *Madonna of Humility* on a blue ground (Milan, Castello Sforzesco). Back in Florence in 1437, he painted the *Madonna and Child* (now in the museum at Tarquinia); and the *Madonna Surrounded by Angels and Saints* for Or San Michele (now Louvre, Paris). In 1442 Fra Filippo was appointed rector and abbot of the parish of S. Quirico at Legnaia, near Florence. His work during this period includes the large *Annunciation* in S. Lorenzo, Florence, and the *Coronation of the Virgin* (Florence, Uffizi), begun before 1442 and finished in 1447. The splendid Bartolini Tondo, a *Madonna and Child with Scenes from the Life of the Virgin* (1452; Florence, Palazzo Pitti), shows great mastery of the organization of space.

About 1452, Filippo Lippi settled in Prato to work on the S. Stefano frescoes, a large and complex series of paintings not completed until 12 years later. In 1456 he was chaplain at the convent of S. Margherita and painted a large altarpiece (Prato, Museum) for the chapel. There he met the nun Lucrezia Buti, who became the mother of his son Filippino, also a painter. In addition to his usual Madonnas, he painted several *Nativities* set in beautiful brown and gold landscapes: one in the convent at Annalena, another for the Camaldolites (both in the Uffizi), and one for the chapel of the Palazzo Medici-Riccardi in Florence (Berlin, Staatliche Museen). His last commission was in Spoleto, where he went in 1466 with his young son to decorate the apse of the cathedral with frescoes, including a grandiose *Coronation of the Virgin*. He died there in 1469.

LIPPOLD, Richard (b. 1915, Milwaukee), American sculptor. He inherited from his father, a distinguished engineer, a sense of precision that he manifested in lengthy calculations of the forces and tensions of his sculptures. His earliest works were "sculptures of lines," made of nickel, brass, or copper wire, and later precious metals—gold and silver—arranged in networks as delicate and complex as spiders' webs.

Lippold's first exhibition in New York, at the Willard Gallery in 1947, consisted of small wire constructions; but his second consisted only of a single huge construction, *Full Moon* (1949–50), which was bought at once by the Museum of Modern Art in New York. The Metropolitan Museum in New York then commissioned another monumental work, *The Sun* (1953–56), made entirely of gold thread. Lippold also executed a number of works in conjunction with architecture, including the *World Tree* (1950), its trunk and conical boughs made of steel rods, for the Harvard University Graduate Center, Cambridge, Massachusetts, and a sheaf of bronze stalactites, suspended from the ceiling, for the bar of the Seagram Building, New York.

LIPTON, Seymour Arthur (b. 1903, New York), American sculptor. He was entirely self-taught. For about 10 years he worked only in wood, producing expressionistic figures with social themes. In 1945 he began to use sheet lead. With his works in molten metal, he was hailed as one of the most promising abstract sculptors in the United States. From 1950 his style began to change again. Using combinations of steel, nickel, and silver, he created knotty forms, which, apparently without representative intention, suggested animals and plants (*Nocturnal Flowering*, 1951; *Flowering in the Jungle*, 1954; *King of the Sea*, 1955, Buffalo, Albright-Knox Art Gallery). The elements of his sculptures are arranged around empty spaces into a capricious, yet sturdy and urgent whole (*Terrestrial Forge*, 1955; Brooklyn, Museum). He received a number of official commissions, including work for Temple Israel at Tulsa, Oklahoma (1954), Temple Beth-El at Gary, Indiana (1955), the Inland Steel Building, Chicago (1957), and Dulles Airport, Washington, D.C. (1964). He received the Logan Medal of the Chicago Art Institute (1957) and the Ford Foundation Award (1961).

Seymour Lipton. *King of the Sea.* 1955. Albright-Knox Art Gallery, Buffalo. *Photo Oliver Baker, New York.*

LISBOA, António Francisco. *See* **ALEIJADHINO.**

LISSITZKY, Eleazar *or* Lazar, *called* El (1890, Smolensk province—1941, Moscow), Russian painter and draftsman, one of the leading representatives of Russian Suprematism and Constructivism. After the Russian Revolution, Marc Chagall invited him to teach architecture and graphic arts at the Vitebsk School of Fine Arts. El Lissitzky was deeply influenced by the Suprematist ideas of Kasimir Malevich, who was also teaching at the school. He combined Malevich's theories with the Constructivist

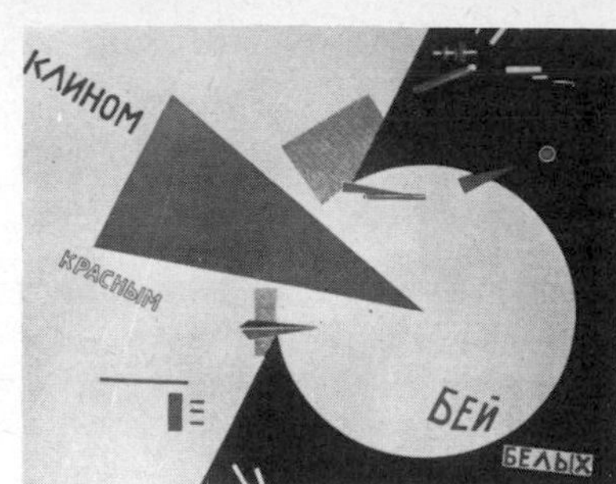

El Lissitzky. *Beat the Whites with the Red Wedge.* 1919–20. Poster.

tendencies then current in Moscow, where, after 1921, he taught at the Academy. In 1919, El Lissitzky was working on a project for a *Speaker's Rostrum* based on a diagonal construction. In 1919 he also began working on a series of abstract paintings and drawings that he called *Proun*; these were compositions of geometric planes that opened out into space, combining painting and relief, and thus representing a shift in El Lissitzky's artistic activity from pictorial to architectural concerns (*Construction—Proun 2*, 1920; Philadelphia, Museum of Art). El Lissitzky also worked on the sets and costumes for an "electromechanical" production of the futuristic opera *Victory Over the Sun*, based on a libretto by the poet and painter Alexei Kruchenik, with music by Matiushin and décor by Malevich. In 1920 he executed the *Story of Two Squares*, a series of six drawings published in Holland in 1922. He also designed the layout and dust jacket for *About This*, a collection of Vladimir Mayakovsky's poems, published in Moscow in 1923, and began creating extremely modern posters in which he ultimately combined painting with photomontage. In 1922 he participated in the Russian Exhibition in Berlin and decorated the Constructivists' section with mural reliefs. In Berlin he became friendly with Theo van Doesburg and, especially, with Laszlo Moholy-Nagy, who transmitted the ideas of Russian Constructivism to the Bauhaus. El Lissitzky was coeditor with the Russian writer Ilya Ehrenburg of several periodicals, notably *Veshch/Gegenstand/Objet* ("Object"), a Constructivist magazine devoted to modern art and published in Russian, German, and French (March 1922–July 1923). He was also interested in exhibition design, and between 1923 and 1928 designed several museum installations in Germany. In 1925 he published *The Isms of Art* with Jean Arp. Then, in 1927, at the request of the art critic Alexander Dorner, director of the Landesmuseum in Hanover, El Lissitzky executed the murals for that museum's famous "Hall of the Moderns," a room devoted to abstract art (destroyed by the Nazis in 1936). In 1928 El Lissitzky returned to the U.S.S.R., and was often given the responsibility for organizing official exhibitions, such as the Soviet pavilions abroad (Cologne, Dresden, Leipzig, Stuttgart, Paris, and New York).

Marcel Lods, Beufé, Honegger, and the Arsène-Henry brothers. Residential complex of Les Grandes Terres, Marly-le-Roi. 1958–60. *Photo Bertrand Weill, Paris.*

LODS, Marcel (b. 1891, Paris), French architect. With his partner Eugène Beaudouin (b. 1898), he played a leading role in the architectural movement of the 1930s. His housing development of Champ-des-Oiseaux at Bagneaux (1931–32), a suburb of Paris, represented the first large-scale application of complete prefabrication. He pursued this experiment in the housing development of La Muette at Drancy (1932–35), where he launched the formula of residential towers. With the open-air school of Suresnes (1935), near Paris, he produced one of the first school buildings to be based strictly on the functional and formal norms of the new architecture. Lods and Beaudouin were also interested in the new possibilities that engineers were opening up in the field of metal construction: in the Maison du Peuple at Clichy (1937–39), they used the remarkable curtain wall developed by Jean Prouvé. Lods's partnership with Beaudouin ended in 1940.

Lods's postwar buildings at Sotteville-lès-Rouen and Fontainebleau were less inventive. The best of his later work is the residential complex of Les Grandes Terres at Marly-le-Roi (with Honegger, Beufé, and the Arsène-Henry brothers, 1958–60), which is particularly remarkable for its shopping center and its network of pedestrian paths.

LOMBARDO, Pietro (*c.* 1435, Carona, Lake of Lugano—1515, Venice), Italian architect and sculptor, active particularly in the design of Venetian palazzi. Pietro employed his talents as both architect and sculptor in Venetia, but the traits that so evidently link him with Bernardo Rossellino and Desiderio da Settignano lead one to suppose that he served his apprenticeship in Florence. The Malipiero monument in S. Zanipolo, Venice, attributed to him, is surmounted by a baldacchino in the Venetian tradition, but the magnificent tombs the artist erected for the doges Marcello (S. Maria Gloriosa dei Frari, Venice) and Pietro Mocenigo (1485; S. Zanipolo) are clearly modeled after Florentine examples. The building to which Pietro Lombardo owes his fame as an architect is the little church of S. Maria dei Miracoli in Venice (1480–89), which stands beside a canal, and with its perfect proportions resembles a precious casket encrusted with polychrome marble.

Pietro's active collaboration with his sons Tullio (1455–1532) and Antonio (1458–1516) makes it difficult to attribute certain works specifically to any one of the three. Tullio is generally credited with the tombs of the doges Vendramin and Giovanni Mocenigo in S. Zanipolo, and with the church of S. Salvatore, Venice. Antonio probably designed the altar of S. Zeno in St. Mark's, and the chapel of the Holy Sacrament in the duomo of Treviso.

LONDON GROUP, English art group founded late in 1913. When Walter Sickert returned to London in 1905, he at once became the center of a group of painters—most notably Lucien Pissarro, Harold Gilman, Charles Ginner, and Spencer Frederick Gore—who looked to Gauguin and the other Postimpressionists for their artistic inspiration. These artists met regularly at Sickert's studio in Fitzroy Street; they took their subject matter from urban and "low life," advocated a light palette and a high color key, and opposed the jury system of selecting pictures for exhibitions. In 1911 (the year following Fry's first Postimpressionist exhibition) the Fitzroy painters finally founded the Camden Town Group, which held its first show at the Carfax Gallery, London, under the presidency of Gore. In late 1913, under the presidency of Gilman, the Camden Group amalgamated with several smaller groups—notably the Vorticists—to form the London Group (the name was suggested by the sculptor Sir Jacob Epstein). This new group held its first exhibition in March 1914 at the Goupil Gallery, London. Among the new members were Epstein, David Bomberg, Sylvia Gosse, Wyndham Lewis, John Nash, Christopher Richard Wynne Nevinson, and Edward Wadsworth; other artists who became associated with the London Group within the next few years were Vanessa Bell, Duncan Grant, Mark Gertler (1891–1939), Bernard Meninsky (1891–1950), and Paul Nash. In the 1960s the London Group had about 90 members, and embraced painters and sculptors of every creed, from the most uncompromising Realism to extreme Abstraction.

LONGHENA, Baldassarre (1598, Venice—1682, Venice), the greatest of the Venetian Baroque architects. He was thirty-three—and had already made a reputation for himself as architect of several patrician residences and of Chioggia Cathedral (1624–47)—when he was commissioned to build S. Maria della Salute in Venice. As the result of a competition, Longhena's plans were accepted and construction proceeded from 1631 to 1648.

Longhena's genius was also expressed in two secular buildings on the Grand Canal, the Palazzo Pesaro (1652/59–1710) and the Palazzo Rezzonico (1660–67), in which the architect developed and enriched the design of Jacopo Sansovino's Libreria Vecchia and Palazzo Corner (both begun 1537), which served as his models. In both buildings, Longhena used rusticated basements to support two stories of colonnades and tall windows.

Longhena's output was considerable. Apart from these three famous buildings, mention should also be made of the following works, all in Venice: the Giustinian-Lolin (after 1625), Marcello-Pindemonte (1624), and Widman-Foscari (1630) palaces; the church of the Ospedaletto (1670–78); the staircase of S. Zanipolo; the nave of S. Maria degli Scalzi (begun 1656), encrusted with gold and with lavender marble; and, in the church of the Frari, the tomb of Doge Giovanni Pesaro (1669), supported by figures of Africans carved out of black marble. On the mainland, the architect built the Villa Widman at Bagnoli, the Villa de Lezze at Rovare, and the Villa Lipomano near Conegliano.

Of all the Italian architects of the 17th century, Longhena remained most faithful to the spirit of the Renaissance, and never sacrificed structural clarity to exuberance of ornament. He himself regarded as one of his masterpieces the staircase of the Venetian monastery of S. Giorgio Maggiore (1643–45), a model of simplicity and elegance.

Baldassare Longhena. S. Maria della Salute, Venice. 1631–48. *Photo Boudot-Lamotte.*

LONGHI, Pietro Falca, *called* Pietro (1702, Venice—1785, Venice), Italian genre painter. Pietro went to Bologna to be taught by Giuseppe Maria Crespi. Back in Venice shortly after 1730, Longhi tried his hand unsuccessfully at decoration in the grand manner (*Fall of the Giants*, completed 1734; Venice, Palazzo Sagredo), and then turned to chronicling the life of his city in cabinet pictures. He prospered in this line, and in 1756 he was elected one of the first members of the Accademia of Venice, where he subsequently taught. A few good portraits disappear, so to speak, in a mass of genre scenes taken both from Venetian low life and from fashionable society: ladies dressing, visiting, and sitting for their portrait in the painter's studio; and family gatherings (*Family Concert*; Milan, Brera). The color is pleasant, very subdued, a little ashen with its mauves and muffled blues.

LOO, van. *See* **VAN LOO.**

LOOS, Adolf (1870, Brno, Czechoslovakia—1933, Vienna), Austrian architect and critic, one of the pioneers of the modern era. After studying at the Professional School at Reichenberg (Bohemia) and at the Dresden Technische Hochschule, he spent three years (1893–96) in the United States. On his return to Vienna, he began to express his ideas in writing with considerable vigor and intransigence, attacking in particular the painters and architects of the Vienna Secession group. Beginning in 1897 he published a series of articles in Vienna's *Neue Freie Presse*, on which his later work would be based. His campaign against ornamentation ran counter to the stylistic philosophy of the day. Loos decided to open a Free School of Architecture (1906), and in 1908 he expounded his convictions once more in his best-known essay, *Ornament und Verbrechen* ("Ornament and Crime"). The year 1910 proved decisive for him; during that time he produced two of his masterpieces: the Goldman and Salatsch buildings, a men's store, in Vienna, conceived as a play of interior volumes in which the essentially practical elements were incorporated into the wall, to compose an undecorated geometric whole; and the Steiner House, also in Vienna, one of the first private houses with the exterior built entirely of reinforced concrete. Again in Vienna, Loos built the Rufer House (1922), the Capua Café (1913), and various shops. From 1923 to 1928 he lived in Paris, where he met the organizers of the periodical *Esprit Nouveau* and became a friend of a number of avant-garde artists, in particular Tristan Tzara, for whom he built a house on Avenue Junot in 1926. In 1931, after his return to Vienna, he published in Innsbruck a collection of articles under the title *Trotzdem* ("Nevertheless"). The previous year he had built his final work, the Müller House, in Prague, which remains an exemplary masterpiece of the work of this precursor.

LORENZETTI, Ambrogio (*c.* 1290, Siena—1348, Siena), Italian painter. His first documented work is a picture dated 1319 (*Madonna of S. Angelo* in Vico l'Abate, near Florence); he is last mentioned in the archives in 1347. During his youth, Ambrogio came under the same influences as his brother Pietro, who was probably his teacher. It is difficult to attribute various unsigned works, such as the *Christ on the Cross*, in the church of S. Marco at Cortona, to one or the other of the two brothers. But Ambrogio's personality soon asserted itself. He was perhaps less powerful and less dramatic than Pietro, but his style had more elegance.

Ambrogio's numerous works are now scattered, but most are still in Siena. First there are the two frescoes in the church of S. Francesco: the *Martyrdom of the Franciscans at Ceuta* and *St. Louis of Toulouse Pronouncing His Vows Before Boniface VIII*. In these large compositions, which still show the influence of Pietro, the scenes take place against an architectural background that stresses successive picture planes. They date from about 1330. The *Presentation in the Temple*, signed and dated 1342 (Florence, Uffizi), and the *Annunciation*, signed and dated 1344 (Siena, Pinacoteca), belong to Ambrogio's mature period, as do the two surprising landscapes "without a sky," the *Town on the Sea* and the *Castle by a Lake* (both Siena, Pinacoteca).

The two frescoes of *Good Government* and *Bad Government* in the Sala dei Nove in the Palazzo Pubblico, Siena, were rightly famous from the time they were painted. Their date is unknown; those suggested range anywhere between 1338 and 1348. In these two compositions (*Good Government* is in a good state of preservation, while the other has deteriorated), subjects are complex, and the ideas are expressed both through symbols and allegories and through realistic scenes of great charm.

LORENZETTI, Pietro (*c.* 1280, Siena—1348, Siena), Italian painter. In 1306 a panel intended for the Palazzo Pubblico in Siena was bought for 100 lire from a certain Petruccio di Lorenzo. It may in fact have been Pietro Lorenzetti, in which case 1306 would be the first documented date in his career. We know little about his life between 1306 and 1320: during this period Pietro remained within the Sienese tradition, that is to say, the Byzantine tradition interpreted and modified by Duccio. The first surviving work that we can attribute to him is the *Virgin* in the Collegiata at Casole d'Elsa. After 1320, traces of his activity are more numerous, and his development is easier to follow. The polyptych in S. Maria della Pieve at Arezzo bears his signature; it is not dated but was commissioned in 1320 and must have been painted then. It shows the combined influences of Gothic miniatures and Giovanni Pisano's sculpture, but reveals above all Pietro's personal temperament and his sense of drama, apparent in the two panels of the Virgin, with the Child and the angel Gabriel. Of the polyptych painted for the church of S. Maria del Carmine in Siena (dated 1329), the central part (the *Virgin and Child*), formerly at Dofana, was reunited with the predella in the Siena Pinacoteca. The wings have been lost.

The frescoes of the Orsini Chapel (Lower Church of S. Francesco at Assisi), attributed by Vasari to Cavallini and Giotto, have now been restored to Lorenzetti and his pupils. If modern art historians agree on the attribution, they disagree on the date, which they situate between 1320 and 1340. The paintings are arranged in three levels: on the lower tier are varied scenes and figures of saints; above, filling the upper part of the wall and the vault, is a *Passion* cycle composed of 11 scenes, with the last 5 (from the *Crucifixion* to the *Descent into Limbo*) by Lorenzetti's own hand. Belonging to the final period are the *Virgin* (dated 1340) and the *Beata Umiltà* polyptych (1341), both in the Uffizi, Florence. The masterpiece of Pietro's last period is the *Birth of the Virgin*, dated 1342 (Siena, Opera del Duomo), in which the violent drama of the Assisi paintings is replaced by a serene spiritual atmosphere.

LORENZO DI CREDI (*c.* 1456, Florence—1537, Florence), Italian painter. He joined Verrocchio's workshop, where, by 1480, he was virtually supervisor of all the painting work and, in his will, Verrocchio put him in charge of all commissions. It is therefore difficult to sort out Lorenzo's youthful work. The difficulty is increased by the fact that his carefully accurate manner does not show much development, although his works extend over a long period; but the *Madonna with Sts. Julian and Nicholas* (Paris, Louvre), dated 1493, provides us with a good point of reference. The *St. Bartholomew* in Or San Michele, Florence, was mentioned by Francesco Albertini in 1510. The *St. Michael* for the vestry of Florence Cathedral was painted in 1523. It is not always easy to place between these known dates the various altarpieces whose precise contours, bright colors, and careful modeling in half tones allow us to attribute them to Lorenzo.

Lorenzo's manner, Vasari tells us, was so close to Leonardo's that their works could be confused; Lorenzo particularly admired Leonardo's "clarity and finish." He studied the modeling of figures on salmon-pink or gray sheets of paper (*carta tinta*), many of which are still extant. In the *Virgin and Child* tondo (Rome, Galleria Borghese), in which he used the pyramidal composition of Leonardo, he added a craftsman's integrity to Classical assurance.

LORENZO MONACO, Piero di Giovanni, *called* (*c.* 1370, Siena—after 1422, Florence), Italian painter. He was brought up in the tradition of the great 14th-century Sienese masters, but his mature period was influenced by the Florentines, particularly Andrea Orcagna. Lorenzo spent part of his time illuminating manuscripts, especially between 1409 and 1413. In his paintings he used the vivid, clear tones of manuscript illumination; but his light effects and his attempt at depth reveal a far wider range. His delicate, weightless figures and decorative backgrounds place his work in the mainstream of the Late Gothic International Style. Apart from the badly preserved frescoes in the Convent of the Oblates in Florence, Lorenzo left mainly altar paintings, now scattered among many Italian and foreign museums. The most famous are in Florence: the *Annunciation* (1408–9) at the Accademia, the *Adoration of the Magi* (1410) and the *Coronation of the Virgin* (1413), both at the Uffizi.

L'ORME, Philibert de (*c.* 1505/10, Lyons—1570, Paris), French architect. He was the son of one of the most highly esteemed master masons of Lyons; therefore, by the time he went to Rome in 1533, he had already become acquainted with the technical difficulties inherent in the art of building. During his stay there De l'Orme studied the Roman remains and

Philibert de l'Orme. Chapel of the château at Anet. 1549–52. *Photo Jean Roubier, Paris.*

made drawings of fragments. He met the great Italian architects of the day, and won the friendship of his first patrons: Marcello Cervino (the future Pope Marcellus II) and Cardinal Jean du Bellay, the ambassador of King François I.

On his return to France in 1536, De l'Orme built a gallery, supported by squinches and divided by Ionic pilasters, in the Lyons residence of Antoine Bullioud, the treasurer of Brittany. Probably on a recommendation from Bullioud, De l'Orme was appointed by François I to inspect the Breton fortresses. His first important commission was for the building of the château of St-Maur-lès-Fossés, near Paris, for Cardinal du Bellay (probably begun about 1541); the building was designed in a classicizing Italianate style, with a single order of Corinthian pilasters inside and out. At the end of 1547 or the beginning of 1548, just after completing St-Maur, De l'Orme was commissioned by Henri II to build the tomb of Henri's predecessor, François I, in the Parisian church of St-Denis. For Henri II he also completed (1548–after 1550) the Sainte-Chapelle at Vincennes in the old Gothic style, and (*c.* 1548) the chapel at Villers-Cotteret, which—like the tomb of François I—was remarkable as an adaptation of Classical Roman design. Another royal commission entailed considerable extensions to the château at Fontainebleau: De l'Orme designed the Cour du Cheval Blanc, with its alternating rhythm of pavilions and recessions; rooms in the Pavillon des Poêles; some alterations in the Galerie d'Ulysse; and the roofing of the Chapelle Haute. All these works were subsequently either destroyed or rebuilt.

For Diane de Poitiers, Henri's mistress, De l'Orme built the château of Anet, near the border between the Île-de-France and Normandy. The two wings were constructed in 1549–51, the chapel in 1549–52, and the entrance pavilion in 1552. Although most of it was demolished after the French Revolution, the parts still standing are among the most admirable extant examples of his work.

Around 1558 De l'Orme reached the peak of a career characterized by rapid success: Henri II had showered him with favors, and on his accession in 1547 had appointed him his official architect. After the king's death in 1559, De l'Orme was replaced in his posts as Superintendent of Buildings and Master of Accounts, and devoted his time to writing.

When Catherine de Médicis became De l'Orme's new patron, she commissioned two works from him: the modeling and extension of the château of St-Maur, which she had bought in 1563 from the heirs of Cardinal du Bellay, and a palace near the Louvre in Paris, on a site known as La Sablonnière, or Les Tuileries. De l'Orme was commissioned to carry out the work in 1563, but only one building—comprising five pavilions linked by galleries—was actually built (demolished 1884).

LORRAIN *or* **LORRAINE,** Claude Gellée, *called* Claude (1600, Chamagne, Vosges—1682, Rome), French painter. In 1613 he accompanied a lace merchant to Rome and then went on to Naples, where it is thought that he joined the studio of the Flemish-born painter Goffredo Wals. Claude returned to Rome around 1619 and entered the service of the Italian landscape painter Agostino Tassi (*c.* 1580–1644). In 1625 he returned to his native Chamagne. He was presented to Claude Deruet (1588–1660), painter to the duke of Lorraine, who employed him on the decoration of the vault in the Carmelite church at Nancy (*c.* 1626; destroyed). But the artist did not care for his task and set off once more for Italy, passing through Lyons and Marseilles. A pen sketch, representing the *Harbor at Marseilles* (1634; Leningrad, Hermitage), is his oldest known drawing.

Claude Lorrain. *Seaport.* Bayerische Staatsgemäldesammlungen, Munich.

In 1627 Claude again arrived in Rome, where he spent the remainder of his long life, traveling tirelessly over the Roman countryside and studying its landscapes. He showed little interest in foreground details, but strove to evoke fleeting horizons, the vibration of the air, the envelopment of light, and everything beyond the middle ground, thereby becoming the master of the "landscape of atmosphere."

In 1637 Philippe de Béthune, the French ambassador to the Vatican, bought two of Claude's paintings: *View of the Campo Vaccino* (1636) and *View of a Seaport: Effect of the Rising Sun* (1636)—both now in the Louvre, Paris—which constitute his early delicate, glowing manner. In 1639 Pope Urban VIII commissioned four others, including a *Seaport at Sunset* and a *Village Fete* (both Louvre). In 1644 Claude began his *Liber Veritatis* ("Book of Truth"), a collection of 195 drawings (portions of which are in the British Museum, London), copied from his paintings and bearing the names of their buyers. The reason for compiling these drawings was that a number of forgeries had been made of his very popular works, and the artist wished to be protected with this register; but it is also thought that these sketches were used by him as a record of the compositions themselves.

Claude's mature period produced a number of serene seascapes glowing with light (*Embarkation of the Queen of Sheba*, 1648; London, National Gallery), and landscapes in which he some-

Claude Lorrain. *Trees and Foliage.* Musée des Beaux-Arts, Besançon. *Photo Giraudon, Paris.*

Lorenzo Lotto. *Young man in a Striped Coat.* 1526. Castello Sforzesco, Milan. *Photo Anderson-Giraudon.*

times used one of his favorite devices: a contrast between the shadows cast by a large central clump of trees and the rays of light. He was also a very original engraver, and in his etchings—the most famous of which include *Sunrise* (1634) and the *Cowherd* (1636)—he succeeded in rendering the same subtle play of light and shade as in his paintings.

With the development of his mature style, Claude tried his hand at historical landscape, using dramatic scenes taken from the Bible (*Marriage of Isaac and Rebecca*, also called the *Mill*, 1648; London, National Gallery) or from mythology (*Ulysses Returning Chryseis to Her Father*, 1647; Louvre). In the mid-1650s he began painting with an accentuated impasto and a vigorous handling. The *Four Hours of the Day* (1667–72; Leningrad, Hermitage) are fine examples of this late style.

LOTTO, Lorenzo (*c.* 1480, Venice—1556, Loreto), Italian painter. Lotto was one of the great portraitists of the Renaissance or, as the critic Bernard Berenson called him, "a psychological painter." His early works include the strange portrait of *Bishop Bernardo de' Rossi*, with pinks and reds on a green background (1505; Naples, Museo di Capodimonte); the *St. Jerome in the Wilderness* (1506; Paris, Louvre), which devotes unusual importance to the landscape; and the large *Recanati Polyptych* (1508; Recanati, Pinacoteca), with its famous scene of the *Annunciation*.

In 1509, Lotto's reputation was high enough for him to be among the first group of artists commissioned to decorate the Vatican Stanze. He was dismissed, along with the others, when Pope Julius II entrusted Raphael with the direction of the works. After a brief return to Venice in 1513, Lotto settled in Bergamo, where he painted a large and grandiose altarpiece of the *Virgin Enthroned* with 10 saints for the church of S. Bartolomeo (1516); the *Virgin with Four Saints*, a fresh and lively work, for S. Spirito (1521); and a *Madonna and Child*, also with four saints, for the church of S. Bernardino (1521). In the frescoes for the Oratorio Suardi in Trescore, near Bergamo (1524), Lotto displays the same taste for popular illustration that was to become more marked in his later work.

The supremacy of Titian in Venice left no place for an old-fashioned artist such as Lotto, who went on painting rather heavily and in cold colors. The artist found more clients in The Marches: his *St. Lucy* altarpiece (1532) was for Iesi; and his *Crucifixion* (1531) was for the church of S. Maria in Telusiano at Monte San Giusto, near Macerata. He gradually stopped trying to paint in the grand style, becoming more direct and more moving, as in the altarpiece depicting the *Madonna of the Rosary* (1539; Cingoli, S. Domenico); or in the *Madonna with Saints* (1546; Ancona, S. Maria della Piazza).

Lotto's many portraits are less uneven than his religious compositions and reveal more clearly his main characteristics: they have the smooth technique and bold effects of the Venetians Giovanni Bellini and Alvise Vivarini, along with velvety accents and a sort of melancholy undertone that becomes increasingly noticeable in the dreamy and anxious faces of his models: the *Young Man in a Striped Coat* (1526; Milan, Castello Sforzesco); *Andrea Odoni* (1527; Hampton Court, Royal Collection); the *Young Man in His Study* (*c.* 1524; Venice, Accademia); and the *Old Man with a Blond Beard* (1542; Milan, Brera). Lotto's landscapes are original and strangely frightening. In *Susanna and the Elders* (1517; Florence, Coll. Contini-Bonacossi) the crowded, asymmetrical effect is particularly marked.

LOUIS, Louis Bernstein, *called* Morris (1912, Baltimore, Maryland—1962, Washington, D.C.), American painter. Louis' work developed in a late Cubist manner until 1953, when he became influenced by the current mode of painterly Expressionism. His work was to become a bridge from this Cubist-based Expressionistic Abstraction to a kind of painting that aimed for an independent and open color expression. His work changed abruptly after 1952, when Louis was introduced to Jackson Pollock's large "drip" paintings of 1947–50, and after an important meeting with the painter Helen Frankenthaler, who showed him how to paint without brushes by staining unsized canvas with poured acrylic paint. The linear overall patterning of his earlier works was transformed into successive vertical waves, stained like translucent curtains into the fabric of the canvas in a series known as the "Veils," done in 1954 and again in 1958 (*Tet*, 1958; New York, Whitney Museum). The plumes and crests of the "Veils" were released into more haphazard floral petals and ribbons in 1960–61 (the "Florals" or "Aleph" series) and into columns and clusters of interweaving color. After 1961, partly in response to the work of his friend Kenneth Noland, Louis painted his "Unfurled" series (*Sigma*, 1961; New York, Priv. Coll.), in which brilliant rivulets of color in parallel streams flow across the lower corners of otherwise blank fields. A further development of this approach appeared in the "Stripe" or "Pillar" paintings from late 1961–62 (*Third Element*, 1962; New York, Museum of Modern Art).

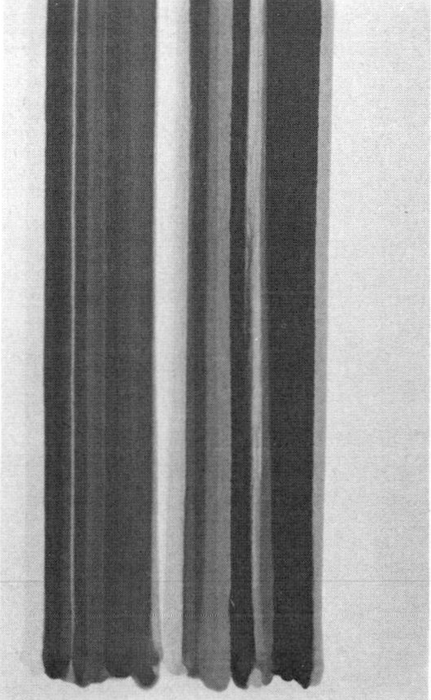

Morris Louis. *Third Element.* 1962. Museum of Modern Art, New York.

LOUIS, Nicolas, *called* Victor (1731, Paris—1800, Paris), French architect. The Hôtel de l'Intendance of Besançon, its fine façade adorned in the center with a circular projection, was his first important contribution (1771–78). It was soon followed by his masterpiece, the Grand Théâtre at Bordeaux (1773–80). This theater, which has a colossal peristyle in front, crowned with 12 figures by the sculptor Pierre-François Berruer (1733–97), is surrounded on the other sides by a vaulted gallery which is interrupted on the back wall by stairways giving access to the stage machinery. Louis also built the Rolly, Saige, Nairac, and Boyer-Fontfrède hôtels; the Château du Bouilh; and many other residences in and around Bordeaux.

When the Duc de Chartres decided to enlarge the Palais-Royal in Paris and to build arcades with shops around the garden, he summoned Louis, a fellow Freemason, to be the architect. This scheme was realized with lightning rapidity. In its succession of precisely similar bays, the ensemble is reminiscent of Roman monuments as well as of Vincenzo Scamozzi's Procuratie Nuove of Venice. This uniformity reigns along the whole length of the building, interrupted only at one corner of the palace by the playhouse (1786–90), which, as the Théâtre-Français, later became the home of the Comédie-Française.

LOUIS XIII STYLE. For some years after the assassination of Henri IV (1610), Marie de Médicis acted as regent and continued her husband's artistic policy.

In 1614 Louix XIII came of age, and 10 years later entrusted the direction of the government to Cardinal Richelieu. The *premier ministre* took a most exalted view of kingship and its duties, urging Louix XIII to patronize artists and to increase the number of official commissions.

When Richelieu and Louis XIII died within six months of each other (December 1642 and May 1643, respectively), the regent, Anne of Austria, was immediately confronted with the problems they left—an endless foreign war and a great number of internal disorders. Her first minister, Jules Mazarin, directed French politics from 1643 until his death in 1661. He was a man of taste and an avid collector; thus the arts flourished during the ministries of Richelieu and Mazarin, although this was largely due to the great rise in the wealth of the middle classes.

For reasons of prestige, Louis XIII commissioned Jacques Lemercier to handle the additions to the Palais du Louvre (Pavillon de l'Horloge, 1624; west wing, 1627), while Richelieu gave him the commission for the Palais Cardinal (1629–36, now Palais-Royal), Paris, as well as for the château and town of Richelieu (both begun 1631), near Tours. Anne of Austria and Mazarin continued this official program: under their aegis the Louvre (north and east wings and the Cour du Sphinx by Lemercier until 1654, then by Louis Le Vau) and the Palais Mazarin (perhaps by François Mansart, begun 1633; now Bibliothèque Nationale) were constructed in Paris. Salomon de Brosse (1565–1629), Lemercier, Le Vau, Pierre Le Muet, and François Mansart devoted much of their time to building châteaux and *hôtels* ("town houses") for the *noblesse d'épée* (old nobility) and the *noblesse de robe* (new "nobility"—the professional class).

The Catholic revival in the early years of the century brought with it a demand for many new churches and monasteries. In Paris, the Jesuits, guided by the architect Father Étienne Martellange, commissioned the church of St-Paul-St-Louis (François Devand [1588–1644], 1627–41) and the chapel of the Maison Professe (designed 1630; today Church of St-Paul), a direct imitation of Il Gesù, the major Jesuit church in Rome. In a similar style of great nobility and severity were St-Gervais (De Brosse, 1616), and the churches of the Sorbonne (Lemercier, 1635–40) and Val-de-Grâce (Mansart, 1645–46; dome and church above first cornice, Lemercier, after 1646), all in Paris. For reasons of economy, the town planning of Louis XIII was less systematic than that of his father. However, he granted sites that were developed very successfully (Île St-Louis, Paris, 1614–30). In painting and sculpture, as well as in architecture, French Classicism developed and matured.

Simon Vouet was by far the most brilliant decorator of the period. In 1627, he became first painter to Louis XIII. He then executed some important decorations (including those for the Louvre and the Luxembourg Palace), which, unfortunately, did not survive, and he received commissions for a large number of altarpieces. Jacques Blanchard (1600–38) also achieved a reputation for his religious compositions. François Perrier painted the gallery of the Hôtel Le Vrillière (*c.* 1645; now Banque de France) in an elegant but powerful style. The Mannerist Claude Vignon, whose use of paint shows the influence of Rembrandt, specialized in literary and Biblical scenes painted in brilliant colors, with theatrical effects (*Washing of the Feet*, 1653; Nantes, Museum).

All the painters so far mentioned studied for a few years in Italy; others were so enamored of Rome that they spent their adult lives there. Poussin loved the landscapes around Rome, which he left for only two years when he returned to Paris to work in the Louvre. His work was taken as the model by all 17th-century Classical artists and by generations of French painters thereafter. Claude Lorrain, the second major talent in French painting of the period, specialized in evoking the lyrical poetry of foliage and the sumptuous harmonies of sunsets over the Italian sea (*Medici Seascape*; Florence, Uffizi). Moïse de Valentin (1591–1632), a disciple of Caravaggio in Rome, used his master's color and chiaroscuro effects, while imbuing his pictures with a grave melancholy (*The Concert*; Louvre).

This sobriety was also dominant in Paris. Philippe de Champaigne, a naturalized Belgian, was an austere religious painter but a robust portraitist. The Le Nain brothers introduced a sense of human dignity into peasant genre scenes. A number of minor Classicists rallied around Charles Le Brun, who was able to obtain the king's approval for a Royal Academy of Painting and Sculp-

Louis XIII Style. François Mansart. Château de Balleroy, Calvados. 1626–36. *Photo Connaissance des Arts, Paris.*

Louis XIII Style. Abraham Bosse. *Gentleman in the age of Louis XIII.* Bibliothèque Nationale, Paris. *Photo Roger-Viollet, Paris.*

ture in 1648. These painters included Laurent de La Hyre, influenced by Poussin; Jacques Stella (1596–1657), whose style is imbued with austere calm; Sébastien Bourdon, who was an able practitioner in all styles and subject matter, from the Biblical picture to the elegant portrait; and Eustache Le Sueur, who decorated the Chambre des Muses of the Hôtel Lambert (1647–49; Louvre). Mention should also be made of Lubin Baugin, with his refined line and subtle color; landscape artists, such as Jacques Fouquier (1580/90–1659) and Jean Lemaire (1598–1659); still-life painters, such as Jacques Linard and Louise Moillon (1610–96); and, finally, the engravers Abraham Bosse, who specialized in scenes from the lives of the bourgeoisie, and Pierre Brébiette (1598–1650), who produced some charming mythological pieces.

In the provinces the prevailing artistic situation was much the same, though modified by local influences and particularly by a stronger penetration of Caravaggism. At Nancy Claude Deruet (1588–1660) and Jacques Callot were active; at Lunéville there was the remarkable and unique Georges de La Tour; at Toulouse there were Friar Ambroise Fredeau (1589–1673), Guy François (1580–1650), and, above all, Nicolas Tournier (1590–after 1660); Philippe Quentin (*c.* 1600–1636) and Richard Tassel practiced in Burgundy.

French sculpture of the 17th century did not attain the heights of architecture and painting, but there was nevertheless a great deal of activity, since the devotional revival of the Counter Reformation demanded an abundance of statues, altars, and tombs. Jacques Sarazin, a Baroque artist while in Italy, became a Classicist in France, where he gathered around him a number of sculptors, including Philippe Buyster (1595–1688), Gérard van Obstal (1594–1668), and Gilles Guérin (1609–78). The latter proved a skillful technician, and Simon Guillain (*c.* 1581–1658) cast the very fine statues of *Louis XIII, Anne of Austria*, and *Louis XIV* for the monument on the Pont-au-Change, Paris (1647; Louvre). The sculptors François (1604–69) and Michel (1612–86) Anguier introduced the style of Alessandro Algardi to France.

Louis XIII Style. Simon Guillain. *Statue of Louis XIII.* 1647. Louvre, Paris. *Photo Alinari.*

LOUIS XIV STYLE. When the young Louis XIV assumed direction of the French state in 1661, he intended to enlist the support of carefully chosen ministers. Accordingly, in 1664, he made Jean-Baptiste Colbert finance minister and superintendent of buildings. Le Brun, protected by Chancellor Séguier and by Colbert, was appointed first painter to the king (1664) and director to the Gobelins tapestry works. In 1648 the Académie Royale de Peinture et de Sculpture was founded; the king protected the new body, gave it a monopoly of teaching, and, through Le Brun, brought it directly under his own patronage. The Academy thus became recognized as an instrument of the royal will. In addition, Louis XIV founded (1666) the Académie de France in Rome, to provide young artists with lodgings and enable them to maintain a constant link with the art of Italy.

The artistic policy of the Sun King was expressed above all in the extraordinary architectural and decorative unity of the Château de Versailles, where Louis XIV wanted to create a uniquely magnificent setting for his own apotheosis. In 1661 Le Vau began to enlarge the small château built by Louis XIII. Louis XIV next ordered the same architect to transform these buildings, which were then surrounded on three sides by a new palace (1668–71), decorated by Le Brun. In 1678 Jules Hardouin-Mansart gave the château its present Classical nobility by the use of the colossal order and the supremacy of horizontal

Louis XIV Style. François Girardon. *Equestrian statue of Louis XIV.* Château de Versailles. *Photo Alinari-Viollet.*

lines. Le Nôtre created an immense park in the formal Classical style, with a complex interplay of vast perspectives and calm artificial lakes accentuating the architectural form.

A vast building program was undertaken at the palace of the Louvre: its quadrilateral was enclosed by Le Vau (1659–64), and the famous Colonnade was built (1667–73) under the supervision of Le Brun and Le Vau. Libéral Bruant built the Hôtel des Invalides (1671–76), a hostel for veteran soldiers, with a long, severe façade and a *cour d'honneur* with a double Tuscan portico. Its famous and magnificently proportioned dome was added later by Hardouin-Mansart (1679–1706). The king's activities in Paris in the sphere of town planning included long avenues with particularly harmonious perspectives, triumphal gates (Nicolas-François Blondel's Porte St-Denis, 1672), and numerous royal squares. The latter included the Place des Victoires (1685–92) and the Place Vendôme (1677–98), both designed by Hardouin-Mansart. Town houses were also built for nobles and rich bourgeois families: Hardouin-Mansart's Hôtel Fieubert (1676–81), Pierre Bullet's Hôtel Le Peletier de St-Fargeau (1687), and René Alexis Delamair's (1675–1745) Hôtel de Rohan (1704–10; today the Archives Nationales).

By 1664, of the Parisian painters who had banded together to create the Academy, only Charles Errard (*c.* 1606–89) and Pierre Mignard remained to rival Le Brun. Errard was offered a gilded exile as director of the Académie de Rome, a coveted post for which Mignard had waited a long time. The death of Colbert, the support of the war minister Marquis de Louvois, and the old age of the king enabled Mignard at last to replace Le Brun in 1690. For 26 years Le Brun was assisted by devoted decorators (the Testelin brothers, Noël Coypel [1628–1707], the Boullongne family, and René Artoine Houasse [1644–1710]), highly skillful landscape painters (Adam François van der Meulen [1632–90]), painters of battle scenes (Joseph Parrocel), and still-life specialists (Jean-Baptiste Monnoyer). Le Brun actively protected his best pupils: they included Charles de La Fosse (fresco in the dome of the Invalides, 1705) and Jean Jouvenet.

In 1671 a quarrel broke out among the members of the Academy over color. In a number of theoretical writings, the critic Roger de Piles attacked the academic doctrines of Poussin, exalting instead the color of Rubens and the Moderns. As a result, the Academy was divided for 30 years between opposing "poussiniste" and "rubeniste" factions. Peace came with the admission of Roger de Piles into the Academy, thus ensuring a victory for the Moderns. The portraitists of the latter part of the century favored brilliant, sometimes mannered effects: Pierre Mignard received a large number of official commissions and was first painter to the king from 1690 to 1695; Hyacinthe Rigaud (*Louis XIV*, 1701; Louvre), Nicolas de Largillière, and François de Troy were also much in demand.

Louis XIV Style *Louis XIV Visiting the Gobelins Factory on October 15, 1667*. Tapestry based on the cartoon by Charles Le Brun. 1673–79. Detail. Mobilier National, Paris.

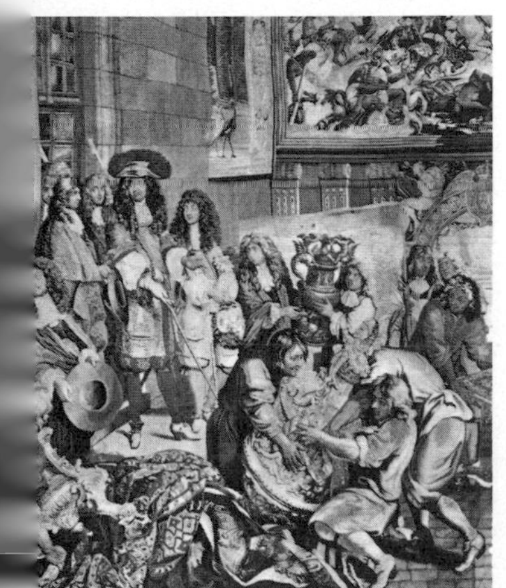

Sculpture, which was an important branch of art under Louis XIV, was strictly controlled by the rules of the Academy. In accord with Le Nôtre, Le Brun chose subjects from the critic Cesare Ripa's *Iconology* (one of the major handbooks of the Baroque period), and provided the sculptors with drawings of the works required. The sculptors working at Versailles included François Girardon (*Apollo Served by the Nymphs*, 1666–75), Gaspard and Balthasar Marsy (*Bassin de Latone*, 1668–71), Martin van den Bogaert Desjardins (*Diana*, 1680), Étienne Le Hongre (*Air*, 1674), and Antoine Coysevox (the *Garonne*, 1686). The same sculptors carved some fine portrait busts, majestic statues of the king, and admirable tombs. Pierre Puget, who worked at Toulon in uncompromising isolation, was much influenced by Bernini (*Milo of Crotona*, 1682; Louvre).

His patronage extending to the minor arts, Louis XIV established (1662) the royal Gobelins factory, under the direction of Le Brun. Royal furniture was made in a spirit of splendor: marble mosaics in the Florentine style, ceremonial furniture in precious metals, carved gilt wood, or (as in examples by the cabinet-maker André Charles Boulle, 1642–1732) sumptuously inlaid with copper and shells.

LOUIS XV STYLE. Louis XV was interested above all in architecture, but he also commissioned a large number of decorative works for his various residences. In this sphere, he left complete power in the hands of his favorite mistress, Madame de Pompadour, whose tastes gave new impetus to Parisian artists. She defended such architects as Jacques-Ange Gabriel, increased the number of royal purchases, and took an active interest in the Sèvres porcelain factory.

In addition to royal patronage, there was growing in Paris an artistic life strongly influenced, as it was to be in the 19th and 20th centuries, by the personalities and theories of intellectuals. There was a proliferation of *salons* and exhibitions, and art criticism made its appearance with Denis Diderot's famous *Salons*. Artists sought to satisfy the needs of their new clientele by producing "attractive" paintings that would fit easily into the decoration of their homes.

Louis XIV Style. Louis Le Vau, Claude Perrault, and others. Colonnade of the Louvre, Paris. 1667–73. *Photo Décor, Paris.*

The return to antiquity, which began around the middle of the 18th century, was therefore at first the work of philosophers, scholars, and archaeologists. Thus, the abandonment of Rococo for the austere Neoclassical style actually began under the reign of Louis XV, before reaching its zenith during that of Louis XVI.

On the whole, architecture rejected the excesses of the European Rococo style and remained faithful to Classical traditions. Louis XV himself took a lively interest in the building of Jacques-Ange Gabriel's Opera House (1753–70) and of his Petit Trianon (1762–68), both at Versailles. This period saw the building of a number of huge town houses, with severe porches, but with harmonious façades overlooking courtyards and gardens—as in the Hôtel Peyrenc de Moras, today the Hôtel Biron (1728–30) by Gabriel and Jean Aubert. Smaller houses were often decorated with remarkable painted paneling, stucco- and plasterwork (Germain Boffrand, Hôtel de Soubise, 1740). The reign of Louis XV was a great period in town planning both for Paris and the provinces. Magnificent royal squares were built: the Place Louis XV in Paris (designed by Gabriel from 1760; known today as the Place de la Concorde); the Place

Louis XV Style. Jacques-Ange Gabriel. Petit Trianon, Versailles. 1762–68. *Photo Courteville-Réalités, Paris.*

Louis XV Style. Jean-Marc Nattier. *Duchesse de Chartres as Hebe.* 1745. Nationalmuseum, Stockholm.

Stanislas (1752–55) in Nancy (formerly called the Place Royale; designed by Héré [1705–63] and decorated by Jean Lamour [1698–1771]); the Place de la Bourse (formerly Place Royale) in Bordeaux by Gabriel. Some provincial cities built new Town Halls—such as those at Metz (Jacques-François Blondel, 1764–75) and at Rennes (Gabriel, 1726–44)—while others erected gateways, fountains, or laid out gardens. Religious architecture was represented by the building of such important churches as Jacques Soufflot's colossal Ste-Geneviève in Paris (after 1754; known today as the Panthéon) or the solemn façade of St-Sulpice, also in Paris (*c.* 1732), by Jean-Nicolas Servandoni (1695–1766).

The situation in painting was much more complex. Charles de La Fosse, with his warm tones, Jean Jouvenet, with his harsh color, and Louis de Boullongne the Younger (1654–1733) were still the king's principal painters. Antoine Coypel (1661–1722) decorated the vault of the royal chapel at Versailles (1709–10); François Lemoyne painted the ceiling of the Salon d'Hercule at Versailles (1733–36); and the great Antoine Watteau employed a Flemish palette for his *fêtes galantes*. The latter influenced a number of minor masters, such as Jean-Baptiste Pater (1695–1736) and Nicolas Lancret (1690–1743), who perpetuated his manner but with a use of fantasy that verges on the vulgar. Jean II Restout (1692–1768) remained strictly a religious painter of great elegance and refinement, while Jean-François de Troy, Carle van Loo, and Charles Natoire (1700–77) painted historical and religious works of great magnificence.

Although there was considerable development in the portrait, works in this genre were generally ceremonial effigies, in which the subject was portrayed in stereotyped attitudes. After Hyacinthe Rigaud and Nicolas de Largillière—both of whom remained faithful to the style of the *Grand Siècle*—came Jean-Marc Nattier, who painted some splendidly elegant, seminude portraits, Jean-Baptiste Santerre, and Jean Raoux. François-Hubert Drouais specialized in producing charming, rather facile portraits of children. Joseph Aved (1702–56), Louis Tocqué (1696–1772), and Joseph Vivien adopted a more realistic and more powerful style. Maurice Quentin de La Tour executed some admirable pastels in which psychology is expressed in exquisite subtleties of color. This painter influenced that vagabond iconographer of the bourgeoisie, Jean-Baptiste Perronneau. François Desportes and Jean-Baptiste Oudry specialized in genre scenes and still lifes, but neither was the equal of Jean-Baptiste Siméon Chardin, the poet of domestic life, and one of the great masters of the still life. Joseph-Marie Vien (1716–1809), who enjoyed the patronage of Madame de Pompadour, took his models from antiquity, and at the Salon of 1761 submitted a *Greek Girl at the Bath* (Priv. Coll.) that was already typical of the Neoclassical style. At the same time, the second half of the 18th century saw the appearance of paintings in which grandiloquent sentiments or moving situations were presented. Jean-Baptiste Greuze (1725–1805) was particularly successful in this genre (the *Village Bride*, 1761; Louvre). The career of Jean-Honoré Fragonard, on the other hand, shows a reaction against this sentimentality and the preference of a large public for the detached manner and intense colors of a skillful painter.

The reign of Louis XV was particularly favored by sculpture. Whole families of sculptors first (until 1760) maintained the traditions of Antoine Coysevox, with the addition of certain Baroque influences; later they turned to a stricter imitation of antiquity. Sculptors were employed principally by the Crown on the decoration of the royal residences at Versailles, Marly, and Bellevue, and their work was largely allegorical or mythological. There flourished a Rococo style of great elegance, as exemplified in the famous *Maria Leszczynska as Juno* (1731; Louvre) by Guillaume Coustou. The Baroque style was particularly successful in funerary sculpture, such as the tomb of Languet de Gergy (1753; Paris, St-Sulpice) by René Michel Slodtz (1705–64) or the mausoleum of Marshal de Saxe by Jean-Baptiste Pigalle (1753–76; Strasbourg, St-Thomas). Edmé Bouchardon, Slodtz, and above all Jean-Baptiste Lemoyne, the sculptor of Louis XV and the creator of some splendid marble and terra-cotta busts (*Montesquieu*, 1761; Bordeaux, Musée des Beaux-Arts), excelled in the realistic portrait, and strove to convey the living expression of the model.

Bouchardon was more of a Classicist than his contemporaries, and in his *Fountain of the Four Seasons* on Rue de Grenelle, Paris (1739–45), he foreshadowed the Neoclassical Louis XVI style. Étienne Falconet created a synthesis of Classical allusion and Rococo prettiness. He was followed in this direction by the talented Pigalle, who was quite capable of carrying realism to the point of paradox (*Nude Voltaire*, 1776; Paris, Institut).

The decorative, highly refined furniture of the period used carved wood (either gilded or painted), veneering with rare essences, inlaid work with exotic woods, japanning or its imitations (Martin varnish), Rococo bronzes, and rich marbles. Tapestry continued to flourish at the Gobelins and at Beauvais under the direction first of Jean-Baptiste Oudry, then of François Boucher. Tapestries were woven from cartoons by Charles-Antoine Coypel (1694–1752), Jean-François de Troy, and Oudry. Carpets were executed at the Savonnerie, delicate silks at Lyons, and chintzes at Jouy. Hard-paste faïence flour-

Louis XV Style. Antoine Coysevox. *Marie Adélaïde de Savoie, Duchesse de Bourgogne.* 1681. Versailles.

Louis XV Style. Edmé Bouchardon. *Summer.* 1739–45. Fountain of the Four Seasons, Paris. *Photo Giraudon.*

Louis XVI Style. Richard Mique. Temple of Love in the garden of the Petit Trianon, Versailles. 1778. *Photo Ciccione-Rapho, Paris.*

ished at Moustiers and at Rouen, soft-paste porcelain at Marseilles, Sceaux, and Strasbourg, while fine china was manufactured at Pont-aux-Choux. Delicate porcelain came above all from the Vincennes factory, which had become the Royal Manufactory of Sèvres.

LOUIS XVI STYLE. When Louis XVI succeeded his father in 1774, the Neoclassical style was already fully developed. In fact, it was inspired above all by the mode of decoration and by the objects discovered by archaeologists at Herculaneum and Pompeii, which Charles-Nicolas Cochin (1715–90) had publicized in France with his *Observations sur les antiquités d'Herculanum* (1754).

Architecture during the reign of Louis XVI still used the Classical orders, but with great sobriety of line and decoration. The king built very little for his own use, but commissioned Richard Mique (1728–94) to build a small Greek-style building, the Temple of Love (1778), and the charmingly rustic Hamlet or Hameau (1780) in the gardens of the Petit Trianon for Marie-Antoinette. Louis XVI was more concerned with town planning: in Paris he ordered the building of the Pont de la Concorde by Jean-Rodolphe Perronet (1786) and the outer walls of the Fermiers Généraux (1784), with its pavilions built by Claude-Nicolas Ledoux. While Jacques-Denis Antoine was completing the Hôtel des Monnaies in Paris (1768–75), the sovereign ordered further building in Paris: the Collège de France by Jean-François Chalgrin (1778) and the École de Chirurgie by Jacques Gondoin (1769–75). The Duc d'Orléans commissioned Victor Louis to surround the gardens of the Palais-Royal with buildings punctuated with arcades and colossal fluted pilasters (1781–84). The provinces could also boast of buildings of the highest order, such as Louis' magnificent Grand Théâtre in Bordeaux (1773–80) and Ledoux's theater at Besançon (1777). And up to the time of the French Revolution, architects in Paris were still building churches influenced by the plan of Roman basilicas, such as St-Philippe-du-Roulle by Chalgrin (1769–84) and St-Louis-d'Antin by Alexandre Brongniart (1781), and, above all, Ste-Geneviève (today the Panthéon), which was begun (1764–80) by Jacques Soufflot and completed (1789–90) by Maximilien Brébion (1716–after 1786) and Jean-Baptiste Rondelet.

Most of the leading artists of the reign of Louis XVI were, in fact, already famous before the king's accession. Jean-Baptiste Greuze (1725–1805), a skillful portraitist, also painted moralizing and sentimental genre scenes, while Jean-Honoré Fragonard excelled in the most varied genres; he was imitated by Nicolas Bernard Lépicié (1735–84), a genre painter and pleasing colorist. With Joseph-Marie Vien (1716–1809), the director of the École de Rome in 1775, Neoclassicism became the official style. Vien sent to the Salons the Greek-style canvases of his pupils Jean Peyron, François-André Vincent, Joseph Benoît Suvée, and the Lagrenée brothers. Louis David was attracted by the austerity of the ancients, and in 1780 presented to the Salon his *Belisarius Begging for Alms* (Lille, Musée des Beaux-Arts), which caused a sensation. The discovery of nature inspired a new school of landscape painters, the principal representatives of which were Joseph Vernet, a specialist in seascapes, and Hubert Robert, the creator of the English-style poetic landscape, dotted with rocks, castles, or Roman ruins. Mention should also be made of Moreau the Elder, Pierre-Antoine Demachy, Jean-Baptiste Hilaire, Jean Pillement, and Henri de Valenciennes. Although the taste for the portrait survived as an inheritance of the previous reign, artists now strove to create a more informal atmosphere and to convey the private

Louis XVI Style. Louis David. *Belisarius Begging for Alms.* Detail. 1780. Musée des Beaux-Arts, Lille.

feelings of the model. Élisabeth Vigée-Lebrun expressed maternal love (*Marie-Antoinette and Her Children*, 1787; Versailles, Museum), and J.-S. Duplessis inspiration (*Gluck*, 1775; Vienna, Kunsthistorisches Museum).

The return to antiquity began in sculpture with the very simple works of Edmé Bouchardon. French artists always mingled a sense of charm and elegance with their love of Greek art. And, in fact, the graceful nudes of Étienne Falconet, of Augustin Pajou or of Jean-Antoine Houdon never break away completely from the Rococo lightness of touch. Similarly, Claude Michel Clodion's (1738–1814) adorable terra-cotta figures and Pierre Julien's groups preserve the elegiac delicacy of that earlier style. In funerary sculpture, however, there were a number of Greek-style sarcophagi and weepers, as in Houdon's tomb of the Comte d'Ennery (1781; Louvre). From 1776 to 1789, the leading sculptors of Louis XVI's reign executed 28 statues of the great men of France, which after 1787 were reproduced in Sèvres biscuit ware and distributed throughout France. But sculpture found its finest expression in portraits by Pajou (*Hubert Robert*, 1789; Paris, École des Beaux-Arts) and above all by Jean-Jacques Caffieri (*Pierre Corneille*, 1777; Paris, Comédie-Française) and Houdon (*Voltaire*, 1781; Comédie-Française).

It was perhaps in the decorative arts that the influence of the Pompeian and Etruscan archaeological discoveries was most felt. In interiors, the paneling was now painted in cold colors and decorated with pilasters and carved motifs of either geometric (Greek) or Classical (garlands, torches, tripods) inspiration. Mique lavished particular attention on the decoration of the small apartments at Versailles (after 1782) for Marie-Antoinette, and the Rousseau brothers decorated the boudoir at Fontainebleau (*c.* 1783–85) with equal verve. Traditional furniture

Louis XVI Style. Jean-Antoine Houdon. *Shivering Girl.* 1783. Musée Fabre, Montpellier.

also adopted sober, rectilinear forms. The tapestry factories of the Gobelins, of Beauvais, and of Aubusson continued to produce tapestries that were exotic, pastoral, historical, and above all allegorical. Hard-paste porcelain was introduced at the royal factory at Sèvres in 1772, then immediately adopted for biscuit ware and ornamental plaques.

LOUIS-PHILIPPE STYLE. Brought to power by the revolution of July 28–29, 1830, the "July Monarchy" of Louis-Philippe (reigned 1830–48) soon set about applying by force a demagogic policy of moderation over French life. In literature and in the arts this spirit of moderation was translated into a definite eclecticism. The "Citizen-King" devoted his fortune to the restoration of the great royal châteaux of Pau, Fontainebleau, and Versailles, which he opened to the public. His reign produced no architectural monuments on a large scale: indeed, the buildings were essentially bourgeois and utilitarian. The sole exception to this is the crypt designed by Ludovico Visconti (1791–1853) for the Invalides (1843), in which the ashes of Napoleon I are housed. Louis-Philippe took a great interest in town planning, and he undertook various projects in Paris. The king and his aides confined themselves to building bridges and fountains, and to completing the Place de la Concorde with its Egyptian obelisk and its magnificent statues. In addition, they built the town hall of the fifth Paris *arrondissement* under Victor Calliat (1801–81), the Palais des Études of the École des Beaux-Arts under Félix Duban (1797–1870), and saw to the completion of the Panthéon and the Arc de Triomphe de l'Étoile under Abel Blouet (1795–1853). Metal architecture found its first rational and aesthetic expression in Henri Labrouste's Bibliothèque Ste-Geneviève (1844–50). In spite of this architectural innovation, however, the reign of Louis-Philippe saw the triumph in France of the Gothic Revival. The government soon realized the risks faced by so many of the great masterpieces of French architecture, and set up the Commission des Monuments Historiques, directed by Prosper Mérimée. The task of this commission was the classification and restoration of the national heritage. This gigantic work was undertaken between 1838 and 1851 by Eugène Emmanuel Viollet-le-Duc, Jean-Baptiste Lassus (1807–57), Félix Duban, and Louis Baltard (1764–1846). In 1837 these men began the restoration of two Paris churches: the Ste-Chapelle and St-Germain l'Auxerrois (completed 1840). The rescue of Notre-Dame was begun in 1845. The restoration quickly extended to St-Denis, Amiens, Vézelay (1840–47), and St-Sernin at Toulouse (1845). Such detailed studies of medieval art, which these restorations made necessary, did much to develop the Neo-Gothic style, as seen in the design for Ste-Clotilde in Paris by François Gau (1790–1853).

Louis-Philippe Style. Ludovico Visconti. Tomb of Napoleon I. 1843. Dome of the Invalides, Paris. *Photo Roger-Viollet, Paris.*

After the 1830 Revolution painting remained, at the Académie des Beaux-Arts, in the hands of Davidian or Romantic masters who had been already eminent under the Bourbons—men such as François-Édouard Picot, Louis Hersent (1777–1860), and Denis Abel de Pujol (1785–1861). "Troubadour" painting, inspired by literature and history, was represented by the work of Joseph Nicolas Robert-Fleury, Eugène Isabey (1804–86), Eugène Deveria (1805–65), and by Hippolyte Delaroche. Historical painters worthy of mention include Léon Cogniet (1794–1880), Jean-François Gigoux, Louis Boulanger, and Ary Scheffer. Romanticism seized on the epic and almost contemporary incidents of the Napoleonic period in paintings by Joseph-Ferdinand Boissard de Boisdenier (1813–66; *Retreat from Russia*, 1835; Rouen, Musée des Beaux-Arts), Auguste Raffet, and Nicolas Charlet (1792–1845). Horace Vernet, on the other hand, was a chronicler of the reign (*Taking of the Smala*, 1845; Versailles, Museum). The ceilings of the Palais-Bourbon (1844) and the Palais du Luxembourg (1847) were decorated by the Romantic master Delacroix, a great lyricist and a colorist of genius. Théodore Chassériau, a pupil of Ingres, but deeply influenced by Delacroix, executed some very refined decoration and some sensual, rather melancholy nudes (*Esther's Toilet*; Louvre). Ingres seemed to react against Romanticism, but with his taste for the arabesque (*Odalisque with Slave*, 1842; Louvre), he was far from being faithful to David; his directorship of the Institut was his main claim to Classicism. This generation also traveled in search of the exotic, the East being a favorite subject of Adrien Dauzats (1804–68), Prosper Marilhat, and Alexandre Gabriel Decamps (1803–60). Beside such Romantic landscape painters as Georges Michel and Paul Huet (1803–69), Jean-Baptiste Camille Corot seems more of a Classicist, close to Poussin. From 1837 an isolated, uncompromising group of landscape painters formed around Théodore Rousseau to paint from nature at Fontainebleau. Thus was begun the Barbizon School, with its realistic studies in deep colors of forests, clearings, moors, and ponds. Realism was born at about the same time with the work of Thomas Couture and Gustave Courbet, who were influenced by Spanish painting, of Jean-François Millet, who painted

Louis-Philippe Style. Jean-François Millet. *Child with a Hoop.* Musée des Beaux-Arts, Grenoble.

peasant subjects, and of Honoré Daumier, a social polemicist. It was also during the reign of Louis-Philippe that a new art form—photography—appeared in competition with painting. In sculpture, Romanticism had not yet become accepted by official artists, who continued to work in the grand tradition, while James Pradier carved Neoclassical female figures for the Place de la Concorde (*Lille* and *Strasbourg*, 1836) and for the crypt of the Invalides. The Salons rejected the independent Romantic sculptors, but these masters, who had already been accepted by the public, still received important commissions for the Citizen-King's main projects: pediments of the Panthéon in 1837 by Pierre-Jean David d'Angers (1788–1856), and of the Chamber of Deputies in 1841 by Jean-Pierre Cortot (1787–1843), and, above all, bas-reliefs for the Arc de Triomphe—François Rude's *The Departure*, 1835–36; Antoine Etex's (1808–88) *Resistance of France to the Coalition of 1814*, and *Peace*, 1835; and Cortot's *Triumph*. Pierre-Jean David d'Angers carved some expressive busts (*Paganini*; Angers, Museum) and excellent medallions; Etex proved a skillful decorator and portraitist, and Antoine Louis Barye an animal sculptor of exceptional sensibility and anatomical observation.

Under Louis-Philippe decorative art had recourse to the systematic pastiche of old forms, mingled with Gothic, Renaissance, and Louis XIII elements. The new industrialization soon overtook the crafts, lowering quality and vulgarizing the models. Louis-Philippe furniture is mainly imitative; paneling was replaced by wallpaper, while the carpets remained very rich. The Gobelins factory repeated old tapestries (such as those of Rubens), or wove historical ones after contemporary designs (Horace Vernet, *Massacre of the Mamelukes*, 1811; Amiens). Bronzes and zincs decorated apartments in abundance, and the goldsmith's work for table settings was particularly splendid. Stained glass was given new impetus with the recreations of the Gothic glassmakers, such as the restoration in 1845 of the stained glass at the Ste-Chapelle by Louis Charles Auguste Steinheil (1814–85), and Antoine Lusson (active to 1872). The number of master glassmakers increased considerably, and their studios produced a great many stained-glass windows based on cartoons by Delaroche, Chassériau, and Ingres. The Sèvres factory produced table services of hard-paste porcelain, richly decorated with royal portraits, while at Fontainebleau, from 1830 on, Jacob-Petit (1796–1868) created unusually colored pieces in an extreme Rococo style.

Louis-Philippe Style. François Rude. *The Departure*. 1835–36. Arc de Triomphe de l'Étoile, Paris.

LOUTHERBOURG, Philip James de (1740, Strasbourg—1812, Chiswick, Middlesex), Alsatian-born landscape painter of the English School. By 1755 he was in Paris, where he studied under Carle van Loo and Francesco Casanova (1727–1802). In 1771 he arrived in London with an introduction to the actor David Garrick, for whom he began working as a painter of scenery at the Drury Lane Theatre in 1773. In 1781 he opened his so-called *Eidophusikon*, which was a spectacle of moving scenery and light shown in a small private theater in London. It proved to be a great success and helped establish the vogue for sensational displays, often protocinematic in character, that lasted throughout the 19th century. De Loutherbourg continued as a painter—he became a Royal Academician in 1781; his theatrical panache gave his works (the *Shipwreck*, 1793, Southampton Art Gallery; *An Avalanche, or Ice-Fall, in the Alps*, 1803, London, Tate Gallery) a certain distinction and force.

LOWRY, Laurence Stephen (1887, Manchester—1976, Manchester), English painter. He studied drawing and painting at the Municipal College of Art, Manchester, between 1905 and 1915. It was not until the period of World War I that he became interested in the life and scenery of the industrial Midlands, where he always lived and found his constant inspiration. Lowry's style changed very little from the early 1920s onward. With its matchstick figures, simplified perspective, and buildings often reduced to gaunt silhouettes, his imagery captures perfectly the starkness and ugliness of the Lancashire urban scene—a physically decaying legacy of the Industrial Revolution. *An Accident* (1926; Manchester, City Art Gallery), which depicts an incident witnessed at Pendlebury in Lancashire, and *River Scene* (1942; Glasgow, Art Gallery and Museum), based on a view of Salford, also in Lancashire, are characteristic examples of his painting. Lowry's work is outside the mainstream of modern art; and he has been called, with some justification, "perhaps the last of the great English eccentrics."

Laurence Stephen Lowry. *An Accident*. 1926. City Art Gallery, Manchester.

LUCAS (HUGENSZ.) VAN LEYDEN (1494, Leiden—1533, Leiden), major Dutch painter and engraver of the Renaissance. Around 1521, he came into contact with Dürer and Jan Gossaert (Mabuse), both of whom had spent considerable time in Venice. As a painter Lucas owes much to Bosch, whose influence is visible in *Lot and His Daughters* (Paris, Louvre) and *Moses Striking the Rock* (1527; Boston, Museum of Fine Arts). The Italianate style of Quinten Massys permeates his fine genre scenes of the *Cardplayers* (Wilton House, Earl of Pembroke) and the *Chess Players* (Berlin, Staatliche Museen).

In Lucas van Leyden the engraver is always superior to the painter. Trained in this field by a goldsmith, Lucas was a master of

Lucas van Leyden. *Return of the Prodigal Son.* Between 1510 and 1517.

the burin at an early age and was technically the equal of Dürer, having the same sharpness of vision but a lighter hand. Although he adopted the more robust touch of Dürer about 1510, Lucas retained his precision and introduced delicate lights, transparent shadows, and a subtle recession of planes through the most sensitive aerial perspective. Two very early engravings, the *Milkmaid* (1510) and the *Story of Joseph* (1510), are entirely successful in this manner. With the brilliant *David Playing Before Saul* (1508), they show Lucas' acute powers of observation and his ability to penetrate character.

Lucas was particularly inclined toward popular genre (The *Beggars*; the *Trickster*; the *Milkmaid*; the *Village Surgeon*) and toward Biblical subjects interpreted in a genrelike manner (*Bathsheba at the Bath; Susanna and the Elders*). His three greatest engravings (1510–17) are the *Prodigal Son, Ecce Homo*, and the *Ascent to Calvary*, in which the title subjects assume secondary interest.

LUCE, Maximilien (1858, Paris—1941, Paris), French painter. His career began as a result of his meeting with the divisionist Paul Signac and his entry into the Salon des Indépendants in 1887. Luce then became one of the Neoimpressionists and took part in the exhibitions of this group in Paris, then with the group known as Les Vingt in Brussels in 1889 and 1892. He loved drawing, and produced an important body of graphic work, including some interesting portraits of Signac and Seurat. In 1935, on the death of Signac, he succeeded to the presidency of the Société des Artistes Indépendants.

For a long time, Luce remained faithful to the divisionist technique. However, he had his own interpretation of the theory, an interpretation that was less mathematical and less rigid than that of Seurat and Signac. Later, his style became more flexible and returned to a more impressionist approach. Luce's urban landscapes and his views of industrial quarters, often depicted at night, are among his most characteristic works. Examples of his work include a *Portrait of Feuillagiste Perrault* (1890; New York, Metropolitan Museum).

Bernardino Luini. *Young Women Bathing.* Villa Pelucca. Brera, Milan. *Photo Anderson-Viollet.*

LUINI, Bernardino (b. *c.* 1490—1532, Milan), Italian painter of the Lombard School. His first authenticated work is a fresco painted in 1512 for Chiaravalle Abbey, representing the *Virgin with Angels* against a landscape background. In 1515 he signed and dated the *Madonna Enthroned with Saints*, now in the Brera, Milan. In 1516 he decorated the Corpus Domini Chapel in S. Giorgio al Palazzo in Milan, and in 1521 he painted additional frescoes in the Busti Chapel of S. Maria di Brera. In 1522 Luini had begun his series of large decorative schemes, sacred and profane, at the Casa Rabia (now divided between Berlin and Washington), at the Villa Pelucca (Brera), at the Greco Milanese Oratory (Paris, Louvre), at the Casa Atellani (Milan, Castello Sforzesco), and the first part of the S. Maurizio cycle with which he entirely decorated the Besozzi Chapel (Church of the Monastero Maggiore, or S. Maurizio) in Milan. In addition to this considerable amount of work as a fresco painter, Luini left many carefully finished easel paintings, mostly religious. The development of his style as seen in his authenticated works shows that he was first influenced by Andrea Solario, then by Bramantino, and also by Bergognone (*c.* 1455–1523/35), whose spontaneous feeling we find in Luini's naive figures and pleasant landscapes.

LUKS, George (1867, Williamsport, Pennsylvania—1933, New York), American painter. While in Europe, where he remained for 10 years, Luks often concentrated on drawing rather than painting, and this experience served him well on his return to America in 1895, when he became an illustrator for the *Philadelphia Press.* As a result of this position, he made the acquaintance of William Glackens, Everett Shinn, and John Sloan, who introduced him to Robert Henri. This meeting had a decisive influence on Luks's art and thinking. In 1895 he began to paint scenes of New York's lower classes and street life with a certain vitality and humor. With broad and quick brushstrokes, Luks depicted street urchins, wrestlers, and coal miners, in such paintings as the *Spielers* (1905; Andover, Mass., Addison Gallery) and *Wrestlers* (1905; Boston, Museum of Fine Arts).

Luks's work clearly reveals the artist's flamboyant personality and robust love of life. Indeed, his temperament and personality typified the dynamism and optimism of early 20th-century America, and his struggles against academicism with his Philadelphian friends, who formed the group called The Eight, demonstrated a new spirit in American art.

LUNDBERG, Gustav (1695, Stockholm—1786, Stockholm), Swedish painter and pastelist. He was a pupil of David von Kraft (1655–1724), and completed his training in Paris under Hyacinthe Rigaud and Nicolas de Largillière. When he came into contact with the late Classicism of the Regency (1715–23), he abandoned the Grand Manner, and tempered the conventional seriousness of the portrait with a gleam of wit. He was soon patronized by court circles in France, and was elected to the Academy of Painting in 1742, three years before his return to Sweden. The two pastel portraits of *François Boucher* (1741; Paris Louvre) and *Jean Marc Nattier* (1741; Louvre) that he presented on the occasion of his admission were typical of his new manner. By means of his sensuous and vigorous touch, Lundberg's color became more transparent, although molded and deepened with highlights and nuances. He gave his female models (*Portrait of Beate Sparre, c.* 1747; Stockholm, Coll. Baron Nordenfalk) a special kind of truthfulness and an elegant, subtle charm. In his royal portraits (*Gustav III, Duke Fried-*

rich Adolf, and Duke Carl, 1750s; Södermanland, Ericsberg Castle, Coll. Count Carl Bonde) he attained a psychological mastery that places him in the same category as Jean-Baptiste Perronneau and Maurice Quentin de La Tour.

LURÇAT, André (b. 1894, Bruyères, Vosges), French architect, brother of the painter Jean Lurçat. Between 1925 and 1935 he made an important contribution to the development of the International Style, which he employed in his first works: the Bertrand and Huggler houses (1924–25) and the Guggenbühl house (1926), all in Paris. The Hôtel Nord-Sud at Calvi (1930), and a complex of dwellings in Vienna (1932), brought his plastic experiments to a high level of maturity. The most successful works of this first period, the Villa Hefferlin at Ville-d'Avray (1932) and the Karl Marx school and stadium complex at Villejuif (1931–32), in which the masses are handled with more restraint, are classics of this period.

When commissioned to rebuild Maubeuge in 1945, Lurçat designed the only coherent town-planning scheme (1945–50) of the immediate postwar years. In the large residential complexes that he built afterward at St-Denis (Cité Paul-Langevin, 1947–50; Cité Paul-Éluard, 1952–58), as well as some community buildings, he returned to much more traditional formulas.

André Lurçat. Villa Hefferlin, Ville-d'Avray. 1932.

LURÇAT, Jean (1892, Bruyères, Vosges—1966, St-Paul-de-Vence, Alpes-Maritimes), French painter and muralist, one of the masters of modern tapestry designing. Lurçat was first influenced by Cubism, and then by Surrealism. Two of his first long trips abroad, one to Spain in 1923, and the other, in 1924, to North Africa, Greece, and Asia Minor, inspired the central theme of many of his paintings: a desertlike environment in which even humanity seems lost (the *Big Cloud*, 1929, Washington, D.C., National Gallery; *Greek Landscape*, 1919, Amsterdam, Stedelijk Museum). His interest in wall decorations such as murals led him to try tapestry designing. From the *Storm* (1927; Paris, Musée National d'Art Moderne) to the *Illusions of Icarus* (1936; The Hague, Royal Palace), he mastered the art of the tapestry cartoon. In 1938 he settled in Aubusson, Creuse, along with the French painters Marcel Gromaire and Toussaint Dubreuil, and together they began to reorganize the weaving industry. Lurçat was a tireless tapestry designer and produced over 1,000 cartoons of varying sizes. Among his most famous creations are the *Four Seasons* (1940) that belongs to the Musées Nationaux; *Liberty* (designed and woven secretly in 1943; Paris, Musée National d'Art Moderne); the *Tapestry of the Apocalypse* (1948; in the choir of the church of Notre-Dame de Toute-Grâce in Plateau d'Assy, Haute-Savoie); *Homage to the Death of the Resistance and Deportation* (1954; Paris, Musée National d'Art Moderne); and the *Song of the World* (1957–64). In addition to paintings and cartoons for tapestries, Lurçat also did illustrations, gouaches, colored lithographs, and designs for ceramics. He wrote poetry and books about tapestry, and also designed the sets and costumes for several theatrical productions.

LURISTAN BRONZES. The small bronzes referred to by this name originated in the valleys and high plains of the Zagros mountains in western Iran. Evidence suggests that the culture of Luristan reached a high point during the 7th and 8th centuries B.C. The bronzes began to appear on the markets of western Iran about 1928. Reliable information regarding their sources is not always available, since almost no excavations were carried out scientifically, but they are said to have been unearthed at the sites of sepulchers and *tepes* (artificial hills marking ancient places of habitation or worship).

Stylistically, the bronzes of Luristan are clearly identifiable and distinct, with contradictory and derivative styles existing side by side. A tendency to abstraction in the standard heads, with their extremely elongated animal shapes, contrasts with the Baroque opulence of the multiform idols. The narrative spirit of the Mesopotamian peoples is quite absent from this art, in which the iconography is rarely used as a narrative adjunct. But the efflorescence of human, and especially animal, forms produced a constantly renewed plastic art, whose creations, even the most fantastic ones, are endowed with an intrinsic life. This unrestrained dynamic vitality is perhaps the principal characteristic of the art of Luristan.

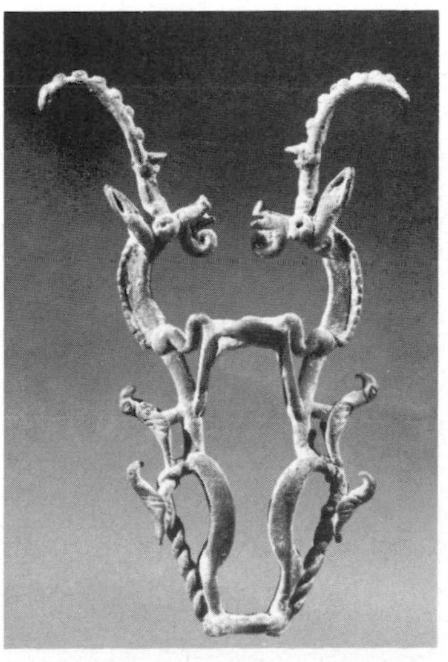

Luristan Bronzes. Votive idol with stylized ibexes and birds. 8th–7th century B.C. Coll. Foroughi, Teheran. *Photo Walter Dräyer, Zurich.*

Sir Edwin Landseer Lutyens. Viceroy's House, New Delhi. 1920–31. *Photo Information Service of India, New York.*

Technically, the bronzes can be divided into two groups, the cast pieces and the beaten plaques and disks. Among the cast bronzes, there is a great variety of objects. The weapons and tools include digitated axes and axes with the blade fashioned like the jaws of wild animals, "halberds," and whetstone handles in the shape of animal heads or protomas (the animal head and neck). Then there are pieces of harness, mainly bits for horses, with the pierced cheek-straps representing real or imaginary animals, chariots and drivers, or animal-slayer heroes. A third group includes hollow standard heads representing gods or fertility goddesses, heroes, wild animals, or heraldic-type monsters rearing face to face. Yet another group includes pins with heads decorated in the same way, and bracelets, torques, and amulets.

The beaten bronzes are of a different and perhaps later style; they are principally plaques for belts, shields, and quivers, or again votive pinheads in disk form. Some of the representations on these pieces seem to be drawn from the religious background of the Medes and Persians. The dating and attribution of the bronzes remain a subject of controversy among scholars. Claude Schaeffer dates most of them from the domination of Mesopotamia by the Kassite mountain people (1500–1200 B.C.). André Godard considers them to be definitely post-Kassite and dates them between 1150 and 700 B.C. On the other hand, Edith Porada sees in them an Elamite influence from the south that probably persisted until the end of the Median period. Certain mythological themes, and more persuasively, the cuneiform inscriptions on some of the bronzes, would lead archaeologists to admit Mesopotamian influences at different periods.

LUTYENS, Sir Edwin Landseer (1869, London—1944, London), English architect, the son of a painter. Influenced by the work of Philip Webb, William Morris, and later by that of Norman Shaw, Lutyens made his name with a series of country houses remarkable for their fusion of disparate styles and for their picturesque character ("The Deanery," Sonning, Berkshire, 1899–1901).

In the period 1900–1910 Lutyens dropped the pseudomedieval elements of his early style in favor of a Classical, Georgian manner. His capacity to design houses that were opulent without being ostentatious, and impressive without seeming austere, made him extremely popular with well-to-do Edwardian clients ("Heathcote," Ilkley, Yorkshire, 1906; or "Nashdom," Taplow, Buckinghamshire, 1905).

Having made his name as a designer of houses, Lutyens turned to architecture of a more ambitious character. Beginning with two churches in the Hampstead Garden Suburb, and the British Pavilion at the Rome Exhibition, 1910 (today the British School at Rome), he went on to design the Viceroy's House, New Delhi (completed in 1930), which is considered his masterpiece, the British Embassy at Washington, D.C. (1926), and the Roman Catholic Cathedral at Liverpool. Lutyens was essentially an eclectic. The exterior of the Viceroy's House, for example, has a decidedly traditional Indian flavor, though many of the interiors are distinctly English Neo-Georgian. But his work is often interesting, and sometimes impressive, because of his feeling for mass. The details are frequently without particular merit, but the relation of the larger units is invariably effective. It was partly for this reason that Lutyens was a good designer of monuments (Cenotaph, Whitehall). Awarded the Royal Institute of British Architects (RIBA) Gold Medal in 1921, Lutyens was President of the Royal Academy from 1938 to 1944.

LYS *or* **LISS,** Jan, *also called* Johann *or* Giovanni (*c.* 1597, Oldenburg, Schleswig-Holstein—1629, Venice), German Baroque painter, usually classified with the Venetian School. He received his training in Amsterdam, Haarlem, and Antwerp around 1615, assimilating the elaborate Mannerist forms of Bartholomaeus Spranger and of the northern Baroque artists through the engravings of Hendrick Goltzius (1558–1617). He journeyed to Venice (1621) and then to Rome (1622), where he mingled with the Bentvueghels, an expatriate group of Flemish genre painters. Lys returned permanently to Venice in 1624, and worked there until his death. He imitated the coloristic and painterly style of the Venetian School, and also drew inspiration from the Flemish art of Rubens and Jordaens. Indeed, many paintings formerly attributed to the latter two artists as well as to Fetti, Strozzi, Piazzetta, and Honthorst have been reassigned to Lys by modern scholars. His works are conceived in an energetic Baroque style that stresses luminosity of color and an extraordinarily loose, impressionistic brushwork. His subjects were drawn from two principal sources: the roisterous life familiar to the northern genre tradition (*Soldiers' Camp, c.* 1625; Nuremberg, Germanisches Nationalmuseum) and the realm of mythology (*Toilet of Venus*, 1625–26; Pommersfelden, Galerie). He also left several religious compositions including the dramatic *Vision of St. Jerome* (1628–29; Venice, S. Nicolò dei Tolentini).

LYTENS, Gysbrecht (active late 16th–early 17th century, Antwerp), Flemish painter, a contemporary of Jan "Velvet" Bruegel, a pupil of Ghislain Vroilynck (d. 1635) in 1598, and a Master in 1617. In 1942 he was identified as the hitherto anonymous Master of the Winter Landscapes. His romantic woodland scenes continued a vein that goes back to Pieter Bruegel the Elder and that was developed throughout the Netherlands—in Holland by Hendrick Avercamp and other 17th-century landscapists, and in Flanders by Josse de Momper and Denis van Alsloot. His works are frequently seen in the paintings of collectors' cabinets by the Franckens. His quality can be judged by the *Winter Landscapes* at Valenciennes (Museum) and in the Nystadt Collection (The Hague), as well as by the *Skaters* (Nantes, Museum).

MABUSE. *See* **GOSSAERT** *or* **GOSSART,** Jan.

MACCHIAIOLI, group of artists in the vanguard of the most important movement of pictorial reform in 19th-century Italy. Their art, in its early phase (1850–55) an outgrowth of the enthusiastic discussions of a group of artists who met in the Caffé Michelangelo in Florence, gathered momentum between 1855 and 1860 and culminated in an exhibition held in Florence in 1861. The leading promoters of the movement were Giovanni Fattori, Telemaco Signorini, and later Silvestro Lega, Adriano Cecioni (1836–86), and Diego Martelli (1839–96), an intelligent and enthusiastic patron. Cecioni's writings show that the Macchiaioli were united in rejecting traditional values in painting. Art, according to Cecioni, is not concerned with form but with the rendering of impressions, or immediate perceptions of reality, by means of *macchie* ("splashes") of bright and dark colors. The Macchiaioli felt they had solved the problem of form by considering it in terms of color values and their relations. It was not by chance that the Macchiaioli were the first in Italy to grasp the significance of Impressionism (through a lecture given by Diego Martelli at Leghorn in 1886 on Manet, Renoir, Degas, Pissarro, and Cézanne) and to spread it throughout the country.

MACDONALD-WRIGHT, Stanton (b. 1890, Charlottesville, Virginia—d. 1973), American painter. In 1907 he made his first trip to France, where he spent most of his time in Paris, studying at the École des Beaux-Arts and the Académie Julian. In 1912 in Paris he met the American painter Morgan Russell. They began experimenting with color in relation to space, and together they developed a style of painting based on Paul Cézanne's artistic principles, which they called Synchromism. Their work became increasingly abstract as they attempted to suggest form by the use of color. Synchromism was closely related to Robert Delaunay's Orphism. This latter movement was, in fact, the Synchromists' *bête noire.* Although Synchromism provoked considerable interest when it first appeared, and there were Synchromist exhibitions in Munich and New York as well as in Paris, it was short-lived and had no lasting repercussions. In 1916 Macdonald-Wright returned to the United States, where the lack of interest in modern art prompted him to give up abstraction in 1920. He embarked on a variety of activities: he was director of the Federal Works of Art Project in California (1935–42), and taught at several universities in California. In 1952–53 he lectured on art in Japan, where he learned both Chinese and Japanese and became interested in Zen Buddhism. When he returned to America in 1953 he revived Synchromism, and an important retrospective exhibition of his work at the Los Angeles County Museum in 1956 was enthusiastically received; it marked the beginning of Macdonald-Wright's second artistic career. A typical example of his later art is his *Song of Victory* (1955; Los Angeles, Priv. Coll.).

MACIVER, Loren (b. 1909, New York), American painter. With the exception of a few childhood lessons at the Art Students League, she was a largely self-taught artist who developed while working under the Federal Art Project during the Depression (*Carey's Backyard*, 1939; New York, Metropolitan Museum), then turned to a decorative abstract style after 1939. Working as an illustrator, Loren MacIver designed magazine and book covers and illustrations, shop windows, murals, Christmas cards, and posters. She especially admired John Marin, but Paul Klee has also been indicated as a source of influence in her work, which ranges in style from realism to figurative and nonfigurative abstraction. Her pictures are always lyrical in feeling, delicately glowing with pastel hues. *Oil Splinters and Leaves* (1950; New York, Coll. Mrs. G. MacCulloch Miller) is notable in this sense for its stylized patterns and atmospherically grayed color harmonies. These delicate harmonies also characterize several paintings that capture her impressions of European cities (*Venice*, 1949, New York, Whitney Museum; *Paris*, 1949, Metropolitan Museum).

MACKE, August (1887, Meschede, North Rhine-Westphalia—1914, Perthes, Seine-et-Marne), German painter. In 1907 and 1908, shortly after leaving the Düsseldorf Academy, Macke paid two visits to Paris, where he discovered the work of the Impressionists, Cézanne, and Seurat. At the end of 1909, he moved to Tegernsee in Bavaria for a year and began painting in a manner influenced by Henri Matisse. He met Franz Marc, Wassily Kandinsky, and Paul Klee in Munich, where he participated in the first exhibition of the Blaue Reiter (December 1911), saw Cubist and Futurist paintings, and was fired with enthusiasm for the art of Robert Delaunay. Finally, in 1912, at Bonn, he began painting his most personal and most enduring works.

He often painted figures strolling, or women looking at window displays of millinery and clothes. With their slim, column-like bodies and elegant carriage, these strollers resemble Seurat's figures; but their bearing is more relaxed, their style less severe, and there is nothing pointillist about their color. The reds, oranges, and yellows clash deliberately with the blues and greens, but the combinations are neither crude nor strident, conveying instead a feeling of well-being, calm, and musing happiness. In April of 1914 Macke went to Tunisia with Klee and the Swiss painter Louis Moilliet, bringing back from his travels a series of watercolors in bright, gay colors (*Market in Tunis I*; Priv. Coll.). A few months later, World War I put an end to his work: at the end of September, he fell in a battle in Champagne.

MACKINTOSH, Charles Rennie (1868, Glasgow—1928, London), Scottish decorator and architect, one of the leaders of the Art Nouveau movement in Great Britain. In 1890, a traveling scholarship enabled him to go to France and Italy. His first work, the corner tower of the Glasgow Herald Building (1894), already showed

Stanton Macdonald-Wright. *Synchromy Yin.* 1930. Santa Barbara Museum of Art, Santa Barbara, California.

Charles Rennie Mackintosh. Glasgow School of Art. 1898–1909. *Photo Annan, Glasgow.*

his rejection of academic tradition. Three years later, he won the competition for the new Glasgow School of Art (1898–1909), which was the first original example of Art Nouveau architecture in Great Britain.

Mackintosh, a stout defender of functionalism in art, soon became interested in the decorative arts. In 1897 he was commissioned to design the furnishings and interior of the Cranston chain of tearooms in Glasgow; he moved toward a curvilinear style, which is well exemplified by the Buchanan Street tearoom (1897–98).

The group of "The Four," comprising Mackintosh, the decorator Margaret Macdonald (1865–1933), whom he married in 1900, her sister Frances (1874–1921), and the latter's husband, the architect Herbert McNair, was founded in 1890. Mackintosh, as leader of the group, entered, in 1901, a competition for the design and interior decoration of the "house of an art lover," organized by the Darmstadt publisher Alexander Koch. Mackintosh was only awarded second prize (M. H. Baillie Scott, 1865–1945, won first place), despite the revolutionary nature of his project. Following the same principles, he designed the library of the Glasgow School of Art (1907–9) on straight lines only; the subtle disposition of horizontal beams and rectangular pillars supporting the galleries punctuated space with a strange rhythm that lifted architecture to the level of poetic abstraction. His last masterpiece, the Cranston tearoom on Ingram Street (1907–11), has this same quality.

Carlo Maderno. Façade of St. Peter's Basilica, Rome. 1607–14. *Photo Leonard von Matt, Buochs.*

MADERNO *or* **MADERNA,** Carlo (1556, Capolago, Lake Lugano—1629, Rome), Italian architect. According to documents dated 1588 and 1591, Maderno came to Rome as a very young man, assisting his uncle, Domenico Fontana, as a stuccoworker. His architectural career, which began only after 1600, became particularly brilliant under the pontificate of Paul V (1605–21). Among his first and most successful designs was the façade of S. Susanna in Rome (1597–1603). Unlike so many Mannerist buildings, there is a clearly readable logic in its façade. By progressively thickening the wall toward the center, Maderno reintroduced to architecture sculptural and chiaroscuro qualities that had been ignored for several generations. In 1603 he was appointed architect to St. Peter's and, in 1607, as official architect to Paul V, was commissioned to remodel the basilica. Maderno has often been criticized for altering Michelangelo's central plan. However, the congregation of cardinals preferred the more traditional plan of a Latin cross, and Maderno had to take their demands into account. Michelangelo's design for the great pronaos was respected but the façade was broadened to meet the wishes of the pope.

Carlo Maderno enjoyed a considerable reputation until his death and, in spite of competition from two younger, and soon prominent architects, Francesco Borromini and Gian Lorenzo Bernini, his activity in Rome never slackened. However, although several important buildings were completed or begun by him, only S. Maria della Vittoria (1608–20) was built entirely according to his design. The reconstruction of the Palazzo Barberini is the chief problem of his career. Although most of the palace was completed by Bernini and Borromini after his death, the unusual H plan and several of the façades were, almost certainly, Maderno's work. Maderno's other works include: the high altar of S. Maria della Pace (1611–14); S. Andrea della Valle (begun *c.* 1590 by Pier Paolo Olivieri, 1551–99, continued by Maderno in 1608, but not completed until long after his death); and the Palazzo Mattei, begun by Domenico Fontana and Francesco da Volterra, whose Classical arcaded courtyard recalls that of the Palazzo Farnese (Maderno worked on the Palazzo Mattei 1606–16).

MAGNASCO, Alessandro, *also called* Il Lissandrino (1667, Genoa—1749, Genoa), Italian painter. He went to Milan around 1680–82 and may have frequented the workshop of Filippo Abbiati (1640–1715). There he acquired a brilliant, quick technique that he used for the rest of his life. Magnasco returned to Genoa in 1703, and subsequently went to Florence as court painter to the Grand Duke of Tuscany. In this latter capacity, he traveled throughout Tuscany and Emilia, with occasional visits to Lombardy. Between 1711 and 1735 he lived mainly in Milan; in 1735 he retired to Genoa, where he died. His art—with its brilliant, fiery technique and its fantastic world of tiny figures bathed in a strange light—is reminiscent of Salvator Rosa, Jacques Callot, Michelangelo Cerquozzi (1602–60), and Pieter van Laer (*c.* 1595–1642).

Magnasco's first signed work, dated 1691 (Milan, Coll. Gallarati Scotti), represented an extraordinary architectural background with ruins and small figures in a style already very much his own. Between 1703 and 1711 he painted *Il corvo ammaestrato* ("The Domesticated Raven") and the *Old Woman and the Gypsies* (both now in the Uffizi, Florence), as well as a *Hunting Scene* commissioned by the duke of Tuscany, which is freer in style, brown in tonality, and which already displays that bizarre poetic feeling that marks his best compositions. Between 1711 and 1735 Magnasco painted a series of pictures for Count Colloredo, the Governor of Lombardy. Between 1735 and 1740 he painted the *Garden Party at Albaro* (Genoa, Palazzo Bianco) and probably the *Christ at Emmaus* for Genoa's Convent of S. Francesco in Albaro (now in the Palazzo Bianco)—his most purely lyrical works. His feeling for sketchiness, movement, and light anticipates the impressionistic style of the Venetian Francesco Guardi.

MAGNELLI, Alberto (b. 1888, Florence), Italian painter. In 1913 he made the acquaintance of the Italian Futurist painters Umberto Boccioni, Carlo Carrà, and the art critic Filippo Marinetti, but never actually joined their movement. The following year he went to Paris, where he was friendly with the Cubists Guillaume Apollinaire, Max Jacob, Pablo Picasso, and Fernand Léger. During this period he painted a series of still lifes and compositions made up of extremely simplified human figures (*Man with a Cart*, 1914). In these works he realized a synthesis of objective and nonobjective forms that enabled him to paint his first completely abstract pictures in Florence in 1915; these were done in bright, flat colors (*Painting No. 0530*, 1915; Coll. artist). Then, for 15 years, Magnelli returned to a semifigurative style. It was not until he went back to Paris in 1933 and produced his stonelike forms that he gradually returned to total abstraction. At that time his ambition was to rediscover forms in their pure, primordial state. Furthermore, he always took great pains to present the abstractions of his mathematical reveries as tangible or sensory forms that are both visually and intellectually stimulating (*Uncomfortable Vision*, 1947, Priv. Coll.; *Point of Hostility No. 1*, 1944, Brussels, Coll. Dotremont). A large body of Magnelli's work consists of montages and collages, techniques that he began to use in 1937 and that he consistently developed ever since.

René Magritte. *Le Grand Siècle*. Galerie Alexandre Iolas, Paris.

MAGRITTE, René (1898, Lessines, Hainaut—1967, Brussels), Belgian painter. He studied at the Academy of Fine Arts in Brussels; in about 1925 Giorgio de Chirico's paintings attracted him to Surrealism and he became its first exponent in Belgium. Although he belonged to the Surrealist group in Paris, and was friendly with the poet Paul Éluard and the writer André Breton, his painting had no connection whatever with Breton's automatism. Magritte's art was, on the contrary, the result of a very conscious process; he took his iconography from the world of objects and, although his choice of colors was somewhat arbitrary, the forms themselves were derived from the meticulous and anachronistic realism of academicians. Magritte valued this realism greatly because his artistic intent was to stir up an uneasy feeling in the observer by means of an unusual or fortuitous juxtaposition of familiar objects (*Threatening Weather*, 1928, London, Coll. Roland Penrose; *The Liberator*, 1947, Los Angeles, County Museum). The disconcerting character of Magritte's paintings is intensified by the titles. These are rarely descriptive, and usually add a new dimension to the pictorial image.

MAIANO, Benedetto. *See* **BENEDETTO DA MAIANO.**

MAILLOL, Aristide (1861, Banyuls-sur-Mer, Pyrénées-Orientales—1944, Perpignan), French sculptor. In 1893 Maillol became friendly with the painters of the Nabis group, which included Pierre Bonnard, Édouard Vuillard, Ker-Xavier Roussel, and Maurice Denis; like them, although with less talent, he tried to bring new life to painting. He soon, however, turned to tapestry making and opened a workshop in Banyuls, where he designed the cartoons (*Bather*, c. 1901) and dyed the wool himself. He discovered his true vocation as a sculptor after an eye disease prevented him from weaving.

Aristide Maillol. *The Mediterranean.* 1902–5. *Photo Walter Dräyer, Zurich.*

There are two surprising facts concerning Maillol's development as a sculptor: the rapidity with which he mastered his style, and the slight amount of change that this style underwent afterward. At the turn of the century, Maillol was still associated with the Nabis and the Art Nouveau artists of the period. A short time afterward, however, he produced an imposing nude of a seated woman, called *The Mediterranean* (1902–5), which possessed the heavy volumes and the architectural structure that thereafter became the distinctive features of his style. About thirty years later, he executed *The Mountain* (1937; Paris, Musée National d'Art Moderne), a variation of *The Mediterranean*, in which the forms were somewhat more refined, firmer, and rather more clearly defined. Maillol's subject range was limited and his style was nearly always the same: namely, a mature and well-built woman whose body had an earthy and timeless quality.

When he was asked about 1905 to do a monument to Louis-Auguste Blanqui, the Socialist who spent nearly half his life in prison because of his revolutionary activities, Maillol produced *Chained Action* (c. 1905; Paris, Musée National d'Art Moderne), a huge feminine nude, who, with her hands bound behind her back, turns around with a fierce and defiant movement. *Night* (1902–9) is a seated female nude whose face is hidden in her arms, which are resting on her drawn-up knees. In the figure for the *Monument to Cézanne* (1912–20: placed in the

Tuileries in 1925), Maillol produced a variation of *Night*. Although there are certain sharp contrasts in his works, there is nothing contorted or dramatic about them. Movement, too, is almost completely absent from his essentially monumental art. Maillol succeeded in reviving Classical idealism in his sculptures, and although they mark an end rather than a beginning of a tradition, they are distinguished by their power, balance, and vitality.

MALEVICH, Kasimir (1878, Kiev—1935, Leningrad), Russian painter. He was the founder of Suprematism, an abstract movement whose principles he enunciated in 1915 in a manifesto called *From Cubism to Suprematism* that was published in the form of a brochure when a large avant-garde exhibition, 0.10, was held in St. Petersburg. Before this, Malevich had gained recognition as the leader of the Russian Cubist movement (*Harvest*, 1912–13; *An Englishman in Moscow, c.* 1914; both in Amsterdam, Stedelijk Museum). Malevich reached the purest form of abstraction in 1913 when he exhibited his famous black square on a white background. This square created a sensation; it was the first element of Suprematism, and was followed soon after by the circle, the cross, and the triangle. Subsequently Malevich painted several compositions based on simple geometrical shapes that were plainly colored on a white background. The acme of simplicity and refinement was his *White Square on a White Background*, which he painted and exhibited in 1919 in Moscow (now in New York, Museum of Modern Art). If his *Self-Portrait* (Moscow, Tretyakov Gallery), painted in the last years of his life, is a reliable indication, the growing hostility of the government forced him to conform to the realistic art of the day. In 1926, however, he was permitted to go to Germany to prepare his book, *Die gegenstandslose Welt*, 1927 ("The Non-objective World," 1954) for publication at the Bauhaus. This was an enlarged version of his 1915 Suprematist manifesto.

Kasimir Malevich. *Harvest.* 1912–13. Stedelijk Museum, Amsterdam.

MALLET-STEVENS, Robert (1886, Paris—1945, Paris), French architect. During the interwar years he shared with the architects Pierre Chareau, Le Corbusier, and André Lurçat the credit for being one of the few defenders of the International Style in France. With them, too, he was one of the founding members of the Union des Artistes Modernes (1930), of which he became president. Mallet-Stevens was an expert builder of private houses, his masterpiece being the group of small private residences (1926–27) along the street that bears his name in the Auteuil section of Paris. Although these houses are built in a Cubist style, they are not reduced to single cubes as are those designed by Le Corbusier; instead, each house is a complex volume created by an interlocking series of secondary volumes into which the architect has dared to introduce a cylinder as a contrast. The interiors are especially remarkable because of their complexity and the free organization of the planes: although Mallet-Stevens unites traditionally separated rooms, he preserves the independence of the new spatial units by placing them on different levels. He designed a few public buildings: the Alfa-Romeo building in Rue Marbeuf, Paris (1925); an imposing block in Rue Méchain, Paris (1930); and several significant although temporary exhibition pavilions. Mallet-Stevens' contribution to modern architecture, although limited in quantity, was of rare quality: he was able to sacrifice the spirit of controversy and an aggressive modernism for the sake of "livability" and aesthetic pleasure.

MANÉ-KATZ (1894, Kremenchug, Ukraine—1962, Tel Aviv), French painter and sculptor of Jewish origin. After attending the School of Fine Arts in Kiev, he went to Paris in 1913. At the outbreak of World War I, he returned to Russia. He went back to Paris in 1921, and became a French citizen in 1927. He volunteered in 1939 and was taken prisoner. When he was freed, he managed to get to the United States, where he spent the rest of the war years; then, in 1945, he returned to France. His best work formed part of the Expressionist revival in the School of Paris, a movement that is especially associated with Jewish artists. Mané-Katz took many of his subjects from the old Testament (*Sacrifice of Abraham*, 1944), Jewish folklore (the *Wailing Wall*, 1938), and contemporary history (*Resistance in the Ghetto*, 1946). His paintings, which have a naive and imaginative quality that is often reminiscent of Marc Chagall's work, communicate a poignant feeling of fatality through their brilliant colors and deliberately distorted forms. Two representative works are *Ecstasy* (1936; Paris, Musée National d'Art Moderne) and *Refugees* (1941; New York, Metropolitan Museum).

MANESSIER, Alfred (b. 1911, St-Ouen, Somme), French painter. A brief stay in 1943 at the Trappist monastery in Soligny-la-Trappe, Orne, left a profound and lasting impression on Manessier; after this, much of his work reflected his intensely religious nature. In the paintings he produced about 1944, such as the *Pilgrims of Emmaus* (1944; Priv. Coll.), the figures are still recognizable, even though the geometricized line and pure color divorce them completely from realistic images. A few years later, however, the expressive power of Manessier's painting was wholly concentrated in abstract color and line (*Magnificat of Harvest Time*; 1952). About 1959, in the paintings inspired by the scenery of Haute Provence, his brushwork became broader and swifter, with serpentine rhythms spreading over the canvas (*Hill at Moissac*, 1959; Paris, Galerie de France). At this time the style of his religious paintings also changed: their structure became less clear, the colors deeper, and the blues seemed to vibrate with mystic and more mysterious overtones (*Et Gloriam Vidi Resurgentis*, 1961; Priv. Coll.). Manessier also did lithographs and designed stained-glass windows in abstract patterns (church at Bréseux, Doubs, 1948).

MANET, Édouard (1832, Paris—1883, Rueil-Malmaison, near Paris), French painter. Manet decided to become a painter at the age of sixteen, but his parents' opposition forced him to choose a naval career. After failing twice the entrance competition for the Naval Academy, he finally obtained his father's permission to enroll in the École des Beaux-Arts, where he studied under Thomas Couture. His independent spirit soon led to friction with his master and, in 1856, he left Couture's studio. In the same year he painted his Baudelairian *Absinthe Drinker* (1858–59; Copenhagen, Ny Carlsberg Glyptotek), which was refused by the official salon despite the support of Eugène Delacroix. In the Salon of 1861 Manet was more fortunate, being awarded an honorable mention for his *Portrait of Monsieur and Madame Auguste Manet* (1860; Paris, Priv. Coll.) and for his *Spanish Singer* (also known as *Le Guitarrero*, 1860; New York, Metropolitan Museum).

By 1862 Manet had gained a reputation as an innovator. In 1863 he exhibited at the Salon des Refusés along with Paul Cézanne, Johan Barthold Jongkind, Camille Pissarro, and J. A. M. Whistler. He submitted three pictures rejected at the 1863 Salon, including *Le Déjeuner sur l'Herbe*, or *Luncheon on the Grass* (1863; Paris, Musée de l'Impressionnisme), which caused a scandal. Manet immediately became the standard-bearer of a new manner of painting and a hero to the younger generation of artists, the future Impressionists. In 1863 he painted the controversial *Olympia* (Musée de l'Impressionnisme) under the direct influence of Titian, but when he exhibited this realistically rendered nude at the Salon of 1865 it drew jeers from the public and sarcasm from the critics. In disgust, Manet made a brief trip to Spain, where he discovered the painting of Velázquez and Goya. After his return to Paris, however, he concentrated on French subjects, while Spanish influences generally became confined to technique and composition.

In 1866 Manet's Salon entry—*The Fifer* (1866; Musée de l'Impressionnisme)—was rejected. The following year his paintings were refused by the Paris Exposition Universelle. In 1868 his *Portrait of Émile Zola* (1868; Musée de l'Impressionnisme) was accepted by the official Salon and, soon after this, he made the acquaintance of Berthe Morisot. Impressed by her charm, he asked her to pose for *The Balcony* (1868; Musée de l'Impressionnisme). During the Franco-Prussian War (1870–71) Manet served as lieutenant in the artillery, but retired to the country during the period of the Commune, returning to Paris only at the end of the insurrection. His portrait of the engraver and lithographer Émile Bellot, called *Le Bon Bock* (1873; Philadelphia, Museum of Art), met with great success at the 1873 Salon. At this time Manet also began to paint masked balls (*Masked Ball at the Opera*, 1873; New York, Coll. Mrs. Doris D. Havemeyer), seascapes, and beach scenes. He also executed his first pastel, a profile of *Madame Manet* (1873; Priv. Coll.). He worked directly from the subject, just as the Impressionists did, and executed several paintings of regattas, notably *Boating* (1874; New York, Metropolitan Museum) and *Argenteuil* (1874; Tournai, Musée des Beaux-Arts). The latter work, showing a masterful technique, was accepted by the Salon of 1875 and was the target of new attacks. At this time Manet's enemies were so numerous that his two entries in the 1876 Salon—*Le Linge* (1874; Merion, Pa., Barnes Foundation) and the *Artist: Portrait of Gilbert-Marcellin Desboutin* (1875; São Paulo, Museu de Arte)—were refused; in 1877 his *Nana* (1877; Hamburg, Kunsthalle) was also rejected. Undiscouraged, Manet painted his dazzling series of beer halls and cafés-concerts (*Waitress*, or *La Servante de Bocks*, 1878; Musée de l'Impressionnisme). In 1879 Manet began to suffer the first attacks of the illness—probably locomotor ataxia—that was to prove fatal. Between treatments and cures he entertained, in his Paris studio, the writers, society figures, and demimondaines he portrayed in pastel: the actress Jeanne de Marsy posed for *Spring: Jeanne de Marsy* (1881, New York, Coll. Mrs. Harry Payne Bingham; sketch in Cambridge, Mass., Fogg Art Museum) and another actress, Méry Laurent, for *Autumn: Méry* (1882; Nancy, Musée des Beaux-Arts). He exhibited the *Bar at the Folies-Bergère* (1881–82; London, Courtauld Institute Galleries) at the Salon of 1882. In 1883 he was paralyzed and confined to bed; he died in April of that year shortly after his leg was amputated.

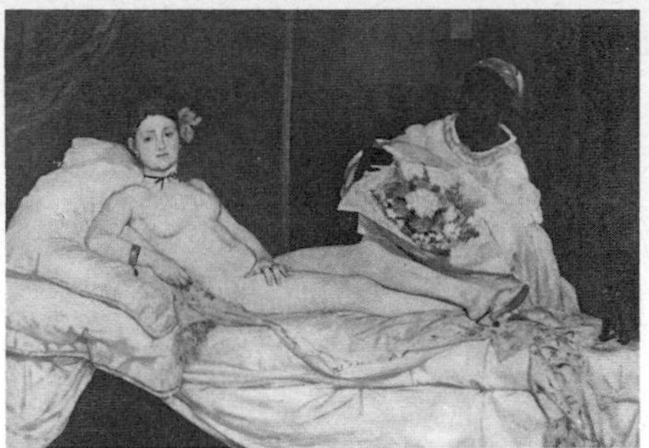

Édouard Manet. *Olympia.* 1863. Musée de l'Impressionnisme, Paris. *Photo Giraudon, Paris.*

Few artists were as controversial in their own time as Manet. In 1876, for instance, he defended himself against his detractors' charge that he had subverted the traditional rules of painting. But, in reality, a large part of his work was derived from old masters. *Le Déjeuner sur l'Herbe* was inspired by Raphael and Giorgione; *Olympia* by Titian's *Venus of Urbino*; the *Old Musician* (1861–62; Washington, D.C., National Gallery) by Velázquez; and *Le Bon Bock* by the drinking and smoking figures of Frans Hals. Manet did not hesitate to borrow a subject from a masterwork or to combine in a single canvas elements he had taken from various sources; thus, *Fishing in St-Ouen* ("La Pêche," *c.* 1858; New York, Metropolitan Museum) recalls Annibale Carracci's *Hunting* and *Fishing* and Rubens' *Landscape with a Rainbow* and *Park of the Château de Steen*. Manet's incalculable contribution to the art of his period stems from his clean linearity, his flattened volumes, his sharp contrasts of light and dark, and the sensual freedom of his brushwork, which imitated that of Velázquez and Frans Hals. His importance also lies in his supremely intelligent style—a style that is both anti-

Édouard Manet. *Spring: Jeanne de Marsy.* 1881. Fogg Art Museum, Harvard University, Cambridge, Mass.

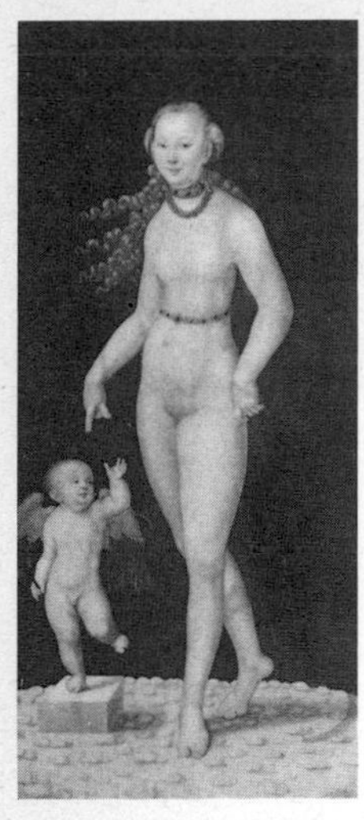

Mannerism. Lucas Cranach the Younger. *Venus and Eros.* Alte Pinakothek, Munich.

intellectual and highly modern, but animated by the teachings of the ancient Japanese masters. In all these respects Manet was a precursor of modern art.

MANGUIN, Henri Charles (1874, Paris—1949, St-Tropez), French painter. He studied with Gustave Moreau at the École des Beaux-Arts in Paris, where he met Henri Matisse, Albert Marquet, Georges Rouault, and Charles Camoin. For some time he took part with them in the Fauvist movement, notably in their famous group exhibition at the Salon d'Automne, which created a scandal in 1905. In the same year he met Paul Signac at St-Tropez, and spent most of his life there. Manguin's paintings are joyful; they vibrate with the warmly colored harmonies of the Mediterranean sun under which most were done (*Fourteenth of July at St-Tropez*, 1905; Paris, Coll. Madame Lucile Manguin). The brightness of his palette justifies his classification with the Fauvists, but while they were inspired by Gauguin, he was more influenced by Cézanne. Manguin loved strong harmonies and luxuriated in the quality of paint; he was also concerned with the treatment of form, which was itself a part of the nature that gave him his taste for life.

MANNERISM. Until comparatively recently this term had a distinctly pejorative connotation. The Italian critic Giorgio Vasari used it as early as 1550 in the sense of "style" or "manner of working" in order to criticize those painters who untiringly repeated the same formulas. In the 17th century the theoreticians Giovanni Pietro Bellori and André Félibien used it to castigate the methodical imitation of the *maniera* of such great masters as Raphael, Titian, and Michelangelo. This way of envisaging Mannerism lasted until 1925. The significance of the term changed and acquired an admirative connotation when 16th-century art was rediscovered in the 20th century. Mannerist painting, which often tended to use strident colors, geometric construction, and eccentric inventions, could not fail to attract a public attuned to Fauvism, Cubism, and especially Surrealism.

Although the interpretations of the term are no longer unfavorable, they are still very varied and confused. The latest critical writings and recent Mannerist exhibitions (Naples, 1952; Amsterdam, 1955) have tried to give a purely historical significance to the term, and have used it to define an entire artistic period stretching over a century, from 1515 to about 1610, throughout Europe. But this historical definition is still ambiguous and cannot logically be applied to German art at the very beginning of the century, which does, in fact, show an exacerbated psychic tension similar to the tormented attitude of the Italians. However, German art did not adopt the Renaissance aesthetic, which was deliberately ignored for an aggravated version of traditional Gothic. This Late Gothic art, with its emotional appeal and contemptuous gracility (Lucas Cranach, *Venus and Eros*, 1531; Brussels, Musées Royaux des Beaux-Arts), had a great influence on such Italian Mannerists as Pontormo and Domenico Beccafumi.

In the violent, sophisticated society of the 16th century, the profane and the sacred were ceaselessly contrasted with each other. The composition of paintings was always unexpected, either decentered along zigzagging diagonals, or fragmented into abrupt masses that are isolated on the sides, in corners, or placed on the frontal plane. The space created by these methods was unstable and suspended between architecture that established an illusion with a phantasmal framework or with clever *trompe-l'oeil* devices. Most of the forms satisfied a taste for the serpentine line, the *figura serpentinata*, which was sometimes transformed into an interrupted line by sudden changes of direction. This hard, jerky method of drawing was also used for rendering fabrics with broken folds and sharp creases. Color was characterized either by discordant tones or dominated by bright orange, strident pinks, and shrill blues or, on the contrary, by faded and acidulous tones, in which pale mauves and grays were mixed with dull greens and light yellows; the unusual search for artificial lighting was in keeping with an attraction toward the bizarre that was universal with the Mannerists.

This immensely rich century can be divided into three periods: the first from 1515 to about 1540, when Mannerism appeared all over Italy with a variety of styles; the second from 1540 to 1570, when Italian art reacted against its first experiments, while these spread to France, Flanders, and Holland; and the last from 1570 to 1610, which saw the rise of an extreme form of Mannerism, verging on Baroque, throughout Europe, while Italy was turning to Classical naturalism. During the first 20 years of the 16th century, a number of contradictory tendencies appeared in Italy. Rosso Fiorentino, working in Florence and Rome, painted tortured scenes in harsh colors. François I invited him to Fontainebleau in 1530, where he covered the Grande Galerie of the château with skillful allegories. Giulio Romano decorated the Palazzo del Tè at Mantua in the same spirit. A refined imitation of Raphael and Correggio led to the experiments of the school of Parma. Parmigianino's style was directly related to them when, with the imagination of a virtuoso, he painted several exquisite Madonnas. The *figura serpentinata* of Michelangelo (*Entombment, c.* 1500; London, National Gallery), and his delicate colored studies influenced Pontormo, whose art was also marked with the strangeness of Northern Gothic (*Visitation, c.* 1530; Carmignano, parish church). Beccafumi, who was attracted by Dürer, was fond of sharp color effects, elongated and undulating silhouettes, and bewildered expressions. Some of the Flemish artists escaped the Gothic style by traveling to Italy to discover the atmosphere of the Renaissance: they included Joos van Cleve (1485–1540); Bernaert van Orley; and Jan Gossaert (called Mabuse).

Mannerism. Marten van Heemskerck. *Erythrean Sibyl.* 1564. Rijksmuseum, Amsterdam.

From 1540 to 1570 a more rational Mannerism flourished in Italy, which was the work of several talented but uninspired painters who leaned heavily on didactic writings. Vasari, a remarkable art historian, as well as painter and architect, published his *Lives of the Most Eminent Painters, Sculptors, and Architects* in 1550. Agnolo Bronzino painted the eminent citizens of Florence with a glacial distinction, and constructed mythological and religious scenes with dry forms. The same intellectual attitude lay behind Vasari's disturbing portraits, and the frescoes he painted in the apartments of the Palazzo Vecchio at Florence, with the help of numerous assistants. The Roman painters followed the various tendencies of Mannerism according to their temperaments. Cecchino Salviati was famous for his erudition and virtuosity (*David Dancing before the Arc*, 1552–54; Rome, Palazzo Sacchetti). Taddeo Zuccaro and his brother Federico decorated the Palazzo Farnese at Caprarola (1559–66) and the Sala Regia in the Vatican (completed 1582). The north contributed such original artists as Pellegrino Tibaldi and Luca Cambiaso, who were both fascinated by the study of geometric volumes and bold foreshortenings. Venetian painting took a different direction with Jacopo Bassano, who preferred his own experiments with light; and with Jacopo Tintoretto, who used the devices, composition, and proportions of his predecessors, but accentuated them and used an original technique for placing the source of light behind objects.

The increasing production of engravings disseminated the early Italian Mannerist style throughout Europe, where it had a profound effect. Francesco Primaticcio, who had been trained at Mantua by Giulio Romano, went to Fontainebleau in 1531 as an assistant to Rosso Fiorentino. Niccolò dell' Abbate often executed frescoes designed by Primaticcio but gave them his own innate sense of color and landscape. Together, these two artists completely transformed the atmosphere of 16th-century French painting by surrounding themselves with numerous Italian, French, and Flemish painters. By about 1560, Fontainebleau was the cynosure of European Mannerism.

Italy also had a pronounced influence on the countries of northern Europe. The work of Jan Sanders van Hemessen is full of restless figures and the linear interplay of dress and gesture. Jan Massys, after visits to France and Italy, painted elegant and chilly nudes against cool-colored perspectives in the Fontainebleau manner. Marten van Heemskerck was following the great models of Italian Renaissance when he painted his religious personages, but he deliberately accentuated the elongated rhythm of their bodies, their contemplative expressions, and the splendor of their strange garments. Jan van Scorel, after three years spent in Italy (1521–24), painted sculptural figures whose slenderness is emphasized by fine hands and exquisite draperies, and architectural settings inspired by Roman churches. Christoph Amberger (1500–61) was the only German painter to turn toward Venice for artistic inspiration, and his portraits of Augsburg dignitaries resemble Bronzino's.

The last phase of Mannerist art—the period from 1570 to 1610—was unconfined by political frontiers or religious differences. French, Flemish, and German artists all met in Rome to share their problems and ideals. Italy produced the oddities of Giuseppe Arcimboldo, the audacities of Antonio Tempesta (1555–1630) and Giovanni Battista Castello (1547–1637), and the more traditional compositions of Federico Zuccaro at the Palazzo Ducale in Venice. In France the so-called Second School of Fontainebleau followed the interval of the religious wars. After the subtle poetry of Toussaint Dubreuil, Ambroise Dubois (*c.* 1543–1614) blended Italian influence with a taste for fluttering draperies and warm colors. At Fontainebleau Martin Fréminet (1567–1619) decorated the Chapelle de la Trinité with tormented, strident frescoes (1608–19). At Nancy, Jacques Bellange (1575–1616) created attenuated figures, trailing extraordinary garments. In Flanders the last generation of Mannerists included Abraham Janssens (1575–1632), Sebastiaan Vrancx, and Marten de Vos; the latter founded the Confraternity of Romanists in 1572, and composed a number of harmonious paintings peopled with figures striking dramatic poses. Holland also had skilled artists: the most famous of them were Abraham Bloemaert, who aggravated the Mannerist atmosphere of his scenes by employing strangely unhealthy flesh tints and sour-sweet faces; and Cornelis Cornelisz. (*c.* 1470–1533), who placed sculptural and sensual figures side by side. The most flourishing school of painting in Europe at the end of the 16th century was at Prague, which attracted German, Flemish, Italian, and Swiss artists. The Fleming Bartholomaeus Spranger worked in Vienna for Emperor Maximilian, and in 1580 followed Emperor Rudolf II to Prague, where his works inaugurated the so-called Prague School of Mannerist paintings. Among German artists working for Rudolf II at Prague were Josef Heintz (1564–1609), who elongated his unquiet figures with their greenish flesh tints; and Hans von Aachen, who was fond of pallid women and rarefied atmosphere. Hans Rottenhammer (1564–1625), an assistant to the Venetian masters Veronese and Tintoretto, filled his paintings with abrupt, colorless

Mannerism. Giovanni Bologna. *Neptune. c.* 1562. Bronze model for the Fountain of Neptune, Bologna. Museo Civico, Bologna. *Photo Alinari-Giraudon.*

shadows. England, which remained only on the fringes of the Mannerist movement, contributed to the 16th-century style through the works of the Flemish-born Hans Eworth and through its finest native-born miniaturist, Nicholas Hilliard. Mannerism appealed considerably to the mystic strain of the Spaniards, who were represented by Luis de Morales (1520/25–86) and especially by El Greco, in whose paintings the use of elongated proportions and dramatic lighting reached their most poignant expression. Italy resisted this last, extreme phase of Mannerism and turned instead toward the Bolognese academicism of Carracci and to the realistic trend represented by Caravaggio and artists working in the Roman studios. Thus, in late 16th-century Italy the ground was prepared for both the restrained French Classicism of Poussin and the vivid Baroque of Rubens, the two opposing impulses present in 17th-century art.

The term Mannerism can also be applied to a certain form of sculpture that first arose in Italy, as an exaggeration of the elegance of Florentine Renaissance work and the plastic strength of Michelangelo. Its early exponents were Benvenuto Cellini, whose works have a delicate distinction; and the Flemish-born Giovanni Bologna, a sculptor of refined subtlety, whose elongated figures and smooth modeling had a profound influence on Pierre Francheville (1548/53–1615), Taddeo Landini (*c.* 1550–96), and Pietro Tacca. This generation of sculptors was fond of extreme proportions, whether embodied in small-scale bronze statuettes and fine pieces of goldsmith's work set off by cameos, or in enormous, almost architectural sculptures whose combination of imaginary figures and rock-garden grottoes gave princely grounds an unusual appearance.

The rest of European sculpture only gradually freed itself from Gothic traditions. The Fleming Hubert Gerhard (*c.* 1540–1620) carved disturbing works influenced by Spranger. His compatriot Adriaen de Vries (*c.* 1546–1626), who worked in turn at the courts of Rudolf II in Prague and Christian IV in Denmark, preferred elegant and sensual forms, a taste that was shared by Johan Gregor van der Schardt (*c.* 1530–after 1581), Hans Reichle, Hans Morinck (d. 1616), and the Dutchman Hendrick de Keyser. In Spain, Alonso Berruguete's sculpture is charged with a restless passion, but the French sculptors vacillated between the somewhat restrained aesthetic principles of Fontainebleau and more exciting, emotional effects. The sense of tragedy is even driven to the point of the macabre with the Lorraine sculptor Ligier Richier (*c.*1500–67).

In recent years art historians have applied the term Mannerist to certain 16th-century works of architecture that share with the painting and sculpture of the period a predilection for effects of exaggerated grace and exuberant fantasy. Characteristics of Mannerist architecture include the use of traditional Classical motifs in untraditional ways or in deliberately ambiguous, often nonfunctional, roles. The Palazzo Zuccaro (today the Biblioteca Hertziana) in Rome's Via Gregoriana, built by Federico Zuccaro in 1593, is perhaps the quintessential Mannerist structure, with its entrance portal and window frames disguised as grotesque heads of monsters with gaping mouths.

As with painting and sculpture, the Mannerist trend in architecture first manifested itself in Italy, in the late works of Michelangelo: the Medici Chapel, 1520–34, and the vestibule of the Laurentian Library, 1523–34, both part of the church of S. Lorenzo in Florence; and the Porta Pia in Rome, built after his designs by assistants (1561–64). Michelangelo's daring architectural innovations were augmented by those of Giulio Romano (Palazzo del Tè, Mantua, 1525–35), Giorgio Vasari (Uffizi, Florence, 1560–74), and Andrea Palladio (Palazzo Valmarana, Vicenza, 1565–66). The Mannerist style spread thereafter to France, especially to the court of François I at Fontainebleau, where Francesco Primaticcio designed the Grotte des Pins (*c.* 1543), which combines imaginative statuary with a form of crude rustication that is another common feature of Mannerist architecture.

MANSART, François (1598, Paris—1666, Paris), French architect. Mansart's career extended from the end of Louis XIII's reign through the minority of Louis XIV. He was one of the founders of French Classicism and began his career auspiciously with a few private dwellings and religious buildings: the church of Ste-Marie de la Visitation (1632–34), and the *hôtels* ("town houses") of La Vrillière (1635–38; now the Banque de France), La Bazinière, and Chavigny (*c.* 1635–41), all in Paris; and the châteaux at Berny (designed 1623) and at Balleroy (begun *c.* 1626; Calvados). In 1635 a large commission came his way, for the Orléans wing of the château at Blois. The château in the Paris suburb of Maisons-sur-Seine (now Maisons-Laffitte), built from 1642 to 1648 for the president René de Longueil, is one of the masterpieces of French architecture. After 1643, during the regency of Anne of Austria and Mazarin's ministry, Mansart was commissioned to build the abbey of Val-de-Grâce. Jacques Lemercier and Pierre Le Muet (1591–1669) intrigued successfully to have the commission transferred to them. However, the Duplessis-Guénégaud family, for whom Mansart had built two town houses, gave him the chance to use his design for the church dome at Val-de-Grâce for their chapel in the château at Fresnes (Seine-et-Marne) instead. The remodeling on the Hôtel d'Aumont (staircase designed 1665) and the reconstruction of the Hôtel Carnavalet (1665), both in Paris, in the Renaissance manner belong to the last part of his career.

Mansart was often faithful to the teaching of his master Salomon de Brosse (1565–1629), and steeped himself in the writings of the Italian theoreticians Sebastiano Serlio and Giacomo Barozzi da Vignola. He designed some interesting variants of the centrally planned church. At Ste-Marie de la Visitation, the rotunda, punctuated by Corinthian pilasters, is contained within a square whose

François Mansart. Château at Maisons-Laffitte. 1642–48. *Photo Bonnefoy-Connaissance des Arts, Paris.*

median axes lead to the entrance drum, the sanctuary, and two lateral chapels, while the diagonal axes terminate in three chapels and the sacristy. Mansart's most accomplished central plans are at Fresnes and in the project for the Chapelle des Bourbons at St-Denis, where he developed the vertical perspective effects that he used again in the stairwells of the châteaux at Blois and Maisons, those two great creations of secular architecture that are landmarks both in the development of French architecture and in Mansart's own work. The château at Maisons stands at a unique point of equilibrium between survivals from the Middle Ages and the early beginnings of Classicism. Like Philibert de l'Orme, Mansart scaled his decoration to the individual story rather than to the entire height of the façade; he preferred the superimposition of orders to the single colossal order. He had the technical virtuosity of the old masters: he used pendentives in the Hôtel de La Vrillière and the staircase at Blois as skillfully as another transition device, the volute, in the Hôtel de l'Aubespine.

MANSART, Jules Hardouin-. *See* **HARDOUIN-MANSART,** Jules.

MANSHIP, Paul (1885, St. Paul, Minnesota—1966, New York), American sculptor. From 1922 to 1926 he lived in Paris. In 1932 he became a member of the Smithsonian Art Commission, of which he was chairman for 20 years. Manship's sculptural style is marked by a strong emphasis on line and design in stylized representations of plant, animal, and human forms, often shown in sweeping movement. His most frequent subjects were mythological and allegorical figures, such as *Centaur and Dryad* (1913; New York, Metropolitan Museum). He also made a number of portrait busts, both in relief and in the round, and executed numerous public commissions, such as *Indian Hunter with Dog* (1926; St. Paul, Minn., Cochran Memorial Park) and the colossal *Prometheus Fountain* (1934; New York, Rockefeller Center).

MANTEGNA, Andrea (*c.* 1431, Isola di Cartura, near Vicenza—1506, Mantua), Italian painter. His name appears on the Paduan registers for the first time in 1441. He is mentioned as the apprentice and adopted son of Francesco Squarcione (1394/97–1468/74), an archaeologist and painter with whom he remained for six years. As early as 1448, Mantegna was one of a group commissioned to decorate the Ovetari Chapel (frescoes badly damaged in 1944) in the Church of the Eremitani in Padua; he worked there until 1456, and the success of the work established his fame. Mantegna's marriage to Nicolosia Bellini, daughter of Jacopo and sister of Gentile and Giovanni, made him a member of the most renowned family of Venetian artists. He painted an altarpiece for S. Zeno, Verona (1456–59), in which eight saints surround an enthroned Madonna under a complex open loggia; the picture was brought to France in 1797, and the predella panels are still there: the *Crucifixion* (Paris, Louvre), the *Agony in the Garden,* and the *Resurrection* (both Tours, Museum).

Called to Mantua by Ludovico Gonzaga, Mantegna became court painter in 1459; he worked on the decoration of the palace chapel (destroyed), which may be represented in three extant engravings of the *Crucifixion, Entombment*, and *Descent into Limbo.* After decorating the *Camera degli Sposi* (Bridal Chamber) at the Palazzo Ducale in Mantua (1473–74), which is a glorification of the reigning Gonzaga family, Mantegna gave complete expression to his genius in the nine large paintings of the *Triumph of Caesar* (before 1486–after 1492), which formed the decoration of a room in the Mantua palace (sold to King Charles I in the 17th century; now in Hampton Court Palace, England; restored in the 1960s).

Meanwhile, Mantegna had produced some important works: the foreshortened *Dead Christ* (Milan, Brera), a bravura piece worthy of the Florentine school, painted about 1465–66; the *St. Sebastian* (*c.* early 1470s; Paris, Louvre); and the small *Madonna of the Rocks* (Florence, Uffizi), which Vasari believed dated from the artist's stay in Rome (1484). Mantegna was again invited to Rome, in 1488, by Pope Innocent VIII, at which time he entirely decorated the little Belvedere Chapel in the Vatican (destroyed in 1780). Back in Mantua, he was still occupied with official commissions, notable among which is the *Madonna della*

Andrea Mantegna. *St. Sebastian. c.* early 1470s. Louvre, Paris. *Photo Giraudon, Paris.*

Vittoria (Louvre), which commemorates Gian Francesco Gonzaga's victory over the French at Fornovo in 1495. Mantegna next worked for Isabella d'Este in Ferrara, and his last period was dominated by the decoration of the princess's study, acquired by Cardinal Richelieu of France and now in the Louvre. It includes the *Parnassus*, which, according to a letter, was painted in 1497; *Minerva Expelling the Vices from the Grove of Virtue*, delivered in 1501–2; and *Comus*, the weakest of all, completed by Lorenzo Costa. The *St. Sebastian* in Venice (Ca' d'Oro) is usually ascribed to the painter's last years.

Squarcione's training gave Mantegna the Paduan taste for antiquities very early, but he must have gone to Venice as early as 1447 and seen the paintings of Antonio Vivarini and Giovanni d'Alemagna (d. 1450), the frescoes of Andrea del Castagno in S. Zaccaria (finished in 1442), and met for the first time Jacopo Bellini and his sons. It was probably in Venice that Mantegna painted most of the *Life of St. James*, particularly the powerful judgment and torture scenes. The landscapes are mere reconstructions of Classical architecture: the human figures, in Roman dress, move through a setting of rocks, blocks of masonry, and flagstones. The draftsmanship gives the sculptural figures a hard, metallic consistency; perspective is used to give impressive views from unusual angles. But his main source was the sculpture of Donatello: the S. Zeno altarpiece imitates the composition and spirit of the altarpiece in S. Antonio, Padua, with its statues inside a sort

Andrea Mantegna. *Portrait of Federigo I Gonzaga.* Detail from the Camera degli Sposi. 1473–74. Palazzo Ducale, Mantua. *Photo Anderson-Giraudon.*

of pilastered loggia. Mantegna was also influenced by the "harsh" style of Andrea del Castagno, particularly when he painted his dramatically foreshortened *Dead Christ,* and he may have had in mind the frescoes of Benozzo Gozzoli in the Palazzo Medici-Riccardi, Florence, when he decorated the *Camera degli Sposi* in Mantua, which remains his masterpiece. His talent for archaeological reconstructions was inimitable; the cartoons of the *Triumph of Caesar* depict an extraordinary frieze filled with pieces of armor, military equipment, and antique vases. It was designed as a long procession, which satisfied the decorative scheme.

In his smaller compositions and predella panels, Mantegna is equally powerful: the three lower scenes in the S. Zeno altarpiece, depicting the *Agony in the Garden*, the *Crucifixion,* and the *Resurrection*, are set in an acid, granite landscape with red rocks, invested with Roman warriors; this obsession with antiquity gave a fresh solemnity to the theme. In the *Madonna* painted in 1497 for the monks of S. Maria in Organo, Verona, the composition is seen from below, and this perspective effect is reinforced by the placing of the saints and the curtain of foliage in the corners. Mantegna's command of composition had never been more masterly.

Mantegna was the "antiquarian" of the Quattrocento. He was probably the only artist of his time to be directly and permanently inspired by the antique fragments found in Italy or brought back from Greece, and he developed a whole system of ornaments directly inspired by Greek and Roman reliefs and medals. They stimulated the imagination of his contemporaries, and, through engravings—of which he was one of the first great masters—they reappeared in all the arts. Mantegna's influence spread throughout northern Italy. Bartolomeo Vivarini had a Mantegnesque period, and so had Giovanni Bellini, for instance in his *Agony in the Garden* (London, National Gallery). Through him also German artists—particularly Albrecht Dürer—discovered Italy, antiquity, and the Renaissance.

MANUEL DEUTSCH, Niklaus (1484, Bern—1530, Bern), Swiss painter and engraver. In 1515 Manuel was commissioned to paint the St. Anne altarpiece (Bern, Kunstmuseum) for the goldsmiths' and painters' confraternities of St. Eligius and St. Luke. His *Temptation of St. Anthony* (1520; Bern, Kunstmuseum) seems to have been influenced by an engraving on the same subject by Martin Schongauer and by Mathias Grünewald's Isenheim Altarpiece.

By the early 1520s Manuel was well established. He also painted his masterpieces, two large tempera paintings: the *Judgment of Paris* (*c.* 1523–24) and *Pyramus and Thisbe* (1529), both in the Basel Kunstmuseum. The first, painted with extremely delicate colors, is a mixture of middle-class domesticity and a kind of Surrealism. An astonishing lyricism in the landscape setting is the outstanding feature of *Pyramus and Thisbe*.

Several of Manuel's drawings have survived, a number of them intended for engraving and often illustrating the history of the Reformation. Late in his career he assumed an increasingly important position in Bern, and was entrusted with diplomatic missions to the other Swiss cantons. He was an exceptional and complex figure, active as a Protestant reformer, soldier, and an outstanding artist as well.

Niklaus Manuel Deutsch. *Lucretia.* 1517. Kunstmuseum, Basel.

MANZÙ, Giacomo (b. 1908, Bergamo), Italian sculptor. He lived for some time in Paris, but in 1930 moved to Milan, where he produced his first really striking work, the *Shulamite* (1930; Bergamo, Coll. Pizzigoni), in colored cement. After retiring to a country house near Selvino, Bergamo, in 1933, he began a remarkable series of portraits of women in bronze, wax, and painted wood (*Portrait of the Artist's Wife*, 1934, Milan, Coll. Carlo Carrà; *Woman Combing Her Hair*, 1935, Rome, Galleria Nazionale d'Arte Moderna). In the late 1930s, Manzù produced his first sculptures of cardinals, a theme that gained him recognition and that was later continued in a number of small and large versions. In 1939 he carved the Passion of Christ in a series of reliefs in which the scenes of the Crucifixion and Deposition reflected his anxieties and melancholy. Manzù's *Self-Portrait with the Model* (1943–46; Milan, Coll. Lampugnami) and his *Portrait of a Woman* (1946; New York, Museum of Modern Art) represent a high point in his career. In 1949, after a competition and an intense controversy, he was commissioned to carve the bronze reliefs on the Porta della Morte ("Door of Death") at St. Peter's in the Vatican (installed in 1964). This was followed in 1955 by the commission for the main door of Salzburg Cathedral in Austria. The stylistic harmony of Classicism and modernity in Manzù's work gives great dignity to his figures, which, whether secular or religious, show a remarkable feeling for the life and elegance of the human body.

MARC, Franz (1880, Munich—1916, Verdun), German Expressionist painter. Although he had discovered his favorite subject, animals, when he was twenty-five, it was not until about six years later that he evolved his personal style. Before his stylistic maturity, he made several studies of single animals of all kinds, and in 1908 actually began painting them. Marc visited Paris twice, in 1903 and 1907; in 1910 he met Wassily Kandinsky, and together they

Franz Marc. *Horses at Rest.* 1912.

prepared a publication that they called *Der blaue Reiter* ("The Blue Rider"), which appeared in 1912. Toward the end of 1911, they organized an exhibition under the same title, which included paintings by August Macke, Heinrich Campendonk, Henri Rousseau, and Robert Delaunay, in addition to their own works. At the time this show took place, a distinct change came over Marc's art. His coloring became bright, and he used colors of the prism instead of local colors to sheathe his forms, which, like the Cubists, Marc tried to purify, geometricize, and synthetize (*Red Horses*, 1911, Essen, Folkwang Museum; *Large White Horses*, 1911, Minneapolis, Walker Art Center).

All Marc's paintings at this period were of animals, but he was not interested in representing them realistically. His animals were dream creatures, symbols and projections of his imagination, appearing idealized and transfigured. Until about the end of 1912, they were painted in the foreground and were detached from the landscape surrounding them, almost in contrast to it. Later they were integrated and partly merged into it, as if the soul of the animal were reflected in the landscape. Another important element in his art at this time was the visit he made to Robert Delaunay in 1912, when Marc first saw Futurist works; this explains the fragmentation of his colors and forms, overlapping in some places and interpenetrating in others (*Deer in the Forest*, 1913–14; Karlsruhe, Staatliche Kunsthalle).

The logical development of his style finally led Marc in 1913–14 to suppress the realistic portrayal of objects entirely. Something dramatic made itself felt, particularly in the landscapes that the Tirol inspired in him (*Unhappy Tirol*, 1913; New York, Guggenheim Museum). In other paintings, the abstraction is total and the titles themselves indicate this trend (*Forms in Combat*, 1914; Munich, Bayerische Staatsgemäldesammlungen). World War I prevented Marc from pursuing this late style for long. He was mobilized in 1914, and was killed two years later at Verdun. His work is among the most significant in German painting at the beginning of the 20th century.

MARCA-RELLI, Conrad (b. 1913, Boston), American painter. He taught in the mural and easel division of the WPA Federal Art Project, where he made the acquaintance of Franz Kline, Willem de Kooning, and John Graham, who introduced him to the principles of European modernism and to the work of Picasso, Miró, and Matisse. After military service during World War II, Marca-Relli resumed painting, working with motifs from circus life and Italian Renaissance architecture. In 1951 Marca-Relli began to paint organic, semi-abstract shapes derived from Surrealist notions of automation, which formally reflected the work of both Miró and Arshile Gorky. In 1952 he began to introduce raw canvas into his paintings through a collage technique, enlarging the medium of collage in a series of restrained and monumental works. Contacts with De Kooning and Pollock in 1953 provided Marca-Relli with a loosened biomorphic vocabulary and balanced his urge for Classical harmony with a freer, more expressive abstraction. His semi-figurative series of *Sleeping Figures* (1953–54) and *Seated Figures* (1962–66), abstract vinyl and metal collages, aluminum reliefs (1962–64), and simplified metal sculptures reflect his characteristic vacillation between an expressionistic mode and a strictly ordered Classical equilibrium.

Marca-Relli's mural-size collages mark an ambitious high point in his career, with such works as *Trial* (1956; Minneapolis, Institute of Arts) or *The Battle* (1956; New York, Metropolitan Museum), which include tautly composed canvas swatches in biomorphic shapes, energetically brushed with black or colored areas of paint. Shallow aluminum reliefs and freestanding sculptures, as well as isolated painted shapes filling a bare field, followed his collages of the early 1960s.

MARCHAND, André (b. 1907, Aix-en-Provence), French painter. He was self-taught and was influenced at first by Cézanne, but he soon turned toward an unusual sort of realism that was related to the work of the Forces Nouvelles group. About 1940, when he went back to Aix, his vision changed completely: he discovered pure color and adopted a "Japanese" kind of composition, stressing pattern and line. He painted several still lifes in this style (*Bottle and Fruit*, 1949; Paris, Musée National d'Art Moderne); huge, powerful, dramatic pictures (*The Fates*, 1944); and a whole series of landscapes of Les Baux in Provence. In the course of his development he peopled his landscapes with large nudes of mythological significance and created an idealized Provence in which woman and the sea were the protagonists in a sort of sacred ballet. After 1955 his vision grew wider, and his paintings of the Camargue (bulls and pink flamingoes) and later of the Breton coast led him to a less directly figurative manner (*Sea Breezes*, 1960).

MARCOUSSIS, Ludwig Casimir Markus, *called* Louis (1878, Warsaw—1941, Cusset, near Vichy), French painter of Polish origin. In 1903 he went to Paris and studied at the Académie Julian, where he met Roger de La Fresnaye. His painting was first influenced by Impressionism and then by Fauvism. In 1910 he became friendly with Georges Braque, Pablo Picasso, and the poets Guillaume Apollinaire and Max Jacob. He exhibited with the Cubists (whose ideas he shared) and, in 1912, contributed to the first exhibition of the Section d'Or, a Cubist group. His collages of 1914 have all the seriousness and compactness of Braque's and Picasso's work in the same medium. Between 1919 and 1928 he completed about 100 paintings

Louis Marcoussis. Etching from *Last Hopes.* 1931. Éditions Jeanne Bucher, Paris.

Marino Marini. *Horseman.* 1952. Walker Art Center, Minneapolis.

on glass—a process that precludes retouching or corrections. These works reveal his strong attachment to the structural principles of Cubism, to which he always remained faithful even though he applied them so as to achieve the delicacy and luminosity that his poetic nature demanded. In 1927, during a visit to Kérity, in Brittany, he painted the *Shells* series and 8 little seascapes (*Port at Kérity*, 1927; Paris, Musée National d'Art Moderne). In 1929 he began a series of *Still Lifes in an Interior* (1929–30), as well as a series of *Figures* (1930–31). Then for a few years he concentrated his activities on engraving, a technique that he mastered admirably (*Last Hopes*, 1931; *Theatrical Etchings for Monsieur Gémier*, 1933; and a series of etchings for Apollinaire's *Alcools*, 1934). He began painting again in 1937. Marcoussis occupies a position in the history of Cubism that comes immediately after the leading names of Braque, Picasso, and Juan Gris.

MARÉES, Hans von (1837, Elberfeld, Wuppertal—1887, Rome), German painter. In 1857 he went to Munich, where he worked with his friend, Franz von Lenbach. In 1864, accompanied by Lenbach, he went to Italy to copy a number of Italian paintings commissioned by his patron, Count Schack. The fundamental principles of his art, however, were not appreciated by his patron, and Marées broke his connection with him. Fortunately, he gained the patronage of the art historian Konrad Fiedler in 1866, and three years later traveled with him to Spain, Holland, and France.

After a stay in Dresden (1872–73), Marées went to Naples, where he painted what are probably his best works: the vast frescoes in the Stazione Zoologica, which include the *Friends of the Artist in a Pergola* (1873). He finally settled in Rome, and for the last years of his life devoted himself to a kind of grandiose, rhythmic painting characterized by a monumentality and plasticity of form. His figures, usually accentuated by a strong chiaroscuro, managed to preserve their isolated, statuesque quality even while being linked organically in space (*Garden of the Hesperides*, 1884–85; Munich, Bayerische Staatsgëmaldesammlungen).

MARIA MARTINS. *See* **MARTINS,** Maria Martins Pereira e Souza.

MARIN, John (1870, Rutherford, New Jersey—1953, Cape Split, Maine), American painter. He attended the Pennsylvania Academy of the Fine Arts (1899–1901), then the Art Students League (1904) in New York. He made his home in Europe from 1905 to 1911. Marin had his first one-man show at Alfred Stieglitz' 291 Gallery in 1909, and exhibited in the Younger American Painters show in 1910 at the same gallery, then in the famous Armory Show of 1913. The Venice Biennale of 1950 paid homage to him in a brilliant retrospective.

Marin's masterly watercolors, more so than his oil paintings, provided the measure of his talent, which was emotional, nervous, and had an original vision that had been influenced by the French Impressionists. He specialized in seascapes (*Maine Islands*, 1922; Washington, D.C., Phillips Collection) that have a brightness of color, a very free treatment of form, an immediacy of sensual expression, and a quivering poetry. Marin excelled in painting raging seas, stormy skies, plains interrupted by mountains, iron bridges, and the buildings of the great American cities (*Lower Manhattan*, 1921; New York, Metropolitan Museum). Never an adherent of artistic theories, he concerned himself only with the unleashing of the elements that drive a man to surpass himself again and again in his impassioned conquest of the material world.

MARINI, Marino (b. 1901, Pistoia, Tuscany), Italian sculptor and graphic artist. A student of painting and sculpture at the Academy of Fine Arts in Florence, he was first influenced by antique sculpture, especially by early Etruscan and Roman figures. To these he brought a disquiet and tension that was typically modern. His early art was somewhat static and included figures that expressed the individual and eternal aspects of human reality (*Blind Man*, 1928; *People*, 1929). His work, however, soon became more dynamic as he concentrated on specific subjects that became his personal themes, and whose significance he constantly deepened. This is evident, for example, in his famous series of *Horses and Riders*, begun in 1936 and developed over the years. In the same way, the combinations of movements in the series of *Jugglers* and *Dancers* were a dialogue between the architecture of the human body and space. In addition to his sculptures, Marini also produced a large body of graphic work and painting, and was an astonishing portraitist. His sculptured portrait busts, in which the individual is also an archetype, include *Campigli* (1940); *Tosi* (1942); *Stravinsky* (1950); and *Henry Miller* (1961).

MARISOL, Marisol Escobar, *called* (b. 1930, Paris), American sculptress. Marisol spent her youth mainly in Los Angeles and in Paris, where she studied art at the École des Beaux-Arts and the Académie Julian. In 1950 she settled in New York and continued her studies at the Hans Hofmann School and the Art Students League; from 1958 to 1960 she worked in Rome.

Marisol began to work primarily in sculpture around 1953. Her early efforts include small playful and erotic terra-cotta figures and roughly carved wood figures of human beings and animals. Her mature work, from the late 1950s and the 1960s, consists of mixed-media assemblages that include juxtapositions of all media—painting, carving, drawing, plaster casts, and found objects. Her skillfully crafted pieces are usually larger than life-size, sometimes conceived as single units, at other times as groups. Characteristic examples of Marisol's work are the *Blacks* (1961–62; mixed media, Coll. Mrs. Eleanor Ward); *Women and Dog* (1964; mixed media, New York, Whitney Museum); and *Dealers* (1965–66; mixed media, New York, Sidney Janis Gallery).

MARKELIUS, Sven (b. 1889, Stockholm), Swedish architect. The first major influence on Markelius was the French architect Le Corbusier, whose ideas he spread in Sweden. In 1930 Markelius collaborated with the Swedish architect Uno Ahrén (b. 1890) in the construction of the Students' Club in the Stockholm Polytechnic School, which was one of the first modern buildings in that city. The large annex Markelius added in 1950 emphasized the functional character of the school even more. His architectural ability progressed steadily from 1932 when he built the Concert Hall in

Hälsingborg, to 1939 when he designed the Swedish Pavilion at the New York World's Fair. The Social Center at Linköping, with its assembly halls, offices, a cinema, and a restaurant, demonstrated the consummate skill with which Markelius could harmonize the different parts of an architectural complex. In 1944 he was appointed director of the Stockholm City Planning Office and, in that capacity, he laid out the satellite town of Vällingby, about six miles from the capital. He coordinated the work of the various architects planning the town and, in 1955, they began constructing its apartment blocks and cultural buildings. The town was completed in 1959.

MARLOW, William (1740, Southwark, London—1813, Twickenham, near London), English painter, mainly of landscapes, although he also did animal studies and marine subjects. Between 1765 and 1768 he traveled in France and Italy. Marlow, who exhibited at the Royal Academy (1788–96; 1807), used the studies that he made abroad as the basis for most of the paintings he executed in later life. He was influenced by Antonio Canaletto, who inspired several of his caprices (*View of St. Paul's Cathedral in a Venetian Setting*, c. 1795; London, Tate Gallery). The *Adelphi under Construction* (c. 1771; London, Coll. Westminster Bank Ltd.) is typical of his mature style. In the mid-1780s Marlow retired from professional practice, but occasionally painted landscapes for his own pleasure.

William Marlow. *View of St. Paul's Cathedral in a Venetian Setting.* c. 1795 (?) Tate Gallery, London.

MAROT, family of French architects and engravers of the 17th century, which included:

JEAN I (c. 1619, Paris—1679, Paris), son of a Huguenot master cabinet-maker. He is best known today for his invaluable series of engravings of the buildings of his time. As an architect, he built two *hôtels* ("town houses") in Paris for Gabriel de Rochchouart, Duc de Mortemart. He is also credited with the design for the famous and splendid wrought-iron grille for the château at Maisons-Laffitte, near Paris, which is now at the entrance to the Galerie d'Apollon in the Louvre, Paris. Jean Marot's large body of engravings, which did much to spread Classicism in Europe, was published in two volumes, in 1727 and 1764. They are commonly known as the *Grand Marot* and the *Petit Marot*.

DANIEL (1663, Paris—1752, Amsterdam), Jean's second son. When he had to leave France at the revocation of the Edict of Nantes (1685), he fled to Holland. He was made chief architect to William of Orange, and was granted a life annuity when the latter became William III of England in 1689. In London, Daniel Marot was probably a consultant in the furnishing of Kensington Palace, and of Windsor Castle, outside London. By 1696 or 1697 he was back in Amsterdam, and spent the remainder of his life in the Netherlands. He was a skilled exponent of the Louis XIV style, which he imported to Holland. Marot's buildings at The Hague include the Stadthuis (1733–39) and part of the Royal Library (1734–38). He published a collection of his engravings in Amsterdam in 1712.

MARQUET, Albert (1875, Bordeaux—1947, Paris), French painter and draftsman. In 1897 he entered the École des Beaux-Arts, where he studied in Gustave Moreau's studio, and where Georges Rouault and Henri Matisse were among his fellow students. Although Marquet was one of the boldest of the Fauves, he was more concerned than the others with the solidity of forms and the harmonious unity of tones. This need for order and equilibrium is manifest in the *Quai des Grands-Augustins* (1905) and the *Beach at Fécamp* (1906), both in Paris, Musée National d'Art Moderne, as well as in *Posters at Trouville* (1906; Priv. Coll.), *Sergeant of the Colonial Troops* (1907; New York, Coll. Robert Lehman), and *Pont St-Michel* (1908; Grenoble, Museum). From an early age Marquet drew assiduously. With a few short, mordant lines he could seize a gesture, a moving animal, the shape of a tree, a boat, or a sail. Once the spirit of Fauvism had subsided in him, he gave up the sturdy portraits, fairgrounds, and acidulous nudes that had been his favorite subjects, and thereafter began painting landscapes exclusively. The paintings he brought back from countless journeys in France and abroad are notable for their fluid, refined technique, pleasing color harmonies, linear conciseness, and for their virtuosity, which was modestly hidden behind a charming nonchalance. More than anything he wanted to give a faithful rendering of reality, and his credo was that of Jean-Baptiste Corot and Gustave Courbet. He found in nature the powers of imagination that he lacked and a sense of renewal that an excessive restraint prevented him from finding in himself.

Albert Marquet. *Woman with an Umbrella.*

MARSH, Reginald (1898, Paris—1954, New York), American painter. The realist tradition of illustration claimed his professional interest for a decade before he turned to painting, and Marsh worked as an illustrator for *Vanity Fair*, *Harper's Bazaar*, and the New York *Daily News*. Marsh was especially attracted by the circus and by the more perverse or lowly aspects of city life. He is well known for his paintings of the crowds and amusement arcades in Times Square and Coney Island, and his careful and loving record of these spots is often quite accurate in detail (*Twenty-Cent Movie*, 1936; New York, Whitney Museum). In 1929 the artist Kenneth Hayes Miller prompted him to turn increasingly to urban scenes, and Marsh painted such inelegant places as the *Bowery* (1930; New York, Metropolitan Museum). The "El" (elevated railway), a typically New York phenomenon, figured in several of his paintings (*Why not use the El?*, 1930; New York, Whitney Museum).

MARSTRAND, Wilhelm Nicolaj (1810, Copenhagen—1873, Copenhagen), Danish painter. He trained at the Royal Academy in Copenhagen, then went to Italy

John Martin. *Project for a Babylonian Triumphal Arch in Regent's Park, London.* 1820. British Museum, London.

(1836–39) and to Munich and Paris in 1840. He returned to Copenhagen, where he remained for the next 15 years before setting off for Italy again, where he stayed from 1855 to 1860. There is a strong narrative element in Marstrand's painting, and most of his subjects are historical or genre scenes (*Two Servant Maids Dressing, with the Third Still Asleep*; Copenhagen, Statens Museum for Kunst). His most representative paintings are to be found at the Kunsthalle, Hamburg, and the Ny Carlsberg Glyptotek, Copenhagen. His frescoes can be seen in the church at Roskilde (Denmark) and in the Aula (assembly hall) of Copenhagen University. The most interesting side of his work is the sketches that he made on the spot and brought back from his travels, particularly the sketches of Roman ruins.

MARTELLANGE, Étienne Ange Martel, *called* (1569, Lyons—1641, Paris), French architect. Martellange became a Jesuit in 1590. His order entrusted him with the building of numerous churches in Paris and the provinces. The Cabinet des Éstampes of the Bibliothèque Nationale in Paris has a notebook containing his plans and projects. Martellange lived in Rome during the period when the Jesuits were expelled from France (1594–1608). He returned to his country in 1604 and was entrusted with the job of inspecting the buildings of his order. His first important undertaking seems to have been the construction of the Jesuit College in Puy, Haute-Loire (1605–7). Martellange adopted as the basic plan for his churches a design that was influenced by the principal Jesuit church in Rome, Il Gesù. Most had a single nave, which was well suited to preaching, and were lined with connecting side chapels that were placed between the buttresses.

Among the numerous churches Martellange designed are the chapels of the Jesuit colleges in La Flèche, Sarthe (1612–21) and Roanne, Loire (1617–26), both of which are characterized by their austere simplicity. In Paris Martellange designed the church of St-Paul-St-Louis (1627–41) in collaboration with the Jesuit architect Father François Derand (1588–1644).

Juan Martínez Montañés. *The Three Kings.* From altarpiece of the Adoration of the Shepherds. 1609–12. Convent of S. Isidoro del Campo, Santiponce. *Photo Mas, Barcelona.*

MARTIN, Homer Dodge (1836, Albany, New York—1897, St. Paul, Minnesota), American painter. He joined the circle of Samuel Palmer in Albany, quickly accepted "the traditional scenic ideal of landscape painting," and emulated the well-balanced compositions of Claude Lorrain. The landscapes of the 1860s are thinly painted and characterized by a delicate touch and simple arrangement of forms. The *Old Mill* (1860; Middlefield, Conn., Coll. Lyman A. Mills) reveals the influence of Thomas Cole. By the early 1870s, Martin became more concerned with color, employing hues not usually found in nature or in academic pictures. Even though his *Raquette Lake* (1869; formerly New York, Coll. M. Knoedler & Co.) is still very traditional in terms of composition, the work sets him apart from his contemporaries. Martin's close relationship with J. A. M. Whistler during his stay in Europe in 1876, as well as his assimilation of the work of the Barbizon painters, considerably influenced his style. His handling became freer, his color more adventurous, and his sketches shifted in medium from pencil to charcoal. He was in Europe again in 1879, remaining there until 1887 and residing mostly in Brittany and Normandy. His complete rejection of the Hudson River School's objectivity is perhaps best seen in the *Harp of the Winds* (1895; New York, Metropolitan Museum).

MARTIN, John (1789, Haydon Bridge, Northumberland—1854, Douglas, Isle of Man), English Romantic painter and engraver. In 1806 Martin went to London, and was employed by a glass manufacturer to paint on glass and china in enamel colors. He first exhibited at the Royal Academy in 1811, and was hailed by overly enthusiastic critics as a rival to Turner. His *Sadak Searching for the Waters of Oblivion* (1812; Southampton, Art Gallery), set in a stupendous rocky landscape, appealed to contemporary Romantic sensibility, as did his *Destruction of Herculaneum* (1822; Manchester, City Art Gallery). Martin continued to paint in this vein, rising to a climax in his illustrations for Milton's *Paradise Lost* (1827) and the Last Judgment series of pictures (the *Great Day of His Wrath*, 1852; London, Tate Gallery), genuine apocalypses that reach a height of Romanticism unique in English art.

Much of his time was taken up with impractical projects for reforming the sewage system of London or "improving the air and water of the metropolis." But in the realm of painting, Martin's extraordinary Babylonian skyscrapers and the sheer volume of his architectural fantasy anticipate the projects of the French architects Étienne-Louis Boullée and Claude-Nicolas Ledoux—especially in his *Project for a Babylonian Triumphal Arch in Regent's Park, London* (1820; London, British Museum).

MARTIN, Kenneth (b. 1905, Sheffield), English painter and sculptor. From 1929 to 1932 he attended the Royal College of Art in London and became known as a painter of landscapes, working directly after nature in accordance with the English Neoimpressionist tradition represented by the Euston Road School. Later his work, like that of Victor Pasmore with whom he allied himself, moved progressively away from figuration, arriving around 1949 at total abstraction. Beginning in 1951 he took up sculpture and worked almost exclusively at mobile constructions in metal. Martin's art champions logic rather than imagination. His most characteristic constructions are composed of metal stalks soldered in spirals or analogous figures, with a rigorously mathematical conception; once suspended, they turn, producing a "perpetual motion" of sinuous and flowing clarity.

MARTÍNEZ MONTAÑÉS, Juan (1568, Alcalá la Real, Andalusia—1649, Seville), Spanish sculptor. One of the greatest masters of polychrome sculpture, his activity centered about the churches, convents, and palaces of Andalusia and Seville. Often Martínez Montañés planned the architectural framework for his altarpieces, and his reputation in this field was such that the design for the magnificent royal chapel (*c.* 1650) in Puebla Cathedral (Mexico) has often been attributed to him. The sculptor provided his assistants with models, reserving the execution of the most important parts to himself. He entrusted skilled painters (including Francisco Pacheco) with the polychromy, but kept them under the strictest supervision.

From the sculptor's formative years date the state of *St. Christopher* (1597) in the church of S. Salvador at Seville; the *St. Jerome* (1597–1604) in the convent of S. Clara at Llerena; and the *Christ of Clemency* (1603–5), a crucifix in Seville Cathedral. The *Infant Jesus* of 1605 in Seville's parish church of the Sagrario not only charms with its childlike grace, but also astounds with its divine majesty.

Notable among the altarpieces of this period is that representing the *Adoration of the Shepherds* (1609–12) on the high altar in the convent of S. Isidoro del Campo at Santiponce; the altarpiece of St. John the Baptist in the convent of S. María del Socorro at Seville (1610–20); and that of S. Miguel at Jerez de la Frontera (*c.* 1617). In the late 1620s, he produced the unusually attractive *Virgin of the Immaculate Conception* ("La Cieguecita") for the tabernacle in Seville Cathedral (1628–31).

Arturo Martini. *Moonlight.* 1932. Middelheim Park Museum, Antwerp.

MARTINI, Arturo (1889, Treviso—1947, Milan), Italian sculptor. He began sculpting around 1905, when he became a pupil of Antonio Carlini in Treviso, and then studied with Urbano Nono (b. 1849) in Venice and, in 1909, with Adolf von Hildebrand in Munich. Although he was influenced by a number of styles and movements ranging from classical statuary to Futurism, he had an imaginative personality that enabled him to fuse and sublimate them. He did numerous terra cottas, such as the *Drinker* (1926; Rome, Galleria Nazionale d'Arte Moderna) and *Moonlight* (1932; Antwerp, Middelheim Park Museum); stone statues, such as the delightful reclining nude called the *Pisan Woman* (1928; Acqui, Piedmont, Coll. Ottolengi), and *Thirst* (1934; Milan, Galleria d'Arte Moderna), which has an exceptional dramatic quality; and high reliefs, including the monument to the *Italian Pioneers of America* (1927–28; Worcester, Mass.), done in collaboration with the American sculptor Maurice Sterne (1878–1957). Martini created a number of sculptures in which the figures are engaged in a specific activity (the *Hundred-Yard Sprinter*, 1935, Venice, Galleria d'Arte Moderna; and *Girl Swimming Under Water*, 1941, Milan, Priv. Coll.). These works had a sense of movement and drama and an expressiveness that culminated in his monumental high relief of *Corporate Justice* (1937; Milan, Palazzo di Giustizia). At the end of his life, Martini produced a distilled version of his artistic experience in his book *La Scultura, lingua morta*, 1945 ("Sculpture: A Dead Language") and in his marble statue of *Palinurus* (1946; Padua University).

MARTINI, Francesco di Giorgio. *See* **FRANCESCO DI GIORGIO MARTINI.**

MARTINI, Simone di Martino, *called* Simone (*c.* 1284, Siena—1344, Avignon), Italian painter. We know nothing about Simone's early works, but his *Maestà* fresco (signed and dated 1315) in the Palazzo Pubblico at Siena suggests earlier works, since such an important commission would not have been given to a beginner. In it the artist displays his debt to Duccio's *Maestà*, but he is more influenced by Gothicisms, replacing the hieratic solemnity of the old master with a refined elegance and a subtle decorative sense. Simone's figures, instead of standing out against a gold background, occupy a space that has been given added dimension by the use of perspective.

In 1317 Simone Martini was at the court of King Robert of Anjou in Naples, where he painted the *Coronation of Robert of Anjou* (1317; Naples, Museo di Capodimonte). His equestrian figure of the medieval condottiere Guidoriccio da Fogliano in the Palazzo Pubblico in Siena (1328) is one of the most surprising examples of Sienese fresco painting. Nothing has survived of the works Simone painted between 1328 and 1333. In the latter year he painted the *Annunciation* altarpiece formerly in the S. Ansano chapel of Siena Cathedral (now in the Uffizi, Florence). This panel painting is one of the highest achievements of Sienese Gothic art.

The date of the frescoes in the chapel of S. Martino, in the Lower Church of S. Francesco at Assisi, is uncertain. Various art historians date them between 1317 and 1339, that is, between the end of the artist's stay in Naples and his departure for Avignon. The paintings seem to be earlier than the Uffizi *Annunciation*, for they show less technical mastery and a less complete assimilation of the Gothic style. The four half-length portraits of saints in the right transept of the Lower Church at Assisi (representing St. Louis of Toulouse, St. Francis, St. Clare, and St. Elizabeth of Hungary) are also attributed to Simone Martini.

In 1339 the artist left Italy to settle permanently in Avignon, which at the time was the seat of

Simone Martini. *St. Louis of Toulouse.* Detail from the Coronation of Robert of Anjou. 1317. Museo di Capodimonte, Naples. *Photo Anderson-Giraudon.*

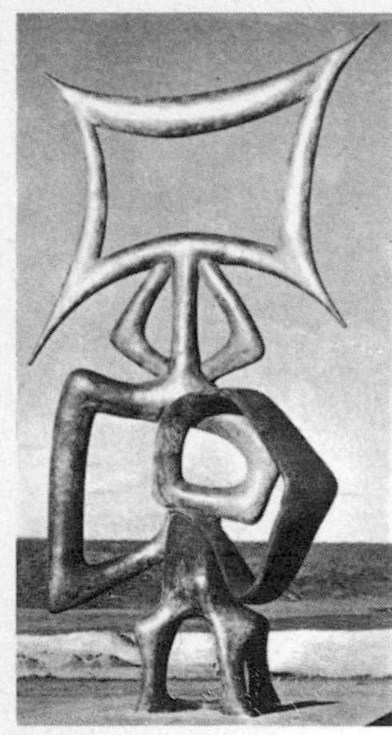

Maria Martins. Bronze statue, gardens of the Presidential Palace, Brasilia. *c.* 1959. *Photo Marcel Gautherot, Rio de Janeiro.*

the Papacy. All that remains of his last works are fragments of frescoes in the porch of Avignon Cathedral.

MARTINS, Maria Martins Pereira e Souza, *called* Maria (b. 1900, Campanha, Brazil), Brazilian sculptress. It was not until 1939 that, on the advice of the sculptor Oscar Jespers, she decided to devote all her time to sculpture. She had her first exhibition in Washington, D.C., in 1940, but it was only in 1946 that her works, exhibited in the Museum of Modern Art in New York, showed the full flowering of her luxuriant style. In 1943 the Valentine Gallery in New York published an album, *Amazonia*, illustrating her group of sculptures of the same name. It included her famous *Cobra Grande* (1943). Her favorite subject was a feminine creature trying to free herself from the clutches of monstrous plants. After Maria won the first prize for sculpture at the São Paulo Bienal (1957), she decorated the Aurora gardens in Brasilia.

MASACCIO, Tommaso di Giovanni, *called* (1401, San Giovanni Valdarno, near Florence—*c.* 1428, Rome), Italian painter. He was, with Donatello and Filippo Brunelleschi, the founder of the heroic style in 15th-century Florence that flourished at the same time as the International Gothic, represented principally by Lorenzo Ghiberti and Gentile da Fabriano. Although no precise chronology has been established for each of Masaccio's works, his oeuvre must date from after 1422, when he entered the Florentine Guild, and before 1428. Masaccio inherited the tradition of Giotto and was the true ancestor of Michelangelo: his influence was felt by most Florentine artists of the 15th century, even though many of them reacted against it, and it was felt chiefly through his frescoes in the Brancacci Chapel in S. Maria del Carmine, Florence. Documents exist for an altarpiece in the Carmelite church in Pisa, painted by Masaccio in 1426, which was described by Giorgio Vasari, but was later dismembered and lost. The main panel, a *Madonna*, was identified, on the grounds of stylistic likeness to some of the frescoes in the Brancacci Chapel and correspondence with Vasari's description, with a panel in the National Gallery, London. A few more panels in Pisa, Berlin, Naples, and Vienna have been identified as coming from the Pisa Polyptych, but much of it is still lost. The polyptych thus recreated can now be used as an authenticated example of Masaccio's mature style to check the style of the Brancacci frescoes. General agreement on the division of these between Masaccio and Masolino has been reached, Masaccio's chief works being the *Tribute Money*, the *Expulsion from Paradise, St. Peter Enthroned, St. Peter Healing the Sick by His Shadow,* and *St. Peter Giving Alms*, together with part of the *Raising of the Praetor's Son* (much of which is by Filippino Lippi). On the basis of the Brancacci frescoes it is possible to attribute to him the fresco of the *Trinity* in S. Maria Novella, Florence. The problem of his relationship to Masolino is complicated by the fact that, in the Brancacci Chapel, they were obviously working together and in some other works attributed to Masolino a very strong influence from Masaccio is unmistakable. The two works in which this extreme similarity of style is most clearly seen are the fresco of the *Baptism of the Neophytes*, in the Brancacci Chapel, and the two panels, now in the National Gallery, London, which come from a large altarpiece, the major parts of which are in Naples. All of this altarpiece appears to be by Masolino, but one panel of *St. Jerome and St. John the Baptist* (London, National Gallery) is very close to Masaccio's style and is attributed to him by many authorities (though not by the Gallery).

The quality for which Masaccio was esteemed by contemporary and later artists was not one that would insure popular success, for he was rigidly grand and uncompromisingly austere in the pursuit of these quasi-scientific aims that distinguish the early, humanist art of 15th-century Florence. The aesthetic purpose of this severity of form and subordination of all the elements of the composition—figures and landscape alike—to an overriding and consistent geometry and illumination was simply that of realism. This heroic style, praised by the architect Leon Battista Alberti in his *Della Pittura* of 1436, was the creation of Brunelleschi, Donatello, and Masaccio, who was by far the youngest of the group. Because he died so young, Masaccio's influence was comparatively small, but his austere rejection of the delights of bright color, gold, and charming detail did even more to cause the younger generation to pay him little more than lip-service. Most of the rest of the 15th century saw a Masacciesque undercurrent, but the increasing Florentine cult of the outline also ran counter to the simple masses and strong chiaroscuro of Masaccio's frescoes. Michelangelo, who made drawings after his frescoes, was probably the first to truly understand Masaccio's art, as he himself had been the first for nearly a century to penetrate the spirit of Giotto's.

Masaccio. *Expulsion from Paradise.* Brancacci Chapel, S. Maria del Carmine, Florence. *Photo Anderson-Giraudon.*

MASEGNE, Jacobello *and* Pier Paolo dalle. *See* **DALLE MASEGNE,** Jacobello *and* Pier Paolo.

MASO DI BANCO (2nd quarter of 14th century, Florence), Italian painter. Maso di Banco, with Stefano Fiorentino and Taddeo Gaddi, is considered one of the closest of Giotto's disciples. He is documented at Florence between 1341 and 1353. It is generally agreed today that he painted at least two of the frescoes in the Bardi II or S. Silvestro Chapel at S. Croce, Florence, illustrating episodes from the legend of St. Sylvester (*Ridolfo dei Bardi at the Last Judgment* and *St. Sylvester and the Dragon*). He is by far the most important of Giotto's followers and, as early as the 15th century, the sculptor Lorenzo Ghiberti, in his *Commentarii*, recognized in him one of the masters of the Trecento. Maso di Banco's art is characterized by the excellence of his draperies, the beauty and expressiveness of the faces, and the attitudes of the figures, which recall the solemn dignity and weightiness of Giotto's.

Masolino da Panicale. *Story of St. Peter: Resurrection of Tabitha and Healing of the Cripple. c.* 1425. Brancacci Chapel, S. Maria del Carmine, Florence. *Photo Anderson-Giraudon.*

MASOLINO DA PANICALE, Tommaso di Cristoforo Fini, *called* (b. 1383, Panicale—d. *c.* 1447), Italian painter. Masolino is first mentioned in 1423, when, according to custom, he was enrolled in the guild of painters, physicians, and apothecaries in Florence. At Empoli, Masolino decorated the St. Helena Chapel in the church of S. Stefano, and painted the imposing *Pietà* for the baptistery of the Collegiate Church. The Uffizi *Madonna* raises the question of his collaboration with Masaccio. About 1425, Masolino began working in the Brancacci Chapel in S. Maria del Carmine, Florence, painting frescoes of the *Story of St. Peter* for Felice Brancacci. He was joined in this commission by Masaccio, and the respective attribution of the frescoes seems to be more or less established; the *Healing of the Cripple* is by Masolino. However, Masolino left Masaccio to complete the work, as he traveled to Hungary with Pippo Spano, the Florentine *condottiere* in the service of King Sigismund. He was back before long and went to Rome about 1430, where he painted the frescoes in S. Clemente (*Story of St. Ambrose; Story of St. Catherine*; and in particular the large *Crucifixion*), in which Masaccio's hand has also been discerned. Two panels with saints (London, National Gallery), which must have belonged to the triptych of the *Miracle of the Snow* (1425–28; Naples, Museo di Capodimonte), painted for S. Maria Maggiore in Rome, caused renewed discussion concerning the work of the two friends in Rome. After a brief stay at Todi, where he painted a *Madonna and Child* for S. Fortunato (1432), Masolino moved to northern Italy with Cardinal Branda Castiglione to execute a remarkable series of frescoes for the baptistery, the Collegiata, and the Cardinal's palace at Castiglione d'Olona. There is no further mention of him after 1447.

MASSON, André (b. 1896, Balagny, Oise), French painter and engraver. After a short period under the influence of the Cubists and Juan Gris (*Card Players*, 1923; Paris, Priv. Coll.), Masson painted his first uncompromisingly symbolic picture, the *Four Elements* (1923–24; Paris, Coll. Dr. Tchernia-Jéramec). He was subsequently drawn into the Surrealist movement, in which he took an active part until 1929. His series of *Fighting Animals* (1927–30) anticipated later paintings that depict the struggles of human beings. This theme was soon superseded by the series of *Massacres* (1931–33), which Masson treated in a number of paintings as well as in 400 drawings executed with sharp, broken lines.

Masson found Spain a congenial land, and lived there from 1934 to 1936, first visiting Andalusia, and then staying at Tossa de Mar in Catalonia, where he painted insects and bullfights. The works produced after the outbreak of the Spanish Civil War affirm his rejection of oppression. In 1941 Masson first took refuge in Martinique, then in North America, where he stayed until 1945. He found a new source of inspiration in Negro and Red Indian myths, and the violence of his expression and brushwork (*There is No Finished World*, 1942; Baltimore, Museum of Art) influenced the stylistic development of many young American painters. During the whole of this period he executed numerous pastels on canvas, as well as sculptures and Surrealistic objects. Upon his return to France, he settled in Aix-en-Provence (1947–56), and once again found an inexhaustible source of inspiration in nature and the elements. He poured into a compact style of strong, strident colors all his previous motifs so that he could glorify the forces of nature and their symbolism all the more effectively (series of *Orgies, Ceremonies*, and *Tutelary Figures*, all 1962–64). Masson's painting was paralleled by his work as a writer and draftsman (*Mythology of Nature, Mythology of Being*, 1936; *Anatomy of My Universe*, 1943; *Nocturnal Notebook*, 1944); as an engraver (*Journey to Venice*, 1951–52; *Féminaire*, 1957); and as an illustrator (André Malraux's *Conquerors*, 1948). Masson also designed the sets and costumes for a number of theatrical productions, notably for *Les Présages* (1933, Ballets Russes de Monte-Carlo), *Numance* (1937) by Miguel de Cervantes, *Hamlet* (1946), *Morts Sans Sépulture* (1946) by Jean-Paul Sartre, *Tête d'Or* by Paul Claudel (1959), and *Wozzeck* by Alban Berg (1963).

MASSYS, MATSYS, *or* **METSYS,** family of Flemish painters of the 15th and 16th centuries.

QUINTEN (1466, Louvain—1530, Antwerp) was trained in the style of Dirk Bouts and became a Master at Antwerp in 1493. Although the inheritor of medieval traditions, he was attracted by the Renaissance style, and was an elegant innovator who introduced a sense of movement into Northern painting. Massys was much impressed by the art of Leonardo da Vinci, whose *sfumato* technique he adop-

André Masson. *Massacres.* 1932–33. *Photo Galerie Louise Leiris, Paris.*

Quinten Massys. *Portrait of Erasmus.* 1517. Galleria Nazionale, Rome. *Photo Anderson-Giraudon.*

ted and whose interest in caricatural expressions he imitated (*Portrait of an Old Man*, 1513; Paris, Musée Jacquemart-André). The works of Massys include a triptych on the *Legend of St. Anne* (1507–9; central panel in Brussels, Musées Royaux des Beaux-Arts, wings in Vaduz, Liechtenstein Collection) and a moving triptych on the *Deposition* (1508–11; Antwerp, Musée Royal des Beaux-Arts) for the Antwerp Carpenters' Guild, a work whose power foreshadows that of Bruegel. Massys' portraits—such as those of his humanist friends *Egidius* (1517; Salisbury, Longford Castle, Coll. Earl of Radnor) and *Erasmus* (1517; Rome, Galleria Nazionale)—are quite original in their presentation of the sitter by means of his function, his work, or his milieu, and they are the forerunners of Holbein's portraits. The *Banker and His Wife* (1514; Paris, Louvre) expresses the new spirit of painting in 16th-century Antwerp.

CORNELIS (*c.* 1510, Antwerp—*c.* 1570, Antwerp), Quinten's son, was a landscapist and one of the most picturesque interpreters of peasant life prior to the time of Pieter Bruegel. Typical are the *Return of the Prodigal Son* (1538; Amsterdam, Rijksmuseum), the *Holy Family at Bethlehem* (1540; formerly Berlin, Kaiser Friedrich Museum), and a *Landscape with Hunters* (Dessau).

JAN (*c.* 1509, Antwerp—1575, Antwerp) was the brother of Cornelis, along with whom he entered the guild in 1531. In 1550 Jan was working in Ghent, and after his return to Antwerp in 1558 helped to introduce the Mannerism of Francesco Primaticcio into Flanders. In his paintings such as *Flora Before the Bay of Naples* (1561; Stockholm, Nationalmuseum); *David and Bathsheba* (1562; Paris, Louvre); *Susanna and the Elders* (1567; Brussels, Musées Royaux des Beaux-Arts); or *Lot and His Daughters* (1565; Brussels, Musées Royaux des Beaux-Arts)—his eroticism differs from that of Frans Floris, being charged with subtle moral intentions. Jan's lines are pure, his color harmonies delicate and rare, and his modeling subdued.

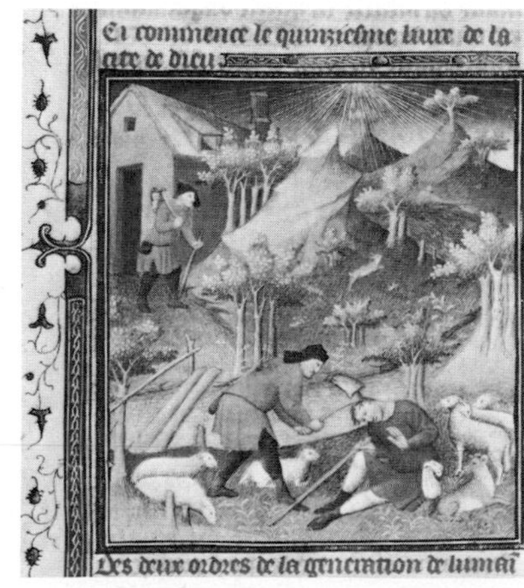

Master of the Boucicaut Hours. *Cain slaying Abel.* Miniature from the second volume of St. Augustine's *La Cité de Dieu.* Walters Art Gallery, Baltimore, Maryland.

MASTER OF THE BOUCICAUT HOURS (early 15th century, Paris), anonymous Franco-Flemish miniaturist, who executed the *Book of Hours* of Jean II Le Meingre, Maréchal de Boucicaut (Paris, Musée Jacquemart-André. It was probably produced between 1405 and 1415, and the artist's hand is recognizable in a large number of other manuscripts illuminated in Paris during the first 20 years of the century (pages from *Dialogues de Pierre Salmon*, 1411/12, Paris, Bibliothèque Nationale and Geneva, Bibliothèque Publique et Universitaire; two Books of Hours, *c.* 1415 and *c.* 1420, Baltimore, Md., Walters Art Gallery). Like the Master of the Duke of Bedford, with whom he collaborated, the Boucicaut Master was a brilliant exponent of an elegant, courtly Gothicism, in line with the taste of his time. He was also a remarkable innovator. He was influenced by Italian art, as were the Limbourg brothers, and through his assimilation of its principles, he opened a new field of vision to French and Flemish artists. The realism he pioneered reached culmination in the work of the Master of Flémalle and the Van Eycks.

Some historians have identified the Master of the Boucicaut Hours with the Bruges artist Jacques Coene (active late 14th–early 15th century), who is known to have worked in Paris in 1398 and, from 1402 to 1404, in Milan Cathedral.

MASTER OF THE CARNATION, name given to a group of anonymous Swiss, German, and Tirolese painters who used carnations as their signatures and were active between the end of the 15th and the beginning of the 16th century. The distinction generally made between the three Masters of the Carnation corresponds to the production of three different workshops.

MASTER OF THE CARNATION OF BERN. He did seven of the panels from the *Altarpiece of St. John the Baptist* for Bern Cathedral, which are now divided between the Bern Kunstmuseum (*Baptism of Christ, c.* 1500), the National Museum in Budapest, and the Zurich Kunsthaus (*St. John the Baptist in the Wilderness* and the *Beheading of St. John the Baptist*). His figures are thickset and impassive, and the settings have an almost geometric simplicity.

MASTER OF THE CARNATION OF ZURICH. He was active in this town between 1490 and 1505 and has often been identified with Hans Leu the Elder (b. 1460). The Zurich Kunsthaus possesses several of his works, notably four panels, two of which are from an altarpiece of St. Michael, and a *Portrait of Hans Schneeberger*. The Berlin Museum's *Feast of Herod* shows a strain of Classicism.

MASTER OF THE CARNATION OF FRIBOURG. He painted the altarpiece in the Cordeliers' Convent in Fribourg (*c.* 1480; Basel, Kunstmuseum), which is remarkable for the freshness of coloring and for a certain solemnity.

MASTER OF THE COEUR D'AMOUR ÉPRIS (active 2nd half of 15th century, Anjou), French miniaturist. This name has been given to the anonymous miniaturist who illustrated the story of *Cuer d'Amours Espris* (*c.* 1460; Vienna, Nationalbibliothek), an allegorical romance written by King René I of Anjou around 1457. The illuminated manuscript, which was dedicated to Jehan II de Bourbon, who had married King René's niece Jeanne de France, is one of the masterpieces of French 15th-century miniature painting. It is especially remarkable for its experiments with the lighting effects of nocturnal settings and sunrises, which are among the earliest known such experiments in European painting. An attempt has been made to identify the Master with the French artist Barthélémy de Clerc (d. *c.* 1476), René of Anjou's valet, who is thought by some to have painted the miniatures in *Le Livre des Tournois du Roi René* (*c.* 1460; Paris, Bibliothèque Nationale).

MASTER OF THE DUKE OF BEDFORD (active 1405–30), anonymous French miniaturist whose name derives from his powerful patron, John of Lancaster, Duke of Bedford, regent of France during the English occupation (1422–35), for whom he did the *Bedford Hours* (1423–30; London, British Museum) and the *Salisbury Breviary* (1424–35; Paris, Bibliothèque Nationale). He belonged to the international artistic circle in Paris and shared a workshop with the Master of the Boucicaut Hours and the Master of the Rohan Hours. The outstanding characteristic of the Master of Bedford's oeuvre is a fine sense of color and a fondness for delicate harmonies, which he used increasingly for atmospheric effects and landscape, perhaps under Italian influence. The Master's fresh tones are present in the very fine *Térence des ducs* (1407–8) and the *Livre de chasse de Gaston de Foix* (both in Paris, Bibliothèque de l'Arsenal).

MASTER E. S. (b. *c.* 1420—d. *c.* 1467), anonymous German Gothic graphic artist, one of the very earliest to practice copperplate engraving and the apparent inventor of the cross-hatch technique. The engravings with which hs is credited are very numerous: over 300 survive, although only 18 actually carry the monogram E.S. His last dated works were executed in 1467, in a clearly mature style, so it is assumed that he died soon afterward.

The Master's subject range was wide, touching on the profane, the sacred, and the fantastic, and he was a ceaseless experimenter. His first engravings are already technically assured, with careful detail work, although they are somewhat diffuse compositionally (*Emperor Augustus and the Tiburtine Sibyl*, *c.* 1440 or 1450; Boston, Museum of Fine Arts). Later his contours become more vigorous, while his figures gain in three-dimensionality. During the Master's mature phase his figures take on further structural robustness, although his compositions never lose the over-all decorative flatness that he stressed throughout his career (*Madonna and Child enthroned with Two Angels*, *c.* 1466; Washington, D.C., National Gallery).

Master of the Duke of Bedford. *Death of St. Edward the Martyr*. Miniature from the *Salisbury Breviary*. 1424–35. Bibliothèque Nationale, Paris.

MASTER OF FLÉMALLE. *See* **CAMPIN,** Robert.

MASTER OF FLORA (mid-16th century), anonymous painter of the school of Fontainebleau to whom the art historian Charles Sterling attributed three paintings: the *Triumph of Flora* (Vicenza, Priv. Coll.), *The Birth of Cupid* (*c.* 1540–60; New York, Metropolitan Museum), and *Abundance* (Ravenna, Accademia). Madame Sylvie Béguin, a French scholar, suggested that this artist should be identified with Rugiero de Rugieri (d. 1596), an Italian painter who in 1557 appeared at Fontainebleau, where he painted the *Life of Hercules* in the Pavillon des Poêles. Although the master evidently based the proportions of his human figures on the Italian Mannerists Primaticcio and Bronzino, he imparted to their supple, elongated, and slightly twisted bodies a more febrile and evanescent quality.

MASTER OF FRANKFURT (active 1480–1530, Antwerp), Flemish painter. He is named after a triptych (*c.* 1505) in the Städelsches Kunstinstitut, Frankfurt, whose central panel depicts the *Crucifixion*; it is flanked by wings showing the donor Claus Humbrecht with three sons and St. Nicholas of Bari, and the donor's wife with her daughter and St. Margaret; an *Allegory of Death* adorns the outside wings. Other paintings attributed to him include the *Adoration of the Magi* (Antwerp, Musée Royal des Beaux-Arts), inspired by Hugo van der Goes; the *Baptism of Christ* (Barcelona); a *Legend of St. Anne* (Berlin); a *Nativity* (Hamburg); and a triptych showing the *Holy Kinship*, the *Birth of the Virgin*, and the *Death of the Virgin* (Frankfurt, Städelsches Kunstinstitut). The Master's *Feast of the Archers in the Guild Garden* (Antwerp, Musée Royal des Beaux-Arts) is curiously archaic, whereas the strong draftsmanship and rather hard coloring of some of his other works indicate that he was a precursor of Quinten Massys. He has been identified with Jan de Vos (1460–1533) and, more convincingly, with Hendrik van Wueluwe (before 1470–1533), who was Master at Antwerp in 1483.

Master of Flora. *Birth of Cupid*. *c.* 1540–60. Metropolitan Museum of Art, New York.

MASTER OF THE GATHERING OF MANNA (active *c.* 1470, Haarlem), Dutch painter. Some art historians identify him with Master Zeno or van Evert Zoudenbalch. He is credited with *Gathering Manna in the Desert* (Douai, Museum) and the *Fire*

Master of the Gathering of Manna. *Jews Gathering Manna in the Wilderness*. *c.* 1470. Musée de la Chartreuse, Dijon. *Photo Giraudon, Paris.*

Master of the Life of Mary. *Servants.* Detail from the Birth of the Virgin. Alte Pinakothek, Munich.

Offering of the Jews (Rotterdam, Museum Boymans-van Beuningen), which form two wings of a large altarpiece probably painted between 1465 and 1475. He is also assumed to have painted *Christ Healing the Blind at Jericho* (Blaricum, North Holland, Priv. Coll.) and a *Crucifixion* (St-Germain-en-Laye, Seine-et-Oise, Priv. Coll.), both of which were probably painted between 1475 and 1485. The Master's compositions are lively, his colors bright, and his drawing is often somewhat caricatural.

MASTER OF THE GROOTE ADORATION (active early 16th century, Antwerp), Flemish Mannerist painter. This master is the assumed painter of various versions of the *Adoration of the Magi.* His name is derived from an *Adoration* that forms the central panel of a triptych, whose wings depict *David and the Messengers* and the *Queen of Sheba*, in the Von Groote collection in Kitzburg, Germany. Among the other works attributed to him are the wings of a triptych whose central panel is missing, illustrating *David and the Ambassadors* and the *Queen of Sheba* (Chicago, Art Institute); a triptych whose center is a *Pietà* (Vienna, Kunsthistorisches Museum); a triptych with the *Last Supper* in the center, *Christ's Farewell to His Mother* on the left wing, and *Christ Washing St. Peter's Feet* on the right wing (Brussels, Musées Royaux des Beaux-Arts); a triptych with the *Last Supper* in the center (New York, Metropolitan Museum); and an *Adoration* (Philadelphia, John G. Johnson Art Collection). The Master loved to paint jewels and he frequently placed his figures in fantastic landscapes strewn with ruins.

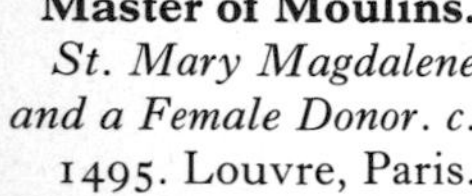

Master of Moulins. *St. Mary Magdalene and a Female Donor. c.* 1495. Louvre, Paris. *Photo Giraudon, Paris.*

MASTER OF THE HOLY KINSHIP (active *c.* 1480–1520, Cologne), German painter. His name derives from a triptych (*c.* 1500; Cologne, Wallraf-Richartz-Museum) representing the Holy Kinship on the central panel and the donors with their patron saints on the wings. The Wallraf-Richartz-Museum also possesses an earlier work by the Master, the fine triptych on the *Legend of St. Sebastian.* Fragments of a youthful work, an altarpiece on the *Seven Joys of the Virgin,* also survive in the Louvre, Paris, and in the Germanisches Nationalmuseum, Nuremberg. Other works attributed to the Master include a *Holy Trinity with the Adoration of the Magi* on the reverse (*c.* 1490; New York, Metropolitan Museum). Around 1490 the Master's style grew closer to the Netherlandish manner; this is evident, for example, in an altarpiece from the church of St. Columba in Cologne, three panels of which are in the Alte Pinakothek, Munich.

MASTER OF THE LEGEND OF ST. BARBARA (active *c.* 1470–1500, Brussels), Flemish painter. He was a pupil of the Flemish painter Rogier van der Weyden. His altarpiece on the *Life of St. Barbara* (*c.* 1475), which is characterized by a marked expression of anxiety on the faces, is now scattered between the Musées Royaux des Beaux-Arts, Brussels; the Musée du Saint-Sang, Bruges; and the Metropolitan Museum, New York. Other paintings attributed to him are the *David Giving a Letter to Uriah* and the *Queen of Sheba Bringing Gifts to Solomon* (both New York, Metropolitan Museum), and two panels depicting the *Story of Job* (Cologne, Wallraf-Richartz-Museum). Some art historians consider the Master of the St. Barbara Legend to be identical with the Flemish master who painted *Two Miracles of St. Nicholas of Bari* (Dublin, National Gallery of Ireland).

MASTER OF THE LEGEND OF ST. URSULA OF BRUGES (active late 15th century, Bruges), Flemish painter. The Master derives his name from the two delightful wings of an altarpiece that depicts the *Legend of St. Ursula* (*c.* 1470; Bruges, Convent of the Black Sisters), and that predates Hans Memlinc's famous version of the same legend. The Master's style is somewhat archaic, but has great subtlety of tone, narrative invention, and a mysticism that is combined with a plebeian gaiety. His other works include *Christ Appearing to His Mother* and *A Donor with St. Paul* (both in New York, Metropolitan Museum), which constitute the wings of an altarpiece; and the *Virgin Suckling the Child*, also in the Metropolitan Museum.

MASTER OF THE LIFE OF MARY, *also known as* **MASTER OF THE LIFE OF THE VIRGIN** (active *c.* 1460–1480/90, Cologne), German painter. He is named after an altarpiece consisting of eight panels illustrating scenes from the life of the Virgin; seven panels are now in the Alte Pinakothek, Munich, and the eighth is in the National Gallery, London. The painter of this altarpiece was one of the most fertile artists of the Cologne School of painting at the end of the 15th century. He was so strongly influenced by the Netherlandish artists, especially by Dirk Bouts and Rogier van der Weyden, that most art historians agree he was trained in a Flemish workshop. He is also credited with the remaining fragments of altarpiece wings, dated 1473, from the church of St. Columba in Cologne, which are now in the Germanisches Nationalmuseum at Nuremberg. Toward the end of his life this charming narrative painter broadened his style in works such as the *Crucifixion with Nicolas of Cusa as Donor* from the hospital church at Bernkastel-Kues, Rhineland-Palatinate, and the triptych of the *Descent from the Cross* (1480; Cologne, Wallraf-Richartz-Museum). The Master's style can also be recognized in stained glass in Cologne and its environs.

MASTER OF THE MAGDALEN (active in Tuscany *c.* 1250), the name given to the unknown Italian painter of a *St. Mary Magdalene* (*c.* 1250) in the Accademia, Florence. It shows a full-length portrait of the saint and, at the sides, scenes from her life. Apart from the influence of Pisa and, through it, of Byzantine art, we find elements of Florentine and Sienese painting in this picture. Many of the paintings attributed to the Master of the Magdalen are not by the same hand, but in the same style and probably from the same workshop. Examples are the altarpieces in the Jarvis Collection, New Haven,

Connecticut, and in the Musée des Arts Décoratifs, Paris, where the central part is occupied by the Virgin and Child between two saints; and the altarpiece in the church of Vico l'Abate, near Florence, particularly interesting for its iconography, with St. Michael enthroned in the center and, on either side, scenes from his legendary life, directly inspired by the *Golden Legend* of Jacobus de Voragine.

MASTER OF THE MÉRODE ALTARPIECE. *See* **CAMPIN,** Robert.

MASTER OF MOULINS (active *c.* 1480—*c.* 1499), French painter. He is named after the triptych in Moulins Cathedral of the *Madonna and Child Surrounded by Angels* (*c.* 1498/99). The closed triptych shows an *Annunciation* painted in grisaille on the two leaves. Inside, on the two wings, are the figures of the donors in princely splendor, Pierre II, Duc de Bourbon, and his wife, Anne de France, the daughter of Louis XI. About a dozen works have been grouped around this triptych, as they appear to have been painted in the same workshop. Beginning with the painting that seems to be the earliest, they include the delightful *Nativity, with Cardinal Jean Rolin* (1480–83; Autun, Museum); two fragments of an altarpiece (central panel lost), *Pierre de Bourbon Presented by St. Peter* and *Anne de France Presented by St. Anne* (1492–93; Paris, Louvre); the *Virgin and Child Surrounded by Four Angels* (*c.* 1490–95; Brussels, Musées Royaux des Beaux-Arts); an *Annunciation* (Chicago, Art Institute) that may be the right panel of a triptych, of which the left may be *Charlemagne and the Meeting at the Golden Gate* (1495–1500; London, National Gallery); *St. Mary Magdalene and a Female Donor* (*c.* 1495; Louvre); and *St. Maurice with a Donor* (who is probably François de Châteaubriant), which scholars date about 1500 (Glasgow, Art Gallery and Museum). Two portraits can be added to this list: *Cardinal Charles II de Bourbon* (*c.* 1483–85; Munich, Alte Pinakothek) and the charming *Young Princess* in the Robert Lehman Collection, New York.

The Master of Moulins remains anonymous. The breadth and simplicity of his compositions, his taste for clearly structured, finely modeled forms, and the nobility with which he endows his sitters make him the last great painter of French Gothicism.

MASTER OF THE NARBONNE ALTAR FRONTAL (active late 14th century, Paris), French painter. The master's name derives from the *Narbonne Altar Frontal* (*c.* 1375; Paris, Louvre), which is drawn in grisaille on silk and illustrates scenes of the Passion. It was discovered in Narbonne Cathedral at the beginning of the 19th century, but there is no doubt that the work was done in Paris around 1375 for King Charles V of France and his wife, Jeanne de Bourbon, who appear on the frontal in the guise of donors. The same master is also credited with some miniatures in the Duc de Berry's *Très Belles Heures de Notre-Dame* (*c.* 1402; Paris, Louvre and Bibliothèque Nationale). After the death (1380) of Charles V, the artist was probably taken into the service of Charles's brother, Jean, Duc de Berry. The Master's style is in the great tradition of the School of Paris miniaturist Jean Pucelle. His linear grace and vivacious expression are typically Parisian, but his iconography and his refined, exact modeling of volumes reveal a direct knowledge of Italian art. His treatment of space, however, is still rudimentary.

MASTER OF THE REGISTRUM GREGORII (late 10th century), German miniaturist who was one of the outstanding artists of the Ottonian renaissance. The *Registrum Gregorii* (*c.* 985) was the masterpiece of the scriptorium founded by Archbishop Egbert at the abbey of St. Maximin in Trier, and was presented by the archbishop to the cathedral of Trier. A fragment is now in the Municipal Library of Trier, with a detailed leaf, representing Otto II receiving homage from the four provinces of Germania, Francia, Italia, and Alemannia, housed in the Musée Condé, Chantilly. The style is similar to that of the Reichenau school, with its typically sumptuous decoration, and the Master also achieved his own vigorous sense of the third dimension. He has also been credited with the important Ste-Chapelle Gospel Book (Paris, Bibliothèque Nationale) and the Lorsch Sacramentary (Musée Condé).

MASTER OF THE ROHAN HOURS (active 1st half of 15th century), anonymous French artist who decorated the manuscript of the *Grandes Heures de Rohan* (*c.* 1420; Paris, Bibliothèque Nationale) with 65 miniatures, 11 of which occupy a full page each. The manuscript is one of the masterpieces of French 16th-century art because of its size and the exceptional quality of the illustrations. In spite of its title, derived from the arms of the Rohan family that appear on the verso of sheet 26, the manuscript was probably executed around 1420 by a French artist (Flemish according to some authorities) attached to the House of Anjou in France. There are also grounds for noting the similarities between the Master of the Rohan Hours and the French painter known as the Master of the Boucicaut Hours. Other works attributed to the Master include the *Heures des Ducs d'Anjou* (Paris, Bibliothèque Nationale), which contain a striking portrait of *King René d'Anjou* on the verso of sheet 81; a panel representing *Apostles and Prophets*, on the back of which there is an *Angel of the Annunciation* (Laon, Museum); a *Book of Hours*, known as the *Cambridge Hours* (before 1420; Cambridge, Fitzwilliam Museum); and the *Pool of Bethesda* (before 1425; Brunswick, Staatliches Herzog Anton Ulrich-Museum).

Master of the Narbonne Altar Frontal. *Appearance of Christ to St. Mary Magdalene.* Detail. *c.* 1375. Louvre, Paris. *Photo Giraudon, Paris.*

Master of St. Sebastian. *St. Sebastian Destroying the Idols.* John G. Johnson Coll., Philadelphia Museum of Art.

MASTER OF ST. GILES (active 1490–1510), painter of unknown identity, probably French. Of his entire output only four panels survive, and they are divided between the National Galleries of London and Washington, D.C. The London panels illustrate episodes from the life of St. Giles and those in Washington the life of St. Remigius. The interest of these panels lies not only in the talent of the artist, but also in their rarely treated subjects. In addition the settings are faithful reproductions of historic French sites: the *Mass of St. Giles* is celebrated before the high altar in the abbey of St-Denis, Paris; the background of *St. Giles and the Hind* is recognizable as the town of Loches, about 20 miles southeast of Tours. The Washington panels, in which St. Remigius is seen baptizing Clovis in Ste-Chapelle, Paris, and blessing the people on the parvis of Notre-Dame, are equally attractive, and all are valuable as documentaries. The portrait of *Philip the Fair* (Winterthur, Coll. Oscar Reinhart) is also attributed to this artist.

MASTER OF ST. SEBASTIAN (active late 15th century, Provence), French painter. He was originally named after seven panels on the *Legend of St. Sebastian*, which are now scattered between the Philadelphia Museum of Art; the Walters Art Gallery, Baltimore; the Hermitage, Leningrad; and the Galleria Nazionale, Rome. The art historian Charles Sterling has since proved that the altarpiece to which the panels belong can be identified with the one commissioned in 1497 from the Flemish painter Josse Lieferinxe and the Italian Bernardino Simondi (d. 1498) by the priors of a confraternity located near the church of Notre-Dame-des-Accoules in Marseilles. Since Simondi died in 1498, before the work was finished, the main responsibility for the painting must be given to Lieferinxe. A large *Calvary* (Paris, Louvre) and several scenes from the *Life of the Virgin*, which were probably painted three or four years earlier than the *Calvary*, have also been attributed to him. Although Lieferinxe's work reveals Netherlandish influences as well as affinities with Lombard and Piedmontese art, the bold clarity of the lighting effects he used to define simple volumes, as well as the calm nobility, the dramatic expression, and the restrained emotion of his style are characteristic of the school of Avignon, of which he was the last great master.

Umberto Mastroianni. *Painted Bronze. 1959. Photo Oscar Savio, Rome.*

MASTER OF THE VIEW OF STE-GUDULE (active *c.* 1470–1500, Brussels), Flemish painter. He is presumed to have been a native of Brussels. The Master's name is derived from a characteristic work, *A Preacher with a View of Ste-Gudule Cathedral in the Background* (*c.* 1490; Paris, Louvre). He also designed tapestry cartoons, and is credited with the *Works of Mercy* (Paris, Musée de Cluny). His paintings include the altarpiece of the *Passion* (Paris, Musée des Arts Décoratifs), the *Virgin in the Temple* and an *Annunciation* (both Brussels, Musées Royaux des Beaux-Arts), the *Adoration of the Magi* (Baltimore, Museum of Art), the *Virgin with St. Mary Magdalene and a Donor* (Liège, Musée Diocésan), and the *Young Man Holding a Prayer Book* (New York, Metropolitan Museum). His paintings are imbued with the animated movement characteristic of 15th-century Gothic Mannerism.

MASTER OF THE VIRGO INTER VIRGINES (active *c.* 1470–1500, Delft), Dutch painter. He owes his name to a fine painting in the Rijksmuseum, Amsterdam, representing the *Virgin and Child with Sts. Catherine, Ursula, Barbara, and Cecilia.* Other works attributed to the Master are a *Crucifixion* (Florence, Uffizi), an *Annunciation* (Rotterdam, Museum Boymans-van Beuningen), an *Adoration of the Magi* (Berlin), an *Entombment* (Liverpool, Walker Art Gallery), a *Lamentation of Christ* (New York, Metropolitan Museum), a portrait of *Hugo de Groot* (New York, Coll. Wildenstein & Co., Inc.), and a *Trinity* (Zagreb). His iconography is very original, and his paintings are either charming or extremely austere. His vast triptych of the *Crucifixion* (*c.* 1495; Durham, Barnard Castle, Bowes Museum) is one of the few Dutch altarpieces of the period that is still complete.

MASTROIANNI, Umberto (b. 1910, Fontana Liri, near Rome), Italian sculptor. He decided to become a sculptor at an early age, and his first one-man show at Genoa in 1931 was followed by many others; these early exhibitions placed him in the Futurist tradition as a successor of Umberto Boccioni. It was only after World War II that Mastroianni broke away from the realism that in general had been the basis of his art until then, and adopted a type of Abstract Expressionism characterized by projections sweeping into space or angular structures (*Winged Apparition*, 1957; *Pegasus*, 1959). His style is very effective on a large scale, as in the *Monument to a Partisan* in Turin's Campo della Gloria (designed in 1946) and the huge *Lovers* (1954) in the central railroad station in Rotterdam. Mastroianni's sculptures, which are single-piece compositions, became progressively more powerful as he succeeded in dramatizing their forms and giving them a flying rhythm.

MATARÉ, Ewald (1887, Aachen—1965, Cologne), German sculptor, painter, and graphic artist. His first desire was to be a painter, and he studied under the painter Lovis Corinth in Berlin in 1907. In 1920, however, he was attracted to sculpture and soon gained recognition as a sculptor of animals. In 1932 Mataré was appointed professor at the Düsseldorf Academy, but was soon dismissed by the Nazis and devoted himself to the applied arts. After World War II he was commissioned to do the bronze doors for the Church of World Peace (1954) in Hiroshima. Among Mataré's other works are the memorial fountain to the German painter Stefan Lochner (1955) outside the Wallraf-Richartz-Museum in Cologne, a gigantic *Phoenix* (1949) in the entrance hall of the Landtag (Parliament building) in Düsseldorf, and numerous woodcuts.

MATHIEU, Georges (b. 1921, Boulogne-sur-Mer), French painter. He gained recognition in the 1947 Salon des Réalités Nouvelles with paintings made of spontaneous splashes and colors that were spread with the fingers, or a rag, or even squeezed straight from the tube. The characteristic calligraphic lines, which he whipped over the plain backgrounds of his paintings with incredible speed, gradually became more taut and concise. Mathieu's most successful works were enormous canvases such as the *Death of Philip III the Bold* (1952), the *Battle of Bouvines* (1954), and *Capetians Everywhere* (1954; Paris, Musée National d'Art Moderne). His retrospective exhibition at the Musée National d'Art Moderne, Paris, in 1963, revealed his stylistic consistency, while his book *Au-delà du Tachisme* ("Beyond Tachism"), published in the same year, proved that he was a perceptive art critic. In 1964 Mathieu gave up his claim of being the "fastest painter in the world" and entered a second phase in which he treated painting as a craft.

MATISSE, Henri (1869, Le Cateau, Nord—1954, Cimiez, Alpes-Maritimes), French Fauvist painter. His first painting was a *Still Life with Books* (1890; Paris, Priv. Coll.). In 1892 his father finally gave him permission to work in Paris, where he studied first at the Académie Julian, then in Gustave Moreau's studio (March 1895) at the École des Beaux-Arts. There Matisse met Charles Camoin, Georges Rouault, and Albert Marquet. During this period, his art was very conservative, and he sent contributions to the Salon of the Société Nationale des Beaux-Arts. Meanwhile on a visit to Brittany, a friend of Monet's introduced Matisse to Impressionism. His palette, which until then had been limited to muted tones, became heightened and varied. Matisse painted a kind of light that brightened tones, sharpened outlines, and made forms more palpable by simplifying them. Cézanne's influence is obvious in still lifes and nudes (*Still Life with Blue Patterned Tablecloth,* 1907, Merion, Pa., Barnes Foundation; *Carmelina,* 1903, Boston, Museum of Fine Arts). This was also the period when Matisse began to do sculpture. The Neoimpressionists inspired various Parisian landscapes as well as a number of compositions painted with a divisionist technique, such as *Luxe, calme, et volupté* (1905; Paris, Priv. Coll.), painted after Matisse had spent the summer of 1904 at St-Tropez with Paul Signac and Henri-Edmond Cross.

Strengthened by all these experiences Matisse was ready for the assertion of his personality and art that was embodied in his new Fauvist manner (*c.* 1905–8). Fauvism was for him an attempt to concentrate the whole art of painting into color and a few other fundamental elements, principally line and rhythm. There were to be no more pictorial transitions; colors were laid boldly side by side and even clashed with each other. But when this clash seemed undesirable, a thick black line was used to surround the forms and separate them. Instead of varying the tones by carefully grading light and shadow, Matisse unified and applied them in large planes, so that color became his unique means of expression; light and form thus became as important as space and depth. These elements, together with the arabesque and rhythm, were the artist's fundamental sources during his Fauvist phase. It was rich with masterpieces such as the *Open Window, Collioure* (1905; New York, Coll. John Hay Whitney), *Still Life with a Red Carpet* (1906; Grenoble, Museum), the *Joy of Living* (1906; Merion, Pa., Barnes Foundation), *Dessert, or Harmony in Red* (1908; Leningrad, Hermitage), the *Dance and Music* (1909–10; both Hermitage), and the *Red Studio* (1911; New York, Museum of Modern Art).

But the influence of Cézanne was bearing more and more heavily on the young generation of artists: Matisse was not the last to abandon Fauvism, although a visit to Morocco in 1911–12 hastened the change, and he produced a number of paintings in which he was evidently fascinated by an austere color range and forms that became harder and stricter until they verged on Cubism: the *Three Sisters* (1906; formerly Coll. Jean Walter-Paul Guillaume), the *Moroccans* (1916; New York, Museum of Modern Art), the *Piano Lesson* (1917; Museum of Modern Art), and the series of studio scenes of which the Musée National d'Art Moderne in Paris possesses the finest (*Painter and Model*, 1916).

The characteristics of his style between 1919 and 1927 were a return to bright color and to a more sinuous line with an enveloping suppleness; the use of a very slight modeling in the figures; and a decorative element that drew on motifs such as branch-patterned hangings in the background, faïence tiles, flowered paper, and Oriental carpets. But Matisse soon tired of this trend, and in 1928 embarked on a new experimental phase: *Decorative Figure Against an Oriental Background* (1927–28; Paris, Musée National d'Art Moderne) and the *Green Sideboard* (1928; Paris, Musée National d'Art Moderne) indicate a turning point in the artist's development.

The synthesis achieved between the complementary tendencies of his genius set its mark on all

Henri Matisse. *The Dance.* 1909–10. The Hermitage, Leningrad.

Henri Matisse. *White Feathers.* 1919. Minneapolis Institute of Art.

Henri Matisse. *Le Tiaré.* 1930. Coll. Ahrenberg, Stockholm. *Photo Walter Dräyer, Zurich.*

Matisse's future works, especially after he executed a vast wall decoration on the theme of the *Dance* for the building housing the collection of the Barnes Foundation in Merion, Pennsylvania (1931–33). After this, he demanded more of color than ever before, whether he chose to juxtapose colors of unprecedented violence (*Rumanian Blouse,* 1940; Paris, Musée National d'Art Moderne), or preferred to establish a chromatic unity, which was often predominantly red, as in *Still Life with a Magnolia* (1941) and *Red Interior* (1948)—both in the Musée National d'Art Moderne, Paris—or even succeeded in transforming black into a color shimmering with light (*Woman Reading Against a Black Background,* 1939, Paris, Musée National d'Art Moderne; *Interior with an Egyptian Curtain,* 1948, Washington, D.C., Phillips Collection). His drawing became both suppler and more taut, concise and suggestive. If the starting point of this synthesis was the decoration of the Barnes Foundation, its final point was the decoration of the chapel of the Dominican convent of Notre-Dame du Rosaire at Vence (1947–51). The chapel was not only an example of Matisse's late style as a painter, but the culmination of experiments he had been conducting for a long time in the various arts.

We must not, in fact, forget Matisse's activities in spheres other than painting. He did a large number of lithographs and etchings, and illustrated about 10 books, notably Mallarmé's *Poésies* (1932), Montherlant's *Pasiphaé* (1944), Baudelaire's *Fleurs du Mal* (1947), and the *Poèmes* of Charles d'Orleans (1950). As a sculptor, Matisse produced an appreciable amount of work which includes some of the outstanding pieces of contemporary sculpture. A special place should be reserved also for his *papiers découpés* ("paper cutouts"), which were the main activity of his last years and which include such masterpieces as the *Negro Boxer* (1947; Paris, Musée National d'Art Moderne), *Zulma* (1950; Copenhagen, Statens Museum for Kunst), and *Melancholy of the King* (1952; Paris, Musée National d'Art Moderne). They are a triumph of pure color and arabesque, perhaps the supreme expression of Matisse's genius.

Mayan Art (Classic period). Corbeled arch with fret decoration. House of the Governor, Uxmal. *Photo Henri Stierlin, Geneva.*

MATSYS. *See* **MASSYS.**

MATTA, Roberto Matta Echaurren, *called* Roberto (b. 1912, Santiago, Chile), Chilean painter of Spanish and Basque descent. In 1934 he worked under the architect Le Corbusier on the latter's plans for the Ville Radieuse ("Radiant City"). The following year in Spain he met Salvador Dali and joined the Surrealist group, which he left in 1948. Matta began painting in 1938. After settling in New York in 1939, he visited Mexico and began a "cosmic symphony," *The Earth is a Man* (completed 1942; Radnor, Pa., Coll. Mr. and Mrs. Henry Clifford). Having returned to Europe after World War II, he lived in Italy until 1954 and then settled in Paris in 1955. He built a multidimensional imaginary world in space in which he suspended invisible mansions, spiral labyrinths, and swirling perspectives, at whose intersections sprout strange chrysalids that are masked with inhumanity (*Eros Precipitate,* 1944; New York, Museum of Modern Art). In Matta's pictorial world, color is no more than the essence of matter volatized in a depth that is translucent and yet impenetrable.

MAULBERTSCH *or* **MAULPERTSCH,** Franz Anton (1724, Langenargen, Lake Constance—1796, Vienna), greatest of the German 18th-century fresco painters. In 1741 he was a pupil of Jakob van Schuppen (1670–1751) at the Vienna Academy, where he became a professor in 1750. Although his debt to Giambattista Piazzetta is obvious, he was haunted throughout his career by the chiaroscuro in Rembrandt's etchings. From 1751 until his death, Maulbertsch painted frescoes in more than 50 places: the Piaristenkirche (1752–53), Vienna; the hall of the Divinity School (*Baptism of Christ, c.* 1766) at the Old University (today the Academy of Sciences), also in Vienna; the abbey church of Heiligenkreuz-Gutenbrunn (*Invention of the Cross,* 1757–58); and the Hall of the Giants in the Hofburg at Innsbruck (*c.* 1775). During the last years of his life, his main field of activity was in Hungary. Maulbertsch was not concerned with giving his illusionistic architecture a semblance of logic or reality, but instead filled his ceilings with marvelously vital flying figures.

MAUVE, Anton (1838, Zaandam, Holland—1888, Arnhem, Holland), Dutch landscape painter and the founder of the school of Laren, which was the Dutch counterpart of the French Barbizon School. He painted dunes, heaths, and marine views (*Fishing Boat Hauled onto a Beach,* 1883; The Hague, Mesdag Museum), but particularly rural scenes of shepherds, cows, and peasants that are endowed with a poetic intimacy (*Return to the Fold*; New York, Metropolitan Museum). Although a cousin of Van Gogh, with whom he lived briefly in 1881, Mauve had no influence on his style, other than suggesting to Van Gogh an interest in the social aspects of Millet's works.

MAYAN ART. The Maya, who founded the most brilliant of the pre-Columbian civilizations, occupied a vast territory to the east and southeast of the Gulf of Mexico. They lived in the most varied geographical conditions, from the chalky, thinly wooded region of Yucatán to the dense, tropical forest of Petén. The evolution of the Maya may be divided into six great periods, covering about 2,500 years altogether. The first, known as the Formative period, began before 500 B.C. (perhaps as early as 1000 B.C.) and terminated about the end of the 3rd century A.D. Our knowledge of this period is derived from its pottery and a few architectural remains (the foundations of a temple at Uaxactún, north of Petén). The succeeding epoch, known as the Ancient, or Classic period, lasted from about A.D. 317 (the first date to figure in an inscription) to the beginning of the 9th century A.D. In spite of a century of decline between A.D. 550 and 650, this was the great period of Mayan art. The third period, the Late Ancient Empire, between A.D. 800 and 925, was marked by a sudden abandonment of the great centers and a widespread shift in population. A period of cultural decline (A.D. 925–75) preceded the fourth, or Mexican period (A.D. 975–1200), during which the invasion of a northern people, the Toltecs, completely overthrew the structure of Maya society. The fifth period (1200–1450) began with a successful uprising of the Maya against their oppressors. An attempt was made to re-establish the old Maya traditions, but the cultural decline became even more rapid despite the fact that a powerful empire, based in the new center of Mayapán (Yucatán), had re-emerged. The last period (1450–1697) began with a revolt against the tyrants of Mayapán. This was followed by the formation of small rival domains in continual conflict with one another. The Spaniards, who had landed in Guatemala in 1523, invaded Yucatán in 1541 and rapidly conquered the whole country. One small Maya group, the Itzas, who had sought refuge on the island of Tayasal in Lake Petén, preserved its independence until 1697.

The Maya economy was entirely agricultural and based very largely on the cultivation of maize. Although they were among the greatest builders in the history of mankind, they never progressed technologically beyond the Stone Age; they understood the metallurgy of gold and copper, but only used these materials to make decorative objects. Another paradox of their history is that they accumulated an enormous body of astronomical knowledge and created the most precise calendar known to man, without the use of scientific instruments. This knowledge enabled the Maya to predict the eclipses of the sun, to make precise calculations of the synodical revolution of Venus, and to formulate a very advanced system of arithmetic (they were the first to use the zero). This obsession with time pervades the whole of their art in the form of figures and symbols. Unfortunately, most of the books—screenfold manuscripts made from fig-bark paper sized with fine lime coating—were destroyed in the 16th century on the order of a Spanish bishop, and only three have survived: the codices of Dresden, Madrid, and Paris. Two of their great sacred texts, the *Popol Vuh*, a sort of Genesis, and the *Chilam Balam*, a collection of prophecies and riddles, have survived in 16th-century versions.

Mayan Art (Classic period). Temple of the Inscriptions, Palenque. 6th century. *Photo Henri Stierlin, Geneva.*

ARCHITECTURE

The Maya, who had developed their religious system and their writing by the end of the Formative period, also possessed at that time one of the essential elements of their architecture, a low platform on which buildings were erected. The only example so far discovered is at Uaxactún (Structure A V). In the Classic period, the Maya built these platforms in the form of huge pyramids, whose mass was counterbalanced by their height, and whose solidity and weight were seemingly rarefied by the play of ascending lines.

Another essential feature of their architecture was the invention of the false, or corbeled vault. This system of building uses slightly cantilevered courses of horizontal stones arranged on top of each other. These courses of stones, superimposed according to two convergent slopes from the supporting walls, created a triangular vault of considerable weight. This required enormously thick supporting walls, which left relatively little space for the rooms themselves. Each building was composed of three parts: a huge base, the building itself (a temple, or later a palace, and its outbuildings), and, finally, an ornamental superstructure. In addition to the superstructure, the entire building was covered with an exuberant stucco decoration; this is the third essential characteristic of Maya architecture. The interiors of the temples were often decorated with frescoes.

The principal buildings at Uxmal (northwest Yucatán) appear to date from shortly after the Classic period, in the 10th century A.D. With its House of the Governor, Nunnery, and Pyramid of the Magician, Uxmal is perhaps the finest of the Maya cities. The Temple of the Inscriptions at Palenque dates from the 6th century A.D. In 1949 a secret staircase was discovered within that pyramid that led to an underground crypt 82 feet from the upper platform. The discovery of this crypt, which contained a sarcophagus and a heavy tombstone over the skeleton of a man aged between forty and fifty, who was literally covered with jewelry and wore a mask of jade mosaic, demonstrates that the Maya pyramids were also used as tombs. During the Toltec period, the domination of the warrior caste meant that palaces were built, rather than temples; Maya art ceased to be exclusively religious,

Mayan Art. Bas-relief at Palenque. Detail. *Photo Henri Stierlin, Geneva.*

becoming more secular. Despite an obvious Toltec influence, the site of Chichén Itzá, with its ball court, its Temple of the Warriors, the so-called Court of the Thousand Columns, and the imposing Castillo pyramid is one of the most impressive ensembles of all Mayan art.

SCULPTURE

A taste for architectural decoration produced a rich body of sculpture, especially bas-relief. In the oldest buildings, the sculpture is free and realistic. Later it developed toward an ever greater degree of stylization, in which the principal motif, a serpent mask, was covered with an abundance of geometric designs. Similarly, the carved human figures were laden with innumerable ornaments (feathers, jewelry, insignia) that obscured the outlines and entirely filled the space.

The best examples of sculpture are found perhaps not so much on the walls of the temples as on the steles and altars. Between A.D. 317 and 550, and again between A.D. 650 and 810, there was a great increase in the practice of erecting steles to mark the passage from one period of time to another. The hieroglyphic inscriptions that cover them refer to celestial phenomena, eclipses, conjunctions of Venus, or other such events, and are very deliberately executed. The altars, enormous carved monoliths, are similarly decorated, with admirable figures of priests and warriors adorned with magnificent ornaments, flanked by hieroglyphs and symbols. The figures are carved in bas-relief, usually in profile; at Copán, however, they are represented fullface and in high relief. Few examples of freestanding sculpture are known. Particularly noteworthy are the many terra-cotta figurines (dating from A.D. 600–950) that have been found in the tombs of the island of Jaina, off the north-west coast of the Yucatán peninsula (state of Campeche). They represent a bewildering variety of characters, faithfully represented with all the insignia of their rank, their clothes, and jewelry.

Mayan Art (late Classic period). *Seated man.* Jaina style. Museo Nacional de Antropología, Mexico City. *Photo Walter Dräyer, Zurich.*

PAINTING

Maya wall painting was no doubt extremely rich, since it is known that the interiors of the temples were painted. Little of it would be known, had it not been for the discovery in 1945 of the city of Bonampak (in Mayan meaning "painted walls"), in the heart of the tropical forests of the Chiapas. At the summit of the pyramid that rises among the ruins, the Temple of the Paintings comprised three halls whose walls were still covered with frescoes dating from the 6th century A.D. Unlike those of Teotihuacán, these works are not entirely religious in subject, but depict the military victory that the foundation of the temple commemorated. These paintings are remarkable for the richness and precision of the detail of the garments, adornments, and headdresses, every one of which is different.

POTTERY AND JEWELRY

Maya ceramic ware was rich and varied. The work can be divided into five great periods: the Mamom period (*c.* 850–500 B.C.), comprising dishes and flat-bottomed vases, striped jars and jugs, and statuettes with pierced eyes; the Chincanel period (500 B.C.–early 1st century A.D.), with multicolored vases and increasing diversification of forms; the Izakol period (1st–3rd century A.D.), which is still relatively unknown; the Tepau period (A.D. 300–600), with polychrome pottery, and dishes on tripod and tetrapod supports; and the Puuc Chenes period (A.D. 600–950), including polychrome vases with supports and crenelated rims, decorated with figures, animals, and liturgical scenes, as well as vases with relief decoration, and dishes with decoration in relief or in champlevé. Maya ornament includes some fine jade figurines and jade plaques decorated with incised scenes. Most of the jewelry and gold dishes known were discovered at Chichén Itzá, which suggests that the Maya were introduced to gold-working by a foreign people, possibly the Toltecs.

Mayan Art. Polychrome ceramic vase. Musée de l'Homme, Paris. *Photo Sougez.*

MAYBECK, Bernard Ralph (1862, New York—1957, Berkeley, California), American architect and teacher. Maybeck studied in Paris at the École des Beaux-Arts (1882–86). In 1886 he returned to New York and worked as a draftsman for the firm of John Mervin Carrère (1858–1911) and Thomas Hastings (1860–1929). With James Russell he formed a brief partnership in Kansas City (1888) and finally settled in Berkeley, California (1889).

Maybeck supervised an international competition for the plan of the University of California's campus, where he designed Hearst Hall (1889). His lifelong interest in creative structure was expressed here in a series of magnificent 54-foot pointed arches. In the Chick House, Berkeley (1913), redwood, patterned shingles, and vertical board-and-batten siding were used in a pleasing contrast. Many of Maybeck's details were eclectic in origin. For example, he used a personal form of Gothic tracery extensively in his Christian Science Church in Berkeley (1910–12). Maybeck's academic training was best expressed in the heavily ornamented Classical rotunda and peristyle of San Francisco's Palace of the Legion of Honor, designed in lath and painted plaster for the Panama-Pacific Exposition of 1915. Despite his Romanticism, Maybeck's use of glass, steel, and concrete placed him in the modern movement.

MAZEROLLES, Philippe de (*c.* 1420, Mazeyrolles, Saintonge?—1479, Bruges), French painter and illuminator. In 1454 he was engaged in business transactions for Charles VII, and in 1466 he was in Bruges working on a *Book of Hours* (Vienna, Nationalbibliothek). In addition to the *Book of Hours*, Mazerolles illuminated a number of manuscripts, including Froissart's *Chronicles* (Wroclaw, formerly Breslau, Civic Library), grisailles for the *Miracles de Notre-Dame* (Paris, Bibliothèque Nationale), and 10 engravings to illustrate the Latin edition of the Bruges Boccaccio, published in 1476 by Colart Mansion, which is famous as one of the oldest books with copperplate engravings. In addition to this varied body of work, Mazerolles may have painted the altarpiece of the *Parlement de Paris*, but this attribution is disputed. The work was executed between 1453 and 1455 for the Grande Chambre of the Parlement de Paris, where it remained, except for a brief period (1796–1808), until 1904, when it was transferred to the Louvre, Paris.

McINTIRE, Samuel (1757, Salem, Massachusetts—1811, Salem), American architect and carver of the Federal period. McIntire was kept busy rebuilding Salem for most of his life, transforming the town with a notable series of public buildings, including: Washington Hall (1792), the Court House (1785), the Branch Church (1804–5), Hamilton Hall (*c.* 1807), and the Archer Building (1809–10). Elias Hasket Derby, the greatest of the Salem merchants, was his lifelong patron, and for the Derby family alone McIntire designed some half dozen houses. Outside Salem only two projects are known: the Lyman House at Waltham, Massachusetts (completed 1798), and a design for the Capitol of the United States entered in the competition of 1792. In 1804 McIntire was engaged to build Salem's South Congregational Church. The fact that he closely copied an earlier church in Newburyport in no way diminished his standing. For, at this time, the skill of an architect was measured by his ability to refine and perfect, not by his originality. In this, McIntire was pre-eminent. The carved ornament of his houses is their particular splendor.

McKIM, MEAD & WHITE, firm of American architects. CHARLES FOLLEN MCKIM (1847, Isabella Furnace, Pennsylvania—1909, St. James, New York), WILLIAM RUTHERFORD MEAD (1846, Brattleboro, Vermont—1928, Paris), and STANFORD WHITE (1853, New York—1906, New York), who became partners in 1879, initially belonged to the Picturesque, medievalizing tradition of the post-Civil War period: McKim and Mead each worked briefly for Russell Sturgis (1838–1909), while McKim and White worked for H. H. Richardson in 1870–72 and 1872–78 respectively.

Their early work is representative of what the American art historian Vincent Scully termed the Shingle Style. This is primarily a domestic, non-urban style, in which the continuity of the exterior skin is emphasized, usually through the use of wooden shingles that were often cut in varied patterns. The firm's commissions from 1879 to about 1885 centered around such seaside resorts as Elberon, New Jersey, Newport, Rhode Island, and Montauk Point, New York. In 1877 McKim and his partners made a study trip to New England, visiting the historic towns of Salem, Marblehead, Newburyport, and Portsmouth to examine Colonial architecture, and the results are seen in the Appleton house at Lenox, Massachusetts (1883–84), where McKim introduced the materials and classicizing details of the Colonial period. Shortly thereafter they moved toward a full-scale Renaissance revival. The Villard houses in New York (1883), which were designed by Joseph Morrill Wells (1853–90) in their office, were the first American examples of this mode.

White was noted for his talent as a decorator and for his facility for picturesque design, characteristics seen already in the dining room he added to Richard Upjohn's Kingscote, Newport (1880–81), and in the firm's Tiffany house, New York (1882–84). McKim, the founder of the firm, was known for his active professional leadership and his skillful composition of large buildings. His work was colder and more correct: he was the architect and planner for the firm's Columbia University on Morningside Heights (1893–1908), and for Pennsylvania Station (1906–9, derived from the Baths of Caracalla), both in New York. His most completely realized extant masterpiece is undoubtedly the firm's Italianate Boston Public Library (1887–98), where he employed such artists as Pierre Puvis de Chavannes, John Singer Sargent, Edwin Austin Abbey, Louis (1854–1913) and Augustus Saint-Gaudens, and Daniel Chester French to execute the ambitious decorative program. McKim was also instrumental in founding the American Academy in Rome. Mead was the stabilizing force in the firm, solving the practical problems and mediating between the two design partners.

The firm participated in the World's Columbian Exposition, Chicago (1893), designing the Agricultural Building. For most of their work through the early 20th century the partners continued to draw on the Italian Renaissance for such competent, though traditionalist, designs as the University Club (completed 1900) and the Knickerbocker Trust (completed 1904), both in New York.

MEIDNER, Ludwig (1884, Bernstadt, Silesia—1966, Darmstadt), German painter and poet. From 1906 to 1907 he attended the Académies Julian and Cormon in Paris, where he became acquainted with Modigliani. Returning to Germany in 1908, Meidner settled in Berlin, where he joined the *Novembergruppe*, and contributed articles to the journal *Aktion*. During the war years 1916 to 1918, when he was serving with the German armed forces, he wrote two books: *Septemberschrei* ("September Cry") and *Im Nacken das Sternenmeer* ("The Starlit Sea Behind"). During the second half of the 1930s, he taught at a Jewish school in Cologne, until he emigrated to London in 1939. Returning to Germany in 1953, he lived first in Frankfurt, and then finally settled in Darmstadt.

During the years immediately preceding World War I, Meidner belonged to the Expressionist avant-garde of Berlin centered around *Der Sturm*. His most important work was produced after 1912, when he painted his apocalyptic landscapes and pictures of burning towns with toppling houses and skies torn by explosions (*I and the City*, 1915; Berlin-Lichterfelde, Coll. Steinhart). After 1918, Meidner's pictures grew less intense and their

Melanesian Art. Male figure. Papuan Gulf, New Guinea. Museum of Primitive Art, New York.

subject matter began to reflect his own growing preoccupation with his Jewish faith. When he returned to Germany in 1953, he painted religious motifs, landscapes, portraits, and self-portraits in a style that reverted to his own early Expressionist period.

MELANESIAN ART. Few regions of the world at a comparable cultural level have produced visual art of such richness and complexity as Melanesia, the group of islands and archipelagoes of the western Pacific, stretching from New Guinea to the Fiji group and inhabited by Oceanic Negroids. When the first Europeans arrived, the whole of Melanesia was at a technological level equivalent to the European Neolithic Age. The principal cutting tools were made of stone or shell and were used for everyday purposes as well as for wood sculpture and for carving masks of great plastic strength. The quality of the art has not benefited from the improvement in working techniques. In so far as the ancient structure has been preserved, the inhabitants of a village or a valley generally govern their own affairs.

RELIGION AND MAGIC

Melanesians have no concept of a single, all-powerful deity. Their world is populated by a host of spirits. Spectacular, often dramatic, ceremonies are performed in their honor, during which they are invited to enter figures and masks that represent them and act as their temporary abodes. Both religion and magic are linked with mana, supernatural power deriving from the spirit world, which can reside in varying degrees in people, nature, and objects. It serves to explain the unusual: the success of a warrior, the wisdom of a notable, the peculiar shape of a stone or root. Through appropriate rites, it can be controlled and imparted to manufactured articles such as canoes or weapons. The sorcerer, who is greatly feared, derives his power from mana. In several Melanesian groups, special houses are built for the men, and the uninitiated and women are not permitted to enter them. In them are kept cult objects, and ceremonies are discussed, planned, and often performed. In some parts these houses are elaborately decorated with carved or painted ornament related to the cult of ancestors or spirits.

STYLISTIC UNITY AND VARIETY

Melanesian art is basically homogeneous, for all its variety of forms and concepts. A number of attempts have been made to link styles or tendencies in Melanesian art with cultural strata. The isolation of styles is a useful tool, but it seems doubtful whether some of the conclusions drawn are valid: whether, for instance, there is a demonstrable connection between the curvilinear style and the Papuan cultural heritage, and whether the beak style in New Guinea and the New Hebrides can be derived ultimately from Ganesh, the Indian elephant god. Certain influences, however, mostly more recent, need not be disputed. Whether the *korwar* style of western New Guinea derives from the Khmer art of Indochina remains to be proved; but it probably represents an influx of influence from Indonesia.

ART AND RELIGION

The union of art and religion is not as complete in Melanesia as it is, for example, in Australia. Thus the stylized heads of frigate birds that decorate nutcrackers and lime spatulas in the Massim district of New Guinea have no ostensible religious connection; but the same motif recurs on canoe prows, the manufacture and decoration of which is accompanied at every stage by ritual considered essential to the safety of the voyage. Aesthetic considerations apply also to articles of definitely religious association.

The most familiar art objects of Melanesia are wood carvings, paintings on wood or bark, masks made of tape (material made from felted bark fibres), pieces modeled in clay, and bamboos and calabashes decorated with incised patterns. Fragility is, however, one of the basic qualities of Melanesian culture, in which the observance of tradition replaces, even abolishes, the concern for eternity.

NEW GUINEA

This is the richest and most artistically complex region. The western half of New Guinea can be divided into three main areas. The western peninsula, Geelvinck Bay, and the offshore islands are the home of an art that owes much to Indonesian influence. Its most notable products are the wood ancestral figures known as *korwar*. The head is enlarged and is sometimes hollowed to hold a skull. Often the statuette holds before it a sort of openwork screen decorated with scrolls and tendril patterns.

Further along the north coast, toward Humboldt Bay, are found canoe prow ornaments and other objects carved in a rounded style. A local style was centered on Lake Sentani, inland from Humboldt Bay. Its best-known manifestations are the standing human figures with elongated faces and rounded limbs, from the chiefs' houses and initiation huts. Sculptured roof ornaments and house posts, with couples and pairs of animals, are of particularly fine workmanship.

The greater part of west New Guinea south of the central mountains forms a clear-cut zone. The great funerary sculptures, the *bis* poles, of the Asmat district commemorate men killed in head-hunting raids. Canoe ornaments are carved in an openwork pattern combined with human figures and turtles. All these are usually finished with white and red pigment. The distinctive character of Asmat art can be seen especially clearly in the shields, whose stylized motifs in champlevé are based on the disintegration of the human figure.

In the art of the Papuan Gulf, in the southeastern part of the island, the human figure is again disintegrated; but while in west Guinea it is the limbs that usually remain recognizable, in the Gulf it is the facial features that persist. Color seems to be the main means of suggestion. The enormous men's houses contain shieldlike votive

Melanesian Art. *Korwar* with child. Western New Guinea. National Museet, Copenhagen.

plaques and flat figures carved in relief, which represent supernatural spirits, not ancestor images.

The islands of Torres Straits and the mainland of western Papua formerly produced notable masks made from plates of tortoise shell drilled along the edges and lashed together, in the form of a human face, a fish, or a crocodile. The islands were also known for small carvings of human beings and sea animals. The wooden foreshafts of arrows were often carved with highly stylized representations of crocodiles or a human figure.

The basin of the Sepik River forms the principal art area of New Guinea. The human face and figure are the most prominent motifs. Masks are made in a number of forms and materials, including wood, basketry, and bark. In the lower Sepik area are produced figures with short, flat noses, but the most common type is the beaked nose, frequently prolonged to the chin or even to the genitals. Faces or figures in similar styles appear on a wide variety of objects. Other subjects that appear commonly are birds and crocodiles. Both are found carved on drums and the prows of dugout canoes. Stools with projecting backs, often in human form, are used by orators in the men's assemblies. In several districts fine paintings are made on wooden boards or on flat sheets of bark or palm spathe. The middle Sepik area produces quite elaborate earthenware finials for the roofs of houses, and large jars for storing sago. Bowls have intricate carved spiral relief patterns that are emphasized by painting in several colors after firing.

In contrast to the vitality and violence of Sepik art, that of Huon Gulf and Tami Island has a static, solid, and even a brooding quality. Its main products, apart from a type of mask made of bark cloth, are of wood: headrests, bowls, scoops, ancestor figures. The human face and figure are treated in an angular manner; the head is set low between the shoulders, and the facial features are more often painted than carved.

In the southeastern part of New Guinea, in the Massim district and the Trobriand Islands, Papuan cultural strains have been greatly modified. The sculpture, produced by specialized craftsmen, is essentially ornamental. Massim art includes neither masks nor ancestor figures. Canoe prows, dance shields, lime spatulas, and many other flat wooden objects are treated in low relief, in a markedly curvilinear style. The motif of the frigate bird is recognizable by its hooked beak, and sea snakes, plants, and the moon are among the other origins ascribed by the carvers to their motifs. A different technique appears on the shields of the Trobriand Islands, the surfaces of which are painted without relief carving.

NEW BRITAIN AND NEW IRELAND

The Bismarck Archipelago is culturally a heterogeneous area in which peoples and influences from the Papuan and Sepik areas of New Guinea as well as from Micronesia and southeast Asia have fused. The two main islands, New Britain and New Ireland, are very rich in art. In New Britain's northern region, a very individual style developed, marked above all by the enormous bark-cloth masks of the Baining tribe, and by those of their neighbors the Sulka, who used a sort of basketry for their masks, usually painted predominantly red. New Ireland is famous for the *malanggan* carvings of the northwest. These are posts of soft wood carved in intricate openwork patterns, representing combinations of human, bird, fish, and snake figures, and painted all over in several colors.

ADMIRALTY AND SOLOMON ISLANDS

In the Admiralty group, surface decoration is of less importance than sculptural quality. The human figure and the crocodile are the most common subjects; they are found on house posts, beds, the handles of wood lime spatulas, daggers, and knives, and below the heads of spears.

The strongly sculptural style of the Solomon Islands is marked by a sober quality. Throughout the area, representations of the human figure predominate, most often carved in wood, and stained black. In the central and southeastern islands, mother-of-pearl inlay emphasizes the sculptural form, while in the northwest (Bougainville and Buka), human figures have bulbous heads often colored red. Prow figures with jutting chins decorate the canoes, and represent spirits of the sea. Fish associated with that cult—dolphins or sharks—are sometimes hollowed to receive the skulls of the dead. In the central islands, large plates of Tridacna (giant clam) shell are carved into grids to close the miniature houses in which the skulls of chiefs are deposited.

Melanesian Art. Dance mask. New Ireland. Tropenmuseum, Amsterdam.

The Santa Cruz group, southeast of the Solomons, is noted for figures of ancestors, painted dance clubs, bowls, and headrests. Probably the outstanding artifacts of the Banks Group, to the north of the New Hebrides, are the abstract masks associated with the Tamate secret society.

NEW HEBRIDES

In some ways the art of the New Hebrides is reminiscent of that of the Sepik Basin. Though not as varied, it gives a similar impression of violence and tension, and uses color extensively. In Malekula, life-size funerary figures are made with the skull of the dead man as the head, the features being modeled in vegetable paste. Wood carving is relatively less important, though there are many examples of notable work in this medium: the large gongs from Ambrym and the pig-killing clubs are examples. In eastern Malekula, canoe prows portraying human faces, birds, and pigs indicate the status of their owner. Large human figures and masks are carved in the fibrous root of tree-ferns. Another type of mask made from palm spathe is lozenge-shaped and is decorated with long hair of plant fibre.

NEW CALEDONIA

In New Caledonian art, wood carving is the most important medium. Though some carvings were colored red, effects are due mainly to fine proportion and to a simplification of form in which certain elements, such as the human nose, are emphasized. The most striking objects are the carved ornaments from the exteriors of chiefs' houses. Masks of black

Melanesian Art. Female figure. Tree fern. Gaua, Banks Islands, New Hebrides. Museum für Völkerkunde, Basel.

Melanesian Art. Ancestor figure. Door frame. Houailou, New Caledonia. Musée de l'Homme, Paris.

wood with large noses, sometimes with actual beaks, may represent water spirits. Ceremonial "axes," consisting of a disk of polished jade fixed to a decorated wood handle covered with tapa, were badges of rank.

FIJI ISLANDS

In the Fiji group, Melanesian and Polynesian strains have been in contact for many centuries. As in western Polynesia, sculpture is rare. A number of fine whalebone figures have been collected in Fiji, but probably originated in the Tonga Islands. Wood figures, however, do seem to be indigenous, although they lack homogeneity of style. The surfaces of clubs are decorated with very delicate carving, often in the form of zigzags between parallel lines. The bark cloth is the finest and most attractive in Melanesia. Formerly strongly influenced by Polynesian styles, it is decorated with motifs painted freehand or printed using a matrix of leaves and strings.

Of the history of Melanesian art before the arrival of Europeans little is known. The stone mortars and pestles that have been found in New Guinea are relics of an earlier tradition. Perhaps some pattern may appear in the form and distribution of petroglyphs when they have been more fully investigated.

Hans Memlinc. *The Seven Joys of the Virgin. c.* 1480. Detail. Alte Pinakothek, Munich.

MELLI, Roberto (1885, Ferrara—1958, Rome), Italian sculptor and painter. He began his career as a sculptor in 1906 at Ferrara, and went to Rome in 1911, where he took an active part in the city's artistic revival. He placed less emphasis on linear movement than on the contrasts of light and shadow, which he tried to achieve in his statues by the alternation of solids and voids. His activity as a sculptor lasted only for a brief period; the best of his work in this field was done between 1911 and 1914, after which he took up painting. The best known of his statues, such as the *Portrait of Vincenzo Costantini* (1913; Rome, Galleria Nazionale d'Arte Moderna), combine Umberto Boccioni's vigor with Medardo Rosso's refined expressiveness. Melli's works were first shown in 1914 at the Secessionist exhibition in Rome. During the interwar years he belonged to the Valori Plastici ("Plastic Values") group, but his art was condemned by the Fascist régime.

MELOZZO DA FORLÌ, Michelozzo degli Ambrogi, *called* (1438, Forlì, near Bologna—1494, Forlì), Italian fresco painter. He was one of the most active of Piero della Francesca's pupils. In Rome Melozzo worked in the church of S. Marco (*c.* 1465–70), painting frescoes of the *Redeemer, St. Mark the Pope,* and *St. Mark the Evangelist.* His fresco of *Sixtus IV Inaugurating the Vatican Library* (1477; Vatican Museum) is a masterly feat in spatial organization. Melozzo's contribution to the Roman church of the SS. Apostoli (*c.* 1480) was probably no less impressive: frescoes of the *Ascension* (Rome, Palazzo del Quirinale) and *Angel Musicians* (Vatican Museum), along with several other recently discovered fragments, have survived from his work there.

It is difficult to determine Melozzo's exact share in the production of two fresco cycles of the mid-1470s that decorated the study of Federigo da Montefeltro in the Ducal Palace at Urbino: the *Illustrious Men* series (now divided between Urbino and the Louvre) and the *Liberal Arts* cycle (two portions in Berlin were destroyed in 1945; remaining is the *Music and Rhetoric* in London's National Gallery). The confusion stems from the fact that the Spaniard Pedro Berruguete worked on them and possibly the Flemish painter Justus of Ghent as well.

Melozzo's influence spread still farther through his work on the sacristy of S. Marco at Loreto (after 1477). His work (*c.* 1493) on the Feo Chapel in the Church of S. Biagio at Forlì (destroyed in 1944) was a final expression of the Quattrocento principles of Piero della Francesca prior to the advent of Roman Classicism.

MEMLINC *or* **MEMLING,** Hans (1435, Memlingen, near Frankfurt—1494, Bruges), German-born painter of the Flemish School. He worked in the style of Rogier van der Weyden, and appears to have been well acquainted with the works of Dirk Bouts, Hugo van der Goes, and contemporary Italian painters. Memlinc was primarily a painter of pious devotional pictures, and the creator of a type of Madonna who radiates a candid grace. He paints with a fineness and an attention to detail equal to Jan van Eyck or Rogier. Memlinc excels in combining sumptuous golds, reds, blues, and violets with the most delicate of half-tones, and in softening his modeling by the use of subtle lighting. His figures seem absorbed in a tranquil devotion, yet an aura of nobility and grandeur is also common in his altarpieces, which usually show the Madonna seated among saints, before a brocade drapery, in the interior of a church or in a landscape (*Donne Triptych,* 1468, London, National Gallery; the *Marriage of St. Catherine,* 1479, Bruges, Hôpital St-Jean). This mixture of nobility and sweetness can be seen in Memlinc's portraits as well, in which the influence of Rogier and Bouts is visible only in the general design. His idealized personages (*Tommaso Portinari,* New York, Metropolitan Museum; *Martin van Nieuwenhove,* 1487, Bruges, Hôpital St-Jean) express the soul of the painter more than that of the sitter. Toward the end of his career, becoming sensitive to Italian influences and to the renewed taste for Van Eyck that spread in Flanders, Memlinc began to show a new vigor in his art. This trend is apparent in the *Virgin of the Annunciation* (1482; New York, Coll. Robert Lehmann); in the *Moreel Triptych* (1484; Bruges, Hôpital St-Jean)—in which Sts. Christopher, Maurice, and Giles are seen as monumental figures against a vast landscape; and in *Bathsheba at the Bath* (*c.* 1485; Stuttgart, Landesmuseum).

MENDELSOHN, Erich (1887, Allenstein, East Prussia—1953, San Francisco), German architect. After training in Berlin and Munich, he spent the first two years of practice (1912–14) chiefly in stage designing and painting. His designs for factories, grain elevators, observatories, and religious buildings showed a sensitive approach to materials (steel and concrete) and an Expressionist use of form to symbolize function. The very sculptural quality of the Einstein Observatory at Potsdam (1919–21) was intended to reveal the plastic possibilities of its projected material (poured concrete), although the actual building employed cement-covered brick. This was followed, in the 1920s, by a series of department stores: the Petersdorff Store at Breslau (1927), and the Schocken Stores at Stuttgart (1927) and Chemnitz (1928). The sweeping curves and marked horizontality of the Schocken Stores reveal the persistence of an Expressionist sensibility. A group of buildings adjoining Kurfürstendamm, Berlin, which includes a dramatic and, again, horizontally-oriented cinema (1928), and the Columbus House (1931) in the Potsdamerplatz, are among Mendelsohn's best works of this period.

When the National Socialist Party rose to power, persecution forced Mendelsohn to leave Germany in 1933. He went first to Brussels, then to London, where he formed a partnership with Serge Chermayeff (b. 1900). His principal work in England was the now-famous De La Warr Pavilion, Bexhill (1934–35), which, with its semicircular stair tower, recalls the earlier Schocken Stores. Mendelsohn's work in Palestine was more extensive, and included two large hospitals, that at Haifa (1937) and the University Medical Center on Mount Scopus, Jerusalem (1937–39); the Palestine Bank, Jerusalem (1938); several large houses, a college, and a library.

In 1941 Mendelsohn went to the United States, settling in San Francisco in 1945. His Maimonides Hospital in San Francisco (1946), with its gently curved, cantilevered balconies, continues his earlier style in a more subdued form. A series of large synagogues and community centers terminated his long career.

Erich Mendelsohn. Façade of Schocken Store, Stuttgart. 1927. *Photo Gerhard Schwab, Stuttgart.*

MENGS, Anton Raphael (1728, Aussig, Bohemia—1779, Rome), German painter, one of the leading personalities of the 18th-century Neoclassical revival. His father was Ismael Mengs (*c.* 1689–1764), director of the Royal Academy of Painting at Dresden, who took him to Rome in 1741. The younger Mengs returned to Dresden in 1745, and became painter to the court of Saxony, producing a large number of portraits, most of them in brightly colored pastels. He settled in Rome in 1751, where the arrival of the German archaeologist Johann Joachim Winckelmann in 1755 was a turning point in his career. In 1761 Mengs finished painting his famous *Parnassus*, a Raphaelesque ceiling fresco in Rome's Villa Albani. In the same year Mengs left for Spain at the invitation of Charles III to become court painter, and soon became the rival of the Rococo decorator Tiepolo. He left Madrid in 1768 and from 1769 to 1772 again lived in Rome, where he decorated the Camera dei Papiri in the Vatican. He then returned to Madrid until 1777, and died of tuberculosis in Rome two years later. His reputation was immense in his own lifetime, but today his decorative painting has few admirers and his theoretical writings, such as *Reflections on Beauty* (1762), interest only specialists. Fortunately the unexpected freedom and sureness of touch in his portraits have saved his reputation from being merely one of historical curiosity.

MENZEL, Adolf von (1815, Breslau—1905, Berlin), German naturalist painter and engraver. He first gained recognition with the wood engravings he did as illustrations for Franz Kugler's *History of Frederick the Great* (1840–42). He produced his best paintings between 1845 and 1870. Menzel frequently depicted interiors (*Room with a Balcony*, 1845, Berlin, Staatliche Museen; the *Artist's Sister with Candle*, 1847, Munich, Bayerische Staatsgemäldesammlungen), exteriors sketched in the open air, or such scenes as the construction of a railway line. The rare refinement of lighting effects achieved in these paintings reveals that Menzel anticipated Impressionism even though he later rejected its theories. His treatment of artificial light in such paintings as the *Théâtre du Gymnase*, painted from memory in 1856, is worthy of Honoré Daumier; *Sunday in the Tuileries* (1867; Dresden, Gemäldegalerie) is reminiscent of Édouard Manet's painting of the same subject. Menzel's passion for the period of Frederick the Great led him to paint eight large canvases, including *Flute Recital at Sanssouci* (1850–52; Berlin, Staatliche Museen) and *Round Table at Sanssouci* (1850; formerly Berlin, Nationalgalerie, destroyed 1945?), in which the figures, Voltaire among them, were all portraits. Some art historians consider his painting of the *Rolling Mill* (1875; East Berlin) to have been a pioneer work that captured the beauty of industrial civilization. Menzel did numerous drawings that have a vital, witty line and, all considered, he was one of the most talented German painters of the 19th century.

MERIAN, family of German engravers of Swiss origin. Their most important members were:

MATTHÄUS, *called* THE ELDER (1593, Basel—1650, Bad Schwalbach, Hesse). In 1617 he entered the service of Johann Theodor de Bry (1561–1623), a print seller and engraver, whose daughter he married in 1618. He had a prosperous business in partnership with his father-in-law in Frankfurt, and they produced enormous quantities of etchings, concentrating on topography (Martin Zeiler's *Topographia*, Frankfurt, 1642). Matthäus was a most skillful draftsman and a number of his prints reach a remarkable artistic level, far beyond what was required by their purely documentary purpose.

MATTHÄUS, *called* THE YOUNGER (1621, Basel—1687, Frankfurt), his son, was both a painter and engraver. In 1640 he trained under Joachim von Sandrart (1606–88) in Holland. He then worked in France with Eustache Le Sueur and Simon Vouet, in Italy with Andrea Sacchi (1599–1661) and Carlo Maratti (1625–1713), and finally in England with Sir Anthony van Dyck. About 1650 he was in Nuremberg, where he painted several portraits, and he was quite successful in this field (*Unknown Man*; London, National Gallery). He painted an equestrian portrait of Leopold I on the occasion of the emperor's coronation in Vienna. His works are difficult to identify because most of them, in fact, are quite similar to Van Dyck's.

KASPAR (1627, Frankfurt—1686, Holland), brother of Matthäus the Younger, was a draftsman and engraver. He was taught by his father and about 1650 went to live in Frankfurt, where he engraved several prints, notably landscapes of the Baden region, seascapes, some portraits, and views.

ANNA MARIA SIBYLLA (1647, Frankfurt—1717, Amsterdam), daughter of Matthäus the Elder, was a draftswoman and miniaturist. Her real interest was natural history, and in 1679 she published the first volume of a work on insects, in which the engraved plates were colored by hand. In 1698 she went to South America and brought back a collection of drawings and watercolors in which she recorded with extraordinary minuteness and refinement the plants, insects, fruits, and birds of that part of the world (London, British Museum; Frankfurt, Städelsches Kunstinstitut); these were used as illustrations for her *Metamorphosis Insectorum Surinamensium* (1705).

MESOPOTAMIAN ART. *See* **AKKADIAN ART; ARAMAEAN ART; ASSYRIAN ART; BABYLONIAN ART; HURRITE ART; KASSITE ART; SUMERIAN ART.**

MESSINA, Antonello da. *See* **ANTONELLO DA MESSINA.**

MEŠTROVIĆ, Ivan (1883, Vrpolje, Yugoslavia—1962, South Bend, Indiana), Yugoslav sculptor. At sixteen, Meštrović went to Vienna, where he studied at the Academy of Fine Arts and contributed to various exhibitions, especially those of the avant-garde Secession group (1902). He also spent some time in France, Italy, and England, but most of his career was passed in Zagreb and in the United States. He taught sculpture (1946–54) at the University of Syracuse in Syracuse, New York, and then at the University of Notre Dame in South Bend, Indiana. In 1954 he became a naturalized American citizen. Meštrović's early sculptures reflect his attachment to poetry, folk songs, and the history of Yugoslavia. His preoccupation with the theme of Serbian freedom is apparent in his famous project for the *Temple of Kosovo* (1907–13); 45 fragments of this wooden model are now in Belgrade's National Museum. Meštrović's fame rests mainly on his many public monuments, the most important of which are: *Monument to the Unknown Soldier* (1935–38; on the Avala hill, near Belgrade); *Monument of Gratitude to France* (1930; Belgrade, Kalemegdan Park); the *Monument to Gregory of Nin*, the 10th-century bishop of Split (*c.* 1927; Split); the memorial church for the Račič family (1920–22; Cavtat, near Dubrovnik); and *Indian with a Bow* and *Indian with a Spear* (both 1926–27; Chicago, Grant Park). A fine example of his nonmonumental sculpture is his marble figure of the *Archangel Gabriel* (*c.* 1924; New York, Brooklyn Museum).

METAPHYSICAL PAINTING, school of Italian painting, developed by Giorgio de Chirico in Paris between 1910 and 1915, and lasting until around 1921. In reaction against the dynamism of the Futurists, the Metaphysical painters revived a nostalgia for antiquity, exalted dream images, and discovered the mystery of apparitions. During his stay in Munich (1906–8), De Chirico read the philosophical works of Nietzsche, Schopenhauer, and Otto Weininger. Without the "mannequins" that peopled De Chirico's paintings at this time, Metaphysical painting would have lacked an essential element in its aesthetic. This idea of the mannequin came to De Chirico from the play *La Chanson de la Mi-Mort* (1913) by his brother Alberto (1891–1952), a painter, poet, and musician known by the pseudonym of Alberto Savinio. Although Metaphysical painting began in Paris, it was in Ferrara, Italy, during World War I, that it became a "school" that could well have taken the mannequin as its emblem. In Ferrara, De Chirico painted his series of *Metaphysical Interiors*, suggested to him by certain shops in the ghetto district, "where one could see cakes and biscuits in extremely strange, metaphysical shapes." The first painter to come under De Chirico's influence was Carlo Carrà, a former Futurist. Carrà painted the same objects as De Chirico but with less sense of fantasy. Savinio claimed that the latter school was a "total representation of spiritual necessities within plastic limits—the ability to express the ghostly side of things—irony." Surprisingly, it was Carrà who fulfilled the third condition, irony, though perhaps unconsciously, by clothing De Chirico's thoughtful mannequins in pleated tunics and by putting tennis rackets and balls in their hands. "We Metaphysical painters have sanctified reality," De Chirico affirmed. The painter who really seems to have sanctified reality was Giorgio Morandi. With three colors and a few very simple lines, he created an atmosphere of mystery.

MÉTEZEAU, a family of French architects whose leading members were:

CLÉMENT I (d. 1550, Dreux, Eure-et-Loire), the founder of the architectural dynasty, was master mason at Dreux, where he worked on the church of St-Pierre.

JEAN (d. 1600, Dreux), his son, finished the south tower of St-Pierre, called St. Vincent's Tower, in 1576 and reconstructed the transept of the church shortly before his death.

THIBAUT (*c.* 1533, Dreux—1593, Paris), Jean's brother, went to Paris in 1570. There he helped to build the Valois tomb (1570) in the church of St-Denis.

LOUIS (*c.* 1562, Dreux—1615, Paris), grandson of Clément I. He was architect to Henri IV, and it is generally agreed that he designed the eastern part of the Grande Galerie of the Louvre. The façades of the Place Royale (now the Place des Vosges), Paris (1605–12), are among the works attributed to him. There is no doubt, however, that he designed the aqueduct at Rungis (1613).

CLÉMENT II (1581, Dreux—1652, Paris), Louis' younger brother, was one of the most celebrated architects of his time. As architect to Charles de Gonzague, the duke of Nevers, he laid out the Place Ducale of the new city of Charleville, near Rheims, in a style similar to that of the Place Royale in Paris. Marie de Médicis sent him to Florence in 1611 to draw the plans for the Palazzo Pitti, so that a palace could be built for her at Paris in the same style. When he returned, we know that he worked under Salomon de Brosse (1565–1629) on the Palais du Luxembourg in Paris (begun 1615). In 1616 he was probably commissioned to build the façade of the Parisian church of St-Gervais, long attributed to Salomon de Brosse. In 1621 Clément II began working on the church of the Oratoire in Paris, which was finished by Jacques Lemercier. At this time he began to serve as architect to Louis XIII. In 1628, during the siege by the forces of Richelieu, he was summoned to the port town of La Rochelle to build the dyke that blockaded the town. He also designed the châteaux at La Meilleraye in Poitou and Chilly (Seine-et-Oise).

METSU, Gabriel (1629, Leiden—1667, Amsterdam), Dutch painter, the most distinguished of the 17th-century minor masters in the intimate Dutch manner. A Master at Leiden in 1648, he came under the influence of Rembrandt, Jan Steen, and Vermeer around 1654 while in Amsterdam. Whether illustrating a romantic conversation (*Soldier and Young Woman*; Paris, Louvre), a musical group (*Violinist and Singer*, 1655; Schleissheim, Staatsgalerie), or a market scene (*Poultry Vendor*, 1662; Dresden, Gemäldegalerie), Metsu takes immense care to link his personages together as though in a play, sometimes with a touching, and sometimes with a malicious effect. By a happy management of solids and voids and contrasted rhythms, he gives Classical grandeur to the *Visit to the Nursery* (1661; New York, Metropolitan Museum). The *Vegetable Market in Amsterdam* (*c.* 1660–65; Louvre) is arranged around the yellow and white outlines of a woman.

METSYS. *See* **MASSYS.**

METZINGER, Jean (1883, Nantes—1957, Paris), French painter. In Paris he attended various academies, where the instruction disappointed him. For Metzinger there could be no real relationship between the physical object constituted by the canvas and the pictorial object represented upon its surface; for him a painting had no value other than the pleasure produced by its combination of forms and colors. Metzinger was influenced by the Neoimpressionists and then by the Fauves, but he was looking for a more coherent compositional construction, and he joined the young painters who from 1908 onward were working along similar lines in the wake of the Cubist innovations of Picasso and Braque. Metzinger took part in the famous Salon des Indépendants of 1911 and in the meetings and exhibitions of the Section d'Or. With Albert Gleizes, he published *On Cubism* (1912), the first theoretical work on this movement to be written by painters who belonged to it. His work, which showed little stylistic change throughout his life, had a sure technique, and a remarkable sense of unity (*Still Life*, 1917, New York, Metropolitan Museum; the *Knitter*, 1919, Paris, Musée National d'Art Moderne).

MEUNIER, Constantin (1831, Brussels—1904, Brussels), Belgian naturalist painter and sculptor. From 1854 to 1857 he was a pupil at the Academy of St. Luke in Brussels. Around 1880, Meunier decisively adopted the working-class themes that were to determine the course of his art—themes he was to advocate as a teacher (1887–95) at the Academy of Painting in Louvain. Meunier's desire was to create a huge epic of man at work, of his creative urge, of his enslavement and revolt, and above all of his links with the soil, the sea, mines, and factories. His scenes of mineshafts and workshops (*Collieries Under Snow*; Brussels, Musée Constantin Meunier) were painted in a somber palette, his heroes being shown in a tragic atmosphere amid smoke, soot, and flames.

As a sculptor Meunier usually worked in bronze, concentrating after 1880 on single figures seen as

Gabriel Metsu. *The Vegetable Market in Amsterdam. c.* 1660–65. Louvre, Paris. *Photo Giraudon, Paris.*

the symbols of their trade (the *Porter*, *c.* 1900, Vienna, Kunsthistorisches Museum; the *Longshoreman*, 1905, Antwerp, Musée des Beaux-Arts). Meunier's culminating sculpture in this vein is his *Monument to Work*, erected in the Place de Trooz at Brussels in 1930. Consisting of four reliefs, four individual statues, and one group, the ensemble summarizes all of the sculptor's intentions in a single vast symbolic and expressionist conception.

MEYER, Hannes (1889, Basel—1954, Crocifisso di Savosa, near Lugano), Swiss architect. Meyer, whose father was an architect, studied at the Basel Technical School and, from 1905 to 1909, was apprenticed to an architectural firm. In 1919 he set up a private practice in Basel, and in 1926 he entered into partnership with the Swiss architect Hans Wittwer. In 1927 they submitted a design in the competition for the League of Nations building in Geneva; their project received third prize. Also in that year, Meyer was appointed lecturer and workshop supervisor at the Dessau Bauhaus; in 1928 he succeeded the German architect Walter Gropius as its director. Meyer's German Trades Union School at Bernau, near Berlin (1928–30), was situated next to a

Constantin Meunier. *The Longshoreman*. Detail. 1905. Musée des Beaux-Arts, Antwerp.

Michelangelo. *Pietà.* 1497–99. Basilica of St. Peter's, Rome. *Photo Jean Roubier, Paris.*

small lake in the heart of a forest; whereas the whole complex harmonized with the landscape, the individual buildings were arranged so that they were functionally related to one another. In 1930 Meyer left the Bauhaus and for the next six years worked in the Soviet Union. He then returned to Switzerland, where he stayed for three years, and in 1939 went to Mexico, remaining there until 1949.

MICHALOWSKI, Piotr (1800, Cracow—1855, Cracow), the leading Polish painter of the 19th century. In Cracow he studied painting with Franz Lampi (1782–1852), a Viennese; eventually he completed his training in Paris (1832) under Nicolas Charlet (1792–1845). Gifted and erudite, he took a vital interest in the government of his country and held important posts in the mining and metallurgical industry. His painting, despite debts to French Romanticism (Théodore Géricault), Van Dyck, and Velázquez, remained profoundly original and shows a complete mastery of form, movement, and color. Michalowski painted battle scenes of great verve (*Battle of Somosierra*; Warsaw, National Museum); studies of peasants (*Portrait of an Old Peasant*; Cracow, National Museum) and Jews with tragic faces; animals (*Two Dogs*; Vienna, Kunsthistorisches Museum); and horsemen (*Napoleon Reviewing His Troops*; Warsaw, National Museum). However, the subject never had more than a secondary importance for him and remained strictly subordinated to plastic values.

MICHAUX, Henri (b. 1899, Namur), Belgian-born French poet and painter. His visual art is wholly concerned with the exploration of the "landscapes of the mind" that were successively revealed to him by the writings of the Comte de Lautréamont, the Flemish mystics, and Asian philosophers, as well as by the painting of Paul Klee and Max Ernst. Michaux the artist was never, however, an illustrator of Michaux the poet; with equivalent plastic means, he captured the fugitive reality that is always just beyond words. The first *Signs* of 1927 were no more than contorted rhythms and convulsive tensions set down in a rapid shorthand. But there ultimately emerged a whole nightmare bestiary, a fantastic monstrous creation: faces twisted in anguish or ecstasy.

Watercolor, with its fluidity, was the perfect medium for Michaux's fundamental theme of the reaching out of the human being. In his wash drawings, the line gave pungency and structure to the evasive substance of color. About 1950, however, black and white predominated. The stain was drawn out and tapered to become an ideogram of movement, or, on the contrary, swelled into disturbing immobility. The hallucinatory drugs with which Michaux experimented from 1956 to 1960 stimulated his vision.

MICHEL, Georges (1763, Paris—1843, Paris), French landscape painter and forerunner of Romanticism. When he was twelve years old, he was apprenticed to the painter of historical subjects, M. Leduc (Le Duc), and when he was fifteen, he was already giving lessons himself. In the company of his friend, the landscapist and engraver Lazare Bruandet (1755–1804), Michel often wandered, sketchbook in hand, through the woods near Paris, at Boulogne and in Meudon. Bruandet influenced him and helped him find his artistic direction. Although Michel's technique was traditional, his approach was new; he disdained paintings of mythological scenes and Italian landscapes and loved to depict the windmills of Montmartre, being, in fact, the first artist to live in Montmartre on the Butte. He also painted suburban townscapes, and excelled in reproducing their romantic aspects, such as the barren stretches of land dominated by the leaden-hued harmonies of the clouds (*Environs of Montmartre*; Paris, Louvre). One of Michel's friends, the wealthy and jealously possessive amateur artist and connoisseur, Baron d'Ivry, spread the rumour that Michel was dead in order to keep his works for himself and to pass them off as his own. Michel died unknown, in a neglect that was partly self-imposed. It is difficult to establish a chronology for his paintings because he always refused to sign or date them on the grounds that the old masters had not done so.

MICHELANGELO, Michelangelo Buonarroti, *called* (1475, Caprese, near Arezzo—1564, Rome), Italian sculptor, painter, military engineer, architect, and poet. Michelangelo was one of the great masters of the Italian Renaissance in whom the ideal of universal excellence was embodied.

The rule of Lorenzo de' Medici was nearing its end when Michelangelo, the scion of an old Florentine family, began his artistic career in the studio of Domenico Ghirlandaio. He then entered the informal school in the Medici gardens near the monastery of S. Marco, where the banking family had gathered together a large collection of ancient sculpture in the keeping of the sculptor Bertoldo di Giovanni, a pupil of Donatello. Michelangelo soon came under the influence of Platonism and the Florentine version of Neoplatonism of Pico della Mirandola and Angelo Poliziano. These scholars had endeavored to form a synthesis of Greek philosophy and the Christian revelation, and had given art the task of embodying this union. After Lorenzo's death in 1492, Florence's political and intellectual pre-eminence was threatened. As a devout Christian, Michelangelo was certainly disturbed by the sermons of the Dominican prior Savonarola, who fulminated against the moral degradation of Florence and formed a new republic after the fall of the Medici. Later on, political upheavals hampered Michelangelo's artistic career for long periods of time. Voluntary exile, quarrels and reconciliations with popes, and projects left half finished—this was to be the pattern of Michelangelo's life as an artist.

A triton drawn by Michelangelo on the wall of his father's villa at Settignano reveals that he was interested at an early age in Antonio Pollaiuolo's dynamic researches into anatomy. Three statuettes for the reliquary of S. Domenico (1494; Bologna, S. Domenico) indicate that Jacopo della Quercia had impressed Michelangelo as much as had Donatello, whose Classically inspired Madonna reliefs he had imitated in the panel of the *Madonna of the Stairs* (*c.* 1492; Florence, Casa Buonarroti). Michelangelo was in Rome between 1496 and 1501, when his first *Pietà* (1497–99; Rome, St. Peter's) was commissioned by the French cardinal Jean de Villiers de la Groslaye. Taking this North European subject, he succeeded in fusing it with a Leonardesque gentleness and a Classical restraint, thereby creating his first masterpiece, conceived by his still serene soul. Now a famous artist, he returned to Florence for four years (1501–5), where he moved quickly toward the Classicism of the tender *Bruges Madonna* (*c.* 1504–6), bought by the merchants of that city for the church of Notre-Dame. His *David* (1501–4) was carved from a damaged block of marble abandoned by Agostino di Duccio because it was considered too narrow for a statue. The *David* was set in position in front of the Palazzo della Signoria, Florence, in 1505 (the original is now in the Accademia and has been replaced by a copy). During this important and creative period in his early career, Michelangelo also did such paintings as the *Doni Tondo* (1503; Florence, Uffizi), with its compact central group of the Holy Family behind which stretches a frieze of nude ephebi who may symbolize the world of paganism at the time of Christ's birth. The cartoon for the *Battle of Cascina* disappeared at an early date, but we know it from a grisaille copy by Bastiano da Sangallo (1481–1551), dated 1542 and preserved in Holkham Hall, Norfolk. Many of the figures, contorted in their struggle and pain, were used again in the fresco of the *Last Judgment*.

Michelangelo. *Doni Tondo (The Holy Family)*. Uffizi, Florence. *Photo Alinari.*

Michelangelo's reputation was such that Pope Julius II, on Giuliano da Sangallo's recommendation, entrusted him with the important project for his tomb. We do not know whether this monument was to have been placed in a chapel in St. Peter's or in a separate building. We do know, however, that its realization was closely connected with work on the new basilica of St. Peter's. In the spring of 1506, while Michelangelo was waiting for the marble he had chosen in Carrara, Julius suddenly gave up the idea for his mausoleum, resulting in the artist's sudden and angry departure from Rome. On five separate occasions following the pontiff's death, Michelangelo returned to the project for the tomb, finally completing the much reduced monument in Julius' titular church, S. Pietro in Vincoli, Rome, between 1542 and 1545.

In March 1508, a few months before inviting Raphael to decorate the Stanze in the Vatican, Julius II commissioned Michelangelo to paint the Sistine Chapel ceiling. At first the artist expected to decorate only the upper part of the vault but, with the pope's permission, he extended the composition to the springing lines where the lunettes alternated with pendentives. During four years of concentrated effort, Michelangelo painted 343 figures within the compartments marked on the vault by a network of illusionistic frames in grisaille. He chose the theme of the history of humanity from the Creation to Noah from the tragedy of the Fall to the promise of redemption. In the arches of the lunettes, half-prostrate figures symbolize the sorrow of fallen humanity. Higher up, the prophets are seated with their radiant, melancholy, or thoughtful faces. Following a medieval tradition, Michelangelo found a place for the

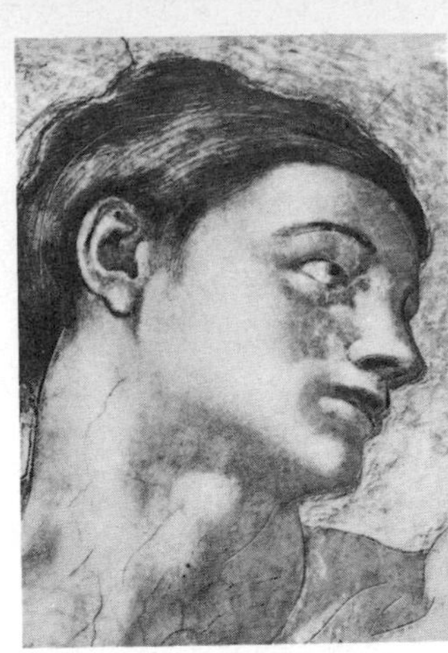

Michelangelo. *Head of Adam*. Detail from the Creation of Man. 1510. Sistine Chapel vault, Rome.

Sibyls, the inspired women of paganism, who were reputed to have foreseen the Christian future of Rome. A long rectangle at the apex of the vault contains nine scenes from Genesis up to and including the story of Noah. As the paintings follow the story back in time, from the *Drunkenness of Noah* to the *Creation of the Stars*, the style becomes essentially broader and more monumental. The *Ignudi*, painted on the cornice that frames the nine scenes, are perhaps archetypes of man's faculties and passions, or may represent the struggle of humanity to release itself from the bonds of the flesh, an interpretation closer to the concepts of Neoplatonism.

When he had completed the Sistine ceiling in 1512, Michelangelo returned for a while to sculpture. He was bound by a contract made in 1513 to the heirs of Julius II, and therefore felt obligated to return to his work on the tomb. The statue of *Moses* (1516; Rome, S. Pietro in Vincoli) was followed by the series of so-called *Bound Slaves* (Florence, Accademia; Paris, Louvre), which communicate a new obsession with unhappiness, the struggle against a hostile fate, against the imaginary powers of oppression whose shackles these men strain to break with all their might.

A final sojourn in Florence from 1516 to 1534 was largely occupied with the funerary chapel for the Medici in the New Sacristy of S. Lorenzo, where the seven figures carved by Michelangelo constitute the largest single ensemble that he left. A statue of the Virgin stands between the two tombs of Giuliano de' Medici, duke of Nemours, and Lorenzo de' Medici, duke of Urbino. At their feet, the personifications of Time (*Day, Night,*

Michelangelo. *Lorenzo de' Medici, Duke of Urbino.* Medici Tomb. 1524–31. New Sacristy of S. Lorenzo, Florence. *Photo Anderson-Giraudon.*

Dawn, and *Twilight*) seem crushed by adversity. After Michelangelo's departure from Florence, the statues were assembled by Giorgio Vasari in the architectural setting designed by the sculptor himself. As in the adjacent sacristy built by Brunelleschi, the bluish color of the architectonic elements stands out from the marble and light plaster of the walls. The lunettes that Michelangelo had intended to paint have remained empty, however.

It was in Rome under the Farnese Pope Paul III that Michelangelo once more began painting, this time the huge *Last Judgment* (1536–41) on the wall behind the altar in the Sistine Chapel. In the upper register, the dominant figure of Christ makes an angry gesture as he pronounces His curse on the damned. The Virgin herself crouches terrified against her Son. In the lower portion of the fresco, the trumpets of angels arouse the dead from their graves. On the left, the elect ascend to heaven. On the other side, the damned are dragged down to a glowing abyss. Saints Peter, Andrew, and John the Baptist stand around Christ, while at His feet are the martyrs Lawrence, Blaise, Sebastian, and Catherine holding the instruments of their torture; St. Bartholomew, flayed and holding his skin round him, bears the features of Michelangelo himself. At the top of the composition, wingless angels carry the instruments of the Passion toward Christ. In this confused scene the elect stand joylessly behind Christ, while the martyrs seem to cry aloud for vengeance. Everything is swept away before the images of punishment: it is the justice of the strong and jealous God of Deuteronomy, now exercised by His Son.

Michelozzo. Convent of S. Marco, Florence. Library. 1437–52. *Photo Alinari-Viollet.*

Michelangelo's long old age was brightened for a few years by his friendship with Vittoria Colonna, the widow of the victor of the Battle of Pavia. In their conversations, which have been recorded, she told him of her interest in North European paintings, whose realistic scenes of Christ's Passion and saintly martyrdoms encouraged her piety. Michelangelo painted two frescoes, the *Crucifixion of St. Peter* and the *Conversion of St. Paul* (1542–45) in the Vatican's Cappella Paolina, at the time of these conversations.

Although Michelangelo's declining strength reduced his sculptural activity, he still pursued his interest in architecture. While the façade of S. Lorenzo in Florence, which Michelangelo had been commissioned to design and for which we possess a fine model (1516), could not be realized, his design for the Biblioteca Laurenziana, also in Florence, was carried out. It was begun in 1524 by Michelangelo himself, and completed according to his plans by Bartolommeo Ammannati in 1560. In Rome, Michelangelo's style achieved an austere majesty in the plan for the three palaces on the Piazza del Campidoglio (1544–52; completed after his death), which are given a severe rhythm by the colossal pilasters that the artist placed beneath very heavy pediments. During his tenure as architect of St. Peter's (1546–64), Michelangelo seldom designed his models with the result that in 1557 the vault of the southern tribune of St. Peter's had to be demolished because a contractor had made a mistake in the curve of a soffit. Built on a light drum of travertine, which Luigi Vanvitelli had to brace with iron in the 18th century, the dome of St. Peter's was at first based upon Michelangelo's wooden model (1558–61). The outer shell, however, was rebuilt and raised by Giacomo della Porta in 1588–90, and no longer conforms to Michelangelo's plan.

The *Pietàs* carved by the artist as death drew near were no longer embodiments of the calmness of his genius, but were expressive of a poignant despair. The manner in which the body of Christ is placed—lying heavily against the Virgin in the *Rondanini Pietà* (1556–64; Milan, Castello Sforzesco) and in the *Palestrina Pietà* (*c.* 1556; Florence, Accademia)—is reminiscent of certain medieval German groups in which Mary clasps her son closely to her.

MICHELOZZO, Michelozzo di Bartolommeo Michelozzi, *called* (1396, Florence—1472, Florence), Italian architect, sculptor, and decorator. He was influenced by his two great contemporaries, Filippo Brunelleschi and Leon Battista Alberti. As a sculptor, he decorated most of his own buildings, and the precious elegance of his work became a model for contemporary ornament.

The Gothic spirit, still retained in the little church of S. Francesco al Bosco in the Mugello (*c.* 1420), is blended with Renaissance Classicism in the curious portal of S. Agostino at Montepulciano (*c.* 1430); the pilasters are Corinthian but the ensemble is crowned with a Gothic gable, while a triangular pediment surmounts the façade. At the convent of S. Marco in Florence (after 1437), Michelozzo created a single nave and a polygonal apse with a flat ceiling, unfortunately spoiled by later decoration. The Ionic order, which Brunelleschi rarely used, appears in the cloister and the friars' library, where two rows of slender columns divide the space into three aisles. The elegance and lucid planning that Giorgio Vasari so admired in this convent are a distinguishing feature of the Palazzo Medici-Riccardi in Florence, Michelozzo's most important urban construction (1444–59). Before later additions were made, the structure was a cubic block, heavily rusticated at the base but becoming progressively smooth on each of the two upper stories, thereby imparting an impression of lightness to the whole building. The ground floor arcades are surmounted by bifurcated windows on the upper floors. A very prominent cornice, decorated, according to Classical models, with ovolos and modillions, projects from the top of the building. The interior court is surrounded by arcades whose arches rest directly on the Corinthian capitals. Near Florence, he built or modernized the Medici villas at Careggi (after 1434), Castello di Trebbio (1427–*c.* 1436), and Cafaggiolo (1451–52).

Michelozzo's sculpture is overshadowed by his architecture, yet in partnership with Donatello from 1423 to 1438, he constructed monuments for the Antipope John XXIII (1421–27; Florence, Baptistery), Cardinal Brancacci (1428; Naples, S. Angelo a Nilo), and the poet Bartolommeo Aragazzi (1427–*c.* 1437; surviving fragments, mostly by Michelozzo, are at Montepulciano and the Victoria and Albert Museum, London). Michelozzo also carved a lunette in his own church of S. Agostino at Montepulciano. This lunette and the silver *St. John the Baptist* (1452; Florence, Museo dell'Opera del Duomo) demonstrate a considerable talent, but Michelozzo was at his best in ornamental sculpture. His medallions, friezes, festoons, and putti decorated buildings of restrained proportions: SS. Annunziata, Florence (1448), where he added the round east end with eight chapels based on the so-called Temple of Minerva Medica, Rome; the sacristy of S. Marco (before 1451), the Chapel of the Crucifix at S. Miniato al Monte (1447–48), and the chapel in the Palazzo Medici-Riccardi (1459), all in Florence; and two tabernacles for the church at Impruneta (1460). In Milan, he embellished the portal of the Medici bank (1455; now in the Castello Sforzesco, Milan) and the Portinari Chapel in S. Eustorgio (1463), which is dominated by a radiant circle of angels suspended at the oculus of the dome.

MICRONESIAN ART. *See* **POLYNESIAN AND MICRONESIAN ART.**

MIES VAN DER ROHE, Ludwig (1886, Aachen, near Cologne—1969, Chicago), German architect and furniture designer, who became an American citizen in 1944. Among the masters of modern architecture, Mies carried rationalism and impersonality to their furthest extremes and achieved the greatest formal purity. His understanding of architectural materials and his respect for detail were derived in part from his artistic education. His earliest training was that of a craftsman. Mies then received professional and cultural training in Berlin, where he was first employed (1905–7) by the architect and noted furniture designer Bruno Paul (1874–1954), and then (1908–11) by the architect Peter Behrens, who introduced him to modern techniques and to the neoclassical art derived from the German architect and painter Karl Friedrich Schinkel.

Although Mies opened his own office in Berlin in 1912, he did not begin to do original architectural work until after World War I. His career can be divided into two phases. The first lasted until 1938 and was spent in Germany. During this time he gained recognition and an international reputation through the publication of his projects, which have since become anthology pieces. He also designed two masterpieces, the German Pavilion at the 1929 International Exhibition in Barcelona, and a private residence, the Tugendhat House (1930) in Brno, Czechoslovakia. Mies designed his first modern projects between 1919 and 1924. The first three illustrate his structural conception of architecture: two sky-scrapers (1919; 1920–21) with a steel frame and glass walls, and an office building (1922) with a concrete framework set back from the façades. His fourth project (1923), for a one-level brick country house, embodied his conception of spatial continuity, while the fifth (1924) was a design for a multi-unit dwelling. During the same period he took an active part in the De Stijl group and financed the modern art magazine *G* (meaning *Gestaltung*, "creative force"), whose aesthetic principles left an indelible mark on his architecture. After 1926 several of his projects were constructed. He built the brick memorial to the revolutionaries Karl Liebknecht and Rosa Luxemburg (1926; Berlin, demolished by the Nazis) and the Wolf House in Guben, Brandenburg. The same year he was also elected vice-president of the Deutscher Werkbund, which brought him the responsibility of organizing the famous outdoor housing exhibition in the Weissenhof quarter of Stuttgart in 1927. This was a model residential quarter for which Mies built a residential block that embodied the concept of flexibility, because the individual flats in the block differed completely from each other by the manipulation of mobile walls. In 1929 he designed his masterpiece, the German Pavilion for the Barcelona International Exhibition. Its structure was utterly bare, and its perfection depended as much on the richness of the materials as on the severe proportions of the De Stijl ideal upon which it was based. During the 1920s he also designed his now classic steel-framed furniture, and produced such pieces as the famous "Barcelona Chair" of steel and leather.

In 1930 Mies succeeded the German architect Walter Gropius as director of the Bauhaus in Dessau. In 1931 the institution was transferred to Berlin and, in 1933, it was closed by the Nazis. From that moment until he settled in the United States in 1938 at the age of fifty-three, Mies devoted his activity to various projects, especially the designing of houses with patios (designs published in 1931 and 1938). As soon as he arrived in America, he was appointed director of the department of architecture at the Illinois Institute of Technology (IIT) in Chicago, a position he held until his retirement in 1955 and in which capacity he trained two generations of American architects.

Ludwig Mies van der Rohe. Crown Hall. 1952–56. Illinois Institute of Technology, Chicago. *Photo Hedrich-Blessing, Chicago.*

Ludwig Mies van der Rohe. Seagram Building, New York. 1956–58.

He was also commissioned to build the vast complex of the Institute itself, whose general plan he completed in 1940–41. The first building was constructed in 1942–43; others built later included the Chemical Engineering and Metallurgy Building (1946), the Engineering Research Building (1946), the Alumni Memorial Hall (1946), the Chemistry Building (1946), the boiler plant (1950), the chapel (1952), and Crown Hall (which houses the School of Architecture, City Planning, and Design; 1952–56). All these buildings were constructed on the same principle, that of a visible steel framework. The fillings were made of brick or glass and the interior spaces were continuous.

Contemporaneously and postdating his activities at IIT, Mies designed several other different types of structures. For instance, he built a series of skyscrapers in which the steel framework was cased in concrete to comply with American fire regulations and in which the primary framework was covered by a secondary one in visible steel. These included several buildings in Chicago: the Lake Shore Drive Apartments (1948–51), the Commonwealth Promenade Apartments (1953–56), and the Esplanade Apartments (1956–57); as well as Lafayette Towers in Lafayette Park, Detroit (1955–63), and, with Philip Johnson, the Seagram Building in New York (1956–58), famous for its bronze façade. He also built some exemplary single-level private houses, the most famous of which is the Farnsworth House in Plano, near Fox River, Illinois (1946–50); museums, especially the one in Houston, Texas (1956); and the home office of the Bacardi Company in Mexico City (1961).

Mies designed very few buildings in Europe during this period. In 1953 his project for the National Theater in Mannheim, Germany, was rejected. In the Mannheim plan he used the principle of exposed girders rising above the plane of the terraces in order to create an interior space free of any kind of support. He returned to this principle in the Houston Museum and the IIT Crown Hall. Although his plans (1960) for the administrative center of the Krupp factories in Essen, Germany, were accepted, the construction of the buildings was postponed.

Mies was certainly the most influential architect of his generation and, after World War II, his were the most frequently copied forms, especially in the United States. He was the leading exponent of the steel and glass architecture of the International Style, although his imitators have generally followed the letter rather than the spirit of his teaching.

Sir John Everett Millais. *Ophelia.* 1852. Tate Gallery, London.

MIGNARD, family of French 17th-century painters, whose most distinguished members were:

PIERRE, *called* LE ROMAIN (1612, Troyes—1695, Paris), portraitist and decorator. He was trained first by Jean Boucher and, then, after spending two years in Fontainebleau, completed his training with Simon Vouet in Paris before going to Rome, where he stayed from 1635 to 1657. In 1658, after a brief stay in Avignon, he returned to the court at Fontainebleau. When he became Painter in Ordinary to the queen mother, Anne of Austria, he was given the important commission of decorating the dome of the Val-de-Grâce, Paris (1663). While engaged in rivalry with Charles Le Brun, whom he succeeded (1690) as director of the Académie Royale de Peinture et de Sculpture, he became the fashionable portraitist of the day (*Marquise de Seignelay as Thetis*, 1691, London, National Gallery; *Louis XIV*, 1673, Turin, Galleria Sabauda). Besides his many portraits and a number of dainty Raphaelesque Madonnas referred to as "Mignardes" (*Virgin with a Bunch of Grapes*, c. 1656; Paris, Louvre), he executed a variety of decorative work, characterized by fresh, bright, strongly contrasted colors. Mignard excelled in portraits of elegant women, whom he had no scruples in flattering (*Madame de Grignan*, 1675; Paris, Musée Carnavalet). His best works were his decorations: those in the gallery and salon of Monsieur, the king's brother, at St-Cloud, and the Cabinet du Dauphin at Versailles are lost, but the *Glory* (representing the Holy Trinity, apostles, prophets, saints, and angels) in the Val-de-Grâce (1663) still survives.

NICOLAS, *called* MIGNARD D'AVIGNON (1606, Troyes—1668, Paris), brother of Pierre. After a stay in Rome (1635–37), he settled at Avignon. He was invited to Paris by Louis XIV, whose portrait he painted in 1660. He decorated the lower apartment of the king in the Tuileries, and was about to decorate the great state room when he died.

PAUL (1639, Avignon—1691, Lyon) *and* PIERRE II, *called* LE CHEVALIER MIGNARD (1640, Avignon—1725, Paris), sons of Nicolas, were both painters. Pierre II was also an architect: he worked at Avignon on the cathedral, the Hôtel-Dieu, and the Hôtel Forbin-Janson.

MILLAIS, Sir John Everett (1829, Southampton—1896, London), vastly successful British painter of genre and portraits. In 1840 he became the youngest student ever to be admitted to the Royal Academy Schools. It was there that he met William Holman Hunt, the earnest idealist, with whom he was later to be associated. During his student years, Millais' art was eminently traditional.

In 1848 Millais, with Holman Hunt, Dante Gabriel Rossetti, and four fellow artists and writers, formed the Pre-Raphaelite Brotherhood to protest against the Royal Academy style and formally to embrace fidelity to nature as the basis for their art. Millais' first essay in this vein, *Lorenzo and Isabella* (1849; Liverpool, Walker Art Gallery) met with modified approval. *Ferdinand and Ariel* (1849; England, Coll. Roger Makins) and *Christ in the Carpenter's Shop* (1850; London, Tate Gallery) were, however, bitterly attacked, especially the latter, which outraged the canon of Victorian propriety and provoked the wrath of Charles Dickens. For some ten years Millais remained faithful to Pre-Raphaelite ideals, although there is a steady leaking away of high purpose in favor of popular anecdote. At their best, Millais' Pre-Raphaelite works can be arresting and strange, as in the *Blind Girl* (1856; Birmingham, City Museum & Art Gallery) or the disturbing and very Mannerist *Bridesmaid* (1851; Cambridge, Fitzwilliam Museum); at their mildest they have the Victorian charm of a nursery story (*Autumn Leaves*, 1856; Manchester, City Art Gallery).

In 1855 Millais married John Ruskin's former wife Effie and thereby lost the support of the critic who had been one of his strongest champions. The British public, however, continued to be enchanted by such works as *My First Sermon* (1863; London, Guildhall), the *Boyhood of Raleigh* (1870; Tate Gallery), and *Bubbles* (1886; Isleworth, Middlesex, Messrs. Pears Soap) which became, quite literally, a household word. Millais was on occasion an opulent portraitist in the style of Alfred Stephens (*Mrs. Bischoffsheim*, 1873; London, National Gallery), and his illustrations of Tennyson and Trollope are quintessential Victorian vignettes. In 1896 he became President of the Royal Academy.

MILLER, Kenneth Hayes (1876, Oneida, New York—1952, New York), American painter. Miller's earliest influences included Arthur B. Davies and Albert Pinkham Ryder, both of whose styles prompted him to work in a Romantic and sentimental manner (*Landscape with Figures*, 1914; New York, Metropolitan Museum). He is best known as a teacher, one of the few to equal the stature and importance of Robert Henri. At his well-known school on Fourteenth Street in New York, Miller was instrumental in reviving the Ashcan School's style and subject matter during the 1920s. Contemporary urban settings were used to express the counterpart of the rural American regionalism that was to dominate the country's painting throughout the 1930s. In search of a methodological tradition, Miller turned to Renaissance theories of composition and to academic techniques of representation that often drained his work of vividness and spirit. Precise detailing and careful composition were maintained in his work even after 1919, when Renoir's influence also became important. In the *Shopper* (1928; New York, Whitney Museum), the meticulously defined, heavy-set woman in middle-class attire appears waxen and stiffly detached before the shop windows, isolated from the bustle around her.

Miller's viewpoint and methods were perpetuated at the Art Students League, where many former Henri pupils studied and where the ideology of regionalism was furthered by such teachers as Thomas Hart Benton.

MILLES, Carl (1875, Lagga, near Uppsala—1955, Lidingo, near Stockholm), Swedish sculptor. After studying for three years at the Technical School of Stockholm, he decided in 1897 to leave for Chile. He stopped in Paris on the way and stayed for eight years. He joined the Académie Colarossi and made the acquaintance of Oscar Wilde and Auguste Rodin. In 1899 he exhibited for the first time at the Paris Salon, and in 1904 went to Munich, where he was deeply influenced by the aesthetic theories of the sculptor Adolf von Hildebrand. When he returned to Sweden (1908), he experimented with monumental sculptures at his studio at Lidingo, which, with its terraces and sheets of water, subsequently became the Milles Museum (Millesgarden). In 1929 Milles first visited the United States. In 1931 he was appointed professor of Sculpture at Cranbook Academy of Art, near Detroit; he became an American citizen in 1945. Milles' sculpture was Expressionistic at first, and gradually turned toward an archaizing Classicism in which the form was boldly simplified into large smooth surfaces. Among his notable works are the *Sun Singer* (1926; bronze, Stockholm); *Gustav Wasa*, a wood carving 23 feet high (1927; Stockholm, Nordiska Museet); the *Orpheus Fountain* (1936; bronze, Stockholm); the onyx *Peace Monument* (1936; St. Paul, Minn., City Hall); and *Man and Nature* (1940), a wooden statue for the Time-Life Building, Rockefeller Center, New York.

MILLET, Jean-François (1814, Gruchy, near Gréville, Manche—1875, Barbizon), French painter of peasant life. Millet studied in Cherbourg (1833–36), and then in Paris with the history painter Paul Delaroche; he soon, however, left Delaroche to study the works of Eustache Le Sueur, Nicolas Poussin, and Rembrandt at the Louvre. In 1840 he exhibited at the Salon for the first time. After marrying in Cherbourg the following year, he returned to Paris in 1842 with his wife and earned a living painting mythological and genre scenes in a flaccid style recalling that of the Rococo age. At the same time, he painted a series of technically assured portraits (*Portrait of a Naval Officer*, 1845; Rouen, Museum). Soon, childhood memories of life in his village oriented him toward humble country scenes, and he developed a style of which the *Winnower* (destroyed; replica in the Louvre, Paris), exhibited at the 1848 Salon, was prototypical. Millet went to Barbizon on the advice of the engraver Charles-Émile Jacque (1813–94), settling near Théodore Rousseau, in a cottage that he was never to leave, so great was his love for this corner of the forest. At the Salon of 1853, he exhibited the *Harvesters Resting* (Boston, Museum of Fine Arts; preliminary painting in the Louvre). The *Gleaners* of 1857 and the *Angelus* of 1858–59 (both Louvre) confirmed the opinion of his admirers.

Jean-François Millet. *The Baker.* 1854. Rijksmuseum Kröller-Müller, Otterlo.

Millet never painted from nature, but always from memory; and, with his original vision, achieved "a rare grandeur and nobility without lessening his rusticity in the least," as Gautier put it. In 1862 Millet produced his masterpiece, the *Man with a Hoe* (1858–62; Hillsborough, Calif., Coll. Mrs. Henry Potter Russell). The fusion of man and his tool, the roothold of the peasant in the earth, had never before been more cogently expressed. During Millet's last years, his palette grew lighter, and he produced landscapes like the *Hamlet of Cousin* (*c.* 1871; Rheims, Musée St-Denis) and the *Spring* (1868–73; Louvre), which were already pierced by rays of Impressionist light. But, just as he was becoming popular, he died and left his widow so poor that the kind-hearted Jean-Baptiste Camille Corot gave her an annuity.

The distinguishing feature of Millet's art is its simplified, synthetized technique—as concentrated as Daumier's—which gives his drawings, so admired by

Van Gogh, the same power as his painting. An exhibition in 1964 at the Musée Jacquemart-André, Paris, stressed a less familiar aspect of his work: the portraits. About 100 were gathered together, including those of his first wife, *Pauline Ono* (*c.* 1841; Cherbourg, Museum), a work brilliant with reds and greens, and *Charles Langevin* (1845; Le Havre, Museum). They were all painted before 1847–48, the date when Millet met the Barbizon painters, and throw a new light on the talent of this controversial artist.

MILLS, Robert (1781, Charleston, South Carolina—1855, Washington, D.C.), American architect. Generally considered to be the first professional trained native American architect, he was graduated from Charleston College in 1800, and then apprenticed himself successively to James Hoban (*c.* 1762–1831), Thomas Jefferson, and Benjamin Latrobe. From the latter Mills acquired a preference for Greek monuments, and became one of the most original interpreters of the Greek Revival style. At the same time, he was one of the first to believe that the United States should develop an indigenous architectural expression, and he worked toward that end in his free adaptations of Classical styles. Mills was especially interested in problems of sound construction, and his Record Office (1822) in Charleston was dubbed the "Fireproof Building" because of its resistance to heat and flame; moreover, it survived the earthquake of 1886.

In his churches Mills evolved novel plans to suit the new need for accommodating the growing congregations of the day. Thus the Sansom Street Church (1808–9) in Philadelphia has an immense circular auditorium, and the Monumental Church (1812) in Richmond, Virginia, has an octagonal interior. Mills designed many public buildings, particularly after his appointment as Federal Architect and Engineer in 1836. In the 1840s he completed the Treasury Building, the U.S. Patent Office, and the former Post Office—all in Washington, D.C. He also executed some charming custom houses, such as those at New Bedford and Newburyport, both in Massachusetts. Mills is probably best known as the designer of the two major American monuments to George Washington. The one in Baltimore (1814–29) consists of a giant column rising from a heavy base and supporting an abacus block surmounted by a statue of the nation's first President. The 555-foot monument in Washington, D.C. (1833–84), rivals the Egyptian obelisks on which it was modeled. In Mills's original design the obelisk rose from a circular Doric colonnade, but this was not included when the monument was finally built, long after his death.

MILNE, David (1882, Paisley, Ontario—1953, Toronto), Canadian painter. As a young man he taught at a country school, later going to New York (*c.* 1904) and studying briefly at the Art Students League. Milne remained in the New York area, and painted in a decorative style that was probably influenced by the Americans Maurice Prendergast and Ernest Lawson. He exhibited at the Armory Show in 1913. After painting a series of watercolors (*Arras Cathedral*; Ottawa, National Gallery) for the Canadian War Memorials in 1919, he returned to the United States and painted for several seasons (1921–23) in the Adirondacks, finally returning to Canada in 1928. His mature work in oils and watercolor was highly personal and sensitive, and often whimsical in expression (*Painting Place*, 1930; Ottawa, National Gallery).

MINGUZZI, Luciano (b. 1911, Bologna), Italian sculptor. He studied at the Bologna Academy of Fine Arts and gave his first exhibition in 1931 at Florence. In his early work, Minguzzi attempted to reconcile the Classical tradition with modern innovations. These initial stylistic preoccupations still appeared in the sculpture he exhibited at the fourth Roman Quadriennale in 1943. Around 1950, however, Minguzzi abandoned the figurative idiom of works such as *Saltimbanco* (1945) and moved toward abstract sculpture (*Dog Among the Reeds*, 1951; New York, Museum of Modern Art). In 1950 he won the grand prize for sculpture at the Venice Biennale and in 1951 he won the sculpture prize at the São Paulo Bienal. Henceforth, he expressed the abstract equivalents of objects (*Stag Beetles*, 1958). In the 1950s Minguzzi continued to refine his style, evolving a linear type of sculpture in which networks of intertwining lines create an elegant effect (*Shadow in the Wood*, 1957).

MINIMAL ART. Minimal art, primary structures, post-painterly abstraction, and hard-edge all have in common a neutral and impersonal quality as opposed to the popular, often satirical aspect of its contemporary trend, Pop art, and the romantic Abstract Expressionist style of the preceding generation. The sources of the new aesthetic stem ultimately from Kasimir Malevich's work of *c.* 1913 (*Black Square on a White Ground*, 1913; Leningrad, State Russian Museum) and Marcel Duchamp's ready-mades, such as the *Fountain* (actually a urinal, 1917; Milan, Gallery Schwarz). The immediate predecessors of the Minimalists were Ad Reinhardt and Josef Albers. There are also roots of this new mode in Abstract Expressionism, particularly in the chromatic abstractions of Barnett Newman, Mark Rothko, and Adolph Gottlieb. The Minimal artists rejected the painterliness and spontaneous emotionalism of their predecessors, but at the same time maintained the primacy of color, all-over composition, scale, and directness in works by the older generation. Ellsworth Kelly's *Red Blue Green* (1963; New York, Sidney Janis Gallery)—with its immaculate surface, pure color, and simple geometric forms executed with razor-sharp precision—is typical of this new aesthetic, as are the shaped canvases of Frank Stella and Charles Hinman (b. 1932) and the pure abstractions of Larry Zox (b. 1936), Robert Huot (b. 1935), and Darby Bannard (b. 1931). Donald Judd's (b. 1928) 1965 untitled work of galvanized iron and painted aluminum (New York, Coll. Philip Johnson) is representative of Minimal sculpture. Also grouped with the minimal artists are Jules Olitski, Kenneth Noland, Jack Youngerman, Larry Poons, and Al Held. The utmost restraint and understatement, mechanical precision, anonymity, and lack of personal involvement characterize this art and indicate both its merits and its limitations.

MINNE, Georges (1866, Ghent—1941, Laethem-St-Martin), Belgian sculptor. At the age of eighteen he began to make

Georges Minne. *Mother and Child.* Middelheim Park, Antwerp.

drawings and sculpture; he always practiced these two arts independently of each other. Two years later, Minne met the Belgian Symbolist writer Maurice Maeterlink, who made a great impression on him and became a close friend, and he began to illustrate Symbolist books, including Maeterlinck's *Serres chaudes* (1889) and Émile Verhaeren's *Villages illusoires* (1894). In 1890 he was invited by Les Vingt to exhibit his work in Brussels, but received bad reviews from the press and was deeply discouraged. At the age of thirty, he suddenly decided to resume his artistic studies and enrolled in the Brussels Academy of Fine Arts. During this period of doubt, he discovered the sculptural theme of the kneeling adolescent (*Le petit agenouillé*, 1896), which left its mark on all his work. In 1910 he experienced a second moral crisis: fearing that his forms had lost their roots in nature, he studied anatomy in the dissection classes at the University of Ghent. He was so conscientious that he made five fresh starts on the maquette for his masterpiece, the *Fountain with Kneeling Figures* (1898; marble, Essen, Folkwang Museum). Minne produced a number of "interior sculptures," which were modeled in clay and generally cast in bronze by two of his sons who were founders. His other favorite subject was the mother and child, which he embodied in moving variations in drawings and sculpture.

MINO DA FIESOLE (1429, Poppi, Casentino—1484, Florence), Italian sculptor. Between 1453 and 1464 he carved a number of portrait busts, including those of Piero and Giovanni de' Medici (1453 and *c.* 1460, respectively; both Florence, Bargello), Niccolò Strozzi (1454; Berlin, Staatliche Museen), and Astorgio Manfredi (1455; Washington, D.C., National Gallery). Their characterization is clearly influenced by the hard realism of antique Roman busts. Mino also executed a number of wall tombs of the typical Florentine type, both in Florence (tomb of Count Ugo, 1471–81, church of Badia) and in Rome (Tomb of Cardinal Riario, after 1474, SS. Apostoli), where he was also employed on sculptures for the Vatican, notably on panels now forming part of the screen in the Sistine Chapel. His work there, however, is difficult to isolate from that of associates. In his use of thinner forms, his sense of decorative pattern, his feeling for grace, and his rather empty modeling, Mino represents a further stage in the reaction—so notable in Florence in the second half of the 15th century—against the forceful drama of Donatello's late style.

MINOAN ART. *See* **CRETAN ART.**

MIR ISKUSSTVA ("The World of Art"), Russian cultural movement founded by Sergei Diaghilev in St. Petersburg in the 1890s and active in the first quarter of the 20th century. It was the outgrowth of a St. Petersburg society called the Nevsky Pickwickians, which flourished in the late 1880s under the leadership of the young Alexander Benois. *Mir Iskusstva* published (1898–1904) a cultural magazine of the same name, organized traveling exhibitions with the aim of placing Russian culture on an equal footing with that of the rest of Europe, and became the main center of the Russian avant-garde.

The periodical *Mir Iskusstva* was the first of its kind in Russia, and it was an extremely active cultural organ for the six years of its existence. Among its numerous contributors were several Russian painters who later designed the sets and costumes for the various productions of Diaghilev's Ballets Russes: Benois himself, Léon Bakst (1866–1924), Alexander Golovine (1863–1930), Konstantin Korovine (1861–1939), and Nicholas Roerich (1874–1947). The magazine's aim was to give an artistic education to the Russian people through its profusely illustrated articles on painting and crafts. While *Mir Iskusstva* introduced Impressionism and Symbolism to its readers, it also concentrated on the artistic treasures of ancient Russia, thus reflecting Diaghilev's interest in Russia's cultural heritage. Although the *Mir Iskusstva* group held exhibitions of contemporary art in St. Petersburg until 1922, the magazine lost its wealthy backers and ceased publication in 1904.

MIRKO, Mirko Basaldella, *called* (b. 1910, Udine), Italian sculptor. He trained first in Venice and Florence, then worked in Arturo Martini's studios in Milan and Monza (1931–34). His entire figural production was profoundly influenced by Martini. In 1937 Mirko visited Paris with his brother, the painter Afro, and became aware of the problems of avant-garde art. About 1947 he began to experiment with abstraction. In the mid-1950s he combined serious and burlesque notes in ritualistic figures of dancers, warriors, and sorcerers. Mirko continued to produce symbolic sculptures, ever more abstract, in the 1960s (*High Priest*, 1964; wood). He worked in a variety of materials—painted plaster, plaques of cut-out copper or brass, and blocks of cement. His masterpiece is the bronze screen for the Ardeatine Graves in Rome (1949–51), dedicated to the memory of 300 Roman hostages of World War II. He also designed the monument to the Italian dead at Mauthausen in Austria, and the fountain with a Venetian glass mosaic in the Piazza Benedetto Brin in La Spezia (1955). Mirko won the grand prize for sculpture at the São Paulo Bienal in 1955 and left for the United States in 1958,

Mino da Fiesole. *Bust of Piero de' Medici.* 1453. Museo del Bargello, Florence.

Joan Miró. *Coffee Mill.* 1918. Galerie Maeght, Paris.

where he accepted a teaching position at Harvard University.

MIRÓ, Joan (b. 1893, Montroig, Catalonia), Spanish painter, potter, and sculptor. Although he began to draw at a very early age, his first paintings date from 1912, and were executed while he was studying at the Galí Art Academy in Barcelona. In 1915, when he had completed his artistic training, he produced paintings that were clearly influenced by Fauvism (*Portrait of E. C. Ricart*, 1917; Chicago, Coll. Mr. and Mrs. Samuel A. Marx). In 1918 he adopted a minutely detailed realism and a light, transparent color (*Coffee Mill*, 1918; Paris, Galerie Maeght). After a series of Montroig landscapes painted in this manner, he began to paint in a method derived from Cubism; his *Self-Portrait* of 1919 (Vauvenargues, Coll. Pablo Picasso) shows a broader, more sustained style, in which the expression is purer and more concise.

Miró maintained contact with the artistic currents in Paris, which he had visited for three months (March–June 1919) and where he found encouragement from his boyhood friend, Pablo Picasso. He made friends with the poets Pierre Reverdy and Max Jacob and attended meetings of the Dada group without actually taking part in them. His interest in Dadaism did not, however, prevent him from returning to the miniaturism of his 1918–19 phase with *The Farm* (1922; formerly Havana, Coll. Ernest Hemingway) and some very simplified still lifes, such as *Table with a Rabbit* (1920; Zurich, Coll. Gustav M. Zumsteg) and the *Ear of Grain* (1923; New York, Museum of Modern Art). In 1923 Miró went through a serious psychological crisis, but he overcame it through the stimulating friendship of the poets who were about to group themselves under the provocative banner of Surrealism. When he returned to Montroig, the inspiration he had received in Paris began to ferment and, with the natural energy he drew from his home, it began to take shape in his paintings. There he painted the *Tilled Field* (1923–24; Radnor, Pa., Coll. Henry Clifford), a significant work in which his genius is clearly evident and already bears traces of his mature style.

Joan Miró. *Harlequin's Carnival.* 1924–25. Albright-Knox Art Gallery, Buffalo.

Miró pursued his adventurous exploration in the realm of the fantastic, the only area in which he felt at ease. His meeting in 1924 with the writer André Breton and with the Surrealists was valuable to him as a justification of his explorations. One of Miró's major works, his famous *Harlequin's Carnival* (1924–25; Buffalo, Albright-Knox Art Gallery), belongs to this period. In 1926–27, at Montroig, he produced a series of "Imaginary Landscapes," and, in 1928, a group of "Dutch Interiors' (*Dutch Interior*, 1928; New York, Museum of Modern Art) that were inspired by the paintings he had seen while visiting Holland. In 1929, while he was painting a series of "Imaginary Portraits" after works by the old masters (Raphael's *La Fornarina*, 1929; New York, Coll. Robert J. Schoelkopf, Jr.), he created his first collages composed of paper and objects. In 1930 he learned lithography, and in the following year exhibited his first "object-sculptures" at the Galerie Pierre in Paris. He designed the sets, costumes, and curtain for Léonide Massine's ballet *Jeux d'Enfants*, produced by the Ballets Russes in Monte Carlo (1932). The same year he also exhibited, together with his Surrealist friends, at the Salon des Surindépendants and, in 1933, he painted his first watercolors. He then produced pastels, paintings on sandpaper, gouaches, watercolors, paintings on copper or masonite, and paintings with objects. In 1937 he painted *The Reaper* (present location unknown), a mural decoration for the Spanish Republic's pavilion at the Universal Exposition in Paris. His activity increased and, as he tried to find a less tense and more restrained manner, his idiom became simpler. In 1939 at Varengéville-sur-Mer, he organized an exhibition of paintings on burlap and, in 1940, he began his admirable series of "Constellations," which he finished at Palma de Mallorca on the Balearic Islands, where he had taken refuge from the Germans.

In 1944, in collaboration with the Spanish ceramist José Llorens Artigas, Miró produced his first ceramics. Again in 1945 and 1946 he began to execute paintings on large canvases and to produce his series of "Women and Birds," including *Woman and Birds in Front of the Sun* (1942; Chicago, Art Institute), *Woman and Bird Beneath the Moon* (1944; Baltimore, Museum of Art), and *Women and Bird in the Moonlight* (1949; London, Tate Gallery). Miró's fame spread; he was given important commissions, such as a mural painting for the Harkness Commons Dining Room in the Graduate Center at Harvard University, Cambridge, Massachusetts (1950), and two ceramic murals for the UNESCO building in Paris (*Wall of the Moon* and *Wall of the Sun*, 1957–59). In 1956 Miró settled in Palma de Mallorca, and in 1960 he began to paint more enthusiastically and in a more diversified manner than ever before. He passed from a forthright graphism to an evasive, almost ethereal style, and then, in 1961–62, he succeeded in creating monumental large-scale paintings merely by tracing a single line over a monochrome background. In 1962 the Musée National d'Art Moderne in Paris organized a retrospective exhibition of his works.

Miró's career offered nothing to attract lovers of the picturesque and unforeseen. He made no attempt himself to add a colorful or romantic touch to his image. His palette is extremely restricted: he uses a few elementary colors—blue, vermilion, yellow, green, and black—with a great economy, but with assurance and infallible accuracy. His is an unexpected, whimsical, droll world of larvae, madrepores, spasmodic amoebas, long and sinuous filaments, and vagrant lines ending with forms that look like bilboquets or mites.

It is a dream world transcribed by a master technician. Miró was a Surrealist quite naturally, with sincerity and humility, and without recourse to artifice or provocative attitudes. He was, in fact, one of those rare Surrealist painters who had no contempt for the resources of his art or for the constraints of his profession.

MIXTEC ART. The Mixtecs appeared about the 8th century A.D. on the high Sierras of the Oaxaca region in Mexico and they called their land Mixteca, meaning "land in the clouds." Their kingdom was fairly extensive since the sites bearing their traces are spread over four Mexican states: Oaxaca, Puebla, Tlaxcala, and Guerrero. The Mixtecs were neighbors of the Zapotecs, whom they often fought and partially dominated. They were divided into chieftainships, each of which was governed by a hereditary ruler. Within this framework, their society was divided into two classes, one comprising the nobles, priests, and merchants, the other craftsmen and peasants. Although it was a warrior society, it excelled in its art, which included jewelry, ceramics, and mosaics. The Mixtecs also left some admirable manuscripts in the form of screenfolds made of deerskin, in which they recorded the elements of their religion, history, genealogy, and legal matters, with painted ideograms that were carefully arranged across the page in separate scenes. Their numeration was vigesimal, as was that of the Maya; they had a calendar and a vast body of astronomical knowledge. There were a great many gods in their religion, including Taandoco, the Sun God, to whom they offered sacrifices of prisoners of war.

It is known from their manuscripts that the Mixtecs built temples, but very little remains of their architecture. Its original quality lay in the decoration—stone mosaics—that covered the exteriors as well as the interior courtyards and rooms. The mosaics that decorate monuments, altars, and the façades of tombs at Mitla, in Zapotec territory, are the most splendid yet discovered. Mixtec sculpture comprises mainly figures carved in greenstone, of men and women standing or seated cross-legged, vessels in alabaster, and little idols of jade and other semiprecious stones.

Mixtec Art. Gold pectoral. Museo Nacional de Antropología, Mexico City. *Photo Henri Stierlin, Geneva.*

The jewelry, pectoral plaques, mouth ornaments, necklaces, rings, orchid-shaped nose ornaments, and earrings were made either by repoussé or by the lost-wax process. In ceramics the Mixtecs developed an original style whose finest wares began to be produced about the 11th century and include especially a form of polychrome pottery decorated with mythological animals and figures, or with simpler designs, closely related to the style of the deerskin manuscripts. The forms of these tripod vessels were varied. Similar shapes appear in the simpler orange-red ware with blackish decoration.

MODERSOHN-BECKER, Paula (1876, Dresden—1907, Worpswede), German painter. She studied at the Berlin Art School from 1896 to 1898, and spent the summer of 1897 in Worpswede, near Bremen, at a newly founded artists' colony. In 1898 she moved into the colony, and in 1901 married a painter of the group, the landscapist Otto Modersohn (1865–1943). During a visit to Paris in 1899–1900 she saw Paul Cézanne's paintings for the first time, and soon introduced his simplified forms, firm construction, and graduated planes into her own paintings. Modersohn-Becker paid three further visits (1903–5; 1906) to Paris and, in the course of the last one, she saw the important Gauguin retrospective at the Salon d'Automne. The exhibition confirmed her in her own method of composition: large, flat areas of color edged with a strong line. She was particularly perceptive in the way she studied and accepted the experiments of the French Postimpressionists before they were widely known in Germany. She frequently painted landscapes, mothers and children, and still lifes, some of the best examples of which are *Peasant Girl* (1904–5; Bremen, Kunsthalle), *Still Life with Flowers* (1905; Bremen, Kunsthalle), *Self Portrait with Camellia Spray* (1907; Essen, Folkwang Museum), *Mother and Child* (1906–7), and *Nude Girl with Flowers* (1907; both Wuppertal, Von der Heydt-Museum der Stadt).

MODIGLIANI, Amedeo (1884, Leghorn—1920, Paris), Italian painter. His mother recognized and encouraged his artistic genius. She took him to museums and sent him to study at the art academies in Florence and Venice. He went to Paris in 1906, but by then his health was already severely undermined by tuberculosis. Aristocratically handsome, unpredictable, temperamental, and always moving from one lodging to another, Modigliani never stopped drawing, painting, and sculpting, and, because of his humanitarian feelings, he generally chose his models from among the poor. He admired the works of Toulouse-Lautrec and Cézanne, and was sincerely interested in the Cubists; he also discovered Negro art, and became friendly with the Rumanian-born sculptor Constantin Brancusi, whose example encouraged him to carve stone figures (*Head*, *c.* 1912, London, Tate Gallery; *Caryatid*, 1913–14, New York, Museum of Modern Art), which, for the most part, remained unfinished. In 1913 Modigliani left Montmartre and settled in Montparnasse, where he was friendly with the Jewish painters Moïse Kisling, Chaim Soutine, and Jules Pascin. Modig-

Mixtec Art. Statuette of a man, from Mitla. Nationalmuseet, Copenhagen.

Amedeo Modigliani. *Head.* *c.*1912. Tate Gallery, London.

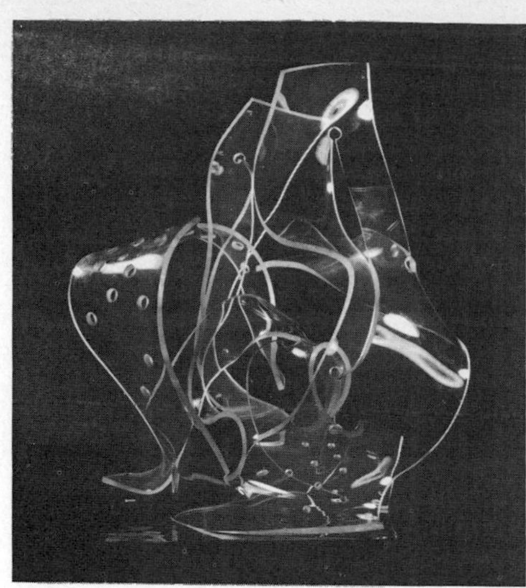

Laszlo Moholy-Nagy. *Double Loop.* 1946. Bayerische Staatsgemäldesammlungen, Munich.

liani wasted his talent and his money, wandering from café to café selling his marvelous drawings, and even his paintings, for a few francs. Fortunately, he was lucky enough to meet some kindly spirits during his life: the English poetess Beatrice Hastings, who supported him from 1914 to 1916; the poet Leopold Zborowski, who gave him money, support, and shelter, and organized exhibitions of his work; and Jeanne Hébuterne, the mistress who bore him a daughter. Finally, he entered the Parisian Hôpital de la Charité, where he died on January 25, 1920. On the day of his funeral, Jeanne Hébuterne committed suicide.

Although deeply committed to the cause of modern art, Modigliani always remained first and foremost a humanist and a Mannerist. His main pictorial subject was the female nude (*Seated Nude*, c. 1917, London, Courtauld Institute; *Reclining Nude*, 1918–19, New York, Museum of Modern Art). He also painted numerous portraits in which he depicted intellectuals, artists, and ordinary men and women. He did many portraits of his friends: *Jacques Lipchitz and His Wife* (1916; Chicago, Art Institute), *Max Jacob* (1916; Paris, Coll. Pierre Roche), *Jean Cocteau* (1917; New York, Coll. Henry Pearlman), *Chaim Soutine* (1917; Paris, Coll. John Netter), and *Moïse Kisling* (1915; Milan, Coll. Dr. Emilio Jesi). His most moving paintings, however, are of children, the poor, or the outcasts of fortune. Modigliani's pity, tenderness, and incurable melancholy pervade their emaciated bodies, listless attitudes, drooping heads, elongated necks, and eyes that seem to be half closed because of some secret grief: *Lolotte* (1917; Paris, Musée National d'Art Moderne), *Poor Girl* (Paris, Priv. Coll.), and *Little Girl in Blue, Jeanne Hébuterne* (1919; Troyes, Coll. Pierre Levy). Although Modigliani's color lacks neither vibrancy nor harmony, it does not actually add anything to his paintings. He was a great draftsman, and it was with line that he interpreted the individuality of his models and expressed his own feelings. In spite of his Expressionistic and Manneristic style, his paintings reveal an unerring taste and chaste restraint.

MOGUL ART. *See* **INDIAN ART; ISLAMIC ART.**

MOHOLY-NAGY, Laszlo (1895, Bacsbarsod, Hungary—1946, Chicago), Hungarian painter, sculptor, teacher, photographer, and writer. He began his artistic career in 1917 by painting portraits and landscapes that were permeated with the spirit of Cubism. In 1920 he settled in Germany, where he met the Russian-born Constructivist painter El Lissitzky, who exerted a strong influence on his art. Moholy-Nagy realized his desire to use modern materials by producing pictures made of papiers collés, reliefs made with real objects, and sculptures made of materials such as sheets of glass, nickel, and wood. In 1923 the German architect Walter Gropius invited him to teach at the Bauhaus in Dessau; there, he supervised the metal workshop and also taught some of the preparatory courses. While at the Bauhaus, Moholy-Nagy produced pictures composed of pure geometric forms set against backgrounds of aluminum, galalith, and other synthetic materials. At the same time, he explored the many artistic possibilities of photography by making photograms, photomontages, and films. In the Bauhaus collection of writings (*Bauhausbücher*), which he edited, he published his *Malerei, Photographie, Film* ("Painters, Photographers, and Film," 1925) and *Von Material zu Architektur* ("Use of Materials in Architecture," 1929), in which he summarized his pedagogical ideas. Moholy-Nagy left the Bauhaus in 1928 and settled in Berlin, where he extended his activities to publicity, typography, and designing extremely modern stage settings (*Tales of Hoffmann*, 1929; *Madama Butterfly*, 1931). After several visits to Paris and a stay in London from 1935 to 1937, he went to the United States. He settled in Chicago in 1937, and founded the new Bauhaus, whose name was changed the next year to the Institute of Design, which he directed until his death.

Moholy-Nagy's interest in the problem of mobility in works of art dates from the publication of his manifesto, the *System of Dynamo-Constructive Forces* (1922). Light became one of the materials with which he created moving volumes in space; around 1930 he constructed a complicated apparatus (*Lichtrequisit*, or "Light-Space Requisite"), a rotating sculpture-machine that displayed light by giving off different intensities of light. This contraption was the forerunner of the *Space Modulators* in which he combined paintings and objects and which he made in London after 1935. In 1940 he began making plexiglass sculptures whose curves intersected in concave-convex movements that were amplified by light projectors. In his book *Vision in Motion*, published posthumously in 1947, Moholy-Nagy described the many artistic concepts and experiences with which he enriched modern art.

MOILLIET, Louis (1880, Bern—1962, Vevey), Swiss painter. A boyhood friend of Paul Klee, he studied from 1900 to 1903 at Worpswede and in 1904 at the Stuttgart Academy. In 1911 he met August Macke and was reunited with Klee in Munich. He introduced Klee to Wassily Kandinsky, who in turn brought him into contact with the artists of the Blaue Reiter. A voyage to Tunisia in April 1914 with Klee and Macke had a profound effect on his work, particularly his watercolors. His early compositions had always been based on a synthetic vision of reality, with a colorism that had much in common with that of Robert Delaunay (*Circus*, 1913–15; Basel, Kunstmuseum). Now, with watercolor, he could seize the evanescent quality of light and suggest a landscape with a subtle play of transparent effects (*Fez*, 1921; Bremgarten, Switzerland, Priv. Coll.). From 1930 until the end of World War II, Moilliet also created stained-glass windows (Lucerne, Lukaskirche, 1934–36).

MOMPER, Josse de *or* Jodocus de (1564, Antwerp—1635, Antwerp), Flemish landscape painter. His works are largely undated and unsigned, thus making a study of his style difficult. Basing his landscapes on those of Pieter Bruegel and the Van Valkenborchs, Momper first produced a number of charming and rather neatly constructed views, as in the undated painting of the *Flight into Egypt* (Oxford, Ashmolean Museum). Gradually his landscapes evolved into artificial Mannerist arrangements of nature, with wild mountain scenery grouped around light-filled valleys, as in the drawing *Landscape with the Fall of Icarus* (1610; Paris, Louvre). Momper also had a taste for the fantastic heritage of Bosch, giving a monstrous and somewhat humorous anthropomorphic character to four strange landscapes of the *Seasons* (Paris, Coll. Lebel).

FRANS (1603, Antwerp—1660, Antwerp), probably his son and pupil. He was in Holland around 1645–50, working at The Hague, Haarlem, and Amsterdam. Frans specialized in landscapes that display the Flemish influence of Jan Bruegel (*Peasants Dancing*; Brussels, Musées Royaux des Beaux-Arts) and the Dutch influence of Jan van Goyen.

MONDRIAN, Pieter Cornelis Mondriaan, *called* Piet (1872, Amersfoort, near Utrecht—1944, New York), Dutch painter and pioneer in the field of abstract art. He was awarded two diplomas (1889; 1892) enabling him to teach drawing in state schools and, in 1892, he enrolled in the Amsterdam Academy of Fine Arts, where he was highly regarded by his masters. The next period in Mondrian's life was a difficult one; he painted a great deal, sold little, and earned a living by making scientific drawings and copies of pictures in museums. A sojourn with the Catholic peasants of Dutch Brabant in 1903 opened new horizons for him. For the most part, he worked in the country around Amsterdam and returned again and again to the same subjects: a farm at Duivendrecht, which he painted in 1905–7, and the banks of the Gein, a stream near Amsterdam (1907–8). Mondrian's first visit to the seaside resort of Domburg on the island of Walcheren in Zeeland, in the summer of 1908, caused him to change his style radically. There he met the Dutch painter Johannes Toorop, whose divisionist method influenced him for a time. On the advice of friends, he went to Paris in late December of 1911. He was immediately influenced by Cubism and worked on a series of *Trees* that are unique in 20th-century painting. The series as a whole reveals a progression from naturalism (*Red Tree*, 1910; The Hague, Municipal Museum) to abstraction (*Apple Tree in Blossom*, 1911; Municipal Museum). In other paintings, such as his series of *Scaffoldings* (1912–14), he attempted to get to the very heart of Cubism and, in so doing, he explored every aspect of the Cubistic experience. Mondrian finally discovered a new realm of painting, in which all elements are transformed into a rhythmic orchestration of lines and colors, unrelated to any association with objective reality. Little by little Mondrian reduced these lines to horizontal and vertical strokes and limited his palette to the three primary colors—red, yellow, and blue—heightened by black and white and, occasionally, by gray.

Mondrian returned to Holland in July 1914, a short while before the outbreak of World War I, and was obliged to remain there for the duration of the war. In Holland he continued his experiments in abstraction (subjects of the *Sea* and *Church Façades*), which in 1915 led to the same pure rhythm of horizontal and vertical lines; these works were an immediate prelude to what Mondrian himself later termed Neoplasticism or Pure Plasticism. In 1915 Mondrian also met the Dutch artist and poet Theo van Doesburg, who later propagated his ideas and helped him to found the magazine *De Stijl*, the first number of which appeared in October 1917. During this period of his life Mondrian published long theoretical articles in *De Stijl*, one of which—*Natuurlijke en abstracte realiteit* ("Natural Reality and Abstract Reality," 1919–20), written in the form of a dialogue—is a pioneer work in the history of abstract art.

Mondrian returned to Paris in February of 1919 and continued his explorations into the theme of the Neoplastic horizontal-vertical. His favorite color was red, and several works of this middle period consisted of a red rectangle occupying two thirds of the painted surface (*Red, Blue, and Yellow Composition*, 1930; New York, Coll. Armand P. Bartos). It was during this period that his ideas influenced Fernand Léger and Willi Baumeister and that he found his first disciples among the younger generation of artists. In 1925 the Bauhaus published his book *Die Neue Gestaltung* ("The New Form"), which was a German translation of a booklet by Mondrian that had been published in 1920 by the Parisian Galerie de l'Effort Moderne under the title of *Le Néo-Plasticisme* ("Neoplasticism"). In 1930 he joined the Cercle et Carré group and in the following year became a member of its successor, the Abstraction-Création group.

Piet Mondrian. *Tree. c.* 1911. Munson-Williams-Proctor Institute, Utica. *Photo Janis Gallery, New York.*

The significance of Mondrian's art rests primarily on his search for plastic purity through the reduction of his artistic means to the simple expression of a relationship, the essence of which lies in two straight lines meeting at right angles. According to Mondrian, the curve, spatial illusion, every accident of the brush, and every process that recalled the techniques of Impressionism had to be rejected. He felt that a canvas—a plane surface—should be filled with a painting that was also strictly plane. Such a painting would become the medium for an idea that was linked neither to time nor space but that controlled both: that idea is relationship. Nevertheless, he always wanted pictorial relationships to be ex-

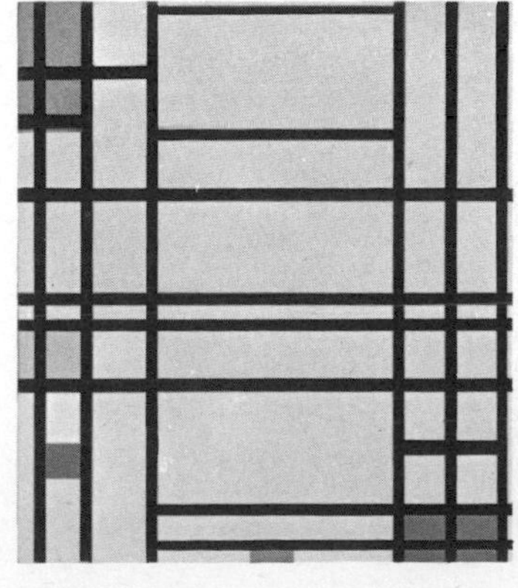

Piet Mondrian. *Composition.* 1939–42. Solomon R. Guggenheim Museum, New York.

Claude Monet. *Women in a Garden.* 1866–67. Musée de l'Impressionnisme, Paris.

pressed dynamically, that is, by an asymmetric equilibrium.

In September 1938, anticipating the outbreak of World War II, Mondrian went to London. In September 1940 he left for the United States, settling in New York, where he finished paintings that he had begun in Paris and London two or three years before, introducing in them an unexpected element, colored squares and lines. The last two years of Mondrian's life brought him more satisfaction than 50 years of incessant toil. A degree of material ease was translated in his works as a greater spiritual ease. Black disappeared, and he painted works such as *New York City* (1942; New York, Coll. Harry Holtzmann), which consists of yellow, red, and blue lines only. In *Broadway Boogie-Woogie* (1942–43; New York, Museum of Modern Art) the lines tend to break up into little rectangles as though under the pressure of a joyful pizzicato. Finally, the unfinished *Victory Boogie-Woogie* (1943–44; Meriden, Conn., Coll. Burton G. Tremaine) is a joyful symphony in which measure and freedom, reserve and exaltation harmonize in a perfect unity; this late work is still ruled, however, by the Neoplastic principle of the horizontal-vertical.

Mondrian's painting occupies an extremely important position in 20th-century art, not only because of his slow progression from naturalism to the most naked abstraction, but even more because of the quality of that progression.

Claude Monet. *Gare St-Lazare.* 1877. Musée de l'Impressionnisme, Paris.

MONET, Claude (1840, Paris—1926, Giverny, Eure), French painter. Around 1858 he met the painter Eugène Boudin, who was impressed by the young man's precocious talent for drawing and encouraged him to paint in the open air. In May of 1859 Monet's father permitted him to go to Paris, where he and Camille Pissarro attended the Académie Suisse. Monet returned to Le Havre in 1862, and began painting landscapes "on the spot" with Eugène Boudin and Johan Barthold Jongkind. Once more in Paris in 1863, he attended the studio of Charles Gleyre, where he met Frédéric Bazille, Renoir, and Sisley. The first painting he sent to the Salon, in 1865, was accepted and won some success. The financial situation of the artist, however, could hardly have been worse: his entire output, 200 canvases in all, was seized by a bailiff and sold for a negligible sum. In desperation he tried to commit suicide, and only Bazille's friendship helped him to overcome his difficulties.

The painting Monet sent to the Salon of 1869 was refused. The same year he went with Renoir to Bougival, where both artists painted the baths of *La Grenouillère* (New York, Metropolitan Museum). When the Franco-Prussian War broke out, Monet left for Trouville, then for London, where he joined Sisley, Pissarro, and Charles-François Daubigny, who introduced him to the art dealer Durand-Ruel. In London the discovery of the art of John Constable and especially of J. M. W. Turner in the museums contributed toward the revelation of a new aspect of light for Monet. It was during his decisive stay in London, in fact, that he painted in smoky, diaphanous tones *Westminster Bridge* (1871; London, Coll. Lord Astor) and *Impression, Sunrise* (1872; Paris, Musée Marmottan), his first two Impressionist paintings. When he moved to Argenteuil (1872–76), where he worked in a studio-boat, Monet's emotional fervor, combined with an almost physical passion for light, led him to transpose the sensations he experienced at viewing all that is most fugitive and fluid in nature. And so a new aesthetic was born, which, under the name of Impressionism, endeavored to seize for all eternity the passing moment and the nostalgia of memory.

At Argenteuil (1873–74), where Renoir and Édouard Manet joined him, Monet painted the bridge over the Seine, the regattas, and the river banks. The principles of the Impressionist movement of which he was already the leader were firmly established. But it is a mistake to think that Monet had deliberately applied a theory and founded his art on a scientific system or a methodical analysis of light phenomena in particular, for not even the slightest intellectual consideration had ever entered his mind. When he painted in an Impressionist manner, he was following his instincts and fulfilling a need that sprang from a fundamentally realistic outlook. In 1874 he sent several paintings, including the famous *Impression, Sunrise*, to the first Impressionist group exhibition at the Parisian studio of the photographer Nadar. A one-man show of Monet's works organized in 1880 by the publisher Charpentier was a fiasco. Weary and disgusted, he refused to join the fifth Impressionist exhibition, and soon drifted away from his friends; this signaled the general disbanding of the group.

Monet went to Fécamp to paint a few seascapes, then in October of 1881 retired to Poissy. He spent the next summer by the English Channel in Normandy, where he often returned to paint: *Fishermen's Nets at Pourville* (1882; The Hague, Gemeentemuseum), *Cliffs at Étretat* (1883; Paris, Musée de l'Impressionnisme). Later he went to the Côte d'Azur with Renoir, then traveled alone to Holland, Brittany, Creuse (1889), London (1891), Norway (1895), Madrid (1904), and Venice (1908). From his various travels he brought back studies of the same subjects painted as the light varied at different times of the day, at different seasons, and in varying atmospheric conditions: the series of *Haystacks* (1890–91), *Poplars* (1891–92), *Rouen Cathedral* (1892–94), the *Banks of the Thames* (1899–1904), and the *Views of Venice* (1908). When fortune smiled on him at last, he bought a house at Giverny whose garden and pond were to become

Claude Monet. *The Studio-Boat. c.* 1874. Rijksmuseum Kröller-Müller, Otterlo.

the inexhaustible source for his masterpieces, the fabulous series of *Water Lilies*, begun in 1899. On the day after his death, a part of the series was placed in the oval room of the Musée de l'Orangerie, Paris, where they were arranged according to the artist's own instructions. Others are in the Tate Gallery in London and the Museum of Modern Art and the Metropolitan Museum, both in New York. Of all Monet's work—indeed, of all the paintings produced in the Impressionist style—the *Water Lilies*, with their exquisite flowers, the shimmering light on their dreamlike pools, the gold and purple glowing in the reflected shade of the trees, will stand as one of the greatest examples of the identification of man with the universe.

MONNOYER, Jean-Baptiste (1634, Lille—1699, London), French painter. Monnoyer was trained at Antwerp and specialized in flower painting. He went to Paris in 1655 and contributed to all the large decorative schemes then in progress: Hôtel Lambert, Hôtel Lauzun, châteaux at Vaux, Vincennes, St-Cloud, Versailles, the Grand Trianon, and Marly. Monnoyer contributed many designs for Gobelins tapestries as well. About 1685 he went to England, where he worked at Montague House and the royal palaces of Windsor, Kensington, and Hampton Court. His still lifes are of the type originated by Jan Davidsz. de Heem: sideboards richly laden with flowers, fruit, rugs, porcelain, etc. *Trompe-l'oeil* and vague literary references were common features of his work (*Flowers, Fruit, and Objets d'Art*, 1665; Montpellier, Musée Fabre).

Monnoyer had two sons, ANTOINE (1670–1747) and BAPTISTE (d. 1714), who followed their father's profession.

MONSÙ DESIDERIO (active 1st half of 17th century, Naples), French painter. For many years two French painters, who came from Metz and who worked together in Naples around 1620, were confused under the single name of Monsù Desiderio. They can now be clearly distinguished as Didier Barra (or Barrat) and François de Nome (or Nomé). Barra, who arrived in Naples around 1608, painted small, clumsy panoramas and vistas (*Panorama of Naples*, 1647; Naples, Museo Nazionale di San Martino); François de Nome, on the other hand, painted works whose mysterious and sometimes disquieting character intrigued the Surrealists in the 1920s and subsequently earned him great popularity. He was apprenticed, while in Rome, to the Flemish painter Balthasar Lauwers (1578–1645) and married Loise Croy, the daughter of another Flemish artist, Jan de Croy (b. 1583). These connections with North European artistic circles probably explain the frequent appearance in his works of dreamlike Gothic buildings (*Church Interior*; Budapest, Hungarian National Gallery). He was also strongly influenced by the many Florentine scenographic engravings that circulated in Naples in the early 17th century. François de Nome was not an isolated or decadent painter, as has often been supposed, but was actually the most brilliant and most imaginative member of a whole group of anonymous Neapolitan artists who painted in a belated Mannerist style and whose works are often mistakenly attributed to him. Only François de Nome, however, had the ability to create livid, unnaturally slender statues in dark, improbable cities that have been burned or destroyed (*Conflagration of Troy,* Rome, Galleria d'Arte L'Obelisco; *Destruction of the Temple*, Cambridge, Fitzwilliam Museum; *Legend of St. Augustine*, 1623, London, National Gallery).

MONTAGNA, Bartolomeo (*c.* 1450, Orzinuovi, near Brescia—1523, Vicenza), Italian painter. In 1482 he was commissioned to paint two Biblical compositions for Venice's Scuola di S. Marco; in 1483 he painted the altarpiece for the Venice Hospital; and in 1487 painted a *St. Sebastian and St. Roch* (Bergamo, Accademia Carrara). His productive period came at the turn of the century, with the *Madonna Enthroned between Four Saints* (1499; Milan, Brera); the *Pietà* (1500) for the basilica of Monte Berico, near Vicenza; and the *Nativity* for the church at Orgiano, which was completed in 1502. In this sequence of monumental works we see the Paduan heritage demonstrated in the firm placement of figures on the ground, the broken draperies, the rusty colors, and leaden tones. Montagna was first and foremost a master of modeling. His compositions are dominated by flagstone pavings and elaborate architectural backgrounds with solid rock foundations, which give them a powerful balance. His son Benedetto (*c.* 1481–1558) painted religious subjects, and was also an engraver.

MONTAÑÉS, Juan Martínez. *See* **MARTINEZ MONTAÑÉS,** Juan.

MONTICELLI, Adolphe (1824, Marseilles—1886, Marseilles), French Romantic painter. In addition to his marvelous landscapes, which anticipated those of the Impressionists, he painted portraits, nudes, still lifes, and erotic scenes that had affinities with the Fauves' color values, Pierre Bonnard's sparkling touch, and Chaim Soutine's swirling paint. In fact, Monticelli's style, which appears to be quite casual, is actually so skillfully controlled that it hides great technical mastery. He transformed forest paths, boats in creeks, fruits on a table, or wild flowers in a vase, into phantasmagorias that appear to give forth gleams, explosions, and steam from smoldering oxides and laval flows. Although Monticelli never troubled to trace a line, a contour, or an intersection of planes on the canvas, he did not neglect his draftsmanship; he created outlines

Adolphe Monticelli. *L'Arlésienne.* 1870–71. Private Coll., Paris. *Photo Bulloz, Paris.*

through his use of color, and his volumes took shape in the effervescent paint. The most characteristic examples of his very personal technique are his portraits, such as that of *Madame René* (1871; Lyons, Musée des Beaux-Arts) and the *Arlesian* (1870–1; Paris, Priv. Coll.), which is one of the finest produced by the French School. Finally, 30 years before the advent of Fauvism, he painted the brilliant *Calanque de Maldormé* (*c.* 1874; Lyons, Musée des Beaux-Arts). Monticelli was held in great esteem by both Eugène Delacroix and Cézanne; Van Gogh even went so far as to write, "I owe everything to Monticelli, who taught me the chromatics of color."

MONTORSOLI, Fra Giovanni Angelo (*c.* 1507, Montorsoli, near Florence—1563, Florence), Italian sculptor and architect. In the 1520s he worked in Florence on the Laurentian Library and the New Sacristy of S. Lorenzo as assistant to Michelangelo. In 1531 Montorsoli entered the Servite order, which commissioned votive portraits of the Medici from him for the church of the SS. Annunziata, Florence. Other works done for the Servites in the decade of the 1530s included a kneeling figure of *Alessandro de' Medici* and statues of *Moses* and *St. Paul*, all for the Annunziata. After 1536 Montorsoli was in Naples, where he collaborated with Bartolommeo Ammannati on the Sannuzaro monument in S. Maria del Parto. In 1539 Montorsoli arrived in Genoa, and in 1543 he began a *Pietà* for the church of S. Matteo, as well as the tomb of Andrea Doria in the crypt. The sculptor left Genoa in 1547 to become master of the works at Messina Cathedral in Sicily. Here he created two of the most beautiful fountains in Italy: the Orion Fountain (1547–50), which stands in the cathedral piazza; and the Neptune Fountain (1551–57), located in the port. After providing the high altar for S. Maria dei Servi (1558–61) in Bologna, Montorsoli returned to his convent in Florence, where he spent the last years of his life.

Montreal School. James E. H. MacDonald. *On the Edge of Winter.* 1928. Musée des Beaux-Arts, Montreal.

MONTREAL SCHOOL. Around 1940, parallel to the emergence of the New York School, an independent movement in Canadian painting developed in Montreal, the cultural center of French Canada. In Montreal there was no question of a wholesale rejection of the European cultural heritage. However, at a time when the postwar generation in Europe was trying to free itself from the influence of the great pioneers of modern art—such as Paul Klee, Wassily Kandinsky, and Pablo Picasso—the Montreal painters were still striving to gain acceptance for the spirit of these masters. This explains the special character of the painting of young artists struggling for recognition in Quebec between 1940 and 1950, and it is mainly in connection with the general drive for emancipation during that decade that it is justifiable to speak of a Montreal school. Yet this so-called school had neither unity of tone nor style and consisted in a variety of tendencies reflecting the general currents of world art. The nature of the school became manifest after the 1950s as a specifically Canadian style spread across the whole country.

The initial phase of the Canadian school lasted from 1910 to 1920 and covered the work of a group of landscapists from Toronto who painted the topography of their own country. Tom Thomson (1877–1917), James E. H. MacDonald (1873–1932), Lawren S. Harris (1885–1970), Arthur Lismer (1885–1969), Frederick Varley (1881–1969), Alexander Young Jackson (1882–1974), and then Franklin Carmichael (1890–1949) and Franz Johnston (1888–1949) freed landscape painting from its superannuated conventions. Their approach was more direct than that of their predecessors, and their bright, sometimes startling coloring was similar to that of the Fauves. After Thomson's death, the latter artists formed an association named the Group of Seven (*q.v.*), which held its first exhibition in 1920 and which dominated the artistic life of Canada. In the 1930s they attracted a number of followers and in 1933 the original group was

Montreal School. Jean Dallaire. *Woman with a Hat.* 1957. *Photo "Société des Arts," Montreal.*

replaced by the Canadian Group of Painters.

At the beginning of World War II two artists, Alfred Pellan and Paul-Émile Borduas, brought the first breath of life to the Montreal School by injecting a radical note into the entrenched academicism of Canadian artistic circles. In 1940 Pellan returned to Montreal after a long stay in Paris. He was thoroughly familiar with Cubist and Surrealist experiments and, with a group of young disciples, he published (1948) a manifesto called the *Prism of the Eye*, which announced a "movement of diverse movements, diversified by life itself," a phrase that could describe the entire Montreal School. This manifesto coincided with an exhibition in which Pellan showed his *Apple Woman* (1943; Toronto, Art Gallery). In this work Pellan advocated a version of Surrealism that was savage, airy, spatial, decidedly "New World."

After the 1940s each member of the Montreal School went his own way. The work of Jacques de Tonnancour (b. 1917) was carefully introspective and discreetly eloquent. Albert Dumouchel (b. 1916) evolved a style similar to that of the Cobra group. In the 1960s he was attracted to New Realism, as shown by such works as *A Moment in Anne's Life* (1966). From a grave, restrained Surrealism, Léon Bellefleur (b. 1910) evolved a fantastic imagery with splashed shapes suggesting a universe in continual expansion (*Reminiscence*, 1962). Roland Giguère (b. 1929) also painted in the Surrealist vein, as did Jean Dallaire (1916–65), who was a master of Magic Realism in the tradition of Paul Klee (*Solar Calculation*, 1957; Ottawa, National Gallery of Canada).

A few months after the appearance of *Prism of the Eye*, a second manifesto, *Global Refusal* (August 1948), was published in Montreal; it was written by Borduas, who was an intransigent theorist and, after 1940, the guiding spirit of the so-called Automatist movement. He represented the other pole of the young school of painting; his work developed with strict painterly logic from figurative painting to Abstract Expressionism (*Sous le Vent de l'Île*, *c.* 1948; National Gallery of Canada) and finally ended in a sort of increasingly bare Tachism (*3+4+1*, 1956; National Gallery of Canada). Automatist painters were Jean-Paul Mousseau (b. 1927), Marcelle Ferron (b. 1924), Fernand Leduc (b. 1916), and Marcel Barbeau (b. 1925), all of whom explored the full potentialities of action painting. The last two evolved a more studied abstraction that brought them nearer to the new Plasticians group, which was formed around 1955.

Before discussing the work of the 1960s, two older painters should be mentioned: Marc-Aurèle Fortin (b. 1888), who pursued his lifelong passion for landscape after 1920, and Jean-Paul Lemieux (b. 1904), a Canadian Balthus whose impressive figures stand out against snowy spaces (*Evening Visitor*, 1956; National Gallery of Canada).

In 1955 the Plasticians developed a simplified idiom based on geometric abstraction and, limiting themselves to two or three colors, produced paintings that were unconfined by the traditional pictorial rectangle. Guido Molinari (b. 1933), who was the main Canadian exponent of hard-edge realism, and Claude Tousignant (b. 1932), Louis Belzile (b. 1929), and Henri Saxe (b. 1937) represented the various tendencies of Plasticism. Jean McEwen (b. 1923), who began as a Tachist, ultimately created carefully arranged colored planes. Jacques Hurtubise (b. 1939) crowded signs into a dense network and controlled his Tachist inventions with a firm rhythm. Yves Gaucher (b. 1933) juxtaposed clashing colors and traced fields of energy with bright tones (*Blue Modulations*, 1965).

It is difficult to speak of a Montreal School in respect to the art of the 1960s. During the 1950s English-speaking Canada had been converted to modern art. The shadow of the Group of Seven faded away in Toronto. Under the leadership of James Williamson Galloway (Jock) Macdonald (1897–1960), Harold Town (b. 1924), Ronald William (b. 1926), Jack Bush (b. 1909), and Kazuo Nakamura (b. 1926) experimented in every kind of abstraction. In Vancouver, British Columbia, Bertram C. Binning (b. 1909) worked in the same vein as Ben Nicholson, while Jack Shadbold (b. 1909) progressed from Surrealism to hard-edge realism. Alex Colville (b. 1920) worked in a monumental, Neorealistic idiom that owed nothing to the past (*To Prince Edward Island*, 1965; National Gallery of Canada).

Montreal artists contributed to the development of sculpture as well. A spirit of free improvisation spread rapidly after around 1955, although the sculptors were more restrained than the painters and do not seem to have been so much at ease with the current of modern art. Louis Archambault (b. 1915), for instance, worked bronze, iron, and terra cotta in an angular style sometimes marked with Surrealism (*Iron Bird*, *c.* 1950; National Gallery of Canada). Armand Vaillancourt (b. 1932) revealed a sensitive feeling for forms in his curtains of hanging stones, which are sometimes reminiscent of Étienne-Martin's work. Robert Roussil's (b. 1925) sculpture is imbued with the powerful spirit characteristic of Riopelle's work, while Françoise Sullivan assembled airy forms with straw. Anne Kahane's (b. 1924) wood sculpture is notable for its sensitivity, while Audrey Taylor built strange structures with imaginary utensils and ironical little Martians.

MOOR VAN DASHORST, Anthonis. *See* **MORO,** Antonio.

MOORE, Henry (b. 1898, Castleford, Yorkshire), major British sculptor of the 20th century. The son of a miner, Moore was about to become a teacher when he was called for military service in 1917. After his demobilization in 1919, he was enabled by an ex-serviceman's grant to study at the Leeds School of Art for two years. In 1921 he won a scholarship that permitted him to attend the Royal College of Art in London, where he was appointed sculpture instructor in 1925 and where he remained until 1932, when he transferred to the Chelsea School of Art, also in London. In 1926 he visited Paris, Rome, Florence, and Ravenna. Moore had his first one-man show at the Warren Gallery in London in 1928. He gave up teaching in 1939 and thereafter lived primarily in the country outside London. During World War II he served as an official British war artist, and his *Shelter Drawings* of 1940 are among his most popular and frequently reproduced works. Moore gained recognition as a central influence in modern art at the 1948 Venice Biennale, where he was awarded the international prize for sculpture.

Few of Moore's early naturalistic sculptures survive, but his productions of the 1920s, done when he was still a student at the Royal College of Art, show that from the very beginning of his career he assimilated three main influences: Egyptian art, African Negro masks and statuettes, and pre-Columbian Mexican sculpture. This third influence bore fruit directly in the *Reclining Figures* based on Yucatán rain deities that he began sculpting in 1929 (*Reclining Figure*, 1929; Leeds, Yorkshire, City Art Gallery) and that he continued to produce throughout his career (*Reclining Figure*, 1957–58, Paris, forecourt of UNESCO headquarters; *Reclining Figure, Lincoln Center Sculpture*, 1963–65, New York, Lincoln Center for the Performing Arts). Moore was also influenced by such modern artists as the Rumanian-born sculptor Constantin Brancusi, the Russian-born sculptor Alexander Archipenko, and Pablo Picasso, as well as by various aspects of Surrealism and Constructivism. By the early 1930s, he stopped using Cubistic block forms and began producing the characteristic undulating swelling shapes that express his belief in a close relationship between man and nature, or what

Henry Moore. *Reclining figure.* 1957–58. UNESCO Building, Paris.

Henry Moore. *Family Group.* 1945–49. Museum of Modern Art, New York.

he called "the organic . . . rather than the geometric." During an abstract period (1933–39), he adopted the practice of piercing his wooden or metal figures with holes, which he sometimes threaded with string or wire. At this time Moore also began, with growing assurance, to search for an equilibrium between the shaped material and the created void. He then returned to a figurative, seminaturalistic sculptural style that he never abandoned. Some of the best-known examples of his work dealing with his most characteristic themes are the *Madonna and Child* (1943–44; Nottingham, St. Matthew's Church), the bronze *Family Group* (1945–49; New York, Museum of Modern Art), the hieratic and mysterious *King and Queen* (1952–53; London, Tate Gallery), and *Standing Figure* (1950; Amsterdam, Coll. Dr. van der Wal). Moore worked in wood, stone (the material with which he was most familiar), and, after about 1950, mostly in bronze. After 1955 he produced a series of *Seated Figures* in which the subject is placed in an architectural setting (*Seated Figure against Curved Wall*, 1956–57; Boston, Museum of Fine Arts). He also did sculptures of animals (*Animal Head*, 1956, Otterlo, Rijksmuseum Kröller-Müller; *Animal Form*, 1959, London, Zoological Society). By the 1960s, his style was still in a state of evolution and he produced two- and three-piece reclining figures that are reminiscent of caves and cliffs (*Two-Piece Reclining Figure No. 1*, 1959, Buffalo, New York, Albright-Knox Art Gallery; *Three-Piece Reclining Figure No. 1*, 1961–62, Montreal, National Bank of Canada), and figures that suggest bones, shells, and knife-edges. Moore has also done numerous drawings.

MOR, Antonis. *See* **MORO,** Antonio.

MORA, family of Spanish sculptors originally from Majorca, who were active in Andalusia in the 17th and early 18th centuries. They produced some of the most convincing examples of Spanish polychrome wood sculpture.

BERNARDO DE (1616, Porreras—1684, Granada), who settled in Granada and married a niece of Alonso de Mena, was, along with Pedro de Mena, a pupil of Alonso Cano. His best-known works, of modest accomplishment, are in Granada: a *St. John of God* in the church dedicated to the saint; a *St. Michael* in the hermitage of S. Miguel el Alto; and an *Ecce Homo* forming part of a reliquary in the Capilla Real, Granada Cathedral.

JOSÉ DE (1642, Baza—1724, Granada), the eldest son of Bernardo, was the most important sculptor in the family. He was influenced at first by his father and by his teacher, Alonso Cano. After moving to Granada in 1650, he went to Madrid three times—first in 1666—where he carved several works, notably a very fine *Purísima* for the cathedral of S. Isidro (since destroyed), and where he was appointed royal sculptor to Charles II. In 1680 he returned permanently to Granada. He was extremely proud and jealous of his art and provided the polychromy for his statues himself, unlike most other Spanish wood carvers. Obsessed by the spiritual life, Mora treated subjects relating to the Passion with a convincing sincerity. The *Virgin of Sorrows* in the monastery of Las Maravillas at Madrid, the *Christ of Mercy* in Granada's church of S. José, and the *St. Bruno* (*c.* 1707) in the Cartuja, or charterhouse, in Granada are among the most impressive examples of his fervent art.

DIEGO DE (1658, Granada—1729, Granada), the younger brother of José, worked independently in his own workshop. His sculpture marks the transition between the tradition derived from Alonso Cano and the 18th-century Baroque style.

MORAN, Thomas (1837, Bolton, Lancashire—1926, Santa Barbara, California), English-born American landscapist, etcher, lithographer, and engraver. He went to America at the age of seventeen and received his first artistic instruction there; he later (1862) returned to England, where the mature works of J. M. W. Turner had a particularly strong influence on him. Jean-Baptiste Camille Corot, Dutch Baroque landscapes, and the paintings of the Hudson River School also affected Moran's later style. When he returned from study in London he began to paint grandiloquent landscapes of Yellowstone National Park, the Grand Canyon, and Yosemite Valley, all of which places he visited on government expeditions. His chief merit was his skill as a colorist, and he is especially known for his Colorado scenes (*Chasm of the Colorado*; Washington, D.C., Capitol), with their steep gorges and cliffs, fiery sunsets, and raging waterfalls. The execution of such paintings as *Western Landscape* (1864; New Britain, Conn., Art Museum of the New Britain Institute) is done with quick strokes of thin pigment, focusing attention on the lively illumination rather than on the modeling of the forms.

MORANDI, Giorgio (1890, Bologna—1964, Bologna), Italian painter and engraver. Morandi, who was an independent and solitary man, was one of the few modern Italian artists who never went to Paris. In 1918–19 he brought Italian Metaphysical painting to its final stage of development, and he did so far from Ferrara, where Giorgio de Chirico and Carlo Carrà had just painted their best-known masterpieces. Although Morandi painted a few beautiful landscapes, only a very few figure studies by him are known, among which is one self-portrait. Morandi created his artistic world with the techniques of still-life painting. A few familiar objects sufficed him: cups, salad bowls, and long-necked bottles that he imprisoned within extremely chaste lines to produce a strange and rarefied atmosphere. He gradually softened the hardness of his contours, and eventually succeeded in finding his own idiom in a delicate compromise between form and color (*Still Life*, 1929; Milan, Coll. Dr. Emilio

Jesi). He could create an atmosphere with three tones and gradually toned down his modulations as if he wanted to reduce painting to the semitones of etching.

MOREAU, family of French artists active in the 18th century.

LOUIS-GABRIEL, *called* THE ELDER (1740, Paris—1806, Paris), engraver and landscapist. His gouaches record walks in the districts of Monceau, Bagatelle, and Beaujon. Moreau apparently was little appreciated in his lifetime because his subject matter and naturalistic style were so different from the academic manner of Nicolas Poussin and Claude Lorrain. In the 20th century, however, he is clearly seen as a precursor of the Barbizon School landscapists, and his work anticipates Jean-Baptiste Camille Corot's fresh vision. Of his rare paintings, the Louvre in Paris possesses one of the finest: *View of the Meudon Hills from the Parc de St-Cloud* (*c.* 1785).

JEAN MICHEL, *called* THE YOUNGER (1741, Paris—1814, Paris), his brother, draftsman and engraver. His student work is known to us through the notebook that he used daily from 1763 (Louvre), which includes nearly 60 pages of sketches, in which he uses a sharp, clear line for body contours, while retaining a Rococo freedom in the representation of drapery. He was appointed draftsman to the Cabinet du Roi and, as the historiographer of his period, there is not a ceremony unrecorded in his graphic oeuvre.

Moreau succeeded Charles Nicolas Cochin as draftsman of the *Menus Plaisirs* ("royal entertainments") in 1790. His reputation today, however, is primarily due to his work as an illustrator, notably for the *Works* of Jean-Jacques Rousseau (1774–83) and for two editions of *Monument du Costume* ("History of Costume"; 1777 and 1783). These fashion plates are masterful records of contemporary manners: *Meeting in the Woods*; *La Grande Toilette*; *It's a Son, Monsieur!* Moreau's heyday came to an end with the régime itself in 1789, and his *Opening of the États Généraux* is one of the last of his 2,400 engravings.

MOREAU, Gustave (1826, Paris—1898, Paris), French painter and draftsman. His real master was the Romantic painter Théodore Chassériau, whom he met in 1848 and with whom he worked for several years. During a visit to Italy (1857–59), he especially admired the paintings of Benozzo Gozzoli, Michelangelo, and Vittore Carpaccio. When he returned to France, Moreau exhibited *Oedipus and the Sphinx* (1864; New York, Metropolitan Museum) in the 1864 Salon. It attracted a great deal of attention, and he was immediately admitted to the Parisian literary circles. Moreau experienced his greatest success in the Salon of 1876 with his famous watercolor, the *Apparition* (1876; Paris, Louvre), which is a brilliant illustration of the Salome legend, a theme to which he returned many times. He subsequently produced the *Unicorns*, the *Return of the Argonauts* (1897), and *Jupiter and Semele* (1896), the only large painting he ever finished. These canvases, as well as most of Moreau's works, are now in his house in Paris, which he left to the nation and which is now the Musée National Gustave Moreau.

Moreau's paintings are the creations of a solitary man, who was immersed in himself and who, for the most part, lived in a world of dreams and fantasies that were to capture the attention of the Surrealists in the 20th century. His work, however, is not condemned to oblivion: his illustrations (1881–85) for La Fontaine's *Fables* are excellent, and even more admirable are the innumerable watercolors and oil sketches that he painted with a freedom and directness completely lacking in his large compositions (*Dead Lyres*, *c.* 1897, and study for the *Chimeras*, 1884; both Musée Gustave Moreau). It is also significant that Fauvism was born in his studio at the École des Beaux-Arts, where he taught from 1892 to 1898 and where some of the greatest painters of the day (Georges Rouault, Henri Matisse, Albert Marquet, Charles Camoin, and Henri Manguin) were trained.

MORETTO DA BRESCIA, Alessandro Bonvicino, *called* (*c.* 1498, Brescia—1554, Brescia), Italian painter. He was, with Giovanni Savoldo and Girolamo Romanino, the leading Brescian painter of the 16th century. He owed much to the Venetian tradition, but at the same time remained faithful to the Lombard heritage of Vincenzo Foppa. Moretto's large altarpieces are generally planned on the same

Giorgio Morandi. *Landscape.* 1937.

Classical composition of two levels, one occupied by the Virgin and Child, the other by a group of three or four saints, with all the figures standing against a blue sky. The types that recur in his oeuvre are austere and realistically treated old men, as well as saints with placid, heavy profiles (*St. Justina*, *c.* 1530–35, Vienna, Kunsthistorisches Museum; *Madonna with St. Elizabeth and Two Donors*, 1541, Berlin, Staatliche Museen). The firmness of the faces is a reminder that Moretto was a remarkable portraitist, who could play skillfully with the floral design of a fabric, its colors, and its textures (*Portrait of a Gentleman*, 1526; London, National Gallery). The quiet strength of his outlines and the peaceful spirituality of his art represent a sort of serene counterpart to the vibrant visual experiments of contemporary Venetian painters. Moretto's portrait style was continued by his pupil, Giovanni Battista Moroni.

MORISOT, Berthe (1841, Bourges—1895, Paris), French Impressionist painter. A great-granddaughter of the French 18th-century painter Jean Honoré Fragonard, she came from a cultured but conventional middle-

Gustave Moreau. *Hydra. c.* 1870. Musée Gustave Moreau, Paris.

Berthe Morisot. *Madame Pontillon Seated on the Grass.* 1873. Cleveland Museum of Art.

class family, and began to study painting when she was fifteen. From 1862 to 1868 she worked with Jean-Baptiste Camille Corot, whose strong influence is recognizable in her delicate and charming landscapes (*Port of Lorient*, 1869; New York, Coll. Mrs. Mellon Bruce). In 1868 she met the painter Édouard Manet (she married his brother Eugène in 1874), who replaced Corot as the major influence on her painting. After joining the Impressionist group, she contributed (*The Cradle*, 1873; Paris, Musée de l'Impressionnisme) to their first exhibition, in 1874, at the studio of the photographer Nadar. She subsequently exhibited at all their shows except that of 1877. Berthe Morisot and Manet exerted reciprocal influences on each other: she did much to convert Manet to plein-air painting, while his influence is especially noticeable in her work of 1875–76 (*Women with a Mirror*, 1875; New York, Coll. Alex M. Lewyt). She concentrated on portraits and interior scenes, which Manet had been the first to paint but to which she added an intimate flavor redolent with her own peculiar sensitivity (*Young Woman Behind a Blind*, 1878; France, Priv. Coll.).

During this mature period, Berthe Morisot's technique was based on large, freely distributed touches of color applied unsystematically and in every direction. Her best works are bathed in a shifting, iridescent light and their range of tones reaches an exceptionally subtle harmony (*The Verandah*, 1882; *Eugène Manet and His Daughter in the Garden*, 1883, Paris, Priv. Coll.). Her watercolors, a genre in which she excelled, have the same airy lightness and spontaneity (*Lady and Child on a Terrace at Meudon*, 1884; Chicago, Art Institute). About 1889, however, she began a new phase that brought her nearer to Renoir's style and that produced, in her last works, a new modeling of considerable suppleness (*Young Girl with a Fan*, 1893, London, Coll. Mr. and Mrs. L. Slotover; *Two Sisters, the Children of Gabriel Thomas*, 1894, Paris, Louvre).

Antonio Moro. *Portrait of a Knight of the Calatrava Order.* Rijksmuseum, Amsterdam.

MORLAITER, Gian Maria (1699/1700, Niederdorf, Tirol—1781, Venice), Italian sculptor. He may well be considered the most important sculptor of the Venetian 18th century, and is at his best in reliefs that translate into marble pictorial effects similar to those used by Giambattista Tiepolo. The two reliefs he contributed to the screen in the Cappella del Rosario in the church of SS. Giovanni e Paolo, Venice, illustrate this essentially pictorial quality (*Adoration of the Magi*; Venice, Palazzo Rezzonico). This Late Baroque treatment, reminiscent of South German Baroque sculpture, often gives way to an elegant and graceful Neoclassicism, which recalls the early sculptures of Antonio Canova. Morlaiter's *bozzetti*—over 100 are in the Donà dalle Rose Collection in Venice—express this pictorial quality even more than his finished works. He worked chiefly for Venetian churches, but also executed commissions for Saxony and Russia. He was, with Tiepolo, one of the founding members of the Venetian Academy in 1756.

MORLAND, George (1763, London—1804, London), English painter. He was the son of Henry Robert Morland (*c.* 1730–97), an accomplished genre painter and picture restorer, and spent most of his youth copying engravings and faking Dutch and Flemish Old Masters. In 1785 Morland set up as a portraitist in Margate, Kent, and exhibited a painting of *Laetitia* at the Royal Academy in London. This painting was one of a series of six (now known only through engravings) illustrating the fall and rehabilitation of a harmless but giddy young girl. Hogarth's influence appears again in the oddly puritanical pair of pictures entitled the *Comforts of Industry* (1835) and the *Miseries of Idleness* (1836; both Edinburgh, National Gallery of Scotland). This note is repeatedly struck in engravings (*Idleness*, 1780; *Industry*, 1780; *Idle Laundress*, 1788 and 1803; *Industrious Cottager*, 1788 and 1803) that were made from his paintings, which he circulated from time to time. Morland is best remembered, however, for his landscapes, characterized by a roughness and approach that were fairly unusual in his period. The best of these were done between 1788 and 1798. Morland obeyed the artistic conventions of his time by including peasant scenes or incidents in his canvases, but made little attempt to make them more picturesque than they actually were (the *Tavern Door*, 1792, Edinburgh, National Gallery of Scotland; *Interior of a Stable*, 1791, London, National Gallery). An unstable character, Morland spent much of his life in financial difficulties, and in 1799 took refuge on the Isle of Wight, where he painted a number of sandy coastal scenes.

MORO, Antonio, *also called* Antonis mor *or* Anthonis Moor van Dashorst (*c.* 1519 Utrecht—1576, Antwerp), Dutch painter. The pupil of Jan van Scorel and a Master at Antwerp in 1547, he was one of the favorite court portraitists of King Philip II of Spain. Moro owed his good fortune to the bishop of Arras (the future Cardinal Granvella), who presented him to the duke of Alba, the Spanish envoy to the Netherlands. The artist made several highly successful visits to the Portuguese and Spanish courts (1552–54), and to the English court (1553); later he returned to Spain (1559–60), and spent his final years in Utrecht, Brussels, and Antwerp. In Spain Moro set the style for court portraiture, and paved the way for Velázquez. He does not flatter his sitters, but portrays them in all their ugliness, hardness, or insignificance. They are depicted against plain backgrounds, with frontal illumination bathing them in a cold and even light, and with extremely smooth surfaces: the *Duke of Alba* (1549; Brussels, Musées Royaux des Beaux-Arts); *Cardinal Granvella* (1549; Vienna, Kunsthistorisches Museum); *Maximilian II* (1550; Madrid, Prado); and *Mary Tudor* (1554; Prado). Moro's late works, painted after his return to the Netherlands, are primarily portraits of the bourgeoisie rather than of the nobility, and their greater looseness of brushwork anticipates the style of Frans Hals.

MORONI, Giovanni Battista (*c.* 1525, Albino, near Bergamo—1578, Bergamo?), Italian painter. He was a pupil of Moretto da Brescia, who strongly influenced his style. The greater part of

Moroni's career was spent in Bergamo, where he was occupied mainly with commissions for altarpieces for churches in the town and its environs. A fair number of these works have remained in their original settings, as, for example, the *Coronation of the Virgin* (1576; Bergamo, S. Allessandro della Croce). His portraits, which earned the approbation of Titian himself during Moroni's lifetime, usually consist of half-length (*Antonio Navagero*, 1565; Milan, Brera) and full-length figures (*Portrait of a Gentleman*, 1563; Florence, Uffizi), in which the simple yet masterly composition is sufficient to convey the nobility of the model. An execution free from preoccupation with details lends distinction to a sober coloring with silvery tones, and yields fine effects from the black of a doublet or the interplay of gray and white (*Portrait of an Old Man, c.* 1565–70; Bergamo, Accademia Carrara). The facial expressions—which are always restrained—are naturally suffused with a delicate melancholy that imparts a genuine poetry to Moroni's portraits.

MORRICE, James Wilson (1865, Montreal—1942, Tunis), Canadian painter. He did not decide to become an artist until 1888, when he resolved to leave for Paris, where he settled in 1890. He spent the rest of his life in France, particularly the south, except for brief visits to Canada and the West Indies, and died in Tunis during one of his frequent wanderings. In the 1890s he painted in the forest of Fontainebleau and on the beaches of Normandy and Brittany. Two visits (1896 and *c.* 1905) to Venice and one (1911) to Tangiers encouraged him to lighten his color range. After the foundation of the Salon d'Automne in 1903, Morrice participated regularly in its exhibitions. He had a gift for capturing the essence of a scene or a landscape with a few simple touches (*Red Houses in Venice*, 1903, and *Racecourse at Vincennes*, 1906; both Montreal, Museum of Fine Arts).

MORRIS, George L. K. (b. 1905, New York), American painter and art critic. During a visit to Paris in 1939, he enrolled in the Académie Moderne, where he worked with the Cubist painters Fernand Léger and Amédée Ozenfant. In Paris he familiarized himself with the problems of modern painting and met the protagonists of the abstract art movement, such as Jean Arp and Piet Mondrian. He held the first of his many one-man shows at the Curt Valentine Gallery, New York, in 1933. Morris helped found two periodicals, *Partisan Review* in New York and *Plastique* in Paris, for which he wrote articles advocating abstract art. In 1936 he was also one of the founders of the American Abstract Artists association, and was its president from 1948 to 1950. Morris' paintings, which are based on decorative motifs, are always enlivened by a sense of movement (*Nautical Composition*, 1937–42; New York, Whitney Museum).

MORRIS, William (1834, Walthamstow, Essex—1896, Kelmscott, Oxfordshire), English designer, poet, and critic. Morris grew up with a passion for the Middle Ages and a feeling for reform that inclined him briefly toward the church. At Exeter College, Oxford, he met Sir Edward Burne-Jones, and together they launched the *Oxford and Cambridge Magazine*. In 1856 he was apprenticed to the architect George Edmund Street (1824–81), but by the end of the year, under the influence of Dante Gabriel Rossetti, he had decided to abandon an architectural career for painting. His career as a painter, however, was also brief; in 1857 he joined Burne-Jones and a group of friends in executing frescoes for the Oxford Union, choosing as his subject *Sir Palomides Watching Tristram and Iseult*. His only easel painting, *La Belle Iseult* (1858; London, Tate Gallery)—actually a portrait of Jane Burden, whom he subsequently married—was also done at Oxford, and shows the same intensely medieval spirit that informs his first collection of poems, *The Defence of Guenevere and other Poems*, published in the same year.

After his marriage in 1859, Morris gave up painting, and with his friend Philip Webb began to build a new home, the Red House, in Upton, Kent; the problem of furnishing it opened to him a future as a master craftsman. The firm of Morris, Marshall, Faulkner & Co., "Fine Art Workmen in Painting, Carving, Furniture, and the Metals," was founded in 1861 "to reinstate decoration down to its smallest details as one of the fine arts." The first Morris wallpapers were produced in 1862, by which time he had a working knowledge of the techniques of dye-staining, weaving, and illumination. In 1866 the firm decorated the Armoury and Tapestry Room at the Victoria and Albert Museum in London. The firm was dissolved in 1875 and reorganized under his control.

William Morris. Wallpaper with floral decoration. *Photo Larousse, Paris.*

The later years of Morris' life were devoted to poetry, printing, and writings on social reform. His interest in Icelandic epics stimulated him to translate a number of the sagas, and his first political poem, *Wake, London Lads*, was published in 1878. His concern for the dignity of the craftsman led him naturally to an idealistic but intensely practical form of socialism, and Morris, an active member of the Social Democratic Federation, wrote, lectured, campaigned, and was arrested on its behalf. Morris' final major artistic undertaking was the Kelmscott Press, founded in 1890 and dedicated to the production of fine books. He died at Kelmscott Manor, the Oxfordshire house that he had originally bought with Rossetti in 1896.

Morris' high seriousness of purpose, his concern with improving the lot of man, and his fresh artistic theories make him an advanced thinker of impressive stature.

MORSE, Samuel Finley Breese (1791, Charlestown, Massachusetts—1872, New York), American painter. He achieved fame as the inventor of the telegraph, but his main concern was painting. In 1811 he went to England to study with the American painters Washington Allston and Benjamin West. His conventional history paintings suffer from weakly drawn, flat, and weightless figures. In a more modern conception (the *Old House of Representatives*, 1822; Washington, D.C., Corcoran Gallery of Art), his scientific bent is evident: 85 informal but accurate portraits people the view of the large hall.

Financial necessity soon forced him to paint portraits, which are his most imposing achievements, often showing a profound insight into personalities. His full-length portrait of the *Marquis de Lafayette* (1824–26; New York, City Hall) is a drama in which a fiery sunset remains subordinated to the extraordinary, almost caricatural face and looming figure viewed from below. In 1826 Morse became the first president of the National Academy of Design in New York, serving in that post until 1845, and again in 1861–62. From 1837 Morse concentrated exclusively on his great invention, the telegraph.

MORTENSEN, Richard (b. 1910, Copenhagen), Danish painter. During a visit to Berlin in 1933, he discovered Wassily Kandinsky's pictures and painted his first abstract works shortly thereafter. Mortensen was an important figure in the Danish art world, both as a theorist and as the founder of the Linien Group, a small circle of abstract painters. In 1947 he settled permanently in France. The striking characteristic of Mortensen's painting is his obvious desire for clarity of expression. This is accentuated by a perfect finish that smoothes away all accidents of the paint and all technical imprecisions. Mortensen's intellectual meticulousness does not, however, exclude an extremely personal dynamism in the articulation of the forms nor an astonishingly fresh range of colors (*Calvados*, 1955; Paris, Coll. Denise René). He also made cartoons for tapestries (*Alata* and *Evisa*, both 1960; Paris, Galerie Denise René) and, after 1944, designed the sets and costumes for theatrical productions.

MOSBRUGGER *or* **MOOSBRUGGER,** Caspar (1656, Au, Bregenzer Wald, Austria—1723, Einsiedeln, Switzerland), the best-known member of a family of Austrian Baroque architects from the Vorarlberg district. Mosbrugger's greatest work was the rebuilding of the pilgrimage church of Einsiedeln. The abbey itself had been largely built (1704–17) from plans by Hans Georg Kuen of Bregenz. Mosbrugger designed the church (1719–23) with a long façade that complements the wooded terrain. He gave the center a Baroque, convex form modeled on the Weingarten abbey church (begun 1715), to which he may have contributed. Einsiedeln's interior combined three different centralized units, which constituted a significant advance beyond the Weingarten church. Indeed the notion of inserting centralized units into a longitudinal building was used most consistently by Mosbrugger. The plans for the rebuilding of the Benedictine abbey of Muri in Aargau canton (built by Giovanni Betini, 1695–98) were probably of his design.

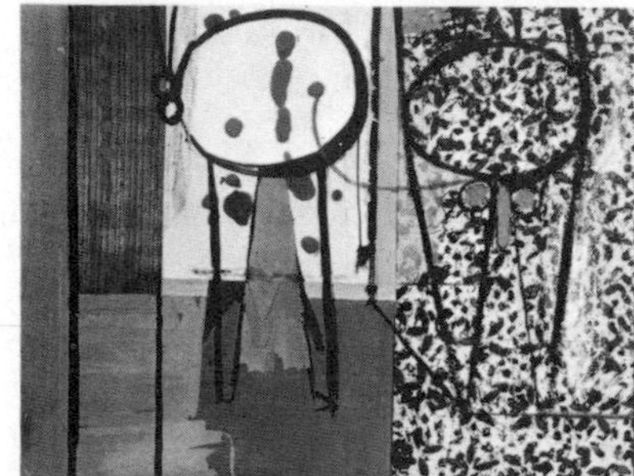

Robert Motherwell. *Pancho Villa Dead and Alive.* 1943. Museum of Modern Art, New York.

MOSES, Anna Mary Robertson, *called* Grandma (1860, Greenwich, New York—1961, Hoosick Falls, New York), American primitive painter. Grandma Moses had been an amateur painter all her life, creating "little pictures for Christmas gifts and things like that," as she described them. At the advanced age of eighty she embarked upon her public career with her first one-man show in New York (October 1940). As she did not die until she was over 100 years old, Grandma Moses had the opportunity to see her works exhibited in the great cities of America and Europe; honors were heaped upon her and she became a celebrated figure.

There is an unusual pleasure in the naive imagery of her works. This simple, tender-hearted old woman painted the people and life of New England with touching sincerity: its valleys, lakes, mountains, and forests; the seasons, which she had seen change so often; picturesque villages with their wooden houses and gaily colored barns; farmyards with stables and children at play; country folk working on the land, amusing themselves or celebrating national holidays (*Thanksgiving Turkey*, 1943; New York, Metropolitan Museum); grazing cows and horse-drawn carts. The drawing is awkward, the composition stereotyped, and the color at times deadened by another placed beside it. The incorrectness, nevertheless, produced some charming effects. Grandma Moses excelled in unfolding a vast panorama, plotting the fertile lands of Vermont in haphazard perspective and finding on her palette the most delicate tones of blue, pink, green, and the range of whites and grays that she used to paint her enchanting winter landscapes. Instinctively she created a limpid, bright, pure world—one in which imagination superseded nature and in which the unreal is so closely linked with the real that the most banal image also seems the strangest.

MOTHERWELL, Robert (b. 1915, Aberdeen, Washington), American Abstract Expressionist painter and art critic. After visiting France (1938–39) he decided to teach part-time while he pursued his artistic training. He attended (1940–41) the Faculty of Fine Arts and Archaeology of Columbia University. In 1941 he also worked in Mexico with the Surrealist painter Roberto Matta, and was considerably influenced by the latter's "psychic automatism." In 1948 he was cofounder with the American painters William Baziotes, Barnett Newman, and Mark Rothko of the "Subjects of the Artist" art school in New York, which eventually became a discussion group for avant-garde artists known as "The Club." He edited *The Dada Painters and Poets* (1950), and was coeditor, with Harold Rosenberg, of the series called *Documents of Modern Art* (1944–51) and, with Ad Reinhardt, of the book *Modern Artists in America* (1951). Until around 1950 his paintings and collages revealed two trends: on the one hand, he seemed to search for themes with an impulsiveness sometimes reminiscent of that of the German painter Kurt Schwitters; on the other, he experimented with the potentialities of color in a way that was partly derived from Matisse (*The Crossing*, 1948; New York, Coll. John D. Rockefeller). In 1951 he painted a mural for a synagogue in Milburn, New Jersey. Around 1954 huge, clearly defined symbols began to appear, for example, in the series of *Elegies to the Spanish Republic* (begun 1947), in which broad, massive forms are applied in flat black paint and are spread across the canvas in a slow, continuous movement that suggests the silhouettes of penitents. After 1959, however,

Motherwell accentuated this simplification of form and color in large-scale compositions whose emotional impact is derived from a vast, homogeneous space that is invaded by symbols.

MOUND BUILDERS, Art of the. The culture of the so-called Mound Builders developed in the east-central United States, in the Mississippi and Ohio river valleys, between the Great Lakes and the Gulf of Mexico. The most interesting sites were discovered in the states of Wisconsin, Ohio (at Hopewell and Adena), and Mississippi. The culture comprised many different tribes, all of which are known for the various types of mounds they built. Their civilization probably began about A.D. 300 and lasted until the end of the 17th century, when the Europeans arrived and the mounds were still being used. New forms of mounds were erected between 1550 and 1650, and it has been suggested that these reflected a new religion imported perhaps by Mexican refugees who fled the Spaniards. The cult objects of this religion, known as the Southern Death Cult, are in fact decorated with motifs similar to Aztec forms, particularly the plumed serpents.

The mounds were built of earth in various sizes and shapes. The strangest are those in the form of animals, such as tortoises and snakes; in the south (Mississippi) are certain ones in the shape of truncated pyramids. They may be as much as 50 or 60 feet high and some 335 feet long. Ramps or stairways led to the top, where there used to be wooden structures; all that remains of these structures are the holes into which the main piers of the framework were driven.

Inside the mounds a very rich array of art was discovered, including copper and ceramic objects, wooden masks, statuettes, basins and pipe bowls in stone, ornaments in bone and mica, and fragments of decorated leather and shells.

The objects found at Hopewell, Ohio, show the most representative and the most highly developed style; the styles of the other regions resemble it—although with local variations—but they are generally poorer. Even the finest copper objects, whether utilitarian or ornamental, cannot stand comparison with the stone carvings, the finest of which were the pipes (145 were found at Hopewell), carved in the shape of human heads, birds, reptiles, and various other animals, with delicate detail and a real concern for expression. The ornamental plaques are both pierced and engraved, with spirals and geometric motifs based on zoomorphic forms, and show a consummate feeling for sculptural values. The art of the Mound Builders was primarily naturalistic; it contained almost no trace of the symbolism and abstract stylization that were common in other pre-Columbian American art.

Mound Builders. Carved pipe from Hopewell, Ohio. Museum of Natural History, Chicago.

MOUNT, William Sidney (1807, Setauket, Long Island, New York—1868, Setauket), American painter. Mount was trained briefly (1824–26) in the sign-painting shop of his brother, Henry Smith Mount (1802–41) in New York, and later at the National Academy of Design, New York (1826–27). He derived his income primarily from portrait painting, for which he was highly acknowledged in his own time, although his reputation now rests more on his genre and landscape paintings. His first genre scenes date from the 1830s and represent the life of his native Long Island, an old settlement that was rich in traditions, a vital outdoor life, and spiritualism. Mount deliberately sought and achieved popularity with his subjects, for he believed that the artist should paint for the public and that the content of a work should be immediately comprehensible. He achieved a mature, convincing style, luminous coloration and frequently interesting compositions (*Eel Spearing at Setauket*, 1845, Cooper-town, New York State Historical Association; *Banjo Player*, 1858, Detroit, Institute of Arts). In the 1850s Mount shown an increasing interest in landscape scenes, which he consistently painted from nature; these are notable for a very loose, painterly style and a pleasing spontaneity (*Fence on the Hill, c.* 1850; New York, Coll. Harry Stone).

MOZARABIC ART. In the late 9th century A.D., while a brilliant Moslem civilization—which gave birth to Hispano-Moresque art—was developing in southern Spain, Christians were resettling the territories to the north. In the 10th and early 11th centuries, Christians who had been hunted out of Andalusia arrived in the kingdom of León, bringing with them an art that took its subject matter from Christianity, some of its structural principles from Late Roman (Early Christian) art, and that was Islamic in design and format. These Christians had been called Mozarabs ("would-be Arabs") while they were living in Moslem territories, and their so-called Mozarabic art spread throughout Spain. Mudejar art, by contrast, was practiced solely in the Catholic areas.

Mozarabic art is almost exclusively religious, and its earliest shrines date from the end of the 9th century. The horseshoe arch, so often used in Cordovan architecture, and the modillion, a characteristic motif of the Great Mosque at Cordova, were taken over without modification. Altar niches were frequently imitations of the mihrabs in Moslem prayer halls.

One of the earliest structures that could be called Mozarab in style is the cruciform church of S. María at Melque, near Toledo (*c.* A.D. 900), in which the horseshoe arches used in the vaulting are combined with Visigothic (the cruciform plan) and Early Christian basilican elements. Perhaps the most successful of Mozarabic

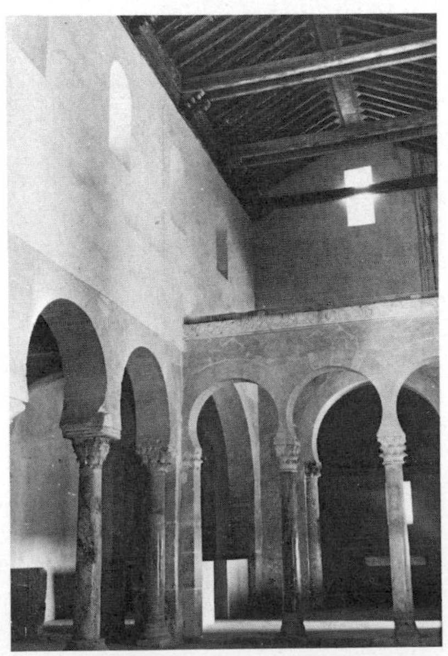

Mozarabic Art. S. Miguel de la Escalada, near León. 10th century. *Photo Mas, Barcelona.*

churches is that of S. Miguel de la Escalada, near León (*c.* A.D. 912), one of the very few Christian buildings of the period that survives near an urban area. The essentially austere basilican feeling is modified by extensive interior use of horseshoe arches; they appear in the side aisle vaulting, over the entrances to the chapels, on the chancel screen, and in the design of the clerestory windows. The interior walls are covered with carved motifs of Moorish origin. On the façades, as on the exteriors of such Mozarabic churches as Santiago de Peñalba (A.D. 919) and S. María de Lebeña (A.D. 924), are carved designs, including spiraling wheels and six-petaled flowers, that are also found on the Great Mosque at Cordova.

Mozarabic art also includes gold-smithery, bronze- and ivory-work, and especially book illumination. The illuminated miniatures appear to derive from both Visigothic and Byzantine sources and are characterized by distinctive designs and strong, bright color: the Beatus Apocalypse of Gerona (executed A.D. 975), preserved in the cathedral archives, is a good example.

MUCHA, Alfons Marie (1860, Ivancice, Moravia—1939, Prague), Czech painter, decorator, and poster designer. In 1887 he went to Paris to complete his artistic education and worked at the Académie Julian, the Académie Colarossi, and in the studio of the painter Jean-Paul Laurens (1838–1921). Mucha was one of the leading designers in the Art Nouveau style and, in his numerous posters, he carried the contemporary taste for the whiplash line to its final exaggeration (*Poster for the Salon des Cent*, 1896). Mucha popularized flowers on slender, twining stems; bizarre undulations of flowing hair; and astral and feminine motifs that earned Art Nouveau its French nickname of *style nouille*, of which his *Poster for Job Cigarette Papers* (1898) is a typical example. He was Sarah Bernhardt's regular poster designer, and in that capacity projected the great tragic actress's personality onto his theater bills (*Gismonda*, 1894; *Lorenzaccio*, 1896; *Medea*, 1898; *Hamlet*, 1899). He also designed the sets and costumes for many of the productions in which she appeared, and he frequently designed jewels for her. In the field of decoration, Mucha did window displays that were arranged with a strange refinement. Between 1904 and 1913 he made six trips to the United States, where he concentrated on painting. He then settled in Prague and resumed his original academic manner. He devoted the rest of his career to painting historical subjects, some of the most notable of which are 20 large paintings illustrating the *Epic of the Slavic People* (1910–28). Mucha donated this cycle, which includes such scenes as the *Abolition of Serfdom in Russia*, to the city of Prague.

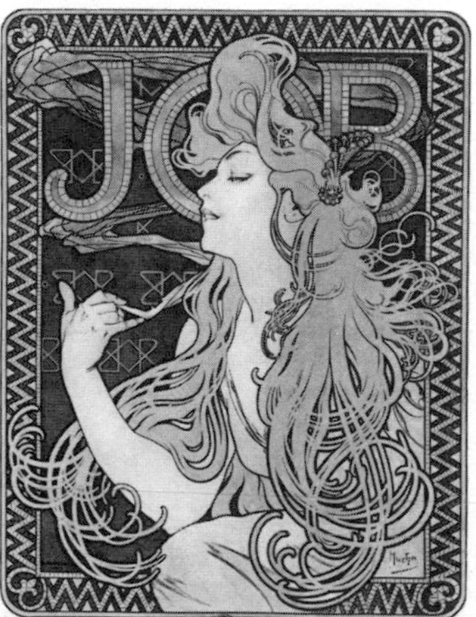

Alfons Marie Mucha. Poster for *Job Cigarette Papers.* 1898. *Photo Guy Gourlay, Paris.*

MUDEJAR ART. The name Mudejar was given, during the Moslem occupation of Spain and its reconquest by the Christian kings, to those Moslems who kept their religion under Christian rule. Mudejar art was made for non-Moslem patrons, either Christian or Jewish, in contrast to Hispano-Moresque art, whose patrons were Islamic. It differs also from Mozarabic art (produced by Christian artists for Moslem patrons), because it flourished in the Christian part of Spain only, but resembles it in being a composite style, which combined—in proportions varying with historic events—Moslem and Christian techniques and ornamental motifs, and followed the development of the rest of European culture from Romanesque to Renaissance. In the middle of the 12th century, in Castile and the kingdom of León, Romanesque architecture borrowed Arabic materials and forms, which produced the brick churches of northern Spain with their Moresque decoration and characteristic outline: S. Cristo de La Luz at Toledo is one of the purest examples of this type. Later Gothic was combined with Moresque, and flourished as much in the great cathedrals (Saragossa and Teruel) as in a crowd of little churches from Cordova to Seville, which were flanked with minarets, faced with colored tiles, or decorated with sculptured interlacings. At the end of the 13th century, and to a greater extent in the 14th century, Mudejar art acquired a more aristocratic manner and became a real court art: the abbey at Las Huelgas at Burgos; the Chapel of San Fernando (1258) in the Great Mosque of Cordova, which had been transformed into a cathedral; the monastery of S. Clara at Tordesillas, founded by Alfonso XI; and the portion of the Alcázar in Seville that was built between 1364 and 1366 by Pedro I (called Pedro the Cruel). It is at Toledo, however, where the presence of Moslem art was everywhere in evidence, that two pure masterpieces can be found: a synagogue built in the 13th century, now the church of S. Maria la Blanca; and the Synagogue del Transito, built in 1357 by Samuel Halevi, King Pedro's financier, and now called S. Maria del Transito. Mudejar art reached its peak in the 15th century, when the Moslems were working on such huge complexes as the monastery of the Hieronymites at Guadalupe in Estremadura, which was not completed until the following century, the castle of Coca (15th century) for the Fonseca family, and the Alcázar in Segovia (largely destroyed

Mudejar Art. Castle of Coca. 15th century. *Photo Martin Hürlimann, Zurich.*

in the 19th century). It enjoyed its final flowering at the beginning of the 16th century, with such works as the doors of the Chapter House of Toledo Cathedral.

MUELLER, Otto (1874, Liebau, Silesia—1930, Breslau), German painter. While still a youth he learned lithography, and then studied at the Dresden Academy from 1896 to 1898. After 10 itinerant years, he visited Berlin in 1908, where he met Erich Heckel. In 1910 he became associated with the New Secession, a protest movement founded by Max Pechstein and Emil Nolde, directed against Impressionism. Although in the same year he also joined the Brücke group, Mueller's painting never had the violence of Ernst Kirchner's or Karl Schmidt-Rottluff's. He simplified forms, outlining them distinctly, but did not resort to aggressive distortions. His coloring was similarly subdued; the materials he used—distemper, and paint mixed with glue and coarse jute canvas—robbed his colorism of any brilliance, flattened his tones, and gave them a faded, ashen quality. Mueller's favorite subjects were nudes, set in paradisiacal primitivistic landscapes; he usually painted adolescent girls with slender, supple bodies, for whom nudity was a natural state (*Nude Standing Among Trees*, 1915; Düsseldorf, Kunstmuseum der Stadt Düsseldorf). After World War I, Mueller made several visits to the Balkans to study the way of life of the gypsies, who provided him with most of his later subjects (*Gypsy with Cat*; Cologne, Wallraf-Richartz-Museum), but his style showed no change.

MÜLLER, Robert (b. 1920, Zurich), Swiss sculptor. In 1954 he had his first one-man show in Paris. He was invited to exhibit his work at the 1956 Venice Biennale and at the 1957 São Paulo Bienal, and steadily gained recognition as one of the most original metal sculptors of his generation. Müller made his sculptures by welding together bits of scrap iron, but in the course of assembling and soldering his material, he obliterated any accidental shapes created by the original objects chosen and completely destroyed their identity. He used found objects to create fabulous animals with formidable carapaces (*Lobster*, 1955; Zurich, Kunsthaus); strange, cruel-looking instruments (*Spit*, 1956; São Paulo, Museu de Arte Moderna); and barbaric steles (*Ex-Voto*, 1957; New York, Museum of Modern Art). Müller's armored sculptures are aggressive forms that follow either a vertical movement in which the thrust of a body springs straight up from the ground (*Mango*, 1956; Saint Gall, Kunstmuseum), or a horizontal movement in which the masses are stretched out and knotted (*Knot*, 1956; Paris, Galerie de France). He sometimes even employed hydraulic power to vitalize his works; these "fountains" are small structures comprising a variety of mobile parts that are set in motion by the circulating water.

MULLER, William James (1812, Bristol—1845, Bristol), English landscape painter. He first exhibited at the Royal Academy in 1833, and shortly afterward left for an extended trip to Germany, Switzerland, and Italy. In 1838–39 Muller went to Egypt and Greece, and in 1843 to Turkey. At the end of 1839 he settled in London, but in 1845 he returned to his native Bristol for reasons of health. Muller exhibited at the Royal Academy from 1833 to 1845, at the Society of British Artists from 1836 to 1841, and at the British Institution during the years 1840–45. He is a minor, though interesting, painter of the Romantic period, and his work falls into two fairly distinctive groups: Middle Eastern scenes and English views. The English paintings, influenced by John Constable and David Cox, are attractive, and are often very fresh in their handling and tone. More exotic, more interesting, and more typically Romantic, however, are Muller's Eastern scenes, such as the *Acropolis, Athens* and the *Pyramids* (both 1843; both Bristol, City Art Gallery). These sometimes reveal, in their composition, the influence of the young J. M. W. Turner.

MULREADY, William (1786, Ennis, Ireland—1863, London), British painter of domestic genre subjects. He became a pupil at the Royal Academy Schools in 1800, making his London exhibition debut in 1804. The first paintings that he showed were landscapes; but the great success of Sir David Wilkie's small scale genre pictures in the Dutch manner made him change his style. After 1807 he began to concentrate on paintings of young boys and peasants, although he occasionally illustrated books, such as *The Vicar of Wakefield* (1840). Mulready's early works clearly show the influence of 17th-century Dutch and Flemish masters, both in subject matter and in technique. Later he was to develop an idiom in which a use of thin glazes achieved a transparency of tone comparable to that of watercolor. Mulready's great popularity, particularly in the 1840s and 1850s, was due to a combination of his style and his subject matter. His style, with its 17th-century overtones, was reassuring to those collectors of conservative taste. In his approach to subject matter, he deftly exploited the picturesque and anecdotal characteristics of 17th-century painting while carefully avoiding its coarseness. Among Mulready's chief patrons was the collector John Sheepshanks, who bequeathed his collection to the Victoria and Albert Museum in 1857. This museum has the most balanced selection of the painter's work: *Giving a Bite* (1836), *the Sonnet* (1839), and *Shooting a Cherry* (1848) are typical.

MULTSCHER, Hans (*c.* 1400, Reichenhofen, Württemberg—1467, Ulm), German painter and sculptor of the Swabian school. He is first recorded in Ulm in 1427, when he was made a citizen of that town. His sculptural activity in Ulm included the decoration of the town hall (*c.* 1427–30) and the cathedral (*Man of Sorrows* on the west portal, 1429). His ability as a painter can be judged by the so-called Wurzach Altarpiece (1437), from the parish church in the South Württemberg town of Wurzach; its central panel has been lost, but eight others are in Berlin's Staatliche Museen. Another important work, the Sterzing Altarpiece (1456–59), demonstrates Multscher's skill as both painter and sculptor and provides ample

Robert Müller. *Lobster*. 1955. Kunsthaus, Zurich.

evidence of the artist's realistic and violently Expressionistic style. The sculptural figures adorning the frame of the shrine and most of the eight panels are considered the work of Multscher himself; some scholars detect a different style in the painted wings, and have attributed them to an anonymous Swabian assistant referred to as the Master of the Sterzing Altarpiece.

Multscher reacted against the idealism of the preceding generation of German artists and imparted to his weighty and overcrowded figures grimacing, brutally caricatural facial expressions.

MUNCH, Edvard (1863, Løten, Hedmark—1944, Ekely, near Oslo), Norwegian painter and graphic artist. Munch's childhood was filled with tragedy and gloom; his mother died when he was five, and one of his sisters when he was thirteen—events that profoundly wounded his spirit. His father was a doctor in a poor district and Munch, whose own health was extremely delicate, grew up in an atmosphere filled with disease, fear, and death. In 1880 he decided to take up painting and studied in Oslo under the guidance of Christian Krohg. Munch made his first trip to Paris in 1885. In 1886 he became a member of "Christiania's Bohemia," an avant-garde group in Christiania (present-day Oslo) that was concerned with contemporary social, political, and moral issues, and in whose antibourgeois atmosphere Munch's nonconformism and revolt against social constraints developed. In 1889 he was awarded a state scholarship that enabled him to return to Paris, where he attended Léon Bonnat's classes for four months before he began working on his own. He was, however, far more interested in the work of Vincent van Gogh and Paul Gauguin than in anything a school could teach him, and it was not long before his style changed. The works painted after his return to Oslo in 1891 show that he was no longer satisfied with painting what he could see: he began to exteriorize his feelings and to express the restlessness of his soul, his preoccupations, and the dark state of his mind. Threatened with illness, he revealed himself, in the paintings of this period, to be panic-stricken, agonized, and beyond all help (*Karl Johans Gate*, 1892, Bergen, Coll. Rasmus Meyer; *The Cry,* 1893, Oslo, Nasjonalgalleriet).

Munch wanted his work to be seen as the outward expression of his conception of the world. This was why, as early as 1889, he planned to group his paintings together under the title of the *Frieze of Life* and why he periodically exhibited his pictures under that label. Although Munch's style was entirely personal, it was influenced to some extent by Symbolism and even by Art Nouveau. He drew out his languorously curving lines in nostalgic perspectives and chose his colors for their expressive values: youth, burning with passion, is painted red; a jealous face is spread with a leprous green (*Jealousy*, *c.* 1893; Nasjonalgalleriet). The section reserved for his paintings at the exhibition of the Association of Berlin Artists (1892) was closed by the organizers themselves. The scandal made him famous overnight and he soon exercised an appreciable influence on the development of painting in Germany, where—except for several trips—he lived until 1908.

In 1894 Munch began to do engravings in which he presented the same subjects and expressed the same feelings as in his paintings. His dry points, etchings, and lithographs are more concise and more striking than his paintings. During a further visit to Paris in 1896, he did a portrait of the French Symbolist poet Stéphane Mallarmé (lithograph and etching), made contact with the members of the Nabis group, exhibited his *Frieze of Life* at the Galerie Art Nouveau, and designed sets for Ibsen's *Peer Gynt* at the Théâtre de l'Oeuvre. In 1897 he exhibited the *Frieze of Life* at the Salon des Indépendants.

Munch was plagued by anxiety all his life, and in 1908 suffered such a severe bout of nervous depression that he entered a Copenhagen clinic. When he left it a few months later, he returned to his native Norway, where he lived for the rest of his life. In his last period of artistic activity, his painting became calmer, his coloring lighter and clearer. In 1914–15 he painted several sun-filled murals for the Great Hall of Oslo University; in 1921–22 he painted murals for the canteen of the Freia Chocolate Factory in Oslo. Munch also painted some very moving self-portraits, such as *Between the Clock and the Bed* (1940; Oslo, Municipal Art Collections), in which he recorded the pitiless work of the passing years. Portraits, in fact, occupied an extremely important place in his work throughout his career: they were generally full-length (*The Frenchman*, 1901; Nasjonalgalleriet), and thus allowed him to make the poses and outlines as eloquent as the face. The Munch-Museet in Oslo contains a large collection of the artist's paintings, prints, and drawings.

Edvard Munch. *The Cry*. 1893. Lithograph.

MUNKÁCSY, Michael von Leib, *called* Mihály (1844, Munkács—1900, Endenich, near Bonn), Hungarian painter. In 1870 he was awarded the Gold Medal of the Salon des Artistes Français in Paris for his painting, *Last Day of a Condemned Man* (1870; Budapest, Hungarian National Gallery). He settled in Paris in 1872, worked at Barbizon in 1874, and contributed regularly to the Salon. In spite of his early training in the manner of the Munich School, Munkácsy was receptive to the ideas of Courbet and the Barbizon painters, and through his work French influence was introduced into Hungarian art. He painted portraits (*Liszt*; Paris, Louvre), landscapes, genre pictures (*Lint Makers*, 1872; Hungarian National Gallery), social documentaries (*At the Pawnbroker's*, 1884; New York, Metropolitan Museum), and religious paintings (*Christ before Pilate*, 1881; Philadelphia, Coll. J. Wanamaker). His vigorous realism, skillful draftsmanship, scrupulous study of form, and mastery of French colorism assured him a high place in Hungarian art of the 19th century.

MURILLO, Bartolomé Esteban (1618, Seville—1682, Seville), Spanish painter. The series of paintings that the young Murillo turned out at first in order to earn his living, either for the Andalusian fairs or for religious houses in the West Indies, gave him a certain ease of execution. Although influenced by Francisco Ribalta and Francisco de Zurbarán, he was perhaps more significantly affected by Flemish and Venetian paintings. A hypothetical visit to Madrid has been suggested as an explanation for these foreign influences. There is, however, no documentary evidence to support this theory, and a more likely explanation can probably be found in contemporary engravings and in the existence of a number of Venetian and Flemish paintings that Murillo could have seen in Seville itself.

After enjoying an immense reputation during his lifetime and, indeed, until the 18th century, Murillo was later accused of insipidity, and has only recently begun to recover from critical neglect. The sometimes mawkish tenderness of his religious sentiments must be viewed as a characteristic of the piety of his times and of his Counter-Reformation patrons; it expressed the sincere faith of a deeply religious man, who worked closely with monasteries, and who interpreted the heavenly world in serene and gentle earthly visions. In fact, Murillo's talent was of the first order; his sense of composition is remarkable, his draftsmanship firm and sure, his coloring exceptional, and the emotional appeal of the atmosphere he created is reminiscent of the pious and beautiful art of Antonio Correggio.

Around 1645–46 he provided 11 paintings for the Franciscans of Seville, including the *Miracle of S. Diego of Alcalá*, also known as the *Angels' Kitchen* (Paris, Louvre). In 1650 he was working for the monastery of Seville's Merced Calzada (*Flight into Egypt*; Genoa, Palazzo Bianco), and in 1655 for Seville Cathedral (*St. Isidore* and *St. Leander*). Canon Don Justino de Neve commissioned him (*c.* 1665) to do a set of paintings for S. Maria la Blanca: the *Triumph of the Immaculate Conception* (Louvre) and the *Dream of the Patrician John* (Madrid, Prado) belong to this series. The *Vision of St. Thomas* (Seville, Museo de Bellas Artes) formed part of a series of paintings (*c.* 1664?) for the Augustinian monastery in Seville. The *Miracle of the Portiuncula* (*c.* 1665–70; Cologne, Wallraf-Richartz-Museum) came from a similar group painted for the Capuchin order.

For the chapel in the Hospital de la Caridad in Seville, Murillo painted (1671–73) some of his finest works: still in place are *St. John of God Carrying an Invalid*, *Moses Striking Water from the Rock*, the *Miracle of the Loaves and Fishes*, and *Plague-Stricken*. A late (1678) painting of the *Immaculate Conception* has a pleasing silvery tonality and vaporous atmosphere. Murillo was probably working in the Convent of the Capuchins at Cadiz (1682) when he fell off a scaffolding and died later in Seville as a result of his injuries. In addition to his religious paintings, he left several genre scenes depicting the street urchins of Andalusia, which display his own very personal blend of realism and tender poetry (*Beggar Boy*, Louvre; *Grape and Melon Eaters*, Munich, Alte Pinakothek). These highly popular works, indebted to similar naturalistic scenes by Caravaggio and Velázquez, have none of the vaporous qualities of his late style, but rather a somber tonality and a precise linearity.

Bartolomé Esteban Murillo. *St. Joseph and the Infant Jesus.* Cabinet des Dessins, Louvre, Paris.

MYCENEAN ART. Mycenean civilization, sometimes called Creto-Mycenean, was that of a military society on the Greek mainland profoundly influenced by the technical accomplishments and aesthetic achievements of neighboring Crete. The Achaeans had reached the tip of the Balkan peninsula at the beginning of the 2nd millennium B.C., and their densest settlements had been on the gulf and in the plain of Argos, at Tiryns and Mycenae, where the most eloquent remains of that age are to be found. But there are also traces of the same civilization at many places in the Peloponnese, in Attica, Boeotia, and Thessaly, as well as further east on Rhodes and Cyprus, and even on the Syrian coast, established during the 14th and 13th centuries B.C., when Mycenean power stretched furthest.

The artistic history of Mycenae cannot be separated from that of Crete, for many of its products—pottery and goldwork for instance—were no more than provincial variants of Minoan art; but the originality of Mycenean architecture stands out clearly. That warlike race of conquerors were organized in a strongly centralized and hieratic society, with a royal family and a king at its head. Their towns' citadels dominated a plain or guarded a pass, and were primarily fortresses. Mycenean town walls are built entirely of great blocks of stone, roughly shaped and arranged not in regular courses but piled together. This manner of building is termed "Cyclopean." Stout bastions protect the ramps of access; enormous monoliths frame the doors, and over the monolithic lintel there is a relieving triangle. That at Mycenae has been carved with the famous confronting lion-

Mycenean Art. Portal of the Lionesses, Mycenae. 14th century B.C. *Photo Van der Heyden—Archives Elsevier.*

Mycenean Art (Minoan inspiration). Bronze poniard incrusted with gold and silver. Royal tombs of Mycenae. 14th century B.C. National Museum, Athens.

esses. Within these outer defenses, the palaces themselves were massive, and their layout was based on the mainland tradition but modified by some elements of Aegean origin. As at Troy, the kernel of the palace was the oblong megaron, but it was larger and more ornate than that at Troy. The central hearth in the main hall was framed by four columns that supported a lantern, and the apertures in that lantern, besides letting out the smoke, provided the only light for the hall. The megaron was not isolated, but had rooms crowded around it. Moreover, at Tiryns the façade of the megaron forms one side of a court surrounded by porticoes; colonnades also add dignity to the various monumental gates pierced in the town wall and leading into the heart of the palace. A stronger and more unified design striving after monumental effects distinguished Mycenean from Cretan palaces. The Aegean elements, such as columns and porticoes, were integrated as decorative motifs, giving the composition life, but not breaking its unity.

The Mycenean taste for monumental architecture is evident too in the beehive tombs, the best example of which are the Treasury of Atreus and the Treasury of Clytemnestra. The earlier burials, where so much goldwork was found, were made level with the ground. About the 15th century B.C., the funeral chamber partially hollowed out of the side of a hillock was turned into a rotunda with a corbeled vault as neat and regular as a beehive. The way up to the actual tomb chambers, the dromos, was flanked by walls with stones in fine regular courses. The monumental door formed by splendid monoliths was decorated with applied architectural motifs carved in colored stone.

In the other arts Cretan influence was much more direct, and the Mycenean product was only a variant, often an impoverished one, of the Minoan tradition. Wall painting only reached the Myceneans in the cold and overly-formal style of the last period. Pottery made use of the motifs of the Palace style, but these very quickly degenerated into geometric patterns. There were also tall vases with superimposed reliefs in a technique learned from the Minoans, but with scenes of siege and combat expressing the ethos of that warlike race of conquerors. The warlike spirit was again in evidence in their splendid weapons inlaid with gold and silver, making the blade of a dagger or a sword into a masterpiece; indeed there are damasked hunting scenes of such vigor and *élan* that it has been thought they must have been imported from Crete. The pomp that surrounded their kings on earth followed them to the tomb, where they were buried with rich accouterments of gold and silver. The German archaeologist Heinrich Schliemann, when he excavated those caskets, jewels, belts, and funeral masks, claimed that they belonged to Agamemnon and his family; but in fact they attest the skill of goldsmiths of the 16th and 17th centuries B.C. The repoussé gold was ornamented with simple geometric patterns: combinations of spirals, rosettes, and net patterns were elegantly disposed to enliven the otherwise slightly monotonous surface of the gold leaf.

MYERS, Jerome (1867, Petersburg, Virginia—1941, New York), American painter. Although poor himself, he was attracted to the slums of New York's Lower East Side, which he began to romanticize in his paintings as early as 1887. Along with that of The Eight (the Ashcan School) and his friend John Sloan, Myers' work was rejected for exhibition by the National Academy in 1907. He then helped to form the Association of American Painters in 1911, and along with Walt Kuhn, the gallery director Henry Fitch Taylor, and the painter Elmer Macrae (1875–1955), Myers helped lay the foundations for the 1913 Armory Show.

Myers' work is both sentimental and romanticizing in its treatment of urban life (*Street Group*; Metropolitan Museum). He thought of New York as a "tapestry of romance" and discovered a world of almost abstract fantasy through his study of the laborers, children, and merchants who populate the slum districts. *The Tambourine* (Washington, D.C., Phillips Collection), with its gay children dancing around an organ-grinder, is characteristic of his view of the poor but happy urchins who snatch a few joyful moments in their otherwise bleak lives.

After 1914 Myers resigned from the Association of American Painters and Sculptors and was honored by acceptance into the National Academy. He maintained his old style even after World War I.

MYTENS, Daniel (*c.* 1590, Delft—before 1648, The Hague), Dutch portrait painter. He was introduced to King James I of England in 1619, and on the death of Paul van Somer (1576–1621) succeeded the latter as portrait painter to the English court. With the accession of Charles I, he was appointed "Picture Drawer to the King." In 1626 he was allowed or possibly instructed to make a visit to the Low Countries for six months, perhaps to study contemporary Flemish portraiture. Mytens returned to Holland in the early 1630s, and in 1637 was acting as Lord Arundel's agent in The Hague.

Mytens was the principal painter at the English court before the arrival of Van Dyck in 1632. His early manner may be seen in the famous portrait of *Lord Arundel in his Sculpture Gallery* (Arundel, Sussex, Arundel Castle, Coll. Duke of Norfolk), painted before 1618. It is a grave and correct portrait, yet of great historical interest because it shows the famous collection of Roman statues that represented Arundel's attempt to import the Italian Renaissance into the English way of life. More successful, exciting, and sophisticated is the portrait of the *Duke of Hamilton* (1629; Coll. Duke of Hamilton, on loan to Edinburgh, National Gallery of Scotland), which shows how much Mytens gained from his visit to the Low Countries. The portrait of *Charles I in Garter Robes* (1633; Coll. Earl Fitzwilliam) is a straightforward and not undignified likeness, but compared with Van Dyck's state portrait of 1636 (Windsor Castle), it appears heavy and devoid of technical interest.

NABIS, group of late 19th-century French painters whose name comes from the Hebrew word for "prophets." The group's origins can be traced to September 1888, when Paul Sérusier met Gauguin at the little art colony of Pont-Aven in Brittany. The meeting was a decisive one: under Gauguin's supervision, Sérusier painted his famous *Landscape of the Bois d'Amour at Pont-Aven* (1888; France, Priv. Coll.) and when, on his return to Paris, he showed his composition to his fellow students at the Académie Julian, they adopted it as their "talisman." An exhibition, held at the Café Volpini in Paris early in 1889, of works by Impressionist and Synthetist painters such as Gauguin, Émile Bernard, and Charles Laval, gave a final impetus to the formation of the group's artistic philosophy. Pierre Bonnard, Henri-Gabriel Ibels (1867–1936), Paul Ranson (1864–1909), and Maurice Denis were converted to the new doctrine. Soon a number of students from the École des Beaux-Arts joined the Nabis: Édouard Vuillard, Ker-Xavier Roussel (1867–1944), René Piot, and, a little later, the Dutch Jan Verkade (1868–1946), the Swiss-born Félix Vallotton, the sculptors Georges Lacombe, Aristide Maillol, and the latter's friend, the Hungarian painter József Rippl-Rónai (1861–1927).

The Nabis met weekly in Ranson's studio and at the art dealer Julien (Père) Tanguy's shop, where they discovered the works of Cézanne and Van Gogh. Their other meeting places included the home of their own art dealer Le Barc de Boutteville, who between 1891 and 1897 devoted most of his exhibitions to their work; the editorial offices of the famous magazine, *Revue Blanche* (in which many works by the Nabis were reproduced), where they met all the important Symbolist writers; and the Symbolist Théâtre de l'Oeuvre, where they worked as costume and stage designers. The Nabis were also influenced by the paintings of Puvis de Chavannes and Odilon Redon, by primitive sculpture and Japanese prints, and to a lesser degree by the paintings of Gustave Moreau and the English Pre-Raphaelites. Denis summarized the group's artistic principles in his theory of two distortions: "The objective distortion that is based upon a purely aesthetic and decorative concept as well as technical principles of color and composition, and the subjective distortion that brings the artist's own perception into play . . ." The Nabis applied these principles not only to easel painting, but also to various decorative techniques and media that they revolutionized and that included painting on cardboard, painting in distemper, stained glass, lithography, posters, stage design, and book illustration.

In 1890 Bonnard, Vuillard, Denis, and Lugné-Poë shared a studio in Place Pigalle, Paris. Later Denis, Sérusier, and Verkade began to adopt a Neoclassical mysticism that was distantly related to the style of the Pont-Aven school. At the same time Bonnard and Vuillard, who were both dedicated Intimists, rebelled against Sérusier's and Gauguin's artistic theories and, along with Roussel, formed a group within a group. In 1899, at Durand-Ruel's Paris gallery, the Nabis exhibited together for the last time. They did so only as an act of homage to Redon, since by this time they had all gone their own ways.

NADELMAN, Elie (1882, Warsaw—1946, New York), Polish-born American sculptor. After leaving Warsaw around 1901, Nadelman went to Munich, where he became familiar with the drawings of Aubrey Beardsley. From 1903 to 1914 he worked and exhibited in Paris, where he gained recognition as a modernist sculptor. In 1914 he went to New York, and by 1918 he had established himself there as a popular sculptor especially in demand for portrait busts. After the Great Depression of the 1930s, however, Nadelman withdrew from the New York art world and stopped exhibiting his works.

Nadelman's major and persistent interest was in relationships of form, which he expressed primarily in simplified curvilinear and balanced human and animal figures. Some of his early work also shows a more Cubistic orientation to form (*Standing Bull* and *Wounded Bull*, both 1915; both bronze, New York, Museum of Modern Art). The major groupings of Nadelman's work are simplified, Impressionistic marble portrait heads, female figures of dancers, and circus performers (*Circus Woman*, c. 1924; Galvano plastique, Riverdale, New York, Coll. Mrs. Elie Nadelman), and small figures caricaturing members of high society.

NAIVE PAINTERS. *See* **PRIMITIVES OF THE TWENTIETH CENTURY.**

NAKIAN, Reuben (b. 1897, College Point, New York), American sculptor. In 1916 he became a studio apprentice to Paul Manship, and from 1920 to 1923 shared a studio with Gaston Lachaise. He began exhibiting in 1923 and held his first one-man show in New York in 1926. Nakian received an important commission in 1961 for decorating the façade of New York University's Loeb Student Center in Washington Square, New York. He believed that the grandeur and elegance of past European art, especially painting, should be an important source of inspiration for the modern sculptor. In the early 1930s Nakian did a series of portraits of artists and government officials, and in 1934 made an 8-foot sculpture of the baseball hero Babe Ruth. Later in the 1930s, and through the next decade, Nakian worked little on sculpture and exhibited rarely, concentrating instead on drawings. He returned to sculpture around 1947, with a series of small works in terra cotta based on mythological themes, which he first exhibited in 1949 and continued developing into the 1960s. With their spontaneity, expressive tactility, and sensuousness, these sculptures are among his most successful works (*Voyage to Crete*, 1949; New York, Coll. Mr. and Mrs. Thomas B. Hess). Nakian also explored mythological themes in both small and monumental bronzes, and in large welded steel constructions; some of the larger works were conceived as group sculptures (*Rape of Lucrece*, 1955–58, welded steel, New York, Museum of Modern Art; *Goddess of the Gold Thighs*, 1964–65, bronze, New York, Egan Gallery).

NANCY, School of, group of French decorative artists formed around 1890 in the city of Nancy. This school was officially founded in 1901 by the Nancy-born glassmaker Émile Gallé (1846–1904) and, according to its statutes, it was a "provincial alliance of the art industries." Its real point of departure was the Exhibition of Earthenware and Glass, organized in Paris in 1884 by the Union Centrale des Arts Décoratifs; Galle's work caused a sensation and made Nancy a particularly active center for Franch crafts. Gallé, who was also a furniture designer, was one of the first craftsmen to promote the Art Nouveau style in France; his work is characterized by a predominance of vegetal forms. He produced some astonishing effects by using layered glass on which he carved reliefs, by engraving it and by introducing gold or silver leaf and air bubbles into its mass of cobalt oxide, thus producing a "moonlight" tone. Following his example, the brothers Auguste (1853–1909) and Jean-Antonin (1864–1930) Daum transformed a factory in Nancy into a glassworks that produced artistic pieces; like Gallé, they produced polychrome crystal (*Gourd-Shaped Vase*, 1900; Paris, Musée des Arts Décoratifs).

The School of Nancy also designed furniture that followed principles of naturalistic decoration. Gallé made such Baroque pieces as the *"Moth" Bed* (1904; Nancy, Musée des Arts Décoratifs), which was decorated with a moth motif. The designs of the cabinetmaker Louis Majorelle (1859–1926) were also based on a direct observation of nature, and the furniture he produced is characterized by its refined marquetry and floral appearance. The architect of the group was Eugène Vallin (1856–1922), who supplied designs for façades to most of the architects of the region. The School of Nancy also revolutionized the art of bookbinding, largely through the work of René Wiener (1856–1939). Assisted by the painter and muralist Camille Martin (1861–98) and Victor Prouvé (1848–1943), Wiener made daring use of pyrogravure designs, produced by burning or scorching wood or leather and leather mosaic. Apart from his work as a bookbinder, Prouvé designed jewelry, embroidery, ironwork, and the famous *Riverside in Spring* (1900; Nancy, Musée des Arts Décoratifs), a dress with Art Nouveau motifs.

In 1903 the School of Nancy organized an exhibition in a hall of the Pavillon de Marsan in the Louvre, Paris. On Gallé's death in 1904, Prouvé took over the direction of the School of Nancy, but in spite of all his efforts it soon declined as an influential forcc in decorative art: in 1936 the firm was dissolved. The school's last important exhibition was in 1909 at the International Exhibition of Eastern France, for which Vallin built a reinforced concrete pavilion that housed the works of his friends.

Nanni di Banco. Detail of one of the *Quattro Coronati. c.* 1410–15. Or San Michele, Florence. *Photo Alinari-Viollet.*

NANNI DI BANCO, Giovanni di Antonio Banco, *called* (*c.* 1387, Florence—1421, Florence), Italian sculptor of the Florentine School. He was an important transitional figure in the development of Italian sculpture from the Gothic to Early Renaissance styles, thus paving the way for the even greater advances made by his contemporary, Donatello. In 1408 Nanni received his first major commission for a life-size marble statue of the prophet Isaiah, to be placed—along with a statue by Donatello—atop the buttresses next to the so-called Porta della Mandorla on the façade of Florence Cathedral. Nanni subsequently received a number of commissions from the various guilds of Or San Michele in Florence to supply the niches for the façade of the church with several sculptured figures. The most important was for the *Quattro Coronati* (*c.* 1410–15), a group of four martyred saints depicted in an increasingly Classicizing style. His last sculpture (begun *c.* 1414) was his relief of the *Assumption of the Virgin* above the Porta della Mandorla; it may have been completed by Luca della Robbia after Nanni's death.

NANNI DI BARTOLO, *called* Il Rosso (active 1419–51), Italian sculptor, an assistant and imitator of Donatello. In 1421 he collaborated with Donatello on the group of *Abraham and Isaac* (Florence, Museo dell'Opera del Duomo). In 1422 he revealed his individual talents in the statue of the *Prophet Obadiah* (Museo dell'Opera del Duomo). After

Napoleon III Style. Victor Baltard. Church of St-Augustin, Paris. 1860–66.

leaving Florence in 1424, Nanni worked for a time in several North Italian cities, including Verona (Brenzoni monument in the church of S. Fermo Maggiore, *c.* 1427–39) and Tolentino (funerary monument of Captain Niccolò Maurizi and portal of the church of S. Nicola, both *c.* 1432–35). In Venice in the 1430s he joined Giovanni and Bartolommeo Buon in the decoration of the Ca' d'Oro, and some critics attribute to him the *Judgment of Solomon* (*c.* 1430), a group of figures situated at the corner of the Palazzo Ducale, opposite the basilica of St. Mark's.

NAPOLEON III STYLE. The name given to art that flourished in France under the reign of Napoleon III (1852–70), also known as the Second Empire. After the disorders of the 1848 Revolution, Napoleon III decided to reorganize Paris, and entrusted this task to Baron Georges-Eugène Haussmann (1809–91), the prefect from 1853 to 1870. As President-Prince, Napoleon III had given immediate encouragement to industry, and, when he became Emperor, supported the Universal Exhibitions of 1855 and 1867, which gave such prominence to French scientific and economic progress. Napoleon III was sufficiently broadminded to recognize both official artists and the avant-garde, supporting the latter by founding the Salon des Refusés in 1863.

The Emperor's major interest was the replanning of Paris. Haussmann systematically destroyed the medieval quarters and opened up broad thoroughfares, such as the boulevards Sébastopol and St-Germain. These roadways were transformed into avenues bordered with blocks of fashionable dwellings. Similarly, Haussmann laid out the arterial roads of the new residential quarters in the west of the city, and a number of huge promenades (Alphand, Bois de Boulogne, 1858). Such a transformation involved the construction of innumerable public buildings (churches, town halls, hospitals, theaters, railway stations, and bridges), often designed in historical styles: Gothic at the church of St-Pierre-de-Montrouge, built in 1863 by Auguster Vaudemer (1829–1914), or Renaissance at the church of the Trinité, 1861–67 (Théodore Ballu) and in the new buildings of the Louvre, 1853–65 (Hector Lefuel). The real innovations, however, were technological ones: iron, cast iron, and glass appeared with Louis Auguste Boileau's (1812–1896) church of St-Eugène (1855), Victor Baltard's (1805–74) church of St-Augustin (1860) and the market building of Les Halles (1854–66), Jacques Ignace Hittorff's Gare du Nord (1863), and especially Henri Labrouste's Salle de Lecture of the Bibliothèque Nationale (1862–68). Among the most successful works in the prevailing Beaux-Arts style was Charles Garnier's Opéra (1862–68).

In painting, the Second Empire saw the triumph of realism. It began with a few landscape painters—Théodore Rousseau, Jules Dupré, Virgilio Narcisso Diaz de la Peña, and Charles-François Daubigny—who worked in the forests and strove to express the eternal quality of nature. For a long time they were turned down by the official Salon. When at last they were accepted, their influence became so great that Rousseau was able to persuade the Emperor to save trees that had been scheduled for cutting down. Their friend Jean-François Millet preferred to paint wide, open plains and peasants at work (*Gleaners*, 1857; Paris, Louvre). Honoré Daumier, on the other hand, portrayed the world of the Parisian workers (*Laundress*, *c.* 1861; Louvre). But the great theoretician of realism was Gustave Courbet, a political and social activist who, as a demonstration of protest, exhibited about 40 paintings in a shed during the Exposition of 1855. Édouard Manet caused even greater scandal with his non-mythologized nudes in contemporary settings. At the same time, the official salons were occupied by the late Romantics, the ageing Eugène Delacroix, Eugène Isabey, and Eugène Devéria (1805–65), as well as Orientalists using vivid color, such as Alexandre Gabriel Decamps (1803–60), Alfred Dehodencq (1822–82), and Eugène Fromentin (*Hawking in Algeria*, 1863; Louvre). Also to be included among the official painters are the realists using traditional techniques, Théodule Ribot (1823–91), Alphonse Legros, Léon Lhermitte (1844–1925), and Rosa Bonheur (1822–99), as well as the masters of large-scale historical painting, exemplified by Élie Delaunay's (1828–91) *Plague in Rome* (1869; Louvre), and the works of Gustave Boulanger (1824–88) and Jean-Léon Gérome (1824–1904). The specialists of the pearly nude, Alexandre Cabanel and Jean-Jacques Henner (1829–1905), should also be included in this category. The religious decorations of Hippolyte Flandrin (1809–64) and Jules Eugène Lenepveu (1819–98) were cold and austere, while those of Paul Baudry were Italianate and as highly colored. François-Xavier Winterhalter (1805–73) portrayed the court; Eugène Emmanuel Amaury-Duval (1808–85), Louis Gustave Ricard (1823–73), and Ernest Hébert (1817–1908) were more subtle and sincere. Interest in military life and a passion for the 18th century favored the genre scene and brought fame to Ernest Meissonier (1815–91). Finally, Constantin Guys (1805–92) became the witty chronicler of the reign through his sketches and caricatures of contemporary types and appurtenances.

Napoleon III Style. Pavillon de l'Empereur, Paris Opéra. 1862–75. *Photo Caroly, Paris.*

Napoleon III Style. François-Xavier Winterhalter. *Empress Eugénie Surrounded by Ladies of the Court.* 1855. Musée National du Palais de Compiègne.

The sculpture of the Second Empire reveals the same eclecticism that prevailed in painting and architecture. It embraces the realism of Daumier, the Romanticism of Jean-Baptiste (called Auguste) Clésinger (1814–83) and Antoine Préault, the lyricism of Barye (*Peace and War*, 1854; Louvre), and Classicism, which still survived in the work of François Jouffroy (1806–82), Pierre Jules Cavelier (1814–94), and Eugène Guillaume (1822–1905). The reign saw the early, elegant works of the so-called Florentines, Paul Dubois (1829–1905), Henri Chapu (1833–91), and Alexandre Falguière (1831–1900), as well as the apogee of the historical Romanticism of Emmanuel Frémiet (1824–1910), who worked on the decoration of the Château de Pierrefonds. But the great sculptor of the reign was Jean-Baptiste Carpeaux.

The abundance of ornamental sculpture, so characteristic of the Second Empire, is also to be found inside buildings where the decorators made lavish use of marbles, golds, and other rich materials. Interior decoration was executed entirely in historical styles (Eugénie's "Louis Seize" apartments or the medieval decoration of Pierrefonds). Around 1865 the "Impératrice" Louis XVI style became fashionable in furniture, porcelain, and goldsmith's work.

NASH, John (1752, London—1835, Cowes, Isle of Wight), English architect. He worked (1767–78) under the Palladian architect Sir Robert Taylor (1714–88) until a legacy enabled him to set up independently as a speculative builder in London. This venture, however, ended in bankruptcy, and he retired to Wales (1783–95), where he developed a substantial local practice. Back in London, Nash resumed his career with a series of country houses. At this time he formed an extremely successful partnership with the landscape gardener Humphrey Repton (1752–1818). Nash's work includes every style that was currently fashionable. His country house career, which lasted from about 1792 until 1812, included twelve large mansions in the Gothic manner, often with Classical interiors; his own castle at East Cowes, Isle of Wight (from 1798); large stuccoed Classical houses (Southgate Grove, 1797); and Italianate villas (Cronkhill, Shropshire, *c.* 1802). In his small picturesque "villas" and cottages (Park Villages, London, *c.* 1824 and 1830; Blaise Hamlet, Gloucestershire, 1811), he developed a type of semidetached house with a unified façade that became extremely popular. Nash's great London project (1810–23), sponsored by the Prince Regent, was the planning of Regent's Park and the construction of Regent Street. But the park was never realized as the urban unit he planned, little remains of the villas, and the superb, full quarter circle of Doric colonnades in Regent Street was demolished in 1848. Park Crescent (begun 1812) and the terraces (including Chester Terrace, 1825; and Cumberland Terrace, 1827) are the only considerable remains of this grand scheme. Brighton Pavilion (1815–21), an architectural extravaganza of Indian, Chinese, and purely imaginary elements, was built for the Prince of Wales, who had been one of his most devoted patrons, and who as George IV commissioned Nash to transform Buckingham House into a suitably magnificent palace; the construction (1825–30) was, however, a fiasco and brought Nash's career to an abrupt end.

NASH, Paul (1889, London—1946, Boscombe, near Bournemouth), English painter. In 1933 Nash was one of the founding members of the group of painters, sculptors, and architects called Unit One. He acted as an official war artist in both world wars, producing stark, angular records of the Western front and more visionary interpretations of the Battle of Britain. The quiet yet disturbing Romanticism of these paintings made him a dominant figure in British painting (*Menin Road*, 1917–19; London, Imperial War Museum). Although Nash felt the impact of a number of influences, his art remained profoundly marked by a Nordic and Celtic strain, the result of a conscious attempt to return to the sources of English art. Technically his roots may be found in the works of John Sell Cotman and J. M. W. Turner; his palette favored the muted colors of the English atmosphere, and even his oils maintained a fluidity and lyricism that relate him to the best traditions of the English watercolorists. He was acutely aware of analogies and correspondences. The sea of German aircraft destroyed in the Battle of Britain suggested to him the waves of a sea of death (*Totes Meer*, 1940–41; London, Tate Gallery), and the tree trunks in *Monster Field* (1939; Durban, South Africa, Art Museum) seem oddly supernatural. In each of his landscapes Nash sought the active element, the drama of an imagined space. In addition to his painting, he executed a fair number of book illustrations (edition of Sir Thomas Browne's *Urne Burial* and *The Garden of Cyrus*, 1932), some textile designs, posters, and theater décor.

John Nash. Cumberland Terrace, Regent's Park, London. 1826. *National Buildings Record, London.*

NASMYTH, Alexander (1758, Edinburgh—1840, Edinburgh), Scottish painter. His paintings of both individuals and groups show the influence of Ramsay, although the emphasis on a landscape background was Nasmyth's personal contribution, seen in his *Neil, Third Earl of Rosebery with His Family* (*c.* 1787; Scotland, Dalmeny House, Priv. Coll.). His most celebrated sitter was *Robert Burns* (1787; Edinburgh, Scottish National Portrait Gallery). Nasmyth later turned to landscape painting, in which he was influenced by 17th-century Dutch masters and by J. M. W. Turner, as is evident in *Winding of the Forth* (Edinburgh, National Gallery of Scotland). He was also active as an architect and landscape gardener. PATRICK (1787, Edinburgh—1831, Lambeth, London), painter, the most distinguished of Alexander's 11 children. Patrick painted meticulously in the Dutch manner, seen in such works as *A View in Hampshire* (London, Victoria and Albert Museum) and *Sir Philip Sidney's Oak, Penshurst Park, Kent* (Victoria and Albert Museum), and was as a result dubbed "the English Hobbema." Other paintings by him include *A Cottage, Formerly in Hyde Park* (1807; London, Tate Gallery), and *Edinburgh* (Richmond, Virginia Museum of Fine Arts, Paul Mellon Collection).

NAST, Thomas (1840, Landau, near Karlsruhe, Germany—1902, Guayaquil, Ecuador), American cartoonist. He arrived in New York as a child in 1846. He became an illustrator for *Frank Leslie's Illustrated Newspaper* (*c.* 1855), and then was associated with the *New York Illustrated News* (1859). In 1862 he joined *Harper's Weekly* as a staff artist, a position he held with considerable influence for nearly 25 years. By 1868 Nast turned from pictorial reporting to cartooning. His best-known campaign in this new field was an exposure of the Tweed Ring and

Tammany Hall, exemplified in his cartoon entitled *Tweed-le-dee and Tilden-dum* (*Harper's Weekly*, October 7, 1876). Nast instituted the use of the dollar sign in cartoon symbolism, as well as the donkey as the emblem of the Democratic Party. He worked for various other periodicals after leaving Harper's, and then published his own *Nast's Weekly* (1892–93). He received the appointment of American consul at Guayaquil, Ecuador, from President Theodore Roosevelt in March 1902.

NATTIER, Jean-Marc (1685, Paris—1766, Paris), French painter. When he was fifteen, his talent was noticed by the architect Jules Hardouin-Mansart, then superintendent of buildings, who gave him a stipend. Shortly afterward, Nattier obtained permission from Louis XIV to draw and then engrave the cycle of paintings by Rubens in the Luxembourg Palace, Paris, glorifying Marie de Médicis. This group of paintings was regarded as one of the marvels of European art, and the publication of the 24 plates of the *Galerie du Palais du Luxembourg* (1710) made Nattier famous. Peter the Great invited Nattier to St. Petersburg. Nattier accepted and went first in 1717 to Amsterdam, where the Czar and his court were staying. He painted portraits of the Czar, the Czarina, and a number of Russian noblemen. At the last moment, however, Nattier decided not to leave his country, but to remain in Paris. His ambition was to be a history painter and it was as such that he entered the Académie Royale de Peinture et de Sculpture in 1718, with his *Perseus Turning Phineus to Stone* (Tours, Museum); but circumstances forced him to remain a portraitist. The fashion was for the historical portrait, in which a living person was represented as a mythological deity. Nattier completely renewed this genre by his ingenuity. His first two successes were *Mademoiselle de Clermont* (1729; Chantilly, Musée Condé) as the goddess of the Waters of Health, and *Mademoiselle de Lambesc* (1732; Paris, Louvre) as Minerva. Fashionable ladies flocked to his studio to be painted as Aurora, Night, a Vestal Virgin, a Naiad, a Muse, and, above all, as Hebe, goddess of youth, holding a goblet from which an eagle is about to drink (*Louise de Bourbon, Duchess of Orléans, as Hebe*, 1744; Stockholm, Nationalmuseum). In 1740 his portraits of the Marquise de Flavacourt as *Silence* and of the Marquise de la Tournelle as *Daybreak* (both destroyed; replicas in Drottningholm Castle, Sweden) won the admiration of Maria Leszczynska, Louis XV's queen, who asked him to paint one of her daughters, Madame Henriette. As a result of this painting (1742; Versailles, Museum), in which he represented his model as Flora, Nattier became the official painter of the queen and of the princesses; he also painted the last portrait that Maria Leszczynska allowed to be made of herself (1748; Dijon, Museum). He exploited his facility and executed every commission; but, when the fashion changed, his artifices were highly criticized, and, at the end of his life, he lost his brilliant clientele.

NATURALISM. Although the concept of Naturalism became familiar in France only after 1870, when, under the Third Republic, it continued and expanded the Realism of the Second Empire, the word had long been in use in the sense given it in the 17th century by the Académie Royale de Peinture et de Sculpture: "The exact imitation of nature in all things." Naturalism, however, only came into its own with the novelist Émile Zola and his friends in the Medan group (so called after their joint publication of *Les Soirées de Medan*, 1880), whose most important members were Guy de Maupassant and Joris Karl Huysmans. The Naturalistic writers supported the Impressionist painters; but it is obvious that they appreciated art above all as a social document, and that their conception of art attached more importance to the modernity of the subject than to plastic experiments. After acting as the apologist of Édouard Manet and Paul Cézanne, Zola, in his "Nouvelle Campagne" of 1896 in the *Figaro*, praised a number of academic painters who, in his opinion, were closer to the Naturalist ideal: Alfred Stevens, painter of society genre, for "his delicate and accurate sincerity"; Alfred Philippe Roll (1846–1919), "the sunny poet of crowds and space"; and even the military painter Édouard Detaille (1848–1912) for his "admirable precision and sharpness!" A better judge, the art critic Louis Édmond

Naturalism. Max Liebermann. *Courtyard of the Amsterdam Orphanage.* 1882. Städelsches Kunstinstitut, Frankfurt.

Duranty, in *La Nouvelle Peinture* (1876), traced the program of Naturalism in art: "What we need is the particular quality of the modern individual, in his clothes, in his social habits, at home, and in the street." Huysmans, who lamented in *L'Art Moderne* (1883), "The Naturalists have so few painters to support!", also felt that painting should deal with every aspect of social life. Disappointed by Manet and despising Gustave Courbet, he praised Jean-François Raffaelli (1850–1924), "the painter of poor people and great skies"; Gustave Caillebotte, "painter of the bourgeoisie at ease, of trade and of finance"; Albert Bartholomé (1848–1928), "one of the few painters who understands modern life"; Jean-Louis Forain (1852–1931), whose watercolors received special praise; Henri Fantin-Latour, whom he reproached only with repeating himself; and above all Degas: "This artist is the greatest we now have in France." Acquiring a new definition, Naturalism in painting was now to be the unembellished description of the human condition, taking as its setting places of work or relaxation. This movement had disciples in various countries. In Germany, the tendency was primarily represented by Adolf von Menzel, who painted workers laboring by the light of the forges (*Rolling Mill*, 1875; Berlin, Staatliche Museen); by Wilhelm Leibl, with his scenes of peasant life; by Max Liebermann, with works like the *Turnip Field Worker* (1875; Hanover, Landesgalerie); in Belgium by Constantin Meunier, with the factory scenes he painted before turning to sculpture; in Russia, by Ilya Efimovich Repin (1844–1930), with the paintings that followed his famous *Volga Boatmen* (1870–73; Leningrad, State Russian Museum); in Hungary, by Mihály Munkácsy, who practiced a melodramatic Naturalism that made excessive use of chiaroscuro; and in Britain, but more timidly, by the Glasgow school, which included Sir John Lavery (1856–1941) before he became an official portrait painter.

NAUEN, Heinrich (1880, Krefeld, near Düsseldorf—1941, Kalkar, near Cleves), German painter. He studied at the academies in Düsseldorf (1898) and Stuttgart (1899–1902), then settled for several years (1902–5) in Laethem-St-Martin, Belgium. In 1911 Nauen settled in Dillborn in the Rhineland. There he joined the circle grouped around Heinrich Campendonk and August and Helmut Macke, and in 1913 contributed to the Rhenish Expressionists exhibition (*Portrait of Helmut Macke*, 1912; formerly Coll. Freiherr von de Heydt). Nauen was in fact one of the leading representatives of Rhenish Expressionism, and the highly luminous effects and violent colors of his early landscapes of the Lower Rhine are strongly reminiscent of Van Gogh and Matisse in his Fauvist period (*Landscape with Plow*, 1907; formerly Berlin, Coll. Prof. Dr. Flechtheim).

Neoclassicism. Antonio Canova. *Venus leaving the Bath.* 1812. Palazzo Pitti, Florence. *Photo Alinari-Giraudon.*

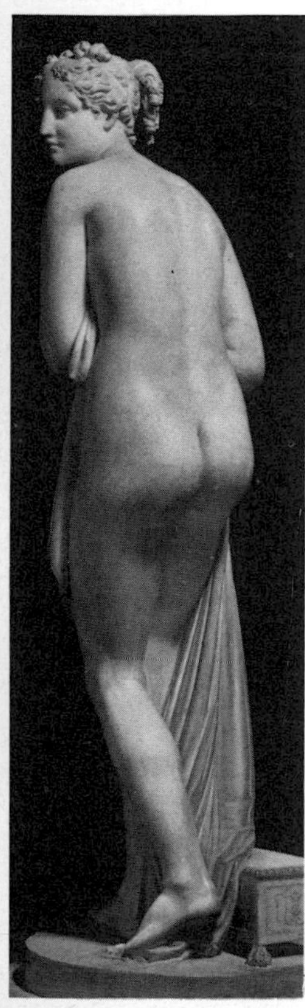

NAY, Ernst Wilhelm (1902, Berlin—1968, Cologne), German painter. His early paintings were influenced by Expressionism. He worked successively in Paris and Rome and, in 1937, was invited by the Norwegian Expressionist painter Edvard Munch to go to Norway. Nay worked in a neo-realistic style until 1948, after which time his painting became increasingly abstract. Even in his most abstract pictures, however, he remains a painter of reality. The principal elements in his compositions are round disks that are sometimes streaked with zigzags or shattered (*Epsilon*, 1959, Coll. artist; *Ecstatic Blue*, 1961, Cologne, Wallraf-Richartz-Museum; *Movement*, 1962, Munich, Coll. Günther Franke). In 1951 Nay settled in Cologne and joined the Zen group, a movement that was founded in 1949 and whose members wanted to introduce mysticism and spiritual values into their abstract art.

NAZARENES, a group of German painters active in Rome in the early 19th century. The Nazarene movement developed as a reaction against the Neoclassical aesthetic advocated by the German art historian Johann Joachim Winckelmann. The group was founded when, under the influence of the German philosopher Friedrich Schlegel's lectures and through the reading of the German art critic Wilhelm Heinrich Wackenroder's *Fantasies on Art* (1799), six foreign students at the Vienna Academy, who called themselves the Brotherhood of St. Luke, opposed the contemporary practice of imitating the works of Greco-Roman antiquity, and advocated instead an art based on the inspiration of primitive Christianity. In 1810 four of these students—Johann Friedrich Overbeck, Franz Pforr (1788–1812), Ludwig Vogel (1788–1879), and Johann Konrad Hottinger (1788–1828)—went to Rome, where they retired to the deconsecrated 16th-century monastery of S. Isidoro, behind the church of Trinità dei Monti. It was only after 1821, when the group left the monastery, that its members became known as the Nazarenes. Aside from its founders, the group also included the artists Peter Cornelius, Wilhelm Schadow, Philipp Veit (1793–1877), Julius Schnorr von Carolsfeld (1794–1872), Josef Führich (1800–76), and the minor painter and art historian Johann David Passavant (1787–1861). Their artistic program was "the revival of fresco painting as it was practiced from the great Giotto to the divine Raphael." In Rome, the Nazarenes collaborated in the production of two large fresco cycles. The first was done in 1816 for the Casa Bartholdy (in the Palazzo Zuccaro, now the Biblioteca Hertziana); these frescoes have been in the Staatliche Museen of East Berlin since 1888. They illustrate the *Story of Joseph*, and the most successful episode is Cornelius' *Recognition of Joseph by His Brothers*. The second group of frescoes was done between 1822 and 1832 for the Villa Massimo, near the church of S. Giovanni in Laterano. These illustrate themes from Dante's *Divine Comedy* (Joseph Anton Koch's *Dante Asleep, Threatened by Wild Beasts and Rescued by Virgil* and *The Ship of Souls and Mount Purgatory*, both 1827–29); scenes from Tasso's *Gerusalemme Liberata* (Overbeck's *Preparation for the Siege of Jerusalem*, 1823–25). These murals are the most successful works the Nazarenes produced in Rome. A few years after the completion of the Villa Massimo frescoes all the Nazarenes, except for Overbeck, left Rome for Germany, and the group disbanded. Art historians regard their works as the principal religious art of the German Romantic movement.

NEBEL, Otto (b. 1892, Berlin), German painter and poet. He attended the classes of Wassily Kandinsky, who influenced him deeply. Nebel's first exhibition took place in 1921; at that time, he was moving toward abstraction, but had not yet found a truly personal style. This came in 1924 with the paintings he called "architectures of light," consisting of a network of straight and curved lines that he set against a plain white background, in order to emphasize their equilibrium. Nebel worked on the review *Der Sturm*, and from 1931 he published several collections of caricatures that reveal a sharp vision of reality developed in the course of extensive travels throughout Europe. The development of his paintings always remained under the influence of the Bauhaus masters; in such paintings as *In Between* (1937; New York, Solomon R. Guggenheim Museum), he tried to reconcile, in a personal synthesis, the passionate rigor of Kandinsky and the poetic fantasy of Paul Klee.

NEGRO ART. *See* **AFRICAN ART.**

NELSON, Paul (b. 1895, Chicago, Illinois), American architect. He is best known for his project for a Suspended House (1938; model in New York, Museum of Modern Art) and for his Franco-American Memorial Hospital in St-Lô (1948–56). The Suspended House was an experimental project, but Nelson felt that it could be built and that it offered possibilities for mass production. The house offers seclusion, flexibility, a great deal of "useless" space, as well as additional aesthetic stimulation through sculpture and painting. Flexibility is provided by a rigid exterior framework from which the exterior walls and individual rooms are suspended. The house can thus be assembled or disassembled at will, and rooms can be added or subtracted. The ground floor, of reinforced concrete and glass brick, was conceived as a service area, the middle floor as a recreation area, and the upper floor, suspended from the roof, as more private, living space. For his hospital at St-Lô, Nelson made a very careful study of functional operations that allowed great economy and efficiency in the final building.

NEOCLASSICISM. The doctrine of the return to antiquity—on which Neoclassicism was based—developed and flourished in the international artistic circles of Rome, from about 1750 to the end of the century. It arose, in part, from the discovery and study of the buried cities of Herculaneum and Pompeii, and received impetus from the work of such antiquaries as the German Johann Joachim Winckelmann, whose *History of the Art of the Ancients* (1764) was the first serious attempt to study the subject. At about the same time, in 1763, James Stuart and Nicholas Revett discovered Greek art and published their findings. Artists and scholars came from all over Europe to add to the intellectual ferment: Italians, such as the architect-engraver Giovanni Battista Piranesi, the architect and archaeologist Francesco Milizia (1725–98), and the painter Pompeo Batoni (1708–87); Frenchmen, such as the sculptor Antoine Houdon and the architects Charles-Louis Clérisseau, Claude-Nicolas Ledoux, and Victor Louis (1735–*c.* 1811); Englishmen, such as the architect-decorator Robert Adam, the painter Gavin Hamilton, and, later, John Flaxman. Added to this list are the German painter Anton Raphael Mengs, a fine portraitist and formidable theoretician; and the Swiss painter Angelica Kauffmann, whose Roman salon was open to artists and travelers.

But the two men who, more than the theoreticians, gave the Neoclassical movement plastic justification were the French painter Louis David and the Italian sculptor Antonio Canova, a favorite of beautiful women, popes, and Emperor Napoleon.

Rococo ornamentation gave way to a more severe style of decoration. In architecture, the column replaced the pilaster, and exterior walls had to obtain their effect without benefit of ornament. Sculptures were based strictly on the Classical statues and bas-reliefs that filled the newly founded museums. In painting, color was de-emphasized in favor of sharp outlines. Sometimes chiaroscuro was abandoned altogether, and attention concentrated exclusively on the line.

From Rome Neoclassicism spread, in the late 18th and early 19th centuries, throughout Europe. In Rome itself one of its most remarkable achievements in the field of town planning was the arrangement of the Piazza del Popolo, the work of Giuseppe Valadier (1814–20; based on plans dating from 1794). In Naples, the Piazza del Plebiscito, with its semicircular colonnade and church of S. Francesco di Paola—begun in 1817 by Pietro Bianchi (1787–1849) and copied from the Pantheon—is an imposing if somewhat cold group.

In France and England Neoclassicism fell on particularly well-prepared ground. In French architecture, it appeared in the work of Jacques-Ange Gabriel and Jacques-Germain Soufflot. On his return from Italy, well before the middle of the century, Gabriel had brought with him an already mature Classicism. As for Soufflot, he submitted his markedly more radical plans for the church of Ste-Geneviève (now the Panthéon) as early as 1755. France produced a whole generation of Neoclassical architects, many of them—such as Étienne-Louis Boullée, Claude-Nicolas Ledoux, Alexandre Brongniart, and Jean François Chalgrin—men of the highest talent. Like Clérisseau, who sold his portfolios to Catherine II, they were prolific craftsmen and produced plans of undeniable grandeur that circumstances, and often their excessive scope, prevented from being executed. Later, Charles Percier and Pierre François Fontaine (1762–1853) had to satisfy the demands of the emperor but they were more practical than the architects of the previous generation, if less exciting. On Napoleon's orders they created commemorative columns, obelisks, and triumphal arches, but the most important of them remained the Arc de Triomphe de l'Étoile, begun in 1806 by Chalgrin. In the field of cabinetmaking, the firm of Jacob-Desmalter produced rather heavy furniture in what is known as the Empire style.

In painting, David had no difficulty in dominating his rivals.

Neoclassicism. Robert Adam. Staircase, Osterley Park, Middlesex. After 1761. *National Buildings Record, London.*

With the *Sabine Women*, exhibited in Paris in 1799, he matched the success of his earlier *Oath of the Horatii* (1784; Paris, Louvre) and made as forceful an aesthetic statement. Even a master such as Baron Antoine-Jean Gros submitted unflinchingly to David's authority. Pierre-Paul Prud'hon, the only artist who can be compared with him, is in fact no less Neoclassical. In sculpture, the most important work was Houdon's nude, *Diana* (1780).

England had remained obstinately attached to the Classical architecture of Andrea Palladio, which had been introduced by Inigo Jones and revived by Lord Burlington. The latter had founded his Classicism well before 1750, and his Chiswick House (*c.* 1725) is a veritable Palladian Villa Rotonda. Colen Campbell's great collection of engravings of Classical architecture, the *Vitruvius Britannicus*, which appeared in three volumes between 1717 and 1725, helped Palladianism attain the authority of a national style. The Neoclassical masters were then the Adam brothers, especially Robert Adam, who had often visited Clérisseau in Rome and

Neoclassicism. Thornton, Hallet, Latrobe, and Bulfinch. Capitol, Washington, D.C. Completed 1863.

Spalato. When he returned in 1758 he became, with his brothers, the leading decorator in the country. From England, Neoclassicism spread to America, where most buildings, especially in the south, were given columned porches (George Washington's residence, Mount Vernon, 1787; Thomas Jefferson's residence, Monticello, 1770–1809). The most thoroughly Neoclassical structures were the state capitols of the new republic: that of Massachusetts in Boston by Charles Bulfinch, that of Virginia at Richmond by Thomas Jefferson, and, most important, that of Washington, D.C., whose construction was extended almost to the end of the 19th century.

As we have seen, the German theoreticians, notably Winckelmann and Mengs, played an important role, even in Rome, in the development of the Neoclassical doctrine. As a result, Neoclassicism left a considerable mark on Germany, especially in Berlin and Munich. The Neoclassical conquest of Berlin is symbolized, as it were, by the Brandenburg Gate (1788–89), built by Carl Gotthard Langhans (1732–1808). But he is eclipsed by Carl Friedrich Schinkel, whose two Berlin masterpieces are the Guard House (1816–18) and the colonnade of the Old Museum (from 1824). In fact, Berlin was the center of a particularly remarkable Neoclassical architecture, which includes the work of Heinrich Gentz (1766–1811), who designed the small Classical temple (1812–13) in Charlottenburg Park. David Gilly (1748–1808) and his son Friedrich (1772–1800) also belonged to this group. Despite his early death, Friedrich Gilly had a great influence on his contemporaries. One of his pupils, Leo von Klenze (1794–1864), was responsible for redesigning Munich: his Königsplatz, flanked by the Glyptothek (1816–30), the Alte Pinakothek (1826–36), and the Propylaea (after 1848), is an impressive Neoclassical group. But the main statement of Klenze's Neoclassical principles is the Walhalla (1830–42), which, despite its German mythological name, is a peripteral Ionic temple built on a high base on a magnificent site near Regensburg.

Neoclassicism was enormously successful in Northern Europe. Thus the architect Johann Carl Ludwig Engel (1778–1840), a pupil of Friedrich Gilly, filled Helsinki with Neoclassical works. Klenze was commissioned to build the Hermitage Museum at St. Petersburg, where the façades by Thomas de Thomon (1743–1813), Vallin de la Mothe (1729–1800), Giacomo Quarenghi, and Carlo Rossi (1755–1849) made that city one of the most magnificent Neoclassical capitals of Europe. In Sweden, the academicism of the sculptor Johan Tobias Sergel (1740–1814) gave his work a certain coldness, but his drawings reveal a more passionate temperament. The father of Danish painting, Nicolai Abraham Abildgaard, was a Classicist, though he was tempted by Romanticism. But the most striking case is undoubtedly that of his fellow-countryman, Bertel Thorvaldsen, to whom a whole museum is devoted in Copenhagen, and who, with Canova, is reputedly the greatest Neoclassical sculptor.

Neoimpressionism. Georges Seurat. *Café-concert.* 1887. Museum of Art, Rhode Island School of Design, Providence.

NEOIMPRESSIONISM, French art movement that developed in the 1880s and early 1890s under the leadership of Georges Seurat, Paul Signac, and their followers. It was based on the scientific study of color and the systematic division of tone. The art critic Félix Fénéon first used the term "Neoimpressionism" in the Brussels magazine *L'Art Moderne*, in the issue of September 19, 1886. It was then repeated by the Parisian art critic Arsène Alexandre in his review (which appeared in the December 10, 1886, issue of *L'Événement*) of Fénéon's famous pamphlet, *Les Impressionnistes en 1886*. The term was given final consecration by Fénéon himself, in *L'Art Moderne* of May 1887, in a decisive essay entitled *Le Néo-Impressionnisme*. In this article he formulated the movement's aesthetic and defined its techniques.

The dispersion of the Impressionist group in 1880 was accompanied by an increasing inflexibility in their method and a return to Classical discipline. In the same year the scientist David Sutter published an important series of articles in the magazine *L'Art* on the *Phenomena of Vision*, in which he outlined 167 rules that prefigured the Neoimpressionist program and concluded with a statement that favored a link between art and science. The psychology and physiology of vision, the problems of optics, and the analysis of light and color became frequent subjects for discussion. Seurat received his artistic training in this climate of theoretical fervor; he was already composing paintings in 1882 with dotted brushstrokes and regular hatchings of vibrant luminosity. In the spring of 1884, together with the artists who had been rejected by the official Salon, Seurat founded the Salon des Indépendants, where he exhibited his first major painting, *Bathing at Asnières* (1883–84; London, National Gallery). The numerous exhibitors included—although they did not yet know each other—Signac, Henri-Edmond Cross, Charles Angrand (1854–1926), and Albert Dubois-Pillet (1846–90). In June of 1884, with Odilon Redon as president, they formed the Société des Artistes Indépendants. In December, at their first exhibition, Seurat once again presented his *Bathing at Asnières*. Signac, whose objectives paralleled those of Seurat, was enthralled by this canvas, and became the latter's most ardent propagandist. In 1885 Signac met Camille Pissarro, whom he introduced to Seurat. Pissarro enthusiastically adopted the new technique as a solution to his need for order and structure, and also interested his eldest son Lucien in the movement. Between 1884 and 1886 Seurat executed his second great composition, *Sunday Afternoon on the Island of La Grande Jatte* (Chicago, Art Institute). It was based on tonal contrasts created in accordance with his newly perfected technique, and on a methodical fragmentation of the brushstroke—a method that he called divisionism and that ultimately became pointillism.

Divisionism, explained Signac, who was the theoretician of the group, "guarantees all the benefits of luminosity, color, and harmony: (1) by the optical mixture of pure pigments (all the colors of the prism and all their tones); (2) by the separation of different elements such as local color, the color of the light, as well as the colors produced by their interactions; (3) by the balancing of these elements and their proportions (according to the laws of contrast, of gradation, and irradiation); (4) by the selection of a brushstroke proportionate to the size of the canvas."

In March of 1886 the art dealer Paul Durand-Ruel went to New York with 300 Impressionist paintings, as well as works by Signac and Seurat, including the latter's *Bathing at Asnières*. That same year, the *Grande Jatte* was the chief attraction at the final Impressionist exhibition, held in Paris from May 15 to June 15. This exhibition marked the breakup, impending since 1880, of the original group, and the official appearance of the Neoimpressionists. Claude Monet, Pierre Auguste Renoir, and Alfred Sisley withdrew; Edgar Degas, on the other hand, accepted the participation of Seurat, Signac, and Camille and Lucien Pissarro, allowing them to exhibit in the same room, but asking that the word "Impressionist" be eliminated from the poster and rejecting the paintings by Angrand and Dubois-Pillet as inadequate. Fénéon's meeting with Seurat and his friends dates from this time. The group exhibited together at the second Salon des Indépendants (August-September, 1886), when Seurat again showed his *Grand Jatte*. In February of 1887 Pissarro, Seurat, and Signac were invited to participate in an exhibition organized by the independent Brussels group known as Les Vingt, who were led by the Belgian lawyer and art critic Octave Maus. The *Grande Jatte* converted several Belgian artists to divisionism, including Henry van de Velde and Théo van Rysselberghe. New divisionists emerged in France—Hippolyte Petitjean (1854–1929), Maximilien Luce, and Lucie Cousturier (1870–1925), to name only the most important—and the movement spread to Italy, where its disciples included Giovanni Segantini, Gaetano Previati (1852–1920), and Angelo Morbelli (1853–1919). Finally, three leading late 19th-century artists were influenced by Seurat and for a time even practiced divisionism, although they never actually belonged to the Neoimpressionist group: they were Paul Gauguin in 1886, Henri de Toulouse-Lautrec in 1887, and Vincent van Gogh for almost the whole of his Parisian period (1886–88).

After Seurat's death in 1891, the Neoimpressionists implored Pissarro to assume leadership of the movement, but he refused—having, in fact, already abandoned divisionism and returned to the freer manner of his earlier works. Only Lucie Cousturier, Cross, and Signac—who in 1899 published his definitive account of Neoimpressionism in *D'Eugène Delacroix au Néo-Impressionnisme*—remained faithful to the spirit of a method that, while being a mere formula for many painters, was the vehicle through which Seurat had expressed his architectonic genius. Henri Matisse established the principles of Fauvism during his pointillist phase in 1899 and then during the summer of 1904, when he met Signac and Cross, with whom he spent the summer painting at St-Tropez. The birth of Cubism was facilitated by the important Seurat retrospective exhibition held at the Salon des Indépendants in 1905.

NEOPLASTICISM, a theory of pure plastic form derived from Cubism by the Dutch painter Piet Mondrian between 1912 and 1917. It proposed the exclusive use of the right angle in a horizontal-vertical position and of the three primary colors plus the "noncolors," black, white, and gray. Mondrian developed the Neoplastic idea after five years (1912–17) of experimentation and active thought with brush or pen in hand. His first disciple was the Dutch artist and poet Theo van Doesburg, whom he met in Amsterdam in 1915 and with whom he published the magazine *De Stijl* (1917–28), which was the main organ of radical Neoplasticism until 1924. Mondrian was assisted in this venture by the Hungarian architect and painter Vilmos Huszar (b. 1884) and the Belgian painter and sculptor Georges Vantongerloo. From 1924 until his death in 1944, he continued to apply the principles of Neoplasticism to his art. Apart from innumerable articles in *De Stijl*, Mondrian developed his ideas in a pamphlet, *Le Néo-Plasticisme* ("Neoplasticism"), published in 1920 by the Parisian art dealer Léonce Rosenberg's Galerie de l'Effort Moderne.

NERI, Manuel (b. 1930, Sanger, California), American sculptor. His work was exhibited widely on the West Coast, where he was a prominent figure in the development of the art of that region.

A former student of Richard Diebenkorn's, Neri began his career as an Abstract Expressionist painter, but later worked primarily in sculpture and occasionally in ceramics. Some of his early sculpture, done in painted plaster (*Loops No. 1*, 1961; Los Angeles, Coll. Peter Voulkos), is characterized by the irreverent, garish style of Funk art that was then gaining popularity in northern California. In the following several years Neri developed a major group of work with his life-size, nude, painted plaster figures, which emit a disturbing and morbid quality through their anonymity, sexlessness, and indeterminate stance (*Figure Standing Around*, 1964). Neri has used color in these images in a fairly decorative, attractive way, but has otherwise left a rough, unfinished-looking form. Around 1966 Neri made a sharp break with his former subject matter and Expressionistic style and began creating geometric abstract constructions (*Untitled*, 1966; San Francisco, Quay Gallery).

NERVI, Pier Luigi (b. 1891, Sondrio, Lombardy), Italian engineer and a leading figure in modern Italian architecture. From the beginning Nervi thought of himself only as a building technician, disavowing any aesthetic preconceptions. When he opened his own firm in 1920, he was able both to plan and supervise the work, and sought to become a large-scale contractor using the most efficient methods he could obtain or develop. His first work was the Augusteo Cinema in Naples (1926–27), but he first attracted attention and praise for his Municipal Stadium in Florence (1930–32). Nervi introduced intuitive hypotheses into his calculations that proved workable in practice, a method he called "static sensibility." He invented a process of prefabrication and a kind of reinforced concrete (*ferro-cemento*), which, because of its extreme flexibility, lends itself to the most varied combinations of forms.

The great Exhibition Hall at Turin (1948–49), with its superb dome, apse, and four inclined supporting arches, consists only of an immense roof with a 250-foot span, made entirely from interlocking, prefabricated units only two inches thick. In the Casino of Ostia Lido (1950), the roof is supported by a central pillar, which gives the ceiling the appearance of an open flower. In the salt warehouse at Tortona (1950–51), a light and spacious area is created by the ingenious use of parabolic vaults. The roof units of the building for the spa of Chianciano (1952) are also used as internal decoration and suggest an enormous rose window. Again, in the tobacco factory at Bologna (1952), the juxtaposition of prefabricated panels by means of special framing produced a surprising checkered ceiling. Finally, the Gatti spinning factory in Rome (1953) has mushroom columns whose ribs follow curves that indicate the directions of imaginary armatures.

From 1946, he was professor of technology at the Rome Faculty of Architecture, and was made doctor *honoris causa* of the University of Buenos Aires. Nervi also worked with some of the best architects of his age. In the Plinary Hall of the UNESCO Building in Paris (1953–57), on which he collaborated with Marcel Breuer and Bernard Zehrfuss (b. 1911), the lightness of the construction is emphasized by the balconies that rest on their own supports, completely free of the walls. In the Pirelli skyscraper in Milan (1955–59, with Gio Ponti), Nervi was responsible for the incomparable effect produced by pillars that divide and taper at their ends. In Rome, he built the domed Palazzetto dello Sport (1957), encircled by V-shaped supports, the larger Palazzo dello Sport (1960), and the Stadio Flaminio (1959), in collaboration with his son, Antonio. Nervi's unfailing virtuosity was again apparent in a later exhibition hall for Turin (1961), a huge square supported on 16 palmlike piers. His first building in the United States was the Port of New York Authority Bus Terminal (1962), built on the axis of the George Washington Bridge and using a similar truss system. Nervi's factory near Mantua (1963), with its suspended roof, and his skyscraper in Montreal, Canada (1966), confirmed his reputation as a creator of elegant solutions to difficult structural problems.

Pier Luigi Nervi and Annibale Vitellozzi. Palazzetto dello Sport, Rome. 1957. *Photo Roger-Viollet, Paris.*

NETSCH, Walter Andrew (b. 1920, Chicago, Illinois), American architect. Netsch worked under Lloyd M. Yost (b. 1908) in Kenilworth, Illinois (1946–47), and eventually joined the firm of Skidmore, Owings & Merrill in their San Francisco office (1947). After four years as an associate in Chicago (1951–55), he became a full partner of the firm in 1955.

After 1951, when he designed the United States Postgraduate School in Monterey, California (1952–55), Netsch was concerned with large-scale campus planning. Several departments at the Naval School, such as mechanical and aeronautical engineering, were housed together because their needs and services were related—a technique that Netsch adopted in later projects. At the United States Air Force Academy, near Colorado Springs, Colorado (1956–62), Netsch again consolidated related activities (administrative, social, and academic) on a strict modular grid. The I- and T-shaped plan in its vast natural setting contrasts with the radial plan of the Circle Campus at the University of Illinois in the dense urban environment of Chicago (first phase completed 1964). Here lecture halls, used by all departments, and a great open plaza above, serve as the academic and social nucleus. Around this center lie classrooms, laboratories, and offices. Circulation is provided at two levels to separate pedestrian and vehicular traffic, with ramps and stairs connecting them.

NEUE SACHLICHKEIT. This term, which means "New Objectivity" and which was coined by the painter G. F. Hartlaub in 1923, refers to the neorealistic style of a number of German painters of the 1920s. Hartlaub, recognizing some affinities in their work, brought their works together in 1925 in an exhibition at the Mannheim Kunsthalle, of which he had been director. These artists never formed a school and never issued a common credo. The New Objectivity can be seen primarily as a reaction against Expressionism, and its emergence prompted the critic Franz Roh to compile the characteristics that he regarded as typical of Expressionism on the one hand and the New Objectivity—which he termed Magic Realism—on the other. Roh's analysis, while illuminating, is also misleading, since the intensity of the German neorealist style would not be possible without Expressionism as a precursor.

Neue Sachlichkeit art developed along two principal lines. The earlier derived partially from the anti-art of Dada, with the important difference that its opponents were strongly committed politically, socially, and morally. The major representatives of this verist strain were George Grosz, the violent satirist of post-World War I German society, and Otto Dix. Both artists had taken part in the Dada movement. At first Grosz's work also showed the influence of Futurism; later he turned to a harder, more brutal descriptive manner, and his comments became, if anything, more trenchant. Dix's was a world of haunted images on morbid themes, realized by the artist with excruciating attention to detail.

The Romantic side of the movement is shown in the work of those artists who, partly under the influence of Pittura Metafisica (*see* METAPHYSICAL PAINTING) and the Italian Valori Plastici aesthetic (a realist movement stressing sculpturesque form, emotional restraint, and geometric precision in the composing and rendering of objects), sought a monumental quality and concentrated their attention on the surface design. Perhaps the best-known artists to display this tendency were the apolitical Georg Schrimpf (1898–1938) and Alexander G. Kanoldt, who was suspected of National Socialist sympathies. In fact, most of the New Objectivity painters were banned by the Nazis and saw their works held up as examples of "degenerate art." Neue Sachlichkeit ceased to be a viable stylistic label after the 1920s, since most of its practitioners, except Grosz, had moved toward a Romantic realism of blunted emotional impact.

NEUMANN, Johann Balthasar (1687, Eger, Bohemia—1753, Würzburg, Franconia), one of the great German Baroque architects. Neumann came to architecture through his career as a military engineer in the service of the Schönborn family, prince-bishops of Würzburg. The deaths, in quick succession, of his three predecessors, Valentino Pezzani (d. 1716), Andreas Müller (d. 1719), and Joseph Greising (1664–1721), enabled Neumann to assume leadership in directing work on the Residenz, the prince-bishop's enormous palace. From 1720 he held a position scarcely subordinate to that of Johann Lukas von Hildebrandt, whom he finally replaced in 1737. He was given the rank of colonel in 1741, and it was in the uniform of that rank that Giambattista Tiepolo portrayed him in his fresco on the ceiling of the grand staircase (1750–53) of the Residenz.

Neumann's style was first formed by study of the engravings of Joseph Furttenbach (1591–1667) and Paul Decker (1677–1713), as well as the writings of Nikolaus Goldman. Architects such as Maximilian von Welsch (1671–1745), Johann Dientzenhofer (1663–1726), and later the Viennese J. B. Fischer von Erlach and Hildebrandt, were also important influences. In 1723 Neumann was sent to Paris to consult with the royal architects Robert de Cotte and Germain Boffrand, to whom he submitted plans for the Würzburg Residenz. He built bridges, aqueducts, and dams, and was as much a skillful engineer as an architect.

The construction of the Würzburg Residenz was begun in 1719, according to the plans of Maximilian von Welsch and Hildebrandt, and was completed by Neumann during the next 30 years. Neumann's individual style is already apparent in the chapel, where alternately Classical and twisted columns support the sinuous projection of the prince's gallery. His touch is even more evident in the Kaisersaal, or imperial hall, an octagonal room that echoes the central projection of the main garden façade. It was also under Neumann's direction that the stuccoworker Antonio Bossi and the painter Johannes Zick (1702–62) decorated the White Hall, the Oval Hall overlooking the gardens, and the Venetian Hall. The place of honor, however, is given to the ceremonial staircase (1734), where a central flight leads up to the landing, turns through 180 degrees, and returns in two flights, allowing a gradual appreciation of the vastness of the hall. It is dominated by the largest fresco in the world, completed by Tiepolo in November 1753, shortly after the architect's death.

A similar arrangement was adopted at Schloss Brühl, which Neumann completed for Clemens-August of Cologne, where the well of the grand staircase (1740) is inundated with light at the end of a dark vestibule. Finally, in Schloss Werneck in Schweinfurt (1733–37), the magnificent staircase, with its surrounding balconies, is reminiscent of the equally famous one built by Johann Dientzenhofer and Hildebrandt at Schloss Weissenstein, Pommersfelden.

It is in his religious architecture, often in country churches, that Neumann reveals one of the dominant characteristics of his art—his mastery of spatial composition. The structure of these fine churches is often based on the complex interpenetration of several circular or elliptical spaces. The boldest expression of these new ideas is to be found in the pilgrimage church of Vierzehnheiligen, Franconia (begun 1743). With the help of the stuccoworker Johann Michael Feuchtmayer and the painter Giuseppe Appiani, Neumann transformed Vierzehnheiligen into one of the most astonishing creations of the Baroque imagination.

In spite of their variety and flexibility, it is possible to reduce the plans of Neumann's churches to a few basic types. A simple nave, preceded by a single tower and bordered by very thick walls, is the model used at Steinbach (1724–25) and in the St. Paulinkirche, Trier (begun 1734). A cruciform plan was used at the Benedictine abbey church of Neresheim (from 1747; with interpenetrating elliptical circular spaces as at Vierzehnheiligen) and

Johann Balthasar Neumann. Residenz, Würzburg. *Photo Kersting.*

at the pilgrimage church of Gössweinstein (1730–39). While the pilgrimage church of Maria Limbach (Hassfurt, 1753–55) has the traditional plan of the "Hallenkirche," a cruciform plan with a flat dome over the transept was used (1741) in the parish church at Etwashausen, Gaibach (1742–45), and in the pilgrimage church of Nikolausberg, near Würzburg (1747–50). Finally, Neumann also adapted a Rococo nave to a Gothic choir, as in the Peterskirche at Bruchsal (1738).

NEUTRA, Richard Joseph (b. 1892, Vienna—d. 1970), American architect of Austrian origin. Neutra completed his studies at the Vienna Technische Hochschule in 1917, and after a further training period in Switzerland, he went to Germany in 1921. The following year, he formed a partnership with Erich Mendelsohn in order to participate in a competition for a business center at Haifa, Israel. They won the first prize, and Neutra was able to go to the United States and study the methods of American architects. He worked in William Holabird's office in Chicago, then did a year's apprenticeship with Frank Lloyd Wright at the architect's studio, Taliesen, in Spring Green, Wisconsin. Neutra became his best pupil, following Wright's principles of the interpenetration of nature and architecture, but replacing the master's sense of fantasy by an austere elegance of his own. In 1924 Neutra began a theoretical study for an urban center of a million inhabitants that he called "Rush City Reformed." He worked out innumerable town-planning and architectural schemes for this imaginary city, and many of the houses he built later are derived from these studies. In 1926 he settled permanently in Los Angeles, where he worked for another Austrian architect, Ru-

Richard Joseph Neutra. Lovell Health House, Griffith Park, California. 1927–29. *Photo Julius Shulman, Los Angeles.*

dolph Schindler (1887–1953), before setting up his own practice. In the same year, he published *Wie baut Amerika*, an excellent analysis of American industrialized methods. In 1928 he invented the "Diatom" prefabricated house, composed of two living units and a garage; each unit had its roof and floor suspended from a central mast. But Neutra's reputation in this area is founded on the Lovell Health House (1927–29) at Griffith Park, near Los Angeles. Its steel framework, composed of speedily assembled elements, was then an innovation. Another highly praised work was the Corona School Bell (1935) at Los Angeles. This was a school based on an "annular" plan, developed in "Rush City Reformed." Throughout his career, Neutra inaugurated many technical innovations: he was one of the first American architects to use radiant heating, to introduce lamination for covering outside walls, and to study the use of sheet metal as a supporting element. With the residence of Josef von Sternberg in the San Fernando Valley (1936), Neutra began a series of luxurious California houses. At the same time, he took a great interest in the problem of a "villa block," that is, a building combining centralized services with the advantages of a single-family house. This led to a series of projects in Los Angeles: Landfair (1937), Strathmore (1938), and above all Kelton (1939), which provided the inhabitants with a maximum of comfort and independence. During World War II, he created "garden cities," the most famous of which was the low-income Channel Heights Housing Project (1942–44) at San Pedro, California.

After the war, his art underwent a dynamic evolution, and a "Neutra school" grew up, composed of young architects who had received their training in his office. Although he was deeply interested in complex programs, such as a group of hospitals and schools in Puerto Rico, Neutra remained above all the architect of the private house. His masterpieces include the Nesbitt House at Brentwood (1942), described as one of the five most beautiful houses in California; the famous Kaufmann "Desert House" at Palm Springs (1946–47); and the Tremaine House at Santa Barbara (1947–48), with its cruciform plan.

NEVELSON, Louise (b. 1900, Kiev, Russia), American painter and sculptress of Russian origin. She grew up in Rockland, Maine, and in 1920 went to live in New York, studying painting with Kenneth Hayes Miller (1878–1952) at the Art Students League (1929–30). In 1931 she went to Munich, where she attended the classes of the German painter Hans Hofmann at the art school he directed. In 1932 and 1933 she worked as an assistant to the Mexican painter Diego Rivera, who employed her to execute his mural paintings. She then began to work as a sculptress, and gave her first exhibition at the Nierendorf Gallery, New York, in 1941. In 1956 she exhibited a series of sculptures in New York on the theme of the *Royal Journey*; then, in 1958, a group of columns and boxes under the general title of *Moon Garden + One*. She later turned to wood carving, at first producing horizontal abstract reliefs that looked like disconcerting elements from unusable furniture. She then created "images of cities," which were constructions consisting of vertical caissons filled with accumulations of architectural debris and meaningless objects that looked like fragments of an unknown civilization, all carefully preserved and arranged (*Wedding Feast at Dawn*, 1959; New York, Museum of Modern Art). In 1959 Nevelson, who also produced lithographs and drawings, was awarded the Grand Prize for sculpture in the ART:USA competition.

NEVINSON, Christopher Richard Wynne (1889, Hampstead, London—1946, London), English painter of figure subjects and landscapes, also active as a lithographer and etcher. In 1912 he went to Paris, where he studied at the Académie Julian and the Cercle Russe, and where he also shared a studio for a time with Amedeo Modigliani. Nevinson was a founding member of the London Group in 1913, and was closely associated with the Futurist movement, publishing the manifesto *Vital English Art* (1914) with the Italian critic and Futurist leader Filippo Tommaso Marinetti. Nevinson was an official war artist in World Wars I and II, and in his World War I work was influenced by the angular, Cubistic stylization common to Futurism and Vorticism. He exhibited in the London Vorticist Exhibition of 1915, but transcended the mannerisms inherent in the idiom through a mixture of imagination and sensitivity, producing as a result some of the most genuinely touching pictures of the war (*Paths of Glory*, *c.* 1916, London, Imperial War Museum; *Column on the March*, 1915, Ottawa, National Gallery of Canada). *La Mitrailleuse* (1915; London, Tate Gallery) is a good example of Nevinson's style in its more angular phase.

NEW ENGLISH ART CLUB, association of British painters formed in 1885, their main intent being to hold exhibitions that would challenge the traditionalism and complacency of the Royal Academy. Their emphasis was on unacademic subject matter, open-air landscape painting, and scenes from middle-class or "low" life. All the paintings exhibited by the club, even works by the members themselves, were chosen by a jury elected by members—a significant departure from the Royal Academy's practice. When Walter Sickert became a member of the club in 1888, he brought with him the Impressionist influence of Edgar Degas, whom he had met in Paris in 1883. Whistler also exerted a strong influence; his famous "Ten O'Clock" lecture of 1885 affected many of the club's artists, urging them to be concerned with purely painterly problems rather than with anecdotal or "literary" pictures. Although Sickert, Philip Wilson Steer, and Frederick Brown (1851–1941) attempted to give unity to the club's work by organizing the London Impressionist Exhibition in 1889 (in which the influence of Whistler was especially apparent), the New English Art Club never constituted a coherent "movement" in English art. Dugald Sutherland MacColl, who wrote

184.

185.

184. **Master of St. Giles.** *St. Remigius Blessing the People on the Parvis of Notre-Dame.* 1490–1510. Samuel H. Kress Coll., National Gallery of Art, Washington, D.C.
185. **Michelangelo.** *Entombment of Christ. c.* 1508. National Gallery, London.
186. **Joan Miró.** *White Lady.* 1950. Private Coll., Paris.
187. **Hans Memlinc.** *Portrait of Martin van Nieuwenhove.* 1487. Hôpital St-Jean, Bruges.
188. **Henri Matisse.** *Open Window, Collioure.* 1905. Coll. John Hay Whitney, New York.
189. **Jean-François Millet.** *The Gleaners.* 1857. Louvre, Paris.

186.

187.

189.

188.

190.

191.

192.

193.

194.

195.

190. **Richard Mortensen.** *Jargeau*. 1953. Coll. Dr. Aronovitch, Stockholm.
191. **Edvard Munch.** *Anxiety*. 1894. Munch-Museet, Oslo.
192. **Amedeo Modigliani.** *Portrait of Chaim Soutine*. 1917. Staatsgalerie, Stuttgart.
193. **Piet Mondrian.** *Farmhouse at Duivendrecht*. *c.* 1906. Coll. Mrs. Isaac Schoenberg, Swarthmore.
194. **Gustave Moreau.** *Rape of Europa*. Musée Gustave Moreau, Paris.
195. **Robert Motherwell.** *Elegy to the Spanish Republic XXXIV*. 1954. Albright-Knox Art Gallery, Buffalo.
196. Opposite: **Claude Monet.** *Terrace at Sainte-Adresse*. Detail. *c.* 1867. Metropolitan Museum of Art, New York.

197.

198.

199.

200.

201.

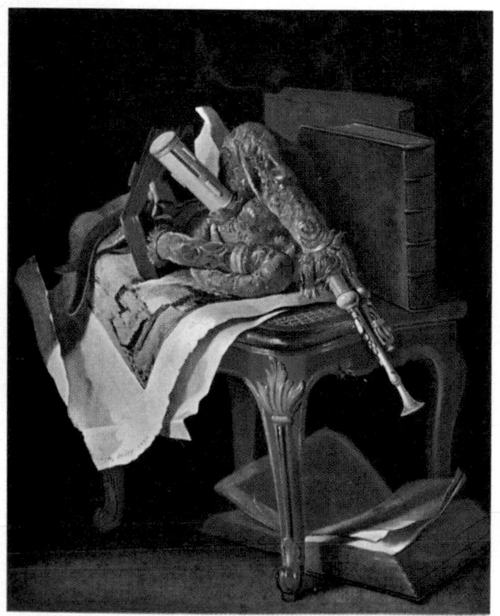

202.

203.

204.

205.

197. **Ben Nicholson.** *May 1957 (Aegina)*. Coll. Stephen M. Kellen, New York.
198. **Jean-Marc Nattier.** *Marquise d'Antin*. 1738. Musée Jacquemart-André, Paris.
199. **Emil Nolde.** *Luncheon Feast*. 1907. Coll. Walter Bareiss, Greenwich, Conn.
200. **Andrea Orcagna.** *Triumph of Death*. Fragment. *c.* 1360s. Museo dell'Opera di S. Croce, Florence.
201. **Isaac Oliver.** *Portrait of a Young Man, said to be Sir Philip Sidney*. Royal Coll., Windsor.
202. **Jean-Baptiste Oudry.** *Before the Fireplace: the Lacquered Footstool*. Coll. Paul Cailleux, Paris.
203. **Roderic O'Conor.** *Marine*. 1895. Oscar Ghez Modern Art Foundation, Geneva.
204. **Piero della Francesca.** *Sinigallia Madonna*. *c.* 1474–78. Galleria Nazionale delle Marche, Urbino.
205. **Parmigianino.** *Madonna of the Rose*. 1528–30. Gemäldegalerie, Dresden.
206. **Perugino.** *Apollo and Marsyas*. *c.* 1496. Louvre, Paris.
207. **Piero di Cosimo.** *Simonetta Vespucci*. Musée Condé, Chantilly.
208. **Francis Picabia.** *Optophone*. 1921. Formerly Coll. H.-P. Roche.
209. **Pinturicchio.** *Portrait of a Young Boy*. Gemäldegalerie, Dresden.

206.

207.

209.

208.

210.

211.

210. **Pisanello.** *Portrait of a Princess of the House of Este* (possibly Ginevra d'Este). *c.* 1443. Louvre, Paris.

212.

213.

214.

215.

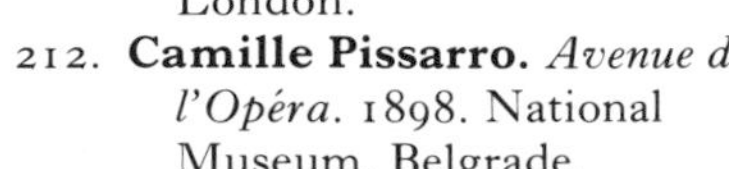

211. **John Piper.** *Somerset Place, Bath.* 1942. Tate Gallery, London.

212. **Camille Pissarro.** *Avenue de l'Opéra.* 1898. National Museum, Belgrade.

213. **Jacopo da Pontormo.** *Deposition.* 1526. S. Felicità, Florence.

214. **Serge Poliakoff.** *Composition Against a Green Background* Coll. Dotremont, Brussels.

215. **Jackson Pollock.** *Shooting Star.* 1947. Galerie Beyeler, Basel.

216. Opposite: **Pablo Picasso.** *La Vie.* Detail. 1903. Hanna Fund, Museum of Art, Cleveland.

217.

218.

219.

220.

221.

222.

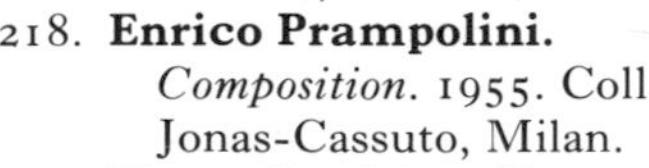

217. **Nicolas Poussin.** *Autumn, or the Spies with the Grapes from the Promised Land.* From the Four Seasons. 1660–64. Louvre, Paris.

218. **Enrico Prampolini.** *Composition.* 1955. Coll. Jonas-Cassuto, Milan.

219. **Pierre-Paul Prud'hon.** *Portrait of Empress Josephine.* 1805. Louvre, Paris.

220. **Pierre Puvis de Chavannes.** *The Poor Fisherman.* 1881. Louvre, Paris.

221. **Alphonse Quizet.** *Rue des Cascades at Belleville.* 1930. Oscar Ghez Modern Art Foundation, Geneva.

222. **François Quesnel.** *Portrait of Henri III. c.* 1575. Louvre, Paris.

for the *Spectator*, became the club's critic and prophet, and the art critics George Moore and Roger Fry supported him in their writings. The club's most vital years were from 1890 to 1914. In 1911 some of its younger members and devotees of Sickert formed the Camden Town Group; in 1913 the latter group, together with such other societies as Wyndham Lewis's Vorticists, merged to form the London Group, which thereafter replaced the New English Art Club in the vanguard of English painting. Nevertheless, the club was still holding exhibitions in the 1960s.

NEW REALISM, term invented by the French art critic Pierre Restany, who in May 1960 published a manifesto under this title at the Galleria Apollinaire, Milan, intended to cover the work of a group of artists who decided to use materials taken directly from everyday life. The group's first real exhibition took place in May 1961 at Restany's Galerie J. in Paris. Its title, "40 Degrees Above Dada," was intended to imply that the participants were also Neo-Dadaists and claimed allegiance to Marcel Duchamp's notion of the ready-made. This group included the French sculptor César, during the period in which he exhibited crushed cars; the French painter Yves Klein, who used a blowtorch to execute "fire paintings" on asbestos sheets; the Swiss sculptor Jean Tinguely, whose "metamechanics" enabled him to construct ironic figures from a seemingly random pile of scrap metal; Armand (Armand Fernandez Arman, b. 1928), who built "accumulations" by assembling piles of discarded objects; Raymond Hains (b. 1926), François Dufrêne (b. 1930), Mimmo Rotella (b. 1918), and Jacques de la Villeglé (b. 1927), all of whom specialized in damaged or "lacerated" posters, torn from walls, which they framed as pictures; Daniel Spoerri (b. 1930), who in his "picture-traps" stuck tables covered with dirty glasses and ashtrays or the remains of a meal together in a random arrangement and then hung them on the wall. Other artists who joined the New Realists included Martial Raysse (b. 1936), who painted *tableaux affreux* ("frightful pictures") and neon-lit landscapes; and the Bulgarian-born Christo (Christo Javacheff, b. 1935), who specialized in *empaquetages* ("packaging") and who in June 1962 went so far as to erect an Iron Curtain in Rue Visconti, Paris, which snarled traffic completely. Gérard Deschamps (b. 1937) assembled rags and wire netting, while Niki de Saint-Phalle (b. 1930) composed reliefs in which she combined plaster statuettes and children's toys.

NEWMAN, Barnett (1905, New York—1970, New York), American painter. In 1947, along with William Baziotes, Mark Rothko, and Robert Motherwell, he helped found a school on Eighth Street, New York, called "Subjects of the Artist," from which the famous "Club" meetings of the Abstract Expressionists developed during the early 1950s. Newman was an associate editor of *Tiger's Eye* (1947–48), a magazine published by these New York painters and dealing with the mythological and aesthetic themes that preoccupied them. With Adolph Gottlieb and Mark Rothko, Newman rebelled against both American regionalism and European geometric abstraction early in the 1940s. Without turning to European models, he sought inspiration in the archetypal creative force and vitality of Northwest Coast Indians and in pre-Columbian art.

The destruction of the void concerned him at first (*Pagan Void*, 1946, and *Genetic Moment*, 1947; both New York, Coll. Mrs. Annalee Newman), and his works were full of darkly eclipsed circular forms and streaks of scrubbed light, with titles evoking, but not illustrating, the myth of primordial creation. Evidence of Newman's concern for *declaring* a space and for establishing a presence appears, for example, in the seminal *Onement I* (1948; New York, Coll. artist). In this painting a band of cadmium red, running vertically down the center of a rectangular plum-colored field, is seen not as a line but as an area where *edges meet*, declaring a vital space that excludes all forms of representation or symbolism. Newman's characteristically grand, empty fields, often saturated with intense color and inflected with one or several vertical stripes of other colors, developed out of this small early work. He forces the viewer to concentrate on the *spatial* experience of sheer color, perceived in purely optical terms. A picture such as *Adam* (1951–52; New York, Coll. Ben Heller), with its close-valued areas of brown-maroon and scarlet, or *Cathedra* (1951; Pasadena, Calif., Museum) demonstrate this notion of powerfully affecting *color space*. This new attitude toward composition and forms exerted an important influence on such younger painters as Larry Poons and Frank Stella.

NICCOLÒ DELL'ABBATE. *See* **ABBATE,** Niccolò dell'.

NICCOLÒ DELL'ARCA *or* **NICCOLÒ DA BARI,** Nicola d'Apulia, *called* (*c.* 1435, Bari—1494, Bologna), Italian sculptor. He worked first in Naples and then went to Bologna, where, in a vein of northern realism, he executed a *Lamentation of Christ* in painted terra cotta with exaggeratedly gesticulating figures for S. Maria della Vita (1463). His reputation derives from the work that occupied him from 1469 for the tomb of St. Dominic at S. Domenico in Bologna. Begun in the 13th century by Nicola Pisano, the tomb was adorned by Niccolò with a roof-shaped crowning, for which he executed a *Christ of Mercy Adored by Two Angels* and various marble statuettes of *Prophets, Saints*, and *Evangelists*. Niccolò also carved the *Madonna with Saints*, a large terra-cotta group, dated 1478, that surmounts the entrance portal of the Palazzo Comunale, Bologna. His art is technically of high quality but reveals an unstable temperament that was hypersensitive to outside influences. This deprives his work of unity, though not of power.

NICHOLSON, Ben (b. 1894, Denham, Buckinghamshire), British painter and sculptor. The son of the painter Sir William Nicholson (1872–1949), he began to paint at a very early age. Nicholson made a series of journeys abroad—to France (1911–12), Italy (1912–13), the Portuguese island of Madeira (1913–14), and California (1917–18). In the course of these trips he sought a personal style, sketching landscapes and buildings in which he captured the structures and rhythms on which he later based his paintings. After 1930 he emphasized a spatial order—especially in his still lifes—that was opposed to all linear perspective and that was in-

Ben Nicholson. *White Relief.* 1939. Coll. Dr. J. L. Martin.

fluenced by Cubism. His meeting with the Dutch Neoplastic painter Piet Mondrian in 1933 gave his work a new and decisive orientation that is evident in the series of reliefs executed toward the end of the year: these are conceived in a Neoplastic spirit, and are composed exclusively of rectangles and squares in slight relief, the most successful examples of which are in white on white. Nicholson then began to take an active part in the avant-garde movement. In 1936 an exhibition of his work was held at the Museum of Modern Art in New York; in 1937 he was a coeditor, along with the English architect J. L. (now Sir Leslie) Martin and the Constructivist sculptor Naum Gabo, of *Circle: International Survey of Constructive Art*. In 1940 he and his wife, the sculptress Barbara Hepworth, went to live at St. Ives in Cornwall, and later in Switzerland.

Although Nicholson began painting in an abstract style around 1923, he never ceased to draw from nature. He felt that figurative and non-figurative art complemented each other, and synthesized these two tendencies in his still lifes, which formed some of his principal and most fertile themes. The brightly colored highlighting with which he formerly gave added power to certain forms (*Winter, November 1950*; Washington, D.C., Phillips Collection) gave way in his later works to warmer, more enveloping tones. He also replaced even applications of color with subtle gradations, and he varied his textures by introducing paint splashed from his brush, rubbings, and scratches. In his later reliefs, a harmony of subtle tones lends poetic reverberations to the sober formal constructions. Nicholson was awarded the Grand Prize of the Guggenheim Foundation in 1956, and the International Painting Prize at the São Paulo Bienal in 1957.

Nicola Pisano. *Nativity* (center), *with the Annunciation and Adoration of the Shepherds.* Detail, pulpit of the Baptistery, Pisa. 1260. *Photo Anderson-Giraudon.*

NICOLA PISANO (b. *c.* 1220/25 or earlier—d. 1284?), Italian sculptor. He is first documented in 1258 at Pisa, where two years later he signed the marble pulpit in the baptistery. With this imposing work, which treats Christian themes with the realism and nobility of Roman Classical art, sculpture re-emerges from its lowly status as part of the decorative detail of a building and becomes once more a grandly independent art that is the forerunner and counterpart of Giotto's oeuvre in painting. When Nicola executed the larger and even more ambitious marble pulpit in Siena Cathedral between 1265 and 1268, he had for his assistants his son Giovanni and Arnolfo di Cambio. The large Fontana Maggiore at Perúgia is Nicola's last work, signed by him and his son and dated 1278; it shows the influence of French Gothic sculpture in its lively detail and in its encyclopedic iconographic program, with its subject matter drawn from the Labors of the Months, the Seasons, the Virtues and Vices, the Signs of the Zodiac, and similar compilations of medieval knowledge.

NIEMEYER, Oscar Niemeyer Soares Filho, *called* Oscar (b. 1907, Rio de Janeiro), Brazilian architect. On leaving the School of Fine Arts at Rio in 1934, he entered the office of Lúcio Costa, with whom he worked on the National Ministry of Education building (1936–43). Since Le Corbusier had been officially invited to supervise the general plan of the ministry, Niemeyer had the opportunity of working with the great architect, and became his most brilliant disciple. Costa eventually gave up the direction of the group commissioned to build the ministry, and Niemeyer was elected unanimously to succeed him.

Niemeyer's first private building was the Obra de Berço Day School (1937) in Rio de Janeiro. Other works in Rio, like his project for a National Athletics Center (1941), or his own house (1942), showed how boldly he rejected the ubiquitous Neo-Colonial style of his contemporaries. Niemeyer's first major large-scale project was for a group of buildings at Pampulha, a recreation center beside an artificial lake near Belo Horizonte, built at the instigation of the town's mayor, Juscelino Kubitschek. In 1942 Niemeyer built the Pampulha Casino, with its onyx columns and satin-covered sun louvers; the "Baile" restaurant, whose undulating lines echo the contours of the embankment; and the Yacht Club, with its double-slope inverted roof. In the following year, he built the Grand Hotel, situated partly in a triangle that projects into the lake; and lastly, the church of S. Francisco.

Niemeyer's work continued to become increasingly lyrical and inventive in the rectangular block of the Cataguazes Boys' Academy (1946); the Boavista Bank in Rio (1946); the United Nations headquarters in New York (1947); and in the buildings for the Duchen Factory, near São Paulo (1950). He also began to take on more complex projects: the Kubitschek Building at Belo Horizonte (1951); and the Copan housing estate at São Paulo (1951), with internal streets containing shops, cabaret, and cinema. At this time, his style was marked by the use of V-shaped supports, long entrance ramps, and consistently curvilinear forms.

While these buildings were still in production Niemeyer, collaborating with other architects, designed a series of permanent pavilions in São Paulo's Ibirapuéra Park, built for an exhibition commemorating that city's fourth centenary. The Palace of Nations and Palace of States (1951), for exhibitions of painting; the Palace of Industry (1953), for exhibitions of machinery; the Palace of the Arts (1954), for sculpture; and the Palace of Agriculture (1955) all belong to this group of pavilions. A concrete marquee, supported on slender columns, tied the ensemble together.

When, in September 1956, President Kubitschek suggested that he build Brasilia, the new capital to be created in sparsely settled territory as an attempt to assist the underdeveloped regions, Niemeyer found an opportunity for demonstrating the full extent of his talent. Not only did he agree to plan the principal buildings, but he also undertook to direct the architectural section of Novacap, an official coordinating body for the entire enterprise. Niemeyer began with the Presidential Palace or "Palace of the Dawn" (officially opened on June 30, 1958), which owes its quality of lightness to a colonnade of sail-shaped roof supports screening the glass façade. But the work that stands out most from the whole group is the Square of the Three Powers. On one side of its base are the Law Courts, on the other the Planalto Palace, and, near its summit, the Houses of Parliament. The latter is a huge horizontal building on three levels housing the two chambers, each differentiated by the treatment of its roof (the Senate with a dome, the Chamber of Deputies with a saucer-shaped roof). A needed counterpoint to the horizontality of the group is provided by two high steel-framed towers, housing the administrative offices.

When President Kubitschek completed his term of office, Niemeyer took on several great national projects outside Brazil. In 1962 he drew up plans for the Tripoli Fair, in Libya. In 1964 he went to Israel, where he designed Haifa University, two complexes for the center of Tel Aviv (the Nordia commercial complex and the Panorama residential complex), and a new city in the Negev Desert.

NINO PISANO (b. *c.* 1315, Pisa?—d. 1368), Italian goldsmith, architect, and sculptor, the son and artistic heir of Andrea Pisano. He is first recorded in 1348–49, when he succeeded his father as master mason of Orvieto Cathedral, a post he held until 1353. In 1357 and 1358 Nino, employed as a goldsmith for the cathedral of Pisa, worked on an altar frontal that was completed later by his son, Andrea II. No works can be attributed to him with any certainty except for two signed versions of the *Madonna and Child*, one in the church of S. Maria Novella in Florence (*c.* 1360), the other forming part of the Cornaro monument in the church of S. Zanipolo, Venice (after 1365). The other attributions to Nino are all controversial, the best-known being the *Madonna del Latte*, which—along with the statues of *St. John the Baptist* and *St. Peter*—was formerly on the altar of S. Maria della Spina in Pisa (all 1365–68; all now in the Museo Nazionale, Pisa).

Oscar Niemeyer. View of the Square of the Three Powers, Brasilia. 1960. Left: Chamber of Deputies; center: administrative offices; foreground: Commemorative Museum. *Photo Marcel Gautherot, Rio de Janeiro.*

NIVOLA, Constantino (b. 1911, Orani, Sardinia), American sculptor. He studied art at the Istituto Superiore d'Arte in Monza, Italy (1930–36), where his teacher was Marino Marini, who was the first to interest him seriously in sculpture. From 1936 to 1939 Nivola was art director of the Olivetti Company. In 1939 he went to New York, where he held his first one-man exhibition of sculpture in 1950. From 1953 to 1957 he was director of the Design Workshop at Harvard University in Cambridge, Massachusetts, and from 1961 to 1963 he taught at Columbia University in New York.

He executed a number of commissions for large architectural reliefs, including one for the Olivetti Company showroom (1953–54) in New York, but also worked on a much smaller and more intimate scale, as in a series of small terra cottas of landscapes and seascapes in the early 1960s. He used nature imagery in a spontaneous, free style, frequently fusing it with figural suggestions (*Summer Day*, 1965; bronze, New York, Byron Gallery). Nivola was especially known for his reliefs in reinforced plaster; these had rich textural surfaces formed with sand and were often painted in bright colors (*Isposso*, 1953; reinforced plaster with sand, New York, Peridot Gallery).

NOGUCHI, Isamu (b. 1904, Los Angeles), American sculptor. After a childhood in Yokohama, he was sent to the United States, where he studied sculpture (1921) with Gutzon Borglum. In 1927, on a grant from the Guggenheim Foundation, he went to Paris, where he worked with Constantin Brancusi. In 1929 and 1930, after his return to New York, he exhibited portraits of friends and abstract sculptures, usually of sheet iron. He then traveled to the Far East (1930–31), staying for a time in Peking, where he learned calligraphic drawing. In 1936 he executed a relief in colored cement for the Rodriguez Public Market in Mexico City. During the interwar years, Noguchi developed his work in solitude, using every possible material to produce works of great formal delicacy. After World War II he rediscovered Japan, and was influenced by primitive *haniwa* sculpture. He produced works revealing an inextricable combination of Eastern and Western styles, and began to specialize in open-air sculpture, conceived as a

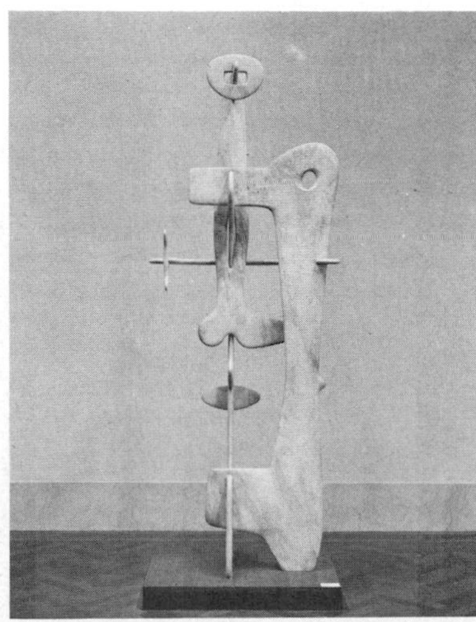

Isamu Noguchi. *Kouros.* 1944–45. Metropolitan Museum of Art (Fletcher Fund, 1953), New York.

ritual art of landscape. Thus he executed two bridges for the Peace Park at Hiroshima (1952), the statues and gardens of the Connecticut General Life Insurance Company in Hartford, Connecticut (1957), the Garden of Peace of the UNESCO Building in Paris (1958), the water garden of the Chase Manhattan Bank Plaza in New York (1964), the Billy Rose Art Garden (1965) of the Israel Museum in Jerusalem, and a colossal metal cube for the plaza of the Marine Midland Grace Trust Company in New York (1968).

NOLAN, Sidney (b. 1917, Carlton, Melbourne), Australian painter. He studied at the National Gallery School in Melbourne, exhibiting first with the Contemporary Art Society there in 1938. In 1942 he designed the sets and costumes for choreographer Serge Lifar's Australian production of *Icarus*, a ballet set to percussion music. In 1946 he began to execute works dealing with the legend of the notorious Australian outlaw, Ned Kelly—a theme that preoccupied him throughout his career (*Kelly*, 1954, London, Coll. Lord and Lady Snow; *Kelly at Glenrowan*, 1955, New York, Museum of Modern Art). Nolan also produced other groups of paintings devoted to such themes as the Australian desert (1949–50) and the drought (1957), which were done in a style of great atmospheric power. His later work included a series devoted to the legend of Leda and the Swan (*Leda and Swan*, 1958; Sydney, Art Gallery of New South Wales). Nolan traveled widely in Europe and North America, and ultimately settled in England.

NOLAND, Kenneth (b. 1924, Ashville, North Carolina), American painter. He studied art with Ilya Bolotowsky (b. 1907) at Black Mountain College in North Carolina (1946), and with Ossip Zadkine at the Zadkine School of Sculpture in Paris (1948–49). Noland's first one-man exhibition was held in 1949 at the Galerie Creuze in Paris, and his work was subsequently shown widely in the United States and in such international exhibitions as the Seattle World's Fair (1962) and the Venice Biennale (1964).

Noland's painting marked a significant departure from the dominating Abstract Expressionist movement in American art by its emphasis on color, untextured surface, and geometric form. An important catalyst for the development of Noland's major style was his introduction, in the early 1950s, to acrylic paints and to the particular way in which they were used by Helen Frankenthaler to stain the canvas. Like his friend Morris Louis, who began using acrylics at the same time, Noland often made large areas of bare canvas part of the total visual image. Central to the development of his art was the relationship between the image and the size and shape of the canvas. In the late 1950s and early 1960s Noland used the motif of concentric, hard-edged rings, precisely centered on a square canvas. Sometimes these rings were ellipsoid and appeared either centered (*Hover*, 1963; Cambridge, Mass., Fogg Art Museum), or above or below center, creating a laterally symmetrical organization of the canvas. Lateral symmetry was at first retained in Noland's next important structural motif, the chevron, which he began to use in 1962. By 1964, however, he had moved the chevrons off center to create an asymmetrical image. With this motif Noland also established a closer relationship between the painted image and the canvas through giving the canvas a diamond shape and having the legs of the chevron paralleling, and sometimes forming, the edges of its two sides (*Away*, 1964; Chicago, Coll. Walter A. Netsch, Jr.). The same fusion of canvas shape and image characterizes the elongated, diamond-shaped canvases of about 1966. In these paintings parallel stripes that rush diagonally across the surface were aligned with two edges of the parallelogram. In about 1967 these stripes lengthened into horizontal bands on extremely long and thin rectangular canvases (*Via Blues*, 1967; New York, André Emmerich Gallery). The essentially dynamic configurations produce a sense of movement along the bands themselves, while another apparent movement is produced by juxtapositions of the color with bare canvas or contrasts of adjacent color bands of the same or different widths. In this respect, as well as for his experiments with the relation of image to canvas, his art was significant in shaping the post-Abstract Expressionist period.

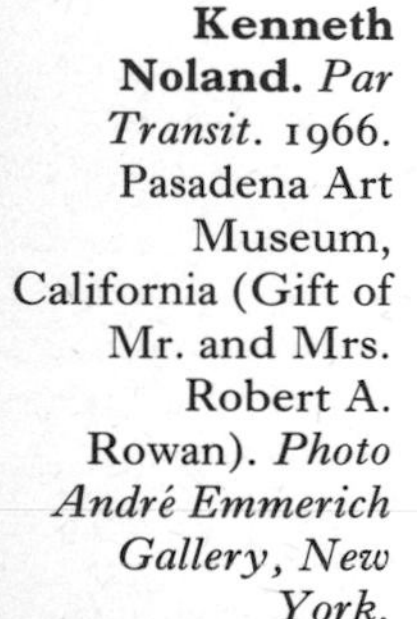

Kenneth Noland. *Par Transit*. 1966. Pasadena Art Museum, California (Gift of Mr. and Mrs. Robert A. Rowan). *Photo André Emmerich Gallery, New York.*

NOLDE, Emil Hansen, *called* Emil (1867, Nolde, Schleswig—1956, Seebüll, Schleswig), German painter. In 1898, while a drawing teacher at St-Gall in Switzerland, he decided to devote his life to painting and went to study with Adolf Hölzel at Dachau, near Munich. He then spent several months in Paris (1899–1900), where he admired above all the works of Honoré Daumier and Édouard Manet. Around 1904, his work was marked by a certain Impressionist influence, and it was not until some years later—through the influence of Edvard Munch and Vincent van Gogh—that he evolved his true style. In 1906 he was invited by the Expressionist painters of the Die Brücke group in Dresden to exhibit with them, but he preferred solitude and independence, and although he spent almost every winter between 1900 and 1940 in Berlin, he always remained a man of the country—rough, untamed, and primitive. He executed most of his work in Schleswig, the barren northern region of Germany, where he was born and where he could be alone with his wild, emotionally charged visions. In 1913–14 Nolde participated in an ethnological expedition to New Guinea, an experience that rein-

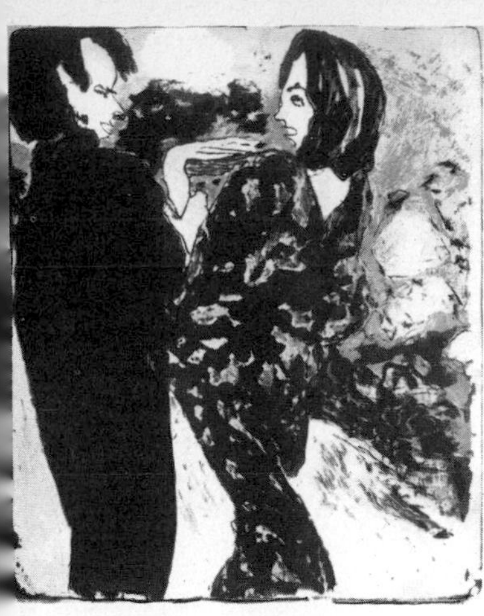

Emil Nolde. *Young Couple*. 1913.

forced his taste for the primitive, for brutal simplifications and distortions of forms, and for vivid colors. His aim, in fact, was to produce not a harmonious and balanced composition, but a searing visual and emotional shock.

The subjects of Nolde's paintings include flamboyant flowers (*Sunflowers*, 1932; Detroit, Institute of Art); stormy, apocalyptic landscapes (*Marsh*, 1916; Basel, Kunstmuseum); exotic Biblical scenes (*Maria Aegyptica*, 1912; Hamburg, Kunsthalle); or themes based on a personal mythology (*Vagabonds*, 1910–15; Cologne, Wallraf-Richartz-Museum). The often crude, almost vulgar element in his oil paintings is less evident in his many watercolors, which, while remaining full of passion and pathos, are usually marked by a delicate yet resonant use of color. Nolde also produced an important body of engraved works, for which he was accorded a prize at the 1952 Venice Biennale. Today the largest collection of his works is contained in the museum of the Ada and Emil Nolde Foundation in Seebüll.

NOLLEKENS, Joseph (1737, London—1823, London), English sculptor. Nollekens was trained in Rome, and worked there for 10 years before returning to London in 1770. His busts of the famous actor David Garrick and of the novelist Laurence Sterne (1765), executed while in Italy, won him immediate acclaim. On returning to London, he became extremely successful as a maker of portrait busts, his sitters including King George III and Dr. Samuel Johnson (both *c.* 1774). Perhaps his most famous works were the busts of the statesmen Charles James Fox and William Pitt. Nollekens is reputed to have made some 74 replicas of the latter. Like his great French contemporary, Antoine Houdon, he excelled as a portraitist, but he also executed statues of subjects from Classical mythology, as well as numerous funerary monuments. The latter include those dedicated to Oliver Goldsmith (died 1774), and to the three naval heroes, Captains Manners, Blair, and Bayne (1782) in Westminster Abbey, London.

NOME *or* **NOMÉ,** François de. *See* **MONSÙ DESIDERIO.**

NORTHCOTE, James (1746, Plymouth—1831, London), English painter. From 1771 to 1775 he was pupil and assistant to Sir Joshua Reynolds. Although he spent three years in Rome (1777–80), not a hint of Italian influence can be discerned in his work; however, the mark of Reynolds is clear in the portraits painted soon after his return to London (*Admiral Lord Hugh Seymour*, 1783; England, Priv. Coll.). In the 1790s Northcote also executed narrative history paintings, such as the *Entry of Richard II and Bolingbroke into London* (1793; Exeter, Royal Albert Memorial Museum). The 19th century brought a wider range of Romantic effects to his work, and his *Emperor Alexander of Russia Rescuing a Boy from Drowning* (1820; London, Royal School of Medicine) is probably the most competent and individual painting he produced. Northcote was also a littérateur and his reputation was enhanced by his friendship with the writer William Hazlitt, whose conversations with the painter were published in book form in 1830.

NORWICH SCHOOL, group of landscape painters active in the first half of the 19th century in Norwich, Norfolk. It is the only English school of painting ever to have developed around a specific geographical area and its formation was accidental, hinging on the fact that the Norfolk landscape painter John Crome preferred to stay at home rather than make his career in London. The Norwich painter John Sell Cotman followed Crome's example. The school was established as the Norwich Society of Artists in February 1803, when a group of artists, meeting at Crome's house in Norwich, announced the formation of a society "for the purpose of an Enquiry into the Rise, Progress, and present state of Painting, Architecture, and Sculpture, with a view to point out the Best Methods of study to attain to Greater Perfection . . ." The group met biweekly to study prints and drawings, holding annual exhibitions from 1805 to around 1840. Crome and Cotman remained the outstanding exponents of the Norwich School of landscape painters; its other members included the sons of both men, Miles Edmund Cotman (1810–58), John Joseph Cotman (1814–78), and John Berney Crome (1794–1842), as well as George Vincent (*c.* 1795–1831), James Stark (1794–1859), John Thirtle (1777–1838), Joseph Stannard (1797–1830), John Middleton (1827–56), Robert Dixon (1780–1815), and Henry Bright (1810–73).

O'CONOR, Roderic (1860, Roscommon, Ireland—1940, Neuil-sur-Layon, Maine-et-Loire), Irish painter. In 1883 he went to France and after 1892 worked at Pont-Aven, Brittany, where he belonged to the group of artists who became Paul Gauguin's disciples on the latter's return from Tahiti in 1893. O'Conor subsequently settled in Paris. He was independently rich and made little effort to sell his paintings. He was also a perceptive collector, and acquired works by Gauguin, Cézanne, Bonnard, Manet, Renoir, and Toulouse-Lautrec. It was only after his death that the public became aware of his achievement and discovered the true importance of his work (the Cézannesque *Still Life with Bottles*, 1892, London, Tate Gallery; *Yellow Landscape, Pont-Aven*, 1892, Isfield, Sussex, Coll. Mrs. Margaret Walker). O'Conor was a friend of Gauguin and Paul Sérusier, and both his oils and woodcuts reveal the influence of Symbolism.

OELZE, Richard (b. 1900, Magdeburg), German painter. From 1921 to 1925 Oelze was at the Bauhaus in Weimar, where he attended Johannes Itten's preliminary course. From 1930 to 1932 he resided in Berlin; he then moved to Paris in 1933, where he became friendly with the Surrealists André Breton, Paul Éluard, Max Ernst, and Salvador Dali. He showed his work at the International Surrealist Exhibition in London (1936) and at the exhibition of Fantastic Art, Dada, and Surrealism held at New York's Museum of Modern Art (1936). He then returned to Germany in 1939 and settled in Worpswede, near Bremen, where he lived until 1940, when he joined the armed forces. Oelze did not come into prominence again until 1959, and he exhibited at the 1968 Venice Biennale.

The art of this solitary man is profoundly Surrealistic and stylized. It has its origins in the German New Objectivity of the early 1920s, and, although initially influenced by the paintings of Max Ernst and René Magritte, his work has remained virtually untouched by subsequent artistic developments. Using earth colors (ochers, ambers, siennas) on a traditional white ground, and employing a transparent varnish applied with very fine brushstrokes, Oelze created a strange world of petrified forests, whose anthropomorphized vegetable forms seem to stare back at the viewer from a thousand ghostly eyes (*In a Church*, 1949–54). A conté crayon drawing, entitled *Frieda* (1935), is in the collection of the Museum of Modern Art in New York.

Josef Maria Olbrich. Marriage Tower on the Mathildenhöhe, Darmstadt. 1907. *Photo Kunstgewerbemuseum, Zurich.*

O'KEEFFE, Georgia (b. 1887, Sun Prairie, Wisconsin), American painter. She began painting in earnest in 1916, when she met the photographer and art collector Alfred Stieglitz, whom she married in 1924 and who gave her enormous encouragement. Her favorite themes were flowers, mountains, bones, and simplified renditions of the architecture of cities (*Black Iris*, 1926, New York, Metropolitan Museum; *Window of Lake George*, 1929, New York, Museum of Modern Art; *Cow's Skull, Red, White, and Blue*, 1931, Metropolitan Museum). She lived in New Mexico for a long time and was greatly influenced by the landscape and light of that state. Georgia O'Keeffe had numerous one-man shows, and important retrospective exhibitions of her paintings were held at the Chicago Art Institute (1943), the Museum of Modern Art in New York (1946), the Dallas Museum of Fine Arts (1953), and the Worcester Art Museum in Worcester, Massachusetts (1960).

OLBRICH, Josef Maria (1867, Troppau, Silesia—1908, Düsseldorf), Austrian architect, a student of Otto Wagner. With Josef Hoffmann, another Wagner pupil, he helped found (1897) the Wiener Sezession, the Austrian counterpart of Art Nouveau. Olbrich's design for the Sezession building in Vienna (1898–99), to house the group's exhibitions, won him immediate acclaim. The heavy floral decoration of the metal cupola is typically Art Nouveau but the blocklike simplicity of the façade looks forward to a new monumentality. In 1899 Olbrich was invited to Darmstadt by the grand duke of Hessen, who was willing to finance the building of an artists' colony. Olbrich built six houses there around a long building with a sumptuous porch, the Ernst-Ludwig Haus (1901). This building, which contained studios and a meeting hall, showed the influence of the Scottish architect Charles Rennie Mackintosh. The Hochzeitsturm ("Marriage Tower," 1907), built in brick and stone, completed the grouping. Its odd "five-fingered" roof shows an incomplete break with the Art Nouveau, but its horizontal window bands, wrapped around the corners, are the first instance of a motif that became nearly universal in the 1920s.

OLDENBURG, Claes (b. 1929, Stockholm, Sweden), American sculptor and environmentalist. His father was a diplomat, and Oldenburg spent much of his early childhood shuttling between the United States, Sweden, and Norway. He graduated from Yale University in 1950, worked as a Chicago reporter on the police beat, then attended the city's Art Institute for two years (1953–54). By 1956 he was doing loosely brushed figurative paintings and had moved to New York. Around 1960 he became involved with a group of New York artists, including Robert Whitman (b. 1935), Jim Dine, Red Grooms (b. 1937), and Allan Kaprow, who initiated a new form of participational art called "happenings." Between 1960 and 1965 Oldenburg conducted many happenings, beginning with "Snapshots from the City" (1960) and "Store Days" (1962), and concluding with such ambitious enterprises as the Los Angeles "Autobodys" (1964), which involved ice cubes, automobiles, and crowds of people as the material for art. During the same year he opened a small storefront on New York's Lower East Side called

"The Store," where he sold painted plaster replicas of food (*Dual Hamburger*, 1962; New York, Museum of Modern Art) and other commodities. With these objects Oldenburg became one of the initiators of Pop art. The images he used derive from the street, home, daily functions, and commerce (*Bedroom Ensemble*, 1963, New York, Sidney Janis Gallery; and *Soft Toilet*, 1966, New York, Coll. Mr. and Mrs. Victor Ganz), and point out the fetishistic nature of common objects (*Giant Light Switches*, 1964; New York, Sidney Janis Gallery and Coll. Leon Kraushar). Oldenburg's interest in the tactile quality of these objects relates him to Abstract Expressionism, as does the messy, loose application of enamel paints on his earlier food replicas. His oversize, stitched-together pieces in such soft materials as vinyl or canvas, stuffed with kapok, were important sculptured innovations. Reversing the expectations of hard sculpture, these huge collapsing objects rely on gravity and chance for their final form.

OLITSKI, Jules (b. 1922, Gomel, Russia), American painter. He studied in New York at the National Academy of Design (1939–42), then in Paris, first at the Académie de la Grande Chaumière (1949–50), then at the Ossip Zadkine School. Olitski's work between 1952 and 1959 was characterized by densely incrusted surfaces built up from rough smears and trails reminiscent of Hans Hofmann (*Diane de Poitiers*, *c.* 1959; Shaftsbury, Vt., Coll. artist). Beginning in 1960 he moved to a stained canvas technique to create a more flexible picture surface. More precise biomorphic and geometric shapes were defined, such as ovals ringing each other or clustering in one area of the field—*The Julius Dmikhovsky Image* (1961; Coll. artist).

By 1963 Olitski was working to obliterate the drawn contours of his shapes through the sheer impact of rich, saturated colors. In a progressive effort to renounce sculptural space and tactile sensations he became more and more antagonistic to the notion of local color and began to spray tiny particles of paint onto soaked, unprimed canvas, masking all linear boundaries (*Prince Patutsky Command*, 1965; New York, Coll. Henry Geldzahler). Later even these faint internal edges disappeared, as defined shape was displaced to the peripheries of the canvas, where thickly brushed bands contrast with the illusory clouds of paint sprayed across the rest of the field. Soft greens, sweet pinks, and ingratiating oranges and purples (*Beyond Bounds*, 1966; Jewett Art Center, Wellesley College, Mass.) delicately sprayed into broad rectangles resist a frontal reading and create an illusory dissolving space, while the thickly painted bands establish the literal existence of the canvas.

OLIVER, Isaac (b. Rouen—d. 1617), English painter of French Huguenot extraction, brought to England by his parents in 1568. He was trained as a miniaturist under Nicholas Hilliard, whom he eventually rivaled in fame and popularity. Compared with the unmistakably English style of Hilliard, Oliver's work has a distinctly Franco-Flemish flavor. He carefully manipulated effects of light and shade to give his figures weight and volume, so that even his smallest miniatures give an impression of size (*Self Portrait*; Coll. Earl of Derby), while his larger miniatures have the air of being reduced full-scale portraits. Such larger works include the well-known *Portrait of a Young Man, said to be Sir Philip Sidney* (Royal Coll.) and the beautiful Mannerist miniature of *Frances Howard, Countess of Essex and Somerset* (Coll. Earl of Derby). The exquisite drawing of a youth, *Henry Frederick, Prince of Wales* (*c.* 1610; Coll. Duke of Buccleuch), has remarkable spaciousness and delicacy. Again differing from Hilliard, Oliver had ambitions to be a history painter, and a few extant drawings of allegorical subjects (*Charity*; London, British Museum) reveal his admiration for the Italian Mannerist painters Parmigianino and Primaticcio.

OLIVIER, Ferdinand (1785, Dessau—1841, Munich), German Romantic painter who, along with his brothers Friedrich (1791–1859) and Heinrich (1783–1848), was one of the founders of the Salzburg school of landscape painting. He studied art in Dresden from 1804 to 1806, and then went to Paris, where he stayed until early in 1810, painting many portraits, including one of Napoleon, and some religious pictures.

Claes Oldenburg. *Hamburger with Pickle and Tomato Attached.* 1963. Coll. Carroll Janis, New York. *Photo Sidney Janis Gallery, New York.*

The philosopher Friedrich Schlegel influenced him to adopt the Nazarene style of painting with its images of primitive Christianity, and he painted many landscapes that included religious figures. At the beginning of a long stay (1812–30) in Vienna he met Joseph Anton Koch (1768–1939) and began to concentrate on historical landscapes. He also painted views of Vienna and its environs (*Quarry near the Church of Matzleinsdorf*, *c.* 1814–16; Vienna, Albertina) and fairly spontaneous landscapes of the Salzburg region, which he visited in 1815 and 1817. During the last decade of his life Olivier increasingly devoted himself to Classical landscapes in the style of Nicolas Poussin.

OLMEC ART. The so-called Olmec people—the term refers to several very early unidentified tribes—flourished in the great coastal plain of the Gulf of Mexico, in particular around the two great sites where their civilization has been studied, Tres Zapotes (Veracruz) and the island of La Venta (Tabasco). Their principal legacy is their art; but the astonishing thing about this art, a highly developed product of a primitive culture, is that nothing has been found that may be said to lead up to it. It is extremely difficult to date the Olmec civilization. La Venta flourished in pre-Classic times, perhaps 800–400 B.C.; Tres Zapotes remained vital several centuries longer (*c.* 400 B.C.–A.D. 600). It is now generally believed that the Olmecs exercised a formative influence on the great Classical civilizations of Mexico—Tajín, Teotihuacán, Maya, and Zapotec.

Olmec Art. Athlete or wrestler. Uxpanapán, Veracruz. Museo Nacional de Antropología, Mexico City.

(There is evidence that they spoke a form of the Maya language.) The Olmecs did not leave any buildings comparable in size to those of the people who came after them. However, they are regarded as the true creators of Mexican sculpture, and they left the earliest remains of carved altars, steles, sarcophagi, pillars, and statues in Mexico. The Olmecs' most unusual creations are the colossal heads, carved of basalt, measuring over 8½ feet high and weighing up to 40 tons. These strange, almost spherical heads were placed on pedestals; their negroid features are realistic and their apparently crude finish is actually a skillfully handled surface texture that causes the facial expression to vary with the light, producing at times a smile, at times a hard impassivity. Ten such heads have been found; they may be dated provisionally at about A.D. 200–300. Giant sculptures of entire figures have also been discovered, some probably actual portraits.

Olmec Art. Colossal head. La Venta, Tabasco. *Photo Henri Stierlin, Geneva.*

The mastery of the Olmec sculptors is equally evident in the numerous blue-green jade figurines attributed to them. These possess the same sensual mouths, drooping at the corners, as the larger works. It might be said that for the Olmecs the body counted far less than the face, with its arresting features and gaze, although anatomical relations and movement are handled with great skill. The faces are of two types: some are like those of the cyclopean heads, but with the curious combination of human and feline features of the jaguar-god; others are elongated and of phallic inspiration.

The Olmecs show a marked taste for deformed figures, such as hunchbacks, dwarfs, and obese children. These strange figures possess an astonishing power of suggestion. The Olmecs also carved out of jade great ceremonial axes decorated with a human face with incised eyes, snub nose, and catlike mouth—again the face of the jaguar-god that reappears constantly in their art, a creature sprung from the legendary union of a woman and a jaguar, which must have been central to the Olmec religion.

Other important Olmec finds are the altars—great slabs of basalt with flat tops, carved with human figures in high and low relief.

The Olmecs were the first to symbolize the four directions of the world by a cross in the shape of a quincunx. They developed a hieroglyphic writing (which appears to be proto-Mayan), a calendar, and an arithmetic using dots and dashes for figures. One of their jade figurines, called the Tuxtla Statuette, bears a date corresponding to A.D. 162. But neither this date, nor the 3rd-century B.C. date deciphered on Stela C of Tres Zapotes, is sufficient evidence to date this art.

OLMSTED, Frederick Law (1822, Hartford, Connecticut—1903, Waverley, Massachusetts), American landscape architect and writer. Olmsted studied in an engineering office from 1837 to 1840, and then spent more than a decade alternately farming and traveling in America and foreign countries. As a result of his travels he published *Walks and Talks of an American Farmer in England* (1852), *A Journey in the Seaboard Slave States* (1856), *A Journey through Texas* (1857), and *A Journey in the Back Country* (1860), which first brought him to public notice. In 1857 Olmsted was appointed superintendent of the new Central Park in New York, and in the same year entered the competition for a new design for the park, in collaboration with Calvert Vaux (1824–95). In 1858 he was appointed chief architect for Central Park. His interests remained wide: he was secretary to the U.S. Sanitation Commission (1861–63), and then went to California, where he assisted in setting up what was to become the Yosemite reservation and designed the grounds of the University of California at Berkeley (1866). Olmsted designed parks for Boston (Franklin Park, 1885), Philadelphia (Fairmount Park, from 1871), Chicago (suburb of Riverside, 1869), and Brooklyn (Prospect Park, 1860), as well as the grounds for the U.S. Capitol in Washington, D.C. (1874–95), and for the World's Columbian Exposition in Chicago (1890–95). Two publications of his later years were *Public Parks and the Enlargement of Towns* (1871) and *A Consideration of the Justifying Value of a Public Park* (1881).

OMMEGANCK, Balthasar Paul (1755, Antwerp—1826, Antwerp), Flemish painter. He studied with the Flemish landscapist Joseph Antonissen (1737–94), and is best known for his pastoral scenes (*Landscape with Cattle, Goats, and Sheep*, 1781, Paris, Louvre; *Landscape with Sheep and Shepherdess*, Amsterdam, Rijksmuseum). Many art historians consider him to have been one of the creators of the Romantic style of landscape painting; he does succeed, in fact, in giving a soul to nature by his treatment of light, which is sometimes gray and melancholy, and sometimes shimmering and golden. Ommeganck was one of the founders (1788) of the Antwerp Society of Artists.

O'NEIL, Henry Nelson (1817, St. Petersburg—1880, London), Russian-born English painter of anecdotal subjects. Like many of his artistic contemporaries in England, he specialized in highly descriptive, often sentimental genre scenes (the *Last Moments of Raphael*, shown 1866; now Bristol, City Art Gallery), but after the success of the Pre-Raphaelites in the early 1850s, he turned to modern themes, producing his greatest success, the widely engraved *Eastward Ho! August 1857* (R.A. 1858; now Elton Hall, near Peterborough, Coll. Proby), which depicts the departure of troops for India at the time of the Sepoy Mutiny of 1857. The sequel, *Home Again* (original formerly London, Leicester Galleries), was exhibited at the Royal Academy in 1859. O'Neil never repeated this success and his later work is often coarse and uneven in quality.

OOST, family of Flemish painters from Bruges.

JACOB VAN, *called* THE ELDER (*c.* 1601, Bruges—1671, Bruges), the most celebrated artist of the family, was trained by his brother FRANS (1595–1625). He had undeniable talent and was strong enough to resist Rubens' great influence. He admired the work of Caravaggio, Titian, and the Carracci, and the resulting eclecticism in his style can be readily seen in such a work as his *Madonna and Saints*, painted in 1648 (Bruges, Musée de l'Église Notre-Dame). Jacob the Elder's ability as a painter is most evident, however, in certain of his genre and religious paintings inspired by Caravaggio, such as the *St. Sebastian* (1646; Bruges, Musée de l'Hôpital de la Potterie) and the *Calling of St. Matthew* (1640; Musée de l'Église Notre-Dame), as well as in his portraits (*Boy with a Muff*, 1650, London, National Gallery; *Family on a Terrace*, 1645, Bruges, Groeningemuseum). These portraits reveal a Dutch influence in their precise delineation, balanced compositions, and bright colors.

JACOB VAN, *called* THE YOUNGER (1639, Bruges—1713, Bruges), son of the above, was also a painter. He studied with his father, then journeyed to Paris (*c.* 1659–61) and to Rome, where he lived for about eight years. His work consists of both genre and religious subjects, such as *Children Drawing in a Studio* (1666; Bruges, Groeningemuseum), and the *Virgin Giving a Stole to St. Hubert* (1668; Bruges, St-Sauveur).

OP ART, a movement in abstract art that developed in the United States around 1960 as a reaction to action painting. Op art (an abbreviated form of the term "optical art") includes visual experiments based on optical illusions and the plastic impressions of movement. It was a sequel to geometrical abstraction, which it claimed to be developing further. It was also partly inspired by the experiments carried out at the Bauhaus, one of whose teachers, Josef Albers, became a professor at Yale University and influenced young American painters through his work, teaching, and his book *Interaction of color* (1963). Op art had various European precursors, but its true spiritual father was the painter Victor Vasarely. In the United States the Op art movement included the Anonima Group, organized in 1960 by Ernest Benkert (b. 1928), Francis Ray Hewitt (b. 1936), and Edwin Mieczkowski (b. 1929). Other Op artists were John Goodyear (b. 1930) and Henry Pearson (b. 1914), both of whom were students of Eastern philosophies; Mon Levinson (b. 1926), whose first exhibition took place in 1960 in New York; and the Polish-born Julian Stanczak (b. 1928), who was a pupil of Albers and later became a teacher at the Cleveland Art Institute. In principle, Op artists believed in the interdependence of art and science, and referred to the work of scientists on the psychology of perception, in particular to the psychologist and art historian Rudolf Arnheim's book *Art and Visual Perception: A Psychology of the Creative Eye*, 1954. Op also tended to embrace all the various European attempts to exploit optics systematically: the Group Zero (founded in Düsseldorf in 1958), which included Heinz Mack (b. 1931) and Günther Uecker (b. 1930); the Groupe de Recherche d'Art Visuel (started in Paris in 1960), of which Julio Le Parc (b. 1928) was the dominant figure; the Italian "N" group in Padua and the "T" group in Milan; and the works of artists such as Agam (Yaacov Gipstein, b. 1928), Hugo Rudolfo Demarco (b. 1932), and Nicolas Schöffer. Although the term "Op art" is a convenient simplification, one must remember that it refers primarily to the American interpretation of an aesthetic that was developed in several countries.

OPIE, John (1761, St. Agnes, near Truro, Cornwall—1807, London), English portrait and genre painter. As a young man Opie was apprenticed to a sawyer, but was rescued from this fate by the satirist Dr. John Wolcot (1738–1819), who wrote under the name of Peter Pindar and who took Opie into his home in 1775. Wolcot, who became Opie's patron and dealer, was an amateur painter and he gave Opie some artistic instruction and a great deal of advice, and sent him out as an itinerant portraitist to country houses in the neighborhood of Truro. Then, noting the boy's vivid grasp of character and sense of the picturesque, he decided to take Opie to London. Accordingly, after a brief period in Devon, Wolcot and Opie arrived in London in 1781; the following year Opie was presented to King George III, who commissioned a picture from him, and from that date he never lacked patrons.

Opie was a highly competent portraitist even before his arrival in London; this can be judged by his portrait of *Dr. John Patch* (1781; Southernhay, East Exeter, Devonshire, Royal Devon and Exeter Hospital). A comparison between this portrait and that of another doctor, *Thomas Glass* (*c.* 1781; Royal Devon and Exeter Hospital), shows how quickly Opie assimilated the sophisticated tastes of London. Within two years of his arrival he was painting highly attractive "fancy pictures" of rustic subjects (*Peasant's Family*, *c.* 1783–85; London, Tate Gallery) in the manner of Gainsborough. By 1786 he was confident enough to undertake seven illustrations for a series called "The Dramatic Works of Shakespeare," published in 1802 by John and Josiah Boydell. These were followed in the 1790s by a number of paintings of historic subjects for a series published in London by Robert Bower in 1806. His masterpiece, *A Gentleman and a Miner with a Specimen of Copper Ore* (1786; England, Coll. Mrs. Warwick Pendarves), is as valuable a document of the Industrial Revolution as Joseph Wright of Derby's *Experiment on a Bird with an Air Pump*.

In the late 1780s, however, his style began to decline, and some flashy but effective female portraits painted in the following decade suggest that he was heavily influenced by Sir Thomas Lawrence's style (*Jane Beetham*, 1790–1800, and *Harriett Beetham*, 1790–1800; both London, Brompton Consumption Hospital). Opie visited France in 1802, and a faint reflection of Louis David's Neo-

Gilles-Marie Oppenord. Decorative architecture. Manufacture de Sèvres.

classical idiom is apparent in his *Self-Portrait* (*c.* 1805; England, Coll. Lady Mander).

OPPENORD *or* **OPPENORDT,** Gilles-Marie (1672, Paris—1742, Paris), French architect and decorator. Oppenord studied with Jules Hardouin-Mansart, and was a pensioner of the king at the French Academy in Rome. On his return to Paris, where he became architect to the regent and a friend of Antoine Watteau, Oppenord played an important role in the development of the Rococo style. His architectural work has almost entirely disappeared, but with the help of his own fine drawings and engravings it has been possible to reconstruct some of his decorative schemes: for example, his paneling (1714) for the former Hôtel de Pomponne, Paris, has been remounted at the Yugoslav embassy in Paris. Narrow panels, in which figures of Fame brandish crowns and trumpets, alternate with broad panels, filled with hunting trophies. The salon of the Château de la Grange-du-Milieu, Seine-et-Oise, has been altered, but the artist's sketches show Oppenord as a discreet decorator, more respectful of symmetry than Juste-Aurèle Meissonnier, and less exuberant than Jean-François de Cuvillies. The Salon d'Angle, or Salon d'Oppenord (1719–20) of the Palais Royal, Paris, embodied the most fluid treatment of space ever attempted, before or after, in France. In its defiance of geometric order, it was a masterpiece of Rococo decoration. Oppenord was also responsible for the major religious work of the time, the completion of St-Sulpice (1725). But of his work on the church (transept façades, nave, choir furnishing, and altar), little survives.

ORBAY, François d' (1631, Paris—1697, Paris), French architect. Around 1648 he entered the firm of the brothers Louis and François Le Vau. D'Orbay's approach appears in work at the Château de Vincennes (from 1654). Between the two wings, dominated by an uninterrupted giant order, a fine triumphal arch was erected, a feature rare in the work of Louis Le Vau. An engraving of the structure, signed by D'Orbay, confirms him as its architect. During the ten years that followed, he became the indispensable collaborator of the Le Vau brothers, both of whom had received commissions for large buildings. The role of D'Orbay became particularly decisive around 1665, during the crisis marked by the decline in France of Italian prestige and the rise of a national Classicism. One difficult task still awaited execution: the completion of the Louvre and the construction of a monumental façade on the side facing St-Germain-l'Auxerrois. A French design was ultimately chosen, first attributed to Claude Perrault, and later to the combined efforts of Perrault, Louis Le Vau, and Charles Le Brun. Recent scholarship indicates that the design that Louis XIV accepted was, in fact, by François d'Orbay (built 1667–73). Placed on a high stylobate, the twin columns of a giant order embrace the two upper floors. They are set in front of a long gallery, which projects in the center and is terminated by lateral pavilions. After Louis Le Vau's death in 1670, the office of chief architect was vacant for eight years, and D'Orbay remained in charge of royal buildings. It was during this period that the great apartments of Versailles, served by the magnificent Ambassadors' Staircase, were decorated. In addition to his functions as architect to the king, D'Orbay accomplished some building projects of his own, most of which have disappeared. The Arch of Peyrou at Montpellier (*c.* 1689), executed to D'Orbay's designs by Charles-Augustin d'Aviler (1653–1701), is still standing. A figure in high relief, set in the wall of a building in Rue de l'Ancienne-Comédie, Paris, is all that is left of the Hôtel des Comédiens Français, built by D'Orbay in 1688.

François d'Orbay. Château de Vincennes. Triumphal arch on the south portico. From 1654. Drawing by the architect, engraved by Marot. Bibliothèque Nationale, Paris.

ORCAGNA, Andrea di Cione, *called* Andrea (active 1344–68, Florence), Italian painter, sculptor, and architect. He was the finest and most versatile Tuscan artist of the mid-14th century generation, which also included his three brothers, Jacopo (active 1362–98), Matteo (active 1358–90), and Nardo de Cione.

From 1354 to 1357, Andrea was engaged on the altarpiece for the Strozzi chapel in S. Maria Novella, Florence, where he partially abandoned the naturalistic tradition of Giotto and returned to the hieratic manner of Roman and Byzantine painting. As the principal artist of the great tabernacle for Or San Michele in Florence (1359), Orcagna employed several assistants, including his brother Matteo. The general arrangement of the tabernacle is indeed striking, although obscured by an excessive profusion of ornaments. The principal parts of the work are attributed to Orcagna. The large relief on the reverse side of the tabernacle, in which the *Dormition* and *Assumption of the Virgin* are represented, is certainly his work. With its gable and numerous pinnacles, the structure as a whole belongs to the Late Gothic style, which is enlivened, however, by the new spirit. In 1359 Orcagna, accompanied by his brother Matteo, went to Orvieto to supervise work on the duomo. He stayed there until 1362, assisting in the execution of the mosaics on its façade. When he returned to Florence, he helped in the designs for the new cathedral,

Andrea Orcagna. *Birth of the Virgin.* Ashmolean Museum, Oxford.

which had been begun in the last years of the 13th century under the direction of Arnolfo di Cambio, but which was radically modified in the 14th century by Francesco Talenti.

Orcagna's painting, which was influenced by Giotto and the Sienese masters, is distinguished by its original flavor and also by its abundance, if the works that have vanished are taken into account, particularly the frescoes at S. Croce admired by Lorenzo Ghiberti. Orcagna's fame was considerable during his own lifetime; and after his death a certain number of paintings, sculptures, and mosaics were attributed to him. Among these works are the *Birth of the Virgin* at Orvieto Cathedral, the loggia of the Piazza della Signoria in Florence, and two large frescoes of the *Triumph of Death* and the *Last Judgment* (an attribution given by Vasari) in the Camposanto at Pisa.

ORDÓÑEZ, Bartolomé (*c.* 1490, Burgos—1520, Carrara, Italy), Spanish Renaissance sculptor. There is evidence that Ordóñez studied in Florence, and it is known that he was in Naples in 1517, where he worked with the Spanish sculptor Diego de Siloe on the altarpiece of the Caraccioli Chapel in the church of S. Giovanni a Carbonara. Shortly afterward he was back in Spain, working on the alteration of the choir of Barcelona Cathedral for the chapter of the Order of the Golden Fleece held in 1519; he decorated the stalls with wood carvings and began work on the *trascoro* (the front part of the choir screen) in Carrara marble, depicting scenes from the life of St. Eulalia (completed 1564). After the death of the Italian sculptor Domenico Fancelli (1469–1519), Ordóñez was asked to take over his unfulfilled commission for the tombs of Cardinal Cisneros (Magistral Church, Alcalá de Henares) and of Joan the Mad and Philip the Handsome (Granada, Capilla Real). For this purpose, he took his workshop to Carrara in 1519, but he died there the following year, leaving the sovereigns' tombs nearly completed, but that of Cisneros unfinished. Ordóñez benefited from the lessons of Italian art and his work was remarkable for its restraint, elegance, and depth of feeling.

ORLEY, Bernaert van (*c.* 1492, Brussels—1541, Brussels), Flemish painter. Van Orley dominated the school of painting at Brussels during the first half of the 16th century, modifying the prevailing traditions set by Rogier van der Weyden and introducing Italian styles. In 1518 he was appointed court painter to Margaret of Austria, Regent of the Netherlands, and in 1532 to Mary of Hungary; under their patronage he painted numerous portraits (*Doctor Georg de Zelle*, 1519, and *Margaret of Austria*; both Brussels, Musées Royaux des Beaux-Arts), *Madonnas*, and large altarpieces, including the triptychs of the *Virtue of Patience* (1521; Brussels, Musées Royaux des Beaux-Arts) and the *Last Judgment* (1525; Antwerp, Musée Royal des Beaux-Arts). There is clear evidence in these works of Raphael's and Michelangelo's influence, which Van Orley absorbed on a visit to Italy and through the many engravings, cartoons, and tapestries after the masters' works that were circulating in Northern Europe.

Van Orley was quite active as a stained-glass (windows for St-Gudule, Brussels, 1537) and tapestry designer. His great 12-part tapestry series called *Hunts*, known as the *Hunts of Maximilian* (1521–30; Paris, Louvre), is a magnificent accomplishment. The scenes have a wonderful vitality and are alive with vibrant colors, with reds glowing amid greens, slate grays, pastel blues, and russet tones. There is a tapestry for each month of the year, showing the meets, the feasting, and the chase after stag and boar over vast stretches of countryside.

ORLOFF, Chana (1888, Konstantinovka, Ukraine—1968, Tel Aviv, Israel), Russian-born French sculptress. In 1904 she left Russia for Palestine, where she lived in Jaffa, and then moved to Paris in 1910. There she attended classes at the École des Arts Décoratifs and the Académie Russe, and was friendly with the leading figures of Montparnasse, including Guillaume Apollinaire and Amedeo Modigliani. During her first period of artistic activity, she carved in wood (*Amazon*, 1916; *Dancer*, 1919; *Fan Dance*, 1921). She then moved toward Cubism and made vigorously stylized figures in cement and marble, with cylindrical bodies and spherical heads (*My Son*, 1923; Grenoble, Museum). Before World War II, her best sculptures were nudes (*Reclining Woman*, 1924; Chicago, Coll. Chonfield) and portraits. From 1945, after a stay in Switzerland, most of her work was executed in bronze and her favorite subjects were birds.

ORME, Philibert de l'. *See* **L'ORME,** Philibert de.

OROZCO, José Clemente (1883, Zapotlán, Jalisco—1949, Mexico City), Mexican painter. In 1908 he entered the Academia San Carlos in Mexico City, where he studied sporadically until 1914. His first exhibition took place in 1915 in the Mexican capital: it consisted of 23 watercolors, drawings, and paintings of scenes from the lives of prostitutes, under the general title of *Casa de Lagrimas* ("House of Tears"). Orozco's unsentimental way of treating his subject earned him the title of "the Mexican Goya." During the Mexican Revolution (1911–17), he published many caricatures in the pro-Revolution periodical *La Vanguardia*, thus giving further weight to this comparison. For revolutionary scenes, he created a violent, somber, purely native

Bernaert van Orley. *Hunts of Maximilian.* 1521–30. Detail. Louvre, Paris. *Photo Giraudon.*

Adriaen van Ostade. *Family Portrait.* 1654. Louvre, Paris. *Photo Alinari-Giraudon.*

style, in which he made frequent use of contrasts of black and white. He had a particular preference for working in fresco, his first effort in this genre being the mural (1923–27) in the National Preparatory School in Mexico City, which contains the first of several versions on the theme of *Maternity*. In 1927 Orozco went to New York, where his exhibition of *Drawings of the Revolution* at the Mary Harriman Gallery was highly successful. He remained in the United States until 1934, and worked on three famous mural series: those at Pomona College in Claremont, California (1930), for which he painted his famous *Prometheus*; those at the New School for Social Research, New York (1931); and those at Dartmouth College in Hanover, New Hampshire (1932–34), which showed his growing receptivity to the great schools of the past. On his return to Mexico, he composed several murals, notably *Catharsis* (1934) for the Palace of Fine Arts, Mexico City, as well as those for the Orphanage, the Governor's Palace, and the University at Guadalajara, Jalisco (1936–40); for the Supreme Court of Mexico City (1941); and for the church of Jesus Nazareno, also in Mexico City (1942). In 1945 he published his autobiography. Orozco's last work was the outdoor mural decoration of the Escuela Normal de Maestros in Mexico City (1947–48).

ORPHISM, a term first used by the French Cubist writer Guillaume Apollinaire in 1912—notably in the lecture he gave in Berlin on the occasion of the Delaunay exhibition at the Der Sturm gallery—to designate an artistic movement favoring the primacy of color in pictorial construction. Apollinaire observed that this movement expressed a desire to escape from the severe color harmonies preferred by Pablo Picasso and Georges Braque, and that it heralded the end of Cubism. Under the name of Orphism, Apollinaire linked the work of Robert Delaunay, Frank Kupka, and the young painters who surrounded them. According to Apollinaire, Delaunay believed that if a simple color does not determine its complementary color, it breaks up in the atmosphere and produces simultaneously all the colors of the solar spectrum. Delaunay himself went on to affirm that the simultaneous contrast of colors would be the only means of producing the dynamism of colors and their construction in the picture. This emphasis on the dynamic role of color led to the emergence of an entirely new art, with its own laws of creation, capable of freeing itself from all objective and visual representation of nature.

OSTADE, Adriaen van (1610, Haarlem—1685, Haarlem), Dutch genre painter. He was a pupil of Frans Hals and developed a predilection for a humorous style that recalls Pieter Bruegel and David Teniers the Younger. Ostade's favorite subjects were smoking dens, tavern scenes, and peasant interiors filled with rowdy incidents in which low types, aroused by wine and feasting, freely indulge in sensual pleasures (*Carousing Peasants in an Interior*, c. 1638, Munich, Alte Pinakothek; *Men and Women in a Tavern*, 1660, Dresden, Gemäldegalerie). Ostade derives his thick, hulking shapes and his simplification of volume from Bruegel, while his suppression of outline and use of chiaroscuro are taken from Rembrandt. This chiaroscuro gives way after 1660 to a somewhat lighter style, more transparent colors, and a less cramped composition. In his finest work, the *Village Fiddler* (1673; The Hague, Mauritshuis), the open-air atmosphere makes for brighter colors and the thickly applied paint takes on the qualities of enamel. Ostade's skill rises above the mere creation of a trivial genre setting, and manages to express the artist's feeling for his fellow men and for life itself.

OTTOMAN ART. *See* **ISLAMIC ART.**

OUD, Jacobus Johannes Pieter (1890, Purmerend, near Amsterdam—1963, Wassenaar, near The Hague), Dutch architect. He worked for a time with the architects Jan Stuyt (1868–1934) and Petrus Cuijpers (1827–1921), as well as with Theodor Fischer (1862–1938) in Munich. Oud met Theo van Doesburg in 1916, and the following year helped to found the review *De Stijl*. The hotel at Noordwijkerhout and the Allegonda villa at Katwijk, the first buildings to reveal his personal style, both date from 1917. Of all the group's members, Oud made the greatest contribution to the development of De Stijl's architectural principles. These were aimed at creating buildings based on "pure plastic" (the "permanent oppositions" obtained through a balance of horizontal and vertical lines) and the use of the primary colors—blue, yellow, and red. De Stijl architects rejected the monumental and preferred a balance between unequal parts to symmetry.

In 1918 Oud was appointed housing architect to the city of Rotterdam, where he built the housing blocks of Spangen and Tussendijken (1920). They were sensational enough for people to speak of a school of Rotterdam, which was sober and functional in contrast to the picturesqueness of the school of Amsterdam, led by Michael de Klerk. In 1921 Oud

J. J. P. Oud. Shell Building, The Hague. 1938.

Jean-Baptiste Oudry. *Swans and a Dog.* 1731. Musée d'Art et d'Histoire, Geneva.

began to move away from the De Stijl group, whose principles no longer seemed sufficiently realistic. He built the housing estates of Oud-Mathenesse (1922) and Hoek van Holland (1924–27) with the greatest care for objectivity. But he still retained the rule of contrasting planes and volumes, which he applied in the Café de Unie (1924–25; destroyed 1940), and especially in the Kiefhoek estate (1925–27), both in Rotterdam. At this period Oud acquired an international reputation through his book, *Höllandische Architektur*, published in 1926 in the "Books of the Bauhaus" series. However, fearing that a too dogmatic functionalism would lead to aridity, Oud began to vary his effects. As a result, the Shell Building in The Hague (1938) seemed to many people an abrogation of his principles. But he never ceased to advocate a pure, simple, and rational architecture. In his last works, like the Bio-Marine Children's Sanatorium, near Arnhem (1952–60), one can see that his development remained faithful to "the search for clear forms for obvious needs."

OUDRY, Jean-Baptiste (1686, Paris—1755, Beauvais), French painter and engraver. He was a pupil of Nicolas de Largillière, and for a time (1713–17) practiced portraiture. But his real talent was as an animal painter, particularly of still lifes based on hunting themes (*Dead Wolf*, 1721; London, Wallace Collection). In 1726 he was appointed painter to the Beauvais tapestry factory, of which he became director in 1734. He held this post without interruption for 20 years, providing cartoons for several series of tapestries, including *Country Pleasures* (1730). But it was the Gobelins factory, whose work he also supervised, that wove the eight tapestries of his renowned *Hunts of Louis XV* (1734–45; Compiègne, Château, and Florence, Palazzo Pitti), which show him to have been a subtle and accurate landscape artist who was particularly sensitive to the beauty of trees and rich foliage.

Oudry was a talented draftsman, as can be seen in the engravings he made for a monumental edition (1755) of La Fontaine's *Fables*. As a painter of still lifes, he showed consummate skill and exceptional delicacy: his famous *White Duck* (1753; London, Coll. Marchioness of Cholmondeley) is an unparalleled tour de force.

OVERBECK, Johann Friedrich (1789, Lübeck—1869, Rome), German painter. With Franz Pforr (1788–1812), he was the founder (1809) of the Lukasbund, or Fraternity of St. Luke, out of which the Nazarene group ultimately developed (1810–12). In 1810 the two artists went to Rome, where they were soon joined by the German painters Peter Cornelius, Philipp Veit (1793–1877), Julius Schnorr von Carolsfeld (1794–1872), and Wilhelm Schadow. Overbeck, who was converted to Catholicism in 1813, exercised considerable influence over the group. With his Nazarene friends, he participated (1816–17) in the decoration of the Roman house of the Prussian Consul-General Jakob Salomon Bartholdy, for which he painted the scene of *Joseph Sold by His Brothers*, which since 1888 has been in the Nationalgalerie of East Berlin's Staatliche Museen. Overbeck also participated in the other collective project undertaken in Rome (1822–32) by the Nazarenes: the mural decorations for three rooms in the villa of Marchese Carlo Massimo. He contributed frescoes illustrating scenes from Tasso's *Gerusalemme Liberata* (*Preparation for the Siege of Jerusalem*, 1823–25). One of his best works is the fresco of the *Miracle of the Roses* (1829) in the Cappella della Porziuncola in the town of Santa Maria degli Angeli, near Assisi. His huge painting of the *Triumph of Religion in the Arts* (1840; Frankfurt, Städelsches Kunstinstitut), on the other hand, is very conventional in its Raphaelesque purity.

Johann Friedrich Overbeck. *Portrait of Vittoria Caldoni.* 1822. Bayerische Staatsgemäldesammlungen, Munich.

OZENFANT, Amédée (1886, St-Quentin, Aisne—1966, Cannes), French painter, one of the founders of Purism. From 1915 to 1917 he expressed his ideas and artistic principles in articles he wrote for *L'Élan*, a magazine he had founded with the Cubist writers Max Jacob and Guillaume Apollinaire. In 1917 he met the architect and painter Charles-Édouard Jeanneret (later known as Le Corbusier), with whom he collaborated in founding the Purist movement and in producing its manifesto, *After Cubism* (1918). From 1920 to 1925 they defended their ideas in their famous periodical *L'Esprit Nouveau*, which provided a platform for the boldest and most diverse tendencies in contemporary art. From 1925 to 1928 Ozenfant devoted himself to the revival of mural painting (*Four Races*, 1928; Paris, Musée National d'Art Moderne) and painted Purist works such as *The Jug* (1926; Providence, R.I., Museum of Art, Rhode Island School of Design). In 1928 he published a work that became a classic: *Art* (Vol. I: *The Balance Sheet of Modern Arts*; Vol. II: *The Structure of a New Spirit*). From 1931 to 1938 he worked on a huge composition called *Life* (Paris; Musée National d'Art Moderne), in which over a hundred figures, handled in the Purist manner, form a chorus in praise of human solidarity. In 1938 he decided to settle in New York, where he founded the Ozenfant School of Fine Arts, which soon became one of the most famous schools of modern art in the United States. He returned to France in 1955, and until his death directed a studio for foreign students in Cannes.

P

PAÁL, László (1846, Zám—1879, Charenton-le-Pont, near Paris), Hungarian landscapist who spent most of his career in France. After studying in Düsseldorf he went to Paris and often worked in Barbizon, where he painted his most successful pictures. He was a plein-air painter, who, for the most part, chose very simple subjects and conveyed the intensity of his feeling for nature through his particularly harmonious use of color. A characteristic work is *In the Forest of Fontainebleau* (1873–76; Budapest, Museum of Fine Arts), in which the great shady trees, penetrated occasionally by tiny shafts of sunlight, dwarf the solitary and defenseless wanderer. Paál was unrecognized during his lifetime and subsisted under drastic circumstances. He died prematurely, yet although his oeuvre is slight, he is justly regarded as one of the masters of the Barbizon School and, with Mihály Munkácsy, as the greatest Hungarian landscapist of the 19th century.

PACHER, Michael (*c.* 1435, Neustift, or Novacella, near Brixen, or Bressanone, North Italy—1498, Salzburg?), Austrian painter and sculptor of altarpieces. Nothing is definitely known of Pacher's early years, but in his first certain works there is stylistic evidence of contact with the altarpieces of Hans Multscher of Ulm, the engravings of Master E.S., and the sculpture of Nicolaus Gerhaerts of Leyden (d. 1473). In the 1470s and 1480s Pacher's work, especially his painting, reveals a direct contact with Italian developments, and it is generally accepted that he studied at first hand the frescoes of Andrea Mantegna in Padua (Ovetari Chapel, Church of the Eremitani).

Michael Pacher. *Coronation of the Virgin.* 1471–81. Detail from altarpiece, church of St. Wolfgang (Salzkammergut). *Photo Gundermann, Würzburg.*

Pacher's first signed and documented altarpiece, executed for the old parish church of Gries, near Bozen (now Bolzano), for which an agreement was drawn up on May 27, 1471, is not the work of an artist at the beginning of his career. The principal subject is the *Coronation of the Virgin*, of which only the carved part survives (preserved not on the church's high altar but in the chapel of St. Erasmus). Evidence of Pacher's reputation is indicated by the fact that in the year of this commission, 1471, the artist concluded an agreement for a larger altarpiece, which is still in its original place in the choir of the pilgrimage church of St. Wolfgang (Salzkammergut). The central subject, as at Gries, is a *Coronation of the Virgin*, but at St. Wolfgang Pacher shows an amazing growth in breadth and flexibility. Here the influence of Mantegna is first apparent: in the solid, volumetric figures, exuding a monumental grandeur, with their broad-planed faces full of gravity. The altarpiece—Pacher's best-known work—was not completed until 1481.

Of his late masterwork, the altarpiece (commissioned in 1484) for the Franciscan church of Salzburg, all that remains is the very fine, although partially damaged, carving of the *Virgin*, which is still in the church, and parts of two painted panels (both in Vienna, Österreichische Galerie). Pacher's so-called Brixen Altarpiece, or the altarpiece of the Fathers of the Church, has unfortunately been dispersed; however, the Alte Pinakothek, Munich, retains the powerful panels of the fathers, which are Pacher's most monumental work in painting, and scenes from the *Life of St. Wolfgang*. These panels reveal that, although Pacher was familiar with theories of perspective, he chose not to follow the mathematically calculated spatial recessions of the Italians, but instead sharpened the diagonal sightlines and squeezed and foreshortened his architectural frameworks, creating deep and dynamic plunges into space. The altar was consecrated in 1465, but the panels were not executed until about 1483.

Pacher's absorption of the style of Mantegna makes his work one of the major factors in the dissemination of Italian art to the North. However, he seems not to have known or to have been unimpressed with Mantegna's use of antique motifs, nor does his sculpture, which achieves its own monumentality and an effective intensity, appear touched by Italian influences.

PAGE, William (1811, Albany—1885, Tottenville, Staten Island), American painter. Page worked as a map engraver's apprentice and was able to study art with Samuel F. B. Morse. He joined a drawing class at the National Academy in 1826, and in 1835 was made its director. During the early 1830s Page painted portraits and historical pictures in Rochester and Albany, and also in Northampton, Massachusetts. As a portraitist, he had a rather romantic and mystical attitude toward his vocation, combining a belief in geometric proportions with a study of phrenology and an artistic approach that sought to avoid pictorial formulas or compositional types. *Portrait of a Young Girl* (New York, Metropolitan Museum) indicates Page's free manner; with its sensitive definition of the face and its loose brushwork, it is quite different from the typical portraits of his time.

In 1849 he set out for Europe to copy paintings by Titian, whose technique he admired greatly. Attempting to emulate the darkened varnish of these old canvases, Page experimented with his materials and, as a result, many of his paintings have since deteriorated from chemical reaction. When he returned from Europe, he settled in New Jersey in order to be near his friend George Inness.

PAINE, James (b. *c.* 1716—d. 1789, France), English architect. Little is known of Paine's early life. He studied drawing at the St. Martin's Lane Academy in London, and architecture under Thomas Jersey (d. 1751). Paine held various high public appointments during his life and, with Sir Robert Taylor (1714–88), was the most sought after architect of his day. He was one of the last of the Palladian architects, although toward the end of his long and prolific career, some parts of his interiors began to show the influence of Robert Adam. The stair well at Wardour Castle, Wiltshire (*c.* 1770–76), the best surviving example of his style, and the library and drawing room ceilings of Brocket Hall, Hertfordshire (*c.* 1760–70) particularly reflect this influence. However, the façades of his buildings, which rely heavily on the work of William Kent, Inigo Jones and, to some extent, Colen Campbell, remained Palladian to the end. His most interesting work is to be found in Stockeld Park, Yorkshire (1758–63); Belford, Northumberland (1754–56); the stables and bridge at Chatsworth, Derbyshire (1758–63); and the Mansion House, Doncaster, Yorkshire (1745–48), which is based on Inigo Jones's palace drawings. Paine was also a well-known bridge designer and planned four of the Thames bridges. He retired to France a few months before his death.

PAJOU, Augustin (1730, Paris—1809, Paris), French sculptor. He was awarded the Prix de Rome in 1748, and was elected to the Académie Royale de Peinture et de Sculpture in 1760. Louis XVI appointed Pajou his official sculptor after he had worked in this capacity for Madame du Barry, executing some 10 busts of her, each with a different headdress. Although he generally aimed for no more than a superficial charm, Pajou's work sometimes possessed profounder qualities, as in the busts of his master *Lemoyne* (terra cotta, 1759; Nantes, Musée des Beaux-Arts), the actor *Carlin* (1763; Paris, Comédie Française) with his jovial plumpness, the painters *Hubert Robert* (terra cotta, 1789; Paris, École des Beaux-Arts), and *Madame Vigée-Lebrun* (1783) in all her youthful radiance. The fine standing figure of *Nathalie de Laborde* (1792) combines the characteristics of the portrait and the decorative statue. Pajou's outstanding success in decorative sculpture was the *Abandoned Psyche* (1785–91; Paris, Louvre), which scandalized the curé of St-Germain-l'Auxerrois in Paris, who was the moral spokesman of the Salon from which it was removed. One of his triumphant achievements was the decoration of the Versailles Opera House (begun 1768), with its green and blue, gold and silver harmonies, and statues in the Classical manner placed all along the double gallery of the auditorium. This magnificent ensemble was completed in 1770 for the marriage of the dauphin, the future Louis XVI.

PALISSY, Bernard (*c.* 1510, Saintes or Lacapelle-Biron, Charente-Maritime—1589/90, Paris), French ceramist, who was also a geologist, physicist, chemist, and philosopher. He is generally regarded as one of the great minds of his time. After studying glass painting and traveling in southwest France, he settled in Saintes around 1540, where, inspired by an ancient ceramic goblet, he devoted 15 years to the study of enamelwork. In 1556 he presented King Henri II with an enameled earthenware bowl. Six years later Anne de Montmorency, High Constable of France, commissioned Palissy to make a rustic grotto for the garden of his château at Écouen. Montmorency died before the work was finished, however, and in 1570 Palissy, badly in need of funds, offered it, in a slightly altered form, to Catherine de Médicis. Palissy himself described the grotto as a large fountain of terra cotta about 40 feet high in the shape of an ocean rock and covered with shells, sea plants, fruits, foliage, animals, and other forms in enamel. The water was ejected through the mouths of carved fishes into a moat surrounding the rock and drained through a hidden canal into the garden opposite. Palissy was in fact considerably ahead of his time in the variety and novelty of his researches and in the primacy he accorded to observation and experiment. His rustic figurines are particularly remarkable for their plant and animal decorations, the molds for which were made on the actual objects—leaves, materials, even cadavers. Above all they are distinguished by the subtlety of their enamels, which are exceptionally clear and transparent.

Richard Boyle, Earl of Burlington. Chiswick House. 1725–29. *Photo Crown Copyright, London.*

PALLADIANISM. This term denotes the movement (*c.* 1720–70) that dominated English architecture, especially in the design of country houses, taking its inspiration from the work of the late Renaissance Venetian architect, Andrea Palladio. Palladianism was tied politically to the Whigs, supporters of the House of Hanover, who associated the Baroque of Sir Christopher Wren and Sir John Vanbrugh with the "unconstitutional" Stuart monarchy.

Several important books initiated and encouraged the movement. In 1712 the Earl of Shaftesbury published his *Letter Concerning Art and Design*, which argued in favor of a more dignified and sober style, reviving the spirit of ancient Rome and avoiding Baroque departure from Classical rule. This was followed in 1715 by the publication of the first volume of a folio of engravings of Classical buildings in Britain, in which the Scottish architect Colen Campbell championed Palladio and his English disciple Inigo Jones.

In the same year Giacomo Leoni (1686–1746), a Venetian architect, began to publish an English version of Palladio's *I quattro libri dell' architettura*, with plates newly drawn by Leoni and a text translated by Nicholas Dubois (*c.* 1665–1735). Both the *Vitruvius* and the *Quattro libri* were dedicated to King George I and are thus clearly Whiggish products. The first Palladian house actually constructed in this early phase of the movement was Wilbury, in Wiltshire. Built in 1710 by architect William Benson

Andrea Palladio. Villa Capra (Villa Rotonda), near Vicenza. 1550–51. *Photo Jean Roubier, Paris.*

(1682–1754), its plan derives ultimately from a design by Jones. In 1718 Wren was deprived of his surveyorship of the Board of Works. Benson was put in his place, and the whole of the Board was filled with Palladians in a sort of architectural *coup d'état.*

Richard Boyle, third Earl of Burlington, was the central figure in the second phase of the Palladian movement. His tastes had sufficiently altered, after an initial tour of Italy (1714–15), for him to entrust the renovation of Burlington House to Campbell, replacing an earlier Baroque architect (probably James Gibbs). In 1719 he again went to Italy, spending some months in Vicenza in order to study Palladio at first hand, and returned to England with many original drawings by Palladio. With his protégé William Kent, Burlington thenceforward dictated the course of the movement until Kent's death in 1748. Burlington's Chiswick House, Middlesex (1725–29), is the most complete expression of Palladianism. It is a free interpretation of Palladio's Villa Rotonda, near Vicenza, with interior details based on work and designs of Inigo Jones.

The style spread throughout England rapidly, the larger houses deriving from Campbell's Wanstead House, Essex (1715–20), and Houghton House, Norfolk (begun 1722), as well as from Kent's Holkham Hall, Norfolk (begun 1734). Inspiration for the smaller houses, or villas, can be traced largely to Chiswick and to Campbell's Stourhead, Wiltshire (designed *c.* 1721). The exteriors of Palladian buildings are austere, with emphasis on unadorned wall space relieved by relatively small windows. The details and architectural motifs derive both from the projects and finished work of Palladio and Jones. Most Palladian buildings have an impressive Classical portico in the middle of the façade. Later Palladian architects include Henry Flitcroft (1697–1769), Isaac Ware (d. 1766), James Paine (*c.* 1716–89), and the John Woods (father and son) of Bath. William Chambers practiced in the style, but in the 1760s and 1770s helped to transform it into something approaching Neoclassicism.

PALLADIO, Andrea di Pietro della Gondola, *called* Andrea (1518, Padua—1580, Vicenza), Italian architect. The Humanist poet Giangiorgio Trissino of Vicenza gave him the name Palladio, derived from Pallas Athena, because it seemed to him that in this young man something of the grace and wisdom of the Greeks had been reborn. Palladio began his career as a stonecutter in his native Padua, and it was among the buildings of antiquity—those of Verona, Istria, and, above all, those of Rome, which he visited three times (in 1541, 1547, and 1549)—that Palladio formed his own style. He also became familiar with Vitruvius and was exposed to both Renaissance (Bramante) and Mannerist (Michelangelo) influences in Rome and in northern Italy, where a number of Roman-trained masters fled after the sack of the city in 1527. The extent to which he absorbed all of these traditions is indicated by his heavy use of ancient motifs, which, however, he handled in a free or idiosyncratic manner.

In 1546 Palladio was chosen from a number of eminent contestants to rebuild the façades of the ancient Palazzo della Ragione in Vicenza, whose renovation posed some delicate problems. Here Palladio employed the familiar design of large arches flanked on either side by two smaller rectangular openings that extended to the level of the springing. The motif is carried out on both stories of the building and is articulated by columns of alternately large and small orders, a treatment that continues around all four sides. The Palazzo della Ragione established an unrivaled position for its architect in Venice as well as Vicenza, and for the next 30 years he received a great number and variety of important commissions.

Because he worked for the nobility, Palladio built many town palaces (palazzi), mostly at Vicenza, and large country homes (villas), throughout the Veneto, and he imposed his style on these two architectural types in particular. He experimented a good deal with the colonnades, handling them either as colossal orders—that is, columns that embrace the entire height of the building (Palazzo Valmarana, 1566, and Loggia del Capitano, 1571; both Vicenza)—or superposed one story on top of another (Palazzo Barbarano or Porto-Barbarano, Vicenza, before 1570). The columns or pilasters either preceded an open loggia or were used as a frame for the bays; the two methods could also be combined, as in the highly individual Palazzo Chiericato, Vicenza (begun 1550). In his designs for country villas, Palladio often applied an ancient pedimented temple front to the central body, but he tempered the solemnity of

Andrea Palladio. Teatro Olimpico, Vicenza. Begun 1580, completed by Vincenzo Scamozzi. Detail of the stage. *Photo Jean Roubier, Paris.*

this arrangement by adding to it lower wings, or *barchesse*, which could be either straight (villas Piovene at Lonedo, *c.* 1538; Emo at Fanzolo, later 1550s; and Barbaro at Maser, *c.* 1555–59), or curved (Villa Badoer at Fratta Polesine, 1554–63).

The Villa Capra, known as the Villa Rotonda (1550–51), in the immediate vicinity of Vicenza, demonstrates a refined handling of academic form. It has a large circular domed hall in the center of a square building, the four identical façades of which are each fronted by an Ionic portico, resulting in an almost completely symmetrical structure. Many of the villas were decorated under Palladio's personal supervision, with the sculpture and stuccowork executed by Alessandro Vittoria, and the fresco paintings by Veronese and his disciples. The most dazzling of these frescoes are found at the Villa Barbaro at Maser (*c.* 1555–59; now the Villa Volpi).

Palladio was particularly interested in theater architecture and decoration. The success of his two temporary wooden theaters, one in the Vicenza Basilica (1561), the other in the Convento della Carità, Venice (1565), led the Olympic Academy of Vicenza to commission Palladio to design the Teatro Olimpico. It too was derived from Roman models; construction began in the year of the architect's death. The most extraordinary feature of the theater is the permanent stage set, originally intended for a production of *Oedipus Rex*, that was executed by his pupil Vincenzo Scamozzi from Palladio's designs. The stage wall, treated as the splendid façade of a palace, opens through three arcades onto streets whose apparent depth is considerably extended by the novel device of "accelerated" perspective—a treatment that makes the actors seem to grow as they withdraw from the stage.

Most of Palladio's secular work is to be seen in and around Vicenza, but his religious and monastic buildings all late works—are mostly in Venice. These include S. Giorgio Maggiore (1566–80) and the refectory of the neighboring monastery, decorated with Veronese's *Marriage Feast at Cana*; the façade of S. Francesco della Vigna (1562); and the church of Il Redentore (begun 1577). The Venetian churches are particularly striking for the beautiful handling of their interior space, yet the adaptation of antique forms on the façades produced somewhat confused but fascinating compositions. A good deal of his success also lies in an insistence on rhythm emanating from his principles of harmonic proportion, which inform all of his buildings, religious and secular, and which are expounded in his published works.

Palladio's style was continued by his immediate followers—Scamozzi, Giovanni Battista Aleotti (1546–1636), Francesco Zamberlan (1529–1606)—and disseminated by his books, the most influential of which was *I quattro libri dell'architettura*, 1570 (*Four Books of Architecture*, published in English in 1738). In the 18th century this style was revived with great success not only in the Veneto, but also in France, Russia, and Sweden. Lastly and above all in England, there flourished what was called Palladianism, which inspired the work of such famous artists as Inigo Jones, James Paine (*c.* 1716–89), Colen Campbell, William Kent, Isaac Ware (d. 1766), and, to a lesser extent, Robert Adam.

PALMA GIOVANE, Jacopo Antonio Negretti, *called* (1544, Venice—1628, Venice), Italian painter, grandnephew of Palma Vecchio. A history painter with Mannerist leanings, he worked, when still young, in the Venetian studio of the aged Titian. During an eight-year stay in Rome, he became familiar with the works of Michelangelo and Raphael. When he returned to Venice in 1568, Palma was attracted by Tintoretto's manner and he imitated it in all his decorations for churches and palaces in Venice, including the sacristy of S. Giacomo dall'Orio (1575). After the fire of 1577 in the Palazzo Ducale, Palma was one of the artists (along with the Bassani, Federico Zuccaro, and Veronese) commissioned to decorate the Sala del Maggior Consiglio and the Sala dello Scrutinio. For the latter he painted a large decorative composition of the *Last Judgment*, showing a medley of figures in vigorous movement. His most typical work is probably the narrative cycle in Venice's Oratorio dei Crociferi (*c.* 1590), which exemplifies the technical dexterity and dynamic confusion of Venetian Mannerism.

Palma Vecchio. *Reclining Venus.* Gemäldegalerie, Dresden. *Photo Alinari.*

PALMA VECCHIO, Jacopo Negretti, *called* (*c.* 1480, Serina, near Bergamo—1528, Venice), Italian painter. In all probability he was never the pupil of Giovanni Bellini, as tradition claims, for his style suggests contacts with the school of Bergamo, which is quite distinct from the Venetian manner practiced by Bellini's circle. Nevertheless, Palma did show considerable interest in the new trends being developed by Titian, Lorenzo Lotto, and other painters of the Venetian Cinquecento, and was one of the first to be influenced by Giorgione, especially in his pastoral compositions of the 1520s (*Three Sisters* or *Three Graces*, before 1525; Dresden, Gemäldegalerie). Palma's ecclesiastical commissions were numerous, and included such large and ambitious *sacre conversazioni* as the altarpieces of *St. Barbara* (*c.* 1522–23; Venice, S. Maria Formosa) and of the *Madonna with St. Roch and St. Mary Magdalene* (*c.* 1512–15; Munich, Alte Pinakothek). Palma's style of portraiture also reflects a Giorgionesque flavor, with lyrically idealized and somewhat dreamy models; his *Portrait of a Lady* (*c.* 1520; Milan, Museo Poldi-Pezzoli) shows the rather robust blond type favored by the artist in his representations of the female figure.

PALMER, Samuel (1805, London—1881, Reigate, Surrey), English watercolorist of intensely mystical and visionary capacities. His incisive style appears to have been based almost exclusively on a study of engravings, mainly those of Claude Lorrain and Adam Elsheimer. In 1822 he met John Linnell (1792–1882), who introduced him to the graphic work of Albrecht Dürer, and in 1824 came a decisive meeting with William Blake. It should be noted, however, that Palmer's visionary streak was already pronounced. In 1827 he retired to Shoreham, a small village in Kent, and in this "valley of vision" he produced his most ecstatic or "excessive" (his own word) watercolors, truly paradisaical images of full moons, sleeping shepherds, unnaturally fertile cornfields and apple trees (*In a Shoreham Garden*, *c.* 1829, London, Victoria and Albert Museum; *Cornfield by Moonlight with the Evening Star*, *c.* 1830, London, Coll. Lord Clark; *Magic Apple Tree*, 1830, Cambridge, Fitzwilliam Museum). The intensity of his vision may be induced from his astonishing *Self-Portrait* (1828; Oxford, Ashmolean Museum). In 1832 he bought a house in London and his mystical identity with the Kentish countryside began to weaken. In 1837 he married John Linnell's daughter Hannah. Sketching tours in Wales (1835, 1836) and a honeymoon in Italy (1837) failed to revive that semi-Christian, semi-Virgilian pastoral strangeness that was the great discovery of his adolescence.

PAN, Marta (b. 1923, Budapest), Hungarian-born French sculptress. She studied painting, drawing, and sculpture in Budapest, then went to Paris in 1947. The forms of her sculpture were at first organic, deriving from plants and shells (7, 1947; plaster), but it was their structure, not their outward appearance, that she tried to capture. In 1953 she produced a series of hinged sculpture whose component parts could be opened and shut, thus assuming entirely different appearances as their positions were shifted. Some of her wooden sculptures (*Le Teck*, 1956) have been used in ballet settings by Maurice Béjart. Marta Pan also designed decorative models in aluminum for mass production, which are specially adapted to modern architectural interiors, as well as a *Floating Sculpture* (1961; Otterlo, Rijksmuseum Kröller-Müller).

Marta Pan. *Floating Sculpture.* 1961. Rijksmuseum Kröller-Müller, Otterlo. *Photo Arno Hammacher, Milan.*

Giovanni Paolo Pannini. *Interior of the Pantheon in Rome.* Samuel H. Kress Coll., National Gallery of Art, Washington, D.C.

PANNINI, Giovanni Paolo (*c.* 1691, Piacenza—*c.* 1765, Rome), Italian painter. Pannini was one of the finest *vedutisti* of the 18th century, and after his arrival in Rome (*c.* 1718) began to specialize in views commemorating the city's official celebrations, public festivals, and historic events (*Interior of St. Peter's with Cardinal de Polignac*, 1729; Paris, Louvre). Conceived as vast urban perspectives with crowds of small animated figures set against sumptuous architectural backgrounds, these compositions are often bathed in light and cut by strong diagonals. In addition to these quasi-documentary scenes of contemporary life, Pannini produced a number of imaginary views (called *capricci* or *vedute ideate*) that combine detailed renderings of actual buildings or landmarks with fantastic ruins; these works anticipate the romantic landscapes of Hubert Robert and Giambattista Piranesi. In his huge companion paintings of *Ancient Rome* and *Renaissance Rome* (both 1757; both New York, Metropolitan Museum) Pannini ingeniously assembled all the major architectural and sculptural monuments of the Eternal City's glorious artistic past.

PAOLO VENEZIANO (b. Venice—d. *c.* 1362, Venice), Italian painter, the most important of the Veneto-Byzantine artists. The art historian Bernard Berenson described his style as "nearly as Byzantine as if trained and working at Constantinople. Influenced somewhat by Italian art." A painting of the *Coronation of the Virgin* in the National Gallery in Washington, D.C. is dated 1324, and is attributed to Paolo. This is the earliest date for his activity, the latest being 1358, on another version of the same theme (New York, Frick Collection), which Paolo signed together with his son Giovanni. Another son, Luca, was also a painter, and all three artists signed the covering that they painted (1345) for the Pala d'Oro in St. Mark's, Venice. Two other paintings are signed by Paolo alone—a polyptych on the *Death of the Virgin* (1333) in the Vicenza Pinacoteca and a *Madonna Enthroned* (1347) in the parish church at Carpineta, near Cesena. Among the dated panels ascribed to him are parts of a dismembered polyptych (1353) whose central panel, representing the Madonna, is in the Louvre, Paris.

PAOLOZZI, Eduardo (b. 1924, Edinburgh), British sculptor of Italian parentage. He studied at the Slade School in London, then traveled to Paris. Paolozzi's first exhibition was in London in 1947, and he was represented among the young British sculptors at the Venice Biennale of 1962, as well as at the São Paulo Bienal in 1957.

Paolozzi, who was young enough to have escaped Henry Moore's dominating influence, rejected the elder sculptor's values of craftsmanship and truth to material, assuming the lead of a new antirational, British movement linked historically with Marcel Duchamp's and Picasso's assemblages of found objects.

Paolozzi's work embodies a search for totemic signs and images in terms of contemporary machine culture. His earlier cement sculptures, which are reminiscent of Giacometti's work in the early 1930s, contain few implications of humanity, suggesting instead a haphazard scatter of marine and insect-like forms in relief upon some central mass or plane. His figures have the quality of semi-animated robots moving awkwardly through the aftermath of an atomic holocaust (*Japanese War God*, 1958; Buffalo, Albright-Knox Gallery). They are marked by the impressions of miscellaneous, but mostly mechanical components that convey, both in surface and structure, the feeling of an industrial, technological, urban environment (*Town Tower*, 1962; London, Marlborough New London Gallery).

PARIS, Harold (b. 1925, Edgemire, New York), American sculptor. In 1954 he studied in Europe on a Guggenheim Fellowship and in 1956 settled in France, where he taught sculpture and built his own foundry. He returned to the United States and settled in the San Francisco Bay area, teaching at the University of California in Berkeley. In the early 1960s Paris was closely associated with Peter Voulkos and other West Coast sculptors in the development of a foundry and a movement in cast-metal sculpture.

Paris' oeuvre is considerably varied and includes terra-cotta reliefs, cast-metal sculpture, and environments. He gained experience in bronze while in Europe and developed his style in the latter medium with bolder, larger works executed in California during the early 1960s. In these he often juxtaposed rectilinear forms with roughly textured Expressionistic forms to create unexpected relationships that are abstract yet suggestive of human experience (*Child*, 1961, bronze; *Voice and Seat*, 1963, cast iron). Around the mid-1960s Paris also became interested in environmental arrangements of objects and, utilizing materials such as rubber, he created unusual tactile effects (*Pantomima Illuma*, 1965–66; plastic, rubber, stainless steel, Coll. artist).

Eduardo Paolozzi. *Japanese War God*. 1958. Albright-Knox Gallery, Buffalo. *Photo David Farrell, London.*

PARIS, School of, name given to a group of foreign painters who gathered in Paris after World War I. The group originally included Amedeo Modigliani, an Italian; Jules Pascin, a Bulgarian; Marc Chagall, a Russian; Moïse Kisling, a Pole; and Chaïm Soutine, a Lithuanian. To these could be added the Polish Léopold Gottlieb (1883–after 1930) and Eugène Zak (1884–1926); Pinchus Krémègne, Michel Kikoïne, and Mané-Katz (Russians); Abraham Mintchine (Ukrainian, 1898–1931); and Max Band (Lithuanian, b. 1900). All these painters belonged to the same generation, and all were Jews, their outlook marked by the melancholy or revolt engendered by common experiences. Although they were contemporaries of the Cubists and were often friendly with them, they did not adopt Cubist theory or practice, but remained emotional, Romantic, and passionately Expressionist in their style. Their Expressionism, however, was very different from the German, Scandinavian, and Belgian manifestations.

Outside France, the term "School of Paris" was broadened to encompass all foreign artists who settled in that city from the beginning of the 20th century, including Pablo Picasso, Juan Gris, Kees van Dongen, and Tsugouharu Léonard Foujita (1886–1968), as well as Chagall, Kisling, and Pascin. The designation eventually became so loose that it became synonymous with the progressive wing of contemporary painting.

PARKER, Raymond, *called* Ray (b. 1922, Beresford, South Dakota), American painter. In 1950 he became acquainted with several New York Abstract Expressionist painters and moved there the following year. Parker's early paintings still manifest Cubist concerns. After 1950 he increasingly explored the possibilities and limitations of color in abstract paintings whose color planes edged each other actively. Subsequent larger canvases became more painterly in treatment and the wide, scrubbed brushstrokes characterized an "Abstract-Impressionist" phase.

Around 1958 Parker was one of several younger painters who reacted against the "academic" imitators of Willem de Kooning and Jackson Pollock. The brushstrokes took on a new discipline, defining legible shapes from the inside out and ordering the structure of the pictures more coherently. *Stack* (1958; New York, Coll. artist), with its three cloud- or loaflike forms suspended one above the other in a vertical rectangular field, is typical of this period. The muted colors are also characteristic of the subtle harmonies Parker chose to explore. By 1962 four or five roughly square or rectangular forms replaced these earlier clouds, now crowding the picture space in parallel vertical or horizontal rows. These clusters were superseded by squares in grid arrangements (*No. 132*, 1964; New York, Kootz Gallery), until the regularity was broken in 1965 by freely cut out shapes in more intense hues, scattered randomly across a neutral ground (*No. 171*, 1966; New York, Coll. artist). Colored fields of Matissean brilliance were contrasted with bending mobile strands in equally bright hues in Parker's paintings of 1967–68.

PARKIN, John Burnet (b. 1911, Toronto), Canadian architect. Parkin established his own practice in Toronto in 1937. He eventually headed the firm of John B. Parkin Associates, Architects and Engineers (organized 1947), one of Canada's largest and most distinguished architectural firms.

Parkin designed a number of small rural elementary schools in Ontario during the 1940s, but after 1950 secured a variety of commissions, particularly at Don Mills, a well-planned satellite community near Toronto. The community includes a 44-acre Shopping Center (1954–60), the brick and timber St. Mark's Presbyterian church (1965), and several industrial buildings. Parkin's own offices—a well-proportioned, glass and steel modular cage—form part of the project.

Engineers within the architectural firm encouraged a wide range of structural expression from the exposure of the rough concrete frame (Ortho Pharmaceutical Plant, Don Mills, 1964) to the use of precast window-wall panels (Imperial Oil Offices, Don Mills, 1963), and folded "tent roof" slabs (Fourth Secondary School, Sault Ste-Marie, 1961).

The smooth glass and mullion skin of the Imperial Oil Engineering Building at Sarnia (1956) closely parallels the International Style architecture of Ludwig Mies van der Rohe and Skidmore, Owings & Merrill.

Other notable examples of Parkin's work are the buildings for Toronto's International Airport (Aeroquay 1 completed 1964); Taylor Instrument Company, North York, 1954; Thomas J. Lipton, Limited, Bramalea, 1966; Humber Memorial Hospital in Weston, near Toronto, 1950–51; Sun Life Offices, Toronto, 1961; and several private homes.

PARLER, family of German (Swabian) masons who worked in Bohemia and throughout southern Germany in the 14th century, and exercised considerable influence on the development of the Late Gothic style in these regions. The best-known members of the family were: HEINRICH THE ELDER, founder of the family, who probably designed the choir of the Kreuzkirche (1351) at Gmünd, a work generally regarded as the earliest example of the Late Gothic style.

PETER (1330, Gmünd—1399, Prague), Heinrich's son, was the most successful member of the family. He was invited by Charles IV to succeed the Frenchman Matthias of Arras (d. 1352) as master mason at Prague Cathedral, where the vaults show an awareness of English work. In addition to his role as architect, Peter directed and probably executed part of the sculptural decoration. Apart from the six royal tombs of the Přemislids family, there are 21 portrait busts placed in the galleries of the triforium (1379–93), which form an almost unique series in German sculpture. Peter was also responsible for the Charles Bridge over the Vltava (begun 1357), as well as for the choir of St. Bartholomew's Church at Kolin (after 1360).

MICHAEL (b. after 1354), Peter's brother, worked on the Cistercian monastery of Goldenkron (Koruna), and on the minster at Ulm (1377–92).

WENZEL (d. 1404), Peter's son, continued his father's work as architect of Prague Cathedral in 1397.

JOHANN PARLER—whose relationship to Peter is unknown—was master mason at Freiburg-im-Breisgau in 1359, where he worked on the choir of the cathedral. He also restored the choir of Basel Cathedral (1357). A certain Heinrich Behaim Balier may have been one of Peter Parler's brothers. He built the eastern part of the choir of St. Sebald at Nuremberg (1361–72), and designed the "Beautiful Fountain" (1385–96) in the market square of the same city.

Parthian Art. *Uthal, king of Hatra.* 2nd century. Mosul Museum.

PARMIGIANINO, Francesco Mazzola, *called* Il (1503, Parma—1540, Castel Maggiore, near Bologna), Italian Mannerist painter. Parmigianino was influenced by Correggio, but this did not prevent him from absorbing the light effects peculiar to Domenico Beccafumi and the violent forcefulness of Giovanni Pordenone. Parmigianino went to Rome in 1524, where he was confronted with a bewildering diversity of styles. He succeeded in fusing these various elements into a highly personal art, delicately fashioned yet powerful, in which the virtuosity he acquired early in life and had ostensibly cultivated (*Self-Portrait in a Convex Mirror*, 1523/24; Vienna, Kunsthistorisches Museum) served an imagination that grew gradually more and more divorced from reality. After the Sack of Rome (1527) he fled to Bologna, where he demonstrated his ability in a powerful and elegantly rhetorical style (*S. Rocco with a Donor*, 1527; Bologna, basilica of S. Petronio), marked by ambiguous opposing rhythms (*Madonna of the Rose*, 1528–30; Dresden, Gemäldegalerie) and minglings of subtle, sensual evocations with ancient ruins and withered leaves (*Madonna with St. Zacharias, St. Mary Magdalene, and St. John*, c. 1530; Florence, Uffizi). Returning to Parma (1531), he painted the frescoes in S. Maria della Steccata (1531–39). With the strange, compelling *Madonna with the Long Neck* (1534–40; Uffizi) he carried the tension of his tapering, elegant lines and unorthodox forms to an extreme. In the last few years of his life, he seemed to be moving toward greater austerity and a style with more solid forms and more accentuated rhythms.

Parmigianino did some remarkable portraits, in which his models were flattered with the most aristocratic reflection of themselves (*Gian Galeazzo Sanvitale*, 1524; Naples, Museo di Capodimonte) and only the pensive melancholy of their inner self remained (*Lady with a Fur*, called *Antea*, 1535–37; Museo di Capodimonte). As a religious painter, he shunned crowd effects and preferred compositions with a few figures, stressing grace and a certain languor in the figures. Some very fine etchings, such as the *Entombment*, quickly brought a widespread reputation for his style; Primaticcio and Niccolò dell'Abbate carried it abroad to France.

PARRIS, Alexander (1780, Hebron, Maine—1852, Pembroke, Massachusetts), American architect of the Federal and Greek Revival periods. In 1816 he built the Sears House, Boston (now the Somerset Club and almost doubled in size)—a remarkably urbane and assured example of the late Federal style. But the building that brought him fame was St. Paul's Church, Boston (1819). This austere stone rectangle, with its hexastyle Ionic portico, marks the beginning of the shift in the artistic sensibility of New England toward the Classical Revival and away from the Federal style of Charles Bulfinch. Bulfinch himself, in 1816, had produced a Classical Revival design for the Massachusetts General Hospital. Parris took over the construction of the hospital and followed it with what is probably his major work, the Quincy Market complex (1824). His use of a post-and-lintel system of granite piers for the building fronts was far in advance of his time. For the next 20 years he was the dominant architect in the Boston area, where he executed the monumental Unitarian church in Quincy (1828), perhaps his finest work.

PARTHIAN ART. After the death of Alexander the Great in 323 B.C., the Persian satrapies were divided among Alexander's Macedonian generals (Diadochi). The Seleucids were the inheritors of the largest part of the Achaemenid empire, and had to confront a new power, that of the Parthians, who had appeared on the eastern frontiers. In fact, around 250 B.C., Arsaces, a nomadic chief, had seized the province of Parthava and had founded the dynasty of the Parthian-Arsacids. This dynasty began to extend its territory westward until it reached the Tigris and then settled in 150 B.C. on the left bank of that river at

Parthian Art. *Nergal with a goddess in majesty.* Hatra, 2nd century. Iraq Museum, Baghdad.

Ctesiphon, opposite Seleucia on the right bank. Greece and the East were now face to face, and the result was a Greco-Iranian culture and art. The arrival of the Romans could do little more than contain an advance that sometimes reached as far as the Mediterranean. This was the case until A.D. 226, the date of the revolt of Ardashir, which finally brought the Parthian dynasty to an end and established the new dynasty of the Sassanians.

Parthian art therefore spans the years between 150 B.C. and A.D. 226. It is a curious fact that our knowledge of it comes mainly from outlying sites: Warka, Ctesiphon, Ashur, and Hatra in what is now Iraq, and, much farther east, Nisa and Kuh-i Khwaja. Examples are also found in sectors of the West, such as Dura-Europos in the mid-Euphrates area and Palmyra in the Syrian desert.

The Parthian palace of Ashur (1st century A.D.) has a façade with three stories and a superposition of columns and niches; in the middle is an imposing, round-arched portal. At Hatra, the palace is composed of the juxtaposition of two *iwans* (porches), with a large portal in the middle, flanked by two smaller ones. Behind one of the *iwans*, and opening onto it, is a square-plan building, surrounded by an ambulatory, which is a temple with a cradle vault.

In the field of freestanding sculpture there are several life-size statues of kings (Uthal, Sanatruq), princesses (Washfari, daughter of Sanatruq; Ubal, daughter of Jabal), dignitaries, priests, and officers, all in ceremonial dress, with their right hands raised in a gesture of welcome. Of the gods, one of the most impressive is the decapitated statue that is thought to be of Baal-Shamim. Among the many reliefs in which an emphasis on frontality appears is one representing a group of three goddesses borne by a lion, with Allat, goddess of war, in the middle; another depicts a bearded Nergal, god of the dead, axe in one hand, and sword in the other, holding watchdogs on leads, with a serpent and a scorpion completing the scene; and finally there is one representing a very beautiful Mithras. Other worthwhile sources of the Parthian style are available: a bearded man's head from Susa (Paris, Louvre); a queen's head, also from Susa; a Parthian prince from Shami, which is probably the most imposing human effigy in metal so far discovered (height: 6 feet 3 inches; 2nd century B.C.; Teheran, Museum).

The Parthian influence is also apparent at Dura-Europos, especially in mural decoration (fresco of the sacrifice of Conon; horseman pursuing an onager, 1st century A.D.), and at Palmyra, where we find the tradition of frontal figuration and the Parthian dress of the wealthy classes. At the other extremity of the Parthian kingdom can be found the astonishing frescoes of Kuh-i Khwaja, with their human figures (king and queen, three gods, etc.). After the fall of the Parthian kingdom, nevertheless, its art continued to exert a powerful influence during the 3rd century A.D., affecting both the early Christian and Sassanian-Persian pictorial and three-dimensional styles.

PASCIN, Julius Mordecai Pincas, *called* Jules (1885, Vidin, Bulgaria—1930, Paris), American painter of Bulgarian origin, a leading member of the School of Paris. Pascin left home at an early age (*c.* 1902) and went first to Vienna, then to Munich, where he attended art school after spending some time in Berlin. He arrived in Paris in 1905 and became one of the legendary figures of Montparnasse. He also did cartoons for the German magazines *Simplicissimus* and *Jugend*. At the beginning of World War I, he emigrated to the United States and became an American citizen. For six years he wandered through Florida, Louisiana, Mexico, and Cuba, recording his travels in witty sketches (*Oyster Bar*, 1917, Columbus, Ohio, Columbus Gallery of Fine Arts; *Morning Toilet in the Pullman*, 1918; *Charleston Bridge*, 1919). On his return to Paris around 1920, his work really began to develop and, for the first time, he produced paintings that were as successful as his drawings. Pascin was primarily concerned with lines and always touched up his figures with diluted, almost pale colors. His principal subject was women and a particularly good example of his sensual nudes is *Madame Julie, the Martinique* (1924; Lausanne, Coll. Paul Josefowitz). He painted such Biblical scenes as the *Prodigal Son* (1921; New York, Coll. Mr. and Mrs. Samuel Josefowitz), a story in which he saw a reflection of his own life, and of which he did many versions. He continued to travel with the obstinacy of a man fleeing from himself; in 1930, after traveling through Spain and Portugal, he returned to Paris and on the day of the private viewing of his exhibition at the Galerie Georges Petit, he hanged himself. Pascin's death tended to accentuate the tragic side of his work. He treated the female body as the image of the supreme recourse against the difficulties of life.

PASMORE, Victor (b. 1908, Chesham, Buckinghamshire), one of Britain's leading modern painters. He was a doctor's son, and worked as an employee of the Public Health Department of the London County Council until 1938. For many years Pasmore was a Sunday painter, influenced by the works of Whistler, Charles Conder, and other English translators of French Impressionist masterpieces (*Parisian Life*, 1936–37, Manchester, City Art Gallery; the *Flower Barrow*, 1938–42, Adelaide, National Gallery of South Australia). He first exhibited as one of "XVII Artists" at the Zwemmer Gallery, London, in 1930 and 1931 and, after 1930, he showed more or less regularly with the London Group, of which he became a member in 1934. In 1937, with the painters Claude Rogers (b. 1907), Graham Bell (1907–43), and William Coldstream, he formed the Euston Road School of Drawing and Painting. Pasmore's misty Whistlerian riverscapes of the 1940s (the *Quiet River : the Thames at Chis-*

Victor Pasmore. *Construction-Relief.* 1966. Marlborough Fine Art Gallery, London.

wick, 1943–44; London, Tate Gallery) are exceptionally attractive works. After around 1947, however, he concentrated on the production of abstract constructions, papiers collés, and reliefs. His artistic activity went so far along this road that his works (*Yellow Abstract,* 1960–61; Tate Gallery) are probably more avant-garde than those of Ben Nicholson, with whom his name must be linked in this context.

PATCH, Thomas (1725, Exeter—1782, Florence), English painter, remembered mainly for his caricatures. In 1747 he traveled on foot to Rome and, except for a trip to the Near East in 1749, remained in Italy for the rest of his life. Patch worked with Claude-Joseph Vernet in Rome from 1750 to 1753. An outspoken and quarrelsome man, he was ordered by the Vatican to leave Rome in 1755, and he settled in Florence. His early works were landscapes of a fairly conventional character, very much like the later *View of Florence from the Cascine Gardens* (1771; Houghton Hall, England, Coll. Marquess of Cholmondeley). Soon after his arrival in Florence, however, he also turned to caricatures, painting in a humorous and kindly manner many of the English residents and visitors there, as in the *Portrait of the Third Duke of Roxburghe* (*c.* 1760; London, National Portrait Gallery), and the *Punch Party* (1760; Altrincham, England, Coll. Earl of Stamford).

PATROON PAINTERS, name given to a group of about six artists, active between 1715 and 1730, who constitute the first clearly recognizable school in American art. The name derives from the patroons, the Dutch land-grant holders who had settled in the Hudson River Valley under the auspices of the Dutch West India Company and who patronized these artists. Despite the personal variations of individual masters, their works show certain common features. Portraits are characterized by flat, weightless figures placed in a spaceless environment. The sitter is often situated before the elaborate stage-like setting of a formal garden. Clear, bright color and the arrangement of formal elements in opposing diagonals enliven the figure with a sense of activity. Among the various styles that have been individuated are the DePeyster Manner, as well as those of the so-called *Aetatis Suae* Painter and the Gansevoort Limner. The DePeyster *Girl with a Lamb* (New York, New-York Historical Society) displays all the patent features of the group. The Gansevoort Limner's *Pau DeWandlaer* (*c.* 1725; Albany, Institute of History and Art), although not expressing any greater aspect of character, establishes a mood of quietude and calm.

PAVIA, Phillip (b. 1912, Bridgeport, Connecticut), American sculptor. From 1930 to 1934 he worked simultaneously in New York at the Art Students League and the Beaux-Arts Institute of Design, and from 1934 to 1937 he studied in Paris and Florence.

In the late 1930s Pavia was strongly affected by John Flannagan and the movement of direct carving in America at that period. For a time he worked in a figurative style, exemplified by a series of simplified, larger than life-size figures of standing men and of colossal plaster heads. In the 1950s Pavia concentrated on abstract bronze sculpture (*Great Jones,* 1958–59; bronze, New York, Coll. Mr. and Mrs. Samuel M. Kootz), in which he was concerned with reflected light, tactility, and weight; his first one-man show of bronzes in New York (1961) was the first major exhibition of abstract bronzes by a New York artist. In the 1960s, however, after a trip to Italy, Pavia returned to stone sculpture, especially marble. His sculpture of this period is abstract and often consists of aggregate compositions of marble cubes juxtaposed in a great variety of colors and textures (*New England Novel,* 1964; Seravezza marbles, New York, Estate of Ethel S. Epstein).

PAXTON, Sir Joseph (1803, Milton-Bryant, Bedfordshire—1865, Sydenham, near London), English architect. The son of a small farmer, he became superintendent of the gardens of the sixth duke of Devonshire at Chatsworth in 1826. Paxton acquired a special place in the history of modern architecture for building, in less than six months, one of the largest buildings of the 19th century—the Crystal Palace. This structure, made entirely of iron and glass, was built in 1851 for the Universal Exhibition in London. Paxton had no training either as an engineer or as an architect. His first experiment (a greenhouse at Chatsworth) dates from 1828, and three years later he invented the principle of the saw-tooth roof, which admits natural light from one direction. Paxton went on to develop a model of a sloping glass roof with a very light wooden frame and a special gutter that formed an integral part of the structure. Hollow iron tubes were to be used for very large spans. It was on this model that Paxton based the great Chatsworth Greenhouse (1836–40), then the Crystal Palace itself, whose entirely prefabricated metal structure (made of mass-produced standard elements) covered more than 753,000 square feet. The materials were used again when the palace was re-erected at Sydenham (1852–54; destroyed by fire in 1936).

PEALE, family of 18th- and 19th-century American painters.

CHARLES WILLSON (1741, Queen Anne's County, Maryland—1827, Philadelphia) was the founder of the family and its most illustrious member. He sired 17 children, a number of whom were named after famous old masters and were also artists, including Rubens Peale (1784–1865) and Titian Ramsay Peale (1799–1885).

Apprenticed at the age of twelve to a saddler, Peale was able to establish his own shop nine years later. Debts soon forced him to expand his services to include watchmaking and portrait painting. He spent two years in London (1767–69) studying art under the American-born history painter Benjamin West. Always enthusiastic about natural science, Peale assembled an extensive collection of specimens and in 1786 established a museum in Independence Hall, Philadelphia. Among the attractions of the museum, which proved to be a financial success, was a portrait gallery of illustrious men. Peale's artistic aim was perfect illusion or tactile realism, achieved by means of an accurate description of forms in diffused light (*Artist in His Museum*, 1822; Philadelphia, Pennsylvania Academy of the Fine Arts). A delightful portrait of two of his sons (*Staircase Group*, 1795; Philadelphia, Museum of Art) is an experiment in *trompe-l'oeil*: the picture frame was a doorway, and an actual step was supposed to have been built in front of the canvas to continue into the real space of the observer the painted staircase upon which the figures stand. Textural realism and cast shadows, as well as the lifelike attitudes of the figures, contribute to the illusion.

RAPHAELLE (1774, Annapolis, Maryland—1825, Philadelphia), his eldest son, learned his craft from his father. His only financial success came between 1803 and 1805, when he exploited the physiognotrace, a profile-making machine invented by the Englishman John Isaac Hawkins. Raphaelle was primarily a painter of still lifes, following Dutch and Flemish prototypes of the 17th century. Characteristically, his art was not especially popular, for portraiture was the only genre of painting considered to be of value to frugal Americans of the period. His best-known work—*After the Bath* (1823; Kansas City, William Rockhill Nelson Gallery of Art)—represents the arm and foot of a girl behind a massive piece of drapery hanging from a rope. The variety of whites, the handling of light and shadow, and the skill of the *trompe-l'oeil* express the level of accomplishment he might have attained sooner had still-life painting been readily accepted by the American public.

Charles Willson Peale. *Staircase Group*. 1795. George W. Elkins Coll., Philadelphia Museum of Art.

REMBRANDT (1778, Bucks County, Pennsylvania—1860, Philadelphia), Raphaelle's brother, was also trained by his father. Unlike Raphaelle, however, he specialized in portraiture and assisted his father in this field. He studied with Benjamin West in London (1802–3) and with François Gérard and perhaps Louis David in Paris. In 1814 he opened Peale's Museum and Gallery of Fine Arts in Baltimore, Maryland. He was president of the American Academy of Fine Arts in New York and founded the National Academy of Design in 1826. Rembrandt is best remembered for his porthole portrait of George Washington, a work first conceived in 1795 but repeated with variations throughout his lifetime. A few landscapes and allegorical works are also included in his oeuvre (*Niagara Falls*, 1832, New London, Conn., Lyman Allyn Museum; and the *Court of Death*, 1820, Detroit, Institute of Arts). His interest in the graphic arts is manifested in *Peale's Graphics* (published in 1835), a manual for the teaching of drawing and writing, and in his pioneering work in the new medium of lithography.

PECHSTEIN, Max (1881, Eckersbach, near Zwickau—1955, Berlin), German Expressionist painter. He was a member of the Brücke in Dresden from 1916, and of all the works produced by this group his were most readily accepted by the public. In fact, although he treated more or less the same subjects as his colleagues—landscapes, portraits, still lifes, beach scenes—and like them, used a bright palette, Pechstein's form and construction were fairly nat-

Max Pechstein. *Seated Female Nude*. 1910. Private Coll.

uralistic (*Green House*, 1909; Cologne, Wallraf-Richartz-Museum). He settled in Berlin in 1908, and about 1912 was painting nudes in a landscape, which revealed the influence of Matisse. The *Red Turban* (1911; Pittsburgh, Museum of Art) is clearly derived from Cézanne in its background details. A journey to the Palau island group (part of the Caroline Islands, western Pacific) in 1914 resulted in a number of paintings with exotic subjects and reinforced Pechstein's already apparent bent toward primitivism. In his later work, which consists of portraits and landscapes, he further tempered his Expressionism, and the more easily acceptable side of his modernism is accentuated (*Sunrise*, 1933; Saarbrucken, Saarland Museum).

PEETERS, Jozef (1895, Antwerp—1960, Antwerp), Belgian painter. In 1913, while a student at the Antwerp Academy, he discovered Futurism, which was to have a strong influence on his work. Peeters' first abstract compositions date from 1919, and he remained a brilliant member of the Flemish avant-garde until 1926. As a defender of pure plasticism, Peeters organized a Conference of Modern Art at Antwerp; coedited, with the painter and art critic Michel Seuphor, the review *Het Overzicht* (1922–25); and published essays and manifestoes (cover for *Het Overzicht*, 1922; Paris, Coll. Michel Seuphor). His own painting was resolutely abstract and geometric (*Composition*, 1923; Coll. Michel Seuphor), and he also executed a considerable body of graphic work, notably linocuts. In 1926, when Expressionism triumphed in Belgium, Peeters abandoned all artistic activity, remaining in retirement until 1954, when his rediscovery as one of the pioneers of Flemish abstract art prompted him to resume painting.

Alicia Penalba. *Large Double.* 1964. Rijksmuseum Kröller-Müller, Otterlo.

PEI, Ieoh Ming, *known as* I. M. (b. 1917, Canton, China), American architect (naturalized 1954) and teacher. Pei immigrated to the United States in 1935, and studied architecture at the Massachusetts Institute of Technology and Harvard University. After teaching design (1945–48), he became Director of Architectural Research for the New York real estate firm of Webb and Knapp (1948). In 1959 he organized his own firm of I. M. Pei and Associates (later I. M. Pei and Partners) in New York.

Pei's projects for Webb and Knapp (Mile High Center in Denver, Colorado, 1955), and later for the Canadian National Railroad (Place Ville Marie, Montreal, 1958–61) are skillfully controlled complexes of high-rise blocks and open plazas. He stressed flexibility, especially in the urban environment, yet he established a strongly felt formal order through his strict axial arrangements. Pei sought high quality (strength, durability, and color) poured-in-place concrete structures. A fair-faced window-wall system was developed for the first Kips Bay Plaza apartment block in New York (1960). Further refinements were carried out for Philadelphia's Society Hill Project (1964), New York's Washington Square East (1964), and M. I. T.'s Center for Earth Sciences in Cambridge, Massachusetts (1964). One significant result of these efforts has been the adoption of a load-bearing screen façade that allows greater plastic, three-dimensional articulation of the traditional rectangular block.

PELLAN, Alfred (b. 1906, Quebec), Canadian painter. In 1926, after studying at the Quebec School of Fine Arts, Pellan won a scholarship to study in Paris. There he immediately acquainted himself with contemporary art, of which very little was then known in Canada, and he met Le Corbusier, Max Ernst, and Fernand Léger. Pellan vacillated between Cubism and Surrealism, and was already moving toward an expressive, violent painting, conceived in relation to the wall space. In 1940, because of World War II, he returned to Canada. He was appointed to a teaching post at the Montreal School of Fine Arts, and his exhibitions provoked fruitful controversy. In 1948, with some friends, he launched the manifesto *Prism of Eyes*, which inaugurated a revival of Canadian painting. Pellan's large, firmly structured, surrealistic compositions (*Flowering*, 1952; Ottawa, National Gallery) also date from this period. After a further stay in Paris (1952–55), he settled at Ste-Rose, near Montreal. Apart from the important series of paintings called *Gardens* (1958), Pellan's later work consists of murals and richly colored stained glass.

PENALBA, Alicia Perez (b. 1918, San Pedro, Buenos Aires prov.), Argentine sculptress and painter. In 1932 she settled in Buenos Aires, where she studied painting at the School of Fine Arts. Her first paintings were exhibited at the Salon Nacional in that city, and were received enthusiastically. In 1948 she went to Paris, and took up engraving for a time before turning to sculpture. For three years she studied sculpture with Ossip Zadkine, and was also influenced by Jean Arp. In 1952 Penalba began her series of *Love Totems* and *Vegetal Liturgies*, both of which employ forms like tree trunks in an imaginary forest. These vertical sculptures were followed by outspread forms, symbolic representations (the *Spark*, 1951), or separate elements arranged in relation to an architectural conception (*Project for a Mirror of Water*, 1961).

PENNELL, Joseph (1860, Philadelphia—1926, Brooklyn), American illustrator. He attended the School of the Pennsylvania Academy of the Fine Arts, where he studied under Thomas Eakins. Pennell began his career as an illustrator in the late 1870s, and by 1881 was producing articles and drawings for such magazines as *Harper's Weekly* and *The Century*. In 1882 he was sent to Florence to do a series of 12 etchings for an article on Tuscany, and traveled to Urbino, Siena, Pistoia, and Venice. In 1884 he returned to Europe, spending time in Rome with Elihu Vedder. When he settled in London in 1885 he met J. A. M. Whistler. Pennell later traveled to Russia (1891–92), and shortly thereafter began his series of the *Jews at Home*. He was working with the editor Henry Harland and Aubrey Beardsley on *The Savoy* by 1893, and two years later became art editor of the *London Daily Chronicle*. In the early years of the 20th century he covered such events as the death of Edward VII, the coronation of George V, and World War I for *The Illustrated London News* and the *London Daily Chronicle*. He returned to settle in New York after the war, and founded the graphics department at the Art Students League, where he taught (1922–26). He is perhaps best known for his publications, among which are *A Life of James McNeill Whistler* (1910), *Etchings and Etchers* (1925), *Lithography and Lithographers* (1915), and *A London Reverie* (1928), as well as illustrated travelogues and pictorial decorations of the war works in England and America.

PERCIER, Charles (1762, Paris—1838, Paris), French architect. His name is inseparable from that of Pierre Fontaine (1762–1853), who was his friend and partner for 30 years.

Percier was a pupil of Antoine-François Peyre and Julien David Le Roy (1724–1803), and had already designed several projects of great boldness when he was awarded the Prix de Rome in 1786. In Rome he renewed his acquaintance with Fontaine, who had been a fellow pupil under Peyre. They greatly admired the ancient Roman buildings, made detailed drawings of them, and published a collection of engravings of the finest residences in Rome and its surroundings. Percier and Fontaine cultivated the Classical decorative elements, as exemplified in the work of Giovanni Battista Piranesi and Charles-Louis Clérisseau, and on their return to France, they displayed their talent in decorative work for the "new men" of the Directoire. This work included not only panels and ceilings, but also the accessories and furniture that occupied extremely elegant interiors. The furniture and ornament was based on ancient Classical and Egyptian forms, a style that had begun under Louis XVI, but now flourished with greater archaeological exactitude in the so-called Empire style. Percier and Fontaine's work in this manner for the Hôtel Chauvelin, Paris (1799) attracted the attention of Joséphine Bonaparte, and launched them on a successful official career that began with the decoration of part of Malmaison

(1800–2). For the ballroom of the Tuileries they designed a flat dome with depressed vaults, surrounded by an Ionic colonnade and terminated by two apses. At the entrance to the Tuileries, they built the Arc de Triomphe du Carroussel (1806–8), which was reminiscent of the arch of Septimius Severus in Rome, and whose dimensions were dictated by the size of the shafts of columns obtained from the marble store at Chaillot. At the Louvre, where they worked from 1802, the staircase of the Salon Carré has disappeared, but the fine Doric vestibule to which it led still dominates the Cour du Sphinx. Percier and Fontaine punctuated the perspective of the Grande Galerie with arches and twinned columns. In the area around the Louvre, Percier, assisted by Claude Étienne Beaumont (1757–1811), re-created the impression of an Italian city, by building the arcades of Rue de Rivoli and Rue de Castiglione (begun in 1806) in designing the "piazzetta" of Place des Pyramides. One of the most elegant of the Empire creations of Percier and Fontaine was the Cabinet (1803–5), made of mirrors, mahogany, and platinum, at the Casa del Labrador (Palacio d'Aranjuez).

Charles Percier and Pierre Fontaine. Arc de Triomphe du Carrousel, Paris. 1806–8. Detail of the western side. *Photo Caroly, Paris.*

PEREDA, Antonio de (*c.* 1608, Valladolid—1678, Madrid), Spanish painter. Perhaps with the aid of his protector, the court architect Giovanni Battista Crescenzi (1577–1660), Pereda received the commission to paint several works for the palace of Buen Retiro in Madrid, including the *Marquis of Santa Cruz Relieving Genoa* (1634; Madrid, Prado). After 1634, however, Pereda was no longer able to secure commissions at court. The paintings of his early period to around 1639 were done in a precise and linear manner, as in the *Marquis of Santa Cruz*, executed with much attention to the rich and even sumptuous detail of fabrics, plumes, and armor. Pereda's *vanitas* paintings of *c.* 1650, one of which is in the Kunsthistorisches Museum, Vienna, are contemplative in nature and suggestive of Dutch influence; they do, however, reveal a softer modeling with less sharp outlines. Pereda also painted a number of specifically religious works, such as an *Annunciation* (1637; Prado), and *St. Dominic in Soriano* (*c.* 1655; Madrid, Museo Cerralbo), and many still lifes (1652; Lisbon, Museu Nacional de Arte Antiga).

PEREIRA, Irene Rice, *called* I. Rice (b. 1907, Boston—d. 1971), American painter. In the 1930s Pereira painted nautical equipment and developed techniques of painting on glass and parchment. In 1937 she turned wholeheartedly to geometric abstraction, coming, to some extent, under the influence of Piet Mondrian. Her austere and complex rectilinear structures seem to float in a fluid space, where light is of primary importance (*White Lines*, 1942; New York, Museum of Modern Art). There is also something intuitive and mystic about Pereira's art, in which color alone can suggest atmospheric effects (*Vanishing Night*, 1951; Dallas, Museum of Fine Arts). She continued to paint on glass in a style whose Romanticism persists within the framework of formal limitations (*Shooting Stars*, 1952; New York, Metropolitan Museum).

PERMEKE, Constant (1886, Antwerp—1952, Ostend), Belgian painter and sculptor, the leading protagonist of Flemish Expressionism in the period between World Wars I and II. From 1912 to 1914 he lived in Ostend, where he began to evolve his own unique style. In 1916, during his evacuation in England, he created the first paintings that reveal the truly original aspects of his idiom. Permeke's mature work is characterized by a massive and powerful human presence; color based mainly on browns and yellows; thickly applied paint; a feeling of gravity, together with a play of light and shade that is reminiscent of Rembrandt, although in a more bitter and more rustic vein (*The Fiancés*, 1923; Brussels, Musée d'Art Moderne). These stylistic characteristics became more marked after 1918, when Permeke returned to Belgium. His draftsmanship became even simpler, his distortions even more brutal, his color more dense, and his figures of fishermen, peasants, and working-class women even more crude and primitive. In 1935–36 Permeke began to execute sculpture, especially torsoes and nudes (*Marie-Lou*, 1935–36; Antwerp, Middelheim Park Museum). Together with his paintings, they show that although he was extremely close to the earth, he was really a visionary at heart and even, in a sense, a mystic. He lends an aura of religious gravity to his *Stranger* (1916; Brussels, Musée d'Art Moderne) or *Black Bread* (1923; Ghent, Coll. G. Vanderhaegen), to a *Sow* (1929; Waalre, Holland, Coll. T. Van Bakel) and her piglets, or a cow in the half-light of a damp *Stable* (1933; Paris, Musée National d'Art Moderne).

Constant Permeke. *Marie-Lou.* 1935–36. Middelheim Park Museum, Antwerp.

PERMOSER, Balthasar (1651, Kammer, Upper Bavaria—1732,

Claude Perrault. Observatoire, Paris. 1668–72. The two domes date from the 19th century. *Photo Doisneau-Rapho.*

Dresden), German sculptor. He received most of his training in Italy, where he was strongly influenced by the sculpture of Bernini. Tradition has it that Permoser remained in Italy for 14 years (*c.* 1671–85), working in Venice, Rome, and other cities. From 1689, when he was made sculptor to the court of Saxony, he lived in Dresden, becoming the city's leading Late Baroque sculptor. Together with the architect Mathaes Daniel Pöppelmann, he helped to create a highly individual and excessively contorted, irrational Baroque style that is exemplified in the Zwinger Palace at Dresden. Permoser is usually credited with the sculptural decoration (1711–18) of the Zwinger. His most famous work is a marble allegorical statue representing the *Apotheosis of Prince Eugene of Savoy* (1718–21; Vienna, Österreichisches Barockmuseum), which he probably executed from a portrait that had been sent to him from Vienna.

PERRAULT, Claude (1613, Paris—1688, Paris), French architect. According to one tradition, he was the sole creator of the Colonnade of the Louvre in Paris. In fact, this seems to have been a collective work, whose principal authorship is highly controversial. Many proposals had been submitted, including plans by Gianlorenzo Bernini, Carlo Rainaldi, and Pietro da Cortona on the Italian side, and Louis Le Vau, François Mansart, and Perrault on the French side. Ultimately, a committee made up of Le Vau, Perrault, and the painter Charles Le Brun was appointed. But in 1666 Louis XIV approved the plans drawn up by Louis Le Vau, with the collaboration of his brother and chief assistant, the brilliant François d'Orbay (who was responsible for the final design). Since Charles Perrault did not include Le Vau in his *Lives of Illustrious Men* (1697–1701), the Colonnade came to be attributed to his brother Claude—an error that was repeated throughout the 18th century. In the 20th century Louis Hautecoeur, the great historian of the Louvre and of French architecture, regarded the Colonnade as the collective work of Le Brun, Perrault, and Le Vau, but the major role was attributed to François d'Orbay by the architect and historian, Albert La Prade. The Colonnade as we know it today (almost all its sculpture is of the 19th century) is not as Perrault intended it. In fact, it was built despite Perrault's suggestions, despite even his initial project, as engraved by Sébastien Leclerc.

Perrault published a translation of Vitruvius and a treatise on *L'Ordonnance des cinq espèces de colonnes selon la méthode des Anciens* (1683). As a scientist, he inspired the plans of the Observatoire, Paris (1668–72), but came up against the objections of the astronomer, Jean Dominique Cassini, from whom Louis XIV had sought advice. The choir of St-Benoît-le-Bétourne (1678) which he restored using Gothic vaults, and the triumphal arch in Place du Trône (both in Paris, 1670; destroyed 1716), are also attributed to him.

PERRÉAL, Jean (*c.* 1460, Paris?—*c.* 1530, Paris or Lyons), French painter. He has been identified as Jean de Paris, an illuminator. We possess no works bearing his signature, and very few that can be attributed to him with complete certainty. From 1483 Perréal resided in Lyons, working as a painter decorator, and as court painter to the Bourbon family, for whom he designed and executed decorations for the entry of Cardinal Charles de Bourbon in 1485. Anne de Bretagne commissioned him to design a sepulcher for her parents (Nantes Cathedral), which was executed in Genoese marble by Michel Colombe. From 1504–6 Perréal acted as the artistic adviser to Margaret of Austria, who gave him a pension. She commissioned him to draw up the decorative program for the church of Brou and to design the tomb of her husband Philibert II of Savoy and her mother-in-law Margaret of Bourbon (built 1509–12). The tomb was finally completed, after much intrigue, from other plans provided by Conrad Meyt. In 1514 Perréal went to England, where he organized the festivities for the marriage of Louis XII and Mary Tudor. Of the many works that have been ascribed to him, only three portraits, executed as illuminations, can be attributed to him with any certainty: these are the portraits of *Charles VIII* and *Anne of Brittany* (*c.* 1495; Paris, Bibliothèque Nationale), and that of the writer *Pierre Sala*, equerry to Charles VIII and close friend of the artist (*c.* 1500–5; London, British Museum), an illumination contained in a collection of Sala's love poems, *Énigmes*. This last painting, with its extensive use of gold in the background, and with its superb craftsmanship, offers an outstanding example of Perréal's style, and serves as the nucleus for a number of other attributions.

Jean Perréal. *Portrait of Philippe de la Platière, called Bourdillon. c.* 1495. Musée Condé, Chantilly.

PERRET, Auguste (1874, Ixelles, near Brussels—1954, Paris), French architect. With his brothers Gustave (1876–1952) and Claude (1880–1960), he built an apartment house in Rue Franklin, Paris (1903). This was the first housing block designed for concrete, and with it Perret became, and remained, an enthusiastic advocate of the rational use of this material. He was commissioned to design the Paris Théâtre des Champs-Élysées (1910–13), which consists, in fact, of three theaters of different sizes. He broke away from the traditional, Italianate theater, with its profusion of gilt and ornamentation, and showed that the exclusive use of reinforced concrete made possible particularly effective and econ-

Auguste Perret. Church of Notre-Dame, Le Raincy. 1922–23. *Photo Chevojon, Paris.*

omic solutions. Above all, Perret showed that this material need not be confined to industrial building, but that it could equal stone in its aesthetic possibilities. Ten years later, he created a similar revolution in ecclesiastical architecture. The church of Notre-Dame, Le Raincy (1922–23), was the first in which all the elements—supports, vault, columns, and ribs—were in reinforced concrete. His most noteworthy achievements include the École Normale de Musique in Paris (1929), a masterpiece of acoustic engineering; artists' houses in Paris; a project for a palace of the Soviets (1931); and the Classical Mobilier National warehouses, also in Paris (1932–35). Perret always tried to improve the composition of the concrete he used in order to enrich and diversify the material. In this way, the Musée des Travaux Publics, Paris (1937), became one of his most attractive achievements. Here he gave full rein to his conception of the *abri souverain* (master shelter), a simple but majestic architectural structure behind which many changing and varied activities could take place.

Mention should be made of his industrial buildings: warehouses at Casablanca (1915); rolling mills at Montataire (1920), and at Issoire (1939); naval laboratories in Paris (1928); and a hangar at Marseilles-Marignane (1950). These buildings solved the problems of the machine age with elegance and honesty. After World War II, in 1945, Perret was appointed director of town planning and reconstruction at Le Havre, the most devastated of all French cities. The new city is based on a very broad north-south axis that links the town hall to the harbor. The church of St-Joseph, whose lantern tower is 350 feet high, is the work of Perret himself.

PERRONNEAU *or* **PERRONEAU**, Jean-Baptiste (1715, Paris—1783, Amsterdam), French painter and pastelist. He studied first with the engraver Laurent Cars (1699–1771) and then with Charles Natoire (1700–77), but soon abandoned engraving for pastels. The competition of Maurice Quentin de La Tour made him travel extensively in search of portrait commissions. In France he visited Orléans, Bordeaux, Angers, Lyons, Toulouse, and Abbeville; he traveled to Italy, Holland, England, Russia, Poland, and Germany as well. Perronneau's first pastels date from 1744: *Madame Desfriches, Mère* (Paris, Coll. Ratouis de Limay) and *Portrait of a Child* (Paris, Coll. Jacques Douret). In 1846, at his first Salon, he entered five portraits of which three were pastels, including one of his brother. He then executed portraits of the engraver *Jacques-Gabriel Huquier* (1747; Paris, Coll. André Lazard), *Mademoiselle Huquier Holding a Kitten* (1746; Paris, Louvre), and his fellow artist *Maurice Quentin de La Tour* (1750; St-Quentin, Musée Antoine-Lécuyer). In 1751 Perronneau executed 12 pastels, including portraits of the amateur draftsman *Aignan-Thomas Desfriches* (Paris, Coll. Ratouis de Limay), the architect *Jean-Michel Chevotet* and his wife *Madame Chevotet* (both Orléans, Museum). Perronneau entered the Royal Academy in 1753 as a portraitist, submitting oil portraits of *Jean-Baptiste Oudry* and the sculptor *Lambert-Sigisbert Adam, called the Elder* (both Louvre). Three of his finest works are in the Louvre: the *Duchesse d'Ayen* (1748), *Madame de Sorquainville* (1749), and *Abraham van Robais* (1767), a linen manufacturer from Abbeville. Perronneau's finished portraits are remarkable for their brilliant use of color, the skillfully executed highlights, and the realistically rendered materials, as well as for the veracity of their lines.

PERSIAN ART. *See* **ISLAMIC ART.**

PERUGINO, Pietro Vannucci, *called* Il (*c.* 1445, Città della Pieve, Umbria—1523, Fontignano, near Perugia), Italian painter, a transitional figure between the Early and High Renaissance. We know nothing of his early years except that he learned the modern technique of oil painting under Andrea del Verrocchio. In 1473 at Perugia he did some work on several panels of the *Life of St. Bernardino*, and an *Adoration of the Magi* attributed to him may date back to 1475 (all in Perugia, Galleria Nazionale dell'Umbria). His first signed work is the *St. Sebastian* fresco of 1478, which he painted in the parish church of Cerqueto. By 1481 he was well enough known to be commissioned to decorate the walls of the Sistine Chapel in the Vatican. Bernardino Pinturicchio was his assistant; his Sistine fresco, *Delivery of the Keys to St. Peter,* made his reputation and marked the beginning of a feverishly productive period. Among his numerous works are the Louvre tondo, the *Virgin and Child Enthroned between Sts. Rose and Catherine* (*c.* 1491–92); the altarpiece of the *Madonna and Saints* (1497) in S. Maria Nuova, Fano; the *Vision of St. Bernard* (1489; Munich, Alte Pinakothek); and the *Nativity* triptych at the Villa Albani in Rome, dated 1491. Between 1493 and 1497, a series of *Madonna and Child* pictures established the sweet, inimitably Peruginesque type. During the same period he painted *Christ in the Garden of Olives* (Florence, Uffizi), the *Pietà* (1495; Florence, Pitti), the Louvre *St. Sebastian,*

Perugino. *Delivery of the Keys to St. Peter.* 1481. Sistine Chapel, Vatican. *Photo Alinari-Viollet.*

the *Crucifixion* fresco in S. Maria Maddalena dei Pazzi, Florence (before 1496), and the altarpiece of the *Virgin and Child with Saints* (*c.* 1495–96; Bologna, Pinacoteca Nazionale). In 1499 he painted an altar triptych (London, National Gallery) for the Certosa di Pavia; in 1500, the Uffizi *Assumption*. At Perugia in 1500 he decorated the audience chamber of the Collegio del Cambio in collaboration with Raphael, and in 1503 he was employed by Isabella d'Este, for whose Mantua residence he painted *Love and Chastity* (1505; Paris, Louvre).

At Cerqueto and in the Sistine Chapel, Perugino's technical mastery is startling. At first in the eyes of his contemporaries he represented the summit of religious art. The S. Maria Maddalena dei Pazzi *Crucifixion* (before 1496), in which three arcades frame three compositions that are admirably simple, shows what he could do and how valuable his work would be for the development of his student, Raphael. He deserves recognition for his airy, clearly organized pictorial space and his feeling for harmonious composition, qualities well seen in both his grandiose *Delivery of the Keys to St. Peter* and his charming small *Apollo and Marsyas* (*c.* 1496; Paris, Louvre).

PERUZZI, Baldassarre (1481, Siena—1536, Rome), Italian architect, painter, and scenographer. Peruzzi left his native city to settle in Rome when he was twenty-two. There he worked with Pietro d'Andrea on the decoration of the church of S. Onofrio (1503; Cappella Maggiore), and assisted Donato Bramante with his designs for St. Peter's. From 1508, the year in which he undertook the building of the Villa Farnesina in Rome, he devoted himself especially to architecture, although he had not yet completely abandoned painting. At the Farnesina itself he painted the ceiling of the Sala di Galatea with astrological motifs, in a manner still reminiscent of Pinturicchio's style. In the garden loggias his nudes (1508–11), painted against a background of false mosaics, show the growing influence of Raphael. The paintings of the Sala delle Colonne (*c.* 1515) demonstrate Peruzzi's love of false perspective and imaginary architecture. Later he collaborated with Raphael on the decoration of the church of S. Maria della Pace, Rome (1516–17), where his work in the Ponzetti Chapel includes the *Presentation in the Temple* and the *Madonna with St. Bridget, St. Catherine, and the donor Ferdinando Ponzetti*. Peruzzi's career as a painter then came to an end without his ever having found a truly personal style.

In architecture, Peruzzi interpreted the lessons of Donato Bramante in a picturesque sense, with particular emphasis on the decorative and illusionistic elements. The Villa Farnesina (1508–11) was built for Agostino Chigi (later acquired by the Farnese family) on the right bank of the Tiber. The main building, flanked by projecting pavilions, was crowned by a boldly carved frieze of *putti* and swags, resting on two superimposed orders of pilasters. Throughout the building and its grounds, Peruzzi proved his talents as a decorator, scenographer, and landscape gardener: pavilions made of foliage, with flowering arcades, harmonize with the building and echo its motifs. In 1520 in Rome he took over the direction of work on St. Peter's, succeeding Bramante and Raphael. Peruzzi's last great work was the Palazzo Massimo alle Colonne, Rome (1532–36), on which he worked until his death. The façade, which follows the curve of the street, is characterized by its contrast between the great depth of the ground floor loggia and the apparent thinness of the upper walls whose small windows are placed in shallow, curiously shaped frames.

Baldassarre Peruzzi. Palazzo Massimo alle Colonne, Rome. 1532–36.

PETEL, Georg (1601/2, Weilheim, Upper Bavaria—1634, Augsburg), the foremost German sculptor of the early 17th century. He carved small figures in ivory, life-size works in wood, and also modeled figures for casting in metal. On his travels he visited Rome (*c.* 1620–22), Genoa (1623–24), and Antwerp (1624). In the latter city, which he revisited in 1627 and 1633, he became acquainted with and was influenced by Rubens, for whom he also worked on a number of occasions.

In Augsburg, Petel received important commissions from the local churches. These included the *Crucifixion* for the Heilig-Kreuz-Kirche (1626–27), the statues of *St. Sebastian* and *St. Roch* (1627–28), *St. Christopher* (1630), and *Salvator Mundi* (1633–34) for the St. Moritzkirche, and the *Ecce Homo* (1630–31) for the cathedral. He also produced an important *Crucifixion with St. Mary Magdalene* for the Niedermünster in Regensburg (1631). In the following year he carved the portrait bust of King Gustavus Adolphus of Sweden (Stockholm, Nationalmuseum).

PETO, John Frederick (1854, Philadelphia—1907, Island Heights, New Jersey), American painter. For much of his life he worked in complete isolation in New Jersey, although it is believed that he studied briefly at the Pennsylvania Academy of the Fine Arts, where he was acquainted with the *trompe-l'oeil* painter William Harnett, his greatest iconographic prototype. From 1875 to 1889 he exhibited at the Pennsylvania Academy.

Peto painted many still lifes on commission, often filling them with banal objects and items that referred to the lives and positions of their purchasers. His favorite subject matter included torn labels, printed advertising cards, photographs, picture portraits of Lincoln (*Lincoln and the Phleger Stretcher*, 1898; Philadelphia, Coll. Mr. and Mrs. Howard Keyser), and metal number templates. He used such items with an obsessive frequency, in a style that aimed at a kind of *trompe-l'oeil* illusionism, although it was not quite as extreme as Harnett's version. The *Old Time Letter Rack* (1894; Boston, Museum of Fine Arts) is one of Peto's most famous works, displaying his looser, almost Baroque method of composition, and his less distinct interest in textural contrast than would be characteristic of Harnett. For Peto both the organization of a composition and the dramatic strength of light and shadow as a design took precedence over precise detailing (*Old Cremona*; New York, Metropolitan Museum). His bold use of pure pictorial values and his interest in American vernacular material link him to such current movements as Pop art; his work bears strong affinities with early productions of such painters as Jim Dine, Jasper Johns, and Robert Rauschenberg.

PETTORUTI, Emilio (b. 1892, Buenos Aires), Argentine painter of Italian parentage. In 1913 he went to Florence to study the Renaissance masters, but he soon became an enthusiastic partisan first of Futurism, then of Cubism. He adopted Cubist subject matter—harlequins, café tables, guitars, and still lifes of fruit—which continued to appear in his works for the next 50 years. He also painted in an arrestingly luminous, flat, and fragmented style (*Green Hat*, 1919, Buenos Aires, Coll. Leonardo Estarico; the superb *Pensierosa*, 1920, Buenos Aires, Coll. Cordova Iturburu; and *Light Burst*, 1916, Paris, Priv. Coll.). While in Paris in 1924, Pettoruti met Juan Gris, with whom he felt a great affinity. Shortly afterward he was forced to return to Argentina, where he was appointed director of the Museum of La Plata, but was dismissed in 1947 by the dictator Juan Perón. He then went back to Europe, settling in Paris in 1953, but he remained almost unknown until the Galerie Charpentier presented a large retrospective of his work in December 1964. It was then seen that he had carried the aims of the Cubists to their ultimate conclusions and had thus achieved a kind of classical form of Cubism (*Quintet*, 1927, San Francisco, Museum of Art; *Verdigris Goblet*, 1934, New York, Museum of Modern Art).

PEVSNER, Antoine (1886, Orel, Russia—1962, Paris), Russian-born French sculptor and painter. In 1911 he left for Paris, where he remained until 1913. Pevsner was impressed by the plastic use of iron in the Eiffel Tower, but was disappointed by Cubism. From 1915 to 1917 he lived in Oslo, where he was joined by his brother Naum Gabo. While still continuing to paint, Pevsner took part in Gabo's plastic experiments, which helped to orient him toward sculpture. Together they laid the foundations of a new type of art that broke with the traditional aesthetic of compact mass and replaced it by that of the void, of depth articulated in space. In March 1917 he returned to Russia. In 1919 Pevsner and Gabo drew up the *Realist Manifesto*, which was printed by the state and displayed all over Moscow in August 1920. The authors' desire to construct their works earned them the name "Constructivists' (*q.v.*). In October 1923 Pevsner left for Paris, where he lived until his death, becoming a French citizen in 1930. Pevsner did not really become a sculptor until 1923, and in his own art he followed the principles laid down in the *Manifesto*. His experiments with perspective, "the annihilation of the flat surface," led him first to fabricate transparent constructions composed of strips of metal and plastic, such as the *Portrait of Marcel Duchamp* (1926; New Haven, Conn., Yale University Art Gallery), a play of open planes that combines thin plates of zinc, copper, and celluloid, cut out and juxtaposed. In some of Pevsner's work the straight line dominates (*Developable Surface Construction*, 1938; *Column*, 1952; and *Peace Column*, 1954), while others are a complex of curves (*Developable Column*, 1942; *Construction in the Egg*, 1948). In yet another group (*World*, 1947; *Seed*, 1949; and *Spectral Vision*, 1959), an almost mystical symbolism pervades the formal structure. But in Pevsner's creations, under the precise effect of light, the apparent mass modulates through inclined planes, volutes, and helixes that are sometimes reminiscent of certain seashells in cross section. Through a continuous spiral movement, Pevsner often creates a seeming *perpetuum mobile* in his work. For the sculptor, light plays the same role as does color for the painter. Each plane breaks, arrests, distributes, or disperses it, thickens it into shadow or radiates it in reflections. Light lends Pevsner's art the immaterial quality of its forms, its fluid rhythms, and complex tensions.

Antoine Pevsner. *Portrait of Marcel Duchamp*. 1926. Yale University Art Gallery, New Haven.

PHILIPPE DE MAZEROLLES. *See* **MAZEROLLES,** Philippe de.

PHOENICIAN ART. The Phoenicians, who were Semites of the Canaanite branch and whose language was closely related to ancient Hebrew, arrived on the eastern shores of the Mediterranean not long before 3000 B.C. They settled on the narrow strip of land dominated by Mt. Lebanon, the Anti-Lebanon range, and Mt. Hermon to the south. The highly irregular coast lent itself to the establishment of small ports, which became urban centers, and even very prosperous cities, as a result of the development of navigation and trade. From north to south, these ports included Ugarit (modern Ras Shamra), Antaradus (Tartus), Marathus (Amrit), Simyra, Botrys (Batrun), Byblos (Jebeil), Sidon (Saida), and Akko. To these should be added the two small islands that became so famous, Aradus (Ruad) and Tyre. Phoenicia remained throughout its history a juxtaposition of small kingdoms, theoretically independent but in fact under the control of the Egyptians, Hittites, Assyrians, and Babylonians. At the

Phoenician Art. *Thunder Baal*. Stele from Ugarit, 14th or 13th century B.C. Louvre, Paris.

fall of Babylon (539 B.C.), the country became a satrapy with a Persian governor, until the arrival of Alexander the Great (332 B.C.), who conquered Tyre and brought to an end its commercial hegemony. On the death of Alexander, a period of decline began, during which Hellenistic culture supplanted that of the indigenous Phoenicians.

Phoenicia was located on a caravan route from Egypt to Asia Minor, and formed the terminus of another route from Mesopotamia. With such a geographical position and history, it is no wonder that Phoenician art and civilization became derivative and composite. Every possible influence made its contribution: Egyptian, Mesopotamian, Anatolian, Hittite, and finally Aegean. The Phoenicians were indeed responsible for at least one discovery of genius, that of the alphabet. Instead of the hundreds of signs used in the Mesopotamian or Egyptian system, their system involved a radically reduced number: 30 in a cuneiform-like alphabetical script at Ugarit and 22 at Byblos, but of the type that was finally adopted in modified form by the Greeks and later the Romans.

Phoenician Art (Mycenean influence). Fertility goddess. Pyxis cover. Ugarit, 14th century B.C. Louvre, Paris.

The Phoenician art of the 3rd and 2nd millennia B.C. is known to us above all from the discoveries made at Ugarit and Byblos. Temples and palaces were built in stone with such taste and skill that Lebanese masons, carpenters, and bronzesmiths were much in demand. At Ugarit, the palace of the kings of the 14th and 13th centuries B.C., with its monumental entrance, corridors, halls, and courtyards, was certainly one of the most luxurious residences in Phoenicia. The walls of the same city, with their ramp and rear entrance built with fine stone slabs, remain an impressive example of fortification. At Byblos there were several temples: one of them was decorated with squared stones; another, with colossal statues at the portal, followed the Egyptian example.

A great many discoveries of Phoenician relief carvings have been made: a limestone stele from Ugarit of the *Thunder Baal* (14th or 13th century B.C.; Paris, Louvre), in which the god of the elements is shown advancing in a costume of Hittite type, with a mace in one hand and a lance in the other; also from Ugarit, a stele carving of *El*, seated on his throne, with an offering bearer (13th century B.C.; Aleppo, Syria, National Museum); the sarcophagus of Ahiram (11th or 10th century B.C.; Beirut, Lebanon, National Museum), containing on one side a procession of servants bearing gifts and marching toward the sovereign, who is seated on a throne.

In the field of metalwork, the most outstanding items are the work of goldsmiths: for example, a gold patera or dish decorated with a hunting scene from Ugarit (between 1450 and 1365 B.C.; Louvre). There are also a number of figurines of deities, the bodies of which are in bronze, plated either with gold or silver: from Byblos, a young beardless man with an alert appearance, who perhaps can be identified as Resheph (2nd millennium B.C.; Beirut, National Museum), and also another figure of Resheph in a very dramatic pose (15th or 14th century B.C.; Louvre). Another example is the seated goddess found at Ugarit (beginning of the 2nd millennium B.C.; Louvre). Both official and unofficial digs have produced innumerable bronze figurines that can be identified with the gods of the Canaanite pantheon (Baals or Astartes).

The Phoenicians also appear to have been among the great ivory workers of the 2nd and 1st millennia B.C. The most famous piece was for a long time the ivory carving on a pyxis cover of the goddess, showing Mycenean influence, which was discovered at Minet el Beida, the port of Ugarit (14th century B.C.; Louvre). Discoveries made in 1952, again at Ugarit, especially of the ornamentation of a ceremonial bed, have shown that there were certainly some very famous workshops in Phoenicia, where ivory was carved in great abundance, which must have rivaled those of Damascus.

The Phoenician art objects received wide distribution to regions where their excellent craftsmanship rather than their religious content found ready acceptance. No great originality could be expected from an art that drew so heavily upon the great traditions flourishing around it, and that was mainly created for export by a mercantile people. It is clear, nevertheless, that the Phoenicians succeeded in an adroit artistic synthesis, giving proof to the sureness of their judgment and to the refinement of their taste.

PIAZZETTA, Giambattista (1682, Venice—1754, Venice), Italian painter of the Venetian School. While in Bologna (*c.* 1703) to complete his artistic education, he was much influenced by the works of Giuseppe Maria Crespi. Piazzetta returned to Venice in 1711 and was soon working on a number of commissions that reflect the somber colors and deep chiaroscuro effects of Crespi (the *Virgin Appearing to St. Philip Neri*, 1725–27; Venice, S. Maria della Fava). In 1727, however, he completed a large canvas for the ceiling of the chapel in SS. Giovanni e Paolo in Venice, in which a lightening of the palette is already evident.

Piazzetta's most brilliant period came between 1740 and 1750, during which he painted the *Fortuneteller* (1740; Venice, Accademia) and the *Idyll on the Seashore* (*c.* 1740; Cologne, Wallraf-Richartz-Museum), two works whose forms are strikingly extravagant and fanciful, yet whose subject matter remains enigmatic despite recent scholarly investigations. Also dating from this decade is his *Rebecca at the Well* (*c.* 1740; Milan, Brera), which treats the old Biblical theme almost in the manner of an 18th-century *galanterie*. Piazzetta also made a considerable contribution in the medium of drawing: in addition to portrait heads and half-length figures, his female nudes, done in a combination of charcoal and chalk, are especially fine, and their soft modeling anticipates the style of Pierre-Paul Prud'hon. He also provided vignettes and illustrations for a number of literary works, including those for a 1745 edition of Torquato Tasso's epic poem, *Gerusalemme Liberata*.

PICABIA, Francis (1879, Paris—1953, Paris), French avant-garde painter. Picabia studied drawing at the École des Arts Décoratifs in Paris and painting at the École des Beaux-Arts, also in Paris. From 1897 to 1908 he executed Impressionistic paintings that were similar to those by Camille Pissarro or Alfred Sisley. In 1909 he turned to Cubism, and then suddenly adopted a Fauvist style. In 1911 he rejoined the Cubistic Section d'Or group, but he left it again the following year, this time to embrace an Orphic conception of painting. In 1915 in New York he met Marcel Duchamp and together they laid the foundations of the Dadaist insurrection. His drawing *Universal Prostitution* (1916–19; New Haven, Conn., Yale University Art Gallery) is a typical example of his Dadaist phase. In 1921, however, Picabia broke with his Dadaist friends and followed André Breton in the creation of the Surrealist movement. In 1924 he designed the sets and costumes for the ballet *Relâche*, for the Swedish Ballet. Then, suddenly, he reverted to figurative art; he returned once more to abstract painting in 1945. He was an individualist always in search of an identity that was inaccessible because it was constantly in the process of formation.

Francis Picabia. *Procession at Seville*. 1912. Coll. Herbert M. Rothschild, New York. *Photo Sidney Janis Gallery, New York.*

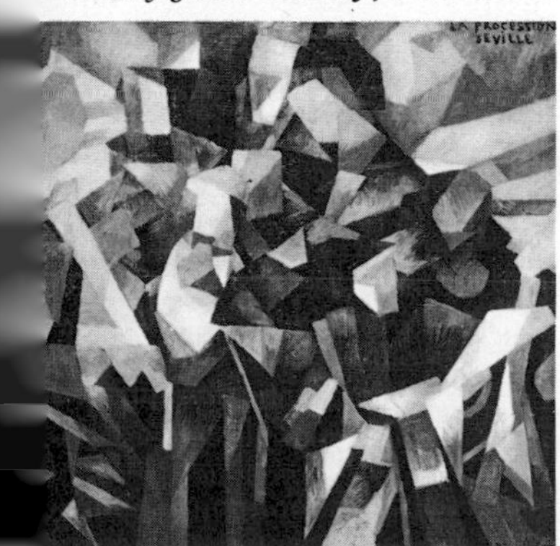

Picabia responded to every aesthetic movement of his time, and even anticipated some, as in certain abstract drawings of 1907. The series of pictures that Guillaume Apollinaire described as "Orphic" were perhaps his most successful works: *Procession at Seville* (1912; New York, Coll. Herbert M. Rothschild), *Udnie*, or the *Dance* (1913; Paris, Musée National d'Art Moderne), and *Edtaonisl* (1913; Chicago, Art Institute). Literature played an important part in Picabia's inspiration and he was fond of producing graphic games containing deliberately absurd inscriptions full of irreverent, Dadaist humor. During World War II Picabia executed a series of works for various occasions in which he openly admitted an academic Mannerism. Then, in 1945, he undertook a series of works characterized by literary affectation and an intentionally outrageous and bizarre quality, which were a constant source of surprise.

Pablo Picasso. *Frugal Repast.* 1904.

PICASSO, Pablo Ruiz (1881, Malaga–1973, Mougins, France), painter, sculptor, ceramist, and engraver of Spanish origin and French nationality. His father was a Castilian art teacher, José Ruiz Blasco, and his mother an Andalusian, Maria Picasso. In 1900 he went to Paris, where in 1901 the art dealer Ambroise Vollard exhibited 75 of his works. Under the influence of the Montmartre painters, especially Henri de Toulouse-Lautrec, Picasso painted street scenes and *café-concerts*. From late 1901 to early 1904, a phase of his artistic evolution known as the Blue Period, he abandoned earlier subjects and expressed his compassion for the tragic condition of the poor, the sick, beggars, mountebanks, prostitutes, and half-starved couples in a series of moving canvases in which various shades of blue predominate: *Life* (1903; Cleveland, Museum of Art), *Célestine* (1903; Paris, Coll. Pellequer), *Woman with a Crow* (1904; Toledo, Museum of Art). In 1904 he moved into a tenement in Montmartre known as the Bateau-Lavoir, which became the meeting place of avant-garde poets, writers, and artists. Early in 1905 he evolved a more supple, even slightly mannered, design, and using a palette dominated by pinks and grays, he painted harlequins, acrobats, and little girls. This came to be known as his Rose Period (*Family of Saltimbanques*, 1905, Washington, D.C., National Gallery; *Mountebanks*, 1905, Chicago, Art Institute; *Mountebank with a Child*, 1906, Zurich, Kunsthaus; *Toilette*, 1906, Buffalo, Albright-Knox Art Gallery). But Picasso soon moved out of this phase: his portrait of *Gertrude Stein* (1906; New York, Metropolitan Museum), his *Self-Portrait* (1906; Philadelphia, Museum of Art), and his earliest sculptures reveal a harder sensibility. The new artistic idiom that appeared in the preparatory sketches for the famous *Demoiselles d'Avignon* (1907; New York, Museum of Modern Art) may be attributed to the influence of ancient Iberian art and to African Negro sculpture: Picasso suddenly renounced sentimentality and illusionistic naturalism and embarked upon a search for a specifically plastic calligraphy and a freer repertoire of forms. In 1908 Picasso and Georges Braque founded Cubism, the movement that caused the greatest artistic re-

Pablo Picasso. *Self-Portrait.* 1906. Philadelphia Museum of Art.

Pablo Picasso. *Three Women at the Fountain.* 1921. Museum of Modern Art, New York.

volution since the Renaissance. During the next few years Picasso produced a succession of masterpieces. From the portraits of *Ambroise Vollard* (1910; Moscow, Pushkin Museum) and *Daniel-Henri Kahnweiler* (1910; Chicago, Art Institute) to the *Aficionado* (1912; Basel, Kunstmuseum) and the *Harlequin* (1915; New York, Museum of Modern Art), a whole line of development is apparent. Picasso's still lifes of the 1910s reveal a similar boldness of abstraction and perhaps an even greater creative freedom.

In 1912 he began executing *papiers collés*, in which fragments of concrete reality were inserted into a picture. This led him to a manner of painting that was less arid, less fragmentary, and more highly colored. This was the period of the *Card Players* (1914; New York, Museum of Modern Art), the many *Guéridons*, the already mentioned *Harlequin* of 1915, and of the still lifes, in which natural elements, either reproduced or in *trompe-l'oeil*, contrast with invented forms.

At the outbreak of World War I in 1914 Picasso was in Avignon, where he was on vacation with Braque and André Derain. Although his thinking was already going beyond Cubism, a number of works produced over the next few years were still Cubist in inspiration, for example, the costumes for the ballet *Parade* (1917) or canvases such as the *Three Musicians* (1921; New York, Museum of Modern Art). In 1918 his various portraits of Olga Koklova, a dancer he married that year, caused a revolution in the art of portraiture. In 1920–21, under the influence of Greco-Roman art, he produced a series of giants and fleshy women, drawn and modeled in a completely Classical manner (*Three Women at the Fountain*, 1921; Museum of Modern Art). Shortly afterward, he painted his finest series of still lifes: *Mandolin and Guitar* (1924; New York, Guggenheim Museum), *Still Life with Mandolin* (1924; Amsterdam, Stedelijk Museum), the *Red Tablecloth* (1924; New York, Priv. Coll.). But in 1925 the series was interrupted by the violently deformed figures of *The Dance* (London, Tate Gallery), which was the first manifestation of an Expressionism that was soon to be justified by subsequent world events. Picasso flirted with Surrealism, but was content to introduce into his paintings fantastic forms, painted in weak colors and with dense volumes, that stand in a space without depth. This was the period of the so-called "metamorphoses" (*Seated Woman*, 1926–27; Museum of Modern Art). Picasso's latent Expressionism, exacerbated by the tragedy of the Spanish Civil War, now became dominant in his art. The emotion that boiled up within him attained its crescendo in *Guernica* (May 1937; Museum of Modern Art), the masterpiece that caused a sensation at the pavilion of the Spanish Republic at the Exposition Universelle (1937) in Paris. The same year, Picasso executed the series of *Weeping Women*, and began the series of *Seated Women* (1937–44). Picasso's inexhaustible energy became more concentrated and less aggressive in the reclining nudes of 1942 (*Aubade*; Paris, Musée National d'Art Moderne) and in the splendid still lifes that followed (*Still Life with Bucrane*, 1942, Düsseldorf, Kunstsammlung Nordrhein-Westfalen; *Enameled Saucepan*, 1945, Musée National d'Art Moderne).

After World War II, Picasso executed a brilliant series of lithographs on which he worked regularly in the Paris studios of the printmaker and lithographer Fernand Mourlot. In 1946 he left Paris and settled on the Côte d'Azur, dividing his time between Golfe-Juan, near Cannes, and the Musée Grimaldi at Antibes, where he had a studio. In four months he painted an impressive collection of works, which he gave to the museum (*Joie de Vivre; Ulysses and the Sirens*). In 1948 he moved to Vallauris, where he took up ceramics with so much enthusiasm and talent that he started a revival in what was then a declining art. With the births of his son Claude in 1947 and of his daughter Paloma in 1949, he produced a number of *maternités* and portraits of his children that overflow with tenderness. Even old age did not reduce the sheer output of Picasso's work, for he executed paintings, engravings, sculpture, pottery, and book illustrations. In 1952 he painted two large panels of *War* and *Peace* for the deconsecrated chapel at Vallauris. In 1957 he painted *La Baignade*, a mural on the theme of the fall of Icarus, for the UNESCO Building in Paris. Meanwhile, he produced landscapes (*Hillside of "La Californie,"* 1959; New York, Coll. Saidenberg), still lifes, and portraits (*Jacqueline*, 1954, New York, Coll. Allan D. Emil; *Sylvette David*, 1954, New York, Coll. Dr. Herschell Carey Walker). He also began a series of paintings based on themes taken from famous pictures: in 1955 Eugène Delacroix's *Women of Algiers* inspired 15 canvases, including one in the Ganz Collection, New York; he also "interpreted" Diego Velázquez' *Maids of Honor* in about 50 variations and from February 1960 to August 1961 produced 27 paintings based on Édouard Manet's *Déjeuner sur l'Herbe*. In 1958 and 1959 Picasso made 45 linocuts of bucolic scenes and bullfights. From 1959 to 1961, at the Château de Vauvenargues in Provence, he painted landscapes, still lifes, and female busts.

Picasso's output was enormous. It includes innumerable sketches and inconclusive experiments, but also highly personal statements and undoubted successes. Indeed, no other artist subjugated his era so despotically, nor attained such fame in his own lifetime as Picasso. He was an unrivaled draftsman, an incomparable engraver (*Minotauromachy*, 1935; *Faun Devouring a Woman*, 1936), and an outstanding sculptor. Examples of his three-dimensional work, which alone would have brought him fame, include the *Bull's Head* (1943; Estate artist), a "metamorphosis" actually consisting of a bicycle saddle and handlebars; the *Man with a Lamb* (1944; Philadelphia, Museum of Art), and *The Goat* (1950; Estate artist). No other artist ever produced such varied and powerful work.

Pablo Picasso. *Bull's Head (Metamorphosis).* 1943. *Photo Chevojon, Paris.*

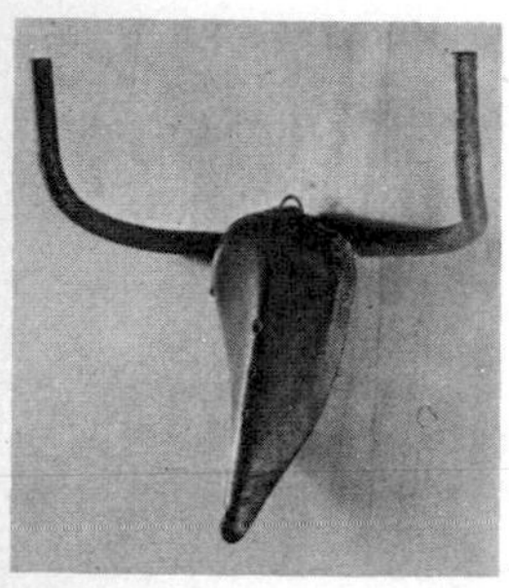

PICKETT, Joseph (1848, New Hope, Pennsylvania—1918, New

Hope), American painter. Pickett was a storekeeper who executed remarkably naive landscapes in the back room of his grocery store. He was not appreciated until after his death, when the art critic Holger Cahill included two of his paintings in an exhibition of "American Primitives" at the Newark Museum, New Jersey (1930). He married and settled down at the age of forty-five, and only began to paint when he was about sixty-five, perhaps as a compensation for the quiet life he led.

Pickett produced only three or four paintings, described by the art critic Dorothy C. Miller as "the most remarkable landscapes ever produced in America." Of these, the best known is *Manchester Valley* (*c.* 1914–18; New York, Museum of Modern Art), an awe-inspiring scene containing furiously cascading perspectives and rigid, geometrical houses having inexorable rows of windows. Two other highly successful landscapes are *George Washington Under the Council Tree* (*c.* 1914–18; Newark, Museum) and *Coryell's Ferry, 1776* (*c.* 1914–18; New York, Whitney Museum). Pickett worked on each of his paintings for years, adding more pigment until he produced the raised surfaces he desired; he also simulated the texture of the objects he painted by adding substances such as sand and shells to the paint. Unlike many American primitives, he avoided the anecdotal and the whimsical; the scenes he depicted are recognizably American but their true locale lies outside the realms of time and space.

PIERO DELLA FRANCESCA (*c.* 1410/20, Borgo San Sepolcro, Tuscany—1492, Borgo San Sepolcro), Italian painter. His name appears for the first time on September 7, 1439, in the accounts of the hospital of S. Maria Novella in Florence, in connection with a sum paid for frescoes (now badly damaged) in the Cappella Maggiore of the church of S. Egidio. He left Florence around the year 1442, never to return. On January 11, 1445, the Confraternity of Mercy at Borgo San Sepolcro commissioned from him an altarpiece which he evidently never finished, leaving parts to be completed by assistants. The central panel of the polyptych, however, is most likely entirely by him (*Madonna of Mercy*; Borgo San Sepolcro, Museo Comunale). During the same period, he painted *Baptism of Christ* (London, National Gallery) for the priory at Borgo San Sepolcro, and *St. Jerome with Donor* (Venice, Accademia). Piero della Francesca was invited to Urbino by Duke Federigo da Montefeltro, and may then have painted the remarkable *Flagellation* (*c.* 1445 or 1456–57; Urbino, Galleria Nazionale), although some art historians tend to ascribe it to a later period. From Urbino, Piero went to Ferrara, where he worked for Lionello d'Este some time before 1450. Unfortunately, the frescoes he painted at that time for the Castello Estense and for the Augustine church of S. Andrea, both in Ferrara, have been destroyed. In 1451 Piero was in Rimini, where he painted the fresco portrait of Sigismondo Pandolfo Malatesta with his patron saint (signed and dated "Petri de Borgo opus 1451") in the Tempio Malatestiano. His most notable project, however, was the decoration of the church of S. Francesco in Arezzo, which had been begun already by Bicci di Lorenzo. Here, from 1452 to 1459, Piero worked on the enormous *Legend of the True Cross* (taken from the *Golden Legend* by Jacobus da Voragine), which was by far the most important work in his career.

The date of Piero's first visit to Rome is unknown. He was there in 1459 to decorate the chamber of Pius II (possibly the room that later became Raphael's Stanza d'Eliodoro). He also worked in S. Maria Maggiore, where a *St. Luke the Evangelist* still survives in one of the chapels. Soon after 1460 Piero left Rome and returned to Umbria. He may have stopped at Perugia, where he painted the *Virgin and Child between Saints* (Perugia, Galleria Nazionale). Between 1460 and 1470, he worked in Borgo San Sepolcro, Urbino, and Arezzo. The *Madonna del Parto* in the chapel of the Campo Santo, a small churchyard in Monterchi, near Borgo San Sepolcro, and the *Resurrection of Christ* (Borgo San Sepolcro, Museo Comunale) date from this period. At the same time Piero also painted a polyptych commissioned by the Augustine Convent in Borgo San Sepolcro, and the *St. Julian* fresco, the latter discovered in 1954 in the deconsecrated church of S. Agostino, which may have been part of a larger composition. He probably painted the famous double portrait of *Federigo da Montefeltro and Battista Sforza* (Florence, Uffizi) during a visit to Urbino in 1465. Between 1474 and 1478 he paid his last visits to Urbino. During that period, Piero painted the *Sinigallia Madonna* for Federigo (Urbino, Galleria Nazionale), a *Nativity* (London, National Gallery) and finally, about 1475, the altarpiece for the church of S. Bernardino (Milan, Brera). He then wrote his treatise on perspective in painting, *De prospectiva pingendi* (before 1482; manuscript in the Biblioteca Palatina in the Museo Bodoniano, Parma) which he dedicated to the Duke of Urbino. Subsequently, after a last visit to Urbino, he wrote a small *Treatise of Arithmetic and Geometry* (manuscript in the Laurenziana Library, Florence) and a small booklet on the proportions of the body (*Libellus de quinque corporibus regularibus*), which Luca Pacioli used in his own book on proportion (*De divina proportione*, 1509). On July 5, 1487, Piero prepared his will; he died blind five years later.

The artistic training of Piero della Francesca took place between 1430 and 1440, during a period remarkable for artistic developments, of which he took full advantage. He was in Florence by the time he was nineteen or twenty, when he was documented as working with Domenico Veneziano in the church of S. Egidio. By the time Piero arrived in Florence, Masaccio had been dead 10 years; but his *Trinity* in S. Maria Novella and the unfinished frescoes of the *Story of St. Peter* in the Brancacci Chapel in S. Maria del Carmine were probably studied carefully by the young Piero. In Ferrara he met Mantegna and later, very likely, Rogier van der Weyden, who was employed by the Este family in 1449; Piero's *Sinigallia Madonna* reveals the possible influence of the Flemish

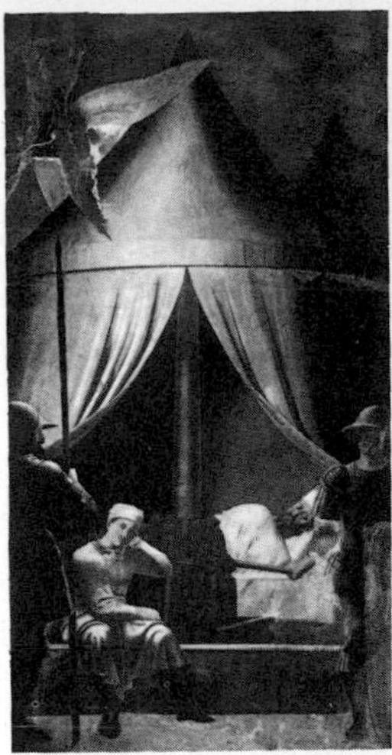

Piero della Francesca. *Dream of Constantine.* 1452–59. S. Francesco, Arezzo.

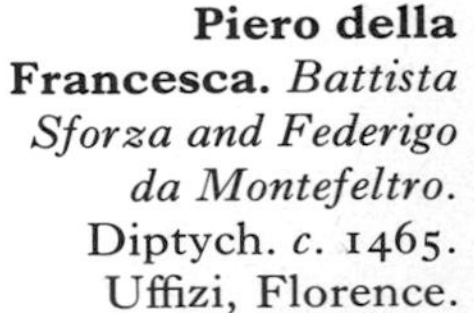

Piero della Francesca. *Battista Sforza and Federigo da Montefeltro.* Diptych. *c.* 1465. Uffizi, Florence.

Piero di Cosimo. *Forest Fire.* Detail. Ashmolean Museum, Oxford.

master, in that it is the first representation of the Virgin in Italian art to be placed in a domestic interior.

The Arezzo *Legend of the True Cross* and the Urbino panels (*Flagellation, Madonna di Sinigallia*) contain a modern, simplified conception of space and color that formed the basis of Piero's art. The *Flagellation* owes its authority and its complete intelligibility to its harmonious architectonic elements. Spatial tension is created by the rhythmic perspective treatment that envelops the figures, and the group in the foreground on the right gives the sensation of depth to the left half of the picture.

Piero della Francesca's meditative cast of mind lent a calm and dignity to his whole oeuvre, qualities that are particularly apparent in the Arezzo frescoes illustrating the *Legend of the True Cross*. Piero has demonstrated here his grasp of essentials by balancing the scenes facing each other on each level without following the iconographic order too closely; instead he has aimed at broad contrasts that possess a truly magnificent eloquence. Each sequence has its own marked rhythm, being divided by a clear, vertical line into two unequal parts, one square and one rectangular. Light floods into these precisely measured sections and creates a pale, clear color, which contains exquisite nuances and which filters into the regular network of spaces.

Piero's style was universal in scope. We can see his mastery and his sense of order in the way he reacted to the Flemish formulas, for instance in the London *Nativity*, where the Child is not unlike Hugo van der Goes' newborn Christ child in the Portinari Altarpiece. In his landscapes the contrasts between light and shade are accented, as in the panorama of the Apennines behind the portraits of Federigo da Montefeltro and his wife (*c.* 1465; Uffizi). Piero's art is even more striking when considered in the context of his period, whose enormous vitality he sums up in a style that is both rustic and courtly, earthy and heroic.

Pietro da Cortona. S. Maria della Pace, Rome. Façade, 1656–57.

PIERO DI COSIMO, Piero di Lorenzo, *called* (1462, Florence—1521, Florence), Italian painter. He studied with Cosimo Rosselli, whose name he adopted, and subsequently (1481) assisted Rosselli in painting some of the frescoes in the Sistine Chapel in Rome. He was attracted by evocative, somewhat strange mythological themes such as the *Death of Procris* (London, National Gallery) and the *Story of Prometheus* (Strasbourg, Musée des Beaux-Arts; Munich, Alte Pinakothek). His masterpiece, *Venus, Cupid, and Mars* (Berlin, Staatliche Museen), is a dreamy landscape filled with delightful details of flowers, butterflies, and animals. *Perseus Freeing Andromeda* (Florence, Uffizi) belongs to the period (early 1500s) in which the groupings of figures and the *sfumato* were inspired by Leonardo, and the landscape by Flemish art. The same characteristics appear in Piero's religious paintings, and are especially notable in the *Madonna and Child with Angels and Saints* (Florence, Ospedale degli Innocenti), the *Immaculate Conception* (Uffizi), the *Madonna and Child Reading a Book* (Stockholm, Royal Palace), and the *Madonna and Child with a Book and a Dove* (Paris, Louvre)—and, according to a recent attribution, the *Madonna and Child with Two Angels* (Venice, Coll. Conte Vittorio Cini), a composition remarkable both for the intensity of its feeling and its technique. Piero's earthiness, combined with his love of the fantastic, gave a sense of conviction to his visions of primitive man and wild life: *The Hunt* (New York, Metropolitan Museum) and the *Battle of the Centaurs and Lapiths* (London, National Gallery). His portraits have an extraordinary immediacy: *Giuliano da Sangallo* and the architect *Francesco Giamberti* (both Amsterdam, Rijksmuseum), and *Simonetta Vespucci* (Chantilly, Musée Condé).

PIETRO DA CORTONA, Pietro Berrettini, *called* (1596, Cortona—1669, Rome), Italian Baroque painter, architect, and decorator, who ranks with Bernini and Borromini as a leader of the High Baroque in Rome. In the 1620s he won favor with the powerful Sacchetti and Barberini families, who assisted him in his career for many years. The fluid virtuosity of his early profane easel paintings—*Triumph of Bacchus* (*c.* 1624) and the *Rape of the Sabine Women* (*c.* 1630; both Rome, Museo Capitolino)—attracted Velázquez on his trip through Italy (1629–31); the promise they contained was later fulfilled in the great decorative cycles executed in Roman and Florentine palaces.

The vast ceiling of the Gran Salone in the Palazzo Barberini (now Galleria Nazionale), Rome, his most important decorative work, was painted between 1633 and 1639 from cartoons that may have been drawn as early as 1628. Following a text supplied by Francesco Bracciolini, the court poet from Pistoia, Cortona illustrated symbolically the virtues and good works of Urban VIII (Barberini) and his family.

While on a brief trip through Florence in 1637, Cortona was detained by Grand Duke Ferdinand II of Tuscany to decorate with frescoes the Camera della Stufa ("stove room") of the Palazzo Pitti. He then began the *Four Ages of Man*, returning in 1640 to finish it and decorate other rooms. In the first floor apartments he undertook ceiling paintings illustrating the accomplishments of Cosimo I in pursuit of glory and immortality. From 1640 to 1647 Cortona was busy with the halls of Mars, Venus, and Jupiter, the last being devoted to the triumph of the prince. His pupil Ciro Ferri painted the halls of Apollo and Saturn.

Pietro worked principally in Rome, dividing his activity between decorative painting and architecture. In recognition of his pre-eminence in both fields he was made a *principe* ("prince") of the Accademia di S. Luca, a position he held from 1634 to 1638, and built a church for the guild dedicated to its patron saint (1635–50), known as the church of SS. Martino e Luca. It is Cortona's earliest full-scale religious structure, but his solutions were in no way those of a tentative beginner. He obtained a stunning articulation of both interior and exterior walls by alternating Ionic pillars and pilasters with stretches of bare wall, which created a gentle, movemented rhythm throughout.

Cortona's architectural roots were in Florentine Mannerism, although his originality often virtually obscured his sources. In the course of his career, in both painting and architecture, he shifted progressively from the exuberance of Mannerism to a more severe, Classicizing style. A new sobriety is apparent in his façade for S. Maria della Pace, Rome (1656–57). Its highly effective and original semicircular portico, projecting between two concave wings, was adopted by Bernini in his religious masterpiece, S. Andrea al Quirinale, Rome (1658–70). His next work, the façade of S. Maria in Via Lata, Rome (1658–62), is still more restrained and monumental, but is related at the same time to the youthful SS. Martino e Luca by its two-storied façade.

He continued to be active as a painter, with decorative cycles for the Gallery of Aeneas at the Palazzo Pamphili (1651–54) and the vaults of the Chiesa Nuova (completed 1665), both in Rome. He also provided cartoons for mosaics in several chapels in St. Peter's, Rome, and painted altarpieces for Arezzo, Imola, Perugia, Venice, and Versailles. His decorative style was to be followed throughout the next hundred years by Francesco Solimena and Giambattista Tiepolo in Italy, Anton Maulbertsch in Austria, and Charles de La Fosse and François Lemoine in France.

PIGALLE, Jean-Baptiste (1714, Paris—1785, Paris), French sculptor. The son of a royal cabinetmaker, he became a pupil of Robert Le Lorrain at eighteen and, after 1734, of Jean-Baptiste Lemoyne the Elder. Pigalle went to Italy at his own expense, residing in Rome from 1736 to 1739. It was there that he modeled in terra cotta the first version (undated; New York, Metropolitan Museum) of his famous *Mercury Fastening His Sandals*, a work full of natural vivacity that owes as great a stylistic debt to Michelangelo and Bernini as to ancient models. In 1744 he presented a marble version (now in the Louvre, Paris) to the Académie Royale de Peinture et de Sculpture as his reception piece. Its popularity led Pigalle to execute a large-scale marble replica in 1748, along with a pendant of *Venus Confiding Her Message to Mercury*. Both were sent by Louis XV to Frederick the Great of Prussia for the emperor's gardens at the palace of Sanssouci in Potsdam; the originals have today been removed to the Staatliche Museen in Berlin.

From 1750 to 1758 Pigalle was employed by Madame de Pompadour, for whom he carved a number of allegorical statues (*Love and Friendship*, 1758; Louvre). Pigalle's masterpiece, in the church of St. Thomas at Strasbourg, is the monumental tomb (1753–76) of the Maréchal de Saxe. Among the sculptor's other works are the *Nude Voltaire* (1776; Louvre); the mausoleum of the Duc d'Harcourt (1774) in the cathedral of Notre-Dame in Paris; a portrait of *Diderot* (1777; Louvre), one of many busts that rank Pigalle among the best representatives of the French realist tradition; and the *Infant with a Bird Cage* (1750; Louvre).

Jean-Baptiste Pigalle. *Denis Diderot*. 1777. Louvre, Paris.

PILON, Germain (*c.* 1530, Paris—1590, Paris), with Jean Goujon, the most famous French sculptor of the 16th century. He worked with Pierre Bontemps (1507–63) on eight figures for the tomb of François I (1557–58; since disappeared). Two years later he was working under Francesco Primaticcio on the monument for the heart of Henri II (Paris, Louvre). Pilon again worked under Primaticcio's direction on the tomb of Henri II and Catherine de Médicis (1563–70; Paris, church of St-Denis). In the kneeling figures above the monument, and in the *gisants* beneath the canopy, Pilon achieved a greater naturalism, skill in execution, and freedom of movement. His work of the 1570s consisted mainly of portrait busts and medals of which the bronze bust of *Bishop Jean de Morvilliers* (after 1577; Orléans, Museum) begins to exhibit the more dramatic style that he developed in the next decade. Around 1583 Pilon began working on several groups commissioned by Catherine de Médicis for the Valois Chapel at the church of St-Denis. The *Resurrection* (fragments in the Louvre and the church of St-Paul-St-Denis, Paris) particularly shows the influence of Michelangelo, while the *St. Francis in Ecstasy* (now in the church of St-Jean-St-François, Paris) avoids Mannerist tension in its almost Baroque quality of relaxed movement. Pilon's last major work was for the tomb of Chancellor René de Birague and his wife, Valentine Balbiani, in the church of Ste-Catherine du Val-des-Écoliers, Paris (1584–85; fragments preserved in the Louvre, Paris). The extant parts, which include a kneeling figure of Birague, a recumbent figure and a relief *gisant* of his wife, as well as a relief *Deposition*, exhibit a new and highly emotional use of naturalism.

PINTURICCHIO, Bernardino di Betto di Biago, *called* (*c.* 1454, Perugia—1513, Siena), Italian painter, active largely in Rome. He worked with the Umbrian master Perugino on the small panels of the *Miracles of S. Bernardino of Siena* (1473; Perugia, Galleria Nazionale); the bright colors of the two panels Perugino painted, *S. Bernardino and the Cripple* and the *Freeing of a Prisoner*, suggest a miniaturist's training. From 1481 until 1483 he again worked with Perugino, this time in Rome's Sistine Chapel; through this association, his own style became lighter (*Circumcision of Moses' Son, Baptism of Christ*). Also in Rome in the 1480s, he painted decorations for the Palazzo Colonna, the apartments of Innocent VIII at the Villa of the Belvedere (partially destroyed), and the Bufalini Chapel at S. Maria in Aracoeli (*Story of S. Bernardino*, soon after 1485). Pope Alexander VI appreciated Pinturicchio's rich, ornate, varied style, commissioning from him the decorations for the Borgia apartments in the Vatican, which the artist painted (1492–94) with the help of many assistants. In Umbria,

Giovanni Battista Piranesi. Etching from the *Carceri d'Invenzioni* series. 1745.

Pinturicchio's major work was the fresco decoration of the Baglioni Chapel in S. Maria Maggiore in Spello, for which he painted a fine self-portrait, dated 1501. In Siena, after completing frescoes of *St. John the Baptist* in the cathedral, he painted a cartoon for the *Fortuna*, one of the designs for the cathedral pavement (1506), and decorated in his lively style the Piccolomini Library of the cathedral with the *Story of Pius II*. Around 1509 Pinturicchio painted the *Story of Ulysses and Penelope* (London, National Gallery) for the palace of Pandolfo Petrucci il Magnifico in Siena, where the aging Luca Signorelli also was at work.

PIOMBO, Sebastiano del. *See* **SEBASTIANO DEL PIOMBO.**

PIPER, John (b. 1903, Epsom, Surrey), English Neo-Romantic watercolorist and topographical painter. Although Piper's artistic temperament was extremely traditional, a visit to Paris in 1933 and contact with such artists as Constantin Brancusi, Georges Braque, Jean Hélion, and Fernand Léger stimulated him to experiment in two-dimensional abstract compositions (*Abstract Painting*, 1935; London, Tate Gallery). During World War II he was an official British war artist and in that capacity produced a number of watercolors depicting the bombed areas of Bath and Coventry, which exemplify his own personal style—a synthesis of Romanticism and topographical accuracy (*Somerset Place, Bath*, 1942; Tate Gallery). Following World War II he worked in the tradition of the sublime and the picturesque, and often reverted to themes painted by such 18th-century artists as James Ward (*Gordale Scar*, 1943; England, Coll. Lord Clark). After 1951 Piper designed the sets and costumes for a number of ballets and plays as well as for several operas by the British composer Benjamin Britten. He also worked as an illustrator and wrote several books.

PIRANESI, Giovanni Battista (1720, Mogliano di Mestre, Venezia—1778, Rome), Italian architect and engraver. He was the son of a mason, and studied perspective and stage design with his uncle, Matteo Lucchesi (1705–76), before going to Rome in 1740, where he studied engraving with Giuseppe Vasi (1710–82). He developed considerable skill in this medium, using the old dry varnish method of Jacques Callot. His first collection of views, *Prime parti di Architetture* (1743), already contains examples of his romantic involvement with Classic ruins, treated in a bold and free manner. From 1748 to his death, Piranesi published 26 collections, comprising 2,000 prints of antiquities—ornaments, vases, statues, and especially buildings—all on an enormous scale. These include the *Vedute di Roma* (from 1748), the *Antichità Romane* (1756), and the *Vedute di Paestum* (1777–78). But among the earliest and greatest of Piranesi's works in this medium are the *Carceri d'Invenzioni* (1745) or "Prisons," in which the artist's passionate and violent temperament transformed the ruins of Roman palaces into a subterranean dream world, filled with ladders, treadwheels, and instruments of torture. Piranesi also wrote and illustrated two theoretical works: *Della Magnificenza ed Architettura de' Romani* (1761) and *Parere sull'architettura* (1765). The first championed the use of the straight line over the curve, and paid tribute to the beauty inherent in simple, unadorned structures, particularly in Roman, Etruscan, and Doric architecture. The *Parere* was more moderate, and accepted the Baroque traditions of ornament and hierarchical order. Piranesi's influence on the development of Neoclassicism was considerable, especially in France, and also in England through Robert Adam, whom he had known and admired in Rome (1750–55).

PISANELLO, Antonio Pisano, *called* Il (b. *c.* 1395, Pisa—d. *c.* 1455), Italian painter, draftsman, and medalist. From 1415 to 1420, under the direction of Gentile da Fabriano, he worked on the decoration (now destroyed) of the Sala del Maggior Consiglio in the Palazzo Ducale at Venice. Pisanello was soon famous, and, after drawing Emperor Sigismondo's portrait in 1432 (Paris, Louvre), he was sought after and welcomed by the courts of Milan (1440), Rimini (1445), Naples (1449), Mantua, and especially Ferrara. A series of portrait medallions illustrates the different stages in his career as a court artist.

In spite of a huge collection of drawings (many of them now in the Louvre, Paris), Pisanello's paintings are known today only in part. There exist for certain four or five small panel paintings in various museums and two frescoes at Verona. The more important panels show portraits of *Lionello d'Este* (*c.* 1441; Bergamo, Accademia Carrara) and one of a *Princess of the House of Este*, possibly Ginevra d'Este (*c.* 1443; Louvre). These portraits stand out from a floral background like tapestry and have an air of fantasy similar to the decorative preciousness of the International Gothic. Yet the precision in the modeling of the faces, seen in profile as on the medallions, proves how earnestly Pisanello tried in his way to reproduce the realistic, third-dimensional quality of his model. Although he came at first under the influence of Stefano da Verona, he is the undisputed heir to Gentile da Fabriano, as evidenced by his elegant and graceful fresco of the *Annunciation* (*c.* 1426; Verona, S. Fermo) and by the delicacy of his pictorial technique. His masterpiece, *St. George and the Princess*, a fresco painted between 1433 and 1438 for the Cappella Pellegrini of S. Anastasia at Verona, epitomizes the ambiguous richness of his style and imagination; in the twilight of the Middle Ages, Pisanello re-created its dreams of chivalry and fantasy with a lighthearted and romantic imagination, but with a vitality in his forms and a thirst for knowledge that are the mark of the modern Renaissance man.

PISANO. *See* **ANDREA PISANO; GIOVANNI PISANO; NICOLA PISANO; NINO PISANO.**

PISIS, Filippo Luigi Tibertelli, *called* Filippo de (1896, Ferrara—1956, Milan), Italian painter. He lived in Paris from 1925 to 1939, but his work aroused little interest, since his preoccupations had nothing in common with those of the other artists of the period. De Pisis seemed to be living in reverse, anxious to hide the poverty of Italian painting of the previous century (*Outskirts of Paris*, 1931; Milan, Coll. Gianni Mattioli). A bright landscape or still life by De Pisis would have pleased Pissarro, Marquet, or Utrillo (*Flowers*, 1932; Milan, Coll. Arturo Jeker). Certainly, the execution may appear sketchy, almost stenographic. De Pisis is clearly not a creator of forms, but a painter of sensations, of unexpected encounters. There were numerous successes among his pictures, which justify the reputation he enjoys in his own country, where he is considered the best Italian landscape painter of the 20th century.

PISSARRO, Camille Jacob (1830, St. Thomas, Virgin Islands—1903, Paris), French Impressionist painter. As a young man Pissarro was sent to study business in Paris, but he was far more interested in sketching than in commerce. Upon his return to the West Indies, his father finally recognized his creative abilities and allowed Camille to return to Paris. When he arrived there in 1855, Pissarro studied at the École des Beaux-Arts and then at the Académie Suisse, where he met Claude Monet. Pissarro became an enthusiastic admirer of Eugène Delacroix's paintings, and took lessons from Jean-Baptiste Camille Corot, who exerted a strong influence on his painting. In 1870, at the outbreak of the Franco-Prussian War, he fled to London, where he found his friend Monet. He also became friendly with the art dealer Paul Durand-Ruel, who later supported the Impressionists and became his patron and dealer.

Camille Pissarro. *Entrance of the Village of Voisins.* 1872. Musée de l'Impressionnisme, Paris.

Pissarro returned to France in June 1871. In 1874, by which time he had completely mastered his own personal style and technique, he took part in the first exhibition of the Impressionist group.

Paradoxically enough, Pissarro, the most steadfast of the Impressionists, was also the most unstable and changeable. In 1875 he painted solidly constructed canvases similar to those of Cézanne. By 1877, however, he had already returned to the luminism characteristic of Monet's style. In 1880 he executed a series of decorative compositions that resembled those of Edgar Degas. In 1885 Pissarro adopted Georges Seurat's and Paul Signac's divisionist method of painting, but it was too rigid for him and he abandoned it in 1890 to resume the more spontaneous, freer style of his early work. He spent the winters in a Paris hotel or apartment. There, looking out of the window, he painted views of Rue St-Lazare, the Tuileries, Avenue de l'Opéra, as well as the main boulevards, all rendered by aerial perspective (*Boulevard Montmartre, Night,* 1897; London, National Gallery). In spite of his weak eyes, he traveled to London, Rouen, Dieppe, Moret, Le Havre and Eragny (he maintained a home there from 1884), where he was delighted to discover his favorite themes of flowering orchards, rustic dwellings, and farm laborers (*La Mère Larchevèque*, 1880, New York, Metropolitan Museum; *Washerwoman at Eragny*, 1893, Metropolitan Museum; *River Banks, Rouen*, 1883, London, Courtauld Institute Galleries; *Orchard*, 1879, Paris, Musée de l'Impressionnisme; *Woman in an Orchard*, 1897, Musée de l'Impressionnisme).

POELZIG, Hans (1869, Berlin—1936, Berlin), German architect. Through his own work and through his teaching, Poelzig was one of the pioneers of modern architecture in Germany. The grouping of cubic elements at his chemical factory at Luban, near Poznan (in present-day Poland), and the continuous horizontal strip windows of the Breslau office building (both 1911–12), prefigured typical architectural motifs of the next decade. But his conversion of the Schumann Circus into the theatrical director Max Reinhardt's Grosses Schauspielhaus, Berlin (1919), was far more visionary. It provided for an arena-shaped stage, surrounded on three sides by stepped rows of seats, and surmounted by a huge dome that, by a system of screens with stalactite-shaped elements, filtered a fantasmagoric light into the auditorium. This extraordinarily imaginative work makes him one of the masters of early 20th-century Expressionist architecture. Later monumental works, such as the large I. G. Farben office building, Frankfurt am Main (1928–31), and the German Broadcasting Company Building, Berlin (1929), were more conventional in style.

POINTILLISM. *See* **NEOIMPRESSIONISM.**

POLIAKOFF, Serge (1906, Moscow—1969, Paris), Russian painter of the School of Paris. As a child, his chief love was music. In 1919 an aunt, the singer Nastia Poliakoff, took him to Constantinople to escape the Revolution. He traveled all over Europe with her before settling in Paris in 1923. He was increasingly attracted to painting, and from 1930 he attended the Académie de la Grande Chaumière, while continuing to earn a living by playing the guitar in the Russian cafés of Paris. In 1937 he met Wassily Kandinsky, and then became a close friend of Otto Freundlich and of Robert and Sonia Delaunay. Around 1937 Poliakoff painted his first nonfigurative compositions. His first one-man show was held at the Galerie l'Esquisse in Paris in 1945. Two years later he was awarded the Kandinsky Prize for painting, after which time his reputation continued to grow.

It is undeniable that Poliakoff succeeded in inventing a pictorial space that is derived neither from Impressionist light theories nor from geometry: his is a two-dimensional space, created through the arrangement of flat forms and the interpenetration of colored planes. His original style combines abstraction and bitter sensuality.

POLLAIUOLO, Antonio (1431/32, Florence—1498, Rome) *and* Piero (1443, Florence—1496, Rome), Italian painters, sculptors, engravers, and goldsmiths. These two brothers, who worked together almost continually after 1460, are fairly representative of a busy 15th-century Florentine workshop in which the activities

Antonio and Piero Pollaiuolo. *Geometry*. Bronze relief from the tomb of Sixtus IV, completed 1493. Grotte Vaticane, Rome. *Photo Leonard von Matt, Buochs.*

were varied and in which the labor was divided and the works produced under a common signature. It is therefore difficult to distinguish the brothers' work with any certainty. Both Antonio and Piero were trained as goldsmiths, and both used a technique requiring a combination of vigor and accuracy of detail. Shortly after 1464, Antonio decorated the Villa della Gallina at Arcetri, near Florence, for a member of the Medici family. For Piero de' Medici he executed three large compositions on the *Labors of Hercules* (*c.* 1460); these are now lost but are known through smaller painted copies (*Hercules and Antaeus, c.* 1465, and *Hercules and the Hydra, c.* 1475; both Florence, Uffizi) and through vigorous bronze statuettes (*Hercules and Antaeus*, Florence, Bargello; *Hercules*, Berlin, Staatliche Museen). The saturated color of *Apollo and Daphne* (*c.* 1470; London, National Gallery)—possibly done in collaboration with Piero—shows an assimilation of Flemish techniques, as does the unusual importance given to landscape in the *Rape of Deianira* (also called *Hercules and Nessus*, before 1467; New Haven, Conn., Yale University Art Gallery).

In 1469 and 1470 Piero was asked to paint the *Six Virtues* (Uffizi) for the council chambers of the Tribunale della Mercanzia in Florence; he also painted the *Coronation of the Virgin* (1483) for the church of S. Agostino in San Gimignano, in the province of Siena. In the meantime, Antonio produced his impressive masterpiece, the *Martyrdom of St. Sebastian* (1475; London, National Gallery). Several extant portraits seem to have been by Antonio's hand (*Profile of a Young Man*, Milan, Museo Poldi-Pezzoli; *Portrait of a Man*, Washington, D.C., National Gallery; *David*, Berlin, Staatliche Museen). In 1484 the two brothers were called to Rome to work on the tomb of Pope Sixtus IV (1484–93) in the Vatican Grottoes of St. Peter's. From then on, they devoted all their time to sculpture, spending the last years of their lives working on the tomb of Pope Innocent VIII (1493–97) in St. Peter's. The first of these works, decorated with reliefs of the Virtues and bas-reliefs of the Liberal Arts, is one of the outstanding works of the first half of the Florentine Renaissance.

Most art historians agree that, after the technical developments of the preceding generation, it was Antonio who made anatomy and landscape features of Florentine art. In accordance with the example of Donatello and the Flemish artists, greater emphasis was placed on the expressive powers of gesture and physiognomy; in short, art gravitated to the opposite pole of Masaccio's stable humanity. In 1466–80 Antonio designed embroideries for liturgical robes which quiver with restless, abrupt motifs. He even questioned the harmony of perspective through his exuberant manner of landscape painting, which is seen in such works as the already mentioned *Labors of Hercules* and the *Rape of Deianira*. All these exciting developments converged in the *St. Sebastian*. After 1460 vitality and movement became the most important aspects of Florentine art, and the Pollaiuolo brothers were two of the most influential protagonists of this new development. This is borne out by the success of Antonio's engravings, in which line became the unique means of expression; his famous *Battle of the Nudes* (*c.* 1470; Uffizi) impressed both Mantegna and Dürer.

Jackson Pollock. *Number 32*. 1950. Kunstsammlung. Nordrhein-Westfalen, Düsseldorf.

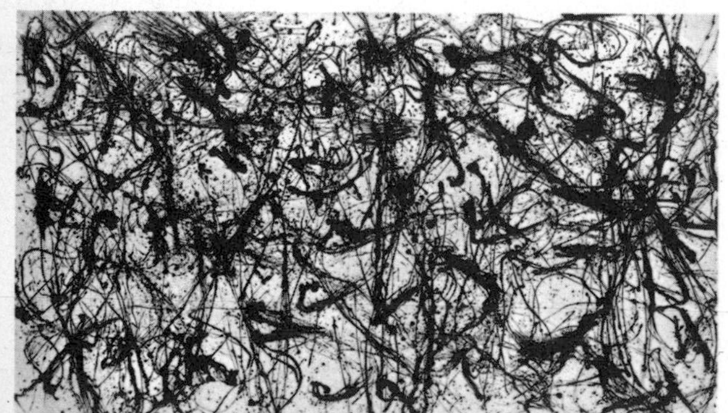

POLLOCK, Paul Jackson, *known as* Jackson (1912, Cody, Wyoming—1956, East Hampton, New York), American painter. With Jackson Pollock the painting of the United States freed itself for the first time from European dominance and finally assumed a leading role in the history of Western art. He became one of the most important members of the Abstract Expressionist movement. Pollock discovered his artistic vocation in 1928, when he joined the Manual Arts High School in Los Angeles. In 1930 he went to New York, where he studied at the Art Students League under Thomas Hart Benton. The early 1930s formed an important phase in Pollock's artistic evolution: he discovered American Indian art and the Mexican mural painters Diego Rivera, José Clemente Orozco, and David Alfaro Siqueiros. Pollock's sketchbooks from this period are filled with drawings after the European masters—Michelangelo, Tintoretto, and El Greco—that show a taste for drama, turbulent movement, and a considerable mastery of Classical draftsmanship.

His first important works date from 1940: highly colored, difficult to understand, and frequently based on sexual or mythological themes, these paintings show the influences of Picasso, Matisse, and even the Surrealists. Nevertheless, such works as *Male and Female* (1942; Haverford, Penn., Coll. Mrs. H. Gates Lloyd), *Pasiphaë* (1943; New York, Coll. Lee Krasner Pollock), *Guardians of the Secret* (1943; San Francisco, Museum of Art), *Totem, Lesson I* (1944; West Redding, Conn., Coll. Mrs. Emily Walker), and *Totem, Lesson II* (1945; Coll. Lee Krasner Pollock) possess a violence as well as a dislocation and conception of space that is peculiarly their own. At this point it is important to clarify the ambiguity that has developed concerning Pollock's connection with the Surrealists. Max Ernst claimed priority in using the "drip" technique, a method of painting with pierced tins through which the paint flows. Pollock in fact devised a method of controlled automatism in order to produce a manual dexterity that would not hinder the immediacy and speed of free expression. "Dripping" was his chosen form of calligraphy. In 1947 Pollock gave his own explanation of his working methods: "My painting does not come from the easel. I hardly ever stretch my canvas before painting. I prefer to tack the unstretched canvas to the hard wall or the floor. I need the resistance of a hard surface. On the floor I am more at ease. I feel nearer, more a part of the painting, since this way I can walk around it, work from the four sides and literally be *in* the painting . . . I continue to get further away from the usual painter's tools such as easel, palette, brushes, etc. I prefer sticks, trowels, knives, and dripping fluid paint or a heavy impasto with sand, broken glass, and other foreign matter added."

From the 1940s until 1950, Pollock produced a series of masterpieces in which violence alternates with tenderness, and brilliant harmonies with more subdued ones: these include *Cathedral* (1947; Dallas, Museum of Fine Arts), *Number 1* (1948; New York, Museum of Modern Art), *Summertime* (1948; Coll. Lee Krasner Pollock), *Number 8* (1949; New York, Coll. Mr. and Mrs. Roy R. Neuberger), *Lavender Mist* (1950; East Hampton, New York, Coll. Alfonso A. Ossorio and Edward F. Dragon), and *Autumn Rhythm* (1950; New York, Metropolitan Museum). In these paintings the whole picture area is filled with a network of lines whose varying thicknesses immediately suggest the rhythm of their duration. This phase ended with the black *Number 29* (1950; Coll. Lee Krasner Pollock), painted on glass with shells, pebbles, and bits of metal grating. Following this, from 1950 to 1952, Pollock gave up color for black and white painting. After reverting to rhythms similar to those in previous paintings (*Number 32*, 1950; Düsseldorf, Kunstsammlung Nordrhein-Westfalen), he returned to an Expressionism that was at the same time more controlled and more frenzied than that of the early 1940s (*Echo*, 1951, New York, Coll. Mr. and Mrs. Ben Heller; *Number 3*, 1952, Coll. Alfonso A. Ossorio and Edward F. Dragon; *Number 7*, 1952, Coll. Lee Krasner Pollock). In 1952, however, Pollock again began to produce large colored canvases: *Convergence* (1952; Buffalo, Albright-Knox Art Gallery) and *Blue Poles* (1953; Coll. Mr. and Mrs. Ben Heller). Nevertheless, he was trying to find a new path, which he discovered with *Deep* (1953; Estate of the artist), showing a black hole on a white background, and in such paintings as *Ocean Greyness* (1953; New York, Guggenheim Museum), in which there is a touching return to the circular forms that had obsessed him in the beginning and had already reappeared in some of the black and white paintings.

POLYNESIAN AND MICRONESIAN ART. The peoples who first colonized the remote Pacific islands of Polynesia and Micronesia 2,000 or more years ago were probably the finest sailors the world has ever known. From the Asiatic mainland they moved eastward over more than 9,000 miles of ocean. Their racial composition is mixed. Both Polynesians and Micronesians are a blend of Caucasoid and Mongoloid, with a slight Negroid strain. Both groups of people are part of the geographical area of Oceania, which also includes Melanesia.

Once they had reached Easter Island and the Marquesas in the eastern Pacific and established outposts in Hawaii to the north and New Zealand to the south, they gradually abandoned long voyages. Once contact was broken among the archipelagoes, cultural variations and distinct regional artistic expressions developed, to a great extent linked to the natural environment of each area.

The islands are mainly of two types. The "high" islands—of volcanic origin—rise steeply from the sea and generally have fertile valleys and adequate rainfall. These conditions have been able to support a relatively dense population, which has in turn been able to develop a cohesive political and social structure. The "low" islands, which are atolls, have poor soil and inadequate rainfall, and water is scarce and often brackish. The only food plant that flourishes is the coconut and life is precarious. New Zealand, the most important Polynesian island, has a temperate climate of continental type, which has influenced the local Maori culture in a very particular way. In all three types of environment, fishing plays an important part in the economy of the coastal areas; for the atoll dwellers it represents the main means of survival.

Like the Melanesians, the Polynesians and Micronesians were at a rudimentary cultural level when first seen by Europeans—a level comparable to the European Neolithic. They used stone or shell for their basic tools, and fishing and farming were their only means of subsistence. In the last several centuries no Polynesians, and only a few Micronesians, practiced the crafts of pottery and weaving.

RELIGIOUS BELIEFS

Polynesians have conceived a hierarchy of gods and goddesses with clearly defined roles in a family structure. The principal deities ruled whole sectors of human activity, including warfare, fishing, and crafts. Natural forces and abstractions, such as the sky and earth, were personified. Of more immediate daily importance were a host of minor deities and deified ancestors. The "idols," which form the most impressive part of Polynesian art, represent these gods and lesser deities as well as the evil spirits from which sorcerers derive their power. Micronesian religious conceptions were less advanced. Their worship was directed to a diversity of spirits—some ancestral—who did not form an organized hierarchy.

SOCIAL STRUCTURE AND ART

The structure of Polynesian society reflected a desire for organization as well as the various beliefs. The office of chief was hereditary, and his powers were in theory very extensive. The noble families traced their descent through a long line of human and mythical ancestors to the gods. The larger Polynesian islands were organized into districts and subdistricts, each under a chief. The mass of the people, the commoners, exercised little political power, and there was also a small class of slaves.

In Micronesia, the societal structure was similar in many ways, with the exception that chiefs were not everywhere regarded as divine. Institutions unknown in Polynesia—notably totemism, the clan, and men's clubhouses in the Caroline Islands—played an important part. The cultural features common to both areas generally seem to be more highly developed in Polynesia. There is much more homogeneity in Polynesian culture than in that of either Micronesia or Melanesia. All Polynesians speak dialects of the same language and are of the same physical type, with only minor local variations; their material

Polynesian and Micronesian Art. Fishermen's god. Rarotonga, Cook Islands. British Museum, London.

Polynesian and Micronesian Art. Female figure. Tonga Islands. Museum of Primitive Art, New York.

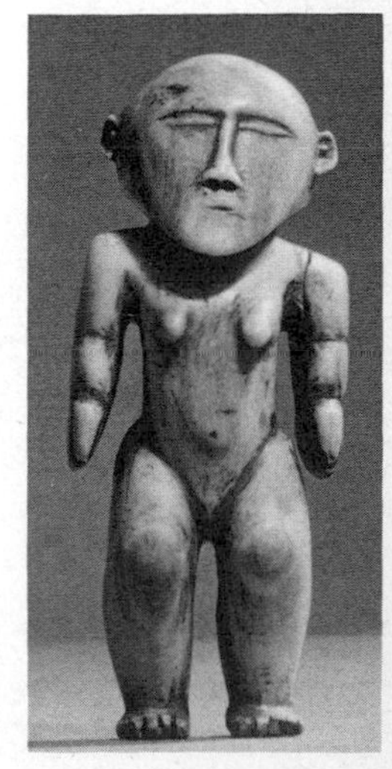

Polynesian and Micronesian Art. Carved head of a club. Marquesas Islands. Musée de l'Homme, Paris. *Photo Sougez, Paris.*

culture, social organization, and religious beliefs all show clear marks of a common origin, which is also clearly seen in their art.

Polynesian art is characterized by a particular attention to line and to technical perfection, a tendency to simplify forms, and indifference to color. Masks are not produced, and carved representations of animals are rare. The subject is usually the human figure, which is sculpted in wood or stone and is always more or less stylized; representations of the great gods are sometimes highly abstract. Polynesians had temples and sacred enclosures, with a priesthood, and in connection with them a tradition of building and carving in stone.

Tonga and Samoa

In western Polynesia figure carving, though not absent, was of minor importance. There was a center of carving in the Haabai group of the Tonga Islands, notable for the production of small figures of whale ivory. Elsewhere in the west figure carvings are even more unusual, though examples are known from Samoa and the Ellice Islands. The Tongans decorated the surfaces of clubs with elaborate geometrical carving that sometimes incorporated small human figures in low relief. Throughout western Polynesia, craftsmen exercised skill in the making of canoes as well as such everyday objects as weapons, fishhooks, mats, and bark cloth.

Society, Austral, and Cook Islands

In the islands of central and eastern Polynesia, art was more diversified. The great gods tended to be represented by highly conventionalized figures or nonrepresentational objects. The Society Islanders made "idols" of plaited coconut fibers over a wood base, covered with red feathers (now usually missing). In Mangaia, Cook Islands, the god Tane, patron of craftsmen, was represented by a stone-bladed adze with elaborate geometric decoration carved on the haft. In Rarotonga, in the same archipelago, enormous rolls of barkcloth wound on carved wood staffs were symbols of the gods; the staffs bore a human head at one projecting end and a phallus at the other. Minor gods and familiar spirits, on the other hand, were given clearly human forms: the fishermen's gods of Rarotonga and the Tahitian sorcerers' images are examples. Polynesian cosmogonic ideas are well illustrated by the figure in London's British Museum, from Rurutu in the Austral group, of the great god Tangaroa creating gods and men. The god is shown in human form, but his facial features are formed by small human figures, and others cover his body. The back is hollowed to contain other small figures.

Marquesas Islands

The art of these islands is distinguished by its technical perfection. The most distinctive products are the stone figures known as tiki—stylized images of the human body, sometimes very large, with large heads and round eyes. Relief carving covered the surface of all everyday objects; noteworthy among these are the wooden bowls, which were covered with fine carving in very low relief. The Marquesans made special forehead ornaments of fretted tortoise shell backed by plates of pearl shell, a form not found elsewhere in Polynesia but common in some Melanesian groups.

Hawaii

After the colonists of the Hawaiian islands lost touch with their homeland in central Polynesia, their culture developed on individual lines. Their great gods, especially Ku, god of war, were represented by large wooden figures with ferocious faces, which were set up in the sacred places. Heads of Ku, made of red and yellow feathers attached to a base of wickerwork, were carried into battle. Smaller wooden figures representing other deities were sometimes furnished with human hair, and teeth and eyes were often of inlaid shell. Wood vessels are often of great beauty, particularly the bowls of polished wood that have as supports squat, grimacing human figures.

Easter Island

The Easter Islanders, who seem to have come originally from the Marquesas, found an environment unfavorable to most of their tropical food and plants. Timber was almost entirely lacking, and only small wood carvings were made—male ancestor figures with protruding ribs, and female ancestral figures in a flattened schematic style. There are also figures with lizards' heads, as well as figures of bird men that represent the god Makemake. It is the large stone carvings, however, that have caught the imagination of travelers and given rise to the numerous fantastic theories about the island. They were cut in the soft tufa of one of the craters and transported to various parts of the island. They are of two types: in one the body tapers, so that they could be set upright in the ground; the others have flat bases and were erected on stone platforms along the coast. The figures apparently represented clan ancestors. A second mystery of the island concerns the petroglyphs and the inscribed wooden tablets, but this enigma is becoming better understood. The "language" seems to be a series of pictographs, or a symbolic script, not merely a system of mnemonics.

New Zealand

Like the Easter Islanders, the colonists who reached New Zealand from Polynesia entered a world quite unlike their tropical homeland, but they found that it offered rich and varied resources to those who were prepared to adapt themselves. The climate imposed new forms of clothing and shelter. For the bark-cloth clothing of the tropics they substituted cloaks and kilts woven from New Zealand flax. The soft and pliant wood of the kauri pine provided timber for substantial homes, as well as wood that was easier to carve than the tropical hardwoods.

Maori carvings are the structural elements of assembly houses, storehouses, and the stockades that protected villages. Human, or at least anthropomorphic, figures predominate, and they were carved in the round or in relief on boards. Usually every space was filled in with spirals, chevrons, or other elements, frequently cut through in openwork. Joints of limbs were indicated by spirals, and often the figures were entirely covered with an engraved pattern resembling tattooing. Elaborate and beautiful openwork prow and stern pieces decorated the large canoes, while the smaller ones had human figures on their prows with the characteristic Maori protruding tongue. Many other objects were similarly decorated—wooden boxes in which feathers were kept, ceremonial clubs, bailers for canoes, and adzes. The decoration of these objects rarely included representations of gods.

The first colonists of New Zealand possessed and developed stone technology. Their descendants discovered a new mat-

Polynesian and Micronesian Art. *Double tiki.* Hawaii. Musée de l'Homme, Paris.

erial, unique in Polynesia: this was nephrite, a hard, veined, green stone similar to jade. It was used by the Maori for making fine adze blades, short clubs, and a variety of ornaments. Of the latter, the best known are the *hei tiki*, pendants in the form of a human figure with the head inclined to one side. Their appearance has led to the belief that they represent the human fetus and were originally fertility symbols. They were greatly valued and were passed down as heirlooms.

Micronesia

Nukuoro, in the Carolines, is famous for its figures of polished wood in which the human body is reduced to its barest essentials: even facial features may be lacking. In the western Carolines, in Palau and to a lesser degree in Yap, the men's houses are decorated with carved and painted gables. In Palau, wooden bowls and tables for offerings are painted dark red and inlaid with white shell to form patterns, sometimes representing birds. The legs of the offering tables are sometimes in the form of human figures, which are more reminiscent of Philippine motifs than of Oceanic ones. Fine carved and decorated canoe ornaments are made in the Carolines, while in the Nomoi (Mortlock) Islands, wooden masks painted black and white represent benevolent spirits.

ORIGINS AND MIGRATIONS

There is little evidence—except the presence of the sweet potato—for any close or continuing connection of Polynesia and Micronesia with the American continent. The evidence of linguistics, physical type, and methods of agriculture, fishing and raising of domestic animals, all point to an origin on the Asiatic mainland. In form, their stone adzes resemble those of Neolithic east and southeast Asia; some of the blades that are thin and flared suggest that the ancestors of the Polynesians were acquainted with metal forms. There are some striking parallels between the sculpture of the island of Enggano, on the southeast coast of Sumatra, and certain Polynesian sculptured works. These local resemblances, however, do not prove the existence of specific links. It has recently been suggested that the movement into the Pacific was initiated by the expansion of the Bronze Age civilization of China in the 2nd millennium B.C. This seems probable, but it was more complicated than a steady and progressive expansion eastward. There must have been both chance voyages and deliberate exploration, as well as movement in a reverse direction.

ARTISTIC FORMS AND TRADITIONS

Among the distinguishing characteristics of Micronesian and Polynesian art are certain ones that seem to result from the persistence of ancient traditions that come to the fore when and where they are favored by historical or environmental circumstances. Simplification of the human form is among the most widespread of those characteristics. This simplification is carried furthest in the figures of two widely separated islands, Nukuoro in the Carolines (Micronesia) and Mangareva, part of the Tuamotus (eastern Polynesia). It is also seen to some extent in the figures of Hawaii, the Society, Cook, and Austral groups, and in the rare Tongan figures.

In New Zealand other traditions prevailed. Though some figures have a static quality, others seem to have been frozen in the midst of violent and contorted movement. Every part of the surface is covered with carved decoration, some of which has significance, but other parts of which are purely ornamental and seem to result from a *horror vacui* on the part of the sculptors. Maori carving is distinguished also by its strongly curvilinear style, which is exceptional in Polynesia and may be a consequence of the use of easily carved soft wood.

Polynesian and Micronesian art comprise not only wood carving: the tradition of stone sculpture is clearly ancient. The great Easter Island statues are famous, but hardly less striking are the stone figures of the Marquesas and the smaller stone figures of the Society and Hawaiian groups. There is also a tradition of building in stone, which is used to make sacred platforms (the *marae* of eastern Polynesia and the *ahu* of Easter Island) and the substructures of chiefs' houses. In the Carolines, remains have been found of cyclopean masonry, as well as stone canals and jetties.

Most Polynesian groups produced fine work in basketry, matting, and bark cloth. The bark cloth of an island or archipelago was often its most characteristic product. The most attractive bark cloth was made in Hawaii, but the Tahitians and the peoples of western Polynesia each had their own methods of production and a clearly recognizable style of decoration.

Although good bark cloth and matting are still made, wood and stone carving in traditional style are practically dead. The early missionaries organized bonfires of idols, and the Polynesians, who were prone to judge their gods according to results, quickly adopted the new religion. In some cases, artifacts were made to meet European demand, after they had ceased to have a function in the native culture.

Polynesian and Micronesian Art. Colossal monolithic images on the slope of Rano-raraku, Easter Island. *Photo American Museum of Natural History, New York.*

POMPEIAN ART. Pompeian art plays such a unique role in the history of Roman art that it deserves a separate place in any study of the forms and history of artistic expression. Pompeii is one of the best-preserved examples of an ancient Roman city known to archaeologists, and it offers a complete record of the social, domestic, and cultural life of its

Polynesian and Micronesian Art. Carved wood plank. New Zealand. Museum of Primitive Art, New York.

Pompeian Art. *Portrait of a baker and his wife.* 1st century A.D. Museo Nazionale, Naples.

citizens from around the 1st century B.C. until the 1st century A.D. From an archaeological and art historical point of view the history of Pompeii begins with the arrival of the Greeks (perhaps as early as the 8th century B.C.). The city, as well as much of the surrounding area along the Bay of Naples, was then dominated by the Samnites, who came from central Italy in the 5th century B.C., and then finally, from 80 B.C., by the Romans. During the Roman period, especially in the reign of Augustus, Pompeii became a fashionable resort. The first indication of disaster was an earthquake that struck the city in 62 A.D. The damage that resulted was still being repaired when Mt. Vesuvius erupted in 79 A.D., completely destroying the city. Archaeological excavation first began at Pompeii in 1748 and has continued ever since.

Pompeian art is an expression of certain unique characteristics in the Roman temperament. In this art one can see the merging of two deep-rooted tendencies: a taste for nature that made Roman citizens introduce landscape and gardens into the plans and decoration of their houses, and a sense for the control of space by means of architectural construction (*see* ROMAN ART). The extant buildings can be dated no earlier than the 5th century B.C.; most of the surviving structures date from the 2nd and 1st centuries B.C., however. There are certain basic characteristics of the typical Pompeian house that are common to most of the houses preserved in the city at the time of its destruction. The House of the Surgeon (so called because a set of surgical instruments was found in it) represents the standard Italic type of house that was built between the 4th and 2nd centuries B.C., before Hellenistic currents appeared in Pompeian architecture. From the entrance or vestibule there is a narrow passage (fauces) leading to a central court or atrium. The latter is covered by a roof that has an opening in the center (compluvium) through which the rainwater drains into a centrally located basin (impluvium). On either side of the atrium are grouped the bedrooms or cubiculae. At the other end of the atrium, opposite the entrance corridor, is the tablinum, which served as an office, where business papers (tabulae) were kept. Beyond the tablinum is the garden. The elaborations and changes include such further additions as two or more atria, a living room (oecus), entertainment hall (exedra), two peristyles—one small and one large—and one or two dining rooms (triclinium). These may be seen in the House of the Faun and the House of the Vettii, among others.

Pompeian Art. Mural painting from Pompeii showing fight between the inhabitants of Nuceria and Pompeii in the amphitheater of Pompeii in A.D. 59. Museo Nazionale, Naples. *Photo Alinari-Giraudon.*

The rooms and porticoes of the typical Pompeian house provided vast areas for decoration. The walls of the atrium and reception rooms in particular were lavishly embellished. Mural painting decorated the walls of shops and public buildings as well as the houses of Pompeii and other cities along the Bay of Naples, such as Herculaneum and Stabiae (present-day Castellammare). The mural decorations expanded the space by illusionistic means, creating the impression of larger or more sumptuously decorated interiors, or by suggesting the opening up or the eliminating of the walls themselves by means of landscape vistas. The Greek influence, which was predominantly academic, is apparent in the dwellings of the upper classes and in the public buildings. The native Italic current finds its outlet in the lower forms of decoration that often appear on the walls of shops. This tradition is comical, caricatural, and expressionistic rather than academic.

Pompeian mural painting has been divided into four styles, each having its own specific characteristics. While the development of these styles represents the stylistic evolution of Pompeian art, all four styles remained in use concurrently, although specific styles were chosen for specific rooms.

The First Style, also known as the "incrusted" or Samnite style, is essentially architectonic in character. It dates from around 150 B.C. to 80 B.C. and imitates costly wall panels made of real marble. The best examples of this style are found in the Samnite House at Herculaneum, in the House of Sallust at Pompeii, and in the peristyle of the House of the Faun, also at Pompeii.

The Second Style appeared in the time of Sulla (about 90–70 B.C.). Its new feature was the introduction of an architectural framework within which or around which the figure scenes and large landscape compositions of the Hellenistic repertoire were organized. The total effect of this style was to create the illusion of spatial penetration. There are many fine examples of the Second Style, including the deservedly famous mural composition at the Villa of the Mysteries, near Pompeii. This mural, which records the various stages of a Dionysiac initiation rite, covers three sides of the room. The individual scenes are separated by a subtle interplay of painted pilasters and columns. This great cycle of paintings dates from the 1st century B.C., and the influence of Hellenistic models can be seen in the way the groups are composed and in the presentation of the scenes, especially in the central picture of Dionysus and Ariadne. On the other hand, the architectural background, the touches of realism, and the individualization of some of the characters are typically Roman in spirit.

The Second Style also contains examples in which the illusion created by the architectural framework has been carried further; for instance, in some cases the wall seems to vanish within the painted frame, and the opening created is filled with further architectural vistas. The great rooms of the villa of Fannius Sinister at Boscoreale, near Pompeii, contain the best examples of this last phase of the

Pompeian Art. Pompeian mosaic showing doves and cat. Museo Nazionale, Naples. *Photo Anderson-Giraudon.*

Second Style in which illusionist landscape and architecture have not yet given way to pure fantasy. Nevertheless, even within the Second Style there are examples of the pure fantasy that is characteristic of later styles.

The Third Style, which first appeared just before the beginning of the Christian era and which lasted until around A.D. 62, was less concerned with hollowing out a wall and thus with giving it depth and developing perspectives, than with simply prettifying it. In the Third Style ornament becomes purely decorative, losing all architectural plastic values, since they are not derived from structural realities. The surfaces are divided by little columns, by slender pillars covered with floral motifs, or by candelabra. Monochrome backgrounds in black, green, or other colors replace the more colorful backgrounds of the previous styles. Excavations of the house of Lucretius Fronto (*c.* A.D. 30) at Pompeii have unearthed splendid examples of this flowery Third Style. The Fourth Style—which appeared around A.D. 63—may be characterized as Baroque because of its opulent, cluttered, and theatrical quality. Among the best examples of this style are the wall decorations in the House of the Vettii at Pompeii, and the fragment of a mural that once adorned a dwelling in Herculaneum (now in the Museo Nazionale, Naples).

It is clear that each of these styles can be defined by the architectural function of the wall that it decorates. In the First and Third the architectonic function of the wall is accentuated by the decoration, whereas in the Second and to a lesser extent in the Fourth, the decoration tends to make the wall disappear in order to make it open onto artificially composed exteriors. The subject matter is always adapted to the different manners of mural painting. The repertoire is large: it includes portraits, still lifes, landscapes, and cycles dealing with Homeric themes and mythological heroes, particularly Hercules, Theseus, and Perseus. Landscapes and still lifes constitute other important categories in the Pompeian repertoire: both express the taste for realistic subjects and reveal an extremely precise observation of the exterior world. The various examples of urban landscapes are particularly prized by urban historians. Stylization and realism are also evident in the presentation of flowers and plants.

In any survey of Pompeian art one cannot neglect mentioning the beautiful mosaics that, in particular, adorn the floors and fountains at Pompeii and Herculaneum. The richness of their coloring, the tonal variations of the blues and yellows, and the refinement of the play of light and shadow in the draperies or skin tones of the figures, as in the portrait of a lady from Pompeii and the depiction of street musicians from the Villa of Cicero in Pompeii (both Naples, Museo Nazionale), reveal an art closely associated with that of painting.

PONT-AVEN, School of. Pont-Aven was popularized through Paul Gauguin's visits and became the center for a school of painting based on the artistic principles he developed in Brittany. Gauguin's first lonely stay at Pont-Aven (June–November 1886) was merely an introduction to the town. His second stay (February–October 1888) was decisive. He took lodgings at the Pension Gloanec, and was immediately recognized as leader by the other artists staying there. The group included the faithful Charles Laval, Gauguin's companion on his trip to Panama and Martinique the preceding year; Henri de Chamaillard (1865–1930), a painter and former lawyer from Quimper, Finistère; Henri Moret (1856–1913); Maxime Maufra (1861–1918); the Swiss Cuno Amiet (1868–1961); and the Irishman Roderic O'Conor. Early in August 1888 Émile Bernard arrived at Pont-Aven from St-Briac, Brittany, with his sister Madeleine, who later became known as the "mystic muse" of Pont-Aven. Under Bernard's stimulus, Gauguin executed the *Vision after the Sermon* (1888; Edinburgh, National Gallery of Scotland), which marked the beginning of his new manner, characterized by cloisonnism and synthetism. The new use of pure color led to the glorification of the decorative plane surface, the raising of the horizon, and the suppression of naturalistic perspectives and space. Synthetism was the direct consequence of this process of simplification and resulted from the need to work not from the subject (as in the past), but from memory. At the end of September 1888, Paul Sérusier (at that time a student at the Académie Julian in Paris) was staying at Pont-Aven and was introduced to Gauguin by Bernard. There, under Gauguin's guidance, Sérusier painted his famous *Landscape at the Bois d'Amour*, also known as *The Talisman* (1888; Paris, Coll. family of Maurice Denis). This was a small board covered with "pure colors assembled in a certain order." When Sérusier triumphantly took it back to his comrades in Paris—the future Nabis—they adopted it as the "talisman" of the new doctrine, which was a decisive revelation for them. The first public show of the Pont-Aven group, held early in 1889 at the Café Volpini in Paris, on the grounds of the Exposition Universelle, bore the name "Exhibition of Painting of the Impressionist and Synthetist Group" and comprised, together with 17 canvases by Gauguin and 23 by Bernard, works by Laval, Anquetin, Schuffenecker, and Émile Fauché (1851–1934), all framed with white rods, which in themselves caused a sensation because of their modernity.

In April 1889, Gauguin returned to Pont-Aven, but was soon exasperated by the throng of

School of Pont-Aven. Paul Gauguin. *Self-Portrait with Portrait of Émile Bernard.* 1888. Stedelijk Museum, Amsterdam.

School of Pont-Aven. Charles Laval. *Self-Portrait Dedicated to Vincent van Gogh.* 1888. Stedelijk Museum, Amsterdam.

painters and tourists and in October moved to the quieter neighboring hamlet of Le Pouldu. Laval, Sérusier, and Armand Séguin spent part of the following summer there in shifts, and Moret, Maufra, and De Chamaillard made frequent visits there.

Although the school of Pont-Aven stirred up a good many ideas and renewed the artistic vision of the late 19th century, the formation of the group was due only to Gauguin's prestige, and the school hardly survived his departure, despite Sérusier's efforts to reform it in 1891 (with Jan Verkade, Séguin, and De Chamaillard) and in 1892 (with Verkade and Mogens Ballin, 1871–1914). Gauguin encountered Séguin again during his final stay at Pont-Aven (April–December 1894)—between his two trips to Tahiti—and wrote the preface for Séguin's 1895 exhibition at the Parisian gallery of Le Barc de Boutteville. Only Filiger and Séguin remained obstinately faithful to Brittany and to the artistic principles of Pont-Aven and Le Pouldu.

PONTI, Gio (b. 1891, Milan), Italian architect. Ponti remained aware of avant-garde tendencies, in particular those of the Movimento Italiano per l'Architettura Razionale ("Italian Movement for Rational Architecture"), and acted as a mediator between the two extremes of functionalism and representative formalism. In this spirit he launched the journal *Domus* (1928), which served to familiarize the public with modern forms of architecture, decoration, and industrial design. In 1933, the year in which he published his book *La Casa all'Italiana*, Ponti became director of the 5th Milan Triennale, an exhibition of great scope that included the Milanese "rationalists" for the first time. Two of Ponti's earliest and most important buildings were the Istituto di Matematica of Rome University (1934), and the Mostra della Stampa Cattolica (1936) in Vatican City. With the office building he designed for the Montecatini Company in Milan in 1936 (he was to build another one for the same firm 15 years later), Ponti came closer to rational architecture. After a series of buildings in Latin America and Europe, he returned to Milan to produce his masterpiece, the Pirelli Tower (1958), a 33-story tower built, in collaboration with Pier Luigi Nervi, on a hexagonal plan with tapering sides. Ponti also collaborated in planning the adjacent area, and is probably Italy's best-known 20th-century architect.

PONTORMO, Jacopo Carucci, *called* Jacopo da (1494, Pontormo, near Empoli—1557, Florence), Italian painter. He was, perhaps, the most sensitive and highly strung representative of the Mannerist trend that, from 1520, led the heirs of the Florentine and Roman High Renaissance beyond or even against the norms of Classicism. Pontormo worked under Mariotto Albertinelli before becoming the pupil and assistant of Andrea del Sarto in 1512. The *Madonna with Four Saints* (1514; Florence, SS. Annunziata) and the *Visitation* (1515–16; cloister of the SS. Annunziata) show the influences of both Sarto and Fra Bartolommeo. The influences of Leonardo da Vinci and Piero di Cosimo reinforced his natural taste for elegant contour as well as unusual motifs and attitudes.

Pontormo was commissioned to decorate the great hall of Lorenzo de' Medici's villa at Poggio a Caiano (1520–21), which had remained unfinished at Lorenzo's death. In one of the side lunettes Pontormo painted a very elegant and lively pastoral scene in which the rustic figures are treated in lightly tinted grays and yellows. Between 1522 and 1525, in the cloister of the Certosa S. Lorenzo al Monte at Galluzzo, south of Florence, he painted a large cycle depicting the Passion (now badly damaged). Pontormo's intentions become clear in his *Deposition* (1526; Florence, S. Felicità), a masterpiece of its kind, painted in light, cool tones of mauve, pink, and green, with undulating figures effectively arranged in a composition built up of sinuous tiers. As a portrait painter, he created a new type, smooth, elongated, and unquiet; the *Gem Engraver* (c. 1516; Paris, Louvre), *Alessandro de' Medici* (c. 1525; Lucca, Pinacoteca Nazionale), and the *Portrait of an Old Lady* (1550–56; Vienna, Belvedere) are all remarkable with their clear colors, the emphasis on the hands, and a draftsmanship that brings the individual into prominence. In the *Visitation* (c. 1530) at the Carmignano parish church, near Florence, he made the central group stand out through its sharp foreshortening and gathered the four figures in one block of faded yellow and red draperies. Finally, under the influence of Michelangelo, he tried to give greater breadth to his compositions, and the contrast between the delicate faces of his models and their huge muscular bodies grew more marked.

POONS, Larry (b. 1937, Tokyo), American painter. A musical composition class with the avant-garde composer John Cage at the New School for Social Research in New York introduced Poons to methods of random composition that were to affect his later paintings considerably. His earliest pictures also involved certain musically rhythmic progressions of geometric forms, recalling the moving syncopated relationship in Mondrian's late work (for example, *Broadway Boogie-Woogie*). Other important influences on his development include the concept of all-over pictorial composition that he found in Jackson Pollock's "drip" paintings, and the broad fields of intense color in Barnett Newman's canvases. Absorbing these influences, Poons added optically activating combinations of color, a distinguishing feature of the paintings he produced between 1963 and 1965. In 1966 he began to work with close-valued combinations of hues that suggested both a great spatial and atmospheric depth, and a seemingly disembodied suspension of the small colored units (*Wildcat Arrival*, 1966; New York, Coll. Albert List). Even though the surface tension of his earlier paintings was neutralized in these later works, the possibility of the field's lateral extension became more apparent and suggestive. In 1967 the influence of such painters as Jules Olitski (b. 1922) could be seen in Poons' loosening of the spatial field and in the increasing range and richness of the color in his work.

POP ART, avant-garde movement that arose in New York around 1959 and that soon spread throughout the United States and Europe. By the late 1950s, despite its success in the United States and despite the high regard enjoyed by Jackson Pollock, Franz Kline, and Willem de Kooning, Abstract Expressionism—or more precisely action painting—was still closely linked with European culture and American artists felt the need for a language of their own. Thus, Pop art (a term coined in the mid-1950s by the English critic Lawrence Alloway) was born. Another important fact concerning Pop art is that it belonged, in its very excess, to a more general tendency of which it wished to be the extreme current, that of a return to figuration.

The everyday environment of the American people provided the repertoire for the first Pop artists, Robert Rauschenberg and Jasper Johns. Although Rauschenberg cannot be regarded in the strict sense of the term as a Pop artist, the members of the Pop art movement claim him as one of the initiators of their school, which included such artists as James Rosenquist, Andy Warhol (b. 1925), Roy Lichtenstein, Claes Oldenburg, Tom Wesselmann, and, to a certain extent, Jim Dine, Robert Indiana (b. 1928), and George Segal (b. 1924). Several of the latter worked as commercial artists and used the techniques of journalism, the poster, printing, and transfers; others carried their naturalistic tendencies to the point of assembling new, worn, or even scrapped objects, while Segal reduced the art of sculpture to the presentation of figures molded from nature and placed in real settings. The aim of such methods is to lay bare objective reality and to discover the modern world of utility and mass production. The school of Pop artists that grew up in Great Britain included Richard Hamilton (b. 1922), David Hockney (b. 1937), Peter Blake (b. 1931), Derek Boshier (b. 1937), Allen Jones (b. 1937), Joe Tilson (b. 1928), Peter Phillips (b. 1939), Richard Smith (b. 1931), and the Anglo-American Ronald B. Kitaj (b. 1932); followers also appeared in other western European countries.

Pop Art. **Tom Wesselmann.** *Bathtub Collage.* 1963. *Photo Galerie Sonnabend, Paris.*

PÖPPELMANN, Matthäus Daniel (1662, Herford, Westphalia—1736, Dresden), one of the greatest German Baroque architects. From 1686 he was working as director of buildings at the court of Dresden. In 1704 he drew up a project for enlarging the Residenz of the elector of Saxony and in 1705 became court architect ("Landbaumeister"). Pöppelmann traveled to Vienna, Rome, and Naples in 1710, seeking advice on the designs for the Dresden Palace. He returned to Dresden to begin his masterpiece, the Zwinger (1711–22; destroyed World War II and since rebuilt), a vast, open-air enclosure of galleries and pavilions intended for court celebrations, and the only part of the projected palace ever built. Covered by an abundance of decoration, including Balthasar Permoser's dramatic sculptures, the Zwinger was the quintessential building of Saxon Baroque. One unfinished side was later filled in by Gottfried Semper's Gemäldegalerie (1847–49). Pöppelmann later worked with the Frenchman Zacharie Longuelune (1669–1748), on the so-called Japanese Palace, Dresden, completed by other architects (from 1715, destroyed World War II). Also with Longuelune, he built the so-called Indian Schloss at Pillnitz (1720–32), with roofs and decoration in the Chinese manner.

Matthäus Daniel Pöppelmann. Entrance pavilion of the Zwinger, Dresden. 1711–22. *Deutsche Fotothek, Dresden.*

PORDENONE, Giovanni Antonio de' Sacchis, *called* (*c.* 1484, Pordenone, near Udine—1539, Ferrara), Italian painter. A probable sojourn in Rome around 1515 or 1516, during which he absorbed Michelangelesque and Raphaelesque influences, accentuated the monumentality of his figures, which is noticeable in his large frescoes in the Malchiostri Chapel in Treviso (*c.* 1519–20) and in Cremona Cathedral (*c.* 1520–22). For the latter Pordenone painted a number of frescoes on the Passion (*Crucifixion*, *Deposition*), which have an almost Germanic sense of drama and Expressionism. After 1525, however, a Manneristic elegance reminiscent of Parmigianino appears in the *St. Gothard between St. Roch and St. Sebastian* (Pordenone, Pinacoteca). Beginning in 1527, Pordenone worked primarily in Venice, where he was Titian's rival and where he painted the organ shutters in the choir of S. Rocco with *St. Christopher* and *St. Martin* (1528–29), and worked also in the cloister of S. Stefano (1532). These late works revert to his earlier monumentality, with huge figures whose energy anticipates that of the last great Venetian master, Tintoretto.

PORTER, Fairfield (b. 1907, Winnetka, Illinois—d. 1975), American painter, critic, and teacher. He was considerably impressed by the works of the revolutionary painters shown at Alfred Stieglitz's 291 Gallery, but his own work reflects the more substantial stylistic influence of Thomas Eakins (on whom he wrote a monograph, published in 1959), Winslow Homer, and Édouard Manet, as well as the brushwork techniques of Frank Duveneck and John Singer Sargent, and the intimism of works by Vermeer, Bonnard, and Vuillard. During the 1930s strong, harshly colored images traced the artist's preoccupation with social and political problems. World War II found Porter employed as government draftsman, an experience that seems to have tightened his style at this time. Porter worked from nature and life, emphasizing light with a strong sense of balance and design in his compositions. Casual, familiar subjects were approached with an unsentimental, almost journalistic eye, opposing the informality of the subject matter with an architectonic ordering of space and composition. Within the portrait interiors, flowers, still lifes or outdoor scenes are subsumed in a sumptuous technique of paint handling and masterful control over the entire visual structure (*Porch in Maine*, 1966; Shawnee Mission, Kansas, Coll. Louis Sosland; and *Ice Coffee*, 1966; New York, Tibor de Nagy Gallery). Porter made the articulation of light one of his main concerns. Light radiates from the spaces between and around shapes and glows on the edges of surfaces and contours.

PORTINARI, Cândido (1903, Brodowski, State of São Paulo—1962, Rio de Janeiro), Brazilian painter. In 1928 he was awarded a scholarship that enabled him to visit Paris. On his return to Brazil, he began illustrating the history of the world in murals executed for some of the finest modern buildings in Brazil. His first major successes were frescoes (1936–45) for the Ministry of Education in Rio de Janeiro, representing the *Working of the Brazilian Soil*, *Children's Games*, and the *Four Elements*. His growing reputation justified an important exhibition of his works in 1940 at the Museum of Modern Art in New York. After decorating (1942) the Hispanic section of the Library of Congress in Washington, D.C., Portinari executed a Biblical cycle for the São Paulo Radio Building (1944), a series of extreme Expressionist violence. He also designed ceramic tiles on the life of St. Francis of Assisi (1944) for the façade of the church of Pampúlha, a suburb of Belo Horizonte; a *Stations of the Cross* (1945) for Belo Horizonte Cathedral; and the two panels on *War* and *Peace* (1953–55) for the United Nations General Assembly Building in New York.

POST, Pieter (1608, Haarlem—1669, The Hague), Dutch architect. Post assisted Jacob van Campen in building the Mauritshuis in The Hague (1633–35), one of the earliest examples of a modest Dutch Classical style; built of brick with stone dressings, it is simply decorated with a giant order of Ionic pilasters. He also worked with Van Campen on the Frederick Henry Palace in the Noordeine section of The Hague (1640), and the Amsterdam Town Hall (begun 1648; now Royal Palace). Post is best known for the Huis ten Bosch, a country house near The Hague (1645), whose impressive central hall is only barely indicated on the modest brick exterior, by a small cupola. His sober, brick shot foundry in The Hague (1665; destroyed World War II), where decoration was slight, is among his most successful works.

POST-PAINTERLY ABSTRACTION, term invented by the American critic Clement Greenberg when he organized an exhibition of contemporary painting at the Los Angeles County Museum of Art in 1964. He used this term to describe the generation of artists (Ellsworth Kelly, Friedel Dzubas, Ray Parker, Kenneth Noland, Frank Stella, Jules Olitski, Edward Avedesian, Darby Bannard, Al Held, Helen Frankenthaler, Sam Francis, Paul Feeley, Gene Davis) who rejected the more extreme painterliness of Abstract Expressionism but still retained some of its features, while also absorbing the influences of its less Expressionistic practitioners (Ad Reinhardt, Mark Rothko, Barnett Newman).

According to Greenberg, modernist painting is defined by the way in which it calls attention to its own limitations—as positive factors of that art. Thus the two-dimensional flatness of the picture support, its specific shape, and its material aspects (e.g. fabric stretched tautly over wooden bars) are openly acknowledged instead of being concealed by illusionistic devices or tricks. The painting is presented as an instantly apprehensible unity. Its hard discrete edges, liquefied and stained or sprayed color fields, definitively structured supports, and repetitive or serialized forms are perceived as a direct and holistic experience. The primacy and pure opticality of color—often appearing in wide saturated expanses (Olitski, Morris Louis, Kelly, Frankenthaler, Larry Poons) or the literal establishment and assertion of the properties of the canvas and its armature (Louis, Olitski, Stella, Noland, Ronald Davis, Bush) are particularly characteristic of the paintings done during the first half of the 1960s.

In the late 1960s many of those artists who had earlier rejected illusionism per se began to emphasize a particularly artificial kind of illusionism in their paintings. Stressing the abstract quality of that illusionism through the use of contradictory perspective devices or patently artificial, man-made surfaces that vary in glossiness, reflectivity, and materials (plastics, metallic pigments, fluorescent colors, etc.), artists such as Stella, Davis, Bannard, and Olitski continued to point out the viability and extensibility of the medium while concentrating on its own limitations.

POUSSIN, Nicolas (1594, Villers, near Les Andelys—1665, Rome), the greatest of the French Classical painters. Poussin went to Paris around 1612, where he met Alexandre Courtois, the curator of the royal picture collection, and through him discovered antique sculpture and the engravings done after Raphael and Giulio Romano that were in the king's collection. He visited Fontainebleau to study Primaticcio's work in the Gallery of Ulysses, and also studied anatomy in a hospital. In 1622 he was commissioned to execute six large tempera paintings on the canonization of St. Ignatius and St. Francis Xavier (now lost) for the Collège de Clermont, the Jesuit college in Paris. These were noticed by Giambattista Marino, an Italian poet who lived at the French court from 1615 to 1623. Marino hired him to work in his own home on historical subjects. The sketches for these works, known as the Massimi drawings, are now in the collection of the library at Windsor Castle and one is in the Budapest Museum of Fine Arts. Marino offered him a room in his house, taught him Italian, and introduced him to Ovid's *Metamorphoses*, of which he made a series of drawings (before 1624; Windsor Castle, Royal Coll.).

Marino suggested that Poussin accompany him to Rome, and the artist, after going first to Venice, where he remained for several months to study the paintings of Titian, arrived in Rome in the spring of 1624 to find the entire colony of French artists there working in Simon Vouet's workshop. At that time Roman artists were divided into two schools: that of the Carracci and that of Caravaggio, the dramatic pioneer of realistic chiaroscuro. Apart from these two groups, there remained only one independent figure: Domenichino, a serious and powerful artist whom Poussin chose as his model. During Poussin's first years (1624–25) in Rome, Marino found the time to introduce him to Marcello Sacchetti, the wealthy collector and banker of Pope Urban VIII, who in turn introduced him to Cardinal Francesco Barberini. Poussin also met Jacques Stella, Claude Lorrain, and François Duquesnoy, a Flemish sculptor who ultimately gained widespread recognition. Poussin worked with enthusiasm—drawing, studying the measurements of ancient statuary with Duquesnoy and Alessandro Algardi, and also studying geometry, optics, and the law of perspective in the library of Cardinal Barberini, who introduced him to his secretary Commendatore Cassiano del Pozzo, who became his patron.

Two important commissions assured his reputation at this time: for Cardinal Barberini, who had just returned from Spain, he painted the *Death of Germanicus* (1628; Minneapolis, Institute of Arts), and for St. Peter's he executed the *Martyrdom of St. Erasmus* (1628–29; now Vatican Museum). He was also still boarding with Jacques Dughet, a pastry cook and caterer whose daughter he married. It was her dowry that enabled Poussin to set up house

Nicolas Poussin. *Nymph, Satyr, Faun, and Cupids.* *c.* 1635. Staatliche Kunstsammlungen, Kassel.

and, finally, to work in peace and security. He painted, for the first time, a picture on a subject of his own choosing: the *Philistines Stricken by the Plague*, or the *Plague at Ashdad* (1630; Paris, Louvre), which he sold to Valguarnera, a Sicilian adventurer who traded in paintings, and for whom he also painted the marvelous *Kingdom of Flora* (1631; Dresden, Gemäldegalerie). His clients—the best known is Del Pozzo—were now Italian and Spanish; and the dealers were buying from him as well.

In 1634–35 Poussin saw a good deal of Domenichino, who, as an ardent music lover, introduced him to Gioseffe Zarlino's *Istituzioni harmoniche* ("Harmonic Institutes"), which provided the basis for the famous theory of modes that he began to apply to his painting. According to this theory, each subject must be treated in a specific manner; thus, brutal subjects were treated harshly and sweet ones gently. Poussin also executed, for Del Pozzo, 23 volumes of drawings—now in the Royal Collection at Windsor—illustrating every aspect of antique art (bas-reliefs, statues, buildings). He borrowed Leonardo da Vinci's *Treatise on Painting* from Cardinal Barberini's library and illustrated it.

In 1635–36 Cardinal Richelieu commissioned a *Triumph of Neptune* (1635–36; Philadelphia, Museum of Art) and four *Bacchanals* for his château. Three of the *Bacchanals* have been identified: the *Triumph of Pan* (*c.* 1637; Gloucestershire, Sudeley Castle, Coll. Simon Morrison), the *Triumph of Bacchus* (original lost; numerous copies extant), and *Triumph of Silenus* (original lost; copy in London, National Gallery). Also linked with this series is a splendid *Bacchanal* in the National Gallery, London, which is also dated around 1637. At just about the same period the artist undertook the *Seven Sacraments* series, commissioned by Del Pozzo and certainly one of Poussin's most important productions. Today five of the *Sacraments* are in the collection of the Duke of Rutland at Belvoir Castle, Grantham; one was destroyed in a fire at the castle in 1816; the seventh is in the Samuel H. Kress Collection at the National Gallery of Art, Washington, D.C. The whole series was most probably painted between

Nicolas Poussin. *Echo and Narcissus.* Before 1630. Louvre, Paris. *Photo Giraudon, Paris.*

1634 or 1638 and 1640, except for the *Baptism* in the Kress Collection, which was not completed until 1642.

Poussin's prestige was now such that Sublet de Noyers, King Louis XIII's superintendent of construction, invited him on behalf of Richelieu to go to France. Still, before leaving Rome Poussin completed one of his finest canvases, the *Dance to the Music of Time* (*c.* 1639–40; London, Wallace Collection), for Cardinal Giulio Rospigliosi, who later became Pope Clement IX. Louis XIII gave Poussin a magnificent reception in Paris and housed him in a wing of the Tuileries Palace. Richelieu asked him to decorate the Grand Cabinet in the Palais Cardinal (later Palais Royal), Paris, with a Biblical theme that could serve as a pretext for the glorification of his political power. The project eventually materialized in a painting of *Moses and the Burning Bush* (1641; Copenhagen, Nationalmuseum), which was hardly worthy of the artist's talent. Louis XIII had large-scale plans for him, too, involving the execution of 40 compositions representing the myth of Hercules for the decoration of the Grande Galerie of the Louvre. The completed fragment of this project was destroyed in the 18th century. The artist, assailed by constantly changing plans and collectors' demands, hastened his departure for Rome, whither he returned (November 1642) never to leave again. His clientele, which had been Italian, now became French. Pointel, the banker, came to Rome and became one of Poussin's most enthusiastic patrons, as did the Duc de Créqui. *The Meeting of Rebecca and Eliezer* (1648; Louvre) was painted for Pointel, and represented—in accordance with his patron's wish—every variety of feminine beauty.

Some of Poussin's canvases—from the *Rape of the Sabines* (*c.*

Nicolas Poussin. *Landscape with the body of Phocion Carried out of Athens.* 1648. Coll. Earl of Plymouth, Oakly Park, Shropshire.

1635, Louvre; *c.* 1637, New York, Metropolitan Museum) or the *Saving of the Infant Pyrrhus* (1637–38; Louvre) to the *Israelites Gathering Manna* (1637/38–39; Louvre) or the *Testament of Eudamidas* (*c.* 1655; Copenhagen, Nationalmuseum)—are conceived as psychological pantomimes. In these works, the great "teller of fables," as Bernini described him, transposed his subjects' feelings into gestures, thereby perfecting the technique of historical painting. Every element in his paintings conveys a message.

The last 15 years of Poussin's life were a veritable apotheosis. Aware of the beauty of nature, he increased (after 1648) his production of landscapes, opposing man's fragile and ephemeral destiny with the eternal fecundity of nature. His paintings are composed with a scrupulous regard for realistic detail, a fact to which his pen and ink sketches and admirable India ink wash drawings attest. Among his masterpieces are the *Landscape with the Body of Phocion Carried Out of Athens* (1648; Oakly Park, Shropshire, Coll. Earl of Plymouth), the *Ashes of Phocion Collected by His Widow* (1648; Knowsley Hall, Lancashire, Coll. Earl of Derby), *Landscape with a Man Killed by a Snake* (1648; London, National Gallery), *Landscape with Orpheus and Eurydice* (*c.* 1650; Louvre), *Landscape with Orion* (1658; New York, Metropolitan Museum), and, finally, the admirable *Four Seasons* series (1660–64; Louvre), which is the artist's final testament.

Nicolas Poussin. *Winter, or the Deluge.* From the series on the Four Seasons. 1660–64. Louvre, Paris.

POWERS, Hiram (1805, near Woodstock, Vermont—1873, Florence, Italy), American sculptor. In the winters of 1834–35 and 1835–36 Powers went to Washington, D.C., where he modeled the heads of General Andrew Jackson (*c.* 1835; New York, Metropolitan Museum), Daniel Webster (1836; Chicago, Art Institute, and Boston, Atheneum), John Quincy Adams (1835; Philadelphia, Pennsylvania Academy of the Fine Arts), John C. Calhoun, and Chief Justice John Marshall. He left America in 1837 for Florence, where he remained for the rest of his life. His marble portrait busts and allegorical female figures are smoothly modeled and reflect the dignity, restraint, and idealized beauty of the Neoclassical style then dominating European and American sculpture. In 1851 Powers received international recognition with his full-length idealized nude, the marble *Greek Slave* (Washington, D.C., National Gallery).

POYNTER, Sir Edward John (1836, Paris—1919, London), English painter, primarily of historical subjects. Occupied at first with decorative work, Poynter soon began to paint the historical subjects—usually set in the ancient world—with which he ultimately became successful and famous. He first gained recognition with *Faithful unto Death* (1865; Liverpool, Walker Art Gallery), yet his best-known painting is probably *A Visit to Aesculapius* (1880; London, Tate Gallery). Poynter combined carefully researched archaeological detail, narrative themes full of anecdotal interest, and highly polished handling. Poynter, who was a competent academic draftsman, brought a certain Continental panache to the debased tradition of English history painting. He was versatile—watercolor came to him as easily as fresco—and made designs for mosaic, stained glass, pottery, and tiles. Also a good administrator, Poynter was the first person to hold the position of Slade Professor at University College, London (1871–75), and was also director of the National Gallery (1894–1904) and president of the Royal Academy (1896–1918).

POZZO, Andrea, *also called* Fra *or* Padre Pozzo (1642, Trento—1709, Vienna), Italian painter, one of the major decorative artists of the Baroque period. On December 23, 1665, under the influence of a sermon, he joined the Jesuit order. In 1676 he decorated the mission church of the Jesuits at Mondovì in Piedmont. The General of the Jesuits summoned him to Rome in 1681, where in 1685 Fra Pozzo began to decorate the interior of the church of S. Ignazio with numerous frescoes, including the celebrated *Triumph of St. Ignatius of Loyola* (1691–94) on the ceiling of the nave. The vertiginous effects of its *sotto in su* illusionism (the view from the ground upward) are intended to open up the infinity of the heavens for the worshipers. Fra Pozzo also designed stage settings for religious festivities, and wrote an influential treatise—*Perspectiva Pictorum et Architectorum* (1693)—that had an enormous success and was translated into English and German. In 1702 Leopold I called him to Vienna, where he provided decorations for the Universitätskirche (1703–4), the Jesuitenkirche (1705), and the Palais Liechtenstein (1704–8). Pozzo's influence was considerable in Vienna, and it was primarily due to his example that the Italian Baroque style of ceiling decoration was disseminated north of the Alps throughout Austria and Bavaria. In Italy itself his art had a profound effect on Francesco Solimena in Naples and Giambattista Tiepolo in Venice.

PRAMPOLINI, Enrico (1894, Modena—1956, Rome), Italian painter, sculptor, and scenographer. Although Prampolini joined the Futurist movement when he was eighteen, he was also influenced by Cubism, Constructivism, and even Dadaism. His architectural sense of space and preference for new materials brought him into close contact with Cubism, particularly with Gino Severini and his friends of the Section d'Or group. During a brief "mechanical" phase that followed this first period, Prampolini designed the sets and costumes for several ballet and theatrical productions; in the course of his career he designed over one hundred such stage settings. In 1929 he signed the Futurist manifesto devoted to "Aeropainting." These paintings contained abstract spatial movements, or "plastic itineraries" (*Plastic Itinerary*, 1929; Milan,

Coll. Dr. Laurini), and they placed Prampolini among the pioneers of non-figurative art. At this time he was also under the influence of Surrealism, but as an active member of the geometric abstractionist Cercle et Carré group (1930), and then of the Abstraction-Création group (1932), Prampolini soon resumed his experiments with the use of new material, finding in them a means of escaping from the traditional limitations of painting. In the late 1930s and early 1940s the horrors of World War II brought about a new phase in Prampolini's artistic development: he lost interest in nature and turned to the study of man and his historical situation (*Woman on the Seashore, c.* 1940; Rome, Priv. Coll.). He also discovered Picasso—the Picasso of *Guernica* and the realistic sculptures, and even wrote a short book about the latter called *Picasso as Sculptor* (1944). Around 1945, however, Prampolini returned to his true path, abstract art, and gained recognition as one of the few painters within the abstract movement who had evolved his own style independently of formulas and fashion, entirely through his own efforts.

PRANDTAUER, Jakob (1660, Stanz, Tirol—1726, Sankt-Pölten, Lower Austria), Austrian Baroque architect and sculptor. In his early years Prandtauer greatly admired the works of Johann Martin Gumpp the Elder (1643–1729) of Innsbruck and those of Enrico Zuccali (1642–1724) in Bavaria, especially the latter's church of the Theatines in Munich, whose plan he later imitated. Prandtauer's most important commission was to build the abbey of Melk, his masterpiece, and one of the greatest creations of Baroque architecture (1701–26). The church is flanked by two long buildings, which, linked by a semicircular gallery, form a terraced forecourt above the river. In the rear are the great cloister and prelates' court placed on an axis with the chevet of the abbey church. In the building that stretches along the right-hand side of the church, a stairway, carved with putti by Lorenzo Mattielli (d. 1748), gives access to the imperial apartments, which are served by a very long corridor. The portal of the church, with giant statues of St. Leopold and St. Coloman, was dominated by two clock towers (rebuilt after a fire in 1738 to a different design with a more bulbous form). The nave, which was also completed after Prandtauer's death, but according to his designs, is flanked by oval chapels and surmounted by galleries whose profane decoration is reminiscent of theater boxes. Antonio Beduzzi's decoration of the high altar is equally dazzling.

Jakob Prandtauer. Melk Abbey. 1701–26. *Photo Helga Schmidt-Glassner, Stuttgart.*

Apart from this masterpiece, Prandtauer's works include several abbeys, abbots' residences, and churches. At the monastery of St. Florian, near Linz, where the Italian Carlo Antonio Carlone had already built the church, Prandtauer designed the entrance building, the staircase, and the great summer refectory (*c.* 1710). He also succeeded Carlone at the monastery of Kremsmünster (from 1708), where he built the entrance court. With the monastery of Herzogenburg, near Sankt-Pölten (completed 1712), the churches of Sonntagsberg, near Weidhofen-am-Ybbs (1706–28), and Ravelsbach (1721–26), Prandtauer made further variations on the plans adopted for the church of Melk and the state rooms of St. Florian. One exception, however, was the church of Christkindl, near Steyr (completed 1708), a rotunda preceded by two bell towers, commissioned by the abbot of Garsten.

PRE-COLUMBIAN ART. The term pre-Columbian applies to the various cultures and civilizations that flourished throughout the American continents before the arrival of Christopher Columbus on October 12, 1492. The two best-known pre-Columbian civilizations are those of the Aztecs in Mexico and the Incas in Peru. But the Aztecs and Incas, masters of the world conquered by the Spaniards, were themselves only recent conquerors whose history dated back at the most only about 200 years; in contrast, it had taken at least 2,000 years to produce the culture of which they were the continuers.

Pre-Columbian Art. Mochica pottery vessel, from Chimbote. *c.* 400–600.

In Peru the oldest traces, those of the primitive hunters, date from about 7000 B.C., but a primitive agriculture did not appear until about 2500, and the first pottery only in about 900 B.C. Then civilizations began to grow—named after the sites on which they were discovered—and their development continued from about the late 9th century B.C. to the arrival of the Spaniards in A.D. 1521. The most noteworthy artistic productions of these civilizations were ceramics (Mochica, Nazca, and others) and weaving. The architecture of Tiahuanaco, of the Chimus (the vast city of Chan Chan), and of the Incas is impressive in size, but in comparison with that of the Mexican builders it lacks imagination. In general the same can be said of sculpture, in which geometric designs and zoomorphic forms are combined with more skill than imagination.

In Mexico the different civilizations gradually formed after the introduction of agriculture in the 2nd millennium B.C. Mexican pottery is very rich, but architecture was the predominant art; it was dedicated to the service of the gods and its most representative form was the pyramid. Sculpture

Pre-Columbian Art. Pyramid of the Sun, Teotihuacán. 1st–3rd century. *Photo Henri Stierlin, Geneva.*

was also of religious inspiration and consisted of symbols of the gods; it was particularly splendid when it was meant to signify the presence of a god.

The other regions of North and South America never knew anything as brilliant as the civilizations of Peru and Mexico. However, the tribal civilizations of Colombia and Ecuador, and the Pueblo and Mound Builders of North America left traces of pottery, goldwork, sculpture, and even architecture that are far from negligible (*see* INDIANS OF NORTH AMERICA, Art of the; INDIANS OF SOUTH AMERICA, Art of the).

The fundamental question is whether the great pre-Columbian civilizations developed independently or derived from some early contact with the Old World. The presence of pyramids and certain other artistic resemblances have led some authoritative scholars to suspect Egyptian influences. Sir Grafton Elliot Smith, misled by imprecise findings in which he thought he could discern elephants, concluded in favor of relations with India. More recently, Robert Heine-Geldern saw a resemblance between the motifs of Central American art and those of Chinese art. But no decisive proof has been established to confirm relations between the New and Old Worlds, except by way of the Bering Strait—which would have occurred only 15,000 years ago—and insignificant contacts between the Eskimos and the Viking immigrants.

Pre-Raphaelite Brotherhood. Edward Burne-Jones. *The Golden Staircase.* 1876–80. Tate Gallery, London.

PRENDERGAST, Maurice Brazil (1859, St. John's, Newfoundland—1924, New York), American painter. In 1884 he had saved enough money to go to Paris, where he studied for three years at the Académie Julian and at the Académie Colarossi. In 1898–99 he visited Europe again, and this time traveled in Italy, settling for several months in Venice, studying the paintings of Vittore Carpaccio and painting such charming scenes as *Ponte della Paglia* (1899; Washington, D.C., Phillips Collection). Robert Henri then invited him to exhibit in the famous show of The Eight held at the Macbeth Gallery in New York (1908). Prendergast left Boston in 1914, and settled in New York for the last 10 years of his life. After assimilating the influence of the Impressionists, he developed a style that is similar to that of the Nabis, but that is also characterized by childlike and romantic qualities. He applied unmixed colors to the canvas with a palette knife, building up a mosaic-like surface in which related tones are arranged in a complicated counterpoint (*Central Park*, 1901; New York, Whitney Museum), and in which the entire composition is reconciled in a formal structure that is at once flat and multidimensional.

PRE-RAPHAELITE BROTHERHOOD, an association of English painters active *c.* 1848, the original members of which were William Holman Hunt, John Everett Millais, and Dante Gabriel Rossetti. They were soon joined by William Rossetti (1829–1919), James Collinson (1825–81), the sculptor and poet Thomas Woolner (1825–92), and the art critic Frederick George Stephens (1828–1907). The Brotherhood evolved as a result of discussions between Hunt and Millais in the autumn of 1848. They disliked the inflated forms and sentiments found in paintings by Raphael's Bolognese followers, and professed instead to see a greater sincerity in the works of the Florentine and Sienese primitives who predated Raphael.

The Pre-Raphaelites held their first meeting in 1848; on that occasion the members studied a volume of engravings by the contemporary Florentine engraver Giovanni Paolo Lasinio (1789–1855) after the 14th- and 15th-century frescoes in the Camposanto at Pisa. They particularly admired those by the 15th-century Italian painter Benozzo Gozzoli, whose cheerful sweetness they considered to be Chaucerian. Dante Gabriel Rossetti was the group's guiding spirit at this time, and the initials P. R. B. (Pre-Raphaelite Brotherhood) first appeared after his signature in 1849, when he exhibited the *Childhood of the Virgin* (London, Tate Gallery) at the Hyde Park Gallery in London. Rossetti was also largely responsible for giving the movement the sultry Catholic overtones evident in such pictures as *Beata Beatrix* (1863; Tate Gallery). Holman Hunt and Millais, on the other hand, represented the "Protestant" phalanx: their painstaking, high-keyed techniques and almost Flemish naturalism were coupled with a puritanical self-denial regarding pictorial glamor.

The Pre-Raphaelites were criticized on many counts. The noted Victorian art critic John Ruskin, however, was their champion throughout the 1850s; in his book, *Modern Painters* (1851–60), Ruskin urged that contemporary painting be reformed by means of a return to nature. The group was short-lived, and by 1852 the original membership had been dissolved. Only Holman Hunt, who spent two years painting in total solitude in Palestine, upheld the group's original ideals and continued to paint in the Pre-Raphaelite style until the end of the 19th century. Other artists who painted in the Pre-Raphaelite manner, without being members of the original group, included William Dyce and Ford Madox Brown. The paintings of Edward Burne-Jones, one of Rossetti's followers, represent the later phase of the Pre-Raphaelite movement and its decline into a recondite symbolism.

PRICE, Bruce (1845, Cumberland, Maryland—1903, Paris),

important late 19th-century American architect whose residential work was especially influential. Although he had studied in Paris, his first works were typically American, in that some reflected the English Queen Anne style, such as a house on 56th Street and one at 600 Madison Avenue, New York City (1885), and some the Richardsonian-Romanesque, such as Osborn Hall at Yale University, and the Windsor Street Station, Montreal (both 1888). But when American taste shifted, in the 1890s, to a more academic and eclectic tradition, his Beaux-Arts training served him well. The Château Frontenac Hotel, Quebec (1890), is still picturesque in its active roof line, but it is in the François I style, and thus has Renaissance details. The American Surety Building (1894–96) and the International Banking and Trust Company (1898–1900) display the blocky outline and Renaissance ornament that characterized New York skyscrapers at the end of the 19th century.

Price's most enduring achievement is undoubtedly the group of remarkable country houses he built at Tuxedo Park, New York, for Pierre Lorillard in 1885. Here he disciplined and formalized the flowing spaces and horizontal masses associated with Shingle Style work, while retaining the naturalistic textures and environmental suitability of those resort retreats. This formality foreshadows a more academic attitude, and there are even explicit revivalistic overtones in one Tuxedo Park house, that for Pierre Lorillard, Jr., which is Neo-Colonial.

Price's domestic work made a deep impression on Frank Lloyd Wright. Not only do many of Wright's plans develop from the Tuxedo Park houses, but the façade of his studio in Oak Park, Illinois (1889), is based on the W. Chandler house.

PRIMATICCIO, Francesco Primaticcio, *called* Il (1504, Bologna—1570, Paris), Italian decorative painter, sculptor, and architect, one of the principal representatives of Mannerism. He was a pupil of Giulio Romano, with whom he worked on the decoration of the Palazzo del Tè at Mantua. When François I invited the assistance of Giulio Romano, the latter sent Primaticcio in his stead (1531). At Fontainebleau, Primaticcio met Rosso Fiorentino, who was working on the decoration of the Galerie François I; he himself was assigned the decoration of the Chambre de la Reine (*c.* 1535). On the death of Rosso in 1540, Primaticcio became supervisor of buildings, a post he held under three French kings: François I, Henri II, and Charles IX. He thus exercised a decisive influence over French art by introducing the Italian Mannerist style, with its very elongated canon of proportion for the figures.

Unfortunately, nothing has survived of the great decorations the artist executed at Fontainebleau. All that remain are his stuccoes (*c.* 1541–45) in the former bedchamber of the Duchesse d'Étampes; a very rich series of drawings on antique themes, inspired by Ovid's *Metamorphoses*, Homer's *Iliad*, and by the exploits of Heracles, Ulysses, and Alexander the Great (Paris, Louvre; Leningrad, Hermitage; Florence, Uffizi; Vienna, Albertina); and tapestries that were woven from his cartoons. After the death of Henri II in 1559, Primaticcio replaced Philibert de l'Orme as superintendent of buildings, and for 10 years, in collaboration with the sculptor Germain Pilon, worked on the tomb of Henri II in the funerary chapel of the Valois family in St-Denis, Paris.

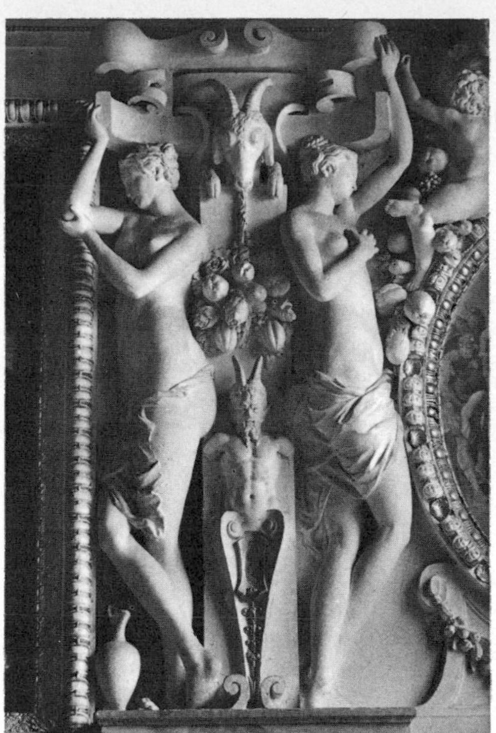

Primaticcio. Stucco decoration in the former bedchamber of the Duchesse d'Étampes. *c.* 1541–45. Château of Fontainebleau. *Photo Verroust, Neuilly.*

PRIMITIVES OF THE TWENTIETH CENTURY. Outside—yet parallel to—the development of the main artistic currents of the Western tradition, there has evolved a craftsmanly approach to painting characterized by the supreme importance given to a minute enumeration of things, people, and events—all rendered at the expense of a true representation in pictorial space, and therefore only partially obeying the laws of perspective. These "naive" methods were adopted after around 1850 by a group of painters who appeared when folk painting was no longer generally practiced. Modern primitive artists usually came from humble backgrounds, and because of their station in life and the frequently belated flowering of their art, they usually remained outside the artistic and spiritual culture of their time. In its deeply original character and rigorously logical development, modern primitive art differs from the creations of earlier naive craftsmen and from children's or madmen's paintings; it does, however, share with the latter types of work certain methods of representation and a primitive vision of things.

The discovery of the Neo-primitives was made in the early years of the 20th century by artists, poets, and a few discerning collectors. The importance of Henri (Le Douanier) Rousseau was recognized around 1905 by the writers Guillaume Apollinaire and Alfred Jarry, the painters Pablo Picasso and Robert Delaunay, as well as by the German art critic and dealer Wilhelm Uhde, who discovered Séraphine in 1912. André Bauchant's main defenders and patrons were the art dealer Jeanne Bucher, Le Corbusier, and Amédée Ozenfant. Public taste for the art of these new primitives increased after the great group exhibitions that took place in the 1920s and 1930s. After World War

Primitives of the 20th century. André Bauchant. *Ulysses and Telemachus.* 1942. Galerie Bucher, Paris. *Photo Joubert.*

II, several comprehensive exhibits of primitive art were held, including one in Rome (1964) and another in Morocco (1964). By the mid-20th century every country claimed its own primitives, including the Polish Teofil Ociepka (b. 1892); the Yugoslavs Ivan Generalič (b. 1914) and Ivan Rabuzin (b. 1919); the Englishman Alfred Wallis (1855–1942); the Belgian Léon Greffe (1881–1957); the Swiss Adolf Dietrich (1877–1957); the Italian Orneore Metelli (1872–1938); the Germans Waldemar Rusche (known as Paps; 1882–1965) and Adalbert Trillhaase (1859–1936); the Spaniard Miguel Vivancos; the Russian Niko Pirosmanichwili (known as Pirosman; 1886–1917); the Greek Theophilos Hadsimichael (known as Theophilos; 1866–1934); and the Israeli Shalom Moskovitz (called Shalom of Safed; b. *c.* 1892). In the United States, artists such as Grandma Moses, Morris Hirshfield, and Joseph Pickett gained widespread recognition. In France after World War II, Jean Ève (b. 1900), Dominique Lagru (1873–1960), Émile Blondel (b. 1893), Jules Lefranc (b. 1887), Louis-Auguste Déchelette (b. 1894), Gertrude O'Brady (b. 1904), André Demonchy (b. 1914), and Aristide Caillaud (b. 1902) became well-known primitive painters.

To this list should be added mention of two primitive architects. In the fantastic Palais Idéal (1879–1912; Hauterives, Drôme) built by Ferdinand Cheval (1836–1924), dreamlike forms are combined with precise references to traditional art in order to create an amazing network of buildings that includes a cascade, a grotto, a Druid's tomb, a Pharaoh's tomb, and a mosque, as well as statues of animals and human beings. Other examples of this type of architecture in France are the carved rocks at Rothéneuf, near St-Malo; these are the work of a little-known builder, Abbé Fouré, who spent 25 years on the project.

Pierre-Paul Prud'hon. *Phrosine and Mélidore*. 1797. Bibliothèque Nationale, Paris.

PROUVÉ, Jean (b. 1901, Nancy), French engineer and builder. Like the great engineers of the 19th century, Prouvé's talent in building with metal derived from an almost instinctive knowledge of the properties of his materials and from a gift for formal and technical invention. In 1934 he designed a prototype for a curtain wall, variations of which were developed to meet the requirements of such particular projects as the Maison du Peuple, Clichy (1937–39; with Eugène Beaudouin [b. 1898] and Marcel Lods); the Centre de la Fédération Nationale du Bâtiment, Paris (1950; with Raymond Gravereaux); the French Pavilion at the Brussels International Exhibition (1958; with Guillaume Gillet). Prouvé designed several prototypes of prefabricated buildings by applying his researches to every element of construction, including shell houses (Meudon, 1949), and the Abbé Pierre House (Beauvallon, 1955). One of his most spectacular designs is the Buvette at Évian (1957; with the architect Maurice Novarina), where the structure seems weightless.

PRUD'HON, Pierre-Paul (1758, Cluny—1823, Paris), French painter. Prud'hon won the Prix de Rome in 1784 and spent three years in Italy (1785–88), where he was particularly impressed by the soft chiaroscuro and *sfumato* effects in the works of Raphael, Correggio, and, above all, Leonardo da Vinci. In Rome the artist became a close friend of the Neoclassical sculptor Antonio Canova, and discovered antique—especially Alexandrine—art, whose languid grace was much to his taste. On his return to Paris, he became active in Jacobin politics; in 1794 he fled from the Thermidorian reaction, settling in Gray, where he executed a series of portraits whose sobriety, tenderness, and fine technique make them worthy of Louis David (*Madame Anthony and her Children*, 1796; Lyons, Museum). Prud'hon returned to Paris at the end of 1796, and at the turn of the century embarked upon his most brilliant period of painting. To these years belong the official portrait of *Empress Josephine* (1805; Paris, Louvre); the allegory of *Justice and Divine Vengeance Pursuing Crime* (1808; Louvre), which was destined for the Palais de Justice in Paris; the *Rape of Psyche* (1808; Louvre), a work of cool eroticism typifying the seductive use of lighting that earned Prud'hon the reputation as "the French Correggio"; and *Venus and Adonis* (1812; London, Wallace Collection), a superb composition bathed in a melting lunar chiaroscuro.

The art of Prud'hon serves as a link between 18th-century Neoclassicism and 19th-century Romanticism. He expressed himself most freely perhaps in his lyrical drawings (collections in the Louvre; Chantilly, Musée Condé; Gray, Museum), frequently executed with black and white pencils on tinted paper, and radiating a mysterious and haunting light that appeals directly to the imagination.

PUCELLE, Jean (active *c.* 1319–27, Paris), French painter. Pucelle was already an established master by 1319, and for over 30 years directed the most active and most original studio for illumination work in Paris. About 15 illuminated manuscripts are known to have been produced in his workshop, including the two masterpieces, the Belleville Breviary (*c.* 1323–26; Paris, Bibliothèque Nationale) and a small Book of Hours (1325–28; New York, Cloisters), which was probably illuminated for Queen Jeanne d'Évreux. These works show that Pucelle was an artistic revolutionary who introduced several new elements into French painting: new effects of modeling (often by the monochromatic grisaille technique), light and shade, and an approach to perspective, all of which belie a direct knowledge of Italian innovations, especially those of Duccio and Giotto. Moreover, he did this without breaking with the tradition of calligraphic elegance established by the illuminator Master Honoré (active 1288–96, Paris; d. before 1318), nor with the Gothic taste for narrative fantasy. With Pucelle the grotesques and drolleries—which in the work of earlier illuminators had been mere marginal embellishments—become integrated with the main illustration, often serving as commentaries on it or on the text, or functioning as caryatids supporting the main picture. These border images show that Pucelle was familiar with the grotesques traditionally used in English and Flemish illustration. For all these reasons, and because his art was influential until the end of the 14th century, Pucelle may be regarded as the true initiator of the International Gothic style that flourished in Northern Europe after 1400.

PUEBLO ART. The Spanish explorers used the term Pueblo to describe groups of Indians whose highly organized villages had impressed them. The territory occupied by these populations covered the southwestern United States (present-day Utah, Nevada, California, Arizona, and New Mexico). Although the ancient inhabitants of this region were related to one another through cultural affinities, they can be divided into three groups: the true Pueblo people, generally known to archaeologists as the Anasazi ("ancient people"); the Hohokam; and the Mogollon. Their descendants are the present-day Zuni and Hopi. The Pueblos were a sedentary, agricultural people; the chronology of their development is uncertain, but it is generally agreed that the first two periods (Pueblo I and II) took place between A.D. 700 and 1100. The years A.D. 1100–1300 (Pueblo III) marked the height of their development in architecture, pottery, and weaving. Subsequently, they entered a period of decline (Pueblo IV and V) that began in the 14th century and is still in evidence.

The originality of the Pueblos had its basis in the agricultural economy, for this gave rise to two forms of habitat: a troglodyte habitat in furnished and fortified caves on cliffs overlooking valleys, and above all a village habitat. The Pueblo villages were constructed within completely closed high adobe or stone walls. The houses backed on to these walls and comprised several stories, each one set back further than the one below to form terraces. Entry from outside the village was gained by climbing rungs set in the wall face and descending on the other side over the roofs of the houses, from terrace to terrace. The plan of these villages was sometimes rectangular, but more often D-shaped, in which case the houses backed only on to the semicircular part and a high wall connected the ends of the semicircle. A central area was always left free, in the middle of which was a large, generally circular chamber dug out of the ground and covered with a flat roof; this was the kiva, and it played an important role in the social and religious life of the community, serving both as meeting place and ceremonial area.

Early Pueblo basketry was of high quality, the women having taken great care to achieve a very close weave. Three basic techniques were used: coiling, twining, and wicker. Designs were often created, but the resulting dark and light patterns do not appear to have had any symbolic meaning. The Pueblos produced textiles and wove various types of bags out of natural fibers. The Navaho loom of today is in fact the one used by the Pueblos in the 8th or 9th century. Sculpture was rather limited, although several examples of small stone carvings are known. Another type of sculpture comprised wooden figurines—the famous *kachina* dolls—that represent beneficent spirits used in ritual ceremonies. Little has survived of Pueblo painting. The walls of the kivas were austerely painted: a mission from the Peabody Museum of Harvard University discovered, in the kiva of the village of Awatovi (in Arizona's Jeddite valley), several successive layers of paintings, the earliest of which represented geometric forms, and the later ones scenes of daily life, treated in a conventional, schematic way.

Like the Hohokam and the Mogollon, the Pueblos attained their fullest artistic expression in painted pottery. Its manufacture was very primitive and was carried out without the aid of a wheel. Different design styles were used with different colors: designs were black on a gray or white ground; red or black on an orange ground; black on red; or black and red on orange. These designs used a repertoire of geometric forms with symbolic meanings (triangles, zigzags, key patterns, undulating lines, ladders), and sometimes associated with them were figures of animals, birds, and plants. The meanings were connected with the cult of water (common among agricultural peoples) and the need to draw it forth and keep it, while the key patterns seem to have represented lightning, the undulating lines clouds, and the vertical or crossed lines rain. The figures of animals, birds, and plants were stylized in an original way, with an intensity that derived from the fantastic or naive elongation of the forms, the inflected position of the body, and the sharp contrast of figure to ground.

Pueblo Art. Zuni vase with geometric decoration, from New Mexico. Museum of the American Indian, New York.

Pueblo Art. Hopi plaque decorated with the figure of the warrior Kipok, from Arizona. Museum of The American Indian, New York.

PUGET, Pierre (1620, Séon, near Marseilles—1694, Marseilles), French sculptor, painter, and architect. He went to Italy, where he worked first in Florence and then (*c.* 1640–43) in Rome in the studio of Pietro da Cortona, the most famous Italian painter of the day. When the municipality of Toulon wanted to replace the old Town Hall, Puget proposed a design for a façade having a portico and caryatids (1656–57), which was enthusiastically accepted. By 1659 his growing reputation reached Paris and the Minister of Finance, Nicolas Fouquet, requested his help for his Château de Vaux, near Melun, at the same time as Jean-Baptiste Colbert asked him to work for Cardinal Jules Mazarin. Puget had the misfortune to accept Fouquet's commis-

Pierre Puget. *Milo of Crotona.* 1682. Louvre, Paris. *Photo Sougez, Paris.*

sion, and the *Gallic Hercules Resting* (1661; Paris, Louvre), which he had carved in Italy, arrived after Fouquet's downfall and was confiscated by his successor, Colbert, for the gardens of his château at Sceaux. Puget then decided to settle in Genoa (1661–67), where he carved, for the church of S. Maria di Carignano, a *St. Sebastian* (*c.* 1661–65) and a *St. Ambrose or St. Alexander Sauli* (*c.* 1661–67); for the oratory of S. Filippo Neri, he carved an *Immaculate Conception* (*c.* 1661–67) that is light, airy, and suffused with youth and purity. On his return to France in 1667, Puget settled in Toulon, where he was appointed director of the studios of naval sculpture at the Arsenal. In the 1670s naval experts persuaded Colbert to abandon almost entirely the practice of decorating ships with wood carving, and Puget was given less and less to do in the shipyards (he was finally dismissed in 1679 and returned to Marseilles). In 1670, however, while walking in the Toulon harbor, he noticed two blocks of marble that were about to be shipped to Versailles via Le Havre. He was so attracted by the beauty of the material that he sent Colbert designs for statues that he proposed to carve from the blocks. Colbert approved the project. It took Puget 10 years to complete the *Milo of Crotona* (1682; Louvre) and *Perseus Rescuing Andromeda* (1684; Louvre). Colbert died in the meantime and was succeeded by the Marquis François Michel Letellier de Louvois, who was favorably disposed toward Puget. Contrary to legend, the *Milo* and *Perseus* were well received and placed in the gardens of Versailles at the entrance of the Tapis Vert, at the center of the park's perspective. Puget's two masterpieces, the colossal bas-reliefs of *Alexander and Diogenes* (1687–92; Louvre) and *St. Charles Borromeo Praying for the End of the Plague in Milan* (1684; Marseilles, Musée des Beaux-Arts) are theatrical and rather confused, but they are so moving that they dispel all criticism.

PUGIN, Augustus Welby Northmore (1812, London—1852, Ramsgate, Kent), English architect and theoretician. He was a precocious and talented draftsman and designer of architectural ornament, and when he became interested in the theater, turned these talents to the design of stage scenery (1831; Gothicizing scenery for the opera *Kenilworth*, London, Covent Garden). In 1833 Pugin had already built a curious house in the Gothic manner for himself near Salisbury. His conversion to Roman Catholicism in the following year also marked a turning point in his critical writing, which gave to the Gothic Revival an ethical and social foundation previously unknown. Pugin's best-known book, *Contrasts: or a Parallel Between the Noble Edifices of the Fourteenth and Fifteenth Centuries, and Similar Buildings of the Present Day: Showing the Present Decay of Taste* (1836), aroused considerable controversy. As a result of this book, as well as of the demand for new Roman Catholic churches following the Act of Emancipation, Pugin received many commissions and produced an incredible number of designs in a relatively short period. His reputation as an architect rests on the elevations, but not the plan, of Sir Charles Barry's Houses of Parliament in London (1836). Pugin himself, however, believed his most successful work to be the private church of St. Augustine, Ramsgate, Kent (1847–51). He was also commissioned to design the Medieval Court for the London Great Exhibition of 1851, but had difficulty accommodating himself to the committee work that such projects entail. Unfortunately, however, Pugin's executed work (St. Chad's Cathedral, Birmingham, 1839–41; St Giles, Cheadle, Staffordshire, 1846; St. Wilfrid, Hulme, Manchester, 1842) was much less successful than his drawings and theories, retaining the two-dimensional, scenery quality of his earlier stage designs.

PUNIC ART. It is well known that the Phoenicians were important navigators and traders in the ancient world. Before the year 1000 B.C., according to tradition, they founded trading stations on the coast of North Africa. In 814 B.C., however, they chose an admirable gulf, protected by hills (the modern Gulf of Tunis) to establish a city that would be more than a mere port of call, rather, a "new capital," which is the meaning of the original name Qart Hadasht, from which the name Carthage is derived. The founding of the city is surrounded with romantic mythology. Its destruction, however, took place in the full light of history in 146 B.C., when the Roman army under Scipio Aemilianus conquered Carthage after a heroic resistance and leveled it completely.

The ruins provide evidence of the fortifications of Carthage, and its extent—the total length of the wall being 22 or 23 miles. The city planning and architecture were, indeed, highly praised by ancient authors. Lagoons were transformed into harbors, one military and one commercial. Long porticoes of Ionic columns bordered the quays. Carthage itself was fairly extensive, and had at the height of its wealth and power a population of 700,000. The city possessed numerous temples, the finest being that of Eshmoun. Only one important example of Punic architecture has survived, the mausoleum of Thugga, which combines a number of different influences, the strongest coming from Asia Minor.

The art of Carthage—called Punic—at first bore the characteristics of the art of Phoenicia, and reflected its spirit (*see* PHOENICIAN ART). This is particularly apparent in the religious iconography, which was confined to abstract symbolism. A single stone was considered sufficient as a symbol, for by analogy its strength was thought to suggest fully the strength of the deity. Moreover, such a stone was believed to be the dwelling place of the god—as, for example, at Beth El. When the cult of the goddess Tanit became dominant, as it remained up to the Roman destruction of the city, her bell-shaped sign began to appear frequently on steles and engraved stones (cippi). During the 4th and 3rd centuries B.C., a strong Hellenistic influence became apparent. The sacred images were not always totally abstract. For example, Baal occasionally was depicted seated in majesty on a throne or standing in the form of a winged sphinx, as seen in a pinax or votive plaque from the Balearic Islands (*c.* 5th century B.C.; Madrid, Museo Arqueologico Nacional). Baal's later humanization recalls the Roman Saturn, with whom he merged after the conquest. Tanit is sometimes clothed in dove's wings and given a lion's head (2nd century B.C.; Tunis, Musée Alaoui).

Carthaginian art, already so marked by Egyptian, Greek, and Etruscan influences, culminated in neo-Punic art, in which the influence of a victorious Rome deeply affected native sculptors and led them to a syncretism that is often delightful in its naiveté. The Ghorfa steles (2nd century A.D.; Musée Alaoui) are of more than archaeological interest; they indicate the persistence of Punic forms in the art of Roman Africa.

Carthaginian superstition was also responsible for works that are far from negligible: masks with magical properties, whose grotesque appearance was intended to chase away evil spirits (examples in Paris, Louvre; Carthage, Musée National; and Musée Alaoui), amulets, pendants made of glass paste worn as necklaces with pearls, and talismans. Craftsmen of Carthage, like those of Phoenicia itself, were highly skilled in the working of glass paste and in the making of jewelry, which found a ready market among the wealthy tradesmen and navigators.

Punic Art. Lion-headed figure of Tanit. Thinissut, 2nd century B.C. Musée Alaoui, Tunis. *Photo Boissonnas, Geneva.*

PURCELL, William Grey (1880, Chicago—1965, Pasadena), *and* **ELMSLIE,** George Grant (1871, Huntly, Scotland—1952, Chicago), American Prairie School architects. Purcell graduated from Cornell University's College of Architecture in 1903, worked briefly under Louis Sullivan in Chicago and John Galen Howard (1864–1931) in Berkeley, California, and eventually formed a partnership (1907–9) in Minneapolis with George Feick (1880–1945). Elmslie emigrated to Chicago from Scotland in 1884, and after experience in the offices of William Le Baron Jenney, Joseph Lyman Silsbee (1848–1913), and Louis Sullivan, he joined Purcell and Feick in 1909. The firm of Purcell, Feick, and Elmslie (1909–13) was renamed Purcell and Elmslie (1913–22) when Feick left the profession in 1913.

The Prairie School architects endeavored to carry the creative spirit of the Chicago movement into the 20th century. It was not surprising that the Roman brickwork and the organic terra-cotta ornament of Purcell and Elmslie's Merchants' Bank in Winona, Minnesota (1911), recalled those forms of Sullivan's firm for the National Farmers' Bank in Owatonna (1907–9).

When the demand for commercial buildings in Chicago declined (the Edison Shop of 1912 was the firm's only commercial commission in the city), Purcell and Elmslie turned to residential architecture in Minneapolis and the rural towns of Minnesota and Wisconsin. The open, cruciform plans, and the long, horizontal elevations of the Edward W. Decker house at Lake Minnetonka (1912–13) and the Harold C. Bradley bungalow at Woods Hole, Massachusetts (1911–12), were common features adopted by the Prairie architects, especially Frank Lloyd Wright.

PURISM, a movement inaugurated in 1915 with the publication of the magazine *Élan*. In this periodical and later writings, Amédée Ozenfant and Édouard Jeanneret—who under the name of Le Corbusier became one of the greatest architects of the 20th century—outlined and developed Purist theories and opposed them to the various aesthetic doctrines current at the time. For example, in 1918 they published the Purist manifesto, *Après le Cubisme* ("After Cubism"). In this work and then in the periodical *L'Esprit Nouveau* (1920–25), Ozenfant and Jeanneret maintained that although Cubism had laid a solid theoretical foundation for the art of painting, it had lost its initial discipline and had reverted to a kind of Impressionism, becoming above all a decorative art. Their aim was to restore art to soundness by removing all fantasy and preciosity from painting, with the intention of restoring objects to their authenticity and architectural simplicity. Thus, a Purist work rejects every accident harmful to the architectural balance of form; its various elements must function as parts of a plastic cohesion that allows no self-indulgence on the part of line and color. Purism, however—no doubt because of its excessive rigor—led to no new developments in painting, and it was only in the architecture of Le Corbusier and his disciples that its theories found a valid field of application.

PURRMANN, Hans (1880, Speyer—1966, Basel), German painter. In 1905 Purrmann settled in Berlin, where he was accepted as a member of the Secession. In 1906 he went to Paris, where he met and became a close friend of Henri Matisse. In 1935 he went to Florence to run the Villa Romana (the German artists' foundation). In the same year his works were removed by the Nazis from public collections in Germany and branded as "degenerate." As a result of Gestapo action in Italy, Purrmann settled in Montagnola, Switzerland, in 1944, where he spent the last years of his life.

The turning point of Purrmann's artistic career was his meeting with Matisse in 1906 in Gertrude Stein's salon; shortly afterward he took over the de-

Punic Art. Ghorfa stele, 2nd century A.D. Musée Alaoui, Tunis. *Photo Boissonnas.*

velopment and direction of the Académie Matisse, where he soon proved that he was more independent and had a more powerful personality than the other German disciples of Matisse, with whom he founded the Café du Dôme group—a group including Rudolf Levy, Oskar Moll (1875–1947), Eugen von Kahler (1882–1911), and the writer Wilhelm Uhde. For Purrmann, Cézanne's teaching was always a factor to be considered. Very close to Matisse's work, however, is Purrmann's *Room with Balcony* (1937; Basel, Coll. Lichtenham). He built up his charming and almost Classical landscapes, still lifes, and figure compositions (*Self-Portrait*, 1953; Darmstadt, Hessisches Landesmuseum) with close-set, chromatic brushwork.

PUVIS DE CHAVANNES, Pierre (1824, Lyons—1898, Paris), French painter. The first of the 19th-century idealists, he was hostile to Impressionism and academicism, and believed that the artist should subordinate nature to the expression of ideas and to the search for ideal beauty. Puvis admired the Neoclassicism of Ingres, and executed conventionally constructed murals in a polished and sober style for such French museums as that at Amiens (*Concordia et Bellum*, 1861), Marseilles (*Massilia, Gateway to the East*, 1867–69), and Lyons (*Sacred Wood*, 1885); for public buildings in Paris, such as the Panthéon (*History of St. Geneviève*, 1874–78; 1898), the Sorbonne (*Sacred Wood*, 1887), and the City Hall (*Summer* and *Winter*, 1891–92); and, lastly, for the Boston Public Library (*Inspiring Muses*, 1894–98). The rigor and nobility of these monumental paintings, their absence of depth, their synthetic composition, and their flat areas of color explain Puvis' influence on Gauguin and Seurat; on the other hand, the idealism and emotional content of his work influenced Redon and the Nabis.

Pierre Puvis de Chavannes. *Summer*. 1891. Cleveland Museum of Art.

The *Poor Fisherman* (1881; Paris, Louvre), the *Shepherd's Song* (1891; New York, Metropolitan Museum), and other easel paintings are somewhat more inspired. The spontaneity of his drawings reveals his genuine personality: their astounding verve, inventiveness, boldness, and assurance clearly indicate that Puvis de Chavannes was a great artistic innovator and a central figure in the Symbolist movement of the 1880s and 1890s.

PUY, Jean (1876, Roanne, Loire—1960, Roanne), French painter. He studied in Paris at the Académie Julian (1897–98) and then at the Académie Carrière (1899–1900), where Henri Matisse was his friend and fellow student. Although he advocated clear painting—his work is characterized by his use of vivid colors—his withdrawn, meditative temperament made him prefer the isolation of his native region or the Breton coast to the excitement of Parisian artistic circles. His *Woman Reading* (1902; Paris, Priv. Coll.), *Nude* (1902; Paris, Priv. Coll.), *Reclining Nude* (1906; Geneva, Oscar Ghez Modern Art Foundation), and *Woman in an Armchair* (*c.* 1924; St-Jeoire, Haute-Savoie, Coll. Dr. Paul Gay) belong to his Fauvist period and reveal a preoccupation with design and volume that were to be paramount in his later development. Puy left a body of work of great vitality: his still lifes, ample nudes, Forez landscapes, and Breton seascapes affirm his desire to express "all that moves the flesh and the mind at once." Puy also executed several mural decorations and designs for ceramics.

QUARENGHI, Giacomo (1744, Bergamo—1817, St. Petersburg), Italian Neoclassical architect who worked primarily in Russia. Quarenghi studied at the Bergamo Academy and in the Roman studio of Anton Raphael Mengs. The exquisite drawings he produced at this time earned him the admiration of Baron Grimm, friend of Catherine II of Russia. When the empress asked Grimm to recommend some Italian architects, the baron suggested Quarenghi. He went to Russia in 1779, where the empress gave him numerous commissions.

Quarenghi's masterpieces are the Alexander Palace at Tsarskoe Selo (1791–96), a gift from Catherine to her favorite grandson, the future Alexander I, and the English Palace at Peterhof (1781–89). The formula of the English Palace—a cubical mass enlivened by a central portico—was repeated at the Academy of Sciences (1783–87) and the State Bank (1783–88), both in St. Petersburg. Quarenghi's Hermitage Theater (1782–85), inspired by Palladio's Olympic Theater in Vicenza, also dates from this period.

With the accession of Alexander I, Quarenghi fell out of favor. One of his last commissions was for the Smolny Institute in St. Petersburg, a school for young noblewomen begun by the Italian Baroque architect Bartolomeo Francesco Rastrelli.

QUATTROCENTO, Italian word used to designate the 15th century in Italian art. While medieval civilization throughout much of Europe was disintegrating in the last throes of the Late Gothic period, a vast movement was developing in Italy during the 15th century, a movement that enabled Italy to command and maintain a dominant artistic position in Europe. This was the Renaissance, which ushered in a new era in literature as well as in the visual arts. The movement eventually spread beyond Italy, where it began and where it found its finest expression, and by degrees covered the whole of Europe, opening the way for the formation of the modern world. (*See* RENAISSANCE ART.)

QUERCIA, Jacopo della. *See* **JACOPO DELLA QUERCIA.**

QUESNEL, François (1533 or 1543/44, Edinburgh—1619, Paris), French painter. He was the eldest son and probably the pupil of Peter Quesnel (d. after 1574), who was painter to King James V of Scotland. In 1572 François left Edinburgh to settle in Paris, where he became a fashionable painter during the reign of Henri III. Primarily a portraitist, Quesnel was less at ease in his oil paintings—such as *Mary Ann Waltham* (1572; Althorp, Northamptonshire, Coll. Earl Spencer), *Madame de Cheverny* (*c.* 1573; Versailles, Museum), and *Madame de Laval* (*c.* 1585; Le Mans, Museum)—than in his pencil drawings. His nearly 200 extant portrait drawings are like a procession of contemporary society: his sitters included the favorites of Henri III, the king himself (Paris, Louvre), and Secretary of Finance Pierre Jeannin (Paris, Bibliothèque Nationale). In 1609, for Henri IV, Quesnel drew the first plan of Paris, which was engraved by Pierre Vallet (*c.* 1575–after 1657) in 12 plates. A self-portrait (1613) is in the Bibliothèque Nationale. Quesnel's two brothers were also artists: Nicolas (d. 1632) was a painter of heraldic shields and Jacques (d. 1624/29) a history painter.

QUIDOR, John (1801, Tappan, New York—1881, Jersey City, New Jersey), American painter. He moved to New York City around 1811 and some time between 1814 and 1822 was, with Henry Inman (1801–46), a student of the portraitist John Wesley Jarvis. Nevertheless, little influence of either teacher or fellow student can be seen in his work. Quidor's earliest known painting, *Dorothea* (1823; Brooklyn Museum), based on Cervantes' *Don Quixote*, shows his characteristic dependence on literary themes. His early style, with its eerie light, gnarled trees, and sense of romanticized folklore emerges in *Ichabod Crane Pursued by the Headless Horseman* (*c.* 1828; New Haven, Conn., Yale University Art Gallery), based on a story by Washington Irving. Between the years 1828 and 1839 he continued to depict episodes from the works of such authors as Irving and James Fenimore Cooper. Heavily applied pigment and a freedom of brushstrokes now became characteristic of his handling, while craggy rocks, sinister trees, and homely caricature-like figures became standard elements of his illustrated stories. His next known work, also inspired by Irving, was *Ichabod Crane at a Ball at Van Tassel's Mansion* (Tarrytown, N.Y., Sleepy Hollow Restorations), dating from 1855. Here a definitive change in Quidor's style is evident: he abandoned his previous use of thickly applied bright color for a restricted palette of amber tones applied in a series of thin glazes; forms are blurred in an amorphous haze, while an underlying calligraphy has replaced his earlier, more solidly modeled forms.

QUIZET, Alphonse (1885, Paris—1955, Paris), French painter. Quizet was born in Montmartre, and became the first and one of the best landscapists of that Parisian quarter. When he was seventeen, he used to accompany Maurice Utrillo, as his guide, and even prepared Utrillo's palette for him. For years inseparable, the two companions often worked together from the same scene, employing the same motif. In 1921 he began painting regularly every Sunday on the banks of the Marne. While Montmartre was naturally one of his favorite subjects (*Rue des Saules at Montmartre*, 1903; formerly Paris, Musée du Luxembourg), the suburbs also furnished Quizet with a number of themes (*Canal de la Villette*, 1923; Neuilly-sur-Seine, Coll. Besson). He painted five large decorative panels in 1943 for the Salle des Mariages at the Town Hall of Pré-Saint-Gervais. Very sensitive to certain popular tastes, Quizet expressed by means of his fine talent as a colorist the all but provincial poetry and serenity of the humbler quarters of Paris.

Giacomo Quarenghi. Colonnade of the Sheremetiev Hospice (now Skifossovsky Hospital), Moscow. 1794–1817. *Photo A.P.N.*

R

RAEBURN, Sir Henry (1756, Stockbridge, near Edinburgh—1823, Edinburgh), Scottish portraitist. When he was about fifteen he was apprenticed to an Edinburgh goldsmith and jeweler named James Gilliland. He may have painted miniatures then, but his earliest dated oil, the portrait of *George Chalmers of Pittencrieff* (1776; Dunfermline, Scotland, Town Hall) is, despite slight faults of anatomy, a remarkably rugged and original work for a young painter. His enchanting *Reverend Robert Walker Skating on Duddingston Loch* (1784; Edinburgh, National Gallery of Scotland), on the other hand, shows a rapid evolution toward maturity that seems to owe nothing to example and everything to native talent.

In 1785 he went to London and visited Sir Joshua Reynolds, who may have been the inspiration behind the slightly rhetorical portrait of *Sir John and Lady Clark* (c. 1790; Coll. Sir Alfred Beit), although its murky Romantic lighting effects seem to be Raeburn's personal modernization of Reynolds' formula. In 1787, Raeburn began to enjoy the unrivaled popularity that was to be his for the next 10 years. His great bravura portraits—*Doctor Nathaniel Spens* (c. 1794; Edinburgh, Hall of Royal Company of Archers), *Sir John Sinclair of Ulbster* (c. 1790; Edinburgh, Scottish National Portrait Gallery), or *The MacNab* (c. 1805–10; London, Coll. Messrs. John Dewar)—date from this period. He became an Associate of the Royal Academy in 1812 and a full member in 1815. In 1822 King George IV visited Scotland and knighted Raeburn; in the following year, he was appointed His Majesty's Limner for Scotland, an honor that he enjoyed for a few months before his death.

Raeburn utilized Reynolds' state portrait formula and gave it an entirely new Romantic luster. *The MacNab*, for example, is a decidedly 19th-century view of an 18th-century attitude. Raeburn's great strength was as the painter of the Northern aristocracy; his temper exactly matched that of his sitters, whom he portrayed without sentimental embellishment. His late portrait of *Mrs. James Campbell* (c. 1805–12; Glasgow, Coll. Colonel P. M. Thomas, on loan to National Gallery of Scotland), a low-toned half-length of a plain old lady in a white cap and a black dress, is a masterly amalgam of objectivity and sympathy.

Carlo Rainaldi. S. Maria in Campitelli, Rome. 1663–67. *Photo Leonard von Matt, Buochs.*

RAINALDI, Girolamo (1570, Rome—1655, Rome), Italian architect. In 1620 he built the church of S. Silvestro at Caprarola, where he used a polychrome decoration that reappeared in several of his later works. He was appointed papal architect himself in 1644, and Pope Innocent X commissioned him to design the façade of the Palazzo Pamphili (1648) in the Piazza Navona, Rome.

CARLO (1611, Rome—1691, Rome), Girolamo's son, was also an architect. Carlo worked in the grand manner, incorporating the Mannerism and Baroque of the Roman tradition with the northern Italian heritage he derived from his father. From 1645 he assisted Girolamo in a number of the buildings in the Piazza Navona commissioned by Innocent X, including designs for S. Agnese (begun 1652; altered by Borromini and completed by others). He later built the Roman church of S. Maria in Campitelli (1663–67), in which he combined several familiar and quite dissimilar devices with highly unusual results.

Rainaldi was simultaneously occupied with the twin domed churches of S. Maria di Monte Santo and S. Maria dei Miracoli on the Piazza del Popolo, which flank the entrance to the Corso, one of Rome's major thoroughfares, forming an urban architectural unit. The façades, with their Classical columns and pediments, may well have been influenced by Bernini, since they are quite unlike Rainaldi's usual treatments, and in any case Bernini altered Carlo's original plans to some extent in 1673.

RAMSAY, Allan (1713, Edinburgh—1784, Dover, Kent), Scottish portraitist. He was the son of the Scottish poet Allan Ramsay and appears to have learned the rudiments of drawing in Scotland, before spending a few months in 1734 in the London studio of the Swedish portraitist Hans Hysing (1678–1752/53). In 1736 Ramsay went to Italy. Unlike many other 18th-century English painters, he went there to learn; he took letters of introduction to Nicolas Wleughels (1668–1737), the director of the French Academy in Rome, and worked under Francesco Fernandi (known as Imperiali) in Rome and with the aged Francesco Solimena in Naples. He was familiar with the current Baroque idiom, as can be seen in his portrait of *Samuel Torriano* (1738; Mellerstain, Berwickshire, Coll. Earl of Haddington), with its bravura drapery and pose, and also in his finer and more mature full-length portrait of *Dr. Mead* (1746; London, Foundling Hospital Art Treasures and Picture Gallery).

By 1739 Ramsay had settled in London, and was painting portraits for a predominantly Scottish clientele. On one of these portraits, that of *Norman, 22nd Chief of MacLeod* (1748; Isle of Skye, Dunvegan Castle, Coll. Mrs. MacLeod of MacLeod) rests one of Ramsay's claims to an important position in the history of British portraiture: he painted his subject in the pose (albeit reversed) of the antique Apollo Belvedere. This naturalization of famous prototypes is the basis of the Grand Style of English portraiture and, although Ramsay was intellectually unwilling or incapable of expanding this manner of painting, as Reynolds did later, he deserves the credit for inaugurating it. Ramsay, however, was by nature an intimist, and his least formal portraits are his most successful. *Hew Dalrymple, Lord Drummore* (1754; Colston, East Lothian, Coll. Lady Broun Lindsay), for example, is a far better painting than the portraits of the Royal Family to which Ramsay devoted his time in the 1760s.

In the latter part of 1754 Ramsay paid a second visit to Italy, during which he refreshed his knowledge of Italian fashions, as is evident in his portrait of *Archibald Campbell, 3rd Duke of Argyll* (1758; England, Albury, Coll. Duke of Northumberland), an adaptation of

Allan Ramsay. *Jean-Jacques Rousseau in Armenian Costume.* 1766. National Gallery of Scotland, Edinburgh.

Solimena's *Self-Portrait* in the Uffizi, Florence. Ramsay's knowledge of, and attraction to, contemporary French painting at this time in his career is of great interest. In a *Dialogue on Taste* that he wrote in 1754, he commends Maurice Quentin de La Tour's realism. Jean-Baptiste Perronneau was the inspiration behind the finely drawn portrait of *Dr. William Hunter* (*c.* 1758–63; Glasgow, Hunterian Museum and University Art Collection), while *Mary Leppell, Lady Hervey* (1762; England, Chevening, Coll. Earl Stanhope) is based quite clearly on Nattier's *Maria Leszczynska.* More important is the generalized tenderness and bloom evident in such female portraits as *Margaret Lindsay, the Artist's Second Wife* (1755–60; Edinburgh, National Gallery of Scotland), *Lady Susan Fox-Strangways* (1761; Earl of Ilchester), and *Elizabeth Montagu* (1762; Scotland, Wemyss Castle, Coll. Captain Michael Wemyss).

The patronage of his fellow Scot, Lord Bute, tutor to the Prince of Wales and Prime Minister in 1762, led Ramsay to court patronage; in 1757 he painted the Prince of Wales and in 1758 Augusta, Princess of Wales (both Mount Stuart, Coll. Marquess of Bute). After the Prince of Wales succeeded to the throne as George III in 1760, he painted full-lengths of the king and queen. In 1761 Ramsay was named Painter-in-Ordinary to the king and announced that he would no longer work for the general public. Happily he broke this rule in 1766 to paint a portrait of the fugitive *Jean-Jacques Rousseau in Armenian Costume* (National Gallery of Scotland) for his friend David Hume. There are no recorded portraits by Ramsay after 1769.

Although Ramsay was not of the intellectual caliber of either William Hogarth or Reynolds, he was more of a European than either and, more important, a modern European. His historical importance as a partial innovator of the Grand Style was not as great as the intrinsic merit of his own style, which is subtler than anything in English portraiture until Gainsborough.

RAMSEYER, André (b. 1914, Tramelan, Bern canton), Swiss sculptor. He received his first training (1932–35) at the École des Beaux-Arts at La Chaux-de-Fonds, near Neuchâtel, and then went to Paris, where he studied (1935–36) with Ossip Zadkine. Ramseyer's early sculpture was Classical and figurative. He then entered a phase in which he interpreted nature freely by transforming simple subjects into flying forms and by stylizing the human body (*Consolation*, 1954; *The Couple*, 1955). He subsequently executed abstract works that harmonized with functional architecture: *Eurhythmy* (1955; Washington, D.C., Swiss Embassy) and *Asteroid* (1957; Lausanne, Park of the Mutuelle Vaudoise). In his abstract sculptures Ramseyer generally dealt with themes connected with growth and birth (*Sap*, 1955; *Germination*, 1957) or with waves, either rising or breaking (*Port of Call*; *Ebb Tide*, 1962).

RAPHAEL, Raffaello Sanzio, *called* (1483, Urbino—1520, Rome), Italian painter. He was the son and pupil of Giovanni Santi, who died when Raphael was eleven. In 1500 Raphael was with Perugino at the Cambio in Perugia, where he probably painted the figures of *Fortitude* and *Justice*. Raphael's delicate treatment is already evident in the small mythological and allegorical compositions of that period: the *Three Graces* (1500; Chantilly, Musée Condé) and the *Knight's Dream* (1500; London, National Gallery). Between 1500 and 1504 he developed his personal style in a number of large-scale religious works: the *Marriage of the Virgin* (1504; Milan, Brera), the *Madonna Conestabile* (1500; formerly Leningrad, Hermitage), the *Coronation of the Virgin* (1502/3; Vatican Museum) for the church of S. Francesco in Perugia, and the serene 1503 version of the *Crucifixion* (National Gallery). By this time he was no longer simply Perugino's pupil, but a master in his own right. During the same period he painted the *Portrait of a Man* (Rome, Galleria Borghese) and the *Christ in Benediction* (1502; Civica Pinacoteca Tosio Martinengo). Another work of this period is the *Madonna and Child Enthroned with Saints* (*c.* 1504; New York, Metropolitan Museum), a finely balanced painting with amply draped figures arranged on either side of the high throne. In 1504 Raphael went to Florence, and there discovered the work of Leonardo da Vinci. This fresh stimulus is evident in the increasing originality and gentleness of such works as the *Madonna del Granduca* (1505; Florence, Palazzo Pitti) and the *Madonna in the Meadow* (1505; Vienna, Kunsthistorisches Museum). The delightful *La Belle Jardinière* (1507; Paris, Louvre) and the monumental *Madonna del Baldacchino* (1507–8; Palazzo Pitti) show the painter's range, which widened considerably with his dramatic *Entombment* (1507; Galleria Borghese), commissioned by Atalanta Baglioni for the church of S. Francesco in Perugia.

Toward the end of 1508 Pope Julius II invited Raphael to decorate the famous Stanze, the old apartments of Pope Nicholas V in the Vatican. A group of Umbrian painters including Perugino, Luca Signorelli, Bartolomeo Bramantino, and Sodoma had already started working there; but the pope, fascinated by the young artist, soon discarded them all. Raphael first decorated the Stanza della Segnatura, which he completed in 1511, and which was a triumph for him. Raphael was then commissioned to decorate the Stanza d'Eliodoro, which he finished in 1514, and in which he painted the pope's portrait. Commissions also came from Roman noblemen: from Sigismondo de' Conti for the *Madonna di Foligno*

Raphael. *School of Athens.* Detail. 1511. Stanza della Segnatura, Vatican. *Photo Anderson.*

(*c.* 1511; Vatican Museum), and from the Sienese banker Agostino Chigi for the decoration of the Villa Farnesina (from 1511). There he painted the magnificent fresco of *Galatea* (1511–12). The most remarkable of Raphael's Madonnas belong to this period: the *Madonna della Sedia* (1514–15; Florence, Palazzo Pitti), with its very effective tondo shape, and the superb *Sistine Madonna*, also known as the *Dresden Madonna* (1513–14; Dresden, Gemäldegalerie).

After Bramante's death in 1514, Michelangelo's departure, and the failure of Leonardo, Raphael was the only one left of the great artists called to Rome by Julius II. He was, therefore, placed in charge of all projects there: the supervision of the architectural work at the Vatican, the decoration of the Vatican Logge, and the execution of 10 cartoons for a series of tapestries to be placed on the lower walls of the Sistine Chapel (*Acts of the Apostles*, 1515–16; London, Victoria and Albert Museum). By June 1514, Raphael had hardly completed the decoration of the second Stanza when he was requested to begin the third, the Stanza dell'Incendio, which he finished in 1517. Yet much of the work was handed over to pupils, particularly to Giulio Romano, since Raphael was occupied with the tapestry cartoons (these were woven from 1517 to 1519 in Brussels, and delivered at the end of 1519 to the Vatican).

In the Logge, Raphael's contribution was limited to general supervision; he introduced the use of grotesques based upon the decoration of the Domus Aurea, which Giovanni da Udine later developed. His architectural work

Raphael. *Madonna della Sedia.* 1514–15. Palazzo Pitti, Florence. *Photo Anderson-Giraudon.*

also demanded much of his time, and since he had succeeded Bramante as architect of St. Peter's, he had to provide a new plan. He also designed a large villa for Giuliano de' Medici, the future Pope Clement VII, on the slopes of Monte Mario (now Villa Madama). At the height of his glory and productivity, the young genius died at the age of thirty-seven.

Having lived and worked in some of the most sophisticated centers of Humanist culture, Raphael remained faithful to the ideals of Humanism. Perugino's art, which was an early influence, suited his temperament. In Raphael's work, however, there is more subtlety and greater strength. It is indeed a triumph of tonal clarity. In his Madonnas, Raphael revealed an even finer touch and more realistic accent. He adopted Leonardo's *sfumato* technique as well as his pyramidal composition in *La Belle Jardinière*, and the Leonardesque harmonization of figure and landscape in the portrait of *Maddalena Doni* (*c.* 1506; Florence, Palazzo Pitti). His portraits changed from busts to half-length figures, also in keeping with Leonardo's practice.

Raphael was not indifferent to the work of Michelangelo, and his study of the great Florentine master's style is apparent in the *Entombment* (1507; Rome, Galleria Borghese), later in the *Fire in the Borgo* (*c.* 1516) at the Vatican, and in the *Sibyls* (1514; Rome, S. Maria della Pace). He was also influenced by some aspects of Venetian painting, and even by Titian himself, whom he knew through Sebastiano del Piombo. This influence is noticeable in the *Mass at Bolsena* (1512) in the Stanza d'Eliodoro, in the *Madonna with the Fish* (*c.* 1513; Madrid, Prado), and in a few portraits such as the *Donna Velata* (*c.* 1514; Palazzo Pitti), and especially the magnificent *Baldassarre Castiglione* (1515–16; Paris, Louvre).

The four wall frescoes in the Stanza della Segnatura (the *Disputa* or *Disputation Concerning the Holy Sacrament*, the *School of Athens, Parnassus*, and the *Law*) illustrate, together with the allegories on the vault, the four great categories of pagan and Christian learning. The Stanza d'Eliodoro is decorated with dramatic episodes from Jewish and Christian history (*Expulsion of Heliodorus from the Temple, Liberation of St. Peter, Leo I Halting Attila Before Rome*, and the *Mass at Bolsena*), which are actually symbolic representations of events in the pontificate of Julius II. The combined influences of Michelangelo and of the Venetian masters are apparent in the grandeur of the conception and style of these dramatic frescoes. The third room, whose theme is the glorification of the pope's power, is called the Stanza dell'Incendio after the most important painting in the room, the *Fire in the Borgo*, which indeed may be the only work there entirely by Raphael's own hand. The Sala di Costantino, finished after the artist's death, completed the decorative scheme with a rhetorical style that was imitated in churches and palaces throughout Italy.

A truly Classical artist, Raphael gave expression to his serene and balanced temperament in some of the most perfectly conceived paintings of the High Renaissance.

RASTRELLI, Bartolomeo Carlo (*c.* 1675, Florence—1744, St. Petersburg), Italian sculptor. He lived for many years in France and in 1715 was a member of the team of French artists and craftsmen recruited by the French architect Jean-Baptiste Le Blond to work in Russia. His rather static equestrian statue of *Peter the Great* (cast in bronze 1744–46? but completed several years earlier) in St. Petersburg, although competent, was eclipsed by the famous statue Étienne Falconet did of Peter 30 years later. In his bronze statue of the *Empress Anna Ivanovna* (1733–34; Leningrad, State Russian Museum), Rastrelli achieved a greater feeling of movement.

BARTOLOMEO FRANCESCO (1700, Paris—1771, St. Petersburg), his son, was trained under the famous Robert de Cotte in Paris, but his entire career was spent in Russia,

Raphael. *Galatea.* 1511–12. Villa Farnesina, Rome. *Photo Anderson-Giraudon.*

where he was chief architect to the Empress Elizabeth (reigned 1741–62), daughter of Peter the Great. In this capacity he supervised all architectural activity in St. Petersburg, which at the time was the cultural and governmental center of the country. His influence was enormous during Elizabeth's life, and he had many pupils and followers, but after 1762 Rastrelli and the Rococo style fell from favor almost instantly as far as royal building was concerned. Partly as a consequence of the shift in official taste, much of his work was drastically altered or destroyed and is now known only from engravings.

One of Rastrelli's earliest commissions from Elizabeth was for the completion of the Anichkov Palace on the Nevski Prospekt (1744). His work there was largely Italianate in conception, although he was beginning to show considerable skill in borrowing some Russian forms, developing the discreet eclecticism with which he created original buildings along traditional lines. Rastrelli next (1747–52) enlarged Le Blond's Peterhof Palace for the empress, inventing outstanding rich interior decorative schemes, including the ornate Merchants' Hall and Staircase.

The colossal size of the Great Palace at Tsarskoe Selo (the imperial village not far from St. Petersburg) suggests that here Rastrelli was trying to rival Versailles (1749–52). An interminable succession of rooms leads to the Grand Staircase and the Throne Room. In the park Rastrelli created three enchanting Rococo pavilions: the Hermitage (1748–52), the Grotto (1755–62), and Mon Bijou (1750), in which his skill with small-scale work and his inventive decoration are seen to excellent advantage.

Nothing could be more imposing than the endless façade of the Winter Palace in St. Petersburg (1754–62), nor pose more of a remodeling problem. Rastrelli tried to unify its length by a beautiful and decorative handling of the windows, but did not succeed in bringing the façade alive. The palaces he built for the nobles were naturally on a smaller scale, but hardly less magnificent. The finest among them are the rather sober Vorontsov Palace (1743–45) and the Stroganov Palace (1750–54).

Rastrelli also turned his fertile imagination to religious architecture. The same skillful organization of architectural masses that he displayed in the Winter Palace and Tsarskoe Selo was used again in the plans for the gigantic Smolny Convent (1748–55) on the banks of the Neva, an immense complex of buildings grouped around a church with five onion domes. Rastrelli attempted a series of individual buildings reminiscent in their silhouette of a Russian medieval monastery. Unfortunately his projected five-story campanile was never executed, and his plans for lively and lavish decoration of both interior and exterior were completely ignored. His masterpiece of religious architecture is the church of St. Andrew at Kiev (1749–56), a Greek-cross plan with five domes, in which the inventive decor does not obscure the particularly harmonious spatial relationships.

Rastrelli, despite his inherently Rococo tendencies, reinforced by the tastes of Elizabeth, did more to create a tradition of Russian Baroque than any other single architect. He also injected a new strain of theatricalism in the architecture of Russia.

RAUCH, Christian Daniel (1777, Arolsen, Hesse—1857, Dresden), German sculptor. During his first visit to Italy (1804–11), Rauch made the acquaintance of the Neoclassical sculptors Antonio Canova and Bertel Thorvaldsen. Having obtained a commission in 1810 to carve the tomb of Queen Louise for the mausoleum at Charlottenburg Palace in Berlin, Rauch executed (1811) at Carrara and at Rome a gracious and appealing statue of the queen, reclining in the Classical manner. This work was followed much later at Charlottenburg Palace by the companion statue of Frederick III (1846). In 1819 Rauch returned to Berlin, where he worked at first in partnership with Karl Schinkel and executed some of the marble sculptures for Schinkel's New Guard House, notably of the generals Friedrich Wilhelm von Bülow and Gerhard von Scharnhorst. In 1820 Rauch went to Weimar to carve a bust of Goethe, and soon afterward drew up plans for a monument to the great poet in Frankfurt. After the six *Victories* (1829–33) for the Valhalla near Regensburg, he began his most famous work, the monument to Frederick the Great on the great boulevard of Unter den Linden in Berlin (1840–51).

RAUCHMILLER *or* **RAUCHMÜLLER,** Mathias (1645, Radolfzell, Baden—1686, Vienna), Austro-German sculptor, ivory carver, and painter. In about 1675 he executed one of his most important works, the marble sepulchral monument for Bishop Karl von Metternich (Trier, Liebfrauenkirche). After 1676 Rauchmiller worked in Vienna, apart from one year spent in Silesia, which was then an Austrian province. During that year (1677–78) he sculpted the tomb of Adam von Arzat (Breslau, Magdalenenkirche) and four statues for the Piast Chapel in Liegnitz. He was also responsible for the restrained Baroque architecture of the chapel as well as for the frescoes of the dome and wall panels. These works won Rauchmiller a reputation as a leading sculptor of

Bartolomeo Francesco Rastrelli. Winter Palace, Leningrad (formerly St. Petersburg). 1754–62. *Photo J. Allan Cash, London.*

sepulchral monuments. Of his many ivory carvings the most striking is a tankard decorated with the *Rape of the Sabine Women* (1676; formerly Vaduz, Coll. Liechtenstein).

RAUSCHENBERG, Robert (b. 1925, Port Arthur, Texas), American painter. Rauschenberg received his real artistic training in the United States—at the Kansas City Art Institute and School of Design (1946–47), under Josef Albers at Black Mountain College, North Carolina (1948–49), and at the Art Students League in New York (1949–50) under Vaclav Vyttacil (b. 1892) and Morris Kantor (b. 1896). Rauschenberg gained recognition around 1953 with his complex collages and assemblages known as "combine paint," in which he introduced real objects and used a mixture of techniques, such as dripped paint, found objects, oil paint, and various materials, including torn posters, children's drawings, and graffiti (*Rebus*, 1955, New York, Coll. artist; *Summer Rental, Number 2*, 1960, New York, Whitney Museum). Rauschenberg stood out in the Neo-Dadaist shows as one of the precursors of Pop art, a movement that he heralded with the violence, irony, and urban imagery of his art. Although he took the contents of his paintings directly from American folklore, he challenged the whole structure of modern civilization and represented one of the transitional elements between the Abstract Expressionism of the 1950s and the new Pop imagery. After 1955 he also designed the sets and costumes for the Merce Cunningham Dance Company. His graphic work is important and includes a noteworthy series of collage illustrations for Dante's *Inferno* (1959–62). His experimentation with silk-screen printing in the 1960s, first in black and white and then with the addition of color, enabled him to bring greater coherence to his work. Rauschenberg won the first prize at the 1964 Venice Biennale.

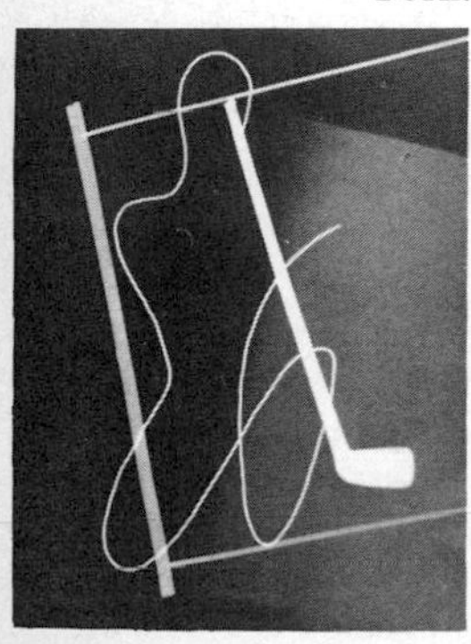

Man Ray. *Rayograph.* 1928. Museum of Modern Art, New York.

RAY, Man (b. 1890, Philadelphia—d. 1976), American painter, sculptor, designer, printmaker, and photographer. He was inspired by the New York Armory Show of 1913 and met most of the avant-garde French artists who came to New York, including Marcel Duchamp and Francis Picabia. With them he founded the New York Dada movement during World War I, and in 1920—together with Duchamp and the American art patron Katherine Dreier—founded the Société Anonyme. In 1921 he went to Paris, and in 1925 he exhibited in the first Surrealist show there. In order to support himself he took up photography, first photographing his friends' paintings and then doing portraits (*Pablo Picasso*, 1933), which quickly became fashionable and assured him a livelihood. Except for the period 1940–51, during which time he lived in California, he made Paris his permanent home.

Man Ray's work presents a number of diverse, almost unrelated aspects; his concern was never to develop a personal style of painting, but rather "to paint as much as possible unlike other painters. Above all to paint unlike myself, so that each succeeding work, or series of works, shall be entirely different from preceding works." From early Cézanne-inspired paintings he progressed rapidly to large, open Dadaist works, such as the *Rope Dancer Accompanies Herself with Her Shadows* (1916; New York, Museum of Modern Art). He also experimented with an airbrush in an attempt to produce paintings that would resemble photographs, and in a further attempt "to create great confusion between the two arts" invented "rayographs"—pictures made by placing objects against photographically sensitive paper. His Surrealist paintings effectively exploit grotesque juxtapositions of unlikely objects, as in the famous *Observation Time—The Lovers* (1932–34; Priv. Coll.), in which an immense pair of lips is placed in a greenish sky over a dark landscape. Man Ray also made several Surrealist films, including *Emak Bakia* (1926), *L'Étoile de Mer* (1926), and *Les Mystères du Château de Des* (1928), as well as numerous mixed media objects.

RAYONISM, avant-garde movement in Russian art, founded in Moscow in 1911–12 by Mikhail Larionov. The Rayonist manifesto, which was not published until 1913, states that a Rayonist painting should give the impression of gliding out of time and space to convey a feeling of a fourth dimension, and that to achieve this end the painter should use parallel or crossed beams of color. The canvases of Larionov and Natalia Goncharova (the only artists who produced Rayonist works) are among the first really abstract works painted in the 20th century, and contain no reminiscences of traditional visual reality.

REALISM. When in the history of European painting representation of the world became intellectualized and remote from outward appearances, a return to close observation of an unsophisticated expression of sense impressions inevitably followed. These almost cyclical reactions, often accompanied by analogous movements in literature and the other arts, are generally described as "realistic." The comparative realism of 17th-century painting, for example, developed in reaction to the highly formal compositional contrivances of 16th-century Mannerism. In Italy the return to realism was initiated with the Carracci, Caravaggio, and their imitators; in Spain with Ribalta, Ribera, Velázquez, and Zurbarán; in Flanders with Rubens (his realism soon changed to Baroque); in Holland with Hals, Vermeer, and Rembrandt; in France with the painters of genre scenes (La Tour, Le Nain, Tournier), portraits (Champaigne, Bourdon), and still lifes (Baugin).

Realistic painting of landscapes and genre scenes became concerned with the scrupulous recording of the present, unembellished by squeamish conventionality. It assumed very different aspects according to the painter's nationality, school, or personal genius. In the work of innumerable minor masters realism was reduced to picturesque scenes treated in a minute, analytical technique that omitted nothing in its anxiety to obtain a meticulous truth. The realism of Caravaggio and his followers, by contrast, is dramatic, with the subject set in a theatrical lighting that prefigures the Baroque.

The more restricted meaning of the term realism denotes the predominantly French movement that took place roughly between 1848 and 1860 in reaction to an outworn Romanticism and to the academicism of the late Neoclassicists. The word was adopted by the defenders of its aesthetic and its enemies, but it remained imprecise. Its chronological limits

Realism. Jules Dalou. *The Reader*. 1878. Louvre, Paris.

were hardly even approximate. Geographically, it was equally fluid; although it was entirely French in origin, it was fed with elements borrowed from England, Holland, and eventually Spain, until it spread throughout Europe. In spirit and form it remained faithful to some characteristics of the academicism it rejected, notably studio painting, the nude as subject matter, and dark colors. Although it appealed to factual observation in opposition to Romantic idealism, it was nevertheless related to the latter in its desire for powerful effect and its humanitarian outlook.

The bourgeois France of Louis-Philippe demanded that contemporary art should reflect a faithful, unadventurous image of itself. This was one aspect of French realism, which was popularized by lithography and in great demand; it was agreeable in the work of Eugène Lami (1800–90), soft and sentimental in the prints and paintings of Octave Tassaert (1800–74), and bitter and moralizing in the caricatures of Gavarni (1804–66). Pictorially, the work of the landscapists was infinitely more powerful. They fought against the historic landscape, as well as the carefully composed landscapes of such Romanticists as Paul Huet, and the picturesque, literary illustrations of travel books. They called for a return to the observation of nature, whose grandeur and mystery they found moving. Technically, their manner derived from the Dutch 17th-century painters and, in more recent times, from the English (the stir caused by Constable's painting at the 1824 Salon is particularly noteworthy in this connection).

The quickened pace of scientific progress provided an increasingly exact understanding of natural reality. The triumphant respect for fact produced the realistic novel, while the 1848 Revolution with its Messianism and fraternal spirit gave the movement its social color. This was far removed from the complaisant art produced under Louis-Philippe. With Daumier, Millet, Courbet, and Corot realism dominated the second half of the 19th century and accomplished its greatest achievements.

Courbet's manner was continued by Alphonse Legros, Guillaume Regamey (1837–75), and by most of the painters of the Salon des Refusés; then, under the leadership of Monet, it inspired the future Impressionists. Corot and his followers—Antoine Chintreuil, Charles Daubigny, Eugène Boudin, and Johan Barthold Jongkind—were, however, the principal forerunners of Impressionism because their vision ultimately became more subtle if not less realistic. In addition to these already distant followers, there were the painters of contemporary life who, like Constantin Guys, then Manet and Degas, added the Baudelairian feeling of modernity—mobility and the ephemeral poetry of the passing world—to their realistic observation.

The portraitists, who imitated the violent forms, vigorous brushstrokes, and dark crude colors of Spanish 17th-century painting, included Théodule Ribot, Thomas Couture, Léon Bonnat, and Carolus-Duran. Sculpture was not deeply affected by the new realistic current, in spite of the abortive efforts of Jules Dalou and the more successful ones of the gifted Constantin Meunier.

In England the Pre-Raphaelites cross-bred realism with a complicated mysticism and an obvious archaism. The Spanish painter Mariano Fortuny (1838–90) mixed a sort of realism with a flashy, superficial *fa presto*. Belgium produced some good realistic works with the artists of the Tervuren School, particularly Charles de Groux (1825–70), the imaginative Henri de Braekeleer, and Alfred Stevens. In Holland, the Hague School combined the manner of the Barbizon School with the national tradition, while a specific, sentimental realism made its appearance with Jozef Israëls (1824–1911) as its outstanding representative and its final phase in Van Gogh's early style. Literary allusion and pastiche predominated over genuine realism in Germany, in spite of Wilhelm Leibl and Hans Thoma (1839–1924). It had a limited effect in Italy where, apart from Antonio Fontanesi (1818–82), it served only as a transitional phase for such future members of the Macchiaioli group as Silvestro Lega and Telemaco Signorini. In the Eastern European countries, where humanitarianism found fertile ground, social realism had a brief career, in spite of the talent of Nicolae Grigoresco and Ion Andreescu (1850–82) in Rumania, Mihály Munkácsy in Hungary, and Ilya Repin (1844–1930) in Russia.

REBEYROLLE, Paul (b. 1926, Eymoutiers, Haute-Vienne), French painter. He began by painting large compositions in which the impact of everyday life was forcefully communicated through the aggressive naturalism of enormous figures and the crudeness of objects and settings. As his command of the techniques of modeling and coloring grew, Rebeyrolle began painting vigorous domestic and rural scenes in dark colors (*Goats*, 1950; Paris, Musée National d'Art Moderne). After being awarded the Prix de la Jeune Peinture in 1950, under controversial circumstances, he gradually developed a freer style, although he never entirely abandoned representation. The landscapes he exhibited in 1964 at the Marlborough Gallery in London contained couples, animals, and nudes defined by large irregular patches of color.

REDON, Odilon (1840, Bordeaux—1916, Paris), French painter and lithographer, one of the outstanding artists of the Symbolist movement. Redon's life had a profound effect on his artistic evolution, and his work can be partly understood through its main events: an ailing and dreamy childhood; a religious crisis at the time of his first Communion; his meeting with the biologist Armand Clavaud, who introduced him to the biological sciences and the avant-garde literature of the day; a passion for music; the influence on him of the Romantic engraver Rodolphe Bresdin; his marriage to Camille Fargue, a Creole like his

Realism. Carolus-Duran. *My Gardener*. 1893. Private Coll. *Photo Giraudon, Paris.*

Odilon Redon. *Portrait of Mademoiselle Violette Heymann.* 1910. Hinman B. Hurlbut Coll., Museum of Art, Cleveland.

own mother; and his close friendships with the poets Stéphane Mallarmé, Francis Jammes, and Paul Valéry. Redon found his artistic inspiration in the subconscious and the aim of his art, in accordance with Symbolist theory, was the expression of ideas through forms. He chose various media through which to express his dreams, but those most suited to them were charcoal, etching, pastel, and especially lithography. His albums of lithographs, in fact, are among the finest of their kind produced in the 19th century: these include *The Dream* (1879), the *Apocalypse of St. John* (1883), *Night* (1886), the *Temptation of St. Anthony* (1888–96), and *Les Fleurs du Mal* (1890). Until he was about fifty Redon used black and white exclusively, and it was only around 1890 that he began to use color to interpret the dream world he had created for himself. He used rare, phosphorescent tones that have a metallic brilliance—for instance, in paintings such as *With Closed Eyes* (Paris, Louvre), *Red Sphinx* (1912–13; Bern, Coll. Hahnloser), *Cyclops* (1895–1900; Otterlo, Rijksmuseum Kröller-Müller), and pastels like the *Birth of Venus* (1912; Paris, Musée du Petit Palais) and the *Shell* (1912; Paris, Coll. Ari Redon). Redon also produced some remarkable portraits late in his career (*Violette Heymann*, 1909–10; Cleveland, Museum of Art) and gaily colored flower studies that are surrounded with a mysterious aura. He also wrote a very fine diary, *À soi-même* ("To Myself," 1922).

Redon's skillful draftsmanship, his fine decorative arabesques, the refined sumptuousness of his coloration, and the unerring pictorial sense with which he interpreted his visions assured him an undying fame. These aspects of his art were studied with profit by Paul Gauguin, Pierre Bonnard, and Henri Matisse.

REDOUTÉ, Pierre Joseph (1759, St-Hubert, near Liège—1840, Paris), French painter and lithographer. He taught drawing to Marie-Antoinette; then to Napoleon's wives, Empress Joséphine and Empress Marie-Louise; and finally to Louis Philippe's wife, Queen Marie-Amélie de Bourbon. Redouté's reputation did not, however, come from his skill as a royal teacher, but from his admirable watercolors of flowers, in which he combined a botanist's precision with the most refined taste. He practiced his art brilliantly into the 19th century and enjoyed considerable popularity even in the 20th century. Besides his illustrations for various botanical volumes, he published several works of his own, notably *Liliacées* ("Liliaceae," 1802–16) and *Les Roses* ("Monograph on Roses," 1817–21). The Musée National d'Histoire Naturelle in Paris possesses about 6,000 watercolors by Redouté.

REGENCY STYLE. *See* **LOUIS XV STYLE.**

REGIONALISM. Although generally applicable to any artist's portrayal of a particular environment, the term is usually reserved for a small group of American artists whose work became popular during the 1930s and early 1940s. The protagonists of regionalism—Thomas Hart Benton, Grant Wood, John Steuart Curry, and sometimes Charles Burchfield—were all from the Midwest and all extolled the virtues of life in the small Midwestern rural communities. Their work is often seen in terms of the fanatical patriotism of the American critic Thomas Craven, who crusaded against contemporary European artists, American expatriates, and the New York School. Craven's chauvinistic approach, however, influenced these artists less than has generally been believed: for much of their work had been produced before he initiated his program, and much of his writing was concerned with criticism of non-regionalists rather than the advocacy of the Midwesterners. The regionalists' success eventually succumbed to the spirit of internationalism that prevailed in American art during and after World War II.

REICHEL, Hans (1892, Würzburg—1958, Paris), German painter. He met Paul Klee in 1919, and the resulting friendship confirmed Reichel's determination to become a painter. After a period of travel, he settled in Paris in 1928, where he remained until his death. Although fascinated by the work of Klee, which was both visionary and lyrical like his own, Reichel was an artist for whom the sense perceptions were as important as the imagination. Imbued with a feeling for German Romanticism, he pursued a very different direction from Klee. Nearly always painting in watercolor, which requires the constant and unpredictable action of both hand and imagination, Reichel created a world in which dream and reality were inextricably and naturally mingled (*Moonlight*, 1948; Paris, Galerie Jeanne Bucher). His last watercolors mark a considerable evolution in his art. He freed these works from the fragile appearance that he had preserved until then, clarifying space, returning to poetry its rights over the dream world, and intensifying his colors by means of an interior light (*Humming*, 1950; Galerie Jeanne Bucher).

REIDY, Affonso Eduardo (1909, Paris—1964, Rio de Janeiro), Brazilian architect. Reidy's first private commission was the Home of Good Will, an institution for the aged (1931–32). In 1936 he was one of the team headed by Lúcio Costa that built the Ministry of Education at Rio. Mature examples of his work in Rio include the Pedregulho housing development, with its long apartment block following the winding contour of a hillside (1947–55), and the Marechal Hermes Community Theater (1950), where an inverted double slope roof was used effectively. Reidy built a few private houses, such as those for Carmen Portinho (1952–54) and Dr. Couto e Silva (1955), but generally preferred larger schemes. The Museum of Modern Art in Rio (1954–57), with its freely flowing spaces, and ingenious lighting techniques, is characteristic of his style. Reidy designed an impressive *brise-soleil* façade for the Rio City Employees Insurance Fund Building (1957–62). Some of his best projects, such as the Experimental School in Asunción that Brazil offered to Paraguay, were never completed. It was begun in 1953 and terminated in

1965, with only the classroom wing completed.

REINHARDT, Ad (1913, Buffalo—1967, New York), American painter. In 1937 Reinhardt joined the American Abstract Artists group, at that time an exciting and important influence on his work. Before and after serving as a Navy photographer during World War II, Reinhardt was a part-time staff artist and art critic for the New York newspaper *PM* (1944–46), and was noted for his sharp, satirical cartoons and articles. He had his first one-man exhibition at New York's Columbia University in 1943, from 1946 exhibited at the Betty Parsons Gallery in New York, and appeared in group exhibitions at the Museum of Modern Art, as well as at the world fairs held in New York, Brussels, and Seattle.

Reinhardt's painting was a very conscious and conceptual process, about which he wrote frequently and dogmatically. His main premise was to separate the areas of life and art. He was consistently an abstract painter; his earlier work reflected several influences, including late Cubism as well as the painting of Stuart Davis and Piet Mondrian, but in the last two decades of his life he attained individualistic solutions that he considered ultimate. Reinhardt's geometric abstractions of the late 1930s (*Untitled*, 1938; New York, Museum of Modern Art) were predominantly bold compositions with hard-edged forms and bright hues, which in the 1940s gave way to a more detailed, softer, over-all style that Reinhardt at first explored in abstract collages, then in oils. Despite his later rejection of Abstract Expressionism, his work was affected by it during the late 1940s: he was close to many of the major exponents of that style and participated, with Robert Motherwell, in editing the publication *Modern Artists in America* (1950), based on discussions among contemporary artists. In 1951 he began to gray his colors and to de-emphasize contrasts; the first geometric, closely valued, red-and-blue paintings developed from 1951 to 1953 (*Abstract Painting, Blue*, 1952; Pittsburgh, Carnegie Institute, Museum of Modern Art); and the first symmetrically trisected paintings, which later became standard for him, appeared around 1952. The first "all black" paintings, with barely distinguishable tonal variations from one rectilinear division to the next, were shown in 1953, and by 1960 Reinhardt had developed his "ultimate" painting: a black, 5-foot square, symmetrically trisected, and evenly painted canvas (*Abstract Painting*, 1960–62; New York, Museum of Modern Art), which he repeated from then on, and which in its exactitude, purity, and impersonality was a herald of the Minimal art of the 1960s.

REMBRANDT HARMENSZ. VAN RIJN (1606, Leiden—1669, Amsterdam), Dutch painter and engraver. After a six-month sojourn in Amsterdam, where he was a pupil of Pieter Lastman (1583–1633), Rembrandt returned to Leiden about 1625, where he worked as an independent master and in association with Jan Lievens (1607–74). Except for the large *Feast of Esther* (*c.* 1625; Raleigh, North Carolina Museum of Art), Rembrandt's early works are all small in size and meticulously executed with much emphasis on detail. He did not paint any commissioned portraits until his last year in Leiden (*c.* 1631) as his interest lay instead in the field of history painting. During this early period, the young Rembrandt was affected by the Italianate motifs that Lastman had employed and that found their way into certain of his own paintings, including *Tobias and His Family* (1626; Lugano, Coll. Thyssen), the *Feast of Esther*, and especially the *Stoning of St. Stephen* (1625; Lyons, Musée des Beaux-Arts), a work that carries, along with the painter's initials, the date 1625, making it his earliest known work.

Two of the most frequent and meaningful subjects that Rembrandt employed throughout his career first appeared during the Leiden period: the depiction of old age and the self-portrait. His mother served as the aged model for Anna in *Tobit and Anna* (1626; Amsterdam, Rijksmuseum) and in *Rembrandt's Mother as the Prophetess Anna* (*c.* 1630; Salisbury, Wilton House, Coll. Earl of Pembroke). The despair of the aged Jeremiah in *Jeremiah Weeping Over the Ruin of Jerusalem* (1630; Rijksmuseum) adds a further dimension to this study of the spiritual depths of old age. Likewise, Rembrandt was drawn to the self-portrait. One of his most powerful youthful self-portraits is the painting he executed about 1629 (Kassel, Staatliche Gemäldegalerie), in which he cast much of his face in shadow, creating a brooding and sensual effect.

Rembrandt. *Jeremiah Weeping Over the Ruin of Jerusalem.* 1630. Rijksmuseum, Amsterdam.

In 1632 Rembrandt left the Calvinist town of Leiden for Amsterdam, and began the most successful and remunerative period of his life. In 1634 he married Saskia van Uylenburgh, the daughter of a wealthy and prominent official. Her first three children died at a very early age, and she herself died of consumption in 1642, one year after their only surviving child, Titus, was born. Upon arrival in Amsterdam, Rembrandt secured a commission from the surgeon Nicolaas Tulp for a group portrait of the members of the Amsterdam Guild of Surgeons. Commonly known as the *Anatomy Lesson* (1632; The Hague, Mauritshuis), this was his first group portrait and it is marked by a dramatic quality and an originality that must have greatly impressed the artist's contemporaries, and that certainly helped to increase his reputation in Amsterdam.

Befriended by the Dutch scientist Christian Huygens and patro-

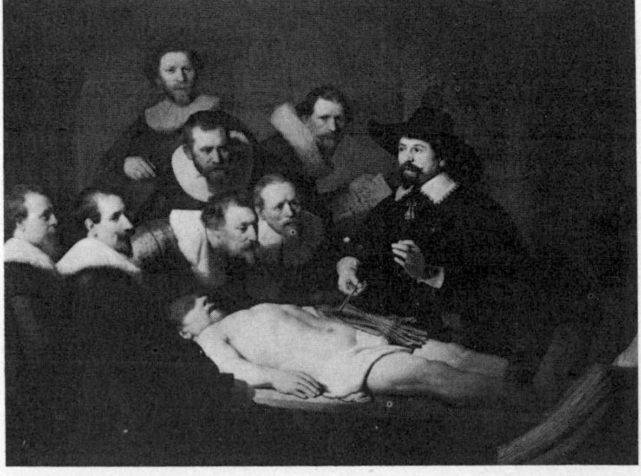

Rembrandt. *Anatomy Lesson of Dr. Tulp.* 1632. Mauritshuis, The Hague.

nized by Frederick of Orange, Rembrandt began to achieve considerable fame in the liberal atmosphere of Amsterdam. His style changed: his handling grew bolder and his palette warmer. The soft tones of his chiaroscuro took on a lyrical effect. Rembrandt executed many portraits that were at times solemn, highly finished, in black and white against a gray background, as is seen in *Marten Soolmans* (1634; Paris, Coll. Rothschild), but more often richly colored, as in *Saskia as Flora* (1634; Leningrad, Hermitage) or in the *Self-Portrait* in official uniform (1634; Paris, Louvre). He was inspired by his great love of life to draw, engrave, and paint a wide variety of subjects, some revealing the influence of Rubens, such as the *Descent from the Cross* (1633; Munich, Alte Pinakothek), some demonstrating his grasp of the full-blown High Baroque style, as in the *Blinding of Samson* (1636; Frankfurt, Städelsches Kunstinstitut), and exhibiting his interest in mythological representations, as the *Rape of Ganymede* (1635; Dresden, Gemäldegalerie). Rembrandt made studies of the nude (drawings of *Adam and Eve*, a *Woman Standing*), creating his most voluptuous nude under the pretext of a Biblical scene already treated by Hendrick Terbrugghen, *Leah Awaiting Jacob*, better known by its traditional title of *Danaë* (1636; Hermitage). His vitality is the driving force behind his masterpiece: the so-called *Night Watch* (1642; Rijksmuseum), a canvas portraying Captain Banning Cocq's militia company. This is possibly the most dramatic painting that Rembrandt executed. He placed in full light only the captain, lieutenant, and flagbearer, depicting their features clearly and vigorously. It is in the careful handling of chiaroscuro, the Baroque rhythm of movement, the lines of force, and the rich golden-brown cast of the colors that one sees the full originality of this magnificent canvas.

Rembrandt. *Supper at Emmaus.* 1648. Louvre, Paris. *Photo Giraudon, Paris.*

The years 1643–56 were first and foremost the period of Rembrandt's greatest drawings and engravings. The artist demanded the same results from etching as from painting. From the time of his youth, he demonstrated a supreme gift for this art, and throughout his career gave it a power of expression that surpassed that of all his predecessors. At times his images are as clear and as simple as the first draft of a drawing (*Baptism of the Eunuch*, 1641) or of a rough sketch (*The Mill*, 1641). Rembrandt's greatest etchings, however, are those conceived as if they were paintings, and because they were often reworked, they are known in several states, giving witness to his feverish effort to carry the effects to their very limits. All of these etchings date after 1643, when Rembrandt began the preliminary work on *Christ Healing the Sick*, the so-called *Hundred Guilders Print* (1643–45). Another important work executed in more than one stage is the *Three Crosses* (1653–60/61).

At the same time, Rembrandt painted a number of superb portraits, such as the masterful *Man with a Golden Helmet* (1650; Berlin, Staatliche Museen), and the intimate and tender *Young Woman with a Broom* (1651; Washington, D.C., National Gallery). His religious paintings of the period evoke a gentle charm, as does the *Holy Family with Angels* (1645; Hermitage), and he achieved a profound spirituality with extremely simple means in such works as the *Supper at Emmaus* (1648; Louvre). His handling became more positive, his color warmer, and his light more golden and lyrical. There developed an increased gravity and solemnity, and a greater maturity in his painting. This change in his style coincided with Hendrickje Stoffels' entry into his life. Two paintings reveal these new characteristics: the beautiful *Portrait of Jan Six* (1654; Amsterdam, Priv. Coll.) and the *Bathsheba* (1654; Louvre). During this productive period, Rembrandt was overwhelmed with troubles. His debts increased steadily, and finally in 1656 he was declared bankrupt, as a result of which he lost his art collection and his home. In 1663

Rembrandt. *Self-Portrait. c.* 1665. Wallraf-Richartz-Museum, Cologne.

Hendrickje died, followed by his son Titus in 1668, and thus Rembrandt's last years were spent in loneliness. Nevertheless, his paintings became increasingly rich in spiritual content. A masterpiece of his late years, and his finest group portrait, is the *Syndics of the Amsterdam Cloth Hall* (1662; Rijksmuseum). Unlike the self-contained and dramatic *Anatomy Lesson* of 1632, it seems to depend upon the spectator for its completion. Another important work of this period is the *Conspiracy of Julius Civilis* (1661–62; Stockholm, Nationalmuseum), Rembrandt's greatest history piece, commissioned by the city fathers for the new Town Hall in Amsterdam. The spiritual strength and lyrical feeling is no less evident in *David and Saul* (*c.* 1658; Mauritshuis), in the *Jewish Bride* (1664; Rijksmuseum), and the *Prodigal Son* (1668–69; Hermitage). Rembrandt's palette is restricted to reds and yellows; his color, often laid on with a knife, is thick and heavily textured.

In contrast to these melancholy images is a remarkable *Self-Portrait* (*c.* 1665; Cologne, Wallraf-Richartz-Museum) that reveals another side of the artist's character. Rembrandt, bent and feeble, stands laughing before a barely visible canvas on an easel. In the face of loneliness and sorrow there is yet a triumph of the spirit.

REMINGTON, Frederic (1861, Canton, New York—1909, Ridgefield, New Jersey), American painter, illustrator, etcher, and sculptor. After 1885 Remington made frequent trips throughout the West and Southwest, in the course of which he stored up in his mind the many scenes and subjects—Indian life, cowboy customs, horses and cattle, soldiers on the frontier—that he later skillfully translated into illustrations, which became famous for their directness and emotional appeal. He gained instant recognition with his first illustrations in *Harper's Weekly* (1886), and in 1890 was assigned as a journalistic illustrator to cover the last Plains Indian War.

From 1905 Remington worked also for *Collier's*, a magazine that featured his illustrations in series. He frequently added imagined details to the realistic memories he painted and designed. His aim was not to document, but to popularize and even romanticize the West in order to recreate its vivid frontier spirit with pictures of Indians, cavalry regiments, cowboys, and animals running across the seemingly limitless expanses of the Great Plains. *Cavalry Charge on the Southern Plains* (1907; New York, Metropolitan Museum) is typical of Remington's choice of subject matter. He was also a noted sculptor of such Western subjects as the *Bronco Buster* (1895), of which there are many bronze replicas, including one in the Metropolitan Museum, New York.

RENAISSANCE ART. During the 15th century, particularly in Italy, there took place a "rebirth," or at least the progressive, contradictory, and finally triumphant resurgence of the Classical substratum, whose ethical and aesthetic values were used once again within the frame of Christian experience and subject to the hazards of contemporary times. In Italy, where the Gothic style had hardly penetrated, the memory of Roman grandeur was not very distant. Countless monuments bore witness to it—despite the ravages of natural forces—and men even before the great wave of archaeological activity uncovered others. Greek thought was revered and its diffusion quickened by the arrival of Greek scholars who fled to the West from Constantinople. The philosophical movement in which the Aristotelian and Platonic traditions confronted each other was accompanied by an immense surge of scholarship, with the discovery and careful editing of numerous manuscripts, the excavation of Roman remains, and the collecting of antiquities. Printing made possible the spread of Classical culture, while libraries—such as that of the Vatican—ensured its preservation.

A new humanism, which extolled man in extolling God and which placed pagan art forms in the service of God and the genius of exceptional individuals at the service of humanity, assumed two fundamental aspects in the world of art: its intellectual aspect was the cult of beauty, which could be integrated from Platonism into Christianity without any danger of heresy; its aesthetic aspect lay in the gradual abandonment of Byzantine forms in favor of modeling, realism, and, in the end, an anthropomorphic ideal that took its models from Greek statuary. The history of the Renaissance may be seen as a progression from the difficult conquest of this realistic form that was stamped with the ideal, through the domination of this ideal, in which formal perfection formed a sort of material reflection of the ideological concepts; and finally, through the decline, when these concepts ended by dominating reality.

The Renaissance was, then, the assertion and then the triumph of a new order, fed by an ancient tradition. Humanism freed the individuality of creative artists and thinkers, but it also had as its basis a wholly intellectual ideal of perfection that was identified with God by an ingenious synthesis. As such, it satisfied the aristocratic and cultivated public, but it held little appeal for the masses, and sometimes resulted, among the artists themselves, in a slight inability to adjust to the new ideas. This lack of adjustment was particularly noticeable in the independent centers where rich artistic traditions were not easily laid aside. In Italy, the cities of Venice and Parma were the most important such centers, and there the intellectualism of the Florentine and Roman humanists competed unsuccessfully with a poetic genius that was sensitive to reality and more inclined to reverie than to the pure delights of the intellect. Outside Italy, the spirit of the Renaissance met with varied acceptance, depending upon the degree to which national traditions could penetrate; France, for instance, and even the Netherlands were more receptive than Germany and the Iberian peninsula.

Several different points of departure have been claimed for the Renaissance. One tradition places its beginning in the late 13th and early 14th centuries with the work of Giotto. According to this argument, Giotto inaugurated the Renaissance by introducing a formal and spiritual flexibility that Masaccio, on the threshold of the Quattrocento, only deepened. The theory is attractive, but it is invalidated by the fact. Far from directly proceeding one from the other, the revolutionary painting of Giotto and that of Masaccio were separated by a wave of the courtly International Style, which preferred the arabesques of miniature painting to the expression of space and the realistic modeling of forms. It was not until a century after Giotto that painters were once again more concerned with form than with line, and that a monumental aesthetic was accepted over that of the miniature. The Renaissance proper did not begin until the threshold of the dazzling Quattrocento, and it was linked to a historical situation: a momentary equilibrium among the separate powers that ruled Italy, a revival of papal power that brought with it the regeneration of Rome's material and spiritual greatness, and the upsurge of humanism. Finally, two phenomena encouraged the flowering of original works, especially in painting: the first was the independence of art centers, and the second was the liberation of individual personalities with the wish to assert themselves more and more, even in group enterprises. This general cohesiveness in the development of the arts and simultaneous fundamental distinctions appeared at once in architecture, sculpture, and painting. Florence, with Brunelleschi, Donatello, and Masaccio, began the movement.

Renaissance Art. Filippo Brunelleschi. Old Sacristy, S. Lorenzo, Florence. 1421–28. *Photo Alinari-Viollet.*

Renaissance Art. Lorenzo Ghiberti. *Jacob and Esau.* Detail from the Doors of Paradise. 1425–52. Baptistery, Florence.

Renaissance architecture was born in Florence with the work of Filippo Brunelleschi, which had been prepared by a tradition that was hostile to Gothic and as faithful as possible to its Roman origins. In this context Brunelleschi's masterpiece, the dome of Florence Cathedral (1420–36), which was entirely Roman in conception, seemed a definite and decisive reaction against medieval architecture. In the churches of S. Lorenzo (begun 1419) and S. Spirito (begun 1436), he showed his uncompromising adherence to the Classical tradition, which laid emphasis on rhythm and the harmony of masses and had a wealth of ornamental motifs adapted to this aesthetic.

The other great early 15th-century architect was Leon Battista Alberti, who was devoted to a Classical culture that he integrated into his own art with the grandeur and elegance of a synthesis peculiarly his own. These qualities link the façade of S. Francesco at Rimini, known as the Tempio Malatestiano (begun *c.* 1446), to the highest Roman traditions. His followers, and to a greater extent those of Brunelleschi, were talented artists who applied and spread their masters' ideas: Michelozzo, who built the Palazzo Medici-Riccardi (begun 1444) in Florence, the prototype of patrician residences; Giuliano da Maiano (*c.* 1432–90), who introduced Brunelleschi's style into southern Italy; his brother Benedetto, who was associated with Il Cronaca in building the Palazzo Strozzi, Florence (1489–1507); Giuliano da Sangallo, who in the 1480s rebuilt the villa at Poggio a Caiano for Lorenzo de' Medici; and Luciano Laurana, an indirect heir of Alberti, and builder of the courtyard and main façade of the Montefeltro palace at Urbino (*c.* 1465–79). Rome at that time inherited the architectural supremacy of Florence, when Bramante finally set Italian architecture on the path of the High Renaissance. It was the Florentine style, however, that inspired the Arsenal at Venice, another center of resistance to Gothic, and that penetrated Bologna, Milan, and Pavia.

The Quattrocento might be called the "Age of Florence," not only for its architecture but also for its painting, at least at the beginning, and especially for its sculpture. Florentine sculpture had then an inimitable truthfulness, guided by a concern for beauty, equilibrium, and style that saved it from the excesses of expressive realism. Two successive generations divided the first and second halves of the century; the first was dominated by Lorenzo Ghiberti and, above all, Donatello, exceptional figures who were imitated by the second generation, for whom grace rather than strength was the primary quality sought.

Nanni di Banco at Florence and Jacopo della Quercia at Siena provided the transition between the art of the Trecento and that of the Quattrocento. Ghiberti's training as a goldsmith had given him a highly finished, precise, and complex style that was at the same time vigorous. The climax of his art came with the extraordinary "Doors of Paradise" (1425–52), the second set of bronze doors he did for the Florentine Baptistery, where the new type of bas-relief, composed like a painting, reached perfection in its supple, elegant realism.

The great figure of the period was Donatello: his work is the high point of the century and is still astonishing in its richness, the variety of its materials and genres, its constant freshness of inspiration, and its unfailing skill. His expressive realism infused a new vigor into the Biblical stories without robbing them of any of their sacred dignity. Because Donatello was steeped in Classical sculpture, he gave this realism, which he shared with his Flemish contemporary Claus Sluter, a deeply conscious sense of style. He introduced into the art of his day a noble, vital synthesis in which ancient traditions were in a way sublimated by his passionate love of life.

After Luca della Robbia, whose work derived from Donatello and Ghiberti but was marked by a peculiar tenderness of expression, there were no more sculptors of equal stature during the Quattrocento. However, there are several lesser masters worthy of mention: Andrea, Giovanni, and Girolamo della Robbia; Agostino di Duccio, whose bas-reliefs are reminiscent of Botticelli's paintings; Desiderio da Settignano, Bernardo and Antonio Rossellino, Mino da Fiesole, Matteo di Giovanni Civitali (1430/35–95), Benedetto da Maiano, Piero and Antonio Pollaiuolo, and finally Andrea del Verrocchio, whose equestrian statue of *Bartolommeo Colleoni* in Venice (left unfinished at his death in 1488) is worthy of comparison with Donatello's *Gattamelata.*

The contribution of Filippo Brunelleschi to architecture and Donatello to sculpture had no equal in painting except in the work of their younger contemporary, Masaccio. He asserted with supreme authority the existence of space in painting, and treated his Biblical subjects with heroic grandeur. The tangible world of reality was rediscovered in Masaccio's painting through a calculated, intellectual approach that brought to art a new and unprecedented grandeur and tension. Like Giotto, Masaccio was the cause of a reaction against his art, pushed to the limits, rather than of a realistic movement. In fact, a Gothic style more or less imbued with Masaccio's manner was continued in the work of Gentile da Fabriano, Benozzo Gozzoli, Fra Filippo Lippi, and Sandro Botticelli. Masaccio's legacy seems to have been divided between artists such as Fra Angelico, who combined it with Gothic characteristics, and his most faithful inheritors: Andrea del Castagno, who used Masaccio's line and color in his own dynamic manner; and Paolo Uccello, for whom space became a purely intellectual obsession and whose mysterious, even fantastic imagination was a world away from Masaccio's religious sentiment. A conflict grew between the primacy of line and the primacy of color that reverberated through the other schools, in Umbria, The Marches, and northern Italy. One painter alone reconciled the two contradictory tendencies and in so

Renaissance Art. Donatello. *St. George.* Detail. *c.* 1420. Museo del Bargello, Florence. *Photo Anderson.*

doing gave a new impulse to the Italian painting he dominated: Piero della Francesca.

In his pictorial world and technique, this master from Arezzo rediscovered Masaccio's powerful equilibrium, which he tempered with a new elegance and freshness. From his combination of line, color, and feeling a new imaginative art was born.

The conquests of Piero della Francesca were decisive. From Mantegna to the impetuous Luca Signorelli, from the suave Perugino and Antonello da Messina (who introduced Flemish features into his paintings) to Giovanni Bellini, with whom Venetian painting attained its first greatness, and to Leonardo da Vinci, Piero's legacy was assimilated by the most varied talents and geniuses. The incoherences of the Quattrocento were resolved in his painting just as they were in Bramante's architecture. The genesis of the Renaissance was ended, and the time had come for its flowering.

The Quattrocento had been the "age of individual achievements"; the 16th century, at least in its beginnings, was the age of general achievements. It was essentially a time of synthesis; artists not only found the solution to earlier conflicts, but went beyond them. The High Renaissance leaves a general impression of fulfillment and grandiose harmony. Whatever tensions had existed in previous artistic explorations, they now relaxed and tended to become absorbed in the general quest for beauty. While each school had its characteristic style, the greatest creations were now gathered in Rome, which attracted artists from other cities and spread their ideas in turn. There is a surprising unison in these works: their splendor, the implied optimism in those produced by a genius as anguished as Michelangelo, and their scale, all these qualities point to the conquest, even though temporary and incomplete, of a superior unity.

Such a unity was the product of a dual development, or more exactly, of a convergence of two artistic currents: one might be termed "objective," and was aimed at achieving a positive, concrete understanding of nature and history through the work of art (Donatello, Masaccio); the other was Neoplatonic, and tried to suggest the sensible reflection of beauty through rhythm and an intellectually conceived geometric harmony. At the end of the Quattrocento, especially in Florence, the second current ran with great force, even with some violence, so that Neoplatonism verged on aestheticism even with such an artist as Botticelli. It is understandable that, under these conditions, Leonardo da Vinci, who had been trained in Florence, should have reacted radically. Beauty still remained for him the aim of art, but it was not the metaphysical idea of beauty that guided him, and certainly not the ideal that could be abstracted from Greco-Roman works. It was only direct study of the visible world and the human phenomenon that interested him. Bramante's attitude was the same; for him beauty was apprehended by experience, or better still, by experimentation. The natural sciences replaced aesthetics, but the aim of every artist remained unchanged. Michelangelo himself, in his absolute quest for an ideal form and in his militant, intransigent return to the Neoplatonic idea, was forced to recognize that that idea was inseparable from the experience of matter: this can be seen in his unfinished sculptures, in which the idea seems to be freed from the inert stone, instead of being incarnated in it. The synthesis of the two conceptions found its highest and most peaceful realization in Raphael's work. It was the apotheosis of the Renaissance, the supreme point of equilibrium of humanism, wherein its contradictory and simultaneous postulations converged, were reconciled, and harmonized.

It was a brilliant synthesis, yet it was threatened. Alongside these grandiose creations were so many failures. Leonardo da Vinci's experiments were short-lived and his method wrecked by faulty techniques as he elaborated it. Michelangelo painted the Sistine Chapel ceiling (1508–12), but the project for the tomb of Julius II was abortive and his measureless dreams gave way to poignant images of despair. Soon, besides the artists' internal conflicts, there was a quickening disintegration of the temporal and spiritual powers, whose order had supported art. Dead were the humanist popes whose patronage had been exercised at the expense of a church crushed by taxation and scandalized by the financial expedients of the curia. The legitimate need for reform brought exasperation, schism in the church, and carried violence in its train.

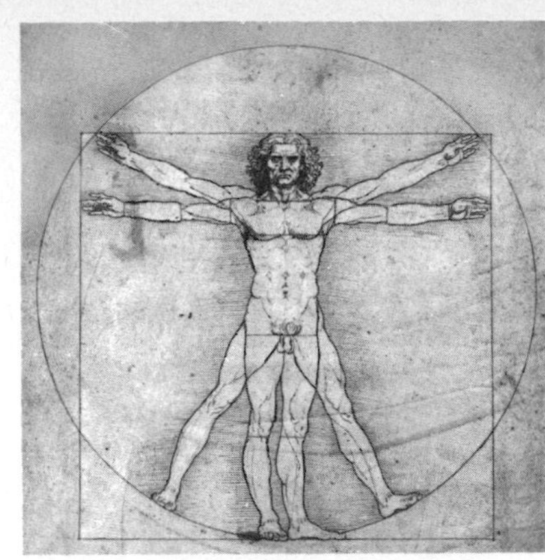

Renaissance Art. Leonardo da Vinci. *Proportions of the human body, after Vitruvius. c.* 1492. Accademia, Venice. *Photo Anderson-Viollet.*

At the same time that the concept of ideal beauty triumphed at Rome and the Renaissance aesthetic spread through Italy and to its neighbors, an art center in the northern part of the peninsula developed a very different aesthetic with equal success: Venice. Its maritime trade had for a long time left it open to the influence of Byzantium, and Venice had only slowly developed an original painting of its own: the Venetian School was not really born until the 15th century, with Vittore Carpaccio, whose work was impregnated with a poetic archaism, and with Giovanni Bellini, who through supple draftsmanship and refined color tried to reflect more and more the changing aspect of form and color in light. When the High Renaissance style reached Venice, there was boundless opposition to its intellectual severity. The dominating mood of art encouraged nuance, in which the tension of the speculative mind dissolved in the enjoyment of music, perspective lines were replaced by distant views enveloped in misty atmosphere, and where form itself was

Renaissance Art. Michelangelo. *Rondanini Pietà.* Detail. 1555–64. Castello Sforzesco, Milan. *Photo Anderson.*

Renaissance Art. Francesco Primaticcio. *Study for the tomb of the Duc de Guise.* After 1550. Louvre, Paris. *Photo Musées Nationaux.*

Renaissance Art. Germain Pilon. *Three Graces.* 1561. Louvre, Paris. *Photo Boitier-Connaissance des Arts.*

Renaissance Art. Philibert de l'Orme and Jean Bullant. Gallery overlooking the Cher River, Château de Chenonceaux. *c.* 1556–81. *Photo Roubier, Paris.*

blurred in the sensitive caress of a brushstroke. All this was resumed in the supreme ease of Giorgione's art, which found its brilliant consummation in Titian's fertile inventions; in the sculpture and architecture of Jacopo Sansovino, who came from Florence but whose name is inseparable from the Venetian Renaissance; and in the architecture of Andrea Palladio. El Greco pushed to its furthest limit that poetic unreality that had even reached the point of the disintegration of form in Tintoretto's painting. Velázquez learned from Venetian painting sensitivity to appearances and a sort of musical poetry of color.

Other centers were also slow to accept the grand style of the Renaissance. In the voluptuous art of Correggio at Parma, ideal beauty was neglected in favor of an expressive, rather soft beauty with an easy appeal to the eye, which anticipated the Baroque. Lombard painting, centered around Leonardo da Vinci, was marked by *sfumato* effects, in which contours dissolved in space, and by an indefinable, irrational charm in the facial expressions of the figures.

France, the northern and eastern countries of Europe, and the Iberian peninsula had been influenced by the spread of humanism, and after the Hundred Years' War, the Reconquista in

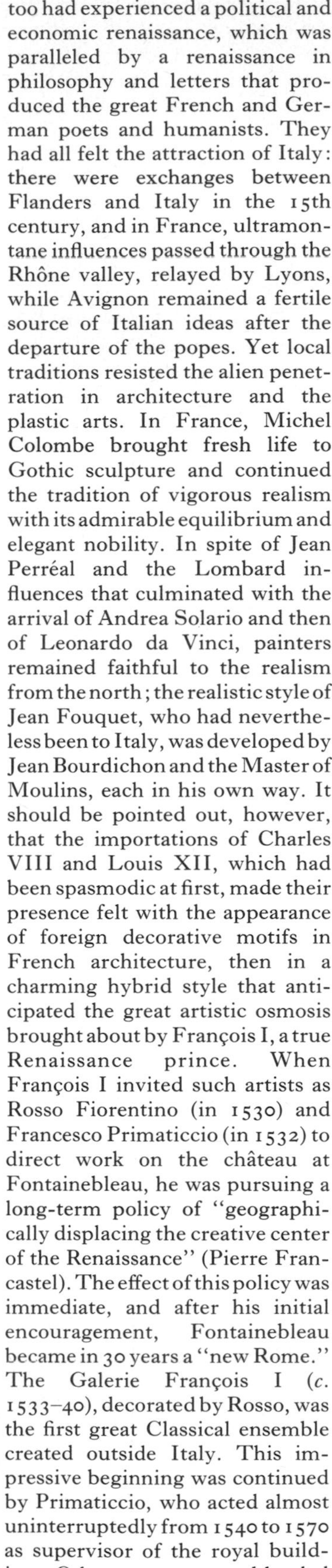

Spain, and the Hapsburg attempt to restore the Roman Empire, they too had experienced a political and economic renaissance, which was paralleled by a renaissance in philosophy and letters that produced the great French and German poets and humanists. They had all felt the attraction of Italy: there were exchanges between Flanders and Italy in the 15th century, and in France, ultramontane influences passed through the Rhône valley, relayed by Lyons, while Avignon remained a fertile source of Italian ideas after the departure of the popes. Yet local traditions resisted the alien penetration in architecture and the plastic arts. In France, Michel Colombe brought fresh life to Gothic sculpture and continued the tradition of vigorous realism with its admirable equilibrium and elegant nobility. In spite of Jean Perréal and the Lombard influences that culminated with the arrival of Andrea Solario and then of Leonardo da Vinci, painters remained faithful to the realism from the north; the realistic style of Jean Fouquet, who had nevertheless been to Italy, was developed by Jean Bourdichon and the Master of Moulins, each in his own way. It should be pointed out, however, that the importations of Charles VIII and Louis XII, which had been spasmodic at first, made their presence felt with the appearance of foreign decorative motifs in French architecture, then in a charming hybrid style that anticipated the great artistic osmosis brought about by François I, a true Renaissance prince. When François I invited such artists as Rosso Fiorentino (in 1530) and Francesco Primaticcio (in 1532) to direct work on the château at Fontainebleau, he was pursuing a long-term policy of "geographically displacing the creative center of the Renaissance" (Pierre Francastel). The effect of this policy was immediate, and after his initial encouragement, Fontainebleau became in 30 years a "new Rome." The Galerie François I (*c.* 1533–40), decorated by Rosso, was the first great Classical ensemble created outside Italy. This impressive beginning was continued by Primaticcio, who acted almost uninterruptedly from 1540 to 1570 as supervisor of the royal buildings. Other currents soon blended with the work of the Italian masters; these were indigenous,

Renaissance Art. Jan Gossaert. *Neptune and Amphitrite.* 1516. Staatliche Museen, Berlin-Dahlem.

more directly inspired by the study of Classical art, and they eventually opened the way to Classicism itself. The leading figures were Pierre Lescot and Philibert de l'Orme in architecture, and Jean Goujon and, to a lesser degree, Germain Pilon in sculpture.

In Flanders, with the late works of Hans Memlinc and particularly the paintings of Gerard David, the school of Bruges gradually moved toward a grace that was perhaps more Lombard than Flemish. Humanist ideas and the science of composition affected the art of Quinten Massys at the new center of Antwerp. But all these marked both the end of the golden age of Flemish painting and an attempt from within to infuse new life into it. In spite of the successful efforts of Jan Gossaert and Lucas van Leyden to inject what they had learned in Italy into this gently stagnating painting, the first Romanists began not a renaissance but a decline that took the form of Brussels Mannerism. In Germany, the arena of the Reformation, artists were divided between German traditions and the appeal of Platonic beauty, and shifted uneasily between the two different tendencies. Grünewald's phantasmagoric style, combining Gothic and northern inspiration, was the medium for the deeply rooted Germanic anguish. The opposite tendency appeared in the work of Lucas Cranach and especially in that of Hans Holbein, who created a major synthesis of northern realism and Italianate vigor and harmony. The dual genius of Albrecht Dürer reunited, without really reconciling, the contradictory aspirations of the new Germany. Italianism certainly made progress in the Iberian peninsula, but it was so intimately involved with composite styles, comprising Christian and Moslem elements, that it assumed the character of a long transition before the peninsula evolved its own art style. The Florentine style affected sculpture; painting was also penetrated with northern and Italian influences: El Greco soon arrived from Crete after visiting Venice.

On the whole, however, Italianism made headway. Europe was open to it, more or less willingly, more or less confusedly. What did it eventually gather from the great flowering of the Renaissance? In Italy itself, during the lifetime of the masters, art was drawn more and more into formalism; unable to find support in the political and moral structure that had once sustained it, it swiftly evolved toward Mannerism. Europe was won over by this systematized and extravagant art that was an eloquent expression of the general confusion of the period. It proliferated new, fantastic forms that would have been foreign to the Renaissance mind; forces that until then had been suppressed rose to the surface. The time had passed for optimism and the proud synthesis of humanism and Christianity. It was only after many confused and painful transitions that the legacy of the Renaissance was once more welcomed with the return of the Classical order.

RENI, Guido (1575, Bologna—1642, Bologna), Italian Baroque painter. He divided his time between Bologna and Rome, where for a brief time he was influenced by Caravaggio (*Crucifixion of St. Peter*, 1604–5; Vatican Museum) before returning to the more balanced Renaissance tradition of Raphael (*St. Andrew Led to Martyrdom*, 1609; Rome, S. Gregorio Magno).

His compositions are deliberately complex, yet the extreme characteristics of the Baroque style are always tempered by a Classical restraint that is typical of the Bolognese School (*Triumph of Samson*, c. 1611; Bologna, Pinacoteca). A superb colorist, Reni employed light tones and transparent flesh tints. In his late style his touch became even lighter, his outlines softer, his tones more silvery, and his brushwork astonishingly free (*Girl with a Wreath*, c. 1635; Rome, Museo Capitolino). His religious compositions were responsible for the immense reputation the artist enjoyed throughout his lifetime, a popularity that was followed inevitably by a long period of neglect. Reni's present reinstatement to critical favor rests rather on his mythological scenes, including the famous fresco of *Aurora* (1613–14) on the ceiling of the Palazzo Rospigliosi in Rome and the *Rape of Helen* (1627–32; Paris, Louvre).

RENOIR, Pierre Auguste (1841, Limoges—1919, Cagnes-sur-Mer), French painter. His father, realizing Auguste's talent for drawing, apprenticed him to a porcelain manufacturer, in whose workshop he decorated plates with flowers and with copies after Rococo paintings. Having diligently saved his money for the tuition, Auguste enrolled in Charles Gleyre's (1806–74) class at the École des Beaux-Arts in 1862. His classmates there included Claude Monet, Frédéric Bazille, and Alfred Sisley. In 1864 Renoir submitted an academic painting, entitled *Esmeralda*, to the Salon, which was accepted; but he destroyed it shortly afterward. Yet, in spite of support from Jean-Baptiste Camille Corot and Charles-François Daubigny, he was rejected by the Salon in 1866. The following year, while working with Monet, he painted a number of Parisian street scenes that were followed by a series of canvases done under the influence of Gustave Courbet, including *Lise with Umbrella* (Essen, Folkwang Museum), accepted by the Salon of 1868, and another painting depicting that same model as *Diana* (1867; Washington, D.C., National Gallery), as well as the *Sisley Family* (1868; Cologne, Wallraf-Richartz-Museum), in which a surprising degree of skill is already apparent. Joining Monet in Bougival, Renoir produced several views of La Grenouillère, a popular bathing spot on the Seine, where he experimented in the representation of reflections and light effects in water, working in rapid, freely applied brushstrokes and employing bright, vivid colors, as can be seen in *La Grenouillère* (1869; Stockholm, National-museum). In a studio lent him by Bazille he painted the *Bather* (1870; São Paulo, Museu de Arte Moderna), exhibited in the Salon of 1870, and an *Odalisque* (1870; Washington, D.C., National Gallery), inspired by Delacroix. In 1872 he rented a studio in Montparnasse, in which his increasing output now included scenes of Paris and landscapes of the Île-de-France region, particularly of Argenteuil, where he frequently went to visit Monet. Examples of his paintings at this time include the *Pont-Neuf* (1872; New York, Coll. Marshall Field), *Meadow* (1873; New York, Coll. Siegfried Kramarsky), *Monet Working in His Garden in Argenteuil* (1873; Georgetown, Conn., Coll. Mrs. A. P. Titzell), and the *Portrait of Monet* (1875; Paris, Musée de l'Impressionnisme). Fortunately for Renoir, the dealer Durand-Ruel began to buy his canvases, thus solving the artist's financial problems. In 1874 Renoir exhibited seven canvases, including the *Loge* (London, Courtauld Institute Galleries) and the *Dancer* (1874; Washington, D.C., National Gallery), at the first Impressionist exhibition at the studio of the photographer Nadar. At this point he began to produce the succession of masterpieces that belong to his Impressionist period: *Le Moulin de la Galette* (1876; Paris, Louvre), the *Portrait of Victor Choquet* (1875; Cambridge, Mass., Fogg Art Museum), the *Swing* (1876; Musée de l'Impressionnisme), and *Bouquet in Front of a Mirror* (1876; Paris, Priv. Coll.), and to paint female nudes bathed in a translucent and dissolving light. By submitting his work to the Salon in order to achieve official recognition, Renoir broke with the Impressionists, allowing his works to be shown only once more, in 1882, in an Impressionist group exhibition, at the request of Durand-Ruel. At

Pierre Auguste Renoir. *Lise as Diana.* 1867. National Gallery of Art, Washington, D.C.

Pierre Auguste Renoir. *Portrait of Claude Monet.* 1875. Musée de l'Impressionnisme, Paris.

that time 25 of his paintings were exhibited, including the superb *Boating Party* (1881; Washington, D.C., Phillips Gallery). In 1881 he traveled to Algiers, and later that same year to Capri, before going to Italy early in 1882.

Although little inclined to innovations, Renoir was both highly intelligent and intensely sensual, and as an artist both naturally spontaneous and extremely skillful. He disdained the mere imitation of nature, learning from Classicism that light, for example, was not an end in itself, but instead must be subordinated to the design and structure of the painting. Accordingly, Renoir began to temper the brightness of his palette, to employ somewhat acid colors, and to purify his line to the point of dryness in a series of canvases, represented by the almost academic *Umbrellas* (*c.* 1884; London, National Gallery). Fortunately, he soon returned to a richer palette when he executed the *Grandes Baigneuses* (1884–87; Philadelphia, Museum of Art), a work that possesses, however, a Classical order and a linear refinement indicating the direction his enthusiasm for Raphael was now leading him.

During this same period, Renoir executed a group of paintings of his wife and new-born son (*Madame Renoir with her son Pierre,* 1885–86, Paris, Coll. Philippe Gangnat; *Mother and Child,* 1885–86, San Francisco, California Palace of the Legion of Honor), which are marked by a simplicity of composition and a certain monumentality of figure type, combined with a linear emphasis so characteristic of his work during his Classical phase.

Renoir's friendship with Paul Cézanne, another former member of the Impressionist group who had turned to a more Classical structural concept of painting, developed during the 1880s. Cézanne's influence can perhaps be seen in Renoir's *Mont St-Victoire* (1880; Merion, Pa., Barnes Foundation). Although refusing to contribute to the eighth and last Impressionist exhibition (1886), Renoir did join the group for the show organized by Durand-Ruel in New York that same year. While continuing to execute canvases of female nudes and landscapes, he painted numerous domestic scenes: *Young Girls at the Piano* (1892; New York, Coll. Robert Lehman), the *Caillebotte Children* (1895; Paris, Coll. Chardeau), and the *Artist's Family* (1896; Barnes Foundation). Renoir's second son, Jean, was born in 1893, the very year the artist engaged a servant named Gabrielle, who was one of his wife's relatives and who was to become his favorite model. It was during this happy period that Renoir's style assumed the monumental breadth and non-linear, painterly qualities that are reminiscent of Rubens rather than of Raphael, and that are so evident in such works as *In the Meadow* (1895; New York, Metropolitan Museum), *Gabrielle and Her Children* (*c.* 1894–96; Paris, Coll. Bernheim-Jeune), and the *Sleeping Bather* (1897; Winterthur, Coll. Oskar Reinhart), as well as such later works as the *Judgment of Paris* (*c.* 1914; Germantown, Pa., Coll. Henry P. McIlhenny).

Renoir began to suffer from arthritis, and for this reason moved to the south of France, first to Grasse, then to Le Cannet in 1902, and finally to Cagnes-sur-Mer in 1905. An exhibition at the second Salon d'Automne in 1904 was a triumph for him. In 1907 he executed a relief medallion of his son Claude (b. 1901), which was his first attempt to give his forms truly three-dimensional treatment; then in 1913 he embarked on his career as a sculptor. Confined to his armchair, he directed the work of a young assistant, guiding his hands over the clay with the aid of a long stick. In this way he executed the *Kneeling Washerwoman* (1917) and the *Victorious Venus* (both Cagnes-sur-Mer, Maison de Renoir). Neither paralysis nor the death of his wife in 1915, however, could inhibit his mental agility, his lyrical force, or his passion for work, which resulted in such paintings as *Woman in White Reading* (1916; Paris, Coll. Philippe Gangnat) and *Seated Nude* (1916; Chicago, Art Institute). The later paintings of Renoir possess a warmth, a massiveness, and a simplicity that stem logically from the earlier works, whose final enrichment and culmination they indeed were.

Pierre Auguste Renoir. *Kneeling Washerwoman.* Detail. 1917. Maison de Renoir, Cagnes-sur-Mer. *Photo Walter Dräyer, Zurich.*

RENWICK, James (1818, New York—1895, New York), American architect. Self-trained as an architect, he won the competition for the new and very fashionable Grace Church in New York (1843—46), whose design—particularly the exterior—is in a very skillfully handled French Gothic style. Immediate professional success followed this first commission, and Renwick pursued a long career as a church architect, although he was the designer of numerous domestic, commercial, and institutional buildings as well. In 1846 Renwick was appointed architect for the new Smithsonian Institution in Washington, D.C. (1848–49), which he designed in a picturesque Romanesque style. In 1860 he designed the Main Hall of Vassar College in Poughkeepsie in a derivative but monumental Second Empire mode, while his most notable work, St. Patrick's Cathedral in New York, was begun in the preceding year. The cathedral was dedicated in 1879 and the spires were completed in 1887, the whole an imposing if highly eclectic compound of French, German, and English Gothic. Not untypical of his period, Renwick's ideas of architectural propriety were directly responsive to the demands of his clients. He worked freely in the Gothic, Romanesque, and French Renaissance styles, handling each with sensitivity and elegance.

RETH, Alfred (1884, Budapest—1966, Paris), French painter of Hungarian origin. He went to Paris in 1905 and began painting in the studio of Jacques-Émile Blanche, who encouraged his experiments in linear construction. From 1907 to 1914 he worked in an orthodox Cubist style (*Nudes and Horses,* 1909; London, Gimpel Fils). He became friendly with the Orientalist Jean Buhot, and was so fascinated by the great cycles of Hindu art that they became as important to him as Negro art was for most Cubists. From his observations of nature, Reth discovered a universal proportion of seven straight lines to one curved line and applied this rule to his interpretation of a subject. He first exhibited at the Salon d'Automne of 1910 and then, with great success, in the Cubist rooms at the Salon des Indépendants in 1911 and 1912. During the 1920s his Cubism became metaphysical, and he covered the surface of his paintings with large rhythmic designs. He made a systematic use, already anticipated in 1914, of unpromising, utilitarian substances such as sand, coal, clinkers, mosaic stones, pebbles, plaster, and egg shells, creating compositions in which he either mixed the materials with color or juxtaposed them without the use of paint. After he had constructed a series of sculptural constructions, *Forms in Space* (1935–39) in wood or metal, he made their counterparts on panels, alternating the built-up portions, which formed the structure of the composition, with planes of pure color. Reth was one of the founding members of the Abstraction-Création movement in 1932 and the Salon des Réalités Nouvelles in 1946.

REYNOLDS, Sir Joshua (1723, Plympton, Devonshire—1792, London), English painter, the most eminent figure in the history of British portraiture. He rose easily and worthily to many official positions and painted highly skilled eclectic portraits that could be appreciated by anyone with a gentleman's knowledge of the great masterpieces of European art.

He received valuable artistic instruction from the portraitist Thomas Hudson (1701–79), whose pupil he became in London (1740). In 1743 Reynolds returned to Plympton and began to paint portraits professionally; from 1744 to 1746 he paid a further visit to London, where he was influenced by the works of William Hogarth and Allan Ramsay, as is evident from his simple but alert portrait of *Lieutenant Roberts* (1747; Greenwich, National Maritime Museum). In 1749 Reynolds set sail from Plymouth to the Balearic Island of Majorca with his friend Commodore (later Admiral) Augustus Keppel; he eventually arrived in Rome in 1750. During the two years Reynolds spent in Rome he gained an understanding of the Grand Style—and became as learned a painter as any on the Continent. He made a prolonged study of the antique, of Raphael, Michelangelo, Carlo Dolci (1616–86), Correggio, and the Carracci, all of whom he was later to "quote" in his mature portraits. His extraordinary ability to translate the works of other artists into his own idiom is apparent in his Rembrandtesque *Self-Portrait* (1753–54; London, National Portrait Gallery), inspired by a *Self-Portrait* by Rembrandt that he had seen in the Corsini Gallery in Rome.

Reynolds returned to England in 1753 via Florence, Parma, Bologna, Venice, and Paris. By that time he was already artistically mature, as is evident from his magnificent portrait of *Commodore Keppel* (1753–54; National Maritime Museum), which portrays a bluff and typically English figure in a manner that is recognizably based on the model of the Apollo Belvedere. This *mise en scène*, in which all the elements contribute to create a heroic illustration of the sitter's personality, is derived from the tradition established by Titian and Van Dyck.

By 1755 Reynolds had painted more than 100 portraits and in 1760, at the first public exhibition of his paintings at the Society of Artists, he emerged as the leader of the British School, his only possible rival, Ramsay, having abstained. He borrowed from various sources: Pietro Longhi (*Charles, 9th Lord Cathcart*, 1753–54; England, Nethway House, Coll. Trustees of the late Earl Cathcart), Ramsay (*Priscilla, Mrs. Panton*, 1757; England, Coll. Earl of Ancaster), and Joseph Aved (*Countess of Albemarle*, 1757–59; London, National Gallery). He created numerous and limpid patterns of his own (*Georgiana, Countess Spencer, and Her Daughter*, 1759–61; Northamptonshire, Althorp, Coll. Earl Spencer). In the 1760s, however, the fantasy and variety in his art began to disappear and a high-minded uniformity became paramount. He painted his female sitters in anonymous Classical draperies (sometimes worn under their peeress's robes), and always included a few learned references to their beauty—generally in the form of doves of Venus, a relief of the Judgment of Paris, or some other respectable allusion. Although Reynolds attempted to establish in England a native tradition of painting in the grand style, he was always prepared to make an exception and paint in a more relaxed and intimate manner; such portraits, usually of his friends (*Dr. Samuel Johnson*, 1772; National Gallery), are among his best.

Sir Joshua Reynolds. *Portrait of Mrs. Thomas Meyrick.* *c.* 1782. Ashmolean Museum, Oxford.

In 1768, when the Royal Academy was founded, Reynolds became its first president. He was knighted the following year and, not unexpectedly, the 1770s mark the climax of his Classical period, during which he turned portraiture into a form of history painting. He reached the climax of this Classical style in his vast *Family of George, Duke of Marlborough* (1778; Oxfordshire, Blenheim Palace, Coll. Duke of Marlborough), a grand and intricate composition. This phase ended with a visit to Flanders and Holland in 1781, in the course of which the influence of Sir Peter Paul Rubens superseded that of the Bolognese masters. A new and delightful naturalism appeared in the portraits of the 1780s: *Mrs. Thomas Meyrick* (*c.* 1782; Oxford, Ashmolean Museum) and *Lady Anne Bingham* (exhibited at the Royal Academy 1786; Coll. Earl Spencer). In these, both women, wearing straw hats and white fichus, are silhouetted against a bright open sky.

Early in 1789 Reynolds lost the sight of one eye. Nevertheless, he managed to paint his magnificent portrait of *Lord Heathfield, Governor of Gibraltar* (1789; National Gallery), a grandiose work in the same spirit as his earlier portrait of Keppel. Reynolds died in 1792, having linked English painting with the mainstream of European art in a way that no previous native-born English painter had ever done. His qualities of calmness, detachment, serenity, and moderation make him the most learned,

Jusepe de Ribera. *Clubfooted Boy.* 1652. Louvre, Paris. *Photo Giraudon.*

although not always the most seductive, painter England ever produced. In the 15 *Discourses* (1769–90) that he delivered first annually and then every two years at the Royal Academy, and that were first printed separately as they appeared and then in their entirety with his own revisions, Reynolds laid down one of the most reasonable and enlightened assessments of the academic position.

RIBALTA, Francisco (1565, Solsona, Lérida—1628, Valencia), Spanish painter. He spent the years from 1582 to 1597 in Madrid, where he seems to have developed an interest in the Caravaggesque technique of chiaroscuro lighting. During this period Ribalta painted a *Christ Nailed to the Cross* (1582; Leningrad, Hermitage), which reveals a precocious talent. Around 1599 the artist settled in Valencia, where he became famous and where he enjoyed the patronage of Archbishop Juan de Ribera, founder of the College of Corpus Christi. Ribalta's best-known painting, the *Last Supper* (*c.* 1610; Valencia, Museum), was one of several altarpieces he provided for the church of that college. He subsequently painted a number of compositions for the Franciscan convent of the Capuchins (the *Angel Appearing to St. Francis*, 1620; Madrid, Prado) and for the Carthusian monastery of Portacoeli, near Valencia (*Christ Embracing St. Bernard*, 1627; Valencia, Museum). The leading master of the Valencian school, Francisco Ribalta passed on his realistic, tenebrous style to his most famous pupil, Jusepe de Ribera.

JUAN (1596, Madrid—1628, Valencia), the artist's son, collaborated with his father and continued in his naturalistic style (*Christ Nailed to the Cross*, 1615; Valencia, Museum).

RIBERA, Jusepe, José *or* Giuseppe de (1591, Játiva, near Valencia—1652, Naples), Spanish-born Baroque painter who became one of the leading artists of the Neapolitan School in Italy. He was a pupil of Francisco Ribalta, although the latter does not seem to have had a great influence over him. At some undetermined date Ribera went to Italy, where he came to be known as *Lo Spagnoletto* ("the little Spaniard"). He lived for several years in Rome, where he studied at the Accademia di S. Luca, becoming a member in 1626 or earlier. Thus in his youth he came under the spell not only of the realistic tradition of Caravaggio but of the Classicism of the Carracci, all of whom had worked in Rome at the turn of the century. Around the year 1616 Ribera arrived in Naples, where he was to spend the rest of his life.

Ribera's considerable reputation was justified by his outstanding talents. His sense of composition, while not equal to that of contemporary Italian painters, was superior to that of his countrymen. His unique technique was characterized by rough surfaces and frequent use of impasto, while his palette grew richer as the years passed.

During the period from 1620 to 1630 Ribera showed a preference for somber colors, dense pigment, and strong Caravaggesque lighting. In these years the artist produced a great number of religious compositions: a *Crucifixion* (1616–20), part of an altarpiece commissioned by the duke of Osuna for the collegiate church of Osuna; a *St. Sebastian tended by St. Irene* (1628; Leningrad, Hermitage); and a *Martyrdom of St. Bartholomew* (*c.* 1630; Madrid, Prado). One of his most remarkable works, both for its almost mystical tenderness and its atmospheric beauty, is *Jacob with the Flock of Laban* (1634; Madrid, Escorial). With almost plebeian vigor he painted the imaginary portrait of *Archimedes* (1630; Prado); the figure of the Greek mathematician is not without some resemblance to one of the drinkers in the *Triumph of Bacchus* (*c.* 1628–29; Prado) by Velázquez, and it must be remembered in this connection that the two Spanish painters met in Naples on the occasion of Velázquez' first visit to Italy (1629–31) as court painter to King Philip IV.

During the years 1635–39 Ribera's colors became brighter, his composition looser, and the landscape elements gained in poetic beauty. The *Trinity* (*c.* 1636; Prado) shows a mingling of mysticism and harsh naturalism typical of much of the Baroque art of the time. In *St. Anthony of Padua and the Infant Christ* (1640; Escorial) certain aspects recall the art of his countrymen Zurbarán and Murillo, while the *Venus and Adonis* (1637; Rome, Palazzo Corsini) reminds one of the Italian Guercino. For the Carthusian monastery of S. Martino, he began in 1637 to paint a *Pietà* and a series of Old Testament figures, which are still in place. The most successful works of this period and those most typical of Ribera's style are undoubtedly *Jacob's Dream* (1639; Prado), with its luminous composition and profound religious feeling; and the *Immaculate Conception* (1635), which occupies the center of the great altarpiece in the Augustinian monastery at Salamanca.

From about 1640 until his death, Ribera continued to give evidence of his striking talent in a late style that is expressed in a number of paintings noted for their magnificent chiaroscuro and compositional effects and for their profound sense of humanity: the *Adoration of the Shepherds* (1650; Paris, Louvre); the *Clubfooted Boy* (1652; Louvre); the *Miracle of S. Gennaro* (1646; Naples Cathedral); and the *Communion of the Apostles* (1651; Naples, S. Martino).

RIBERA, Pedro de (*c.* 1683, Madrid—1742, Madrid), Spanish architect. His work is typical of Madrid architecture in the second quarter of the 18th century. Ribera became assistant to Teodoro Ardemáns (1664–1726), chief architect to the Madrid Municipal Council, and succeeded to his functions when Ardemáns died. As the latter's influence on his work declined, it matured into an ornate Baroque, more tormented than his master's, but becoming relatively restrained in its final phase. The design for the pagodalike catafalque of the Duke and

Duchess of Burgundy (1712) was borrowed in part from Ardemáns, but the decoration, with its contorted lines and lacy appearance created by the mass of candles, is more personal. In Ribera's later designs for the catafalques of Louis XIV (1716) and Luis I of Spain (1724), the ornament tends to obliterate the lines of the architecture. The structure again became more distinct in the catafalque for Victor-Amédée II of Savoy (1732–33). An equally audacious expression of this taste remains only in the main entrances of some buildings, which he treated like altarpieces and in which the exuberant decoration contrasts with the bare walls and geometric rooms surrounding them. Among the finest examples of this genre are the portals of the Guard House (1720) and the Hospicio de S. Fernando (begun 1722; now Madrid, Museo Municipal). The Fountain of Fame (1731–32), now installed near the Museo Municipal in Madrid, is in the same decorative style.

The Marquis del Vadillo, Ribera's patron, was crown governor of Madrid from 1715 to 1729, and Ribera benefited from the remarkable town planning program that the marquis undertook, which included the riverside park of the Virgen del Puerto. Del Vadillo was buried in this park in Ribera's hermitage (1718), a church with the silhouette and proportions of a park pavilion. In 1719 Ribera presented his plans for the Toledo bridge over the Manzanares River (1723–24). Several of his projects remained unfinished. These included Montserrat (1720), with its pure and powerful moldings, and S. Cayetano, which would have subordinated the towers to an immense crossing dome (projects of 1722 and 1737). Outside Madrid, he designed the large gothicizing tower of the new Salamanca Cathedral (1733–38; rebuilt after the earthquake of 1755) and the chapel of Nuestra Señora de la Portería in the church of S. Antonio at Ávila (1731).

Pedro de Ribera. Hermitage of the Virgen del Puerto, Madrid. 1718. *Photo Mas, Barcelona.*

Ribera could have studied Italian architecture from treatises and engravings, but French influence, which predominated at the Spanish court, had only an intermittent effect on his work. His Baroque style was largely the local version practiced in Madrid and the provinces.

RICCIO, Andrea Briosco, *called* Andrea (between 1470 and 1475? Padua—1532, Padua), Italian Renaissance sculptor in stone and bronze, also a goldsmith. Padua at the time was a center of Humanistic studies, and it is understandable that Classicism was more pronounced in the art of the region than in the rest of Italy. In 1506 Riccio was commissioned to do two bronze reliefs for the basilica of S. Antonio, Padua, both illustrating Old Testament subjects. These he finished in 1507, the year his design for the Paschal Candlestick was accepted, also for S. Antonio (presbytery). Executed over a nine-year period, this unique piece is the most elaborate sculpture of its kind produced during the Italian Renaissance. Probably a little before 1511, Riccio did four bronze reliefs, depicting the *Histories of the Cross*, for S. Maria dei Servi, Venice. These works, along with the high-relief bronze of the *Meeting of St. Martin and the Beggar*, are now in the Galleria Giorgio Franchetti, Ca' d'Oro, Venice. The major production of the artist's maturity is the tomb of the Humanist scholar Girolamo della Torre (1516–21; Verona, sacristy of S. Fermo Maggiore), an unusual work in which, appropriately, Riccio avoided Christian iconography and represented Della Torre as a Greek philosopher, with his journey through life culminating in his attainment of the Elysian Fields. The National Gallery in Washington, D.C., owns an important collection of Riccio's bronze reliefs, including a large *Entombment*, parts of which resemble the reliefs on the Paschal Candlestick.

Henry Hobson Richardson. The Crane Library at Quincy, Massachusetts. 1880–83.

RICHARDSON, Henry Hobson (1838, St. James Parish, Louisiana—1886, Boston), American architect. After studying at Harvard University, he went to Paris (1859–65), where he worked in Henri Labrouste's office. French rationalistic planning remained an important influence throughout his career. When he returned to the United States, Richardson settled in New York, although most of his activity was centered in Boston. His style was somewhat derivative at first (French in plan and form, English in picturesque massing and detail), but in the 1880s it became increasingly original. The formality of regular façades was replaced by asymmetrical but rational planning, and by a fresh use of old materials such as shingle (John Bryant House, Cohasset, Mass., 1880). Charles F. McKim and Stanford White were both Richardson's assistants, and their firm of McKim, Mead & White became a leading exponent of the "Shingle Style," a direct outgrowth of Richardson's domestic architecture. Richardson's last great house, built for J. J. Glessner in Chicago (1885–87), was his finest expression of intelligent and well-articulated planning in masonry.

Richardson's public work included churches, libraries, colleges, and government buildings. His libraries (Crane Library, Quincy, Mass., 1880–83) embodied the same principles of asymmetrical, functional planning as his houses. Trinity Church, Boston (1872–77) is in a more archaeological Romanesque style. The elegantly planned red brick

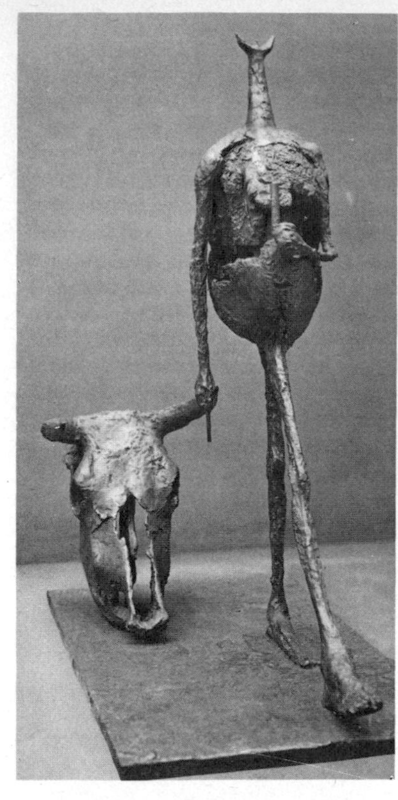

Germaine Richier. *Tauromachia.* 1953. *Photo Marc Vaux, Paris.*

Sever Hall at Harvard College in Cambridge, Mass. (1878–80) harmonizes beautifully with its 18th-century neighbors without being a pastiche of Colonial forms. The Piranesian jail he built in Pittsburgh, Pennsylvania (1885), epitomizes his genius in the expressive use of masonry.

In Chicago, where Richardson's influence was most profound, he built the massive Marshall Field Warehouse (1885–86; demolished 1930). His last commercial structure, The Ames-Pray Building in Boston (1886), was in the same spirit. Through a highly personal interpretation of the Romanesque, Richardson developed a truly original style that enabled the 19th century to free itself of Romantic historicism, and launched the modern movement.

RICHARDSON, Jonathan (1665, London—1745, London), English artist, the principal portrait painter of the period between Sir Godfrey Kneller and Thomas Hudson (1701–79). Richardson studied with John Riley (1646–91) from 1688 to 1691, but his own style is a slacker and more passive version of Kneller's (*Mary, Duchess of Roxburghe*, 1716, Floors Castle, Coll. Roxburghe; *Lord Chancellor Cowper*, *c.* 1710, Firle Place, Sussex, Coll. Viscountess Gage; *George Vertue*, 1738, London, National Portrait Gallery). His only great virtue, however, was competence. In 1740, having amassed a fine collection of old master drawings, he stopped painting, but continued to exert considerable influence through his books, *The Theory of Painting* (1715) and *An Account of Some of the Statues, Bas-Reliefs, Drawings, and Pictures in Italy* (1722), a guidebook written in collaboration with his son Jonathan the Younger (1694–1771), and widely used by Englishmen making the Grand Tour of the Continent.

RICHIER, Germaine (1904, Grans, near Arles—1959, Montpellier), French sculptress and graphic artist. She went to Paris in 1925 and took lessons with Antoine Bourdelle. The works included in Richier's first exhibition, held in 1934 at the Galerie Max Kaganovich in Paris, were Classical in style; during the 1940s she turned almost exclusively to animal sculpture, and her most characteristic subjects were spiders, owls, bats, and toads. Richier's style changed gradually: in *Storm* (1947–48; Paris, Musée National d'Art Moderne), *Hurricane* (1948–49; Musée National d'Art Moderne), *The Ogre* (1951; Priv. Coll.), and *The Hydra* (1954; London, Coll. Hanover Gallery), there is a sort of organic, visceral symbolism grafted onto realistic details, whose morbid Expressionism shocked the public. Her *Crucified Christ* (1960; church of Notre-Dame-de-Toute-Grâce, Assy) created a heated controversy. Among her notable later works are *Tauromachia* (1953; Paris, Galerie Berggruen), one of her masterpieces; the series of *Bird-Men* (1953–55); and *The Mountain* (1956; Musée National d'Art Moderne), a disquieting composition of bone and plant elements heaped together.

Germaine Richier also modeled graceful figurines in gilt bronze, set with enamel and Baroque agglomerations of lead and colored stones (1952), and large polychrome plasters (1957–58) in which she shed her obsessions and offered a more conciliatory face to the public. She also did illustrations, such as engravings for Arthur Rimbaud's *Une Saison en Enfer* (1949).

RICHTER, Hans (1888, Berlin—1976, Locarno, Switzerland), German-born American painter and film maker. He was influenced by Cubism and in 1914 began to contribute to the Berlin avant-garde periodical *Die Aktion* ("Action"). In 1916, the year of his first one-man show in Munich, he joined the Zurich-based Dada group. He also worked in an Expressionistic style, producing portraits of friends such as *Dr. Udo Rukser* (1914; Quilota, Chile, Coll. Rukser) and about 100 *Visionary Portraits* (1917). He then executed black and white paintings inspired by the spirit of Dadaism (*Balcony*, 1916, Turin, Museo Civico; *Head I*, 1918, Chicago, Coll. Ludwig Mies van der Rohe). In 1919 he painted the first of his scroll paintings, *Praeludium* (New Haven, Conn., Yale University Art Gallery), to express the "principle of continuity in a formal motif." These were long rolls on which he executed a sequence of abstract drawings, which he put through a succession of transformations and developed like a musical theme. Richter's first scroll paintings were a link between painting and film, and with the experience he had gathered from them, he shot one of the first abstract films ever made, *Rhythm 21*, in 1922. In 1940 Richter emigrated to the United States, and in 1942 was appointed director of the Film Institute of the City College of New York. His film, *Dreams that Money can Buy* (1944–47), which he produced with the assistance of the painters Max Ernst and Marcel Duchamp, is—in spite of its abstract parts—a classic of the Surrealist cinema. Another memorable film was *8 × 8* (1955–58), which he shot with friends and associates such as Jean Arp, Alexander Calder, and Jean Cocteau, as well as with Ernst and Duchamp. Richter called it "A Chess Sonata in Eight Episodes for Film."

RICKEY, George (b. 1907, South Bend, Indiana), American sculptor and painter. Rickey spent his childhood and youth in Scotland. His extensive education in history, art, and art history included studies at Balliol College, Oxford; the Ruskin School of Drawing and of Fine Art, Oxford (1928–29); the Académie André Lhote and Académie Moderne, Paris (1929–30); New York University (1945–46); and the Institute of Design, Chicago (1948–49). His first one-man exhibition of paintings was held at the Caz-Delbo Gallery,

New York, in 1933, and, of sculpture, at the John Herron Art Institute, Indianapolis, in 1953.

Rickey's development began with painting: in the 1930s and 1940s he worked particularly with murals in tempera, for which he received numerous commissions (United States Post Office, Selinsgrove, Pennsylvania, 1938; Knox College, Galesburg, Illinois, 1940–41). He made his first mobile in 1945, and began to work extensively in kinetic sculpture around 1950. Rickey's early kinetic constructions are fairly complicated and agitated and depend strongly on natural imagery, as indicated by titles such as *Silverplume, II* (1951; Ghent, New York, Coll. Mr. and Mrs. Larry Gelbart) and *Waterplant* (1959–61; Andover, Mass., Addison Gallery of American Art). His later work, though still sometimes suggestive of natural phenomena, tends to be simpler and more geometrical and abstract (*Sedge II*, 1961, stainless steel, Hanover, New Hampshire, Dartmouth College; *Two Red Lines*, 1966, painted steel, Coll. artist).

RIEMENSCHNEIDER, Tilman (*c.* 1460, Osterode—1531, Würzburg), German Late Gothic sculptor. He was first trained as a stone sculptor in Erfurt, where he was also exposed to religious sculpture in alabaster. He later spent time in Strasbourg and then went to Ulm to learn wood carving, probably under Michel Erhart. He appears in the Würzburg records of 1478 or 1479 and settled there in 1483.

Tilman Riemenschneider. Tomb of Bishop Rudolf von Scherenberg. 1496–99. Detail. Würzburg Cathedral. *Photo Gundermann.*

Although Riemenschneider's style is connected with the carvings of the Syrlin family at Ulm, his work is extremely individual. In particular his refined treatment of the female body was rare at the time in Germany. The life-size sandstone statue of *Eve* (1491–93; Würzburg, Mainfränkisches Museum) that Riemenschneider carved for the south porch of the Marienkapelle at Würzburg is an example of this delicacy.

In 1496–99 he carved the proudest of his funerary monuments, that of Prince Bishop Rudolf von Scherenberg, his patron, in Würzburg Cathedral, whose deeply wrinkled face has an admirable dignity. A *St. Jerome and the Lion* (1505–10; Cleveland, Museum of Art) shows his mastery of alabaster and his gift for realistic observation. From 1499 to 1513 he was occupied with the impressive memorial monument to Emperor Henry II and his wife Kunigund in Bamberg Cathedral. After 1519 he executed the tomb of another patron, Bishop Lorenz von Bibra (Würzburg, Cathedral).

While work was continuing on these monuments, his workshop was sending altarpieces throughout the region, inspired by the fine examples of wood carving in the graphic work of Martin Schongauer. Riemenschneider's manner is apparent in such carvings as the St. Magdalen altarpiece (1490–92) at Münnerstadt, fragments of which are in the Bayerisches Nationalmuseum, Munich; the famous Altar of the Holy Blood (1501–5) in St. Jakob, Rothenburg; and the Altar of the Virgin (*c.* 1505) at Creglingen. One of his late works is the altarpiece for the nunnery church at Maidbronn, depicting the *Lamentation*, of which a small wooden model of the center section—the *Pietà*—is owned by the museum of the Rhode Island School of Design at Providence.

Riemenschneider's work can be seen as a summation of German and Netherlandish Gothic tendencies, and his influence was considerable.

RIETVELD, Gerrit Thomas (1888, Utrecht—1964, Utrecht), Dutch architect. In 1918, when he was designing and building his first wooden furniture, Rietveld became associated with the founders of the De Stijl group and shared in their activities until the group's dissolution in 1931. In 1923 he worked with Theo van Doesburg and Cor van Eesteren (b. 1897) on a series of architectural projects, which were exhibited at the Galerie Léonce Rosenberg, Paris, and were accompanied by the publication of his manifesto *Vers une construction collective* ("Toward Group Building"). The Rietveld-Schröder House at Utrecht, which Rietveld built in 1924 and furnished with the help of the decorator T. Schröder-Schräder, conformed strictly to De Stijl principles. He repeated the experiment in his mass-produced houses at Utrecht (1931–34), but with less striking contrasts. The popularity of the academic Delft school curtailed his activity in Holland, and after building the Vreeburg Cinema at Utrecht (1936), he confined himself to furniture designing. When World War II ended, interest in Rietveld's work revived, and he received a number of important commissions: the Dutch Pavilion at the Venice Biennale (1953–54); the De Ploeg Textile Works at Bergeijck (1956); and the Zonnehof Cultural Center at Amersfoort (1959).

RIGAUD, Hyacinthe Rigau y Ros, *called* Hyacinthe (1659, Perpignan—1743, Paris), French painter. He was the most distinguished portraitist during the reign of Louis XIV. He worked in the studio of Charles Le Brun and was awarded the Prix de Rome in 1682; Le Brun, however, advised him to remain in Paris, where a brilliant career awaited him. Louis XIV twice sat for his portrait—in 1694 and 1701. The second version (Paris, Louvre), showing the monarch in his sumptuous coronation robes, is a forceful image of the royal majesty, and remains the artist's most famous portrait. After this success, Rigaud's reputation began to extend beyond France; the most distinguished patrons sat for him, including ambassadors, princes, clerics (*Bossuet*, 1702, and *Cardinal de Polignac*, 1715; both Louvre), financiers, courtiers, artists, and writers.

Rigaud's ideal was the art of Sir Anthony van Dyck. His studio was like a highly specialized factory, in which faithful assistants each fulfilled a particular task: Charles Parrocel the battle scenes, Jean-Baptiste Monnoyer the flowers, François Desportes the landscapes and still lifes. Nevertheless,

Hyacinthe Rigaud. *Portrait of the Artist's Mother.* 1695. Louvre, Paris. *Photo Giraudon, Paris.*

Rigaud planned the general conception of his own compositions and reserved certain parts for himself, especially the faces. One portrait, however, holds a place of importance in his oeuvre—that of the artist's mother (1695; Louvre). The head is shown in three views, one full-faced and two in profile, and was intended as a sculptor's model. Its simplicity and restraint doubtlessly place it among the best of his works. It has been said that Rigaud's art marked the transition from the 17th to the 18th century. In fact, its grandeur and instinct for impressive poses derive from the Louis XIV style, but the gracefulness of his portraits—particularly evident in that of the young Louis XV (1715; Versailles, Museum)—is characteristic of the 18th century.

RIMMER, William (1816, Liverpool, England—1879, South Milford, Massachusetts), American sculptor. Rimmer came to the United States as a child (1818) and lived most of his life in the Boston area. In 1847, to teach himself medicine, he began dissecting corpses at the Massachusetts Medical College; a few years later he began practicing medicine and in 1855 he was licensed by the Suffolk Medical Association. After *c.* 1864, when he opened a private drawing school and published his *Elements of Design*, Rimmer became a well-known though controversial teacher of art anatomy. His publication, *Art Anatomy*, appeared in 1877.

As in medicine, Rimmer was self-taught in drawing, painting, and sculpture. He began carving in granite in 1855. In 1861 he executed the *Falling Gladiator* (plaster, Boston, Museum of Fine Arts; 1906, two bronze copies: Boston, Museum of Fine Arts and New York, Metropolitan Museum), which is often considered the greatest example of his romantic, turbulent style and of his characteristic nude male figures in tension and struggle. The two other major sculptures among the few that have survived are the *Dying Centaur* (1871, plaster, Boston, Museum of Fine Arts; 1907, bronze, Metropolitan Museum) and *Fighting Lions* (*c.* 1871, plaster, Boston Art Club; 1907, bronze, Metropolitan Museum). An especially expressive example of Rimmer's painting is *Flight and Pursuit* (1872; Philadelphia, Museum of Art).

RIOPELLE, Jean-Paul (b. 1923, Montreal), Canadian painter. In 1944 he was cofounder with Paul-Émile Borduas of the Automatist movement in Montreal. In 1945 he went to Paris, where he met the leading exponents of Tachism, or action painting, including Wols (Wolfgang Schulze), Camille Bryen (b. 1907), and Georges Mathieu. In August 1948, during a brief visit to Canada, he signed the manifesto of the Borduas group, *Refus global* ("Total Refusal"), which was a vehement expression of the anger of Canada's French-speaking artists and intellectuals against the established authorities as well as a proclamation of their aspirations for an independent Quebec. His watercolors have the impulsiveness typical of the medium and his gouaches are reflective; oil painting, on the other hand, offered him a wider field of action and encouraged abstraction. In 1950 Riopelle began squeezing paint straight out of the tube onto the canvas, the paint gradually forming itself into broad, thick areas of flaming color. After 1952 he applied his paint in short or long serried strips that followed a circular pattern, producing paintings that were like mosaics of light in which all the power and poetry of the Canadian forests seemed to be concentrated. In 1956 Riopelle's manner changed again and his painting became less dense; large white areas that were closely worked now formed a part of the canvas, giving it a freer, more spacious feeling (*Preo*, 1964; Buffalo, Albright-Knox Art Gallery).

RIVERA, Diego (1886, Guanajuato—1957, Mexico City), Mexican painter. He entered the School of Fine Arts of Mexico City in 1899, and won a scholarship to Europe at the age of twenty-one. Rivera went first to Spain and then to Paris, where he remained until 1920, following with great interest the development of the Cubist painters who were his friends. When he returned to Mexico City, Rivera decorated the Bolivár Amphitheater in the University with a painting of the *Creation* (1922), which was the first modern mural painting in Mexico. Rivera painted huge allegorical or historical frescoes for the Ministry of Education in Mexico City (1923–28), the National School of Agriculture at Chapingo (1927), the Cortés Palace at Cuernavaca (1930), and the National Palace in Mexico City (1930–35). In 1931 he was invited to New York, where the Museum of Modern Art organized an exhibition of his work, and he painted several frescoes in Rockefeller Center in New York (never completed and since destroyed), San Francisco, and Detroit; these works provoked considerable controversy because of his introduction of "dialectical materialism into the technique of painting." Again in Mexico City, from 1936 to 1940, he executed many easel paintings of landscape and portrait subjects. He returned to mural paintings with a series of "portable" murals for the National Institute of Cardiology (1943–44) and for the National Palace (1950).

RIVERA, José de (b. 1904, West Baton Rouge, Louisiana), American sculptor. He began making sculpture in the early 1930s and received his first major commission in 1938 for Newark Airport in New Jersey (*Flight*, aluminum; now owned by the Newark Museum). His first one-man show was held in New York in 1946.

De Rivera began to work in a modernist direction in the early 1930s with simplified, stylized, and highly polished metal sculptures. In the late 1930s he became familiar with the work of Piet Mondrian and Constantin Brancusi, whose emphasis on elemental form and color was influential on his own style, as were the Constructivists' principles of movement, space, and time. From the beginning, De Rivera was interested in using rotation in his sculpture to produce a slow, controlled movement and a changing relationship of forms in space, and to increase and complicate the play of light on the polished metal surfaces. Around 1939 he began making constructions of abstract and simply shaped aluminum sheets painted in primary colors (*Blue and Black*, 1951; New York, Whitney Museum). The other, but related, line of development in De Rivera's work is found in the series of highly polished stainless steel constructions of curvilinear and continuous forms (*Homage to the World of Herman Minkowski*, *c*. 1955, chrome, nickel, and stainless steel, New York, Metropolitan Museum; and *Construction 34*, 1954, chrome, nickel, steel, New York, Grace Borgenicht Gallery).

RIVERS, Larry (b. 1923, New York), American painter and sculptor. Rivers is also known for his poetry, stage design, graphics, and illustrations. A year in Europe (1950), where he carefully observed the work of Bonnard and Soutine, convinced him that the modern painter could still work creatively in a realistic, figurative mode. As an early admirer of Willem de Kooning's Abstract Expressionist style, Rivers was to adapt the latter's spontaneous brushwork and subjective focus to a montagelike combination of images taken from the urban and commercial environment. Indirect suggestions of sociopolitical themes were combined with painterly execution and accomplished draftsmanship in such works as *Washington Crossing the Delaware* (1953; New York, Museum of Modern Art) and the *Dutch Masters Series* (1963; New York, Dwan Gallery), which refer to reproductions of other paintings or commercial trademark images. Portraits of his mother-in-law are notable for their unabashed realism and candidness (*Double Portrait of Birdie*, 1955; New York, Whitney Museum), while works containing popular images and insignia (1954–55 and after 1961) are treated in blurred, multiple views.

By giving banal themes and materials a tactile surface treatment, Rivers offered an alternative to that first independently American style of the 20th century. From 1963 he worked predominantly on constructions, collages, prints, shaped-canvas constructions, and painted figural sculptures. Polemical as well as sentimental motivations remained apparent in his versatile work (*Throwaway Dress: New York to Nairobi*, 1967; New York, Marlborough-Gerson Gallery).

RIZZO, Antonio (*c*. 1430, Verona—after 1499, Foligno, near Perugia), Italian sculptor and architect. He is the outstanding sculptor of the Venetian School in the 15th century. Rizzo worked first at Pavia, where he is recorded in 1465, and sculptured the cornerstones in the great cloister of the Certosa. He then settled in Venice, where, with the assistance of Antonio Bregno, he finished the majestic Foscari portico at the entrance to the Doges' Palace. The Foscari arch (begun by the Buon brothers) bears statues of *Adam* and *Eve* (after 1491) attributed to Rizzo. After the fire of 1483, he was appointed master of the works at the palace, and built the monumental Staircase of the Giants (1491; completed by Pietro Lombardo). His masterpiece, in the Venetian church of S. Maria Gloriosa de' Frari, was the tomb of the Doge Niccolò Tron (1476–before 1483?). Rizzo also executed two other funerary monuments in Venice: the tomb of the Doge Antonio Barbarigo (between 1483 and 1493; convent of the Carità), and the tomb of Giovanni Emo (after 1483) for the convent of S. Maria dei Servi (now dispersed between Vicenza and the Louvre, Paris).

ROBBIA, Luca della (1399/1400, Florence—1482, Florence), Italian sculptor and ceramicist, famed as the inventor of glazed terra cotta, usually of white figures on a blue background but occasionally polychromatic, which became the basis of a flourishing factory production carried on by his nephew Andrea and other members of this Florentine family. The prolific production of this material has somewhat obscured the fact that as a young man he was one of the leading marble sculptors of the Early Renaissance in Florence. His most important marble work is the *Cantoria* (*Singing Gallery*), made for Florence Cathedral between 1431 and 1438. The *Cantoria* consists of music-making angels in relief supported on consoles with additional reliefs between them. Two bronze angels that originally formed part of the *Cantoria* are now in the Musée Jacquemart-André in Paris. The first payment for the *Cantoria* was made in 1431 and the last in 1438; it is therefore clear that Luca's reliefs were being worked on before Donatello made his own *Cantoria* on the opposite side of the cathedral. Luca's figures, like Donatello's, derive from Classical sarcophagi and are firmly and solidly modeled. Most of the rest of Luca's work is in glazed terra cotta: the *Resurrection* and *Ascension* lunettes on the doors of the north and south sacristies of Florence Cathedral and the figures in roundels in the Pazzi Chapel; but the monument to Bishop Federighi in S. Trinita, Florence, has a splendid marble recumbent figure of the bishop, with figures of the dead Christ, the Virgin, and St. John above, and two angels below. This is framed by an enamel terracotta surround of flowers and leaves.

ANDREA (1435, Florence—1525, Florence), Luca's nephew and pupil, continued the production of glazed terra cottas; his best-known works are the *Bambini*, roundels of foundlings, on the façade of Brunelleschi's Spedale degli Innocenti in Florence. His sons included:

GIOVANNI (1469, Florence—1529, Florence), perhaps the most gifted of all, at least in his early work (lavabo in S. Maria Novella, Florence, 1497).

GIROLAMO (1488, Florence—1566, France), after working in the family enterprise, spent the better part of his career in France, where he was employed on the terra-cotta decoration of the châteaux of Madrid in the Bois de Boulogne (*c*. 1527–47) and Fontainebleau (1559–66). He also executed the tombs of Charles IV and Catherine de Médicis at St-Denis (1563–65).

ROBERT, Hubert (1733, Paris—1808, Paris), French painter. He specialized in view paintings of real and imaginary ruins, for which he earned the nickname of *Robert des ruines* ("Robert of the ruins"). Robert was a close friend of Jean-Honoré Fragonard, and in 1761 the two artists toured the region around Naples, making innumer-

Antonio Rizzo. *Eve*. *c*. 1491. Doges' Palace, Venice. *Photo Anderson.*

Luca della Robbia. *Music-Making Angels*. Detail of the Cantoria. 1431–38. Museo dell'Opera del Duomo, Florence. *Photo Alinari-Giraudon.*

Hubert Robert. *Tivoli Gardens.* Musée des Beaux-Arts, Pau. *Photo Giraudon.*

able landscape sketches. During his 11-year sojourn in Italy, Robert became fascinated by the works of the *vedutisti*, particularly Giambattista Piranesi and Giovanni Paolo Pannini. When he returned to Paris in 1765, he was received into the Académie Royale de Peinture et de Sculpture with a *View of Rome from the Port of Ripetta* (1766; Paris, École des Beaux-Arts).

Like Pannini, Robert frequently combined actual architectural or sculptural landmarks with imaginary settings and figures engaged in ordinary activities, but preferable to these are his paintings on the real life of his times, depicting a variety of places (*Pont du Gard*, 1787, Paris, Louvre; *Felling Trees on the Tapis Vert*, 1775, Versailles, Museum). Even more interesting are the visual records he left of the changing scene in 18th-century Paris (*Demolition of the Houses on the Pont Notre-Dame*, 1786, Paris, Musée Carnavalet; *Project for the Rearrangement of the Grande Galerie of the Louvre*, *c.* 1796, Louvre).

Robert's love of parks and gardens, which he so often painted, won him the appointment in 1788 of draftsman to the king's gardens. In this capacity, he planned the grounds at Méréville for the financier Laborde, and was commissioned to transform the copse of the Bains d'Apollon in the gardens at Versailles. He is also remembered as one of the first curators of the Louvre, a post he was awarded in 1784.

ROBERTI, Ercole de' (*c.* 1450, Ferrara—1496, Ferrara), Italian painter. The third artist of genius of the Ferrarese Quattrocento, after Cosimo Tura and his teacher Francesco del Cossa. His originality is already apparent in the series of frescoes (1470) on the Months in the Palazzo Schifanoia at Ferrara, on which Ercole seems to have worked in close collaboration with Cossa. He then followed his master to Bologna, where around 1473 he painted the predella and pilasters of Cossa's Griffoni Altarpiece (Vatican Museum). In this predella Ercole depicted the *Miracles of St. Vincent Ferrer* with stupendously inventive brio and a setting of weird buildings. The same uneasy feeling pervades Roberti's *St. John the Baptist* (Berlin, Staatliche Museen), in which the emaciated prophet stands against a distant seascape. This rather bitter sharpness is relieved in the admirable altarpiece (*Virgin and Child Enthroned with Four Saints*) the artist painted in 1480 for the church of S. Maria in Porto in Ravenna (now in Milan, Brera). Roberti articulated this composition with a new sense of color harmony and balance of light, thus allying himself with the most modern and classicizing Italian artists of the period—Piero della Francesca, Antonello da Messina, and Giovanni Bellini.

Ercole worked in Bologna for the court of the Bentivoglio, painting (*c.* 1480) the companion portraits of *Giovanni II Bentivoglio* and his wife *Ginevra Bentivoglio* (both Washington, D.C., National Gallery). He settled permanently in Ferrara in 1486, where he entered the service of the Este family and succeeded Tura as their official artist. Although his decorative works, like those of Tura, have disappeared, the mastery of his style can be judged from a series (after 1480) of small panels including the *Gathering of Manna* (London, National Gallery), the *Pietà* (Liverpool, Walker Art Gallery), and the *Way to Calvary* (Dresden, Gemäldegalerie). Roberti here attains a combination of ferociousness and bitter serenity unparalleled by his contemporaries.

ROBERTS, David (1796, Stockbridge, near Edinburgh—1864, London), English landscape painter. After working as a painter of backdrops for a traveling circus, Roberts was appointed as a painter of stage sets at Drury Lane in London, later transferring to Covent Garden Opera House. He specialized in architectural subjects, which he treated in a characteristically Romantic style: he was especially fond of depicting picturesque ruins and churches. At his best Roberts had a feeling for space and light similar to that of the 17th-century Dutch painters on whose example many of his works depended. The Victoria and Albert Museum in London houses representative works, in particular the fine *Interior of Milan Cathedral.* Other examples include *Interior of the Cathedral at Burgos* (1835; London, Tate Gallery), *Choir of the Church of St. Paul at Antwerp* (1848; Tate Gallery), and *Sundown over the Cloister of San Onofrio in Rome* (1856; Edinburgh, National Gallery of Scotland).

ROBERTS, William (b. 1895, London), English painter. Having won a London County Council scholarship, he studied at the Slade School of Fine Art from 1910 to 1913, alongside Edward Wadsworth, Stanley Spencer, and Paul Nash. Roberts, who joined Roger Fry's Omega Workshop for a brief period from 1913 to 1914, was fully alive to the new forces, as is evident in such pictures as the *Toe Dancer* (1914; London, Victoria and Albert Museum), although he was never to reject narrative content. He signed the Vorticist Manifesto (1914), and took part in the Vorticist Exhibition at the Doré Galleries (1915). In 1918 he worked as an official war artist, producing the large, morbidly Romantic *First German Gas Attack at Ypres* (Ottawa, National Gallery).

Roberts' style altered little after the early 1920s, by which time he had evolved a highly personal form of Cubism, with its narrative detail, high viewpoint, indeterminate space, and simplified angular treatment of the figure. Typical of his later style are the *Palm Foretells* (1937; Bristol, City Art Gallery), *Hampstead Fair* (1951; Coll. London Transport Board), and the evocative *Vorticists at the Restaurant de la Tour Eiffel: Spring, 1915* (1962; London, Tate Gallery), which includes portraits of Ezra Pound, Wynd-

William Roberts. *The Vorticists at the Restaurant de la Tour Eiffel: Spring 1915.* 1961–62. Tate Gallery, London.

ham Lewis, and Edward Wadsworth.

ROCHE, Eamonn Kevin (b. 1922, Dublin, Ireland), *and* **DINKELOO,** John Gerard (b. 1918, Holland, Michigan), American architects. Roche and Dinkeloo, with others, were brought together by Eero Saarinen in 1950 to complete the costly General Motors Center commission (1948–56) in Warren, Michigan. After Saarinen's death the firm of Eero Saarinen Associates survived until 1966, when Roche and Dinkeloo organized Kevin Roche-John Dinkeloo and Associates in Hamden, Connecticut.

Roche-Dinkeloo, following Saarinen's example, moved away from the universal space containers of the 1950s toward specific spatial solutions based on individual program needs. The steel-and-glass building of the Cummins Engine Company in Darlington, England (1966), however, closely paralleled the work of Mies van der Rohe. The Oakland Museum in California (under construction in 1968) is laid out on layers of profusely planted terraces and courts. The Air Force Museum at Wright-Paterson Air Force Base near Dayton, Ohio, occupies eight acres of exhibition area covered by a suspended steel roof that is supported from four massive pylons. Similar structural boldness was displayed in offices for the Ford Foundation in New York (completed 1967), and for the Knights of Columbus in New Haven, Connecticut (begun 1967).

ROCKLIN, Raymond (b. 1922, Moodus, Connecticut), American sculptor. Rocklin completed his artistic education with a stay in Italy (1952–53), during which he clarified his ideas and moved toward a modern equivalent of the Italian Baroque style. His first one-man show took place at the Tanager Gallery, New York, in 1956, after which he taught for some time at the University of California at Berkeley (1959–60). Rocklin generally worked with sheets of copper or brass, which he cut out and assembled into strange, leafy plant forms (*Battle Hymn of the Republic*, 1957). The edges of the sheets are carefully trimmed into twisted lines so that the separating intervals leave an impression of depth. Although he belonged to the Abstract Expressionist current of American art, his version of the style was softened with his own imaginative feeling.

ROCOCO STYLE. According to the historian Fiske Kimball (*Creation of the Rococo*, 1943), the word Rococo was used in a pejorative sense in painters' studios at the end of the 18th century to describe works of the previous period. In the later, and strict sense, it is applied to the style of ornament that came into vogue around 1730–35. Rococo ornament was characterized by the use of asymmetrical motifs, particularly in cartouches, the interplay of curves and countercurves; and a profusion of detail, particularly shell forms. Fiske Kimball denied that the style's origins were Italian and maintained that it grew naturally out of the arabesques of Jean Bérain the Elder (1639–1711), transformed by Pierre La Pautre, Gilles-Marie Oppenord, and Louis-Claude Vasse (1716–72). This opinion, however, is not generally accepted. Asymmetrical cartouches are frequently found in the work of the Italian Agostino Mitelli (1609–60), and even in that of Gian Lorenzo Bernini. The commonest use of Rococo ornament in architecture was in decorating interior surfaces such as walls and ceilings, while its application to exteriors was confined to such details as decorative keystones. Robert de Cotte was a practitioner of the style, but it was another architect, Germain Boffrand, who produced one of the masterpieces of Rococo interior decoration in the Oval Salon (*c.* 1735–40) at the Hôtel de Rohan-Soubise in Paris.

The historian Hans Sedelmayr divided the development of the Rococo into four phases: a preliminary period at the end of Louis XIV's reign, a second phase under the Regency, a third lasting to the middle of Louis XV's reign, and a final phase covering the end of his reign. This scheme practically equates the Rococo with French art, although Sedelmayr did add that it was only one among many 18th-century styles.

In France, where the Rococo style undoubtedly developed, its most characteristic expression in painting can be found in the work of Antoine Watteau and François Boucher. The first imbued the graceful but merely ingenious arabesque of Bérain with a tender melancholy, indissociable from the elegance of his figures, whose dress seems to be part of their very substance. Boucher's art is less subtle, but he too was fond of such Rococo motifs as shells, coral, and chinoiserie. The courtly genre scenes of Jean-Honoré Fragonard, painted in a light mood, and with a suitably delicate brushstroke, also capture the spirit in which the Rococo style flourished. In sculpture, Jean-Jacques Caffieri's vital modeling illuminated the characters of those who sat for his now famous portrait busts, while the sensitive, fluid forms of Étienne Falconet portrayed the ideal feminine nude, descended from the type introduced by the School of Fontainebleau in the 16th century.

In Lorraine, French Rococo found favorable conditions for expansion: the finest buildings, such as the fragile, ephemeral châteaux of King Stanislas, or the admirable town-planning complex of the Place Stanislas (1752–55) and the Place de la Carrière, Nancy, were all the work of Emmanuel Héré de Corny (1705–63). In Lorraine there are even examples of Rococo religious buildings, which are rare in France: the church of Bon Secours in Nancy (completed 1745) by Héré and the church of St-Jacques at Lunéville (1730–47) by Boffrand.

It would be a mistake to think that the French type of Rococo swept all Europe. Italian Rococo, for example, was an extremely

Rococo Style. Germain Boffrand. Hôtel de Rohan-Soubise, Paris. *c.* 1740. *Photo Verroust.*

Rococo Style. Étienne Falconet. *Bather.* Private Coll., Paris.

Rococo Style. François Boucher. *Madame Bergeret.* 1746. National Gallery of Art, Washington, D.C.

Rococo Style. Jean-François de Cuvilliés. Amalienburg Pavilion in the park surrounding Nymphenburg Palace, Munich. 1734–39. *Photo Helga Schmidt-Glassner.*

brilliant manifestation, almost entirely concentrated in Venice. Like its French counterpart, Venetian Rococo has an all-embracing character; everything fashioned in the style was perfectly integrated into a life as sophisticated as that in France, but less artificial. Venice enjoyed the services of a superb decorative painter, Giambattista Tiepolo, whose great wall and ceiling paintings, exhibiting inventiveness, gay color, vital movement, and spacious atmosphere grace many churches and palaces. The landscapes of Francesco Guardi and Antonio Canale (called Canaletto) have the elegance of Watteau's paintings without his melancholy poetry. In a less elegant vein, the rather stiff, almost clumsy genre pictures of Pietro Longhi go beyond traditional formulas to document, however naively, contemporary Venetian society. Another and quite original style of Rococo appeared in Turin with the decoration of the hunting lodge at Stupinigi by Filippo Juvarra (begun 1729).

Spain seems to have been less hostile to the Rococo than is commonly supposed. Admittedly, it was primarily an art imported from France, entering the country with Philip V and the Bourbon dynasty. The sculpture and garden layout in the park of La Granja and part of that at Aranjuez have a distinctly French flavor. A series of tapestries woven from cartoons by Francisco José de Goya y Lucientes between 1776 and 1780 depict a style of life that could be called Rococo.

Although Latin American Rococo is often difficult to distinguish from Baroque and popular art, churches such as the cathedral of Mexico City, S. Clara at Queretaro, and the Rosary Chapel in S. Domingo at Oaxaca clearly fall within this category. A Latin American whose work reveals French Rococo elements is the extraordinary Brazilian sculptor and decorator Aleijadhino.

England, as usual, was an exceptional case. During the Rococo period, its architecture remained Palladian and painting, however brilliant, returned to the portrait tradition of Sir Anthony van Dyck. The art of Thomas Gainsborough, however, particularly the landscape backgrounds of his portraits, shows considerable French Rococo influence. The painter who perhaps comes closest to the Rococo spirit is William Hogarth, whose treatise on aesthetics (*Analysis of Beauty*, 1753), extols the value of sinuous lines. The Rococo style in English domestic decoration appears in the work of William Vile (d. 1767) and Thomas Chippendale (1718–79), who, in their more elaborate designs for luxury furniture, often containing Gothic or Chinese motifs, were influenced by the French Rococo. The conversation pieces of the painter Johann Zoffany may also be taken as examples of the English Rococo.

The importance of the countries of Central Europe for the history of the Rococo is almost as great as that of France. In these countries, religious art and the art of the court form two distinct currents. Court architecture and decoration drew its inspiration directly from France; in the Rhineland the Elector of Cologne employed the services of Robert de Cotte, and in Bavaria the Elector Maximilian, returning from exile in 1715, brought Josef Effner (1687–1745) with him, a pupil of Boffrand, who organized workshops of French decoration. The principal artist of the elector's successor, Karl Albert, was Cuvilliés, an engraver originally from Hainaut, who published his designs simultaneously in Germany and France. Cuvilliés' decoration covers the Amalienburg pavilion (1734–39) in the park surrounding Nymphenburg Palace in Munich, the Reichen Zimmer ("rich rooms," 1730–37) of the Residenz at Munich, and the marvelous theater in the Residenz, which was inaugurated in 1753 and restored after almost complete destruction during World War II.

Rheno-Franconian Rococo was largely due to an architect of genius, Johann Balthasar Neumann. After 1719 Neumann was in charge of building the Würzburg Residenz, among the most perfect examples of Rococo architecture, with frescoes by Tiepolo along the main staircase. Saxony developed a type of Rococo quite independent of the French version, although its principal architect, Matthäus Daniel Pöppelmann, had visited Paris. His style shows great freedom in the Zwinger at Dresden (1711–22), a sort of precinct for court festivals, surrounded by low galleries with pavilions and onion domes, and embellished with the contorted statues executed by Balthasar Permoser in a style more Baroque than Rococo. In contrast, Prussian Rococo was thoroughly French in character. The style, often referred to as Frederician Rococo, was introduced by the painter Antoine Pesne, whose manner was similar to Watteau's. Its French character is most apparent in the palace of Sanssouci (built 1745–53 by Georg Wenzeslaus von Knobelsdorff), the favorite residence of Frederick the Great, and at the palace of Potsdam (1763–66; since destroyed).

Perhaps the most striking and original art of 18th-century Germany is to be found in the churches. Those erected by the Bavarian architect Johann Michael Fischer were generally decorated by stuccoworkers from the old abbey of Wessobrunn who formed a specialized colony. The genius of German architects, and especially stuccoworkers, lay in using French motifs in a highly plastic, architectural manner. This is apparent in sanctuaries such as

Rococo Style. Johann Ferdinand Dietz. *Mercury*. After 1763. Mainfränkisches Museum, Würzburg. *Photo Gundermann, Würzburg.*

Rococo Style. Johann Michael Fischer. Church at Diessen, near Ammersee. 1732–39. *Foto Marburg.*

Fischer's Ottobeuren (1737–66), as well as in Steinhausen (1727–33) and Die Wies (1746–54), both by Dominikus Zimmermann. From Bavaria the Dientzenhofer family of architects carried the style to Bohemia. The work of these artists, particularly that of Josef Anton Feuchtmayer (1696–1770) and Ignaz Günther (1725–75), is extremely free and graceful and occasionally even comic, as in the stuccowork of Ferdinand Dietz (d. *c.* 1780). The only painter of real genius was Franz Anton Maulbertsch, whose work in Saxon, Hungarian, and Bohemian buildings exhibits a masterly grasp of chiaroscuro. The sculpture of Georg Raphael Donner (1693–1741) combined the force of Venetian Baroque with the gracefulness of Austrian Rococo.

No survey of the Rococo is complete without mentioning a craft that was common to every country—the manufacture of porcelain. After 1709—when Johann Friedrich Böttger (1682–1719) discovered the secret of making porcelain, previously unknown outside China—the process spread throughout Europe. The Meissen factory, the cradle of the industry, was founded in 1710, followed by one at Vienna in 1719, Hoechst in 1749, Berlin in 1750, Frankenthal in 1755, Furstenberg in 1757, Ludwigsburg in 1758, Nymphenburg the same year, and Fulda in 1764. In Italy, the Capodimonte factory was founded in 1743, after which the art was carried to Spain to the Buen Retiro factory in Madrid. In France, Sèvres became a royal factory in 1760, while Chantilly had been active since 1725. Soft-paste porcelain was mainly produced in England, at Chelsea from 1745 to 1784, and at Derby from 1750.

Although magnificent table services were produced by many factories, it is with the production of figurines that one associates the best of Rococo porcelain. Within this realm the two most important Modellmeisters were Johann Joachim Kändler (1706–75) of the Meissen factory and Frans Anton Bustelli (1723–63) of the Nymphenburg factory.

RODCHENKO, Alexander (b. 1891, St. Petersburg), Russian painter, the founder of Non-objectivism. By 1914 he was producing his first abstract pictures, which were composed of strictly geometric designs traced with a compass. When Kasimir Malevich founded Suprematism, Rodchenko tried to surpass the latter movement with his Non-objectivism, which upheld approximately the same principles but which claimed to take them much further. In 1918–19, in answer to Malevich's famous *White Square on a White Background*, Rodchenko painted *Black on Black*, consisting of dark circles. In Moscow later, the two painters confronted each other in an exhibition (1919) devoted to Suprematism and Non-objectivism. Vladimir Tatlin joined Rodchenko and discussed with him the spatial problems that had haunted him. In 1920, when Tatlin was creating his "counter-reliefs" of glass, wire, and metal, Rodchenko developed his spherical "hanging sculptures," which were the first of their kind. Rodchenko's innovations were incorporated into Constructivism by El Lissitzky, Naum Gabo, and Antoine Pevsner. In 1922 he gave up painting and sculpture for industrial design, photography, and typography.

RODIN, Auguste (1840, Paris—1917, Meudon, Seine-et-Oise), French sculptor and draftsman, one of the greatest artists of the 19th century. He belonged to a universal sculptural tradition, and embodied a whole set of aspirations that found their culmination and most powerful expression in his work, which was at once a fervent product of late Romanticism and the herald of modern art. Rodin was as much a realist as Gustave Courbet, but he was akin to the Impressionists in his ability to capture the most fleeting instants of life and to perpetuate their ephemerality in sculptures that live beyond the momentary action they reflect.

In 1854 Rodin joined the free drawing school, later to become the École Nationale des Arts Décoratifs. Horace Lecoq de Boisbaudran (1802–97) taught him drawing and Carpeaux instructed him in modeling. Later, he tried to enter the École des Beaux-Arts, but was refused three times. In 1864 he became an assistant of the sculptor Albert Carrier de Belleuse (1824–87) at the Sèvres porcelain factory, where more skillful work was required of him. Rodin also shared in some of Carrier de Belleuse's

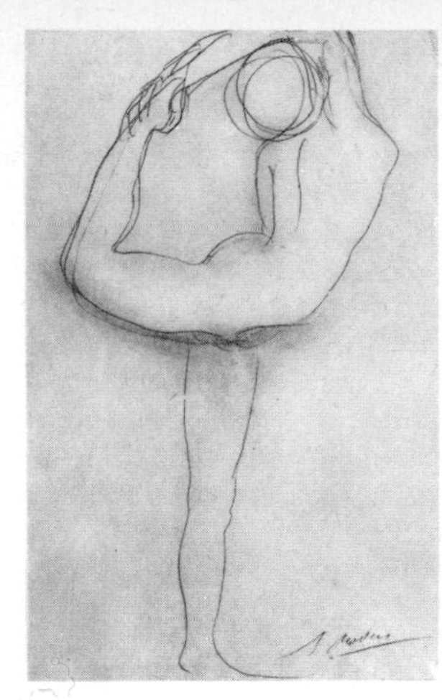

Auguste Rodin. *Crayon study of a dancer.* Musée National Rodin, Paris.

important commissions for decorating such buildings as the Marquise de Païva's house in the Champs-Élysées. In 1864 he sent a work to the Salon for the first time—*Man with a Broken Nose*—but the sculpture was rejected. After the Franco-Prussian War of 1870–71 he went back to his post with Carrier de Belleuse, who had important contracts in Belgium, some of which he entrusted to Rodin. Accordingly, Rodin went to Brussels and stayed there for more than five years (1871–77). Carrier de Belleuse returned to Paris in 1872, and Rodin entered into partnership with the Belgian sculptor Antoine Joseph van Rasbourg (1831–1902), and in that capacity decorated several monuments and buildings in Brussels. These include the Stock Exchange, the Palais des Académies, and several houses on the Boulevard Anspach. In 1875 Rodin went to Italy to study its art, and was particularly influenced by Michelangelo, who helped him to free himself from academicism. The work Rodin sent to the Salon

Auguste Rodin. *The Kiss.* 1886. Musée National Rodin, Paris. *Archives photographiques, Paris.*

of 1877, the *Age of Bronze* (1876), was the target of a lively controversy.

Rodin's supporters became more and more numerous until, in 1880, the Under Secretary of the Ministry of Fine Arts commissioned him to do the door of the Musée des Arts Décoratifs in Paris. This project was the origin of the *Gate of Hell* (1880–1917), a monumental work that occupied Rodin for the rest of his life, and that ultimately included 186 figures. In the *Gate of Hell*, Rodin either gradually incorporated single figures that he had treated independently (*Adam*, 1880; *The Thinker*, 1880; *Paolo and Francesca*, 1887), or withdrew individual subjects (*Lechery*, 1882; the *Prodigal Son*, before 1889) or whole groups (*Fugit Amor*, before 1887; *The Kiss*, 1886) that had originally been conceived as part of the project. The *Gate of Hell* is an extraordinary revelation of the continuity of Rodin's thought and the reflection of an indeflectible purpose within him.

All through his life, in poverty and fame, Rodin worked relentlessly and with unflagging creativity. Every idea immediately took concrete shape and became a living form for him. This probably explains why so many of his works are memorable images in the popular mind: *Eternal Spring* (1884), *La Belle Heaulmière* (c. 1885), *Danaid* (1885), *Eternal Idol* (1889), *Orpheus* (1892), the *Hand of God* (before 1898), *The Secret* (1910), and *The Kiss*, which has already been mentioned. His numerous watercolors communicate the same passionate immediacy as his sculptures. They suggest volume and movement with the economy of a few pencil lines and a few touches of color.

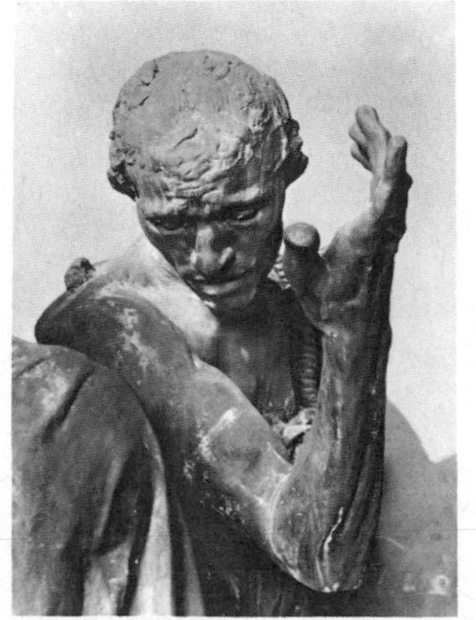

Auguste Rodin. *Pierre de Wiessant.* Detail from the Burghers of Calais. 1884–86. Musée National Rodin, Paris. *Photo Sougez.*

Around 1880 Rodin's life became easier. A young painter, Maurice Haquette, who was a brother-in-law of the Under Secretary at the Ministry of Fine Arts, intervened on Rodin's behalf, with the result that a large studio at the government's marble repository in Rue de l'Université, Paris, was placed at his disposal. For a long time, however, several of Rodin's sculptures caused violent controversies, particularly his *Victor Hugo* (1893) and his famous *Balzac*. It was not until 1939 that the figure was cast in bronze (by private subscription) and placed in a worthy position at the intersection of Boulevard Raspail and Boulevard Montparnasse in Paris. Rodin had better luck with the *Burghers of Calais* (1884–86), commissioned by the municipality of Calais: the monument was finally erected in 1895 in front of the Calais Town Hall. After 1900, when Rodin held an important retrospective exhibition of his work in the Place de l'Alma in Paris, he suddenly became famous and his genius was no longer questioned. In 1916 he bequeathed his works to the French nation; thus, thanks to his legacy, wonderfully complete collections of his work can be seen at the Musée National Rodin (housed in the Hôtel Biron) in Paris or at the Rodin Museum in Meudon. In the United States, the Rodin Museum in Philadelphia, a branch of the Philadelphia Museum of Art, also contains a comprehensive collection of his work.

RODRÍGUEZ TIZÓN, Ventura (1717, Ciempozuelos, near Madrid—1785, Madrid), Spanish Baroque architect. He began training in 1731 at the castle of Aranjuez under the French military engineer Étienne Marchand (d. 1733). However, his subsequent association, which began in 1735, with the Italian architects of the Palacio Real in Madrid—Filippo Juvarra and his pupil and successor, Giovanni Battista Sacchetti—was more important to his development.

At the age of fourteen Rodríguez entered the service of King Philip V as a draftsman in connection with the work on the Palacio Real, Madrid. A pronounced Baroque strain appears in his early drawings, those for the catafalques of Cardinal Molina (1744) and Philip V (1746; Madrid, Museo Municipal), a strain that is even more marked in his architectural designs, in which he infuses the Italian Baroque with a distinctly Spanish flavor. Rodríguez' first major work, the church of S. Marcos in Madrid (1749–53), shows the influence of Juvarra's S. Filippo Neri in Turin (plan 1715?) and of Francesco Borromini's S. Carlino in Rome (1638–41). To the same period belong the ingenious remodeling of the Rococo Pilar church at Saragossa (1750), the church of S. Norberto in Madrid (1754; destroyed), and the uncharacteristically restrained interior decoration for the Church of the Incarnation, also in Madrid (1755).

With the accession of Charles III in 1759, Rodríguez was deprived of his position as palace architect and released from the royal retainership he had held for 28 years. For the second half of his career he was forced to depend for his livelihood on minor commissions and teaching at the Real Academia de Nobles Artes, Madrid.

In their simplicity and strict functionalism, the works of this second period (1759–85) are comparable to those of Juan de Herrera. More important to Rodríguez, however, was the new, functionalist architectural theory already spread abroad in France and Italy by Carlo Lodoli (1690–1761) and Jacques-François Blondel. He was by no means dogmatic in following theory, however, as is evident in his convent for the Agustinos Filipinos at Valladolid (1760), which owes something to Bonavia's S. Antonio chapel; in his highly functionalist Barcelona Royal College of Surgeons (1761), with its stark exterior; in his graceful palace for his protector, the Infante Don Luis, at Baodilla del Monte, near Madrid (before 1776); and in his façade for Pamplona Cathedral (1783), in which he gave full vent to his feeling for antiquity on a massive scale.

ROGERS, Isaiah (1800, Marshfield, Massachusetts—1869, Cincinnati, Ohio), American architect. Rogers, together with Alexander Parris and Solomon Willard (1783–1861), dominated Boston architecture after Bulfinch's departure for Washington. But much of Rogers' life was spent outside of Boston: in New

York, Washington (as supervising architect of the Treasury Department), and Cincinnati. His first major work was the Tremont House in Boston (1828–29). This was a radical departure in hotel design, initiating a new standard of luxury and functional planning, as well as technological innovations like indoor plumbing. Built in the Greek Revival style, the Tremont House nevertheless showed Rogers' independence of stock formulas. It won him acclaim, and a series of commissions for increasingly grand hotels, including the Bangor House at Bangor, Maine (1832) and the St. Charles in New Orleans (1851). The most famous of all was the Astor House in New York (1832–36). While in New York, he designed perhaps his greatest work, the Merchants' Exchange (1836–42). This rectangular block, with its monumental Ionic colonnade and impressive recessed porch, masks a grand and unexpected interior rotunda. In buildings such as the Bank of America in New York (1835), as well as Brazer's in Boston (*c.* 1842), Rogers handled the vocabulary of Romantic Classicism imaginatively, and brought a new grandeur to the streets of American cities.

ROHNER, Georges (b. 1913, Paris), French painter. He trained under Lucien Simon (1861–1945) at the École des Beaux-Arts in Paris, and with Robert Humblot (1907–62) was a founder member of the Forces Nouvelles group. Simon, Humblot, and Rohner were among the painters who, about 1935–36, contributed to a type of realistic art in which style was disciplined to the point of asceticism, and purely plastic values were of primary importance. Rohner carried the style further than anyone else in the group (*Christ Meeting the Prisoners*, 1941). Classical purity and restraint take on a modern touch of the bizarre in his still lifes, where the extreme realism sometimes verges on pure fantasy, and in such symbolical compositions as the *Tiber Valley* (1967). His ability to manipulate space pictorially is shown in *Kitchen Dish Cloth*, in which a towel appears suspended in mid-air.

ROMAN ART. In recognition of the diversity of artistic expressions that existed under that epithet, separate articles shall cover the Roman art produced in the East, Africa, and the West. In this way, due importance can be given to the influences of the diverse sources of origin. After a long period during which Roman art had subsisted on nothing but borrowings, that city had a part to play in adapting such forms and structures, in architecture particularly, to Roman needs and ways of thought; in later centuries, all Europe drew inspiration from that style.

From the start, Rome was wedged between two peoples with very original artistic styles—the Etruscans to the north and the Greeks to the south. The people of Latium borrowed from their neighbors the few elements they required to make life agreeable, since their own society of peasants, soldiers, and priests lacked that class of craftsmen from which artists arise. If under the monarchy Rome enjoyed a period of brilliance, it was due entirely to the Etruscans: the Romans' adoption of Etruscan art is proved by the scanty archaeological remains, and suggested by Livy's account. It is not by chance that the first artists known in Rome were Etruscans and Greeks. Among the former was the sculptor Vulca (late 6th century B.C.), whose Capitoline Jupiter was enthroned in the cella of the temple dedicated to that most venerable Roman deity; the temple itself was even built on the Etruscan plan. Among the Greek artists were Damophilos and Gorgasos, who in the early 5th century B.C. painted the walls of the temple dedicated to Dionysus, Demeter, and Core.

ARCHITECTURE

General Characteristics

It was not until the time of Augustus that the Roman spirit sought new forms of artistic expression that were based on motifs borrowed from the Hellenic tradition, but adapted and modified to suit a new civilization. However, the situation was not the same in architecture, which began to adapt itself to peculiarly Roman ways of seeing at least two centuries earlier.

Roman architecture was primarily urban in nature: the very power of Rome required for its expansion the development of cities. From that point of view it is easy to understand certain traditional aspects of the typical Roman city plan, which cannot be explained solely as a solution to military concerns nor linked to the original elements of the military camp. That plan is based on a rectangular division of the site, in which the grid has its axes along the cardo and the decumanus, and forms the fundamental nucleus. Within the network, practical rather than aesthetic considerations determined the place that was set aside for several large groups of monuments. The forum was laid out along one of the axes in such a way as to facilitate easy circulation and at the same time to give the capitol and basilica a space large enough to allow them a monumental situation. The theater constituted another point of attraction; its role was presented particularly clearly in the imperial cities of Lepcis Magna and Sabratha (both in Tripolitania).

In their encounter with other civilizations, the Romans sought to give a grandiose and monumental expression to their new sense of power and were able to derive something fresh from traditional techniques and forms. It is entirely characteristic that it was the most Roman of Romans, Cato the Elder, who decided on his return from Greece in 184 B.C. to build the first great basilica in the Forum (called the Basilica Porcia after his family name).

It is interesting to note how the Romans first brought originality to their architecture and transformed the tradition they inherited. They used Hellenistic methods of construction, but profoundly modified them in two respects. The systematic use of the modular principle had impoverished Hellenistic architecture, but the architects themselves had never broken with the Classical conception that form expressed structure, and that the former should not become a secondary or ornamental feature. So it was a revolutionary change when Roman architects separated form from structure. Their practical and economical sense led them first to

Roman Art. *Capitoline Wolf.* Wolf, early 5th century B.C., Etruscan; figures of the twins Romulus and Remus added during Renaissance. Museo dei Conservatori, Rome.

Roman Art. Canopus. Hadrian's Villa, Tivoli. A.D. 125–135. *Photo Yvan Butler, Geneva.*

turn their attention exclusively to structure, with no regard for aesthetic considerations. Thus economical techniques were rapidly developed; mortared masonry replaced large blocks shaped to fit, pilasters came more into fashion, and, most important, there was wide use of vaulting, undoubtedly learned from their Etruscan neighbors. The traditional forms and motifs inherited from the Greeks were applied to the structure only afterward as ornaments, and this led to the development of the decorative orders (Ionic and especially Corinthian), applied columns, sham pediments, and revetments, of marble, stucco, or plaster; the last alternative was the determining factor in the development of wall painting. The spread of rapid and economical building methods opened up extraordinary possibilities of handling great masses.

Roman Art. Arch of Constantine, Rome. A.D. 312–315. *Photo Leonard von Matt, Buochs.*

Such great Romans as Sulla, Pompey, and Caesar had a feeling for the architectural expression of political power, and in this they were understood by their architects, who even went so far as to modify the shape of the landscape to increase the monumental effect. The Tabularium at Rome was an example of this, as were the Temple of Fortuna at Praeneste (Palestrina) and the Forum of Trajan at Rome. The result was a new architectural conception, with the building no longer respecting the landscape but dominating it. This new spirit was manifest in the palaces on the Palatine, at Hadrian's Villa in Tivoli, in the gardens and parks that enlivened the towns, and even in the style of wall paintings.

A few examples will suffice to show the profound transformation in architecture brought about by the Romans.

Architectural Types

The first type of building in the Forum to be adapted to the commercial and judicial needs of the Roman citizenry was the basilica. In the early 2nd century B.C., first the Basilica Porcia and then the Basilica Aemilia enhanced the monumental character of the Roman Forum. The basilican plan was divided internally into three or five aisles separated by colonnades; the two central rows of columns supported an attic that was higher than the side aisles and whose windows illuminated the whole building. Terminal apses provided the area for the tribunals; on the exterior of the longer sides there was sometimes a portico, or else shops reminiscent of the tabernae in which merchants formerly conducted business. The Basilica Ulpia in Trajan's Forum is the masterpiece of this type; it derived even greater emphasis from its position in the ensemble designed by Apollodorus of Damascus: around it were large areas bounded by porticoes laid out in subtle rhythms of curves and straight lines.

The first great architectural ensembles date from the time of Sulla (late 2nd–early 1st century B.C.). In the first place, there was the Tabularium at Rome, which joined the two hills of the Capitol with its high three-story façade some 230 feet long, and formed a magnificent backdrop for the Forum. It consisted of a massive substructure crowned by two galleries, the first with arcading above pilasters decorated with Doric half-columns, and the second with a more open Corinthian colonnade. But the Temple of Fortuna at Praeneste (*c.* 80 B.C.) was the real masterpiece of this landscape-dominating type of architecture. A pyramid of steps, terraces, and covered ramps, including a semicircular esplanade surrounded by porticoes, was dominated by the imposing mass of the round temple. All the buildings were arranged with strict symmetry along a vertical axis that passed through the center of the rotunda. The shrine of Jupiter at Terracina and that of Hercules at Tivoli showed the same intention, but they were simpler in conception. The introduction of niches in buttressing walls, of which a good example is the large portico of Herodes Atticus on the southern flanks of the Athenian Acropolis, was part of this taste for movement, for a rhythmic vibration of space.

By the emperor's own will, the age of Augustus (27 B.C.–A.D. 14) marked an end to the architecture of prestige and splendor; the role of art was indeed to glorify the ruler and his family, but it was pervaded by a sense of proportion and Classical simplicity. Among the buildings that belonged to this period were the first state of the Pantheon in Rome (27 B.C.), the Temple of Augustus and Livia at Vienne, the Maison Carrée at Nîmes (16 B.C.), the Pont du Gard near Nîmes, and several fine town gates in Italy and Gaul. At Rome, Augustus continued work on the Forum of Caesar and built the palace on the Palatine. In the

Roman Art. Mausoleum of Hadrian (now Castel Sant' Angelo), Rome. A.D. 132–139. *Photo Leonard von Matt, Buochs.*

Roman Forum, the temple of Mars Ultor (2 B.C.)—which was of marble, something quite new—was surrounded simply by a portico; everything else was sacrificed for the sake of a gallery of ancestral portraits of the dynasty, placed in half circles and niches. The plan of temples, placed on a podium and with prostyle façade and engaged columns, as well as the style of decorative detail, and the Corinthian type of column that was used at this time all derived from Hellenistic tradition and have a boldness and richness that are related to Pergamene art. However, it is perhaps in triumphal arches that the plastic quality of Augustan architecture comes out most clearly. The slender and harmonious arch of Susa in Piemonte (9 B.C.) is one of the masterpieces of this type, with its single, well-proportioned arch opened in the massive rectangular structure ornamented with marble revetments imitating the Classical orders. Subsequent triumphal arches, perhaps imitating town gates, became decidedly larger and came to include three vaulted passageways, while the decoration was much more elaborate; but the elegance and delicacy of the arch of Susa was never recaptured.

The interest in creating a harmonious relationship between architecture and nature did not diminish, however, and Augustus, like his contemporaries, was a great admirer of carefully arranged gardens. Pompey (106–48 B.C.) built a portico on the Campus Martius, and Agrippa (63–12 B.C.) added another that opened onto a huge garden filled with statues and bordered by baths and by the Euripos, in which the youth of Rome came to bathe. These vast open areas contrasted sharply with the urban "landscape" of imperial Rome, whose buildings began to be built taller as a result of the growth in population. The tall urban dwellings of five or six stories were entered through one or two narrow doorways that opened onto dark stairways. The windows upstairs were sometimes given balconies, whose projection was regulated by town laws. The same type of house was built in the great provincial towns.

In the 2nd century A.D., with the reigns of Trajan and Hadrian, the monumental possibilities of Roman architecture were exploited in grandiose works that reflected the might of the Empire. The first of these monuments were at Rome, but later the Severan emperors erected the most splendid and powerful of them in the provinces, in Tripolitania and Libya. At Rome, the final stage of the Pantheon, the Forum of Trajan designed by Apollodorus of Damascus, as well as Hadrian's Villa at nearby Tivoli, his mausoleum at Rome (A.D. 132–139), and later, the Baths of Caracalla, are all elaborate, skillful, and varied creations in which surfaces and volumes are enclosed and broken up to form an endless variety of compositions. Hadrian's Villa (*c.* A.D. 125–138) is a veritable encyclopedia of Roman architectural themes and forms in its lavish array of baths, porticoes, and halls, to which are joined all other elements. For strict composition and sure handling of space, perhaps nothing excells the great Baths of Caracalla (*c.* A.D. 215), buildings that fulfilled perfectly both the practical requirements of urban public life and the 3rd-century A.D. emperors' taste for ostentation.

The constancy in Roman architecture is still conspicuous in one of the last great works of imperial architecture, Diocletian's palace at Spalato (early 4th century A.D.), which is enclosed in a quadrilateral extending some 594 feet along the Adriatic and just over 700 feet inland. It was first and foremost a military fortification, with a square tower at each corner and round towers on either side of the gates; the interior is divided in the manner of a camp, by two perpendicular axes, with military installations occupying an important area. Along the shore, on the south, the living quarters were arranged as well as the shrines of divinities and a funerary *heroon*. The capacity of Roman architects to plan and master space produced felicitous results in other buildings, too: the Pantheon at Rome, with its great dome, and the theaters of Orange in the West (early 1st century A.D.), Aspendus in the East (*c.* A.D. 165), and Sabratha in Africa (early 3rd century A.D.) are all, with slight variations, based on the same fundamental concept of a great semicircular sweep contrasted with an imposing rectangular façade backing the stage. The great amphitheaters of elliptical plan, uniquely constructed of closed curves (early 1st century A.D.)—the Colosseum at Rome (A.D. 72–80), and the arenas at Arles and Nîmes—are sometimes heavy but always imposing and a credit to Roman powers of building.

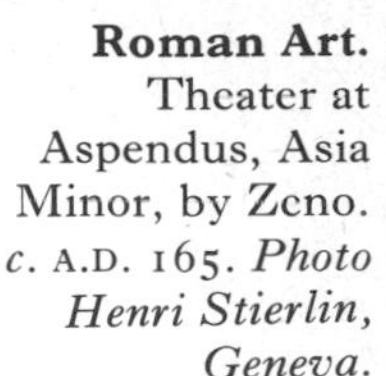

Roman Art. Theater at Aspendus, Asia Minor, by Zeno. *c.* A.D. 165. *Photo Henri Stierlin, Geneva.*

SCULPTURE

Portraits

A practical spirit and taste for naturalism, combined with particular religious requirements, favored the development of portraiture. As in architecture, both the style and the artists came from Etruria, where a tradition of funerary effigies of astounding lifelikeness was still active in the 2nd century B.C. The Romans also liked to record a dead man's features, sometimes even in the very realistic form of the death mask, and so they were quite ready

Roman Art. Colosseum, or Flavian amphitheater, Rome. A.D. 72–80. *Photo Leonard von Matt, Buochs.*

Roman Art. Statue of Augustus from Prima Porta. Detail. *c.* 20 B.C. Vatican Museum. *Photo Leonard von Matt, Buochs.*

to make use of that type of statue; indeed, there is often no perceptible difference between an Etruscan and a Roman portrait. Another source was Greece, where there was a tradition of portraiture from the 4th century B.C. The influence of the Hellenistic tradition persisted in Roman portraiture through the last years of the Republic, although the best works of that period betrayed the intense individuality and powerful personality of the sitter. The portraits of Pompey, Cicero, and Caesar reveal the emphatic characteristics of those historical personalities, particularly the sharp features, bony facial structure, hard, closed lips, and great eyes under a bare forehead. Certain portraits of Caesar are the incarnate expression of the determination, ambition, and love of power that motivated the conqueror of Gaul.

In the Augustan age, the classic taste that led to a search for generalization in architecture also modified the expression of any excessive individuality in the numerous portraits of the emperor that were made at various stages of his life, and in those of his family. The standing portrait in the Louvre, signed by Cleomenes, is a good example of such idealization; the emperor's face is represented in the guise of Mercury, and only a few details, such as the hair, the wrinkles at the bridge of the nose, and the shape of the mouth give individuality to the figure.

Roman Art. *Procession of priests and senators.* Bas-relief from the Ara Pacis. 13–9 B.C. Uffizi, Florence.

After the time of Augustus, portraiture wavered between these two tendencies; the taste for realism and the picturesque often dominated when it was not modified by a Classical revival. The age of Hadrian produced fine portraits: the image was systematically pared down to essentials, and the dry, clear, vigorous style brought out the structure of the face by supporting and placing every element very precisely. Thereafter, technique came to be neglected, and in the numerous portraits of the 3rd and 4th centuries A.D. a roughness and tendency to simplify were meant to make up for this.

Museums are crowded with Roman statuary, but the works of real originality are few. Greek originals brought to Rome at the time of the Republic were copied over and over, gaining nothing in the process. Even when they had a precise commission to fulfill, Roman sculptors were easily satisfied to copy a Greek type and dress it in a toga, limiting their original work to the head. Rare are such statues as the Augustus from Prima Porta (*c.* 20 B.C.; Vatican Museum), which has a strong originality. The emperor is represented standing and wearing a breastplate; his *paludamentum* is gathered around his body and draped over his left arm, while his right arm is outstretched as though to mark the beginning of a speech. The stance is that of 5th-century B.C. athletes, with the weight on the right leg, the left extended behind and resting on the very tip of the toes. However, the sculptor was not at all interested in these problems of pose, but only in the creation of a historical personage. The breastplate is completely covered with figures symbolizing the power of the young emperor and master of the world. In a way that was typically Roman, the historic moment is identified by the scene represented on the breastplate: the Parthian king is shown handing back to Tiberius the eagles captured from the legions of Crassus and Antony.

Historical Reliefs

The use of a work of art as a historic document was a practice congenial to the Roman temperament; thus the historical relief was another original element in Roman sculpture. As early as the 4th century B.C., Roman victories were celebrated in pictures; during the 3rd century B.C. the practice developed of carrying in the triumphal procession accorded a conquering general a number of paintings of the main episodes in his victorious campaign. When sculpture came to be used as a decorative adjunct to architecture, such scenes of military life were carved in relief, and later scenes of civilian life were similarly treated. One of the finest and earliest examples was the Ara Pacis ("Altar of Peace") erected by Augustus at Rome in 13 B.C. (dedicated in 9 B.C.), on his return from conquering provinces in the East, Spain, Gaul, and on the Rhine. The building was of modest proportions, the substructure measuring about 38 by 34 feet. A wall with openings on the east and west surrounded the altar and was decorated with reliefs whose themes were those that were being celebrated simultaneously in the poems of Horace and Virgil. On the longer sides was represented an official procession of the people and their magistrates paying homage to the goddess of peace. The reliefs on either side of the portals recorded mythological and allegorical themes connected with the founding of Rome.

By borrowing from the style of pictorial reliefs, historical ones rapidly evolved as a more realistic and more complete form of expression. The illusionist style that was also found in painting made a more varied representation possible and, most important, introduced pictorial elements into what had previously been a mere neutral ground against which the figures moved in procession in the manner of Greek art. A freedom in the choice of poses, the introduction of such natural elements as trees and houses, and an accentuation of the model all gave depth to the ground, enabling the figures to be spaced more freely within it. Once sculptors mastered this new technique suitable for representing the various scenes and places of the emperor's exploits, they developed the practice of integrating reliefs into various types of monuments, particularly triumphal arches. An original scheme was adopted for Trajan's Column (A.D. 113) and used again for that of Marcus Aurelius (*c.* A.D. 180): the scenes follow one another in a spiral around the column, making it possible to represent all the aspects of a campaign or a conquest.

PAINTING

The divorce between architectural form and structure and the taste for superimposed ornament favored the development of wall painting to the point where it became an essential feature of architecture, particularly of the Roman house. The two conceptions of the three-dimensional quality of the house and the decorative role of the wall painting were never separated. The town of Pompeii provides splendid illustrations of this fact, and therefore a discussion of Roman painting is reserved to the article on Pompeian Art.

Roman Art in Africa. Ruins of Timgad, Algeria. Founded A.D. 100 by Trajan. Foreground: Arch of Trajan. Rear: Theater, and to its left, the Forum. *Photo Ray-Delvert.*

ROMAN ART IN AFRICA. While Roman art in the capital tended to rigidify due to an increasing reliance upon academic formulas, that of the provinces was often enriched and invigorated by contact with a relatively unsophisticated native tradition. This is true, to varying degrees in the several arts, of the North African provinces. The Romans encouraged the existing agricultural economy, and since this was often dependent upon the use of waterworks, many reservoirs and aqueducts remain. Roman urban constructions in these regions are among the best-preserved and the most numerous in the empire. Where new cities were founded, either independently or alongside existing ones, the Roman axial rectangular plan was used. Public buildings—including a basilica, temple, and curia—were grouped around the porticoed forum. The basilica, an elongated rectangle, often had its apse on the longitudinal side. The curia might assume a simple rectangular form (Thamugadi) or a temple form (Lepcis Magna). Temples themselves were either of Italo-Roman design, built on a high podium—sometimes unusually so—or of a regional type in which the old Punic divinities were worshiped under the guise of Roman names. Baths on the Roman model were extremely common, arranged on a central axis with identical rooms on either side including the piscina, frigidarium, and caldarium. These were often magnificently decorated with sculpture, paintings, and mosaics. Theaters again are in the Italic-Roman tradition, although their monumental scale may be judged by the fact that temples and sanctuaries were often included within their precincts.

The great architectural ensembles from the time of the Severi at Lepcis Magna are the finest expressions of this rich and vigorous style. To an old native town of twisting narrow streets in which no element stood out clearly, Septimius Severus added a forum and basilica as the main features of a monumental scheme. The forum, the arches of whose portico rested directly on Corinthian capitals, served to frame a great temple raised on a podium at one end of it; at the other end the forum was filled by a monumental basilica based on the same scheme as that built in the Forum of Trajan at Rome by Apollodoros of Damascus and imitated in other provinces—especially Gaul.

ROMAN ART IN THE EAST. *See* **GRECO-ROMAN ART IN THE MIDDLE EAST.**

ROMAN ART IN THE WEST. The encounter of the Greco-Roman Classical tradition with the styles, beliefs, customs, and social organization of each large province stimulated the growth of local styles that expressed native conceptions through the adaptation of Classical formulas. In the West, in spite of local variations, the Gallo-Roman civilization stretching from the Rhine to Spain had a true unity.

Though the Celts were familiar for centuries with Mediterranean art, they adopted neither its forms nor its spirit. It seems to have been architecture, introduced along with the urban way of life imposed by the victors, that opened the eyes of the Gauls to plastic values. The Gauls seem to have been quick to appreciate the practical and aesthetic value of the durable stone architecture that took the place of their primitive wood and daub huts. They soon developed a taste for mass and volume, as the Roman builders erected arches, monumental gates, and temples in their land. And they erected buildings in which the elements of Classical architecture were adapted to serve native needs and beliefs. The shrine at Sanxay (near Poitiers), the so-called Temple of Janus at Autun, the Moulin du Fâ near Royan, and the ensemble at Petinesca in Switzerland all show the skill of these apprentice builders and the use they made of foreign formulas. The type of temple they built had a cella that was square, hexagonal, or round, neatly arranged on one or two levels; this central element was surrounded by a gallery, generally with a portico, supported against the cella walls.

In the new cities of Gaul, which were often laid out on the same regular plan as the cities of Italy, the monumental groups of the forum and theater were given their functional places. But here, too, the Gallo-Romans modified traditional schemes. An original type of forum found both at Paris and at Alesia (Alise-Ste-Reine), in which there was a court with porticoes, a basilica, and a shrine for divinities, became common in the 2nd century A.D. The plan of the theater was also modified. A complete

Roman Art in the West. Amphitheater, Nîmes. Early 1st century A.D. *Photo Yan, Toulouse.*

type, unlike the great Provençal theaters of Orange, Arles, and Vaison, and which was a cross between a theater and an amphitheater, began to spread through central and northern Gaul at the time of Augustus. The *cavea* was like that of an amphitheater in that it was more than a semicircle; but some of the stage buildings adopted from the theater were fitted into the elliptical shape of the amphitheater. It was mainly in the 2nd century A.D. that large architectural groups began to appear within the urban complexes, in the form of baths and palaces. The clearest expression of this trend is preserved in the baths at Trier, whose regular, symmetrical plan is skillfully contrived to allow for the harmonious association of the various functional elements in this vast building. Its basilica later held an important place in the development of Christian architecture. The Porta Nigra (A.D. 313–316), in the same town, also attested the Gauls' feeling for monumentality, which had been rather timidly set forth in the earlier gateways at Autun (early 1st century A.D.).

Perhaps the originality of the Gallo-Romans is best seen in their funerary architecture, in which they skillfully adapted and modified foreign elements, some of which came from provinces at the very eastern end of the Empire. The well-known monument of the Julii (Caius and Lucius Caesar) at St-Rémy in Provence (*c.* A.D. 5) and, on a smaller scale, the pillars that once stood at Neumagen, on the Mosel (2nd and 3rd centuries A.D.), recall the style of Roman Syria. Spain remained faithful to the massive, round mausoleum type such as was erected in Rome on the Via Appia, and in the African provinces. Germany, on the other hand, built such monuments as those at Igel and Neumagen (3rd century A.D.), which undoubtedly bore the influence of an Orientalizing tradition.

The Greco-Roman tradition does not seem to have succeeded in giving Gallo-Roman sculptors a new sense of form. The traditional taste of the Celtic clientele led them to prefer funerary and votive reliefs. The sarcophagi at Arles stand comparison with the best Italian work. Even outside of Provence and the Rhône valley, works were produced that show an exacting sense of the proper balance of mass and volumes, and a good knowledge of anatomy and the play of the muscles of a body in motion; such a work is the splendid mythological frieze in the museum at Sens. But most of these were the work of foreign artists who came in numbers in the wake of the Roman legions. Native sculpture showed the usual strong tendency toward linearity and lack of volume, with juxtaposed figures that stood out very little from the background. At the beginning of the 4th century, when Roman influence weakened, native traditions reasserted themselves. Portraiture developed in certain western regions, particularly in Spain, where the official art did not kill the very powerful realist style that produced a fine group of portraits of private citizens.

A strong sense of form was evident in works made by craftsmen rather than by artists, such as the vases of terra sigillata whose ornament was stamped on by molds. This type of pottery was at first imported from Italy, the district around Arezzo in particular; but it soon became a speciality of Gallic workshops and spread continually from the south to the north. Mythological themes and scenes of daily life appeared along with a great variety of decorative motifs that were often peculiar to particular potters, whose names have been preserved in signatures stamped in the clay. They provide useful material for a study of the decorative talent of the Gallo-Romans. In the western part of the Empire, mosaic production flourished. While certain regions—Spain, for example (Ampurias and Barcelona)—based their first works in the 1st century A.D. on Italian examples, Gaul and Germany (Trier) had their own workshops and tended more toward geometric than floral decoration, with sober colors. Mosaics of quality and diversity continued to be popular until the 4th century A.D.

ROMANESQUE ART. The term "Romanesque" was coined about 1825, after the term "Gothic," and it is just as misleading, but it has been firmly established by usage. In this article two distinct periods will be considered: the Carolingian period, sometimes called pre-Romanesque, which includes the late 8th and all the 9th and 10th centuries, and the Romanesque period proper, which covers all of the 11th century and a major part of the 12th.

ARCHITECTURE

Carolingian Religious Architecture

In most buildings of this period the early basilican plan was retained, but with modifications that affected three parts of the church, one of which was the choir and apses. The principal apse increased in size, especially in monastic churches, and the choir, which had to accommodate a large community of monks, was frequently lengthened by one bay. Absidioles, or subsidiary apses, were added to the right and left of the central apse and opening onto the aisles of the nave. Another innovation, which did not appear until the last quarter of the 10th century, was the ambulatory, a semi-circular gallery surrounding the choir. The second modification that occurred was the addition of a transept. The third change was the introduction of a narthex. This was not a new invention, but a feature inherited from Classical Greece that was employed with increasing frequency after the year 1000.

Besides buildings on a basilican (rectangular) plan, there were also Carolingian structures of central and radiating plan—circular, square, and polygonal. Here again, throughout the Empire the emphasis was on the imitation of Classical and Eastern models; moreover, that imitation was imperfect as a result of deficient technique. The builders always used small units of masonry, either stone or brick. In churches of rectangular plan the roofing was of timber except in the apses. Use was made of materials salvaged from older buildings; as these became increasingly rare, missing columns were often replaced by piers, or columns and piers were alternated. Examples of this kind of imitation and reconstruction are found in two sanctuaries on a central plan, the Palatine Chapel (or Minster) and the oratory at Germigny-des-Prés (Loiret). The chapel at Aachen, called the Palatine because it belonged to the Imperial palace, was built on an octagonal plan by the architect Eudes of Metz, between A.D. 792 and 805. The octagonal central space, marked out by massive piers connected by semicircular arches, was surrounded by an annular aisle.

Built in A.D. 806 for Theodulph, bishop of Orléans from A.D. 798 to 818, the oratory at Germigny-des-Prés was completely restored in the 19th century. The original plan, however, is known: four piers at the corners of a square central space supported a dome and were connected by four arches that opened onto four small barrel-vaulted galleries, each ending in an apse.

Few Carolingian churches survive, and these have been entirely restored or partly rebuilt. Among them are Vaison Cathedral (Vaucluse), with its three Carolingian horseshoe apses; Notre-Dame-de-la-Couture at Le Mans; and the crypts of St-Aignan at Orléans (begun *c.* 1018) and of St-Savinien at Sens. Outside France are S. Satiro in Milan (A.D. 876), which, like Germigny-des-Prés, reflects Armenian models; and, in Catalonia, the churches at Tarrasa (9th century A.D.).

Romanesque Religious Architecture

At the turn of the 10th and 11th centuries an immense number of churches were built in which are apparent several characteristics of Romanesque art. In France, the long period of unrest and misery during the last reigns of the Carolingian dynasty was followed by happier times, toward the end of the 10th century, and a number of churches were consecrated or founded before the year A.D. 1000. St-Bénigne at Dijon, of which nothing remains but the lower floor of the rotunda, was not founded until A.D. 1001, under Abbot William of Volpiano (A.D. 989–1017). But in Paris, the rebuilding of St-Germain-des-Prés under Abbot Morard was quite certainly undertaken before the year 1000. The influence of Benedictine abbeys, which grew in strength during the 11th century, had begun to assert itself in the mid-10th century. The abbey church of Cluny, erected by the coadjutor St. Mayeul between A.D. 955 and 981, already conformed to the "Benedictine plan" of a choir opening into the side aisles, which were continued beyond the transept. In Roussillon, St-Michel-de-Cuxa was consecrated in A.D. 974. At St-Trophîme in Arles (later altered) the transept was vaulted about A.D. 952.

These churches had for the most part a very simple plan, comprising a single nave, or a nave and two aisles ending in three apses—the cella and two absidioles—and had neither transept nor narthex (St. Pierre at Cassrès, Catalonia, *c.* 1006; Saorge, Alpes-Maritimes, 11th century). Methods of construction remained those of the Carolingian period. Exterior decoration, when it was applied at all, was reduced to a series of flat vertical strips: ornamental, not functional, they covered the wall with light and dark stripes connected under the eaves by a pattern of small arches forming a blind arcade.

These strips are known as Lombardic pilasters; the architecture of this period is called Lombardic because it first appeared in northern Italy in the 8th century A.D., and no doubt also because of the reputation of Lombard masons—notably the *comacini*—who were in great demand in many parts of the West. The Lombardic style covered northern and central Italy, the south and east of France (Provence, the Rhône valley, and Burgundy), Catalonia, and Dalmatia; it even took root later in eastern Europe but did not spread to the north or the Atlantic seaboard.

The pre-Romanesque, or First Romanesque, period was mostly concerned with the imitation of earlier models, and its architecture retained a cosmopolitan and imperial character. This preparatory phase was fruitful, not only because of the sheer number of buildings that proliferated both before and after the year A.D. 1000, but also because of their diversity, which was the result of a first tentative attempt to free art from Carolingian uniformity and to create a new style. In Auvergne, a regional style began to emerge about the mid-10th century in monuments that had in common enough traits found only among themselves to warrant their being identified as a group. The old cathedral of Clermont-Ferrand (of which only the crypt survives), consecrated in A.D. 946, contained one of the first examples of a chevet with the ambulatory opening onto

Romanesque Art. Carolingian oratory at Germigny-des-Prés. A.D. 806. *Archives photographiques, Paris.*

Romanesque Art. Palatine Chapel, Aachen. Carolingian period, A.D. 792–805. *Foto Marburg.*

radiating chapels. This type of chevet appeared at the end of the same century in Touraine, as well as in Maine and Orléanais. On the other hand, Catalan architecture showed tendencies characteristic of its own Romanesque style. Lombardy and Burgundy, too, had found styles of their own.

The decisive step was taken in the course of the 11th century. While stylistic elements evolved toward their final forms, technical progress brought about important changes in the design and construction of churches. The art of dressing stone, which had been lost for a long time, was revived, so that vaulting, previously confined to apses, became increasingly common in naves. The abbey church of St-Philibert at Tournus, begun about A.D. 950, had a nave covered with a wooden roof, which was not replaced by a vault until the 11th century. The situation was also helped by improved methods of transport. As long as waterways were almost the only really practicable arteries, each province was restricted to its own resources, and therefore nature dictated the manner of construction and even the style of building. But the rapid progress made during the 11th century in the training of horses and oxen for draft work reduced this dependence considerably. Thus Flanders, lacking stone and limited to the use of brick, became able to avail herself of Boulonnais limestone.

Romanesque Art. Abbey church of St-Philibert, Tournus. *c.* 960–1120. *Photo Jean Roubier, Paris.*

General Characteristics of the Romanesque Church

Because of the diversity among surviving monuments, it is impossible to describe the typical Romanesque church. But distinctive characteristics can be enumerated that are common, if not to all buildings, at least to a great many of them.

The Plan. The two ancient plans—radiating and rectangular—that had been maintained throughout the Carolingian period remained in favor. Churches and chapels on a central plan were still numerous in Italy, Germany, and France: the baptistery of Florence, the old cathedral in Brescia, and the church of Charroux (Vienne), the octofoil chapel of St-Michel-d'Entraigues (Charente), and Neuvy-St-Sépulcre (Indre). However, the rectangular plan remained by far the more prevalent. The sanctuary, at the opposite end from the main entrance, ended in either a flat wall or a semicircular apse. The apse was sometimes furnished with absidioles, either parallel (as at St-Saturnin, Puy-de-Dôme) or radiating, which was the usual type. To allow space for the choir, one or more bays separated the apse from the transept. The ambulatory, which began to appear in the 10th century, was used in most structures in the 11th and was customary in pilgrimage churches. The transept, which forms the arms of the Latin cross, is hardly ever lacking in Romanesque churches. Of the many types, some are very wide with aisles of their own; the arms usually end in straight walls, but some end in apses, as in Rhenish churches. Even among churches with aisled naves, there are some without transepts (Berzé-le-Sec, Aisne); others have double transepts, which may both be at the sanctuary end (as in Cluny III), or, in churches with apses facing both east and west, at opposite ends of the nave (as in St. Godehard, at Hildesheim). The nave was either simple, that is, aisleless, or flanked by single or double aisles. The most usual plan consisted of a nave with a single aisle on either side; in France, the aisleless nave appeared most often in the southern provinces (Stes-Maries-de-la-Mer, Bouches-du-Rhône); at the other extreme, St-Sernin at Toulouse provides a remarkable example of double side aisles. The narthex of early basilicas—a large porch or vestibule adjoining the façade—was retained in the Romanesque period but was not always considered indispensable. Among the most famous are those of St-Bénoit-sur-Loire (Loiret) and Vézelay (Yonne); in Germany, that of the imperial cathedral at Speyer; in Catalonia, that of S. Vicente at Cardona.

The Façade. In these very organic buildings, the façade was never a mere addition, separate from and unrelated to the rest of the plan; it was rather an integral part of the whole, echoing the transverse axis and by its proportions anticipating the interior volumes. Whether the church had aisles or not, the façade was surmounted by a gable; the only difference in appearance was that in churches with aisles the façade was divided in thirds by buttresses or half-columns, so that there were three separate doorways. This general scheme lent itself to many variations. Often above the central doorway was a great window illuminating the nave. Over the side portals, the wall was either left bare or pierced by an opening, as at St-Jouin-des-Marnes (Deux-Sèvres), or it was adorned with sculptured motifs, as at Notre-Dame-la-Grande in Poitiers.

Piers and Vaults. Supports for the roof were of infinite variety, and

Romanesque Art. Abbey church of St-Benoît-sur-Loire. Begun *c.* 1060; completed 12th century. *Photo G. de Miré.*

included cylindrical columns, piers of similar form but built up in superimposed layers of small units of masonry (as at St-Philibert at Tournus), square piers, and piers with engaged half-columns. Just as the façade was adapted to the framework of the building, so were the piers related in a subordinate sense to the vault.

The earliest pre-Romanesque churches were still roofed with timber. The extension of the stone vault from the half-dome of the apse to the nave was one of the great advances of 11th-century architecture; the danger of fire was thereby considerably reduced. The three principal types of vault were the tunnel or barrel vault, the groined vault, and the domical vault. The tunnel vault has been defined as a semi-circular arch prolonged indefinitely. Its disadvantage is that it exerts a very strong lateral thrust that tends to force outward the walls on which it rests. If the said walls are high and pierced by openings, this thrust is proportionately stronger and more dangerous. This is why the first tunnel-vaulted churches were low and admitted little light. Aisleless churches were given thicker walls reinforced here and there with buttresses. In churches with aisles, the nave was buttressed by the aisles, which were also propped by buttresses. The aisles themselves might be tunnel-vaulted or half-tunnel-vaulted. Transverse arches were erected before the tunnel vault to sustain it: they reinforced it at each bay.

The intersection at right angles of two tunnel vaults of equal diameter produces the groined vault, divided into four quarters or cells. The groins are simply the lines where the cells intersect; the place where the groins meet at the apex is called the crown. Romanesque architects hardly ever used the groined vault except for covering side aisles. The ribbed vault, the use of which became standard in Gothic times, developed out of the groined vault and appeared first at the end of the 11th century in Durham Cathedral in England, and in the 12th century in Normandy (nave of Ste-Trinité at Caen, 1130). The rib is an additional arch placed under the line of the groin.

The Dome. This is a hemispherical or oval vault whose base should rest on a wall of the same shape. If it covered a rotunda, its construction posed no problem; but since in most cases it had to cover a square or rectangular area—the transept crossing or a bay of the nave—it was necessary to form a transition from the square plan to a circular or polygonal one. Two means were used: squinches and pendentives. The latter are concave triangles set into the four corners of the square to be covered, sloping outward as they rise and thus forming a circular or polygonal base on which the dome may rest. Squinches, similarly placed, are small arches built across the interior corners of the square, by means of which the dome no longer rests on four but on eight arches. Both methods were used in France. Domes on squinches were sometimes octagonal and sometimes hemispherical on an octagonal drum. Domes on pendentives were very common in Périgord and Angoumois.

Regional Schools

Romanesque architecture covered a vast geographical area in Europe. It embraced France, Italy, Germany, the British Isles, and the northern part of the Iberian peninsula; it even extended beyond western Europe to parts of Poland (Cracow), Scandinavia (Trondheim), Yugoslavia, and Hungary. An attempt has been made to divide this very extensive area into architectural provinces, and such an attempt seems justifiable enough if one accepts the fact that the Carolingian period (in which a uniform imperial art prevailed) was succeeded by an era of local differentiation, above all in construction methods, representing original solutions to architectural problems (vaults, arrangement of buttresses, lighting). Even the plans of churches varied from region to region.

Region does not mean school, but two facts seem equally obvious: one is that within the same region many monuments display stylistic resemblances; the other is that regional boundaries are often exceeded and that similar architectural conceptions appear in widely scattered places. In short, it is difficult to deny the existence of groups of workshops operating in a common tradition and applying similar techniques. The existence of regions—and of regional customs—is even less disputable; but school and region are two distinct ideas and ought not to be confused.

Romanesque Art. Church of Ste-Trinité, Caen. 1062–66. *Photo Jean Roubier, Paris.*

Pilgrimage Roads

A master merely had to move his center of operations for the limits of a regional style to move along with him. By this means the Burgundian architectural style found its way to Bourbonnais (at Souvigny), and Auvergne's building conceptions appeared in the former county of Forez (at Champdieu). These were only cases of excursions slightly beyond the home ground. But there were also long journeys, notably those along the pilgrimage routes that led to Jerusalem, Rome, and Santiago de Compostela. All along the "way of St. James" there arose monasteries and churches in vast numbers. These great thoroughfares facilitated not only all types of exchanges, but also the spread of architectural styles from one province to another and from one country to another.

Cluniac Art

The vast body of literature on Cluniac art attests the fact that few questions have been more hotly debated. At Cluny itself, the deplorable destruction wrought between 1811 and 1823 left standing only a few remnants of the extensive group of buildings (church, abbey, and outbuildings) that could still be admired in the 18th century and even survived the Revolution. Several archaeological research projects, of which the most important were organized between 1928 and 1934, enable one to form some idea of what formerly existed. Of the three churches that were built in succession, Cluny I and II belonged to the 11th century, while Cluny III was started about 1088; it was completed in 1118, but in 1125 the nave collapsed. Building was resumed after 1125, during the abbacy of Peter

Romanesque Art. Tower "of the Blessed Water". Abbey church of Cluny. 1088–1118. *Photo Josef Jeiter, Hadamar.*

the Venerable (1122–56), and culminated in a new consecration in 1130. Cluny III had a nave with two side aisles on either side and a double transept; the sanctuary was surrounded by an ambulatory with radiating chapels. The nave had a pointed tunnel vault (a system that became very popular) with a transverse arch of the same form at each bay; it was much taller than the side aisles and could thus be lit by clerestory windows opening immediately below the vault. The narthex was of later date, and was not finished until 1220. The abbey church of Cluny was, in its time, the largest church in Christendom; it was much admired and served as a model for a number of other churches, especially in Burgundy and adjacent regions.

In Burgundy, the Romanesque period gave rise to at least three types of religious buildings: churches reminiscent of Cluny, those that were similar to Vézelay, and those with windowless naves. In more remote provinces, the lack of agreement between religious affiliation and style of building is still more noticeable.

Cistercian Art

The Cistercian order, which was a reformed branch of the Benedictines, conformed to a very strict rule. Its founder, St. Bernard, condemned Benedictine "luxury" and would not countenance painted or sculptured decorations in monastic churches. This trend toward complete austerity appeared also in architecture, in the form of simplification of plan (reverting as far as possible to that of primitive churches) and suppression of towers as well as of all superfluous ornament. The order was founded in 1099, and on the death of St. Bernard (1153) it already numbered 150 monasteries. They were to become much more numerous in the 13th century. The earliest Cistercian church was Fontenay (Côte d'Or), built between 1139 and 1145. Its plan, based on the Latin cross, is entirely composed of straight lines and right angles. The chevet has a square end; the nave, with single aisles, is separated from the choir by a wide transept; there are no windows in the nave, which has a pointed tunnel vault, buttressed by transverse barrel vaults over the aisles.

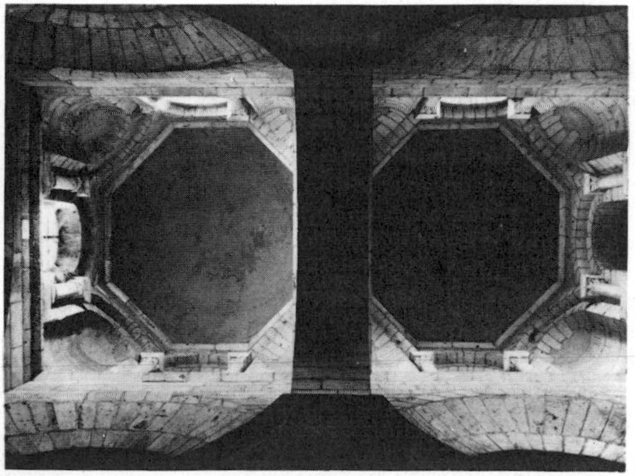

Romanesque Art. Domes of the tower, Cathedral of St-Front, Périgueux. 1120–73. *Photo Lagrange, Périgueux.*

Religious Architecture in France

Morienval (Oise). Like Champagne and the northern provinces, the Île-de-France was very rich in Romanesque churches. They were nearly all rebuilt in the Gothic period. The abbey church at Morienval, although disfigured by restorations, gives one an idea of these former churches of northern France, with their porches surmounted by a gallery and a square tower and their twin towers framing the chevet.

Marmoutier (Bas-Rhin). The churches of Alsace were within the Rhenish sphere of influence, where, from the 9th century, a powerful and enduring regional style prevailed, with the result that monuments of the Romanesque period still reflected the fidelity of their builders to Carolingian traditions and Lombardic influences. In the abbey church at Marmoutier, the 12th-century façade decorated with Lombardic arcades and pilasters, the two hexagonal towers flanking it, and the porch and inner vestibule surmounted by a gallery and a square tower bear admirable witness to the church in its original state.

Caen (Calvados). Ste-Trinité at Caen, the church connected with the Abbaye-aux-Dames, is a typical product of the Norman school. Norman architecture was not only distinguished very early by characteristics of its own, but it also extended its influence to Brittany, Picardy, Maine, the west of the Île-de-France, England, Sweden, Sicily, and southern Italy. Ste-Trinité was built over a very extensive crypt that probably was part of an earlier building. Begun in 1062, the work was finished in 1066, the date of the consecration. The aisles have groined tunnel vaults; the apse, with its half-dome, has two stories of windows that are framed by semicircular arches carried on freestanding columns; the ambulatory, scarcely more than rudimentary, does not encircle the sanctuary; two towers flank the façade, and a third rises above the crossing of the transept.

Tournus (Saône-et-Loire). The abbey church of St-Philibert is one of the few important pre-Romanesque churches that have been preserved intact. The huge two-story narthex is divided by massive piers into three aisles each consisting of three bays. At the chevet, the ambulatory gives access to three rectangular radiating chapels. The church was first begun in the second half of the 10th century. At first roofed in timber, it was later (late 11th–early 12th century) roofed with transverse tunnel vaults on diaphragm arches, which buttressed each other like the spans of a bridge. The aisles have groin vaulting. In the lower story of the narthex the reverse is true: the central space is groin-vaulted and the aisles have transverse tunnel vaults. In the upper story of the narthex, the very tall nave, which is lit by large windows, is tunnel-vaulted, while the aisles have half-tunnel vaults that rest on the nave wall below the clerestory.

Vézelay (Yonne). Built about 1100, damaged but not destroyed by a fire in 1127, and provided with a large two-story narthex at the beginning of the 12th century, La Madeleine at Vézelay was finally completed in the early 13th century by the addition of a Gothic choir over a Romanesque crypt that still survives. The nave has a groined tunnel vault with transverse arches; it comprises two stories and is lit by clerestory windows above the aisles. The façade was fundamentally altered in the 13th century by the addition of the final story of the south tower and the completion of the central window decorated with statues.

Clermont-Ferrand (Puy-de-Dôme). Notre-Dame-du-Port (12th century) is very characteristic of the Romanesque style of lower Auvergne. The choir of Notre-Dame-du-Port is surrounded by an even number of absidioles with no axial chapel: four radiating absidioles open off the ambulatory, and two parallel ones at the side open off the transept. The nave has a tunnel vault without transverse arches, and is buttressed by quadrant vaulting over the aisles. A narthex the width of the façade gives access to the nave. The octagonal belfry that surmounts the transept crossing rests on oblique lintels that take the place of squinches across the interior corners.

Le Puy (Haute-Loire). Unlike Notre-Dame-du-Port, the cathedral of Notre-Dame at Le Puy is unique, not only in its own region but throughout France: it is one of those monuments that defy any sort of classification and surpass the limits of a provincial style. The oldest parts—the choir, the transept, and the last two bays of the nave—go back to the late 11th century, while the porch and the first two bays date from the 12th. The nave is covered by a series of domical vaults carried on squinches. The freestanding belfry situated behind the church is of Limousin type. The black and white striped façade rises boldly against the slope of the Corneille rock; its decorative elements (cusped arches, alternating black and white voussoirs) attest Moorish influence.

Poitiers (Vienne). Notre-Dame-la-Grande (*c.* 1130–45) is the most famous example of an architectural style whose distribution extends beyond Poitou, as far north as Anjou and as far south as Guienne. The building belongs to the three-aisled type, or hall church (the German *Hallenkirche*). The façade, notable for its sculptured ornament, is framed by two clusters of engaged columns surmounted by lantern turrets, which are roofed with imbricated stone tiles in a fish-scale pattern. The nave, which is typical of this region, has a tunnel vault with transverse arches. It has no clerestory but is lit from the aisles and by the great window in the façade, over the portal. At the end of the nave is the ambulatory with radiating chapels. The axis of the chevet is inclined slightly to the left. Over the crossing rises a square tower surmounted by a cylindrical belfry with a small conical spire.

Périgueux (Dordogne). Like Notre-Dame-la-Grande, the cathedral of St-Front at Périgueux represents a regional style. Characteristic of the style are domes carried on pendentives and supported by heavy piers (which may be square or flanked by engaged columns) connected by wide transverse and longitudinal arches without ornament. These churches are generally without aisles, but St-Front, their prototype, is distinguished by its narrow aisles. Its five domes rise over each arm and at the center of the Greek-cross plan. Erected on the site of an older cathedral destroyed by fire in 1120, St-Front was completed in 1173. It was severely damaged during the religious wars and restored several times. As the cathedral was almost entirely rebuilt in the 19th century, it is difficult to reconstruct this monument in its original state.

Toulouse (Haute-Garonne). The church of St-Sernin was founded about 1077 or 1083; construction went on for about a century and a half. The oldest parts are the choir, consecrated in 1096, and the nave and aisles, completed in 1119. Work continued until the 13th century, at which time the belfry was given its present form. A pilgrimage church situated on one of the great routes to Santiago de Compostela, it has two crypts that were intended for the display of relics and nine chapels—five radiating chapels off the ambulatory and two opening off each arm of the transept. There are double side aisles; the nave, covered by a tunnel vault with transverse arches, is strengthened by the quadrant vaults of the aisles, which are themselves supported by buttresses.

Arles (Bouches-du-Rhône). The former cathedral of St-Trophîme was built before the year 1000 on the site of a 5th-century basilica dedicated to St. Stephen. In the course of years, it has received additions and undergone alterations. The great portal on the central part of the façade, notable for its sculptured ornament, dates from the late 12th century; the belfry that rises above the crossing of the transept belongs to the same period. The Gothic choir is of the 15th century.

Religious Architecture in Italy

A great many churches were built or rebuilt in Italy in the course of the 11th and 12th centuries. Among the most celebrated were the basilica of S. Ambrogio in Milan, of which several Romanesque parts have survived; S. Maria Maggiore at Bergamo; S. Zeno at Verona; and St. Mark's in Venice. In Emilia there were the cathedrals of Piacenza, Parma, and Modena; in Tuscany, the baptistery of Florence (the former cathedral of S. Giovanni, octagonal in plan, with an apse added in the 13th century) and the church of S. Miniato al Monte, also in Florence; the cathedral and baptistery at Pisa; and the church of S. Michele at Lucca. The last is interesting, because it furnishes an example—rare in the Middle Ages, even in Italy—of a lack of cohesion between exterior forms and the interior structure; the façade, with its tiers of arcades superimposed in the Pisano-Lucchese style, is more like a piece of scenery than a gable end, for the upper part is just a wall with nothing behind it. In central Italy, mention should be made of the two churches at Tuscania (formerly called Toscanella) that were originally built before the year 800 and

Romanesque Art. Portal, former Cathedral of St.-Trophîme, Arles. Late 12th century. *Photo Josef Jeiter, Hadamar.*

Romanesque Art. Façade, Church of S. Miniato al Monte, Florence. 1062 and 12th century. *Foto Marburg.*

Romanesque Art. Façade and bell tower, Church of S. Zeno, Verona. *c.* 1123 and later. *Photo Josef Jeiter, Hadamar.*

later reconstructed: S. Pietro at the end of the 11th century and S. Maria Maggiore in the 12th. In Rome, S. Maria in Trastevere, although dating from the Romanesque period, is not Romanesque in style but is modeled on the older basilicas; in the same city are S. Clemente and S. Maria in Cosmedin. In the south is the cathedral of Bari; in Sicily, those of Palermo (with a 12th-century apse), Monreale, and Cefalù—the last two in the Norman style.

Verona. The church of S. Zeno, the building of which was begun twice, in the 5th and 9th centuries A.D., was given its final form in the first part of the 12th century, between about 1120 and 1138. The campanile is contemporaneous with the main structure. The church is not vaulted but has a timbered Gothic trefoil roof. A noticeable feature is the alternation of slender columns with massive compound piers, the latter being extended by tall engaged columns on the walls of the nave. The portal, framed by two columns supported on lions, is typical of Italian Romanesque.

Pisa. Pisa Cathedral, which set the pattern for Pisano-Lucchese religious architecture, constitutes with its baptistery and its campanile (the Leaning Tower) one of the most remarkable monumental groups in Italy. Built on a very marked Latin-cross plan, the church has double aisles on either side of the nave and three aisles in the transept, which is wide and projects boldly from the main axis of the building. A round apse, without an ambulatory, prolongs the nave; almost all 68 columns are re-used antique monoliths. The crossing of the transept is covered by an oval dome; the exterior walls, intended to be viewed from all angles, had as much careful workmanship lavished on them as the façade with its four stories of colonnettes. Begun in 1063, the work was supervised by the architect Buschetus (or Boschetto); the consecration took place in 1118. Work was taken up again in the second half of the 12th century by Rainaldus, who designed the façade, and continued until toward the end of the 13th century (when the apse was remodeled). The baptistery and campanile were begun somewhat later than the church, in 1153 and 1173 respectively, and were not finished until the 14th century.

Religious Architecture in Spain

Spanish Romanesque architecture extended throughout the northern half of the country, from Catalonia to Galicia, in other words through all the Christian kingdoms, and including Portugal. The sites of the principal monuments, starting with the west, are: Santiago de Compostela; Coimbra, whose old cathedral (late 12th century) is a simplified edition of Santiago; Zamora; Salamanca (the old cathedral); Oviedo; León (S. Isidoro); and Jaca. In Castile there are Silos; Avila (S. Vicente); Segovia (S. Martin and S. Esteban); and Toledo. Catalonia includes Ripoll, Tahull, whose church of S. Clemente (consecrated in 1123), with its timber-roofed nave and its decoration of blind arcades, represented a late example of the First Romanesque style. Everywhere, Visigothic and Mozarabic traditions mingle in varying proportions with foreign influences (those of Lombardy, Auvergne, and Languedoc).

Ripoll. The monastery of S. Maria at Ripoll, one of the oldest in this region, was founded in the 6th century A.D.; destroyed by the Moors, rebuilt in the 11th century, and destroyed again in 1835, nothing remains except the church, which was restored in accordance with its original 11th-century character. It is especially notable for its plan in the form of a tau cross. The double aisles are separated from the nave by robust square piers. The nave and its four aisles culminate in a very prominent transept, onto which seven parallel absidioles open directly. The largest of these, in the center, houses the sanctuary. The sculpture on the portal dates from the 12th century.

Santiago de Compostela. Begun in 1074 or 1075, Santiago de Compostela was the ideal pilgrimage church. It was thus almost exactly contemporaneous with the old parts of St-Sernin at Toulouse (begun *c.* 1077). Certain architectural features are common to both buildings—chevet with nine radiating chapels, dome carried on squinches, blind arcading on the façade—but Santiago has single side aisles, the chancel is longer, and the upper gallery extends all around the apse. The narthex with its Pórtico de la Gloria, and the south façade, named after the silversmiths' quarter (Puerta de las Platerias), date from the 12th century. The Churrigueresque west façade (18th century) contrasts with the sobriety of the rest of the structure.

Religious Architecture in England

In England as in Spain, a local

Romanesque Art. Church of the Benedictine Abbey of Santa Maria, Ripoll. 11th century. *Archives photographiques.*

223. **Raphael.** *Marriage of the Virgin.* 1504. Brera, Milan.

223.

224.

225.

224. **Henry Raeburn.** *Portrait of Mrs. Eleanor Urquhart.* c. 1795. National Gallery, Washington, D.C.

225. **Man Ray.** *Rope Dancer Accompanies Herself with Her Shadows.* 1916. Museum of Modern Art, New York.

226. **Odilon Redon.** *Birth of Venus.* Petit Palais, Paris.

227. **Robert Rauschenberg.** *Tracer.* 1963. Coll. Mr. and Mrs. Frank Titelman, Altoona, Pennsylvania. Photo Galerie Sonnabend, Paris.

228. **Hans Reichel.** *Watercolor.* 1954. Photo Galerie Bucher, Paris.

226.

227.

228.

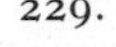

229.

230.

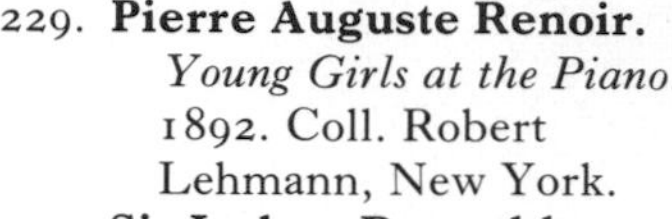

229. **Pierre Auguste Renoir.** *Young Girls at the Piano.* 1892. Coll. Robert Lehmann, New York.

230. **Sir Joshua Reynolds.** *Master Francis George Hare.* 1788. Louvre, Paris.

231. **Guido Reni.** *St. Jerome.* *c.* 1635. Kunsthistorisches Museum, Vienna.

232. **Hyacinthe Rigaud.** *Louis XIV.* 1701. Louvre, Paris.

233. **Diego Rivera.** *The Arums.* Private Coll.

234. **Jusepe de Ribera.** *Jacob's Dream.* 1639. Prado, Madrid.

235. Opposite: **Rembrandt.** *Self-portrait.* Detail. *c.* 1669. Iveagh Bequest, Kenwood House, London.

231.

232.

233.

234.

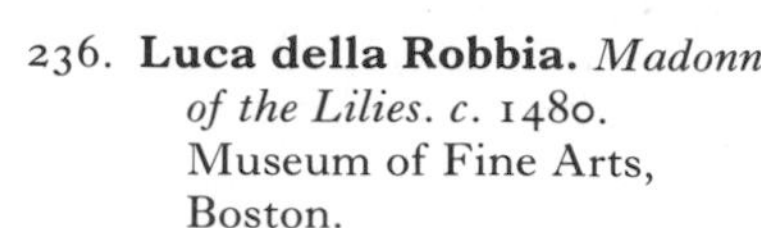
236. **Luca della Robbia.** *Madonna of the Lilies. c.* 1480. Museum of Fine Arts, Boston.

237. **George Romney.** *Portrait of Mrs. Davenport.* 1782–84. National Gallery of Art, Washington, D.C.

236.

237.

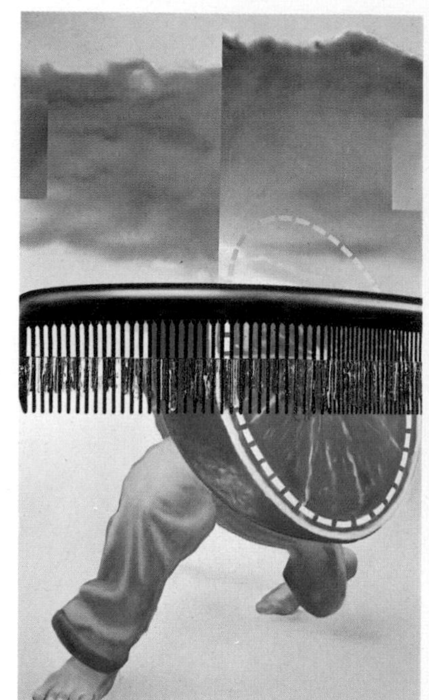
238.

239.

240.

241.

238. **James Rosenquist.** *Early in the Morning.* 1963. Coll. Mr. and Mrs. Robert C. Scull, New York.

239. **Hubert Robert.** Pont du Gard. 1787. Louvre, Paris.

240. **Théodore Rousseau.** *The Little Fisherman.* 1848–49. Louvre, Paris.

241. **Georges Rouault.** *The Apprentice Worker (Self-Portrait).* 1925. Musée National d'Art Moderne, Paris.

242. **Mark Rothko.** *Sassrom.* 1958. Coll. Cardazzo, Venice.

242.

243. **Dante Gabriel Rossetti.** *Reverie.* Victoria and Albert Museum, London.
244. **Peter Paul Rubens.** *Rape of the Daughters of Leucippus. c.* 1618. Alte Pinakothek, Munich.
245. **Jacob van Ruisdael.** *The Wheat Field. c.* 1670. Metropolitan Museum of Art, New York.
246. **Salomon van Ruysdael.** *View of a River in the Province of Gelderland.* 1644 or 1647. Mauritshuis, The Hague.

243.

244.

245.

246.

247.

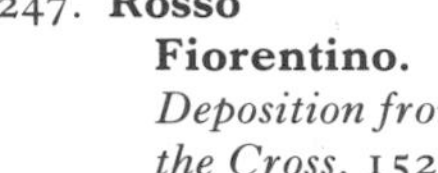

247. **Rosso Fiorentino.** *Deposition from the Cross.* 1521. Pinacoteca, Volterra.
248. **Henri Rousseau.** *The Snake Charmer.* 1907. Musée de l'Impressionnisme, Paris.

248.

249.

250.

251.

249. **Sassetta.** *Mystic Marriage of St. Francis.* 1437–44. Musée Condé, Chantilly.
250. **Egon Schiele.** *Self-Portrait.* 1911. Private Coll.
251. **Jan van Scorel.** *Portrait of a Young Student.* 1531. Museum Boymans-van Beuningen, Rotterdam.
252. **Karl Schmidt-Rottluff.** *Resting in the Studio.* 1910. Kunsthalle, Hamburg.
253. **Gino Severini.** *Dancer.* 1913. Eric Estorick Coll., London.
254. **Sebastiano del Piombo.** *Dorothea.* *c.* 1513. Staatliche Museen, Berlin-Dahlem.
255. **Kurt Schwitters.** *Collage in Blue and White.* 1926. Private Coll.

252.

253.

256. Opposite: **Georges Seurat.** *Sunday Afternoon on the Island of La Grande Jatte.* Detail. 1886. Art Institute of Chicago.

254.

255.

258.

257.

259.

257. **Walter Richard Sickert.** *Interior of St. Mark's, Venice.* 1901–3. Tate Gallery, London.
258. **Jan Sluyters.** *Self-Portrait.* 1924. Stedelijk Museum, Amsterdam.
259. **Luca Signorelli.** *Life of St. Benedict.* 1497–98. Detail. Monastery of Monte Oliveto Maggiore, Asciano.
260. **Ben Shahn.** *Handball.* 1939. Museum of Modern Art, New York.
261. **Paul Signac.** *Port of St-Tropez.* 1894. Musée de l'Annonciade, St-Tropez.
262. **Alfred Sisley.** *Snow at Louveciennes.* 1878. Musée de l'Impressionnisme, Paris.

260.

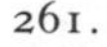

261.

262.

tradition (in this case Saxon) and a foreign element (namely Norman) coexisted. Norman architects were working in England even in the 11th century, before the Conquest of 1066, after which their influence became stronger. The plan of English churches—largely a Benedictine plan—without an ambulatory, was that of Norman churches. A square lantern tower was customary at the crossing of the transept. There also occurred a rapid evolution toward the Gothic mode. Numerous imposing buildings—cathedrals more often than monasteries—rose up at the end of the 11th century and during the 12th: Winchester, Ely, Durham, Chichester, Gloucester, and Norwich. The oldest example of the Anglo-Norman style is the chapel of St. John in the Tower of London, with a tunnel-vaulted nave and groined vaults over the two aisles. The former abbey, now the cathedral, of St. Albans (1077) is typically Norman in plan, with its seven graduated absidioles.

Durham. Durham Cathedral, begun in 1093 at the same time as the adjoining monastery, is one of the masterpieces of Romanesque architecture in England; it is also one of the earliest examples of a transition from Romanesque to Gothic, of which it may indeed be the prototype. The nave, divided into sections of double bays by alternating single cylindrical piers and massive grouped piers, was covered with a ribbed vault between 1110 and 1113, before that of St-Denis. The wide projecting transept has an aisle on one side only; the choir, which is without an ambulatory and is divided into two double bays, ends in an apse flanked by two absidioles. In elevation the nave is of three stories of diminishing height. Two square towers frame the façade; another square tower, still more impressive, rises over the transept crossing.

Ottonian and Franconian Religious Architecture

The name Austrasia, taken from Carolingian political geography, denotes a vast area that embraced Flanders, the Netherlands, Switzerland, and Western Germany, as well as the frontier provinces of France. There the Carolingian tradition was still very strong in Romanesque times, and Carolingian models—such as the church of St-Riquier (or Centula; *c.* 800)—continued to be copied in the Rhineland. The characteristic features of Romanesque architecture in Germany are the presence of an apse at the western as well as at the eastern end of the church, and a double transept with rounded extremities sometimes surmounted by lantern towers (as in St. Michael at Hildesheim; 1014–34). Trefoil chevets, such as are found in St. John at Münster in Switzerland (early 11th century) and St. Mary in Capitol at Cologne (1040–69), suggest a Lombardic influence. Naves were originally roofed in timber, although after the 12th century stone vaults were used as they were everywhere else. The imperial cathedral at Speyer, originally timbered, was given groin vaulting after 1106. The Rhenish churches, so dominating in presence with their towers framing each of two apses and a fifth tower at the crossing of the transept, give some idea of what the great Carolingian abbey churches were like. Apart from Speyer Cathedral, the most notable in Germany are the abbey of Maria Laach (1093–1156), with a transept at each end surmounted by a belfry, and the cathedrals of Trier, Mainz, and Worms; in Switzerland, the cathedral of Basel; in Belgium, Tournai Cathedral (*c.* 1110 and 1165), with apses at both ends and a trefoil sanctuary, the churches of St. Gertrude at Nivelles (dedicated 1046) and St. Barthélemy at Liège; and in the Netherlands, St. Servaas at Maastricht. There were also some exceptions: new influences, notably Burgundian, sometimes came to counterbalance the regional tradition. Thus the church of Romainmôtier in Switzerland offers striking parallels with St-Philibert at Tournus.

Outside the regions and provinces enumerated above, Romanesque religious architecture spread through the Danube basin, Scandinavia, and Christian settlements in Syria and Palestine.

Civil Architecture

Only a small number of public monuments (town halls, bridges, fountains) have survived from Romanesque times, while dwellings—both convents and private houses—have nearly all disappeared. In the absence of complete groups of buildings, it is the abbeys that form the most important remains. In properties where space was not restricted, numerous buildings with varied functions were set up around the cloister and the sanctuary. The plan of these complex structures was like that of the Roman villa, the cloister taking the place of the central atrium. Of all this nothing remains but scanty traces, and even in the best-preserved sites these are usually obscured by later Gothic and Baroque additions. There are stillrooms at Clairvaux (Aube) and Vincelotte (Yonne), and Romanesque parts in the abbeys of Mont-St-Michel, of Fontenay (Côte d'Or)—which is unusually well preserved and the oldest extant Cistercian complex—of Noirlac (Cher), Ganagobie (Basses-Alpes), Silvacane, Le Thoronet, and Sénanque. Outside France is Poblet, in Catalonia, which retains certain 12th-century elements, notably the chapter house and the fountain in the cloister; and Maulbronn in Württemberg, begun about 1150; the Cistercian foundation of Fossanova, near Rome, dates from the first years of the 13th century.

Romanesque Art. Façade with transept towers, Ely Cathedral. *c.* 1090–1180.

Romanesque Art. Abbey church of Maria Laach. 1093–1156. *Photo Ars Liturgica.*

Romanesque Art. The Ramparts of Ávila. *c.* 1090–1100. *Photo Martin Hürlimann, Zurich.*

Better than the monuments themselves is the famous plan that has been preserved of the abbey of Saint Gall in Switzerland. This 9th-century document gives a clear indication of Romanesque monastic building, and reveals the persistence of Classical traditions into the medieval Christian world.

Very few traces remain of public works carried out before the 13th century. The Pont St-Bénézet at Avignon (1177–85) is among the surviving examples. Even municipal buildings are rare, and the oldest go back no further than the late 12th century; examples in France include the town hall at La Réole, and in Italy, the Palazzo della Ragione at Verona (1194). Residences of the upper and middle classes, some of which date back to the first half of the 12th century, are a little more numerous. In France, the best example of these is the Episcopal Palace at Auxerre, built for Bishop Hugues de Montaigu (1116–36). There one notices the unbroken succession of semicircular open bays that characterizes all the dwellings of the period. This feature is also found in England, Germany, and Italy (in the oldest of the Venetian *palazzi*, Palazzo Dona and Palazzo Loredano). Some ancient towns laid out on a rectilinear plan have been unusually well preserved, such as Villefranche-de-Conflans (Pyrénées-Orientales); these give some idea of urban development before the rise of the "new towns" in the 13th century.

Military Architecture

Massive, solid, and designed for defensive purposes, military buildings withstood destructive forces better than other forms of architecture, although they were also exposed to more. All castles until the end of the 10th century, and nearly all until the 12th, were built of wood like the praetorian towers in Roman camps. The stone keep can therefore be regarded as a Romanesque invention. In France, the oldest is that of Langeais (*c.* A.D. 992–94), built for Fulke Nerra, count of Anjou. Until the end of the 11th century, fortified castles were nothing more than keeps, which were quadrangular in plan—for example Loches, Beaugency, and the Tower of London. The special characteristic of Norman strongholds was that the principal tower was flanked by another smaller square tower. This arrangement was also used in England and Sicily. From the 12th century, military architecture benefited from new ideas acquired by the crusaders as a result of their contact with Eastern cultures. In Palestine, the Krak des Chevaliers (destroyed by an earthquake and rebuilt in the late 12th century) and the Château de Saône were a source of inspiration for Western military architecture. Round towers appeared, and keeps with round turrets at the corners were no longer unusual in the 12th century (Houdan, Seine-et-Oise, 1100; Étampes, *c.* 1140).

Nearly all the town ramparts known belong to the Gothic period; some, however, go back to the 12th century. The oldest fortified enclosure in western Europe, that of Ávila, was inspired by Moorish models and was built in the last years of the 11th century (*c.* 1090–1100). The walls surround the town with a rectangle of ramparts topped by some 2,500 embrasures and flanked by 88 semicircular towers.

SCULPTURE

Romanesque ornament, which is extremely rich and complex, reveals at a glance the multiplicity of its origins: its elements are derived from Classical, Gallo-Roman, barbaric, Oriental, and Islamic art. From Islam it took horseshoe arches and cusped arcading; from the art of the steppes, fantastic beasts and monsters of all kinds, animals confronted, interlaced, or joined together with one head. The sculpture born in the Carolingian period was not concerned with the human figure, but it did serve to maintain a tradition of craftsmanship. The figure had remained a familiar feature of the other arts, and in the first quarter of the 11th century it reappeared in sculpture. The precisely dated (1020–21) lintel at St-Genis-des-Fontaines (Pyrénées-Orientales) represents Christ in Glory in a double aureole supported by two angels, with three standing Apostles on his right hand and three on his left, each standing in a bay of an arcade with head enshrined in a horseshoe arch. Even in these early works the most constant characteristic of Romanesque monumental sculpture is evident: its assimilation into the architectural setting. The carving, whether a single figure or a narrative sequence, is never a mere addition. It is part of the structure and emphasizes its elements—lintel, tympanum, capitals, archivolts, and even supports.

The lintel at St-Genis, the related one at St-André-de-Sorède, and other figures set in arcading such as those at Azay-le-Rideau are scarcely articulate expressions, but in spite of their clumsiness they mark the dawn of a new era. From that time the rediscovered human figure continued to acquire importance. Before the end of the 11th century, historiated capitals increased in number, while at the beginning of the 12th century major sculpture appeared on doorways. The history of Romanesque sculpture can be divided into three phases with necessarily vague transitional dates: the first, a period of somewhat tentative experiments occasionally inspired by painting and the minor arts, was followed by a peak period in the last decade of the 11th century and the first half of the 12th. After 1150 a third phase was the transition toward the Gothic and the decadence of Romanesque art as such. The great Romanesque sculpture—that of the best period—flourished in certain favored regions in northern Spain, Italy, and central and southern France (Burgundy, Languedoc, Provence, Auvergne, and Poitou).

Sculpture in France

Burgundy and Adjacent Regions—When the abbey church of Cluny was destroyed at the beginning of the 19th century, some capitals from the choir were spared; they are preserved in the Musée Lapidaire du Farinier and were probably carved about 1095, the date of the consecration of the choir.

Romanesque Art. *Scene from the Life of St. Martin.* Church of La Madeleine, Vézelay. *c.* 1120–40. *Foto Marburg.*

Romanesque Art. Gislebertus. *The Last Judgment.* *c.* 1135–1140. St-Lazare Cathedral, Autun. *Photo Marburg.*

Romanesque Art. Gislebertus. *Nativity. c.* 1135–1140. Cathedral of St-Lazare, Autun. *Photo Boudot-Lamotte, Paris.*

Romanesque Art. Bernard Gilduin. *Christ in Majesty.* Detail from the mensa of an altar. 1096. Church of St-Sernin, Toulouse. *Photo Yan, Toulouse.*

These capitals, in which the influence of ivory carving is evident, represent the eight modes of the Gregorian chant (personified by figures), the Virtues, the Seasons, the Earth and its labors, the Arts, the rivers of Paradise, and the Garden of Eden.

In La Madeleine at Vézelay, on capitals in the nave (*c.* 1120–40), secular allegories appear as well as scenes from the Old Testament and the lives of the saints. Of the same period as those at Vézelay if not a little earlier, the capitals in St-Lazare at Autun are magnificent in style and ambitious in scheme.

Even more than capitals, sculptured tympanums testify to the vitality of Burgundian workshops. At Vézelay, the central portal of the façade was damaged during the Revolution and restored by Viollet-le-Duc, but the majestic composition of the interior portal between the narthex and the nave has survived intact (*c.* 1120).

Another masterpiece of Burgundian sculpture is the tympanum over the entrance to the cathedral of St-Lazare at Autun, executed about 1140 by Gislebertus, one of the few artists known from that period. Sculpted portals of the second half of the 12th century, which are sometimes excessively refined, are notable not only for their lively and picturesque scenes (for instance, the Last Supper at Charlieu) but also for their profusion of carved ornament, which is like stone lacework. The most striking examples of this new style are the portals of Charlieu (Loire), Avallon (Yonne), and St-Julien-de-Jonzy (Saône-et-Loire).

Languedoc and Aquitaine. In these provinces, which profited from a constant flow of exchanges with northern Spain, Romanesque art flowered early. Its earliest monuments at Toulouse and Moissac, although different in style from those in Burgundy, share with them an origin in the late 11th century as well as signs of a continued tradition. In St-Sernin at Toulouse, the mensa of an altar carved in low relief by Bernard Gilduin is dated 1096; behind the choir, the reliefs in the ambulatory, which are Classical in style, obviously belong to the same period. The sculptures on the doorway known as the Porte de Miègeville cannot be of much later date (*c.* 1100–10).

At Moissac (Tarn-et-Garonne), the cloister of the abbey church of St-Pierre was finished in 1100, the approximate date of the carved piers and of most of the 88 capitals. The tympanum of the church is slightly later. The jambs and *trumeau* are also sculpted (the striking figure of the prophet Jeremiah is on the right). A series of portals carved in the course of the 12th century evidence the spread of Moissac's influence—in Ste-Foi at Conques (Aveyron; *c.* 1124), on the borders of Auvergne, one of the most beautiful examples of Romanesque sculpture; and the cathedral of St-Étienne at Cahors, of about 1140.

Provence. Romanesque sculpture appeared in Provence later than it did in Languedoc and Burgundy—only in the second half of the 12th century. This art of the Rhône valley produced notable monuments, of which only two have been preserved—the priory church of St-Gilles-du-Gard and St-Trophîme at Arles. The abbey church of St-Gilles has a triple portal on its west façade, but only the central doorway is contemporaneous with the old part of the building (*c.* 1170). The French-style lateral doorways, added in the early 13th century, were the work of artists from the Île-de-France.

The former cathedral of St-Trophîme, built in the 10th century on the site of an earlier cathedral, was completed at the end of the 12th century by the addition of a Classical-style porch, whose sculptured decoration is reminiscent of that of St-Gilles. The cloister, with its carved piers, dates in part from the 12th century (north and east walks) and in part from the 14th (south and west walks). The unity of style of the historiated capitals is further evidence of the prolonged survival of Romanesque formulas in Provence.

Poitou and Adjacent Regions. Between the Loire and the Garonne stretches a region where sculpture was widely practiced. Sculptured façades are numerous there, as are decorative and historiated capitals. The pattern of these façades is rather distinctive: the tympanum is often bare or even absent, and it is the archivolts that receive the main decorative elements. Above the portals, a profusion of statues and decorative motifs makes the façades of Poitou, Saintonge, and Angoumois seem like illustrated pages from some great stone book.

The numerous ornamental and historiated capitals in this western region are striking in the diversity of their styles, the wide variety of their decorative motifs and the bold range of iconography: at St-Hilaire in Poitiers, the *Nativity* was depicted complete with the bathing of the Child, as was the *Flight into Egypt*; at Chavigny, in the ambulatory of the church of St-Pierre was carved a whole series of haunting images drawn from Scripture (such as the *Temptation of Christ*) and from some bestiary of monsters.

Auvergne. By the 12th century the sculpture of Auvergne, which had established a tradition during Carolingian times, had not reached a stage of development comparable with that of Poitevin sculpture. Great carved façades are not found there, and the portals, with their triangular lintels and small tympanums, do not provide the sculptor with a surface favorable to important sculpture. The originality typical of Auvergne sculpture shows best in historical capitals. The most notable are those in St-Nectaire and in St-Paul at Issoire; within Puy-de-Dôme one finds them also in the church at Ennezat, in St-Pierre at Mozat, and at Clermont-Ferrand. Certain scenes are represented in a vivid manner and sometimes with rather heavy-handed humor. Thus, in the famous *Expulsion from Eden* at Notre-Dame-du-Port, Adam is seen stamping his foot at Eve while an angel drags him along by the beard.

Other Parts of France. As early as the mid-12th century, the northern provinces of France witnessed the birth and rapid development of Gothic sculpture, and Romanesque art—sculpture as much as architecture and painting—was superseded earlier and left fewer traces. In the Île-de-France, the church of St-Étienne at Beauvais has a complex group of ornamental motifs on the façade of the north transept that is comparatively rare. In Lorraine, the portal at Pompierre (Vosges), a Burgundian work or strongly influenced by that style, stands out for its rich iconography, which includes the *Massacre of the Innocents*, the *Annunciation to the Shepherd*, the *Adoration of the Magi*, and the *Entry into Jerusalem*. In Alsace, the portal at Andlau (Bas-Rhin) is adorned with scenes from Genesis and a *Foundation of the Church* in an archaic style that has been thought to reveal Lombardic influence.

Sculpture in Italy

As in France, and at about the same time, the art of sculpture seems to have reawakened in Italy after a period of oblivion. This Romanesque renaissance began in Lombardy and Emilia, and one associates it with the name of a certain Wiligelmo or Guglielmo, who worked at Modena and later at Cremona in the first years of the 12th century. He was responsible for scenes from Genesis and figures of prophets in niches on the portal of the cathedral at Modena. The date of this fine work is disputed: some have assigned it to the end of the 11th century (about 1099), making Italy the home of the first sculptured portals. Two pupils of Wiligelmo, Guglielmo of Verona and Master Niccolò, are credited with the carvings on the doorway of S. Zeno at Verona (*c.* 1138), with the sculpture of St. Zeno on the tympanum and scenes from the Old and New Testament carried out in five registers of low relief on either side of the door. Of an earlier date (late 11th century) are the curious bronze plates fixed on wood, from the same portal; they may be of Germanic origin, as their style is close to that of the Rhenish metalworkers. The handsome doors at S. Zeno inspired those of the cathedrals of Pisa (1180) and Monreale (1186), both of which were works of Bonannus of Pisa a century later. At the end of the 12th century a new workshop appeared, that of Benedetto Antelami, whose works at Parma (the cathedral in 1178, and the baptistery, begun in 1196) betray without a doubt the influence of French sculpture.

Sculpture in Spain

Problems of dating have found expression in controversies over the relative ages of monuments. There has been much dispute over whether the sculptures in the cloister at Silos were executed before or after those in the cloister at Moissac (*c.* 1100). It is known from documentary evidence that important works were carried out at Silos in the mid-11th century (between 1042 and 1073) and again 100 years later. A debate of the same kind is raised regarding the relative dates of the sculptures of St-Sernin at Toulouse and of Santiago de Compostela. The relationship between them is ob-

Romanesque Art. *Adoration of the Magi.* Early 12th century. Church of La Charité-sur-Loire. *Photo Jean Roubier, Paris.*

vious in certain details: on both the Puerta de las Platerias at Santiago and the Porte de Miègeville at St-Sernin one can see the same figure of St. James the Greater between two tree trunks.

Besides Santiago and Silos, there are sculptured portals of the abbey church of S. Maria at Ripoll (1st half of the 12th century) and the cathedral of Zamora (1152–74). Fundamentally different from the portals of French churches, the one at Ripoll is set in a framework of sculpture in low relief arranged in six registers, and is somewhat reminiscent of S. Zeno. After 1150 Romanesque sculpture proliferated: at Estella, in the church of S. Miguel, the sculpture is arranged in horizontal courses as at Ripoll; the celebrated narthex known as the Pórtico de la Gloria at Santiago dates from about 1170.

Ottonian and Franconian Sculpture
In the countries of northern Europe, sculpture scarcely existed before the Gothic period. Romanesque churches in Germany, with apses at both ends, had no portals to decorate. On the other hand, Romanesque elements, adopted late, survived longer and were still employed in the 13th century.

PAINTING

In painting one is impressed by the evidence of a continuity not merely of the art, but of great art. From the few surviving Carolingian paintings, it would appear that those works were not inferior to paintings of the 11th and 12th centuries; and although earlier vestiges are still more rare, their importance and value are known from descriptions left by historians.

Romanesque painting developed from a combination of many varied influences. Immediately connected with the Carolingian and Ottonian art that preceded it, it preserved something of the vivacity of the former and serene gravity of the latter. Its more remote origins go back to Early Christian times, to the catacombs, and to barbaric art; these contributions mingled in proportions that varied from country to country, and they were adapted everywhere to the local character. Finally, the impressive example of Byzantium exerted a very important influence. Byzantine art invaded the West in successive waves over a prolonged period and by several routes. Italy, favored by its geographical situation, remained during the 12th and 13th centuries the chosen soil of Byzantinism and the center for its expansion throughout the West. The 16th-century Italian painter and critic Giorgio Vasari regarded all painting prior to Giotto as part of "the Greek style."

In such circumstances, it is difficult to assign precise chronological limits to Romanesque painting. Its beginnings are rendered elusive by the rarity of surviving works, and although its final manifestations are certainly easier to date, the dates of these last works are different in each region.

The technique of Romanesque painting was not an invention of the period; it derived from three principal methods, all of which were inherited from Classical antiquity. The first, true fresco, or *buon fresco*, was used especially in Italy. The paint was applied with water on a freshly plastered wall, which absorbed the color, hardened in drying, and acquired the solidity of stone. This kind of painting was very durable but demanded speed in execution and a great sureness of touch. The second technique, known as *à la grecque*, was more complex. On a dry foundation composed of at least six coats of plaster, a dark ground was applied; over that, the mat colors and then the glossy were painted. The third method, mat painting on a light ground, was the one most often employed in France in the Romanesque period. It consisted of a single application of color on plaster that had already dried and was remoistened at the time of painting. The result was similar to true fresco in appearance; the same rapidity was required and retouching was impossible in this case also. Whether Romanesque painters used cartoons is a disputed question. It is certain, however, that they sketched outlines on the wall to mark the contours of the figures and to guide the application of color.

The style of wall decoration varied from one site to another. This diversity undoubtedly reflected that of the origins of Romanesque art, from the very beginning; but workshop traditions and individual temperaments also played their part. However, certain characteristics common to even the most dissimilar groups of paintings make it possible to define the pictorial style of the Romanesque period. First and foremost is Classical simplicity: the minimal number of figures and almost complete absence of accessories in Romanesque painting distinguished it from the Gothic painting that followed. When the scene did not unfold against a plain background, the setting consisted of nothing more than a series of parallel horizontal bands. If it was necessary to pinpoint the location of the action, the artist introduced a symbolic object—a seat if an interior was to be suggested, as in the *Annunciation* (for the angel "came in unto" Mary); a tree or, more precisely, a simplified plant form that was little more than a diagram, to indicate a field or garden (as in the *Earthly Paradise* at St-Savin); a background of roofs or bricks to suggest the proximity of a town. The painter scrupulously observed a sort of grammar of shapes and used an alphabet whose letters were folds of garments and facial features. There were variations in this alphabet, but they were limited in number, and each master remained faithful to his chosen formula. This system of pictography resulted in a striking resemblance among all the figures in the same composition.

The purely decorative parts of wall paintings—borders and

Romanesque Art. Bonanno. *Massacre of the Innocents.* 1180. S. Ranieri portal, Pisa Cathedral.

Romanesque Art. *Apostles.* End of 11th century. Santo Domingo de Silos. *Photo Leonard von Matt, Buochs.*

bands across the background—conformed just as rigidly to the accepted code. The motifs varied, but all were traditional, having been inherited from preceding centuries or Classical antiquity: Greek-key patterns, hollow cubes, half-moons placed back to back, unwinding scrolls and ribbons, and, under the lower registers of larger works, painted draperies.

Finally, the essential and least varying stylistic quality of Romanesque frescoes was, to quote art historian Henri Focillon, "respect for the wall." This means not only that the painting was adapted to its architectural setting, but also that there was a ready acceptance of the flat surface. The painter was careful not to betray the building he decorated by opening false windows onto fake distances. He scorned the *trompe-l'oeil* of perspective and the modeling that gave an illusion of volume. His range of colors was limited. In the western provinces of France, yellow and red ocher, green, black, and white were almost the only pigments used; blue was rare and reserved for halos. Elsewhere, vermilion, gray, and several shades of red and blue were employed.

Although it was of wide range, the iconography of Romanesque painting was not as rich as that of Gothic painting. Without being subservient to the very letter of Scripture, the Romanesque painter took care to preserve what he believed to be historic truth. Thus the earliest pictorial interpretations (Syro-Palestinian and Hellenistic) of numerous subjects taken from the Old and New Testament and the Apocrypha continued until the 12th century. Sometimes the manner of representing a given subject had undergone changes in pre-Romanesque times. In such cases the painter (or sculptor) of the 12th century, unaware of the forgotten prototypes, followed precedents established by usage in his own time. Thus, in Romanesque interpretations of the *Ascension*, Christ is seen standing in a mandorla supported by angels, while the earliest representations of the scene show Him climbing a mountain and lost in clouds, in accordance with Scripture. Literary texts sometimes determined at an early date the form a theme would subsequently take.

The principal subjects of Romanesque wall painting, for the most part drawn from the Bible, were as follows: from the Old Testament, Genesis provided scenes of the Creation, the Earthly Paradise, the Deluge, the Tower of Babel, and the stories of Abraham and Joseph; Exodus, the story of Moses; Kings, the David cycle; from the New Testament came cycles on the Life of Christ (Annunciation, Visitation, Nativity, Public Ministry, Passion and Resurrection, Ascension, and Pentecost), apocalyptic visions (the Last Judgment; Christ in Glory, either surrounded by the symbols of the Evangelists or not, and nearly always placed in the apse). The destiny of the soul was shown in scenes of the conflict between Good and Evil, and the battle of Virtues and Vices, more or less inspired by the *Psychomachia* of Prudentius. The lives of the saints included the Apostles, the first martyrs, and also a few contemporary saints.

Wall Painting in France

The finest extant group in western France is that found in the abbey church of St-Savin-sur-Gartempe (Vienne). The foundation of the abbey dates back to the 9th century; the construction of the present building was undertaken by Abbot Eudes about 1060 and finished about 1115. The painted decoration was in five places: nave, sanctuary, crypt, belfry porch, and the gallery above the porch; the dates of each are a subject of controversy but it is agreed that the whole group can be attributed to the early 12th century. The iconographic scheme is among the most comprehensive. The paintings in the crypt of the church of St-Nicolas at Tavant (Indre) and those in the church of St-Martin at Nohant-Vic (Indre-et-Loire) are generally attributed to the last years of the 11th century or the beginning of the 12th. These two works, of different inspiration but equal intensity—and both notable for the lively attitudes of their figures—provide some insight into the probable nature of Carolingian wall painting. At St-Aignan at Brinay (Cher), dating from the mid-12th century, the most striking qualities are the harmony of the composition, the subtle tonality, the serenity, and the soothing moderation with which even the most dramatic episodes, such as the *Massacre of the Innocents*, are treated. The Chapelle de Liget (Chemillé-sur-Indrois, Indre-et-Loire), built about 1170, was decorated at much the same time with painted scenes from the lives of Christ and the Virgin, and figures of saints. The palette is limited but used with considerable skill; the colors are soft and luminous. In Burgundy, the most notable group is that in the Monks' Chapel of the Cluniac priory at Berzé-la-Ville (Saône-et-Loire), an example of glossy painting on a blue background. The date is disputed, and may be from the late 11th century to the mid-12th, the years 1103–9 being the most likely. During the whole Romanesque period, the paintings produced throughout lower Auvergne and Velay, from Le Puy to Brioude, followed the dark-ground technique and a style inspired by Byzantine traditions, Eastern influences, and echoes of Carolingian art. Although geographically close to Auvergne, the frescoes in the church of St-Léger at Ébreuil (Allier) are in the light-ground technique and, as far as repainting allows one to judge, gray tones predominate, which is rather rare.

Wall Painting in Spain

In Spain the actual paintings have been detached from the walls, remounted on canvas, and transferred to museums in Madrid, Vich, Solsona, and, most important, Barcelona. Their original sites were in the northern provinces of Spain—Catalonia, León, and Old Castile. Their present location, regrettable in a sense, has the advantage of providing a concentration of this forceful art, whose principal characteristics, in addition to fresh and lively color, are firm and strongly emphasized line, ignorance or total neglect of perspective, and a certain stiffness of attitude. Differences are apparent among the works as a result of varying degrees of absorption of Mozarabic traditions, Byzantine contributions, and French and Italian influences; but there is a strong affinity between them in their reflection of the local character. In Catalonia, the chief wall paintings come from Bohi (S. Juan; early 12th century) and Tahull (churches of S. Maria and of S. Clemente, province of Lérida, 1st half of 12th century; now in Barcelona, Museum of Catalan Art), from S. Quirce at Pedret (Barcelona, same period as above; partly in Episcopal Museum, Solsona), from Seo de Urgel (church of S. Pedro, now in

Museum of Catalan Art); from Osormort (church of S. Saturnino, now in Episcopal Museum, Vich). The frescoes from the Ermita de la Vera Cruz at Maderuelo (province of Segovia) and from S. Baudelio, Berlanga (province of Soria), have been transferred to the Prado in Madrid. The paintings in the narthex of S. Isidoro at León, known as the Panteón de los Reyes, were executed during the reign of Ferdinand II of León (1157–88), and are still in their original position.

Wall Painting in Italy

In Italy the art of fresco developed everywhere simultaneously, encouraged by lively local traditions and the proximity of Greek models. Chronologically, its scope was very extensive: *arte romanica*, with roots deep in the Early Christian past, continued until the mid-13th century. In northern Italy, the collegiate church of S. Pietro and S. Orso at Aosta, a building that goes back to the time of Bishop Anselm (990–1025), retains part of a decoration painted in the 11th century that is notable for its excellent technique, vivid color, and well-proportioned figures. The church of S. Vincenzo at Galliano (south of Como), consecrated in 1007 and decorated with frescoes at about the same time, and the abbey church of S. Pietro al Monte (Civate, province of Como), 100 years later, remain as evidence of a flourishing Lombard school of painting in the 11th and 12th centuries. In Rome, the frescoes in S. Clemente (in the nave of the lower church, *c.* 1100) and in S. Giovanni a Porta Latina (*c.* 1200) attest not only the way Roman painting evolved in the course of a century, but also the persistence of its narrative style. The groups of paintings at Castel S. Elia and at Ferentillo belong to the 12th century; those in the crypt at Anagni are still Romanesque in feeling in spite of their very late date (*c.* 1250). The excellent and varied decoration in S. Angelo in Formis (near Capua) is in itself a history of painting in southern Italy from the 11th century to the beginning of the 13th; Byzantine influence, apparent in the oldest parts, wanes in the later parts as the local style affirmed itself.

Wall Painting in Germany

Toward the end of the 10th century, Ottonian Germany was the scene of a renaissance that affected every branch of culture. That the wall painting at that period was of high quality is suggested by both contemporary evidence and those works that have survived: unfortunately, these are very rare and are often rendered unrecognizable as a result of repainting. The most interesting sites are in three areas that have as their centers Lake Constance, Regensburg, and Salzburg. The chapel of St. Sylvester, situated at Goldbach on the shores of Lake Constance, is decorated with paintings that were discovered only in the present century, and that have thus escaped the drastic restorations of the preceding period. In the nave are the Miracles of Christ, arranged in two registers, and, in the choir, the Twelve Apostles. The much retouched paintings in the church of St. George at Oberzell (on the island of Reichenau) are similar in iconographic content. Both works date from about 1000 (Oberzell from the late 10th century, and Goldbach from the early 11th). Near Regensburg, the abbey church of St. Emmeram retains fragments of a decoration that can be assigned to the mid-10th century; it comprises figures of saints and scenes from the lives of St. Peter and St. Denis. The abbey church at Prüfening and the chapel of All Saints in the cloister of Regensburg Cathedral were painted about 1150. The paintings in the abbey church of Lambach, north of Salzburg, date from the end of the 11th century, and those in the convent of Nonnberg in Salzburg are from the mid-12th.

Wall Painting in England

The importance of English painting in the Romanesque period is vouched for by illuminated manuscripts; very little remains of the wall paintings, which must have been quite numerous. Canterbury Cathedral retains two examples. The decoration in the crypt (the chapel of St. Gabriel) was certainly done prior to 1174, for it was spared by the fire that severely damaged the cathedral at that date; the other, in the ambulatory south of the choir (chapel of St. Anselm) is later, but probably dates from only shortly after the fire. In the chapel of St. Anselm the only fragment still visible, but exceptionally well preserved, represents St. Paul and the viper, a rather unusual subject taken from the Acts of the Apostles. Also in a perfect state of preservation, the paintings in the chapel of St. Gabriel (the Heavenly Jerusalem, and scenes from the life of Christ) reveal a strong Byzantine influence. The frescoes in the church of St. Botolph at Hardham (Sussex), which date from the 12th century, are connected rather with Carolingian models. Those in the church of St. Mary at Copford (Essex) are related to English manuscripts of the same period.

MANUSCRIPT ILLUMINATION

Manuscripts, whether painted or merely decorated with outline drawings heightened with color, are a precious source of information for the historian of medieval art, as they are very well preserved. Merovingian Gaul and the British Isles possessed several lively and productive centers of illumination, such as Luxeuil and Corbie, Canterbury and Winchester; thus the development of this art in Western Europe at the end of the 8th century was not, properly speaking, a renaissance. It might more accurately be called a florescence.

Throughout the Empire scriptoria multiplied and great schools were established. In the first rank were the palace school at Aachen and that of Trier; in France, these included the schools of the Loire (Tours, Fleury) and those of Rheims, Metz, and St-Amand. One of the most beautiful productions of the Aachen palace school is the *Évangéliaire de Charlemagne* (*c.* 781; Paris, Bibliothèque Nationale), also called that of Godescalc, from the name of its artist. It is a lavish manuscript with gold characters on purple vellum, the first pages of which are adorned with paintings of Christ in Majesty and the Evangelists. The scriptorium of St-Martin at Tours produced, among other works, the *Évangéliaire de Lothair* (*c.* 845), featuring a portrait of that prince; and the Bible presented to Charles the Bald by Abbot Vivien (*c.* 850), adorned with eight fine full-page paintings.

Political conditions in France during the late 9th and 10th centuries caused a period of inactivity after the fine Carolingian era; thus for a period of about 100 years after 950 it was the empire of the Ottos and Henrys that became the center of Western culture. The most celebrated scriptoria at this time were at Fulda, Hildesheim, the lower Rhine valley (Cologne), and those regions already referred to as the principal sites of wall paintings: Regensburg, Salzburg, and Reichenau. This coincidence can be explained by the manifold activities of the great abbeys, and it provides evidence of reciprocal influences between wall painting and manuscript illumination.

In the 11th century, a new period of expansion was initiated. While previously, clearly defined schools imposed their style over a restricted geographical area, the art of the 11th century extended all over Europe and comprised a variety of styles. In France, many scriptoria were formed or burst into new activity: in the north, in Paris (St-Germain-des-Prés), St-Denis, and Poitiers, and further south at Limoges (where illumination came under the influence of enameling), Albi and St-Sever. The paintings of Beatus of Liebana (*Commentaries on the Book of Revelation*, *c.* 786), who worked at the abbey of St-Sever in the mid-11th century, have a Spanish flavor. Their haunting forms are unforgettable, and—in the complete absence of figures—the skillful distribution of areas of brilliant color is enough to render the work a masterpiece of abstract painting.

At the end of the 11th century, the so-called *bibbie atlantiche*, or "Atlas" Bibles, began to appear in central Italy (from the scriptoria of Rome, Latium, and Umbria); they are of large size, in several volumes, and all are adorned with paintings. The one known as the *Pantheon Bible*, produced at Rome in the first third of the 12th century (Vatican Library), is a typical example. On the reverse side of the third folio is represented the story of Adam up to the Expulsion from Eden; the narrative is unfolded in four registers; the whole work has the air of a fresco reproduced on a small scale, and in some places it is reminiscent of the cycle of Adam at Ferentillo (in the abbey church of S. Pietro a Valle, from the late 12th century). Among works produced in southern Italy, where the manuscripts are distinguished primarily by their form of script (*scriptura beneventana*), one must mention the Exultet Rolls in which the paintings, alternating with the text, follow each other on a scroll intended to be unrolled before the eyes of the faithful (11th and 12th centuries).

In England, where the tradition of manuscript painting was among the most lively, activity did not slacken. Among other centers, Winchester maintained a school of the highest rank, producing the *Psalter of Henry of Blois* (mid-12th century; London, British Museum).

WORK IN PRECIOUS MATERIALS

A legacy from ancient cultures, works of art in precious materials continued to be produced in the 10th, 11th, and 12th centuries. A few masterpieces have survived, including the golden reliquary of Ste-Foy, an impressive cult image made at Conques in the 10th century in a workshop where activity continued until the 13th century. The art of sculpture in bronze was carried on in Saxony (Hildesheim, 10th and 11th centuries), in Wallonia (baptismal font in St. Bartholomew at Liège, 1113), and in Champagne (paschal candlestick at Rheims). Enamel work flourished at Limoges: one of the finest achievements of the Limousin enamelers is the plaque bearing a portrait of Geoffrey Plantagenet, who died in 1151; it comes from his tomb in Le Mans Cathedral and is now in the museum at Le Mans. Ivory sculpture, practiced in Charlemagne's time in Austrasia, Germany, and France, is particularly interesting because it provided models for the monumental sculpture that was revived in the 11th century. Ottonian Germany retained in the 12th century the traditions of the old workshops of Metz and Liège. The most famous example of needlework is the so-called Bayeux Tapestry formerly attributed to Queen Matilda; a vast hanging embroidered in wool, approximately 230 feet long and nearly 20 inches wide, it is an Anglo-Norman work of the late 11th century (*c.* 1088–92). Stained glass, already known among the Gauls in the 6th century, according to Gregory of Tours and Fortunatus, only reached its full flower in the second half of the 12th century, when the new style of architecture encouraged its development.

ROMANINO, Girolamo di Romano, *called* Il (*c.* 1484, Brescia—after 1559, Brescia), Italian painter of the Lombard School. Romanino's formative period was probably influenced by Giorgione and Titian, the great masters of the Venetian Renaissance, whose spirit is seen in his altarpiece of *St. Justina* (1513; Padua, Museo Civico). Even in his mature style there remained evidence of the subtlety of Venetian coloring: his fondness for silvery and rosy tones is seen in the late *Mystic Marriage of St. Catherine* (*c.* 1530; Washington, D.C., National Gallery). A sort of romantic disquiet invests Romanino's portraits (*Portrait of a Man*; Bergamo, Accademia Carrara) and imparts a genuine pathos to his religious scenes (*Christ at Emmaus*; Brescia, Pinacoteca). Dramatic incidents, heightened to the point of expressionism, as well as the most sensual or worldly associations, appear in his large decorative paintings, such as the frescoes with scenes from the Passion in Cremona Cathedral (1519). Romanino's frescoes in the Castello del Buon Consiglio at Trento (*c.* 1531–32) enliven the walls of that austere palace with beautiful mythological figures and familiar incidents from daily life. His bold experimentation with candlelight effects in *St. Matthew and the Angel* (1521–24) seems directly to prefigure the art of another Lombard, Caravaggio, and is today responsible for recalling critical attention to this once-underestimated painter.

ROMANTICISM. The chief characteristics associated with Romanticism include the importance given to sensibility, imagination, and fantasy as against reason and order; the replacement of a Greco-Roman ideal by an admiration for the Middle Ages; values that were national and Christian, even primitive; and a return to what was considered "real" nature. In the visual arts, however, these characteristics did not inevitably imply the use of a new idiom. In fact, at certain periods and in some countries, Romanticism was content to use the Neoclassical idiom. A vague notion of the primitive, associated with both the pre-Classical Etruscans and the Middle Ages, to some extent united these apparently contradictory expressions of Romanticism.

GERMANY

The Nazarene painters, whose outstanding members were Peter Cornelius and Johann Friedrich Overbeck, have a special interest for this ambiguous Romanticism in Neoclassical trappings. Their two group enterprises, the Biblical paintings at the Casa Bartholdi and those celebrating the great Italian poets at the Villa Massimi, place them unequivocally in the Romantic tradition, but the affected naiveté of their manner, which imitated Raphael and Perugino, was fundamentally graphic and Classical with little emphasis on color. These characteristics apply as well to the minor German Romantics, including such provincial painters as Philipp Otto Runge (1777–1810) and Erwin Speckter; the allegorical figures of the first and the decorations of the second, which are among the best of the period, were derived directly from Pompeian murals.

In Caspar David Friedrich, German Romanticism produced a unique kind of landscape painting. The style is cold, but the subject matter is tragic and literary. His lunar landscapes, crosses on mountain summits, Gothic ruins, and snowy clearings had few imitators.

The Neoclassical architect Karl Friedrich Schinkel contributed to the renaissance of the Gothic style with his cathedral designs and Gothic houses at Potsdam (*c.* 1800). The most influential propagandists for the Gothic style were the brothers Sulpice and Melchior Boisserée, whose engravings of Cologne Cathedral, published in 1823, were the result of years of study. At the same time, they gathered a collection of primitive paintings that, when acquired by Ludwig I of Bavaria, made this period fashionable again.

ENGLAND

There is no doubt that England was the leading country in this rebirth of the Gothic style, both through the scholarly and practical activities of intellectuals and artists. The systematic study of medieval cathedrals, first in England, then of those within easy reach across the Channel, was begun by the English, who founded the first antiquarian societies. In 1750 the antiquarian Horace Walpole began Gothicizing the little house he had bought in Strawberry Hill, Twickenham. An almost unbroken chain of works followed throughout the country, of which the most notable in London are the Guildhall (1787) by George Dance and the Houses of Parliament at Westminster, begun in 1840 on the designs of Charles Barry and A. W. N. Pugin.

The English contribution to the graphic arts was equally important. William Blake and the Anglo-Swiss Henry Fuseli, both of whom represent the visionary and fantastic aspect of Romanticism, are particularly noteworthy. Blake, a poet and precursor of Romanticism, began engraving his drawings for the Bible and the *Divine Comedy* in 1787. Fuseli was a much more sophisticated artist and his graphic work is Neoclassical. Nothing in Blake or Fuseli gave an inkling of the revival in painting that was about to take place in England. The natural conservatism of the English, which is noticeable in the 18th-century portraitists, contributed to this revival. In some of William Hogarth's paintings (*Shrimp Girl*; London, National Gallery) freshly colored flesh tints, impregnated with light, have been brushed broadly onto the cheeks, replacing the cool Neoclassical palette. A contributory factor to this lightening of painters' colors was the art of the watercolor, which had never been treated with such a light, bold touch. Robert Cozens, Thomas Girtin, and John Sell Cotman were some of the distinguished painters in this medium. Bonington learned the delicacy of his landscapes from them and Turner, in the course of his travels in France and the British Isles, added his own veils of light to the watercolor. John Crome painted his Norfolk landscapes in oils and Constable gave his paintings a luminosity that inspired the whole of the Romantic landscape school.

FRANCE

Romanticism was slow in coming to France. The closing years of the 18th century had its "troubadour" style, patriotic tragedies, and Gothic buildings set in fashionably laid out parks—all of which can be seen as Rococo rather than Romantic manifestations. After the Revolution and the Empire, royalist tastes were even more inclined toward the Middle Ages and knight errantry. But in painting Louis David's grip over the Neoclassical School took long to weaken. The first revolt was made by Baron Gros, who dared to confess his admiration for Rubens. Géricault, 20 years younger than Gros, effected a more permanent revolution. A sound Classical training was apparent in his nudes and pen and ink drawings, but it was the impetuosity of his Michelangelesque draftsmanship in the *Raft of the Medusa* (1819; Louvre) that won victory for Romanticism.

Eugène Delacroix stood at the confluence of all French Romantic currents: he took the palette of Rubens from Gros, the lightness and freshness of English coloring from his friend Bonington, and tried to discover the secret of Constable's scintillating light. While Delacroix's position as leader of French Romanticism is undeniable, the position of Ingres, on the other hand, was very ambiguous. In some of his small historical paintings he was attracted by medieval illumination, although fundamentally he remained a Neoclassicist. But his pupil, Théodore Chassériau, could claim a place among the Romantics through his fascination for the East, as well as the warm light and strange poetry of his paintings. The only one of the Romantics who could rival Delacroix was Honoré Daumier. The intensity of feeling and the style of his draftsmanship was Romantic, but since he was not interested in the past and stormy emotions left him indifferent, Daumier should perhaps be classed with the Realists who followed him rather than with Romanticism.

The other glory of French art of the period was landscape painting. Paul Huet (1803–69) tried to paint an emotional vision of nature that could be qualified as Romantic, while Corot learned much from such Neoclassicists as Michallon and Bertin. Such painters of the

Romanticism. Horace Walpole. Strawberry Hill, Twickenham. 1750–70. *Photo Country Life, London.*

Romanticism. Théodore Chassériau. *Venus of the Sea.* 1838. Louvre, Paris. *Archives photographiques, Paris.*

Romanticism. Francisco Goya. *"Volaverunt."* 1796–99. Aquatint from the *Caprichos.*

Barbizon School as Théodore Rousseau, and Daubigny, the painter of water, depicted the pleasant side of nature. The religious strain in Jean-François Millet touched on a sterner side of life in the country.

Géricault was not only a distinguished painter, he also produced some incomparable pieces of sculpture. Daumier cultivated this facet of his genius as well. But the great Romantic sculptors were François Rude, Antoine Barye, and Antoine Préault.

The essence of Romanticism may well be found in an isolated Spaniard, part of whose career fell before the Romantic movement and whom the Romantics hardly knew—Francisco de Goya. His life and art summarize the whole history of Romanticism. His brilliant portraits certainly derive something from the English School, but the series of engravings called the *Caprichos* show, before the end of the century, that he was haunted by the monsters engendered by the "sleep of reason." He was the prototype of Romantics, perhaps because he was fiercely individualistic and in revolt against his surroundings.

ROMNEY, George (1734, Dalton-in-Furness, Lancashire—1802, Kendal, Westmorland), English portraitist. In 1757 Romney established himself as a portrait painter in Kendal and Lancaster. In 1762 he went to London, where he rapidly built up a busy practice. His tastes at this time were narrow but consistent: he aimed at a simplified version of the Classical ideal and, although he lacked the erudition of Sir Joshua Reynolds, he evolved a style of harmonious, almost feminine fluidity, based on his admiration for Roman sculpture. He also had a flair for pictorial economy that gives his portraits a quality of distinction markedly superior to those of such contemporaries as Francis Cotes.

Although Romney had a successful practice in London, he abandoned it in 1773 to go to Italy, where he stayed for 18 months, returning to England by way of Florence, Bologna, and Venice. He spent much of his time in Italy diligently copying Raphael's paintings, but it was Guido Reni's influence that, together with that of his friend John Flaxman, was to be most noticeable in his mature style and in the portraits painted between 1775 and 1790. He reduced the settings in his paintings to a tree in the background or a sketchy Classical reference (*Lady Louisa Stormont*, 1776, England, Nethway House, Coll. Earl Cathcart; the *Leveson-Gower Children*, 1776–77, London, Coll. Duke of Sutherland). Romney made little reference to the sitter's background or profession, but he did imbue his portraits with a tranquillity and a sensibility that, allied to his extremely clear sculptural modeling, occasionally enabled him to achieve a remarkable poetry that is lyrical in contrast to the rhetoric of Reynolds or the romance of Thomas Gainsborough (*Mrs. Carwardine and Son*, 1775; Northamptonshire, Wakefield Lodge, Coll. Lord Hillingdon).

The influence of Emma Hart (later Lady Hamilton), with whom he fell deeply in love some time after 1781, seems to have disrupted this moment of equilibrium. He painted her many times and in various guises: as *Prayer* (1782–86; London, Kenwood, Lord Iveagh Bequest), as a *Spinstress* (1787; Kenwood), and as *Ariadne* (1785; Greenwich, National Maritime Museum). His rougher portrait sketches (*Study of Lady Hamilton, c.* 1786; London, National Gallery) have an ardor and freedom, together with an overtly theatrical emotionalism. Also in the 1780s, Romney produced numerous drawings of Shakespearian subjects, of which there are many examples in the Fitzwilliam Museum at Cambridge. In the early 1790s a nervous instability became more pronounced, and he was probably insane for some time before his death.

Romney's reputation rests on the sketchy simplicity of his best portraits, notably his *Self-Portrait* (1780; London, National Portrait Gallery), and his clarity of design, which links him with the Neoclassical style that was then emerging on the Continent.

ROOT, John Wellborn (1850, Lumpkin, Georgia—1891, Chicago), major American architect of the Chicago School. In 1864 he was sent to Liverpool, where he studied architecture and music. He received a bachelor's degree in civil engineering from New York University in 1869 and became a draftsman in the office of the Gothic Revivalist James Renwick. Root moved to Chicago in 1872 to work for Peter Bonnett Wight (1838–1925). There he met Daniel Burnham and the two formed a partnership that proved to be extremely productive. Unfortunately, only three of the firm's 27 buildings in downtown Chicago survive: the Rookery (1885–86), the Commerce Building (1885–86), and the Monadnock Block (1889–91).

Root's affinities with H. H. Richardson and his invention of rich, stylized decoration may be seen in the Rookery, a building that incorporates some local structural innovations. The treatment of the ground floor exterior, alternating sturdy supporting columns and window walls, anticipates the base of Sullivan's Guaranty Building in Buffalo (1894–95).

But it is primarily Root's noncommercial work that is Richardsonian; his business commissions are often emphatically utilitarian. The Montauk Block (1881–82) in Chicago has been praised as an epochal office building for its straightforward approach to the creation of economical, fireproof office space as well as for its "floating-raft" foundations, which helped solve the problem of erecting tall buildings on Chicago's marshy soil. Its design and that of the second Rand McNally building (1889–90), Chicago, which had steel-frame street walls, look ahead to the more direct, if monotonous, horizontal expression of frame construction so prevalent in the 20th century. His masterpiece is the Monadnock Block. The first design, conceived in 1884, drew on Egyptian sources, but Root gradually planed away all ornamental detail. The ranks of projecting bay windows not only increase the amount of interior light but, by providing a vertical emphasis and a strong surface modulation, enhance the building's austere magnificence.

ROSA, Salvator (1615, Arenalla, near Naples—1673, Rome), Italian painter and engraver, also a poet, musician, and actor. Rosa was particularly influenced by the battle scenes of Aniello and by those of Michelangelo Cerquozzi, as well as by Ribera's tenebristic scenes of torture. He was in Rome in 1635, then in Naples again two years later. For nine years, from 1641 to 1649, he lived in Florence, where he was in the service of the Medici court before settling finally in Rome in 1649. Salvator was a restless creative genius, with astonishing imaginative gifts and a wild romantic fancy, who favored fiery depictions of battles (*Battlepiece*, 1652; Paris, Louvre), and above all highly picturesque landscapes with rocky settings in which tiny figures of witches, soldiers, brigands, gods, and saints wander (*St. Onofrio*, mid-1660s; Milan, Brera). He also produced a number of macabre allegories, one of the finest being *Human Fragility* (*c.* 1657; Cambridge, Fitzwilliam Museum).

ROSENQUIST, James (b. 1933, Grand Forks, North Dakota), American painter. Influenced in spirit by the Surrealists Salvador Dali and René Magritte, as well as by his fellow Pop artists Jasper Johns and Robert Rauschenberg, Rosenquist traces his stylistic origins to the billboard painting by which he supported himself during his first years in New York (1955–60). The technique of photographic enlargement used in this trade served Rosenquist in his own art: he developed a method of splicing and combining fragmentary blown-up images taken from commercial advertising along with the motifs of our industrial culture so that the effect is often as abstract and disconcerting as cinemascope movie close-ups.

Rosenquist's iconography of the recognizable includes images that are used for their specific contemporary associations as well as for their more abstract qualities: big swirls of canned spaghetti, rubber tires, atom bomb clouds, automobile parts, human faces, food, clothing, and light bulbs. In his largest three-panel mural *F-111* (1965; New York, Coll. Mr. and Mrs. Robert Scull) he interweaves these images with the fuselage of a giant airplane, painted in luridly harsh billboard color. By 1962 Rosenquist had also extended this montage-enlargement method to single panel paintings, so that the fragmentary images (more collagelike in earlier work, but single cutouts in the later canvases) were almost beyond recognition due to their scaling (*Above the Square*, 1963; Coll. Mr. and Mrs. Robert Scull). He uses the materials of our modern industrial complex inventively in many of his works—plastic sheeting, Plexiglas, neon light, simulated metal. Freestanding constructions have also occupied the artist for several years (*Capillary Action II*, 1963; New York, Leo Castelli Gallery).

ROSSELLI, Cosimo (1439, Florence—1507, Florence), Italian painter. A pupil of Neri di Bicci (1373–1452) and Benozzo Gozzoli, he popularized a calm and clear style, which may be seen in his groups of the *Virgin and Child with Saints* (1471; East Berlin), the *Annunciation with Four Saints* (1473; Paris, Louvre), and in his fresco on the *Vocation of S. Filippo Benizzi* (1476; Florence, SS. Annunziata). In 1481 Cosimo was, along with Sandro Botticelli, Domenico Ghirlandaio, and others, one of the team of artists commissioned by Pope Sixtus IV to decorate the Sistine Chapel in the Vatican. His share of the work there (*Moses Destroying the Tablets of the Law*, the *Sermon on the Mount*, and the *Last Supper*, all 1482) is indebted to Ghirlandaio in respect to the figures, their grouping, and even the colors. After his return to Florence, Rosselli painted frescoes (1484–86; now lost) in the monastery and church of S. Ambrogio. Still extant, in the church, is the scene of the *Miracle of the Holy Sacrament*, with a clear but rather overcrowded composition in the manner of Gozzoli.

ROSSELLINO, family of 15th-century Florentine artists whose principal members were:

BERNARDO (1409, Settignano, near Florence—1464, Florence), Italian Renaissance architect and sculptor. We encounter Bernardo first in his work on the façade of the church of the Misericordia in Arezzo (1433), where he executed a relief of the Virgin. The tomb of Leonardo Bruni (begun 1444; Florence, S. Croce) is typical of his extensive work in funeral monuments between 1435 and 1454. His monument to the Blessed Villana (1451; Florence, S. Maria Novella) is in a less modern idiom. At the same time he became assistant to the famous Florentine architect Leon Battista Alberti, to whose designs he built the Palazzo Rucellai in Florence (1446–53). Rossellino seems to have played an important part in the construction of the Palazzo Venezia in Rome, built to the orders of Pietro Cardinal Bembo, the future Pope Paul II. Rossellino's outstanding contribution was in the field of town planning, an art uncultivated since Roman times. This aspect of his career began when Pope Nicholas V asked him to prepare plans for the Borgo district in Rome, and for the approaches to St. Peter's. Later, the Piccolomini pope, Pius II, required his talents to raise his birthplace, Pienza, to the status of a city. The center of the town was intentionally planned as a single unit based on the cathedral. The cathedral lies on the main axis of a plaza whose sides converge toward a town hall at the north end. The east and west sides are flanked by the bishop's palace and the Palazzo Piccolomini.

Cosimo Rosselli. *Pietà.* Philadelphia Museum of Art.

Bernardo Rossellino. Pienza Cathedral. 1461–62. *Photo Alinari-Giraudon.*

Antonio Rossellino. *Stoning of St. Stephen.* 1473. Prato Cathedral. *Photo Alinari-Giraudon.*

Rossellino is thought also to have been the architect of the Palazzo Piccolomini at Siena, which has affinities with the Pienza palace, both deriving from the Palazzo Rucellai.

ANTONIO (1427, Settignano—1479, Florence), unlike his brother Bernardo, practiced sculpture exclusively. His first signed and dated work (1456) is a bust of the Humanist physician Giovanni Chellini (London, Victoria and Albert Museum), which may have been taken from a life mask and which shows the influence of Desiderio da Settignano. Antonio's first known commissioned work was a splendid tomb for the cardinal of Portugal (1461–66; Florence, S. Miniato), a masterpiece of Florentine refinement. Earlier Antonio had collaborated with his brothers Bernardo and Giovanni on the shrine of Blessed Marcolino da Forlì (1458; Forlì, Museum) and on the tomb of Neri Capponi (Florence, S. Spirito). Antonio also executed many fine busts of children and men, notably of *Matteo Palmieri* (1468; Florence, Bargello), the *Young St. John* (*c.* 1470; Washington, D.C., National Gallery), and a very beautiful statue of *St. Sebastian* for the Collegiata d'Empoli. In 1473 he executed three reliefs for the throne of Prato Cathedral. His style shows a sensitivity toward light and shade, and subtle modulations of surface detail.

ROSSETTI, Gabriel Charles Dante, *called* Dante Gabriel (1828, London—1882, Birchington-on-Sea, Kent), English poet and painter, one of the founders of Pre-Raphaelitism. From 1846 to 1848 he studied in the Antique School of the Royal Academy in London and later, briefly, with Ford Madox Brown and William Holman Hunt. With Hunt and John Everett Millais he was part of the original nucleus of the Pre-Raphaelite Brotherhood, whose members also included literary figures: his *Girlhood of Mary Virgin* (1849; London, National Gallery), exhibited in the Free Exhibition at the Hyde Park Gallery in London, was the first picture to bear the initials PRB. In pictures such as *Ecce Ancilla Domini* (1850; London, Tate Gallery) and *Found* (begun 1853, left unfinished; Wilmington, Del., Bancroft Foundation), he painted mournful Botticellian allegories with a note of social protest.

In 1857 Rossetti worked with William Morris and Edward Burne-Jones on the frescoes for the Union Debating Society in Oxford and inspired them to become part of the Brotherhood. His association with Morris was prolonged through his love for Morris' wife Jane, whose face Rossetti reproduced time and time again in the guise of *Queen Guinevere* (pen-and-ink drawing, 1858; Dublin, National Gallery of Ireland), *Proserpina* (1877; Tate Gallery), and many others. The inspiration for his early works, such as *Mary Magdalene at the House of Simon the Pharisee* (1858; Cambridge, Fitzwilliam Museum), was Elizabeth Siddall, a neurotic beauty whom he married and who died of an overdose of laudanum in 1862. In a fit of grief Rossetti buried a manuscript volume of poems with his wife; these were exhumed in 1869 and published as *Poems* in 1870.

The brooding pensiveness, the compositional clutter, the chilly discomfort, and the medieval details in such watercolors as the *Wedding of St. George and the Princess Sabra* (1857; Tate Gallery) connect him with the escapist strain in Pre-Raphaelitism. His preference for watercolor and his preoccupation with Dante (in 1861 he published translations from Dante and the early Italian poets) are singularly reminiscent of Blake. Rossetti may thus be regarded as a late Romantic.

ROSSI, Gino (1884, Venice—1947, Venice), Italian painter. In 1907 he went to Paris with the sculptor Arturo Martini, and—after seeing the works of Gauguin, Van Gogh, and the Cubists—realized that he wanted to become a painter. He returned to Paris in 1912; unfortunately, however, his artistic career was terminated in 1926 when an attack of insanity necessitated his confinement in an asylum, where he remained for the rest of his life. In 1948, a year after his death, a retrospective of about 50 of his works, organized at the Venice Biennale, revealed his important position in the history of Italian painting. Rossi's oeuvre includes such pictures as *Young Girl with a Flower* (1908; Spresiano, Treviso, Coll. Giuseppe Fanna) and *Fisherman in a Green Beret* (1913; Johannesburg, Coll. Marcello Bernabò), which both show the influence of Gauguin's Pont-Aven period. He also produced Cubist compositions, such as *Still Life with Violin and Bottles* (1922; Milan, Coll. De Romans), *Still Life with a Revolver* (1922; Coll. Marcello Bernabò), and *Village on a Hill* (1923; Venice, Galleria Internazionale d'Arte Moderna), which has a completely Cézannesque structure. Rossi's art shows a conscientious and original experimentation.

ROSSO, Medardo (1858, Turin—1928, Milan), Italian sculptor. Rosso visited Paris in 1884 and 1886. When he returned there in 1889, the exhibition of his work at the Exposition Universelle met with a gratifying success, particularly in avant-garde circles that included Auguste Rodin, Edgar Degas, the collector Henri Rouart (whose portrait Rosso modeled in 1890; Rome, Galleria Nazionale d'Arte Moderna), and Émile Zola. During this period Rosso executed some of his finest works: *Little Girl Laughing* (1890; Barzio, Rosso Museum), *Lady with a Veil* (1893;

Medardo Rosso. *Ecce Puer.* 1910. Musée National d'Art Moderne, Paris. *Archives photographiques, Paris.*

Galleria Nazionale d'Arte Moderna), and *Yvette Guilbert* (1894; Venice, Galleria Internazionale d'Arte Moderna di Ca' Pesaro). Rosso spent his last years in Milan, where he enjoyed an increasing reputation: Umberto Boccioni even hailed him as a precursor of Futurist sculpture in his *Technical Manifesto of Futurist Sculpture* (1912).

At first Rosso had a pictorial vision of reality, then he moved quite naturally toward a sculpture with delicate surface effects that rendered the quivering life of forms and the sheath of light that enveloped them. Rosso often used wax because its malleability and fluidity could render these effects better than any other material. In spite of their modernistic qualities, the melancholy, twilight feeling of Rosso's figures suggests that his sculpture represents the final phase of the 19th-century tradition, rather than Rodin's work.

ROSSO FIORENTINO, Giovanni Battista di Jacopo, *called* (1494, Florence—1540, Paris), Italian painter and decorator. He was a striking exponent of the sophisticated and neurotic style known as Mannerism, which became an international phenomenon partly through his agency. One of his early works in Florence was the *Assumption of the Virgin* (1517; SS. Annunziata), the last of a series of frescoes begun by Andrea del Sarto. This work, which reveals the influence of Albrecht Dürer, is not yet overtly Mannerist, but the strange and inhuman expressions of his faces depart radically from Renaissance precedent. The disturbing, almost hysterical expressions of the *Assumption* appear also in the *Madonna with Four Saints* (1518; Florence, Uffizi), painted for the rector of S. Maria Novella. In the *Madonna with Two Saints* (1521; Villamagna), the faces have become even more inhuman but now his rebellious anticlassicism has begun to mature into a more positive statement, visible in his sure handling of the faceted, angular drapery. This maturity is even more apparent in the *Deposition* (1521; Volterra, Pinacoteca), whose hallucinatory quality results in part from his extraordinary treatment of light. Rosso was the first artist to treat this subject according to Scripture, as a nocturnal event, illuminated only by the moon. The unreal atmosphere is enhanced by the abstract angularity of figures and drapery, as well as by the strangeness of coloring, attitudes, and expressions. Rosso's next two paintings in Florence, the pala for the Dei family (1522; S. Spirito) and the *Marriage of the Virgin* (1523; S. Lorenzo), continue this development. He went to Rome in 1524, where he painted the relatively unsuccessful frescoes of the *Creation of Eve* and the *Fall of Man* (S. Maria della Pace), and studied the works of Michelangelo and Raphael. While in Venice in 1530, Rosso received an invitation from François I to decorate the Grande Galerie (called the Galerie François Ier) at Fontainebleau. The paintings and elaborate stucco decorations that he devised for the gallery helped to establish the Mannerist style in France.

ROSZAK, Theodore (b. 1907, Poznan, Poland), American sculptor and painter. In 1909 his parents emigrated from Poland and settled in Chicago. Roszak held his first one-man exhibition of paintings and lithographs in Chicago (1928). In 1931 he settled in New York, where he continued drawing and painting and began to model sculpture in plaster. In his paintings, he oscillated at first between realism, fantasy, and abstraction, but the influence of Laszlo Moholy-Nagy helped him to find his own sculptural idiom. From about 1936 to 1945 Roszak went through a period of pure Constructivism and made structures in plastic, steel, and wood that were reminiscent of the practical exercises done by the Bauhaus students (*Bipolar Form*, 1940, Chicago, Coll. Mrs. Aniel Lunetto; *Spatial Construction*, 1943, New York, Coll. artist). The strictly geometric reliefs and forms, based on the line and cone, gave way around 1946 to metal sculptures that were freer and more suggestive. The *Specter of Kitty Hawk* (1946–47; New York, Museum of Modern Art) was his first work in the intensely dramatic style in which he ultimately excelled. Insects and plants provided the themes for many of the sculptures he did in the 1950s and 1960s (*Sea Sentinel*, 1956; New York, Whitney Museum). The birth of his daughter prompted him to execute a figure suggesting the budding of a flower (*Thorn Blossom*, 1947; Whitney Museum), while the *Whaler of Nantucket* (1952–53; Chicago, Art Institute) was the result of his reading of Herman Melville's *Moby Dick*.

Theodore Roszak. *Specter of Kitty Hawk.* 1946–47. Museum of Modern Art, New York.

ROTHKO, Mark (1903, Dvinsk, Latvia—1970, New York), American painter of Russian origin. Rothko's parents emigrated to the United States in 1913 and in 1925 he settled in New York, where he began painting while attending Max Weber's courses at the Art Students League. In 1936–37 he worked for the WPA Federal Art Project. In 1948 he joined William Baziotes, Robert Motherwell, and Barnett Newman in founding an art school in New York called "Subjects of the Artist," which developed into a discussion group called "The Club." Rothko was influenced by Surrealism until around 1947; it helped to free him from the Expressionism characteristic of his first paintings, and enabled him to create a transparent aquatic world inhabited by a flora and fauna with tentacular excrescences (*Prehistoric Memories*, 1946; New York, Betty Parsons Gallery). As he gradually developed his own style, he tried to release color from the constraints of form and literary allusion and to create a kind of chromatic plain chant (*Number 24*, 1949; New York, Coll. Mr. Joseph H. Hirshhorn). Around 1950 his images began to fade away into a colored haze and then, in a general process of simplification, he transformed his shapes into imprecise, diffuse rectangles that almost filled the area of the canvas (*Number 2*, 1962; New York, Coll. Mrs. Albert

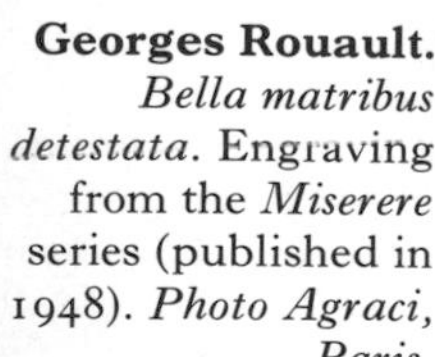

Georges Rouault. *Bella matribus detestata.* Engraving from the *Miserere* series (published in 1948). *Photo Agraci, Paris.*

D. Lasker). Rothko created spaces of varying depths by an almost imperceptible cadence of colors, which established infinite gradations in the intensity of the light (*White and Greens on Blue*, 1957; New York, Coll. Nelson A. Rockefeller). However strong their resonances might be, his blues, yellows, reds, and greens never fragment his dazzling and absolute space, but diversify the nature of its unity.

ROTTMANN, Carl (1797, Handschusheim, near Heidelberg—1850, Munich), German painter. Rottmann, the most important landscape artist working in Munich in the early 19th century, studied under his father Franz (1768–1816), and also with Johann Christian Xeller (1784–1872) in Heidelberg. The landscapes he painted in Italy (1826–27) further enhanced his youthful reputation, and he was able to persuade King Ludwig I of Bavaria to commission a cycle of Italian landscape frescoes for the western arcades in the Munich royal gardens. The 28 frescoes (1830–33) were painted after a second trip to Italy in 1828. In 1834 Ludwig sent him to Greece to make studies for a Greek cycle, placed in a special hall of the Neue Pinakothek, Munich (1838–50).

Although Rottmann was influenced by the early Romantics in his youthful landscapes, he subsequently evolved a highly individual style in expansive, open-ended views that showed great understanding of geological structure and historical atmosphere. Rottmann was highly influential through his Italian cycle—the first monumental landscape series in 19th-century German painting—and his Greek cycle, which virtually discovered the Greek landscape for German art.

ROUAULT, Georges (1871, Paris—1958, Paris), French painter and engraver. His father, a carpenter, apprenticed him at the age of fourteen to a stained-glass maker, and in the evening the boy attended classes at the École des Arts Décoratifs. In December 1890 Rouault was admitted to the École des Beaux-Arts in Paris and to the studio of Élie Delaunay (1828–91). After the latter's death, the studio was directed by Gustave Moreau, whose favorite pupil Rouault soon became. He was awarded the Chenavard Prize for his *Christ Among the Doctors* (1894; Colmar, Musée d'Unterlinden), and exhibited several times at the Salon des Artistes Français. After the death of his master, he was appointed curator of the Musée Gustave Moreau in 1903, but his salary was not adequate. Along with his financial difficulties there developed an artistic crisis of major proportions. For a short period he aligned himself with the Fauvists, a group that included some of his fellow students in Moreau's studio—Henri Matisse, Albert Marquet, and Henri-Charles Manguin, with whom he founded the Salon d'Automne in 1903. He never felt, however, that their ideas were congenial to his own. It was his meeting with the writer Joris-Karl Huysmans (a recent convert to Catholicism) in 1901, and with the Catholic writer Léon Bloy in 1904 that strengthened the religious cast of his ideas and helped him discover the significance of his own creativity as well as the plastic means appropriate to it. In some of the clowns he painted in these years, his drawing was already simplified to its essential lines, and color to its most restrained tones.

The spectacle of humanity expiating original sin aroused both Rouault's pity and his anger. The imperfections of man that betrayed themselves in egoism, complacency, pride, hypocrisy, and debauchery filled Rouault with horror, as is evident in *Monsieur and Madame Poulot* (1905; Hem, Coll. Philippe Leclercq), inspired by Léon Bloy's novel *La Femme Pauvre*; in the *Prostitute Before a Mirror* (1906; Paris, Musée National d'Art Moderne), *Massacred Heads* (1907–8; London, Tate Gallery), *Monsieur X* (1911; Buffalo, Albright-Knox Art Gallery), and later in the *Three Judges* (1913; New York, Museum of Modern Art). He had no use for modeling, chiaroscuro, and toned color, with the result that the impact of his images became even more powerful. Hard, opaque brushstrokes, thick outlines resembling the lead in stained glass, savage slashes of color, and massive caricatural forms set against ominous shadows: these were the technical means Rouault employed in the creation of his highly distinctive and expressive style. His workmen worn out with privation and toil (*Suburb of Endless Sorrow*, 1911; Paris, Musée d'Art Moderne de la Ville de Paris), the circus clown who suppresses his grief as he makes others laugh (*Old Clown*, 1917; New York, Coll. Stavros Niarchos), and exhausted peasants, all give witness to his compassion for the poor and disinherited of the world. In his youth he had painted religious subjects, and in 1913 he returned to them with greater determination. There followed a period (1917–27) during which he executed a series of book illustrations (*Reincarnations of Père Ubu*, published by Ambroise Vollard), and the *Miserere* engravings. Afterward, with the exception of the series of *Pierrots* (1937–38), he painted nothing but the Passion of Christ, repentant prostitutes, Virgins of Consolation, Biblical scenes, and landscapes: *The Veronica* (1933; Musée National d'Art Moderne), *Setting Sun* (1937; Worcester, Art Museum), *Christian Nocturn* (1952; Musée National d'Art Moderne), and *Sarah* (1956; Paris, Priv. Coll.).

Rouault's desire for near perfection in his work and a scrupulous regard for craftsmanship sometimes led to unfortunate results, as in his practice of working the paint on some of his pictures with an excessive patience and care until it had the consistency of enamel. His drawings, etchings, and watercolors are often preferable to these overworked oils. He did little, in fact, that can stand comparison with the 58 plates of the *Miserere*. For it was in the austerely monochromatic discipline of these exceptionally large copperplates that Rouault's obsessions and the simplicity of his vision found their most valid expression.

ROUBILIAC, Louis François (1702/5, probably Lyons—1762, London), French sculptor. He spent his working life in London, where he arrived around 1732/5. He visited Italy in 1752 and was much impressed by Bernini's work as well as by antique sculpture. Roubiliac first gained recognition with his statue of *George Frederick Handel*, done in 1738 for the Vauxhall Pleasure Gardens, London (the original statue now belongs to Messrs. Novello, London, and the terra-cotta model is in the Fitzwilliam Museum, Cambridge). During the 1740s and 1750s he made numerous portrait busts, all of a high quality, including those of his friend *William Hogarth* (*c.* 1740; London, National Portrait Gallery) and the series in Trinity College, Cambridge. His fame as a monumental sculptor was established by his *Monument to John, Duke of Argyll* (1745–49; London, Westminster Abbey); he also executed several additional tombs there and in other English churches (*Monument to Bishop Hough*, 1746; Worcester Cathedral). Two of Roubiliac's latest and finest monuments in Westminster Abbey are those to *Handel* (1761) and *Lady Elizabeth Nightingale* (1761), which is very dramatic, with a figure of Death derived from Bernini's *Alexander VII* in St. Peter's.

ROUSSEAU, Henri Julien Félix, *called* Le Douanier (1844, Laval, Mayenne—1910, Paris), French painter. A tinker's son, he attended school in Laval, and in 1863 joined the army. He was demobilized in 1868, married, and in 1871 obtained a post as a toll officer of the Customs and Excise Department in Paris. Rousseau began painting regularly when he was about forty, although he did not retire from the toll office until 1893.

Behind the façade of a humble, middle-class existence, Rousseau pursued an artistic activity that was as original as it was prolific. He copied pictures in the Louvre, and exhibited assiduously at the Salon des Indépendants and the Salon d'Automne. As early as 1886 he attracted the attention of Paul Signac, Camille Pissarro, Odilon Redon, and Henri de Toulouse-Lautrec, and soon counted among his friends the poets Alfred Jarry, Guillaume Apollinaire, and Max Jacob, and the painters Robert Delaunay, Fernand Léger, Georges Braque, and Pablo Picasso. He was a great painter who developed his work day after day with an awareness of his craftsmanship and a perseverance that was certainly not typical of an amateur artist guided solely by his instinct. A number of disturbing questions are prompted by his prolific and varied production, in which the arrangements of pictorial motifs are as strict as they are unexpected; in which the light, the relationships of the tones, and the perspective and rhythmic interplay of proportions show a consummate technique and a style that is both noble and familiar (*War*, 1894, Paris, Musée de l'Impressionnisme; *Sleeping Gypsy*, 1897, New York, Museum of Modern Art; *The Orchard*, 1898, Paris, Priv. Coll.; the *Cart of Père Juniet*, 1908, Paris, Louvre). His still lifes, for instance, have a sublime humility, and fabulously exotic compositions (*Virgin Forest at Sunset*, 1907, Basel, Kunstmuseum; the *Snake Charmer*, 1907, Musée de l'Impressionnisme; *The Jungle*, 1908, New York, Priv. Coll.' and *The Dream*, 1910, Museum of Modern Art), while his portraits are characterized by their hieratic dignity.

Rousseau was no more a "primitive" painter than Paul Cézanne, nor was he a "folk artist" or "Sunday painter": he was a painter who had learned nothing and knew everything, who had an exact understanding of his means and aims, who belonged to no school and dominated them all. Rousseau's extraordinarily limpid skies, his magnificent vegetation that blends every shade of green, his long flowers swaying their white and pink corollas, and his figures that seem to have escaped from some ineffable rustic epic are enough to convince the sceptic that such skill has nothing in common with the results of a Sunday pastime or an untutored dream.

An additional argument against the notion that Rousseau was a primitive is his way of juxtaposing the most disparate objects and the least logically connected things in nature: the sofa in the middle of the jungle in *The Dream*; the lion holding a proclamation and crouching among the artists in *Liberty Inviting the Artists to Participate in the 22nd Salon des Indépendants* (1906; Zurich, Coll. Dr. Franz Meyer). These incongruities would seem comical, the associations would appear preposterous, even a little mad, if Surrealism had not accustomed us to the juxtapositions that Rousseau did not calculate but that he found naturally in the reality of his heart.

Henri Rousseau. *Cart of Père Juniet.* 1908. Louvre, Paris.

ROUSSEAU, Théodore Pierre Étienne (1812, Paris—1867, Barbizon), French painter. He was the leader and most important artist of the Barbizon School. His ambition, pursued with an almost scientific curiosity, became to express the innermost nature of the countryside, its light and structure. Accordingly, Rousseau began a tour of the country, starting with the Auvergne in 1830 (*Valley of Saint-Vincent, c.* 1830, London, National Gallery; *Village in a Valley, c.* 1830, New York, Metropolitan Museum). In 1832 we find him in Normandy, and the paintings of this period reveal the influences of Jan van Goyen and Salomon van Ruysdael in their mellow, monochromatic skies (*Market in Normandy, c.* 1833; Leningrad, Hermitage). His first visit to the forest of Fontainebleau in 1833 was an experience that had the impact of a revelation. The stormy *Plain of Montmartre* (*c.* 1835; Paris, Louvre) dates from this period and reveals the influence of John Constable. In Nantes, as the guest of the painter Charles Le Roux, Rousseau painted the famous *Avenue of Chestnut Trees* (*c.* 1835;

Théodore Rousseau. *Landscape.* Musée des Beaux-Arts, Bescançon. *Photo Bulloz, Paris.*

Thomas Rowlandson. *Drawing Class from the Living Model at the Royal Academy, London. c.* 1808. Museum of Fine Arts, Boston.

Louvre). Although one of his most successful works, it was rejected twice by the Salon, and after the second rejection in 1837, Rousseau left Paris for a cottage at Barbizon. There he was joined by Antoine Barye, the critic Théophile Thoré, Virgilio Narcisso Diaz de la Peña, and Jules Dupré (1811–89). After one particularly fruitful trip to the Landes with Dupré, in 1844, Rousseau returned with the *Plain at the Foot of the Pyrenees* (Louvre) and a series of sketches that later formed the basis of his *Marsh in the Landes* (1852; Louvre). After the revolution of 1848 his work was more generally accepted, and the state commissioned his masterly *Outskirts of the Forest of Fontainebleau at Sunset* (1848–50; Louvre). In 1855 he received official recognition when a whole room was reserved for his work at the Exposition Universelle. It was Rousseau's new vision of nature, as well as his technique of tiny, systematically applied brushstrokes, that set the stage for the Impressionists.

ROWLANDSON, Thomas (1756, London—1827, London), English artist, one of the most brilliant and prolific draftsmen in the history of British art. He studied art at the Royal Academy Schools in London, and spent two vital years (1771–73) in Paris—a visit that had a profound effect on his style. Around 1780 he discovered his personal idiom—the gently satirical portrayal of contemporary life—and remained faithful to it until his death. His artistic ability neither grew nor diminished over the years, and his style remained fixed; compare, for example, *A Coffee House* (*c.* 1780–85; Aberdeen, Art Gallery and Industrial Museum) with *The Mall, St. James's Park* (*c.* 1815–20; London, London Museum). His work was extremely popular with his contemporaries and he found a ready market for his drawings with the London printsellers S. W. Fores, Thomas Tegg, and Rudolph Ackermann. In his later years Rowlandson became dependent on Ackermann, who commissioned him to illustrate a number of popular texts, including a series called *The Tour of Dr. Syntax in Search of the Picturesque*, which appeared in Ackermann's *Poetical Magazine* in 1809 with a text by the humorist William Combe. It was followed by a series of books with colored plates, for which Rowlandson supplied the original watercolors, whose outlines he then etched on copperplate. Many of Rowlandson's drawings evoke comparison with those of artists whose work was far removed from the normal English canon: his *Vauxhall Gardens* (1784; Torquay, Devon, Coll. Alfred E. Pearson) bears traces of Gabriel de Saint-Aubin's (1724–80) style; his *Sir Peter Paul Rubens Setting His Palette* (Edinburgh) is similar to certain works by Jean-Honoré Fragonard; and his *Skaters on the Serpentine* (*c.* 1786; London Museum) can be compared to the work of Aert van der Neer. Rowlandson's caricatures have stylistic overtones that reveal the influence of the Italian artist Pier Leone Ghezzi (1674–1755), and it was his easy assimilation of foreign idioms and his lack of true indignation or satirical bite that distinguish Rowlandson's art from that of William Hogarth, with whom he shared many superficial similarities.

ROY, Pierre (1880, Nantes—1950, Milan), French painter. In 1908 he became associated with the Fauves and the poets who supported them, such as Guillaume Apollinaire and Max Jacob. With his painting of *Adrienne Fishing* (1919; Paris, Priv. Coll.), which he considered the real beginning of his career, Roy began to evoke the marvelous in everyday life. In 1920 he allied himself with the founders of Surrealism but, although he contributed to their first group exhibition in Paris in 1925, he remained on the fringe of their activities and was associated with them only because he shared certain affinities with them—for example, their fondness for evocative, dreamlike subjects. He illustrated Jules Supervielle's *Enfant de la haute mer* (1946) with lithographs and also designed sets for the Ballets des Champs-Élysées (*Jeux de cartes*, 1945) and the Copenhagen Opera. In his paintings Roy cultivated the unusual (*Day in the Country*, 1937; Paris, Musée National d'Art Moderne) and frequently, within a single composition, assembled disparate objects, which he painted with a minute realism, creating *trompe-l'oeil* effects that emphasized the poetic strangeness of their juxtapositions.

RUBENS, Peter Paul (1577, Siegen, Westphalia—1640, Antwerp), Flemish painter. Otto van Veen's (1556–1629) Late Mannerist-Classicist style influenced Rubens' earliest work. In 1598 Rubens became a master in the Antwerp Guild of St. Luke. Two years later the young artist traveled to Italy, where he remained for eight years. While in Venice Rubens met a man employed by Vincenzo I Gonzaga, Duke of Mantua, through whom he was able to enter the duke's service. Rubens executed relatively few works for his patron (*Baptism of Christ*, 1605, Antwerp, Musée Royal des Beaux-Arts; *Gonzaga Family in Adoration of the Most Holy Trinity*, 1605, Mantua, Palazzo Ducale; *Transfiguration*, 1605, Nancy, Musée des Beaux-Arts), concentrating more on making copies of other works, and participating in 1603 in a diplomatic mission to Spain, where he studied the magnificent royal collection of paintings (especially the Titians) in Madrid, and where he painted an important equestrian portrait of Philip III's favorite, the *Duke of Lerma* (Madrid, Capuchin Fathers of Castilla). During his Italian sojourn Rubens spent much time in Rome, executing a *Lamentation of Christ* (1601–2; Rome, Galleria Borghese) and his first public commission, the three

Peter Paul Rubens. *Jupiter and Semele.* Musées Royaux des Beaux-Arts, Brussels. *Photo A.C.L.*

Peter Paul Rubens. *Self-Portrait*. Detail from *Self-Portrait with Isabella*. 1609. Alte Pinakothek, Munich.

altarpieces for the church of S. Croce in Gerusalemme: *St. Helena, Elevation of the Cross*, and *Crowning with Thorns* (1601–2; now Grasse, Hôpital du Petit-Paris). These works reveal the strong impact of Italian painting upon Rubens during this important period of his development. Titian, Veronese, and Tintoretto made an especially lasting impression upon him. He recalled these masters when he painted the Doria and Spinola family portraits in Genoa (*Portrait of Brigitte Spinola Doria*, 1606, Dorsetshire, Kingston Lacy, Coll. Ralph Bankes; *Portrait of Caterina Grimaldi, c.* 1606, Coll. Ralph Bankes), the Gonzaga portraits in Mantua, and revealed as well the influence of such other artists as Taddeo Zuccaro and Jacopo Bassano in his final works in Rome: the S. Maria in Vallicella Altarpiece (left unfinished 1607; Grenoble, Musée de Peinture et de Sculpture) and the *Adoration of the Shepherds* (1608; Fermo, Pinacoteca Comunale). By the time he returned to Antwerp, Rubens was obliged at first to paint in accordance with the prevailing Flemish taste in spite of the fact that he was patronized by the Burgomaster Rockox, appointed official painter to Archduke Albert and Archduchess Isabella in 1609, and had gained entrance into Humanist circles through his marriage to Isabella Brandt in 1609. Rubens was hesitating at that time between Tintoretto's violent intensity (*Raising of the Cross*, 1610; *Descent from the Cross*, 1611–14; both Antwerp Cathedral) and Janssens' sense of balance; the results may be seen in his *Self-Portrait with His Wife Isabella* (1609–10; Munich, Alte Pinakothek) and the *Incredulity of St. Thomas* (1615; Antwerp, Musée Royal des Beaux-Arts).

During the period from 1610 to 1618, Rubens executed religious works on a great scale, such as the *Resurrection* triptych in Antwerp Cathedral (1612), the *Assumption of the Virgin* (*c.* 1615–16; Brussels, Musées Royaux des Beaux-Arts), the *Adoration of the Magi* altarpiece (1617–19; Mechlin, SS. Jean-Baptiste et l'Évangéliste), as well as smaller, more intimate representations of religious themes, such as *Susanna and the Elders* (1613; Stockholm, Nationalmuseum), the *Flight into Egypt* (1613; Kassel, Staatliche Kunstsammlungen), and *Samson and Delilah* (Cologne, Coll. Gottfried Neuerburg). His mythological paintings range from the calm and Classical *Jupiter and Callisto* (1613; Staatliche Kunstsammlungen) to the dramatic *Rape of the Daughters of Leucippus* (*c.* 1618; Alte Pinakothek).

Unlike many of his paintings, which were often partially painted by assistants, Rubens' ink and color sketches were always by his hand and represent his style in a more personal way. The ink wash and black chalk drawing of the *Entombment* (*c.* 1615; Amsterdam, Rijksmuseum), for example, although revealing the influence of the Caravaggio *Entombment* in the Vatican, indicates his maturity following his Italian trip.

From 1616 to 1625 Rubens gradually abandoned the Classicist elements and surrendered entirely to the full impact of the Baroque. His magnificent *Last Judgment* (1616; Alte Pinakothek) derives from Michelangelo but replaces the *terribilità* of the Sistine Chapel work with a majestic triumph. The *Fall of the Damned* (Alte Pinakothek) possesses an overwhelming imaginative force. Between 1618 and 1620, the *Miracles of St. Ignatius* (1619; Vienna, Kunsthistorisches Museum), *Miracles of St. Francis Xavier* (1619; Kunsthistorisches Museum), *Last Communion of St. Francis of Assisi* (1619; Antwerp, Musée Royal des Beaux-Arts), and the remarkable *Christ on the Cross* (1620; Musée Royal des Beaux-Arts) make up the masterpieces of this period of powerful Baroque creations. This same expressiveness characterizes the historical paintings, such as the series on the history of *Decius Mus* (*c.* 1618; Vaduz, Coll. Liechtenstein), and the mythological works, such as *Atalanta* (Madrid, Prado), the various versions of the *Drunkenness of Silenus* (*c.* 1618; Alte Pinakothek), and the *Battle of the Amazons* (*c.* 1618; Alte Pinakothek). This Baroque style is evident to an equal degree in the great *Hunts* in Dresden (1618–20; Gemäldegalerie), Leningrad (1616–17; Hermitage), and Munich (1616–17; Alte Pinakothek), as well as in the *Adoration of the Magi* (*c.* 1625; Antwerp, Musée Royal des Beaux-Arts), in the *Flight of Lot* and *Virgin Among the Angels* (both Louvre), and particularly in the series of paintings on the *History of Marie de Médicis* for the Luxembourg Palace in Paris (1622–25; Louvre).

From 1627 to 1630 Rubens carried out a number of diplomatic missions to the courts of Madrid, Paris, and London for Archduchess Isabella, his patroness. This painter and diplomat also proved himself to be a man of extensive learning. A linguist and connoisseur of antiquities, he had a wide range of interests, displaying an erudition and versatility that amazed his contemporaries.

At the age of fifty-three Rubens married a young girl of seventeen, Hélène Fourment, and embarked on a new phase of his career. His unique gifts are revealed in the sketches based upon passages in Ovid's *Metamorphoses* for the decoration of the hunting lodge of Philip IV, the Torre de la Parada (1637–38). Rubens revealed in this work both a freshness of imagination and an ease of design: the *Fall of Icarus, Abduction of Proserpina, Milky Way*, and the *Birth of Venus* number among the most

Peter Paul Rubens. *Entombment. c.* 1615. Rijksmuseum, Amsterdam.

Peter Paul Rubens. *The Artist with Hélène Fourment in Their Garden*. *c*. 1631. Alte Pinakothek, Munich.

beautiful of these studies. Hélène Fourment often served as his model and appears in a number of religious works, such as the *Mystical Marriage of St. Catherine* (*c*. 1630; Berlin, Coll. Koppel), *David and Abigail* (*c*. 1635; Detroit, Institute of Arts), and the *Holy Family* (Madrid, Prado). She also appears in some of his Dionysian scenes (*Feast of Venus*, Vienna, Kunsthistorisches Museum; *Judgment of Paris, c*. 1638–39, Prado), the *Three Graces* (*c*. 1636–40; Prado), and his *Garden of Love* (*c*. 1634; Prado)—these being the first examples of *fêtes galantes*. But most often he painted her in various costumes, posing alone or with their children, and seated or walking about the park of their estate. The most beautiful of these portraits are in the Louvre (*Hélène Fourment with Two of Her Children, c*. 1636–37) and in Munich's Alte Pinakothek (*Hélène Fourment in a Wedding Dress, c*. 1631; *Hélène Fourment and Her Son François, c*. 1635). His treatment of Bacchanalian themes (*Nymphs and Satyrs, Peasant Dance*, 1638–40; Prado) and of the Kermesse is both exuberant and lusty. Indeed, this style reaches perfection in the Louvre *Kermesse* with its carnal earthiness and vitality. Yet the crowning glory of Rubens' art may be found in his splendid paintings of the female nude. Following Titian, although working in a more systematic fashion, Rubens achieved a veritable triumph in his depiction of women.

RUDE, François (1784, Dijon—1855, Paris), French sculptor. He won the Grand Prix de Rome in 1812, but did not go to Rome because the Frémiet family, with whom he was living, left Paris for exile in Brussels—due to their political opinions—and Rude, who was in love with and later married their daughter Sophie, left with them. He opened a workshop in Brussels and also taught sculpture. The last work he executed in Belgium was a bust of *Louis David* (1826; Paris, Louvre). He returned to Paris in 1827 and sent *Mercury Tying His Heel-Wings* (Louvre) to the Salon the following year; in 1831, he sent the plaster *Neapolitan Fisherboy with Tortoise*. The statesman Louis Adolphe Thiers, who admired Rude and was anxious to finish the Arc de Triomphe de l'Étoile in Paris, commissioned Rude to execute one of the four trophies on the piers. This was the *Departure of the Volunteers of 1792* (1835–36), better known as *La Marseillaise* because of the furious figure of the Motherland urging on the soldiers of the Revolution with her song. In spite of the strong Classical elements in this sculpture, it shocked Rude's contemporaries so much that his application to enter the Academy was rejected three times. Among his finest sculptures are the statue of the mathematician *Gaspard Monge* (1846–48; Beaune, near Dijon, Place Gaspard Monge); the tomb of Godefroi de Cavaignac (1847; Paris, Montmartre Cemetery), in which the figure, wrapped in a shroud, is as moving as a recumbent Gothic effigy; and the statue of *Maréchal Michel Ney* (1852–53; Paris, Avenue de l'Observatoire), a masterpiece of expressive intensity and truthfully observed movement that was greatly admired by Rodin. The best illustration of Rude's passion for the truth is the bust he made, after a studio wager, of the lawyer *Dupin the Elder* (1835; copy in Dijon, Musée Rude). Another of his masterpieces is *Napoleon Awaking to Immortality* (1847; model in Louvre), commissioned by Claude Noisot, a captain of the grenadiers and former officer of the Emperor's Guard, for his park at Fixin, near Dijon, where the bronze original still stands.

François Rude. *Statue of Maréchal Michel Ney*. 1852–53. Avenue de l'Observatoire, Paris.

RUDOLPH, Paul (b. 1918, Elkton, Kentucky), American architect. A pupil of Walter Gropius at Harvard University, he demonstrated a free and unstandardized style at first (Cultural Center, Wellesley College, Massachusetts, 1955–59), with the form of a building developing from its function. As chairman of the department of architecture at Yale University from 1958, he exercised a great influence over young architects, both through his teaching and his own work, which was often marked by a boldly sculptural handling of concrete. The school complex at Sarasota, Florida (1957–60), was the first of his works to demonstrate a clear break with his earlier composite style. The multistoried garage at New Haven, Connecticut (1959–62), a handsome cantilevered concrete structure; a project for a motel of closely interlocking blocks at Waverly, New York (1961); the Arts and Architecture buildings at Yale University in New Haven (1960–64); and the Endo Laboratories on Long Island, New York (1960–64), established Rudolph's position as a leader in the field. He also designed the chapel, on a radiating plan, for the Tuskegee Institute, Alabama (begun 1960).

RUISDAEL, Jacob van (1628/29, Haarlem—1682, Haarlem), Dutch landscape painter. Ruisdael, nephew of the landscapist Salomon van Ruysdael, towers above all his contemporaries in his erudition, freedom of expression, tremendous interest in the elements of nature, and in his skill at successfully rendering the close and consistent relationship of water, earth, and sky that is present only in Holland. His earliest paintings still adhere to the Dutch realist tradi-

Jacob van Ruisdael. *Windmill at Wijk. c.* 1665. Rijksmuseum, Amsterdam.

tion (*Cottages under the Trees*, 1646; Leningrad, Hermitage), but his style very soon became more relaxed and imbued with a profound respect for nature. Often the artist confined his palette to browns and greens, tempered with beige or brightened with touches of yellow and red. His sensitive exploitation of atmospheric values and his feeling for form and movement are quite exceptional. The *Jewish Cemetery* (*c.* 1660; Dresden, Gemäldegalerie) is one of his most dramatic canvases, a vision of despair that depicts the raging fury of nature; *Wheatfields* (*c.* 1670; New York, Metropolitan Museum) is suffused with a wild but poetic atmosphere. This sometimes stormy and melancholy mood prefigures 19th-century Romanticism; indeed, Ruisdael exerted a strong influence upon such German landscapists as Caspar David Friedrich. By contrast, certain peaceful scenes (*Windmill at Wijk, c.* 1665; Amsterdam, Rijksmuseum) are evocations of the more familiar flat topography of the Dutch countryside, with harmonious lines and subtle color variations. Ruisdael's predilection was for forms in violent movement, forms that disintegrate and vanish—winds, storm-tossed clouds, contrasts of light and shadow.

Jacob van Ruisdael. *Sandy Path.* Rijksmuseum, Amsterdam.

RUSH, William (1756, Philadelphia—1833, Philadelphia), American sculptor. One of the earliest American sculptors, predating the 19th-century Neoclassicists, Rush developed his art out of the Colonial tradition of functional art. He earned his reputation and livelihood as a carver of ship figureheads, using as subjects both allegorical figures and representations of famous men (*Genius of the United States* for the frigate *United States*; figures of Jean-Jacques Rousseau, Benjamin Franklin, and William Penn for other vessels). Although Rush's oeuvre includes many portrait busts, his full-length ideal figures are usually the more expressive and accomplished aspect of his work, as in the over life-size figures of *Comedy* and *Tragedy* (both 1808; painted wood) commissioned for the first Chestnut Street Theater in Philadelphia, and now in the Edwin Forest Home, Philadelphia. Rush's draped wood figures are generally carved in a sweeping, decorative, and linear manner, showing an interesting combination of the Rococo and American Colonial figurehead styles.

RUSSELL, Morgan (1886, New York—1953, Broomall, Pennsylvania), American painter. After studying with Robert Henri he went to France at the age of nineteen, where he met Henri Matisse, Guillaume Apollinaire, Amedeo Modigliani, and the art patron Leo Stein, who gave him financial assistance. But his most decisive meeting was with Stanton Macdonald-Wright, with whom he founded the Synchromist movement partly as a reaction to Orphism. Russell's *Synchromy in Green*, shown at the Salon des Indépendants in 1913, was the first Synchromist work. In 1916 he went to New York for a month to participate in the avant-garde Forum Exhibition at the Anderson Galleries. When he returned to France he lost interest in Synchromism, adopting a Classical, rather conventional figurative style. Occasionally, however, he reverted to abstraction in works such as the *Life of Matter* (1925; Paris, Coll. Michel Seuphor), which is in the best Synchromist tradition. Except for several winters in Rome and a trip to California in 1931, Russell lived in France from 1916 to 1946, mostly in Burgundy; in 1946 he returned to America. Deeply religious, he turned late in his career to a number of large-scale Biblical works in a severe Classical style, and spoke of his early abstractions as belonging to his "kindergarten period."

The most important aspect of Russell's artistic production is his Synchromist work. Although his painting is related to that of Macdonald-Wright, it is less suave and harmonious, and more abrupt. Russell's paintings are in fact inhabited by a rude strength; rough-hewn geometrical shapes, often trapezoidal, are crammed and crumpled into a kinetic image that contrasts with the lyrical undulations of form in the work of his colleague.

RUSSOLO, Luigi (1885, Portogruaro, Veneto—1947, Cerro Lago Maggiore, near Laveno), Italian painter. In March 1910, together with Umberto Boccioni, Giacomo Balla, Carlo Carrà, and Gino Severini, he signed the first *Manifesto of Futurist Painters*. Russolo came nearer to abstraction than perhaps any other artist of the group, and soon left realistic subjects (*Revolt*, 1911; The Hague, Gemeentemuseum). In *Plastic Synthesis of the Actions of a Woman* (1912; Grenoble, Musée des Beaux-Arts), he gave his own interpretation of the Futurist concept of motion. He was particularly concerned with the relations of solid objects to the space around them, and in his paintings the latter ceases to take a merely passive role, assuming a reality of its own (*Solidity of Fog*, 1912, Milan, Coll. Dr. Gianni Mattioli; and *Interpenetration of Houses + Light + Sky*, 1912–13, Basel, Kunstmuseum). Russolo became increasingly interested in music: he introduced noise into the vocabulary of musical sound, and invented an instrument called the rumorharmonium, with which he organized concerts. He also published a manifesto on the art of noise, or Bruitism, translated by N. Slonimsky as *Music since 1900*.

Luigi Russolo. *Interpenetration of Houses + Light + Sky.* 1912–13. Kunstmuseum, Basel.

RUYSDAEL, Jacob van. *See* **RUISDAEL,** Jacob van.

RUYSDAEL, Salomon van (*c.* 1600, Naarden—1670, Haarlem), Dutch landscape painter, the uncle of Jacob van Ruisdael. Ruysdael spent the greater part of his life at Haarlem, where he settled around 1616 and where he entered the painters' guild in 1623. His stylistic development may be traced from early landscapes of the 1630s, imitating the calm, dark-hued, and tightly drawn manner of Van de Velde's pupil Jan van Goyen, through a lightened palette in the 1640s, to, finally, a looser compositional format and broader handling in the 1660s. Ruysdael was a precise and sensitive observer of reality, his favorite subjects being riverbanks and streams flowing through peaceful meadows, with an occasional village bell tower providing a dramatic contrast to a wind-filled sail on the horizon. Examples of his work include a *River Landscape* (*c.* 1630; Amsterdam, Rijksmuseum), the *Ferry near Gorcum* (1646; New York, Metropolitan Museum), and the *Halt at an Inn* (1649; Budapest, Museum of Fine Arts).

RYDER, Albert Pinkham (1847, New Bedford, Massachusetts—1917, Elmhurst, New York), American painter. Ryder was largely self-taught and was refused admission to the National Academy of Design, New York, but was finally admitted after informal study with the portraitist William E. Marshall (1837–1906). He exhibited first at the National Academy in 1873, and later with the rival Society of American Artists, of which he was a founder. During the 1870s he produced landscapes and pastoral scenes, but after 1880 he began concentrating on imaginary subjects and scenes inspired by the Bible, Chaucer, Shakespeare, and the 19th-century Romantic poets and writers. In 1877 he went to England; then in 1882 he traveled to Europe, visiting France, Holland, Italy, Spain, and Tangier, but the art of the past seems to have made little impression on him. In 1887 and 1896 he made two further journeys to Europe, chiefly for the sea voyage; both times he remained for a short time in London before returning to New York. Ryder's work became increasingly popular, but after 1900 his eyesight—which had always been poor—declined, and so did the quality of his paintings.

Moody, romantic, a hermit in the modern metropolis, Ryder occupies a position in American painting similar to that of Edgar Allan Poe or Herman Melville in literature. He painted dreamlike scenes of dark boats adrift in moonlit seas (*Toilers of the Sea*, 1884; New York, Metropolitan Museum), or forest landscapes filled with unearthly light (*Forest of Arden*, 1897, Metropolitan Museum; *Siegfried and the Rhine Maidens*, 1875–91, Washington, D.C., National Gallery; the *Flying Dutchman*, before 1890, Washington, D.C., National Collection of Fine Arts). At times his imagery recalls that of Odilon Redon, as in the *Race Track* (1895, Cleveland, Museum of Art), which shows a scythe-bearing skeleton on horseback. But it is difficult to compare Ryder with other painters, for he was not very interested in the work of other artists and looked to his inner world for inspiration.

RYSBRACK, Michael (1694, Antwerp—1770, Antwerp), Flemish Baroque sculptor active in England. The son of the landscape painter Peter Rysbrack (1655–1729), he settled (*c.* 1720) in London, where he began to carve monuments from designs supplied by the architect James Gibbs. In 1723, for instance, Rysbrack executed a *Monument to Matthew Prior* (London, Westminster Abbey), which was placed in a setting designed by Gibbs. His most famous monument is that to *Sir Isaac Newton* (1731; Westminster Abbey), in which he collaborated with the architect William Kent. While many of Rysbrack's portrait busts, such as his *James Gibbs* (1726; London, St. Martin-in-the-Fields), are of the usual Late Baroque type, he had carved as early as 1723 his *Daniel Finch, Earl of Nottingham* (Rutland, Ayston Hall, Coll. G. S. Finch) in Roman Republican style, with Classical drapery and short hair. The latter style was popular with the English nobility, and Rysbrack adopted it frequently. Several of his busts combine Baroque and Classical elements (*Alexander Pope*, 1730; London, Atheneum). He carved relatively few statues, but his *Hercules* (*c.* 1743; Stourhead, Wiltshire, National Trust) shows the influence of the *Farnese Hercules* combined with the sculptor's personal observations of prize fighters. Rysbrack also carved 10 freestanding life-size figures, including that of *Sir Hans Sloane* (*c.* 1737; London, Chelsea Physic Garden), and executed large statues, of which his best is the Baroque-inspired bronze equestrian figure of *King William III* (1735; Bristol, Queen Square).

RYSSELBERGHE, Théo van (1862, Ghent—1926, St-Clair, Provence), Belgian painter. After a trip to Spain and Morocco in 1884, he helped the art critic Octave Maus to found Les Vingt, a group of 20 artists whose aim was to encourage artistic exchanges between Belgium and France. Rysselberghe then went to Paris, where he became friendly with Georges Seurat and, along with Paul Signac, Henri-Edmond Cross, and Camille Pissarro, was converted to Neoimpressionism. Rysselberghe applied their divisionist theories to his landscapes (*The Walk*, 1901, and *Fantasia Arabe*, 1884; both Brussels, Musée d'Art Moderne) and his portraits (*Octave Maus*, 1885, and *Madame Maus*, 1890, both Musée d'Art Moderne; *Maria Sethe*, Antwerp, Musée des Beaux-Arts). Around 1895 he participated in Henry van de Velde's crusade for the revival of the decorative arts and designed posters, furniture, typographical designs, and jewelry. Visiting Paris again in 1898, he became a familiar figure in Symbolist literary circles: *A Reading* (1903; Ghent, Museum voor Schone Kunsten) is a group portrait of writers, including André Gide and Maurice Maeterlinck, with the poet Émile Verhaeren in the middle. Rysselberghe eventually retired to St-Clair in Provence, where he abandoned divisionism, brightened his palette, broadened his brushstrokes, and let his brush play freely over the canvas.

SAARINEN, Eero (1910, Kirkkonummi, near Helsinki—1961, Birmingham, Michigan), American architect. His father was the architect and town planner Eliel Saarinen, with whom he emigrated to the United States in 1923. When his studies at Yale University were finished (1930–34), Eero settled at Cranbrook, Michigan, working as his father's partner (1936) until the latter's death in 1950. His first major commission was for the General Motors Technical Center (1948–56) at Warren, Michigan. This consisted of a complex of 25 buildings around a central lagoon, of steel framework construction, and façades of brick and glass. The General Motors Center, with its gables in multicolored glazed bricks and splendid park and fountains, became a symbol of industrial success and developed a style that dominated American architecture through the decade.

In the following years Eero constructed a number of very different buildings. The first was the Kresge Auditorium for the Massachusetts Institute of Technology at Cambridge, Massachusetts (1955), with a shell-domed concrete roof, which has been criticized for using a very simple exterior envelope that belies its complex internal arrangements. In 1958 he designed a very dramatic suspended roof for the hockey rink at Yale University. The roof was centrally supported by steel cables anchored in the lateral walls and radiating from a slender concrete arch. The IBM factory at Rochester, built in the same year, employed a steel framework constructed on an expandable plan. Its laminated aluminum façade contrasted with the earlier Milwaukee War Memorial Hall (1957), whose raw concrete finish, sculptural pilotis, and spectacular overhang produced a decidedly expressionistic effect. The same taste for the dramatic is noticeable in the TWA Terminal at Kennedy Airport, New York (1956–62), and in the Dulles International Airport near Washington, D.C. (1958–62). Eero was usually at his best in planning vast uncluttered spaces, but sometimes less successful when limited by a more urban and traditional setting, as in the American embassies in Oslo (1959) and London (1955–60).

He justified the lack of consistent style in his work by the variety of projects it had to serve. Eero's approach, however, was not without method, and involved detailed functional analysis of the problem, as well as the construction of a series of maquettes, which he preferred to drawings. One invention that resulted from this approach was a mobile waiting room for Dulles Airport, which greatly facilitated passage between the building and the plane. In addition to his architectural work, he designed furniture (from 1941) in association with Charles Eames (b. 1907), remarkable for its elegant use of plastic materials. His molded pedestal tables and chairs are internationally known and admired. Finally, he was exceptional in the encouragement he gave to contemporary art by commissioning painting and sculpture, either as an additional embellishment (sculptures of Antoine Pevsner, Seymour Lipton, and Theodore Roszak), or as part of a building's very conception (especially sculpture for the Massachusetts Institute of Technology Chapel by Harry Bertoia).

SAARINEN, Eliel (1873, Rantasalmi, Kuopio, Finland—1950, Ann Arbor, Michigan), American architect. He formed a partnership with two other Finnish architects, Herman Gesellius (1874–1916) and Armas Lindgren (1874–1929), and together they designed the Finnish Pavilion at the Paris Exposition Universelle (1900). Saarinen's first really personal work was the central station at Helsinki (designed 1904; built 1910–14), distinguished by its clarity, boldness, and strongly articulated masses. Saarinen gained the attention of a wider public when he won the second prize in 1922 for the Chicago Tribune skyscraper. Commissions came from the United States and he decided to emigrate there the following year. He settled at Bloomfield Hills, near Detroit, Michigan, where from 1925 he designed the main building of the Cranbrook Foundation. The Cranbrook Academy itself (1940) is in the dry, modernized, Neoclassical style that characterized much of international architecture in the preceding decade. In 1936 he took his son, Eero Saarinen, as a partner, and a number of works produced by their office showed Eero's growing contribution (Kleinhans Music Hall, Buffalo, 1938; Christ Lutheran Church, Minneapolis, 1949–50).

SAENREDAM, Pieter Jansz. (1597, Assendelft—1665, Haarlem), Dutch painter. He pursued a career in Haarlem as a painter of architecture, specializing in church interiors. Between 1629 and 1663 he painted views of the churches of Utrecht (*St. Mary's Square and St. Mary's Church at Utrecht*, 1663; Rotterdam, Museum Boymans-van Beuningen), of Haarlem (*Interior of St. Bavo at Haarlem*, 1600; Worcester, Mass., Art Museum), and of other Dutch cities. Saenredam made his sketches on the spot and

Eero Saarinen. Technical Center of General Motors, Warren, Michigan. 1950–55. *Photo General Motors—Ezra Stoller.*

then transposed them according to his own calculations of proportion and perspective, developing shadows and lights in an abstract manner, raising the height of vaults and pillars, and diminishing the size of his very few figures in order to give an impression of vast space, emptiness, and silence. Saenredam's paintings are generally austere and cold in tone. Nevertheless, they appeal not only to the mind because of their strict geometrical calculations, but to the eye as well, due to a kind of rigorous and tangible poetry emanating from the subtleties of his art.

SAINT-GAUDENS, Augustus (1848, Dublin—1907, Cornish, New Hampshire), Irish-born American sculptor. Saint-Gaudens went to the United States as an infant. In 1867 he went to Paris, which was then becoming the foremost European center of training and inspiration for American artists; he earned his living there by cutting cameos while attending the École des Beaux-Arts. In 1875, following a visit to Rome, Saint-Gaudens was back in the United States.

Acknowledged as the leading sculptor of his day, Saint-Gaudens received numerous public commissions and was especially renowned for his subtle low-relief panels, such as those on the base of the *Memorial to Admiral David Farragut* (1880; bronze, New York, Madison Square) or the *Memorial to Robert Louis Stevenson* (1887–92; bronze, Edinburgh, St. Giles' Cathedral). Major examples of Saint-Gaudens' three-dimensional sculptures include the standing *Lincoln* in heroic size (1887; bronze, Chicago, Lincoln Park) and the expressive *Memorial to Mrs. Henry Adams* (1891; bronze, Washington, D.C., Rock Creek Cemetery).

Augustus Saint-Gaudens. Adams Memorial, Rock Creek Cemetery, Washington, D.C.

SAINT-SAËNS, Marc (b. 1903, Toulouse), French painter. Saint-Saëns became particularly interested in the problems of mural painting, and executed several frescoes for the Palais du Travail in Narbonne and the public library in Toulouse. When he met the painter and designer Jean Lurçat, he turned to tapestry designing, and painted his first cartoon in 1934. He taught at the École des Arts Décoratifs in Paris from 1946, and divided his time between teaching and designing numerous tapestries that were woven by the Association des Peintres-Cartonniers. The symbolism of myths and legends has an important place in the work of Saint-Saëns. Examples of his designs can be seen in his Picassoesque *Theseus and the Minotaur* (1943; Paris, Musée National d'Art Moderne) and in his *Velázquez and Quevedo* (1959; Madrid, Casa Velázquez).

SALMON, Robert (*c.* 1775, England—*c.* 1848, Boston), American painter. When he went to Boston from Liverpool in 1828, Salmon was already noted as a painter of seascapes and marine subjects. His journals indicate that he painted over 300 works during his Boston years (1828–41). His paintings, such as *View of Boston and the Harbor* (1829; Boston, Harrison Gray Otis House), were done in tempera or oil on canvas or board in an extremely detailed manner, accurately reproducing the building and bay area of the city. Such views are of special historical value because of their faithfulness to actual appearance. In many of his paintings, Salmon also revealed his rather extensive knowledge of ship construction. Indeed, his scrupulously realistic rendering of ships resulted in his being commissioned to paint records of naval fires for insurance companies. In all Salmon is said to have painted about 800 pictures, of which 70 are still extant and in the Museum of Fine Arts, Boston, the Boston Public Library, and the Peabody Museum in Salem, Massachusetts.

SALVATOR ROSA. *See* **ROSA,** Salvator.

SALVIATI, Francesco de' Rossi, *called* Cecchino (1510, Florence—1563, Rome), Italian painter. He was a pupil of Andrea del Sarto, in whose studio he worked in 1529. He received his surname from Cardinal Salviati, who took him into his service in 1531. The resulting sojourn in Rome brought him into contact with the Mannerist movement that grew out of the styles of Michelangelo and Raphael. He also became familiar with the work of Parmigianino, whose elegant and flexible grace he imitated. After a visit to Bologna, he went back to Rome in 1541 to decorate a chapel in S. Maria dell'Anima (1541–44). On his return to Florence in 1544, he was commissioned to paint the important cycle in the Sala dell'Udienza of the Palazzo Vecchio, illustrating the story of Camillus. Salviati had been invited to France as early as 1542, but did not make the journey until 1554–55. Unfortunately, nothing remains of his painting there, except for the *Incredulity of St. Thomas* (Paris, Louvre) that he executed for the Chapel of the Florentines at Lyons. When he returned to Rome in 1555, Salviati decorated one of the rooms in the Palazzo Farnese.

SALZILLO *or* **ZARCILLO,** Francisco (1707, Murcia—1783, Murcia), Spanish sculptor.

Salzillo was one of the last important polychrome sculptors, although his colorism lacks the subtlety of the greatest 17th-century polychrome works. In his early period (1727–46) he continued the Italian Baroque traditions of his father, as seen in the *Pietà* in the church of S. Bartolomé, Murcia, and in the *Virgen de la Leche* relief in Murcia Cathedral. His mature work includes a realistic *Penitent St. Jerome* at La Nora, near Murcia, which is perhaps his finest piece, and his notable *pasos* (processional figures for Holy Week), preserved in the Ermita de Jesús, Murcia, which houses the Museo Salzillo: *Christ's Fall on the Road to Calvary* (1752), *Christ on the Mount of Olives* (1754), the *Last Supper*, and the *Betrayal of Judas* (1763). Of his last period, the *paso* of the *Flagellation* (1777; Museo Salzillo) and the *Belén*, or Neapolitan-style crèche, with 556 figures of people and 372 animals, should be mentioned (Murcia, Museo Provincial de Bellas Artes).

Much of Salzillo's inspiration is profoundly original, but more important, his work is quintessentially Spanish. His *pasos* re-create entire scenes from local daily life, animated by the consuming faith typical of the Spanish people.

SANDBY, family name of two brothers from Nottingham, England, active as topographical draftsmen and watercolorists in the 2nd half of the 18th century. Both brothers went to London in 1742 and were employed in the Drawing Office in the Tower (now the Ordnance Survey Department).

THOMAS (1721, Nottingham—1798, London), architect as well as draftsman. In 1743 he became draftsman to the Duke of Cumberland, whom he accompanied on the Continental military campaigns of 1743 and 1745 and on those against the Young Pretender in England and Scotland; he was employed mainly to draw camps and fortifications. He ultimately turned to architecture, becoming professor of architecture at London's Royal Academy in 1768. Thomas was appointed Deputy Ranger of Windsor Forest and was responsible for the layout of the park, the forest, and of Virginia Water.

PAUL (1725, Nottingham—1809, London), a watercolorist and landscape painter, was attached to the Government Drawing Office for 10 years. After the subjection of Scotland in the 1745 rebellion, he made numerous topographical sketches of Edinburgh and its environs, enlivening them by the introduction of small genre figures drawn in the manner of Francis Hayman (1708–76), such as *In the Grounds of Herriot's Hospital, Edinburgh* (*c.* 1756; Berkshire, Windsor Castle, Royal Art Collection). Around 1752 he returned to England and lived at Windsor Great Park with his brother Thomas. Paul was a committee member of the Society of Artists and a founding member of the Royal Academy.

Whereas Thomas Sandby's drawings are those of an architect and landscape gardener, Paul did much to facilitate the acceptance of the topographical watercolor as a work of art. He worked mainly in gouache and transparent watercolor and produced unpretentious works that reflect many influences, notably those of Canaletto (*North Terrace of Windsor Looking East*; England, Coll. H.R.H. Princess Royal), Richard Wilson (*Romantic Castle*; Nottingham, Castle Museum and Art Gallery), Thomas Gainsborough (*Rainbow*; Castle Museum and Art Gallery), and Hayman (*Kitty Fisher as a Milkmaid, c.* 1758–60; Royal Art Collection).

SANGALLO, family of Italian architects active in the 15th and 16th centuries.

GIULIANO GIAMBERTI, *called* GIULIANO DA SANGALLO (1445, Florence—1516, Florence), began his career as a skilled cabinetmaker and sculptor; by the end of his life he was acknowledged as one of the most inspired masters of Italian architecture of the late Quattrocento. In his hands some of the elements of Brunelleschi's architecture were elaborated and given new strength, and, with his archaeological knowledge, his travels, and his activities in several Italian cities, he did much to diffuse contemporary Florentine ideas in the early years of the 16th century.

Giuliano, who would prove his artistic ability in the Sassetti tombs (1491; Florence, Sassetti Chapel, S. Trinita), and his skill as a military engineer in the fortress of Ostia (begun 1483), was forty years old when, in 1485, he was entrusted with the work that is considered his masterpiece, the church of the Madonna delle Carceri ("Madonna of the Prisons") in Prato. The plan adopted by Sangallo was that of the Greek cross, with slightly projecting arms covered by a barrel vault. The broad arches and the pendentives between them support the dome, which is pierced by round openings, or oculi, near its base line. Sangallo's innovation does not lie in the rhythmic divisions of the walls, which are less subtle than Brunelleschi's, but in the powerful effect of spatial unity; there is no point in the interior where the observer cannot take in the whole in one glance. A little later, for the sacristy of S. Spirito in Florence (1489–92), he created an octagonal space that is hardly less coherent and beautiful than that of the Madonna delle Carceri.

The villa that Lorenzo de' Medici wanted to build at Poggio a Caiano (1480–85), in the countryside, gave Sangallo a chance to design another masterpiece. Here a rectangular base, surrounded by arcades, supports a terrace that encircles the building. A flat roof covers the two-story structure. In the center of the main façade, a loggia opens behind an Ionic colonnade, crowned by a triangular pediment. The large central hall, reminiscent of the Roman bath, is lighted by narrow openings in the lateral façades. To overcome Lorenzo's apprehension about the technical difficulties involved in covering such a vast space, Sangallo designed a barrrel vault of poured concrete with richly decorated coffers—a system that he and his brother Antonio the Elder would experiment with again in their house in the Borgo Pinti, Florence.

Other works by Sangallo should be mentioned here: the fortresses at Poggio Imperiale, near Pog-

Francisco Salzillo. *The Last Supper. c.* 1780. Salzillo Museum, Murcia. *Photo Yan, Toulouse.*

Giuliano da Sangallo. Villa Medici, Poggio a Caiano. 1480–85. *Photo Alinari-Giraudon.*

Giuliano da Sangallo. Courtyard of the Palazzo Gondi, Florence. 1490–94. *Photo Brogi-Giraudon.*

gibonsi (1488), and Borgo San Sepolcro (1502), which rivaled Francesco di Giorgio Martini's work in military architecture; the colonnaded courtyard of the Palazzo Gondi, Florence (1490–94), with its wells, its capitals decorated with a variety of subjects, and its staircase with Donatellian balustrades; and the austere cloister of S. Maria Maddalena dei Pazzi, Florence (*c.* 1480).

Giuliano da Sangallo was a learned antiquarian and he identified the *Laocoön* sculpture group as soon as it was excavated in 1506. Two of his manuscripts, the *Tacuino senese* (Siena, Biblioteca Comunale) and the *Codex Barberinus* (Vatican Library), along with an illustrated copy of Dante's *Divine Comedy* (Rome, Biblioteca, Vallicelliana), are revelations of his skill as a draftsman, his technical interests, and his passion for archaeology.

ANTONIO, Giamberti da Sangallo, *called* THE ELDER (1455, Florence—1534/35, Florence), his brother. With the death of Giuliano da Sangallo in 1516, Antonio emerged from his brother's shadow. Until then, he had been associated with work in military architecture and gave a foretaste of his style in civilian building with the church of SS. Annunziata at Arezzo (begun 1506), built on the Latin-cross plan and delicately decorated. In Florence, when Pope Leo X wanted to complete the Piazza dell' Annunziata, Antonio, with Baccio d'Agnolo (1462–1543), designed a replica (1517) of the famous portico of the Ospedale degli Innocenti in Florence, built by Brunelleschi and Francesco della Luna (b. 1376). It was in the small Tuscan town of Montepulciano, however, that Antonio produced his major works, which included the travertine marble palaces of Contucci, Cervini, Tarugi, and Del Pecora. Halfway between the town and the valley beneath it, Antonio built one of the most beautiful churches in Italy, the Madonna di S. Biagio (1518–28).

Antonio da Sangallo the Younger. *Model for St. Peter's, Rome.* After 1536. Vatican Museum.

ANTONIO, Cordiani da Sangallo, *called* THE YOUNGER (1483, Florence—1546, Terni), the nephew of Giuliano da Sangallo and Antonio da Sangallo the Elder. After some work of secondary importance done under the influence of Bramante, he built S. Maria di Loreto (1507) in Trajan's Forum, Rome, perhaps with the collaboration of Giuliano. The high quality of this work may have attracted the attention of Cardinal Farnese, who faithfully supported the great architect for many years. The construction of the huge Palazzo Farnese in Rome began in 1510, following the younger Antonio's plans, which were extended after the cardinal became Pope Paul III in 1534. The Farnese became the model for Roman palaces for three centuries. Among several other urban buildings, Antonio erected the Zecca (now the Banco di S. Spirito, 1523–24) and the Florentine-style Palazzo Palma, both in Rome.

The only military engineer who could rival him during the Renaissance was his pupil Michele Sanmicheli. Antonio built the massive octagonal and circular bastions of Civitavecchia (1515), and extended the defenses of Parma, Piacenza, Nepi, and Ancona (1537). At Perugia he laid out the colossal Rocca Paolina with its wonderful balcony, from which there is a view over the whole of Umbria. At Orvieto he designed the Well of S. Patrizio (1527–37), with its two intricate spiral staircases lit by 72 small windows.

Antonio became chief architect of St. Peter's at the death of Baldassare Peruzzi (1536) and drew up a feasible but complicated plan, which can be studied in the wooden model preserved in the Vatican Museum. It won the favor of the papal court, but was dropped at Antonio's death.

Following the example of Pius II in Pienza, the Farnese family commissioned their architect to lay out the city of Castro in Umbria, which, however, was razed during the reign of Pope Innocent X. Among the vast number of works produced by Antonio during his most prolific period were the churches of S. Maria in Porta Paradiso and the chapel of the Alborensi (*c.* 1520) in S. Giacomo degli Spagnuoli, both in Rome, as well as the Cappella Paolina and the rooms for public consistories in the Vatican.

SANMICHELI, Michele (1484, Verona—1559, Verona), Italian Mannerist architect. Between 1510 and 1524 Sanmicheli worked on the Gothic façade of Orvieto Cathedral, then entered the pope's service in 1526 to design the fortifications of Piacenza and Parma. Fortifications for the Venetian state, where he settled after the Sack of Rome in 1527, form a large part of his output and influenced the character of his nonmilitary architecture as well. His work in this capacity—which includes the Porta Nuova, Verona (1539–50), the Forte di S. Andrea a Lido, Venice (1535–49), the Porta S. Zeno, Verona (1542), and the Porta Palio, Verona (1557)—is marked by boldly rusticated gateways and an economical but expressive use of ornament. Although his early Palazzo Pompei in Verona (*c.* 1529) is firmly based on the work of Donato Bramante and Raphael, Sanmicheli soon developed his own style of emphatically contrasted light and shade in façades articulated by complex rhythms (Palazzo Canossa, Verona, *c.* 1537). This complication of the façade attained its peak in the Palazzo Bevilacqua, Verona (*c.* 1530), where his Mannerism is visible not only in the complexity of rhythms, the abundance of ornament, and the opposition of disjunctive shapes, but in the conscious misuse of the Classical vocabulary, especially in the projection of triglyphs to form

Michele Sanmicheli. Palazzo Bevilacqua, Verona. *c.* 1530. *Photo Alinari-Giraudon.*

consoles for a balcony. In the palaces of his later years (Palazzo Grimani, Venice, begun 1556), Sanmicheli enlarged the window area greatly with a corresponding de-emphasis of the wall surface. His work as a military engineer is sometimes evident in his churches as well as his palaces, especially in the fortress-like S. Maria in Argano, Verona (1547).

SANSOVINO, Jacopo Tatti, *called* Jacopo (1486, Florence—1570, Venice), Italian sculptor and architect. Adopted by his master, the sculptor Andrea Contucci da Monte Sansovino (*c.* 1467–1529), whose name he took, Jacopo Tatti won fame as a sculptor while still young. He went to Rome in 1505, where he came into contact with the architect Giuliano da Sangallo, distinguished himself in Bramante's eyes, and won the favor of Pope Leo X and later Clement VII. In this period he concentrated on sculpture, executing *Bacchus* (*c.* 1514; Florence, Bargello), *St. James the Major* (Florence, Duomo), the tombs of *Cardinal Giovanni Michiel* and *Bishop Orso* (both *c.* 1519; Rome, S. Marcello), and the majestic *Madonna del Parto* (1519–21; Rome, S. Agostino), all of which were direct products of Classicizing Renaissance Rome.

After a first visit to Venice in 1523, he established himself there permanently in 1527. He soon became the major architect and sculptor in Venice, and, thanks to the support of Cardinal Grimani, was appointed to superintend the building projects of the Republic in 1529. His large and magnificent Palazzo Corner, called the Ca' Grande (designed 1532, cornerstone laid 1537; now the Prefettura), established a standard style for Venetian houses that would be followed for many years. To a Bramantesque rusticated basement, Sansovino added a majestic façade in harmony with Venetian tradition. Another major work was the church of S. Francesco della Vigna (1534; completed by Palladio), which Sansovino designed in collaboration with the geometrician Francesco Giorgi.

In 1536, to shelter the precious manuscripts bequeathed to Venice by Petrarch or saved from the Turkish invaders by Cardinal Bessarion, Sansovino began the construction of the Libreria Vecchia, or Old Library, in the Piazzetta S. Marco, which is his masterpiece (completed 1583–88 by Vincenzo Scamozzi). In imitation of the Roman basilica, and with a nod toward Bramante, he built two orders of columns—Doric below, supporting an unusually heightened Ionic—framing two rows of arcades. In the upper gallery, between large columns that support the entablature, smaller ones bear the spring of the arches. This design is repeated below, except that the arch supports are piers. It was this arrangement, equally familiar to Serlio, that Palladio later used in his Basilica at Vicenza (1549).

For Sansovino sculpture was an integral part of the building it adorned. He designed particularly rich decoration for the Loggetta (1537–40; rebuilt after collapse, 1902), a portico placed at the base of the Campanile of S. Marco to allow for the meetings of the Procuratori in bad weather, adopting unusual proportions for the building to accommodate the large amount of sculpture on the exterior. Sansovino's ability to create dynamic contrasts of highlight and shadow with his carving is an outstanding feature of the Libreria Vecchia as well. The sacristy doors and choir galleries of St. Mark's, the monument to the Doge Francesco Venier in S. Salvatore (1561), the *Mars* and *Neptune*, symbolizing the dominance of Venice, at the head of the Staircase of the Giants in the Doges' Palace (1554)—perhaps his most famous works—the gracious *Madonna and Child* at the Arsenal (1534), and the many other sculptures with which he adorned his adopted city retained Sansovino's early-formed High Renaissance style, but increased in power and sensuousness, and, particularly in the sacristy doors, in drama, while maintaining Classical equilibrium.

Another major architectural achievement in Sansovino's career is La Zecca (the Mint), also on the Piazzetta S. Marco (completed 1545). Since the building was the depository for Venice's bullion reserves, Sansovino gave it a heavy, strong exterior, which he may have derived from Giulio Romano's Palazzo del Tè, Mantua (1526–34), introducing the rusticated column into Venetian architecture. The Palazzo Delfino (1562), the oval church of the Hospital for Incurables, the chur-

Jacopo Sansovino. Palazzo Corner, or Ca' Grande, Venice. Designed 1532; construction begun 1537. *Photo Alinari-Giraudon.*

ches of S. Giorgio dei Greci and S. Geminiano (the latter replaced by the Napoleonic wing of the Procuratie Nuove after 1807) are only some of the many buildings he erected in Venice during the second part of his long career.

SANT'ELIA, Antonio (1888, Como—1916, near Monfalcone, Gorizia), Italian architect. He was the brightest hope in town planning of the Futurist generation, but his premature death prevented him from carrying out any of his original ideas. Sant'Elia studied architecture in Milan and then Bologna. After 1912 he worked in several architects' offices, and devoted his leisure time to developing his own projects. Instead of studying the problems of the individual block, he grappled with the entire layout of a visionary city of the future, the Città Nuova, a huge project for which he drew precise, detailed plans of both its general form and individual parts. He presented his work to the Milanese public in 1914 at the first exhibition of the Nuove Tendenze group to which he belonged. In the introduction to the catalogue Sant'Elia expressed his socialist, utopian views with a perfectly clear idea of the necessary reforms. Sant'Elia did hundreds of drawings for his city; stylistically, they have much in common with Russian Constructivism. The dominant idea was of a large metropolis conceived in terms of its functions as the setting for movement within it; primary importance was given to vertical and horizontal movement systems for people and traffic. Elevators were built outside buildings and ran up and down the façades; iron footbridges with swiftly moving platforms linked the houses at various levels; the houses themselves were built of concrete, glass, and iron, and were stripped of decoration; the upper stories were sometimes stepped to admit more light to the streets below. Sant'Elia was called up in World War I as an officer and was killed in action. The War Memorial at Como was later erected from his designs, although altered in many details, and his works are on permanent exhibition at the Villa Olmo near Como.

SANTOMASO, Giuseppe (b. 1907, Venice), Italian painter. Santomaso began as a figurative painter, influenced by Pio Semeghini (1878–1964) and by Medardo Rosso. His experience was broadened by visits to Holland and France, in both of which he held exhibitions (in Amsterdam in 1937 and in Paris in 1939). After 1942 his increasing abstractionism became more elaborate, although traces of figural painting remained in his forms with merged outlines. After World War II he belonged in turn to the Fronte Nuovi delle Arti (New Artistic Front; 1947) and to the Eight Italian Painters group (1952); his work at that time was described as "abstract-concrete," or Concrete Art, an intellectual style in which representative images were suppressed, although references to traditional art were not completely erased. Santomaso's pictures, whose titles generally allude to his travels, are frequently impressions of particular places vibrating with light, the intensity of which he sought to capture in color (*At the Concerts of Arzignano*, 1953, Brescia, Coll. Achille Cavallini; *Fisherman's Net*, 1954, Paris, Coll. Mme. Niomar Bittencourt). His work appears to owe something to both Braque and Jean Lurçat. Santomaso also painted frescoes, made pottery and lithographs, and illustrated the poems of Paul Éluard with drawings. In 1959 he was awarded the International Marzotto Prize.

SANZIO, Raffaello. *See* **RAPHAEL.**

SARAZIN *or* **SARRAZIN,** Jacques (1588, Noyon, Oise—1660, Paris), French sculptor. He was the most important French sculptor of the mid-17th century, virtually creating the style that dominated this period and training many important sculptors of the next generation in his studio. Sarazin studied first under Nicolas Guillain (d. 1639), then spent many years in Rome (1610–*c.* 1627). Roman influence is evident in his early work at Cardinal Aldobrandini's villa at Frascati, and—after his return to France—at the château and nymphaeum at Wideville (1630–32). Sarazin's caryatids, executed for the Pavillon de l'Horloge at the Louvre, Paris (1636), may be considered the first instances of French Classicism in sculpture, parallel to the work of François Mansart in architecture and Nicolas Poussin in painting. Sarazin's next commission was the decorative scheme for Mansart's Château de Maisons, near Paris (1642–50), for which he supplied small models and generally supervised the program. His last great work was the monument to Henri de Bourbon, Prince de Condé (begun 1648).

SARGENT, John Singer (1856, Florence—1925, London), American expatriot painter. Sargent traveled widely, studying in Florence, Holland, and Spain, and settled in Paris in 1874, first as an art student, absorbing the prevailing influences of Gustave Courbet and the Impressionists, and then as a professional artist. He was highly precocious, exhibiting first in 1877.

In the Salon of 1884, Sargent showed the portrait of a celebrated beauty, Madame Gautreau (*Madame X*; New York, Metropolitan Museum), whom, in a strikingly simple composition, he depicted as a vain and socially conscious woman. The unfavorable publicity resulting from this realistic treatment caused the artist to settle in London, where he later took over the studio of J. A. M. Whistler. Like Whistler, Sargent was capable of skillful and unusual compositional arrangements,

Sassanian Art. Palace of Shapur I and the Arch of Khosrau, Ctesiphon. A.D. 241–272 or 6th century A.D. *Photo Enrico Mariani, Como.*

structured by light, shadow, and color. Often he used brilliant and seemingly capricious illumination to obliterate details, soften edges, and articulate shapes unexpectedly without destroying solid form. He revealed his mastery of composition and light in his tribute to a Spanish dancer, *El Jaleo* (1882; Boston, Isabella Stewart Gardner Museum), and particularly in the group portrait of the same year, the *Daughters of Edward D. Boit* (Boston, Museum of Fine Arts), in which his handling of figures in space is extraordinary. Sargent specialized in portraits, most often of society leaders, and attained great popularity. His mercurial watercolors, mostly travel sketches, are an important part of his oeuvre, executed with the same technical mastery but with greater intimacy than his oils. Toward the end of his life he painted murals for the Boston Museum of Fine Arts (1916–21), the Widener Library at Harvard University, Cambridge, Massachusetts, and the Boston Public Library (begun 1890s).

SARMATIAN ART. *See* **STEPPES ART.**

SARTO, Andrea del. *See* **ANDREA DEL SARTO.**

SASSANIAN ART. It was during the reign of the Parthian king Artabanus that a petty king named Ardashir I, grandson of Sassan, a priest of the temple of the goddess Anahita at Istakhr, rebelled against his suzerain. After a conflict lasting several years, Ardashir and Artabanus met in the battle of Hormizdagan (A.D. 224), which resulted in the Parthian king's defeat and death. Two years later, the rebel chief appeared before the city of Ctesiphon in present-day Iraq, took possession of it, and had himself crowned king, proclaiming the fall of the Parthian dynasty and the founding of the Sassanid (A.D. 226). It marked the beginning of a new period in the history of Iran, which lasted until A.D. 642, the date of the battle of Nahavend that heralded the supremacy of the Arabs, and the introduction of Islam into Persia.

Sassanid culture was inspired by a dynastic ideal, reflected in its art, which seems primarily concerned with the glorification of the king and with bearing witness to his power. In the capital, Ctesiphon, a huge palace was constructed (either A.D. 241–272 or 6th century A.D.), possibly by Ardashir's successor, Shapur I. Little remains of it except for the so-called Arch of Khosrau, which was built over what may have been an audience hall, and which still soars majestically above the desert. Another palace, constructed for Shapur I in the 3rd century A.D., is at Bishapur. It was originally covered by a dome, and had niches cut into its walls, which were adorned with painted stucco and covered with mosaics.

The masterpieces of Sassanid art are, however, the fine rock sculptures. The rocks at Naqsh-i-Rustam, near Persepolis, are carved with a relief depicting the investiture of Ardashir by the god Ahuramazda. At Bishapur and Naqsh-i-Rustam, there are a number of reliefs commemorating the triple triumph of Shapur I over the three Roman Emperors Gordian III, Philip the Arab, and Valerian, who was made prisoner with many of his soldiers in A.D. 260. At Bishapur, Bahram I is represented in a scene of his investiture; at Naqsh-i-Rustam, Bahram II appears surrounded by his family. In another relief, Hormizd II charges and unhorses his adversary. The kings desired that their hunting exploits be celebrated as well; these are seen in such examples as the reliefs in the large grotto of Taq-i-Bustan, near Kermanshah, Iran, which contain detailed representations of mounted elephants herding boars and stags toward swamp thickets, where the royal hunters awaited them. One of the most impressive pieces of Sassanid sculpture is unquestionably the colossal statue of Shapur I, discovered lying on the floor of the grotto at Bishapur, which gives one an impression of superhuman grandeur.

Craftsmen of the minor or decorative arts seem to have been even more prolific than the stone carvers. The period of their greatest activity was during the reigns of Khosrau I and II (6th–7th centuries A.D.). The cup of Khosrau I in gold, rock crystal, rubies, and glass (6th century A.D.; Paris, Cabinet des Médailles), decorated in the center with an image of the monarch seated on his throne, is only one of the many extant examples of the refined and exceedingly difficult technique of these Sassanian artisans. Their extraordinary skill is also evident in carvings of animals, such as the horse's head in the Louvre, made of silver picked out with gold (4th century A.D.), the chair and table legs in the shapes of griffins (New York, Coll. David Weill), or the rhytons (drinking bowls) shaped into the heads of gazelles (New York, Coll. Guennol).

Sassanian Art. *A royal hunt*. Rupestrian relief at Taq-i-Bustan. 5th century. *Photo Rostamy, Teheran.*

Another product of Sassanian craftsmen was the numerous textiles that were used to wrap precious relics and have fortunately survived. Some of the motifs of stucco decoration were repeated in these fabrics, which found their way to the West, reappearing in the Romanesque art of Europe.

SASSETTA, Stefano di Giovanni di Consolo, *called* (*c.* 1392, Asciano or Cortona—1451, Siena), Italian painter. Little is known of his life, but his activity in Siena between 1425 and 1450 is recorded by many contracts. Sassetta kept alive, in the 15th century, the religious ideals of the Trecento masters and the tradition of the Sienese Gothic style, while giving free rein to his

Sassanian Art. *Colossal statue of Shapur I*. Detail. 2nd half of 3rd century. Grotto of Mudan, Bishapur. *Photo Rostamy, Teheran.*

own imagination and love of the marvelous.

Among the surviving works of Sassetta, the earliest are fragments of a dismembered and partly destroyed altarpiece painted between 1423 and 1426 for the Arte della Lana Chapel, such as the *St. Thomas Aquinas Praying* (Budapest, National Gallery) and the *Vision of St. Thomas* (Vatican). The architectural backgrounds with perspective effects are reminiscent of those of Pietro and Ambrogio Lorenzetti. On the other hand, in the *Last Supper* (fragment from the predella in Siena, Pinacoteca), the architectural background is no longer Gothic, but consists of semicircular arcades, which reveal a knowledge of Filippo Brunelleschi's innovations, surprising in Siena at that time. Between 1430 and 1432, Sassetta painted the *Madonna della Neve* ("Madonna of the Snow") altarpiece (Florence, Coll. Contini Bonacossi) for Siena Cathedral. During the same period ending in 1437, he painted numerous works, including the polyptych in S. Domenico, Cortona.

In 1437 the artist was commissioned to paint a polyptych for the main altar of the church of S. Francesco at Borgo San Sepolcro. The altarpiece had a predella and pinnacles, painted on both sides. In 1752 it was taken from the altar and dismembered. The central panel (*Virgin and Child*) and two wings with figures of saints are now in Bordeaux (Priv. Coll.); the other two wings and the central panel from the back (*St. Francis in Ecstasy*) are in Settignano (Coll. Berenson); seven of the eight scenes on the back are in London (National Gallery) and one in Chantilly (Musée Condé). We only know of one scene from the predella (Berlin, Staatliche Museen). The Chantilly panel (*Mystic Marriage of St. Francis*) is one of the most charming paintings of the declining Sienese Gothic style, and possesses all the poetic feeling of the waning Middle Ages.

SAURA, Antonio (b. 1930, Huesca, Aragon), Spanish painter. He was attracted, then disappointed by the activities of a Surrealist group with whom he was associated during his first trip to Paris, where he stayed for two years (1953–55). In Madrid he joined several other artists of his generation, including Manolo Millares (b. 1926), Rafael Canogar (b. 1934), and Luigi Feitó (b. 1929), to found the El Paso group and the review of the same name (1957–60), whose various exhibitions left no doubt about their critical attitude toward the Franco régime. As early as 1954, Saura had drifted away from Surrealism and evolved a violently Expressionistic style derived from Picasso and the unlimited space of Jackson Pollock. He concentrated on abstractions of the human body, allowing nothing peripheral or irrelevant to distract him from his single purpose. The *Priests, Imaginary Portraits* (*Goya*, 1959–60; *St. Teresa of Ávila*; the *Duchess of Alba*; *Brigitte Bardot*), and then the aggressively sexual *Nudes*, and the *Crucifixions* (1959, 1960, New York, Matisse Gallery; 1963, Paris, Galerie Stadler; and others), were his means of avenging the outrage done to man.

SAVOLDO, Giovanni Girolamo (*c.* 1480, Brescia—after 1548, Venice?), Italian painter. Much of his career remains obscure: his inscription in the guild of Florentine painters in 1508 proves that he was in Tuscany for a time, while another document records that he was in Venice in 1521, where he spent most of his life. The protection of Duke Francesco II Sforza would suggest that Savoldo lived in Milan from 1529 to 1535; a will drawn up in 1526 reveals that the painter was married to a Dutch woman, which probably allowed him to establish connections with the artistic currents of Northern Europe.

In his rather dreamy portraits Savoldo continues the poetic mood of Giorgione (*Portrait of a Man*, 1510, Milan, Brera; *Portrait of a Knight*, Washington, D.C., National Gallery). His religious compositions include a *Nativity* (1527; Middlesex, Hampton Court Palace) and an altarpiece in the church of S. Maria in Organo at Verona (1533). Savoldo's preoccupation with light, with its reflection on forms and its transformation of tonal values, is no doubt the result of Flemish influence, particularly that of Jan van Eyck: thus, the *Adoration of the Shepherds* (1540; Venice, S. Giobbe) attempts a skillful nocturnal effect by framing a moonlit shepherd in a window, while *Tobias and the Angel* (*c.* 1540; Rome, Galleria Borghese) envelops its realistically conceived figures and landscape in an amber atmosphere.

SCAMOZZI, Vincenzo (1552, Vicenza—1616, Venice), Italian architect and theoretician. He is considered one of the last great Renaissance architects. Scamozzi worked on Sansovino's unfinished Libreria Vecchia, Venice (begun 1537; completed by Scamozzi 1583–88), and brought to completion three of Palladio's major undertakings, the Teatro Olimpico (1579–80) and Villa Rotonda (begun 1550), both in Vicenza, and S. Giorgio Maggiore, Venice (1565); however, he deviated from the original plans to some degree.

As an architect, Scamozzi is best known for the Procuratie Nuove in the Piazza S. Marco, Venice (1584–1640; completed by Baldassarre Longhena), which was to complement Sansovino's adjacent Libreria. However, in reaction to Sansovino, Scamozzi designed a building with three stories of moderate height instead of two very tall ones, and produced a plan of more academic correctness.

Of his original works, the majority of which show a strong dependence on Palladio, the most

Vincenzo Scamozzi. Procuratie Nuove, Venice. 1586–1611 (second order modified by Longhena, 1640). *Photo Alinari-Giraudon.*

Gottfried Schadow. *Princesses Louisa and Frederica of Prussia.* 1797. Staatliche Museen, Berlin-Dahlem.

important is the Villa Pisani ("La Rocca") at Lonigo, designed in 1576 and begun two years later. He designed several Venetian palaces, of which the most famous is the Continari degli Scrigni (1609), and a number of other residences, including the Villa Nani-Mocenigo, Canda (1580–84). Perhaps the least Palladian of his works is the beautiful Teatro all'Antica at Sabbioneta, based on Classical designs, which he executed for Vespasiano Gonzaga (1588–89).

He was a great traveler, visiting Poland, Germany, Nancy, and Paris in addition to Austria, and his diary is full of interesting comments on contemporary architecture. His most influential piece of writing, *Idea dell'architettura universale* (Venice, 1615), is a classic work dealing primarily with architectural theory. It was translated into English, French, Dutch, and German soon after its initial appearance.

SCHADOW, Gottfried (1764, Berlin—1850, Berlin), German sculptor. Schadow lived in Rome from 1785 to 1787, where he met Antonio Canova. When he returned to Berlin, he worked at first in the Porcelain Factory, and then succeeded Tassaert in 1788 as court sculptor. He now began his brilliant association with the architects who were transforming Berlin, particularly with Carl Gotthard Langhans (1732–1808), who built the Brandenburg Gate. In 1790 Schadow carved, as his first major project, the graceful tomb of Alexander von der Mark in the Dorotheenkirche. Possibly his most important works, however, were the quadriga (destroyed in World War II) and bas-reliefs on the Brandenburg Gate. In 1797 he executed his most admired statues, full-figure portraits of the princesses Louisa and Frederica of Prussia (Berlin, Staatliche Museen), in which he combined a realistic drapery style with much grace and charm. Although Schadow never quite reached these heights again, his monuments to Field Marshal Gebhard Blücher at Rostock (1819) and to Martin Luther at Wittemberg (1821) are impressive and dignified in their simplicity.

WILHELM (1789, Berlin—1862, Düsseldorf), a painter, was the son of Gottfried. He was one of the Nazarenes who, in 1816–17, decorated the Palazzo Zuccaro in Rome (the frescoes are now in East Berlin, Staatliche Museen) for the Prussian Consul-General Jakob Bartholdy. In 1826 Wilhelm succeeded Peter Cornelius as head of the Düsseldorf Academy. During his lifetime, he enjoyed a high reputation as a leading painter, an opinion not generally shared today.

SCHAMBERG, Morton Livingston (b. 1881, Philadelphia—d. 1918), American painter. He went to Paris in 1906, and upon his return shared a studio in Philadelphia with the photographer and Precisionist painter Charles Sheeler, a close friend, with whom he later returned to Europe (1908–9). Schamberg himself did some portrait photography in 1913, the same year that his arbitrarily colored landscapes appeared in the Armory Show in New York. First influenced by the works of Matisse and the Cubists that he had seen in Paris, Schamberg subsequently became acquainted with Marcel Duchamp and Francis Picabia, French Dada artists and aesthetic theorists. Around 1912 Schamberg began to paint partially abstract pictures, using machine-like forms and motifs from American folk themes. Between 1913 and 1918 he and Sheeler spent time collecting and sketching early American furniture and handicrafts in the Pennsylvania Dutch regions. His interest in machines as subject matter was an extension of this concern with extremely simplified, precisely crafted forms, a logical development of the analytical still-life mode native to American art from its early period. Schamberg was interested also in the forms of Cubism which he used in a modified version to express the pristine clarity and functionalism of the machine age. Although he sometimes mocked modern mechanisms, as in *Telephone* (1916; Columbus, Ohio, Gallery of Fine Arts), his approach to the machine was more directly pictorial than that of his European Dadaist contemporaries. Nevertheless, Schamberg's *291 Machine* (1916; New Haven, Yale University Art Gallery) is not unlike Picabia's 1916–17 drawings of meshing gears (*Machine Tournez vite*), but Schamberg's aim was quite different from that of the French artist. Like Léger, Schamberg saw hope rather than ruin in the machine, and his early death cut short a promising artistic development based upon this positive notion.

SCHAROUN, Hans (b. 1893, Bremen), German architect. He was the leading representative of the "organic architecture" movement in Germany and his unrealized projects influenced the younger generation as much as those which were built. In 1920 Scharoun took part in the architectural discussions of the November group, led by Bruno Taut (1890–1938) at Berlin. In 1925 he

Morton L. Schamberg. *Machine.* 1916. Yale University Art Gallery, New Haven, Conn.

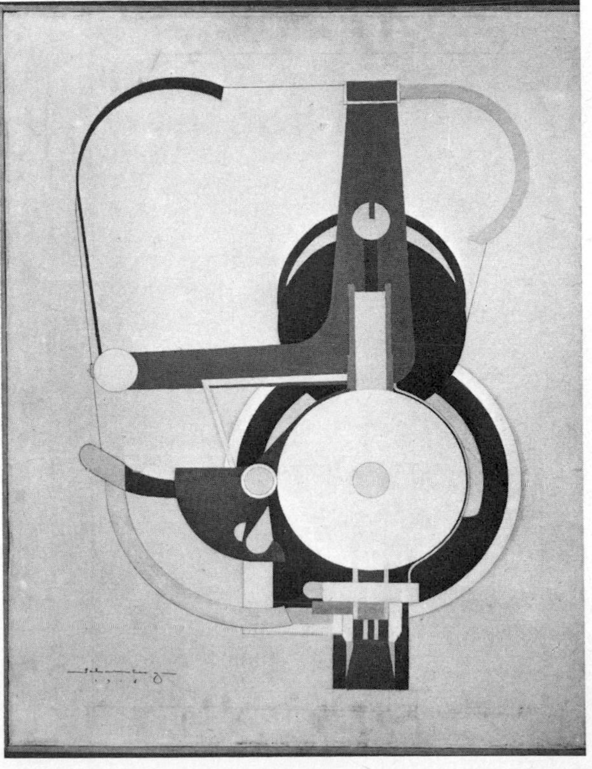

Hans Scharoun. Villa Schminke, Löbau. 1932.

joined the Berlin architectural association of Der Ring, formed by leading architects of the day to defend modern ideas against official conformism. When the Weissenhof estate was built at Stuttgart for the Deutscher Werkbund exhibition in 1927, Scharoun was invited by its director, Ludwig Mies van der Rohe, to build a house along with such other European masters as Le Corbusier and J. J. P. Oud. The first projects that won him acclaim were a home for the aged at Breslau (1929) and the terrace houses of the Berlin-Siemensstadt estate (1930). His work began to embody the conception that the elements of a house should, like the parts of an organism, function cooperatively to satisfy the fundamental need of its occupants. He gave an interesting application of the idea in the Schminke House at Löbau in Saxony (1932), an elegant steel structure whose free form made it seem suspended in the countryside. After World War II he was made head of the Berlin Department for Building and Housing to rebuild the shattered city. He formed the Berliner Kollektiv group, which presented an astonishing town planning project for the capital (1946). The large-scale projects for rebuilding the Hansa district in Berlin (1954) and the housing estate built at Charlottenburg-Nord (1955–61) that occupied him during this period were more concerned with the problems of urban planning space than with particular architectural forms. Some of his most famous projects were the Kassel Theater and the primary school at Darmstadt, which he discussed at the Darmstadt Conference in 1951 in his lecture on "Man and Space." Scharoun's unrealized projects were more numerous than those actually built, but they were no less controversial or influential. The Romeo and Juliet double blocks of flats at Stuttgart (1963), built in collaboration with Wilhelm Frank, and the Geschwister Scholl High School at Lünen, Westphalia (1955–62), are among his more controversial works. The concert hall he built for the Berlin Philharmonic Orchestra (1963) gave substance to the powerful imagination embodied in projects for individual buildings and town planning schemes.

SCHIAVONE, Andrea Meldolla, *called* Andrea (between *c.* 1500–3 and 1522, Zara, Dalmatia—between 1563 and 1582, Venice), Italian painter and engraver. Schiavone went to Venice around 1530, and in 1540 or 1541–42 the art historian Giorgio Vasari commissioned a painting from him (now lost) depicting the *Battle Between Charles V and the Moslem Leader Barbarossa II* that had taken place in 1535. Schiavone was first influenced by Bonifazio Veronese, and was the protégé of Titian and Tintoretto in Venice: Titian's influence is evident in the *Adoration of the Shepherds* (Vienna, Kunsthistorisches Museum), and Tintoretto's in the *Condemnation of Midas* (Middlesex, Hampton Court Palace). Whereas the latter two artists profoundly influenced his painting, his style of drawing owes much to Parmigianino, particularly in respect to the themes. Several of his paintings—which are difficult to date—are in Venetian churches and museums: they include the *Circumcision, Adoration of the Magi, Adoration of the Shepherds*, and the *Annunciation*, which are in the church of S. Maria del Carmine; and the *Christ on the Way to Emmaus* in the church of S. Sebastiano. The Kunsthistorisches Museum in Vienna also has a large collection of his works, including a *Self-Portrait*. His mannered drawing and rich, luministic coloring are characteristic of Late Renaissance painting and foreshadow the Baroque style. Schiavone also executed numerous engravings, including a signed engraving of the *Rape of Helen by Paris* (1547).

SCHIELE, Egon (1890, Tulln, near Vienna—1918, Vienna), Austrian painter. He received his training at the Vienna Academy of Fine Arts (1906–9), and then met Gustav Klimt, whose linear style profoundly influenced his work. In 1909 Schiele helped found the *Neukunstgruppe* (New Art Group), which held an exhibition in Vienna. The human figure was the main subject of his work, drawn with a sharp, febrile line, accented with intense color, and exhibiting an emaciated, lonely eroticism. Although called up for military service in 1915, he continued to paint nudes, dreamlike images of towns and trees, and anguished groups of figures, such as *Woman with Two Children* and

Karl Friedrich von Schinkel. Altes Museum, Berlin. 1823–30. *Photo Kunstgeschichtliche Bildstelle Humboldt-Universität, Berlin.*

The Family (both *c.* 1917; Vienna, Österreichische Galerie). Schiele died from Spanish influenza when he was twenty-eight years old, just after enjoying a prominent position at the Secession exhibition in Vienna.

SCHINKEL, Karl Friedrich von (1781, Neuruppin, Brandenburg—1841, Berlin), German architect. He entered the offices of Friedrich Gilly, a greatly talented architect of the Classic Revival and an important formative influence. Schinkel then spent some years in Italy (1803–5), but found on his return that the defeat of Prussia had created very unfavorable conditions for architectural developments.

He began his public career as assessor in the Public Works Department (1810) and later as state architect (1815), which gave him a certain control over all new construction in Berlin. His first major commissions were not received until 1816, when he began work on three Berlin masterpieces: the New Guard House (1816–18), a modified Doric temple flanked by massive end walls superbly proportioned and sculptured according to his own program; the Theater (designed 1818; built 1819–21), where Schinkel's nationalistic handling of Greek elements is most apparent; and finally the Altes (Old) Museum with its long, majestic Ionic colonnade (1823–30). Outside Berlin, where his influence was profound, he built many villas and churches.

The buildings actually completed by Schinkel are few compared to the number he designed. He left an enormous collection of plans and projects, among which we may mention two grand schemes: a palace for King Otto of Greece on the Acropolis, Athens (1834), and the castle of Orianda for the empress of Russia in the Crimea (1838). With the possible exception of the English architect Sir John Soane, Schinkel was perhaps the most refined exponent of Romantic Classicism in northern Europe.

SCHLAUN, Johann Conrad (1695, Norden—1773, Münster), German architect. The beauty of his work, characterized by the simplicity with which he handled Baroque forms and a respect for materials atypical for the period, is particularly apparent in two early Capuchin churches at Brakel (1715–18) and Münster (1724–29). While in the service of Clemens August of Bavaria, Schlaun studied with Balthasar Neumann at Würzburg (1720–21), went to Rome to study the works of Bernini and Borromini (1722), and to Munich, where he made careful observations of the Nymphenburg and Schleissheim palaces (1724). When he became Chief Architect and Engineer to Clemens August, Elector of Cologne, Schlaun was commissioned to enlarge Schloss Brühl (1725–28). His masterpiece of this early period, the hunting lodge of Clemenswerth near Sögel, was built for the elector between 1736 and 1749. Although influenced by Marly-le-Roi, with eight pavilions grouped around a central block, Clemenswerth was much simpler, with plain brick surfaces articulated by wall strips, heightened only by sculptured garlands in stone. After 1740 Schlaun's studies of Borromini began to bear fruit, particularly in the house of the Brethren of Mercy at Münster (1745–53) and the chapel of St. Johannes Nepomuk, near Rietberg (1744–48). To this mature period belong the architect's country house, Rüschhaus, near Münster (1745–48), and his town house at Münster (1753–55). But his last years were occupied by the Schloss at Münster (1767–73), where he remained consistently Baroque, especially in the forward-curving central pavilion.

SCHLEMMER, Oskar (1888, Stuttgart—1943, Baden-Baden), German painter and sculptor. He first studied at the Stuttgart Academy under Adolf Hölzel, then went to Berlin (1910–11), where he had a chance to see examples of French painting, notably by Paul Cézanne and Georges Seurat. Schlemmer returned to Stuttgart and began painting landscapes in muted colors and geometricized forms. These tendencies were accentuated during the following years, although in 1915 he painted figures that were no more than silhouettes defined by the interplay of curves and countercurves. The same fondness for geometry appears in the reliefs Schlemmer did in 1923 for the Bauhaus at Weimar (destroyed by the Nazis in 1930), where he had taught painting, sculpture, and stage design (1920–29). In his painting, Schlemmer constantly returned to the same mechanistic figures, with their simplified forms, regular gestures and expressionless faces. Only the attitudes, the arrangements in an ambiguous space, and the light were varied (*Fourteen Figures in an Imaginary Architecture*, 1930, Cologne, Wallraf-Richartz-Museum; *Bauhaus Staircase*, 1933, New York, Museum of Modern Art).

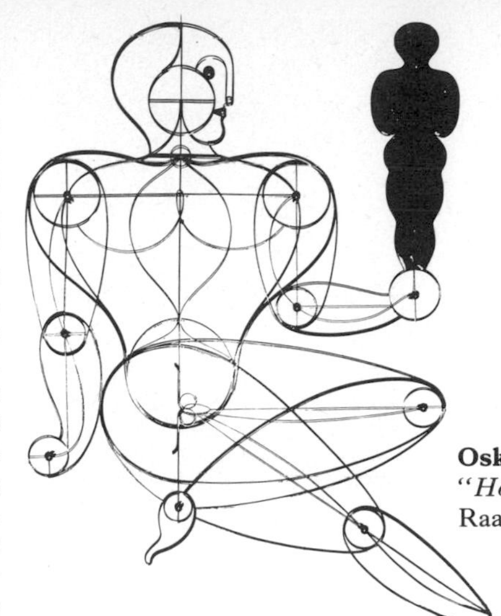

Oskar Schlemmer. *"Homo."* 1931. Coll. Raabe, Zwenkau.

In his *Treader Ballet* (partly conceived in 1916, first performed at Stuttgart's State Theater in 1922) the dancers' heads and limbs were encased in the same stiff cylindrical shapes that characterized his painted figures. In his last years, his forms lost a little of their precision, his composition became less limpid, the contrasts between light and dark grew sharper, and an uneasy nervousness appeared in his color and brushwork (series of *Windows*, 1942; Stuttgart, Coll. Frau Tut Schlemmer).

SCHLÜTER, Andreas (between 1662 and 1669, Danzig or Hamburg—1760, St. Petersburg), greatest Baroque sculptor of Germany, and also active as an architect. When he arrived in Berlin from Warsaw in 1694, he already demonstrated a profound knowledge of Italian art and possibly also of French and Dutch art. He almost certainly went to France in the course of his studies and there must have seen the new sculptures of Antoine Coysevox, Martin Desjardins, and François Girardon. On returning to Berlin in 1696, Schlüter began to prepare the design for an equestrian monument to Frederick III, but the subject was altered to portray the Great Elector Friedrich-Wilhelm (now in Charlottenburg Castle).

Andreas Schlüter. *Head of a Dying Warrior. c.* 1696. Arsenal, Berlin. *Foto Marburg.*

He soon attained an eminent position and, in 1698, he was commissioned to supervise the building of the Arsenal, which had been started in 1695. Schlüter had already carved the magnificent masks of dying warriors to adorn the courtyard, but his architectural scheme was beset with problems. He tried to erect a heavy attic above the entablature and this weakened the construction. After an enquiry in 1699 he was removed from this position but remained in charge of the building of the "New Palace," a responsibility he had also assumed in 1698. In 1703 his great equestrian statue of the Elector was installed. Schlüter's Mint Tower also suffered from structural failings and had to be pulled down in 1706, which put an end to his successful career.

Although he received very few commissions after this Schlüter did build the Kamecke Palace in Berlin (1711–12; destroyed World War II), and in 1714 accepted an invitation to St. Petersburg, where he died in obscurity.

SCHMIDT-ROTTLUFF, Karl Schmidt, *called* Karl (b. 1884, Rottluff, near Chemnitz), German painter. In 1905 he was one of the painters who founded the Brücke at Dresden (the name was supplied by Schmidt-Rottluff), Germany's first modern artistic movement. For the rest of his life he practiced a vigorous Expressionism, coarser than the work of Ernst Ludwig Kirchner, yet more sturdy and vehement than that of Erich Heckel. His palette in 1910 was bright, and his drawing loose and deliberate. Then he painted a series of Norwegian landscapes (1911) in which heavily saturated colors, stimulated by Fauvism, clashed violently with each other (*Landscape*; Feldafing, Coll. Buchheim). Like the other members of the Brücke, Schmidt-Rottluff settled in 1911 in Berlin, where he remained for the rest of his life. The influence of primitive art and probably of Kirchner and Heckel on his work of *c.* 1913 produced forms of geometric simplicity in landscapes and figures informed by a mystical quality (*Nude Figures in the Open Air*, 1913; Hanover, Städtische Galerie). The mystical character of his work is especially apparent in a series of religious woodcuts (*Road to Emmaus*, 1918). After World War I his drawing lost some of its stiffness, and his work became more lyrical (*Summer at the Sea*, 1919; formerly Essen, Folkwang Museum). The precise, primitive qualities of Schmidt-Rottluff's many woodcuts (from 1910) influenced much of his painting.

SCHNABEL, Day (b. 1905, Vienna), American sculptress of Austrian origin. After training at the Vienna Academy of Fine Arts, she went to Holland to study sculpture and architecture, becoming especially interested in the De Stijl movement. Following a visit to Italy, she went to Paris, where she studied under Marcel Gimond and Charles Malfay (1887–1940). During World War II, she emigrated to the United States and worked in Ossip Zadkine's New York studio. She returned to Paris in 1947, at which time she abandoned figurative art. Her sculpture became abstract, although sometimes suggestive of a specific theme, as in *Flight* (1950)—which was the maquette for a monument in honor of aviation—or of pure construction, as in *Transformations* (1956; New York, Whitney Museum), in which masses are juxtaposed in harmony or contrast.

SCHNEIDER, Gérard (b. 1896, Ste-Croix, Switzerland), French painter of Swiss origin. In 1916 he went to Paris, studying at the École des Arts Décoratifs (1916–18) and in Fernand Cormon's (1845–1924) studio at the École des Beaux-Arts (1918–20). Schneider then returned to Neuchâtel, where he had his first one-man show in 1920. In 1924 he returned to Paris, and settled there permanently. He worked as a picture restorer and showed his own paintings at the Salon d'Automne (1926) and at the Salon des Surindépendants (1936; 1939). At this point in his career, however, he still wavered between Cubism and Surrealism. Before World War II, he dabbled cautiously with abstraction, but it was not until 1944 that he wholeheartedly devoted himself to abstract painting (*Composition*, 1944; Paris, Musée National d'Art Moderne). The canvases he produced during the first phase of his development are characterized by groups of bold, well-defined forms that he subjected to a constant graphic discipline. Subsequently, his forms flowed in waves of color over vast areas, creating minutely orchestrated pictorial symphonies (*Cérak*, 1955; New York, Coll. Raymond Mindlin). He never made any reference to the exterior world, or even suggested the contents of a painting by giving it a specific title. In 1957 Schneider won the International Prize for Abstract Painting at Lissone, Italy. An exhibition of his paintings at the Galerie Arnaud in Paris (1967) was a credit to his constantly renewed inventiveness and mastery in the exploration of the world of forms and colors.

SCHÖFFER, Nicolas (b. 1912, Kalocsa, Hungary), French sculptor of Hungarian origin. He went to Paris in 1936 and attended classes at the École des Beaux-Arts. Schöffer held his first one-man show in Paris in 1948; at that time he gained recognition in the art world with his invention of "spatiodynamism," which he defined as "the constructed and dynamic integration of space into plastic work." His spatiodynamic sculpture consisted of a strictly geometric metal framework onto which disks of Plexiglass or thin metal were attached at odd intervals. These plates in turn projected images onto a screen. Schöffer constructed several such

Nicolas Schöffer. *Lux 4.* 1957. *Photo Hervochon.*

sculptures in the shape of towers, including the one—over 166 feet high—that broadcasts concrete music and that was commissioned by the Salon des Travaux Publics (1954; Paris, Parc de St-Cloud). In 1956 he harnessed cybernetics in the service of his art and, with the help of engineers, invented *Cysp I* (Paris, Galerie Denise René), a robot-sculpture. In 1957 he perfected "luminodynamism" (*Lux I*, 1957–58; Paris, Musée National d'Art Moderne), whose novelty consisted in using sculptures supplied with mobile reflectors, filters, and screens to produce luminous effects in space. "Chronodynamism" appeared in 1959 with *Chronos I*, which combined music (in the form of chromatic variations) with effects of light and color intensity. Schöffer's experiments then continued with *Anamorphous Reliefs* (1961), in which rotating elements in Plexiglass were reflected as anamorphoses on a polished concave surface; the *Musiscope* (1960), a pictorial organ with an electronic keyboard, which projected endless combinations of colored forms on a screen; the *Light Wall* (1962), which was designed for mass production and consisted of a translucent panel behind which luminodynamic cells created a constantly changing pattern; and finally the *Teleluminoscope* (1961), which was like a television set that produced abstract images.

SCHONGAUER, Martin (*c.* 1450—d. 1491, Breisach, near Freiburg), German painter and engraver, the son of Caspar Schongauer, an Augsburg goldsmith. Before Albrecht Dürer, who had a great admiration for him, Schongauer was unquestionably the greatest artist that Germany produced. The only painting that can be attributed to him with certainty is the *Virgin in the Rose Bower* (1473; Colmar, church of St-Martin), in which the influence of Rogier van der Weyden is evident. A small *Nativity* (Munich, Alte Pinakothek) may be attributed to Schongauer on stylistic grounds, but the panels of an altarpiece painted about 1475 for the Dominicans (now in Colmar, Musée d'Unterlinden) are only workshop products. This leaves the engravings, of which there are no fewer than 115, as the principal legacy of his genius. Two engravings deserving special mention are the charming small *Virgin seated in a Courtyard* and the *Temptation of St. Anthony* (*c.* 1475). Schongauer's Late Gothic style has Mannerist qualities; the figures with their long, pointed shoes hardly touch the ground. Yet he engraved such Passion scenes as the great *Christ Carrying the Cross* with such thoughtfulness and profundity that Dürer could do no better than imitate him.

SCHWITTERS, Kurt (1887, Hanover—1948, Ambleside, Westmorland), German painter. His early work was rather academic but, about 1917–18, he painted and drew portraits and landscapes with an abstract tendency, which reflected the influence of the German Expressionists and the French Cubists. In the following year Schwitters inserted *papiers collés* into his compositions, and executed his first group of *Merz* pictures, made of discarded items (bits of wood, rags, wire, nails, string, etc.) mixed with printed words that had been picked at random and arranged without regard for their meaning. Schwitters exhibited these pictures at Herwarth Walden's Sturm Gallery in Berlin (1918), and published poems in the review of the same name (1919).

In 1922, he went to Holland, where he met Theo van Doesburg, who introduced him to the ideas of the De Stijl movement. De Stijl influences can be seen on some of his later collages. Schwitters elaborated his experiments in a more architectural way, and for years was engaged in building his famous *Merzbau*, a huge construction in which the most heteroclite and provocative objects were combined. Along with his artistic activities, he published (1923–32) a magazine called *Merz*, in which he defended the Dadaists, then in 1924 he produced a special number on Neoplasticism and Russian Constructivism. He worked at the time with El Lissitzky, who was living in Hanover, and shared his interests in typography and the advertising arts. In 1937 he founded with Willi Baumeister, César Domela-Nieuwenhuis (b. 1900), and Friedrich Vordemberge-Gildewart the *Ring neuer Werbegestalter* (New Advertising Designers' Circle). Later that year Schwitters fled from the Nazis to Norway, and constructed a second *Merzbau* at Lysaker, near Oslo. As the Germans invaded Norway he fled again, this time to England, where he was at first interned as a German citizen. When he was released, Schwitters began a third *Merzbau* on an isolated farm near Ambleside, in the Lake District, but death interrupted his labors.

Kurt Schwitters. "*Schnurchel en largeur.*" 1923. Coll. Hannah Höch, Berlin.

SCIPIONE, Gino Bonichi, *called* (1904, Macerata, The Marches—1933, Arco, Trento), Italian painter. In spite of his unusually brief period of creative activity, Scipione was regarded as the leader of the Roman School, which he founded in 1928 in collaboration with Mario Mafai (b. 1902). In his early painting he conveyed meaning through symbols, then made a direct approach to reality with a highly personal combination of Expressionism and Romanticism (*Roman Prostitute*, 1930, Milan, Coll. G. Mattioli; *Piazza Navona*, 1930, Rome, Coll. G. Bottai). The mixture of brutality and fantasy in his style earned him widespread recognition. A retrospective exhibition, held in 1954 at the Galleria d'Arte Moderna in Rome to mark the fiftieth anniversary of his birth, showed that his originality held its own alongside all the modern artistic tendencies.

SCOREL *or* **SCHOOREL,** Jan van (1495, Schoorl, near Alkmaar—1562, Utrecht), Dutch painter, architect, engineer, poet, and musician. He established Humanism and the Italian style in Holland, just as his teacher Jan Gossaert did in Brussels. In 1517 or 1518 he was in Utrecht with Gossaert, but remained there only a short time before beginning a long journey that took him through Germany and Switzerland to Carinthia (1520), then to Venice, from where he began a pilgrimage (1520–21) to Jerusalem. On his return from the Holy Land he reached Rome during the brief pontificate (1522–23) of the Utrecht-born Pope Adrian VI, who appointed him keeper of the papal collections. Scorel finally returned to Holland around 1523. These extensive travels were responsible for the diversity of his style. One can follow his artistic development by comparing his triptych of the *Holy Kinship* (1520; Obervallach, Carinthia, parish church), which is typically Dutch and primitive, with his *Tobias and the Angel* (1521; Priv. Coll.), which is a landscape in the style of Joachim Patinir; with his *Presentation in the Temple* (Vienna, Kunsthistorisches Museum), which reveals the influences of Raphael and Bramante; and with his *Bathsheba in Her Bath* (*c.* 1530–38; Amsterdam, Rijksmuseum), in which the figure is depicted before an exotic landscape and Italianate palaces. His religious works are historical and Classical in conception (*Baptism of Christ*, Paris, Coll. Hevezy; *Sermon of St. John the Baptist*, The Hague, Coll. Thurkow). Scorel also executed several portrait friezes depicting *Pilgrims to Jerusalem*, in which the figures are wooden but full of character. The panel showing *Twelve Jerusalem Pilgrims* (1520s; Haarlem, Frans Halsmuseum) reveals his portraiture at its best. There is a more relaxed air, more life, and more tenderness in his portraits of a *Young Scholar* (1531; Rotterdam, Museum Boymans-van Beuningen), a *Magistrate* (*c.* 1550; Wilton House, near Salisbury, Coll. Earl of Pembroke), *Pope Adrian VI* (1523; Louvain, Brabant, Rectorate of the University), a *Jerusalem Pilgrim* (1525–30; Bloomfield Hills, Mich., Cranbrook Academy of Art Galleries), and his portrait of his mistress, *Agatha van Schoonhoven* (1529; Rome, Galleria Doria Pamphili). His religious paintings were more important from an art historical point of view; in them, he included untraditional elements such as nudes, drapery in the ancient Classical style, stately Roman architecture, and immense composite landscapes.

Sebastiano del Piombo. *Pietà. c.* 1515 or *c.* 1517. Museo Civico, Viterbo. *Photo Anderson-Viollet.*

SCOTT, Sir George Gilbert (1811, Gawcott, Buckinghamshire—1878, London), English architect. In 1835 he went into partnership with W. B. Moffatt (1812–87), a relationship that lasted many years. Scott attracted considerable attention in 1844 by winning the international competition for St. Nicolas's Church, Hamburg. This marked the beginning of an enormously successful practice, which included the building or restoration of over 730 cathedrals, churches, and public and private buildings. Scott's sheer industry made him the most representative figure of the Gothic Revival, the style that had captured Victorian taste. His preference for the decorated style (practiced 1307–77) did sometimes lead him to substitute it, quite inappropriately, and his work on Sir Christopher Wren's St. Michael's, Cornhill, amounted to vandalism. Some characteristic examples of his work include St. Giles, Camberwell (1844), the Martyrs' Memorial, Oxford (1841), the Albert Memorial, London (1863–72), and St. Pancras Station Hotel, London (1868–74), a vigorous and sumptuous Gothic extravagance.

SCYTHIAN ART. *See* **STEPPES ART.**

SEBASTIANO DEL PIOMBO, Sebastiano Luciani, *called* (*c.* 1485, Venice—1547, Rome), Italian painter. He was the friend and pupil of Giorgione, and early in his career was closely associated with the great Venetian master, whose melancholy gentleness he imitated in his *Death of Adonis* (*c.* 1512; Florence, Uffizi). The influence of Giorgione's last manner, however, is even more marked in the large figures Sebastiano painted in the niches of the church of S. Bartolomeo, or in *St. John Chrysostom* (Venice, S. Giovanni Crisostomo), painted in a typically Venetian style. As soon as Sebastiano arrived in Rome, his style developed rapidly. In 1511 Agostino Chigi asked him to share in the decoration of the Villa Farnesina, where he painted a *Polyphemus*, among other frescoes, and the lunettes in the loggia. He was a member of Raphael's circle, as we can see from his subtle portraits: *La Fornarina* (1512; Uffizi), the *Young Violinist* (*c.* 1515; Paris, Coll. Rothschild), and the portrait of *Dorothea* (*c.* 1513; Berlin, Staatliche Museen).

Sebastiano's art became heavier in his final Roman phase, when he came under the strong influence of Michelangelo, who corresponded with him in a series of very interesting letters, and who gave him sketches and cartoons to develop. Michelangelo's impact may be seen in the powerful *Pietà*, dated by various scholars at *c.* 1515 or *c.* 1517 (Viterbo, Museo Civico), with its superbly sculptural figure of the dead Christ, so isolated from that of the Virgin. It is also evident in the *Resurrection of Lazarus* (1519; London, National Gallery). Sebastiano was at his best in his portraits, such as those of *Andrea Doria* (1526; Rome, Galleria Doria Pamphili) and *Clement VII* (1526; Naples, Museo di Capodimonte). After the Sack of Rome, he wandered through Italy, working for the Gonzaga family for some time in Mantua, then returning to Venice. Back in Rome, Sebastiano was given (1531) the lucrative post of Keeper of the Papal Seal—*il Piombo*—hence his nickname. After this he painted only a few rather cold portraits and some large religious works, such as the *Birth of the Virgin* (begun 1532; Rome, S. Maria del Popolo), left unfinished at his death.

SECESSION, name given to a number of avant-garde artistic movements founded in Germany and Austria at the end of the 19th and the beginning of the 20th centuries.

The earliest, the Munich group, was founded in 1892 by Franz von Stuck (1863–1928), Wilhelm Trübner (1851–1917), and Fritz von Uhde (1848–1911). From 1893 it held important exhibitions, including the works of Arnold Böcklin, Jean-Baptiste Camille Corot, Gustave Courbet, Max Liebermann, and Jean-François Millet. Although it supported the Impressionist movement, its avant-garde character was less pronounced than that of the Berlin Secession. The latter's foundation in 1899, under the presidency of Max Liebermann, was in fact the result of a long aesthetic controversy that went back to 1892, the date of an exhibition of the *Verein Berliner Künstler* (Association of Berlin Artists), from which

Secession. Ernst-Ludwig Kirchner. Poster for an exhibition of the New Secession in Berlin. 1910.

Edvard Munch had been obliged to withdraw a group of 55 paintings that he had submitted. This scandal caused a complete split among the artists. Munch and his supporters found allies in the literary circles of the capital, where they soon formed strong ties, and it was out of their discussions that the Berlin Secession arose. Although the sympathies of the group were initially with Impressionism, it was not long before the great Neoimpressionist masters, the Nabis and the Fauves, were regularly exhibited. In 1902 a brilliant exhibition presented to the public 28 paintings of Munch, including his series called *Frieze of Life* (begun *c.* 1891), Ferdinand Hodler's *William Tell* (1903; Soleure, Coll. Kottmann), and three works by Wassily Kandinsky. However, in 1910, the Secession jury refused the work of 27 avant-garde artists, notably Emil Nolde's painting, *Pentecost* (1909; Bern, Kunstmuseum). The rejected artists immediately organized themselves into a rival association, called the New Secession, under the presidency of Max Pechstein. Besides Kandinsky, Alexej von Jawlensky, and Alfred Kubin, the most important members were the Brücke artists.

The Viennese Secession, founded in 1897 under the presidency of Gustav Klimt, its moving spirit, played a decisive part in spreading the Jugendstil. Besides regularly publishing its review, *Ver Sacrum*, it organized a series of provocative exhibitions: 1902, Klimt's *Beethoven* frieze for Max Klinger's exhibition; 1903, French Impressionists and Neoimpressionists; 1904, Hodler's paintings. It was in this distinguished circle, where artists, poets, musicians, architects, and decorators met, that Oskar Kokoschka received his early training. His exhibition in 1908 marked both the culmination and the disintegration of the Secession movement.

SECTION D'OR ("golden section"), group of French Cubist painters active in the 1st quarter of the 20th century. The year 1912 marked the passage from Analytic Cubism to Synthetic Cubism and witnessed the movement's widespread propagation. In the same year Albert Gleizes and Jean Metzinger published *Du Cubisme*, the first doctrinal work on the new movement. Also in that year, from October 10–30, the historic exhibition of paintings by the Section d'Or group was held at the Galerie La Boétie in Paris. The exhibition included works by Juan Gris, Fernand Léger, Gleizes, Metzinger, André Lhote, Robert Delaunay, Louis Marcoussis, Roger de La Fresnaye, Marcel Duchamp, Jacques Villon, André Dunoyer de Segonzac, Luc-Albert Moreau (1882–1948), and Jean Marchand (1883–1940). The painter and engraver Jacques Villon provided the initiative and the title of this exhibition, which created a considerable stir in Parisian artistic circles. In Villon's studio, a number of artists passionately interested in problems of rhythm and proportion met on Sunday afternoons, among them the Cubist theoreticians Gleizes and Metzinger, as well as Francis Picabia, Léger, and La Fresnaye. At these meetings Villon developed his pyramidal theory of vision based on theories developed by Leonardo da Vinci; Villon also suggested the title of "Section d'Or," which he borrowed from the treatise *Divine Proportion* by the Bolognese monk Luca Pacioli, which had been published in Venice in 1509 and illustrated by Leonardo himself.

Formulated by Vitruvius and taken up again during the Renaissance, the golden section or divine proportion is the ideal relation between two magnitudes, expressed numerically in the following manner:

$$\frac{1}{0.618} = \frac{1.618}{1}$$

and demonstrated in many masterpieces in the various arts, being applied consciously or, more often, by instinct. Although the golden section was not the only constant to which the Cubists referred for the mathematical organization of their canvases, it reflected the profound need for order and measure that they felt more through sensibility and reason than as a result of calculation.

SEGALL, Lasar (1891, Vilna, Lithuania—1957, São Paulo), naturalized Brazilian painter of Russian origin. He was attracted by Germany and attended classes at the Berlin Academy of Fine Arts from 1906 to 1909. He then went to Dresden, where he soon entered artistic circles and was given his first one-man exhibition (1910). The paintings he did between 1912 and 1923 were directly influenced by German Expressionism, but their haggard, starved, and pitiful figures, defined by angular lines and subdued colors, suffer from structural weakness and an obvious need for technical discipline (*Eternal Wanderers*, 1918; Dresden, Gemäldegalerie). At the end of 1923 he left Germany for São Paulo, where he acquired Brazilian citizenship (1924) and gained a reputation as the leading painter of the Brazilian school. The obsessions of Segall's youth never disappeared from his art: his emigrants, wandering prostitutes, and poor families are the moving conceptions of a hard-working, intense, and wounded man. His Expressionist paintings, such as *Pogrom* (1936–37), the *Emigrants' Ship* (1939–41), and *Exodus* (1947; New York, Jewish Museum), reveal his lacerated soul, but the artist can be better appreciated in his many variations of the "forest" theme (begun as early as 1910, but primarily exploited 1950–55), in his watercolors impregnated with the naiveté of the common man, and in his drawings and prints, which are remarkable for their economy of means and indifference to calculated effect.

SEGANTINI, Giovanni (1858, Arco, near Trento—1899, Schafberg, Engadine), Italian painter. Segantini rebelled against the academic artistic instruction he had received at the Brera Academy and for some time was a member of the bohemian circles in Milan. But in 1886 his love of country life made him turn to painting the

Giovanni Segantini. *Homecoming*. Before 1898. Kunstmuseum, Bern.

peaceful hills of Switzerland. Segantini became the leading Neoimpressionist painter in Italy. His colors were bright at the time and he valued divisionism as a means of rendering the luminous atmosphere of the Alpine landscapes that enchanted him (*Haymaking*, 1899; St-Moritz, Musée Segantini). Unfortunately, his carefree vein gave way toward the end of his life to a deliberately literary symbolism that destroyed the best aspects of his art. The great triptych of *Life, Nature, and Death* (Musée Segantini) is an example of the painter's final manner.

SEGHERS, Hercules Pietersz. (*c.* 1590, Haarlem?—1640, The Hague), Dutch landscape painter and engraver, known particularly for his fantastic etchings. Only four of his paintings are signed, but 15 paintings and about 50 etchings are attributed to him. Seghers' visionary genius was slow to develop. His early paintings either possess the same anecdotal appeal as Josse de Momper's, or they depend on the Dutch compositional formula of three color planes—brown, green, and blue. However, his extreme originality began to reveal itself about 1620. His mature landscapes express a mind in torment. Nature, particularly mountains, was his sole subject matter: man appears only as a passerby lost in the storm or as a solitary peasant driving his flock homeward (*Mountain Landscape*, 1630–35; Florence, Uffizi). If the scene is one of calm, large pools of shadow fill it with an atmosphere of uneasiness, or, as in the *Valley* (*c.* 1625; Rotterdam, Museum Boymans-van Beuningen), imaginary foliage spreads out under the clouds, blanketed by a thick fog. In *View of Rhenen* (before 1630?; Berlin, Staatliche Museen), the vibrant tones of the red roofs and an emerald green strip on the horizon add a harsh note to his strange, exotic harmony.

Seghers was perhaps even more original in his etchings. His wildness and Baroque temperament are suggested by his stippling and broken, thick, dynamic lines. Among his contemporaries he was virtually alone in his constant experimentation with graphic techniques. He sometimes printed his etchings on colored paper, heightening the effect with watercolor, and he is believed to have been the first to use aquatint. Today Seghers is accepted as the foremost genius of 17th-century Dutch painting before Rembrandt.

SELIGMANN, Kurt (1900, Basel—1962, New York), American painter of Swiss origin. He held his first exhibitions at Basel and Bern in 1918 and 1932. He also produced a collection of 15 etchings, *Cardiac Protuberances* (1934), with an introduction by Anatole Jakowski. Seligmann lived in Paris and joined the Surrealist movement in 1937. He contributed to the international exhibition organized by André Breton in 1938, where his *Ultra-Furniture*, a footstool with its four feet shaped like the legs of a woman, caused a sensation. He emigrated to New York in 1939. Paintings of this period, soon after his arrival, include *Souvenir of America* (1943; Buffalo, Albright-Knox Gallery) and *Sabbath Phantoms* (1939; New York, Museum of Modern Art). He had a passion for the occult and made a collection of spells, which he used to write his book *The Mirror of Magic* (1948). Classical mythology was the inspiration of his later work, including a series of etchings called the *Myth of Oedipus* (1944).

SEMPER, Gottfried (1803, Hamburg—1879, Rome), German architect. He studied the humanities before turning his interest to architecture in Munich. In 1826 he went to Paris, where he was the assistant of Gau and Hittorff. From 1830 to 1833 he traveled in the south of Italy and in Greece, where he studied the polychromy of the antique temples. His principal field of activity was first at Dresden, where he built the Opera (1837–41; rebuilt after the fire of 1869) and the Gemäldegalerie (begun 1847). In 1849 he was obliged to return to Paris, where he worked until 1851, at which time he went to London, there winning the favor of the Prince Consort. A theoretician of the highest order (*Style in the Technical and Tectonic Arts,* 1860–63), he emphasized the character of building materials and advocated a sort of functionalism before its time. In this respect he had a profound influence, his ideas being similar to those developed by Viollet-le-Duc in France at the same time. Summoned to Vienna in 1871, Semper prepared the plans for the Burgtheater (1874–88) and for the two great imperial museums; he then went to Rome, where he died.

Gottfried Semper. Dresden Opera. 1837–41. *Deutsche Fotothek, Dresden.*

SEQUEIRA, Domingos António de (1768, Belem, Lisbon—1837, Rome), Portuguese painter. He was an outstanding draftsman and portraitist, and in his handling of light and color he was a precursor of Impressionism. Sequeira was given a scholarship to Rome, where he studied from 1788 to 1795. He became First Court Painter in Lisbon in 1802 and in this capacity executed works for the palaces of Ajuda, near Funchal, and Mafra, not far from Lisbon. Sequeira was an acute political observer; because of his liberal views he left Portugal permanently during the absolutist counter-revolution of 1823. He went first to Paris, exhibiting the *Last Days of Camões* in the Salon of 1824, for which he won a gold medal. He then settled in Rome, where he spent the rest of his life.

While a student in Rome and when he was first at court, Sequeira painted in an academic style; however, even these pictures anticipated the intense and dramatic works of his later years, when he was able to use chiaroscuro to highly expressive purposes. Until the early 1820s he concentrated on penetrating and surprisingly informal portraits, developing an increasingly deft touch in his handling of light and shadow (*Gregório Francisco de Queirós, c.* 1823, drawing; Lisbon, Priv. Coll.), and on allegories of contemporary political events, in which he revealed his ability to organize groups of figures.

After his flight from Lisbon, Sequeira developed a more Impressionistic manner and turned his attention to religious themes. His *Mocking of Christ* (*c.* 1830; Lisbon, Museu Nacional de Arte Antiga), executed in a severely restricted palette, achieves a new immediacy through his earthy approach. Many of his finest late works are drawings or lithographs. His charcoal and chalk drawing of the *Last Judgment* (1832–33; Museu Nacional de Arte Antiga) reveals a visionary dimension in his sensibility. Sequeira must be considered a major European rather than Portuguese painter. His life and work have often been compared with Goya's.

SERLIO, Sebastiano (1475, Bologna—*c.* 1554, Fontainebleau), Italian architect. Serlio was one of the artists who introduced Italian art to 16th-century France, both through his theoretical writings, and through his work at the court of Fontainebleau. He studied architecture in the Roman studio of Baldassarre Peruzzi (*c.* 1514–27), who bequeathed him drawings and plans that appeared later in his book, *L'Architettura*. Serlio did not leave any notable building in Italy, but his intellectual activities familiarized him with the current High Renaissance concepts before he introduced them into France, where he spent the last 13 years of his wandering career. His writings, contained in *L'Architettura*, were more important than his work as painter or architect. Its influence was particularly great since its aim was practical rather than theoretical. Book IV, which described the antiquities of Rome, and Book III, in which the five orders were systematized for the first time, were published at Venice in 1537 and 1540. Books I, II, and V, which dealt with geometry, perspective, and temples (that is, churches), were printed in Paris in 1545 and 1547. The *Libro Extraordinario*, a treatise on portals, published at Lyons in 1551, replaced the unpublished Book VI in the standard edition. The fantastic designs with which the *Libro Extraordinario* was illustrated had enormous influence on French Mannerism. Book VII appeared in 1575, long after Serlio's death, and Book VIII on military architecture has never been published. The book was criticized by Italian theorists, but French artists and architects such as Philibert de l'Orme and Jean Goujon praised him for having "illuminated" the doctrines of Vitruvius.

When Serlio went to France at the age of 65 (1540), François I nominated him "Painter and Architect in Ordinary of our buildings and edifices at Fontainebleau." However, Serlio's advice was disregarded. An Italian, the Cardinal of Ferrara, commissioned Serlio to build his residence near Fontainebleau, the Hôtel du Grand Ferrara, whose famous rusticated portal is all that remains today. He also built the château of Ancy-le-Franc in Yonne (*c.* 1546). The building was planned around a square courtyard, supported at the angles by projecting pavilions. Pilasters of the same order were superimposed on the façades, Doric outside and Corinthian in the courtyard, where they frame the loggias. Serlio here showed his liking for slate roofing, casement and dormer windows, and exterior stairs, which he thought were the most graceful features of French buildings. He also treated French traditions with a respect that other Italians lacked.

Domingos António de Sequeira. *Mocking of Christ.* Museu Nacional de Arte Antiga, Lisbon. Courtesy of Ministério da Educação Nacional, Direcção-Geral do Ensino Superior e das Belas Artes. *Photo Francisco Marques, Lisbon.*

SERODINE, Giovanni (*c.* 1600, Ascona, Ticino—1630, Rome),

Sebastiano Serlio. Château of Ancy-le-Franc. Begun *c.* 1546. *Photo Jean Roubier, Paris.*

José Luis Sert. Fondation Maeght, St-Paul-de-Vence. 1962–64.

Italian painter. He was one of the most independent and original followers of Caravaggio, and certainly the most brilliant colorist among them. Serodine arrived in Rome in 1615, nine years after Caravaggio's departure from that city and five years after his death, so that the latter's influence could be absorbed only through his work. Caravaggio's manner is evident in the early *Calling of the Sons of Zebedee* (*c.* 1622; Ascona), but in his masterpiece, the moving *Almsgiving of St. Lawrence* (*c.* 1625; Rome, Galleria Nazionale), Serodine's personal style was already emerging. His qualities are even more pronounced in the *Portrait of His Father* (1628; Lugano, Museo Civico). One of Serodine's last works, *St. Peter in Prison* (Rancate, Coll. Züst), uses the candlelit setting developed by Gerrit van Honthorst, but the heavy impasto technique recalls Rembrandt's mature style.

SERT, José Luis (b. 1902, Barcelona), Spanish architect. He was trained at the Escuela Superior de Arquitectura of Barcelona, and later was profoundly influenced by his experience in Le Corbusier's studio in Paris (1929–30). In 1939, after the Spanish Civil War, Sert emigrated to the United States. He held the presidency of the CIAM (Congrès Internationaux d'Architecture Moderne) from 1947 to 1956, and was appointed Dean of the Harvard Graduate School of Design in 1958. His predecessor at Harvard was Walter Gropius, but Sert's training was opposed to the strict functionalism of Gropius, as well as to the formalism of Ludwig Mies van der Rohe. Sert's own buildings include the Harvard Health Center (1957–61), the U.S. Embassy in Baghdad (1955–63), and the New England Gas and Electricity company headquarters at Cambridge, Massachusetts (completed 1964). His Fondation Maeght at St-Paul-de-Vence in the Alpes-Maritimes (1962–64; in association with Joan Miró) was particularly successful, both functionally and visually. When the two Catalonians planned this garden of architecture, they must have had in mind the powerfully Expressionistic work of that other Catalonian, Antonio Gaudí. As a town planner, Sert developed a plan for the expansion of Bogotà, Colombia, in association with Le Corbusier and Paul Lester Wiener (1895–1967), and, with Wiener, the new Motor City in Baixada Fluminense, Brazil. He was commissioned by CIAM to write *Can Our Cities Survive* (3rd ed., Cambridge, Mass., 1947), a comparative analysis of the development of modern cities.

Michel Seuphor. *Rondo II.* 1957. "Lacuna drawing."

SÉRUSIER, Paul (1865, Paris—1927, Morlaix, Finistère), French painter. His friendship with Paul Gauguin, whom he had met at Pont-Aven in 1888, gave added glamor to his vastly cultured life. He was *massier*, or "student in charge of the studio" at the Parisian Académie Julian, where he had a profound influence over his fellow students, Pierre Bonnard, Maurice Denis, Paul Ranson (1864–1909), Édouard Vuillard, and Félix Vallotton—the members of the future Nabis group, whose theorist he became. In 1889–90 he joined Gauguin again at Le Pouldu, near Pont-Aven, and in 1895 accompanied Maurice Denis on a visit to Tuscany. In 1897 the painter Jan Verkade, a former fellow student who had become a monk under the name of Dom Willibrod, introduced him to the school of religious art in the Benedictine abbey of Beuron, Württemberg-Baden. Its teaching, based on the "sacred proportions," obsessed Sérusier for the rest of his life. He returned to Beuron several times, notably in 1903, taught at the Académie Ranson in Paris, and finally retired to Brittany in 1914. During the last years of his life, Sérusier was deeply affected by a mysticism nourished by his passion for Celtic poetry, Breton calvaries, and Gothic tapestries. Apart from a few successful canvases (*Still Life*, 1891; Paris, Coll. Henriette Boutaric), his painting was far less convincing than his theories. His artistic treatise, the *A.B.C. of Painting* (1921), is an intelligent as well as an idealistic work.

SERVRANCKX, Victor (1897, Diegem, near Brussels—1965, Vilvoorde, near Brussels), Belgian painter. He was one of the pioneers of abstract art (*Opus 47*, 1923; Elewijt, Mechlin, Priv. Coll.). He studied at the Académie Royale des Beaux-Arts in Brussels (1912–17), where he was brilliantly successful. His first show in Brussels (1917) was also the first exhibition of nonfigurative painting in Belgium. Servranckx at first practiced the "pure plastic," or geometrical, form of abstraction, but then produced abstract whirling forms and experimented with the texture of paint; at the same time, however, he also produced figurative work. In 1936 his fresco for the Salon de la Radio at Brussels was described by Fernand Léger as "a milestone in the history of modern mural decoration." After his retrospective exhibition at the Palais des Beaux-Arts in Brussels in 1947, Servranckx returned to pure plasticism, but in a freer and more flexible style than in his earlier work.

SEUPHOR, Michel (b. 1901, Antwerp), French writer and painter of Belgian birth. He founded the review *Het Overzicht* in Antwerp, which for four years (1921–25) opened its columns to the pioneers of abstract art. After several visits to Paris he decided to settle there in 1925 and became the friend and later the principal biographer of Piet Mondrian, as well as Robert Delaunay and Jean Arp. In 1929 Seuphor and Joaquin Torrès-Garcia (1874–1949) founded the

Cercle et Carré group and a review of the same name to defend functional architecture and nonfigurative painting. He also wrote novels, poetry, and books of aphorisms. Notable among his writings are those on abstract art, which are careful documents of its developments: *Abstract Art, Its Origins and First Masters*, 1949; *Dictionary of Abstract Painting*, 1957; *The Sculpture of This Century*, 1959; *Abstract Painting, Its Genesis and Development*, 1962; and *Style and Utterance*, 1965. Seuphor continued drawing while he pursued these literary activities. His first efforts go back to 1932, but after 1951 he produced several "lacuna drawings" in pen and ink. In these drawings the spaces are filled with freely drawn black, horizontal lines, while geometric motifs suggesting limitless horizons wherein forms might proliferate in the void are left blank (*Province of Space*, 1952; *Orpheus*, 1964). At the same time he was working on collages (*The Nations of Heaven*, 1955; Newark, N.J., Newark Museum), and after 1959 on large-scale assemblages of drawings, which he used as sources for tapestry cartoons and ceramic decoration for the Manufacture de Sèvres (after 1964).

SEURAT, Georges (1859, Paris—1891, Paris), French Neoimpressionist painter. In 1878 he entered the École des Beaux-Arts, where he studied for two years under Henri Lehmann (1814–82), a student and follower of J. A. D. Ingres. Although his temperament was basically Classical and he was naturally inclined to discipline, he nevertheless bestowed his admiration upon Delacroix, in whose work he had found confirmation of the physical laws of color as set forth in the treatise by the chemist Michel Eugène Chevreul, which influenced him profoundly.

In November 1880, after completing a year's term of military service in Brest, Seurat returned to Paris, where for two years he devoted himself exclusively to drawing, stressing the study of values, contrasts, and shading. In 1883 the Salon accepted his drawing of his friend, the painter Edmond-François Aman-Jean (1882; New York, Metropolitan Museum). That same year he also began painting his first major composition, *Bathing at Asnières* (1883–84, reworked *c.* 1887; London, National Gallery). It was refused by the Salon of 1884, but was later exhibited in the first Salon of the Société des Artistes Indépendants, of which Seurat was a founding member. In the course of the first meetings of the Indépendants, he came to know Odilon Redon, Henri-Edmond Cross, Albert Dubois-Pillet (1846–90), Charles Angrand, and Paul Signac. It was only with the latter two, however, that he developed a deep friendship. Signac immediately adopted Seurat's ideas, and they exchanged the results of their artistic experiments.

In 1884 Seurat began to do drawings and studies of landscapes and of the crowds in the park on the island of La Grande Jatte, near Asnières. Because of his inflexible and methodical way of working, he accumulated 23 drawings and 38 painted panels in the course of each morning's preparatory work on the site. He spent his afternoons and part of his evenings in his studio completing each preliminary picture. *Sunday Afternoon on the Island of La Grande Jatte* (1886; Chicago, Art Institute) created a scandal when Seurat presented it, together with six seascapes that he had brought back from Grandcamp in October 1885, at the last Impressionist exhibition in 1886. Apart from the Symbolist writers Émile Verhaeren and Félix Fénéon, the majority of the artists and critics reacted with indignation.

Through scientific experimentation, Seurat had discovered an optical law of color effects; experiment, however, was not responsible for the comparably logical system of linear and spatial organization that he developed. According to the art critic John Rewald, Seurat found the solution to this particular problem in the work of a young scientist named Charles Henry, who had written a treatise on the expressive value of line. When Seurat met Henry in 1886 he had already completed the *Grande Jatte* and the preparatory studies that led up to that masterpiece. On the other hand, although he had already discovered the rules of color harmony through experimentation and his reading of scientific literature, it was in the use of the endless resources of line, formal structure, and architectonics that he displayed his creative genius. Far from subordinating line to color, he used it as a controlling factor, restoring simplicity and purity to line so that it could withstand the busy effect created by the pigmentation and the corrosive appearance of the stippling. The majestic calm, the perfect balance, and the Classical conception of the *Grande Jatte* and of the important paintings that followed it—*La Parade* (1887–88; Metropolitan Museum), *Les Poseuses* (final version 1886–88; Merion, Pa., Barnes Foundation), *Le Chahut* (1889–90; Otterlo, Rijksmuseum Kröller-Müller), and the *Circus* (unfinished, 1890–91; Paris, Musée de l'Impressionnisme)—represent the victory of construction over analysis, of the permanent over the ephemeral, and of order over dispersion.

Seurat's summer visits to the ports of the Channel coast—Honfleur (1886), Port-en-Dessin (1888), Le Crotoy (1889), and Gravelines (1890)—inspired him to paint some extraordinary seascapes. One is entitled to imagine all that Seurat's work might have gained had he not died as a result of a severe infection at the age of thirty-two. He was a painter-theoretician, engaged in the most highly intellectualized kind of adventure, and sought from scientific method what other artists demand of instinct. In fact, science brought him only the certainties that his inventive mind needed: neither his intellectuality nor his theories managed to stifle his lively imagination, which broke through the limits imposed by will and emotional discipline.

Georges Seurat. *Le Chahut*. 1889–90. Rijksmuseum Kröller-Müller, Otterlo.

Georges Seurat. *Woman Powdering Herself*. 1889–90. Courtauld Institute of Art, London.

SEVERINI, Gino (1883, Cortona—1966, Paris), Italian painter. In 1901 he was in Rome, where he met Umberto Boccioni and then Giacomo Balla, who became his first teacher. In 1906 Severini went to Paris, where he discovered Georges Seurat's works and became friendly with the Cubist painters and writers Picasso, Max Jacob, Pierre Reverdy, and Guillaume Apollinaire. In 1910 his name appeared among the signatories of the first Futurist manifesto and the following year in Paris he was instrumental in introducing Boccioni, Carlo Carrà, and Luigi Russolo to Picasso, Georges Braque, Juan Gris, and Robert Delaunay. Severini took part in the first Futurist exhibition, which was held at the Galerie Bernheim-Jeune in Paris (February, 1912). His painting *Dancing the Pan-Pan at the Monico* (1909–11; original destroyed, artist's 1960 reconstruction in Paris, Musée National d'Art Moderne) was one of the masterpieces of Futurism.

In all his paintings, Severini struggled to re-create "dynamic sensation itself" by the interpenetration of colors and rhythms; *Dynamic Hieroglyphic at the Bal Tabarin* (1912; New York, Museum of Modern Art) and the series of *Dancers* (1912–14) are striking examples. These paintings, executed in the pure colors used by Seurat, were in striking contrast to the severe grays and browns of the Cubists.

In 1918 Severini met the Parisian art dealer Léonce Rosenberg, to whom he had been introduced by Juan Gris, and who became his agent. Severini joined Rosenberg's avant-garde group, L'Effort Moderne, which exhibited at his gallery of the same name. Severini's new work as well as his investigation of the Section d'Or (the Golden Mean theory of proportion) soon led him from Cubism—which he practiced from about 1916 to 1921—to a type of Classicism. In 1922 he did a series of frescoes for the poet Sir George Sitwell's castle of Montefugoni, near Florence. Severini was then invited to Switzerland, where he decorated several churches with frescoes and mosaics. He also executed mosaics in Italy (including the entrance hall of the Milan Triennale, 1933) and in France. After 1948 he entered a new phase of his artistic development: this was characterized by a return to the fantasy of his early work, and was based on a combination of Cubistic and Futuristic elements (*Yellow Buffet*, 1948; Rome, Coll. Monaco). He also produced ceramic sculptures, illustrated books, and, besides his plastic art, wrote several theoretical works in French (*du Cubisme au Classicisme*, 1921) and Italian. Severini was one of the acknowledged pioneers of modern art.

Richard Norman Shaw. Old Swan House, Chelsea, London. 1876. *Photo Kersting, London.*

SHAHN, Ben (1898, Kovno, Lithuania—1969, New York), Russian-born American painter. In 1906 he emigrated to the United States with his family, and later became a naturalized American citizen. Shahn worked as a lithographer's apprentice to earn enough money to study successively at New York University, the City College of New York, the National Academy of Design, New York (1922), and the Art Students League, New York. After two visits to Europe in 1927 and 1929, he gave up his purely aesthetic experiments and began painting subjects with a social purpose. His first important works date from 1930; the series of gouaches on the Sacco and Vanzetti case were painted between 1931 and 1932 (the *Passion of Sacco and Vanzetti*, 1931–32; New York, Whitney Museum).

Shahn's favorite medium was tempera, which was admirably suited to his precise graphic style (*Handball*, 1939, and *Willis Avenue Bridge*, 1940; both New York, Museum of Modern Art). His paintings are generally peopled by figures with extremely stylized features and outlines, when they are not actually caricatured. They are set against landscapes, painted in modulated tones, and sometimes contain a considerable wealth of detail. The complete absence of perspective; the use of clear, bright colors; the play of contrasting primaries; as well as the meticulously descriptive detail that is always taken from the concrete reality surrounding the painter—all these traits are reminiscent of the Italian primitives, who made a deep impression on Shahn during his visits to Europe. His very personal combination of realism and abstraction creates an apparent naiveté that is used for social protest and sometimes even a rather black humor. After 1950 Shahn introduced more or less regular geometric designs into his compositions, which give them a satirical and ironical overtone; *Ave* (1950; Hartford, Conn., Wadsworth Atheneum) is a notable example.

SHAW, Richard Norman (1831, Edinburgh—1912, London), English architect. Shaw drew his inspiration from a number of different historic styles. After a Gothic essay in the church of the Holy Trinity at Bingley, Yorkshire (1864–68), and the English church at Lyons (1868), he turned to the Queen Anne style for the Convent of the Sisters of Bethany, near Bournemouth (1874), and the Swan House, Chelsea, London (1876). Shaw artfully combined elements from several periods in the same building, especially mid-17th century brick houses of Dutch inspiration. He applied this technique to country houses, as well as to such public and commercial buildings as the two blocks of Scotland Yard, London (1887–90), and the earlier New Zealand Chambers, also in London (1872). At the end of his career he turned to a grandiose Classicism with Baroque details in the Piccadilly Hotel, London (1905). Both his mature (Queen Anne) and late styles had a considerable influence abroad, especially in the United States.

SHEELER, Charles (b. 1883, Philadelphia—d. 1965), American painter. Sheeler was trained in the Munich School's tradition of rapid, virtuoso brushwork. A trip to Italy in 1909 changed his artistic point of view as for the first time he saw the "architectural" possibilities of planned paintings and timeless subjects. Seeking a livelihood upon his return home, he became a self-taught photographer. This new medium gave Sheeler a sense of freedom, and instinctively he turned to fresh subjects: the unembellished, utilitarian architecture of barns, ships, factories, and machines. When he began painting a few years later, he synthesized his original photographic experiences. Sheeler's paintings of the 1920s and 1930s (a masterpiece is *Upper Deck*, 1929; Cambridge, Mass., Fogg Art Museum) respect the integrity of composite forms, intensifying their identity by clarifying lines and shapes, and emphasizing their sculptural character by means of strong lighting. A stay in New England in 1946 deeply affected Sheeler's art: form and color acquired independent existences beyond actuality; lines and forms became more arbitrary, more obviously arranged. *Ballardvale* (1948; Andover, Mass., Addison Gallery of American Art) marked the turning point in his style. Subsequently, a synthesis was achieved in which architectural elements themselves were transformed into abstract shapes, often transparent and superimposed (*Architectural Cadences*, 1954; New York, Whitney Museum).

SHINN, Everett (1876, Woodstown, New Jersey—1953, New York), American painter. While in Philadelphia, he joined John Sloan, George Luks, and William Glackens at Robert Henri's studio, where they were able to discuss the arts in a free and tolerant atmosphere. The group later banded together with Henri in New York to form a school of brashly realistic painting known as The Eight. The style of Shinn's paintings accorded easily with the rapid, spontaneous manner and earthy subject matter that Henri had passed on to Glackens, Luks, and the others. Shinn treated such themes as the *Sixth Avenue El After Midnight* (1899; New York, Coll. Arthur G. Altschul) with both expressiveness and facility. In time he detached himself from the group and became more interested in the world of the theater and music hall, concentrating on such subjects as the *London Hippodrome* (1902; Chicago, Art Institute) or the performers in a musical *Revue* (1908; New York, Whitney Museum) before the glow of the bright stage footlights.

In about 1907, Shinn was hired to decorate the Stuyvesant (later Belasco) Theater in New York, which prompted many portrait commissions from theater people, as a result of which he painted such well-known figures as Julia Marlowe, Ethel Barrymore, and David Warfield. Another commission in 1911, which forced Shinn to revert to a more traditionally realistic style, was that for murals in the City Hall at Trenton, New Jersey, portraying the industrial landscape of the state's capital.

SIAMESE ART. The cultural history of Thailand begins in the middle of the 6th century A.D. when the Mon people from lower Burma became the ruling class of the empire of Dvāravatī. The earliest Siamese Buddhist sculpture of the 6th and 7th centuries A.D. displays a direct dependence on Indian prototypes. At the same time we can recognize certain unmistakable Siamese characteristics. The heads are usually disproportionately large, and the suggestion of a Siamese ethnic type asserts itself in the broad faces, flat noses, and full lips. The arrangement of the body and the simplified carving of the sheath-like robe reveal that the prototypes for these earliest Siamese statues were the icons of the Gupta period at Sārnāth. The first period of Siamese civilization came from a Khmer invasion in the 10th century and the establishment of a vice-royalty at Lopburi, north of Bangkok. The art of this period in Siam is a provincial version of the Classic Khmer style of Angkor. The straight overhanging brows, pointed noses, and prominent chins of the Lopburi heads served to distinguish them from contemporary work in Cambodia. A truly national Siamese dynasty was established in the 13th century at Chiengmai with the ascendancy of the Thai people, who as early as the 9th century had invaded northern Siam from Yunnan. In the typically Siamese style of Chiengmai the heads of the Buddhas are marked by sharp arched eyebrows, exaggerated almond eyes with decoratively curved lids, a sharp hooked nose and tiny, softly modeled lips (*Seated Buddha*, 14th century, Sukhodaya style; Bangkok, Peñcamapabitra Monastery). In the last 700 years of Siamese art, the earlier styles continued to be repeated with innumerable local variations. The development of the Buddha image became increasingly stylized, culminating in the elegant attenuated formula achieved at Ayudhya in the 17th century. Familiar aspects of this style are the flame finial, the svelt, unmodeled smoothness of torso and tubular limbs, the pliant curves of elongated fingers, and the masks whose features form a decorative repetition of arcs and curves.

Siamese Art. Wat Sra Sri, Sukhōthaï. 13th–14th century. *Photo Louis Frédéric, Paris.*

The development of architecture in Siam exactly parallels the evolution of sculpture. The earliest structures of the 6th and 7th centuries A.D. may be described as Indian colonial and are succeeded by buildings in Khmer and later in Burmese styles. The earliest buildings of monumental importance are the sanctuaries at Lopburi, which, as might be expected in this period of Khmer domination, are closely related to the Classic buildings at Angkor. Such elements as the bombshell-shaped towers and the richly carved lintels bear a resemblance to the architecture of Angkor Wat, but the plan of Wat Mahādhatu is more directly related to the arrangement of Indian temples of the Gupta period and later. Derivations from the pyramidal temple-mountain of Khmer architecture are occasionally found in Siamese shrines: at Chiengmai, Wat Chet Yot (1455–*c.* 1470) is a copy of the Mahābodhi Temple at Pagān, which was itself derived from the famous temple at Bodhgayā.

The ruins of Ayudhya, which served as the capital from 1350 until its destruction by the Burmese in 1767, contained many typical Siamese developments of the stupa. These *prachedis*, erected as shrines to Buddhist holy men

Siamese Art. *Head of Buddha.* Style of Sukhōthaï. 13th–14th century. Museum, Sukhōthaï.

Siamese Art. Wat Arun, Bangkok. 19th century. *Photo Martin Hürlimann, Zurich.*

and Siamese kings, are round in plan, with a series of rings leading up to the bell-shaped dome from which springs a tapering onion-shaped finial.

The last phase of Siamese architecture is represented by the numerous palaces and temples built in Bangkok since 1782. The *bots* (sanctuaries) are built almost entirely of wood with elaborately carved bargeboards and gables. The decorative elements of these late buildings, including the octavanārāma at Bangkok (early 19th century), are a jumble of borrowings from ancient Siamese and modern Chinese sources. Although their overlapping roofs recall the galleries of Angkor Wat, this form actually descends from early wooden buildings in Cambodia and Siam. The gilded, towering *prachedis* that fill the courtyards of temples and palaces in Bangkok are the modern descendants of the ruined shrines of Ayudhya.

SICKERT, Walter Richard (1860, Munich—1942, Bathampton, near Bath), English landscape, portrait, and genre painter. In 1868 Sickert's family settled in England, where as a young man he was equally attracted by acting and painting: he was on the stage for several years before he became a student at London's Slade School of Art in 1881. A meeting with Whistler led to an apprenticeship (1882–83) in Whistler's studio, where he was given a thorough training in engraving and etching. In 1883 Sickert went to Paris to deliver Whistler's *Portrait of the Artist's Mother* to the Salon, and while there he began a friendship with Edgar Degas that lasted until the latter's death in 1917.

In the 1890s Sickert exhibited in London with the New English Art Club, and in 1893 opened the first of his many schools of art in Chelsea. The Parisian art dealer Bernheim gave him exhibitions in 1907 and 1909, but English dealers did not notice him until the late 1920s, when he had one-man shows at the Saville, Leicester, and Redfern galleries in London.

Degas was certainly the main artistic influence in Sickert's life. Both painters shared a natural passion for the theater: for Sickert, however, the theater was the democratic and inelegant world of the English music hall and, although he painted it in the brilliant and elliptical manner of Degas (*Le Lion Comique, c.* 1888; London, Coll. Lord John Cottesloe), he created earthier and darker effects than Degas. Sickert's skill as a painter was entirely French, yet the content of his works was, paradoxically, unswervingly English (*The Mantelpiece, c.* 1907, Southampton, Hampshire, Art Gallery; *The Old Bedford, A Corner of the Gallery, c.* 1897, Liverpool, Walker Art Gallery). In the genre scenes painted during his stay in London's Camden Town area (1908–14), Sickert almost lost the painterly detachment he had learned from Degas and enthusiastically immersed himself in sordid scenes, such as nudes on iron bedsteads and lower-class couples off to the pub or simply stifling in the boredom of a Sunday afternoon (*Ennui, c.* 1913; London, Tate Gallery). At the end of his life, however, he reverted to the decorative style of his youth: paintings such as *Sir Thomas Beecham Conducting* (*c.* 1930; New York, Museum of Modern Art) are similar to the works of the Nabis in their simplicity. Sickert's overwhelming interest in his subject matter led him to neglect purely technical considerations; at their best his pictures have a rough, rich, dark, and genuinely exciting quality.

SIEBERECHTS, Jan (1627, Antwerp—1700/3, Antwerp), Flemish painter. He was unique among Antwerp painters in that his primary influence came from such Italianate Dutch masters of the period as Jan Both (d. 1652) and Karel Dujardin, whom he may have met on an early trip to Italy. This influence is visible in *Spring* (1653; Berlin, Staatliche Museen). His personal style began to develop in the 1660s, when motifs involving coaches or herdsmen in shallow water or on flooded roads were explored (*Market Cart with Animals at a Ford,* 1671; Dublin, National Gallery). Nevertheless, Sieberechts' landscapes have a majestic, monumental quality closer in spirit to French landscape painting than to Dutch. He also ventured into other motifs in *Sleeping Peasant Girls* (Munich, Bayerische Staatsgemäldesammlungen) and *The Cradle* (1671; Copenhagen, Statens Museum for Kunst). Sieberechts went to England about 1672, where he specialized in such country house "portraits" as those of *Chevely* (1681; now at Belvoir Castle, Leicestershire) and *Longleat* (1675/76; Longleat, Wiltshire, Coll. Marquess of Bath). He had a profound influence on the development of English landscape painting.

SIGNAC, Paul (1863, Paris—1935, Paris), French pointillist painter and chief theorist of Neoimpressionism. In 1884 he was one of the founders of the Société des Artistes Indépendants and contributed to all nine of the group's exhibitions between 1884 and 1893. There he met Georges Seurat, whom he initiated into the techniques of Impressionism; Seurat, in exchange, converted Signac to his theory of simultaneous contrast, and together they perfected pointillism, the Neoimpressionist technique of painting. The similarity of their thinking and artistic methods was so strong for several years that the attribution of canvases to one or the other artist became difficult.

Paul Signac. *Two Milliners.* 1885. Coll. Emil G. Bührle, Zurich.

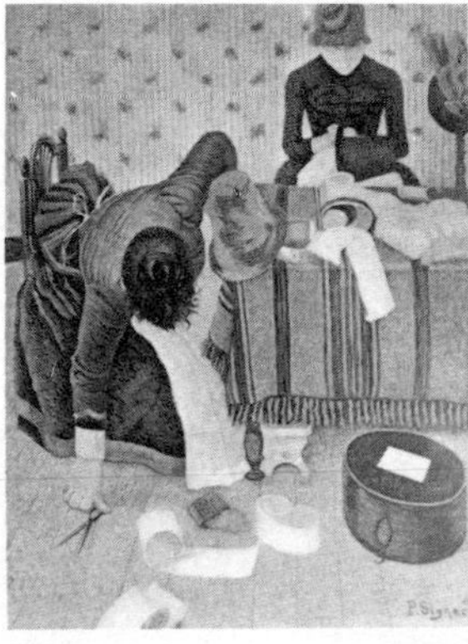

Signac's lyricism eventually led him to use colors of greater intensity; after about 1900 he changed his technique and, abandoning the round dots of pointillism, he began to use square spots of primary colors. His favorite subjects were port views (*View of the Port of Marseilles*, 1905; New York, Metropolitan Museum), and the canvases he painted on the coasts of the Channel, the Atlantic, and the Mediterranean resemble carefully disposed mosaics. These paintings were actually painted in his studio after watercolors done outdoors. Less of a constructor than Seurat and far more attentive to color than to composition, Signac is not always completely convincing in his artistic output, which nevertheless originated in firm conviction. After Seurat's premature death in 1891, he assumed the leadership of the Neoimpressionist movement. In 1908 he became president of the Société des Artistes Indépendants, and for 27 years never failed to encourage young artists or to fight for new ideas, even when they contradicted his own.

Signac was an accomplished writer, and his book *From Eugène Delacroix to Neoimpressionism* (1899) is a masterly presentation of Neoimpressionist theory. His monograph on Johan Barthold Jongkind (1927), his important article "Les besoins individuels et la peinture" for the *Encyclopédie Française* (1935), as well as excerpts from his journal are extremely interesting documents.

SIGNORELLI, Luca (1441/50, Cortona, Tuscany—1523, Cortona), Italian painter. According to reliable witnesses such as Luca Pacioli and Giorgio Vasari, Luca Signorelli was a pupil of Piero della Francesca. There is additional evidence for this in Signorelli's fresco of *St. Paul*, painted in 1474 for the Bishop's Palace in Città di Castello, near Florence (now in Città di Castello, Pinacoteca Comunale), and in his three *Madonnas* (Boston, Museum of Fine Arts; Oxford, Christ Church; Rome, Coll. Count Cini). In Signorelli's later works the figures became less stable and the contrasts more pronounced: in the *Annunciation* fresco, originally in a chapel in an isolated cottage at Casa da Monte, near Gragnano (now Arezzo, Church of S. Francesco), in the *Madonna Lactans* (*c.* 1470–80; Milan, Brera), and in the sharply drawn *Flagellation* (*c.* 1475; Brera). Signorelli obviously met Antonio and Piero Pollaiuolo and saw the frescoes by Fra Filippo Lippi in the duomo at Prato, near Florence. His Florentine leanings became more marked in the frescoes in the sacristy of St. John in the sanctuary of the Holy House at Loreto, in the province of Ancona. These were painted between 1476 and 1479 and are imbued with the artist's very personal feeling for back-lighting effects and shadows. In 1481 he was one of the painters invited by the pope to decorate the Sistine Chapel in the Vatican: his main contribution there was a masterful fresco on the *Testament and Death of Moses* (1482). Signorelli had a gift for strong compositions, as may be seen in his *Adoration of the Magi* (1482; Paris, Louvre), done for the church of S. Agostino in Città di Castello. He painted in quick succession for Lorenzo the Magnificent a *Madonna* (*c.* 1490; Florence, Uffizi) and the *Realm of Pan* (*c.* 1488; formerly Berlin, destroyed in 1945). At the same time, Signorelli painted the *Holy Family* (1491; Florence, Uffizi); an *Annunciation* (1491; Volterra, Pinacoteca Comunale) for Volterra Cathedral; and a *Circumcision* (*c.* 1492; London, National Gallery) for the church of S. Francesco in Volterra. In 1493–94 he painted another *Adoration of the Magi* (Paris, Louvre) for the church of S. Agostino in Città di Castello; in 1496, a *Nativity* (London, National Gallery) for the church of S. Francesco in Città di Castello; and, in 1498, the *Martyrdom of St. Sebastian* (Città di Castello, Pinacoteca Comunale). All these works are characterized by a well organized composition and a great number of figures. Signorelli produced his best work for large-scale decoration: in 1497–98 he painted eight frescoes illustrating the *Life of St. Benedict* in the cloister of the monastery of Monte Oliveto Maggiore at Asciano, near Siena, and in 1499 he was invited by the chapter of Orvieto to complete the decoration of the chapel of S. Brizio in Orvieto Cathedral, a project started by Fra Angelico and Benozzo Gozzoli in 1477. In 1500, when his work on the vaults had been accepted, he suggested a complete scheme for six walls of the chapel on a theme that was unusual in Italy at that time, the Last Judgment. The walls were probably completed in 1502, although he received his final payment in 1504. Between 1509 and 1513 Signorelli executed several fresco panels in the palazzo of Pandolfo Petrucchi (now called the Palazzo del Magnifico) in Siena.

Luca Signorelli. *Realm of Pan. c.* 1488. Formerly Kaiser-Friedrich Museum, Berlin.

The elements that Signorelli inherited from Piero della Francesca were the sculptural style of his figures and his dramatic feeling. Already in his Brera *Flagellation* he used a strong oblique lighting that was later accentuated in the Loreto frescoes with their interesting contrasts. Stylistically, this type of lighting resulted in very symmetrical compositions with rather stereotyped contrasts in colors and facial types. Signorelli's interest in nudes and in draperies that reveal the movements of the human body is exemplified in his *Testament and Death of Moses* in the Sistine Chapel, in which he painted the contemporary costumes with striking ease and dignity. His powerful *Realm of Pan* was one of the most extraordinary compositions of the late Quattrocento and was particularly remarkable for the plastic harshness of its style. It was the most daring contemporary painting of nudes and had a powerful symbolic significance. It was conceived on the model of a *sacra conversazione*, with figures grouped around a central throne and with a gravely religious atmosphere. The landscape in the *Realm of Pan*, with its dark rocks and architectural motif, is very reminiscent of the Uffizi *Madonna* in which a round temple, a ruined archway, and shepherds evoke the pagan world. The background of the *Portrait of a Lawyer with a Red Cap* (*c.* 1500; Berlin, Staatliche Museen) and the plain, strewn with buildings, of the Urbino *Crucifixion* (Urbino, Galleria Nazionale) are similar.

Through his impetuosity and *terribilità*, Signorelli was, apart from Michelangelo, the last of the great Tuscan fresco painters of the 15th century.

SIGNORINI, Telemaco (1835, Florence—1901, Florence), Italian painter. He gave up his academic studies in 1852 to devote himself to painting and through 1855 frequented the Caffé Michelangelo in Florence, where he became the chief theorist of the Macchiaioli group. Signorini lived in Venice the following year, traveled through Northern Italy, Paris, and London, and eventually returned to Florence. He then joined the school of Pergentina with Silvestro Lega and Odoardo Borrani (1834–1905). Signorini's restless temperament is revealed in some paintings of the 1860s (*Insane Ward at S. Bonifacio, Florence*, 1865; Venice, Galleria Internazionale d'Arte Moderna), but it did not prevent him from pursuing his experiments with determination and perseverance. His figure studies and atmospheric effects reveal the influence of the Impressionists, particularly of Edgar Degas (*November*, 1870; Galleria Internazionale d'Arte Moderna). Meanwhile, the tachist technique of the Macchiaioli had yielded to a freer conception of plein-air painting, which evolved from the innovations introduced by Signorini and the school of Pergentina.

SILOÉ, Diego de (*c.* 1495, Burgos—1563, Granada), one of the foremost Spanish Renaissance architects and sculptors, presumed to have been the son of Gil de Siloé. He first studied at Burgos, where his father worked, and while still very young traveled in Italy when Michelangelo's career was at its height. His first great creative period unfolded in Burgos between 1519 and 1528. During this time he united his knowledge of Classical form and ornament, which he had acquired in Italy, with Spanish realism and pathos. The plan for the tower of S. María del Campo at Burgos (1527), built by his pupil Juan de Salas, and the plans for the gateway and courtyard of the Irish college at Salamanca, built by Juan de Álava (1529–34), both date from this fruitful period. In Burgos Cathedral, however, Siloé worked more as a sculptor than as an architect. His tomb for Bishop Don Luis de Acuña (1519), in the St. Anne Chapel, reproduces Pollaiuolo's model for that of Sixtus IV. His work from 1519 to 1523 has an entirely different significance: the Escalera Dorada ("gilded staircase"; 1519–26) at the end of the north transept combined strength and grace in the arrangement of the steps and its ornamentation of putti, coats of arms, foliage, and fantastic objects. In the High Constable's chapel, Siloé collaborated with the Burgundian Felipe Vigarny (*c.* 1470–1543) on the main altarpiece (1523) and on that of St. Peter (*c.* 1523). Michelangelo's influence is noticeable in the group of *St. Anne, the Virgin, and the Child Jesus* that adorns the center of the small altarpiece in the Acuña Chapel (1523), while the artist's personal sense of pathos is more evident in the *Christ at the Pillar* from the altarpiece of S. Tecla.

Diego de Siloé. Escalera Dorada, Burgos Cathedral. 1519–26.

In 1528 Siloé went to Granada, where he carved the marble tomb of Don Rodrigo de Mercado (actually installed at Oñate). When he arrived, the cathedral walls were just above ground level. He was commissioned to continue the building in the Renaissance manner and designed a twin-towered façade combining a rotunda, ambulatory, triumphal arch, and basilican nave, using a Corinthian order. The medallion of the *Virgin with Child* at the gateway to the large sacristy as well as the carvings of the Virtues and angels in the Puerta del Perdón are particularly noteworthy. Siloé's statues of King Ferdinand of Aragon and Queen Isabella of Castile were installed in the earlier Capilla Real adjacent to the cathedral, built by Enrique de Egas.

Gil de Siloé. Tomb of Juan de Padilla. Detail: statue of the deceased. Museum, Burgos.

The style of Granada Cathedral appears again at Malaga Cathedral, on which Siloé may have collaborated, and also in the tower and chevet of Guadix Cathedral, for which his intervention in 1541 has been established. In addition to the sculpture already discussed, there is a relatively important series at Castile and Granada. The altarpiece in the chapel of the Licentiate Gómez de Santiago in the church at Santiago de la Puebla (Salamanca province), on which he collaborated with Vigarny, the *Holy Family with St. John* (Valladolid, Museum), and the *Virgin* of the S. Salvador gate at Granada (1546) belong to this noteworthy group.

SILOÉ, Gil de (b. *c.* 1450–d. early 16th century), Spanish Late Gothic sculptor, possibly of Flemish origin, whose work also shows traces of Rhenish influence. He is documented in Burgos from 1486 to 1501, and nearly all his known work is preserved in or near this town.

The most important group left by Siloé is in the church of the Charterhouse of Miraflores at the gates of Burgos; it comprises the gilded wooden altarpiece for the great high altar (1496–99), executed with the collaboration of Diego de la Cruz (documented late 15th century), and two tombs in alabaster (designed 1486; executed 1489–93), the first of John II of Castile and his wife Isabella of Portugal, placed in front of the altar, and the second of their son Don Alfonso, built in a wall recess. The recumbent figures of the king and queen, richly dressed and as finely carved as goldsmith's work, are mounted on an octagonal star-shaped pedestal, decorated with the *Virtues, Evangelists,* and *Saints.*

The tomb of Don Alfonso shows the young man kneeling in prayer against a background of intricately carved panels and framed by still more elaborate stylized leaves and tendrils. In addition to the praying effigy, there are well-characterized figures of the Apostles, an *Annunciation* scene, and scores of domestic and fantastical animals.

Siloé's masterpiece is the tomb of Juan de Padilla, which he executed for the church of Fresdelval Monastery, near Burgos (*c.* 1500–1505; Burgos, Museo Provincial). The work bears a richly carved plinth supporting the statue of the dead man kneeling under a great arch, a composition similar to that of the Don Alfonso tomb. The background panels are less intricate than usual in the work of Siloé: deeply carved motifs contrast with areas left completely smooth. Two statues from the Padilla tomb are preserved in the Museum of Fine Arts, Boston, and three are in the Metropolitan Museum, New York. Siloé is also credited with the *Tree of Jesse* altarpiece in the Capilla S. Ana (*c.* 1486–92) and the Altarpiece of St. Anne in the Capilla del Condestable (*c.* 1500–1505), both in Burgos Cathedral.

SIMONE MARTINI. *See* **MARTINI,** Simone.

SINGHALESE ART. According to the Mahavamsa, or the Great Chronicle of Ceylon, the beginnings of civilization on this island date back to the 5th century B.C. The Mahavamsa dates the foundation of the Buddhist confraternities and even the creation of statues of the Buddha as early as the reign of Devānampiya Tissa (247–207 B.C.). It seems highly improbable, however, that the buildings that have survived to our own time date from earlier than the 2nd or 3rd century A.D., and these have been extensively rebuilt or restored.

The first capital of the kingdom, the city of Anuradhapura, was the political and religious center of the island from the 3rd century B.C. to the 8th century A.D., when it was destroyed by Tamil invaders from southern India. One can still see the great stupas or dagobas rising from the thick dark forest that has submerged the ancient Buddhist city. Some of the buildings, now completely covered with vegetation, indeed resemble small mountains. One of the most impressive of all is the Ruvanväli, the third largest dagoba in Ceylon, which dates back to the reign of Duttha Gāmani (A.D. 101–177). A relic chamber inside the dome contained at one time a large number of statues and various objects made of precious metals. Another characteristic detail to be found in most of the dagobas is the presence of an altar, or *vāhalkada*, decorated with carved animals and located around the building at the four cardinal points. The decoration is of a kind that is found in the earliest Indian buildings, such as the Maurya column of Sārnāth. However, the Singhalese dagobas are differentiated from their Indian models by the absence of sculptural ornaments and by the fact that they possess no trace of the balustrade so typical of Hindu stupas.

One of the earliest buildings in Anuradhapura was the Lohapāsāda or Bronze Palace of King Duttha Gāmani, a famous monument described at length in the Mahavamsa, of which nothing remains unfortunately but the foundations, a forest of almost 1,600 granite pillars. It was probably a nine-story royal monastery. The superstructure was made of wood and the roof was covered with copper.

Innumerable full-length effigies of the Buddha have been discovered in the immediate vicinity of the Ruvanväli dagoba, but these have been restored in such a crude fashion that it is only possible to gain a clear idea of their original appearance by referring to photographs taken at the time of their excavations at the beginning of the 20th century. It then becomes immediately apparent that these statues are an adaptation of the type of Buddha created in India at Amaravati during the last Andhra dynasty. The resemblance of the drapery treatment is particularly striking. The Buddhist sculptural tradition at Amaravati and Nagarjunakonda lasted, according to some scholars, until the 5th, and, to others, until the 7th and 8th centuries A.D. The Singhalese work, therefore, may date from the 5th to the 8th century.

A characteristic type of Singhalese sculpture is the semicircular relief, which has come to be known as a moon stone and which decorated the threshold of most sanctuaries. The composition of these reliefs was unchanging and consisted of an arrangement of concentric motifs, including four

Singhalese Art. Ruvanväli dagoba at Anuradhapura. Founded *c.* 150 B.C. Restored. *Photo Aerofilms Ltd., London.*

Singhalese Art. *Reclining statue of Buddha entering Nirvana.* Carved in the rock of Gal Vihāra, Polonnaruva. Late 12th century. *Photo Pietro Francesco Mele-Rapho, Paris.*

animals symbolizing the cardinal points (they also appear on the Maurya column of Sārnāth), and a frieze containing wild ducks (connected with the Hindu deity Brahma). These sculptures, some of which date from the 4th or 5th centuries A.D., perpetuated the Classical style of the Indian sculpture from the Mauryan period.

The earliest surviving Singhalese paintings are frescoes found in a cave of the huge rock of Sigiriya, on which King Kassapa (A.D. 511–529) built the fortress and palace, whose remains can still be seen. The frescoes depict two female deities surrounded by their attendants. Both the drawing and the color have an astonishing vigor, and although the technique is Indian, the types represented are undoubtedly Singhalese.

The last important manifestation of Singhalese art took place at the capital of Polonnaruva. Situated in the heart of the jungle that occupies the northeast portion of the island, this city became a great artistic center during the reign of King Parākramabāhu (1164–97). The most noteworthy work of this period is a group of statues carved out of the rock of the Gal Vihāra at Polonnaruva. This group includes a gigantic recumbent figure of the Buddha entering Nirvana, a work on a monumental scale taken from an iconographic type that originated in Anuradhapura. More original is the enormous Potgul Vehera effigy carved out of the rock that overlooks Lake Topawewa: it is the portrait of a Buddhist sage or king, perhaps even of Parākramabāhu himself.

The most important architectural achievement at Polonnaruva is the group of temples or monasteries included in the complex of buildings known as the Great Quadrangle, which formed the center of the city. The most beautiful of these buildings is undoubtedly the Hata-da-ge, the House of the Sixty Relics, which is built entirely out of closely fitting blocks of sandstone. The outer walls are devoid of any decoration, but the main façade has a *hamsa* frieze and two recessed panels bearing inscriptions. At the foot of the wall runs a podium decorated with crouching lions, while the entrance itself is marked by the usual moon stone, flanked here by two guardian Nagas.

Not far from the Hata-da-ge is one of the finest examples of Singhalese architecture, the Vatadāgē, or Shrine of the Sacred Tooth, a round temple built by Parākramabāhu that was originally covered by a wooden roof resting on several concentric rows of pillars, which have survived.

SINGIER, Gustave (b. 1909, Warneton, West Flanders), Belgian-born French painter. He began painting in 1923. He studied art for three years and then worked until 1936 as a designer in a shop-fitting business while continuing to paint. Around 1945 Singier's style developed in the same direction as that of the abstract artists Alfred Manessier and Jean Le Moal, but his coloring and artistic vision remained individual. His paintings are filled with an enchanting, often flickering light; at first the objects in them were fragmented, then they dissolved in an interplay of rhythmic lines, and finally even the lines disappeared to make way for a free evocation of the exterior world. In his abstract paintings, Singier used flat areas of color that were overlaid at first with geometric forms, which were drawn with a touch of fantasy and humor (*Navigable Space*, 1954; Basel, Galerie Beyeler); then, around 1960, these areas were enlivened with simple, capricious lines that resembled ripples of water undulating beneath a light breeze. The sensuousness and preciousness of Singier's art is accentuated by the paint itself, which frequently has the appeal of fine ceramic. In 1946 he also began creating designs for tapestries.

SIQUEIROS, David Alfaro (b. 1896, Chihuahua), Mexican painter. He was one of three founders of the modern school of mural painting (Diego Rivera and José Clemente Orozco were the others) that grew up in Mexico after the revolution. His first mural, the *Elements*, for the National Preparatory School of Mexico City, was done in 1922 side by side with Orozco's first frescoes. Siqueiros' work as an artist is inseparable from his militant political activities, which on several occasions have ended in imprisonment or driven him into exile, first in Argentina (1932–33), then in the United States, where he founded a workshop in New York (1935) for experimenting with materials suitable for mural painting. When he returned to Mexico in 1939, Siqueiros was accused of complicity in an attempt to assassinate Leon Trotsky and was arrested. He went into exile again and did some vast mural compositions in Chile (*Death to the Invader, c.* 1942; Chillan, Escuela Mexico), and then in Cuba (*Allegory of Racial Equality*, 1943). As soon as he returned to his country, Siqueiros began decorating several public buildings and produced easel paintings as well. Among these is the fresco of the *Mexican Revolution* for the Museo Nacional de Antropología and the *Theater in the Life of the Community* for the theater of the National Association of Actors, both in Mexico City. They were begun about 1960, interrupted when the artist was again arrested in 1961, and only finished after his release in 1965. After that he worked on a huge interior and exterior decoration, the *Progress of Humanity*, for the then projected Congress Hall of Mexico City. Sculpture and painting were combined in daring experiments with contemporary industrial materials, and swept into a single monumental creation. An ideological realism, which is essentially humanist, is always present in his art, whose wild intoxication of form and movement has immense power and vitality.

SIRONI, Mario (1885, Tempio Pausania, Sardinia—1961, Milan), Italian painter. He became friendly with Umberto Boccioni and was involved in the Futurist movement. After 1914 Sironi lived and worked mainly in Milan. His driving artistic impulse was the desire to express the condition of man in society and the tragic grandeur of modern times. He was fond of somber colors and dark spaces crossed with lambent lights, and often used a technique that brought him close to Expressionism. In 1920 Sironi began a series of *City Outskirts*, images of deserted, sooty suburbs and factories, two of the best examples being *Urban Landscape* (1924; Rome, Galleria Nazionale d'Arte Moderna) and the *Gasometer* (1943; Milan, Coll. Jucker). Sironi also executed several large frescoes, including *Law Between Justice and Strength* (1936; Milan, Palace of Justice), as well as paintings in which he used a thick, rough paint that made his canvases look as if they were carved out of living rock.

SISLEY, Alfred (1839, Paris—1899, Moret-sur-Loing, Seine-et-Marne), French painter. He came from a wealthy English family who resided in Paris, and was able to follow his artistic bent at an early age because of his father's encouragement. When he was twenty-three, Sisley entered Charles Gleyre's (1806–74) studio at the École des Beaux-Arts in Paris, where he became friendly with Jean-Frédéric Bazille, Claude Monet, and Auguste Renoir. All four artists left the school in 1863 and worked together at Chailly in the forest of Fontainebleau; in 1865 Sisley accompanied Renoir to Marlotte, also in Fontainebleau. He exhibited for the first time at the Salon of 1866, but his work was refused the following year and again in 1869. His father was ruined by the Franco-Prussian War of 1870, after which time Alfred had to support his family unaided. He pursued his career in the face of indifference by public and dealers alike, except for the Parisian art dealer Paul Durand-Ruel, who bought Sisley's pictures because he was sorry for him. Sisley was first influenced by Gustave Courbet, then more profoundly by Jean-Baptiste Camille Corot, and it was through Monet that he evolved an Impressionistic style. Except for brief visits to England and Normandy, he never left Paris and its environs, working for a long time in and around Louveciennes (*Snow at Louveciennes*, 1878; Paris, Musée de l'Impressionnisme).

Sisley was the most modest, the most retiring, and the poorest of the Impressionists, but he perhaps also had the most richly endowed imagination. His painting was more even than that of his friends, and he always strove for perfection. He generally confined himself to landscapes and it was only late in his life that their simplicity, distinction, and unity was appreciated (*Flood at Port Marly*, 1876; Musée de l'Impressionnisme).

Alfred Sisley. *Ferry in the Floods*. 1876. Musée de l'Impressionnisme, Paris. *Archives photographiques, Paris.*

SKIDMORE, OWINGS & MERRILL, large and important firm of American architects. It was founded in 1935 by Louis Skidmore (1897–1962) and Nathaniel A. Owings (b. 1903). They were joined the following year by John O. Merrill (b. 1896). The firm's influence did not make itself felt until after World War II, when one of its most talented associates, Gordon Bunshaft, created the highly influential Lever House in New York (1952). Its elegant, sheer surface of glass over a steel frame, heavily influenced by the work of Mies van der Rohe, set the style for the 1950s. Several other office buildings by the firm follow Lever House in style and quality: the Inland Steel Company Building in Chicago (1954); the Connecticut General Life Insurance Building, near Hartford (1957), again of steel and glass; the Pepsi-Cola Building (1959); Union Carbide Corporation offices (1960); and the headquarters of the Chase Manhattan Bank (1957–61), all in New York.

Although the Skidmore, Owings & Merrill style of the 1950s may be seen as the final phase of the International Style of the 1920s, the firm's work began to take new directions. The interfaith chapel of the Air Force Academy at Colorado Springs (1959–61), for example, was an extraordinary design, built on a tetrahedral plan. The emphatically curved pilotis of the John Hancock Building in San Francisco (1960) marked a return to Expressionism. Skidmore, Owings & Merrill varied its style again in the First National City Bank, New York, an airy steel structure faced with white marble. This was further explored in the Banque Lambert, Brussels (1960–61), and the Beinecke Rare Book and Manuscript Library of Yale University, New Haven, Connecticut (1962–63).

Skidmore, Owings & Merrill. Chapel of the Air Force Academy, Colorado Springs. 1959–61. *Photo U.S. Air Force.*

SLEVOGT, Max (1868, Landshut—1932, Neukastell, Palatinate), German painter and illustrator, who was—with Max Liebermann and Lovis Corinth—one of the leading representatives of German Impressionism. In 1901 Slevogt went to Berlin, and it was around this time that his style became influenced by French naturalism, especially the art of Millet, Courbet, and Manet. The latter's manner is particularly evident in one of Slevogt's best-known works, the *Portrait of D'Audrade as Don Giovanni* (1902; Stuttgart, Staatsgalerie), in which the visible brushstrokes are dashingly handled in order to render a dynamic and ephemeral moment on stage. In 1913–14 Slevogt traveled in Egypt, and in 1917 he received a teaching appointment at the Berlin Academy. In addition to being an accomplished painter, he was an excellent book illustrator and graphic artist, his drawings often appearing in *Simplizissimus* and *Jugend*.

SLOAN, John (1871, Lock Haven, Pennsylvania—1951, Hanover, New Hampshire), American painter. He began working as a newspaper illustrator for the Philadelphia Press, together with George Luks, Everett Shinn, and William Glackens. These artists all met at the studio of Robert Henri, whom Sloan had met in 1891, and who became the foremost influence on his work. As an illustrator, Sloan had developed great skill at capturing the essential elements of a situation with speed and accuracy in a dry, unsentimental style. He specialized in genre scenes of ordinary life in a palette dominated by grays, the color of the city. Sloan remained a studio painter, however realistic, being particularly concerned with the social implications of art, and with the development of a peculiarly American style. When newspaper work became scarce in Philadelphia, he and his friends migrated to New York. Refused by the academic establishment, they formed an independent group known as The Eight, and organized an exhibition in 1908 at the Macbeth Gallery in New York. The show, which included Sloan's *Hairdresser's Window* (1907; Hartford, Conn., Wadsworth Atheneum), was criticized for its earthy subject matter. Sloan painted typical New York phenomena such as Coney Island, Union Square, and the Bowery, in addition to domestic genre scenes (*The Cot*, 1907; Brunswick, Maine, Bowdoin College Museum of Art). He participated in the famous Armory Show of 1913, where he exhibited *Sunday, Women Drying their Hair* (1912; Andover, Mass., Phillips Academy, Addison Gallery of American Art). Although a socialist throughout his career and a longtime illustrator for the *Masses*, Sloan refused to countenance any necessary relation between propaganda and art.

Claus Sluter. *Philip the Bold with St. John the Baptist.* 1391–97. From the portal of the Chartreuse de Champmol, Dijon.

SLUTER, Claus (*c.* 1350, Haarlem—1406, Dijon), Franco-Flemish sculptor. This powerful and expressive artist, whose traditional style bridged the Late Gothic tradition and the first stirrings of the Renaissance, founded the Burgundian school of sculpture. Nothing is known of his work outside the 21 years he spent at Dijon in the service of Philip the Bold, duke of Burgundy: even this can only be appreciated from the remains of his work for the Carthusian monastery, or Chartreuse, at Champmol, near Dijon, which was founded by Philip, who wanted to be buried there. Sluter first appeared at Champmol in 1385 as one of the assistants to the master sculptor Jean de Marville, whom he replaced in 1389 as head of the ducal workshops.

Sluter's initial project at the monastery was the group of statues for the portal (1391–97), depicting the presentation of the donors to the Virgin by two saints: on one side, Duke Philip kneels beside St. John the Baptist; on the other, his wife, Margaret of Flanders, is accompanied by St. Catherine. On the pier of the entrance, the Virgin bends protectingly over the Child, who is looking up at the cherubs of the central dais. Sluter marked the beginning of a new tradition by the perspective effect he created in this group, by his realistic treatment of the figures, and by the well-defined relationships between them. In 1395–1403 he sculptured another monumental work, a *Calvary* for the main courtyard of the monastery, of which only the hexagonal base, known as the *Well of the Prophets* or the *Well of Moses*, remains, and is decorated with life-size statues of Moses and five prophets. Sluter lavished the finest of his artistic abilities on these figures, of which the most majestic and admirable are *Moses* and *Zachariah*. In 1404 Philip the Bold died and Sluter retired to the abbey of St-Étienne in Dijon. Philip's successor John the Fearless then asked Sluter to finish Philip's cenotaph (begun 1385; now Dijon, Musée des Beaux-Arts) as quickly as possible. It is a remarkable work, showing the recumbent figure of the duke lying on a slab of black marble, with a lion at his feet and two angels holding his helmet at his head. In an open arcade at the side, 40 alabaster figures of *pleurants* ("weepers") form a mournful procession. Sluter devoted the rest of his life to this tomb, but died before it was finished; it was finally completed in 1410 by his nephew Claus de Werve and by his former assistant Hennequin de Prindale.

SLUYTERS, Jan (1881, 's Hertogenbosch—1957, Amsterdam), Dutch painter. Sluyters soon revealed an eclectic predilection as he began to adapt himself to various movements of his time, working in both Impressionist and Neoimpressionist styles. Gauguin was an especially important influence. It was the advent of Fauvism, however, that enabled Sluyters to arrive at a more personal means of expression, when he adopted its bright colors, as in his *Vase of Flowers* (1912; Otterlo, Rijksmuseum Kröller-Müller). The time that he spent at Overijssel (1915–16) brought about the further development of his style, resulting in what is perhaps his best work. He spurned the rustic and idyllic vision of The Hague school, and sought a determinedly Expressionist mode in order to better reveal the tragic reality of the Dutch peasantry. Sluyters subsequently returned to a less dramatic but no less vigorous style, which he retained for the remainder of his career and which is evident in such works as his *Self-Portrait* (1924; Amsterdam, Stedelijk Museum).

SMET, Gustave de (1877, Ghent—1943, Deurle, near Laethem-St-Martin), Belgian painter. He lived for a time with his brother Léon (b. 1881), also a painter, at the village and art colony of Laethem-St-Martin, near Ghent. During World War I he took refuge in Holland, where he became friendly with the

Dutchman Jan Sluyters and the Frenchman Henri Le Fauconnier (1881–1946), both of whom helped him to form his personal style in 1916. When he returned to Belgium in 1922 De Smet developed a mature Expressionist style that brought his painting closer to that of his friends Frits van den Berghe (1883–1939) and Constant Permeke, who, like him, painted country scenes in muted colors. De Smet's own painting is characterized by a calm atmosphere, refinement, and a soft coloring dominated by chestnut browns, red brick, dull pinks, and ocher; it is also distinguished by a concern for strict geometry and a careful composition that made him a distant inheritor of the Cubist tradition (*Green Girl*, 1927; Basel, Kunstmuseum). During the 1930s De Smet's stylistic Mannerism became less obtrusive, his drawing more flexible, and his forms less taut; nevertheless, it is the restrained sympathy and the quiet appeal of his muted tones that make his paintings particularly appealing.

SMIBERT, John (1688, Edinburgh—1751, Boston), Scottish-born American painter. He moved to London in about 1709, and found employment as a coach painter. Following a brief return visit to Edinburgh in 1717, Smibert spent three years in Italy. There he perfected his technical skill through studying the works of Titian, Raphael, Rubens, and Van Dyck (he made a copy of the latter's *Cardinal Bentivoglio* while in Florence). Smibert returned to London in 1720, and for the next seven years produced between 15 and 30 portraits a year, mainly of relatively unknown people. His reputation changed considerably in the unsophisticated society of the New World. He sailed with Bishop George Berkeley (whom he had met in Italy) in 1728, landing in Newport, Rhode Island, early in 1729. The portrait of *Dean Berkeley and His Entourage* (1729; New Haven, Yale University Art Gallery), based on drawings made at sea, is one of the few paintings actually executed in Newport. This work represents a high point in the artist's career, and was to have significant influence on the group portraits by such artists as Joseph Blackburn, Robert Feke, and America's finest Colonial portraitist, John Singleton Copley. Later in 1729 the artist moved to Boston, where he was enthusiastically received, since he was the first London artist with a knowledge of Italy to arrive in that city. A lack of serious rivals, as well as poor health and failing eyesight, account for the increasing deterioration of his style after his first few years in Massachusetts. The portrait of *Sir William Pepperell* (1747; Salem, Mass., Essex Institute) typifies his late manner with its static, wooden quality, and awkward handling of the full-length figure. In addition to painting portraits, he established the first "color shop" in Boston where art prints as well as artists' supplies were sold. He revealed his architectural capabilities in his design for Faneuil Hall (1740–42), the public market in Boston.

SMIRKE, Sir Robert (1781, London—1867, Cheltenham), English architect. He was one of the most important architects of the Greek Revival. Smirke was apprenticed briefly to Sir John Soane. He traveled through Greece and Italy (1801–5), and on his return published his sketches of ancient buildings in *Specimens of Continental Architecture* (1806). He established his reputation with Covent Garden Theater (1808; since destroyed), London's first building in the Doric style. The theater was highly influential, and together with his considerable business skills, led to his appointment as architect to the Board of Works (1813). Smirke's masterpieces include the British Museum (1823–47) and the General Post Office (1824–29; destroyed), both in London. The immense scale of the museum's colonnade is imposing if not ingenious, and reveals a sure, scholarly handling of Greek forms. Smirke retired from practice in 1845.

SMITH, David (1906, Decatur, Indiana—1965, Bolton Landing, New York), American sculptor. Smith, perhaps the foremost American sculptor of the mid-20th century, began as a painter, studying at the Art Students League in New York with the Czech Cubist Jan Matulka (b. 1890). Smith made the transition from painting to sculpture between 1930 and 1933, having been inspired to try welded-metal sculpture by reproductions of work by Julio Gonzalez and Pablo Picasso that used this technique. During the Depression years he executed a series of *Medals for Dishonor* (1937–40), powerful indictments of the social ills of that period. During World War II Smith worked as a welder in a defense plant, but returned to sculpture in the late 1940s with a group of works in which the influence of Alberto Giacometti predominates (*Blackburn—Song of an Irish Blacksmith*, 1950; estate of the artist). From these works, Smith developed his technique of "drawing-in-space," using linear metal elements to describe a complex rhythm within a two-dimensional plane (*Hudson River Landscape*, 1951; New York, Whitney Museum). Also in the 1950s he began to produce series of works based on relations of the human form ("Agricola" and "Tank Totem"). These yielded to a more geometric, less organic style at an architectural scale in the latter part of the decade, and culminated in the "Zig" and "Cubi" series. The former retained curvilinear, if geometric, forms with painted surfaces (*Zig VII*, 1963; New York, Marlborough-Gerson Gallery), but the "Cubi" pieces consisted primarily of burnished metallic cubiform elements joined at odd angles and suspended on high bases.

David Smith. *Cubi XVIII*. 1964. Coll. Stephen D. Paine, Boston.

SMITH, Sir Matthew (1879, Halifax, England—1959, London), English painter. After studying at the Manchester School of Art and later at the Slade School in London, Smith obtained his father's permission to go to France. Attracted by the Gauguin legend, he went first to paint at Pont-Aven. When he finally got to Paris, Smith enrolled at Henri Matisse's academy, but unfortunately, it closed a month after his arrival. In 1914 he adopted the Fauvist manner, which he retained throughout his

Frans Snyders. *Still Life with Game and Fruits.* 1613. Museum, Kassel.

career, enriching it with increasingly brilliant arabesques and using rich, oily color dominated by sonorous reds (*Lilies*, 1913–14; Leeds, City Art Gallery). Although Smith excelled in still lifes, especially flowers, he applied himself as well to figure painting (*Model Turning*, 1924; London, Tate Gallery), landscapes (*Landscape, Evening, Cagnes, c.* 1935; London, British Council), and portraits (*Marshal of the Royal Air Force Sir John Salmond, c.* 1947; Coll. Sir John Salmond). Sir Matthew, a member of the London Group, occupies an important position in 20th-century English painting: as the ambassador of French art he aroused among his compatriots an interest in "pure" painting and restored to the profession a dignity unknown since William Turner's day.

SMITH, Tony (b. 1912, South Orange, New Jersey), American sculptor. Smith worked from about 1938 to 1960 as an architect, assisting Frank Lloyd Wright during the first two years. He began working in sculpture around 1940, although it was not until 1960 that he devoted himself exclusively to this medium. Smith emerged then as one of the most prominent sculptors of the 1960s, and the forerunner and chief influence on the minimal sculpture of this period. Smith's aesthetic derives in part from his architectural sensibilities, particularly a long-time interest in the primitive geometric architecture of the Pueblos. Although his work often begins from modular units (model for the *Maze*, 1967; New York, Finch College Museum of Art), his sculptures rarely preserve the symmetry evident in other minimal sculpture (*Night*, 1966; New York, Fischbach Gallery). Like that of his contemporaries, however, Smith's work is often large in scale, severe (usually painted black), and geometrical (*Die II*, 1967; Fischbach Gallery). Occasionally allusions are made to objects or persons (*Cigarette*, 1967; Fischbach Gallery).

Sir John Soane. Bank of England, London. 1788–1833. *National Buildings Record, London.*

SMYTHSON, Robert (b. *c.* 1536–d. 1614, Wollaton, Nottinghamshire), English architect. He was the most important architect of the Elizabethan period, developing a peculiarly English style out of Italian and Flemish Renaissance forms within a Romantic, sham castle framework. Smythson is first known to have worked as a mason at Longleat, Wiltshire (1568–75), but his masterpiece, Wollaton Hall in Nottinghamshire, was a later work (1580–88). It was a highly original, symmetrically planned building, with corner towers and a central hall, probably substituted for a courtyard in a plan derived from Sebastiano Serlio. The carved ornament is particularly exuberant, and the tracery in the high tower windows that light the internal hall gives the huge pile a medieval look, heightened by the four-tower plan. Smythson is believed to have contributed to the design of Hardwick Hall, Derbyshire (1590–97), as well as to several other houses in the Midlands.

SNYDERS, Frans (1579, Antwerp—1657, Antwerp), Flemish painter. He was the friend and frequent collaborator of Peter Paul Rubens, and the first painter to specialize in animal still lifes. His early works, including *Fruit and Game* (1603; Brussels, Gallery Willems) and *Vegetable and Game Dealer* (1610; Brussels, Priv. Coll.), are unadventurous and unskilled compositions in the manner of Pieter Aertsen and Joachim Beuckelaer. Snyders' mature style can be seen in the *Four Markets* series (*c.* 1615–20; Leningrad, Hermitage) painted for Alexander Triest. Great craftsmanship and simple construction combine to produce a powerful composition divided into rectangular sections. The Baroque device of diagonal construction appeared only in Snyders' later works. He also helped Rubens on many great pictures, especially with the still-life elements and animals (*Miracle of the Fishes*, 1618; Mechlin, Notre-Dame au delà de la Dyle). Snyders may also have contributed to some of the figure painting in other works executed with Rubens (*Hunt with Samson*; Rennes, Musée des Beaux-Arts). He seems, however, to have been indebted to a drawing by Rubens for the motif of a dead swan that appears in many of his later paintings (*Larder with Swan, Asparagus, and Young Man in Kitchen*; Ottawa, National Gallery). The sense of vitality and movement with which Snyders infused his hunting scenes (*Boar Hunt*; Poznan, Muzeum Narodowe) carried over even into his still lifes (*Fish Stall*; Hermitage).

SOANE, Sir John (1753, Goring-on-Thames, Oxfordshire—1837, London), English architect. The king, impressed by several prizes he had won, granted Soane a traveling scholarship, and he set out for Italy in 1778. In 1788 he was appointed architect to the Bank of England, an office that brought him both financial security and professional prestige, and that he maintained until 1833. Soane's architecture is a highly personal interpretation of Neoclassicism. With his work in London on the Bank of England, Soane's characteristic mannerisms began to develop, particularly in his interiors: broad arches and shallow domes; vaulted ceilings intersected by decorated ribs (No. 12 Lincoln's Inn Fields, London; 1792–94); unusual clerestory lighting; and, on the exterior, the striking effect of irregular skylines. Typical of this period are the Dulwich Gallery and Mausoleum (1812), where the bold but carefully articulated masses of the buildings are covered by a roof system made picturesque by groupings of stone cinerary urns and coffers. At Dulwich too,

Soane's unique system of ornament is particularly well used. His interest and skill in creating visual effects can be seen in his London house at No. 13 Lincoln's Inn Fields (1812–13), now the Soane Museum, where, through a system of well-placed mirrors, the illusion of considerable depth is maintained in a relatively small space. But the masterpiece of his career remains his work on the Bank of England (1788–1833). The functional demands of this complex of offices and halls would not have permitted the proportions necessary for the successful application of Classical orders. Soane's ornament, which he developed at the bank, was flexible enough to overcome this problem, and his brilliant handling of space marks him as one of England's most original architects.

SOCIAL REALISM, movement in American painting associated with the 1930s Works Progress Administration (WPA). Many of the artists involved had in fact worked on that federal project, often influenced in their protests by artists of the Mexican Revolution. Nevertheless, many works with socio-political content were done before the WPA had come into existence. The Depression years turned many American painters to the consideration of such social problems as labor-management struggles, the miseries of poverty and unemployment, middle-class materialism, lawmakers and law enforcers, and racial discrimination. Pictures of poverty and the underworld by such an artist as Jack Levine (*Feast of Pure Reason*, 1937; New York, Museum of Modern Art) made treatments of similar themes by The Eight seem relatively Romantic. Along with Levine and such other Americans as Philip Evergood (*Railroad Men*, *c.* 1935; present location unknown) and William Gropper (*Old Tree and Old People*, 1939; New York, Whitney Museum), many European artists who fled to America in the 1930s produced socially oriented, often satirical art.

SOCIÉTÉ ANONYME. In 1920 Marcel Duchamp, Man Ray, and the abstract artist and patron Katherine S. Dreier (1877–1952) decided to found an organization that would awaken the American public to the latest currents in the arts. The title was provided by Man Ray, who had been fascinated by the term "Société Anonyme" ever since Duchamp had told him that it meant "incorporated" in French. They decided to name their organization "Société Anonyme, Incorporated."

The first works in the Société's collection were six paintings by Man Ray, contributed by John R. Covert, who had just given up a promising career as an abstract painter to go into business. Henceforth the collection grew rapidly, and when in 1941 its founders decided to donate it to the Yale University Art Gallery, New Haven, Connecticut, it included works by 169 artists from 23 countries. Since the collection often borrowed works from private collections for its exhibitions, there were gaps in it that were subsequently filled by the Yale Art Gallery: by the 1960s it was one of the most important and representative collections of modern art in the world.

SODOMA, Giovanni Antonio Bazzi, *called* (1477, Vercelli, Piedmont—1549, Siena), Lombard painter. Sodoma came under the influence of Umbrian painters, particularly Luca Signorelli and Raphael, and probably worked with Leonardo, whose art left a profound impression on his work. In 1503 he painted the frescoes in the refectory of the Olivetan monastery of S. Anna in Campana, near Pienza. Shortly afterward Sodoma painted one of his most famous series, in the monastic cloister of Monte Oliveto Maggiore; from 1505 to 1508 he completed 31 frescoes, continuing the *Life of St. Benedict* begun earlier by Signorelli. These light, open compositions show a remarkable gift for the grouping of figures, as well as an almost morbid beauty in the faces and attitudes. In 1512 he decorated the façade of the Palazzo Agostino Bardi in Siena, and the same year went to Rome to paint *Alexander and Roxana* at the Villa Farnesina. Other works in Siena include frescoes for the Confraternity of S. Sebastiano (*c.* 1518), and the decoration of the St. Catherine Chapel in S. Domenico (1526), one of his masterpieces. During the same period Sodoma painted the touching and graceful *St. Sebastian* (Florence, Palazzo Pitti). He also worked in Volterra and Pisa. His numerous works all have a very personal style; notwithstanding a certain affectation, they are marked by beautiful color, subtle light effects, and a poetic feeling for landscape.

Sodoma. *Wedding of Alexander and Roxana.* 1512. Farnesina, Rome. *Photo Anderson.*

SOFFICI, Ardengo (1879, Rignano sull'Arno—1964, Forte dei Marmi, Tuscany), Italian painter, polemicist, and writer. He took an active part in contemporary Italian movements from Futurism to the Novecento. After living for some years in Paris (1900–7), where he was acquainted with Apollinaire, Max Jacob, and other notable figures of the time, he settled in Florence and became, along with Giovanni Papini, one of the group active in the creation of the avant-garde review *La Voce*. This review defended the Futurists in particular, for whom Soffici organized an exhibition in 1913 on the publication's premises. The same year he founded the review *Lacerba* with Papini. Soffici's most successful paintings date from this period, during which he applied the principles he had learned from Paul Cézanne and from Cubism: the influence of the latter movement is clearly evident in his *Fruit and Wine Bottle* (1915; Milan, Coll. Frua de Angeli). Soffici's devotion to these modern trends, however, was short-lived, and in February 1915 he broke with the Futurist movement altogether. Returning to representational painting, characterized by an excessive simplification of the subject, he came under the influence of Giovanni Fattori. His later paintings include the moody and somber *Landscape* (1943; Milan, Coll. Mario Carletti).

SOLARIO *or* **SOLARI,** Andrea (b. *c.* 1470, Milan—d. 1520), Italian painter of the Lombard school, the brother of Cristoforo Solario, and one of the most distinguished pupils of Leonardo da Vinci. Together the brothers went to Venice in 1489: Andrea's *Holy Family with St. Jerome* (1495; Milan, Brera) shows the influence

Cristoforo Solario. *Recumbent figure of Lodovico il Moro.* 1497–99. Certosa di Pavia. *Photo Alinari-Viollet.*

of the Venetians on his style. Invited to Normandy in 1507, Andrea worked there until 1509 on frescoes for the cardinal of Amboise's chapel in Gaillon Castle. Among the artist's works, two are justly famous: the *Virgin with the Green Cushion* (*c.* 1500), formerly in the refectory of the Franciscan cloister at Blois, and the *Head of St. John the Baptist* (1507), both in the Louvre, Paris. According to Vasari, Andrea died in 1520 while working on an *Assumption of the Virgin* for the sacristy of the Certosa di Pavia. His remarkable sense of color derives from the Venetian School, while to Leonardo he owes the softness and gentleness of his facial types, notably his Madonnas.

SOLARIO *or* **SOLARI,** Cristoforo (*c.* 1460, Angera, Lago Maggiore—1527, Milan), Italian sculptor and architect. He worked at first in Venice (1489) with his brother Andrea before being invited to Milan (1495) by Lodovico il Moro, who commissioned from Cristoforo marble funerary statues (1497–99) of himself and of Beatrice d'Este for the church of S. Maria delle Grazie (they are now in the Certosa at Pavia). Cristoforo was later appointed sculptor to Milan Cathedral, for which he carved the statues of *Adam* and *Eve* (1502) that adorn the façade. Solario was quite active as an architect in Milan, where he built the dome (1511) of S. Maria della Passione and probably the church of S. Maria della Fontana. His art was thoroughly imbued with the new spirit of the Renaissance and he evidently learned from and was receptive to the architectural innovations of Bramante.

SOLIMENA, Francesco, *called* L'Abate Ciccio (1657, Canale di Serino, near Naples—1747, Barra), Italian decorative painter, the leading representative of the Late Baroque style in 18th-century Naples. Solimena worked at Rome, Monte Cassino, and in Spain, but his most valuable legacy may be found in the churches of Naples, where he left huge frescoes crowded with dynamic figures that are broadly painted and cast in a dramatic tenebristic light (*Fall of Simon Magus*, 1690, S. Paolo Maggiore; *Expulsion of Heliodorus from the Temple*, 1725, Gesù Nuovo; others in S. Maria Donnaregina, 1684, and in the sacristy of S. Domenico Maggiore, 1709). One of Solimena's most impressive compositions is the large-scale preparatory sketch for the *Massacre of the Giustiniani at Chios* (Naples, Museo di Capodimonte), which was intended for the Senate Chamber at Genoa. Unrivaled as the most successful Italian painter of the 18th century, Solimena became the leader of an influential academy in Naples, which numbered among its pupils Francesco de Mura (1696–1784), Sebastiano Conca (1679–1764), Giuseppe Bonito (1707–89), Corrado Giaquinto (1703–65), and the Scottish Allan Ramsay, who carried Solimena's grand manner of portraiture (*Self-Portrait*; Florence, Uffizi) back to the British Isles.

Jacques-Germain Soufflot. Interior view of the cupola of the Panthéon, Paris. 1756–80. *Photo Boudot-Lamotte.*

SOUFFLOT, Jacques-Germain (1713, Irancy, Yonne—1780, Paris), French architect. At the age of eighteen he went to Rome, where his enthusiasm for drawing ancient monuments won him entry to the French Academy (1734). On his return to France, Soufflot lived in Lyons. The façade of the Hôtel-Dieu on the Rhône (1745) and the Loge du Change (1747) belong to this period. In 1749 Madame de Pompadour appointed Soufflot to accompany the young Marquis de Vandières, her brother and future director of royal buildings, on a trip to Italy. During this second trip, Soufflot drew the ruins of the temples of Paestum near Naples, which revealed the Greek Doric order to architects of his generation.

Soufflot soon returned to Lyons, where he built the Hôtel de Lacroix-Laval (1751), the chapel of La Charité at Mâcon (1751), the Maison Merlino in the Île Barbe (1752–53), and the Grand Théâtre (1753–56; destroyed). The Doric order, so appreciated by Soufflot at Paestum, was used in the crypt of his most important work, the Parisian church of Ste-Geneviève (1755), commissioned by Louis XV and known since the Revolution as the Panthéon. In this church, which is centrally planned on a Greek cross, Soufflot was rash enough to sacrifice solidity to elegance, taking structural risks in supporting the dome and its huge drum, whose weight rested largely on four groups of three columns. The Panthéon is unique in its combination of strict regularity and monumental Roman detail with a lightness usually associated with Gothic architecture. During his career in Paris, Soufflot also built the Hôtel de Marigny au Roule (1768–71; since destroyed), the École de Droit (1771–83), the Fontaine de l'Arbre-sec (1775), and the nymphaea of the Château de Menars and the Château de Chatou.

Soufflot lived at the very end of the Baroque period and was a leader of the Neoclassical reaction. The somewhat austere aspect of the Panthéon even looks forward to the Napoleonic style.

SOULAGES, Pierre (b. 1919, Rodez, Rouergue), French painter. He began painting independently when very young, and

Pierre Soulages. *Painting*. 1947. Private Coll., Paris.

became interested in the Romanesque buildings and megaliths of his native Rouergue. It was not until he moved to Paris after World War II that his painting became completely abstract. In 1938 he began painting austere winter landscapes, filled with bare, dark trees with twisted branches; these were followed in 1946 by calligraphic paintings in black or brown on a white ground. The strict discipline and strength of their lines provided the framework for powerful compositions based on the varying tensions between white and black. The broad, precise, heavy rhythms of Soulages' brushstrokes induced a sense of arrested movement and pent-up energy in his later paintings. Their impact lay in the dynamic communication of vertical, horizontal, and transverse rhythms, confronting and intersecting one another (*Painting*, 1951; Turin, Galleria d'Arte Moderna). Dryness was avoided in this concentrated idiom by means of light, transparent transitions interrupted by bright color that, shortly after 1950, often replaced browns and gave depth to the black (*Composition*, 1954; Munich, Moderne Galerie Otto Stangl).

SOUTINE, Chaim (1894, Smilovichi, near Smolensk—1943, Paris), Russian Lithuanian painter of the School of Paris. In 1911 he arrived in Paris, where Marc Chagall, Jacques Lipchitz, and Blaise Cendrars were among his friends. Soutine soon became a familiar figure in Montparnasse, where he was encouraged by Amedeo Modigliani. He often went to Les Halles to buy sides of meat, which—like his great artistic mentor, Rembrandt—he then painted in various stages of decomposition.

Always restless and dissatisfied with others and himself, he experienced alternating periods of complete sterility and frenetic work: in 1922, for instance, after spending three years at Céret in Provence, he returned to Paris with 200 still lifes and landscapes, about 100 of which were bought the following year by the American collector, Dr. Albert C. Barnes of Merion, Pennsylvania, where they now form part of the Barnes Foundation's holdings. In 1940 France was invaded and Soutine had to flee Paris; he retired to a village in Touraine, where he painted a few more fine landscapes.

Comparatively few works survive from Soutine's first phase before his sojourn at Céret, but they are nonetheless attractive (*Still Life with Herrings*, 1916; Paris, Coll. Katia Granoff) in their simple lines and restrained colors. Nevertheless, his reputation has been established by his later compositions, of an Expressionistic fury akin to that of his contemporary, Georges Rouault. Dislocated forms and torrents of thick paint—primarily incandescent reds, milky whites, and deep blues—became the hallmarks of his feverish style. His usual subjects were psychologically revealing portraits; tempestuous landscapes with precipitous paths, wildly tossing trees, and dark clouds (*Windy Day at Auxerre*, 1939; Washington, D.C., Phillips Gallery); valets, bakers (*Pastry Cook*, 1922; Paris, Louvre), acolytes (*Choir Boy*, 1927; Louvre); or flayed sides of beef, skinned rabbits, blood-spattered ducks, and dressed poultry (*Cock, c.* 1926; Chicago, Art Institute) with their outspread tails, scarlet crests, and black plumage streaked with green. Soutine was wholly possessed by his anguish, and was indifferent to the experiments of the Fauves and Cubists. Although he despised the painting of his contemporaries, he admired Cézanne, Van Gogh, and Rembrandt above all. A poor draftsman, to whom emotional intensity of paint mattered more than line or composition, Soutine did not create a new idiom, preferring rather to paint his own unique temperament.

Chaim Soutine. *Pastry Cook*. 1922. Louvre, Paris.

SPENCER, Niles (1893, Pawtucket, Rhode Island—1952, Dingman's Ferry, Pennsylvania), American painter. After studies at the Rhode Island School of Design, he went to New York, where he studied with George Bellows and Robert Henri. Spencer then traveled in France and Italy (1921–22 and 1928–29), and also sojourned frequently in New England, first in Ogunquit, Maine, and later in Provincetown, Massachusetts. His work of the 1920s is in the prevailing Cubist-Realist style, with land- or cityscapes reduced to their geometrical components (*Seventh Avenue*, 1927, New York, Whitney Museum; *Ordinance Island, Bermuda*, 1928, New York, Museum of Modern Art).

In the late 1940s and early 1950s, Spencer's works became increasingly two-dimensional, with frequent abstract passages, although always with roots in the man-made geometry of modern urban life. Such paintings as *Apartment Tower* (1944; Whitney Museum) and *In Fairmont* (1951; Museum of Modern Art) live up to his Purist ideal.

SPENCER, Sir Stanley (1891, Cookham, Berkshire—1959, Cookham), English religious painter. Spencer's cast of mind was remarkably similar to that of William Blake or Samuel Palmer, while the formal influences on his deliberately primitive style were most probably those of Masaccio and Wyndham Lewis. Spencer studied in London at the Slade School of Fine Art from 1908 to 1912, but many art critics feel that even without an academic training he would have achieved precisely the same willfully innocent style, drawing his inspiration, as he did throughout his life, from his home in the village of Cookham-on-Thames (*Nativity*, 1912; London, Slade School of Fine Art, University College). During World War I he served with the British army in Macedonia and translated his experiences with the Royal

Nicolas de Staël. *Drawing.* 1947. Private Coll.

Army Medical Corps into paintings such as *Travoys Arriving with wounded at a Dressing Station in Smol, Macedonia* (1919; London, Imperial War Museum) and the mural decorations for the Oratory of All Souls at Burghclere, Berkshire (1922–33). His *Resurrection of the Soldiers* (1928–29), a fresco on the altar wall of the Burghclere memorial church, and his huge *Resurrection : Cookham* (1923–27; London, Tate Gallery) are two of the most intense and memorable examples of his religious art. During World War II Spencer was officially commissioned to paint a series of shipyards in the port of Glasgow. After the war he returned to the Resurrection theme and painted many more religious works. There have been several retrospective exhibitions of Spencer's paintings, including one at the Arts Council Gallery in London (1955).

SPRANGER, Bartholomaeus (1546, Antwerp—1611, Prague), Flemish Mannerist painter. Spranger found genuine masters in Italy, where he was a painter to Pope Pius V and Cardinal Farnese after his arrival in Rome in 1567. His admiration for the elegant eroticism of Parmigianino and Correggio resulted in a similar quality of preciosity and voluptuousness in his own style of painting, which gave rise to an entire school of Mannerism in Central Europe after his appointment to the courts of Emperor Maximilian II in Vienna (1575) and Emperor Rudolf II in Prague (1584). For the latter Spranger produced two of his most typical and best-known paintings, the companion pieces of *Vulcan and Maia* and *Hercules and Omphale* (both *c.* 1590; both Vienna, Kunsthistorisches Museum). Produced on copper, they exemplify his taste for slender proportions, mannered poses, affected facial expressions, and unusual coloristic effects in which pearly flesh tints and accents of topaz, acid green, and carmine predominate. Spranger produced an important body of drawings whose verve and spontaneity of handling are in striking contrast to the minute detail of his paintings.

STACKPOLE, Ralph (b. 1885, Williams, Oregon), American sculptor. At sixteen Stackpole began studies at the Art School of California in San Francisco; two years later he went to Paris, enrolling at the École des Beaux-Arts (1906–7). After returning to the United States, he studied painting with Robert Henri (1911). Again in Europe from 1921 to 1923, he lived in Italy and in Paris. Stackpole then returned to the United States to live in California. In 1941 he was appointed by President Roosevelt to the Fine Arts Commission in Washington, D.C., but in 1949 he returned to France, where he settled permanently.

Stackpole was a carve-direct sculptor with a preference for massive, large-scale sculpture in hard and enduring materials, such as granite, although he also occasionally carved in wood; a significant influence on his work was the ancient monumental sculpture of South America. He had a particular interest in architectural sculpture, and in the United States he executed a number of public monuments (*Pacifica*, 1939; San Francisco, commissioned for the Golden Gate International Exhibition), although he was also noted for portrait busts and smaller, more individualistic sculptures (*Force de jeunesse*, 1958; granite, Coll. artist).

STAËL, Nicolas de (1914, St. Petersburg—1955, Antibes), French painter of Russian birth. He fled Russia as a child after the Revolution, was orphaned at an early age, and raised in Belgium. De Staël attended the Royal Academy of Fine Arts in Brussels in 1932, after which he traveled through Europe, visiting many museums. He served in the Foreign Legion during World War II, married, and returned to painting in Nice in 1940, concentrating on still lifes and portraits of his wife, Jeannine. He turned to abstract painting in 1942, with work based on the geometrical constructions of Synthetic Cubism. The death of his wife had a powerful emotional impact, but his work progressed, becoming much more dynamic and impressive (*Composition*, 1946, New York, Knoedler Gallery; and *Painting*, 1947, New York, Museum of Modern Art). In his paintings of the late 1940s greater depth and luminosity was imparted through exquisite color, embodied in rhythmically structured blocks and cubes (*Jour de Fête*, 1949; Basel, Galerie Beyeler). These rhythmic structures then began to lose their purely abstract quality, evoking architecture (*Roofs*, 1952; Paris, Musée National d'Art Moderne), space, and landscapes (*Figures by the Sea*, 1952; Galerie Beyeler). This figurative trend in his work became increasingly explicit, particularly in his series of football players (*Footballers*, 1951; London, Coll. Estorick) and musicians (*Jazz Players, in Memory of Sidney Bechet*, 1952; Paris, Priv. Coll.). Finding his work moving inevitably back toward representationalism, De Staël felt himself in the midst of an insoluble conflict, and committed suicide.

STAHLY, François (b. 1911, Constance, near Schaffhausen), German-born French sculptor. In 1931 he went to Paris, where he studied at the Académie Ranson under Charles Malfray, and in 1936 he helped to found the Témoignage group at Lyons. He worked in wood at first (*House of*

François Stahly. Fountain for Golden Gateway Park, San Francisco. 1964.

Tears, 1952; *Budding*, 1953) and gave his sculptures the complexity of knotted or splayed roots—organic forms that preserved the inherent qualities of the medium. When he later used stone and metal, Stahly's sculpture was conceived in relation to architecture and its social surroundings. In 1960 he was invited to the United States, where he continued the same experiments at the Aspen School of Contemporary Art in Colorado, then at Washington University in Seattle. The forests in the American North-west left a deep impression and gave him the idea of making high wooden sculptures like totem poles, which could be assembled into porticoes similar to the construction at the Maison de la Radio in Paris (1962–63). Stahly realized the same conception in stone and bronze for fountains, which are among his finest works of the 1960s.

STAMOS, Theodoros (b. 1922, New York), American painter. The son of Greek immigrants, Stamos was educated in New York. He began to paint at home in 1937, and at the age of twenty-two had his first one-man show of oils and pastels at the Wakefield Gallery in New York (1943). After this he began to evolve a more distinctive style, at first realistic, then abstracting and distorting from such subjects as beach debris, shells, driftwood, or starfish forms arranged in broad symbolic patterns. Like his older colleagues Adolph Gottlieb and William Baziotes, Stamos has been called a "poetic symbolist" because of his preference for lyrically abstract biomorphic forms, and for the subtle moods and tones that are both the content and the characteristic look of his paintings.

In 1948–49 a European tour that included France, Italy, and Greece was perhaps responsible for the more Classical basis of Stamos' painterly reveries. By 1952 a more consolidated abstract structure began to replace the earlier allusive imagery. Stamos often worked in series, and by 1958 had embarked on a group of pictures such as *High Snow, Low Sun, No. 3* (1957; New York, André Emmerich Gallery), which established cosmically radiant color presences, suggesting without describing the kinetic effects of atmosphere and weather. Later works continued this intention of gently evoking climatic moods and effects through color: *Day of Two Suns* (1963; Minneapolis, Minn., Walker Art Center), or *Aegean Sun Box No. 2* (1965; André Emmerich Gallery), still find their sources in the colors, air, and light of nature.

Richard Stankiewicz. *Sculpture. 1959. Photo Stable Gallery, New York.*

STANFIELD, Clarkson (1793, Sunderland, near Newcastle—1867, Hampstead, London), English marine painter. After a career in the British Navy, Stanfield turned to scenery painting, working at London's Drury Lane Theatre after 1822. In 1834, however, he gave up this work in order to concentrate on oil and watercolor painting, invariably choosing marine subjects (*Off the Dogger Bank*, 1846; London, Victoria and Albert Museum). He was made a full academician in 1835, and won a gold medal at the Paris Exhibition of 1855. Many of his paintings were based on sketches made in the course of his frequent visits to the Continent (*Lake Como*, 1825; *Entrance to the Zuyder Zee, Texel Island*, before 1844; *Canal of the Giudecca with the Church of the Gesuati, Venice,* 1863; all London, Tate Gallery). Stanfield, whose work is decorative, highly effective, and rather artificial, was highly esteemed by the art critic John Ruskin, who called him "the leader of the English realists."

STANKIEWICZ, Richard (b. 1922, Philadelphia), American sculptor. Stankiewicz settled in New York and studied at the Hans Hofmann School of Fine Arts (1948–49). In 1950 he went to Paris, where—still undecided whether to become a painter or sculptor—he worked first with Fernand Léger and then with Ossip Zadkine. He returned to New York in 1951. Stankiewicz's sculptures employ scrap metal, particularly the detritus from machines, exploiting the contrast between the found material and the created form. His skillfully assembled abstract works are often witty (*Kabuki Dancer*, 1956; New York, Whitney Museum) or evocative (*City Bird*, 1957; New York, Museum of Modern Art).

STEEN, Jan (1625/26, Leiden—1679, Leiden), Dutch painter. He ranks with Adriaen van Ostade as the most popular of all Dutch genre painters, and was probably the most imaginative. Steen was a brewer's son who became a pupil of the landscapist Jan van Goyen in 1648; he worked at The Hague, Delft, and Haarlem, then returned to Leiden around 1670, where from 1672 he operated a tavern. As a result of his training with Van Goyen, he was a landscape painter at first (*Skittle Players Outside an Inn*, *c.* 1660–63; London, National Gallery), but later he began imitating Pieter de Hooch's studies of middle-class life (the *Morning Toilette*, 1663; London, Buckingham Palace). From 1660 he tried to combine Frans Hals' realism and Jacob Jordaens' vivacity in such scenes as the *Merry Company* (*c.* 1663; The Hague, Mauritshuis) or the *Feast of St. Nicholas* (*c.* 1667; Amsterdam, Rijksmuseum). Later still, he drew inspiration from his own tavern for his more large-scale paintings of the rowdy Dutch populace making merry (*Twelfth Night*, 1668; Kassel, Staatliche Gemäldegalerie). This satirist was a fine painter, arranging his compositions in a lively harmony and never missing an opportunity to place some beautiful object—such as a pewter tankard, a hat, or a wineglass—well in evidence. Steen painted in a bright light that emphasized shapes, gestures, and facial expressions, and achieved infinitely subtle gradations of cold color—chiefly shimmering pink, pastel blue, lemon yellow, and ash gray.

STEENWIJK *or* **STEENWYCK THE ELDER,** Hendrik van (*c.* 1550, Steenwijk, Holland—1603, Frankfurt, Germany), Dutch painter. Hendrik specialized in architectural scenes: in most of his works, he chose aerial views, looking down into the nave of a church or into the open square of a town in

Hendrik van Steenwijk the Elder. *Interior of Antwerp Cathedral.* Kunsthalle, Hamburg.

order to develop his perspective effects more fully. His style is characterized by distinct outlines, bright colors, and an attention to detail, as in his *Market Place at Aachen* (1598; Brunswick, Herzog Anton Ulrich-Museum), which contains many carefully delineated figures engaged in various activities. More typical of Hendrik's work, however, is the superb *Interior of Antwerp Cathedral* (Hamburg, Kunsthalle), in which the figures are quite insignificant compared to the overpowering architectural setting. His use of light to clarify the structure and use of perspective to create the sensation of great spatial penetration had a great influence on other artists handling the same themes.

HENDRIK VAN, *called* THE YOUNGER (1580, Antwerp—*c.* 1649, London), his son, was also a painter of architectural settings. He worked in a style very close to that of his father, as is evident in his *Interior of a Gothic Church* (1605; Vienna, Kunsthistorisches Museum). Some of Hendrik the Younger's imaginary scenes, such as the *Open Square with Figures* (1614; The Hague, Mauritshuis), are softer in outline and more subtle in execution than his father's paintings.

STEER, Philip Wilson (1860, Birkenhead, Cheshire—1942, London), English painter of landscapes, portraits, and genre pictures. He studied at the Gloucester School of Art, and then (1882–84) in Paris at the Académie Julian and the École des Beaux-Arts. There, he was profoundly impressed by the works of Edgar Degas, whose influence is clearly visible in Steer's more serious portraits (*Mrs. Raynes*, 1922, and *Mrs. Cyprian Williams and Her Daughters*, 1891; both London, Tate Gallery).

During the late 1880s Steer was one of the founding members of the New English Art Club and exhibited with that group as well as with the London Impressionists. He had a nostalgia for the 18th century that inspired him to paint portraits and genre scenes in the style of Thomas Gainsborough and Jean Honoré Fragonard, while his more finished landscapes (*Richmond, Yorkshire*, 1906; Oxford, Ashmolean Museum) have a heavy coruscating surface that reveals his admiration for John Constable and Adolphe Monticelli. Only in his watercolors and lighter plein-air seascapes—notably his many scenes of the beach at Walberswick, East Suffolk (*Girls Running: Walberswick Pier*, 1894; Tate Gallery)—does Steer emerge as a painter of vitality and freshness.

STELLA, Frank (b. 1935, Malden, Mass.), American painter. Although his earliest work was oriented toward Abstract Expressionism, the first paintings shown publicly were a rigorous group of black canvases (1958–59) in which parallel stripes, outlined by bare canvas, reiterated or inverted the pattern of their framing edges. By means of the stripes "generated" by the edges of the canvas, structure was deduced from the literal format rather than depicted within a field, thus emphasizing the painting's existence as an object. Stella's choice of particularly artificial metallic or fluorescent colors also heightened the man-made, artificial quality of the painting. Stella, always a prolific painter, tended to work in series, varying the solutions to particular problems of structure, color, or shape while extending the range and variables of his work as a whole.

Between 1960 and 1963 he worked on three series of metallic aluminum, copper, and magenta paintings in multiple geometric shapes (including trapezoids with cutout centers, octagons, pentagons, and parallelograms) with concentric parallel striations. In 1962 a group of multicolored paintings, in which concentric bands of graded values created depth illusions like camera bellows, served as a kind of antidote to the monochrome and formal rigor of the other series. Between 1964 and 1965 Stella worked simultaneously on two series, one of zigzags and irregular V-shaped stripes in metallic polychrome (*Empress of India*, 1965; Los Angeles, Coll. Irving Blum) and another of pinwheels in fluorescent alkyd stripes. At the same time he departed from the stripe technique in a series of eccentrically shaped paintings whose internal shapes coincided only partially with the silhouette of the canvas. Later he worked on an intricate sequence of interlacing circles, arcs, and fanning protractor shapes (1966–67). Although still concerned with formal problems, Stella's notion of structure became increasingly complex through the interaction of shapes and synthetic but sensuous colors.

STELLA, Joseph (1877/79, Muro Lucano, near Potenza—1946, New York), American painter of Italian origin. He went to New York in 1896 to study medicine, which he soon abandoned for painting. During a trip to Europe in 1909–12 he met the Italian Futurists, and on his return to America he began translating his impressions of the new continent into Futurist terms. Stella gained recognition with his ambitious *Battle of Lights: Coney Island* (1913; New Haven, Conn., Yale University Art Gallery), in which he transformed the amusement park into a kaleidoscopic panorama of shifting, glittering fragments. Shortly thereafter in his famous painting of *Brooklyn Bridge* (1917–18; Yale University Art Gallery), he developed this Futurist style into a more personal one. With this work, the hectic dynamism of Futurism disappeared from Stella's idiom; instead, he selected certain details of the bridge and the city behind it, arranging them in a stable composition that still retained the surging movement of his earlier work. This style became more schematic in the effective series of five panels entitled *New York Interpreted* (1920–22; Newark, Museum).

STEPPES ART. A vast area of steppes and desert stretches from the Danube to Manchuria, bordered on the north by forests and on the south by plateaus that spread from the Balkans to Tibet and the Chinese plains. For centuries nomadic peoples of horsemen and shepherds lived there, wandering from place to place without cultivating the land and nearly always without building any permanent dwellings. Although, as a result of this, the nomads developed no monumental architecture or sculpture, they created an artistic portable metalwork of remarkable boldness.

The Iranian-speaking tribes, who ranged the western steppes during the so-called Indo-European period (prior to the expansion of the Altaic peoples), were already working bone, wood, and later on gold and bronze.

The existence of gold plaques decorated with animal motifs has been known since the 17th century, when they were found in Siberia by the prospectors of Peter the Great. Modern Soviet researchers continue to make new discoveries, while theories on the origins of Steppes art, its distribution, influence, and eventual disappearance increase proportionately. Its finest examples possess a nervous vitality and tension that are particularly attractive.

ZOOMORPHIC STYLE

There is general agreement that the zoomorphic style does not date from the beginning of the nomadic spread. The historians Minns and Borovka have related its origins to a very ancient tradition of horn- and bonework that was common among the hunters of the northern forests, while Rostovtzeff stresses its affinities with primitive Chinese art. More recently, scholars have paid greater attention to the importance of the Karasuk culture, which was also connected with China and appeared in eastern Siberia about 1100 B.C. Minns again, followed by Godard and Ghirshman, emphasized the contribution of the Near and Middle East (Assyria, Urartu, Anatolia, and Iran) to the Scythian art of southern Russia. Ghirshman, Jettmar, and Artamonov, however, defined the theory of an "Iranian unity" in the linguistic and ethnic sense of the term, which embraced the peoples living on the Iranian plateau, including the Medes and Persians, as well as the nomadic tribes who remained on the northern steppes. In spite of variations owing to historical differences, their relationship is evident, not only in their language, but also in every phase of their artistic development.

Cimmerians and Scythians

Southern Russia played a dominant part in this development because of its proximity to the civilizations of the Middle East and also because the zoomorphic style evolved there very early. It was the homeland of the Scythians and, before them, of the Cimmerians who, in the 7th century B.C., invaded Media, north-west of Iran, and other neighboring regions. No strictly Cimmerian form of Steppes art has so far been found.

Iranian and even Syrian influences are, on the other hand, already obvious in the bone plaques found in the tombs of Zhabotin, which belong to the archaic Scythian style of the 7th century B.C. During the following period, the Ziwiye treasure, which may date from the end of the 7th century, is of great importance. This lucky find threw fresh light on the Asiatic phase of Scythian art. On the gold leaves of Ziwiye, the composition and range of nomadic animals, recumbent deer, and heads of birds of prey appear side by side with the fabulous bestiary of Mesopotamia and Urartu. There is an obvious link with the archaeological sites of Kuban and the Dnieper valley, which for a long time have been regarded as a branch of the mature Scythian art of the 6th century. The products of Kuban were steeped in Middle Eastern influences and are found side by side with objects that have obviously been imported from the south. They imitated Greek models more and more closely, at first in the Archaic and then the Classical styles, and have been excavated with works of purely Greek origin. Toward the end of the 5th century B.C. Scythian art degenerated rapidly. Around the Black Sea, it was replaced by Classical forms, while in the steppes a new race, the Sarmatians, became dominant and began to impose their own version of the zoomorphic style.

In Siberia the styles of Altai and the Minusinsk basin were practically contemporary with the spread of the Scythian style in Russia and were closely related to it. In the Minusinsk region, near ancient Karasuk, the art of Tagar is like a rough copy of Scythian models. The Altaic culture of Maiemir, further south, represents an early phase of the zoomorphic style. In the group of Pazyryk tombs on the heights of Altai, the harness ornaments, saddle cloths, and objects in wood, felt, or leather that were found have an unmistakably Scythian character, mixed with some well-assimilated Achae-

Steppes Art (Scythian). Panther. Kelermes, Kuban. 8th century B.C. The Hermitage, Leningrad.

Steppes Art (Kuban culture). Bronze deer. Kasbek, Caucasus. 6th–5th century B.C. Museum of Russian History, Moscow. *Photo Walter Dräyer, Zurich.*

Steppes Art (Scytho-Altaic). Harness ornament: stylized heads of elk. 5th century B.C. The Hermitage, Leningrad.

Steppes Art (Scytho-Altaic). Tracing of a tattooed pattern. Pazyryk tombs, 5th–4th century B.C.

Steppes Art (Sarmatian). *Combat between a tiger and a griffin.* Perforated gold plaque. Siberia, 3rd century B.C. The Hermitage, Leningrad.

menid and Chinese influences, but quite untouched by Greek elements. The fantasy and ingenuity of Scythian carving and metalwork appear with fresh vigor in these historically precious objects.

The historical link between Pazyryk and southern Russia is difficult to establish in the absence of works of a similar style in the intermediary regions. There probably were exchanges, connected perhaps with the trading of gold, rather than with a migration or any political domination, since in the 5th century B.C. the Scythians in Europe were driven toward the west by newer tribes and had no empire east of the Don.

Sarmatians

In the basin of the upper Ob in western Siberia, prospectors found gold plaques that Peter the Great collected and that are now attributed to the Sarmatians. Their style is marked by Mede, Achaemenid, and Saka elements that also characterize the "treasure of the Oxus" of Bactrian provenance. The plaques and bracelets of this princely treasure are covered with zoomorphic motifs, including felines, birds of prey, and griffins, but while the earliest are partly decorated with cloisonné work, the latest have only reliefs and cavities in which jewels and coloured glass must have been inserted. This tradition from eastern Iran replaced the old Scythian heritage and was carried west by the Sarmatians during the last centuries before the Christian era, as far as European Russia and later on into the Danube basin.

Ordos Bronzes

At the other extremity of the steppes, where the Gobi Desert and the Ordos plateau skirt the Great Wall of China, plaques and small bronzes, generally of unknown provenance, have been found. This scattered, still ill-defined group presents different aspects of the zoomorphic style.

The tombs of Noin Ula, near Lake Baikal at the northern limit of the vast territory where the Ordos bronzes were found, also contained a few plaques, but a more important relic than these are the woollen carpets and embroidered felt blankets, which have been dated to the beginning of the Christian era. Some are decorated in the zoomorphic Steppes style, others with Chinese motifs.

Sarmatian zoomorphic art survived, although with considerable changes, among the successors of the Iranian nomads; it existed during the late Classical period and during the great invasions of the Teutons, Avars, and other Turkish peoples of the steppes, as well as among some Tibetan tribes.

NON-ZOOMORPHIC ART

The steppes craftsmen sometimes turned from animal representations to scenes of human life, anthropomorphic divinities, mythical and epic tales. There are Scythian plaques from southern Russia illustrating wrestlers challenging each other, two warriors swearing an oath of friendship while they drink from the ritual goblet, a great goddess enthroned among her worshipers, and a rider worshiping the goddess. A similar scene decorates a felt hanging from Pazyryk. The Sarmatians of the Black Sea frequently depicted warriors in the act of beheading their enemies or carrying their heads in triumph. A Sarmatian plaque from Siberia is decorated with a hunter chasing a boar on horseback; another with a hero reclining with his head in a woman's lap, while his groom sits on the ground holding the horse's reins. Battle scenes appear on some Ordos bronzes and a hero of Sarmatian type driving a chariot on others. Medals found in southern Russia and the Danube valley bear human images, but Greek influence is more apparent in these.

TECHNIQUE AND STYLE

All through its history, Steppes art preserved a number of specific characteristics that were determined by its origins and the conditions of nomadic life. As the first materials it used were bone or horn, which were small and of about the same shape, the outstanding feature of zoomorphic carving was distortion of the body according to certain set conventions: paws bent back or tucked under the stomach, antlers displayed ornamentally, and outlines that are truncated, shortened, and curved into a ring or a slanting S. This style continued even when a less restricted surface was available to the craftsman, as on the gold leaves covering the *goryti* (wooden or leather cases to contain a bow and arrows).

An element of fantasy is inseparable from zoomorphic art. It was already implicit in the choice of motifs, which mixed griffins and monsters with the fauna of the steppes. In addition to this, the artist was always ready to elaborate the original animals with apparently superfluous and fabulous decorations. Yet in spite of these alterations and contortions, the character of the animals was never lost.

EXTERNAL INFLUENCES

The nomads, who lived on the frontiers of nearly all the great agricultural civilizations, borrowed ideas and motifs from them, which they then carried to territories remote from their original centers in the course of their migrations. The Scythian, Sarmatian, Saka, and Siberian styles of Altai and Noin Ula diverged precisely because of these external influences. The mosaic of these exchanges and displacements often makes attribution hazardous. We do know, however, that griffins with the head of an eagle or a lion and animals locked in combat can be found, well before the great Steppes period, in the art of the Middle East. Similarly, rectangular frames and pierced work in some Sarmatian objects and their copies from Ordos existed in Luristan bronzes, which were appreciably earlier.

Steppes Art (Sarmatian). *Grape harvest.* Medallion on a bowl. Novocherkassk tombs, 1st century B.C. Regional Museum, Rostov. *Photo Walter Dräyer, Zurich.*

Steppes Art (Ordos bronzes). *Two men wrestling in a forest.* Perforated plaque. 100 B.C.–A.D. 100. Victoria and Albert Museum, London.

In southern Russia, the Scythians soon eliminated Assyrian and Urartian influences. Yet Greek art began to destroy the native style, even when the motifs reproduced remained traditional. In the Altai foreign influences were resisted. The massive monsters of the Middle East took on a slender shape, a springing step, and a more vivacious air. Among the Altaic finds of foreign provenance, there exist a large carpet, decorated with a procession of horsemen and deer, and a textile embroidered with feminine figures, both of which are Achaemenid in origin. A felt decoration for a tent depicting swans and another embroidered with the phoenix and flowers are Chinese in character.

Fewer distortions appear in Sarmatian art from Russia and Siberia than in the styles discussed above; even the monsters have a more natural appearance. Animal fights are commoner and more dramatic, and the supple undulating outlines are reminiscent of Altaic art. Plant decoration, treated in a summary but effective way, appears for the first time.

In the Far East, standard heads and bronze plaques sometimes present rather clumsy versions of Scythian and Sarmatian styles. Others are strongly marked by Chinese influence and some archaeologists include the earliest examples in the style of the Warring States period. Throughout the whole region, Chinese influence of the Han period was pervasive.

It is difficult to appreciate the spirit that informed Steppes art at its inception. With the exception of a few domestic scenes, the Steppes artist seems to have turned from depicting everyday life to follow a symbolic treatment. It has been suggested that zoomorphic art grew out of totemism, which was the basis of tribal organization well before they began a nomadic way of life. It is possible that the zoomorphic style was a survival of a prenomadic era and was connected with a hunting economy. If this is true, the image of the animal that was the ancestor and protector of the tribe would have evolved until it had become for the nomads the supernatural guide of the shamans and souls of the dead. Inadequate knowledge prevents us from reaching a final decision. One fact, however, is beyond dispute: the importance of the steppes tradition should not be underestimated, for it transmitted to the European Middle Ages a sense of asymmetry, a dynamic disequilibrium, and the interplay of forms that is commonly called "barbarian."

STEVENS, Alfred (1817, Blandford, Dorset—1875, London), English painter and sculptor. He received no formal art training in England, and in 1833 went to Italy, where he remained for nine years, working and studying in Naples, Rome, Florence, Milan, and Venice. Stevens went to London, where he obtained a teaching post at the School of Design (1845–47). He devoted much of his time to the conception and execution of decorative designs, and was the chief artist for a Sheffield firm that specialized in bronze and metalwork. In 1856 Stevens entered the competition for the memorial to the Duke of Wellington that was to be erected in St. Paul's Cathedral, London, and he spent the last 19 years of his life attempting to complete the monument in the face of hostility, official indifference, and lack of funds. The *Wellington Monument* (1856–75)—his most important work—has been justly described as the last monument in the Renaissance tradition, a description that also underlines Stevens' fundamental lack of originality. He remains, nevertheless, the most important English sculptor of the 2nd half of the 19th century. Stevens was also an extremely competent painter, and it is unfortunate that he destroyed a large number of his own canvases. His finest extant paintings are the portraits of *Mrs. Young Mitchell and Her Baby, Mary* (1851), *Mrs. Mary Ann Collman* (1854), and *King Alfred and His Mother* (*c.* 1848), all in London's Tate Gallery.

STIEGLITZ, Alfred (1864, Hoboken, New Jersey—1946, New York), American photographer, art dealer, and theorist. He was one of the first to maintain the independent artistic status and potential of the photograph as distinct from painting and sculpture; but he was also a pioneer in these latter fields, opening a succession of galleries in New York that championed modern art in America. With the help of his friend and photographic colleague Edward Steichen, who was on the Continent shortly after 1900, Stieglitz provided the sole outlet for American expatriates serving their modernist apprenticeships in Europe and European innovators of the new styles. After he returned to America in 1890, Stieglitz was a vital patron and uncompromising moral supporter of many American artists. The sales and exhibitions at his various galleries, in

Alfred Stevens. *Mary Ann, wife of Leonard Collman.* *c.* 1854. Tate Gallery, London.

addition to such publications as *291* and *Camera Work* (1902–17), helped maintain and publicize the painters Sheeler and Hartley, as well as the writings of Gertrude Stein, and such critics as Sadakichi Hartmann and Marius de Zayas. Stieglitz understood the modern artist's disenfranchized position, and his belief in art-for-art's sake did sustain many artists who had to face an unsympathetic public and a hostile critical press. His own contribution to the history of photography was vital (*The Terminal*, 1893; Rochester, N.Y., George Eastman House). An exponent of straightforward pictorial expression, Stieglitz supported and printed the work of Paul Strand, Sheeler, and Steichen in the pages of *Camera Notes*, *291*, and *Camera Work* (noted for the high quality of its reproductions).

In New York Stieglitz ran the Photo-Secession or "291" Gallery (1905–17), showing Paul Cézanne, Rodin's drawings, Picasso, and Brancusi, as well as the Americans Oscar Bluemner, his future wife Georgia O'Keeffe, Sheeler, Dove, Hartley, Gaston Lachaise, and Elie Nadelman (1882–1946). At the Intimate Gallery housed in the Anderson Galleries (1925–29) and later at the American Place (1929–34), he continued to show radical examples of modern art.

STIJL, De. In October 1917, the first number of the Dutch review *De Stijl* ("Style") appeared at Leiden. Its foundation was the outcome of the meeting between Piet Mondrian and Theo van Doesburg. A group formed around them that included the painters Bart Anthony van der Leck (b. 1876), Georges Vantongerloo from Antwerp, the Hungarian Vilmos Huszar (1884–1960), and the Italian Gino Severini; the architects J. J. P. Oud, Robert van't Hoff (b. 1887), Jan Wils (b. 1891), and shortly afterward, G. T. Rietveld; the poet Antonie Kok, and then, in 1921, the German film maker Hans Richter. With the heritage of Cubism, their familiarity with Futurism and Kandinsky's first abstractions, the group tried to evolve a plastic idiom that would be equally applicable to painting, architecture, and the decorative arts. This was Neoplasticism, whose principles were described by Mondrian and Van Doesburg in the first numbers of the review. The members of the group rejected individualism and all its manifestations, whether Impressionist or Expressionist, stripping forms of all accidentals and all traces of past traditions. This distillation inevitably led to pure geometrical abstraction in which the equilibrium of the work rested on the relationship of horizontals and verticals alone. Color was limited to the three primaries—red, yellow, and blue—used without any mixture or alteration, and to the "non-colors"—black, gray, and white.

Apart from Mondrian's work, which illustrated and transcended the principles of Neoplasticism, their most successful application was in architecture. The basis of their construction was the cube and the parallelepiped, which were alone considered the elementary forms of space. These forms did not in any way limit the Neoplastic architects; each geometric element was inseparable from the whole, and extended into every part of the structure.

Mondrian wrote four essays between 1917 and 1919 on the new aesthetic, which were substantially reprinted in a booklet, *Le Néo-Plasticisme*, which appeared in Paris in 1920. The group, however, soon began to show signs of breaking up. After visiting the Bauhaus, Van Doesburg joined Walter Gropius and Mies van der Rohe; then in 1922 he was attracted to Dada and added a supplement to *De Stijl* called *Mecano*, in which appeared the names of Kurt Schwitters, Jean Arp, Tristan Tzara, Georges Ribemont-Dessaignes, and Man Ray. In the following year an exhibition, "De Stijl Architecture and Painting," was held in Paris, which was the swan song of the movement.

While the Bauhaus took over and popularized some of the ideas of De Stijl, the review was discontinued in 1928. At the same time the painters of the group joined the Cercle et Carré movement, then the Abstraction-Création group in Paris.

De Stijl. Robert van't Hoff. Ter Heide House, Utrecht. 1916. *Photo G. Abstede, Utrecht.*

STILL, Clyfford (b. 1904, Grandin, North Dakota), American painter. He taught at the Washington State College of Pullman (1933–41), and then at the California School of Fine Arts (1946–50), where he exercised an important influence on the development of Abstract Expressionism. He moved to New York in 1950, teaching there at Hunter and Brooklyn colleges. He was prominent among the exhibitors in the "15 Americans" show held at the Museum of Modern Art, New York, in 1952.

In Still's paintings of the late 1940s, where large streaked fields are broken by raw patches of irregular color, there are indirect reminiscences of an earlier Surrealistic mode (*Jamais*, 1944; Venice, Coll. Peggy Guggenheim). Although the pigment is applied thickly, there is no sense of superimposition; the colored areas break in upon one another without becoming locatable in terms of depth (*1948–D*, 1948; New York, Coll. William Rubin). In the 1950s Still continued, in the style he had developed in the previous decade, to fill large canvases with vibrating sheets of color (*Untitled*, 1957; Basel, Kunstmuseum).

STONE, Edward Durell (b. 1902, Fayetville, Arkansas), American architect. Frank Lloyd Wright was impressed by his work on the Mandel House at Mount Kisco, New York, which he built in 1930.

Edward Durell Stone. United States Embassy. New Delhi. 1958.

Nine years later he designed the sober and tasteful Museum of Modern Art in New York, in association with Philip L. Goodwin (1885–1958), one of the earliest buildings in the United States in the International Style. Subsequently, Stone developed a more decorative manner, often using a screen of profilated bricks or tiles in front of a glass façade that functioned as a *brise-soleil* in tropical countries. Its finest expression came in the American Embassy in New Delhi, India (1958). In 1958 he was commissioned to design the immense, circular American pavilion for the International Exhibition in Brussels. He returned to his earlier style in the rather mannered Gallery of Modern Art, New York (1962), consisting of a composite tower reminiscent of the white, windowless walls of a mosque, mounted on arched pilotis.

STORRS, John Bradley (1885, Chicago—1956, Mer, France), American sculptor. His art education included studies in Germany (1907–8); at the Chicago Academy of Art and the Pennsylvania Academy of the Fine Arts (1908–10); at the Académie Julian in Paris (1910–12); and with Auguste Rodin (1912–14). Between 1907 and 1928 he traveled extensively in Europe, the Near East, Egypt, Canada, and Mexico; after 1920 he lived primarily in France, but made frequent visits to Chicago until the mid-1930s. In the 1940s he worked almost solely on drawings and a few small paintings, and in the early 1950s returned to figurative sculpture.

From 1914 to 1938 Storrs gained recognition as a leading American abstract sculptor, working mainly in a Cubistic style (*Composition Around Two Voids*, 1932; stainless steel, New York, Whitney Museum). His work includes carved stone and wood sculpture, bronze casts, stainless steel assemblage reliefs, and polychromed terra-cotta pieces in which the colors are used to emphasize the relationships of the planes (*Dancer*, 1922; New Haven, Yale University Art Gallery).

STOSS, Veit (1438/47, Horb, Swabia—1533, Nuremberg), German sculptor. Stoss's name appears in the documents when he surrendered his Nuremberg citizenship and went to Cracow, where from 1477 to 1489 he executed one of his major works, the painted high altar for the church of St. Mary. This monumental work, with its delicate polychromy, owes less to Nuremberg sculpture than to Flemish and Danubian art and perhaps also to the sculpture of Nicolaus Gerhaerts of Leyden. During his stay in Poland, the sculptor also carved the stone tomb of King Casimir Jagiello (1492) in the cathedral on the Wawel in Cracow, and several other tombs, including that of Archbishop Zbigniew Oleśnicki (d. 1493) in the cathedral of Gniezno. Stoss returned to Nuremberg in 1496, and regained his citizenship. In 1499 he carved three stone reliefs of scenes from the Passion: the *Last Supper, Christ on the Mount of Olives*, and the *Arrest of Christ*, which were donated by Paul Volckamer to the church of St. Sebald. One of Stoss's masterpieces is the *Angelic Salutation* (1517–18), placed within a garland of sculptured wood and suspended from the triumphal arch in the church of St. Lorenz in Nuremberg. Several crucifixes date from the last period of his life: one in the church of St. Lorenz, another in the Germanisches Museum, and a third in St. Sebald (*c.* 1500), which is both realistic in its anatomical structure and clear in its basic sculptural form. Another work, perhaps the most important work of his late period, is the Bamberg Altar (1520–23; Bamberg Cathedral), commissioned originally for the Carmelite monastery by his son Andreas, who was then prior of the monastery.

The influence of Veit Stoss on Nuremberg sculpture was considerable. Wood was his favorite material, which he carved with consummate virtuosity. In this medium, Stoss achieved an expressiveness of form that makes him one of the most characteristic and certainly one of the greatest artists of the Late Gothic style in Germany.

STOTHARD, Thomas (1755, London—1834, London), English book illustrator and painter. In 1779 he began his remarkable career as a book illustrator with his pictures for the *Poems of Ossian* and Augustus John Hervey's *Naval History*. He drew his subject matter from a wide variety of sources—including Shakespeare, Pope, Byron, Burns, Spencer, Fielding, Smollett, Richardson, Sterne, Defoe, and Milton—and it is said that over 3,000 of his designs were actually engraved. Stothard's style was slightly academic, revealing the influence of the decorative artists Giovanni Battista Cipriani (1727–85) and Angelica Kauffmann; it is best illustrated in domestic and sentimental scenes, in which the episodes portraying children are particularly successful. His paintings are invariably small and his handling is somewhat sketchy; his colors are often reminiscent of those of Titian, Rubens, and Watteau, artists whom he particularly admired.

Veit Stoss. *Death of the Virgin.* Detail, high altar of St. Mary's Church, Cracow. 1477–89. *Photo Art Institute, Warsaw.*

Thomas Stothard. *Design for the Wellington Shield.* Apsley House, London. *Photo Victoria and Albert Museum, London.*

The *Vintage* (exhibited 1821; London, National Gallery) is probably his most important oil painting. In 1822 he painted the cupola of the upper hall of the Advocates' Library in Edinburgh, and in 1814 he won the competition for the design of the *Wellington Shield* (London, Apsley House, Wellington Museum), which was presented to the Duke of Wellington by the merchants and bankers of London.

STRICKLAND, William (1788, Navesink, New Jersey—1854, Nashville, Tennessee), American Greek Revival architect. His first important building, the Masonic Hall in Philadelphia (1810; destroyed 1819), was a large but awkward mixture of Gothic and Federal forms. In 1818, he won the competition for the Second Bank of the United States in Philadelphia. This building, with its great porticoes and its brilliantly conceived plan, proved that buildings of Greek inspiration could effectively answer modern needs. The bulk of his work for the next 25 years was in the Philadelphia area: the United States Naval Home (1826), the First Unitarian Church (1828), the United States Mint (1829), and the Merchants' Exchange (1834). He also built the Athenaeum at Providence, Rhode Island (1836) and the mints in Charlotte, North Carolina (1835), and New Orleans (1835–36). Most of this work is in the Greek style, although he did occasionally venture into Gothic (St. Stephen's, Philadelphia; 1822) and Egyptian (Laurel Hill Cemetery project, *c.* 1835) modes. Engineer as well as architect, Strickland built breakwaters and bridges, and in 1825 was sent to England to study railroads and canals. In 1844 he went to Nashville to build the state capitol, and while there designed the monumental First Presbyterian Church (1848–51) in the Egyptian style.

STRINDBERG, August (1849, Stockholm—1912, Stockholm), Swedish writer and painter. Although he left a large body of works, his painting was nevertheless a marginal activity beside his drama and novels. Impressionism came to him as a revelation when he visited Paris in 1871 (*Strandparti*, 1873; Stockholm, Coll. Fru Elsa Ahgren), but his style, in which Romantic vehemence is combined with a hallucinatory Expressionism and visionary power, was not derived from any school. In the passionate landscapes that he himself called "symbolist," in which man-made structures and natural phenomena merge ambiguously into an imaginary reality, a distant light is captured in somber, tormented impastos (*Flying Dutchman*, 1892, Copenhagen, Statens Museum for Kunst; *Staden, c.* 1900, Stockholm, Coll. Gustaf Jonsson). This art of the fortuitous, depending on the ambivalence of form, is closely connected with the fundamental equivocation of Strindberg's great plays, where, as he said himself, action, setting, and actors "divide, multiply . . . and volatize into the superior consciousness that dominates them all, that of the dreamer."

STUART, Gilbert Charles (1755, North Kingstown, Rhode Island—1828, Boston), American painter. His first teacher was Cosmo Alexander (active 1763–1770s), who took the youth to his native Scotland in 1772. When Stuart returned home the following year, he was apparently unaffected by European art and began painting portraits in the somewhat stylized Colonial manner, placing his subjects in unpretentious settings. At the outbreak of the American Revolution in 1775, he went to London. From 1777 to 1782 he was a pupil in the London studio of the American history painter Benjamin West. Stuart remained in London until 1787, then went to Dublin, and in 1793 returned to America to set up a studio in New York. Thereafter he maintained studios in Philadelphia (1794–96), Washington, D.C. (1803–5), and finally Boston (1805–28).

In England Stuart's unadorned style underwent a change as the result of his admiration for the facile brushwork and richly impasted surfaces of the great Baroque portraitists of the day—Gainsborough, Reynolds, Hoppner, Ramsay, and Romney. Stuart's mature style of portraiture captures a quality of lifelike immediacy that was achieved by engaging his sitters in animated conversation as he painted them. The reserved George Washington was an especially difficult subject, and Stuart labored over three versions of his portrait: the full-length Lansdowne type, commissioned by the Marquis of Lansdowne (1796; Philadelphia, Pennsylvania Academy of the Fine Arts); the half-length Vaughan type, probably bought by the English merchant Samuel Vaughan (1795; original lost); and the Atheneum Head, commissioned by Martha Washington (1796; Boston, Museum of Fine Arts).

Many of his renderings of lesser-known figures (*Ann Penn Allen, c.* 1795, and *Mrs. Joseph Anthony, c.* 1798; both New York, Metropolitan Museum), with their delicate images, are probably more worthy of recognition.

STUBBINS, Hugh Asher (b. 1912, Birmingham, Alabama), American architect and teacher. Stubbins worked for Royal Barry Wills (1895–1962) and the firm of Miller, Martin, and Lewis. He formed a brief partnership (1937–39) with Marc Peter in Boston, then accepted an offer from Walter Gropius to teach architectural design at Harvard University (1940–52), and eventually became department chairman (1953). He returned to his own practice, Hugh Stubbins and Associates (organized 1940), in 1954.

Stubbins' early houses in Concord, Brockton, and Hingham expressed in native New England wood and fieldstone construction the clear, straightforward design approach taught by Gropius and Marcel Breuer at Harvard. His buildings maintain a quiet unity and personal scale, even the later and larger commissions often executed in brick and poured-in-place concrete, such as the Senior

Residences for Dana Hall School in Wellesley, Massachusetts (1963–65) and the Bowdoin College Senior Center in Brunswick, Maine (1965–66). In contrast, the sweeping arches of the Berlin Congress Hall (1957) create a dramatic, active gesture appropriate to its function as a public exhibition, theater, and convention hall.

Architecture, Stubbins stressed, must be integrated with the total environment. He followed this philosophy at Princeton University by harmonizing his new Dormitory Quadrangle (completed 1964) with the Gothic Revival buildings around it through irregular massing and broken silhouettes. At Harvard the powerful Countway Library of Medicine (completed 1963) works well with the monumental Neoclassical Medical School buildings nearby.

STUBBS, George (1724, Liverpool—1806, London), English animal painter. He is recorded as painting portraits in several northern cities—Wigan (1744), Leeds, York (1746–52), Hull, and Liverpool—but it seems clear that he undertook this work solely in order to support himself while he pursued his favorite study, that of anatomy. In 1746 Stubbs gave private lectures on human anatomy to the pupils at York Hospital. With masterly clarity, he drew and etched a human embryo for a book on midwifery by Dr. Burton of York, published in 1751. His masterpiece, the *Anatomy of the Horse* (published 1766), on which he worked for four years (1756–60) in a farmhouse in Horkstow, Lincolnshire, is a great work of natural science and one that won him a European reputation.

In 1754 Stubbs went to Rome, to prove to himself that "nature is superior to art." He returned to England via Ceuta, where he is said to have seen a lion attack a horse, an incident that greatly impressed him and that bore fruit in one of his most celebrated pictures, *Horse Frightened by a Lion* (1770; Liverpool, Walker Art Gallery). After his arrival in London in 1760, Stubbs exhibited with the Society of Arts (1761–74), rising to the rank of president in 1773. His exhibits consisted entirely of equestrian portraits, race horses, and hunters, and sporting conversation pieces, such as *Molly Longlegs with a Jockey* (1762; Walker Art Gallery). He became an Associate of the Royal Academy in 1774 and a full Academician in 1775. In the 1790s Stubbs, who enjoyed the favor of the Prince of Wales, painted one of his most exquisite pictures: the *Prince of Wales' Phaeton* (1793; Windsor Castle, Royal Collection). In 1802 he began another great anatomical study, a *Comparative Exposition of the Structure of the Human Body with that of a Tiger and Common Fowls*, which was left unfinished at his death.

Stubbs is unique in English art, indeed in European art, in that he approached the business of painting as a scientist, with a complete lack of emotional or intellectual preconceptions. He was primarily an anatomist and a recorder of a narrow range of facts about the physical world. Nothing moves in his calm, airless pictures: even his racehorses are demonstrations of the mechanics of movement rather than illustrations of the act itself, yet these literal recordings occasionally achieve great beauty. His independence and integrity of vision place him on a par with William Hogarth and Joseph Wright of Derby rather than with the long train of animal painters among whom his name is often found.

George Stubbs. *Mares and Foals.* Tate Gallery, London.

SUGARMAN, George (b. 1912, New York), American sculptor. In 1955–56 Sugarman studied in Paris at the Zadkine School of Sculpture; and after 1960 he taught at Hunter College, New York. His sculpture from the late 1950s and early 1960s included small wood pieces suggesting abstracted figural presences and larger, polychromed piled-up Cubistic constructions (*Criss-Cross*, 1963; laminated and polychromed wood, New York, Stephen Radich Gallery). In the following years the development of his sculpture shows an increasing preoccupation with form and space. This interest became distinctly and successfully defined in Sugarman's creation of sculptural groups of physically separate pieces that are loosely disposed in an extended space and in his use of bold color, which he considered fundamentally important to his sculpture, both for its emotional impact and for its ability to articulate the form in space (*Two in One*, 1966, polychromed wood, and *Two Fold*, 1968, polychromed wood; both New York, Fischbach Gallery).

SULLIVAN, Louis Henry (1856, Boston—1924, Chicago), leading American architect of the Chicago School. From the historical point of view, Sullivan's work lies between that of H. H. Richardson, who inspired Sullivan through his free and highly original interpretations of Romanesque forms, and that of his pupil Frank Lloyd Wright. After studying at the Massachusetts Institute of Technology (1870–73), Sullivan worked for a year in William Le Baron Jenney's office, then traveled to Europe. He settled in Chicago when he returned to the United States, entered the firm of Dankmar Adler, and became a partner in 1881. His theoretical observations on architecture are contained in two books written in solitude and obscurity during the latter part of his life: *Kindergarten Chats* (1901) and *Autobiography of an Idea* (1922).

The Adler and Sullivan partnership lasted until 1895. To this period belong the Auditorium Building in Chicago (1886–89); the Wainwright Building in St. Louis (1890–91), the first steel-

Louis Henry Sullivan and Dankmar Adler. Wainwright Building, St. Louis, Missouri. 1890–91.

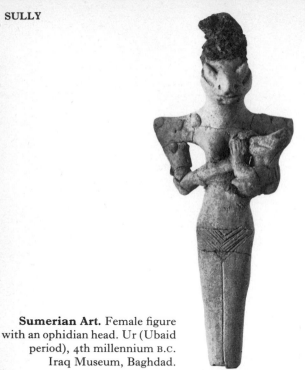

Sumerian Art. Female figure with an ophidian head. Ur (Ubaid period), 4th millennium B.C. Iraq Museum, Baghdad.

framed skyscraper built by the firm; the Schiller Building in Chicago (1892), a tower block built on a U-shaped plan; the Guarantee Building in Buffalo (1894–95); and the Prudential Building in Buffalo (1895). The separation between the two partners coincided with the crisis of progressive architecture at the World's Columbian Exposition in 1893 at Chicago, when a return to a heavy-handed Classical style gained dominance. Sullivan only designed two more Chicago buildings after this: the Gage Building (1898) and the Carson Pirie Scott Department Store (1899–1904), whose horizontal emphasis was unusual in his style of architecture.

Sullivan's work, which was especially concerned with commercial architecture, presents two very different aesthetic aspects. On the one hand he contributed to the development of the office block as a separate category of building through his constant search for the formal expression of function. But this designer of simple, logical structures also had a taste for elaborate decoration, and developed a highly original and beautiful system of ornament to which he attached great importance as an expression of artistic personality. This ornament was employed most effectively in the gilt decoration of the Auditorium and on the spandrels of the Wainwright Building.

SULLY, Thomas (1783, Horncastle, Lincolnshire—1872, Philadelphia), English-born American painter. He came to America in 1792 with his parents, who were in the theater. In 1798 Sully was in Philadelphia, where he set up a studio. On a trip to England (1809) he met Benjamin West and was strongly influenced by Sir Thomas Lawrence. Sully returned to Philadelphia in 1810, and established the most famous and productive portrait studio in the nation. His portrait of *Samuel Coates* (1812; Philadelphia, Pennsylvania Hospital) is typical of his early style, having a greater solidity of form and more intense interest in the light and atmosphere surrounding the figure than his later, more spontaneous manner. From the 1820s until his death, Sully was the most popular portraitist in America, carrying on the role formerly played by Stuart. He portrayed nearly every president from Washington through Lincoln (*George Washington Wearing the Order of the Cincinnati*, 1840; New York, Metropolitan Museum) as well as Benjamin Franklin, Daniel Boone, Edgar Allan Poe, Washington Irving, and other notable Americans. Typical of his mature manner is the full-length portrait of *Queen Victoria* (1839; Philadelphia, Society of the Sons of St. George), which captures the rather elegant, reflective, and romantic quality of the young queen. Sully's late works tend to be slightly weak in structure, but the bravura and accomplishment of technique redeem even the most quickly executed of his more than 2,500 paintings.

SUMERIAN ART. Sumer is the name given to the region in the Lower Mesopotamian Valley that produced one of the most brilliant civilizations in the ancient Middle East, from the end of the 4th millennium to the beginning of the 2nd millennium B.C. Although the point is still disputed, some scholars believe that the Sumerians, who were non-Semitic in race and language, arrived in the region about 3200 B.C., while others date their arrival at *c.* 4000 B.C. or even earlier. The first signs of artistic activity were discovered at Jarmo, in the form of terra-cotta figurines of animals and especially images of what was obviously a prototype of the mother-goddess. This beginning can probably be dated to the early 5th millennium.

Sumerian Art. Tablet with pictograms. Jemdet Nasr. *c.* 3000 B.C.

Sumerian protohistory is divided into several phases named after the sites where they appeared for the first time. The earliest culture in northern Mesopotamia is named after Hassuna, whose inhabitants were already making decorated pottery. The decoration was nonfigurative, and either painted or incised, or sometimes both. The Samarra period, named after Samarra on the Tigris river, was evidently more advanced not only technically but also artistically. The Hassuna was succeeded by the Halaf culture, from Tell Halaf in Syria, during which it is possible that the Al Ubaid people migrated from southwest Persia to southern Mesopotamia. The Halaf culture produced figurines of a type of mother-goddess with exaggerated forms and heavy breasts. The Al Ubaid culture, which replaced the Halaf, produced figurines of mother-goddesses that were more slender and delicate, and quite different from earlier examples. Masculine figures with more or less simplified contours, and made of terra cotta, were also manufactured.

Mesopotamia enjoyed a burst of surprising creativity in the second half of the 4th millennium B.C., during the Warka (Uruk) and Jemdet Nasr periods. Architecture, sculpture, stone vessels, and glyptics all point to a prodigious activity covering every aspect of life. Writing was invented: pictographic at first, then linear, and finally cuneiform, bringing to an end the protohistoric period. At this time the typical Sumerian political unit was developed: the city state, along with which appeared the earliest ziggurats.

It is usual to distinguish two periods in Sumerian art and civilization: the Early Dynastic or pre-Sargonic, so called because it preceded and ended with the advent of Sargon of Akkad; and the

263.

264.

265.

263. **Veit Stoss.** *Head of St. Peter.* Detail from the high altar. 1477–89. St. Mary's Church, Cracow.
264. **Nicolas de Staël.** *Little Footballers.* 1952. Private Coll.
265. **Gilbert Stuart.** *Mrs. Richard Yates.* 1793. National Gallery of Art, Washington, D.C.
266. **Frank Stella.** *Ifafa II.* 1964. Coll. Mr. and Mrs. Robert C. Scull, New York. Photo Castelli Gallery, New York.
267. **Chaim Soutine.** *Portrait of Maria Lani. c.* 1929. Museum of Modern Art, New York.
268. **Sir Matthew Smith.** *Apples in a Plate.* 1919. Tate Gallery, London.

266.

267.

268.

269.

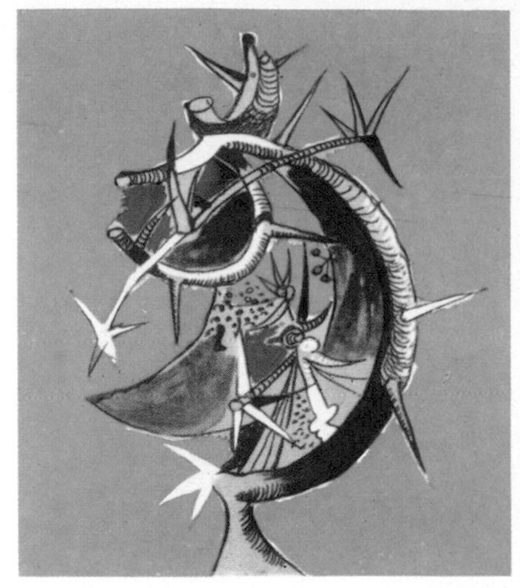

270.

271.

272.

269. **George Stubbs.** *Couple in a Phaeton.* 1787. National Gallery, London.

270. **Graham Sutherland.** *Head of Thorns.* 1946. Private Coll., New York.

271. **Giandomenico Tiepolo.** *Peasants Resting.* 1757. Villa Valmarana, near Vicenza.

272. **Hendrick Terbrugghen.** *Flute Player.* 1621. Gemäldegalerie, Kassel.

273. **Dorothea Tanning.** *A Strict Intimacy.* 1965. Galerie "Le Point Cardinal," Paris.

274. **Gerard Terborch.** *Woman Writing.* c. 1665. Mauritshuis, The Hague.

275. Opposite: **J. M. W. Turner.** *The 'Fighting Téméraire' tugged to her last berth to be broken up.* Detail. 1838. National Gallery, London.

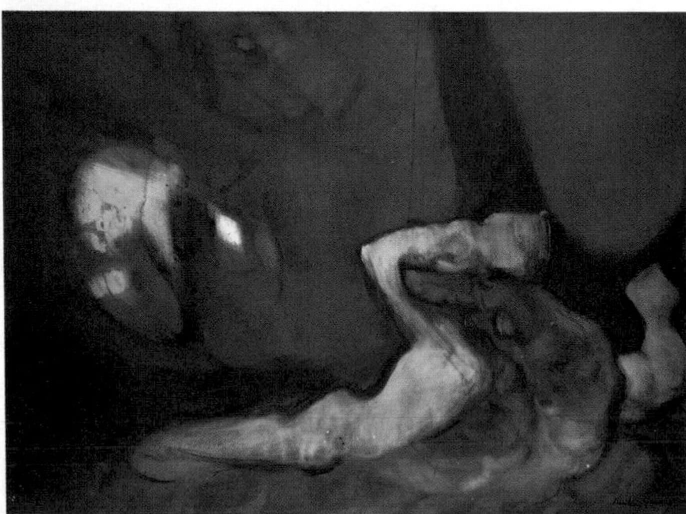

273.

274.

276.

277.

278.

279.

276. **Tintoretto.** *Christ Washing the Disciples' Feet. c.* 1550. Prado, Madrid.
277. **Titian.** *Venus and Adonis.* Detail. *c.* 1554. Metropolitan Museum of Art, New York.
278. **Bradley Walker Tomlin.** *Number 20.* 1949. Museum of Modern Art, New York.
279. **Cosimo Tura.** *Portrait of a Member of the Este Family. c.* 1451. Metropolitan Museum of Art, New York.
280. **Henri de Toulouse-Lautrec.** *Dance at the Moulin Rouge.* 1890. Coll. Henry P. MacIlhenny, Philadelphia.
281. **Maurice Utrillo.** *Moulin de la Galette.* Private Coll., Paris.
282. Opposite: **Paolo Uccello.** *St. George and the Dragon.* Detail. *c.* 1440. National Gallery, London.

280.

281.

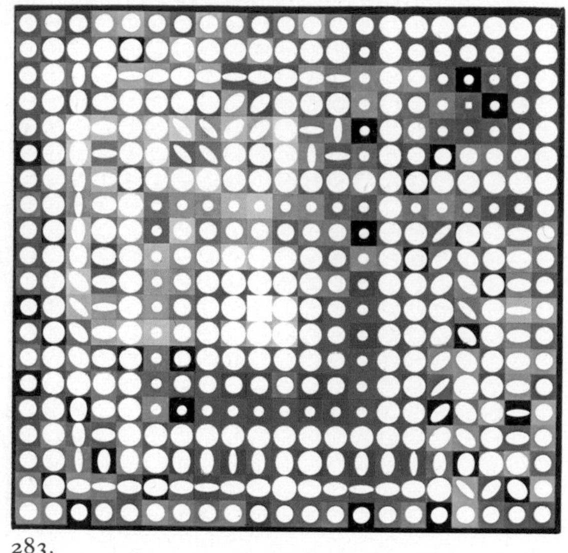

283.

284.

285.

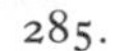

286.

287.

288.

283. **Victor Vasarely.** *Orion.* 1961. Photo Galerie René, Paris.

284. **Diego de Velázquez.** *Infanta Margareta Teresa. c.* 1660. Prado, Madrid.

285. **Jan Vermeer.** *The Lace Maker. c.* 1664. Louvre, Paris.

286. **Paolo Veronese.** *Feast in the House of Levi.* 1573. Accademia, Venice.

287. **Willem van de Velde the Younger.** *Cannon Shot. c.* 1660. Rijksmuseum, Amsterdam.

288. **Jacques Villon.** *Seated Woman.* 1914. Photo Galerie Carré, Paris.

289.

290.

289. **Édouard Vuillard.** *Annette's Supper*. 1900. Musée de l'Annonciade, St-Tropez.
290. **Maurice de Vlaminck.** *The Painter's House at Valmondois, or the Clapboard House*. 1920. Musée National d'Art Moderne, Paris.
291. **Andrea del Verrocchio.** *Madonna and Child*. Metropolitan Museum of Art, New York.
292. **Rogier van der Weyden.** *Virgin and St. John. Christ Crucified*. c. 1455–59? Johnson Coll., Philadelphia Museum of Art.
293. **Edward Alexander Wadsworth.** *Signals*. 1942. Tate Gallery, London.
294. **Antoine Watteau.** *Meeting for the Hunt*. c. 1720. Wallace Coll., London.
295. **James McNeil Whistler.** *Portrait of Mrs. Leyland*. 1872–3. Frick Coll., New York.

291.

292.

295.

293.

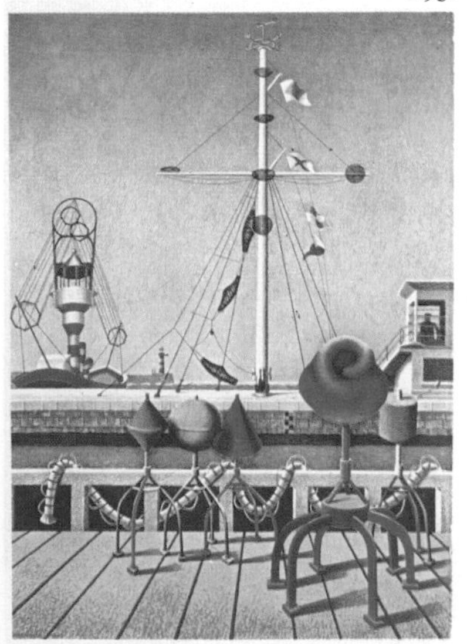

294.

296.

297.

298.

299.

301.

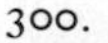

300.

296. **Richard Wilson.** *Cader Idris. c.* 1774. National Gallery, London.
297. **Konrad Witz.** *Crucifixion.* Before 1435. Staatliche Museen, Berlin-Dahlem.
298. **Grant Wood.** *American Gothic.* 1930. Art Institute of Chicago.
299. **Andrew Wyeth.** *Christina's World.* 1949. Museum of Modern Art, New York.
300. **John Xceron.** *Radiant.* 1945.
301. **Francisco de Zurbarán.** *St. Marina.* Museo Provincial de Bellas Artes, Seville.

Neo-Sumerian, which designates the period following the Akkadian interlude and the Guti period, after which the Sumerians returned in force and resumed power and control over Lower Mesopotamia. They remained in the region until the 21st century B.C., when they finally disappeared under the attacks of the Babylonian Amorites.

Pre-Sargonic Sumerian art, particularly when it originated in the southern part of the country, is austere and powerful. All of their statuary was created expressly for religious purposes. Ten figures found at Tell Asmar (beginning of the 3rd millennium B.C.; Baghdad, Iraq Museum) are among the most important examples to survive from the pre-Sargonic or Early Dynastic period. Of the ten, two are cult statues, differentiated from the remaining figures of worshipers by their greater height and by the large, deeply cut pupils of their eyes (possibly to hold inset stones). The two deities, one male and one female, have been identified as Abu, Lord of Vegetation, and the mother goddess, in the base of whose statue can be seen a tiny figure representing her child (only the feet and lower legs remain). Their bodies are depicted in rigid conical forms (except for the goddess, whose body is more cylindrical), their shoulders and arms forming rectangles that extend to the waist, where the arms bend inward, hands clasped—or grasping a bowl—over the chest or abdomen.

A beautiful head carved in marble, dated to the beginning of the 3rd millennium (Iraq Museum) and found in Uruk, reveals the high degree of sensitivity achieved by the Sumerian sculptors. Most striking is the deeply arched groove suggesting the eyebrows and the sockets for the eyes, again perhaps to hold inset stones. Sumerian sculptors showed their concern for clarity by dividing their relief compositions, whether religious or historical, into registers. An example is the 26th-century B.C. stele, called the *Stele of the Vultures* (Paris, Louvre), commemorating the victory of Eannatum, king of Lagash, over the hostile city of Umma. The chronology of the story is strictly observed, and from top to bottom two phases of the combat can be seen, the funerals of the friendly soldiers and the counting of prisoners. It was in provinces that were penetrated by Sumerian culture but inhabited by a people who were predominantly Semitic that sculpture became noticeably gentler in character, as can be seen in such examples as the smiling faces from Khafaje, Agrab, and particularly Mari (*The Steward Ebihil*, 1st half of the 3rd millennium B.C., Louvre; *Ur-Nina the Great Musician*, 1st half of the 3rd millennium, Damascus, National Museum).

Along with their remarkably original sculptures, the Sumerians developed an architecture that had a great influence on later Mesopotamian civilizations. The ziggurat became the dominant form of religious structure and continued to be used by successive peoples long after the Sumerians had vanished, appearing in Babylon and the Assyrian capitals. In their underground tombs, the Sumerians employed the corbeled vault, which, however, they did not use in their religious or domestic buildings (they did use the arch over the doorways of their houses). The Sumerian temple complexes contained a court, as in the temple at Khafaje, and at times a monumental entrance with two flanking towers. Since there was no stone for building, all of these massive structures were constructed of mud bricks.

No survey of pre-Sargonic Sumerian art is complete without mention of the splendid metal art objects and inlay work from the so-called royal tombs of Ur. The gold helmet from Meskalamdug, a dagger with a filigree sheath, the adornments of Queen Shubad of Ur, the figure of a ram caught in a bush (made of gold, lapis lazuli, and silver; 1st half of 3rd millennium B.C., London, British Museum), figures from the necks of harps, and the so-called Standards from Ur and Mari are among the most remarkable of Sumerian artifacts. The Standard of Ur (1st half of 3rd millennium B.C.; British Museum), whose purpose is not yet known, is made up of two inward slanting panels. The trapezoidal-shaped sides are decorated with mythological figures and the panels themselves contain representations of a military victory and the celebration that followed. One of the most interesting examples of Sumerian inlay work is found on the Philadelphia harp sound box (1st half of 3rd millennium B.C.; University Museum).

Sumerian Art. Head of a Woman. Uruk, Early 3rd millennium B.C. Iraq Museum, Baghdad.

Sumerian Art. Goddess, one of ten figures found at Tell Asmar. Early 3rd millennium B.C. Iraq Museum, Baghdad.

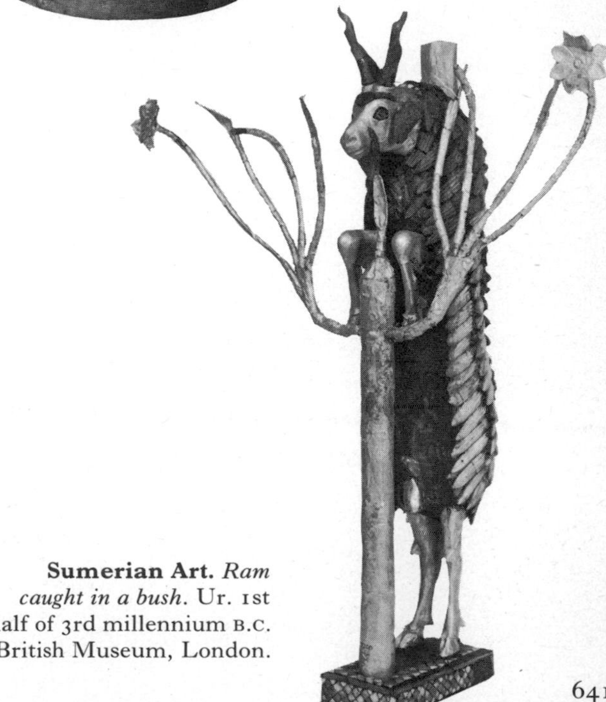

Sumerian Art. *Ram caught in a bush.* Ur. 1st half of 3rd millennium B.C. British Museum, London.

Sumerian Art. Sound box of a harp. Ur. 1st half of 3rd millennium B.C. University Museum, Philadelphia.

The top register shows a hero with two rampant figures of human-headed bulls; the second and third registers contain scenes of a banquet, in which animals both serve and are served, while an ass plays the harp. In the lower register are represented a gazelle and a "scorpion man," mentioned in the *Epic of Gilgamesh* (the great Mesopotamian epic based upon Sumerian sources, and possibly dealing with legends surrounding a Sumerian king of Uruk who ruled during the first half of the 3rd millennium). No satisfactory interpretation of these scenes has as yet been given.

After the Akkad period and the domination of the Guti, the Sumerians resumed power in their former territory. The Neo-Sumerian period began with the primacy of Uruk, followed by the third dynasty of Ur, with kings such as Urnammu, who brought about an exceedingly brilliant civilization and art. The city of Lagash (modern Tello) became an extraordinary art center as a result of the activities of its ruler Gudea. Although he had no royal title, this priest-king commissioned sculptors to make about 30 statues of him; notable among these are the *Turbaned Head of Gudea* (22nd century B.C.; Paris, Louvre), the *Statue of Gudea* (British Museum), *Gudea as a Builder* (Louvre), and a representation of his wife, known as the *Woman with a Scarf*, and their son Ur-Ningirsu (head in the Louvre; body in New York, Metropolitan Museum). Power, simplicity, realism and volume are the qualities of these works.

The work of the painters and architects was an equally valuable aspect of Neo-Sumerian culture: the mural paintings at Mari, the temples, palaces (the one at Mari covered about 5 acres), and the ziggurats, such as the great Ziggurat of Ur (22nd–21st century B.C.). This magnificent building represents perhaps the final development of the ziggurat form made by the Sumerians. As reconstructed by Leonard Woolley, this structure consisted of a huge rectangular platform, upon which six smaller platforms were built, at the top of which was the shrine (to the moon god), rebuilt, according to ancient sources, in glazed blue brick by Nebuchadnezzar. Three imposing flights of stairs led to the first stage, while the remaining stages were reached by staircases flanking the walls. About 2015 B.C., the Sumerian power began to crumble before the Elamites and the Amorites, who settled in Babylon (their most famous king was Hammurabi, 1790–1750 B.C.). Afterward nothing remained of the Sumerians except their speech, which survived as a sacred language, their literature, and their magnificent art.

Neo-Sumerian Art. Ziggurat of the IIIrd dynasty of Ur. 22nd–21st century B.C. *Reconstructed by Leonard Woolley.*

Neo-Sumerian Art. *Turbaned head of Gudea.* Tello. 22nd century B.C. Louvre, Paris.

SUPREMATISM, name given by the Russian painter Kasimir Malevich to the style of geometric abstraction he derived from Cubism in about 1913. The formal elements of the Suprematist style were the rectangle, the circle, the triangle, and the cross. Although the first public appearance of the movement's work took place in 1913, when Malevich exhibited his perfect square (black on a white background), its manifesto was not published until 1915 (*From Cubism to Suprematism*, St. Petersburg). Almost simultaneously Vladimir Tatlin originated the Constructivist movement, and Alexander Rodchenko formulated the principles of Nonobjectivism, both closely related to Suprematism. However, it was chiefly through the activity of the painter, draftsman, and graphic designer El Lissitzky that Constructivist and Suprematist ideas were introduced in 1922 into Germany where, in Bauhaus circles, they encountered the Neoplastic current brought from Holland by Theo van Doesburg during the same period. While Neoplasticism has more deeply affected the art of our time, it is Malevich to whom credit must be given for having gone farthest in the shortest time, by leaping from Cubism to Suprematism in the space of a few months and starting anew on an entirely different and quite simple basis (*Suprematist Composition, White on White, c.* 1918; New York, Museum of Modern Art).

SURREALISM. Its international ramifications, duration, high ideals, and the caliber of the artists to whom the term is ascribed have made Surrealism one of the most important movements of the first half of the 20th century. Surrealism attempted to establish a way of life and a conception of the world that its painters, sculptors, writers, and film makers explored from a common point of view. Growing out of the earlier Dada movement, it transformed the latter's negative attitudes into constructive action. As Dadaists, the leaders of Surrealism had battled for what they called "artistic free-thinking." By the end of 1922, however, the force of Dada was declining; its members, grouped around the review *Littérature* (founded in 1919), dreamed of throwing life itself—meaning the world of secret desires that issue spontaneously from the unconscious—in the face of academicism. They were fascinated by abnormal mental states and with the theories of psychoanalysis and metaphysics. It was during this "period of sleep" that the first attempts at automatic writing were made. The Surrealist adventure had begun.

The official date of its birth was 1924, the year that Breton published the *Manifeste du Surréalisme* and that the first number of *La Révolution Surréaliste* appeared with the inscription: "We must formulate a new *Declaration of the Rights of Man.*" Surrealism preserved Dada's destructive attitudes and attacked the human world as a whole, especially its criteria of coherence. The concept of a reality knowable through evidence, reason, and logical structure was, according to the Surrealists, nothing but a crude enticement that should be avoided. In exchange they offered not a vague, unrealistic idealism, but a concrete sense of a superior, absolute, and fabulous reality. This "surreality" depended less on nature than on the human imagination that interpreted it. When he was developing these ideas, Breton exhorted poets and artists to create a modern supernatural world in which chance and their instinctive impulses would be essential elements. Hence his now classic definition: "*Surrealism*, n. Pure psychic automatism through which the real functioning of thought may be expressed either verbally, or in writing, or in any other manner. Dictation of thought completely uncontrolled by reason and independent of all aesthetic or moral preoccupation." There was not a single Surrealist painter who would not have countersigned De Chirico's resounding declaration: "It should never be forgotten that a painting should always reflect a profound feeling and that profound means strange and that strange means hardly known or completely unknown." De Chirico's porticoes, ghosts, dummies, and metaphysical interiors, painted between 1910 and 1917, offered a model of oneiric art to the Surrealists. But the first of the Surrealist painters was undoubtedly Max Ernst, whose *Reunion of Friends* (1922; Hamburg, Priv. Coll.) portrayed the Surrealist group when it was first formed, and whose collage of *Two Children Threatened by a Nightingale* (1924; New York, Museum of Modern Art) was the pictorial equivalent of a manifesto. André Masson's *Trees* (1923; Paris, Priv. Coll.) indicated his allegiance to the new attitude. In 1924 Miró joined the Surrealist movement with his *Ploughed Land* and *Harlequin's Carnival* (Buffalo, Albright-Knox Art Gallery), adding the mischievous spirit of his exuberant and delicious imagination.

In 1925 the first group exhibition of Surrealist painting took place in Paris at the Galerie Pierre. It included works by De Chirico, Paul Klee, Arp, Ernst, Ray, Miró, Picasso, and Pierre Roy. In the same year an "Office of Surrealist Experiments" was founded. The succeeding years saw the opening of a Surrealist gallery in Rue Jacques-Callot, Paris; the invention of *frottage* ("rubbing") by Ernst (*She Keeps Her Secret*, 1925; London, Priv. Coll.; from the *Histoire Naturelle* series, published 1926); Tanguy's early efforts, such as the *Extinction of Useless Lights* (1927; New York, Museum of Modern Art); the inception of the Belgian Surrealist group around René Magritte; and the important publication of Breton's book, *Le Surréalisme et la Peinture* (*Surrealism and Painting*, 1928). Shortly afterward the writer Louis Aragon, in his *La Peinture au défi* (*The Challenge of Painting*, 1930), insisted that the subject of collages, which were considered the most characteristic expression of Surrealist painting, should preferably be scandalous: "The marvelous is always the embodiment of a moral symbol in violent opposition to the morality of the world whence it arises."

In 1929 Surrealist activity became even more intense; as a result of a break with various members of the group, Breton published the *Second Manifeste du Surréalisme*, then began publishing a review, *Le Surréalisme au service de la Révolution* (1930–33). The movement was strengthened by an exceptional recruit in the person of Salvador Dali, coproducer with Luis Buñuel of the films *Un chien andalou* (1929) and *L'Âge d'or* (1930). Dali practiced a "paranoic-critical activity" in his behavior, writings, and paintings, all of which involved the use of hallucinatory phenomena. Even in his youthful paintings (*Lugubrious Game*, 1929, Paris, Priv. Coll.; *Persistence of Memory*, 1931, New York, Museum of Modern Art), Dali introduced a breath of extravagance into the shared Surrealist ideal. Alberto Giacometti joined the movement in 1931 and began his astonishing object-sculptures (*Palace at Four o'Clock in the Morning*, 1932–33; Museum of Modern Art). He was followed by Victor Brauner, who at that time was passing through a phase of social fantasy typified by the *Strange Case of Monsieur K.* (1933; Paris, Priv. Coll.). Other artists swelled the ranks: Hans Bellmer (b. 1902), whose disturbing "dolls" initiated many refined and perverse drawings; Wolfgang Paalen (1907–59), whose activities were intellectual as well as artistic, and who later wrote books on ethnology; Oscar Dominguez (b. 1906), who invented the automatic "decalcomania" process in 1936; and Kurt Seligmann, an enthusiast for the occult sciences. Surrealist groups sprang up in every country from Czechoslovakia to Japan. In 1936 a large exhibition was organized in London by Roland Penrose and the English Surrealists, among whom were David Gascoyne (b. 1916), Humphrey Jennings (b. 1907), Henry Moore, Paul Nash, and Robert Read (b. 1893). In 1937 Breton opened the Galerie Gradiva in Rue de Seine, Paris. The outstanding event was the International Exhibition of Surrealism held in January 1938 at the Galerie des Beaux-Arts in Paris, where the group proved that an exhibition was not simply a question of hanging pictures on a wall, but the creation of a particular imaginative atmosphere. The rooms were lighted by braziers and named with fantasy street signs (such as Rue Faible, Rue aux Lèvres, Rue de la Vieille-Lanterne). Duchamp, who organized the exhibition, had the idea of transforming the main room into a grotto vaulted with 1,200 sacks of coal, with a carpet of dead leaves on the floor and a pool decorated with reeds and lilies in the corner. In 1938, while Breton was on a visit to Mexico, he signed the manifesto *For an Independent Revolutionary Art* with Leon Trotsky and Diego Rivera, and then founded the FIARI (International Federation of Independent Revolutionary Artists),

Surrealism. Max Ernst. *Reunion of Friends*. 1922. Private Coll., Hamburg. *Photo Walter Dräyer, Zurich.*

Surrealism. Alberto Giacometti. *Suspended Ball*. 1930. *Photo Marc Vaux.*

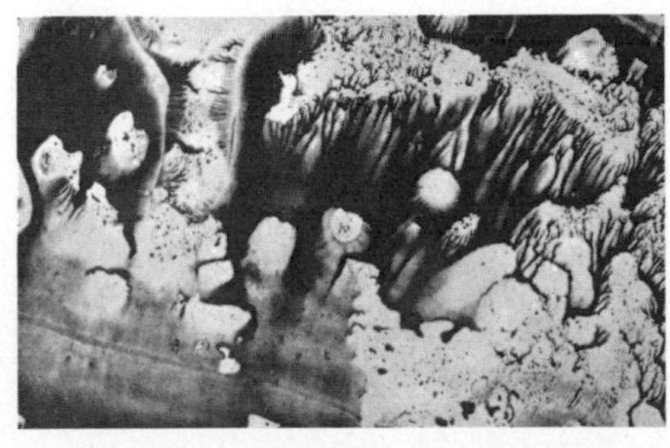

Surrealism. Oscar Dominguez. *Decalcomania without an Object*. Reproduced in the review *Minotaure*. 1936.

whose activities were interrupted by World War II.

In 1941 Breton emigrated to the United States, where he found Masson, Ernst, and Duchamp, and where the "voice of Surrealism" continued to be heard through the review *VVV* (1942–44). The Cuban painter Wifredo Lam produced disquieting impressions of the jungle after he had met Breton; Roberto Matta painted immense canvases whose cosmic spaces seemed inhabited by terrifying extraterrestrial creatures; Arshile Gorky began the experiments that had such an influence on American Abstract Expressionism; the sculptors Alexander Calder and David Hare were also associated with Surrealism. When he returned to Paris in 1946, Breton longed to instill the movement with a fresh vigor. The International Exhibition of Surrealism in 1947 at the Galerie Maeght provided a powerfully symbolic setting with its 21 steps made of book spines, the curtain of rain, and the Room of Superstitions planned by the architect Frederick Kiesler, and containing 12 altars dedicated to mythical beings. Although the activity of the Surrealist group after World War II lacked its former impact, its presence was felt, and the work of the painters and sculptors who had been its first masters won worldwide recognition. Others were discovered and presented to the public when the Compagnie de l'Art Brut, founded in 1947 by Breton, Jean Paulhan (b. 1884), and Jean Dubuffet, collected the productions of the mentally abnormal, including Adolf Wölfli (1864–1930) and the medium Scottie Wilson. Reviews such as *Medium, Le Surréalisme même, Bief*, and *La Brèche*, which succeeded each other, reflected the changing spirit of Surrealism and reported the invention of new games. The third International Exhibition of Surrealism, held in 1959 at the Galerie Daniel Cordier in Paris under the sign of Eros, was an attempt to revive the scandalous spirit of its early days. The last significant enterprise of the movement was the 1965 International Exhibition of Surrealism at the Galerie de l'Oeil in Paris, held under the title of the "Absolute Separation." The year 1966 can be considered the terminal date of Surrealism: it began with the deaths of Giacometti and Brauner and ended with the death of Breton, in whom the movement lost the irreplaceable guarantor of its authenticity.

Surrealism. Pablo Picasso. *Portrait of André Breton.*

SUTHERLAND, Graham (b. 1903, London), English painter. After studying at the Goldsmiths' School of Art, he concentrated on etching and produced landscapes and illustrations of a hallucinatory character. His art then underwent the influence of William Blake and of his disciple Samuel Palmer and of the Surrealists as well. Following a stay he made in the County of Pembroke in 1936, Sutherland's style showed a marked change. From that time on, his vision expanded and his work acquired greater expressiveness. He discovered new forms of life, tinted with hitherto unknown colors. Strange vegetable and mineral forms, insects metamorphosed into totems look out from his canvases on to a mental universe teeming with hidden forces. They take possession of the spectator as their strange message slowly filters into his consciousness. In Sutherland's work, art reaches back to its primal nature: it inspires in man a mixture of fear, joy, and ecstasy.

Sutherland is, without doubt, one of the leaders of the contemporary English School of painting. In 1944, asked to decorate a church at Northampton, he created a *Christ on the Cross* that makes one think of certain Spanish primitives, of totems, and, again, of the works of such an artist as Grünewald. Following this, he devoted considerable time to portraits. The head of a man calls forth from him the same qualities of analysis and synthesis as the phenomena of nature. Thus a portrait dominated by a pair of shrewd, cruel eyes, even though painted in accordance with all laws of realism, seems, at times, not very far from belonging to the plant world, the insect world, or the reptile kingdom.

In 1951 Sutherland was commissioned to paint a large panel for the Festival of Britain on the theme of "The Origins of the Earth." In 1952 he represented England at the Biennale in Venice, where he was awarded the acquisition prize of the Museum of Modern Art, São Paulo. His most important commission was for the tapestry of *Christ in Majesty*, measuring about 14 by 40 feet, for Coventry Cathedral, where it was placed in 1962. Byzantine influence is strongly marked in it. His work is well represented in the collections of the Tate Gallery in London and in the Museums of Modern Art of New York and Paris.

SYMBOLISM is the name given to a movement in literature and the plastic arts that developed around 1885. The Symbolist painters and poets no longer aimed at a faithful representation of the world, but at an imaginative suggestion of their dreams through symbolic allusion and luxuriant decorative form. The year 1886—with the appearance of Arthur Rimbaud's *Illuminations*, the arrival of Vincent van Gogh in Paris, and Paul Gauguin's first stay in Brittany—confirmed the break with Impressionism and marked the official birth of Neoimpressionism on the one hand, and of Symbolism, in opposition to it, on the other. The movement first appeared in literature: in the manifesto he published in an issue of *Figaro* in 1886, the poet Jean Moréas put forward the name Symbolism "as the only word capable of adequately describing the current tendency of the creative spirit in art." His principal formula was meant to have validity for all the arts: "To clothe the idea in a sensitive form." Soon after there appeared a number of journals that propagated the new aesthetic doctrine: in 1886 *La Pléiade, Le Décadent, La Vogue, Le Symboliste*; in 1889 Albert Aurier's *Le Moderniste* and *La Plume*; in 1890 *Le Mercure de France*; and in 1891 *La Revue Blanche*. The *Poésies* of Stéphane Mallarmé appeared in 1887; in 1889 the *Parallèlement* of

Paul Verlaine, the *Essai sur les Données Immédiates de la Conscience* of Henri Bergson and the famous work of Édouard Schuré, *Les Grands Initiés*, which discussed the mystical and theosophical current of Symbolism. The same year witnessed the appearance of Symbolism in painting on the occasion of the exhibition at the Café Volpini of the "Impressionist and Synthetist Group" (Gauguin and the school of Pont-Aven).

The young critic Albert Aurier, an enthusiastic admirer of Gauguin, defined Symbolist painting in an article in the *Mercure de France* (1891): "The work of art," he proclaimed, "must be: 1. *Ideist*, since its only goal will be expression of the idea; 2. *Symbolist*, since it will express the idea in forms; 3. *Synthetic*, since it will transcribe the forms in a mode of general comprehension; 4. *Subjective*, since the object will never be considered in it as an object, but as the sign of the idea perceived by the subject; 5. (as a consequence) *Decorative*, for decorative painting properly so called, as the Egyptians and very likely the Greeks and the Primitives conceived it, is nothing but a manifestation of an art that is at once subjective, synthetic, symbolist, and ideist." These characteristics, which put emphasis upon Ideist Symbolism and the tendency toward decorative abstraction, applied particularly to Gauguin and the school of Pont-Aven, as well as to the Nabis group, but they were already evident, in an intuitive and rather literary form, in three isolated artists with whom the Symbolist generation claimed kinship: Gustave Moreau, Puvis de Chavannes, and Odilon Redon. Gustave Moreau was, in some respects, the French equivalent of the English Pre-Raphaelites who were discovered in France at the Universal Exhibition of 1855. Moreau's influence was widely felt—not only by decadent writers like Joris-Karl Huysmans and Jean Lorrain, but also by the Nabis.

While the work of Puvis de Chavannes, in spite of its nobility and undeniable harmony, now appears more closely related to an academic allegorism than to authentic Symbolism, its influence was also considerable, and all contemporary artists from Gauguin to the Nabis claimed him as a precursor. Odilon Redon, a contemporary of Impressionism, which he thought "too low-ceilinged," was a friend of Mallarmé and the young Symbolist writers André Gide, Paul Valéry, and Francis Jammes, and following the example of Moreau and Puvis, whom he greatly admired, sought in his works "human beauty with the glamor of thought." Redon succeeded in creating the plastic counterpart of his dreams. He is the Symbolist painter par excellence.

Symbolism was perhaps less a school than the atmosphere of a period. The extent of the movement can be measured in a book by André Mellerio, *The Idealist Movement in Painting* (1896), which distinguished four groups: the Chromo-Luminarists, the Neoimpressionists, the Synthetists, and the Mystics.

Although the Symbolist movement found its finest expression in France, it spread all over Europe. There were hardly any artists who remained untouched by the Symbolist mystique: Eugène Carrière and Henri Fantin-Latour in France, James McNeill Whistler in England, James Ensor in Belgium, who began in the Impressionist manner but in 1890 discovered in the mask an expression for his fantastic and ironic vision. In Germany, amid a climate of Wagnerian romanticism, Symbolism was represented by the poet Stefan George and ended by merging with Expressionism, to which it gave a new profundity, as in the works of Ferdinand Hodler and Edvard Munch.

SYNCHROMISM. This movement, which expressed the independence of form from volume by creating a plastic space through emotionally valued color, was founded in Paris in 1912 by two American painters, Stanton Macdonald-Wright and Morgan Russell. Its primary influences, including Impressionism, the work of Cézanne and Matisse, had been assimilated by that year, and were furthered in their development by the catalytic example of Robert Delaunay's Orphism. Russell had absorbed Monet's manner by 1908. But his greatest source was Cézanne, who inspired him to create solid forms through light, via the modulations of warm and cool colors.

Symbolism. Odilon Redon. *Rider in Flight.* Rijksmuseum Kröller-Müller, Otterlo.

Macdonald-Wright was equally impressed by Cézanne, especially by the latter's watercolors; his interest in light, however, derives from Renoir, while his interest in color theory (by 1910) followed his exposure to Cubism and Pointillism. Two other Americans, Patrick Bruce and Arthur B. Frost, Jr., also joined the movement. Bruce, initially attracted by the color compositions of Matisse, came increasingly under Cézanne's influence. Frost's influences are more difficult to specify.

The group held an exhibition in Paris at the Galerie Bernheim-Jeune in 1913, then in Munich and at the Armory Show in New York, also in 1913. Both its originators abandoned the style by 1916, although Macdonald-Wright revived it in 1953 and was given a retrospective exhibition at Los Angeles in 1956.

SYNTHETISM. *See* **PONT-AVEN.**

T

TAC (The Architects' Collaborative), American architectural firm organized in 1945 around Walter Gropius. The original partners included Jean B. Fletcher (1915–65), Norman C. Fletcher (b. 1917), John C. Harkness (b. 1916), Sarah P. Harkness (b. 1914), Robert S. McMillan (b. 1916), Louis A. McMillan (b. 1916), and Benjamin Thompson (b. 1918). The latter resigned in 1965 in order to establish his own practice.

TAC (as the name implies) operates on co-operative teamwork wherein all members participate in weekly criticism of the firm's current work. To preserve individual creativity and project coherence, however, final design decisions rest with one partner-in-charge, a "team captain," thus fostering the best of both systems. At Six Moon Hill (1948), an early TAC housing project in Lexington, Massachusetts, all partners except Gropius participated in a community development experiment.

TAC has contributed numerous elementary and secondary schools to the great Boston area. At Phillips Academy in Andover, spatially flexible studios, classrooms, and laboratories were designed within a strong structural framework for the new Arts and Communication Center (1959) and the Evans Science Building (1959). Dormitories and dining facilities, such as the Greylock Residential Houses at Williams College in Williamstown, Massachusetts (1965), are among several college and university commissions.

Other outstanding projects include the Harvard University Graduate Center (1949); the United States Embassy in Athens (1956); and the University of Baghdad in Iraq (under construction in 1968). TAC acted as consultant, along with Pietro Belluschi, on the controversial Pan American Building in New York (1958).

The Architects' Collaborative. Pan American Building, New York. *Photo by courtesy of Theo Crosby, London.*

TACCA, Pietro (1577, Carrara—1640, Florence), Italian sculptor. Beginning in 1592, he was an assistant of Giovanni Bologna in Florence, where he completed his master's equestrian statue of Grand Duke Ferdinand I of Tuscany (1608) in the Piazza SS. Annunziata. Tacca was also responsible for the completion of the equestrian statues of Philip III of Spain in Madrid's Plaza Mayor (1606–13) and of Henri IV of France, formerly on the Pont-Neuf in Paris (1613; destroyed 1792). His own masterpiece is the set of four bronze *Slaves* (1615–24) on the base of Giovanni Bandini's (1540–99) monument to Ferdinand I in the Piazza della Darsena at Leghorn. These figures combine a Mannerist type of twisted pose with a naturalism of detail and a clarity of design that herald the Baroque. This transitional style is also perceptible in Tacca's bronze equestrian monument to Philip IV in the Plaza de Oriente, Madrid (*c.* 1634–40). In Florence he was responsible for the colossal statues of Ferdinand I and Cosimo II (1626–34) above their tombs in S. Lorenzo's Cappella dei Principi, and for the two bronze fountains with marine monsters in the Piazza SS. Annunziata (1627).

TACHISM, term invented by the French art critic Pierre Guéguen, who used it for the first time in 1951 in a lecture given at Menton, Alpes-Maritimes, to describe the free tendency in abstract painting that had developed in opposition to geometric abstraction. In 1954, in an article in the magazine *Art d'aujourd'hui*, Guéguen expanded on the background and definition of the word, which is derived from *tache* (touch or spot); it applied, he said, not so much to a new movement as to a pictorial tendency that had evolved slowly. Having served as a justification for the abstract Surrealism of such painters as Simon Hantai (b. 1922), Nejad (b. 1923), and Jean Degottex (b. 1918), the term Tachism soon replaced labels such as lyrical abstraction and informal art to describe the results obtained by such different processes as Wols's "coulures," Jackson Pollock's "dripping," and Georges Mathieu's "tubism" (squeezing the paint from the tube directly onto the canvas). It was applied to such fundamentally distinct idioms as that of Camille Bryen (b. 1907) or Jean-Paul Riopelle in France; Clyfford Still, Sam Francis, or Willem de Kooning in the United States; Bernard Schultze (b. 1915) in Germany; Antonio Tàpies in Spain; Alberto Burri in Italy; and Alan Davie (b. 1920) in Britain.

TAEUBER-ARP, Sophie (1889, Davos, Switzerland—1943, Zurich), Swiss painter. After studying applied art in Saint Gall (1908–10), Munich (1911; 1913), and Hamburg (1912), she taught textile design for 13 years (1916–29) at the Zurich School of Arts and Crafts. With Jean Arp, whom she met in 1915 and married in 1921, she belonged (1916–20) to the Dadaist movement. Beginning in 1916 she began painting gouaches and nonfigurative, geometric oils, which sometimes included small ornamental motifs (*Vertical-Horizontal Composition on White Background*, 1916; Paris, Coll. François Arp). She also used these motifs in embroidery and collages, two media she chose because of their impersonal character (*Embroideries*, 1922; Zurich, Kunstgewerbemuseum). From 1928 to 1940 she lived in Meudon, near Paris, and participated in the abstract movements of Cercle et Carré (1930) and Abstraction-Création (1931–36). She also founded the magazine *Plastique*, which was published from 1937 to 1939. During World War II she took refuge in Grasse, where she executed colored lithographs in collaboration with Arp, Sonia Delaunay, and Alberto Magnelli.

Sophie Taeuber-Arp was one of the important figures in the abstract art movement of the years between World Wars I and II. She always remained faithful to an artistic order and sense of proportion based on the harmony of colors and the clarity of forms, but this sobriety excluded neither freedom of inspiration nor richness of invention. In her later years, a growing freedom, transmitted by the movement of the line, announced innovations that her accidental death suddenly interrupted. Sophie Taeuber-Arp also executed sculptures (*Portrait of Jean Arp*, 1918; Zurich, Coll. Erika Schlegel), geometric constructions, and reliefs.

TALENTI, Francesco (b. *c.* 1300–d. 1369, Florence), Italian architect. Talenti's principal works, which include the completion of Giotto's Campanile and the enlargement and redesigning of the Duomo in Florence, are in a Late Italian Gothic style that is difficult to characterize. Talenti's work, coming as it does at the very end of the Gothic period and the beginning of the Renaissance, has many Classical qualities, in spatial treatment as well as in details, while remaining within the Gothic tradition. Giotto's Campanile was begun in 1334, but only the lower stories were completed within the designer's lifetime, and the work was continued first by Andrea Pisano and then by Talenti. Both successors kept Giotto's decorative, geometric marble facing, but lightened the upper stories by enlarging the openings. Talenti succeeded Pisano in the 1340s and was working on the Campanile in the following decade when he was named Capomaestro of the Duomo (1350). Little work had been done on the cathedral since the death of its first architect, Arnolfo di Cambio, in 1302. Talenti was asked to redesign the building and produce a wooden model in 1355. In 1366 a commission of artists and laymen approved the plan and the final model was begun in the following year. This last version retained Arnolfo's basic type of an aisled, vaulted nave with a dome over the crossing, a vaulted choir, and transepts of equal length. The pointed arches formed by the rib vaults are Gothic, but the frontal pilasters on the piers, as well as the architrave and cornice separating the capitals from the arches, are quite Classical. The mixture of styles, however difficult to describe, is not at all discordant, and the effect produced is at once powerful and tranquil.

TAMAYO, Rufino (b. 1899, Oaxaca, Mexico), Mexican painter. After studying (1917–21) at the Academia de Arte de San Carlos in Mexico City, he was appointed (1921) head of the ethnographical drawing section of the National Museum of Anthropology of Mexico. In 1933 he was commissioned to execute a large fresco on the theme of *Music* for the Academy of Music in Mexico City. In 1950 he went to Europe and exhibited at the Venice Biennale, which was a personal triumph. He had gained international recognition, and within a few years was given a series of important commissions for mural decorations, in his own country (*Mexico Today* and the *Birth of Nationality*, both 1952–53; Mexico City, Palacio de Bellas Artes), in the United States (*Nature and the Artist*, 1943, Northampton, Mass., Smith College, Hillyer Gallery; *America*, 1955, Houston, Second National Bank of Houston; *Prometheus*, 1957, San Juan, Puerto Rico, University of Puerto Rico), and in Europe (*Prometheus Bringing Fire to Man*, 1958; Paris, UNESCO building, Conference Hall).

Tamayo attempted to combine Mexican folk themes with a diversity of European styles that included borrowings from Picasso, reminiscences of Cubism, Expressionism, and Surrealism. His forms, alternately diluted and articulated, are outlined in sharp zigzags and drowned in salmon reds, pale mauves, or dark blues; they are either naturalistic or symbolic, sometimes blending into the canvas surface, sometimes exploding into dashing arabesques and sudden disintegration. Tamayo is one of the few Mexican artists of his generation to have departed from the epic style that began with the 1910 Revolution in his country. His instinctively poetic vision followed private paths, which led him to a rediscovery not of myths, but of the true pictorial values of his people (*Singer*, 1950; Paris, Musée National d'Art Moderne).

TANGUY, Yves (1900, Paris—1955, Woodbury, Connecticut), French-born American painter. His naval career took him to England, Spain, Portugal, Africa, and South America. On his return to Paris in 1922, he became friendly with the Surrealist poet Jacques Prévert and spent the next two years in anxious search of his vocation. Finally a painting by Giorgio de Chirico, which he saw in the window of the Galerie Paul Guillaume in Paris, inspired him to take up painting. In 1925 he joined the Surrealist movement and took part in all their exhibitions. In 1942 he settled in Woodbury, Connecticut. He became an American citizen in 1948.

Of all the Surrealists, Tanguy possessed the strongest intuition of a reality independent of that perceived by the senses, of a pristine, limpid world. Although he employed the most traditional, at times even academic, artistic means to express his dreams and anxieties, his work disturbs and attracts the viewer; for Tanguy filled the undefined space and the radiant light of his canvases with strange, spectral forms that seem to have emerged from a seabed or from the arid surfaces of some distant star (*Days of Slowness*, 1937; Paris, Musée National d'Art Moderne). Tanguy was Surrealism personified. Shortly before his death, he began working on large canvases in which vast, stony surfaces and calcareous structures rise in defiance of the horizon, expressing the terrifying inertness of mineral life (*Multiplication of Arcs*, 1954; New York, Museum of Modern Art).

TANNING, Dorothea (b. 1913, Galesburg, Illinois), American painter. In 1935 she went to New York, where she discovered Surrealism through the comprehensive exhibition "Fantastic Art, Dada, and Surrealism" that took place in 1936–37 at the Museum of Modern Art. In 1942 she met Max Ernst (whom she married in 1946), and in 1944 she held her first one-man show in New York at the Julien Levy Gallery. In the 1940s she painted in a strictly Surrealistic style in which the forms were extremely clear and the imagery taken from the subconscious (*Birthday*, 1942; Coll. artist). Lit-

Francesco Talenti. Campanile of Florence. Begun by Giotto, completed *c.* 1359. *Photo Brogi-Giraudon.*

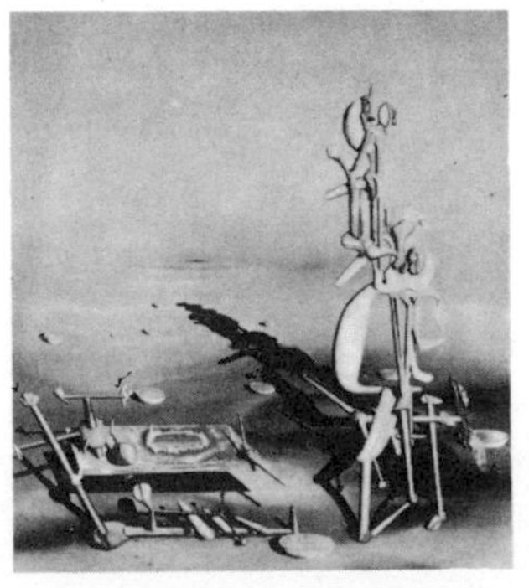

Yves Tanguy. *"Divisibilité Indéfinie."* 1942. Albright-Knox Art Gallery, Buffalo.

tle girls and their fantasies are the principal themes of Dorothea Tanning's Surrealistic paintings (*Interior Scene Accompanied by Sudden Joy*, 1951, New York, Coll. Copley; *Eine Kleine Nachtmusik*, 1946, London, Coll. Roland Penrose). In the 1950s her area of concentration shifted from the subconscious to the real world, and she portrayed in an expressionistic manner maternity, birth, love, and death (*Family Portrait*, 1951; Coll. artist). After 1954 her canvases were invaded by shimmering mists that revealed glimpses of nude Bacchantes, and she depicted ritual operations involving fantastic animals and characters (*Distractedly*, 1961; Paris, Priv. Coll.). Her brushstrokes became more volatile, and she created a greater sense of movement (*Sotto Voce, I,* 1957, London, Tate Gallery; *Yellow Storm*, 1955, New York, Coll. Jacobs). In the course of her career, Dorothea Tanning also designed the sets and costumes for a number of ballet and theatrical productions.

TÀPIES, Antonio (b. 1923, Barcelona), Spanish painter. In 1946, after abandoning law studies, Tàpies decided to devote himself exclusively to painting. During the first two years of his artistic career he concentrated on collages (*Collage*, 1947; Paris, Coll. Henry Lazard). In 1948 he began to execute paintings in which generally earth-colored and smoke-stained colors predominated and in which the scratchings and graffitic figures characteristic of his subsequent work appeared for the first time. In 1948 Tàpies helped found the Barcelona-based group and magazine *Dau al Set*. Its members and contributors included the painters Joan Ponç (b. 1927), Juan-José Tharrats (b. 1918), and Modesto Cuixart (b. 1925), the poet Joan Brossa, and the art critics Arnaldo Puig and Juan-Eduardo Cirlot. From 1949 to 1953 Tàpies abandoned all attempts to achieve his effects through the actual quality of the paint, and began to construct canvases whose backgrounds were made up of subtly differentiated tonal values on which he superimposed or engraved geometric signs or deformed letters ("*Mudrc*," 1949; Barcelona, Coll. José Luis Samaranch). After 1954 Tàpies partially returned to earlier experiments with materials; for instance, he used such austere and skillful combinations as oil paint mixed with crushed marble, powdered pigment, and latex. With these diverse materials he created huge desolate surfaces covered with fossil-like imprints, creases, incisions, and thin, crude colors that seem to have been washed and denatured by the weather (*Painting*, 1960; Paris, Coll. Galerie Stadler). Throughout his career Tàpies continued to simplify his compositional principles.

TATLIN, Vladimir Evgrafovich (1885, Kharkov, Ukraine—1953, Novodevichye), Russian Constructivist painter and sculptor. His first pictures reflected two influences: ancient Russian icons and the art of Paul Cézanne. During a brief stay in Paris in 1912, he paid a visit to Picasso's studio, whereby he completely changed his artistic direction. He was most inspired by a wooden relief in the form of a still life and composed of various objects; it gave him the idea for the *Painting Reliefs* and *Relief Constructions* on which he began working in 1913–14 after his return to Russia. Using a variety of materials such as wood, metal, cardboard, plaster, cement, and tar, he covered the surfaces of these reliefs with coatings and glazes on which he sprinkled powder and broken glass. Tatlin eliminated all figuration from his art and, confining himself in this way to the creation of simple geometric forms, was an early exponent of abstract art and opened the way that ultimately led to Constructivism.

Tatlin first showed his reliefs in his Moscow studio during the winter of 1913–14, and then at the "Tramway V" exhibition in St. Petersburg. Tatlin continued his experiments with his series of *Corner Counter-Reliefs* (1915), which were constructions without either a plinth or a background and which thus had to be suspended by wire or hung in a corner. A whole room was reserved for these *Counter-Reliefs* at 0.10, the "Latest Futurist Painting Exhibition," held in St. Petersburg in December 1915.

Vladimir Tatlin. *Counter-Relief.* 1914–15.

At the beginning of the Russian Revolution, Tatlin was appointed to a teaching post at the Higher Artistic-Technical Studios ("Vkhutemas"). He became the leader of a group of artists who called themselves the "Productivists" and who, in opposition to Kasimir Malevich, advocated the application of art to utilitarian ends. In 1919, overcome with political enthusiasm, Tatlin created his project for a *Monument to the Third International* (never constructed), one of the first buildings conceived entirely in abstract terms. After nonfigurative art was discredited by the Soviet government in 1920, Tatlin left Moscow for Leningrad, where from 1922 he taught at the Research Institute for Artistic Culture ("Inkkuk"), specializing in the study of materials. In 1927 he returned to Moscow and to his teaching post at the newly reorganized State Studios, where he was put in charge of the ceramics section.

TCHELITCHEW, Pavel (1898, District of Kaluga, near Moscow—1957, Grottaferrata, near Rome), American painter and scenographer of Russian origin. Tchelitchew studied art at the Kiev Academy (1918–20), where he became acquainted with Cubism and Constructivism. In 1921 he went to Berlin, where he continued painting and designing sets and costumes for theatrical productions, notably for the opera-ballet *Le Coq d'Or* (1923; Berlin, State Opera). In 1923 he settled in Paris. He turned wholeheartedly to easel painting, and produced numerous portraits and landscapes in which realistic subjects predominated. From 1925 to 1927 he tackled the problem of simultaneity with his series of "multiple images" and "laconic compositions," often painted in a mixture of gouache, sand, and coffee grounds. He then (1927) began concentrating on circus scenes (*Circus Figure, c.* 1928;

David Teniers the Younger. *Books and a Globe.* Musées Royaux des Beaux-Arts, Brussels.

Washington, D.C., formerly Coll. Lord Clark) and children. Among the most successful scenographic designs of Tchelitchew's Paris years were those for the ballets *Ode* (1928; Paris, Diaghilev Ballets) and *Nobilissima Visione, St. Francis* (1938; London, Ballets Russes de Monte Carlo), as well as that for Louis Jouvet's production of Jean Giraudoux's play *Ondine* (1939–40; Paris). In 1935 he made his first trip to the United States, where he subsequently settled and obtained citizenship. After the mid-1930s, Tchelitchew became increasingly preoccupied with the problems of perspective and metamorphosis. In *Portrait of My Father* (1939; Los Angeles, Coll. Mr. Edward James), for instance, a winter landscape becomes a Bengal tiger holding a black snake in its mouth; and the children in his famous symbolic canvas *Hide-and-Seek* (1941; New York, Museum of Modern Art) become a gnarled tree. In 1943 he began his series of "interior landscapes," or anatomical paintings in which he depicted figures whose skeleton or veins showed through their skin (*Golden Leaf*, 1943, New York, Coll. Mr. and Mrs. J. Russell Lynes; *Living Shell*, 1944, New York, Priv. Coll.). During the last years of his life (1950–56), Tchelitchew created strictly geometrical studies of the human head (*Head from Side*, 1951; New York, Coll. Mr. and Mrs. R. Kirk Askew, Jr.) and of abstract concepts (*Itinerary of Light*, 1955; New York, Coll. Mr. and Mrs. Zachary Scott), in which the forms are made up of spheres, cones, and lines.

TENIERS THE YOUNGER, David (1610, Antwerp—1690, Brussels), Flemish painter. The son of the Antwerp painter David Teniers the Elder (1582–1649), who was also his teacher, he became a Master in 1632. Teniers was a close friend of Rubens, a member of the most select artistic circles, and court painter to Archduke Leopold Wilhelm, for whose painting collection he was made conservator. He started his artistic career by imitating the fantastic style of Herri met de Bles (1500–54) and Josse de Momper, as in his *Temptation of St. Anthony* (*c.* 1633–36; Brussels, Musées Royaux des Beaux-Arts) and the much later *Alchemist* (1680; Munich, Bayerische Staatsgemäldesammlungen). He then attempted to compete with Adriaen Brouwer by painting genre scenes purged of vulgarity, as in his *Boors' Carouse* (1644; London, Wallace Collection), *Cabaret Interior* (1645; Paris, Louvre), and *Smokers and Drinkers in an Alehouse* (1650; Munich, Priv. Coll.). Finally, along with these other themes, he began to paint a number of *Kermessen*. He often demonstrated some very attractive qualities: a harmony of light colors (blue, red, or creamy white set amidst gray), excellent light effects, and the use of transparent shadows. Examples dated between 1640 and 1660 are the *Village Fete with Cauldrons* (1643; London, National Gallery), the *Prodigal Son at a Table Outside an Inn* (1644; Louvre), *Archduke Leopold Wilhelm at a Village Fete* (1647; Madrid, Prado), *Peasant Wedding* (Munich, Alte Pinakothek, and New York, Metropolitan Museum), and *Village Merry-making* (1649; London, Royal Collection). Teniers' somewhat anecdotal paintings are not as highly regarded as they once were. The private cabinet pieces that represent the *Archduke Leopold Wilhelm in His Picture Gallery*—with versions in Brussels (1651; Musées Royaux des Beaux-Arts), Madrid (Prado), Munich, and Vienna (Kunsthistorisches Museum)—are preferred today by many critics.

TEOTIHUACÁN, Art of. Teotihuacán was an early ceremonial center for agrarian rites that later became the holy city of the Mexican plateaus, ruled by priests; but unlike the other great centers of pre-Columbian Mexico, it was inhabited: its 4 square miles of ruins include traces of private dwellings and poor quarters beside the remains of pyramids and temples. Teotihuacán, which is about 7,000 feet above sea level and 25 miles northeast of Mexico City, was built on a longitudinal axis that was later called the Miccaotli, or Road of the Dead. The power of the city extended only over the high plateaus, where it was the center of an empire whose traces have been discovered in the present-day Mexican states of Tlaxcala, Puebla, Michoacán, and Guerrero. Its history has been divided into four phases: Teotihuacán I, from 300 B.C. to the beginning of our era; stage II, from the year A.D. 1 until 300; stage III, about A.D. 300–650; and stage IV, from about A.D. 650 to 900. The peak of its civilization was stage III, but the details of its history are unknown. Only its art survives, including the faces of the gods: Huehueteotl, God of Fire; Xipe, God of the Spring and Vegetation; Xipe Totec, "Our Lord the Flayed One"; Quetzalcoatl, the Plumed Serpent; and Tlaloc, God of Rain, who brought life to the earth. All these were modeled, engraved, and carved in a great variety of materials: porphyry, andesite, slate, jadeite, basalt, mica, serpentine, quartz, bone, clay, horn, wood, and obsidian. They were also painted in the frescoes of the temple walls and on the outside of vases. The figurines of Teotihuacán I are realistic but already show a tendency toward simplification that transforms the figure into a symbol and conveys a presence rather than a face. The influence of a migration from the Gulf of Mexico that brought the tradition of a geometric, symbolic art increased this tendency during Teotihuacán II and III. Pottery, which was made in molds at an early period, was exported as far as Guatemala, and survives in fairly large quantity. The most characteristic form is a cylindrical tripod vessel, generally decorated with symbols of the gods in a champlevé or cloisonné technique.

Art of Teotihuacán. Effigy vessel of Tlaloc. A.D. 300–650. Museo Nacional de Antropología, Mexico City. *Photo Walter Dräyer, Zurich.*

Art of Teotihuacán. Head of a serpent. Ciudadela, inner face of central pyramid. Before A.D. 500. *Photo Gisele Freund.*

Art of Teotihuacán. Pyramid of the Sun, with platforms of the Pyramid of the Moon courtyard. *Photo Henri Stierlin, Geneva.*

The anthropomorphic vases and human figurines in terra cotta are impressive because a sort of hieratic majesty and serenity informs even the most ordinary attitudes.

The major art of Teotihuacán is its architecture, built on a gigantic scale and comprising a series of incomparable pyramids, some of them truncated with a stairway on one side, others with stages formed by alternating vertical and sloping walls. The most famous are the Ciudadela, the Temple of Quetzalcoatl (or South Pyramid), the Pyramid of the Sun (216 ft. high on a square base measuring 761 by 721 ft.) and the Pyramid of the Moon (some 140 ft. high on a base measuring about 490 by some 385 ft.). The city area, scattered with these temples, preserves within itself an ideal image of cosmic equilibrium, reflecting its original function as a geomantic position for observing the earth's relation to the sun.

TERBORCH *or* **TER BORCH,** Gerard (1617, Zwolle—1681, Deventer), Dutch painter. A superb painter of the bourgeois life of Holland, Terborch began his career with low-life genre (*Camp Scene with Soldiers Playing Cards, c.* 1642/43, Berlin, Staatliche Museen; *Boy Defleaing a Dog, c.* 1655, Munich, Alte Pinakothek), and then achieved recognition for his intimate, homely scenes and for his virtuosity in the handling of fine fabrics such as silk and satin (*The Unwelcome Message*, 1653, The Hague, Mauritshuis; *Reading Lesson, c.* 1653, Paris, Louvre; *Music Lesson*, 1667–68, London, National Gallery; and the so-called *Paternal Admonition, c.* 1654–55, Berlin, Staatliche Museen). As a result, he secured for himself a unique place among such masters of genre as Jan Vermeer, Frans Mieris the Elder, and Pieter de Hooch. Yet his importance as one of the earlier Dutch portraitists should not be overlooked. Not only did he have the probity of the Haarlem portraitists, and something of the vivacity of Frans Hals, but he also painted his models with insight and a rare poetic feeling. Terborch chose to place his figures against a neutral background, completely devoid of furnishings or accessories, thus creating the effect of a dream-like vision (*Helena van der Schalke as a Child, c.* 1644; Amsterdam, Rijksmuseum). One of his most remarkable paintings is his *Swearing of the Oath of Ratification of the Treaty of Münster* (1648; London, National Gallery), which he executed while in Westphalia to commemorate the peace treaty between Spain and Holland, and the recognition of Holland as an independent kingdom. This small work, considered his masterpiece, is in the tradition of the group portraits by Frans Hals and Bartholomeus van der Helst.

TERBRUGGHEN *or* **TER BRUGGHEN,** Hendrick (1588, Deventer—1629, Utrecht), Dutch painter of the Utrecht school. A pupil of Abraham Bloemaert, he went to Italy in 1604, remaining until 1614, and like his countrymen Gerrit van Honthorst and Dirck van Baburen (1570–1623), came under the spell of Caravaggio and the Italian Caravaggisti. His earliest known paintings executed upon his return to Utrecht (*Calling of St. Matthew, c.* 1617; Le Havre, Musée du Havre) demonstrate the extent of this impact. This early work, however, also reveals the retention of 16th-century motifs and the color schemes of his master Bloemaert. Not until after 1620 did Terbrugghen fully develop the Caravaggesque elements in his style, possibly under the influence of Honthorst and Baburen, both of whom returned from Italy about that time. The youthful *Flute Player* (1621; Kassel, Gemäldegalerie) recalls the young dandy, seen from the back, in Caravaggio's *Calling of St. Matthew* in the church of S. Luigi dei Francesi in Rome, and the figure types, gestures, and general arrangement of pictorial elements in Terbrugghen's 1621 version of the *Calling of St. Matthew* (Utrecht, Centraal Museum) suggests the actual working from the Caravaggio painting, or more likely, from an engraving made after this work, in which the pictorial elements have been reversed. The strong chiaroscuro effects that Terbrugghen created in the paintings of this later period also demonstrate an indebtedness to the great Italian master. There is, however, a clearer and softer light in his work than is found in Caravaggio's paintings, or in the paintings of Honthorst. Terbrugghen's originality as a painter lies not only in the kind of lighting he employed, but also in the imaginative and poetic feeling he achieved and in the sense of almost classic grandeur he created.

THAULOW, Frits (1847, Oslo, Norway—1906, Volendam, Netherlands), Norwegian painter. He was the only true Scandinavian Impressionist. Following several visits to France, he finally settled there in 1892. He was a member of the jury of the 1889 Universal Exhibition, where his painting *Winter in Norway* (1887) was acquired by the French State for the Palais du Luxembourg, Paris. Like Claude Monet and Alfred Sisley, he enjoyed creating the effects of rain and mist and even attempted night scenes which he treated with a great deal of virtuosity. He also produced many winter scenes (*Snow*; Boston, Museum of Fine Arts). Thaulow chose his subjects from the French countryside and was particularly fond of canal and river banks and small villages, all of which he portrayed in an unusual lighting (*Canal Scene in Winter*, 1894; *Landscape*, 1895, Philadelphia, Museum of Art). His earliest work, on the other hand, represents the landscapes of his native Norway.

THAYER, Abbott Henderson (1849, Boston—1921, Monadnock, New Hampshire), American painter. In the early 1870s Thayer took a studio in New York and attended the National Academy of Design, where he annually exhibited two or three canvases; by the time he married in 1875, he had

Frits Thaulow. *Street in Kragerö.* 1882. Nasjonalgalleriet, Oslo.

Louis Thévenet. *Coat Stand.* 1917. Musées Royaux des Beaux-Arts, Brussels. *Photo A.C.L.*

made a name for himself as an animal painter. In the same year he went to Paris, studying at the École des Beaux-Arts. Although he did not give up animal painting entirely, Thayer concentrated his efforts on portraiture and figure painting when he returned to America. *The Sisters* (1884; New York, Brooklyn Museum) is one of his best-known works. His *Florence Protecting the Arts* (1893–94; Brunswick, Maine, Bowdoin College Museum of Art) constitutes his introduction to mural painting. In the late 1890s he again became interested in natural history and began writing essays on his newly discovered law of concealing coloration. These camouflage discoveries were published in 1909, and were illustrated with examples of his precisely delineated animal paintings. Thayer's pencil sketches of the period are indicative of his mastery of draftsmanship and subtle modeling (*Gladys*, 1897; Providence, Rhode Island School of Design). In his last years, landscapes became a growing concern: *Winter Sunrise, Monadnock* (1918; New York, Metropolitan Museum) is handled with a quick, impetuous stroke and an Impressionist's flatness of space, while affording the viewer a vivid sense of locale.

THEOTOKOPOULOS, Domenikos. *See* **GRECO,** El.

THÉVENET, Louis (1874, Bruges—1930, Hal, near Brussels), Belgian painter. In 1903 Thévenet began to show his paintings: he took part in the exhibitions of the Libre Esthétique group (1904) and frequented a few bourgeois salons. In 1914, however, he retired to the village of Hal, in the province of Brabant, where he lived out the rest of his life in solitude. He was an Intimist, and painted a great many interiors and still lifes, and only a few landscapes. Thévenet expressed his feeling for the human setting, for furniture, and everyday objects with great simplicity (*Eggs in the Pan*, 1911; Brussels, Coll. Madame D. van Haelen). There are few figures of human beings in his pictures, although sometimes a little girl appears (*Coat Stand*, 1917; Brussels, Musées Royaux des Beaux-Arts); more frequently the memory of the absent one reigns alone over the objects (*Monsieur is Going Out*, 1916; *Open Commode*, 1918, Brussels, Priv. Coll.). Thévenet's paintings have a very original abstract quality, created by an internal geometry that governs the arrangement of the planes, volumes, and colors.

THORNHILL, Sir James (1675, Melcombe Regis, Dorset—1734, Thornhill Park, Dorset), English painter. He was the only English decorative painter to work in the scenic Baroque tradition. Thornhill's earliest recorded commission was to paint the scenery for Thomas Clayton's opera *Arsinoe, Queen of Cyprus*, which was first performed on January 16, 1705. In the same year he executed mural decorations at Stoke Edith, Herefordshire (destroyed by fire in 1927), and in 1706 he worked on the decoration of the Sabine Room at Chatsworth, the Duke of Devonshire's home in Bakewell, Derbyshire. A note, dating from 1707, in the minute book of the governors of Greenwich Hospital (now the Royal Naval College), near London, indicates that Thornhill had already received a commission to decorate the Painted Hall there. Thornhill, in fact, executed several mural decorations for the hospital: the Upper Hall has been called the most complete realization of Baroque scenography in an English interior. He was also working simultaneously on the ceiling of the Prince of Wales' bedroom at Hampton Court (1715), the decoration of the chapel of All Souls, Oxford (1713–14), the ceiling of the Great Hall at Blenheim Palace, Oxfordshire (1716), as well as the eight huge grisaille decorations illustrating stories from the *Life of St. Paul* (1716–19) for the cupola of St. Paul's Cathedral, London. In 1716 he became governor of Sir Godfrey Kneller's Academy of Painting in London; in 1718 he was appointed History Painter in Ordinary to His Majesty; in 1720 he became Sergeant Painter to His Majesty, was made Master of the Painter-Stainers' Company, and received a knighthood; and in 1723 he was made a Fellow of the Royal Society. His last two commissions were the chapel of Wimpole Hall, Cambridgeshire (1721–24) and the decoration of Moor Park, Hertfordshire (1720–28). In 1732 he resigned his office as Sergeant Painter in favor of his son John (active 1730–60). Although Thornhill's decorative painting was probably inferior to that of Kent, he was the first Englishman to master the large-scale decorative idiom and thereby effectively ended the hegemony of foreign practitioners of that genre in England.

THORVALDSEN, Bertel (1768, Copenhagen—1844, Copenhagen), Danish Neoclassical sculptor. With Antonio Canova, Thorvaldsen was the most representative exponent of the Classical Revival in sculpture. In 1781 he entered the Royal Academy of Fine Arts in Copenhagen. He was so successful that in 1796 he was awarded a scholarship enabling him to go to Rome. In 1802 he gained recognition with his marble model of *Jason* (1803–28; Copenhagen, Thorvaldsens Museum). This was followed by such statues as *Cupid and Psyche* (1807), *Venus with the Apple* (1813–16), and the *Shepherd Boy* (1817). In 1808 he joined the Accademia di S. Luca, and in 1812, on the occasion of a projected visit from Napoleon, he executed a frieze on the subject of

Bertel Thorvaldsen. *Three Graces and Cupid.* 1819. Thorvaldsens Museum, Copenhagen.

the *Triumphant Entry of Alexander the Great into Babylon* (gesso model, Rome, Palazzo del Quirinale; cast, Thorvaldsens Museum). Thorvaldsen's authority grew so great that in 1816 he was entrusted with the restoration of the recently excavated archaic statues from Aegina, Greece, destined for the Munich Glyptothek. In 1818–19 he returned to Denmark, where he was commissioned to execute statues of *Christ* (1821) and the *Twelve Apostles* (1821–27) for the church of Our Lady of Copenhagen, as well as a number of other monuments. When he returned to Rome he received so many commissions that he had to employ assistants in order to fulfill them. Among his most famous works are the *Tomb of Pope Pius VII* (1824–31; Rome, St. Peter's) and the *Lion of Lucerne* (1819–21; Lucerne, Gletscherpark). He spent the last years of his life in Copenhagen, where he was accorded great honors, including the establishment during his own lifetime of the Thorvaldsens Museum, which contains most of his sculptures, both originals and casts.

TIBALDI, Pellegrino, *also called* Pellegrino de' Pellegrini (1527, Puria di Valsolda, near Milan—1596, Milan), Italian painter, architect, and sculptor. Tibaldi went to Rome (1547), where he greatly admired the work of Michelangelo, as is evident in such works as his *Adoration of the Christ Child* (1549; Rome, Galleria Borghese) and the fresco depicting battle scenes (*c.* 1550) in the S. Dionigi Chapel of the church of S. Luigi dei Francesi, Rome. In Rome Tibaldi also decorated the Sala Paolina in the Castel S. Angelo with frescoes on the lives of various saints (1552–53). He also executed frescoes (*c.* 1555) in the Poggi Chapel in the church of S. Giacomo Maggiore, Bologna. Later he went to Milan, where he was almost exclusively concerned with architecture, especially after 1567, when St. Charles Borromeo made him supervisor of works at the cathedral. He designed several parts of the duomo, including the choir, and also found time to fulfill commissions in other Italian cities. In 1586 he went to Spain to work at the Escorial, where his typically Mannerist attempt to reduce form to geometric shapes reached an extreme in his decorations (allegories of the *Liberal Arts*, 1590–92) for the Palace Library.

Tibetan Art. *Yama, god of death.* Musée Guimet, Paris. *Photo Roger-Viollet, Paris.*

TIBETAN ART. Situated between India and China, Tibet appears to share some of the characteristics of these two mother civilizations of Asia: she derived her iconography and her religion from the first, and decorative motifs of an essentially secular nature from the second. Tibetan art is pre-eminently a religious art, and has found no need to renew its forms. Every stage of composition as well as the choice of colors is laid down in the sacred texts, which provide exact instructions even as to the slightest detail in the postures, the dimensions, and the dress of the deities depicted, which the painter-monk or sculptor-monk had to make concrete through meditation and scrupulous work. It is an anonymous, mystical art, and is itself a ritual act. There is no form of Tibetan art known prior to the introduction of Buddhism into the country (7th century A.D.) and its transformation into Lamaism through the merging of the Bon cult (the original local religion) and Mongolian Shamanism with Tantric rites belonging to Indian Sivaism, under the influence of the monk Padmasambhava (8th century A.D.).

The architecture consists mainly of monastic palaces, which form whole villages capable of accommodating thousands of monks. The buildings are grouped around a sanctuary that consists of a very high central nave housing the statue of the deity, and low, dark side aisles generally built of wood. The entire group of buildings is surrounded by solid stone or brick walls that are very thick at the base and narrow toward the top: the profile of the unit takes the form of a trapezium. Within these outer walls are the houses. Those of the important lamas are built of stone and plaster, and often comprise several stories. The terraces sometimes have tiled Chinese-style roofs. Inside these buildings are wood or stone columns surmounted by corbels and carved capitals of an Indian type. The decoration adopts Chinese motifs, accompanied by friezes of dicta written in Tibetan characters. Bright colors are widely used. The oldest known buildings (although restored several times) are Ribok'ang Cathedral in Lhasa, founded, according to legend, by King Srong-tsan-gam-po (7th century A.D.), and the monastery of Bsam-yas, which is believed to have been built by Padmasambhava in about A.D. 770. The famous Potala Palace at Lhasa is later, and was begun in 1643 by the fifth Dalai Lama. It is built entirely in stone and roofed only with terraces. Also typically Tibetan is the chorten, a cylindrical

Tibetan Art. Potala Palace, Lhasa. Begun 1643. *Photo Harrer, Kitzbühel.*

structure placed on a domed, terraced square base, and ending in a pinnacle. The chorten is derived from the Indian stupa and is adapted to a number of different uses, including those of outer gateway, tomb, reliquary, signal, commemorative monument, and votive object.

The frescoes, painted temple banners (*tankas*), and scrolls are always religious in intention. The composition is unchanging, as are the colors, which are symbolic. These are not so much paintings as colored drawings, whether they are divine images or geometric compositions known as the Magic Circle (*mandala*). There are at least two distinct schools of painting: that of the southeast, whose themes are close to the Indo-Nepalese tradition (notably at Shigatse), and that of the northeast, in which a Chinese influence predominates (at Derge). The art of the woodcut (for book illustrations, pamphlets, prayers) escapes to some degree the rigidity of the religious rules and often provides small pictures of great charm, invention, and fantasy.

Sculpture was subject to the same restrictions as painting and is highly expressive: almost invariably it depicts the various deities. The technique of casting bronze by the lost-wax method was used for most of the works. The statues were lacquered, gilded, and often inlaid with precious stones. Their style remains closely related to that of the Sena and Pala dynasties of Bengal, but is complicated with "Baroque" elements borrowed from Chinese sculpture. The deified lamas are represented seated, and are strongly realistic. A freer, more popular art is found in many terra-cotta votive plaquettes, usually molded, in which the details are picked out with great skill.

Masks for use in ritual dances were made of wood, papier-mâché, and metal that was painted and gilded. Goldwork seems to have been the one field in which the Tibetan artist freed himself from his constraints. The virtuosity and artistic genius of the craftsmen is to be found in reliquaries, prayer mills, pots, trumpets, jewelry, and decorative motifs.

TIEPOLO, Giambattista (1696, Venice—1770, Madrid), Italian decorative painter, the major artist of the Venetian Rococo. Tiepolo's early paintings show the influence of the late work of Giambattista Piazzetta, although he inherited his brilliant palette, his appreciation of women and their finery, as well as his lightness and festive air from Paolo Veronese. In 1719 he married Giovanni Antonio and Francesco Guardi's sister Cecilia, who gave him nine sons, two of whom—Giandomenico and Lorenzo (1736–76)—were accomplished painters in their own right. In 1726 Tiepolo was invited to Udine, where he decorated (1726) the chapel of the Sacrament in the duomo and executed several frescoes (*c.* 1726) in the episcopal palace. His commissions were so varied and numerous that it is difficult to establish a strict chronology for them, no more than a bare mention of his main decorative works being possible here. In Venice he decorated several churches, notably S. Maria del Rosario dei Gesuati (1737–39), where the ceiling frescoes contain more illusionistic architecture than is usual for him; S. Maria degli Scalzi, whose vast ceiling (1743–44), representing the *Miracle of the Holy House of Loreto*, was destroyed by a bomb in 1915, although two fragments are conserved in the Accademia, Venice; and the Chiesa della Pietà (1754–55), where his frescoes have delicate colors and a harmonious style. In Venice he also decorated the main hall of the Scuola dei Carmini (1740–44); several rooms (*c.* 1745–50) of the Palazzo Labia, the principal hall of which contains the story of Antony and Cleopatra, including the famous *Meeting of Antony and Cleopatra* and *Banquet of Antony and Cleopatra*; as well as several frescoes in the Palazzo Rezzonico, where his most famous work is *Merit Between Nobility and Virtue*, also known as the *Apotheosis of the Poet Quintiliano Rezzonico* (*c.* 1758), done with the help of his son Giandomenico. In the environs of Venice his works included the fresco on the *Reception of Henry III at the Villa Contarini alla Mira* (1754; originally in the Villa Contarini at Mira, near Venice, and now in Paris, Musée Jacquemart-André) and the fresco depicting the *Apotheosis of the Pisani Family* (1761–62) on the ceiling of the ballroom in the Villa Pisani at Strà on the Brenta Canal.

Tiepolo was also commissioned to paint ceiling frescoes (the *Course of the Sun on Olympus*, 1740) at the Palazzo Clerici, Milan; and the ceiling of the ballroom (*Triumph of Hercules*, 1761) at the Palazzo Canossa, Verona. His reputation soon became universal, and in 1750 the Prince-Bishop of Würzburg, Carl Philipp von Greiffenclau, summoned him with his sons Giandomenico and Lorenzo to Würzburg in order to decorate the Residenz. There he decorated the Kaisersaal (1752); the gigantic ceiling of the Grand Staircase, where his *Olympus with the Quarters of the Earth* (1743) is perhaps his most enthralling work; and the chapel (1752). Among Tiepolo's other works, the most complete and attractive are the frescoes (1757) at the Villa Valmarana, outside Vicenza, showing scenes taken from Homer, Virgil, Ariosto, and Tasso. In 1762, in answer to an invitation from the king of Spain, Tiepolo went to Madrid, where he remained until his death. There, in the Royal Palace, he painted frescoes in the Throne Room (*Apotheosis of Spain*, 1764), the Guardroom (*Aeneas Conducted to the Temple of Venus*, 1764–66), and the Queen's Anteroom (*Apotheosis of the Spanish Monarchy*, 1764–66).

Tiepolo's ceilings, painted in fresco with luminous tones, are suffused with an even clarity, and are filled but not overcrowded with

Giambattista Tiepolo. *Rinaldo and Armida. c.* 1750–55. Art Institute of Chicago.

Giambattista Tiepolo. *Aurora Dispersing the Clouds of Night. c.* 1755–60. Boston Museum of Fine Arts.

fresh-complexioned women and angels. Tiepolo was the master of airborne figures, and was also a good perspectivist. This also applies to his easel paintings devoted to mythical themes (*Danaë*, 1736; Stockholm, University Museum), fables (*Telemachus and Mentor*, *c.* 1740; Amsterdam, Rijksmuseum), or everyday life in Venice. Although most at home when dealing with the latter subjects, he was also an effective translator of human nature; for example, his portrait of the *Procurator Giovanni Querini* (*c.* 1749 or later; Venice, Galleria Querini-Stampalia) reveals the ugly sitter's cunning disposition, while his scenes from the *Passion* (*c.* 1738–40; Venice, church of S. Alvise) are the embodiment of genuine emotion.

As an engraver, he is equally surprising: his *capricci*, which are executed with extremely fine strokes, reveal a mysterious side of his nature; in them serpents, dead men, tombs, or punchinellos make unexpected appearances, and there is a total absence of logic, yet the overall effect is not tragic.

TIEPOLO, Giandomenico (1727, Venice—1804, Venice), Italian Rococo painter, draftsman, and engraver, son and principal assistant of Giambattista Tiepolo. In 1749 he executed frescoes on the *Life of S. Girolamo Emiliani* for the chapel of Villa Duodo at Zianigo, near Venice, which was subsequently acquired by the Tiepolo family. These frescoes, now in Venice's Ca' Rezzonico, depict punchinellos engaged in various forms of merriment. Giandomenico collaborated with his father for the first time during a stay (1750–53) in Würzburg, where they both worked on a decorative cycle in the Residenz. Giandomenico received independent commissions, such as the overdoors for the Residenz, where he executed representations of Justinian, St. Ambrose, and the emperors Theodosius and Constantine. In Germany he also executed a considerable number of other works on Biblical themes, such as *Christ Healing the Blind Man* (1752; Hartford, Wadsworth Athenaeum). In 1757 he again collaborated with his father, this time on the important fresco cycle at Villa Valmarana, Vicenza. Giandomenico worked on the carnival scenes—of which he was very fond—in the *forestria*, or guesthouse; elsewhere in the villa he expressed his true personality with lively, often bizarre and exotic scenes. Nevertheless, despite his reputation as a painter of gaily idyllic genre scenes and of *commedia dell'arte* themes, he occasionally struck an unexpectedly macabre note in his drawings, which are akin in spirit to those of Goya. Giandomenico—who was active (1762–70) as a draftsman in Madrid while Goya was in that city—actually anticipated the Spaniard's style.

TIFFANY, Louis Comfort (1848, New York—1933, New York), American painter, decorator, and craftsman. He first studied art with the landscape painters George Inness and Samuel Coleman. Tiffany's oils and watercolors nostalgically recalled exotic Oriental scenes (*Mosque of Mohammed Ali and Tombs of the Mamelukes, Cairo*; New York, Brooklyn Museum). Travels in Europe made him aware of the arts and crafts revival movements current in England and on the Continent, and stimulated his interest in relating the decorative arts to architecture. Upon his return to New York, the Louis Comfort Tiffany Foundation was founded in 1878 (adjunct to his father's Tiffany and Co., silversmiths and jewelers) in order to promote an integrated approach to architecture and the design and production of furniture, lighting, glassware, and jewelry.

Tiffany was especially inspired by glassware, and attempted to recreate the effect of oxidized, long-buried vessels through a chemically treated glass-blowing process of his own invention. Designed in fantastic organic or flowing forms, the glass was made in great quantity and may still be seen in many shops, as well as private and museum collections (New York, Museum of Modern Art and Metropolitan Museum). The curving arabesques, fluid spirals, and graceful floral forms of the glass objects also characterize the light fixtures, bronze and silver work, wooden chairs, and stained-glass windows created by the Tiffany Studios in New York. The international Art Nouveau style that blossomed simultaneously in Europe and America around 1900 was one of the contributing factors to this mode of design and ornament, but Tiffany himself was one of its innovators. He was one of the major figures in the movement to revive Gothic attitudes toward fine craftsmanship, but the objects and furnishings made by his studios were also mass produced, if unique in design.

TINGUELY, Jean (b. 1925, Fribourg), Swiss sculptor. From 1940 to 1944 he attended the Basel School of Fine Arts, where he studied painting. He then (*c.* 1945–52) produced abstract paintings and worked on strange concepts, such as edible structures in grass and constructions in wire, metal, wood, and paper. In 1952 he settled in Paris, where he began to construct his first *Métamécaniques*, a name he invented and meaning "beyond the machine." These are animated, robotlike structures made of wire and sheet metal, which perform various operations in space and often contain sound- and odor-producing devices. Tinguely first showed his *Métamécaniques* in 1954. Then he completed (1955) various *Machines à peindre* ("painting machines"). After this constructive phase, he conceived (1959) his *Homage to New York*, a machine-happening that destroyed itself as it functioned in the garden of New York's

Jean Tinguely. *Armored Car.* 1965. Galerie Iolas, Paris. *Photo André Morain, Paris.*

Tintoretto. *Discovery of the Body of St. Mark.* 1562–66. Brera, Milan.

Museum of Modern Art on March 17, 1960. His first *Study for the End of the World* (1961) was the prelude for a series of aggressive, self-destroying monster sculptures covered with tinsel that expressed his "joyful," anarchic view of the world. In Tinguely's art a basic conception of great power is always combined with an original approach to rhythm and execution. With his productions of the 1960s (*Eureka*, 1964, Lausanne, Swiss National Exhibition; *Armored Car*, 1965, Paris, Galerie Iolas), he entered a hallucinatory phase, in which he confronted the spectator with a ritual of majestic beauty.

TINTORETTO, Jacopo Robusti, *called* (1518, Venice—1594, Venice), Italian painter, the leading representative of Venetian Mannerism. The son of a dyer (whence his nickname), Tintoretto probably trained with such Mannerists as Bonifacio Veronese, Andrea Schiavone, or Paris Bordone (1500–70/71). His first works, the *Last Supper* (1547; Venice, S. Marcuola) and *St. Mark Rescuing a Slave* (1548; Venice, Accademia), are quite in the Venetian tradition, with its fondness for crowding elements of equal importance into the foreground. The latter, painted for the Scuola di S. Marco, is directly inspired by Michelangelo's *Conversion of St. Paul,* showing the same contrast between the prostrate and standing figure. The former reveals both an affinity for and a rejection of Titian's art. Its outstanding quality is a new sense of drama, with a rare sweep and authority, but its carefully drawn buildings are still in the tradition of the Bellini and Carpaccio. A change is evident in *Christ Washing the Disciples' Feet* (*c.* 1550; Madrid, Prado), originally in the church of S. Marcuola; its striking perspective effects were to become the hallmark of the artist's style. With the large painting of *St. Augustine Healing the Plague-Stricken* (*c.* 1549; Vicenza, Museum), Tintoretto displayed his virtuosity in producing dramatic effects: the figures are posed obliquely or in diagonals with astonishing foreshortenings that punctuate the scene in every direction. Tintoretto is closer to Titian in the *Fall of Man* (1550–53; Venice, Accademia) and to Veronese in the admirable *Susanna and the Elders* (*c.* 1560–70; Vienna, Kunsthistorisches Museum). His late style developed the characteristics of Mannerism with an inconceivable energy and speed, permitting him to reveal its prodigious powers of invention for the first time by means of attenuated, sinuous figures, an oblique composition, and a transparent, dematerializing light that accentuates the dramatic effect of his scenes. His colossal conception of the human form (which is essentially Michelangelesque) is given full expression in the cycle of three canvases in the *Miracles of St. Mark* (1562–66), painted for the Confraternity of S. Marco.

The immense cycle of paintings in the Scuola di S. Rocco, on which Tintoretto worked for 23 years (1564–87), represents the peak of his visionary achievement. Beginning with scenes from the *Life of Christ* in the upper hall, he used light and color to give a direct emphasis to the figures, as in the white form of *Christ before Pilate.* The visual orchestration reaches perfection in the huge *Road to Calvary* and *Crucifixion,* in both of which swirling crowds gather on the fringes of the central action, and yet are drawn into it by the eerie and unrealistic light. The realms of heaven and earth mingle confusedly in the *Ascension* and *Baptism of Christ*, but the contrast between the colorless, silvery silhouettes and the purple and orange robes of the protagonists is sufficient to indicate distance and scale. Tintoretto's most lyrical and inventive paintings are the *Flight into Egypt*, with its astonishing palmy landscape of darkness, and the complex *Mary Magdalene in the Wilderness*, from the *Life of the Virgin* in the lower hall (1584–87).

The vast S. Rocco project was followed by the paintings in the Palazzo Ducale in Venice, where he took on enormous projects in the Sala del Collegio; the Sala del Senato, where the ceiling is decorated with the famous *Triumph of Venice as Queen of the Seas* (1581–84); and the huge *Paradise* (1588) in the Sala del Maggior Consiglio, said to be the largest painting in the world.

Tintoretto. *Mars and Venus Surprised by Vulcan.* Alte Pinakothek, Munich.

It was in the art of portraiture that Tintoretto remained most faithful to the Venetian tradition. His portraits are as numerous as his decorative paintings, for Titian alone could not satisfy the needs of his prosperous Venetian clientele. Tintoretto added a greater brilliance and a more studied intensity to Titian's fine portrait style, contrasting the intense faces of his sitters with their somber costumes and backgrounds (*Alvise Cornaro*, mid-1550s; Florence, Palazzo Pitti).

Except for a brief visit to Mantua in 1580, Tintoretto never left Venice in the course of his long life. He was the embodiment of the city's cultural energies and extended its artistic horizons far beyond the limits of reality and the probable. A feeling of irresistible power, drawn from the *terribilità* of Michelangelo, contributed to the humanity and grandeur of his art, which transcended the Renaissance and anticipated the Baroque.

TITIAN, Tiziano Vecellio *or* Vecelli, *known in English as* (*c.* 1485, Pieve di Cadore, Belluno—1576, Venice), Italian painter. When he was nine or ten years old, he was taken to Venice and apprenticed to Sebastiano Zuccato (d. 1527), who later sent him to the studio of Gentile Bellini. Titian finally became a pupil of Giorgione, assisting the latter with the frescoes on the façade of the Fondaco dei Tedeschi; these are now lost, but are known from drawings. He moved to Padua in December 1510, shortly after the death of Giorgione. In 1511, still at Padua, he was paid for three frescoes on

Titian. *Sacred and Profane Love.* *c.* 1515. Galleria Borghese, Rome.

the *Miracles of St. Anthony of Padua*, executed for the Scuola del Santo, where they remain. When he returned to Venice in 1513, he painted the first of his *sacre conversazioni* and the famous allegory of *Sacred and Profane Love* (*c.* 1515; Rome, Galleria Borghese). He opened a workshop and in 1516 received the commission for an *Assumption of the Virgin* for the church of S. Maria Gloriosa dei Frari (the work is still *in situ*). It proved so popular that commissions flowed in: the *Virgin Appearing to St. Francis, St. Aloysius, and a Donor* (Ancona, Pinacoteca) was painted in 1520 for the church of S. Francesco in Ancona, followed two years later by the so-called Brescia Polyptych for SS. Nazaro e Celso in Brescia (*in situ*). In 1523 Titian's connections with Duke Federico II's court at Mantua began, and he painted the *Virgin and Child with St. Catherine*, known as the *Virgin with the Rabbit* (*c.* 1530; Paris, Louvre). In the meantime, however, he continued to work for Venetian churches: between 1519 and 1526 he painted the *Pesaro Madonna*, an altarpiece at the Frari commemorating Jacopo Pesaro's victory over the Turks at Santa Maura; in 1530 he provided the huge altarpiece of *St. Peter Martyr* for S. Zanipolo (destroyed by fire in 1867), which marks the end of the quiet balance of his style of the 1520s and the beginning of a more dynamic proto-Baroque manner.

Titian. *Landscape.* *c.* 1516. Cabinet des Dessins, Louvre, Paris. *Photo Musées Nationaux.*

In 1530 Cardinal Ippolito de' Medici invited the artist to Bologna to paint the portrait of Emperor Charles V (now lost). During a subsequent visit to Bologna in the winter of 1532–33, the master painted a second portrait of Charles V (Madrid, Prado). In 1533 Titian was appointed court painter to the Holy Roman Emperor. A series of portraits painted at this time indicate that the most eminent figures of the day solicited his services: *Cardinal Ippolito de' Medici* (1533; Florence, Palazzo Pitti), *Isabella d'Este* (1534; Vienna, Kunsthistorisches Museum), *Francesco Maria della Rovere, Duke of Urbino*, and his wife, *Eleonora Gonzaga* (both 1536–38; both Florence, Uffizi), *Alfonso d'Avalos, Marchese del Vasto* (1536; Paris, Coll. De Ganay). He also painted, for Guidobaldo II, the famous *Venus of Urbino* (1538; Uffizi), one of the finest achievements of his maturity.

At the same time Titian continued to work in Venice, where—between 1534 and 1538—he executed the huge painting of the *Presentation of the Virgin* (now in the Accademia, Venice) for the Scuola della Carità. It was followed by the ceiling frescoes in S. Maria della Salute (1543–44), with such Biblical subjects as *David and Goliath* and *Cain Slaying Abel*, and by the portraits of *Cardinal Pietro Bembo* (*c.* 1542; Washington, D.C., National Gallery), *Clarice Strozzi as a Child* (1542; Berlin, Staatliche Museen), *Pope Paul III* (*c.* 1543; Naples, Museo di Capodimonte), and *Pietro Aretino* (1545; Palazzo Pitti). In the mid-1540s Titian left for Rome and was welcomed there as the guest of Paul III. During his stay in the Vatican, he painted a group of portraits for the Farnese family (*Pope Paul III and his Grandsons*, 1546; Museo di Capodimonte), and the voluptuous mythological canvas of *Danaë* (*c.* 1545; Museo di Capodimonte).

Titian's style changed at this time, his late manner growing freer and his activity more widespread. At the invitation of Charles V, he went to Augsburg to paint a number of portraits, among others one of the emperor himself seated in an armchair (1548; Munich, Alte Pinakothek) and another showing him in full armor on horseback on the battlefield at Mühlberg (Prado). During his second visit to Augsburg (1550–51), he worked at other

Titian. *Emperor Charles V.* 1548. Alte Pinakothek, Munich.

court portraits, notably those of *King Philip II of Spain* (Prado and Museo di Capodimonte) and of *Johann Friedrich, Elector of Saxony* (1550; Kunsthistorisches Museum). The last illustrious visitors to his workshop were King Henri III of France and Giorgio Vasari. Titian died in Venice during an epidemic of plague, and was buried with honors in the church of the Frari. At the time of his death he left unfinished a *Pietà* (begun 1573; Venice, Accademia) that was intended for his own family chapel there; it was completed by Palma Giovane. As early as the Paduan frescoes, Titian's forms are stronger and his color areas more clearly defined than Giorgione's, his style soon depending on the interplay of luminous color tones alone. An impressive development may be observed in his religious painting, from the Renaissance serenity and balance of the Bellini-like *Madonna of the Cherries* (*c.* 1510–20; Vienna, Kunsthistorisches Museum) to his masterpiece of dramatic style, the Frari *Assumption*, in which groups of figures, without any architectural background, are the only means used to organize space.

After 1530 Titian became increasingly concerned with portraiture, but already in the early Giorgionesque *Man with a Glove* (Paris, Louvre) his characteristic clarity and refinement appear. Between 1530 and 1540 his portraits are numerous and varied, the color becoming richer, more sumptuous, and varied by a fine gradation of tones (*La Bella*, 1536, Palazzo Pitti; the *Girl in a Fur*,

Vienna, Kunsthistorisches Museum). After 1540, he began to simplify his late style even further. His color became more vibrant, and such works as the *Annunciation* (*c.* 1565) for the church of S. Salvatore at Venice possess a new warmth. In his last works, particularly the *Pietà*, the new element of pathos added a personal and poignant accent to the grandeur expressed by Titian's art.

TOBEY, Mark (1890, Centerville, Wisconsin—1976, Basel, Switzerland), American painter. Sometimes called the least American of American painters, Tobey worked neither in a violent nor in an Expressionistic manner. His paintings are remarkable for the meticulous care of their execution and the refinement of their color—a result of the almost exclusive use of the techniques of watercolor, tempera, and pastels.

Mainly self-taught, Tobey settled in New York in 1911 and achieved some commercial success as a portraitist, somewhat in the Sargent tradition. In 1922 he moved to Seattle, where he taught at the Cornish School. After traveling widely until 1931, he moved to England. During his sojourn there, Tobey made several trips to the Orient, where he studied Chinese calligraphy with his friend Teng Kwei in Shanghai, and Zen Buddhism in Japan, thus completing his years of training. By 1935 he had developed a unique technique that he called "white writing," which consisted of a network of calligraphic markings in white ink against a colored ground, by means of which he delineated images of city streets, as in *Broadway* (1936; New York, Metropolitan Museum). In this painting the countless trajectories of passers-by and vehicles and the myriad lights of Times Square form an inextricable tangle of white lines that represents the artist's own inner vision, in Zen Buddhist terms, of the urban scene that both excited and disturbed him greatly. The reference to the physical world is nonetheless clearly visible. *City Radiance* (1944; New York, Coll. Feininger), however, is totally nonobjective and is made up of an elaborate web of lines that possesses an intricacy and delicacy absent in the earlier work.

During the last years of the 1930s, Tobey was employed on a WPA project in Seattle, remaining in that city throughout the 1940s. It was during the 1950s, however, that Tobey achieved international recognition as one of America's foremost painters. In 1958 he became the first American since Whistler to receive first prize at the Venice Biennale. Examples of Tobey's work during this period are *Street* (1954) and the lyrical *Search* (1954), both in the collection of Jeanne Bucher, Paris.

Mark Tobey. *Street.* 1954. *Photo Galerie Jeanne Bucher-Luc Joubert, Paris.*

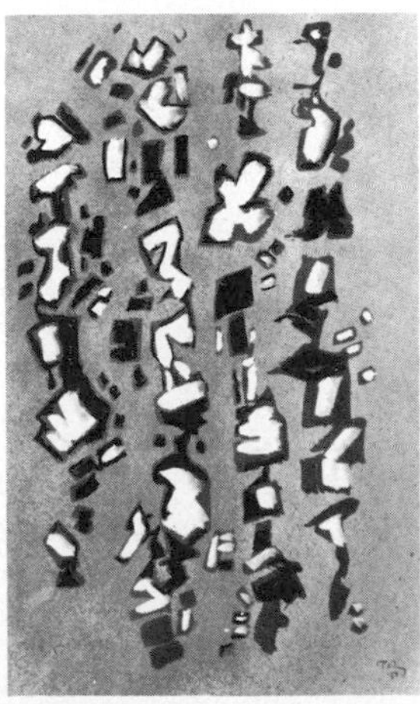

TOLTEC ART. The Toltecs occupied the region covered by the present Mexican states of Tlaxcala, Hidalgo, Morelos, and Puebla, and their principal center was the city of Tula, northwest of both Teotihuacán and Mexico City. Their civilization probably emerged during the 9th century A.D. and developed from A.D. 850 to 1250. One of the important features of their history is that in the 10th century A.D. they seized the northern areas of the Maya country and produced a synthesis of the two civilizations, the finest examples of which are found at Chichén Itzá in Yucatán. It was long believed that the Toltecs were the founders of Teotihuacán, but in fact they arrived much later and were merely its heirs, or destroyers. Although they were known as Toltecs, that is to say, builders, they were essentially a militarist people, and it was they who created the first Mexican society in which the warrior caste had precedence over the priests.

The architecture of the Toltecs was inspired by that of Teotihuacán, but there is a certain dryness about its forms that suggests poverty of inspiration rather than purity of conception. Tula, like Teotihuacán, was a ritual center without fortifications, containing the traditional terraced pyramids, colonnaded porticoes, and courts. No major structural innovations are evident, however, although the Toltecs did invent an original element: the Atlantean figures, composed of several blocks of carved stone assembled with the help of tenons, and used either as supports or for decoration. Another characteristic element of Toltec sculpture was the Chacmool, a semi-recumbent figure bearing on its belly a receptacle for offerings; this type spread throughout the territories under Toltec influence. The steles, glyphs, friezes of warriors, and reliefs of jaguars, eagles, and coyotes reveal, as do the Atlantean figures and Chacmool, an art that is above all decorative. The Toltec gods are hieratic and laden with ornaments: they do not possess the haunting, hypnotic quality of the Maya gods, but they have a calm gravity, and although they are less grandiose than the Maya figures, they are no less strange.

Toltec Art. Detail of Atlantean figure. North pyramid, Tula. 13th century. *Photo Henri Stierlin, Geneva.*

Toltec Art. *Chacmool.* Chichén Itzá, 13th century. Museo Nacional de Antropología, Mexico City. *Photo Walter Dräyer, Zurich.*

Jacopo Torriti. *Coronation of the Virgin.* 1296 (?). Apse of S. Maria Maggiore, Rome.

TOMLIN, Bradley Walker (1899, Syracuse, New York—1953, New York), American painter. In 1923 he went to England and then to Paris, where he was more interested in the work of Cézanne, Van Gogh, and Gauguin than in that of Picasso, Matisse, or Braque. In 1926–27 he again visited England, Italy, and Paris, where he shared Rodin's former studio with his close friend, the painter Frank London (1876–1945). He did not, in fact, evolve a truly personal style until the late 1930s, possibly as a result of the famous exhibition of "Fantastic Art, Dada and Surrealism" held in 1936 at the Museum of Modern Art in New York. During the late 1930s and early 1940s Tomlin produced semi-abstract still lifes, some of which were reminiscent of Braque, while others included Surrealist props. The elegiac note in his work grew even deeper and more somber in *To the Sea* (1942; New York, Coll. Mr. William Benton) and *Burial* (1943; New York, Metropolitan Museum), both of which are montages of abstract forms, architectural details, and real objects (a ship's figurehead, a laurel-crowned athlete's head).

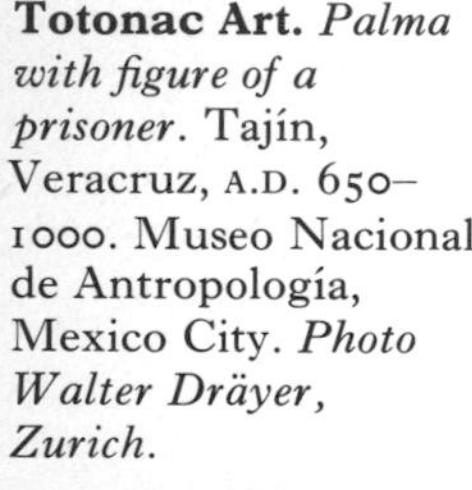

Totonac Art. *Palma with figure of a prisoner.* Tajín, Veracruz, A.D. 650–1000. Museo Nacional de Antropología, Mexico City. *Photo Walter Dräyer, Zurich.*

Tomlin did not, however, emerge as a truly important and original artist until the last five years of his life, when he came under the influence of Abstract Expressionist painters. Two important transitional works—*Arrangement* (*c.* 1944; Urbana, Ill., Krannert Art Museum, University of Illinois) and *The Armor Must Change* (1946; New York, Coll. Mr. and Mrs. Ben Wolf)—show the extent and gradualness of this change. The ribbonlike outlines of *Number 3* (1948; U.S.A., Coll. John E. Hutchins) and especially of *Tension by Moonlight* (1948; New York, Betty Parsons Gallery), which consists of six white bands on black, were the acutest realization of Tomlin's desire to do away with subtleties.

Interesting as they are, these lyrical works are not completely typical of Tomlin. He soon returned to the architectural complexities that haunted him, this time, however, using an expanded version of the abstract vocabulary with which he had just been experimenting. Works such as *Number 20* (1949) and *Number 9: In Praise of Gertrude Stein* (1950), both in New York's Museum of Modern Art, represent an architectural and intellectual apprehension of multiple experiences, a vision that Pollock was simultaneously translating in another way.

In 1952–53 Tomlin produced his greatest works; the tremendous tension characteristic of his earlier canvases disappeared as he attained the unified lyricism and inward harmony toward which he had perhaps always been working.

TOOKER, George (b. 1920, Brooklyn, New York), American painter. In the early 1940s he worked under the New York urban realist Kenneth Hayes Miller, and later studied privately with the illustrator and painter Paul Cadmus, who taught him to use his favorite medium, egg tempera. Tooker's style, in which realistically drawn scenes of figures are defined with a polished and deliberate precision, has been termed "Magic Realism." The contrast between the careful execution and the unsettling psychological implications of his subject matter sets up a particularly compelling tension. Tooker deals with themes of alienation and dehumanization in contemporary settings. His manner also refers to early Italian painting and to the Surrealistic associations of works by René Magritte and Balthus, both of whom were important influences. In his well-known *Government Bureau* (1956; New York, Metropolitan Museum) Tooker comments upon the machine-like sterility of modern bureaucracy as he shows identical-looking people lined up in front of booths containing strange, staring, and hostile officials. In *Box* (*c.* 1967; Coll. artist), he again emphasizes the concern with psychological discomfort that pervades his work. Its subject is a nude figure cramped into a shallow, illusionistic, box-like frame.

TORRITI, Jacopo, *also called* Jacopo da Torrida (active late 13th century, Rome), Italian painter and mosaicist. Few records remain of his life, and his fame rests entirely on the Roman apsidal mosaics in the churches of S. Giovanni in Laterano and S. Maria Maggiore, as well as on the frescoes attributed to him in the church of S. Francesco at Assisi. The Assisi frescoes were undertaken in about 1280 in the upper church of the basilica, in collaboration with Cimabue (the two may have met in Rome in 1272), but the individual contributions of each artist, as well as dates, are difficult to determine. The S. Giovanni mosaics (*c.* 1291) are even more problematic. The existing work is actually a careful 19th-century copy of the 13th-century work, which itself was probably a copy or restoration of a 4th- or 5th-century mosaic. Fortunately the original of Torriti's work survives at S. Maria Maggiore (1296?), a mosaic in which he took a greater role. The general scheme is based on that of Pietro Cavallini's mosaic in S. Maria in Trastevere, Rome (early 1290s?), with the *Coronation of the Virgin* occupying the most prominent position. Torriti's great innovation consisted in placing the *Death of the Virgin* under the Coronation, thus breaking the chronological sequence and linking the upper and lower zones both decoratively and thematically. The *Coronation* itself, surrounded by saints and angels, seems to be Torriti's original invention.

TOSI, Arturo (1871, Busto Arsizio, Lombardy—1956, Milan), Italian painter. He was almost exclusively a landscape painter, one of the most spontaneous and lyrical in modern Italian art. Belonging at first to the tradition established in 19th-century Lombardy by the painters of the Scapigliatura, Tosi then turned to French Postimpressionism, the influences of which he assimilated without imitating any particular artist. Although he was one of the founders of the reactionary Novecento in the early 1920s, he was too fond of Cézanne and Bonnard to be confined within the Neoclassicism of the movement. When Tosi was well past eighty, his freshness of approach and his brilliant, rigorous technique were still as apparent as ever. An example of his work is the very lyrical landscape entitled *Lake Iseo* (1952; Milan, Coll. Giovanardi).

TOTONAC ART. The Totonacs inhabited the western coastal plain of the Gulf of Mexico, where they developed a major civilization, the principal center of which was the city of Tajín, whose ruins still stand in the present State of Veracruz. Their civilization is also frequently referred to as that of Tajín. Its origins date back to the 10th century B.C., and in the 7th century A.D. it assimilated the influences of the Olmecs, Teotihuacán, and the Maya. About the year A.D. 1450, the Totonacs were defeated and conquered by the Aztecs.

Totonac sculptors produced some large reliefs, such as those of the pelota court at Tajín that represent the ball games and the sacrifice of one of the players, but they excelled above all in three very special kinds of work: the so-called yokes, *palmas*, and *hachas*. The term yokes has been given to the u-shaped carvings that, according to historian Raoul d'Harcourt, "represent, translated into stone for ritual purposes, the thick wickerwork belts worn as protection by the pelota players." These yokes carved from polished hard stone (diorite, jadeite, green granite, porphyry) are decorated with an animal or human figure. The *palmas*, so named because of their palmate form, were also based upon the pelota player's equipment; they were carved in limestone, the decorations being at times abstract, but more often figurative, containing depictions of men, gods, or symbolic animals. The *hachas* were ax-head gods—ceremonial axes with heads carved in profile. These extremely well-finished works of sculpture avoid coldness by being stylized with great simplicity and purity. Terracotta sculpture was more realistic, and depicted figures of gods, warriors, and musicians in more correctly observed postures.

Totonac Art. *Hacha with profile of a man.* A.D. 650–1000. Museum für Völkerkunde, Munich. *Photo Walter Dräyer, Zurich.*

Totonac architecture is equal to the greatest achievements of ancient Mexico. It succeeded in finding an original mode of expression somewhere between the austere Classicism of Teotihuacán and the Baroque opulence of the Maya. Its masterpiece is the truncated Pyramid of the Niches (*c.* A.D. 700–800) at Tajín, which has seven terraces, with rectangular walls pierced by niches (364 in all, corresponding to the days of the Totonac year), surmounted by a cornice that balances the whole.

TOULOUSE-LAUTREC, Henri-Marie Raymond de Toulouse-Lautrec-Monfa, *called* Henri de (1864, Albi, Tarn—1901, Malromé, near Bordeaux), French painter. A descendant of the counts of Toulouse, who had acquired their title during Charlemagne's reign, he was a sickly but bright child, and spent his early years at his family's estate near Albi. In 1873 his parents moved to Paris, where he attended the Lycée Fontanes (now the Lycée Condorcet). Lautrec then continued his studies in Albi under his mother's vigilant and affectionate supervision. Unfortunately, in two consecutive falls (1878 and 1879), he broke both his thighs and remained a cripple for the rest of his life. He grew into a grotesque little man, barred from the ordinary pleasures of life but determined to fight adversity with the courage he had inherited from his ancestors.

His first paintings—*Soldier Saddling His Horse* (1879), the *Falconer: Comte Alphonse de Toulouse-Lautrec* (1881; both Albi, Musée Toulouse-Lautrec), and *Comte Alphonse de Toulouse-Lautrec Driving His Four-in-Hand to Nice* (1881; Paris, Musée du Petit Palais)—revealed his staggering virtuosity and precocious feeling for modern art. In 1882 he enrolled in Léon Bonnat's class in Paris, then (1883) in that of Fernand Cormon. Bored with academic discipline and fascinated by the work of Édouard Manet and Edgar Degas, he cut most of Cormon's classes. It was there, nevertheless, in 1886, that he met Vincent van Gogh, of whom he did a pastel portrait (1887; Laren, Holland, Coll. V. W. van Gogh). The two painters became friendly and Lautrec influenced the Dutch painter to leave Paris for Provence. In 1885 Lautrec decided to leave home and live the life of a Montmartre artist in complete independence. At the Moulin de la Galette, the Moulin Rouge, and at Aristide Bruant's cabaret, the Mirliton, he frequently spent whole nights drinking and sketching all sorts of music hall stars and even royalty who had wandered astray into this demimonde. By the time he was twenty-five he had already mastered his technique, as may be seen in such works as the *Ball at the Moulin de la Galette* (1889; Chicago, Art Institute), the *Dance at the Moulin Rouge* (1890; Philadelphia, Coll. Henry P. MacIlhenny), *Mademoiselle Dihau at the Piano* (1890; Musée Toulouse-Lautrec), and *La Goulue* (1891; Musée Toulouse-Lautrec).

Henri de Toulouse-Lautrec. *"A la mie."* 1891. Museum of Fine Arts, Boston.

For a brief period (1886–87), Lautrec was influenced by the Impressionists, especially by Manet, Camille Pissarro, and Auguste Renoir, but most of all by Degas (*In Batignolles: Portrait of a Montmartre Model*, 1888, London, Coll. Andrew Goeritz; *Portrait of the Comtesse de Toulouse-Lautrec in the Salon at Malromé*, 1887, Musée Toulouse-Lautrec; *At the Moulin Rouge*, 1892, Chicago, Art Institute), and he even exhibited with them in 1889 at the Salon des Indépendants. Nevertheless, after about 1888, his work took a direction quite different from that of Impressionism. In 1891 he designed his first posters, an art form he mastered from the start. Their simplified forms, their bold, flat areas of color, and their striking layouts had a decisive effect upon his painting. Using quick, sure

Henri de Toulouse-Lautrec. *Portrait of G.-H. Manuel.* 1891. Coll. Bührle, Zurich.

Henri de Toulouse-Lautrec. *"Au salon de la rue des Moulins."* 1894. Musée Toulouse-Lautrec, Albi. *Photo Giraudon, Paris.*

brushstrokes and applying pure color mixed with turpentine, he produced the dazzling series of pictures that have the spontaneity of sketches and the authority of oil paintings: *Jane Avril Dancing* (1892; Paris, Louvre), *Woman Pulling Up Her Stocking* (1894; versions in Paris, Musée de l'Impressionnisme, and Albi, Musée Toulouse-Lautrec), *Two Friends* (1894; Musée Toulouse-Lautrec), and *At the Bar: the Chlorotic Cashier* (1898; Zurich, Kunsthaus). During the 1890s he also contributed humorous drawings to such periodicals as *Le Rire, Le Courrier Français, Le Figaro, La Revue Blanche*, and *La Plume*. In 1895 he visited London, and in 1896 Holland and Spain. In 1898 he returned to London for an exhibition of his works at the Goupil Gallery. Excessive drinking and the strain of night life had so deeply undermined his health that in 1899, on his return to Paris, he was committed to a clinic for disintoxication. While there he drew his famous series of *Circus* scenes. Sensing that the end was in sight, he had himself transported to his mother's side at Malromé, where he died on September 9, 1901. In 1922 she offered the paintings remaining in her son's studio to the town of Albi, where today they are exhibited at the Musée Toulouse-Lautrec in the Palais de la Berbie.

The dominant themes of Lautrec's painting—the actresses, clowns, dancers, lesbians, the circus scenes, café-concerts, brothels, race tracks, in sum all the creatures and spectacles of a pleasure-loving Paris—are similar to those portrayed by Degas, who had considered Lautrec an equal. Lautrec's draftsmanship is, however, more concise, and more biting than the former's, his color more sober and his movement swifter. In spite of the triviality and futility of its subject matter, it communicates the proud distinction, verve, and disillusionment behind which Lautrec masked his tragedy with touching reserve. Lautrec also outstripped Paul Gauguin's attempt at "synthesis": his use of the arabesque was more than merely supple, firm, and sensitive; it was completely unsentimental and unliterary. He learned a great deal from Japanese prints. This Japanese influence, combined with that of poster design, led him away from Impressionism and Symbolism in the direction of the monumental art of placards and panels, such as those with which he decorated La Goulue's booth at the Foire du Trône (1895). Lautrec's noble spirit, imprisoned as it was within his ugly body, masked his humiliation: the most gifted artist of his time hid the secret of his genius from curious outsiders with a wisecrack.

TOWN, Ithiel (1784, Thompson, Connecticut—1844, New Haven), American architect. He was a member of the Connecticut Academy of Arts and Sciences, and with his friend Samuel F. B. Morse was a founder of the National Academy of Design. In 1825 Yale awarded him an honorary master's degree, and in 1836 he was made an honorary member of the Royal Institute of British Architects.

Town's commissions were so often associated with other men that it is hard to assess his individual contribution. His first known work was the building of Center Church, New Haven (1813), designed by Asher Benjamin. Immediately afterward he built the nearby Trinity Church (1814–15), one of the first Gothic Revival churches in America. During these years he invented the famous Town Lattice Truss, a bridge truss that he patented and marketed throughout Europe and the United States.

In 1825 Town settled in New York, where he formed a partnership with Martin E. Thompson (1789–1877). Simultaneously in that year they produced two landmarks of the early Greek Revival: Thompson's Phenix Bank in New York and Town's Eagle Bank in New York (not completed and demolished after the bank's failure). The firm was soon joined by Alexander Jackson Davis, continuing as Town and Davis after Thompson's departure. The arrangements within the firm varied, and today it is almost impossible to assess the individual contributions of each partner. The following list of attributions therefore is only tentative. The Bowery Theater in New York (Town, 1825), with its massive Greek Doric portico, was followed by the Connecticut State Capitol, New Haven (Town, 1829), the first Greek Doric temple in New England. In 1833 Town and Davis built the New York Customs House (now Subtreasury), a combination of Greek temple and Roman dome that the firm particularly favored. New York University (begun 1833) belongs to the period of Town's partnership with Thompson. The North Carolina Capitol (1833–40), built in collaboration with Davis, achieves a monumental quality in spite of its modest size. The Wadsworth Athenaeum in Hartford, Connecticut (1842), also in collaboration with Davis, was one of Town's last efforts. Town retired in 1835 (collaborating occasionally thereafter), and built for himself a magnificent Greek Revival house in New Haven, designed to hold his great library.

TRECENTO ART, the art of the 14th century in Italy. The holy year 1300 was marked by the magnificent jubilee of Pope Boniface VIII (reigned 1294–1303), whose dream it was to unite in his person both spiritual and temporal power. The archbishop of Bordeaux, elected pope in 1305 as Clement V, soon moved his court to Avignon (1309), which remained the papal residence for almost 100 years. The transfer of the Holy See was the basic reason for one of the peculiar features of the Trecento, the absence of artistic activity in Rome. When in 1367 Pope Urban V (reigned 1362–70) attempted to rebuild Rome, he had to call on a Sienese architect, Giovanni di Stefano, to restore S. Giovanni in Laterano and erect an enormous tabernacle there. Two other factors had important consequences for the art of this century: the abandonment of the imperial policy of unifying Italy, and the rebirth of humanism. Among the local dynasties that began to arise, prefiguring those of the Quattrocento, there appeared such patrons as Can Grande della Scala, imperial vicar of Verona (1291–1329), the first Lombard tyrant to take an interest in artists. Robert of Anjou, king of Naples from 1309 to 1343, declared that he felt more pride in being a poet than in being a king. Everywhere artists were given commissions, so that the painters, who previously had been obliged to belong to the guild of physicians and pharmacists, were allowed to form their own guild, in 1349 at Florence and in 1355 at Siena.

With the rebirth of humanism in the Trecento, the cult of antiquity was introduced. Dante, who was exiled from Florence about 1302 and wandered from city to city until his death in 1321, took the examples for his *Divine Comedy* (begun *c.* 1307) as much from the ancient world as from Christianity. Petrarch, who was crowned with laurels at the Capitol in 1341, turned the attention of his contemporaries to epigraphy and archaeology. Boccaccio, who is known today primarily as the author of the ribald *Decameron* (1348–53), was above all a popularizer of ancient culture, notably in his treatise on mythology, *De Genealogiis Deorum Gentilium* (1351–60). Such a moral climate inevitably influenced painting: in the Arena Chapel at Padua Giotto painted the allegorical figure of Hope in a Classical costume; his followers represented figures wearing the Greek *chlamys*, a cloak fastened at the shoulder.

In painting, the Trecento was the century of Giotto: even the Sienese School, which was then at its height, was reduced to second place by the work of the Florentine master. His frescoes in the Arena Chapel at Padua (1304–1312/13) revolutionized the art of his time. His fame was such that he soon became an almost legendary artist, whose methods seemed definitive. Among his immediate pupils, who were active in the first half of the Trecento, the most famous was his godson Taddeo Gaddi, who painted the frescoes of the *Life of the Virgin* in the Baroncelli Chapel (1332–38) of S. Croce, in Florence. The school also often copied the master's figures instead of devising its own from nature. Certain artists escaped from these conventions, including Maso di Banco, whose work is marked by strongly sculptured effects (*Life of St. Sylvester*, Bardi Chapel, S. Croce); Bernardo Daddi (*c.* 1290–1355), who painted with rather sentimental delicacy; and Giovanni da Milano, whose painting shows a feeling for picturesque detail. In the second half of the Trecento, the most prolific of the Giottesque painters was Agnolo Gaddi, son of Taddeo, a painter, architect, and mosaicist. In Florence there were two other painters distinguished by their personal interpretation of the accepted principles: Andrea da Firenze (2nd half of the 14th century), in his decoration of the Spanish Chapel at S. Maria Novella (begun 1365), and Andrea Orcagna, whose altarpiece in the Strozzi Chapel of the same church (1354–57) showed that painting and sculpture were for him a single art.

Trecento Art. Bonino da Campione. Equestrian statue of Can Grande della Scala, Verona. Begun before 1375.

Giotto's influence was not confined to the city in which he had his workshop; it spread into every province. Tommaso da Modena (1325/26–before 1379) adopted his manner and spread it in the course of his travels. At Naples, the frescoes in S. Chiara and those in the Incoronata, the chapel founded in 1352 by Queen Jeanne, were purely Giottesque. Altichiero da Zevio (1369–90) and Jacopo Avanzo (2nd half of the 14th century) at Padua and Francesco Traini (active 1321–63) at Pisa were worthy continuators of Giotto's style. At Arezzo this role was played by Spinello Aretino (*c.* 1346–1410), the most ardent Giottesque artist of the late Trecento (*Life of St. Benedict, c.* 1386; Florence, sacristy of S. Miniato). The only city to which Giotto's influence did not spread was Venice, which remained faithful to Byzantine tradition through Paolo da Venezia and Nicoletto Semitecolo (active 1353–70).

Painting developed in Siena outside the mainstream deriving from Giotto, and followed original ways first developed by Duccio di Buoninsegna. Because he broke less abruptly with the Greek (Byzantine) manner than did artists of the Florentine School, he fixed the norms of a pictorial idealism in which a taste for bright colors and elegant forms, and a feeling for luxury and poetic evocation remained predominant. This conception appeared also in the work of his disciple Simone Martini, who combined poetic imagination with a care for exactitude (*Condottiere Guidoriccio da Fogliano*, 1328; Siena, Palazzo Pubblico). The Lorenzetti brothers nurtured the same qualities, but worked with different aims: Pietro excelled in tragic realism, relieved by a certain brightness; Ambrogio, a painter of encyclopedic knowledge, strove to place his narrative skill at the service of ambitious symbols (*Allegories of Good and Bad Government, c.* 1340; Palazzo Pubblico). Barna da Siena succeeded in coming close to the innovative style of Simone Martini in the scenes of the *Life of Christ* that he painted in the collegiate church of S. Gimignano, variously dated in the early 1350s or, according to some, 1381.

In sculpture, the Trecento saw the flowering of the Pisan School and the beginnings of the Florentine School. In 1301 Giovanni Pisano, son of Nicola Pisano, signed the marble pulpit of the church of S. Andrea at Pistoia. He was appointed master builder of Pisa Cathedral and there carved a monumental pulpit (1302–10) whose supports included groups of figures forming caryatids; this was an innovation. Among Giovanni Pisano's many pupils, only two are worthy of note: Giovanni di Balduccio (b. 1317/18), whose principal work is the reliquary (1335–39) at S. Eustorgio, Milan—called the Arca di S. Pietro Martire—that was intended to house the relics of St. Peter of

Trecento Art. Giovanni Pisano. *Adoration of the Magi.* Detail of pulpit. 1302–10. Duomo, Pisa.

Trecento Art. S. Maria della Spina, Pisa. Enlarged after 1323. *Photo Anderson.*

Verona; and Tino di Camaino (*c.* 1285–1337), a specialist in funerary sculpture (tomb of Antonio degli Orsi, bishop of Florence, in that city's cathedral, 1321), who settled in Naples and there carved the mausoleum of Mary of Hungary (1324–25) at S. Maria Donna Regina.

Florentine sculpture was revived by Andrea Pisano, who completed a set of bronze doors for the baptistery in 1336. He succeeded Giotto as architect of the Campanile and directed the creation of the master's 54 bas-reliefs. There was one principal work in the new style, the polychromed tabernacle of Or San Michele (1352–59) by Andrea Orcagna, whose work in marble was strongly related to goldwork. Besides the work of the Florentine and Sienese schools, the Trecento produced that of the Campionesi, a family of marble workers who worked mostly in Verona and Milan. Two brothers of Venetian origin, Jacobello and Pier Paolo dalle Masegne, also gained some renown at Bologna, where they carved the marble polyptych for the main altar of S. Francesco (1388–92).

Trecento architecture was marked by composite adaptations of Gothic. Until 1330 Lorenzo Maitani (*c.* 1275–1330) was master mason of Orvieto Cathedral, which had been begun in the preceding century on a Romanesque plan and was continued in the Gothic style. In Florence, work on the cathedral had been suspended, until Francesco Talenti enlarged the nave about 1358. But the great project at this time was Or San Michele, on which work continued without interruption from about 1337. Two works that were begun during the Trecento were not completed until later centuries: Milan Cathedral, which from 1386 was the object of disputes between various master masons, and the church of S. Petronio at Bologna, begun in 1390 by Antonio di Vicenzo. In Venice, two churches were built in the style of Flamboyant Gothic: S. Maria della Carità and the Madonna del Orto, each with a nave and no transept. In the 1330s S. Maria Gloriosa dei Frari was begun.

Trecento Art. Palazzo Vecchio, Florence. Founded 1299.

Secular architecture was not marked by many notable differences from religious buildings. The most striking buildings are the *palazzi comunali*, which usually preserve a fortress-like appearance. A notable exception is the Doges' Palace in Venice, whose elegant façade along the quay was built in the second half of the century. During the Trecento the loggias acquired a truly Italian style: these were buildings open on two or three sides, with arcades; they were sometimes used as markets. The loggia of the castle of Boniface VIII at Anagni and the Loggia dei Lanzi (1376) in Florence are the best examples.

TRIBOLO, Niccolò Pericoli, *called* (1500, Florence—1550, Florence), Italian sculptor, architect, and engineer. He was taught by Jacopo Sansovino, and was a friend of Michelangelo. In 1525 he was in Bologna, where he executed some sculptural decoration for the façade of S. Petronio. Ten years later he carved a marble relief representing the *Assumption of the Virgin* (1536–37; now Bologna, S. Petronio) for the church of the Madonna di Galliera, also in Bologna. During 1533 he went to Florence to assist Michelangelo in the Medici Chapel, but their collaboration ended upon the death of Pope Clement VII in 1534 (it was resumed briefly in 1545, when Tribolo installed certain of Michelangelo's statues for the

Trecento Art. Doges' Palace, Venice. 2nd half of 14th century.

tombs). Whatever merits he had as a sculptor, Tribolo was a better engineer and landscape gardener: it was he who designed the Boboli Gardens in Florence, a rustic arrangement of paths and steps, in which statues and fountains were employed to provide an agreeable setting. Similarly, he designed the gardens of the Villa Reale di Castello near Florence, and those of the Medici villa at Petraia, which he decorated with fountains surmounted by statues by Bartolomeo Ammannati and Giovanni Bologna. The two fountains that Tribolo designed and executed for the Villa di Castello (Fountain of the Labyrinth, Fountain of Hercules) are considered his most important works.

TRISTÁN, Luis (*c.* 1586, Toledo—1624, Toledo), Spanish painter. He studied (1603–7) under El Greco, whose pictures he occasionally copied (*Grand Inquisitor Cardinal Fernando Niño de Guevara*, 1612; Toledo, Seminario), but he was even more influenced by Orazio Borgianni (1578–1616). Tristán's *Holy Family* (1613; Florence, Coll. Count Contini-Bonacossi), for example, shows something of El Greco's influence but owes more to Borgianni in its treatment of color, composition, modeling, and light. Velázquez is known to have seen and admired several of Tristán's paintings in Seville, and the treatment of lighting, composition, and draperies in such works as *St. Louis of France Giving Alms* (1620; Paris, Louvre) and the *Last Supper* (1616; church of Yepes) are likewise apparent in Velázquez' style. Other paintings in Seville that Velázquez may have seen include the *St. Francis* (Alcázar) and the *Trinity* (1624; Cathedral). The *Adoration of the Shepherds* (c. 1620; Bilbao, Museum) has also been attributed to Tristán, and places him in the vanguard of early Baroque painting in Spain.

TROGER, Paul (1698, Welsberg, Pustertal—1762, Vienna), Austrian Baroque painter, one of the leading ceiling decorators of the 18th century. In 1741 he went to Italy to study under Giuseppe Alberti (1640–1716). While in Venice he came into contact with Giambattista Piazzetta's extremely dramatic chiaroscuro lighting, which became a predominant characteristic of Troger's own style (*Descent from the Cross*, 1722, Kaltern, Tirol, Church of the Holy Cross; *Agony in the Garden, c.* 1728, Salzburg, Peterskirche). Another lasting influence came as the result of a visit to Naples, where he absorbed the style of Francesco Solimena. In 1728, upon his return to Austria, he painted the dome of the Kajetanerkirche in Salzburg, and later decorated the library and the so-called Marble Room in the monastery at Melk (1731–32). Troger's ceiling frescoes adorn many churches in Austria, including St. Lambert at Altenburg (1732–33) and the chapel of Schloss Heiligenkreuz-Gutenbrunn (1739). From 1748 to 1750 he decorated the cathedral at Bressanone (called Brixen in German).

TROY, family of French painters active in the 17th and 18th centuries whose most important members were:

JEAN III DE (1638, Toulouse—1691, Montpellier). On his return from the traditional visit to Rome, he settled at Montpellier, where he opened an academy.

FRANÇOIS DE (1645, Toulouse—1730, Paris), brother of Jean III. In 1674 he entered the Académie Royale de Peinture et de Sculpture, and in 1708 he became its director. François was primarily a portrait painter and enjoyed a great reputation in his day. His best works include the *Duchesse d'Orléans* (Versailles, Museum); the *Duchesse du Maine* (1694; Orléans, Museum); *Jean de Jullienne* (1722; Valenciennes, Museum); *Mouton the Lutanist* (1690; Paris, Louvre); and a portrait of *Mansart* (Versailles, Museum).

JEAN FRANÇOIS DE (1679, Paris—1752, Rome), son of François and the most famous member of the family. During a stay in Rome (1698–*c.* 1704), he was attracted by the work of the great colorists Titian and Rubens. Jean François was elected to the Académie at the age of twenty-nine and distinguished himself as a decorator, portraitist, and genre painter. He achieved prominence in the Salons with what were then called *tableaux de mode*, mirrors of the gay, elegant life under the Regency. His paintings provide some piquant glimpses of the kind of life he led: *A Reading from Molière* (1710; London, Coll. Sir Philip Sassoon); *Luncheon with Oysters* (1735; Chantilly, Musée Condé); and the "quartet" of 1725: the *Declaration* (Berlin), the *Unfastened Garter*, the *Game of Pied-de-boeuf* (copy in London, National Gallery), and *Lunch in the Country*. Of equal note are the splendid *Gathering in a Park* (1731; Berlin) and the *Hunt Breakfast* (1737; London, Wallace Collection). For collectors he painted a number of the less sacred Biblical subjects: the *Bath of Susanna* (1727; Rouen, Museum); *Bathsheba* (Leningrad, Hermitage; 1727, Angers, Museum); and *Lot's Daughters* (1722; Orléans, Musée de Peinture et de Sculpture), his favorite subject; or the more engaging mythological ones, such as the *Repose of Diana* (1726; Nancy, Museum). He was also given official commissions, notably the *Luncheon with Oysters* for the dining room of Louis XV's private apartments at Versailles and designs for a tapestry in seven tableaux of the *Story of Esther and Mordecai* (1737–42; Paris, Musée des Arts Décoratifs), which was one of the greatest successes of the Gobelins workshops. In 1738 he was appointed director of the Académie de France in Rome, where he displayed an ambassadorial pomp and was admired because of his affable generosity. He was as great a portrait painter as Nicolas de Largillière and Hyacinthe Rigaud, as skillful a decorator as François Boucher; but he was unique as a painter of social life under the Regency.

Jean-François de Troy. *Luncheon with Oysters.* 1735. Detail. Musée Condé, Chantilly. *Photo Giraudon, Paris.*

Tribolo (after plans by). Boboli Gardens, Florence, 1550. *Photo Martin Hürlimann, Zurich.*

TRUMBULL, John (1756, Lebanon, Connecticut—1843, New York), American history and portrait painter. He was the son of Governor Jonathan Trumbull of Connecticut, and in 1773 completed his education at Harvard. He interrupted his artistic career, however, to serve (1775–77) during the American Revolution in

Washington's Continental Army. One of his finest works of this period is the full-length portrait of *George Washington* (1780) now in the Metropolitan Museum in New York.

After an initial trip to London in 1780, Trumbull crossed the Atlantic again in 1784, spending the next five years at the Royal Academy, in the studio of the famed American expatriate history painter, Benjamin West. During this period he painted *Priam Returning with the Body of Hector* (1785; Boston, Atheneum) and one of his most popular canvases, the *Battle of Bunker's Hill* (1786; New Haven, Yale University Art Gallery). He returned to America permanently in 1816 and a year later received his most important commission: a series of four monumental paintings on Revolutionary themes (*Washington Resigning His Commission; Surrender of Cornwallis; Surrender of Burgoyne; Signing of the Declaration of Independence*) for the Rotunda of the U.S. Capitol in Washington, D.C. In these works, which he completed in 1824, one notes the great debt the artist owes to Rubens and to the grandiloquent Baroque narrative tradition. Among his most memorable portraits are a half-length of *Thomas Jefferson* (1787) and a full-length of *Washington Before the Battle of Trenton* (1792), both in the Metropolitan Museum.

John Trumbull. *George Washington.* 1780. Metropolitan Museum of Art, New York (bequest of Charles Allen Munn, 1924).

Cosimo Tura. *Dead Christ Supported by Two Angels. c.* 1475. Kunsthistorisches Museum, Vienna.

Trumbull's considerable influence on American art of the early 19th century was augmented by his role as President of the American Academy of Fine Arts, a post he held from 1816 to 1835. His *Autobiography*, published in 1841, provides the most complete account of his life and work. The largest collection of his paintings in America is at New Haven, in the Yale University Art Gallery, to which the artist donated his canvases in 1831.

TURA, Cosimo (*c.* 1430, Ferrara—1495, Ferrara), Italian painter of the Ferrarese school. Throughout his entire artistic career (*c.* 1451–*c.* 1485), Tura seems to have been the official painter of the Ferrarese princes, Duke Borso d'Este and his successor, Ercole I. Numerous documents mention that he executed portraits of princes: decorative paintings (probably 1459–63) at the castle of Belfiore on the outskirts of Ferrara; standards and banners; as well as designs for tapestries, embroidery, furniture, gold and silver ornaments, and robes for state occasions or tournaments. Only a few examples of his work remain in Ferrara: namely, a *St. George and the Dragon* and an *Annunciation* (both 1468–69; now Museo della Cattedrale) for the organ shutters of Ferrara Cathedral; two fragments from the *St. Maurelius Altarpiece*—the *Condemnation of St. Maurelius* and the *Execution of St. Maurelius* (probably *c.* 1470; formerly in the church of S. Giorgio fuori le Mura, now in the Pinacoteca); and the frescoes (probably 1469–71) in the Palazzo Schifanoia, which Tura painted in collaboration with other artists, principally Ercole de' Roberti. Some 30 paintings can be attributed to him with certainty, most of which belonged to polyptychs that have been dispersed since the 15th century. Several surviving documents have enabled art historians to date three of these works with some certainty: the already mentioned organ shutters from Ferrara Cathedral; the great *Roverella Polyptych* painted for the church of S. Giorgio fuori le Mura (*c.* 1474; now divided between London, National Gallery; Paris, Louvre; Rome, Galleria Colonna; and San Diego, Cal., Museum of Fine Arts); and the *St. Anthony of Padua* (1484; originally in the church of S. Niccolò, Ferrara; now Modena, Galleria Estense). But it is often difficult to date precisely the other pictures not mentioned in documents due to the consistency of Tura's artistry and the unity of his oeuvre. He evolved an extremely original style in which graphic sharpness and the fantasy of the courtly Gothic tradition are fused with plastic strength of the Donatellian milieu of Padua as well as Piero della Francesca's ornamental clarity. Moreover, works such as the *Pietà* (possibly 1472; Venice, Museo Correr) show that he had understood Rogier van der Weyden's dramatic naturalism. The diversity of Tura's paintings links him with the followers of Francesco Squarcione (1394/97–1468/74), whom he probably knew personally in Padua. He nevertheless excelled all of Squarcione's followers, except Andrea Mantegna, in the power of his poetic inventions and the intensity of his Expressionism. Tura's superiority is also evident in the exceptional mastery of his style: his figures, placed in their settings with sculptural authority, are worthy of the Florentine innovators; he emphasized relief effects with great force, and knew how to compose his most elaborate compositions with an extremely modern conception of spatial cohesion. For all these reasons Tura is considered to have been the founder of the Ferrarese school, whose strangeness and rather disturbing poetry were to a great extent derived from his example.

TURKISH ART. *See* **ISLAMIC ART.**

TURNER, Joseph Mallord William (1775, London—1851, Chelsea), English painter. There is still very little known of his education, but it is certain that in 1788 he was given lessons in perspective by the watercolorist Thomas Malton (1726–1801), and that from 1789 he attended classes at the Royal Academy. In 1790 Turner presented a drawing of the *Archbishop's Palace, Lambeth* at the Academy Exhibition; in 1791 he submitted two drawings. In successive years, Turner continued to present works at the Academy exhibitions that brought him increasing notice from the public. In 1793 he was befriended by the art lover Dr. Thomas Monro, chief physician at Bethlehem Hospital. Turner copied in the doctor's house a great many sketches of the landscape artist John Cozens and assimilated the latter's poetic manner. At this time the *Copper Plate Magazine* commissioned him to make a series of drawings of historic sites in England: for several summers he traveled in Wales, Kent, Cheshire, Shropshire, Cumberland, and the Midlands—drawing cathedrals, old castles, ruined abbeys, rivers, and bridges with a deep awareness of the variations of light. From 1796 he also exhibited oil paintings, such as *Morning on Coniston Edge* (1798; London, Tate Gallery).

Between 1800 and 1819 Turner's output increased considerably both in quantity and variety. *Aeneas and the Sibyl* (*c.* 1798; Tate Gallery) was the first of a series of mythological landscapes. In 1802 he visited France and Switzerland for the first time. This journey resulted in the famous *Calais Pier* (1803; London, National Gallery) and in a great many studies of Chamonix, Bonneville, and Lake Geneva. In 1804 he built a gallery behind his house in Harley Street, which was intended for the permanent exhibition of his works. This was later enlarged, then transferred to another building in Queen Anne Street. It contained the collection of paintings and drawings that he refused to sell or that he later bought back in order to leave them to his country. In 1807 Turner was appointed professor of perspective at the Royal Academy, but did not begin teaching until 1811. In 1807 he began his *Liber Studiorum*, for which he made 100 sepia drawings, of which 71 were engraved in mezzotint. He divided the plates into "pastoral scenes," "historical scenes," "seascapes and mountain scenes," and "epic pastorals." Turner was now at the height of his powers, and attained an originality that confounded his critics and earned him the admiration of such men as Sir Thomas Lawrence. He painted the pictures of his mature style, such as the *Death of Nelson* (1806–8), *London Seen from Greenwich* (1809), and *Frosty Morning* (1813; all Tate Gallery), made innumerable drawings for book illustrations, and created a systematic topography of Britain in his pictures of the *South Coast* and *Provincial Antiquities of Scotland* by Sir Walter Scott (1826). During a three-week tour of the Rhine Valley in 1817, Turner executed 50 large-scale sketches. Whereas his watercolors and designs for engravings are as precise as miniatures, the drawings for his paintings are sketchy and unfinished.

In 1819 a five-month journey to Italy marked the beginning of a new period, which lasted until 1840. His taste for intense light and glowing colors had already resulted in Turner and his imitators being called the "white painters." From this period date *Ulysses Mocking Polyphemus* (1829; National Gallery) and the paintings executed from 1829 to 1837 at Petworth, the home of his patron Lord Egremont (*Park at Petworth*, 1829; Tate Gallery). From 1833 Turner exhibited his famous dreamlike views of Venice, such as the *Grand Canal* (1835; New York, Metropolitan Museum) or the *View of the Piazzetta* (*c.* 1835; Tate Gallery).

J. M. W. Turner. *Crossing the Stream.* 1815. Tate Gallery, London.

J. M. W. Turner. *Shipwreck.* 1805. Tate Gallery, London.

Finally, from 1840 to 1850, the tendencies already noted in Turner's work became further exaggerated. His primary preoccupation had long been to express the imponderable effects of light and movement; he now showed a growing interest in the conflict of the elements and cosmic cataclysms. With the sole aim of observing all the nuances of atmosphere, and in order to paint a *Snowstorm at Sea* (1842; National Gallery), he had himself tied for four hours, at the age of sixty-seven, to the bridge of the steamboat "Ariel," which set out in bad weather from Harwich. *The "Sun of Venice" Leaving Port* (1843; Tate Gallery) and above all the famous canvas called *Rain, Steam, and Speed* (1844; National Gallery) show him to be a forerunner of Impressionism. His work was mocked and abused, but he found an enthusiastic defender in John Ruskin, whom he met in 1840, and who praised his work in his *Modern Painters* (1843). Turner's last works, such as *Angel Standing in the Sun* (1846; Tate Gallery), reveal the "exuberant Romanticism" with which Claude Monet reproached him.

TWACHTMAN, John Henry (1853, Cincinnati—1902, Gloucester, Massachusetts), American Impressionist painter. He studied at the Munich Academy as well as in Italy and France. Twachtman settled near Greenwich, Connecticut, where the countryside around his home furnished him with the subjects for his art. His early work was done under the influence of Frank Duveneck, also a native of Cincinnati who had studied and painted in Munich and Italy. When Twachtman went to Paris, where he studied with Louis Boulanger at the Académie Julian, he was still under the sway of Duveneck's manner. His early paintings show that he was a skillful craftsman, but not yet a startlingly original artist. It was only after his return to America (1885) that he became interested in the Impressionists' theories of color, light and atmosphere. With Theodore Robinson (1852–96), Twachtman was one of the first Americans to experiment with these French pictorial theories and methods. For some time the result did not meet with public favor, and although Twachtman was popular with such fellow artists as Childe Hassam and Weir, his work had no ready market during his lifetime.

As he grew older, Twachtman became more and more spiritual and poetic, and this spiritual quality is reflected in his later paintings. They are no longer objective or purely Impressionistic, but are instead pastel-colored, dreamlike landscapes. His *Winter Landscape* (*c.* 1900; Albany, Coll. Fillin) is painted in an Impressionistic technique, with very closely meshed pale tones typical of this late period.

TWORKOV, Jack (b. 1900, Biala, Poland), Polish-born American painter. He came to the United States in 1913, studied at Columbia University (1920–23), and at the National Academy of Design (1923–25). During the Depression, like many of his New York artist colleagues, Tworkov worked for the Public Works Art Project (1934) and later for the WPA (1937–41). Cézanne's work was a great and pervasive influence for Tworkov, and summer contacts at Provincetown with the painter Karl Knaths encouraged this interest, also introducing him to the work of Joan Miró, Paul Klee, and Wassily Kandinsky. His early work included figurative paintings, landscapes, and still lifes. He met Willem de Kooning while working for the government art project in 1934, and later banded together with him and other Abstract Expressionist painters to form the New York School in the 1940s and early 1950s. During World War II Tworkov worked as a tool designer, and when he returned to painting in 1946 he began to explore an abstract automatic method based on an interest in Surrealism's experiments with the unconscious. In 1947 he abandoned still lifes for the figure (*Figure*, 1948–9; Hartford, Conn., Wadsworth Athenaeum). The Virginia landscape offered Tworkov the inspiration for more painterly compositions while he taught at the American University in Washington, D.C. (1948–9). He also taught at Black Mountain College, North Carolina, Queens College and Pratt Institute in New York, and at the University of Minnesota.

By 1954 the color and flamelike diagonal strokes had become the components of a more subtle atmospheric style, creating shimmering, transparent fields of textured pigment as in *Watergame* (1955; New York, Coll. Mr. and Mrs. Lee V. Eastman). In 1962 a series of red, white, and blue canvases occupied Tworkov, as he dealt with balancing quantities of pure tube color in gridlike arrangements, more taut than the flickering façades of his previous work, and without the chromatic modulations characteristic of the freer style. Although he was one of the exponents of an Expressionistic mode during the high point of Abstract Expressionism in the mid-1950s, the control he exercised distinguished his paintings from the rawness of a De Kooning.

TYTGAT, Edgard (1879, Brussels—1957, Brussels), Belgian painter. Tytgat painted in an Impressionist manner until after World War I; he then began to paint the delightful scenes and spiritual narrative pictures with which his name was ultimately associated. Tytgat's narrative manner is also highly individual, for he gave his stories an atmosphere of legend, and sometimes even recounted well-known tales. His forms are naively simplified, his colors delicately muted (*Inspiration*, 1926; Courtrai, West Flanders, Coll. Tony Herbert), and the human beings in his pictures usually belong to an unreal world. Yet there is a touching sincerity in the meetings of Tytgat's lovers (*The Charming Vanquished and the Handsome Conqueror*, 1927; Brussels, Priv. Coll.), and a sympathetic wonderment and humorous understanding in his descriptions of the circus with its merry-go-round horses, stalls, and fairgrounds. There would be something missing from Belgian Expressionism if, besides the impetuosity and energy of Constant Permeke, the calmness of Gustave de Smet's compositions, and the emotional restlessness of Frits van den Berghe (1883–1939), there were not also Tytgat's humor, his tender ingenuity, and malicious, gentle smile.

UBAC, Raoul (b. 1910, Malmedy), Belgian painter and sculptor. He went to Paris in 1929, where around 1934 he made contact with the Surrealist group. Under the influence of Man Ray he then turned to photography, while at the same time he learned etching in Stanley Hayter's studio. But it was not until 1942 that Ubac found his true path. Beginning with large-scale pen or pencil drawings, he turned successively, from 1945 onward, to gouache, slate sculpture, and oil painting. His early work was strictly realistic, but he soon adopted a nonfigurative approach. The canvases of his landscapes (*Forest*, 1953; New York, Guggenheim Museum) and still lifes are divided into parallel layers, while in more figurative works, man seems to be caught in a radiographic vision (*Horseman*, 1951, Liège, Coll. Graindorge; and *Two Persons at a Table*, 1950, New York, Museum of Modern Art). Few paintings give the feeling of such an identity of the mineral and the living—the living taking on the static qualities of stones, and the mineral awakening to a secret, silent life of its own (*Calvary*, 1958; Paris, Galerie Maeght).

UCCELLO, Paolo di Dono, *called* Paolo (1397, Florence—1475, Florence), Italian painter. He was an unusual and slightly eccentric figure, and in addition to being a painter, was also a mosaicist, worker in marquetry, decorator, and one of the most skilled and conscientious craftsmen of his time. Uccello was mentioned in 1407 as being a *garzone di bottega* (workshop assistant) in Lorenzo Ghiberti's workshop, where he remained until around 1414–15. In 1425 he was in Venice, where he was employed at St. Mark's as a master mosaicist. Uccello returned to Florence in January 1431, and probably began the four frescoes (*Creation of the Animals and Creation of Adam, Creation of Eve and the Fall of Man, The Deluge,* and *Noah's Sacrifice and the Drunkenness of Noah*; all *c.* 1431–50) in the Chiostro Verde of the church of S. Maria Novella before receiving the commission for the equestrian portrait of *Sir John Hawkwood*, called Giovanni Acuto (1436; Florence Cathedral). In 1443, again for the cathedral, Uccello decorated the clockface on the west wall and then provided three cartoons for the stained-glass circular windows in the cupola, representing the *Ascension, Resurrection,* and *Nativity*; they were followed (1444) by a fourth cartoon of the *Annunciation*. The only design rejected was the *Ascension*; a cartoon by Ghiberti on the same theme was preferred. Another fresco series, mentioned by Vasari, on *Scenes from the Life of Monastic Saints* (Florence, upper cloister of the church of S. Miniato al Monte), probably dates from the 1440s or earlier.

Uccello lived in Padua between 1445 and 1448; during this time he introduced the virile, monumental Tuscan style into the North with a series of large figures—they are said to have impressed Andrea Mantegna—called *Illustrious Men* or *Giants* (originally in the Casa Vitaliani; now lost). The three panels, illustrating Niccolò da Tolentino's *Victory over the Sienese at the Battle of San Romano in 1432* (*c.* 1455–60; Florence, Uffizi; Paris, Louvre; London, National Gallery), were originally hung in the great hall of the Palazzo Medici-Riccardi in Florence. His *St. George and the Dragon* (*c.* 1440–50, Paris, Musée Jacquemart-André; *c.* 1440, London, National Gallery) gives us an idea of two lost works, *Battle of the Dragons and Lions*, which was originally in the Palazzo Medici (now Medici-Riccardi) and the *Four Elements*, a fresco on the ceiling of a hall in the Palazzo Peruzzi, Florence, in which the elements are represented as animals. In 1465 Uccello went to Urbino, where the Confraternity of the Corpus Domini commissioned him to paint the altarpiece depicting the *Legend of the Profanation of the Host* (*c.* 1468; Urbino, Galleria Nazionale delle Marche). Uccello, however, was getting old, and the altarpiece was completed (1473–74) by Justus of Ghent, after Piero della Francesca had refused the task. Uccello's astonishing *Hunt* (Oxford, Ashmolean Museum), considered by some to be a fragment of a decoration commissioned by Federigo da Montefeltro, was one of his last works. His point of departure was the monumental style developed by Masaccio after 1424 on the walls of the Brancacci Chapel in the church of S. Maria del Carmine, Florence, but he went beyond this. In Venice Uccello discovered the decorative painting that Gentile da Fabriano had completed around 1409 (now destroyed) in the Palazzo Ducale. Upon his return to Florence, he produced his masterpiece, the frescoes in the Chiostro Verde, which were executed under Masaccio's influence. The equestrian portrait of *Sir John Hawkwood*, intended to take the place of a marble statue, is like the demonstration of an optical exercise. The system of perspective is just as important in the three panels of the *Battle of San Romano*, in which Uccello's genius expressed itself above all in the profusion of details and curious forms and in the marvelously fanciful backgrounds that are stylistically reminiscent of the Urbino altarpiece. Uccello's animal battles were popularized abroad through engravings, and his geometrical drawings are regarded as expressions of the fine intellectuality characteristic of the artists of the Florentine Renaissance, all of whom had a lasting influence on modern art.

UPJOHN, family of architects, originally from England, who settled in the United States in the 19th century and whose principal members were:

RICHARD (1802, Shaftesbury, England—1878, Garrison, New York). In 1829 he emigrated to the United States and in 1830 settled in New Bedford, Massachusetts, where he worked as a draftsman before moving to Boston in 1834. There Upjohn worked as an architect both on his own and in the office of Alexander Parris until 1839, in which year he was commissioned to design Trinity Church in New York, where he established permanent residence. Trinity Church was completed in 1846 in a rather Puginian Gothic mode and received considerable acclaim, ensuring for its designer a long series of church commissions, including the Church of the Ascension (1840–41), the Church of the Holy Communion (1844–46), and Trinity Chapel (1852–55), all in

Paolo Uccello. *Panel from the Legend of the Profanation of the Host. c.* 1468. Galleria Nazionale delle Marche, Urbino. *Photo Alinari-Giraudon.*

Jorn Utzon. New Opera House, Sydney. Project of 1956; completed 1968.

New York. Although best known as a designer of Gothic churches, he was also responsible for commercial buildings (Corn Exchange Bank, New York, 1854), as well as numerous houses. He was the author of *Upjohn's Rural Architecture* (1852), and a founding member and first president (1857–76) of the American Institute of Architects.

RICHARD MICHELL (1828, Shaftesbury, England—1903, New York), son of the preceding architect. He entered his father's office in 1846, and after spending a year in Europe (1851–52), returned to become his father's partner. Although he too designed many churches, he was equally well known for his commercial and institutional projects. The most notable of these was the State Capitol in Hartford, Connecticut (1873–85), which remains one of the largest and most distinctive examples of the High Victorian Gothic in America.

UTRILLO, Maurice (1883, Paris—1955, Le Vésinet, near Paris), French painter. The illegitimate son of Suzanne Valadon, he was adopted by the Spanish architect and writer Miguel Utrillo y Molins in 1891. Utrillo had an excessive love of alcohol even as a schoolboy, and had to be admitted to the mental hospital of Ste-Anne in 1900. When he was released, his mother authoritatively placed a paint brush in his hand in an effort to distract him from his obsession; his first paintings, with their rough texture and dark colors, soon revealed his remarkable gifts (*Roofs*, 1906–7; Paris, Musée National d'Art Moderne). His palette gradually grew brighter and his drawing firmer. Then followed the best period of Utrillo's incredible career, the so-called white period, which ended in 1914. His work possessed a sensitivity that transformed the most banal subjects through a splendid poetry: the monotony of the narrow streets, the melancholy of courtyards, dreary suburbs, stunted trees, and the crumbling façades of Montmartre's slums (*L'Impasse Cottin*, *c.* 1910, Paris, Musée National d'Art Moderne; *Rue Norvins*, 1912, Zurich Kunsthaus). An indefinable grace transfigures the humblest chapel or the smallest country church (*Church of Mourning*, or the "*Little Communicant*," 1912; Paris, Coll. Paul Pétridès). He had an unerring sense of color values and of tonal relationships. His grays, pale blues, and greens, his flashes of vermilion, and especially his milky whites defy analysis (*Place du Tertre*, 1911–12, London, Tate Gallery; *Moulin de la Galette*, Paris, Priv. Coll.).

Utrillo learned his method of outlining forms from Suzanne Valadon. After 1914 he heightened the register of his palette and accented his realism. In 1923 Sergei Diaghilev commissioned him to design the sets and costumes for his ballet, *Barabau*. In 1934 he married Lucie Valore, who installed him in a comfortable villa at Le Vésinet, where he continued to paint. Unfortunately, his late works were very often not much more than a pastiche of his earlier canvases.

UTZON, Jørn (b. 1918, Copenhagen), Danish architect. After studying at the Copenhagen School of Architecture (1937–42), Utzon spent three years in Stockholm, where the work of Gunnar Asplund established an important influence. In 1946 he went to Helsinki and became a trainee in the office of Alvar Aalto. Aalto's influence, together with the inspiration of Frank Lloyd Wright, formed Utzon's principles of an organic architecture using materials in accordance with their own properties. His own house at Hellebaek (1952) was innovative for its spaciousness and open planning, and was followed by a house at Holte (1952–53), in which Japanese influence predominates. Utzon attained international stature when he won first prize in a competition for the new Sydney Opera House in 1956. This daring and dramatic composition consists of immense shells housing the opera house, concert hall, and foyers, surmounting a stepped platform containing an experimental theater, vehicular access, and additional space. Less dramatic but equally expressive of human needs are the two housing estates of Kingoshusene near Helsingør and the Danish Cooperative Building in Fredensborg (1957–60).

V

VALADON, Maria Clémentine, *called* Suzanne (1867, Bessines, Haute-Vienne—1938, Paris), French painter. It was in 1883, the year her son Maurice Utrillo was born, that she did her first drawings. Suzanne was then 15 years old. Her father was a bricklayer, her mother a laundress, and her early years were spent in poverty. After working as an acrobat (a fall made her leave circus life), she became a painter's model. Puvis de Chavannes, Henri de Toulouse-Lautrec, Auguste Renoir, and Edgar Degas were among the artists who painted her. Degas was as enthusiastic about her artistic abilities as he was about her qualities as a model. In 1908 she began painting landscapes and still lifes, which are remarkable for their sound composition and the depth of their coloring. Her favorite subjects, however, were nudes and faces, which she painted with an unflinching, even brutal realism that sometimes took on aspects of the trivial. Suzanne's contour line, which encircled forms in such a way as to recall the leading in stained glass (*Netfishing*, 1914; Paris, Musée National d'Art Moderne), is remarkably expressive and concise.

VALDÉS LEAL, Juan de (1622, Seville—1690, Seville), Spanish painter. He was a pupil of Antonio del Castillo (1616–68), and was educated in Cordova, where he remained until 1653. Valdés Leal's pictures of these early years reveal the influence of Castillo. He then settled in Seville (1656), where he painted his first mature works for the Hieronymite convent of Buenavista, including the *Temptation of St. Jerome* and the *Flagellation of St. Jerome* (both 1657; Seville, Museum). The use of harsh colors and a new, radiant light characterizes another work of this period, the *Pietà* (*c.* 1657–60; New York, Metropolitan Museum), whose dramatic realism was carried over into Valdés Leal's last great work in Cordova, the main altar of the church of the Carmelites (1658), to which the *Presentation of the Virgin* (Madrid, Prado) is related. His religious temperament is revealed in the *Allegory of Vanity* (1660; Hartford, Connecticut, Wadsworth Athenaeum), filled with symbols of human weakness and decay. His *Via Crucis* of the following year (New York, Hispanic Society) is a stronger version of a youthful work (Cordova, church of S. Jaime) in which the light is handled with great skill. His *Assumption of the Virgin* (*c.* 1659; Washington, D.C., National Gallery) and *St. Thomas Villanueva giving Alms* (*c.* 1665–70; New York, Kress Foundation) both reveal a light, sparkling manner. Among his last and most famous works were the *Finis Gloriae Mundi* and the *Triumph of Death* (both 1672; Seville, Caridad). Valdés Leal's last great work was the *Christ in the Temple* (1686; Prado), which again reveals his violence, energy, and brilliant, almost theatrical coloring.

VALLOTTON, Félix (1865, Lausanne—1925, Paris), French painter of Swiss origin. His entire career was spent in Paris, where he arrived at the age of seventeen and entered the Académie Julian. Vallotton became a friend of Paul Sérusier, Pierre Bonnard, Maurice Denis, and Paul Ranson (1864–1909), and was intimately connected with the Nabis group that centered around *La Revue Blanche*. Then, for a brief period, he was tempted by the pointillist technique (*Waltz*, 1893; Paris, Galerie Mouradian et Vallotton), but ultimately adopted a position between Neoimpressionism and a purified Neoclassicism. At one period it might even be said that he worked against the current, opposing a general concern for a free interpretation of visual appearance with a meticulous, sometimes cruel realism. Vallotton's sense of abstraction raised the quality of his work above that of merely accurate rendering. The caustic quality of his vision, so marked in his drawings and engravings—*Burial*, 1891; *Assassination*, 1893; *Execution*, 1894—many of which were published in book form (*Intimacies*, 1897–98; *Crimes and Punishments*, 1902), finds expression in his painting in a certain acidity of color, especially in his treatment of nudes (*Unfinished Study of a Nude, Académie Julian*, 1885; France, Priv. Coll.). On the other hand, Vallotton is more tender in intimate scenes and, through the rigor of his style, reveals great depth of feeling in numerous landscapes.

VANBRUGH, Sir John (1664, London—1726, London), English Baroque architect. He had already established a reputation as a dramatist (*The Provok'd Wife*, 1697) when, at a relatively late age, he took up the art of building to design Castle Howard for the Earl of Carlisle. His influence became even greater when, as Comptroller of the Office of Works, he became Sir Christopher Wren's most important colleague in 1702. Vanbrugh's design for Castle Howard, Yorkshire (1699–1714), owes much to Wren's first plan for Greenwich Hospital. An open courtyard bordered by low wings that house kitchens and a chapel precedes the main body of the building, which is dominated by the great hall and staircases of honor, and which is joined to the wings by a curved arcade. At the back the building widens out to house the huge apartments, oriented toward the park. Similar arrangements were adopted at Blenheim Palace, Oxfordshire, the residence that Queen Anne had built from 1705 for the Duke of Marlborough in gratitude for his victory over the French at Höchstädt-Blenheim. This building has a majesty and powerful interplay of volumes quite foreign to Wren's more Classical discipline.

Sir John Vanbrugh. Castle Howard, Yorkshire. 1699–1714. *Photo Kersting, London.*

Vanbrugh's own castellated house at Greenwich (1717), which foreshadowed the Gothic Revival, was inspired by medieval fortresses. Seaton Delaval in Northumberland (*c.* 1720–28), equally medieval in its massing although Classical in its elements, has a cyclopean grandeur unequaled anywhere in Europe. When the Duke of Marlborough was relieved of his command by the Tories, Vanbrugh lost his comptrollership. The poor state of his relations with the Duchess of Marlborough forced him to withdraw in 1711, and the huge building was completed by Nicholas Hawksmoor. Vanbrugh was reinstated as Comptroller after the death of Queen Anne, and was knighted in 1714.

VANDERLYN, John (1775, Kingston, New York—1852, Kingston), American painter. Vanderlyn was sent to Paris (1796) by his patron, Aaron Burr. He returned to America, and between 1801 and 1803 made many sketches of Niagara Falls, intending to have engravings made after them to sell abroad. In 1803 he was again sent to Europe, this time by the Academy of Arts of the City of New York, to select casts and copies of the old masters for the use of the Academy. He spent two years in Rome and eight years in Paris. Vanderlyn was strongly influenced by the current Neoclassical style in France. His penchant for this academic mode is reflected in *Marius Amid the Ruins of Carthage* (San Francisco, M. H. de Young Memorial Museum) as well as in *Ariadne on Naxos* (1814; Philadelphia, Pennsylvania Academy of the Fine Arts). In 1815 he returned to New York, where he later exhibited panoramas of the *Palace and Gardens of Versailles* (1833; New York, Metropolitan Museum) in a specially constructed building. Aside from a commission to decorate the Capitol Rotunda in Washington, D.C. (1837), which depicted the *Landing of Columbus*, his work from the 1820s until his death was confined largely to portraiture. Vanderlyn approached this genre with the same slow, deliberate execution as his earlier history painting, requiring innumerable sittings of his subjects. That the amount of time expended was not, however, in vain is witnessed by the clear, sure drawing and strong characterization of such a portrait as the *Wife and Child of Colonel Marinus Willett* (1801/2; Metropolitan Museum).

Georges Vantongerloo. *Construction.* 1917. Philadelphia, Museum of Art.

VAN DER WEYDEN, Rogier. *See* **WEYDEN,** Rogier van der.

VAN LOO, family of French painters of Dutch origin. Apart from Jacob (*c.* 1614, Sluis, Zeeland—1670, Paris), the founder of the family, and Abraham-Louis, his son, the principal members were:

JEAN-BAPTISTE (1684, Aix-en-Provence—1745, Aix-en-Provence), son of Abraham-Louis. He was both a portraitist and a historical painter. He achieved recognition for his portrait of Louis XV (1723), and later he was given the task of restoring Primaticcio's frescoes at Fontainebleau. From 1737 to 1741, Jean-Baptiste was in London, where he painted members of the court (*Portrait of Sir Robert Walpole*, 1740; Gatschina, Palace). His two most admired paintings are the *Institution of the Order of the Holy Ghost by Henri III* (Paris, Louvre) and the *Triumph of Galatea* (Leningrad, Hermitage). Other paintings include the *Vision of the Archbishop of Rouen* (New York, Museum of the New-York Historical Society).

CHARLES ANDRÉ, *called* CARLE (1705, Nice—1765, Paris), was brought up by his brother Jean-Baptiste, whose junior he was by 21 years. Carle was awarded the Prix de Rome in 1724, and lived for a time in Rome, then in Turin (1732–34), where the King of Sardinia gave him several important commissions for decorations, including 11 compositions for his palace on the theme of *Jerusalem Delivered*. Carle tried to compete with the *petite manière* of François Boucher, but he was not at ease with these precious subjects and *scènes galantes*, preferring grander themes, such as those in his six paintings on the *Life of St. Gregory* (Leningrad, Hermitage), intended as decorations for the Invalides chapel. He also worked in St-Sulpice, where one can still see his *Annunciation, Visitation, Adoration of the Shepherds*, and *Presentation in the Temple*. Other works on a smaller scale include a *Self-Portrait* (1762; Hermitage) and *Sultana taking Coffee* (1755; Paris, Musée des Arts Décoratifs).

LOUIS-MICHEL (1707, Toulon—1771, Paris) was a pupil of his father Jean-Baptiste. A particularly fashionable society portraitist, he is best-known for such family portraits as the *Family of Carle Van Loo* (1757; Paris, Musée des Arts Décoratifs).

VANTONGERLOO, Georges (1886, Antwerp—1965, Paris), Belgian sculptor and painter. He had already acquired a reputation as a sculptor when, in 1917, he created his first nonfigurative works—"constructions within the sphere" and compositions of rectangular volumes (*Construction*, 1917; Philadelphia, Museum of Art). In the same year he published his *Reflections* on an art freed from the subject and capable of conveying the notion of space, in the review *De Stijl*, founded by Theo van Doesburg and Piet Mondrian. Parallel with them, Vantongerloo was trying to base his art only on the relations between vertical and horizontal lines. These experiments, which he pursued for 20 years, culminated in paintings in which the colors are subtly harmonized, and in boldly balanced sculptures of wood and metal (*XY=K Green and Red*, 1929; New York, Museum of Modern Art). His pamphlet, *Art and Its Future*, was published at Antwerp in 1924. In 1930 he took part in the *Cercle et Carré* exhibition, and, with Auguste Herbin, founded the Abstraction-Création group in the following year. From 1937 curves entered his work, at first intermingled with straight lines, but later in a freer form (*Composition Green-Blue-V=Black No. 105*, 1937; New York, Guggenheim Museum). In steel or nickel wire the movement of the curve extended into space to envelop a solid nucleus. This desire to go beyond the limitations of three dimensions, to integrate the work of art with the universe, resulted in

Plexiglass constructions through which light is refracted.

VANVITELLI, Luigi (1700, Naples—1773, Naples), Italian architect. He was the son of Gaspar van Wittel (1653–1736), a Dutch painter who settled in Italy, and himself practiced painting before turning to architecture. His first important works were done at Ancona, where, commissioned by Pope Clement XII, he built several utilitarian buildings as well as the church of Il Gesù (1743–45). King Charles IV of Naples then commissioned him to design the royal palace at Caserta, near Naples (1752–74). A sort of Neapolitan Versailles, and the largest building of the 18th century, this huge quadrilateral is intersected by two arms of a cross, forming four rectangular courtyards of equal size, reduced at the corners by cut-off walls. Placed in one of the arms of the cross, a magnificent staircase leads to a large octagonal vestibule. This room, at the center of a palace that contains some 1,200 rooms, is particularly impressive, providing vast and dramatic perspectives. These Baroque scenographic effects are balanced in the elevations by a strict Classicism. Vanvitelli's Chiesa dell'Annunziata in Naples (1761–82) is more thoroughly Baroque. His Classicism is again apparent in the Foro Carolino, Naples (1757–65; now Piazza Dante). Vanvitelli's considerable talents are equally evident in the cavalry barracks (1753–74) near Naples and the great Acquedotto Carolina (1752–64), also near Naples, which rivals Roman works in grandeur and engineering skill.

Luigi Vanvitelli. Ceremonial Staircase, Royal Palace, Caserta, near Naples. 1752–74. *Photo Alinari-Giraudon.*

VARLEY, John (1778, London—1842, London), English painter. Like J.M.W. Turner and Thomas Girtin, Varley also studied at the London house of Dr. Thomas Monro, an amateur artist and art patron. He then became a specialist in watercolor. Visits to North Wales in 1799, 1800, and 1802 introduced him to the scenery that inspired his finest creations. Varley was never a particularly original artist, but his best work is soundly and conventionally designed and gracefully executed (*Market Place, Leominster*, exhibited 1801; Hereford, City Museum and Art Gallery). He exhibited at the Royal Academy from 1798 to 1804 and then almost every year between 1825 and 1841. He also showed at the Old Water-Colour Society in London. He was an influential and popular teacher, whose pupils included William Holman Hunt and John Linnell. CORNELIUS (1781, London—1873, London), John's younger brother, was an optical and electrical inventor as well as a watercolorist. In 1804 he was a founding member of the Old Water-Colour Society. Cornelius produced carefully finished Classical and architectural subjects, and worked in Ireland and Wales (*First View of Cader Idris*, 1803; Hereford, City Museum and Art Gallery). His pencil study of *J. M. W. Turner* (after 1811) is in the Graves Art Gallery, Sheffield: it was done with the graphic telescope, a device that was invented by Varley in 1811 and that reproduces—on a piece of paper—the object observed, in order that its outlines may be traced.

VASARELY, Victor (b. 1908, Pécs, Hungary), French painter of Hungarian origin. In 1930 Vasarely settled in Paris. While working in advertising and decoration, he continued to develop his own painting, which was Constructivist in inspiration, culminating in his *Harlequins, Chessboards, Martians, Zebras, Improvisations on Tracings and Cellophanes*, and *Photographisms*. He then painted a great deal on cellophane, later superposing several sheets on top of each other in order to achieve effects of depth by means of transparency—a technique he called "multidimension." He became increasingly preoccupied with the animation of surfaces, noting on the back of his pictures in what light they should be seen and whether they could be looked at in two, three, or four different ways (*Yellan*, 1950; Galerie Denise René). In 1955, Vasarely launched "Kineticism," a style of abstract painting in which an impression of movement is created by optical illusion (*Ondho*, 1956–60; New York, Museum of Modern Art). Basing his approach on the principle of the identity of form and color, which he called "plastic unity," Vasarely provided himself with the basis of a language whose endless resources he continued to exploit.

VASARI, Giorgio (1511, Arezzo—1574, Florence), Italian Mannerist painter and architect, one of the leading theoreticians of art in the 16th century. In Florence he knew Michelangelo and Andrea del Sarto, then in 1529 at Arezzo he met Rosso Fiorentino, whose influence is apparent in the plan of Vasari's several versions of the *Descent from the Cross*, notably that painted in 1536 for S. Domenico at Arezzo (now Arezzo, SS. Annunziata). In 1532 Vasari entered the service of Cardinal Ippolito de' Medici in Rome; later in Florence Alessandro de' Medici became his

Victor Vasarely. *Zebra*. 1935. Study.

Giorgio Vasari. Uffizi, Florence. 1560–80. *Photo Brogi-Giraudon.*

patron. These connections led to the painting of several portraits, including those of *Alessandro* and *Lorenzo de' Medici* (both 1534; both Florence, Uffizi). Vasari's other works include an *Assumption of the Virgin* (1539; Monte San Savino, S. Agostino), an *Allegory of the Conception* (1540–41; Florence, SS. Apostoli), as well as a *Leda* for Francesco Rucellai and a *St. Jerome*, both of which were painted in 1541. After 1546 he traveled throughout Italy, gathering a prodigious amount of information, which he published in 1550 in the first edition of his famous book, *Lives of the Most Eminent Painters, Sculptors, and Architects*. In 1555 he entered permanently into the service of Cosimo de' Medici, and in this capacity his main task was to renovate and make habitable Cosimo's residence, the ancient Palazzo della Signoria, or Palazzo Vecchio, which dated from the 1300s. Vasari redesigned and rebuilt the interior and also made some changes in the exterior, notably the entrance courtyard; his most important undertaking at the Palazzo Vecchio was the execution of the fresco decorations, which he did between 1555 and 1572. In his first period of work on the palace (1555–62) he decorated the apartments, namely the Quartiere degli Elementi, the six rooms of the Quartiere de Leone X, and the Quartiere di Eleonora. Then in a second period of activity (1563–72) he transformed the decorations in the Sala Grande or Salone dei Cinquecento, working on the ceiling first (1563–66) and then (1566–72) on the walls. Meanwhile (1560–80) Vasari built the Uffizi, which the Medici family used for their administrative offices, and in 1562 was one of the founders of the Accademia del Disegno in Florence. In 1568 he partly rewrote and enlarged his *Lives*. Vasari's portraits sometimes have an air of melancholy seriousness and his allegories are complicated and curious.

Vecchietta. *Risen Christ*. 1476. Church of S. Maria della Scala, Siena.

VECCHIETTA, Lorenzo di Pietro, *called* (*c*. 1412, Castiglione d'Orcia, near Siena—1480, Siena), Italian painter, sculptor, architect, and military engineer. Vecchietta studied under Sassetta, and between 1433 and 1439 worked with Masolino on the frescoes in the Collegiata at Castiglione Olona. Vecchietta then returned to Siena, where he worked for nearly 10 years on several decorations in the Spedale di S. Maria della Scala: frescoes (*Vision of the Beato Sorore* and three scenes from the *Story of St. Tobias*, 1441) in the Pellegrinaio, or Infirmary Hall; paintings (1445; now in the Siena Pinacoteca) for the Reliquiera, a cupboard in which relics were kept; and frescoes (1446–49) in the sacristy of the church of S. Maria della Scala. Between 1450 and 1453 Vecchietta painted a series of frescoes illustrating the *Articles of Faith* for the vault of the baptistery of Siena Cathedral. In 1461 he produced his masterpiece, the sculpturesque fresco of *St. Catherine of Siena* in the Palazzo Pubblico, Siena. He continued to paint altarpieces, the most remarkable of which is the triptych in the cathedral of Pienza, in Siena province, on the *Assumption of the Virgin* (1461–62). Vecchietta spent his last years executing sculptures in marble, wood, and bronze. Although his wood carvings have a touch of the medieval style (*St. Bernardino*, 1475; Florence, Bargello), his bronzes bear no trace of the Gothic idiom (*Risen Christ*, 1476; Siena, S. Maria della Scala).

VECELLIO, Tiziano. *See* **TITIAN.**

VEDDER, Elihu (1836, Schenectady, New York—1923, Rome, Italy), American painter. In 1865 he studied under François-Édouard Picot in Paris (*African Sentinel*, 1865; New York, Metropolitan Museum); he then traveled to Florence in order to acquaint himself with the masters of the High Renaissance (*Alchemist*, 1868; New York, Brooklyn Museum). Four years later he returned to America. In 1886 Vedder was elected a member of the National Academy, but he decided to return to Europe, where he settled in Rome.

Vedder's works range from Romantic paintings, rich in color and surface texture, to pictures derived in style and subject matter from the High Renaissance works he had studied in Italy (*Rome, Representative of the Arts*, 1894; Brooklyn Museum). He is well known for his illustrations of the *Rubaiyat of Omar Khayyám* and for his mural decorations in the Library of Congress in Washington, D.C. *Fisherman* (1865; Albany, Coll. Fillin) shows Vedder combining Classicist and Romantic tendencies in a universal "type" figure dominated by a sentimental mood. The *Lair of the Sea Serpent* (1864; Boston, Museum of Fine Arts) also exemplifies Vedder's Romantic side, with its fascination for mysterious sea monsters realistically portrayed.

VEDOVA, Emilio (b. 1919, Venice), Italian painter. Vedova was able to achieve recognition as an artist at the age of sixteen, thanks to the efforts of an uncle in Rome. His career really began, however, when he joined the Corrente movement in Milan in 1942. One of the founders of the Fronte Nuovo delle Arti in 1946, Vedova took part in this group's two exhibitions in Milan (1947) and Venice (1948). He was also one of the group of Eight Italian Painters who took common action at the Venice Biennale in 1952. Whether figurative or totally abstract, Vedova's painting seems to be haunted by the image of a limited and compressed universe. At times it evokes an oppressively enclosed space, seen in his study for *Revolt*

(1951; Priv. Coll.), or possesses a tumultuous movement that suggests a desire for escape, as in his *Europa 1950* (Venice, Galleria Internazionale d'Arte Moderna) and *Imprisoned Spirit* (1951; Vicenza, Coll. Festa).

VELÁZQUEZ, Diego Rodríguez de Silva y (1599, Seville—1660, Madrid), Spanish painter. According to tradition, he studied first with Francisco de Herrera the Elder (*c.* 1590–1665), then with Francisco Pacheco (1564–1654) from 1610 until 1616. The latter, who specialized in the portrait, instilled in Velázquez an abiding interest in portraiture, with the result that he became one of the greatest portraitists of all time. Pacheco realized that his pupil, who became a master in 1617 and who the following year married his daughter Juana, deserved a better career than Seville could offer, and he was able to secure for Velázquez letters of introduction to important individuals close to the king in Madrid. In 1622 the young artist visited Madrid briefly for the first time, without any definite results. A second visit of longer duration in 1623 with Pacheco was crowned with success, however: Velázquez painted some portraits, one of which, a portrait of the king, was given the honor of a public exhibition, after which he was appointed court painter. During this first period Velázquez' style was characterized by a choice of popular, even plebeian subjects or models, an almost architectural firmness of composition, and the contrast of somber and brightly lit surfaces. In particular, there were genre pictures called *bodegónes*, which combined the still life with figures. The most remarkable of his early works are the *Three Musicians* (*c.* 1619; Berlin, Staatliche Museen), *Peasants at Table* (*c.* 1617; Leningrad, Hermitage), the *Old Woman Frying Eggs* (1618; Edinburgh, National Gallery), and the *Water Carrier of Seville* (*c.* 1619; London, Apsley House, Wellington Museum). His liking for familiar domestic themes caused him to incorporate them in certain of his religious paintings (*Christ in the House of Mary and Martha, c.* 1622, London, National Gallery). During this same period Velázquez executed a number of excellent portraits. The most astonishing of these is undoubtedly that of the Franciscan nun *Doña Jerónima de la Fuente* (1620; Madrid, Prado); others include the portrait of *Don Cristóbal Suarez de Ribera* (Seville, S. Hermengildo) and that thought to be of *Francisco Pacheco* (1623; Prado). The portrait of the poet *Luis de Gongora* (1622; Boston, Museum of Fine Arts) was painted at Pacheco's request in Madrid during the artist's first visit.

Diego de Velázquez. *Three Musicians. c.* 1619. Staatliche Museen, Berlin-Dahlem.

Once he had settled in Madrid, Velázquez became not only painter to the king, but also an increasingly important official in the palace. He appears to have attached much importance to this latter role, probably for the social advantages it gave him. The paintings in the royal collections enabled him to deepen his knowledge of Italian painting, especially of the Venetians, who revealed to him the pictorial possibilities of the nude and of sumptuous materials presented in the proper lighting. At this time Velázquez executed some admirable portraits of the *Infante Don Carlos* (*c.* 1626; Prado), *Philip IV* (Prado; Metropolitan Museum), and the *Count-Duke of Olivares* (1625; New York, Hispanic Society). The *Expulsion of the Moriscos* (destroyed in 1734) enabled him in 1627 to win a competition in which Vicente Carducho (1576–1638) and Angelo Nardi (1584–1663/65) also participated. The *Triumph of Bacchus* (the *Drunkards*, 1629; Prado), however, is the masterpiece of this period. Painted for the king's bedchamber, it is a combination of a Classical theme from Ovid's *Metamorphoses* and the Sevillian *bodegónes*, in which peasant types gather about a rather fleshy and youthful Bacchus. Rubens, visiting Madrid in the fall of 1628, recognized the great ability of the Spanish artist and befriended him, even sharing his studio. It was probably Rubens' advice that prompted Velázquez to undertake a journey to Italy in 1629.

He set sail from Barcelona, landed at Genoa, and visited Venice, Ferrara, Bologna, Florence, Rome, and Naples, where he met Jusepe de Ribera, before returning to Madrid in 1631. It was in Italy that he painted the portrait of *Mary of Hungary* (Prado), *Joseph's Coat Brought to Jacob* (1630; Escorial), and the *Forge of Vulcan* (1630; Prado). During the years 1631–36 his brush gained not only in richness, but also in expressiveness, as can be seen in the *Temptation of St. Thomas Aquinas* (*c.* 1631–32; Orihuela, Cathedral Museum) and especially in the *Christ on the Cross* (*c.* 1631–32; Prado), one of his most profound religious paintings. Some of his finest portraits date from this period: the *Court Jester Calabazas* (*c.* 1635), a *Sibyl*, which is thought to be the artist's wife, *Doña Antonia de Ipeñarrieta* and her husband *Don Diego del Corral* (all four in the Prado); *Philip IV* in embroidered court dress (London, National Gallery); *Queen Isabella of Bourbon* (Vienna); and *Prince Baltasar Carlos* (1633; London, Wallace Collection). Velázquez painted for the Salon de Reinos or Hall of Realms at the Buen Retiro Palace in Madrid some of his most celebrated works (now in the Prado); these were the *Surrender of Breda* (*Las Lanzas*, 1634) and the equestrian portraits of *Philip IV* and *Prince Baltasar Carlos*. The *Surrender of Breda* is the most important painting of this group, and indeed one of his finest achievements. Velázquez' equestrian portrait of *Don Gaspar de Guzman, Count-Duke of Olivares* (*c.* 1634; Prado) on the other hand is certainly one of the finest of the portraits of this period.

During the years 1636–43, Velázquez' superb series of portraits continued, painted in a palette dominated by various shades of gray: the *Jester Sebastian de Morra* (Prado), *Francesco I d'Este* (1638; Modena, Galleria Estense), the standing *Prince Baltasar Carlos* (1640–42; Vienna, Kunsthistorisches Museum), and the sculptor *Martínez Montañés* (1638; Prado). Hunting, which played an essential role in the life of the court, naturally played a similarly important part in Velázquez' painting. The artist depicted hunting episodes in *Philip IV Hunting Wild Bear* (*La Tela Real*; London,

Diego de Velázquez. *Luis de Gongora.* 1622. Museum of Fine Arts, Boston.

Diego de Velázquez. *The Infanta Margarita.* 1656–57. Kunsthistorisches Museum, Vienna.

National Gallery) and represented *Prince Baltasar Carlos* (1635–36) and the *Infante Don Fernando* (*c.* 1632–35; both Prado) in hunting clothes. Lastly, for the royal hunting lodge, the Torre de la Parada, he executed an *Aesop* and a *Menippus* of extraordinary vigor (both *c.* 1638–41; Prado). The portraits that Velázquez continued to produce in great abundance in the years 1643–49 reveal a new richness of color; examples include *Cardinal Pamphili* (Hispanic Society), the *Lady with a Fan* (*c.* 1648; Wallace Collection), and *Philip IV at Fraga* (1644; New York, Frick Collection), painted during the French campaign. He then paid a second visit to Italy in order to purchase additional art objects for the king's collection, especially for that of the Alcázar, where he had designed the octagonal salon in imitation of the Tribuna in Florence. During this second Italian trip (1649–51), Velázquez visited Genoa, Venice, Naples, and Rome. In Naples he purchased antique statuary, and in Venice he bought such paintings as Tintoretto's *Paradise* (Prado) for Philip IV. While in Rome, Velázquez executed the magnificent portrait of *Pope Innocent X*, which possesses an extraordinary psychological insight into the sitter's character (1650; Rome, Palazzo Doria; copy possibly by artist, Washington, D.C., National Gallery). Also painted in Italy, the *Toilet of Venus* (1649–51; London, National Gallery) is an exceptional subject for a Spanish painter during the 17th century, and reveals the influence of Titian and Rubens. Back in Madrid, he painted a bust of *Philip IV* (Prado), various portraits of *Queen Maria-Anna*, the king's second wife (Prado; Paris, Louvre), and her children *Prince Philip Prosper* (1659; Vienna, Kunsthistorisches Museum) and the *Infanta Margarita* (1656–57; Kunsthistorisches Museum). The latter is the principal figure in *Las Meniñas* (1656; Prado), the masterpiece of Velázquez' final period. In this painting, surrounded by her maids and dwarfs, the Infanta stands in the room of the Alcázar where Velázquez portrays himself painting the king and queen (seen in the mirror directly behind her head). The *Spinners* (*Las Hilanderas, c.* 1657; Prado), which represents the myth of Arachne and Athena, possesses a complex iconography.

Diego de Velázquez. *The Spinners. c.* 1657. Prado, Madrid. *Photo Giraudon.*

During Philip IV's journey to Fuenterrabia and to Pheasant Island in the spring of 1660 for the wedding of Louis XIV and the Infanta Maria Teresa, Velázquez took on the vast project of decorating the pavilion where the royal families of France and Spain would meet. On his return to Madrid, he fell seriously ill and died very shortly thereafter.

VELDE, family of 17th-century Dutch painters, of whom the most important members were:

ESAIAS VAN DE (*c.* 1591, Amsterdam—1630, The Hague), a genre painter with Caravaggesque tendencies (*The Assault*, 1616; Amsterdam, Rijksmuseum) and a portraitist in the service of the Princes of Orange. Above all he was an excellent landscape painter, the creator of calm, accurately drawn, and sensitively observed scenes, usually in small format (*Dunes*, 1629; Rijksmuseum).

WILLEM VAN DE, *called* THE ELDER (1611, Leiden—1693, London), a precise and meticulous painter of ships and naval battles. Willem the Elder preferred the grisaille technique, and a large number of grisailles executed during the 1650s can be found in the National Maritime Museum and the Wallace Collection in London and in the Rijksmuseum in Amsterdam. In 1658 Willem temporarily joined the Dutch fleet so that he could sketch naval battles at first hand while they were in progress. Some of his battle pieces, however, were done from descriptions years after their occurrence, such as the *Battle of the Downs* of 1639 (1659; Rijksmuseum) and the *Battle of Scheveningen* of 1653 (1655; National Maritime Museum). When Charles II sailed to England to claim his throne in 1660, Willem was among those who accompanied the king, whose service he later entered.

WILLEM VAN DE, *called* THE YOUNGER (1633, Leiden—1707, London), Willem the Elder's son, was also a painter of ships and seascapes. He studied first with his father, then with Simon de Vlieger (*c.* 1600–53), and like his father entered the service of Charles II, settling in England in 1674. His earliest known work was executed in 1652. In many ways a better painter than his father, Willem the Younger developed a fine painterly style, which is evident in such works as the *Port of Amsterdam* (1686; Rijksmuseum) and the *Cannon Shot* (*c.* 1660; Rijksmuseum). Toward the end of his career, he drew a series of small studies of shipwrecks that were delicately rendered in pencil or pen.

ADRIAEN VAN DE (1636, Amsterdam—1672, Amsterdam), brother of Willem the Younger, was a painter of landscapes and animals, as well as of *staffage* (small-scale figures and animals in a landscape) for such artists as Jacob van Ruisdael, Meindert Hobbema, and Jan van der Heyden. Adriaen also did a number of effective and well-executed rustic landscapes, such as the *Farm* (1666; Berlin, Staatliche Museen), *Painter Sketching* (Dresden, Gemäldegalerie), and atmospheric beach scenes, such as the *Beach at Scheveningen* (1658; Kassel, Gemäldegalerie).

VELDE, Henry Clemens van de (1863, Antwerp—1957, Zurich), Belgian painter, architect, and decorator. Attracted at first to painting, he went to Paris to study with Carolus-Duran in 1884. On his return to Belgium two years later, Van de Velde helped to found the Antwerp *Als ik Kan* group. He later moved to Brussels, where in 1889 he joined the avant-garde group Les Vingt, through which he learned of the English Arts and Crafts movement and the work of William Morris. Van de Velde turned his attention to applied art, specifically to illustration and furniture design, his latter work being well received at the Dresden Exhibition of Applied Arts in 1897. In 1895 at Uccle, near Brussels, he designed and built himself a house, the Bloemenwerf, for which he not only drew up the plans, but also designed the furniture, carpets, curtains, lamps, heating equipment, cooking utensils, and crockery. In 1896 the dealer Siegfried Bing commissioned him to decorate his shop, the Maison de l'Art Nouveau, in Paris, which gave its name to the new style emanating from Belgium. Van de Velde's fame spread, especially in Germany, where he went on a lecture tour in 1900–1. He decorated and equipped the Folkwang Museum at Hagen (1900–2), employing a full-blown Art Nouveau ornamentation. Meanwhile, he was called by the grand duke of Saxe-Weimar to become the artistic adviser to the court in 1901, and to assist in the development of an awareness of good design in local industry. As a result, Van de Velde set up the School of Arts and Crafts (Kunstgewerbeschule) at Weimar, which became a laboratory of Art Nouveau work. The building he designed for the school (1906) was a kind of manifesto of his teaching.

The war interrupted his career in Germany, and in 1917 he left for Switzerland, later going to Holland, where the Kröller-Müller family commissioned him to design the museum at Otterlo that bears their name (completed only in 1937–54), an exemplary work perfectly adapted to its function.

Henry van de Velde. Folkwang Museum, Hagen. 1900–2. Central hall. *Photo Franz Stoedtner.*

On his return to Belgium in 1926, Van de Velde was given the task of setting up the Institut des Arts Décoratifs de la Cambre, a school of architecture and decorative arts, which he led until 1935. The original spirit of this school was reflected in the Belgian exhibition pavilions organized by Van de Velde and his team for the Paris (1937) and New York (1939) Expositions. At the same time, he was appointed professor of architecture at Ghent University, where he designed the library block (1936), one of the finest buildings of his late period.

VENEZIANO, Domenico. *See* **DOMENICO VENEZIANO.**

VERMEER, Johannes, *called* Jan (1632, Delft—1675, Delft), Dutch painter. He was one of the greatest Dutch painters of the 17th century, surpassing in quality all others who dealt with the same subject matter, mainly interior genre scenes. His oeuvre was extremely small, probably due to his slow, painstaking method of working, and of the less than 40 works that can be assigned to him, only two are dated—the *Procuress* (1656; Dresden, Gemäldegalerie) and the *Astronomer* (1668; Paris, Priv. Coll.). In the early years (*c.* 1655–66) his work shows the influence first of the Utrecht Caravaggisti, then of Carel Fabritius. In the later 1660s Vermeer attained his classic phase in a series of cool, balanced, and perfectly harmonious compositions. Paintings of the last period (1670s) tended toward an exaggeration of perspectival and decorative elements.

The earliest paintings, and the only ones that deal with Biblical or mythological subjects, are the *Diana and her Companions* (The Hague, Mauritshuis) and *Christ at the House of Mary and Martha* (Edinburgh, National Gallery of Scotland), both of which date from around 1655. Both reveal the Baroque character of Vermeer's early work, equally visible in the *Procuress*. That he was familiar with the Utrecht painters is evidenced by the inclusion of Dirck van Baburen's (1570–1623) *Procuress* in two of Vermeer's pictures—the *Concert* (Boston, Isabella Stewart Gardner Museum) and the *Lady Seated at the Virginals* (London, National Gallery). The warmth of reds and yellows in Vermeer's *Procuress* also indicates an awareness of the work of Rembrandt and

Jan Vermeer. *Christ at the House of Mary and Martha. c.* 1655. National Gallery of Scotland, Edinburgh.

his followers. The same warmth pervades the *Girl Asleep at a Table* (*c.* 1657; New York, Metropolitan Museum). The space is opened by a view into another room, and this is a unique example, in Vermeer's work, of a device favored by Pieter de Hooch and other Delft painters of interiors. In the equally anecdotal *Soldier and a Laughing Girl* (*c.* 1657; New York, Frick Collection), Vermeer continues to emphasize the figures, and has not yet attained the total spatial clarity that would mark his classic phase. Although the *Lady Reading a Letter at an Open Window* (*c.* 1658; Dresden, Gemäldegalerie) belongs to the last years of this early phase, the relation between the figure and the space is still unclear, and the warm colors and intense light are conveyed through a grainy textured paint. The *Kitchen Maid* (*c.* 1658; Amsterdam, Rijksmuseum) is transitional between his early and his middle periods.

In his mature work, Vermeer achieved a classic balance in compositions of great structural simplicity, where the existence of forms in space was expressed with the utmost clarity in generally cool tones (*Woman Reading a Letter, c.* 1665, Amsterdam, Rijksmuseum; and *Maid Handing a Letter to Her Mistress, c.* 1665, Frick Collection). *The Young Woman with a Water Jug* (Metropolitan Museum) exemplifies Vermeer's abandonment of Baroque chiaros-

Jan Vermeer. *Young Woman with a Water Jug. c.* 1660. Metropolitan Museum of Art, New York.

Jan Vermeer. *Head of a Girl. c.* 1665. Mauritshuis, The Hague.

curo for a bright, daylight atmosphere, with a new interest in transparency and reflected light. The paint is now handled with a beautiful smoothness, as in the *Woman Weighing Pearls* (*c.* 1665; Washington, D.C., National Gallery). A superb group of very small paintings of women's heads also belongs to this classic phase, including *Head of a Girl* (*c.* 1665; Mauritshuis); the *Lace Maker* (*c.* 1665–68; Paris, Louvre); *Girl with a Flute* (*c.* 1665–70); and *Woman with a Red Hat* (both Washington, D.C., National Gallery). Vermeer's only two landscapes (actually townscapes) also date from the 1660s: the *Street in Delft* (*c.* 1660; Amsterdam, Rijksmuseum), and the *View of Delft* (*c.* 1662; Mauritshuis).

Whereas in his early work the figure dominated the space, and in the middle years a perfect accord was reached between the two, in Vermeer's last phase it is the space that dominates the figure. In these rich compositions depth is increased by the juxtaposition of a dark foreground with a more intense, yet subtle light in the distance (*Allegory of the Art of Painting, c.* 1670; Vienna, Kunsthistorisches Museum; *Lady at the Virginals with a Gentleman Listening, c.* 1668–70, London, Buckingham Palace; the *Letter, c.* 1670, Amsterdam, Rijksmuseum; and the *Concert*, Boston, Isabella Stewart Gardner Museum).

Paolo Veronese. *Donna Giustiniani-Barbaro and Her Servant.* 1563. Villa Barbaro (today Villa Volpi), Maser.

VERNET, family of French painters of the 18th and 19th centuries: JOSEPH (1714, Avignon—1789, Paris), who specialized in landscapes. In 1734 he went to Italy, where he remained for almost 20 years. From this period date the *Ponte Rotto* and the *Vues du Château Saint-Ange* (both 1745; both Paris, Louvre), two masterpieces whose elegance and luminosity prefigure Corot. On his return to France in 1753, Joseph was received into the French Academy. The Marquis de Marigny, the Superintendent of Buildings, commissioned him to paint a series of 24 pictures representing the principal ports of France; he painted only 14 of them, and these took up nine years of work. The finest is probably the *View of Toulon* (*c.* 1755–56; Musée de la Marine), which is given the added attraction of a pleasure party in a blockhouse. In the last period of his career, Vernet allowed himself to repeat in his studio the interchangeable storm scenes requested by English collectors, and the women bathers that were preferred by his French patrons.

CARLE (1758, Bordeaux—1836, Paris), a painter and engraver. The Directoire, which governed France from 1795 to 1799, inspired him to become a cartoonist, a fitting prelude to his work as a lithographer, which resulted in over 800 prints. During the period of the Empire, Carle painted numerous military parades and battle scenes (*Morning of the Battle of Austerlitz,* 1803; Versailles). Some of his finest drawings are of race courses, hunts, and the elegant life of Restoration Paris (*Foule de Chevaux*; Newport, R.I., Coll. Forsyth Wickes).

HORACE (1789, Paris—1863, Paris), Carle's son, was gifted with great facility and enjoyed enormous success as a painter of seascapes and battle pieces. When his friend, the Duc d'Orléans, became King Louis-Philippe, Horace executed most of his work at Versailles, where the king created a museum to the glories of France. It was there that Vernet painted his most popular works, representing the victories of the revolutionary armies (*Napoleon at the Battle of Wagram*) and the African campaigns (*Capture of the Smalah of Abd-el-Kader,* 1845). Later, for a few years before his death, he became the official painter of the Second Empire.

VERONESE, Paolo Caliari, *called* Paolo (1528, Verona—1588, Venice), Italian painter and decorator. His rather transparent colors and fondness for bright tones was part of his Veronese artistic heritage. Among the artist's first known works, dating from his Veronese period, are the Bevilacqua (1548; Verona, Museo Civico) and Gonzaga (1552; Mantua, Pinacoteca) altarpieces, and the *Temptation of St. Anthony* painted for Mantua Cathedral (1553; Caen, Museum).

Veronese settled in Venice in 1553 and rarely left the city, except to go to Rome in 1560. Among his first commissioned works in Venice were three ceiling frescoes (1553) in the Palazzo Ducale, including the famous representation of *Juno Bestowing Her Gifts on Venice* (Paris, Louvre). In 1555 the prior of the convent of S. Sebastiano in Venice commissioned from him a *Coronation of the Virgin* for the sacristy's ceiling. The *trompe-l'oeil* was treated with such ease that Veronese was soon commissioned to paint a cycle on the *Life of Esther* (1556) and a *Life of St. Sebastian* (1558) in the choir.

When Veronese went to Rome in 1560 he could not fail to have found in the work of Raphael and Michelangelo a strong encouragement to continue painting in the Grand Manner. On his return to Venice, official commissions were abundant: he collaborated with Titian's son, Orazio Vecelli, on the decoration of the Sala del Maggior Consiglio in the Palazzo Ducale (1562); painted huge canvases of sacred festivals, including the *Marriage at Cana* (1562; Louvre), commissioned by the monks of S. Giorgio Maggiore for their refectory; the *Feast in the House of the Pharisee* for the Servites (before

Paolo Veronese. *Finding of Moses.* 1570–80. Prado, Madrid. *Photo Anderson.*

Andrea del Verrocchio. *David.* 1473–75. Museo del Bargello, Florence. *Photo Alinari-Giraudon.*

1573; Louvre); the *Banquet of St. Gregory the Great* for the sanctuary of Monte Berico (1572); and the *Feast in the House of Levi* (1573; Venice, Accademia) for the Dominicans of S. Zanipolo.

Veronese, who had become the great "impresario" of painting, completely rejected the dramatic effects of Tintoretto. The decorations at the Villa Barbaro (today Villa Volpi) at Maser, near Treviso (1563) are treated with a sort of intoxicated illusionism, in which buildings, landscapes, false doors, and a procession of mythological figures cover all the walls. In the large religious compositions, crowds of figures are highlighted and stretch across the canvas in splendid costumes and settings (*Adoration of the Magi*, 1573, London, National Gallery; *Mystic Marriage of St. Catherine*, *c.* 1575, Venice, Accademia). As early as 1560 Veronese had painted several of the allegorical tondi for the large hall in the Libreria Vecchia in Venice. He was later given the task of glorifying Venice in a ceiling fresco in the Sala del Maggior Consiglio in the Palazzo Ducale. One of the finest and best contrived works of the time, which clearly anticipated the Baroque, the *Triumph of Venice* is an allegorical depiction of the Republic between Justice and Peace. Voluptuous mythological canvases such as the *Mars and Venus* (1576–84; New York, Metropolitan Museum) also date from this period. Veronese's tone becomes more serious in the *St. Pantaleon Healing a Sick Boy* (1587; Venice, S. Pantaleone), which has a pathos that was increasingly noticeable in the painter's final manner. He left an enormous workshop and several pupils. His brother, Benedetto, and his two sons, Carlo and Gabriele, put the final touches to his last works.

His unique contribution to painting was a sumptuous, serenely balanced, yet rather superficial style of decoration to counterbalance the tormented inner drama of Tintoretto. With a gift for scenography equaled only by Tiepolo, Veronese organized teeming compositions full of figures and little episodes, yet managed to unify and control them because he possessed in the highest degree the art of representing panoramic spectacles without any confusion. This is evident in the *Family of Darius before Alexander* (*c.* 1565; London, National Gallery), in which the masses converge to emphasize the essential elements in the scene.

Veronese has long been praised as the representative of Venetian Classicism. He has also won the reputation of being overbearingly grandiose and superficial, and yet his artistic personality is never other than brilliant: the vast orchestration of his paintings is made up of sound vital elements and is organized around a central core that is generally well constructed and conceived. He left an immense heritage: Nicolas Poussin and Claude Lorrain learned from him the value of architecture in a landscape; Rubens and Charles Le Brun learned the secret of compositional breadth. In addition to influencing the 17th-century artists in France, he inspired the *fêtes galantes* and voluptuous mythologies of the entire 18th century.

VERROCCHIO, Andrea di Michele Cioni, *called* Andrea del (1435, Florence—1488, Venice), Italian sculptor, painter, and goldsmith. Although most Florentine artists of the Renaissance were proficient in most media and techniques, Verocchio's versatility was exceptional; as early as 1460 he anticipated Leonardo da Vinci's universality. In 1472 he completed the superb marble and porphyry sarcophagus of Piero and Giovanni de' Medici in the Old Sacristy of S. Lorenzo, Florence. He then worked on the marble cenotaph to Cardinal Niccolò Forteguerri (1478–83; Pistoia Cathedral), commissioned in 1476. Verrocchio revealed the full measure of his creative powers with the sculptural group of *Christ and St. Thomas* (1467–83; Florence, façade of Or San Michele), which had been commissioned in 1463. It was an extraordinarily bold conception because the saint's figure stands well out from its niche and his back is half turned to the observer. In sculpture, Verrocchio also reinterpreted—but with more refinement and complexity—Donatello's two main themes: the nude youth (*David*, 1473–75; Florence, Bargello) and the equestrian statue (*Monument to Bartolommeo Colleoni*, 1479–88; Venice, Campo dei SS. Giovanni e Paolo). Verrocchio received the commission for the monument in 1479, sent his model to Venice for approval in 1481, and went to Venice to execute the statue in 1483. He died before completing the monument, and it was finished in 1496 by the sculptor Alessandro Leopardi (d. 1522/23).

It is difficult to establish an exact catalogue of Verrocchio's paintings, particularly for his *Madonnas* (Berlin, Staatliche Museen; London, National Gallery; New York,

Andrea del Verrocchio. *Monument to Bartolommeo Colleoni.* 1479–88. Campo dei SS. Giovanni e Paolo, Venice. *Photo Alinari-Giraudon.*

Maria Elena Vieira da Silva. *Bridge Over the City.* 1962–64.

Metropolitan Museum; Frankfurt am Main, Städelsches Kunstinstitut). The height of his activity as a painter was during the period 1470–80, after which time he seemed to have concentrated on sculpture. His most famous painting is the *Baptism of Christ* (after 1470; Florence, Uffizi) in which Leonardo da Vinci's hand can be recognized in the curly-headed angel on the left. Verrocchio's style appears to better advantage in the *Madonna and Child with St. Donatus and St. John the Baptist* (completed after 1485; Pistoia Cathedral), which is characterized by a new simplicity of composition and by the remarkable strength of the figures. Another masterpiece, the *Madonna and Child* in the Staatliche Museen, Berlin, was painted before 1470 (the museum owns two Verrocchio *Madonnas*).

Verrocchio was an active, cultivated, and accomplished workshop director. He was not only the master of Leonardo, but of most of the Italian artists active around 1490. Among the sculptors who passed through his studio were Benedetto Buglioni (1461–1521) and Giovanni Francesco Rustici (1474–1554); among the painters were Perugino, Lorenzo di Credi, and Francesco Botticini.

VERTUE, VARTU, *or* **VERTEWE,** family of English master masons.

ROBERT (active 1475–1506) was the son of Adam Vertue, with whom he worked on Westminster Abbey (1475–80; after 1482). He probably became master mason to the king about 1487, and in 1499 was in charge of the royal works at Greenwich. In 1501 he was at the Tower of London, and later worked on the Bath Abbey Church (1501–after 1503) with his brother William. He was probably the chief designer of Henry VII's Chapel at Westminster, of which the foundation stone was laid in 1501/2. In 1506 he was described as one of the king's three master masons, but he died before the end of that year.

WILLIAM (active 1501–27) is first mentioned in the records with his brother Robert at Bath Abbey Church in 1501. He worked on Henry VII's Chapel at Westminster, and by 1506 (or as early as 1502) was involved in the building of St. George's Chapel at Windsor. In 1510 he was appointed the king's master mason at the Tower of London, and was connected there with the rebuilding of St. Peter's Chapel after a fire in 1512. William paid several visits to King's College Chapel, Cambridge, perhaps to give advice on the fan vaulting. In 1511 he received a second contract at Windsor to finish St. George's Chapel. Soon afterward he began to design and supervise the building of Corpus Christi College, Oxford (1512–18). William was working at Woking Palace in 1515, and at Eton College the following year. The cloister and cloister chapel of St. Stephen in the Palace of Westminster (completed under Henry Redman) are late works. The style of the Vertues represented the culmination of English Gothic.

VEZELAY, Paule (b. 1893, southern England), English painter, engraver, and designer. Attracted by the abstract work of Jean Arp and Joan Miró, she undertook her first nonfigurative works between 1927 and 1928. Vezelay became a member of Abstraction-Création in 1934 and was associated with a number of other groups in Paris—the Salon des Surindépendants (1929–39); the Salon des Réalités Nouvelles from its formation in 1946; the Groupe Espace in Paris from 1953, and in Britain from 1955, becoming president of the latter in 1957. She was also made a Fellow of the Society of Industrial Artists and Designers.

Paule Vezelay first became known as a book illustrator, and practiced as a designer of carpets and textiles as well. Sculpture, collages, constructions of wire, plastic, and string (these date from 1936), engraving, pastels, and oils have all at different times formed her media. The titles of her paintings (*Menacing and Placed Object; Harmonious Tranquility; Luminous Forms; Dancing Shapes*) exactly represent their blend of abstract clarity and visual content.

Vezelay first exhibited at London's Dorien Leigh Gallery in 1921 and held many one-man shows in Paris and London thereafter. Her work was acquired by the Arts Council of Great Britain and is to be found in many private collections.

VIEIRA DA SILVA, Maria Elena (b. 1908, Lisbon), French painter of Portuguese origin. She took up painting in 1919 and sculpture in 1924, going to Paris for the first time in 1928, where she studied sculpture with Antoine Bourdelle and Charles Despiau. A year later, Vieira da Silva worked with the painters Charles Dufresne, Othon Friesz, and Fernand Léger, and with the graphic artist Stanley William Hayter. A work from this period, entitled *Composition* (1934; Paris, Priv. Coll.), contains seemingly iridescent green, blue, violet, and orange lines, placed in random diagonal formations or woven into net-like patterns and set against a neutral background. Both the use of muted color

Giacomo da Vignola. Palazzo Farnese, Caprarola. 1547–59. Plan.

contrasts and the linear structures placed against somewhat amorphous grounds continued to be a stylistic factor in certain later works, such as *Golden City* (1956; Paris, Coll. Pierre Granville).

In the works she produced during World War II, she juxtaposed a multitude of squares, rectangles, and lozenges, arranging them in such a way that the surface of the canvas seems to twist and turn, as in the *Card Players* (1942; Coll. Louis Franck) and in the later *Library* (1949; Paris, Musée National d'Art Moderne). Yet her paintings are not disturbing; the light that fills them is exceedingly gentle and the color is soft, often dominated by tones of grays and whites.

VIGÉE-LEBRUN, Élisabeth-Louise (1755, Paris—1842, Paris), French portrait painter. Her wit and beauty did much to further the very rapid professional success she achieved even before her marriage to the dealer Jean-Baptiste Lebrun (1776). Madame Vigée-Lebrun executed portraits of many leading social figures, but it was her friendship with Queen Marie-Antoinette that especially assured her reputation. Among about 20 portraits of the queen, particular mention should be made of *Marie-Antoinette and Her Children* (1787; Versailles). In these pictures, and in her *Self-Portrait* (*c.* 1791; Florence, Uffizi), Vigée-Lebrun expressed a Rousseauist sensibility, tinged with an 18th-century grace and sense of decorum. One of her most famous paintings, *Madame Vigée-Lebrun and Her Daughter* (1789; Paris, Louvre) combines the cult of "simplicity" and a search for purity of style, even in the treatment of costumes. In 1789 she left the country and traveled in Italy, Austria, and Russia, painting portraits of *Mademoiselle Porporati* in Italy (1792; Turin, Museum), *Grand Duchess Elizabeth Alexeyevna* in Russia (1792; Montpellier, Museum), and *Madame de Staël as Corina* in Switzerland (1808; Geneva, Musée Rath).

VIGNOLA, Giacomo Barozzi da Vignola, *called* Giacomo da (1507, Vignola, Emilia—1573, Rome), Italian architect. Since he studied under the architectural scholar Sebastiano Serlio in an atmosphere of learned Classicism, Vignola's interest soon took a theoretical turn. His influential study, *Regola delli cinque ordini di architettura* (1562), is heavily indebted to Serlio's own treatise, although more restricted in scope.

This theoretician, who might be called the father of academic architecture, showed himself to be quite free and original in his own buildings. In 1554, he built S. Andrea in Via Flaminia, Rome, the earliest example of a church with an oval dome and the archetype of many later oval plans. The Villa Giulia (1550–55) for Pope Julius III was Vignola's first major commission. On his next commission, the Villa Caprarola for the Farnese family (1559–73), Vignola had to build on the foundations already laid (*c.* 1520) by Antonio da Sangallo the Younger and Baldassare Peruzzi in the form of a pentagon. Vignola tempered the severity of the exterior in the central courtyard, where the pentagon becomes a circle: to the two stories of the villa correspond two circular galleries, where tall arcades alternate with smaller openings. In the upper gallery, a row of engaged Ionic columns punctuates this strict alternation and adds a feminine note.

During the third quarter of the 16th century, Vignola's influence dominated in central Italy. He built palaces in Rome, Piacenza, Rieti, and Velletri, as well as fountains at Viterbo and Vetralla. His Mannerism is apparent in his published drawings of gates and doorways, which show great imagination and vitality. In Rome Vignola built the smaller cupolas of St. Peter's, and during the last years of his life planned Il Gesù, the Roman church for the Society of Jesus (founded 1540), whose design is considered an important stage in the artistic and spiritual development of Catholicism. Owing much to Leon Battista Alberti in plan and elevation, Il Gesù is in the form of a Latin cross. The long nave is crossed by a broad domed transept, a combination of longitudinal and central plans developed by Alberti in S. Andrea at Mantua. The sides of the wide nave are lined by two rows of chapels that absorb the thrust of the barrel vault covering the nave. A building of this shape is admirably suited for preaching (an important feature in Counter Reformation religious life) and for the performance of individual Masses required by the order.

Viking Art. Sculptured ornament. Detail of a horse collar found at Søllested. National Museum, Copenhagen.

VIKING ART. The history of the Vikings, a Scandinavian people whose pirate bands were formed of Danish, Swedish and Norwegian warriors, stretches from the 8th to the 11th century A.D. They made their presence felt for the first time in A.D. 793, when they sacked the monastery of Lindisfarne, off the coast of Northumberland; through similar attacks they established their power throughout the 9th century A.D. In A.D. 839 the Viking chief Turgeis, or Thorgest, conquered Ireland and proclaimed himself king; other chiefs took possession of the Isle of Man and the Orkneys, obtained the duchy of Normandy in the 10th century, and set off to attack England; while under the leadership of Eric the Red in the late 10th century they colonized Ireland and Greenland. The disappearance of the Vikings after the death of such chiefs as Canute the Great in 1053 (b. 994?) and Ingvar Vittfarne in 1041 (b. 1016) was caused by the growth of Christianity and particularly the development of the Western states.

Their artistic sense expressed itself in every sphere of life, and their art is distinguished by a number of original features. There is not a trace of flower nor plant motifs in their ornament, and the human figure was seldom represented, except sometimes in the form of a mythological hero. The favorite motifs were animals—especially dragons, swans, horses, and snakes. The most commonly recurrent decorative element was strapwork, which is similar to the interlacing used by Irish miniaturists in the 7th and 8th centuries except that the Viking strapwork has a more elongated spiral and more fantastic animal forms.

The Viking ships were among their finest achievements. The craft

Viking Art. Ship unearthed at Oseberg, Norway. *c.* A.D. 850. Detail of prow. Universitetets Oldsaksamling, Oslo.

Viking Art. Animal head. Oseberg, Norway. 9th century. Universitetets Oldsaksamling, Oslo.

that became legendary through their raids was the *drakkar*, a warship with a prow shaped like a dragon, which was driven by oars or by a rectangular sail. Different parts of the ship, especially the stem and stern, were sometimes carved with animals in relief. At their extremities were fixed ensigns in gilded bronze. The tomb of a high-ranking Viking was a ship, which was buried in a tumulus with the prow turned toward the sea, the dead man sealed in a funerary chamber behind the mast and surrounded by propitiatory objects. The most characteristic of these ship burials, which have given us a fuller understanding of Viking culture, are in Norway: at Gokstad, excavated in 1880, with its gunwale protected on each side by many round shields painted black and yellow; and at Oseberg, unearthed in 1904, which contained the remains of two women, possibly Queen Asa and one of her attendants (Oslo, Universitetets Oldsaksamling). The Oseberg ship was full of furnishings and utensils, as well as sledges, a cart, caskets, and sculptured posts of unidentified purpose.

The best Viking art is perhaps the sculpture. The runic stones, irregular blocks of sandstone or granite bearing runic inscriptions commemorating an event, show skill in exploiting the harsh material and in elegantly distributing the characters over the surface. The Jelling stone that Harold Bluetooth erected about 958 in memory of his parents is engraved on one side with a *Christ in Glory*, surrounded by strapwork, and on another with an extraordinary emblematic quadruped (found at Jelling, Denmark; now in Copenhagen, National Museum). The monument at Lärbro, on the island of Gotland, is decorated with high reliefs narrating the exploits of the Icelandic hero Hild. Certain artists signed their work. The most notable was Gaut, who worked on the Isle of Man, where two signed stones were found that have led to the identification of other sculpture in his style. Wood carving in oak, pine, and birch was carried to the point of virtuosity, and a delicacy was attained that is reminiscent of the filigree work. The Oseberg ship burial (Universitetets Oldsaksamling) contains the most striking examples of wood carving, which decorate the body and runners of the sleighs, the shafts and panels of the cart (part of which illustrates Gunnar in the snake pit), a bedstead terminating in the heads of two fabulous beasts, and other objects.

The architecture of the Vikings, though less advanced than their boat building, had a distinctive style. The most important building of any settlement was the *langhallr*, a large communal house with several dependent units, where a high-ranking person lived and public meetings took place. It consists of a stone basement, triangular gables, and pitched roof of birchbark covered with turf, supported by a double row of wooden columns; the whole building was divided into compartments and a rectangular hearth was set in the center. Domestic dwellings were rectangular and made of wood, and the longitudinal walls curved outward like the sides of a ship. The Vikings were famed as military engineers for their circular camps with an impeccable geometric layout; the one at Trelleborg in Denmark, west of Zealand, is an example. One of their fortifications was Danevirke in Jutland, which had ramparts made of blocks of granite, over 9 miles long and 18 feet high.

Goldwork included sword handles with chased guard and pommel, spurs, and jewelry in a variety of metals. The women wore oval brooches in the form of convex bronze plaques covered with decoration: fine specimens are those found in the tombs at Birka, on an island in Lake Malar, Sweden. Bracelets, sometimes made of three twisted rods, and bracteates, or medallions with signs in relief on one face, were at one time made of gold; but after the Vikings began trading with the Arabs, they preferred silver. Their goldsmiths excelled in making necklaces of braided silver, in which as many as eight wires were spun into a spidery filigree.

In spite of certain unchanging aspects, the variety of Viking art has led some historians to postulate the existence of schools. At the beginning there was the Vestfold school during the reign of Queen Asa. Its strong individual character can be appreciated in the works from the Oseberg ship. Then came the Gotland school, whose zoomorphic art was particularly ebullient. The Gokstad school followed in the 10th century, characterized by a combination of

Viking Art. The Jelling stone. A.D. 958. National Museum, Copenhagen.

Viking Art. Tombstone from Tängelgarda, Gotland, Sweden. 8th century. Nationalmuseum, Stockholm. *Photo A.T.A., Stockholm.*

Viking Art. Gold bracteate. 7th–8th century. Nationalmuseum, Stockholm. *Photo Antikvarisk-Topografiska Arkivet, Stockholm.*

abstraction and representation in its zoomorphism; it was in turn succeeded by the Jelling school, which borrowed certain elements from Christian art, and the Søllested and Mammen schools, whose dominant feature was strapwork. In the 11th century the Ringerike school and the various British ones were distinguished by their eclecticism and the complexity of their motifs.

VILLANUEVA, Carlos Raúl (b. 1900, Croydon, England), Venezuelan architect. He was the leading figure in modern Venezuelan architecture, not only through his own work, but also through his action in the Banco Obrero, the co-ordinating building organization of his country. After executing a number of personal variations on Latin American colonial styles, Villanueva drew inspiration from contemporary international architecture and attempted to adapt new technical and stylistic innovations to several large-scale programs (residential buildings at Caracas). But his major work remains the buildings of Caracas University, including the Olympic Stadium (1950–51), the Aula Magna, the Plaza Cubierta (1952–53), library, clinic, and lecture halls. The Aula Magna (auditorium) is an especially beautiful hall whose curved white ceiling is broken by shaped, colored acoustic panels designed by Alexander Calder. Throughout the entire complex, Villanueva showed great imagination in diversifying the plans and in using the resources of reinforced concrete. This group of buildings, decorated by Jean Arp, Fernand Léger, Alexander Calder, and Victor Vasarely, is a particularly successful example of synthesis in the arts.

VILLANUEVA, Juan de (1739, Madrid—1811, Madrid), Spanish architect. Villanueva spent seven years in Rome as a scholar at the Academy (1759–65), during which time he disavowed Rococo principles. Upon his return to Spain, he became the most successful representative of the new Classicism at the Spanish court. In 1770 he designed the vestry and the Palafox Chapel in the cathedral of Burgo de Osma. Here he developed a motif later used at the Prado in Madrid, with pairs of freestanding columns, beneath straight entablatures, forming a screen around the rotunda. As new buildings were needed to accommodate the court, he built the Casita de Abajo and the Casita de Arriba at the Escorial (both 1773), and later the Casita del Principe at El Pardo (1784). These three small villas are masterpieces of his style—the Spanish equivalent of Jacques-Ange Gabriel's Petit Trianon at Versailles, and owing something to French Neoclassicism. In 1785 Villanueva was commissioned to build the Prado, originally conceived as a natural history museum in connection with the civic improvement of Madrid. His last works in Madrid were the Academy of History (1788), the Oratory of the Caballero de Gracia (1789), and the Observatory (1790). The latter, a first essay in Greek Revival forms, and the expression of function through geometric variation, opened a new era in Spanish architecture.

VILLON, Gaston Duchamp, *called* Jacques (1875, Damville—1963, Puteaux, near Paris), French painter and engraver. During the difficult times of his early career, when Toulouse-Lautrec was a formative influence, Villon earned his living by contributing to humorous periodicals, notably *Le Rire* and *L'Assiette au Beurre*, and designing posters for the Montmartre cabarets. Although Impressionism and then Fauvism attracted him at first, his taste for analysis eventually drew him toward an unorthodox interpretation of Cubism. In 1912 Villon began holding regular meetings in his studio at Puteaux with such artists as Robert Delaunay, Frank Kupka, Roger de la Fresnaye, Fernand Léger, Albert Gleizes, his sister Suzanne, and his two brothers, the sculptor Raymond Duchamp-Villon and the painter Marcel Duchamp.

Jacques Villon. *Portrait of Walter Pach.* 1932–47. Minneapolis Institute of Arts.

After World War I, his pictures were painted in a relatively restrained range of colors, dominated by browns and grays (*Game*, 1919; Coll. Louis Carré). In the 1930s the geometric forms of his paintings became increasingly luminous, with imbricated, spectral colors (*Architecture*, 1931, and *Joy*, 1932; both Coll. Louis Carré). Later works (*Windows*, 1932–33; Coll. Louis Carré) even more strikingly create depth through the expressive manipulation of color planes. Although most of Villon's work had been in the realm of abstraction, in 1935 he returned to portraits (*The Draftsman*, 1935; Coll. Louis Carré), scenes from everyday life, and landscapes, which interested him increasingly. During World War II he retired to the Tarn, where he painted many pictures of the countryside (*Garden with Pumpkins*, 1942, and the *Three Orders*, 1944; both Coll. Louis Carré) that were exhibited after the war. The high quality of the paintings was maintained in succeeding years: *Unfathomed Depths* (1945; Coll. Louis Carré), *Corn Mill* (1946; Oslo, Coll. Ragnar Moltzau), and *Woman Scything* (1950; Milwaukee, Art Center). Magnificent landscapes (*The Seine in the Valley of La Haye*, 1960; Paris, Galerie Louis Carré) furnished further evidence of the elegant precision of his style. In the course of his long career Villon had managed to reconcile French Impressionism and Cubism, analysis and synthesis, realism and abstraction. In his last years, Villon's theories regarding the division of planes, the pyramidal creation of space, and the prismatic separation of tones were mastered, and became the vehicles of a vital expressive force.

VINCI, Leonardo da. *See* **LEONARDO DA VINCI.**

VINGT, Les, Belgian art movement of the late 19th century. In 1881 the Belgian lawyer Octave Maus (1856–1919) founded the review *L'Art Moderne* with the help of his colleague, Edmond Picard (1836–1924). Two years later, when the official jury refused the work of about 20 young painters, Maus founded the Association des Vingt, a group of 20 Belgian painters and sculptors. Beginning in 1884, they held annual exhibitions in Brussels to which they invited many foreign and often unknown artists.

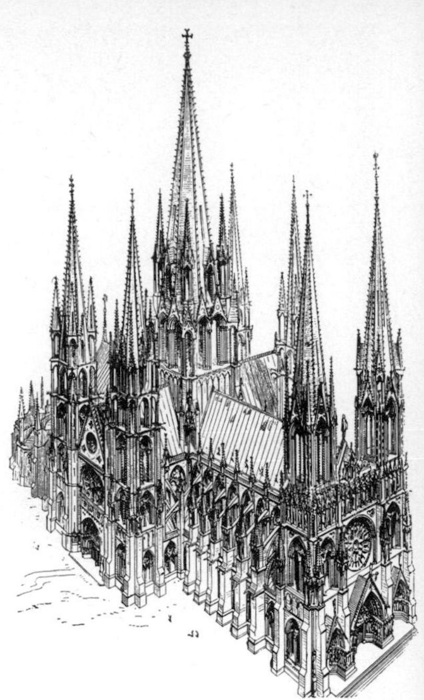

Eugène-Emmanuel Viollet-le-Duc. *Reconstruction of the ideal cathedral.*

The guest artists, who were generally only invited every other year to avoid repetition or favoritism, presented a choice that was all the more remarkable because most of them had not yet been requested to exhibit anywhere. The most distinguished names were Auguste Rodin and J. A. M. Whistler in 1884; Claude Monet, Pierre Auguste Renoir, Odilon Redon, and Adolphe Monticelli (1824–86) in 1886; Berthe Morisot, Lucien Pissarro, and Georges Seurat in 1887; Henri de Toulouse-Lautrec and Paul Signac in 1888; Henri-Edmond Cross, Paul Gauguin, Monet, Pissarro, and Seurat in 1889; Paul Cézanne, Redon, Renoir, Signac, Alfred Sisley, Toulouse-Lautrec, and Van Gogh in 1890; Gauguin, Pissarro, Seurat, and Vincent van Gogh (retrospective) in 1891; Mary Cassatt, Maurice Denis, Toulouse-Lautrec, and Seurat (retrospective) in 1892. After 1887 Seurat and his friends were regularly represented at Brussels and several members were converted to divisionism.

The periodical *L'Art Moderne*, now the organ of Les Vingt, published informed articles on new tendencies and outstanding personalities of contemporary art by such authors as Octave Mirbeau, Félix Fénéon, Joris-Karl Huysmans, and Émile Verhaeren. In addition, the annual exhibitions were accompanied by lectures given by Catulle Mendès, Villiers de l'Isle-Adam, Stéphane Mallarmé, Gustave Kahn, Henry van de Velde, and Paul Verlaine.

The number of members in the group did not always remain at 20; internal quarrels, resignations, and elections changed its composition frequently. Among those who later won international reputations were James Ensor, Georges Minne, Félicien Rops (1835–98), Théo van Rysselberghe, and Van de Velde. Toward the end, a few foreigners were elected, such as the Dutchman Jan Toorop and the Frenchmen Rodin and Signac. In 1893 the dissolution of the society was effectively voted.

VIOLLET-LE-DUC, Eugène-Emmanuel (1814, Paris—1879, Lausanne), French architect. In the course of a number of journeys through France and Italy (1835–39), he became so knowledgeable about medieval architecture that Prosper Mérimée, then inspector of historical buildings, entrusted him at the age of twenty-six with the task of restoring the ruinous abbey of Vézelay (1840). There are few medieval buildings in France that he did not restore. These included the abbey church of St-Denis, the cathedrals of St-Sernin, Toulouse, and Notre-Dame in Paris, as well as those of Amiens, Chartres, and Rheims. He worked on the ramparts of Carcassonne and undertook a detailed restoration of the Château de Pierrefonds as a residence for Napoleon III. On the basis of a narrowly rationalistic conception of medieval architecture, he proceeded to innumerable questionable and much criticized restorations. But his theoretical writings exercised considerable influence, not only on his contemporaries (*Dictionnaire raisonné de l'architecture française du XIe au XVIe siècle*, 1854–68), but also on such different architects as Auguste Perret, Frank Lloyd Wright, Hendrik Berlage, Victor Horta, and even Le Corbusier. His formula that "any form without an explicable purpose cannot be beautiful" contains within itself the whole process of 20th-century functional architecture.

VISCHER, family of German sculptors and bronzesmiths. Their Nuremberg studio produced tombstones and funerary monuments that were used throughout Central and Eastern Europe from the mid-15th to the mid-16th century. The family comprises: PETER, *called* THE ELDER (*c.* 1460–1529). An early work, and one of Peter's most important, is the bronze figure called the *Branch Breaker* (1490; Munich, Bayerisches Nationalmuseum), once attributed to Adam Kraft. The handling of anatomical features is exceptionally detailed and realistic, and shows considerable advance over other German works of this type, in which drapery obscures the actual form of the human figure. Somewhat more conventional, but still masterful in conception and handling, is the bronze statue of *Archbishop Ernst von Sachsen* (1495; Magdeburg Cathedral), created as part of the archbishop's tomb monument. Peter the Elder's most famous work, however, is the reliquary shrine for St. Sebald (first plan drawn up 1488; Vienna, Akademie der bildenden Künste) in the church of St. Sebald at Nuremberg. This monumental shrine is in the form of a canopy; it is essentially Gothic in style, but in the course of execution, from 1507 to 1519, it was covered by a luxuriant embroidery of Renaissance ornamentation that included figures of Sirens and Hercules; candelabra; and statuettes of the 12 apostles placed in front of the piers and draped in a somewhat Classical style. Included among the figures is a *Self-Portrait* by Peter the Elder. An inscription on the shrine indicates that he was assisted in this work by his three sons: HERMANN THE YOUNGER (*c.* 1486–1517), PETER THE YOUNGER (1487–1528), and HANS (*c.* 1489–1550), who were probably largely responsible for the Italianate character of the work. Other commissions executed by the studio include a cloister gate completed in 1522 and originally intended for the funerary chapel of the Fuggers at Augsburg (now at the Château de Montrottier in Savoy), and two statues cast in 1513 for the tomb of Emperor Maximilian at the Hofkirche in Innsbruck. In addition to these works, the studio continued to produce innumerable tombstones of unrivaled technical mastery, including the tomb of Frederick the Wise in the castle church at Wittemberg, generally attributed to Peter the Younger. Other works include three reliefs of *Orpheus and Eurydice* (*c.* 1515–20; Hamburg, Museum für Kunst und Gewerbe; Berlin, Staatliche Museen; Washington, D.C., National Gallery).

Peter Vischer the Elder. *Self-Portrait.* Detail from the shrine of St. Sebald. 1507–19. Church of St. Sebald, Nuremberg. *Photo Lala Aufsberg.*

Peter Vischer the Younger. *Orpheus and Eurydice.* *c.* 1515–20. Staatliche Museen, Berlin.

VITTORIA, Alessandro (1525, Trent—1608, Venice), Italian sculptor. He had had some training before he went to Venice in 1543 to enter the workshop of Jacopo Sansovino. Vittoria's first signed work was an unfinished *St. John the Baptist* in the Venetian church of S. Zaccaria (1550). In 1552 he competed with Sansovino for a colossal *Hercules* for Ercole II d'Este, but their rivalry was resolved in 1553 when Sansovino commissioned him to do two caryatid figures (completed 1555) for the door of the Libreria Vecchia in Venice. Vittoria also executed numerous fine medals, and worked on monuments, religious commissions, and stucco decorations—particularly for the architect Andrea Palladio—in the cities and villas of the Veneto region, as well

Alessandro Vittoria. *St. Jerome. c.* 1569. Church of S. Maria dei Frari, Venice. *Photo Alinari-Giraudon.*

as in the Doges' Palace at Venice (for which he provided a superb stucco ceiling on the Scala d'Oro, *c.* 1560). During the mid-1560s he designed the stucco decorations that accompany Paolo Veronese's frescoes in the Villa Barbaro (today Villa Volpi) at Maser, near Treviso, built by Palladio. His best-known work is the *St. Jerome* (*c.* 1569) in the Chiesa dei Frari in Venice. Fire in the Doges' Palace in 1577 led to his being employed on its redecoration, for which he carved the figures of *Justice* and *Venice* (completed 1579) surmounting the great central windows on the façade facing the Piazzetta and the lagoon, and—on the doorway between the Antecollegio and the Collegio—the allegorical figures that paraphrase Michelangelo's Medici Chapel figures. In his statues and reliefs Vittoria shows the marked influence first of the antique and of Sansovino, and then, from the 1560s onward, of Michelangelo and Parmigianino. His portrait busts (*Domenico Duodo*, 1596; Venice, Ca' d'Oro) are highly naturalistic and derive their peculiar excellence from the dignity and distinction with which they invest individual characteristics.

After Sansovino, Vittoria ranks as the best Venetian sculptor; a close friend of Titian and Tintoretto, he formed with them and with Michele Sanmicheli, Palladio, and Veronese one of the group of great artists who represent the Venetian equivalent of the High Renaissance in Central Italy.

VIVARINI, family of Italian painters active in Venice, whose workshop nearly rivaled that of the Bellini family for over half a century. The hallmarks of their style were a feeling for fine materials, enamel-like color, and a carefully balanced composition.

ANTONIO (*c.* 1415, Murano—1476/84, Venice), the eldest member of the family, worked regularly from 1440 to 1450 with Giovanni d'Alemagna. They collaborated on a *Coronation of the Virgin* (1444; Venice, S. Pantaleone) that is remarkable for its rich and congested composition. Antonio's *Madonna* in S. Tomaso at Padua, in spite of all the flowers and flourishes of Gothic decoration, is nevertheless more elegant. After 1448 his space became more articulated, his outlines more animated, and a solemn grace appeared in his paintings. The panels of *St. Catherine Casting Out a Pagan Idol* (Washington, D.C., National Gallery, Kress Collection) and of *St. Peter Martyr* (New York, Milan, etc.) have caused such art historians as Roberto Longhi to consider Antonio as a sort of "Venetian Masolino."

BARTOLOMEO (*c.* 1432, Murano—1499, Murano), Antonio's younger brother, had a more energetic style than Antonio. His first works (1450–62) were done in the shadow of his brother, but he reacted strongly to Mantegna's manner and soon developed a polished and rather sharp style of his own. The *Madonna with Saints* (1465; Naples, Museo di Capodimonte) is flowery in style, while a sense of volume characterizes the *Madonna della Misericordia* (1473; Venice, S. Maria Formosa); at times a sort of Gothic linearism reappears, as in a triptych containing the *Madonna and Child Between St. Andrew and St. John the Baptist* (1478; Venice, S. Giovanni in Bragora) and in a *St. George* (1485; formerly Berlin, destroyed 1945). There is greater simplicity and a colder feeling in a large polyptych of 1490 (Florence, Coll. Contini-Bonacossi), whose central panel depicts *Christ as a Pilgrim.*

ALVISE (*c.* 1446, Venice or Murano—1503/5, Venice), Antonio's son, was probably the pupil of his uncle Bartolomeo, judging at least from the rather strained style of his *Montefiorentino Polyptych* (1475; Urbino, Galleria Nazionale), which is his first known work. Alvise learned how to achieve tonality in painting from Antonello da Messina; this skill is evident in the *Sacra Conversazione with St. Louis of Toulouse and St. Anthony of Padua* (1480; Venice, Accademia). The *Madonna with Four Saints* (formerly Berlin, destroyed 1945), with its architectural superstructure, and *St. Ambrose* (Venice, Chiesa dei Frari) show fairly close affinities with the style of Giovanni Bellini. Some portraits (one of them, *Portrait of a Gentleman*, painted in 1497; London, National Gallery), done in a smooth, restrained style, have been attributed to Alvise and reveal the influence of Giorgione and Titian.

VLAMINCK, Maurice de (1876, Paris—1958, Rueil-la-Gadelière), French painter. It was not until he met André Derain in 1900 that Vlaminck began to paint seriously. He was at first attracted by the Impressionists, then by Van Gogh. The influence of the latter and the 15 months he worked at Chatou with Derain were decisive for his highly spontaneous early manner. Fauvism, which was already a powerful reality in the work of Vlaminck and Derain, became an official movement when they joined the circle that formed around Albert Marquet and Henri Matisse. Some of Vlaminck's best work dates from this period when the group exhibited at the Salon des Indépendants, then at the Salon d'Automne in the famous *cage aux Fauves* ("cage of the wild beasts"). It includes *Bridge at Chatou* (1905; Paris, Priv. Coll.), *Bateaux-lavoirs* (1905; Paris, Priv. Coll.), *Street at Marly-le-Roi* (1905–6), and *Red Trees* (1906; both in Paris, Musée National d'Art Moderne). These paintings, together with others in the same vein, were bought in a block by the dealer Ambroise Vollard. Then came a crisis when Vlaminck felt he had "reached a maximum intensity." Under Cézanne's in-

Maurice de Vlaminck. *Still Life with Lemons.* 1913–14. National Gallery of Art, Washington, D.C.

fluence he gave up his surging lines and shrieking colors and, from 1908 to 1914, painted strong, well-defined forms in dark colors, including *Bougival* (1910; Paris, Musée d'Art Moderne de la Ville de Paris) and his *Self-Portrait* (1912; Paris, Priv. Coll.), a successful work in harmonies of black and green.

After World War I Vlaminck's realism became more marked. Just as he had turned from the tempestuous interpretations of his Fauvist period, so now he abandoned the style and stability he had derived from Cézanne and worked in the manner of the Flemish Expressionists and Dutch naturalists. The abuse and rancor in his books, *Tournant Dangereux* ("Dangerous Turning," 1929), *Poliment* ("Good Manners," 1931), and *Portraits avant décès* ("Portraits before Decease," 1943), reflect the increasing disillusionment of his last years.

VORDEMBERGE-GILDEWART, Friedrich (1899, Osnabrück, Lower Saxony—1963, Ulm), German painter. In 1924 Vordemberge-Gildewart founded Group K, and maintained close ties with the De Stijl group in Leiden (*Construction No. 3*, 1924; Meudon, Coll. Nelly van Doesburg). He joined the Circle et Carré group in 1930, and later became a founding member of the Abstraction-Création group in Paris (1932). Although Vordemberge-Gildewart's compositions remained in the tradition of Neoplasticism, he preferred triangular shapes and diagonals to its rectangles and strict horizontal-vertical format (*Composition No. 121*, 1940; New York, Guggenheim Museum). In 1938 he settled in Amsterdam, where in 1948 he ran the publishing house of Duwaer. During the 1950s De Stijl rectangles and colors occasionally recurred (*Composition No. 181*, 1951; Zurich, Coll. Max Bill). He moved to Ulm in 1955, where he taught at the Hochschule für Gestaltung. A large retrospective exhibition of Vordemberge-Gildewart's work was held at the Ulm Museum in 1963.

VORTICISM, an English anti-Impressionist movement similar to Cubism in France and, more comparably, to Futurism in Italy since it accepted and sought out the forms of the machine world. These forms, highly abstracted, were treated as flat, plan-like systems of arcs and angles, and organized radically on a vortex principle, which had the effect of sucking the spectator into a whirling recession (Wyndham Lewis, *Composition*, 1913; London, Tate Gallery). Vorticism is thus of historical interest as one of the several independent manifestations of the drive to abstraction that became apparent in Europe between 1910 and 1912.

The movement could be said to have lasted from 1912 to 1915; it is perhaps straining the word to call it a movement at all, for not merely did it revolve around the figure of Lewis—it was all but contained by him. His circle included the writers Ezra Pound, who coined the word "vorticist" in 1913 and whose portrait Lewis painted in 1938 (Tate Gallery), and Richard Aldington; T. E. Hulme, the anti-Romantic philosopher; the sculptors Jacob Epstein and Henri Gaudier-Brzeska (1891–1915); and the painters William Roberts, Edward Wadsworth, and C. R. Nevinson. Apart from its purely historical significance, Vorticism is remembered for its generally vitalizing influence in British art. The first (and last) Vorticist exhibition took place at the Doré Gallery, London, in June 1915. But, although a number of painters were subsequently to employ Vorticism's precise, metallic handwriting to record aspects of the war upon which Europe was embarked—and for which those forms seemed peculiarly fitted—none maintained Vorticism's short-lived burst of non-figurative painting.

VOUET, Simon (1590, Paris—1649, Paris), French painter. At the age of 14 he was invited to England to paint the portrait of a high-ranking French lady. He came to the notice of the French ambassador in Turkey and left with him for Constantinople in 1611. Vouet stayed there a year, then left for Venice and went on to Rome at the beginning of 1614. He made the acquaintance of several artists there and contrived to win powerful protectors, among whom was Cardinal Barberini. He opened a school in Via Ferratina and, at this period, was considered the leader of the colony of French painters in Rome. In 1623 his protector, Cardinal Barberini, was elected Pope Urban VIII and Vouet's fortunes prospered as a result; he was nominated prince of the Accademia di S. Luca and was given several important commissions (*Last Supper*, 1625; Loreto, Palazzo Apostolico). At about this time (before 1627) Vouet painted his last picture in the Tenebrist manner, *Intelligence, Memory, and Will* (Rome, Museo Capitolino), and his first picture with the clear, diffused lighting characteristic of his final manner, an *Allegory of the Fine Arts* (Rome, Galleria Nazionale). Louis XIII and Cardinal Richelieu, who planned to put him in charge of several extensive decorative programs, invited him back to Paris. On his arrival in 1627, Vouet was appointed First Painter to the King and given living accommodation in the Louvre. He began working on large decorative paintings, most of which have unfortunately been destroyed, in the Palais Cardinal (*c.* 1635) and the châteaux of Chessy (early 1630s), Chilly (1630–32), and St-Germain-en-Laye (begun early 1630s) and the hôtels of Bullion (1630) and Séguier (from 1638) in Paris. The Nymphaeum of the château at Wideville is one of the few to survive intact. Vouet's best works in the Classical Baroque style include *Time Conquered* (1627; Madrid, Prado), *The Presentation* (1641; Paris, Louvre), and the *Allegory of Peace* (*c.* 1648; Chatsworth, Derbyshire, Coll. Duke of Devonshire). In 1642, Vouet decorated the Palais Royal (1643–47) in Paris and the château at Fontainebleau (1644).

VOULKOS, Peter (b. 1924, Bozeman, Montana), American sculptor. His earliest major interest was in ceramics; in 1952 he received an M.F.A. degree from the California College of Arts and Crafts in Oakland, and rapidly gained an international reputation as an ex-

Vorticism. Henri Gaudier-Brzeska. *Standing Birds*. 1914. Museum of Modern Art, New York.

Simon Vouet. *Lot and His Daughters*. Musée des Beaux-Arts, Strasbourg. *Photo Giraudon, Paris.*

cellent ceramicist. Voulkos' innovative approach enabled him to develop the clay medium in new directions that led to a renewal of clay sculpture. While in Los Angeles (1954–59), he experimented freely with the form and surface of clay as expressive means in themselves. During these years he created multipart forms, which he joined with epoxies, and began to use epoxy paints together with glazes. Around 1958 Voulkos made a definite shift, using boldly piled up cylinders of clay as armatures for large-scale, massive ceramic sculptures (*Little Big Horn*, 1959; Oakland, Art Museum). After moving to the San Francisco Bay area in 1959, he turned primarily to bronze. Together with other sculptors living in the vicinity, he built a foundry where he did his own casting. Voulkos cast separate slabs of bronze, bent or broke them up, and then welded or bolted them together in bold, rugged constructions, sometimes contrasting geometric platformlike blocks with dynamic, Expressionistic forms (*Bad Day at Shattuck, II, c.* 1964; bronze and wood, Los Angeles, Coll. David Stuart Galleries). In the mid-1960s, however, Voulkos abandoned this style of juxtaposition and executed such harmonious, clear-cut geometrical constructions as *Hiro* (1964–65; aluminum and bronze, Los Angeles, County Museum of Art).

VOYSEY, Charles Francis Annesley (1857, Hessle, Yorkshire—1941, Winchester), English architect. He set up practice in 1882 and produced graceful designs for decorative art, which rivaled those of William Morris but were more reminiscent of the work of Arthur Mackmurdo (1851–1942). His ornamental objects and wallpapers (*Cereus*, 1886; London, Victoria and Albert Museum) were even more fashionable than his furniture. Voysey's architecture, largely country houses, had simple lines in reaction to heavily ornamented Victorian historicism. The private houses he built in Kensington are all distinguished by large bays and elegant brick bonding. Voysey's country houses ("The Orchard," Chorleywood, Hertfordshire, 1900–1; Annesley Lodge, Hampstead, 1895) combined the charm of the past with a functional modern planning.

VUILLARD, Édouard (1868, Cuiseaux, Saône-et-Loire—1940, La Baule), French painter. He studied at the Lycée Condorcet in Paris and planned to attend the military academy of St. Cyr, but his fellow pupil, Ker-Xavier Roussel (1867–1944), who later became his brother-in-law, persuaded him to take up painting. The academic teaching at the École des Beaux-Arts soon revolted him and he joined the Académie Julian (1888), where Paul Sérusier was the student-in-charge and Pierre Bonnard became his friend. Vuillard was fascinated by the linear technique and flat colors of Japanese prints. The best of his work, whose Intimist character became more marked with the years, reflects this Oriental influence.

Gauguin's brief influence on Vuillard can be seen in his painting *In Bed* (1891; Paris, Musée National d'Art Moderne), while some portraits of Misia Natanson and her brother Cipa Godebski bear the unmistakable stamp of the Japanese print. Vuillard's interiors and family scenes reflect his fondness for dimly lit well-heated rooms and cozy boudoirs cluttered with curtains and knick-knacks, where the daylight can hardly penetrate (*Sitting Room with Three Lamps*, 1899; Zurich, Coll. Zumsteg). He delighted in painting his family, especially his mother to whom he was devoted (*Annette's Supper*, 1900; St-Tropez, Musée de l'Annonciade). Vuillard also attempted mural painting in his 10 scenes of the Tuileries, painted in tempera on the walls of the Natansons' dining room (1894; three in Paris, Musée National d'Art Moderne), or in his series of *Interiors* for Dr. Vaquez (1896; Paris, Petit-Palais). His decorations for the foyer of the Théâtre des Champs-Élysées (1912–13), the Palais de Chaillot (1938), and the League of Nations building in Geneva (1939) were less successful.

W

WADSWORTH, Edward Alexander (1889, Cleckheaton, Yorkshire—1949, London), English painter and engraver. Wadsworth exhibited with the Vorticists, and after service with the navy (1915–17) was engaged upon dazzle camouflage work on shipping at English ports. His interests were thus established early: to an overriding passion for the sea and ships were joined a lively sense of pictorial structure and pattern making, and an instinctive leaning toward precision of expression. The drawings and prints he made toward the end of and immediately after World War I are genuine documents of their time. In 1920 Wadsworth published a book of drawings of *The Black Country*, with an introduction by Arnold Bennett, followed six years later by a book of copper engravings, *The Sailing Ships and Barges of the Western Mediterranean and Adriatic*. Thereafter he applied himself almost entirely to tempera. For the rest of his life he developed and refined an idiom in which can be found echoes of Fernand Léger and the Cubists on the one hand, of Giorgio de Chirico, Pierre Roy, and the Surrealists on the other (*Little Western Flower*, 1938). Still lifes of heterogeneous objects were typical of his later works (*The Bleached Margin*, 1937). Wadsworth was at different times a member of the London Group, X Group, the New English Art Club, and Unit One; he was elected an Associate of the Royal Academy in 1943. In 1945 he delivered a paper to the Royal Institute of Civil Engineers on *The Aesthetic Aspect of Civil Engineering Design* (it was subsequently published). Wadsworth executed a number of public mural decorations, notably for the Canadian War Museum in Ottawa, the RMS *Queen Mary*, and the De La Warr Pavilion, Bexhill. His work is represented in London's British Museum and Tate Gallery (memorial exhibition 1951), and in the Stedelijk Museum at Amsterdam.

WAGNER, Otto (1841, Penzing, near Vienna—1918, Vienna), Austrian architect, the undisputed leader of the Austrian architectural revival at the end of the 19th century. At the beginning of his career in Vienna, Wagner distinguished himself with a project for a Kursalon in the municipal park (1863). In 1894 he was appointed to a teaching post at the Vienna Academy, where—in classes that had a profound effect on the rising generation of architects—he taught that the architect should try to harmonize his techniques with recently discovered materials. These ideas were published in his book, *Moderne Architektur* (1895), but were not immediately embodied in his practical work, which followed the aesthetic forms of the Jugendstil. This is evident in the Karlsplatz Station for the Vienna underground railway (1899–1901), and in the Majolika Haus (1898), a block of flats with moderate rents, whose façade of ceramic tiles and ironwork balconies attempted to bring art into ordinary people's lives. Wagner soon adopted a more radical attitude and insisted on the "absolute primacy of structure over decoration." Two Viennese buildings mark this development: the church of St. Leopold at the top of the Steinhof (1905–7), and the Post Office Savings Bank (1904–6), where the use of steel and glass create an effect of linear purity and restraint. This mature phase of Wagner's architecture became an important influence in the development of the International Style.

WALKOWITZ, Abraham (1880, Tunen, Siberia—1965, Brooklyn, New York), Russian-born American painter. He was brought to the United States during early childhood, and spent a number of years alternately traveling and studying between 1907 and 1914. The work done after his return to America in 1914 shows the influence of Henri Matisse, the Fauves, and Wassily Kandinsky. In an expressive personal manner, Walkowitz portrayed the industrial and urban phenomena that had been Robert Delaunay's inspiration in Paris (*New York*, 1917; New York, Whitney Museum). He first showed at Stieglitz' gallery between 1912 and 1917, and was included in the famous Forum Exhibition at the Anderson Gallery in New York. Walkowitz, like Kandinsky and the Fauves, was especially interested in children's drawings, whose qualities of freshness and freedom were captured in his own watercolors. He did many sketches of figurative subjects (*Bathers*, 1910; New York, Coll. Mr. and Mrs. Lawrence B. Karter), as well as scenes of New York's buildings tangled in webs of abstract lines. During the 1920s he continued to work on figurative abstractions (*Dance Rhythms*, 1920; New York, Zabriskie Gallery).

WALLIS, Henry (1830, Sutton, near London—1916, Croydon, near London), English painter. He was a pupil at Cary's Academy, at the Royal Academy Schools, and in the studio of Charles Gleyre (1806–74) in Paris. Wallis is chiefly remembered for the *Death of Chatterton* (exhibited 1856; London, Tate Gallery), which although belonging to the type of carefully reconstructed historical genre that he had been painting before, revealed a new, strong Pre-Raphaelite influence in coloring and precision of detail. It was painted

Otto Wagner. Post Office Savings Bank, Vienna. 1904–6. View of the main hall. *Photo Kunstgewerbemuseum, Zurich.*

Henry Wallis. *Death of Chatterton.* 1856. Tate Gallery, London.

in the actual attic where the poet had died, and was highly praised by John Ruskin. The model for Chatterton was the young George Meredith, with whose wife Wallis eloped to Capri in 1858. Wallis exhibited regularly at the Royal Academy until 1877, and produced several books on Italian and Persian ceramics. His masterpiece, and one of the most beautiful of all Pre-Raphaelite paintings, is the *Stonebreaker* (Birmingham, City Museum and Art Gallery), a small panel of 1857, which was shown at the Academy in 1858 with a quotation from Carlyle's *Sartor Resartus* printed in the catalogue.

WALTER, Thomas Ustick (1804, Philadelphia—1887, Philadelphia), American architect. He was raised in the building trades, and apprenticed at the age of fifteen to the Greek Revival architect William Strickland. After an interruption of seven years, during which he studied painting and science, he returned permanently to architecture at the age of twenty-four. In 1833 Walter won the competition for Girard College in Philadelphia, and the great peripteral temple that he built was a major monument of the Greek Revival. Girard College established his place in Philadelphia, and earned him the patronage of Nicholas Biddle, whose house, Andalusia, Walter remodeled with a Doric portico based on the temple of Hephaestus in Athens. The climax of his career, and the work for which he is best known, is the great cast-iron dome of the United States Capitol in Washington, D.C., and the new House and Senate wings (1851–65), with which he transformed the existing building into a vast composition of almost Baroque character. Walter became pre-eminent in the field and was elected second president of the American Institute of Architects, of which he was a founding member.

WARD, James (1769, London—1859, London), English painter of landscapes, portraits, animals, and historical subjects. As a young man (*c.* 1781–82) he was apprenticed to the engraver John Raphael Smith (1752–1812); in the late 1780s he began painting. He modeled his first pictures after those by his brother-in-law George Morland, whose rural manner he emulated (*Farmyard Scene*, 1790; England, Coll. Countess of Munster). By 1795 George Stubbs replaced Morland as the main influence on Ward's art. Gradually, his animals took on a Romantic aspect. Paintings such as the *Boa Serpent* (1803; destroyed) and *Bulls Fighting, with a View of St. Donat's Castle, Glamorganshire, in the Distance* (1803–4; London, Victoria and Albert Museum) were greatly admired by Théodore Géricault and Eugène Delacroix. The major influence on Ward's mature style was Rubens, whose *Château de Steen* was the direct inspiration for the *Bulls Fighting*. Between 1811 and 1821 Ward was occupied with *Gordale Scar, Yorkshire* (1811–15; London, Tate Gallery), an enormous landscape; and with an allegorical painting celebrating the British victory at Waterloo. It is an immense canvas, whose full title is *The Genius of Wellington on the Car of War, Supported by Britannia and Attended by the Seven Cardinal Virtues, Commanding Away the Demons Anarchy, Rebellion, and Discord, with the Horrors of War* (1818–22; London, Chelsea, Royal Hospital). Ward's fortunes began to decline around 1820, although he managed to execute several admirable and dramatic paintings after that date, notably that of Napoleon's charger *Marengo* (1826; England, Coll. Duke of Northumberland), in which the horse is portrayed against a darkening sky.

WARD, John Quincy Adams (1830, near Urbana, Ohio—1910, New York), American sculptor. In 1859 he went to Washington, D.C., where he modeled several busts of statesmen, and in 1861 he settled in New York City. In 1893 he became the first president of the National Sculpture Society, a position he held until 1905.

Although Ward believed strongly in the study of Classical Greek sculpture for models, he also believed that American artists should render American subjects, as is evident in his *Indian Hunter* (1864; bronze, New York, Central Park) and *Freedman* (1865; bronze, Boston, Athenaeum), both of which were internationally acknowledged at the Paris Exposition of 1867. Ward's work is marked by qualities of robustness and masculinity (*Horace Greeley*, 1890, bronze, New York, City Hall Park; equestrian statue of *General Thomas*, 1878, bronze, Washington, D.C.).

WASMANN, Friedrich (1805, Hamburg—1886, Merano), German painter. In 1829 Wasmann received a traveling scholarship and went to Munich (1829–30; 1835–39) and to Rome (1832–35), where he became associated with the Nazarenes, especially Johann Friedrich Overbeck. After his conversion to Catholicism in 1835, he returned to Munich before settling in Bolzano in 1839. It was there that he acquired his reputation as a portraitist—a field in which he surpassed his contemporaries in sensitive draftsmanship and psychological insight (*Head of a Dead Woman, c.* 1842; Munich, Staatliche Graphische Sammlung). Although he always regarded himself as one of the Nazarenes, Wasmann was only a peripheral member of their group. The characteristic features of his remarkable proto-Impressionist landscapes are his use of bright, luminous colors and his rather heavy brushwork, in which the paint is built up layer upon layer (*Vineyard at Meran, Autumn, c.* 1831; Winterthur, Oskar Reinhart Foundation).

WASTELL, John (active 1485–1515), English mason. From 1490 he worked at King's College, Cambridge, where he was responsible for the magnificent fan vault of the chapel (begun 1446 by Reginald of Ely; completed 1515). In April 1496 Wastell was appointed master mason at Canterbury Cathedral, where he built "Bell Harry," a central tower that is one of the masterpieces of the Perpendicular Style. We next find him in Cambridge (1502–14), working at King's Hall and at Great St. Mary's, where he may have designed the tower. Although there is no documentary evidence that he built the eastern chapels of Peterborough Cathedral (*c.* 1500), they closely resemble his authenticated work. Other buildings that reflect his style are Lavenham Church in Suffolk, the gate tower at St. John's College in Cambridge, and the tower of Fotheringhay Castle in Northamptonshire. On stylistic evidence we may assume that he designed the church of St James (now the cathedral) at Bury St. Edmunds. Although Wastell knew the work of the Vertue brothers and was not unaffected by it, his style was quite distinct from the "royal school" of which they were the leaders.

WATTEAU, Antoine (1684, Valenciennes—1721, Nogent-sur-Marne), French painter. In Paris, where he arrived before 1702, he made the acquaintance of the print dealers Jean and Pierre Mariette, who introduced him to the painter Claude Gillot, with whom he worked from 1703 to 1707, absorbing that painter's style and interest in subjects from the Italian Comedy. Although none of Watteau's paintings are dated, it is thought that those depicting the Italian Comedy, and its French counterpart, including *Mezzetin* (New York, Metropolitan Museum) and *Italian Comedians* (Washington, D.C., National Gallery), date from the period of his stay with Gillot.

Watteau's first sound training was obtained during his stay with Claude Audran III (1708–9). During this time, Watteau was able to study the works of Rubens, and assisted Audran as well, developing the light, supple line that characterizes his style. He was admitted to the Academy in 1712, but from this date until 1715, little is known of his career.

Between 1715 and 1716 Watteau stayed with the art patron Pierre Crozat, where he made the acquaintance of the painter Charles de Lafosse and was able to study Crozat's collection of Venetian masters. His paintings of this period (*La Conversation*, 1716; Paris, Priv. Coll.) depict what are probably Crozat's friends in the quiet setting of the park at Montmorency. Watteau then returned to Paris, where—between 1716 and 1719—his greatest paintings were executed, including the famous *Embarkation for Cythera* (1717; Paris, Louvre). A brief visit to London in 1719, where he painted *L'Amour paisible* (formerly New York, Coll. Balback), left a strong impression on the colony of French artists living there. Watteau, whose health was always delicate, returned to France, retiring eventually to Nogent-sur-Marne, where he died at the home of Philippe Le Fèvre, one of Louis XIV's courtiers.

Antoine Watteau. *The Dance.* Staatliche Museen, Berlin.

WATTS, George Frederick (1817, London—1904, Compton, Surrey), English painter and sculptor. At the age of twenty he exhibited the *Wounded Heron* (Compton, Watts Gallery), in the style of Sir Edwin Landseer, at the Royal Academy, London. In 1843 he won first prize in a competition for the decoration of the Houses of Parliament with his cartoon *Caractacus Led in Triumph Through the Streets of Rome.* He used the money to go to Italy, where he was an avid student of fresco and monumental painting, interests he drew on later in his career. In 1867 he was elected both Associate and full member of the Royal Academy. His fame dates from his first one-man exhibition in London in 1881; this was followed by a show at the Metropolitan Museum, New York, in 1884–85.

Antoine Watteau. *Embarkation for Cythera.* 1717. Louvre, Paris. *Photo Giraudon.*

Watts first won notice for his portraits, although *Lady Holland* (1843; Royal Coll.) and *Lady Powerscourt* (1850s; England, Coll. Mrs. Michael Chapman) give little indication of the quintessential Victorianism he was to achieve in such later male portraits as *Sir Edward Burne-Jones* (1870; Birmingham, City Museum and Art Gallery). Here he revealed a real gift for characterization. His projected series, *The House of Life*, was to be a symbolic history of mankind; less ambitious ventures, such as the *Irish Famine* (Watts Gallery) and *Fata Morgana* (London, Leger Galleries Ltd.), have their full measure of Victorian pathos and lubricity. In the 1860s Watts turned to sculpture, in which he was amazingly competent (*Clyte, c.* 1868; London, Tate Gallery). In his later years he evolved a type of ambiguous moral allegory on a vast scale. Examples of such work include *Mammon* (1884–85; Tate Gallery) and *Hope* (late version, 1886; Tate Gallery), which became his best-known work, despite its undeniably *retardataire* conception.

WEBB, Philip (1831, Oxford—1915, Worth, Sussex), English

George Frederick Watts. *Hope.* 1886. Tate Gallery, London.

domestic architect. He worked at first in the office of George Edmund Street (1824–81), a leading Gothic Revival architect of the period. There he met William Morris, who made him one of his associates. Webb's first important building, the Red House at Bexley Heath in Kent (1859–60), was built for Morris and his wife, with Morris himself designing all the furniture and interior decoration. Webb planned the house in a functional spirit, refusing to sacrifice interior comfort to exterior symmetry. But the details of the design were eclectic; the pointed arches and high pitched roofs are Gothic, while the sash windows are imitated from the period of William and Mary and Queen Anne. He subsequently built a number of town houses in London (No. 1 Palace Green, 1868; and No. 19 Lincoln's Inn Fields, 1868–69), and such country houses as Goldwyns in Surrey (1873) and Smeaton Manor in Yorkshire (1877–79). Webb's production ceased with his retirement in 1901.

WEBER, Max (1881, Bialystok, Russia—1961, Great Neck, New York), American painter of Russian origin. After his arrival in New York with his family at the age of ten, he took painting and drawing lessons at Pratt Institute (from 1897). In 1905 he was in Paris, where he worked first at the Académie Julian, then under the direction of Matisse. Upon his return to the United States, he exhibited at Alfred Stieglitz' 291 Gallery (1909 and 1911). Influenced at first by the Fauves and Cubists, he often approached abstraction between 1912 and 1917 (*New York at Night*, 1915); but he soon returned to a more realistic style, quite close to that he had formulated since 1911 in a canvas such as *The Geranium* (New York, Museum of Modern Art). In fact, Weber could never renounce for long the fund of lyricism that constituted his true nature. Toward 1945 he again submitted to the tendency toward Abstract Expressionism. But this was only a brief interlude, and his work remained basically outside the postwar mainstream of American art, as did that of Rouault in France.

WEIR, Julian Alden, *called* J. Alden (1852, West Point, New York—1919, New York), American painter. In 1873 he went to Paris, where he studied with Jean-Léon Gérôme (1824–1904) at the École des Beaux-Arts, but he was not comfortable with the academic routine and style, and after a trip to Spain in 1876 was attracted to the works of Velázquez. He returned to America and produced paintings that were predominantly dark in tone, richly painted, and solidly constructed. His portraits and still lifes won him recognition, and culminated in his election to the National Academy in 1886.

In 1883 Weir made a second trip to Europe. During this sojourn he was occupied with the significant commission of buying paintings for the Erwin Davis collection in New York, and his selection of two large canvases by Édouard Manet (*Boy with a Sword, c.* 1861, and *Woman with Parrot*, 1866; both New York, Metropolitan Museum) reveals the change in his taste. In 1891 Weir began to paint in a definitely Impressionistic style. This was a vital step in the history of Impressionism in America, for when a painter of Weir's caliber clearly advocated the latter style, it was automatically endorsed as an acceptable manner of painting. In 1893 he and John Twachtman gave a joint exhibition at the American Art Galleries in New York, which also included canvases by Claude Monet and Émile Bernard; in 1898 Weir, Twachtman, Childe Hassam, and other American Impressionists exhibited together as The American Ten in an attempt to promote native Impressionism. *Landscape* (Albany, Coll. Fillin), a pastel on paper that was probably executed after 1891, is a fine example of his mature work. After the Armory Show of 1913 Weir was impressed with the new uses of form and color being explored by the younger French artists, and began to move away from Impressionism and to use larger color areas.

WEST, Benjamin (1738, Springfield, Pennsylvania—1820, London), American history painter. In 1756 West set himself up as a portraitist in Philadelphia and in 1758 he worked in New York. Late in 1759 he went to Italy, where he spent three years. In Rome he made the acquaintance of Anton Raphael Mengs and Gavin Hamilton, and in an astonishingly short period of time mastered the current Neoclassical idiom as propounded by these two masters. Visits to Florence, Bologna, and Venice added nothing to his style, which remained dull throughout his vastly successful career.

In 1763 West set up as a portraitist in London, painting in a style that combined characteristics of Mengs, Pompeo Batoni (1708–87), and Sir Joshua Reynolds. Although his talent was limited, his flair was enormous, and his versatility can be judged by comparing the uneasily grouped *Duke of Cambridge with Princesses Charlotte and Augusta* (1778; London, Royal Collection) with the more polished wedding portrait of *Mr. and Mrs. John Custance* (1778; Kansas City, Mo., Nelson Gallery of Art).

It was as a history painter, however, that West made his mark. In 1764 he sent two pictures to the Society of Artists, and in 1768 was introduced to King George III by Robert Drummond, Archbishop of York, on the strength of his painting of *Agrippina Landing at Brindisium with the Ashes of Germanicus* (1768; New Haven, Conn., Yale University Art Gallery). This picture induced the king to appoint West his historical painter (1772) and to commission for the Royal Collection a picture of the *Departure of Regulus from Rome* (*c.* 1767; London, Kensington Palace, Royal Collection), which was a very skillful work.

West, who was not a Classicist by inclination, soon evolved a historical formula best suited to his talents. In 1771 he exhibited a picture at the Royal Academy of the *Death of Wolfe* (1771; Ottawa, National Gallery of Canada), in which Wolfe is wearing contemporary dress. The picture was a tremendous success. West made vast sums of money from the sale of engravings of the work and then from a series of "contemporary" or "fashionably" medieval subjects. In *Penn's Treaty with the Indians* (1778; Philadelphia, Pennsylvania Academy of the Fine Arts) he also exploited the Red Indian motif, but the *Death of Bayard* (1773; London, Royal Collection) and the *Battle of Crécy* (1778; Royal Collection), although dull as pictures, present an interesting parallel with similar developments on the Continent, notably in the chivalrous subjects of Nicolas-Guy Brenet (1728–92) and Nicolas-Bernard Lépicié (1735–84).

West's reputation was so great that in 1792 he succeeded Reynolds as president of the Royal

Academy. In 1802 he visited Paris, where he was hailed as the representative of the avant-garde in painting. In the first decade of the 19th century he painted a series of religious pictures that mark a great advance on his earlier style. His best-known work in this mode—his masterpiece according to some—is *Death on a Pale Horse* (1814; Pennsylvania Academy of the Fine Arts), which was a combination of an apocalyptic subject and Romantic confusion. Rather more interesting is his *Christ Rejected by Caiaphas* (1814; Pennsylvania Academy of the Fine Arts), which is one of the vast, crowded compositions that he manipulated so well.

West was essentially a fashionable phenomenon, but the interest of his paintings is confined almost entirely to the topicality of their subject matter. He was also an extremely influential figure in the history of American painting because, for more than 50 years, his London studio was the training ground for some of the most important American artists of the period—Gilbert Stuart, John Singleton Copley, Robert Fulton (1765–1815), Charles Willson Peale, and John Trumbull, to name only a few.

WESTERMANN, Horace Clifford (b. 1922, Los Angeles), American sculptor. He began to work in sculpture around 1953, and during the 1950s and the 1960s developed a highly individualistic style that is based on irony and paradox through unexpected uses of materials and the resulting ambiguous—or startlingly precise—meanings. Thus *A Rope Tree* (1964; wood, Milwaukee, Coll. Dr. and Mrs. A. Melamed) is a piece of wood carved into a twisted shape that simultaneously resembles a rope and a tree, while *Walnut Box* (1964; mixed media, Chicago, Coll. Mr. and Mrs. E. A. Bergman) is precisely what it is labeled—a walnut wood box filled with walnuts. In the early 1950s he dealt with the imagery of war and death; around 1956 he began a series of eccentric and ambiguous "houses" and "towers" with such titles as *Madhouse, Mysteriously Abandoned New House*, and *Suicide Tower*; in the late 1950s he produced a number of figurative-architectural personages (*Angry Young Machine*, mixed media). In the early 1960s he became more interested in the paradoxical possibilities of materials themselves and in more abstract concepts.

WEYDEN, Rogier van der (b. 1399/1400–d. 1464, Brussels), Flemish painter. His place of birth has not been determined and the events of his youth, including his apprenticeship, are in great dispute. The most controversial period of Rogier's life occurs in the years before 1427. Many of the works that might be assigned to this period have been attributed by a number of historians to the so-called Master of Flémalle, now identified with Robert Campin, and to Campin's pupil Jacques Daret (*c.* 1404–*c.* 1470). Rogier also seems to have worked in Campin's studio, although probably not as an apprentice *per se*. Arguments have been advanced, however, for reattributing these works to Rogier on the basis of style and iconography. Although these arguments are by no means definitive, their conclusions will be assumed here as the basis for a discussion of Rogier's earliest period. Despite the fact that no surviving works are signed, many can be identified through documentary evidence, and through these the corpus of his work can be tentatively reconstructed.

Rogier's earliest period (before *c.* 1430) reveals the influence of Jan van Eyck, although his coloring is colder and more heavily applied. These qualities characterize the rather stiff *Madonna in the Meadow* (*c.* 1420; Berlin, Staatliche Museen) and the awkwardly composed *Marriage of the Virgin* (*c.* 1425; Madrid, Prado). In the two *Annunciations* executed between 1425 and 1430 (Prado; and Brussels, Musées Royaux des Beaux-Arts) there is a noticeable softening of Rogier's style. Certain motifs appear in his paintings of *c.* 1430 that recur often in his later works. In the *Madonna with Sts. Peter, Benedict, and Augustine* (Aix-en-Provence, Musée Granet), as in the Prado *Marriage of the Virgin*, a figure appears in the foreground seen from the back.

In his mature period (1430–50), Rogier became increasingly concerned with the Passion and with the Virgin's role in those events. He often places her in an architectural setting that lends depth to the picture (*Seated Virgin*, *c.* 1435, Lugano, Coll. Thyssen-Bornemisza; and *Standing Virgin*, Vienna, Kunsthistorisches Museum). Contemporary church portals form the architectural setting for the divided triptych of the Virgin, painted in the 1440s, of which the central panel (*Pietà*) and left wing (*Nativity*) are in the Royal Chapel of Granada Cathedral and the right wing (*Resurrected Christ Appearing to His Mother*) is in the Metropolitan Museum, New York. These paintings also begin to reveal significant differences between Rogier's and Van Eyck's approaches. Rogier tended to make greater use of chiaroscuro, thus emphasizing the figure at the expense of other objects within the setting (*St. Luke Painting the Virgin*, *c.* 1435; Boston, Museum of Fine Arts).

Rogier van der Weyden. *Calvary triptych. c.* 1440–45. Kunsthistorisches Museum, Vienna.

Rogier's treatment of the Passion lends a mysterious, tragic beauty to the suffering Christ and his companions, especially in his three *Crucifixions* of around 1440 (Vienna, Kunsthistorisches Museum; Berlin, Staatliche Museen; Zurich, Coll. Abegg). A confined architectural setting and gilt background (a 14th-century device that Rogier revived) places the emotionally charged figures in high relief in his masterly *Descent from the Cross* (Prado). The use of a gilt background also occurs in the related *Last Judgment* altarpiece (*c.* 1443–46; Beaune, Hôtel-Dieu), commissioned by Chancellor Nicolas Rolin for the chapel he built there. Rogier also invested his portraits of this period with the same intensity and mystery that appears in his treatment of the Passion (*Head of Robert de Masmin* and *Portrait of a Young Lady*, both Staatliche Museen).

Rogier's last period (1450–64) began with a Holy Year pilgrimage to Rome, and his contact with the Italian Renaissance considerably softened and humanized his Northern mysticism. The change is

Rogier van der Weyden. *St. Mary Magdalene.* Braque triptych. *c.* 1452. Louvre, Paris.

noticeable both in his secular work, as the portrait of *Francesco d'Este* (New York, Metropolitan Museum), and in religious paintings, such as his many pictures of the *Virgin and Child* (Chicago, Art Institute; San Marino, California, Huntington Library & Art Gallery), and especially in the *Adoration of the Magi*, also known as the *St. Columba Triptych* (Munich, Alte Pinakothek). Among the most important works of this period are the *Nativity* triptych or Middelburger Altar (Staatliche Museen) and the *Seven Sacraments* triptych (Antwerp, Musée Royal des Beaux-Arts), commissioned by Jean Chevrot, Bishop of Tournai.

Rogier's influence was extremely profound during his lifetime and for a long time afterward, not only on Flemish painting but throughout Europe.

WHEATLEY, Francis (1747, London—1801, London), English painter of portraits, conversation pieces, and sentimental genre pictures, best remembered for his *Cries of London*, engraved in 1795 (the originals are now in the Royal Academy, London, and the Bearsted Collection, Upton House, Banbury, Oxfordshire). Wheatley was employed in the decoration of London's Vauxhall Gardens, and first exhibited at the Society of Artists in 1765. In 1779 he went to Ireland for five years, painting views of country seats and a number of documentary pictures, such as the *Interior of the Irish House of Commons* (1780; London, Coll. Sir Avery Douglas Frederick Gascoigne). After his return to London in 1784, he began to submit genre pictures to the Royal Academy on the themes of charity or married felicity. That Wheatley knew the sentimental work of Jean-Baptiste Greuze (1725–1805) can be seen from his picture of *John Howard Relieving Prisoners* (*c.* 1788; Sanden Hall, Staffordshire, Coll. Earl of Harrowby), based on elements from *La Mort du Paralytique* and *La Dame de Charité*. In 1792 he made his contribution to the serial story in painting with his *Life of a Country Girl* (Bearsted Coll.), consisting of four episodes: *Maidenhood, Courtship, Marriage,* and *Married Life*. The very real charm of Wheatley is due to the sincerity of his feeling and the clarity of his technique.

J. A. M. Whistler. *Arrangement in Black and Gray No. 1 : the Artist's Mother*. 1871–72. Louvre, Paris.

WHISTLER, James Abbott McNeill (1834, Lowell, Massachusetts—1903, London), American painter and graphic artist. Active in both Paris and London, Whistler developed a style that, despite its similarities with contemporary developments in French painting, strikes a singularly English compromise between innovation and restraint. In 1855 he went to Paris, where he led a determinedly bohemian life and worked intermittently in the studio of Charles Gleyre (1806–74). Whistler began his career as an etcher, and after a journey to Alsace and the Rhineland, published *Twelve Etchings from Nature* (Paris, 1858). As a painter, the first major influence on his work was that of Gustave Courbet, to whom he was introduced by Henri Fantin-Latour in the same year. Courbet's dark and heavy style is apparent in Whistler's early portraits, notably the man in the foreground of *Wapping* (1861; New York, Coll. John Hay Whitney), a picture painted after his move to London in 1859. His first important painting, *At the Piano* (1859; Cincinnati, Art Museum), however, contains a simplification of outline and a deliberate asymmetry of form.

Whistler's significance as a European artist became apparent in 1864, the date of his *Rose and Silver : La Princesse du Pays de la Porcelaine* (Washington, D.C., Freer Gallery), which with its fan, screen, and kimono is as important a manifesto of the contemporary Japanese taste as Manet's *Portrait of Émile Zola* or Claude Monet's *Woman with a Fan*. This superficial *japonaiserie* was to deepen into something far more original and mature, an instinctive appreciation for Japanese composition, which reached its full power in such pictures as the *Nocturne in Blue and Gold: Old Battersea Bridge* (*c.* 1872–75; London, Tate Gallery).

Other influences on Whistler's work were those of Dante Gabriel Rossetti and Armand Gautier (1825–94), who contributed equally to the image of the long-jawed beauty in a white dress posed against a white curtain and known as the *Symphony in White No. 1 : the White Girl* (1862; Washington, D.C., National Gallery), which was hung in the Salon des Refusés (Paris) in 1863, or to the more delicate *Little White Girl* (1864; Tate Gallery). The technique of silhouetting a figure against an almost blank ground remained Whistler's standard practice for his greatest portraits, notably those of the *Artist's Mother* (1871–72; Paris, Louvre), *Miss Cicely Alexander* (1871–72; Tate Gallery), *Mrs. F. R. Leyland* (1873; New York, Frick Collection), and *Thomas Carlyle* (1872–73; Glasgow, Art Gallery). These later portraits, however, bear elaborate subtitles that introduce us to the second phase of Whistler's art: the phase of Arrangements, Harmonies, and Nocturnes. The portrait of his mother, for example, was originally entitled *Arrangement in Black and Gray No. 1 : the Artist's Mother*. In 1877 he exhibited his *Nocturne in Black and Gold : Falling Rocket* (*c.* 1874; Detroit, Institute of Art) at the Grosvenor Gallery.

Whistler's growing fame as a wit and eccentric coincided with his decline as a painter. Several waspish exchanges with Oscar Wilde, whom he met in 1881, added to his legend, which was crowned when he delivered his famous Ten O'Clock lecture, later translated into French by his close friend, the poet Stéphane Mallarmé, in 1885. A collected edition of his early writings entitled *The Gentle Art of Making Enemies*, published in 1890, established him as the innovator whom Ruskin had attacked. In 1888 he married Beatrix Godwin; shortly afterward the couple moved to Paris, where Whistler's art was enthusiastically supported by the critics Théodore Duret, Gustave Geffroy, and Roger Marx. In November 1891 the portrait of his mother was bought for the French nation and placed in the Louvre. Eleven years later, Whistler died in London.

WHITE, Stanford. *See* **McKIM, MEAD & WHITE.**

WHITTREDGE, Worthington (1820, Springfield, Ohio—1910,

Summit, New Jersey), American painter. He went to Europe in 1849 to see the Barbizon School painters in France, and went on to study in Düsseldorf until 1854. He was in Rome from 1854 to 1859, but soon began to feel that his work was a betrayal of his native sensibility, and returned to New York. There, at the New-York Historical Society, he first saw the grandiloquent mountain landscapes of Thomas Cole and Asher B. Durand, and was impressed and inspired by their passionately American, forceful style. He moved to the Catskills in an attempt to recapture his own original vision of the native countryside. His pictures were moody scenes of fields or woods (*Evening in the Woods*; New York, Metropolitan Museum), seacoast views, or meadows and mountains, painted with a fresh and glowing range of colors and usually containing genre elements suggesting the nearness of civilization (*Camp Meeting*, 1874; New York, Metropolitan Museum). The *House on the Sea* (Los Angeles, County Museum) is typical of Whittredge's treatment of the outdoors, depicting farmers near their haycart and a peasant woman tending her garden. A *Boating Party in Central Park* (New York, Coll. Paul Lane) also adds picturesque genre elements to the natural scene, reminiscent of the artist's European training rather than of his indigenous inspiration.

WIERTZ, Antoine (1806, Dinant, Namur—1865, Brussels), Belgian Romantic painter. He was a pupil of the portraitist and history painter, Mathieu-Ignace van Bree (1773–1839), whose bombastic naturalistic style was passed on to other pupils as well, including Gustaaf Wappers (1803–74), Ferdinand de Braekelaer (1792–1883), and Nicaise de Keyser (1813–87). These painters, who formed a distinct school, came of age at a critical moment when Belgium attained independence (1830), and of them Wiertz was the most idiosyncratic. He traveled to Paris in 1829, where he won the Prix de Rome (1832), visited Italy in 1834, and returned to Liège. In 1844 he settled in Brussels, where the government built a studio for him (now the Musée Wiertz), large enough to accommodate his enormous paintings. Wiertz's almost perverse delight in the morbid and the monstrous is reflected in many

Antoine Wiertz. *La Belle Rosine*. 1847. Musée Wiertz, Brussels. *Photo A.C.L., Brussels.*

of his titles: *Revolt of Hell against Heaven* (1842), *One of the Giants of the Earth* (1860), *Buried Alive* (1854), and *Thoughts and Visions of a Severed Head* (1853)—all in the Musée Wiertz. These horrors were conveyed with great naturalism in a style derived from a study of Peter Paul Rubens and Michelangelo, as in *La Belle Rosine* (1847; Musée Wiertz), in which a quite sensual, amber-colored nude confronts a highly realistic skeleton. Some of his paintings, equally violent but less macabre, were inspired by patriotism (*Blow from the Hand of a Belgian Lady*, 1861; Musée Wiertz).

WILKIE, Sir David (1785, Cults, near Edinburgh—1841, at sea near Gibraltar), Scottish painter of genre scenes, Romantic histories, and portraits. In 1805 after a short period during which he painted portraits in Fife, Wilkie went to London with a letter of introduction to the Earl of Mansfield, for whom he painted his *Village Politicians* (1806; London, Coll. Earl of Mansfield), a skillful but very obvious translation of his Dutch and Flemish prototypes. The note of slightly forced comedy, which is also apparent in his *Alfred in the Neatherd's Cottage* (1806; Coll. Commander A. F. Armitage, R.N.), soon gave way to greater sweetness and seriousness, in which resolutely "Pauper" subjects—such as the *Blind Fidler* (1807; London, National Gallery), *Blind Man's Buff* (1812; England, Royal Collection), *Distraining for Rent* (1815; Coll. Countess of Swinton), and the *Penny Wedding* (1818; Royal Collection)—are treated with as much care and finesse as if they were historical subjects. Wilkie's refusal to sentimentalize, his solid Scottish good sense, his thin and brilliant handling all combine to add a new weight and depth to the tradition of Hogarthian genre painting.

It is a measure of Wilkie's stature as an artist that, despite the immense popularity of these works, he experimented with more adventurous idioms. The first note of increased seriousness appears in the *Chelsea Pensioners Reading the Gazette of the Battle of Waterloo* (1822; London, Apsley House, Wellington Museum), which was a genuine attempt to depict a contemporary event without the usual trappings of history painting. Also evident, in the figure of the woman waving a handkerchief, is a broader, looser, more generalized and European type of figure. This increasingly Baroque tendency becomes magnificently clear in the two pictures that commemorate King George IV's state visit to Scotland in 1822. The portrait of *George IV in Highland Dress* (1830; Royal Collection) is a startlingly Romantic conception weakened only by the resolutely amiable visage of the king himself. Even more impressive is the *Entry of George IV into Holyrood House* (1830; Royal Collection).

In 1824 Wilkie experienced a series of personal misfortunes that brought on a severe nervous illness, and in 1825 he set out on a prolonged tour of Italy and Spain. He was the first English artist to visit Madrid, where he stayed for six months and was much impressed by the paintings of Velázquez and Murillo. On his return to London in 1829 he exhibited three Italian and four Spanish subjects at the Academy. The most famous of the Spanish pictures, the *Defense of Saragossa* (1828; London, Buckingham Palace, Royal Collection) is a Romantic manifesto similar to Delacroix's *Liberty Leading the People*. During the 1830s Wilkie continued to produce genre paintings but they lacked seriousness. His exquisite *Bride's Toilet* (1838; Edinburgh, National Gallery of Scotland), for example, is a version of Bonington's work. Perhaps his most impressive attempt at the Romantic ideal is his portrait of *William IV in the Uniform of the Grenadier Guards* (1833; Royal Collection).

Wilkie was knighted in 1836 and set out on another long journey in

Jens Ferdinand Willumsen. *Stone Breakers.* 1891. Bronze, stucco and wood. Statens Museum for Kunst, Copenhagen.

1840, this time via The Hague, Cologne, Munich, and Vienna to Cairo, Jerusalem, and Alexandria. The portrait sketches of this period (*Sultan Abdul Meedgid*, 1841; London, Buckingham Palace, Royal Collection) are reminiscent of Delacroix's Moroccan sketchbook. In June 1841 Wilkie died at sea of a fever said to have been brought on by eating ices in Malta. In England his death was treated as a national calamity: J. M. W. Turner's *Peace—Burial at Sea of Sir David Wilkie* (1841–42; London, Tate Gallery) is the most celebrated of the many tributes paid to him.

WILKINS, William (1778, Norwich—1839, London), English architect. After studying at Cambridge, he went to Greece, Asia Minor, and Italy (1801–4) to gather material for his *Antiquities of Magna Graecia* (1807), which became an authoritative source on the subject. Shortly afterward he was appointed professor of architecture at the Royal Academy, where, in teaching and in practice, he pioneered the Greek Revival in England. He used the Ionic order from the Erechtheum in Athens for Downing College, Cambridge (1806–10). For University College, London (1827–28), he designed the main block, whose imposing portico was unfortunately poorly integrated with the rest of the composition. Wilkins also designed Haileybury College, Hertford (1806–9), and the Gothic Revival New Court of Trinity College, Cambridge (1821–23). His most important commission, for the National Gallery in London (1832–38), was also his greatest failure, for its broken and disunified façade seemed to many critics unworthy of its prominent position.

WILLIAM OF WYNFORD (active 1360–1403; d. 1411/12), English mason, possibly a native of Winford, Somerset. In 1364/65 he was master mason at Wells Cathedral, where he began the southwest tower. In 1372 he was granted a life pension by Edward III but began to undertake more work for ecclesiastical patrons. Wynford worked at Abingdon Abbey (1375–76) and, on stylistic grounds, is credited with the design of New College, Oxford (begun 1380), founded by William of Wykeham. It is certain that he worked for Wykeham at Winchester, where the foundation stone of the college was laid in 1367.

In 1394 Wynford began to transform the nave of Winchester Cathedral in the Perpendicular Style. In 1400–2 he was active in rebuilding the hall of Queen's College, Oxford. In addition to his architectural work, Wynford supervised the carving of tombs and other sculpture, and was responsible for the chantry of his patron, Wykeham, in Winchester Cathedral. He was one of the first architects to plan a specifically domestic type of building, and was the founder or leader of a school in the south and west of England. Wynford was probably the chief influence for the splendid church towers of Somerset, among the finest in England.

WILLUMSEN, Jens Ferdinand (1863, Copenhagen—1958, Cannes), Danish painter and sculptor. He studied at the Academy of Fine Arts in Copenhagen, then went to Spain and France, where he lived in Paris (1890–94). Willumsen's meeting with Gauguin and Paul Sérusier at Pont-Aven (1890) attracted him to Synthetism (*Two Women Walking, Brittany*, 1890; Coll. Ernst Mathiasen). His personal and decorative interpretation of this style is evident in the first sketch of his *Large Relief*, later executed in gilt bronze and marble (1923–28; Copenhagen, Statens Museum for Kunst), which dates from this period. After 1900 an occasional sense of anxiety betrayed a fundamentally Expressionist nature. These qualities became more pronounced after 1910 (*Evening Soup*, 1918; formerly coll. artist). The landscapes he painted in Spain and Algeria had great spontaneity, and their bright colors became even more intense in his Venetian works (1929–30). At the end of his life Willumsen expressed the isolation of old age in an impressive trilogy of self-portraits called *Titian Dying* (1935–38; Fredriksund, Willumsen Museet).

WILSON, Richard (1714, Penegoes, Montgomeryshire, Wales—1782, Llanberis, Denbighshire, Wales), British painter who introduced European Classicism to native English landscape painting. He was apprenticed to the portraitist Thomas Wright in London and worked there as a portraitist in the 1740s, achieving a brisk semi-Rococo competence that almost equaled that of William Hogarth (*Admiral Thomas Smith, c.* 1746, Greenwich, National Maritime Museum; another version of 1744 at Hatley Hall, England). In 1746 he submitted two landscapes to the art collection of the Foundling Hospital, London. In 1750 he went to Venice and in 1752 he arrived in Rome; there he met the French landscapist Joseph Vernet, who encouraged him to give his full attention to landscape painting. His immediate model for Italianate landscapes was Claude Lorrain, whom he emulated in such paintings as *Et in Arcadia Ego* (1755; Kent, Wrotham Park, Coll. Lady Elizabeth Byng). On his return to London in 1758 Wilson specialized in Italian scenes (*Hadrian's Villa*; Manchester, City Art Gallery), English scenes treated in his new Classical manner (*Snowdon*; Liverpool, Walker Art Gallery), and commissioned views of country seats (*View of Croome Court, near Worcester*, 1758–59; Birmingham, City Art Gallery). In 1776, on the death of Francis Hayman (1708–76), he applied for and obtained the post of librarian at the Royal Academy. In 1781 he retired to Colomendy Hall, near Llanberis, where he died the following year.

Richard Wilson. *Holt Bridge on the River Dee. c.* 1762. National Gallery, London.

Wilson's position in the history of British landscape painting is comparable to that of Sir Joshua Reynolds in the field of portraiture: both took over a respectable but limited native genre and gave it a quasi-European status. In Italy he learned a more dramatic and condensed formula for depicting a scene, a generalized and intellectual vision that was basically Latin and ideal. Even his most specific scenes (*Cader Idris*; London, National Gallery) are characterized by a rigorous grandeur in which the emphasis is on form rather than emotive detail.

WITTE, Emmanuel de (1616/18, Alkmaar, near Amsterdam—1692, Amsterdam), Dutch painter. He is considered the finest of Dutch architectural painters, although he created historical pictures, portraits, harbor scenes, and genre pictures as well. He began to turn to architectural themes around 1650. De Witte's paintings of church interiors are much richer and more interesting than those of his contemporaries, since he would freely borrow from several actual buildings for the sake of the mood and composition of a painting (*Interior of a Church*, 1668; Rotterdam, Boymans-van Beuningen Museum). He endowed his interiors with an atmosphere of quiet solemnity that is both moving and convincing. His genre scenes are also notable for their attractive color and rich detail (*Fish Market*, 1672; Boymans-van Beuningen Museum).

WITZ, Konrad (1400/10, Rottweil—*c.* 1445, Basel or Geneva), one of the greatest of the pre-Renaissance German (Swabian) painters. His career, of which few personal details are known, is marked by two major works: the *Heilspiegelaltar* ("Redemption Altarpiece," *c.* 1435–36) and his only signed and dated work, the *Altarpiece of St. Peter* (commissioned 1444). Of the surviving panels of the *Heilspiegelaltar*, nine are in the Basel Kunstmuseum, one is in Berlin (Staatliche Museen), and two at Dijon (Musée des Beaux-Arts). The work, probably intended for the monastery of the Augustinian canons of Basel, shows evidence of Flemish influence. Witz had evidently studied the work of Jan van Eyck, but his modeling is stronger and more sculptural than that of the Flemish master. He was capable of skillful perspective renderings, although the effect does not seem to have been obtained by a mathematical calculation.

The central panel of the *Altarpiece of St. Peter* has disappeared, but the Musée d'Art et d'Histoire at Geneva has two panels, painted on each side, one with a *Portrait of the Donor, François de Mies, kneeling before the Virgin* and the *Deliverance of St. Peter*, the other with the *Adoration of the Magi* and the *Miraculous Draft of Fishes*. An unprecedented feature of the latter is the faithful recording of a landscape, which is quite clearly the shore of Lake Geneva dominated by the Salève mountain. It is one of the first attempts of a painter to record the landscape before him and may well be the first in the history of easel painting.

In addition to these two altarpieces, there are a number of smaller pictures by Konrad Witz: *Joachim and Anna* in the Basel Kunstmuseum; the delightful painting of *St. Catherine and St. Magdalen* in Strasbourg (Musée des Beaux-Arts); Nuremberg has an *Annunciation* (Germanisches Nationalmuseum), and Naples a *Virgin with Several Saints* (Museo di Capodimonte), which may have been his first work; a badly damaged *Dance of Death* in the cemetery of the Dominicans at Basel has also been attributed to Witz. His art is an important landmark in the conquest of reality that was pursued by painters throughout the 15th century.

WOESTIJNE, Gustave van de (1881, Ghent—1947, Brussels), Belgian painter. He settled in the village of Laethem-St-Martin in 1899. There he became a member of the artists' colony that, rejecting Impressionism, turned for inspiration to Fra Angelico and the Flemish primitives. Woestijne's work of this period can be divided into two categories: idyllic landscapes reminiscent of Maurice Denis' paintings (*Sunday Afternoon*, 1914; Brussels, Musées Royaux des Beaux-Arts); and portraits and peasants' heads, which reveal Bruegel's influence in their tense expression and incisive lines (*Portrait of the Artist's Wife*, 1910, and *Young Peasant*, 1913; both Ghent, Musée des Beaux-Arts). During the 1920s Woestijne's forms became increasingly geometric, involving forceful coloring and dramatic expression (*To Give Hospitality to a Stranger*, 1920; Waregem, fresco on the façade of Villa Rozenhuis). His religious works, especially the grief-stricken faces of Christ, were among his most successful (*Our Saviour Jesus Christ in the Garden of the Fountains*, 1907, Ghent, Coll. A. Vyncke; and *Jesus Christ Offering Us His Blood*, 1925, Ghent, Musée des Beaux-Arts).

Gustave van de Woestijne. *The Beggar Violinist.* 1920. Musée des Beaux-Arts, Liège.

WOLLASTON, John (active 1736—d. 1770), British-American painter. He was the son of a London artist of the early 18th century, and was himself painting in that city as early as 1736. Information concerning his activity in America is relatively precise, in spite of the fact that he moved frequently, spending time in New York (1749–52), Maryland (1753–54), Virginia (*c.* 1755–57), and Philadelphia (1758). His portrait of *Richard Randolph, Jr.* (Williamsburg, William and Mary College) is typical of his male figures, which were placed against abstract backgrounds; the female subjects were usually more fancifully located in landscape settings, accompanied by fountains or still lifes. The artist went to India in 1758 with the East India Company, returning to Charleston, South Carolina, in 1767. His portrait of *Ann Gibbs* (Worcester, Mass., Art Museum) shows a strong change in style. The hands are no longer so obviously flaccid and the physiognomy reveals a sense of character and vivacity. Few portraits were painted during his brief stay in Charleston, and nothing is known of his subsequent career in London.

WOLS, Wolfgang Schülze, *called* (1913, Berlin—1951, Paris), German-born French painter. He was raised in Dresden, where he became an excellent violinist. After studying briefly at the Berlin

Bauhaus under Mies van der Rohe and Laszlo Moholy-Nagy, he went to Paris in 1932. Wols began painting his first watercolors during this period, and became acquainted with Joan Miró, Alexander Calder, Tristan Tzara, and Max Ernst. In 1940, the Betty Parsons Gallery held the first exhibition of his works in New York; in 1945 Wols returned to Paris. His watercolor *Nearby Star* (*c.* 1944; Paris, Coll. Mme. Monique Cuturier) resembles a single-celled animal more than an astral body. Later watercolors broke the contained, oval shape of *Nearby Star* to assume more rectangular forms, as in *Explosion of the Cathedral* (*c.* 1947; Paris, Coll. Mme. Henri-Pierre Roché) and *Four Corners* (*c.* 1948–49; Paris, Coll. Michel Cuturier). René Drouin organized two exhibitions without his permission in Paris: one in 1945 of his gouaches and watercolors, the second in 1947 of his paintings. It eventually became evident that these exhibitions marked a significant stage in action and calligraphic painting (*Composition on Yellow Ground*, Meudon, Coll. Heursant; and *Blue Phantom*, 1951, Milan, Coll. Dr. R. Jucker).

WOOD, Christopher (1901, Knowsley, near Liverpool—1930, London), English painter. Wood was an artist of great, although not altogether fulfilled, promise by the time of his suicide at twenty-nine. In the 1920s he led a restless, migratory existence, moving from one European city to another and changing from style to style; he was influenced in turn by Van Gogh, Modigliani, Picasso, and the Cornish "primitive" Alfred Wallis (1885–1942). In this period Wood abandoned an important commission from Sergei Diaghilev to design the costumes for a production of the ballet *Romeo and Juliet*, and it was only in the last months of his life that he began to produce the paintings on which his reputation rests. These are mostly landscapes of the Breton and Cornish coasts, painted with great freshness of color and form. The best of these (*Boat in the Harbor, Brittany*, 1929, London, Tate Gallery; *Drying Nets: Treboul Harbor*, 1930, Toledo, Museum of Art) convey an impression of simplicity and innocence without, however, seeming quaint or falsely naive.

WOOD, Grant (1891, Anamosa, Iowa—1942, Iowa City), American painter. A lifelong resident of Iowa, he was one of the exponents of regionalism, a form of realism common in America during the 1930s and based on the desire of native artists to end America's cultural dependence on Europe by finding inspiration for art in everyday local experiences. Wood's painting, however, always remained strongly individual. He made several trips to Europe in the 1920s, and painted landscapes in a sketchy, impasto manner influenced by Impressionism. In Munich in 1928 he studied the German and Flemish primitives and this encouraged a complete transformation of the style and content of his art. Upon his return to the United States, he painted in a crisp, firmly delineated, and precisely modeled style that was clearly derived from that of the Gothic and early Renaissance masters he had studied in Europe. His subjects were the Iowa people and places with which he was familiar. His most famous canvas, *American Gothic* (1930; Chicago, Art Institute), brought him immediate recognition. In landscapes such as the *Midnight Ride of Paul Revere* (1931; New York, Metropolitan Museum) Wood simplified rolling hills into smooth, bulbous forms, and placed them in a space he had dramatized by extreme and sudden diminution of size and exaggerated linear perspective. He regularized all objects into solid, almost geometric forms that cast precise shadows; the resulting unreal quality is enhanced by an airless clarity.

WOOD THE ELDER, John (b. 1704–d. 1754, Bath), English architect. At the beginning of his career, he worked in the north of England and in London, then moved to the fashionable spa of Bath. There he began planning an architectural scheme in which modest but elegant houses are linked architecturally to form an integrated complex of streets and squares. He attempted to restore Bath's former Roman grandeur with projects for a forum and arenas in Classical style, but only lived long enough to supervise the construction of the Palladian Queen Square (1729–36), and South Parade (begun 1743), which, with the North Parade, was part of an unfinished project for a forum. Shortly before he died, Wood began the Circus, a vast oval precinct intersected by three streets, and inspired by the three superimposed orders of the Colosseum in Rome. Wood's work shows an excellent handling of the Palladian vocabulary (Prior Park, near Bath, 1735–48).

JOHN, *called* THE YOUNGER (1728–1782) continued his father's work at Bath. He completed the Circus and then built the highly original Royal Crescent (1767–75), a semicircle of houses linked by a uniform façade. Wood's skill and taste in using the Palladian style of his father is evident in the Assembly Rooms (1769–71) and in the Hot Baths (1773–78).

WOODVILLE, Richard Caton (1825, Baltimore—1855, London), American painter. He went to Düsseldorf in 1845 to study with Karl Friedrich Lessing (1808–80). After 1851 he lived as an expatriate

Christopher Wood. *Boat in Harbor, Brittany.* 1930. Tate Gallery, London.

in Paris and London. Woodville painted relatively few works, and most of those that remain are purely genre scenes, such as *Reading the News* (1846; New York, National Academy of Design), although his *Politics in the Oyster House* (1848; Baltimore, Walters Art Gallery) and *War News from Mexico* (1848; National Academy of Design) deal with historical subjects. He executed a number of homely narratives and anecdotal genre scenes (*Sailor's Wedding, c.* 1855; formerly Baltimore, Coll. W. T. Walters), in which a multitude of incidental and sentimental details are employed to narrate a pictorial drama.

Woodville's compositions recall certain 17th-century masters: paintings such as the *Cavalier's Return* (1847; exhibited Washington, D.C., Corcoran Gallery), with their Gothic interiors, refer quite clearly to the works of the Dutch 17th-century genre painters, especially Pieter de Hooch and Gerard Terborch.

WOOTTON, John (d. 1756, London), English painter. The date of his birth is unknown, but he was certainly a pupil of the Dutch battle painter Jan Wyck (1640–1700) in the 1690s. He soon emerged as the first distinguished sporting artist in England. His favorite composition consisted of a horse in profile, held by a groom, with generalized buildings in the background. His style developed very little and he was extremely prolific, evolving out of his basic formula such variations as the sporting conversation piece and the hunt group. Most of his pictures are less than life-size, although he did at times paint on that scale (*Scarr with His Groom*, 1714; Chatsworth, Derbyshire, Coll. Duke of Devonshire). Wootton also collaborated occasionally on equestrian portraits (*Henry Hoare*, 1726; Stourhead, Wiltshire, with the figure by Michael Dahl and the horse by Wootton). Two very grand series of sporting scenes by him are at Longleat, Wiltshire (Coll. Marquess of Bath) and Althorp, Northamptonshire (Coll. Earl Spencer). The latter series dates from about 1733.

WOTRUBA, Fritz (b. 1907, Vienna), Austrian sculptor. He received his initial training as an engraver and only gradually turned to sculpture. In 1925 Wotruba became a pupil of the sculptor Anton Hanak (1875–1939), but soon left to work on his own. The strength of his craftsmanship won him immediate acclaim, and Aristide Maillol refused to believe that his *Torso of a Man*, seen at the exhibition of Austrian art in Paris in 1929, was the work of a young man of 22. Wotruba's *Crouching Man* (1931; Vienna) won him even wider public recognition. In 1938 political events forced him to emigrate to Switzerland and he did not return to Vienna until 1945, when he was appointed to teach at the Academy of Fine Arts. Although his style developed along Classical lines during the years spent in Basel and Bern, he began to produce astonishing variations on the structure of the human body after World War II (series of *Human Cathedrals*, 1946–49). Wotruba continued to experiment with half-abstract, half-figurative forms, which he treated as caryatids, built up with angular blocks in skillful equilibrium (*Large Reclining Figure*, 1951), as cylindrical shafts (*Torso*, 1955), or as reliefs.

WPA/FAP (Works Progress Administration/Federal Art Project). The program was established by the U.S. government in August 1935 and grew out of three previously existing New Deal projects that had been initiated to aid artists during the Depression. The first of these, the Public Works of Art Project (December 1933–June 1934) was established to aid unemployed artists through the winter of 1933–34. Approximately 2,500 artists, working at "plumbers'" wages, were employed by the project, producing over 15,000 oil paintings, murals, sculptures, watercolors, etchings, and drawings to decorate public buildings. The Treasury Section of Painting and Sculpture (October 1934–June 1943) employed artists by contract rather than by weekly salary to produce paintings, murals, and architectural sculpture for the embellishment of federal buildings. The third division, the Treasury Relief Art Project (July 1935–June 1939), was a complement of the Treasury Section. Works of art were produced for both new and old buildings, while payments for the Treasury Section's projects came from the building funds of new edifices. The Federal Art Project (August 1935–April 1943), like the

Fritz Wotruba. *Rock-Woman.* 1947–48. Middelheim Park Museum, Antwerp.

other projects, provided employment, encouraged the growth of artistic expression, promoted a broader interest in American art, and established centers for art education. Artists were hired to produce works of art in all media for distribution to tax-supported institutions.

Perhaps the most significant, and sometimes most disappointing works of these projects, were the murals. The artists were inspired by the Mexican muralists José Clemente Orozco and Diego Rivera, but lacked the daring of their Latin colleagues; in fact their murals tended to be more conservative than their pre-WPA paintings. The change in style is especially evident in the works of abstract artists such as Arshile Gorky and Karl Knaths. Though atypical, works by such artists as Ben Shahn (*Worker with Electric Drill*, 1938; study for Bronx Central Post Office mural, College Park, Md., Coll. University of Maryland) and Kindred McLeary (*Lower East Side*, 1939; New York, Madison Square Post Office) reveal some of the fine achievements of the WPA murals. Nearly every known artist of the period, except those who were teaching, was in some way connected with the WPA.

WREN, Sir Christopher (1632, East Knoyle, Wiltshire—1722, Hampton Court, Middlesex), English architect. Although among the greatest English architects, Wren first won fame as a distinguished mathematician and did nothing before the age of 34 to suggest his exceptional and prolific career as a builder. He was made professor of astronomy in London (1657) and at Oxford (1661), but his interest extended to the applied sciences as well. His two first buildings, Pembroke College Chapel, Cambridge (1663–65), and the Sheldonian Theatre, Ox-

Fritz Wotruba. *Standing Figure.* 1953–55. Musée National d'Art Moderne, Paris.

Sir Christopher Wren. Church of St. Stephen, Walbrook. 1672–77. East Side. *Photo Kersting, London.*

ford (1664–69), attracted the attention of the Royal Society. In 1663 Charles II appointed him to the commission for the restoration of St. Paul's Cathedral in London. He spent eight or nine months (1665–66) studying architecture in France.

The reconstruction that followed the Great Fire in London opened a vast field of opportunity to architects. Six days before the disaster in September 1666, Wren presented the king with a plan for rebuilding St. Paul's, which is known as the First Model. Six days after the flames had died down, he submitted a plan for rebuilding the City based on a centralized principle. Wren was able to put his name to one colossal undertaking, the reconstruction of St. Paul's Cathedral and 51 parish churches, which lasted from 1670 to 1711. The most frequently adopted plan was longitudinal, which preserved the memory of the destroyed churches (St. James's, Piccadilly, 1682–84; St. Bride's, 1670–84), and the central plan, which was suspect because of its Roman Catholic associations, only rarely appears (St. Mary, Hill, 1670–71). A compromise between the two was made at St. Mary, Aldermanbury (1670–71), and at St. Stephen, Walbrook (1672–77), where the vaulted octagonal plan anticipated the transept of St. Paul's. Although Wren conceded little importance to façades, his use of inverted consoles and contrasting arcades and oculi produced some notable successes at St. Peter, Cornhill (*c.* 1677), and St. Mary, Aldermanbury. The porch of St. Mary-le-Bow (*c.* 1680) contains a motif borrowed from François Mansart's Hôtel de Contin in Paris. Belfries offered Wren opportunities for some ingenious variations with galleries and onion domes that pierce the mists of London with their points (St. Bride's, St. Magnus the Martyr, 1705; St. Vedast, 1697).

Sir Christopher Wren. St. Paul's Cathedral, London. 1675–1711. *Photo National Building Record, London.*

Wren examined several possibilities for St. Paul's which began with a plan for preserving the ruins. The most elaborate, which has survived as a wooden maquette and is known as the Great Model, is a very original version of the radial plan. However, Wren had to abandon it and returned to the Latin cross, but inserted a large octagonal space and a dome into the transept, which was surmounted rather strangely with a spire. A royal decree of 1675 authorizing the project, called the Warrant Design, left Wren free to introduce his own modifications in the details and decoration. It was a prudent measure that made allowances for changes in taste over the long period of its construction. In fact, it took 36 years to build and by that time the old architect had ample opportunity to improve on the elevations of the Warrant Design. The spire proposed in the original plan was replaced by an elegant lantern. Among a number of original features, the system of buttresses is notable. They were built above the side aisles to support the thrust of the nave, but are concealed from view; of the two superimposed orders that decorate the periphery of the church, the second is no more than a modern and deceptive screen for this medieval arrangement.

Wren made a distinction between the absolute beauty inherent in geometric figures and the relative beauty of forms that familiarity has made acceptable. He claimed that both were equally respectable, which explains how he could keep Gothic forms for the interior of St. Mary, Aldermanbury, and Tom Tower over the entrance to Christ Church, Oxford (1681). The variety of Wren's secular buildings is a reflection of this adaptable and tolerant attitude. Dutch influence and a sort of middle-class good nature characterize his buildings erected under William and Mary (Fountain Court at Hampton Court, completed after 1698; and London's Kensington Palace, 1689–1702). Paradoxically, it was in such university buildings as Trinity College Library, Cambridge (1676–84), or the barracks at Chelsea Hospital (1682–92) and Greenwich Hospital (1696–1702) that Wren achieved his most impressive effects. The magnificent naval hospital at Greenwich was Wren's last great undertaking. He had been ennobled in 1675 and had outlived two wives. After the accession of George I, he was forced to give up his office of Surveyor General of the King's Works and retired in 1718.

WRIGHT, Frank Lloyd (1867/69, Richland Center, Wisconsin—1959, Phoenix, Arizona), American architect. He began studying engineering at Wisconsin University, but his interest in architecture led him to Chicago (1887), where he joined the office of Dankmar Adler and Louis Sullivan as a designer. He left the office in 1893, but always referred to Sullivan as his "well-beloved master." Wright's early houses were characterized by free planning, long horizontal lines, windows treated not as openings in the façade but as surfaces integrated into the whole, and overhanging roofs with deep eaves (Willets House, Highland Park, Ill., 1902; Heurtley House, Oak Park, Ill., 1902). Wright himself designed the furniture, often built into the walls in the Japanese manner, for a particular house (Martin House, Buffalo, New York, 1904; Coonley House, Riverside, Ill., 1908; and especially Robie House, Chicago, 1909). The stained-glass windows

..e designed for these houses, sometimes using opalescent glass in geometric patterns, were among the few adornments he would allow. Materials appeared only in their "natural" state: unvarnished wood, unfaced stone, brick as it comes out of the kiln. The feeling for nature that led him to use these materials made Wright initially unsympathetic to city architecture but extremely successful in building for rural living. During this period he produced several innovative designs for office buildings (Larkin Building, Buffalo, N.Y., 1904) and churches (Unitarian Church, Oak Park, Ill., 1906). Reinforced concrete, then a relatively new material, was used in both buildings.

He lived in Japan from 1916 to 1922, where he was impressed by the purity of traditional architectural forms, and was commissioned to build the Imperial Hotel, Tokyo (1922). This was one of the few buildings that withstood the great earthquake of 1923, and Wright attributed its resistance to the cantilevered wooden floor blocks he invented for the building. In 1936 he built the famous "Falling Water," Edgar J. Kaufmann's house at Bear Run in the woods of Pennsylvania. It is a dramatic ensemble of cantilevered projections, suspended over a waterfall and strikingly related to the landscape. The S. C. Johnson Wax Company then asked him to design a large administrative building at Racine, Wisconsin (1936–39). The exterior brick walls are nearly all concave and windowless, while inside slender concrete columns spread out into a corolla to support a luminous ceiling. Wright returned 13 years later to build an extraordinary glass tower (1949–51) with rounded corners and circling bands, in which the laboratories were installed. His last great and highly controversial work was the Solomon R. Guggenheim Museum in New York (1956–59), designed as an immense spiral.

WRIGHT, Michael *or* John Michael (*c.* 1617, London—1700, London), English artist. He was the most interesting portrait painter of Sir Peter Lely's generation. In 1648 he became a member of the Academy of St. Luke in Rome, which indicates that he was a Roman Catholic, and thus must have known Poussin and Velázquez. A fine linguist, Wright became a connoisseur and antiquary and was eventually appointed antiquary to Archduke Leopold Wilhelm of Flanders, who was Governor General of the Netherlands. He returned to England in 1656 when the archduke resigned this position. His portrait of Oliver Cromwell's daughter *Mrs. Claypole* (1568; London, National Portrait Gallery) is filled with learned Italianate iconographical references, as is his *Thomas Chiffinch* (National Portrait Gallery), one of the most truly Baroque portraits painted in England in the 17th century. Throughout the 1660s, Wright painted portraits that are similar to those of William Dobson (*Sir William Bruce*, 1665; Edinburgh, Scottish National Portrait Gallery). In 1670 he was commissioned to paint various Justices of the Common Pleas and King's Bench (Inner Temple) and the Barons of the Exchequer. The 22 portraits he painted of these men gained him considerable recognition from his contemporaries. The Baroque strangeness of his style can best be appreciated in his full-length portrait of the Irish chieftain *Sir Neil O'Neill* (1680; London, Tate Gallery); it is full of Manneristic conceits, including a full set of Japanese armor, that create a powerful yet anachronistic effect.

WRIGHT OF DERBY, Joseph Wright, *called* (1734, Derby—1797, Derby), English painter, particularly noted for his unique philosophical genre pieces. He trained as a portrait painter under Thomas Hudson (1701–79) from 1751 to 1753 and resumed his studies in 1756. Born at the threshold of the Industrial Revolution, Wright worked primarily in and around the manufacturing town of Derby, where the atmosphere of industrial progress suited his own vigorous spirit of amateur scientific enquiry.

As an artist he matured rapidly. His best-known works are also his earliest and most individual: scenes articulated by strong chiaroscuro, generally derived from a single artificial light source, depicting scientific discoveries or experiments (*Alchemist in Search of the Philosopher's Stone Discovers Phosphorus*, 1771–95, Derby, Museum and Art Gallery; *Academy by Lamplight*, *c.* 1769, London, Royal College of Surgeons). His masterpiece of this type is undeniably his *Experiment with the Air Pump* (1768; London, Tate Gallery), in which purely painterly

Frank Lloyd Wright. Administrative buildings of the S. C. Johnson Wax Company, Racine, Wisconsin. 1936 and 1949.

Joseph Wright of Derby. *Experiment with the Air-Pump.* 1768. Tate Gallery, Lon

James Wyatt. Bowden Park, Wiltshire. *Photo National Buildings Record, London.*

considerations are painlessly combined with the shrewd detailed range of portrait heads.

Wright also attempted literary genre, with less remarkable results. However, in *The Dead Soldier* (1787; London, Coll. Louis Meir) after a poem by John Langhorne, the stark Romantic scenery and Wright's own Tenebrist inclinations create a masterly evocation of the contemporary mood.

In 1773 he went to Italy, where he stayed for two years. He was impressed by the moonlight scenes of Claude Joseph Vernet, whose style is reflected with some lessening of formality in Wright's scenes of his native Derbyshire (*Moonlight Landscape*, 1780s; Alfreton Hall, Derbyshire, Coll. R. C. A. Palmer-Morewood).

After a brief excursion to Bath in 1775, Wright settled in Derby in 1777 and there spent the rest of his life. A notable portrait of his later years is that of *Sir Brooke Boothby* (1781; Tate Gallery), an elegant gentleman captured in a meditative moment as he relaxes in a woodland setting. His unique quality as a painter lies in his ability to express the spirit of the Enlightenment without sentimentality or pretension.

WYATT, James (1746, Weeford, Staffordshire—1813, Marlborough, Wiltshire), English architect. James Wyatt was the most distinguished member of a dynasty of architects. His design for the Pantheon (a rendezvous for masquerades) in Oxford Street, London (1770–72; destroyed 1792) brought him immediate success and made him one of the most fashionable architects of the day, with a reputation rivaling that of the Adam brothers. His Classical designs for country houses, as well as additions and alterations to several colleges at Oxford and Cambridge, are unexceptional. His interiors, however, particularly the decorative work, are often a skillful refinement. He was also responsible for "restoration" work on Lichfield, Salisbury, Hereford, and Durham cathedrals (1787–97), in the unscholarly manner of the time. He built several country houses in the fashionable 18th-century Gothic style originated by Horace Walpole (1717–97) at his house, Strawberry Hill. Lee Priory, Kent (1783–90), built for a friend of Walpole, was the first such house, and was far more accurate in its handling of Gothic motifs than Strawberry Hill. Perhaps the most extravagant building of the early Gothic Revival was Fonthill Abbey, Wiltshire (1796–1813), built for the millionaire Gothic novelist William Beckford. Wyatt's last house in the Gothic manner, Ashridge in Hertfordshire (begun 1806), has a symmetrical plan and thus differs from the extravagant irregularity of Fonthill.

WYETH, Andrew (b. 1917, Chadds Ford, Pennsylvania), American painter. He won acclaim at the age of 12 with his illustrations for the Brandywine edition of *Robin Hood*. Wyeth's style is characterized by a minute, precise realism, undoubtedly influenced by photography in its exactness of detail and use of unusual viewpoints. Wyeth lived at Chadds Ford, Pennsylvania, and spent summers at Cushing, Maine. Both locations, in addition to his family and neighbors, form the typical subjects of his work—deserted landscapes and scenes conveying the conflicts of solitude. This sense of loneliness and spiritual malaise relates Wyeth's work to that of Edward Hopper and Ben Shahn (*Chambered Nautilus*, 1956; New York, Coll. Mr. and Mrs. Robert Montgomery). But he adds an even more disturbing element by depicting such emotional themes in the slick style of magazine illustration (*Christina's World*, 1949; New York, Museum of Modern Art). An ambiguous and subtle symbolism that links the subject's personality with the elements of his environment is particularly apparent in *Albert's Son* (1959; Oslo, Nasjonalgalleriet) and *Karl* (1948; New York, Coll. Mr. and Mrs. John D. Rockefeller III).

X Y Z

Henry Yevele. Westminster Abbey. *Photo Kersting, London.*

XCERON, John (1890, Isari, Greece—1967, New York), Greek-born American painter. He emigrated to the United States in 1904 and did his preliminary training at the Corcoran Art School, Washington, D.C. (1910–16). Xceron continued his studies in New York, then went to Paris (1927) for 10 years, exhibiting at the Salon des Surindépendants in 1931 (*Violin No. 7*, 1931; New York, Coll. Mary Dorros Xceron). Although these works from the 1920s and early 1930s show Cubist influences, Xceron's work became increasingly geometric and abstract. His first one-man show was held in New York (1935), where he returned permanently in 1937 (*Composition No. 242*, 1937; New York, Guggenheim Museum). Xceron painted geometric figures and grills suspended in an airy, vibrant space. An imaginative fantasy is blended with solid composition in balanced paintings marked by great spatial freedom (*Painting No. 293*, 1946; New York, Guggenheim Museum). Greater freedom of composition, as well as the use of curved elements, mark his later work (*Painting II, No. 436*, 1961; Priv. Coll.).

YEVELE, Henry (*c.* 1320–*c.* 1400), major English medieval architect. His name (variously spelled) indicates that his family originated in Yeaveley, Derbyshire, and he himself was almost certainly a native of the Midlands. He was admitted a freeman of London in 1353, and rapidly reached the top of his profession. In 1357–58 he was working for the Black Prince, and in 1360 was placed in charge of royal works at Windsor Castle. Yevele was employed at the Tower of London (the "Bloody Tower") and also at the Palace of Westminster, where he directed work on the clock tower (1365). He received a contract for the London Charterhouse in 1371, and for a bridge between Chelmsford and Moulsham, Essex, the following year. In 1375 he was working for John of Gaunt at the Savoy, and in 1377 he probably designed the tomb of Edward III at Westminster Abbey. In 1386 he was overseer on the cathedral close at Canterbury. He carried out work at Old St. Paul's in 1387–88, and possibly several years before.

Yevele became master mason at Westminster by 1388, and in 1390 was commissioned, with William of Wynford and Hugh Herland, to carry out repairs at Winchester Castle. Toward the end of 1394 he was designing the new Westminster Hall, of which the vault of the north porch was his last certain work.

In addition to the buildings already mentioned, Yevele was responsible for work at Eltham, Gravesend, Queenborough Castle, and Barnard Castle. We know that he worked at Canterbury, and, on stylistic grounds, it seems certain that he designed the nave of the cathedral and the West Gate of the city. Other works that may be attributed to him with some confidence are the nave, west cloister, abbot's house, and a number of tombs in Westminster Abbey.

YOUNGERMAN, Jack (b. 1926, Louisville, Kentucky), American painter. He studied at the University of Missouri, then received his only formal training at the École des Beaux-Arts, Paris, where, from 1949, he studied under the G.I. Bill. He simplified lyrical, broadly defined free-form areas that derive from real forms. Jagged but flowing contours, flat bright colors, and large scale characterized his work from 1954. He then became involved with the creation of new and varied shapes (*Anajo*, 1962; New York, Betty Parsons Gallery) that operate in an ambiguous space. Since figure and ground interlock and exchange roles, as in *Red and White* (1962; Parsons Gallery) where the white "background" becomes part of the red "figure," the picture plane becomes unified rather than divided into multiple levels. Primary colors make these sharp-edged images, softened by curving contours, seem hard and their impact forceful. Youngerman's many silk screens and lithographs further explore saturated, brilliant color combinations and inventive, crisply drawn shapes, reminiscent in feeling of Matisse's late paper-cutout compositions.

ZADKINE, Ossip (1890, Smolensk—1967, Paris), French sculptor of Russian origin. When he was sixteen, Zadkine was sent to Sunderland, a small English town, to finish his education. There he joined evening classes in drawing and sculpture. Soon afterward, he went to London, then in 1909 to Paris, where he began to work in a Cubist mode. In spite of Zadkine's success with Cubist sculpture (*Woman with a Fan*, 1918), the

Ossip Zadkine. *The Destroyed City.* 1948–51. Leuvehaven Quay, Rotterdam.

Zapotec Art. Funerary urn in the form of the jaguar-god. Museum für Völkerkunde, Berlin. *Photo Walter Dräyer, Zurich.*

strictness and formality of the style was not suited to his poetic temperament, and in about 1920 he began working in a more lyrical, personal manner. His sculpture became increasingly Baroque as he began to experiment with more complex groups and varied forms, and with compositions of greater movement, which were executed in the more flexible medium of plaster (*Maenads*, 1934; *Homo-sapiens*, 1935–36).

Shortly before 1940, Zadkine's forms became lighter, perforated by openings that yielded a multiplicity of points of view. His work became increasingly expressive—the embodiment of emotion and concepts. *Prisoner* (1943), for example, which he did during World War II in the United States, is not a woman confined behind bars: it is an idea trying to escape and proclaim its existence outside. *Orpheus* became in the 1948 version, just like the *Poet* of 1956, not so much a human form as a melody that unfolds in space and suggests a conception of time. Zadkine exercised a considerable influence on modern sculpture through his work and through teaching in Paris, both at the Académie de la Grande-Chaumière and in his own studio.

ZAPOTEC ART. The Zapotecs occupied the high valleys of Oaxaca, Etla, Tlacolula, and Zimatlán, in the middle of the area between the southern part of the Gulf of Mexico and the shores of the Pacific. There, between the peoples of the Teotihuacán region and the Mayas, they developed a theocratic culture that probably had its roots in very early times, since by about the beginning of the Christian era the Zapotecs possessed a considerable knowledge of astronomy, an accurate calendar, and a glyphic writing. At its beginning, the Zapotec civilization was influenced by the Olmecs and Mayas; then it assimilated cultural elements from the conquering Mixtecs (*c.* 7th century A.D.), before it was finally crushed by the Aztecs in the 15th century. Zapotec art, like that of other pre-Columbian Mexican cultures, was closely tied to religion. The cult of the dead is believed to have held an important place in it, because the finest specimens of Zapotec art, especially the terra-cotta funerary urns, have been found in graves on Monte Albán, near Oaxaca. The urns are in anthropomorphic forms that combine realistic figures and attitudes with a profuse baroque decoration; the mask of Cosijo, God of Rain and Lightning, whose features combine those of a serpent and jaguar, is often set amid a clay mass of floral motifs, feathers, and a variety of ornaments. Zapotec tombs were either hollowed out of the living rock or had flat stone roofs, and were sealed with a slab carved with fine reliefs. The walls were generally covered with frescoes. Besides the urns, the tombs have also yielded pottery of varied forms and decorations, as well as terra-cotta figures, which have come to represent the quintessence of this vanished civilization. A lively realism characterizes some of the figures carved in relief on monumental stone slabs found at Monte Albán. On such slabs the figure is accompanied by glyphs designating the name of the personage represented and the date of the event.

ZEHRFUSS, Bernard (b. 1911, Angers), French architect. Zehrfuss began his career in Tunis, where between the years 1942 and 1954 he built a variety of administrative buildings, a hospital complex, an ophthalmic center, and the Sadiki College. His name is connected with two of the most outstanding buildings erected in Paris since World War II: the CNIT Building (National Center of Industry and Technology, 1958), whose vast shell-concrete roof, resting on three points, is one of the largest in the world; and the UNESCO Building (1953–58), in partnership with Marcel Breuer and Pier Luigi Nervi. Zehrfuss also supervised the construction of the new underground buildings needed for the expansion of UNESCO (1963–65). His buildings for industry include the Renault factory at Flins (1951), and the Mame Printing Works at Tours (1952).

ZIMMERMANN, Dominikus (1685, Gaispoint, near Wessobrunn—1766, Wies, Upper Bavaria), German architect. Zimmermann was trained in the technique of decorative stuccowork before he turned his attention to architecture, in which for 40 years he showed signal ability. The splendor of his abbeys and churches bears witness to his skill, as well as to the wealth of the Bavarian clergy under the prosperous electorship of Karl-Albrecht von Wittelsbach. Zimmermann holds a place of primary importance in the history of Baroque architecture in Bavaria.

The plans for the monasteries of Maria-Mödingen (1716–28) and Siessen (1726–33) prepared Zimmermann for work on his first masterpiece, the pilgrimage church at Steinhausen (1727–33), near Schussenried. Its style was repeated (1736–39) in the Liebfrauenkirche at Günzburg.

The results of experiments undertaken by Zimmermann in

Bernard Zehrfuss, Robert Camelot, and Jean-Jacques de Mailly. CNIT Building, Paris. 1958. *Photo Jean Roubier.*

these two churches were incorporated later into his designs for the famous pilgrimage church at Die Wies (1745–54), near Steingaden. The large oval nave is unusual in that its main axis is at right angles to the façade. A gallery runs around this entire oval space, opening onto it by means of 16 arcades supported on 32 pillars. This gallery is enclosed to left and right by corniced walls, emerging in front below the drum of the cupola and at the back in the chancel. The latter is surrounded by an ambulatory behind which rises the belfry. All these architectonic factors contribute to the enhancement of the decoration, in which the Rococo polychromy achieves a wonderful brilliance. The great stucco artist has here applied the Italian technique of *scagliola*, a form of alabaster that imitates the effect of marble, and whose colors may be infinitely varied.

JOHANN BAPTIST (1680, Gaispoint—1758, Munich), the brother of Dominikus, was primarily a decorator and stuccoworker. They frequently collaborated, as in the churches at Die Wies and Steinhausen. Johann Baptist's great ceiling fresco at Steinhausen (1730–31) is one of the masterpieces of Bavarian decorative painting, typically gay and sensuous. He also provided the decoration for the Gallery of Ancestors (1728–30) in the Munich Residenz and for the church of Piren (1736) in Upper Bavaria, and did the stuccowork for the Hall of Mirrors in Munich's Amalienburg, a pavilion situated in the park of Nymphenburg Palace.

ZOFFANY, Johann (1734/35, Frankfurt—1810, London), German-born English Rococo painter of portraits, interiors, and theatrical genre scenes. The portrait of *Sir Richard Neave* (Coll. Sir Arundel Neave), puzzlingly dated 1751, suggests not only that Zoffany was a competent portrait painter by this early date but that he was accomplished in the English style. He arrived in England in about 1760. By 1762 he was working under David Garrick's protection and was commissioned by that actor to paint a number of "theatrical conversation pieces," such as *Garrick and Mrs. Cibber as Jaffier and Belvidera* (1763; England, Coll. Earl of Durham). Perhaps his finest picture of this type is *Parsons, Bransby, and Watkyns in "Lethe"* (*c.* 1766; Birmingham, City Museum and Art Gallery).

Zoffany's ability as a portraitist has not received its due. His *George III* (Windsor Castle, Royal Collection; exhibited at the Royal Academy in 1771), showing the monarch informally seated against a plain background, is a welcome contrast to the grandeur of Reynolds and Gainsborough. Equally remarkable for its note of domestic intimacy is the picture of *Queen Charlotte with the Two Elder Princes* (1766–67; Windsor Castle, Royal Collection), in which Zoffany included the first of his brilliant Rococo interiors.

From 1772 to 1776 Zoffany was in Florence painting the *Tribuna of the Uffizi* (Windsor Castle, Royal Collection) on commission from Queen Charlotte. This picture, which shows a group of connoisseurs, admiring pictures and statues, ushers in the second phase of his work, in which he concentrated on the cluttered and overcrowded documentary. Zoffany went to India in 1783 and stayed there to paint appealing but not particularly incisive genre scenes until 1789. Little is known of the output of his last years, but he remains England's most professional painter in the Rococo style. In addition, his work is important as the most complete delineation on record of upper middle-class life in the latter half of the 18th century.

ZORACH, William (1887, Eurburg, Lithuania—1966, Bath, Maine), American sculptor. His family emigrated to the United States in 1891 and lived in Cleveland. Zorach studied painting at the National Academy of Design in New York (1907–8), and then settled in Paris in 1910. He exhibited at the Salon d'Automne (1911), then at the Armory Show (1913), on his return to New York. Although his first sculpture was done in 1917, he continued painting until 1922. Zorach's painting had been Cubist, but his sculpture was inspired by the archaic art of Egypt and Greece. The greater part of his output included heads, torsos, nudes, and animals carved directly from stone or wood (*Floating Figure*, 1922; Buffalo, Albright-Knox Art Gallery), but he also executed bas-reliefs and monumental sculpture for public buildings (*Spirit of Dance*, 1932; New York, Radio City Music Hall).

Dominikus Zimmermann. Pilgrimage church at Die Wies, near Steingaden, Upper Bavaria. 1745–54. *Photo Retzlaff.*

ZUCCARO *or* **ZUCCARI,** Taddeo (1529, Sant'Angelo in Vado, near Urbino—1566, Rome) *and* Federico (1542, Sant'Angelo in Vado—1609, Ancona), Italian Mannerist painters. Taddeo worked primarily in Rome, where prior to 1556 he executed mythological frescoes for the Villa Giulia and where with his brother he painted frescoes (completed 1582, after his death) in the Vatican's Sala dei Palafrenieri. From 1559 to 1566 Taddeo executed frescoes (*François I Receiving Charles V in Paris*) and stucco decorations at the Palazzo Farnese in Caprarola.

After Taddeo's death, Federico pursued his brilliant career as a decorator, working at Venice in the Sala del Maggior Consiglio of the Palazzo Ducale (*Barbarossa and Alexander III*, 1582), and at Florence, where he completed (1575–79) the frescoes in the dome of the cathedral of S. Maria del Fiore, which had been begun by Giorgio Vasari. He traveled in France (1572–74) and was later in England (1575) and Spain (1585–89; decorations for the high altar of the Capilla Mayor at the Escorial). One of the prime theorists of Mannerism, Federico

William Zorach. *Moses*. 1935. Columbia University, New York. *Photo Baker, New York.*

Federico Zuccaro. *Taddeo Zuccaro Sketching the Laocoön.* Uffizi, Florence. *Photo Alinari, Florence.*

maintained an academy at his house in Rome, located in Via Gregoriana. This residence, the Palazzo Zuccaro (today housing the Biblioteca Hertziana), was designed in 1593 by Federico himself. The interior is richly adorned with his frescoes. In 1607 he wrote *L'Idea de' pittori, scultori, ed architetti*, a treatise summarizing his teachings regarding Mannerist principles; it was successfully reissued in 1768.

The Zuccari belonged to the last generation of Mannerists in Rome, and their vast decorative cycles anticipate the Baroque style of the 17th century.

ZURBARÁN, Francisco de (1598, Fuente de Cantos, Badajoz—1664, Madrid), Spanish painter. His first signed work is an *Immaculate Conception* (1616; Bilbao, Coll. Felix Valdés), which already shows his originality in its use of tonal contrasts and its understanding of the life of the spirit. Zurbarán did not remain in the Andalusian capital, but in 1617 set up his studio at Llerena, where he continued to live until 1628. He portrayed religious personages in a tenebrist and monumental style, thus making up for his inability to compose scenes by his skillful contrasts of light and shade, by the sculpturesque attitudes of his figures, and by his astonishingly intuitive understanding of monastic life. For the Dominican monastery of S. Pablo el Real (today called S. Magdalena) he painted the *Life of St. Dominic* in 14 scenes, of which two have remained in place. Also for S. Pablo he produced seven portraits of the *Doctors of the Church* (three are today in Seville, Museo Provincial de Bellas Artes), and, for the oratory of the sacristy, a *Christ on the Cross*. The latter work (now Chicago, Art Institute) won him immediate fame for the consummate skill of its chiaroscuro effects and for its intense pathos. At the Merced Calzada, Zurbarán's series on the *Life of St. Peter Nolasco* originally adorned the small cloister (two of the most famous paintings in the series—*St. Peter Nolasco Dreaming of the Heavenly Jerusalem* and the *Apostle Peter Appearing to St. Peter Nolasco*, both dated 1629—are today in Madrid's Prado). The *St. Serapion* (1628; Hartford, Wadsworth Athenaeum) from the same convent epitomizes two recurring characteristics of Zurbarán's art: a noble restraint in the depiction of martyrdom, and a masterly display of crisp white draperies. From S. Buenaventura comes the well-known scene of *St. Bonaventure on his Bier* (1629; Paris, Louvre).

In 1629 Zurbarán was officially invited by the municipality of Seville to take up residence in that city, and it was there—between 1630 and 1639—that he produced his most remarkable works: still-life studies (*Still Life with Oranges*, 1633; Florence, Coll. Count Contini-Bonacossi) and especially religious pictures for the churches, monasteries, and seminaries of the city. Among the greatest religious works of his Seville period are the *Vision of the Blessed Alonso Rodríguez* (1630; Madrid, Academia de S. Fernando), from the sacristy of the Jesuit church; the *Apotheosis of St. Thomas Aquinas* (1631; Seville, Museo Provincial de Bellas Artes); and *St. Hugo of Grenoble Visiting the Refectory of the Carthusians* (*c.* 1633; Museo Provincial de Bellas Artes), from the Carthusian monastery of Las Cuevas at Triana, a suburb of Seville. In 1634 Zurbarán was called to Madrid, to take part in the decoration of the Salón de Reinos (Hall of Realms) in Buen Retiro Palace, where in fact his contribution consisted of some very mediocre works (*Labors of Hercules*; Madrid, Prado). The magnificent series painted in 1638–39 for the Carthusian monastery of Nuestra Señora de la Defensión at Jerez de la Frontera has been scattered; the pictures of the great reredos are divided among the museums of Grenoble (*Adoration of the Shepherds*; Musée de Peinture et de Sculpture), Cadiz (*Angel with Censer*; Museo Provincial de Bellas Artes), and New York (*Battle of El Sotillo*; Metropolitan Museum).

By the 1640s Zurbarán's position of leadership in Sevillian art circles was being challenged by the younger Bartolomé Esteban Murillo. It was difficult for him to adapt himself to the changing fashion in painting, although he attempted (rather unsuccessfully) to imitate Murillo's style in works of the 1650s and 1660s. Zurbarán tried, apparently without much success, to re-establish his reputation by returning to Madrid, but he died there in great poverty in 1664.

ZWOBADA, Jacques (1900, Neuilly-sur-Seine, near Paris—1967, Paris), French sculptor. Rodin's influence is evident in the lyricism of two early public monuments (*Monument to André Caplet*, 1926, Le Havre; and *Monument to Simon Bolivar*, 1933, Quito). Zwobada later left representational art to sculpt monolithic abstract works that suggested movement through the voids with which it was pierced. For 15 years he abandoned sculpture to teach and practice drawing. His inspiration returned in about 1948, when his work again assumed lyrical, semifigurative qualities (*Dance*, 1952). Zwobada began to teach at the Paris School of Applied Arts in 1953, but at the premature death (1956) of the woman who had been his inspiration, he devoted the last years of his life to her funerary monument in the Campo Santo Mentana, near Rome. It was executed from drawings and contains his finest works, including *Night Ride* (1963), which guards the entrance, the tragic *Orpheus* (1954), and *The Couple* (1956).

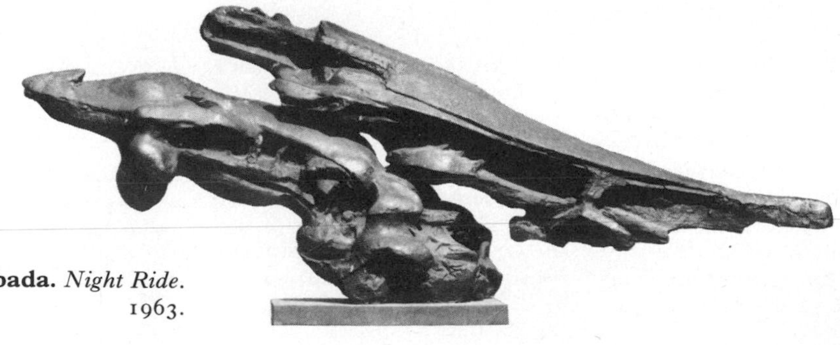

Jacques Zwobada. *Night Ride.* 1963.